Christopher

THE OXFORD
COMPANION TO
ENGLISH
LITERATURE

The Oxford Companion to English Literature

COMPILED AND EDITED BY

SIR PAUL HARVEY

FOURTH EDITION REVISED

BY DOROTHY EAGLE

OXFORD UNIVERSITY PRESS

Oxford   New York

PREFACE TO THE FOURTH EDITION

THE main work in preparing this new edition has been to bring the entries for the twentieth century up to date. Many new writers have become established since Harvey first wrote, and a few who were accorded only brief entries then are now recognized as major figures. New articles have been written for these and old ones have been expanded. The rest of the book has been revised with a very light hand. Here and there a minor gap has been filled, and as far as possible the latest or best editions of important works have been noted, as well as recent biographies or editions of correspondence. A few alterations in the text have been made where modern scholarship has thrown new light (in Old English or Shakespearian studies for example), but in the main the book is still the same companion that is familiarly known to so many readers simply as 'Harvey'.

In order to make room for new material a certain amount of weeding and pruning has been done: some of the entries concerning common allusions seemed no longer significant—either the subject-matter had become too well known or it had passed out of currency—and these have been dropped: others that looked disproportionately long have been cut down.

I cannot in the limited space mention by name all those who have helped and advised, but I want to thank the many readers who have written over the past twenty-five years and whose critical suggestions have contributed to the work of revision. I should also like to acknowledge the kindness of Professor Deb, formerly of the University of Allahabad, who supplied a detailed criticism of the entire book. My thanks are also due to the experts whom I consulted, in particular Mr. James D. Hart of the University of California for his survey of the articles concerned with American literature, and to Professor D. Grant for the revision of this section, to Professor C. R. Cheney for the revision of the article on the Calendar in the appendix, and also to Dr. J. Corson, Mr. John Heath-Stubbs, and many others, including the staff of the Bodleian Library.

D. S. E.

June 1967

From the
PREFACE TO THE THIRD EDITION

THE text has again undergone revision, and many articles have been amended or rewritten. To many kind critics who have helped me with corrections and suggestions, and in particular to Dr. C. T. Onions, Professor Ernest Weekley, and the late Sir John Fox, I owe acknowledgements and thanks.

H. P. H.

August 1946

PREFACE TO THE SECOND EDITION

IN this edition a general revision has been made and new entries have been added where these were felt to be necessary. Appendices are included, consisting of articles on the Censorship of the press and drama and on Copyright, and of a Perpetual Calendar, which it is hoped may be of value to students.

In the general work of revision I wish to acknowledge the help which I have received from many reviewers and correspondents. I am particularly indebted to Mr. R. P. Jago and to Dr. Eis of Brünn for a number of corrections and observations, and to Mr. A. E. Stamp, C.B., F.S.A., of the Public Record Office, for advice in the preparation of the Perpetual Calendar. Sir Frank MacKinnon was good enough to contribute the article on Copyright which bears his signature.

H. P. H

September 1936

PREFACE

THIS volume will serve its purpose if it proves a useful companion to ordinary everyday readers of English literature. It is necessarily a work of compilation and selection, because the range of the possible subject-matter is so great. English literature has a continuous history of over a thousand years, it has been produced in many lands, and there is no subject on which it does not touch. Completeness in a moderate compass, and the equipment of a specialist at all points, are therefore impossible.

According to the general scheme of the work, as designed by the publishers, two main elements are included, in alphabetical arrangement. The one is a list of English authors, literary works, and literary societies which have historical or present importance. Under an author's name is given a selection of facts—especially dates—bearing on his life and literary activity. Under the title of a work there is some indication of its nature, and for the greater works of fiction of the past—whether poetry, prose, or drama—there is usually a brief sketch of the plot. American literature is an essential part of the literature of our language, and a certain number of American authors and of their works, those best known in this country, have been treated on the above lines. Original literary appreciation is not attempted, and comments verging on aesthetic criticism are intended to give rather a conventional view of the importance and distinctive qualities of the author or work under discussion. In this part of the volume, where a compiler must often plead for the indulgence of experts, living authors present the hardest problem. Contemporary judgement is notoriously fickle and tends to be impassioned. I could have wished to exclude all living authors; yet some have established reputations that can hardly be ephemeral, and some may claim at least a place beside the popular favourites of other days. I have therefore, on advice, given very brief entries to a limited number of living authors and recent works; but without finding a criterion of choice that satisfies me. I must apologize to those whose merits I have unintentionally neglected, and ask readers to pass lightly over errors of selection on this difficult borderland. After all, it comprises only one of some fifty generations of English authors.

The other element is the explanation of allusions commonly met with, or likely to be met with, in English literature, in so far as they are not covered by the articles on English authors and works. The selection is limited to allusions which contain a proper name, with a few special exceptions: some literary terms, some names of wines, and names of old coins like 'gold moidores' and 'pieces of eight', which are more than mere common nouns to readers of English. Even among proper names the number of possible entries is huge. Apart from the characters of English fiction, one must reckon with names from several mythologies, with saints, heroes, statesmen, philosophers, men of science, artists, musicians, actors, with literary forgers and impostors—in short, with every kind of celebrity. In order to restrict the field of choice

I have had to bear in mind that this is not a dictionary of mythology, or history, or science, or music, but a companion to English literature, and therefore to look at all such special subjects through the mirror of English literature. It is sometimes a distorting mirror. Thus foreign authors are included as matter of allusion in English, not on any scale of merit which would satisfy students of those literatures. Eustache Deschamps, for instance, appears because of his relations with Chaucer, though many great figures in French literature are passed over. In the selection of place-names, the grounds of choice are similar. A volume of this size would not hold all the places referred to in English writers of some standing. But Grub Street and Fleet Street have associations which greater thoroughfares do not share; Harvard and Yale have claims to inclusion over and above their merits as universities; Mount Helicon must be preferred to Everest.

If these general principles of selection win approval, it still remains true that no two persons would agree on their application in detail. But I hope I have included a large proportion of entries which would be admitted by common consent, and have contrived to provide many signposts that will direct the inquirer to fuller knowledge. Some of the entries may appear unnecessary from the very familiarity of the subject; but it must be remembered that what is familiar to residents in this country may not always be so to readers in other lands which have a common heritage in our literature.

In a compilation such as this, the debt to previous writers is necessarily very great, coextensive in fact with the book itself. I must, to begin with, acknowledge my special indebtedness to certain sources of general literary information. These are: the *Cambridge Histories of English Literature* and *of American Literature*; the various works of Professor Saintsbury (including the *Periods of European Literature* issued under his general editorship); the *Surveys* of Professor Elton; and A. C. Ward's *Twentieth-Century Literature*. The biographies of British authors in the following pages are mainly, but not exclusively, based on the *Dictionary of National Biography*. Many definitions are adapted and much miscellaneous literary information derived from the *Oxford English Dictionary*. I have, in addition, profited by the labours of the innumerable editors, biographers, and commentators of authors whose works are dealt with herein. It would be impossible to name them all, but I should perhaps mention my special debt to such outstanding biographers as J. G. Lockhart and Sir E. K. Chambers.

The articles on classical mythology are based, in the main, on Homer, Hesiod's *Theogony*, the Greek tragedians, Virgil, and Ovid, with much guidance and assistance from the *Classical Dictionaries* of Sir William Smith and Lemprière. Those on Scandinavian mythology are founded on the *Poetic Edda* and the *Heimskringla*; those on Celtic mythology, on the *Hibbert Lectures* of Professor John Rhys and the *Mythology of the British Islands* of C. Squire; and the few notes on Indian and Muslim theology and mythology on W. J. Wilkins's *Hindu Mythology*, Sale's *Koran*, and Duncan Forbes's *Mohammedan Mythology*. In matters of archaeology and ancient religion and philosophy, I should mention the assistance I have had from the encyclopaedic writings of M. Salomon Reinach, and in respect of English philosophy from Professor J. Seth, *English Philosophers and Schools of Philosophy*. As regards early English romances, I am particularly indebted to J. E. Wells, *Manual of the Writings in Middle English*.

It would be impossible to enumerate within the compass of a short preface the works that I have had recourse to when dealing with special subjects such as Old London, the history of journalism, London clubs, etc. I have endeavoured to draw my information from the authors best qualified to give it, and I hope that my acknowledgements in this general form will be accepted.

I have also consulted on particular points a number of works of reference such as the *Encyclopaedia Britannica* (11th and 14th editions), the *Century Cyclopaedia of Names*, and Haydn's *Dictionary of Dates*, from which I have taken a few facts and dates; also *Notes and Queries*, and its French counterpart, the *Intermédiaire des Chercheurs*; and the invaluable *Dictionary of Phrase and Fable* and *Reader's Handbook* of Dr. Brewer.

I should not omit to mention the assistance I have had from the ever instructive pages of the *Times Literary Supplement*, from the staff of the London Library, and from friends and correspondents in England, Ireland, France, and America. I owe a special debt of gratitude to Mr. C. R. L. Fletcher, who has read and commented on the whole of the proofs; and to the staff of the Oxford University Press for general guidance and detailed help in the preparation of the work. Mr. B. R. Redman, who read the proofs with that object, has added a number of short articles to fill gaps in the treatment of American authors and subjects. The suggestions and corrections of these helpers have contributed immensely to whatever standard of completeness and accuracy has been achieved. I only regret that considerations of space and the limited scope of the work have made it impossible to incorporate all the additions that they proposed. For the blunders that may have escaped their scrutiny, I alone am responsible.

H. P. H.

October 1932

NOTE

THE names of AUTHORS, at the head of articles, are printed in capitals (e.g. **KEATS**, JOHN); the TITLES OF LITERARY WORKS in bold italics (e.g. ***Lycidas***); other subjects of articles, in ordinary bold type (e.g. **Gotham**, WISE MEN OF).

CHARACTERS IN FICTION and PERSONS IN REAL LIFE are entered under their surnames, e.g. 'Samuel Weller' under 'Weller'; John Dryden under 'Dryden'; unless the two names form in current use an indissoluble whole, or the surname is little known. Thus 'Peter Pan' appears under 'Peter', 'Little Nell (Trent)' under 'Little Nell'. As regards names such as Thomas of Erceldoune, William of Malmesbury, the entry in the *D.N.B.* has in each case been followed.

Where the TITLE OF A WORK consists of a Christian name and a surname, it is entered under the Christian name, e.g. 'Barnaby Rudge' under 'Barnaby'.

Cross-references have been added where it appeared advisable. In comparatively rare cases, especially when a play or novel is mentioned in connexion with some minor character in it, '(q.v.)' after the name of the novel or play signifies no more than that an article will be found on it; the article may contain no reference to the character in question.

ABBREVIATIONS

a.	= *ante*, before.		l., ll.	= line, lines.
ad fin.	= *ad finem*, near the end.		LXX	= Septuagint.
b.	= born.		ME.	= Middle English
B.M. Cat.	= *British Museum Catalogue.*		M.Gk.	= Modern Greek
c.	= *circa*, about.		MHG.	= Middle High German
c. or ch.	= chapter.		N. & Q.	= *Notes and Queries.*
cent.	= century.		N.T.	= New Testament
cf.	= *confer*, compare.		OE.	= Old English (Anglo-Saxon).
C.H.A.L.	= *Cambridge History of American Literature.*		OED.	= *Oxford English Dictionary.*
			OIr.	= Old Irish.
C.H.E.L.	= *Cambridge History of English Literature.*		ON.	= Old Norse.
			op. cit.	= *opus citatum*, work quoted.
d.	= died.		O.T.	= Old Testament.
D.N.B.	= *Dictionary of National Biography.*		P.E.L.	= *Periods of European Literature.*
E.B.	= *Encyclopaedia Britannica.*		pron.	= pronounced.
ed.	= edition or edited by.		q.v.	= *quod vide*, which see.
E.E.T.S.	= Early English Text Society.		qq.v.	= *quae vide*, both which, or all which, see.
et seq.	= *et sequentes*, and following.			
fl.	= flourished.		*sc.*	= *scilicet*, understand or supply.
Gk.	= Greek.			
I.D.C.	= *Intermédiaire des Chercheurs* (the French counterpart of *Notes and Queries*).		S.P.E.	= Society for Pure English.
			s.v.	= *sub verbo*, under the word.
			T.L.S.	= *Times Literary Supplement.*
L.	= Latin.		tr.	= translation or translated by.

A

À BECKETT, GILBERT ABBOTT (1811–56), educated at Westminster School, and called to the bar at Gray's Inn, was the first editor of 'Figaro in London' and on the original staff of 'Punch' (q.v.). He was for many years a leader-writer on 'The Times' and 'Morning Herald', and was appointed a Metropolitan police magistrate in 1849. He wrote a large number of plays and humorous works, including a 'Comic History of England' (1847–8), a 'Comic History of Rome' (1852), and a 'Comic Blackstone' (1846).

His son, GILBERT ARTHUR À BECKETT (1837–91), educated at Westminster School and Christ Church, Oxford, was, like his father, a regular member of the staff of 'Punch' from 1879. He wrote, in collaboration with Sir W. S. Gilbert (q.v.), the successful comedy, 'The Happy Land' (1873).

A la recherche du temps perdu, by Marcel Proust (q.v.), a long, complex novel in seven sections, the last three published posthumously. It springs from a particular metaphysical conception of the unreality and reversibility of time, the power of sensation ('involuntary memory') rather than intellectual (or 'voluntary') memory to recover the past, and the subject's consequent power to cheat time and death. The chief character, 'Marcel', is also the narrator of the book. Each section represents a phase or experience of his life, forgotten, or deadened by the years, then jerked back to his consciousness by some trivial sensation. This he now reconstitutes, reassessing significances in the light of the intervening years, switching from past to present or merging one in the other, seeking reality behind illusion (and finding it in the last section 'Le Temps retrouvé').

Remarkable features of the work are: its analysis of human behaviour and emotion; its studies of disintegrating personalities and a changing social order (in which change is hastened by the First World War); a wonderful gallery of portraits; also the author's poetic feeling and his descriptive and evocative powers.

An English translation by C. K. Scott-Moncrieff and (the last section) Stephen Hudson was published between 1922 and 1931, entitled 'Remembrance of Things Past'. The titles of the sections are: 'Du Côté de chez Swann' ('Swann's Way'); 'A l'ombre des jeunes filles en fleurs ('Within a budding grove'); 'Le Côté de Guermantes' (The Guermantes Way'); 'Sodome et Gomorrhe' ('Cities of the Plain'); 'La Prisonnière' ('The Captive'); 'Albertine disparue' ('The Sweet cheat gone'); 'Le Temps retrouvé' ('Time regained').

A per se, the letter A when standing by itself, hence the first, chief, most excellent, most distinguished, or unique person or thing. 'The floure and A per se of Troie and Grece' (Henryson, 'Testament of Cresseid').

Abaddon, the Hebrew name of Apollyon, the angel of the bottomless pit (Rev. ix. 11).

Abana and **Pharpar,** the rivers of Damascus referred to by Naaman as better than all the waters of Israel (2 Kings v. 12).

Abaris, a Scythian priest of Apollo, who is said to have visited Greece, and to have ridden through the air on an arrow, the gift of the god.

Abbasides, a dynasty of Caliphs, descendants of Abbas (uncle of Mohammed), who ruled from A.D. 750, when the Umayyads (q.v.) were finally defeated, to 1258. Among them the most famous was Haroun-al-Raschid (q.v.). The sultans of Turkey derived their claim to the Caliphate from this family.

Abbey of Thelema, see *Thelema.*

Abbey Theatre, Dublin, THE, opened in 1904 with W. B. Yeats's 'On Baile's Strand' and Lady Gregory's 'Spreading the News'. In 1903 Miss A. E. Horniman, a friend and admirer of Yeats, had been brought by him into contact with the Fays' National Theatre Company, which had been producing Yeats's early plays, and decided to build a theatre in Dublin to serve as a permanent home for the company. She took over the hall of the Mechanics' Institute in Abbey Street (built on the site of the old Theatre Royal, burnt down in 1880) and an adjoining building, and there erected the Abbey Theatre. Yeats and Lady Gregory were the initial directors and their company, led by F. J. and W. G. Fay, Arthur Sinclair, and Sara Allgood was by 1907 well enough established to weather the storm provoked by the first night of Synge's 'The Playboy of the Western World' (q.v.). The Fays, dissatisfied with the way the theatre was developing, left in 1908, and in 1910 Miss Horniman withdrew her subsidy, making the theatre over to the company. Many new playwrights appeared, such as Lennox Robinson (q.v., who succeeded Yeats as manager), St. John Ervine, Sean O'Casey (q.v.), Brinsley MacNamara and George Shiels: and there were successful tours of England, Ireland and the United States. The Abbey received a grant from the new Government of Eire in 1924, so becoming the first State-subsidized theatre in the English-speaking world. In 1951 the theatre was burnt down. While rebuilding was in progress the company played in the Queen's Theatre and the new Abbey opened on 18 July 1966.

ABBO OF FLEURY (945?–1004), a French theologian, author of an 'Epitome de Vitis Romanorum Pontificum' and of lives of the saints, one of the sources utilized by Ælfric (q.v.).

Abbot, The, a novel by Sir W. Scott (q.v.), published in 1820, a sequel to 'The Monastery' (q.v.).

The work is concerned with that period of the life of Mary Queen of Scots which she spent in imprisonment at Lochleven Castle, her escape, the rally of her supporters and their defeat at the battle of Langside, and her withdrawal across the border to England. With these historical events is woven the romantic story of Roland Graeme, or Roland Avenel, a spirited but hare-brained youth, over whose parentage hangs a certain mystery. After being brought up in the castle of Avenel as page to the Lady of Avenel, he is sent by the Regent Murray to act as page to Mary Stuart in her imprisonment, with directions to watch and report any attempt at escape. These directions he is prevented from carrying out both by his own chivalrous loyalty, by the influence of his fanatical grandmother, Magdalen Graeme, and by his love for Catherine Seyton, one of the queen's attendant ladies. Instead, he becomes an active agent in devising the queen's flight. The mystery of his birth is explained and he is found to be the heir of the house of Avenel. He is pardoned by the Regent and marries Catherine Seyton. The novel takes its title from the abbot of Kennaquhair, Edward Glendinning (Father Ambrose), brother of Sir Halbert Glendinning, the knight of Avenel (see *Monastery*).

Abbot of Misrule, see *Misrule*.

Abbotsford, the name of Sir W. Scott's property near Melrose on the Tweed, purchased in 1811.

Abbotsford Club, The, was founded in 1834, in memory of Sir Walter Scott, for the purpose of publishing materials bearing on the history or literature of any country dealt with in Scott's writings. It ceased its publications in 1865.

Abdĕra, a Greek city on the coast of Thrace, birthplace of Democritus(q.v.), Protagoras the sophist, and Anaxarchus the philosopher; in spite of which its inhabitants were proverbial for stupidity.

Abdiel, in Milton's 'Paradise Lost', v. 805 and 896, the loyal seraph, who resists Satan's proposal to revolt: 'Among the faithless, faithful only he.'

ABÉLARD or ABAILARD, PIERRE (1079–1142), a brilliant disputant and lecturer at the schools of Ste Geneviève and Notre Dame in Paris, where John of Salisbury (q.v.) was among his pupils. He was an advocate of rational theological inquiry and the founder of scholastic theology. He fell in love with Héloïse, the niece of an old canon of Notre Dame, one Fulbert, in whose house he lodged, a woman of much learning to whom he gave lessons. Their love ended in a tragic separation, and in a famous correspondence. Abélard was much persecuted for alleged heresy, in particular by St. Bernard (q.v.), but was sought out by students. Héloïse died in 1163 and was buried in the same tomb as her lover.

Pope's poem 'Eloisa to Abelard' was published in 1717; G. Moore's 'Héloïse and Abélard' was published in 1921.

Abencerrages, The, a legendary Moorish family of Granada, at enmity with the Zegris, another family of Moors. This feud and the destruction of the Abencerrages by Abu Hassan, Moorish king of Granada, in the Alhambra, have been celebrated by Spanish writers, and form the subject of a romance by Chateaubriand (q.v.). The Abencerrages and Zegris figure in Dryden's 'Conquest of Granada' (q.v.).

ABERCROMBIE, LASCELLES (1881–1938), poet and critic. His chief published works were: 'Interludes and Poems' (1908), 'Emblems of Love' (1912), 'Deborah' (1912), all poetry; 'Thomas Hardy, a Critical Study' (1912), 'The Epic' (1914), 'Theory of Art' (1922), all critical; 'Collected Poems' (in the 'Oxford Poets', 1930).

Abershaw, LOUIS JEREMIAH or JERRY (1773?–95), highwayman, the terror of the roads between London, Kingston, and Wimbledon. Hanged on Kennington Common.

Abessa, in Spenser's 'Faerie Queene', 1. iii, the 'daughter of Corceca slow' (blindness of heart), and the personification of superstition.

Abigail, in 1 Samuel xxv, the wife of Nabal and subsequently of David. The name came to signify a waiting-woman, from the name of the 'waiting gentlewoman' in 'The Scornful Lady' by Beaumont and Fletcher (q.v.), so called possibly in allusion to the expression 'thine handmaid', so frequently applied to herself by Abigail in the above chapter.

Abingdon Law. It is said that Maj.-Gen. Browne at Abingdon, during the Commonwealth, first hanged his prisoners and then tried them.

Abora, MOUNT, in Coleridge's 'Kubla Khan', is perhaps to be identified with Milton's Mt. Amara (q.v.). See J. L. Lowes, 'The Road to Xanadu' (1927), pp. 374–5.

Abou Ben Adhem, may his tribe increase, the first line of a poem by Leigh Hunt (q.v.). Abou Ben Adhem sees a vision of an angel writing in a book of gold the names of those who love the Lord. His own name is not included. He prays that he may be written down as one who loves his fellow men. The next night the angel returns and Abou Ben Adhem's name then heads the list.

Abou Hassan, in the 'Arabian Nights' (q.v., 'The Sleeper Awakened'), a merchant of Baghdad, carried while intoxicated to the palace of Haroun-al-Raschid, and persuaded when he woke up that he was the Caliph. Cf. the incident of Christopher Sly in the Induction of Shakespeare's 'The Taming of the Shrew'.

Abracadabra, a cabalistic word intended to suggest infinity, which first occurs in a poem by Q. Severus Sammonicus, 2nd cent. It was used as a charm and believed to have the power, when written in a triangular arrangement and worn round the neck, to cure agues, etc. Fun is made of it in 'A Lay of St. Dunstan' in Barham's 'Ingoldsby Legends' (q.v.).

Abraham, the Hebrew patriarch, figures largely in Arabian and Muslim legend. It is said, for instance, that King Nimrod sought to throw him into a fiery furnace, whence he was rescued by the grace of God. This legend is referred to by Moore in 'Lalla Rookh' (q.v., 'Fire-Worshippers'). Again, the black stone in the Kaaba (q.v.), which had fallen from Paradise, was given by Gabriel to Abraham, who built the Kaaba.

Abraham-man, ABRAM-MAN, one of 'a set of vagabonds, who wandered about the country, soon after the dissolution of the religious houses; the provision of the poor in those places being cut off, and no other substituted' (Nares). The OED. suggests that the name is possibly in allusion to the parable of the beggar Lazarus in Luke xvi. Brewer states that inmates of Bedlam who were not dangerously mad were kept in 'Abraham Ward', and were allowed out from time to time in a distinctive dress and permitted to beg. The 'Abraham-man' is referred to in Awdeley's 'Fraternitye of Vacabones' (1561) and frequently in the dramatists of the 16th–17th cents. Hence, *to sham Abram,* to feign sickness. 'When Abraham Newland was cashier of the Bank of England, and signed their notes, it was sung: "I have heard people say That sham Abraham you may, But you mustn't sham Abraham Newland"' (J. C. Hotten, 'Dict. Slang').

Absalom, the son of King David, who rebelled against his father, and whose death occasioned David's lament in 2 Sam. xviii. 33.

Absalom and Achitophel, a satirical poem, in heroic couplets, by Dryden (q.v.), published in 1681. The poem deals in allegorical form with the attempt by Lord Shaftesbury's party to exclude the Duke of York from the succession and to set the Duke of Monmouth in his place. It was written at the time when Shaftesbury's success or failure hung in the balance, and was designed to influence the issue by showing, under their scriptural disguise, the true characters of the various political personages involved. Chief among these are: Monmouth (Absalom); Shaftesbury (the false tempter Achitophel); the Duke of Buckingham (Zimri), who, as responsible for the 'Rehearsal' (q.v.), was particularly obnoxious to Dryden; Charles II (David); Titus Oates (Corah); and Slingsby Bethel, sheriff of London (Shimei).

The poem, which was immensely popular, was followed in 1682 by a second part, which was in the main written by Nahum Tate (q.v.), but revised by Dryden, who moreover contributed 200 lines, entirely his own, containing, among a number of savagely satirical portraits, the famous characters of Og (Thomas Shadwell, q.v.) and Doeg (Elkanah Settle, q.v.). The lines in question begin

Next these a troop of busy spirits press,

and end with

To talk like Doeg, and to write like thee.

Absentee, The, a novel by M. Edgeworth (q.v.), published in 1812.

Lord Clonbrony, the absentee landlord of Irish estates, lives in London to please his extravagant wife, who is ashamed of her Irish origin, and is mocked by the society into which she forces her way by her lavish expenditure. Lord Clonbrony becomes heavily indebted and is threatened with an execution. Meanwhile his son, Lord Colambre, a sensible young man, has gone incognito to visit his father's estates, and his eyes are opened to the evils of absenteeism. He helps his father to discharge his debts on condition that he returns to his estates, a condition to which Lady Clonbrony is with difficulty brought to consent; and the story closes with the promise of a happier era.

Absolute, SIR ANTHONY, and his son CAPTAIN ABSOLUTE, characters in Sheridan's 'The Rivals' (q.v.).

Abt Vogler, a poem by R. Browning (q.v.). The Abbé Vogler (1749–1814), the subject of the poem, was court chaplain at Mannheim and inventor of improvements in the mechanism of the organ. Vogler has been extemporizing upon the musical instrument of his invention, calling up a vision of pinnacled glory. He laments that this palace of beauty has disappeared with the music. But presently he takes comfort in the thought that there is no beauty, nor good, nor power, whose voice has gone forth, but survives the melodist. It is enough that God has heard it.

Abu Bakr, the first Caliph elected after the death of Mohammed.

Abu Ibn Sina, commonly known as Avicenna (q.v.).

Abus, THE, the Roman name of the river Humber, mentioned in Spenser's 'Faerie Queene', II. x. 16.

Abȳdos, a city of Asia, on the shores of the Hellespont, famous for the loves of Hero and Leander. For Byron's poem see *Bride of Abydos.* See also *Sestos.*

Abȳla, one of the Pillars of Hercules (q.v.).

Acadēmus, a Greek who revealed to Castor and Pollux (q.v.), when they invaded Attica to recover their sister Helen, the place where Theseus had concealed her. See *Academy.*

Academy or ACADEME, from *Academia,* a grove near Athens, sacred to the hero Academus (q.v.), near which Plato (q.v.) had a house and garden and in which he opened his school of philosophy. The second Academy, where a modified Platonic doctrine was taught, was founded by Arcesilaus about 250 B.C.; the third by Carneades about 213 B.C. Together with the School of Athens, the Academy was finally closed by Justinian.

Academy, The, a periodical, was founded in 1869 as 'a monthly record of literature, learning, science, and art', by Charles Edward Cutts Birch Appleton. In 1871 it was converted into a fortnightly, and in 1874 into a weekly review. It included Matthew Arnold, T. H. Huxley, Mark Pattison, and John Conington, among its early contributors. After several vicissitudes 'The Academy' was absorbed by 'The English Review' in 1922.

Academy, THE BRITISH, a society, incorporated in 1902, for the promotion of the study of the moral and political sciences, including history, philosophy, law, political economy, archaeology, and philology. It publishes Proceedings, administers endowments for a number of annual lectures, encourages archaeological and oriental research, etc. Its first secretary was Sir Israel Gollancz.

Academy, THE DELLA CRUSCA, see *Della Crusca.*

Academy, THE FRENCH (*Académie française*), was founded by Cardinal Richelieu in 1635. It is essentially a literary academy. One of its principal functions is the compilation and revision of a dictionary of the French language. The first edition of this appeared in 1694, and there have been numerous subsequent editions. A work that has been approved by the Academy is said to be 'crowned' by it. See *Immortals.*

Academy of Arts, THE ROYAL, was founded under the patronage of George III in 1768, for the annual exhibition of works of contemporary artists and for the establishment of a school of art. It was housed at first in Somerset House, then in the National Gallery, and finally removed to Burlington House in 1869. Sir Joshua Reynolds was its first president. It is occasionally referred to as 'The Forty', from the number of the Academicians.

Acadia, now known as *Nova Scotia,* was discovered by the Cabots (1497) and first settled by the French at the end of the 16th cent., who gave it the name of Acadia. The French inhabitants were attacked by the Virginians in 1613, and the country was in 1622 occupied by Scotsmen under Sir William Alexander, who obtained a grant of it from James I. Its possession was finally confirmed to England by the Treaty of Utrecht. The sufferings of the French Acadians, when expelled in the 18th cent., are recounted in Longfellow's 'Evangeline' (q.v.).

Acapulco ship, THE, another name for the 'Manila ship', one of the Spanish royal ships that sailed annually from Manila in the Philippines for Acapulco on the coast of Mexico, and brought back from that port the output of the Mexican mines. They were regarded as valuable prizes by the English privateers of the 17th–18th cents. Anson (q.v.) is said to have taken the equivalent of £500,000 in the Acapulco ship that he captured (see his 'Voyage round the World', c. viii). See also, e.g., Woodes Rogers, 'Cruizing Voyage'.

Acatalectic, 'not *catalectic*' (q.v.), a term applied to a verse whose syllables are complete, not wanting a syllable in the last foot.

'Stern daughter of the voice of God!' is an iambic dimeter (see *Metre*) acatalectic.

Aceldama (pron. Acel′da-mah), a Hebrew word, the 'field of blood', the name given to the 'potter's field' purchased with Judas's thirty pieces of silver, to bury strangers in. See Matt. xxvii. 8 and Acts i. 19.

Acestes, in Virgil's 'Aeneid' (v. 525), a Sicilian who shot an arrow with such swiftness that it caught fire from friction with the air.

Achātēs, usually styled 'Fidus Achates', a friend of Aeneas (q.v.), whose fidelity was so exemplary as to become proverbial.

Achĕron, a river of Hades, interpreted as ὁ ἄχεα ῥέων the river of woe. See *Styx.*

Achilles, son of Peleus and Thetis (qq.v.), the bravest of the Greeks in the Trojan War. During his infancy Thetis plunged him in the Styx, thus making his body invulnerable, except the heel, by which she held him. He was educated by the centaur Cheiron, who taught him the arts of war and of music. To prevent him from going to the Trojan War, where she knew he would perish, Thetis sent him to the court of Lycomēdēs, where he was disguised in female dress among the king's daughters. As Troy could not be taken without the help of Achilles, Odysseus went to the court of Lycomedes disguised as a merchant, and displayed jewels and arms. Achilles discovered his sex by showing his preference for the arms and went to the war. He was deprived by Agamemnon of Briseis, who had fallen to his lot in a division of booty. For this affront he retired in anger to his tent, and refused to appear in the field, until the death of his friend Patroclus recalled him to action. In armour made for him by Hephaestus, he slew Hector, the champion of Troy, and dragged his corpse, tied to his chariot, to the Greek ships. He was wounded in the heel by Paris as he solicited the hand of Polyxena, a daughter of Priam, in the temple of Athena. Of this wound Achilles died.

The TENDON OF ACHILLES, the tendon by which the muscles of the calf of the leg are attached to the heel, is so called from the above story of the vulnerable heel of Achilles.

Achilles' spear: Telephus, a son-in-law of Priam, and king of Mysia, attempted to prevent a landing of the Greeks on their way to Troy, and was wounded by Achilles. Learning from an oracle that he would be cured only by the wounder, he sought the camp of the Greeks, who had meanwhile learnt that they needed the help of Telephus to reach Troy. Achilles accordingly cured Telephus by applying rust from the point of his spear. Shakespeare ('2 Henry VI', v. 1) and Chaucer ('Squire's Tale', 232) refer to this power of the spear of Achilles both to kill and cure.

The plant ACHILLEA (milfoil) is supposed to have curative properties.

Achilles and the Tortoise, a paradox propounded by the philosopher Zeno (q.v.). Achilles and a tortoise have a race. Achilles runs ten times as fast as the tortoise, which has a hundred yards start. Achilles can never catch the tortoise, because when Achilles has covered the hundred yards, the .tortoise has covered ten; while Achilles is covering these ten, the tortoise has gone another yard; and so on.

Achitophel, see *Absalom and Achitophel.* Ahithophel (2 Sam. xv–xvii, spelt 'Achitophel' in the Vulgate and Coverdale's version) conspired with Absalom against David, and his advice being disregarded, hanged himself.

Acīdālĭa, a surname of Aphrodite, from the well *Acidalius* near Orchomenos in Boeotia.

Acis, see *Galatea.*

Ackermann, RUDOLPH (1764–1834), German lithographer who opened a print shop in the Strand in 1795. He published Annuals, including 'Forget-me-not', 1825, and the 'Repository of Arts, Literature, and Fashions' 1809–28, 'The Microcosm of London', 1808, by William Combe, illustrated by Rowlandson and A. C. Pugin, and other topographical works.

Acrasia, in Spenser's 'Faerie Queene', ii. xii, typifies Intemperance. She is captured and bound by Sir Guyon, and her Bower of Bliss destroyed.

Acre or ST. JEAN D'ACRE, a seaport on the coast of Palestine, was captured by the Crusaders of the Third Crusade in 1191, Richard Cœur de Lion contributing by his energy to its fall. It was the last stronghold held by the Christians in the Holy Land. It was successfully defended in 1799 against Buonaparte by a Turkish garrison aided by Sir Sidney Smith. It was captured from Mehemet Ali in 1840 by the allied fleet under Sir Robert Stopford, with Sir Charles Napier (1786–1860) as his second in command.

Acres, BOB, a character in Sheridan's 'The Rivals' (q.v.).

Acrisius, see *Danaë.*

Actaeon, according to Greek legend a famous hunter, who saw Artemis and her attendants bathing, or, according to another version, boasted himself superior to her in the chase. For this he was changed into a stag, and devoured by his own hounds.

Actes and Monuments of these latter perilous times touching matters of the Church, popularly known as the BOOK OF MARTYRS, by Foxe (q.v.), first published at Strasburg in Latin in 1559, and printed in English in 1563.

This enormous work, said to be twice the length of Gibbon's 'Decline and Fall', is a history of the Christian Church from the earliest times, with special reference to the sufferings of the Christian martyrs of all ages, but more particularly of the protestant martyrs of Mary's reign. The book is, in fact, a violent indictment of 'the persecutors of God's truth, commonly called papists'. The author is credulous in his acceptance of stories of martyrdom and partisan in their selection. The work is written in a simple homely style, and enlivened by vivid dialogues between the persecutors and their victims. The title of the Latin version is 'Rerum in Ecclesia Gestarum . . . maximarumque per Europam persecutionum, etc.'

Action française, L', an extreme right-wing political group which flourished in France between 1900 and 1940, monarchist, anti-semitic, and Roman Catholic. The newspaper 'L'Action française', its organ, was founded and edited by two literary journalists and polemical writers, Charles Maurras (1868–1952) and Léon Daudet (1867–1942). The latter was a son of Alphonse Daudet.

ACTON, SIR JOHN EMERICH EDWARD DALBERG, *first Baron Acton* (1834–1902), was born at Naples of a Shropshire Roman Catholic family, and educated at Paris, Oscott, and privately at Edinburgh. He studied history and criticism at Munich under Döllinger from 1848 to 1854, and with him visited Italy in 1857. He was Whig M.P. for Carlow (1859–65) and formed a friendship with Gladstone. In the 'Rambler' (converted under his direction to the 'Home and Foreign Review') he advocated Döllinger's proposed reunion of Christendom, but stopped the 'Review' on the threat of a papal veto. He was strenuous in his opposition to the definition by the Catholic Church of the dogma of papal infallibility, publishing his views in his 'Letters from Rome on the Council' (1870). In 1874, in letters to 'The Times', he criticized Gladstone's pamphlet on 'The Vatican Decrees'. His literary activity was great, and took the form of contributions to the 'North British Review', the 'Quarterly Review', and the 'English Historical Review' (which he founded), besides lectures and addresses. Lord Acton was appointed Regius professor of modern history at Cambridge in 1895, on which occasion he delivered a remarkable inaugural lecture on the study of history (reprinted in 'Lectures on Modern History', 1906). One of his principal works was the planning of the 'Cambridge Modern History' (1899–1912), for which he wrote the opening chapter. His other published works include 'Historical Essays and Studies' (1907), 'The History of Freedom' (1907), and 'Lectures on the French Revolution' (1910). He had planned early in life a history of liberty, 'the marrow of all modern history' in his view, and for this he collected much material, but only fragments of it, as above, were published.

Ada Clare, one of the two wards in Chancery in Dickens's 'Bleak House' (q.v.).

Adah, in Byron's 'Cain' (q.v.), Cain's wife.

Adam, the name given in the Bible to the first man, the father of the human race, 'the goodliest man of men since born' of Milton's 'Paradise Lost' (iv. 323). Hence the phrase *the Old Adam*, the unregenerate condition or character.

Adam, the designation of a 12th-cent. Norman-French dramatic representation of scriptural history (the Fall, the death of Abel, and the prophets of the Redemption), in eight-syllabled verse, probably written in England, important in the evolution of the drama in England from its liturgical origins.

Adam, in Shakespeare's 'As You Like It' (q.v.) the faithful old servant who accompanies Orlando in exile.

Adam, ROBERT (1728–92), architect, the second son of William Adam (1689–1748), a Scottish architect. He went to Italy in 1754 and published drawings of the ruins of Diocletian's palace at Spalato (Split) in Dalmatia (1764). He established himself in London in 1758 with his two younger brothers, James, also an architect, and William, the business manager of the firm. The brothers acquired on a 99-year lease the land on the north bank of the Thames on which was built the Adelphi (ἀδελφοί, 'brothers'), a terrace of houses raised on vaulted warehouses. The scheme was a financial failure. Adam designed the Admiralty Screen and houses in London and Edinburgh, as well as public buildings and country houses. He brought about a revolution in interior decoration, using a light and elegant style which was applied to all the details of the room, including the furniture and carpets. 'The Works in Architecture of Robert and James Adam' was published in three volumes in 1773, 1779, and 1822.

Adam Bede, a novel by G. Eliot (q.v.), published in 1859.

The plot is founded on a story told to George Eliot by her aunt Elizabeth Evans, a Methodist preacher and the original of the Dinah Morris of the novel, of a confession of child-murder, made to her by a girl in prison. Hetty Sorrel, pretty, vain, and selfish, is the niece of the genial farmer, Martin Poyser. She is loved by Adam Bede, a stern high-minded village carpenter, but is deluded by the prospect of the position which marriage with the young squire, Arthur Donnithorne, would give her, and is seduced by him, in spite of the efforts of Adam Bede to save her. Arthur breaks off relations with her, and Hetty, broken-hearted, presently consents to marry Adam. But before the marriage, Hetty

discovers that she is pregnant, flies from her home to seek Arthur, fails to find him, is arrested and convicted of the murder of her child, and is transported. After a time Adam discovers that he has won the heart of Dinah Morris, a deeply religious young Methodist preacher, whose serene influence pervades the whole story, and whom Adam's brother, the gentle Seth, has long loved hopelessly, and now with a fine unselfishness resigns to him.

The work is remarkable for the characters of the two brothers; of Dinah and Hetty; of the garrulous Mrs. Poyser; the kindly vicar, Mr. Irwine; and the sharp-tongued schoolmaster, Bartle Massey. Also for its pleasant descriptions of scenery, and particularly of the Poysers' farm.

Adam Bell, Clym of the Clough (or CLEUGH), and **William of Cloudesley,** three noted outlaws, as famous for their skill in archery in Northern England as Robin Hood and his fellows in the Midlands. They lived in the forest of Engelwood, not far from Carlisle, and are supposed to have been contemporary with Robin Hood's father. Clym of the Clough is mentioned in Jonson's 'Alchemist', I. ii; and in D'Avenant's 'The Wits', II. i. There are ballads on the three outlaws in Percy's 'Reliques' ('Adam Bell') and in Child's collection. In these, William of Cloudesley, after having been captured by treachery, is rescued by his comrades. They surrender themselves to the king and are pardoned on William's shooting an apple placed on his little son's head.

Adam Blair, see *Lockhart*.

Adam Cast Forth, a dramatic poem (1908) by C. M. Doughty (q.v.), dealing with the separation of Adam and Eve after the expulsion, and their reunion.

Adam Cupid, in Shakespeare's 'Romeo and Juliet', II. i. 13, perhaps alludes to Adam Bell (q.v.), the archer.

Adam, or EDOM, **o' Gordon,** a Berwickshire freebooter, subject of a Scottish ballad included in Percy's 'Reliques'.

Adam's Ale, a humorous expression for water, as the only drink of our first parents.

Adamastor, in the 'Lusiads' (v. li) of Camoëns (q.v.), the spirit of the Cape of Storms (now known as the Cape of Good Hope), who appears to Vasco da Gama and threatens all who dare venture into his seas. 'Adamastor' is the title of a poem by Roy Campbell (q.v.).

Adamites, in ecclesiastical history, the name of sects who affected to imitate Adam in respect of his nakedness. 'An enemy to Clothes in the abstract, a new Adamite' (Carlyle, 'Sartor Resartus').

ADAMNAN, ST. (c. 625–704), abbot of Iona from 679. The life of St. Columba is generally attributed to him.

Adams, PARSON ABRAHAM, a character in Fielding's 'Joseph Andrews' (q.v.).

ADAMS, HENRY BROOKS (1838–1918), American man of letters and grandson and great-grandson of presidents of the United States. He published, among other writings, an ambitious 'History of the United States during the Administrations of Jefferson and Madison' (9 vols., 1889–91), and illustrated his dynamic theory of history in two distinguished and complementary works: 'Mont-Saint-Michel and Chartres' (1904), a study in 13th-cent. unity, and 'The Education of Henry Adams' (1907), an autobiographical account of 20th-cent. multiplicity.

ADAMS, SARAH FLOWER (1805–48), is remembered as a writer of hymns, including 'Nearer, my God, to Thee'. She also wrote 'Vivia Perpetua', a dramatic poem (1841).

ADAMSON, ROBERT (1852–1902), educated at Edinburgh University, became professor of philosophy and political economy at Owens College, Manchester, and subsequently at Aberdeen and Glasgow. His chief works, 'On the Philosophy of Kant' (1879), a monograph on Fichte (1881), 'The Development of Modern Philosophy' (1903), and 'A Short History of Logic' (1911, the reprint of an earlier article), show a gradual reaction from idealism to realism.

ADDISON, JOSEPH (1672–1719), the son of a dean of Lichfield, was educated at the Charterhouse with Steele, and at Queen's College, Oxford, and Magdalen, of which he became fellow. He was distinguished as a classical scholar and attracted the notice of Dryden by his Latin poems. He travelled on the Continent from 1699 to 1703, having been granted a pension for the purpose, with a view to qualifying for the diplomatic service. His 'Dialogues upon the usefulness of Ancient Medals' (published posthumously) were probably written about this time. In 1704 he published 'The Campaign', a poem in heroic couplets, in celebration of the victory of Blenheim. He was appointed under-secretary of state in 1706, and was M.P. from 1708 till his death. In 1709 he went to Ireland as chief secretary to Lord Wharton, the Lord Lieutenant. He formed a close friendship with Swift, Steele, and other writers, and was a member of the Kit-Cat Club (q.v.). Addison lost office on the fall of the Whigs in 1711. Between 1709 and 1711 he contributed a number of papers to Steele's 'Tatler' (q.v.), and joined with him in the production of the 'Spectator' (q.v.) in 1711–12. His tragedy 'Cato' was produced with great success in 1713, and during the same year he contributed to Steele's periodical, the 'Guardian', and during 1714 to the revived 'Spectator'. His prose comedy, 'The Drummer' (q.v., 1715), proved a failure. On the return of the Whigs to power, Addison was again appointed chief secretary for Ireland, and started his political newspaper, the 'Freeholder' (1715–16). In 1716 he became a lord commissioner of trade, and married the countess of Warwick. In 1718 he retired from office with a pension of £1,500. His last year was marked by increasing tension in the relations between him and Steele, of which several papers by Addison in the 'Old Whig' are evidence. Addison was buried in Westminster Abbey, and lamented in a noble elegy by Tickell (q.v.). He was satirized by Pope in the character of 'Atticus' (q.v.).

Addison of the North, see *Mackenzie (H.)*.

Addled Parliament, THE, the parliament summoned by James I in 1614 in the hope of obtaining money. Being met by a demand that Impositions (duties raised by the sole authority of the king) should be abolished and the ejected clergy restored to their livings, the king dissolved the parliament, which, having passed no act and granted no supplies, received the above nickname.

Adeline, LADY, in Byron's 'Don Juan' (q.v.), the wife of Lord Henry Amundeville.

Adelphi, THE, see *Adam (R.)*.

Adicia, in Spencer's 'Faerie Queene', v. viii, the wife of the Soldan (Philip of Spain), the symbol of injustice.

Aditi, in the Veda (q.v.), the impersonation of infinity, or of all-embracing nature. In post-Vedic Hindu mythology, the mother of the gods.

Admētus, the husband of Alcestis (q.v.).

Admirable Crichton, THE, see *Crichton*.

Admiral Hosier's Ghost, a party song, written by R. Glover (q.v.), on the taking of Porto Bello from the Spaniards in 1739. Hosier had been sent in 1726 in command of a squadron to the West Indies, but was reduced by his orders to long inactivity, during which his men perished by disease, and he himself is said to have died of a broken heart. The ballad is in Percy's 'Reliques'.

Adonai, the Supreme Being, a Hebrew word signifying 'my Lords'. It is one of the names given in the O.T. to the Deity, and is substituted by the Jews, in reading, for the 'ineffable name', Yahweh or Jehovah.

Adonais, An Elegy on the Death of John Keats, a poem in Spenserian stanzas by P. B. Shelley (q.v.), published in 1821.

The death of Keats moved Shelley not only to sorrow for one whom he classed among the writers of the highest genius of the age, but to indignation at the savage criticisms on Keats's work which he believed had hastened his end. In this elegy (in form resembling classical elegies such as Bion's lament for Adonis), the poet pictures the throng of mourners, the Muse Urania, Dreams and Desires, Sorrow and Pleasure, Morning and Spring, and the fellow-poets, all bringing their tribute to the bier of Adonais. The lament then changes to a triumphant declaration of the poet's immortality.

Adōnis, the son of Cǐnўras, king of Cyprus, and Myrrha; a beautiful youth beloved by Aphrodite. He received a mortal wound from a wild boar, and the flower anemone was said to have sprung from his blood. Proserpine restored him to life, on condition that he should spend six months with her and the rest of the year with Aphrodite, a symbol of winter and summer. His death and revival were widely celebrated (in the East under the name of his Syrian equivalent, *Thamuz*; cf. 'Paradise Lost', i. 446–52). As a feature in this worship, the image of Adonis was surrounded with beds of plants in flower, whose rapid withering symbolized the cycle of life and death in the vegetable world. 'Gardens of Adonis' are referred to in Shakespeare, '1 Henry VI', I. vi; also in Milton, 'Paradise Lost', ix. 440, and in Spenser's 'Faerie Queene', III. vi. 29, though in the latter passages the similarity is only in the name.

An ADONIS in the 18th cent. was a particular kind of wig ('a fine flowing adonis'; Graves, 'Spiritual Quixote', III. xix).

See also *Venus and Adonis*.

Adramelech, in Milton's 'Paradise Lost', vi. 365, one of the rebel angels.

Adrastus, king of Argos, leader of the expedition of the 'Seven against Thebes' (see *Eteocles*), and of the second expedition against Thebes, known as the war of the Epigoni.

Adriana, in Shakespeare's 'The Comedy of Errors' (q.v.), the jealous wife of Antipholus of Ephesus.

Adriano de Armado, a character in Shakespeare's 'Love's Labour's Lost' (q.v.).

Adriatic: the annual ceremony of the wedding of the Doge of Venice to the Adriatic, the *Sposalizio del Mar*, was symbolical of the sea power of Venice. Traces of the ceremony are found as early as the 11th cent. The Doge, in his state barge, the Bucentaur, proceeded to sea on Ascension Day and dropped a ring into the water.

Adullamites, a name applied to a group of liberal M.P.s, including Edward Horsman, Robert Lowe, and Earl Grosvenor, who seceded from the Reform party in 1866 and opposed the Franchise Bill. The name was first given by John Bright to Horsman, who, he said, 'had retired into what may be called his political cave of Adullam, to which he invited everyone who was in debt, and everyone who was discontented'. (1 Sam. xxii. 1–2.)

Advancement of Learning, *The*, a philosophical treatise by Francis Bacon (q.v.), published in 1605. Unlike most of Bacon's philosophical works, it appeared in English and not in Latin. After disposing of the various objections to learning and enunciating its advantages, the author considers the various methods of advancing knowledge and the defects in present practice. After which, the divisions of knowledge—history, poetry, and philosophy—are enumerated and analysed. This work was later expanded in Bacon's 'De Augmentis'.

Adventurer, *The*, a periodical conducted

during 1752–4 by John Hawkesworth (1715?–73), to which Samuel Johnson and Joseph Warton (qq.v.) contributed many papers.

Adventures of a Guinea, Chrysal, or the, a satirical narrative by Charles Johnstone (1719?–1800?), published in 1760–5, in which a guinea is made to describe its various owners. Several chapters are given to an account of the 'Hell-fire Club' (q.v.).

Adventures of a Younger Son, The, a novel by E. J. Trelawny (q.v.), published in 1831.

The work, which is partly autobiographical, is the story of the life of a wild Byronic character, a lawless daredevil, warped in youth by the harshness of his father, who deserts from the navy and takes to a life of piracy in the Indian Ocean, encountering many exciting adventures. These are told with much vigour and freshness, and there are good descriptions of Eastern scenes.

Adventures of an Atom, The, see *Atom*.

Adventures of Philip, The, see *Philip*.

Advice to a Painter, see *Instructions to a Painter*.

Advocates' Library, THE, in Edinburgh, founded by Sir George Mackenzie of Rosehaugh (1636–91), king's advocate, and opened in 1689. It was presented to the nation by the Faculty of Advocates in 1924, and endowed by Sir A. Grant with £100,000. It became the National Library of Scotland in 1925, and is one of the libraries that receive a copy of all works published in Great Britain.

Advocatus Diaboli, or *Devil's Advocate*, the popular name for the *Promotor Fidei*, who, in a proposal for canonization before the Sacred Congregation of Rites in the R.C. Church, advances what there is to be said against the candidate's claim.

Æ, AE, or **A.E.,** see *Russell (G. W.)*.

Aëdon, see *Itylus*.

Aegëon, see *Briareus*.

Aegeon, in Shakespeare's 'The Comedy of Errors' (q.v.), the Syracusan merchant who is father of the Antipholus twins.

Aegeus, a mythical king of Athens and father of Theseus (q.v.).

Aeginëtan Marbles, THE, from the temple of Aphaea (see *Britomartis*) in the island of Aegina. They represent groups of warriors fighting, with a figure of Athena or Aphaea standing in the centre. The Marbles were bought in 1812 by the Crown Prince Louis of Bavaria and placed in the Glyptothek at Munich.

Aegir, in Scandinavian mythology, the chief of the sea-giants. He represents the peaceful ocean. His wife, Ran, draws mariners down to her abode in the deep. They have nine daughters, the stormy billows. A banquet given by Aegir to the gods is a prominent incident in this mythology.

Aegisthus, according to Greek legend, was the son of Thyestes (the son of Pelops) and his daughter Pelopia. As a result of the feud between Thyestes and his brother Atreus (q.v.), Aegisthus murdered Atreus. When the sons of Atreus, Agamemnon (q.v.), king of Argos, and Menelaus, king of Sparta, went to the Trojan War, Aegisthus seduced Agamemnon's wife Clytemnestra (q.v.), and with her murdered Agamemnon on his return from Troy. Orestes (q.v.), the son of Agamemnon, with the assistance of his sister Electra, subsequently avenged his father by killing Aegisthus and Clytemnestra.

Aeglamour, the 'Sad Shepherd' in Ben Jonson's pastoral drama of that name (q.v.).

Aeglogue, an obsolete spelling of 'Eclogue' (q.v.), associated with a fanciful derivation from αἴξ, goat (as if 'discourse of goat-herds').

Aegyptus, see *Danaides.*

Ælfred, see *Alfred.*

ÆLFRIC, called GRAMMATICUS (*d. c.* 1020), was a monk at Winchester and Cerne and abbot of Eynsham. His chief works are Catholic Homilies (990–2), largely drawn from the works of St. Augustine, St. Jerome, St. Gregory, and other Latin writers, and 'Lives of Saints' (993–6), a series of sermons in alliterative rhythms. His Paschal homily against transubstantiation was published in 1566 under ecclesiastical patronage as 'A Testimonie of Antiquitie'. Several other works of his survive, including a Latin grammar; a 'Colloquy' between the teacher, the pupil, and various persons, a ploughman, a shepherd, a hunter, &c.; a paraphrase in the vernacular of the first seven books of the Bible (not all of it his own work); and a treatise, 'De Veteri et de Novo Testamento', an introduction to the Testaments. Ælfric is a most prominent figure in Anglo-Saxon literature, and the greatest prose writer of his time; his writings are important from their illustration of the belief and practice of the early English Church.

Ælfthryth (ELFRIDA) (*c.* 945–1000), the daughter of Ordgar, ealdorman of Devon, the second wife of King Eadgar, and mother of Æthelred the Unready. She was believed to have caused the death of her stepson, Eadward the Martyr. According to William of Malmesbury's mainly fabulous account of her life, King Eadgar, hearing of her beauty, sent Æthelwald, ealdorman of East Anglia, to see her. Æthelwald falling in love with her, reported disparagingly on her appearance, in order to marry her himself. Eadgar subsequently discovered the deceit, caused the death of Æthelwald, and took Ælfthryth to wife.

Ælla, *Songe to,* one of the 'Rowley Poems' of Chatterton (q.v.).

Aenēas, the son of Anchises and Aphrodite, and the husband of Creūsa, daughter of Priam, king of Troy, by whom he had a son, Ascanius. When Troy was in flames at the end of the Trojan War, he carried away upon his shoulders his father Anchises and the statues of his household gods, leading his son by the hand and leaving his wife to follow behind. But she was separated from him in the confusion and lost. His subsequent adventures are told by Virgil in the 'Aeneid' and by other Latin authors, who, in a spirit of flattery, traced the descent of the Roman emperors to Aeneas. Leaving Troy with a fleet of twenty ships, he was shipwrecked near Carthage, where he was kindly entertained by Dido the queen, who fell in love with him. But Aeneas left Carthage by order of the gods, and Dido in despair took her own life. Coming to Cumæ, Aeneas was conducted by the Sibyl to the nether world, that he might hear from his father's shade the facts of his posterity. After a voyage of seven years, and the loss of thirteen ships, he reached the Tiber, where he married Lavinia, the daughter of King Latinus, having slain in single combat Turnus, king of the Rutulians, his rival for her hand. Aeneas succeeded his father-in-law as king of the Latins and after a short reign was killed in a battle with the Etruscans. He is known as 'pious Aeneas' for his filial piety and fidelity to his mission.

AENEAS SILVIUS PICCOLO'MINI (1405–64), Pope Pius II from 1458, was a patron of letters, and author of a romance, 'Eurialus and Lucretia', of treatises on many subjects, and of Commentaries on his times.

Aeneid, *The,* a poem in Latin hexameters by Virgil (q.v.), recounting the adventures of Aeneas (q.v.) from the fall of Troy.

Aeŏlus, the god of the winds. In the 'Odyssey' (x. 1 et seq.) Aeolus was the ruler of a floating island in the west, on whom Zeus had conferred dominion over the winds. When Odysseus was returning to Ithaca, Aeolus gave him, confined in a bag, all the winds unfavourable to his voyage; but the companions of Odysseus out of curiosity untied the bag and released the winds. In consequence his ships were driven back.

AESCHYLUS (525–456 B.C.), the great Athenian tragic poet, was present in the Athenian army at the battle of Marathon, and may have been present at that of Salamis. He was defeated by his younger rival Sophocles in 468 B.C. He visited Syracuse more than once at the invitation of Hieron I, and died at Gela in Sicily. Legend attributes the manner of his death to the fall of a tortoise which an eagle let drop, mistaking his bald pate for a rock. Of the large number of tragedies that he wrote only seven have come down to us: 'The Persians' (on the triumph of Greece over the Persian invaders), 'The Seven against Thebes' (the story of Eteocles and Polyneices), the 'Prometheus Bound', 'The Suppliants' (i.e. the fifty daughters of Danaus), and the great trilogy on the story of Orestes, the 'Agamemnon', the 'Choephori', and the

'Eumenides'. Aeschylus may be regarded as the founder of Greek tragedy, having introduced a second actor (where there had previously been only one actor and the chorus), and subordinated the chorus to the dialogue.

Aesculāpius (ASCLEPIUS), son of Apollo and Coronis, was taught the art of medicine by Cheiron (q.v.), the Centaur. At the prayer of Artemis he restored her favourite, Hippolytus (q.v.), to life. Zeus, angered at this interference, struck Aesculapius with lightning. After his death he was honoured as the god of medicine, and was represented holding in his hand a staff, round which is wreathed a serpent, a creature peculiarly sacred to him. Among his children was a daughter, Hygieia (q.v.). His principal temple was at Epidaurus; patients who slept in the temple were cured in the night or learnt in a dream the method of cure.

Æsir, THE, in Scandinavian mythology the collective name of the gods, of whom the chief are Odin, his wife Frigga, and his sons Thor, Balder, Tyr, Vali, Vidar, Bragi, Hödur, and Hermod (qq.v.). Loki (q.v.) was also one of the Æsir, but an evil spirit. Their dwelling was known as Asgard. See also *Vanir* and *Ragnarök*.

Aeson, king of Iolchus and father of Jason (q.v.). He was restored to youth by the arts of Medea (q.v.).

AESOP (6th cent. B.C. ?), the fabulist, a semi-legendary person, said to have been originally a slave, who received his freedom from his master Iadmon, a Thracian. The fables attributed to him are probably a compilation of those of many authors. The story that Aesop was ugly and deformed appears to have originated with Maximus Planudes, a 14th-cent. monk, who wrote a life of the fabulist. Landor has two 'Imaginary Conversations' between Aesop and his fellow slave Rhodope.

Aesthetic Movement, a movement during the eighties of the last century in which the adoption of sentimental archaism as the ideal of beauty was carried to extravagant lengths and accompanied by affectation of speech and manner and eccentricity of dress. It was much ridiculed, e.g. in 'Punch' and in Gilbert and Sullivan's opera 'Patience'.

Æthelflæd (*d. c.* 918), the 'Lady of Mercia', daughter of King Alfred, and wife of Æthelred, ealdorman of Mercia. She was a great warrior, and aided her brother Eadward to subdue the Danish parts of England as far north as the Humber.

Æthelred, king of Wessex, 866–71.

Æthelred the Unready, king of England, 979–1016. 'Unready' is properly 'Rede-less', the man without counsel.

Æthelstan, king of England, 925–40. In his reign considerable progress was made towards the unification of the English people, and his policy tended to bring England into closer contact with the Continent. Many of the cultural changes which are commonly attributed to the Norman Conquest can be traced back to Æthelstan's reign.

Æthelwald, see *Ælfthryth*.

ÆTHELWOLD or **ETHELWOLD, ST.** (908?–984), born at Winchester, entered the monastery of Glastonbury, of which St. Dunstan was abbot, and became dean thereof. He subsequently re-established a monastic house at Abingdon, introducing the strict Benedictine rule from Fleury; and when Eadgar became king of England and Dunstan primate, was appointed bishop of Winchester. He co-operated with Dunstan and Oswald (qq.v.) in reforming religion, expelling the secular clergy from Winchester, Chertsey, Milton, and Ely, and substituting monks. He rebuilt the church of Peterborough, and built a new cathedral at Winchester. He exerted his influence also for the revival of learning. He was author of a collection of the regulations and customs of Benedictine convents entitled 'Regularis Concordia'. He is commemorated on 1 August.

Aethiopica, a Greek romance by one Heliodorus of Emesa in Syria (? 3rd cent., improbably stated to have been a Christian bishop). Chariclea is the daughter of Persine, wife of the king of Ethiopia, and was born white owing to the effect of a marble statue on her mother while pregnant. The mother, in fear of the accusations to which this might give rise, entrusts the child to Charicles the Pythian priest, and Chariclea becomes priestess of Apollo at Delphi. Theagenes, a Thessalian, falls in love with her and carries her off. After many adventures they reach Ethiopia, and Chariclea is about to be immolated when she is discovered to be the daughter of the king of the country. Sidney drew on this romance in his 'Arcadia' (q.v.). An English version by Thomas Underdowne (1569?) is included in the Tudor translations.

Aetion, in Spenser's 'Colin Clouts come home againe', possibly represents Shakespeare.

Aëtius, the Roman general who in A.D. 451, in conjunction with Theodoric, defeated Attila and the Huns near Châlons. He was murdered by Valentinian in 454.

Affectionate Shepherd, *The*, see *Barnfield*.

Affery, see *Flintwinch*.

Afrasiab, in the 'Shahnameh' of Firdusi (q.v.), the king of Turan who carries on a long warfare with the kings of Iran, and is killed by Kaikhosru (q.v.).

Afreet, EFREET, AFRIT, AFRITE, an evil demon or monster of Muslim mythology.

Agag, in Dryden's 'Absalom and Achitophel', i. 675, is generally supposed to represent Sir Edmond Berry Godfrey, the Middlesex magistrate who took the depositions of Titus Oates and was soon after found murdered in the fields near Primrose Hill.

'And Corah [Titus Oates] might for Agag's murder call
In terms as coarse as Samuel used to Saul.'
The reference is to 1 Sam. xv.

Agamēdēs, see *Trophonius.*

Agamemnon, king of Argos, the son or grandson of Atreus (q.v.). He married Clytemnestra (q.v.) and was elected commander of the Greek host that went to Troy to recover Helen, the wife of his brother Menelaus, carried off by Paris (qq.v.). The Greek fleet was detained at Aulis, where Agamemnon sacrificed his daughter Iphigenia (q.v.) to appease Artemis, whose favourite stag he had killed. After the fall of Troy, Cassandra (q.v.) fell to his share and foretold that his wife would put him to death. On his return to Argos, he was murdered by Clytemnestra and her paramour Aegisthus (q.v.). See *Aeschylus* and *Browning (R.).*

Aganippe, a fountain on Mt. Helicon (q.v.), sacred to the Muses.

Agapē, in Spenser's 'Faerie Queene', IV. ii. 41, the Fay, mother of Priamond, Diamond, and Triamond, who, seeking to obtain for her children from the Fates
'Long life, thereby did more prolong their pain'.
The word in Greek means affection, charity,

Agapēmonē, meaning 'abode of love', an institution founded in 1845 at Charlinch near Bridgwater, Somerset, by one Henry James Prince, where he and his followers lived on a communist basis, professing certain spiritual doctrines. (See Hepworth Dixon, 'Spiritual Wives' (1868), c. xxii et seq.)

Agdistes, in Spenser's 'Faerie Queene', II. xii. 48, the porter of the Bower of Bliss.

Agdistis, a Phrygian nature-goddess, sometimes identified with Cybele (q.v.), and connected with the legend of Attis (q.v.).

Age of Reason, The, by Thomas Paine (q.v.), published as a whole in 1795. The first part appeared in 1793, but no copies are extant. This work, which sets forth Paine's 'thoughts on religion', was written in Paris at the height of the Terror.

Agincourt, a village in the north of France where, on St. Crispin's day, 25 Oct. 1415, Henry V of England defeated a superior force of French.

Aglaia, one of the Graces (q.v.).

Agnes, ST., the patron saint of virgins, martyred in the persecution of Diocletian and commemorated on 21 Jan. It was a popular belief that by performing certain ceremonies on St. Agnes's Eve, one would dream of the person whom one was destined to marry. Tennyson wrote a poem, 'St. Agnes' Eve'.
For Keats's poem see *Eve of St. Agnes.*

Agnes Grey, a novel by Anne Brontë (q.v.), published in 1847. It is the story of a rector's daughter who takes service as a governess, and is ill-treated and lonely. She experiences kindness from no one but the curate, Mr. Weston, whom she finally marries. With her modest demeanour is contrasted the conduct of Rosalie Murray, her eldest charge, a heartless coquette.

Agnes Wickfield, a character in Dickens's 'David Copperfield' (q.v.).

Agni, in the religion of the Vedas (q.v.), the god of fire, an immortal who has taken up his abode among men, the lord and protector of the household.

Agramant, in the 'Orlando Innamorato' and the 'Orlando Furioso' (qq.v.), the emperor of Africa, suprême ruler of the infidels, a descendant of Alexander the Great, who leads his hosts against Charlemagne.

Agravain, SIR, in Malory's 'Morte Darthur', the son of King Lot and brother of Gawain, Gaheris, and Gareth; he conspires against Launcelot, and discloses to King Arthur Launcelot's love for Guinevere.

Agrican, in the 'Orlando Innamorato' (q.v.), the king of Tartary to whom the hand of Angelica (q.v.) has been promised. He besieges her in Albracca, and is slain by Orlando.

Agricŏla, GNAEUS JULIUS (A.D. 37–93), was Roman governor of Britain and subdued the whole country with the exception of the highlands of Scotland. Tacitus the historian, his son-in-law, wrote his life.

Agrippa, see *Herod Agrippa I.*

AGRIPPA, HENRICUS CORNELIUS, of Nettesheim (1486–1535), a scholar and writer on the occult sciences. He wrote 'De Occulta Philosophia libri tres' (1529) and 'De Vanitate Scientiarum' (1530), and argued against the persecution of witches. Jacke Wilton and the earl of Surrey meet him in the course of their travels (Nash, 'The Unfortunate Traveller', q.v.). He is said to be the astrologer, Her Trippa, of Rabelais's Third Book.

Aguecheek, SIR ANDREW, in Shakespeare's 'Twelfth Night' (q.v.), a ridiculous foppish knight.

Ahab, CAPTAIN, a character in Herman Melville's 'Moby Dick' (q.v.)

Ahania, in the mystical poems of Blake (q.v.), the wife of Urizen, symbolical perhaps of physical desire.

Ahasuerus, see *Wandering Jew.*

Ahmed, Prince, and the Fairy Peri-Banou, the subject of one of the 'Arabian Nights' (q.v.). The three sons of a king were in love with his niece, the princess Nur-al-Nihar. The king, embarrassed to choose between them, promised her to whichever son should bring him the greatest marvel. Hussein, the eldest, secured a flying carpet which would transport whoever sat on it wherever he wished; Ali, the second, a spying-tube which permitted one to see whatever one desired; and Ahmed, the youngest, a magical apple the scent of which cured all disorders. The brothers met at an appointed place. The spying-tube revealed Nur-al-Nihar dying of a disorder; the carpet transported them to her presence; and the apple cured her. The king, still embarrassed, proposed a shooting match, in which Ahmed's arrow travelled so far that it could not be found, and Nur-al-Nihar was assigned to one of the other brothers. But Ahmed, seeking his arrow, encountered the beautiful fairy Peri-Banou, fell in love with her and married her.

Aholah and **Aholibah**, in Ezek. xxiii, personifications of Samaria and Jerusalem as harlots, whom the prophet reproves for their adulterous intercourse with false religions. There is a poem entitled 'Aholibah' in Swinburne's 'Poems and Ballads, 1st Series' (1866).

Aholibamah, a character in Byron's 'Heaven and Earth' (q.v.). For the scriptural Aholibamah see Gen. xxxvi. 2.

Ahriman or ANGRA MAINYU, in the Zoroastrian system, the principle of evil, in perpetual conflict with Ormazd, the god of goodness and light.

Ahura Mazda, see *Ormazd.*

Aidoneūs, a name of Pluto or Hades (q.v.).

Aids to Reflection, a philosophical treatise by S. T. Coleridge (q.v.) in the form of a series of aphorisms and comments, published in 1825.

The principal philosophical doctrine advanced in this is the distinction between Understanding and Reason. Understanding is the faculty by which we reflect and generalize from sense-impressions; while Reason either predetermines experience or avails itself of a past experience to supersede its necessity in all future time. The appropriate sphere of the Understanding is the natural not the spiritual world. By Reason, on the other hand, we have knowledge (and herein Coleridge parts company with Kant) of ultimate spiritual truths. Morality and Prudence in turn are distinguished by the fact that the former flows from the Reason and Conscience of man, the latter from the Understanding. The above doctrine is to be gathered in the main from the part of the work entitled 'Aphorisms on Spiritual Religion'.

AIKEN, CONRAD POTTER (1889–   ), poet and novelist, born in Georgia. He was resident for many years in England. He published the first of his several volumes of verse, 'Earth Triumphant', in 1914, and 'Selected Poems' in 1929. A 'Collected Poems' appeared in 1953. He has published five novels, of which the first, 'Blue Voyage' (1927), and the autobiographical 'Ushant' (1952) are the best known. His short stories were collected in 1960, and his criticism, 'Reviewer's ABC', in 1958. His edition (1924) of the poetry of Emily Dickinson (q.v.) did much to make her known.

Aimwell, a character in Farquhar's 'The Beaux' Stratagem' (q.v.).

AINGER, ALFRED (1837–1904), educated at King's College and at Trinity Hall, Cambridge, became canon of Bristol (1887–1903) and master of the Temple (1894 till his death). He was a popular lecturer and preacher, and author of a life of Charles Lamb (1882), a life of Crabbe (1903), and 'Lectures and Essays' (published posthumously, 1905); he also edited Lamb's Works (1883–8).

Aino, in the 'Kalevala' (q.v.), the sister of Youkahainen, whom Wainamoinen wins for a bride, and who to avoid him drowns herself.

AINSWORTH, WILLIAM HARRISON (1805–82), educated at Manchester Grammar School, published his first novel 'Rookwood', which was immediately successful, in 1834. He edited 'Bentley's Miscellany', 1840–2, and 'Ainsworth's Magazine', 1842–53, and then acquired the 'New Monthly Magazine'. He wrote thirty-nine novels, chiefly with some historical basis, of which the best known are 'Crichton' (1837), 'Jack Sheppard' (1839), 'The Tower of London' (1840), 'Old St. Paul's' (1841), 'Guy Fawkes' (1841), 'The Miser's Daughter' (1842), 'Windsor Castle' (1843), 'The Lancashire Witches' (1848), and 'The South Sea Bubble' (1868).

Ajax, (1) son of Telamon, king of Salamis, was, after Achilles, the bravest of the Greek host that besieged Troy. After the death of Achilles, Ajax and Odysseus contended for the arms of the dead hero. When they were allotted to Odysseus, Ajax, maddened with rage, slaughtered a flock of sheep, thinking them the sons of Atreus who had given the preference to Odysseus, and stabbed himself. From his blood sprang a purple flower (perhaps the iris or the hyacinth). He was known as *Telamonian Ajax* to distinguish him from (2) *Ajax son of Oïleus,* king of Locris, who led forty ships to the Trojan War, having been one of the suitors of Helen (q.v.). On his return homewards, his ship was wrecked, but Poseidon brought him to a rock, and he would have been saved if he had not boasted that his escape was due to his own efforts. Whereupon Poseidon split the rock with his trident and Ajax was drowned. According to Virgil's account, Ajax was struck by lightning after the shipwreck, having incurred the anger of Athene.

Akbar Khan, the great Mogul emperor of Hindustan, who reigned 1556–1605.

AKENSIDE, MARK (1721–70), the son of a butcher of Newcastle-upon-Tyne, and a physician who rose to eminence in his profession. He was the author of 'The Pleasures of Imagination' (q.v.), published in 1744 (rewritten and published in 1757 as 'The Pleasures of the Imagination'); also of a number of odes and minor poems, of which the best is the 'Hymn to the Naiads' (q.v.), written in 1746 and published in Dodsley's 'Collection of Poems' (1758).

Akhnaton, Amenhotep IV, king of Egypt, who came to the throne about 1375 B.C., and introduced a new religion, in which the sun-god Ra (designated as 'Aton') superseded Amon. He himself assumed the office of high-priest, and left Thebes, which was identified with the worship of Amon, for a new capital, Tell-el-Amarna. He was succeeded by his son-in-law, Tutankhamen (q.v.).

AKSAKOV, SERGEI TIMOFEYEVICH (1791–1859), Russian author, who drew his inspiration from Gogol (q.v.) and depicted family life in a rural community, showing a passionate sympathy with nature. His chief works are: 'Chronicles of a Russian Family' (1856), 'Recollections' (1856), 'Years of Childhood' (1858); they are autobiographical.

Al Asnam, Zayn, the subject of a tale in the 'Arabian Nights' (q.v.). Zayn was a prodigal king of Basra, who wasted his substance and ruined his city. When reduced to poverty he consulted a sheikh, and by his advice dug in the grounds of his palace near his father's tomb and there came upon a cavern in which were eight female statues made of precious stones; the pedestal for a ninth statue was vacant. He was told that this missing statue was twenty-fold more precious, and that in order to secure it he must first find a maiden of immaculate purity. For this purpose he was given a mirror which revealed any secret blemish. After long search he discovered the perfect damsel and fell in love with her. On proceeding to the cavern, he found that the damsel herself was the missing statue and occupied the ninth pedestal.

Al Sirat, in the Muslim creed, the bridge, 'stretched over the back of Hell, sharper than a sword and finer than a hair. The feet of the unbelievers slip upon it, by the decree of God, and fall with them into the fire. But the feet of believers stand firm upon it, by the grace of God, and so they pass to the Abiding Abode.' (A short creed by Al-Ghazzali, in Macdonald, 'Muslim Theology'.)

Alabama, The, the name of a war-steamer built at Birkenhead for the Confederates during the American Civil War, which wrought much havoc among the Federal mercantile shipping. The British government was charged with breach of neutrality in allowing the 'Alabama' to sail (1862) from a British port, and heavy damages were awarded by arbitration against it.

ALABASTER, WILLIAM (1567–1640), an Elizabethan divine and Latin poet, was educated at Westminster and Trinity College, Cambridge. Between 1588 and 1592 he produced two notable poems in Latin; an unfinished epic on Queen Elizabeth, which has been preserved in manuscript, and of which Spenser said 'Who lives that can match that heroick song?' ('Colin Clouts come home againe'); and the tragedy 'Roxana', which Dr. Johnson thought contained the best

Latin verse written in England before Milton. In 1596 Alabaster became chaplain to Robert Devereux, Earl of Essex, and sailed with him to Cadiz. In 1597 he became a Roman Catholic (influenced by the same priest who temporarily converted Ben Jonson) and was arrested and deprived of Anglican orders. His sonnets (first published in 1959) were probably written about this time. · Often written in the dramatic Petrarchan form, they are among the earliest metaphysical poems of devotion and seem to have been composed during the course of a profound religious experience. It was, however, as a theologian that Alabaster was chiefly known in his own day. His first major essay in mystical theology, 'Apparatus in Revolutionem Iesu Christi', was written in exile in the Low Countries and declared heretical by the Holy Office. He revolted from the Roman Church and by 1613–14 was again a Protestant, later becoming a doctor of divinity at Cambridge and chaplain to the king. In 1618 he married Katherine Fludd, a widow, and became stepfather to the celebrated physician and alchemist, Robert Fludd (q.v.). After twenty years of vicissitudes his life now became settled and he devoted his later years to theological studies: 'De Bestia Apocalyptica' (Delft, 1621), 'Ecce Sponsus Venit' (1633), 'Spiraculum Tubarum' (? 1633). In 1635 he published a scholarly abridgement of Schindler's Hebrew lexicon.

Aladdin and the Wonderful Lamp, an oriental tale generally regarded as belonging to the 'Arabian Nights' (q.v.), but not contained in any MS. of the collected tales.

Aladdin, the scapegrace son of a poor tailor in China, is employed by a Moorish sorcerer to obtain for him, from a subterranean cavern, a lamp possessing magic powers, but disappoints the sorcerer by retaining the lamp for himself. Discovering its power, he acquires great wealth and marries Bedr-el-Budur, the Sultan's daughter, for whom by means of the lamp he constructs a wonderful palace. The sorcerer, disguised as an itinerant merchant, recovers the lamp by offering 'new lamps for old', and whisks palace and princess off to Africa. Aladdin, pursuing, kills the magician, regains the lamp, and conveys palace and bride back to China.

Alaham, a tragedy by Fulke Greville (q.v.), Lord Brooke, posthumously published in 1633.

Alaham, second son of the king of Ormus, deposes his father, and orders him as well as his elder brother Zophi to be blinded. They are taken to places of refuge by Caelica, the king's daughter. Alaham causes search to be made for them, threatens Caelica with the rack, and finally orders all three to the stake. A messenger relates their death and the popular discontent that follows. The tragedy might, as Charles Lamb remarked, with more propriety be termed a political treatise than a play.

Alastor, or The Spirit of Solitude, a poem by
P. B. Shelley (q.v.), published in 1816.
'Alastor' is Greek for 'avenger'.

This was the poet's first important work.
It is an allegory in which the idealist is
depicted happy in the contemplation of high
thoughts and visions of beauty. Presently he
seeks in reality the counterpart of his dreams.
He meets with frustration, is plunged into
despair, and dies. The poem is a condemnation of self-centred idealism, and at the same
time a lament for a world in which 'many
worms and beasts and men live on', while
'some surpassing spirit' is borne away leaving
pale despair and cold tranquillity' behind.

Alban, St. (*d. ?* 304), the first British martyr,
who is said to have been put to death under
the edicts of Diocletian. While still a pagan,
he had sheltered in his house a Christian
cleric by whom he was converted. The cleric
was traced to Alban's house, and Alban,
wrapped in the cleric's mantle, was arrested
in his place. His identity having been discovered, he boldly declared himself a Christian and was ordered to immediate execution.
The prodigies that attended his removal so
impressed the executioner that he too declared
himself a Christian, and another soldier had
to be found to take his place. St. Alban was
put to death on the hill overlooking the town
of Verulam (q.v.). He is commemorated on
22 June.

Albany, Albainn, Albin, Albania, ancient
poetic names of Gaelic origin for the northern
part of Britain.

Albany, Duke of, a character in Shakespeare's 'King Lear' (q.v.).

Albany, The, Piccadilly, originally a single
mansion, so called from the second title of
the duke of York who owned it at the end
of the 18th cent., subsequently divided into
bachelor chambers. Lord Byron, Macaulay,
George Canning, 'Monk' Lewis, and Bulwer
Lytton (qq.v.) lived there.

Alberich, in Scandinavian mythology the
king of the elves. In the 'Nibelungenlied'
(q.v.) he guards the treasure of the Nibelungs,
and is robbed of it by Siegfried. In Wagner's
version of the story he is the Nibelung who
steals the gold of the Rhine maidens and
makes it into a ring.

ALBERICUS GENTILIS, see *Gentilis.*

Albert Memorial, The, erected in Hyde
Park in memory of the Prince Consort (*d.*
1861), was designed by Sir Gilbert Scott,
whose idea, as quoted by Mr. Lytton Strachey
('Queen Victoria'), 'was to erect a kind of
ciborium to protect the statue of the Prince
... designed in some degree on the principles
of the ancient shrines'. It includes a frieze
containing 170 life-size figures, besides statues representing the virtues and sciences,
and took some seven years to complete (1872).
The statue of the prince, by J. H. Foley, was
not finished till some years later.

ALBERTI, Leon Battista Degli
(1404–72), Italian architect and writer on
painting and sculpture ('Della Pittura Libri')
and architecture ('De Re Aedificatoria';
English translation by G. Leone, 1726). His
theories had a profound influence on Renaissance and subsequent architecture.

ALBERTUS MAGNUS (1193–1280), a native of Swabia, a Dominican friar, and a great
scholastic philosopher. He was an interpreter
of Aristotle, whose doctrine he expounded
at Cologne and Paris. Thomas Aquinas was
among his pupils. His wide learning earned
for him the name of *Doctor Universalis.*

Albigenses, a Christian sect living in Provence in the 12th cent., who took their name
from the town of Albi, and were conspicuous
in a dissolute age for their extravagant
asceticism. They were accused of holding
Manichaean (q.v.) doctrines. Pope Innocent
III preached a crusade against them, which
was conducted with extreme cruelty by
Simon de Montfort (1208–13) and resulted
in the fall of Count Raymond of Toulouse,
the ruler of Provence, thus beginning the subjection of the southern provinces of France
to the central government in Paris. There is
an interesting passage on the Albigenses in
Bridges, 'The Testament of Beauty', iii. 680
et seq.

Albinus, see *Alcuin.*

Albion, an ancient poetical name for Britain,
perhaps derived from its white (Latin, *albus*)
cliffs, visible from the coast of Gaul.

Albion's England, see *Warner.*

Alboin, see *Albovine.*

Albovine, a tragedy by D'Avenant (q.v.),
printed in 1629, the author's first play.

Albovine (Alboin), king of the Lombards,
having triumphantly entered Verona, marries
his captive, Rhodolinda, whose royal father
he has conquered and killed. In drunken
exaltation at the marriage feast he requires
Rhodolinda to drink a health from a cup
formed of her father's skull. In revenge she
determines on his death, and is assisted by
her favourite, Hermegild, to whom she
promises herself and the kingdom. For this
purpose they make use of Paradine, the king's
minion, making him believe that the king has
dishonoured his bride Valdaura. Paradine
kills Valdaura, and then the king. The truth
being revealed to him, he kills Rhodolinda
and Hermegild. The story, drawn from the
history of the Lombards by Paulus Diaconus,
is told in a novel by Bandello, translated by
Belleforest ('Histoires tragiques'). The same
subject is treated in 'The Witch' (q.v.) by
Middleton, and in Swinburne's 'Rosamund,
Queen of the Lombards'.

Albracca, in the 'Orlando Innamorato'
(q.v.), the capital of Galafron, king of Cathay,
in which Angelica is besieged by Agrican
(qq.v.).

Albumazar, an Arabian astronomer (805–85), author of astronomical works. He is the subject of a play by Tomkis (q.v.), acted in 1615 before James I at Cambridge. In this, Albumazar is a rascally wizard, who transforms the rustic Trincalo into the person of his absent master with absurd consequences. The play was subsequently (1668) revived, and Dryden wrote a prologue for it, in which he wrongly charged Ben Jonson with adopting it as the model for his 'Alchemist' (q.v.). It was again revived by Garrick.

ALCAEUS (*fl. c.* 611–580 B.C.), a celebrated lyric poet of Mitylene in Lesbos, author of hymns to the gods, and songs of war and love, of which only a few fragments survive in Athenaeus. He was the inventor of the ALCAIC metre, a stanza of four lines, as follows:

$$--\cup-- \mid -\cup\cup-\cup\underset{\smile}{} \text{ (twice)}$$
$$--\cup---\cup--$$
$$-\cup\cup-\cup\cup-\cup-\cup$$

Tennyson experimented in this metre:

O mighty-mouthed inventor of harmonies,
O skill'd to sing of Time or Eternity,
   God-gifted organ-voice of England,
      Milton, a name to resound for ages.

Alceste, see *Misanthrope*.

Alcestis, in Greek mythology, the wife of Admetus, king of Pherae. She gave her life to redeem her husband from death (see under *Apollo*), but was rescued by Hercules from the envoy of Hades—the subject of one of the plays of Euripides. See *Balaustion's Adventure*.

Alchemist, The, a comedy by Jonson (q.v.), first acted in 1610 and printed in 1612, by many considered the greatest of his plays. Love-wit, during an epidemic of the plague, leaves his house in London in charge of his servant, Face. The latter, with Subtle, the Alchemist, and Dol Common, his consort, use the house as a place for deluding and cheating gullible people, by holding out to them promise of the philosophers' stone. Among their victims are Sir Epicure Mammon, a greedy, voluptuous knight; Tribulation Wholesome, and Ananias, puritans; Dapper and Drugger, a clerk and a tobacconist; and Kastril, the quarrelsome lad who wants a good match for his sister Dame Pliant. Surly, the gamester, who sees through the fraud, attempts to expose it, by presenting himself disguised as a Spaniard; and the unexpected return of Love-wit puts Subtle and Dol to sudden flight. Face makes peace with his master by resourcefully marrying him to Dame Pliant.

Alcīdes, a name of Hercules (q.v.), who was the stepson of Amphitryon (q.v.), the son of Alcaeus (son of Perseus, q.v.).

Alcīna, in the 'Orlando Innamorato' and the 'Orlando Furioso' (qq.v.), a witch who was mistress of an enchanted garden, and changed her lovers into beasts, stones, or trees. Astolfo and Rogero were among her prisoners.

Alcinöus, the prosperous king of Phaeacia and father of Nausicaa (q.v.), who hospitably entertained Odysseus when cast upon his coast, on his return from Troy.

ALCIPHRON, a Greek writer of about A.D. 200, author of letters purporting to be by Athenians of various classes, depicting Athenian life in the 4th cent. B.C.

Alciphron, or The Minute Philosopher, a philosophical treatise in the form of dialogues by Berkeley (q.v.), composed in America, published in 1732.

There are seven dialogues, in which the interlocutors are Euphranor and Crito on the one side, and Alciphron and Lysicles, the 'minute philosophers', on the other. The 'minute philosophers' are the free-thinkers, who have rejected the ancient methods of philosophy and adopted new views of religion and morality. In the dialogues the free-thinkers are discussed as atheists, libertines, metaphysicians, etc. The setting is pleasant, and the polemic vigorous, with occasional touches of the Socratic method.

Alcmaeon, son of Amphiarāus and Erĭphȳlē. His mother, induced by the present of the fatal necklace of Harmonia (q.v.), engaged her husband, Amphiaraus, to take part in the expedition against Thebes. Amphiaraus, knowing that he would perish in it, enjoined on Alcmaeon to slay his mother. This he did, and was punished by the gods with madness, Alcmaeon's wife, Callirrhoë, also desired to possess the necklace, and his attempt to procure it for her was the cause of his own death.

ALCMAN, a Greek lyric poet of the second half of the 7th cent. B.C., born at Sardis, who came to Sparta and there composed choral lyrics for the festivals. Of these his *parthenia* (choral songs for maidens) were especially celebrated. Only fragments of his work survive, one of them a part of a parthenion.

Alcmena, see *Amphitryon*.

ALCOFRIBAS NASIER, the pseudonym under which François Rabelais (q.v.) published his 'Gargantua' (q.v.); an anagram of the author's name.

Alcor, see *Alioth*.

ALCOTT, LOUISA M. (1832–88), American author of books for girls, among which 'Little Women' (q.v., 1868) enjoyed a very wide popularity.

ALCUIN or ALBINUS (English name EALHWINE) (735–804), theologian, man of letters, and coadjutor of Charlemagne in educational reforms. He was born at York and educated in the cloister school of York under Archbishop Egbert. He met Charlemagne at Parma in 781, and settled on the Continent, becoming finally abbot of Tours. He wrote liturgical, grammatical, hagiological, and philosophical works and numerous letters and poems, including a Latin elegy on the destruction of Lindisfarne by the Danes.

Alcuin Club, THE, founded to encourage and assist in the practical study of ceremonial, and the arrangement of churches, their furniture, and ornaments, in accordance with the rubrics of the Book of Common Prayer, strict obedience to which is the guiding principle of the Club. The first publication of the Club ('English Altars', by W. H. St. John Hope), for the years 1897–8, was issued in 1899.

Alcyon, in Spenser's 'Daphnaida' and 'Colin Clout', is Sir Arthur Gorges, on whose wife's death the 'Daphnaida' is an elegy. Gorges commanded the 'Warspite', Ralegh's flagship on the Islands Voyage, 1597, and was a poet and translator. He died in 1625.

Alcyone, see *Halcyone*.

Aldebaran, the Arabic name of a star of the first magnitude in the constellation of Taurus (α Tauri).

Aldersgate, originally EALDREDESGATE, one of the old gates of London. From the old gatehouse John Day (q.v.) issued his editions of Ascham's 'The Scholemaster', Foxe's 'Book of Martyrs', and some of Tyndale's works.

Aldgate, the principal east gate of the ancient city of London. Its earlier name was ALEGATE or ALGATE, the derivation of which is doubtful. The gatehouse was at one time occupied by Chaucer.

ALDHELM, ST. (640?–709), the first titular of the bishopric of Sherborne, was educated under Theodore (q.v.) at Canterbury and was foremost in the intellectual movement led by him. He was author of a number of Latin works (including treatises in prose and verse on the merits of virginity, with illustrious examples of chaste living), which reveal a wide knowledge of classical and Christian authors. His ornate and difficult vocabulary shows the influence of Irish models. He was abbot of Malmesbury and built churches at Malmesbury, Bruton, and Wareham, and monasteries at Frome and Bradford. He is commemorated on 25 May. The best edition of his 'Opera' is that by Rudolph Ehwald for the 'Monumenta Germaniae Historica' (1913–19).

Aldiborontiphoscophornio, see *Chrononhotonthologos*.

Aldine Press, see *Aldus Manutius*.

Aldingar, SIR, the subject of a ballad included in Percy's 'Reliques', the treacherous steward of King Henry, who brings a false accusation against Queen Eleanor.

ALDINGTON, RICHARD (1892–1962), poet and novelist. He began writing early and by 1913 was literary editor of the 'Egoist', the Imagist periodical. He published several volumes of poetry, as well as critical and biographical work, but was best known for his novels: 'Death of a Hero' (1929), 'The Colonel's Daughter' (1931), and 'All Men are Enemies' (1932). 'Portrait of a Genius,

But . . .' (1950) is a biography of D. H. Lawrence which praises his writing but sometimes seems less than fair to the man. 'Lawrence of Arabia' (1955) is a bitter denigration of T. E. Lawrence and his career.

ALDRICH, THOMAS BAILEY (1836–1907), a New England author, born at Portsmouth, New Hampshire, who edited the 'Atlantic Monthly' (q.v.) from 1881 to 1890. His best-known work is 'The Story of a Bad Boy' (1870). Other prose works are 'Marjorie Daw' (1873), 'Prudence Palfrey' (1874), 'The Stillwater Tragedy' (1880). He also wrote verse, especially *vers de société*.

Aldus Manutius (1449–1515), scholar, printer, and publisher. Originally a teacher, he founded an academy at Venice for the study of Greek and Latin, and began editing and printing grammars and classical texts (many for the first time). His roman and italic type cut by Francesco da Bologna and his Greek types greatly influenced the design of printers' letters. He popularized the use of small formats for learned books.

Alectryon, a youth set by Ares to watch against the approach of the sun, during his amour with Aphrodite. But Alectryon fell asleep, and Ares and Aphrodite were discovered. Ares, in his wrath, changed Alectryon into a cock, who still heralds the dawn (Lucian, 'Alectryon').

Alessandria, the city founded by the Lombard League in the 12th cent. to defy Frederick Barbarossa, who had destroyed Milan.

Alexander, a name borne by Paris (q.v.), son of Priam, king of Troy.

ALEXANDER, SIR WILLIAM, *Earl of Stirling* (1567?–1640), a courtier, and a friend of Drummond of Hawthornden (q.v.). He was secretary of state for Scotland from 1626 till his death. His chief poetical works are a collection of sonnets called 'Aurora' (1604), a long poem on 'Doomsday' (1614) in eight-lined stanzas, a 'Paraenesis' to Prince Henry, and four tragedies on Darius, Croesus, Alexander, and Caesar, similar, but inferior, to those of Fulke Greville (q.v.), Lord Brooke.

Alexander VI, see *Borgia (Rodrigo)*.

ALEXANDER OF HALES (d. 1245), a native of Gloucestershire, studied at Paris, and taught theology there. For a short time he held various ecclesiastical appointments in England and became archdeacon of Coventry. Returning to Paris he entered the Franciscan order and continued to teach theology, the first holder of the Franciscan chair of theology in the University. He was the author of glosses on the 'Sententiae' of Peter Lombard. The 'Summa Theologiae' which goes under his name was put together by other Franciscan theologians, partly drawing on his teachings. In the later Middle Ages he was known as the *Irrefragable Doctor*.

Alexander the Great (356–323 B.C.), son of Philip II of Macedon and Olympias, born at

Pella, and educated by Aristotle, became king of Macedon in 336 B.C. He caused the Greek states to nominate him to conduct the war against Persia and in 334 crossed the Hellespont. He captured the family of Darius and extended his conquests to Egypt, where he founded Alexandria; and, after completely defeating the Persians at the battle of Arbela in 331, to India. He married Roxana, the captive daughter of Oxyartes, a Bactrian prince, and a second wife, Barsine, daughter of Darius and Statira. He is said to have destroyed Persepolis, the capital of the Persian empire, at the instance of the courtesan Thais (331). He died of fever at Babylon in 323 when only 32 years old. His horse was named Bucephalus. See also *Clitus, Diogenes, Parmenio, Perdiccas*.

Alexander was made the centre of a cluster of medieval legends, comparable to those of the Carlovingian and Arthurian cycles. The chief of the romances concerning him are the great French 'Roman d'Alexandre' of the 12th cent., some 20,000 alexandrines, and the English 'King Alisaunder' of the 13th cent., 8,000 octosyllabic verses. The story of the rivalry of his two wives forms the subject of Nathaniel Lee's tragedy, 'The Rival Queens' (q.v.).

Alexander and Campaspe, see *Campaspe*.

Alexander and Lodowick, 'the Two Faithful Friends, who were so like one another that none could know them asunder; wherein is declared how Lodowick married the Princess of Hungaria in Alexander's name and each night laid a naked sword between him and the princess, because he would not wrong his friend', an old ballad in Evans's collection. There was also a play written by Martin Slaughter, called 'Alexander and Lodowick' (Dyce). The story is referred to in Webster, 'The Duchess of Malfi', I. ii.

Alexander's Feast, see *Dryden*.

Alexandria, the capital of Egypt under the Ptolemies, was founded by order of Alexander the Great in 331 B.C.

Alexandrian Library, THE, was formed at Alexandria during the reign of the Ptolemies (beginning with Ptolemy Soter, 323–283 B.C.). It is said to have contained at one time about 400,000 manuscripts, of which a part were accidentally burnt when Julius Caesar was besieged in Alexandria. The story that the library was destroyed by order of the Caliph Omar is without foundation.

Alexandrine, an iambic line of six feet, which is the French heroic verse, and in English is used, e.g., as the last line of the Spenserian stanza, or as a variant in a poem of heroic couplets. The name is derived from the fact that certain 12th- and 13th-cent. French poems on Alexander the Great were written in this metre.

Alfheim, in Scandinavian mythology, the home of the Elves (*Alfar*), and of the god Frey or Freyr (q.v.).

ALFIERI, VITTORIO (1749–1803), Italian dramatist, born in Piedmont. He was the devoted lover of the countess of Albany, wife of the Young Pretender. Between 1777 and 1789 he wrote nineteen tragedies, remarkable for their severe conciseness and austerity of form. Most of them derive their subjects from classical history or legend (e.g. 'Antigone', 'Virginia'), but some draw on modern history (e.g. 'Maria Stuarda'), whilst Alfieri's finest creation is the protagonist of his biblical tragedy 'Saul'. The clash of opposing wills and passions in the tragedies gives them a certain affinity with the works of the German 'Stürmer und Dränger'. Alfieri's autobiography is the earliest example of romantic self-portraiture in Italian.

ALFRED (ÆLFRED) (849–901), king of the West Saxons (871–901), is important in the history of literature for the revival of letters that he effected in the west of England. He first translated into English the 'Cura Pastoralis' of Pope Gregory, with a view to the spiritual education of the clergy. A copy was sent to each bishop. The preface to this translation refers to the decay of learning in Wessex and indicates Alfred's intention of restoring it. He then translated the 'Historia adversus Paganos' of Orosius (q.v.), inserting the latest geographical information at his disposal, notably accounts of the celebrated voyages of Ohthere to the White Sea and of Wulfstan in the Baltic, which he received direct from the explorers. He had a translation made of Bede's 'Historia Ecclesiastica' (q.v.), with some omissions, but giving a West-Saxon version of the hymn of Cædmon (q.v.). He also translated the 'De Consolatione Philosophiae' of Boethius (q.v.), with some original additions. The West-Saxon version of Augustine's 'Soliloquia' is also probably the work of Alfred. He composed a code of laws, drawing on the Mosaic and earlier English codes. The 'Anglo-Saxon Chronicle' (q.v.) may represent in part his work or inspiration.

Alfred, a masque, containing 'Rule, Britannia', see *Thomson (J., 1700–48)*.

Alfred, *Proverbs of*, see *Proverbs of Alfred*.

Alftruda, a character in C. Kingsley's 'Hereward the Wake' (q.v.).

Algarsife, one of the two sons of King Cambuscan, in Chaucer's 'Squire's Tale' (see *Canterbury Tales*).

Algrind, in Spenser's 'Shepheards Calender' (q.v.), Edmund Grindal, archbishop of Canterbury, 1576–83.

Alhambra, THE, from the Arabic *al-hamrā*, 'the red house', the palace of the Moorish kings at Granada, built in the 13th cent. 'The Alhambra' is the name of a work by Washington Irving (q.v.).

Ali, the first cousin and son-in-law of Mohammed (q.v.). He was the fourth Caliph; but the Shia (q.v.) sect consider him the first, regarding his three predecessors as interlopers. His descendants, the ALIDS, include Ali's sons Hasan and Hoseyn, the Fatimid dynasty of Egypt, the sherifs of Morocco, and other rulers of parts of the Muslim world. Ali was assassinated A.D. 660.

Ali Baba and the Forty Thieves, an oriental tale generally regarded as one of the 'Arabian Nights' (q.v.), but not included in any MS. of these. The source from which Galland drew it is unknown.

Ali Baba and Kassim were two brothers in a town of Persia. Ali Baba one day, while collecting wood in the forest, observed forty robbers getting access to a cave by pronouncing the words, 'Open, Sesame!', whereupon a door in the rock opened. Using the same password he presently entered the cave, found it full of the robbers' treasure, and brought home some sacks full of gold. He was soon compelled to reveal his discovery to Kassim, who in turn went to the cave, but forgot the password after entering it, and was unable to get out. He was discovered in the cave by the robbers, cut in quarters, and hung up in the cave. Ali Baba, coming to seek him, conveyed the body home, and in order to simulate a natural death, sent for an old cobbler to sew the quarters of the body together. Through this cobbler the thieves, determined to destroy the person who still knew their secret, eventually traced the house of Ali Baba, though at first their purpose was defeated by the ingenuity of Morgiana, Ali Baba's servant, who placed chalk-marks on the neighbouring doors similar to that by which the thieves had sought to recognize her master's. At last the captain of the thieves brought his men concealed in leather oil-jars to the house of Ali Baba, intending to kill him in the night, but was again defeated by Morgiana, who destroyed them with boiling oil, and finally killed the captain himself.

Alice, or The Mysteries, see *Ernest Maltravers.*

Alice Brand, a ballad in the 4th canto of Scott's 'Lady of the Lake' (q.v.), telling how Urgan, 'a christened man', who has been carried off by the Elfin king and changed into a dwarf, is re-transformed into 'the fairest knight' by Alice Brand and is found to be her lost brother.

Alice's Adventures in Wonderland, a story for children by Lewis Carroll (see *Dodgson*), published in 1865.

Alice is a little girl who dreams that she pursues a White Rabbit down a rabbit-hole, and there meets with strange adventures and odd characters, the Duchess and the Cheshire Cat, the Mad Hatter and the March Hare, the King and Queen of Hearts, and the Mock Turtle. See also *Through the Looking-Glass.*

Alids, see *Ali.*

Alifanfaron, in medieval romance, the pagan emperor of Taprobane (q.v.), in love with the daughter of Pentapolin, the Christian king of the Garamantes. Don Quixote (q.v.) takes two flocks of sheep for their opposing armies, and attacks what he supposes to be the forces of Alifanfaron.

Alioth and Alcor, two stars in the constellation of the Great Bear.

Alisaunder, King, the legendary story of Alexander the Great, a verse romance of the early 14th cent., some 8,000 lines in octosyllabic couplets. According to the legend, Nectanabus, king of Egypt, had tricked Olympias, wife of Philip of Macedon, by magic and begotten Alexander. The poem deals with the birth and youth of Alexander, his succession to Philip's throne, the conquest of Carthage and other cities, and his wars with Darius. The latter part of the poem relates Alexander's perils and conquests in the Far East (describing the geography and wonders of those regions), his seduction by Candace, and his death by poison.

ALISON, SIR ARCHIBALD (1792–1867), educated at Edinburgh University, and called to the Scottish bar, was a frequent contributor to 'Blackwood's Magazine', and the author of a 'History of Europe during the French Revolution' (1833–42), and its sequel, 'Europe from the Fall of the First to the Accession of the Third Napoleon' (1852–9). He also wrote a 'History of Scottish Criminal Law' (1832–3) and an 'Autobiography' (edited by his daughter in 1883).

Alison Wilson, in Scott's 'Old Mortality' (q.v.), the housekeeper of Silas Morton of Milnwood.

Alken, HENRY THOMAS (1785–1851), draughtsman of sporting prints and illustrator of books by C. J. Apperley ('Nimrod') and Surtees.

All Fools, a comedy by George Chapman (q.v.), first published in 1605, but probably produced in 1599. The plot is adapted from the *Heautontimorumenos,* and some of the characters from the *Adelphi,* of Terence. It deals with the fooling of Gostanzo, a dictatorial and conceited father, who is made instrumental in promoting the love-affairs of his son and daughter.

All Fools' Day, see *April Fool's Day.*

All for Love, or The World well lost, an historical tragedy by Dryden (q.v.), published in 1678.

In this, his finest play, Dryden abandoned the use of the rhymed couplet, and adopted blank verse. The plot deals with the story of Antony and Cleopatra, but, as compared with Shakespeare's treatment of it, Dryden gains simplicity and concentration by confining his play to the last phase of Antony's career, when he is besieged in Alexandria, and to the struggle between Ventidius his general, Dolabella his friend, and Octavia his wife, on the one hand, and Cleopatra on the other, for the soul of Antony. The former are on the point of success, and a composition is to be made with Caesar (Octavianus, afterwards Augustus) involving the separation of Antony from Cleopatra, when Antony falls into jealous suspicion that Dolabella will supplant him in Cleopatra's affections. Meanwhile the forces of Caesar are pressing him hard. The defection of the Egyptian fleet seems the final blow. On a false report that Cleopatra has taken her life, Antony falls on his sword. Cleopatra finds him dying, and applies the asp to her arm.

All for Love, or A Sinner well saved, a poem by Southey (q.v.) published in 1829. The story is taken from a life of St. Basil, and tells how a freedman, Eleëmon, makes a compact with Satan to forgo his hope of heaven if he may have his master's daughter, the high-born Cyra, for his wife. They live happily married for twelve years, after which the compact is revealed by the ghost of Cyra's father. Eleëmon in agony of spirit flies to St. Basil, who imposes a penance on him. When Satan claims the fulfilment of his compact, Basil meets him in argument and proves the bond invalid.

All-Hallows' Day, All Saints' Day, 1 Nov. ALL-HALLOW EVE, or *Hallow-e'en*, 31 Oct., was in the old Celtic calendar the last night of the old year, the night of all the witches, the new year beginning on 1 Nov. Many superstitious and ancient customs, such as bobbing for apples, attached to it. See Burns's 'Halloween' for Scottish customs. Mary Avenel, in Scott's 'The Monastery' (q.v.), being born on All-Hallow Eve, is supposed to be gifted with second sight.

All Saints' Day, 1 Nov., the festival on which there is a general celebration of the saints, instituted early in the 7th cent., when Pope Boniface IV transformed the heathen Pantheon at Rome into a church dedicated to the Christian martyrs.

All Souls College, Oxford, was founded by Henry VI in 1438, with Archbishop Chichele (1362?–1443), by whom the college was endowed, as co-founder, to pray for the souls of all the faithful and especially of those who fell in the wars against France. It is a unique foundation, consisting of a Warden and Fellows (originally 40), and no undergraduates.

All Souls' Day, 2 Nov., the festival on which prayers are offered for the souls of all the faithful deceased. It is said to have been instituted at Cluny at the end of the 10th cent.

All the Talents Administration, formed after the death of Pitt, in 1806, by William, Lord Grenville, Pitt's cousin. It was said to contain 'all the talents, wisdom, and ability of the country', and the term was used derisively by its opponents.

All the Year Round, see *Dickens*.

All's Lost by Lust, a tragedy by W. Rowley (q.v.), printed in 1633.

This was Rowley's principal play. According to the argument prefixed to it, Roderigo, king of Spain, deeply enamoured of Jacynta, daughter of Juliano his principal general, and urged on by Lothario, a gentleman of better fortunes than condition, sends Juliano to fight against Mulymamen, king of Barbary, and in his absence ravishes Jacynta. She escapes to her father, and he to avenge her induces Mulymamen to join him in ousting Roderigo from his kingdom. This they do, and Mulymamen now demands the hand of Jacynta, but she scorns him. The infuriated barbarian and Juliano fight with one another. Mulymamen snatches Jacynta before him as Juliano rushes to the attack, so that the father slays his own daughter and is presently himself slain by the Moor. Cf. Landor's 'Count Julian' and Southey's 'Roderick' (qq.v.).

All's Well that Ends Well, a comedy by Shakespeare (q.v.), composed at an uncertain date, placed by some as early as about 1595, by others as late as about 1604 (E. K. Chambers, 1602–3), first printed in the folio of 1623.

The plot is drawn from Painter's 'Palace of Pleasure' (No. xxxviii). Bertram, the young count of Rousillon, on the death of his father is summoned to the court of the king of France, leaving his mother and with her Helena, daughter of the famous physician Gerard de Narbon. The king is sick of a disease said to be incurable. Helena, who loves Bertram, goes to Paris and effects his cure by means of a prescription left by her father. As a reward she is allowed to choose her husband, and names Bertram, who unwillingly obeys the king's order to wed her. But under the influence of the worthless braggart Parolles, he at once takes service with the duke of Florence, writing to Helena that until she can get the ring from his finger 'which never shall come off', and is with child by him, she may not call him husband. Helena, passing through Florence on a pilgrimage, finds Bertram courting Diana, the daughter of her hostess there. Disclosing herself as his wife to these, she obtains permission to replace Diana at a midnight interview with Bertram, having that day caused him to be informed that Helena is dead. Thereby she obtains from Bertram his ring, and gives him one that the king had given her. Bertram returns to his mother's house, where the king is on a visit. The latter sees on Bertram's finger the ring he had given Helena, suspects Bertram of having destroyed her, and demands an explanation on pain of death. Helena herself now appears, explains what has passed, and claims that the conditions named in Bertram's letter have been fulfilled. Bertram, filled with remorse, accepts her as his wife.

Allan-a-Dale, one of the companions of Robin Hood (q.v.), and the subject of a song in the 4th canto of Scott's 'Rokeby' (q.v.).

Allecto, one of the Furies (q.v.).

Allegory, a figurative narrative or description, conveying a veiled moral meaning; an extended metaphor.

Allegra, daughter of Byron and Claire Clairmont, Mary Shelley's step-sister.

Allegro, L', a poem by Milton (q.v.), written in 1632. The Italian title means 'the cheerful man', and this idyll is an invocation to the goddess Mirth to allow the poet to live with her, first amid the delights of rustic scenes, then amid those of 'towered cities' and the 'busy hum of men'. Cf. *Penseroso (Il)*.

Allen, BENJAMIN and ARABELLA, characters in Dickens's 'The Pickwick Papers' (q.v.).

Allen, ETHAN (1738–89), a famous soldier in the American Revolution, who was born in Connecticut, but who removed to New Hampshire in 1769. His name is inseparably associated with the 'Green Mountain Boys' (q.v.), whose leader he was. At the outbreak of the Revolution he captured Ticonderoga with a small force, demanding the surrender of the British garrison, it is said, 'in the name of the great Jehovah and the Continental Congress', words which have become historic (though perhaps never spoken).

Allen, RALPH (1694–1764), of Prior Park, Bath, the correspondent of Pope, and benefactor of Fielding. He was deputy postmaster at Bath, and devised and managed a system of cross-posts for England and Wales by which he amassed a large fortune. He gave large sums in charity and was one of the models from whom Fielding drew Squire Allworthy in 'Tom Jones' (q.v.).

> Let humble Allen, with an awkward shame,
> Do good by stealth, and blush to find it fame.

(Pope, Epilogue to 'Satires', Dial. i. 135–6.)

Alleyn, CHIEF DETECTIVE INSPECTOR, the hero of Ngaio Marsh's detective stories.

Alleyn, EDWARD (1566–1626), an actor (Richard Burbage's chief rival) and partner of Philip Henslowe, with whom he built the Fortune Theatre, Cripplegate. There he acted at the head of the Lord Admiral's company, playing among other parts the hero in Marlowe's 'Tamburlaine', 'Jew of Malta', and 'Faustus'. He acquired great wealth, bought the Manor of Dulwich, and built and endowed Dulwich College. His first wife was Henslowe's stepdaughter, his second the daughter of Dr. Donne. He was a patron of Dekker, John Taylor, and other writers.

Alliteration, the commencement of two or more words in close connexion with the same letter or the same sound. Alliteration was the basis of versification in OE. and other Germanic poetry, and among moderns is conspicuous in that of Swinburne.

Allworth, TOM and LADY, characters in Massinger's 'A New Way to pay Old Debts' (q.v.).

Allworthy, SQUIRE and BRIDGET, characters in Fielding's 'Tom Jones' (q.v.). The character of Squire Allworthy was drawn from Fielding's benefactors Ralph Allen and Lord Lyttelton (qq.v.).

Alma, a river in the Crimea, scene of the first battle in the Crimean War, 1854, in which the allies under Lord Raglan and Marshal St. Arnaud defeated the Russians under Prince Menschikoff.

Alma (in Italian meaning 'soul', 'spirit'), in Spenser's 'Faerie Queene', II. ix and xi, represents the virgin soul. She is the Lady of the House of Temperance, where she is visited by Prince Arthur and Sir Guyon, and defended against her enemies by the former.

Alma, the title of a poem by Matthew Prior (q.v.).

Alma Mater, 'bounteous mother', a title given by the Romans to several goddesses, especially to Ceres and Cybele, and applied in England to universities and schools in respect of their relation to their pupils.

Almack's Assembly Rooms stood in King Street, St. James's, and were celebrated in the 18th and early 19th cents. as the scene of social functions. They were founded by one William Almack (*d.* 1781), who appears to have come to London as valet to the duke of Hamilton. Almack's was replaced as a social centre after 1863 by Willis's Rooms, and these were afterwards applied to other purposes. Almack was also founder of a gaming club, since converted into Brooks's (q.v.).

Almagest (from Arabic article *al* and Greek μεγίστη, greatest), the name applied to the great astronomical treatise of Ptolemy (see *Ptolemy, Claudius*).

Almanach de Gotha, see *Gotha*.

Almansur, 'the victorious', a title assumed by many Muslim princes, notably by the Amir Mohammed of Cordova (939–1002), an enlightened ruler, who became king of Andalusia in 996 and greatly extended the Muslim power in Spain and Africa.

Almanzor and Almahide, see *Conquest of Granada*.

Almayer's Folly, a novel by Joseph Conrad (q.v.), published in 1895.

Almeria, the heroine of Congreve's 'The Mourning Bride' (q.v.).

Almesbury, in the Arthurian legend, is the modern Amesbury in Wiltshire.

Alnaschar, in the 'Arabian Nights' (q.v., 'The Barber's Fifth Brother'), a beggar who inherited a hundred pieces of silver, invested them in a basket of glassware, and then indulged in visions of the riches and grandeur that would come from successive trading ventures. These culminated in the dream that he had married the daughter of the chief Vizier, and haughtily spurned her with his foot, 'Thus!'—whereupon he kicked the basket, and scattered all his wares.

Alonzo the Brave and the Fair Imogine, a ballad by M. G. Lewis (q.v.).

Aloysius, ST., see *Eloi.*

Alph, in Coleridge's 'Kubla Khan' (q.v.), the sacred river in Xanadu. For its connexion with the river Alpheus and with the Nile, see J. L. Lowes, 'The Road to Xanadu' (1927).

Alpha and Omĕga, the first and last letters of the Greek alphabet, 'the beginning and the end', originally said of the Divine Being (Rev. i. 8).

Alphēus, one of the largest rivers in Greece, rising in Arcadia and flowing through Elis. Milton refers to it in 'Lycidas': 'Return, Alpheus; the dread voice is past that shrunk thy streams.' See also *Arethusa.*

Alphonsine Tables, astronomical tables by Arab and Spanish astronomers, collected under the direction of Alphonso X of Castile, in 1253. Also called TOLETAN TABLES, from the fact that they were adapted to the city of Toledo. They are referred to under the latter name by Chaucer, 'Franklin's Tale', 545.

Alsatia, a cant name given to the precinct of Whitefriars in London, which, until its privileges were abolished in 1697, was a sanctuary for debtors and lawbreakers. These privileges, which were confirmed by James I in a charter of 1608, had their origin in the exemption from the ordinary jurisdiction enjoyed by the establishment of Carmelite friars that originally occupied the precinct. See Shadwell, 'The Squire of Alsatia', and Scott, 'The Fortunes of Nigel', where the turbulent society of Alsatia is described. The name is taken from Alsace, the 'debatable land' between France and Germany.

Altamont, a character in Rowe's 'The Fair Penitent' (q.v.).

Altamont, FREDERICK, in Thackeray's 'Memoirs of Mr. C. J. Yellowplush' (q.v.), a handsome young gentleman who keeps a tilbury and disappears during the day on some business in the City, which turns out to be sweeping a crossing.

Altamont, COLONEL JACK, *alias* AMORY, *alias* ARMSTRONG, a character in Thackeray's 'Pendennis' (q.v.).

Althaea, in Greek mythology, see *Meleager.*

Althea, To, a poem by R. Lovelace (q.v.).

Altisidora, in 'Don Quixote' (q.v.), the duchess's wanton damsel, who made love to the don, and then accused him of stealing her garters. She finally admitted that she was like the man who searched for the mule on which he was riding.

Alton Locke, Tailor and Poet, a novel by C. Kingsley (q.v.), published in 1850.

The hero, the son of a small London tradesman, educated by a puritanical widowed mother, is brought into contact with the misery of the working classes by being apprenticed to a sweating tailor, and becomes imbued with Chartist ideas. His poetical gift leads to his being befriended first by a humorous old Scotch bookseller, Saunders Mackaye, and then by a benevolent dean, his beautiful daughter Lillian (with whom he falls hopelessly in love), and her cousin Eleanor Staunton. Under their influence he momentarily consents to the emasculation of his revolutionary poems before publication, a weakness that he bitterly regrets. Roused by the taunts of his Chartist comrades, he undertakes a mission that involves him in a riot, and is sentenced to three years' imprisonment. On emerging from this he learns that Lillian is engaged to his prosperous time-serving cousin, falls ill of typhus, is nursed by Eleanor and brought by her to a saner understanding of the grievances of the poor and of the teaching of Christianity. He emigrates to America and dies on the voyage.

Altruria, a Utopian land created by William Dean Howells (q.v.) in 'A Traveller from Altruria', published in 1894.

Amadis of Gaul (*Amadis de Gaula*), a Spanish or Portuguese romance, written in the form in which we have it by Garcia de Montalvo in the second half of the 15th and printed early in the 16th cents., but taken from 'ancient originals', now lost, perhaps by Joham de Lobeira (1261–1325), or by Vasco de Lobeira (*d.* 1403), the materials of the story being of French source. Many continuations were written relating to the son and nephew of Amadis, Esplandian and Florisando.

Perion, king of Gaul (Wales?), falls in love with Elisena, daughter of Garinter, king of Lesser Britain; their child Amadis is placed in an ark on the river, and until his identity is revealed, is known as the 'Child of the Sea'. He becomes the flower of chivalry and achieves wonderful feats of arms. He loves Oriana, daughter of Lisuarte, king of Great Britain, who is sought in marriage by the emperor of Rome and granted to him by her father, but rescued by Amadis. Whence arises a great conflict. The emperor arrives with his fleet, but is defeated and killed. Amadis then comes to the succour of Lisuarte, reconciliation follows, and all ends happily.

The romance was translated into French by Herberay des Essarts in 1540, and an abridged version of it was published (1803) by R. Southey (q.v.). 'Amadis of Gaul' and 'Palmerin of England' were two of the works specially excepted from the holocaust of romances of chivalry carried out by the curate and the barber in 'Don Quixote' (q.v.).

Amadis of Greece, a Spanish continuation of the seventh book of 'Amadis of Gaul' (q.v.), of which Lisuarte of Greece, the grandson of Amadis, is the hero. The work is probably by Feliciano de Silva (16th cent.).

Amaimon, a devil of medieval demonology.

Amalthēa, the nymph who nursed the infant Zeus (q.v.) in Crete. According to the legend, she fed him with the milk of a goat. It was a horn of this goat that Zeus endowed with the power of producing whatever the possessor wished, and gave to Amalthea and her sisters. This horn of Amalthea was the 'horn of plenty' or cornucopia, the symbol of abundance. It is also called the 'Ammonian Horn', from the identification of Zeus with Ammon. In another version Amalthea was the name of the goat.

Amara, MT., a place in Abyssinia, where the kings of that country secluded their sons, to protect themselves from sedition (Milton, 'Paradise Lost', iv. 28). It figures as 'Amhara' in Johnson's 'Rasselas' (q.v.).

Amarant, a giant slain by Sir Guy of Warwick on his way to the Holy Land, the subject of a ballad in Percy's 'Reliques', which is part of a longer poem by Samuel Rowlands (1649).

Amaryllis, the name given to a shepherdess by Theocritus, Virgil, and Ovid. Spenser, in his 'Colin Clouts come home againe', uses the name to signify Alice, one of the daughters of Sir John Spencer of Althorpe. She became the countess of Derby for whom Milton wrote his 'Arcades' (q.v.).

Amāsis, see *Polycrates*.

Amaurote, the capital of Sir Thomas More's 'Utopia' (q.v.). Rabelais (II. xxiii) uses the name 'Amaurotes' for an imaginary people invaded by the Dipsodes.

Amazing Marriage, *The*, a novel by G. Meredith (q.v.), published in 1895.

Carinthia Jane and her brother Chillon are children of old Captain John Peter Kirby, the 'Old Buccaneer', who carried off the countess of Cresset under her husband's nose, and married her when the earl conveniently died a fortnight later. On the old buccaneer's death they are left not far from destitute, and at the mercy of a miserly old uncle, Lord Levellier. Carinthia is a fine elemental creature, a 'beautiful Gorgon', brought up in the wilds of the Austrian mountains. Lord Fleetwood, spoilt by his immense wealth and parasitical companions, tyrannical and impulsive, proposes to her in the course of a quadrille the first day he sees her, and is accepted by the artless girl. He soon repents of his mad freak, and trusts that the girl has done the same. But he is held to his engagement by Lord Levellier, anxious to be rid of the charge of his niece. Fleetwood, priding himself on being a man of his word, consents to marry her, meets her at the church door, drives her straight to a prize-fight, which he forces her to witness, leaves her indefinitely at an inn, and goes on with his ordinary avocations, refusing to see her and treating her with every circumstance of insult, in order to punish her for forcing his hand. The birth of her child only increases his resentment. Circumstances have brought her for refuge to the home in Whitechapel of the Woodseers, the father a minister among the poor, the son

Gower Woodseer (drawn perhaps from R. L. Stevenson), a penniless philosopher, with flashes of wit and a 'broad playfulness'. While walking in the Alps he has met Carinthia and Fleetwood, has become the devoted admirer of the first and friend of the second, and now strives to bring about a change of heart in Fleetwood. This comes at last, with the discovery of what a treasure he has lost. For Carinthia's heart has changed likewise, and when Fleetwood belatedly does penance and comes to woo his wife, he finds that she is no longer to be won. She accompanies her brother, as an army nurse, to an insurrectionary war in Spain, leaving Fleetwood to turn Roman Catholic monk and die of his austerities.

Amazon, RIVER, see *Orellana*.

Amazons, a race of female warriors alleged by Herodotus to exist in Scythia. They figure also in mythology in the legends of Troy (see *Thersites*), Hercules, Theseus (qq.v.), etc.

The word is explained by the Greeks from ἀ privative and μαζός a breast (in connexion with the fable that they destroyed the right breast so as not to interfere with the use of the bow), but this is probably the popular etymology of an unknown foreign word. [OED.]

Ambassadors, *The*, a novel by H. James (q.v.), published in 1903.

This is one of the novels in which, with much humour and delicacy of perception, the author depicts the reaction of different American types to the European environment. Chadwick Newsome, a young man of independent fortune, the son of Mrs. Newsome of Woollett, Mass., a widow of overpowering virtue and perfection, has been living in Paris and is reported to have got entangled with a wicked woman. Mrs. Newsome has decided to send out an ambassador to rescue Chad and bring him home. This ambassador is the elderly, amiable, guileless Strether, dependent on Mrs. Newsome, for whom he entertains prodigious respect and to whom he has allowed himself to become engaged. The story describes Strether's evolution in the congenial atmosphere of Paris, his desertion to the side of Chad and the bewitching comtesse de Vionnet (he is convinced that the relation between them is virtuous), and his own mild flirtation with the pleasant cosmopolitan Maria Gostrey. Meanwhile his attitude and the disquieting report of Waymarsh, Strether's stolid and conscientious American friend, have caused dismay at Woollett, and Mrs. Newsome sends out a fresh ambassador in the person of her daughter, the coldly glittering Sarah Pocock. The attempts to bamboozle Sarah utterly fail, and she presents her ultimatum—immediate return to America—to the delinquents Chad and Strether. Chad, exhorted by Strether, refuses to abandon the lady; and poor Mr. Strether is accordingly notified that all is over between him and Mrs. Newsome. Then, and then only, an accident throws Strether unexpectedly into the company of Chad and Mme de Vionnet in circumstances which leave no doubt as to the nature of their real relations. Sadly disillusioned, but still insisting on the necessity of Chad's loyalty to Mme de Vionnet, Strether from a sense of duty turns his back on Paris.

Amber Witch, *Mary Schweidler, The,* a novel by Meinhold (q.v.), published in 1843 and translated from the German by Lady Duff Gordon.

It is a story, remarkable for its simplicity and realism, told by a pastor of the island of Usedom, in the time of the Thirty Years War, of the fearful sufferings of the people, and of their belief in witchcraft. Mary Schweidler, the amiable daughter of the pastor, has the misfortune to attract the attention of the unscrupulous sheriff of the district, who, unable to obtain possession of her otherwise, causes her to be suspected of witchcraft, arrested, and subjected to a cruel trial, without being able to bend her to his will. At last, on the way to the stake, the girl is rescued by a sensible young nobleman who disbelieves in witchcraft, the sheriff meets a fearful death, and all ends well.

Ambree, MARY, a legendary English heroine, supposed to have taken part in the siege of Ghent in 1584, when that town was held by the Spaniards. A ballad about her is included in Percy's 'Reliques', and she is referred to by Ben Jonson ('Epicœne', IV. ii, 'Tale of a Tub', I. iv, and 'Fortunate Isles') and other Elizabethan dramatists.

Ambrose, FATHER, in Scott's 'The Abbot' (q.v.), Edward Glendinning, abbot of Kennaquhair.

AMBROSE, ST. (*c.* 340–97), born at Trèves, was a celebrated bishop of Milan (elected against his will by the people when still a catechumen), one of the Fathers of the Church, and a vigorous opponent of the Arians. He developed the use of music in the services of the church, restoring its ancient melodies and founding what is known as the Ambrosian chant (as opposed to the Gregorian chant introduced two centuries later by Pope Gregory the Great). He composed several hymns, including, according to one tradition, the 'Te Deum' (q.v.).

Ambrose Lamela, see *Don Raphael.*

Ambrose's Tavern, the supposed scene of the 'Noctes Ambrosianae' (q.v.). 'The Street or Lane in which Ambrose's Tavern is situated derives its name of Gabriel's Road from a horrible murder which was committed there' (Lockhart, 'Peter's Letters to his Kinsfolk', 1819, vol. ii, p. 197). 'This locality, which still bears the name by which it was so bloodily baptised, is situated in the vicinity of West Register Street, at the back of the east end of Princes Street, and close to the Register Office.... But a too literal interpretation is not to be given to the scene of these festivities. Ambrose's Hotel was indeed "a local habitation and a name", and many were the meetings which Professor Wilson and his friends had within its walls. But the *true* Ambrose must be looked for only in the realms of the imagination—the veritable scene of the "Ambrosian Nights" existed nowhere but in their author's brain, and their flashing fire was struck out in solitude by genius independent of the stimulus of companionship' (Preface to Professor Ferrier's edition of John Wilson's 'Works').

Ambrosian Library, THE, at Milan, founded in 1609, was originally the private library of Cardinal Borromeo (1564–1631), archbishop of Milan, and was bequeathed by him to public uses. It was named after St. Ambrose, bishop of Milan.

Ambrosio, the hero of M. G. Lewis's 'The Monk' (q.v.).

Amelia, the heroine of the episode of Celadon and Amelia in the book on 'Summer' of Thomson's 'The Seasons' (q.v.).

Amelia, a novel by H. Fielding (q.v.), published in 1751.

This is the last of Fielding's novels and the story is less successfully told than that of 'Tom Jones'. A good deal of the book is devoted to exposing various social evils of the time, such as the defects in the law of debt, and the scandals of the sponging-houses and prisons. William Booth, a penniless young officer, with little to recommend him beyond a good person and physical courage, has run away with the virtuous Amelia, against her mother's wishes. The poverty of the couple, Booth's folly and weakness of character, and the beauty of his wife, involve the couple in the series of misfortunes with which the story is occupied. Booth himself succumbs to the charms of Miss Matthews, whom he meets in prison, but his infidelity, when it subsequently comes to the knowledge of Amelia, is generously forgiven. Amelia becomes the object of the illicit pursuits of various unscrupulous admirers. The couple are reduced to the utmost misery, and the long-suffering devotion of Amelia is prolonged, until the situation is saved by the discovery that the will by which her sister inherited her mother's property is forged and Amelia is the true heiress. Among the pleasant features of the book are some of the minor characters, the faithful Sergeant Atkinson; the benevolent Dr. Harrison, a sort of second Squire Allworthy; the pair of Colonels, James the unprincipled, and Bath, whose bravery is only equalled by his punctiliousness; and the admirably drawn women, Mrs. Atkinson and Miss Matthews.

American, The, a novel by H. James (q.v.), published in 1877.

American Democrat, *The, or Hints on the Social and Civic Relations of the United States of America,* by J. F. Cooper (q.v.), published in 1838. In this vigorous work Cooper examined and set forth, to the offence of his countrymen, the defects and dangers of democracy as it flourished in America.

American Fabius, THE, a name bestowed on George Washington because his tactics resembled those of Fabius Maximus (q.v.).

American Taxation, On, a speech by E. Burke (q.v.), made in 1774 on a motion for the repeal of the American Tea Duty.

After dealing with the narrower arguments regarding the expediency of the proposal, Burke turns to a broad historical view of the subject, going back to the Navigation Act and explaining the course of British policy. He shows that the Tea Duty is at variance with the declarations of ministers and an 'exhaustless source of jealousy and animosity' without practical benefit. He exhorts the Government to abandon it. 'Do not burden the Americans with taxes. You were not used to do so from the beginning. Let this be your reason for not taxing. These are the arguments of states and kingdoms. Leave the rest to the schools.'

Amerigo Vespucci (1451–1512), a Florentine merchant who settled at Seville and sailed in 1499 in an expedition to the West under Ojeda, and again in 1501 in the service of the king of Portugal. In the summary account of his travels addressed in 1504 to Duke René of Lorraine, which appeared in a book published in 1507 at St. Diez in Lorraine, he claimed to have made a voyage in 1497 in which he discovered 'Terra Firma', the mainland of S. America. His name was given to the continent of America in virtue of this claim, which is not substantiated by evidence. The matter is discussed at length in an appendix to Washington Irving's 'Life of Columbus'.

Amhara, see *Amara.*

Amharic, the principal language spoken in Abyssinia. It is partly Semitic, partly Hamitic, in origin.

Amiatinus Codex, the best extant MS. of the Vulgate, so called from the abbey of Monte Amiata, to which it was presented. It was discovered in the 19th cent. to have been written in England, early in the 8th cent., at Wearmouth or Jarrow. It was probably copied from an Italian original. It is now in the Laurentian Library at Florence.

Amidas, in Spenser's 'Faerie Queene', v. iv, the brother of Bracidas. Their dispute over their inheritance is solved by Sir Artegall.

AMIEL, HENRI-FRÉDÉRIC (1821–81), Swiss author. His remarkable diary was published first in part in 1883 ('Fragments d'un journal intime', 2 vols.) and translated by Mrs. Humphry Ward in 1885. It has since been re-edited and augmented.

Amiens, THE TREATY OF, concluded in 1802 between the British and French governments. Great Britain abandoned her recent conquests with the exception of Ceylon and Trinidad, while France retained her conquests in Europe. War was renewed in 1803. It was by this treaty that the royal title of France, borne by English kings since · Edward III, was dropped.

Amintor, the hero of Beaumont and Fletcher's 'The Maid's Tragedy' (q.v.).

Amis and Amiloun, a metrical romance of the Middle English period, in which the virtue of friendship is exalted. It is adapted from the French 13th-cent. romance, 'Li amitiez di Ami et Amile'.

Amis and Amiloun, two noble foster-brothers, are bound in close friendship. Amiloun takes the place of Amis in a trial by combat, for which piece of guileful devotion he is punished with leprosy. Amis, discovering his friend in this grievous plight, at the bidding of Raphael sacrifices his own children in order to cure the leprosy. But the gods do not allow the sacrifice to be realized. Amis and his wife Belisante go to see the dead bodies of their children and find them only sleeping. This noble and pathetic tale finds a place in one of Pater's 'Studies in the History of the Renaissance', and has been told in prose by W. Morris; both use the form 'Amis and Amile'.

Amlet, MRS. and DICK, characters in Vanbrugh's 'The Confederacy' (q.v.).

Ammon, or more correctly AMON or AMUN, the supreme god of the Egyptians in the Theban religion. His worship spread to Greece, where he was identified with Zeus, and to Rome, where he was known as Jupiter Ammon. His oracle in Africa became famous after Alexander the Great had visited it.

Ammonian Horn, see *Amalthea.*

Amon, see *Ammon.*

Amoret, in Spenser's 'Faerie Queene', III. vi and xii, and IV. vii, daughter of the nymph Chrysogone and twin sister of Belphoebe. She is 'of grace and beauty noble Paragon', and has been married to Sir Scudamour, but carried off immediately after by the enchanter Busirane and imprisoned by him until released by Britomart. Timias (q.v.) loves her, but being reproved by Belphoebe leaves her. This incident refers to the displeasure of Queen Elizabeth at the relations of Sir W. Ralegh (q.v.) with Elizabeth Throgmorton.

Amoretti, a series of eighty-eight sonnets by Spenser (q.v.), which have been thought to illustrate the course of his wooing of Elizabeth Boyle, the lady whom he married. These were printed with the 'Epithalamion' (q.v.) in 1595.

Amory, BLANCHE, a character in Thackeray's 'Pendennis' (q.v.).

AMORY, THOMAS (1691 ?–1788), a writer of Irish descent, the author of two eccentric works of fiction, 'Memoirs of several Ladies of Great Britain', published in 1755, and 'The Life of John Buncle, Esq.', published in

1756–66. Eighteen imaginary ladies were to be the subjects of the 'Memoirs', but the author confines himself to one, Mrs. Marinda Benlow, adding disquisitions on a great many miscellaneous subjects, among others, the doctrines of Athanasius. 'John Buncle' (q.v.) is virtually a sequel of the 'Memoirs', but is a good deal more entertaining. Amory was an ardent Unitarian, and a student of medicine, geology, and antiquities, and in his rambling narratives and digressions he gives a mass of information on these subjects.

Amos Barton, The Sad Fortunes of the Rev., see *Scenes of Clerical Life*.

Amphibology, AMPHIBOLY, a sentence that may be construed in two distinct senses; ambiguity arising from the uncertain construction of a sentence.

Amphibrach, a foot consisting of a long between two short syllables.

Amphictionic Council, in Greek history, an association of Greeks worshipping at the shrine of the same god. The most important was that of Delphi, which included many of the principal peoples of Greece. It exercised as a rule little political influence, but Philip of Macedon used it to further his schemes. See also *Sacred Wars*.

Amphīon, son of Zeus and Antiope, was a harper of such skill that when he and his brother Zethus were fortifying Thebes the stones moved of their own accord and formed a wall. See also *Antiope*.

Amphitryon, a Theban prince, who obtained the promise of the hand of Alcmena, daughter of Electryon, king of Mycenae, on condition that he should avenge the death of that king's sons, who had been killed by the Teleboans. Zeus, captivated with the charms of Alcmena, borrowed the features of Amphitryon while he was gone to the war, and introduced himself to her as her victorious husband. The son of Zeus and Alcmena was Hercules. This legend is the subject of plays by Plautus, Molière, Dryden (see below), and Giraudoux. Amphitryon's connexion with gastronomy arises from a line in the play of Molière. The servant of Amphitryon, perplexed by the resemblance of the two who claim to be his master, hears Jupiter invite some friends to dinner, and is thereby convinced that he is the genuine Amphitryon—'Le véritable Amphitryon est l'Amphitryon où l'on dîne'.

Amphitryon, a comedy by Dryden (q.v.), published in 1690.

The play is adapted from the comedies of Plautus and Molière on the subject of Amphitryon (see above), who, expecting to arrive at home on the morrow from a successful campaign, sends his slave Sosia in advance to announce his return to his wife, Alcmena. Jupiter, in order to enjoy the favours of Alcmena, assumes the form of Amphitryon, and forestalls her husband; at the same time ordering Mercury to take the form of Sosia, and keep out the true Sosia. The comedy consists in the complications arising from the successive arrival at Amphitryon's palace of two indistinguishable Amphitryons, and two indistinguishable Sosias, and the final confrontation of the two Amphitryons.

Amram, the father of Moses (Exod. vi. 20). There is a reference to 'Amram's son' in Milton, 'Paradise Lost', i. 339.

Amrita, a Sanskrit word meaning 'immortal'; in Hindu mythology, the water of life or ambrosia, procured by the gods by churning the ocean.

Amundeville, LORD HENRY, a character in Byron's 'Don Juan' (q.v.), whose house is the scene of part of the last three cantos.

Amurath (Murad), the name of several Turkish Sultans in the 14th–16th cents. 'Not Amurath an Amurath succeeds, But Harry Harry'; Shakespeare, '2 Henry IV', v. ii.

Amyas, in Spenser's 'Faerie Queene', 'the Squire of low degree'. See *Poeana*.

Amyas Leigh, the hero of C. Kingsley's 'Westward Ho!' (q.v.).

Amymōnē, one of the daughters of Danaus (see *Danaïdes*). Mentioned by Milton, 'Paradise Regained', ii. 188, as a 'beauty rare'.

Amyntas, in Spenser's 'Colin Clouts come home againe', is Thomas Watson (q.v.).

AMYOT, JACQUES (1513–93), a French writer, whose version of Plutarch was translated into English by Sir T. North (q.v.).

Amys and Amylion, see *Amis and Amiloun*.

Āna, neuter plural termination of Latin adjectives in -*ānus* (e.g. *Virgiliana*), a term used of a collection of the sayings of some person, or anecdotes or literary gossip about him.

Anabaptist, one who baptizes over again, as the due performance of a rite ineffectually performed in infancy; the name of a sect that arose in Germany in 1521. There was a revolt of Anabaptists in 1534 at Münster, under John of Leyden, who founded a theocracy, and was executed in 1536. The name is applied (more or less opprobriously) to the Protestant religious body of the Baptists.

Anabasis, see *Xenophon*.

Anacharsis, a Scythian who went to Athens about 594 B.C., made the acquaintance of Solon, and became famous for his wisdom, in contrast to the stupidity and ignorance of his fellow countrymen.

Anacharsis, Le Voyage du Jeune, an historical romance by the Abbé Jean-Jacques Barthélemy (1716–95), descriptive of Greece in the time of Pericles. It was published in 1788.

Anacharsis Clootz, see *Clootz*.

Anacoluthon, Greek, 'wanting sequence'; a sentence in which a fresh construction is adopted before the former is complete.

ANACREON (6th cent. B.C.), a famous lyric poet of Teos in Ionia, author of many melodious verses on love and wine. He lived chiefly at Samos, but went to Athens at the invitation of the tyrant Hipparchus. He is said to have died choked by a grape-stone. Of his poems only a few genuine fragments have survived, many songs that bear his name being by other authors. T. Moore (q.v.) published in 1800 a translation of the 'Odes of Anacreon' into English verse. Byron calls Moore 'Anacreon Moore'.

Anacrusis, 'striking up', an additional syllable at the beginning of a verse before the normal rhythm, e.g. the 'and' in the second of the following lines:

Till danger's troubled night depart
And the star of peace return.

Anadyŏ'mĕnĕ, see *Venus*.

***Analogy of Religion**, Natural and Revealed, to the Constitution and Course of Nature, The*, a treatise in defence of the Christian religion, by J. Butler (q.v.), published in 1736.

The treatise is directed against the views of the Deists, which were very prevalent at that time. The author takes as starting-point the assumption, which was common ground to him and his adversaries, 'that there is an intelligent Author of Nature, and natural Governor of the world'. Proceeding from that part of the Divine government over intelligent creatures which comes under our view, to the larger and more general government which is beyond it, and comparing the acknowledged dispensations of Providence with what religion teaches us to believe and expect, he finds that the two are analogous and of a piece, and that the latter must reasonably therefore be accepted. On these lines the author discusses the credibility of a future life, of miracles, of revelation, and other religious doctrines.

Ananias, (1) the Jewish high-priest before whom Paul was brought and who caused him to be smitten on the mouth (Acts xxiii); (2) the husband of Sapphira who was struck dead because he 'lied unto God' (Acts v); (3) a character in Jonson's 'The Alchemist' (q.v.).

Anapaest, Greek, 'reversed'; a reversed dactyl, a metrical foot composed of two short followed by a long syllable.

Anaphora, 'carrying back', the repetition of the same word or phrase in several successive clauses; for instance, 'Awake up, my glory; awake, lute and harp; I myself will awake right early.'

Anarchy, The Masque of, a poem by P. B. Shelley (q.v.), 'written on the occasion of the Massacre of Manchester' (the Peterloo (q.v.) affair, August 1819).

Anastasius, a picaresque novel by T. Hope (q.v.), published in 1819.

The story, told in the form of an autobiography, is that of a Greek of Chios, a man of courage and ability, but utterly unscrupulous, who lived in the latter part of the 18th cent. It takes the reader to Greece, where the hero fights with prowess against the rebellious Albanians; to Constantinople, where he lives by his wits, and turns Muslim to escape the consequences of detection in an amour with a Turkish lady; to Egypt, where he enters the service of the Mamelukes and rises temporarily to a position of some eminence; to Smyrna, where he behaves atrociously to an amiable and trustful young lady; and to Arabia, where he lives for a time among the Wahabis. Notwithstanding the great variety of the adventures recounted and of the places whose oriental customs are depicted, the book, which is very long, is monotonous. It enjoyed, however, considerable popularity.

Anatomie of Abuses, The, see *Stubbes*.

Anatomy of Melancholy, The, a treatise by Robert Burton (q.v.), published in 1621.

In purpose the treatise is a medical work. The introduction sets out that melancholy is 'an inbred malady in every one of us'. Part i deals with the definition, causes, symptoms, and properties of melancholy; part ii, with its cure; part iii, with the melancholy of love, and the melancholy of religion. But the subject is expanded until it covers the whole life of man; and social and political reform, as well as bodily and mental health, are brought within its purview. The treatment is marked by a sense of humour and pathos, and a tolerant spirit in religion. In the exposition and illustration of his argument, Burton uses quotation (or paraphrase) to an extreme degree, drawing on a very wide field of literature, from the Bible and the Fathers, through Greek and Latin classics, to the Elizabethan writers. His book thus becomes a store-house of the most miscellaneous learning, and is apt to be regarded in that light rather than as a medical treatise.

Ancaeus, the steersman of the ship 'Argo' (see *Argonauts*), who is said to be the occasion of a well-known proverb. He had been told by a seer that he should not live to taste the wine of his vineyard. A cup of his own wine being set before him, he laughed at the seer, who replied, πολλὰ μεταξὺ πέλει κύλικος καὶ χείλεος ἄκρου, 'There's many a slip between the cup and the lip'. At that moment Ancaeus was told that a wild boar was near. He went out to pursue it and was killed.

Anchises, a Trojan prince, who enjoyed the favour of Venus, and became by her father of Aeneas (q.v.).

Ancien régime, a French expression signifying the old order of things before the French Revolution.

Ancient Mariner, The Rime of the, a poem by S. T. Coleridge (q.v.), which first appeared in 1798 in Wordsworth's and Coleridge's 'Lyrical Ballads' (q.v.), and subsequently in the latter's 'Sibylline Leaves', published in 1817.

An ancient mariner meets three gallants on their way to a marriage feast and detains one to recount his story. He tells how his ship was drawn towards the South Pole by a storm. When the ship is surrounded by ice, an albatross comes through the snow-fog and is received with joy and hospitality, but is presently shot by the mariner. For this act of cruelty a curse falls on the ship. She is driven north to the Line, and becalmed. The crew die of thirst except the mariner, who by the light of the moon beholding God's creatures of the great calm and their beauty, blesses them in his heart. The spell breaks and the ship is brought back to England, but the mariner for penance is condemned ever to travel from land to land and to teach by his example love and reverence to all God's creatures. J. L. Lowes, in 'The Road to Xanadu', traces the process by which Coleridge built up the poem from various sources.

Ancient of Days, a scriptural title of God; Dan. vii. 9.

Ancients and Moderns, Quarrel of the, see *Battle of the Books.*

Ancrene Riwle, or *Ancrene Wisse, The,* a devotional manual in prose written for the rule and guidance of certain English recluses. The author is unknown. Besides the Middle English copies, which vary considerably, there are French and Latin versions. The work, which is animated by a 'lofty morality and infinite tenderness' (C.H.E.L.), belongs to the early Middle English period (c. 1200–50).

ANDERSEN, HANS CHRISTIAN (1805–75), Danish poet and author of dramas, novels, and books of travel, is chiefly known in England by his series of fairy tales, of which the first volume appeared in 1835. They were first translated into English by Mary Howitt (1846), and by Caroline Peachey in the same year.

ANDERSON, SHERWOOD (1876–1941), American writer, born in Ohio. He came to prominence as a leading naturalistic writer with his third book, 'Winesburg, Ohio' (1919), a collection of stories illustrating life in a small town. He excelled in the short story and published three more collections, 'The Triumph of the Egg' (1921), 'Horses and Men' (1923), and 'Death in the Woods' (1933), in which he continued to illustrate the frustrations of contemporary life, a theme also explored in his novels. His best novels are 'Poor White' (1920) and 'Dark Laughter' (1925). He published an autobiographical narrative, 'A Story-Teller's Story' (1924), and drew upon his own experience in several other later books.

Andouillets, ABBESS OF, the subject of an episode in vol. vii of Sterne's 'Tristram Shandy' (q.v.).

Andrea del Sarto, a poem by R. Browning (q.v.), included in 'Men and Women', published in 1855.

Andrea del Sarto (1486–1531) was called 'The Faultless Painter'. The poet presents him as reflecting, in a monologue addressed to Lucrezia, his wife, on his deficiencies: his inferiority in inspiration to Raphael; his faithlessness to his patron Francis I; his neglect of his parents; his weak devotion to Lucrezia, who is, in fact, unworthy. But he is peaceful and resigned. Perhaps in the New Jerusalem there will be four walls to be decorated, by Leonardo, Raphael, Michelangelo, and himself.

Andrea Ferrara, a celebrated maker of swords, probably a Venetian, of the 16th cent. The name came to be frequently used to signify a broadsword. According to the author's notes on 'Waverley' (q.v.), it is generally believed that Andrea Ferrara was brought over by James IV or V to instruct the Scots in the manufacture of sword-blades.

Andrea of Hungary, Giovanna of Naples, and *Fra Rupert,* three plays forming a trilogy, by W. S. Landor (q.v.), published in 1839–40.

These plays deal with the marriage of Andrea, brother of King Lewis of Hungary, to Giovanna, queen of Naples, in the 14th cent.; his assassination at his wedding-feast owing to the intrigues of the Hungarian monk Fra Rupert; the accusation brought against Giovanna of causing her husband's murder; the attempts, finally successful, to oust her from her throne; and the exposure at the last of Fra Rupert.

Andreas, an OE. poem formerly attributed by some to Cynewulf (q.v.), included in the 'Vercelli Book' (q.v.). It recounts a mission of St. Andrew to the Mermedonians, Ethiopian savages, among whom St. Matthew was in danger. It is remarkable for its description of a sea voyage.

Andrée, SALOMON AUGUST (1854–97), the Arctic explorer, born at Grenna in Sweden, and educated as an engineer. With Nils Strindberg and Knut Fraenkel, he attempted in 1897 to cross the North Polar regions in a balloon. They started on 11 July from Danes Island, Spitsbergen, but their balloon was driven down in 83° N. lat. Their remains, diaries, etc., were accidentally found on White Island off the NE. coast of Spitsbergen by a Norwegian expedition in August 1930 and the Diaries published in 1931.

ANDREW OF WYNTOUN, *see Wyntoun.*

ANDREWES, LANCELOT (1555–1626), educated at Merchant Taylors' School and Pembroke Hall, Cambridge, was bishop successively of Chichester, Ely, and Winchester. He was renowned for his patristic learning, wrote theological works, and was first on the list of the divines appointed to make the 'Authorized Version' of the Bible.

Androcles, or *Androclus, and the Lion,* a story told by Aulus Gellius (v. 14) of a slave who, running away from a cruel master and concealing himself in a cave in Africa, was confronted by a lion. The animal presented to him a swollen paw, from which he extracted a thorn. Androcles was subsequently captured and sentenced to fight with a lion in the arena. It chanced that this lion was the same that he had relieved. The lion recognized its benefactor and, instead of attacking him, showed every sign of affection and gratitude. Bernard Shaw wrote a play 'Androcles and the Lion' (1912).

Andrŏ'măchē, the wife of Hector (q.v.) and mother of Astyanax. Her parting with Hector before a battle is the most pathetic passage in Homer's 'Iliad' (Book VI). After the capture of Troy she fell to the share of Neoptolemus, and after his death married Helenus (q.v.), a brother of Hector. Aeneas met with her in Epirus ('Aeneid', iii).

Andrŏ'mĕda, a daughter of Cepheus, king of Ethiopia, and Cassiopea. Cassiopea boasted herself (or her daughter) more beautiful than the Nereids. Whereupon Poseidon in anger sent a sea-monster to ravage the country. To abate his wrath, Andromeda was exposed on a rock to the monster, but was rescued by Perseus (q.v.), who, returning through the air from the conquest of the Gorgons, changed the monster to a rock by showing it the Medusa's head. Charles Kingsley (q.v.) wrote a poem on this myth, entitled 'Andromeda'.

Andronicus Comnenius, see Wilson (J., 1627–96).

Andvari, in Scandinavian mythology, a dwarf who was forced by Loki to give up his treasure and the magic ring with which he could make gold (known in German romance as the Ring of the Nibelungs). It passed into the possession of Fafnir, was taken from him by Sigurd, and by Sigurd given to Brynhild.

Aneirin, The Book of, see Aneurin.

Anelida and Arcite, a poem in rhymeroyal by Chaucer (q.v.), belonging to his early period. It is the lament of Queen Anelida for the falseness of Arcite her lover.

ANEURIN or **ANEIRIN** (fl. 600?), a Welsh bard whose compositions are contained in a MS. 'Book of Aneirin' of the 13th cent. This contains the 'Gododin', an elegy on the Welsh chieftains who fell at Cattraeth at the hands of the Saxons.

Angel, from the Greek word ἄγγελος, a messenger, used in the LXX to translate the Hebrew *Malak*, in full *malak-yehowah*, 'messenger of Jehovah', whence the name and doctrine of angels passed into Latin and the modern languages. [OED.] The angels in the Scriptures are prominent chiefly in the apocalyptic books, e.g. Revelation and the apocryphal Book of Enoch (q.v.). The latter (c. xxi) enumerates seven archangels: Uriel, Raphael, Raguel, Michael, Sariel, Gabriel, and Jerahmeel. But the names vary in other passages. According to the late 5th-cent. work attributed to Dionysius the Areopagite, the heavenly beings are divided into three

hierarchies, each containing three orders or choirs, viz. seraphim, cherubim, thrones; dominions, virtues, powers; principalities, archangels, angels. The Koran (q.v.) names four chief angels: Gabriel, who writes down the divine decrees; Michael, the champion of the faith; Azrael, the angel of death; and Israfel, who will sound the trump at the resurrection.

Angel, the coin, see Noble.

Angel in the House, The, see Patmore.

Angelic Doctor, THE, Thomas Aquinas (q.v.).

Angelica, in the 'Orlando Innamorato' (q.v.) and 'Orlando Furioso' (q.v.), the daughter of Galafron, king of Cathay, the object of Orlando's love and the cause of his madness. For the story see under the above-named poems. Cf. Milton, 'Paradise Regained', iii. 341.

Angelica, the heroine of Congreve's 'Love for Love' (q.v.).

Angelico, FRA (c. 1387–1455), born GUIDO DI PIETRO. He became Fra Giovanni, a Dominican friar of Fiesole, and was known as 'Il Beato Angelico'. He painted religious subjects, including about fifty frescos in the convent of S. Marco, Florence.

ANGELL, SIR NORMAN (1874–), writer and lecturer on politics and economics, was awarded the Nobel Peace Prize in 1933. His most famous work was 'The Great Illusion' (1910), which demonstrated the futility of war.

Angelo, a character in Shakespeare's 'Measure for Measure' (q.v.).

ANGELO, HENRY (1760–1839?), a fencing-master patronized by the fashionable, and especially by Byron. In 1830 he published his 'Reminiscences'.

Angles, THE, one of the Low German tribes that settled in Britain, where they formed the kingdoms of Northumbria, Mercia, and East Anglia, and finally gave their name to the whole English people. The name in its origin signifies the people of Angul, a district of Holstein, so called from its angular shape. [OED.]

Anglo-Catholic, see Catholic Church.

Anglo-Norman (or Anglo-French, as some scholars have called it) designates the French language as spoken and written in the British Isles from the Norman Conquest until roughly the end of the 14th cent. It was basically a Western type of French. Transplanted to Britain it developed characteristics of its own at an ever-increasing though not uniform rate. The earliest A.-N. work of real literary merit, the 'Voyage of St. Brendan' (q.v.), composed in the first half of the 12th cent., shows relatively few insular traits, whereas the French of the 'Contes Moralisés' of Nicole Bozon, of the early 14th cent., illustrates the wholesale disintegration of later Anglo-

Norman; yet the French of John Gower (q.v.), writing half a century later, could pass for Continental French, thanks to the special advantages he enjoyed.

Although nearly all the literary genres practised in France are represented, A.-N. literature is particularly rich in didactic and religious or moralizing works, in chronicles and pseudo-historical 'Bruts' (q.v.), and in manuals or treatises of a practical nature, many such works being based upon Latin originals. The first outstanding dramatic production French has to show, the 12th-cent. semi-liturgical play of 'Adam' (q.v.), was almost certainly written in England.

Further evidence of the vogue of French is furnished by the large number of Continental French works which were transcribed and of which A.-N. MSS. provide superior and sometimes unique texts, e.g. the 'Song of Roland' (q.v.).

An A.-N. type of French continued to be used for official documents and in courts of law long after it had ceased to be a 'living' language.

Anglo-Saxon, originally a collective name for the Saxons of England as distinct from the 'Old Saxons' of the Continent, was extended to the entire Old English people and language before the Conquest. After the Conquest, natives and new incomers were at first distinguished as English and French; but as the latter also became in a few generations English politically and geographically, the name could no longer be applied distinctively to the people of Edward the Confessor and Harold. Hence the extended use of the name Anglo-Saxon. [OED.] In this book the English language before the Conquest is referred to as *Old English* (see *English*). See also *Angles* and *Saxon*.

Anglo-Saxon Chronicle, The, compiled by monks working at different centres, notably Winchester, Canterbury, and Peterborough, is, in the main, a dry chronological record, in vernacular, of events in England from the beginning of the Christian era to the middle of the 12th cent. It contains, however, some vivid and more detailed passages, notably the account of the struggle with the Danes during the period 893–7, and of the misery of the common people during the civil wars of the reign of Stephen. In the portion of the 'Chronicle' relating to the 10th cent. are inserted some important poems, among others the 'Brunanburh' (q.v.). The earlier part of the 'Chronicle', down to 892, may represent the work or inspiration of King Alfred.

Anima Poetae, a collection of aphorisms, observations, reflections, and other literary material, extracted from the numerous notebooks of S. T. Coleridge (q.v.), and published by Ernest Hartley Coleridge in 1895.

Animal Farm, a novel by George Orwell (q.v.), published in 1954. It is a satire in fable form on Revolutionary and post-Revolutionary Russia, and, by extension, on all revolutions. The animals of Mr. Jones's farm revolt against their human masters and drive them out, the pigs becoming the leaders. Eventually the pigs, dominated by Napoleon, their chief, become corrupted by power and a new tyranny replaces the old. The ultimate slogan runs 'All animals are equal but some animals are more equal than others'. Napoleon, ruthless and cynical, represents Stalin, and Snowball, the idealist whom he drives out, Trotsky. Boxer, the noble carthorse, stands for the strength, simplicity, and good nature of the common man.

Anitra, in Ibsen's 'Peer Gynt' (q.v.), an unscrupulous Arab damsel, with whom the hero flirts when masquerading as a prophet.

Anna Christie, a play by Eugene O'Neill (q.v.), first produced in 1921, which was one of the playwright's early successes.

ANNA COMNENA (*b.* 1083), daughter of the emperor Alexius Comnenus, and author of the 'Alexiad' (a history in fifteen books, mainly of her father's life). She figures in Scott's 'Count Robert of Paris' (q.v.).

Anna Karenina, a novel by Tolstoy (q.v.).

Annales Cambriae, ancient annals of Wales, of which the earliest extant MS. dates from the second half of the 10th cent. They have a special literary interest on account of their reference to the 'Battle of Badon, in which Arthur carried the cross of our Lord Jesus Christ on his shoulders, and the Britons were victors', placing it in the year 518. They also refer to the battle of Camlan in 539, 'in which Arthur and Medraut [Modred] fell'. We have here one of the sources of the subsequent Arthurian legend.

Annalia Dubrensia, see *Cotswold Games.*

Annals of the Parish, a novel by Galt (q.v.), published in 1821, in which the Rev. Micah Balwhidder chronicles, with quaint simplicity and unconscious humour, the events, great and small, that affected the homely lives of the parishioners of Dalmailing in Ayrshire during the period 1760–1810. The scene of the death of Mr. Cayenne (ch. xlvii) has been declared by a competent authority 'one of the greatest things in all literature'.

Anne, queen of England, 1702–14.

Anne of Geierstein, or *The Maiden of the Mist,* a novel by Sir W. Scott (q.v.), published in 1829.

The period of the story is the reign of Edward IV. The earl of Oxford and his son Arthur de Vere, exiled from England after the victory of the Yorkist party at Tewkesbury, are travelling on the Continent engaged in intrigues in the Lancastrian interest, under the name of Philipson and in the guise of merchants. Passing through Switzerland and overtaken by a storm in the mountains, they are hospitably entertained by Arnold Biederman, the Landamman or chief magistrate of Unterwalden, whose niece, the young countess Anne of Geierstein, rescues Arthur from death. The business of the Philipsons being with Charles the Bold, duke of Burgundy, they accompany Biederman and other Swiss delegates who are setting out to remonstrate with the latter against the outrageous proceedings to which the Swiss have been subject at his hands. The Philipsons are seized by the cruel Archibald of Hagenbach, the duke's governor of the citadel of Brisach, and narrowly escape death, a fate only averted by a rising of the citizens against Hagenbach and his condemnation by the Vehmgericht (q.v.) and execution. The story is then occupied with the negotiations between Philipson (or Oxford), the duke of Burgundy, and Margaret of Anjou (Henry VI's queen), of which the object is to secure the duke's assistance to the Lancastrian cause in return for the cession to him of Provence. These negotiations are interrupted by the utter defeat of the duke by the Swiss at Granson and Morat. After the duke's death at Nancy, Oxford and his son return to Geierstein, where Arthur marries Anne.

Apart from the vivid portrait of Charles the Bold, and the picture of the court of René, the king of Troubadours, the most interesting feature in the book is the description of the secret tribunal of the Vehmgericht, of which Anne's father, Count Albert of Geierstein (*alias* the Black Priest of St. Paul's), is for the time being the chief figure. For this description Scott drew on Goethe's 'Goetz von Berlichingen', which he had translated.

Annot Lyle, a character in Scott's 'Legend of Montrose' (q.v.).

Annual Register, The, an annual review of events of the past year, founded by Dodsley (q.v.) in 1758, which still survives.

Annus Mirabilis, a poem by Dryden (q.v.), published in 1667, and probably written at Charlton in Wiltshire, where the poet lived during the plague and fire years. It is written on the model of 'Gondibert' (q.v.) in quatrains, of which the first 200 deal with the sea-fight against the Dutch at Bergen on 3 August 1665, the indecisive four days' battle of June 1666, and the victory over the Dutch off the N. Foreland on 25 July of the same year. The remaining hundred quatrains relate the Fire of London (2–7 Sept. 1666).

ANOUILH, JEAN (1910–), French dramatist, many of whose plays have been translated and produced in England and the United States. They include: 'Le Bal des Voleurs' (1938, 'Thieves' Carnival', Lond. 1952), 'Léocadia' (1942, 'Time Remembered', Lond. 1954), 'Eurydice' (1942, 'Point of Departure', Lond. 1950), 'Antigone' (1946, Lond. 1949), 'L'Invitation au Château' (1948, 'Ring Round the Moon', Lond. 1950), 'L'Alouette', an historical play, about St. Joan of Arc (1953, 'The Lark', Lond. 1955).

ANSELM, ST. (1033–1109), a native of Aosta in N. Italy, and a pupil of Lanfranc at the abbey of Bec in Normandy. He made the monastic profession and became in time abbot of Bec. While he held this office he visited England, where William Rufus had left the see of Canterbury vacant for four years. In a fit of sick-bed repentance, Rufus appointed Anselm archbishop (1093), a responsibility which the latter reluctantly accepted. The king resumed his tyrannous course and in 1097 Anselm withdrew to Rome. He returned to England as archbishop under Henry I. Anselm wrote many theological and philosophical works, including the famous 'Monologion', 'Proslogion', and 'Cur Deus Homo'. He is commemorated on 21 April.

Anselmo, see *Curious Impertinent*.

Anson, GEORGE, *Baron Anson* (1697–1762), who became first lord of the Admiralty, made his famous voyage round the world in 1740–4. The account of it, compiled by his chaplain, R. Waters, was published in 1748. It is a stirring narrative of the sea. The seven vessels of the squadron were reduced by storms to three. Of these, two sailed refitted from Juan Fernandez, attacked and destroyed the town of Paita, and captured the Manila galleon with a vast treasure. Anson finally reached home with a single ship.

ANSON, SIR WILLIAM REYNELL (1843–1914), Warden of All Souls, M.P. for the University of Oxford, and a learned writer on the Law and Custom of the Constitution (1879–86) and on Contracts (1879).

Anster Fair, see *Tennant*.

ANSTEY, CHRISTOPHER (1724–1805), educated at Eton and King's College, Cambridge, is remembered as the author of the 'New Bath Guide' (1766), a series of letters in anapaestic verse, describing the adventures of the 'Blunderhead Family' at Bath, and depicting the manners of the place and time with much good humour and drollery.

ANSTEY, F., the pseudonym of THOMAS ANSTEY GUTHRIE (1856–1934), who was author of many novels and dialogues, including 'Vice Versa' (q.v., 1882), 'The Giant's Robe' (1883), 'The Tinted Venus' (1885), 'A Fallen Idol' (1886), 'The Pariah' (1889), 'Voces Populi' (1890), 'Tourmalin's Time Cheques' (1891), 'The Talking Horse' (1892), 'The Man from Blankley's' (1893), 'Mr. Punch's Pocket Ibsen' (1893), 'Baboo Jabberjee, B.A.' (1897), 'The Brass Bottle' (1900), 'Salted Almonds' (1906). He was on the staff of 'Punch' from 1887 to 1930.

Antaeus, a giant, son of Poseidon and Gē (the Earth), and a mighty wrestler. Hercules attacked him, and as Antaeus drew new strength from his mother whenever he touched the earth, Hercules lifted him in the air and squeezed him to death in his arms.

Ante-Nicene and **Post-Nicene Fathers,** terms applied respectively to Christian literature from the time of the Apostles to the Council of Nicaea (A.D. 325), and from the Council of Nicaea to Pope Gregory I (*d.* 604).

Antĕnor, a wise counsellor of Priam (q.v.), king of Troy. In post-Homeric legend he is a traitor, who plans to surrender the city and the palladium (q.v.), to the Greeks.

Anthology, The Greek, a collection of some 6,000 short elegiac poems, inscriptions, etc., by more than 300 writers (7th cent. B.C.–10th cent. A.D.), originating in a collection by Meleager of Gadara (the 'Garland of Meleager', *c.* 60 B.C.), which grew by successive additions. In its present form it is substantially the collection of Constantinus Cephalas, a Byzantine of the 10th cent. A.D., known as the 'Palatine Anthology' because it was discovered (by the French scholar Salmasius (q.v.) at the age of 19) in the Palatine Library of Heidelberg.

Anthropo'phagi, in Greek legend, a people of Scythia that fed on human flesh.

Antichrist, the archetypal personal opponent of Christ and His Kingdom, expected by the Early Church to appear before the end of the world, and much referred to in the Middle Ages. The term was at one time applied by some (e.g. Wycliffe) to the Pope or the Papal power. 'Antichrist' is mentioned in 1 John ii. 18, 22, and 2 John vii, and variously referred to as the *Man of Sin* (2 Thess. ii. 3), the *Beast* (Revelation), etc.

Anti-Corn-Law League, see *Corn Laws*.

Antĭgŏnē, a daughter of Oedipus (q.v.) and Jocasta. When the strife between her brothers Eteocles (q.v.) and Polyneices had led to the death of the latter, she buried his body by night, against the order of King Creon, and was ordered by him to be buried alive. She took her own life before the sentence was executed, and Haemon, the king's son, who passionately loved her, killed himself on her grave. The incident was made the subject of one of the tragedies of Sophocles.

Antigŏnus, (1) a character in Shakespeare's 'The Winter's Tale' (q.v.); (2) a character in Beaumont and Fletcher's 'The Humorous Lieutenant' (q.v.); (3) the name of one of Alexander's generals, who on Alexander's death received certain provinces of Asia, and of some of his descendants, kings of Macedonia.

Anti-Jacobin, The, a journal founded by Canning (q.v.), to combat the subversive principles of philosophy and politics that were current at the end of the 18th cent., and to deride their supporters. It was edited by Gifford (q.v.), and included among its contributors, besides Canning, Ellis (q.v., a converted author of 'Rolliad' satires), and Frere (q.v.). In addition to ordinary news, the journal published satirical verse, mainly in the form of parody, of which 'The Needy Knife-grinder', a parody of Southey, and 'The Loves of the Triangles', a parody of Erasmus Darwin's 'The Loves of the Plants', are famous examples. 'The Rovers' was an amusing burlesque of contemporary German

drama. Its final and most important satire was 'The New Morality' by Canning, a denunciation of the French propaganda and an exhortation to maintain the old English institutions. The 'Anti-Jacobin' came to an end in 1798, but its crusade, in feebler form, was continued by 'The Anti-Jacobin Review and Magazine'. 'The Poetry of the Anti-Jacobin' was reprinted in 1852, with explanatory notes by Charles Edmonds.

Antilia, see *Seven Cities*.

Antinomian, one who maintains that the moral law is not binding upon Christians, under the 'law of grace'. A sect appeared in Germany in 1535 which was alleged to hold this opinion. See *Hutchinsonians*.

Antĭnŏus, a youth of remarkable beauty, who was a favourite of the Emperor Hadrian. He was drowned in the Nile in A.D. 122.

Antiŏpē, a daughter of Nycteus, king of Thebes, was beloved by Zeus, by whom she became mother of Amphion and Zethus. To avoid her father's anger she fled to Epopeus, king of Sicyon, or was carried off by him. Nycteus made war on Epopeus and in dying entreated his brother Lycus to continue the war and recover his daughter. This Lycus did and married Antiope. But Dirce, the first wife of Lycus, imprisoned and tormented Antiope. The latter escaped to her sons, who undertook her revenge. They killed Lycus and tied Dirce to the horns of a bull, which dragged her till she died. A fountain in the neighbourhood of Thebes which bore her name sprang from her blood.

Antipholus, the name of the twin brothers, sons of Aegeon, in Shakespeare's 'The Comedy of Errors' (q.v.).

Antiquaries, THE SOCIETY OF, was founded about the year 1572 at the instance of Archbishop Parker, but was suppressed on the accession of James I. The present Society was founded in Jan. 1717–18, with Peter Le Neve as president. Its 'Archaeologia' was first printed in 1770.

Antiquary, The, a novel by Sir W. Scott, (q.v.), published in 1816.

A gallant young officer, known as Major Neville, on whose birth there is supposed to be the stain of illegitimacy, falls in love in England with Isabella Wardour, who, in deference to the prejudices of her father, Sir Arthur Wardour, repulses him. Under the assumed name of Lovel, he follows her to Scotland, falling in on the way with Jonathan Oldbuck, laird of Monkbarns, a learned and garrulous antiquary, and a neighbour of Sir Arthur. Lovel saves the lives of Sir Arthur and his daughter at the peril of his own, fights a duel with Hector M'Intyre, Oldbuck's impetuous nephew, and saves Sir Arthur from the ruin that his credulity and the impositions of the German charlatan Dousterswivel have brought on him. He finally turns out to be the son and heir of the earl of Glenallan, and all ends happily. The charm of the book, Scott's 'chief favourite among all his novels', lies in the character of the Antiquary, drawn according to Scott from a worthy friend of his boyish days (George Constable), but in which we may recognize a portrait or caricature of Scott himself; and in that of old Edie Ochiltree, the king's bedesman, shrewd, ironical, and kindly, who is instrumental in routing the rascally Dousterswivel, and in bringing events to a satisfactory termination.

Antiquary, The, a comedy by Shackerley Marmion (q.v.).

Antiquities of Warwickshire, see *Dugdale.*

Antisthĕnēs, the founder of the Cynic school of philosophy. He was an Athenian, lived in the 5th cent. B.C., and was a pupil of Socrates. He taught in the Cynosarges, for which reason probably his pupils were called Cynics, though others attribute the name to their surliness (from κύων, a dog). He despised art and learning, and the luxuries and comforts of life, and taught that virtue consists in the avoidance of evil and independence of needs. Diogenes (q.v.) was the most famous of his pupils.

Anti'strŏphē, meaning 'turning about', in a Greek chorus, the response to the *strophe* (q.v.), recited as the chorus proceeded in the opposite direction to that followed in the strophe. The metre of *strophe* and *antistrophe* was the same.

Antonīnus Pius (A.D. 86–161), Roman emperor from 138 to 161. He devoted himself to promoting the happiness of his people and his reign was an exceptionally peaceful and prosperous one. The WALL OF ANTONINUS, or Antonine Wall, was built in the course of the reign by the prefect Lollius Urbicus between the Forth and the Clyde to strengthen the protection of the province of Britain against invasions from the North.

Antonio, (1) the Merchant of Venice, in Shakespeare's play of that name (q.v.); (2) the brother of Prospero in 'The Tempest' (q.v.); (3) a sea-captain in 'Twelfth Night' (q.v.); (4) the brother of Leonato in 'Much Ado about Nothing' (q.v.); (5) the father of Proteus in 'Two Gentlemen of Verona' (q.v.).

Antonio and Mellida, a tragedy by J. Marston (q.v.), printed in 1602, and probably acted two years earlier, is interesting as having provided Ben Jonson with materials for his ridicule of Marston in the 'Poetaster' (q.v.). In Part I of the play, Antonio, son of Andrugio, duke of Genoa, is in love with Mellida, daughter of Piero, duke of Venice. The two states are at war and Genoa has been defeated, and a price set in Venice on the heads of Antonio and Andrugio. Antonio, disguised as an Amazon, comes to Piero's court to seek Mellida. Mellida flees with Antonio but is captured. Andrugio offers himself as a victim to Piero, who appears to relent, and assents to the marriage of Antonio and Mellida, and the first part closes joyfully.

In Part II Piero reveals his true character. He kills Andrugio, contrives the dishonour of Mellida in order to prevent the match, plots the death of Antonio, and gains the hand of Andrugio's widow. Mellida dies brokenhearted. Antonio, urged by the ghost of his father, assumes the disguise of a fool, and kills Piero.

Antony and Cleopatra, an historical tragedy by Shakespeare (q.v.), probably written about 1606–7, and first printed in the folio of 1623. In it the poet closely follows North's 'Plutarch'.

The play presents Mark Antony, the great soldier and noble prince, at Alexandria, enthralled by the beauty of the Egyptian queen, Cleopatra. Recalled by the death of his wife Fulvia and political developments, he tears himself from Cleopatra and returns to Rome, where the estrangement between him and Octavius Caesar is terminated by his marriage to Octavia, Caesar's sister, an event which provokes the intense jealousy of Cleopatra. But the reconciliation is short-lived, and Antony leaves Octavia and returns to Egypt. At the battle of Actium, the flight of the Egyptian squadron is followed by the retreat of Antony, pursued to Alexandria by Caesar. There, after a momentary success, Antony is finally defeated. On the false report of Cleopatra's death, he falls upon his sword. He is borne to the monument where Cleopatra has taken refuge and dies in her arms. Cleopatra, fallen into Caesar's power, but determined not to grace his triumph, takes her own life by the bite of an asp.

See also *Cleopatra.*

Anūbis, an ancient Egyptian deity, ruler of the dead, whom he conducts to the shades. He was represented by the Egyptians with the head of a jackal, and by the Romans with that of a dog.

Anushirvan, see *Khusrau I.*

Anville, MISS, the name borne by the heroine of Miss Burney's 'Evelina' (q.v.), until she is recognized by her father.

Aonia, a part of Boeotia (q.v.) which includes Mt. Helicon and the fountain Aganippe, sacred to the Muses. Hence Milton speaks of 'the Aonian Mount' ('Paradise Lòst', i. 15), and Thomson ('Castle of Indolence', II. ii) refers to poets as 'the Aonian hive'.

Apache (pron. 'apa′sh'), the name of a tribe of Red Indians, applied in recent times to the hooligans of Paris. Cf. *Mohock.*

Apelles (4th cent. B.C.), Greek painter from Colophon in Ionia. He painted portraits, e.g. 'Alexander wielding a thunderbolt' and 'Campaspe' (q.v.), mythical subjects, e.g. 'Aphrodite Anadyomene', and allegories, e.g. 'Calumny'. He is said never to have let pass a day without practising with his pencil; hence the proverb, *nulla dies sine linea.* He wrote a book on painting. Descriptions of his works were studied by the Italian painters of the Renaissance.

APELLES AND THE COBBLER: a cobbler, having found fault with the drawing of a shoe-latchet in one of the pictures of Apelles, proceeded to criticize the drawing of the legs. To which Apelles replied, 'ne supra crepidam judicaret', or according to another version, 'ne sutor ultra crepidam', of which the modern equivalent is 'the cobbler should stick to his last'. Hazlitt coined the word 'ultracrepidarian' for a critic who goes beyond the sphere of his knowledge, with reference to William Gifford (q.v.), at one time a shoe-maker's apprentice.

Apemantus, the 'churlish philosopher' in Shakespeare's 'Timon of Athens' (q.v.).

Aphaeresis, the suppression of a letter or syllable at the beginning of a word.

Aphorism, a term transferred from the 'Aphorisms of Hippocrates' to other sententious statements of the principles of physical science, and later (e.g. in Coleridge's 'Aids to Reflection' (q.v.), which are divided into 'Aphorisms' and 'Comments') to statements of principles generally. Thence it has come to mean any short pithy statement into which much thought or observation is compressed. J. S. Mill wrote a fragment on aphorisms, and John Morley a short discourse on the same subject.

Aphrŏdītē, see *Venus*.

Apicius, MARCUS GABIUS, a gourmet who lived in the reign of Tiberius. Having squandered his fortune till it was reduced to about £80,000, he hanged himself from despair at having so little left to live on. Some of his receipts were written down, but the work on cookery which bears the name of Caelius Apicius is thought to be a compilation of later date.

Apis, an ancient Egyptian deity, the incarnation as a bull of Ptah, the god of the sun, identified with Osiris (q.v.). Apis was represented as a bull with the disk of the sun between his horns.

Apocalypse, from a Greek verb meaning 'to disclose', the 'revelation' of the future granted to St. John in the isle of Patmos; the book of Revelation in the N.T.

Apocrypha, THE, in its special sense, those books included in the Septuagint and Vulgate versions of the O.T. which were not originally written in Hebrew and not counted genuine by the Jews, and which, at the Reformation, were excluded from the Sacred Canon by the Protestant party, as having no well-grounded claim to inspired authorship. They are Esdras (I and II), Tobit, Judith, the Rest of Esther, the Wisdom of Solomon, Ecclesiasticus, Baruch (with the Epistle of Jeremiah), the Song of the Three Holy Children, the History of Susanna, Bel and the Dragon, the Prayer of Manasses, Maccabees (I and II).

The texts of the Apocryphal Gospels, Acts, Epistles, and Apocalypses are printed in 'The Apocryphal New Testament', translated by M. R. James (1924).

APOLLINAIRE, GUILLAUME (1880–1918), the name taken by the French poet WILHELM APOLLINARIS KOSTROWITZKY, who was closely associated with the early Cubist painters (writing about them in 'Les Peintres cubistes', 1913). He was one of the first writers to try and produce similar effects of dislocation and simultaneity in poetry. The two collections 'Alcools' (1913) and 'Calligrammes' (1918) contain his best work.

Apollo, called also PHOEBUS, often identified with the sun, was the son of Zeus and Latona (q.v.). He was the god who brings back sunshine in spring, who sends plagues, and who founds states and colonies. He was the god of music and poetry (cf. Shelley's 'Hymn of Apollo') and had the gift of knowing the future, so that his oracles were in high repute. He was the type of manly youth and beauty, and was represented in the famous Colossus (q.v.) at Rhodes. When his son Aesculapius (q.v.) had been killed by the thunders of Zeus, Apollo in his resentment killed the Cyclops who had fabricated the thunderbolts. Banished by Zeus from heaven for this act, he hired himself to Admetus, king of Pherae, as one of his shepherds and served him for nine years. He rewarded the kind treatment of Admetus by obtaining for him the boon that he might be redeemed from death, if another would die in his place (see *Alcestis*). See also *Delos, Delphi*. The BELVEDERE APOLLO is a Greek statue, ? 2nd cent. B.C., in the Vatican (the *Belvedere* is part of the Vatican palace, originally a garden pavilion).

Apollonius of Tyana in Cappadocia (*b. c.* 4 B.C.), a Pythagorean philosopher who attained so great a fame by his pretended magical and wonder-working powers that divine honours were paid to him. His life was written by Philostratus.

Apollonius of Tyre, the subject of a popular medieval romance. See *Pericles* (Shakespeare's drama).

APOLLONIUS RHODIUS, a poet and grammarian of Alexandria, who wrote at the end of the 3rd and beginning of the 2nd cents. B.C. His 'Argonautica', a poem in the Homeric style on the expedition of the Argonauts (q.v.), lacked the epic fire and was the occasion of a literary feud between him and Callimachus (q.v.). He spent part of his life at Rhodes and is said to have subsequently become chief librarian at Alexandria.

Apollyon, 'The Destroyer', the angel of the bottomless pit (Rev. ix. 11). He figures in Bunyan's 'Pilgrim's Progress' (q.v.).

Apologia pro Vita sua, see *Newman*.

Apologie for Poetrie, The, or *Defence of Poesie,* a prose essay by Sir P. Sidney (q.v.), probably written at Wilton in 1580 during the queen's temporary displeasure with him. A treatise by Stephen Gosson (q.v.), entitled the 'Schoole of Abuse, conteining a pleasant invective against Poets, Pipers, Players, Jesters, and Such like Caterpillers of a Commonwealth', dedicated to Sidney, was probably the occasion. The 'Apologie' was published in 1595 after Sidney's death, in two editions, one of which bore the first of the above titles, the other the second.

It is a methodical examination of the art of poetry and a critical discussion of the state of English poetry in the author's time, such as had not before appeared in English. Starting with the essential nature of poetry, the art of imitation or representation, the author classifies the various kinds of poetry, discusses their relation to philosophy and history, the objections (including Plato's) that have been raised to poetry, and English poetry from Chaucer to his own day. He next deals with the principles that should be observed in tragedy and comedy, laments the poverty of English lyrical poetry and the affectation of the current English style. Lastly, he deals with prosody in its special relation to the English language.

Apologue, a fable conveying a moral lesson.

Apology for Smectymnuus, see *Smectymnuus.*

Apology for the Life of Mr. Colley Cibber, see *Cibber.*

Apology for . . . the People called Quakers, by Robert Barclay (1648–90), published in 1678.

Apophthegm, a terse pointed saying, embodying an important truth in a few words (OED). Bacon's 'Apophthegms new and old' is a collection of anecdotes embodying such sayings, '*mucrones verborum*, pointed speeches' as he describes them.

Aposiopēsis, a rhetorical artifice, in which the speaker comes to a sudden halt in the middle of a sentence, as if unable or unwilling to proceed.

Apostles, THE, a group of young men at Cambridge in the late 1820s, whose members included Arthur Hallam, Monckton Milnes, Tennyson, and R. C. Trench (qq.v.).

Appeal from the New to the Old Whigs, see *Burke* (E.).

APPERLEY, CHARLES JAMES (1779–1843), a Shropshire squire, educated at Rugby, wrote, under the pseudonym 'Nimrod', 'Memoirs of the Life of John Mytton' (1837) and 'The Life of a Sportsman' (1842), both illustrated by Henry Alken. He was a contributor to 'The Sporting Magazine' and a member of the staff of 'The Sporting Review'.

APPIAN, an historian born at Alexandria, who lived at Rome in the first half of the 2nd cent. A.D. He wrote in Greek narratives of the various Roman wars from the earliest times to the accession of Vespasian. A part of his work survives.

Appian Way, THE, the first great public road made by the Romans. It was begun in the censorship of Appius Claudius Caecus (312 B.C.) and ran from Rome to Capua and thence to Brundusium (Brindisi).

Appius, see *Virginia.*

Appius and Virginia, (1) a tragedy commonly attributed to J. Webster (q.v.), by some authorities to J. Heywood (q.v.), in whole or part (T.L.S. 30. vii. 31). The date of production is uncertain. It appears not to have been printed until 1654. The plot is taken from the classical legend (see *Virginia*), which forms one of the stories in Painter's 'Palace of Pleasure' (q.v.).

(2) A tragedy by John Dennis (q.v.).

April Fools' Day, 1 April, the celebration of which is probably the survival of ancient festivities formerly held at the spring equinox, from 25 March (old New Year's Day) to 1 April.

APULEIUS (*b. c.* A.D. 114), of Madaura in Africa, educated at Carthage and Athens, was author of the 'Metamorphoses seu de Asino Aureo', 'The Golden Ass' (q.v.).

Aqua Toffana, a slow-acting transparent odourless poison, probably arsenical, invented in the 17th cent. by an Italian woman named Toffana, who lived at Palermo and Naples, and used to sell it in vials labelled *Manna di S. Nicola di Bari*. Several poisoners, headed by an old hag named Spara, who had the secret from Toffana, were arrested in 1659, and five of them were executed.

Aquarius, a constellation that gives its name to the eleventh sign of the zodiac, which the sun enters on 21 Jan. It is represented by the figure of a man pouring water from a pitcher.

Aquilo, see *Boreas.*

AQUĪNAS, ST. THOMAS (*c.* 1225–74), of Aquino in Italy, Italian philosopher and Dominican friar, a compound of the seeker after truth and the Christian apologist. He represents in his writings, and notably in his 'Summa Totius Theologiae', the culmination of scholastic philosophy, the harmony of faith and reason. The above work, which remained unfinished, was a vast synthesis of the moral and political sciences, brought within a theological and metaphysical framework, one of the greatest monuments of the medieval intellect. St. Thomas Aquinas was known as the 'Angelic Doctor', and by his school companions as 'the Dumb Ox'. His followers were called THOMISTS. He is commemorated on 7 March.

Ara vos prec, the title of a work by T. S. Eliot (q.v.), taken from Dante, 'Purgatorio', xxvi. 145. The words are Provençal, 'Now I do pray you'.

Arabesque, the Arabian or Moorish style of mural decoration, composed in flowing lines of branches, leaves, and scroll-work fancifully intertwined. Representations of living creatures were excluded from it. But in the arabesques of the Renaissance human and animal figures, both natural and grotesque, were freely introduced.

Arabia Deserta, Felix, Petraea, in ancient geography, the several parts of the desert region between Egypt, Syria, and the Euphrates. ARABIA PETRAEA included the peninsula of Mt. Sinai and the country N. and NE. of it, and was named after its capital Petra. ARABIA DESERTA included the Syrian desert and part of the Arabian peninsula. ARABIA FELIX (i.e. *fertile*, as it was supposed to be) included the more southerly parts of the peninsula.

Arabia Deserta, see *Doughty.*

Arabian Nights' Entertainments, or *The Thousand and One Nights,* is a collection of stories written in Arabic which were made known in Europe early in the 18th cent. by the translation into French of Antoine Galland. They were translated into English by Edward William Lane in 1839–41, with some omissions, and an unexpurgated version was published by Sir Richard Burton in 1885–8. There is a French translation by J. C. Mardrus (1899 and subsequent years).

The source of the tales is uncertain. The framework (that is, the story of the king who killed his wives successively on the morning after the consummation of their marriage, until he married the clever Scheherazade, who saved her life by the tales she told him) is of Persian origin. It is mentioned by Mas'udi (A.D. 944) and in the 'Fihrist' (A.D. 987) as occurring in a book called the 'Hezār Afsāne' or 'Thousand Tales', attributed to a Princess Homai, the daughter according to tradition of Artaxerxes I. But the stories themselves told by Scheherazade are, for the most part, not Persian but Arabian in character, and were probably collected in Egypt by a professional story-teller at some time in the 14th–16th centuries.

Arabin, THE REV. FRANCIS, a character in Trollope's 'Barchester Towers' (q.v.) and subsequent Barsetshire novels, a protégé of Dr. Grantly, vicar of St. Ewold's and afterwards Dean of Barchester. He marries the widow, Eleanor Bold.

Arachne, a woman of Colophon in Lydia, so skilful a weaver that she challenged Athene (q.v.) to a contest. She depicted in her work the amours of the gods, thereby arousing the wrath of Athene, who tore the work in pieces. Arachne in despair hanged herself, but was changed into a spider.

Arafa or ARAFAT, a hill near Mecca, the scene of certain ceremonies in the course of the Mohammedan pilgrimage (such as pelting a cairn with stones), no doubt the survival of heathen rites, explained by legends relative to Adam and Eve, to Abraham's sacrifice, and the like.

ARAGON, LOUIS (1897–   ), French novelist, poet, and essayist, a one-time leader of the Surrealists ('Mouvement perpétuel', 1926, poems; 'Le Paysan de Paris', 1926, a novel; 'Traité du Style', 1928, essay). Later prose writings reflect his politically committed attitude of 'social realism' and include novels of life in Paris and the provinces after 1900, e.g. the trilogy 'Le Monde réel' (1933–42, 'Les Cloches de Bâle', 'Les Beaux Quartiers', 'Les Voyageurs de l'impériale'), 'Aurélien' (1945), and the essay 'Pour un réalisme socialiste' (1934). He was one of the poets of the French Resistance during the 1939–45 war and reached a wide public with the lyrics and *chansons* of 'Le Crève-cœur', 'Les Jeux d'Elsa', 'La Diane française.'

Aramis, see *Three Musketeers.*

Arbāces, (1) the legendary founder of the Median empire (see *Sardanapalus*); (2) a character in Beaumont and Fletcher's 'A King and No King' (q.v.); (3) a character in Bulwer Lytton's 'The Last Days of Pompeii' (q.v.).

ARBER, EDWARD (1836–1912), began his career as an Admiralty clerk, 1854–78, but studied English Literature at King's College, London and in 1881 became professor of English at Mason College, Birmingham. He produced 'English Reprints' (1868–71), 'Transcripts of the Registers of the Company of Stationers of London, 1554–1640' (1875–94), and 'Term Catalogues, 1668–1709' (1903–6).

Arbiter elegantiae, see *Petronius.*

Arblay, MADAME D', see *Burney.*

ARBUTHNOT, JOHN (1667–1735), was M.D. of St. Andrews and physician in ordinary to Queen Anne. He formed a close friendship with Swift and was acquainted with Pope and most of the literary men of his day, and earned general praise both for his medical science, his wit and humour, and his kind heart. His 'History of John Bull' (q.v.), a collection of pamphlets issued in 1712 advocating the termination of the war in France, was included in Pope and Swift's 'Miscellanies' of 1727. The first of these pamphlets was called 'Law is a Bottomless Pit, exemplified in the case of the Lord Strutt, John Bull, Nicholas Frog, and Lewis Baboon, who spent all they had in a Law Suit'. This work was the origin of JOHN BULL, the typical Englishman. Dr. Arbuthnot was the principal author of the 'Memoirs of Martinus Scriblerus' (q.v.), which were published with Pope's 'Works' in 1741. He also wrote medical works, which proved him to be in advance of his age in medical science. Of these the most interesting is 'An Essay concerning the nature of Aliments' (1731), in which he urges the efficacy of appropriate diet in disease, and 'An Essay concerning the effect of Air on Human Bodies' (1733). In 'A Sermon preached to the People at the Mercat Cross, Edinburgh' (1706), he advocated the union of Scotland with England. His 'Essay on the Usefulness of Mathematical Learning' (1701) is said to be an excellent work. He wrote one poem, an ethical study, '*ΓΝΩΘΙ ΣΕΑΥΤΟΝ, Know Thyself*' (1734).

Arc, JOAN OF, see *Joan of Arc*.

A'rcădes, Part of an Entertainment presented to the Countess-Dowager of Derby at Harefield by some noble persons of her Family, by Milton (q.v.), written about 1633. It was probably composed at the request of Henry Lawes, the musician, while Milton was at Horton.

The piece is short, and consists of a song by nymphs and shepherds as they approach the seat of state of the countess, an address to them by the Genius of the Wood, in decasyllabic couplets, describing his occupations and praising music, and two further songs, one by the Genius, the other by the chorus.

Arcadia, a mountainous district in the Peloponnese, the domain of Pan, the shepherd's god, taken as an ideal region of rustic contentment. *Arcades ambo*, 'Arcadians both', is applied by Virgil (Ecl. vii. 4) to Corydon and Thyrsis, young shepherds and poets. The phrase *Et in Arcadia ego* is first found in a picture by Guercino (1590–1666). It shows a skull, which shepherds have discovered, with those words inscribed below it, meaning 'Even in Arcady there am I' (sc. 'Death'). The phrase is sometimes misinterpreted, or altered to *Et ego in Arcadia* [*vixi*], 'I too have lived in Arcady', to express the idea of a supreme happiness now lost. See E. Panofsky in 'Philosophy and History: Essays presented to E. Cassirer', 1936.

Arcadia, a series of verse eclogues connected by prose narrative, published in 1504 by Sannazar (q.v.), occupied with the loves, laments, and other doings of various shepherds in Arcadia. The work, which was immensely popular, was a link between the pastorals of Theocritus and Virgil and those of Montemayor, Sidney, Spenser, and later writers.

Arcadia, Greene's, see *Menaphon*.

Arcadia, The, a prose romance by Sir P. Sidney (q.v.), including at the end of each book a pastoral eclogue. It was begun in 1580 for the amusement of his sister, the countess of Pembroke, but not published until 1590, after Sidney's death. Sidney had no high opinion of the work and is said to have asked when dying that it should be destroyed. But it has importance in the history of English literature. The chief incidents were dramatized in 'The Arcadia' (1640) by James Shirley (q.v.).

The scene is laid in Arcadia, with its flowery meads, where 'shepherd boys pipe as tho' they would never be old'. The main thread of the story is as follows. Pyrocles and Musidorus, son and nephew of the king of Macedon, gallant knights and devoted friends, are wrecked on the coast of Laconia. Pyrocles is carried off by pirates, Musidorus rescued by shepherds and carried to Arcadia, whose king,

Basilius, in consequence of an oracle, has retired with his young wife Gynecia and his beautiful daughters Pamēla and Philoclea into a forest. Pyrocles seeing Philoclea in the forest falls in love with her, disguises himself as a woman (Zelmane), and is admitted by Basilius to his household. Basilius falls in love with Zelmane, while both Philoclea and her mother Gynecia, seeing through the disguise, also fall in love with him.

Musidorus discovers Pyrocles, falls in love with Pamēla, and obtains employment as servant to Dametas, who has charge of Pamēla. He makes love to Mopsa, daughter of Dametas, to veil his affection for Pamēla. The pathetic story is here introduced of the true Zelmane, daughter of the wicked Plexistus, who from love of Pyrocles had followed him as a page, fallen sick, and died. (The character of Bellario in Beaumont and Fletcher's 'Philaster' is borrowed from this Zelmane.) Cecropia, who had been heiress to the crown of Arcadia until Basilius married and had daughters, now carries off Pamēla, Philoclea, and the disguised Pyrocles. She is besieged in the castle where she holds them captive, trying by the most cruel devices to make one or other of the sisters marry her son Amphialus. (Pamēla's prayer during imprisonment acquired celebrity; Charles I on the scaffold handed a copy of it to Bishop Juxon, incurring thereby the censure of Milton.) Finally, after deeds of valour by the disguised Pyrocles, the stirring narrative of which is unfortunately unfinished, the sisters are delivered.

The sisters and Pyrocles return to the forest, where finally Musidorus runs away with Pamēla, and Pyrocles, pestered by both Basilius and Gynecia, gives to each an assignation in a cave on the same night, thus confronting husband and wife with each other. On this occasion Basilius drinks a love potion intended by Gynecia for Pyrocles, and falls apparently dead. Pyrocles is found in Philoclea's chamber and arrested; Musidorus is captured. Gynecia confesses that she is the cause of Basilius's death. Pyrocles and Musidorus are sentenced to death, Gynecia to be buried alive, Philoclea to a nunnery. At this moment a stranger arrives, who reveals the identity of Pyrocles and Musidorus as princes of Macedon and Thessaly, and Basilius comes to life again, his potion proving to have been only a sleeping draught. A general pardon and clearing up follow.

The miscellaneous poems printed with the 'Arcadia' contain little that is comparable to Sidney's other work, but they include the splendid dirge 'Ring out your bells, let mourning shews be spread', and the song 'My true love hath my heart'.

Archangel, an angel of the highest rank, a title generally applied in Christian legend to Michael (q.v.). For the seven archangels enumerated by the Book of Enoch, see under *Angel*.

Archdeacon Singleton, *Letters to*, see *Singleton*.

Archer, a character in Farquhar's 'The Beaux' Stratagem' (q.v.).

Archer, ISABEL, the heroine of H. James's 'The Portrait of a Lady' (q.v.).

ARCHER, WILLIAM (1856–1924), educated at Edinburgh University, was a distinguished dramatic critic, and is remembered for his editing and translation of the plays of Ibsen. He also wrote a life of Macready (1890), a study of Henry Irving (1883), and other works, including the play, 'The Green Goddess'.

Arches, COURT OF, the ecclesiastical court of appeal for the province of Canterbury, formerly held at the church of St. Mary-le-Bow or 'of the Arches' (so called from its arched crypt).

ARCHILŎCHUS of Paros (*fl.* 648 B.C.), 'one of the great original forces in Greek literature' (Jebb), especially celebrated for his satirical iambic verses, and proverbial for his bitterness. It is said that when Neobulē, who had been promised to Archilochus in marriage, was given by her father to a wealthier man, the poet's satire drove her and her sisters to suicide.

Archimago or ARCHIMAGE, in Spenser's 'Faerie Queene', is the great enchanter, symbolizing Hypocrisy, who deceives Una by assuming the appearance of the Red Cross Knight (I. i). His deceits are exposed and Archimago is 'laid full low in dungeon deep' (I. xii. 36). From this he emerges in Book II to seek vengeance on Sir Guyon for what he has suffered at the hands of the Red Cross Knight, and employs Braggadochio (q.v.) for the purpose.

Archimēdēs (287–212 B.C.), a famous mathematician of Syracuse, many of whose works are extant, including the treatises 'De Sphaera et Cylindro', 'Circuli Dimensio', etc. He is said to have constructed a kind of orrery representing the movements of the heavenly bodies, to have invented the screw for raising water which bears his name, and to have set on fire with lenses the ships of the Roman consul Marcellus that were besieging Syracuse. When the town was taken, the Roman general gave strict orders that Archimedes should not be hurt and offered a reward to whoever should bring him alive. But a soldier, not knowing who he was, killed Archimedes, who was engaged in solving a problem and refused to follow him. 'Give me where to stand and I will move the earth' is a saying attributed to him. See also *Eureka*.

Arch-poet, the name given to the anonymous German Latin poet, whose patron was Rainald of Dassel, arch-chancellor of Frederick Barbarossa and archbishop of Cologne (1161–7). His best-known poem is the 'Confession' in which occur the lines later used as a drinking song:

> meum est propositum taberna mori,
> ut sint vina proxima morientis ori.
> tunc cantabunt letius angelorum chori:
> 'sit deus propitius huic potatori.'

This term is also applied in Philemon Holland's translation of Camden's 'Britannia' to 'Henrie of Aurenches, Archpoet to King Henrie the Third', and used by Pope and Fielding as equivalent to poet laureate (q.v.).

Arcīte, see *Palamon and Arcite*.

Ardashir Babagan, a Persian employed by the Parthian king Ardawan, who, as told in the 'Shahnameh' of Firdusi (q.v.), eloped with Ardawan's favourite wife, made himself master of Persia, and became the founder of the Sasanian dynasty. In A.D. 226 he occupied Ctesiphon and took the title of king of the Iranians.

Arden, a large forest in the Midlands, centred in Warwickshire, which figures frequently in Elizabethan literature. The scene of the greater part of Shakespeare's 'As You Like It' is laid there. Drayton in 'Polyolbion', xiii. 15, makes it extend from the Severn to the Trent.

Arden of Feversham, *The Tragedy of Mr.*, a play published in 1592, of which the author is unknown. It has been attributed by some to Shakespeare. It deals with the persistent attempts, finally successful, of Mistress Arden and her paramour, Mosbie, to murder Arden, for which purpose they hire two murderers, Black Will and Shakbag. The crime is discovered and Mosbie and Mrs. Arden are executed. The play is founded on a murder actually committed in February 1550/1 and recorded by Holinshed. A play on the same subject was written by Lillo (q.v.).

Ardenne, THE FOUNTAIN OF, in Boiardo's 'Orlando Innamorato' (q.v.), had the power of changing to hate the love of those who drank its waters.

Ardennes, THE WILD BOAR OF THE, William de la Marck, the third son of John I, count of La Marck and Aremberg, so called because of his ferocity and acts of rapine. He was beheaded in 1485 by order of the Emperor Maximilian. He figures in Scott's 'Quentin Durward', where the historical facts regarding him are perverted.

Areopagitica: a Speech of Mr. John Milton *for the Liberty of Unlicensed Printing to the Parliament of England*, by Milton (q.v.), published in 1644. The title is derived from *Areopagus* (q.v.).

In this discourse Milton, addressing the 'Lords and Commons of England', attacks their recent order 'that no book . . . shall be henceforth printed unless the same be first approved and licensed by such . . . as shall be thereto appointed'. He shows, first that licensing has been chiefly the practice of those whom the Presbyterian Government most detest, viz. the Papacy and the Inquisition; while Moses, Daniel, St. Paul, and the

Fathers, by precept or example, enjoin freedom in the pursuit of learning. Next, that promiscuous reading is necessary to the constituting of human virtue. And thirdly, that the attempt to keep out evil doctrine by licensing is like 'the exploit of that gallant man who thought to pound up the crows by shutting his park gate'. Not only will licensing do no good, but it will be a grave discouragement and affront to learning; and he quotes the case of the imprisoned Galileo. Milton ends with a magnificent exhortation to the 'Lords and Commons of England' to consider 'what nation it is whereof ye are, and whereof ye are the governors: a nation not slow and dull, but of a quick, ingenious and piercing spirit'. He compares it to an 'eagle mewing its mighty youth', and urges that it should not be shackled and restricted. 'Give me the liberty to know, to utter, and to argue freely, according to conscience, above all liberties.'

Areopagus, the hill of Ares (Mars), near the Acropolis at Athens. It was the place of meeting of the 'Upper Council', the highest judicial tribunal of the city, with general supervision in political and religious matters.

Ares, the god of war of the ancient Greeks, identified by the Romans with Mars. He was said to be the son of Zeus and Hera, and to have been detected by Hephaestus (Vulcan) in an amorous intrigue with Aphrodite, caught in a net, and exposed to the ridicule of the assembled gods.

Arĕthūsa, a fountain in Ortygia (the island in the harbour of Syracuse). Legend relates that the river-god Alpheus (q.v.) fell in love with the nymph Arethusa when she bathed in his stream. She fled from him to Ortygia, where Artemiş transformed her into a fountain. But Alpheus, flowing under the sea, was united with the fountain. The myth is the subject of Shelley's poem 'Arethusa', and Milton refers to it in 'Arcades'.

Arethusa, a character in Beaumont and Fletcher's 'Philaster' (q.v.).

ARETINO, PIETRO, or the ARETINE (1492–1556), born at Arezzo in Italy, whence his name. He was author of five comedies and a tragedy, and also of satires and other works of a scandalous or licentious character. He is frequently mentioned in English works of the Elizabethan and later periods and differently appreciated, from 'It was one of the wittiest knaves God ever made' of Nash ('The Unfortunate Traveller') to 'that notorious ribald of Arezzo' of Milton ('Areopagitica').

Argalia, in Boiardo's 'Orlando Innamorato', the brother of Angelica (q.v.).

Argan, the *malade imaginaire* in Molière's comedy of that name.

Argante, (1) in the Arthurian legend, Morgan le Fay (q.v.), the fairy queen to whom Arthur, after the last battle, is borne to be healed of his wounds; (2) in Spenser's 'Faerie

Queene' (III. vii), a mighty and licentious giantess, typifying lust, daughter of Typhoeus the Titan; (3) a character in Molière's 'Les Fourberies de Scapin'.

Argantes, in Tasso's 'Jerusalem Delivered' (q.v.), a fierce Circassian, a champion on the pagan side, finally killed by Tancred.

Argenis, see *Barclay (J.).*

Argentile and Curan, a story in the 'Albion's England' of Warner (q.v.), reprinted in Percy's 'Reliques'. King Adelbright on his death-bed leaves his daughter Argentile to the care of King Edel, who, hoping to get her kingdom, keeps her from the sight of princely suitors. Curan, son of a Danish prince, takes service in Edel's household as a kitchen drudge in order to woo her, and Edel, to further his own plans, encourages his suit. The indignant Argentile flees, and Curan in despair becomes a shepherd. He falls in love with a neatherd's maid, who turns out to be Argentile. They are married, and Curan, claiming his wife's kingdom, conquers and kills Edel and becomes king of Northumberland.

Argentina or ARGENTORATUM, in imprints, Strasburg.

Argestes, the Latin name for the west-south-west, or according to Pliny the west-north-west, wind.

Argonauts, the name given to the heroes who accompanied Jason (q.v.) on board the ship 'Argo' to Colchis to recover the Golden Fleece. The cause of this expedition was as follows: Phrixus and Helle, pursued by the hatred of their step-mother Ino (q.v.), fled from Thebes to the court of Aeëtes, king of Colchis, on the back of a ram who had a golden fleece and wings. On the way, Helle became giddy and fell into the part of the sea called, in consequence, the Hellespont; but Phrixus arrived safely, sacrificed the ram to Zeus, and dedicated the golden fleece. Aeëtes, to obtain possession of the fleece, murdered Phrixus. When Jason, some time after, demanded of his uncle Pelias the kingdom of Iolchos, which Pelias had usurped, Pelias to get rid of him said he would surrender the kingdom if Jason would first avenge the death of their relation Phrixus. Jason undertook the expedition, embarked on the 'Argo' with the bravest of the Greeks, and after many adventures reached Colchis. Aeëtes promised to surrender the fleece, which had been the cause of the death of Phrixus, if Jason performed certain difficult tasks. These included the sowing of a dragon's teeth, from which armed men would arise whose fury would be turned against Jason. With the help of Medea (q.v.), the king's daughter, who fell in love with Jason and possessed a knowledge of enchantments, the tasks were successfully accomplished, and Jason and Medea returned to Iolchos with the golden fleece.

The story is the subject of one of Pindar's best odes (Pyth. iv), of the 'Argonautica' of

Apollonius Rhodius (q.v.), and of W. Morris's 'Life and Death of Jason' (q.v.).

Argos or ARGUS, (1) a monster with a hundred eyes. Hera, jealous of Io (q.v.), whom Zeus had changed into a heifer, sent Argos to watch her rival. But Hermes by order of Zeus slew him, having lulled him to sleep with his lyre. Hera put the eyes of Argos in the tail of the peacock, a bird sacred to her; (2) the dog of Odysseus (q.v.), who recognized his master on his return from Troy after an absence of twenty years.

Argyle, ARCHIBALD CAMPBELL, *eighth earl, first marquess of* (1598–1661), who took a prominent part in the events in Scotland that contributed to the downfall of Charles I, figures in Scott's 'The Legend of Montrose' (q.v.), where his character is contrasted with that of his great rival, the earl of Montrose. Beheaded 1661.

Argyle, JOHN CAMPBELL, *second duke of* (1678–1743), a prime agent in bringing about the union of England and Scotland, and a distinguished military commander (he suppressed Mar's rising of 1715), figures in Scott's 'The Heart of Midlothian' (q.v.).

Ariadne, daughter of Minos (q.v.), king of Crete, fell in love with Theseus (q.v.), who had come to deliver the Athenians from the tribute of youths and maidens sacrificed to the Minotaur (q.v.). With her help he penetrated the Labyrinth where the monster was confined and destroyed it. He carried away Ariadne, but when they arrived at the island of Naxos, forsook her. Ariadne in despair hanged herself, or according to another legend was found by Dionysus (Bacchus), who took her to wife.

Arian heresy: 'under Constantine the emperor about three hundred years and upward after Christ, Arius a priest in the church of Alexandria, a subtle-witted and a marvellous fair-spoken man, but discontented that one should be placed before him in honour, whose superior he thought himself in desert, became through envy and stomach prone unto contradiction, and bold to broach at the length that heresy, wherein the deity of our Lord Jesus Christ contained but not opened in the [Apostles'] creed, the co-equality and co-eternity of the Son with the Father, was denied' (Hooker, 'Eccles. Polity', v. xlii). The heresy was repudiated in the Nicene Creed and in the Athanasian Creed. One of the most interesting points about this heresy is that all the 'barbarian' tribes who overran the western Roman Empire in the 4th, 5th, and 6th cents. had been converted by Arian preachers (except the Franks, who were heathens till the time of Clovis, and the Angles and Saxons). The result was that the Franks were Catholics from the first, and had inducement to fight the Arian tribes.

Ariel, (1) in Shakespeare's 'The Tempest' (q.v.), an airy spirit whom the witch Sycorax has imprisoned in a cloven pine and whom

Prospero by his magic releases and employs to give effect to his designs; (2) in Milton's 'Paradise Lost' (vi. 371), a rebel angel; (3) in Pope's 'The Rape of the Lock' (ii. 53 et seq.), the chief of the sylphs 'whose humbler province is to tend the fair'.

Aries, see *Ram*.

Arimanes, Ahriman (q.v.), the form of that name used by Byron in his 'Manfred' (q.v.).

Arimaspians, a Scythian people, of whom Herodotus (iv. 27) relates that they had only one eye, and that there were gold-guarding gryphons in their country; a legend that probably relates to the presence of gold in the Urals.

Arioch, in Milton's 'Paradise Lost' (vi. 371), one of the rebel angels.

ARION (7th cent. B.C.?), a semi-mythical poet and musician of Lesbos, whose principal achievement was to perfect the dithyramb or hymn to Dionysus. He is said to have spent the greater part of his life at the court of Periander, tyrant of Corinth, and also to have visited Italy, where he amassed much wealth. On his return he was thrown overboard by the sailors, who desired to acquire his treasure. But a dolphin, charmed by the song he had been allowed to sing before his death, carried him to land.

Arion, a fabulous horse, the son of Poseidon and Demeter. It belonged to Adrastus (q.v.), and its swiftness enabled him to escape after the failure of his expedition against Thebes.

ARIOSTO, LUDOVICO (1474–1533), born at Reggio, spent the greater part of his life at Ferrara and for many years was in the service, first of Cardinal Ippolito, and then of Duke Alfonso I, of Este. This family he exalted in his poem, the 'Orlando Furioso' (q.v.), published in its final form in 1532, the greatest of Italian romantic epics. There is a portrait by Titian, said to be of Ariosto, in the National Gallery.

Ariosto of the North, so Byron calls Sir W. Scott ('Childe Harold's Pilgrimage', iv. 40).

Aristaeus, an ancient divinity worshipped in many parts of Greece, as the protector of flocks and herds, and vines and olives. He is generally described as the son of Apollo and Cyrene. Virgil in the fourth Georgic relates how Aristaeus, having angered the Dryads and lost all his bees in consequence, was able with the advice of Proteus to conciliate the nymphs and obtain new swarms from the carcasses of bulls. He was father of Actaeon (q.v.).

Aristarchus of Samos, who lived about 280 B.C., was an eminent astronomer and mathematician; he lived at Alexandria. Going beyond Pythagoras (q.v.), he maintained that the earth revolved round the sun, and that this was the cause of the seasons.

Aristarchus of Samothrace, a celebrated grammarian and critic, who was head of the

Alexandrian Library from *c.* 180 to *c.* 145 B.C. His principal work was the revision of the text of Homer's 'Iliad' and 'Odyssey'.

Aristīdes, an Athenian general and statesman, surnamed 'The Just', who commanded his tribe at the battle of Marathon (490 B.C.) and was archon in 489. He was the advocate of a quiet and conservative policy as opposed to the 'strong navy' policy of Themistocles. The struggle between the leaders became acute and Aristides was ostracized (see below) in 482, but fought at the battle of Salamis, and commanded the Athenian contingent at the battle of Plataea. He died about 468 B.C., so poor that his funeral could not be paid for from his estate. Ostracism (from οστρακου, potsherd) was effected by popular vote, the voters writing on a potsherd or tablet the name of the person they desired to be sent into exile. Plutarch relates that an illiterate voter asked Aristides (not knowing him) to write 'Aristides' upon his tablet. The good man, surprised, asked whether Aristides had ever injured him. 'No,' replied the voter, 'but it vexes me to hear him everywhere called the Just.'

Aristippus, of Cyrene, a disciple of Socrates and founder of the Cyrenaic school of philosophy. He regarded pleasure as the only absolute good in life. But he was not a sensualist, and held that the pleasant was identical with the good, and must be obtained by self-control.

Aristippus, or the Joviall Philosopher, see *Randolph (T.).*

ARISTOPHANES (*c.* 448–*c.* 380 B.C.), the great Athenian comic poet, whose comedies are of historical value for their caricatures of the leading personages of the time and their comments on current affairs. The following are his extant comedies: the 'Acharnians' (an attack on the war-party), the 'Knights' (an attack on the demagogue Cleon), the 'Clouds' (a criticism of the new spirit of philosophical inquiry), the 'Peace' (advocating peace with Sparta), the 'Wasps' (an attack on demagogues), the 'Birds' (general political satire), the 'Frogs' (Euripides and Aeschylus contending for the tragic prize among the dead), the 'Plutus' (an allegory on the coming of wealth to the worthy), the 'Lysistrata' and 'Ecclesiazusae' (dealing with government by women), and the 'Thesmophoriazusae' (Euripides tried and convicted at the female festival of the Thesmophoria).

Aristophanes, THE ENGLISH, Foote (q.v.).

Aristophanes' Apology, a poem by R. Browning (q.v.), published in 1875.

Balaustion (see *Balaustion's Adventure*) is returning to Rhodes, with Euthukles her husband, after the fall of Athens and the death of Euripides. She relates the events of the night on which the news of the death of Euripides was received. Aristophanes, half-drunk and flushed with the triumph of his 'Thesmophoriazusae', had come to their

house, and a discussion had followed, which forms the substance of the poem, between Aristophanes and Balaustion: the former defending comedy as the representation of real life and attacking the ascetic and unnatural Euripides; the latter maintaining the superior value of the tragic poet, and supporting her view by reading his 'Herakles'.

ARISTOTLE (384–322 B.C.), the great Greek philosopher, was born at Stageira in Chalcidice (Macedonia). His father was Nicomachus, the physician of Amyntas II, king of Macedonia. Aristotle studied at Athens under Plato, and stayed there for twenty years. He was subsequently appointed by Philip of Macedon to be tutor to his son Alexander. On the accession of the latter to the throne (335), Aristotle returned to Athens, where in the shady paths surrounding the Lyceum he lectured to many scholars, while walking up and down (περιπατῶυ), whence his school came to be known as the Peripatetic. He remained thus occupied for thirteen years, and here composed the greater part of his works. After the death of Alexander in 323 Aristotle came under political suspicion and retired to Chalcis in Euboea, where he died. His works (in the main notes or summaries of his oral lectures), which had an immense influence on thought and some of which serve as text-books today, cover an extraordinarily wide field: logic, moral philosophy, metaphysics, poetry, physics, zoology, politics, and rhetoric. He created Logic, the science of reasoning. He surveyed the whole range of zoology, adopting broad classifications which have been accepted by later science. His most famous treatises are his 'Ethics', an introduction to moral philosophy (he was the first to point out that virtue is a state of the will, and not of the reason), 'Poetics', and 'Politics', though the scope of this last is limited to the city-state of his day. He was made known in the Middle Ages by Latin versions and by the works of Arabian philosophers, such as Avicenna and Averroës (qqv.).

Ark, The, Sir W. Ralegh's ship at the battle with the Spanish Armada.

Arlotto Mainardo (1396–1484), the curate or *piovano* of S. Cresci di Maciuoli, near Fiesole, a witty and jovial priest, who made several journeys to Flanders and is said even to have visited England, where he obtained the favour of Edward IV. The witticisms attributed to him were collected in 'Facetie Piacevoli' (1500), which were frequently reprinted.

Armachanus, the Latin title of the archbishops of Armagh; see *Fitzralph.*

Armada, THE INVINCIBLE, consisting of some 130 ships (besides smaller vessels), was collected by Philip II of Spain and dispatched in 1588 under the duke of Medina Sidonia. It was to sail to Flanders to transport thence to England the Spanish army of the duke of Parma. It was defeated and dispersed by the

English fleet under Lord Howard of Effingham and such captains as Drake, Frobisher, and Hawkins.

Armadale, a novel by Wilkie Collins (q.v.), published in 1866.

Armado, Don ADRIANO DE, a character in Shakespeare's 'Love's Labour's Lost' (q.v.).

Armageddon, in Rev. xvi. 16, the place where the Kings of the Earth are to be gathered together for 'the battle of that great day of God Almighty'.

Armida, in Tasso's 'Jerusalem Delivered' (q.v.), the niece of Hidraotes, king of Damascus, a powerful magician. She offered her services to the defenders of Jerusalem when it was besieged by the Christians under Godfrey de Bouillon, and going to the Christian camp lured away by her beauty many of the principal knights. She inveigled them by magic power into a delicious garden, where they were overcome by indolence. Among her captives were Rinaldo of Este and Tancred (qq.v.).

Armine, FERDINAND, the hero of Disraeli's 'Henrietta Temple' (q.v.).

Arminianism, the doctrine of James Arminius or Marmensen (d. 1609), a Dutch protestant theologian, who put forth views opposed to those of Calvin, especially on predestination, refusing to hold God responsible for evil. In 1618–19 his doctrines were condemned by the synod of Dort; but they spread rapidly and were embraced, in whole or in part, by large sections of the Reformed Churches.

Arminius (latinized form of HERMANN) (B.C. 18–A.D. 19), the chief of the German tribe of the Cherusci, who incited his countrymen to rise against the Romans and destroyed the army of Varus in A.D. 8. He also conducted the resistance to Germanicus.

ARMSTRONG, JOHN (1709–79), a physician and poet, author of 'The Art of Preserving Health' (1744), a surprisingly pleasant poem in spite of its unattractive title; also of 'Taste', a satirical epistle of literary criticism.

Armstrong, WILLIAM, known as KINMONT WILLIE (*fl.* 1596), a border moss-trooper, whose nickname is taken from his castle of Kinmont in Canonby, Dumfriesshire. He was captured in 1587 but escaped; he was imprisoned in 1596 at Carlisle, but was rescued by the Scottish warden. His fate is unknown. He is the hero of the ballad, 'Kinmont Willie', included in Scott's 'Border Minstrelsy'.

Arnaut, an Albanian.

Arno, the river on which stands Florence, the city where Dante was born and the home of Boccaccio, the Medici, etc.

Arnold, in Byron's 'The Deformed Transformed' (q.v.), the ugly son of Bertha, who is miraculously transformed into the shape of Achilles.

ARNOLD, SIR EDWIN (1832–1904), educated at King's College, London, and University College, Oxford, was principal of the Poona College, Bombay Presidency, 1856 to 1861, when he joined the staff of the 'Daily Telegraph'. The fruit of his Indian experience is seen at its best in 'The Light of Asia, or The Great Renunciation' (q.v., 1879), a poem of which Buddha is the subject. He wrote a number of other poems, some of them translations from the Sanskrit.

ARNOLD, MATTHEW (1822–88), son of T. Arnold (q.v.), the great head master of Rugby, was educated at Rugby, Winchester, and Balliol College, Oxford, where he won the Newdigate Prize. He became fellow of Oriel College, and an inspector of schools, a post which he held from 1851 till 1883. He was professor of poetry at Oxford from 1857 to 1867. His first volume of poems, 'The Strayed Reveller and other Poems', appeared in 1849. It contained 'The Forsaken Merman', 'The Sick King in Bokhara', and the sonnet on Shakespeare. 'Empedocles on Etna [q.v.], and other Poems', containing 'Tristram and Iseult' (q.v.), followed in 1852. Both these volumes were shortly afterwards withdrawn from circulation. In 1853 appeared a volume of 'Poems' containing extracts from the earlier books, 'Sohrab and Rustum' and 'The Scholar-Gipsy' (qq.v.); also the 'Church of Brou', 'Requiescat', the 'Memorial Verses to Wordsworth' and the 'Stanzas in Memory of the Author of Obermann'. 'Poems, Second Series', including 'Balder Dead' (q.v.), appeared in 1855; 'Merope, a Tragedy' (q.v.) in 1858; and 'New Poems', including 'Thyrsis' (q.v.), 'Rugby Chapel', 'Heine's Grave', 'A Southern Night' (a lament for one of his brothers), and other well-known pieces, in 1867.

The bulk of Matthew Arnold's prose works appeared after 1860. The most important of these were the 'Essays in Criticism' (1865 and 1888), in which he gave literary criticism an unusually wide scope, extending it to an attack on the 'philistinism' or 'provinciality' then, in his opinion, prevailing in England. He also published lectures, 'On Translating Homer' (1861) and 'The Study of Celtic Literature' (1867). His 'Culture and Anarchy', a criticism of English social and political life, appeared in 1869; and this was followed by various works of religious criticism, 'St. Paul and Protestantism' (1870), 'Literature and Dogma' (1873), 'God and the Bible' (1875), and 'Last Essays on Church and Religion' (1877).

Special reference is due to Arnold's attempts to secure the improvement of education, and particularly secondary education, in England. He was sent in 1859, and again in 1865, to study educational systems on the Continent, and his reports, 'The Popular Education of France' (1861) and 'Schools and Universities on the Continent' (1868), drew attention to our deficiencies in this respect. There are

41

further references to his views on education in other writings, e.g. 'Culture and Anarchy' (1869), and the 'Letters on Compulsory Education' in 'Friendship's Garland' (1871).

ARNOLD, THOMAS (1795–1842), educated at Winchester and Corpus Christi College, Oxford, is principally remembered as the headmaster (1828–42) who raised Rugby to the rank of a great public school. He was author of an unfinished 'History of Rome' (1838–42), inspired by Niebuhr (q.v.), and of an edition of Thucydides (1830–5). He was appointed Regius professor of modern history at Oxford in 1841. His 'History of the later Roman Commonwealth' appeared posthumously in 1845.

ARNOLD, SIR THOMAS WALKER (1864–1930), a learned writer on the Caliphate, Legacy of Islam, &c.

Arnold of Brescia (d. 1155), an Italian Augustinian, an eloquent ascetic, who vigorously condemned the temporal power and abuses of the clergy and papacy. He gathered round him a following known as Arnoldists, and fomented the revolution by which the Roman republic of 1145 was instituted. Arnold fled from Rome in 1155, was seized by order of Frederick Barbarossa, handed over to the pope, Adrian IV (Nicholas Breakspear), and executed.

Arraignment of Paris, The, a pastoral play in verse by G. Peele (q.v.), published in 1584.

It was written for and played before Queen Elizabeth, whose beauty and virtue are duly celebrated. Paris is tending his flocks on Ida, with Oenone his wife, when he is called on to decide to which of the three goddesses, Juno, Pallas, or Venus, the golden apple shall be awarded. He decides in favour of Venus, who carries away Paris, leaving Oenone disconsolate. Juno and Pallas arraign Paris before the gods of partiality in his judgement. The case is referred to Diana. She evades the delicate choice by awarding the apple to the nymph Eliza, 'our Zebeta fair'.

Arria, see *Paetus.*

ARRIAN (c. A.D. 95–175), of Nicomedia in Bithynia, an officer in the Roman army who became consul under Antoninus Pius, wrote a history of the Asiatic expedition of Alexander the Great, with a supplementary account of India, including the voyage of Nearchus, Alexander's general, from the mouth of the Indus to the Persian Gulf; also a manual of the philosophy of Epictetus, and other works.

Arrowsmith, Martin, a novel by Sinclair Lewis (q.v.), published in 1925.

Arsăcēs, the founder of the Parthian empire and the first of the Arsacid rulers. He revolted against the Seleucids about 250 B.C.

Arsis, in modern acceptation, the strong or accented syllable in English metre. The precise meaning of the word in Greek is uncertain.

Art Nouveau, architecture and decoration of the turn of the 19th cent. using unclassical proportions and forms of plants, etc., in an attempt to get away from the formality of academic tradition.

Art of Dining, see *Hayward (A.).*

Art of English Poesy, *Observations on the,* an attack on the use of rhyme in English poetry by Thomas Campion (d. 1619), to which S. Daniel (q.v.) replied in his 'Defence of Rhyme'.

Art of Rhetorique, see *Wilson (T.).*

Artaxominous, the king in 'Bombastes Furioso' (q.v.).

Arte of English Poesie, see *Puttenham.*

Artegal, a legendary king of Britain, son of Gorbonian, deposed for his crimes and replaced by his brother Elidure. When Artegal returned from exile, Elidure restored him to the throne. The story, which is in Geoffrey of Monmouth, is the subject of a poem, 'Artegal and Elidure', by Wordsworth.

Artegall, SIR, in Spenser's 'Faerie Queene', Bk. v, the champion of Justice. Britomart (q.v.), to whom his image has been revealed by a magic mirror, is in love with him, and her quest of him ends in their union. Symbolizing Lord Grey de Wilton, he undertakes the rescue of Irena (Ireland) from the tyrant Grantorto. Jointly with Prince Arthur he slays the Soudan (Philip II of Spain).

Artemis, see *Diana.*

Artemisia, (1) a queen of Halicarnassus in Caria, who accompanied Xerxes in his invasion of Greece and fought with distinction at the battle of Salamis. This is 'the Carian Artemisia' referred to by Tennyson in 'The Princess', ii; (2) the sister, wife, and successor of Mausōlus, king of Caria. Her grief at his death was so great that she mixed his ashes with her drink and built in his memory at Halicarnassus the Mausoleum, which passed for one of the seven wonders of the world. She reigned 352–350 B.C.

The name 'Artemisia' is given to the genus of plants that includes wormwood or absinth, either from the goddess Artemis, because of their medicinal properties, or from the above queen, who mixed her husband's ashes with her drink.

Artful Dodger, THE, a character in Dickens's 'Oliver Twist' (q.v.).

Arthur, KING. The romantic figure of King Arthur has probably some historical basis, and there is reason to think that, as Nennius (q.v.) states, he was a chieftain or general (*dux bellorum*) in the 5th or 6th cent. The 'Annales Cambriae' (q.v.) place the battle of Mount Badon, 'in which Arthur carried the cross of our Lord Jesus Christ on his shoulders', in 518, and the 'battle of Camlan, in which Arthur and Medraut fell', in 539. The contemporary chronicler Gildas (q.v.) makes no mention of Arthur (though he refers to the battle of Badon), nor do some of the principal Welsh bards of the 6th and 7th cents. But there is mention of him in certain ancient poems contained in the 'Black Book of Carmarthen' and more especially in the ancient Welsh romance 'Kilhwch and Olwen' (q.v.), where he figures with Kay, Bedivere, and Gawain (Gwalchmei). But this Arthur is a king of fairyland, and the author of the tale is building, in Matthew Arnold's words, with the 'materials of an older architecture, greater, cunninger, and more majestical'. In fact, Arthur and several other characters in the Arthurian legend can be traced to figures in the ancient Celtic pantheon (Rhys, 'Studies in the Arthurian Legend', 1901), but their working up and fashioning was, in the wide sense of the word, English (Saintsbury, 'The Flourishing of Romance' in P. E. L.). Rhys suggests that there were originally two Arthurs, the British god and the human general, whose characters have become blended in legend.

Arthur first takes definite form as a romantic hero in the 'Historia Regum Britanniae' of Geoffrey of Monmouth (q.v.), a work in which the author's imagination played a very large part. In this narrative Arthur is the son of Uther Pendragon (Welsh = chief leader in war) and Ygaerne (Igraine), wife of Gorlois of Cornwall, whom Uther wins by the help of Merlin's magic. The elves bestow on him long life, riches, and virtues. At the age of 15 he becomes king of Britain and wars against Scots, Picts, and Saxons. With his sword 'Caliburn' (Excalibur) he slays Childric, defeats the heathen, and conquers Scotland, Ireland, Iceland, and the Orkneys. He marries Guanhamara (Wenhaver, Guinevere), a lady of noble Roman family. He conquers many lands on the Continent. His court is at Caerleon on Usk. He is summoned to pay tribute to the Emperor Lucius of Rome, resists, and declares war. Guanhamara and the kingdom are left in Modred, his nephew's, charge. On his way to Rome he slays the giant of St. Michael's Mount. Walwain (Gawain), his ambassador, defies the emperor and bears himself bravely in the ensuing combat. Arthur is about to enter Rome when he receives warning that Modred has seized Guanhamara and the kingdom. He returns with Walwain, who is slain on landing. Modred retreats to Cornwall, and in a final battle on the Camel, is slain with all his knights. Arthur is mortally wounded, and is borne to the island of Avalon for the healing of his wounds. Guanhamara takes the veil.

This story was developed by the Norman writer Wace (q.v.), who added many details. The 'Round Table' is first mentioned by him, a device to settle the disputes as to precedence among Arthur's knights. The wounded king is expected to return from Avalon and resume his kingdom. Wace's work served as the basis of the 'Brut' of Layamon (q.v.), the first English record of the 'noble deeds of England', which adds many romantic details, and

a fairy element, to the story. Elves are present at Arthur's birth, his sword and spear are of magic origin. After the final battle at Camelford, Arthur is borne off to Argante (Morgan le Fay, q.v.) in Avalon, in a magic boat.

The Arthurian story was also developed in the French *Matière de Bretagne*, by such writers as Marie de France and Chrétien de Troyes, and later by Robert de Baron. Arthur became the centre of a mass of legends in various tongues. A number of these, dealing with various personages, Merlin, Launcelot, Tristram, etc., were gradually associated with him. He is the central figure only in the narratives of his earlier years and of his final battles and death. In the other tales his court is merely the rallying-point for the various adventurous knights. He ceases to be the model of purity and valour, and yields in importance to Gawain and Launcelot.

The story of Arthur, as summarized above, is the foundation of Malory's 'Morte Darthur' (q.v.), but the greater part of this work is occupied with the exploits of the Knights of the Round Table, the quest of the Holy Grail, the loves of Launcelot and Guinevere and of Tristram and Iseult. For Tennyson's presentment of the story see *Idylls of the King*. See also *William of Malmesbury*; and *Glastonbury* for Arthur's alleged burial there.

Arthur, PRINCE, in Spenser's 'Faerie Queene', symbolizes 'Magnificence' (? Magnanimity), in the Aristotelian sense of the perfection of all the virtues. He enters into the adventures of the several knights and brings them to a fortunate conclusion. His chief adventures are the slaying of the three-bodied monster Gerioneo (Philip II of Spain) and the rescue from him of Belgè (the Netherlands) (Bk. v. x and xi); and, jointly with Artegall, the slaying of the Soudan (Philip II) in his 'chariot high' (the Armada) (v. viii). Whether Spenser had in mind any particular living person in his description of Arthur is uncertain; perhaps the earl of Leicester is indicated.

Articles of Confederation and Perpetual Union, THE, were the thirteen Articles, agreed to by the Continental Congress in 1777, which provided for a union of the American Colonies to be known as the United States of America. The Articles were subject to ratification by the individual States, and it was not until 1781, when Maryland finally agreed to the Articles, that ratification was complete. Once the Articles were effective, the old Continental Congress proceeded to act as the Congress of the Confederation.

Articles of Religion, THE, or THE THIRTY-NINE ARTICLES, the thirty-nine statements to which those who take orders in the Church of England subscribe. In 1553 forty-two Articles were published. These were modified and reduced by Convocation to thirty-nine and received parliamentary sanction in 1571.

Arts Council of Great Britain, THE, was incorporated by royal charter in 1946 for the purpose of developing greater knowledge, understanding, and practice of the fine arts and to increase their accessibility to the public. It grew out of the war-time Council for the Encouragement of Music and the Arts, which began in 1940 with a grant of £25,000 from the Pilgrim Trust. The first chairman was Lord Macmillan; the vice-chairman and prime mover Dr. Thomas Jones, C.H. Lord Keynes (q.v.) was chairman from 1942 to 1945.

Arundel Marbles, THE, part of a collection of statuary, pictures, gems, and books made by Thomas Howard, 2nd earl of Arundel (1585?–1646), a patron of learning and the arts. The marbles and many statues were given by his grandson, the 6th duke of Norfolk, to the University of Oxford. The marbles include the 'Parian Chronicle' (q.v.).

Arundines Cami, a collection of Cambridge Latin verses, projected and published in 1841 by Henry Drury (1812–63).

Arvalan, the son of Kehama, in Southey's 'Curse of Kehama' (q.v.).

Arveragus, in Chaucer's 'Franklin's Tale' (see under 'Canterbury Tales'), the husband of Dorigen.

Arviragus, in Shakespeare's 'Cymbeline' (q.v.), one of the king's sons.

Aryan, a term applied by some to the great division or family of languages which includes Sanskrit, Zend, Persian, Greek, Latin, Celtic, Teutonic, and Slavonic, with their modern representatives; also called Indo-European and Indo-Germanic. Also applied to a member of the Aryan family, one belonging to or descended from the ancient people who spoke the parent Aryan language. [OED.]

As You Like It, a comedy by Shakespeare (q.v.), probably produced about 1599, not printed till the folio of 1623. It is a dramatic adaptation of Lodge's romance 'Rosalynde' (q.v.), with the addition of the characters of Jaques and Touchstone, the humorous scenes, and other minor alterations.

Frederick has usurped the dominions of the Duke his brother, who is living with his faithful followers in the forest of Arden (q.v.). Celia, Frederick's daughter, and Rosalind, the Duke's daughter, living at Frederick's court, witness a wrestling match in which Orlando, son of Sir Rowland de Boys, defeats a powerful adversary, and Rosalind falls in love with Orlando and he with her. Orlando, who at his father's death has been left in the charge of his elder brother Oliver, has been driven from home by Oliver's cruelty. Frederick, learning that Orlando is the son of Sir Rowland, who was a friend of the exiled Duke, has his anger against the latter revived, and banishes Rosalind from his court, and Celia accompanies her. Rosalind assumes a countryman's dress and takes the name Ganymede;

Celia passes as Aliena his sister. They live in the forest of Arden, and fall in with Orlando, who has joined the banished Duke. Ganymede encourages Orlando to make love to her as though she were his Rosalind. Oliver comes to the forest to kill Orlando, but is saved by him from a lioness, and is filled with remorse for his cruelty. He falls in love with Aliena, and their wedding is arranged for the morrow. Ganymede undertakes to Orlando that she will by magic produce Rosalind at the same time to be married to him. When all are assembled in presence of the banished Duke to celebrate the double nuptials, Celia and Rosalind put off their disguise and appear in their own characters. News is brought that Frederick the usurper, setting out to seize and destroy his brother and his followers, has been converted from his intention by 'an old religious man' and has made restitution of the dukedom.

Jaques, a lord attending on the banished Duke, a contemplative character, compounded of humour and melancholy, and Touchstone, a cynical philosopher in the garb of a buffoon, who marries the country wench, Audrey, are among the delightful minor characters of the play.

Asaph, in the part of 'Absalom and Achitophel' (q.v.) written by Tate, is Dryden, and refers to the Asaph of 1 Chron. xvi. 4–7 and xxv. 1, and the hereditary choir, the 'Sons of Asaph', who conducted the musical services of the Temple.

Asaph, ST. (*d. c.* 600), a pupil of St. Kentigern (q.v.) in his monastery at Llanelwy, and his successor as its prior. He was the first bishop of that see, which took his name. He is commemorated on 1 May.

Ascalaphus, see *Proserpine.*

Ascanius, the son of Aeneas (q.v.).

Ascapart, the giant conquered and converted by 'Bevis of Hampton' (q.v.).

Ascendant, see *House* (Astrological).

ASCHAM, ROGER (1515–68), was educated at St. John's College, Cambridge, where he distinguished himself in classics and became Greek reader in 1538. He published in 1545 'Toxophilus', a treatise in English in dialogue form on archery, urging the importance of physical training in education. He succeeded Grindal as tutor to Princess Elizabeth in 1548, and travelled on the Continent as secretary to Sir Thomas Morison, English ambassador to Charles V, in 1550–3. In the latter year he became Latin secretary to Queen Mary, being specially permitted to continue in his profession of Protestantism. In 1558 he was appointed private tutor to Queen Elizabeth. In his 'Scholemaster', published after his death, he dealt with the education of boys of position both at school, of which he criticized the prevailing discipline, and after leaving it, pointing out the dangers of idle attendance at court and of Italian travel. By his 'Toxophilus' and 'Scholemaster' and by his 'Letters' he contributed notably to the development of a simple English prose style. His love of sport is interesting. According to Camden ('Annales', 1568), he lived and died a poor man, owing to his addiction to dicing and cock-fighting. Whatever may be the truth about his gambling (which he condemns in 'Toxophilus'), he acknowledges in the 'Scholemaster' his interest in cock-fighting.

ASCLEPIADES, a lyric poet of Samos, of the 3rd cent. B.C., to whom is attributed the invention of the Asclepiadic metre (a spondee, two or three choriambs, and an iambus).

Asclepius, see *Aesculapius.*

Asfandiyar, see *Isfendiyar.*

Asgard, in Scandinavian mythology, the region, in the centre of the universe, inhabited by the gods.

Ash Wednesday, the first day of Lent, so called from the practice in the Roman Catholic Church of marking the foreheads of penitents with ash on that day.

Ash Wednesday, the title of a book of poems by T. S. Eliot (q.v.).

Ashfield, FARMER and MRS., characters in Morton's 'Speed the Plough' (q.v.).

Ashkenazim, see *Sephardim.*

Ashley Library, a private library collected by Thomas James Wise (q.v.), remarkable for its first editions of famous English poets and dramatists from Jacobean times, i.e. from Ben Jonson downwards. It was acquired by the British Museum in 1937. The catalogue of the library (11 volumes) appeared in 1922–30.

ASHMOLE, ELIAS (1617–92), antiquary and astrologer, studied physics and mathematics at Brasenose College, Oxford. He joined the Royalists and held several government appointments. He presented his collection of curiosities (based on the collection given to him by John Tradescant, q.v.) to Oxford University, to which he subsequently bequeathed his library. He wrote or edited antiquarian and Rosicrucian works.

Ashtaroth, see *Astarte.*

Ashton, SIR WILLIAM, LADY, and LUCY, characters in Scott's 'Bride of Lammermoor' (q.v.).

Asia, PAMPERED JADES OF, see under *Tamburlaine the Great.*

Asiento Treaty, a treaty between Great Britain and Spain, accompanying the Treaty of Utrecht of 1713, by which Great Britain obtained the exclusive right for a period of years of importing negro slaves into the Spanish colonies in America, and also the right of sending each year one cargo of goods to Portobello.

Aslauga's Knight, a romance by De La Motte Fouqué (the author of 'Undine', q.v.) translated by Carlyle in 'German Romance'.

Aslauga was the daughter of Sigurd and wife of Ragnar Lodbrog. The Knight Froda, long afterwards reading of her, elects her as the lady of his heart and his helper in fight and song. Aslauga appears to him from time to time and controls his destiny, and finally carries him off to the land of spirits.

Asmadai, in Milton's 'Paradise Lost', vi. 365, one of the rebel angels, vanquished by Raphael. The name is the same as 'Asmodæus' (q.v.).

Asmodæus, in Tobit iii. 8, the evil spirit who loved Sarah, daughter of Raguel, and slew the seven husbands given to her in succession. The spirit was driven away to Egypt by the smoke made by the heart and liver of a fish laid on the ashes of incense, according to instructions given by the angel to Tobias; after which the latter was able to marry Sarah in peace.

Asmodeus is the name given by Le Sage in his 'Diable Boiteux' (q.v.) to the demon companion of Don Cleofas.

Asoka, emperor of India, 264–228 B.C. Inscriptions state that he abandoned a career of conquest by the sword in order to spread the religion of Buddha. He sent missionaries far and wide for this purpose, and is highly venerated by Buddhists.

Asolando, the title of the collection of the last poems of R. Browning (q.v.), published on the day of Browning's death, 12 Dec. 1889. It contains some of the author's most beautiful short pieces, and ends with the well-known 'Epilogue'—'At the midnight in the silence of the sleep-time'. The title is derived from a word ascribed to Cardinal Bembo, *asolare,* 'to disport in the open air, amuse oneself at random'.

Aspasia, the famous Greek courtesan, daughter of Axiochus of Miletus, came to Athens, where she acquired fame by her beauty, culture, and wit. She so captivated Pericles (q.v.), that he made her his lifelong companion. See *Pericles and Aspasia.*

Aspatia, a character in Beaumont and Fletcher's 'The Maid's Tragedy' (q.v.).

Asphodel, a genus of liliaceous plants, mostly native of Southern Europe. The poets make it the flower of the Elysian fields (Homer, 'Odyssey', xi. 539) and connect it with the legend of Proserpine (q.v.). The word 'daffodil' is a corruption of 'asphodel'.

Aspramont, Aspramonte in Calabria, which figures in the Charlemagne legends as the scene of a fictitious campaign against the Saracen king.

Asrael, see *Azrael.*

Assassins, THE, a fanatical sect whose religion was compounded of Magianism and Islam, founded in Persia at the end of the 11th cent. by Hasan-ben-Sabbah, known as the 'Old Man of the Mountain', from the castle of Alamút in the mountains south of the Caspian which was his stronghold. The Assassins migrated to the Lebanon and were notorious for the secret murders that they carried out at the orders of their chief. It was said that before they attacked an enemy they intoxicated themselves with hashish, whence their name, which means 'hashish-eaters'.

For the story of Hasan-ben-Sabbah's relations with Nizam-ul-Mulk and Omar Khayyám, see under *Nizam-ul-Mulk*.

Asseneth, in a variant of the story of Joseph and Potiphar's wife, is Potiphar's daughter, whom Joseph consents to marry if she will renounce her gods, which she does. An angel signifies approval and Pharaoh gives a feast to celebrate the nuptials. The story, perhaps of early Christian invention, was made the subject of a French prose romance, early in the 14th cent., by Jean de Vignay.

ASSER (*d.* 909?), a monk of St. David's, who entered the household of King Alfred and studied with him for six months in each year (*c.* 885). He received the monasteries of Amesbury and Banwell, and later a grant of Exeter and its district, and was bishop of Sherborne. He wrote a Latin life of Alfred and a chronicle of English history between 849 and 887. The authenticity of these has been disputed. The 'Life' is important as 'the earliest biography of an English layman'. The classic edition is by W. H. Stevenson (1904, 1959).

Assiento Treaty, see *Asiento*.

Assonance, the correspondence or rhyming of one word with another in the accented and following vowels, but not in the consonants, as, e.g., in Old French versification.

Assur, ASHUR, or ASSHUR, the local god of the city of the same name, which was the metropolis of the first Assyrian kingdom. He became the supreme god of the Assyrians, the god of war, the protector of the people, represented in a horned cap, shooting an arrow from his bow. His wife was Belit.

Astarte, ASHTAROTH, ASHTORETH, ISHTAR, the eastern equivalent of the Greek Aphrodite, the goddess of love and fruitful increase.

ASTARTE is the name under which Augusta (Byron's half-sister) figures in his poem 'Manfred' (q.v.). The story of Byron and Astarte is told in 'Astarte', by Ralph Milbanke, earl of Lovelace (issued privately in 1905 and for general sale in 1921).

Astley, SIR JACOB, *Baron Astley* (1579–1652), a Royalist who served as major-general with distinction in the Civil War. He was 'hurt' at Edgehill. His prayer before the Battle of Edgehill is famous: 'O Lord! Thou knowest, how busy I must be this day: if I forget Thee, do not Thou forget me.'

Astley, PHILIP (1742–1814), the famous equestrian performer and circus-owner, joined General Elliott's light horse in 1759 and became breaker-in and sergeant-major.

He opened an exhibition of horsemanship at Lambeth, and in 1770 a wooden circus at Westminster. Subsequently he established in all nineteen equestrian theatres, including Astley's Royal Amphitheatre, London.

Astolat, in Malory's 'Morte Darthur' (Ascolet in 'Le Morte Arthur', q.v.), is, according to Malory, Guildford in Surrey. For the 'Fair Maid of Astolat' see *Elaine le Blank*.

Astolfo, in the 'Orlando Innamorato' and the 'Orlando Furioso' (qq.v.), a courteous and graceful English knight, one of the suitors of Angelica (q.v.), and at one time a prisoner of Alcina (q.v.). He receives from Logistilla (q.v.) a magic horn, the blast of which fills its hearers with panic, and a book that tells him all he wishes to know. He gets possession of the hippogriff of Rogero, and, with an Englishman's partiality for travel, flies about the world, relieves Prester John in Nubia of his troubles with harpies, visits Paradise, whence St. John carries him in a chariot to the moon. There, in a valley, are collected all the things that are lost on earth, lost kingdoms, lost reputations, lost time, and in the heap he finds the lost wits of Orlando, which he restores to the crazy hero. As regards his description as an English knight, it appears that in the earlier French *chanson* he figures as *Estout de Langres*, or *Lengrois*, corrupted into *Lenglois* and *l'Englois* (F. J. Snell in P.E.L., 'The Fourteenth Century').

Astraea, a daughter of Zeus and Themis. According to the poets, she lived on earth during the golden age and was a source of blessing to men; but their impiety drove her to heaven during the brazen and iron ages, and she was placed among the constellations of the zodiac, under the name Virgo.

ASTRAEA in line 290 of Pope's 'Imitations of Horace', Ep. II. i,

'The stage how loosely does Astraea tread',

is Mrs. Behn (q.v.).

Astraea Redux, a poem on the Restoration of Charles II, by Dryden (q.v.), published in 1660.

Astrée, see *Urfé*.

Astrophel, a pastoral elegy, written by Spenser (q.v.) in 1586 on the death of Sir Philip Sidney, who was mortally wounded in that year at Zutphen. Spenser again lamented him in 'The Ruines of Time' (q.v.).

Astrophel and Stella, the series of sonnets in which Sir P. Sidney (q.v.), according to the common account, expressed his love for Penelope Devereux, daughter of the 1st earl of Essex. In 1580 she was married against her will to Lord Rich, and Sidney's disappointment and passion are supposed to have found voice in these poems. It appears, however, that Penelope was in love before her marriage with Charles Blount, earl of Devonshire, whom she married after her divorce from Lord Rich. This renders the theory of Sidney's devotion to her improbable, but not impossible. The sonnets were not published until 1591, after Sidney's death, and their chronological order is uncertain. Eleven songs, originally printed after the Sonnets, were interspersed among them in the 'Arcadia' of 1598.

Asuras, in later Hindu mythology, evil demons, the enemies of the gods. In the Vedas, the term is frequently applied to the gods themselves.

Asyniur, in Scandinavian mythology, the collective name of the goddesses (see *Æsir*).

Atabalipa, in Milton's 'Paradise Lost', xi. 409, is Atahualpa, the Inca of Peru who was conquered by Pizarro.

Atala, see *Chateaubriand*.

Atalanta, according to legend the daughter of Iasus and Clymene, who was exposed by her father and suckled by a she-bear. She lived in celibacy, but her beauty gained her many admirers. She required her suitors to run a race with her. If any reached the goal before her, he was to be her husband; but all whom she distanced were to be killed with her dart. As she was almost invincible in running, many suitors perished in the attempt, till Milanion presented himself. Aphrodite had given him three golden apples from the garden of the Hesperides, and as soon as he had started on his course he cunningly threw down the apples, and Atalanta, charmed at the sight, stopped to gather them, so that Milanion arrived first at the goal. (According to another version, the successful suitor was Hippomenes.) Atalanta was present at the hunting of the Calydonian Boar, which she was the first to wound. She received its head from Meleager (q.v.). For Swinburne's 'Atalanta in Calydon' see *Swinburne*. 'Atalanta's Race' is the first poem in W. Morris's 'The Earthly Paradise' (q.v.).

Atalantis, *The New*, see *Manley*.

Atē, in Greek mythology, a daughter of Zeus, the goddess of evil, who incites men to wickedness and strife.

Atellan or OSCAN FABLES, *Atellanae Fabulae*, so called from Atella, a town of the Osci in Campania. They were 'a comic but not wanton kind of popular farce' (Lewis and Short), apparently representing scenes in the life of country towns. They were at first performed not by professional actors, but by amateurs. They were written in the Oscan language of southern Italy, which resembled Latin.

Athalie, the name of Racine's greatest play, which deals with the story of Athaliah, daughter of Ahab and Jezebel, and wife of Joram, king of Judah. She put to death all the children of the house of David, save Joash, who escaped and was hid in the house of the Lord. After six years Joash was proclaimed king, and Athaliah slain (2 Kings xi).

Athamas, see *Ino*.

Athanasian Creed, THE, the creed *Quicunque vult*, called in some manuscripts the creed of St. Athanasius (q.v.). Its origin has been the subject of much controversy. It is perhaps the work of Caesarius (*d.* 542), bishop of Arles.

Athanasius, ST. (*c.* 296–373), a famous bishop of Alexandria in the reign of the emperor Constantine, and a vigorous opponent of the Arian heresy. He was in consequence much attacked by the Arians, and persecuted by Constantine and his successor Constantius. For the creed that bears his name see previous entry. He was repeatedly driven into exile and concealment, but remained steadfast in his faith. He is commemorated on 2 May.

Atheism, *On the Necessity of*, see *Shelley* (*P.B.*).

Atheist's Tragedie, *The*, a tragedy by Tourneur (q.v.), printed in 1611.

D'Amville, the 'atheist', desiring, from the wish to increase the wealth of his family, to marry his son to Castabella, who is betrothed to Charlemont, the son of Montferrers, his brother, arranges that Charlemont shall go abroad on military service. During his absence, D'Amville and Belforest, Castabella's father, achieve their purpose, and Castabella is married to the sickly Rousard. D'Amville then murders Montferrers. Charlemont, falsely reported dead, and exhorted by the ghost of his father to 'leave vengeance to the King of Kings', now returns. D'Amville endeavours to secure his murder, but vengeance comes upon him in the death of his two sons. Finally, when himself about to carry out the execution of Charlemont, he dashes out his own brains by accident, and Charlemont is united to Castabella.

Athelstane of Coningsburgh, a character in Scott's 'Ivanhoe' (q.v.).

Athelston, a verse romance of about the year 1350, of some 800 lines. Four messengers meeting by chance in the forest swear brotherhood. One, Athelston, becomes king of England, and makes one of the brothers archbishop of Canterbury, one earl of Dover, and one earl of Stane and husband of Athelston's sister. Dover secretly accuses Stane and his wife of plotting against the king. Athelston imprisons them. The queen intercedes, but the king brutally kicks her and kills her unborn child. The archbishop, interceding in turn, is ordered to give up his office, but excommunicates the king, who submits on a threat of popular rising. Stane is tried by ordeal and exculpated. The king declares the son of the countess of Stane (St. Edmund) his heir. Dover is exposed by ordeal and executed.

Athenae Oxonienses, see *Wood* (*A.*).

Athenaeum, *The*, a literary and artistic review founded in 1828 by James Silk Buckingham (q.v.). It rose to eminence under the editorship of Charles Wentworth Dilke (q.v.), and many of the greatest English writers of the nineteenth century were among its contributors. 'It was full of the most awful swipes about poetry and the use of globes. . . . Golly, what a paper!' (John Finsbury in 'The Wrong Box' by R. L. Stevenson and Lloyd Osbourne, 1889, ch. xv). 'The Athenaeum' was incorporated in 'The Nation and Athenaeum' in 1921, and this in turn in 'The New Statesman' in 1931.

Athenaeum Club, The, in London, was founded in 1824 as an association of persons of literary, scientific, and artistic attainments, patrons of learning, etc. Among its founders were the earls of Liverpool and Aberdeen, the marquess of Lansdowne, Scott, Davy, Faraday, Cröker, Lawrence, and Moore. (There was an 'Athenaeum' at Rome, a university on the Capitoline, founded by the emperor Hadrian, for the promotion of science and literature.)

Athēnē, the Greek goddess of wisdom, industry, and war, identified by the Romans with their goddess Minerva. She was the daughter of Zeus and Metis, and sprang fully grown and armed from the brain of her father, who had swallowed Metis when pregnant, fearing that her child would be mightier than he. Athene quarrelled with Poseidon for the right of giving the name to the capital of Cecropia (see under *Cecrops*). The assembly of the gods settled the dispute by promising the preference to whichever gave the more useful present to the inhabitants of the earth. Thereupon Poseidon struck the ground with his trident, and a horse sprang up. But Athene produced the olive, was adjudged the victor, and called the capital Athenae. The meaning of her other name *Pallas* is unknown. It was perhaps the name of a goddess of some other religion with whom the Greeks identified Athene. She is represented generally with a countenance marked by masculine firmness and composure rather than by softness and grace. In one hand she holds a spear, in the other a shield with the head of Medusa (q.v.) displayed upon it. See also *Arachne, Marsyas.*

Athenian Gazette, The (afterwards known as the 'Athenian Mercury'), 'resolving all the most Nice and Curious Questions', was a penny weekly sheet issued from 1689/90 to 1695/6, a precursor of 'Notes and Queries'. It was published by Dunton (q.v.).

Athens of the North, a term applied sometimes to Edinburgh, sometimes to Copenhagen.

ATHERTON, GERTRUDE FRANKLIN (1857–1948), American writer, born at San Francisco. She wrote many novels, several of them based on the history of her native California. Among her more important works are 'The Conqueror' (1902), a fictional biography of Alexander Hamilton, 'Julia France and Her Times' (1912), 'Black Oxen' (1923),

and 'Adventures of a Novelist' (1932), her autobiography.

Athos, Mt., the 'Holy Mountain', the easternmost of the three Chalcidic peninsulas projecting into the Aegean Sea from Macedonia. It has been occupied since the Middle Ages by various communities of monks.

Athos, Porthos, and **Aramis,** the 'Three Musketeers' (q.v.) in Alexandre Dumas's novel of that name.

Atkins, Thomas or **Tommy,** see *Tommy Atkins.*

Atlantic Charter, the name commonly given to the joint declaration, issued on 14 July 1941 by President Roosevelt and Mr. Churchill, of certain common principles in the national policies of their countries. These may be roughly summarized as follows. The U.S. and Britain (i) seek no aggrandizement; (ii) desire no territorial changes not wished for by the peoples concerned; (iii) respect the right of all peoples to choose their form of government and desire restoration of sovereign rights and self-government to those who have been deprived of them; (iv) will promote access on equal terms by all States to trade and raw materials; (v) will aim at collaboration of all nations to secure improved economic conditions and social security; (vi) desire, after the destruction of Nazi tyranny, a peace providing security for all nations and freedom from want and fear for all men, and (vii) enabling all to traverse the seas without hindrance; (viii) believe that, pending the establishment of a permanent system of general security, the disarmament of the aggressor nations is essential.

Atlantic Monthly, The, an American, and more particularly a New England, magazine of literature, the arts, and politics, founded in 1857. J. R. Lowell (q.v.) was its first editor (1857–61), and W. D. Howells and T. B. Aldrich (qq.v.) were among his distinguished successors (1871–81 and 1881–90 respectively). ˎAlthough no longer in the pre-eminent place it held in the 19th cent. it maintains its traditions and includes many leading American men of letters among its contributors.

Atlantis, a fabulous island in the ocean west of the Pillars of Hercules, a beautiful and prosperous country, the seat of an empire which dominated part of Europe and Africa. But owing to the impiety of its inhabitants, it was swallowed up by the sea. The story is told by Plato in the 'Timaeus'.

Atlantis, New, see *New Atlantis.*

Atlas, one of the Titans (q.v.). As punishment for his part in the revolt of the Titans he was employed to support the heavens with his head and hands somewhere in the west of the earth. He was changed into a mountain by Perseus (q.v.), who, being refused hospitality by Atlas, turned the eyes of the Medusa upon him. According to Lucian ('Charon')

Hercules visited Atlas and for a time relieved him of his burden. Atlas was father of the Pleiades, Hyades, and Hesperides (qq.v.).

Atli, in W. Morris's 'Sigurd the Volsung' (q.v.), the Attila of history.

Atom, The History and Adventures of an, a satire by Smollett (q.v.), published in 1769.

The Atom, having in the course of its transmigrations lived in the body of a Japanese, relates to one Nathaniel Peacock his experiences in Japan. Japan stands for England, and the various Japanese personages referred to in the story represent prominent characters in the recent political history of England (e.g. Yak-strot, the earl of Bute). The satire is of the utmost coarseness.

Atossa, (1) wife of Darius and mother of Xerxes, the Persian king whose attempt in the 5th cent. B.C. to subjugate Greece met with disaster. She is a prominent figure in Aeschylus's tragedy of 'The Persians'; (2) see *Moral Essays*.

Atreūs, according to Greek legend, a son of Pelops (q.v.) and king of Argos. The tragedy associated with his name does not appear in Homer. The post-Homeric poets relate that Atreus, to revenge himself on his brother Thyestes for seducing his wife, invited Thyestes to a banquet and served him the flesh of his children to eat. Thyestes fled in horror, cursing the house of Atreus, which was visited by various calamities. Thyestes became the father of Aegisthus (q.v.) by his own daughter Pelopia. Aegisthus slew Atreus, who had ordered him to kill Thyestes, and restored Thyestes to the throne of which Atreus had deprived him. Atreus was the father of Agamemnon and Menelaus (qq.v.).

Atropos, see *Parcae*.

ATTERBURY, FRANCIS (1662–1732), educated at Westminster and Christ Church, Oxford, became bishop of Rochester, after holding various important preferments. He engaged in the Phalaris (q.v.) controversy and in the political and theological disputes of the day. He was imprisoned in 1720 for alleged participation in a plot to restore the Stuarts, and subsequently left the country and threw in his lot definitely with the Jacobites. In religion he was a strong supporter of the Church of England, and opposed to the Latitudinarians (q.v.). He was a notable preacher and a trenchant political writer. His 'Sermons' were published in 1740, and his 'Miscellaneous Works' in 1789–98. His 'Discourse occasioned by the Death of Lady Cutts' appeared in 1698.

Attic, a dialect of ancient Greek spoken at Athens and in the surrounding country (Attica). As an epithet, it is applied to a pure, simple, polished style, as being characteristic of the best Greek writers.

ATTIC SALT, refined, delicate, poignant wit, of a kind characteristic of the ancient Athe-

nians. From the Latin *sal atticum*, the word *sal* meaning both 'salt' and 'wit'.

See also *Order*.

Attic boy, THE, in Milton's 'Il Penseroso' (q.v.); see *Cephalus*.

Atticus, the character under which Pope (q.v.) satirized Addison (q.v.) in lines published in 1723 in a miscellany entitled 'Cythera, or poems upon Love and Intrigue', and reprinted in 'Miscellanies, the last Volume', 1728. The lines, much altered, reappeared in Pope's 'Epistle to Dr. Arbuthnot' (193–214), 1735.

The original of the character, T. Pomponius Atticus (109–32 B.C.), was a Roman *eques* (a member of the order of 'Knights', who held a middle rank between the Senate and the Plebs). His surname was given him on account of his long residence in Athens and knowledge of Greek literature. He was a close friend of Cicero, whose letters to him still exist.

Attila, king of the Huns. He ravaged the Eastern Empire during the years 445–50, and after making peace with Theodosius, invaded the Western Empire and was defeated at Châlons by Aëtius in 451. He died in 453. The terror he inspired is shown in the name given to him, the 'Scourge of God' (*flagellum Dei*). In German heroic legend he figures as ETZEL, and in Norse legend as ATLI.

Attis, a Phrygian deity connected with the myth of the 'Great Mother', Rhea, Cybele, or Agdistis. Attis was the beautiful son of Nana, daughter of the river-god Sangarius; she conceived him after gathering the fruit of an almond tree sprung from the blood of Agdistis. Agdistis fell in love with Attis, and because he wished to marry the daughter of the king of Pessinus, drove him mad so that he mutilated himself. His spirit passed into a pine tree and violets sprang up from his blood. His death was mourned for two days, after which his recovery was celebrated, a symbol of the death and revival of plant life.

AUBREY, JOHN (1626–97), antiquary, educated at Trinity College, Oxford, was author of a 'Perambulation of Surrey', which was included in Rawlinson's 'Natural History and Antiquities of Surrey' (1719); of a collection of 'Lives' of eminent persons, much used by Anthony à Wood (q.v.), and subsequently published in 1813 (fuller editions in 1898 and 1931); and of 'Miscellanies' (1696), a book of stories and folk-lore.

Auburn, see *Deserted Village*.

Aucassin and Nicolette, a 13th-cent. legend of Provence, which has been translated or adapted by F. W. Bourdillon, Swinburne, Andrew Lang, and Eugene Mason. With 'Amis and Amile' (see *Amis and Amiloun*) it forms the subject of one of Pater's 'Studies in the History of the Renaissance'. The original is in prose interspersed with songs.

Aucassin, son of Count Garins of Beaucaire, loves Nicolette, a beautiful Saracen captive. The father forbids their marriage and immures Nicolette in a tower, and subsequently, after further dissension with his son, imprisons Aucassin himself. The damsel escapes and is followed by Aucassin, and the story is concerned with their simple adventures and faithful love, which is finally rewarded.

Auchinleck (pron. 'Affleck'), the name of the family estate of James Boswell (q.v.).

AUDEN, WYSTAN HUGH (1907–), born at York and educated at Gresham's School, Holt, and Christ Church, Oxford, where he was already known as a leader of the young poets of his generation. He lived for a time in Berlin under the Weimar Republic, when Nazism was already becoming a threat. His early work was verse of social criticism and protest and showed the influence of psychoanalytical as well as of Marxist ideas. After his return to England he worked as a schoolmaster and with documentary films. He published 'Poems' (1930) and 'The Orators' (1932) and, with Louis MacNeice, 'Letters from Iceland' (1937). He also experimented, in collaboration with his friend Isherwood, in drama, including 'The Dog Beneath the Skin' (1935) and 'The Ascent of F6' (1936). Also written with Isherwood was 'Journey to a War', a travel book about China. During the Spanish Civil War Auden served on the Republican side as a stretcher-bearer. He emigrated to the United States in 1939, and later became an American citizen. Since the Second World War, however, he has lived much in Italy and Austria, and was professor of poetry at Oxford from 1956 to 1961. Auden's later verse, including 'New Year Letter' (1941), 'The Age of Anxiety' (1948), 'The Shield of Achilles' (1959), 'Homage to Clio' (1960), and 'About the House' (1966) to some extent abandons his earlier ideas and is written from a standpoint of Christian commitment. His collected criticism, 'The Dyer's Hand', appeared in 1963.

Audhumla, in Scandinavian mythology, the cow that fed the giant Ymir (q.v.) with her milk.

Audrey, in Shakespeare's 'As You Like It' (q.v.), the country wench wooed and won by Touchstone.

Audrey, St., St. Etheldreda, daughter of Anna (king of East Anglia) and patron saint of Ely. She is commemorated on 23 June.

TAWDRY LACE, a silk 'lace' or neck-tie much worn by women in the 16th and early 17th cents., appears in the earliest quotation as *St. Audrey's lace*. It is told by Baeda that St. Audrey died of a tumour in the throat, which she considered to be a just retribution because in her youth she had for vain show worn many splendid necklaces. Harpsfield, archdeacon of Canterbury in the 16th cent., thinks that the silk neck-tie may have been worn in memory of this. Skinner in his

'Etymologicon' (1688) explains *tawdry lace* as 'ties . . . brought at the fair held at the fane of St. Etheldreda'. There is no discrepancy between the two statements. 'St. Audrey's laces' would naturally be largely offered for sale at her fair, and this doubtless led to the production of cheap and showy qualities of the article, which at length gave to *tawdry* its later meaning. [OED.]

AUDUBON, JOHN JAMES (1785–1851), an American ornithologist of French descent, noted for his remarkable pictures of birds. The colour prints of his 'Birds of America' were issued serially in London in 1827–38, and the accompanying text, 'Ornithological Biography', in which he was assisted, in 1831–9. He also published, again with assistance, 'Viviparous Quadrupeds of North America' (plates, 1842–5; text 1846–54). His important 'Journal' appeared in 1929.

Aufidius, a character in Shakespeare's 'Coriolanus' (q.v.).

Augēan Stables. Augeas, king of Elis, had an immense herd of oxen, whose stables had never been cleansed. Their cleansing in one day was one of the labours imposed on Hercules (q.v.) by Eurystheus. Hercules undertook the task for a reward of a tenth part of the herd, and accomplished it by changing the course of the river Alpheus so that it should flow into the stables. Augeas refused the promised payment on the pretext that Hercules had made use of artifice. Hercules thereupon conquered Elis and put Augeas to death.

Augsburg, INTERIM OF, a statement of religious doctrine prepared at the bidding of Charles V in 1548, which was in the nature of a compromise, adopting from the Roman Catholic position such doctrines as transubstantiation and papal supremacy, and from the Protestant position justification by faith and the marriage of priests.

Augsburg Confession, a statement of the Protestant position drawn up by Melanchthon for the Diet of 1530.

Augusta, the name of several Roman towns colonized by Augustus or otherwise considered worthy of the title. Thus *Augusta Emerita* (Merida) in Lusitania was colonized by Augustus with veterans of the fifth and tenth legions, and *Augusta Praetoria* (Aosta) with men of the praetorian guard.
  Ammianus Marcellinus (*fl.* A.D. 390) refers to Londinium (the Roman London) as a city on which the title *Augusta* had been conferred. Thomson in his 'Seasons' ('Spring') uses the name for London.

Augusta, in imprints, Augsburg.

Augusta Leigh, Byron's half-sister, see *Leigh.*

Augusta Trebocorum, in imprints, Strasburg. See also *Argentina.*

Augusta Treverorum, in imprints, Trèves.

Augusta Trinobantum, in imprints, London.

Augusta of Berkely, THE LADY, the heroine of Scott's 'Castle Dangerous' (q.v.).

Augustan Age, a period of literary eminence in the life of a nation, so named because during the reign of the Emperor Augustus (27 B.C.–A.D. 14) Virgil, Horace, Ovid, Tibullus, &c., flourished. The term is applied in the history of English literature to the period of Pope and Addison, or limited to the reign of Queen Anne, or extended backwards to include Dryden. In French literature the term is applied to the period of Corneille, Racine, and Molière. Goldsmith has an essay on the 'Augustan Age in England' in 'The Bee'; he identifies it with the reign of Queen Anne. See also Saintsbury's 'The Peace of the Augustans', a survey of 18th-cent. English literature (1916).

Augustin or AUSTIN FRIARS, a religious order of mendicant friars, formed in the 13th cent. to bring together under the single rule of St. Augustine a number of small congregations of hermits. Many houses of the order were swept away by the Reformation. Austin Friars Church in London (Old Broad Street) formed part of the priory founded in 1253, when the first friars of the order had recently reached England. At the dissolution, the church was transferred to the Dutch Protestants, who still possess it.

AUGUSTINE, ST., OF HIPPO (345–430), was born at Tagaste in Numidia (Constantine), his mother being Monica, a devout Christian. He was trained as a rhetorician, formed an irregular union, and was father of a son (Adeodatus). He was for a time a Manichaean, but was converted after hearing the sermons of Ambrose, bishop of Milan, where Augustine was a teacher of rhetoric. The scene of his conversion is vividly described in his 'Confessions'. He became bishop of Hippo, and was engaged in constant theological controversy, combating Manichaeans, Donatists, and Pelagians. The most famous of his numerous works is the 'De Civitate Dei' ('City of God'), a treatise in vindication of the Christian Church. His 'Confessions' contain a striking account of his early life. His sermons were used throughout the Middle Ages. Augustine died during the siege of Hippo by the Vandals. His principal tenets were the immediate efficacy of grace, and absolute predestination; he furnished the doctrinal basis of the revolt of Luther and Calvin, and of the Jansenist heresy. He is commemorated on 28 August.

Augustine, ST. (d. 604), first archbishop of Canterbury. He was prior of Pope Gregory I's monastery of St. Andrew at Rome, and was sent by that pope with forty monks to preach the Gospel in England. He was favourably received by King Ethelbert, who was afterwards converted. Augustine was consecrated 'bishop of the English' at Arles.

He founded the monastery of Christ Church at Canterbury. St. Augustine's, also at Canterbury, was a Benedictine abbey, named from its founder, and is now used as a missionary college. St. Augustine is commemorated on 26 May.

Augustinian Canons, an order of canons regular of the Roman Catholic Church, who adopted the rule of St. Augustine in the 11th cent. The order spread to various parts of Europe, including England, during the later Middle Ages.

Augustus, GAIUS JULIUS CAESAR OCTAVIANUS (63 B.C.–A.D. 14), the nephew of Julius Caesar, and first Roman emperor, occupying the throne from 27 B.C. till his death. The title of Augustus was conferred on him in 27 B.C. by the senate and people as a mark of their veneration. It was borne by all subsequent Roman emperors; even Charlemagne used it, and several of his successors in the Holy Roman Empire.

Auld Lang Syne, a song whose words were contributed by Burns (q.v.) to the fifth volume of James Johnson's 'Scots Musical Museum' (1787–1803). It was not entirely of Burns's composition, but was taken down by him, according to his own account, 'from an old man's singing'. But, in fact, the refrain, at least, had long been in print. The original version has been attributed to Sir Robert Aytoun, an ancestor of W. E. Aytoun (q.v.).

Auld Reekie, a term familiarly applied to the old town of Edinburgh, in allusion to its smoky atmosphere.

Auld Robin Gray, see under *Lindsay* (*Lady A.*).

Aulic Council, a sovereign court in the Holy Roman Empire, instituted in 1506, which sat at Vienna. It heard appeals from the courts of the Germanic states.

AULUS GELLIUS, see *Gellius*.

Aurelia Allobrogum, in imprints, Geneva.

Aureng-Zebe, a tragedy by Dryden (q.v.), published in 1676.

This was Dryden's last rhymed play, and he subsequently adopted the use of blank verse. The plot is remotely based on the contemporary events by which Aureng-Zebe wrested the empire of India from Shah Jehan, his father, and from his brothers. But it turns on the attempt first of the old emperor, then of Morat, one of his sons, to take from Aureng-Zebe, by violent means, Indamora, a captive queen, his affianced bride. The attempt is defeated by the constancy of Indamora and the generous qualities displayed by Aureng-Zebe and by Arimant, the governor of Agra, aided by the jealous rivalry of Nourmahal, the empress.

Aurignac, in the Haute-Garonne, France, gives its name, from the flint implements found there, to an industry or culture, the AURIGNACIAN, which is believed to have prevailed in France from about 11,500 to 10,000 B.C. 'Throughout all this time Aurignacian men continued to carve figures and engrave small objects, and to decorate the walls of the caves which they inhabited' (Peake and Fleure, 'Hunters and Artists'). The three principal types of man of this culture are the Grimaldi, Cro-Magnon, and Combe Capelle.

Aurōra, the Greek *Eos*, a daughter of Hyperion (q.v.) and the goddess of the dawn. She is represented by the poets as rising in the east from the couch of her husband Tithonus, drawn in a rose-coloured chariot, preceding the sun, pouring the dew upon the earth, and making the flowers grow.

Aurora Leigh, a romance in blank verse by E. B. Browning (q.v.), published in 1856.

Aurora Leigh tells the story of her life. She is left an orphan, studious and poetical by nature, and is brought up in the uncongenial home of an aunt. She is often with her rich cousin, Romney Leigh, a man wrapped up in philanthropic schemes, but arrogant and dogmatic. He proposes to her, but his proposal, suggestive that he wants a 'helpmate not a mistress', wounds her pride and she refuses him. She goes to live· in London, earning her bread by her pen. Romney rescues a poor outcast daughter of a tramp, Marian Erle, and offers to marry her. But the project is defeated. Later, when misfortune has overtaken Romney, his philanthropic plans have failed, his Hall has been burnt down and himself blinded, he and Aurora come together. The story is made the vehicle for the expression of the author's views on a variety of subjects, social, literary, and ethical.

Aurora Raby, a character in the last three cantos of Byron's 'Don Juan' (q.v.), a beautiful and innocent young heiress.

Aurungzebe, see *Aureng-Zebe.*

Ausonia, a name applied by poets to Italy, from the *Ausones,* an ancient, perhaps Greek, name for the inhabitants of middle and southern Italy.

AUSONIUS, DECIMUS MAGNUS (*c.* A.D. 310–90), a Roman poet, born at Bordeaux, near which he also died. He taught grammar and rhetoric, and acquired such reputation that he was appointed tutor to Gratian, son of the Emperor Valentinian, and in Gratian's reign rose to high official position. Among his many poems was one on the Moselle, its wine and trout.

AUSTEN, JANE (1775–1817), was born at Steventon in Hampshire, of which her father was rector, and lived an·uneventful life at her birthplace, at Bath, Southampton, Chawton (near Alton), and Winchester, where she died and is buried. Of her completed novels (for which see under their titles) 'Sense and Sensibility' appeared in 1811, 'Pride and Prejudice' in 1813, 'Mansfield Park' in 1814, 'Emma' in December 1815, 'Northanger Abbey' and

'Persuasion' posthumously in 1818. The order in which they were written is somewhat different. 'Pride and Prejudice', in its original form and entitled 'First Impressions', was begun in 1796, refused by a publisher in 1797, and revised before ultimate publication. 'Sense and Sensibility' was begun in 1797 but apparently left unfinished for many years. 'Northanger Abbey' was begun in 1797, sold to a publisher in 1803, but not then published. The manuscript was recovered in 1816, and may have been revised, but appears to represent the earliest of her work as we have it in the six published novels. 'Mansfield Park' was begun in 1811, 'Emma' in 1814, and 'Persuasion' in 1815. Besides these Jane Austen was author of two works which she did not publish, 'Lady Susan' (the story, written about 1805, and told in letters, of a designing coquette, the widow Lady Susan Vernon) and a fragment, 'The Watsons' (q.v.). These were published by J. E. Austen-Leigh in the second edition of his 'Memoir of Jane Austen' (1871). A further fragment, written in 1817, known to her family as 'Sanditon', was published in 1925. The standard edition of Jane Austen is that of R. W. Chapman, 1923–54; Letters, 1932, 1952.

Auster, see *Notus.*

AUSTIN, ALFRED (1835–1913), of a Roman Catholic family, was educated at Stonyhurst and Oscott College. He became a barrister, but soon abandoned the legal profession for literature. He was much interested in foreign politics and a devoted follower of Disraeli. In 1883 he became joint-editor with W. J. Courthope of the newly founded 'National Review', and was its sole editor for eight years after the latter's resignation in 1887. Between 1871 and 1908 he published twenty volumes of verse, of little merit. A prose work, 'The Garden that I love', published in 1894, proved very popular, and in 1896 Austin was made poet laureate, shortly afterwards publishing in 'The Times' an unfortunate ode celebrating the Jameson Raid. Some of his pleasantest work is to be found in his prose writings, on the garden of his Kentish home (Swinford Old Manor) and kindred subjects. His 'Autobiography' appeared in 1911.

AUSTIN, JOHN (1790–1859), was called to the bar at the Inner Temple after serving in the army, was professor of jurisprudence at the London University, 1826–32, and while holding this post wrote his famous 'Province of Jurisprudence Determined' (1832). His 'Lectures on Jurisprudence' were published in 1863.

AUSTIN, JOHN LANGSHAW (1911–60), educated at Shrewsbury and Balliol College, Oxford, White's professor of moral philosophy in the University of Oxford (1952–60). Though he published only a few technical articles in his lifetime, he had great influence as an exponent of the philosophical method which takes as its starting-point the careful elucidation of the ordinary, non-philosophical use of language. Two of his most important courses of lectures, 'Sense and Sensibilia' and 'How to Do Things with Words', were published posthumously.

AUSTIN, SARAH (1793–1867), *née* Taylor, wife of John Austin (q.v.), translated Ranke's 'History of the Popes' (1840), 'The History of the Reformation in Germany' (1845), and 'Germany from 1760 to 1814' (1854); also F. W. Carové's 'Story without an End' (1834).

Austin Friars, see *Augustin Friars*.

Authorized Version, see *Bible* (*The English*).

Authors, THE SOCIETY OF, a non-profit-making organization founded in 1884, controlled by its Members and devoted to protecting and promoting their rights and interests at home and abroad, and helping and advising them through its Secretariat on legal and practical problems connected with their literary work. Its quarterly publication is *The Author*.

Auto-da-fé, a Portuguese expression (Spanish, *auto-de-fe*), meaning 'Act of Faith', an act or decision of the Holy Inquisition, and its execution; hence popularly applied to the burning alive of heretics.

Autocrat of the Breakfast–Table, The, see *Holmes* (*O. W.*).

Autŏlўcus, (1) in Greek mythology, a son of Hermes, celebrated for his craft as a thief, who stole the flocks of his neighbours and mingled them with his own. In this he was outwitted by Sisyphus (q.v.); (2) the witty rogue and pedlar in Shakespeare's 'The Winter's Tale' (q.v.).

Autŏmĕdon, the charioteer of Achilles (q.v.). Hence a name used to signify a coachman.

Autun, THE BISHOP OF, sometimes used to designate Talleyrand (Charles Maurice de Talleyrand-Périgord, 1754–1838), the French diplomatist who played a great role as minister under Napoleon I and Louis XVIII. He had been appointed bishop of Autun in 1788. He accepted the Civil Constitution of the Clergy, but afterwards put off his orders.

Avalon, AVALLON, or AVELION, in the Arthurian legend, a place in the 'Isle of the Blessed' of the Celts, a mythical land like the Fortunate Isles (q.v.). It is to Avalon that Arthur is borne after his death. See *Glastonbury* for its identification with that place.

Avare, L' ('The Miser'), one of Molière's most famous comedies. Harpagon, the miser, and his son Cléante are rivals for the hand of Mariane. Cléante gets possession of the casket containing the miser's treasure, and gives his father, whom his loss has reduced to frenzy, the choice between Mariane and the casket. The old man chooses the latter and abandons Mariane to his son.

Avars, a Tartar tribe who migrated to the region about the Don, the Volga, and the Caspian Sea in the 6th cent. Thence they extended their dominion westward to the Danube, were subdued by Charlemagne, and disappeared from history in the 9th cent. They built stockades of wood and earth round their settlements, known as AVAR RINGS, of which traces still remain. In one of these, in 796, Charlemagne, after defeating the Avars, captured an immense treasure, the fruit of the pillage of the Greek Empire by the Avars.

Avatar, in Hindu mythology, the descent of a deity to the earth in incarnate form; hence loosely, a manifestation, display, phase.

Ave atque vale, Latin, 'hail and farewell!', as a farewell to the dead, notably in the poem of Catullus in memory of his brother, to which Tennyson refers in his poem 'Frater, ave atque vale'.

Ave Maria, 'Hail Mary!', the angelic salutation to the Virgin (Luke i. 28) combined with that of Elizabeth (v. 42), used as a devotional recitation, with the addition (in more recent times) of a prayer to the Virgin, as Mother of God; so named from its first two words.

Avebury, Wiltshire, the site of Early Bronze Age monuments, c. 1800 B.C. The remains of two stone circles are enclosed in a huge circular bank and ditch with a circle of probably 100 standing stones on its inner edge. An avenue of standing stones leads to Overton Hill, where there was another monument of the same age. The stones were first recorded in detail in the 18th cent.

AVELLANEDA, ALONSO FERNANDEZ DE, the name assumed by the author of the false Part II of Cervantes's 'Don Quixote', issued in 1614. Cervantes's own Part II appeared in 1615.

Avenel, MARY, a character in Scott's 'The Monastery' and 'The Abbot' (qq.v.), and JULIAN, her uncle, a character in the former. ROLAND AVENEL is the hero of the latter work. The WHITE LADY OF AVENEL is a supernatural being introduced in 'The Monastery'.

Aventine, THE, the most southerly and one of the highest hills of Rome. On it was a temple of Diana, the sanctuary of runaway slaves and of plebeians.

Avernus, a lake of Campania, filling the crater of an extinct volcano. From its surface mephitic vapours arose, which led the ancients to regard it as the entrance to the infernal regions.

AVERROËS (ABUL WALID MOHAMMED BEN AHMED IBN ROSHD) (1126–98), a Muslim doctor born at Cordova, and a philosopher, the author of a famous commentary on Aristotle. He is mentioned with Avicenna (q.v.) by Dante, 'Averrois, che il gran comento feo' ('Inferno', iv. 144).

Avesta, the sacred writings of the Parsees, usually attributed to Zoroaster (q.v.). As we have them, they are the fragmentary and composite relic of an ancient priestly literature said to have been destroyed by Alexander the Great at Persepolis. In its present form it probably dates from the Sasanian period, but the oldest extant manuscript is of comparatively recent date (13th cent.).

AVIĀNUS, FLAVIUS, probably of the 4th cent. A.D., the author of fables in Latin elegiacs, which were much used as a school book in the Middle Ages.

Avice Caro, in Hardy's 'The Well-Beloved' (q.v.), the name of the three women, mother, daughter, and granddaughter, loved in succession by Jocelyn Pierston.

AVICENNA (ABU IBN SINA) (980–1036), a Persian physician and philosopher and commentator on Aristotle. He is mentioned by Dante ('Inferno', iv. 143).

Avignon, a city on the Rhône in France. Clement V removed the papal seat to Avignon in 1308, and there it remained until 1377. It was sold by Joanna I, queen of Naples, to Pope Clement VI in 1348, Provence being then the inheritance of the Angevin kings of Naples. After the outbreak of the papal schism in 1378, two anti-popes, Clement VII and Benedict XIII, resided successively in Avignon, the latter being expelled from the town in 1408. The city remained, with interruptions, in the possession of the popes until annexed by the French National Assembly in 1791. Avignon is also famous for its connexion with Petrarch (q.v.).

Avon, THE SWAN OF, Shakespeare, born at Stratford-on-Avon, so called by Jonson ('To the Memory of Shakespeare').

Awkward Age, The, a novel by Henry James (q.v.), published in 1899.

Awntrys (Adventures) of Arthure at the Terne Wathelyne, an alliterative verse romance of the 14th cent., containing two parts. In the first, Arthur and his court go from Carlisle to 'Tarn Wathelyne' (Tarn Wadling near Hesket in Cumberland) to hunt. Queen Guinevere is entrusted to the care of Gawain. During a storm, a fearful figure, the spirit of Guinevere's mother, appears to Guinevere and Gawain, reproaches her for her evil life, exhorts her to penance and amendment, and prophesies the destruction of King Arthur and the Round Table. The second part relates a fight between Gawain and Sir Galleron of Galway, who seeks to recover his lands taken by Arthur and given to Gawain. Arthur stops the fight, makes Gawain lord of Wales, and restores to Galleron his former territory.

Ayala's Angel, a novel by A. Trollope (q.v.), published in 1881.

Lucy and Ayala Dormer, after having been brought up in an artistic and luxurious home, are left penniless orphans. The romantic Ayala is taken into the family of her aunt Emmeline, the vulgar and purse-proud wife of the city millionaire, Sir Thomas Tringle; while Lucy goes to the home of her uncle Dosett, a civil servant of small means, and his conscientious but depressing wife. Trouble soon follows. Lucy rebels against the drab conditions of life in the small house at Notting Hill, and Ayala shows a lack of proper deference for her wealthy aunt and cousins. An exchange is effected, and Ayala goes to Notting Hill. But this does not mend matters. Lucy falls in love with an impecunious artist; and Ayala, with equal perversity, refuses three eligible suitors: Tom Tringle, her cousin, who tries to charm her by a display of his jewellery, and shows his disappointment by knocking the breath out of a policeman and other outrageous proceedings; Colonel Jonathan Stubbs, an Admirable Crichton but for his red hair and large mouth; and the absurd Captain Batsby, who thinks the possession of a very pretty little place of his own down in Berkshire a sufficient claim to her affections. In the end, however, Ayala discovers that Stubbs is the 'Angel' after all, and sufficient means of subsistence are found for Lucy and her artist. Many amusing situations are also furnished by the love affairs of the two Tringle daughters.

Ayenbite of Inwit, 'Remorse of Conscience', a prose translation from a French moral treatise, made by Dan Michel of Northgate, Canterbury, about 1340, and chiefly of philological interest.

AYER, ALFRED JULES (1910–   ), educated at Eton and Christ Church, professor of the philosophy of mind and logic in the University of London (1946–59), Wykeham professor of logic in the University of Oxford (1959–   ). He is the author of 'Language, Truth and Logic' (1936), which was the first exposition of logical positivism in the English language, 'The Foundations of Empirical Knowledge' (1940), and 'The Problem of Knowledge' (1956), as well as volumes of philosophical essays.

Ayesha, the favourite wife of Mohammed (q.v.). To her loss of a necklace under conditions regarded as suspicious may broadly be traced, it is said, the seclusion of Muslim women down to the present times.

Ayesha, (1) a novel by Morier (q.v., 1834), which introduced the Turkish word 'bosh' into English; (2) a novel by Sir Rider Haggard (q.v.).

Aylwin, a novel by W. T. Watts-Dunton (q.v.).

Aymon, The Four Sons of, a medieval French romance. See *Rinaldo.*

Ayrshire Legatees, The, a novel by Galt (q.v.), published in 1820.

It takes the form of letters recording the proceedings of a worthy Scottish minister and his family in the course of a visit which they pay to London in order to take possession of a legacy. Their naïve comments on their experiences, and the comments of their friends in Scotland on the letters themselves, make an entertaining miscellany.

AYTOUN, WILLIAM EDMONDSTONE (1813–65), a descendant of the poet Sir Robert Aytoun (1570–1638) who was the reputed author of the lines on which Burns based his 'Auld Lang Syne', was educated at Edinburgh Academy and University. He divided his life between law and literature, becoming professor of Belles-Lettres at Edinburgh in 1845, and sheriff of Orkney in 1850. He is chiefly remembered for his share in the 'Bon Gaultier Ballads' (q.v., 1845), for his 'Lays of the Scottish Cavaliers' (q.v., 1849), and for his 'Firmilian, or the Student of Badajoz' (1854), a mock-tragedy, in which he parodied and ridiculed the poems of the so-called 'Spasmodic School' (q.v.). The hero of 'Firmilian', a student at the university of Badajoz, is engaged in writing a tragedy on the subject of Cain. In order to equip himself for his task, to learn 'the mental spasms of the tortured Cain', he embarks on a career of crime, with absurd results.

Azaria and Hushai, see *Pordage.*

Azazel, see *Scapegoat.* In Milton's 'Paradise Lost' (i. 534), Azazel is the 'Cherub tall' who raises the standard of the host of Satan.

Azim, the hero of 'The Veiled Prophet of Khorassan', one of the tales in Moore's 'Lalla Rookh' (q.v.).

Azo, in Byron's 'Parisina' (q.v.), the marquis of Este.

Azoth, the alchemists' name for mercury, and the universal remedy of Paracelsus (q.v.).

Azrael, in Jewish and Muslim mythology, the angel who in death severs the soul from the body.

Aztecs, a native American people first known as inhabitants of the valley of Mexico. They became important and extended their conquests in the 15th cent., their most successful leader being Montezuma I (1440–69). The Aztecs were conquered by the invading Spaniards under Cortez, early in the 16th cent. They figure in Dryden's heroic drama, 'The Indian Emperor' (1665), and in Southey's 'Madoc' (q.v.).

Aztlan, in Southey's 'Madoc' (q.v.), the capital of the Aztecas. The word means 'place of the heron' and is, in Aztec legend, the original home of the Aztec race.

B

B.B.C., THE, the BRITISH BROADCASTING CORPORATION, the national broadcasting authority, constituted in 1927. It succeeded the British Broadcasting Company, which had been formed in 1922.

Baal, name of the chief god, or in the plural (BAALIM) of the gods, of the Phoenician and Canaanitish nations; hence, a false god. The name appears in various forms and combinations, e.g. BEL, the Baal of Babylon; BAAL-ZEBUB, the 'fly-god', etc.

Bāb, THE, or GATE, the name given to Mirza Mohammed Ali, a Shiite, who began to preach a reformed Muslim religion in Persia in 1845 and was executed in 1850. His followers were called the BABIS, and his religion BABISM. The Babis were expelled from Persia after an attempt on the life of the Shah.

The Bāb was succeeded in 1866 by Abdul-Baha, who preached a revised form of Bābism, in which the Koran is recognized, but its finality as a revelation is denied. The BAHAIS are now a flourishing sect, with their centre at Haifa.

Bab Ballads, a collection of humorous ballads by W. S. Gilbert (q.v.), published in 'Fun' in 1866–71 and in volume form in 1869 and ('More Bab Ballads') 1873. Several of the Gilbert and Sullivan operas (q.v.) owed their origin to the 'Ballads', e.g. 'Patience', 'Iolanthe', 'Ruddigore', and 'The Yeomen of the Guard'. This matter is fully dealt with in I. Goldberg's 'The Story of Gilbert and Sullivan' (1929).

Babbage, CHARLES (1792–1871), educated at Peterhouse, Cambridge, a mathematician and scientific mechanician. He was a founder, secretary, and later, member, of the Astronomical Society. He devoted thirty-seven years of his life and much of his fortune to the perfection of a calculating machine of his invention.

Babbitt, a novel by S. Lewis (q.v.), published in 1922.

George F. Babbitt, a self-satisfied, ebullient, and prosperous house-agent and citizen of Zenith, a typical mid-western American town, from fully accepting, comes gradually to question and rebel against the ideals and conventions of middle-class business society. He is ostracized for his behaviour, but the loneliness and unhappiness that follow, as well as disillusionment with his new bohemian and socialist friends, reconcile him to his family duties and Zenith's way of life.

The novel was extraordinarily successful both in America and abroad, and 'Babbitt' and 'Babbittry' have been adopted into the language as identifying a social type and its ideals.

BABBITT, IRVING (1865–1933), American critic and professor at Harvard, born in Ohio. He was, with Paul Elmer More, a leader of the New Humanist movement in the 1920s, and a fierce critic of romanticism. Among his works are 'The New Laokoon' (1910), 'Rousseau and Romanticism' (1919), 'Democracy and Leadership' (1924); and 'On Being Creative' (1932).

Babel, Hebrew word in the Old Testament for BABYLON (q.v.).

For the story of the TOWER OF BABEL see Gen. xi.

Babes in the Wood, see *Children in the Wood.*

Bābism, see *Bāb.*

Baboo, see *Babu.*

Baboon, LEWIS, see *John Bull.*

Babu, a Hindu title of respect answering to our Mr. or Esquire; hence, a native Hindu gentleman; also (in Anglo-Indian use) a native clerk or official who wrote English; sometimes applied disparagingly to a Hindu, or more particularly a Bengali, with a superficial English education.

Babylon, a magnificent city, once the capital of the Chaldee empire; also the mystical city of the Apocalypse; whence in modern times applied polemically to Rome or the papal power, and rhetorically to any great and luxurious city.

THE WHORE OF BABYLON is a term applied to the Roman Catholic Church by the early puritans, with reference to Rev. xvii.

The HANGING GARDENS OF BABYLON ranked as one of the seven wonders of the world. One tradition attributes them to the Assyrian queen Semiramis, but the builder may have been Nebuchadnezzar (king of Babylon 605–562 B.C.), who married Amyitis, daughter of Astyages the Mede and is said to have built a series of terraced gardens near the palace to remind her of her native hills and forests.

Babylon, an old ballad, of which the plot is known 'to all branches of the Scandinavian race', of three sisters, to each of whom in turn an outlaw proposes the alternative of becoming a 'rank robber's wife' or death. The first two choose death and are killed by the outlaw. The third threatens the vengeance of her brother 'Baby Lon'. This is the outlaw himself, who thus discovers that he has unwittingly murdered his own sisters, and thereupon takes his own life. The ballad is in Child's collection (1883–98).

Babylonian Captivity, the period (c. 603–536 B.C.) during which the Jews were captive in Babylon. Nebuchadnezzar, having subdued Judaea, removed the inhabitants to Babylon, whence they were released by Cyrus. 'By the waters of Babylon we sat down and wept, when we remembered thee, O Sion'; Ps. cxxxvii. 1.

'Babylonian Captivity' is also applied to the period of the residence of the popes at Avignon, under French influence, beginning with Clement V in 1308.

Bacbuc, in Rabelais, IV. i, and v. xxxiv et seq., the oracle of the Holy Bottle, consulted by Panurge on the question whether he should marry (see *Pantagruel*).

Bacchanalia, the mysteries or orgies celebrated in ancient Rome in honour of Bacchus (q.v.). They were attended by such licentiousness that they were suppressed in 186 B.C., but the evidence of excesses is now discredited by some and the suppression attributed to political motives.

Bacchanals, priests, priestesses, or votaries of Bacchus (q.v.).

Bacchantes, priestesses of Bacchus, represented with dishevelled hair and garlands of ivy, carrying a thyrsus, and clashing cymbals.

Bacchus, a name of the Greek God Dionysus (q.v.).

BACCHȲLĪDĒS, the most important Greek lyric poet after Pindar, since the publication by F. G. Kenyon (1897) of extensive fragments of his works discovered in the Oxyrhynchus papyri. He lived about 470 B.C., a native of Iulis in Ceos, and was a nephew of Simonides.

Bach, JOHANN SEBASTIAN (1685–1750), born at Eisenach, of a family that included many musicians, was one of the greatest composers of all time. He was for many years musical director of two churches at Leipzig, where he composed most of his music. Much of this is of a sacred character, highly intellectual, and showing a supreme command of counterpoint and fugue.

Back Kitchen, THE, in Thackeray's 'Pendennis' (q.v.), was 'The Cyder Cellars' in Maiden Lane, frequented by Porson, Maginn, Charles Dickens, etc.

Backbite, SIR BENJAMIN, one of the scandalmongers in Sheridan's 'School for Scandal' (q.v.).

Backwell, EDWARD (*d.* 1683), a London goldsmith and banker at the Unicorn in Fleet Street, probably the chief originator of the system of bank-notes. He had financial dealings with Cromwell and Charles II, and was ruined by the closing of the exchequer by the latter in 1672. There are frequent references to him in Pepys's 'Diary'.

Bacon, FRIAR, see *Friar Bacon and Friar Bungay.*

BACON, FRANCIS, *first Baron Verulam* and *Viscount St. Albans* (1561–1626), was the younger son of Sir Nicholas Bacon, Lord Keeper in Queen Elizabeth's reign. He was born at York House, in the Strand, London, and educated at Trinity College, Cambridge. He was admitted to Gray's Inn and went through the various steps of the legal profession. He entered Parliament in 1584 as member for Melcombe Regis, and subsequently represented other constituencies. He then wrote papers on public affairs, including a 'Letter of Advice to Queen Elizabeth' urging strong measures against the Catholics. He made the acquaintance of the earl of Essex, who treated him with generosity and endeavoured to advance him in his career. Nevertheless, having been appointed to investigate the causes of Essex's revolt in 1601, he was largely responsible for the earl's conviction. He married Alice Barnham in 1606, became Solicitor-General in 1607, Attorney-General in 1613, Lord Keeper in 1617, and Lord Chancellor in 1618. In 1621 he was charged before the House of Lords with bribery, and confessed that he had been guilty of 'corruption and neglect' but denied that he had ever perverted justice. He was deprived of the great seal, fined, condemned to confinement during the king's pleasure, and disabled from sitting in parliament. He remained in the Tower only a few days, the fine being subsequently assigned by the king to trustees for Bacon's own use. The remaining years of his life were spent in literary and philosophical work. Pope described him as 'the wisest, brightest, meanest of mankind'.

Bacon's works may be divided into three classes, the philosophical (which form by far the greatest portion), the literary, and the professional works. The principal and best known of the philosophical works are: (1) the 'Advancement of Learning' (q.v.), published in English in 1605; (2) the 'Novum Organum' (q.v.), published in Latin in 1620, under the general title 'Francisci de Verulamio . . . Instauratio Magna', with a second title (after the preface) 'Pars secunda operis, quæ dicitur Novum Organum sive indicia vera de interpretatione naturæ'; and (3) the 'De Augmentis', published in Latin in 1623 with the title 'Opera F. Baconis de Verulamio . . . Tomus primus, qui continet de Dignitate et Augmentis Scientiarum libros ix'. It was Bacon's ambition to create a new system of philosophy, based on a right interpretation of nature, to replace that of Aristotle; the 'Novum Organum' describes the method by which the renovation of knowledge was to be achieved, and is thus the keystone to the whole system. The 'Advancement of Learning', of which the 'De Augmentis' may be regarded as an enlarged edition, was included in the 'Great Instauration' or Renewal of the Sciences as a preliminary review of the present state of knowledge. Of Bacon's literary works, the most important are the 'Essays' (q.v.), first published in 1597, and issued in final form in 1625; 'De Sapientia Veterum', published in 1609; 'Apophthegms New and Old', published in 1624; the 'New Atlantis' (q.v.) in 1626; and the 'History of Henry the Seventh' in 1622. The largest and most important of his professional works are the treatises entitled 'Maxims of the Law' and 'Reading on the Statute of Uses'.

Bacon wrote much in Latin, and always endeavoured to clothe in that language the works to which he attached importance, with a view, as he supposed, to their greater permanence. Yet he was capable of varied and beautiful styles in English, and there is a peculiar magnificence and picturesqueness in much of his writing. Many of the sentences in the 'Essays' have assumed almost the character of proverbs. But he is sometimes obscure. The standard edition of Bacon's 'Works' is that of James Spedding (q.v.), published in 1857–9, followed by the 'Life and Letters' in 1861–74.

BACON, ROGER (1214?–94), philosopher, studied at Oxford and Paris, where he may have graduated doctor, returned to England c. 1250, and probably remained at Oxford till c. 1257, when he incurred the suspicion of the Franciscan order, to which he belonged. He was sent under surveillance to Paris, where he remained in confinement ten years. He produced at the request of Pope Clement IV Latin treatises on the sciences (grammar, logic, mathematics, physics, and modern philosophy)—'Opus Majus', and, perhaps, 'Opus Secundum' and 'Opus Tertium'. He was again in confinement for his heretical propositions, c. 1278–92, and is said to have died and to have been buried at Oxford. He wrote also on chemistry and alchemy. By the public of his day he was regarded as a necromancer, and was believed to have constructed a brazen head capable of speech.

Roger Bacon may be described as the founder of English philosophy. Like his more famous namesake of the 17th cent., he advocated the substitution of an appeal to experience for the scholastic method of argument from general premises based on authority. Like him, he begins by stating the chief causes of error (*offendicula*)—authority, custom, the opinion of the ignorant many, the concealment of ignorance under a show of knowledge. But, unlike Francis Bacon, he attached importance to mathematics, and his scientific method, by recognizing the value of deduction, is better than that of his namesake. At the same time, Bacon's outlook remained medieval and mystical. His attack on the methods of scholasticism was taken up again and developed by William Ockham (q.v.) in the next century. Bacon was a man of great learning: he had a wide knowledge of the sciences, was an accomplished Greek scholar, and knew Hebrew and Aramaic. As a practical scientist he invented spectacles, and indicated the manner in which a telescope might be constructed.

Bacon and **Bungay**, (1) the rival publishers in Thackeray's 'Pendennis' (q.v.); (2) see *Friar Bacon and Friar Bungay*.

Baconian Theory, the theory that Francis Bacon (q.v.) wrote the plays attributed to Shakespeare. It was started, apparently, in the middle of the 18th cent., and is based partly on (supposed) internal evidence in Shakespeare's plays (the knowledge displayed and the vocabulary), and partly on external circumstances (the obscurity of Shakespeare's own biography, and the assumption that the son of a Warwickshire husbandman was unlikely to be capable of such skilful creations). Some holders of the theory have found in the plays cryptograms in support of it, e.g. in the nonce-word 'honorificabilitudinitatibus' in 'Love's Labour's Lost' (v. i), which has been rendered in Latin as 'These plays, F. Bacon's offspring, are preserved for the World'; the word, however, is found elsewhere as early as 1460.

Among prominent supporters of the theory may be mentioned Lord Penzance ('Judicial Summing Up'), Sir T. Martin (Shakespeare or Bacon?'), I. Donnelly ('The Great Cryptogram'), Mrs. E. W. Gallup ('Bi-Literal Cypher'), Sir G. Greenwood ('Shakespeare Problem re-stated'), and Sir E. Durning-Lawrence ('Bacon is Shake-speare', 1910; 'The Shakespeare Myth', 1912). The American cryptologists, W. S. and E. F. Friedman, ('The Shakespearean Ciphers Examined', 1957) have convincingly shown that none of the cipher 'evidence' supports the theory.

Badajoz, SIEGE OF, in Spain, undertaken by Wellington in 1811. Badajoz and Ciudad Rodrigo were two strong fortresses which barred Wellington's advance from Portugal into Spain. Badajoz was stormed in April 1812 with very heavy losses to the British troops, and the capture was attended with acts of great cruelty and outrage.

Badinguet, a nickname of Napoleon III.

Badman, The Life and Death of Mr., an allegory by Bunyan (q.v.), published in 1680.

The allegory takes the form of a dialogue, in which Mr. Wiseman relates the life of Mr. Badman, recently deceased, and Mr. Attentive comments on it. The youthful Badman shows early signs of his vicious disposition. He beguiles a rich damsel into marriage and ruins her; sets up in trade, swindles his creditors by fraudulent bankruptcies, and his customers by false weights; breaks his leg when coming home drunk, and displays a short-lived sickbed repentance. His wife dies of despair, and Badman marries again, but his second wife is as wicked as he is, and they part 'as poor as Howlets'. Finally Badman dies of a complication of diseases. The story is entertaining as well as edifying, and has a place in the evolution of the English novel.

Badon, MOUNT, the scene of a battle connected with the legends of Arthur. It is first mentioned by Gildas (q.v.), but without reference to Arthur. The 'Annales Cambriae' (q.v.) give the date of the battle as 518, and state that Arthur bore the cross of our Lord Jesus Christ there and the Britons were victorious. Badon is identified by some authorities with Bath, by others with Badbury near Wimborne. For a discussion of the question see E. K. Chambers, 'Arthur of Britain'.

Badour or BADOURA, PRINCESS, see *Camaralzaman.*

Badr-ed-Din or BEDR-ED-DIN, HASSAN, see *Nur-ed-Din.*

Badroulboudour or BEDR-EL-BUDUR ('moon of moons'), in 'Aladdin and the Wonderful Lamp' (q.v.), the daughter of the Sultan of China.

Baedeker, KARL (1801–59), editor and publisher, of Essen, Germany. He started the issue of the famous guide-books in Coblenz, and this was continued by his son, Fritz, who transferred the business to Leipzig.

Baetica, a Roman province of Spain, of which Corduba (Cordova) was the capital, deriving its name from the river *Baetis* (Guadalquivir), whence 'Baetic vale'.

Baffin, WILLIAM (*d.* 1622), navigator and discoverer. He was pilot in the Muscovy Company's expeditions of 1615 and 1616 in search of the North-West Passage, which resulted in the discovery of the bay which has since been given his name. He was killed at the siege of Kishm in an expedition against the Portuguese in the Persian Gulf. He wrote accounts of most of his voyages.

BAGE, ROBERT (1728–1801), a papermaker by trade, was author of six novels, 'Mount Henneth' (1781), 'Barham Downs' (1784), 'The Fair Syrian' (1787), 'James Wallace' (1788), 'Man as he is' (1792), and 'Hermsprong or Man as he is not' (1796). Scott included the first, second, and fourth in his 'Ballantyne novels'. Bage was a materialist, and 'Hermsprong', the best of his works, the story of a 'natural man' without morals or religion, is written to expound his views.

BAGEHOT, WALTER (1826–77), of Langport, Somerset, educated at Bristol and at University College, London, was a banker and shipowner, joint-editor with R. H. Hutton of the 'National Review' after 1855, and editor of the 'Economist' from 1860 till his death. His remarkable insight into economic and political questions is shown in his 'The English Constitution' (1867), 'Lombard Street' (1873), and 'Economic Studies' (1880, ed. Hutton). His 'Physics and Politics' (1876) is an 'application of the principles of natural selection and inheritance to political society'. In his 'Literary Studies' (1879) were republished papers contributed by him to the 'National Review'.

Bagford Ballads, The, illustrating the last years of the Stuarts' rule and the last years of the 17th cent., were published by the Ballad Society in 1878. They were assembled by John Bagford (1651–1716), originally a shoemaker, a book-collector who made for Robert Harley, first earl of Oxford, the collection of ballads that was subsequently acquired by the duke of Roxburghe, and at the same time made a private collection for himself.

Bagnet, Mr. and Mrs., characters in Dickens's 'Bleak House' (q.v.).

BAGNOLD, ENID (Lady Jones), author of 'National Velvet' (1935) and other works.

Bagstock, MAJOR JOE, a character in Dickens's 'Dombey and Son' (q.v.).

Bahais, see *Bāb*.

Bahram I, the king of Persia who put to death Mani, the founder of Manichaeism (q.v.), in A.D. 274.

Bahram Gur, or the 'Wild Ass', a national hero of Persia, who came to the throne in A.D. 420, celebrated as a hunter in the 'Rubáiyát' of Omar Khayyám (q.v.).

Baiae, a town on a small bay near Naples, in beautiful surroundings and possessing warm mineral springs, a favourite resort of the Romans, who built many palaces and villas there. Its site is now covered by the sea.

Baiardo, in the 'Orlando Furioso' (q.v.), the horse of Rinaldo. See *Bayard*.

Bailey, THE OLD, on the site of Newgate gaol, the seat of the Central Criminal Court in London, so called from the ancient *bailey* or *ballium* of the city wall between Lud Gate and New Gate, within which it was situated. (A *bailey* is an external wall enclosing the outer court of a feudal castle, forming the first line of defence.)

BAILEY, NATHAN or NATHANIEL (*d.* 1742), author of an English dictionary (1721), the forerunner of Johnson's and very popular.

BAILEY, PHILIP JAMES (1816–1902), was privately educated at Nottingham and matriculated in Glasgow University with a view to the Presbyterian ministry, but soon renouncing this intention, studied law in a solicitor's office and became a barrister of Lincoln's Inn. Deeply impressed by Goethe's 'Faust' and feeling compelled to give his own version of the legend, he retired in 1836 to the seclusion of his father's house at Old Basford, near Nottingham, where in three years he wrote the original version of his 'Festus' (q.v.), published in 1839. A second, much enlarged edition appeared in 1845. The final edition of 1889, which exceeded 40,000 lines, incorporated the greater part of three volumes of poetry that had appeared separately in the interval: 'The Angel World' (1850), 'The Mystic' (1855), and 'The Universal Hymn' (1867). Bailey is often regarded as the father of the 'Spasmodic School' (q.v.). In 1856 he received a civil list pension. In 1858 he published 'The Age', a colloquial satire.

***Bailiff's Daughter of Islington,** The,* the title of an old ballad, included in Percy's 'Reliques'. A squire's son loves the bailiff's daughter of Islington (probably the place of that name in Norfolk), but his friends send him to London bound as an apprentice. After seven years the lovers meet again and are united.

BAILLIE, JOANNA (1762–1851), Scottish dramatist and poetess, published in 1798 her first volume of 'Plays on the Passions', containing 'Basil' and 'De Monfort'; the latter was produced by Kemble and Mrs Siddons in 1800. A second volume appeared in 1802, and a third in 1812. Her most successful drama, 'The Family Legend', was produced in 1810. 'Miscellaneous Plays' appeared in 1836. Miss Baillie's poems ('Fugitive Verses', 1790, and 'Metrical Legends', 1821) show sprightly humour. She was a close friend of Sir Walter Scott, who much admired the 'Plays on the Passions'.

BAILLIE, ROBERT (1599–1662), Scottish Presbyterian divine, minister of Kilwinning, Ayrshire, and subsequently professor of divinity (1642) and principal (1660) of Glasgow University. He was with the Covenanters' army at Dunse Law, 1639, and in 1640; and was sent to London to draw up accusations against Laud, 1640. His 'Letters and Journals' (Bannatyne Club, 1841–2) are of importance for the history of the Civil War.

Bailly, HENRY, in Chaucer's 'Canterbury Tales' (q.v.), the host of the Tabard Inn.

BAIN, ALEXANDER (1818–1903), born in Aberdeen of humble parents, left school when eleven years old to work as a weaver, but continued his studies and obtained a bursary at Marischal College. He visited London and made the acquaintance of Mill and Carlyle. In 1860 he was appointed professor of logic at Aberdeen. In 1876 he founded the periodical 'Mind'. His two principal philosophical works were 'The Senses and the Intellect' (1855) and 'The Emotions and the Will' (1859). His other works include 'Mental and Moral Science' (1868), 'Logic' (1870), 'Mind and Body' (1872), and 'James Mill, a Biography' and 'J. S. Mill, a Criticism with Personal Recollections' (1882). Bain was one of the first exponents of a scientific psychology based on a physiological method that traces psychological phenomena to nerve and brain. He elaborated Mill's doctrine that the mind is to be explained by experience and association of ideas, extending this view from the intellect to the will and emotions. Though a Utilitarian in general, he accepted the existence in the human mind of 'motives that pull against our happiness', and held that purely altruistic conduct is possible.

Baines, CONSTANCE and SOPHIA, characters in Bennett's 'The Old Wives' Tale' (q.v.).

Bairam, the name of two Muslim festivals— the LESSER BAIRAM, lasting three days, which follows the fast of Ramadan (q.v.), and the GREATER BAIRAM, seventy days later, lasting four days.

Bajazet or BAJAYET, ruler of the Ottomans (1389–1402), overran the provinces of the Eastern empire and besieged Constantinople, but was interrupted by the approach of Timour (Tamerlane), and was defeated and taken prisoner by him. He figures in Marlowe's 'Tamburlaine the Great' and Rowe's 'Tamerlane' (qq.v.).

BAKER, Sir SAMUEL WHITE (1821–93), traveller and sportsman, whose explorations contributed to the knowledge of the sources of the Nile. He discovered and named Albert Nyanza (Lake Albert). He was appointed in 1869 for four years governor-general of the Equatorial Nile basin. His best-known works are 'Rifle and Hound in Ceylon' (1853), 'The Nile Tributaries of Abyssinia' (1872), and 'Ismailia' (1874).

Balaam, requested by Balak, king of Moab, to curse the invading Israelites, but warned by God not to do so, yet went on his ass with the princes of Moab. He would have been killed by an angel standing in the way if his ass had not saved him. When he beat the ass, the Lord opened her mouth, and she reproved him. Finally Balaam, inspired by God, foretold the happiness of Israel (Num. xxii–xxiv).

Balaam, Sir, the subject of a pungent satire in Pope's 'Moral Essays', Ep. iii. 339 et seq., a religious, punctual, frugal citizen tempted by the Devil through wealth, who becomes a corrupt courtier. He takes a bribe from France and is hanged:

The Devil and the king divide the prize;
And sad Sir Balaam curses God and dies.

Balaclava, a small seaport on the coast of the Crimea, near Sebastopol, was the scene in the Crimean War of the famous charge of the Light Brigade (26 Sept. 1854), celebrated in Tennyson's poem. The Russians, about 12,000 strong under General Liprandi, had captured certain redoubts held by a small force of Turks, and thus threatened the port. They had next attacked the English and been repulsed by the Heavy Brigade under General Scarlett. Owing to a misconception of Lord Raglan's orders, Lord Lucan then ordered Lord Cardigan with the Light Cavalry to charge the Russian army, which had reformed with artillery in front. The charge was heroically carried out, but out of 673 officers and men who took part in it, 247 were killed or wounded.

Balade of Charitie, The, one of the 'Thomas Rowley' poems, see *Chatterton.*

Balafré, Le, Henri de Guise (1550–88), a leader of the *Ligue* directed against the Protestants in France and one of the authors of the massacre of St. Bartholomew, so called from a scar on his face. He conspired to oust Henri III from the throne of France, but the latter caused him to be assassinated at the château of Blois. Scott gives this nickname, in his 'Quentin Durward' (q.v.), to Ludovic Lesly, the hero's uncle, one of the Scottish Archers of the Guard.

Balan, see *Balin and Balan.*

Balance, The, see *Libra.*

Balaustion's Adventure, a poem by R. Browning (q.v.), published in 1871.

Balaustion, a Rhodian girl, a deep admirer of the Athenian poet Euripides, persuades her kinsfolk to leave Rhodes when that island joins the Peloponnesian league against Athens. Her ship is pursued by a pirate into the harbour of Syracuse, the bitter enemy of Athens, where refuge is denied them. The hostility of the Syracusans is however changed to welcome when Balaustion recites to them Euripides' play, the 'Alkestis', in which their god Herakles is celebrated. Browning 'transcribes' the play, putting his comments in the mouth of Balaustion.

Balaustion appears again in 'Aristophanes' Apology' (q.v.).

Balbec, the name used by Proust (q.v.) for the seaside resort (Cabourg) in Normandy which is the scene of many of the incidents of 'À la recherche du temps perdu' (q.v.).

Balboa, Vasco Nuñez de (1475–1517), one of the companions of Cortez, the conqueror of Mexico. He is said to have joined the expedition of 1510 to Darien as a stowaway. It was he who first, in 1513, discovered the Pacific Ocean, not Cortez, as Keats supposed when he wrote:

Or like stout Cortez when with eagle eyes
He stared at the Pacific.

(Nor was Balboa silent on this occasion, as Keats makes Cortez. He exclaimed 'Hombre!') Balboa was beheaded by Pedrarias, governor of Darien, on a charge of treason.

Balchristie, Jenny, in Scott's 'The Heart of Midlothian' (q.v.), the housekeeper of the laird of Dumbiedikes.

Balclutha, in the Ossianic poem 'Carthon' (q.v.), a town on the Clyde, burnt by Combal, father of Ossian, in one of his raids.

Balder or Baldur, in Scandinavian mythology, a son of Odin (q.v.), the god of the summer sun, beloved by all, but threatened with death. Frigga, his mother, has persuaded all things to vow not to injure him, but has overlooked the mistletoe. Loki (q.v.) induces the blind god Hödur to throw a branch of mistletoe at Balder, and this kills him. In another legend Hödur is the rival of Balder for the beautiful Nanna, and has obtained possession of the irresistible Miming (q.v.) sword 'Mistelteinn' (mistletoe). For the legend of Hermod's journey to hell to recall Balder to the upper world, see *Balder Dead.*

Balder, a dramatic poem by Dobell (q.v.), published in 1854.

A poet has taken his young bride to live in 'a tower gloomy and ruinous'. He is engaged in mystic meditations, and believes himself selected to conquer the secret of the universe. Meanwhile she pines, but is for a time comforted by the presence of her infant child. Presently the child sickens and dies, and the mother goes mad. The poet conjures the doctor to cure her, threatening him with death if he fails. Finally, unable to witness his wife's sufferings and to listen to her prayers for death, he kills her.

The poem, which contains some fine passages, but is hardly readable today as a whole, is the most notable production of the 'Spasmodic School' (q.v.).

Balder Dead, a poem by M. Arnold (q.v.), published in 1853.

Balder (q.v.) has been slain by the blind Hödur through the scheming of Loki. The poem tells of the lament of the gods for him, and of Hermod's journey to the shades to persuade Hela to give him up. Hela consents if all things on earth will weep for Balder. This they all do except Loki, who, in the guise of an old hag, refuses. Hermod returns and relates his failure to Balder, who is reconciled to his lot, and holds out the hope of a happier world, after the destruction of Odin and the gods at Ragnarök.

Balderstone, CALEB, a character in Scott's 'Bride of Lammermoor' (q.v.).

Baldur, see *Balder.*

Baldwin, the name of four of the Christian kings of Jerusalem (and a nominal Baldwin V, an infant), including the successor of Godfrey de Bouillon, who figures in Tasso's 'Jerusalem Delivered' as one of the leaders of the Christian host, and also in Scott's 'Count Robert of Paris' (q.v.).

BALDWIN, WILLIAM, see *Mirror for Magistrates.*

BALE, JOHN (1495-1563), bishop of Ossory, author of several religious plays, a history of English writers, and numerous polemical works in favour of the cause of the Reformation. He is notable in the history of the drama as having written 'King John', the first English historical play, or at least a bridge between the interlude and the historical play proper.

BALFOUR, ARTHUR JAMES, *Earl of* (1848-1930), a distinguished statesman, educated at Eton and Trinity College, Cambridge, notable in a literary connexion as the author of 'A Defence of Philosophic Doubt' (1879), 'The Religion of Humanity' (1888), 'Essays and Addresses' (1893), 'The Foundations of Belief' (1895), 'Questionings on Criticism and Beauty' (Romanes Lecture, 1909), 'Theism and Humanism' (Gifford Lectures, 1915), 'Essays Speculative and Political' (1920), 'Theism and Thought' (Gifford Lectures, 1923), and 'Opinions and Argument' (1927).

Balfour, DAVID, a character in R. L. Stevenson's 'Kidnapped' (q.v.) and 'Catriona'.

Balfour of Burley, JOHN, a leader of the Cameronian sect, who figures in Scott's 'Old Mortality' (q.v.).

Balibari, THE CHEVALIER DE, in Thackeray's 'Barry Lyndon' (q.v.), the uncle of the hero.

Balin and Balan, one of Tennyson's 'Idylls of the King' (q.v.), published in 1885 with 'Tiresias'. See *Balin le Savage and Balan.*

The poem is described in the original edition as 'an introduction to Merlin and Vivien'. Balin, a violent, choleric, but honest man, a knight of Arthur's court, is filled with humble devotion to Queen Guinevere. Disturbed by a glimpse that he gets of the intrigue between Launcelot and the queen, he leaves the court. His suspicions are finally confirmed by the perfidious Vivien. Possessed with fury at the shattering of his idol, he defaces the queen's crown on his shield and flings it from him. His brother Balan, another knight of Arthur's court, who has been given the quest of a demon, passing at the moment and thinking that this mad knight must be the demon of whom he is in search, attacks him. The two brothers fall, mortally wounded by each other.

Balin le Savage and **Balan,** two brothers, 'marvellous good knights' whose deeds and death at each other's hands unwittingly are told in Malory's 'Morte Darthur', Bk. II; also in Swinburne's 'Tale of Balen' (1896). They appear to have had their origin in Belinus and Bran (qq.v.), gods of the sky and nether world respectively in Celtic mythology (J. Rhys, 'Studies in the Arthurian Legend').

Baliol, MRS. BETHUNE, in the introduction to Scott's 'Chronicles of the Canongate' (q.v.), the friend of Chrystal Croftangry, on whose recollections the latter draws for his stories.

Baliol, JOHN DE (d. 1269), father of John de Baliol, king of Scotland (1292-6), founded Balliol College, Oxford, about 1263, as an act of penance imposed for having 'vexed and damnified' the churches of Tynemouth and Durham.

Balkis, or BELKIS, the name given by the Arabs to the queen of Sheba who visited Solomon (1 Kings x). The Koran (c. xxvii) contains an allusion to the story that Solomon, having heard a report that her legs and feet were covered with hair, invited her into a court of which the floor was covered with glass. The queen, mistaking this for water, lifted her robe in order to pass through it, thus giving Solomon an opportunity of ascertaining the truth of the report. According to some legends Balkis (on her return to Ethiopia) bore a son to Solomon whom she named David and who became king of Abyssinia.

See also the song 'Balkis was in her marble town' in 'Emblems of Love' (Pt. III, 'Virginity and Perfection') by Abercrombie (q.v.).

Ball, JOHN, a leader of the Peasants' Revolt of 1381. He was a priest. He is the subject of W. Morris's romance 'The Dream of John Ball'.

Ballad, originally a song intended as the accompaniment to a dance; hence a light, simple song of any kind, or a popular song, often one celebrating or attacking persons or institutions. From this last is derived the modern sense in which a ballad is a simple spirited *poem* in short stanzas in which some popular story is graphically narrated. [OED.] In this sense of the word oral tradition is an essential element. There has been much discussion as to the origin and composition of the old English ballads. They appear to date, mostly, from the 15th cent. (See 'The Ballad of Tradition', by G. H. Gerould, 1932.)

Ballad of Bouillabaisse, a ballad by W. M. Thackeray (q.v.), published in 'Punch' in 1849. The author muses on the sad memories recalled by the old accustomed corner in the Paris inn, where with his young wife and friends he used to eat *bouillabaisse*.

Ballade, strictly, a poem consisting of one or more triplets of seven- or (afterwards) eight-lined stanzas, each ending with the same line as refrain, and usually an envoy addressed to a prince or his substitute; e.g. Chaucer's 'Compleynt of Venus'. More generally, a poem divided into stanzas of equal length, usually of seven or eight lines.

Balladino, ANTONIO, in Jonson's 'The Case is Altered' (q.v.), the character under which Munday (q.v.) is ridiculed.

Ballantyne, JAMES (1772–1833), at first a solicitor, then a printer in Kelso, printed Sir W. Scott's 'Minstrelsy of the Scottish Border' in 1802, and thenceforth continued to print Scott's works. He transferred his press from Kelso to Edinburgh in 1802 and Scott became a secret partner in 1805. In 1809 he took a quarter-share in the bookselling business of John Ballantyne & Co. started by Scott. He was ruined by the bankruptcy of Constable & Co. in 1826. Scott nicknamed him 'Aldiborontiphoscophornio' from the character in Carey's 'Chrononhotonthologos' (q.v.).

Ballantyne, JOHN (1774–1821), brother of James Ballantyne (q.v.), became in 1809 manager of the publishing firm started by Sir Walter Scott. He was nicknamed by Scott 'Rigdumfunnidos' from the character in Carey's 'Chrononhotonthologos' (q.v.). Scott planned Ballantyne's Novelist's Library, 1821-4, solely for his financial benefit but only one volume was published before his death.

BALLANTYNE, ROBERT MICHAEL (1825–94), writer of stories for boys, was a nephew of James and John Ballantyne (qq.v.). He worked with Hudson's Bay Company and in Constable's printing firm before turning to literature as a career. His popular books include 'The Young Fur Traders', 'The Coral Island', 'The Dog Crusoe', 'Erling the Bold', etc.

Balliol College, Oxford, was founded by John de Baliol (q.v.) in 1263, and his foundation was much increased by his widow, Devorguilla. Among famous masters of this college have been John Wycliffe and Benjamin Jowett (qq.v.), and among its many distinguished members Humphrey (q.v.), duke of Gloucester, Adam Smith (q.v.), and a large proportion of the British statesmen of the last hundred years.

Balm in Gilead, an allusion to Jer. viii. 22, where the prophet, lamenting the sorry state of the Jews, exclaims, 'Is there no balm in

Gilead? Is there no physician there?' See also Gen. xxxvii. 25. *Balm of Gilead* is a modern term denoting an oleo-resin formerly esteemed for its medical properties.

Balmawhapple, THE LAIRD OF, FALCONER by surname, a character in Scott's 'Waverley' (q.v.).

Balnibarbi, in 'Gulliver's Travels' (q.v.), the country, subject to the king of Laputa, of which Lagado is the capital, where in every town there is an academy of projectors, engaged on projects for increasing the welfare of mankind, none of which come to perfection.

Balor, the chief of the Fomors (q.v.) of Gaelic mythology. One of his eyes had the power of destroying whatever it looked on. The eye was put out and Balor himself slain by Lugh, the sun-god, at the great battle of Moytura.

Balthazar ('possessor of treasure'), one of the three Magi (q.v.) or 'wise men of the East'. He is represented as king of Chaldea.

BALTHAZAR is the name assumed by Portia as a lawyer in Shakespeare's 'Merchant of Venice' (q.v.).

Baltic, The Battle of the, see *Campbell (T.)*.

Balwhidder, THE REV. MICAH, in Galt's 'Annals of the Parish' (q.v.), the minister of Dalmailing.

BALZAC, HONORÉ DE (1799–1850), French novelist, author of the great collection of romances entitled 'La Comédie humaine' in which he endeavoured to represent, faithfully and minutely, the whole complex system of French society, Parisian and provincial. The design is expounded in his famous 'General Preface' (1842). He has been considered by many authorities (including Henry James) the greatest of all novelists, and has powerfully influenced later writers of fiction. Though born in Tours, Balzac spent most of his life in Paris, living in a garret during his early years as a writer, and seldom at any time out of financial difficulties. He first attained success by 'Le Dernier Chouan' (1829), and more conspicuously by 'La Peau de Chagrin' (1831). These were followed by a number of masterpieces, 'Eugénie Grandet', 'Le Père Goriot', 'Le Cousin Pons', etc. His 'Contes Drolatiques', a Rabelaisian work, published in 1832–7, and a few comedies, stand apart from the main body of his work.

Bamboccio (cripple), the nickname of Pieter van Laar (1613–74?), Dutch painter of scenes of low life, whence the name BAMBOCHADES for genre pictures of this kind.

Bampton Lectures, THE, on theological subjects, are delivered at Oxford annually, the cost being defrayed out of the proceeds of the estate left for the purpose by the Rev. John Bampton, of Trinity College, Oxford, and a prebendary of Salisbury, who died in 1751. Among notable Bampton lecturers have been Whately, Milman, Mansel, Liddon, and Rashdall.

Ban, in the Arthurian legends, king of Brittany and father of Launcelot (q.v.).

Banastaire, HUMFREY, in Sackville's 'Complaint of Buckingham' (q.v.), the dependant of Buckingham who betrayed him.

Banbury, a town in Oxfordshire, formerly noted for the number and zeal of its Puritan inhabitants. Whence 'Banbury man' is used by Ben Jonson and others for a sanctimonious fellow.

BANBURY CAKES were known to Gervase Markham ('English Huswife', II. ii, 1615), and are still famous.

BANBURY CHEESES were thin, and Bardolph in Shakespeare's 'Merry Wives' (I. i) addresses Slender as 'You Banbury cheese!'

BANBURY CROSS, destroyed by the Puritans, has been restored in recent times. It is the subject of a well-known nursery rhyme.

BANCROFT, GEORGE (1800–91), American historian and diplomat, born in Massachusetts, and educated at Harvard College and Göttingen. The 'History of the United States from the Discovery of the American Continent' appeared from 1834 to 1876. Two supplementary volumes, 'History of the Formation of the Constitution of the United States', appeared in 1882.

BANDELLO, MATTEO (1485–1561), a Lombard who fled to France and was made bishop of Agen by Francis I, was the best Italian writer of short stories in the 16th cent. Many of his tales were translated by Belleforest into French (1564–82), and thirteen of these French versions were rendered into English by Geoffrey Fenton in his 'Tragical Discourses' (1567). Painter's 'Palace of Pleasure' (q.v.) includes twenty-five of Bandello's tales, nine translated from the Italian and sixteen from Belleforest.

Bandusia, a fountain celebrated by Horace, probably on his Sabine farm.

Bangorian Controversy, a church controversy of the early years of the reign of George I. The Anglican Church, which was committed to the hereditary principle of monarchy, found itself in a difficulty when the claims of the Stuarts were set aside on the death of Queen Anne and a parliamentary king brought in from Hanover. Strict churchmen refused the oaths of allegiance to the new king, and there was strong feeling between the non-jurors and the rest. Benjamin Hoadly, bishop of Bangor and the king's chaplain, published a pamphlet and preached a sermon in 1717 reducing Church authority to a minimum and making sincerity the chief test of true religion. These gave rise to the 'Bangorian controversy', in which a great number of pamphlets were issued, the most important among them being the 'Three Letters to the Bishop of Bangor' of W. Law (q.v.).

BANIM, JOHN (1798–1842), the 'Scott of Ireland', novelist, dramatist, and poet, is chiefly remembered for the pictures of Irish life and character, drawn with greater fidelity than by earlier novelists, and with more attention to the sombre side, contained in his 'Tales by the O'Hara Family' (first series, 1825). In some of these he was assisted by his brother, MICHAEL BANIM (1796–1874), who also wrote 'Father Connell' (1842), 'Clough Fion', and 'The Town of the Cascades'.

Bank of England, THE, was founded on the basis of a scheme put forward by William Paterson (1658–1719, who also conceived the unfortunate Darien project, q.v.), with a view to raising money for William III's foreign campaigns. The charter, after violent opposition in Parliament, was granted in 1695. Sir John Houblon was appointed the first governor, with Michael Godfrey (a nephew of Sir Edmund Berry Godfrey), one of the most active promoters, as deputy-governor. The bank began its operations in the Grocers' Hall. Leading works on the subject are 'A History of the Bank of England', by A. Andréadès (1909), and 'The Bank of England', by Sir John Clapham (1944). 'The Bank of England from Within, 1694–1900', by W. Marston Acres (2 vols., 1931), may also be consulted. In this work the financial side of the Bank is subordinated to internal affairs and the human element in the Bank's history.

Banker Marks, see *Freemasons.*

Banks, SIR JOSEPH (1743–1820), an eminent explorer and natural historian, and a great pioneer of science, who studied the flora of Newfoundland in 1766, and accompanied Cook in his expedition round the world in the 'Endeavour', subsequently visiting Iceland. He made valuable natural history collections, which are preserved in the British Museum. He was president of the Royal Society, 1778–1820. Banks left a narrative of Cook's voyage.

Banks's or BANKES'S HORSE, see under *Marocco.*

Bankside, the right bank of the Thames at Southwark (q.v.), noted in the 16th and 17th cents. for its theatres and disreputable haunts.

Bannatyne Club, THE, was founded in 1823, with Sir Walter Scott as president, for the publication of old Scottish documents (see Lockhart's 'Scott', lviii). The club was dissolved in 1861. George Bannatyne (1545–1608), in whose honour it was named, was the compiler in 1568 of a large collection of Scottish poems.

Bannockburn, near Stirling, the scene of the great battle in 1314, when Robert Bruce utterly routed the English under Edward II, and all Scotland was lost to the latter. The battle is described in Scott's 'Lord of the Isles', vi.

Banquo, in Shakespeare's 'Macbeth' (q.v.), a general of the king of Scotland's army. Though mentioned by Holinshed, he is not regarded as an historical character.

Banshee, a supernatural being supposed by the peasantry of Ireland and the Scottish Highlands to wail under the windows of a house when one of the inmates is about to die. Certain families of rank were reputed to have a special 'family spirit' of this kind. The word is a phonetic spelling of the Irish 'bean sídhe', from OIr. 'ben síde', a female spirit or elf. [OED.]

Bantam, ANGELO CYRUS, in Dickens's 'Pickwick Papers' (q.v.), Grand Master of the Ceremonies at Bath.

Baphomet, the alleged name of the idol that the Templars were accused of worshipping. According to l'Abbé Constant, quoted by Littré, this word was cabalistically formed by writing backwards *tem. o. h. p. ab.*, abbreviation of *templi omnium hominum pacis abbas*, 'abbot of the temple of peace of all men'.

Barabas, the 'Jew of Malta', in Marlowe's play of that name (q.v.).

Barabbas, the notable robber, released instead of Jesus (Matt. xxvii. 16–26).

Baralipton, a mnemonic term in scholastic logic constructed to represent by its first three vowels a syllogism in which the two premisses are universal affirmatives, and the conclusion a particular affirmative (see *Barbara*).

Barataria, in 'Don Quixote' (q.v.), the island of which Sancho Panza is made governor.

Barathron or BARATHRUM, a deep chasm behind the Acropolis at Athens, into which criminals' corpses were thrown.

Barbara, in logic, a mnemonic term designating the first mood of the first figure of syllogisms, the three A's signifying that the major and minor premisses and the conclusion are universal affirmatives. In this system, E signified a universal negative proposition, I a particular affirmative, O a particular negative. Of the possible combinations of these four letters in groups of three, only nineteen are valid syllogisms, which are enumerated in a well-known mnemonic verse, beginning:
BarbaraA, cElArEnt, dArII, fErIOque prioris.
(See Aldrich, 'Artis Logicae Rudimenta'.)

Barbara Allan, a Scottish ballad included in Percy's 'Reliques', on the subject of the death of Sir John Grehme for unrequited love of Barbara Allan, and her subsequent remorse. 'Barbara Allen's Cruelty', another ballad on the same theme, is also in the 'Reliques'.

Barbarossa, the nickname ('Red-Beard') of Frederick I, emperor of the Holy Roman Empire (1152–90). He made five expeditions into Italy for the purpose of its subjugation, and entered Rome. But the last expedition was opposed by the Lombard League and was a failure. Barbarossa was drowned in a river in the course of the Third Crusade (having gone by land to avoid the perils of the sea), but legend says that he still sleeps in a cavern in the Kyffhäuser mountain, with his companions about him and his beard grown round a stone table, until the need of his country shall summon him forth. This legend appears to have been transferred from Charlemagne to Barbarossa, and from Barbarossa to his grandson, Frederick II.

Barbary Corsairs, the cruisers of Barbary (the Saracen countries along the N. coast of Africa), to whose attacks the ships and coasts of the Christian countries were incessantly exposed.

Barbason, the name of a demon mentioned by Shakespeare in 'The Merry Wives', II. ii, and 'Henry V', II. i.

BARBAULD, MRS. ANNA LETITIA (1743–1825), *née* AIKIN, was author of miscellaneous poems and prose essays, including nature studies entitled 'Hymns in Prose'. She is chiefly remembered for her fine lines beginning:
Life! I know not what thou art.

Barbican, an outer fortification to a city or castle. The Barbican in London (Aldersgate Street) was, according to Stow, the site of an old watch-tower 'whence a man might behold the whole Citie toward the South, as also into Kent, Sussex, and Surrey'. In the street named after it lived Gondomar, the Spanish Ambassador, and John Milton (1645–7).

Barbizon School, a group of French painters, including Théodore Rousseau (1812–67) and J. F. Millet (1814–75), who worked at Barbizon in the Forest of Fontainebleau in the mid-19th cent., painting landscapes *en plein air* and peasant scenes.

BARBOUR, JOHN (1316?–95), Scottish poet, was archdeacon of Aberdeen in 1357. He probably studied and taught at Oxford and Paris. He was one of the auditors of exchequer, 1372, 1382, and 1384. He composed his poem 'The Bruce' (q.v.), celebrating the war of independence and deeds of King Robert and James Douglas, about 1375. Other poems which have with reasonable certainty been ascribed to him are the 'Legend of Troy' and 'Legends of the Saints', being translations from Guido da Colonna's 'Historia Destructionis Troiae' and the 'Legenda Aurea'.

Barchester Towers, a novel by A. Trollope (q.v.), published in 1857.
This is the second in the Barsetshire series, the sequel to 'The Warden' (q.v.). To the characters included in that work are now added Dr. Proudie, the new bishop of Barchester, henpecked by the masterful Mrs. Proudie, and the bishop's chaplain, the intriguing and hypocritical Mr. Slope. 'Barchester Towers' is mainly occupied with the struggle between Mr. Slope and Mrs. Proudie for the control of the diocese, and in particular for the disposal of the wardenship of Hiram's Hospital as between the two candidates, Mr. Harding, the former warden, and Mr. Quiverful, the incumbent of a small

living and the father of fourteen children, a struggle in which the lady comes out triumphant. Mr. Slope's manœuvres are dictated partly by his rivalry with Mrs. Proudie, partly by his desire to win the hand of the widowed Mrs. Bold, Mr. Harding's daughter, while at the same time he is smitten with a violent passion for the Signora Vesey-Neroni, the daughter of Canon Stanhope, a lady in an equivocal matrimonial position. Mr. Harding's candidature for the wardenship is defeated, in spite of the strenuous advocacy of Archdeacon Grantly and his allies; but the tables are turned by the offer to him of the vacant deanery of Barchester, which Mr. Slope had hoped to obtain. Mr. Slope, defeated by Mrs. Proudie, disappointed of his hope of the deanery, rejected with contumely by Mrs. Bold, publicly exposed by the Signora Neroni, is unceremoniously bundled out of his chaplaincy and disappears from view. Mrs. Bold marries Mr. Arabin (q.v.).

Barchino, in imprints, Barcelona.

BARCLAY, ALEXANDER (1475?–1552), poet, scholar, and divine, probably of Scottish birth, was successively a priest in the college of Ottery St. Mary, Devonshire, a Benedictine monk at Ely, a Franciscan at Canterbury, and rector of All Hallows, Lombard Street, London. He translated Brant's 'Narrenschiff' into English verse as 'The Ship of Fools' (q.v., 1509), and wrote his 'Eclogues' (q.v.) at Ely (1515–21). He also translated a life of St. George from Baptist Mantuan, and Sallust's 'Bellum Jugurthinum' (c. 1520).

BARCLAY, JOHN (1582–1621), a Scot born at Pont-à-Mousson in France, author of 'Argenis' (1621), a Latin political and historical romance, in which there is reference, more or less precise, to recent events on the Continent, notably to the wars of the League, and the characters have some resemblance to actual personages, such as Henri IV of France. He also wrote 'Euphormionis Satyricon', a satire on the Jesuits in the form of a picaresque novel, in Latin, in two parts, published in 1603?–7.

Bard, The, a Pindaric ode by Gray (q.v.), published in 1757.

The ode is based on a tradition current in Wales that Edward I, when he completed the conquest of that country, ordered all the bards that fell into his hands to be put to death. It is a lamentation by a Welsh bard, and a curse pronounced by him and the ghosts of his slaughtered companions on Edward's race, whose misfortunes are foretold. Then the bard sings of the glories that will come with the house of Tudor, and of the poets of that age.

Bardell, Mrs., in Dickens's 'Pickwick Papers' (q.v.), Mr. Pickwick's landlady, who sues him for breach of promise.

Bardolph, in Shakespeare's 'Henry IV' and 'Henry V' (qq.v.), one of Falstaff's disreputable boon companions. He is 'white-livered and red-faced, by means whereof a' faces it out and fights not'. He is hanged for looting in the French war. In Shakespeare's 'Merry Wives of Windsor' (q.v.) we find him discarded by Falstaff and employed as tapster by the host of the Garter Inn.

Bareacres, EARL and COUNTESS OF, characters in Thackeray's 'Vanity Fair' (q.v.).

Barebones Parliament, the assembly summoned by Cromwell in 1653, consisting of 133 members, so called from one of its members, Praise-God Barbon, an Anabaptist leatherseller in Fleet Street.

BARETTI, GIUSEPPE MARC' ANTONIO (1719–89), born at Turin, came to London and opened a school for teaching Italian in 1751. His 'Italian and English Dictionary' was published in 1760. He was a friend of Johnson and Thrale.

BARHAM, RICHARD HARRIS (1788–1845), educated at St. Paul's School and Brasenose College, Oxford, took orders and held various preferments, including that of a minor canon of St. Paul's. His 'Ingoldsby Legends', written in the latter part of his life and first published in 'Bentley's Miscellany' and 'The New Monthly Magazine', were reissued in 1840, and by their humour, felicity of verse, narrative power and variety of subject, became immensely popular, though charges of irreverence and the like have been made against them. He was particularly successful in the grotesque or frankly comic treatment of medieval legend.

BARING, MAURICE (1874–1945), poet and novelist, entered the Diplomatic Service but abandoned it for journalism. His early verse included 'Pastels and Other Rhymes' (1891) and 'The Black Prince' (1902) and his 'Collected Poems' were published in 1925. His plays, 'Diminutive Dramas' and 'The Grey Stocking' appeared in 1910 and 1912 respectively. Later he turned to novels, short stories, and essays, of which the best-known titles are 'C' (1924), 'Cat's Cradle' (1925), 'Tinker's Leave' (1927), and 'In the End is my Beginning' (1931).

BARING-GOULD, SABINE (1834–1924), educated at Clare College, Cambridge, was rector of Lew Trenchard in Devon, and author of a large number of religious and other works, and novels. The latter include 'Mehalah' (1880), 'John Herring' (1883), 'Court Royal' (1886), 'Richard Cable' (1888), etc. He also wrote 'Curious Myths of the Middle Ages' (1866–8).

BARKER, GEORGE GRANVILLE (1913–), born in Essex of an English father and Irish mother. He taught in a Japanese university in 1939 and lived in America from 1940 to 1943. He then returned to England, though for further periods living in America and Italy. He published 'Thirty Preliminary Poems' in 1933 and early attracted the admiration of W. B. Yeats. Other volumes include 'Eros in Dogma' (1944), 'News of the World' (1950), and 'The True Confession of George Barker' (1950). His 'Collected Poems' appeared in 1957. They are marked by a rhetorical and dionysiac style and a preoccupation with human suffering and guilt.

BARKER, HARLEY GRANVILLE GRANVILLE-, see *Granville-Barker* (*H. G.*).

Barkis, in Dickens's 'David Copperfield' (q.v.), the carrier, who sent a message by David to Clara Peggotty that 'Barkis is willin' '.

Barlaam and Josaphat, a medieval religious romance, interesting as a christianized version of the legend of Buddha. It appears first in the works of John of Damascus (8th cent.), then in the 'Lives of the Saints' of Symeon Metaphrastes, a celebrated Byzantine hagiographer, and subsequently was widely disseminated.

Josaphat was, according to the story, the son of an Indian king, Abenner, who persecuted the Christians. A glorious and prosperous reign was foretold for Josaphat, but in a higher kingdom; and it was said that he would become a Christian. Abenner, perturbed by the prophecy, for a time secluded his son from the world, but yielding to his entreaties at last allowed him freedom. Barlaam, a holy man, now visited India, conversed with Josaphat, and converted him to Christianity. His father having failed to shake him in his faith, associated him in the kingdom, was himself converted, and then died. Josaphat handed over the kingdom to Barchias, sought out Barlaam, and died a hermit.

Barleycorn, JOHN, the personification of barley, as the grain from which malt liquor is made.

BARLOW, JOEL (1754–1812), American poet and diplomat, born in Connecticut, who is remembered as the author of 'The Columbiad' (q.v.) and the mock epic 'Hasty Pudding' (1796), and as one of the 'Hartford Wits' (q.v.).

Barmecide, the patronymic of a family of princes ruling at Baghdad just before Haroun-al-Raschid, concerning one of whom the story is told in the 'Arabian Nights' (q.v., the story of the Barber's Sixth Brother) that he put a succession of imaginary dishes before a beggar pretending that they contained a sumptuous repast. The beggar, entering into the spirit of the jest, pretended to be intoxicated by the imaginary wine offered him, and fell upon his entertainer. Hence 'Barmecide' is used of one who offers illusory benefits. See also *Jaffar*.

Barn Elms, at Barnes, near London, had in the 17th–18th cents. a fashionable promenade, favoured by Evelyn, and notorious for the duels fought there. Referred to in Congreve's 'Love for Love' (q.v.), II. ii.

Barnaby Bright, or LONG BARNABY, St.

Barnabas' Day, 11 June, in the old style reckoned the longest day of the year.

Barnaby Rudge, a novel by Dickens (q.v.), published in 1841, as part of 'Master Humphrey's Clock'. This was the earlier of Dickens's two historical novels (for the other see *Tale of Two Cities*), the period dealt with being that of the Gordon anti-popery riots of 1780. Reuben Haredale, a country gentleman, has been murdered, and the murderer has never been discovered. Geoffrey Haredale, his brother, a Roman Catholic, and Sir John Chester are enemies. Chester's son Edward is in love with Haredale's niece, Emma; and the elders combine, in spite of their hatred, to thwart the match. The Gordon riots supervene, fomented secretly by the smooth villain Chester. Haredale's house is burnt, and Emma carried off. Edward saves the lives of Haredale and Emma, and wins Haredale's consent to his marriage with the latter. Haredale discovers the murderer of his brother, the steward Rudge, the father of the half-witted Barnaby and the blackmailer of the unhappy Mrs. Rudge. Rudge pays the penalty of his crime. Chester is killed by Haredale in a duel.

The principal interest of the book lies in the vivid descriptions of the riots, which held London terrorized for several days, and in the characters accessory to the above plot: the pathetic figure of Barnaby; the sturdy locksmith Gabriel Varden, with his peevish wife, and the incomparable Dolly, his coquettish daughter; Simon Tappertit his apprentice, small in body but aspiring and anarchical in soul, and Miss Miggs, his mean and treacherous servant; John Willet, host of the Maypole Inn, and Joe his gallant son; Hugh the savage ostler, who turns out to be Chester's son, and Dennis the Hangman; and lastly Grip, Barnaby's raven.

Barnacle, a character in Shirley's 'The Gamester' (q.v.).

Barnacles, THE, in Dickens's 'Little Dorrit' (q.v.), types of government officials in the 'Circumlocution Office'.

BARNARD, LADY ANNE, see *Lindsay* (*Lady A.*).

Barnard's Inn, one of the old Inns of Chancery (q.v.). It was bequeathed by John Mackworth (*d.* 1451), dean of Lincoln, the owner, to the Dean and Chapter of Lincoln. It was at the time occupied by one Barnard and became a law students' Inn, but remained the property of the Dean and Chapter until 1894, when it was sold to the Mercers' Company, who established their school there. (G. R. Stirling Taylor, 'Historical Guide to London'.)

Barnardine, in Shakespeare's 'Measure for Measure' (q.v.), a prisoner 'that apprehends death no more dreadfully but as a drunken sleep; careless, reckless, and fearless of what's past, present, or to come'.

Barnavelt, Sir John van Olden, an historical tragedy, probably by J. Fletcher (q.v.), acted in 1619. This remarkable play was discovered by Mr. A. H. Bullen among the MSS. of the British Museum and was printed in his 'Old English Plays' (1883).

The play deals with events in the contemporary history of Holland. Barnavelt, the great advocate, disturbed by the growing power of the Prince of Orange and the army, under cloak of a religious movement conspires against him and raises companies of burghers in the towns to resist the army. The plot is discovered, the companies disarmed, and Barnavelt's principal associates are captured. One of these, Leidenberch, confesses. Barnavelt, who by virtue of his great position is still left at liberty though suspect, upbraids him and tells him that death is the only honourable course left to him. Leidenberch, in remorse, takes his own life. The Prince of Orange, who had hitherto counselled moderation, now convinced of the gravity of the conspiracy, advises severe measures. Barnavelt is arrested, tried, and executed.

BARNES, BARNABE (1569?–1609), educated at Brasenose College, Oxford, was a voluminous writer of verse. He issued (perhaps privately) 'Parthenophil and Parthenophe, Sonnettes, Madrigals, Elegies, and Odes' in 1593, and 'A Divine Centurie of Spirituall Sonnets' in 1595. He also wrote an anti-popish tragedy, 'The Devil's Charter'.

BARNES, WILLIAM (1801–86), the son of a farmer in Blackmoor Vale, Dorset, entered St. John's College, Cambridge, in 1838, took orders, and became rector of Came in 1862, where he remained till his death. He wrote a number of poems in the Dorset dialect, marked by pleasant sentiment and a strong perception of the charms of the country ('Poems of Rural Life', three series, 1844, 1859, and 1863).

Barney, in Dickens's 'Oliver Twist' (q.v.), a Jew, associate of Fagin.

BARNFIELD, RICHARD (1574–1627), educated at Brasenose College, Oxford, published 'The Affectionate Shepherd' (1594), 'Cynthia, with certain Sonnets' (1595), and other poems (1598), including two pieces, which appeared in the 'Passionate Pilgrim' (q.v., 1599), and were long attributed to Shakespeare, the better known of these being the ode, 'As it fell upon a day, In the merry month of May'. 'The Affectionate Shepherd' is a pastoral, based on the second eclogue of Virgil and dedicated to Lady Rich (Sidney's 'Stella'). In 1598 Barnfield published 'The Encomion of Lady Pecunia', a satirical poem on the power of money.

Barnum, PHINEAS TAYLOR (1810–91), the great American showman, began his career by exhibiting a bogus nurse of George Washington, alleged to be aged 161. He then started the American museum, containing curiosities and monstrosities. He conducted Tom Thumb to Europe in 1844, and Jenny Lind to America in 1850. In 1881 he combined forces with the keenest of his rivals, launching the firm of Barnum and Bailey, which visited Olympia (London) in 1889. He acquired the elephant Jumbo in 1882.

Barnwell, George, see *George Barnwell.*

Baroque, a word adapted from the Portuguese *barroco,* Spanish *barrueco,* meaning a rough or imperfect pearl; originally a term of abuse applied to 17th-cent. Italian art and that of other countries, especially Germany, influenced by Italy. It is characterized by the unclassical use of classical forms, and by the interpenetration of architecture, sculpture, and painting to produce grandiose and emotional effects.

BARRÈS, MAURICE (1862–1923), French writer and politican who is best known outside France for his extreme Nationalism, the almost mystical fervour of his patriotism, and the fame he acquired by his daily articles (later collected and published) to the newspaper 'L'Echo de Paris' during the 1914–18 war. Among his own countrymen his reputation was of longer standing, and was more purely literary. By birth he was a Lorrainer, and the love of his own particular corner of France was really the living heart of his fervent gallicism. At his death he may be said to have ranked with Anatole France as one of the representative figures of the literature of 19th and early 20th century France. His best-known books are: 'Un Homme libre' (1889), 'Le Jardin de Bérénice' (1891), 'Les Déracinés' (1897, the first volume of a trilogy 'Le Roman de l'énergie nationale'), 'Colette Baudoche' (1909), 'La Colline inspirée' (1913), 'Les Amitiés françaises' (1903), etc.

BARRIE, SIR JAMES MATTHEW (1860–1937), educated at Dumfries Academy and Edinburgh University, was in his early days a journalist (his experiences in this profession are reflected in his 'When a Man 's Single', 1888). Among the best of his earlier works are the biography of his mother, 'Margaret Ogilvy' (1896), and such sketches as 'A Window in Thrums' (1889). As a dramatist his most original work is to be found in 'Quality Street' (1901), 'The Admirable Crichton' (1902), 'What Every Woman Knows' (in which he pricks the bubble of male self-sufficiency, 1908), and 'The Twelve-Pound Look' (the exposure of a pompous egoist, 1910); while he gained immense popularity with 'Peter Pan' (q.v., 1904). His other writings included: 'Better Dead' (1887), 'Auld Licht Idylls' and 'An Edinburgh Eleven' (1888), 'My Lady Nicotine' (1890), 'The Little Minister' (1891, the play was produced in 1897), 'Sentimental Tommy' (1896), 'Tommy and Grizel' (1900), 'The Little White Bird' (1902), 'Peter Pan in Kensington Gardens' (1906), and 'Peter and Wendy'

(1911). Also a number of dramatic works, among others, 'The Professor's Love Story', produced in 1894; 'The Little Minister' (1897), 'Little Mary' (1903), 'Alice Sit-by-the-Fire' (1905), 'Dear Brutus' (1917), 'Mary Rose' (1920). See *Kailyard School*.

Barrington, DAINES (1727–1800), lawyer, antiquary, and naturalist, is said to have induced Gilbert White (q.v.) to write his 'Natural History of Selborne'.

Barrington, GEORGE (*b.* 1755), whose real name was WALDRON, was a famous pickpocket, who was ultimately transported to Botany Bay. He moved in good society and robbed Prince Orloff of a diamond snuff-box said to be worth £30,000. He published a description of his voyage to Botany Bay and is chiefly remembered for the lines attributed to him (when a convict):

True patriots we, for be it understood,
We left our country for our country's good.
But these are now said to be by another hand (see R. S. Lambert, 'The Prince of Pickpockets').

BARROW, ISAAC (1630–77), educated at Charterhouse, Felsted, and Peterhouse, Cambridge, was successively professor of Greek at Cambridge, of geometry at Gresham College, and of mathematics at Cambridge, resigning the latter appointment in 1669 in favour of his pupil, Isaac Newton. He became master of Trinity in 1672. He wrote an 'Exposition of the Creed, Decalogue, and Sacraments' (1669), 'Euclidis Elementa' (1655), 'Archimedis Opera' (1675), and a treatise on 'The Pope's Supremacy' (published 1680). His sermons rank among the best in the English tongue; they are written with great smoothness and lucidity, but are extremely long. Coleridge ('Anima Poetae') refers to Barrow's 'verbal imagination', in which he 'excels almost every other writer of prose'.

Barrow, SIR JOHN (1764–1848), accompanied Lord Macartney on his missions to China and the Cape of Good Hope. He became assistant secretary to the Admiralty, and revived the projects to explore the Arctic for a NW. passage, which had been dropped since the failure of Baffin (q.v.). His 'Autobiographical Memoir' (1847) contains an interesting account of his travels. He also published a 'History of Voyages into the Arctic Region' (1718) and other books of travel.

Barry, ELIZABETH (1658–1713), a celebrated actress who owed her entrance to the stage to the patronage of the earl of Rochester. She 'created' more than one hundred roles, including Monimia in Otway's 'The Orphan', Belvidera in 'Venice Preserved', and Zara in 'The Mourning Bride'. Otway was passionately devoted to her, but she did not return his affection.

BARRY CORNWALL, see *Procter (B. W.)*.

Barry Lyndon, *The Luck of, a Romance of*

the Last Century, by Fitzboodle, a satirical romance by Thackeray (q.v.), published in 'Fraser's Magazine' in 1844, subsequently entitled 'The Memoirs of Barry Lyndon Esq., by Himself'.

It takes the form of the autobiography of Redmond Barry, an impudent Irish adventurer, who flies from Ireland under the delusion that he has killed (at the age of fifteen) his adversary in a duel, serves in the English and Prussian armies, and then turns gamester and man of fashion, a career in which he meets with such prodigious success that he becomes well-to-do, and by his effrontery is able to bully the wealthy widow, the countess of Lyndon, into marrying him; whereupon he assumes the name of Lyndon. He dissipates her fortune and grossly maltreats her until she is rescued by her relatives. He now falls on evil days and ends his life in the Fleet prison. In spite of being a thorough blackguard, his courage and frankness retain the reader's interest. And his old rascal of an uncle, the Chevalier de Balibari, is likewise an entertaining figure.

Barsetshire Novels, The, of A. Trollope (q.v.) are the following: 'The Warden', 'Barchester Towers', 'Doctor Thorne', 'Framley Parsonage', 'The Small House at Allington', and 'The Last Chronicle of Barset' (qq.v.).

Barthélemy, JEAN JACQUES, see *Anacharsis (Le Voyage du Jeune.)*

BARTHOLOMAEUS ANGLICUS (*fl.* 1230–50), also known as BARTHOLOMEW DE GLANVILLE, though the addition 'de Glanville' is most uncertain; a Minorite friar, professor of theology at Paris, and author of 'De proprietatibus rerum', an encyclopaedia of the Middle Ages first printed *c.* 1470. A 14th-cent. English version by John Trevisa was issued by Wynkyn de Worde, *c.* 1495.

Bartholomew, MASSACRE OF ST., the massacre of Huguenots throughout France ordered by Charles IX at the instigation of his mother Catherine de Médicis, and begun on the morning of the festival, 24 Aug. 1572.

Bartholomew Fair was held, at least from Henry II's time, within the churchyard of the priory of St. Bartholomew, Smithfield, London, at Bartholomew tide (24 Aug., O.S.), attended by the 'Clothiers of all England and drapers of London' (Stow), and 'a Court of pie-powders (q.v.) was daily during the fair holden for debts and contracts'. The fair was continued as a pleasure-fair until 1855. For a description of the fair in the 17th cent. see Ben Jonson's 'Bartholomew Fayre': see also H. Morley, 'History of Bartholomew Fair' (1858).

Bartholomew Fayre, a farcical comedy by Jonson (q.v.), produced in 1614. The play, the plot of which is very slight, presents, with much humour and drollery, if somewhat coarsely, the scenes of a London holiday fair, with its ballad-singers, stall-keepers, bullies, bawds, and cut-purses. Bartholomew Cokes, the perfect simpleton, visits the fair and is successively robbed of his purses, his cloak and sword, and finally of his future wife, whom he is to marry against her will; while his servant, the self-confident and arrogant Waspe, is robbed of the licence which is to marry them, and is put in the stocks for brawling. The puritan, Zeal-of-the-land Busy, is ridiculed for his hypocrisy, and likewise gets put in the stocks. Overdo, the Justice of the Peace, who attends the fair in disguise to discover its 'enormities', is taken for a pickpocket and subjected to the same humiliation.

Bartholomew Pig, a pig sold at Bartholomew Fair (q.v.). 'Little tidy Bartholomew boar-pig' is a name applied by Doll Tearsheet to Falstaff ('2 Henry IV', II. iv.)

Bartholomew's Day, ST.: on this day (24 August) in 1662 some 2,000 of the English clergy resigned their cures, refusing to assent to everything contained in the Book of Common Prayer, as required by the Act of Uniformity.

Bartholomew's Hospital, ST., see *Rahere*.

Bartolist, a student of Bartolo, an eminent Italian jurist (1313–57); hence, a person skilled in the law.

Barton, SIR ANDREW, the subject of a ballad in two parts, included in Percy's 'Reliques'. He was a Scottish sea officer who lived in the 16th cent. He obtained letters of marque to make reprisals against the Portuguese for damage suffered at their hands by his father, and availed himself of them to interfere with English ships. The earl of Surrey fitted out two ships under his sons Sir Thomas and Sir Edward Howard, who after an obstinate engagement, in which Barton was killed, captured the two Scottish vessels.

Barton, ELIZABETH (1506–34), the NUN or MAID OF KENT, was a domestic servant, and at one time subject to trances. She attributed her utterances during these trances to religious inspiration. She was induced by Bocking, a monk of Canterbury, to anathematize all opponents of the Roman Catholic Church, and inveighed against Henry VIII's divorce from Catharine of Aragon, prophesying that he would die in a month after his marriage with Anne Boleyn. She was executed with her accomplices at Tyburn. The story is told by Froude in his 'History'.

BARTRAM, WILLIAM (1739–1823), American Quaker naturalist and traveller, author of 'Travels through North and South Carolina . . .' (1791), whose descriptions of nature influenced Coleridge and Wordsworth.

Baruch, a book of the Apocrypha, attributed in the text to Baruch the scribe of Jeremiah (Jer. xxxvi), a composite work containing a confession of sin, an exhortation to wisdom, and a song of comfort, probably written after A.D. 70.

Bas Bleu, see *Blue Stocking*.

Bashan, a kingdom beyond the Jordan conquered (with its King Og) by the Israelites under Moses (Num. xxi. 33). The mention of 'fat bulls of Basan' is in Ps. xxii. 12.

BASHKIRTSEFF, MARIE (1860–84), a Russian diarist, whose 'Journal', written in French and published posthumously in 1887, attained a great vogue by its morbid introspection and literary quality, and was translated into several languages (Engl. translation, 1890, by Mathilde Blind).

Basil, Pot of, see *Isabella or the Pot of Basil*. The word 'basil' is derived from the Greek βασιλικόν, 'royal', perhaps because the plant was 'used in some royal unguent bath or medicine' (Prior). For the many Greek and Italian traditions concerning this plant and its dual character, erotic and sinister, see Gubernatis, 'Mythologie des Plantes', vol. ii. The belief among the Creoles of Louisiana in its power of attracting love is referred to in 'The Grandissimes', by G. W. Cable (c. ix).

Basilea, in imprints, Basle.

Basilikon Doron, see *James I (1603–25)*.

Basilisco, a braggart knight in 'Solyman and Perseda' (perhaps by Kyd, q.v.), referred to in Shakespeare's 'King John', I. i.

Basilisk, a fabulous reptile, also called a cockatrice, alleged to be hatched by a serpent from a cock's egg. According to ancient authors its breath, even its look, was fatal. According to Pliny, it was so called from a spot resembling a crown on its head. Medieval authors furnished it with 'a certain combe or coronet'. In the 16th cent. the name was given to a kind of large brass cannon.

Basilius, (1) a character in Sidney's 'Arcadia' (q.v.); (2) in 'Don Quixote', the rival of Camacho (q.v.).

Baskerville, JOHN (1706–75), English printer, first a writing-master in Birmingham. By 1754 he had established a printing office and type-foundry in Birmingham. His books are notable for the quality of presswork, type, and paper. His first book was a Latin Virgil, 1757, followed by a Milton in 1758. He was the first to use 'wove' (extra smooth) paper, and gave his pages a gloss by hot-pressing them after printing. In order to print the Book of Common Prayer (3 editions, 1760–2) and the Bible (1763), Baskerville bought a nomination as supernumerary Printer to the University of Cambridge. His books are among the masterpieces of English printing; but they did not sell, and after his death his types were sold to Beaumarchais (q.v.) for his edition of Voltaire.

Baskett, JOHN (d. 1742), king's printer, was printer to the University of Oxford, 1711–42. He printed editions of the Book of Common Prayer, and the 'Vinegar Bible' (q.v.) in two volumes (1716–17), of which it was said that it was 'a basketful of errors'.

Basoche, the guild of clerks attached to the

French courts of justice under the old régime, which at one time possessed certain privileges, appointed a king (*roi de la basoche*), held parades, and gave dramatic performances.

Basrig or BACSECG, the Danish king defeated and killed at the battle of Assendon (Æscesdun) in 871 by the English under Æthelred.

Bassae, near Phigalia in the south-west of Arcadia, the site of a famous temple to Apollo Epicurius, built by Ictinus (one of the architects of the Parthenon) and described by Pausanias as one of the most beautiful in the Peloponnese. Its ruins are still standing. The frieze of the inner cella, representing the combat of the Centaurs and the Lapithae, was acquired for the British Museum in 1814.

Bassanio, in Shakespeare's 'Merchant of Venice' (q.v.), the lover of Portia.

Bassett, COUNT, a character in Vanbrugh and Cibber's 'The Provok'd Husband' (q.v.).

Bassianus, a character in Shakespeare's 'Titus Andronicus' (q.v.).

Bastard, The, see *Savage (R.)*.

Bastard, PHILIP THE, son of Sir Robert Faulconbridge, in Shakespeare's 'King John'.

Bastard, WILLIAM THE, in English history, is William the Conqueror, the natural son of Duke Robert of Normandy and of the daughter of a tanner of Falaise.

Bastîle, THE, in Paris, was built as a fort under Charles V and Charles VI of France, in 1370–82, and was later used as a State prison. It was destroyed by the populace of Paris on 14 July 1789. The anniversary of its fall, as marking the end of the old régime, is the national holiday of republican France.

Batavia, the Netherlands, formerly inhabited by a Celtic tribe called the BATAVI. Also the capital of the Dutch East Indies.

Bates, MISS, a character in Jane Austen's 'Emma' (q.v.).

Bates, CHARLEY, in Dickens's 'Oliver Twist' (q.v.), one of the pickpockets in Fagin's gang.

BATES, HENRY WALTER (1825–92), naturalist, who visited Pará with Alfred Russell Wallace in 1848 and the Amazons in 1851–9. His researches revealed over 8,000 species new to science. He published his 'The Naturalist on the Amazons' in 1863.

Bates, JOHN, in Shakespeare's 'Henry V' (q.v.), one of the English soldiers with whom the king converses before the battle of Agincourt.

Bath, in Somerset, is the site of a Roman spa, AQUAE SULIS, probably built in the 1st and 2nd cents. A.D. The legendary prince Bladud was said to have discovered the hot springs. Much of the extènsive·Roman baths have been excavated, and fragments of a temple, as well as tombs, altars, etc., have been found. The King's Bath was built in 1597 and during the 17th cent. it was used for medicinal purposes.

In the 18th cent. Bath was transformed into a social resort by Richard ('Beau') Nash (q.v.), who became Master of Ceremonies, Ralph Allen (q.v.), who promoted the development of the city, and John Wood, father and son, who designed the Palladian public buildings and houses. It is the subject of very frequent literary allusion, having been visited among many others by Smollett, Fielding, Sheridan, Fanny Burney, Goldsmith, Southey, Landor, Jane Austen, Wordsworth, Cowper, Scott, Moore, and Dickens. Its ruins seem to be the subject of the OE. poem 'Ruin' (q.v.). It was once a cloth-making centre, and is mentioned in this connexion by Chaucer ('Canterbury Tales', Prologue 447, concerning the 'Wife of Bath').

Bath, COLONEL, a character in Fielding's 'Amelia' (q.v.).

Bath, KING OF, see *Nash (R.)*.

Bath, ORDER OF THE, an order of British knighthood, so called from the bath which preceded installation, instituted in 1399.

Bath, Wife of, see *Canterbury Tales*.

Bath Guide, The New, see *Anstey (C.)*.

Bathos, Greek, 'depth'. The current usage for 'descent from the sublime to the ridiculous' is due to Pope's satire, 'Bathos, the art of sinking in Poetry' ('Miscellanies', 1727–8). The title was a travesty of Longinus's essay, 'On the Sublime'.

Bathsheba Everdene, a character in Hardy's 'Far from the Madding Crowd' (q.v.).

Bathyllus, a beautiful youth of Samos, loved by Anacreon (q.v.).

Batrachomyomachia, or *Battle of the Frogs and the Mice*, a mock-heroic Greek poem, at one time erroneously attributed to Homer. It describes in Homeric style a battle between the tribes of the mice and the frogs, the cause of hostilities being the destruction of a mouse while visiting a frog. Zeus and Athena deliberate as to the sides that they shall take. The frogs are at first defeated, but Zeus intervenes and having failed with thunderbolts sends crabs to quell the strife.

Thomas Parnell (q.v.) wrote a satirical 'Homer's Battle of the Frogs and the Mice' (1717), directed against Theobald and Dennis.

Battle, SARAH, the subject of one of Lamb's 'Essays of Elia' (q.v.), 'Mrs. Battle's Opinions on Whist', a character drawn from Mrs. Burney, the wife of Admiral Burney, and sister-in-law of Fanny Burney (q.v.).

Battle of Alcazar, The, a play in verse by Peele (q.v.), published in 1594. It deals with the war between Sebastian, king of Portugal, and Abdelmelec, king of Morocco, who had recovered his kingdom from a usurper, Muly Mahamet. The latter invokes the assistance of Sebastian, offering to give up the kingdom of Morocco to him and to become his tributary. Sebastian sails with his fleet to Morocco, and at the battle of Alcazar is killed, as are also Abdelmelec and Muly Mahamet, the latter being drowned while fleeing from the field. Sebastian is assisted in his expedition by the adventurer Stukeley (q.v.), who is likewise killed at the battle (which was fought in 1578).

Battle of Britain, the name popularly given to the series of encounters over London and S.E. England between the R.A.F. and the German Air Force in 1940 in which British victory ended the threat of German invasion. The prime minister, Winston Churchill, in his survey of the air warfare in the House of Commons on 20 August said: 'Never in the field of human conflict was so much owed by so many to so few.'

Battle of Dorking, The, an imaginary account of a successful invasion of England, designed to draw attention to the lack of adequate military preparation, published in 'Blackwood's Magazine', May 1871, by General Sir G. T. Chesney.

Battle of Lake Regillus, The, the title of one of Macaulay's 'Lays of Ancient Rome' (q.v.). Lake Regillus lay east of Rome in the territory of Tusculum and on its banks was won the great victory of the Romans over the Latins under Tarquin *c.* 496 B.C.

Battle of Maldon, see *Maldon.*

Battle of Otterbourne, see *Otterbourne.*

Battle of the Books, The, a prose satire by Swift (q.v.), written in 1697, when Swift was residing with Sir W. Temple, and published in 1704.

Temple had written an essay on the comparative merits of 'Ancient and Modern Learning' (the subject at that time of an animated controversy in Paris), in which by his uncritical praise of the spurious Epistles of Phalaris he had drawn on himself the censure of William Wotton and Bentley. Swift, in his 'Battle of the Books', treats the whole question with satirical humour. The 'Battle' originates from a request by the moderns that the ancients shall evacuate the higher of the two peaks of Parnassus which they have hitherto occupied. The books that are advocates of the moderns take up the matter; but before the actual encounter, a dispute arises between a spider living in the corner of the library and a bee that has got entangled in the spider's web. Aesop sums up the dispute: the spider is like the moderns who spin their scholastic lore out of their own entrails; the bee is like the ancients who go to nature for their honey. Aesop's commentary rouses the books to fury, and they join battle. The ancients, under the patronage of Pallas, are led by Homer, Pindar, Euclid, Aristotle, and Plato, with Sir W. Temple commanding the allies; the moderns by Milton, Dryden, Descartes, Hobbes, Scotus, and others, with the support of Momus and the malignant deity, Criticism. The fight is conducted with great spirit. Aristotle aims an arrow at Bacon but

hits Descartes. Homer overthrows Gondibert. Virgil encounters his translator Dryden, in a helmet nine times too big. Boyle transfixes Bentley and Wotton. On the whole the ancients have the advantage, but a parley ensues and the tale leaves the issue undecided.

Battle of the Frogs and the Mice, see *Batrachomyomachia.*

Battle of the Spurs, a name given (1) to the battle of Courtrai (1302) in which the Flemings defeated Robert, count of Artois, on account of the number of gilt spurs the victors collected; (2) to the battle of Guinegatte (1513) in which Henry VIII with the Emperor Maximilian defeated the French, on account of the hurried flight of the latter.

Battle Abbey Roll, THE, was probably compiled about the 14th cent. purporting to show the names of families that came over to England with William the Conqueror. The roll itself is not extant. We have only 16th-cent. versions by Leland, Holinshed, and Duchesne, all said to be imperfect and to contain names which have obviously no right there. [E.B.]

Battle Hymn of the Republic, a patriotic hymn of the Federal party in the United States of America, written by Julia Ward Howe (1819–1910). She visited the army of the Potomac in 1861, and was invited to provide dignified words for the popular marching tune, 'John Brown's body lies a-mouldering in the grave' (q.v.). The fine stanzas beginning 'Mine eyes have seen the glory of the coming of the Lord' were the result of her effort. The poem was first published in the 'Atlantic Monthly' (q.v.) in 1862.

Battledore-book, see *Horn-book.*

Battus, a shepherd of Arcadia, who saw Hermes steal the flocks of Admetus. He was bribed by the god not to tell, but broke his promise, and was turned into a stone.

Baucis, see *Philemon.*

BAUDELAIRE, CHARLES (1821–67), French poet. 'Les Fleurs du Mal', his famous collection of 1857, was remarkable for prosodic beauty and for a novel sense of the musical and evocative power of language. The feeling for morbid beauty which it also showed was equally novel in 1857 and after a court case six poems were banned from this and subsequent (French) editions. The ban was lifted in 1945. Baudelaire also wrote literary and art criticism, more fully appreciated since his death, 'Curiosités esthétiques' (1868), 'L'Art romantique' (1868).

Baviad, The, see *Gifford.*

Bavieca, the horse of the Cid (q.v.).

BAXTER, RICHARD (1615–91), a presbyterian divine, who sided with parliament and was a military chaplain during the Civil War. 'A pious, useful, irrepressible heresiarch' (Saintsbury), he was the author of 'The Saint's Everlasting Rest' (1650, the book that Mrs.

Glegg, in 'The Mill on the Floss', used to favour in a domestic crisis), and of 'Call to the Unconverted' (1657). He contributed powerfully to the Restoration and had a bishopric offered to him; but soon after refusing it he suffered much ill-treatment under Charles II and James II, being imprisoned in 1685–6, and fined by Judge Jeffreys on the charge of libelling the Church in his 'Paraphrase of the New Testament' (1685). His numerous writings include a lengthy autobiography, 'Reliquiae Baxterianae', published in 1696.

Bayard or BAIARDO, the magic horse given by Charlemagne to Renaud, son of Aymon, or Rinaldo (q.v.), which figures in 'The Four Sons of Aymon', the 'Orlando Innamorato', and the 'Orlando Furioso' (qq.v.). Bayard was formerly used as a mock-heroic allusive name for any horse, and also as a type of blind recklessness. [OED.]

Bayard, PIERRE DU TERRAIL, SEIGNEUR DE (c. 1473–1524), the 'chevalier sans peur et sans reproche', born in the Dauphiné, a famous captain in the Italian campaigns of Charles VIII, Louis XII, and Francis I, killed after the battle of Romagnano. He won his first laurels fighting against the 'Great Captain', Gonsalvo de Cordova (q.v.), at the Garigliano in the kingdom of Naples.

Bayes, the name under which Dryden is ridiculed in Buckingham's 'The Rehearsal' (q.v.). The name is taken from the bay laurel, sprigs of which were woven into a wreath to crown a conqueror or poet.

Bayeux Tapestry, THE, an embroidered strip of linen, about 80 yards long by 19 inches wide, belonging to Bayeux in Normandy. It was probably commissioned by Bishop Odo of Bayeux and made in Kent, c. 1070–80. It depicts the events leading up to and including the Norman Conquest.

Bayham, FRED, 'huge, handsome, and jolly', a character in Thackeray's 'The Newcomes' (q.v.).

BAYLE, PIERRE (1647–1706), French philosopher, author of the 'Dictionnaire historique et critique' (1697–1702), a pioneer work in scientific biography and in criticism of religion and legend. There were English editions in 1710, 1734–8, 1734–41, and 1826.

BAYLY, THOMAS HAYNES (1797–1839), educated at Winchester and St. Mary Hall, Oxford, produced songs, ballads, and dramatic pieces, including 'I'd be a butterfly', 'She wore a wreath of roses', and 'Perfection' (a successful farce). Becoming involved in financial difficulties, he in a short time produced thirty-six pieces for the stage. His verse has been the object of a good deal of ridicule.

Baynard Castle, Blackfriars, London, perhaps a royal residence in pre-Conquest times (see W. R. Lethaby, 'London before the Conquest'), took its name from Baynard, a follower of William the Conqueror, to whom the estate was granted. From him it passed to the Fitzwalters, by whom it was transferred to the Black Friars. A later Baynard's Castle, further east (Upper Thames Street), was an important residence of the dukes of York in the 15th cent. It was destroyed in the Great Fire.

Baynes, GENERAL, MRS., and CHARLOTTE, characters in Thackeray's 'The Adventures of Philip' (q.v.).

Bayona, see Namancos.

Bazzard, MR., in Dickens's 'Edwin Drood' (q.v.), Mr. Grewgious's clerk.

Beaconsfield, EARL OF, see Disraeli.

Beagle, H.M.S., see Darwin (C. R.).

Bean Lean, DONALD, in Scott's 'Waverley' (q.v.), a Highland marauder.

Bear, THE, AT THE BRIDGE FOOT, a tavern that stood just outside the Great Gate at the Southwark end of old London Bridge (q.v.). It is frequently mentioned by Pepys, e.g. 26 Oct. 1664; 24 Feb. 1666–7.

Bear, THE GREAT: for its mythological origin see Callisto.

Bear and Ragged Staff, THE, a crest of the earls of Warwick, borne before the Conquest by the Saxon earls of Warwick, and derived from the chivalrous Guy of Warwick (q.v.).

Beardsley, AUBREY VINCENT (1872–98), black-and-white illustrator whose fantastic, mannered style was highly individual yet typical of art nouveau (q.v.). He became art editor of the 'Yellow Book' in 1894, and the next year he started 'The Savoy', to which he contributed three poems and a prose fragment, 'Under the Hill'. He illustrated Oscar Wilde's 'Salome', 'The Rape of the Lock', and other books, achieving a remarkable output before his early death from tuberculosis.

Beast, NUMBER OF THE, in Revelation xiii. 18. The precise figures composing the number are uncertain, 666 or 616, but the former are generally adopted. It has been suggested that since each digit in 666 falls short by one of the perfect number seven, the number thereby symbolizes Antichrist. But it is more probably a cryptogram, of which no interpretation commanding general assent has yet been offered. One of the most likely rests on the fact that the letters of the name 'Nero Caesar' written in Hebrew represent numbers which added together make 666, or 616 if the name Nero is written as in Latin without a final n. Least probable are attempts to make the cipher represent some conspicuous character of modern history (Swete, 'Apocrypha').

Beatrice, DANTE'S, see Dante.

Beatrice, a character in Shakespeare's 'Much Ado about Nothing' (q.v.).

BEATTIE, JAMES (1735–1803), professor of moral philosophy at Marischal College,

Aberdeen, and poet, is remembered as the author of 'The Minstrel', a poem in Spenserian stanzas, tracing the development of a poet in a primitive age. The work remained unfinished. Book I appeared in 1771, Book II in 1774.

Beau Beamish, a character in Meredith's 'The Tale of Chloe' (q.v.).

Beau Brummel, see *Brummel*.

Beau Nash, see *Nash (R.)*.

Beau Tibbs, a character in Goldsmith's 'The Citizen of the World' (q.v.); an absurd creature, poor and unknown, but boasting of familiarity with the nobility and affecting the airs of a man of fashion. His wife is at once a slattern and a coquette, who washes her husband's shirts while her talk is of countesses.

Beauchamp's Career, a novel by G. Meredith (q.v.), published serially in 1875, in volume form in 1876.

Nevil Beauchamp's career begins in the navy, where he shows himself a gallant officer and a chivalrous if somewhat Quixotic gentleman. In spite of subversive views on political and social questions, he earns the approval of his rich aristocratic uncle, the Hon. Everard Romfrey, a medieval baron in ideas and a hater of radicals and the like. After the Crimean War, Nevil plunges into politics, stands unsuccessfully as a radical candidate for parliament, and comes under the influence of Dr. Shrapnel, an enthusiastic servant in the cause of humanity, but a republican, a free-thinker, and everything that is detestable in the eyes of Mr. Romfrey and his friends. Induced by misrepresentations, Romfrey goes so far as to horsewhip Shrapnel, thereby incurring the fierce indignation of his nephew, who makes it a point of honour to force his proud uncle to apologize to the radical. This apparently hopeless enterprise becomes an obsession with Nevil, whose love affairs are likewise a source of distress to him. He is torn between his early passion for Renée de Croisnel, now the unhappy wife of an elderly Frenchman, and his love for her utter contrast, the ideal English girl, Cecilia Halkett. He resists the temptation which the flight of Renée from her husband places in his way; but he loses Cecilia, whom her father and her friends conspire to marry to Nevil's more humdrum cousin. Harassed and unhappy, Nevil falls desperately ill and lies at death's door. His danger effects the miracle, and Romfrey comes to Shrapnel's cottage, where the sick man lies, and tenders his apology. Nevil recovers and marries Shrapnel's ward, Jenny Denham, a kindred soul. But after a few months' happiness, Beauchamp's career is prematurely closed. He is drowned while trying to rescue a child from the sea.

Beaumains, in Malory's 'Morte Darthur', the nickname given to Sir Gareth by Sir Kay, the steward.

Beaumanoir, in Disraeli's 'Coningsby' (q.v.), represents Belvoir Castle.

Beaumanoir, Sir Lucas, in Scott's 'Ivanhoe' (q.v.), Grand Master of the Knights Templars.

BEAUMARCHAIS, PIERRE AUGUSTIN CARON DE (1732–99), son of a Paris watchmaker named Caron. He obtained admission to the court as music-master to the daughters of Louis XV, became popular and wealthy, had many adventures, and took the name of Beaumarchais from a small property belonging to his wife. He was author of the famous comedies 'Le Barbier de Séville' (1775) and its sequel 'Le Mariage de Figaro' (1784), the latter a keen satire on French society.

BEAUMONT, FRANCIS (1584–1616), was born at Grace-Dieu in Leicestershire of an ancient family. He was educated at Broadgates Hall, Oxford, and was entered at the Middle Temple in 1600. He made the acquaintance of Jonson, for several of whose plays he wrote commendatory verses, and of Drayton. He collaborated with John Fletcher in dramatic works from about 1606 to 1616 (for a list of the plays so produced see under *Fletcher, J.*). 'The Woman-Hater' (1607), a comedy showing the influence of Jonson and based on the 'humour' of the principal character, is probably the work of his sole pen. Dryden states that Beaumont was 'so accurate a judge of plays that Ben Jonson, while he lived, submitted all his writings to his censure, and 'tis thought used his judgement in correcting, if not contriving, all his plots'. And this superior faculty for the construction of plots is discernible in some of the plays that he wrote in collaboration with Fletcher. Beaumont was buried in Westminster Abbey, near Chaucer and Spenser.

Beauty and the Beast, a fairy tale of which the best-known version appears in the French 'Contes' of Mme de Villeneuve (1744). A somewhat similar story is included in the 'Piacevoli Notti' of Straparola (1550).

Beauty ('la Belle') is the youngest and favourite daughter of a merchant, who suffers reverses. He sets out on a journey in the hope of restoring his shaken fortunes. Unlike her sisters, Beauty asks him to bring her back only a rose. The journey proves a failure, but on his return, in the beautiful garden of an apparently uninhabited palace, he plucks a rose for Beauty. The Beast, an ugly monster, to whom the palace belongs, threatens him with death as the penalty for his theft unless he gives him his youngest daughter. Beauty sacrifices herself and goes to the Beast's palace and lives there. She is gradually filled with pity and affection for the Beast and finally consents to marry him, whereupon he turns into a beautiful prince, having been released from a magic spell by her virtue and courage.

BEAUVOIR, SIMONE DE (1908–   ), French novelist and essayist, with J.-P. Sartre (q.v.) one of the leading Existentialist writers, author of: 'L'Invitée' (1943), 'Le

Sang des Autres' (1944), 'Les Mandarins' (1954), etc., novels; 'Le Deuxième Sexe' (1949) and other essays, including travel literature; also 'Mémoires d'une Jeune Fille rangée' (1958) and subsequent volumes of autobiography.

Beaux' Stratagem, The, a comedy by Farquhar (q.v.), produced in 1707.

Aimwell and Archer, two friends who have run through their estate, arrive at the inn at Litchfield, in search of the adventure that will rehabilitate their fortunes. Archer for the nonce passes as Aimwell's servant. There is much speculation as to who they are, and Boniface the landlord concludes that they are highwaymen. This curiosity is shared by Dorinda, daughter of the wealthy Lady Bountiful, who has fallen in love with Aimwell at first sight—in church, and Mrs. Sullen, wife of Lady Bountiful's son, a drunken sot. Aimwell, thinking Dorinda a suitable prey, gets admission to Lady Bountiful's house on a pretext, with Archer, between whom and Mrs. Sullen a mutual attraction has sprung up. An attack by rogues on the house is the occasion of the rescue of the ladies by Aimwell and Archer, and they both press the advantage thus gained. But Aimwell, who has passed himself off as his elder brother, Lord Aimwell, smitten with remorse in presence of the trustfulness of Dorinda, confesses the fraud. At this moment Mrs. Sullen's brother opportunely arrives, to rescue his sister from the brutality of Sullen. He brings news of the death of Aimwell's elder brother and of the accession of Aimwell to title and fortune. Sullen at the same time willingly agrees to the dissolution of his marriage, so that Mrs. Sullen is free to marry Archer, and all ends happily.

Beazeley, OLD TOM and YOUNG TOM, characters in Marryat's 'Jacob Faithful' (q.v.).

Beck, MADAME, a character in Charlotte Brontë's 'Villette' (q.v.).

Becket, a tragedy by A. Tennyson (q.v.), published in 1884.

The subject of the play is the bitter quarrel that arose between Henry II and Thomas à Becket when the king had appointed the latter, already his chancellor, to be archbishop of Canterbury against his wish, culminating in the words of the king which authorized the four knights to seek out Becket at Canterbury and kill him in the Cathedral. With this is woven the story of the love of Henry for Fair Rosamund, whom he entrusts to Becket's protection; of Queen Eleanor's finding her way to Rosamund's bower with intent to kill her; and of Rosamund's rescue by Becket and relegation to Godstow nunnery.

Becket, THOMAS À, see *Thomas à Becket.*

BECKETT, SAMUEL BARCLAY (1906–), novelist and dramatist, born in Dublin. He went to Paris about 1928 to study and teach and has lived there since 1938. He was a friend of James Joyce (q.v.) and at one time his secretary. Many of Beckett's works were written first in French. They include: some poetry; an early study of Proust (1931); the novels (written for the most part in the form of interior monologues) 'Murphy' (English 1938, author's French translation 1947), 'L'Innommable' (1953, 'The Unnameable' 1959), 'Molloy' (Fr. 1951, Eng. 1959), 'Malone meurt' (1951, 'Malone dies' 1958), 'Watt' (Eng. first published in Paris 1958, London 1964); and a number of short plays, notably 'En attendant Godot' (1952, 'Waiting for Godot', prod. London 1956), 'All that fall' (1957, 'Tous ceux qui tombent', 1957), 'Fin de partie' (1957, 'End Game', 1958), 'Krapp's last tape' and 'Embers' (1959, 'La Dernière Bande' and 'Cendres', 1960).

BECKFORD, PETER (1740–1811), master of foxhounds and scholar, was author of the famous 'Thoughts upon Hare and Fox Hunting' and 'Essays on Hunting' (1781), which marked an era in the history of hunting. Beckford also wrote 'Familiar Letters from Italy' (1805).

BECKFORD, WILLIAM (1759–1844), son of William Beckford (1709–70) the alderman and lord mayor in the days of Wilkes, was a man of great wealth, M.P. successively for Wells and Hindon, who spent large sums in collecting works of art and curios, and in the building and extravagant decoration of his mansion of Fonthill, where he lived in almost complete and somewhat mysterious seclusion from 1796. He is remembered chiefly as the author of the fantastic oriental tale 'Vathek' (q.v.). But many readers will derive more pleasure from his two books of travel, 'Dreams, Waking Thoughts, and Incidents' (1783, revised 1834), and 'Recollections of an Excursion to the Monasteries of Alcobaça and Batalha' (1835).

Bed of Ware, THE GREAT, an oak bed 10 ft. 9 in. in length and breadth, with a richly carved headboard, columns, and canopy, of the 16th cent., whose first home may have been Ware Park. It was transferred to the Saracen's Head Inn at Ware, apparently before the end of the 16th cent. It is referred to by Shakespeare ('Twelfth Night', III. ii); Jonson ('Epicœne', V. i); and Farquhar ('The Recruiting Officer', I. i). It is now in the Victoria and Albert Museum.

BEDDOES, THOMAS LOVELL (1803–49), educated at Charterhouse and Pembroke College, Oxford, went abroad to study medicine and settled at Zürich in 1835, living thereafter mostly abroad. He published in 1821 'The Improvisatore' and in 1822 'The Bride's Tragedy'. His most important work, 'Death's Jest-Book' (q.v.), a play in the Elizabethan spirit, was begun in 1825 and repeatedly altered at various times, not being published until 1850, after his death by suicide. Beddoes showed in his work, besides a taste for the *macabre* and supernatural, a capacity for occasionally fine blank verse, and more especially a poignant lyrical gift, displayed in his dirge for Wolfram in 'Death's Jest-Book', in his beautiful 'Dream Pedlary' ('If there were dreams to sell, What would you buy?'), and in many other short pieces. His poetical works were edited by Gosse in 1890 and 1928. See also H. W. Donner, 'T. L. Beddoes' (1935).

BEDE or **BÆDA** (673–735), historian and scholar, was when young placed under the charge of Benedict Biscop, abbot of Wearmouth. Thence he went to the monastery of Jarrow, where he spent the greater part of his life. He appears from his writings to have been wise, learned, and humble. He was a diligent teacher, and a Latin and Greek scholar, and found many pupils among the monks of Wearmouth and Jarrow. He was buried at Jarrow, but his bones were taken to Durham during the first half of the 11th cent. The epithet 'Venerable' was first added to his name in the century following his death. His 'Historia Ecclesiastica Gentis Anglorum' (q.v.) was brought to an end in 731, and by that year he had written nearly forty works, chiefly biblical commentaries. The treatise 'De Natura Rerum', one of his earliest works, contains such physical science as was then known, and has the merit of referring phenomena to natural causes.

BEDE, CUTHBERT, *see* BRADLEY (E.).

Bedford Coffee-house, THE, stood at the north-east corner of Covent Garden. It was frequented by actors and others, including Garrick, Foote, Sheridan, Hogarth, and Fielding.

Bedivere, SIR, in Malory's 'Morte Darthur,' one of Arthur's knights. He and his brother Sir Lucan, with Arthur, alone survived the last battle, and it was he who at Arthur's bidding threw Excalibur into the water, and bore the king to the barge that carried him away to Avalon.

Bedlam, a corruption of Bethlehem, applied to the Hospital of St. Mary of Bethlehem, in Bishopsgate, London, founded as a priory in 1247, with the special duty of receiving and entertaining the clergy of St. Mary of Bethlehem, the mother church, as often as they might come to England. In 1330 it is mentioned as 'an hospital', and in 1402 as a hospital for lunatics. In 1346 it was received under the protection of the City of London, and on the dissolution of the monasteries, it was granted to the mayor and citizens. In 1547 it was incorporated as a royal foundation for the reception of lunatics. In 1675 a new hospital was built in Moorfields, and this in turn was replaced by a building in the Lambeth Road in 1815. The hospital has now been transferred to Monks Orchard, Eden Park, Beckenham.

From Bedlam are derived such expressions as TOM o' BEDLAM (q.v.) and BESS o' BEDLAM, for wandering lunatics, or mendicants posing as lunatics.

Bedr-ed-Din, HASSAN, see under *Nur-ed-Din*.

Bedr-el-Budur, see *Badroulboudour*.

Bee, *The*, see *Goldsmith*.

BEECHER, HENRY WARD, see *Stowe*.

Beef Steaks, THE SUBLIME SOCIETY OF, was founded in 1735 by John Rich, the manager of the Covent Garden Theatre. The society, which included many eminent persons, used to meet and dine in a room at the theatre, the name being derived from the beef-steaks served. When Covent Garden Theatre was burnt, the Society moved to the Bedford Coffee-house (q.v.), and later to the Lyceum Theatre.

Beef-steak Club, THE, was founded about 1876; the members used to dine in a room at Toole's Theatre, and moved, when this was demolished, to Green Street, Leicester Square. There was an earlier club of the same name. These are not to be confused with the 'Sublime Society of Beef Steaks'.

Beefeater, an eater of beef, a popular appellation of the Yeomen of the Guard in the household of the Sovereign, instituted at the accession of Henry VII in 1485; also of the Warders of the Tower, who were named Yeomen Extraordinary of the Guard in the reign of Edward VI. (The conjecture that the word has some connexion with the French *buffet* is historically baseless.) [OED.]

Beefington, a character in 'The Rovers' (see *Anti-Jacobin*).

Beelzebub, adapted from the Latin word used in the Vulgate to render both the Greek βεελζεβούλ of the received text of the N.T., and the Hebrew 'baal-zᵉbub', 'fly-lord', mentioned in 2 Kings i. 2 as 'God of Ekron'. The word βεελζεβούλ represents the Assyrian for 'lord of the high house', but was understood in N.T. times as 'lord of the underworld'. In Matt. xii. 24 Beelzebub is spoken of as 'prince of the devils'. Milton gives the name to one of the fallen angels, next to Satan in power ('Paradise Lost', i. 79).

BEERBOHM, SIR MAX (1872–1956), educated at Charterhouse and Merton College, Oxford, a critic, essayist, and caricaturist, published his first book, 'The Works of Max Beerbohm', in 1896. A master of wit, irony, and satire, and of a polished and incisive style, he directed his criticism at literary mannerisms and social pretences. He succeeded Bernard Shaw as dramatic critic of the 'Saturday Review' in 1898. One of the best known of his critical works is 'A Christmas Garland' (1912), a series of parodies of contemporary authors, Wells, Bennett, Conrad, Chesterton, etc. 'Zuleika Dobson' (1911) is an amusing story of the devastating effect on the youth of Oxford of a beautiful adventuress. His other principal works are: 'More', 'Yet Again', 'And Even Now' (essays); 'Seven Men' (stories); also volumes of caricatures, among others—

'The Poet's Corner' (1904), 'A Book of Caricatures' (1907), 'Rossetti and his Circle' (1922).

Bees, Fable of the, see *Mandeville* (*B. de*).

Beethoven, LUDWIG VAN (1770–1827), born at Bonn in Rhenish Prussia, of Dutch descent, the famous German musical composer. He studied under Haydn. He became afflicted with deafness in 1802, which increased until it became complete, but did not arrest his creative genius. Beethoven died in Vienna. His principal achievement was the introduction into the art of music of something other than the mere development of musical themes. His musical conceptions have an intellectual and moral quality that was previously unknown. He perfected the symphony. His compositions included one opera ('Fidelio'), two masses, nine symphonies, and a large number of concertos, sonatas, quartets, and trios.

BEETON, MRS. ISABELLA MARY (1836–65), *née* Mayson, author of a famous book of cookery and domestic economy, first published in 1859–61 in 'The Englishwoman's Domestic Magazine' and in book form in 1861 ('The Times', 3 Feb. 1932).

Befana, an Italian corruption of EPIPHANIA, Epiphany, an Italian female Santa Claus, who fills children's stockings on Twelfth Night. Her name is also used as a bogy to frighten children.

Beggar's Bush, according to Ray's 'Proverbs' (p. 244, ed. 1768), 'a tree notoriously known on the London Road from Huntington to Caxton', frequented by beggars.

Beggars Bush, The, a drama by J. Fletcher (q.v.), and perhaps Massinger, probably produced in 1622.

Florez, the rightful heir of the earldom of Flanders but ignorant of his rights, and living as a rich merchant at Bruges, is in love with Bertha, who is heiress of Brabant, but has been stolen away and placed with the Burgomaster of Bruges and is equally ignorant of her rights. Gerrard, father of Florez, who has been driven from Flanders, has concealed himself among the beggars near Bruges, is their king, and watches over the interests of Florez. Wolfort, the usurper, proposes to marry Bertha and restore her to her rights, thus obtaining possession of Brabant. He sends Hubert, one of his nobles, who is in love with Jacqueline, Gerrard's daughter, to effect his purpose. Hubert, however, joins the beggars, among whom Jacqueline is living, and plots with Gerrard to get Wolfort into their power. In this they are successful. The identity of Florez and Bertha is revealed and they are married. The play is interesting by reason of its examples of early thieves' cant, and its realistic picture of vagabond life.

Beggar's Daughter of Bednall Green, The, a ballad written in the reign of Elizabeth and included in Percy's 'Reliques'.

Bessee is the fair daughter of a blind beggar, employed at the inn at Romford and courted by four suitors, a knight, a gentleman of good birth, a merchant of London, and the innkeeper's son. They all withdraw their suit on being referred by her to her father, except the knight. The old beggar gives her as dowry three thousand pounds, two pounds for every one the knight puts down. It now appears that the beggar is Henry, son of Simon de Montfort, who has assumed the disguise of a beggar for safety.

The story forms the basis of Chettle and Day's 'Blind Beggar of Bednal Green' (1600, printed 1659). J. S. Knowles (q.v.) also wrote a comedy called 'The Beggar's Daughter of Bethnal Green'; and R. Dodsley (q.v.) wrote a musical play, 'The Blind Beggar of Bethnal Green'.

Beggar's Opera, The, a musical play by J. Gay (q.v.), produced in 1728.

The play arose out of a suggestion by Swift to Gay that a Newgate pastoral 'might make an odd pretty sort of thing'. The principal characters are Peachum, a receiver of stolen goods, who also makes a living by informing against his clients; his wife, and his pretty daughter, Polly; Lockit, warder of Newgate, and his daughter Lucy; and Captain Macheath, highwayman and lighthearted winner of women's hearts. Polly falls desperately in love with Macheath, who marries her. Her father, furious at her folly, decides to place her in the 'comfortable estate of widowhood' by informing against Macheath, who is arrested and sent to Newgate. Here he makes a conquest of Lucy's heart, and there is a spirited conflict between Polly and Lucy, the rival claimants to his affection ('How happy could I be with either, Were t'other dear charmer away!'). In spite of her jealousy, Lucy procures the escape of Macheath. The play was a great success and Gay is said to have made £800 by it. (It was said to have made Gay rich, and Rich—the producer—gay.)

Beghard, a name derived like BÉGUINE (q.v.) from the surname of Lambert Bègue, given to members of certain lay brotherhoods which arose in the Low Countries early in the 13th cent. in imitation of the *béguine* sisterhoods. From the 14th cent. the beghards were denounced by Popes and Councils and persecuted, and such as survived in the 17th cent. were absorbed in the Tertiarii of the Franciscans. [OED.]

Béguine, a name derived from the surname of Lambert Bègue or le Bègue ('the stammerer'), a priest of Liége in the 12th cent., given to the members of certain lay sisterhoods which began in the Low Countries in the 12th cent.; they devoted themselves to a religious life, but were not bound by strict vows. They were protected by Pope John XXII when he persecuted the Beghards (q.v.), and are still represented by small communities in the Netherlands. [OED.]

Behemoth, an animal mentioned in Job xl. 10, probably a hippopotamus. Used in modern literature as a general expression for one of the largest and strongest animals.

> Behémoth, biggest born of earth.
> (Milton, 'Paradise Lost', vii. 471.)
> The might of earth-convulsing béhemoth.
> (Shelley, 'Prometheus Unbound', iv. i. 310.)

The OED. supports Milton's accentuation.

Behistun Inscription, THE, a cuneiform inscription in the three languages of the Persian empire, on a lofty rock between Hamadan and Kirmanshah, recounting the events of the reign of Darius. It was copied and deciphered by Sir Henry Rawlinson.

Behmenism, see *Boehme.*

BEHN, MRS. AFRA, APHRA, APHARA, or AYFARA (1640–89), daughter of John and Amy Amis, lived as a child in Surinam, Guiana. She returned to England in 1658, and married Behn, a city merchant. She was employed by Charles II as a spy in Antwerp on the outbreak of the Dutch war. Between 1671 and 1689 she produced fifteen plays, of which the most popular was 'The Rover' (in two parts, 1677–81), dealing with the amorous adventures in Naples and Madrid of a band of English cavaliers during the exile of Charles II. 'The City Heiress' (q.v.), 1682, is one of her typical coarse comedies of contemporary London life. She also wrote poems (including the beautiful 'Love in fantastic triumph sat'), and novels, of which her 'Oroonoko, or the History of the Royal Slave' (q.v.) is the best known. It is the first English philosophical novel containing dissertations on abstract subjects, such as the religion of humanity. Afra Behn was buried in the east cloister of Westminster Abbey.

Bel and the Dragon, one of the apocryphal books of the O.T., detached from the Book of Daniel. Bel was an idol worshipped by the Babylonians (the word is equivalent to *Baal*), and the story tells how Daniel convinced King Astyages that it was a mere image of brass. The dragon was a living animal, which was also worshipped. Daniel disproved its divine character by giving it lumps of pitch, fat, and hair to eat, so that it burst asunder.

Belarius, a character in Shakespeare's 'Cymbeline' (q.v.).

Belch, SIR TOBY, in Shakespeare's 'Twelfth Night' (q.v.), a roistering humorous knight, uncle to Olivia.

Belcher, a neckerchief with blue ground and large white spots having a dark blue spot or eye in the centre, named after the celebrated pugilist Jim Belcher (1781–1811).

Belial, adapted from the Hebrew words *beli-ya'al,* means literally 'worthlessness' and 'destruction', but in Deut. xiii. 13, and elsewhere, in the phrase 'sons of Belial', it is retained untranslated in the English version, as a proper name. It has thus come to mean the spirit of evil personified, and is used from early times as a name for the Devil or one of the fiends, and by Milton ('Paradise Lost', i. 490) as the name of one of the fallen angels.

Belinda, (1) the heroine of Pope's 'The Rape of the Lock' (q.v.); (2) a character in Vanbrugh's 'The Provok'd Wife' (q.v.); (3) the title of a novel by Maria Edgeworth (q.v.); (4) the niece of Mr. John Jorrocks, who promised her (on her marriage) £1,000 every time she should have twins.

Belinus, the name of a Celtic sun-god, and of a legendary British king (perhaps the same as Cassibelaunus) who built a tower and made a haven for ships at what was afterwards London. Billingsgate (q.v.) is thought by some to be connected with his name.

Belisarius, the great military commander during the reign of Justinian (527–63), was a native of Illyria and of humble birth. After successful campaigns against the Vandals, Goths, and Bulgarians, he was in 563 accused of conspiring against the emperor. His eyes, according to tradition, were put out, and he was reduced to wandering, a beggar, about the streets of Constantinople. But, in fact, he appears to have been only imprisoned for a year.

Belit, see *Assur.*

Belkis, see *Balkis.*

Bell, ADAM, see *Adam Bell.*

Bell, ALEXANDER GRAHAM (1847–1922), born at Edinburgh and educated at Edinburgh and London Universities, went to Canada in 1870, and thence to Boston, U.S.A., where he became professor of vocal physiology. He exhibited in 1876 his invention of the means of transmitting sound by electricity, which, when perfected, became the telephone.

BELL, CLIVE (1881–1964), writer on art and literature. In 'Art' (1914) he stated his theory that 'significant form', independent of subject, was the essential quality of a work of art. His critical work includes 'Civilization' (1928) and 'Proust' (1929).

BELL, CURRER, ELLIS, and ACTON, see *Brontë C., E., and A.*).

Bell, JOHN, see *Egan.*

Bell, LAURA, the heroine of Thackeray's 'Pendennis' (q.v.).

Bell-the-Cat, Archibald Douglas, fifth earl of Angus (1449?–1514), who earned the nickname by declaring to his confederates that he would 'bell the cat', i.e. kill Robert Cochrane, earl of Mar, the hated favourite of James III. He figures in Scott's 'Marmion' (q.v.).

Bell's Life in London, see *Egan.*

Bella Wilfer, a character in Dickens's 'Our Mutual Friend' (q.v.).

Bellafront, in Dekker's 'The Honest Whore' (q.v.), the repentant courtesan and exemplary wife of the worthless Matheo.

Bellair, a character in Etherege's 'The Man of Mode' (q.v.).

Bellamira, a comedy by Sir C. Sedley (q.v.), produced in 1687.

It is a coarse but lively play, founded on the 'Eunuchus' of Terence, reflecting the licentious manners of Sedley's day. Dangerfield, a braggart and a bully, whose cowardice is exposed in an adventure similar to that of Falstaff at Gadshill, is an amusing character.

BELLAMY, EDWARD (1850–98), American novelist and political theorist, born in Massachusetts, whose fame rests upon his popular Utopian romance, 'Looking Backward' (1888).

The hero of 'Looking Backward' falls asleep in 1887 and awakes in Boston, in the year 2000, to find great social changes. The squalor and injustices of 1887 have disappeared, private capitalism has been replaced by public, and everyone works for and is a member of the state. The moral, social, and cultural benefits of the new system are everywhere apparent. The work had an immense vogue; a Nationalist Party was formed to advocate its principles; and Bellamy's ideas are still of considerable influence in the United States.

Bellario, (1) the name assumed by the heroine of Beaumont and Fletcher's 'Philaster' (q.v.) when disguised as a page; (2) in Shakespeare's 'The Merchant of Venice', Portia's lawyer cousin.

BELLARMINE, ROBERTO FRANCESCO ROMOLO (1542–1621), an Italian cardinal and a powerful defender of the Roman cause against the Protestants, was author of 'Disputationes de Controversiis Christianae Fidei adversus hujus temporis haereticos' (1581–93).

The name 'Bellarmine' was given to a large glazed drinking-jug with capacious belly and narrow neck, originally designed by the Protestant party in the Netherlands as a burlesque likeness of their great opponent, the cardinal. [OED.]

Bellaston, LADY, a character in Fielding's 'Tom Jones' (q.v.).

Belle or ISOPEL **Berners,** a character in Borrow's 'Lavengro' (q.v.), a sturdy wandering lass, who acts as second to Lavengro in his fight with the Flaming Tinman.

Belle Dame sans Merci, La, a ballad by Keats (q.v.), written in 1819.

The knight-at-arms, enthralled by an elf, wakes from the dream of his lady, not to find his dream realized, but the cold hill's side, where 'no birds sing'. The poem is, says Oliver Elton, 'a touchstone' for this kind of composition. 'La Belle Dame sans Merci' is also the title of a poem, in rhyme royal and octaves, translated from Alain Chartier, attributed at one time to Chaucer, but now thought, on manuscript authority, to be the work of Sir Richard Ros.

Belle Sauvage, or BELL SAVAGE, **Inn,** THE, stood on Ludgate Hill, and dated at least from the 15th cent. In a deed of 1453 it is described as 'Savages Inn' or the 'Bell-on-the-Hoop'; and the name 'Bell Savage' perhaps arose from the association of the name of the proprietor with the sign of the Bell. Dramatic performances and bull-baiting took place in its yard in the 16th and 17th cents., and it was a starting-place for coaches in the 18th cent. Sir Thomas Wyatt's march on London came to an end there. The site is now occupied by the publishing house of Cassell, whose publisher's design interprets the name as meaning 'the beautiful savage woman'.

Belle's Stratagem, The, a comedy by Mrs. H. Cowley (q.v.), produced in 1780.

Doricourt returns from his travels to marry Letitia Hardy, whom he has not seen since his childhood, the match having been arranged by their parents. He finds her beautiful but lacking in animation; she falls in love with him at once. Distressed by his cold reception, she determines to win him by first disgusting him through the assumption of the manners of a country hoyden, and then conquering his heart by her sprightliness at a masquerade, and this scheme she successfully accomplishes. The sub-plot is concerned with Sir George Touchwood, a doting husband, who brings his wife, Lady Frances, to London for the first time in her life; the attempt of Courtall to seduce her at the masquerade by assuming the same disguise as her husband; and the defeat of the plot by her old admirer, Saville.

BELLENDEN, or BALLENDEN, JOHN (*fl.* 1533–87), Scottish poet and translator into Scots of Livy.

Bellenden, LADY MARGARET, EDITH, and MAJOR, characters in Scott's 'Old Mortality' (q.v.).

Bellĕrŏphon, son of Glaucus, king of Corinth. He was banished for a murder, and fled to the court of Proetus, king of Argos, where Anteia, the king's wife, fell in love with him. As he slighted her passion, she accused him to her husband of an attempt on her virtue. Proetus, unwilling to violate the laws of hospitality by killing Bellerophon under his roof, dispatched him to his father-in-law, Iobates, bearing a letter signifying that he should be killed (whence the expression *Bellerophontis litterae*). Iobates accordingly sent Bellerophon against the monster Chimaera (q.v.); but Bellerophon, with the aid of the winged horse Pegasus (q.v.), overcame it. He afterwards destroyed assassins sent by Iobates, and was successful in an expedition against the Amazons. Thereupon Iobates, despairing of killing the hero, gave him his daughter to wife and the succession to his throne. Other legends relate that he attempted to fly to heaven on Pegasus, but that Zeus by means of a gadfly caused the horse to throw its rider.

Bellerophon, H.M.S., the ship (Captain Maitland) on board of which Napoleon surrendered himself in 1815.

Bellerus, the name of a fabulous person introduced by Milton in his 'Lycidas' to account for *Bellerium* or *Bolerium*, the Roman name of Land's End, in Cornwall.

Bellini, a family of Venetian painters, JACOPO (*c.* 1400–70/1), his sons and pupils, GENTILE (active *c.* 1460–1507) and GIOVANNI (active *c.* 1459–1516). Giovanni made significant contributions to the development of Venetian painting in its depiction of light and rendering of emotion, and in his technique. Much of his enormous *œuvre* may be the work of assistants.

Bellisant or BELLISANCE, in the tale of 'Valentine and Orson' (q.v.), the sister of king Pepin, and wife of the emperor of Constantinople, mother of Valentine and Orson.

BELLOC, JOSEPH HILAIRE PIERRE (1870–1953), born in France, educated at the Oratory School, Edgbaston, and Balliol College, Oxford, was a versatile writer of essays, novels, verse, travels, history, biography, and criticism. Among his best works is 'The Path to Rome' (1902), the description of a tramp from Toul in the north of France, through Switzerland and northern Italy, to Rome, with divagations on innumerable subjects. His other best-known writings include: 'Hills and the Sea' (1906), 'The Bad Child's Book of Beasts', 'More Beasts for Worse Children', 'The Modern Traveller', 'Cautionary Tales' (all light verse); 'The Girondin', 'The Green Overcoat', 'Mr. Clutterbuck's Election', 'A Change in the Cabinet' (novels); 'The Four Men' (fantastic travel); 'Marie Antoinette' (history); 'The Servile State' (sociology); 'British Battles'; 'History of England'; and books of essays on 'Nothing', 'Something', 'Everything', etc.

Bellona, the Roman goddess of war.

Bells, The, a dramatic adaptation by L. Lewis of 'The Polish Jew' of Erckmann-Chatrian, the story of a burgomaster haunted by the consciousness of an undiscovered murder that he has committed. It provided Sir H. Irving with one of his most successful parts.

Bells and Pomegranates, the title under which a series of poems was published by R. Browning (q.v.) between 1841 and 1846, including 'Pippa Passes', 'Dramatic Lyrics' ('The Pied Piper', 'Waring', etc.), 'The Return of the Druses', 'A Blot in the 'Scutcheon', 'Colombe's Birthday', 'Dramatic Romances' ('How they brought the good news', etc.), and 'Luria' (qq.v.). The entire series was then issued in one volume under the above title (1846).

Bellyn, in 'Reynard the Fox' (q.v.), the name of the ram.

Belmont, Portia's house in Shakespeare's 'The Merchant of Venice' (q.v.).

Belmont, SIR FRANCIS, the heroine's father in Miss Burney's 'Evelina' (q.v.).

Belphegor, the LXX and Vulgate form of the Moabitish 'Baal-Peor' mentioned in Num. xxv.

In Machiavelli's 'Novella di Belfagor' (probably written *c.* 1518), the name is given to an archdevil sent by Pluto to the world to investigate the truth of the complaints made by many souls reaching hell, that they have been sent there by their wives. Belphegor has orders to take a wife, arrives in Florence well provided with money and a retinue of devils as servants, and marries. But he is unable to put up with his wife's insolence, and prefers to run away from her and return to hell. We have echoes of this legend in one of the stories of Barnabe Rich's 'Farewell to the Military Profession' (1581), and in Jonson's 'The Devil is an Ass' (1616). John Wilson (? 1627–96) produced a tragicomedy, 'Belphegor, the Marriage of the Devil', in 1690.

Belphoebe, in Spenser's 'Faerie Queene', the chaste huntress, daughter of the nymph Chrysogone, and twin sister of Amoret (q.v.); she symbolizes Queen Elizabeth. Belphoebe puts Braggadochio (q.v.) to flight (II. iii), finds herbs to heal the wounded Timias ('whether it divine Tobacco were, or Panachea, or Polygony', III. v), and rescues Amoret from Corflambo (q.v., IV. iii).

Belshazzar's Feast, the feast made by Belshazzar, the son of Nebuchadnezzar and the last king of Babylonia, at which his doom was foretold by writing on the wall, as interpreted by Daniel (Dan. v). Belshazzar was killed in the sack of Babylon by Cyrus (538 B.C.). He is the subject of dramas by Hannah More and Milman, of Robert Landor's 'Impious Feast', and of a poem by Lord Byron (qq.v.).

Beltane, the Celtic name of the first of May, the beginning of summer, used for old May Day in Scotland, where anciently it was one of the quarter-days. It is also the name of an ancient Celtic anniversary celebration on May Day, in connexion with which great bonfires were kindled on the hills. Cormac's Glossary explains *belltaine* as 'two fires which the Druids used to make, and they used to bring the cattle [as a safeguard] against the diseases of each year to those fires'. [OED.]

Beltenebros, the name assumed by Amadis of Gaul (q.v) when he retired to the wilderness to do penance, being in disgrace with Oriana.

Beltham, SQUIRE and DOROTHY, characters in Meredith's 'Harry Richmond' (q.v.).

Belton Estate, The, a novel by A. Trollope (q.v.), first published in 'The Fortnightly Review' in 1865, and reprinted separately in 1866.

The Belton property in Somerset, belonging to Mr. Amedroz, is entailed, in default of any son of his own, on a distant cousin, Will Belton. Charles, the son of Mr. Amedroz, commits suicide, and Clara his sister is menaced with destitution when her father shall die. Will Belton, a warm-hearted, self-confident young farmer, hardly known to the Amedroz family, comes forward on the death of Charles with offers of assistance, wins the affection of the feckless Mr. Amedroz, forcefully puts his affairs in order, and is welcomed as a brother by Clara. He promptly proposes to her and is rejected, because Clara is already in love with Captain Aylmer, her cold-blooded, mean-spirited relative, whose true character she has not gauged. In compliance with a promise that he has given to his aunt on her death-bed, Aylmer proposes to Clara and is accepted. But his meanness and tyrannical disposition soon come to light, as also those of his odious mother and sister, and arouse the resentment of Clara. She breaks off her engagement and is finally married to Will Belton.

Belvedere Apollo, see *Apollo*.

Belvidera, the heroine of Otway's 'Venice Preserv'd' (q.v.).

Bembo, PIETRO (1470–1547), Italian humanist, became bishop of Bergamo, a cardinal, and historiographer of Venice. He wrote in Latin and Italian, in prose and verse. He was a devoted admirer of Lucrezia Borgia (q.v.), and figures prominently in the 'Cortegiano' of Castiglione (q.v.).

Ben, BIG, the great bell in the Clock Tower of the Houses of Parliament at Westminster, named after Sir Benjamin Hall, Chief Commissioner of Works (1855–8), during whose term of office it was cast.

Ben Hur: *A Tale of the Christ,* an historical novel about the early days of Christianity, by Lewis Wallace (American novelist, 1827–1905), published in 1880.

Ben trovato, from the Italian phrase 'se non è vero, è ben trovato' (if it is not true it is well invented), sometimes used as an epithet of a good story, etc.

BENAVENTE Y MARTINEZ, JACINTO (1866–1954), Spanish playwright and critic, who was awarded the Nobel Prize in 1922. He was the author of many light and pleasant comedies of which the following are the best known in English translations: 'Saturday Night' (1903), 'Rose of Autumn' (1905), 'Vested Interests' (1907), 'Brute Force' (1908).

Benbow, JOHN (1653–1702), a gallant British admiral, master of the fleet in the battle off Beachy Head (1690) and at Barfleur and La Hogue (1692), and commander of the bombarding flotilla at Saint Malo and Dunkirk (1693-4-5). He was later commander-in-chief in the West Indies, where, badly supported by the ships of his squadron, he endeavoured to bring Du Casse, the French admiral, to an engagement off Santa Marta. He here had his right leg shattered by a chain shot, but after having had the wound dressed, returned to the quarter-deck. He died of his wounds at Port Royal.

Benedick, a character in Shakespeare's 'Much Ado about Nothing' (q.v.). The name is used (also erroneously in the form 'Benedict') of an apparently confirmed bachelor who marries.

Benedict Biscop, ST. (628?–690), a thegn of Oswiu, king of Northumbria, who after making two pilgrimages to Rome retired to the Isle of Lérins, where he adopted the monastic life. After two years he again went to Rome, and was directed by the pope, Vitalian, to accompany Theodore of Tarsus from Rome to Canterbury. He was then appointed abbot of St. Peter's, Canterbury (669), resigning the dignity two years later to visit Rome once more. During this journey he collected and brought back many volumes and relics. On his return he founded (in 674) the monastery of St. Peter at the mouth of the river Wear, importing workmen to build a church of stone and to glaze the windows. Once more he went to Rome, bringing back a further store of books and relics. After this he founded the sister monastery of St. Paul at Jarrow. He was buried in his church at Wearmouth, having left directions for the careful preservation of his library. He is regarded as one of the originators of the artistic and literary development of Northumbria in the next century. He is commemorated on 12 Feb.

Benedictines, the order of monks, also known from their dress as 'Black Monks', established by St. Benedict (480–543) about the year 529, when he founded the monastery on Monte Cassino in Campania; the first in time, as in fame, of the great Western Church orders. It became noted for its wealth and for the learning of its members. Among its offshoots were the Cluniacs and Cistercians. Battle Abbey in Sussex was built for them by William I where the battle of Hastings was fought. As regards their valuable literary work see *Maurists*.

Benengeli, see *Cid Hamet Ben Engeli*.

BENÉT, STEPHEN VINCENT (1898–1943), American poet, born in Pennsylvania. He is known chiefly for his narrative poem on the Civil War, 'John Brown's Body' (1928). He wrote a section of a projected epic poem on the American westward migration, 'Western Star' (1943). His collected 'Ballads and Poems' appeared in 1930. He also wrote several novels and the libretto for the folk-opera, 'The Devil and Daniel Webster' (1943).

BENÉT, WILLIAM ROSE (1886–1950), American poet, and brother of S. V. Benét. He published many volumes of romantic verse and two verse novels, the best of which is the autobiographical 'The Dust Which Is God' (1941).

Benicia Boy, nickname of John Heenan (1835–73), an American pugilist, who fought Thomas Sayers, the champion of England, in 1860. Heenan was a much bigger and stronger man than Sayers, but the latter was more skilful. The desperate fight between them was interrupted, and a silver belt awarded to each.

Benjamin, used of a youngest and favourite son, in allusion to the youngest son of Jacob (Gen. xxxv. 8; xlii, etc.).

Benjamin, A, in the first half of the 19th cent., was an overcoat of a particular shape (according to Brewer from the name of a tailor).

BENJAMIN OF TUDELA (*fl. c.* 1150), a Spanish Jew and traveller in the East, whose itinerary 'Masaoth', printed at Constantinople in 1543 and at Ferrara in 1556, was translated into English in 1840 by A. Asher. Benjamin visited Constantinople, the Aegean, Damascus, Jerusalem, Baghdad, Basra, Aden, Assuan, and Egypt, of which Saladin was then vizier.

BENLOWES, EDWARD (1605?–76), a Caroline poet whose chief work, 'Theophila, or Love's Sacrifice' (1652), caused him to be ridiculed by Samuel Butler, Pope, and Warburton. The poem, which shows a feeling for theological mysticism, is written in successive triplets of ten, eight, and twelve syllables, and uses curious coinages of word and phrase.

Bennet, MR., MRS., JANE, ELIZABETH, MARY, KITTY, and LYDIA, characters in Jane Austen's 'Pride and Prejudice' (q.v.).

BENNETT, (ENOCH) ARNOLD (1867–1931), born near Hanley in Staffordshire, spent his childhood in modest surroundings, and was educated locally and at London University. He became a solicitor's clerk in London and in 1893 assistant editor and subsequently editor of the periodical 'Woman'. After 1900 he devoted himself exclusively to writing, theatre journalism being among his special interests.

His fame as a novelist rests chiefly on 'The Old Wives' Tale' (q.v., 1908) and the 'Clayhanger' series ('Clayhanger' (1910), 'Hilda Lessways' (1911), 'These Twain' (1916), reprinted as 'The Clayhanger Family' (1925)). The 'Five Towns' which figure prominently in these works are Tunstall, Burslem, Hanley, Stoke-upon-Trent, and Longton, centres of the pottery industry; and the features, often ugly and sordid, of this background are skilfully woven into stories of lives which he presents dispassionately, with an infinite delight in significant detail, but without comment or protest. 'Riceyman Steps' (1923) is another of Bennett's pictures of life in drab surroundings in which the novelist is seen at his best. It is the story of a miser, a second-hand bookseller in Clerkenwell, who not only starves himself to death, but infects his wife with his passion for economy and brings her also to an untimely end. Among Bennett's other best-known works are: 'The Grand Babylon Hotel' (1902), 'The Grim Smile of the Five Towns' (short stories, 1907), 'Mile-

stones' (play, with E. Knoblock), and 'The Matador of the Five Towns' (short stories, 1912).

BENOIT DE SAINTE-MAURE, a 12th-cent. *trouvère*, born probably at Sainte-Maure in Touraine and patronized by Henry II of England, for whom he composed a verse history of the dukes of Normandy. His best-known work is the 'Roman de Troie', based on the writings of Dares Phrygius and Dictys Cretensis (qq.v.). The 'Roman' was translated into Latin prose by Guido da Colonna (q.v.), and thus served as a source on which many subsequent writers drew, including Boccaccio, followed by Chaucer and Shakespeare, in the story of 'Troilus and Cressida'.

Bensalem, the name of the imaginary island in Bacon's 'New Atlantis' (q.v.).

BENSON, EDWARD FREDERIC (1867–1940), noted as the author of the popular novel 'Dodo' (1893), and many other stories.

BENTHAM, JEREMY (1748–1832), educated at Westminster and Queen's College, Oxford, was called to the bar at Lincoln's Inn, but never practised, and turned his mind to physical science and political speculation. He published anonymously in 1776 his 'Fragment on Government', in form a criticism of Blackstone's 'Commentaries', in which he first sketches his theory of government. While in Russia, during 1785–8, he wrote his 'Defence of Usury' (1787) and a series of letters on a 'Panopticon' (1791), a scheme for improving prison discipline. In 1789 he published his 'Introduction to Principles of Morals and Legislation' (which had been first printed in 1780). Besides these he produced a number of works on ethics, jurisprudence, logic, and political economy, his influence proving greatest in the first two of these spheres. In the dissemination of his views, Bentham was greatly assisted by his devoted disciple, Étienne Dumont of Geneva, who compiled a number of treatises based on Bentham's manuscripts and published them, between 1802 and 1825, in French. A considerable part of Bentham's published works are retranslations of Dumont.

It is in the 'Fragment on Government' and more fully in the 'Principles of Morals and Legislation' that we have enunciated the political and ethical theory (rather than philosophical doctrine) of 'Utility' by which Bentham is principally remembered. 'It is the greatest happiness of the greatest number that is the measure of right and wrong'. Pain and pleasure are the 'sovereign masters' governing man's conduct; 'it is for them alone to point out what we ought to do'. Pleasures and pains can be quantitatively measured according to their intensity, duration, certainty, and propinquity. When the pleasures and pains resulting from any act to all the members of the community affected have been measured by these standards, we are in a position to determine the moral quality of the act. The criterion of the goodness of a law is this principle of Utility, the measure in which it subserves the happiness to which every individual is equally entitled. The *motive* of an act being always self-interest, it is the business of law and education to make the sanctions sufficiently strong to induce the individual to subordinate his own happiness to that of the community. Bentham worked out the quantitative value of pains and pleasures as motives of action with extraordinary minuteness, with the object of giving scientific accuracy to morals and legislation.

Bentham did not share the theoretical views of the French Revolutionists, and he criticized the 'Declaration of the Rights of Man' in his 'Anarchical Fallacies' (included in his collected works). His democratic views are expressed in his 'Constitutional Code' (1830). His 'Chrestomathia', a series of papers on education, appeared in 1816. He also propounded a number of valuable reforms in the administration of English justice, which have since his time been applied. In 1824 Bentham, with the assistance of James Mill (q.v.), founded the 'Westminster Review', the organ of the philosophical radicals, which lasted until 1907.

BENTLEY, E. C., see *Clerihew*.

BENTLEY, RICHARD (1662–1742), born at Oulton in Yorkshire, was educated at St. John's College, Cambridge, and appointed by Stillingfleet, bishop of Worcester, tutor to his son, remaining six years in his household. He was brought into great repute as a scholar by his 'Epistola ad Millium' in 1691, a critical letter in Latin on the Greek dramatists, contributed to John Mill's edition of Malelas, a medieval chronicler. In 1692 Bentley delivered the first Boyle lectures, entitled 'A Confutation of Atheism', seeking for part of his argument the assistance of Isaac Newton (q.v.). He became keeper of the king's libraries in 1694. During 1697–9 he was engaged in the famous controversy relating to the 'Epistles of Phalaris' (see *Phalaris, Epistles of*), which he proved to be spurious. In 1699 he was appointed Master of Trinity College, Cambridge, which he ruled with such despotic power that he was brought before the bishop and nominally, though not effectually, deprived of his mastership. Among his greatest critical works were his bold revisions of the text of Horace and Manilius. His arbitrary revision of Milton's 'Paradise Lost', on the other hand, was a venture in a field unsuited to his genius. Bentley is caricatured by Pope in the 'Dunciad' (Bk. IV. 201 et seq.). His son Richard (1708–82) was a correspondent of Horace Walpole (q.v.). Jebb (q.v.) wrote a life of Bentley (1882).

Bentley, RICHARD (1794–1871), publisher, the founder of 'Bentley's Miscellany' (1837) with Charles Dickens as editor. His issue at a low price of 127 volumes of 'Standard Novels' was not only a successful but, from the public standpoint, a beneficial venture. He was succeeded in the business by his son GEORGE BENTLEY (1828–95), who introduced many notable novelists to the public, including Wilkie Collins, Mrs. Henry Wood, and Miss Rhoda Broughton.

Benvolio, in Shakespeare's 'Romeo and Juliet' (q.v.), a cousin and friend of Romeo.

Beowulf, the name given to an Old English poem of some 3,200 lines, perhaps the earliest considerable poem in any modern language. The manuscript, of the late 10th cent., formed part of the collection of Sir Robert Bruce Cotton, whence it passed into the British Museum.

The poem opens with praise of the deeds of the Danes, Scyld their king, and his descendants. One of these, Hrothgar, builds a great hall, Heorot. The monster Grendel enters the hall at night and carries off thirty of Hrothgar's thanes, and haunts the hall for twelve years, accomplishing more murders. Beowulf, the nephew of Higelac, king of the Geats (a tribe living in the south of Sweden), hearing of the trouble, comes with fourteen companions across the sea to give assistance, and is welcomed by Hrothgar, but taunted by Unferth, one of Hrothgar's followers, for his defeat by Breca in a swimming-match. Beowulf tells the true story and retorts on Unferth for not facing Grendel. Beowulf and his men sleep in the hall; Grendel breaks in and devours Hondscio, one of these, and seizes Beowulf, who unarmed wrestles with him and tears out his arm. Grendel, mortally wounded, makes off to his lair. Hrothgar rewards Beowulf, and Unferth is silenced. The minstrel sings the tragic tale of the blood-feud which brings about the death of Finn, King of the Frisians. Grendel's mother, a water-hag, enters the hall to revenge her son, and carries off Aeschere, the counsellor of Hrothgar. Beowulf prepares to attack her. Unferth, recognizing the greater prowess of Beowulf, lends him his sword. Beowulf dives into the mere, and reaches a cave where the witch's lair is, and fights with her, but the sword fails to wound her. She nearly kills him, but his woven armour, with God's assistance, saves him. He sees an old sword, made by giants, among the armour in the cave, and with this cuts off the witch's head, and also the head of Grendel, who is lying in the cave. But their blood melts the sword, of which only the hilt remains. With this and the head of Grendel, Beowulf returns to Heorot. Hrothgar praises him, but warns him against pride. Beowulf and his Geats return to their own land. Beowulf surrenders the gifts he has received to Higelac, his king, and receives in return the sword of Hrethel and a part of the kingdom.

After the death of Higelac and Heardred his son, Beowulf succeeds to the kingdom, where he reigns for fifty years. A dragon which has been guarding a treasure finds that it has been robbed, and devastates the country. Beowulf and eleven companions go out to meet it. The dragon issues from its mound breathing out fire. All the companions, save Wiglaf, fly to a wood. Beowulf's sword breaks, and the dragon sets its teeth in Beowulf's neck. Wiglaf wounds it, and its strength wanes. Beowulf kills it, but is mortally wounded. He bids Wiglaf bring the treasure out of the mound, that he may see it. He directs that a barrow be built for him on the Whale's Headland, and dies. Wiglaf rebukes his companions and sends word of Beowulf's death. The messenger warns the people of coming troubles. Beowulf's body is burnt on a pyre, with his armour and the treasure.

Many of the persons referred to in Beowulf are known to us from other sources, and it is possible to fix the date of the historical events in the first part of the 6th cent. The date of the composition of the poem is uncertain; it has been strongly argued that it is the work of a Christian poet of the 8th cent.

There is a good edition of the poem by F. Klaeber (1922) and a number of translations, one of them by William Morris in collaboration with A. J. Wyatt (1892).

Beppo: A Venetian Story, a poem by Lord Byron (q.v.), published in 1818.

The poem tells, in the mock-heroic style, with much gaiety and gentle irony, the story of a Venetian carnival, at which a lady's husband, Beppo (short for Giuseppe), who has been absent for many years, returns in Turkish garb, and confronts her and the *cavaliere servente* whom she has taken to herself. No tragedy follows, but reconciliation over a cup of coffee.

BÉRANGER, PIERRE JEAN DE (1780–1857), French poet, the author of very popular light verse (*chansons*), usually cheerful satire of contemporary society and events.

Berenīcē, the wife of Ptolemy III Euergetes. When her husband invaded Syria to avenge the death of his sister (also named Berenice) who had been murdered by her husband Antiochus, king of Syria, she dedicated a lock of her hair as a votive offering for his safe return. This lock mysteriously disappeared and was said to have become the constellation *Coma Berenices* (near the tail of *Leo*). Callimachus wrote a poem in celebration of it, which Catullus translated. Berenice was put to death by her son, Ptolemy IV Philopator, in 221 B.C.

Berenīcē, daughter of Agrippa I (grandson of Herod the Great), and wife of her uncle Herod, king of Chalcis. After his death in A.D. 48, she lived with her brother Agrippa II. She is the Bernice of Acts xxv. Titus during his campaigns in Judaea fell in love with her and she accompanied him on his return to Rome. But the Romans disapproved of the connexion and he dismissed her. The rupture of their relations is the subject of Racine's 'Bérénice' and of Otway's 'Titus and Berenice'.

BERENSON, BERNARD (1865–1959), art historian and philosopher, born in Lithuania and educated in America. In 1887 he settled in Europe. In his 'Italian Painters of the Renaissance' (first published as separate essays, 1894–1907) he developed the theory that the 'tactile values' of a work of art, i.e. its ability to communicate a sense of form, stimulated in the spectator a state of increased awareness or 'life enhancement'. 'Italian Pictures of the Renaissance' (1932) is a list of attributions and locations of all important Italian paintings of the Renaissance. He also wrote on history, aesthetics, and politics.

Bergamask or BERGOMASK, the name of a dance 'framed in imitation of the people of Bergamo (a province in the state of Venice), ridiculed as clownish in their manners and dialect' (Nares), referred to in Shakespeare's 'Midsummer Night's Dream', v. 360.

BERGERAC, CYRANO DE (1619–55), a French soldier and duellist, whom a wound in the Spanish War turned into a dramatist and novelist. He is the subject of a highly successful play by the French dramatist, Edmond Rostand (1898).

BERGSON, HENRI (1859–1941), French philosopher, the son of a Jewish father (a musician) and an English mother, taught philosophy at various schools and universities in France and was elected in 1900 to a professorship in the Collège de France. His principal works appeared as follows: 'Essai sur les données immédiates de la conscience' (Eng. transl. entitled 'Time and Free Will') in 1888; 'Matière et mémoire' in 1896; 'L'Évolution créatrice' in 1907; and 'Les Deux Sources de la morale et de la religion' in 1932. 'Le Rire, essai sur la signification du comique' appeared in 1900.

Bergson's importance lies in the fact that he stated the problem of philosophy afresh. Whereas Kant thought of science as mathematical physics, Bergson examined the non-mathematical sciences (biology, physiology, and psychology) and sought in them a fresh approach to metaphysical problems. He observed that philosophers in describing change have taken time into account only in the sense of a conventional measure, spatial in character, and have ignored real duration, what each of us is conscious of, the indivisible continuity of change, and that this must be recognized as a reality. He saw in psychical life, besides various causal elements, an element of spontaneity or freedom (a subject treated in his first work), which expresses itself in action, introducing something new and unpredictable amid the general laws of nature. Mind thus acts on matter, and does so in a mysterious way, which Bergson examined in 'Matière et mémoire'.

The body, he contends, and particularly the brain, is solely an instrument of action. The brain, in perception, receives certain impulses from without and places these in relation with motor mechanisms selected with more or less freedom. Above all, memories are not stored in the brain. Pure memory (as distinct from habit-memory) is a psychical, not a physiological, function. The past has not ceased to exist and past psychical states have the same sort of independent survival as the material world. In relation to pure memory the function of the brain is to shut out from consciousness the greater part of our past, only letting through that small segment of it which is relevant to the practical activity of the moment; and it is at this point of connexion between memory and perception that spirit influences matter.

Proceeding from this, by a survey of the field of biology, Bergson was led to consider various theories of evolution. This is the theme of 'L'Évolution créatrice'. Having shown reason for thinking that evolution cannot be wholly due to the preservation and accumulation of chance variations, he finds in an original impulse of life, *l'élan vital*, a common effort on the part of individual organisms, that psychological factor in evolution which is the profound cause of transmitted variations.

Bergson's conception of the world as a whole, set out in the same work, is of the existence of two opposing currents: on the one hand inert matter pursuing its downward course; on the other, organic life striving upwards, overcoming the obstacles that matter places in its way, displaying a single original impulse, but following divergent lines of development.

Bergson was interested in scientific psychical research. He was president of the London Society for Psychical Research in 1913, and his presidential address (published in the Society's proceedings for that year) is perhaps the most interesting of his shorter writings.

Berinthia, a character in Vanbrugh's 'The Relapse' and Sheridan's 'A Trip to Scarborough' (qq.v.).

Berkeley, *The Old Woman of*, a poem by Southey (q.v.).

BERKELEY, GEORGE(1685–1753), philosopher, was born at Dysert Castle, in Kilkenny county, and educated at Kilkenny and Trinity College, Dublin. He came to England in 1713, and became associated with Steele, Addison, Pope, Swift, and others. He travelled abroad and in 1728 went for three years to America in connexion with his abortive scheme for a missionary college in Bermuda. He was dean of Derry in 1724 and bishop of Cloyne in 1734, where he remained till 1752. He then retired to Oxford, where he died.

His chief works were the 'Essay towards a New Theory of Vision' (1709) on the independence of the ideas derived from sight and feeling and their 'arbitrary' though constant connexion; the 'Principles of Human Knowledge' (1710); and the 'Dialogues between Hylas and Philonous' (1713). These embody his earlier system of philosophy. He pub-

lished his dialogues of 'Alciphron' (q.v.) in 1732, his 'Theory of Vision' in 1733, and 'Siris', a miscellany on the virtues of tarwater for the body and of a more mystical philosophy than that of his earlier years for the soul, in 1744. In 1713 he contributed to the 'Guardian' (q.v.) essays against the freethinkers; in 1734 he published the 'Analyst', a criticism of the new mathematical positions; and in 1735–7 the 'Querist', dealing with questions of social reform. His 'Commonplace Book' was discovered and published in 1871.

Berkeley takes up the evolution of English philosophy where Locke left it (see *Essay concerning the Human Understanding*), and his work is primarily a destructive criticism of Locke's external, material reality. Only particular things exist, and since these are only a complex of sensations, if we abstract from them that of which we have perception, nothing remains. The 'support' of ideas or sensations is percipient mind. The *esse* of material things is *percipi*. Locke's distinction between the primary and secondary qualities of objects has no validity. Both are exclusively mental. Locke's dualism of spirit and matter, like that of Descartes, leads, in Berkeley's view, to scepticism and atheism (of which Hobbes (q.v.) is the prominent example), and these Berkeley was specially concerned to combat. According to him, spirit is the only real cause or power. Of the existence of our own percipient mind we have knowledge from experience. The existence of other finite spirits is at least probable, principally because they speak to us. For the same reason we believe in the existence of God, who speaks to us in the whole system of nature, through the sense-experiences produced in our minds in a regular and uniform manner.

In his 'Alciphron' Berkeley, through the medium of pleasant Platonic dialogues, combats the views that he attributes to the deists, discusses the nature of virtue, finds proof of the existence of God in the theory of vision, etc. In his last work, 'Siris', his idealism takes a more transcendental form, and the intellectual processes are exalted at the expense of the senses. Berkeley was a master of English prose; he is remarkable for his lucidity, grace, and dignity of expression.

During his stay in America he wrote, besides 'Alciphron', a set of 'Verses on the prospect of planting arts and learning in America', in which occurs the often quoted line, 'Westward the course of empire takes its way'.

Berlin Decree, see *Orders in Council*.

Bermoothes, THE, in Shakespeare's 'The Tempest', 1. ii, are the Bermuda islands, discovered by Juan de Bermudez, a Spaniard, in 1515, and rediscovered by English explorers in 1609.

Bermudas, *The*, see *Marvell*.

'THE BERMUDAS', also called 'The Streights'

(Straits), was a cant term for certain obscure courts and alleys near St. Martin's Lane, frequented by thieves, debtors, knights of the post, etc.

Bernadotte, JEAN-BAPTISTE-JULES (1763–1846), the ancestor of the reigning Swedish dynasty, was the son of a French attorney. He had a brilliant career with the Revolutionary armies and in 1804 was one of Napoleon's first promotion of marshals. In 1810 the Diet of Sweden elected him heir to the throne of Sweden. After this he fought against the French (and changed his Christian names to Charles-Jean). In 1818 he became King Charles XIV of Sweden.

BERNARD, ST. (1091–1153), a great French ecclesiastic, founder of the abbey of Clairvaux, one of the 'Latin Fathers', the glory of the Cistercian Order, and practically dictator of Christendom. In the schism of 1130 between Anacletus and Innocent II, Bernard vigorously supported Innocent. He preached the second Crusade. He was an adversary of Abelard (q.v.). He left some remarkable letters and theological treatises, and was one of the founders of Latin hymnody.

BERNARD OF MORLAIX, a Benedictine monk of the monastery of Cluny in Burgundy, lived in the 12th cent., and was author of the beautiful Latin poem, 'De Contemptu Mundi', of which Archbishop Trench (q.v.) published extracts in his 'Sacred Latin Poetry' and which inspired the hymn, 'Jerusalem the Golden', by Neale (q.v.).

Bernardines, see *Cistercians.*

Bernardo del Carpio, a semi-legendary hero of Spanish chivalry, the son of a secret marriage between the Count de Saldaña and the sister of Alfonso the Chaste. His father was imprisoned by the king, and Spanish ballads deal with Bernardo's attempts to get his release, his rebellion after the Count's death in prison, and his other achievements. He lived in the 9th cent., but according to one legend he pressed Roland to death in his arms at Roncesvalles (see 'Don Quixote', I. xxvi). The legend of Bernardo del Carpio is a kind of rejoinder by the Spaniards to the *chansons* of French prowess associated with Charlemagne and Roland.

Berners, BELLE or ISOPEL, see *Belle Berners.*

BERNERS, JOHN BOURCHIER, *second Baron* (1467–1533), statesman and author. He was chancellor of the exchequer in 1516 and attended Henry VIII at the Field of the Cloth of Gold. He translated the 'Chronicles' of Froissart (q.v., 1523–5); 'Huon of Bordeaux' (q.v., probably printed in 1534); Guevara's 'El Relox de Principes' under the title of the 'Golden Boke of Marcus Aurelius' (1535); and another Spanish work, the 'Castell of Love' (printed 1540).

BERNERS, JULIANA, see *Book of St. Albans.*

Bernhardt, SARAH (ROSINE BERNARD) (1844–1923), a celebrated French actress, partly of Jewish descent. Her earliest successes, during the period 1867–77, were in Victor Hugo's 'Ruy Blas', as Zanetto in Coppée's 'Le Passant', as Doña Sol in Hugo's 'Hernani', and as Phèdre in Racine's tragedy. They were largely due to her beautiful voice and magnetic personality. She was frequently seen in London. The loss of a leg, late in her life, owing to an accident, did not diminish her activity, and she acted at the front during the war of 1914–18.

BERNI, FRANCESCO (1496/7–1535), a Tuscan poet, author of facetious, burlesque compositions, whose style was imitated by Byron in his 'Don Juan' and 'Beppo'. Berni also wrote a recast of Boiardo's 'Orlando Innamorato' (q.v.), which for a long time was regarded as superior to the original.

Bernstein, BARONESS, see *Virginians (The).*

Berosus (BAR-OSEA), a priest at Babylon in the reign of Antiochus Soter (280–262 B.C.), author of chronicles of Chaldea, known to us only through 'quotations at second or third hand' (Sayce).

The 'Berosi Antiquitatum libri quinque', forged by Annius, a monk of Viterbo (15th cent.), were long accepted as genuine.

Berowne or **Biron,** in Shakespeare's 'Love's Labour's Lost' (q.v.), one of the three lords attending on the king of Navarre.

Berserk, BERSERKER, from an Icelandic word of disputed etymology, a wild Norse warrior of great strength and ferocious courage, who fought in the battlefield with a frenzied fury known as the 'berserker rage'. It often means a lawless bravo or freebooter. [OED.] The word is sometimes explained as equivalent to 'baresark', one who fought without armour, in his bare shirt.

Berthe au grand pied (*d.* 783), the wife of Pépin le Bref and mother of Charlemagne. She is the subject of an early French *chanson de geste.*

Bertram; *or the Castle of St. Aldobrand,* a play by Maturin (q.v.), produced in 1816, highly successful in its time, but rendered unreadable today by its overwrought sentiment and passion.

Bertram, COUNT OF ROUSILLON, a character in Shakespeare's 'All's Well that Ends Well' (q.v.).

BERTRAM, CHARLES (1723–65), sometimes self-styled CHARLES JULIUS, literary forger, English teacher in a school for naval cadets at Copenhagen. He produced between 1747 and 1757 an alleged transcript of a manuscript work on Roman antiquities by Richard of Cirencester (q.v.), together with a copy of an ancient itinerary of Britain, at many points supplementing and correcting the itinerary of Antoninus. He also published works of Gildas and Nennius, with the text of his forgery and a commentary on it, at Copenhagen, 1757, and several philological works. His imposture was finally exposed by B. B. Woodward in the 'Gentleman's Magazine', 1866–7.

Bertram, HARRY, a character in Scott's 'Guy Mannering' (q.v.).

Bertram, SIR THOMAS and LADY, and their sons and daughters, characters in Jane Austen's 'Mansfield Park' (q.v.).

Bertram Risingham, a character in Scott's 'Rokeby' (q.v.).

Besant, MRS. ANNIE (1847–1933), *née* Wood, an ardent supporter of Liberal causes, became a pupil of Mme Blavatsky and a member of the Theosophical Society (q.v.) in 1889. She was President of the Society in 1907. In 1917 she was President of the Indian National Congress and was active in the cause of Indian self-government.

BESANT, SIR WALTER (1836–1901), was educated at King's College, London, and Christ's College, Cambridge. He published 'Early French Poetry' in 1868 and 'The French Humourists' in 1873, was secretary to the Palestine Exploration Fund, 1868–86, and with E. H. Palmer wrote 'Jerusalem' (1871). As a contributor to 'Once a Week', he became acquainted in 1869 with James Rice, with whom he collaborated in several novels, including 'Ready-Money Mortiboy' (1871), 'The Golden Butterfly' (1876), 'By Celia's Arbour' (1878), and 'The Chaplain of the Fleet' (1881). From 1882 he continued to write fiction without collaboration, chiefly based on historical incident, e.g., 'Dorothy Forster' (1884) and 'For Faith and Freedom' (1888). 'The Revolt of Man' (1882) is a satirical romance, in which Besant shows himself a critic of women's claims to political power. In 'All Sorts and Conditions of Men' (1882) and 'Children of Gibeon' (1886), he called attention to social evils in East London, and stimulated the foundation of 'The People's Palace', Mile End, for intellectual improvement and rational amusement (1887). He helped to found the Society of Authors (1884), and edited 'The Author' (1890). He defined the financial position of authors in 'The Pen and the Book' (1899). In 1894 Besant commenced the 'Survey of London', which he unfortunately left unfinished (the work appeared in 1902–12), but published 'London' in 1892, 'Westminster' in 1895, and 'South London' in 1899. His other works include 'The Eulogy of Richard Jefferies' (1888), 'Captain Cook' (1889), and (with W. J. Brodribb) 'Constantinople' (1879). His 'Autobiography' appeared in 1902.

Bess o' Bedlam, see *Bedlam*.

Bess of Hardwick, Elizabeth Talbot, countess of Shrewsbury (1518–1608), daughter and co-heir of John Hardwick of Hardwick, Derbyshire. She is described as 'a woman of masculine understanding and con-duct, proud, furious, selfish, and unfeeling' (Lodge). To her care and to that of her husband, the sixth earl of Shrewsbury, Mary Queen of Scots was entrusted in 1569 at Tutbury. She married her daughter to Charles Stuart, younger brother of Darnley (Arabella Stuart was the issue of the marriage), and was imprisoned in the Tower in consequence. She was herself four times married and inherited the fortunes of her four husbands, her income being estimated at £60,000. She built Chatsworth (not the present building) and Hardwick Hall.

Bessus, in Beaumont and Fletcher's 'A King and no King' (q.v.), a cowardly braggart.

The historical Bessus was Satrap of Bactria under Darius III. After the defeat of the latter by Alexander the Great at Arbela, Bessus murdered Darius, assumed the title of king, was betrayed to Alexander, and put to death.

Bessy, the name given to one of the stock characters, a man dressed as a woman, in the medieval sword-dance (q.v.) and in the Mummer's Play (q.v.).

Bestiaries, medieval treatises derived from the Greek PHYSIOLOGUS, which was a collection of some fifty fabulous anecdotes from natural, mostly animal, history, of a moralizing and symbolical character. It was translated into many languages. In the 12th cent. additions began to be made to the Latin version from the popular Encyclopaedia of the Middle Ages, the 'Etymologiae' of Isidore of Seville (q.v.). The bestiaries were often richly illustrated with miniatures, especially those written in England in the 12th and 13th cents.

'The Book of Beasts' (1954) is a translation from a Latin bestiary of the 12th cent., made and edited by T. H. White.

Bethgelert, meaning 'grave of Gelert'. According to a story traditional in the village at the foot of Snowdon, where Llewelyn the Great had his abode, Gelert was a hound given by King John to Llewelyn. On one occasion this favourite hound was missing when Llewelyn went to the chase. On his return he found the hound smeared with blood, his child's bed in disorder, while the child was not to be seen. Thinking that the hound had devoured the child, the father killed Gelert with his sword. The child, awakened by the hound's dying yell, cried out from under a heap of coverings, and under the bed was found a great wolf which the hound had slain.

The story is the subject of a ballad by W. R. Spencer (1811). Similar stories are found in other places and in the 'Gesta Romanorum', and Baring-Gould ('Curious Myths') traces their origin to Indian sources.

Bethnal Green, see *Beggar's Daughter of Bednall Green*. Bethnal Green was a hamlet separated from London by fields when Pepys drove there by coach to dine at Sir W. Rider's

(16 June 1663), at the house said to have been built by the 'Blind Beggar'.

BETJEMAN, JOHN (1906–   ), a poet whose work reflects the contemporary scene with perceptive wit. His books of verse include 'Mount Zion' (1933), 'Continual Dew' (1937), 'Old Lights for New Chancels' (1940), 'New Bats in Old Belfries' (1944), and 'A Few Late Chrysanthemums' (1954). His 'Collected Poems' were published in 1958, and 'Summoned by Bells', an autobiography in verse, in 1960. He has inspired a new enthusiasm for Victorian architecture.

Betrothed, The, a novel by Sir W. Scott (q.v.), published in 1825.

Though styled one of the 'Tales of the Crusaders', it has in fact little to do with these. The scene is laid in the Welsh Marches, in the reign of Henry II. Eveline Berenger, the sole child of a Norman baron, finds herself in grave peril when the fierce Welsh prince, Gwenwyn, besieges her father's castle of Garde Douloureuse, and the old warrior himself is killed in an imprudent sally. She is rescued by Hugo de Lacy, Constable of Chester, and under the influence of gratitude and of a vow made in the moment of danger, consents to be affianced to him, though his age commands her respect rather than her love, and he is under pledge moreover to set off immediately to the Crusade. Left to the care of his nephew, the gallant Damian, whom she secretly loves, and exposed not only to malicious tongues but to the machinations of Randel, another de Lacy kinsman, Eveline spends the years of his absence in a position of much difficulty and danger. Hugo's return is only just in time to extricate Eveline and Damian from a position of the utmost peril; for they are charged with high treason, and accused moreover of taking a disloyal advantage of his absence to indulge their mutual love. The old Constable clears up the situation, releases Eveline from her pledge to him, and places her hand in that of Damian.

Betteredge, GABRIEL, in Wilkie Collins's 'The Moonstone' (q.v.), steward in Lady Verinder's house and narrator of parts of the story.

BETTERTON, THOMAS (1635?–1710), actor and dramatist, joined Sir John D'Avenant's company at Lincoln's Inn Fields in 1661, and was associated in the management of the Dorset Garden Theatre from 1671. He opened a 'theatre in Little Lincoln's Inn Fields' in 1695, producing Congreve's 'Love for Love', and in 1705 the theatre erected by Sir John Vanbrugh in the Haymarket. His impersonations included Hamlet, Mercutio, Sir Toby Belch, Macbeth, Bosola (in the 'Duchess of Malfi'), and Heartwell (in Congreve's 'The Old Bachelor'). His dramas include the 'Roman Virgin', acted 1670, adapted from Webster's 'Appius and Virginia'; the 'Prophetess', 1690, an opera from the 'Prophetess' of Beaumont and Fletcher;

'King Henry IV', 1700 (in which he played Falstaff), from Shakespeare; the 'Amorous Widow', *c.* 1670, from Molière's 'George Dandin'; and the 'Bondman', printed in 1719, from Massinger. He was a man of high character, and was much esteemed as an actor by his contemporaries.

Betterton, MRS. (*d.* 1711), the wife of Thomas Betterton (q.v.), at first known on the stage as Mrs. Saunderson, the first notable actress on the English stage (until 1660 female parts were taken by men or boys). Mrs. Betterton was the first woman to act a series of Shakespeare's great female characters, such as Lady Macbeth, Ophelia, and Juliet.

BETTI, UGO (1892–1953), Italian dramatist and poet. The plays 'Frana allo scalo nord' ('Landslip at the North Freight Yard'), published in 1935, and 'Corruzione al palazzo di giustizia' ('Corruption in the Palace of Justice', 1949), exemplify his preoccupation with justice, guilt, and responsibility. Symbolism and allegory are important in many of his dramas, of which he wrote twenty-five between 1926 and 1953. The best are perhaps 'La regina e gli insorti' ('The Queen and the Rebels', 1951) and 'L'aiuola bruciata' ('The Burnt Flower-bed', 1953).

Betty, MISS, in Fielding's 'Amelia' (q.v.), the spiteful and rapacious sister of the heroine.

Betty, WILLIAM HENRY WEST (1791–1874), actor, called the 'Young Roscius'. He played Romeo at Belfast, and Hamlet and Prince Arthur at Dublin in 1803, when only twelve. He appeared in London in 1804–5. He subsequently went to Christ's College, Cambridge, returned to the stage in 1812, and finally retired in 1824.

Betty Martin, ALL MY EYE AND, a colloquial expression meaning 'all humbug', occurs in Grose's 'Classical Dictionary of the Vulgar Tongue' (1785). The shorter form, 'all my eye', occurs in Goldsmith, 'The Good-natured Man' (1768). The fanciful derivation, from an imaginary Latin prayer, 'Ah, mihi, beate Martine', has no authority.

Beulah, LAND OF, see Isaiah lxii. 4. In Bunyan's 'Pilgrim's Progress', it lies 'beyond the valley of the Shadow of Death and also out of the reach of Giant Despair'. Here the pilgrims were in sight of the Heavenly City, 'they heard continually the singing of birds and saw every day the flowers appear in the earth'.

Beuves de Hanstone, a 12th-cent. French *chanson de geste*, of which Bevis of Hampton (q.v.) is the subject.

Beverly of Graustark, see under *Graustark*.

Bevis of Hampton, a popular verse romance of 4,000 lines, of the early 14th cent. The mother of Bevis, wife of Guy, earl of Southampton, having procured the murder of her husband by Mordure, son of the emperor of Germany, marries the murderer. Bevis is sold as a slave and given to the king of Armenia, who offers him his daughter Josian as wife. Bevis, as a Christian, at first refuses the union, but saves Josian from an unwelcome suitor, Brademond; and finally accepts Josian on her promise to become a Christian. The king, misled as to the lovers' relations, sends Bevis with a sealed letter to Brademond, who imprisons him for seven years. Josian is married first to Yvor, king of Mombrant, then to Earl Miles, whom she hangs on the wedding night. Bevis rescues her from the stake, and takes her to England. He defeats and slays the emperor and Yvor. After various adventures, in the course of which he converts the giant Ascapart or Asclopard, he and Josian return to the East.

The story is told in Drayton's 'Polyolbion' (ii. 259). The sword of Bevis was called 'Morglay'.

Bewick, THOMAS (1753–1828), wood-engraver, apprenticed to, and subsequently partner of, Ralph Beilby. He engraved blocks for Gay's 'Fables' (1779), 'Select Fables' (1784), 'General History of Quadrupeds' (1790), 'History of British Birds' (1797 and 1804) and 'Fables of Aesop' (1818). The text of the 'British Birds' was by the Rev. Mr. Cotes, of the 'Quadrupeds' by R. Beilby.

BEYLE, HENRI, see *Stendhal.*

Bezae, CODEX, see *Bible (The).*

Bezonian, from Italian *bisogno,* Spanish *bisoño,* a raw recruit, a needy beggar, base fellow, knave, rascal. 'Under which king, Bezonian? speak or die' (Shakespeare, '2 Henry IV', v. iii. 116).

Bhagavad-gítā, one of the principal sacred writings of the Hindus, an episode in the great epic Mahābhārata in which Krishna instructs and exhorts Arjuna before the battle of Kuruksetra. It is a product of the Bhāgavata or Vāsudeva sect who worshipped Krishna as one of the principal incarnations of the supreme god Vishnu. It is probably to be dated about the 1st or 2nd cent. A.D. Since then it has remained one of the most esteemed and influential works of the religious literature of India.

Bianca, (1) a character in Shakespeare's 'The Taming of the Shrew' (q.v.); (2) in his 'Othello' (q.v.), the mistress of Cassio.

Bianchi and **Neri,** 'White' and 'Black', the name of two factions formed by the citizens of Florence after the expulsion of the Ghibellines in the 13th cent. The Bianchi, refusing to submit to the directions of Pope Boniface, and threatened by the approach of Charles of Valois, fled from the city (among them Dante and the father of Petrarch) in 1301, and ultimately joined the Ghibellines.

BIAΘANATOΣ [Biathanatos], A Declaration of that Paradoxe or Thesis that Self-Homicide is not so Naturally Sinne that it may never be otherwise, by John Donne (q.v.), published in 1624.

Bible, THE. (1) THE OLD TESTAMENT. The oldest Hebrew text that we possess of this (*Codex Babylonicus Petropolitanus*) is comparatively recent, dating only from 916 A.D. It is a Masoretic text, i.e. one prepared by the guild of scholars called *Masoretes* (see *Masora*). Of much earlier date (5th cent. B.C.) is the Samaritan text of the Pentateuch. We have also the *Targums* or Aramaic paraphrases, written at various times subsequent to the date when Aramaic superseded Hebrew as the language spoken by the Jews (shortly before the Christian era). The Greek version, known as the *Septuagint* (q.v.), of the 3rd cent. B.C. is of far greater importance. Other translations into Greek were made in the 2nd cent. A.D. and were collected in parallel columns, together with the current Hebrew text and a revised text of the Septuagint, by Origen in his *Hexapla.* This has perished with the exception of the revised Septuagint, of most of which we possess an 8th-cent. copy. In addition to the above, there was an old Latin version (known as *Vetus Itala*) of an early Greek translation, of which fragments alone remain, and which was superseded by Jerome's Latin text, known as the *Vulgate* (q.v.).

(2) THE NEW TESTAMENT. Of this we possess manuscripts in Greek, and manuscripts of translations from the Greek into Latin, Syriac, and Coptic. The most important of these are the Greek, of which the chief are the *Codex Vaticanus* and the *Codex Sinaiticus,* uncial manuscripts of the 4th cent.; the *Codex Bezae,* containing the Greek text on the left-hand page and the Latin on the right, probably earlier than the 6th cent.; and the *Codex Alexandrinus,* an uncial of the 5th cent. Of the Latin versions there were, before Jerome undertook their revision in the Vulgate, two main types current respectively in Africa and Europe. Several manuscripts of these survive. Of the Vulgate text there are a large number of manuscripts, of which the best are Northumbrian (based on Italian originals), Irish, and Spanish. (See in this connexion *Amiatinus Codex* and *Lindisfarne Gospels.*)

See also *Bible (The English), Mazarin Bible, Zürich Bible, Polyglot Bible, Complutensian Polyglot, Luther, Gutenberg,* and *Ulfilas.*

Bible, THE ENGLISH. Apart from paraphrases attributed to Cædmon (q.v.) and the translation by Bede (q.v.) of part of the Gospel of St. John, the earliest attempts at translation into English of the Holy Scriptures are the 9th- and 10th-cent. glosses and versions of the Psalms, followed by the 10th-cent. glosses and versions of the Gospels (the 'Durham Book' or 'Lindisfarne Gospels', q.v., and the 'West-Saxon Gospels'), and Ælfric's translation of the O.T. at the close of the same century. After this little was done until the time of Wycliffe (q.v.), to whom and his followers we owe the two 14th-cent. versions associated with his name, the first complete renderings into English of the Scriptures. Of these two versions, taken from the Latin text, which appeared about 1382 and 1388, it is doubtful how much was Wycliffe's own work. The second, or revised version, was a great improvement on the first, and is a readable and correct translation.

William Tyndale (q.v.) was the first to translate the N.T. into English from the Greek text; this he probably did in Wittenberg, the translation being printed first at Cologne, and when this was interrupted, at Worms (1525-6). In 1530 his translation of the Pentateuch was printed at Marburg, followed by a translation of the Book of Jonah. These translations were made from the Hebrew, with reference also to the Vulgate, Erasmus's Latin version, and Luther's Bible. Our Authorized Version (see below) is essentially the text of Tyndale. The complete English Bible that bears the name of Miles Coverdale (q.v.) was printed in 1535. It is not a translation from the original texts, but probably from Luther's version, the Zürich Bible, and the Vulgate, with assistance from Tyndale's version. A second edition was issued in 1537. The Prayer Book text of the Psalms is largely Coverdale's version.

'Matthew's Bible' was issued in 1537, under the pseudonym of John Matthew, by John Rogers (1500?-55). He was a friend of Tyndale, was converted to Protestantism, and prepared and annotated his version for publication. Rogers was burnt at Smithfield in Mary's reign.

'Taverner's Bible', prepared by Richard Taverner (1505?-75), was a revision of Matthew's. It appeared in 1539. Richard Taverner was a religious author who was patronized by Wolsey and Cromwell, was sent to the Tower on the latter's fall, but subsequently obtained the favour of Henry VIII.

The 'Great Bible', also called 'Cranmer's Bible', was brought out in 1539 under the auspices of Henry VIII; Coverdale was placed by Cromwell in charge of its preparation. The printing of it was begun in Paris and finished in London.

Towards the end of Henry VIII's reign, there were interdictions on the use of the Bible. During Mary's reign, the reformers took refuge, some in Frankfort-on-the-Main, some in Geneva, where in 1560 appeared the Genevan or 'Breeches' (q.v.) Bible. It had a marginal commentary which proved agreeable to the Puritans.

In 1568 was published the 'Bishops' Bible', an edition promoted by Archbishop Parker to counteract the popularity of the Calvinistic Genevan Bible; while Romanists made a translation, known as the Rheims and Douai version, which appeared, the N.T. in 1582, the O.T. in 1609-10. It is characterized by the frequent use of Latinisms.

The 'Authorized Version' arose out of a conference at Hampton Court, convened by James I in 1604, between the High Church and Low Church parties. The undertaking was proposed by Dr. Reynolds, president of Corpus Christi College, Oxford, and was supported by the king. The revisers were forty-seven in number, divided into companies dealing with various sections of the Bible, and were drawn from the most eminent scholars and divines of the day. They were instructed to follow the text of the 'Bishops' Bible' wherever they could. The work of revision and retranslation occupied three years and a half, and the so-called 'Authorized Version' (it was not authorized by any official pronouncement) appeared in 1611. It is practically the version of Tyndale with some admixture from Wycliffe. Two issues of it were made in 1611, known respectively as the 'He Bible' and the 'She Bible', because in the first the words in Ruth iii. 15 read 'and he went into the citie', and in the second 'and she went into the citie'. Modern bibles are based with slight variations on the 'She Bible'. Various editions of the Bible are named after eccentricities of wording or mistakes in the printed text; a few of the more important of these, such as 'Breeches Bible' and 'Vinegar Bible', are dealt with under their respective names.

In 1870 the Convocation of Canterbury appointed a committee to consider the question of revision, and as a consequence of their report two companies were constituted to revise the authorized versions of the O.T. and N.T. respectively. The Revised Text was published, of the N.T. in 1881, of the O.T. in 1885. That of the N.T. was unfavourably received, owing to many irritating and apparently unnecessary alterations of familiar passages. The Revised Version of the O.T., though not altogether free from these, was in many respects an improvement on the Authorized text. In 1922 the Revd. James Moffatt, Washburn Professor of Church History in the Union Theological Seminary, produced a 'New Translation of the New Testament', and in 1924 'The Old Testament, a new Translation', both of which caused some controversy. The Rt. Revd. Monsignor Ronald Knox (q.v.) published a new translation of the Bible based on the Vulgate text; the N.T. in 1945 and the O.T. in 2 vols. in 1949.

In 1947 a new translation of the Bible into modern English, to be known as the New English Bible, was undertaken by a Joint Committee of all the Churches (except the Roman Catholic) in the British Isles. The work was to be carried out by panels of translators for the O.T., Apocrypha, and N.T., with the help of literary advisers, and published by the University Presses of Oxford and Cambridge. The new translation of the N.T. was published in March 1961.

Bible in Spain, *The*, a narrative of travel, by Borrow (q.v.), published in 1843.

Borrow travelled in Spain as colporteur

of bibles for the British and Foreign Bible Society from 1835 to 1840, and this book purports to be an account of the adventures that he met with in that country, at a time of great disturbance owing to the Carlist troubles. It is impossible to say how far the various incidents recounted actually occurred; but the vivid picture that the author gives of Spain is unquestionably true, and the work is one of the best of English books of travel.

Bibliographical Society, THE, founded in 1892. Its 'Transactions' were first published in 1893 (merged with 'The Library' (q.v.) in 1920). The Society publishes also separate monographs, and in 1926 issued the invaluable 'Short-Title Catalogue of English Books, 1475–1640'.

Bibliography, WORKS OF, see under *Bohn, Brydges, Dewey, Dibdin (T. F.), Hazlitt (W. C.), Lang, Lowndes, McKerrow, Quaritch, Watt (R.)*, and previous entry.

Bickerstaff, ISAAC, a fictitious person invented by Swift (q.v.). A cobbler, John Partridge, claiming to be an astrologer, had published predictions in the form of an almanac. Swift in the beginning of 1708 produced a parody entitled 'Predictions for the ensuing year, by Isaac Bickerstaff', in which he foretold the death of Partridge on 29 March. On 30 March he published a letter giving an account of Partridge's end. Partridge indignantly protested that he was still alive, but Swift retorted in a 'Vindication' proving that he was really dead. Other writers took up the joke, and Steele, when he launched 'The Tatler' in 1709, adopted the name of Bickerstaff for the supposed author.

BICKERSTAFFE, ISAAC (*d.* 1812?), an Irish playwright, who produced many successful comedies and opera libretti, including the popular comic operas 'Love in a Village' (1762), 'The Maid of the Mill' (1765), 'The Padlock' (q.v., 1768). 'The Hypocrite' (1769, adapted from Molière's 'Tartuffe' and Cibber's 'The Non-Juror') contains the well-known character of a hypocrite, 'Mawworm'. His 'Lionel and Clarissa', successfully produced in 1768, later appeared as 'The School for Fathers'. Bickerstaffe fled the country in 1772 suspected of a capital crime.

Bidpai or *Pilpay, The Fables of*, or *Kalilah and Dimnah*, is the title of the Arabic version of a lost original of the 'Panchatantra', a celebrated Sanskrit collection of fables, the source of much European folklore. 'Bidpai' is a corruption of 'bidbah', the appellation of the chief scholar at the court of an Indian prince.

Biedermeier, a German style of furniture, showing the pseudo-classical taste of the late French 'Empire'. It takes its name from a political caricature in 'Fliegende Blätter', and was in vogue from about 1815 to 1848.

Biederman, ARNOLD, a character in Scott's 'Anne of Geierstein' (q.v.).

BIERCE, AMBROSE (1842–1914?), American writer, born in Ohio. He served in the Civil War and afterwards became a prominent journalist, living and working for a time in England (1872–6). He returned to San Francisco, and later worked as a correspondent in Washington. He published much, and collected his writings together in 12 vols. (1909–12), but is best known for his short stories, realistic, sardonic, and strongly influenced by E. A. Poe (q.v.). They were published in 'Tales of Soldiers and Civilians' (1891), a title which was changed to 'In the Midst of Life' (1892; rev. edn. 1898). Tired of life and America, he travelled to Mexico in 1913 and mysteriously disappeared, it is thought in the fighting of the Civil War.

Bifröst, in Scandinavian mythology, the bridge by which the gods cross from heaven to earth, the rainbow. It is guarded by Heimdal, and at its summit sit the Norns (qq.v.).

Big Brother, in Orwell's 'Nineteen Eighty-four' (q.v.), is the head of the Party, who never appears in person, but whose dominating portrait in every public place, with the caption *Big Brother is watching you*, is inescapable.

Big-endians and Little-endians, see *Gulliver's Travels.*

Biglow Papers, see *Lowell (J. R.).*

Bilbo, apparently from Bilbao in Spain (long called in English Bilboa), a sword noted for its elasticity and temper. 'Bilbow blades' could be bent till point met hilt.

Bilboes, of uncertain derivation, but, like the preceding, usually referred to Bilbao on the alleged ground that many of these instruments were manufactured there consisted of a long iron bar with sliding shackles to confine the ankles of a prisoner, and a lock by which to fix one end of the bar to the floor. [OED.]

Bildad, one of the three friends of Job (q.v.).

Bill of Rights, see *Rights, Bill of.*

Billickin, MRS., in Dickens's 'Edwin Drood' (q.v.), a cousin of Mr. Bazzard, who lets lodgings in Bloomsbury.

BILLINGS, JOSH, see *Shaw (H. W.).*

Billingsgate, the name of one of the gates of London on the river side, and hence of the fish market there established. It is perhaps derived from a personal name, Billing (cf. Billingshurst), and according to fable from Belinus (q.v.), a legendary British king. There are frequent references in 17th-cent. literature to the abusive language of the Billingsgate market; hence foul language is itself called 'billingsgate'.

Bills of Mortality, official returns of the deaths in a certain district, which began to be published weekly by the London Company of Parish Clerks in 1592 for 109 parishes in and around London. Hence this district (the precise limits of which were often modified) became known as 'within the bills of mortality'. [OED.]

Billy Budd, Sailor, a short novel by H. Melville (q.v.), published posthumously in 1924. Billy Budd, a handsome and innocent sailor in an English naval ship, is persecuted by a malevolent petty officer, Claggart. Billy strikes Claggart and unintentionally kills him, and Captain Vere, though recognizing his true character, has no alternative but to have him hanged. Benjamin Britten wrote an opera (1951) to a libretto from the story, written by E. M. Forster (q.v.) and Eric Crozier.

Billy Taylor, the subject of an old song. He is pressed and sent to sea and followed by his true love, disguised as a sailor, who shoots him when she finds him unfaithful to her, and is made first lieutenant of the 'Gallant Thunderbomb'. The text is in Oliver's 'Comic Songs' (2nd ed. 1825?, according to B.M. Cat.).

Bingen, BISHOP OF, otherwise known as *Bishop Hatto* (q.v.).

BINGHAM, JOSEPH (1668–1723), fellow of University College, Oxford. He withdrew from the university, being unjustly charged with preaching heretical doctrine. He was author of 'Origines Ecclesiasticae, or the Antiquities of the Christian Church' (1708–22), a very learned work, which long retained its authoritative character.

Bingley, CHARLES, a character in Jane Austen's 'Pride and Prejudice' (q.v.).

Binks, SIR BINGO and LADY, characters in Scott's 'St. Ronan's Well' (q.v.).

BINYON, LAURENCE (1869–1943), poet, for forty years (until 1933) an official in the British Museum, where he became Keeper of prints and drawings, noted as an authority in many branches of art, especially Oriental painting. He was the author of many volumes of poems, of which the first was 'Lyric Poems' (1894), and of some plays. Among his publications may be mentioned 'Auguries' (1913), 'The Anvil and other Poems' (1916), the drama 'Arthur' (1923). His poem 'For the Fallen' (1914) contains the lines

> They shall not grow old, as we that are left grow old:
> Age shall not weary them, nor the years condemn.
> At the going down of the sun and in the morning
> We will remember them.

Binyon also translated Dante's 'Divina Commedia' (q.v.) ('Inferno', 1933; 'Purgatorio', 1938; 'Paradiso', 1943).

Biographia Literaria, a literary autobiography by S. T. Coleridge (q.v.), published in 1817.

The autobiographical thread is slender. The work consists in the main of a discussion of the philosophy of Kant, Fichte, and Schelling, and a criticism of Wordsworth's poetry. (For Coleridge's philosophical doctrines see under *Aids to Reflection*.)

BION (*c.* 100 B.C.?), a pastoral poet of Smyrna, who ended his life in Sicily, where he was poisoned. He is best known for his lament for Adonis, on which Shelley partly modelled his 'Adonais'. Moschus (q.v.) called himself the pupil of Bion.

Birch, HARVEY, the mysterious pedlar and spy in 'The Spy', a novel of the American Revolution, by J. F. Cooper (q.v.).

Birdcage Walk, in St. James's Park, London, so called from the cages for birds and beasts kept there for the amusement of Charles II.

Birds of America, see *Audubon, John James*.

Birnam Wood, see *Macbeth*.

Biron or BEROWNE, in Shakespeare's 'Love's Labour's Lost' (q.v.), one of the three lords attending on the king of Navarre.

Biron, a character in Southerne's 'The Fatal Marriage' (q.v.).

BIRRELL, AUGUSTINE (1850–1933), President of the Board of Education, 1905–7; chief secretary for Ireland, 1907–16; author of 'Obiter Dicta' (1884, 1887, 1924), 'William Hazlitt' (1902), 'Andrew Marvell' (1905).

Bishop Blougram's Apology, a poem by R. Browning (q.v.), included in 'Men and Women', published in 1855.

The poem is a casuistical apology for the position of a beneficed priest whose belief does not extend to all the doctrines of the Roman Catholic religion. Though a monologue in form, it is in fact an argument between the bishop and Mr. Gigadibs, his critic, in which the bishop succeeds, at least, in silencing the critic. But Browning has the last (crushing) word. Cardinal Wiseman was the model from whom Bishop Blougram was drawn.

Bishop Hatto: a legend of the 10th cent. relates that Hatto, archbishop of Mainz, at a time of famine (970) assembled a company of poor people in a barn and burnt them to death, that there might be more food for the rich. He was pursued by an army of mice, took refuge in a tower on the Rhine still known as the Mäuseturm, and was there devoured by them. The legend is told in 'Coryat's Crudities', and in a poem by Southey (q.v.).

The historical Bishop Hatto was not guilty of this atrocity, and the Mäuseturm was in fact erected for the collection of tolls on river traffic. The legend is said to arise from an erroneous derivation of Mäuseturm from *Mäuse* (mice). Similar legends of men devoured by mice or rats are widely prevalent among northern nations; Baring-Gould ('Curious Myths') attributes their origin to the heathen practice of human sacrifice in times of famine.

Bishopsgate, the principal north gate of the ancient city of London. It is mentioned as *porta episcopi* in Domesday, but the particular bishop with whom it was connected is unknown. Loftie thinks it may have been Erkenwald or St. Botolph. Burbage's first theatre was just outside Bishopsgate.

Bismarck, OTTO EDUARD LEOPOLD, PRINCE VON (1815–98), afterwards duke of Lauenburg, known as 'The Iron Chancellor', born at Schönhausen in Prussia, became Prussian prime minister in 1862, and under his administration were fought the war against Denmark of 1864 and the war against Austria of 1866. Bismarck became chancellor of the North German Federation in 1867, and in 1870–1 ensued the war with France, in which the southern states co-operated with Northern Germany. The German Empire was constituted in 1871 and Bismarck was its first chancellor. He presided at the Congress of Berlin in 1878 and concluded the Triple Alliance in 1883. Having incurred the displeasure of the Emperor William II, he resigned in 1890.

BLACK, WILLIAM (1841–98), a native of Scotland, war correspondent of the 'Morning Star' during the Franco-Prussian War, and subsequently sub-editor of the 'Daily News', is remembered for some of his novels: 'A Daughter of Heth' (1871), 'A Princess of Thule' (1873), 'Macleod of Dare' (1879), stories of his native country; and 'The Strange Adventures of a Phaeton' (1872), which combines romance with descriptions of English localities.

Black Agnes, Agnes, countess of Dunbar (1312?–69), daughter of the first earl of Moray and wife of the tenth earl of Dunbar, remembered for her spirited defence of Dunbar Castle against the English (1339).

Black Beauty, see *Sewell.*

Black Bess, the celebrated mare of Dick Turpin (q.v.).

Black Book of Carmarthen, THE, a Welsh manuscript of the 12th cent., containing a collection of ancient Welsh poetry, interesting among other things for references to King Arthur.

Black Book of the Admiralty, an ancient code of rules for the government of the navy, said to have been compiled in the reign of Edward III.

Black Brunswickers, a military mounted force raised by Frederick William, duke of Brunswick (1771–1815, killed at Quatre Bras), for service against the French in the Napoleonic wars. There is a famous picture by Millais representing 'The Black Brunswicker'. See also *Hussars.*

Black Death, THE, the name now commonly given to the Great Pestilence or visitation of the Oriental Plague, which devastated most countries of Europe near the middle of the 14th cent., and caused great mortality in England in 1348–9; sometimes also including the recurrences of the epidemic in 1360 and 1379. The epithet 'black' is of uncertain origin and not known to be contemporary. It is first found in Swedish and Danish 16th-cent. chroniclers. [OED.]

Black Douglas, see *Douglas (The Black).*

Black Dwarf, The, a novel by Sir W. Scott (q.v.), in the first series of the 'Tales of My Landlord', published in 1816.

The principal character in the story, who gives it its title, is a dwarf of extraordinary ugliness and strength who takes up his abode in a lonely spot in southern Scotland at the beginning of the 18th cent., builds himself a hovel of mighty stones, and acquires a reputation for supernatural powers. He is called Elshender the Recluse, or Elshie of the Mucklestanes, and his acrimonious speech suggests an excessively misanthropical disposition. Yet the story, of which the plot is slender, tells of his beneficent influence on events in his neighbourhood. A robber carries off Grace Armstrong, to the distress of her lover, the young farmer Hobbie Elliot, but she is immediately restored on the dwarf's intervention. His intervention prevents the marriage of Isabella Vere with Sir Frederick Langley, to which her unwilling consent has been wrung by her father, the laird of Ellieslaw, for his own ends. It turns out that the Dwarf is the rich Sir Edward Manley, the near kinsman of Isabella, a man embittered by his deformity and by his unhappy love for Isabella's mother; he has long been supposed dead, and Ellieslaw is deeply indebted to him.

Black-eyed Susan, see *Burnand (Sir F. C.), Gay (J.).*

Black Friars, members of the order of the Dominicans, founded at the beginning of the 13th cent. by St. Dominic, so called from the colour of their dress. They had a convent in the part of the City of London that still bears their name. The buildings were surrendered to the Crown in Henry VIII's reign, and the case for his divorce from Queen Catherine was heard there by the papal legate. For Burbage's theatre in the precincts of the old monastery, see *Blackfriars Theatre.*

Black Hole of Calcutta, the punishment cell of the barracks in Fort William, Calcutta, into which, by order of Suraja Dowlah, 146 Europeans were thrust for a whole night in 1756, of whom only twenty-three survived till the morning.

Black Hussars, see *Hussars.*

Black Letter, type reproducing the *Jexbura* book-script used for liturgical and other formal writing from the 12th until the 15th cent., the most elaborate of the scripts known as 'Gothic'.

Black Maria, popular name for a prison van.

Black Michael, nickname of Sir Michael Hicks Beach (1837–1916), chancellor of the exchequer, 1885 and 1895–1902), from Black Michael, the king's wicked brother in 'The Prisoner of Zenda' (q.v.).

Black Monks, the Benedictines (q.v.), so called from the colour of their dress.

Black Prince, THE, a name given (apparently by 16th-cent. chroniclers) to Edward, the eldest son of Edward III (1330–76). The origin of the appellation is a matter of conjecture, and published sources, says the OED., afford no evidence. It was perhaps due to 'his dreaded acts in battle', or to his wearing black armour.

Black Rod, short for 'Gentleman Usher of the Black Rod', so called from his black wand of office, is the Chief Gentleman Usher of the Lord Chamberlain's department of the royal household, who is also usher to the House of Lords and to the Chapter of the Garter.

Black Watch, THE, the Royal Highland Regiment of the British Army, so called from the colour of their uniform, a dark tartan.

Blackacre, THE WIDOW, a character in Wycherley's 'The Plain Dealer' (q.v.).

Blackfriars Theatre, THE, an apartment in the dissolved monastery of the Black Friars (q.v.) purchased by James Burbage (q.v.) in 1596 and adapted for a play-house. Owing to local opposition, it was handed over to the Children of the Chapel see *Paul's*, (*Children of*) but reverted to Richard Burbage (q.v.) in 1608. Shakespeare had a share in the theatre and his company acted there. Its site is marked by Playhouse Yard near 'The Times' office (Loftie).

BLACKMAN, BLAKMAN, or **BLAKE-MAN,** JOHN (*fl.* 1436–48), fellow of Merton College, Oxford, chaplain and contemporary biographer of Henry VI, our main authority for his piety, etc.

BLACKMORE, SIR RICHARD (*d.* 1729), physician to Queen Anne, produced some indifferent poems of great length, heroic and epic, and 'The Creation, a philosophical poem demonstrating the existence and providence of God' (1712), which was warmly praised by Dr. Johnson.

BLACKMORE, RICHARD DODDRIDGE (1825–1900), educated at Blundell's School, Tiverton, and Exeter College, Oxford, published some volumes of verse and a number of novels, of which the most famous was 'Lorna Doone' (q.v., 1869). Among the others were 'Clara Vaughan' (1864), 'Cradock Nowell' (1866), 'The Maid of Sker' (1872), 'Alice Lorraine' (1875), 'Cripps the Carrier' (1877), 'Christowell' (1881), and 'Springhaven' (1887). The last is a pleasant tale of adventure and romance centring in a small southern port in the days of the Napoleonic wars, and presenting Wellington, Napoleon, and George III.

Blackpool, STEPHEN, a character in Dickens's 'Hard Times' (q.v.).

Blackstick, FAIRY, see *Rose and the Ring.*

BLACKSTONE, SIR WILLIAM (1723–80), educated at Charterhouse School and Pembroke College, Oxford, was a fellow of All Souls and the first Vinerian professor of English law at Oxford. His fame rests on his 'Commentaries on the Laws of England' (1765–9), a comprehensive picture of the English law and constitution as a single organic structure. The work was criticized by Bentham ('Fragment on Government') and others, but exercised a powerful influence. It was translated into French, German, Italian, and Russian. Blackstone published a collection of 'Law Tracts' in 1762. He was made a judge in 1770.

Blackwood's Edinburgh Magazine, a monthly periodical started in 1817 by William Blackwood (1776–1834) the publisher, as a rival to the 'Edinburgh Review' (q.v.), of a less ponderous kind than the 'Quarterly' (q.v.). It had John Wilson, J. G. Lockhart, and James Hogg (qq.v.) on its staff. The number for October 1817 contained the famous satire on Edinburgh notabilities which took the form of a pretended 'Chaldee MS.' 'Blackwood's' was then Tory in politics, and the avowed enemy of the 'Cockney School' in literary matters, i.e. Lamb, Hazlitt, and in particular Leigh Hunt. In 1819 William Maginn (q.v.) was added to the staff. He was perhaps the originator of the 'Noctes Ambrosianae' (q.v.), which shortly began to appear in 'Maga', as 'Blackwood's' was familiarly called. De Quincey was also among the early contributors.

Mrs. Oliphant's interesting 'Annals of a Publishing House: William Blackwood and his Sons' appeared in 1897.

Bladud, a legendary king of Britain, father of Lear, and founder of the city of Bath.

BLAIR, ERIC, see *Orwell.*

Blair, HUGH (1718–1800), Scottish divine and professor of rhetoric, is remembered for his famous sermons (5 vols., 1777–1801) and 'Lectures on Rhetoric'. He belonged to a distinguished literary circle which included Hume, A. Carlyle, Adam Smith, and Robertson.

BLAIR, ROBERT (1699–1746), educated at Edinburgh and in Holland, was ordained minister of Athelstaneford in East Lothian in 1731. He published in 1743 'The Grave', a didactic poem of some 800 lines of blank verse, in which he celebrates death, the solitude of the tomb, and the anguish of bereavement. The poem compares favourably with the somewhat similar 'Night Thoughts' (q.v.) of Edward Young, with which it was almost exactly contemporary. It was illustrated by William Blake (q.v.).

Blaize, Elegy on Mrs. Mary, a burlesque elegy by Goldsmith (q.v.), published in 'The Bee'.

Blaize, FARMER, in Meredith's 'The Ordeal of Richard Feverel', Lucy Feverel's uncle.

BLAKE, WILLIAM (1757–1827), the son of a London hosier, did not go to school, but was apprenticed to James Basire, engraver to the Society of Antiquaries. His earliest poems are contained in 'Poetical Sketches', published in 1783 at the expense of his friends, Flaxman and Mrs. Mathew. In 1789 he engraved and published his 'Songs of Innocence', in which he first showed the mystical cast of his mind. Their underlying theme is the all-pervading presence of divine love and sympathy, even in trouble and sorrow. 'The Book of Thel' appeared in the same year, and its theme is similar: the maiden Thel laments the vanity and transience of life, and is answered by the lily, the cloud, the worm, and the clod; they explain the principle of mutual self-sacrifice and that death means a new birth. 'Tiriel' belongs to the years 1788–9. It is the story of a tyrant and his rebellious children, the symbolic meaning of which is obscure. In 1790 Blake engraved his principal prose work, the 'Marriage of Heaven and Hell', in which, with vigorous satire and telling apologue, he takes up his revolutionary position, of which the main features are the denial of the reality of matter, the denial of eternal punishment, and the denial of authority. In 'The French Revolution' (1791), 'America' (1793), and the 'Visions of the Daughters of Albion' (1793), his attitude of revolt against authority is further developed. He creates a mythology of his own, with Urizen, the deviser of moral codes, and Orc, the arch-rebel, for central figures. The 'Songs of Experience' (1794) are in marked contrast with the 'Songs of Innocence'. The brightness of the earlier work gives place to a sense of gloom and mystery, and of the power of evil. We find again a protest against restrictive codes and an exaltation of the spirit of love. The 'Songs of Experience' include the famous 'Tiger! Tiger! burning bright'. In 'The Book of Urizen' (1794), 'The Book of Ahania', 'The Book of Los' (1795), Blake pursues, in mythological form, his exposure of the errors of the moral code. By an inversion of the Miltonic story, it is Urizen, the author of moral law, who is expelled from the abode of the Eternals, and obtains control over the human world. In 'Europe' (1794) and 'The Song of Los' (1795), Enitharmon is the giver of restrictive morality, on behalf of Urizen, to the sons of men; Los, a changing and perplexing character, appears to be the personification of Time, a champion of light, but held in bondage; Orc rises in rebellion, a symbol of the French Revolution. In 'Vala' (1797), subsequently in great part re-written and re-named 'The Four Zoas', the symbolism is exceptionally difficult to follow, but we still have the opposition of Urizen and Orc, representing authority and anarchy; the condemnation of the oppressive code of morality; the ultimate triumph of Orc and of liberty. In the later version (the 'Four Zoas') there is a new element, the revelation of forgiveness through Jesus Christ. In 1804 Blake began to engrave his final symbolic works, 'Milton' and 'Jerusalem'. Milton returns from eternity to correct the error to which he had given currency, and enters into Blake, who preaches the doctrine of Jesus, of self-sacrifice and for-giveness. In 'Jerusalem' we have expounded Blake's theory of Imagination, 'the real and eternal world of which the Vegetable Universe is but a faint shadow'; 'the world of imagination is the world of eternity. It is the divine bosom into which we shall all go after the death of the vegetated body.' In 'The Ghost of Abel' (1822), a short dramatic dialogue, Blake, referring to Byron's 'Cain', combats the view that the curse of Cain was uttered by Jehovah, and attributes it to Satan. His later minor poems include some beautiful lyrics, such as 'The Morning' and 'The Land of Dreams'; also the fragmentary 'The Everlasting Gospel', his own interpretation of the Gospel of Christ.

Blake engraved his poems on plates, in many surrounding the text with illustrations which he coloured by hand. He designed, and sometimes engraved, illustrations of works by other poets, notably Young's 'Night Thoughts' and Blair's 'Grave', and he made large watercolour illustrations, e.g. for the Book of Job, and the 'Divina Commedia', as well as colour-printed drawings, produced by a special process of his own devising. The same symbolic and imaginative qualities are evident in his drawings as in his poems. There is a good edition of 'The Poetical Works of William Blake' by John Sampson, Oxford, 1905. A 'Life of Blake' by Alexander Gilchrist was published in 1863 (2nd ed., 1880; new ed., 1906). See also Northrop Frye's study of Blake, 'Fearful Symmetry' (Princeton, 1947).

[In the preparation of the above summary of Blake's symbolic poems, much help has been obtained from vol. xi, ch. ix, of the C.H.E.L.]

Blakesware, in Hertfordshire, the 'Blakes-moor' of the 'Essays of Elia' (q.v.), the great house where Mary Field, Lamb's grand-mother, was housekeeper.

Blanchefleur or BLANCHEFLOUR, see *Flores and Blancheflour*.

Blandamour, in Spenser's 'Faerie Queene', Bk. IV, a 'jolly youthful knight', 'his fickle mind full of inconstancie', who consorts with Paridell and Duessa (qq.v.).

Blank Verse, verse without rhyme, especially the iambic pentameter or unrhymed heroic, the regular measure of English dramatic and epic poetry, first used by the earl of Surrey (q.v.).

Blanketeers, a body of workmen who met at the so-called Blanket Meeting in St. Peter's Field, Manchester, on 10 March 1817, provided with blankets or rugs, in order to march to London and press their grievances on the attention of the government.

Blankley's, The Man from, a play by F. Anstey (q.v.); originally one of the 'Voces Populi' in *Punch*.

Blarney, a village near Cork. In the Castle of Blarney there is an inscribed stone in a position difficult of access. The popular saying is that any one who kisses the 'Blarney stone' will ever after have 'a cajoling tongue and the art of flattery or of telling lies with unblushing effrontery' (Lewis, 'Topographical Dictionary of Ireland', quoted in OED.).

Blarney, LADY, in Goldsmith's 'Vicar of Wakefield' (q.v.), one of the fine ladies introduced to the Primroses by Squire Thornhill.

Blatant Beast, THE, in Spenser's 'Faerie Queene' (VI. xii), a monster, the personification of the calumnious voice of the world, begotten of Envy and Detraction. Sir Calidore (q.v.) pursues it, finds it despoiling monasteries and defiling the Church, overcomes it and chains it up. But finally it breaks the chain, 'and now he raungeth through the world again'. Cf. *Questing Beast*, below.

Blattergowl, MR., in Scott's 'The Antiquary' (q.v.), the minister of Trotcosey and a neighbour of Mr. Oldbuck.

Blavatsky, MADAME HELENA PETROVNA (1831–91), a Russian, who in 1873 became connected with spiritist research in New York, and there, with Col. H. S. Olcott and W. Q. Judge, founded the Theosophical Society. In 1879 she transferred her activities to India, where the Theosophical Society was organized on a new basis (see *Theosophy*).

Blazed Trail, The, a popular novel of the Michigan lumber camps, published in 1902, by the American writer, Stewart Edward White.

Bleak House, a novel by Dickens (q.v.), published in monthly parts in 1852–3.

The book contains a vigorous satire on the abuses of the old court of Chancery, the delays and costs of which brought misery and ruin on its suitors. The tale centres in the fortunes of an uninteresting couple, Richard Carstone, a futile youth, and his amiable cousin Ada Clare. They are wards of the court in the case of Jarndyce and Jarndyce, concerned with the distribution of an estate, which has gone on so long as to become a subject of heartless joking as well as a source of great profit to those professionally engaged in it. The wards are taken to live with their kind elderly relative John Jarndyce. They fall in love and secretly marry. The weak Richard, incapable of sticking to any profession and lured by the will-o'-the-wisp of the fortune that is to be his when the case is settled, sinks gradually to ruin and death, and the case of Jarndyce and Jarndyce comes suddenly to an end on the discovery that the costs have absorbed the whole estate in dispute.

When Ada goes to live with John Jarndyce, she is accompanied by Esther Summerson, a supposed orphan, one of Dickens's saints, and the narrative is partly supposed to be from her pen.

Sir Leicester Dedlock, a pompous old baronet, is devotedly attached to his beautiful wife, Lady Dedlock. The latter hides a dreadful secret under her haughty and indifferent exterior. Before her marriage she has loved a certain Captain Hawdon and has become the mother of a daughter, whom she believes dead. Hawdon is supposed to have perished at sea. In fact the daughter lives in the person of Esther Summerson, and Hawdon in that of a penniless scrivener. The accidental sight of his handwriting in a legal document discovers to Lady Dedlock the fact of his existence, and its effect on her awakens the cunning old lawyer Tulkinghorn to the existence of a mystery. Lady Dedlock's inquiries bring her, through the medium of a wretched crossing-sweeper, Jo, to the burial-ground where her former lover's miserable career has just ended. Jo's unguarded revelation of his singular experience with this veiled lady sets Tulkinghorn on the track, until he possesses all the facts and tells Lady Dedlock that he is going to expose her next day to her husband. That night Tulkinghorn is murdered. Bucket, the detective, presently reveals to the baronet what Tulkinghorn had discovered, and arrests a former French maid of Lady Dedlock, a violent woman, who has committed the murder. Lady Dedlock, learning that her husband knows her secret, flies from the house in despair, and is found dead near the grave of her lover, in spite of the efforts of her husband and Esther to save her.

Much of the story is occupied with Esther's devotion to John Jarndyce; her acceptance of his offer of marriage from a sense of duty and gratitude, though she loves a young doctor, Woodcourt; Jarndyce's discovery of the state of her heart; and his surrender of her to Woodcourt.

There are a host of interesting minor characters, among whom may be mentioned Harold Skimpole (drawn 'in the light externals of character' from Leigh Hunt), who disguises his utter selfishness under an assumption of childish irresponsibility; Mrs. Jellyby, who sacrifices her family to her selfish addiction to professional philanthropy; Jo, the crossing-sweeper, who is chivied by the police to his death; Chadband, the pious, eloquent humbug; Turveydrop, the model of deportment; Krook, the 'chancellor' of the rag and bone department, who dies of spontaneous combustion; Guppy, the lawyer's clerk; Guster, the poor slavey; the law-stationer Snagsby; Miss Flite, the little lunatic lady who haunts the Chancery courts; and Jarndyce's friend, the irascible and generous Boythorn (drawn from Walter Savage Landor).

The case of 'Jarndyce and Jarndyce' was suggested by the celebrated proceedings arising from the intestacy of one William Jennings, who died in 1798, leaving property at Birmingham worth many millions.

Bleeding Heart Yard, London, in Dickens's 'Little Dorrit' (q.v.), the abode of Pancks, the Plornishes, etc. It stood on the south side of Charles Street, Hatton Garden. The author of the 'Ingoldsby Legends' (q.v.) tells in 'The House-Warming' of the carrying off of Lady Hatton, wife of Sir Christopher, by the Devil, with whom she had a compact, and of the finding of her heart in this locality.

Blefuscu, in Swift's 'Gulliver's Travels' (q.v.), an island separated from Lilliput by a narrow channel.

Bleise or BLEYS, in Malory's 'Morte Darthur' and Tennyson's 'Coming of Arthur' (qq.v.), is described as the master of Merlin. He dwelt in Northumberland.

Blemmyes, a people of Africa, who, according to fable (Herodotus, iv. 85), had no heads, but eyes and mouth placed in the breast.

Blenheim, BATTLE OF (sometimes called battle of Hochstedt), in Bavaria, in 1704, in which Marlborough, having marched to the Upper Danube and joined Prince Eugene, defeated the French and Bavarians under Marshal Tallard. For poems on the battle see *Addison* and *Southey*.

Blenheim Palace, the mansion at Woodstock, Oxfordshire, erected by the nation for the duke of Marlborough after the battle of Blenheim (1704). It was designed by Vanbrugh (q.v.). Blenheim Park is part of the old 'Royal Chase' in which Woodstock Manor House stood. It was laid out by 'Capability' Brown.

Blessed Damozel, *The,* a poem by D. G. Rossetti (q.v.), of which the first version appeared in 'The Germ' (q.v., 1850); many revised versions appeared subsequently.

In this poem the maiden, 'one of God's choristers', leans out from the rampart of heaven, sees the worlds below and the souls mounting up to God, and prays that she may be united once more with the lover whom she has left on earth and whose own comments are introduced parenthetically into the poem.

BLESSINGTON, MARGUERITE POWER, *Countess of* (1789–1849), after an unhappy first union, married the earl of Blessington, and travelled on the Continent with him and Alfred, Count d'Orsay, with whom she ultimately lived. She published 'A Journal of Conversations with Lord Byron' in 1832, 'The Idler in Italy' and 'The Idler in France', and a number of novels.

Blifil, in Fielding's 'Tom Jones' (q.v.), a character representing the extreme of cunning hypocritical meanness.

Bligh, WILLIAM (1754–1817), the commander of H.M.S. 'Bounty' (q.v.) who was cast adrift by her mutinous crew. He was appointed governor of New South Wales (1805), and was forcibly deposed and imprisoned by disaffected military officers. He became vice-admiral of the Blue.

Blimber, DR., and his daughter CORNELIA, characters in Dickens's 'Dombey and Son' (q.v.).

Blind Beggar of Bethnal Green, see *Beggar's Daughter of Bednall Green.*

Blind Harry, see *Henry the Minstrel.*

Blithedale Romance, *The,* see *Hawthorne.*

BLOK, ALEXANDER ALEXANDRO-VICH (1880–1921), outstanding Russian Symbolist poet, one of a number of young poets influenced by the philosopher Vladimir Solovyov, from whom Blok took the central theme of his earlier poetry, Sophia, the feminine personification of Divine Wisdom. Later this exaltation turned to gloom and pessimism from which eventually a new positive theme of the love of Russia emerged. Blok at first welcomed the 1917 Revolution and his masterpiece 'The Twelve' (1918; tr. C. Bechhofer, 1920) is a mystical interpretation of it. Blok's other major works are 'Verses about the Beautiful Lady' (1904), 'Earth's Bubbles' (1905), 'The City' (1906), 'The Field of Kulikovo' (1908), 'The Scythians' (1918). Other translations appear in anthologies from 1929 onwards.

Blondel de Nesle, French poet, in legend a friend of Richard Cœur de Lion. Richard, on his return from the Holy Land in 1192, was imprisoned by the duke of Austria. According to Favine's 'Theatre of Honour and Knighthood' (translated from the French, London, 1623), Blondel set out to find him, for no news of him had reached England for a year Coming to a certain castle in Austria he heard that a single prisoner was detained there, but could not learn his name. Accordingly he sat under a window of the castle, and sang a song in French that he and the king had composed together: half-way through the song he paused, and Richard took up the other half and completed it. So Blondel returned to England and reported where the king was.

Blood, THOMAS (1618?–80), an adventurer who, among other exploits, headed an unsuccessful attempt to take Dublin Castle from the Royalists in 1663, and tried to steal the Crown jewels from the Tower in 1671. He figures in Scott's 'Peveril of the Peak' (q.v.).

Bloody Assizes, THE, the name given to the assizes held in 1685 in the west of England by Judge Jeffreys (q.v.) for the trial of the supporters of the duke of Monmouth after his defeat at Sedgemoor. Some 300 persons are said to have been executed and 1,000 sent as slaves to the American plantations.

Bloody Brother, *The,* or *Rollo, Duke of Normandy,* a play by J. Fletcher (q.v.), Jonson (q.v.), and perhaps other collaborators, produced about 1616.

The duke of Normandy has bequeathed his dukedom to his two sons Rollo and Otto. Rollo, the elder, a resolute and violent man, in order to secure the whole heritage, kills his brother and orders to immediate execution all who refuse to further his ends, including his old tutor Baldwin. The latter's daughter, Edith, pleads for his life, and her beauty captivates Rollo, but his order to stay the execution comes too late. Edith determines to avenge her father's death, and prepares to kill Rollo when he comes to woo her. His apparent repentance shakes her determination. While she hesitates, the brother of another of Rollo's victims enters and kills the tyrant. The scene between Latorch, Rollo's favourite, and the Astrologers was probably written by Jonson, as also part of Act IV, sc. i.

Bloom, LEOPOLD, a character in James Joyce's 'Ulysses' (q.v.).

Bloomer, a form of female attire that originated in America about 1850, being adopted for a time by some of the American pioneers of the movement for women's rights. 'It was invented by Mrs. Elizabeth Smith Miller, the daughter of Gerrit Smith, a prominent abolitionist, a great landowner in western New York. . . . Mrs. Miller wanted a dress in which she could easily take long walks about her country home. It consisted of a small jacket, a full skirt descending a little below the knee, and trousers down to the ankle. It was not beautiful, but was very comfortable and convenient and entirely modest. Mrs. Amelia Bloomer, editor of the "Lily", the first woman's paper, was much pleased with it, and advocated it warmly in her paper, and thus it became associated with her name.' (A. S. Blackwell, 'Lucy Stone: Pioneer of Woman's Rights', Boston, 1930.)

BLOOMFIELD, ROBERT (1766–1823), of humble origin, worked as an agricultural labourer and then as a shoemaker under his brother George in London, enduring extreme poverty. He is remembered as author of the poem, 'The Farmer's Boy', published in 1800, of which it is said that 26,000 copies were sold in less than three years. The similarity of his circumstances to those of John Clare (q.v.) leads to their being frequently compared, but the talent of Bloomfield was inferior to that of Clare.

Bloomsbury Group, the name given to a number of friends who began to meet about 1906 and included, among many others, John Maynard Keynes, Lytton Strachey, Virginia and Leonard Woolf, Vanessa and Clive Bell, David Garnett, Duncan Grant, E. M. Forster, and Roger Fry. The association, which was based on friendship and interest in the arts, derived its philosophy from the central passage of G. E. Moore's 'Principia Ethica': 'By far the most valuable things . . . are . . . the pleasures of human intercourse and the enjoyment of beautiful objects; . . . it is they . . . that form the rational ultimate end of social progress.'

Bloomsbury Square, near the British Museum, was one of the first squares to be laid out in London (by the earl of Southampton in 1665). Bloomsbury, part of the old manor of Rugmere, was so called from one Blemund, owner of the land in the time of King John. Sir Charles Sedley, Steele, Disraeli, and other notable persons lived there.

Blossom's Inn or BOSOM'S INN, an inn in Lawrence Lane, Cheapside, occasionally referred to by Elizabethan writers.

'Our jolly clothiers kept up their courage and went to Blossom's Inn, so called from a greasy old fellow who built it, who always went nudging with his head in his bosom winter and summer, so that they called him the picture of old Winter.' (Deloney, 'History of Thomas of Reading', c. ii; in the rest of the tale the name is given as 'Bosom's Inn'.)

Blot in the 'Scutcheon, A, a tragedy in three acts, by R. Browning (q.v.), performed at Covent Garden Theatre in 1843.

The events take place in the 18th cent. Lord Henry Mertoun loves Mildred, the sister and ward of Lord Tresham, and delays to ask her hand of him until he has already become intimate with her. Lord Tresham willingly gives his consent, but, warned by a retainer that some man has access to Mildred's chamber, obtains from her an admission of her guilt, but not a confession of her lover's name. Lord Tresham surprises Mertoun and kills him, but is filled with despair by the youth's story of his love, error, and remorse, and the sense that he has ruined his sister's happiness. Mildred dies of a broken heart and Lord Tresham takes poison.

Blougram, BISHOP, see *Bishop Blougram's Apology.*

Blount, MARTHA (1690–1762), the friend of Pope to whom he dedicated his 'Epistle on Women' ('Moral Essays') and his Epistles 'To a Young Lady with the Works of Voiture' and 'To the same on her leaving the Town' (in which occurs the character of Zephalinda).

Blouzelinda, a shepherdess in 'The Shepherd's Week' of J. Gay (q.v.).

Blue and the Gray, THE, familiar names for the armies of the North and South during the American Civil War, referring to the fact that the first wore blue uniforms and the second gray.

Blue and Yellow, The, the 'Edinburgh Review' (q.v.), so called from the colours of its cover, which were the election colours of the Whig party when the Review was started.

Blue Beard, a popular tale in an oriental setting, from the French of Perrault (q.v.), translated by Robert Samber (1729?).

A man of great wealth, but disfigured by a blue beard, and of evil reputation because he has married several wives who have disappeared, asks for the hand of Fatima, the younger of the two daughters of a neighbouring lady of quality. At last she is prevailed on to marry him. Blue Beard, called away on business, leaves the keys of all his treasures to his young wife, but strictly enjoins her not to make use of the key of a particular room.

Overcome by curiosity, she opens this room and finds in it the bodies of Blue Beard's previous wives. Horror-struck, she drops the key, which becomes indelibly stained with blood. Blue Beard returns, discovers her disobedience, and orders her to death. She begs for a little delay, 'Sister Anne' sees her brothers arriving, and Blue Beard is killed before he can execute the sentence.

Andrew Lang, in his 'Perrault's Popular Tales', discusses the many parallel stories found in other countries. Blue Beard is identified by local tradition in Brittany with Gilles de Retz (q.v.).

Blue Stocking, a woman having or affecting literary tastes. The origin of the term is to be found in the evening parties held about 1750 in the houses of Mrs. Vesey, Mrs. Montagu, and Mrs. Ord, who endeavoured to substitute for card-playing, which then formed the principal recreation, more intellectual modes of spending the time, including conversations on literary subjects in which eminent men of letters often took part. Many of those who attended eschewed 'full dress', among them Benjamin Stillingfleet, who habitually wore blue worsted, in lieu of black silk, stockings. In reference to this, Admiral Boscawen is said to have dubbed the coterie the 'Blue Stocking Society' [OED.]. There is an account of the 'Blue-stocking Clubs' in Boswell, under the year 1781, and Hannah More (q.v.) wrote a poem 'Bas Bleu, or Conversation' on the same subject. Mrs. Chapone (q.v.) was another member of the coterie.

Blue-coat School, a charity school of which the pupils wear the almoner's blue coat. Of these schools there are many in England, the most noted being Christ's Hospital (q.v.), formerly in London, founded by Edward VI, whose uniform is a long dark blue gown fastened at the waist by a belt, and bright yellow stockings.

Bluemantle, one of the four Pursuivants attached to the English College of Arms (see *Heralds' College*).

Blue-nose, a nickname for a native of Nova Scotia (the term frequently occurs in Haliburton's 'Sam Slick'); also applied to Nova Scotian ships.

Blues, THE, the Regiment of Royal Horse Guards, originally the Royal Regiment of Horse, one of the New Model regiments disbanded in 1660 and immediately raised afresh, so called from the colour of its uniform.

Bluffe, CAPTAIN, a character in Congreve's 'The Old Bachelor' (q.v.).

Blumine, in Carlyle's 'Sartor Resartus' (q.v.), the lady with whom Herr Teufelsdröckh falls in love (probably based on a Miss Margaret Gordon, whom Carlyle knew and admired before he met Jane Welsh).

BLUNDEN, EDMUND CHARLES (1896–), poet and scholar, educated at Christ's Hospital and Queen's College, Oxford. He served with the Royal Sussex during the war of 1914–18, and his 'Undertones of War' (1928) is an outcome of this experience. After his own poetry (collected edition, 1930; later poems, 1940), his greatest service to poetry has been the researches into and discovery and publication of the hitherto unpublished poems of John Clare (q.v.). He has also published the first adequate biography of Leigh Hunt (1930), and 'Shelley, a Life Story' (1946). He was elected professor of poetry at Oxford in 1966.

Blunderbore, a giant in the tale of 'Jack the Giant-killer' (q.v.).

BLUNT, WILFRID SCAWEN (1840–1922), poet and publicist, author of 'The Love Sonnets of Proteus' (1880) and other volumes of poetry (complete edition, 1914). His political life and writings were all in defence of nationalism, Irish, Egyptian, and Indian.

Boadicea, BONDUCA, misspellings for BOUDICCA, queen of the Iceni in the east of Britain, who led a revolt against the Romans, but was finally defeated by Suetonius Paulinus in A.D. 61 and took her own life.

'Boadicea' is the title and subject of a poem in galliambics by Tennyson; also of a fine ballad by W. Cowper. See also *Bonduca*.

Boanerges, 'sons of thunder', the name given by Jesus Christ to James and John (Mark iii. 17), because they offered to call down fire from heaven to consume the inhospitable Samaritans (Luke ix. 54).

Boar of the Ardennes, THE WILD, William Count de la Marck, who figures in Scott's 'Quentin Durward' (q.v.).

Boar's Head Inn, THE, celebrated in connexion with Falstaff (Shakespeare's 'Henry IV'), was in Eastcheap, where the statue of William IV now stands. The inn existed until 1831. It is the subject of a paper in Washington Irving's 'Sketch Book'. One of the best of Goldsmith's essays is his 'Reverie in the Boar's Head Tavern at Eastcheap'.

Boaz and **Jachin,** the names of the two pillars set up by Solomon in the porch of the Temple (1 Kings vii. 21).

Bob and wheel: in prosody the *wheel* is a set of short lines forming the concluding part of a stanza, usually five in number, varying in form and length, but generally having the first line rhyming with the last, and often the intervening lines rhyming with each other; the first line in some types is very short, and is then called the *bob* [OED.].

Bob Logic, in 'Life in London', by Egan (q.v.), the Oxonian associate of Jerry Hawthorn and Corinthian Tom.

Bobadill, CAPTAIN, a character in Jonson's 'Every Man in his Humour' (q.v.), an old soldier, vain, boastful, and cowardly, notable among the braggarts of comedy for his gravity and decorum.

FRANCESCO BOBADILLA was the Spanish governor of Hispaniola, appointed in 1499, who put Columbus and his brother in chains, and sent them back to Spain.

BOABDIL, a corruption of Abou Abdullah, was the last Moorish king of Granada (1482–92), a pathetic figure in Washington Irving's 'Conquest of Granada'.

Bobby, a slang nickname for a policeman, probably an allusion to the name of Mr. (afterwards Sir) Robert Peel, who was home secretary when the new Metropolitan Police Act was passed in 1828. Cf. *Peelers*.

BOCCACCIO, GIOVANNI (1313–75), Italian writer and humanist, was born at or near Florence, the son of a Florentine merchant. His formative years, from about 1325 until 1340, were spent in Naples, where he began his literary studies and wrote some of his first works. His outlook was greatly conditioned by the aristocratic society in which he moved and especially by his contacts with the Angevin court, but the tradition that he fell in love with Maria d'Aquino, illegitimate daughter of King Robert of Naples, is now discredited. He returned to Florence in 1340, and witnessed the ravages of the Black Death in 1348, described in the introduction to the first day of the 'Decameron' (q.v.). From 1350 onwards the municipality of Florence employed him on various diplomatic missions. His friendship with Petrarch (q.v.)—whom he first met in 1350—gave a powerful impetus to his classical studies, and his house became an important centre of humanist activity. He wrote a Life of Dante (q.v.) and was the first to deliver a course of public lectures on the text of the 'Divine Comedy' (1373–4). Boccaccio's chief works, apart from the 'Decameron' were: 'Filocolo', a prose romance embodying the story of 'Flores and Blancheflour' (q.v.); 'Filostrato', a poem on the story of Troilus and Cressida; 'Teseida', a poem on the story of Theseus, Palamon, and Arcite, which was translated by Chaucer; 'Ameto', a combination of allegory and pastoral romance, partly in prose, partly in verse; the 'Amorosa visione', an uncompleted allegorical poem; 'Fiammetta', a psychological romance in prose, in which the woman herself recounts the various phases of her unhappy love; the 'Ninfale fiesolano', an eponymic idyll translated into English (from a French version) by an Elizabethan, John Goubourne. He also wrote a number of encyclopaedic works in Latin: the 'Genologia deorum gentilium'; the 'De casibus virorum illustrium'; the 'De claris mulieribus', etc.

Boccaccio is an important figure in the history of literature, particularly of narrative fiction, and among the poets who found inspiration in his works were Chaucer, Shakespeare, Dryden, Keats, Longfellow, and Tennyson.

Boche, a French popular and contemptuous name for a German which came into vogue in England in 1914–18.

Bodle, a Scottish copper coin of the value of two pennies Scots or (*c*. 1600) one-sixth of an English penny. The name is reputed to be derived from the name of a mint-master *Bothwell*, but no documentary evidence is cited. [OED.]

Bodleian Library, see *Bodley*.

Bodley, SIR THOMAS (1545–1613), was educated at Geneva, whither his parents had fled during the Marian persecution, and subsequently at Magdalen College, Oxford. After being for some time a lecturer in that university, he travelled abroad, and from 1588 to 1596 was English diplomatic representative at The Hague. He devoted the rest of his life and most of his resources to founding at Oxford the great library that bears his name. It was opened in 1602. In 1609 Bodley endowed it with land in Berkshire and houses in London, and in 1610 the Stationers' Company undertook to give to the library a copy of every book printed in England. It received also important gifts of books, in its early days, from Laud, Oliver Cromwell, and Robert Burton (author of the 'Anatomy of Melancholy'). Among other considerable accessions may be mentioned John Selden's library, received in 1659, and the Tanner, Rawlinson, Gough, Malone, Douce, and Hope collections of books and MSS., and John Nichols's collection of newspapers in more recent times. The Canonici MSS. were purchased in 1817 and the Oppenheimer Collection of Hebrew books in 1829. Many of the MSS. of John Locke were acquired in 1947. The Bodleian shares with the Cambridge University Library, the National Library of Scotland (see *Advocates' Library*), the Library of Trinity College, Dublin, and (with limitations) the National Library of Wales, the right, under the Copyright Act (1911), to receive on demand a copy of every book published in the United Kingdom. Macray's 'Annals of the Bodleian' (1868, 1890) and Sir Edmund Craster's 'History of the Bodleian Library, 1845–1945' (1952) are standard works on the Library.

BOECE, see *Boëthius*.

BOECE or BOËTHIUS, HECTOR (1465?–1536), a native of Dundee and a student in the University of Paris, where he became a professor. He published Latin lives of the bishops of Mortlach and Aberdeen (1522), and a Latin history of Scotland to the accession of James III (1526), the latter including many fabulous narratives, among others that of Macbeth and Duncan, which passed into Holinshed's chronicles and thence to Shakespeare.

BOEHME, JACOB (1575–1624), a peasant shoemaker of Görlitz in Germany, a mystic. The essential features of his doctrine were that will is the original force, that all manifestation involves opposition, notably of God and nature, that existence emerges from a process of conflict between pairs of contrasted principles (light and darkness, love and anger, good and evil, and so forth) and that in this way the universe is to be seen as the revelation of God. The doctrine of Boehme strongly influenced W. Law (q.v.). English translations of Boehme's works, by various hands, appeared in 1645–62. A reprint of the works in English, ed. C. J. Barker, was published in 1910–24.

Boeotia (pron. Bē-ō′shia), a country in central Greece, surrounded by mountains, containing the valleys of the Cephissus and Asōpus, and having Thebes for its capital. Its inhabitants were proverbial for dullness of intellect, but the country gave birth to many illustrious men, such as Hesiod, Pindar, Plutarch, and Democritus (qq.v.). 'Boeotian' has come to be used as a derogatory adjective, synonymous with boorish, dull-witted.

BOËTHIUS, ANICIUS MANLIUS SE-VERINUS, frequently referred to as 'Boece' in the Middle Ages, born at Rome between A.D. 470 and 475, was consul in 510 and in favour with Theodoric the Great; but incurring his suspicion of plotting against the Gothic rule, was imprisoned and put to death in 525. In prison he wrote the celebrated work, 'De Consolatione Philosophiae', which was translated by King Alfred (q.v.). Two versions of the translation exist, in one of which the metrical portions of the original are rendered in prose, in the other in verse. The 'De Consolatione' was also translated by Chaucer under the title 'Boethius', by Queen Elizabeth, and by others.

Boffin, MR. and MRS., characters in Dickens's 'Our Mutual Friend' (q.v.).

Boggley Wallah, THE COLLECTOR OF, Jos Sedley, a character in Thackeray's 'Vanity Fair' (q.v.).

Bogle, *The Rhyme of Sir Lancelot,* see *Bon Gaultier Ballads.*

Bogomils, a sect which arose in the 13th cent. in Bulgaria, holding heretical views on the divine birth of Christ, on the sacraments, and on other points of dogma. They held Manichaean (q.v.) opinions on the dual origin of good and evil.

Bohème, *Scènes de la vie de,* a well-known romance of Paris student life, by Henry Murger (1822–61), published in 1848; Puccini's opera 'La Bohème' was founded on it.

Bohemia, SEA COAST OF: in Shakespeare's 'The Winter's Tale', III. iii, Antigonus says, 'our ship hath touched upon the deserts of Bohemia'. Sometimes quoted as one of the rare instances where Shakespeare failed in general knowledge, since Bohemia is an entirely inland country.

Bohemia, *Story of the King of,* told by Corporal Trim in vol. viii of Sterne's 'Tristram Shandy' (q.v.).

Bohemian is frequently used in the sense of a gipsy of society, especially an artist, literary man, or actor, who leads a free, vagabond, or irregular life, and despises conventionalities. In this sense the term was adopted from French, in which *bohème, bohémien,* have been applied to the gipsies since their first appearance in the 15th cent., because they were thought to come from Bohemia. The word, with this meaning, was introduced into English by Thackeray. [OED.]

BOHN, HENRY GEORGE (1796–1884), publisher, and author of the 'Guinea Catalogue' of old books (1841), a valuable early bibliographical work. Among Bohn's many publications ('Standard Library', 'Classical Library', 'Scientific Library', &c.) may be specially mentioned his 'Antiquarian Library' (1847 onwards).

BOHR, NIELS HENRIK DAVID (1885–1962), Danish theoretical physicist. He came to Manchester in 1912 to work in Rutherford's laboratory and in 1916 was appointed professor of theoretical physics at Copenhagen. He applied the quantum theory to the problem of atomic structure and became the leader of theoretical atomic physics. He was awarded the Nobel Prize for Physics in 1922. His researches led to the theory of nuclear fission and the development of the atomic bomb. After the German occupation of Denmark in the Second World War he escaped to Sweden, then to England, and finally to the United States, where he took part in work on the atomic bomb. He was deeply concerned about the implications of the bomb in world politics and appealed for mutual confidence among the great powers and for interchange of knowledge between scientists. In 1957 he was awarded the first Ford 'Atoms for Peace' prize. His publications include 'Theory of Spectra and Atomic Constitution' (1922) and 'Atomic Theory and Description of Nature' (1935).

BOIARDO, MATTEO MARIA (1441 ?–94), an Italian poet of the old chivalry, who drew on the legends of Arthur and Charlemagne for his materials. His principal work was the unfinished 'Orlando Innamorato' (q.v.).

BOILEAU (DESPRÉAUX), NICOLAS (1636–1711), French critic and poet, the friend of Molière, La Fontaine, and Racine, who by his 'Satires', 'Épîtres', and 'Art Poétique', remarkable for discrimination and good sense, did much to form French literary taste, previously vitiated by Spanish and Italian influences. He was known as the *législateur du Parnasse.*

Bois-Guilbert, SIR BRIAN DE, the fierce Templar in Scott's 'Ivanhoe' (q.v.).

Boke of the Duchesse, *The,* a poem of some 1,300 lines by Chaucer, written in 1369. It is an allegorical lament on the death of Blanche of Lancaster, first wife of John of Gaunt. In a dream the poet joins a hunting party of the Emperor Octovien. He comes upon a knight in black who laments the loss of his lady. The knight tells of her virtues and beauty and their courtship, and in answer to a question declares her dead. The hunting party reappears, a bell strikes twelve, and the poet awakes, with the story of Ceyx and Halcyone, which he had been reading, in his hand.

Bold, JOHN, a character in Trollope's 'The Warden' (q.v.). Mrs. Bold, his widow, figures prominently in its sequel, 'Barchester Towers' (q.v.), and in 'The Last Chronicle of Barset', where she is the wife of Dean Arabin.

Bold Stroke for a Wife, A, a comedy by Mrs. Centlivre (q.v.), produced in 1718. Colonel Fainall, to win the consent of Obadiah Prim, the Quaker guardian of Anne Lovely, to his marriage with the latter, impersonates Simon Pure, 'a quaking preacher'. No sooner has he obtained it than the true Quaker arrives and proves himself 'the real Simon Pure', a phrase that has become proverbial.

BOLDREWOOD, ROLF, pseudonym of T. A. BROWNE (q.v.).

Boldwood, FARMER, a character in Hardy's 'Far from the Madding Crowd' (q.v.).

Bolingbroke, son of John of Gaunt, the future Henry IV, figures in Shakespeare's 'Richard II' (q.v.).

BOLINGBROKE, HENRY ST. JOHN, *first Viscount* (1678–1751), educated at Eton and perhaps Christ Church, Oxford, a supporter of Harley and the Tory party in parliament, became secretary of state in 1710, was created Viscount Bolingbroke in 1712, and was in charge of the negotiations which led to the treaty of Utrecht (1713). He founded the 'Brothers' Club' (q.v.) in 1711. He was dismissed from office on the accession of George I, was attainted, and his name was erased from the roll of peers. He fled to France and was secretary of state to James the Pretender, from whose service he was dismissed in 1716. He was pardoned and returned to London in 1725, and settled at Dawley, Middlesex. It is to the following period that his principal political and philosophical writings belong. He contributed to the 'Craftsman' (q.v.) from 1727 to 1735 a number of virulent attacks on the Whig government under Walpole and Townshend, notably in the 'Remarks on the History of England' (1730–1) and in 'A Dissertation upon Parties' (1735). In 1735 he retired to Chanteloup in Touraine, and there wrote his 'Letters on the Study and Use of History' (1752), in which he points out the failure of English historical literature to produce either a general history, or particular histories, comparable to those of foreign nations. In 1736 he wrote 'A Letter on the Spirit of Patriotism' (q.v.), and in 1738 'The Idea of a Patriot King' (q.v.). In politics he advocated a kind of democratic Toryism, anticipating that of Disraeli. Pope was responsible for the

printing of a private edition of the 'Letters on History' (1738) and for another of 'The Idea of a Patriot King' (1740). He also had printed, probably unknown to the author, a larger edition of the 'Patriot King' which later fell into Bolingbroke's hands and prompted his attack on Pope in the authorized edition (1749).

After Bolingbroke's death David Mallet published the 'Letters on History' (1752), the 'Letter to Sir William Windham' (q.v., written 1717) together with two other short pieces (1753), and, in 1754, his collected works including a number of essays of a deistical tendency. These were probably written in connexion with Pope's 'Essay on Man' (q.v.).

Bolivar, SIMON (1783–1830), 'The Liberator', the leader of the revolution of Venezuela against Spain. He founded the republic of Colombia, uniting Venezuela, New Granada (the modern Colombia), and Ecuador; became dictator of Peru; and formed the republic of Bolivia. Peru and Bolivia turned against him in 1826, and the republic of Colombia broke up soon after his death.

Bollandists, Belgian Jesuits who publish the 'Acta Sanctorum', legends of saints arranged according to the days of the calendar. The work was begun at Antwerp by John Bolland, a Flemish Jesuit of the 17th cent., the first volume appearing in 1643, and the last volume of the original series in 1786 after the dispersal of the Jesuits. The Bollandists were re-established in Brussels in 1837 and continue their hagiographic studies, but in a more historical spirit. Their quarterly review ('Analecta Bollandiana') was founded in 1882.

Bolt Court, Fleet Street, contained the home of Dr. Johnson from 1776 to 1784. Cobbett (q.v.) published his 'Political Register' there.

Bolton, FANNY, a character in Thackeray's 'Pendennis' (q.v.).

Bomba, KING, Ferdinand II (of the Bourbon dynasty) of Naples, whose treacherous and tyrannical reign extended from 1830 to 1859, so called on account of his bombardment of Messina in 1848.

Bombastes Furioso, a burlesque by William Barnes Rhodes (1772–1826), published in 1810, with illustrations by G. Cruikshank. The name is applied to a person who talks in a bombastic way. (The word 'bombast' originally means cotton-wool, hence cotton-wool used as padding, and so inflated language.)

The characters in the burlesque are King Artaxominous, Fusbos, his minister, General Bombastes, and Distaffina. The king is divided in his affections between his queen Griskinissa and Distaffina, who is beloved by Bombastes. He is discovered in Distaffina's cupboard by Bombastes and prepares to hang himself, but decides to hang up his boots instead. Bombastes fights with and kills the king, and is in turn wounded by Fusbos:

> Here lies Bombastes, stout of heart and limb,
> Who conquer'd all but Fusbos—Fusbos him.

Fortunately the dead revive and all join hands and dance.

Bombastus, in Butler's 'Hudibras' (II. iii, q.v.), refers to Paracelsus (q.v.).

Bon Gaultier Ballads, a collection of parodies and light poems by W. E. Aytoun (q.v.) and Sir T. Martin (q.v.), published in 1845. Among the authors parodied are Tennyson (notably his 'Locksley Hall', in the 'Lay of the Lovelorn'), Macaulay, Lockhart, and Mrs. Browning (in 'The Rhyme of Sir Lancelot Bogle').

'Bon Gaultier' was the pseudonym under which Sir Theodore Martin contributed to 'Tait's' and 'Fraser's' magazines. It is taken from Rabelais (Prologue to 'Gargantua'), who uses the words in the sense of 'good fellow' or 'good companion' ('Gaultier' is a proper name generalized).

Bond Street, London, named after Sir Thomas Bond, who began its construction about 1688. Sterne, Sir T. Lawrence, and Boswell (qq.v.) lived there at various times. It has long been famous for its shops.

Bonduca (Boadicea), a tragedy by J. Fletcher (q.v.), produced some time before March 1619 (the date of the death of Richard Burbage, who acted in it).

The tragedy is based on the story of Boadicea (q.v.) as given by Holinshed. But the principal character in the tragedy is Caratach (Caractacus), the sagacious and patriotic soldier, a generous enemy, and a wise counsellor to the impetuous British queen. The play presents the battles in which Boadicea is defeated and killed, her daughters take their lives, and Caratach is taken prisoner. Incidents worked into the general action are the love of the Roman officer Junius for Bonduca's daughter, and her treachery; and the disobedience of Poenius Postumus to his general's orders, expiated by his suicide.

Boniface, the landlord of the inn in Farquhar's 'The Beaux' Stratagem' (q.v.); whence taken as the generic proper name of innkeepers.

Boniface, ABBOT, in Scott's 'The Monastery' (q.v.), the abbot of Kennaquhair.

Boniface, ST. (680–755), the apostle of Germany, born at Kirton or Crediton in Devonshire, was educated in a monastery at Exeter and at Nursling, near Winchester. He went to Rome in 718, and with authority from Pope Gregory II, proceeded to Germany, where he preached, established monasteries, and organized the Church. He was slain with his followers by pagans at Dokkum on the Bordau. He is commemorated on 5 June.

His original name is said to have been *Wynfrith.*

Bonnivard, see *Prisoner of Chillon.*

Bonny Dundee, Graham of Claverhouse (q.v.).

Bontemps, ROGER, the subject of a song by P. J. de Béranger (q.v.), the type of cheerful contentment.

Bonthron, ANTHONY, in Scott's 'Fair Maid of Perth' (q.v.), a villainous cut-throat, employed by Sir John Ramorny to murder Henry Smith and the duke of Rothsay.

Booby, SIR THOMAS and LADY, and SQUIRE BOOBY, characters in Fielding's 'Joseph Andrews' (q.v.).

Boojum, in Lewis Carroll's 'The Hunting of the Snark', an imaginary creature, a dangerous variety of the snark.

Book of Kells, see *Kells.*

Book of Martyrs, see *Actes and Monuments.*

Book of Mormon, see *Mormons.*

Book of St. Albans, The, was the last work issued (1486) by the press that was set up at St. Albans about 1479, soon after Caxton had begun to print at Westminster. It contains treatises on hawking, hunting, and heraldry, and its authorship is attributed to a certain Juliana Berners, whom tradition represents as prioress of the nunnery of Sopwell in Hertfordshire. The book is a compilation and probably not all by one hand. An edition printed by Wynkyn de Worde in 1496 also included a treatise on 'Fishing with an Angle'.

Book of Snobs, The, see *Snobs of England.*

Book of the Duchess, The, see *Boke.*

Booksellers' Row, a name that was given to the old Holywell Street, which ran parallel to the Strand between St. Clement Dane's and St. Dunstan's, before the formation of Aldwych at the end of the 19th cent.; so called from the number of second-hand booksellers that had shops there.

Boone, DANIEL (1735–1820), American pioneer, explorer, and Indian fighter, who played a notable part in the opening up and settlement of Kentucky and Missouri. His name is a synonym for pioneering courage, sagacity, and endurance. Byron devotes to him seven stanzas in the eighth canto of 'Don Juan'.

Boötes, from the Greek word meaning ploughman, wagoner; a northern constellation, 'the Wagoner', situated at the tail of the Great Bear and containing the bright star Arcturus. See *Icarius.*

BOOTH, CHARLES (1840–1916), a successful shipowner, was author of a monumental inquiry into the condition and occupations of the people of London, of which the earlier part appeared as 'Labour and Life of the People' in 1889, and the whole as 'Life and

Labour of the People in London' in seventeen volumes (1891–1903). Its object was to show 'the numerical relation which poverty, misery, and depravity bear to regular earnings and comparative comfort, and to describe the general conditions under which each class lives'. The passing of the Old Age Pensions Act in 1908 was largely due to Booth's advocacy of this reform.

After an interval of forty years a 'New Survey of London Life and Labour' on the lines of Booth's inquiry was undertaken in 1928 by the London School of Economics with Sir Hubert Llewellen Smith as Director. It was completed in 9 vols. in 1935.

Booth, WILLIAM (1829–1912), popularly known as 'General' Booth, famous as the founder of the Salvation Army (q.v.), was born in a suburb of Nottingham, the son of a speculative builder. He joined the Methodists, and became a travelling preacher of Methodism, but broke with his Church and turned independent revivalist. He started his Christian Mission in Whitechapel, the nucleus of the Salvation Army, in 1865. Though entirely ignorant of theology, and a man of narrow prejudices, he became, by his sympathy for the degraded poor, by his fervour, and by his gift for advertisement, a considerable force in the religious life of the country.

Booth, WILLIAM, the hero of Fielding's 'Amelia' (q.v.).

Bör or BORR, in Scandinavian mythology, the son of Buri (the first man, made by the cow Audhumla licking the salt stones), and father of Odin (q.v.).

Borachio, a large leather bottle or bag used in Spain for wine or other liquors; hence a drunkard, a mere 'wine-bag'. Shakespeare used the word as the name of one of the characters in his 'Much Ado about Nothing' (q.v.), and it occurs in Congreve, Middleton, etc., to signify a drunkard.

Borak, AL, the winged horse of Mohammed, on which he was, in a vision, borne to Jerusalem and to heaven.

Borderers, The, a tragedy by Wordsworth (q.v.), composed in 1795–6.

The gentle Marmaduke, leader (in the reign of Henry III) of a band of Borderers whom he has collected to protect the innocent, is induced by the perfidy of the villainous Oswald to cause the death of the blind old Baron Herbert, whose daughter Idonea he loves, being led to believe that her father intends to sell her into infamy.

Boreas, the North wind, regarded as a divine being by the ancient Greeks, and brother of the other winds, Zephyrus and Notus. Identified with the Aquilo of the Romans.

Borgia, CESARE (1476–1507), favourite son of Pope Alexander VI, notorious for his violence and crimes, at the same time a man of great military capacity, and one of the early believers in the unity of Italy. He per-

haps murdered his brother Giovanni, duke of Gandia, and he instigated the murder of Alfonso of Aragon, his sister Lucrezia's husband. He conquered Romagna, but his position was shaken by a conspiracy of the dispossessed or threatened nobles (the Orsini, Baglioni, etc.). Borgia decoyed them to his house, had them arrested, and two of them strangled. His power came to an end after the death of his father. Julius II had him arrested, but he was released on condition of surrendering his castles in Romagna. Borgia fled to the court of Navarre (he had married Charlotte, sister of the king of Navarre), and was killed in the service of the king. He is, to a considerable extent, the 'hero' of Machiavelli's 'Il Principe'.

Borgia, LUCREZIA (1480–1519), daughter of Pope Alexander VI and sister of Cesare Borgia (q.v.). She was married when very young to Don Gasparo de Procida, but the marriage was annulled by her father, and she was betrothed to Giovanni Sforza. This engagement was also cancelled by her father for political reasons, and Lucrezia was married to Alfonso of Aragon, a relative of the king of Naples. Alfonso was murdered by direction of Cesare Borgia, and Lucrezia then married Alfonso d'Este, heir to the duke of Ferrara, being at the time 22. Her life henceforth was peaceful, and when her husband reached the throne, her court became a centre for artists, poets, and men of learning, such as Ariosto, Titian, and Aldus Manutius (qq.v.).

Borgia, RODRIGO (1431–1503), Pope Alexander VI, a Spaniard by birth, the father of Cesare and Lucrezia Borgia (qq.v.), elected to the pontificate in 1492. His policy was mainly directed to the recovery of the Papal States and the unscrupulous promotion of the interests of his family. The tradition that the Borgias possessed the secret of a mysterious and deadly poison, which they used against their enemies, has not been substantiated by historical research. It may be accounted for by the hostility of contemporary chroniclers and by the tendency to attribute to poison any unexplained and sudden death.

BORON or BORRON, ROBERT DE, a 12th–13th-cent. French poet, who composed a trilogy—'Joseph d'Arimathie', 'Merlin', and 'Perceval', in which he developed the early story of the Holy Grail (q.v.) and linked it with the Arthurian tradition. Of the trilogy only the first poem and part of the second survive.

Borough or **Burrough,** STEPHEN (1525–84) and his brother William (1536–99), navigators, remembered especially for their exploratory voyages to Russia round the North Cape.

Borough, THE, London, signifies Southwark (q.v.).

Borough, The, a poem by Crabbe (q.v.), published in 1810, in twenty-four 'Letters' describing life and character as seen by the poet in Aldeburgh. Among the most striking of the tales are those of 'Peter Grimes', 'Ellen Orford', and 'Clelia' (qq.v.).

Borr, see *Bör*.

BORROW, GEORGE (1803–81), was educated at Edinburgh High School and at Norwich and articled to a solicitor, but adopted literature as a profession. He assisted in compiling the 'Newgate Calendar' (q.v.), and then travelled through England, France, Germany, Russia, Spain, and in the East, studying the languages of the countries he visited. In Russia and Spain he acted as agent for the British and Foreign Bible Society, and in the latter country as correspondent for 'The Times'. Finally he settled near Oulton Broad in Suffolk, where he became celebrated for his promiscuous hospitality. He published a number of books based in part on his own life, experiences, and travels: 'The Zincali, or an account of the Gypsies in Spain' (1841), 'The Bible in Spain' (q.v., 1843), 'Lavengro' (q.v., 1851), 'The Romany Rye' (q.v., 1857), and 'Wild Wales' (1862). His novels have a peculiar picaresque quality, graphically presenting a succession of gipsies, rogues, strange characters, and adventures of all kinds, without much coherence, the whole permeated with the spirit of the 'wind on the heath' and of the unconventional. 'Lavengro' and 'The Romany Rye' are largely autobiographical, but the border-line between autobiography and fiction in them is hard to trace.

Bors de Ganis, SIR, in Malory's 'Morte Darthur', one of the knights of the Round Table, and cousin of Sir Launcelot. He takes part in the quest of the Holy Grail.

BOSCAN, JUAN (*c.* 1490–1542), a Spanish poet born at Barcelona, who did much to introduce Italian verse forms into the poetry of his country. He was an intimate friend of another Spanish poet, Garcilasso de la Vega (q.v.), and the two are mentioned together by Byron in 'Don Juan' (i. 95).

Boscobel, a farm near Shifnal in Shropshire, where Charles II lay in hiding after the battle of Worcester. The 'royal oak', which stood near it, has now disappeared. See also *Pendrell*.

Bosola, a character in Webster's 'The Duchess of Malfi' (q.v.).

Bosom's Inn, see *Blossom's Inn*.

Bosphorus, or more correctly BOSPORUS, the channel between the Black Sea and the Sea of Marmora, said to be so called from the legend of Io (q.v.).

BOSSUET, JACQUES BÉNIGNE (1627–1704), French divine and famous preacher, one of the leading figures at the court of Louis XIV, of whose son, the Dauphin, he was tutor, and bishop of Meaux. His fame rests principally on his eloquent funeral orations on great personages of the reign. His 'Discours sur l'histoire universelle' (1681) is a summary of history in which the divine intervention is traced at each stage. He also wrote an 'Histoire des variations des Églises protestantes' (1688). Bossuet was a rigidly dogmatic theologian; he entered into controversy with Fénelon (q.v.) on the subject of Quietism (q.v.) and secured the condemnation of his adversary's doctrines by the court of Rome.

Boston Tea Party, the name given to the act of violence by which the American colonists in 1773 manifested their objection to the tea duty imposed by parliament. A large quantity of tea shipped to Boston was on arrival seized and thrown into the harbour by a number of young men disguised as Red Indians.

Bostonians, The, a novel by Henry James (q.v.), published in 1866.

BOSWELL, JAMES (1740–95), born at Edinburgh, the son of Alexander Boswell, Lord Auchinleck, a Scottish judge who took his title from the family estate in Ayrshire. He was educated at Edinburgh High School and University, and reluctantly studied law at Edinburgh, Glasgow, and Utrecht, his ambition being directed to literature or politics. He made the acquaintance of Samuel Johnson (q.v.) in London in 1763. After his sojourn at Utrecht (1763–4) he travelled on the Continent until 1766, and was introduced to General Paoli in Corsica. As a result he became absorbed in Corsican affairs, and published 'An Account of Corsica' in 1768, and 'Essays in Favour of the Brave Corsicans' in 1769. Boswell paid frequent visits to Johnson in London (from Edinburgh, where he practised at the bar) between 1772 and 1784, and made a tour in Scotland and the Hebrides with Johnson in 1773. He was elected a member of the Literary Club in 1773, succeeded to his father's estate in 1782, was called to the English bar in 1786, and was recorder of Carlisle in 1788–90. In 1789 he came to reside in London. His 'Journal of a Tour to the Hebrides' appeared in 1785. He had been storing up materials for his great work, the 'Life of Samuel Johnson', since 1763, and after Johnson's death in 1784 he applied himself to the task under pressure from Malone. The book appeared in 1791, and proved Boswell's extraordinary aptitude and talent as a biographer. While Johnson owes much to Boswell, Boswell's devotion to Johnson was the source of his own fame. G. Birkbeck Hill's edition of the 'Life' has been revised by Dr. L. F. Powell (1934–50). Much information concerning his life may be obtained from his letters to the Rev. W. J. Temple, published in 1857 (new ed., with other letters of Boswell, by C. B. Tinker, Oxford, 1924). Boswell's London and Continental journals, as well as other private papers, many discovered at Malahide Castle, have been edited by F. A. Pottle. See also under *Zélide*.

Bosworth, BATTLE OF, in Leicestershire, the last battle of the Wars of the Roses, fought in

1485, when Richard III was defeated by the earl of Richmond (Henry VII) and killed.

Botanic Garden, The, see *Darwin (E.).*

Botany Bay, a bay on the eastern coast of New South Wales, where a penal settlement was established in 1787–8.

Botany Bay Eclogues, early poems by Southey (q.v.), written at Oxford in 1794. They take the form of monologues and dialogues by transported felons.

Bothie of Tober–na–Vuolich, The, a poem in English hexameters by Clough (q.v.), published in 1848 as 'The Bothie of Toper-na-Fuosich'.

The poem, described as 'A Long-vacation Pastoral', tells the story of the love of Philip Hewson, a young Oxford radical on a reading-party in Scotland, for Elspie, the daughter of a Highland farmer.

(A 'bothie' is a hut or cottage.)

Bothwell, James Hepburn, *fourth earl of* (1536?–78), husband of Mary Queen of Scots, is the subject of an historical poem by W. E. Aytoun (q.v., 1856), and of a tragedy by Swinburne (q.v., 1874).

Bothwell, Sergeant, in Scott's 'Old Mortality', a soldier in Claverhouse's force, who claims the name of Francis Stewart.

Botolph or Botulf, St. (*d.* 680), an Englishman who studied in Germany and became a Benedictine monk. He founded a monastery at Ikanho (perhaps near the present town of Boston), which was destroyed by the Danes. He died, with a high reputation for sanctity, at Botolphstown (Boston). Four churches in London are dedicated to him, and he is also commemorated in Botolph's Lane and Botolph's wharf.

Bo-tree, the *ficus religiosa* or pipal tree (from *bodhi,* 'perfect knowledge'), the sacred tree of the Buddhists. It was under a tree of this kind that Gautama attained the enlightenment which constituted him 'the Buddha'. It is regarded as the embodiment of universal wisdom and in some sort identified with Buddha himself.

Botticelli, Sandro (*c.* 1445–1510), Florentine painter, son of Mariano Filipepi, probably a pupil of Fra Filippo Lippi. He was called Botticelli ('little tub'), the nickname of his elder brother. He belonged to the circle of scholars and artists at the court of Lorenzo de' Medici, and many of his paintings reflect the humanist and classical interests of the time. He made a series of drawings illustrating Dante. His mythological subjects, such as the 'Primavera' and 'Birth of Venus', are complex allegories. He was perhaps influenced in his late works by the teachings of Savonarola (q.v.).

Bottom, Nick, the weaver in Shakespeare's 'A Midsummer Night's Dream' (q.v.).

A 'droll', 'The Merry Conceits of Bottom

the Weaver', adapted from Shakespeare's play, was printed in 1646.

BOUCICAULT (originally BOURCI-CAULT), DIONYSIUS ('DION') LARD-NER (1820?–90), educated at London University, was a skilful adapter of plays from plays or novels by other hands. He produced 'London Assurance' in 1841, 'The Corsican Brothers' (from the French) in 1848, 'The Colleen Bawn' in 1859, 'Arrah-na-Pogue' in 1864, and 'The Shaughraun' in 1875.

Bouillabaisse, see *Ballad.*

Bouillon, Godefroi de, duke of Lower Lorraine, leader of the 1st Crusade and proclaimed 'Protector of the Holy Sepulchre' in 1099. He died in 1100. He figures in Scott's 'Count Robert of Paris' (q.v.).

Boulle, André Charles (1642–1732), French cabinet-maker, who has given his name to marquetry in brass, tortoise-shell, and other materials, also called Boule or Buhl.

Bouncer, Mr., a character in 'The Adventures of Mr. Verdant Green'; see *Bradley (E.).*

Bounderby, Josiah, a character in Dickens's 'Hard Times' (q.v.).

Bountiful, Lady, a character in Farquhar's 'The Beaux' Stratagem' (q.v.).

Bounty, The Mutiny and Piratical Seizure of H.M.S., a narrative by Sir J. Barrow (q.v.), published in 1831.

H.M.S. 'Bounty', a ship of about 215 tons, which had been sent to the South Sea Islands to collect breadfruit trees, left Tahiti early in 1789 for the Cape of Good Hope and the West Indies. On 28 April of that year, Fletcher Christian, Alexander Smith (the John Adams of Pitcairn Island), and others seized Lt. Bligh, the commander, and placed him and 18 of the crew in an open boat and cast them adrift. These eventually reached Timor. The 'Bounty' then sailed east with 25 of the crew to Tahiti, where 16 were put ashore. These were subsequently arrested and many of them were drowned in H.M.S. 'Pandora'. Fletcher Christian and 8 others with some Tahitians went on and settled at Pitcairn Island. There they founded a colony, of which John Adams became the leader, and which was subsequently taken under the protection of the British government. These events form in part the basis of Lord Byron's poem 'The Island' (q.v.).

Bourbons, The, a branch of the royal family of France, the descendants of Robert de Clermont, sixth son of Louis IX, who in 1272 married Béatrix de Bourbon, in the Bourbonnais, one of the old provinces in the centre of France. The Bourbons ascended the throne in the person of Henri IV in 1589, and retained it, apart from the Revolutionary and Napoleonic periods, until 1830, or indeed, taking Louis Philippe (Bourbon-Orléans) into account, until 1848. The Bourbons also furnished kings to Naples, and to Spain, through the duke of Anjou, grandson of Louis XIV.

Bourdaloue, LOUIS (1632–1704), a celebrated French divine and preacher of the reign of Louis XIV.

BOURGET, PAUL (1852–1935), French novelist, whose novels of psychological analysis are also notable for the discussion of (usually moral) problems of his day, e.g. 'Cruelle Enigme' (1885), 'André Cornélis' (1887), 'Le Disciple' (1889), 'L'Étape' (1903).

BOURNE, VINCENT (1695–1747), Latin poet, was one of Cowper's masters at Westminster School. He published 'Poemata, Latine partim reddita, partim scripta' (1734), some of which were translated by Cowper and Lamb.

Boustrophedon, from the Greek words meaning 'ox turning', written alternately from right to left and left to right, like the course of the plough in successive furrows, as in various ancient inscriptions in Greek and other languages.

Bouts-rimés, 'The bouts-rimez were the favourites of the French nation for a whole age together. . . . They were a List of Words that rhyme to one another, drawn up by another Hand, and given to a Poet, who was to make a poem to the Rhymes in the same Order that they were placed upon the list.' Addison, 'Spectator', No. 60.

Bovary, Madame, the chief work of Flaubert (q.v.).

Bow Bells, the bells of Bow Church, i.e. St. Mary-le-Bow, formerly 'Seyn Marie Chyrche of the Arches', in Cheapside, London, so called from the 'bows' or arches that supported its steeple. This church having long had a celebrated peal of bells, and being nearly in the centre of the City, the phrase 'within the sound of Bow-bells' has come to be synonymous with 'within the City bounds' [OED.].

Bow Street, a street in London near Covent Garden, in which the principal Metropolitan police court is situated. Hence 'Bow Street Runner' was used in the first half of the 19th cent. for a police officer. Henry Fielding (q.v.) was magistrate here. Will's Coffee-house (q.v.) was at No. 1 Bow Street. Waller, Wycherley, Garrick, Mrs. Woffington, at various times lived in this street.

BOWDLER, THOMAS (1754–1825), M.D. of Edinburgh, published his 'Family Shakespeare', an expurgated edition of the text, in 1818; and prepared on similar lines an edition of Gibbon's 'History'. His works gave rise to the term, 'to bowdlerize'.

BOWEN, ELIZABETH DOROTHEA COLE (1899–   ), novelist and short story writer, born in Dublin. Her novels include 'The Last September' (1929), 'To the North' (1932), 'The House in Paris' (1935), 'The Death of the Heart' (1938), 'The Heat of the Day' (1949), and 'A World of Love' (1955). She has published a number of volumes of

short stories, including 'Encounters' (1923), 'The Cat Jumps' (1934), and 'The Demon Lover' (1945).

Bower of Bliss, THE, in Spenser's 'Faerie Queene', II. xii, the home of Acrasia (q.v.), demolished by Sir Guyon.

Bowery, THE, a street in the lower (southern) part of New York, said to have been so called because it ran through Peter Stuyvesant's *bouwerij* or farm (see W. Irving's 'Knickerbocker's History of New York'). It was formerly notorious as a haunt of the criminal classes. Its present population is cosmopolitan.

Bowge of Court, The, an allegorical poem in seven-lined stanzas by Skelton (q.v.), satirizing court life. The word 'bowge' is a corrupt form of 'bouche', meaning court-rations, from the French 'avoir bouche à cour', to have free board at the king's table.

BOWLES, WILLIAM LISLE (1762–1850), educated at Winchester and Trinity College, Oxford, was vicar of Bremhill in Wiltshire from 1804 to 1850, and a canon of Salisbury. He is remembered chiefly for his 'Fourteen Sonnets' published in 1789, the first of any merit that had appeared for a long period. They stimulated Coleridge and Southey, and the former made many manuscript copies of them for his friends. In 1806 Bowles published an edition of Pope, which aroused a controversy, with Byron and Campbell as participants, about the value of Pope's poetry.

Bowling, LIEUTENANT TOM, in Smollett's 'Roderick Random' (q.v.), Roderick's generous uncle and protector.

Bowling, TOM, the subject of a well-known song by C. Dibdin (q.v.), included in his 'Oddities' performed at the Lyceum in 1788–9, is said to represent his brother Tom Dibdin, who died at Cape Town on his way home from India in 1780.

Bows, MR., in Thackeray's 'Pendennis' (q.v.), the first fiddler in the orchestra of Mr. Bingley's company, and instructor of Miss Fotheringay in acting.

BOWYER, WILLIAM (1699–1777), 'the learned printer', was printer of votes of the House of Commons (1729), printer to the Royal Society (1761), and to the House of Lords (1767). He published his 'Origin of Printing' in 1774.

Bowzybeus, a drunken swain, the subject of the last pastoral in the 'Shepherd's Week' of J. Gay (q.v.).

Box and Cox, a farce by J. M. Morton (q.v.), adapted from two French vaudevilles, and published in 1847. Box is a journeyman printer, Cox a journeyman hatter. Mrs. Bouncer, a lodging-house keeper, has let the same room to both, taking advantage of the fact that Box is out all night, and Cox out all day, to conceal from each the existence of the other. Discovery comes when Cox unexpectedly gets a holiday. Indignation follows, and complications connected with a widow to whom both have proposed marriage; and finally a general reconciliation. See also *Cox and Box.*

Boxers, THE, the name (a translation of Chinese words meaning 'fist of harmony') of a secret Chinese association in which popular discontent took an anti-foreign form at the end of the 19th cent. The Boxers besieged the legations at Pekin early in 1900. The latter were relieved by an international force in August of that year.

Boxiana, see *Egan.*

Boy and the Mantle, The, a ballad included in Percy's 'Reliques', which tells how a boy visits King Arthur's court at 'Carleile', and tests the chastity of the ladies there by means of his mantle, a boar's head, and a golden horn. Sir Cradock's (Caradoc's) wife alone successfully undergoes the ordeal.

Boy Bishop, THE, one of the choir-boys formerly elected at the annual 'Feast of Boys' in certain cathedrals, to walk in a procession of the boys to the altar of the Innocents or of the Holy Trinity, and perform the office on the eve and day of the Holy Innocents, the boys occupying the canons' stalls in the cathedral during the service. Provision for this is made in the Sarum Office (see E. K. Chambers, 'The Mediaeval Stage', App. M). This custom dates from the 13th cent. and lasted until the Reformation. Boy Bishops were appointed also in religious houses and in schools.

Boycott, CHARLES CUNNINGHAM (1832–97), agent for Lord Erne's estates in Co. Mavo, came into conflict with the Irish Land League and suffered annoyances which in 1880 gave rise to the word 'boycott'.

BOYER, ABEL (1667–1729), a French Huguenot who settled in England in 1689. He published a yearly register of political and other occurrences (1703–13) and a monthly periodical, the 'Political State of Great Britain' (1711–29). He also brought out an English-French and French-English Dictionary, a 'History of William III'(1702), and a 'History of Queen Anne' (1722). He translated into English the 'Memoirs of Gramont' (q.v.) and Racine's 'Iphigénie'.

Boyg, THE, in Norwegian folk-lore and in Ibsen's 'Peer Gynt' (q.v., II. vii), a vague, impalpable, ubiquitous, and invulnerable troll-monster.

Boyle, CHARLES, *fourth earl of Orrery* (1676–1731), editor of the spurious Epistles of Phalaris which led to the Phalaris (q.v.) controversy.

BOYLE, JOHN, *fifth earl of Orrery* (1707–62), son of Charles Boyle (q.v.), was an intimate friend of Swift, Pope, and Johnson (qq.v.). His 'Remarks on the Life and Writings of Dr. Jonathan Swift' were written in a series of letters to his son Hamilton at Christ Church, Oxford, and published in 1751. These letters give a critical account of Swift's character, his life, his relations with Stella and Vanessa, and his friendship with Pope and others—Gay, Dr. Delany, and Dr. Young, 'his intimate friends, whom he loved sincerely'. Orrery discusses Swift's work: poetry, political writings, letters, 'Gulliver's Travels', 'The Tale of a Tub', etc. Although he deplores Swift's misanthropy 'which induced him peevishly to debase mankind, and even to ridicule human nature itself' (Letter VI), he says that the character at which Swift aimed and which he deserved was that of 'an enemy to tyranny and oppression in any shape whatever' (Letter XVII).

BOYLE, ROGER, *first earl of Orrery* (1621–79), author of 'Parthenissa' (1654–65), a romance in the style of La Calprenède and Mlle de Scudéry (qq.v.), which deals with the prowess and vicissitudes of Artabanes, a Median prince, and his rivalry with Surena, an Arabian prince, for the love of Parthenissa. Boyle also wrote a 'Treatise on the Art of War' (1677) and some rhymed tragedies.

Boyle Lectures, THE, (1) BOYLE LECTURE SERMONS, on religion, established in 1691 under the terms of the will of the Hon. Robert Boyle (1627–91), son of the first earl of Cork, natural philosopher and chemist, one of the founders of the Royal Society. He was also deeply interested in theology, and studied Hebrew, Greek, Chaldee, and Syriac. (2) BOYLE LECTURES, founded by the Oxford University Junior Scientific Club in 1892. Both series of lectures are described, listed, and dated in the Oxford Bibliographical Society's 'Proceedings and Papers', iii. 1.

Boyne, BATTLE OF THE, fought in 1690 on and across the river Boyne in Ireland. William III and the Protestant army defeated James II, who fled to Kinsale and escaped to France.

Boythorn, a character in Dickens's 'Bleak House' (q.v.).

BOZ, the pseudonym used by Dickens (q.v.) in his contributions to the 'Morning Chronicle' and in the 'Pickwick Papers', 'was the nickname of a pet child, a younger brother, whom I had dubbed Moses, in honour of the Vicar of Wakefield; which being facetiously pronounced . . . became Boz'. (Dickens, Preface to 'Pickwick Papers', ed. 1847.)

Bozzy and Piozzi, see *Wolcot.*

Brabançonne, THE, the national anthem of Belgium, composed by F. Campenhout at the time of the revolution of 1830.

Brabantio, in Shakespeare's 'Othello' (q.v.), the father of Desdemona.

Bracegirdle, ANNE (1663?–1748), a famous and enchanting actress, the friend of Congreve, to the success of whose comedies on the stage she largely contributed. She also created Belinda in Vanbrugh's 'Provok'd Wife', and played Portia, Desdemona, Ophelia, Cordelia, and Mrs. Ford, in Shakespearian adaptations. She was finally eclipsed by Mrs. Oldfield in 1707 and retired from the stage in consequence.

Bracidas, in Spenser's 'Faerie Queene', v. iv, the brother of Amidas, whose dispute over their inheritance from their father Milesio is settled by Sir Artegall.

BRACKENRIDGE, HUGH HENRY (1748–1816), American writer, born in Scotland, whose satirical novel 'Modern Chivalry' (1792–1815) gives a good description of men and manners during the early days of the American Republic.

Brackyn, see *Parnassus Plays* and *Ignoramus*.

BRACTON, BRATTON, or BRETTON, HENRY DE (*d.* 1268), a judge and ecclesiastic, was author of the famous treatise 'De Legibus et Consuetudinibus Angliae', the first attempt at a complete treatise on the laws and customs of England. He also left a 'Note-book' containing some two thousand legal cases with comments.

Bracy, SIR MAURICE DE, in Scott's 'Ivanhoe' (q.v.), one of Prince John's knights, a suitor for the hand of Rowena.

Bradamante, in the 'Orlando Innamorato' and 'Orlando Furioso' (qq.v.), a maiden warrior, sister of Rinaldo. She fights with the great Rodomont (q.v.). Rogero (q.v.) comes to her assistance, and falls in love with her. For the sequel see under *Rogero*.

BRADDON, MARY ELIZABETH (MRS. MAXWELL) (1837–1915), became famous by her novel 'Lady Audley's Secret', first published in 'The Sixpenny Magazine' and issued separately in 1862. She contributed to 'Punch' and 'The World', wrote plays, and edited magazines, including 'Temple Bar' and 'Belgravia'. But she is best known by her novels, which, though criticized on the score of their sensationalism, have merits which commend them to good judges.

BRADLAUGH, CHARLES (1833–91), famous as an advocate of free thought, was a private soldier in the army, 1850–3, then a solicitor's clerk, and proprietor of the 'National Reformer' from 1862. He was elected M.P. for Northampton in 1880, but unseated, having been refused the right to affirm instead of swearing on the Bible. He was re-elected in 1881 and a prolonged struggle ensued, ending in 1886, when he was at last allowed to take his seat. Bradlaugh engaged in several lawsuits to maintain the freedom of the press, published pamphlets on various subjects, and during 1874–85 was associated with the work of Mrs. Besant (q.v.).

BRADLEY, ANDREW CECIL (1851–1935), brother of F. H. Bradley (q.v.), and literary critic, especially noted for his contributions to Shakespearian scholarship. His best-known works are 'Shakespearean Tragedy' (1904) and 'Oxford Lectures' (1909). He was professor of poetry at Oxford, 1901–6.

BRADLEY, EDWARD (1827–89), educated at University College, Durham, and rector of Stretton, Rutland, is remembered as the author of the 'Adventures of Mr. Verdant Green, an Oxford Freshman' (1853–7). Under the pseudonym 'Cuthbert Bede' he contributed extensively to periodicals, and published works in verse and prose, some of which he illustrated himself. He also drew for 'Punch'.

BRADLEY, FRANCIS HERBERT (1846–1924), brother of A. C. Bradley (q.v.), and fellow of Merton College, Oxford, published 'Ethical Studies' in 1876, and 'Principles of Logic' in 1883. His 'Appearance and Reality' (1893) was considered an important philosophical work of profound criticism of contemporary metaphysical thought. Bradley's 'Essay on Truth and Reality', a book less negative in character than its predecessors, appeared in 1914.

BRADLEY, DR. HENRY (1845–1923), philologist, is principally remembered for his work on the 'Oxford English Dictionary' (q.v.). He first gave help, while still in London, with the letter B; then undertook in 1889 the independent editing of the letter E, and removed to Oxford in 1896. He succeeded Sir James Murray (q.v.) as chief editor. He also wrote a successful book on 'The Making of English' (1904). A memoir on him by R. Bridges (q.v.) is prefixed to 'Collected Papers of Henry Bradley' (1928).

BRADSHAW, HENRY (1831–86), educated at Eton and King's College, Cambridge, scholar and antiquary, was librarian of his university, 1867–86. He published treatises on typographical and antiquarian subjects, some containing original discoveries.

Bradshaw's Railway Guide was first published in 1839 in the form of 'Railway Time Tables' by George Bradshaw (1801–53), a Quaker, engraver, and printer. These developed into 'Bradshaw's Monthly Railway Guide' in 1841 and continued to be published until May 1961.

BRADSTREET, ANNE (*c.* 1612–72), American poet, was born in England but emigrated to Massachusetts in 1630. Her poems were published without her knowledge in London in 1650, under the title of 'The Tenth Muse Lately Sprung Up in America', and a 2nd edition, with her own additions and corrections, appeared in Boston in 1678. She belongs to the tradition of Quarles (q.v.), and was highly praised in her own time. Her poems—at least her shorter pieces, in prose as well as verse—are interesting in themselves, but are important as the first literary work of any significance to come out of New England.

Bradwardine, THE BARON OF, and ROSE, characters in Scott's 'Waverley' (q.v.).

Braes of Yarrow, THE, see *Yarrow*.

Braggadochio, in Spenser's 'Faerie Queene', the typical braggart. His adventures and final exposure and humiliation occur in Bks. II. iii; III. viii; and v. iii.

Bragi, in Scandinavian mythology, son of Odin, and god of poetry and eloquence. It is he who welcomes the heroes as they enter Valhalla. He is the husband of Idun (q.v.).

Bragwaine or BRANGWAINE, in the Arthurian legend, the maid-attendant of Isoud of Ireland. See *Tristram*.

Brahe, TYCHO (pron. Teeko Brah'è) (1546–1601), a famous Danish astronomer, who built for Frederick II of Denmark the great observatory on the island of Hven, known as the Uraniborg. He made important astronomical discoveries, but did not accept the Copernican system.

Brahma, the supreme God of post-Vedic Hindu mythology, and in the later pantheistic systems, the Divine reality, of which the entire universe of matter and mind is only a manifestation. The personal god Brahma, the creator, is evolved from the above abstraction, and with Vishnu, the preserver, and Siva, the destroyer, forms the TRIMURTI, the great Hindu triad. Brahma is now less worshipped by Hindus than the other members of the triad.

A BRAHMIN or BRAHMAN is a member of the highest or priestly caste among the Hindus.

Brahms, JOHANNES (1833–97), born at Hamburg, a great composer of the classic type, author of many beautiful songs, of examples of every kind of chamber music, and of four symphonies.

Braille, LOUIS (1809–52), the French inventor, himself blind, of a system of reading for the blind. This consists of embossed characters printed on special paper, recognizable by touch, and formed by varying combinations of six dots.

Brainworm, a character in Jonson's 'Every Man in his Humour' (q.v.).

Bramble, MATTHEW and TABITHA, characters in Smollett's 'Humphry Clinker' (q.v.).

Brambletye House, see *Smith (Horatio)*.

Bramine, see *Draper (Mrs. E.)*.

Bran, in Macpherson's Ossianic poem 'Temora', Fingal's dog, which is found lying on the broken shield of Fillan, before the cave where the hero lies dead.

Bran, the Blessed, a son of Llyr (q.v.). His tale is told in the 'Mabinogion' (q.v.). In Celtic mythology he was a god of the underworld, who later assumed the character of a hero, and finally was made the father of Caractacus, a convert to Christianity, and an introducer of that religion to Britain.

Bran, The Voyage of, an early Irish work, partly in prose, partly in verse, originally written, according to Kuno Meyer, in the 7th cent. and copied in the 10th.

Bran, son of Febal, is summoned by a woman bearing a silver apple-tree branch to Emain, the 'Happy Otherworld', a distant island in the western ocean. He sets out upon the sea with three companies of nine men. They first touch at the Island of Joy, then at the Land of Women. The chief of the Women draws Bran ashore with a magic clew and keeps him with her for, it seems, a year. Longing seizes one of the band to return. All accompany him, and on their arrival in Ireland they find they have been absent so long that their departure is forgotten save in the ancient stories. Bran tells his adventures and disappears again from mortal ken; his companion who touches the Irish soil is reduced to ashes. (See Alfred Nutt, 'The Voyage of Bran'.)

Brand, a lyrical drama by Ibsen (q.v.), published in 1866.

Brand, a young Norwegian clergyman, filled with contempt for the timorous practical compromising spirit of the religion of his countrymen, and an ardent conviction that 'all or nothing' should be the principle of faith, goes at the call of duty to a town on a distant sunless fiord. Unbendingly he practises his principle and enforces it on others, though it costs him the life of his child and of his wife. Finally the people whom he has sacrificed himself to elevate turn against him and drive him out into the snow, and he is reduced to despair. An avalanche overwhelms him as he makes his last appeal to the Deity, and receives the answer, 'He is the God of Love'.

Brandan, ST., see *Brendan*.

Brandon, COLONEL, a character in Jane Austen's 'Sense and Sensibility' (q.v.), who marries Marianne Dashwood.

Brandon, MRS., the 'Little Sister' in Thackeray's 'The Adventures of Philip' (q.v.), who had previously figured in his 'A Shabby Genteel Story'.

Brandon, RICHARD (*d.* 1649), the executioner of Charles I and various distinguished Royalists. He was the son of Gregory Brandon, common hangman of London.

Brandt, see *Gertrude of Wyoming*.

Brandt, MARGARET, the heroine of Reade's 'The Cloister and the Hearth' (q.v.).

Branghtons, THE, in Miss Burney's 'Evelina' (q.v.), the heroine's vulgar relations.

Brangwaine, see *Bragwaine*.

BRANTÔME, PIERRE DE BOURDEILLES, *Abbé* and *Seigneur de* (*c.* 1534–1614), French author of memoirs, a soldier who fought in many countries and was for a time chamberlain to Henri III. An excellent witness to the vices of his age, being moved neither by shame nor indignation, he left a series of memoirs, much of them of a scandalous character, which were not published until after his death (1665–6). These include: 'Les Grands Capitaines français', 'Les Grands Capitaines étrangers', 'Vie des dames illustres francaises et étrangères', and 'Vie des dames galantes', titles given by the booksellers.

Branwen, see *Mabinogion*.

Brasenose College, Oxford, was founded in 1509, replacing an earlier Brasenose Hall. In 1344 a part of the students of Oxford migrated for a time to Stamford, where they occupied a house known as Brasenose Hall, on the door of which was a brass knocker shaped like a nose. The knocker remained at Stamford until 1890, when it was acquired by the College. It was this knocker which probably gave its name to the Hall, although it has been maintained that the origin of Brasenose is to be sought in 'brasinium', a brewery.

Brasidas, a famous Spartan general in the Peloponnesian War, killed in 422 B.C. For the story of Brasidas sparing the mouse that bit his finger, for its show of fight, see Bridges, 'Testament of Beauty', l. 531.

Brasil, see *Brazil*.

Brass, a character in Vanbrugh's 'The Confederacy' (q.v.).

Brass, MAN OF, see *Talus*.

Brass, SAMPSON, and his sister SALLY, characters in Dickens's 'The Old Curiosity Shop' (q.v.).

Brave New World, a novel by A. Huxley (q.v.), published in 1932. It is a fable about a world state in the 7th cent. A. F. (after Ford), where social stability is based on a scientific caste system. Human beings, graded from highest intellectuals to lowest manual workers, hatched from incubators, and brought up in communal nurseries, learn by methodical conditioning to accept their social destiny. The action of the story develops round Bernard Marx, an unorthodox and therefore unhappy Alpha-Plus (something had presumably gone wrong with his antenatal treatment), who visits a New Mexican Reservation and brings a Savage back to London. The Savage is at first fascinated by the new world, but finally revolted, and his argument with Mustapha Mond, World Controller, demonstrates the incompatibility of individual freedom and a scientifically trouble-free society.

In 'Brave New World Revisited' (1958) Huxley reconsiders his prophecies and fears that some of these may be coming true much sooner than he thought.

Brawne, FANNY, the lady whom Keats (q.v.) met in 1818 and with whom he fell in love. She was young and lively, and was kind and constant to her lover, but appears to have little understood what manner of man he was. His passion is reflected in one or two of his sonnets, notably 'The day is gone', and 'I cry your mercy'. His letters to her were published in 1878 (ed. H. B. Forman) and in the collected edition (1935). Her letters to his sister were published in 1937.

Bray, MADELINE, a character in Dickens's 'Nicholas Nickleby' (q.v.).

Bray, *Vicar of,* see *Vicar of Bray*.

Brazen, CAPTAIN, a character in Farquhar's 'The Recruiting Officer' (q.v.).

Brazil, a word of unknown origin, perhaps a corruption of an oriental name of the dyewood originally so called. On the discovery of an allied species, also yielding a dye, in S. America, the territory where it grew was called *terra de brasil* 'red-dye-wood land', afterwards abbreviated to *Brasil*, 'Brazil'.

The name *Brasil* figures in connexion with the legendary 'Island of the Blest' in the Western Ocean ('O'Brazil, the Island of the Blest' is a poem by Gerald Griffin).

Bread and Cheese Club, THE, a New York literary society founded by J. F. Cooper (q.v.).

Bread Street, off Cheapside, was at one time the chief bread market in the City of London. In the time of Stow (q.v.) it was 'wholly inhabited by rich merchants, and divers fair inns be there'. John Milton was born in Bread Street.

BRECHT, BERTOLT (1898–1956), German dramatist and poet. After emigration from Nazi Germany, he returned and settled in 1959 in East Berlin, where he founded and directed the Berlin Ensemble (since his death it has been directed by his widow, Helene Weigel). Brecht's early plays (e.g. 'Baal', 1922, and 'Drums in the Night', 1922) show kinship with Expressionism, and at this stage Brecht was associated with the left-wing theatre of Piscator. 'Man is Man' (1927) anticipates Brecht's later systematic development of the 'alienation effect', and his version of 'The Beggar's Opera' ('Three-penny Opera') was one of the theatrical successes of Weimar Germany, not least in the bourgeois circles which he satirized. His theory of 'epic theatre' rejected Aristotelian principles, regarded a play as a series of loosely connected scenes, dispensed with the traditional 'dramatic' excitement, and used songs as an integral element. The theory is illustrated in its most significant form in 'The Life of Galileo' (1937–9), 'The Good Woman of Setzuan' (1938–41), 'Mother Courage' (1941) (based on a story by Grimmelshausen, q.v.), 'Puntila and His Servants' (1948) and 'The Caucasian Chalk Circle' (1948). All these plays call for a highly stylized acting which, like his general theory of drama (expounded in its most mature form in his essay 'Little Treatise on the Theatre', 1949), discards the notion that drama should seek to create the illusion of reality. Some of Brecht's plays (like 'St. Joan of the Stockyards') have a particularly direct anti-capitalist theme, and others (like 'The Preventible Rise of Arturo Ui') combine this with the theme of Hitlerism. The didactic plays of the period around 1930 ('He who said Yes/He who said No', 'The Measures Taken') are closely connected with the interests of the Communist Party, with which

Brecht was intimately associated from the late 1920s. He was never a member of the Party, however, and his relations with it, even in his last years in East Germany (during which his dramatic output virtually ceased), became rather uncertain. Brecht was also an outstanding lyrical poet.

Breck, ALAN, a character in R. L. Stevenson's 'Kidnapped' (q.v.) and 'Catriona'.

Breeches Bible, THE, a name given to the edition of the English Bible printed at Geneva in 1560 (see *Bible, the English*), in allusion to the version adopted therein of Gen. iii. 7, 'They sewed fig leaves together, and made themselves breeches'.

Breitmann, HANS, see *Leland* (*C. G.*).

Brendan, BRANDAN, or BRENAINN, ST. (484–577), of Clonfert in Ireland, perhaps made a journey to the northern and western isles which formed the basis of the 'Navigatio Sancti Brendani', now generally accepted as a Christianized *imram* or story of an adventurous sea-voyage, an old Irish literary genre which flourished between the 6th and 12th cents. and of which 'The Voyage of Bran' and 'Maeldune' (qq.v.) are representative. The Anglo-Norman versified form (by a certain Benedict), 'The Voyage of St. Brendan', is based on one of the forms of the 'Navigatio', of which the oldest extant version dates from not later than the 10th cent. It has been repeated in many languages at various times, and recently by Matthew Arnold and Sebastian Evans. The saint, sailing in search of the earthly Paradise, which at last he reaches, meets with fabulous adventures. Of these the best known is his meeting with Judas on a lonely rock on Christmas night, where the traitor is allowed once a year to cool himself, in recompense for a single act of charity in his lifetime. St. Brendan visited Brittany between 520 and 530, and is said to have accompanied St. Malo there. He is commemorated on 16 May.

(There was another St. Brendan, almost contemporary, of Birr, disciple of St. Finnian of Clonard, to whom the voyage to Brittany is by some attributed.)

Brengwaine, see *Bragwaine*.

Brennus, the Gaulish chief who in 390 B.C. defeated the Romans at the Allia and took Rome, all but the Capitol, holding the city to ransom. See *Vae Victis*.

Brentford, Two KINGS OF, see *Rehearsal*.

Brer Fox and Brer Rabbit, the chief characters in 'Uncle Remus'. See *Harris* (*J. C.*).

BRETON, NICHOLAS (1545?–1626?), educated at Oxford, was author of a miscellaneous collection of satirical, religious, romantic, and pastoral writings in verse and prose. His best work is to be found among his short lyrics in 'England's Helicon' (q.v.), and in his pastoral volume 'The Passionate

Shepheard' (1604). His other writings include (in verse) 'The Pilgrimage to Paradise' and 'The Countess of Penbrooke's Love' (1592), 'Pasquil's Mad-cappe' (earliest known copy, 1626), 'The Soules Heavenly Exercise' (1601), 'The Honour of Valour' (1605); and (in prose) an angling idyll entitled 'Wits Trenchmour' (1597), 'The Wil of Wit, Wit's Will or Wil's Wit.' (1599), 'Crossing of Proverbs' (1616), 'The Figure of Foure' (first published *c.* 1597), 'A Mad World, my Masters' (1603, a dialogue), and 'The Fantasticks' (1626, a collection of observations on men and things arranged calendar-wise according to seasons, days, and hours).

Breton Lays, in English literature of the ME. period, are short stories in rhyme like those of Marie de France (q.v.), taken from Celtic sources. For examples see *Orfeo* and *Launfal*.

Bretton, MRS. and JOHN, characters in Charlotte Brontë's 'Villette' (q.v.).

Bretwalda, a title given in the Old English Chronicle to King Egbert, and (retrospectively) to seven earlier kings of various Old English states, said to have held superiority, real or titular, over their contemporaries; also occasionally assumed by later Old English kings. Its sense can only be 'lord (or ruler) of the Britons' or 'of Britain' [OED.].

Brewer's Dictionary of Phrase and Fable, first published in 1870 (revised 1952 and subsequently), a useful work containing explanations of English phrases, cant and slang terms, characters of fiction and romance, etc., by the Revd. Ebenezer Cobham Brewer (1810–97).

Brian Boru (926–1014), having become king of Munster, started on a career of conquest, in which he defeated the Danes, and gradually extended his dominion to the whole of the island, until he became chief king of Ireland. He gained a great victory over the Danes at Clontarf in 1014, but was slain in his tent after the battle.

Briana, in Spenser's 'Faerie Queene', VI. i, the mistress of a castle who takes a toll of ladies' locks and knights' beards to make a mantle for her lover Crudor.

Briareüs (also known as *Aegeon*), according to Greek mythology, one of three hundred-handed giants, sons of Uranus and Gë. He is generally represented as, with his brothers (Cottus and Gyes), helping the gods in their war with the Titans.

Bridal of Triermain, The, a poem by Sir W. Scott (q.v.), published in 1813. It is a romance of love and magic, telling of the quest of Roland de Vaux, lord of Triermain, for the maid Gyneth, daughter of King Arthur and the fay Guendolen, and her rescue from the spell that Merlin has laid on her.

Bride of Abydos, The, a poem by Lord Byron (q.v.), published in 1813.

Zuleika, daughter of the Pasha Giaffir, is,

by her father's order, to be the reluctant bride of the rich bey of Karasman, whom she has never seen. She confesses her grief to her beloved brother Selim. The latter reveals to her that he is not her brother, but her cousin, the son of her father's brother, murdered by her father. Moreover he is a pirate chief, and he asks Zuleika to share his lot. At this moment Giaffir, waving his sabre, comes upon them. Selim is killed and Zuleika dies of grief.

Bride of Lammermoor, The, a novel by Sir W. Scott (q.v.), published in 1819 (in the third series of 'Tales of My Landlord').

Lord Ravenswood, deprived of his title for the part he had taken in the Civil War of 1689, and dispossessed of his estate in East Lothian by the legal chicanery of Sir William Ashton, a clever upstart lawyer who has attained the office of Lord Keeper, dies in a fit of fury against the man whom he regards as the author of his ruin. His son, the fiery sombre Master of Ravenswood, inherits his hatred, and, as sole possession, the ruinous tower of Wolf's Crag. Chance leads to his saving the life of his enemy, Sir William Ashton, and of Lucy Ashton, his daughter, and he falls deeply in love with the latter and she with him. Political changes raise the friends of Ravenswood to power, and the timid Sir William thinks it advisable to conciliate Ravenswood, which he does so effectually that the latter overcomes his desire for vengeance and becomes secretly betrothed to Lucy Ashton. Lady Ashton, a woman of violent and domineering character, who has hitherto been absent from her home, now returns, learns the state of affairs, and contemptuously dismisses Ravenswood, who proceeds on a foreign mission after having renewed his pledge to Lucy. Lady Ashton now sets about breaking her daughter's spirit and obliging her to marry a husband of her own choice, the Laird of Bucklaw, by a course of cruel oppression. To this the gentle Lucy appears at last to yield, only stipulating that she shall write to Ravenswood and obtain his release from her pledge. The letter is intercepted by her mother, and Lucy in despair consents to the fixing of the wedding day, convinced that her lover has abandoned her. Immediately after the ceremony Ravenswood, at last apprised of what is going forward, appears, and challenges Lucy's brother and her husband to duels on the morrow. The same night, Lucy stabs her husband and is found insane and shortly after dies. Ravenswood, galloping furiously along the shore to meet his antagonists, is swallowed up in a quicksand.

One of the characters in the book is Caleb Balderstone, the old butler of Ravenswood, determined to maintain in the eyes of the world the fallen dignity of the family, who resorts for this purpose to the most absurd devices.

Bride of the Sea, Venice, see *Adriatic*.

Bridehead, SUE, a character in Hardy's 'Jude the Obscure' (q.v.).

Bridewell, originally the name of a royal palace in London, which stood on the bank of the Thames at the mouth of the river Fleet and near a well of St. Bride. This palace was rebuilt by Henry VIII for the reception of the Emperor Charles V. It is the scene of the third act of Shakespeare's 'Henry VIII'. It was given by Edward VI for a hospital, and afterwards converted into a house of correction. It was in great part destroyed in the Fire of London.

Bridge of Sighs, THE, at Venice, the bridge connecting the Palace of the Doge with the State prison, across which prisoners were conducted from judgement to punishment.

Bridge of Sighs, The, a poem by T. Hood (q.v.), published in 1846.

This was one of Hood's most popular works and shows his power of pathos at its highest. Its subject is the finding of the drowned body of a woman, an outcast of society, who has sought refuge from life in the gloomy river.

Bridgenorth, MAJOR and ALICE, characters in Scott's 'Peveril of the Peak' (q.v.).

BRIDGES, ROBERT (1844–1930), born at Walmer, was educated at Eton and Corpus Christi College, Oxford, and studied, and for a time practised, medicine. His reputation as a poet was made by the successive volumes of his 'Shorter Poems', published in 1873, 1879, 1880, 1890, and 1893. He also published some longer poems: 'Prometheus, the Firegiver' (1884), 'Eros and Psyche' (1894), and 'Demeter' (1905). 'Eden', an oratorio, appeared in 1891. An edition of the 'Poetical Works of Robert Bridges' appeared in 1898–1905, which contained in addition the sonnet sequence 'The Growth of Love' (first form 1876), the Purcell Commemoration ode, some reprints of poems from magazines, and his eight plays (published between 1885 and 1893): 'Nero' (two parts), 'Palicio', 'The Return of Ulysses', 'The Christian Captives', 'Achilles in Scyros', 'The Humours of the Court', and 'The Feast of Bacchus' (partly from the 'Heautontimorumenos' of Terence). The Oxford Press edition of the 'Poetical Works' (1912) first made the author known to the world in general. In 1913 Bridges was appointed poet laureate. In 1914 he issued privately 'October, and other Poems', subsequently published, with some war poems added, in 1920. In 1916 he published 'The Spirit of Man', a collection of prose and verse extracts from various authors, having special bearing on the spiritual needs of the time, and in 1925 a volume of 'New Verse'. Bridges also wrote much prose, including essays on 'Milton's Prosody' (1893), 'John Keats' (1895), and on 'The Influence of the Audience on Shakespeare's Drama'. He was one of the founders of the Society for Pure English (q.v.) and edited its series of Tracts.

The author of many beautiful lyrics and a remarkable metrist, Bridges was perhaps too subtle and severe a poet to appeal to a very wide public. But his great philosophical poem in 'loose Alexandrines', 'The Testament of Beauty' (1929), a compendium of the wisdom, learning, and experience of an artistic spirit, went through fourteen editions or impressions in its first year.

Bridges was intimately associated with the Oxford University Press, taking an active interest in questions of type, spelling, and phonetics, and did much to encourage taste and accuracy in printing. He was also interested in Church music, and collected 'Chants for the Psalter' (privately printed in 1899) and the Yattendon Hymnal.

Bridget or BRIGIT or BRIDE, ST. (453–523), a patron saint of Ireland. She was born, it is said, at Faugher, near Dundalk,'the daughter of Dubhtach by his bondmaid Brotsech. She took the veil and was probably invested with rank corresponding to that of bishop. She was the founder of the church of Kildare, and is commemorated on 1 Feb. Other authorities see in her a survival of Birgit, the Gaelic goddess of fire, an origin attested by the sacred flame in her shrine at Kildare, and other attributes (C. Squire, 'Mythology of the British Islands').

Bridgewater Treatises: the Revd. Francis Henry, 8th earl of Bridgewater (1756–1829), left £8,000 for the best work on 'The Goodness of God as manifested in the Creation', which was divided among the eight authors of the 'Bridgewater Treatises' (Sir Charles Bell, Dr. T. Chalmers, Dr. John Kidd, Dean Buckland, Dr. William Prout, Dr. Peter M. Roget, Dr. William Whewell, and the Revd. William Kirby).

BRIDIE, JAMES, the pen-name of OSBORNE HENRY MAVOR (1888–1951), playwright, who was born and educated in Glasgow, qualified as a doctor, and served in the R.A.M.C. in both world wars. His best-known plays are 'The Anatomist' (1930), 'Tobias and the Angel' (1930), 'Jonah and the Whale' (1932), 'A Sleeping Clergyman' (1933), 'Susannah and the Elders' (1937), 'Mr. Bolfry' (1943), 'Dr. Angelus' (1947), 'Daphne Laureola' (1949), and 'The Queen's Comedy' (1950). He was a founder of the Glasgow Citizens' Theatre.

Bridlegoose, in Rabelais, III. xxxix, et seq., the judge who decided causes by throw of dice.

BRIEUX, EUGÈNE (1858–1932), French dramatist, author of plays on social themes, 'Les trois filles de M. Dupont' (1897), 'Les Avariés' ('Damaged Goods', 1901), 'Les Hannetons' (1906), 'Blanchette' (1892), 'La Robe Rouge' (1900), etc. Brieux became known to English readers in general through G. B. Shaw's introduction to Mrs. Shaw's translation of three of his plays.

Brigadore, in Spenser's 'Faerie Queene', the horse of Sir Guyon, stolen by Braggadochio (v. iii. 34).

Brigantes, THE, a powerful British tribe, who occupied most of the country from the Humber to the Roman Wall. Their capital was Eborācum (York). They were not thoroughly subdued by the Romans until the reign of Hadrian.

Briggs, a character in Miss Burney's 'Cecilia' (q.v.), drawn in some respects from the sculptor Nollekens.

Briggs, MISS, a character in Thackeray's 'Vanity Fair' (q.v.).

Bright, JOHN (1811–89), son of a Rochdale miller, famous as a leading agitator against the Corn Laws, and as an orator. He was M.P. successively for Durham (1843), Manchester, and Birmingham, and held various posts in Mr. Gladstone's governments (1868 onwards). Bright and Cobden (q.v.) were the two leading representatives of the emergence of the manufacturing class in English politics after the Reform Act of 1832.

Brigliadoro, the horse of Orlando (q.v.).

Brigs of Ayr, THE, the Old and New Bridges across the river Ayr at Ayr, celebrated by Burns in his poem of that name.

BRILLAT - SAVARIN, ANTHELME (1755–1826), French magistrate and writer, author of the famous gastronomic work, 'La Physiologie du Goût'.

Brīsēis, daughter of Brises of Lyrnessus, fell into the hands of Achilles (q.v.) when her country was conquered by the Greeks, but was taken from him by Agamemnon when the latter was obliged to surrender Chryseis (q.v.). This was the occasion of the wrath of Achilles and of his prolonged withdrawal from the Trojan War.

Brisk, FASTIDIOUS, a character in Jonson's 'Every Man out of his Humour' (q.v.).

Brisk, a voluble coxcomb in Congreve's 'The Double Dealer' (q.v.).

Bristol Boy, THE, Chatterton (q.v.).

Bristol-diamond or BRISTOL STONE, a kind of transparent rock-crystal, found in the Clifton limestone near Bristol, and alluded to by Spenser in the 'Faerie Queene' (IV. xi. 31):

> But Avon marched in a more stately path,
> Proud of his Adamants with which he shines
> And glisters wide.

Bristol Milk, Sherry wine shipped to Bristol, or, according to Macaulay ('Hist. of England', I. iii), 'a rich beverage made of the best Spanish wine'.

Britannia, the Latin name of Britain, and a poetic name for Britain personified. For the figure of Britannia on the copper coinage of 1672, the earliest modern coin on which it appears, Frances Teresa Stuart or Stewart, duchess of Richmond, was probably the model.

Britannia, or according to the sub-title, '*a chorographical description of the flourishing Kingdoms of England, Scotland, and Ireland from the earliest antiquity*', by W. Camden (q.v.), was published in Latin in 1586, the sixth (much enlarged) edition appearing in 1607. It was translated in 1610 by Philemon Holland (q.v.). It is in effect a guide-book of the country, county by county, replete with archaeological, historical, physical, and other information.

Britannia's Pastorals, see *Browne (W.).*

British Academy, see *Academy (The British).*

British Association for the Advancement of Science, THE, held its first meeting at York in 1831. Its object is the promotion and diffusion of science, and the encouragement of intercourse of scientists.

British Magazine, The, founded in 1759 by Newbery (q.v.), with Smollett (q.v.) for editor, and Goldsmith (q.v.) among its contributors.

British Museum, THE, Bloomsbury, occupies the site of the old Montagu House, which was acquired in 1753 to house the library and collection of curiosities of Sir Hans Sloane (q.v.). These were from time to time enormously increased, notably by the purchase of the Harleian MSS., the gift by George II and George IV of royal libraries, the purchase of the Elgin Marbles (q.v.), and the acquisition of Egyptian antiquities (including the Rosetta Stone, q.v.) and of the Layard Assyrian collections. The new buildings, designed by Sir Robert Smirke, were erected in 1823–47, and the great reading-room, designed by Antonio Panizzi, the librarian, was opened in 1857.

Britomart, the heroine of Bk. III of Spenser's 'Faerie Queene', the daughter of King Ryence of Brittany and the female knight of chastity. She has fallen in love with Artegall (q.v.), whose image she has seen in a magic mirror, and the poet recounts her adventures in her quest for him.

Britomartis, in classical mythology, was a Cretan goddess, probably of fertility; known also as *Dictynna,* goddess of nets, and in Aegina, whither she was said to have fled from the pursuit of Minos (q.v.), as *Aphaea.*

Briton, The, a weekly periodical conducted in 1762 by Smollett (q.v.) in Lord Bute's interest. Wilkes's 'North Briton' (q.v.) was started in opposition to it.

Britten, (EDWARD) BENJAMIN (1913–), composer, educated at Gresham's School, Holt, and at the Royal College of Music. He became Musical Director of the English Opera Group in 1947, and founded, with Peter Pears and Eric Crozier, the Aldeburgh Festival in 1948. Among his early publications were many choral works and solo songs, but serious acclamation was first given to his 'Variations on a Theme by Frank Bridge' (1937). His works include arrangements of folk songs, orchestral compositions, and, especially since 1945, operas: 'Peter Grimes' (1945), 'The Rape of Lucretia' (1946), 'Albert Herring' (1947), a new version of 'The Beggar's Opera' (1948), 'Let's Make an Opera' (for children, 1949), 'Billy Budd' (with E. M. Forster and Eric Crozier, 1951), 'The Turn of the Screw' (1954), and 'Curlew River' (1964). Other notable compositions are 'A Young Person's Guide to the Orchestra' (1946), 'The Spring Symphony' (1949), and 'A War Requiem', with words from the *Missa pro Defunctis* and the poems of Wilfred Owen (commissioned to celebrate the consecration of St. Michael's Cathedral, Coventry, May 1962).

Broad Stone of Honour, The, a work by Kenelm Henry Digby (1800–80), first published in 1822 (re-written and enlarged 1826–7).

It is a study of chivalry, which is defined as 'that general spirit and state of mind which disposes men to heroic and generous actions and keeps them conversant with all that is beautiful and sublime in the intellectual and moral world', and is considered historically, in its relation to Christianity, knighthood, women, etc. In the preface to the work the author says: 'I have enterprized . . . to frame and imprint a book . . . which I call The Broad Stone of Honour, seeing that it will be a fortress like that rock upon the Rhine where coward or traitor never stood, which bears this proud title, and is impregnable.' The reference is to the fortress of Ehrenbreitstein, of the name of which the title is the English translation.

Broadside, a sheet of paper printed on one side only, forming one large page; a term generally used of ballads, etc., so printed.

Brobdingnag, see *Gulliver's Travels.*

Broceliande, in the Arthurian cycle, a legendary region, adjoining Brittany, where Merlin lies enchanted by Vivien. There is a forest of Brécilieu in Brittany, in which a legendary tomb of Merlin is shown.

Brocken, SPECTRE OF THE, a natural phenomenon, first observed in 1780 on the Brocken in the Harz mountains (North Germany), in which an enlarged shadow of the spectator is thrown by the rays of the evening sun on a bank of cloud opposite him. Goethe uses the Brocken as the scene, in 'Faust', of the Witches' Sabbath.

Brodie, WILLIAM (*d.* 1788), deacon of the Incorporation of Edinburgh Wrights and Masons, and a town councillor, became the head of a gang of burglars which operated in Edinburgh, 1787–8. One of the gang turned King's Evidence; Brodie fled, but was at last found in Amsterdam. He was executed on 1 Oct. 1788. He is the subject of a play by R. L. Stevenson and W. E. Henley (qq.v.), 'Deacon Brodie, or the Double Life'.

Broken Heart, The, a tragedy by J. Ford (q.v.), printed in 1633.

The scene is Laconia. Penthea, who was betrothed to Orgilus, whom she loved, has been forced by her brother Ithocles to marry the jealous and contemptible Bassanes, who makes her life so miserable that presently she goes mad and dies. Ithocles returns, a successful general, from the conquest of Messene and is honourably received by the king. He falls in love with Calantha, the king's daughter, and she with him, and their marriage is sanctioned by the king. Orgilus, to avenge the fate of Penthea, of which he has been the witness, entraps Ithocles and kills him. During a feast, Calantha hears in close succession the news of the death of Penthea, of her father, and of Ithocles. She dances on, apparently unmoved. When the feast is done, she sentences Orgilus to death, and herself dies broken-hearted.

BROME, RICHARD (*d.* 1652?), was servant or perhaps secretary to Jonson, whose friendship he afterwards enjoyed and in conjunction with whose son he wrote a comedy, 'A Fault in Friendship' (1623), which has not survived. 'The Northern Lass' (q.v.), his first extant play, was printed in 1632. 'The Sparagus Garden' (a place to which more or less reputable persons resorted to eat asparagus and otherwise amuse themselves), a comedy of manners, was acted in 1635. 'The City Witt' (q.v.) was printed in 1653. 'The Joviall Crew' (q.v.), his masterpiece and latest play, was acted in 1641. His other plays (fifteen in all of his plays have survived) include 'The Queen's Exchange' (printed 1657) and 'The Queen and Concubine' (printed 1659), romantic dramas. Some of the plays, particularly 'The City Witt', show the marked influence of Jonson, others that of Dekker.

BRONTË, ANNE (1820–49), sister of Charlotte and Emily Brontë (qq.v.), was part author with her sisters of 'Poems, by Currer, Ellis, and Acton Bell', and author, under the pseudonym Acton Bell, of 'Agnes Grey' (q.v., 1847), and of 'The Tenant of Wildfell Hall' (q.v., 1848).

BRONTË, CHARLOTTE, afterwards NICHOLLS (1816–55), daughter of Patrick Prunty or Brontë, an Irishman, perpetual curate of Haworth, Yorkshire, from 1820 till his death in 1861. Charlotte's mother died in 1821, leaving five daughters and a son. Four of the daughters were sent to a clergy daughters' boarding-school (of which Charlotte gives her recollection in the Lowood of 'Jane Eyre'), an unfortunate step which may have hastened the death of Charlotte's two elder sisters. In 1831–2 Charlotte was at Miss Wooler's school at Roehead, whither she returned as a teacher in 1835–8. She was subsequently a governess, and in 1842 went with her sister Emily to study languages at a school in Brussels, where during 1843 she was employed as teacher. In the next year Charlotte was back at Haworth, and in 1846

appeared a volume of verse entitled 'Poems by Currer, Ellis, and Acton Bell', the pseudonyms of Charlotte, Emily, and Anne. 'The Professor', Charlotte's first novel, was refused by Messrs. Smith Elder and other publishers, and was not published until 1857; while Emily's 'Wuthering Heights' (q.v.) and Anne's 'Agnes Grey' were accepted by J. Cantley Newby in 1847 and published in 1848. Charlotte's 'Jane Eyre' (q.v.) was published by Smith Elder in 1847 and achieved immediate success. Fresh sorrows now descended on the author: her brother, whose vicious habits had caused the sisters much distress, died in September 1848, Emily before the end of the same year, and Anne in the following summer, and Charlotte alone survived of the six children. She produced 'Shirley' (q.v.) in 1849, and 'Villette' (q.v.), founded on her memories of Brussels, in 1853; both stories, as well as 'Jane Eyre', appeared under the pseudonym Currer Bell. 'Emma', a fragment, appeared in the 'Cornhill Magazine' in 1860, after her death. Charlotte married in 1854 the Revd. A. B. Nicholls, her father's curate, but died a few months later.

BRONTË, EMILY (1818–48), sister of Charlotte and Anne Brontë (qq.v.), was part author with her sisters of 'Poems by Currer, Ellis, and Acton Bell' (1846), and author, under the pseudonym of Ellis Bell, of 'Wuthering Heights' (q.v.). 'Last Lines' and 'Remembrance' are among her finest poems. She was, at her best, a great poet.

Brontë, (PATRICK) BRANWELL (1817–48), the brother of Charlotte, Anne, and Emily. He was a clerk on the Leeds and Manchester railway, and was dismissed for culpable negligence. He was subsequently tutor to a family. He took to opium and died of consumption.

Brontë, DUKE OF, see *Nelson*.

Brontës or BRONTEUS, see *Cyclopes*.

Brook, MASTER, in Shakespeare's 'Merry Wives of Windsor' (q.v.), the name assumed by Ford when Falstaff is making love to his wife.

Brook Farm Institute, see *Transcendental Club*.

Brooke, LORD, see *Greville (Fulke)*.

Brooke, DOROTHEA and MR., characters in G. Eliot's 'Middlemarch' (q.v.).

BROOKE, HENRY (1703–83), born in Ireland and educated at Trinity College, Dublin, lived most of his life in Ireland. He is principally remembered as the author of the curious novel 'The Fool of Quality' (q.v., 1760–72). His other novel 'Juliet Grenville' (1774) is of less importance. He published in 1739 a tragedy entitled 'Gustavus Vasa', on the delivery of the Swedes from the Danish yoke in 1521 by the valour of Gustavus. The performance of this play was prohibited, owing to the fancied resemblance of the villain in it to Sir Robert Walpole. Brooke publicly advocated the relaxation of the penal laws against Roman Catholics. His philosophical poem, 'Universal Beauty', was published in 1735.

BROOKE, RUPERT (1887–1915), the son of a Rugby master, was educated at Rugby School and King's College, Cambridge. He began to write poetry while at Rugby, and his first volume of verse was published in 1911. During 1913–14 Brooke travelled in America and the South Seas. When war broke out in 1914, he took part in the unsuccessful defence of Antwerp, and early in 1915 was sent to the Mediterranean. He died and was buried at Scyros on 23 April of that year. His 'Collected Poems' (1918), including the '1914' group of sonnets (published in 1915) caught the mood of romantic patriotism of the early war years before it turned to disillusionment. His 'Letters from America' appeared in 1916, with an introduction by Henry James.

Brooks of Sheffield, in Dickens's 'David Copperfield' (q.v.), an imaginary person invented by Mr. Murdstone to indicate David to his friend Quinnion.

Brooks's, a club founded by Almack (q.v.) in the middle of the 18th cent. It was originally in Pall Mall, and the present club-house dates from 1778. In its early days it was a noted gambling centre, and was much associated with the names of C. J. Fox and Sheridan. Horace Walpole writes of it to Sir Horace Mann on 2 Feb. 1770, 'The young men of the age lose five, ten, fifteen thousand pounds in an evening there'.

Brother Jonathan, the nickname of the American nation, as John Bull is of the British. The origin is unknown. It is attributed by some, without historical evidence, to Jonathan Trumbull (1710–85), Governor of Connecticut during the American War of Independence, a friend and counsellor of Washington, to whom Washington is said to have referred familiarly as 'Brother Jonathan'.

Brothers, The, a comedy by Cumberland (q.v.), produced in 1769.

The younger Belfield has been dispossessed of his estate by his brother, and driven from his sweetheart, Sophia, whom that brother is now courting, having forsaken his wife Violetta. A privateer is wrecked on the coast, on board of which are the younger Belfield and Violetta. Their unexpected arrival frustrates the designs of the elder brother.

Brothers' Club, THE, founded by St. John (Bolingbroke) in 1711 at the inspiration of Swift 'to advance conversation and friendship' and assist deserving authors and wits. It was composed of members of the Tory Ministry and some of their supporters, and included Swift, Prior, Arbuthnot, Harley's son, Lord Orrery, and others.

Brou, CHURCH OF, at Bourg-en-Bresse, near Lyons, a beautiful church built (1511–36) by Margaret of Austria, wife of Philibert II, duke of Savoy. It contains exquisite tombs of Philibert, his wife, and his mother, Margaret of Bourbon. It is celebrated in a poem by M. Arnold (q.v.).

Brough, the swindling philanthropist in Thackeray's 'The Great Hoggarty Diamond' (q.v.).

BROUGHAM, HENRY PETER, *Baron Brougham and Vaux* (1778–1868), educated at Edinburgh High School and University, rose to be Lord Chancellor. Best known as a parliamentary orator and the advocate of Queen Caroline, in the history of literature he is remembered principally as one of the founders, with Jeffrey and Sydney Smith, of the 'Edinburgh Review' (q.v.) in 1802. He also wrote 'Observations on the Education of the People' (1825), 'Historical Sketches of Statesmen in the time of George III' (1839–43), 'Demosthenes upon the Crown, translated' (1840), and 'Life and Times of Lord Brougham', published posthumously in 1871. Brougham is said to have been the author of the article on 'Hours of Idleness' in the 'Edinburgh Review' (January 1808) which provoked Byron's 'English Bards and Scotch Reviewers'. He was a man of amazing activity, effected considerable improvements in the court of chancery, took an important part in founding London University (1828), and sat constantly in the supreme court of appeal and judicial committee of the privy council. His features lent themselves to caricature in 'Punch'. Of the many squibs written on him the most famous is the description of him in Peacock's 'Crotchet Castle' (q.v., in the chapter 'The March of Mind'), where he figures as 'the learned friend'.

The BROUGHAM, a one-horse closed carriage, with two or four wheels, was named after him.

Brougham Castle, *Song at the Feast of*, a poem by Wordsworth (q.v.), composed in 1807. See under *Shepherd (Lord Clifford, the)*.

BROUGHTON, RHODA (1840–1920), novelist. When Miss Broughton started to write she had a reputation for audacity of which a younger generation deprived her— much to her private amusement. She once said of herself, 'I began my career as Zola, I finish it as Miss Yonge'. Her best-known books are: 'Cometh up as a Flower' (1867), 'Not Wisely but too Well' (1867), 'Doctor Cupid' (1886), 'A Waif's Progress' (1905).

Browdie, JOHN, in Dickens's 'Nicholas Nickleby' (q.v.), a bluff, kind-hearted Yorkshireman, who befriends Nicholas and Smike.

Brown, CAPTAIN and JESSIE, characters in Mrs. Gaskell's 'Cranford' (q.v.).

Brown, FATHER, in G. K. Chesterton's detective stories, a Roman Catholic priest, highly successful in the detection of crime by intuitive methods.

BROWN, CHARLES BROCKDEN (1771–

1810), the first professional American author, was born in Philadelphia. He wrote the four Gothic novels by which he is remembered, within the space of two years: 'Wieland', the most successful, in 1798, and 'Arthur Mervyn', 'Ormond', and 'Edgar Huntly' in 1799. Although faulty and obviously indebted to Godwin and Mrs. Radcliffe (qq.v.), they are of undoubted power and of interest in their attempt to set the Gothic in the American scene. Brown was admired in England, but has a special importance in his own country as a pioneer of the native literary tradition.

BROWN, GEORGE DOUGLAS (1869–1902), novelist, born in Ayrshire, is remembered for his novel, 'The House with the Green Shutters' (1901), written from the standpoint of realism in contrast to the sentimentalization of the 'Kailyard School' (q.v.).

Brown, JOHN, 'of Osawatomie' (1800–59), the anti-slavery leader commemorated in the well-known marching song 'John Brown's body lies a-mouldering in the grave', migrated in 1855 from Ohio to Kansas, where he became a leader of the anti-slavery movement. On the night of 16 October 1859, at the head of a small party of his followers, he seized the arsenal of Harper's Ferry, Virginia, intending to arm the Negroes and start a revolt. He was quickly captured, tried by the authorities of Virginia, and hanged at Charlestown, Virginia.

The author of the song is unknown; it was set to an old Methodist hymn-tune and became the most popular marching-song of the Federal forces. See also *Battle Hymn of the Republic*.

BROWN, DR. JOHN (1810–82), educated at Edinburgh High School and University, practised as a physician in Edinburgh with success, and was author of essays published under the title 'Horae Subsecivae' ('odd hours', vol. I, 1858; vol. II, 1861; vol. III, 1882), including in the second series the beautiful dog story 'Rab and his Friends', 'a flawless example of pathos in a brief compass' (Elton); and of an essay on Marjorie Fleming (q.v.).

Brown, JOHN (1826–83), for over thirty years a favourite and devoted Scottish attendant of Queen Victoria, who enjoyed a singularly privileged position, and became 'almost a State personage'. (See Lytton Strachey, 'Queen Victoria', pp. 272–3.)

Brown, LANCELOT (1716–83), landscape architect, called 'Capability Brown' because he was reputed to say, when consulted on the landscaping of an estate, that it had capabilities.

BROWN, THOMAS (1663–1704), satirist, educated at Christ Church, Oxford, where he wrote the famous 'I do not love thee, Dr. Fell' (see *Fell*). He afterwards settled in London as a hack writer and translator. His 'Amusements Serious and Comical' (1700)

contain entertaining sketches of London life. His collected works appeared in 1707.

BROWN, THOMAS EDWARD (1830–97), born in the Isle of Man and educated at King William's College, Isle of Man, and Christ Church, Oxford, was a fellow of Oriel College, and second master at Clifton from 1864 to 1893. He published 'Betsy Lee, a Foc's'le Yarn' in 1873, 'Foc's'le Yarns' in 1881, and other books of verse. His collected poems were issued in 1900, and there is a selection of the best of them in the 'Golden Treasury' series. The greater part of his poems are in the Manx dialect and deal with the life of the humble inhabitants of the island. They have found very warm admirers, who rank Brown high among the English poets of the 19th cent.

Brown Bess, the name familiarly given in the British army to the old flint-lock musket. BROWN MUSKET was in earlier use; both names existed long before the process of 'browning' the barrel, and apparently referred to the brown walnut stock. [OED].

Brown, Jones, and Robinson, see *Doyle* (*R.*).

BROWNE, CHARLES FARRAR (1834–67), American humorous moralist, born in Maine, who wrote under the pseudonym of ARTEMUS WARD. He purports to describe the experiences of a travelling showman, and like 'Josh Billings' (H. W. Shaw, q.v.) uses his own phonetic spelling. He contributed to 'Punch' and died in England.

Browne, HABLOT KNIGHT (1815–82), under the pseudonym 'Phiz', illustrated some of the works of Dickens, Surtees, Smedley, etc.

Browne, ROBERT, see *Brownists*.

BROWNE, SIR THOMAS (1605–82), was born in London and educated at Winchester and Broadgates Hall, Oxford. He studied medicine at Montpellier, Padua, and Leyden, and graduated at this last university as doctor. In 1637 he settled at Norwich, where he practised physic. He was knighted in 1671 on the occasion of a royal visit to Norwich. His 'Religio Medici' (q.v.) appeared in 1643, though written some years earlier; his 'Pseudodoxia Epidemica', better known as 'Vulgar Errors' (q.v.), appeared in 1646; 'Urn Burial' (q.v.) and 'Garden of Cyrus' in 1658; his 'Christian Morals' was not published till 1716, after his death, and was later (1756) edited by Samuel Johnson. The best edition of his collected works is by G. Keynes (6 vols., 1928–31, 1964).

BROWNE, THOMAS ALEXANDER (1826–1915), best known under his pseudonym 'Rolf Boldrewood', an Australian squatter and police magistrate, and a warder of gold-fields, was author of the very popular 'Robbery under Arms' (1888), the story of a bush-ranger, Captain Starlight; also of 'The Miner's Right' (1890). The 'Squatter's Dream' and 'A Colonial Reformer' appeared in the same year, giving excellent pictures of the life of the Australian squatter.

BROWNE, WILLIAM (1591–1643), was a Devonshire man educated at Exeter College, Oxford. He published 'Britannia's Pastorals', a fluent but desultory narrative poem, dealing with the loves and woes of Marina, Celia, and the like, in couplets interspersed with lyrics, Bk. I in 1613, Bk. II in 1616; but Bk. III remained in manuscript till 1852. His 'Shepherd's Pipe', written in conjunction with Wither (q.v.), appeared in 1614. Among various epitaphs he wrote the well-known lines on the dowager countess of Pembroke, 'Sidney's sister, Pembroke's mother' (attributed however to Ben Jonson in Whalley's edition of that poet, 1756). His poetry is characterized by a genuine love of nature, and influenced Milton, Keats, and Mrs. Browning. His works were collected by W. C. Hazlitt in 1868.

Brownie, a benevolent spirit or goblin, of shaggy appearance, supposed to haunt old houses, especially farmhouses, in Scotland, and sometimes to perform useful household work while the family were asleep. [OED.]

BROWNING, ELIZABETH BARRETT (1806–61), whose father's name Moulton was changed to Barrett on succeeding to an estate, married Robert Browning in 1846. Her 'Essay on Mind; with other Poems' appeared in 1826; 'Prometheus Bound, translated from the Greek of Aeschylus; and Miscellaneous Poems in 1833; 'The Seraphim and other Poems' (including 'Cowper's Grave') in 1838; a volume of 'Poems' (including 'The Cry of the Children') in 1844; 'Sonnets from the Portuguese' in 1850; 'Casa Guidi Windows' (recording political events in Italy and manifesting Mrs. Browning's enthusiasm for the cause of Italian liberty) in 1851; 'Aurora Leigh' (q.v.) in 1857; and 'Poems before Congress' in 1860. 'Last Poems' appeared posthumously in 1862. After her marriage Mrs. Browning lived mostly in Italy, and died at Florence. Her best work is contained in the 'Sonnets from the Portuguese', where the form restricted her tendency to prolixity. Mrs. Browning's romance is the subject of 'Miss Barrett's Elopement' by Mrs. Carola Lenanton (Oman), 1929, and of the successful play 'The Barretts of Wimpole Street', by Rudolf Besier, 1930.

BROWNING, OSCAR (1837–1923), historian. He was a pupil of W. J. Cory (q.v.) at Eton and from 1860 to 1875 was himself an assistant master there. Later he was a history lecturer at King's College, Cambridge, and finally President of the British Academy of Arts in Rome, where he wrote 'A History of the Modern World, 1815–1910' (1912), 'A General History of the World' (1913), and 'A Short History of Italy' (1917).

BROWNING, ROBERT (1812–89), the son of a clerk in the Bank of England, had little formal education, apart from a year studying Greek at University College, London. His first poem, 'Pauline' (q.v.), appeared in 1833 and he first visited Italy in 1834. 'Paracelsus' (q.v.), which attracted the friendly notice of Carlyle, Wordsworth, and other men of letters, appeared in 1835. He next published 'Strafford' (q.v.), a tragedy, which was played at Covent Garden in 1837. 'Sordello' (q.v.) followed in 1840. 'Bells and Pomegranates' (including 'Pippa Passes', 'The Return of the Druses', 'A Blot in the 'Scutcheon', 'Colombe's Birthday', 'Luria', 'A Soul's Tragedy', qq.v., and other pieces) appeared during 1841–6. In 1846 he married Elizabeth Barrett (see under *Browning, E. B.*), and lived with her mainly in Italy at Pisa, Florence, and Rome, until her death in 1861, after which Browning settled in London. In 1850 he published 'Christmas Eve and Easter Day' (q.v.), and in 1855 'Men and Women' (q.v.). 'Dramatis Personae' (q.v.) appeared in 1864, and in 1868–9 the long poem 'The Ring and the Book' (q.v.). His chief remaining works appeared as follows: 'Balaustion's Adventure' (q.v.) and 'Prince Hohenstiel-Schwangau' (q.v.) in 1871, 'Fifine at the Fair' (q.v.) in 1872, 'Red Cotton Nightcap Country' (q.v.) in 1873, 'Aristophanes' Apology' (q.v.) and 'The Inn Album' (q.v.) in 1875, a translation of the 'Agamemnon' of Aeschylus in 1877, 'Dramatic Idyls' in two series in 1879–80, 'Jocoseria' (containing the fine dramatic, monologue 'Cristina and Monaldeschi') in 1883, 'Ferishtah's Fancies' in 1884, and 'Parleyings with certain People' in 1887. His last volume of poems, 'Asolando' (q.v.), was published on the day of his death. He was buried in Westminster Abbey. Two volumes of his correspondence with Mrs. Browning were published in 1899.

Brownists, adherents of the ecclesiastical principles of Robert Browne (1550?–1633?), who preached c. 1578 denouncing the parochial system and ordination, whether by bishops or by presbytery. About 1580 he, with Robert Harrison, collected a congregation at Norwich, which they called 'the church', but which was familiarly known as 'the Brownists'. He finally submitted to the bishop of Peterborough and became for forty years rector of Achurch in Northamptonshire. He is regarded as the founder of congregationalism.

Brownlow, MR., a character in Dickens's 'Oliver Twist' (q.v.).

BRUCE, JAMES (1730–94), educated at Harrow, African traveller, was author of an interesting narrative of his 'Travels to discover the source of the Nile' (he discovered that of the Blue Nile), and of his visit to Abyssinia, published in 1790. His veracity was long doubted, but established by Burton, Speke, and Baker.

Bruce and the Spider : according to legend, Bruce, while lying concealed from the English in the island of Rathlin, one day watched a spider making repeated attempts to fix its web to a beam of the ceiling, and at last succeeding. Encouraged by this example, he left the island in 1307, landed at Carrick with a small band of followers, and gradually drove the English from Scotland.

Bruce, The, an epic poem by Barbour (q.v.), written about 1375.

The author relates the story of King Robert the Bruce and James Douglas, and of the war of independence, mingling anecdote with substantially accurate history. It contains some good descriptive passages, notably of the Battle of Bannockburn, and a frequently quoted outburst on freedom, beginning
          'A! Fredome is a noble thing!'

Brugglesmith, the title of a short story by Kipling (q.v.), included in 'Many Inventions', of an amusing midnight adventure in the streets of London with a drunken man. (He gives his address as 'Brugglesmith', interpreted by a policeman as 'Brook Green, Hammersmith'.)

Bruin, meaning 'brown', the name of the bear in 'Reynard the Fox' (q.v.), whence it has come to signify a bear in general.

Brumaire, from French *brume*, mist, the name of the second month of the year in the French revolutionary calendar. It extended from 22 (or 23) Oct. to 20 (or 21) Nov. The 18th Brumaire of the year VIII (9 Nov. 1799) was the day on which the French Directory fell and the supreme power was entrusted to Napoleon Buonaparte, as first Consul, with Sieyès and Roger-Ducos as his associates.

Brummagem, a local vulgar form of the name of the town of Birmingham, hence (contemptuously) an article of Birmingham manufacture; used especially of cheap jewellery and the like. The old spelling of 'Birmingham', e.g. in Clarendon, is often 'Bromwicham', which would naturally be pronounced 'Brummagem'.

Brummel, GEORGE BRYAN (1778–1840), generally called BEAU BRUMMEL, a friend of the prince regent (George IV) and leader of fashion in London. He died in poverty at Caen.

Brunanburh, a poem in Old English, included in the Anglo-Saxon Chronicle (q.v.) under the year 937, dealing with the battle fought in that year at Brunanburh between Æthelstan with an English army and the Northmen, supported by the forces of Scotland and Wales. The site of the battle is unknown. It is a song of triumph recounting the deeds of Æthelstan and his brother Eadmund, and the rout and slaying of the invaders. J. H. Frere (q.v.) and A. Tennyson wrote translations of the poem.

Brunehaut, BRUNHALT, see *Thierry and Theodoret.*

Brunel, SIR MARC ISAMBARD (1769–1849), born in Normandy and educated for the Church, served in the French navy and emigrated to America in 1793. There he practised as a surveyor and engineer. He came to England in 1799, where he had a distinguished career as an inventor and engineer, having charge, among other important works, of the construction of the Thames tunnel (1825–43).

His son ISAMBARD KINGDOM BRUNEL (1806–59), also a distinguished engineer, designed Clifton suspension bridge (1831), built the Great Western Railway (1833 onwards), and did much marine building, e.g. the 'Great Eastern' (1852–8) and other steamships. He was also concerned in the buildings for the Great Exhibition of 1851.

Brunelleschi, FILIPPO (1377–1446), the first Italian architect of the Renaissance to study classical buildings and introduce classical forms into his designs; the inventor of linear perspective.

Brunhild, see *Brynhild.*

Bruno, GIORDANO (?1548–1600), Italian philosopher (who saw God as the unity reconciling spirit and matter), born at Nola. He was in early life a Dominican friar, but broke from his order and wandered about Europe teaching his philosophical doctrines, which are obscure, or embodying them in dialogues and verse (some of them dedicated to Sir P. Sidney, under whose auspices he visited Oxford) of great fire and vigour. He finally quarrelled with one of the Mocenigos, by whom he was employed at Venice, was denounced to the Inquisition, arrested, condemned to death, and burnt (whether in reality or in effigy is not quite certain).

Brut, meaning 'chronicle', is a transferred use of *Brut = Brutus,* the legendary founder of Britain, as in the French title, 'Roman de Brut', and in the 'Brut' of Layamon (q.v.).

Brut of Layamon, see *Layamon.*

Brute or BRUTUS, legendary founder of the British race. Geoffrey of Monmouth (q.v.) states that Walter, Archdeacon of Oxford, gave him an ancient book in the British tongue, containing an account of the kings of Britain from Brutus to Cadwallader. This Brutus was son of Sylvius, grandson of Ascanius and great-grandson of Aeneas. Having had the misfortune to kill his father, he collected a remnant of the Trojan race and brought them to England (uninhabited at the time 'except by a few giants'), landing at Totnes. He founded Troynovant or New Troy (later known as London) and was the progenitor of a line of British kings including Bladud, Gorboduc, Ferrex and Porrex, Lud, Cymbeline, Coel (Cole, the 'merry old soul'), Vortigern, and Arthur. The name 'Troynovant' is a back-formation from 'Trinovantes', the name of the powerful British tribe that lived north and east of London. Drayton, in his 'Polyolbion' (i. 312), relates the legend, and Selden, in his 'Illustrations' to that work, discusses its probability.

Brute, SIR JOHN and LADY, characters in Vanbrugh's 'The Provok'd Wife' (q.v.).

Brutus, DECIUS, a character in Shakespeare's 'Julius Caesar' (q.v.).

Brutus, LUCIUS JUNIUS, the legendary first consul of Rome. His brother was murdered by Tarquinius Superbus, and he escaped the same fate only by simulating idiocy—whence the name Brutus. After the death of Lucretia (see *Lucrece*), he stirred the Romans to expel the Tarquins and was elected to the consulship. He put to death his two sons for conspiring to restore the Tarquins.

Brutus, MARCUS JUNIUS (85–42 B.C.), joined Pompey in the civil war (49), but after the battle of Pharsalia was pardoned by Caesar. He nevertheless joined the conspirators who assassinated Caesar, in the hope of restoring republican government. On the occasion of Caesar's murder, the dying man uttered the famous words, '*Et tu, Brute*'. In the subsequent war between Brutus and Cassius on the one hand and Octavian and Antony on the other, the former were defeated at Philippi (42), and Brutus took his own life. His wife was Porcia, daughter of Cato of Utica.

BRYAN, SIR FRANCIS (*d.* 1550), poet, soldier, and diplomatist, was Henry VIII's permanent favourite, held various court posts, and was sent on diplomatic missions. He behaved discreditably in the matter of the execution of his cousin, Anne Boleyn, and accepted a pension vacated by one of her accomplices. Cromwell, in writing of this circumstance to Gardiner and Wallop, calls him 'the vicar of hell', which became a popular nickname. It is to this, no doubt, that Milton in the 'Areopagitica' refers when he writes, 'I name not him, for posterity's sake, whom Henry VIII named in his merriment his vicar of hell'. Bryan contributed to 'Tottel's Miscellany' and his poetry was highly valued in his day, but is now undiscoverable.

BRYANT, WILLIAM CULLEN (1794–1878), American poet, born in Massachusetts. He first practised law, but entered journalism and was for fifty years editor of the New York 'Evening Post'. He began to make a name as a poet as early as 1817, with the publication of 'Thanatopsis', and confirmed his reputation as the leading American poet of the day with his 'Poems' (1821). A new collection of 'Poems', containing substantially his best work, appeared in 1832. He was a limited poet, deeply indebted to Wordsworth, but often wrote with great dignity and power, as in the well-known lyric 'To a Waterfowl'.

BRYCE, JAMES (1838–1922), *Viscount Bryce*, educated at the High School and University of Glasgow, at Trinity College, Oxford, and at Heidelberg, was Regius professor of civil law at Oxford, 1870–93, and held a number of high political and diplomatic posts, including those of chief secretary for Ireland (1905–6) and ambassador at Washington (1907–13). His publications include two classical works: 'The Holy Roman Empire' (1864) and 'The American Commonwealth' (1888), besides a number of other writings on various subjects: 'Impressions of South Africa' (1897), 'Studies in History and Jurisprudence' (1901), 'Studies in Contemporary Biography' (1903), 'South America: Observations and Impressions' (1912), 'Modern Democracies' (1922).

BRYDGES, SIR SAMUEL EGERTON (1762–1837), bibliographer, published his valuable 'Censura Literaria' in 1805–9 and 1815, 'The British Bibliographer' in 1810–14, and 'Restituta: or Titles, Extracts, and Characters of old books in English Literature Revived' in 1814–16.

Brynhild or BRUNHILD, one of the principal characters in the 'Volsunga Saga' (see under *Sigurd the Volsung*) and in the 'Nibelungenlied' (q.v.).

Brythons, a Welsh name used to distinguish the branch of the Celtic race which was ultimately driven into Wales and Cornwall, from the Goidels (q.v.).

Bubastis, the Greek name of the Egyptian goddess PASHT, identified by the Greeks with Artemis (q.v.), and represented under the form of a cat. The town of Bubastis, on the Pelusiac branch of the Nile, was the chief seat of the worship of this goddess.

Buccaneer, from the French *boucanier*, originally 'one who hunts wild oxen' (Littré) from *boucan* (a S. American name for a hurdle on which meat was roasted or smoked over a fire), a barbecue, *boucaner*, to dry meat on a barbecue. Thus the word was used to mean one who dries and smokes flesh on a *boucan* after the manner of the Indians. The name was first 'given to the French hunters of St. Domingo, who prepared the flesh of the wild oxen and boars in this way'. Hence it was extended to 'piratical rovers who formerly infested the Spanish coasts in America' (E. B. Tylor, quoted in OED.). See *Esquemeling*.

Bucentaur, see *Adriatic*.

Bucephalus, the horse of Alexander the Great.

BUCHAN, JOHN, *first Baron Tweedsmuir* (1875–1940), author. Private secretary to the high commissioner of S. Africa, 1901–3; on H.Q. staff of British Army, France, 1916–17; director of information under the prime minister, 1917–18; governor-general of Canada, 1935–40. Among his writings are: 'Montrose' (1913, 1928), 'Sir Walter Scott' (1932), 'Julius Caesar' (1932), 'Oliver Cromwell' (1934). His novels include: 'The Thirty-Nine Steps' (1915), 'Greenmantle' (1916), 'Mr. Standfast' (1919), 'Midwinter' (1923), 'Dancing Floor' (1926), 'The Blanket of the Dark' (1931), 'Gap in the Curtain' (1932).

BUCHANAN, GEORGE (1506–82), born at Killearn in Stirlingshire, studied at St. Andrews and Paris, and became tutor to a natural son of James V. He satirized the

Franciscans, thus provoking Cardinal Beaton, and was imprisoned at St. Andrews. Escaping thence he went to the Continent, became a professor at Bordeaux, where he had Montaigne among his pupils, and in 1547 was invited to teach in the university of Coimbra, but was imprisoned by the Inquisition, 1549–51. After some years in France he returned to Scotland and professed himself a protestant. He became a bitter enemy of Mary, in consequence of the murder of Darnley, and vouched that the Casket Letters were in her handwriting. He wrote his 'Detectio Mariae Reginae' in 1571. He was tutor to James VI and I during 1570–8. Chief among his many writings are his Latin poem 'De Sphaera', an exposition of the Ptolemaic system as against that advocated by Copernicus, and his Latin 'Rerum Scoticarum Historia' (1582), which for long was regarded as a standard authority. His first elegy 'Quam misera sit conditio docentium literas humaniores Lutetiae', describes the hard lot of the student at Paris.

BUCHANAN, ROBERT WILLIAMS (1841–1901), poet and novelist, the son of a socialist and secularist tailor who owned several socialistic journals in Glasgow. He came to London in 1860, and made his reputation by 'London Poems' in 1866, 'Master Spirits' (1874), and 'Ballads of Life, Love, and Humour' (1882). He satirized Swinburne and others in 'The Session of the Poets' in the 'Spectator' (1866), and attacked the Pre-Raphaelites (q.v.) in the 'Contemporary' (1871) in a pseudonymous article entitled 'The Fleshly School of Poetry', which led to a prolonged controversy. Of his novels (all now forgotten) the principal are 'The Shadow of the Sword' (1876) and 'God and the Man' (1881). He wrote many plays, of which the chief successes were 'Alone in London' (1884), 'A Man's Shadow' (1889), 'The Charlatan' (1894), 'The Strange Adventures of Miss Brown' (1895).

Buchanan and **Targe**, in J. Moore's 'Zeluco' (q.v.), the Scotsmen who quarrel about Mary Queen of Scots.

Bucket, INSPECTOR, the detective in Dickens's 'Bleak House' (q.v.).

BUCKHURST, LORD, see *Sackville* (*T.*) and *Sackville* (*C.*).

Buckingham: the line, 'Off with his head! So much for Buckingham', occurs, not in the Shakespearian text, but in Colley Cibber's version of 'Richard III' (III. i).

Buckingham, *Complaint of,* see *Complaint of Buckingham.*

Buckingham, GEORGE VILLIERS, *first duke of* (1592–1628), the favourite of James I, by whom he was familiarly known as 'Steenie', figures in Scott's 'The Fortunes of Nigel' (q.v.). He was assassinated by John Felton.

Buckingham, GEORGE VILLIERS, *second duke of* (1628–87), a prominent figure in the reign of Charles II and an influential member of the Cabal, was the Zimri of Dryden's 'Absalom and Achitophel' (q.v.). He was author of the burlesque 'The Rehearsal' (q.v.), 1671, and of other verses and satires. He figures in Scott's 'Peveril of the Peak' (q.v.).

BUCKINGHAM, JAMES SILK (1786–1855), author and traveller, and founder of the 'Athenaeum' (q.v.).

Buckingham Palace, in London, stands on the site of an old mulberry garden planted in 1609 by order of James I, which became a favourite place of popular resort. It was bought in 1703 by the duke of Buckingham, who built, or rebuilt, a house in the garden. It was bought in 1762 by George III (and then known as 'Queen's House'), and the house was rebuilt for George IV, by Nash (q.v.), whose gateway, known as 'Marble Arch', was transferred to its present position in 1847 when the eastern range was built by Blore. The façade was refronted in stone by Sir Aston Webb in 1913. Queen Victoria made Buckingham Palace the most usual royal residence in London.

BUCKLAND, FRANCIS TREVELYAN (1826–80), naturalist, educated at Winchester and Christ Church, Oxford, published 'Curiosities of Natural History' and kindred works, and started 'Land and Water' in 1866.

Bucklaw, THE LAIRD OF, Frank Hayston, a character in Scott's 'The Bride of Lammermoor' (q.v.).

BUCKLE, HENRY THOMAS (1821–62), received no school or college training and devoted himself to travelling on the Continent, where he acquired the principal languages. The first volume of his 'History of Civilization in England' appeared in 1857 and the second in 1861. These were only to be introductory portions of a far larger work, which the author's premature death at Damascus prevented him from executing. Buckle criticized the methods of previous historians and sought to adopt a more scientific basis, with special regard to the physical conditions of various countries, such as their climate and soil. In the second volume he illustrated his method by applying it to the history of Spanish civilization from the 5th to the 19th cent., and of Scottish civilization to the 18th cent.

Bucklersbury, a street off Cheapside, in the City of London. Stow says that its western end was 'possessed of Grocers and Apothecaries', which explains the following:

'Like a many of these lisping hawthorn-buds, that come like women in men's apparel, and smell like Bucklersbury in simple-time.'

(Shakespeare, 'Merry Wives', III. iii. 87.) The name was originally BUCKERELSBURY, from the name of an old city family.

Bucolic, from Greek βουκόλος, herdsman, means pastoral; and the plural, BUCOLICS, pastoral poems.

Buddha, 'the Enlightened', the title given by the adherents of one of the great Asiatic religions, thence called BUDDHISM, to the founder of their faith, Sakyamuni, Gautama, or Siddartha, who flourished in northern India in the 5th cent. B.C. Sakyamuni is regarded as only the latest of a series of Buddhas or infallible religious teachers, which is hereafter to be continued indefinitely. [OED.] He was the son of the king of Kapilavastu (at the foot of the mountains of Nepal). Finding salvation neither in the teaching nor in the austerities of the Brahmans, he developed by long meditations, his own religion, which he expounded at various places in India, making many disciples. The principal doctrines of Buddhism are, that suffering is inseparable from existence, which is an evil; that the principal cause of suffering is desire; that the suppression of suffering can be obtained by the suppression of desire, and this in turn by Buddhist discipline, of which *nirvana* is the reward. *Nirvana* is the extinction of individual existence and absorption into the supreme spirit.

BUDGELL, EUSTACE (1686–1737), a cousin of Addison, a miscellaneous writer who contributed to the 'Spectator' and is alluded to by Pope in 'The Dunciad'.

Buffalo Bill, the name under which William Cody (1846–1917) obtained a world-wide fame. He was born in Iowa, worked as a herder in the western plains, and served as hospital orderly in the Civil War. His fame as a scout, slayer of Indians, and terror of bandits was largely fictitious, the result of the works of the American novelist Ned Buntline and of the press campaign of John Burke. He achieved great success in Europe with his 'Wild West Show' and was lionized in England in consequence of his spurious fame and striking appearance. But the tide of prosperity passed away, and though Cody struggled on gamely to the last, he died in poverty and comparative obscurity. The T.L.S. of 17 Oct. 1929 contains an interesting article on the 'Legend of Buffalo Bill', from which the above facts are taken.

Buffle, SIR RAFFLE, a character in Trollope's 'The Small House at Allington' and 'The Last Chronicle of Barset', John Eames's blustering official chief.

BUFFON, GEORGES LOUIS LECLERC DE (1707–88), French naturalist, was keeper of the king's botanical garden, and author of a remarkable 'Histoire Naturelle' in thirty-six volumes (1749–88), a pioneer work, in which he deals not only with natural history, but with mineralogy and such questions as the origin of the earth.

Buffone, CARLO, in Jonson's 'Every Man out of his Humour' (q.v.), 'a public scurrilous profane jester', perhaps intended to designate John Marston (q.v.).

Our word BUFFOON is derived through the French 'bouffon' from the Italian 'buffone',

a jester (*buffa,* a jest, *buffare* to puff, either in the sense of something light and frivolous, or with reference to puffing out the cheeks as a comic gesture).

Buffs, THE, the East Kent Regiment, the old 3rd Foot regiment of the line, so called from the buff facings of its uniform.

Bufo, a character in Pope's (q.v.) 'Epistle to Dr. Arbuthnot' (ll. 230–48). It is uncertain whom it represents.

Bug Bible, a name given to versions of the English Bible (Coverdale's and Matthew's) in which the words in Psalm xci. 5 are translated 'thou shalt not be afraid for any bugs by night'.

Buhl, see *Boulle.*

Bukton, a friend of Chaucer, to whom he addressed an 'Envoy', of some interest for the light it throws on the author.

Bulbo, PRINCE, a character in Thackeray's 'The Rose and the Ring' (q.v.).

Bulbul, a bird of the thrush family, much admired in the East for its song; hence sometimes called the 'nightingale' of the East.

Bull, from Latin *bulla,* the leaden seal attached to the Pope's edicts, and hence a papal or episcopal edict. The word is applied to a non-episcopal edict in 'the Golden Bull', a decree issued by Charles IV in 1356 to regulate the election and coronation of an emperor.

Bull, an expression containing a manifest contradiction in terms or involving a ludicrous inconsistency unperceived by the speaker. The origin of the term is unknown. No foundation appears for the guess that it originated in a contemptuous allusion to papal edicts or for the assertion of the 'British Apollo' (1708, no. 22) that 'it became a Proverb from the repeated Blunders of one Obadiah Bull, a Lawyer of London, who lived in the reign of K. Henry the Seventh' (OED.). Often associated with the Irish.

Bull, JOHN, see *John Bull.*

Bull, DR. JOHN (1563?–1628), composer, singing-man of the Chapel Royal (1585), and professor of music at Gresham College (1597–1607). He was subsequently (1617–28) organist of Antwerp Cathedral. See *National Anthem.*

Bull Run, the name of a small river or creek in eastern Virginia, the scene of two important battles in the American Civil War, in 1861 and 1862. The Federals were severely defeated in both battles.

Bulldog Drummond, see *Sapper.*

Bull-dogs, the colloquial name of the 'University Police', the Proctors' attendants at the Universities of Oxford and Cambridge.

Bulls of Basan, see *Bashan.*

Bully Bluck, see *Magog Wrath.*

Bulstrode, MR., a character in George Eliot's 'Middlemarch' (q.v.).

Bultitude, MR. and DICK, characters in F. Anstey's 'Vice Versa' (q.v.).

Bumble, the beadle in Dickens's 'Oliver Twist' (q.v.), a type of the consequential, domineering parish official.

Bumby, MOTHER, a fortune-teller frequently alluded to by the Elizabethan dramatists. Lyly (q.v.) wrote a play entitled, 'Mother Bombie' (1594), which is, says Hazlitt, 'very much what its name would import, old, quaint, and vulgar', 'little else than a tissue of absurd mistakes, arising from the confusion of the different characters one with another, like another Comedy of Errors, and ends in their being (most of them) married . . . to the persons they most dislike'.

Bumper, SIR HARRY, in Sheridan's 'School for Scandal' (q.v.), one of Charles Surface's convivial companions, who sings the famous song:
'Here's to the maiden of bashful fifteen.'

Bumppo, NATTY, see *Cooper (J. Fenimore)*.

Bunbury, an imaginary character introduced by Wilde (q.v.) in his play 'The Importance of being Earnest', where Bunbury serves as an excuse for visits to various places.

BUNBURY, HENRY WILLIAM (1750–1811), a Norfolk squire, is remembered as a great caricaturist, and as the author of the 'Academy for Grown Horsemen . . . by Geoffrey Gambado', 'Master of the Horse to the Doge of Venice', a humorous work illustrated by his own comic plates, and an early example of the literature of sport.

Bunce, JACK, *alias* ALTAMONT, ex-actor and pirate in Scott's 'The Pirate' (q.v.).

Bunce, PETER, one of the bedesmen in Trollope's 'The Warden' (q.v.).

Bunch, MOTHER, an ale-wife of London, well known in the 16th cent. There is a reference to her in Nash's 'Pierce Penniless', in Dekker's 'Satiromastix' (l. 1178), and in 'The Weakest goeth to the Wall' (attributed to Webster). The name of 'Mother Bunch' was adopted in the title of many 17th-cent. books of anecdotes and jests.

Buncle, John see *John Buncle.*

Bungay and **Bacon,** the rival publishers in Thackeray's 'Pendennis' (q.v.). Bungay is there proprietor of the (fictitious) 'Pall Mall Gazette'.

Bungay, THOMAS, known as 'Friar Bungay' (*fl.* 1290), a Franciscan, who was divinity lecturer of his order in Oxford and Cambridge. He was vulgarly accounted a magician and is frequently referred to in that capacity. See *Friar Bacon and Friar Bungay.* FRIAR BUNGAY, an astrologer, figures in Lytton's 'The Last of the Barons' (q.v.).

Bungay Castle, in Suffolk. When Hugh Bigot in Henry II's reign 'added fortifications to his Castle of Bungay, he gave out this rhyme, therein vaunting it impregnable:

Were I in my castle of Bungey
Upon the river of Waveney
I would ne care for the King of Cockney.'
Ray's 'Proverbs', p. 251 (ed. 1768).

Bunion, ROSA, in Thackeray's 'Mrs. Perkins's Ball' (q.v.), poetess, author of 'Heartstrings', 'Passion Flowers', etc., who loves waltzing even beyond poesy, and lobster salad as much as either.

Bunker's Hill, more correctly Breed's Hill, a height near Boston in America, where in 1775 an English force, after severe fighting, compelled the withdrawal of the American insurgents.

Bunkum, BUNCOMBE, empty claptrap oratory, from *Buncombe*, the name of a county in N. Carolina, U.S. The use of the word originated near the close of the debate on the 'Missouri Question' in the 16th congress, when the member for this district rose to speak, and persevered in spite of impatient calls for the 'Question', declaring he was bound to *make a speech for Buncombe.* [OED.]

Bunsby, CAPTAIN JOHN, a character in Dickens's 'Dombey and Son' (q.v.), a friend of Captain Cuttle.

Bunthorne, REGINALD, the principal male character in Gilbert and Sullivan's comic opera 'Patience', 'a fleshly poet' in whose person the 'Aesthetic Movement' of the eighties was caricatured.

BUNYAN, JOHN (1628–88), born at Elstow, near Bedford, the son of a tinsmith, learned reading and writing at the village school and was early set to his father's trade. On completing his sixteenth year he was drafted into the parliamentary army and was stationed at Newport Pagnell from 1644 to 1646 under the command of Sir Samuel Luke, an experience perhaps reflected in his 'The Holy War'. In 1653 he joined a Nonconformist church in Bedford, preached there, and came into conflict with the Quakers, against whom he published his first writings, 'Some Gospel Truths opened' (1656), and 'A Vindication' thereof (1657). He had profited by two religious books belonging to his first wife (who died *c.* 1656, leaving four young children) and devoted himself to reading the Bible. 'I was never out of the Bible either by reading or meditation.' He married his second wife, Elizabeth, *c.* 1659, and was arrested in November 1660 for preaching without a licence. Refusing to comply with the law, he was kept in prison for twelve years, until Charles II's Declaration of Indulgence. During the first half of this period he wrote nine of his books, the principal of which was his 'Grace Abounding to the Chief of Sinners' (q.v., 1666). In the same year appeared 'The Holy City, or the New Jerusalem', inspired by a passage in the book of Revelation. After this he wrote no more until, in 1671, he published 'A Confession of my Faith, and a Reason of my Practice'. After his release in 1672 he was appointed pastor to the same church in Bedford, but was again imprisoned for a short period, during which he wrote the first part of 'The Pilgrim's Progress from this World to that which is to come' (q.v.). The second part, with the whole work, was published in 1678. His other principal works are 'The Life and Death of Mr. Badman' (q.v., 1680), and 'The Holy War' (q.v., 1682). Bunyan preached in many places, but was not further molested. He was buried in Bunhill Fields, London.

Burana Carmina, see *Carmina Burana.*

Burbage, JAMES (*d.* 1597), actor, was a joiner by trade. He was one of the earl of Leicester's players in 1574. He leased land in Shorèditch (1576), on which he erected, of wood, the first building in England specially intended for plays. In 1596 he acquired a house in Blackfriars, and converted it into the 'Blackfriars Theatre' (q.v.). He lived in Halliwell Street, Shoreditch, 1576–97. The first English playhouse is mentioned in an order of council, Aug. 1577, and was known as 'The Theatre'; the fabric was removed, *c.* Dec. 1598, to the Bankside and set up as the Globe Theatre (q.v.).

Burbage, RICHARD (1567?–1619), actor, was son of James Burbage (q.v.), from whom he inherited a share in Blackfriars Theatre and an interest in the Globe Theatre. He acted as a boy at the Theatre in Shoreditch and rose to be an actor of chief parts, 1595–1618, in plays by Shakespeare, Ben Jonson, and Beaumont and Fletcher. He excelled in tragedy. Burbage lived in Halliwell Street, Shoreditch, 1603–19. He is known also as a painter in oil-colours.

Burbon, SIR, in Spenser's 'Faerie Queene', v. xi, represents Henry of Navarre.

Burchell, MR., in Goldsmith's 'Vicar of Wakefield' (q.v.), the name assumed by Sir William Thornhill.

Burden of a song, from the Romantic *bourdon,* the continuous bass or 'drone' of a bagpipe, is the refrain or chorus, a set of words recurring at the end of each verse.

In the English Bible (e.g. Isa. xiii. 1, 'The burden of Babylon') 'burden' is used to render the Hebrew *massa,* which Gesenius would translate 'lifting up (of the voice), utterance, oracle'. But it is generally taken in English to mean a 'burdensome or heavy lot or fate' [OED.].

BURGOYNE, SIR JOHN (1722–92), nicknamed 'Gentleman Johnny', remembered principally as the general who was forced to capitulate to the Americans at Saratoga in 1777, was the author of a clever and successful comedy 'The Heiress' (1786), in which the vulgarity of the rich Alscrip family is contrasted with the native good breeding of Clifford, Lord Gayville, and his sister; while the temporary humiliation of the virtuous heroine, Miss Alton, who is driven to take

service in the Alscrip family, until she is discovered to be an heiress and Clifford's sister, provides a sentimental interest. He also wrote 'The Maid of the Oaks' (1774), a cheerful little comedy of country life. He figures in G. B. Shaw's play 'The Devil's Disciple' (1900).

Burial of Sir John Moore, The, see *Wolfe.*

Buridan, a French scholastic philosopher of the end of the 12th cent. to whom is attributed the sophism of the ass equally pressed by hunger and thirst and placed between a bundle of hay and a pail of water, who must die of hunger and thirst, having no determining motive to direct him to one or the other. 'Like Buridan's ass between two bundles of hay' is said of a person undecided between two courses of action, who adopts neither. According to tradition Buridan was thrown into the Seine in a sack (Villon, 'Ballade').

Burke, 'A Genealogical and Heraldic History of the Peerage and Baronetage of the United Kingdom', first compiled by John Burke and published in 1826. Since 1847 it has been published annually.

BURKE, EDMUND (1729–97), the second son of a Dublin attorney, who was a Protestant married to a Catholic wife. He was brought up as a Protestant, and educated at Trinity College, Dublin. He entered the Middle Temple in 1750. His first published works, 'A Vindication of Natural Society' (q.v.) and 'A Philosophical Inquiry into the Sublime and Beautiful' (q.v.), appeared in 1756. In the same year he married Jane Nugent. He started the 'Annual Register' in 1759, and contributed to it till 1788. He became private secretary to the marquis of Rockingham in 1765, who from time to time helped him by advances of money and at his death directed that the bonds should be destroyed. Burke entered parliament as member for Wendover in the same year, and first spoke in the House in 1766 on the American question. During the following years he vehemently attacked the Tory government. He participated in stock-jobbing operations and remained in consequence involved in financial difficulties for the rest of his life, but bought an estate at Beaconsfield in 1768, before the crash came. He published his 'Observations on "The Present State of the Nation" ' (q.v.) in 1769, and 'Thoughts on the Present Discontents' (q.v.) in 1770. He became M.P. for Bristol on the invitation of the citizens in 1774, and made his speeches 'On American Taxation' and 'On Conciliation with the Colonies' in 1774 and 1775. His 'Letter to the Sheriffs of Bristol' (q.v.) was written in 1777, and his great speech against employing Indians in the war was made in 1778. His speech on economical reform was made in February 1780. His championship of free trade with Ireland and of Catholic emancipation lost him his seat at Bristol in 1780, and his 'Two

Letters . . . to Gentlemen in the City of Bristol' (1778) and his 'Speech at the Guildhall, in Bristol' (1780), form a noble vindication of his attitude. He became M.P. for Malton in Yorkshire in 1781. By his attacks on the conduct of the American War he contributed powerfully to North's resignation of office. He became paymaster of the forces in 1782 but retired from the ministry with Fox, returning to the same post in 1783 under the coalition government. His sympathy with the Irish Catholics is shown by his letters 'To a Peer of Ireland on the Penal Laws' (1782) and 'To Sir Hercules Langrishe' (1792). He took an active part in the investigation of the affairs of the East India Company and became the relentless enemy of Warren Hastings (q.v.). His famous speeches on the East India Bill and 'On the Nabob of Arcot's Private Debts' were delivered in 1783 and 1785. He opened the case for the impeachment of Warren Hastings in 1788, and supported Wilberforce in advocating the abolition of the slave-trade in 1788–9. His 'Reflections on the Revolution in France' (q.v.) appeared in 1790, followed by 'A Letter . . . to a Member of the National Assembly' (1791), and by 'An Appeal from the New to the Old Whigs' in 1791, a defence against the charge of inconsistency between his attitude towards the American colonies and his denunciation of the French Revolution. In the same year appeared 'Thoughts on French Affairs'; 'Remarks on the Policy of the Allies' in 1793; and the 'Letters on a Regicide Peace' (q.v.) in 1795–7. He retired from parliament in 1794 and received a pension from the ministry, for which he was criticized, chiefly by the duke of Bedford and earl of Lauderdale. He defended himself in his 'Letter to a Noble Lord' (q.v.) in 1796. His collected works were published in 1792–1827.

Burke's political life was devoted to five 'great, just, and honourable causes': the emancipation of the House of Commons from the control of George III and the 'King's friends'; the emancipation (but not the independence) of the American colonies; the emancipation of Irish trade, the Irish parliament, and the Irish Catholics; the emancipation of India from the misgovernment of the East India Company; and opposition to the atheistical jacobinism displayed in the French Revolution. An historical study of Burke was published by Lord Morley in 1867, and a life by him in the English Men of Letters series in 1879.

Burke, WILLIAM, the name of a notorious criminal executed at Edinburgh in 1829 for smothering many persons in order to sell their bodies for dissection (his accomplice was William Hare). Hence 'to burke' is to murder as Burke did, and, figuratively, to smother, 'hush up', suppress quietly.

Burleigh or **Burghley,** WILLIAM CECIL, LORD (1520–98), lord treasurer under Queen Elizabeth and her chief minister. He had

previously been secretary to Lord Protector Somerset; secretary of state, 1550–3; and employed in negotiations by Queen Mary. He is introduced in Sheridan's 'The Critic' (q.v.), where, in Puff's tragedy, he comes on the stage and shakes his head, being too much occupied with cares of state to talk, whence the expression, 'Burleigh's nod'.

Burlesque, from Italian *burla*, ridicule, mockery, literary composition or dramatic representation which aims at exciting laughter by the comical treatment of a serious subject or the caricature of the spirit of a serious work. Notable examples of burlesque in English literature are Butler's 'Hudibras', and 'The Rehearsal' (qq.v.).

Burman, MRS., in Meredith's 'One of our Conquerors' (q.v.), Victor Radnor's wife.

BURNABY, FREDERICK GUSTAVUS (1842–85), cavalry officer and traveller, commanded the 3rd household cavalry, 1881–5; killed in the attempt to relieve Khartoum. He was author of 'A Ride to Khiva' (1876).

BURNAND, SIR FRANCIS COWLEY (1836–1917), educated at Eton and Trinity College, Cambridge, had a vocation for the stage which manifested itself in the production of a large number of burlesques, notably 'Black-eyed Susan' (1866), 'Cox and Box' (1867), and 'The Colonel' (1881). He contributed to 'Punch' from 1863 and joined the staff; his 'Happy Thoughts' (1866) proved one of the most popular series in that periodical. He was editor of 'Punch', 1880–1906.

Burne-Jones, SIR EDWARD COLEY (1833–98), painter and designer. His romantic subjects, such as 'King Cophetua and the Beggar Maid', usually portray women with a characteristic willowy beauty. He designed tapestry and stained glass for Morris and Co., and illustrations for the Kelmscott Press.

Burnell the Ass, the hero of the 'Speculum Stultorum' of Wireker (q.v.). Burnell, an ass who wishes to acquire a larger tail, goes to Salerno and to Paris to study, meets with various adventures, and finally loses his tail altogether. In the course of these travels he hears the story to which Chaucer alludes in the 'Nun's Priest's Tale' (l. 492):

I have read well in Dan Burnell the Ass,
Among his verse, how that there was a cock,
For that a priestès son gave him a knock
Upon his leg, while he was young and nice,
He made him for to lose his benefice.

The story is that Gundulf, driving some chicks from the granary, struck a cockerel and broke its leg. The cock bided its time. On the day on which Gundulf was to receive his father's benefice, he was to start at cock-crow for the town where the installation was to take place. But the cock that day failed to crow; Gundulf was late, and lost his benefice. In the main narrative, the Ass represents the monk who is discontented with his lot.

BURNET, GILBERT (1643–1715), educated at Marischal College, Aberdeen, was a popular preacher and was offered four bishoprics before he was 29. These he refused, and in 1674 was dismissed from the post of king's chaplain for remonstrating with Charles II for his profligacy. He was chaplain to Mary when she was still Princess of Orange. He became bishop of Salisbury in 1689 under William III. He published his account of the death-bed repentance of Rochester (q.v.), 'Some passages in the Life and Death of the right honourable John Wilmot Earl of Rochester', in 1680, and his 'History of the Reformation in England', vol. i in 1679, vol. ii in 1681, vol. iii in 1714. His 'Exposition of the Thirty-nine Articles' appeared in 1699, and his best-known work, 'The History of My Own Times', posthumously (1724–34). Other notable works by Burnet were the 'Memoires of the . . . Dukes of Hamilton' (1677), the 'Life of Sir Matthew Hale' (1682), and the 'Journal of Lord Russell's last week' (first published in the 'General Dictionary', 1739, and subsequently in the 'Life of William Lord Russell', 1819).

BURNET, THOMAS (1635?–1715), a Yorkshire divine and master of the Charterhouse. He was the author of 'The Sacred Theory of the Earth' (1684–90), an imaginative and romantic cosmogony, suggested to him by a voyage across the Alps. It contains, particularly in the third book, descriptive passages that are highly sonorous and magniloquent. The work was much praised by Addison in No. 146 of the 'Spectator'.

BURNETT, FRANCES ELIZA HODGSON (1849–1924), writer of popular stories, born in Manchester, emigrated to the United States in her youth. Best known as the author of 'Little Lord Fauntleroy', first published as a novel (1886) and later dramatized (1888). The hero, Cedric Errol, comes to England at the age of 7 with his American mother, a widow, upon becoming heir to his grandfather, an earl. He has been beautifully bred in both character and manner to play the part. He wins the affection of his crusty old grandfather and, after defeating a pretender to the estate, reconciles him and his mother.

BURNEY, DR. CHARLES (1726–1814), organist and minor composer, was the friend of Garrick, Reynolds, and Dr. Johnson and his circle. He was the author of a 'History of Music', published in 4 vols. between 1776 and 1789. He also wrote accounts of his travels in France, Italy, Germany, and the Low Countries, which he made in order to collect material for the work.

Burney, CHARLES (1757–1817), son of Dr. Burney (q.v.), was famous in his day as a classical scholar. After his death the British Museum bought his library of over 13,000 vols. which, besides classical books and manuscripts, included the largest extant collection of early English newspapers.

BURNEY, FRANCES, MADAME D'ARBLAY (1752–1840), daughter of Dr. Burney, the historian of music, lived during her youth in the midst of that literary society which included Dr. Johnson and Burke. In 1778 she published her first novel 'Evelina' (q.v.) anonymously, but the revelation of its authorship brought her into prominence, and she was appointed second keeper of the robes to Queen Charlotte (1786). Being broken in health, she with difficulty obtained permission to retire. In 1793 she married General d'Arblay, a French refugee in England. From 1802 to 1812 she was interned by Napoleon and lived in France. The last part of her life was spent in England. Her second novel 'Cecilia' (q.v.) was published in 1782, 'Camilla' (q.v.) in 1796, 'The Wanderer' in 1814. She edited her father's 'Memoirs' in 1832. Her 'Early Diary' (1768–78), with pleasant sketches of Johnson and Garrick, was published in 1889, and her later 'Diary and Letters' (1778–1840), which gives an interesting account of her life at court, in 1842–6. Miss Burney was the originator of the simple novel of home life, taking as her theme the entry into the world of a young girl of virtue and understanding, but inexperienced, and exposing her to circumstances and incidents that develop her character, and display the various droll persons with whom she comes in contact.

Burning Babe, The, see *Southwell*.

BURNS, ROBERT (1759–96), born at Alloway in Ayrshire, was the son of a cottar, and was educated by his father. Set to work as a farm labourer, he early developed an inclination for literature, and also a tendency to dissipation. From 1784 to 1788 he farmed 118 acres in partnership with his brother Gilbert at Mossgiel, and during this period wrote some of his best work: 'The Cotter's Saturday Night', 'The Twa Dogs', 'Hallowe'en', 'The Jolly Beggars' (a cantata descriptive of a vagabond's festival), 'To a Mouse', 'To a Mountain Daisy', and some of his keenest satires, 'Death and Dr. Hornbook' (against a village apothecary) and 'Holy Willie's Prayer' (against a self-righteous elder of Mauchline). In 1786, in order to obtain the passage-money for a voyage to Jamaica, where a post on a plantation had been offered him, he published the Kilmarnock edition of his early poems. It made him famous, and took him for a time to Edinburgh, where his modesty, the charm and ease of his conversation, and his conviviality, made him very popular. The second edition of his poems (published by William Creech) brought him £500 and enabled him to settle down on a small farm at Ellisland and to marry Jean Armour, one of his many loves (another had been Alison Begbie, 'Mary Morison', who rejected him; and another Mary Campbell, a Glasgow skipper's daughter, who died, and was the subject of his 'To Mary in Heaven'). Burns also received an exciseman's place, which after the failure of his farm was his principal means of support. Apart from songs, he now wrote little of importance ('Tam o' Shanter', q.v., and 'Captain Matthew Henderson' are the chief exceptions). He contributed some 200 songs, new or adapted, to the successive volumes of James Johnson's 'Scots Musical Museum' (1787–1803), among others the famous 'Auld Lang Syne' (q.v.), 'Scots wha hae', 'A Red, Red Rose', and 'It was a' for our Richtfu' King'. In 1792 he also accepted an invitation from George Thomson to supply songs for his 'Scottish Airs with Poetry'. Among his many beautiful lyrics may be mentioned 'John Anderson, my Jo', 'Comin' thro' the Rye', 'The Banks of Doon', and 'Mary Morison'. In a different category fall the humorous vernacular 'Address to the Deil', 'To a Louse', and 'The Auld Farmer's New Year Salutation to his Mare Maggie', a delightful retrospect of a long association between man and beast.

The sympathy that Burns had at first manifested for the French revolutionaries brought him into bad odour with the authorities and nearly cost him his place; while his inclination to convivial living undermined his health. In the last two years of his life he began to see through the aims of France. His last ballad, 'Does haughty Gaul invasion threat?' shows his patriotic spirit; he joined the Dumfriesshire Volunteers in 1794 and was buried with military honours. See also *Sylvander*.

Burrough, STEPHEN and WILLIAM, see *Borough*.

BURTON, JOHN HILL (1809–81), educated at Aberdeen, wrote much for Edinburgh booksellers, reviews, and newspapers, and made his mark by a life of David Hume (1846). He published a 'History of Scotland' (1853, 1867–70), 'The Book-hunter' (1862), 'The Scot Abroad' (1864), and many other treatises and editions, chiefly historical.

BURTON, SIR RICHARD FRANCIS (1821–90), after leaving Trinity College, Oxford, without graduating, joined the Indian Army in 1842. He wrote over eighty books on his travels in India, Africa, and the Americas, perhaps the most noted of which is his 'Personal Narrative of a Pilgrimage to Al Madinah and Mecca' (1855–6), a pilgrimage which he, as one of the first Englishmen to visit Mecca, had to make in disguise. An excellent swordsman, he also wrote works on the bayonet and the sword. He translated the 'Lusiads' of Camoëns (q.v.), but is best known for his translation of the 'Arabian Nights' (q.v., 1885–8) and of 'Kama Sutra' (1883), 'The Perfumed Garden' (1886), and other works of Arabian erotology. He was consul at Damascus, 1869–71, and at Trieste (1872), where he died.

BURTON, ROBERT (1577–1640), educated at Nuneaton and Sutton Coldfield schools, and at Brasenose College and Christ Church, Oxford, became vicar of St.

Thomas's, Oxford, and rector of Segrave, Leicestershire. He was author of the 'Anatomy of Melancholy' (q.v.).

BURY, RICHARD DE (1281–1345), named from his birthplace, Bury St. Edmunds, was tutor to Edward III when Prince of Wales, became bishop of Durham, and is celebrated as a patron of learning. He was an ardent collector of books, employing for this purpose members of the mendicant orders. He founded a library in Durham College, Oxford, and was author of 'Philobiblon', the autobiographical sketch in Latin of a lover of letters, first printed in 1473. An English translation was published in 1832.

Busby, RICHARD (1606–95), educated at Westminster and Christ Church, Oxford, was a famous headmaster of Westminster School from 1638 to 1695. Among his pupils were Dryden, Locke, Atterbury, and Matthew Prior.

Busirane, in Spenser's 'Faerie Queene', III. xi and xii, the 'vile Enchaunter' symbolizing unlawful love. He is stricken down by Britomart in his castle and forced to release Amoret. On the door of one of the rooms of the castle was written:

'*Be bold, be bold,* and every where, *Be bold*';

but on another iron door,

'*Be not too bold.*'

Busīris, a mythical king of Egypt, son of Poseidon, who sacrificed all strangers who came to the country. He was slain by Hercules. There was a city of Busiris (Abousir) in the Delta. Milton attributes the name Busiris to the Pharaoh of the Exodus ('Paradise Lost', i. 306).

Busīris, King of Egypt, a tragedy by Edward Young (q.v.).

Buskin, a word existing in many European languages, whose ultimate derivation is unknown. The special source of the English word is likewise uncertain. It is the word used for the high thick-soled boot (*cothurnus*) worn by actors in ancient Athenian tragedy, frequently contrasted with the 'sock' (*soccus*) or low shoe worn by comedians. Hence it is applied figuratively to the style or spirit of tragedy, the tragic vein. *To put on the buskins,* to write tragedy. [OED.]

Bussy D'Ambois, a tragedy by Chapman (q.v.), published in 1607, and the most famous of the author's plays. It was severely criticized by Dryden.

Bussy D'Ambois (in real life, Louis de Bussy-d'Amboise), a man of insolence and fiery courage, is introduced to the court of Henri III of France by Monsieur, brother of the king, his protector. He quarrels with the king's courtiers, of whom he kills three in an encounter, and even with the Duc de Guise. He wins the favours of the wife of the count of Montsurry (Montsoreau), and when Monsieur, who is also enamoured of the lady, discovers this fact he reveals it, from jealousy, to Montsurry. The latter forces his wife by torture to send a letter summoning Bussy to her. On his arrival, Bussy is overpowered and killed.

The story is the same as that told by Dumas in 'La Dame de Montsoreau'. It is interesting that both writers make the same alteration of the actual fact, which was that, not Monsieur, but the king, who detested Bussy, revealed Bussy's amour to Montsoreau.

Bussy D'Ambois, The Revenge of, a tragedy by Chapman (q.v.), composed in 1610 or 1611, printed in 1613. The play is a sequel to the tragedy 'Bussy D'Ambois' (q.v.).

Clermont D'Ambois, brother of Bussy, a courageous stoical gentleman, close friend of the Duc de Guise, being urged by the ghost of his dead brother to avenge his murder, will only do so by the honourable method of a duel, for which he sends a challenge to the cowardly Montsurry, who evades it. Urged again by the ghost, he introduces himself to Montsurry's house, forces him to fight, and kills him. He then learns the assassination of his patron Guise, and refusing to live amid 'all the horrors of the vicious time', kills himself. The similarity of the play in certain respects to Shakespeare's 'Hamlet' is evident.

Busybody, The, a comedy by Mrs. Centlivre (q.v.), produced in 1709.

Sir George Airy and Miranda are in love with one another, but her guardian, Sir Francis Gripe, has the design of marrying her himself and believes that she loves him. The devices by which his intentions are defeated, and those by which Charles, Gripe's son, secures the hand of Isabinda, whom her father intends for a Spanish merchant, occupy the play. The character of Marplot, whose well-meant but misdirected interference constantly endangers the course of true love, has enriched the language with a name for the blundering busybody.

Butcher, THE BLOODY, a term applied to the duke of Cumberland, second son of George II, on account of the cruelty with which, after Culloden, he suppressed the rebellion of 1745.

BUTLER, ALBAN (1711–73), educated at Douai, where he was subsequently professor of philosophy and divinity. In 1746 he was sent to England and became chaplain to the duke of Norfolk. He was president of the English college at St. Omer, 1768–73. He was author of 'The Lives of the . . . Principal Saints' (1756–9).

BUTLER, JOSEPH (1692–1752), was son of a Presbyterian linen-draper at Wantage, and was educated at Oriel College, Oxford. He was made rector of Haughton-le-Skerne in Durham in 1722, and in 1725 of Stanhope in the same county. In 1736 he was brought into prominence by being appointed clerk of the closet to the queen, and in 1738 bishop of Bristol, from which he was translated to Durham in 1750. In 1726 he published 'Fifteen Sermons' preached at the Rolls Chapel, in which he defines his moral philosophy, affirming an intuitional theory of virtue. While recognizing benevolence and a due degree of self-love as elements in virtuous conduct, he regards conscience as governing and limiting them by considerations, not of happiness or misery, but of right and wrong. In 1736 appeared his 'Analogy of Religion' (q.v.), a defence of the Christian religion against the Deists by showing that their natural religion is open to the same objections as revelation. To this was added his essay, 'Of the Nature of Virtue'.

Butler, THE REVD. REUBEN, a character who marries Jeanie Deans in Scott's 'The Heart of Midlothian' (q.v.).

BUTLER, SAMUEL ('Hudibras' Butler) (1612–80), born at Strensham in Worcestershire, the son of a farmer, and educated at the King's School, Worcester. As attendant on Elizabeth, countess of Kent, he became acquainted with Selden (q.v.). Nothing further is known of his life until 1661, when he was employed by the earl of Carbery. About 1673 he enjoyed the patronage of George Villiers, second duke of Buckingham, who, however, is satirized in his 'Characters' (on the model of those of Theophrastus, q.v., published in his 'Genuine Remains' in 1759) and his 'Hudibras' (q.v.). Of the latter work, Pt. I was published in 1663, Pt. II in 1664, and Pt. III in 1678. It was highly approved by Charles II, who gave the author £300 and later a pension of £100 a year; but Butler was perhaps for a time neglected, and was said to have died in penury. This is commemorated in the epigram on the monument erected to his memory in Westminster Abbey:

> The Poets Fate is here in emblem shown:
> He asked for Bread and he received a
>   Stone.

Butler's verse also includes 'The Elephant in the Moon', a satire directed against Sir Paul Neale, of the Royal Society. The elephant turns out to be a mouse, which has got into the telescope. Butler's 'Genuine Remains in Verse and Prose' were edited in 1759 by Robert Thyer, and more completely by A. R. Waller and R. Lamar in 1908–28.

BUTLER, SAMUEL ('Erewhon' Butler) (1835–1902), the grandson of Dr. Samuel Butler (1774–1839), the great headmaster of Shrewsbury School and bishop of Lichfield, was educated at Shrewsbury and St. John's College, Cambridge. He abandoned the intention of taking holy orders and went to New Zealand in 1859, where he succeeded as a sheep-breeder, as recounted in his 'A First Year in Canterbury Settlement' (1683). He returned to England in 1864 and settled in Clifford's Inn. In 1872 he published 'Erewhon' (q.v.) and in 1873 'The Fair Haven', an ironic defence of Christian evidences. 'A

Psalm of Montreal', a short satirical presentation of the conflict between Greek art and modern gospels, evoked by the discovery of a plaster cast of the Discobolus in a Montreal lumber-room, was written in Canada in 1875 and published in 1884. He next wrote a series of works of scientific controversy, 'Life and Habit' (1877), 'Evolution Old and New' and 'God the Known and God the Unknown' (1879), 'Unconscious Memory' (1880), 'Luck or Cunning' (1887), and 'The Deadlock in Darwinism'. His general attitude in these was one of protest against the Darwinian banishment of mind from the universe; and he maintained the transmissibility, by heredity, of acquired habits. He published in 1881 'Alps and Sanctuaries of Piedmont and the Ticino', a delightful travel-book combining wit and humour with a keen appreciation of beauty of scenery and the character of the people; and in 1888 'Ex Voto', on the Sacro Monte of Varallo-Sesia. In 1896 appeared his 'Life and Letters of Dr. Samuel Butler', his grandfather. Meanwhile Butler had developed a keen interest in Homer, which led to his theory of the feminine authorship of the 'Odyssey' and its origin at Trapani in Sicily. On the latter subject he published an article in 1893; 'The Authoress of the Odyssey' appeared in 1897, and translations of the 'Iliad' and the 'Odyssey' into a vigorous homely prose in 1898 and 1900. 'Shakespeare's Sonnets Reconsidered' appeared in 1899, and 'Erewhon Revisited' (q.v.) in 1901. Butler's autobiographical novel, 'The Way of All Flesh' (q.v.), was published posthumously in 1903, and selections from his note-books in 1912, under the title, 'The Note-books of Samuel Butler'.

Butler was pre-eminently a satirist, who waged war against the torpor of thought, the suppression of originality, the hypocrisies and conventions, that he saw around him.

Button's Coffee-house, the rival of Will's (q.v.), stood in Russell Street, Covent Garden. It was frequented by Dryden, Addison, Steele, and Pope. Button was an old servant of Addison's.

Buzfuz, MR. SERJEANT, in Dickens's 'Pickwick Papers' (q.v.), counsel for the plaintiff in Bardell v. Pickwick.

Bycorne, see Chichevache.

By-Ends, MR., in Bunyan's 'Pilgrim's Progress' (q.v.), 'a very arch fellow, a downright hypocrite; one that would be religious, which way ever the world went: but so cunning, that he would be sure never to lose or suffer for it'.

Byng, ADMIRAL JOHN (1704–57), was sent in 1756 to relieve Port Mahon in Minorca, which was threatened by a French fleet. He was repulsed, sentenced by court-martial for neglect of duty, and shot at Portsmouth. Voltaire wrote, in 'Candide' (1759), 'Il est bon de tuer de temps en temps un amiral pour encourager les autres'.

BYRD, WILLIAM (1538?–1623), was organist of Lincoln, 1563, and joint-organist of the Chapel-Royal, 1569. He was granted the monopoly of issuing printed music and music-paper in 1575. In 1588 he composed the first English madrigals, and published 'Psalmes, Sonets, and Songs' (1588), 'Songs of Sundrie Natures' and 'Liber primus Sacrarum Cantionum' (1589), 'Liber secundus' (1591), 'Gradualia' (1607), and 'Psalmes, Songs, and Sonnets' (1611).

Byrhtnoth's Death, see Maldon (Battle of).

BYROM, JOHN (1692–1763), educated at Merchant Taylors' School and a fellow of Trinity College, Cambridge. He taught shorthand in Manchester, where he chiefly lived, and elsewhere, and wrote, besides a quantity of religious verse, a pleasant anapaestic 'Pastoral' celebrating the daughter of Richard Bentley (q.v.), with whom he fell in love. He was a Jacobite and an enthusiastic admirer of W. Law (q.v.) and turned some of his teaching into verse, introducing the anapaest with strange effect. His 'Private Journal and Literary Remains' throw much light on Law's character. Byrom wrote the hymn, 'Christians, awake! Salute the happy morn'.

BYRON, GEORGE GORDON, sixth Baron (1788–1824), son of Captain John Byron, a profligate, and Catherine Gordon of Gight, was born in London and came into the title when 10 years old. He had unexpectedly become heir-presumptive in 1794, in consequence of the fifth baron's grandson falling in action in Corsica. He was educated at Harrow and Trinity College, Cambridge. While at Cambridge he printed his 'Hours of Idleness' (at first named 'Juvenilia'), published in 1807, which were severely criticized in the 'Edinburgh Review'. To this criticism he replied, in 1809, in 'English Bards and Scotch Reviewers' (q.v.). From 1809 to 1811 he travelled abroad, visiting Portugal, Spain, Greece, and the Levant, and addressing 'Maid of Athens' to Theresa Macri. On his return he took his seat in the Lords, and in 1812 published the first two cantos of 'Childe Harold' (q.v.). During the next four years appeared 'The Giaour', 'The Bride of Abydos', 'The Corsair', 'Lara', 'Parisina', 'The Siege of Corinth', and 'Hebrew Melodies' (all dealt with under their titles), also 'The Dream', a beautiful visionary poem in blank verse. In 1815 Byron married Anne Isabella Milbanke, an heiress, from whom he was separated in 1816. He thereupon left England, never to return, embittered by the strictures of what he regarded as a hypocritical society. In company part of the time with the Shelleys, he travelled to Switzerland and Venice, which, with Ravenna, Pisa, and Genoa, became his headquarters. Canto iii of 'Childe Harold' appeared in 1816, canto iv in 1818. In 1817 appeared 'The Lament of Tasso', a dramatic soliloquy, expressing the poet's passionate love and regret, as he lies in prison, for Leonora d'Este. Byron wrote the first five cantos of 'Don Juan' (q.v.) in 1818–20; 'Beppo' (q.v.) appeared in 1818. In 1819 began his connexion with Teresa, Countess Guiccioli, who lived with him for a time at Venice, and whom he followed to Ravenna. While there and subsequently at Pisa he wrote his dramas, the principal of which are 'Manfred', 'Cain', 'Marino Faliero', 'The Two Foscari', 'Sardanapalus', 'Heaven and Earth' (dealt with under their titles); also 'Mazeppa' (q.v.), 'The Prophecy of Dante' (a dramatic soliloquy embodying the poet's vision of the future liberation of Italy), and the later cantos of the unfinished 'Don Juan'. In 1822 Byron and Leigh Hunt joined in the production of 'The Liberal' magazine. The first number contained Byron's 'The Vision of Judgment' (q.v.), an outcome of his feud with Southey. The second contained 'Heaven and Earth'; and the fourth, Byron's translation of the first canto of Pulci's 'Morgante Maggiore'. No further numbers appeared. In 1823 Byron set out to join the Greek insurgents, and died of fever at Missolonghi in April 1824. His last works include the tragedy 'Werner' (q.v., 1822), the beautiful romantic verse tale 'The Island' (q.v., 1823), 'The Age of Bronze' (1823), a satirical poem inspired by the Congress of Verona, and 'The Deformed Transformed' (q.v.), an unfinished drama (1824). Byron's body was brought home from Greece and buried at Hucknall Torkard, in Nottinghamshire, near his family seat.

Byron's poetry, though much criticized on moral grounds, was immensely popular at home, and also abroad, where it exerted great influence on the Romantic movement. This popularity it owed to the author's persistent attacks on 'cant political, religious, and moral', to the novelty of his oriental scenery, to the romantic character of the Byronic hero (constantly reappearing in successive works), and to the ease and fluency, and (very frequently) the real beauty, of his verse.

Byron, HARRIET, the heroine of Richardson's 'Sir Charles Grandison' (q.v.).

BYRON, JOHN (1723–86), as a midshipman on the 'Wager', one of the ships of Lord Anson's squadron in his famous voyage, was wrecked on an island off the coast of Chile in 1741. His 'Narrative' of the shipwreck, published in 1768, was used by his grandson, Lord Byron, in his description of the storm and wreck in 'Don Juan'.

Byron, *The Conspiracy and Tragedy of Charles Duke of*, a double play by Chapman (q.v.), published in 1608.

The play deals with the intrigues of Charles Gontaut, Duc de Biron, a brave soldier who had fought successfully and been nobly rewarded by Henri IV of France, but whose overweening ambition made him disloyal to the king. His plots are discovered, he asks forgiveness and is pardoned. But his restless ambition makes him prepare a new conspiracy, which is revealed to the king. He is arrested and condemned to death. He professes his innocence and is reduced to frenzy and despair when he realizes that he is to die.

Byronic, characteristic of or resembling Lord Byron (q.v.) or his poetry, that is to say, contemptuous of and rebelling against conventional morality, or defying fate, or possessing the characteristics of Byron's romantic heroes, or imitating his dress and appearance; 'posturing statuesque pathetic', as Meredith describes it; 'a man proud, moody, cynical, with defiance on his brow, and misery in his heart, a scorner of his kind, implacable in revenge, yet capable of deep and strong affection' (Macaulay, 'Byron').

BYWATER, INGRAM (1840–1914), educated at University College School and King's College School, London, and at Queen's College, Oxford, and a fellow of Exeter College, was an eminent Greek scholar. He succeeded Jowett as Regius professor of Greek in 1893. He had acquired a European reputation by his edition (1877) of the Fragments of Heraclitus. His monumental edition of the 'Poetics' of Aristotle appeared in 1909. He made important contributions to the OED., and guided the critical methods of the editors of the long series of Oxford Classical Texts.

Byzantine, the word used to designate the art, and especially the architecture, developed in the Eastern division of the Roman Empire. This Eastern division endured from the partition of the Empire between the two sons of Theodosius in A.D. 395 to the capture of Constantinople, its capital, formerly known as Byzantium, by the Turks in 1453. The Byzantine architecture is distinguished by its use of the round arch, cross, circle, dome, and rich mosaic ornament. St. Mark's at Venice is a prominent example.

The 'Byzantine historians' are those who lived in the Eastern Empire from the 6th to the 15th cents.

C

C.I.D., the Criminal Investigation Department of Scotland Yard.

C.S.C., see *Calverley*.

Ça ira, the name of a celebrated French revolutionary song, of which the refrain is

Ah! ça ira, ça ira!
Les aristocrates à la lanterne!

It is said to have originated in the hopeful reply, 'Ça ira', of Benjamin Franklin to a question about the prospects of the American republic in the War of Independence.

Caaba, see *Kaaba*.

Cabal, from the Hebrew word *qabbalah* (see *Cabbala*), a secret intrigue of a sinister character formed by a small body of persons, or a small body of persons engaged in such an intrigue; in British history applied specially to the five ministers of Charles II who signed the treaty of alliance with France for war against Holland in 1672; these were Clifford, Arlington, Buckingham, Ashley, and Lauderdale, the initials of whose names thus arranged happened to form the word *cabal*. [OED.]

Cabbala, from the Hebrew *qabbalah*, tradition, a Jewish tradition of the mystical interpretation of the Scriptures, a reaction from the rationalism of the school of Maimonides (q.v.), developed between the 9th and 13th cents., comprising the 'Sepher Yezirah' ('Book of Creation') and the 'Zohar' ('Splendour'). These mystic doctrines included the existence of 'Sephiroth', realized abstractions or emanations, by which the infinite entered into relations with the finite; and the belief that the letters of the biblical text, converted into numbers, may be manipulated in such a way as to reveal hidden truths. There is perhaps a trace of this in the number of the Beast in Rev. xiii. 18.

CABELL, JAMES BRANCH (1879–1958), American novelist, born in Virginia. Many of his stories are set in an imaginary country, Poictesme, which is described in the course of the series. 'Jurgen' (1919), the best known of the 18 titles published in the 'Storisende Edition' (1927–30), came under fire for immorality. 'The Cream of the Jest' (1917) is another of his better novels. He also published several volumes of criticism and poetry.

CABLE, GEORGE WASHINGTON (1844–1925), American novelist, author of some charming stories of the old Creole society of Louisiana, including 'Old Creole Days' (1879), 'The Grandissimes' (1880), and 'Madame Delphine' (1881).

Cabot, JOHN (Giovanni Caboto) (1450–98), Italian navigator in the English service. In 1497, accompanied by his son (see below), he sailed from Bristol to try to find a north-west passage to India, discovering Cape Breton Island and Nova Scotia. He made further expeditions in the following years.

Cabot, SEBASTIAN (1474–1557), son of the above, born at Bristol, a celebrated navigator, who sailed with his father in the expedition of 1497. He was pilot-major to the Emperor Charles V, 1519–26 and 1533–44, in which position he made important explorations in South American seas. He returned to Bristol in 1547 and was pensioned by Edward VI. He promoted the Company of Merchant Adventurers for the discovery of the North-East Passage to China and supervised the north-east expeditions to China of 1553 and 1556.

Cacodemon, from the Greek word meaning an evil spirit, in which sense it is used in Shakespeare's 'Richard III', i. iii. In astrology the name is applied to the Twelfth House in a figure of the Heavens, so called from its baleful influence.

Cacus, in Roman legend, a monster or brigand who lived in a cave on the Aventine (q.v.) hill. As Hercules was driving home the oxen of Geryon (q.v.), Cacus stole some of them, and dragged them backwards into his cave to escape discovery. Hercules departed without perceiving the theft, but the lowing of his other oxen was answered by those in the cave. Hercules thereupon attacked Cacus, slew him, and recovered his oxen.

Cade, JACK, REBELLION OF, a political movement in 1450 by the men of Kent against the misrule of Henry VI and his council. It was headed by Jack Cade, an Irish adventurer who took the name of Mortimer. With a large mob he marched on London, entered the city in triumph and beheaded Lord Say, the lord treasurer. After a fight on London Bridge, the insurgents deserted Cade, who was pursued into Sussex and slain.

Cadenus and Vanessa, a poem by Swift (q.v.), written in 1713 for Esther Vanhomrigh ('Vanessa'), and published after her death by her request. It is the narrative, in mock classical form, of the author's relations with 'Vanessa' and an apology for his conduct. 'Cadenus' is an obvious anagram of 'Decanus'. Miss Vanhomrigh evidently took no exception to his statement of the facts, since she preserved the poem and desired it to be published.

Cadmean victory, 'a victory involving one's own ruin' (Liddell and Scott), usually associated with some incident in the story of Thebes, of which Cadmus (q.v.) was the legendary founder. Cf. *Pyrrhic Victory*.

Cadmus, son of Agenor, king of Phoenicia, was sent by his father in search of his sister Europa (q.v.), whom Zeus had carried away. His companions were devoured by a dragon, which he attacked and overcame by the assistance of Athene. He sowed its teeth in the plain, upon which armed men sprang up. He threw a stone in the midst of them, whereupon they turned their arms against each other, till all perished except five, who helped Cadmus to found the city of Thebes in Boeotia. Cadmus married Harmonia, a daughter of Aphrodite. Owing to the misfortunes of their children (Ino, Semele, qq.v., etc.), whom Hera persecuted, Cadmus and Harmonia entreated the gods to relieve them of the miseries of life, and were turned into serpents. Cadmus was reputed the first to introduce the use of letters into Greece.

Cadogan, a mode of knotting the hair behind the head, said to be derived from the first earl of Cadogan (d. 1726). It was popular among French ladies in the 18th cent.

Cadoudal, GEORGES (1771–1804), a leader of the Chouans (q.v.), executed for plotting against the life of Napoleon Buonaparte.

Cadūcĕus, the wand carried by an ancient Greek or Roman herald, and specially the fabled wand carried by Hermes (q.v.) as messenger of the gods. It is usually represented with two serpents twined round it. As Hermes was thought to have the power of bringing sleep to men, Milton ('Paradise Lost', xi. 132) speaks of 'the pastoral reed of Hermes, or his opiate rod'.

Cadwal, in Shakespeare's 'Cymbeline' (q.v.), the name borne by Arviragus while he lived in the woods.

Cadwallader, the son of Cadwallon and last king of the Britons, who reigned in the 7th cent. He defended Wales against the Saxons, and Merlin prophesied his return at some future time to expel them. He joined Penda, king of Mercia (an Angle), against Eadwine, the Angle king of Northumbria.

CADWALLADER is also the name of a character in Smollett's 'Peregrine Pickle' (q.v.), and a *Mrs. Cadwallader* figures in George Eliot's 'Middlemarch' (q.v.).

CÆDMON (corruptly CEDMON) (*fl.* 670), entered the monastery of Streaneshalch (Whitby) between 658 and 680, when already an elderly man. He is said by Bede to have been an unlearned herdsman, who received suddenly, in a vision, the power of song, and later put into English verse passages translated to him from the Scriptures. The name Cædmon cannot be explained in English, and has been conjectured to be Celtic (an adaptation of the British Catumanus). In 1655 François Dujon (Franciscus Junius) published at Amsterdam from the unique Bodleian MS. Junius 11 (*c.* 1000) long scriptural poems, which he took to be those of Cædmon. These are 'Genesis', 'Exodus', 'Daniel', and 'Christ and Satan' (qq.v.). Modern scholarship denies them to Cædmon. The only authentic fragment of his work that survives is his first Hymn, which Bede quotes.

Caelestina, a character in Dekker's 'Satiromastix' (q.v.). See also *Celestina.*

Caelia, in Spenser's 'Faerie Queene' (q.v.), i. x, the Lady of the House of Holiness, mother of Fidelia, Speranza, and Charissa (Faith, Hope, and Charity).

Caelica, a collection of sonnets and songs by Sir Fulke Greville (q.v.).

Caerleon, see *Carlion.*

Caermarthen, Black Book of, a Welsh MS. of the 12th cent., containing poems attributed to the great traditional bards of Wales.

CAESAR, the name of a patrician family of Rome, which GAIUS JULIUS CAESAR (102?–44 B.C.), the conqueror of Gaul and dictator, raised to the highest eminence. He was not only a great general and statesman, but an orator and historian. The only work of his that has come down to us is his 'Commentarii', the history of the first seven years of the Gallic War, and of part of the Civil War.

The name Caesar was assumed by his adopted son, Octavianus, on whom the Senate conferred the title 'Augustus', and by Tiberius as the adopted son of Augustus. Both names were used by successive emperors, whether of the family of Caesar or not. 'Caesar' survived as a title in *Kaiser* and *Tsar.*

Caesar's Wife: Julius Caesar divorced his wife Pompeia, who was accused of an intrigue with Clodius, not because he thought her guilty, but because Caesar's wife must be above suspicion.

Caesar and Cleopatra, a play by G. B. Shaw (q.v., 1901).

Caesar and **Luath,** Burns's 'Twa Dogs'.

Caesar and Pompey, a Roman tragedy by Chapman (q.v.), published 1631, but written at an earlier date.

It deals with the contention of Caesar and Pompey, the events leading up to the battle of Pharsalus (48 B.C.), the murder of Pompey, and the suicide of Cato of Utica. The latter is the real hero of the play, of which the motto is 'Only a just man is a free man'.

Caesaraugusta, in imprints, Saragossa.

Caesarean or CAESARIAN **operation** or SECTION, the delivery of a child by cutting through the walls of the abdomen, as was done according to Pliny in the case of the original ancestor of the Caesars.

Caesarion, son of Gaius Julius Caesar (q.v.) and Cleopatra (q.v.). He was executed by order of Augustus.

Caesūra, in Greek and Latin prosody, the division of a metrical foot between two words, especially in certain recognized places near the middle of the line; in English prosody, a pause about the middle of a metrical line, generally indicated by a pause in the sense.

Cagliostro, COUNT ALESSANDRO (1743–95), whose real name was Giuseppe Balsamo, was a charlatan born at Palermo. After a dissolute and criminal youth, he travelled in the East and studied alchemy. He then wandered about Europe selling drugs and philtres, and acquired a great reputation. He visited London several times and was received in the best society, but finally underwent a period of imprisonment in the Fleet. In 1785 he was implicated in the affair of the 'Diamond Necklace' (q.v.). He was acquitted in this connexion, but imprisoned on other grounds. He was arrested in Rome in 1789 as a heretic (on the denunciation of his wife, Serafina) and sentenced to death, but this was commuted to perpetual imprisonment.

Cahors, in the S. of France, a famous seat of Italian money-changers and financiers in the Middle Ages; whence the name CAORSIN for a money-dealer from Cahors. The Caorsins were expelled from England by Henry III in 1240, readmitted on the intervention of the pope in 1250, and again proscribed and imprisoned in 1251 'on account of their unbounded and detestable usury' [OED.]. Dante couples Cahors with Sodom in 'Inferno' xi. 50.

Cain: A Mystery, a tragedy by Lord Byron (q.v.), published in 1821.

Cain, revolting against the toil imposed upon him as the consequence of another's fault, and puzzled to reconcile what he sees with what he has been taught of the Omnipotent God, becomes a pupil of Lucifer, and questions him about the problems of existence. Lucifer's teaching intensifies the revolt of Cain against the conditions he endures, and in a fit of passion at Abel's devotion to Jehovah, he strikes his brother and kills him. Remorse and punishment follow, and Cain goes out into exile. The audacity of the poem aroused intense indignation, and evoked many attacks on the author.

Cain, The Wanderings of, see *Wanderings*.

Cain-coloured, of the reputed colour of the hair of Cain, to whom, as to Judas Iscariot, a red or reddish-yellow beard was attributed.

He hath but a little wee face, with a little yellow beard, a Cain-coloured beard.
(Shakespeare, 'Merry Wives', 1. iv. 22.)

CAINE, SIR THOMAS HENRY HALL (1853–1931), of Manx and Cumberland parentage, was befriended by D. G. Rossetti (q.v.), whom he first met in 1880. Caine was Rossetti's housemate from 1881 till the latter's death. He was author of a number of novels of wide popularity, many of them centred in the Isle of Man, including 'The Shadow of a Crime' (1885), 'The Deemster' (1887), 'The Bondman' (1890), 'The Scapegoat' (1891), 'The Manxman' (1894), 'The Christian' (1897), 'The Eternal City' (1901), 'The Prodigal Son' (1904), 'The White Prophet' (1909), 'The Woman Thou Gavest Me' (1913). Several of the above have been dramatized. 'My Story', a narrative of the early years of Caine's literary career, appeared in 1908.

Cairbar, in Macpherson's Ossianic poems, a lord of Connaught, who rebels against King Cormac, murders him and usurps the crown. It is he who slays, and is slain by, Oscar, son of Ossian.

CAIRD, EDWARD (1835–1908), educated at Greenock Academy, Glasgow and St. Andrews Universities, and Balliol College, Oxford, which he entered in 1860. An older man than his fellow undergraduates at Balliol, he found his most intimate associates among graduates, notably T. H. Green (q.v.). Jowett was his tutor. He became fellow and tutor of Merton College, and in 1866 professor of moral philosophy at Glasgow. In 1893 he succeeded Jowett as master of Balliol College. In his 'Philosophy of Kant' (1868), 'The Critical Philosophy of Immanuel Kant' (1889), and his monograph on Hegel (1883), he produced brilliant expositions and criticisms of the systems of these two philosophers. In 1893 he published his Gifford lectures on 'The Evolution of Religion'.

CAIRD, JOHN (1820–98), principal of the University of Glasgow, and elder brother of Edward Caird (q.v.); author of 'An Introduction to the Philosophy of Religion' (1880), in which he discusses the evolution of religion, and shows ground for thinking that the organic development of Christianity is not inconsistent with its divine or supernatural origin.

Caius (pron. 'Keys') **College,** Cambridge (full title, Gonville and Caius College), was formerly Gonville Hall, which was founded by Edmund Gonville in 1348. John Caius or Kay (1510–73), scholar and physician to Edward VI and Mary, who was educated at Gonville Hall, refounded and enlarged it as Caius College in 1557, and was master, 1559–73.

Caius, DR., a character in Shakespeare's 'The Merry Wives of Windsor' (q.v.).

Calais was taken by Edward III in 1347, the lives of the principal burgesses being spared at Queen Philippa's intercession. It was recaptured in Mary's reign by the duke of Guise (1558), to the deep mortification of the queen. During her last illness she told a lady-in-waiting, 'When I am dead and opened, you shall find Calais lying upon my heart' (Holinshed).

Calandrino, a foolish credulous fellow, to whom many ludicrous misfortunes happen in the 'Decameron' (q.v.) of Boccaccio (e.g. viii. 3, viii. 6, ix. 3).

Calantha, the heroine of Ford's 'The Broken Heart' (q.v.).

CALDERÓN DE LA BARCA, PEDRO (1600–81), a great Spanish dramatist, and the successor of Lope de Vega (q.v.). Eight of his plays were translated into English by FitzGerald (q.v.). The best known is 'La Vida es Sueño'. Dryden, Goethe, Shelley, Bridges, among others, were under obligations to him. Besides some 120 plays, Calderón wrote more than 70 *autos*, dramatic presentations of the Mystery of the Holy Eucharist, in which his genius is said to be seen at its best (Magnus, 'Dict. of European Literature').

CALDERON, GEORGE (1868–1915), English dramatist, was educated at Rugby and Trinity College, Oxford. His plays include: 'The Fountain' (1909), 'The Little Stone House' (1911), 'Revolt' (1912), and a tragedy in blank verse, 'Cromwell: Mall o' Monks' (in his collected plays, 1921–2).

Caleb Balderstone, a character in Scott's 'The Bride of Lammermoor' (q.v.).

Caleb Williams, Adventures of, a novel by W. Godwin (q.v.), published in 1794.

This work is interesting as an early example of the propagandist novel and the novel of crime and its detection. It was designed to show 'the tyranny and perfidiousness exercised by the powerful members of the community against those who are less privileged than themselves'. The first part of the book deals with the misdeeds of Tyrrel, an arrogant and tyrannical country squire, who ruins a tenant on his estate, Háwkins, for refusing to yield to one of his whims, and drives to the grave his niece, Miss Melville, for refusing to marry a boor of his selection. In the course of these doings he comes into conflict with Falkland, a neighbouring squire of high-minded and benevolent disposition, knocks him down in public, and is shortly after found murdered. Suspicion falls on Falkland as the murderer, but is diverted to Hawkins and his son, who are tried and executed. From this time Falkland becomes eccentric and solitary. Caleb Williams, the self-educated son of humble parents, is appointed his secretary, and presently becomes convinced that Falkland is in fact the murderer of Tyrrel. The remainder of the book is taken up with the unrelenting persecution of Williams by Falkland, in spite of Williams's devotion to his employer, and his refusal to betray the latter's secret. By Falkland's cunning dispositions, Williams is imprisoned on a charge of robbing his employer. He escapes from prison, but is tracked from concealment to concealment by Falkland's agents, until, driven to desperation, he lays a charge of murder against Falkland, is confronted with him, and although he has no proof to offer, by the generosity and sincerity of his statement, wins from the murderer a confession of his own guilt.

Caledonia, the Roman name for the northern part of Britain. Hence used poetically for Scotland.

Calendar, the system according to which the beginning and length of the year are fixed.

The JULIAN CALENDAR is that introduced by Julius Caesar in 46 B.C., in which the ordinary year has 365 days, and every fourth year is a leap year of 366 days, the months having the names, order, and length still retained. This was known as 'Old Style' when the Gregorian Calendar was introduced.

The GREGORIAN CALENDAR is the modification of the preceding, adapted to bring it into closer conformity with astronomical data and the natural course of the seasons, and to rectify the error already contracted by its use. This modification was introduced by Pope Gregory XIII in 1582, and adopted in Great Britain in 1752. It was known as 'New Style'. The error, due to the fact that the Julian year of 365¼ days (allowing for leap years) was 11 minutes 10 seconds too long, amounted in 1752 to 11 days, and in order to correct this, 2 Sept. was in that year followed by 14 Sept., while for the future the years 2000, 2400, 2800, were to be reckoned as leap years, but the other hundredth years, 1800, 1900, 2100, &c., were to be ordinary years. See *Year*.

The CHINESE year begins at the first new moon after the sun has left Capricorn, i.e. some time between 21 Jan. and 19 Feb.

Dates used to be given according to the year of the Emperor's reign, and sometimes a sexagenary cycle was used, but modern dates are calculated from the founding of the Republic in 1912. The Gregorian calendar is now used for official purposes, as also in modern Japan, where it has existed side by side with the National Calendar, which takes as its starting-point the supposed accession-date of the first Emperor (660 B.C.), and a method of dating by era names.

The FRENCH REPUBLICAN CALENDAR made the year begin at the autumnal equinox, and was in use in France from 22 Sept. 1792, date of the proclamation of the Republic, until 1 Jan. 1806. Its twelve months of thirty days (supplemented by five intercalary days) were *Vendémiaire* (Sept.–Oct.), *Brumaire* (Oct.–Nov.), *Frimaire* (Nov.–Dec.), *Nivôse* (Dec.–Jan.), *Fluviôse* (Jan.–Feb.), *Ventôse* (Feb.–March.), *Germinal* (March–April), *Floréal* (April–May), *Prairial* (May–June), *Messidor* (June–July), *Thermidor*(July–Aug.), *Fructidor* (Aug.–Sept.). The names were invented by Fabre d'Églantine (1755–94), the French poet, and the chronological arrangement devised by Gilbert Romme (1750–95).

The JEWISH CALENDAR combines solar years with lunar months, an additional month being intercalated in each of seven years in every cycle of nineteen years. It reckons from the creation of the world (3760 B.C.). The months are *Nisan* (normally March–April), *Iyar* (April–May), *Sivan* (May–June), *Tammuz* (June–July), *Ab* (July–Aug.), *Elul* (Aug.–Sept.), *Tishri* (Sept.–Oct.), *Cheshvan* (Oct.–Nov.), *Kislev* (Nov.–Dec.), *Tebeth* (Dec.–Jan.), *Shebat* (Jan.–Feb.), *Adar* (Feb.–March), *2nd Adar* (intercalary month). The new year begins on the first and second days of the month *Tishri*. Thus A.D. 1932 = A.M. 5692–3, *Tishri* 1 of A.M. 5693 falling on 1 Oct. 1932.

In the MUSLIM CALENDAR the year consists of twelve lunar months of alternately 30 and 29 days each, dating from A.D. 622, the year of the Hijra (q.v.). The Calendar is known as the era of the Hijra, usually abbreviated in English in the Latin form, A.H. (Anno Hijrae), and is based solely on the phases of the moon, taking no account of the solar year, in relation to which it recedes approximately eleven days each solar year. The months are *Muharram*, *Safar*, *Rabi 'Al-Awwal*, *Rabi 'Al-Akhir*, *Jumada Al-Ula*, *Jumada Al-Ukhra*, *Rajab*, *Sha'ban*, *Ramadhan*, *Shawwal*, *Dhu Al-Qa'da*, *Dhu Al-Hijja*. Tables of conversion of Muslim and Christian dates can be consulted in G. S. P. Freeman-Grenville's 'The Muslim and Christian Calendars' (1963).

See also *Calends, Nones, Ides, Newgate Calendar*, and Appendix III.

Calender or KALENDER, one of a mendicant order of dervishes in Turkey and Persia.

Calends or KALENDS, the first day of any month in the ancient Roman calendar. The

Romans reckoned the days forward to the Calends, Nones, or Ides next following. Thus 27 May was described as the sixth day before the Calends of June.

See also *Greek Calends*.

Calenius, WALTER (*d.* 1151), a name used by John Bale (q.v.) for an undefined writer who was archdeacon of Oxford, 1115–38. This Walter, according to Geoffrey of Monmouth (q.v.), brought from Brittany the Celtic chronicle which Geoffrey professed to translate. 'Calena' being, in the bastard Latin of the 16th cent., used for Oxford, Bale by 'Calenius' meant only Walter of Oxford. He is sometimes confused with later archdeacons of Oxford, Walter of Coutances (1183) and Walter Map (q.v.).

CALEPINO, AMBROSIO (*d.* 1511), an Italian Augustinian monk, author of a Latin dictionary, whence the French word *calepin* (note-book). 'Calepin' occurs in English literature in the sense of 'book of reference'.

Cales, KNIGHT OF: 'Cales [Cadiz] knights were made in that voyage [1596] by Robert, earl of Essex, to the number of sixty; whereof (though many of great worth) some were of low fortunes: and therefore Queen Elizabeth was half offended with the Earl for making knighthood so common' (Fuller, *Worthies* (*Kent*), II. 121.)

Caliban, in Shakespeare's 'Tempest' (q.v.), the misshapen evil-natured monster, son of the witch Sycorax; 'an attempt to reduce to one common denominator the aboriginal type whom the dramatist had seen [brought to England from America by travellers and exhibited] or of whom he had heard or read' (Sir S. Lee).

Caliban upon Setebos, a poem by R. Browning (q.v.), included in 'Dramatis Personae' (q.v.).

Caliban (q.v.), lying in the mud in a cave, while Prospero and Miranda believe him at work, thinks out, from a savage's point of view, the problem of the creation of the world by his god Setebos (q.v.). He speaks in the third person. Setebos, dwelling 'in the cold of the Moon', himself subordinate to a higher deity 'The Quiet', has made the world as a plaything to amuse himself, just as Caliban himself would make a clay bird, and throw it in the air and laugh if its leg were broken. Setebos is like Caliban in other respects also, neither kind nor cruel, good in the main, but jealous. In the fancied security of his cave Caliban expresses a hope that Setebos may some day come to an end. But a thunderstorm brings him promptly to order: 'Lo! 'Lieth flat and loveth Setebos!'

Caliburn, see *Excalibur*.

Calidore, SIR, the Knight of Courtesy, the hero of Bk. VI of Spenser's 'Faerie Queene'. He pursues and chains the 'Blatant Beast' (q.v.).

Caligula, GAIUS CAESAR, son of Germanicus, so called from his wearing, when a boy, *caligae* or soldiers' boots, was Roman emperor A.D. 37–41. The cruelties and vices that marked his reign were perhaps due to his madness. He considered himself a god and erected a temple in his own honour. He proposed to raise his horse ('Incitatus') to the consulship, and committed other outrageous eccentricities. He was finally murdered. Horace Walpole, in his letters to Mann, ii. 103, refers to the 'Caligulisms' of Frederick, Prince of Wales.

Caliphate, the rule of the Caliphs ('vice-regents') who succeeded Mohammed (q.v.). The first four were Abu Bakr, Omar, Othman, and Ali. These were followed by the Umayyad and the Abbasid (qq.v.) Caliphs. The Abbasid dynasty came to an end with Mu'tasim, the last Caliph of Baghdad, in 1258. The title of Caliph was subsequently assumed by the Ottoman sultans. The Caliphate practically ceased to exist after the abolition of the sultanate in 1922. There were also Fatimite Caliphs in Egypt (see *Fatima*) in the 10th–12th cents. Various other Muslim dynasties have from time to time assumed the dignity of the Caliphate. The chief of these is perhaps that of the sultans of Morocco, who, under the title of Grand Sherifs, are still revered as Caliphs by their subjects.

Calipolis, in Peele's 'Battle of Alcazar' (q.v.), the wife of Muley Muhamet, the Moorish king, frequently quoted as typical of a sweetheart (e.g. Shakespeare, '2 Henry IV', II. iv). Sir W. Scott writes the name, 'Callipolis'.

Calista, the heroine of Rowe's 'The Fair Penitent' (q.v.), in which the 'gay Lothario' figures as her lover.

Calisto, see *Callisto*.

Some beauty rare, Calisto, Clymene.
   (Milton, 'Paradise Regained', ii. 186.)

Calisto and Melibea, see *Celestina*.

Call of the Wild, The, the story of the dog Buck, by Jack London (q.v.), published 1903.

CALLIMACHUS (*b. c.* 310 B.C.), a celebrated poet of Alexandria, who was perhaps chief librarian of the library of that city. Some of his poems survive and justify Ovid's comment, 'quamvis ingenio non valet, arte valet'. His epigram on his friend Heraclitus of Halicarnassus has been translated in a well-known poem by W. J. Cory (q.v.). He also wrote a poem on the 'Lock of Berenice' (q.v.), which Catullus translated.

Calliŏpē, the muse (q.v.) of epic poetry.

Callipolis, see *Calipolis.*

Callirrhoë, the wife of Alcmaeon (q.v.). Callirrhoe is also the name of the heroine of the romance 'Chaereas and Callirrhoe' (q.v.).

Callista, a religious novel by J. H. Newman (q.v.), published in 1856.

Callisthĕnēs, a nephew and pupil of Aristotle, who accompanied Alexander the Great on his expedition. He became obnoxious to the monarch, was accused of being privy to a plot against him, and was put to death in 327 B.C. Landor has an 'Imaginary Conversation' between Callisthenes and Aristotle.

Callisto, a nymph, the daughter of Lycaon (q.v.), the companion of Artemis and a huntress, was beloved by Zeus and became the mother of Arcas (the eponymous hero of Arcadia). She was metamorphosed into a she-bear by the design of the jealous Hera, and was on the point of being slain by her son in the chase, when both were turned into constellations, Callisto into the Great Bear.

Calpē, the modern Gibraltar, one of the Pillars of Hercules. The 'Calpe foxhounds' is a celebrated pack, hunting the country inland from La Linea.

CALPRENÈDE, GAUTHIER DE COSTES DE LA, see *La Calprenède*.

Calvary (from Latin *calvaria*, skull, used to translate the Aramaic *gogulpo*, Heb. *gulgolep*, which in Gk. N.T. becomes 'Golgotha'), the name of the mount of the Crucifixion, near Jerusalem. Hence 'a Calvary' is a life-size representation of the Crucifixion, in the open air, or a series of representations, in a church or chapel, of the scenes of the Passion.

CALVERLEY, CHARLES STUART (1831–84), educated at Harrow and Balliol College, Oxford, whence he migrated to Christ's College, Cambridge, became a barrister of the Inner Temple, but suffered grievously in health from an accident in 1867, which impaired his power of work. He published 'Verses and Translations' in 1862 and 'Fly Leaves' in 1866, becoming famous under the initials 'C. S. C.' for his parodies (of Browning, Macaulay, Tupper, among others) and for the wit and scholarship of his verse.

Calves' Head Club, an association formed at the end of the 17th cent. to ridicule Charles I, calves' heads being used to represent the monarch and his courtiers on the anniversary of his execution. The club was suppressed in 1735.

CALVIN (from *Calvinus*, the latinized form of the family name *Cauvin*), JEAN (1509–64), the great French theological writer and reformer, was born at Noyon in Picardy. He settled at Geneva in 1536, where he became dictator of a kind of theocracy, and caused Servetus (q.v.) to be burnt in 1553. His great work was the 'Institution de la religion chrétienne', written first in Latin (Basel, 1535) and afterwards in French, in which he expounded his doctrine of original sin, of predestination and election, and his anti-Roman views, and showed himself a master of prose. He was the spiritual father of John Knox and the originator of the dogma of Scottish Presbyterianism. Wherever Protestantism has had to fight for its life, it has sought strength in the discipline of Calvinism.

The 'Calvinistic Methodists' are the section of the Methodists who follow the Calvinistic opinions of Whitefield (q.v.) as opposed to the Arminian (q.v.) opinions of J. Wesley (q.v.).

Calydon, an ancient town and district of Aetolia. See *Meleager*.

Calypso, one of the daughters of Atlas, a nymph who reigned in the island of Ogygia. When Odysseus (q.v.) was shipwrecked on her coasts, she received him hospitably and offered him immortality if he would remain with her. The hero refused, and after seven years' delay was allowed to depart.

Cam and **Isis,** the rivers on which Cambridge and Oxford stand, sometimes used to signify these universities. But there is no real river Isis: the Romans called the river *Thamesis* from source to sea. The corruption, as old as Leland's time, arose from the 'Thame stream' coming in at Dorchester. Hence 'Thame' and 'Isis' are bred out of real name *Thamesis*.

Cama, see *Kama*.

Camacho, in 'Don Quixote' (q.v., II. xx, xxi), a rich farmer of La Mancha, who prepares a splendid feast in anticipation of his wedding with Quiteria; of whom, however, he is deprived, by means of a stratagem, by his rival Basilius.

Camaralzaman ('Moon of the Age'), in the 'Arabian Nights' (q.v.), the prince who marries Badoura, daughter of the king of China. They were brought together secretly one night by the intervention of the jinn, fell in love with one another and exchanged rings. Then the jinn separated them, and they were lost to one another, but were ultimately reunited.

Camarina, a town on the southern coast of Sicily, a colony of Syracuse. In its neighbourhood was a marsh which the inhabitants drained, in defiance of the advice of an oracle, thus opening a way for their enemies to attack them. In the 1st Punic War, Camarina was captured by the Romans and the inhabitants sold into slavery. Whence the proverb: μὴ κίνει Καμαρίναν, *ne moveas Camarinam* (Don't disturb Camarina), quoted by Dominie Sampson in Scott's 'Guy Mannering', c. viii.

Cambal, CAMBALLO, one of the two sons of King Cambuscan, in Chaucer's 'Squire's Tale' (see *Canterbury Tales*; see also *Cambell* for the continuation of his story in Spenser's 'Faerie Queene').

Cambell or CAMBELLO, the name given by Spenser in 'The Faerie Queene', IV. iii, to Cambal (q.v.), whose tale he borrows from 'Dan Chaucer, well of English undefyled', and completes. Cambell is brother of Canace, for whom there are many suitors. It is arranged that the strongest of these, three brothers, shall fight with Cambell, and the lady be awarded to the victor. Two of the brothers are defeated; the contest between the third, Triamond, and Cambell is undecided, each wounding the other. They are reconciled by Cambina, Triamond's sister; Canace is awarded to Triamond and Cambell marries Cambina. The magic ring of Canace in the 'Squire's Tale' reappears in the 'Faerie Queene', with the power of healing wounds.

Camber, according to legend, one of the sons of Brute (q.v.), the legendary first king of Britain. Camber is supposed to have given his name to Cambria (Wales), but this is in fact a latinized derivative of *Cymry* (Welshmen).

Cambrai, THE ARCHBISHOP OF, a tèrm used to designate Fénelon (q.v.).

CAMBRENSIS, GIRALDUS, see *Giraldus de Barri.*

Cambria, see *Camber.*

Cambridge, in Old English *Grantebrycg,* was according to legend made the seat of a school by Sigebert, king of the East Angles, about 630. The first historical trace of Cambridge as a university (*studium generale*) is in 1209, its first recognition in a royal writ to the chancellor of Cambridge in 1230, the first papal recognition in 1233. The process of development of the prerogatives of the University was slow, the chancellor's jurisdiction reaching its full extension in 1383. (See H. Rashdall, 'Universities of Europe'.)

Cambridge (Mass., U.S.A.), near Boston, is the seat of Harvard University.

Cambridge Platonists, see *Platonists.*

Cambridge University Press. Books were first printed at Cambridge in 1521–2 by John Siberch (John Lair of Siegburg), a friend of Erasmus. A charter was granted to the University by Henry VIII in 1534 authorizing the printing of books there, but not until 1583 was the first university Printer, Thomas Thomas, appointed. The undertaking was opposed by the Stationers' Company as an infringement of their privilege, but the University finally vindicated its rights. The activity of the Press was developed under the influence of R. Bentley (1662–1742, q.v.), and many notable books were produced by it in the 18th cent. Among these were four Prayerbooks and a Bible printed by Baskerville (q.v.). The Pitt Press Building was erected early in the 19th cent. out of the surplus contributions for the statue to Pitt in Hanover Square.

Cambuscan, in Chaucer's 'Squire's Tale' (see *Canterbury Tales*), a king of Tartary.

Cambȳses, KING, subject of a tragedy (1569) by Thomas Preston (q.v.), which illustrates the transition from the morality play to the historical drama. It is founded on the story of Cambyses (king of Persia) in Herodotus; its bombastic grandiloquence became proverbial, and is referred to in '1 Henry IV', II. iv: 'I must speak in passion, and I will do it in King Cambyses' vein'. Among the characters are three comic villains, Ruff, Huff, and Snuff,

who figure again in the 'Martin Marprelate Controversy' (q.v.) in the course of Lyly's 'Pappe with an Hatchet'.

CAMDEN, WILLIAM (1551–1623), antiquary and historian, was educated at Christ's Hospital, St. Paul's School, and Magdalen College and Christ Church, Oxford. He was appointed headmaster of Westminster School in 1593. He made tours of antiquarian investigation up and down England, and published his 'Britannia' (q.v.) in 1586, of which the sixth (greatly enlarged) edition appeared in 1607. He published in 1615 'Annales . . . regnante Elizabetha . . . ad annum 1589', largely a panegyric of Queen Elizabeth; the second part was printed posthumously in 1627. He founded a chair of history in Oxford University. He wrote principally in Latin, but his 'Britannia' was translated into English by Philemon Holland (q.v.) in 1610, and his 'Annales' in 1625, 1628, and 1635 by other hands.

Camden Society, founded in 1838 in honour of W. Camden (q.v.), for the purpose of publishing documents relating to the early history and literature of the British Empire.

The CAMBRIDGE CAMDEN SOCIETY was founded by Neale (q.v.) in 1839 for the study of ecclesiology. Its name was afterwards changed to 'The Ecclesiological Society'.

Cameliard, in Malory's 'Morte Darthur', the realm of King Leodogran, father of Guinevere.

Camelot, in the Arthurian legend, the place where King Arthur held his court, is stated by Malory to be Winchester. But there was a Camelot in Somersetshire, which still survives in Queen's Camel, and Leland found traditions of Arthur there. Drayton, in the 'Polyolbion' (3rd Song, l. 395), refers as follows to the river Ivel in Somersetshire:

> The nearest neighbouring place to Arthur's ancient seat,
> Which made the Briton's name through all the world so great.
> Like Camelot what place was ever yet renowned?

On which Selden (in his 'Illustrations' to the 'Polyolbion') observes: 'By South Cadbury is that Camelot, a hill of a mile compass at the top, four trenches circling it, and twixt every of them an earthen wall.' There is something of the sort there.

Cameronians, the followers of Richard Cameron (*d.* 1680), a noted Scottish Covenanter and field preacher, who rejected the indulgence granted to nonconforming ministers and formally renounced allegiance to Charles II. His followers afterwards constituted the body called the 'Reformed Presbyterian Church of Scotland'. The Cameronians figure prominently in Scott's 'Old Mortality' (q.v.).

The CAMERONIAN REGIMENT (the old 26th Regiment of Foot, now the 1st battalion of the Scottish Rifles), was formed originally from the Cameronians and other Presbyterians who rallied to the cause of William III and fought at the battle of Killiecrankie.

Camilla, a Volscian princess, dedicated when young to the service of Diana. She was so fleet of foot that she could run over a field of corn without bending the blades, and over the sea without wetting her feet (Virg. 'Aen.' vii. 808 et seq.). She helped Turnus against Aeneas (q.v.) and died of a wound she received from Aruns.

Camilla, or a Picture of Youth, a novel by F. Burney (q.v.), published in 1796.

The story deals with the matrimonial concerns of a group of young people, Camilla Tyrold and her sisters, the daughters of a country parson, and her cousin Indiana Lynmere; and centres round the love-affair of Camilla herself and her eligible suitor, Edgar Mandlebert. Its happy consummation is delayed over five volumes by intrigues, contretemps, and misunderstandings. The book, especially in its earlier chapters, contains some of the comic situations and absurd characters in which Miss Burney excelled. Among the latter are Sir Hugh Tyrold, Camilla's good-natured but unpractical uncle; the grotesque tutor, Dr. Orkborne, so wrapt up in his own studies that he can give no attention to the duties for which he is engaged; and the fop Sir Sedley Clarendel. But the drollery soon gives place to overstrained romance.

Camillo, a character in Shakespeare's 'Winter's Tale' (q.v.).

Camiola, the heroine of Massinger's 'The Maid of Honour' (q.v.).

Camisard (from *camisa*, a shirt), a name given to the Calvinist insurgents of the Cevennes during the persecution (the 'dragonnades') which followed the revocation of the Edict of Nantes by Louis XIV in 1685.

Camlan, according to the 'Annales Cambriae' (q.v.) the scene of a battle in 539 'where Arthur and Medraut fell', is perhaps Slaughter or Bloody Bridge on the Camel near Camelford in Cornwall, or a site on the Cam near Cadbury. Malory places the last battle on a down beside Salisbury and not far from the sea.

CAMOËNS, LUIS DE (1524–80), a Portuguese poet, who lost an eye in service against the Moors and suffered other misfortunes, including a shipwreck off the coast of Cochin China, in which he is said to have lost all his property, swimming to shore with one hand while he held his poems in the other. He died miserably in Lisbon. He was the author of 'Os Lusiadas', the 'Lusiads', an epic poem on the descendants of Lusus, the legendary hero of his country, and more particularly on the exploits of Vasco da Gama (q.v.), the great Portuguese navigator. This was published in

1572. There is a close translation in English by Aubertin, and Sir Richard Burton also wrote a version.

Camorra, a secret society of lawless malcontents in Naples and other Neapolitan cities, which existed during the 19th cent.

Campagna, THE ROMAN, the plain surrounding Rome, extending from the sea on the West to the Sabine hills.

Campaign, THE, see *Addison*.

Campaigner, THE, see *Newcomes*.

Campaspe, Alexander and, a prose comedy by Lyly (q.v.), published in 1584. Alexander the Great, enamoured of his Theban captive Campaspe, gives her freedom and engages Apelles to paint her portrait. Apelles and Campaspe fall in love with each other, and when the portrait is finished, Apelles spoils it, so as to have occasion for further sittings. Alexander suspects the truth and by a trick makes him reveal it. He surrenders Campaspe to Apelles and returns to his wars, saying 'It were a shame Alexander should desire to command the world, if he cannot command himself'. The play includes the charming lyric, 'Cupid and my Campaspe playd,/At cards for kisses. . .'. The story of Alexander, Campaspe, and Apelles is told in Pliny's 'Natural History', xxxv. 36.

Campbell, the family name of the earls of Argyle (q.v.), celebrated in the song 'The Campbells are coming'. The chief of the house is styled in Gaelic Mac Calain More, after its ancestor, Sir Colin Campbell, surnamed More or Great, for his achievements in war.

CAMPBELL, ROY (1902–57), born in Durban. He came to Europe in 1919 and lived partly in England, partly in the South of France, and partly in Spain. During the Spanish Civil War he supported General Franco's side and in the Second World War he volunteered with the British Army and served in East and North Africa. Some years after the war he settled in Portugal, where he was killed in a car crash. His poetry, vigorous and often aggressively satiric as well as lyrical, includes 'The Flaming Terrapin' (1924), 'Adamastor' (1930), and translations of St. John of the Cross, Baudelaire, and Calderón. His 'Collected Poems' appeared in two volumes in 1949 and 1959, and his autobiography 'Light on a Dark Horse' in 1951.

CAMPBELL, THOMAS (1777–1844), son of a Glasgow merchant, was educated at Glasgow University. He published 'The Pleasures of Hope' (q.v.) in 1799, 'Gertrude of Wyoming' (q.v.) in 1809, 'Theodric' and other poems in 1824, and 'The Pilgrim of Glencoe' and other poems in 1842. He is principally remembered for his splendid war-songs, 'Hohenlinden', 'The Battle of the Baltic', and 'Ye Mariners of England'; for 'The Soldier's Dream', 'Lord Ullin's Daughter', 'Lochiel's Warning', and 'Lines on Revisiting a Scene in Argyllshire'; and also for some single lines that have become proverbial, such as 'Like angel-visits, few and far between' ('Pleasures of Hope', Pt. II), taken from Blair's 'Like angels' visits, short and far between'.

Campeador, EL, a surname of the Cid (q.v.), meaning 'the Champion'.

Camperdown, a village on the coast of the Netherlands, off which in 1797 the British fleet under Duncan defeated the Dutch under De Winter, thereby preventing a projected invasion of Ireland.

Campion, EDMUND (1540–81), fellow of St. John's College, Oxford (1557), went to Douai in 1571 and graduated there, and joined the Jesuits in 1573. He returned to England in 1580, preached privately in London, was arrested in 1581, sent to the Tower, examined under torture, and executed.

CAMPION, THOMAS (d. 1619), mentioned as a 'doctor in phisicke', published in 1595 a volume of Latin 'Poemata', and in 1602 'Observations in the Art of English Poesie' directed 'against the vulgar and unartificial custom of riming'. He wrote masques for presentation at court, a treatise on music, a volume of songs on the death of Prince Henry and four 'Books of Ayres' (1610–12), containing pleasant lyrics (some set to music by Campion himself), including the beautiful 'There is a garden in her face'.

Campo-Basso, COUNT OF, an Italian captain in the army of Charles the Bold of Burgundy, who figures in Scott's 'Quentin Durward' and 'Anne of Geierstein' (qq.v.).

Camulodunon, the Old British name of Colchester.

CAMUS, ALBERT (1913–60), French writer, born in Algeria, author of two notable short novels: 'L'Étranger' (1942) and 'La Peste' (1947); a number of plays, including 'Le Malentendu', 'Caligula', and 'Les Justes'; also of essays and other prose writings, e.g. 'Le Mythe de Sisyphe' (1942) and 'L'Homme révolté' (1951). His name is associated with a 'philosophie de l'absurde' bearing some resemblance to Existentialism (q.v.). In 1957 he was awarded the Nobel Prize for literature.

Canace (pron. Can'ǎsē), the daughter of King Cambuscan (q.v.), in Chaucer's 'Squire's Tale' (see *Canterbury Tales*), and in Spenser's 'Faerie Queene' (Bk. IV).

Canaletto (Canale), ANTONIO (1697–1768), Venetian architectural painter. He worked for Joseph Smith, English Consul in Venice (whose collection is now in the Royal Collection), and other English patrons, working in England from 1746 to c. 1756. He painted views of Whitehall and the Thames.

Cancel, in printing, a new page or sheet substituted for one cancelled or suppressed.

Cancer, (1) the zodiacal constellation of the Crab, lying between Gemini and Leo; (2) the fourth of the signs of the zodiac, which the sun enters on 21 June. The sign originally coincided with the constellation.

Candǎcē, (1) title of the queens of the Ethiopians in Hellenistic and Roman times. The treasurer of one of them was converted and baptized by Philip (Acts viii. 27–39). Another Candace invaded Egypt in 22 B.C. (2) A legendary queen of Tarsus who, in an episode of the legends attaching to Alexander the Great (q.v.), lures the conqueror by her fascination to a life of sloth.

Candaules, a legendary king of Lydia. See *Gyges*.

Candida, one of the 'pleasant' plays in G. B. Shaw's 'Plays, Pleasant and Unpleasant' (q.v.).
   It deals with the conflict between 'a higher, but vaguer timider vision . . . an incoherent mischievous even ridiculous unpracticalness', represented by the poet Eugene Marchbanks, and 'the clear bold sure sensible benevolent salutarily shortsighted Christian Socialist ideal', represented by the Hackney parson Morell. Candida is Morell's wife.

Candide, a philosophical tale by Voltaire (q.v.), satirizing the optimism of Rousseau and Leibniz.

Candlemas, 2 Feb., the feast of the Purification of the Virgin Mary, celebrated with a great display of candles. Brand ('Popular Antiquities') quotes Becon ('Reliques of Rome') as tracing this ceremony of candle-bearing to an ancient Roman custom of carrying torches in honour of Juno Februata. Candlemas Day is one of the quarter-days in Scotland.

Candor, see *Public Advertiser*.

Candour, MRS., one of the scandal-mongers in Sheridan's 'School for Scandal' (q.v.), rendered peculiarly odious by her assumption of a love of truth.

Cane'phŏrus, in ancient Greece, one of the 'maidens who carried on their heads baskets containing the sacred things used at the feasts of Demeter, Bacchus, and Athena' (Liddell and Scott); hence applied to figures of young persons carrying baskets on their heads.

Canicular Days, the days immediately preceding and following the heliacal rising of the dog-star (either Sirius or Procyon), about 11 Aug.; the dog-days.

Canicular Year, the ancient Egyptian year, which was reckoned from one heliacal rising of Sirius to the next.

Canicular period, see *Sothic Cycle*.

Canidia, a Neapolitan courtesan whom Horace once loved, and whom, after her desertion of him, he holds up to contempt as a sorceress. (Horace, Epodes v and xvii, also Satires, I. viii.)

Cannae, the site, in Apulia, of the memorable defeat of the Romans by Hannibal in 216 B.C.

CANNING, GEORGE (1770–1827), statesman and author, was educated at·Eton and Christ Church, Oxford. He was appointed foreign secretary in 1822 and premier in 1827. Apart from his political speeches (published in 1828), he is remembered in a literary connexion as founder of and contributor to 'The Anti-Jacobin' (q.v.); his 'Poems' were published in 1823.

Canon's Yeoman's Tale, The, see *Canterbury Tales.*

Canongate, Chronicles of the, see *Chronicles of the Canongate.*

Canonical Hours, stated times of the day appointed by the canon of the Catholic Church for prayer and devotion. The Canonical Hours have been fixed since the 6th cent. as follows: Lauds, Prime, Terce, Sext, None, Vespers, Compline (Mass is celebrated normally between Terce and Sext). Also the hours (now from 8 a.m. to 6 p.m.), within which marriage can legally be performed in a parish church in England.

Canōpic Vase (from *Canopus,* a town of ancient Egypt), a vase used in Egypt, chiefly for holding the entrails of embalmed bodies. Its distinctive feature was that its lid was in the form of an emblematic head. The town CANOPUS was supposed to derive its name from Canopus, the helmsman of Menelaus, who died in Egypt on the return from Troy.

CANOPUS is also the name of the bright star α in the southern constellation Argo.

Canossa, in the district of Modena, a castle of Matilda, countess of Tuscany, where in 1077 the emperor Henry IV submitted to penance and humiliation imposed by Pope Gregory VII; hence 'to go to Canossa' implies a reconciliation, real or feigned, with the pope.

Cantab, an abbreviation of CANTABRIGIAN, of or belonging to the University of Cambridge.

Cantabrian (from *Cantabri,* a people who lived in the north of Spain), means Spanish or Biscayan.

Cantacuzene, a noble Byzantine family, a member of which, John, the historian, became emperor of the East in 1341.

Canterbury Pilgrims, THE, a name given to the Anglican settlers who founded Christchurch in New Zealand in 1851. See also next entry.

Canterbury Tales, The, Chaucer's greatest work, designed about 1387, and written for the most part in heroic couplets (about 17,000 lines). The main *Prologue* is especially interesting for the vivid picture it presents of contemporary life. A party of twenty-nine[1]

[1] So the prologue states, but there are, including Chaucer himself, thirty-one. It has been suggested that the words *and preestes three* (Prol. 164) are not Chaucer's. But evidently Chaucer changed his mind as the work proceeded, and left it unfinished when he died.

pilgrims are assembled at the Tabard Inn in Southwark, about to travel to the shrine of Becket at Canterbury, and of each of these the poet draws a striking portrait. They are:

1. Knight;
2. Squire;
3. Yeoman (servant);
4. Prioress;
5. Nun;
6, 7, 8. Three Priests;
9. Monk;
10. Friar;
11. Merchant;
12. Clerk of Oxford;
13. Sergeant of Law;
14. Franklin (freeman and freeholder);
15. Haberdasher;
16. Carpenter;
17. Webbe (weaver);
18. Dyer;
19. Tapicer (maker of tapestry);
20. Cook;
21. Shipman(sailor);
22. Doctor of Physic;
23. Wife of Bath;
24. Parson (parish priest);
25. Ploughman;
26. Miller;
27. Manciple (steward);
28. Reeve (bailiff);
29. Summoner (officer of ecclesiastical court);
30. Pardoner (seller of indulgences);
31. Chaucer himself.

After supper the host proposes that they shall shorten the way by telling each two stories on the way out and two on the way back. The teller of the best stories shall have a free supper on his return. The host will accompany them and act as guide. The pilgrims agree and the tales follow, preceded each of them by a short prologue. But the plan by which each pilgrim would tell four tales was apparently curtailed. Even the reduced plan was not completed, and the work contains only twenty-three tales:

1. *The Knight's Tale,* a shortened version of the 'Teseida' of Boccaccio, the story of the love of Palamon and Arcite, prisoners of Theseus, king of Athens, for Emilia, sister of Hippolyta, queen of the Amazons, whom Theseus has married. The rivals compete for her in a tournament. Palamon is defeated, but Arcite, the favourite of Mars, at the moment of his triumph is thrown and injured by his horse through the interposition of Venus and Saturn, and dies. Palamon and Emilia, after prolonged mourning for Arcite, are united.

2. *The Miller's Tale,* a ribald story of the deception, first of a husband (a carpenter) through the prediction of a second flood, and secondly of a lover who expects to kiss the lady's lip and avenges himself for his disappointment with a hot coulter.

3. *The Reeve's Tale,* connected with the French *fabliau,* 'De Gombert et ses deux Clers', and the 'Decameron', D. x, N. 6, an indecent story of two clerks who are robbed by a miller of part of their meal, and revenge themselves on the miller's wife and daughter. (The Reeve, who had been a carpenter, thus retorts upon the Miller.)

4. *The Cook's Tale* (another tale of 'harlotrie' as Chaucer calls it) is imperfect and omitted in some manuscripts. It is followed by the *Cook's Tale of Gamelyn* (not by Chaucer), for the substance of which see under *Gamelyn.*

5. *The Man of Law's Tale*, related to a story in Gower's 'Confessio Amantis', B. ii, is the story of Constance, daughter of a Christian emperor, married to the Soldan on condition that he shall become a Christian, and by the device of the Soldan's mother cast adrift on the sea. Her subsequent misfortunes are very similar to those told in the verse romance 'Emaré' (q.v.).

6. *The Wife of Bath's Tale* is preceded by a long prologue, in which Chaucer places in her mouth a condemnation of celibacy in the form of an account of her life with her five successive husbands. The Tale is like Gower's story of Florent in 'Conf. Amant.' B. i, but is transferred to the court of King Arthur. It relates how a knight who is required, in order to avoid execution, to answer correctly within a twelvemonth the question, what do women love most, is told the right answer—'sovereignty'—by a foul old witch on condition that he marries her. He reluctantly complies and finds the witch restored to youth and beauty.

7. *The Friar's Tale* tells how a Summoner meets the devil dressed as a bailiff, who confides to him his methods in dealing with men. The Summoner attempts to extort a gift from a widow, who commends him to the devil. The devil thereupon hales him off to hell.

8. *The Summoner*, in retaliation, relates how the manœuvres of a greedy and hypocritical friar by a sick-bed were unsavourily defeated.

9. *The Clerk's Tale*, which the poet states he learnt from Petrarch, was translated by the latter into Latin from the 'Decameron', D. x, N. 10. It tells how the marquis of Saluces married the humble Griselda, and of her virtues and patience under trials. (The same story is treated in Dekker's 'Patient Grissil', q.v.)

10. *The Merchant's Tale*, of an old man and his young wife. The old man becomes blind; the wife and her lover take advantage of this in a pear-tree. Pluto suddenly restores the husband's sight, but Proserpine enables the wife to outwit him. The precise source of the story has not been traced.

11. *The Squire's Tale*, of Cambuscan, king of Tartary, to whom on his birthday an envoy from the king of Arabia brings magic gifts, including a ring for the king's daughter Canace, which enables her to understand the language of birds. A female falcon tells Canace the story of her own desertion by a tercelet. The poet promises the continuation of the tale, but it is incomplete. (See under *Cambell* for the continuation in Spenser's 'Faerie Queene'.) The tale is referred to by Milton in 'Il Penseroso':

Or call up him who left half-told
The story of Cambuscan bold,
Of Cambal and of Algarsife
And who had Canace to wife.

Cambal and Algarsife are Cambuscan's sons. The origin of the tale is unknown.

12. *The Franklin's Tale*, of a woman, Dorigen wife of Arveragus, who to escape the assiduity of her lover, the squire Aurelius, makes her consent depend upon an impossible condition, that all the rocks on the coast of Brittany be removed. When this condition is realized by the aid of a magician, the lover, from a generous remorse, releases her from her promise. Chaucer states that the tale is taken from a 'British Lay', but this is lost. Similar stories are found in Boccaccio's 'Filocolo', B. v, and 'Decameron', D. x, N. 5.

13. *The Second Nun's Tale*, in rhyme-royal, is perhaps translated from the life of St. Cecilia in the Golden Legend of Jacobus a Voragine. It describes the miracles and martyrdom of the noble Roman maiden Cecilia and her husband Valerian.

A certain canon and his yeoman having joined the party at Boughton-under-Blee, we next have

14. *The Canon's Yeoman's Tale*, an exposure of the follies and rogueries of the Alchemists.

15. *The Doctor's Tale*, of the death of Virginia by her own wish at her father's hands, to save her from the designs of the wicked judge Apius, who has conspired to get possession of her. Chaucer quotes Livy as the source, but has followed fairly closely the version of the story in the 'Roman de la Rose'.

16. *The Pardoner's Tale* has an analogue in an Italian miscellany known as the 'Cento Novelle Antiche', N. lxxxii. The Pardoner discourses on the evils of Gluttony and Drunkenness, Gambling and Swearing. This theme is illustrated by the story of three revellers who in plague-time set out on a search for Death, who has killed one of their comrades. An old man tells them they will find him under a certain tree. There they discover a heap of gold. Each designs to get sole possession of the treasure, but they only succeed in killing one another.

17. *The Shipman's Tale*. There is a similar story in the 'Decameron', D. viii, N. 1. The wife of a niggardly merchant asks the loan of a hundred francs from a priest to buy finery. The priest borrows the sum from the merchant and hands it to the wife, and the wife grants him her favours. On the merchant's return from a journey the priest tells him that he has repaid the sum to the wife, who cannot deny receiving it.

18. *The Prioress's Tale*, the source of which is unknown, is the legend of a widow's child murdered by Jews because he sings 'O alma Redemptoris mater' when passing through the Ghetto at Lincoln on his way to school. He miraculously continues his song after his throat is cut and the body is in consequence discovered. This tale is in rhyme-royal.

19. Chaucer's own contribution follows, in the form of the *Tale of Sir Thopas*, in which he slyly ridicules the romances of knight-errantry by contemporary rhymers. It contains phrases from 'Isumbras', 'Li Beaus

Desconus' (qq.v.), and refers to Sir Bevis, Sir Guy, etc. It is soon interrupted, and Chaucer then gives the *Tale of Melibeus*, a prose translation of a French romance, 'a moral tale vertuous'. It is a long and (to us) tedious disputation between Melibeus and his wife Prudence on the most judicious method of dealing with enemies who have done them grievous injuries.

20. *The Monk's Tale* is composed of a number of 'tragedies' of persons fallen from high estate, taken from different authors and arranged on the model of Boccaccio's 'De casibus virorum illustrium'. The tale is in eight-lined stanzas.

21. *The Nun's Priest's Tale*, perhaps developed from one of the episodes in the French story of Reynard the Fox, tells of a fox that beguiled a cock by praising his father's singing, and was beguiled in turn to let the cock escape.

22. *The Manciple's Tale* is the fable of the Crow, which had been treated by many authors from Ovid onwards. A certain Phebus has a crow that is white and can counterfeit any man's speech. It thus reveals to Phebus his wife's infidelity. Phebus in a fury kills his wife, and then, in remorse, plucks out the crow's white feathers, deprives it of its speech, and throws it out 'unto the devil', which is why crows are now black.

23. *The Parson's Tale*, a dissertation in prose on penitence, the character of each kind of sin, and the appropriate remedy. It is probably the raw material on which Chaucer proposed to work, rather than his finished tale.

Tyrwhitt's famous text of the 'Canterbury Tales', with introductory discourse, was published in 1775–8.

Canute or CNUT, a Dane, king of England, 1016–35. The old story of Canute and the sea is told in Holinshed, VII. xiii. Being on the seashore near Southampton, he sat down close to the rising tide and bade it go no further. When it advanced and wetted him, he said to his courtiers that they called him king, but that he 'could not stay by his commandment so much as this small portion of water'. This he did to reprove their flattery. Cf. Thackeray's satirical ballad on the subject in 'Rebecca and Rowena' (q.v.).

Canute, The Song of, a famous early English ballad stated to have been composed and sung by the king as he rowed past Ely, and recorded by a monk of Ely in 1166. It begins:

Merie sungen the munechis binnen Ely
Tha Cnut ching rew ther by.

Canute's or CANUTUS BIRD, the Knot. The derivation of the name of this bird from King Canute (mentioned by Camden and Drayton) is said by the OED to be without historical or even legendary foundation.

Caorsin, see *Cahors*.

Cap of Liberty or PHRYGIAN BONNET, the conical cap placed in Roman times on the head of a slave on his emancipation. It was adopted as a symbol of liberation (the *bonnet rouge*) by the French Revolutionary Jacobins in April 1792, when the Swiss survivors of the mutiny at Nancy of Aug.–Sept. 1791 were released from the galleys; for the red 'Phrygian bonnet' was the head-dress of the galley slaves at Marseilles, where these men had been confined.

'Capability' Brown, see *Brown (L.)*.

Capaneūs, one of the seven heroes who marched from Argos against Thebes (see under *Eteocles*). He was struck with a thunderbolt by Zeus when scaling the walls of Thebes, because he defied the god.

Cape of Storms, *Cabo Tormentoso*, the name given to the south-western cape of Africa by its discoverer, Bartholomew Diaz, in 1487; subsequently changed by John II of Portugal to Cape of Good Hope.

CAPELL, EDWARD (1713–81), Shakespearian commentator. His edition of Shakespeare in 10 vols. in 1768 was the first to be based on complete and careful collations of all the old copies, and it is his arrangement of the lines that is now usually followed. His Commentary ('Notes and Various Readings to Shakespeare'), begun in 1774, was published in 3 vols. in 1783.

Capet, the name of the French dynasty founded by Hugo Capet in 987, which ruled until 1328, when it was succeeded by the House of Valois. Louis XVI was described as Louis Capet when tried before the Convention in 1793. The origin of the surname of Hugo I is uncertain.

CAPGRAVE, JOHN (1393–1464), an Augustinian friar, who resided most of his life in the friary at King's Lynn. He wrote, in Latin, sermons, theological tracts, and commentaries on many books of scripture. His chief Latin historical works are 'Nova Legenda Angliae', 'De illustribus Henricis', and 'Vita Humfredi Ducis Glocestriae'. In English he wrote lives of St. Gilbert of Sempringham and of St. Catharine of Alexandria, also a chronicle of English history extending to A.D. 1417, of some importance as an early English prose work.

Capitol, THE, in ancient Rome, that summit of the Capitoline hill on which stood the magnificent temple of Jupiter. In this temple were kept the Sibylline books, and here the consuls took the vows on entering upon office. It was to this temple also that victorious generals were carried in triumph to render thanks to Jupiter.

In modern Rome the term is applied to the Piazza del Campidoglio, in the depression between the two summits of the Capitoline hill, where Brutus made his speech after the murder of Caesar. In the centre of the Piazza stands the bronze equestrian statue of Marcus Aurelius. On one side is the Palace of the Senator, where it is said that Petrarch (q.v.)

was crowned and Rienzi (q.v.) ruled as tribune.

In Washington the Capitol is the seat of the National Congress. It is built in Renaissance style, and surmounted by a great dome. It was completed in 1830.

Capitolinus, MARCUS MANLIUS, see *Manlius Capitolinus.*

Capitulary, a collection of ordinances, especially those made by the Frankish kings.

Caponsacchi, CANON GIUSEPPE, one of the principal characters in Browning's 'The Ring and the Book' (q.v.).

Capricorn, (1) the zodiacal constellation of the He-goat, lying between Sagittarius and Aquarius; (2) the tenth of the signs of the zodiac, which the sun enters about 21 Dec. The sign originally coincided with the constellation.

Captain, THE GREAT, see *Cordova.*

Captain Kettle, see *Kettle.*

Captain Nemo, see *Nemo.*

Captain Singleton, *Adventures of,* see *Singleton.*

Capua, an ancient city of Campania, famous for its wealth. It is said that the soldiers of Hannibal were enervated by its luxury when moved to winter quarters there after the battle of Cannae.

Capuchin, a friar of the order of St. Francis, of the new rule of 1528, so called from their sharp-pointed capuches or hoods.

Capulets, THE, in Shakespeare's 'Romeo and Juliet' (q.v.); also in a the noble Veronese house (the Cappelletti) to which Juliet belongs, hostile to the family of the Montagues (the Montecchi).

Caput Mortuum ('dead head'), in alchemy, the residuum remaining after the distillation or sublimation of any substance, good for nothing but to be thrown away, all virtue having been extracted.

Carabas, MARQUESS OF, a character in the fairy tale of 'Puss in Boots' (q.v.); also in a song by Béranger (q.v.); in B. Disraeli's 'Vivian Grey' (q.v.); and in Thackeray's 'Book of Snobs'.

Caractacus or CARADOC, king of the Silures in the west of Britain during the reign of Claudius, was defeated by the Romans and fled to Cartimandua, queen of the Brigantes, who betrayed him. He was taken a prisoner to Rome in A.D. 51, where his noble spirit so pleased the emperor that he pardoned and released him. He figures as Caratach in Beaumont and Fletcher's 'Bonduca' (q.v.). W. Mason (1724–97), the friend of Gray, wrote a play 'Caractacus'.

Caradoc, see *Caractacus.*

Caradoc or CRADOCK, SIR, see *Boy and the Mantle.*

Caran d'Ache, adapted from a Russian word meaning 'pencil', the pseudonym of Emmanuel Poiré (1858–1909), a celebrated French humorous illustrator, who employed the method of silhouettes outlined by a single continuous line.

Carausius, see *Caros.*

Carbine, a famous horse, brought by the duke of Portland from Australia in 1895. He won thirty-three out of his forty-three races in Australia, and was only once unplaced.

Carbonari ('charcoal-burners'), the name of a secret political association formed in the kingdom of Naples, during the French occupation under Murat, with the design of introducing a republican government. It lasted during part of the 19th cent. Louis Napoleon was a Carbonaro in his youth.

Carbonek, in the legend of the Holy Grail, the enchanted castle where the Grail is found.

Cardan, JEROME (GIROLAMO CARDANO) (1501–76), a famous Italian mathematician, and writer on medicine and occult sciences.

Cardenio, in 'Don Quixote' (q.v.), the lover of Lucinda, who, driven mad by the loss of her, haunts the Sierra Moreña, and is finally reunited with her.

Cardinal's Snuff-Box, *The,* a novel by Henry Harland (q.v.), published in 1900.

Cardinall, *The,* a tragedy by James Shirley (q.v.), produced in 1641, and printed in 1652.

This is one of the best of Shirley's plays. The cardinal, urged by ambition, designs that the Duchess Rosaura, the widowed daughter-in-law of the king of Navarre, shall marry his nephew Columbo, general of the army, and obtains the support of the king. The duchess is betrothed to Columbo accordingly, although she loves the Count Alvarez. While Columbo is at the wars she obtains the king's consent to her marriage with Alvarez. On the wedding night, Columbo murders Alvarez. Hernando, a colonel who has been affronted by Columbo in the field, plots with the duchess to be revenged, she promising him her hand if he succeeds. Hernando kills Columbo in a duel. The cardinal, suspecting the complicity of the duchess, plans to ravish and kill her. Hernando, concealed behind the arras, kills the cardinal, but not before the latter by a trick has effected the poisoning of the duchess. Hernando takes his own life.

Cardoile, CARDUEL, in the Arthurian romances, perhaps Carlisle, but in the History of Merlin said to be in Wales.

CARDUCCI, GIOSUÈ (1835–1907), Italian poet and scholar, professor of Italian literature at Bologna University from 1860 to 1904, winner of the Nobel prize for literature in 1906. He was the greatest poet of the Risorgimento (q.v.). Much of his poetry is inspired by the greatness and endurance of Italy's classical heritage. Some of his best poems are in 'Rime nuove' (1861–7) and

'Odi barbare' (1873–89), the metrical forms of the latter being derived from various types of Horatian ode.

Careless, in Sheridan's 'School for Scandal' (q.v.), one of the companions of Charles Surface. Also a character in Congreve's 'The Double Dealer' (q.v.).

Careless Husband, The, a comedy by Cibber (q.v.), printed in 1715.

Sir Charles Easy, who neglects his wife and carries on an intrigue with her woman and with Lady Graveairs, is brought to contrition by discovering that his wife's gentle and friendly treatment of him is due not to ignorance of his infidelities, but to her virtue and sense of duty. The coquette, Lady Betty Modish, is led to accept the suit of her honourable lover, Lord Morelove (with whom is contrasted the boastful lady-killer, Lord Foppington), by a plot to excite her jealousy and to persuade her that Morelove, weary of her contempt, is about to give her up.

CAREW (pron. 'Carey'), THOMAS (1598?–1639?), a son of Sir Thomas Carew, a master in Chancery, was educated at Corpus Christi College, Oxford, and became secretary to Sir Dudley Carleton at Venice and subsequently for a short time at The Hague. He won the favour of Charles I, was appointed to an office at court, and received an estate from him. He was, in poetry, a disciple of Ben Jonson, and wrote a fine elegy on Donne. His principal works are a masque, 'Coelum Britannicum' (1634), 'The Rapture' (a fine but licentious amatory poem), and numerous graceful songs and lyrics.

CAREY, HENRY (d. 1743), is remembered as the author of the burlesque 'Chrononhotonthologos' (q.v.), as the inventor of the nickname of Ambrose Philips (q.v.), and principally as the author of the words and music of 'Sally in our Alley'. He also wrote a burlesque opera, 'The Dragon of Wantley' (1734).

Carfax (Latin *quadrifurcus*, four-forked), a place where four roads meet, the intersection of two principal streets in a town, as at Oxford and Exeter. The crossing of the great streets of medieval London at Leadenhall market (q.v.) was called the 'Carfukes of Leadenhall' in 1357 (Lethaby).

Carinthia Jane, the heroine of Meredith's 'The Amazing Marriage' (q.v.).

Carker, JAMES, a character in Dickens's 'Dombey and Son' (q.v.).

Carleton, Memoirs of Captain, see *Memoirs of Captain Carleton.*

CARLETON, WILLIAM (1794–1869), born in Tyrone, the son of a poor peasant, was the author of a number of remarkable stories of Irish peasant life, of which he paints the melancholy as well as the humorous side. His 'Traits and Stories of the Irish Peasantry' were collected and published in 1832 (first contributed to 'The Christian Examiner'), a

second series following in 1833, and 'Tales of Ireland' in 1834. The best of his longer stories was 'Fardorougha, the Miser' (q.v.), 1839.

CARLIELL, ROBERT (d. 1622?), poet. His 'Britaines Glorie: or an Allegorical Dreame, with the Exposition thereof', a poem published in 1619, in praise of the Protestant Church in England, is a picturesque diatribe against the Church of Rome and the evils ascribed to the Papists. In particular he contrasts the benefit of printing the Bible in English with the 'subtile deceit of the Pope, to have the word of God set forth in the Latin Tongue, which the common people could not understand . . . being forced to receive the word from the Priests'. The poem ends with the description of the three 'thick-set hedges' to guard the country from Popery: (1) the Nobility, Gentry, and Commonaltie; (2) the Beagles: subordinate officers and ministers; and (3) the Bishops.

Carlion, in Malory's 'Morte Darthur' (q.v.), the city where Arthur was crowned and held his court, probably Caerleon-upon-Usk, though in places Carlisle appears to be meant.

CARLISLE, FREDERICK HOWARD, *fifth earl of* (1748–1825), Chancery guardian to Lord Byron and attacked by him in 'English Bards and Scotch Reviewers'. His tragedy, 'The Father's Revenge', was praised by Johnson and Walpole.

Carlos, DON, the deformed son of Philip II of Spain. The marriage of the latter with Elizabeth of France, who had been affianced to Don Carlos, forms the subject of Otway's tragedy 'Don Carlos' (q.v.).

Carlovingians or CAROLINGIANS, the second royal dynasty of the Franks, of which Pepin, the father of Charlemagne, was the first king (751). It was succeeded by the Capetian line in 987.

Carlton Club, THE, was founded in 1831 by the duke of Wellington and his political friends. It is a political club for men of Conservative opinions. Its present house in Pall Mall, replacing an earlier one built in 1836, was opened in 1855.

Carlton House, London, from which Carlton House Terrace is named, was built for Henry Boyle, Baron Carleton (d. 1725), and sold to the Prince of Wales in 1732. It became famous as the home of George IV when Prince of Wales.

CARLYLE, ALEXANDER (1722–1805), nicknamed 'Jupiter', educated at Edinburgh University, Glasgow, and Leyden, a minister and leader of the Scottish 'Broad Church' party, was author of an interesting autobiography which refers to various notable events and personalities of the period (printed in 1860).

Carlyle, JANE BAILLIE WELSH (1801–66), wife of Thomas Carlyle (q.v.). Collections of her letters were published in 1883, 1924, and 1931.

CARLYLE, THOMAS (1795–1881), was born at Ecclefechan, in Dumfriesshire, of peasant stock. He was educated at the parish school, then at Annan Academy, and at the age of 15 entered Edinburgh University. He was subsequently a schoolmaster at Annan and Kirkcaldy, but soon took to literary work, contributing to Brewster's 'Edinburgh Encyclopaedia', studying German literature, and writing his 'Life of Schiller', which appeared in the 'London Magazine' in 1823–4 and was separately published in 1825. His translation of 'Wilhelm Meister's Apprenticeship' appeared in 1824, followed by that of 'Wilhelm Meister's Travels' (included in 'German Romance', 1827). In 1826 he married Jane Welsh, a Scottish lady of strong character and shrewd wit, one of the best letter-writers in the English language, and retired to her farm at Craigenputtock, on the lonely moors of Nithsdale. He contributed essays on German literature to the 'Edinburgh' and other reviews, wrote 'Sartor Resartus' (q.v.), which was published by 'Fraser's Magazine' in 1833–4, and the first part of the 'French Revolution' (q.v.). He removed to Cheyne Row, Chelsea, in 1834. The manuscript of the first volume of the 'French Revolution' was accidentally burnt while in J. S. Mill's keeping, but Carlyle re-wrote it and the work finally appeared in 1837. In the same and following years he gave several courses of popular lectures, the most successful, that 'On Heroes, Hero-Worship, and the Heroic in History', being published in 1841. In his 'Chartism' (1839) and 'Past and Present' (1843) he turned his attention to political problems of the day, and the present and future of Labour, expressing his contempt for the teachings of political economy and democratic nostrums. Salvation, according to him, was to be sought in a return to medieval conditions and the rule of the strong just man, who was not to be got by popular election. The same views, in an exaggerated form, are to be found in his 'Latter-Day Pamphlets' (1850). Carlyle's second great work, 'Oliver Cromwell's Letters and Speeches', was published in 1845, and the 'Life of John Sterling' in 1851. After this he spent fourteen years on the preparation of the 'History of Frederick the Great' (published 1858–65), of which, though it is the most entertaining of his works, the result is generally considered disproportionate to the labour spent on it. Mrs. Carlyle died in 1866, and after this he wrote little of importance. 'The Early Kings of Norway' appeared in 1875. His 'Reminiscences' appeared in 1881, and his 'Life' was written with more frankness than judgement by his friend and disciple, James Anthony Froude (q.v.). Several volumes of his letters have been published: 'Early Letters of T. Carlyle' (1886), 'Correspondence between Goethe and Carlyle' (1887), 'Letters of T. Carlyle' (2 vols., 1888), ed. C. E. Norton; 'Letters of T. Carlyle to His Youngest Sister (1899), ed. C. T. Cope-

land; 'New Letters of T. Carlyle' (2 vols., 1904), 'The Love Letters of T. Carlyle and Jane Welsh' (2 vols., 1909), 'Letters of T. Carlyle to J. S. Mill, John Sterling and Robert Browning' (1923), ed. A. Carlyle; 'T. Carlyle: Letters to his wife' (1953), ed. T. Bliss; 'The Correspondence of Emerson and Carlyle' (1964), ed. J. Slater.

Carmagnole, a kind of dress much worn in France from 10 Aug. 1792. It was the southern name for a long waistcoat worn by the Marseillais 'Fédérés' who came to Paris at that date and helped to storm the Tuileries. The name was extended to a lively song and dance popular among the revolutionists in 1793.

CARMAN, BLISS (1861–1929), Canadian poet, born in New Brunswick; one of the group of poets that came to maturity after the Confederation and expressed the developing national consciousness. His earlier poems are among his best, especially those in 'Low Tide on the Grand Pré' (1893). Among his other works are 'Songs from Vagabondia' (in collaboration with Richard Hovey, 1894) and 'Sappho' (1904).

Carmathians, see *Karmathians*.

Carmelites, an order of mendicant friars (called also, from the white cloak which forms part of their dress, WHITE FRIARS) and nuns, who derive their origin from a colony founded on Mt. Carmel by Berthold, a Calabrian, in the 12th cent.

Carmilhan, a spectre ship, the subject of one of Longfellow's 'Tales of a Wayside Inn'. She brings disaster to whatever ship meets her. The captain of the 'Valdemar' derides the legend, but encounters the 'Carmilhan' (with Klaboterman, the Kobold of the sea, on board) in a storm, and the 'Valdemar' is sunk.

Carmina Burana, a collection of Goliardic poems (see *Golias*) from the Benedictine monastery of Benedictbeuern in Bavaria. The best edition is by A. Hilka and O. Schumann, of which the first two volumes were published in 1930.

Carnegie, ANDREW (1835–1919), the son of a damask-linen weaver of Dunfermline, was taken when a child to America by his parents, who emigrated thither during the 'hungry forties'. At the age of 13 he began work in a cotton factory. Later, by his energy and shrewd speculative investment, he became enormously rich and one of the foremost ironmasters in the United States. In 1900 he published his 'Gospel of Wealth' maintaining that a 'man who dies rich dies disgraced', and in 1901, retiring from business, set about the distribution of his surplus wealth. The most important of his benefactions from a literary standpoint was his provision of public libraries in Great Britain and the United States, on condition that the local authorities provided site and maintenance. He also instituted a trust for the universities of Scotland, and several trusts for the advancement of research and education in the United States. In 1910 he founded the Carnegie Peace Fund for the promotion of international peace.

Carol, a word whose etymology is obscure, and of which the earliest meaning appears to be a round dance; thence a song, originally the song accompanying the dance, and especially a song of joy sung at Christmas time in celebration of the Nativity. The first collection of Christmas carols that we possess was printed by Wynkyn de Worde in 1521.

Caroline, a term applied to the dramatists, authors, etc., of the period of Charles I.

Caroline, QUEEN, (1) consort of George II, figures in Scott's 'The Heart of Midlothian' (q.v.) and is prominent in the memoirs of the time; (2) consort of George IV, figures in Byron's poems, etc.

Caroline Gann or BRANDON, see *Brandon*.

Caroline Minuscule, a style of writing developed at Tours under Charlemagne, and perpetuated in our modern hand.

Carolingians, see *Carlovingians*.

Caros, in Macpherson's Ossianic poem of that name, is the Carausius of history. He was the commander of a fleet charged to protect the coast of Gaul in the reign of Maximian, but becoming suspect to the emperor, crossed to Britain, assumed the title Augustus, and was finally acknowledged by Diocletian and Maximian as their colleague in Britain, where he continued to rule until murdered in 293. In the Ossianic poem he is attacked by Oscar and his troops put to flight.

Carpathian wizard, see *Proteus*.

CARPENTER, JOHN (1370?–1441?), town clerk of London, 1417–38, compiled the 'Liber Albus', a valuable collection of records of the city of London (printed in the Rolls Series, 1859, translated by Riley, 1861). He left lands for educational purposes, from which the City of London School was founded.

Carpet, MAGIC, see *Ahmed* for that described in the 'Arabian Nights'. According to Muslim legend Solomon had a carpet which transported him and his army, the wind carrying it wherever he wished to go. See Koran, c. xxi, and Sale's notes to c. xxvii.

Carpet-bagger, in U.S. political slang, a scornful term applied after the American Civil War of 1861–5 to immigrants from the northern to the southern states, whose 'property qualification' consisted merely of the contents of the carpet-bag which they had brought with them. Hence applied approbriously to all northerners who went south and tried, by the Negro vote or otherwise, to obtain political influence; and generally to anyone interfering in the politics of a locality with which he is thought to have no genuine or permanent connexion.

Carpio, BERNARDO DEL, see *Bernardo del Carpio*.

Carrasco, SAMSON, in 'Don Quixote' (q.v.), a bachelor of the University of Salamanca, a little mirth-loving man, who, in order to cure Don Quixote of his folly, disguises himself as the Knight of the Mirrors, overcomes him in combat, and requires him to return home and abstain from chivalric exploits for a year. He boasted to Don Quixote that he had fixed Giralda, the weathercock on the cathedral of Seville.

CARROLL, LEWIS, see *Dodgson*.

Carson, KIT (1809–68), famous American trapper and guide, whose activities were mainly in the Rocky Mountains region.

Cartaphilus, see *Wandering Jew*.

CARTER, ELIZABETH (1717–1806), daughter of a Kent clergyman, and a member of the Blue Stocking (q.v.) circle, was a friend of Richardson and of Dr. Johnson, who had a high opinion of her abilities and to whose 'Rambler' she contributed two numbers. She published a translation of Epictetus in 1758. Her letters to Miss Talbot, Mrs. Vesey, and Mrs. Montagu were published after her death (1809–17).

Cartesianism, see *Descartes*.

Carthage, a famous city of the ancient world, situated about the centre of the coast of N. Africa, whose power in the latter part of the 3rd cent. B.C. under the leadership of Hannibal, gravely threatened Rome. The Punic Wars (as the wars between Rome and Carthage were called[1]), which lasted 265–242, 218–201, and 149–146 B.C., ended in the destruction of the latter city. Its restoration was begun by Julius Caesar, and it became an important post of the Roman province of Africa. For the phrase 'delenda est Carthago', see *Cato the Censor*. See also *Marius among the ruins of Carthage*.

Carthon, the title of one of Macpherson's Ossianic poems. Clessammor, the uncle of Fingal, being driven to Balclutha by a storm, has married Moina, daughter of a local chief, but has been driven away, and left his bride behind him, and she, after giving birth to Carthon, has died. Combal, father of Fingal, has burnt Balclutha. Carthon, who was carried off to safety by his nurse, when grown to man's estate invades Morven to revenge the destruction of Balclutha. He is slain in single combat by his own father, Clessammor, who does not know him, but dies from grief on discovering that he has killed his son.

Carthusians, an order of monks founded in the Dauphiné by St. Bruno in 1086, remarkable for the severity of their rule. The name is derived 'from *Catursiani Montes*, or from *Catorissium*, *Chatrousse*, a village in the

[1] *Punic*, from L. *Punicus*, earlier *Poenicus*, from Gk. φοῖνι, Phoenician. The epithet is applied to Carthage because it was a Phoenician colony. Phoenicia was an ancient country consisting of a narrow strip of land on the coast of Syria, containing the cities of Tyre and Sidon. There were many Phoenician colonies on the coast of the Mediterranean.

Dauphiné, near which their first monastery was founded' [Littré] (not from *La Grande Chartreuse*, which was named after the order). See also under *Charterhouse*.

Carton, SYDNEY, a character in Dickens's 'A Tale of Two Cities' (q.v.).

CARTWRIGHT, WILLIAM (1611–43), poet and dramatist, one of the 'sons' of Ben Jonson (q.v.). His most successful play, 'The Royal Slave', was performed before Charles I at Oxford in 1636. His 'Comedies, Tragicomedies, with other Poems' were published in 1651.

Caruso, ENRICO (1873–1921), the famous Italian operatic singer, a tenor, was born at Naples. He first came into prominence by his singing in 'La Bohème' in 1894, in which as Rodolfo he subsequently achieved one of his greatest successes. He sang only in Italian and French opera. From 1903 till his death he was the leading tenor of the Metropolitan Opera House, New York.

Carvel, Hans, see *Hans Carvel*.

CARY, ARTHUR JOYCE LUNEL (1888–1957), novelist, born at Londonderry, was educated at Clifton and Trinity College, Oxford, and studied art in Edinburgh and Paris. He took part in the Balkan War, 1912–13, joined the Nigerian political service in 1913, and served with a Nigerian regiment in the Cameroons campaign, 1915–16. In 1920 he returned to Oxford and devoted himself to his family and to writing. His early 'African' novels, 'Aissa Saved' (1932), 'An American Visitor' (1933), 'The African Witch' (1936), and 'Mister Johnson' (1939), show, with shrewd sympathy, the relations between Africans and their British administrators. Two novels are studies of childhood, 'Charley is my Darling' (1940) and 'House of Children' (1941); and two of women, 'The Moon-light' (1946) and 'A Fearful Joy' (1949). His greatest work consists of two trilogies: 'Herself Surprised' (1941), 'To Be a Pilgrim' (1942), and 'The Horse's Mouth' (1944), concerned mainly with art; and 'Prisoner of Grace' (1952), 'Except the Lord' (1953), and 'Not Honour More' (1955), a study of politics. Each novel of these trilogies is narrated in the first person by one of the three main characters. Cary also wrote political studies, 'Power in Men' (1939), 'The Case for African Freedom' (1941), and 'The Process of Real Freedom' (1943); poems, 'Marching Soldier' (1945) and 'The Drunken Sailor' (1947); a study in aesthetics, 'Art and Reality' (1958); short stories, 'Spring Song' (1960); and a novel with a religious theme, 'The Captive and the Free' (1959).

CARY, HENRY FRANCIS (1772–1844), educated at Christ Church, Oxford, was an assistant librarian at the British Museum from 1826 to 1837. He translated Dante's 'Divina Commedia' ('Inferno', 1805–6; 'Purgatorio' and 'Paradiso', 1814); and wrote a series of articles on the early French poets in the 'London Magazine' (collected 1846).

Carya'tids (a word meaning 'maidens of Caryae', a town in Laconia, where, at the annual festival of Artemis, it was customary for bands of girls to perform ritual dances), female statues in long drapery used instead of columns to support the entablature of a temple. One of the Caryatids from the Erechtheum in Athens is now in the British Museum.

CARYLL, JOHN (1625–1711), diplomatist, secretary to Mary of Modena, queen of James II, and author of 'Sir Solomon Single', a comedy. He was a friend and correspondent of Pope, to whom he suggested the subject of 'The Rape of the Lock' (q.v.).

Casabianca, LOUIS (1755–98), a Corsican who commanded the French vessel 'l'Orient' at the battle of Aboukir, where he is said to have blown up his ship to prevent its falling into the hands of the English, and perished with his little son. This incident is the subject of the well-known poem by Mrs. Hemans (q.v.).

CASANOVA DE SEINGALT, GIACOMO (1725–98), an Italian adventurer, whose Memoirs, written in an imperfect but lively French, describe, with shameless frankness, his rogueries, adventures, and amours in most countries of Europe, and provide an entertaining picture of 18th-cent. European society and of the very singular author. Casanova's veracity has been much questioned, and no doubt it is rather in the main outlines of the picture than in its details that he is to be trusted. The work by which Casanova hoped to achieve immortality was his novel 'Icosameron', a distant precursor of the works of Jules Verne and of 20th-cent. science fiction. The English hero and heroine are precipitated into the imaginary Utopian realm of the *Megamicri* in the interior of the earth.

Casaubon, MR., a leading character in G. Eliot's 'Middlemarch' (q.v.).

CASAUBON, ISAAC (1559–1614), a French Huguenot scholar and theologian, born in exile at Geneva, who resided in London from 1610 to 1614. His chief work was his criticism of the 'Annales Ecclesiastici' of Baronius, in his 'De rebus sacris et ecclesiasticis exercitationes' (1614). He published critical editions of a number of classical authors of the early Christian era. He was too learned and too critical a scholar to find rest in any of the churches of the day. A life of Casaubon was written by Mark Pattison (q.v., 1875).

Casby, CHRISTOPHER and FLORA, characters in Dickens's 'Little Dorrit' (q.v.).

Casca, one of the conspirators in Shakespeare's 'Julius Caesar' (q.v.).

Case is altered, The, a comedy by Jonson (q.v.), printed in 1609, but written before 1599.

Count Ferneze, who has lost an infant son, Camillo, when Vicenza was captured by the French general Chamont, sees his elder son Paulo go off to the wars against this same Chamont, under the special care of his general Maximilian. Paulo is taken prisoner, but on the other hand Maximilian brings back Chamont and his friend Gasper captive. It is agreed that Gasper shall return and effect an exchange between Paulo and Chamont, but Gasper personates Chamont, and Chamont himself departs. The trick is discovered, and Ferneze is on the point of executing Gasper, when Chamont returns with Paulo, and it is moreover discovered that Gasper is Ferneze's lost son Camillo. The other elements of the play are more amusing: the attempts made by various parties to secure the daughter and the treasure of the beggar Jaques de Prie (neither of them his by rights), and the fun made of Antonio Balladino, a character in which Anthony Munday (q.v.) is ridiculed.

Caseldy, a character in Meredith's 'The Tale of Chloe' (q.v.).

Cask of Amontillado, The, a tale by Edgar Allan Poe (q.v.).

Casket Letters, THE, letters supposed to have passed between Mary Queen of Scots and Bothwell, and to have established her complicity in the murder of Darnley. They were repudiated by the queen as forgeries (and some have suspected George Buchanan, q.v., as the forger), but it was threatened that they would be used as evidence against her. They disappeared before the end of the 16th cent. and have never been recovered.

Caslon, WILLIAM (1692–1766), was the first English typefounder to make a complete range of Roman and Italic types of his own design, besides cutting Greek and exotic scripts. From 1725 onwards his types superseded those hitherto imported from abroad in English printing, and are still in use. His foundry was carried on by his descendants until 1872. The firm of Caslon was acquired in 1936 by Stephenson, Blake and Co. Ltd., of Sheffield, who now supply Caslon's Roman and Italic types.

Cassandra, daughter of Priam, king of Troy, received the gift of prophecy from Apollo, who was enamoured of her. But as she slighted him, the god contrived that no trust should be placed in her predictions. After the fall of Troy she fell to the lot of Agamemnon (q.v.), who took her back to Greece and to whom she foretold the calamities that awaited him. She was murdered by Clytemnestra (q.v.).

Cassandre, a romance by La Calprenède (q.v.). It was translated into English in the middle of the 17th cent. and is said to have been read by Charles I in prison.

Cassibellaun (CASSIBELAN in Shakespeare's 'Cymbeline'), or CASSIVELLAUNUS, the ruler of the country north of the Thames, who was given the chief command of the British forces that resisted Caesar's second invasion (54 B.C.). He was defeated and obliged to sue for peace. Legend makes him brother and successor of Lud (q.v.).

Cassim, the brother of Ali Baba (q.v.).

Cassio, MICHAEL, in Shakespeare's 'Othello' (q.v.), the Moor's lieutenant.

CASSIODŌRUS, MAGNUS AURELIUS (c. A.D. 480–575), of Scylacēum in Bruttium (the modern Squillace in Calabria), a distinguished statesman who governed for many years the Ostrogothic kingdom under Theodoric the Great and his successors, and a man of exceptional learning for his period. He spent the last years of his life at the monastery at Viviers which he had founded. There he set his monks to copy classical (Latin) manuscripts; much would have been lost but for this. He was author of several works in Latin, of which the most important is a collection of state papers known as 'Variarum Epistolarum Libri XII'.

Cassiŏpēa, wife of Cepheus, king of Ethiopia, and mother of Andromeda (q.v.). She boasted herself (or her daughter) more beautiful than the Nereids, thus incurring the wrath of Poseidon. She was changed into a northern constellation, the 'starr'd Ethiop queen' of Milton's 'Il Penseroso'.

Cassitĕrĭdes, the 'tin islands' of the ancient Greeks; possibly Cornwall, where there are tin mines, or islands off the Spanish coast, near Finisterre.

Cassius, in Shakespeare's 'Julius Caesar', the friend of Brutus and leader of the conspiracy against Julius Caesar.

Castalia, the name of a spring on Mt. Parnassus, sacred to Apollo and the Muses, said to be so called from Castalia (daughter of Achelous), who plunged into it to escape the pursuit of Apollo.

Castalio, a character in Otway's 'The Orphan' (q.v.).

Castara, see *Habington.*

CASTIGLIONE, BALDASSARE (1478–1529), Italian humanist, chiefly known for his prose dialogue, 'Il Cortegiano' (1528), translated in 1561 into English by Sir Thomas Hoby (1530–66). In this dialogue, which takes place at the court of Urbino, and is presided over by the duchess, all the qualifications of the ideal courtier, ethical and intellectual, as well as military, sporting, and elegant, are set out and discussed. The work had much influence on the literature of England, e.g. on Surrey, Wyatt, Sidney, and Spenser.

Castle Dangerous, a novel by Sir W. Scott (q.v.) published in 1831, in the fourth and last of the 'Tales of My Landlord'.

The story deals with the defence in 1306 of Douglas Castle by Sir John de Walton, assisted by the young knight Aymer de Valence, on behalf of the king of England, against the forces of Robert the Bruce and Sir James Douglas ('The Black Douglas'). The Lady Augusta of Berkeley, a noble and beautiful young Englishwoman, has offered her hand and fortune to the English knight who will hold it for a year and a day. In a spirit of light-hearted frolic she herself goes in disguise, with an aged minstrel, Bertram, to the neighbourhood of the castle. Here she is in danger of being treated as a spy by Sir John, before he discovers her identity, and then is captured by the Douglas, and is offered to Sir John in exchange for the castle. Sir John's embarrassment is solved by the arrival of orders to surrender the castle, and the lady is restored to her lover.

Castle of Bungay, see *Bungay Castle.*

Castle of Indolence, The, a poem in Spenserian stanzas by J. Thomson (1700–48, q.v.), published in 1748.

This, the most polished and musical of Thomson's works, was begun in 1733. It consists of two cantos, of which the first describes the castle of the wizard Indolence, into which he entices the weary pilgrims of this earth. Once there, a torpor steals over them, and they sink into idleness amid delightful sights and sounds. With a light touch of caricature various real persons, including the poet himself, inhabitants of the castle, are sketched in. Presently, becoming diseased and loathsome, the inmates are thrown into a dungeon and left there to languish. The second canto describes the conquest of the wizard and the destruction of his castle by the knight of Arms and Industry.

Castle of Otranto, The, a Gothic Story, a novel by H. Walpole (q.v.), published in 1764.

This work purported in the first edition to be a translation from the Italian, but its authorship was acknowledged in the second edition. The events related are supposed to have occurred in the 12th or 13th cents. Manfred, prince of Otranto, the villain of the story, is the grandson of a usurper of the realm, who had poisoned Alfonso, the rightful lord. It had been prophesied that the line of the usurper should continue to reign until the rightful owner had grown too large to inhabit the castle and as long as male issue of the usurper remained to enjoy it. When the story opens, Manfred is about to marry his only son to the beautiful Isabella, but on the eve of the wedding the son is mysteriously killed. Terrified lest he should be left without male descendants, Manfred determines to divorce his wife and marry Isabella himself. Isabella escapes with the assistance of Theodore, a young peasant, bearing a singular resemblance to the portrait of Alfonso, and already under suspicion of some connexion with the death of Manfred's son. Theodore is imprisoned, but is released by Matilda, Manfred's daughter, with whom he falls in love. Manfred, suspicious of an amour between Theodore and Isabella, and learning that Theodore and a lady from the castle are together by night at Alfonso's tomb, hurries there and stabs the lady, only to find that he has killed his daughter, Matilda. The supernatural element that has pervaded the story now brings it to an end. The ghost of Alfonso (a mysterious gigantic figure that haunts the castle), in accordance with the prophecy has grown too big for the edifice, and throws it down, and terror forces Manfred to reveal the usurpation. Theodore turns out to be the heir of Alfonso and the rightful prince, and marries Isabella.

Castle Perilous, in Malory's 'Morte Darthur' (the story of Beaumains or Sir Gareth), the castle of the Lady Lyones. See *Gareth and Lynette.*

Castle Rackrent, a novel by M. Edgeworth (q.v.), published in 1801.

Thady Quirk, steward to the Rackrent family, tells the story of the family since he has known it. He begins with the hard-drinking Sir Patrick who dies singing his favourite song:

He that goes to bed, and goes to bed sober,
Falls as the leaves do . . .

Next comes the litigious Sir Murtagh, who 'out of forty-nine suits which he had, never lost one but seventeen'. Then follows the quarrelsome Sir Kit, who marries a 'Jewish', and locks her up for seven years. Last comes Sir Condy, who tosses up whether he shall marry the rich Miss Moneygawl or the pretty Judy Quirk, and runs through the remainder of the Rackrent property, much of which passes into the hands of Attorney Quirk, Thady's son, a sharp-witted rascal. The book gives a vivid picture of the reckless living which in the 18th cent. brought many Irish landlords to ruin.

Castlereagh, Robert Stewart, *second marquis of Londonderry,* better known as *Viscount Castlereagh* (1769–1822), was chief secretary for Ireland 1799–1801, and secured the passing of the Act of Union by the Irish parliament. He was subsequently president of the board of control and in charge of the war and colonial offices. He sent Wellesley to Portugal and was responsible for the Walcheren expedition. He fought a duel with Canning in 1809, wounded him, and resigned office. He was foreign secretary from 1812 to 1822, and took a leading part in the European settlement at the Congress of Vienna and after Waterloo, restraining the allies from retaliation on France. His mind became affected by work and responsibility and he committed suicide. Shelley (q.v.) in his 'Masque of Anarchy' (provoked by the Peterloo, q.v., affair) wrote:

I met Murder on the way—
He had a face like Castlereagh.

Castlewood, Thomas, *third Viscount,* and his wife Isabel; Francis, *fourth Viscount,* his wife Rachel, and his daughter Beatrix; Francis, *fifth Viscount*; characters in Thackeray's 'Esmond' (q.v.). Also Eugène, *Earl of*

Castlewood, in Thackeray's 'The Virginians' (q.v.), son of the last named.

Castor and Pollux, twin brothers, known as the DIOSCURI, sons of Zeus by Leda (q.v.). They took part in the expedition of the Argonauts (q.v.), in the course of which Pollux defeated and slew Amycus in the combat of the cestus, and was thereafter reckoned the god of wrestling and boxing. Castor distinguished himself in the management of horses. The twins were also regarded as the friends of navigators, having the power to calm storms. They were made a constellation known as *Gemini* or the Twins.

Castor is a name given to the phenomenon known as a *Corposant* (see *Elmo's Fire*). When two corposants were seen together, they were called *Castor* and *Pollux* and were thought to portend the cessation of a storm.

Castriot, GEORGE, see *Scanderbeg*.

Castruccio Castracani, The Sword of, a poem by E. B. Browning. He was a famous soldier of the 14th cent. and a leader of the Ghibellines. His sword, which had been kept till some patriot should arise and free Italy, was offered to Victor Emmanuel, who exclaimed, 'Questa è per me'.

Catachrēsis, application of a term to a thing it does not properly denote; misuse of words.

Catacomb, a word of uncertain etymology, (1) representing the Latin *catacumbus*, used as early as the 5th cent. in connexion with the subterranean cemetery under the Basilica of St. Sebastian on the Appian Way near Rome, in or near which the bodies of the apostles Peter and Paul were said to have been deposited: this is the only sense in which the word is used in English before the 17th cent. (2) In later times applied (in the plural) to all the subterranean cemeteries lying around Rome (some of which, after having long been covered up and forgotten, were accidentally discovered in 1578). The word is also extended to similar subterranean works elsewhere. Scott in 'Old Mortality', c. ix, uses it for a compartment in a cellar.

Cataian, variant of CATHAIAN, a man of Cathay or China; 'used also to signify a sharper, from the dexterous thieving of those people' [Nares], and so used by Shakespeare in 'The Merry Wives of Windsor', II. i.

Catalectic, said of a verse whose last foot is truncated and has only one syllable, or is altogether cut off; e.g. 'Best and brightest, come away'. Cf. *acatalectic*.

Caterans, Highland irregular fighting men, marauders.

Catharine of Alexandria, ST., a princess in the 3rd cent., who embraced the Christian religion by divine inspiration, and converted all with whom she came in communication, including the wife of the Emperor Maxentius and his general Porphyrius. She was beheaded in 307, after other methods of putting her to death, including that of the wheel which bears her name (a diabolical engine consisting of four wheels armed with knives and teeth turning different ways), had failed owing to divine interposition. Her body was conveyed by angels to Mount Sinai, where it was said to have been discovered *c*. 800. She is commemorated on 25 Nov.

A CATHERINE WHEEL is a kind of firework which rotates while burning; or a lateral somersault.

CATHARINE OF GENOA, ST. (*b*. 1447), born at Genoa of an illustrious family. She felt an early vocation to a convent life, but was refused on account of her youth. Her marriage to Giuliano Adorno was unhappy. She became an outstanding mystic, and wrote 'Dialogues of the Soul and Body' and a 'Treatise on Purgatory'. She is commemorated on 15 Sept.

Catharine of Siena, ST. (1347–80), an Italian saint. Her holiness of life and gift of diplomacy were so famous that she was called upon to mediate between Pope Urban VI and the Florentines in 1378. It was through her persuasion that Gregory XI returned from Avignon to Rome. Her extensive correspondence with popes and princes, instinct with religious fervour, was published in 1860. She is commemorated on 30 April.

Cathay ('Khitai'), the name under which China was known under the Mongol dynasty, the Khitans being a people of Manchu race to the NE. of China who established an empire over north China during two centuries ending in 1123. See 'Cathay, and the way thither, or the medieval geography of Asia' by Sir Henry Yule (1866), which includes the narratives of the voyages of Friar Odoric of Pordenone early in the 14th cent., of Ibn Batuta of Tangier (1325–55), and of Benedict Goës, a Jesuit born about 1561 in the Azores, who was one of the missionaries sent to Akbar in 1594; he proceeded from India to China early in the 17th cent.

CATHER, WILLA SIBERT (1876–1947), American novelist, born in Virginia, but brought up in Nebraska. She used her knowledge of pioneer life in her early novels: 'Alexander's Bridge' (1912), 'O Pioneers' (1913), 'The Song of the Lark' (1915), 'My Antonia' (1918), and 'One of Ours' (1922), though in the later novels of this group the leading characters escape from their narrow environment into a wider world of thought and action. Miss Cather's next group of novels includes her greatest: 'A Lost Lady' (1923), a moving lament for the passing of the pioneering era of the West, 'The Professor's House' (1925), in which the same theme is transferred on to an intellectual and personal plane, and 'Death Comes for the Archbishop' (1927), a chronicle of the early Catholic mission in New Mexico. 'Shadows on the Rock' (1931), a tale of 17th-cent. Quebec, is more sentimental and mannered than her best work, but no less finely written. She also published short stories, some criticism, and an early volume of poems, 'April Twilights' (1903).

Catherine, a novel by Thackeray (q.v.), published in 1839–40, and written under the pseudonym 'Ikey Solomons, junior'. It is an ironical tale of a criminal life, designed to discredit the practice of ennobling crime in fiction. Catherine Hayes, from whom 'Catherine' was drawn, was executed for the murder of her husband in 1726.

Catherine de Bourgh, LADY, a character in Jane Austen's 'Pride and Prejudice' (q.v.).

Catholic Church, a term first applied to the whole body of Christian believers, as distinguished from an individual congregation or particular body of Christians. After the separation of the Eastern and Western Churches, 'Catholic' was assumed by the latter as its descriptive epithet, and 'Orthodox' by the former. At the Reformation the term 'Catholic' was claimed as its exclusive right by the body remaining under the Roman obedience, in opposition to the Protestant or Reformed Churches. These however also retained the term, giving it, for the most part, a wider and more ideal and absolute sense. In England it was claimed that the Church, even as Reformed, was the national branch of the 'Catholic Church' in its proper historical sense. As a consequence, in order to distinguish the unreformed Latin church, its chosen epithet of 'Catholic' was further qualified by 'Roman'. On this analogy 'Anglo-Catholic' has been used by some, since about 1835, of the Anglican Church, in preference to 'Protestant' [OED.]. In the latter part of the 19th and in the 20th cents., the term Anglo-Catholic has been applied in a more special sense to the present high church element in the Anglican Church, which was associated with the Oxford Movement (q.v.) and emphasizes the Catholic as distinct from the Protestant character of that Church.

The OLD CATHOLICS are a religious party who separated from the Roman Catholic communion in Germany after the Vatican Council of 1870–1.

Catholic King, HIS CATHOLIC MAJESTY, a title assumed by the kings of Spain. It was given first to Isabella (by Alexander VI), then to her and her husband Ferdinand.

Catiline, a Roman tragedy by Jonson (q.v.), first acted in 1611. The play is based on the events of the year 63 B.C., when Catiline organized a conspiracy to overthrow the existing government and to renew with the aid of Sulla's veterans the scenes of bloodshed which Rome had recently seen. Cicero and Antonius were elected consuls, and Catiline, secretly encouraged by Caesar and Crassus, prepared for a rising. Cicero, however, warned by Fulvia, the mistress of Curius, of the intention to assassinate him as a first step in the movement, summons the senate and accuses Catiline, who leaves Rome and joins the troops raised by his adherents at Faesulae. Cicero

obtains evidence of the guilt of the conspirators through the ambassadors of the Allobroges, and submits it to the senate, which resolves that they shall be put to death. Catiline falls in the decisive engagement between his troops and those of the government commanded by Petreius.

Catnach, JAMES (1792–1841), a publisher in Seven Dials, London. He issued at a very low price a large number of chap-books, ballads, and broadsides, many of them about crimes, highwaymen, and executions, which throw much light on his period.

Cato, a tragedy by Addison (q.v.), produced in 1713.

It deals with the last phase of the life of Marcus Porcius Cato the republican, who is besieged in Utica by Caesar (46 B.C.). He is betrayed by Sempronius, a senator, and by Syphax, a Numidian ally, but faithfully supported by Juba, the Numidian prince. Further resistance to Caesar being useless, he provides for the escape of his friends and takes his own life rather than surrender to the dictator. A love interest is added to the play in the devotion of Juba to Cato's daughter Marcia, and in the rivalry of the two sons of Cato for the hand of Lucia, a rivalry resolved by the death of one of them while bravely resisting the traitor Syphax.

The political excitement at the moment when the play was produced—Anne's health was failing and the question of the succession was acute—contributed to the success of a drama dealing with Cato's last stand for liberty.

Cato the Censor (234–149 B.C.) was famous for his opposition in that office to the prevalent fashions of luxury. Having been sent on a mission to Africa, he was so struck with the reviving prosperity of Carthage that he became convinced that Rome would never be safe until Carthage was destroyed. Therefore whenever called upon to vote in the senate, and whatever the subject, his final words (according to Florus) were 'Delenda est Carthago'.

Cato Street Conspiracy, a plot by a certain Thistlewood (q.v.) and some thirty other persons in 1820 to murder the ministers of the Crown at a cabinet dinner, provoked by the repressive measures taken by the government against the advocates of reform. The conspirators met in a stable in Cato Street near the Edgware Road. The conspiracy was betrayed and the leaders executed.

Catriona, see *Kidnapped*.

CATULLUS, GAIUS VALERIUS (c. 84–c. 54 B.C.), a great Roman poet and epigrammatist, born in or near Verona. The Lesbia celebrated in his poems was Clodia, the notorious sister of Publius Clodius. He had a country house at Sirmio on the Lacus Benacus (Lake of Garda), the Sirmione of Tennyson's 'Frater, ave atque vale'.

Caucus, a word of obscure origin, which arose in New England, said to have been used in Boston (U.S.) before 1724. In the U.S. it signifies a private meeting of the representatives of a political party previous to an election or to a general meeting of the party, to select candidates for office or to concert other measures for furthering the party's interests. In English newspapers since 1878 it has been generally misused and applied opprobriously to a committee or organization charged with seeking to manage the elections and dictate to the constituencies, but which is in fact usually a representative committee popularly elected for the purpose of securing concerted political action in a constituency. [OED.]

Caudine Forks, narrow passes in the mountains of Samnium where the Roman army surrendered to the Samnites in 321 B.C., and were obliged to pass under the yoke (a spear supported transversely by two others placed upright) to symbolize their subjugation.

Caudle Lectures, see *Mrs. Caudle's Curtain Lectures.*

Cauline, SIR, the subject of a ballad included in Percy's 'Reliques', a young knight at the court of the king of Ireland, who falls in love with Christabelle, the king's daughter, is banished, returns in disguise and slays a grim 'Soldan' giant who is a suitor for the princess, but is himself mortally wounded. Christabelle dies of a broken heart.

Caurus, Latin name of the NW. wind.

Causeries du lundi, see *Sainte-Beuve.*

CAVAFY, CONSTANTINE (1863–1933), a Greek poet who lived in Alexandria. His poems (154 in all) were translated by Professor John Mavrogordato and published in England in 1951. E. M. Forster speaks of him as 'a very wise, very civilized man', the extent of whose ambition was 'to be understood in Alexandria and tolerated in Athens'.

Cavalier, Memoirs of a, see *Memoirs.*

Cavaliers, a name given to the adherents of the king in the Civil War of the 17th cent. It was originally reproachful and given to the swashbucklers on the king's side, who hailed the prospect of war.

CAVALIER LYRICS, a term applied to the lyrical poetry of which there was a remarkable outburst during the reign of Charles I, and of which the court was the centre, though Robert Herrick, the chief of these lyrists, was not a courtier. The principal other Cavalier lyrists were Thomas Carew, Sir John Suckling, and Richard Lovelace (qq.v.).

Cave, EDWARD (1691–1754), the son of a Rugby cobbler, became a London printer and published many journals and books, but is chiefly remembered as the founder of the 'Gentleman's Magazine' (q.v.), which he conducted from 1731 until his death.

Cave of Adullam, see *Adullamites.*

Cave of Harmony, THE, in Thackeray's 'The Newcomes' (q.v.), was drawn from Evans's Tavern at the NW. corner of Covent Garden piazza, frequented by Douglas Jerrold, G. A. Sala, Leech, etc.; and from the 'Coal Hole' in Fountain Court, Strand.

Cave of Mammon, see *Mammon.*

Cavelarice, see *Markham (G.).*

CAVENDISH, GEORGE (1500–61?), a gentleman of Thomas Wolsey's household, and author of a remarkable biography of the cardinal ('The Life and Death of Thomas Woolsey'), in which with much art he contrasts the magnificence of the cardinal's life with his subsequent disgrace, and indicates 'the wondrous mutability of vain honours . . . and the fickle trust to worldly princes'. It was first printed in 1641, but was previously circulated in manuscript.

Cavendish, HENRY (1731–1810), natural philosopher, grandson of the second duke of Devonshire, educated at Peterhouse, Cambridge. He discovered the constitution of water and atmospheric air, and experimented on electricity and the density of the earth. His name is commemorated in the CAVENDISH LABORATORY at Cambridge for physical research, founded in 1874 by the seventh duke of Devonshire.

Cavendish, THOMAS (1560–92), fitted out three ships in 1586 and circumnavigated the globe, reaching Plymouth on his return in September 1588. His ship was the 'Desire'. In the course of his voyage he captured the great treasure-ship off the coast of California. He began another voyage in 1591 with Capt. John Davis, but died at sea.

Cavendish on Whist, 'The Principles of whist, stated and explained by Cavendish' (the pseudonym of HENRY JONES, 1831–99), published in 1862. Jones was a member of the Cavendish Whist Club.

Cavour, CAMILLO BENSO, *Count di* (1810–61), was prime minister in the Sardinian government, 1852–9 and 1860–1. He caused Sardinia to join the western allies against Russia in 1855 and sent a Sardinian force to the Crimea under La Marmora. Having thus enhanced the international status of Sardinia, he secured in 1858 an alliance with Napoleon III, which led to the successful campaign of 1859 against Austria. He resigned office in anger on learning the terms of peace settled by the two emperors at Villafranca and accepted by Victor Emmanuel, by which Sardinia acquired only Lombardy. On his return to office in 1860 he effected the annexation of Tuscany, and after Garibaldi's adventurous, and at times embarrassing, expedition to Sicily and Naples, the annexation of southern Italy. His statesmanship thus brought about, before his death, the unification of the greater part of Italy.

Cawdor, THANE OF, see *Macbeth.*

Caxon, JACOB, in Scott's 'The Antiquary' (q.v.), hairdresser at Fairport, employed by Jonathan Oldbuck.

CAXTON, WILLIAM (c. 1421–91), the first English printer, and a merchant and man of affairs. He was apprenticed to a London merchant and then spent thirty years in the Low Countries. From 1465 to 1469 he was governor of the English merchants at Bruges, and successfully negotiated commercial treaties with the dukes of Burgundy. He began translating the 'Recuyell of the Historyes of Troye', but, becoming secretary to the household of Margaret, duchess of Burgundy, sister of Edward IV, in 1469, he did not complete the work until he was in Cologne in 1471. There he probably worked in a printing house. Returning to Bruges, Caxton gave his book to the duchess, subsequently, c. 1475, printing it on a press set up with Colard Mansion, a calligrapher who was probably his pupil. He also printed in Bruges 'The Game and Playe of the Chesse' (q.v.), c. 1475. He established a press at Westminster in 1476—his first dated book printed there is 'The Dictes or Sayengis of the Philosophres', 1477—and printed about 100 books, a number of them his own translations from the French. He used eight founts of type, the first of which he brought from Bruges; he began to use woodcut illustrations c. 1480. His importance in the history of English literature is by no means confined to his work as a printer, for he contributed by his translations to the formation in the 15th cent. of an English prose style.

Caxtons, The, a novel by Bulwer Lytton (q.v.), published in 1849.

Pisistratus Caxton narrates, with gentle humour, the simple annals of the Caxton family. He gives a pleasant picture of his father, a kindly scholar absorbed in a great work; his uncle Jack, who pursues his mania for speculative enterprises with results disastrous to the family; and his other uncle, Roland, an old warrior in whose opinion Sir William Caxton who fought at Bosworth is a more creditable ancestor than Caxton the printer. The only considerable incident in the story is the attempt of the Byronic youth Vivian, who turns out to be the reprobate son of Roland, to carry off Fanny Trevanion, the rich heiress. Pisistratus, who has been in love with her and secretary to her father, emigrates to Australia and eventually marries his cousin Blanche.

Cayster, a river in Lydia, falling into the Aegean Sea near Ephesus, and according to the poets celebrated for its swans.

Cebes, a Greek philosopher, of Thebes, who figures in Plato's 'Phaedo'. The 'Picture' or 'Table' (πίναξ), a work once attributed to him, a symbolical representation of the life of man, is now held to be by a later author.

Cecial, TOM, in 'Don Quixote' (q.v.), Sancho Panza's neighbour, who engages himself as mock-squire to the bachelor Samson Carrasco (q.v.) when the latter masquerades as the Knight of the Mirrors.

Cecilia, ST., a Christian martyr who died at Rome in 230. She is said to have been forced to marry, in spite of her vows of celibacy, a certain Valerian. She converted him to Christianity, and both suffered martyrdom. Through a medieval misinterpretation of a sentence in her Acts ('Cantantibus organis in corde suo soli domino decantabat') she came to be associated with church music and in particular with the organ, which she was supposed to have played. When the Academy of Music was founded at Rome in 1584 she was adopted as the patroness of Church Music. Her story is told in Chaucer's 'Second Nun's Tale' (see *Canterbury Tales*). Dryden (q.v.) wrote a 'Song for St. Cecilia's Day', and Pope (q.v.) an 'Ode for Music on Saint Cecilia's Day'. She is commemorated on 22 Nov.

Cecilia, or Memoirs of an Heiress, a novel by F. Burney (q.v.), published in 1782.

This was the second of Miss Burney's novels, and was at once successful. Cecilia Beverley has inherited a large fortune on the sole condition that her husband must take her name. Until she comes of age she is required to live with one of her three guardians. The first of these is Harrel, a gambler, who, failing in his attempt to exploit her, and to save himself from ruin, commits suicide. The second is the impossibly vulgar and avaricious Briggs. Cecilia goes to stay with the third, the Hon. Compton Delvile, a man of overweening family pride, 'arrogant without merit, imperious without capacity'. She and Mortimer Delvile, his son, fall deeply in love with one another; but old Delvile treats Cecilia with contempt, and is furious at the idea that his son should exchange his name for hers. A marriage is nevertheless arranged between the young couple on the basis that Cecilia shall renounce her fortune and Delvile keep his name. But this plan is defeated by the machinations of the crafty Monckton, whom Cecilia has always regarded as a trusty friend, but who, being married to a woman much older than himself, hopes to win Cecilia and her fortune when his own wife dies. Monckton's treachery is exposed, Cecilia and Mortimer Delvile are married, and after further tribulations old Delvile is reconciled to the match. There are many admirably drawn subsidiary characters, notably the mischievous rattle, Lady Honoria Pemberton.

Cecilia Halkett, a character in Meredith's 'Beauchamp's Career' (q.v.).

Cecrops, the legendary first king of Attica, which was called CECROPIA after him, and founder of Athens. See *Athene*.

Cedilla, a mark (ș), derived through the letter z from the Arabic letter *şād*, written, especially in French and Portuguese words, under the letter c, to show that it has the soft sound in positions in which the hard sound would be normal, as before *a*, *o*, *u*.

Cedric the Saxon, one of the principal characters in Scott's 'Ivanhoe' (q.v.).

Ceix and Alceone, a tale in bk. v of Gower's 'Confessio Amantis' (q.v.). See *Halcyone*.

Celadon and Amelia, the hero and heroine of an episode included in Thomson's 'Seasons' (q.v.) in the book on 'Summer'. Amelia is killed by lightning in her lover's arms.

Celaeno, one of the Harpies (q.v.).

Celestial City, THE, in Bunyan's 'Pilgrim's Progress' (q.v.), signifying Heaven.

Celestial Empire, THE, the translation of one of the native names for China.

Celestina, or the Tragi-Comedy of Calisto and Melibea, a novel in dialogue which has had several stage adaptations. The first known edition appeared about 1499, in sixteen acts, and a later version, in 1502, in twenty-one acts. It is reasonably certain that Acts II–XVI were written by Fernando de Rojas (q.v.), although the authorship of Act I and the later additions is still disputed.

The work takes the form of a dialogue, but is essentially dramatic, and marks an important stage in the literary history of Spain and of Europe. Though, as Mabbe, its translator, observes, 'some part of it seemeth somewhat more obscene than may suit with a civil style', it is an extremely vivid, entertaining work, one of the first to present romance in everyday life. The reader is brought into disreputable, but admirably depicted, company. The principal interlocutors are these: Calisto, a young gentleman of birth and fortune; Melibea, a modest and romantic young lady; Celestina, a crafty wise old bawd; Parmeno and Sempronio, the rascally braggart servants of Calisto; and Elicia and Areusa, two wenches. The plot is briefly as follows. Calisto casually meeting Melibea falls violently in love with her, but is, from her modesty, sharply repulsed. On the advice of one of his servants he calls in the aid of Celestina, who interposing in the affair deflects Melibea from the path of virtue and brings about a general catastrophe. Celestina is murdered by Parmeno and Sempronio for a share in the reward that she has received, and these are punished with death for their crime. Calisto is killed in one of his secret meetings with Melibea, and she in despair takes her own life.

An excellent and racy, if exuberantly diffuse, translation into English prose, 'The Spanish Bawd', was made by James Mabbe (q.v.), and published in 1631. It has been reissued in the Tudor Translations. The early part of 'Celestina' was translated into English verse by John Rastell, provided with a happy ending, and published, about 1530, as 'A new comodye in englysh in maner of an interlude', better known as 'An Interlude of Calisto and Melebea'. It is one of the first English dramatic works that approach true comedy.

A new translation was made by P. Hartnoll in 1959 (Everyman).

Rojas's borrowings from Petrarch are discussed in A. D. Deyermond's 'The Petrarchan Sources of *La Celestina*' (1961).

Celia, one of the principal characters in Shakespeare's 'As You Like It' (q.v.). See also *Caelia*.

Célimène, see *Misanthrope*.

CELLINI, BENVENUTO (1500–71), a Florentine goldsmith and sculptor, and author of one of the most vivid and interesting autobiographies ever written. It was first published (dedicated to Richard Boyle) at Naples in 1730; English translations include that by T. Roscoe (1791–1871), and by J. A. Symonds (q.v.), published in 1888. Cellini combined the characters of artist and bravo; he was arrogant, passionate, conceited, and vainglorious. His autobiography gives a vivid account of the personalities and events of his time, including the Sack of Rome (1527), in which he took part; he also describes artistic techniques such as bronze casting. He went to France and worked for Francis I.

Celt, a name applied in modern times to peoples speaking languages akin to those of the ancient Galli or Gauls, including the Bretons in France, the Cornish, Welsh, Irish, Manx, and Gaelic of the British Isles. Also a name applied to flint implements of the Stone Age.

Celtic Twilight, The, a collection of stories by Yeats (q.v.), published in 1893, illustrating the mysticism of the Irish and their belief in fairies, ghosts, and spirits. It has since become a generic phrase (slightly ironical) for the whole Irish literary revival movement.

Cenci, The, a tragedy by P. B. Shelley (q.v.), published in 1819.

Count Francesco Cenci, the head of one of the noblest and richest families in Rome under the pontificate of Clement VIII, after a life of wickedness and debauchery, conceived an implacable hatred against his children, which towards one daughter Beatrice took the form of an incestuous passion. Beatrice, after vain attempts to escape from her miserable situation, plotted with her stepmother Lucretia, and her brother Bernardo, the murder of their common tyrant. It was done by two hired assassins. Circumstances having aroused suspicion against them, the Cenci were arrested, and by dint of examinations and torture, the facts were discovered, and the Cenci sentenced to death. In spite of the compassion aroused by their lamentable tale, the executions of Beatrice, her stepmother, and one of her brothers were carried out by order of the pope. These events occurred in the year 1599, and are made the subject of Shelley's play.

Censorship, *see* Appendix I.

Cent Nouvelles Nouvelles, Les, a collection of French tales, probably related to a real

Court audience, of the jokes and intrigues of burghers and their dames and serving-maids, licentious in character, and showing Italian influence (e.g. of the 'Decameron'). It was presented by its author to Philippe duke of Burgundy in 1462.

Centaurs, THE, a fabulous people of Thessaly, half men and half horses (see *Ixion*). The legend of their existence perhaps arose from the ancient inhabitants of Thessaly having tamed horses and appearing to their neighbours mounted on horseback. The celebrated battle of the Centaurs and the Lapithae (q.v.) occurred in consequence of a quarrel at the marriage of Hippodamia and Peirithous, king of the Lapithae. The Centaurs, who had been invited to the feast, intoxicated with wine, offered violence to the women. The Lapithae, resenting the injury, drove the Centaurs from the country. Famous among the Centaurs was Cheiron (q.v.).

CENTLIVRE, SUSANNAH (1667?–1723), actress and dramatist, married in 1706 Joseph Centlivre, cook to Queen Anne. She wrote eighteen plays, chiefly comedies, between 1700 and 1722. 'The Wonder! a Woman Keeps a Secret' (1714) provided Garrick with one of his most successful parts, and 'The Busybody' (q.v., 1709) and 'A Bold Stroke for a Wife' (q.v., 1718) are tolerably good.

Cento (Latin *cento*, a garment of patchwork), a literary composition made up of scraps from various authors, or, more loosely, a 'string' or farrago.

Cephalus, (1) the husband of Procris, daughter of Erechtheus. Eos (see *Aurora*) fell in love with him, and caused dissension between husband and wife. Artemis gave Procris a dog called Laelaps ('Storm') and a spear that never missed its aim. These Procris gave to Cephalus and a reconciliation followed. But Procris was still jealous, and watched her husband, hidden in a bush, when he was hunting. Cephalus, thinking that he heard some animal stirring in the bush, hurled the spear and killed Procris. There is a reference to this myth in the 'Shafalus' and 'Procrus' of Pyramus and Thisbe (Shakespeare, 'Midsummer Night's Dream', v. i). Milton refers to Cephalus as 'the Attic boy' in 'Il Penseroso' (q.v.). (2) The father of Lysias (q.v.), the old man in Bk. I of Plato's 'Republic'.

Cephissus, THE, the chief river of Attica, flowing from Mt. Pentelicus past Athens.

CEPOLA or **CEPOLLA,** BARTOLOMÉ (*d. c.* 1477), an Italian jurist born at Verona, author of various legal works. His 'Cautelae juris utilissimae' (Venice, 1485) or 'Devices' and tricks for evading the law are often alluded to (e.g. Rabelais, II. x).

Cerberus, the dog of Pluto (q.v.), who had fifty heads according to Hesiod, and three according to other authors. He was stationed at the entrance of Hades, to prevent the living from descending to the infernal regions, and the dead from escaping. The heroes who in their lifetime visited Pluto's kingdom appeased him with a cake, for instance Aeneas ('Aen.' vi. 417), whence the expression 'a sop to Cerberus'; Orpheus (q.v.) lulled him to sleep with his lyre.

Cercōpes, cunning thievish gnomes who tried to steal the weapons of Hercules in his sleep, and were changed by Zeus into monkeys.

Cerdic (*d.* 534), a Saxon ealdorman, who according to the tradition landed near Southampton in 495, defeated the Britons, and acquired South Hampshire, and subsequently the Isle of Wight. He took the title of king of the West Saxons, and was the ancestor of the English royal line.

Cerdon, a cobbler, one of the bear-baiters in Butler's 'Hudibras' (q.v.).

Ceres, see *Demeter*.

CERVANTES SAAVEDRA, MIGUEL DE (1547–1616), the great Spanish novelist and dramatist, was born at Alcalà of an ancient but impoverished family, and was wounded and lost for life the use of his left hand at the battle of Lepanto (1571). He was taken by pirates in 1575, and spent the next five years as a prisoner at Algiers. The remainder of his life was, for the greater part, occupied with a struggle to earn a livelihood from literature and humble government employment. His greatest work 'Don Quixote' (q.v.) was published, the first part in 1605, the second in 1615. He also wrote a number of plays (sixteen of which survive), a collection of short stories ('Novelas Ejemplares'), and a tale of adventure, 'Persiles y Sigismunda'. Fletcher drew largely on these last two for the plots of his plays.

Cestus, the girdle of Aphrodite or Venus, which had the power of awakening love. Also the name for the leather thongs which were bound round the hands of Greek and Roman boxers to make their blows more effectual.

Cestus of Aglaia, The, articles by Ruskin on the laws of art, originally published in the 'Art Journal' (1865–6).

Ceyx, see *Halcyone* and *Ceix*.

Cézanne, PAUL (1839–1906), French painter, born at Aix-en-Provence. He was a friend of Zola until the publication of Zola's novel 'L'Œuvre' (1886) in which Cézanne and the Impressionists (q.v.) were slighted. At first closely connected with the Impressionists, Cézanne became more and more concerned with the rendering of solidity by the simplification of forms. His work was the starting point for the development of Cubism (q.v.).

Chabot, The Tragedy of, a tragedy by Chapman (q.v.), probably revised and added to by Shirley, published in 1639. The date of its composition is uncertain.

Philip de Chabot, High Admiral of France under Francis I, a loyal servant of the king, incurs the enmity of Montmorency, the High Constable, Poyet the Chancellor, and their faction. By fearless insistence on his innocence he infuriates the king, is accused on trumped-up charges, and found guilty of high treason by the judges under pressure from the chancellor. The king pardons him and discovers the abusive conduct of the chancellor, who is tried and sentenced. But Chabot's heart is broken by the unjust treatment he has suffered, and he dies.

Chace, The, see *Somerville (W.)*.

Chadband, a character in Dickens's 'Bleak House' (q.v.).

Chaereas and Callirrhoe, a Greek romance by Chariton (? 2nd cent.), one of the sources on which Sidney drew in his 'Arcadia'.

Chaffanbrass, MR., the skilful barrister in A. Trollope's 'The Three Clerks', 'Orley Farm', and 'Phineas Redux' (qq.v.).

Chainmail, MR., a character in Peacock's 'Crotchet Castle' (q.v.). He believes the 12th cent. to be the best period in English history.

Chaldean, a native of Chaldea, especially one skilled in occult learning, astrology, etc. Hence generally a seer, soothsayer, astrologer.

Chaldee MS., see *Blackwood's Magazine*.

CHALKHILL, JOHN (*fl.* 1600), the author of a pastoral 'Thealma and Clearchus', published in 1683 by Izaak Walton, and reproduced in Saintsbury's 'Caroline Poets', vol. ii (1906), and of other verse included in the 'Compleat Angler'. Nothing definite is known about his life.

Challenger, PROFESSOR GEORGE EDWARD, hero of 'The Lost World' and other stories by Sir A. Conan Doyle (q.v.), a distinguished zoologist and anthropologist of great vitality and violent temper.

Challenger Expedition, THE, for deep-sea exploration, in which H.M.S. 'Challenger' was employed, 1872–6. It was conducted by Sir Charles Wyville Thomson (1830–82), the naturalist, who published 'The Voyage of the Challenger' in 1877.

CHALMERS, THOMAS (1780–1847), educated at St. Andrews, where he was professor of moral philosophy, 1823–8. He was subsequently (1828–43) professor of divinity at Edinburgh, and an active pioneer of the movement which led to the disruption of the Scottish Established Church and the formation of the Free Church. He was a great preacher and author of many theological and philosophical treatises, including 'The Adaptation of External Nature to the Moral and Intellectual Constitution of Man' (Bridgewater Treatise, 1833).

Cham, an obsolete form of the word *Khan*, formerly applied to the rulers of the Tartars and the Mongols, and to the emperor of China. Smollett, in a letter to Wilkes, 16 March 1759 (in Boswell), refers to Johnson as 'that great Cham of literature'.

Chamade, through French and Portuguese from L. *clamare*, to call, a signal by beat of drum or sound of trumpet inviting to a parley.

CHAMBERLAYNE, EDWARD (1616–1703), educated at St. Edmund Hall, Oxford, tutor to the duke of Grafton and to Prince George of Denmark, was author of 'Angliae Notitia, or the Present State of England' (1669), a handbook of social and political conditions, which met with extraordinary success, and was enlarged by his son, John Chamberlayne.

CHAMBERLAYNE, WILLIAM (1619–89), was a physician at Shaftesbury in Dorset. He published a play entitled 'Love's Victory' in 1658, but is remembered for his 'Pharonnida' (1659), an heroic poem in five books of rhymed couplets. It deals with the romantic tale of Argalia, a kind of knight errant, rescued from the Turks on the coast of the Morea; threatened with execution for nearly slaying Almanzor, the villain of the story, but reprieved; falling in love with Pharonnida, the king's daughter; and after many vicissitudes united to her. The style is obscure and involved, and the tale somewhat incoherent; but the poem is not without beauties. It is in Saintsbury's 'Caroline Poets', vol. i (1905).

CHAMBERS, SIR EDMUND KERCHEVER (1866–1954), civil servant (Education) and literary critic. He is best known for the critical exactness and range of his history of the Elizabethan drama down to and including Shakespeare. His publications include: 'The Medieval Stage' (1903), 'The Elizabethan Stage' (1923), 'William Shakespeare' (1930).

CHAMBERS, EPHRAIM (*d.* 1740), published his 'Cyclopaedia' (the first English Encyclopaedia, which has no connexion with the current 'Chambers's Encyclopaedia') in 1728. See *Encyclopédie*.

CHAMBERS, ROBERT (1802–71), founded with his brother the publishing firm of W. and R. Chambers, Edinburgh, and wrote and issued a number of books on Scottish history, biography, and literature. He established 'Chambers's Journal' in 1832, and wrote and published anonymously in 1844 'Vestiges of Creation' in which he maintained a theory of evolution of species in animal life and prepared the way for the modern scientific view of the history of the earth. His 'Book of Days', an antiquarian miscellany, appeared in 1862–4.

Chambers's Encyclopaedia was begun in 1859 and completed in 1868, by the firm of W. and R. Chambers (see preceding entry). There have been many subsequent editions.

CHAMISSO, ADELBERT VON (1781–1838), German zoologist and poet, chiefly remembered for his 'Peter Schlemihls Wunderbare Geschichte'. See *Schlemihl*.

Chamont, one of the principal characters in Otway's 'The Orphan' (q.v.).

Champagne, the name of a former province in eastern France, through which flows the Marne. Its wine ranks highest among those of France. The best known is sparkling and straw-coloured, but other varieties are still, rose-coloured or red. Its fame dates far back. It is related for instance that Wenceslaus, king of Bohemia, coming in 1397 to Rheims to negotiate a treaty with Charles VI, found the wine so much to his taste that he spun out the discussion to the utmost, getting drunk daily before dinner. It is mentioned by Butler in 'Hudibras', II. i (1664); and in Etherege's 'Man of Mode' (1676), IV. i, occur the lines,

> Then sparkling Champaigne
> Puts an end to their reign.

Champion, The, a periodical issued thrice a week in 1739–41, mainly written·by H. Fielding (q.v.). The essays in it centre round an imaginary group, the Vinegar family.

Champion of the King, or OF ENGLAND: his office is, at the coronation, to ride armed into Westminster Hall, and challenge to combat anyone who disputes the king's title. The office is attached to the manor of Scrivelsby, formerly held by the Marmion family, and is now held by the Dymoke family. The last performance was at the coronation of George IV.

Champollion, JEAN FRANÇOIS (1790–1832), a French Egyptologist, who was the first to interpret Egyptian hieroglyphics. See also *Wilkinson.*

Chancellor, RICHARD (d. 1556), navigator, pilot-major to Sir Hugh Willoughby's (q.v.) expedition to the North-East in 1553. He made a second expedition to Russia in 1555 and was wrecked off the coast of Aberdeenshire on his return. The narrative in Hakluyt of his first visit to Moscow is the first account of some importance in English of the Russian people.

Chances, The, a play by J. Fletcher, with perhaps some contributions by another hand. (The prologue and epilogue are not by Fletcher.) The date of the play is uncertain. The prologue refers to a production after Fletcher's death. The plot is based on a novel of Cervantes, and the 'Chances' are the coincidences by which Constantia, who is eloping with the duke of Ferrara, and the duke himself, are brought into a number of complications, from which they are extricated by Don John and Don Frederick, two Spanish gallants, Dame Gillian their landlady at Bologna, and Vecchio, a professional wizard. The dialogue shows Fletcher at his best.

CHANDLER, RAYMOND (1888–1959), American writer of mystery stories, born in Illinois. His best-known books, distinguished for their style, are 'The Big Sleep' (1939), 'Farewell, My Lovely' (1940), and 'The Little Sister' (1949).

Chandos, SIR JOHN (d. 1370), English soldier, 'the flower of all chivalry' (Froissart). He fought at the siege of Cambrai, 1337, at Crécy, 1346, and at Poitiers, 1356, where he saved the life of the Black Prince. Edward III granted him a manor in Lincolnshire and lands in the Coutantin, and in 1360 appointed him his regent and lieutenant in France. He died of wounds in a battle near Poitiers and the French king declared that Sir John alone could have made the peace permanent between England and France.

Sir John was one of the founders of the Order of the Garter, and one of the twenty-five original knights.

Changeling, The, a tragedy by T. Middleton (q.v.) and W. Rowley (q.v.), printed in 1653, but acted as early as 1623.

Beatrice-Joanna, daughter of the Governor of Alicant, is ordered by her father to marry Alonzo de Piracquo. She falls in love with Alsemero, and in order to avoid the marriage imposed on her, employs the ill-favoured villain De Flores, whom she detests but who cherishes a passion for her, to murder Alonzo. To the horror of Beatrice, De Flores exacts the reward he had lusted for. Beatrice is now to marry Alsemero. To escape detection she arranges that her maid Diaphanta shall take her place on the wedding night; and to remove a dangerous witness, De Flores then kills the maid. The guilt of Beatrice and De Flores is revealed to Alsemero, and they are both brought before the governor, whereupon they take their own lives. The title of the play is taken from the sub-plot, in which Antonio disguises himself as a crazy changeling in order to get access to Isabella, wife of the keeper of a madhouse. The main plot is taken from John Reynolds's 'God's revenge against Murther' (1621).

CHANNING, WILLIAM ELLERY (1780–1842), an American Unitarian clergyman, much involved in the Unitarian controversy c. 1815. He exercised a marked influence on American intellectual life, and can be considered a forerunner of the Transcendentalists. His 'Remarks on American Literature', calling for a literary Declaration of Independence, appeared in 1830.

His nephew, WILLIAM ELLERY CHANNING (1818–1901), poet and transcendentalist, is chiefly remembered for his friendship with Emerson. His 'Poems' appeared in 1843–7. Thoreau (q.v.) called his style 'sublimoslipshod'.

Chansons de geste, epic poems in Old French embodying legends which had grown up about earlier historical figures. The earliest extant versions are of the 12th cent., and use the legends to embody problems and difficulties of feudal society: either the stresses within the feudal system itself caused by conflicting loyalties, as in the 'Raoul de Cambrai' and 'Girart de Roussillon'; or those caused by the impact of the crusades on feudalism, as in the 'Chanson de Guillaume' and above all in the 'Chanson de Roland' (q.v.). These epics gradually grew into three cycles: the *geste du roi,* those dealing with the legendary Charlemagne and his knights; the William of Orange cycle; and the cycle of the rebellious vassals. The genre followed the usual development of narrative literature during the old French period: the earliest poems, the 'Roland' and 'Gormont et Isembart', are heroic in tone; the 12th cent. poems with William as their hero, are more realist; the later poems have courtly and marvellous elements in them, and lose the tragic seriousness of the early works: they also become more elaborate in style, the early poems being written in a simple, formulaic style of great dramatic force.

Chanticleer, the cock, figures in 'Reynard the Fox' (q.v.) and in Chaucer's 'Nun's Priest's Tale' (see *Canterbury Tales*).

Chaonia, a district of Epirus where the doves, 'Chaonian birds', were said to deliver oracles. Cf. *Dodona*.

Chap-book, a modern name applied by book-collectors and others to specimens of the popular literature which was formerly circulated by itinerant dealers or chapmen, consisting chiefly of small pamphlets of popular tales, ballads, tracts, etc. They were illustrated with wood-blocks, and consisted of sixteen pages octavo or twenty-four pages duodecimo, and were sold generally at a penny to sixpence. They reproduced old romances, such as 'Bevis of Hampton' and 'Guy of Warwick', or such stories as John Gilpin, Robinson Crusoe, or nursery rhymes and fairy tales. They were issued in great numbers throughout the 18th cent.

Chapel, CHILDREN OF THE, see *Paul's (Children of)*.

Chaplin, CHARLES SPENCER (1889–   ), film comedian ('Charlie Chaplin'), was born in London, but made his career in Hollywood, California.

CHAPMAN, GEORGE (1559?–1634?), born probably near Hitchin in Hertfordshire, and educated at Oxford. He is chiefly known for his translation of Homer, animated by 'a daring fiery spirit' (Pope) and commemorated in Keats's sonnet, 'Much have I travelled in the realms of gold'; but Swinburne and others have drawn attention to the remarkable quality of his dramatic works. He was renowned as a scholar and is perhaps the 'rival poet' of Shakespeare's 'Sonnets'.

He published the obscure poem 'The Shadow of Night' in 1594, 'Ovid's Banquet of Sence' in 1595, and a continuation of Marlowe's 'Hero and Leander' in 1598. His principal tragedies were published at the following dates: 'Bussy D'Ambois' (q.v., 1607), 'The Conspiracy and Tragedy of Byron' (q.v., 1608), 'The Revenge of Bussy D'Ambois' (q.v., 1613), 'Caesar and Pompey' (q.v., 1631), 'The Tragedy of Chabot' (q.v., 1639). His principal comedies were published at the following dates: 'The Blind Beggar of Alexandria' (1598), 'An Humorous Day's Mirth' (1599), 'All Fools' (q.v., 1605), 'May-Day' (1611),

'The Gentleman Usher' (q.v., 1606), 'Monsieur D'Olive' (q.v., 1606), 'The Widow's Tear's (1612), 'Eastward hoe!' (q.v., 1605). This last play was written in collaboration with Ben Jonson and Marston, and contains a flippant allusion to the Scots, which gave offence at Court, and led to the temporary imprisonment of the authors. Chapman published a specimen of his rhyming fourteen-syllable version of the 'Iliad' in 1598, and the whole 'Iliad' in 1611, adding the 'Odyssey' (rhyming ten-syllable) in 1614–15, and the hymns etc. in 1616. Translations by him from Petrarch appeared in 1612, from Musaeus in 1616, Hesiod's 'Georgicks' in 1618, and a satire of Juvenal in 1629. He wrote also copies of verses for his friends' books, court poems, and a masque (1614). His collected works appeared in 1873–5, with an essay by Swinburne.

CHAPONE, HESTER (1727–1801), *née* Mulso, a friend of Samuel Richardson and Gilbert White, published verses and tales (1750–3) and essays (1773–7). She wrote part of No. 10 of the 'Rambler'. Her 'Works' and 'Posthumous Works' appeared in 1807. Her 'Letters on the Improvement of the Mind' (1774) were highly esteemed in her day. She was a member of the 'Blue Stocking' (q.v.) coterie.

Character of a Trimmer, see *Savile (G.)*.

Characteristics of Men, Manners, Opinions, Times, see *Shaftesbury*.

Charalois, the hero of Massinger's 'The Fatal Dowry' (q.v.).

Charge of the Light Brigade, THE, see *Balaclava*.

Charicles, see *Aethiopica*.

Charing Cross, London: the site of what was the hamlet of Charing in the time of Edward I, who set up there one of the Eleanor Crosses (q.v.).

CHARING CROSS ROAD has replaced Holywell Street (see *Bookseller's Row*) as the home of secondhand booksellers.

Charitie, The Balade of, see *Balade*.

Charivari (from 14th-cent. French and medieval Latin words of unknown origin), a serenade of 'rough music' with kettles, pans, tea-trays, and the like, used in France in derision of unpopular marriages, and unpopular persons generally. Hence a confused medley of sounds. [OED.] 'Charivari' was taken as the name of a satirical journal in Paris, and adopted in 1841 as part of the title of the London 'Punch' (q.v.).

Charlemagne (742–814), king of the Franks (768) and emperor of the West (800), the son of Pepin. He and his paladins are the subject of numerous *chansons de geste*, of which the 'Chanson de Roland' is the most famous (see *Roland*). Legend relates that he is not dead, but sleeping in the Odenberg in Hesse, or in the Untersberg near Salzburg, whence he will emerge when the persecutions of Antichrist are completed, to avenge the blood of the saints.

Charles I, king of England, 1625–49.

Charles II, king of England, 1660–85. He figures in Scott's 'Peveril of the Peak' and 'Woodstock' (qq.v.), and many other works.

Charles XII, king of Sweden, 1682–1718, and a great military commander, who led his forces successfully against the northern coalition. He captured the capital of Poland from Augustus the Elector of Saxony, and invaded Russia, defeating Peter the Great at Narva (1700) and being in turn totally defeated at Poltava in 1709, after which he retreated to Turkey. He returned in 1714 to Stralsund, which alone remained to him of his continental possessions, but was driven thence to Sweden. He was killed at Frederikshald in a war with Norway. His life was written by Voltaire. Johnson ('Vanity of Human Wishes') says of him:

> He left the name at which the world grew pale,
> To point a moral or adorn a tale.

See also *Mazeppa.*

Charles Edward Stuart (1720–88), the Young Pretender, figures in Scott's 'Waverley' and 'Redgauntlet' (qq.v.).

Charles the Bold, duke of Burgundy (1467–77), married Margaret of York, sister of Edward IV. He was severely defeated by the Swiss at Granson and Morat, and killed in an engagement with them before Nancy. He figures in Scott's 'Anne of Geierstein' and 'Quentin Durward' (qq.v.).

Charles's Wain, the constellation comprising the seven bright stars in *Ursa Major,* known also as 'The Plough' and 'The Dipper' (U.S.A.). The name appears to rise out of the verbal association of the star-name *Arcturus* with Arthur, and the legendary association of Arthur with Charlemagne; so that what was originally the wain of Arcturus became at length the wain of Charlemagne. [OED.; but the association of Arthur with Charlemagne does not appear to be well founded.]

Charley, CHARLIE, the name colloquially given in former times to a night-watchman. The origin is unknown: some have conjectured 'because Charles I in 1640 extended and improved the watch system in the metropolis'.

Also a small triangular beard extending from the under lip to a point a little below the chin: as seen in portraits of Charles I. [OED.]

Charley's Aunt, a highly popular farcical comedy by Brandon Thomas, produced in 1892 and still frequently played.

Charmian, in Shakespeare's 'Antony and Cleopatra' and Dryden's 'All for Love' (qq.v.), the attendant of Cleopatra. The name, given as Charmion, is in Plutarch's 'Antony'.

Charmond, FELICE. a character in Hardy's 'The Woodlanders' (q.v.).

Charon, in Gk. mythology, the ferryman of Hades, who, for an obolus, ferried the souls of the dead over the rivers Styx and Acheron to the infernal regions. It was usual among the ancients to place a piece of money under the tongue of the deceased for the purpose of this payment.

CHARRIÈRE, MADAME DE, see *Zélide.*

Charterhouse, THE, near Smithfield, London, was one of the houses of the Carthusian (q.v.) order in England. It was built in 1371, and at the dissolution of the monasteries under Henry VIII was taken from the monks with circumstances of great cruelty. It passed through the hands of various nobles, and was finally sold to Sir Thomas Sutton, merchant, who converted it into a school and a house for the aged poor. The school became famous and numbered Steele, Addison, Wesley, Leech, and Thackeray among its pupils. The home for poor brethren is the scene of Colonel Newcome's last days and death in Thackeray's 'The Newcomes' (q.v.). The old school has been removed to Godalming, and the school of the Merchant Taylors took its place until 1933.

Charteris, SIR PATRICK, the provost of Perth, in Scott's 'Fair Maid of Perth' (q.v.).

Chartist, one of the body of political reformers (chiefly of the working classes) who arose in 1837 and who made certain demands embodied in the 'Six Points' of the document called the 'People's Charter', viz. Universal Suffrage, Vote by Ballot, Annual Parliaments, Payment of Members, Abolition of the Property Qualification, and Equal Electoral Districts. The 'Chartists', as such, disappeared after 1848.

Charybdis, a dangerous whirlpool on the coast of Sicily, in the straits of Messina, opposite Scylla (q.v.). It threatened destruction to the fleet of Odysseus. It was said that Charybdis was an avaricious woman, who stole the oxen of Hercules, for which theft she was struck with a thunderbolt by Zeus, and turned into a whirlpool.

Chase, The, see *Somerville (W.).*

Chaste Maid in Cheapside, A, a comedy by T. Middleton (q.v.), printed in 1630.

The play centres round the attempt of the dissolute Sir Walter Whorehound to pass off his mistress as his niece (the 'Chaste Maid') and to marry her to the foolish pedantic son of Yellowhammer, a rich goldsmith; while Whorehound himself is to marry Yellowhammer's daughter, Moll. The first part of the plot succeeds, but the second fails. For Moll and the resourceful young Touchwood are in love with one another, and their attempts to evade the parents and get married, though repeatedly foiled, are finally successful.

Chastelard, a tragedy by Swinburne (q.v.), published in 1865, on the subject of Mary

Queen of Scots, and Chastelard, a grandson of Bayard, who fell desperately in love with her and followed her to Scotland. He was discovered in her room, sentenced to death, and executed.

Chatauqua, see *Chautauqua*.

Château d'Amour, see *Grosseteste*.

Château Gaillard, a fortress built by Richard I on the height of Les Andelys overlooking the Seine, for the purpose of his war with the French king. It was lost by John (1204).

CHATEAUBRIAND, FRANÇOIS RENÉ, *Vicomte de* (1768–1848), one of the pioneers of the French romantic movement. His most famous work was 'Le Génie du Christianisme' (1802), a work of Christian apologetic, based on the emotional and imaginative appeal of religion to the deepest instincts in man's nature. 'Of all religions that have ever existed' —thus the author sums up his thesis—'the Christian religion is the most poetical, the most favourable to freedom, art, and letters; the modern world owes all to it, from agriculture to the abstract sciences.' From this work Chateaubriand detached and published in advance two fragments, 'Atala', the romance of a young Red Indian, Chactas, and an Indian maiden, Atala; and 'René', the story of a young European, the author himself under a thin disguise, devoured by a secret sorrow, who flees to the solitudes of America. Both were enthusiastically received. Of Chateaubriand's later works, besides the romances 'Les Martyrs' (1809), a prose epic of early Christianity, and 'Le Dernier Abencérage' (1826), a tale of 16th-cent. Spain, the best known is the autobiographical 'Mémoires d'Outretombe' (1849–50). Between 1793 and 1800 Chateaubriand lived in exile in England, mainly in London. Under Louis XVIII, during a political phase of his career, he was again in London, as French ambassador.

Chatham, EARL OF, see *Pitt*.

Chatsworth, the famous mansion in Derbyshire of the dukes of Devonshire. The original house was built by Sir William Cavendish, husband of Bess of Hardwick (q.v.). This was rebuilt in 1688 by the first duke of Devonshire.

CHATTERTON, THOMAS (1752–70), son of a writing-master who was a lay clerk of Bristol Cathedral, while still at school at Colston's Hospital wrote a notable satire 'Apostate Will', 1764, and other verses. In 1768 he published a pseudo-archaic description of the mayor of Bristol's passing over the 13th-cent. bridge, and met William Barrett, an antiquarian surgeon who was writing a history of Bristol, George Catcott, and Henry Burgum, pewterers, for all of whom he fabricated documents, pedigrees, poems, of which he claimed to possess the originals. He also fabricated a number of poems purporting to be the work of an imaginary 15th-cent. Bristol

poet, Thomas Rowley, a monk and friend of William Canynge, an historical Bristol merchant. He offered some of these to Dodsley, the publisher, and sent a history of painting in England (supposed to be by Rowley) to Horace Walpole, who was temporarily deceived. The fraud was exposed by T. Tyrwhitt in his 'Poems supposed to have been written . . . by Thomas Rowley', 1777 and 1778; but the poems are none the less work of a poetical genius. 'Elinoure and Juga', published in the 'Town and Country Magazine', 1769, was the only 'Rowleian' piece to appear in Chatterton's life-time, and editions of the poems of 'Thomas Rowley' were published in 1778 and 1782. In 1770 he came to London, and his burlesque opera 'The Revenge' was successfully produced in that year. Reduced to despair by his poverty, he poisoned himself with arsenic, 24 Aug. 1770, at the age of 17. His collected works appeared in 1803, and have been several times reprinted.

CHAUCER, GEOFFREY (prob. 1345–1400), was son of John Chaucer (*d.* 1366), vintner, of London. The date of his birth has been matter for much discussion. In 1357 he was employed in the service of Lionel, afterwards duke of Clarence. In 1359 he was in the army with which Edward III invaded France, was taken prisoner, but shortly ransomed. He married Philippa, probably daughter of Sir Payne Roet, and sister of John of Gaunt's third wife. He evidently enjoyed John of Gaunt's patronage. Philippa died apparently in 1387. Chaucer held various positions at court and in the king's service, and was sent on a mission to Genoa and Florence in 1372–3, when he perhaps met Boccaccio and Petrarch. He was sent on secret service to Flanders in 1376 and 1377, and was attached to embassies to France and Lombardy in 1378. In 1374 he was appointed controller of customs in the port of London and leased the dwelling-house over Aldgate. He was knight of the shire for Kent in 1386, and went the Canterbury pilgrimage in April 1388. About this time he 'was clerk of the king's works at various places, including Westminster Abbey, living close to St. Margaret's. He received pensions from Edward III, John of Gaunt, Richard II, and Henry IV. He was buried in Westminster Abbey, a monument being erected to him in 1555.

Chaucer's writings fall into three periods: (1) The period of French influence (1359–72), in which he uses the octosyllabic couplet. To this period belong 'The Boke of the Duchesse', 1369, and the 'Romaunt of the Rose', so far as written by Chaucer. (2) The period of Italian influence, especially of Dante and Boccaccio, 1372–86, in which he leaves off the octosyllabic couplet, uses mainly the 'heroic' stanza of seven lines, and begins to use the heroic couplet. To this period belong 'The Hous of Fame'; 'The Parlement of Foules'; 'Troylus and Cryseyde'; 'The Legende of

Good Women'; and the first drafts of some of his tales. (3) The period of his maturity, 1386–1400, in which he uses the heroic couplet. To this period belong the 'Canterbury Tales', designed about 1387. His various poetical works will be found referred to under their several titles. His prose works include a translation of Boethius, and a 'Treatise on the Astrolabe' compiled for 'little Lewis my son', in English, 'for Latin ne canst thou yet but small, my little son'.

The Ellesmere MS., owing to its regularity and general good quality, is the usual basis of the text of Chaucer. It is the only MS. of the 'Canterbury Tales' illustrated throughout and has been published in collotype facsimile. It is now in the Huntington Library in the United States.

Chaucer's well-known portrait was made from memory by Occleve on the margin of one of his works. The 'Canterbury Tales' were first printed by Caxton in 1478(?); the collected works were first issued by W. Thynne in 1532. The fullest edition is that of W. W. Skeat, with introductions and notes, Oxford, 7 vols. (1894–7). See also *Tyrwhitt*.

Chaucer Society, THE, founded in 1868 by Furnivall (q.v.), for the purpose of collecting materials for the study of Chaucer.

Chaucerians, SCOTTISH, name given to a group of 15th–16th-cent. Scottish writers who show in a greater or less degree the influence of Chaucer. See *James I* (of Scotland), *Henryson, Dunbar, Douglas (Gawin)*.

Chautauqua, sometimes incorrectly spelt *Chatauqua*, an American literary institution developed in 1874, at first confined to summer literary classes held on Lake Chautauqua, New York State; later extended to a Reading Circle with a series of textbooks arranged for home study; and now also to travelling entertainments of an educational nature, concerts, and drama. Its object is the general diffusion of education.

Chauvinism, an exaggerated and bellicose patriotism, a word derived from one Nicholas Chauvin of Rochefort, a veteran French soldier of the First Republic and Empire, whose demonstrative patriotism was celebrated and at length ridiculed by his comrades. Chauvin figured in the 'Soldat laboureur' of Scribe, and his name was especially popularized by Cogniard's famous vaudeville, 'La Cocarde tricolore' (1831).

Chaworth, MARY ANNE, later Mrs. Chaworth-Musters, the lady with whom Byron fell in love in his youth, and to whom he proposed in 1803. She is celebrated in Byron's poem, 'The Dream'.

Cheapside ('cheap' is from Old English *céap*, buying and selling) was a busy market in medieval London, and a place for pageants and sports, and occasionally for executions (until Tudor times, there were no buildings on the north side, so that more space was available than now). It was surrounded by streets whose names suggested the trade of the locality, Bread Street, Poultry, Ironmonger Lane, Honey Street, Milk Street, etc.

Cheddar Caves, stalactite caves in the cliffs of the Mendip Hills, near the village of Cheddar. CHEDDAR CHEESE, for which this district is also famous, is mentioned as early as 1666. Bailey in his dictionary of 1721 mentions (s.v. *Cheddar*) that 'the milk of all the town cows is brought every day into one common room', duly recorded, 'and one common cheese made with it'.

Cheeryble Brothers, THE, Ned and Charles, characters in Dickens's 'Nicholas Nickleby' (q.v.).

Cheiron or **Chīron**, a centaur (q.v.), the son of Cronos (q.v.) and Philȳra, famous for his knowledge of medicine, music, and archery. He taught mankind the use of medicinal herbs, and was the instructor of many heroes and the friend of Hercules. He was accidentally wounded by Hercules in the knee when the latter fought with the Centaurs. Hercules went to his assistance, but as the wound was incurable, Cheiron, to escape from the pain, gave up his immortality to Prometheus.

CHEKE, SIR JOHN (1514–57), fellow of St. John's College, tutor to Edward VI, and subsequently professor of Greek at Cambridge. He was imprisoned by Queen Mary, 1553–4. He was an eminent scholar, and though he wrote little in the vernacular (but many Latin translations from the Greek), was influential in promoting a simple style of English prose. He is referred to ('O soul of Sir John Cheeke') in Milton's Sonnet XI, 'A Book was writ of late'.

CHEKHOV, ANTON PAVLOVICH (1860–1904), Russian dramatist and short-story writer. He studied medicine in Moscow, where he began writing short humorous stories for journals. Though he never abandoned this genre, many of his later stories are longer and more serious: 'Ward No. 6' (1892), 'A Dreary Story' (1889). Chekhov's first successful play 'Ivanov' (1887) was followed by the better known 'The Seagull' (1896), 'Uncle Vanya' (1897), 'The Three Sisters' (1901), and 'The Cherry Orchard' (1904), of which the last two were written for the Moscow Art Theatre, with which Chekhov was closely associated. Since 1903 the greater part of Chekhov's work has been translated. The major translation is that of C. Garnett: 'The Tales of Tchehov' (1916–22) and 'The Plays of Tchehov' (1923–4).

Chelsea, meaning, according to the 'Oxford Dictionary of English Place-names', 'landing-place for chalk or lime-stone', was a separate village until gradually absorbed into London in the 18th–19th cents. Here (on the site of the present Danvers Street) Sir Thomas More (q.v.) had his residence, where he received Erasmus. In the 17th and 18th cents. Chelsea was much patronized by Cockneys and was famous for its bun-house (see below; see also Congreve's 'Love for Love', II. ii). The manor of Chelsea was purchased in 1712 by Sir Hans Sloane (q.v.), who founded there the Botanic Garden. The Cremorne Gardens (q.v.) were in Chelsea. Chelsea has a reputation as a home of painters: Rossetti, Whistler, and many others lived there.

Chelsea, SAGE OF, T. Carlyle (q.v.).

Chelsea Bun-house, THE, famous in the 18th cent., and kept in its palmy days by one Richard Hand, stood in Jew's Row (now Pimlico Road). It was demolished in 1839. Swift (q.v.) writes to Stella about the 'r-r-rare Chelsea buns'.

Chelsea Hospital, for disabled soldiers ('Chelsea Pensioners'), was founded by Charles II and built from the designs of Sir Christopher Wren. Fanny Burney's father was for many years organist there.

Chemos or CHEMOSH, a Moabite god (1 Kings xi. 7), ranks after Moloch in Milton's hierarchy of hell ('Paradise Lost', i. 406).

CHÉNIER, ANDRÉ (1762–94), French poet and one of the earliest figures in the French Romantic movement. Inspired by the spirit of the Greek anthologists, he wrote idylls, eclogues, and elegies marked by pastoral simplicity and freshness. At first a revolutionary, he was presently alienated by the excesses of the Terror and wrote a fine ode in defence of Charlotte Corday. He was arrested early in 1794 and after some months in prison was guillotined on the 7th Thermidor, immediately before the fall of Robespierre.

His brother, MARIE-JOSEPH CHÉNIER (1764–1811), was a dramatic poet, and author of the 'Chant du Départ', a famous Revolutionary song, still heard on national occasions.

Chequers, a Tudor mansion near Princes Risborough, Bucks., presented to the nation in 1917 by Lord and Lady Lee of Fareham for the purpose of serving as the country seat of the Prime Minister of England while in office.

Cherith, the name of the brook where Elijah was fed by ravens (1 Kings xvii).

Cherry and **Merry**, in Dickens's 'Martin Chuzzlewit' (q.v.), Pecksniff's daughters, Charity and Mercy.

Cherry and the Slae, The, see *Montgomerie*.

Cherubim, a Hebrew word of uncertain derivation. In the O.T. they are living creatures with two or four wings, but the accounts of their form are not consistent. They first appear in Gen. iii. 24, as guardians of the tree of life. The Divine Being is frequently stated to dwell or sit between (or above) the cherubim. Their inclusion among the angels appears to belong to Christian mysticism. According to Dionysius the Areopagite they form the second of the nine orders of angels. See *Angel*.

Cheshire Cat, *To grin like a*: no satisfactory explanation of the allusion has been put forward. It has been attributed to the fact that Cheshire cheeses were at one time moulded in the shape of a cat; and to the attempts of a sign-painter to represent a lion rampant on the signs of many of the Cheshire inns. (N. & Q., 1st series, ii. 412; v. 402). The Cheshire Cat figures in Lewis Carroll's 'Alice in Wonderland' (q.v.).

Cheshire Cheese, THE, a hostelry in Wine Office Court, off Fleet Street, London, rebuilt shortly after the Restoration and still in existence.

CHESNEY, SIR GEORGE TOMKYNS (1833–95), a distinguished Indian officer, published in 'Blackwood's Magazine' in 1871 'The Battle of Dorking' (q.v.), which created a sensation, and in 1876 'The Dilemma', a powerful story of the Mutiny, besides other novels.

Chester, SIR JOHN, and EDWARD his son, characters in Dickens's 'Barnaby Rudge' (q.v.).

Chester Plays, see *Miracle Plays*.

CHESTERFIELD, PHILIP DORMER STANHOPE, *fourth earl of* (1694–1773), statesman and diplomatist, was ambassador at The Hague, 1728–32, and entered the Pelham ministry in 1744. His tolerance as lord lieutenant of Ireland in 1745–6 kept that country quiet. He was a wit and an orator, wrote political tracts, and contributed to the 'World', but is remembered as a writer principally for his 'Letters' to his natural son, Philip Stanhope. These were written almost daily from 1737 onwards and were designed for the education of the young man. They are full of sensible instruction, admirably expressed, more particularly in matters of good breeding (for the boy was exceptionally awkward and ungraceful), but have been reprobated on account of a few passages contrary to good morals, in which he commended intrigue while condemning vulgar vice. The letters to his son were followed by letters to his godson, also named Philip Stanhope. These letters are on the same lines as their predecessors. The letters to his son were published (by the son's widow) in 1774; those to his godson, by Lord Carnarvon, in 1890. A complete edition of all Chesterfield's letters, by B. Dobrée, appeared in 1932. Chesterfield is also remembered in connexion with Johnson's 'Dictionary'. Johnson had addressed the 'Plan' of that work to Chesterfield, but it was received with neglect (unintentional according to the latter). On the publication of the Dictionary, Chesterfield wrote two papers in the 'World' in commendation of it. Thereupon on 7 Feb. 1755 Johnson addressed to Chesterfield the famous letter, in which he bitterly rejected a notice which 'had it been early, had been kind; but it has been delayed till I am indifferent, and cannot enjoy it; till I am solitary, and cannot impart it; till I am known, and do not want it'. Lord Chesterfield also wrote some 'Characters of

Eminent Persons' which contain valuable historical matter. Everyone feared him because he was believed to be writing his own Memoirs, which would brand most people severely. He gave his name to a kind of overcoat and to a kind of couch.

CHESTERTON, GILBERT KEITH (1874–1936) educated at St. Paul's School, essayist, critic, novelist, and poet, among whose best-known writings are: (novels and short stories) 'The Napoleon of Notting Hill', 'The Man who was Thursday', 'The Flying Inn', 'The Ball and the Cross', 'The Innocence of Father Brown', 'The Wisdom of Father Brown'; (poetry) 'The Ballad of the White Horse', 'Wine, Water, and Song', 'Poems';(essays)'Heretics','GenerallySpeaking', 'What's Wrong with the World'; (biography)'RobertBrowning','CharlesDickens'; (criticism) 'G. F. Watts', 'William Blake'.

CHESTRE, THOMAS, see *Launfal.*

CHETTLE, HENRY (*d.* 1607?), the son of a London dyer, was apprenticed to a stationer, and was for a time a partner in a printing business. Upon its failure he took to writing plays, of which he is reputed the author of thirteen, and the joint-author of considerably more (including 'The Blind Beggar of Bednal Green', with J. Day (q.v.)). The only extant play attributed to him alone is 'The Tragedy of Hoffman' (1602), dealing with the story of a Danish pirate who is executed, and the revenge and execution of his son. He edited Greene's 'Groatsworth of Wit' (q.v.) in 1592, and wrote two satirical pamphlets, 'Kind-Hart's Dreame' (1592?) and 'Pierce Plainnes Prentiship' (1595). He also published 'Englande's Mourning Garment', an elegy on Queen Elizabeth, in 1603.

Chevalier, THE YOUNG, Charles Edward Stuart (1720–88), the Young Pretender.

Chevalier de St. George, James Francis Edward Stuart (1688–1766), the Old Pretender, called by the Jacobites 'King James III and VIII'.

Chevy Chase, The Ballad of, one of the oldest of the English ballads, probably dates in its primitive form from the 15th cent. Its subject is the rivalry of the neighbouring families of Percy and Douglas, heightened by the national quarrel between England and Scotland. Percy, earl of Northumberland, has vowed to hunt for three days across the Scottish border 'maugre the doughty Douglas'. The two parties meet and fight, there is great slaughter on both sides, and both Percy and Douglas are killed. (Cf. *Otterbourne.*) The ballad was printed in Capell's 'Prolusions' in 1760 and is included in Percy's 'Reliques'.

Cheyne Row and **Walk,** in Chelsea, named from Lord Cheyne, who sold the manor to Sir Hans Sloane (q.v.). Carlyle lived in Cheyne Row; George Eliot, Count d'Orsay, D. G. Rossetti, Turner, in Cheyne Walk.

Don Saltero's coffee-house (q.v.) stood in Cheyne Walk.

Chiaroscuro, meaning originally the style of pictorial art in which only the light and shade, and not the various colours, are represented, is used figuratively of poetic and literary treatment in the sense of mingled clearness and obscurity, light and gloom, praise and blame, etc.; but is still used chiefly for pictorial art.

Chiasmus, a figure of speech by which the order of the words in the first of two parallel clauses is reversed in the second, e.g. 'He saved others; himself he cannot save.'

Chichele or **Chicheley,** HENRY (1362?–1443), archbishop of Canterbury, son of a yeoman of Higham Ferrers, Northamptonshire. He was educated at Winchester and New College, Oxford, and became archbishop in 1414. He founded the Chichele chest in Oxford University for the relief of poor students, built a house for Cistercians in Oxford, and was co-founder, with Henry VI, of All Souls College (q.v.).

Chichevache, a perversion of the French *chiche face,* 'thin-face', the name of a fabulous monster said to feed only on patient wives, and hence, from scarcity of the diet, to be always lean and hungry. Her spouse, the Bycorne, on the contrary grew fat on his abundant diet of patient husbands.

> O noble wyves, ful of heigh prudence,
> Let noon humilitie your tonges nayle . . .
> Lest Chichevache you swolwe in her entrayle. (Chaucer, 'Clerk's Tale', 1132.)

Chiffinch, WILLIAM (1602–88), the confidential agent of Charles II, page of the bedchamber, figures in Scott's 'Peveril of the Peak' (q.v.).

CHILD, FRANCIS JAMES (1825–96), American scholar, born in Massachusetts. While professor of English at Harvard University he published his great collection of 'English and Scottish Popular Ballads' (1883–98).

Childe, in 'Childe Harold', 'Childe Roland', etc., signifies a youth of gentle birth, and is used as a kind of title. In the 13th and 14th cents. 'child' appears to have been applied to a young noble awaiting knighthood.

Childe Harold's Pilgrimage, a poem in Spenserian stanzas by Lord Byron (q.v.), begun in Albania in 1809, of which the first two cantos appeared in 1812, canto iii in 1816, canto iv in 1818.

The poem purports to describe the travels and reflections of a pilgrim who, sated and disgusted with a life of pleasure and revelry, seeks distraction in foreign lands. The first two cantos take the reader to Portugal, Spain, the Ionian Isles, and Albania, and end with a lament on the bondage of Greece. In the third canto the pilgrim passes to Belgium, the Rhine, the Alps, and the Jura. The historical associations of each place are made the poet's theme, the Spanish war, the eve of Waterloo and Napoleon, and more especially Rousseau and Julie. In the fourth canto the poet abandons his imaginary pilgrim and speaks in his own person, of Venice, Arqua and Petrarch, Ferrara and Tasso, Florence and Boccaccio, Rome and her great men, from the Scipios to Rienzi.

Childe of Elle, the subject of an old ballad included in Percy's 'Reliques', who loves the fair Emmeline, runs away with her, slays the foremost of the pursuers, and is finally forgiven by the baron her father.

Childe Roland, in an old Scottish ballad, a son of King Arthur. His sister, Burd Ellen, is carried away by the fairies to the castle of the king of Elfland. Aided by the instructions of Merlin, Childe Roland makes his way into the castle and rescues his sister.

> Child Rowland to the dark tower came,
> His word was still 'Fie, foh, and fum,
> I smell the blood of a British man.'
>   (Shakespeare, 'King Lear', III. iv.)

Halliwell ('Nursery Rhymes') thinks that Shakespeare is here quoting from two different compositions, the first line from a ballad on Roland, the second and third from the story of Jack the Giant-killer (q.v.).

Childe Roland to the Dark Tower Came, a poem by R. Browning (q.v.), included in 'Dramatic Romances', published in 'Men and Women' in 1855.

A brave knight is attempting an adventure, in which all who have previously undertaken it have failed. He reaches the tower just when he despairs of succeeding. Around him he sees the figures of the 'lost adventurers'. He sounds his horn to announce that he has come. We may see in the dreamlike narrative an allegory of life.

Childe Waters, one of the most beautiful of the old ballads, celebrating the constancy of Ellen to Childe Waters, her heartless lover, whom she serves as a page, receiving cruel and degrading treatment. Her child is born in a stable, where she is tending her master's horse. He hears her singing a lullaby and wishing herself dead, relents, and marries her. The ballad is in Percy's 'Reliques'.

Childermas, the festival of the Holy Innocents (28 Dec.), commemorating the slaughter of the children by Herod (Matt. ii. 16).

Children in the Wood, THE, the subject of an old ballad (apparently written in 1595), which is included in Percy's and Ritson's collections. A gentleman of Norfolk on his death-bed leaves his property to his infant son and daughter, and gives the charge of them to his brother. The brother designs to get possession of the property by making away with the children. He hires two ruffians to slay them in a wood. One of these, more tender-hearted than the other, repents and kills his fellow, and then abandons the children in the wood. The children perish and the Robin-redbreast covers them with leaves. The wrath of God falls upon the wicked uncle, who loses his sons and his goods, and dies in gaol. The surviving ruffian is arrested for robbery, condemned to death, and confesses the deed.

A similar story is the subject of the second of 'Two lamentable Tragedies; the one the murder of Maister Beech, a chandler in Thames Street. The other of a young child murthered in a wood by two ruffins, with the consent of his unkle. By Robt. Harrington, 1601, 4to'.

Children of the Chapel, CHILDREN OF PAUL'S, see *Paul's (Children of)*.

Chillingworth, ROGER, in Hawthorne's 'The Scarlet Letter' (q.v.), the name assumed by Hester Prynne's husband.

CHILLINGWORTH, WILLIAM (1602–44), a scholar and fellow of Trinity College, Oxford, embraced Romanism and went to Douai in 1630, but abjured that creed in 1634. He was one of the literary coterie that gathered round Lord Falkland at Great Tew, and was the author of the controversial work, 'The Religion of the Protestants a safe Way to Salvation' (1638).

Chillip, DR., in Dickens's 'David Copperfield' (q.v.), the physician who attended Mrs. Copperfield at the hero's birth.

Chillon, The Prisoner of, see *Prisoner of Chillon*.

Chiltern Hundreds, hundreds (i.e. subdivisions of a county, having their own courts) in Oxfordshire and Buckinghamshire which contain the Chiltern Hills. The manorial rights of these belonged to the Crown, which appointed over them bailiffs and stewards. These offices are now obsolete, but the stewardship of the three Buckinghamshire hundreds (Stoke, Desborough, and Burnham) has been retained for a special purpose. No member of parliament may by law resign his seat so long as he is duly qualified; on the other hand a member who accepts an office of profit under the Crown must vacate his seat subject to re-election. Therefore a member who desires to resign applies for the 'Stewardship of the Chiltern Hundreds' or other similar post, which is, by a legal fiction, held to be such an office; the appointment entails his resignation, and having thus fulfilled its purpose, is itself vacated. [OED.]

Chimaera, according to Greek legend, a monster, offspring of Echidna (q.v.), with a lion's head, goat's body, and dragon's tail; the head continually vomited flame. It was overcome by Bellerophon (q.v.), mounted on the winged horse Pegasus.

According to Rabelais (II. vii), among the books found by Pantagruel in the library of St. Victor was a treatise on the very subtle question, debated for seventy days at the Council of Constance, 'utrum chimaera in vacuo bombinans possit comedere secundas intentiones', a formula in which the author sums up the inanities of decadent scholasticism.

Chimène, or XIMENA, the wife of the *Cid* (q.v.).

Chimes, The, a Christmas book by Dickens (q.v.), published in 1845.

It is the story of a nightmare or vision in which Toby Veck, porter and runner of errands, under the influence of the goblins of the church bells and a dish of tripe, witnesses awful misfortunes befalling his daughter, a vision happily dissipated at the end; together with some social satire on justices, aldermen, and the like, in the persons of Sir Joseph Bowley and Mr. Chute.

Chingachgook(pron. 'chi′ca′go'), the Indian chief in the 'Leatherstocking' series of tales of Indian life of J. F. Cooper (q.v.).

Chinoiserie, decoration in imitation of the Chinese style. It came into fashion in the late 17th cent. with the importation of Chinese porcelain and lacquer, was used to decorate porcelain, furniture, and occasionally rooms and even buildings during the 18th cent., culminating in the extravagant orientalism of the Royal Pavilion, Brighton, built by Nash (q.v.), 1815–21.

Chios, an island in the Aegean Sea, one of the reputed birthplaces of Homer. It was celebrated for its wine.

Chippendale, THOMAS (1718–79), cabinetmaker. 'The Gentleman and Cabinet-Maker's Director,' published in 1754, spread throughout the country his designs in 'Gothic, Chinese, and Modern taste'.

Chivery, MR. and 'YOUNG JOHN', characters in Dickens's 'Little Dorrit' (q.v.).

Chloe, see *Daphnis and Chloe*. 'Chloe' is the name by which Pope ('Moral Essays', ii. 157) refers to Lady Suffolk, mistress of George II. Matthew Prior has several poems to 'Chloe'.

The 'Chloe' or 'Cloe' mentioned in several of Horace Walpole's letters was the duke of Newcastle's French cook, Clouet.

Chloe, The Tale of, see *Tale of Chloe*.

Choice, The, see *Pomfret*.

Choice of Hercules, THE, see *Hercules*.

Choliamb, see *Scazon*.

Chopin, FRÉDÉRIC FRANÇOIS (1809–49), pianist and composer, was born near Warsaw of a French father and a Polish mother. He composed two concertos, and a large number of pianoforte solo compositions, études, mazurkas, preludes, nocturnes, etc. His romantic connexion with George Sand (q.v.) is recorded in her 'Lucrezia Floriani', where Chopin figures as Prince Karol.

Chopine, a kind of shoe raised by a cork sole or the like, worn about 1600 in Spain and Italy, and on the English stage. 'Your lady-ship is nearer heaven than when I saw you last, by the altitude of a chopine' (Shakespeare, 'Hamlet', II. ii), which implies that the boy-actor (who took female parts) had grown.

Chops of the Channel, the entrance into the English Channel from the Atlantic.

Choriamb, a metrical foot of four syllables, the first and last long, the two others short. A Choree is a Trochee (q.v.).

Chouans, a name given to irregular bands who maintained in the west of France (the Vendée and Brittany) a partisan war against the Republic and the first empire, after 1793; hence a polemical name for partisans of the Bourbons. The word is perhaps from the name of Jean Chouan, said to be one of their leaders, or from *chouan* an older form of *chat-huant*, a species of owl. Probably the coincidence suggested the appellation. [OED.] It is said that the Chouans imitated the hoot of an owl as a rallying-cry. See *Balzac* for his novel 'Le Dernier Chouan'.

CHRÉTIEN DE TROYES, a writer of courtly romances for the French feudal aristocracy in the second half of the 12th cent.: his extant works are 'Erec and Enide' (c. 1160), 'Cligès' (c. 1162), 'Yvain and Lancelot' or the 'Chevalier de la Charete' (c. 1170, for the Countess Marie de Champagne), and 'Perceval' or 'Le Conte du Graal' (c. 1180, for Count Philip of Flanders), which he left unfinished at his death, and which was the starting-point for the cycle of Grail romances. His works were very popular, and exercised a great influence both in France and abroad.

Christ and Satan, an OE. poem, or perhaps three poems, contained in the Junius MS. (see *Caedmon*). It has been described as 'a set of lyric and dramatic amplifications of a number of Biblical and legendary themes'— Satan's lament for his fall, the Harrowing of Hell, and the Temptation of Christ.

Christ Church, Oxford, a college begun by Cardinal Wolsey (it was to be called 'Cardinal College'), and taken over after his fall and established by Henry VIII in 1546. Among famous men educated there were Locke, John Wesley, Dr. Pusey, and Gladstone. Christ Church is at the same time the cathedral of Oxford, the cathedral being within the walls of the college and serving as its chapel.

Christ's Hospital, London, also known as the BLUECOAT SCHOOL (q.v.), founded under a charter of Edward VI as a school for poor children, in buildings that before the dissolution had belonged to the Grey Friars. Here were educated Coleridge, Lamb, and Leigh Hunt. The school was removed to Horsham.

Christs Teares over Jerusalem, a tract by T. Nash (q.v.), published in 1593. Abandoning his contentious and vituperative writings, Nash here figures as a religious reformer. He applies Christ's prophecy of the fall of Jerusalem as a warning to sinful London.

He analyses with his usual vigour the vices and abuses of contemporary society.

Christs Victorie and Triumph, the principal poem of Giles Fletcher (q.v.).

Christabel, a poem by S. T. Coleridge (q.v.), published in 1816.

The poem is unfinished. The first part was written at Stowey in Somerset in 1797, the second at Keswick in Cumberland in 1800 after the poet's return from Germany. Christabel, daughter of Sir Leoline, praying at night in the wood for her betrothed lover, finds a lady in distress, the fair Geraldine, and brings her to the castle, where she is hospitably received. She claims to be the daughter of Lord Roland de Vaux, who had once been the friend of Sir Leoline before they were estranged by a quarrel, and to have been forcibly abducted from her home. In reality she is a malignant supernatural creature who has assumed the form of Geraldine in order to work evil, and Christabel has seen through her disguise, but is forced to silence by a spell. Sir Leoline sends his bard to Lord Roland to tell him that his daughter is safe and to offer reconcilement.

The poem, apart from introducing a new metre, is important as one of the most beautiful in English poetry.

Christian, the hero of Bunyan's 'The Pilgrim's Progress' (q.v.).

Christian, EDWARD, a character in Scott's 'Peveril of the Peak' (q.v.).

Christian, FLETCHER, see *Bounty.*

Christian Hero, The. An Argument proving that no Principles but those of Religion are Sufficient to make a great Man, a treatise by Steele (q.v.), published in 1701.

Finding, as the author tells us, 'Military life exposed to much Irregularity', he wrote this little work 'with a design to fix upon his own Mind a strong Impression of Virtue and Religion, in opposition to a stronger Propensity towards unwarrantable Pleasures'. In it he inculcates the value of the Bible as a moral guide and the failure of the old philosophy. The treatise ends with a comparison between Louis XIV and William III, and includes a significant passage recommending, in contrast with the immorality that pervaded most of the writings of the day, a chivalrous attitude towards women. The work is important as one of the first signs of a change of tone in the English literature of the period.

Christian King, MOST, a title of the kings of France since the middle of the 15th cent., or even, according to some authorities, since Pepin le Bref (Larousse).

Christian Morals, see *Browne (Sir T.).*

Christian Year, The, a collection of sacred poems by Keble (q.v.), published in 1827. The book attained great popularity both because of the beauty of much of the verse and owing to its connexion with the Oxford

Movement (q.v.), of which it expressed the sentiment.

Christiana, in the second part of 'The Pilgrim's Progress' (q.v.), the wife of Christian.

Christianity, An Argument against abolishing, see *Swift.*

CHRISTIE, AGATHA (MRS. M. E. L. MALLOWAN) (1891–   ), prolific writer of detective fiction and plays, including: 'The Mysterious Affair at Styles' (1920, which introduced the Belgian detective Hercule Poirot), 'The Murder of Roger Ackroyd' (1926), 'Murder on the Orient Express' (1934), 'Ten Little Niggers' (1939), 'The Mousetrap' (1952), etc.

Christie Johnstone, a novel by C. Reade (q.v.), published in 1853. It is a romantic story, not devoid of humour, telling how the gallant large-hearted Christie, a Scottish fisher-girl, proved herself more than worthy to marry the weak-willed artist, Charles Gatty, and, by saving him from drowning, won over even his dour mother.

Christie's: Christie, Manson, and Woods, King Street, St. James, fine art auctioneers. James Christie, the elder (1730–1803), was an auctioneer in London (1766–1803). His eldest son, James Christie, the younger (1773–1831), took over his father's business, and moved to the present premises in 1824. He wrote on the antiquity of chess, Greek vases, etc.

Christis Kirk on the Green, an old Scottish poem, doubtfully attributed to James I or James V of Scotland, in nine-lined stanzas with a 'bob' after the eighth line, descriptive of the rough fun, dancing, and love-making of a village festival or 'wappinshaw'. Two additional cantos were composed by Allan Ramsay (q.v.).

Christmas-box, originally a box, usually of earthenware, in which contributions of money were collected at Christmas by apprentices, etc., the box being broken when full and the contents shared. Now, a present given at Christmas to employees and tradespeople. Hence 'Boxing Day'.

Christmas Carol, A, a Christmas book by Dickens (q.v.), published in 1843.

Scrooge, an old curmudgeon, receives on Christmas Eve a visit from the ghost of Marley, his late partner in business, and beholds a series of visions of the past, present, and future, including one of what his own death will be like unless he is quick to amend his ways. As a result of this he wakes up on Christmas morning an altered man. He sends a turkey to his ill-used clerk, Bob Cratchit, positively enjoys subscribing to Christmas charities, and generally behaves like the genial old fellow that he has become.

Christmas Eve and Easter Day, two distinct poems under one title, by R. Browning (q.v.), published in 1850.

In the first the narrator recounts a spiritual experience, a vision in which he is taken first to a dissenting chapel, then to St. Peter's Church at Rome, then to a lecture-room where a German professor is investigating the origin of the Christian myth, and finally back to the dissenting chapel. He concludes that his 'heart does best to receive in meekness' this last mode of worship, where earthly aids are cast aside and God 'appears serene with the thinnest human veil between'.

In 'Easter Day' a Christian and a sceptic are disputing. The Christian narrates a vision from which he has learnt the value of life, with its limitations, but with the hope remaining 'to reach one eve the Better Land'.

Christopher, St., meaning 'Christ-bearer', a Christian martyr of the 3rd cent., said to have lived in Syria and to have been a man of exceptional size and strength. As a penance for his past sins he used to carry pilgrims over a river. Jesus Christ, the legend says, came to him in the form of a child, to be carried over, but before Christopher reached the other side, the burden became so heavy that he nearly failed. 'Marvel not', said Christ, 'for with me thou hast carried the sins of all the world.' The saint is commemorated on 25 July. He is the patron saint of wayfarers.

CHRISTOPHER NORTH, a pseudonym used by J. Wilson (1785–1854, q.v.).

Christopher Robin, a small boy who figures in the nursery tales of A. A. Milne. 'The Christopher Robin Story Book' appeared in 1929.

Christopher Sly, see *Taming of the Shrew.*

Christy Minstrels, a troupe of minstrels imitating Negroes, originated in the 19th cent. by one George Christy of New York. The name was afterwards extended to any similar company with blackened faces who sing Negro melodies interspersed with jokes.

Chronicles, see under *Anglo-Saxon Chronicle, Annales Cambriae, Asser, Bede, Camden (William), Capgrave (John), Cirencester, Eadmer, Fabyan (Robert), Flodoard, Florence of Worcester, Geoffrey of Monmouth, Gesta Francorum, Gildas, Giraldus Cambrensis, Hall (Edward), Harrison (William), Hayward (Sir John), Holinshed (Raphael), Hoveden (Roger), Jocelin de Brakelond, Nennius, Peterborough Chronicle, Richard III (History of), Robert of Gloucester, Speed (John), Stow (John), Vergil (Polydore), Wace of Jersey, William of Malmesbury, William of Newburgh, Wyntoun (Andrew of).*

Chronicles of the Canongate, *The,* an inclusive title for certain of Sir W. Scott's novels, 'The Highland Widow', 'The Two Drovers', and 'The Fair Maid of Perth' (qq.v.), to which the author attached the fiction that they were written by Mr. Chrystal Croftangry, who draws on the recollections of his old friend, Mrs. Bethune Baliol, a resident in the Canongate, Edinburgh. Mr. Croft-

angry's own story, notable among Scott shorter sketches, forms an introduction to the Chronicles.

Chrononhotonthologos, a burlesque of contemporary drama by Henry Carey (q.v.), 'the Most Tragical Tragedy that ever was Tragediz'd by any Company of Tragedians', acted in 1734. Chrononhotonthologos is king of Queerummania, and two of the characters are Aldiborontiphoscophornio and Rigdum-Funnidos, names which Scott gave to James and John Ballantyne, on account of the pomposity of the one and the fun and cheerfulness of the other.

Chrysal, *or the Adventures of a Guinea,* see *Adventures of a Guinea.*

Chrysaor, in Spenser's 'Faerie Queene', v. i. 9 and v. xii. 40, the sword of Justice, wielded by Sir Artegal. The Chrysaor of Greek mythology was a son of Poseidon and Medusa.

Chrȳsēis, daughter of Chryses, a priest of Apollo. She had been taken prisoner and allotted to Agamemnon. Chryses came to the Greek camp to win his daughter's freedom, but was received by Agamemnon with contumely. Thereupon the god sent a plague on the Greek host. To avert this, Achilles urged that Agamemnon should follow the advice of Calchas, the seer, and surrender the damsel. This he finally was obliged to do, but in his wrath he took from Achilles the girl Briseis (q.v.), thereby causing Achilles to retire for a time from the Trojan War.

CHRYSOSTOM, ST. JOHN (*c.* 345–407), one of the Greek Fathers of the Church, was born at Antioch in Syria of a noble family. Under his mother's influence he was baptized in 370, and spent ten years in the desert, leading an ascetic life and studying theology. He became bishop of Constantinople, and applied the revenues of the see to charitable purposes. He was a most eloquent preacher, and his sermons, directed against the vices of the capital and of the leading personages of the empire (including the empress Eudoxia), coupled with his disciplinary measures, aroused much hostility. He was condemned by a packed synod (*Ad Quercum*), banished to Nicaea, recalled, and deposed by a second synod. He was sent to Cocysus on the slopes of Mount Taurus; but his energy was unquelled, and he was again removed to more distant regions, but died on the way at Comana. In his writings he emphasized the ascetic element in religion and the need for personal study of the Scriptures. His voluminous works include, notably, commentaries on the Gospel of St. Matthew and on the Epistles to the Romans and Corinthians. The name 'Chrysostom' means 'golden-mouth' and was given to him on account of his eloquence.

Chuang-tzu, see *Taoism.*

Chucks, Mr., a character in Marryat's 'Peter Simple' (q.v.).

Chuffey, in Dickens's 'Martin Chuzzlewit' (q.v.), Anthony Chuzzlewit's old clerk.

Chump, MRS., a character in Meredith's 'Sandra Belloni' (q.v.).

CHURCH, RICHARD WILLIAM (1815–90), dean of St. Paul's, was author of lives of St. Wulfstan (1844) and St. Anselm (1870), and of Spenser and Bacon (1879 and 1884) in the English Men of Letters series. He also wrote a notable history of the 'Oxford Movement' (1891) and an essay on Dante, of whom he was a devoted student; this was republished with a translation of Dante's 'De Monarchia' in 1878. He published a large number of essays, sermons, and addresses, and an interesting little book on 'The Beginnings of the Middle Ages' (1877).

Church of England, the English branch of the Western Church, which at the Reformation repudiated the supremacy of the Pope, and asserted that of the Sovereign over all persons and in all causes, ecclesiastical as well as temporal, in his dominions. [OED.]

Church. of Scotland, the Church established in Scotland in 1560 and confirmed in 1689. It is presbyterian (see *Presbyterianism*).

CHURCHILL, CHARLES (1731–64), educated at Westminster School. He went to St. John's College, Cambridge, but his university career was interrupted by his marriage at the age of 18. He became famous by his satire on contemporary actors, 'The Rosciad', published in 1761, and his violent satire on Bute and the Scots, 'The Prophecy of Famine', published in 1763. He attached himself to John Wilkes (q.v.) and contributed largely to his paper 'The North Briton'. He wrote other political and social satires (notably 'The Author', against Smollett; 'The Epistle to William Hogarth' and 'The Duellist', 1763; 'The Times', 1764; and 'The Candidate', directed against 'Jemmy Twitcher', Lord Sandwich, 1764), but died young at Boulogne, on his way to visit Wilkes in France.

Churchill, FRANK, a character in Jane Austen's 'Emma' (q.v.).

CHURCHILL, RT. HON. SIR WINSTON (LEONARD SPENCER) (1874–1965), eldest son of Lord Randolph Churchill (third son of the seventh duke of Marlborough). He entered the army in 1895 and served in Cuba, India, Tirah, and Egypt; was present as a war correspondent at Spion Kop, Diamond Hill, etc.; and served in France at Lieut.-Col. in 1916. He was under-secretary of state for the colonies, 1906–8; president of the board of trade, 1908–10; home secretary, 1910–11; first lord of the Admiralty, 1911–15; secretary of state for war, 1918–21; for the colonies, 1921–2; chancellor of the exchequer 1924–9; prime minister, 1940–5 and 1951–5. Among his publications are: 'The Story of the Malakand Field Force' (1898), 'The River War' (1899), 'London to Ladysmith via Pretoria' (1900), 'Ian Hamilton's March'

(1900), 'Lord Randolph Churchill' (1906–7), 'My African Journey' (1908), 'Liberalism and the Social Problem' (1909), 'The World Crisis' (4 vols. 1923–9), 'My Early Life' (1930), 'Marlborough' (1933–8), 'War Speeches, 1940–5' (1946), 'The Second World War' (6 vols., 1948–54), and 'A History of the English-speaking Peoples' (4 vols., 1956–8).

CHURCHILL, WINSTON (1871–1947), American novelist, was born in Missouri. Among his chief works, mostly historical romances, are: 'Richard Carvel' (1899), 'The Crisis' (1901), 'The Crossing' (1904), 'Coniston' (1906), 'Mr. Crewe's Career' (1908), and 'A Far Country' (1915).

CHURCHYARD, THOMAS (1520?–1604), at one time page to Henry, earl of Surrey, the poet, lived a wandering life, partly as a soldier in Scotland, Ireland, France, and the Low Countries, partly as a hanger-on of the court and the nobility. He published, before 1553, 'A myrrour for man'. Between 1560 and 1603 he issued a multitude of broadsheets and small volumes in verse and prose, several containing autobiographical pieces and notices of current events. His best-known works are 'Shore's Wife' (1563), in the 'Mirror for Magistrates' (q.v.), and the 'Worthines of Wales' (1587). Among his narrative poems are the 'Wofull Warres in Flaunders' (1578) and the 'General Rehearsall of Warres' (1579), in which he made use of his own experience as a soldier. Spenser in his 'Colin Clout' refers to Churchyard as 'Old Palaemon that sung so long until quite hoarse he grew'.

CIBBER, COLLEY (1671–1757), son of Caius Cibber the sculptor, was educated at Grantham School and became an actor in 1690. He brought out his first play 'Love's Last Shift' in 1696, of which Congreve said that 'it has only in it a great many things that were like wit, that in reality were not wit', a criticism applicable to his numerous other plays, in which he showed skill as a playwright rather than the qualities of a man of letters. Sir Novelty Fashion in 'Love's Last Shift' suggested Vanbrugh's Lord Foppington in 'The Relapse' (q.v.). One of the best of Cibber's plays was 'The Careless Husband' (q.v.), printed in 1705. Cibber was made poet laureate in 1730, and was fiercely attacked in consequence by other writers. Pope made him the hero of the 'Dunciad' (q.v.) in the final edition of that poem. Cibber published in 1740 an autobiography entitled 'Apology for the life of Mr. Colley Cibber, Comedian'. By this he is principally remembered, on account of the admirable theatrical portraits, of Betterton, Mrs. Bracegirdle, Nokes, etc., that it contains.

CICERO, MARCUS TULLIUS (106–43 B.C.), sometimes referred to in English literature as *Tully*, was born near Arpinum. After studying law and philosophy he came forward as a pleader. His success in this capacity opened the way for him to the highest offices, and he became consul in 63. His political fame is chiefly based on his vigorous action against the conspiracy of Catiline. Owing to the enmity of Clodius he was banished in 58 for a short time. In the civil war between Caesar and Pompey he joined the party of the latter, but after Pharsalia was pardoned by Caesar. After Caesar's assassination he took the lead of the republican party and vigorously attacked Mark Antony in his Philippic orations. On the formation of the triumvirate he was proscribed, and put to death in 43. His works consist of writings on the art of rhetoric (of which the 'De Oratore' is the chief); on political philosophy ('De Legibus' and 'De Republica'); on moral philosophy ('De Officiis', 'De Senectute', and 'De Amicitia'); and on theology ('De Natura Deorum'); of a large number of orations (including the Verrines and the Philippics) and epistles (many of them to his friend Atticus).

Cicisbeo (pron. tchi-tchiz-bay'-o), the name formerly given in Italy to the recognized gallant of a married woman. The word, whose origin is uncertain, is also used for a knot of ribbon tied to a sword-hilt, walking-stick, etc.

Cid, The, the favourite hero of Spain, in the account of whom history and myth are difficult to disentangle. Rodrigo Díaz de Bivar, el Cid Campeador ('el Seyd', the lord, 'Campeador', champion), of a noble Castilian family, born c. 1030, rose to fame by his prowess in the war between Sancho of Castile and Sancho of Navarre, and in conflicts with the Moors. Having incurred the jealousy of Alphonso, king of Castile, he was banished and became a soldier of fortune, fighting at times for the Christians, at others for the Moors. His principal feat was the capture of Valencia from the Moors after a siege of nine months. He died of grief at the defeat of his force, in 1099.

In myth his character has been glorified into a type of knightly and Christian virtue and patriotic zeal. His achievements are narrated in the 'Poema del Cid' of the 12th cent. (the most important of early Spanish poems, some 3,700 irregular lines), in the Spanish Chronicle of the 13th cent., and in numerous ballads. The chronicles relating to him were translated by R. Southey (q.v., 1808). The Cid is the subject of the most famous drama of Corneille (q.v.). The Cid's horse was called Babieca.

Cid Hamet Ben Engeli, an imaginary Arabian author to whom Cervantes attributes the story of Don Quixote (q.v.).

Cider: for J. Philips's poem, see *Cyder.*

Ci-devant, a French term meaning 'formerly', signifies, in the language of the French Revolution, a man of rank, i.e. one formerly such, the Republic having suppressed distinctions of nobility.

Cimabue, Giovanni (c. 1240-1302?), Florentine painter. Vasari (q.v.) tells how his Madonna, painted for Santa Maria Novella, Florence (now attributed to Duccio), excited such enthusiasm that it was carried in procession to the church. Few of his paintings can be authenticated.

Cimmerian, of or belonging to the Cimmerii, a people fabled by the ancients to live in perpetual darkness; hence proverbially used as a qualification of dense darkness. The historical Cimmerii lived on the Sea of Azov, and the word Crimea is derived from their name.

Cimon and Iphigenia, see *Cymon and Iphigenia.*

Cincinnātus, Lucius Quinctius, a type of old-fashioned integrity and frugality in the annals of the Roman republic. He was called in 458 B.C. from the plough, with which he cultivated his own land, to deliver the Roman army from the peril in which it stood in its conflict with the Aequians. Having successfully done this and held the command for only 16 days, he returned to his plough.

Cinderella, a fairy tale, from the French of Perrault (q.v.), translated by Robert Samber (1729?).

The gentle Cinderella is cruelly used by her stepmother and two stepsisters, and when her household drudgery is done, sits at the corner of the hearth in the cinders, whence her name. Her stepsisters having gone to a ball, she is left crying at home. Her fairy godmother arrives, provides her with beautiful clothes, a coach made out of a pumpkin, and six horses transformed from mice, and sends her to the ball, on condition that she returns before the stroke of twelve. The prince falls in love with her. She hurries away at midnight, losing one of her tiny glass slippers (*pantoufle de verre*; perhaps *verre* should be *vair*, minever), and resumes her humble garb at the fireside. The prince has search made for her and announces that he will marry her whom the slipper fits. To the discomfiture of the stepsisters the slipper is found to fit only Cinderella, who produces the fellow to it from her pocket, and marries the prince. Andrew Lang, in his 'Perrault's Popular Tales', discusses the analogous stories which exist in the folk-lore of various countries.

Cinque Ports, a group of seaports (originally five, Hastings, Dover, Sandwich, Romney, Hythe, to which were added the two 'ancient towns', Rye and Winchelsea, and many associated towns) having jurisdiction along the south-east coast from Seaford in Sussex to Birchington in Kent. In ancient times they furnished the chief part of the English navy, in consideration of which they received many important privileges and franchises. These were mostly abolished in 1832 and 1835, and the Lord Wardenship is now chiefly an honorary dignity. Each of the associated towns above referred to was called a 'limb' of one of the ports, and contributed its ship to the tale of fifty-seven which the ports had to furnish in the 13th cent. The origin of the group is unknown; no real charter was granted before Edward I.

Cinquecento, a term applied in Italy to the 16th cent., and to that style of art and architecture, characterized by a reversion to classical forms, which arose about 1450.

CINTHIO, GIAMBATTISTA GIRALDI (1504–73), born at Ferrara, the author of the 'Hecatommithi' or a hundred tales, told after the manner of Boccaccio's 'Decameron' (q.v.) by ten ladies and gentlemen sailing to Marseilles after the sack of Rome in 1527. Some of these were incorporated by Painter in his 'Palace of Pleasure' (q.v.) and provided the plots of Shakespeare's 'Othello' and 'Measure for Measure', and of plays by Beaumont and Fletcher and Shirley. His nine tragedies and his treatise on tragedy had a decisive influence on the development of 16th-cent. drama in Italy.

Circassian, the name of the inhabitants of a region in the NW. of the Caucasus, formerly known as Circassia (now Kuban). They were finally subjugated, after a long struggle, by the Russians in 1864, after which many thousands migrated to Turkish territory. They were notable for beauty of form and feature. Circassian fathers used to sell their daughters to Turkish merchants for Turkish harems.

Circē, celebrated for her knowledge of magic and venomous herbs, inhabited an island called Aeaea. Odysseus, returning from the Trojan War, visited this island. His companions were changed by Circe's potions into swine. Odysseus, fortified against her enchantment by the herb called *moly*, demanded from Circe, sword in hand, the restoration of his companions. Circe complied, and Odysseus remained with her for a year, becoming by her the father of Telegonus, or according to Hesiod of Agrius and Latinus. See also *Scylla* and *Gryll*.

Circumcellion, 'a name given to the Donatist fanatics in Africa during the 4th cent. from their habit of roving from place to place' ('Dict. of Christian Antiquities'), extended to vagabond monks generally.

Circumlocution Office, THE, the type of a government department, satirized in Dickens's 'Little Dorrit' (q.v.).

CIRENCESTER, RICHARD OF (d. 1401?), a monk of St. Peter's, Westminster, who compiled a 'Speculum Historiale', A.D. 447–1066. See *Bertram (Charles)*.

Cirrha, a seaport on the Corinthian Gulf, near Delphi and Mt. Parnassus. The region was sacred to Apollo.

Cistercians, the name of a monastic order, an offshoot of the Benedictines, founded at Cistercium or Cîteaux in 1098 by Robert, abbot of Molesme. St. Bernard (q.v.) was

a Cistercian; his *Bernardines* were a branch of the Cistercians with reformed rules.

Cities of the Plain, THE, see *Sodom and Gomorrah*.

Citizen of the World, The, by Goldsmith (q.v.), a collection of letters purporting to be written by or to an imaginary philosophic Chinaman, Lien Chi Altangi, residing in London. They first appeared as 'Chinese Letters' in Newbery's 'Public Ledger', most of them in the course of 1760. They were republished under the title of 'The Citizen of the World' in 1762. They are in effect a series of whimsical or satirical comments on English customs and peculiarities, on the mental and moral characteristics of the race, and on literary subjects, together with character-sketches and episodes, the whole strung on a slender thread of narrative. The best-known character-sketches in the book are those of the 'Man in Black' (q.v.) and 'Beau Tibbs' (q.v.).

City, THE, short for *the City of London*, that part of London which is under the jurisdiction of the Lord Mayor and Corporation; more particularly, the business part of this, in the neighbourhood of the Exchange and Bank of England. It substantially represents the ancient city that was enclosed in the Roman wall, with the addition of the wards of Farringdon Without and Bishopsgate Without. 'The City' is used metaphorically of business interests or business men.

City Heiress, The, a comedy by Aphra Behn (q.v.), produced in 1682.

Sir Timothy Treat-all, 'an old seditious knight, who keeps open house for Commonwealthsmen', has disinherited his Tory nephew, Tom Wilding. Wilding is courting Charlot, the city-heiress, and introduces his mistress Diana to Sir Timothy, as Charlot. Sir Timothy, under this deception, arranges a marriage with her. During an entertainment at his house, he is visited by a strange nobleman who offers him the crown of Poland. The same night, however, his house is burgled and his papers stolen, and himself and the strange lord bound fast. It turns out not only that Sir Timothy has married his nephew's mistress, but that the Polish Ambassador was Wilding in disguise, and the burglars his associates, who have got possession of Sir Timothy's treasonable correspondence, and of the papers relating to his estate. Wilding is united to Charlot. The plot is complicated by another intrigue, in which Wilding and his friend Sir Charles Merriwill seek the favour of the rich widow, Lady Galliard.

City Madam, The, a comedy by Massinger (q.v.), acted in 1632 and printed in 1659.

The wife and daughters of Sir John Frugal, a rich merchant, are grown extravagant and presumptuous as a result of their wealth. The girls repel their suitors, Sir Maurice Lacy and Mr. Plenty, by attaching intolerable conditions to the grant of their hands. To teach them a lesson, and at the same time to test his brother, Luke, a ruined prodigal whom he has taken into his house (where he occupies a servile position and feigns virtue and humility), Sir John pretends to retire into a monastery and to hand over his property and the management of his family to Luke. Being placed in this position, the brother acts with great harshness to Lady Frugal and her daughters, and to Sir John's creditors and apprentices. Luke's hypocrisy is exposed, the return of Sir John is welcomed by his family, and his daughters gladly promise submission to their suitors.

City of Destruction, THE, in Bunyan's 'The Pilgrim's Progress' (q.v.), typifies the state of the worldly and irreligious.

City of Dreadful Night, *The,* see under *Thomson* (*J.,* 1834–82) and *Kipling.*

City of Refuge, in the Mosaic dispensation, a walled town set apart for the protection of those who had accidentally committed manslaughter. See Deut. iv. 41–43.

City of Seven Hills, THE, Rome. The seven hills are the Palatine, Aventine, Capitoline, Caelian, Esquiline, Viminal, and Quirinal.

City of Dreaming Spires: M. Arnold ('Thyrsis') refers to Oxford as 'that sweet city with her dreaming spires'.

City of the Tribes, THE, Galway, so called from the fourteen families or 'tribes' whose ancestors settled there about 1270.

City of the Violet Crown, THE, Athens, see *Violet-crowned City.*

City Witt, *The,* or *the Woman wears the Breeches,* a comedy by Brome (q.v.), printed in 1653.

This is the brightest and most amusing of Brome's comedies. Crasy, a young citizen, has been ruined by his generous and easy-going disposition, and is cursed moreover with a virago for a mother-in-law, Mrs. Pyannet Sneakup. From her he gets no mercy in his misfortune, and the friends whom he has helped in the past turn from him when he comes to them for assistance. His wife indulges her amorous proclivities as soon as he leaves her. He determines to show them all that his past good-nature was not due to want of wit, and disguising himself in various characters plays on their several vices to extort from them the money and jewels he has lent them or they have stolen from him. Aided by his servant Jeremy, who passes himself off as the rich widow Tryman, he contrives a marriage between the latter and his malignant brother-in-law, a drubbing for each of his wife's would-be lovers, and humiliation for his mother-in-law. The pedant, Sarpego, with his comically apposite snatches of Latin, who refuses to repay him a loan of ten pounds, does not escape his share of punishment.

Civil War, THE, in English history, the war between Charles I and Parliament, which began in 1642 and ended virtually in 1646. It was followed by the second Civil War of 1648–51, which was terminated by the battle of Worcester.

In American history, the Civil War or War of Secession (1861–5) was caused by the secession of the eleven southern or Confederate (q.v.) States (as a result of the anti-slavery agitation and the growth of the doctrine of state sovereignty) and was terminated by the surrender of their armies.

Civil Wars between the two Houses of York and Lancaster, an epic poem by S. Daniel (q.v.), of which the first four books appeared in 1595. The complete work, comprising eight books, was published in 1609. It contains some 900 eight-lined stanzas, of a grave and philosophic cast, and marked by strong patriotism. The first book deals with the period from the Conquest to Hereford's rising against Richard II, the remaining seven with that from the Wars of the Roses to the accession of Edward IV and his marriage with Lady Elizabeth Grey.

Clack, MISS, in Wilkie Collins's 'The Moonstone' (q.v.), a niece of Sir John Verinder, and narrator of part of the story.

Claimant, THE, Arthur Orton; see *Tichborne.*

Clairmont, CLAIRE (CLARA MARY JANE) (1798–1879), daughter of Mary Clairmont who became William Godwin's (q.v.) second wife. She accompanied Mary Godwin on her elopement with Shelley (q.v.), and in spite of pursuit remained with them on the Continent, giving rise to most of the calumnies directed against Shelley. She returned to London with the Shelleys and in 1816 obtained an introduction to Byron, becoming so intimate with him that when he went to Switzerland the Shelleys were induced to follow him. Her child Allegra was born in 1817, and for nearly three years lived with Byron. In 1821 Allegra was placed in a convent near Ravenna much against the will of Claire, and died in 1822 as the result of a fever. Claire's subsequent life was spent in Russia, Italy, and Paris. She died in Florence in 1879.

Clan na Gael, 'brotherhood of Gaels', an Irish secret society, which had its origin in 1870 among the Fenians (q.v.), and represented the party of extreme violence in the movement for Irish independence.

Clandestine Marriage, *The,* a comedy by Colman the elder and Garrick (qq.v.), produced in 1766.

This entertaining comedy was suggested by Hogarth's pictures of 'Marriage-à-la-Mode'. Lovewell, the clerk of Mr. Sterling, a wealthy and purse-proud London merchant, has secretly married his employer's younger daughter, Fanny, but dares not brave the father's anger by a disclosure. The father, ambitious to ally himself with a noble family, has arranged a marriage between his elder daughter and Sir John Melvil, nephew of Lord Ogleby, who accept the alliance as a way out of their pecuniary difficulties. Lord Ogleby and Melvil arrive at Sterling's house to make the final arrangements, when Melvil suddenly reveals his aversion for the match with the elder Miss Sterling and his passion for the more attractive Fanny. The latter with embarrassment repels his advances, but hesitates to reveal her marriage. Melvil turns to Mr. Sterling and induces him, for a financial consideration, to agree to the transfer of his affections to the younger daughter. But now Mrs. Heidelberg, Mr. Sterling's wealthy sister, strongly resents the proposed affront to the family, and orders Fanny to be packed off from the house. Fanny in despair applies to Lord Ogleby, an amorous old beau, who, mistaking her inarticulate confession for a declaration of love for himself, announces that he will himself marry her, thereby further increasing the perplexity of Lovewell and Fanny. Finally a lover is discovered in Fanny's bedroom, and the household assemble outside the door for the exposure of the villain. When he turns out to be Lovewell, Lord Ogleby good-naturedly intervenes on behalf of the guilty couple, offers to take Lovewell under his own protection, and appeases Sterling's wrath.

Clara Douglas, the heroine of Bulwer Lytton's comedy 'Money' (q.v.).

Clara Middleton, the heroine of Meredith's 'The Egoist' (q.v.).

Clare, a nun of the order instituted at Assisi, c. 1212, by St. Clare, who was inspired by admiration for St. Francis of Assisi. The sisters are also called 'Poor Clares' and 'Minoresses'.

CLARE, JOHN (1793–1864), the son of a Northamptonshire labourer, and himself at various times a herd-boy, militiaman, vagrant, and unsuccessful farmer, who became insane in 1837. He published in 1820 'Poems Descriptive of Rural Life', 'The Village Minstrel' in 1821, 'The Shepherd's Calendar' in 1827, and 'The Rural Muse' in 1835. Other poems of his were published after his death (ed. A. Symons, 1908), and an edition of his poems by Blunden and Porter appeared in 1920. An autobiography of his early years was edited by Edmund Blunden in 1931.

Clarenceux, the second king-of-arms in England (see *Heralds' College*), whose office is to marshal and arrange the funerals of all baronets, knights, and esquires south of the river Trent. He was formerly called *Surroy* as opposed to *Norroy* the northern king-of-arms. The name Clarenceux is derived from the English dukedom created for Lionel, second son of Edward III, when he married the heiress of Clare in Suffolk. [OED.]

Clarendon, CONSTITUTIONS OF, enacted at a council summoned in 1164 by Henry II to meet at Clarendon in Wiltshire. Their object was to check the power of the clergy. The most important of the sixteen articles declared that beneficed clergy should not leave the realm without the king's leave; that no tenant-in-chief should be excommunicated without the king's knowledge; that a criminous clerk should be tried in the king's court; and that after conviction he should not be protected by the Church from punishment. After the murder of Becket, Henry was compelled to give up the Constitutions of Clarendon.

CLARENDON, EDWARD HYDE, *earl of* (1609–74), was educated at Magdalen Hall, Oxford, and practised law. As M.P. for Wootton Bassett in the Short Parliament and for Saltash in the Long Parliament, he at first sided with the opposition, but, as a strong Anglican, from 1641 onwards he was one of the chief supporters and advisers of the king. He followed the Prince of Wales in his exile to Scilly and Jersey, where he began his 'History'. He was lord chancellor and chief minister to Charles II from 1658, retaining this position at the Restoration. The future James II married his daughter, Anne Hyde. He subsequently became unpopular, partly owing to the ill-success of the Dutch war; and being impeached, he fled to France in 1667 and lived at Montpellier and Rouen, dying at the latter place. At Montpellier he composed his 'Life', part of which he incorporated with the 'History'.

The 'History'—'The True Historical Narrative of the Rebellion and Civil Wars in England'—was first printed from a transcript under the supervision of Clarendon's son in 1702–4, the original manuscript (now in the Bodleian) being first used in Bandinel's edition (1826). But Bandinel either deciphered it badly or garbled it, and the first true text is that of Dr. Macray (Oxford, 1888). The 'Life of Clarendon', by himself, appeared in 1759, the 'History of the Irish Rebellion and Civil Wars in Ireland' in 1721 (subsequently incorporated in the 'History'), and selections from his correspondence ('Clarendon State Papers'), edited by Scrope and Monkhouse, in 1767–86.

Clarendon was chancellor of the University of Oxford from 1660 until his fall. His works were presented to the University by his heirs, and from the profits of the publication of the 'History' a new printing-house, which bore his name, was built for the University Press (q.v.).

Clarendon Press, see *Oxford University Press*.

Clarendon type, a thick-faced, condensed type, in capital and small letters.

Clarendon's History of the Rebellion and Civil Wars in England, see *Clarendon (Edward Hyde)*.

Clarinda, the name used by Mrs. Agnes Maclehose (*née* Craig) in her correspondence with Burns (q.v.), who signed himself Sylvander.

Clarissa, one of the principal characters in Vanbrugh's 'The Confederacy' (q.v.).

Clarissa Harlowe, a novel by Richardson (q.v.), of which two volumes were issued in 1747 and five in 1748.

This was the second of Richardson's novels and, as in the others, the story is told by means of letters, written by the heroine Clarissa to her friend Miss Howe, and by the other principal character, Robert Lovelace, to his friend John Belford. Clarissa, a young lady of good family, 'of great Delicacy, mistress of all the Accomplishments, natural and acquired, that adorn the Sex', is wooed by Lovelace, an attractive and versatile but unscrupulous man of fashion. Clarissa's family oppose the match because of his doubtful reputation, and Clarissa for a time resists his advances. But she is secretly fascinated by him, and he succeeds in carrying her off. Clarissa dies of shame, and Lovelace is killed in a duel by her cousin, Colonel Morden. The novel, as the title-page shows, was intended as a warning of 'the Distresses that may attend Misconduct both of Parents and Children in relation to Marriage', and was thus in some sort a complement of 'Pamela'.

CLARK, JOHN WILLIS (1833–1910), educated at Eton and Trinity College, Cambridge, registrary of Cambridge University from 1891 till his death, is remembered for his 'Architectural History of the Colleges of Cambridge' (with Robert Willis, 1886), his 'Barnwell Priory' (1897, 1907), and his admirable history of libraries, entitled 'The Care of Books' (1901).

CLARKE, CHARLES COWDEN- (1787–1877), the schoolmaster and friend of Keats (q.v.), and author of 'Recollections of Writers' (with Mary Cowden-Clarke, 1878), etc.

CLARKE, MARCUS ANDREW HISLOP (1846–81), emigrated to Victoria in 1863, and wrote a number of plays and novels, of which the best known is 'For the Term of his Natural Life' (1874), a vivid and gloomy tale of a penal settlement.

CLARKE, MARY VICTORIA COWDEN- (1809–98), wife of Charles Cowden-Clarke (q.v.), is remembered as the author of the 'Complete Concordance to Shakespeare', which she published in monthly parts, 1844–5.

CLARKE, SAMUEL (1675–1729), educated at Caius College, Cambridge, metaphysician, moralist, and opponent of the Deists. His view of morality was that there exists, in the nature of things, an immutable agreement or harmony of certain things and circumstances with certain others, an aspect of reality, like its causal relations, apparent to the understanding. Clarke's principal works were his Boyle Lectures (1704 and 1705), 'A Demonstration of the Being and Attributes of God'

and 'A Discourse concerning the Unchangeable Obligations of Natural Religion'.

Classic, in relation to literature, is defined by Sainte-Beuve as what is very good and is made to last. The OED. defines it as (1) 'Of the first class, of the highest rank or importance; approved as a model; standard, leading. (2) Of or belonging to the standard authors of Greek and Latin antiquity. (3) In the style of the literature of Greek and Latin antiquity.' Cf. *Romantic.*

Classical art is the art of classical antiquity; or that in which the Orders of architecture (q.v.) are used with the purpose of emulating classical art; or that which, though not using classical forms, expresses classical ideals. Neo-classicism is the style of the late 18th and early 19th cent. based on an antiquarian study of classical, especially Greek, buildings.

Claude (1807–80), the chief of the Paris police 1859–75, who acquired celebrity in many criminal affairs. Entirely apocryphal memoirs of Claude (10 vols.) appeared in 1881–3.

Claude Lorraine (1600–82), CLAUDE GELLÉE, called Le Lorrain, French landscape painter who spent most of his life in Rome. His compositional formulae influenced the Picturesque movement.

Claude Melnotte, the hero of Bulwer Lytton's 'The Lady of Lyons' (q.v.).

CLAUDEL, PAUL (1868–1955), French poet, dramatist, and essayist. He was also a diplomat and spent many years abroad. His poetry includes 'Cinq grandes odes' (1910) and 'La Cantate à trois voix' (1931). His poetic dramas, his best-known work, include 'Tête d'or' (1890), 'Partage de midi' (1906, prod. 1948), 'L'Otage' (1911), 'L'Annonce faite à Marie' (1912), 'Le Soulier de Satin' (1925–8). In all of them religious and mystical fervour mingle or conflict with human passion and emotion.

CLAUDIAN (CLAUDIUS CLAUDIANUS), the last great poet of ancient Rome, was a native of Alexandria. He lived in Rome c. A.D. 395–404, where he enjoyed the favour of Stilicho and praised him in official poems. The best known of his shorter works, the idyll on the 'Old Man of Verona', was translated by Cowley.

Claudio, (1) the lover of Hero in Shakespeare's 'Much Ado about Nothing' (q.v.); (2) a character in his 'Measure for Measure' (q.v.).

Claudius, in Shakespeare's 'Hamlet' (q.v.), the king of Denmark.

Claus, see *Santa Claus.*

CLAVELL, JOHN (1603–42), was a highwayman who was condemned to death and then pardoned (1627). He published a metrical autobiography, 'Recantation of an ill led Life' (1628), which begins arrestingly '*Stand and deliver* to your observation Right serious thoughts . . .' and proceeds to describe the highway law and organization of thieves. He warns thieves about the miseries of prison life, and travellers and innkeepers about the ways and appearance of thieves.

Claverhouse, GRAHAM OF, see *Graham of Claverhouse.*

Clavering, SIR FRANCIS and LADY, characters in Thackeray's 'Pendennis' (q.v.).

Claverings, The, a novel by A. Trollope (q.v.), published in 1867.

Harry Clavering and Julia Brabazon have been in love, but the latter, having debts and expensive tastes, throws over her impecunious lover and marries the wealthy Lord Ongar, a worn-out debauchee. He dies within a year, having led her a terrible life and contrived to asperse her honour. Meanwhile Harry Clavering has become engaged to Florence Burton, daughter of the engineer in whose house he has lived as a pupil, a young lady of amiable character but modest charms. Julia returns to London, a social outcast, and Harry becomes entangled with her, at last finding himself in the position of having promised to marry both Florence and the widow. Finally, under gentle pressure from various quarters, Harry decides to be faithful to Florence. The story includes various repellent characters, Julia's brother-in-law Sir Hugh Clavering, and Count Pateroff and his sister Mme Gordeloup, whose proceedings intensify the punishment meted out to Julia for her worldly choice of a husband.

Clavijo, DON, in 'Don Quixote' (q.v., II. xxxviii, et seq.), a gentleman who is transformed into a crocodile by Malambruno, and released from the enchantment by Don Quixote.

Clavileño, in 'Don Quixote' (q.v., II. xli), the wooden horse supposed to possess magic properties, on which Don Quixote mounts to achieve the adventure of Trifaldi and Malambruno, and which, being full of combustibles, blows up on a match being applied to its tail.

Clayhanger, see *Bennett (E. A.).*

Claypole, NOAH, in Dickens's 'Oliver Twist' (q.v.), a fellow apprentice of the hero in the establishment of Mr. Sowerberry, the undertaker; and subsequently one of Fagin's gang of thieves.

Cleanness, an alliterative poem of 1,800 lines, of the period 1300–60, exalting purity and the delights of lawful love. It deals with three subjects from the Scriptures, to enforce its moral: the Flood, the destruction of Sodom and Gomorrah, and the fall of Belshazzar. It includes passages of great power, such as the denunciation of Sodom and the description of the destruction of Babylon. It is attributed to the same author as 'Pearl' and 'Patience' (qq.v.).

Cleishbotham, JEDEDIAH, schoolmaster and parish clerk of Gandercleugh, who, by a fic-

tion of Sir W. Scott, sold to publishers the 'Tales of My Landlord' (q.v.). These were supposed to have been composed by his assistant schoolmaster Peter Pattieson from the stories told by the landlord of the Wallace Inn at Gandercleugh. (See the introduction to 'The Black Dwarf'.)

CLELAND, JOHN (1709–89), novelist and journalist, educated at Westminster School. He was for a time consul at Smyrna, and later employed by the East India Company. His novel 'Fanny Hill: Memoirs of a Woman of Pleasure' (published in two vols. in 1748 and 1749) was suppressed as pornography in 1749, since when it has enjoyed a persistent surreptitious publication. An unexpurgated edition published openly in England in 1963 was seized by the police. Cleland also wrote 'Memoirs of a Coxcomb' (1751) and other novels and dramatic pieces.

Clelia or CLOELIA, a Roman maiden who, being among the hostages given to Porsena (q.v.), escaped and swam across the Tiber to Rome. The Romans returned her to Porsena, who from admiration of her courage released her. Her story is the basis of the 'Clélie' of Mlle de Scudéry (q.v.).

Clelia, the coquette whose gradual decline to the almshouse is described by Crabbe (q.v.) in one of the tales of 'The Borough'.

CLEMENS, SAMUEL LANGHORNE, who wrote under the pseudonym MARK TWAIN (1835–1910), born in Missouri of a Virginian family, was apprenticed in boyhood to a printer, became a pilot on the Mississippi in 1857 and a newspaper correspondent in 1862, being at that time in Nevada. He then adopted as pseudonym the leadsman's call which had become familiar to him on the Mississippi. He first came into prominence as a writer with his 'Jim Smiley and his Jumping Frog' in 1865, and shortly after became a popular lecturer. He went on a cruise to the Mediterranean in 1867, and his gaily irreverent reactions to the Old World were published to great acclaim in 'The Innocents Abroad' (1869). He published 'Roughing It', the story of his life in Nevada, in 1872, and, in the same humorous and realistic style, 'A Tramp Abroad' (1880), an account of other adventures in Europe. He collaborated with Charles Dudley Warner in a novel satirizing contemporary life in 1873, and its title, 'The Gilded Age', has been given to the post Civil War epoch in American history. He went to English history for 'The Prince and the Pauper' (1882), a story of Edward VI as a boy changing places with Tom Canty, a beggar, and also for 'A Connecticut Yankee in King Arthur's Court' (1889), a disturbing fantasy which satirizes both the past and the present. But his own life provided the material for his greatest books: 'The Adventures of Tom Sawyer' (q.v., 1876), a re-creation of his childhood on the banks of the Mississippi, 'Life on the

Mississippi' (1883), memorable for its account of his life as a river pilot, and 'The Adventures of Huckleberry Finn' (q.v., 1884), his masterpiece and an epic of the Mississippi. He increasingly lost direction as a writer after 1889, and dissipated time and money on chimerical business enterprises; and his irrational pessimism and bitterness were increased by the death of his wife and two of his three daughters. But some of his later work is to be remembered, especially 'The Tragedy of Pudd'nhead Wilson' (1894), a study in miscegenation, and the two sombre tales, 'The Man that Corrupted Hadleyburg' (1900) and 'The Mysterious Stranger' (1916). He dictated his autobiography during his last years and large sections have been published. He was made a D.Litt. of Oxford in 1907.

CLEMENT I, a bishop of Rome of the 1st cent., of whom little is known with certainty. According to Eusebius and Jerome he died in the third year of the reign of Trajan. Two 'Epistles to the Corinthians', probably spurious, are attributed to him. These were highly regarded in the early centuries of the Christian era, then disappeared, and were rediscovered by Patrick Young (Patricius Junius, 1584–1651, librarian to James I and Charles I), in the Alexandrian codex of the LXX.

CLEMENT OF ALEXANDRIA, a Greek Father of the Church, probably born at Alexandria, c. A.D. 160. Four of his works have come down to us. He was the first to apply Greek culture and philosophy to the exposition of the Christian faith.

Clementina Porretta, a character in Richardson's 'Sir Charles Grandison' (q.v.).

Clementine Decretals, see *Decretals*.

Clementine Vulgate, see *Vulgate*.

Clennam, ARTHUR and MRS., characters in Dickens's 'Little Dorrit' (q.v.).

Cleofas Zambullo, DON, the hero of 'Le Diable Boiteux' (q.v.) of Le Sage.

Cleombrŏtus, a philosopher of Ambracia, who is said, after reading the 'Phaedo' of Plato, to have leapt into the sea and drowned himself to exchange this life for a better.

'Ha! Cleombrotus! And what salads in faith did you light on at the bottom of the Mediterranean?'
(Charles Lamb, 'All Fools' Day'.)

Cleon, an Athenian general and demagogue, originally a tanner, an opponent of Pericles and after his death leader of the party that opposed peace in the Peloponnesian War. He achieved military fame by taking prisoner in 424 B.C. the Spartans in the island of Sphacteria. He was subsequently defeated by Brasidas and killed in battle (422).

Cleon, a character in Shakespeare's 'Pericles' (q.v.).

Cleon, a poem by R. Browning (q.v.), published in 1855.

Cleon is supposed to be one of the poets to whom St. Paul in Acts xvii. 28 refers in the words, 'As certain also of your own poets have said, For we are also his offspring'. Cleon believes in Zeus as the one God, but sees no warrant for the belief in immortality. He states the case to King Protus: his sense of the inadequacy of this life, and his conception of another in which realization shall be as ample as unrealized desire is on earth. But Zeus has not revealed such a life, and Cleon grieves in consequence.

Cleopatra, eldest daughter of Ptolemy Auletes, king of Egypt, was born in 68 B.C. She was named by her father heir of the kingdom, in conjunction with her brother Ptolemy, but was driven from the throne by his guardians Pothinus and Achillas. She was restored to the throne with her brother by Julius Caesar, and when her brother perished in the Alexandrine War became sole ruler of Egypt. By Caesar she had a son named Caesarion. After Caesar's death in 44 B.C. she met Antony in Cilicia and gained his heart by her beauty and fascination. In the war between Antony and Octavian she followed her lover, and the defection of her fleet at the battle of Actium (31 B.C.) hastened his defeat. Despairing of Antony's fortunes, she retired to her mausoleum at Alexandria and caused a report to be spread of her death. Thereupon Antony stabbed himself. To escape being carried captive to Rome by Octavian, Cleopatra took her own life (30 B.C.). The story of her relations with Antony has been made the theme of three famous plays, Shakespeare's 'Antony and Cleopatra' (q.v.), Dryden's 'All for Love' (q.v.), and Samuel Daniel's 'Cleopatra' (see below). Her relations with Caesar are the theme of a play by G. B. Shaw (q.v.), 'Caesar and Cleopatra'.

The granite obelisks called CLEOPATRA'S NEEDLES have nothing to do with that queen, but were erected at Heliopolis by Thothmes III about 1600 B.C. That which stands on the Thames Embankment was brought to England in 1878.

Cleopatra, a tragedy in blank verse by S. Daniel (q.v.), published in 1594. It is on the Senecan model, and deals with the story of Cleopatra after the death of Antony. Octavius Caesar endeavours to persuade her to leave the monument that she had caused to be built, in order that he may have her to grace his triumph. Feigning to yield, she asks permission first to sacrifice to the ghost of Antonius. After the performance of the rites she dines with great magnificence, and by her order a basket of figs is brought her which contains an asp. With this she does herself to death. Her son Caesarion about the same time is murdered at Rhodes and the race of the Ptolemies becomes extinct.

Cleopatra, in Dickens's 'Dombey and Son' (q.v.), the name by which Mrs. Skewton (q.v.) was known, from the title of a sketch of her when young, reclining in her barouche like

Cleopatra in her galley. In old age she continued to preserve the attitude in a bath chair kept for this purpose.

Cléopâtre, see *La Calprenède.*

Clerihew, an epigrammatic verse-form invented by Edmund Clerihew Bentley (1875–1956), consisting of two rhymed couplets, usually dealing with the character or career of a well-known person, e.g.

Sir James Jeans
Always says what he means;
He is really perfectly serious
About the Universe being Mysterious.

Clerimond, in the tale of 'Valentine and Orson' (q.v.), the sister of the giant Ferragus.

Clerk of Chatham, THE, the schoolmaster in Shakespeare's '2 Henry VI', who in Act IV. ii is haled before Jack Cade.

Clerk's Tale, The, see *Canterbury Tales.*

CLERK-MAXWELL, JAMES (1831–79), was the first professor of experimental physics at Cambridge. His best-known researches relate to electricity and magnetism, and his theories with regard to these were fully propounded in a treatise published in 1873. Its fundamental ideas have been generally accepted and have formed the basis of much subsequent work. They contributed to the development of the theory of the Conservation of Energy.

Clerkenwell, in London, a district that took its name from a well at which the parish clerks of London used each year to perform a miracle play. The Knights Hospitallers (q.v.) of St. John had their house and church in this district.

Cleveland, CAPTAIN CLEMENT, a character in Scott's 'The Pirate' (q.v.).

CLEVELAND, JOHN (1613–58), one of the most popular poets of the mid-17th cent. He was an active royalist and much of his writing was political satire which is lost on the modern reader. The most celebrated work is 'The Rebel Scot', a satire on the Scottish invasion of 1644. His poetry shows extreme examples of metaphysical conceits.

Cliché, French, 'a stereotype block', a stock expression which by constant use has become hackneyed and lost its sharp edge.

Clichy, a suburb of Paris. The CLICHIENS were a royalist club that met there after the Terror.

Clifford, LORD, THE SHEPHERD, see *Shepherd (Lord Clifford, the).*

CLIFFORD, WILLIAM KINGDON (1845–79), educated at King's College, London, and Trinity College, Cambridge, professor of applied mathematics at University College, London. He wrote some philosophical treatises ('Seeing and Thinking', 1879; 'Lectures and Essays', 1879), conceiving consciousness as built up out of simple elements

of 'mind-stuff'. His contributions to philosophy were cut short by his early death.

Clifford's Inn, one of the old Inns (q.v.) of Chancery, situated in the corner of Fleet Street and Chancery Lane, and said to have derived its name from a Robert Clifford, to whom Edward II granted the property in 1310 (Stow). The Society of law students who came into possession of it was dissolved at the beginning of the 20th cent., and the Inn has now been demolished.

Clink, THE LIBERTY OF THE, in Southwark, a precinct surrounding the London house of the bishops of Winchester. The Clink itself was a noted prison. The liberty enjoyed exemption from the ordinary jurisdiction; and here stood some of the early theatres, the bear-gardens, and the stews (G. R. Stirling Taylor, 'Historical Guide to London'). Hence the slang expression 'in clink' for 'in prison'.

Clio, the Muse (q.v.) of history.

C L I O were the letters with one or other of which Addison signed all his papers in the 'Spectator'.

Clitus or CLEITUS, a friend and general of Alexander the Great, who saved Alexander's life at the battle of Granīcus (334 B.C.). Taunted by Clitus at a banquet in 328, Alexander, who was heated with wine, killed him with a javelin, and was then inconsolable for his loss.

CLIVE, MRS. CAROLINE ARCHER (1801–73), *née* Meysey-Wigley, published, chiefly under the initial V, verses and novels, including 'Paul Ferroll' (q.v., 1855). She was accidentally burnt to death.

Clive, CATHERINE, commonly known as KITTY CLIVE (1711–85), actress, and friend of Horace Walpole, by whom she was pensioned.

Clive, ROBERT, *Baron Clive of Plassey* (1725–74), obtained an ensign's commission in the East India Company's service in 1747. He showed his bravery and military gifts by the capture of Arcot in 1751 and his subsequent defence of that city against a vastly superior force of French and natives. In 1757 he avenged the tragedy of the Black Hole of Calcutta (q.v.) by defeating Suráj ud Dowlah in the great victory of Plassey. He became governor of Bengal in 1758, and a second time (after a visit to England) in 1765. He resigned owing to ill health in 1767. His conduct was subjected in 1772–3 to a parliamentary inquiry, which resulted substantially in his favour. He died by his own hand.

Clockmaker, Sam Slick, the, see *Haliburton.*

Cloddipole, one of the rustics in Gay's 'Shepherd's Week' (q.v.).

Cloister and the Hearth, The, an historical romance by C. Reade (q.v.), published in 1861, enlarged from the slight story, 'A Good Fight', which had appeared in 'Once a Week' in 1859.

The story, which is laid in the 15th cent., was inspired by the author's reading of the 'Colloquies' and life of Erasmus, and the writings of Froissart and Luther. Gerard, the hero, the son of a mercer of Tergou, is destined for the Church, but falls in love with Margaret Brandt, the daughter of a poor scholar, suspected of sorcery. He abandons his career and betroths himself to her, but the anger of his father, the hostility of the burgomaster, and the envy of his two wicked brothers succeed in preventing the marriage, and Gerard is imprisoned. He escapes to Margaret, but is presently pursued and obliged to flee the country. The story now proceeds through a series of exciting incidents and vivid scenes in monasteries, taverns, and palaces, as Gerard travels through the disturbed countries of Germany and Burgundy to Italy. Here, by the cruel device of his enemies, he receives false news of the death of Margaret, and in despair gives himself up to a life of debauchery, and then takes the cowl. Meanwhile Margaret gives birth to a son and is reduced to despair by the loss of all trace of Gerard. Finally, as a Dominican preacher, he returns to his native town, is astounded to discover Margaret alive, and is at length persuaded, through the agency of his little son, to return to her and accept the living of Gouda. This same son, the close of the story indicates, is the future Erasmus (q.v.).

Clootie, a name for the Devil, as popularly represented with a cloven hoof (probably derived from an old word meaning 'claw').

O thou! whatever title suit thee,
Auld Hornie, Satan, Nick or Clootie.
(Burns, 'Address to the Deil'.)

Clootz, ANACHARSIS, Jean Baptiste Clootz (1755–94), a Prussian, who migrated to Paris, took the name Anacharsis (q.v.), adopted revolutionary views, but was purged from the Jacobins and guillotined (see Carlyle, 'French Revolution', I. iii and VI. i).

Clorin, the 'Faithful Shepherdess' in Fletcher's drama of that name (q.v.).

Clorinda, in Tasso's 'Jerusalem Delivered', a leader of the pagan forces, the daughter of the king of Ethiopia, who had been lost as a babe in the forest and suckled by a tigress. Tancred, who has fallen in love with her, slays her unwittingly in a night attack.

Cloten, a character in Shakespeare's 'Cymbeline' (q.v.).

Clotho, see *Parcae*.

Cloud-cuckoo-land, see *Nephelococcygia*.

Cloudesley, WILLIAM OF, see *Adam Bell*.

CLOUGH, ARTHUR HUGH (1819–61), son of a Liverpool cotton merchant, and educated at Rugby and Balliol College, Oxford, became a fellow of Oriel and, after throwing up his fellowship, principal of University Hall, London. He was subsequently an examiner in the Education Office. He died at Florence, and Matthew Arnold's 'Thyrsis' was written to commemorate his death. He is chiefly remembered as the author of the hexameter poem, 'The Bothie of Tober-na-Vuolich' (q.v., 1848), and of some fine lyrics, including the well-known 'Say not the struggle nought availeth', which bear the mark of the spiritual agitation caused by religious doubts. His longer poems, published posthumously, include 'Dipsychus' (q.v., 1869), 'Amours de Voyage' (like the 'Bothie' in hexameters), and 'Mari Magno', a series of tales (1862).

Clove, a character in Jonson's 'Every Man out of his Humour', who makes a pretence to learning by a display of long words and abstruse terms.

Club, THE, see *Johnson (Samuel)*.

Clumsy, SIR TUNBELLY, a character in Vanbrugh's 'The Relapse' and Sheridan's 'A Trip to Scarborough' (qq.v.).

Cluniacs, an order of monks which developed from the Benedictine abbey of Cluny, near Mâcon in France, and separated from the parent order in the 11th cent. Its church at Cluny, largely wrecked in the Revolution, was second in size only to St. Peter's in Rome.

Clutha, in Macpherson's Ossianic poems, the river Clyde.

Clutterbuck, CAPTAIN CUTHBERT, a fictitious personage supposed to be concerned with the publication of some of Sir W. Scott's novels, e.g. 'The Monastery'.

Clym of the Clough, see *Adam Bell*.

Clym Yeobright, a character in T. Hardy's 'The Return of the Native' (q.v.).

Clymĕnē, (1) daughter of Oceanus and Tethys, and mother of Atlas and Prometheus; (2) daughter of Minyas, and mother of Phaethon by the Sun.

Some beauty rare, Calisto, Clymene.
(Milton, 'Paradise Regained', ii. 186.)

Clytemnestra, daughter of Tyndareus, king of Sparta, and Leda (q.v.), and wife of Agamemnon (q.v.), king of Argos. On the return of Agamemnon from the Trojan War, she, with her paramour Aegisthus (q.v.), murdered her husband, and was in turn slain by Orestes, Agamemnon's son.

Clytia or CLYTIĒ, a nymph, daughter of Oceanus, who was loved by Apollo. She was deserted by him, pined away, and was changed into a sunflower, which constantly turns its head to the sun.

Cnut or CANUTE (q.v.), king of England, 1016–35.

Coal Hole, THE, a tavern in Fountain Court, Strand, from which Thackeray in part drew his 'Cave of Harmony' (q.v.).

Coart, COUWAERT, or CUWAERT, in 'Reynard the Fox' (q.v.), the name of the hare. It is the same word as our 'coward'.

Coatel, a character in Southey's 'Madoc' (q.v.).

Coavinses, in Dickens's 'Bleak House'(q.v.), see *Neckett.*

COBBE, FRANCES POWER (1822–1904), philanthropist and religious writer, published anonymously 'The Theory of Intuitive Morals' in 1855–7. She was associated with Mary Carpenter in her ragged school and reformatory work, and occupied herself with relief of destitution and workhouse philanthropy. Her voluminous writings include 'Broken Lights'(1864), 'Darwinism in Morals' (1872), 'The Duties of Women' (1881), and an autobiography (1904). She was an early advocate of women's suffrage and opponent of vivisection.

COBBETT, WILLIAM (1763–1835), the son of a labourer at Farnham, and self-educated, enlisted as a soldier and served in Florida from 1784 to 1791. He obtained his discharge, brought an accusation of peculation against some of his former officers, and in 1792 retired to America to avoid prosecution. There he published pro-British pamphlets under the pseudonym of 'Peter Porcupine'. He returned to England in 1800 and became a Tory journalist, editing 'Cobbett's Political Register', a weekly newspaper, from 1802. Soon he adopted popular opinions and wrote from 1804 in the radical interest. He published 'Parliamentary Debates', afterwards taken over by Hansard, and 'State Trials', wrote an 'English Grammar' (1817) and a number of books on economics and other subjects. He also farmed in Hampshire and subsequently in Surrey. From 1817 to 1819 he was in America. His 'History of the Protestant "Reformation" in England and Ireland' appeared in 1824; his 'Advice to Young Men' in 1829. He became M.P. for Oldham in 1832. He wrote with exceptional perspicuity and vigour, and showed good sense and sound observation in agricultural matters. But his honesty and shrewdness are marred by an arrogant and quarrelsome attitude, and by wrong-headed prejudices. His 'Rural Rides' (q.v.), collected in 1830, are today the most interesting of his writings. His 'Political Register', which attained a very large circulation, was continued until his death. See G. D. H. Cole, 'The Life of Cobbett' (1924; 1927).

Cobden, RICHARD (1804–65), son of a Sussex farmer, settled in Manchester in 1832. He was a foremost leader of the Anti-Corn Law League, and M.P. for Stockport (1841–7), for the West Riding of Yorkshire (1847–57), and for Stockdale in 1859. By his strenuous advocacy he powerfully contributed to the repeal of the Corn Laws (1846). He negotiated the commercial treaty with France, 1859–60.

COCCAI, MERLIN; see *Folengo.*

Cock-and-bull story, an expression that apparently had its origin in some tale or fable,

means a long idle rambling story; or a concocted, incredible story.

'Some mens whole delight is . . . to talk of a cock and a bull over a pot.'
(Burton, 'Anatomy of Melancholy', II. ii. 4.)

Cock and Pie, used in asseverations, is perhaps for 'God and Pie', where 'Pie' is the table of rules of the Roman Catholic Church governing the offices for each day.

'By cock and pie, you shall not choose, sir! come, come.'
(Shakespeare, 'Merry Wives', I. i.)

Cock Lane Ghost, a supposed ghost to which were attributed mysterious noises heard at No. 33 Cock Lane, Smithfield, of which the object was said to be the detection of a crime. They were discovered in 1762 to be due to an imposition practised by one William Parsons, his wife, and daughter, but not before the report had created much excitement. Dr. Johnson took part in the investigation of the mystery (see Boswell's 'Life', 1763). See A. Lang, 'Cock Lane and Common Sense' (1894), and D. Grant, 'The Cock Lane Ghost' (1965).

Cock of the North, George, fifth duke of Gordon (1770–1836), who raised the regiment now known as the Gordon Highlanders and commanded it (1795–9) in Spain, Corsica, Ireland, and Holland, where he was severely wounded. 'Cock of the North' is also the name of a well-known tune on the pipes.

Cockatrice (from Latin *calcatrix*, apparently a medieval translation of the Greek ἰχνεύμων, ichneumon), a serpent identified with the basilisk (q.v.), fabled to kill by its mere glance, and to be hatched from a cock's egg. In heraldry, it is a hybrid monster with the head, wings, and feet of a cock, terminating in a serpent with a barbed tail.

Cockayne or COCKAIGNE, LAND OF, the name of a fabulous country, the abode of luxury and idleness. The origin of the term has been much discussed but remains obscure. Baring-Gould ('Curious Myths') regards it as originally a nickname for the 'Fortunate Isles' (q.v.). The word in its derivation is connected with 'cook' or 'cake'. The OED. gives a quotation *c.* 1305, from which it appears that the houses in Cockayne were covered with cakes.

COCKBURN, HENRY THOMAS, *Lord Cockburn* (1779–1854), was educated at the Edinburgh High School and University. He shared with Jeffrey (q.v.) the leadership of the Scottish Bar for many years, became solicitor-general for Scotland in 1830, Lord Rector of Glasgow University in 1831, and judge of the Court of Sessions in 1834. His 'Memorials of His Times' (1856) gives lively accounts of literary circles in Edinburgh and descriptions of Brougham, Jeffrey, John Wilson, Sydney Smith, and the founding of the 'Edinburgh Review' (q.v.), to which he contributed an article on the Parliamentary

Representation of Scotland (1830). His 'Life of Jeffrey' was published in 1852.

Cocke Lorell's Bote, a popular satire of the 16th cent., in verse, in which types of the various tradesfolk take ship and sail through England. The captain of the 'Bote' is Cocke Lorell, a tinker and probably an historical personage. It is an interesting picture of low life.

COCKER, EDWARD (1631–75), a teacher of arithmetic and writing in London, whose treatise on arithmetic attained great popularity and gave rise to the expression 'according to Cocker'.

Cockney, from Middle English *coken-ey*, 'cocks' egg', of which the original meaning was perhaps one of the small or misshapen eggs occasionally laid by fowls. It came to mean 'a cockered child', an effeminate fellow or milksop, and so was used derisively for a townsman in contrast to the hardier inhabitants of the country, and finally for one born in the city of London (always more or less in a contemptuous or bantering sense). Hence it was extended to the London dialect or accent.

The Cockney School was a nickname given by Lockhart to a set of 19th-cent. writers belonging to London, of whom Leigh Hunt and Hazlitt were representative members.

Cockpit, The, the name of a theatre in London in the 17th cent., referred to by Pepys (11 Oct. 1660 and 5 Jan. 1662–3). Also the name of a block of buildings near Whitehall erected by Henry VIII as government offices.

The Cockpit of Europe is an expression applied to Belgium as the scene of many wars (a cockpit being the scene of cock-fights).

Co'clēs, Publius Horatius, a Roman who at first with two companions and then alone opposed the whole army of Porsena, king of Etruria, at the head of the bridge leading into Rome, while his companions behind him were cutting off communication with the other shore. When the bridge was destroyed, Cocles, though wounded, leapt into the Tiber and swam across it with his arms. The feat is the subject of one of Macaulay's 'Lays of Ancient Rome'.

Cocoa-tree Club, The, in St. James's Street, originally a chocolate house of the same name, dating from the early 18th cent. After being a Tory centre and subsequently, in 1745, a resort of the Jacobite party, it became a fashionable club where, as Horace Walpole's letters attest, there was gambling for high stakes. 'At the Cocoa-tree Lord Stavordale, not one-and-twenty, lost eleven thousand last Tuesday, but recovered it by one great hand at hazard' (1770).

COCTEAU, JEAN (1889–1963), French author. His numerous works belong mainly to the period between the two world wars

when he was prominently associated with modernist groups in literature, art, music, and the cinema. They include: poetry; novels; sketches for ballet; drama, e.g. modernizations of classical myths ('Orphée', 'La Machine Infernale', etc), a psychological drama 'Les Parents terribles', and in 1946 a romantic drama 'L'Aigle a deux têtes', translated for the English theatre as 'The Eagle has Two Heads'.

Cōcȳtus, the 'river of lamentation', from κωκύω, I howl; a river of Epirus, and by the poets regarded as a river of Hades. See *Styx.*

Codille, a term used in the game of ombre, when the adversaries of ombre win the game.

> Just in the jaws of ruin, and Codille.
> (Pope, 'Rape of the Lock', iii. 93.)

Codlin and **Short**, in Dickens's 'Old Curiosity Shop' (q.v.), travel about the country with a Punch and Judy show. Thomas Codlin was a surly misanthrope; Short (whose real name was Harris, but was familiarly known as 'Short Trotters') was a cheerful little man. Codlin, who suspects that Little Nell and her grandfather have run away from their friends and is anxious to get the reward for their discovery, assures Nell that 'Codlin's the friend, not Short'.

Codrington, Christopher (1668–1710), born in Barbados, and educated at Christ Church, Oxford, became captain-general of the Leeward Islands in 1697. He spent the last years of his life in study on his Barbados estates, which he bequeathed to the Society for the Propagation of the Gospel, for the foundation of a college in Barbados. He also left his books and £10,000 to All Souls College, Oxford, a bequest out of which was founded the Codrington Library.

Cœlebs in Search of a Wife, a novel by Hannah More (q.v.), published in 1809. It is a collection of social sketches and precepts, strung together on the thread of the hero's search for a young woman who shall possess the qualities stipulated for by his departed parents.

Coffee-houses were first introduced in London in the time of the Commonwealth and were much frequented in the 17th and 18th cents. for political and literary discussion, circulation of news, etc. There is an interesting description of them in Macaulay's 'History of England', c. iii. See *Button's, Will's, Grecian, Garraway's.*

Cogglesby, Andrew and Tom, characters in Meredith's 'Evan Harrington' (q.v.).

COKE, Sir EDWARD (1552–1634), educated at Norwich and Trinity College, Cambridge, and a barrister of the Inner Temple, was advanced by Burghley's influence to be attorney-general, to the disappointment of Francis Bacon (q.v.), whose lifelong rival he was. He became chief justice of the Common Pleas in 1606, of the King's Bench in 1613. Here he quarrelled incessantly with the Court of Chancery and was dismissed by the king in 1616. Gardiner calls his dismissal a 'turning point' in the relations of king and parliament. Coke's fame as a legal author rests on his eleven volumes of 'Reports' (1600–15), and his 'Institutes' (1628–44) in which he recast, explained, and defended the common law rules. The first part of the 'Institutes' is the commentary on the 'Tenures' of Littleton (q.v.), whence the term, now obsolete, *Coke-upon-Littleton*, a cant name for a mixed drink.

Coke, LADY MARY (1726–1811), a daughter of John, duke of Argyll, the wife of Edward Viscount Coke. Her entertaining 'Letters and Journals' have been privately printed (1889–96).

Cokes, BARTHOLOMEW, a character in Jonson's 'Bartholomew Fayre' (q.v.).

Colbek, THE DANCERS OF, the subject of a story in Robert Mannyng's 'Handlyng Synne' (q.v.).

A band of 'fools' led by Bovo and Gerlew come to Colbek (Kölbigk in Anhalt, Saxony) and dance and sing in the churchyard, enticing the priest's daughter to dance with them. The priest, about to begin mass, bids them desist, but they continue. He curses them and prays that they may be obliged to dance for a twelvemonth. This they do in obedience to the curse, and although the others survive the ordeal, the priest's daughter falls dead at the end, and the priest dies soon after.

The circumstances (perhaps an epidemic of St. Vitus's dance) from which the story sprang appear to belong to 1021. Two letters narrating the event were circulated as credentials by pretended survivors of the band. One of these, the letter of Theodric, makes Bruno, bishop of Toul (afterwards Pope Leo IX), vouch for the facts. Theodric was miraculously cured at the shrine of St. Edith of Wilton, and the letter was preserved in the Acts of St. Edith, and Mannyng had it before him.

Colbrand, in the romance of 'Guy of Warwick' (q.v.), the Danish giant slain by Sir Guy. The story is also told in Drayton's 'Polyolbion', xii. 130 et seq.

Cold Harbour or COLD HARBOROUGH, an ancient building in the parish of All Hallows the Less, in Dowgate Ward, London, at one time the College of Heralds, and subsequently the residence of Bishop Tunstall (1474–1559). It was removed by the earl of Shrewsbury, who erected small tenements in its place, where debtors and others took sanctuary, a character that the locality enjoyed perhaps owing to its connexion with the bishop. The name is also applied to derelict houses (perhaps destroyed in the Saxon and Angle invasions of Britain) and is borne by several localities in England.

Coldbath Fields, in Clerkenwell, London, famous for a prison established there in the reign of James I, now closed.

Cole, KING, the 'merry old soul' of the nursery rhyme, was Coel, one of the legendary kings of Britain enumerated by Geoffrey of Monmouth (q.v.) in his 'Historia Regum Britanniae'. Some authorities trace him even further back to the god Camulus, whose name is seen in Camulodunon (Colchester). There is a poem about him by Masefield (q.v.) in 'King Cole and other Poems' (1923).

COLENSO, JOHN WILLIAM (1814–83), started life as a poor Cornish boy, became a sizar of St. John's College, Cambridge, a master at Harrow, and ultimately bishop of Natal. Besides text-books on arithmetic and algebra, he published 'Ten Weeks in Natal' in 1854; a 'Commentary on the Epistle to the Romans' (1861), which attacked the sacramental system and evoked much opposition; and a 'Critical Examination of the Pentateuch', (1862–79), concluding that these books were post-exile forgeries. He was deposed and excommunicated by Bishop Gray of Capetown (who had no jurisdiction over him), but confirmed in the possession of his see by the law courts (1866).

COLERIDGE, HARTLEY (1796–1849), eldest son of Samuel Taylor Coleridge (q.v.), educated at Ambleside and Merton College, Oxford, was appointed a probationer fellow of Oriel College, but dismissed in 1820 on a vague charge of intemperance. He tried work as a schoolmaster, with little success, contributed to the 'London Magazine' and 'Blackwood's', and lived mainly at Grasmere. His longest work is the 'Biographia Borealis' or 'Lives of Northern Worthies' (1833–6, 1852). His poems include some beautiful sonnets, notably those 'On Prayer', 'To Homer', 'To Shakespeare', and that on himself—'When I review the course that I have run', and some pieces marked by a singular melancholy charm, such as 'She is not fair to outward view', and 'She pass'd away like morning dew'. His collected poems were issued in 1851, and his essays and some of his notable marginalia in the same year, by his brother Derwent.

COLERIDGE, MARY ELIZABETH (1861–1907), belonged to the same family as her great namesake; for her grandfather, Francis George Coleridge, was the nephew of S. T. Coleridge (q.v.). She was author of some remarkable poetry. Her 'Poems Old and New' (1907) and 'Gathered Leaves' (1910) were published posthumously. Her first novel, 'The Seven Sleepers of Ephesus' (1893), was praised by R. L. Stevenson. 'The King with Two Faces', an historical novel centring round Gustavus III of Sweden, appeared in 1897.

COLERIDGE, SAMUEL TAYLOR (1772–1834), son of the vicar of Ottery St. Mary, Devon, was educated at Christ's Hospital (Lamb, in his Elia essay, describes the impression that Coleridge, some years his senior there, made upon him) and at Jesus College,

Cambridge. Thence for an unknown reason he betook himself to London and enlisted in the 15th Dragoons, but was discharged after a few months and returned to Cambridge. He made the acquaintance of Robert Southey (q.v.), and the pair devoted themselves to 'Pantisocracy', a form of communism which they contemplated realizing on the banks of the Susquehanna. He married Sara Fricker in 1795, Southey marrying her sister.

He contributed verses to the 'Morning Chronicle' as early as 1793-5, and in 1794 wrote and published in conjunction with Southey 'The Fall of Robespierre'. In 1796 he started a newspaper, 'The Watchman', which lasted for only ten numbers. In 1795 he made the acquaintance of Wordsworth, and the two poets, between whom there sprang up a deep friendship, lived in close intercourse for about a year at Nether Stowey and Alfoxden in Somerset. Their 'Lyrical Ballads' (q.v.) containing Coleridge's 'Ancient Mariner' (q.v.) appeared in 1798. Coleridge wrote the first part of 'Christabel' (q.v.) and 'Kubla Khan' (q.v.) in 1797, and contributed some of his best poems to the 'Morning Post' during 1798-1802. 'France, an Ode', a retractation of his faith in the revolutionary movement, appeared in 1798. 'Dejection' was written in 1802. After his visit to Germany in 1798-9, he published (1799-1800) his translations of Schiller's 'Piccolomini' and 'The Death of Wallenstein' under the title 'Wallenstein'. He settled for a time (1800-4) at Keswick, where he wrote the second part of 'Christabel'. In 1804 he travelled to Malta and Italy, returning in 1806 broken in health and a prey to the use of opium. In 1808 he gave lectures on the English poets at the Royal Institution, which were imperfectly reported, and in 1809 he launched his second periodical, 'The Friend', 'a literary, moral, and political weekly paper', subsequently re-written and published as a book (1818). In this appeared the grim ballad-tale of 'The Three Graves', written some twelve years previously. He spent much of the latter part of his life in the houses of friends, notably of John Morgan at Hammersmith and subsequently at Calne, and after 1816 of a kindly surgeon, James Gillman, at Highgate. He had been given annuities of £75 each by Josiah and Thomas Wedgwood, but Josiah's was withdrawn in 1811. In 1817 appeared his 'Biographia Literaria' (q.v.) or literary autobiography, and in 1825 his 'Aids to Reflection' (q.v.), in the first of which he did much to introduce German philosophy to English thinkers, though some of his philosophical doctrines were arrived at independently. He also wrote three plays, 'The Fall of Robespierre' (1794), 'Zapolya' (1817), and 'Osorio'. This last, written before 1798, was acted, under the title 'Remorse', at Drury Lane in 1813. Coleridge's finest poems, 'The Ancient Mariner', 'Kubla Khan', and 'Christabel', are characterized by the sense of mystery that he suggests. His gift in a lighter mood is seen in such a poem as

'The Devil's Thoughts' (q.v.), written with Southey.

Apart from his poetry, Coleridge did valuable work in literary criticism, maintaining that the true end of poetry is to give pleasure 'through the medium of beauty'. The 'Biographia' contains much of this criticism, in particular of the poems of Wordsworth. In philosophy, he courageously stemmed the tide of the prevailing doctrines derived from Hume and Hartley, advocating a more spiritual and religious interpretation of life, based on what he had learnt from Kant and Schelling. 'Anima Poetae' (q.v.), edited from his unpublished notebooks in 1895 by E. H. Coleridge, contains some of his most interesting work in this sphere. Mention must also be made of his 'Confessions of an Enquiring Spirit', edited by H. N. Coleridge in 1840, letters revealing his attitude to the question of Biblical inspiration. In political philosophy, to which he paid much attention, he declared himself the heir of Burke and an enemy of Jacobinism, though constructively he had little to offer. There are biographies by J. Dykes Campbell (1894) and E. K. Chambers (1938). His 'Letters' are being edited by E. L. Griggs. Vols. I and II were published in 1956 and Vols. III and IV in 1959.

COLERIDGE, SARA (1802-52), daughter of S. T. Coleridge (q.v.) and wife of Henry Nelson Coleridge, was author of 'Phantasmion' (1837), an elaborate romantic fairy-tale, with a host of characters, among whom figure Oloola, the spirit of the storm, and Valhorga, the earth spirit. Even Potentilla, the special protectress of Prince Phantasmion, is a fairy of no mean powers, for she is able to convert him into a sort of flying sea-serpent, for the discomfiture of the pirates who infest his shores. The story, which is concerned with the love of Phantasmion for Iarine, whom after many adventures he wins from his rivals Karadan and the wicked king Glandreth, is told with much charming fancy, and interspersed with many pleasant lyrics. Sara Coleridge also helped her brother Derwent to edit their father's poems, and her husband to edit her father's philosophical writings. Her interesting 'Letters' were published in 1873.

COLET, JOHN (1467?-1519), dean of St. Paul's and the principal Christian humanist of his day in England. He studied at Oxford and in Italy, and lectured on the New Testament at Oxford from 1496 to 1504, Erasmus being among his hearers. As dean of St. Paul's, he founded and endowed St. Paul's School, for which he wrote a Latin accidence, W. Lily supplying the syntax. This book, revised by Erasmus, ultimately developed into the 'Eton Latin Grammar'. Colet was a pioneer of the English Reformation, famous as a preacher and lecturer. His 'Exposition of St. Paul's Epistle to the Romans' and 'Exposition of St. Paul's First Epistle to the Corinthians' (ed. by J. H. Lupton, Cambridge

University Press) throw light upon his method of exegesis. There is an interesting picture of Colet and his school in Erasmus, Ep. 1211 (in Allen's ed.; translation by J. H. Lupton, 1883).

COLETTE, SIDONIE-GABRIELLE (1873–1954), the foremost French woman author of her day, wrote novels and other prose works notable for their sensitive understanding and descriptions of nature (human and animal) and of country life. The 'Claudine' series (1900–3) made her name, but her outstanding novels include: 'La Vagabonde', 'Chéri', 'La Chatte', etc. 'Sido' (1929), reminiscences of young days in the Burgundian country, is remarkable for the portrait of her mother. 'Les Vrilles de la Vigne' (1908) and 'Dialogues de Bêtes' (1904) may also be mentioned.

Colin and Lucy, see *Tickell.*

Colin Clout, the name adopted by Edmund Spenser (q.v.) in the 'Shepheards Calender' and 'Colin Clouts come home againe' (qq.v.). COLIN CLOUT is also the name of a rustic in Gay's 'Shepherd's Week' (q.v.). See also *Colin Cloute.*

Colin Clouts come home againe, an allegorical pastoral written by Spenser (q.v.) on his return to Kilcolman after his visit to London of 1589–91. It was dedicated to Sir Walter Ralegh 'in part paiment of the infinite debt in which I acknowledge my selfe bounden unto you, for your singular favours and sundrie good turnes, shewed to me at my late being in England'. The poem describes in allegorical form how Ralegh visited Spenser in Ireland, and induced him to come to England 'his Cynthia to see'—i.e. the queen. There is a charming description of the sea voyage; after which the poet tells of the glories of the queen and her court, and the beauty of the ladies who frequent it. Then follows a bitter attack on the envies and intrigues of the court. The poem ends with a tribute to 'Rosalind' in spite of her cruelty to the poet. Of the characters mentioned in the work, Cynthia is Queen Elizabeth, Hobbinol is G. Harvey (q.v.), Amyntas is T. Watson (q.v.), the Shepheard of the Sea is Sir W. Ralegh (q.v.).

Coliseum, THE, see *Colosseum.*

Colkitto, 'or MACDONNEL, or GALASP', in Milton's first 'Tetrachordon' sonnet, was the lieutenant-general of the marquis of Montrose in his campaign on behalf of Charles I. He was called *Alexander Macdonnel, Mac-Colkittoch, Mac-Gillespie,* that is to say Alexander Macdonnel, the son of Colkittoch, the son of Gillespie (or Galasp). He figures in Scott's 'Legend of Montrose' (q.v.).

Colleen Bawn, The (Anglo-Irish, meaning 'The Fair Girl'), the title of a play by Dion Boucicault (1859), founded on Gerald Griffin's 'The Collegians' (q.v.).

College of Arms, see *Heralds' College.*

Collegians, The, a novel by Griffin (q.v.), published in 1829.

It is a sombre, sensational story of the injudicious secret marriage of young Hardress Cregan with a girl of lower station than his own, repented when he finds himself loved by a woman of no less beauty and greater refinement. He allows himself to become affianced to the latter under strong pressure from an imperious mother, and connives at the removal, in fact at the murder, of his innocent young wife. He is arrested on the eve of his marriage with his second love. The tragedy is relieved by some amusing scenes of Irish life, quiet humour, and good ballads. Dion Boucicault's play 'The Colleen Bawn' was founded on this novel.

Collegiate Ladies, in Jonson's 'Epicœne' (q.v.), a group of dissolute women 'between courtiers and country madams, who live from their husbands and give entertainment to all the wits and braveries [beaux] of the time'.

COLLIER, JEREMY (1650–1726), educated at Ipswich and Caius College, Cambridge, was rector of Ampton, Suffolk, 1679–85. He publicly absolved on the scaffold two of those executed for the assassination plot, in 1696, and was in consequence outlawed. He became a nonjuring bishop in 1713. He is chiefly remembered for his 'Short View of the Immorality and Profaneness of the English Stage', 1698, in which he particularly attacked Congreve and Vanbrugh (qq.v.). The work created a great, if temporary, impression. Congreve and D'Urfey were prosecuted, Betterton and Mrs. Bracegirdle were fined, and some of the poets replied, though not very effectively. But the futility of Collier's attack is shown by the continued success of the type of play that he inveighed against. Collier published a learned 'Ecclesiastical History of Great Britain' in 1708–14.

COLLIER, JOHN PAYNE (1789–1883), author of 'Notes on Rare English Books' (1865) and editor of the 'Roxburghe Ballads' (1847) as well as of many papers for the Camden, Percy, and Shakespeare societies; remembered also for his falsifications of ancient documents, notably for forgeries of marginal corrections of the text of Shakespeare in the 'Perkins folio'.

COLLINGWOOD, ROBIN GEORGE (1889–1943), philosopher and archaeologist. He was educated by his father before going to Rugby and University College, Oxford, and in 1935 became professor of metaphysical philosophy in Oxford. He combined philosophy with the history and archaeology of Roman Britain. His chief work in the latter field was 'Roman Britain and the English Settlements' (with J. N. L. Myres, 1936). In his vigorous 'Autobiography' (1939) and 'The Idea of History' (1946) he maintained the identity of philosophy and history. Earlier books include an 'Essay on Philosophical Method' (1933) and 'The Principles of Art' (1938).

COLLINS, ARTHUR (1690?–1760), a bookseller in London, was author of the 'Peerage of England' (1709, enlarged editions, 1735 and 1756), and of the 'Baronetage of England' (1720).

COLLINS, JOHN CHURTON (1848–1908), was educated at King Edward's School, Birmingham, and Balliol College, Oxford. He was greatly interested in English literature and long agitated, with ultimate success, for its academic recognition at Oxford. He was a frequent contributor to the 'Quarterly Review', 'The Saturday Review', and other periodicals, and became professor of English at the University of Birmingham. He edited Cyril Tourneur's works (1878), Lord Herbert of Cherbury's poems (1881), and Robert Greene's works (1905); and published 'Ephemera Critica' (1901), 'Studies in Shakespeare' (1904), 'Studies in Poetry and Criticism' (1905), and 'Voltaire, Montesquieu, and Rousseau in England' (1905). Churton Collins was found drowned at Oulton Broad, near Lowestoft.

COLLINS, WILLIAM (1721–59), the son of a Chichester hatter, educated at Winchester and Magdalen College, Oxford. He was an exquisite lyrical poet, but his verse was unfortunately small in quantity, and some of it (the 'Ode on the Music of the Grecian Theatre', written in 1750, and 'The Bell of Aragon', his last ode) is lost. He published his 'Persian Eclogues' as an undergraduate in 1742, and in 1747 his 'Odes'. The best known of these are the 'Ode to Evening', the 'Ode to Simplicity', and the 'Ode written in 1746' ('How sleep the brave'). The charming 'Dirge in Cymbeline' must also be mentioned. His long 'Ode on the popular Superstitions of the Highlands', containing some magnificent verse, was written in 1749 and published posthumously. He became insane and died in his sister's house at Chichester.

Collins, WILLIAM, in Jane Austen's 'Pride and Prejudice' (q.v.), a pompous, silly, and self-satisfied young clergyman, excessively obsequious to persons of high social station. The solemn letter of thanks that he addresses to Mr. Bennet (c. xxiii, though the text is not given) after his stay with the family has led to his name being colloquially associated with such letters.

COLLINS, WILLIAM WILKIE (1824–89), was called to the bar in 1851, but adopted literature as a profession. He made the acquaintance of Dickens and contributed to 'Household Words' from 1855. It was in this periodical that he published in 1860 'The Woman in White' (q.v.), by which his fame was established as practically the first English novelist who dealt with the detection of crime. His other works include: 'Antonina, or the Fall of Rome' (1850), 'Hide and Seek' (1854), 'The Dead Secret' (1857), 'My Miscellanies' (1862), 'No Name' (1862), 'Armadale' (1866), 'The Moonstone' (q.v., 1868), 'Man and Wife'

(1870), 'Poor Miss Finch' (1872), 'The New Magdalen' (1873), 'A Rogue's Life' (1879), 'Little Novels' (1879), 'The Black Robe' (1881). For the collaboration of Collins with Dickens, see *Dickens*.

COLMAN, GEORGE, the elder (1732–94), born in Florence, where his father was British envoy, was educated at Westminster and Christ Church, Oxford. He was manager of the Covent Garden Theatre, 1767–74, and of the Haymarket Theatre, 1777–89. He was a friend of Garrick and collaborated with him in writing the excellent comedy, 'The Clandestine Marriage' (q.v., 1766). He wrote or adapted some thirty dramatic pieces, edited Beaumont and Fletcher (1778), and translated Terence (1765) and Horace's 'Art of Poetry' (1783). His most effective plays were 'Polly Honeycombe' (1760) and 'The Jealous Wife' (1761, an adaptation of Fielding's 'Tom Jones').

COLMAN, GEORGE, the younger (1762–1836), son of George Colman the elder (q.v.), educated at Westminster School, Christ Church, Oxford, and Aberdeen University, made his name as a dramatist by the romantic comedy 'Inkle and Yarico' (q.v., 1787). His comedy 'The Heir-at-Law' (1797) is famous for its presentation of Dr. Pangloss, the greedy, pompous pedant. 'John Bull' (1803) contains the supposed type of the British character, Job Thornberry. 'The Iron Chest' (1796) is a dramatization of 'Caleb Williams' (q.v.). Colman's other pieces are less important.

Colmekill, in Shakespeare's 'Macbeth', II. iv, is *I-Colm-kill* (the island of Columba of the Church), the modern Iona (q.v.).

Cologne, see *Ursula* and *Colonia*.

Cologne, THREE KINGS OF, or Wise Men of the East: the Magi, Gaspar, Melchior, and Balthazar, whose bones the Emperor Barbarossa is said to have brought from Milan and deposited in Cologne Cathedral.

Colombe's Birthday, a play by R. Browning (q.v.), published in 1844 and acted in 1853.

Colombe is duchess of Juliers and Cleves, liable however to be ousted under the Salic Law by her cousin Prince Berthold. The latter claims his rights, and offers the young duchess marriage, employing her advocate Valence to convey his offer. But Valence himself loves Colombe, and finally wins her by his loyalty and self-denial.

Colonel Jack, *The History and Remarkable Life of Colonel Jacque, Commonly Call'd,* a romance of adventure by Defoe (q.v.), published in 1722.

The supposed narrator, abandoned by his parents in childhood, falls into bad company and becomes a pickpocket. His profession grows distasteful to him, and he enlists, and presently deserts to avoid being sent to serve in Flanders. He is kidnapped, sent to Virginia, and sold to a planter. He is promoted to be an overseer, is given his liberty, becomes himself a planter, and acquires much wealth. He returns home, has a series of unfortunate matrimonial adventures, but finally ends in prosperity and repentance.

Colonia, COLONIA AGRIPPINA, COLONIA CLAUDIA, or COLONIA UBIORUM, in imprints, Cologne. Colonia is also an imprint for Naples.

Colonia Allobrogum, in imprints, Geneva.

Colonia Munatiana, in imprints, Basle.

COLONNA, VITTORIA (1490–1547), granddaughter of Frederick, duke of Urbino, and devoted wife of the marquis of Pescara, was a woman remarkable in a dissolute age for her stainless character and the admiration she inspired among great men, among others Michelangelo. Her writings, largely religious, include some notable sonnets.

Colophon, from Gk. κολοφών, summit, 'finishing touch', the inscription or device, sometimes pictorial or emblematic, placed at the end of a book or manuscript, and containing the title, the scribe's or printer's name, the date and place of printing, etc.

Colosseum, THE, or Flavian amphitheatre, in Rome, was begun by Vespasian in A.D. 72 and inaugurated by Titus, after his return from the conquest of Jerusalem. It was the scene, during four centuries, of countless gladiatorial combats and of the martyrdom of many Christians. It was reduced to its present ruinous condition partly by earthquakes, partly by being used as a quarry for building-stone.

Colossus of Rhodes, bronze statue of Apollo by the Greek sculptor Chares, 250 B.C., which passed for one of the seven wonders of the world.' According to an unfounded tradition, its feet rested on two moles, which formed the entrance of the harbour, and ships passed between its legs. It is said by Pliny to have been seventy cubits high. It was demolished by an earthquake in 224 B.C.

COLUMBA, ST., otherwise COLUMCILLE or COLUMBANUS (521–597), son of Feidilmid, an Ulster chief, and a pupil of St. Finnian, became a recluse at Glasnevin, and built churches at Derry and other places. He went to Scotland in 563, founded the monastery of Hy (Iona), and preached to the Picts. His relics were translated to Ireland in 878, but were destroyed by the Danes in 1127. Several books believed to have been written by him were long venerated in Ireland. He is commemorated on 9 June.

Columban, ST. (543–615), born in Leinster and a monk under St. Comgall at Bangor, Down, resided in Burgundy, 585–610. There he built monasteries at Anegray and Luxeuil, for which he drew up a monastic rule, afterwards common in France, until replaced by that of St. Benedict. He was expelled from Burgundy by Theodoric II and preached to the heathen Germans and Suabians. He founded the monastery of Bobbio in the Piedmont and died there. He is commemorated on 21 Nov.

Columbiad, The, a lengthy epic poem by Joel Barlow (q.v.), which surveys the panorama of early American history, as revealed in a vision to Columbus. After bringing his history up to date, the author launches into prophecy. First published as 'The Vision of Columbus' (1787), the poem was renamed 'The Columbiad' in 1807.

Columbine, a character in Italian comedy, the daughter of Pantaloon and mistress of Harlequin, which has been transferred to our pantomime or harlequinade.

Columbus, CHRISTOPHER (c. 1445–1506), in Spanish CRISTÓVAL COLÓN, a Genoese navigator, the discoverer of America. He is said to have first proposed his expedition of discovery to the Genoese republic and other powers, but to have been rebuffed. He finally obtained the favour of Queen Isabella of Castile and embarked on his first voyage in 1492. He met with much ingratitude and persecution, but made in all four voyages to the West Indies. His object was to reach the Cathay of Marco Polo, and he remained under the impression that the regions he discovered were the fringes of the Asiatic continent.

> A Castilla y a León
> Nuevo mundo dió Colón,

is his epitaph in the cathedral of Seville.

Columbus's Egg : after the return of Columbus from his successful voyage of discovery he was invited to a banquet by Cardinal Mendoza. 'A shallow courtier present, impatient of the honours paid to Columbus, abruptly asked him whether he thought that in case he had not discovered the Indies, there were not other men in Spain who would have been capable of the enterprise. To this Columbus made no immediate reply, but taking an egg, invited the company to make it stand on end. Everyone attempted it, but in vain. Whereupon he struck it upon the table so as to break the end and left it standing on the broken part; illustrating in this simple manner that when he had once shown the way to the New World nothing was easier than to follow it.' (W. Irving, 'Life of Columbus', v. vii, on the authority of the Italian historian Benzoni; but the story, Prof. S. E. Morison states in 'The Atlantic Monthly' for Jan. 1942, occurs earlier, in a biography of the Italian architect Brunelleschi.)

COLUMELLA, LUCIUS JUNIUS MODERATUS, a native of Gades in Spain. He was a contemporary of Seneca and the author of a work (c. A.D. 65) on the various forms of agriculture, the keeping of livestock and bees, etc. The 'Columella' referred to by Jane Austen in 'Sense and Sensibility' is the hero of a tale by Richard Graves (q.v.).

COLVIN, Sir SIDNEY (1845–1927), educated at Trinity College, Cambridge, became Slade Professor of Fine Art at Cambridge (1873–85), and keeper of the prints and drawings at the British Museum (1884–1912). Besides numerous contributions to periodicals, chiefly on the history and criticism of art, he published lives of Walter Savage Landor (1881) and Keats (1887) in the English Men of Letters series; 'A Florentine Picture Chronicle' (1898); 'Early Engraving and Engravers in England' (1905); 'Drawings by Old Masters at Oxford' (1902–8). Colvin edited the 'Letters of Keats', 1887, the Edinburgh edition of R. L. Stevenson's works (1894–7), and the 'Letters of R. L. Stevenson' (1899 and 1911). He published 'John Keats, his Life and Poetry' in 1917, 'Memories and Notes of Persons and Places' in 1921.

Colyn Cloute, a satirical poem by Skelton (q.v.), directed against ecclesiastical abuses, and written about 1519. See also *Colin Clout.*

Comala, the title of one of the Ossianic poems of Macpherson (q.v.). Comala, daughter of Sarno, king of Inistore, is in love with Fingal, and follows him, disguised as a youth. Her romantic passion so much recommends her to the king that he is about to marry her, when the invasion of Caracul (Caracalla) intervenes. Comala sees the battle from a neighbouring hill, and on the victory of Fingal, dies from the revulsion to joy from terror.

COMBE, WILLIAM (1741–1823), educated at Eton, published a number of metrical satires, including 'The Diaboliad' (1776, directed against Simon, Lord Irnham). He is specially remembered for the verses that he wrote to accompany Rowlandson's drawings of the adventures of 'Dr. Syntax'. The first of these works, 'Dr. Syntax in search of the Picturesque', a parody of the popular books of picturesque travels of the day (and particularly of those of William Gilpin, q.v.), appeared in the 'Poetical Magazine' in 1809 (reprinted in 1812). Dr. Syntax is the grotesque figure of a clergyman and schoolmaster, who sets out during the holidays, on his old horse Grizzle, to 'make a Tour and Write It', and meets with a series of amusing misfortunes. This was followed in 1820 by 'The Second Tour of Dr. Syntax in search of Consolation' for the loss of his wife, and in 1821 by 'The Third Tour of Dr. Syntax in search of a Wife'. Combe also wrote the letterpress for Rowlandson's 'Dance of Death' (1815–16), 'Dance of Life' (1816), 'Johnny Quae Genus' (1822), and for 'The Microcosm of London' (1808).

Comberback, Silas Tomkyn, name assumed by S. T. Coleridge on joining the Dragoons.

Combray, the name used by Proust for the country town (Illiers, near Chartres) described in the early volumes of 'A la recherche du temps perdu' (q.v.).

Comédie humaine, La, see *Balzac.*

Comedy, from κωμῳδός = κωμαοιδός singer in the κῶμος or comic chorus, a stage play of a light and amusing character with a happy conclusion to its plot. Also, that branch of the drama which adopts a humorous or familiar style, and depicts laughable characters and incidents. [OED.] Greek comedy originated in the festivals of Dionysus (q.v.), celebrated with song and merriment at the vintage. See also *Sentimental Comedy.*

Comedy, The Divine, see *Divina Commedia.*

Comedy of Errors, The, a comedy by Shakespeare (q.v.), acted in 1594 (and perhaps as early as 1592), and first printed in the folio of 1623. This is one of the earliest and crudest of his plays and is, in the main, an adaptation of the 'Menaechmi' of Plautus.

Syracuse and Ephesus being at enmity, any Syracusan found in Ephesus is put to death unless he can pay a ransom of a thousand marks. Aegeon, an old Syracusan merchant, has been arrested in Ephesus, and on the duke's order explains how he came there. He and his wife Aemilia had twin sons, exactly alike and each named Antipholus; the parents had purchased twin slaves, also exactly alike, and each named Dromio, who attended on their sons. Having in a shipwreck been separated, with the younger son and one Dromio, from his wife and the other son and slave, Aegeon had never seen them since. The younger son (Antipholus of Syracuse) on reaching manhood had gone (with his Dromio) in search of his brother and mother and had no more been heard of, though Aegeon had now sought him for five years over the world, coming at last to Ephesus.

The duke, moved by this tale, gives Aegeon till evening to find the ransom. Now, the elder Antipholus (Antipholus of Ephesus), with one of the Dromios, has been living in Ephesus since his rescue from shipwreck and is married. Antipholus of Syracuse and the other Dromio have arrived there that very morning. Each twin retains the same confusing resemblance to his brother as in childhood. From this the comedy of errors results. Antipholus of Syracuse is summoned home to dinner by Dromio of Ephesus; he is claimed as husband by the wife of Antipholus of Ephesus, the latter being refused admittance to his own house, because he is supposed to be already within; and so forth. Finally Antipholus of Ephesus is confined as a lunatic, and Antipholus of Syracuse takes refuge from his brother's jealous wife in a convent.

Meanwhile evening has come and Aegeon is led to execution. As the duke proceeds to the place of execution, Antipholus of Ephesus appeals to him for redress. Then the abbess of the convent presents Antipholus of Syracuse, also claiming redress. The simultaneous presence of the two brothers explains the numerous misunderstandings. Aegeon recovers his two sons and his liberty, and the abbess turns out to be his lost wife, Aemilia.

COMESTOR, PETRUS, of Troyes, in Champagne, of the 12th cent., so named on account of his voracity in the matter of books. He was the author of a 'Historia Scholastica', a collection of scriptural narratives with commentary. His work was apparently known to Chaucer. Dante places him among the Doctors of the Church in the Heaven of the Sun, 'Paradiso', xii. 134.

Comhal, in Macpherson's Ossianic poems, the father of Fingal (q.v.).

Comical Revenge, The, or Love in a Tub, a comedy by Etherege (q.v.) acted in 1664, important as the first example of English prose comedy, as afterwards seen in Congreve and Sheridan; while the serious portions are written in rhymed heroics. The play shows the author's acquaintance with the early comedies of Molière.

The serious part of the plot deals with the rivalry of Lord Beaufort and Colonel Bruce for the hand of Graciana. A duel ensues. Bruce is defeated, tries to kill himself in despair, is cured of his wound, and consoled with Graciana's sister. The comic and farcical part has only a slender plot and centres about the French valet Dufoy, who for his impudence is confined by his fellow servants in a tub. His master, Sir Frederick Frolick, the fine gentleman of the times, is courted by a rich widow; he cajoles her out of £200 and finally marries her. There is a foolish country knight, Sir Nicholas Cully, whom two rogues cozen out of a thousand pounds. The knaves and the fool are exposed, and for punishment married off against their will and expectation.

COMINES, PHILIPPE DE, see *Commines*.

Coming of Arthur, The, the first of Tennyson's 'Idylls of the King' (q.v.), published in 1869.

Arthur, newly crowned and setting out to conquer his rebellious barons, sees and falls in love with Guinevere, daughter of King Leodegran of Cameliard; and after his success sends to ask her hand. Leodegran hesitates, owing to the mystery that surrounds the birth of Arthur, but after hearing the advice of Bellicent, wife of King Lot of Orkney, consents. Lancelot comes to fetch Guinevere, and Arthur and she are married. An indication is given of the purpose that Arthur sets before himself in his kingdom: to

Have power on this dark land to lighten it,
And power on this dead world to make it live.

Coming Race, The, a romance by Bulwer Lytton (q.v.), published in 1871.

The narrator describes his visit to a subterranean race that in distant ages took refuge from inundations in the bowels of the earth. Owing to the discovery of Vril, a form of energy embodying all the natural forces, this race has reached a high degree of civilization and scientific invention. Their country is a Utopia in which there is neither war nor crime, neither poverty nor inequality. The inhabitants regard with contempt the type of society which they describe as 'Koom-Posh— viz. the government of the ignorant upon the principle of being the most numerous', which leads to rivalry, misery, and degradation. Their women are physically stronger than their men, and it is the women who choose their spouses, a custom that involves the narrator in grave embarrassment and finally in danger of his life, from which he is saved by the devotion of his host's daughter and restored to the upper regions of the earth.

Commander of the Faithful, a title of the Caliphs (q.v.).

Commedia dell'Arte, in the history of Italian drama, improvised drama performed by professional actors, developed in the 16th cent. from the popular character comedy, and having its origin in the Atellan (q.v.) farces. It is said to have been invented by Francesco Cherea, a favourite actor of Pope Leo X.

COMMINES, PHILIPPE DE (*c.* 1445–1511), of a Flemish family, first served Philip of Burgundy and his son Charles the Bold, and then entered the service of the French king Louis XI, whose counsellor he became. He wrote remarkable chronicles of Louis XI and Charles VIII, which were translated into English by Thomas Danet (1596), and inspired Sir W. Scott's 'Quentin Durward' (q.v., in which Commines himself figures). Commines was the first critical and philosophical historian since classical times.

Common, DOL, a character in Jonson's 'The Alchemist' (q.v.).

Common Prayer, The Book of, was evolved in the 16th cent. to meet the popular need for aids to devotion (not entirely satisfied by the *Primers*, q.v.) and the demand for the use of the vernacular in church services. Its development was gradual. The Sarum breviary was reissued in 1541 and ordered to be used throughout the province of Canterbury in 1542. The reading in churches of a chapter of the Bible in English, and the Litany in English (probably the work of Cranmer, q.v.), were introduced in 1544, and an English communion service in 1548. About the same time the Primers were revised, and the King's Primer issued in 1545 in the interests of uniformity; it included the English Litany. Cranmer and a commission each drafted a scheme for a prayer book, and these were discussed in Edward VI's reign, leading to the successive issue of the Prayer Books of 1549 and 1552. In the latter the form of the Book of Common Prayer was practically settled, though a revision was made under Elizabeth (1559), minor changes under James I, and the final text is that of 1662. As it stands the Prayer Book represents largely the work of Cranmer; Nicholas Ridley (q.v.) may perhaps claim some share.

Common Prayer, The Revised Book of, embodied the proposals which, after prolonged discussion, the bishops, presided over by Archbishop Randall Davidson, laid before

Convocation in 1927. It consisted of the Prayer Book of 1662, with a permissive alternative version as regards Holy Communion, Baptism, Confirmation, and Matrimony, and numerous additional occasional prayers. Opposition arose in regard to the revision of the office for Holy Communion, and when the Revised Book was submitted to Parliament at the end of 1927, it was rejected by the House of Commons though passed by the House of Lords. It was again submitted in the following year with certain modifications, but again rejected.

Though without formal authority, the 1928 Book is available in editions for liturgical use. It is used in many churches, particularly for Baptisms, Marriages, and other occasional offices.

Common Sense school of philosophy, see *Reid (T.,* 1710–96).

Communism, a theory that advocates a state of society in which there should be no private ownership, all property being vested in the community and labour organized for the common benefit of all members, each working according to his capacity and receiving according to his wants. [OED.]

For the social order established in Russia by the Bolshevik party, see *Lenin.*

COMNENA and **COMNENUS,** see *Anna Comnena.*

Comparini, PIETRO and VIOLANTE, the putative parents of Pompilia, in Browning's 'The Ring and the Book' (q.v.).

Complaint, The, or Night Thoughts on Life, Death, and Immortality, see *Night Thoughts.*

Complaint of Buckingham, The, a poem by T. Sackville (q.v.), contributed by him to the 'Mirror for Magistrates' (q.v.).

Henry Stafford, duke of Buckingham, after his rebellion against Richard III, takes refuge with a dependant, Humfrey Banastaire. Banastaire betrays him to the king, and Buckingham is executed. As his corpse lies on the ground, it raises its head and heaps curses on Banastaire and his children.

Complaint of Deor, see *Deor.*

Complaynt to the King, see *Lindsay (Sir D.).*

Compleat Angler, The, or the Contemplative Man's Recreation, a discourse on fishing by I. Walton (q.v.), first published in 1653, the second edition in 1655. The fifth edition, containing Cotton's continuation, appeared in 1676.

It takes the form of a dialogue, at first between the author 'Piscator' (a fisherman), Auceps (a fowler), and Venator (a hunter), each commending his own recreation, in which Auceps is silenced, and Venator becomes a pupil of the angle; then between Piscator and Venator alone. In the course of this, after a short spell with the otter-hounds, the author instructs his pupil in the mode of catching all the various kinds of freshwater fish, with directions for dressing some of them for the table. There are observations on rivers and fish-ponds, and directions for the making of artificial flies and fishing-line. The instruction is given as they fish along the river Lea near London, and there are pleasant interludes of verse and song. But Walton, though a proficient angler, knew little of fly-fishing, and what he tells about it is admittedly in the main at second hand. The continuation, supplied by Charles Cotton (q.v.), takes the form of conversations between 'Piscator' and 'Viator' (a traveller, who turns out to be Venator of the earlier part), as they fish along the river Dove, which divides the counties of Derby and Stafford. 'Piscator' instructs 'Viator' in fishing 'fine and far off' for trout and grayling; and opportunities are taken to indicate the rocky and picturesque scenery of the district. There are also fuller directions for the making of artificial flies than had appeared in Walton's work.

Complutensian Polyglot Bible, THE, the earliest complete polyglot Bible, containing the Hebrew, Septuagint, and Vulgate texts, a Hebrew dictionary, etc., prepared at the expense of Cardinal Ximenes in the early part of the 16th cent., at Alcala in Spain (of which town *Complutum* is the ancient name). The special Greek type used has formed the basis of modern Greek type-design (Proctor types and others). It has been called the finest Greek type ever designed.

Composite Order, the most ornate order of Roman architecture, the capital combining the acanthus leaves of the Corinthian with the volutes of the Ionic orders.

COMPTON-BURNETT, IVY (1892–), a novelist whose stories are told within the strict conventions of her own style. The plots, often concerned with crime and violence in Edwardian upper middle class society, emerge mainly through the prolonged conversations of the characters. Her first novel, 'Dolores', appeared in 1911 and was followed by 'Pastors and Masters' in 1925, 'Men and Wives' (1931), 'A House and its Head' (1935), 'Parents and Children' (1941), 'Mother and Son' (1955), and many others.

COMTE, AUGUSTE (1798–1857), French philosopher, was in early life secretary to the socialist C. H. de Saint-Simon (q.v.), by whom he was influenced, but whom he subsequently repudiated. He was the chief exponent of the positivist philosophy, which excludes metaphysics and revealed religion, and substitutes the religion of humanity and sociological ethics, based on history and designed for the improvement of the human race. Comte's principal work was the 'Cours de Philosophie Positive' (1830–42), in which he worked out the three stages of knowledge, the theological, the metaphysical, and the positive, and classified the sciences according to their decreasing generality and increasing complexity: mathematics, astronomy, physics, chemistry, biology, sociology. In his later work, 'Système de Politique Positive' (1851–4), he attempted to frame a positivist religion which is a sort of parody of Roman Catholicism, with sacraments, prayers, etc. His principal English disciple was F. Harrison (q.v.), but he also influenced J. S. Mill (q.v.).

Comus, *A Masque, presented at Ludlow Castle, 1634, before the Earl of Bridgewater, Lord President of Wales,* by Milton (q.v.). Though described as a 'masque', it is strictly a pastoral entertainment.

This work was, like the 'Arcades' (q.v.), written at the request of Henry Lawes, the musician, while Milton was at Horton. The occasion was the celebration of the earl of Bridgewater's entry on the presidency of Wales and the Marches. The name 'Comus' was not included in the title in the first three printed editions, but is taken from one of the characters, a pagan god invented by Milton, son of Bacchus and Circe, who waylays travellers and tempts them to drink a magic liquor which changes their countenances into the faces of wild beasts. A lady and her two brothers are benighted in a forest. The lady, separated from her companions, and attracted by the revelry of Comus and his rout, comes upon Comus, in the guise of a shepherd, who offers to lodge her in his cottage, and leads her off. The brothers appear and are told what has happened by the good Attendant Spirit, who has taken the form of the shepherd Thyrsis. He warns them of the magic power of Comus and gives them the root of the plant Haemony as a protection. The scene changes, and Comus, with his rabble round him, is discovered pressing the lady to drink from a glass, while she, strong in her purity, resists his enticements. The brothers burst in and disperse the crew. Unfortunately they have not secured the wand of Comus, and are unable to release the lady from the enchanted chair in which she sits. Thyrsis thereupon invokes Sabrina, goddess of the neighbouring river Severn, who comes attended by water-nymphs, and frees the lady. After an ode of thanks to Sabrina, the lady and her brothers return safely to Ludlow Castle.

Conachar, in Scott's 'Fair Maid of Perth' (q.v.), the Highland apprentice of Simon Glover.

Conan, in the legends relating to Finn (Fingal), 'in some respects a kind of Thersites (q.v.), but brave and daring even to rashness' (Author's notes to 'Waverley'). Having visited the infernal regions, he received a cuff from the Arch-fiend, which he instantly returned with the words 'blow for blow'.

Conary, a poem by Ferguson (q.v.), published in 1880, and based on the old Irish bardic tale of the 'Destruction of the Guesthouse of Da Derga': Conary is a king of Ireland. Three lawless brothers banished for their crimes, and joined by the brothers of the king, roam the seas. They make a piratical raid on Ireland and attack the guesthouse, where the champions of Ireland are assembled under the king. Learning that the king himself is there, two of his brothers take their own lives; the third is killed. But Conall, the mighty champion, is led away by fairies, and Conary, left almost alone, is killed.

Conchobar or CONCHUBAR, in the Ulster cycle of Irish mythology, king of Ulster. See *Cuchulain* and *Deirdre*.

Conciliation with America, *Speech on,* by E. Burke (q.v.), made in the House of Commons on 22 March 1775.

This was a last effort by Burke to find a peaceful solution of the difference with the American colonies, and is one of his greatest speeches, and a literary masterpiece. Burke's proposal is to restore order and repose to the empire 'by restoring the former unsuspecting confidence of the colonies in the mother country'. He rejects the use of force, as temporary and uncertain in its effects, as impairing what it is sought to preserve, as contrary to experience in our colonial administration, and as inapplicable to the 'fierce spirit of liberty' prevailing in the English colonies. He traces the 'capital sources' from which this spirit has grown up, descent, religion, remoteness of situation; and propounds three alternatives, to change this spirit, to prosecute it as criminal, to comply with it as necessary. He shows the first two courses to be impossible or inexpedient. He dismisses American representation in parliament as impracticable. He finds the solution in the taxation of America through grants by the local legislatures and not by imposition. His trust is in America's interest in the British constitution: 'My hold of the colonies is in the close affection which grows from common names, from kindred blood, from similar privileges, and equal protection.' 'Freedom they can have from none but you. This is the commodity of price, of which you have the monopoly.' 'Magnanimity in politics is not seldom the truest wisdom; and a great empire and little minds go ill together.'

Concordat, an agreement between Church and State, especially between the Roman See and a secular government relative to matters that concern both. One of the most famous of such agreements was that made in 1801 between Napoleon and Pius VII.

Condell, HENRY, see *Heming*.

CONDORCET, JEAN ANTOINE NICOLAS CARITAT, *Marquis de* (1743–94), see *Philosophes*.

Conduct of the Allies . . ., *The,* title of a pamphlet by Swift (q.v.), composed in Nov. 1711 in favour of peace.

Confederacy, *The,* a comedy by Vanbrugh (q.v.), produced in 1705, adapted from d'Ancourt's 'Les Bourgeoises à la mode'.

Gripe and Moneytrap, two rich usurers, are niggardly husbands, and Gripe's wife, Clarissa, in order to pay her debts, is obliged to pawn her necklace with Mrs. Amlet, a seller of paint and powder and the like to ladies. Mrs. Amlet has a knave of a son, Dick, who passes himself off as a colonel, and is trying to win by fair means or foul the hand of Gripe's daughter Corinna, assisted in the plot by his confederate Brass, who acts as his footman, and by Flippanta, Clarissa's maid. Meanwhile Gripe falls in love with Money-trap's wife, and Moneytrap falls in love with Gripe's wife. This the ladies communicate to each other and contrive to turn to their mutual advantage. By their directions, Brass and Flippanta, who act as go-betweens, extract two hundred and fifty pounds apiece from the would-be lovers to relieve their ladies' immediate necessities. An amusing scene follows in which the two couples are at tea together, very cheerful, each of the four pleased with the course of events, when the pawned necklace brings about a general exposure. Clarissa has told her husband that she has lost it, and he has warned the goldsmiths to look out for it. Dick has stolen it from his mother and sent Brass to try and sell it. The goldsmith to whom Brass offers it now brings it to Gripe. Dick's true character and the pawning of the necklace are thus brought to light. Clarissa, to silence her husband, alludes to the £250 given to Mrs. Moneytrap; and the latter, to silence hers, to the like present to Clarissa. However, as Corinna is prepared to take Dick in spite of all, and Mrs. Amlet to endow him with £10,000, roguery meets with some measure of success.

Confederate States of America, the name assumed by the eleven Southern States (Virginia, Georgia, North and South Carolina, Alabama, Tennessee, Louisiana, Arkansas, Mississippi, Florida, Texas) which seceded from the American Union in 1860–1 and formed a confederacy. After their defeat in the Civil War (q.v., 1865) they were forced into reunion with the Northern States.

Confederation of the Rhine, the union of certain German states under the protection of the French Empire from 1806 to 1813; it was an interesting reversion to the policy of Cardinal Richelieu (q.v.).

***Confessio Amantis,** The,* is the principal English poem of Gower (q.v.). It exists in three versions completed probably between 1386 and 1390. The first version is dedicated to Richard II, the second to Henry IV. Caxton's edition (1483) follows the second version and is the basis of Professor Morley's text (1888). This version omits passages in praise of Richard II and Chaucer that had appeared in the first. The poem contains 34,000 lines in short couplets.

The poet tells how he, a lover weary of life, appealed to Venus, who required him to make full confession to Genius, her priest.

This the lover does, and the priest instructs him concerning each of the seven deadly sins and its remedy, exemplifying each point with one or more stories. Venus reappears, shows the poet his grey hairs in a mirror, and dismisses him from her court as too old for love, giving him a pair of black beads marked 'pour reposer'. The stories are taken from classical and medieval sources and include the tale of Florent (told also by Chaucer's 'Wife of Bath') and that of Constance (Chaucer's 'Man of Lawes Tale'). The poem shows the influence of Chaucer, and the language is substantially the same as his.

Confession of Rakow, see *Socinianism.*

Confessions, see *Augustine* and *Rousseau.*

Confessions of an English Opium Eater, by De Quincey (q.v.), published in 1822 (enlarged edition 1856).

This book, which established De Quincey's literary reputation, after an account of his early years and his rambling life in Wales, relates how he was led by physical suffering and nervous irritation first to take opium, and then to increase his consumption of it, until he reached the large quantity of 8,000 drops of laudanum a day. He describes the fearful effects, chiefly in the form of tumultuous dreams, brought about by this abuse of the drug, continued during eight years, until, alarmed at the prospect of imminent death, he determined to conquer the habit. The narrative ends with the account of the gradual reduction that he effected in his daily dose, a reduction itself attended by great suffering, but finally in the main successful.

Confessions of an Enquiring Spirit, see *Coleridge (S. T.).*

Confucius, the Latinized form of K'ung Fu-tzu (551–479 B.C.), meaning 'Master K'ung', who has been revered by the Chinese as their greatest sage.

He was born in the state of Lu in present-day Shantung. Little is known for certain about his life. He felt that the remedy for the moral and political evils of a divided China lay in conserving the culture of the sage founders of the Chou dynasty (1030–256 B.C.). Failing to secure acceptance of his doctrines at any of the courts he visited, he became a teacher of moral and political wisdom, mainly to young men who were potential statesmen. He has been revered not only for his lofty ideals, but also because he was traditionally (but mistakenly) regarded as author or editor of the oldest among the Thirteen Classics, which later provided China with her staple educational diet and became required reading for aspirants to the mandarinate. This heterogeneous corpus of history, poetry, ethics, and works on ritual, divination, etc. includes the *Analects,* which contains the most authentic of the Master's sayings, and the *Book of Mencius,* comprising the teachings of the most famous later Confucian.

CONFUCIANISM became systematized during the Han dynasty (206 B.C. to A.D. 220). Despite the rivalry of Taoism (q.v.) and Buddhism (which entered China in the 1st cent. A.D.), it formed the dominant ideology of China throughout most of its history down to the close of the empire in 1911. Dominating the educational system, it moulded moral beliefs and political practices. Although Confucius's own teachings were entirely secular and largely concerned with goodness, justice, loyalty, filial piety, and other virtues practised in human relationships, a cult of Confucius developed. The term Confucianism has sometimes also been loosely applied to religious practices coloured by Confucianist ritual (e.g. ancestor-worship) or sponsored by the Confucian state (e.g. the religious functions of the Emperor).

CONGREVE, WILLIAM (1670–1729), born at Bardsey, near Leeds, of an ancient family. Owing to the fact of his father's commanding the garrison at Youghal, he was educated at Kilkenny school and Trinity College, Dublin, at both of which he was a fellow student of Swift. He entered the Middle Temple, but soon gave up law for literature, published a feeble novel of intrigue, 'Incognita' (1692), and in 1693 suddenly achieved fame by his comedy 'The Old Bachelor' (q.v.). Of his other comedies, 'The Double Dealer' (q.v.) appeared in 1694, 'Love for Love' (q.v.) in 1695, and 'The Way of the World' (q.v.) in 1700. In these Congreve shows himself the supreme master of the artificial comedy or comedy of manners, displaying the narrow world of fashion and gallantry. His one tragedy 'The Mourning Bride' (q.v.) was produced in 1697. He replied in that year to the attack made on him in the 'Short View' of Jeremy Collier (q.v.). Congreve gave up writing for the stage in consequence, it is said, of the comparative failure of his last comedy. But he was then in moderately affluent circumstances, holding more than one government post, and enjoying general admiration and the friendship of men like Swift, Steele, and Pope. He was visited by Voltaire, and was closely attached to the duchess of Marlborough. He was throughout the friend of the enchanting Mrs. Bracegirdle (q.v.). He was buried in Westminster Abbey.

Coningsby, or The New Generation, a political novel by Disraeli (q.v.), published in 1844.

The background of the story is formed by the political events from the passage of the Reform Bill in 1832 down to the fall of the Melbourne ministry in 1841. These provide the author with opportunity for expounding his own political creed, his contempt for the Conservatism without principles which he attributed to the party of Peel; his hostility to the Whigs and Utilitarianism; his condemnation of the new poor law and the unimaginative treatment of the peasantry. The existing system of government with its self-seeking politicians like Rigby, and its Tadpoles and Tapers (the typical party wire-pullers), must be amended, and the representation of the people obtained. Against this background we have the story of the early life of Harry Coningsby, a generous and intelligent lad, the orphan grandson of the wealthy marquess of Monmouth. Young Coningsby, whose parents had incurred Lord Monmouth's displeasure by their marriage, is now restored to his grandfather's favour, and sent to Eton, where he becomes the friend and saves the life of Oswald Millbank, son of a rich Lancashire manufacturer, who is Lord Monmouth's bitterest enemy. The story traces Coningsby's career at Eton and Cambridge, the development of political views contrary to those of his grandfather, and his falling in love with Edith, the daughter of Millbank. The discovery by Lord Monmouth of these deplorable tendencies in his grandson leads to a crisis in the hero's fortunes. On the death of Lord Monmouth it is found that Coningsby has been disinherited. He bravely renounces his life of ease and sets to work as a barrister. But Millbank, the manufacturer, who had been no less hostile than Lord Monmouth to Coningsby's marriage with Edith, impressed by the young man's proof of character, now relents, and the story ends with Coningsby's election to parliament for Millbank's constituency, his marriage to Edith, and his restoration to fortune.

Lord Monmouth is drawn from the same Lord Hertford who provided the model for Thackeray's Lord Steyne (q.v.), but without the latter's more repellent features. Rigby is a caricature of Croker (q.v.). Sidonia, the Jew superman, who figures again in 'Tancred' (q.v.), here makes his first appearance.

Conington, JOHN (1825–69), educated at Rugby and Magdalen College, Oxford, and fellow of University College, Oxford, was the first professor of Latin at Oxford (1854–69). He edited Virgil and Persius, published verse translations of Horace (1863–9), the 'Aeneid' (1866), and half the 'Iliad' (1868).

Connecticut Wits, see *Hartford Wits.*

Connoisseur, The, a periodical conducted in 1754–6 by George Colman the elder and Bonnell Thornton, contained some early papers by W. Cowper (q.v.).

CONNOLLY, CYRIL (1903–), became a journalist and regular contributor to the 'New Statesman' and from 1942 to 1943 was literary editor of the 'Observer'. He founded the literary review 'Horizon' with Stephen Spender in 1939. His one novel, 'The Rock Pool', was published in 1935, and collections of essays have appeared later, including 'Enemies of Promise' (1938), 'The Unquiet Grave' (1944), 'The Condemned Playground' (1944), and 'Ideas and Places' (1953).

Conquest of Granada, The, or Almanzor and Almahide, a heroic play in rhymed couplets, in two parts, by Dryden (q.v.). It appeared in 1670.

The play was very famous in its day, and besides much rant and bombast, contains some good verse and pleasant lyrics. It was one of the principal objects of satire in the 'Rehearsal' (q.v.). The plot is much embroiled and not worth giving in detail. The background is the quarrels of the rival factions of Moors, the Abencerrages and the Zegrys, under Boabdelin the last ruler of the kingdom of Granada, and the war in which that kingdom fell to Ferdinand and Isabella. Almanzor is a valiant soldier who aids the Moors against the Spaniards, but finally turns out to be the long-lost son of the duke of Arcos, a noble Spaniard. Almahide is the betrothed of Boabdelin, with whom Almanzor falls in love. She returns his love, but is faithful to her promise to Boabdelin, who throughout the play is torn between jealousy of Almanzor and need for his strong arm. Almanzor's suit remains unsuccessful until after the death of Boabdelin in the last act. A second love interest is provided by the rivalry of Abdalla, the king's brother, and Abdelmelich, chief of the Abencerrages, for the hand of the imperious Lyndaraxa, sister of the chief of the Zegrys; and a third, by the troubled course of the love of Ozmyn, a brave young Abencerrage, for Benzayda, a Zegry maiden.

Conquest of Granada, The, a romantic history in satirical vein, by Washington Irving (q.v.), published in 1829.

Conrad, the pirate chief in Lord Byron's 'The Corsair' (q.v.).

CONRAD, JOSEPH (1857–1924), whose full name was Teodor Josef Konrad Korzeniowski, was born of Polish parents in the Ukraine. He accompanied his parents when they were exiled (in consequence of revolutionary activities) to Vologda in Northern Russia, where his mother died; was subsequently for a time at school at Cracow; and in 1874 became member of the crew of a French vessel, thus satisfying a long-felt craving for a seafaring life. In 1878 he joined an English merchant ship, and in 1884 gained his Board of Trade certificate as a Master and was naturalized as a British subject. He left the sea in 1894 and devoted himself to literature.

The sea provides the setting of most of his works, and his devotion to it is seen at its best in his 'Mirror of the Sea' (1906). His earlier novels, 'Almayer's Folly' (1895) and 'An Outcast of the Islands' (1896), reveal Conrad struggling with the difficulties of a language and a technique unfamiliar to him. But he achieved success in 'The Nigger of the Narcissus' (1898), and 'Lord Jim' (1900), the tale of a young Englishman who in a moment of panic deserts his apparently sinking ship, loses his honour, and finally retrieves it by an honourable death. In 'Youth', 'Heart of Darkness', and 'Typhoon' (1902) Conrad

produced three of his finest short stories. Among his other best-known works were 'Nostromo' (1904), 'The Secret Agent' (1907), 'Under Western Eyes' (1911), 'Chance' (1914), 'Within the Tides' (1915), and 'The Rescue' (1920).

Conrade of Montserrat, a character in Scott's 'The Talisman' (q.v.), based on the historical Conrad of Montferrat.

Conscience, MR., in Bunyan's 'The Holy War' (q.v.), the Recorder of the city of Mansoul, deposed from his office during the tyranny of Diabolus.

Conscious Lovers, The, a comedy by Steele (q.v.), based on the 'Andria' of Terence, produced in 1722. This was Steele's last play, and in it he illustrates his views on duelling, the proper attitude of men to women, etc.

Young Bevil is, at his father's desire, about to marry Lucinda, daughter of the wealthy Mr. Sealand. But he has fallen in love with Indiana, an orphan, whom he has found destitute and friendless in a foreign town and has honourably supported; she loves him in return. Not wishing openly to oppose his father's wishes, he makes known to Lucinda his aversion to the proposed marriage, the more readily because his friend Myrtle loves her, while she is also sued by an avaricious pedant, Cimberton. In doing this he offends Myrtle, is challenged to a duel, declines, and exhibits the folly of duelling. Indiana turns out to be the lost daughter, by a former marriage, of Mr. Sealand, who is happy to bestow her on Bevil in place of Lucinda. As the latter's dowry is now halved in consequence of the discovery of her sister, Cimberton renounces his suit, and Myrtle successfully asserts his claim.

Conscript Fathers, a collective title by which the Roman senators were addressed; used also as a title by the Venetian senate.

CONSTABLE, HENRY (1562–1613), was educated at St. John's College, Cambridge, embraced Roman Catholicism, and withdrew to Paris. He published 'Diana', a volume of sonnets, in 1592; it was republished in 1594 with additions, many of them by other poets. He was sent as papal envoy to Edinburgh in 1599 and pensioned by the French king. He came to London in 1603, was imprisoned in the Tower in 1604 and released the same year. He died at Liège. Verses by him were embodied in various collections, among others in 'England's Helicon' (q.v.). His collected works were published in 1859. Many of his sonnets are modelled on or translated from sonnets by Desportes.

Constable, JOHN (1776–1837), landscape painter, born at East Bergholt, Suffolk, the son of a miller. He entered the Academy Schools in 1799, but was largely self-taught. He was elected a Royal Academician in 1829. His interest in transient effects of light and his rural subjects, often with East Anglian settings, departed from the standards of classical landscape, and his genius at first met with little recognition in England, though he had considerable success in Paris, being acclaimed by Delacroix (q.v.) and influencing the Barbizon School (q.v.). 'The Life of John Constable' by his friend C. R. Leslie, R.A., was published in 1843 (ed. A. Shirley, 1937).

Constance, (1) the heroine of 'The Man of Lawes Tale' in 'The Canterbury Tales' (q.v.); (2) in Shakespeare's 'King John' (q.v.), the mother of Arthur, the king's nephew.

Constance of Beverley, a character in Scott's 'Marmion' (q.v.).

Constant, a character in Vanbrugh's 'The Provok'd Wife' (q.v.).

Constant Couple, The, *or a Trip to the Jubilee,* a comedy by Farquhar (q.v.), produced in 1700.

The play, which is coarse and farcical, was very successful, owing chiefly to the amusing character of Sir Harry Wildair, 'an airy gentleman, affecting humorous gaiety and freedom in his behaviour'. It had a less successful sequel in 'Sir Harry Wildair' (1701).

CONSTANT DE REBECQUE, BENJA-MIN (1767–1830), French novelist, philosopher, politician, and orator, born at Lausanne of a family of French Protestant refugees, had his university education in Germany (Erlangen) and at Edinburgh. He was intermittently in Paris after 1795, but was exiled by Napoleon. His political career began after the Restoration. He is remembered partly by the political and religious treatises of 'De la religion considerée dans sa source . . .' (1824–31), but much more by his short novel of psychological analysis, 'Adolphe' (first published in London in 1816) and by his intellectual and passionate friendships with women, notably Mme de Charrière and Mme de Staël (qq.v.). At many points 'Adolphe' reflects his own liaison with Mme de Staël.

Constantia Durham, a character in Meredith's 'The Egoist' (q.v.).

Constantine the Great, Roman Emperor, A.D. 306–37. He was converted to Christianity, it is said, by seing a luminous cross in the sky with the words ἐν τούτῳ νίκα (*in hoc signo vinces*) before the battle (312) in which he defeated his rival Maxentius. He transferred the capital of the empire to Byzantium, which he renamed Constantinople. See *Helena (Saint), Eusebius, Donation of Constantine, Labarum.*

Contarini Fleming, *a Psychological Romance,* by Disraeli (q.v.), published in 1832.

The book takes the form of an autobiography, showing the development of a poetic character. Contarini Fleming is the son of a Saxon nobleman and a Venetian lady of ancient lineage. A child of an imaginative and melancholy disposition, he is wretched at school, from which he runs away, and is introduced into social and political life, for which he shows precocious aptitude, by his father, who has a sympathetic understanding of his peculiar temperament. His first attempts at literature are crude or ill-judged. He realizes the chief desire of his youth by visiting Venice, where he falls madly in love with a cousin, Alceste Contarini, whom he marries, but loses within a year. He then travels in Spain and the Levant, finally takes up his abode in Rome, and devotes himself to 'the amelioration of his kind' and 'the study and creation of the beautiful'.

Contemporary Review, The, was founded in 1865, and edited for many years by Sir Percy Bunting.

Continental system, THE, the plan of Napoleon Buonaparte for cutting off Great Britain from all connexion with the Continent, by forbidding to his subjects and allies the importation of British goods. This was proclaimed by the 'Berlin Decree' of 19 Nov. 1806.

Conversation, *A complete Collection of polite and ingenious,* by Swift (q.v.), published in 1738.

In this entertaining work Swift good-humouredly satirizes the stupidity, coarseness, and attempted wit of the conversation of fashionable people as he had observed it. In three dialogues he puts into the mouth of various characters, Lord Sparkish, Miss Notable, Lady Smart, Tom Neverout, etc., samples of questions and answers, proverbial sayings, and repartees, fitted, as he explains in the amusing introduction, 'to adorn every kind of discourse that an assembly of English ladies and gentlemen, met together for their mutual entertainment, can possibly want'. The work was published under the pseudonym of 'Simon Wagstaff, Esq.'

COOK, ELIZA (1818–89), poet. Her complete collected poems were published in 1870. The most popular of these was 'The Old Arm Chair', which had appeared in 1837. She conducted 'Eliza Cook's Journal', 1849–54.

COOK, JAMES (1728–79), the celebrated circumnavigator, published his 'Sailing Directions' in 1766–8. He left records of his three principal voyages: the first, round the Horn and the Cape of Good Hope, 1768–71 (an account of this was compiled by J. Hawkesworth from the journals of Cook and his botanist Joseph Banks, q.v., and published in 1773; Cook's own journal was edited by Wharton in 1893); the second, 'A Voyage towards the South Pole and round the World in 1772–5', published in 1777; the third, 'A Voyage to the Pacific Ocean in 1776–80', published in 1784 (the third volume by Capt. T. King). Cook touched at Hawaii in 1779, was driven off by a storm, and on putting back to refit was murdered by the natives.

Cook's Tale, The, see *Canterbury Tales.*

Cooling Card, apparently a term of some unknown game, applied figuratively to anything that 'cools' a person's passion or enthusiasm. The expression is frequent in Elizabethan literature, e.g. in Lyly's 'Euphues' and Shakespeare's '1 Henry VI', v. iii. 84.

COOPER, JAMES FENIMORE (1789–1851), born in New Jersey, spent his youth partly on the family estate at Cooperstown on Otsego Lake (N.Y.), partly in the merchant marine (after dismissal from Yale), partly in the American navy. He then settled down as a country proprietor and a writer of novels. His second book 'The Spy' (1821), a stirring tale of the American Revolution, brought him into prominence. He travelled abroad in Europe with his family, 1826–33. His other best-known works are: 'The Pioneers' (1823), 'The Pilot' (1823) and 'The Red Rover' (1827), two notable early tales of adventure at sea; 'The Last of the Mohicans' (1826), 'The Prairie' (1827), 'The Pathfinder' (1840), and 'The Deerslayer' (1841). The last four, with 'The Pioneers', form a series, 'The Leatherstocking Tales', dealing with Indian life in the forest and the wilderness, and centring in the adventures of Natty Bumppo; they furnish not only exciting incidents, but a vivid picture of the Red Indian and his surroundings in a period that has passed away. Cooper's 'England, with Sketches of Society in the Metropolis', a sarcastic account of English society, appeared in 1837. He was also, however, deeply critical of American democracy, and expressed his conservative opinions directly in 'The American Democrat' (1838) and fictionally in 'Homeward Bound' and 'Home as Found' (1838). Among his many other works, the scholarly 'History of the Navy of the United States' (1839), 'Satanstoe' (1845), a fine historical novel of manners, and 'The Crater' (1848), a Utopian romance, could be mentioned to illustrate his fertility and variety.

Cooper's Hill, see *Denham*.

Copenhagen, the duke of Wellington's famous horse, which carried him in the Peninsular War and at Waterloo.

Copenhagen, THE BOMBARDMENT OF, by Nelson (under Sir Hyde Parker) in 1801, was undertaken in order to break up the Northern Confederacy (Russia, Sweden, and Denmark) against Britain. It was in the course of this that Nelson, placing his telescope to his blind eye, declared that he could not see the signal of recall hoisted by Admiral Parker.

Copernicus, latinized form of the surname of NICOLAS KOPPERNIK (1473–1543), a native of Thorn in Prussian Poland and a canon of Frauenburg, a celebrated astronomer, who propounded the theory that the planets including the earth move in orbits round the sun as centre, in opposition to the older theory of Ptolemy (q.v.) that the sun and planets move round the earth. His 'De revolutionibus' was published in 1543, but a brief popular account of his theory was circulated in manuscript from 1530.

Cophetua, KING, a legendary king in Africa, who cared not for womankind, until he saw a beggar maid 'all in gray', with whom he fell in love. He married her and together they lived 'a quiet life during their princely reign'. The tale is told in one of the ballads included in Percy's 'Reliques', where the maid's name is given as Penelophon. Shakespeare in 'Love's Labour's Lost' (IV. i) gives it as Zenelophon. There are other references to the story in Shakespeare's 'Romeo and Juliet' (II. i) and '2 Henry IV' (v. iii), in Jonson's 'Every Man in his Humour' (III. iv), and in Tennyson's 'The Beggar Maid'.

Copmanhurst, CLERK OF, otherwise Friar Tuck (q.v.), in Scott's 'Ivanhoe' (q.v.).

COPPARD, ALFRED EDGAR (1878–1957), short story writer and poet. He was almost entirely self-educated, having become a shop-boy at the age of 9, and began writing while an accountant at Oxford. His collections of stories include: 'Adam and Eve and Pinch Me' (1921), 'Clorinda Walks in Heaven' (1922), 'Fishmonger's Fiddle' (1925), and 'The Dark-Eyed Lady' (1947). His 'Collected Poems' were published in 1928 and 'Cherry Ripe' in 1935.

Copt, a native Egyptian Christian belonging to the Jacobite sect (Monophysites, q.v., who take their name from Jacobus Baradaeus of Edessa, a 6th-cent. heresiarch). The word is probably a form of Αἰγύπτιος (Egyptian), though some refer it to *Coptos*, the name of an ancient city in Upper Egypt. Coptic, a descendant of ancient Egyptian, has become a dead language, but is much studied because there are Coptic versions of the Scriptures.

Copyright, *see* Appendix II.

Coranto, or current of news, the name applied to periodical news-pamphlets issued between 1621 and 1641 (their publication was interrupted between 1632 and 1638) containing foreign intelligence taken from foreign papers. The Corantos were one of the first forms of English journalism, and were followed by the 'newsbook' (q.v.).

CORANTO or COURANTE was also the name of a dance formerly in vogue, distinguished by a running or gliding step.

Corbaccio, a character in Jonson's 'Volpone' (q.v.).

CORBETT (or CORBET), RICHARD (1582–1635) was the son of Vincent Corbet, a Surrey gardener, of whom Ben Jonson said in an elegy 'His mind as pure and neatly kept As were his nourseries . . .'. Richard was educated at Westminster and Christ Church, Oxford, became chaplain to James I and, later, bishop first of Oxford and then of Norwich. He was generous, witty, and eloquent, and his poetry—'Certain Elegant Poems' (1647) and 'Poetica Stromata; or a collection of sundry peices in poetry' (1648)—ranges from the entertaining traveller's story of 'Iter Boreale' and the ironical verses on 'The Distracted Puritane' to the charming little poem 'To his son, Vincent Corbet' on his third birthday. He also addressed some amusing lines to Thomas Coryate (q.v.) after the latter's return from his journey in France, Savoy, Italy, etc. He pronounced the funeral oration for Sir Thomas Bodley (q.v.).

Corceca, in Spenser's 'Faerie Queene', I. iii. 18, 'blindness of heart', an old blind woman, mother of Abessa (Superstition).

Cordelia, in Shakespeare's 'King Lear' (q.v.), the youngest daughter of the king.

Cordelier, a Franciscan friar of the strict rule, so called from the knotted cord worn round the waist. The 'Cordeliers' was the name of a political club in the French Revolution, which met in an old convent of this order. It included Danton and Marat among its members, and represented the most advanced revolutionary faction. See *Jacobin.*

Cordon Bleu, the sky-blue ribbon worn by the Knights Grand Cross of the French order of the Holy Ghost, the highest order of chivalry under the Bourbon kings. The name is extended to a person distinguished in his profession, e.g. to a first-class cook.

Cordova, GONSALVO HERNANDEZ DE (1453–1515), a famous Spanish general known as the 'Great Captain', who, under Ferdinand the Catholic, fought against Portugal and the Moors, and drove the French out of Naples. See *Bayard.*

Corduba, Cordova in Spain, the birthplace of the two Senecas and Lucan (qq.v.).

CORELLI, MARIE, pen-name of MARY MACKAY (1855–1924), popular novelist of her day. Her publications include: 'A Romance of Two Worlds' (1886), 'Barabbas' (1893), 'Sorrows of Satan' (1895), 'The Mighty Atom' (1896), 'The Master Christian' (1900), 'Temporal Power' (1902), 'The Young Diana' (1917), 'The Secret Power' (1921).

Corflambo, in Spenser's 'Faerie Queene', IV. vii and viii, 'a mighty man, Ryding upon a Dromedare on hie, Of stature huge and horrible of hew', symbolizes lust. He carries off Amoret, who is released from him by Timias and Belphoebe. He is slain by Prince Arthur.

CORIAT, THOMAS, see *Coryate.*

Corineus, see *Gogmagog.*

Corinna, (1) a Greek poetess of Tanagra in Boeotia of the 6th c. B.C. She is said to have given instruction to Pindar; (2) Ovid's flame.

Corinne, the title of a novel by Mme de Staël (q.v.).

Corinthian, from the proverbial luxury and licentiousness of ancient Corinth, a gay licentious man.

'I am . . . a Corinthian, a lad of mettle, a good boy.'
(Shakespeare, '1 Henry IV', II. iv. 13.)

In the first half of the 19th cent., 'Corinthian' was used for a man of fashion about town.

It was applied by M. Arnold to an over-brilliant literary style.

Corinthian Order, one of the orders of classical architecture, more ornate than Doric and Ionic, having capitals decorated with acanthus leaves.

Corinthian Tom, a character in Pierce Egan's 'Life in London'. See *Egan.*

Corinthians, THE, a well-known amateur Association Football club, founded in 1882.

Coriolanus, a Roman historical drama, by Shakespeare (q.v.), probably written about 1608. It was printed in the folio of 1623. The story is taken from North's Plutarch.

Caius Marcius, a proud Roman general, performs wonders of valour in a war against the Volscians, and captures the town Corioli, receiving in consequence the surname Coriolanus. On his return it is proposed to make him consul, but his arrogant and outspoken contempt of the Roman rabble makes him unpopular with the fickle crowd, and the tribunes of the people have no difficulty in securing his banishment. He betakes himself to the house of Aufidius, the Volscian general, his enemy of long standing, is received with delight, and leads the Volscians against Rome to effect his revenge. He reaches the walls of the city, and the Romans, to save it from destruction, send emissaries, old friends of Coriolanus, to propose terms, but in vain. Finally the mother, wife, and son of Coriolanus come and beseech him to spare the city. He yields to their prayers, makes a treaty favourable to the Volscians, and returns with them to Antium, a Volscian town. Here the Volscian general turns against him, accusing him of betraying the Volscian interests, and with the assistance of conspirators of his faction, slays Coriolanus in a public place.

Cormac, in the Ossianic poems of Macpherson (q.v.), the king of Ireland during whose minority Cuthullin commands the Irish forces, Swaran invades Ireland, and Fingal comes to the rescue. Cormac is murdered by Cairbar.

Cormoran, a Cornish giant slain by Jack the Giant-killer.

Corn Laws, THE, restricting the importation of foreign corn, were a subject of acute controversy during the first half of the 19th cent. The principal of these, Robinson's Act of 1815, permitted importation only when the price of wheat reached 80s. a quarter. A sliding-scale act was passed in 1828. The Corn Law was abolished by Peel in 1846, as a consequence of the agitation of the Anti-Corn Law League of Bright and Cobden, the distress prevalent in England, and the Irish famine of 1845.

CORNEILLE, PIERRE (1606–84), French dramatist. He was in his early days one of the group of authors who wrote plays under the direction of the Cardinal de Richelieu. His genius was first shown in his tragedy

'Médée' (1635), followed by his masterpiece 'Le Cid' (q.v., 1637), based on a Spanish play concerning the youth of that hero. The other great works by which he founded classical tragedy in France were 'Horace' and 'Cinna' (1640), 'Polyeucte' (1641?), 'La Mort de Pompée' (1643?), and 'Rodogune' (1644?). His fine comedy 'Le Menteur' (1643) is adapted from the Spanish of Alarcón. His later plays are less important, and he was eclipsed by the growing fame of Racine. The characteristic of his tragedies is the nobility and grandeur of his heroes and heroines and the dignity of his style, often declamatory, sometimes rising to passionate ardour, and marked here and there by splendid lines. 17th-cent. English translators of Corneille include Mrs. Katherine Philips (q.v.), the 'Matchless Orinda'.

Cornelia, 'Mother of the Gracchi' (2nd cent. B.C.), was the daughter of Publius Scipio Africanus the elder. She married Tiberius Sempronius Gracchus and became mother of the famous tribunes, Tiberius and Gaius. When a lady once made a show of her jewels at Cornelia's house, and asked to see Cornelia's, the latter produced her two sons, saying 'These are my jewels'.

Cornelia, the wife of Pompey in Kyd's tragedy 'Pompey the Great' (q.v.); also in Masefield's 'Tragedy of Pompey the Great'.

Cornhill, in the city of London, 'a corn-market time out of mind', says Stow. Here there were stocks and a pillory.

Cornhill Magazine, The, a monthly periodical, was founded in 1860 with Thackeray (q.v.) as first editor. His last two novels, 'The Adventures of Philip' and 'Denis Duval', were published in it, as were also contributions from Ruskin and Matthew Arnold, Mrs. Gaskell's 'Cousin Phillis' and 'Wives and Daughters', and some of Trollope's novels. Sir Leslie Stephen (q.v.) was editor from 1871 to 1882, and subsequently James Payn, J. St. Loe Strachey, and R. J. Smith. 'Our storehouse being in Cornhill', writes Thackeray in the preface to the first number, 'we date and name our magazine from its place of publication.'

Corn-law Rhymer, see *Elliott (E.).*

Cornubia, a Roman name for Cornwall.

Cornucopia, see *Amalthea.*

CORNWALL, BARRY, see *Procter (B. W.).*

Corny, KING, Cornelius O'Shane, 'King of the Black Islands', a character in Maria Edgeworth's 'Ormond' (q.v.).

Coronach (from the Irish *coranach*, Gaelic *corranach*), a funeral dirge.

Corōnis, (1) the daughter of Phlegias, loved by Apollo, by whom she became mother of Aesculapius (q.v.); (2) the daughter of Phoroneus, king of Phocis, who was changed by Athene into a crow.

Corot, JEAN-BAPTISTE CAMILLE (1796–1875), French landscape-painter, associated with the Barbizon School (q.v.).

Corporate, CHRISTOPHER, in Peacock's 'Melincourt' (q.v.), the solitary elector of the borough of Onevote, which returns two members to parliament.

Corposant, see *Elmo's Fire.*

Corpus Christi, the Feast of the Blessed Sacrament or Body of Christ, observed on the Thursday after Trinity Sunday. It was instituted by Pope Urban IV about 1264, and at many places (e.g. York and Coventry) was celebrated by the performance of sacred plays (see *Miracle Plays*).

Corpus Christi College, Cambridge, founded in 1352 by a guild of Cambridge townsmen. It contains the library of Archbishop Parker (q.v.), one of the most famous collections of manuscripts in England.

Correggio, ANTONIO (1494 or 1489–1534), Italian painter, called after his birthplace in Lombardy. He worked chiefly in Parma in a style which foreshadows the baroque.

Corroboree, the native dance of the Australian aborigines, of a festive or warlike character, danced at night by moonlight or a bush fire.

Corsair, the name, in the languages of the Mediterranean, for a privateer, chiefly applied to the cruisers of Barbary, which preyed on the shipping and coasts of Christendom. The word is often treated as identical with *pirate,* though the Barbary corsairs, who chiefly sailed from N. African ports, were licensed by the Turkish government at Constantinople.

Corsair, The, a poem in heroic couplets by Lord Byron (q.v.), published in 1814.

Conrad, a pirate chief in the Aegean Sea, a man of many vices and one virtue (a certain sense of chivalry), receives warning that Seyd, the Turkish Pacha, is preparing a fleet for a descent on his island. He determines to anticipate him, takes leave of his beloved Medora, arrives at the Pacha's rallying-point at night, and introduces himself to his presence as a dervish escaped from the pirates. The premature firing of the Pacha's galleys by Conrad's men gives warning of the intended *coup,* which is only partially successful. Conrad is wounded and taken prisoner, but not before he has rescued Gulnare, the chief slave in the Pacha's harem, from imminent death. She becomes enamoured of him, obtains the postponement of his execution, and finally brings him a dagger wherewith he may kill Seyd in his sleep. From this act he revolts, whereupon she herself kills the Pacha, and escapes with Conrad. But she has now become repulsive to him. They arrive at the pirate island, where Conrad finds Medora dead from grief at the reported slaying of her lover. Conrad disappears and is never heard of more.

Corsican, THE, the CORSICAN UPSTART, GENERAL, etc., Napoleon Buonaparte, born at Ajaccio in Corsica in 1769.

Corsican Brothers, The, a play translated by Boucicault (q.v.) from the French, and produced in 1848.

Cortegiano, Il, see *Castiglione.*

Cortes, THE, the legislative assemblies of the Spanish and Portuguese kingdoms.

Cortese, GIACOMO, Italian scholar, in 1884 described a page of a palimpsest fragment which he had found in the binding of Ovid's 'Metamorphoses'. He gave a reproduction of the page, and attributed the fragment to Cornelius Nepos. The attribution and date were actively discussed by scholars, and the piece, which contained a reference to Ennius, passed into the histories of Latin literature as 'Anonymus Cortesianus'. In 1904 L. Traube (q.v.) showed that Cortese (by this time professor of classical philology at Rome) had invented the text and fabricated the reproduction by taking all the letters from Angelo Mai's plate of a palimpsest part of Cicero's 'De Republica', published in 1822.

Cortez, HERNANDO (1485–1547), the conqueror of Mexico. He entered Mexico City in 1519. It was not he, but Balboa (q.v.), who first of all Europeans gazed on the Pacific (see Keats's sonnet 'On first looking into Chapman's Homer').

Corvino, a character in Jonson's 'Volpone' (q.v.).

CORVO, BARON, see *Rolfe (F. W.).*

CORY, WILLIAM JOHNSON (1823–92), educated at Eton and King's College, Cambridge, was an assistant master at Eton and changed his name from Johnson to Cory in 1872. He published some educational works, but is remembered as the author of two volumes of poems, notably his 'Ionica' (1858) containing the well-known translation of the epigram on Heraclitus of Halicarnassus by the Alexandrian poet Callimachus, 'They told me, Heraclitus, they told me you were dead'. His 'Letters and Journals' (1897, edited by F. Warre-Cornish) is a classic.

CORYATE, THOMAS (1577?–1617), the son of a rector of Odcombe, educated at Gloucester Hall, Oxford, travelled in 1608 through France, Italy, Switzerland, Germany, and Holland, mainly on foot. He published in 1611 a narrative of his travels, entitled 'Coryats Crudities' and 'Coryats Cramb'. 'The Odcombian Banquet', a reprint of verses prefixed to the 'Crudities', appeared in the same year. In 1612 he set out overland to India, travelling through Constantinople, Palestine, Mesopotamia, and reaching Agra in 1616. He died at Surat. A letter of his from the court of the Great Mogul is printed by Purchas, and this and another letter from the East are included in a compilation called 'Thomas Coriate Traveller for

the English Wits: Greeting' (1616). Coryate wrote in a strange and extravagant style. See 'The Life and Adventures of Thomas Coryate', by M. Strachan (1962).

Corybantes, the priests of Cybele (q.v.), who in the celebration of their festivals beat their cymbals and behaved as if delirious. The infant Zeus (q.v.) was entrusted to their care, and with their cymbals they drowned his cries and prevented Cronos from finding where he was concealed.

Corycian Cave, THE, on Mt. Parnassus, derived its name from a nymph Corycia, beloved of Apollo. The Muses are sometimes called Corycian Nymphs.

Corydon, a shepherd who figures in the 'Idylls' of Theocritus and the 'Eclogues' of Virgil, and whose name has become conventional in pastoral poetry.

Coryphǣus, the leader of a chorus in the Attic drama.

Cosmos, see *Humboldt.*

Costard, a clown in Shakespeare's 'Love's Labour's Lost' (q.v.).

Costigan, CAPTAIN and EMILY (Miss Fotheringay), characters in Thackeray's 'Pendennis' (q.v.).

COTGRAVE, RANDLE (*d.* 1634?), author of a famous French-English Dictionary published in 1611. He was a scholar of St. John's College, Cambridge. He had a wide knowledge not only of French and French literature, but of the slang of the day, and also of natural history. Urquhart relied largely upon his dictionary for the translation of Rabelais.

Cotman, JOHN SELL (1782–1842), landscape-painter, chiefly in watercolour, a leading member of the Norwich School (q.v.).

Cotswold Games, public athletic contests held, from an uncertain antiquity, on the open rounded hills of the Cotswolds. They were revived and organized about 1604 by Captain Robert Dover, who lived in the Cotswolds, and were made the subject of 'Annalia Dubrensia, or Celebration of Captain Robert Dover's Cotswold Games', a collection of poems by thirty-three writers, including such well-known names as Drayton, Ben Jonson, Randolph, and Heywood. The games continued to be held during Whitsun-week until the end of the 18th cent. 'Dover's Games' are the scene of Wildgoose's first exploit in Graves's 'The Spiritual Quixote' (q.v.). 'Dover's Hill' is the name of the flat top of the Cotswold escarpment above Chipping Campden.

Cotswold, LION OF, i.e. a sheep. John Heywood, in the 16th cent., refers to someone who was as fierce 'as a lion of Cotswold'.

Cotter's Saturday Night, The, a poem by Burns (q.v.).

Cottle, JOSEPH (1770–1853), a bookseller of Bristol, who published works of Southey,

Coleridge, and Wordsworth, and wrote poems of little literary merit. His brother AMOS SIMON COTTLE (1768?–1800) translated in metre the Edda of Saemund (1797).

COTTON, CHARLES (1630–87), of Beresford Hall, Staffordshire, is chiefly remembered as the author of the dialogue between 'Piscator' and 'Viator' written in 1676, which forms the second part in the fifth edition of Izaak Walton's 'Compleat Angler' (q.v.). He also wrote many pleasant verses, including the 'New Year Poem' praised by Charles Lamb, burlesques of Virgil (1664) and Lucian (1665), and a translation of Montaigne's 'Essays' (1685), closer but less racy than Florio's (q.v.).

COTTON, SIR ROBERT BRUCE (1571–1631), educated at Westminster School and Jesus College, Cambridge, was an antiquary and collector of manuscripts and coins. He gave the free use of his library to Bacon, Camden, Ralegh, Selden, Speed, Ussher, and other scholars, and sent a gift of manuscripts to the Bodleian Library on its foundation. He joined the parliamentary party and published various political tracts. The COTTONIAN LIBRARY, largely composed of works rescued from the dissolved monasteries, was left to the nation by Sir John Cotton (1621–1701), grandson of Sir Robert; it was placed in Essex House, then in Ashburnham House, where it suffered severely from fire in 1731. It was removed to the British Museum in 1753. It includes such treasures as the Lindisfarne Gospels (q.v.) and other splendid biblical MSS. such as the Codex Purpureus, and the MSS. of 'Beowulf', 'Pearl', and 'Sir Gawain and the Green Knight' (qq.v.).

Cottys or COTTUS, a hundred-handed giant, brother of Briareus (q.v.) and Gyes.

Cotytto, a Thracian goddess, associated with Cybele, worshipped with licentious rites, whose cult spread widely.

COUCH, SIR ARTHUR THOMAS QUILLER-, see *Quiller-Couch.*

Coué, ÉMILE (1857–1926), a chemist of Troyes in France, who developed a system of psychotherapy by which he claimed that persons, through auto-suggestion, could counteract a tendency to disease. His formula, 'Every day, in every way, I am becoming better and better', had a wide vogue.

Coulin, a British giant mentioned in Spenser's 'Faerie Queene', II. x. 11.

Council of Trent, an 'oecumenical' council of the Roman Catholic Church which sat, with considerable intervals, at Trent in the Tyrol, 1545–63, settling in a coherent form the doctrines of that Church in opposition to those of the Reformation. Its decisions are the recognized Roman Catholic authority on matters of faith and discipline.

Count Julian, a tragedy by Landor (q.v.), published in 1812.

It deals with the story of the vengeance taken by Count Julian, a Spanish nobleman, on Roderigo the king, who has dishonoured Julian's daughter; and Julian's fate. The subject is also treated in Southey's 'Roderick' (q.v.), and in a different form by Rowley in his 'All's Lost by Lust' (q.v.).

Count Robert of Paris, a novel by Sir W. Scott (q.v.), published in 1831, the year before the author's death. This was one of the 'Tales of my Landlord', fourth series, the last of the Waverley Novels. It was written in ill health and betrays the decline of his powers.

The scene is laid in Constantinople in the days of the Emperor Alexius Comnenus (1081–1118), and the story centres in the arrival there of the first crusaders, and in a plot of Nicephorus Briennius, the husband of Anna Comnena (q.v.), to dethrone his father-in-law. Anna Comnena herself figures largely in the novel and provides some of its best pages. Count Robert of Paris, a proud and valiant Frankish knight, and his Amazonian wife Brenhilda, are among the crusaders. On the occasion of the homage done by these to the emperor, Count Robert grossly insults the latter by seating himself on his throne. He thereby arouses the wrath of Hereward, an English soldier of the emperor's Varangian (q.v.) guard. The count and his wife, by a device of the emperor's, are detained as hostages for the crusaders when these cross to Asia; the count is thrown into prison, and rescued thence by the chivalrous Hereward. Meanwhile his wife Brenhilda is exposed to the unwelcome attentions of Briennius, and challenges him to a duel, agreeing to surrender herself to him if defeated. When the time for the duel comes, Count Robert presents himself in her stead, and as Briennius fails to appear, Hereward fights on his behalf. He is defeated, but his life is spared by the count in consideration of his past services. Hereward attaches himself to the count, having discovered his old Saxon love, Bertha, in the countess's waiting-woman.

Counter-Reformation, a movement in the Roman Catholic Church in opposition to the Protestant Reformation. It developed in the latter part of the 16th cent., after the Council of Trent (1545–63) and the peace of Cateau-Cambrésis (1559) between Philip II and Henri II of France. In the course of the repressive measures which, together with reforms and reorganization, formed part of this movement, Giordano Bruno (q.v.) was burnt as a heretic.

Countess Cathleen, The, a play by Yeats, published in 1892, one of the two plays with which the Irish national theatre started on its course (see *Yeats, W. B.*).

The scene is laid 'in Ireland in old times' at a period of famine. The people sell their souls to the demons for food. The countess does all she can to relieve their needs, till the demons steal her wealth. Finally she sells her own soul to the demons for a great sum, sacrificing her hope of salvation for the people. But at the end she is forgiven, for her intention was good.

Country Wife, The, a comedy by Wycherley (q.v.), produced in 1675.

This is one of the wittiest of Wycherley's plays, but the manners depicted are coarse and indecent. The plot illustrates the folly both of excessive jealousy and of excessive credulity in lovers. Mr. Pinchwife, having occasion to come to London for the marriage of his sister, Alithea, brings with him his artless young country wife, and the excess of his suspicion puts ideas into her head, which are the cause of his undoing. Sparkish, who was to marry Alithea, from the opposite excess of confidence and credulity loses her at the last moment to a new wooer; while Horner, a witty young libertine, who has spread a false report about himself in order to facilitate his amours, is able to satisfy Pinchwife of his wife's innocence.

This play was adapted by Garrick as 'The Country Girl'.

County Palatine, in England, a county of which the earl or lord had originally royal privileges, with the right of exclusive civil and criminal jurisdiction. The counties palatine are now Cheshire and Lancashire. The word Palatine meant originally 'of or belonging to the imperial palace of the Caesars'.

Coup de théâtre, an unexpected and sensational turn in a play.

Courcy, LORD and LADY DE, and their sons and daughters, characters in A. Trollope's Barsetshire (q.v.) series of novels, types of a worldly, self-seeking, heartless aristocracy.

Courier, The, a newspaper that attained considerable importance in the early part of the 19th cent., under the management of Daniel Stuart (q.v.). Coleridge and Wordsworth were among its contributors. Galt (q.v.) was at one time its editor.

Courier of Lyons, The, see *Reade.*

Court of Arches, see *Arches (Court of).*

Court of Love, an institution said to have existed in Provence and Languedoc in the Middle Ages, a tribunal composed of lords and ladies for deciding questions of gallantry.

Court of Love, The, an allegory (1,400 lines in rhyme-royal) attributed doubtfully to Chaucer, in which the poet visits the Court of Venus, converses with those who frequent it, and reads its twenty statutes. He is assigned as 'servant' to a damsel, named Rosiall, and witnesses various allegorical scenes, notably the picture of those who have voluntarily renounced love. The poem ends with a charming concert of the birds on May-day, when they sing descants on the opening words of psalms. Linguistic peculiarities suggest that this poem was of later date than Chaucer, or was extensively re-written. It purports to

be the work of one 'Philogenet, of Cambridge, clerk'. In spirit it is thoroughly Chaucerian.

Court of Pie-Powder, see *Piepowder Court.*

COURTELINE, the name by which GEORGES MOINAUX (1860–1929) is generally known: French humorist and satirist, who ridiculed French officialdom, civil and military, and French legal absurdities, in a number of sketches and short plays, e.g. 'Messieurs les Ronds-de-Cuir' (1893), translated as 'The Bureaucrats', 'Les Gaîtés de l'Escadron' (1886), 'Le Train de 8 h. 47' (1888), 'Un Client sérieux' (1897).

COURTHOPE, WILLIAM JOHN (1842–1917), educated at Harrow, and Corpus Christi College and New College, Oxford, became a civil service commissioner and professor of poetry at Oxford. His chief works are the last five volumes of the standard edition of Pope's works, including a 'Life' (1871–89); and a 'History of English Poetry' (1895–1910). In 1884 he contributed a volume on Addison to the English Men of Letters series. His other works include 'Ludibria Lunae' (1869), and the delightful Aristophanic 'Paradise of Birds' (1870, in which a philosopher and a poet are tried for the crimes of mankind against the birds and are barely acquitted). 'The Country Town and other Poems', published in 1920 after his death, contain many pieces of great charm.

Courtier, The ('Il Cortegiano'), see *Castiglione.*

Courtly Love, a conception of love which first developed in the feudal courts of the south of France in the first half of the 12th cent., and is the chief theme and inspiration of the troubadours in their chansons; it is essentially aristocratic, its basic situation of humble lover, haughty lady and tale-bearing slanderers (*losengiers*) being modelled on the relation of vassal to overlord in feudal society: the lady must be the epitome of feudal social virtues, the lover must remain true in spite of cruelty and scorn, must be guided in all things by his love of his lady (*domna*), serve and study to deserve her, and be completely absorbed in his devotion. Treated as an elegant and entertaining social and literary game of gallantry in the Midi, courtly love passed into the north of France in the second half of the 12th cent., where, especially in the hands of writers like Chrétien de Troyes (q.v.), and *clercs* like Andreas Capellanus, it developed into a more serious code of social morality.

Courtoys, the name of the hound in 'Reynard the Fox' (q.v.).

Courtship of Miles Standish, see *Miles Standish.*

Cousine Bette, La, a novel by Balzac (q.v.).

Couwaert, see *Coart.*

Covenant, THE, or NATIONAL COVENANT, a protestation signed all over Scotland in 1638, in which the subscribers swore to defend the Protestant religion and to resist all contrary errors and corruptions. A COVENANTER (in Scotland traditionally pronounced *covenan'ter*) was a subscriber or adherent of the above.

Covenant, THE SOLEMN LEAGUE AND, a treaty between the English and Scottish nations concluded in 1643, stipulating the preservation of the reformed Church in Scotland, the reformation of religion in England, the extirpation of popery and episcopacy, and peace between the kingdoms.

Covent Garden, in London, the old Convent Garden of Westminster. At the dissolution of the monasteries, it passed into the hands of the Russell family, who built Bedford House north of the Strand and laid out the garden for building, with the market as the centre. Inigo Jones built St. Paul's Church there, and the piazza that runs along two sides of the market-place. Many celebrated people lived in Covent Garden (Sir Kenelm Digby, Sir Godfrey Kneller, Sir Peter Lely, Zoffany, Lady Mary Wortley Montagu, among others), and the Bedford Coffee-house and those of Will and Button (qq.v.) were in the neighbourhood. Covent Garden is frequently mentioned in 17th- and 18th-cent. literature, generally as a centre of dissipation. It is still the principal wholesale market in London for vegetables, fruit, and flowers.

The first COVENT GARDEN THEATRE was opened by Rich in 1732. It was burnt down in 1808, and its successor in 1856. In these, many famous actors were seen, including Garrick, Munden, the Kembles, Braham, Mrs. Siddons, and Macready. The new theatre (by Barry) opened in 1858 has been the principal home in England of English and Italian opera.

Covent Garden Journal, a periodical issued twice a week during 1752 by H. Fielding (q.v.), under the pseudonym of Sir Alexander Drawcansir, containing essays on literature and manners. It contained an attack on Smollett's 'Peregrine Pickle' and 'Roderick Random', to which that author replied in a scurrilous pamphlet, 'A Faithful Narrative of . . . Habbakuk Hilding, Justice, Dealer, and Chapman' (1752).

Coventry, TO SEND TO, to exclude a person from the society of which he is a member, on account of objectionable conduct. The origin of the expression is perhaps indicated, in the opinion of the OED., by the following quotation:

'At Bromingham a town so generally wicked that it had risen upon small parties of the king's, and killed or taken them prisoners and sent them to Coventry' [then strongly held for the parliament]. Clarendon, 'History of the Rebellion', VI, § 83.

COVENTRY, FRANCIS (*d.* 1759?), educated at Magdalene College, Cambridge, author of the 'History of Pompey the Little' (1751), a satire in the form of the picaresque

narrative of the life of a lap-dog, who undergoes many vicissitudes, passing from one owner to another of very diverse stations.

Coventry Miracle Plays, see *Miracle Plays*.

COVERDALE, MILES (1488–1568), studied at Cambridge, was ordained priest in 1514 and adopted Lutheran views. He translated at Antwerp, apparently in the pay of Jacob van Meteren, the Bible and Apocrypha from German and Latin versions with the aid of Tyndale's New Testament. His translation was first printed perhaps by Christopher Froschouer of Zürich. A modified version was issued in 1537. Coverdale also superintended the printing of the 'Great Bible' of 1539 (see under *Bible, The English*). He was bishop of Exeter in 1551–3, and was allowed to leave England in 1554 after Queen Mary's accession. He was in England again in 1559, published his last book, 'Letters of Saintes', in 1564, and was rector of St. Magnus, London Bridge, from 1563 to 1566. His collected works, which include translations of theological tracts and German hymns, were published in 1844–6. If he was in fact (which has been questioned) the translator of the version of the Bible attributed to him, he is entitled to the credit for much of the noble language of the Authorized Version, and in particular for the Prayer-book version of the Psalter.

Coverley, SIR ROGER DE, a character described by Addison (q.v.) in the 'Spectator' (q.v.). He is a member of the Spectator Club, 'a gentleman of Worcestershire, of ancient descent, a baronet. His great-grandfather was inventor of that famous country-dance which is called after him. He is a gentleman that is very singular in his behaviour, but his singularities proceed from his good sense, and are contradictions to the manners of the world, only as he thinks the world is in the wrong. . . . It is said, he keeps himself a batchelor, by reason he was crossed in love by a perverse beautiful widow of the next county to him.' He figures in a number of the 'Spectator' papers (both by Addison and Steele), being depicted at home, at church, at the assizes, in town, at the play, at Vauxhall, etc.

COWARD, NOËL (1899–   ), actor, dramatist, and composer. His plays of the 1920s, which matched the contemporary mood of smart sophistication, established his popularity, and his continuing production of plays, revues, musical plays, operettas, and films, spiced with wit and sweetened with sentimentality, has added to it. Among his best-known plays are: 'Private Lives' (1930), 'Cavalcade' (1931), 'Design for Living' (1933), and 'Blithe Spirit' (1941). 'Bitter Sweet', an operetta (1929), had a long run of success in London and New York.

COWLEY, ABRAHAM (1618–67), was son of a wealthy citizen of London, king's scholar at Westminster, and scholar and fellow of

Trinity College, Cambridge. His amazing precocity is shown by the fact that, when 10 years of age, he composed an epical romance of 'Pyramus and Thisbe', followed two years later by the epic 'Constantia and Philetus' (both included in 'Poetical Blossoms' published in 1633). 'Love's Riddle', a pastoral drama, appeared in 1638; 'Naufragium Joculare', a Latin comedy, in the same year; and 'The Guardian', reissued as 'The Cutter of Coleman Street', a comedy directed against the Puritans, in 1641. Ejected from Cambridge in that year as a result of the Civil War, he went first to Oxford and thence in 1646 to Paris, where he became cipher-secretary to Queen Henrietta Maria and was employed on delicate diplomatic missions. He came as a Royalist spy to England in 1655, was imprisoned, released on bail (his release occasioned suspicions of his honesty), and studied medicine at Oxford. After the restoration, a competence was provided for him by the earl of St. Albans and the duke of Buckingham, and he received a grant of the manor of Oldcourt (Nethercot).

His principal works, besides those mentioned above, are 'The Mistress', a love-cycle, 1647; 'Miscellanies' including four books of the 'Davideis', an epic in decasyllabic couplets on the biblical history of David, 1656; odes on the Restoration and against Cromwell, 1660–1; 'Verses on several occasions', 1663. In his 'Pindarique Odes', included in the 'Miscellanies', he introduced the fashion of the rhetorical ode, in irregular verse, imitated by Dryden and others. His prose works, marked by grace and simplicity of style, include a tract on 'The Advancement of Experimental Philosophy' (1661), a 'Discourse by way of Vision concerning Oliver Cromwell' (1661), and some 'Essays', notably one 'Of Myself', containing interesting particulars of his early life.

COWLEY, Mrs. HANNAH (1743–1809), née Parkhouse, wrote a number of comedies between 1776 and 1795, including 'The Runaway' (1776) and 'A Bold Stroke for a Husband' (1783), of which the most successful was 'The Belle's Stratagem' (q.v.), produced in 1780. She contributed weekly sentimental verses to the 'World' as 'Anna Matilda'.

COWPER (pron. 'Cooper'), WILLIAM (1731–1800), son of a rector of Great Berkhampstead, was educated at a private school (where he was bullied) and at Westminster School. He was then articled to a solicitor (1750–2), in 1752 took chambers in the Middle Temple, and was called to the bar in 1754. He suffered from fits of depression, which, when he was offered a clerkship in the House of Lords in 1763, developed into mania, and he tried to commit suicide. From his mania he recovered, but he thereafter lived in retirement. In 1765 he became a boarder in the house of Morley Unwin at Huntingdon, where the cheerful simple life perfectly suited him.

After Unwin's death, he removed with Mary, Unwin's widow, to Olney, coming under the influence of Newton, the evangelical curate of the place, at whose instance he contributed to the collection of 'Olney Hymns' (published in 1779), his contributions including such well-known hymns as 'Hark, my soul! it is the Lord', and 'God moves in a mysterious way'. He became engaged to Mrs. Unwin, but suffered another outbreak of mania in 1773. In 1779, the influence of the strenuous Newton being withdrawn, Cowper entered upon the most peaceful period of his life, and began to write much poetry. In 1781 he published 'Anti-Thelyphthora', a reply to a book by his cousin Martin Madan advocating polygamy. At the suggestion of Mrs. Unwin he wrote eight satires: 'Table Talk', 'The Progress of Error', 'Truth', 'Expostulation', 'Hope', 'Charity', 'Conversation', and 'Retirement'. These were published in 1782. The volume included some shorter poems, among others the well-known 'Boadicea' and 'Verses supposed to be written by Alexander Selkirk'. In 1782 he wrote 'John Gilpin' (q.v.) and in 1784 'The Task' (q.v.). The volume which contained these (published in 1785) also included 'Tirocinium', a vigorous attack on public schools as Cowper knew them. In 1786 he moved, with Mrs. Unwin, to Weston, where he wrote some short poems published after his death, including 'Yardley Oak' (1791), the verses 'On the Loss of the Royal George', the sonnet 'To Mrs. Unwin', the beautiful lines 'To Mary', and 'The Poplar Field'. In 1785 he undertook the translation of Homer, published in 1791, which was not successful. He received a pension in 1794. Mrs. Unwin died in 1796, and her loss left Cowper shattered in mind and body. He wrote the fine but gloomy poem 'The Castaway' shortly before his death.

Cowper's admirable letters, of which several editions have been published, throw light on his simple, gentle, and humane personality. His poetry is notable as heralding a simpler and more natural style than the classical style of Pope and his inferior imitators.

Cox and Box, an operetta by Sir F. Burnand, music by Sir A. Sullivan (qq.v.), produced in 1867. See also *Box and Cox.*

Cox's Museum : James Cox, jeweller and clockmaker in Shoe Lane, had a museum in Spring Gardens, of which catalogues for 1772 and 1774 figure in the Catalogue of the British Museum. The East India Co. ordered two clocks from him to be sent to the emperor of China. But the museum did not prosper, and the stock was disposed of by a lottery. See Mrs. Ellis's notes in Mackinnon's edition (1930) of Miss Burney's 'Evelina', in which book there is a reference to the museum.

Crab, in Shakespeare's 'Two Gentlemen of Verona' (q.v.), Launce's dog.

CRABBE, GEORGE (1754–1832), was born at Aldeburgh in Suffolk, where his father was collector of salt-duties. He was apprenticed to a doctor, and subsequently practised medicine at Aldeburgh. During his apprenticeship he made the acquaintance of Sarah Elmy, whom he married ten years later. In 1780 he went to London, where he was generously befriended by Edmund Burke and on his advice published 'The Library' in 1781, a poem in the manner of Pope containing the author's somewhat commonplace reflections on books and reading. In the same year he took orders and became curate of Aldeburgh, and from 1782 to 1785 was chaplain at Belvoir to the duke of Rutland. In 1783 appeared, after revision by Burke and Johnson, 'The Village' (q.v.), a poem in heroic couplets. A long interval followed during which Crabbe published nothing of importance. In 1807 appeared a volume containing among other poems 'The Parish Register' (q.v.), which first revealed the gifts of Crabbe as a narrative poet. The same volume contained 'Sir Eustace Grey', the terrible account, in eight-lined stanzas, by a patient in a madhouse, of his decline from happiness and prosperity. In 1810 he published 'The Borough' (q.v.), a poem in twenty-four 'letters', in which he illustrates by various stories the life of a country town. This was followed in 1812 by 'Tales', twenty-one stories in which the poet again shows his power of narrative and character-drawing. The best known of these is 'The Frank Courtship', the comedy of the wooing of the worldly Sybil by the puritan Josiah. This and other 'Tales', notably 'The Patron' and 'The Gentleman Farmer', reveal Crabbe's somewhat grim sense of humour. In 1814 Crabbe was appointed vicar of Trowbridge, and in 1819 he published 'Tales of the Hall', stories again, terrible, humorous, or sad. This was the last volume published in his lifetime, but the collected edition of his works issued by his son in 1834 contained some fresh tales of considerable merit, such as 'The Equal Marriage' and 'Silford Hall'. A complete collection of Crabbe's poems, edited by A. W. Ward, was issued by the Cambridge University Press in 1905–7. Crabbe was a realistic describer of life as he saw it, in all its ugliness—'Though nature's sternest painter yet the best', as Byron called him—and rarely rose to the higher flights of poetry. He visited Scott at Edinburgh in 1822 (there is a pleasant account in Lockhart, lvi), and the two authors, though their outlook was so different, appear to have enjoyed each other's poetry. Scott calls him the 'English Juvenal' in 'Waverley' and the 'British Juvenal' in 'The Heart of Midlothian'.

Cracherode, CLAYTON MORDAUNT (1730–99), scholar and collector of books. The inheritance of ample means enabled him to acquire a fine collection of books and prints, which he bequeathed to the British Museum. His special interest was in early editions of the classics and the Silver Age of Latin, as well as in early printing as an art.

Cradock, SIR, see *Boy and the Mantle*.

Craftsman, The, a periodical started in Dec. 1726 by Nicholas Amhurst ('Caleb D'Anvers'), to which Bolingbroke (q.v.) contributed his 'Remarks upon the History of England' (Sept. 1730–May 1731) and his 'Dissertation upon Parties' (1733). William Pulteney, later earl of Bath, was another leading contributor. Its title was intended to indicate Sir Robert Walpole as a 'man of craft'; and its essence (so far as it was political) lay in its opposition to Walpole and his cabinets. The journal ran for about ten years.

Craigdallie, in Scott's 'The Fair Maid of Perth' (q.v.), the bailie of Perth.

Craigenputtock, see *Carlyle (T.)*.

CRAIK, MRS., see *Mulock*.

CRANE, HART (1899–1932), American poet, born in Ohio. He published two volumes of verse, 'White Buildings' (1926) and 'The Bridge' (1930), in which the force of genius is fully apparent. He combined a wide knowledge of modern poetry with a mystical perception of America as an ideal, something in the manner of Whitman (q.v.), and though his vision, especially in 'The Bridge', is not always coherent, it is among the most arresting in modern American verse. He committed suicide on his way home from Mexico. A 'Collected Poems', which added some new work, appeared in 1933.

Crane, ICHABOD, see *Sleepy Hollow*.

CRANE, STEPHEN (1871–1900), American writer, born in New Jersey. He published his first book 'Maggie: A Girl of the Streets' in 1893, and made his name with 'The Red Badge of Courage: An Episode in the American Civil War' (1895), a brilliant realistic and psychological novel of an inexperienced soldier (Henry Fleming) and his reactions to battle. Crane served abroad as a war correspondent in Mexico and Cuba (1896) and later in Greece, and twice lived for some time in England. He published, among other work, two volumes of free verse, and two fine collections of short stories, 'The Open Boat' (1898) and 'The Monster' (1899).

Cranford, a novel by Mrs. Gaskell (q.v.), published in 'Household Words' in 1851–3, republished in 1853.

'Cranford' is a prose idyll, in which the authoress, drawing in part on her experiences of Knutsford, describes with much tenderness, and a just blend of humour and pathos, life in a quiet Cheshire village in the early 19th cent. Gentility is the predominant note in Cranford, and the ladies (there are hardly any gentlemen) practise 'elegant economy'. Mrs. Gaskell draws delightful portraits of these ladies, from the Honourable, but dull and pompous, Mrs. Jamieson (with her butler, Mr. Mulliner, who resembles 'a sulky cockatoo') to Miss Betty Barker, the old clerk's daughter. But the principal characters are the daughters of a former rector, Matilda Jenkyns (the gentle Miss Matty) and her stern elder sister Miss Debōrah, who thinks 'Pickwick' by no means equal to Dr. Johnson. We have sketches of the tragedy of the genial Captain Brown, run over by a train while deep in the perusal of a number of the obnoxious 'Pickwick'; of Miss Matty's unhappy little love story; of the panic caused in the village by a succession of purely imaginary robberies; of the flutter due to the visit of Lady Glenmire, widow of a Scottish baron, and still more to her marriage with the rather vulgar Mr. Hoggins, the surgeon; and so forth, ending with the ruin of Miss Matty through the failure of a bank, the kindly devices of her friends to help her, and the fortunate return from India of her long-lost brother Peter, who describes how he once 'shot a Cherubim'.

Cranion, in Drayton's 'Nymphidia' (q.v.), Queen Mab's charioteer.

CRANMER, THOMAS (1489–1556), archbishop of Canterbury, was a fellow of Jesus College, Cambridge. He propounded views in favour of the divorce of Henry VIII from Catharine of Aragon, was appointed to the archbishopric in 1533, and maintained the king's claim to be the supreme head of the Church of England. He supervised the production of the first prayer-book of Edward VI, 1549; prepared the revised prayer-book of 1552; and promulgated the forty-two articles of religion (afterwards reduced to thirty-nine) in the same year. To meet the need for suitable sermons, he contributed to and probably edited the first book of 'Homilies' issued in 1547. In Queen Mary's reign he was condemned for heresy by Cardinal Pole, recently appointed archbishop of Canterbury, and degraded in 1556. He signed six documents admitting the supremacy of the pope and the truth of all Roman Catholic doctrine except transubstantiation, in vain, and was burned at the stake repudiating these admissions on 21 March 1556, at Oxford, holding his right hand (which had written his recantation) steadily in the flames, that it might be the first burnt. He compiled a 'Reformatio Legum Ecclesiasticarum' (1550), which never saw the light, and wrote on Anglican discipline and theology; but his chief title to fame is that of being the principal author of the English liturgy.

For CRANMER'S BIBLE see under *Bible* (*The English*).

Crapaud or JOHNNY CRAPAUD, a derisive term at one time in use for a Frenchman. According to Guillim and Peacham, 17th-cent. writers on heraldry, the ancient arms of France were three *crapauds* or toads. Strange as it may seem, it appears uncertain whether this is true or not. There is much discussion of the subject in the 'I.D.C.' A statue of King Clovis at Frankfort-on-Main shows, it is said, three toads on his shield, and a 14th-cent. tapestry in Rheims Cathedral likewise shows

toads as his device. On the other hand it is argued that heraldic emblems were adopted in France only after the first crusade, much later than Clovis. On the whole it appears that the so-called toads are rudely executed attempts to represent fleurs-de-lis, or lance-heads.

CRASHAW, RICHARD (1612?–49), the son of a noted anti-papal preacher, was educated at Charterhouse and Pembroke Hall, Cambridge, and was a fellow of Peterhouse from 1635 to 1643. He entered the Roman Catholic Church and went to Paris, and appears to have been introduced to Queen Henrietta Maria by his friend Cowley (q.v.), her secretary. She in turn introduced him to Cardinal Pallotto, the governor of Rome, who appointed him his private secretary, and subsequently procured him a benefice in the Basilica-church of Our Lady of Loretto in 1649, where he died shortly after his arrival.

His principal poetical work was the 'Steps to the Temple' (1646), a collection of religious poems showing great devotional ecstasy, and the influence of Marino and also, as Gosse has pointed out, of the Spanish Mystics. To this was attached a secular section, the 'Delights of the Muses', containing the well-known 'Music's Duel', a paraphrase of the Latin of Strada, in which the nightingale and the lute-player contend until the former, 'unable to measure all those wild diversities of chatt'ring strings', fails and dies; and also the pretty 'Wishes. To his (supposed) Mistresse', beginning 'Whoe'er she be'. His poem, 'The Flaming Heart', a hymn to St. Teresa, belongs to the period before he became a Roman Catholic. The posthumous 'Carmen Deo Nostro' (1652) included reprints of many of his best earlier poems besides new works.

Cratchit, BOB, a character in Dickens's 'A Christmas Carol' (q.v.).

Craven Fellowships and scholarships at Oxford, and Craven scholarships and studentships at Cambridge, were founded by John, Baron Craven of Ryton (d. 1649).

CRAWFORD, FRANCIS MARION (1854–1909), was born of American parents at Bagni di Lucca in Tuscany, and was educated at Harvard, Heidelberg, and Rome. He edited for a time the 'Indian Herald' at Allahabad. His first novel, 'Mr. Isaacs, a tale of Modern India', was published in America in 1882. He returned to Italy in 1883 and thereafter lived principally at Sorrento. He travelled extensively and his novels reflect his knowledge of foreign lands. Thus four have Rome for their scene: 'Saracinesca' (1887), 'Sant' Ilario' (1889), 'Don Orsino' (1892), and 'Corleone' (1896); one has Constantinople, 'Paul Patoff' (1887); three have the East, 'Zoroaster' (1885), 'Khaled' (1891), 'Via Crucis' (1898); and three have Germany, 'Dr. Claudius' (1883), 'Greifenstein' (1889), and 'The Cigarette-maker's Romance' (1890); while the scene of others is laid in England or America.

Crawford, HENRY and MARY, characters in Jane Austen's 'Mansfield Park' (q.v.).

CRAWFORD, ISABELLA VALANEY (1850–86), Canadian poet, was born in Dublin, and from the age of 8 lived in Canada. Her collected poems, which show a considerable lyrical gift, were published in 1905.

Crawford, LORD, in Scott's 'Quentin Durward' (q.v.), the commander of the Scottish Archers of the Guard.

Crawley, THE REV. JOSIAH, and his daughter GRACE, characters in A. Trollope's 'Framley Parsonage' and 'Last Chronicle of Barset' (qq.v.).

Crawley, SIR PITT, his sister MISS CRAWLEY, his brother the REV. BUTE, and MRS. BUTE, and his sons, PITT and RAWDON, leading characters in Thackeray's 'Vanity Fair' (q.v.).

Craye, COL. HORACE DE, a character in Meredith's 'The Egoist' (q.v.).

CRAYON, GEOFFREY, pseudonym of W. IRVING (q.v.).

Crazy Kate, the subject of a digression in 'The Sofa', the first part of Cowper's 'The Task' (q.v.).

Creakle, in Dickens's 'David Copperfield' (q.v.), the bullying headmaster of the hero's first school.

Credo, 'I believe', the first word of the Apostles' and Nicene Creeds in Latin. Hence a name for either of these creeds. Also used for the short space of time in which a man might say his Creed.

CREEVEY, THOMAS (1768–1838), was whig M.P. successively for Thetford and Appleby. The 'Creevey Papers' published in 1903, consisting of letters to his stepdaughter, Elizabeth Ord, extracts from his journal, and letters to Creevey from various important persons, are interesting for their gossip, and the light they throw on the characters of prominent persons and on the society of the later Georgian era. In Creevey's old age, when the Whigs were in power, he held office as treasurer of Ordnance, and afterwards as treasurer of Greenwich Hospital. Charles Greville (q.v.) in his 'Memoirs' (20 Feb. 1838) refers to Creevey's cheerful and sociable disposition; he was at once 'perfectly happy and exceedingly poor'.

CREIGHTON, MANDELL (1843–1901), fellow of Merton College, Oxford, held the living of Embleton in Northumberland until appointed in 1884 to the chair of ecclesiastical history at Cambridge. He was the first editor of the 'English Historical Review', surrendering the post on his selection for the bishopric of Peterborough in 1891, whence he was transferred to that of London in 1897. His important 'History of the Papacy during the Reformation' appeared in 1882–94. His other historical works include 'The Tudors and the Reformation' (1876), 'The Age of Elizabeth' (1876), and biographies of Simon de Mont-

fort (1876), Cardinal Wolsey (1888), and Queen Elizabeth (1896). His 'Life and Letters' was published by his widow in 1904.

Cremona, a town in Lombardy where the art of violin-making reached its highest excellence in the 17th and early 18th cents. The two Amatis, Stradivarius, and Guarnerius lived there. Its celebrity occasioned the famous quotation of Dean Swift, when a lady's mantua knocked over a violin:
'Mantua vae miserae nimium vicina Cremonae' (Virgil, 'Eclogues', ix. 28).

Cremorne Gardens, in Chelsea, were a popular place of entertainment during the middle of the 19th cent., but became notorious for irregularities and were closed in 1877.

Creon, (1) brother of Jocasta (see Oedipus and Sphinx) and later king of Thebes (see Antigone); (2) king of Corinth (see Creüsa).

Crescent and the Cross, The, the narrative of an eastern tour by Bartholomew Elliott George Warburton (1810–51), an Irish barrister, generally known as 'Eliot Warburton'. The book, which covers much the same ground as Kingslake's 'Eothen' (q.v.), had great success.

Cresseid, The Testament of, the chief work of the Scottish poet Henryson (q.v.), was printed in 1593. It is written in rhyme-royal. The poet describes in the prologue how he took up a book
    Written by worthie Chaucer glorious
    Of fair Cresseid and lusty Troilus,
and proceeded to tell the retribution that came upon the fickle Cressida.

Diomede, wearied of Cressida, repudiates her; she takes refuge with her father Calchas and bitterly reproaches Venus and Cupid. A council of the gods discusses the punishment for her blasphemy. Finally Saturn deprives her of joy and beauty, and the Moon strikes her with leprosy. As she sits by the wayside, with her leper's cup and clapper, Troilus rides by, with a party of victorious Trojans;
    Then upon him she cast up baith her ene;
    And with ane blenk it come into his thocht
    That he sumtime hir face before had seen;
    But she was in sic plye he knew her nocht.
Nor do her dim eyes recognize him; but she receives his alms, and learns who he is, and dies after sending him a ring he once had given her.

Cressida, see Troilus and Cressida, also Cresseid.

Creüsa, (1) or Glaucē, a daughter of Creon, king of Corinth. When she was about to marry Jason (q.v.), she put on a garment given her by Medea, whom Jason had abandoned. This garment was poisoned, and set her body on fire, so that she died in torment; (2) a daughter of Priam, king of Troy, and the wife of Aeneas (q.v.) and mother of Ascanius. In the flight after the fall of Troy she became separated from her husband, who never recovered her. According to Virgil, she appeared to Aeneas in a dream and predicted the calamities and eventual fame that awaited him.

CRÈVECŒUR, J. HECTOR ST. JOHN DE (1735–1813), French soldier and explorer, who settled and farmed in New York State and became naturalized as an American citizen. He published his famous 'Letters from an American Farmer' in 1782, a work greatly liked by the English romantics. He returned to France in 1790, where he died.

Creweian Oration, THE, at Oxford, commemorates the benefactions to the University and to Lincoln College of Nathaniel Crewe, third Baron Crewe (1633–1721), bishop of Oxford and subsequently of Durham, who was rewarded with the deanery of the Chapel Royal for his subserviency to James II. He was excepted from the general pardon of 1690, but retained his see of Durham. The Creweian Oration has come to include all other benefactions during the preceding year, and is delivered, in alternate years, by the public orator and the professor of poetry.

Crewler, THE REVD. HORACE and **MRS.,** characters in Dickens's 'David Copperfield' (q.v.), the parents of SOPHY, whom Traddles marries.

CRICHTON, JAMES, 'THE ADMIRABLE' (1560–85 ?), son of Robert Crichton of Eliock, was educated at St. Andrews, and travelled to Paris, 1577, where he is said to have disputed on scientific questions in twelve languages. He served in the French army, and visited Genoa, Venice, and Padua, where he successfully challenged the university in discussion. He was a staunch Catholic and a good swordsman. He was killed in a brawl at Mantua. His authentic and extant works consist mainly of odes and orations addressed to Italian nobles and scholars. His title of Admirable originated in Sir Thomas Urquhart's narrative of his career, 1652.

For the play 'The Admirable Crichton', see *Barrie.* See also Harrison Ainsworth's 'Crichton' (1837).

Cricket on the Hearth, The, a Christmas book by Dickens (q.v.), published in 1846.

John Peerybingle, carrier, and his much younger wife, Dot, are as happy a couple as possible, although the venomous old Tackleton, who himself is about to marry the young May Fielding, throws suspicion on Dot's sincerity. This suspicion appears to be disastrously verified when an eccentric old stranger takes up his abode with the Peerybingles and is discovered one day by John, metamorphosed into a bright young man by the removal of his wig, in intimate conversation with Dot. By the fairy influence of the Cricket on the Hearth John is brought to the decision to pardon her offence, which he attributes to the incompatibility of their ages and temperaments. But there turns out to

be no occasion for forgiveness, for the bright young man is an old friend, the lover of May Fielding, believed dead, who has turned up just in time to prevent her marrying Tackleton. Among the other characters are Caleb Plummer and his blind daughter, Bertha, the toy-makers; and Tilly Slowboy, most loving and incompetent of nurses.

Crimsworth, WILLIAM, the hero of Charlotte Brontë's 'The Professor' (q.v.).

Crippen, DR. HAWLEY HARVEY (1862–1910), murderer whose arrest at sea was due to the first use of wireless telegraphy in a criminal case.

Cripplegate, one of the gates of the city of London, of which there is record as early as the year 1000. The name is probably derived from an OE. word *crepel,* meaning a burrow or narrow passage, and indicates that the gate was a narrow and less important one. Stow repeatedly refers to it as a postern, but attributes the name to the number of cripples who resorted there.

Crisparkle, THE REVD. SEPTIMUS, a character in Dickens's 'Edwin Drood' (q.v.).

Crispin and **Crispinian, SAINTS,** brothers, members of a noble Roman family, according to tradition, who left Rome for Soissons to preach Christianity and supported themselves there by shoemaking. They were ordered by the Emperor Maximian to be put to death, but survived various attempts to kill them, until their heads were cut off. They are the patron saints of shoemakers, and are commemorated on 25 Oct., date of the battle of Agincourt. See Shakespeare's 'Henry V' IV. iii. 40: 'This day is call'd the feast of Crispian', etc.

Crispinus, in Jonson's 'The Poetaster' (q.v.), represents the dramatist Marston.

Critic, The, or a Tragedy Rehearsed, a comedy by R. B. Sheridan (q.v.), produced in 1779.

In this play Sheridan satirized, after the manner of Buckingham's 'Rehearsal' (q.v.), not only the sentimental drama, but also the malignant literary criticism of the day. We have first Dangle and Sneer, the spiteful critics; Sir Fretful Plagiary, the poetaster (a caricature of Richard Cumberland); and Puff, the unscrupulous advertiser of literary wares, who has reduced the puff to a science. But Puff himself has written a tragedy, 'The Spanish Armada', to the rehearsal of which he takes Sneer and Dangle. This is an absurd historical drama with an admixture of the sentimental element, written in bombastic style, in which Sir Walter Ralegh, Sir Christopher Hatton, the earl of Leicester, and Lord Burleigh are presented, at the moment when the Armada is approaching; while Tilburina, the daughter of the governor of Tilbury Fort, is in love with Don Ferolo Whiskerandos, a Spanish prisoner. The discussion of the play by the author and the two critics, as the rehearsal proceeds, make as highly entertaining caricature of the dramatic art.

Criterion, The, a literary periodical of critical essays and reviews, founded by T. S. Eliot in 1922 and edited by him until it ceased publication in 1939.

Critical Review, The, a Tory and Church paper, founded in 1756 by Archibald Hamilton, an Edinburgh printer, in opposition to the 'Monthly Review' (q.v.). It was edited during 1756–9 by Smollett (q.v.) and supported by Johnson and Robertson. It came to an end in 1817.

Croaker, a character in Goldsmith's 'The Good-natured Man' (q.v.).

CROCE, BENEDETTO (1866–1952), Italian philosopher, historian, and critic. His writings on aesthetic theory (the branch of philosophy which he most cultivated) and his essays on contemporary literature, published in his journal 'La Critica' from 1903 to 1944, profoundly influenced aesthetic thought and critical method in Italy during the first half of the 20th cent. He continually revised his ideas, but the article on 'Aesthetics' in the 14th edition of the 'Encyclopaedia Britannica' contains the chief elements of his mature thought, including his definition of art as 'lyrical intuition'. His numerous works include 'Estetica come scienza dell'espressione e linguistica generale' ('Aesthetics as the Science of Expression and General Linguistics'), the 'Storea dell'età barocca in Italia', and 'La litteratura della nuova Italia'.

Crockett, DAVID (1786–1836), American politician and Congressman. He was transformed for political ends by skilful Whig journalists into an eccentric, humorous, shrewd frontier hero, and has remained a mythical figure. He died in the defence of Alamo.

Crockford, 'Crockford's Clerical Directory', first published in 1857. A book of reference for facts relating to the clergy and the Church of England.

Crockford's, a famous gambling club established in 1827 at 50 St. James's Street, London, by William Crockford (1775–1844). Crockford was originally a fishmonger; he amassed £1,200,000 out of the club in a few years.

Crocodile's Tears: the crocodile was fabulously said to weep, either to allure a man for the purpose of devouring him, or while devouring him. Whence many allusions in literature. Sir John Mandeville (xxviii) says, 'In that contre . . . ben gret plentee of Cokadrilles. Theise serpents sleu men, and thei eten them wepynge'. 'Sir J. Hawkins' Voyage' in Hakluyt, iii, has this passage: 'In this river we saw many Crocodils. . . . His nature is ever when hee would have his prey, to cry and sob like a Christian

body, to provoke them to come to him, and then hee snatcheth at them.'

Crocus, in mythology, the lover of the maiden Smilax. The pair were changed into the plants that bear their names.

Croesus, the last of the kings of Lydia, who passed for the richest of mankind. In conversation with Solon he claimed to be the happiest of men, but the philosopher replied that no man should be deemed happy until he had finished his life happily. When Croesus had been conquered by Cyrus and was about to be burnt alive, he thrice called on the name of Solon. Cyrus asking the reason for this, was moved at the explanation and at the recollection of the inconstancy of human affairs, and released Croesus, whom he made his friend.

Croft, ADMIRAL and MRS., characters in Jane Austen's 'Persuasion' (q.v.).

Croftangry, CHRYSTAL, see *Chronicles of the Canongate*.

CROKER, JOHN WILSON (1780–1857), educated at Trinity College, Dublin, was secretary to the Admiralty and a prominent Tory politician. He is the supposed original of Rigby in Disraeli's 'Coningsby' (q.v.). He was a contributor to the 'Quarterly Review', and became notorious for his scathing criticism of Keats's 'Endymion'. He edited Boswell's 'Life of Johnson' (1831) and was severely criticized by Macaulay, whose 'History of England' (first two volumes) he in turn attacked in 1849. His works include 'An Intercepted Letter from Canton' (1804, a satire on Dublin society), 'Military Events of the French Revolution of 1830' (1831), and 'Essays on the Early Period of the French Revolution' (1857). The 'Croker Papers', published in 1884, are interesting for the light they throw on the political life of Croker's period of office (1808–32), and for the letters they include from the duke of Wellington and others. It was Croker whom Macaulay said he 'detested more than cold boiled veal'.

CROKER, THOMAS CROFTON (1798–1854), author of 'Researches in the South of Ireland' (1824), 'Fairy Legends and Traditions' (1825–8), 'Legends of the Lakes' (1829), afterwards called 'Killarney Legends', and 'Popular Songs of Ireland' (1839). Croker's 'Legends', which are the work of an accomplished antiquary and earned the enthusiastic admiration of Scott, are a storehouse of information on Irish folklore.

CROLY, GEORGE (1780–1860), educated at Trinity College, Dublin, and rector of St. Stephen's, Walbrook, was author of 'Salathiel' (1829), a weird romance of the wandering Jew, Rome under Nero, and the siege of Jerusalem by Titus; 'Marston' (1846), a romance of which the French Revolution and the Napoleonic wars provide the background; 'Catiline' (1822), a tragedy; and numerous narrative and romantic poems. Byron ('Don

Juan', xi. 57) refers to him as the 'Revd. Rowley Powley'.

Cromagnon, the name of a cave near Les Eyzies in the Dordogne, where in 1868 were discovered four skeletons in association with objects of the Aurignacian (q.v.) period. They were of a tall race with large low skulls, the face short and broad, the eye-sockets low, and the nose narrow and prominent, and form one of the three main types of man of the Aurignacian culture.

Crome, JOHN (1768–1821), landscape painter, known as 'Old Crome' to distinguish him from his son, also a painter. Of humble origin, he spent his life in Norwich, founding the Norwich School in 1803.

Cromwell, The True Chronicle Historie of the whole life and death of Thomas Lord, a play published in 1602 and stated in the title to have been 'written by W. S.' It was included in the 3rd and 4th Shakespeare folios (1663 and 1685). The play has little merit and is certainly not by Shakespeare.

Cromwell, OLIVER, Lord Protector, 1653–8. He figures in Scott's 'Woodstock' (q.v.). His name was pronounced 'Crumwell', whence the Royalist toast, 'God send this *crumb well* down!'

Cromwell, RICHARD, Lord Protector, 1658–9.

Cromwell, THOMAS, *Earl of Essex* (1485?–1540), secretary to Cardinal Wolsey and subsequently to Henry VIII, and his chief adviser in ecclesiastical matters. He was the principal promoter of the dissolution of the monasteries. He negotiated Henry's marriage with Anne of Cleves. The failure of this match and of the policy that underlay it, coupled with the intense unpopularity of the minister, led to his downfall. A bill of attainder was passed and Cromwell was executed.

Cronos or KRONOS, in Greek mythology, one of the Titans, a son of Uranus and Gē, and father by Rhea of Hestia, Demeter, Hera, Poseidon, Hades, and Zeus. The children of Uranus conspired against their father, who immediately after their birth had confined them in Tartarus, and Uranus was castrated and divided from Gē by Cronos (a widely diffused cosmogonic myth; see A. Lang, 'Custom and Myth'). Cronos succeeded Uranus as ruler of the universe, and was in turn dethroned by Zeus. The Saturn (q.v.) of the Romans was identified with him.

Crop-ears or **Crop-eared,** terms applied to the Puritans or 'Roundheads' (q.v.) by their opponents, and probably intended to associate them with those whose ears had been cut off as a punishment. [OED.]

Crosbie, ADOLPHUS, a character in A. Trollope's 'The Small House at Allington' (q.v.).

Crosby Hall, in Bishopsgate, London, a splendid mansion built by alderman Sir John Crosby (*d.* 1475) about 1466. It was an important feature of 16th-cent. London. Sir Thomas More lived there about 1520, and the countess of Pembroke, 'Sidney's sister', in 1609. It is mentioned in Shakespeare's 'Richard III', I. iii, and III. i. The Hall, after a chequered career, was re-erected in 1908 on a site in Chelsea. It is now the centre of the Federation of University Women.

Crossjay Patterne, a character in Meredith's 'The Egoist' (q.v.).

Crotchet Castle, a novel by Peacock (q.v.), published in 1831. As in most of Peacock's novels, the story includes an assembly of oddities at a country house, Mr. Skionar (Coleridge), Mr. MacQuedy (a Scottish economist), Mr. Firedamp (a meteorologist), Mr. Chainmail (typifying medieval romance), and others. This is varied by a trip by river and canal to Wales, reminiscent of a trip taken by Peacock with Shelley up the Thames. The best character is the Revd. Dr. Folliott, a man 'both learned and jolly', of robust common sense, an improvement on Dr. Gaster and a forerunner of Dr. Opimian (qq.v.). The plot is extremely slight, and is supplied by young Mr. Crotchet's unfortunate love affairs with Miss Touchandgo and Lady Clarinda.

Crowdero, the one-legged fiddler (*crowd,* an old English word for fiddle) and leader of the bear-baiters in Butler's 'Hudibras' (q.v.).

Crowe, CAPTAIN, the Sancho Panza of Sir Launcelot Greaves in Smollett's (q.v.) novel of that name.

CROWE, WILLIAM, see *Lewesdon Hill.*

Crowland, see *Croyland.*

Crown of Thorns, THE, the crown that the soldiers put on the head of Jesus Christ before the Crucifixion (Matt. xxvii. 29).

Crown of Wild Olive, The, four lectures by Ruskin (q.v.), delivered in 1866; the first on 'War', delivered at the Royal Military Academy; the second on 'The Future of England', at the Royal Artillery Institution; the third on 'Work', to a working men's institute, dealing in particular with the objects, sometimes wasteful or futile, to which capital directs labour; the fourth, in the Bradford Town Hall, on 'Traffic' (in the sense of buying and selling), in which he discussed architecture in its relation to religion, and the false ideals of wealth.

A crown of wild olive was the only prize at the Olympic Games (q.v.). Ruskin used it as a title in allusion to the importance of not working for a false idea of reward.

CROWNE, JOHN (1640?–1703?), probably the son of William Crowne, an emigrant to Nova Scotia. He returned to London by 1665, when his romance 'Pandion and Amphigenia' was published. His first comedy, 'The Country Wit', appeared in 1675, containing the character of Sir Mannerly Shallow, the pompous fool, subsequently developed by him into Sir Courtly Nice in the play of that name. Three dull tragedies followed, and then his best comedies 'City Politiques' (1683), a satire on the Whigs, and 'Sir Courtly Nice' (q.v.) in 1685. He wrote three further tragedies (including 'Thyestes', 1681) and two comedies: 'The English Frier' (1690), a satire on the Catholic priests who had been prominent at the court of James II; and 'The Married Beau' (1694), founded on the story of 'The Curious Impertinent' (q.v.) in 'Don Quixote'.

Croyland or CROWLAND, a famous abbey in Lincolnshire founded by Æthelbald of Mercia in the 8th cent., near the tomb of St. Guthlac. It figures prominently in C. Kingsley's 'Hereward the Wake' (q.v.).

Croyland or *Crowland History, The,* a chronicle of the 14th or 15th cent., printed by Savile in 1596, and for long erroneously attributed to Ingulf, Abbot of Croyland (*d.* 1109), secretary to William the Conqueror. It was shown by Sir Francis Palgrave and others to be a forgery of the 15th cent.

CRUDEN, ALEXANDER (1701–70), a bookseller in the Royal Exchange and corrector of the press, who in 1737 published his 'Biblical Concordance'. He suffered periodical attacks of insanity, and once believed himself divinely appointed to reform the nation.

Cruikshank, GEORGE (1792–1878), illustrator and caricaturist, son of Isaac Cruikshank, also a caricaturist. His caricatures were published in periodicals, including 'The Scourge' (1811–16) and 'The Meteor' (1813–14), and he illustrated Pierce Egan's 'Life in London', Grimm's 'German Popular Stories', Dickens's 'Sketches by Boz' and 'Oliver Twist', novels by Harrison Ainsworth, Thackeray's 'Legend of the Rhine', etc. From 1835 for some years Cruikshank issued the 'Comic Almanack', one of the predecessors of 'Punch'.

Crummles, MR. VINCENT, MRS., and NINETTA ('the infant phenomenon'), characters in Dickens's 'Nicholas Nickleby' (q.v.).

Cruncher, JERRY, a character in Dickens's 'A Tale of Two Cities' (q.v.).

Crusoe, ROBINSON, see *Robinson Crusoe.*

Crutched, CROUCHED, or CROSSED **Friars** (*Fratres cruciferi*), a minor order of friars so called from their bearing or wearing a cross. Their house stood at the corner of Seething Lane and Crutched Friars Street in the City of London. After their dissolution in 1539 and the destruction of the monastic buildings, the Navy Office was constructed on part of the site. There Samuel Pepys lived and conducted his business ('Diary', 18 July 1660, etc.).

Cry of the Children, The, one of the best known of the poems of E. B. Browning (q.v.), published in 1843 in 'Blackwood's Magazine'. It is the lament of the children in factories

and mines, the victims of industrial development.

Crystal Palace, see *Exhibition.*

Cubism, a movement in art developed by Picasso (q.v.) and Georges Braque (1882–1963): the first Cubist pictures were exhibited in 1907. In Analytical Cubism forms are broken down into simple geometric shapes, various views of an object being shown together. In Synthetic Cubism, which developed *c.* 1912, fragments of objects, such as newspapers and matches, are often incorporated in the paintings (collages).

Cuchulain (pron. 'Cuhoo'lin'), one of the principal heroes of the Ulster cycle of Irish mythology, the nephew or ward of Conchubar, king of Ulster. He is supposed to have lived in the first century of the Christian era. His birth was miraculous, and he showed his strength and prowess at an early age. While still a child he killed the terrible watch-dog of the Smith Culan, and compensated the owner by undertaking to guard his house in the dog's place, whence the name Cuchulain, signifying 'Culan's hound'. Of his numerous feats of valour, which won him the love of many women, the chief was his defence of Ulster, single-handed, against Medb or Maeve, queen of Connaught, who attacked it in order to carry off the Brown Bull of Cuailgne (pron. Cooley). Cuchulain was killed, when 27, by Lugaid, son of a king of Ulster, and the daughters of Calatin the wizard, in vengeance for their fathers whom Cuchulain had slain.

A series of the legends about him have been translated by Lady Gregory (q.v., 'Cuchulain of Muirthemne'). He figures in Macpherson's Ossianic poems as 'Cuthullin' (q.v.).

Cuckold's Haven or **Point,** a spot on the Thames riverside, a little below Rotherhithe, so called, according to tradition, because in King John's reign a miller there had a beautiful wife, who attracted the king's favour. The miller was compensated, says the tale, by a grant of as much land on that side as he could see from his house.

Cuckoo–Song, The, see '*Sumer is icumen in*'.

Cuddie Headrigg, in Scott's 'Old Mortality' (q.v.), the ploughman in Lady Margaret Bellenden's service.

Cuddy, a herdsman or shepherd, in the 'Shepheards Calender' of Spenser, and in the 'Shepherd's Week' of Gay (qq.v.).

CUDWORTH, RALPH (1617–88), educated at Emmanuel College, Cambridge, was one of the leading members of the Cambridge Platonists. He was successively master of Clare, professor of Hebrew, and master of Christ's. His principal works were 'The True Intellectual System of the Universe' (1678); and a 'Treatise concerning Eternal and Immutable Morality', published after his death (1731). His style is lucid, but has not the vigorous and striking quality of that of Hobbes.

The characteristic feature of the philosophy of Cudworth and the other Platonists is its reaction against the narrow Puritan dogmatism, and against the materialism of Hobbes and Descartes. They were idealists, and maintained the spiritual constitution of the universe. Sense can reveal only appearance; reality consists in 'intelligible forms', which are 'not impressions printed on the soul without, but ideas vitally protended or actively exerted from within itself'. As moralists they held that reason and religion are in harmony; truth and true goodness cannot be disunited; morality is based upon reason.

Cuff, SERGEANT, the detective in Wilkie Collins's 'The Moonstone' (q.v.).

Cufic, a variety of Arabic writing attributed to the scholars of Cufa or Kufa, an ancient city near Babylon, the residence of the Caliphs before the building of Baghdad, and a great seat of Muslim learning. Cufic differs from ordinary Arabic writing in the angular form of many of the letters and the general rigidity of the strokes.

Culdee, from the Old Irish *céle dé*, associate or servant of God, member of an ancient Scoto-Irish religious order, found from the 8th cent. onwards. The name appears to have been first given to solitary recluses; these were afterwards associated in communities of anchorites; and finally brought under the canonical rule along with the secular clergy by the end of the 11th cent. [OED.]

Culling, MRS., afterwards LADY ROMFREY, a character in Meredith's 'Beauchamp's Career' (q.v.).

Cullŏ'den, near Inverness, the site of the battle in which in 1746 the duke of Cumberland defeated the force of the Young Pretender.

CULVERWEL, NATHANAEL (*d.* 1651?), educated at Emmanuel College, Cambridge, was one of the Cambridge Platonists (q.v.). His 'Light of Nature', in which he sought to apportion the respective spheres of reason and faith, was published in 1652. His early death, probably when only 32, prevented the execution of a larger design, the reconciliation of the teaching of the Gospel with reason.

CUMBERLAND, RICHARD (1732–1811), educated at Westminster School and Trinity College, Cambridge, was author of a number of sentimental comedies, of which 'The West Indian' and 'The Brothers' (qq.v.) are the best; some tragedies; two novels, 'Arundel' (1789) and 'Henry' (1795), and a translation of the 'Clouds' of Aristophanes; also of an interesting autobiography. Cumberland caricatured by Sheridan as Sir Fretful Plagiary in 'The Critic' (q.v.).

Cumberland, WILLIAM AUGUSTUS, *duke of* (1721–65), third son of George II, and in command the English of army at Culloden (1746); known as 'the Butcher' on account of the severity with which he stamped out disaffection among the Highlanders. He figures in Scott's 'Waverley' (q.v.).

CUMMINGS, E. E. (1894–1962), American poet, born in Massachusetts. He published the first of his many volumes of verse, 'Tulips and Chimneys', in 1924. 'Poems 1923–54' appeared in 1954. Cummings's experiments with typography and punctuation helped to give his verse a greater air of modernity than it in fact possessed; but several of his lyrics prove the strength and genuineness of his talent. He was imprisoned in a French military camp on a false charge in 1917, and his account of his experience, 'The Enormous Room' (1922), is a masterpiece of its kind.

Cumnor, LORD and LADY, and their daughter, LADY HARRIET, characters in Mrs. Gaskell's 'Wives and Daughters' (q.v.).

Cunctator, see *Fabius.*

CUNNINGHAM, ALLAN (1784–1842), a native of Dumfriesshire, was at first a stonemason and subsequently secretary to Francis Chantrey, the sculptor. He supplied to R. H. Cromek much of the material (fabricated by himself) of Cromek's 'Remains of Nithsdale and Galloway Song'. He published 'Traditional Tales of the English and Scottish Peasantry' in 1822, 'The Songs of Scotland, Ancient and Modern' (including the famous 'A Wet Sheet and a Flowing Sea') in 1825, and 'Lives of the most eminent British Painters, Sculptors, and Architects' in 1829–33. Many of Cunningham's short pieces and imitations of ancient ballads, such as 'Hame, Hame, Hame' and 'The sun rises bright in France', gained much popularity.

CUNNINGHAM, JOHN (1729–73), author of the successful farce 'Love in a Mist' (1747), and of much tuneful contemplative verse, not all of it included in his 'Poems, chiefly Pastoral' (1766).

CUNNINGHAME GRAHAM, ROBERT BONTINE (1852–1936), the son of a Scottish laird, educated at Harrow, a man of varied career, during which he was an M.P., a leader of the Dock Strike in 1887, an anarchist, and a traveller in remote parts of the world, particularly in the interior of Spanish America, where he gained an intimate knowledge of gaucho life and of the older civilization surviving from the period of Spanish rule. His writings include remarkable stories of travel and descriptions of strange scenes and people, and tales of Scotland, notably in 'Mogreb-el-Acksa' (Morocco, 1898), 'Thirteen Stories' (1900), 'Success' (1902), 'Hernando de Soto' (1903), 'Scottish Stories' (1914), 'The Horses of the Conquest' (1930).

Cunobelin (Cymbeline), a king of Britain in the early years of the Christian era, and father of Caractacus (q.v.).

Cup, *The,* a tragedy by A. Tennyson (q.v.), produced in 1881. Camma, the wife of Sinnatus, tetrarch of Galatia, poisons the pro-Roman traitor Synorix (who has killed her husband and tried to seduce her), and takes her own life.

Cupid, identified by the Romans with the Greek EROS, the god of Love. He is generally represented to be the son of Venus (Aphrodite), but his father is variously stated to be Jupiter, Mars, or Mercury. He is pictured as a winged infant, armed with a bow, a quiver full of arrows, and torches.

Cupid's Revenge, see *Fletcher (J.).*

Cupid and Campaspe, see *Campaspe.*

Cupid and Psyche, an allegorical episode in the tale of the 'Golden Ass' (q.v.) of Apuleius. Cupid becomes enamoured of Psyche, daughter of a king, and visits her every night, but remains invisible and forbids her to attempt to see him. Her sisters tell her that her lover is a serpent and will finally devour her. One night she takes a lamp and looks at Cupid while he sleeps, and agitated by the sight of his beauty lets fall a drop of hot oil on his shoulder. The angry god departs and leaves Psyche solitary and remorseful. She wanders over the earth in search of her lover, subjected by Venus to hardships and trials until Jupiter, taking pity on her, makes her immortal and reunites her to Cupid.

This fable was the subject of a poem by Shackerley Marmion (q.v.), 1637; of another by William Morris in the 'Earthly Paradise' (q.v.); and there is a version of it in Pater's 'Marius the Epicurean' (q.v.) and in the 'Eros and Psyche' of Bridges (q.v.).

Curé de Meudon, Rabelais (q.v.).

Cure for a Cuckold, A, a comedy by J. Webster (q.v.) and W. Rowley (q.v.), brought out in 1661.

It deals with the love-affairs of two couples, Bonville and Annabel, and Lessingham and Clare; and contains a notable duel scene on Calais sands. It cannot be called a satisfactory play; but there are scenes in it which, on internal evidence, Gosse showed to be attributable to Webster; and these, if separated from the inferior matter provided by Rowley, form a complete and charming idyll, which Gosse proposed to call 'Love's Graduate'. Under this name they were issued in 1884, edited by S. E. Spring-Rice.

Curfew (from French *couvre-feu*), originally a regulation in force in medieval Europe by which at a fixed hour in the evening, indicated by the ringing of a bell, hearth-fires were to be covered over or extinguished, the probable object of the regulation being the prevention of conflagrations. Hence it has come to mean the practice of ringing a bell at a fixed hour in the evening, continued after the original purpose was obsolete. [OED.]

Curie, MARIE (1867–1934), *née* Slodowska, born at Warsaw, the wife of Pierre Curie, a professor of physics at the Sorbonne. With her husband she discovered radium in 1898 and contributed greatly to the knowledge of radio-activity. M. and Mme Curie received the Nobel prize for physics in 1903, and Mme Curie (who succeeded her husband in his professorship after his death in 1906) received in 1911 that for chemistry also.

Curious Impertinent (or *The Fatal Curiosity*), an episode in 'Don Quixote' (q.v.), which provided the plot for more than one of the English 17th-cent. dramas. Anselmo having married the beautiful Camilla, urges his friend Lotario to test the virtue of the latter by making love to her. Lotario, at first reluctant, yields to the constant pressure of his friend, with results disastrous to all concerned. The lapse of Camilla encourages the licentiousness of her maid Leonela, and this leads to the discovery of her mistress's infidelity, the death of Anselmo and Lotario, and Camilla's retirement to a convent.

Curius Dentatus, MARCUS, Roman consul in 290, 275, and 274 B.C., celebrated as a type of old Roman frugality and virtue. After repeatedly defeating the enemies of Rome, he retired to his small farm and cultivated the land with his own hands. Compare *Cincinnatus.*

CURLL, EDMUND (1675–1747), a bookseller and pamphleteer, chiefly remembered for the controversy about the publication of Pope's correspondence (see under *Pope, Alexander*), and on account of his literary frauds and indecent publications (Pope refers to 'Curl's chaste press' in 'The Dunciad', i. 40). Curll is also mentioned in Swift's poem 'On the Death of Dr. Swift'.

CURRER BELL, see *Brontë (C.).*

Curryfin, LORD, a character in Peacock's 'Gryll Grange' (q.v.).

Curse of Kehama, The, a poem by Southey (q.v.), published in 1810.

The peasant Ladurlad kills Arvalan, son of the mighty Raja of the world, Kehama, to protect his daughter Kailyal from Arvalan's lust. Ladurlad and Kailyal are brought before the infuriated Kehama for punishment. Kailyal clings for protection to the statue of the goddess Marriataly, falls into the river, and is borne away. Kehama pronounces a curse on Ladurlad, charming his life, so that he cannot be harmed by disease or weapons or age, but at the same time is denied water and the fruits of the earth. Kailyal and Ladurlad, in his misery, are reunited. Then follow a succession of incidents in which the fate of this unfortunate pair is subjected to the influence of the various powers, good and evil, of the complicated Hindu mythology, while the revengeful spirit of Arvalan seeks again to get possession of Kailyal. The curse of Kehama turns into a blessing, for by his immunity from death, Ladurlad is able to save his daughter from the dangers that threaten her. Finally Kehama, who has obtained dominion over Swerga or heaven, aspires also to the throne of Paladon or hell. He drinks the 'amreeta' or cup of immortality, to find that he has drunk immortal death and punishment, and becomes the fourth supporter of the throne of Yamen the lord of hell. Kailyal also drinks it, and is borne to the Bower of Bliss, to enjoy immortal life. Ladurlad sinks to rest and awakes in heaven.

Cursive, writing done without lifting the pen, so that the characters are joined together.

Cursor Mundi, a poem in Northern Middle English of some 30,000 lines, mainly in eight-syllabled couplets, of the early 14th cent. It recounts, with many divagations, traditions, and fragments of hagiology, the Bible history from the creation onwards. The author, whose name is unknown, shows skill in popularizing religious instruction. Many copies of the poem survive, indicating the favour in which it was held.

Curtain, THE, one of the earliest of the London theatres, built, soon after the Theatre (see *Burbage, J.*), in Shoreditch. The Chamberlain's company, which included Richard Burbage and Shakespeare, probably acted there from 1597 to 1599.

Curtana, the pointless sword carried before the sovereign of England at the coronation, emblematic of the sword of mercy.

Curtius, LACUS: according to legend a chasm appeared in the Roman forum in 362 B.C., which the soothsayers declared could only be filled if Rome's greatest treasure were thrown into it. Whereupon Marcus Curtius, saying that Rome could have no greater treasure than arms and valour, mounted his steed in full armour and leapt into the chasm, which thereupon closed over him.

Curule Chair, in Roman antiquity, was a chair inlaid with ivory and shaped like a camp-stool, used by the highest magistrates.

CURZON, ROBERT, *fourteenth Baron Zouche* (1810–73), educated at Charterhouse and Christ Church, Oxford, was author of a 'Visit to the Monasteries of the Levant' (1849), a fascinating record of travels, undertaken in search of manuscripts, to Mount Athos, Greece, Palestine, and Egypt; also of 'Armenia' (1854), and of an 'Account of the most celebrated Libraries of Italy' (1854).

CURZON OF KEDLESTON, GEORGE NATHANIEL, *Marquess* (1859–1925), as a young man travelled in India, Persia, and the Far East; was viceroy of India from 1899 to 1905, chancellor of Oxford University from 1907, and secretary of state for foreign affairs, 1918–22. His chief publication was 'Persia and the Persian Question' (1892), a monumental survey of the country, remarkable for its range, accuracy, and first-hand information. As viceroy Lord Curzon devoted great care to the neglected ancient monuments of India, and created the post of director-general of archaeology. Lord Curzon's immense powers of work, combined with a certain

aloofness of demeanour and preference for splendour and formality in official life, gave rise to numerous legends, many of them of a humorous character.

Custance, the widow in Udall's 'Ralph Roister Doister' (q.v.).

Custaunce or CONSTAUNCE, the heroine of Chaucer's 'The Man of Law's Tale' (see *Canterbury Tales*).

Custom of the Country, The, a romantic drama by J. Fletcher (q.v.) and P. Massinger (q.v.), composed between 1619 and 1622, derived from the 'Persiles y Sigismunda' of Cervantes. The play is disfigured by the indecency of some of its scenes.

Count Clodio, an Italian governor, is suitor to Zenocia, but she loves Arnoldo, the younger of two brothers, and marries him. Zenocia and the two brothers forcibly oppose Clodio's claim to the 'custom of the country' (by which he may spend the bridal night with every bride), and escape by sea. Zenocia is captured by a Portuguese captain, and placed in the service of Hippolita at Lisbon, where Arnoldo also arrives. Hippolita falls in love with Arnoldo, who endeavours to recover Zenocia. A meeting between them is witnessed by the jealous Hippolita, who orders Zenocia to be strangled; but this is prevented by the governor of Lisbon, to whom the repentant Clodio has applied for her release. Hippolita now has recourse to the witch Sulpitia, who causes Zenocia to waste away, by melting a waxen image of her. But Arnoldo wastes away in sympathy. Hippolita, moved to remorse, cancels the charm, and resigns Zenocia to Arnoldo. There is an underplot concerned with the adventures of Arnoldo's elder brother Rutilio.

Custos Rotulorum, the principal justice of the peace in a county, who has custody of the rolls and records of the sessions of the peace.

Cute, ALDERMAN, a character in Dickens's 'The Chimes' (q.v.), said to be intended for Sir Peter Laurie, the City magistrate.

Cuthbert, ST. (*d.* 687), in his youth kept sheep on the hills near the Lauder, a tributary of the Tweed. He entered the monastery of Melrose, of which he became prior. In course of time he was sent to fill the post of abbot of Lindisfarne, on which the monastery of Melrose then depended; and after several years, feeling himself called to a life of perfect solitude, he retired to the small island of Farne. In 684, at a synod held under St. Theodore, archbishop of Canterbury, he was selected for the see of Lindisfarne, and to overcome his unwillingness to accept it, King Egfrith himself, accompanied by the bishop of the Picts, visited him on his island. After two years, feeling death approaching, he retired to the solitude of his island, and died in his cell. His body, which was said to have remained for many years in a state of incorruption and was carried away by the monks when they were driven by the Danes from

Lindisfarne, was finally buried in Durham cathedral. He is commemorated on 20 March.

St. CUTHBERT'S BEADS is a popular name, originating on Holy Island and the Northumbrian coast, for the detached and perforated joints of the encrinites (a fossil lily-like marine animal) there found.

CUTHBERT BEDE, see *Bradley (E.)*.

Cuthullin, in the Ossianic poems of Macpherson (q.v.), the Irish hero Cuchulain (q.v.), transposed in time so as to be contemporary with Finn (Fingal). See *Fingal*.

Cutpurse, MOLL, see *Moll Cutpurse*.

Cutter of Coleman Street, The, see *Cowley (A.)*.

Cuttle, CAPTAIN EDWARD, a character in Dickens's 'Dombey and Son' (q.v.). His favourite expression is, 'When found, make a note of'.

Cutty Sark, (1) see *Tam o' Shanter*; (2) the name of a famous clipper ship built in 1869 for the China tea trade. She sailed 363 miles in one day. She now lies in a concrete bath beside Greenwich Pier to serve as an educational centre for the Merchant Marine.

Cutty Stool, formerly in Scotland, a particular seat in church where offenders against chastity, etc., had to sit during divine service and receive a public rebuke from the minister.

Cuvier, GEORGES (1769–1832), a great French naturalist, and a founder of the sciences of comparative anatomy and palaeontology.

Cuwaert, see *Coart*.

Cuyp, AELBERT (1620–91), Dutch landscape painter, whose study of light influenced English painters.

Cyanean Rocks or SYMPLEGĂDES, two rocks at the entrance of the Euxine Sea, which were believed to clash together, crushing vessels that passed between them. The Argonauts (q.v.) narrowly escaped them.

Cybĕlē, an Asiatic goddess representing the fecundity of nature, worshipped especially in Phrygia. Thence her cult passed into Greece, where she was known as RHEA. According to mythology she became enamoured of the shepherd Attis (q.v.), a legend connected with the productivity of the earth.

Cyclădes, a group of islands in the Aegean sea, regarded as lying in a circle round Delos.

Cyclic poets, a group of Greek epic writers whose writings collectively formed a sort of legendary history of the world from the earliest times, and supplied themes to Greek dramatic and lyric poets. Nothing is known with certainty about the authors.

Cyclōpes, a race of giants having but one eye, in the middle of the forehead, who inhabited the island of Sicily. When Odysseus visited the island, Polyphemus (q.v.) was chief among them. The most solid walls and impregnable fortresses were attributed to their work, and

as they lived near Mt. Etna, they were supposed to be the workmen of Hephaestus and to fabricate the thunderbolts of Zeus. Among the Cyclopes mentioned by name in English literature are Brontēs (or Bronteus) and Pyracmon.

Cyder, a poem in blank verse, in two books, by J. Philips (q.v.), published in 1708, on the cultivation of cider apples, and the manufacture and virtues of cider, written in imitation of Virgil's Georgics.

Cyllēnē, one of the highest mountains in the Peloponnese, fabled to be the birthplace of Hermes (q.v.).

Cymbeline, a play by Shakespeare (q.v.), acted in 1610 or 1611, first printed in the folio of 1623. It combines a fragment of British history, freely adapted from Holinshed, with the story of Ginevra from Boccaccio's 'Decameron' (ii. 9).

Imogen, daughter of Cymbeline, king of Britain, has secretly married Leonatus Posthumus, an accomplished gentleman. The queen, Imogen's stepmother, desirous that her son Cloten should marry Imogen, reveals this secret marriage to the king, who banishes Posthumus. The latter, at Rome, boasts of the virtue of Imogen, and enters into a wager with Iachimo that if he can win Imogen's favour he shall have a diamond ring that Imogen had given Posthumus. Iachimo, repulsed by Imogen, by a stratagem gets admission to her chamber at night, brings back to Posthumus evidence that convinces him of her infidelity, and receives the ring. Posthumus writes to Pisanio, his servant at the court, directing him to kill Imogen. Pisanio from compassion spares her, provides her with a man's apparel, and leaves her in a forest, where she is kindly entertained by Bellarius and the two sons of Cymbeline, whom he had stolen in their infancy. A Roman army invades Britain. Imogen falls into the hands of the Roman general and becomes his page. In the ensuing battle Cymbeline is captured and then rescued, and the general and Imogen are taken prisoners, as also Iachimo, thanks to the valour of Bellarius, of the king's sons, and also of Posthumus, who has returned from Rome to fight for Cymbeline. He now surrenders himself for execution as having returned from banishment. The Roman general asks Cymbeline to spare Imogen. The king moved by something familiar in her appearance, spares her life and grants her a boon. She asks that Iachimo be forced to tell how he came by the ring that he wears on his finger. Iachimo discloses his treachery. Posthumus, learning that his wife is innocent and believing her dead, is in despair, till Imogen reveals herself. The king's joy at recovering his daughter is intensified when Bellarius restores to him his two lost sons, and the scene ends in a general reconciliation. The play contains the beautiful dirge, 'Fear no more the heat o' the sun'.

Cymochles in Spenser's 'Faerie Queene', II. v, vi, and viii, 'a man of rare redoubted might', 'given all to lust and loose living', the husband of Acrasia (q.v.) and brother of Pyrochles (q.v.). He sets out to avenge on Sir Guyon the supposed death of his brother. But Phaedria (q.v.) intervenes. He is finally slain by Prince Arthur.

Cymŏdŏcē, one of the Nereids. Cymodoce is the name of the mother of Marinell in Spenser's 'Faerie Queene', IV. xii. Swinburne's 'Island of Cymodoce' in 'Songs of the Springtides' is the island of Sark.

Cymon ,and Iphigenia, one of Dryden's 'Fables', taken from the 'Decameron' (v. i) of Boccaccio.

Cymry, the Welsh. The word, which is Welsh, probably means 'the compatriots'.

CYNEWULF, probably a Northumbrian or Mercian poet of the late 8th or 9th cent. At one time a great many OE. poems were attributed to him, but modern scholarship is inclined to restrict the canon of his works to four poems contained in the 'Exeter Book' and the 'Vercelli Book' (qq.v.). The epilogues of these are 'signed' with runic characters corresponding to the letters that compose the name Cynewulf. The poems are 'St. Juliana', 'Elene', the story of the discovery of the true cross by the Empress Helena, mother of Constantine, the 'Fates of the Apostles', a very brief martyrology of the apostles, and a poem on the Ascension which is placed in the 'Exeter Book' between a poem on the Incarnation and one on the Last Judgement. Of the four, the finest is the 'Elene'.

Cynics, see *Antisthenes.*

Cynosure, 'dog's tail', the constellation *Ursa Minor,* which contains in its tail the Pole star; hence a centre of attraction.

Cynthia, (1) a surname of Artemis or Diana (q.v.), from Mt. Cynthus in Delos, where Artemis was supposed to have been born; (2) Spenser, in 'Colin Clouts come home againe', uses the name to designate Queen Elizabeth; (3) in Congreve's 'The Double Dealer'(q.v.), the daughter of Sir Paul Plyant, affianced to Mellefont.

Cynthia, a poem by R. Barnfield (q.v.).

Cynthia's Revels, a comedy by Jonson (q.v.), printed in 1601, satirizing some court types. These figure under the names of Amorphus, a traveller who has drunk of the fountain of self-love; Asotus, a foolish young gallant; Hedon the voluptuous; Anaides the impudent; Philautia, self-love; Argurion, money; Moria, folly. Cynthia is Queen Elizabeth. Actaeon alludes to Essex; Cupid and Mercury in disguise are pages at her court. The plot is extremely slight, and the play is tedious and of little interest at the present day. The song of Hesperus in Act v, sc. iii, 'Queen and huntress, chaste and fair', is one of Jonson's most beautiful lyrics.

Cypress, a coniferous tree, often regarded as symbolic of mourning, frequently planted in cemeteries of southern Europe, and its branches or sprigs used at funerals (the 'invisae cupressi' of Horace, Od. II. xiv). For the triple signification of the cypress among the ancients, as a symbol of generation, of death, and of immortality, see De Gubernatis, 'Mythologie des Plantes', s.v. *Cyprès.*

In Shakespeare's 'Twelfth Night', II. iv ('in sad cypress let me be laid'), 'cypress' in the opinion of Aldis Wright means a coffin of cypress wood, or a bier strewn with cypress branches; but in III. i, of the same play, 'a cypress, not a bosom, hideth my heart', the word means 'cypress lawn' or crape. Cf. Milton, 'Il Penseroso', 'sable stole of cypress lawn'. In the latter sense the word is derived from the name of the island of Cyprus.

Cypress, MR., a character in Peacock's 'Nightmare Abbey' (q.v.), a caricature of Byron.

Cypresse Grove, THE, see *Drummond of Hawthornden.*

Cyprian, belonging to Cyprus, an island famous in ancient times for the worship of Aphrodite or Venus. Hence the word is used in the sense of 'lewd' or 'licentious', and in the 18th–19th cents. was used to signify a prostitute.

CYPRIAN, ST. (*c.* A.D. 200–58), bishop of Carthage and a Father of the Church, author of 'De Unitate Catholicae Ecclesiae' and other theological works, beheaded under the Emperor Valerian.

Cyrano de Bergerac, see *Bergerac.*

Cyrenaic School of philosophy, see *Aristippus.*

Cyrus, Le Grand, see *Scudéry.*

Cythēra, an island (Cerigo) on the coast of the Peloponnese, sacred to the goddess Aphrodite, who was thence surnamed Cythĕrēa.

D

Dacier, THE HON. PERCY, a character in Meredith's 'Diana of the Crossways' (q.v.).

Dactyl, a metrical foot consisting of one long followed by two short syllables, or of one accented followed by two unaccented (de- rived from the three joints of the finger, δάκτυλος). See *Metre.*

Dada, a movement in art and literature founded *c.* 1916 in Zürich and more or less simultaneously in New York. It lasted until

1922, with Paris as its centre from 1920. The name (meaning 'hobby-horse') was chosen at random from the dictionary; the aim of Dada was destructive, denying sense and order.

Daedălus, an ingenious Athenian craftsman. Having murdered his nephew Talus, as likely to prove his rival in ingenuity, he fled with his son Icărus to Crete, where he constructed the famous labyrinth for King Minos (q.v.). Having incurred the king's displeasure, he was imprisoned, and escaped with Icarus by means of wings. But Icarus flew too high, and the heat of the sun melted the wax wherewith the wings were fastened, so that he fell into the sea west of Samos (hence called the Icarian Sea) and was drowned. Daedalus made his way to Sicily.

Dagobert I, the son of Clotaire II and king of the Franks (628–39). St. Eloi (q.v.) was his treasurer.

Dagon, the national deity of the ancient Philistines, represented as half man, half fish (Judges xvi. 23; 1 Sam. v. 1–5; Milton, 'Paradise Lost', i. 462).

Dagonet, in Malory's 'Morte Darthur', King Arthur's fool.

Daguerreotype, an early photographic process invented by Louis Jacques Daguerre (1789–1851) in 1839.

Daily Courant, The, the first English daily newspaper, started in March 1702. It contained foreign intelligence, translated from foreign newspapers. It lasted till 1735.

Daily News, The, was founded by Dickens (q.v.), as a Liberal rival to the 'Morning Chronicle', in 1846. But Dickens soon abandoned the editorship to John Forster (q.v.). Among notable contributors and members of its staff at various times may be mentioned Harriet Martinaeu (q.v.), Andrew Lang (q.v.), and the eminent war correspondent, Archibald Forbes (1839–1900). It became 'The News Chronicle', having absorbed 'The Daily Chronicle' in 1930.

Daily Telegraph, The, founded in 1855, was the first daily paper to be issued in London at a penny. Its enterprising character and rather highly coloured style proved so successful that for a time it enjoyed a larger circulation than any other English newspaper. Among famous members of its staff have been George Augustus Sala (q.v.), Sir Edwin Arnold (q.v.), and Edward Dicey (1832–1911).

Dairyman's Daughter, The, a moral tale by Legh Richmond (1772–1827), rector of Turvey, published in 1809. This tract had an enormous circulation, reaching two million copies.

Daisy, SOLOMON, see *Solomon Daisy.*

Daisy Miller, one of H. James's (q.v.) most popular stories, published in 1879, and dramatized by James in 1883. Daisy Miller travels to Europe with her wealthy, common-

place mother, and in her innocence and audacity offends convention and seems to compromise her reputation. She dies in Rome of malaria. She is one of the most notable and charming of James's portrayals of 'the American girl'.

Dale, LAETITIA, a character in Meredith's 'The Egoist' (q.v.).

Dale, LILY, the heroine of A. Trollope's 'The Small House at Allington' (q.v.). Her sister, Bell, her uncle the Squire, and her cousin, Bernard, are other important characters in this novel.

D'Alembert or DALEMBERT, JEAN LE ROND (1717–83), see *Philosophes* and *Encyclopédie.*

Dalgarno, LORD, a character in Scott's 'Fortunes of Nigel' (q.v.).

Dalgetty, DUGALD, a character in Scott's 'Legend of Montrose' (q.v.).

Dame Durden, the subject of a well-known song, who kept five men-servants 'to use the spade and flail', and five women servants 'to carry the milken-pail'.

Damien, FATHER JOSEPH (1841–89), a Belgian priest at Honolulu, went in 1873 to the neglected leper settlement on the island of Molokai. There he spent the rest of his life ministering, single-handed for the first twelve years, to the spiritual and material welfare of 700 lepers. In 1885 he contracted the disease, but continued to work until his death. R. L. Stevenson wrote an account of him, 'Father Damien', in 1890 ('Chambers's Biographical Dictionary').

Damiens, ROBERT FRANÇOIS (1714–57), a madman who attempted the life of Louis XV. He was executed after having been, it is said, chained on a steel bed that was heated. Hence the reference in Goldsmith's 'The Traveller' (q.v.) to 'Damiens' bed of steel'.

Damocles, one of the flatterers of Dionysius the elder, tyrant of Syracuse. He pronounced Dionysius the happiest of men, whereupon Dionysius invited him to experience the happiness of a monarch. He placed him at a banquet, where presently Damocles perceived a naked sword hanging over his head by a single hair.

Damoetas, (1) a shepherd in the 'Idylls' of Theocritus and 'Eclogues' of Virgil; (2) a character in Sidney's 'Arcadia' (q.v.); (3) and an old shepherd in Milton's 'Lycidas' (q.v.).

Damon, a shepherd singer in Virgil's eighth 'Eclogue'; a name adopted by poets for a rustic swain. Cf. 'Epitaphium Damonis' of Milton (q.v.), his Latin elegy on his friend Charles Diodati (q.v.).

Damon and Musidōra, two lovers, who are the subject of an episode in Thomson's 'Seasons' (q.v., 'Summer').

Damon and Pythias, a rhymed play by R. Edwards (q.v.), acted probably in 1564, printed in 1571. Damon and Pythias, Pythagorean Greeks, visit Syracuse, and the former is presently arrested on a baseless charge of spying and conspiring against Dionysius the tyrant of Syracuse, who orders his execution. Damon obtains a respite of two months to return home in order to settle his affairs, Pythias offering himself as security for his return. Damon is delayed and arrives when Pythias is just about to be put to death. They contend which shall be executed, each striving to save the other. Dionysius, impressed with their mutual loyalty, pardons Damon and asks to be admitted to their brotherhood.

In the original classical legend it is Phintias (of which 'Pythias' is a corruption), not Damon, who is sentenced, and Damon who goes bail for him.

DAMPIER, WILLIAM (1652–1715), buccaneer, logwood-cutter, privateer, and explorer, visited in the course of his activities many parts of the world, the Spanish Main, Yucatan, the Pacific, Australia, and the East Indies. He published accounts, in a vivid and straightforward style, of his travels and observations, in his 'Voyages' (1697), 'Voyages and Descriptions' (1699), and 'A Voyage to New Holland' (1703–9). Dampier also figures in Woodes Rogers's journal of his privateering expedition (see *Rogers, W.*).

Dan to Beersheba, FROM, i.e. from one end of the land to the other, an expression said to be first used by Sterne (q.v.) in the 'Sentimental Journey' (cf. Judges xx. 1). The city Dan was at the extreme north of the land of Canaan, Beersheba at the extreme south.

DANA, RICHARD HENRY (1815–82), born in Massachusetts, an American jurist and politician, shipped in 1834 as a sailor for a voyage in the Pacific. He published in 1840 a record of this experience under the title 'Two years before the Mast'.

Danaë, the daughter of Acrisius, king of Argos. An oracle foretold that the king would be killed by his daughter's son, and Acrisius therefore confined her in a brazen tower. Zeus, who was enamoured of her, visited her there in a shower of gold. Their son was Perseus (q.v.). Danae and the child were cast adrift on the sea in a boat and borne to the island of Seriphos, where they were kindly treated by the King Polydectes. See *Perseus*.

Danaïdes, the fifty daughters of Danaus, king of Argos, were promised in marriage to their fifty cousins, the sons of Aegyptus. Danaus, who had quarrelled with Aegyptus, made his daughters promise to slay their husbands on their wedding night. This they all did except Hypermnestra, who suffered her husband Lynceus to escape. The others were condemned in Hades to try for ever to fill a sieve with water.

Dance of Death, *The*, or *Danse macabre* (or *Danse macabré*) gave expression to the sense, especially prominent in the 15th cent. (perhaps as a consequence of the plague and the preaching of the mendicant friars), of the ubiquity of Death the leveller. The Dance appears to have first taken shape in France, as a mimed sermon, in which figures typical of various orders of society were seized and haled away each by its own corpse (not, as later, by the personification of Death). The earliest known painting of the Dance, accompanied by versified dialogues between living and dead, was made in 1424 in the cemetery of the Innocents in Paris, and the German artists (including Holbein) who later depicted it appear to have drawn inspiration from French sources. The origin of the word *macabre* or *macabré* has been the subject of many conjectures.

Dancer, DANIEL, a famous miser (1716–94), in whose wretched hovel large sums of money were found after his death.

Dandie Dinmont, in Scott's 'Guy Mannering' (q.v.), a sturdy hospitable Liddesdale farmer, and the owner of a special breed of terriers. After the novel was published the name Dandie Dinmont was generally given to James Davidson, farmer of Hindlee in Teviotdale, who possessed a celebrated race of terriers, named Mustard and Pepper according to their colours, without other individual distinctions, except 'old', 'young', and 'little'. Davidson was not the prototype of Dandie Dinmont, Scott never having met Davidson till after the publication of the novel although he had been told the story of the Mustards and Peppers.

Dandin, GEORGE, the hero of a comedy of that name by Molière (q.v.), a tradesman who marries a noble's daughter and suffers many humiliations in consequence. 'Vous l'avez voulu, George Dandin', is his frequent comment on his situation.

Dandiprat, a small coin current in England in the 16th cent., worth three-halfpence. Hence a small, insignificant, or contemptible fellow.

Danegeld, an annual tax imposed at the end of the 10th cent. or in the 11th cent., originally (as is supposed) to provide funds for the protection of England from the Danes, and continued after the Norman Conquest as a land-tax. [OED.]

Dane-law, the part of England over which Danish law prevailed, being the district NE. of Watling Street ceded by the treaty of Wedmore (878), or perhaps the Northumbrian territory in Danish occupation. [OED.]

Dangerfield, a character in Sedley's 'Bellamira' (q.v.); also a character in Sir W. Scott's 'Peveril of the Peak' (q.v.).

Dangle, a character in Sheridan's 'The Critic' (q.v.).

Daniel, an OE. poetical paraphrase of the Biblical story, found in the Junius MS. (see *Caedmon*).

Daniel, CHARLES HENRY OLIVE (1836–1919), scholar, fellow, and Provost of Worcester College, Oxford, is remembered for his lifelong interest in printing. He established a private press at Oxford, where he revived the use of the Fell type (see *Fell*), and produced some fine examples of typography, including plays and poems of Robert Bridges.

The DANIEL MARK, sometimes called the *Misit* Mark, the special note of the press, represents Daniel in the lions' den with the motto: 'Misit Angelum suum' ('He sent his Angel').

DANIEL, SAMUEL (1562–1619), the son of a music-master, entered Magdalen Hall, Oxford, in 1579, and after visiting Italy became tutor to William Herbert, third earl of Pembroke, and later to Annè Clifford, daughter of the countess of Cumberland. He is mentioned in Spenser's 'Colin·Clout' (q.v.) as the 'new shepherd late up sprong'. He published 'Delia', a collection of sonnets inspired by Tasso and Desportes, in 1592; the 'Complaynt of Rosamond', in which Fair Rosamund confesses and laments her relations with the king, also in 1592; and 'Cleopatra' (q.v.), a Senecan tragedy, in 1594. 'Musophilus, or Defence of all Learning' (q.v.) appeared in 1599; the 'Defence of Rhyme' in 1602 (?), in which he maintained, in reply to Thomas Campion's 'Art of English Poesy', the fitness of the English language for rhymed verse; 'Philotas' (q.v.), a Senecan tragedy, in 1605. He issued in 1609 a new edition of his 'Civil Wars' (q.v.), which had first appeared in 1595. He composed numerous masques for court festivities, including 'Tethys Festival', 1610, and 'Hymen's Triumph', 1615. He was inspector of the children of the queen's revels from 1615 to 1618. His poems were sharply criticized by Ben Jonson, with whom he was 'at jealousies', but praised for their 'sweetness of ryming' by Drummond of Hawthornden, and for their purity of language by Sir John Harington and S. T. Coleridge. William Browne (q.v.) calls him 'well-languaged Daniel'.

Daniel come to judgement, A, a quotation from Shakespeare's 'The Merchant of Venice', IV. i, in allusion to Susanna, 45 et seq.

Daniel in the lions' den, a reference to the story in Dan. vi of Daniel being cast, by order of King Darius, into the den of lions, and of their mouths being shut by the angel of God, so that they did not hurt him.

Daniel Deronda, a novel by G. Eliot (q.v.), published in 1876, the last of her novels.

Gwendolen Harleth, high-spirited, self-confident, and self-centred, marries Henleigh Grandcourt, an arrogant selfish man of the world, for his money and position, to save her mother and herself from destitution, and in spite of the fact that she knows of the existence of another woman and children to whom Grandcourt is in honour bound. She comes under the influence of the high-souled Daniel Deronda, and her dependence on his guidance increases as the brutality of her husband drives her to revolt and even to thoughts of murder. Daniel's own parentage is enveloped in mystery, which is gradually revealed by his attraction to the noble Jew, Mordecai, and his gentle sister, Mirah, and the final disclosure of his Jewish birth. Grandcourt's tragic death, of which Gwendolen feels herself partly guilty, leaves her with Daniel as her only hope. This is changed to despair when she learns his intention of devoting himself to the cause of a national centre for the Jewish race, and of marrying Mirah, a despair that gradually gives place to resignation. Klesmer, the musician, whose genius and devotion to his art atone for his personal deficiencies, is notable among the minor characters.

Dannisburgh, LORD, a character in Meredith's 'Diana of the Crossways' (q.v.), drawn from Lord Melbourne.

D'ANNUNZIO, GABRIELE (1863–1938), Italian poet, novelist, and playwright. In the First World War he effectively urged the entry of Italy on the side of the Allies, and himself took part in some spectacular exploits on the sea and in the air. In 1919, with a small volunteer force, he occupied Fiume, where he remained as dictator until 1921. His flamboyance, his grand passion for Eleanora Duse, the erotic and decadent aspects of some of his works, and their Nietzschean content, made him the subject of controversy, both as man and writer. His best play is 'La figlia di Iorio' (1904). His best poetry is in 'Alcione' (1904), one of the four completed books of his 'Laudi' ('Praises of the Sky, the Sea, the Earth, and Heroes').

Dansker, a Dane.

'Inquire me first what Danskers are in Paris.'

(Shakespeare, 'Hamlet', II. i. 7.)

DANTE ALIGHIERI (1265–1321) was born at Florence of a Guelf family. The circumstances of his early life are obscure, but we know that in 1277 he was formally betrothed to his future wife, Gemma Donati, and that in 1289 he took part in military operations against Arezzo and Pisa. During this early period of his life he fell in love with the girl whom he celebrates under the name of Beatrice in the 'Vita nuova' and the 'Divina Commedia'. Her identity has been much discussed, but the generally accepted view is that she was Bice Portinari, who became the wife of Simone de' Bardi. When she died, in 1290, Dante was grief-stricken and sought consolation in the study of philosophy. In 1295 he became active in the political life of Florence. In June 1300 he was one of the municipal priors who banished the leaders of the White and Black Guelf factions (see *Bianchi and Neri*), and in Oct. 1301 he was one of three envoys sent to Rome to negotiate with Boniface VIII. He was never to set foot in Florence again, for during his absence the Blacks seized power, and Dante (whose sympathies were with the Whites) became the victim of political reprisals. He was falsely accused of barratry, his property was confiscated, and he went into exile. For the rest of his life he led a wandering existence, being twice the guest of the Della Scala family at Verona and staying once with the Malaspina in the Lunigiana region of the Apennines. It is probable that his wanderings took him as far afield as Paris. For the last few years of his life he found refuge with Guido Novello da Polenta at Ravenna, where he died.

The precise dating of Dante's works presents many problems, as yet unsolved. The first in order of composition (apart from his earliest lyric poems) was the 'Vita nuova', written in the period 1290–4. In it Dante brings together thirty-one poems, most of them relating directly or indirectly to his love for Beatrice. A linking prose narrative and commentary tells the story of his love and interprets the poems from the standpoint of one who has come to see his beloved as the instrument of his spiritual salvation. The 'Convivio', or 'Banquet', is an unfinished philosophical work, planned as a series of fourteen treatises, each in the form of a prose commentary on one of Dante's own *canzoni*. The four completed treatises, written between 1304 and 1308, draw on numerous philosophical sources, but principally on Aristotle. The first book contains a defence of the Italian language. The main topics of the other three books are respectively: science, philosophy, and nobility. The fourth book also discusses imperial authority. The Latin treatise 'De vulgari eloquentia', begun shortly before the 'Convivio', is also unfinished. The completed part consists of an inquiry into the form of vernacular language most suitable for lofty poetry, followed by the beginning of a discussion of the technique of the *canzone*. It is a pioneering work in the field of linguistic history. The 'Monarchia', written in the period 1309–12, is a Latin treatise on the universal empire and the relations between emperor and pope. The first book argues that a universal empire is necessary for the well-being of mankind; the second that the Roman Empire was divinely ordained; the third that the emperor should have complete autonomy in the temporal sphere, his authority being derived directly from God and not from the pope. It is very uncertain when Dante began his masterpiece, the 'Divina Commedia' (q.v.). It may have been begun as early as 1307, or possibly not until 1314 or later. It was finished just before his death.

Danton, JACQUES (1759–94), a celebrated French statesman of the Revolution, a member of the Convention and of the first (Dantonist) Committee of Public Safety, which gave place to the 'Great [Robespierrist] Committee' in July 1793. He finally came into conflict with Robespierre and was guillotined.

Danu, in Gaelic mythology, the mother of the gods (the *Tuatha dè Danann*).

Daphnaïda, an elegy by Spenser (q.v.). See *Alcyon*.

Daphne, according to mythology, a daughter of the river Penēus, of whom Apollo became enamoured. Daphne fleeing from his importunities entreated the assistance of the gods, who changed her into a laurel. Hence the laurel became the favourite tree of Apollo.

Daphnis, a son of Hermes, who was brought up by the nymphs, was taught by Pan to play on the flute, and became a shepherd on the slopes of Mt. Aetna. He was regarded as the inventor of pastoral poetry. According to one form of the legend, he was struck with blindness for infidelity to the Naiad whom he loved.

Daphnis and Chloe, a Greek pastoral romance, one of the earliest works of its kind, sometimes attributed to an author Longus, of whom nothing is known. Its date is uncertain, perhaps the 2nd cent. A.D. It is the story of two infants discovered respectively by Lamon and Dryas, shepherds of Mitylene, and brought up by them to tend their sheep and goats, and tells of their love and adventures, and final union, after the discovery of their wealthy parents. G. Moore (q.v.) wrote a translation ('The Pastoral Loves of Daphnis and Chloe'), published in a limited edition in 1924.

Dapper, a character in Jonson's 'The Alchemist' (q.v.).

D'ARBLAY, MME, see *Burney* (F.).

Darby and Joan, a jocose appellation for an attached husband and wife, especially in advanced years and humble life. The 'Gentleman's Magazine' of 1735, v. 153, has, under the title 'The joys of love never forgot: a song', a mediocre copy of verses containing a reference to 'Old Darby, with Joan by his side', who 'are never happy asunder'. This has usually been considered the source of the names, and various conjectures have been made both as to the author and as to the identity of 'Darby and Joan', but with no valid results. [OED.]

Darcy, FITZWILLIAM, one of the principal characters in Jane Austen's 'Pride and Prejudice' (q.v.).

Dares, the boxer at the funeral games, in Virgil, 'Aeneid' v. 369 et seq.

Dares Phrygius, in Homer's 'Iliad', v. 9, a priest of Hephaestus among the Trojans. A work in Latin purporting to be the translation of an account by him of the destruction of Troy, known as the *De Excidio Trojae*, was popular in the Middle Ages and one of the sources of Trojan legend. It dates perhaps from the 5th cent. A.D. See *Dictys Cretensis*.

Darien Scheme, THE, a scheme proposed by William Paterson (1658–1719), the projector of the Bank of England, for a Scottish settlement on the isthmus of Panama. An expedition for the purpose set out in 1698, but proved unsuccessful, and the scheme was abandoned in 1700. Practically the whole circulating capital of the Scottish people was invested in the scheme; and so, at the Union (1707), a sum of money was paid by England in compensation for the losses sustained by Scotland.

Darius the Great, son of Hystaspes, was king of Persia 521–485 B.C. According to Herodotus (iii. 85), he and six other chiefs, having slain the usurper of the throne, Gomates, agreed that that chief should be king whose horse neighed first, and in this way Darius was chosen, thanks to the ingenuity of his groom. He greatly extended the Persian empire and in his reign began the great war between the Persians and the Greeks. His army was defeated at Marathon, and before he was able to renew the struggle he died, leaving the execution of his schemes to his son Xerxes. Darius is referred to in Daniel v. 31, and the following chapters.

Dark Ages, in modern use, refers to the period between the break-up of the Roman Empire and the end of the 10th cent.

DARLEY, GEORGE (1795–1846), an Irish poet and mathematician, educated at Trinity College, Dublin. He was a member of the staff of the 'London Magazine' and wrote the pleasant pastoral drama 'Sylvia' (1827) and the poem 'Nepenthe', besides a good deal of other verse, including 'The Errors of Ecstacie' (1822), which shows his considerable lyrical power. Some of his prose tales were collected in 'Labours of Idleness' (1826).

Darley Arabian, a bay Arab stallion from whom the best English race-horses are descended, imported about 1700 by Mr. Darley of Yorkshire. 'Flying Childers' (q.v.) was his son, and 'Eclipse' (q.v.) his great-great-grandson.

DARLING, FRANK FRASER (1903–   ), naturalist, author of 'Wild Country' (1938), 'A Naturalist on Rona' (1939), and other descriptions of wild life in the British Isles.

Darling, GRACE, daughter of James Darling, keeper of the Outer-Farne lighthouse, off the coast of Northumberland, who with her father in 1838 gallantly put out in a coble in a heavy sea and rescued several passengers of the wrecked 'Forfarshire' steamer.

Darnay, CHARLES, a character in Dickens's 'A Tale of Two Cities' (q.v.).

D'Artagnan, one of the heroes of Alexandre Dumas's 'The Three Musketeers' (q.v.).

Dartle, ROSA, a character in Dickens's 'David Copperfield' (q.v.).

DARWIN, CHARLES ROBERT (1809–82), born at Shrewsbury, grandson of Erasmus Darwin (q.v.), was educated at Shrewsbury, Edinburgh University, and Christ's College, Cambridge. He embarked in 1831 as naturalist on the 'Beagle', bound for South America on a scientific expedition. He returned in 1836, and published in 1839 his 'Journal of Researches into the Geology and Natural History of the various countries visited by H.M.S. Beagle'. His 'Structure and Distribution of Coral Reefs' appeared in 1842, 'Geological Observations on Volcanic Islands' in 1844, and 'Geological Observations on S. America' in 1846. His great work, 'On the Origin of Species by means of Natural Selection', appeared in 1859. Darwin had received in 1858 from Dr. A. R. Wallace (q.v.) a manuscript containing a theory of the origin of species identical with his own. This he had published with a letter of his own, addressed to Dr. Asa Grey in 1857, containing a sketch of his theory. Darwin's book gave rise to intense opposition, but found distinguished supporters in Huxley, Lyell, and Sir Joseph Hooker. It was followed by 'The Variation of Animals and Plants under Domestication' (1868), and 'The Descent of Man' (1871). Among Darwin's other works were 'The Fertilisation of Orchids' (1862), supplemented by 'Cross and Self-Fertilisation' (1876); 'The Movements and Habits of Climbing Plants' (1864); 'The Expression of the Emotions in Man and Animals' (1872); 'Insectivorous Plants' (1875); 'The Power of Movement in Plants' (1880), in which was formulated his theory of circumnutation; and 'Formation of Vegetable Mould through the action of Worms' (1881). The 'Life and Letters of Charles Darwin', edited by his son Francis Darwin, appeared in 1887, and 'More Letters of Charles Darwin', by Francis Darwin and A. C. Seward, in 1903.

DARWIN, ERASMUS (1731–1802), educated at St. John's College, Cambridge, spent much of his life as a physician at Lichfield, where he established a botanical garden. He embodied the botanical system of Linnaeus in a poem 'The Botanic Garden', of which Pt. II, 'The Loves of the Plants', appeared in 1789, and Pt. I, 'The Economy of Vegetation', in 1791. The poem is in heroic couplets, in imitation of Pope. The goddess of Botany, descending on earth, holds forth on various natural phenomena throughout the four cantos of Pt. I, while Pt. II describes 'the Ovidian metamorphosis of the flowers, with their floral harems', stamens and pistils figuring as beaux and belles. The work was ridiculed by Canning and Frere in 'The Loves of the Triangles'. In his 'Zoonomia', published in 1794–6, Darwin expounds the laws of organic life on the evolutionary principle.

DASENT, SIR GEORGE WEBBE (1817–96), Scandinavian scholar, educated at Westminster and Magdalen Hall, Oxford. He was the interpreter of Icelandic sagas to us, publishing many translations, 'Popular Tales from the Norse' (1859), 'The Story of Burnt Njal' (1861), etc.

Dashwood, ELINOR and MARIANNE, the principal characters in Jane Austen's 'Sense and Sensibility' (q.v.). JOHN DASHWOOD is their stepbrother.

Datchery, DICK, the name assumed by one of the characters in Dickens's 'Edwin Drood' (q.v.); his identity is not revealed when the fragment ends.

DAUDET, ALPHONSE (1840–97), French novelist, for long best known in England by his charming sketches of Provençal life ('Lettres de mon Moulin', 1869) and as the creator of the amusing type of Provençal Frenchman, 'Tartarin de Tarascon'. His other early works include the semi-autobiographical 'Le Petit Chose' (1868) and 'Contes du Lundi' (1873, tales of the Franco-Prussian war. The bulk of his output consists of long, much more naturalistic novels, such as 'Fromont Jeune et Risler Aîné' (1874), 'Jack' (1876), 'Le Nabab' (1877), 'Numa Roumestan' (1880), etc. The influence of Dickens and Thackeray has been remarked in some of these.

Daumier, HONORÉ (1808–79), French painter and lithographer. More than 4,000 of his political and satirical cartoons were published in 'Charivari', 'Caricature', and 'Le Figaro'.

Dauphin, the title of the eldest son of the king of France from 1349 to 1830. According to Littré, the title *Dauphin* borne by the lords of the Viennois was a proper name *Delphinus* (the same word as the name of the fish, dolphin), whence the province subject to them was called the Dauphiné. When Humbert III, the last lord of the Dauphiné, ceded the province to Philip of Valois in 1349, he made it a condition that the title should be perpetuated by being borne by the eldest son of the French king. [OED.]

The edition of the Latin classics *ad usum Delphini* (1674) was prepared for the son of Louis XIV.

D'AVENANT, SIR WILLIAM (1606–68), was born at Oxford and educated there. He is said to have been Shakespeare's godson. His earliest drama 'The Tragedy of Albovine' (q.v.) was published in 1629, 'The Cruel Brother' (a tragedy) in 1630, 'The Platonick Lovers' (tragicomedy) in 1636, his comic masterpiece 'The Wits' (q.v.) in the same year, 'The Unfortunate Lovers' in 1643 (acted in 1638), and 'Love and Honour' in 1649 (acted in 1634). D'Avenant was made poet laureate in 1638. He actively supported the cause of Charles I, and was knighted by him in 1643 at the siege of Gloucester. He was imprisoned in the Tower, 1650–2, and is said to have been saved by Milton. His romantic epic 'Gondibert' (q.v.) appeared in 1651. He practically founded English opera by his 'Siege of Rhodes' (q.v., 1656). After the Restoration he and Thomas Killigrew (q.v.) obtained patents from Charles II giving them the monopoly of acting in London. His charter for the theatre known as the Duke's House was later transferred to Covent Garden. In conjunction with Dryden he

adapted Shakespeare's 'The Tempest' in 1667. With Dryden and others he is satirized in the 'Rehearsal' (q.v.).

David, in Dryden's 'Absalom and Achitophel' (q.v.), represents Charles II.

David, KING, the second king of Israel, the youngest son of Jesse of the tribe of Judah. In his youth he slew the Philistine giant Goliath (1 Sam. xvii). On the death of Saul he became king of Judah and, after the murder of Ishbosheth, of the whole of Israel (2 Sam. ii and v). His last years were darkened by the rebellion and death of his son Absalom (2 Sam. xv–xviii). See also *David and Jonathan* and *Psalms*.

David, ST. (6th cent.), the son of a prince of south Wales, is said to have received his education from St. Paulinus, at Whitland, Carmarthenshire. Returning to his native province, he established monasteries in the vale of the Ross near Menevia. He became bishop, and removed the see from Caerleon to Menevia (St. David's). He is the patron saint of Wales and is commemorated on 1 March.

David, Song to, see *Smart.*

David and Bethsabe, The Love of King, a play in blank verse by Peele (q.v.), printed in 1599. The title sufficiently indicates the subject of the play, which contains the well-known lines:

> To joy her love I'll build a kingly bower,
> Seated in hearing of a hundred streams.

David and Jonathan, types of loving friends; 'the soul of Jonathan was knit with the soul of David, and Jonathan loved him as his own soul' (1 Sam. xviii. 1). Jonathan was the son of Saul, David was Saul's appointed successor as king of Israel.

David Copperfield, a novel by Dickens (q.v.), published in 1849–50. 'Of all my books,' wrote Dickens, 'I like this the best.' It is (in some of its details) Dickens's veiled autobiography.

David Copperfield is born at Blunderstone (of which the original is the village of Blundeston) in Suffolk, soon after the death of his father. His mother, a gentle weak woman, marries again, and her second husband, Mr. Murdstone, by cruelty disguised as firmness, and abetted by Miss Murdstone his sister, drives her to an early grave. Young Copperfield, who has proved recalcitrant, is sent to school, where he is bullied by the tyrannical headmaster, Creakle, but makes two friends in the brilliant and fascinating Steerforth and the good-humoured plodding Traddles. Thence he is sent to menial employment in London, where he lives a life of poverty and misery, enlivened by his acquaintance with the mercurial and impecunious Mr. Micawber and his family. He runs away and walks penniless to Dover to throw himself on the mercy of his aunt, Betsey Trotwood, an eccentric old lady, who had renounced all interest in him from his birth, because, contrary to her firm expectation, he had been born a boy instead of a girl. He is kindly received and given a new home, which he shares with an amiable lunatic, Mr. Dick. This poor gentleman is perpetually engaged on a memorial regarding his affairs, but is unable to complete it owing to the inevitable intrusion into it of King Charles's head. Copperfield continues his education at Canterbury, living in the house of Miss Trotwood's lawyer, Mr. Wickfield, whose daughter, Agnes, a girl of exceptionally sweet and high-minded disposition, exercises a powerful influence on the rest of his life. He then enters Doctors' Commons, being articled to Mr. Spenlow, of the firm of Spenlow and Jorkins. Meanwhile he has come again into touch with Steerforth, whom, ignorant of his true character, he introduces to the family of his old nurse, Clara Peggotty, married to Barkis, the carrier. This family consists of Mr. Peggotty, a Yarmouth fisherman, his nephew Ham, and the latter's cousin, Little Em'ly, a pretty simple girl whom Ham is about to marry. The remaining inmate of Mr. Peggotty's hospitable home is Mrs. Gummidge, another dependant and a widow, whose peevish laments for her forlorn condition are patiently borne by Mr. Peggotty. Steerforth induces Em'ly to run away with him, thereby producing intense misery in the Peggotty household. Mr. Peggotty sets out to find her, following her through many countries, and finally recovering her after she had been cast off by Steerforth. The latter's crime also brings unhappiness to his mother, and to her protégée, Rosa Dartle, who has long loved Steerforth with all the suppressed violence of a passionate nature. The tragedy finds its culmination in the shipwreck and drowning of Steerforth, and the death of Ham in trying to save him.

Meanwhile Copperfield, blind to the affection of Agnes Wickfield, marries Dora Spenlow, a pretty empty-headed child, and becomes famous as an author. Dora dies after a few years of married life, and Copperfield, at first disconsolate, gradually awakens to the mistake he has made in rejecting such a treasure as Agnes. Her father has fallen into the toils of a villainous and cunning clerk, Uriah Heep, who, under the cloak of fawning humility, has obtained complete control over him, reduced him to the verge of imbecility, and nearly ruined him. Uriah also aspires to marry Agnes. But his misdeeds, which include forgery and theft, are exposed by Micawber, employed as his clerk, with the assistance of Traddles, now a barrister. Uriah is last seen in prison, under a life sentence. Copperfield marries Agnes. Mr. Peggotty, with Em'ly and Mrs. Gummidge, is found prospering in Australia, where Mr. Micawber, relieved of his debts, appears finally as a much-esteemed colonial magistrate.

David Simple, *The Adventures of, in Search of a Real Friend*, a romance by Sarah Fielding (q.v.), published in 1744.

The hero, disillusioned by the discovery that his beloved brother has attempted to rob him of his inheritance by means of a forged will, sets out on a journey to discover a human creature capable of friendship. His experiences are such as to convince him of the base and mercenary motives by which the world is actuated, until he meets Cynthia, who has unjustly been excluded from a share in her father's fortune and cruelly treated by the lady to whom she is companion; also a distressed brother and sister, Valentine and Camilla, who have been ousted from their father's affection by the machinations of a stepmother. These deserving people he relieves, and the four spend their time telling and listening to stories, wandering about London and moralizing on what they see; until the hero and Camilla, and Valentine and Cynthia, after a sufficient delay to prove the delicacy of all concerned, become betrothed. Valentine and Camilla are reconciled to their father, the hero decides to share his fortune with the others, and all live together as a happy community.

Davideis, an epic poem by A. Cowley (q.v.).

DAVIDSON, JOHN (1857–1909), was a schoolmaster in Scotland from 1872 to 1889. He settled in London in the latter year, having previously published 'Scaramouch in Naxos' (1889) and other plays. His 'Perfervid', a novel, appeared in 1890. His 'Fleet Street Eclogues' (1893) proved his genuine poetic gift, followed by 'Ballads and Songs' (1894), 'A Second Series of Fleet Street Eclogues' (1896), 'New Ballads' (1897), and 'The Last Ballad' (1899). Between 1901 and 1908 he wrote a series of 'Testaments' expounding (in blank verse) a materialistic and rebellious philosophy, described very fully in the introduction to 'The Theatrocrat' (1905). He committed suicide in 1909, leaving an unfinished poem 'God and Mammon'.

Davies, CHRISTIAN, *alias* MOTHER ROSS (1667–1739), a female soldier, born in Dublin, who enlisted under the name of Christopher Welsh, c. 1693. She fought in Flanders and at the battle of Blenheim, 1704. She was wounded at Ramillies, 1706, and her sex having been revealed, was dismissed the service, but still followed the army. She was pensioned in 1712. She was thrice married, all her husbands being soldiers.

DAVIES, JOHN (1565?–1618), of Hereford, poet and writing-master. He published 'Microcosmos' (1603), 'Humours Heau'n on Earth. . . . As also The Triumph of Death' (1605), being a description of the plague of 1603), the 'Holy Roode' (1609), 'Wittes Pilgrimage (by Poeticall Essaies)' (1611), 'The Muse's Sacrifice', containing the author's famous 'Picture of an Happy Man' (1612), and 'Wit's Bedlam' (1617). He also issued an 'Anatomy of Fair Writing' (1633). Some of his epigrams, most of which are contained in 'The Scourge of Folly' (undated), are valuable for their notices of Ben Jonson, Fletcher, and other contemporary poets.

DAVIES, SIR JOHN(1569–1626), a Wiltshire man of good family, educated at Winchester and Queen's College, Oxford, solicitor- and attorney-general for Ireland, and subsequently appointed lord chief justice of the King's Bench in England as a reward for maintaining the legality of Charles I's forced loans. He died before taking up this office. His 'Orchestra', a poem in seven-lined stanzas, of the school of Spenser, in which natural phenomena are reduced to an ordered motion or 'dancing', was published in 1596. 'Astraea', a collection of acrostics on the name Elizabeth, appeared in 1599, and 'Nosce Teipsum' (highly praised by Coleridge), a philosophical poem on the nature of man and on the nature and immortality of the soul, in the same year.

DAVIES, WILLIAM HENRY(1871–1940), poet and author of the 'Autobiography of a Super-tramp' (1908). He went to America at the age of 22 and led a vagrant life both there and after his return to England. His collected poems were published in 1943.

DAVISON, FRANCIS (1575?–1619?), son of William Davison, secretary of state to Queen Elizabeth; educated at Gray's Inn, and befriended by Essex. He issued, with his brother Walter, a 'Poetical Rapsody' (q.v.) 'containing divers sonnets, odes, elegies, madrigals, and other Poesies' in 1602, 2nd edition in 1611, 3rd edition, 1621.

Davus Sum (Byron, 'Don Juan', XIII. xiii):

But I'm not Oedipus and Life's a Sphinx;
I tell the tale as it was told, nor dare
To venture a solution, *Davus sum,*

is a quotation from Terence, 'Andria' (I. ii), where the slave Davus, in answer to a question, says, 'Davus sum, non Oedipus', alluding to the fact that Oedipus alone was able to solve the riddle of the Sphinx (q.v.).

DAVY, SIR HUMPHRY (1778–1829), natural philosopher, was professor of chemistry at the Royal Institution, and greatly advanced the knowledge of chemistry and galvanism. He invented the miner's safety-lamp. His collected works, prose and verse, with a memoir by his brother, were published in 1839–40. Mention may be made of his little dialogue 'Salmonia, or Days of Fly-fishing, by an Angler' (1828), which in its form and style reminds the reader of Izaak Walton. Davy was a friend of Sir W. Scott, and there is a pleasant account in Lockhart of Davy's visits to Abbotsford.

Davy Jones, in nautical slang, the spirit of the sea, the sailor's devil. DAVY JONES'S LOCKER, the grave of those who perish at sea.

DAVYS, JOHN (1550?–1605), navigator, made three Arctic voyages in search of the North-West Passage and gave his name to Davis Strait. He wrote the narrative (in Hakluyt) of the second of these voyages and was also author of 'The Seaman's Secrets' (1594) and 'The Worlde's Hydrographical Description' (1595).

Daw, SIR JOHN, in Jonson's 'Epicœne' (q.v.), a braggart cowardly knight, who pretends to learning.

Dawes Plan, THE, an arrangement evolved by an international committee of financial experts set up at the end of 1923 to consider the question of the Reparations to be paid by Germany. Germany had declared it impossible to pay the annuities fixed by the Allies in 1921 (£100,000,000 plus 26 per cent. of exports) and France had begun the occupation of the Ruhr. The Committee, presided over by General Charles G. Dawes of the United States, comprised two representatives each for Great Britain, France, Italy, Belgium, and the United States. They reported in April 1924, making recommendations for the stabilization of the German currency, the reorganization of the Reichsbank, and the establishment of a Transfer Committee to receive payments in marks from Germany and carry out transfers of these to the Allies. They also drew up a schedule of annuities ranging from 1,000 million to 2,500 million gold marks, secured on taxes, railways, and industrial securities. The plan was put into operation, but was superseded by the Young Plan (q.v.).

Dawks's Letter, a newspaper of the late 17th cent., printed in written characters to resemble a manuscript letter.

Dawson, BULLY, a notorious character in the 17th cent. Addison in the 'Spectator', No. 2, writes: 'Sir Roger was what you call a fine gentleman, had often supped with my Lord Rochester and Sir G. Etherege . . . and kicked Bully Dawson in a public coffeehouse for calling him youngster.' Charles Lamb refers to Bully Dawson in the 'Essays of Elia' ('Popular Fallacies').

Dawson, JEMMY, the hero of a ballad by Shenstone (q.v.). He was one of the Manchester rebels who supported the Young Pretender, and was drawn, hanged, and quartered on Kennington Common in 1746.

Dawson, PHOEBE, the heroine of one of the tales in Crabbe's 'The Parish Register', ii (q.v.).

Day, FANCY, the heroine of Hardy's 'Under the Greenwood Tree' (q.v.).

Day, DAYE, or DAIE, JOHN (1522–84), the foremost English printer of the reign of Elizabeth I. He published Protestant devotional books under Edward VI and was imprisoned by Queen Mary; later he held lucrative monopolies for the psalms in metre, the catechism, and the A.B.C., printed the first church music book in English (1560), and the first English edition of Foxe's 'Martyrs' (1563). He was patronized by Archbishop Parker, at whose behest he was the first to print Old English, having type made for it.

DAY, JOHN (*fl.* 1606), was educated at Caius College, Cambridge. He collaborated with Dekker and others in a number of plays. Of his own extant works, 'The Isle of Gulls', suggested by Sidney's 'Arcadia', appeared in 1606, 'Law Trickes' in 1608, and 'Humour out of Breath' in the same year. His best work, 'The Parliament of Bees' (q.v.), appeared perhaps in 1607, though the earliest extant copy is of 1641. His works were collected by A. H. Bullen in 1881. See also *Parnassus Plays*.

DAY, THOMAS (1748–89), educated at Charterhouse and Corpus Christi College, Oxford, and a barrister of the Middle Temple, devoted himself largely to works of moral and social reform. He was the author of the 'History of Sandford and Merton' (1783–9, see *Sandford and Merton*), in which he attempted to reconcile Rousseau's naturalism with a sounder morality.

Day of Doom, The, a poem by Michael Wigglesworth (q.v.), published in New England in 1662, with the sub-title: 'A Poetical Description of the Great and Last Judgment.'

DAY-LEWIS, CECIL (1904–), born in Ireland and educated at Wadham College, Oxford, where he became associated with a group of young left-wing poets of which Auden (q.v.) was the acknowledged leader. He worked as a schoolmaster and was for some time an active member of the Communist Party. His early verse reflects this affiliation but he later turned to personal and pastoral themes, in which the influence of Hardy is notable. During the Second World War he worked in the Ministry of Information, and was professor of poetry at Oxford from 1951 to 1956, the first poet of distinction to hold this post since Matthew Arnold. His verse includes 'Collected Poems 1929–36' (1938) and 'Collected Poems' (1954), translations of Virgil, and a number of detective stories written under the pseudonym of Nicholas Blake. He has also published an autobiography, 'The Buried Day' (1960).

De Augmentis, see *Bacon (Francis)*.

De Bourgh, LADY CATHERINE, a character in Jane Austen's 'Pride and Prejudice' (q.v.).

De Craye, COLONEL, a character in Meredith's 'The Egoist' (q.v.).

De Croye, ISABELLE and **HAMELINE,** characters in Scott's 'Quentin Durward' (q.v.).

DE LA MARE, WALTER (1873–1956), educated at St. Paul's Cathedral School, and for some years engaged in business in London, was the author of many poems in which dreams and reality, fairies and humble natural creatures, are delightfully blended. His works include 'The Listeners' (1912), 'Peacock Pie' (1913), 'The Veil' (1921), 'The Burning-Glass' (1945), 'Winged Chariot' (1951), all poems; 'Collected Poems' (1920), 'Poems 1919–1934' (1935), 'Collected Poems' (1942);

'Henry Brocken' (1904), 'The Return' (1910), 'Memoirs of a Midget' (1921), (novels); 'Collected Stories for Children' (1947). His early books were published under the name of Walter Ramal.

DE LA RAMÉE, MARIE LOUISE, see *Ouida*.

DE LA ROCHE, MAZO (1885–1961), Canadian novelist, born in Ontario, best known as the author of the 'Jalna' novels, so named after the first of the series, 'Jalna' (1927).

DE MORGAN, WILLIAM FREND (1839–1917), educated at University College, London, at first devoted his attention to art and in particular to the production of stained glass and glazed pottery, working for a time in association with his friend William Morris (q.v.). He was particularly successful with decorative tiles, but ill health brought his activities in this direction to an end, and in the latter part of his life he turned to the writing of fiction. 'Joseph Vance', his masterpiece, appeared in 1906, 'Alice-for-Short' (1907), 'Somehow Good' (1908), 'It never can happen again' (1909), 'An Affair of Dishonour' (1910), 'A Likely Story' (1911), and 'When Ghost meets Ghost' (1914). 'The Old Madhouse' (1919) and 'The Old Man's Youth' (1921), left unfinished by De Morgan, were skilfully completed by his widow. De Morgan also wrote two treatises on the craft of pottery (Society of Arts Journal, vol. xl, and a 'Report on the Feasibility of a Manufacture of Glazed Pottery in Egypt', 1894).

De Nugis Curialium, see *Map*. This is also the sub-title of the 'Policraticus' of John of Salisbury (q.v.).

De Profundis, 'Out of the depths', the first two words of the Latin version of Psalm cxxx. It is the title of the prose apologia of Oscar Wilde (q.v.).

DE QUINCEY, THOMAS (1785–1859), the son of a Manchester merchant, was educated at Manchester Grammar School, and after leading for some time a rambling life, went to Worcester College, Oxford, but took no degree. He here first began opium-eating. He was one of the early members of the staff of 'Blackwood's Magazine' (q.v.), for which he wrote the 'Confessions of an English Opium Eater' (q.v., 1822, enlarged ed. 1856), and 'On Murder as one of the Fine Arts' (1827). De Quincey produced a great deal of miscellaneous literary work, including the translation of a German novel ('Walladmor'), an original novel 'Klosterheim' (1832), 'The Logic of Political Economy' (1844), and a large number of essays on a great variety of subjects. Mention should be made of his 'Autobiographic Sketches' (1834–53), his articles on Wordsworth, Coleridge, Lamb, and others, his dream visions ('Suspiria de Profundis', 'Savannah-La-Mar', 'Levana and Our Ladies of Sorrow', 'The English Mail-

Coach'), and his tales, 'The Spanish Military Nun' and 'The Revolt of the Tartars'. Of his critical work, his essay 'On the Knocking at the Gate in Macbeth' is best remembered. He wrote an ornate prose, sometimes marked by splendid imagery (as in passages of 'Our Ladies of Sorrow', the 'Confessions', and the 'Autobiography') and humour. His works have been more than once collected. An edition by D. Masson in fourteen volumes appeared in 1889–90.

De Rerum Natura, the great philosophical poem by Lucretius (q.v.).

De Sublimitate, the Latin title given to the critical Greek treatise (Περὶ ὕψους) attributed to Longinus (q.v.).

DE TABLEY, LORD, see *Warren(J. B. L.).*

De Vere, ARTHUR, *alias* ARTHUR PHILIPSON, son of the earl of Oxford, a character in Scott's 'Anne of Geierstein' (q.v.).

DE VERE, AUBREY THOMAS (1814–1902), the son of Sir Aubrey de Vere (1788–1846, himself a poet), was educated at Trinity College, Dublin. He came early under the influence of Coleridge and Wordsworth. He was a friend of Tennyson, and a lifelong friend and advocate of Sir Henry Taylor, as poet and dramatist. Later friends included Robert Browning and R. H. Hutton. He published 'The Waldenses and other Poems' in 1842, and 'English Misrule and Irish Misdeeds', displaying Irish sympathies, in 1848. In 1851 he was received into the Roman Catholic Church. His voluminous works include 'The Legends of St. Patrick' (1872), 'Critical Essays' (1887–9), 'Recollections' (1897), and dramas. He is the subject of a 'Memoir' by Wilfrid Ward (1904).

De Veritate, the principal philosophical work of Lord Herbert of Cherbury (q.v.).

Dead Sea Scrolls, *The,* the popular name for the remains of the once considerable collection of Hebrew and Aramaic MSS. discovered in caves at the NW. end of the Dead Sea between 1947 and 1956. Although no one MS. is intact and many exist only in fragments, nearly all the books of the canonical O.T. are represented, as well as apocryphal books and some works not previously known. The Scrolls belonged to the library of the Jewish community at Qumran about the beginning of the Christian era, and it is probable that most of them were written there, between 20 B.C. and A.D. 70. It is presumed that they were hidden in the caves for safety. The Scrolls are important in being almost the only surviving MS. material in Hebrew and Aramaic from this period and have a valuable bearing on the study of O.T. texts. They also provide a first-hand account of Jewish life and thought contemporary with the beginning of Christianity.

Dead Souls, see *Gogol.*

Dean of St. Patrick's, THE, Swift (q.v.).

Deane, MR. and LUCY, characters in G. Eliot's 'The Mill on the Floss' (q.v.).

Deans, DAVID, and his daughters JEANIE and EFFIE, the principal characters in Scott's 'The Heart of Midlothian' (q.v.).

Dearbhorgil, see *Devorguilla* (2).

Death and Dr. Hornbook, a satirical poem by Burns (q.v.). Dr. Hornbook was a fictitious village schoolmaster who eked out his salary by the sale of drugs.

Death of Blanche, *The,* see *Boke of the Duchesse.*

Death's Jest-Books, or *The Fool's Tragedy,* a play by Beddoes (q.v.), begun by him in 1825 and altered and touched up by him until the end of his life. It was published, after his death, in 1850. Three distinct manuscript versions of the play exist.

Wolfram and Isbrand have entered the service of Melveric, the duke of Munsterberg, in disguise, to take vengeance on him for the death of their father and the dishonour of their sister; Wolfram in the character of a knight, Isbrand of a court-fool. Wolfram, of a generous and forgiving temper, is sent to rescue Melveric from captivity among the Moors, and chivalrously carries out his mission. He finds Melveric in love with Sibylla, a fellow captive, whose affection has already been given to Wolfram. Contention arises, in which Wolfram's generosity is repaid first with a poisoned cup and then with death by Melveric's sword. Melveric returns to his country, where many troubles await him and where he is haunted by the ghost of Wolfram. There follows a strange medley of conspiracy, murder, and charnel-house scenes, with an element of the supernatural, which ends in the death of all the principal characters, the ghost of Wolfram leading off Melveric to the sepulchre as the curtain falls. The play contains some fine blank verse and beautiful lyrics, notably the dirge for Wolfram, beginning

> If thou wilt ease thy heart
> Of love and all its smart.

Debatable Land, a tract of country between the Esk and the Sark on the borders of Cumberland, claimed before the Union by both England and Scotland, and the scene of frequent conflicts.

Debrett, the peerage of the United Kingdom first published in 1802 by John Debrett, under the title 'Peerage of England, Scotland, and Ireland, containing an Account of all the Peers'. Now issued annually.

Decameron, *The,* a collection of tales by Boccaccio (q.v.), written probably over many years, but assembled in their definitive form between 1349 and 1351. The setting of the tales, which are drawn from many sources, is as follows. Florence being visited by the plague in 1348, seven young ladies and three young men leave the city for neighbouring villas, the beauty of which is described, and spend part of each of ten days (whence the name) in diverting one another with stories, each person telling one tale on each day, so that there are one hundred tales in all. The work had much influence on English literature, notably on Chaucer, and many of the tales were incorporated in Painter's 'Palace of Pleasure' (q.v.).

Declaration of Independence, THE, the document signed 4 July 1776, whereby the American Congress declared the United States of North America to be independent of the British Crown. Thomas Jefferson, John Adams, Roger Sherman, Robert R. Livingstone, and Benjamin Franklin drew up the Declaration, which was signed by eleven States.

Declaration of Indulgence, THE, was issued by Charles II in 1672 suspending the penal laws in ecclesiastical matters in such a way as to give religious liberty to Roman Catholics and Dissenters. It was recalled in 1673 under pressure from the Commons. A fresh Declaration of Indulgence was issued by James II in 1687; and a third in April 1688. It was for refusing to compel their clergy to read the last that the seven bishops were brought to trial. Three successive Declarations of Indulgence were published in Scotland, 1662–4, to the advantage of moderate Presbyterianism.

Decline and Fall of the Roman Empire, The, an historical work by Gibbon (q.v.), of which vol. i of the first (quarto) edition was published in 1776, vols. ii and iii in 1781, and the last three volumes in 1788.

This, the greatest of historical works in English literature, falls into three divisions, as defined by the author in the preface: from the age of Trajan and the Antonines to the subversion of the western Empire; from the reign of Justinian in the East to the establishment of the second or German Empire of the West, under Charlemagne; from the revival of the western Empire to the taking of Constantinople by the Turks. It thus covers a period of about thirteen centuries, and comprehends such vast subjects as the establishment of the Christian religion, the movements and settlements of the Teutonic tribes, the conquests of the Muslims, and the crusades. It traces in fact the connexion of the ancient world with the modern.

The history is marked by lucidity, completeness, and substantial accuracy, though in the latter respect it has been superseded by later works written in the light of fuller knowledge. (It is supplemented by notes in the editions of J. B. Bury, 1896–1900, 1909–13.) The principal criticism to which it is open is a certain lack of proportion, and a want of sympathy with man in his nobler impulses. History was to Gibbon 'little more than the crimes, follies, and misfortunes of mankind'.

Decretals, epistles of the popes on points of doctrine or ecclesiastical law. The first collection of decretals was that of Gregory IX in five books (1234), followed by a sixth book in 1298, by the CLEMENTINES of Clement V in 1313, and by the EXTRAVAGANTS of John XXII and his successors. The decretals constitute the 'new' canon law as distinguished from the 'old' canon law contained in Gratian's 'Decree' of 1150.

The FALSE or ISIDORIAN DECRETALS are a collection of decretals, made in the 9th cent., containing certain spurious documents supporting the papal claim to temporal power. The author takes the name of Isidore, archbishop of Sevile (d. 636). The forged documents contain about a hundred letters purporting to be from early popes, and include the famous 'Donation of Constantine' (q.v.). They were finally shown to be spurious by Laurentius Valla, the great humanist, in the 15th cent.

Dedalus, STEPHEN, a character in James Joyce's 'Ullysses' (q.v.).

Dedlock, SIR LEICESTER, LADY, and VOLUMNIA, characters in Dickens's 'Bleak House' (q.v.).

Dee, MILLER OF THE, see *Miller of the Dee.*

DEE, DR. JOHN (1527–1608), mathematician and astrologer, was educated at St. John's College, Cambridge, and became a fellow of Trinity College, Cambridge, where the stage effects he introduced into a performance of the 'Peace' of Aristophanes procured him his lifelong reputation of being a magician; this was confirmed by his erudition and practice of crystallomancy and astrology. He wrote numerous learned works, including 'De Trigono' (1565), 'Navigationis ad Cathayam . . . delineatio Hydrographica' (1580), and a 'Treatise on the Rosie Crucian Secrets'.

Deerbrook, a novel by Harriet Martineau (q.v.), published in 1839.

Deerslayer, The, a novel by J. F. Cooper (q.v.), published in 1841.

Defarge, M. and **MME,** characters in Dickens's 'A Tale of Two Cities' (q.v.).

Defence of All Learning, see *Musophilus.*

Defence of Poesie, see *Apologie for Poetry.*

Defence of Poetry, see *Shelley (P. B.).*

Defender of the Faith, DEFENSOR FIDEI, a title conferred on Henry VIII by Leo X in 1521, in recognition of Henry's 'Defence of the Seven Sacraments'. The Bull is in Rymer's 'Foedera', vi, and in an Appendix to Roscoe's 'Leo X'.

Deffand, MME DU, MARIE DE VICHY-CHAMROND (1697–1780), a French literary hostess, whose *salon* was frequented by Montesquieu, D'Alembert, and others, and who became blind in later life. Horace Walpole was her close friend, and a large number of her letters to him survive (edited by Mrs. Paget Toynbee, 1912). Walpole's letters to her were destroyed by his request.

DEFOE, DANIEL (1660?–1731), born in London, the son of James Foe, a butcher. He changed his name to Defoe c. 1703. He married Mary Tuffley in Jan. 1683/4, being at that time a hosiery merchant in Cornhill, and having apparently travelled in Spain, Italy, Germany, and France. He took part in Monmouth's rebellion, and joined William III's army in 1688. In 1701 he published 'The True-born Englishman', a satirical poem combating the popular prejudice against a king of foreign birth. In 1702 appeared 'The Shortest Way with the Dissenters', a notorious pamphlet in which Defoe, himself a dissenter, ironically demanded the total suppression of dissent, at any cost, to show the absurdity of ecclesiastical intolerance. For this he was fined, imprisoned (May–Nov., 1703), and pilloried. Although he was regarded as a hero by the people, the sense of his unjust treatment appears to have affected his character. Under the influence of this and of pecuniary distress— he attributed his ruin to his imprisonment— he became shifty and mercenary in public affairs. He wrote his 'Hymn to the Pillory', a mock-Pindaric ode, while imprisoned, and started his newspaper 'The Review' (q.v.) in 1704. In the same year appeared his pamphlet 'Giving Alms no Charity', and in 1706 his 'True Relation of the Apparition of one Mrs. Veal', a vivid piece of reporting of a current ghost story. During the following years he was employed as a secret agent of Harley and Godolphin, largely in Scotland, in support of the union, but his fidelity to his employers is questioned. Certain ironical anti-Jacobite pamphlets in 1712–13 led to his prosecution by the Whigs for treasonable publications and to a brief imprisonment. He now started a new trade journal, 'Mercator', in place of 'The Review'. In 1715 he was convicted of libelling Lord Annesley, but escaped punishment by the favour of Lord Townshend, the Whig secretary of state, to whom he sold his services as a secret agent and journalist.

He published the first volume of his best-known work 'Robinson Crusoe' (q.v.) in 1719, the 'Farther Adventures' of his hero following a few months later. The next five years saw the appearance of his most important works of fiction, as follows: 'Life and Adventures of Mr. Duncan Campbell', the deaf and dumb conjurer, and 'Captain Singleton' (q.v.), in 1720; 'Moll Flanders' (q.v.), 'A Journal of the Plague Year' (q.v.), 'The History of Peter the Great', and 'Colonel Jack' (q.v.) in 1722; 'Roxana' (q.v.),the 'Memoirs of a Cavalier' (q.v., not quite certainly by Defoe), his tracts on Jack Sheppard (q.v.), and 'A New Voyage round the World', in 1724; 'The Four Voyages of Capt. George Roberts' in 1726. The 'Memoirs of Captain George Carleton' (q.v.), which appeared in 1728, were probably largely by his hand. His 'Tour through the Whole Island of Great Britain', a delightful guide-book, in three volumes, appeared in 1724–7. During the last six years of his life (1715–31) his principal works were 'The Complete English Tradesman' (1726), 'Augusta Triumphans, or the Way to make London the Most Flourishing City in the Universe' (1728), 'A Plan of the English Commerce' (1728), and 'The Complete English Gentleman', not published until 1890. In addition to the works mentioned above, Defoe produced a vast number of pamphlets on all sorts of subjects; in all he published over 250 works. He died in his lodgings in Ropemaker's Alley, Moorfields, and was buried in what is now Bunhill Fields. Defoe, apart from the political shiftiness above alluded to, was not only an extraordinarily prolific and versatile, but a liberal, humane, and moral writer.

Deformed Transformed, *The*, an unfinished drama by Lord Byron (q.v.), written in 1822.

Arnold is a hideous hunchback and miserable in consequence of his deformity. A stranger, the Devil in disguise, offers to change his shape, and calls up the forms of Caesar, Alcibiades, and others to tempt him. Arnold chooses the form of Achilles, and this the stranger confers upon him, assuming in exchange the hunchback shape of Arnold, whom he thereafter follows as an attendant. Part II presents the sack of Rome in 1527, in the course of which Arnold distinguishes himself. At this point the fragment ends.

Degare or **Degore,** *Sir*, a metrical romance of some 900 lines, of the early 14th cent. The daughter of a king of England, who has been ravished by a knight, secretly bears a son. She abandons him in the forest with a purse of money, a letter of directions, and a pair of gloves designed to indicate the lady he is to marry. The poem relates the prowess of the son in numerous adventures encountered in his search for his father. The name is supposed to be a corruption of *L'égaré*, and is the origin of 'Diggory'.

Degas, EDGAR (1834–1917), French painter and sculptor of ballet and racecourse scenes, and studies of figures in characteristic actions, such as women bathing or ironing clothes. He was friendly, though not in sympathy, with the Impressionists.

Deïănira, a daughter of Oeneūs, king of Aetolia. Her beauty gained her many admirers and her father promised to give her to him who proved the strongest. Hercules obtained the prize and married Deianira. As they travelled together, they were stopped by the swollen stream of the Evenus, and the centaur Nessus offered to carry her safely to the opposite shore. Hercules consented, but no sooner had Nessus reached the opposite bank than he offered violence to Deianira. Hercules, seeing this, shot a poisoned arrow and mortally wounded Nessus. To avenge himself the latter gave Deianira his tunic, stained with blood infected by the poisoned arrow, telling her that it had the power to reclaim a husband from unlawful loves. When Hercules was unfaithful to her, Deianira sent him the centaur's garment, which caused his death.

Deïdămīa, a daughter of Lycomēdēs, at whose court Achilles (q.v.) spent some time in concealment. She bore to Achilles a son, Neoptolemus.

Deil, *Address to the,* a poem by Burns (q.v.).

Deïphŏbus, a son of Priam of Troy, who married Helen (q.v.) after the death of his brother Paris. He was betrayed by her and slain by Menelaus. He figures in Shakespeare's 'Troilus and Cressida' (q.v.).

Deirdre, the heroine of the tale of 'The Sons of Usnach' (pron. 'Usna'), one of the 'Three Sorrowful Stories of Erin'. She was the daughter of Fedlimid, harper to King Conchobar of Ulster, and Cathbad the Druid prophesied that her beauty would bring banishment and death to heroes. Conchobar destined her for his wife and had her brought up in solitude. But she accidentally saw and fell in love with Naoise (pron. 'Naisi'), the son of Usnach, who with his brothers carried her off to Scotland. They were lured back by Conchobar and treacherously slain, and Deirdre took her own life. (See Lady Gregory, 'Cuchulain of Muirthemne', and the dramas on Deirdre by G. W. Russell, Synge, and Yeats.)

Deism, or 'natural religion', the belief in a Supreme Being as the source of finite existence, with rejection of revelation and the supernatural doctrines of Christianity.

The Deists, who came into prominence at the end of the 17th and during the 18th cents., were a group of writers holding the above belief, of whom the chief were Charles Blount (1654–93), John Toland (1670–1722), Matthew Tindal (1657–1733), Anthony Collins (1676–1729), Thomas Chubb (1679–1747), and the third earl of Shaftesbury (q.v.). Their views derived from those of Lord Herbert of Cherbury (q.v.).

DEKKER, THOMAS (1570?–1632), was born, and mainly lived, in London, the manners of which his writings vividly illustrate. He suffered from poverty and was long in prison for debt, but appears to have been a man of happy and lovable temperament. He was engaged about 1598 by Philip Henslowe (q.v.) to write plays (most of which are now lost) in collaboration with Drayton, Ben Jonson, and many others. He published 'The Shoemaker's Holiday' (q.v.) and 'Old Fortunatus' (q.v.), comedies, in 1600. Having been ridiculed, jointly with Marston, by Ben Jonson in the 'Poetaster', he retorted in 'Satiromastix' (q.v.), a play produced in 1602. His other principal plays are 'The Honest Whore' (q.v.), of which Pt. I appeared in 1604, and Pt. II in 1630; 'Patient Grissil' (q.v.), written in collaboration with Chettle and Haughton,

1603; the 'Witch of Edmonton' (q.v.), written in collaboration with Ford and Rowley, 1623. He also collaborated with Middleton in the 'Roaring Girl' (q.v.), 1611, and Massinger in the 'Virgin Martyr' (q.v.), 1622. He published a tragicomedy 'Match Mee in London', 1631. He wrote a number of pamphlets, as follows: 'The Wonderful Yeare 1603', containing a poignant description of London during the plague of that year; 'The Seuen deadly Sinnes of London', and 'Newes from Hell', an imitation of Nash, 1606; 'The Belman of London', a social satire, 1608. He produced 'The Guls Hornebooke' (q.v.), 1609, and 'Fowre Birds of Noahs Arke', a prose devotional work, 1609. 'The Batchelors Banquet', a tract founded on 'Les Quinze Joyes de Mariage', has been wrongly attributed to him. His dramatic works were collected by R. H. Shepherd in 1873, and his miscellaneous works by Dr. Grosart in 'The Huth Library'. His writings are marked by a sunny simplicity and sympathy for the poor and oppressed (including animals tortured for man's amusement).

Delacroix, EUGÈNE (1798–1863), French painter, a leader of the Romantic Movement. His 'Journal' (published 1893–5) gives a vivid account of his personality, his methods of work, and the artistic life of Paris.

DELANE, JOHN THADDEUS (1817–79), educated at King's College, London, and Magdalen Hall, Oxford, the famous editor of 'The Times' (q.v.), 1841–77.

DELANY, MRS. MARY (1700–88), of the Granville family, the wife (after the death of her first husband) of Dr. Patrick Delany (the friend of Swift), left a voluminous correspondence ('Autobiography and Correspondence', 1861–2; see also 'Mrs. Delany at Court', R. Brimley Johnson, 1925), throwing much light on the mode of life among people of quality in the 18th cent. Mrs. Delany introduced Fanny Burney at court.

Delectable Mountains, THE, in Bunyan's 'The Pilgrim's Progress' (q.v.), 'Emmanuel's Land', within sight of the Celestial City.

Delenda est Carthago, see *Cato the Censor.*

Delĭa, a name of Artemis or Diana, who was said to have been born in the island of Delos.

Delia, a collection of sonnets by S. Daniel (q.v.), published in 1592.

Delilah (DALILA in Milton's 'Samson Agonistes', q.v.), in Judges xvi, a woman of the valley of Sorek, loved by Samson; she persuaded him to tell her the secret of his strength and (by cutting off his hair) betrayed him to the Philistines.

Della Crusca, ACCADEMIA, literally academy of the bran or chaff, the name of an academy established at Florence in 1582, mainly with the object of sifting and purifying the Italian language; whence its name, and its emblem, a sieve. The first edition of its dictionary appeared in 1612.

The name Della Cruscan is also applied to a school of English poetry, at once silly and pretentious, started towards the end of the 18th cent. It was taken from the Florentine Academy, to which Robert Merry (1755–98), one of the members of the school, in fact belonged. The Della Cruscan poets were attacked by W. Gifford (q.v.) in his 'Baviad' and 'Maeviad'.

Della Robbia, LUCA, see *Robbia, Luca della.*

Delmour, COLONEL, and his brother MR. DELMOUR, characters in S. E. Ferrier's 'The Inheritance' (q.v.).

DELONEY, THOMAS (1543?–1600?), ballad-writer and pamphleteer, was by trade a silk-weaver. He wrote ballads and broadsides (three on the Spanish Armada, 1588). But his three chief works, written between 1596 and 1600, are prose narratives relating respectively to the clothier's craft ('Thomas of Reading'), the weaver's craft ('Jack of Newbury'), and the shoemaker's craft ('The Gentle Craft'). This last includes the story of 'Simon Eyre', the shoemaker's apprentice who became lord mayor and founder of Leadenhall (a story adapted by Dekker in 'The Shoemaker's Holiday', q.v.); and that of 'Richard Casteler' in which figures Long Meg or Meg of Westminster (q.v.). In these works the author, with considerable humour, portrays the life of the middle classes of Elizabethan times, and gives vivid pictures of London scenes.

Deloraine, WILLIAM OF, a character in Scott's 'Lay of the Last Minstrel' (q.v.).

Delos, an island in the Aegean, one of the Cyclades, supposed to have been raised from the sea, as a floating island, by Poseidon, and anchored to the bottom of the sea by Zeus, to be a resting-place for Latona (q.v.). It contained temples of Apollo and Latona. The whole island was declared sacred by the Greeks, and was made the treasury of the Greek confederacy against the Persians. It was the transfer of this treasury to Athens that provoked the jealousy of other Greek states, and thus contributed to bring about the Peloponnesian War.

Delphi, situated in Phocis, in a deep rocky cleft on the south-west slopes of Mt. Parnassus, was the seat of a temple to Apollo and of an oracle of world-wide fame. The oracles were delivered by a priestess of Apollo called the PYTHIA, who was supposed to be inspired by the sulphurous vapours issuing from a cavity in the ground within the temple. It was customary for those who consulted the oracle to give large presents to the god; whence were derived the immense treasures of the temple. The oracle was in existence in the Mycenaean age and did not finally disappear until the 4th cent. A.D. But its period of greatest influence was in the 8th to 5th cents. B.C. It was looted by Sulla and sank into decay during the 1st cent. A.D. There

was a revival under Hadrian and the final flicker came under Julian (A.D. 360).

The PYTHIAN GAMES were held in the neighbourhood of Delphi every four years, in the interval between the Olympic Games (q.v.), in the third year of each Olympiad.

Delphi, in imprints, Delft.

Delphin Classics, *ad usum Delphini,* see *Dauphin.*

Delvile, MORTIMER, the hero of F. Burney's 'Cecilia' (q.v.).

Dēmēter, known as CERES to the Romans, was the Greek goddess of the corn-bearing earth and of agriculture. Mythology made her the daughter of Cronos and sister of Zeus, but she does not figure among Homer's Olympian deities. Persephone (Proserpine, q.v.) was her daughter. She instructed Triptolemus, the son of Celĕus, king of Attica, in the arts of agriculture, and lent him her chariot, wherein he travelled all over the world bringing corn to the inhabitants. After the carrying off of Proserpine by Pluto (see under *Proserpine*), she endeavoured in vain to recover her daughter, and so great was her grief that Jupiter granted Proserpine to spend part of the year with her mother and the remainder with Pluto. This myth, symbolical of the sowing of the seed (the sojourn of Proserpine with Pluto in the nether regions) and growing of the corn (her return to the upper world), and perhaps also of the death of man and his future life, was celebrated in the great Eleusinian mysteries.

The myth has been treated by Tennyson in his 'Demeter and Persephone', and by Robert Bridges in his mask 'Demeter' (1905).

Demetrius, the silversmith of Ephesus, who stirred up his fellow craftsmen against Paul; see Acts xix. 24 et seq.

Demetrius, a character in Shakespeare's 'A Midsummer Night's Dream' (q.v.); also in Jonson's 'The Poetaster' (q.v.), where Demetrius represents the poet Marston; also in Fletcher's 'The Humorous Lieutenant' (q.v.).

Demetrius, PSEUDO-, an impostor who usurped the Russian throne in 1605–6, and was assassinated in Moscow in the latter year. He was a monk, Otrefief·by name, who pretended to be Demetrius, the son of the Tsar Ivan whom Boris the usurper had put to death.

Demiurge, in the Platonic philosophy, the maker or creator of the world; in certain later systems, as the Gnostic, a being subordinate to the Supreme Being, and sometimes conceived as the author of evil.

Demŏcrĭtus, a celebrated Greek philosopher, born at Abdera about 460 B.C. He wrote on the natural sciences, mathematics, morals, and music. He advanced (with Leucippus) the theory that the world was formed by the concourse of atoms, the theory subsequently expounded by Lucretius, and confirmed and developed by recent scientific discovery. Juvenal speaks of him as ever laughing at the follies of mankind, and he is sometimes known as the 'laughing philosopher' in opposition to the melancholy Heraclitus (q.v.).

DEMOCRITUS JUNIOR, pseudonym of ROBERT BURTON (q.v.).

Demogorgon, the name of a mysterious deity, first mentioned, so far as is known, by the scholiast (Lactantius?) on Statius's 'Thebais'; also mentioned by the scholiast on Lucan's 'Pharsalia'; perhaps a mistake for Demiurgus, the Creator. Demogorgon is described in the 'Genealogia Deorum' of Boccaccio as the primeval god of ancient mythology, and this appears to be the sense of the word in modern literature (Spenser, Milton, Shelley, etc.). [OED.] In Shelley's 'Prometheus Unbound' (q.v.) Demogorgon is an eternal principle or power which ousts the gods of a false theology. The countess of Saldar's 'Demogorgon' (in Meredith's 'Evan Harrington', q.v.) is tailordom.

Demon-lover, THE, see *Lenore*.

Demŏ'phŏon or **De'mŏphon,** (1) son of Celĕus, king of Eleusis, and brother of (or identical with) Triptolemus (q.v.). Celeus hospitably received Demeter (q.v.) when she was wandering about the world in search of her daughter, and she, to mark her gratitude, tried to make Demophoon immortal by placing him in the flames, in order to purge away his mortal elements. But his mother, Metanīra, was terrified and intervened; (2) son of Theseus (q.v.) and Phaedra, and lover of Phyllis, daughter to Sithon, king of Thrace. He left her to go for a time to Athens but prolonged his absence, and Phyllis, thinking herself abandoned, took her own life and was changed into a tree.

DEMOSTHĒNĒS (*c.* 383–322 B.C.), the Athenian orator, born in the Attic deme of Paeania. His fame, won by his eloquence and personality in spite of lack of wealth and position, rests principally on the orations delivered to rouse his countrymen to the danger of the subjugation of Greece by Philip of Macedon (hence the word 'philippic'). After the defeat of the confederate Greeks, Antipater, one of the successors of Alexander, demanded the surrender of Demosthenes, who, pursued by the Macedonian emissaries, took poison and died.

Dempster, MR. and JANET, characters in G. Eliot's 'Janet's Repentance' (see *Scenes of Clerical Life*).

DENHÁM, SIR JAMES STEUART, see *Steuart*.

Denham, JENNY, a character in Meredith's 'Beauchamp's Career' (q.v.).

DENHAM, SIR JOHN (1615–69), was born in Dublin and educated at Trinity College, Oxford. He took part in public affairs on the king's side and was forced to surrender Farnham Castle, of which he was governor, to Sir William Waller in 1642. His chief poetical work is the topographical poem 'Cooper's Hill' (1642), combining description of scenery with reflections, moral, historical, and political, and containing the well-known quatrain on the River Thames, which begins 'O could I flow like thee'. Denham published 'The Sophy', an historical tragedy of the Turkish court, in 1641; also a paraphrase of part of the 'Aeneid', and occasional verses and satires.

Denis, ST., first bishop of Paris and patron saint of France, decapitated in 280 with two companions on the hill of Montmartre. Legend (which also identifies Denis with Dionysius the Areopagite of Acts xvii) relates that they carried their heads in their hands to the spot where subsequently the abbey of Saint-Denis, near Paris, was built.

Denis Duval, an unfinished novel by Thackeray (q.v.), published in the 'Cornhill Magazine' in 1864. This was Thackeray's last work of fiction.

The principal scene of the fragment is Rye in the second half of the 18th cent., with its colony of French refugees, and its widespread smuggling activities. Here Denis Duval, a descendant of French Protestant pastors, lives with his grandfather, a barber and smuggler, and his Alsatian mother. He tells the story of his life, how in early youth he fell in love with Agnes, the daughter of Mme de Saverne, a Frenchwoman who had fled to England from the tyranny of her half-crazy husband, under the evil influence of the Chevalier De la Motte, a sinister person who subsequently kills her husband. De la Motte settles in Rye and joins in the smuggling business, and (with Lütterloh, a German associate) in more treasonable practices, which Denis Duval is the means of bringing to light. Denis incurs the fierce enmity of the smuggling confederacy of Rye, is vigorously persecuted, escapes great dangers, and takes to the sea. And here the fragment breaks off. But we know from Thackeray's notes that it was intended that Denis should go through a long course of adventures in the naval service, from the sea-fight with Captain Paul Jones to the defeat of Admiral Grasse's squadron; that De la Motte should endeavour forcibly to marry Agnes to Lütterloh; that De la Motte was hanged, and that Lütterloh went down on the 'Royal George', on board of which he had gone to receive payment for his work as a spy.

Dennis, in Dickens's 'Barnaby Rudge' (q.v.), the hangman and one of the leaders of the No-Popery riots.

DENNIS, JOHN (1657–1734), educated at Harrow and Caius College, Cambridge, was author of 'Rinaldo and Armida' (1699) and other tragedies, one of which, 'Appius and Virginia' (1709), was satirized for its bombast by Pope ('Essay on Criticism', iii. 585–8). To this Dennis replied in his 'Reflections, Critical and Satirical' (1711). Pope retorted in his 'Narrative of Dr. Robert Norris, concerning the strange and deplorable Frenzy of Mr. J. Denn— an officer in the Custom-House' (1713), an employment held by Dennis. He is best known for his critical works, which include 'The Advancement and Reformation of Modern Poetry' (1701), 'The Grounds of Criticism in Poetry' (1704), 'An Essay on the Genius and Writings of Shakespeare' (1712).

Dennison, JENNY, in Scott's 'Old Mortality' (q.v.), the attendant on Edith Bellenden.

Denouement, the unravelling of the plot, the final solution, in a drama or novel; Aristotle's λύσις.

Deodand, a thing forfeited to God; specifically in English law a personal chattel which, having been the immediate occasion of the death of a human being, was forfeited to God as an expiatory offering, i.e. forfeited to the Crown to be applied to pious uses. Deodands were abolished by statute in 1846.

Deor, Complaint of, an OE. poem of 42 verses, divided into stanzas. It is included in the 'Exeter Book' (q.v.). Deor is a minstrel who has fallen out of favour and been supplanted by another minstrel, Heorrenda, and consoles himself by considering the misfortunes of others, Wayland the Smith, Theodoric, Hermanric, etc. Each stanza ends with the refrain 'That passed; this also may'.

'Deputy', in Dickens's 'Edwin Drood' (q.v.), the nearest thing to a name acknowledged by the imp who attends on Durdles.

Derby, COUNTESS OF, wife of the seventh earl, who as 'queen' of the Isle of Man figures in Scott's 'Peveril of the Peak' (q.v.).

Derceto, the fish-goddess of Ascalon in Syria, the legendary mother of Semiramis (q.v.).

Derrick, a noted hangman at Tyburn, c. 1600, the origin of the word 'derrick', a crane.

Derriman, FESTUS, the braggart yeoman in Hardy's 'The Trumpet-Major' (q.v.).

Dervish, a Muslim friar, who has taken vows of poverty. Some sects of Dervishes are known by their fantastic practices of *dancing* or *whirling*, and *howling*.

Desborough, LUCY, a character in Meredith's 'The Ordeal of Richard Feverel' (q.v.).

DESCARTES, RENÉ (1596–1650), a French mathematician, physicist, and philosopher, the founder of the school of philosophy known as CARTESIAN. He lived a great part of his life in Holland, and was invited by Queen Christina to Sweden, where he died. The starting-point of his philosophy, expounded in his chief work 'Le Discours de la Méthode' (1637), .was the famous phrase *cogito, ergo sum,* 'I think, therefore I am', and the distinction between spirit and matter. Rejecting philosophical authority and tradition, he relied exclusively on reason, and

adopted a quasi-mechanical conception of the universe, which he reduced to space, matter, and motion, operating under mathematical laws. He did not, however, explain the interaction of spirit and matter, while some of his principal physical theories were upset by Newton's discoveries. But his influence on the development of philosophy and science was immense. It extended to literature, where the impulse he gave to the rule of reason is manifested in the writers of the 17th cent. The chief ethical work of Descartes was his 'Traité des Passions' (1649).

DESCHAMPS, EUSTACHE, surnamed MOREL (*b. c.* 1346), French poet, one of the creators of the *ballade*. He addressed a complimentary poem to Chaucer, whom he styled 'great translator'.

Desdemona, the heroine of Shakespeare's 'Othello' (q.v.).

Deserted Village, The, a poem by Goldsmith (q.v.), published in 1770, of which the theme is the superiority of agriculture to trade in the national economy. The poet revisits Auburn, a village hallowed by early associations, and marks its depopulation and the inroads of monopolizing riches, which have driven the peasants to emigration. He laments a state of society where 'wealth accumulates and men decay'. The poem contains charming descriptions of village life and character. Boswell attributes the last four lines to Johnson. Goldsmith's pictures of a happy rural community provoked a protest in Crabbe's 'The Village'.

Despair, GIANT, in Bunyan's 'The Pilgrim's Progress' (q.v.), imprisons Christian and Hopeful in Doubting Castle.

Desperate Remedies, a novel by T. Hardy (q.v.), published in 1871.

This was the first of Hardy's published novels, and belongs in his classification to the group of 'novels of ingenuity', with the best claim to that description of the three novels of that group. It is a tale of 'mystery, entanglement, surprise, and moral obliquity', in which Cytherea Graye, beloved by and loving a young architect, Edward Springrove, is forced by poverty to accept a post as lady's maid to the eccentric Miss Aldclyffe, the woman whom her father had loved but had been unable to marry. Miss Aldclyffe's machinations, the discovery that Edward is already engaged to a woman whom he does not love, and the urgent need of supporting a sick brother, drive Cytherea to accept the hand of Aeneas Manston, Miss Aldclyffe's illegitimate son, a passionate villain, whose first wife is believed to have perished in a fire. No sooner is the wedding ceremony performed than Cytherea discovers that Edward is free from his entanglement and that there is reason to think that Manston's first wife is still alive, and she escapes from his clutches. Ingenious detective work brings to light the fact that Manston has murdered his first wife, in order to gain Cytherea. He hangs himself in his cell, and the lovers are finally united.

Destiny, a novel by S. E. Ferrier (q.v.), published in 1831.

The story deals with the fortunes of the various members of the Malcolm family: Glenroy, a typical Highland chief, married, after the death of his first wife, to the London-bred Lady Elizabeth Waldegrave, who finds conditions of life in her husband's home so intolerable that she separates from him; Glenroy's poor but worthy cousin Captain Malcolm and his son Ronald; another cousin, the misanthrope Inch-Orran, who disappoints Glenroy by leaving his estate to Ronald and his father; Glenroy's nephew Reginald, who plights his troth to Edith, the chief's daughter by his first wife, and jilts her to marry her half-sister; Ronald, who voluntarily disappears after a shipwreck to leave his father in possession of the Inch-Orran property, and returns after years to marry the jilted Edith. The story of their vicissitudes, somewhat artificial, is relieved by one or two good characters, notably that of the boorish minister, the Revd. Duncan M'Dow.

Detectives in Fiction, see *Alleyn, Brown (Father), Bucket, Cuff, Dupin, Fortune, French, Hanaud, Holmes, Lecoq, Lupin, Maigret, Poirot, Tabaret, Thorndyke, Trent, Vance, Wimsey (Lord Peter).*

Deucalion, a son of Prometheus (q.v.), and ruler of part of Thessaly. Jupiter, angered by the impiety of mankind, covered the earth with a deluge. Deucalion and his wife Pyrrha saved their lives by taking refuge on the top of Parnassus, or, according to some, by building a ship as advised by Prometheus, in which they were carried to the top of that mountain. After the flood had subsided, Deucalion and Pyrrha consulted the oracle of Themis on the question how to repair the loss of mankind and were told to throw stones behind them. The stones thrown by Deucalion became men, and those thrown by Pyrrha women.

Deuceace, THE HON. ALGERNON PERCY, youngest son of the earl of Crabs, a character in Thackeray's 'The Memoirs of Mr. C. J. Yellowplush' (q.v.).

Deuceace is an unscrupulous gambler and swindler, who, after ruining the simpleton Dawkins, overreaches himself in the pursuit of the large fortune left by Sir George Griffin to his pretty young widow and his crook-backed daughter by an earlier marriage, on conditions which are unknown. Uncertain which to marry, Deuceace determines to have two strings to his bow. His design is discovered by the widow and her bitter vindictiveness aroused. She lures him first into a duel, in which he loses a hand, and then into a marriage with the humpback, to discover too late that the latter is penniless, and that he has been outwitted by his own father—a cleverer scoundrel—who has married the widow and secured the fortune.

Deus ex machina, 'God from the machine', an unexpected event or intervention in a play or novel, which resolves a difficult situation. When a god was introduced in the ancient Greek drama, he was brought on to the stage by some mechanical device (μηχανή).

Deuteronomy (from Greek δεύτερος second, and νόμος law), the title of the fifth book of the Pentateuch, originating in a mistranslation of the Hebrew words in Deut. xvii. 18, which mean 'a copy or duplicate of this law'. The book contains a repetition, with comments, of the Decalogue and most of the laws contained in Exodus xxi–xxiii and xxxiv. Some authorities regard it as the 'book of the law' discovered by Hilkiah, the high priest, in the house of the Lord, during the reign of Josiah (2 Kings xxii. 8).

Deva, one of the good spirits of Hindu mythology.

Deva, the river Dee in Cheshire.

Where Deva spreads her wizard stream.
                                    (Milton, 'Lycidas'.)

Devi, in Hindu mythology, 'the goddess', the wife of Siva (q.v.).

Devil, THE (from the Greek διάβολος, 'distorter, traducer', the word used by the Septuagint to translate the Hebrew word 'Satan'), in Jewish and Christian theology, the name of the supreme spirit of evil, subordinate to the Creator, but possessing superhuman powers of access to, and influence over, men. [OED.] The conception of the Devil may be traced to the idea widely diffused among men, of the dual principles of good and evil in the scheme of things, an idea expressed, for instance, in the Ormazd and Ahriman of the Persians. In the Jewish religion this conception is personified at first in the serpent, a malignant and treacherous creature. The word 'devil' is also applied to malignant beings of supernatural powers, of whom Satan is the prince, clothed, in medieval conception, in grotesque and hideous forms, with horns, tails, and cloven hoofs, derived from figures of Greek and Roman mythology (Pan, the satyrs); thence it is transferred to malignantly wicked or cruel men. It is finally applied colloquially to a junior legal counsel who does professional work for his leader, a literary hack, and generally one who does work for which another receives credit or remuneration or both. A *Printer's devil* is the errand-boy in a printer's office; but Johnson (in Boswell, 20 April 1781) speaks of a man having married a printer's devil.

Devil is an Ass, The, a comedy by Jonson (q.v.), first acted in 1616, ridiculing the 'projectors' or monopolists, and exposing the pretended demoniacs and witch-finders, of the day. Fitzdottrel, a 'gull' or simpleton, is cheated out of his estate by Meercraft, a 'projector', who parades various ridiculous schemes for making money and deludes him with the promise that he will make him duke of Drowndland through a project for land reclamation. When Fitzdottrel finds he has made over his estate to the wrong person, he consents to pretend to be bewitched:

It is the easiest thing, Sir, to be done,
As plain as fizzling: roll but with your eyes
And foam at the mouth. A little castle-soap will do it,

and deceives a justice by the simple fraud. Pug, 'a less devil' who has been allowed by Satan to try his hand at iniquity on earth for one day, finds himself completely outwitted by human knaves, outdone in wickedness, and finally sent to Newgate.

Devil upon Two Sticks in England, The, a continuation by W. Combe (q.v.), published in 1790, of Le Sage's 'Diable Boiteux' (q.v.). Foote (q.v.) also wrote a farce called 'The Devil upon Two Sticks', produced in 1768, satirizing the College of Physicians and quack doctors.

Devil's Advocate, see *Advocatus Diaboli*.

Devil's Island, THE, the *Île du Diable*, one of the three small *Îles du Salut* of the coast of French Guiana, part of the French penal settlement in that colony.

Devil's Thoughts, The, a humorous satirical poem by S. T. Coleridge and Southey (qq.v.) describing the Devil going a-walking and enjoying the sight of the vices of men as they follow their several avocations. The poem was imitated by Byron in his 'Devil's Drive', and by Shelley in his 'Devil's Walk'. Some lines in it have become familiar, such as

And the Devil did grin, for his darling sin
Is pride that apes humility.

Devorguilla, (1) the wife of John de Baliol, founder of Balliol College, Oxford. After his death she increased the endowment of the college. In fact, the college was founded out of Devorguilla's property. She was a great heiress in Galloway. John de Baliol had little land of his own; (2) or **Dearbhorgil**, wife of O'Ruark, prince of Meath. Dermot MacMurchad, king of Leinster, during the absence of O'Ruark on a pilgrimage, eloped with her to his capital, Ferns. Roderick of Connaught, high king of Ireland, came to O'Ruark's assistance. Dermot fled to England and received help from Henry II. This was the occasion of the Anglo-Norman invasion of Ireland in 1170. The story is told by Giraldus Cambrensis ('History of the Conquest of Ireland', ch. i et seq.).

DEWEY, JOHN (1859–1952), American philosopher, one of the leaders of the Pragmatist school, and educationist, born in Vermont. His chief works are: 'Critical Theory of Ethics' (1891), 'Studies in Logical Theory' (1903), 'Democracy and Education' (1916), 'Human Nature and Conduct' (1922).

Dewey, MELVIL (1851–1931), American librarian. He was the originator of the 'Decimal system of classification for library cataloguing'.

Dewy, DICK, the hero of Hardy's 'Under the Greenwood Tree' (q.v.).

Dhu'lkarnain, the name under which Alexander the Great figures in the Koran (c. xviii), and builds the wall against the irruptions of Gog and Magog (q.v.). The word means 'two-horned' (see *Dulcarnon*), and various reasons are given for the name being applied to Alexander, such as that he was king of the East and of the West.

Diable Boiteux, Le ('The Lame Devil'), a romance by Le Sage (q.v.), published in 1707.

Asmodeus (q.v.), a demon released by Don Cleofas Zambullo from a bottle in which he has been imprisoned by a magician, diverts his benefactor by lifting the roofs off houses and showing him what is passing within, thus providing a series of satirical pictures of Parisian society. He assists Don Cleofas in a number of adventures and finally effects his union with his beloved Serafina. See *Devil upon Two Sticks*.

Diacritic, from διακρίνειν to separate, a sign or mark above or under a letter used to distinguish its various sounds or values, e.g. ö, é, ç, å.

Diadochos, meaning 'successor' (plural, Diadochi), the name given to the Macedonian generals among whom the empire of Alexander the Great was divided after his death.

Diaeresis, from διαιρέειν to divide, (1) the separation of a diphthong into two separate vowels; (2) the sign [¨] placed over the second of two vowels, which otherwise make a diphthong or single sound, to indicate that they are to be pronounced separately.

Diafoirus, a doctor in the 'Malade Imaginaire' of Molière (q.v.).

Dial, The, the literary organ of the American Transcendental movement (see *Transcendental Club*), which appeared 1840–4, and of which R. W. Emerson (q.v.) was for a time editor. It contained contributions from Thoreau (q.v.).

Dial, The, (1880–1929), a literary journal which began in Chicago and moved (1918) to New York. It championed the modern movement in letters, and published many of the most distinguished writers of the day.

Diall of Princes, the title of the translation by Sir T. North (q.v.) of Guevara's 'El Relox de Principes', published in 1577, which provided much of the material for Lyly's 'Euphues' (q.v.).

Dialogues of the Dead, Four, by Prior (q.v.), imaginary conversations on the model set by Lucian (q.v.) and perhaps directly suggested by Fénelon's 'Dialogues des morts'. The first is between 'Charles the Emperor and Clenard the Grammarian' on the relative character of greatness; the second is between 'Mr. John Lock and Seigneur de Montaigne'; the third between 'The Vicar of Bray and

Sir Thomas Moor'; and the fourth between 'Oliver Cromwell and his Porter'.

George, Lord Lyttelton (q.v.), also wrote 'Dialogues of the Dead' (1760).

Dialogues concerning Natural Religion, a treatise on natural theology, by Hume (q.v.), published in 1779.

There are three interlocutors in the Dialogues, whose attitudes are indicated by Hume when he contrasts 'the accurate philosophical turn of Cleanthes' with 'the careless scepticism of Philo' and 'the rigid inflexible orthodoxy of Demea'. Hume intends to make Cleanthes the hero of the dialogue; his position is that of a philosophical theism, in which divine intelligence and goodness are inferred from evidences of purpose in the world as we know it. But in the course of the dialogue the scepticism of Philo makes considerable impression upon his opponent.

The subject of the Dialogues is the nature of God (the existence of God is considered unquestionable). Philo attacks the anthropomorphism of the theologians, who see in the nature of God a counterpart of that of man. The discussion brings Philo and Cleanthes into agreement on the existence of the evidences of design in the works of God. But as regards the inferences to be drawn thence, Philo will not go beyond the inference of a divine intelligence. He cannot accede to the inference of divine goodness. Divine goodness may be compatible with the misery that we see in the world, but is assuredly not to be inferred thence.

Dialogus de Scaccario, or *Dialogue of the Exchequer*, is the work of Richard Fitz-Nigel, treasurer of England from 1195 or 1196 to 1198, and bishop of London 1189–98. It takes the form of a dialogue in Latin between teacher and pupil, and is one of the principal sources of our knowledge of the Norman administration in England prior to Magna Carta.

Diamond Necklace, AFFAIR OF THE, the name given to the plot, successfully carried out in 1783–4, of Jeanne de St. Remy de Valois, the descendant of an illegitimate son of Henri II and wife of a self-styled Comte de Lamotte, to get possession of a diamond necklace from the jewellers who had made it, on the pretence that Queen Marie Antoinette had consented to purchase it. Jeanne de Valois had persuaded the Cardinal de Rohan, her dupe, who was desirous of dispelling the disfavour in which he was held at court, that she was in favour with the queen; she had even effected an interview between him and a woman who personated the queen. The cardinal was next led to believe that the queen wished to purchase the necklace and to employ him as intermediary. By this means, and a forged document purporting to signify the queen's acceptance of the terms of purchase, Jeanne got possession of the necklace. It was broken up, and the Comte de Lamotte fled to England with most of the jewels. The

cardinal and Jeanne were arrested; the cardinal was acquitted, Jeanne was whipped and branded. She escaped from the Salpétrière, where she was imprisoned, came to England, wrote her memoirs, and died in 1791. Though the innocence of the queen is now established, much suspicion and discredit clung to her for a time. (See A. Lang, 'Historical Mysteries', and T. Carlyle, 'The Diamond Necklace'.)

Diamond Pitt, see *Pitt (T.)*.

Diana, a Roman goddess identified with the Greek ARTEMIS. The latter was the daughter of Zeus and Leto, and the twin sister of Apollo. She lived in perpetual celibacy and was the goddess of the chase. She also presided over child-birth, and in post-Homeric literature was identified with the moon, in which character she frequently occurs in English literature. There was a famous temple of Diana or Artemis at Ephesus, but here her characteristics were different, and were those of an Eastern nature-goddess. Her statue at Ephesus, which was supposed to have fallen from heaven, was a many-breasted idol, symbolizing the productive forces of nature. 'Great is Diana of the Ephesians' was the cry of the silversmiths of Ephesus, when they found their trade in shrines for Diana threatened by the preaching of Paul (Acts xix. 24 et seq.).

Diana, a character in Shakespeare's 'All's Well that Ends Well' (q.v.).

Diana, a volume of sonnets by H. Constable. (q.v.), first published in 1592.

Diana Enamorada, see *Montemayor*.

Diana Merion, the heroine of Meredith's 'Diana of the Crossways' (q.v.).

Diana of the Crossways, a novel by Meredith (q.v.), published in 1885. The story has some historical foundation, but not in respect of the central incident of the betrayal of a political secret with which the name of the Hon. Mrs. Norton, Sheridan's granddaughter, was falsely connected.

The beautiful and witty Irish girl, Diana Merion, marries Mr. Warwick, 'a gentlemanly official', a man of limited intelligence, quite incapable of understanding the exceptional qualities of his wife. Her innocent indiscretions awaken his jealousy and he brings an action for divorce against her, citing Lord Dannisburgh, an eminent statesman (drawn from Lord Melbourne), which he loses. Husband and wife then live apart. Percy Dacier, a rising young politician, falls in love with her and she with him, and under stress of persecution by her husband she is on the point of accepting his protection, when the dangerous illness of her devoted friend, Lady Dunstane, recalls her to her senses. Dacier perseveres in his attentions, and she is once more on the point of yielding to his importunities when he discovers that an important political secret confided by him to her has been communicated, from mixed motives, among others pecuniary embarrassment, to the editor of a London newspaper. This produces a final breach between them. At this point Diana's husband dies. After a time she gives her hand to her steady faithful adorer, Thomas Redworth, who, without brilliancy, has sufficient wit to understand and appreciate her.

DIAPER, WILLIAM (1686?–1717), poet. In his 'Nereides: or, Sea-Eclogues' (1712) the speakers are mermen and mermaids. He translated Part I of Oppian's 'Halieuticks', a Greek didactic poem on fish and fishing.

Diarmid or DIARMAIT **O'Duibhne**, in the legends relating to the Irish hero Finn, the lover of Grainne (q.v.).

Diary of a Country Parson, The, see *Woodforde*.

Diary of a Nobody, The, by George and Weedon Grossmith, published in 1892. It originally appeared in 'Punch'. It is the diary of Charles Pooter, of The Laurels, Holloway, an assistant in a mercantile business, and recounts with an amusing simplicity his domestic, social, and business troubles, and their satisfactory issue.

DIBDIN, CHARLES (1745–1814), dramatist and song-writer, is best remembered for his nautical songs, including 'Tom Bowling'. He published a 'History of the Stage' (1795), and produced several plays at the Haymarket and Lyceum theatres.

DIBDIN, THOMAS FROGNALL (1776–1847), nephew of Charles Dibdin (q.v.), educated at St. John's College, Oxford, a famous bibliographer, was librarian to Lord Spencer at Althorp. He published his 'Introduction to the Knowledge of Rare and Valuable Editions of the Greek and Latin Classics' in 1802, his 'Bibliomania' (a 'bibliographical romance', in which the study of bibliography is recommended as a cure for bibliomania) in 1809, 'A Bibliographical, Antiquarian, and Picturesque Tour in France and Germany' in 1821, his 'Library Companion' in 1824, 'Reminiscences of a Literary Life' in 1836, and his 'Bibliographical, Antiquarian, and Picturesque Tour in the Northern Counties of England' in 1838.

DICEY, ALBERT VENN (1835–1922), educated at Balliol College, Oxford, fellow of All Souls, and Vinerian professor of law. He was author of an 'Introduction to the Study of the Law of the Constitution' (1885) and other legal works.

Dick, MR., the amiable lunatic in Dickens's 'David Copperfield' (q.v.).

Dick Amlet, a character in Vanbrugh's 'The Confederacy' (q.v.).

DICKENS, CHARLES (1812–70), the son of a government clerk, underwent in early life, as the result of his family's poverty (his father was imprisoned in the Marshalsea), experiences similar to some of those depicted in 'David Copperfield', and received little education. He became reporter of debates in the Commons to the 'Morning Chronicle' in 1835, and contributed to the 'Monthly Magazine' (1833–5), to the 'Evening Chronicle' (1835), and other periodicals, the articles that were subsequently republished as 'Sketches by Boz, Illustrative of Every-Day Life and Every-Day People' (1836–7). These were immediately followed by 'The Posthumous Papers of the Pickwick Club', of which the publication in twenty monthly numbers began in April 1836 (the author being then 24). In this work Dickens suddenly reached the plenitude of his powers as a humorist and achieved success and financial ease. 'Oliver Twist' (q.v., 1837–8) followed in 'Bentley's Miscellany', and 'Nicholas Nickleby' (q.v., 1838–9) in monthly numbers. His next two novels, 'The Old Curiosity Shop' (q.v.) and 'Barnaby Rudge' (q.v.), Dickens published as parts of the serial 'Master Humphrey's Clock' (1840–1), an unnecessary device which he soon abandoned. In 1842 he went to America, where he advocated international copyright and the abolition of slavery. The literary results of the voyage were 'American Notes' (1842) and 'Martin Chuzzlewit' (q.v., 1843–4). 'A Christmas Carol' appeared in 1843, a Christmas book that was followed in each of the succeeding years by 'The Chimes', 'The Cricket on the Hearth', 'The Battle of Life', and 'The Haunted Man', works described by him as 'a whimsical sort of masque intended to awaken loving and forbearing thoughts', which added greatly to his popularity. He paid a long visit to Italy in 1844, which produced the 'Pictures from Italy' contributed to the 'Daily News' in 1846 (Dickens was the founder and for a short time editor of this paper), and to Switzerland in 1846, where he wrote 'Dombey and Son' (q.v.), published in 1848. In 1850 Dickens started the weekly periodical 'Household Words', succeeded in 1859 by 'All the Year Round', and this he carried on until his death. In these he published much of his later writings, including the Christmas stories that replaced the earlier Christmas books. 'David Copperfield' (q.v.), appeared in monthly numbers in 1849–50, 'Bleak House' (q.v.) in 1852–3, the unsuccessful 'Child's History of England' in 1852–4, 'Hard Times' (q.v.) in 1854, 'Little Dorrit' (q.v.) in 1855–7, 'A Tale of Two Cities' (q.v.) in 1859, 'Great Expectations' (q.v.) in 1860–1, and 'Our Mutual Friend' (q.v.) in 1864–5. Dickens had begun to give public readings in 1858, which he continued during his second visit to America in 1867–8. After his return he began, in 1870, 'Edwin Drood' (q.v.), but died suddenly before finishing it. Among minor works of his later years should be mentioned 'Hunted Down' ('New York Ledger', 1859, 'Household Words', 1860), 'Holiday Romance' (1868), 'The Uncommercial Traveller' series (q.v., 1861). Dickens collaborated with Wilkie

Collins in various stories which appeared in 'Household Words' and 'All the Year Round' (e.g. 'The Wreck of the Golden Mary', 'A Message from the Sea', and 'No Thoroughfare'). The standard biography of Dickens is that of John Forster (1872–4; memorial edition, 1911); see also that by Edgar Johnson, 'Charles Dickens: His Tragedy and Triumph' (1952). His Letters are being published in the Pilgrim Edition, ed. M. House and G. Storey (vol. i, 1965–).

DICKINSON, EMILY (1830–86), American poet, was born at Amherst, Massachusetts, and passed her life there in seclusion. Only two of her poems were published—without her consent—during her life, but she left over a thousand in manuscript. Two volumes of selections appeared in 1890–1, and others followed, but not until Thomas H. Johnson's definitive edition of 1955 was it possible to assess fully the range of her extraordinary genius. Her lyrical, paradoxical, gnomic verse, treating of love and death, is marked as much by wit and a keen sense of domestic realities as by mysticism. Her letters are the best commentary on her life and work and were edited by Thomas H. Johnson in 1958.

Dictionary of National Biography, see *National Biography*.

Dictionary of the English Language, A, by S. Johnson, see *Johnson's Dictionary*.

DICTYS CRETENSIS, the reputed author of a diary of the Trojan War. A Latin translation of what purported to be a Greek version of this diary has come down to us. According to the preface to this work Dictys was a Cretan of Cnossos who accompanied Idomeneus to the Trojan War. This and the narrative of Dares Phrygius (q.v.) are the chief sources of medieval Trojan legends.

Diddler, JEREMY, the chief character in James Kenney's farce 'Raising the Wind' (1803). Jeremy's characteristic methods of 'raising the wind' by continually borrowing small sums which he does not pay back, and otherwise sponging on people, probably gave rise to the current sense of the verb 'diddle'—to cheat or victimize. [OED.]

DIDEROT, DENIS (1713–84), French philosopher, dramatist, and critic, the son of a cutler, chiefly remembered in England as one of the founders of the 'Encyclopédie' (q.v.) and principal director of that great enterprise. He was the author of philosophical essays, such as the 'Lettre sur les aveugles' (1749) and the 'Pensées sur l'interprétation de la nature' (1754), of works of dramatic and art criticism, of novels ('La Religieuse', 'Jacques le Fataliste'), of the amusing character sketch 'Le Neveu de Rameau', and of two sentimental comedies, 'Le Fils Naturel' (1757) and 'Le Père de Famille' (1758).

Dido, also called ELISSA, the daughter of a Tyrian king. She was married to her uncle, Sychaeus, who was murdered for the sake of his wealth. But Dido sailed secretly from Tyre with his treasure. Arriving on the coast of Africa, she obtained the grant of so much land as could be covered with the hide of a bull. But she had the hide cut into thin strips and enclosed a space which became the fort of Carthage. Threatened by the neighbouring King Iarbas, who demanded her in marriage, she erected a funeral pile and took her own life. Virgil makes Dido a contemporary of Aeneas (q.v.). She falls in love with him when he is shipwrecked on the coast of Carthage. When Aeneas, by order of the gods, forsakes her, Dido kills herself. There is an opera, 'Dido and Aeneas', by Henry Purcell (q.v.).

Dido, The Tragedy of, a tragedy by Marlowe and Nash (qq.v.), published in 1594.

Die-hard, one that resists to the last; an appellation of the 57th regiment of Foot in the British army, earned by their gallant conduct at the battle of Albuera (D.N.B., s.v. *Inglis, Sir William*); now frequently applied in a political sense to those who are ultra-conservative in their general views or in reference to some particular subject of controversy.

Dies Irae, 'day of wrath', the first words of the greatest among medieval Latin hymns, the authorship of which is attributed to Thomas of Celano (*fl. c.* 1225).

Dietrich of Bern, the name given in the 'Nibelungenlied' (q.v.) to Theodoric, a great king of the Ostrogoths (c. 454–526), who invaded Italy and decisively defeated Odoacer at Verona (Bern) in 489. He was the hero of the German epics of the 13th cent. and of the Teutonic race in general, and the centre round which clustered many legends.

Dieu et mon droit, 'God and my right', said to be the password given by Richard I at the battle of Gisors (1198), in which he defeated the French. It has been the motto of the sovereigns of England since the time of Henry VI.

DIGBY, SIR KENELM (1603–65), was educated at Gloucester Hall (Worcester College), Oxford. This versatile man was an author, a naval commander (who defeated the French and Venetian fleets in Scanderoon harbour, 1628), and a very rash diplomatist. He was interested in physical science (he discovered the necessity of oxygen to the life of plants, and was a member of the council of the Royal Society). He published a criticism of Sir T. Browne's 'Religio Medici' in 1643, and wrote 'Of Bodies' and 'Of the Immortality of Man's Soul' in the same year. His 'Private Memoirs' (an account, under disguised names, of his wooing and wedding of Venetia Stanley) were published in 1827–8.

DIGBY, KENELM HENRY (1800–80), educated at Trinity College, Cambridge, and converted to Roman Catholicism, was author of 'The Broad Stone of Honour' (q.v., 1822), 'Mores Catholici' (1831–40), etc.

Digest of Justinian, see *Pandects*.

Dilettanti, SOCIETY OF THE, originally founded about 1732 as a dining society by some gentlemen of wealth and position who had travelled in Italy, soon devoted itself to the patronage of the fine arts. It has chiefly encouraged the study of classical archaeology. See Lionel Cust's 'History' of the society (1898).

DILKE, SIR CHARLES WENTWORTH (1843–1911), liberal statesman, was author of 'Greater Britain' (1868), the record of a tour through many parts of the British Empire. He treated more fully questions connected with the empire in his 'Problems of Greater Britain' (1890). He published anonymously in 1874 a lively satirical brochure, 'The Fall of Prince Florestan of Monaco'. He was proprietor of the 'Athenaeum' and 'Notes and Queries'.

DILLON, WENTWORTH, *fourth earl of Roscommon* (1633?–85), author of a blank-verse translation of Horace's 'Ars Poetica' (1680) and an 'Essay on Translated Verse' (1684). He was the first critic who publicly praised Milton's 'Paradise Lost'.

Dimeter, see *Metre*.

Dimmesdale, The REVD. ARTHUR, a character in Hawthorne's 'The Scarlet Letter' (q.v.).

Dinadan, SIR, in Malory's 'Morte Darthur', one of King Arthur's knights and in the opinion of Sir Tristram 'the best joker and jester, and a noble knight of his hands, and the best knight that I know'.

Dinarzade, in the 'Arabian Nights' (q.v.), the sister of Scheherazade (q.v.).

Dinas Vawr, The War-Song of, see *Misfortunes of Elphin*.

Dingley Dell, in Dickens's 'Pickwick Papers' (q.v.), the home of the hospitable Mr. Wardle.

Dinmont, see *Dandie Dinmont*.

Diocletian (245–313), born of obscure parents in Dalmatia, rose to distinction in the army, and was proclaimed Roman emperor in 284. In consequence of the attacks to which the empire was exposed in many directions, he shared the rule first with Maximian, and subsequently with two other Caesars, taking the East for his own share. In 305 he abdicated and retired to his native Dalmatia, where he built the magnificent palace, the ruins of which, still known as SPALATO, inspired Robert Adam's design of the Adelphi. The Christians were subjected to severe persecution in his reign (303). He was the first Roman emperor to establish the joint rule system on a permanent basis.

Diodati, CHARLES (*d.* 1638), son of an Italian Protestant who had settled in London and married an English wife, the schoolfellow and close friend of Milton. Milton addressed to him two of his Latin elegies, and lamented

his death in the pastoral 'Epitaphium Damonis'.

DIODŌRUS SICŬLUS, a Greek historian born in Sicily, who flourished in the latter half of the 1st cent. B.C. He wrote a history of the world in forty books, of which we possess i–v (dealing with the early history of Egypt, Assyria, Ethiopia, and Greece) and xi–xx (from the Persian invasion of Greece to 302 B.C.).

DIOGENES LAERTIUS, of Laerte in Cilicia, an author of the 2nd or 3rd cents. A.D., who wrote in Greek ten books of 'Lives of the Philosophers', which have survived.

Diogenes the Cynic, a Greek philosopher born at Sinope in Pontus about 412 B.C., who, after a dissolute youth, practised at Athens the greatest austerity, finally taking up his residence, it is said, in a large earthenware jar. He censured all intellectual pursuits, such as astronomy, not directed to some obvious practical advantage. He was taken prisoner by pirates, and sold as a slave at Corinth, but soon received his freedom. Here occurred his famous interview with Alexander the Great, who asked him whether he could oblige him in any way, and was told 'Yes, by standing out of my sunshine'. It is said that Alexander was so struck with his independence that he said, 'If I were not Alexander, I should wish to be Diogenes.' When Philip of Macedon was threatening Corinth and the inhabitants feverishly set about strengthening the defences, Diogenes, not to be outdone in activity, trundled his tub to and fro (Lucian, 'De Historia Conscribenda', 3).

Diomēdēs, son of Tydeus and king of Argos, was one of the Greek princes who joined in the expedition against Troy, and, next to Achilles, was the bravest in the host. Athene aided him in battle and enabled him to wound even Ares and Aphrodite. According to post-Homeric legend he helped Odysseus to carry off the palladium (q.v.) from Troy.

There was another Diomedes, king of the Bistones in Thrace. He owned famous mares, which he fed on human flesh. He was killed by Hercules.

Diōnē, according to Homer, the mother of Aphrodite by Zeus; according to Hesiod, the daughter of Oceanus. In early Greek mythology she was probably the supreme goddess, the female counterpart of Zeus (her name is from Διός, genitive of Ζεύς).

Dionysius, the ELDER and YOUNGER, were tyrants of Syracuse (405–367 B.C., and 367–343 B.C. respectively). The elder made himself master of half Sicily, beautified Syracuse, had a taste for literature, and was visited by Plato. He became very suspicious in his later years, and is said to have made a subterranean cave, known as DIONYSIUS' EAR, with peculiar acoustic properties, from which he could hear what was said by prisoners whom he held in confinement. (This is referred to in Scott's 'Fortunes of Nigel'.)

The younger was twice driven from the throne, and finally was, it is said, reduced to support himself at Corinth as a schoolmaster. To this Byron refers in his 'Ode to Napoleon':

> That Corinth's pedagogue hath now
> Transferr'd his by-word to thy brow.

Dionysius of Halicarnassus (1st cent. B.C.), Greek rhetorician, author of a history of Rome and of works of literary criticism.

Dionysius the Areopagite, a disciple of St. Paul (Acts xvii. 34). A writer of the late 5th cent. who sought to introduce certain mystical elements into Christianity from Neoplatonism claimed to be Dionysius the Areopagite, and successfully imposed on medieval Christendom.

Dionȳsus, a Greek god, also known as BACCHUS, the son of Zeus and Semele (q.v.), a god of the fertility of nature, a suffering god, who dies and comes to life again, particularly a god of wine, who loosens care and inspires to music and poetry. Hence his connexion with the dithyramb, tragedy, and comedy. Elements of ecstasy and mysticism are found in his cult. Zeus, to save the infant Dionysus from the jealousy of his wife Hera, conveyed him to Mt. Nysa, where he was brought up by the nymphs. He was persecuted by unbelievers and took vengeance on them (see, e.g., *Pentheus*). He made an expedition to Eastern lands, teaching mankind the elements of civilization and the use of wine. In this connexion he is frequently represented drawn in a chariot by tigers, and accompanied by a rout of votaries, male and female (Satyrs, Sileni, Maenads, Bassarids).

Dionyza, a character in Shakespeare's 'Pericles' (q.v.).

Dioscuri, or 'sons of Zeus', a name given to Castor and Pollux (q.v.).

Diotīma, a priestess of Mantinea, reputed teacher of Socrates in philosophy, referred to in the 'Symposium' of Plato.

Diplomatic, originally meant 'of or pertaining to official or original documents' (from Greek δίπλωμα, a doubling, a folded paper, a letter of recommendation), and the diplomatic science was the science of palaeography, in which sense it is used in the title of the great work of Mabillon (q.v.), 'De re diplomatica'. The transition to its later meaning appears to have arisen from the title 'Corps Universel Diplomatique du Droit des Gens' of Dumont (1726), where, as the subject matter was *international* relations, 'corps diplomatique', though used in its original sense, came to be taken as meaning 'having to do with international relations'. [OED.]

Dipsas, a serpent whose bite was fabled to produce raging thirst.

> Cerastes horn'd, Hydrops, and Ellops drear,
> And Dipsas.
> (Milton, 'Paradise Lost', x. 526.)

Dipsodes, 'the thirsty ones', the people whose conquest by Pantagruel (q.v.) is related by Rabelais (Bk. II. xxiii, xxviii, et seq.).

Dipsȳchus, a poem by Clough (q.v.), published posthumously. The poem, which represents the 'conflict between a tender conscience and the world', takes the form of dialogues between Dipsychus and an attendant Mephistophelean spirit, 'a compound of convention and impiety', who endeavours to persuade him to adopt a worldly standard of conduct. The scene is set in Venice.

Dircē, see under *Antiope*. The fountain Dirce being near Thebes, the epithet DIRCEAN is used by poets as equivalent to Theban or Boeotian, and applied to Pindar ('the Dircean Swan') and others.

Discoverie of Witchcraft, The, see *Scott* (*Reginald*).

Discoveries made upon Men and Matter, see *Timber*.

Dismal Science, THE, political economy; so named by T. Carlyle ('The Nigger Question', 'Miscellaneous Essays', vii. 84).

Dismas, or DYSMAS, or DIMAS, the legendary name of the Penitent Thief crucified by the side of Jesus Christ. The name of the Impenitent Thief was Gestas.

Disowned, The, a novel by Bulwer Lytton (q.v.), published in 1828. It is the story of a young man, Clinton L'Estrange, who is repudiated by his father Lord Ulswater (from a mistaken suspicion that he is not in fact his son), but is finally rehabilitated. The villain Crauford is drawn from Henry Fauntleroy, the banker and forger, who was executed in 1824.

Dispensary, The, see *Garth*.

DISRAELI, BENJAMIN, *first earl of Beaconsfield* (1804–81), eldest son of Isaac D'Israeli (q.v.), received his literary training chiefly in his father's library, and was never at a university. He entered Lincoln's Inn in 1824, and published his first novel 'Vivian Grey' (q.v.) in his twenty-second year (1826–7). He was much hampered by debt during his early years, but he made the grand tour. He published 'The Young Duke' in 1831, 'Contarini Fleming' (q.v.) in 1832, 'Alroy' and 'Ixion in Heaven' (q.v.) in 1833, 'The Infernal Marriage' (q.v.) in 1834, 'The Rise of Iskander' in 1834, 'Henrietta Temple' (q.v.) in 1837, and 'Venetia' (q.v.) in the same year. In that year also he entered parliament as member for Maidstone. 'Coningsby' and 'Sybil' (qq.v.) appeared in 1844 and 1845, 'Tancred' (q.v.) in 1847. For many years after this political affairs absorbed his energies, and it was not until 1870 that his next famous novel 'Lothair' (q.v.) was published. He was prime minister from Feb. to Dec. 1868, and again from 1874 to 1880. He became the intimate friend of Queen Victoria. He published his last novel, 'Endymion' (q.v.), in the latter year. His principal merit as a novelist is his skill in presenting political and social types and the motives by which they are actuated, as a rule with a kindly humour. Many of his characters are drawn from personages of his time. Among Disraeli's writings outside fiction, the best is his 'Lord George Bentinck: a Political Biography' (1852). He also wrote a 'Vindication of the English Constitution' (1835), 'The Letters of Runnymede' (mostly vigorous attacks on contemporary politicians) and 'The Spirit of Whiggism' (1836). Disraeli's 'Correspondence with his Sister, 1832-52' was published in 1886, and 'Home Letters and Correspondence' in 1887, both edited by Ralph Disraeli. His 'Letters to Lady Bradford and Lady Chesterfield' appeared in 1929. His Life has been written by W. F. Monypenny and G. E. Buckle (revised edition, 1929).

D'ISRAELI, ISAAC (1766–1848), descended from a Jewish family which had fled from Spain to Venice in time of persecution, the father of Benjamin Disraeli (q.v.), was the author of several discursive collections of literary and historical anecdotes, of which the first, and best, was 'Curiosities of Literature' (1791–3 and 1823). He also wrote 'Calamities of Authors' (1812–13), 'Quarrels of Authors' (1814), and 'Amenities of Literature' (1841).

Dissertation upon Parties, *A*, see under *Bolingbroke (Viscount)*.

Distaff's or ST. DISTAFF's **Day,** the day after Twelfth Day or the Feast of the Epiphany (7 Jan.), on which women resumed their ordinary employments after the holidays. Also called *rock-day*, the 'rock' being the staff of a hand spinning-wheel.

Distaffina, a character in Rhodes's 'Bombastes Furioso' (q.v.).

Dithyramb, a Greek choric hymn, originally in honour of Dionysus or Bacchus, vehement and wild in character.

Dittany, the name of a plant reputed to have the power of drawing weapons from wounds and healing these, so called from Mt. Dicte in Crete, where it grew.

Diurnalls, see *Newsbooks*.

Divan, a word, originally Persian, meaning a fascicle of written sheets, hence a collection of poems, an account-book, an office of accounts, a tribunal of revenue or justice, a council of state, a council-chamber, a cushioned bench.

Diversions of Purley, Ἔπεα πτερόεντα *or*, see *Tooke*.

Dives, a Latin word meaning 'rich man', which occurs in the Vulgate version of the parable of Lazarus (Luke xvi), and has come to be used generically for 'rich man'.

Divina Commedia, the greatest work of Dante (q.v.), comprising the 'Inferno', the 'Purgatorio' and the 'Paradiso', in *terza rima* (lines of eleven syllables, arranged in groups of three and rhyming a b a b c b c d c).

The 'Inferno' is a description of Hell, conceived as a graduated conical funnel, to the successive circles of which the various categories of sinners are assigned. The 'Purgatorio' is a description of Purgatory, a mountain rising in circular ledges, on which are the various groups of repentant sinners. At the top of the mountain is the Earthly Paradise, where Dante encounters Beatrice. In his visit to Hell and Purgatory, Dante has for guide the poet Virgil, and there he sees and converses with his lost friends or former foes. The 'Paradiso' is a vision of a world of beauty, light, and song, where the Poet's guide is Beatrice. The poem is not only an exposition of the future life, but a work of moral edification, replete with symbolism and allusions based on Dante's wide knowledge of philosophy, astronomy, natural science, and history.

Among well-known translations are those of Binyon, Longfellow, and H. F. Cary (qq.v.).

Divine Legation of Moses, see *Warburton (William)*.

Divine Sarah, Sarah Bernhardt (q.v.).

Divio, in imprints, Dijon.

Divorce, The Doctrine and Discipline of, the first of Milton's Divorce Tracts. See *Milton*.

Dixie, the name of an American national song, composed in 1859 by Daniel Decatur Emmett (1815–1904), musician and composer of Negro melodies to Bryant's Minstrels, New York. It made a special appeal to the army of the Confederate States in the American Civil War, and still enjoys great popularity. 'Dixie' in the song signifies the Southern States; it is 'de land ob cotton'. It occurs in many other Southern songs which the Civil War produced. The origin of the name is obscure. Some refer it to Jeremiah Dixon, who with Charles Mason in 1763-7 surveyed the boundary between Maryland and Pennsylvania, which later separated the slave States from the free States; and there are various other explanations, none of them convincing.

DIXON, RICHARD WATSON (1833–1900), educated at King Edward's School, Birmingham, and Pembroke College, Oxford, became the intimate friend of Burne-Jones, William Morris, R. Bridges, and G. M. Hopkins, held various preferments, and was canon of Carlisle for many years. He published an elaborate 'History of the Church of England from the Abolition of Roman Jurisdiction' (1877–1900) and several volumes of poems, of which the longest (in *terza rima*) is 'Mano, or a poetical history . . . concerning the adventures of a Norman Knight' in the 10th and 11th cents. (1883); the best are included in the selection of 'Poems' issued with a memoir by R. Bridges in 1909.

Dizzy, familiar abbreviation of the name of Benjamin Disraeli (q.v.).

Djinn, see *Jinn.*

Dobbin, CAPTAIN, afterwards COLONEL, WILLIAM, a character in Thackeray's 'Vanity Fair' (q.v.).

Dobbs, DOMINE, a character in Marryat's 'Jacob Faithful' (q.v.).

DOBELL, SYDNEY THOMPSON (1824–74), who was privately educated, published in 1850 'The Roman', a dramatic poem inspired by sympathy with oppressed Italy, and in 1854 'Balder' (q.v.). Under the influence of the Crimean War he issued in 1855 'Sonnets on the War' (jointly with Alexander Smith), and in 1856 'England in Time of War'. Two volumes of his poetical works appeared in 1875. Dobell was a leading member of the 'Spasmodic School' ridiculed by Aytoun (q.v.). His best-known pieces are 'Tommy's Dead', the lament of a father over his son; and the ballad with the refrain 'Oh, Keith of Ravelston', included in 'A Nuptial Song'.

DOBSON, HENRY AUSTIN (1840–1921), educated at Beaumaris Grammar School and at a gymnase at Strasbourg, then a French city, entered the Board of Trade, where he served from 1856 to 1901. He was an accomplished writer of verse of the lighter kind, some of his best work appearing in 'Vignettes in Rhyme' (1873), 'Proverbs in Porcelain' (1877), and in 'Old World Idylls' (1883). A further volume 'At the Sign of the Lyre' (1885) was extremely popular. Dobson had a wide knowledge of the 18th cent., testified by his prose biographies of William Hogarth (1879, extended 1891), Steele (1886), Goldsmith (1888), Horace Walpole (1890), Samuel Richardson (1902), Fanny Burney (1903). Under the title of 'Four Frenchwomen' (1890) he published essays on Charlotte Corday, Madame Roland, the Princesse de Lamballe, and Madame de Genlis. He also published three series of 'Eighteenth-Century Vignettes' (1892–4–6), besides several volumes of collected essays.

Doch-an-doris or DOCH-AN-DOROCH (Gaelic), a stirrup-cup, or a final drink at night.

Doctor, *The,* a miscellany by Southey (q.v.), published in 1834–47. It is a collection of articles on a great variety of subjects, differing from a common-place book in that they are connected together, somewhat loosely, by the story that runs through them of an imaginary Dr. Daniel Dove of Doncaster and his horse Nobs. It contains the nursery story of The Three Bears, and its humour is occasionally Rabelaisian.

Doctor ANGELICUS, Thomas Aquinas (q.v.); INVINCIBILIS, William Ockham (q.v.); IRREFRAGABILIS, Alexander of Hales (q.v.); MIRABILIS, Roger Bacon (q.v.); SUBTILIS, Duns Scotus (q.v.); UNIVERSALIS, Albertus Magnus (q.v.).

Doctor Faustus, *The tragical history of,* a drama in blank verse and prose by Marlowe (q.v.), published apparently in 1604, though entered in the Stationers' Register in 1601, and probably produced in 1588. It is perhaps the first dramatization of the medieval legend of a man who sold his soul to the Devil, and who became identified with a Dr. Faustus, a necromancer of the 16th cent. The legend appeared in the 'Volksbuch' published at Frankfurt in 1587, and was translated into English as 'The History of the Damnable Life and Death of Dr. John Faustus'. Marlowe's play follows this translation in the general outline of the story, though not in the conception of the principal character, who, under the poet's hand, from a mere magician, becomes a man athirst for infinite power, ambitious to be 'great Emperor of the world'.

Faustus, weary of the sciences, turns to magic and calls up Mephistopheles, with whom he makes a compact to surrender his soul to the Devil in return for twenty-four years of life; during these Mephistopheles shall attend on him and give him whatsoever he demands. Then follows a number of scenes in which the compact is executed, notable among them the calling up of Paris and Helen, where Faustus addresses Helen in the well-known lines: 'Was this the face that launched a thousand ships. . . .' The anguish of mind of Faustus as the hour for the surrender of his soul draws near is poignantly depicted. Both in its end and in the general conception of the character of Faustus, the play thus differs greatly from the 'Faust' of Goethe (q.v.).

Doctor Fell, see *Fell.*

Dr. Syntax, see *Combe.*

Doctor Thorne, a novel by A. Trollope (q.v.), published in 1858, one of the Barsetshire group of novels.

Dr. Thorne, a man of good family, is the medical practitioner at the village of Greshamsbury. His brother, Henry Thorne, has seduced the sister of Roger Scatcherd, a stonemason, and been killed by him. Roger Scatcherd has been imprisoned and liberated, his sister has emigrated and married, and her child, known as Mary Thorne, has been brought up by Dr. Thorne; but the circumstances of her birth are not generally known. Scatcherd, in spite of a propensity to drink, has become a wealthy contractor. Mr. Gresham, squire of Greshamsbury, has been impoverished by extravagant expenditure, partly due to his aristocratic wife, a member of the De Courcy family; he is gravely embarrassed and his property is largely mortgaged to Scatcherd. Frank Gresham, his son, falls in love with the obscure and penniless Mary Thorne. The novel is occupied mainly with the attempts of his family to induce him to abandon Mary, and to 'marry money', in particular Miss Dunstable, the heiress of wealth made by a patent unguent, and a sensible and entertaining person, though somewhat elderly. Their efforts are defeated, and when Mary is found to be the heiress of old Scatcherd, all obstacles to her union with Frank are removed.

Dr. Wortle's School, a novel by A. Trollope (q.v.), published in 1881.

Dr. Wortle is the proprietor of a highly successful private school patronized by the nobility. He engages as assistant master a certain Mr. Peacocke, a former fellow of Trinity, Oxford, a man in holy orders, who has spent five years in the United States and there married. Though he and his wife (as the matron) are thoroughly efficient and agreeable, there is some mystery about their past, and suspicion arises that they are not married. Their union was in fact not regular, for their marriage had taken place when Mrs. Peacocke's first husband, a brutal drunkard, was, without their knowledge, still alive. The scandal increases, fomented by an enemy of Dr. Wortle, and he receives what he considers an impertinent admonition from the bishop. Dr. Wortle, who has a good deal of the sturdy independence of Archdeacon Grantly (q.v.), moved by compassion for the unfortunate couple and annoyance at the interference of the bishop and the complaints of various sanctimonious parents, obstinately takes his assistant's side, in spite of the threatened ruin of his school. Matters are put right by the death of the first husband, and Dr. Wortle triumphs.

Doctors' Commons, originally the common table and dining-hall of the College of Doctors of Civil Law in London; hence the name is applied to the buildings occupied by these, and now to their site, to the south of St. Paul's Cathedral. The society was formed in 1509, and in their buildings were held the Ecclesiastical and Admiralty courts. The society was dissolved in 1858 and the buildings taken down in 1867. Literary allusions to Doctors' Commons in later times generally relate to marriage licences, probate and registration of wills, and divorce proceedings, presumably because such matters were dealt with there.

Doctors of the Church, certain early 'fathers', distinguished by their learning and sanctity: especially, in the Western Church, Ambrose, Augustine, Jerome, Gregory; in the Eastern Church, Athanasius, Basil, Gregory of Nazianzus, and Chrysostom.

Doctor's Tale, The, see *Canterbury Tales.*

DODD, WILLIAM (1729–77), a forger, educated at Clare Hall, Cambridge, and rector of Hockliffe and vicar of Chalgrove (1772). He forged a bond for £4,200 in the name of his former pupil, the fifth Lord Chesterfield, and was executed, in spite of many petitions on his behalf, one of them written by Dr. Johnson. Dodd's numerous publications include 'Beauties of Shakespeare' (1752).

DODDRIDGE, PHILIP (1702–51), a nonconformist divine, was a celebrated hymnwriter and author of 'The Rise and Progress

of Religion in the Soul' (1745), a work notable for its literary as well as its devotional quality. He also published in 1747 'Some Remarkable Passages in the Life of Col. James Gardiner', the reformed rake and colonel of dragoons (1688–1745) who became a religious enthusiast, was killed at Prestonpans, and figures in Scott's 'Waverley' (q.v.).

DODGSON, CHARLES LUTWIDGE (1832–98), celebrated under his pseudonym LEWIS CARROLL, was educated at Rugby School and Christ Church, Oxford. He was mathematical lecturer at Oxford from 1855 to 1881. Dodgson wrote books for children that had the advantage of appealing by their humour, logic, and inventive absurdity to grown-up people also. His most popular works were 'Alice's Adventures in Wonderland' (1865), and 'Through the Looking-glass' (1872), both illustrated by Sir John Tenniel. His other publications include 'Phantasmagoria and other poems' (1869), 'The Hunting of the Snark' (q.v., 1876), 'Rhyme? and Reason?' (1883), and 'Sylvie and Bruno' (1889), besides various mathematical treatises of which the most valuable is 'Euclid and his Modern Rivals' (1879).

DODINGTON, GEORGE BUBB (1691–1762), a time-serving politician who attained high office and a peerage (as Baron Melcombe), was author of a 'Diary', published posthumously in 1784, which throws much light on the venal politics of his day.

Dōdōna, in Epirus, the seat of a celebrated oracle of Zeus, the oldest in Greece. The will of the god was signified by the rustling of the wind in the oak trees.

Dods, MEG, in Scott's 'St. Ronan's Well' (q.v.), the landlady of the Cleikum Inn.

DODSLEY, ROBERT (1703–64), while a footman in the service of the Hon. Mrs. Lowther, published 'Servitude, a Poem' (1729, afterwards reissued as 'The Footman's Friendly Advice to his Brethren of the Livery'). He became a bookseller and wrote several plays, including a tragedy 'Cleone' (1758), a musical play, 'The Blind Beggar of Bethnal Green' (1741), and 'The Toyshop, a dramatic Satire' (1735). But he is chiefly remembered as the publisher of works by Pope, Johnson, Young, Goldsmith, and Gray, and of the 'Select Collection of Old Plays' (1744) and 'A Collection of Poems by several hands' (1748–58), revised and continued by Pearch (1775). In 1758 he founded, in conjunction with Edmund Burke, the 'Annual Register', which still appears. His place of business was at 'Tully's Head' in Pall Mall.

Dodson and Fogg, in Dickens's 'Pickwick Papers' (q.v.), Mrs. Bardell's attorneys.

Doe, JOHN, see *John Doe.*

Dogberry and **Verges,** in Shakespeare's 'Much Ado about Nothing' (q.v.), constables. Dogberry is a precursor of Mrs. Malaprop in his gift for misapplying words.

Dog-Latin, bad, unidiomatic Latin. '"Nescio quid est materia cum me", Sterne writes to one of his friends (in dog-Latin, and very sad dog-Latin too)'; Thackeray, 'Eng. Hum.' vi. Cf. *Doggerel.*

Dogs, famous in History, Myth, and Fiction:

Actaeon's hounds, see *Actaeon.*

Alcibiades' dog. Plutarch relates that Alcibiades had an uncommonly large and beautiful dog, whose principal ornament was his tail. Yet he caused the tail to be cut off, that the Athenians should talk of this piece of eccentricity rather than find something worse to say of him.

Argos, q.v. (2).

Beau, Cowper's spaniel.

Bevis, in Scott's 'Woodstock', Sir Henry Lee's greyhound.

Boatswain, Byron's favourite dog; the inscription on a monument to him at Newstead states that he possessed 'Beauty without vanity, Strength without insolence, Courage without ferocity, and all the Virtues of man without his Vices'.

Bounce, a Danish dog belonging to Pope.

Boy, a favourite dog of Prince Rupert's, his companion in imprisonment at Lintz, suspected of being his master's familiar spirit, and famous in pamphlet warfare. His death at Marston Moor was greeted with exultation by the Puritans.

Bran, q.v., Fingal's dog.

Bull's-eye, in Dickens's 'Oliver Twist', Bill Sikes's dog.

Cerberus, q.v.

Crab, in Shakespeare's 'Two Gentlemen of Verona' (q.v.), Launce's dog.

Dash, Thomas Hood's dog and later Charles Lamb's; he provides some amusing passages in Lamb's letters.

Diogenes, in Dickens's 'Dombey and Son', the dog that Toots gives to Florence Dombey.

Flush, Mrs. Browning's dog, the gift of Miss Mitford.

Garryowen, the Citizen's mangy old mongrel in Joyce's 'Ulysses' (q.v.).

Geist, a dachshund belonging to Matthew Arnold, celebrated in the poem, 'Geist's Grave'. Geist was succeeded by other dachshunds, Max and Kaiser.

Gelert, see *Bethgelert.*

Jip, in Dickens's 'David Copperfield', Dora's dog.

Katmer, q.v.

Keeper, Emily Brontë's bulldog.

Labës, in Aristophanes' 'Wasps', the dog who is tried for stealing a cheese.

Laelaps, see *Cephalus.* This hound was fated to catch whatever it pursued. A difficulty seemed likely to arise when it was set to hunt an uncatchable fox which was devastating the Theban territory; but Zeus evaded the problem by turning both into stone.

Luath, q.v.

Lufra, in Scott's 'The Lady of the Lake' (v. 25), Douglas's hound.

Lycas, the subject of an epitaph attributed to Simonides (q.v.), translated as follows by F. L. Lucas:

Although beneath this grave-mound thy white bones now are lying,
Surely, my huntress Lycas, the wild things dread thee still.
The memory of thy worth tall Pêlion keeps undying,
And the looming peak of Ossa, and Cithaeron's lonely hill.

Maera, see *Icarius.*

Maida, a favourite hound of Sir Walter Scott's.

Margarita, a hunting dog to which a tombstone, now in the British Museum, was erected by its Roman master and mistress.

Math, King Richard II's favourite greyhound. According to Froissart, ii, ch. 238 [241], it forsook Richard at the castle of Flint, when his deposition was imminent, and attached itself to Henry of Lancaster.

Mauthe dog, a spectral dog, of which an account is given in a note to Scott's 'Peveril of the Peak', reputed to have haunted Peel Castle in the Isle of Man.

Montargis, Dog of, q.v.

Music, a favourite dog of Wordsworth's, on which he wrote two poems.

Mustard and *Pepper,* in Scott's 'Guy Mannering', the terriers of Dandie Dinmont (q.v.).

Orthrus, see *Geryon.*

Peritas, a dog belonging to Alexander the Great, after which he is said to have named a city.

Pomero and *Giallo,* Pomeranian dogs belonging to W. S. Landor.

Quoodle, in Chesterton's 'The Flying Inn', 'a sort of mongrel bull-terrier'.

Rab and his Friends, see *Brown (Dr. J.).*

Roswal, in Scott's 'The Talisman' (q.v.), Sir Kenneth's hound.

Tartar, in Charlotte Brontë's 'Shirley' (q.v.), Shirley's dog, 'of a breed between mastiff and bull-dog'.

Theron, q.v.

Theseus' hounds, in Shakespeare's 'A Midsummer Night's Dream' (q.v.), 'bred out of the Spartan kind . . . slow in pursuit, but match'd in mouth like bells'.

Tobias's dog, which accompanies Raphael and Tobias on their journey (Tob. v. 16).

Toby, q.v.

Xanthippus' dog, the dog of Xanthippus (the father of Pericles) which swam by his master's galley to Salamis when the Athenians were obliged to abandon their city, and was buried by his master on a promontory known as Cynossëma (Dog's Grave).

There are some good stories of sheep-dogs in Hudson's 'A Shepherd's Life', and dog-stories of another kind in Jack London's 'The

Call of the Wild', 'White Fang', and 'Jerry of the Islands'.

Dog-Star, the star Sirius, in the constellation of the Greater Dog, the brightest of the fixed stars. Also applied to Procyon (the Lesser Dog-Star), a star of the first magnitude in the Lesser Dog.

The days about the time of the heliacal rising of the Dog-Star are known as the DOG-DAYS (in current almanacs 3 July to 11 Aug.). The name arose from the pernicious 'influence' attributed to the Dog-Star, but it has long been popularly associated with the belief that at this season dogs are most apt to run mad. [OED.]

Doge of Venice : for his wedding with the sea, see *Adriatic*.

Doggerel, comic or burlesque, or trivial, mean, or irregular verse. The derivation is unknown, but cf. *Dog-Latin*. [OED.]

Doggett, THOMAS (*d.* 1721), actor and joint-manager of the Haymarket, and subsequently of Drury Lane, theatres, and friend of Congreve and Colley Cibber, instituted in 1716, in honour of the anniversary of the accession of George I, a prize, known as DOGGETT'S COAT AND BADGE, for a rowing competition among Thames watermen, which is still held.

Doit, an old Dutch coin, the eighth of a stiver, worth about half a farthing in English money.

Dol Common, in Jonson's 'The Alchemist' (q.v.), the female confederate of Subtle and Face.

Dolabella, a character in Shakespeare's 'Antony and Cleopatra' (q.v.), and in Dryden's 'All for Love' (q.v.).

DOLBEN, DIGBY MACKWORTH (1848–67), was educated at Eton. Even at school he displayed Roman Catholic tendencies as well as a marked poetic gift. He became an Anglican Benedictine monk in 1864. He was accidentally drowned in the river Welland in his twentieth year, when preparing to go up to Oxford. His poems, many of them religious and devotional, were edited with a memoir by Robert Bridges in 1915.

Doll Common, see *Dol Common*.

Doll Tearsheet, a character in Shakespeare's '2 Henry IV' (q.v.).

Dollalolla, QUEEN, a character in Fielding's 'Tom Thumb' (q.v.).

Dollar, the English name for the German *thaler*, a large silver coin, of varying value, current in the German states from the 16th cent.; especially the unit of the German monetary union (1857–73) equal to 3 marks (about 2s. 11d.). The word *thaler* is short for *Joachimsthaler*, literally '(gulden) of Joachimsthal' (in Bohemia), where they were coined in 1519 from a silver mine opened there in 1516.

DOLLAR is also the English name for the peso or *piece of eight* (i.e. eight reales), worth about 4s. 6d., formerly current in Spain and the Spanish American colonies, and marked with the figure 8. The dollar is now the standard unit of coinage of the United States, and the name is also applied to various foreign coins of a value more or less approaching that of the Spanish or American dollar. The dollar sign $ is perhaps a corruption of *ps*, the Spanish contraction for *peso*; or a corruption of the two pillars (symbolizing the Pillars of Hercules) on Spanish coins, with the scroll about them; or of the figure 8 and the pillars.

Döllinger, JOHANN JOSEPH IGNAZ VON (1799–1890), a great German Church historian, a Liberal, and the head of the 'Old Catholic' party in the Roman Church. He opposed the declaration relating to papal infallibility, and was excommunicated by the archbishop of Munich in 1871.

Dolly Dialogues, The, by Anthony Hope (Hawkins), published in 1894, reprinted from the 'Westminster Gazette'. They are amusing and witty conversations, hung on a slight thread of story, in which figure Samuel Travers Carter, a middle-aged bachelor, and the attractive Dolly Foster, with whom he has flirted at Monte Carlo, and whose marriage to Lord Mickleham is understood to have caused Carter much unhappiness.

Dolly Varden, a character in Dickens's 'Barnaby Rudge' (q.v.). Also the name of a picture hat.

Dolon, a Trojan who went by night as a spy to the Greek camp and was slain by Odysseus and Diomedes ('Iliad', x). In Spenser's 'Faerie Queene', v. vi, Dolon is 'a man of subtill wit and wicked mind', who tries to entrap Britomart.

Dolores, a poem in anapaests by Swinburne (q.v.) included in the first series of 'Poems and Ballads'. It is addressed to 'Our Lady of Pain' and in it the poet sings of forbidden pleasures and the weariness and satiety that follow them.

Dom, a shortened form of the Latin *dominus*, prefixed to the names of Roman .Catholic ecclesiastical and monastic dignitaries, especially of Benedictine and Carthusian monks.

Dombey and Son, Dealings with the Firm of, a novel by Dickens (q.v.), published in 1847–8.

When the story opens Mr. Dombey, the rich, proud, frigid head of the shipping house of Dombey and Son, has just been presented with a son and heir, Paul, and his wife dies. The father's love and hopes are centred in the boy, an odd, delicate, prematurely old child, who is sent to Dr. Blimber's school, under whose strenuous discipline he sickens and dies. Dombey neglects his daughter, Florence, and the estrangement is increased by the death of her brother. Walter Gay, a frank, good-hearted youth in Dombey's employment, falls in love with her, but is sent to the West Indies by Dombey, who disapproves of their relations. He is shipwrecked on the way and believed to be drowned. Dombey marries again—a proud and penniless young widow, Edith Granger, but his arrogant treatment drives her into relations with his villainous manager, Carker, with whom she flies to France, fiercely repelling, however, the natural view he takes of the situation. They are pursued, Carker meets Dombey in a railway station, falls in front of a train, and is killed. The house of Dombey fails; Dombey has lost his fortune, his son, and his wife; his daughter has been driven by ill-treatment to fly from him, and has married Walter Gay, who has survived his shipwreck. Thoroughly humbled, he lives in desolate solitude till Florence returns to him and at last finds the way to his heart.

Among the other notable characters in the book are Solomon Gills, the nautical instrument-maker and uncle of Walter Gay, and his friend Cuttle, the genial old sea-captain; Susan Nipper, Florence's devoted servant; Toots, the innocent and humble admirer of Florence; Joe Bagstock, the gouty retired Major; and 'Cousin Feenix', the good-natured aristocrat.

Domdaniel, apparently from the Greek or Latin words meaning 'hall or house of Daniel'; a fictitious name introduced in the French 'Continuation of the Arabian Nights' by Dom Chaves and M. Cazotte, 1788–93, whence adopted by Southey in 'Thalaba' (q.v.), and so by Carlyle. It is not clear whether 'Daniel' is intended to refer to the Hebrew prophet or to 'a great Grecian Sage' of that name who appears in the tale of 'the Queen and the Serpents' in the 'Arabian Nights'. Domdaniel is a fabled submarine hall where a magician or sorcerer met with his disciples. [OED.]

Domesday Book, where 'Domesday' is a Middle English spelling of 'Doomsday', day of judgement, is the name applied since the 12th cent. to the record of the Great Inquest or survey of the lands of England, made by order of William the Conqueror in 1086. It contains a record of the ownership, area, and value of these lands, and of the numbers of tenants, livestock, etc. Its title originated in a popular name given to the book, as a final and conclusive authority on all matters connected with land-tenure. The MS. is in the Public Record Office.

DOMETT, ALFRED (1811–87), educated at St. John's College, Cambridge, and a barrister of the Middle Temple, emigrated to New Zealand. He was a friend of R. Browning, who lamented his departure in 'Waring' (q.v.). Domett was author of 'Ranolf and Amohia, a South Sea Day Dream' (1872) and 'Flotsam and Jetsam' (1877). Of these poems the former is a story of Maori life, and contains beautiful descriptions of New Zealand scenery.

Dominicans, an order of mendicant friars instituted in 1215 by the Spanish ecclesiastic, Domingo de Guzman, also called St. Dominic. They were known in England as the Black Friars from the colour of their dress.

Dôn, the British equivalent of the Gaelic *Danu* (q.v.), the mother of the gods.

Don Carlos (1788–1855), second son of Charles IV of Spain, a claimant to the Spanish throne, deprived of the position of heir presumptive by the abolition of the Salic law (pragmatic sanction of 1830). His son and grandson were likewise claimants. CARLIST risings in their favour are frequently referred to.

Don Carlos, a tragedy by Otway (q.v.), in rhymed verse, produced in 1676.

Philip II, king of Spain, having married Elizabeth of Valois, who had been affianced to his son Don Carlos, is stirred to jealousy by their mutual affection. This jealousy is inflamed by the machinations of Ruy Gomez and his wife the duchess of Eboli, till he believes in their guilty relations; he causes the queen to be poisoned and Don Carlos takes his own life, the king discovering too late their innocence.

Don John of Austria, see *John.*

Don Juan, according to a Spanish story first dramatized by Gabriel Tellez (1571–1641, who wrote under the pseudonym of Tirso de Molina) in 'El Burlador de Sevila', and subsequently by Molière in 'Le Festin de Pierre', and in Mozart's great opera 'Don Giovanni', was Don Juan Tenorio, of Seville. Having attempted to ravish Doña Anna, the daughter of the commander of Seville, he is surprised by the father, whom he kills in a duel. A statue of the commander is erected over his tomb. Juan and his cowardly servant Leporello visit the tomb, when the statue is seen to move its head. Juan jestingly invites it to a banquet. The statue comes, seizes Juan, and delivers him to devils. Don Juan is the proverbial heartless and impious seducer. His injured wife is Elvira.

Don Juan is the theme of a play by Shadwell (q.v.), 'The Libertine'; and of a poem by Lord Byron (see below). For R. Browning's Don Juan, see *Fifine at the Fair*; and for G. B. Shaw's, see *Man and Superman.*

Don Juan, an epic satire in *ottava rima*, in sixteen cantos by Lord Byron (q.v.), published in 1819–24.

Don Juan, a young gentleman of Seville, in consequence of an intrigue with Donna Julia, is sent abroad by his mother at the age of 16. The vessel in which he travels is wrecked and crew and passengers take to the long-boat. After much suffering, in the course of which first Juan's spaniel, then his tutor, are eaten by the crew, Juan is cast up on a Greek island. He is restored to life by Haidée, the beautiful daughter of a Greek pirate, and the pair fall in love. The father, who is thought dead, returns, finds the lovers together, and cuts down Juan, who is placed in chains on one of the pirate's ships. Haidée goes mad and dies, and Juan is sold as a slave in Constantinople to a sultana who has fallen in love with him. He has the misfortune to arouse her jealousy, is menaced with death, but escapes to the Russian army which is besieging Ismail. In consequence of his gallant conduct at the capture of the town, he is sent with dispatches to St. Petersburg, where he attracts the favour of the Empress Catharine. The latter sends him on a political mission to England. The last cantos (the poem is unfinished) are taken up with a satirical description of social conditions in England, and in a less degree with the love-affairs of Juan. With the story are intermingled innumerable digressions on every sort of subject, treated in a mocking vein; and with attacks on the victims of Byron's scorn or enmity, Southey, Coleridge, Wellington, Lord Londonderry, and many others. The lovely lyric, 'The Isles of Greece', occurs in canto iii. Don Juan himself is a charming, handsome, and unprincipled young man, who delights in succumbing to the beautiful women he meets, but he is little more than the connecting thread in a vast social comedy intershot with Byron's passionate wit. The form of the poem was inspired by the 'Whistlecraft' of J. H. Frere (q.v.).

Don Quixote de la Mancha, a satirical romance by Cervantes (q.v.), published in 1605, a second part appearing in 1615.

Cervantes gave to this work the form of a burlesque of the romances of chivalry, which were already losing their popularity with his countrymen. But he soon ceased to write mere burlesque; the character of the hero gradually deepens and the work becomes a criticism of life, which Spaniards accept as permanent and universal. The substance of the story is as follows. Don Quixote, a poor gentleman of La Mancha, a man of amiable character, and otherwise sane, has had his wits disordered by inordinate devotion to such tales, and imagines himself called upon to roam the world in search of adventures, on his old horse (Rosinante), and accoutred in rusty armour, accompanied by a squire in the rustic Sancho Panza, a curious mixture of credulity and shrewdness, whom he lures with the prospect of the governorship of an island. He conforms to chivalric tradition in nominating a good-looking girl of a neighbouring village to be mistress of his heart, under the style of Dulcinea del Toboso, an honour of which she is entirely unaware. To the disordered imagination of the knight the most commonplace objects assume fearful or romantic forms, and he is consequently involved in the most absurd adventures with distressing consequences to himself. Finally one of his friends, the bachelor Samson Carrasco, in order to force him to return to his home, disguises himself as a knight, overthrows Don Quixote, and requires him to abstain for a year from chivalrous exploits. This period Don Quixote

resolves to spend as a shepherd, living a pastoral life, but, falling sick on his return to his village, after a few days he dies.

The above story, as has been said, consists of two parts. After the first had been published, a continuation was issued by a writer who styled himself Alonso Fernandez de Avellaneda. This forgery, which Cervantes appears to have resented, stimulated him to write his own Part II. The book was translated into English, as early as 1612, by Thomas Shelton, and in 1700–3 by Motteux (qq.v.); and the plots of several 17th-cent. English plays have been traced to it.

Don Raphael and **Ambrose Lamela,** in Le Sage's 'Gil Blas' (q.v.), a pair of cunning rogues who appear from time to time in the course of the story, and are finally among the victims at an *auto-da-fé*.

Don Saltero's Coffee-house, founded by John Salter about 1690, stood in Cheyne Walk, Chelsea. It was still in existence when Carlyle moved into Cheyne Row in 1834. There is at present on its site a house called Don Salteros.

Don Sebastian, a tragicomedy, by Dryden (q.v.), published in 1691.

The play is based on the legend that Sebastian (q.v.) king of Portugal survived the battle of Alcazar. He is presented as a captive of Muley Moluch, the Moor, together with Almeyda, a princess of the royal house, with whom Sebastian is in love. Muley Moluch, moved by Sebastian's courage and dignity, spares his life; but on learning that he has used his liberty to marry Almeyda (of whom Muley Moluch has become violently enamoured), orders his execution. The person charged to carry it out is Dorax, a noble Portuguese, who, in consequence of what he considers unjust treatment by Don Sebastian in the past, has turned renegade and is now governor of the fortress. Dorax, however, saves Sebastian, desiring a more honourable revenge. Muley Moluch is killed in a revolt, and Almeyda and Sebastian are established in control of the kingdom. But, horrified at the discovery that they have the same father, Sebastian becomes an anchorite and Almeyda takes the veil. There is a fine scene where Dorax, after having saved Sebastian, reveals himself as the aggrieved Don Alonzo, and demands satisfaction; a scene which ends in a display of generosity on each side and reconciliation. The author uses the character of the Mufti to ridicule the Christian clergy.

Donatello (1386–1466), Italian sculptor, the first and most influential artist of the Early Renaissance. With Brunelleschi (q.v.) he developed linear perspective, which he used in his low reliefs. He studied classical sculpture in Rome, and produced the first equestrian bronze statue, the 'Gattemelata', since the Roman period.

Donation of Constantine, The, the supposed grant by the Emperor Constantine to

Pope Silvester of temporal power over Rome and Italy, in gratitude for his own conversion to Christianity. The grant, which was probably forged at Rome in the 8th cent., is included in the False Decretals (q.v.).

Donatists, a Christian sect which arose in North Africa in A.D. 311 out of a dispute concerning the election of a bishop of Carthage. They maintained that their own party was the only true Church, and that the baptisms and ordinations of others were invalid. Their name was derived from Donatus, a supporter of Majorinus (the bishop elected by the Donatists), or from Donatus the Great, who succeeded Majorinus as bishop. [OED.]

DONĀTUS, AELIUS, a grammarian who taught at Rome in the 4th cent. and had St. Jerome among his pupils. He was the author of a Latin grammar, 'Ars Grammatica', known as the 'Donet' or 'Donat', which has served as the basis of later works. A 'Donet' is hence used for an introduction to, or the elements of, any art or science. It is mentioned in 'Piers Plowman', A, v. 123, and other early English works. The original 'Donat' is ridiculed by Rabelais as one of the works in which Thubal Holofernes instructed the youthful Gargantua (q.v., i. xiv).

Donet or DONAT, see *Donatus.*

DONNE, JOHN (1571 or 1572–1631), the son of a London ironmonger and of a daughter of J. Heywood (q.v.) the author, was educated both at Oxford and Cambridge, and was entered at Lincoln's Inn. He was in the early part of his life a Roman Catholic. He was secretary to Sir T. Egerton, keeper of the great seal from 1598 to 1602, but alienated his favour by a secret marriage with Anne More, niece of the lord keeper's wife. He sailed in the two expeditions of Essex, to Cadiz and to the Islands, in 1596 and 1597, an episode of which we have a reflection in his early poems 'The Storm' and 'The Calm'. He took Anglican orders in 1615 and preached sermons which rank among the best of the 17th cent. From 1621 to his death he was dean of St. Paul's and frequently preached before Charles I.

In verse he wrote satires, epistles, elegies, and miscellaneous poems, distinguished by wit, profundity of thought and erudition, passion, and subtlety, coupled with a certain roughness of form ('I sing not Syren-like to tempt; for I am harsh'). He was the greatest of the writers of 'metaphysical' poetry, in which passion is interwoven with reasoning. Among his more important poems is the satirical 'Progresse of the Soule', begun in 1601, in which, adopting the doctrine of metempsychosis, he traces the migration of the soul of Eve's apple through the bodies of various heretics. But he left the work uncompleted. His best-known poems are some of the miscellaneous ones, 'The Ecstasie', 'Hymn to God the Father', the sonnet to Death ('Death, be not proud'), 'Go and catch

a falling star', etc. They include also a fine funeral elegy (in 'Anniversaries') on the death of Elizabeth Drury, and an 'Epithalamium' on the marriage of the Count Palatine and the Princess Elizabeth, 1613. Thomas Carew described him as

a king who ruled as he thought fit
The universal monarchy of wit,

and Ben Jonson wrote of him that he was 'the first poet in some things'.

Imperfect collections of his poems appeared in 1633–49, and 'Letters' by him in 1651. His poems were edited by Dr. Grosart in 1872–3, by C. E. Norton in 1895, by E. K. Chambers in 1896, and by H. J. C. Grierson (Oxford English Texts, 1912; Oxford Poets, 1929), the standard edition. A biography of Donne was written by Izaak Walton, published in 1640, another by E. Gosse in 1899. His name is usually pronounced and was frequently spelt 'Dunne'.

Donnithorne, ARTHUR, a character in George Eliot's 'Adam Bede' (q.v.).

Donnybrook, a village near Dublin, famous for its fair, the scene of much riotous jollity, dating from the time of King John, and suppressed in the 19th cent.

Donzel, from Latin *dominicellus,* diminutive of *dominus,* a young gentleman not yet knighted, a squire or page. 'Damsel' is the feminine form.

Dooley, MR., see *Dunne.*

Doolin of Mayence, the subject of a French *chanson de geste* of the 13th cent., and of a prose romance of the 15th cent. He was reputed an ancestor of Ogier the Dane (q.v.).

Doomsday Book, see *Domesday Book.*

Doomster, in a Scottish court of law, the officer (usually the executioner) who formerly read or repeated the sentence.

Doorm, EARL, a character in Tennyson's 'Idylls of the King' ('Geraint and Enid', q.v.).

Dora, the popular name for the Defence of the Realm Act, 1914, under which many regulations restrictive of liberty were issued.

Dora Spenlow, in Dickens's 'David Copperfield' (q.v.), the hero's 'child-wife'.

Dorastus and Fawnia, see *Pandosto.*

Dorax, a character in Dryden's 'Don Sebastian' (q.v.).

Dorcas Society, a ladies' association, connected with a church, for the purpose of making clothes for the poor; called after the Dorcas mentioned in Acts ix. 36.

Dorian Mode, in music, one of the ancient Greek modes, of a simple and solemn character, a minor scale appropriate to earnest or warlike melodies (Jebb).

Doric, derived from *Doris,* a small country in Greece, south of Thessaly, the home of the Dorians, one of the principal Hellenic races. From Doris the Dorians migrated to the Peloponnese (Herodotus i. 56). The word is used to signify rustic, as in

> With eager thought warbling his Doric lay.
> (Milton, 'Lycidas'.)

It is used also of a 'broad' or rustic dialect of English, as that of the north of England, and Scotland.

DORIC ORDER, in architecture, the simplest, and sturdiest of the three Grecian orders. The Roman Doric column, unlike the Grecian, may have a base and be unfluted.

Doricourt, a character in Mrs. Cowley's 'The Belle's Stratagem' (q.v.).

Dorigen, the heroine of the Franklin's Tale, in Chaucer's 'Canterbury Tales' (q.v.).

Dorimant, a character in Etherege's 'The Man of Mode' (q.v.).

Dorothea, the heroine of 'Hermann and Dorothea', a poem by Goethe (q.v.).

Dorothea, ST., a Christian martyr who suffered in the persecution under Diocletian (303). She is commemorated on 6 Feb. Her story forms the subject of Massinger's 'The Virgin-Martyr' (q.v.).

Dorothea Brooke, the heroine of G. Eliot's 'Middlemarch' (q.v.).

D'Orsay, COUNT ALFRED GUILLAUME GABRIEL (1801–52), a Frenchman who, coming to London in 1821, soon made himself famous as a wit, a dandy, and an artist. He was adopted by the earl and countess of Blessington. In 1823, with his benefactors, he travelled to Genoa, where he met Byron and made a rapid pencil sketch of the poet which has survived. In 1827 he married Lady Harriet Gardiner, Lord Blessington's daughter by a former marriage, but a separation took place almost immediately. He was prominent in the society of Gore House, at which Lady Blessington entertained all literary, political, and artistic London.

Dorset, EARL OF, see under *Sackville* (C.) and *Sackville* (T.).

DOS PASSOS, JOHN (1896–   ), American novelist, born at Chicago. His first important novel was 'Three Soldiers' (1921), and he has since published many others, as well as poetry, plays, essays, and books of travel. He is best known for his novels 'Manhattan Transfer' (1925), a collective portrait of life in New York City, and 'U.S.A.' (1938), a trilogy composed of 'The 42nd Parallel' (1930), '1919' (1932), and 'The Big Money' (1936). 'U.S.A.' tries to capture, by its use of all the devices open to a novelist, the variety and multiplicity of American life in the 20th cent., which is viewed critically from the standpoint of an idealist and individualist.

DOSTOEVSKY, FEODOR MIKHAILOVICH (1821–81), Russian novelist. His first novel 'Poor People' (1846) was followed by a number of stories and the 'Memoirs from the House of the Dead' (1861-2) based on his impri-

sonment and exile in Siberia for alleged revolutionary activity. His major novels are 'Crime and Punishment' (1866), 'The Idiot' (1866), 'The Devils' (1871), and 'The Brothers Karamazov' (1880). Dostoevsky's novels are notable for their depth of character analysis, preoccupation with abnormal psychology, and the humour of the absurd. In his socioreligious themes Dostoevsky advanced his own mystical view of Russian Christianity as an antidote to rationalism and socialism. A number of his novels appeared in English in the 1880s, but their full impact on English readers was due to the translation by C. Garnett, 'The Novels of Feodor Dostoevsky' (1912–20).

Dotheboys Hall, in Dickens's 'Nicholas Nickleby' (q.v.), the school conducted by Mr. Squeers.

Douai Bible, see *Bible* (*The English*).

Double Dealer, The, a comedy by Congreve (q.v.), produced in 1694.

Mellefont, nephew and prospective heir of Lord Touchwood, is about to marry Cynthia, daughter of Sir Paul Plyant. Lady Touchwood, a violent dissolute woman, is in love with Mellefont, but as he rejects her advances, determines to prevent the match and ruin him in Lord Touchwood's esteem. In this design she finds a confederate in Maskwell, the Double Dealer, who has been her lover, pretends to be Mellefont's friend, and aspires to cheat him of Cynthia and get her for himself. To this end he leads Plyant to suspect an intrigue between Mellefont and Lady Plyant, and Touchwood an intrigue between Mellefont and Lady Touchwood; and contrives that Touchwood shall find Mellefont in the latter's chamber. Mellefont is disinherited and Cynthia is to be made over to Maskwell. The latter's plot, however, here goes wrong. Lord Touchwood informs Lady Touchwood of Maskwell's intention to marry Cynthia. This awakens her jealousy. She finds Maskwell and upbraids him, and is overheard by Lord Touchwood, who now perceives Maskwell's treachery, and defeats his final attempt to carry off Cynthia.

Double Deceit, The, or, The Cure for Jealousy, a lively comedy by William Popple (1701–64), produced in 1735. Two young men, whom it is proposed to marry to two heiresses who are unknown to them, conspire to defeat the project. They arrange to exchange places with their valets, who are to court the ladies. The ladies, apprised of the trick, exchange places with their maids. But the pseudo-valets fall in love with the pseudo-maids, and all ends well.

Doubloon, a Spanish gold coin, originally double the value of a pistole (q.v.), i.e. = 33 to 36 shillings English.

Doubting, Castle in Bunyan's The 'Pilgrim's Progress' (q.v.), the castle of Giant Despair.

Doucepers, see *Douzepers*.

DOUGHTY, CHARLES MONTAGU (1843–1926), educated at Caius College, Cambridge, is principally remembered for his remarkable record of 'Travels in Arabia Deserta' carried out in 1876–8, first published in 1888 (republished in 1920 and 1921). It is notable for its style, in which Chaucerian and Elizabethan English is mixed with Arabic. Doughty also wrote a number of poems: 'The Dawn in Britain' (6 vols., 1906), 'Adam cast forth' (a sacred drama, 1908), 'The Cliffs' (1909), 'The Clouds' (1912), 'The Titans' (1916), 'Mansoul, or the Riddle of the World' (1920).

Douglas, a romantic tragedy by J. Home (q.v.), based on a Scottish ballad, and acted in 1756.

Old Norval, the shepherd, brings up the infant son of Douglas and Sir Malcolm's daughter, who after his birth has married Lord Randolph. The child has been exposed owing to Sir Malcolm's hatred. Known as Young Norval, he saves the life of Lord Randolph, and is given a commission in the army. Hated and traduced by Glenalvon, Lord Randolph's heir-presumptive, he is waylaid, slays Glenalvon, but is himself killed by Lord Randolph. His identity is discovered, and his mother in despair takes her own life.

DOUGLAS, LORD ALFRED BRUCE (1870–1945), poet and friend of Oscar Wilde (q.v.), whose 'Salome' he translated from French into English. His published verse includes 'The City of the Sorel' (1899), 'Sonnets' (1909), 'In Excelsis' (1924), and 'Lyrics' (1935). He edited the 'Academy' (q.v.) from 1907 to 1910.

Douglas, ARCHIBALD, *fifth earl of Angus* (Bell-the-cat, q.v.), figures in Scott's 'Marmion' (q.v.).

Douglas, THE BLACK, a name applied to two of the Douglases:

(1) Sir James Douglas (1286?–1330), who in 1319, in the days of Robert Bruce and Edward II, invaded England and plundered many towns and villages in the North. 'It was said that the name of this indefatigable and successful chief had become so formidable that women used in the northern counties to still their froward children by threatening them with the Black Douglas' (Scott, 'History of Scotland', ch. xi). He three times destroyed an English garrison in his castle of Douglas, which he burnt twice (see *Douglas Larder*), and it is on one of these incidents that Scott bases the story of his 'Castle Dangerous' (q.v.). After the conclusion of peace with Edward III, James Douglas set out on a pilgrimage to the Holy Land, carrying the heart of Bruce, but was killed on the way, fighting the Moors in Andalusia.

(2) Sir William Douglas, lord of Nithsdale (*d.* 1392?), illegitimate son of Archibald, third earl of Douglas. He married a daughter of Robert II and received the lordship of Niths-dale in 1387. In 1388 he made a retaliatory raid on Ireland, burning Carlingford and plundering the Isle of Man.

Douglas, ELLEN, heroine of Scott's 'Lady of the Lake' (q.v.).

DOUGLAS, GAWIN or GAVIN (1474?–1522), Scottish poet and bishop of Dunkeld, was third son of Archibald, fifth earl of Angus. He wrote two allegorical poems, 'The Palice of Honour' (first published 1553?) and 'King Hart' (first printed 1786); also a translation of the 'Aeneid' with prologues (1553), which constitutes him the earliest translator of the classics into English; probably there were earlier editions published both of the 'Aeneid' and of 'The Palice of Honour'. There is an edition of Douglas's works by John Small of Edinburgh (1874).

Douglas, SIR JAMES and SIR WILLIAM, see *Douglas* (*The Black*, (1) and (2)).

DOUGLAS, KEITH (1920–44), poet of the Second World War, killed during the invasion of Normandy. His poems, of which those written on active service in the Middle East are the most important, appeared in periodicals and war-time anthologies, but were not published in full until 1951.

DOUGLAS, NORMAN (1868–1952), novelist and essayist. Among his works are: 'Alone' (1921), 'South Wind' (1917), 'In the Beginning' (1928), 'Three of Them' (1930).

Douglas Larder, THE: the English in the time of Edward I had placed a garrison in Douglas Castle and stored it with provisions for the English army. Sir James Douglas (q.v.) surprised the garrison on Palm Sunday 1306–7 and got possession of the castle. He broke up the barrels of provisions, killed his prisoners and threw in their dead bodies; and then set fire to the castle. (Scott, 'Tales of a Grandfather', ch. ix.)

Douglas Tragedy, *The*, a ballad included in Scott's 'Border Minstrelsy', the story of the carrying off of Lady Margaret by Lord William Douglas. They are pursued by her father and seven brothers, who fall in the ensuing fight. But Lord William dies of his wounds, and Lady Margaret does not survive him.

Dousterswivel, HERMAN, a character in Scott's 'The Antiquary' (q.v.).

Douzepers, DOUCEPERS, in the Carlovingian romances, the twelve peers or paladins of Charlemagne, said to be attached to his person as being the bravest of his knights. Spenser in the 'Faerie Queene', III. x. 31, likens Braggadochio to 'a doughty Doucepere'.

Dove Cottage, a short distance from the NE. shore of Grasmere Lake, taken by Wordsworth and his sister at the end of 1799 when they migrated to the Lakes. They occupied it till the end of 1807.

Dover, CAPTAIN ROBERT, see *Cotswold Games*.

DOWDEN, EDWARD (1843–1913), educated at Queen's College, Cork, and Trinity

College, Dublin, became professor of English literature at the latter in 1867. He was noted as a Shakespearian scholar, publishing in 1875 'Shakspere, his Mind and Art', and his 'Shakspere Primer' in 1877, followed by editions of many single plays. He wrote a number of other volumes of criticism, the standard 'Life of Shelley' (1886), and short biographies of Southey, Browning, and Montaigne.

Dowel, Dobet, Dobest, characters in 'Piers Plowman' (q.v.), Passus IX.

DOWLAND, JOHN (1563?–1626?), lutanist and composer, published three books of 'Songes or Ayres of Foure Partes with Tableture for the Lute' (1597, 1600, and 1603). He dedicated his 'Lachrymae' to Anne of Denmark, and was lutanist to Charles I, 1625.

Down with Knavery, see *Hey for Honesty.*

Downing, Sir George (1623?–84), soldier, diplomat, and politician, was scout-master-general of Cromwell's army in Scotland in 1650 and headed the movement for offering Cromwell the crown. He was British resident at The Hague both under Cromwell and Charles II, and M.P. for Morpeth in 1670.

Downing Street, Westminster, No. 10 of which is the official residence of the prime minister, is named after the above. The street also contains the official residence of the chancellor of the exchequer, and the foreign and commonwealth offices stand on its S. side. So that 'Downing Street' is often used to signify the British government.

Sir George Downing (1684?–1749), the grandson of the above, left estates from the proceeds of which, after much litigation, Downing College, Cambridge, was founded.

Dowsabel, an English form of the Latin female name *Dulcibella,* used generically for a sweetheart.

DOWSON, ERNEST (1867–1900), author of a book of remarkable poems (1896), of which the best known is 'Non sum qualis eram . . .' with the refrain 'I have been faithful to thee, Cynara! in my fashion'.

DOYLE, Sir ARTHUR CONAN (1859–1930), educated at Stonyhurst and Edinburgh University, adopted the profession of medicine and practised at Southsea, 1882–90. He will be remembered chiefly for his creation of the amateur detective, Sherlock Holmes (q.v.), embodied in a cycle of stories ('The Adventures of Sherlock Holmes' (1891), 'The Memoirs of Sherlock Holmes' (1894), 'The Hound of the Baskervilles' (1902), and others), and of his friend and foil Dr. Watson. Doyle's first work of fiction, 'A Study in Scarlet' (also a Holmes story), appeared in 1887, and was followed by a series of historical and other romances for half a century. Notable among them may be mentioned 'Micah Clarke' (1889), 'The White Company' (1891), 'The Exploits of Brigadier Gerard' (1896), 'Rodney Stone'

(1896), 'The Lost World' (1912), the first of the Professor Challenger stories. His patriotism was shown in his pamphlet 'The Great Boer War' (1900), designed to place the true facts of that war before the world. His 'Story of Waterloo', a one-act play (1900), originally 'A Straggler of '15', furnished Sir Henry Irving with one of his most successful parts. He wrote a 'History of Spiritualism' (1926), a subject in which during his later years he was much interested.

DOYLE, Sir FRANCIS HASTINGS CHARLES (1810–88), second baronet, was educated at Eton and Christ Church, Oxford, and became fellow of All Souls and professor of poetry at Oxford. He published several volumes of verse, including ballads on military subjects ('The Loss of the Birkenhead', 'The Red Thread of Honour', and 'The Private of the Buffs').

Doyle, RICHARD (1824–83), illustrator. He worked for 'Punch' (1843–50) and designed its cover. He illustrated chiefly fairy stories and published books of annotated drawings, including 'The Foreign Tour of Brown, Jones, and Robinson' (1854), whose comic adventures in England and on the Rhine he had depicted in 'Punch'.

Drachenfels, a mountain in the Siebengebirge on the Rhine, in which is the Drachenhöhle or dragon's cave, the lair of the dragon killed by Siegfried (q.v.).

Draco, a celebrated lawgiver of Athens, whose code (621 B.C.) was noted for its severity; hence the adjective 'draconian' = 'severe'.

Dracula, the story of a vampire, written in 1897 by Bram Stoker (1847–1912). The fiendish activities of Count Dracula, told in dramatic diary form by the principal characters, begin and end in the mountains of Transylvania, the traditional home of vampire lore. The objects of Dracula's blood-lust are two young and beautiful women, and the men who try to defend them call in the help of a Dutch professor, Van Helsing, who is described as 'a philosopher and a metaphysician, and one of the most advanced scientists of his day'. The horror and the tension of the struggle increase until the climax on the last pages of the book.

Dragon of Wantley, The, a humorous ballad, probably of the 17th cent., satirizing the old verse romances. It tells of a Yorkshire dragon that devoured children and cattle, and was killed by More of More Hall. The ballad is included in Percy's 'Reliques', the editor of which provides the following key: Wantley is Wharncliffe, in the parish of Penniston, Yorks. A conflict having arisen between the parishioners and Sir Francis Wortley (the dragon) with regard to the tithes, More of More Hall as attorney or counsellor conducted the suit, which was decided in favour of the parishioners. For another explanation see Lockhart's 'Scott', ch. xii.

A burlesque opera called the 'Dragon of Wantley' by Henry Carey (q.v.) was produced in 1734. The inn at Barchester mentioned by Trollope (*passim*) is 'The Dragon of Wantley'.

Dragon's Teeth, see *Cadmus.*

Dragonnades, a series of persecutions directed by Louis XIV against the Protestants of France, so called because dragoons were quartered upon them. Hence the word 'dragonnade' is applied to any persecution with the help of troops.

Drake, SIR FRANCIS (1540?–96), circumnavigator and admiral, was born at Tavistock, Devonshire. His early sea-career is uncertain, but he was undoubtedly engaged in the Guinea trade with Sir John Hawkins. He commanded the 'Judith' in Hawkins's ill-fated expedition to San Juan de Ulloa of 1567, and made three voyages to the W. Indies in 1570–2. In 1577 he set out in the 'Pelican' (afterwards renamed 'The Golden Hind') for the river Plate, sailed through the Straits of Magellan (after executing Thomas Doughty, one of his officers, on a charge of conspiracy), plundered Valparaiso, rounded the Cape of Good Hope, and completed the circumnavigation of the world. He was knighted by Elizabeth on his return in 1581. Under a commission from Elizabeth he plundered St. Iago and burnt Vigo in 1585, and took San Domingo and Cartagena. In 1587 he destroyed a Spanish armament in the harbour of Cadiz, unaware that the order to commit acts of war, in so far as it extended to Spanish territory, had been withdrawn. Drake, as vice-admiral, commanded one of the divisions of the English fleet against the Armada, which he defeated off Gravelines and pursued to the north of Scotland. He was subsequently associated with Sir John Norris in an expedition which in 1589 plundered Coruña and destroyed much Spanish shipping. Drake died in Jan. 1596 off Portobello in the course of an unsuccessful expedition with Sir John Hawkins to the W. Indies; Hawkins had died on the same expedition a few weeks before Drake. The narratives of some of his expeditions figure in Hakluyt and Purchas, and he became the hero of many legends.

Drama of Exile, *A*, a poem by E. B. Browning (q.v.).

Dramatis Personae, a collection of poems by R. Browning (q.v.), published in 1864, three years after his wife's death. The collection includes 'Abt Vogler' (q.v.), 'Prospice', 'Rabbi Ben Ezra' (q.v.), 'A Death in the Desert', and the longer pieces 'Caliban upon Setebos' (q.v.) and 'Mr. Sludge, "The Medium"' (q.v.).

Draper, MRS. ELIZA (1744–78), wife of Daniel Draper (an official in the service of the East India Company), with whom Sterne (q.v.) had one of his love-affairs. She is the 'Eliza' and the 'Bramine' of the 'Journal to Eliza' and of the 'Letters from Yorick to Eliza'.

Draper, RUTH (1884–1956), American diseuse. Her dramatic sketches, written by herself, which delighted audiences throughout the English-speaking world, were witty and lively, frequently ironical, sometimes touching. She not only portrayed women of every age and class, but also created other characters on the stage so vividly that they could almost be seen and heard as she moved among them. As a young woman she received advice and encouragement from Henry James (q.v.).

***Drapier's Letters,** The*, published by Swift (q.v.) in 1724. The word 'Drapier' = 'Draper'.

A patent had been granted to the duchess of Kendal for supplying copper coins for use in Ireland, and by her had been sold to a certain William Wood for £10,000. The profit on the patent would have been apparently some £25,000. In 1723 the Irish houses of parliament voted addresses protesting against the transaction. Swift took up the cudgels on behalf of the Irish. Writing in the character of a Dublin draper, he published a series of four letters in which he prophesied ruin to the Irish if 'Wood's half-pence' were admitted into circulation. The letters produced an immense effect, and the government was forced to abandon the project and compensate Wood.

Drawcansir, a character in Buckingham's 'The Rehearsal' (q.v.), parodying Almanzor in Dryden's 'Conquest of Granada' (q.v.).

DRAWCANSIR, SIR ALEXANDER, pseudonym of H. FIELDING (q.v.).

DRAYTON, MICHAEL (1563–1631), born at Hartshill in Warwickshire, but of the details of whose life little is known, produced a vast quantity of historical, topographical, and religious verse, besides odes, sonnets, and satires. His earliest work was a volume of sacred verse, the 'Harmonie of the Church', paraphrases of songs and prayers from the O.T. and Apocrypha, published in 1591. In 1593 he published 'Idea, the Shepheards Garland', eclogues in the tradition of Spenser, praising Elizabeth, lamenting Sir P. Sidney, etc., and containing pleasant songs. These were republished with alterations as 'Eglogs' *c.* 1605 in 'Poems Lyrick and Pastoral', and as 'Pastorals' in 1619. Drayton's 'Ideas Mirrour', a series of sonnets, many of them inspired by French originals, and including the magnificent 'Since there's no help, come let us kiss and part', was published in 1594. The lady referred to under the name 'Idea' was probably Anne, second daughter of Sir Henry Goodere, an early patron of Drayton. 'Endimion and Phœbe', a pastoral, was written about 1595.

Drayton's great topographical poem on England, 'Polyolbion' (q.v.), was completed in 1622. 'The Owle', a satire, appeared in 1604; and 'Poemes Lyrick and Pastorall', containing the splendid 'Ballad of Agincourt' ('Fair stood the wind for France'), the ode 'To the Virginian Voyage', and some other

notable odes on the Anacreontic model, *c.*
1605. 'Nimphidia' (q.v.) and other poems,
including two pleasant pastorals and the
interesting autobiographical and critical letter
in verse 'To Henery Reynolds', appeared in
1627.

Drayton's chief historical poems were 'Piers
Gaveston', *e.* 1593; 'Matilda', 1594; 'The
Tragicall Legend of Robert, Duke of Nor-
mandie', 1596; 'Mortimeriados', republished
as 'The Barrons Wars', 1603; and the 'Legend
of Great Cromwell', included in the 1610 edition of the 'Mirror for Magistrates' (q.v.).
In 1597 appeared his 'England's Heroicall
Epistles', imaginary letters in verse exchanged
by historical personages, of whom there are
twelve couples in the first edition of the work,
such as Henry II and Fair Rosamund, Edward IV and Jane Shore, Lord Guildford
Dudley and Lady Jane Grey. Drayton was
buried in Westminster Abbey.

Dreadnought, the name of a large battleship, the first of its class (having ten 12-inch
guns in five turrets, turbine engines, and other
innovations), built for the British navy in
1905. It was the name of a queen's ship in
Elizabeth I's reign. A ship of the same name
was engaged at the battle of Trafalgar and
subsequently served as a hospital for seamen
of all nations, now replaced by the Seamen's
Hospital at Greenwich.

Dream, The, a poem by Lord Byron (q.v.),
written in 1816 and inspired by his love for
Mary Chaworth.

Dream of Fair Women, A, a poem by A.
Tennyson (q.v.).

Dream of Gerontius, see *Newman.*

Dream of the Rood, The, an OE. poem,
formerly attributed by some to Cædmon
(q.v.), by others to Cynewulf (q.v.). It consists of a narrative introduction, relating the
vision of the cross, and the poet's emotions in
its presence; followed by the address of the
visionary cross to the poet, telling of the
crucifixion and resurrection, and reflections
thereon.

The poem is included in the 'Vercelli
Book' (q.v.) and parts of it are inscribed in
runes on the Ruthwell Cross in Annandale.

Dreams, GATES OF, according to Greek
legend, the ivory gate and the gate of horn,
through which false and true dreams respectively issue. There is a reference to them in
the 'Odyssey', xix. 562, and in the 'Aeneid',
vi. 894 et seq.

DREISER, THEODORE (1871–1945),
American novelist, born in Indiana. He was
brought up in poverty and became a journalist. His first novel, 'Sister Carrie' (1900), was
withheld from circulation on the grounds of
immorality, and he did not make a name for
himself until his second, 'Jenny Gerhardt'
(1911). Both novels have working-class girls
as their heroines and describe the impact of
wealth and society upon them. A similar
theme is illustrated in the career of Cowper-
wood, a business magnate, the hero of the
'Trilogy of Desire'—'The Financier' (1912),
'The Titan' (1914), and the greatly inferior
'The Stoic' (1947). Dreiser's naturalistic
philosophy was also powerfully expressed in
'The "Genius"' (1915), a study of an artist in
which much of Dreiser's own experience is
involved, and 'An American Tragedy' (1925),
an indictment of American business and
society. Dreiser became a socialist in the
1920s and expressed his beliefs in several
books, notably 'Tragic America' (1931). He
was an ungainly stylist but this disability
counts for little in view of his passionate
sincerity and concern for the facts of American life.

Dreme, The, see *Lindsay* (*Sir D.*).

Dresden China: Augustus, elector of
Saxony (1670–1733), formed a collection of
Chinese and Japanese porcelain and established experimental pottery works at Dresden. Here Böltger discovered how to make a
porcelain resembling the Chinese ware, first
exhibited in 1710. The manufacture was
conducted with extreme secrecy at Meissen
near Dresden, where the factory remained
until the 19th cent., its products being known
as Dresden china. Here Kandler, the chief
modeller of the factory from 1731 to 1775,
produced the little statuettes and groups
particularly associated with the name.

Dreyfus, ALFRED (1859–1935), an officer in
the French army, famous owing to the judicial miscarriage which caused his imprisonment and the fierce controversy which
preceded his rehabilitation. In 1894 a letter
(known as the *bordereau* or schedule), addressed
to the German military attaché in Paris and
enumerating a number of documents which
were to be sent to the latter, was purloined
from the German embassy and handed to the
French Ministry of War. Owing to the similarity of the handwriting of this unsigned letter
to that of Dreyfus, who held an appointment
at the ministry, he was arrested, tried, and
convicted, and sent to the Devil's Island off
the coast of Guiana. In 1896 Col. Picquart
came accidentally upon evidence indicating
that the true criminal was a certain Major
Esterhazy. But the strongest opposition, involving the use of forgery, intimidation, and
a violent anti-semitic press campaign, was
raised to the reopening of the question of the
guilt of Dreyfus. In the course of this controversy, Émile Zola published his famous letter,
entitled 'J'accuse', in 'L'Aurore' (Jan. 1898),
and was condemned in consequence to a
year's imprisonment. It was not until 1906
that the sentence condemning Dreyfus was
finally quashed by the Court of Appeal. The
controversy gave rise to the term DREYFUS-
ARD, to signify a supporter of the innocence
of Dreyfus. Extracts from the papers of Col.
Schwartzkoppen, the German military attaché
in Paris at the time, confirming Esterhazy's
guilt, appeared in 1930.

DRINKWATER, JOHN (1882–1937), poet and dramatist, is perhaps best known for his fine historical play 'Abraham Lincoln' (1918). His published works include other historical plays on 'Oliver Cromwell' (1921), 'Mary Stuart' (1921), and 'Robert E. Lee' (1923), several volumes of verse, an edition of Sir Philip Sidney's poems, studies of William Morris (1912) and Swinburne (1913), etc. He published in 1930 a life of Pepys. His autobiography was published in 1931–2.

Droeshout, MARTIN (*fl.* 1620–51), engraver; see *Shakespeare*.

Droit d'aubaine, a right claimed by French kings, in default of treaty to the contrary, to the property of any alien who died in their country. It was abolished in 1790, re-established by Napoleon I, and finally annulled in 1819. The etymology of *aubaine* is uncertain; Hatzfeld and Darmesteter refer *aubain*, an alien, to a presumed late Latin form *alibanum*, from *alibi*.

Drolls or DROLL-HUMOURS, in Commonwealth days, when various devices were employed to evade the ordinance of 2 Sept. 1642 forbidding stage plays, were farces or comic scenes adapted from existing plays or invented by the actors, and produced generally on extemporized stages at fairs and in taverns. Among the subjects of such 'drolls' were Falstaff, the grave-diggers' colloquy in 'Hamlet', and Bottom the Weaver.

Dromio, the name of the twin slaves in Shakespeare's 'The Comedy of Errors' (q.v.).

Drows, see *Trows*.

Drugger, ABEL, a character in Jonson's 'The Alchemist' (q.v.). One of Garrick's most famous parts.

Druidism, a religious system that prevailed among the ancient Celts of Gaul and Britain. According to Caesar the Druids were a learned and priestly class. They believed in the immortality and transmigration of the soul. Their rites were conducted in oak-groves, and the oak and mistletoe (q.v.) were objects of veneration to them. In Irish and Welsh legend they figure as magicians and soothsayers. After their defeat in Mona (Anglesey) by the Romans under Suetonius Paulinus, there is no further mention of their existence in England and Wales, but they survived in Ireland and north Britain.

The modern 'Druids' are a Friendly Society founded in England in 1781, and since extended to America and Australia.

Drum ecclesiastic, the pulpit, from the stanza in Butler's 'Hudibras' (q.v., I. i):

When Gospel trumpeter, surrounded
With long-eared rout, to battle sounded;
And pulpit, drum ecclesiastic,
Was beat with fist instead of a stick.

Drum's Entertainment, JACK or TOM, a rough reception, turning an unwelcome guest out of doors; 'to bale a man in by the head,

and thrust him out by both the shoulders' (Holinshed). The expression occurs in Shakespeare, 'All's Well that Ends Well', III. vi.

Drummer, *The,* a comedy by Addison (q.v.), produced in 1715. Sir George Truman, supposed to have been killed in the wars, returns after twelve months' captivity and ousts the suitors of Lady Truman, including one who, in order to forward his plans, has assumed the disguise of a ghostly drummer.

DRUMMOND, HENRY (1851–97), theological writer, author of 'Natural Law in the Spiritual World' (1883), 'Ascent of Man' (1894).

DRUMMOND, WILLIAM HENRY (1854–1907), Canadian poet, was born in Ireland and went to Canada with his family at the age of 11. He is the poet of the French-Canadian *habitant* and *voyageur*, and treats in simple homely verse of their oddities and backwoods life. He published 'The Habitant' (1897), 'Johnny Courteau' (1901), 'The Voyageur' (1905), 'The Great Fight' (1908).

DRUMMOND OF HAWTHORNDEN, WILLIAM (1585–1649), was born at the manor of Hawthornden near Edinburgh. He was educated at Edinburgh University, and travelled abroad. He was a friend of Drayton and an acquaintance of Ben Jonson, a Royalist and episcopalian, and he wrote pamphlets and verses in the Royalist cause. He had an unhappy love story: Mary Cunningham of Barns, to whom he was affianced, died on the eve of their wedding, and inspired many of his sonnets and songs. He also wrote elegies, satires, and hymns.

Drummond lamented Prince Henry in 'Tears on the Death of Mœliades' in 1613, and published 'Flowers of Zion' (religious verse) and 'The Cypresse Grove', his finest work, a prose meditation on death, in 1623. He wrote a 'History of Scotland' from 1423 to 1524, which was first printed in 1655. He also left manuscript notes (printed in 1832) of a visit that Ben Jonson paid him. The first collected edition of his poems was issued in 1656, his complete works were printed in 1711, and there have been in the 19th cent. editions by Laing, by the Maitland Club, and a life of him by David Masson. There is a critical edition of the poems by L. E. Kastner, 1913.

Drury Lane, London, was so called from the Drury family, who had a large house there from Tudor times. The theatre of that name was originally a cock-pit in the Lane, converted into a theatre in James I's time. It was rebuilt by Thomas Killigrew (1612–83, q.v.), to whom Charles II granted a patent in 1662, again by Wren in 1674, and again in 1812. The reopening of the theatre on this last occasion was celebrated in 'Rejected Addresses' (q.v.). Booth, Garrick, Mrs. Siddons, Kemble, and Kean are among the famous actors who have been seen there. In the 19th cent. it was the great house of Christmas pantomimes.

Druses, or DRUZES, a political and religious sect, inhabiting the region round Mt. Lebanon, and the Hauran in Syria. They are believed to derive their name from Ismail al-Darazi, who in 1040 supported the claim of the tenth Fatimite Caliph, Hakim Biamrillahi, to be a divine incarnation, and introduced this belief to the Lebanon. [OED.] Darazi was, however, declared apostate by Hamzah ibn Ali ibn Hamzah, who is regarded as the founder of their faith. The religious tenets of the Druses, a singularly exclusive body, are sedulously veiled in obscurity. See also *Return of the Druses.*

Dryads and Hamadryads, in the belief of the Greeks and Romans, were the nymphs (q.v.) of trees, and were thought to die with the trees that had been their abode.

Dryasdust, DR. Jonas, a fictitious character, a prosy antiquarian, to whom Sir W. Scott addresses the prefaces of some of his novels.

DRYDEN, JOHN (1631–1700), was born at the vicarage of Aldwinkle All Saints, between Thrapston and Oundle in Northamptonshire. He was educated at Westminster, under Busby, and at Trinity College, Cambridge. He had a small competence and is said to have attached himself to his wealthy cousin, Sir Gilbert Pickering, Cromwell's chamberlain. In 1658 he wrote his remarkable 'Heroic stanzas' (quatrains) on the death of Cromwell; 'Astraea Redux' in 1660, on the return of Charles II, in which he first showed his mastery of the heroic couplet; and a 'Panegyric' on the Restoration in 1661. His early plays, 'The Wild Gallant' (in prose, acted in 1663) and 'The Rival Ladies' (acted in 1664), are not of great importance, except that the latter is an early example of the use of the rhymed couplet in dramatic verse. 'The Indian Emperor' (1665) (an heroic play dealing with the conquest of Mexico by Cortez, the love of the Emperor Montezuma's daughter for Cortez, and the death of father and daughter) was very popular and is one of the best of its kind. In 1663 Dryden married Lady Elizabeth Howard, eldest daughter of the earl of Berkshire. The marriage appears not to have been altogether a happy one, though there is no evidence of actual disunion. His wife survived him until 1714. In 1667 Dryden published his 'Annus Mirabilis' (q.v.). He was appointed poet laureate in 1668 and historiographer in 1670, and wrote some fourteen plays between 1668 and 1681. Of these the most important are the following: 'Tyrannic Love or the Royal Martyr' (q.v., 1669), and 'Almanzor and Almahide or the Conquest of Granada' (q.v., 1670); 'Amboyna', a tragedy in prose and blank verse produced in 1673, designed to exasperate the English against the Dutch by reviving the story of the massacre of some Englishmen at that place (in the Moluccas) by the Dutch in 1623; 'Aurengzebe'

(q.v.), his last rhymed tragedy, 1676; the 'Spanish Fryar', 1681, an attack on the papists (Elvira with the aid of a friar carries on an intrigue with Lorenzo, who is discovered to be her brother). His best play and his first drama in blank verse, 'All for Love' (q.v.), a version of the story of Antony and Cleopatra, appeared in 1678. Of his earlier comedies the best is 'Marriage-à-la-Mode' (q.v.), produced in 1673; the 'Mock Astrologer' (1668), adapted from a play by Thomas Corneille, contains four fine songs. In 1679 he wrote an adaptation of 'Troilus and Cressida' (q.v.), 'which might', said George Saintsbury, 'much better have been left unattempted'. Dryden makes Cressida kill herself because her fidelity to Troilus is doubted; and Troilus kills Diomede, and is in turn killed by Achilles; a commonplace solution.

In 1671 appeared the 'Rehearsal' (q.v.), attributed to Buckingham, satirizing the rhymed heroic plays of Dryden, D'Avenant, and others. In 1673 Dryden was engaged in a literary controversy with Elkanah Settle (q.v.), author of a series of bombastic dramas which enjoyed considerable popularity. In 1679, having incurred the ill-will of John Wilmot, second earl of Rochester, on account of a passage in the earl of Mulgrave's anonymous 'Essay on Satire', which was attributed to Dryden, the latter was attacked and beaten, at Rochester's instigation, by masked men in Rose Alley, Covent Garden.

Dryden wrote a number of critical pieces which generally took the form of prefaces to his plays; but one, the 'Essay of Dramatick Poesie' (q.v.), was an independent work. It was published in 1668. His 'Defence of the Epilogue' at the end of the 'Conquest of Granada' contains a criticism of Fletcher and of certain aspects of Shakespeare's writing; and the Dedication to 'Examen Poeticum' (vol. iii of 'Miscellany Poems') is another notable piece of critical work.

In 1680 began the period of Dryden's satirical and didactic poems. 'Absalom and Achitophel' (q.v.) appeared in 1681; 'The Medal' (q.v.) in 1682; 'Mac Flecknoe' (q.v.) piratically in 1682 (authorized ed. 1684, probably written *c.* 1679); 'Religio Laici' (q.v.) also in 1682; 'The Hind and the Panther' (q.v.) in 1687, after his conversion to Roman Catholicism in 1686. His Pindaric ode on the death of Charles II 'Threnodia Augustalis' and his much finer 'Ode to the Memory of Mrs. Anne Killigrew' (pronounced by Johnson to be the finest in the language) appeared in 1685 and 1686. His later dramas include two operas, 'Albion and Albanius' (1685) and 'King Arthur' (1691); 'Don Sebastian' (q.v.), a tragicomedy, and 'Amphitryon' (q.v.), a comedy, both of the year 1690; and 'Cleomenes', a tragedy based on Plutarch's account of the Spartan hero, 1692. His last play was 'Love Triumphant', a tragicomedy on the lines of 'Marriage-à-la-Mode', 1694.

Dryden refused to take the oaths at the Revolution and was deprived of the laureateship and of a place in the Customs that he had held since 1683. The last part of his life was occupied largely with translations, many of which appeared in 'Miscellany Poems' (1684 and later years). He translated in verse Persius and the Satires of Juvenal (1693), the whole of Virgil (the complete work appeared in 1697), and parts of Horace, Ovid, Homer, Theocritus, and Lucretius. The translation of Virgil was very successful, and according to Pope brought him in £1,200. The translation of Juvenal and Persius was prefaced by a 'Discourse concerning the Original and Progress of Satire' (1693). Dryden also paraphrased the Latin hymn 'Veni Creator Spiritus' ('Creator Spirit, by whose aid'), and Scott further attributed to him a version of the 'Te Deum' and of a hymn for the Nativity of St. John the Baptist. He wrote his famous second ode for St. Cecilia's day (the first 'Song for St. Cecilia's Day' was published in 1687), entitled 'Alexander's Feast', for a musical society in 1697; he thought it the best of all his poetry. His last great work was the collection of paraphrases of tales by Chaucer, Boccaccio, and Ovid, called 'Fables, Ancient and Modern' (q.v.), with a delightful preface, published late in 1699, shortly before his death in April 1700. He was buried in Westminster Abbey, in Chaucer's grave, and twenty years later a monument to him was erected there by John Sheffield, Lord Mulgrave (duke of Buckingham).

Dryden's published works were very numerous; in addition to those referred to above, mention may be made of the following:

Poems—'Upon the death of Lord Hastings' (1649), contributed to 'Lachrymae Musarum' when Dryden was at Westminster; verses prefixed to John Hoddesdon's 'Sion and Parnassus' (1650); lines 'To My Lord Chancellor' Clarendon (1662) and 'Verses to Her Royal Highness the Duchess of York', Clarendon's daughter (1665); 'Britannia Rediviva: a Poem on the Birth of the Prince' (1688); 'Eleonora; a Panegyrical Poem to the Memory of the Countess of Abingdon' (1692); 'An Ode, on the Death of Mr. Henry Purcell' (1696); the 'Secular Masque', prologue and epilogue, written for the revival of Fletcher's play, 'The Pilgrim' (1700). In addition Dryden wrote a large number of prologues and epilogues for his own plays and those of other authors, or to be spoken on special occasions.

Plays—'Secret Love, or the Maiden-Queen' (1668); 'Sir Martin Mar-all, or the Feign'd Innocence' (1668); 'The Tempest', an adaptation of Shakespeare's play by D'Avenant and Dryden (1670); 'The Assignation, or Love in a Nunnery' (1672); 'The State of Innocence, and Fall of Man', a dramatic version of Milton's 'Paradise Lost' (1677); 'Oedipus' (with Nathaniel Lee, 1679); 'The Kind Keeper, or Mr. Limberham' (1680); 'The Duke of Guise' (with Nathaniel Lee, 1683). Dryden also contributed to Sir Robert Howard's 'Indian Queen' (1665).

Prose Works—A life of Plutarch, prefixed

to a translation of Plutarch's 'Lives' 'by several hands' (1683); part of 'A Defence of the Papers Written by the late King and Duchess of York' (1686); the 'Character of St. Evremont' in 'Miscellaneous Essays by St. Evremont' (1692); the 'Character of Polybius and his writings' in 'The History of Polybius translated by Sir H. S.' (1693–8); 'Life of Lucian', written in 1696 for a projected translation of Lucian's 'Dialogues' (1711). Also translations of 'The History of the League', by Maimbourg (1684); 'The Life of St. Francis Xavier', by Bouhours (1686); and 'De Arte Graphica', by Du Fresnoy (1695).

The standard edition of Dryden's collected works is that of Sir W. Scott, published in 1808, and revised and corrected by George Saintsbury in 1882. A collection of Dryden's 'Critical Essays', by W. P. Ker, was published in 1900. There is a life of Dryden by G. Saintsbury in the English Men of Letters series (1881).

Du Barry, JEANNE BÉCU, *Comtesse* (1743–93), mistress of Louis XV, executed during the Terror.

DU BARTAS, GUILLAUME SALLUSTE, SIEUR (1544–90), a French poet and soldier, who was mortally wounded at the battle of Ivry. As a poet he was less appreciated in France than in Britain, where he was received by James VI of Scotland and by Queen Elizabeth, and welcomed by Sir Philip Sidney. He published in 1578 an epic on the creation of the world, called 'La Semaine', which was translated into English by Joshua Sylvester (1592–9, collective ed. 1605). He may have influenced Spenser and Donne; and Milton, in writing the 'Paradise Lost', had perhaps, here and there, Sylvester's translation in mind.

DU CANGE, CHARLES DU FRESNE, SIEUR (1610–88), French man of letters, author of a valuable 'Glossarium ad scriptores mediae et infimae latinitatis' (1678), and editor of Joinville's and Villehardouin's chronicles.

DU MAURIER, GEORGE LOUIS PALMELLA BUSSON (1834–96), born in Paris, where he was educated, was the author of three novels, 'Peter Ibbetson' (1891), 'Trilby' (1894), and 'The Martian' (published posthumously in 1896). They are rendered interesting by the author's recollections of early days as an art student in Paris and Antwerp, but are somewhat marred by sentimentalism and melodrama. He contributed occasional drawings to 'Punch' from 1860, and joined its regular staff in 1864, in succession to John Leech. His drawings chiefly satirize upper and middle-class society in the spirit of Thackeray. He also contributed verse and prose to the same periodical from 1865, including 'The History of the Jack Sprats'.

Dualism, a philosophical system that recognizes two ultimate and independent principles in the scheme of things, such as mind and matter, or good and evil. It is opposed to *monism* and to *pluralism*.

Dubric or DUBRICIUS, ST. (*d.* 612), the reputed founder of the bishopric of Llandaff, said by Geoffrey of Monmouth to have crowned Arthur king of Britain and to have been archbishop of Caerleon. He is mentioned in Tennyson's 'The Coming of Arthur' (q.v.).

Ducat, from Italian *ducato*, late Latin *ducatus*, used as the name of a silver coin issued in 1140 by Roger II of Sicily, bearing the superscription R DX AP, i.e. *Rogerus Dux Apuliae*, to which, according to Du Cange, 'Glossarium', 'Ducatus nomen imposuit'. In 1284 the first gold ducat (worth about 9s.) was struck at Venice under the doge John Dandolo, with the legend 'Sit tibi Christe datus quem tu regis iste ducatus'. This, though it did not originate, may have contributed to spread the name. [OED.] The silver ducat was worth about 3s. 6d.

Duccio di Buoninsegna (active 1278–1319), the first painter of the Sienese school to infuse deep feeling and narrative power into his painting. His 'Maestà' was acclaimed and carried in procession to the Siena cathedral.

Ducdame, ducdame, ducdame, in Shakespeare's 'As You Like It', II. v, perhaps a transposition for *duc ad me*, 'bring to me' (Hanmer, also Johnson), or mere jargon.

Duchess of Malfi, The, a tragedy by J. Webster (q.v.), published in 1623, but played before 1614. The story is taken from one of Bandello's *novelle*, through Painter's 'Palace of Pleasure' (q.v.), and also shows the influence of Sidney's 'Arcadia' (q.v.).

The duchess, a spirited and high-minded woman, a widow, in a charming scene reveals her love for the honest Antonio, the steward of her court. They are secretly married, in spite of the warning of her brothers, the cardinal and Ferdinand, duke of Calabria, that she must not remarry; a warning induced by consideration for their 'royal blood of Arragon and Castile', and, as Ferdinand afterwards confesses, by desire to inherit her property. They place in her employment, to spy upon her, the ex-galley-slave Bosola, who betrays her to them. The duchess and Antonio fly and separate. The duchess is captured and is subjected by Ferdinand and Bosola to fearful mental tortures and finally strangled with two of her children. Retribution comes upon the murderers; Ferdinand goes mad, the cardinal is killed by the remorseful Bosola, and Bosola by the lunatic Ferdinand. Bosola has already killed Antonio, mistaking him for the cardinal. The often-quoted dramatic line 'Cover her face. Mine eyes dazzle. She died young', occurs in Act IV, sc. ii.

DUCK, STEPHEN (1705–56), was born in Wiltshire of humble parentage and began his life as a farm labourer. Almost entirely self-educated, he took to writing verse, and

through Lord Macclesfield came to the notice of Queen Caroline, who gave him a pension and made him a Yeoman of the Guard in 1733. In 1746 he took Holy Orders and became rector of Byfleet in 1752, but drowned himself four years later in a fit of despondency. His best-known poem 'The Thresher's Labour' was published in 'Poems on Several Occasions' in 1736.

Ducrow, ANDREW (1793–1842), a celebrated equestrian performer, the son of a Flemish 'strong man'. He was the chief equestrian at Astley's (q.v.) circus and the originator of many feats of horsemanship still seen at circuses. He subsequently became proprietor of Astley's with William Best.

Dudon, in the 'Orlando Innamorato' and 'Orlando Furioso' (qq.v.), son of Ogier the Dane, is captured by Rodomont and sent a prisoner to Africa, where he helps to destroy the fleet of Agramant.

Duenna, The, a comic opera by R. B. Sheridan (q.v.), produced in 1775.

Don Jerome, an obstinate irascible father, is determined that his daughter Louisa shall marry an odious little Jew, Isaac, but she is in love with Antonio. Jerome discovers that the duenna is acting as intermediary between Louisa and Antonio, dismisses the duenna, and locks up Louisa. Louisa disguised as the duenna escapes from the house, leaving the duenna to take her place. The Jew is fooled into marrying the duenna and into bringing Antonio and Louisa together.

Duessa, in Spenser's 'Faerie Queene', the daughter of Deceit and Shame, Falsehood in general, in Book I signifies in particular the Roman Catholic Church, and in Book v. ix, Mary Queen of Scots (the reference causing great offence to the king of Scotland).

DUFF, JAMES GRANT (1789–1858), a distinguished Anglo-Indian official, was author of an important 'History of the Mahrattas' (1826).

DUFFY, SIR CHARLES GAVAN (1816–1903), Irish nationalist, is remembered in a literary connexion as having started with Thomas Osborne Davis, in 1842, 'The Nation', a journal for which he gathered a brilliant staff of 'Young Irelanders'. 'The Nation' was suppressed on political grounds in 1848–9. Duffy emigrated to Australia in 1855 and rose to political eminence there. He wrote 'Young Ireland, 1840–50' (1880–3), 'Life of Thomas Davis' (1890), 'Conversations with Thomas Carlyle' (1892), and 'My Life in Two Hemispheres' (1898).

DUGDALE, SIR WILLIAM (1605–86), garter king-at-arms, and author of 'The Antiquities of Warwickshire', a topographical history that showed a great advance in respect of fullness and accuracy on previous works of the same kind. It was published in 1656. Dugdale's 'Monasticon Anglicanum', written in collaboration with Roger Dodsworth, an account of the English monastic houses, appeared in three volumes in 1655–73. In 1658 he published his 'History of St. Paul's Cathedral', and in 1662 'The History of Imbanking and Drayning of divers Fenns and Marshes', in which he strays beyond the limits of his subject to give much information of antiquarian and historical interest. He also wrote 'Origines Juridicales' (1666), a history of English laws, law-courts, and kindred matters, and 'The Baronage of England' (1675–6).

Duke, THE IRON, the duke of Wellington, so called from his firm will.

Duke of Exeter's Daughter, the name given to a rack in the Tower of London, of which the invention is attributed to John Holland, duke of Exeter, constable of the Tower in 1420.

Duke of Milan, The, a tragedy by Massinger (q.v.), printed in 1623, one of his earliest and most popular plays.

Ludovico Sforza, duke of Milan, has, in the war between the Emperor Charles and the French, allied himself with the latter. On their defeat, he goes to surrender himself to Charles, but in fear of his fate, first gives a written instruction to his wicked favourite Francisco to put his beloved wife Marcelia to death if anything untoward happens to himself. Francisco, in order to make Marcelia yield to his lust, reveals this warrant to her, but fails to move her chastity and only incenses her against the duke, so that on his return after his reconciliation with Charles she receives him coldly. This, coupled with accusations from various quarters of his wife's intimacy with Francisco, makes him suspicious of her. Francisco, to avenge himself for his failure, now tells the duke that Marcelia has made amorous advances to him, which so inflames the duke with anger that he stabs her to death; but dying, she reveals the truth and the duke is distracted with remorse. Francisco, a price being put on his head, returns to court in the disguise of a Jewish doctor, and undertakes to restore Marcelia to life. He is discovered and tortured, but not before he has poisoned the duke.

Duke's Children, The, see *Phineas Finn.*

Dukeries, THE, a district in Nottinghamshire containing several ducal estates, Welbeck (duke of Portland), Clumber (duke of Newcastle), Worksop (formerly belonging to the duke of Norfolk), Thoresby (Earl Manvers, formerly belonging to the duke of Kingston).

Dulcarnon, from an Arabic word meaning 'two-horned' (see *Dhu'lkarnain*), a dilemma; *at dulcarnon,* non-plussed. Chaucer has

I am, til God me bettere mynde sende,
At dulcarnon, right at my wittes ende.

('Troylus and Cryseyde', iii. 881.)

Dulce domum, a Latin poem, the school song of Winchester, of which the author is unknown. According to tradition 'he was a child belonging to the school who was kept at Winchester during the holidays for having committed some serious offence'. Its date is also uncertain, some authorities assigning it to the 16th, others to the 17th cents. The tune is generally accepted as the composition of John Reading, organist of Winchester College 1681–92.

Dulcinea del Toboso, the name given by Don Quixote (q.v.) to the peasant girl Alonza Lorenzo, whom he elects to be mistress of his heart. Hence the English use of the name Dulcinea for a sweetheart.

Dumaine, in Shakespeare's 'Love's Labour's Lost' (q.v.), one of the three lords attending on the king of Navarre.

DUMAS, ALEXANDRE (1803–70), French dramatist and novelist, known generally as 'Dumas père', was the son of a mulatto general of the Empire. His fame rests chiefly on 'Le Comte de Monte-Cristo' (1844–5), a novel of mystery, adventure, and vengeance, and on the long series of romantic novels in which he dealt with many periods of European history. His backgrounds are less solidly constructed than Scott's, and his characters less elaborate, but in vigour and vitality his work compares with the best of Scott's historical novels. His chief series fall into three famous 'groups': (1) the d'Artagnan group ('Les Trois Mousquetaires', 'Vingt ans après', 'Le Vicomte de Bragelonne', etc.); (2) the Chicot group ('La Dame de Monsoreau'—known in England as 'Chicot the Jester', 'Les Quarante-cinq', 'La Reine Margot'); (3) the Revolution group ('Mémoires d'un médecin', 'Le Collier de la reine', 'La Comtesse de Charny', 'Le Chevalier de Maison Rouge'). But Dumas wrote countless books: novels (frequently with assistants to supply his historical material), travel sketches, a cookery book, interesting memoirs, and also many very successful plays.

DUMAS, ALEXANDRE, known as 'Dumas fils' (1824–95), son of A. Dumas the novelist (1803–70, q.v.), was the author of some highly successful social dramas, of which the best known are 'La Dame aux camélias', 'Le Demi-Monde', 'Francillon', and 'Denise'.

Dumb Ox of Cologne, Thomas Aquinas (q.v.), so called by his fellow monks, because of his taciturnity.

Dumbello, LADY, in A. Trollope's Barsetshire series of novels, the married name of Griselda, daughter of Archdeacon Grantly (q.v.).

Dumbiedikes, THE LAIRD OF, in Scott's 'The Heart of Midlothian' (q.v.), (1) the grasping landlord of the widow Butler and Davie Deans; (2) Jock Dumbie, his son, Jeanie Deans's silent suitor.

Dun Cow, Book of the, an Irish manuscript of the 11th cent. containing mythological romances. A fragment of it survives, containing in particular many of the feats of Cuchulain (q.v.).

Dun Cow of Dunsmore, a monstrous animal slain by Guy of Warwick (q.v.).

Dun in the Mire, where 'Dun' (originally a dun horse) is a quasi-proper name for any horse, is the name of an old Christmas game (also called 'drawing Dun out of the mire'), in which the horse in the mire is represented by a heavy log, and the players compete to lift and carry it off.

If thou art Dun, we'll draw thee from the mire.

(Shakespeare, 'Romeo and Juliet', I. iv. 41.)

DUNBAR, WILLIAM (1465?–1530?), Scottish poet, was possibly M.A. of St. Andrews, and for a time a Franciscan friar. He was wrecked off Zealand while carrying out a diplomatic mission for James IV. He was pensioned in 1500. He wrote 'The Thrissill and the Rois', his first great poem, in 1503; 'The Dance of the Sevin Deidly Synnis' between 1503 and 1508; 'The Goldyn Targe', the 'Lament for the Makaris', and 'The Twa Maryit Women and the Wedo', about 1508; and numerous minor pieces. Dunbar wrote a poem 'In Honour of the City of London', inspired by his visit with the ambassadors to the court of Henry VII during the negotiations for the marriage of Margaret Tudor. He described Queen Margaret's visit to the north of Scotland in 'The Quenis Progress at Aberdeen'. He is supposed by some to have fallen at Flodden (1513), by others to have written the 'Orisone' after 1517.

'The Thrissill and the Rois' (Thistle and the Rose) is a political allegory in rhymeroyal; the Rose is Margaret Tudor, married to James IV (the Thistle). 'The Twa Maryit Women and the Wedo' (widow), a conversation in which the three interlocutors relate their experiences of marriage, is a satire on women reminiscent of the 'Wife of Bath'. 'The Goldyn Targe' is an allegory in which the poet, appearing in a dream before the court of Venus, is wounded by the arrows of Beauty in spite of the shield of Reason. In 'The Dance of the Sevin Deidly Synnis', the poet in a trance sees the fiend Mahoun call a dance of unshriven outcasts, who are depicted with extreme vigour. The 'Lament for the Makaris' (makers = poets) is a splendid elegy, suggestive of Villon, with a refrain *Timor mortis conturbat me*, in which he bewails the transitoriness of things, and the deaths of his predecessors (beginning with Chaucer) and contemporaries. His works show much Rabelaisian humour, satirical power, and imagination.

Duncan, in Shakespeare's 'Macbeth' (q.v.), the king of Scotland murdered by Macbeth.

Duncan Gray, a poem by Burns (q.v.).

Dunciad, The, a satirical poem by Pope (q.v.), of which three books were published anonymously in 1728. Its authorship was acknowledged in 1735. The 'New Dunciad' was published in 1742, and this forms the fourth book of the complete work as it ap-

peared in 1743. The poem had been under preparation for some years and its issue was determined by the criticisms of Pope's edition of Shakespeare contained in Theobald's 'Shakespeare Restored'. Theobald (q.v.) was made the hero of the poem in its earlier form, but in the final edition of 1743 Cibber (q.v.) was enthroned in his stead. The satire is directed against Dulness in general, and in the course of it all the authors who have earned Pope's condemnation are held up to ridicule. But the work is not confined to personal abuse, for literary vices receive their share of exposure. The argument of the poem is as follows.

Book I. The reign of Dulness is described. Bayes (i.e. Cibber) is shown debating whether he shall betake himself to the church, or gaming, or party-writing, but is carried off by the goddess and anointed king in the place of Eusden, the poet laureate, who has died.

Book II. This solemnity is graced by games, in which poets, critics, and booksellers contend. There are races, with divers accidents, in which booksellers pursue the phantom of a poet; exercises for the poets; and finally a test for the critics, to decide whether they can hear the works of two authors read aloud without sleeping. But presently spectators, critics, and all, fall fast asleep.

Book III. The king, slumbering with his head on the lap of the goddess, is transported to the Elysian shades, where, under the guidance of Elkanah Settle (q.v.), he sees visions of the past and future triumphs of the empire of Dulness, how this shall extend to the theatres and the court, the arts and the sciences.

Book IV. The realization of these prophecies is described, and the subjugation of the sciences and universities to Dulness, the growth of indolence, the corruption of education, and the consummation of all in the restoration of night and chaos.

Dundreary, LORD, a character in 'Our American Cousin' (1858) by Tom Taylor (q.v.), an indolent brainless peer, a part developed and acted with great success by E. A. Sothern in New York. His long drooping whiskers became proverbial.

Dunedin, a poetic name for Edinburgh (q.v.). 'Dun' is Gaelic for fortress, or indeed for any hill. Edinburgh is the hill on which King Edwin of Northumbria built his castle, 'Edwinsburgh'.

Dunkirk, EVACUATION FROM. The German army having in May 1940 invaded Holland and Belgium and broken through the French defences on the Meuse, got round the right and rear of the Allied armies in the north (which had entered Belgium) and reached Boulogne and Calais. The British army retired to Dunkirk and its beaches, and in spite of fierce German attacks on land, continuous air bombardment, torpedoes and mines, was withdrawn under the protection of the R.A.F.

The withdrawal was completed on 3–4 June, and was effected by 222 light warships and 665 other vessels, making repeated trips during four or five days. The number of men brought off (British and French) was 335,000.

Dunmow Flitch, THE, according to an ancient custom of the manor of Dunmow in Essex, was given to any married couple who after twelve months of marriage could swear that they had maintained perfect harmony and fidelity during that time. The antiquity of the custom is shown by the reference to it in the Prologue to Chaucer's 'Wife of Bath's Tale':

The bacoun was nought fet for hem, I trowe,
That some men fecche in Essex at Dunmowe.

The custom is said to have been instituted by Robert Fitz-Walter in 1244 and is still observed.

DUNNE, FINLEY PETER (1867–1936), American author, remembered as the creator of 'Mr. Dooley', whose shrewd and humorous sayings helped to steady American public opinion during and after the Spanish-American War of 1898.

DUNS SCOTUS, JOANNES, known as the DOCTOR SUBTILIS (1265?–1308?), a Franciscan, who entered the order at Dumfries in 1278. He lectured on the 'Sententiae' of Peter Lombard at Oxford, probably 1300–4, and at Paris, 1304–7. He died at Cologne, probably on 8 Nov. 1308. Duns was the author of 'Quaestiones subtilissimae' on the Metaphysics of Aristotle, of 'Quaestiones quodlibetales', and of the 'Opus Oxoniense', his commentary on the 'Sententiae' (printed Opera Omnia, Paris 1891–5). An extreme realist in philosophy, he borrowed from Ibn Gebirol (*fl.* 1045) the theory of a universal matter, the common basis of all existences, while, by attacking the validity of 'natural theology'; he was one of the first to undermine the harmony of faith and reason, which was an essential point in the doctrine of Thomas Aquinas. He was a vigorous supporter of the doctrine of the Immaculate Conception, and of the freedom of the will.

His followers, the SCOTISTS, were a predominating scholastic sect until the 16th cent. when the system was attacked, first by the humanists, and then by the reformers, as a farrago of needless entities and useless distinctions. The DUNSMEN or DUNSES, on their side, railed against the 'new learning', and the name DUNS or DUNCE, already synonymous with 'cavilling sophist', soon passed into the sense of 'blockhead incapable of learning or scholarship'.

DUNSANY, EDWARD JOHN MORETON DRAX PLUNKETT, *eighteenth Baron* (1878–1957), writer of plays, prose, and verse, of fantasy and myth. His stories include 'The Gods of Pegana' (1905), 'Time and the Gods'

(1906), 'The Sword of Welleran' (1908), 'A Dreamer's Tales' (1910), and 'The Book of Wonder' (1912). His first play, 'The Glittering Gate' was produced at the Abbey Theatre in 1909 and was followed by many others, published under the titles 'Five Plays' (1914), 'Plays of Gods and Men' (1917), 'Plays of Near and Far' (1923), 'Plays for Earth and Air' (1937), &c. He also published volumes of verse and a series of autobiographies.

Dunstable, the name of a town in Bedfordshire, used in such expressions as 'plain as Dunstable way', apparently referring to the road from London to Dunstable, a part of the ancient Roman Road called Watling Street, notable for its long straight stretches, and general evenness. [OED.]

Dunstable, MISS, a character in A. Trollope's 'Dr. Thorne' and 'Framley Parsonage' (qq.v.).

Dunstan, ST. (924–88), born at Glastonbury of a noble family, was educated by the Irish scholars who had settled at that place. He became a favourite of King Æthelstan, but was expelled from the court on an accusation of being a wizard. He spent part of the period of his disgrace with Ælfheah (Elphege), bishop of Winchester, by whom he was persuaded to take the monastic vows. He is also said to have practised the arts of metal-working, painting, and transcribing. Dunstan was restored to favour by King Eadmund and appointed by him abbot of Glastonbury. He restored the abbey materially and spiritually and made it a famous school. He became one of the chief advisers of kings Eadmund and Eadred, but when King Eadwig succeeded, he incurred his disfavour by rebuking him for his vicious propensities and retired to Flanders in disgrace in 956, Count Arnulf assigning him a residence at Ghent. Eadgar recalled Dunstan to him and appointed him bishop of Worcester (957), bishop of London (959), and archbishop of Canterbury (961). Dunstan devoted his energies to restoring and reforming English monasteries and to making the Danes an integral part of the nation. He averted civil war by crowning Eadward in 975, and foretold to King Æthelred the calamities by which the nation would expiate Eadward's murder. His festival is kept on 19 May. There is a famous late story of the Devil appearing in the form of a woman to tempt Dunstan, who seized the apparition by the nose with red-hot smith's tongs.

DUNTON, JOHN (1659–1733), a publisher and bookseller, who in 1690–6 issued the 'Athenian Gazette' (afterwards 'Athenian Mercury') dealing with philosophical and other abstruse matters, and was the author of a large number of political pamphlets, and of 'The Life and Errors of John Dunton' (1705).

Duodecimo, generally abbreviated '12mo', a book in which each leaf is one-twelfth of a whole sheet. Hence applied to a person or thing of diminutive size.

Dupin, the detective in the detective tales of Poe (q.v.).

Durandal, see *Durindana*.

Durandarte, a hero of Spanish legend and ballad, killed at Roncesvalles. See 'Don Quixote', Pt. II, ch. xxiii. He is the subject of a ballad by M. G. Lewis (q.v.).

Durden, DAME, see *Dame Durden*.

Durdles, the stone-mason in Dickens's 'Edwin Drood' (q.v.).

Dürer, ALBRECHT (1471–1528), German painter and engraver, the son of a Hungarian goldsmith who had settled in Nuremberg. He was deeply impressed by the Italian Renaissance and introduced to the North the ideals and forms which he encountered in his visits to Italy. He wrote treatises on proportion and artistic theory, as well as a diary of a visit to the Netherlands, and he engraved and published series of woodcuts and copper engravings, including the 'Great' and 'Little Passion' and the 'Knight, Death, and the Devil'.

D'URFEY, THOMAS (1653–1723), a French Huguenot by descent, familiarly known as Tom Durfey, wrote a large number of songs, tales, satires, melodramas, and farces. He was a scurrilous fellow, but the familiar friend of everyone, including Charles II and James II. He replied to the strictures of Jeremy Collier (q.v.) in his 'The Campaigners', a comedy, 1698. Among his other comedies may be mentioned 'Madame Fickle' (1677) and 'The Virtuous Wife' (1680). His 'Wit and Mirth, or Pills to purge Melancholy', 1719, is an interesting collection of songs and ballads.

Durga, see *Siva*.

Durham, CONSTANTIA, a character in Meredith's 'The Egoist' (q.v.).

Durham Report, *The,* 'on the Affairs of British North America', 1839, was made by the first earl of Durham, governor-general of the British provinces in N. America and high commissioner for the adjustment of important questions in Lower and Upper Canada. It is said to have been mostly written by his secretary, Charles Buller; it was notable for its liberal character and determined the policy of Durham's successors. There is a good life of Lord Durham ('Radical Jack') by Chester W. New (Oxford, 1929).

Durindana or DURANDAL, the sword of Roland or Orlando, which had been that of Hector of Troy.

DURRELL, LAWRENCE GEORGE (1912–), poet and novelist. The Eastern Mediterranean, where he spent a large part of his life, forms the background to much of his writing. His poetry includes 'Private Country' (1943), 'Cities, Plains, and People' (1946), 'On seeming to Presume' (1948), 'The Tree of Idleness' (1955), and 'Selected Poems' (1956). 'The Alexandria Quartet' (completed in 1960) comprises four novels, 'Justine', 'Balthazar', 'Mountolive', and 'Clea'.

Dutch, MY OLD, the title of a famous music-hall song, put in the mouth of a coster-monger; the word 'Dutch' is an abbreviation of 'Dutchess' (old spelling of 'Duchess') and is slang for 'wife'.

Dutch courage, courage induced by liquor, an allusion to the drinking habits ascribed to the 'Dutch' (meaning perhaps little more than 'foreigners').

Dutch Courtezan, *The,* a comedy by Marston (q.v.), printed in 1605.

Young Freevill, being about to marry Beatrice, daughter of Sir Hubert Subboys, determines to break his connexion with Franceschina, the Dutch Courtezan. He introduces the latter to his self-righteous friend Malheureux, who becomes violently enamoured of her. She consents to gratify his passion if he will kill Freevill, and bring proof of the deed in the shape of a ring given by Beatrice to Freevill. Malheureux discloses the situation to Freevill, who consents to help him. A pretended quarrel is arranged, Freevill disappears, Malheureux takes the ring to Franceschina, who hastens to communicate the news to old Freevill and Sir Hubert Subboys. Malheureux is arrested for the murder of Freevill and sentenced to death. At the last moment Young Freevill appears, and begs forgiveness for the device that he has adopted to cure his friend of his passion. Franceschina is condemned to the whip and gaol.

Duval, CLAUDE (1643–70), a highwayman notorious for his daring and gallantry. He was born in Normandy, came to England, took to the road, and was executed. His death was the subject of a satiric ode by Samuel Butler.

Dwarf, in Scandinavian mythology, the name of a class of supernatural beings sprung from the decaying body of Ymir (q.v.). They were of diminutive form, dwelt under the earth, and their nature partook of good and evil. They were particularly skilful in working metals. It is they who kill Kvasir, from whose blood the Odhaerir (q.v.) or poetic mead is made, and who forge the chain (Gleipnir) with which Fenrir (q.v.) is bound.

Dyck, SIR ANTHONY VAN (1599–1641), Flemish painter, born in Antwerp. He began to work in Rubens's studio when a youth, and soon became his chief assistant. He spent a short time in the winter of 1620–1 in the service of James I, but returned to Flanders and was in Italy from 1621 to 1625. In 1632 he came to England as court painter to Charles I. He was knighted and had great success, painting many portraits of the royal family and the Court. He married a lady of the Scottish house of Ruthven in 1640. In England there was little patronage for religious and history painting, and Van Dyck's output was almost exclusively portraits. But, a painter of international repute with a knowledge of the best continental work, he widened the horizons of English art and set the style of the grand portrait for nearly two centuries. Though courtly and sophisticated, his portraits show a keen understanding of character. He died in England and was buried in Old St. Paul's.

DYER, SIR EDWARD (d. 1607), was educated either at Balliol College or Broadgates Hall, Oxford. He was introduced by the earl of Leicester at court, where he held various official positions. His most famous poem is the description of contentment, beginning, 'My mind to me a kingdom is'. Meres mentions him as 'famous for elegy', and according to Collier he translated part of Theocritus. Sir Philip Sidney's pastoral, 'Join, mates, in mirth with me', is addressed to him and Sir Fulke Greville.

DYER, GEORGE (1755–1841), educated at Christ's Hospital and Emmanuel College, Cambridge, usher at Dedham Grammar School, and subsequently in a school at Northampton, and author of poems and critical essays. He is remembered principally as the friend of C. Lamb (q.v.), who speaks of him as a gentle and kindly eccentric. He was nearly drowned in the New River while in a fit of abstraction. See 'Amicus Redivivus' in the 'Essays of Elia'.

DYER, JOHN (1699–1758), a Welshman remembered as the author of 'Grongar Hill', a poem descriptive of the scenery of the river Towy, published in 1726. His later didactic poems, 'The Ruins of Rome' (1740) and 'The Fleece' (1757, on the unpromising subject of sheep and the wool trade), merit less notice.

Dymoke, see *Champion of the King*.

Dynasts, The, *An Epic-Drama of the War with Napoleon, in three Parts, nineteen Acts and one hundred and thirty Scenes*, by Thomas Hardy (q.v.), was published in 1904–8: Part I in 1904, Part II in 1906, and Part III in 1908.

This great work is written mainly in blank verse, partly in a variety of other metres, partly in prose. The stirring events of history with which it deals are recounted in the descriptive passages and stage directions. The whole centres round the tragic figure of Napoleon. Part I opens with the year 1805, and Napoleon's threat of invasion. It presents the House of Commons discussing the repeal of the Defence Act, Napoleon's coronation at Milan, the preparations at Boulogne for invasion, the battles of Ulm and Austerlitz, Trafalgar, the death of Nelson, and the death of Pitt.

In Part II we have the defeat of the Prussians at Jena, the meeting of Napoleon and Alexander at Tilsit, the battle of Wagram, the fall of Godoy and the abdication of the king of Spain, and war in Spain (Coruña, Talavera, Torres Vedras), the divorce of Josephine, and Napoleon's marriage with Marie Louise.

Part III presents the Russian expedition of 1812, the British victories in the Pyrenees, the battle of Leipzig, Napoleon's abdication, his return from Elba, the ball in Brussels, Quatre-Bras, and Waterloo. By the side of the major scenes are little 'patches of life' seen at close quarters, episodes showing how these great events affected English rustics in Wessex, private soldiers, camp-followers, and other humble folks. And above them all, 'supernatural spectators of the terrestrial action', are 'certain impersonated abstractions or Intelligences, called Spirits', the Ancient Spirit of the Years, the Spirit of the Pities, the Spirits Sinister and Ironic, the Spirit of Rumour, with their respective choruses; also the Shade of the Earth, and the Recording Angels. At the head of them is the Immanent Will, the force, unconscious and heedless, that moves the world. They are introduced not, as the author is careful to point out in his preface, 'as a systematized philosophy warranted to lift "the burthen of the mystery" of this unintelligible world', but to give by their comments a universal signification to the particular events recounted.

Dysmas, see *Dismas*.

E

Eadgar, king of England 959–75. In 957 Eadgar, the younger of the two brothers, divided the realm with Eadwig: Eadwig died in 959, and Eadgar united the whole realm till his death in 975.

EADMER (d. 1124?), a monk of Canterbury, who wrote a Latin chronicle of the events of his own time down to 1122 ('Historia Novorum in Anglia'), and a biography of his friend and leader Anselm.

Eadmund (841–70), see *Edmund*.

Eadmund, king of England, 940–6.

Eadmund Ironside, king of England in 1016. After dividing the realm with Canute the Dane, he died suddenly (probably murdered by Canute).

Eadred, king of England, 946–55.

Eadward the Confessor, king of England, 1042–66.

Eadward the Elder, king of England, 901–24.

Eadward the Martyr, king of England, 975–9.

Eadwig, king of England, 955–9, see *Eadgar*.

Eagle, SOLOMON, a crazy fanatic in Ainsworth's 'Old St. Paul's'.

Eagle of Meaux, THE, Bossuet (q.v.).

Eames, JOHNNY, a character in A. Trollope's 'The Small House at Allington' and 'Last Chronicle of Barset' (qq.v.).

Earine, (1) in Jonson's 'The Sad Shepherd' (q.v.), the shepherdess loved by Æglamour; (2) in G. Moore's 'Aphrodite in Aulis', the girl who marries the sculptor Rhesus and inspires him with his ideal figure of Aphrodite.

EARLE, JOHN, see *Microcosmographie*.

Early English Text Society, founded in 1864 by Frederick James Furnivall (q.v.), for the publication of Early and Middle English texts.

Earnscliff, a character in Scott's 'The Black Dwarf' (q.v.).

Earnshaw, HINDLEY and HARETON, characters in Emily Brontë's 'Wuthering Heights' (q.v.).

Earthly Paradise, THE, see *Paradise*.

Earthly Paradise, The, a poem by W. Morris (q.v.), published in 1868–70, consisting of a prologue and twenty-four tales, in Chaucerian metres.

The prologue tells how a company of Norsemen, fleeing from the pestilence, set sail in search of the fabled Earthly Paradise 'across the western sea where none grow old'. They are disappointed of their quest and return after long wanderings, 'shrivelled, bent and grey', to a 'nameless city in a distant sea' where the ancient Greek gods are still worshipped. They are hospitably received and there spend their remaining years. Twice in each month they meet their hosts at a feast and a tale is told, alternately by one of the elders of the city and one of the wanderers. The tales of the former are on classical subjects (Atalanta, Perseus, Cupid and Psyche, Alcestis, Pygmalion, the Apples of the Hesperides, Bellerophon, etc.), those of the latter from Norse and other medieval sources. Among the wanderers' tales, 'The Lovers of Gudrun' (q.v.), a version of the Icelandic Laxdæla Saga, is the most striking. Between the tales of each month are interpolated lyrics in which the author gives expression to his sense of the effect of the changing year on the English landscape.

East India Company, THE, or the 'Company of Merchants trading to the East Indies', was incorporated in 1600, and from 1773 had the chief part in the political administration of Hindustan, until 1858. After the Mutiny the government was assumed by the Crown. It was familiarly known as 'John Company', an appellation taken over from the name JAN KOMPANIE by which the Dutch East India

Company, and now the Dutch government, are known to natives in the East.

East Lynne, a novel by Mrs. H. Wood (q.v.).

Easter Day, one of the great festivals of the Christian Church, commemorating the Resurrection of Christ, and corresponding to the Jewish Passover. It is celebrated on the first Sunday after the calendar full moon which happens on or after 21 Mar. The name Easter is derived from the Saxon goddess EOSTRE, originally the dawn-goddess, whose festival was celebrated at the vernal equinox.

Easter Island, in the S. Pacific, probably discovered by Capt. Davis in 1687, but first visited by the Dutch navigator Roggeveen on Easter Day 1722, and later by Capt. Cook, when it was uninhabited. It is noted for its remarkable monolithic statues facing seawards, some of them 20 feet and more in height, erected, according to Roggeveen, for protection from enemies coming from the sea. There were, he says, special priests who served the idols. The idols had long ears, and the people had their ears dragged down to their shoulders. The date of the idols is unknown. The inhabitants of the island also used a pictographic script engraved on wooden tablets.

Eastern Church, see *Orthodox Church*.

Eastern Empire, the more easterly of the two parts into which the Roman Empire was divided in A.D. 395. Its capital was Byzantium (Constantinople), which was taken by the Turks under Mahomet II in 1453.

Eastward hoe, a comedy by G. Chapman, Jonson, and J. Marston (qq.v.), printed in 1605, having been previously performed by the Children of the Revels at the Blackfriars. The literary controversy between Jonson and Marston had for the time ceased. A passage derogatory to the Scots (III. iii. 40–47) gave offence at court, and the three authors were imprisoned, but released on the intercession of powerful friends. The play is particularly interesting for the light it throws on London life of the time. Like Dekker's 'Shoemaker's Holiday', it gives a sympathetic picture of a tradesman.

The plot contrasts the careers of the virtuous and idle apprentices, Golding and Quicksilver, of the goldsmith Touchstone; and the fates of his two daughters, the modest Mildred, who marries the industrious Golding, and the immodest Gertrude who, in order to ride in her own coach, marries the penniless adventurer Sir Petronel Flash. Golding soon rises to the dignity of a deputy-alderman, while Sir Petronel, having sent off his lady in a coach to an imaginary castle of his, and filched her dowry, sets off for Virginia, accompanied by the prodigal Quicksilver, who has robbed his master. They are wrecked on the Isle of Dogs, and brought up before Golding, the deputy-alderman. After some days in prison, where their mortifications lead them to repent, they are released at Golding's intercession.

Eatanswill, the scene of the parliamentary election in Dickens's 'Pickwick Papers' (q.v.).

Ebionites, a body of heretics of the 1st and 2nd cents. who held that Jesus was a mere man and that the Mosaic law was binding upon Christians. [OED.]

Eblana, in imprints, Dublin.

Eblis, in the Muslim religion, the Devil, the chief of the apostate angels, who refused to worship Adam. He figures in Beckford's 'Vathek' (q.v.).

Eborācum, in imprints, York.

Ebuda, in the 'Orlando Furioso' (q.v.), the island on which Angelica was exposed to the Orc.

Ecbatana, the ancient capital of the Medes (q.v.). Its site is now occupied by Hamadan.

Ecce Homo, 'Behold the man' (John xix. 5), hence used for a picture representing Christ wearing the crown of thorns. See also *Seeley*.

Eccles, ROBERT, a character in Meredith's 'Rhoda Fleming' (q.v.). (He calls himself Robert Armstrong in the early stages of the story.)

Ecclesiastes (Greek rendering of the Hebrew *Koheleth*, preacher), one of the books of the O.T., formerly ascribed to King Solomon, but now thought to be of later date, probably of the 3rd cent. B.C. The author exhorts to wisdom, industry, and the fear of God; but the book concludes, as it begins, sombrely: 'Vanity of vanities, saith the Preacher; all is vanity.'

Ecclesiastical History of Bede, see *Historia Ecclesiastica.*

Ecclesiastical Politie, Of the Laws of, see *Laws of Ecclesiastical Politie.*

Ecclesiastical Sonnets: see *Wordsworth.*

Ecclesiasticus, meaning the 'Book of the Church', a name given to it in the African Church owing to its use as a book of instruction, is a book of the Apocrypha otherwise known as 'The Wisdom of Jesus the son of Sirach'. It is a collection of moral and practical maxims, dating probably from the first half of the 2nd cent. B.C.

Echidna, in Greek mythology, a monster, half woman and half snake. She was the mother of various other monsters of antiquity, such as Chimaera, Orthrus the formidable dog of Geryon, Cerberus, the Sphinx, the Hydra (qq.vv.). In Spenser's 'Faerie Queene' (VI. vi), she is the mother of the Blatant Beast (q.v.).

Echo, according to Ovid was an Oread (q.v.) whose loquacity caused Juno to change her into an echo, something which cannot speak until someone else has spoken, and then must repeat the words it hears. She fell in love with Narcissus and pined away for love of him till only her voice remained.

Eckermann, JOHANN, see *Goethe.*

Eckhart or **Eckhard,** JOHANNES, known as MEISTER ECKHART (1260?–1327?), a German philosopher and mystic. He was a Dominican and received the degree of Doctor from Boniface VIII. He was subsequently summoned before the Inquisition and made a partial recantation of his doctrines. He is regarded as the founder of German mysticism.

Eckhart, TRUSTY, the subject of a German legend and of a tale by Ludwig Tieck (translated by Carlyle). In the latter he is a follower of the duke of Burgundy who gives his son to save his master's life. He incurs unjust suspicion, and another of his sons is killed by the duke. He is reconciled with the duke as the latter lies dying and is made guardian of his children.

In the German legend of Holle or Holde (Venus) he is an old man who appears on Maundy Thursday to warn people against the monsters that rush through the streets in Holle's train on that night; or sits outside the Venusberg to warn passing knights of its dangers.

Eclectics, a class of philosophers who neither attached themselves to any school, nor constructed independent systems, but 'selected such doctrines as pleased them in every school' (Liddell and Scott). In modern use the term 'eclectic' has both the same signification and a vaguer sense of one unfettered by a narrow system in matters of opinion or practice.

Eclipse, the famous race-horse, born during an eclipse, died in 1789, aged 25 years. He was never beaten. He was the property of Colonel O'Kelly, an Irish adventurer, who, born in humble circumstances, became a count of the Holy Roman Empire. The saying 'Eclipse first and the rest nowhere' arose on the occasion of Eclipse's first race, the Queen's Plate at Winchester, when O'Kelly made his famous bet of placing the horses in order, and won it by running Eclipse first and the rest nowhere.

Eclogue, from Greek ἐκλογή, a selection, is a short poem, especially a pastoral dialogue, such as Virgil's 'Bucolics'.

Eclogue, Virgil's Fourth, see *Virgil.*

Eclogues, The, of A. Barclay (q.v.), written about 1515, are interesting as the earliest English pastorals, anticipating Spenser. They are moral and satirical in character, dealing with such subjects as the evils of a court life and the happiness of the countryman's lot. They are modelled upon Baptist Mantuan and the 'Miseriae Curialium' of Aeneas Sylvius (qq.vv.).

Economist, The, a weekly financial and commercial review founded in 1843. James Wilson was its first editor. It advocated free trade and the repeal of the corn laws and took up a sound attitude in opposition to the reckless railway speculation of the middle of the century. Among its later editors was Bagehot (q.v.), Wilson's son-in-law.

Economy of Vegetation, The, see *Darwin (E.).*

Ector, Sir, in Malory's 'Morte Darthur' (q.v.), the knight to whom the infant King Arthur was entrusted. He was father of Sir Kay (q.v.), the seneschal.

Ector de Maris, Sir, in Malory's 'Morte Darthur' (q.v.), a knight of the Round Table and brother of Sir Launcelot. It is he who, in the last chapter of the work, finds Sir Launcelot dead and utters his great lament over him.

Edda, an old Norse name of two distinct Icelandic books:

(*a*) The *Prose* or *Younger Edda.* A summary of Odinic mythology, followed by two treatises on poetic composition, the whole forming a manual of instruction for poets. This work is attributed to Snorri Sturlason (q.v., *c.* 1230).

(*b*) The *Poetic* or *Elder Edda.* A collection (made *c.* 1200) of old Norse poems on cosmogony, mythology, and traditions of Norse heroes. The name of 'Edda of Sæmund' was applied to this work, from an erroneous attribution of the compilation to Sæmund.

The Eddas are the chief source of our knowledge of Scandinavian mythology.

EDDINGTON, Sir ARTHUR STANLEY (1882–1944), educated at Owens College, Manchester, and Trinity College, Cambridge, and professor of astronomy at Cambridge, a distinguished astronomer, noted for his researches into the stellar system and the internal constitution of stars; also for his contributions to the theory of Relativity and the popularization of modern physical theory ('The Expanding Universe', 1933).

EDDY, Mrs. MARY BAKER GLOVER (1821–1910), born at Bow, New Hampshire, the founder of Christian Science, of which she expounded the doctrine in 'Science and Health' (1875).

Eden, in Dickens's 'Martin Chuzzlewit' (q.v.), a dismal pestilential settlement in the United States, promoted by swindlers, where even Mark Tapley finds it creditable to be jolly.

Eden, Garden of, in the Biblical narrative, the first abode of man, a region from which issued the four rivers, Hiddekel (Tigris), Euphrates, Pison, and Gihon, which point to some locality in the neighbourhood of Mesopotamia (Gen. ii. 8 et seq.). The word Eden means 'delight', and the term is used figuratively to signify a paradise.

EDEN, EMILY (1797–1869), daughter of William Eden, first baron Auckland, accompanied her brother, governor-general of India, to that country, and published 'Portraits of the People and Princes of India' (1844), 'Up the Country' (1866), and 'Letters from India' (1872); also two novels, 'The Semi-detached

House' (1859) and 'The Semi-attached Couple' (1860).

EDEN, RICHARD (1521?–76), translator, a precursor of Hakluyt (q.v.) in disseminating information about early navigations and discoveries. He translated Münster's 'Cosmography' (1553), Peter Martyr's 'Decades of the Newe Worlde or West India' (1555), and 'The Art of Navigation' from the Spanish of Martin Cortes (1561).

Eden Bower, a poem by D. G. Rossetti, included in his 'Poems' of 1870. Lilith (q.v.), Adam's mythical first wife, persuades Satan to let her personate him in the temptation of Eve, the woman who has ousted her.

Eden Hall, Luck of, see *Luck of Eden Hall.*

Edgar, (1) a character in Shakespeare's 'King Lear' (q.v.); (2) master of Ravenswood, the hero of Scott's 'Bride of Lammermoor' (q.v.).

Edgar Huntly, a Gothic novel of the American frontier, published in 1799, by C. B. Brown (q.v.).

Edge-hill, see *Jago.*

EDGEWORTH, MARIA (1767–1849), daughter of Richard Lovell Edgeworth (1744–1817), an Irishman and an educationist, who wrote jointly with his daughter 'Practical Education' (1798), a work which shows the influence of Rousseau's ideas. Maria Edgeworth was a successful novelist, and a friend of Sir W. Scott, who admired her work. Her principal novels, devoted in great part to depicting Irish life, were 'Castle Rackrent' (q.v.), published in 1800; 'Belinda' (1801), a picture of society at the end of the 18th cent., commended by Jane Austen in 'Northanger Abbey' (q.v.); 'The Absentee' (q.v.), published in 1812, one of a series of 'Tales of Fashionable Life'; 'Ormond' (q.v.), published in 1817. She is also remembered for the excellent presentation of child life in 'The Parent's Assistant' (1796–1801), 'Early Lessons' (1801), 'Moral Tales' (1801), 'Popular Tales' (1804), 'Frank' (1822), and 'Harry and Lucy' (1825).

Edict of Nantes, issued by Henri IV of France in 1598, granting liberty of conscience to the Protestants, certain facilities for worship, access to public offices, permission for Protestant schools, &c. The Edict was revoked by Louis XIV in 1685.

Edinburgh, the capital of Scotland, was originally a military station established by Edwin, the first Christian king of Northumbria (617–33), from whom it takes its name. It was made a royal burgh by charter of David I (1124–53) and became the capital in the 15th cent. 'Dunedin' and 'Edina' are poetical names for Edinburgh.

Edinburgh Castle was the residence of King Malcolm II (d. 1034) and the earliest building still standing, St. Margaret's chapel, may have been built by the wife of Malcolm

III, St. Margaret, who died in the castle in
1093. In the 14th cent. it was held for seventeen years by the English. The Old Parliament Hall was the scene of the Black Dinner
of 1440 when the earl of Douglas and his
brother were murdered. James VI of Scotland and I of England was born in the 'Old
Palace', built in 1555. The Castle is crowned
by the Scottish War Memorial, built by Sir
Robert Lorimer in 1927. 'Mons Meg', a
15th-cent. cannon, perhaps made at Mallance
in Galloway, stands on the ramparts.

Edinburgh Review, The, a quarterly periodical established in Oct. 1802 by Francis Jeffrey,
Henry Brougham, and Sydney Smith (qq.v.),
and published originally by Messrs. Constable. It initiated a new era in literary
criticism, adopting a higher and more independent tone than its predecessors. Though
Tories (including at first Sir W. Scott) wrote
for it, it assumed gradually a completely
Whig attitude. It was notable for its condemnation of the school of Lake poets. Among
famous contributors to it were Macaulay,
Carlyle, Hazlitt, Arnold, Arthur Stanley, Sir
J. Stephen, and Gladstone. 'The Edinburgh
Review' came to an end in 1929.

There was an earlier 'Edinburgh Review'
of 1755, but although it had distinguished
contributors (including Adam Smith), only
two numbers of it appeared.

Edison, THOMAS ALVA (1847–1931), born
in the United States of mixed Dutch and
Scottish ancestry, had a very limited education and became a newsboy on the railways
at 12, and afterwards a telegraph operator,
devoting his spare time to study and experiments. His first patent was taken out in 1868
and this was followed by a number of inventions, among others one that contributed
an important element to the Bell telephone.
His most important inventions were the
'phonograph', or original of the gramophone,
in 1877, and the incandescent electric lamp
in 1879. He also devised a 'kinetoscopic
camera' for taking moving pictures, and did
much to develop the transmission and storage
of electrical power.

Edith Granger, see *Granger.*

Edith of Lorn, the heroine of Scott's 'Lord
of the Isles' (q.v.).

Edith Plantagenet, THE LADY, kinswoman
of Richard I, a character in Scott's 'The
Talisman' (q.v.).

Edith Swan-neck, mistress of Harold II,
king of England. Harold had three sons and
two daughters, probably by her. When he was
dead, she was fetched to identify the body,
which she did not by the face, for that was
mangled, but by some marks known only
to her.

Edmund or EADMUND (841–70), king of the
East Angles, martyr and saint, was born at
Nuremberg, the son of King Alkmund, and
adopted by Offa, king of the East Angles,

about 854. He succeeded to Offa's throne
in 855. He was defeated by the Danes at
Hoxne, bound to a tree, scourged, shot at
with arrows, and beheaded on refusing to
renounce Christianity. He was interred at
Hoxne, and subsequently enshrined at Bury
St. Edmunds. He is commemorated on 20
Nov.

Edmund, in Shakespeare's 'King Lear'
(q.v.), the bastard son of the earl of Gloucester.

Edom o' Gordon, see *Adam o' Gordon.*

Edward, a fine old Scottish ballad of domestic tragedy, included in Percy's 'Reliques' and
beginning:

Why does your brand sae drop wi' blude,
                                Edward, Edward?

Edward the Confessor, see *Eadward.*

Edward the Martyr, see *Eadward.*

Edward I, king of England, 1272–1307.

Edward II, king of England, 1307–27.

Edward II, an historical drama in blank
verse by Marlowe (q.v.), produced in 1593.
It deals with the recall by Edward II, on his
accession, of his favourite, Piers Gaveston;
the revolt of the barons, and the capture and
execution of Gaveston; the period during
which Spenser (Hugh le Despenser) succeeded Gaveston as the king's favourite; the
estrangement of Queen Isabella from her
husband; her rebellion, supported by her
paramour Mortimer, against the king; the
capture of the latter, his abdication of the
crown, and his murder in Berkeley Castle.
'The death-scene of Marlowe's king', wrote
Charles Lamb, 'moves pity and terror beyond
any scene, ancient or modern, with which I
am acquainted' ('Specimens of the English
Dramatists').

Edward III, king of England, 1327–77.

Edward III, The Raigne of, an historical
play, published in 1596, of uncertain authorship, attributed by some, at least in part, to
Shakespeare.

The two first acts are concerned mainly
with the dishonourable wooing of the countess of Salisbury by the king, who is finally
brought to a sense of shame by her determination to kill herself if he pursues his suit.
The rest is occupied with the French wars.

Edward IV, king of England, 1461–83.

Edward V, king of England in 1483, in
which year he was deposed and murdered.
See *Princes in the Tower.*

Edward VI, king of England, 1547–53.

Edward VII, king of England, 1901–10.

Edward VIII, king of England, 20 Jan.–
11 Dec. 1936.

Edwardian, characteristic of the early years
of the present century (roughly, the reign
of Edward VII), a term frequently used in
contrast with 'Victorian' (q.v.), as implying a

reaction from some of the tendencies of the Victorian age, notably its self-satisfaction and unquestioning acceptance of authority in religion, morality, and literature. The Edwardian age is in the main an age of criticism, of questioning, and of refusal to accept established institutions. This tendency is seen, for instance, in the works of G. B. Shaw, H. G. Wells, and Arnold Bennett. From another point of view the Edwardian age appears as a time of great prosperity and glitter, of social stability and spacious ease, the halcyon period before the storm.

EDWARDS, JONATHAN (1703–58), born in Connecticut, the philosopher, ardent divine, and formidable preacher who provoked the movement of religious revival and exaltation in New England known as the 'Great Awakening'. In his 'Treatise concerning Religious Affections' (1746) he nicely discriminated between the state of grace and the state of worldliness. His attempt to make this distinction a criterion of fitness to receive the Eucharist led to his dismissal from the charge of the church of Northampton, Mass., in 1750. He then became for six years a missionary to the Indians. His principal philosophical work, 'A Careful and Strict Enquiry into the Modern Prevailing Notions of . . . Freedom of Will' (1754), in which he combated from a predestinarian standpoint the Arminian view of liberty, occasioned Boswell's remark that 'the only relief I had was to forget it', and Johnson's aphorism, 'All theory is against freedom of the will; all experience for it'. (Boswell, 'Life of Johnson', under the year 1778, ed. G. B. Hill, iii. 291.)

EDWARDS, RICHARD (1523?–66), of Corpus Christi College and Christ Church, Oxford, was master of the children of the Chapel Royal, 1561. He composed 'Palamon and Arcite' (now lost) for Queen Elizabeth's entertainment at Oxford, 1566. The 'Excellent Comedie of . . . Damon and Pithias' (q.v., 1571) is his only extant play. He was the compiler of the 'Paradise of Daynty Devises' (q.v.), published after his death (1576).

Edwin and Angelina, see *Hermit.*

Edwin Drood, *The Mystery of,* an unfinished novel by Dickens (q.v.), published in 1870.

The fathers of Edwin Drood and Rosa Bud, both of them widowers, have before their deaths betrothed their young children to one another. The orphan Rosa has been brought up in Miss Twinkleton's school at Cloisterham (Rochester), where Edwin, also an orphan, has an uncle, John Jasper, the precentor of the cathedral, to whom he is devoted and who appears to return the devotion. It is understood that the two young people are to marry as soon as Edwin comes of age, although this very understanding has been fatal to love between them. Jasper, a sinister and hypocritical character, gives Rosa music-lessons and loves her passionately, but inspires her with terror and disgust. There now come

upon the scene two other orphans, Neville and Helena Landless. Neville and Edwin at once become enemies, for Neville admires Rosa and is disgusted at Edwin's unappreciative treatment of her. This enmity is secretly fomented by Jasper and there is a violent quarrel between the young men. On the last of Edwin's periodical visits to Cloisterham before the time of his anticipated marriage, Rosa and he recognize that this marriage will not be for their happiness, and break off the engagement. But Edwin postpones telling his uncle Jasper. That same night Edwin disappears under circumstances pointing to foul play and suggestive of the possibility that he has been murdered by Neville Landless, a theory actively supported by Jasper. But Jasper receives with uncontrollable symptoms of dismay the intelligence that the engagement of Edwin and Rosa had been broken off before Edwin's disappearance, and this betrayal of himself is noted by Mr. Grewgious, Rosa's eccentric good-hearted guardian. Neville is arrested, but as the body of Edwin is not found, is released untried. He is ostracized by public opinion and is obliged to hide himself as a student in London. The remainder of the fragment of the novel is occupied with the continued machinations of Jasper against Neville and his pursuit of Rosa, who in terror of him flies to her guardian in London; with the countermoves prepared by Mr. Grewgious, assisted by the amiable minor canon Mr. Crisparkle, and a new ally, the retired naval officer, Mr. Tartar; also with the proceedings of the mysterious Mr. Datchery, directed against Jasper. Of the solution or catastrophe intended by the author no hint exists, beyond those which the fragment itself contains, and the statement as to the broad lines of the plot given by John Forster, the biographer of Dickens. There have been many conjectures, turning mainly on two points: whether Edwin Drood had in fact been murdered or had miraculously survived; and who was Datchery. With regard to the latter it has been suggested for instance that Datchery was Drood himself, or Grewgious, or Grewgious's clerk Bazzard, or Helena Landless, in disguise.

Besides the persons above referred to, mention should be made of some notable characters: the fatuous Mr. Sapsea, auctioneer and mayor; Mr. Honeythunder, the bullying 'philanthropist'; the grim stonemason Durdles, and his attendant imp 'Deputy'.

Efreet, see *Afreet.*

Égalité, the name assumed by Philippe, Duc d'Orléans, in 1792. He was a member of the Constituent Assembly and Convention, gave his vote for the death of Louis XVI, and was himself arrested and executed in 1793. He was the father of King Louis Philippe.

EGAN, PIERCE, the elder (1772–1849), is remembered as the author of 'Life in London; or the Day and Night Scenes of Jerry Hawthorn and his elegant friend Corinthian

Tom', issued in monthly numbers from 1820 (the completed book in 1821), illustrated by George and Robert Cruikshank. The book is a description of the life of the 'man about town' of the day, interesting for the light it throws on the manners of the period and for the many slang phrases it introduces. In 1824 Egan began the issue of a weekly paper, 'Pierce Egan's Life in London and Sporting Guide', which subsequently developed into the well-known sporting journal 'Bell's Life in London'. The title of this periodical was taken from John Bell (1745–1831), printer, publisher, and journalist, one of the founders of the 'Morning Post' and proprietor of 'Bell's Weekly Messenger', whose fame and popularity had given his name a commercial value (see Stanley Morison, 'John Bell', 1930). 'Bell's Life' was in 1859 incorporated in 'Sporting Life'. Egan was also author of the successful 'Boxiana; or Sketches of Antient and Modern Pugilism' (founded on an earlier work by George Smeeton), published first in parts in 1812–13, then reprinted in volumes and added to in 1815–29 (five volumes in all).

EGAN, PIERCE, the younger (1814–80), novelist, son of the preceding and associated with him in several of his works. He wrote a vast number of novels and is accounted a 'pioneer of cheap literature'.

Egdon Heath, the scene of Hardy's 'The Return of the Native' (q.v.).

Egĕria, an Italian goddess of fountains, who had a sacred spring near the Porta Capena of Rome. According to Roman legend she was the counsellor and wife of King Numa (the successor of Romulus), who, in order that he might commend his laws to the people, declared that they were previously sanctified and approved by her.

EGERTON, SIR THOMAS, *Baron Ellesmere* and *Viscount Brackley* (1540?–1617), was lord chancellor from 1603 till his death. He befriended Francis Bacon. John Donne was his secretary for four years (1596–1601), and Samuel Daniel and John Owen addressed poems to him. He left judicial and legal treatises in manuscript.

EGGLESTON, EDWARD (1837–1902), itinerant Methodist preacher and author, born in Indiana, U.S.A. His fame rests upon 'The Hoosier Schoolmaster' (1871), in which the author sought to depict, faithfully and realistically, the men and women of the backwoods of his native state.

Egil, in Scandinavian legend, a brother of Völunder (see *Wayland*). He was a skilled workman and archer, and, like the William Tell of later legend, was required by King Nidhud to shoot an arrow at an apple placed on his son's head.

Egil Skallagrimsson, the hero of the Egla Saga (see *Saga*).

EGINHARD, see *Einhard*.

Egla Saga, see *Saga*.

Eglantine or EGLENTYNE, MADAME, the Prioress in Chaucer's 'The Canterbury Tales' (q.v.).

Eglinton Tournament, THE, an attempt to revive the ancient tourney, made in 1839 at the suggestion of the thirteenth earl of Eglinton. The tournament was held at Eglinton Castle, Ayrshire. There is a good description of it in Disraeli's 'Endymion', cc. 59 and 60.

Egoist, The, a novel by Meredith (q.v.), published in 1879.

It is 'a comedy in narrative' of which the central figure is Sir Willoughby Patterne, rich and handsome, with a great position in the country, but insufferably selfish and fatuously conceited. Laetitia Dale, a lady with brains, but poor and shy, has long cherished a romantic passion for him, which he has not discouraged. But he has proposed to and been accepted by Constantia Durham, 'the Racing Cutter', as Mrs. Mountstuart Jenkinson, a clever neighbour with a gift for descriptive phrases, calls her. Constantia soon finds out the true Sir Willoughby, and one day during the courtship it is learnt that she has eloped with an officer of hussars—Willoughby's first humiliation. Presently he discovers the qualities needed for a Lady Patterne in Clara Middleton, the daughter of an epicurean professor, and the 'dainty rogue in porcelain' of Mrs. Mountstuart, and wins her hand in a whirlwind courtship. Clara's liberation is a longer affair than that of her predecessor, and is the main theme of the book. For Clara is a woman of greater delicacy than Constantia, and Willoughby fights hard against a second jilting. He cunningly wins her father's powerful support by the charm of Patterne port, 'an aged and a great wine'. On the other side are the scholar Vernon Whitford ('Phoebus Apollo turned fasting friar'), and young Crossjay, son of Lieutenant Patterne, a gallant officer of marines and poor relative of Willoughby, whose shabby appearance has drawn on him an unforgettable insult from the baronet. Crossjay, a jolly little lad, is finally the instrument of her release, for he unintentionally overhears Willoughby, seriously threatened by Clara's recalcitrance, seeking a line of retirement by a proposal to Laetitia Dale, which the latter, with a remnant of pride, refuses. So Willoughby finds himself once more and doubly humiliated; though in the end, by sheer pressure of persistence, he obtains the hand of the reluctant Laetitia. Clara marries Vernon Whitford. Dr. Middleton was drawn from T. L. Peacock (q.v.), and Vernon Whitford from Leslie Stephen (q.v.).

Egoist, The, originally 'The New Freewoman: An Individualist Review', founded by Miss Harriet Shaw Weaver and Miss Dora Marsden. It published articles on modern poetry and the arts, and from being a feminist paper became, under the influence of Ezra Pound and others, a mouthpiece for the Imagist poets (see *Imagism*). It ran from 1914 to the end of 1919, first fortnightly and then monthly, with Richard Aldington as assistant editor, followed by T. S. Eliot in 1917. Miss Marsden and Miss Weaver succeeded each other as nominal editors and it was due to Miss Weaver that Joyce's 'Portrait of the Artist as a Young Man' was published serially in the magazine in 1914–15.

Egremont, CHARLES, the hero of Disraeli's 'Sybil' (q.v.).

Egyptian thief, THE, in Shakespeare's 'Twelfth Night' (v. i. 112), is from the story of Theagenes and Chariclea in the 'Aethiopica' of Heliodorus. They were carried off by Thiamis, an Egyptian pirate, who fell in love with Chariclea, and, being pursued, shut her up in a cave with his treasure. When escape seemed impossible, being determined that she should not survive him, he thrust her through, as he thought, with his sword (Aldis Wright).

Eidothea, according to Homer (Od. iv) the daughter of Proteus (q.v.). She teaches Menelaus how to seize and question her father.

Eighteenth Century, an age associated in England, in a literary connexion, with the names of Swift, Pope, Defoe, Goldsmith, Richardson, Sterne, Johnson, Bolingbroke, Berkeley, Burke, and Young; an age of prose rather than poetry, of lucidity, simplicity, and grace, rational and witty rather than humorous, and somewhat lacking in intensity.

Eikon Basilike, *the Pourtraicture of His Sacred Majestie in His Solitudes and Sufferings,* a book by Dr. Gauden (q.v.), purporting to be meditations by King Charles I, and accepted as such at the time, published about the date of his execution, 30 Jan. 1649 (1648 O.S.). The book appealed to the popular sentiment of the moment so strongly that forty-seven editions of it were published, and the parliament thought it necessary to issue a reply, in the form of Milton's 'Eikonoklastes', published in 1649. 'Eikon Basilike' means 'royal image', and 'Eikonoklastes', 'image-breaker'. 'Eikonoklastes' takes the 'Eikon' paragraph by paragraph, and purports to refute it, but does so in a tedious and unworthy manner.

Eikonoklastes, see *Eikon Basilike.*

EINHARD, or EGINHARD (770?–840?), a Frankish noble in the service of Charlemagne and subsequently of Louis le Débonnaire. He wrote a biography of Charlemagne (*Vita Caroli Magni*) and was, according to (false) tradition, his son-in-law.

EINSTEIN, ALBERT (1879–1955), born at Ulm in Würtemberg of German-Jewish parents, and educated at Munich and in Switzerland, became in 1902 an engineer in the Swiss Patent Office, where he remained until 1909. It was during this period that he evolved some of his principal theories, the Special Theory of Relativity, the Inertia of Energy, etc. His General Theory of Relativity followed some years later (1915–17). From 1909 to 1911 he was professor at Zürich,

Prague, and finally at the Prussian Academy of Science. He is chiefly famous for his revolutionary theory of the nature of space and time, known as the Theory of Relativity, which entirely upset the Newtonian conception of the universe; but he also did important work in other branches of physics, e.g. by providing a mathematical theory of the Brownian movement of molecules. He was awarded the Nobel Prize for Physics in 1926 for his theory of the photo-electric effect which first formulated the photon concept.

The *Special* or *Restricted Theory of Relativity* states broadly that natural phenomena run their course according to the same general laws in respect of two observers of whom one is moving in a uniform rectilinear manner in respect of the other. This theory appears to be substantially in accord with our observation of natural phenomena; but it conflicts with the law of the propagation of light, viz. that this takes place, *in vacuo,* in straight lines at a velocity of 300,000 km. a second. If it does this for one observer, it cannot do so for another observer moving, e.g., away from him with a certain additional velocity. But this conflict is based on two assumptions: (1) that the time-interval between two events is independent of the condition of motion of the observer; (2) that the space interval between two points of a rigid body is independent of the condition of motion of the observer. To maintain the theory of relativity these assumptions must be abandoned and a formula sought by which the quantities noted by the first observer may be made to correspond with the quantities noted by the second observer, so that the law of the transmission of light shall hold good for both. This formula Einstein finds in the equations of what is known as the 'Lorentz Transformation', from which it results that relatively to a stationary observer, a metre rod laid in the axis of a moving system is not one metre long but only $\sqrt{1-v^2/c^2}$ of a metre, where v is the velocity of the moving system, and c that of light; and similarly that the intervals between the beats of a clock in a moving system are not of one second but slightly more. This surprising conclusion cannot be verified by ordinary experience because the differences cannot be detected with ordinary velocities, but it is confirmed by certain experiments. The Restricted Theory of Relativity thus requires that every general law of nature must be so constituted that it applies when, instead of the space-time data of one observer, we substitute those of another *in uniform rectilinear motion.* And the theory so stated is borne out by many optical and electro-magnetic facts of experience.

But it appears unlikely that the laws of nature should hold good only in relation to observers in particular states of motion. The *General Theory of Relativity* avoids this improbability by adopting a physics such that the laws of nature hold good in all cases; in other words by such an interpretation of the properties of space and gravitational fields as will admit the general extension of the recognized laws of nature. Under this interpretation, space loses its Euclidean characteristics, and in the vicinity of matter becomes curved, gravitation and inertia become indistinguishable, the 'force' of gravitation appears an illusion, the curved path of projectiles being due to their effort to keep a straight track in a curved space. The applications of this General Theory, unlike those of the Restricted or Special Theory of Relativity, have so far all been astronomical. The best confirmed effect predicted is that the elliptical orbit of a planet rotates in the same plane as the planet moves and in the same sense. The theory also predicts that stars near the sun's position in the sky will be seen during solar eclipse to be displaced from their predicted positions because of the gravitational bending of light rays passing near the sun.

Einstein's pioneer application of his theory to cosmology in 1917 revolutionized the science and is one of his most far-reaching achievements, despite later modifications entailed by the discovery of the expansion of the universe. It introduced an unexpected revival, *mutatis mutandis*, of the idea of a finite universe. Space in the Einstein universe is closed but unbounded, and its geometry is not that of Euclid (Einstein, 'Relativity, A Popular Exposition', trans. by R. W. Lawson; Eddington, 'Space, Time, and Gravitation'; Max Born, 'Einstein's Theory of Relativity', rev. ed., 1962).

Eisteddfod, a Welsh word meaning 'session', the congress of Welsh bards held annually.

El Dorado, the name of a fabulous country or city, 'The Great and Golden City of Manoa', which was believed by the Spaniards and Sir Walter Ralegh (q.v.) to exist on the banks of the Amazon or the Orinoco. It was supposed to abound in gold, whence the name, which means 'the gilded one', perhaps applied to the king of that country.

El Greco, see *Greco, El*.

Elagăbălus or HELIOGABALUS, VARIUS AVITUS BASSIANUS (*c.* 201–22), born at Emesa, became a priest of the Syro-Phoenician sun-god Elagabalus, whose name he took. Through the intrigue of his grandmother, Julia Maesa, who pretended that he was the son of Caracalla, the troops in Syria were induced to proclaim him Roman emperor. His reign, notable for its profligacy, lasted from 218 to 222, when he was slain by the troops.

Elaine, in Malory's 'Morte Darthur', (1) ELAINE LE BLANK, the daughter of Sir Bernard of Astolat and known as the FAIR MAID OF ASTOLAT, who falls in love with Launcelot and dies for love of him (see under *Launcelot of the Lake*; also *Lancelot and Elaine*); (2) the daughter of King Pelles and the mother, by Launcelot, of Galahad; (3) the wife of King Nentres (Malory, I. ii); (4) the wife of King Ban (IV. i); (5) the daughter of King Pellinore

(III. xv). Some or all of these may derive from the Elen, wife of Myrddin (Merlin), of British mythology.

Elberich, see *Alberich*.

Elder Brother, The, a drama by J. Fletcher (q.v.), assisted probably by Massinger (q.v.), and completed about 1635 (after the former's death).

Lewis, a French lord, proposes to marry his daughter Angelina to one of the sons of Brisac, a country gentleman. Charles, the heir of Brisac, devoted to study, declines marriage; and Brisac thereupon proposes that Angelina shall marry the younger brother, Eustace, and that Charles shall be induced to surrender the bulk of his inheritance to Eustace, who eagerly falls in with the proposal. The plan is in a fair way of accomplishment, when Charles sees Angelina and they mutually fall in love. Eustace, a poor-spirited courtier, is routed, and after various complications the lovers are united.

Eldon, JOHN SCOTT, *first earl of* (1751–1838), fellow of University College, Oxford, lord chancellor 1801–6 and 1807–27, famous as one of the greatest of English lawyers: famous also for the delays of his court.

Eleanor Crosses, crosses erected by Edward I at the places where the funeral cortège of his queen, Eleanor of Castile, who died in 1290 at Harby, Notts., rested between Lincoln and Westminster, where she was buried. Three remain, at Hardingstone and Geddington in Northants. and Waltham Cross. Others were at Lincoln, Woburn, Stony Stratford, Dunstable, St. Albans, Cheapside, and Charing Cross, and there may have been two more.

Eleatic, the name used to describe the philosophy of Parmenides (*d. c.* 450 B.C.) and Zeno (*fl. c.* 460 B.C.), who lived or were born at Elea, an ancient Greek city on the west coast of south Italy. These philosophers held that the real universe is a single, indivisible, eternal, unchanging whole, and the only subject of knowledge; what is mutable and perishable, and phenomena such as motion, are illusions, and about them we can have only conjectures.

Elector Palatine, the ruler of a State of the old German Empire, including two territories: one on both sides of the Rhine, just south of Mainz; the other in (later) Bavaria, just north of the Danube and south of the Upper Main. He was one of the seven original electors of the empire (see *Holy Roman Empire*). The word 'palatine', from Lat. *palatium*, signified an officer of the palace or court of the German emperors.

Electra, a daughter of Agamemnon (q.v.). She incited her brother Orestes (q.v.) to avenge their father's death by assassinating Clytemnestra (q.v.). Orestes gave her in marriage to his friend Pylades. She is the subject of plays by Sophocles and Euripides.

Elegant Extracts, see *Knox (V.)*.

Elegiac, (1) in prosody, the metre consisting of a dactylic hexameter and pentameter (qq.v.), as being the metre appropriate to elegies; (2) generally, of the nature of an elegy, which according to Coleridge 'is the form of poetry natural to the reflective mind'. It may treat, he adds, of any subject, if it does so with reference to the poet himself. In a narrow sense, an elegy is a song of lamentation for the dead.

Elegy in a Country Churchyard, a meditative poem in quatrains of ten-syllabled lines by Gray (q.v.), published in 1750, having been begun in 1742.

The churchyard referred to is perhaps that of Stoke Poges. The poet in a reflective and melancholy mood gives expression to the thoughts called up in his mind by the sight of the tombs of the 'rude forefathers of the hamlet', and compares their humble lot with the great careers from which their fate excluded them. The poem ends on a personal note, with the supposed death of the author, his burial in the churchyard, and the epitaph on his grave.

Elene, see *Cynewulf.*

Elephant in the Moon, see *Butler (Samuel,* 1612–80).

Eleusinia, the Eleusinian mysteries, the most famous of the religious ceremonies of Greece, celebrated in honour of Demeter and Persephone, at Eleusis near Athens. They arose from an agrarian festival and appear to have been originally a feast of purification and fertility having reference to the autumn sowing of the corn. With this came to be connected the idea of the gods of the lower world, the descent into Hades, and the future life. The mysteries culminated in a rite carried out in a darkened hall, where the worshippers were shown visions in flashes of light.

Eleven Thousand Virgins, THE, see *Ursula.*

Elf, the name of a class of supernatural beings, in Teutonic mythology supposed to possess magical powers, which they used variously for the benefit or injury of mankind. They were believed to be of dwarfish form, to cause nightmares and diseases, to steal children, etc. In modern literature *elf* is a mere synonym of *fairy*, which generally denotes a more playful and less terrible creature than the 'elf' as originally conceived. Spenser applied the word 'elf' to the knights of his allegorical 'faerie land'.

Elfrida, see *Ælfthryth.*

Elgin Marbles, THE, sculptures and architectural fragments from Athenian buildings, chiefly from the frieze and pediment of the Parthenon, the work of Phidias (q.v.). They were collected by the earl of Elgin (1766–1841) when envoy to the Porte (1799–1803), conveyed to England (the ship containing them was wrecked near Cerigo), and sold to the British government. They were placed in the British Museum in 1816.

Elia, see *Essays of Elia.*

Elidure, a legendary king of Britain, see *Artegal.*

Elijah, a Hebrew prophet in the reign of Ahab. He was miraculously fed by ravens at the brook Cherith; raised the dead son of the widow of Zarephath; confuted the prophets of Baal; and was carried to heaven in a chariot of fire (1 Kings xvii et seq.).

ELIOT, SIR CHARLES (1863–1931), educated at Balliol College, Oxford, was a distinguished diplomatist, vice-chancellor of Sheffield University from 1905, and principal of the University of Hong-Kong, 1912–18. He was author of 'Turkey in Europe' (published in 1901 under the pseudonym 'Odysseus'), a learned and entertaining account of Macedonia and its various races under the old régime; of 'Letters from the Far East' (1907); and of 'Hinduism and Buddhism' (1921).

ELIOT, GEORGE (MARY ANN CROSS, *née* EVANS) (1819–80), spent the early part of her life in Warwickshire, where her father was agent for an estate. From somewhat narrow religious views she was freed by the influence of Charles Bray, a Coventry manufacturer, and devoted herself to completing a translation of Strauss's 'Life of Jesus' (1846). In 1850 she became a contributor to the 'Westminster Review' (q.v.) and in 1851 its assistant editor, resigning the post in 1853. In 1854 she published a translation of Feuerbach's 'Essence of Christianity' and about the same time joined George Henry Lewes (q.v.) in a union, without legal form, that lasted until his death. 'Amos Barton', the first of the 'Scenes of Clerical Life', appeared in 'Blackwood's Magazine' in 1857, followed by 'Mr. Gilfil's Love-Story' and 'Janet's Repentance' in the same year; these at once excited admiration of her talent as a novelist. 'Adam Bede' (q.v.) was published in 1859, 'The Mill on the Floss' (q.v.) in 1860, and 'Silas Marner' (q.v.) in 1861. In 1860 and 1861 she visited Florence, where the story of 'Romola' (q.v.) was conceived; it was published in the 'Cornhill' in 1862–3. 'Felix Holt' (q.v.), her only novel that deals with English politics, appeared in 1866. She travelled in Spain in 1867 and her dramatic poem, 'The Spanish Gipsy', appeared in 1868. 'Middlemarch' (q.v.) was published in instalments in 1871–2, and 'Daniel Deronda' (q.v.), her last great work, in the same way in 1874–6. Among her less important writings may be mentioned the satirical 'Impressions of Theophrastus Such' (1879) and the poems, 'How Lisa loved the King' (1867), 'Agatha' (1869), 'Armgart' (1870), 'The Legend of Jubal' (1870).

In May 1880 she married John Walter Cross, but died in December of the same year. Her novels reveal an exceptional sense of the humour and pathos of human life, a deep religious conviction of the purifying effect of human trials, and wide and varied learning.

ELIOT, THOMAS STEARNS, O.M., (1888–1965), a major figure in English literature since the 1920s. He was born at St. Louis, Missouri, and educated at Harvard, the Sorbonne, and Merton College, Oxford. He settled in England in 1915. His first volume of verse 'Prufrock and Other Observations' was published in 1917, and was followed by 'Poems' in 1919, hand-printed by Leonard and Virginia Woolf at the Hogarth Press. During this time he was assistant editor of the 'Egoist' (q.v.), to which he contributed some of his early criticism, and in 1922 he founded the 'Criterion' (q.v.), in which 'The Waste Land' was first published, dedicated to Ezra Pound. This cryptic and allusive poem, the masterpiece of Eliot's earlier manner, expressed powerfully, through the use of ancient myths translated into contemporary social life, man's need for salvation. It was generally read as giving voice to the disillusionment of the post-war world.

In 1927 he became a British subject and a member of the Anglican Church, and in 'Ash Wednesday' (1930) and the series of Ariel Poems he developed a less taut, more lyrical style in which to treat the experience of the discovery of faith. The masterpiece of this new style was 'The Four Quartets', first published as a whole in New York in 1943, the different parts having been published separately from 1936. In these highly original poems, meditations on time and eternity, the personal and the general, and man's place in nature and in history, he first reached a wide public and succeeded in communicating in a modern idiom the fundamentals of Christian faith and experience. With 'Sweeney Agonistes' in 1932 Eliot began his attempt to revive poetic drama, continued with 'Murder in the Cathedral' (1935), 'The Family Reunion' (1939), and three 'comedies': 'The Cocktail Party' (1950), 'The Confidential Clerk' (1954), and 'The Elder Statesman' (1958). These last were not wholly successful attempts to clothe profound ideas in the garb of a conventional West End play. He also produced a minor masterpiece in 'Old Possum's Book of Practical Cats' (1939), a classic among books of poetry for children.

Eliot was highly influential as a critic and in his combination of literary and social criticism may be called the Arnold of the twentieth century. Among his works may be mentioned: 'The Sacred Wood: Essays on Poetry and Criticism' (1920), 'The Use of Poetry and the Use of Criticism' (1933), 'Elizabethan Essays' (1934), 'The Idea of a Christian Society' (1940), 'Notes towards the Definition of Culture' (1948), 'Poetry and Drama' (1951), 'Essays on Poets and Poetry' (1957). In 1948 he was awarded the Nobel Prize for Literature and received the Order of Merit.

Eliphaz, one of the three candid friends of Job (q.v.).

Elisha, the successor as prophet of Elijah (q.v.), whose mantle he received; the children that mocked him were destroyed by bears (2 Kings ii). For his miracles (the Shunammite's son, Naaman's leprosy, etc.) see 2 Kings iii et seq.

Elision, the suppression of a vowel or syllable in pronouncing.

Elissa, (1) a name borne by Dido (q.v.); (2) in Spenser's 'Faerie Queene', II. ii, one of the two 'froward sisters' of the sober Medina (q.v.).

Elivagar, see *Hvergelmir*.

Eliza, in Sterne's 'Journal to Eliza' and 'Letters from Yorick to Eliza', was Mrs. Eliza Draper (q.v.).

Elizabeth I, queen of England, 1558–1603.

Elizabeth II, queen of England, 1952–

Elizabeth and her German Garden, an amusing and successful novel by Elizabeth Mary, Countess Russell, by her first marriage Countess von Arnim, published in 1898.

Elizabeth of Bohemia, daughter of James I. See under *Queen of Hearts* and *Wotton*.

Elizabeth of Hungary, St., the wife of Louis, Landgrave of Thuringia (1207–31), the subject of the dramatic poem 'The Saint's Tragedy', by C. Kingsley (q.v.).

Elizabethan Literature, a name often applied vaguely to the literature produced in the reign of Elizabeth I and the first Stuarts.

Ellen, the heroine of the ballad of 'Childe Waters' (q.v.).

ELLEN ALLEYNE, the pseudonym under which C. Rossetti (q.v.) produced her earlier poems.

Ellen Douglas, the 'Lady of the Lake' in Scott's poem of that name (q.v.).

Ellen Orford, one of the tales in Crabbe's 'The Borough' (q.v.). It is the melancholy story of a woman who, after a neglected childhood, is seduced and abandoned; her child turns out an idiot; she marries, her husband dies, and his death is followed by the tragic end of their children; she herself is stricken with blindness, but finds consolation in her trust in God.

Ellesmere, Lord, see *Egerton (Sir T.)*.

Ellieslaw, Richard Vere, *laird of*, and his daughter Isabella, characters in Scott's 'The Black Dwarf' (q.v.).

Elliot, Hobbie or Halbert, a character in Scott's 'The Black Dwarf' (q.v.).

ELLIOT, JANE (1727–1805), third daughter of Sir Gilbert Elliot, of Minto, was author of the most popular version of the old lament for Flodden, 'The Flowers of the Forest', beginning, 'I've heard them lilting at our ewe-milking'.

Elliot, SIR WALTER, his daughters ELIZABETH, ANNE, and MARY, and his heir presumptive WILLIAM WALTER ELLIOT, characters in Jane Austen's 'Persuasion' (q.v.).

ELLIOTT, EBENEZER (1781–1849), became a master-founder at Sheffield, and is remembered as the 'Corn-law Rhymer'. As poet he attracted the attention of Southey. He bitterly condemned the bread-tax, to which, in his 'Corn-Law Rhymes' (1828), he attributed all national misfortunes. His other principal long poems are 'The Village Patriarch' and 'Love', but he also wrote some lyrics of much beauty, and the well-known political 'Battle Song'. His verse was collected in 1846.

Elliott, KIRSTIE, ROBERT, GILBERT, CLEMENT, and ANDREW, characters in R. L. Stevenson's 'Weir of Hermiston' (q.v.).

Ellipsis, the leaving out from a sentence words necessary to express the sense completely.

ELLIS, GEORGE (1753–1815), was one of the founders with Canning of the 'Anti-Jacobin' (q.v.), after having previously taken a hand on the other side in the 'Rolliad' (q.v.). He published in 1805 his valuable 'Specimens of Early English Romances in Metre'. He was a friend of Sir W. Scott. His 'Poetical Tales by Sir Gregory Gander' appeared in 1778.

ELLIS, HENRY HAVELOCK (1859–1939), writer and scientist, born at Croydon. After some years spent as a teacher in Australia, he returned to England and qualified as a physician, but devoted himself to science and literature. He edited the 'Mermaid Series' of Elizabethan dramatists (1887–9) and the 'Contemporary Science Series'. His principal works, in which he showed independence of thought and ardour for scientific social progress, were: 'The New Spirit' (1890), 'Man and Woman' (1894), 'Studies in the Psychology of Sex' (1897–1910; the first vol. published in England led to a prosecution, after which the publication was transferred to the U.S.), 'Affirmations' (1898, studies of Nietzsche, Zola, and other writers), 'The Soul of Spain' (1908), 'The Task of Social Hygiene' (1912), and some volumes of verse.

Ellwood, THOMAS (1639–1713), Quaker and friend of Milton (q.v.), to whom he suggested by a chance remark the writing of 'Paradise Regained' (q.v.).

Elmo's Fire, ST., or CORPOSANT, the ball of light sometimes seen about the masts or yard-arms of a ship in a storm. This St. Elmo is said to have been Pedro Gonzalez of Astorga (1190–1240), a Dominican who devoted himself to preaching to the mariners of Galicia.
    The St. Elmo of ST. ELMO'S CASTLE at Naples is said to be a corruption of St. Ermo, or St. Erasmus, an Italian bishop martyred under Domitian and a patron of sailors in the Mediterranean.

Elohim, in Hebrew a plural form signifying 'gods', but often construed as singular, with the sense 'God'. The words 'Elohimic' and 'Elohistic' are applied to passages of the Hebrew scriptures characterized by the use of the word 'Elohim' instead of the word 'Yahveh' (Jehovah, whence *Jahvistic* or *Jehovistic*).

Eloi or ELOY (ELIGIUS), ST. (588–659), a skilful goldsmith, who was treasurer of the French kings Clotaire II and Dagobert I, and became bishop of Noyon. He is the patron of craftsmen. 'By Seint Eloy' was the 'greatest oath' of Chaucer's Prioress. He is commemorated on 1 Dec.

Eloisa or HÉLOÏSE, see *Abélard*.

ELPHINSTONE, MOUNTSTUART (1779–1859), governor of Bombay from 1819 to 1827, was author of a classic 'History of India' (1841) and of 'The Rise of the British Power in the East' (1887).

Elshender the Recluse, CANNY ELSHIE, or the WISE WIGHT OF MUCKLESTANE-MOOR, the 'Black Dwarf' in Scott's novel of that name (q.v.).

Elsinore, a seaport in Denmark, on the Sound, the scene of Shakespeare's 'Hamlet' (q.v.). Now called Helsingör.

ELTON, OLIVER (1861–1945), author of 'The Augustan Ages' in 'Periods of European Literature' (1899), and of three 'Surveys of English Literature', viz. 1780–1830 (1912), 1830–80 (1920), and 1730–80 (1928).

Elton, THE REVD. PHILIP, in Jane Austen's 'Emma' (q.v.), the conceited young vicar of Highbury. He marries the rich ill-bred Miss Hawkins of Bristol, sister of Mrs. Suckling of Maple Grove.

ÉLUARD, PAUL (1895–1952), French lyric poet whose published collections include: 'L'Amour, la Poésie' (1929), 'La Vie immédiate' (1932), 'Les Yeux fertiles' (1936), 'Poésie et Vérité' (1942), 'Choix de Poésies' (1946). He was an early leader of the Surrealists, but like Aragon (q.v.) he reached his widest public with poetry written during the Second World War.

Elvira, (1) the wife of Don Juan (q.v.); (2) the heroine of Dryden's 'The Spanish Fryar' (see under *Dryden*); (3) the mistress of Pizarro in Sheridan's 'Pizarro' (see under *Sheridan, R. B.*); (4) the heroine of Victor Hugo's 'Hernani' (q.v.).

Elvire, the wife of Browning's 'Don Juan' in 'Fifine at the Fair' (q.v.).

Ely Place, see *Holborn*. It is also sometimes mentioned in allusion to Sir G. Lewis, of a famous firm of solicitors which has its offices there.

ELYOT, SIR THOMAS (1499?–1546), author of the 'Boke named the Governour', published in 1531, a treatise on education and politics, which displays the influence at this time of the classics, and Plato in particular, and illustrates the evolution of English prose. To this book Elyot owed his appointment as ambassador to Charles V. He wrote a number of other works, including 'The Doctrine of Princes' (translated from Isocrates, 1534), 'The Image of Governance' (translated from a Greek manuscript of Eucolpius, the secretary of the Emperor Alexander Severus, and first published 1540), and Platonic dialogues and compilations from the Fathers. His translations did much to popularize the classics in England. His 'Dictionary' (Latin and English, 1538) was the first book in England to bear this title.

Elysium, a place or island in the western ocean, where, according to Greek mythology, the souls of the virtuous enjoy complete happiness and innocent pleasures. Virgil places it in Hades.

Elzevir or ELSEVIER, a family of publishers, booksellers, and printers in the Netherlands. LOUIS, born at Louvain *c.* 1546, worked as a bookbinder in Antwerp, but migrated to Holland for religious reasons and began publishing and bookselling in Leyden in 1583. His descendants carried on in Utrecht, Leyden, Amsterdam, and The Hague. His grandson, Isaac, began a printing business at Leyden in 1617 (and became printer to the university). The press, which continued until 1712, is famous for its editions in small format, which have been highly prized by collectors.

Emaré, a 14th-cent. verse romance of 1,000 lines. Emaré is the daughter of the Emperor Artyus. By the order of her unnatural father, she is cast adrift in a boat, clothed in a robe beautifully embroidered with four legends. She is found on the coast of Galys and married by Sir Cador, king of that country. Her son Segramour is born. By the wiles of the king's mother she is again cast adrift with her son and robe, and reaches Rome, where she is succoured by a merchant and works embroidery. For seven years her husband laments her, and coming to Rome to do penance is reunited with her.

Emathia, a region of Macedonia, the original seat of the Macedonian monarchy. Hence 'Emathian conqueror' for Alexander the Great in Milton's sonnet, 'When the assault was intended to the City'.

Ember Days, four periods of fasting and prayer appointed by the Church to be observed respectively in the four seasons of the year. By the Council of Placentia (1095) they were appointed to be the Wednesday, Friday, and Saturday next following (1) the first Sunday in Lent, (2) Whit-Sunday, (3) Holy Cross Day, 14 Sept., (4) St. Lucia's Day, 13 Dec. The word *Ember* appears in the 'Laws of Æthelred' as *ymbren*, perhaps a corruption of OE. *ymbrine*, period, revolution of time. But it may be due to popular etymology working upon some vulgar Latin corruption of *quatuor tempora*; cf. German *quatember* Ember-tide. [OED.]

Emblem-book, a book containing pictorial representations whose symbolic meaning is expressed in words. This kind of literature was begun by Alciati, a Milanese, whose 'Emblematum Libellus' appeared in 1522. The best known of his English followers were Quarles and Wither (qq.v.). Emblematic verses sometimes also took the form of verses themselves shaped in various forms, such as crosses, altars, bottles, etc. Wither, for instance, wrote a rhomboidal dirge.

Emblems, a book of short devotional poems by Quarles (q.v.), published in 1635.

The poems are in various metres, each based on some scriptural text, followed by appropriate quotations from the Fathers, and an epigram, and illustrated by quaint engravings, mostly by William Marshall (*fl.* 1630–50), and some of them taken from Herman Hugo's 'Pia Desideria'. Some of the poems take the form of dialogues, e.g. between Eve and the Serpent, between Jesus and the Soul, and between the Flesh and the Spirit.

A 'Collection of Emblemes' was also published by Wither (q.v.), similarly illustrated, in 1634–5.

Emblems of Love, a volume of poems in dramatic form by Abercrombie (q.v.).

Emelye, see *Emilia*.

Emerald Isle, Ireland, so called on account of its verdure. Dr. W. Drennan claimed to have first used the expression in his poem 'Erin' (1795).

EMERSON, RALPH WALDO (1803–82), American philosopher and poet, was born in Massachusetts, inheriting from his parents strong religious and spiritual tendencies. He was educated at Harvard, studied theology, was ordained, and became pastor at Boston, but resigned his charge owing to his views on the nature of the sacrament, which he was unable to regard 'as a divinely appointed, sacred ordinance of religion'. He came to Europe and visited England in 1833, meeting Coleridge, Wordsworth, and Carlyle (with whom followed a long friendship and correspondence). On his return to America he lectured on literature, biography, history, and human culture, and settled at Concord in 1835. Emerson's prose essay 'Nature', on the relation of the soul to nature, was published in 1836, and earned for his philosophical doctrine the epithet 'transcendental' (q.v.), which signifies that he was an idealist with a tinge of mysticism: 'Nature is the incarnation of thought. The world is the mind precipitated.' Emerson delivered his influential address 'The American Scholar' at Harvard in 1837, in which he urged America to assert its intellectual independence. He was editor of the idealist periodical 'The Dial' (q.v.) until 1844. In this appeared his poems, 'The Problem', 'Wood-notes', 'The Sphinx', and 'Fate'. In 1841 was published the first volume of his 'Essays', the second in 1844, and a collection of poems in 1847. The first volume of the

'Essays' contains his important discourses on 'Self-reliance', 'Compensation', and 'The Over-Soul'. He again came to England in 1847 and delivered lectures in the following year. 'Representative Men' was published in 1850, and 'English Traits' in 1856. During this period he took an active part in the anti-slavery campaign. From 1857 he contributed poems and prose (including 'The Roman Girl', 'Terminus', etc.) to the 'Atlantic Monthly' (q.v.). 'The Conduct of Life', a series of essays on Worship, Fate, Power, Wealth, etc., appeared in 1860; the poem 'May-Day' in 1867; the essay 'Society: Solitude' in 1870; 'Letters and Social Aims' in 1876. 'Miscellanies' and 'Lectures and Biographical Sketches' were published posthumously. His 'Journals', published in 1909–14, contain records of his self-communion and observations on men and books, as well as chronicles of daily events.

Emilia, (1) the lady loved by Palamon and Arcite, the EMELYE of the 'Knight's Tale' (see *Canterbury Tales*), who figures also in Fletcher's 'Two Noble Kinsmen' (q.v.); (2) in Shakespeare's 'Othello' (q.v.), the wife of Iago.

Emilia in England, see *Sandra Belloni*.

Emilia Viviani, see *Epipsychidion*.

Em'ly, LITTLE, a character in Dickens's 'David Copperfield' (q.v.).

Emma, a novel by Jane Austen (q.v.), begun in 1814 and published in 1816.

Emma, a clever and very self-satisfied young lady, is the daughter, and mistress of the house, of Mr. Woodhouse, an amiable old valetudinarian. Her former governess and companion, Miss (Anne) Taylor, beloved of both father and daughter, has just left them to marry a neighbour, Mr. Weston. Missing her companionship, Emma takes under her wing Harriet Smith, parlour-boarder at Mrs. Goddard's school in the neighbouring village of Highbury, the natural daughter of some person unknown, a pretty but foolish girl of 17. Emma's active mind sets to work on schemes for Harriet's advancement, and the story is mainly occupied with the mortifications to which Emma is subjected as a result of her injudicious attempts in this connexion. She first prevents Harriet from accepting an eligible offer from Robert Martin, a young farmer, as being beneath her; much to the annoyance of Mr. Knightley, the bachelor owner of Donwell Abbey, Martin's landlord, the friend of the Woodhouses, and one of the few people who can see faults in Emma. She has hopes of effecting a match between Harriet and Mr. Elton, the young vicar, only to find that Elton despises Harriet, and has the presumption to aspire to her own hand. Frank Churchill, the son of Mr. Weston by a former marriage, an attractive but thoughtless young man, now appears on the scene. Emma at first fancies him in love with herself, but presently thinks that Harriet might

attract him, and encourages her not to despair, encouragement which Harriet applies not to Frank Churchill, of whom she has no thought, but to the great Mr. Knightley himself, with whom Emma is unconsciously in love. Emma has the double mortification of discovering, first that Frank Churchill is already secretly engaged to Jane Fairfax, niece of Miss Bates, the kindly garrulous daughter of a former vicar of Highbury, and secondly that Harriet has hopes, which appear to have some foundation, of supplanting her in Mr. Knightley's affections. But all ends well, for Mr. Knightley proposes to a humiliated and repentant Emma, and Harriet is easily consoled with Robert Martin, on his proposing to her a second time.

Empĕdŏclēs, a learned and eloquent philosopher, of Agrigentum in Sicily, who flourished about 444 B.C. It is said that his curiosity to visit the crater of Etna proved fatal to him, a legend to which Milton refers in 'Paradise Lost', iii. 471, Lamb in 'All Fools' Day', and Meredith in 'Empedocles'. Matthew Arnold (q.v.) also wrote a dramatic poem 'Empedocles on Etna' (first published anonymously in 1852), in which the philosopher, once powerful in Sicily, but now 'the weary man, the banished citizen', climbs to the summit of the mountain resolved to die. He muses on man's mediocre lot and his own happier days, and speculates on the fate of the soul after death, before plunging into the crater.

Empedocles on Etna, see *Empedocles*.

Empire, (1) the ROMAN, a term applied to the period of the rule of, or to the territories ruled by, the Roman Emperors, beginning with Augustus Caesar (27 B.C.). The Roman Empire was divided into Eastern and Western (qq.v.) Empires in A.D. 395; see also *Holy Roman Empire*; (2) the FIRST, of France, Napoleon I emperor, 1804–15; (3) the SECOND, of France, Napoleon III emperor, 1852–70; (4) the INDIAN, instituted in 1876, when Queen Victoria was proclaimed Empress of India; and many others.

EMPSON, WILLIAM (1906–), born in Yorkshire and educated at Winchester and Magdalene College, Cambridge, where he studied mathematics. He taught in universities in China and Japan and subsequently became professor of English at Sheffield University. He published two volumes of verse, 'Poems' (1935) and 'The Gathering Storm' (1940). His criticism includes 'Seven Types of Ambiguity' (1930), 'The Structure of Complex Words' (1951), and 'Milton's God' (1961). Empson's poetry is extremely difficult, making use of analytical argument and imagery drawn from modern physics and mathematics, but together with his criticism it has proved widely influential on younger writers.

Empyrean, THE, in ancient cosmology, the highest heaven, the sphere of the pure element fire (from the Greek ἔμπύριος, fiery).

In Christian use, the abode of God and the angels.

Enceladus, one of the Giants of Greek mythology, sons of Gē, who rose against the gods but were defeated. Enceladus was imprisoned under Mt. Etna.

Encyclopaedia Britannica. The word *encyclopaedia* means instruction in the whole circle of learning. Among early precursors of the E.B. may be mentioned the 'Grand Dictionnaire' of Moréri (1643-80), the 'Dictionnaire historique et critique' of Bayle (1647-1706), the 'Cyclopaedia' of Ephraim Chambers (q.v., 1728), and the great French 'Encyclopédie' (q.v.) of the 18th cent.

The first 'Encyclopaedia Britannica' was issued by a 'Society of Gentlemen in Scotland' in numbers (1768-71), the editor being William Smellie, a printer, afterwards secretary of the Society of Scottish Antiquaries. It was a dictionary of the Arts and Sciences. The second edition (1777-84), in ten volumes, added history and biography. The third edition, in fifteen volumes, appeared in 1788-97; and the fourth edition, in twenty volumes, in 1801-10. The undertaking was taken over by Constable in 1812, and the copyright sold after the failure of that house in 1826. After some further editions it passed to Cambridge University for the publication in 1910-11 of the eleventh edition in 28 volumes. [E.B.] The tenth and eleventh editions were by Hugh Chisholm. The fourteenth edition, under the editorship-in-chief of Mr. J. L. Garvin, was published in London and New York, in 1929. Since then a system of continuous revision has replaced the making of new editions. See also *Chambers's Encyclopaedia.*

Encyclopaedists, the collaborators in the *Encyclopédie* (q.v.) of Diderot and D'Alembert.

Encyclopédie, L', an encyclopaedia published under the direction of Diderot and (until 1758) of D'Alembert (qq.v.), in 35 volumes, between 1751 and 1776. It originated in a proposal to translate Ephraim Chambers's 'Cyclopaedia' (1728). Its contributors included Voltaire, Montesquieu, J. J. Rousseau, Buffon, Turgot, and other brilliant writers. It embodied the philosophic spirit of the 18th cent., and its attempt to give a rational explanation of the universe is marked by love of truth and contempt for superstition. Its sceptical tendencies brought upon it the hostility of the clergy and official classes, and its publication was twice prohibited.

Endeavour, The, Captain Cook's ship on his first voyage to the Pacific.

Endimion, The Man in the Moone, an allegorical prose play by Lyly (q.v.), published 1591. Endimion abandons Tellus (the earth) in consequence of a hopeless passion for Cynthia (the moon). Tellus conspires with the witch Dipsas against Endimion, who is sent to sleep for forty years. Cynthia breaks the spell and releases Endimion with a kiss. The dramatic element is slight, the allegory perhaps relating to the rivalry between Elizabeth (Cynthia) and Mary Queen of Scots (Tellus), and the favour of Elizabeth for Leicester (Endimion). This is supplemented by subordinate allegories in the quarrel of the witch Dipsas and her husband Geron (the earl and countess of Shrewsbury), and the relations of Eumenides (perhaps Sir Philip Sidney) with Semele (perhaps Lady Rich).

Endor, THE WITCH OF, the woman with 'a familiar spirit' consulted by Saul, when forsaken of God and threatened by the Philistines. At her request she calls up Samuel, who prophesies the death of Saul and the destruction of his army (1 Sam. xxviii).

Endymion, a beautiful shepherd, of whom Selene (Diana) became enamoured when she saw him sleeping on Mt. Latmos. She caused him to sleep for ever that she might enjoy his beauty, whence the proverb, 'Endymionis somnum dormire', to signify a long sleep. According to another version he obtained from Zeus eternal youth and the gift of sleeping as long as he wished.

Endymion, a poem in four books, by Keats (q.v.), published in 1818.

The poem tells, and develops with a wealth of invention, the story of Endymion, the 'brain-sick shepherd-prince' of Mt. Latmos, with whom the moon goddess (Cynthia, Phoebe) falls in love, and whom, after luring him, weary and perplexed, through 'cloudy phantasms', she bears away to eternal life with her. With this story are mingled legends of Venus and Adonis, of Glaucus and Scylla, and of Arethusa. The poem includes in Bk. I the great 'Hymn to Pan', and in Bk. IV the beautiful roundelay 'O sorrow'.

In his preface, Keats described this work as 'a feverish attempt rather than a deed accomplished'. It is the work of an immature genius, the product of sensation rather than thought. The allegory, which is somewhat obscure, represents the poet pursuing ideal perfection and distracted from his quest by human beauty. The poem was violently criticized in 'Blackwood's Magazine' and the 'Quarterly'.

Endymion, a novel by Disraeli (q.v.), published in 1880.

This was the last of the author's novels. Endymion and Myra are the twin children of William Pitt Ferrars, a rising politician, who, when on the point of reaching cabinet rank, is overtaken by misfortune, and, after a period spent in retirement, dies penniless. Endymion is withdrawn from Eton and obtains a clerkship at Somerset House; Myra becomes companion to Adriana, the daughter of the rich and genial banker Adrian Neuchatel (subsequently Lord Hainault). The author traces the rise to social eminence of Myra, a beautiful, proud, ambitious, and determined woman, and to political eminence of Endymion, a clever and amiable, but more passive character. Myra's success is due to her captivating and marrying first Lord Roehampton, the foreign secretary, and secondly the parvenu monarch, King Florestan. Endymion owes his success less to his own ability than to the support given him by his brother-in-law, Lord Roehampton, and to the influence exerted on him by his imperious sister and by Lady Mountfort, a leader of political society, whom he marries on the death of her first husband. The story provides a succession of cleverly drawn characters and of entertaining pictures of life in high social and political spheres. The period dealt with is, in the main, that of the administrations of Lord Melbourne and Sir Robert Peel (1834–41), and Lord Roehampton is a thinly veiled portrait of Lord Palmerston.

England expects that every man will do his duty, Nelson's famous signal before the battle of Trafalgar.

England's Helicon, a miscellany of Elizabethan verse, published in 1600, edited by Bullen in 1887 and included in Arber's 'English Scholar's Library'. It is the best collection of lyrical and pastoral poetry of the Elizabethan age, and includes pieces by Sidney, Spenser, Drayton, Greene, Lodge, Ralegh, Marlowe, and others.

England's Parnassus, a collection of extracts from contemporary poets, by R. Allot, published in 1600.

English, originally the dialect of the Angles (the first to be committed to writing), and extended to all the dialects of the vernacular, whether Anglian or Saxon. OLD ENGLISH or ANGLO-SAXON is the English language of the period which ends about 1100–50; followed by MIDDLE ENGLISH during the period to about 1500; and after this by MODERN ENGLISH, which derives from the East Midland dialect, especially that of London. KING'S or QUEEN'S ENGLISH is correct grammatical English.

Abusing of God's patience and the king's English.

(Shakespeare, 'The Merry Wives of Windsor', I. iv. 5.)

English Association, THE, founded in 1906 to promote the teaching and advanced study of the English language and of English literature, and to unite all those who are interested in these subjects.

English Bards and Scotch Reviewers, a satirical poem in heroic couplets by Lord Byron (q.v.), published in 1809.

Nettled by a contemptuous criticism of his 'Hours of Idleness' in the 'Edinburgh Review', Byron wrote this vigorous satire, in which he attacks not only Jeffrey, the editor of the 'Review', but Southey, Scott, Wordsworth, and Coleridge, and tilts indiscriminately at all the poets and poetasters of the romantic school, while holding up to admira-tion Dryden and Pope, and their followers, Campbell and Rogers, in the classical tradition.

English Place-Name Society, THE, founded in 1923 to carry out the survey of English place-names inaugurated under the auspices of the British Academy in 1922. The Survey is published county by county.

English Poets, Lives of the, originally entitled 'Prefaces biographical and critical to the Works of the English Poets. By Samuel Johnson' (q.v.), published in 1779–81.

The work was undertaken at the request of certain London booksellers, to serve as biographical prefaces to a reprint, which they contemplated, of the works of the English poets. The selection of the poets was made by them, and includes authors of very different merit, and no poet earlier than Milton. The 'Lives' contain much interesting biographical matter, but are not always trustworthy and have been superseded in this respect. The criticism is unequal. At its best, it is some of the finest in the language; it is at its worst when Johnson is dealing with authors with whom he is out of sympathy, such as Milton and Gray. His condemnation of Milton's 'Lycidas' on the grounds of its artificiality and insincerity is well known.

English Traveller, The, a romantic drama by T. Heywood (q.v.), printed in 1633.

Geraldine, returning from his travels, finds that the lady whom he loves has been married to Wincot, a worthy old gentleman, to whom he is under obligations. He and the lady bind themselves, she that she will marry him after Wincot's death, he that he will remain single till then. A base plot by his treacherous friend Delavil leads to Geraldine's discovery that Delavil has seduced Wincot's wife. Heartbroken, Geraldine decides to leave the country. Before doing so he attends a farewell feast given him by Wincot. Wincot's wife hypocritically taxes him with his desertion of her, whereupon he reveals his discovery and upbraids her as an adulteress. She, in contrition and despair, dies.

There is a humorous under-plot, borrowed from the 'Mostellaria' of Plautus: the prodigal son who wastes his father's substance during the latter's absence on a voyage, the father's unexpected return, the tricks of a resourceful servant to postpone the discovery of the prodigal's doings, and the final pardon and general reconciliation.

Enid, see Geraint and Enid.

Enitharmon, in the mystical poems of Blake (q.v.), a minister of Urizen (q.v.); she conveys his moral laws to mankind. In some parts she is the equivalent of Space, and nearly always the feminine counterpart of Los (q.v.).

Enjambment, a technical term in verse, signifying the carrying on the sense of a line or couplet into the next.

Enna, the name of the vale in Sicily in which Proserpine (q.v.) was gathering flowers when she was carried off by Pluto.

Enneads, see *Plotinus*.

ENNIUS, QUINTUS (239–169 B.C.), born at Rudiae in Calabria, a town in touch with Hellenism. He was the originator of Roman epic poetry, introducing the hexameter and the Homeric mode of treatment, in which he was followed by Virgil. His most important work was 'Annalium Libri xviii', a history of Rome from the arrival of Aeneas in Italy, in the form of an epic poem. Of this and of his tragedies only fragments survive.

Enobarbus [Domitius Ahenobarbus], in Shakespeare's 'Antony and Cleopatra' (q.v.), Antony's follower.

Enoch, the sixth in descent from Adam and father of Methuselah; he did not die, but was translated to heaven (Gen. v. 24). To his authorship are ascribed two apocryphal works, the 'Book of Enoch' and the 'Book of the Secrets of Enoch'. The former is an important collection of Pharisaic fragments, dating from the 2nd or 1st cent. B.C. The second is of later date and was perhaps written by a Hellenistic Jew of Alexandria. These writings deal with a multitude of subjects, astronomical, physical, historical, and apocalyptic.

Enoch Arden, a poem by A. Tennyson (q.v.), published in 1864.
Enoch Arden, Philip Ray, and Annie Lee are children together in a little seaport town. Both the boys love Annie, but Enoch, more resolute, wins her, and they live happily for some years, till Enoch, under temporary adversity, accepts an offer to go as boatswain in a merchantman. He is shipwrecked and for more than ten years nothing is heard of him. Annie is reduced to poverty, and Philip, who has faithfully loved her throughout, convinced of the death of Enoch, renews his wooing and finally makes her his wife. Then Enoch, rescued from a lonely island, returns. He witnesses, unknown, the happiness of Annie and his children and Philip. Broken-hearted, he finds strength to resolve that they shall not know of his return until after his death.

Enquiry concerning Human Understanding, by Hume, see *Treatise of Human Nature*.

Enquiry concerning the Principles of Morals, by Hume, see *Treatise of Human Nature*.

Enquiry into the Present State of Polite Learning, An, a treatise by Goldsmith (q.v.), published in 1759.
This was Goldsmith's first considerable piece of writing, but the subject was hardly suited to his genius. In it he examines the causes of the decline of polite learning from ancient times, through the dark ages, to its present state in France, Italy, Holland, Germany, and England. He attributes the exist-

ing literary decay in England to the pedantry, solemnity, and lack of naturalness of poets, to the restrictions to which dramatic writers are subject, and to the defective system of the English universities.

Entail, The, a novel by J. Galt (q.v.), published in 1823, the story of the iniquitous disinheritance, by Claud Walkinshaw, a successful packman, of his eldest son in favour of his second son, a 'natural', because he is enabled thereby to reconstitute the ancestral property of the Walkinshaws. The disastrous consequences of this act recoil on himself, and on his children and grandchildren. The melancholy story is enlivened by many racy and humorous passages, such as the description of the judicial inquiry into the fatuity of the 'natural', and by the admirable portraits of the Walkinshaw family.

Entelechy, an Aristotelian term meaning the realization or complete expression of some function; used by later writers to signify that which gives perfection to anything, the informing spirit, the soul. In Rabelais, v. xix, 'Entelechy' is the kingdom of the lady Quintessence.

Entente Cordiale, THE, the political understanding between Great Britain and France established about 1904. It was rendered possible by the agreement arrived at in that year on certain outstanding subjects of dispute, notably Egypt and Morocco.

Eolus, see *Aeolus*.

Éon, CHEVALIER D' (1728–1810), a French political adventurer, who assumed at times the dress of a woman and was employed by Louis XV as a secret agent at the court of Elizabeth of Russia and later in London. Havelock Ellis has introduced the word *Eonism* into psycho-pathology as the generic term for cases of Transvestism, or the mania of men for wearing women's clothes.

Eos, see *Aurora*.

Eōthen, see *Kinglake*.

Ephesians, inhabitants of Ephesus, a word used by Shakespeare ('2 Henry IV', II. ii, 'The Merry Wives of Windsor', IV. v) for boon companions. Shakespeare uses 'Corinthian' (q.v.) in much the same sense.
For 'Diana of the Ephesians' see *Diana*.

Ephesus, SEVEN SLEEPERS OF, see *Seven Sleepers of Ephesus*.

Ephialtes, a demon supposed to cause nightmare, probably derived from a Greek verb meaning 'to leap upon'.

Epic, a poem that celebrates in the form of a continuous narrative the achievements of one or more heroic personages of history or tradition. Among the great epics of the world may be mentioned the 'Iliad', 'Odyssey', and 'Aeneid' of classical, and the 'Mahabharata' and 'Ramayana' of Hindu literature; the 'Chanson de Roland'; the 'Poema del Cid';

Milton's 'Paradise Lost'; Boiardo's 'Orlando Innamorato'; Ariosto's 'Orlando Furioso'; Tasso's 'Gerusalemme Liberata'; and Camoën's 'Lusiads' (qq.v.).

Epic of Hades, The, a poem in blank verse by Sir L. Morris (q.v.), published in 1876–7.

It consists of monologues put in the mouths of some of the principal characters of Greek mythology, such as Marsyas, Helen, Psyche, Andromeda, Narcissus, Laocoon, whom the poet encounters as he visits successively Tartarus, Hades, and Olympus.

Epic of the Wheat, The, see *Norris (F.)*.

Epicede or EPICEDIUM, a funeral ode.

Epicœne, or The Silent Woman, a comedy by Jonson (q.v.), first acted in 1609, and one of the most popular of his dramas. Morose, an egotistic bachelor with an insane aversion to noise, proposes to disinherit his nephew Sir Dauphine Eugenie, whom he suspects of ridiculing him, and to marry, if he can find a Silent Woman. Cutbeard, his barber, has found such a one in Epicœne. Immediately after the marriage Epicœne recovers the vigorous use of her tongue, to the dismay of Morose, which is increased by the arrival of his nephew and friends, with a party of 'Collegiate Ladies' and musicians to celebrate the bridal. Driven frantic by the hubbub, and having in vain consulted a pseudo-divine and a canon lawyer as to possible grounds of divorce, he accepts his nephew's offer to rid him of Epicœne for five hundred pounds a year and the reversion of his property. Whereupon Sir Dauphine pulls off Epicœne's peruke and reveals her as a boy whom he has trained for the part (the word 'Epicene' means 'with characteristics of either sex').

Among the characters who contribute to the humour of the play are Captain Otter, who always speaks under correction when his wife is present; Sir Amorous La-Foole, a braggart and coward; the Collegiate Ladies (q.v.), and Sir John Daw, a braggart knight, who pretends to learning and collects the titles of classical works without knowing their contents.

Epictētus, Stoic philosopher (*c.* A.D. 60–140) of Hierapolis in Phrygia, a freedman of Epaphroditus, himself a freedman of Nero. He taught at Rome and subsequently at Nicopolis in Epirus, and is said to have been lame and poor. He wrote nothing himself, and the 'Enchiridion', or collection of his principles, was compiled by his disciple Arrian (q.v.). According to Epictetus, virtue consists in endurance and abstinence. Riches and honours are foreign to man and independent of him; but the true good and evil of life are within his control.

Epicurean, The, a prose romance by T. Moore (q.v.), published in 1827.

This is the story of Alciphron, a Greek Epicurean philosopher, who goes to Egypt in A.D. 257 to learn the secret of eternal life. He there assists a young Egyptian priestess,

Alethe, who is secretly a Christian, to escape. By her and by an anchorite he is converted to Christianity. Alethe suffers martyrdom, and Alciphron himself is sentenced to hard labour and dies in the mines.

EPICŪRUS (341–270 B.C.), the founder of the school of philosophy that bears his name, was the son of an Athenian father. He was brought up in Samos, and after teaching philosophy in various places finally established his school in Athens. His will and some fragments of his writings survive, but his philosophy may be best read in the 'De Rerum Natura' of Lucretius. He adopted the atomic theory of Democritus (q.v.), concerning the universe, and in ethics regarded the absence of pain—ἀταραξία, or repose of mind—as the greatest good. Since virtue produces this repose, it is virtue that we should pursue.

Epidaurus, a town on the NE. coast of the Peloponnese and a centre of the worship of Aesculapius (q.v.), whom Milton refers to as 'the God in Epidaurus' ('Paradise Lost', ix. 506).

Epĭgŏnī, 'the Descendants', the name given in Greek mythology to the sons of the seven heroes who perished in the expedition against Thebes (see *Eteocles*). Ten years after this expedition the Epigoni, led by Adrastus (q.v.), attacked Thebes to avenge their fathers, and razed it to the ground. The name is also applied to the heirs of Alexander the Great's successors (the Diadochi).

Epigram, originally an inscription, usually in verse, e.g. on a tomb; hence a short poem ending in a witty turn of thought; hence a pointed or antithetical saying.

EPIMĔNĬDĒS, a semi-mythical Cretan poet and soothsayer, who is said to have visited Athens in the 6th cent. B.C. to purify the city from the taint of a sacrilege. Legend relates that while tending his father's flocks in his boyhood, he one day entered a cave, fell asleep, and did not awake for 57 years, when to his surprise he found his brother grown an old man. The quotation in Titus i. 12, Κρῆτες ἀεὶ ψεῦσται, etc., is said to be from his works.

Epimētheūs, in Greek mythology, brother of Prometheus (q.v.). Less wise than his brother, he married Pandora (q.v.) and opened her box, whence issued the train of evils which have since vexed mankind.

Epiphany, THE, meaning 'manifestation', the festival commemorating the manifestation of Christ to the Gentiles in the persons of the Magi; observed on 6 Jan. Hence 'Twelfth-night', the festival of the 'Three Kings'.

Epipsychidion, a poem by P. B. Shelley (q.v.), published in 1821.

The poem is addressed to Emilia Viviani, a lady in whom the poet thought he had found the visionary soul in perfect harmony with his own ('Epipsychidion' would mean 'a soul upon a soul', that is 'a soul that is complementary to a soul'). The poem is an exposition and defence of free love, not only Platonic but passionate.

Epistolae Obscurorum Virorum ('Epistles of Obscure Men'), published in 1515–17, are an anonymous collection of letters in medieval Latin purporting to be written by various bachelors and masters in theology to Ortuinus Gratius, a famous opponent of the new learning, in which they incidentally expose themselves to ridicule and to scurrilous charges. The letters are attributed principally to Ulrich von Hutten (1488–1523), soldier, humanist, and supporter of Luther, and were written in connexion with the celebrated Reuchlin–Pfefferkorn (qq.v.) controversy.

Epithalamion, a splendid hymn by Spenser (q.v.), perhaps in celebration of his marriage with Elizabeth Boyle in 1594. The poem was printed with the 'Amoretti' (q.v.) in 1595. The name is Greek, 'upon the bride-chamber'.

Epode, (1) a kind of lyric poem invented by Archilochus, in which a long line is followed by a shorter one, in metres different from the elegiac (q.v.), as in Horace's 'Epodes'; (2) the part of a lyric ode sung after the strophe and antistrophe (q.v.).

Eponymous, that gives his name to anything, used especially of the mythical 'personages from whose names the names of places or peoples are reputed to be derived.

Epopee, an epic poem, or the epic species of poetry.

Eppie, in G. Eliot's 'Silas Marner' (q.v.), the daughter of Cass and adopted child of Silas (abbreviation of Hephzibah, 'if it's nowise wrong to shorten the name').

Eppur si muove, see *Galileo.*

Epstein, SIR JACOB (1880–1959), sculptor, born in New York of Russian–Polish parents. He settled in London in 1905. He modelled portraits in bronze and carved and modelled large figures, often of religious subjects.

Er the son of Armenius, The Myth of, in the 10th book of Plato's 'Republic' (q.v.). Er, having been killed in battle, came to life again on the twelfth day and related what he had seen in the other world. The story is told to illustrate the rewards that await the just after death.

ERASMUS, DESIDERIUS (1466–1536), the great Dutch humanist, was born at Rotterdam. Under pressure of his guardians he became an Augustinian monk, but thanks to the protection of the bishop of Cambrai was allowed to leave the cloister and travel extensively in Europe. He came more than once to England, where he was welcomed by the great scholars of the day, More, Colet, and Grocyn, and was induced by Fisher to lecture at Cambridge on Greek (he was appointed Lady Margaret Reader) from 1511 to 1514.

He received from Archbishop Warham the benefice of Aldington in Kent, and on his resigning it, a pension which was continued until his death. His principal works were the 'Novum Instrumentum', a new Latin version of the New Testament, with a commentary (1516); 'Encomium Moriae' ('The Praise of Folly', 1509, a satire written at the suggestion of Sir Thomas More, principally directed against theologians and Church dignitaries); 'Enchiridion Militis Christiani' (1503, a manual of simple piety according to the teaching of Jesus Christ, which was translated by Tyndale into English, and also into other languages), 'Institutio Christiani Principis' ('Education of a Christian Prince'), the vivid and entertaining 'Colloquia' and letters furnishing autobiographical details and pictures of contemporary life, which have been drawn upon by C. Reade in 'The Cloister and the Hearth' (q.v.) and by Sir W. Scott in 'Anne of Geierstein' (q.v.). His 'Adagia', a collection of Latin and Greek proverbs, traced to their source with witty comments, one of the first works of the new learning (1500), was much drawn upon by Rabelais among others. Erasmus prepared the way for the Reformation by his writings—his version of the New Testament, the scathing comments on Church abuses that accompanied it, and his 'Encomium Moriae'. With the movement itself he sympathized at first. But he refused to intervene either for or against Luther at the time of the Diet of Worms, although invoked by both sides. He urged moderation on both and disclaimed sympathy with Luther's violence and extreme conclusions, and at a later stage (1524, in his tract on 'Free Will') entered into controversy with him. The standard edition of the 'Letters' of Erasmus is edited by P. S. and H. M. Allen.

Erastian, a name applied to the doctrine, attributed to Erastus, of the subordination of the ecclesiastical to the secular power. Erastus, or Liebler, was a physician of Heidelberg in the 16th cent. His actual efforts were mainly directed against the use of excommunication, which was exercised tyrannically by the Calvinistic churches. [OED.]

Eràto, one of the Muses (q.v.), who presided over love-poetry.

ERCELDOUNE, THOMAS OF, called also the RHYMER and LEARMONT (*fl.* 1220?–97?), seer and poet, is mentioned in the chartulary (1294) of the Trinity House of Soltra as having inherited lands in Erceldoune, a Berwickshire village. He is said to have predicted the death of Alexander III, king of Scotland, and the battle of Bannockburn, and is the traditional fountain of many (fabricated) oracles, one of which 'foretold' the accession of James VI to the English throne. He is the reputed author of a poem on the Tristram story, which Sir Walter Scott considered genuine; it probably emanated from a French source. The romance of 'True Thomas' and the 'ladye gaye', popularly attributed to him, may be placed after 1401 (edited by Dr. J. A. H. Murray; 1875).

ERCKMANN-CHATRIAN, the joint name adopted by ÉMILE ERCKMANN (1822–99) and ALEXANDRE CHATRIAN (1826–90), French authors of a series of novels, set in Alsace and treating of the wars of the French Revolution and the Napoleonic period, as seen from the standpoint of the humble soldier. The best known are the 'Histoire d'un conscrit' (1864), 'Waterloo' (1865), and 'Histoire d'un paysan' (1868). 'L'Ami Fritz' (1876), which falls outside this cycle, was also a successful work.

Erebus in Greek mythology, (1) a place of nether darkness, on the way to Hades; (2) the god of darkness.

Erebus, The, and **The Terror,** the ships of Sir John Franklin's expedition, which sailed in 1845 in search of the North-West Passage. They were abandoned in 1848 after having been for 18 months beset in the ice. Both ships had been employed by Sir James Clark Ross in his Antarctic voyage of 1839–41.

Erechthēus, a mythical king of Athens, either identical with, or the grandson of, the equally mythical Erichthonius. In a war of the Athenians against the Eleusinians and their ally Eumolpus, son of Poseidon, he was advised by the Delphic oracle that in order to be victorious he must sacrifice one of his daughters, which he did. The Eleusinians were defeated, but Poseidon in anger destroyed Erechtheus and all his house. This legend is the subject of a tragedy in the Greek form by Swinburne (q.v.).

Erewhon (pronounced as three short syllables, 'ĕ-rĕ-whŏn'), a satirical romance by S. Butler (1835–1902, q.v.), published in 1872.

The narrator, having crossed an unexplored chain of mountains in a remote part of a colony (Butler had in mind New Zealand), comes upon the land of Erewhon (an anagram of 'nowhere'). The institutions that he finds there and describes are a vigorous satire on the hypocrisy, compromise, and mental torpor that Butler was ever inveighing against. The most notable feature in the Erewhonian system is the paradoxical substitution for moral obliquity of physical ailment as a proper subject for punishment. Whereas pulmonary consumption is a crime, embezzlement is a matter for condolence and curative treatment. In the Musical Banks, the Birth Formulae, etc., we have satires on ecclesiastical institutions and parental tyranny. There is an ingenious description of the development of machinery to the point when it had to be completely abolished lest it should 'take charge' and overwhelm the inhabitants. Finally the narrator escapes from the country in a balloon of his own construction, accompanied by an Erewhonian lady with whom he has fallen in love.

Erewhon Revisited, a sequel to 'Erewhon' (q.v.) by S. Butler (1835–1902, q.v.), published in 1901.

Higgs (to adopt the name by which the narrator of Erewhon was known to the Erewhonians), driven by an overmastering desire to revisit that country, does so after an interval of twenty years, to discover that his ascent in a balloon has been held miraculous, that a religious myth has grown up round it, that he is himself now worshipped as the child of the sun, and that a great temple is on the point of being dedicated to him. The way in which public credulity has been exploited by the professors Hanky and Panky, and the new religion adopted by the 'musical banks', is told with consummate irony. Horrified at the mischief he has done, and goaded by Hanky's sermon at the dedication, Higgs reveals himself, but is hustled away by friendly hands. An amusing conference follows between all concerned to decide what is to be done about 'Sunchildism', as the new religion is called; Higgs is then smuggled out of the country.

Eric, a legendary king of Sweden, who could control the direction of the wind by turning his cap.

Eric, or Little by Little, an edifying story of school life by Frederic William Farrar (1831–1903, dean of Canterbury), published in 1858. The book, which was written when Farrar was a master at Harrow, proved highly popular.

Erĭdănus, originally a river-god, mentioned by Hesiod and Herodotus as a northern river in which amber was found. But Latin poets identify Eridanus with the river Po. See also *Phaeton.*

ERIGĔNA, see *Scotus.*

Erĭgŏnē, see *Icarius.*

Erin, the ancient name of Ireland.

Erin go bragh! 'Ireland for ever!', the refrain of 'The Exile of Erin', a poem by T. Campbell (q.v.).

Erīnÿes, see *Furies.*

Erkenwald, see *Paul's Cathedral.*

Erl-King, the German *Erl-könig* (alderking), an erroneous rendering of the Danish *eller-konge,* king of the elves, a malignant goblin, who in German legend, and in Goethe's poem on the subject, haunts the Black Forest, and lures people, particularly children, to destruction. Goethe's poem was the foundation of one of Schubert's best-known songs ('Erlkönig', written in 1816), and was translated by Sir W. Scott.

Ermeline, in 'Reynard the Fox' (q.v.), Reynard's wife.

Ermensul, see *Irminsul.*

Ermine Street or ERMING STREET or ERMYN STREET, the name of a road corresponding in parts with the old Roman road from London through Huntingdon to Lincoln. The derivation is uncertain. Dr. Guest connected it with the names of the Ermings or Fenmen. It has been suggested that it is from 'Irmin', the Teutonic god whose name appears in 'Irminsul' (q.v.).

Ernani, see *Hernani.*

Ernest Maltravers, and Alice, or The Mysteries, a novel and its sequel by Bulwer Lytton (q.v.), published in 1837 and 1838.

The author, in his preface, states that he is indebted to Goethe's 'Wilhelm Meister' for the idea of a moral education set forth in these books. Ernest Maltravers, a young man of wealth and position, benighted on a moor, seeks refuge in the hovel of Luke Darvil, a villainous cut-throat. He is saved from murder and robbery by Darvil's daughter Alice, a beautiful, uneducated, and morally undeveloped child, who at the same time escapes from her father's cruel treatment. Touched by her helplessness, Ernest constitutes himself her protector, but finally yields to his passion for her. Alice thereafter remains faithful to Ernest, though circumstances separate them for many years. During these Ernest loves a number of women, and twice becomes engaged, but the marriages are prevented by the designs of his unscrupulous enemy, Lumley Ferrers. Finally Ernest is reunited and married to Alice. With this story is woven the tragedy of the unfortunate Castruccio Cesarini, the disappointed Italian poetaster, who becomes the tool and finally the murderer of Ferrers.

Ernulf or ERNULPHUS (1040–1124), bishop of Rochester, and author of the 'Textus Roffensis', a collection of laws, papal decrees, and documents relating to the church of Rochester. The comprehensive curse or excommunication of Ernulphus figures in Bk. III, chs. x, xi of Sterne's 'Tristram Shandy' (q.v.).

Eros, see *Cupid.* Eros in Shakespeare's 'Antony and Cleopatra' (q.v.) is the faithful attendant of Antony, and kills himself to avoid killing his master. An aluminium statue of a winged figure, called Eros, by Alfred Gilbert, surmounting a fountain in Piccadilly Circus, was erected in 1893 as a memorial to the Earl of Shaftesbury (1801–85), the philanthropist.

Erostrătus, or ERATOSTRATUS, see *Herostratus.*

Erotokritos, of Vincenzo Kornaros, a medieval Greek epic, edited (1929) by J. Mavrogordato.

ERRA-PATER, the assumed name of the author of an astrological almanac first published in 1535, referred to by Butler in 'Hudibras', I. i, and by Congreve in 'Love for Love' (qq.v.).

Erse, a term used to designate (1) Irish Gaelic; (2) in 18th-cent. practice, the Gaelic language of Scotland (which is in fact of Irish origin).

Esau, see *Jacob and Esau.*

Esculapius, see *Aesculapius.*

Escurial or ESCORIAL, THE, a vast and gloomy edifice on the Sierra NW. of Madrid, designed as a palace, a convent, and a tomb by Philip II, who erected it in accomplishment of a vow made in a moment of panic at the battle of St. Quentin (1557). San Lorenzo, to whom the vow was made, was burnt to death on a slow fire, and the plan of the building resembles a gridiron. Philip II died there (1598), after having lived there fourteen years. The origin of the name is uncertain.

Esdras, the reputed author of two of the books of the Apocrypha: the first mainly a compilation from Chronicles, Nehemiah, and Ezra; the second a record of angelic revelations and visions, pointing to the destruction of the wicked and the salvation of the righteous.

Esmond, The History of Henry Esmond, Esquire, a novel by Thackeray (q.v.), published in 1852.

The History is narrated by Henry Esmond himself. He is the son (supposed to be illegitimate) of the 3rd Viscount Castlewood, who was killed fighting for King James at the battle of the Boyne. Henry then comes under the protection of the 4th viscount, in whose household he serves as page. He is kindly treated by Lord Castlewood, and particularly by Lady Castlewood, for whom he conceives a profound devotion. He has the misfortune to bring the small-pox into the household, by which Lady Castlewood loses some of her beauty, and in consequence much of her husband's love. The unprincipled Lord Mohun takes advantage of the estrangement between them to attempt to seduce Lady Castlewood. This attempt is discovered by Lord Castlewood, and in spite of Henry's endeavour to take the quarrel on himself, a duel follows, in which Lord Castlewood is mortally wounded. On his death-bed he reveals to Henry that the 3rd viscount was married to Henry's mother and that Henry is the rightful owner of the title and property. Henry decides to sacrifice himself and not claim his rights, so as not to injure Lady Castlewood and her son Frank. But Lady Castlewood, in her passionate grief for her lord's death, bitterly upbraids Henry for allowing the duel to take place, and banishes him from her house.

Henry joins the army and serves with distinction in Marlborough's campaigns, from Blenheim to Malplaquet. In the course of his service he returns to England, and hearing a false rumour that Lady Castlewood is about to marry her chaplain, the square-toed Tom Tusher, hurries to see her. The scene of their reunion, in Winchester Cathedral, is one of the most touching and dramatic passages in Thackeray's works. In spite of her petulance, Lady Castlewood has given her heart to

Henry, and henceforth loves him tenderly. But meanwhile her two children, Frank, the present viscount, and Beatrix his sister, have grown up. The latter is a girl of extraordinary beauty, but vain of her beauty and ambitious. Henry falls deeply in love with her, but she is too proud to consider an alliance with one whom she regards as of illegitimate birth. She becomes affianced to the duke of Hamilton, but he is murdered by Lord Mohun before the marriage can take place. Finally she causes the failure of a scheme promoted by Henry for the proclamation of the Pretender, by flirting with the prince and luring him to Castlewood at the moment when his presence in London is necessary. Completely disillusioned, Henry abandons her and marries Lady Castlewood, his act of self-sacrifice having before this become known both to her and to her son and daughter. Henry and his wife migrate to Virginia and their subsequent history in that country is referred to in 'The Virginians' (q.v.). Beatrix, it appears from the latter work, subsequently married Tom Tusher (who became a bishop) and, after his death, Baron Bernstein. Thackeray gives a vivid picture of English society in the early years of the 18th cent., introducing Dick Steele and his Prue, Marlborough and his Duchess, Swift, and Addison.

Esmond, BEATRIX, one of the principal characters in Thackeray's 'Esmond' and 'The Virginians' (qq.v.).

Esop, see *Aesop.*

Esotĕ'ric, a word used by Lucian, who attributes to Aristotle a classification of his own works into 'esoteric', i.e. designed for, or appropriate to, an inner circle of advanced or privileged disciples, and 'exoteric', i.e. popular, untechnical. Later writers use the word to designate the secret doctrines said to have been taught by Pythagoras to a select few of his disciples.

Esperanto, a universal language introduced in 1887 by Dr. L. L. Zamenhof, and now somewhat widely used.

Esplandian, the son of Amadis of Gaul (q.v.) and Oriana. In his childhood he was suckled by a lioness by which he had been carried off, but being recovered by his parents became a doughty knight, performed great exploits against the Turks, and married Leonorina, the daughter of the Greek emperor.

Espriella, *Letters of,* see *Southey.*

Esprit d'escalier, French, a tardy wit, which thinks of a smart retort or witticism too late, when its owner is going downstairs, on his way out of the house.

ESQUEMELING, EXQUEMELING, or OEXMELIN, ALEXANDER OLIVIER, a Dutch physician, who lived with the buccaneers (q.v.), 1668–74, and published an account of them (including Morgan) and their doings. This was translated into Spanish, French, and English.

Essay concerning Human Understanding, a philosophical treatise by Locke (q.v.), published in 1690 (2nd edition, 1694; 4th, 1700; 5th, 1706; each with large additions).

The Essay is an examination into the nature of knowledge, as calculated to guide us to the proper use of our understanding. Locke begins by refuting the doctrine of 'innate ideas', and maintaining that all knowledge is of empiric origin. The materials or objects of understanding are termed by him *ideas,* and after giving an account of the origin, sorts, and extent of our ideas, he considers what knowledge the mind derives from them. The source of ideas is *experience,* the observation of external objects or the internal operations of the mind, i.e. sensation or reflection. Sensation is always of a quality. Qualities are either primary—extension, figure, mobility, and number; or secondary—not really belonging to things, but imputed to them, depending on our subjective perception, and inscrutably connected with the primary qualities, which alone really belong to things. A number of simple ideas being constantly found to go together, the mind is led to suppose a substratum for them, and this we call *substance,* but have no other idea of its nature. We are equally ignorant of spiritual substance, the substratum of the operations of the mind. We do not even know whether material and spiritual substance are the same or different. The idea of cause or power is derived from experience, principally of the workings of the mind. The idea of infinity is a negative idea derived from experience of the absence of any limit to the power of imagination to extend space, time, or number.

Knowledge consists in the perception of the agreement or disagreement of ideas, and is either intuitive and direct, or demonstrative (through the interposition of a third idea). Knowledge in matters of real existence is limited to two certainties, of our own existence, by intuition, and of the existence of God, by demonstration. For, as regards the latter, we have intuitive certainty that bare nothing cannot produce any real being. Therefore from eternity there has been something to which thinking perceiving beings owe their powers, that is God, Eternal Mind.

We have a lesser degree of certainty of the existence of finite beings without us, of which the mind perceives nothing but its own ideas, and cannot know that they agree with the things themselves. Locke advances various arguments for the objective validity of sensitive knowledge, but points out that even if we admit its validity, this knowledge is narrowly limited: we know only of the existence together, here and now, of collections of simple ideas; we cannot demonstrate the necessity of their coexistence. There are therefore very few general propositions, carrying with them undoubted certainty, to be made concerning substances; a perfect science of natural bodies is unattainable. Experience and history is all we can attain to, from which we may derive advantages of ease and health. Still less can we attain to 'scientifical' knowledge of spirits. Knowledge at once general and real must be, not of the relations of ideas to reality, but of ideas to each other, e.g. mathematics, and also moral science (though on the latter point he is more doubtful in his 'Reasonableness of Christianity'). The faculty that God has given us in place of clear knowledge is judgement, whereby the mind takes a proposition to be true or false without demonstration. Locke discusses the relations of faith and reason. Unlike Bacon and Hobbes, he holds that faith is nothing but the firm assent of the mind, which cannot be accorded to anything except on good reason. Revelation must be judged by reason. But the field of knowledge being so limited, it must be supplemented by faith, and this is the basis of Locke's 'Reasonableness of Christianity' published in 1695.

Essay of Dramatick Poesie, by Dryden (q.v.), published in 1668, and probably written at Charlton, near Malmesbury, in Wiltshire, whither the poet betook himself during the plague.

It takes the form of a dialogue between four interlocutors, Eugenius (Dorset), Crites (Sir Robert Howard), Lisideius (Sir Charles Sedley), and Neander (Dryden himself). The four friends have taken a boat on the Thames on the day of the engagement between the English and Dutch fleets in the mouth of the river (3 June 1665). At first the friends are mainly occupied with this stirring event, but presently, as the sound of firing becomes more distant, their talk turns to literary subjects, and they discuss the comparative merits of the English and French drama, and of the old and the new English drama. The Essay is largely concerned with a defence of the use of rhyme in drama. It also contains an admirable appreciation of Shakespeare.

Essay on Criticism, a didactic poem by Pope (q.v.), in heroic couplets, published anonymously in 1711. It begins with an exposition of the rules of taste and the authority to be attributed to the ancient writers on the subject. The laws by which a critic should be guided are then discussed, and instances are given of critics who have departed from them. The work is remarkable as having been written when Pope was only 21.

Essay on Man, a philosophical poem in heroic couplets by Pope (q.v.), published in 1732–4.

It consists of four epistles, addressed to Henry St. John, Lord Bolingbroke, and perhaps to some extent inspired by his fragmentary philosophical writings. It is part of a larger poem projected but not completed. Its object is to vindicate the ways of God to man; to prove that the scheme of the universe is the best in spite of appearances of evil, and that our failure to see the perfection of the whole is due to our limited vision. Epistle I treats of the nature and state of man

with respect to the universe; Epistle II, of man with respect to himself as an individual; Epistle III, of man with respect to society; Epistle IV, of man with respect to happiness. Dugald Stewart expressed the view that the Essay is 'the noblest specimen of philosophical poetry which our language affords' ('Active and Moral Powers', Works, 7. 133), a judgement which would now hardly be endorsed. Dr. Johnson's verdict was very different: 'Never were penury of knowledge and vulgarity of sentiment so happily disguised.'

Essays and Reviews, a collection of essays on religious subjects from a broad church standpoint, published in 1860. The editor was the Revd. Henry Bristow Wilson (author of 'The Communion of Saints', 1851), and the other contributors were Frederick Temple (the future archbishop), Mark Pattison (q.v.), Jowett (q.v.), Rowland Williams, Baden Powell, and C. W. Goodwin.

The essays, which were, in general, critical of doctrine, and in some instances provocative in form, occasioned much offence. Wilson and Williams were tried in the Court of Arches (q.v.) and found guilty of heresy, but were acquitted on appeal. The only essay that has much interest today is Pattison's, on the 'Tendencies of Religious Thought in England, 1688–1750'.

Essays, or Counsels, Civill and Morall, The, of F. Bacon (q.v.), are collections of reflections and generalizations, and extracts from previous authors, woven together, for the most part, into counsels for the successful conduct of life and the management of men.

Three editions of the essays were published in Bacon's lifetime. The first, that of 1597, contained ten essays; the second, that of 1612, contained thirty-eight essays; and the third, that of 1625, contained fifty-eight. Of these some deal with questions of state policy, such as the essay on 'Greatness of Kingdoms'; some with personal conduct, such as those on 'Wisdom for a Man's Self' and 'Cunning'; some on abstract subjects, such as 'Truth', 'Death', and 'Unity'; while some reveal Bacon's delight in Nature, such as the pleasant essay on 'Gardens'.

Essays contributed to the Edinburgh Review, Critical and Historical, by T. B. Macaulay (q.v.), a collection published in 1843 and later editions.

The 'Essays' deal with the following subjects (the date of original publication is appended): Milton (1825), Machiavelli (1827), Hallam's Constitutional History (1828), Southey's Colloquies on Society (1830), Robert Montgomery's Poems (1830), Southey's Edition of the Pilgrim's Progress (1830), Civil Disabilities of the Jews (1831), Moore's Life of Byron (1831), Croker's Edition of Boswell's Life of Johnson (1831), Lord Nugent's Memorials of Hampden (1831), Burleigh and his Times (1832), War of the Succession in Spain (1833), Horace Walpole (1833), the Earl of Chatham (1834), Mackintosh's History of the Revolution (1835), Lord Bacon (1837), Sir William Temple (1838), Gladstone on Church and State (1839), Lord Clive (1840), Ranke's History of the Popes (1840), Comic Dramatists of the Restoration (1841), Lord Holland (1841), Warren Hastings (1841), Frederic the Great (1842), Madame d'Arblay (1843), Addison (1843), the Earl of Chatham (second article, 1844). They take, as a rule, the form, not so much of a review of the books named at the head of each, but of a general survey, biographical, political, or literary, of the subject of that book. They are occasionally truculent, as that on Croker's 'Boswell', and misleading (it is said), as those on Bacon and Hastings. The best are those on Chatham, Clive, and Sir William Temple.

Essays in Criticism, see *Arnold* (M.).

Essays of Elia, *The,* miscellaneous essays by C. Lamb (q.v.), of which the first series appeared in the 'London Magazine' between 1820 and 1823, and were republished in a separate volume in the latter year. The second series was published in 1833. Lamb adopted the pseudonym Elia to save the susceptibilities of his brother John, still a clerk in the South-Sea House, which is the subject of the first of the 'Essays'. The name was that of an Italian clerk formerly in the service of that institution. Lamb appears to have pronounced it 'Ellia', but see 'The Pronunciation of *Elia*', by G. L. Barnett in 'Studies in Romanticism', v. i, Autumn 1965.

The 'Essays' are largely autobiographical; they deal with mankind at large as seen through the medium of Lamb's own experiences and impressions. They present, with exquisite humour and pathos, and in a brilliant and inimitable style, characters that the author has known (such as Samuel Salt, his father's employer, in 'Some of the Old Benchers of the Inner Temple'), recollections of childhood (as in 'Christ's Hospital' and 'Blakesmoor') or of later life (as in 'The South-Sea House'), personal experiences (as in 'The Superannuated Man'), the productions of a playful or melancholy fancy (as in 'A Dissertation upon Roast Pig' and 'Dream Children'), and general comments and criticism.

Essenes, a Jewish sect, dating from before the Christian era, whose name is perhaps derived from a Syriac word meaning 'pious'. They held certain speculative opinions, grafted on their Judaism, regarding the soul and the future life, and offered prayers to the sun. They lived a monastic and ascetic life, renouncing marriage, and had community of goods.

Este, HOUSE OF, one of the most celebrated of the princely families of Italy. Albert Azzo, lord of Este in Italy, born about 996, said to be descended from Odoacer, king of Italy (476), married first Cunegonda of the house of Guelf, by whom he became the ancestor of the houses of Brunswick and Hanover, and secondly Gersonda, whose descendants were

the Estes, lords of Ferrara and Modena. The house of Este is exalted in Ariosto's 'Orlando Furioso' (q.v.), where Ruggiero (Rogero, q.v.) is represented as its ancestor.

See also *Leonora d'Este.*

Estella, a character in Dickens's 'Great Expectations' (q.v.).

Esther Lyon (or BYCLIFFE), the heroine of G. Eliot's 'Felix Holt' (q.v.).

Esther Summerson, a character in Dickens's 'Bleak House' (q.v.), and narrator of part of the story.

Esther Waters, a novel by G. Moore (q.v.), published in 1894.

It is the story of the life of a religiously minded girl, a Plymouth Sister, driven from home into service at 17 by a drunken stepfather. She obtains a situation at Woodview, the house of the Barfields, where a racing-stable is kept, and all above- and below-stairs (except Mrs. Barfield, a Plymouth Sister like Esther) are wrapt up in gambling on races. There, in a moment of weakness, she is seduced by a fellow servant and deserted. She has to leave her place, though kindly treated by Mrs. Barfield. Then follows a poignant tale of poverty, hardship, and humiliation: the lying-in hospital, service as wet-nurse, other miserable situations, even the workhouse, in the mother's brave struggle to rear her child. Her seducer re-enters her life, marries her, and makes a good husband. But he is a book-maker and public-house keeper; exposure to weather at the races ruins his health, and trouble with the authorities over betting at his house causes the latter to be closed. He dies, and leaves his wife and son penniless. Finally Esther returns to Woodview, where she finds peace at last, with Mrs. Barfield, now a widow, living alone and impoverished in a corner of the old house.

Estienne (STEPHANUS), the name of a family of French printers of the 16th cent. Henri Estienne (*d.* 1520), of a Provençal family, came to Paris in 1502 and started printing. Of his sons, Robert (1503–59), a scholar as well as a printer, who adopted the device of the olive tree, printed a number of important works, a critical Latin New Testament (1523), a Latin Bible (1528) and a 'Thesaurus linguae Latinae' (1532, the best Latin dictionary of the time). Robert was the first to number the verses of the N.T. (in Greek, 1550) and later of the whole Bible. He printed several important works in Greek in Garamond's (q.v.) types besides Eusebius, 'Historia Ecclesiastica', 1544, and was King's Printer in Latin, Greek, and Hebrew. He moved to Geneva in 1551. Henri Estienne (1531–98), the son of Robert, did valuable work in collecting and collating manuscripts in Italy. He printed at Geneva works of Greek authors and a 'Thesaurus Graecae Linguae' (1572).

Estmere, KING, the subject of an ancient legend preserved in one of the ballads in Percy's 'Reliques' (q.v.).

King Estmere is a king of England who with his brother Adler goes to the court of King Adland to ask the hand of his daughter, but learns that Sir Bremor, 'a foule paynim', king of Spain, has forestalled him. The lady, however, accepts him. While preparations are being made for the wedding, the king of Spain arrives and claims his bride. Estmere returns disguised as a harper, slays the king of Spain, drives off the 'Kempery men' (i.e. the fighting men), and marries the lady.

Esto Perpetua Club, THE, founded in 1784, consisted of supporters of Fox against Pitt, including Dr. French Laurence, George Ellis, the antiquary, General Richard Fitzpatrick, and Lord John Townshend. The idea of 'The Rolliad' (q.v.) originated with this club.

Estotiland, a mythical tract in North America, supposed to lie near the Arctic circle, east of Hudson Bay. It is mentioned by Milton, 'Paradise Lost', x. 686.

Estrildis, a German maiden brought to England by King Humber (q.v.), loved by Locrine, king of Britain, and mother by him of Sabrina. She and her daughter were drowned in the Severn by Locrine's angry queen, Gwendolen. The story is told by Geoffrey of Monmouth and reappears in Spenser's 'Faerie Queene' (II. x), also in Swinburne's 'Locrine'. In Wace and Layamon, the name of Æstrild's daughter is *Abren*, and she is drowned in the river *Auren*, which Sir F. Madden (note in his edition of Layamon, l. 2498) thinks is the Avon (flowing into the sea at Christchurch). The Welsh name of the Severn is *Havren*.

Etĕŏclēs, son of Oedipus (q.v.) and Jocasta, and brother of Polyneices. After their father's death it was agreed that the brothers should reign in Thebes in alternate years; but Eteocles refused to give up the throne at the appointed time. Polyneices, assisted by Adrastus, king of Argos, and the Argive army headed by seven heroes, marched against Thebes, and was opposed by Eteocles. After indecisive fighting, it was decided that the struggle should be settled by the brothers in single combat. In this they slew each other. The Argive chiefs were slain with the exception of Adrastus. This war was known as that of 'The Seven against Thebes', the subject of a tragedy by Aeschylus.

Ethelburga's, ST., one of the earliest extant churches in London. Ethelburga (*d.* 676?) was sister of Erkenwald, bishop of London (*d.* 693), and was herself abbess of Barking.

Ethelfleda, see *Æthelflæd*.

Ethelred, see *Æthelred*.

Ethelwold, ST., see *Æthelwold*.

ETHEREGE or **ETHEREDGE,** SIR GEORGE (1634?–91?), perhaps son of Capt. George Etheredge, an early planter in the Bermudas, spent part of his early manhood in France. He produced 'The Comical Revenge, or Love in a Tub' (q.v.) in 1664.

The serious portions are in rhymed heroics, setting a fashion that was followed for some years, while the comic underplot in prose with its lively realistic scenes was, as Gosse has pointed out, the foundation of the English comedy of Congreve, Goldsmith, and Sheridan. In this Etherege drew his inspiration from Molière. In 1668 he produced 'She would if she could', and in 1676 'The Man of Mode' (qq.v.), two further comedies. Etherege, thanks to the protection of Mary of Modena, was sent in 1685 as envoy to Ratisbon, where he remained for some years, a period of his life on which his manuscript 'Letter-book', discovered by Sir Edmund Gosse (and since published), throws an interesting light.

Etherington, EARL OF, a character in Scott's 'St. Ronan's Well' (q.v.).

Ethiop queen, THE STARR'D, in Milton's 'Il Penseroso' (q.v.), is Cassiopea (q.v.).

Étienne (STEPHANUS), the printer, see *Estienne*.

Eton College, near Windsor, was founded by Henry VI, as a preparatory school for King's College, Cambridge, the charter of foundation being dated 1440 and followed by various charters of endowment. The College included, in addition to some 300 sons of noblemen and gentlemen, 70 king's scholars on the foundation, who passed by seniority to King's College, Cambridge (see also under *Montem*). In 1443 Waynflete, headmaster of Winchester, was induced by the king to migrate to Eton, and was accompanied by five fellows and thirty-five scholars of Winchester.

Among the many names eminent in literature, connected with Eton, may be mentioned those of Edward Hall, the historian, Thomas Tusser, Sir Henry Wotton, Edmund Waller, Henry More, Bishop Pearson, Bolingbroke, Henry Fielding, Thomas Gray, Horace Walpole, George Canning, Richard Porson, Shelley, Praed, Gladstone, Hallam, Milman, Swinburne, and Robert Bridges (qq.v.).

Etruria, see *Wedgwood*.

Etruscans, THE, a people of uncertain origin, who inhabited in early times a portion of NW. Italy and in the 8th cent. B.C. developed a system of powerful city states and a flourishing civilization of which many remains have been discovered. Their language, known to us in inscriptions, is still unread except for some names and isolated words. The Etruscans formed a small ruling class in most of the cities they dominated; at the height of their power in the 7th cent. B.C. their influence extended from the Po to Campania, Rome being governed during some part of the time by the Etruscan family of the Tarquinii. After 500 B.C. the political strength of the Etruscans began to decline, though the influence of their more highly developed art and civilization continued to be felt in Rome.

Ettarre, see *Pelleas and Ettarre*.

Ettrick Shepherd, THE, see *Hogg (J.).*

Etzel, the name given in German legend to Attila, king of the Huns.

EUCLID (EUCLEIDĒS), the celebrated geometrician, lived at Alexandria in the reign of the first Ptolemy (323–283 B.C.), but the place of his birth is not known. His great work on elementary geometry and arithmetic survives. It was Euclid who told Ptolemy that there was no 'royal road' to geometry.

Euclio, in the 'Aulularia' of Plautus, an old miser, on whom Molière modelled his Harpagon (in 'L'Avare').

Eugene Aram, a novel by Bulwer Lytton (q.v.), published in 1832. It is based on the story of Eugene Aram, a schoolmaster of Knaresborough, a man said to have been of unusual ability and gentle disposition, who in 1759 was tried and executed at York for the murder of one Clarke.

In the novel Eugene Aram is represented as a romantic character, who under pressure of dire poverty consents to the murder, which is done by his accomplice Houseman. From this moment Aram suffers the torments of remorse. He settles in a remote village and falls in love with Madeline Lester, a woman of noble character. Their marriage is about to take place when Houseman reappears and betrays Aram, who is imprisoned, tried, and sentenced to death, while Madeline succumbs to the shock.

Eugene Aram, The Dream of, a poem by Hood (q.v.), based on the same story as the preceding.

Eugénie Grandet, a novel by Balzac (q.v.).

Eugenius, a character in Sterne's 'Tristram Shandy' (q.v.), the friend of Yorick. He represents John Hall Stevenson (q.v.).

EUHĒMĒRUS, a Sicilian in the service of Cassander of Macedonia (311–298 B.C.). He wrote a 'Sacred History' in which he advanced the theory (for which he professed to have found documentary evidence in an imaginary island in the Indian Ocean) that the Greek gods were human kings or heroes, deified after their death by those whom they had ruled over or benefited. This method of explaining mythological stories was called after him EUHEMERISM.

Eulenspiegel, TILL, the name of a German, born according to tradition about 1300, the son of a peasant, and the subject of a collection of satirical tales, German or Flemish in origin, published in 1519 (Flemish version 1520–1). He is a scapegrace whose knaveries and escapades are carried on under a pretence of simplicity and stupidity, and are directed against noblemen, priests, tradesmen, and innkeepers. One of these incidents figures in Chaucer's 'Summoner's Tale'. The book was translated into many languages, among others into English in an abridged form by William Copland, under the title of 'Howleglass', about 1560. See 'The Marvellous Adventures . . .

of Master Tyll Owlglass', transl. by K. R. H. Mackenzie, 1860.

Eumaeus, the faithful swineherd of Odysseus (q.v.), who on the latter's return from the Trojan War helped him to destroy the suitors of Penelope.

Eumĕnĭdes, see *Furies.*

Euphelia and **Cloe,** the subjects of a frequently quoted ode by Prior (q.v.):

Euphelia serves to grace my measure,
But Cloe is my real flame.

Euphemism, the substitution of a less distasteful phrase or word for a more accurate but more offensive one.

Euphorion, in Pt. II of Goethe's 'Faust' (q.v.), represents, at one stage of the drama, Lord Byron, whom Goethe laments in a famous dirge.

Euphormionis Satyricon, see *Barclay (J.).*

Euphrŏsynē, one of the Graces (q.v.).

Euphues, a prose romance by Lyly (q.v.), of which the first part, 'Euphues: the Anatomy of Wit', was published in 1578, and the second, 'Euphues and his England', in 1580. The plot of each is very slender and little but a peg on which to hang discourses, conversations, and letters, mainly on the subject of love. The work is largely based on North's 'Diall of Princes' (q.v.). In the first part Euphues, a young Athenian, visits Naples, where he makes the acquaintance of Philautus, an Italian, and a friendship develops between them. None the less Euphues proceeds to oust Philautus from the affections of Lucilla, to be in turn ejected by one Curio. Euphues and Philautus, after upbraiding one another, unite in holding Lucilla 'as most abhominable', and part friends, Euphues returning to Greece and leaving behind him a pamphlet of advice to lovers, which he terms 'a cooling Carde for Philautus'.

In Pt. II Euphues and Philautus travel to England, where their adventures are even less entertaining than at Naples. They are largely concerned with the love-affairs on which Philautus embarks, in spite of the advice of Euphues to use circumspection in his dealings with English ladies; and much space is occupied by a discussion on such questions as 'whether in love be more required secrecie or constancie'. Finally Euphues is recalled to Greece. From Athens Euphues addresses a letter to the ladies of Italy, 'Euphues' glass for Europe', in which he describes England, its institutions, its ladies, its gentlemen, and its queen; and a final letter of general advice from Euphues to Philautus completes the work.

'Euphues' is famous for its peculiar style, to which it has given the name 'Euphuism'. Its principal characteristics are the excessive use (1) of antithesis, which is pursued regardless of sense, and emphasized by alliteration and other devices; and (2) of allusions to historical and mythological personages and to natural history (probably drawn from the writings of Erasmus). Scott has satirized Euphuism in the character of Sir Piercie Shafton in 'The Monastery' (q.v.), and C. Kingsley has defended 'Euphues' in 'Westward Ho!' (q.v.).

The work is interesting for its place in the evolution of the English novel, and it had a stimulating effect on the writers of the age, such as Lodge and Greene.

Euphues Golden Legacie, see *Rosalynde.*

Euphuism, see *Euphues.*

Eurēka, a Greek word (more correctly 'heurēka') meaning 'I have found it', the exclamation uttered by Archimedes (q.v.) when he discovered, by observing in his bath the water displaced by his body, the means of testing (by specific gravity) whether base metal had been introduced in Hiero's crown.

EURIPĪDĒS (480–406 B.C.), the youngest and most 'modern-minded' of the three great Attic tragedians, said to have been born at Salamis on the day of the defeat of the Persians in the naval battle off that island. The characteristics of his plays are their human quality (men and women are represented in them as they are in everyday life), their poignant realism, and the frequent introduction, to conclude the drama, of a god *ex machina.* His extant plays, the survivals of some ninety that he is said to have written, are the following: 'Alcestis', 'Medea', 'Hippolytus', 'Hecuba', 'Andromache', 'Ion' (the founder of the Ionian race), the 'Suppliants' (the refusal of Creon of Thebes to bury the Argive warriors), the 'Heracleidae' (the children of Heracles persecuted by Eurystheus), the 'Mad Heracles', 'Iphigenia among the Tauri', the 'Trojan Women', 'Helen', the 'Phoenissae' (the story of Eteocles and Polyneices, with a chorus of Phoenician maidens), 'Electra', 'Orestes', 'Iphigenia at Aulis', the 'Bacchae' (the destruction of King Pentheus by the Bacchantes), and the 'Cyclops', a 'satyr play' dealing with the story of Odysseus and Polyphemus. Euripides was made much fun of by the comic poet Aristophanes.

Eurōpa, daughter of Agēnor, king of Phoenicia, of whom Zeus became enamoured. He assumed the shape of a beautiful bull and mingled with the herds of Agenor. Europa caressed him and sat upon his back. Zeus thereupon carried her off to Crete, where she became the mother of Minos, Rhadamanthus, and Sarpēdon (qq.v.).

Eurus, the East wind.

Euryǎlus, see *Nisus.*

Eurŷdice, see *Orpheus.*

Eurysthēus, a king of Argos, in whose service Hercules (q.v.) executed his twelve labours.

EUSDEN, LAURENCE (1688–1730), poet

laureate from 1718 until his death. He had celebrated the marriage of the duke of Newcastle, who gave him the laureateship. Pope refers to him in 'The Dunciad' (q.v.):

> Know Eusden thirsts no more for sack or praise;
> He sleeps among the dull of dead days.

EUSEBIUS of Caesarea in Palestine (A.D. 265–340), bishop of Caesarea, and a celebrated historian and theologian. His 'Chronicle' in Greek (of which we have a Latin version by Jerome) contains an epitome of universal history and chronological tables, the foundation of much of our knowledge of the dates of events in Greek and Roman history. He was involved in the Arian controversy, was one of the leaders at the Council of Nicaea, and voted for the 'Nicene formula'. He was a voluminous writer, and a valuable authority on the early church, showing diligence and sincerity. His 'Ecclesiastical History', which earned him the title of 'Father of Church history', was completed *c.* 325. His 'De Vita Constantini', often tacked on to the 'History' but evidently written earlier, is of especial interest; for the question whether Constantine was ever actually baptized rests upon Eusebius.

Eustace, FATHER, a character in Scott's 'The Monastery' (q.v.), the energetic sub-prior of Kennaquhair.

Eustace Diamonds, The, a novel by A. Trollope (q.v.), reprinted from the 'Fortnightly Review' in 1873.

Lizzie Greystock, the daughter of old Admiral Greystock, beautiful but grasping, and a clever, unscrupulous liar, wins the hand of the wealthy Sir Florian Eustace, who soon leaves her a widow. He has given her a diamond necklace that has been for generations in his family, and is worth £10,000. The story centres on this necklace, which the lawyer of the Eustace family is determined to recover as an heirloom, while Lizzie is equally determined to retain it. She intends at the same time to marry the worthy Lord Fawn, who insists on the surrender of the necklace. Lizzie is finally exposed, and having failed to catch any of her other admirers is reduced to marrying Mr. Emilius, a popular preacher, but suspected to be a Bohemian Jew, with a wife already at Prague.

Euterpē, the Muse (q.v.) of lyric poetry.

Euxine, the ancient Greek name of the Black Sea. The word signifies 'hospitable' and the name was given in a euphemistic sense, on account of its rough and stormy character.

Evadne, a character in Beaumont and Fletcher's 'The Maid's Tragedy' (q.v.).

Evalak or EVELAKE, king of Sarras in the legend of the Grail (q.v.).

Evan Harrington, a novel by Meredith (q.v.), published in 1861.

Evan Harrington is the son of Melchizedek Harrington, the glorified tailor of Lymport, 'the great Mel', 'the Marquis', as he is known, a man of distinguished appearance and fine manners. Evan's sisters have married, one an officer of Marines, one a rich brewer, Andrew Cogglesby, and one a Portuguese nobleman, the Count de Saldar. The sisters are all anxious to forget their connexion with tailordom—'Demogorgon' as the countess calls it—and to establish Evan in a good position by a grand marriage. Evan has been staying with the countess in Lisbon, has been employed as temporary secretary to the British envoy, the Hon. Melville Jocelyn, and has fallen in love with his niece Rose. Evan's father has just died, leaving heavy debts. The novel tells the story of the gallant fight made by the countess, with endless resource and audacity, to launch Evan in 'high life' and conceal the undesirable connexion, in the face of the honest Evan's reluctance, of the determination of their mother, 'a woman of mark and strict principle', that Evan shall carry on the tailoring business, and of various disconcerting incidents. The whole truth of course comes out, but Evan has by that time confessed to Rose and won her heart. And now the countess overreaches herself. She adopts a dishonourable device for the discomfiture of Ferdinand Laxley, Evan's rival and enemy, of which Evan feels in honour bound to assume the guilt. He is dismissed the house and his engagement with Rose broken off. Meanwhile Juliana Bonner, the sickly cousin of Rose, and immediate heiress of the Jocelyn property, has fallen in love with Evan, whose innocence she discovers. Rejected by him, on her death-bed she makes the truth known to Rose, and bequeaths the whole Jocelyn property to Evan. His renunciation of this in favour of the Jocelyn family, coupled with the clearing of his character and the financial support of his eccentric old bachelor uncle, Tom Cogglesby, leads to a happy conclusion of the story. Among the minor characters may be mentioned Evan's friend, Jack Raikes, the butt of old Cogglesby's farcical humour.

It should be remembered that Meredith was himself the grandson of a famous Portsmouth tailor.

Evandale, LORD, a character in Scott's 'Old Mortality' (q.v.).

Evangelical, a term applied from the 18th cent. to that school of Protestants which maintains that the essence of 'the Gospel' consists in the doctrine of salvation by faith in the atoning death of Christ, lays more stress on faith than on works or on sacramental grace, and upholds the verbal inspiration of the Bible. As a distinct party designation, the term came into general use, in England, at the time of the Methodist revival; and it may be said, with substantial accuracy, to denote the school of theology which that movement represents.

Evangeline, a narrative poem in hexameters, by Longfellow (q.v.), published in 1847.

Gabriel Lajeunesse and Evangeline Bellefontaine, son and daughter of two well-to-do peasants of Grandpré in Acadia, have recently been betrothed, when the inhabitants are driven from their homes for disaffection to the English rule. By accident the lovers embark on different ships and are carried to widely distant destinations. Gabriel and his father become prosperous farmers in Louisiana. Evangeline, her father having died of grief, travels to seek Gabriel, and at length reaches his farm, only to find that he has migrated to the western prairies. After years of fruitless search she becomes a sister of mercy and tends the sick. At length she finds Gabriel, at the point of death, in an almshouse, and the lovers are united as he dies. The poem is notable for its descriptions of American scenery and its idyllic simplicity.

EVANS, SIR ARTHUR JOHN (1851–1941), son of Sir J. Evans (q.v.), educated at Harrow and Brasenose College, Oxford, and at Göttingen, was made keeper of the Ashmolean Museum in 1884, and from 1893 was engaged on archaeological investigations in Crete, which resulted in the discovery of the pre-Phoenician script and an entire new civilization. From 1900 he devoted himself to the excavation of the Palace of Knossos, Crete. His chief publications were: 'Through Bosnia, etc.' (1895), 'Antiquarian Researches in Illyricum' (1883–5), 'Cretan Pictographs and Pre-Phoenician Script' (1896), 'Further Discoveries of Cretan and Aegean Script' (1898), 'The Mycenaean Tree and Pillar Cult' (1901), 'Scripta Minoa' (vol. i, 1909), and 'The Palace of Minos at Knossos' (1922–35).

Evans, SIR HUGH, a Welsh parson in Shakespeare's 'The Merry Wives of Windsor' (q.v.). He is the 'Sir Hugh' referred to in Lamb's 'Amicus Redivivus' ('Essays of Elia').

EVANS, SIR JOHN (1823–1908), archaeologist and numismatist, was president of the Geological, Numismatic, and Antiquarian Societies, and was author of several learned works: 'Flint Implements of the Drift' (1860), 'The Coins of the Ancient Britons' (1864), 'The Ancient Stone Implements, Weapons, and Ornaments of Great Britain' (1872), and 'The Ancient Bronze Implements, Weapons, and Ornaments of Great Britain and Ireland' (1881).

EVANS, MARY ANN, see *Eliot (G.).*

EVANS, SEBASTIAN (1830–1909), brother of Sir J. Evans (q.v.), educated at Emmanuel College, Cambridge, was editor of the 'Birmingham Daily Gazette', 1867–70, and part founder and editor of the 'People', 1878–81. He was also an artist and exhibited at the Royal Academy. In literature he is remembered as an ardent medievalist, as the author of 'Brother Fabian's Manuscripts' (1865), 'Songs and Etchings' (1871), 'In the Studio' (1875), and as translator of 'The High History of the Holy Graal' (1898–1903, 1910); he also wrote an original study of the Grail ('In quest of the Holy Grail', 1898).

Evans's, in the NW. corner of the Piazza, Covent Garden, originally the residence of the earl of Orford (*d.* 1727), converted into an hotel in 1774. In 1844 it passed under the management of one Paddy Green and became famous for its musical parties and suppers. Thackeray's 'Cave of Harmony' is partly drawn from it. It was subsequently, for a time, the home of the National Sporting Club.

Eve, the name given by Adam to his wife (Gen. iii. 20), the first woman. 'The fairest of her daughters, Eve' (Milton, 'Paradise Lost', iv. 324).

Eve of St. Agnes, The, a poem by Keats (q.v.) written in 1819. Madeline has been told the legend that on St. Agnes' Eve maidens may have visions of their lovers. Her lover Porphyro is of hostile lineage, and she is surrounded by 'hyena foemen, and hot-blooded lords'. Yet he steals in on this night, and when she wakes from dreams of him, she finds him by her bedside. Together they escape from the castle.

Tennyson (q.v.) also wrote a poem, 'St. Agnes' Eve', describing the rapture of a nun in her convent garden on that night.

Evelina, a novel by Fanny Burney (q.v.), published in 1778.

Sir John Belmont, disappointed of the fortune which he expected to receive with his wife, abandons her and their child Evelina, who is brought up in seclusion by a guardian, Mr. Villars. Evelina, who has grown up a beautiful and intelligent girl, goes to visit a friend, Mrs. Mirvan, in London, where she is introduced into society and falls in love with the handsome and dignified Lord Orville, but is exposed to much mortification by reason of her vulgar grandmother, Mme Duval, her ill-bred relatives, and the pursuit of her pertinacious lover, Sir Clement Willoughby. An attempt is made to induce Sir John Belmont to recognize Evelina as his daughter, which is met by the surprising announcement that his daughter had been conveyed to him by the woman who had attended Lady Belmont in her last illness and had been in his care since infancy. It is now discovered that this nurse had passed her own child off on Sir John. Evelina is recognized as his heir, and marries Lord Orville.

EVELYN, JOHN (1620–1706), educated at Balliol College, Oxford, was a man of means, of unblemished character, and a dilettante, who helped to advance English civilization. He published in 1661 'Fumifugium or The inconvenience of the Air and Smoke of London dissipated'; in 1662, 'Sculptura', a book on engraving; 'Sylva', a book on practical arboriculture, which exerted great influence, in 1664; 'Navigation and Commerce' in 1674; and a number of translations from the French on architecture, gardening, etc. He is remembered principally by his 'Diary', describing

his travels on the Continent and containing brilliant portraits of his contemporaries; it covers his whole life. It was first published in 1818, but not printed in full until the edition of 1955 by E. S. de Beer. Evelyn's 'Life of Mrs. Godolphin' was first printed in 1847, and various other minor works have been published in recent times.

Evening, Ode to, see *Collins (William).*

Everard, COLONEL MARKHAM, a character in Scott's 'Woodstock' (q.v.).

Evergreen, The, see *Ramsay (A.).*

Every Man in his Humour, a comedy by Jonson (q.v.), performed at the Curtain Theatre (with Shakespeare in the cast) in 1598.

Kitely, a merchant, is the husband of a young and pretty wife, and his 'humour' is jealousy. His house is resorted to by his young brother with a crowd of riotous but harmless gallants, and these he suspects of designs on his wife. One of these young men is Edward Knowell, whose father's 'humour' is excessive solicitude for his son's morals. Dame Kitely, though not suspicious by nature, becomes highly credulous when her suspicions are aroused. Bridget, Kitely's sister, is merely a young woman easily wooed and won. Bobadill, one of Jonson's greatest creations, a 'Paul's man' (q.v.), is a boasting cowardly soldier, who associates with the young gallants above mentioned. Out of these elements, by the aid of the devices and disguises of the mischievous Brainworm, Knowell's servant, an imbroglio is produced in which Kitely and his wife are brought face to face at a house to which each thinks the other has gone for an improper purpose; Bobadill is exposed and beaten; young Knowell is married to Kitely's sister; and poetasters and 'gulls' are held up to ridicule. The misunderstandings are cleared up by the shrewd and kindly Justice Clement.

The prologue contains an exposition of Jonson's dramatic theory.

Every Man out of his Humour, a satirical comedy by Jonson (q.v.), first acted in 1599 at the Globe Theatre, in which the poet holds up to ridicule various absurd characters and fashions of the day: Fastidious Brisk, the spruce fashionably dressed courtier; Fungoso, a student, whose aim in life is to be a courtier, but who is always behind the fashion; Sordido, his father, a countryman, whose recreation is reading almanacs and his felicity bad weather, because his barns are full; Sogliardo, Sordido's brother, whose ambition is to be taken for a man of quality; Deliro, who dotes absurdly on his wife; Puntarvolo, a vainglorious knight, who makes a ridiculous insurance on the safe return of his cat and dog from a voyage to Constantinople. They are all put 'out of humour' with their various predilections.

Everyman, the title of a popular morality (q.v.) of the 15th cent., of Dutch origin.

The characters are God, Messenger, Death, Everyman, Fellowship, Kindred, Good Deeds, Goods, Knowledge, Beauty, Strength, and similar abstractions. The theme is the summoning of Everyman by Death. Everyman finds that no one of his friends except Good Deeds will accompany him.

Everyman's Library, a series of reprints of the world's masterpieces of literature; the series also includes some original works of reference.

Evidences of Christianity, see *Paley.*

Evil, THE, see *King's Evil.*

Ewart, NANTY, captain of the smuggler's brig in Scott's 'Redgauntlet' (q.v.).

EWING, MRS. JULIANA HORATIA (1841–85), *née* GATTY, a notably successful writer of books for the young. Among these may be mentioned 'A Flat Iron for a Farthing' (1873), 'Lob-lie-by-the-Fire' (1873), 'The Miller's Thumb' (in 'Aunt Judy's Magazine', 1873, republished as 'Jan of the Windmill', 1884), 'Jackanapes' (1884), 'The Story of a Short Life' (1885).

Ex pede Herculem, 'judge the size of Hercules from his foot'. Aulus Gellius (I. i) quotes Plutarch as stating (in a work now lost) that Pythagoras calculated the stature of Hercules by comparing the length of the stadium of Olympia with the stadia in other parts of Greece. The former was 600 ft. in length as measured by Hercules; the latter 600 ft. as measured by ordinary men. Cf. the similar expression, 'ex ungue leonem' ('judge the lion from its claw').

Examination of Sir William Hamilton's Philosophy, a treatise by J. S. Mill (q.v.), published in 1865, and amplified in subsequent editions.

The most important part of the work is the doctrine developed by Mill in regard to the external world (expressed in the famous phrase 'permanent possibility of sensation') and the mind or self. 'If we speak of the Mind as a series of feelings, we are obliged to complete the statement by calling it a series of feelings which is aware of itself as past and future; and we are reduced to the alternative of believing that the Mind, or Ego, is something different from any series of feelings, or possibilities of them, or of accepting the paradox, that something which *ex hypothesi* is but a series of feelings, can be aware of itself as a series.' 'I ascribe a reality to the Ego—to my own Mind—different from that real existence as a Permanent Possibility, which is the only reality I acknowledge in Matter.'

Examiner, The, a Tory periodical started by Viscount Bolingbroke (q.v.), in the autumn of 1710, and conducted by Jonathan Swift until June 1711. Prior was a contributor. Some forty numbers appear to have been published. It engaged in controversy with Steele's 'Guardian' (q.v.) and Addison's 'Whig Examiner'.

Examiner, The, a weekly periodical launched in 1808 by John Hunt and his brother Leigh Hunt (q.v.), dealing with literature and politics, which by its independent attitude exercised a considerable influence on the development of English journalism. From 1821 to 1849 it was edited by Albany Fonblanque, a radical; then by John Forster and Henry Morley. It lasted until 1880.

Excalibur, a corrupt form of 'Caliburn' (the name used in Geoffrey of Monmouth), was King Arthur's sword, which he drew out of a stone when no one else could draw it (Malory, I. iv), or which was given him by the Lady of the Lake (Malory, II. iii). Malory says that the word is equivalent to 'cut-steel'. 'The Welsh form in the Mabinogion is *Caledvwlch,* which has a resemblance, that cannot well be accidental, to *Caladbolg,* the name of a famous sword in Irish legend'. [OED.] When Arthur was mortally wounded in the last battle, he ordered Sir Bedivere to throw Excalibur into the water. A hand rose from the water, caught the sword, and vanished.

Excelsior, Latin 'higher', the motto adopted (in defiance of Latin grammar) by the State of New York in 1778; used by Longfellow (as an expression of incessant aspiration after higher attainment) for the refrain of a well-known poem.

Exchange, THE LONDON STOCK, for the sale and purchase of securities (shares, stocks, and bonds) was originally conducted at Jonathan's coffee-house in Change Alley, and subsequently in a room taken by the brokers in Sweeting's Alley, which was given the name of the Stock Exchange Coffee House. In 1801 joint stock capital was raised to provide premises on the present site of the Stock Exchange in Capel Court. These premises have since been extended.

Exchange, THE NEW, a bazaar on the south side of the Strand, a popular resort in the 17th–18th cents., frequently referred to in the drama of the period.

Exchange, THE ROYAL, London, was originally founded by Sir T. Gresham (q.v.) in 1566 and opened by Queen Elizabeth. It was destroyed in the Great Fire of 1666. Its successor was likewise burnt in 1838. The present building was opened in 1844.

Excursion, The, a poem in nine books by Wordsworth (q.v.), published in 1814. This is the middle portion of a great philosophical poem 'on man, on nature and on human life', in three parts, designed by the author, but of which this alone was completed. The whole work was to be entitled 'The Recluse', 'as having for its principal subject the sensations and opinions of a poet living in retirement'. It was planned in 1798, when Wordsworth was living at Alfoxden, near Coleridge.

The story is very slight. The poet travelling with the Wanderer, a philosophic pedlar, meets with the latter's friend, the pessimistic Solitary. The source of the latter's despondency is traced to his want of religious faith and of confidence in the virtue of man, and is reproved in lengthy arguments. Another character, the Pastor, is introduced, who illustrates the harmonizing effect of virtue and religion by narratives of the lives of persons interred in his churchyard. They visit the pastor's house, and the Wanderer draws his general philosophical and political conclusions from the discussions that have passed. The last two books deal in particular with the industrial expansion of the early part of the century and the degradation of the humbler classes that followed in its train. The remedy is found in the provision of proper educational facilities for the children. Book I embodies the beautiful 'Story of Margaret' or 'The Ruined Cottage', originally written as a separate poem.

Exeter Book, THE, a famous collection of old English poems, copied about 975, given by Bishop Leofric (*d.* 1072) to Exeter Cathedral, where it still remains. The book contains many important works, including 'Christ', 'Guthlac', 'The Phoenix', 'Juliana', 'The Wanderer' (q.v.), 'The Seafarer' (q.v.), 'Widsith' (q.v.), 'Deor' (q.v.), and the 'Riddles'.

Exeter Hall, a large hall in the Strand, London, opened in 1831, for meetings of religious and philanthropic bodies, concerts, etc. It was noted for the religious services held there in 1856 by the Revd. C. Spurgeon (q.v.). It was for many years the centre of the Young Men's Christian Association. The name is used allusively of Evangelicalism.

Exhibition, THE GREAT, the first international exhibition of the products of industry, promoted by Prince Albert, and held in 1851 in Hyde Park in the Crystal Palace (afterwards removed to Sydenham).

Existentialism, the name commonly given to a group of somewhat loosely associated philosophical doctrines and ideas which have found contemporary expression in the work of such men as Sartre, Heidegger, Marcel, Camus, and Jaspers. Though the theories advanced by different existentialist writers diverge widely in many important respects, so that it would be misleading to speak of a philosophical 'school' or 'movement', certain underlying themes can be singled out as characteristic. Existentialists tend, for example, to emphasize the unique and particular in human experience; they place the individual person at the centre of their pictures of the world, and are suspicious of philosophical or psychological doctrines that obscure this essential individuality by speaking as if there were some abstract 'human nature', some set of general laws or principles, to which men are determined or required, by their common humanity, to conform. Each man is what he chooses to be or make himself; he cannot escape responsibility for his character or his deeds by claiming that they are the predetermined consequence of factors beyond his power to control or resist, nor can he justify what he does in terms of external or 'objective' standards imposed upon him from without. Sartre, in particular, insists upon the notion of the individual as the source of all value, and as being obliged to choose for himself what to do and what standards to adopt or reject: consciousness of such freedom is a condition of 'authentic' existence, as opposed to the type of behaviour stigmatized as springing from 'bad faith' (*mauvaise foi*), whereby people deceive themselves into thinking that they are bound to act in certain ways, play certain roles. Thus existentialists typically give priority to sincerity and creativity in the moral life, and sometimes appear to regard any decision as justified if it is made in perfect honesty and with absolute inner conviction. Critics have pointed out that existentialist ethics seems to provide little guidance to practical choices; the bare reference to 'authenticity' is hardly helpful in the assessment of the relative merits of alternative courses of action. Again, it has been argued that, through their romantic preference for 'extreme situations', existentialists have been led to overlook or distort the character of more everyday moral perplexities and problems. Even so, in their psychological explorations they have often shown an impressive insight and introduced interpretative concepts which have greatly extended the area of moral self-knowledge and self-awareness. This, perhaps more than anything, explains the wide appeal of their writings.

Exodus, an OE. poetical paraphrase of the Biblical story, contained in the Junius MS. (see *Cædmon*). The style is lively and vigorous, and there is a famous description of the destruction of the Egyptians in the Red Sea.

Exoteric, see *Esoteric.*

Expansion of England, The, see *Seeley.*

Expressionism, an art movement developed in Germany in the early 20th cent. Artists of the first Expressionist group, *Die Brücke,* founded in 1905, influenced by Van Gogh, Munch, and primitive art, expressed emotion by distortion of form and violent colour. The artists of the second group, *Der Blaue Reiter,* founded in 1911, were more concerned with the evocative qualities of colour and pattern, unrelated to content, and from this abstract expressionism developed.

Extravagants, see *Decretals.*

Extravaganza, a composition, literary, musical, or dramatic, of an extravagant or fantastic character.

Eyck, JAN VAN (active 1422–41), Flemish painter. The existence of his elder brother

Hubert is disputed. The discovery of oil painting has been attributed to the brothers, but probably Jan only developed a technique which was already in existence. Jan was Court painter to the duke of Burgundy and made secret missions to Spain and Portugal on his behalf.

Eyrbyggja Saga, see *Saga.*

Eyre, SIMON, see *Simon Eyre.*

F

FABER, FREDERICK WILLIAM (1814–63), educated at Shrewsbury, Harrow, and Balliol College, and a friend of Coleridge and Newman. He was received into the Roman Catholic Church in 1845, having previously been rector of Elton. With Father Hutchison he founded the London Oratory. He published many hymns (including 'Pilgrims of the Night' and 'The Land beyond the Sea') and devotional treatises.

Fabian, in Shakespeare's 'Twelfth Night' (q.v.) a servant of Olivia, who joins in the schemes against Malvolio and Sir Andrew Aguecheek.

FABIAN, ROBERT, see *Fabyan.*

Fabian Society, a society founded in 1884 consisting of socialists who advocate a 'Fabian' policy (see *Fabius*) as opposed to immediate attempts at revolutionary action. The 'Fabian Essays' of the society were issued in 1889. The names of Sidney Webb and Mrs. Webb, and of G. B. Shaw (q.v.), are especially associated with it.

Fabiola, *or the Church of the Catacombs,* a novel of early church history published in 1854, by Nicholas Wiseman (1802–65), the cardinal archbishop of Westminster.

Fabius, Quintus Fabius Maximus, nicknamed *Cunctator* or 'the delayer', was appointed dictator at Rome after the great victory won by Hannibal over the Romans in 217 B.C. He carried on a defensive campaign against Hannibal, avoiding direct engagements, and harassing the enemy. Hence the expressions, 'Fabian tactics', 'Fabian policy'.

Fable of the Bees, *or Private Vices, Public Benefits,* see under *Mandeville (B. de).*

Fables, *Ancient and Modern,* by Dryden (q.v.), published in 1699.

They are verse paraphrases of tales by Chaucer, Boccaccio, and Ovid. From Chaucer Dryden took 'Palamon and Arcite', 'The Cock and the Fox', 'The Wife of Bath's Tale', and the 'Character of the Good Parson'; from Boccaccio, 'Sigismonda and Guiscardo', 'Theodore and Honoria', 'Cymon and Iphigenia'; from Ovid he took some of the 'Metamorphoses'.

Fabliau, a short tale in verse, almost invariably in octosyllabic couplets, dealing for the most part from a comic point of view with incidents of ordinary life (Saintsbury). The *fabliau* was an important element in the French poetry of the 12th–13th cents.

Fabricius, Gaius Fabricius Luscinus, who was consul in 282 and 278 B.C., was, like Cincinnatus (q.v.), a typical example of ancient Roman honesty, simplicity, and frugality. As censor in 275 he was distinguished for the severity with which he endeavoured to repress the growing tendency to luxury.

FABYAN, ROBERT (*d.* 1513), chronicler, was sheriff of London in 1493. He expanded his diary into 'The Concordance of Histories', a compilation extending from the arrival of Brutus in England (see *Brute*) to the death of Henry VII (first printed, 1516; edited by Ellis in 1811). His chronicles are of importance with respect to the history of London.

Face, a character in Jonson's 'The Alchemist' (q.v.).

Factotum, see *Johannes Factotum.*

Fadladeen, the pompous chamberlain in Moore's 'Lalla Rookh' (q.v.).

Faerie Queene, *The,* the greatest work of Spenser (q.v.), of which the first three books were entrusted to the printer in Nov. 1589, and the second three were published in 1596.

The general scheme of the work is expounded in the author's introductory letter addressed to Sir Walter Ralegh. By the Faerie Queene the poet signifies Glory in the abstract, and Queen Elizabeth in particular (who also figures under the names of Belphoebe, Mercilla, and Gloriana). Twelve of her knights, the 'patrons' or examples of twelve different virtues, undertake each an adventure, on the twelve successive days of the Queen's annual festival. Prince Arthur symbolizes 'magnificence', in the Aristotelian sense (says the author) of the perfection of all the other virtues (he must have meant not 'magnificence' but 'magnanimity', μεγαλοψυχία, or 'gentlemanliness', καλοκαγαθία). Arthur has a vision of the Faerie Queene, and, determining to seek her out, is brought into the adventures of the several knights and carries them to a successful issue. But this explanation, given in the introduction, does not appear from the poem itself; for the author starts at once with the adventures of the knights, intending to give his account of their origin in the last of the twelve books which the work was to contain, but this was never written. Spenser published only six books, of which the subjects are as follows:

(i) the adventures of the Red Cross Knight of Holiness (the Anglican Church), the protector of the Virgin Una (truth, or the true religion), and the wiles of Archimago (q.v.) and Duessa (q.v.);

(ii) the adventures of Sir Guyon, the Knight of Temperance, his encounters with Pyrocles and Chymocles, his visit to the cave of Mammon and the House of Temperance and his destruction of Acrasia (q.v.) and her Bower of Bliss. Canto x of this Book contains a chronicle of British rulers from Brute to Elizabeth;

(iii) the legend of Chastity, exemplified by Britomart and Belphoebe;

(iv) the legend of Triamond and Cambell, exemplifying Friendship; together with the story of Scudamour and Amoret;

(v) the adventures of Artegall, the Knight of Justice, in which allegorical reference is made to various historical events of the reign of Queen Elizabeth: the defeat of the Spaniards in the Netherlands, the recantation of Henri IV of France, the execution of Mary Queen of Scots, and the administration of Ireland by Lord Grey de Wilton;

(vi) the adventures of Sir Calidore, exemplifying Courtesy.

We have also a fragment on Mutability, being the sixth and seventh cantos of the legend of Constance, which was to have formed the seventh Book. This fragment contains a charming description of the Seasons and the Months.

The work as a whole, modelled to some extent on the 'Orlando Furioso' of Ariosto, suffers from a certain monotony, and its chief beauties lie in the particular episodes with which the allegory is varied and in descriptions, such as those of the Cave of Mammon and the temptation of Sir Guyon by the Lady of the Idle Lake, in Book ii. The meaning of many of the allusions, which must have added to the interest of the work for contemporaries, is now lost. The poem is written in the stanza invented by Spenser (and since utilized by Thomson, Keats, Shelley, and Byron), in which a ninth line of twelve syllables is added to eight lines of ten syllables, rhyming a b a b b c b c c.

Fafnir, in the Volsunga Saga (q.v.), the dragon who guards the Nibelungs' hoard of gold, and is slain by Sigurd.

Fag, Captain Absolute's servant in Sheridan's 'The Rivals' (q.v.).

Fagin, a character in Dickens's 'Oliver Twist' (q.v.).

Fainall and **Mrs. Fainall,** characters in Congreve's 'The Way of the World' (q.v.).

Fainéant, French word meaning 'do-nothing'. *Rois fainéants* is a designation of the later Merovingian kings, whose authority was superseded by that of the 'Mayors of the Palace'.

Fair Maid of Perth, *Saint Valentine's Day, or the,* a novel by Sir W. Scott (q.v.), published in 1828, as the second of the 'Chronicles of the Canongate'.

The scene is laid at Perth in the turbulent times at the close of the 14th cent. when the mild Robert III was king of Scotland; and the story opens with an attempt by the profligate young duke of Rothsay, the king's son, aided by his villainous Master of the Horse, Sir John Ramorny, to break into the house of an honest burgher, Simon Glover, and carry off his daughter Catharine, the Fair Maid of Perth. The attempt is defeated by the sturdy armourer, Henry Smith or Gow, who, in the affray, hacks off the hand of Ramorny. Henry is as strong and skilful in the use of weapons as in their forging, and his addiction to fighting mars his prospect of winning the hand of the gentle Catharine, though he has a vigorous advocate in her father. This incident is followed by the endeavours of Ramorny to wreak his vengeance first on the armourer, in which he is unsuccessful, then on his patron Rothsay, by whom he considers himself betrayed. At the instigation of the crafty duke of Albany, the king's ambitious brother, the unfortunate Rothsay is lured by Ramorny, with Catharine as bait, to the Castle of Falkland, where he is done to death. Meanwhile a Highland apprentice of Simon Glover, the fiery youth Conachar, has become, by the death of his father, chief of the clan Quhele. He passionately loves Catharine, and bitter enmity has arisen between him and the armourer. A feud between the clan Quhele and the clan Chattan is to be settled by mortal combat between thirty representatives of each clan, among whom the chiefs are necessarily included. But here enters a tragic element; for Conachar's hot temper is strangely blended with constitutional cowardice, of which the youth is grievously conscious. One of the champions of the clan Chattan having at the last moment defaulted, his place is taken by the armourer, who eagerly grasps the opportunity of finding himself face to face with Conachar. After a fearful battle during which Conachar has been protected by the devotion of his foster-father, Torquil of the Oak, and his eight sturdy sons, most of the combatants lie dead or wounded on the field, and Conachar is finally confronted by Henry Smith. His courage, hitherto painfully maintained, now gives way, and he turns and flees, to hide his disgrace in suicide. Henry, sickened with the carnage, vows to hang up his broadsword for ever, and is accepted by Catharine.

Fair Maid of the West, The, or *A Girle worth Gold,* a comedy of adventure, in two parts, by Heywood (q.v.), printed in 1631.

The play opens with a vivid scene at Plymouth, where Essex's expedition is on the point of sailing for the Azores (1597), and gallant Master Spencer has the misfortune to kill a man while protecting Besse Bridges, 'the flower of Plymouth', from insult. He has to fly the country, but first makes provision for Besse, by handing over to her the Windmill Tavern at Fowey, which she subsequently conducts with equal spirit and decorum. Meanwhile Spencer, who has sailed to the Azores, is wounded to the point of death in trying to stop a quarrel. He sends a message to Besse, bidding her adieu and devising all his property to her. Besse employs part of this to fit out a privateer, in which she sets sail to bring home his body. Instead she rescues Spencer himself, who has recovered and been captured by Spaniards. After many adventures Besse is finally united to her lover. The first part, at least, makes a breezy and entertaining melodrama.

Fair Penitent, The, a tragedy in blank verse by Rowe (q.v.), produced in 1703.

The plot of the play is that of Massinger and Field's 'Fatal Dowry' (q.v.), shortened and somewhat modified at the end. Charalois becomes Altamont; Beaumelle, Calista; Rochfort, Sciolto; Romont, Horatio; and Novall, Lothario. The play was extremely successful and was constantly revived until the early 19th cent. The 'haughty, gallant, gay Lothario' has become proverbial, and was the model on which Richardson drew Lovelace in his 'Clarissa Harlowe' (q.v.). In revivals of the play Garrick acted Lothario, and subsequently Mrs. Siddons, Calista. Johnson said of it that 'there is scarcely any work of any poet at once so interesting by the fable, and so delightful by the language'. He observes, however, with reference to the title of the play, that Calista 'may be reasonably suspected of feeling pain from detection rather than from guilt'.

Fair Quarrel, A, a comedy by Middleton (q.v.) and W. Rowley (q.v.), published in 1617.

Captain Ager receives from a fellow officer an insult which reflects on his mother's virtue. A duel is arranged, but Ager is too conscientious to fight unless he is satisfied that his cause is a just one. He tells his mother of the accusation, which she at first indignantly denies, but presently, in order to prevent the duel, admits to be true. Ager then declines to fight, and is branded by his adversary as a coward. Having now what he considers an adequate reason, he fights and defeats his enemy. They are reconciled and all ends well. The offensive under-plot of the play calls for no special notice. The treatment by the authors of the problem presented in the main plot was made the subject of a warm eulogy by Charles Lamb in his 'Specimens'.

Fair Rosamond, see *Rosamond.*

Fairchild Family, The, see *Sherwood.*

Fairfield, LEONARD, a character in Bulwer Lytton's 'My Novel' (q.v.).

Fairford, ALAN, a character in Scott's 'Redgauntlet' (q.v.).

Fairservice, ANDREW, in Scott's 'Rob Roy' (q.v.), a gardener at Osbaldistone Hall, employed as servant by Francis Osbaldistone, a sanctimonious, self-important, cowardly rascal, who by his loquacity and disloyalty adds to his master's difficulties.

Faithful, in Bunyan's 'The Pilgrim's Progress' (q.v.), the companion of Christian; he is put to death at Vanity Fair.

To deal faithfully is to treat in the manner in which Faithful dealt with Talkative; Christian observes 'There is but little of this faithful dealing with men nowadays, and that makes religion to stink so in the nostrils of many as it doth'.

Faithful, JACOB, see *Jacob Faithful.*

Faithful Shepherdess, The, a pastoral play by J. Fletcher (q.v.), printed not later than 1610.

It deals with the love-affairs of various shepherds and shepherdesses. Clorin, the Faithful Shepherdess, skilled in simples and strong in her chastity, has vowed fidelity to her dead lover and lives by his tomb. Thenot is in love with her, but only so long as she remains faithful to her dead lover. Perigot is in love with Amoret, and Amarillis with Perigot. Amarillis being repulsed, enlists the services of the Sullen Shepherd to cross Perigot's love for Amoret. The wanton Cloe, seeking a lover, finds Daphnis too coy, and makes an assignation with Alexis.

The various couples assemble at night in the forest, and Amarillis, by dipping in a magic well, assumes the form of Amoret. Complications follow, and are finally resolved. Though without much dramatic interest, the play is full of passages of poetic beauty, and ranks, as a pastoral, with Ben Jonson's 'Sad Shepherd' and Milton's 'Comus' (qq.v).

Falconer, ALGERNON, a character in Peacock's 'Gryll Grange' (q.v.).

FALCONER, WILLIAM (1732–69), author of 'The Shipwreck', a poem in three cantos recounting the wreck of a ship on the coast of Greece, which had considerable vogue in its day. It appeared in 1762 (revised versions in 1764 and 1769). Falconer was drowned at sea.

Falernian, a wine celebrated among the ancient Romans, made from the grapes of the Falernian territory in Campania.

Falkland, one of the principal characters in Godwin's 'Caleb Williams' (q.v.). See also *Faulkland.*

Falkland, LUCIUS CARY, *second Viscount* (1610?–43), a famous Royalist, 'a man learned and accomplished, the centre of a circle [at Great Tew, near Oxford] which embraced the most liberal thinkers of his day, a keen reasoner and an able speaker, whose convictions still went with the Parliament, while his wavering and impulsive temper, his love of the Church, his passionate longings for peace, led him to struggle for a king whom he distrusted, and to die for a cause that was not his own' (J. R. Green). He fell at Newbury.

Falkland Islands, THE, were seen by Davis in 1592, and by Hawkins in 1594. Capt. Strong in 1690 sailed through the sound between them, naming it Falkland Sound. In 1764 De Bougainville took possession of the islands for France, which subsequently ceded them to Spain. Meanwhile Commodore Byron had occupied one of the small islands of the group. Spain renounced her claim in favour of Great Britain in 1771. The neighbouring ocean was the scene of the naval action of 8 Dec. 1914, in which the squadron of Admiral von Spee was (with the exception of one ship) destroyed by the British squadron commanded by Sir Doveton Sturdee.

Fall of Robespierre, The, a drama (1794) written by Coleridge (Act I) and Southey (Acts II and III) in collaboration, of little value.

Falls of Princes, see *Lydgate.*

False One, The, a tragedy attributed to J. Fletcher (q.v.), in which Massinger may also have had a share, printed in 1647; the date of production is uncertain.

The play deals with the joint occupation of the throne of Egypt by Ptolemy and his sister Cleopatra, and the intrigues of Photinus relating thereto; the treacherous murder of Pompey by Septimius; the entanglement of Caesar by the charms of Cleopatra; the revolt of the Alexandrians; the further treachery and hanging of Septimius ('The False One'); the suppression of the revolt by Caesar; the death of Ptolemy; and the reconciliation of Caesar with Cleopatra.

Falstaff, SIR JOHN, in Shakespeare's 'Henry IV' (q.v.), a fat, witty, good-humoured old knight, loving jests, self-indulgent, and over-addicted to sack; a braggart who, when exposed, has presence of mind and resource enough to find some shift to save his face; he seems to exaggerate and boast his vices in order to bring out their humorous side. The Falstaff of Shakespeare's 'Merry Wives of Windsor' (q.v.), written to command, presents a very different character. A mere designing knave, with but few sparks of his former ingratiating humour, he cuts a sorry figure in the indignities and mortifications to which his vices expose him. The character was originally called Oldcastle, but objection was taken by Lord Cobham, a descendant of the original Sir John Oldcastle (q.v.), 'for he died a martyr'.

Falstaff, Original Letters of Sir John, and his Friends; now first made public by a Gentleman, a Descendant of Dame Quickly, by James White (1775–1820), a friend of C. Lamb, who collaborated in their production. They were published in 1796.

Familiar Letters, see *Howell (J.).*

Fancyfull, LADY, a character in Vanbrugh's 'The Provok'd Wife' (q.v.).

Fanny, Lord, see *Hervey (John).*

Fanny's First Play, a comedy by G. B. Shaw (q.v.), published in 1911.

Fanny's Way, PRETTY, see *Parnell (T.).*

FANSHAWE, ANNE, LADY (1625–80), wife of Sir Richard Fanshawe, who was a devoted adherent to, and sufferer for, the Royalist cause, and after the Restoration was ambassador to Portugal and subsequently to Spain. Lady Fanshawe shared her husband's wanderings and wrote interesting 'Memoirs', first printed in 1829.

FANSHAWE, CATHERINE MARIA (1765–1834), poetess, remembered on account of her riddle on the letter H, which has often been attributed to Byron. The opening line originally ran ' 'Twas in heaven pronounced, and 'twas muttered in hell'; but the accepted reading—and the alteration is generally assigned to James Smith (q.v.)—now is ' 'Twas whispered in heaven, 'twas muttered in hell'.

Far from the Madding Crowd, a novel by Hardy (q.v.), published in 1874.

The theme, which recurs in other of Hardy's novels, is the contrast of a patient and generous devotion, with selfish unscrupulous love and with violent passion. Gabriel Oak, the shepherd, serves the capricious Bathsheba Everdene for many years with a humble unselfish devotion. Sergeant Troy, the gallant fascinating soldier, who deserts Fanny Robin and lets her die in childbed in a workhouse, wins Bathsheba for his wife and then ill-treats her. Troy is murdered by Farmer Boldwood, who is impelled by a furious longing for Bathsheba. Boldwood becomes a lunatic, and Gabriel and Bathsheba are at last united.

FARADAY, MICHAEL (1791–1867), the eminent physicist, was the son of a blacksmith and was apprenticed as a bookbinder. He attracted the attention of Sir H. Davy (q.v.) and was engaged by him as an assistant in 1812. Faraday made notable contributions to nearly all branches of physical science; but his greatest achievement was the discovery of magneto-electricity. He propounded the theory of 'lines of force', developed electrochemistry, and originated the theory of the atom as a 'centre of force'. His 'Experimental Researches in Electricity', reprinted from 'Philosophical Transactions', were published in 1839–55; his 'Life and Letters' in 1870. It was said that 'Sir H. Davy's greatest discovery was Michael Faraday'.

Farce (from a metaphorical use of the word *farce,* stuffing), was originally applied to explanatory or additional matter introduced into the liturgy; thence to the impromptu buffoonery which the actors were wont to insert in the text of religious dramas. It now means a dramatic work designed solely to excite laughter. It should be distinguished from Extravaganza (q.v.), with which it is sometimes confused.

Fardorougha, the Miser, a novel by W. Carleton (q.v.) published in 1839.

It is a powerful study of an Irish farmer torn between the passion of avarice and the love for a son who has come late in his married life. The villainous Bartle Flanagan, to revenge himself on the old usurer, who has been the cause of his ruin, enters his service and cunningly fixes the guilt of a crime he has committed on Fardorougha's son, Conor, and gets him transported; finally attempting, with the help of the lodge of Ribbonmen (q.v.) to which he belongs, to abduct his victim's sweetheart. He overreaches himself, and is hanged, but not before he has, in the terror of death, exculpated Conor. There are many humorous passages in this sombre tale.

Farmer George: George III was caricatured as 'Farmer George' on account of the simplicity of his tastes and his interest in agriculture.

Farmer's Boy, The, see *Bloomfield.*

Farnese, the name of an Italian family which rose to importance through the elevation of Alexander Farnese to the papal see as Paul III (1534). He created the duchy of Parma for his son Pietro.

The FARNESE BULL is a group of statuary by the brothers Apollonius and Tauriscus of Tralles (*c.* 150 B.C.) showing Dirce tied to a wild bull by Zethus and Amphion (see under *Antiope*). The sculpture was found in the Baths of Caracalla and placed in the Farnese palace.

The FARNESE HERCULES is a statue by the Athenian sculptor Glycon (1st cent. B.C.) of the hero leaning on his club, perhaps copied from an original by Lysippus.

FARQUHAR, GEORGE (1678–1707), was a sizar at Trinity College, Dublin, and after being an officer in the army became an actor, but gave up the stage in consequence of accidentally wounding a fellow player. He took to writing comedies, and produced 'Love and a Bottle' in 1699, 'The Constant Couple, or a Trip to the Jubilee' (q.v.) in 1700, 'Sir Harry Wildair' in 1701, 'The Inconstant' and 'The Twin Rivals' in 1702, 'The Stage Coach' (with Motteux, q.v.) in 1704, 'The Recruiting Officer' (q.v.) in 1706, and 'The Beaux' Stratagem' (q.v.) in 1707. The last two are the best of his plays, and are marked by an atmosphere of reality and genial merriment very different from that of the artificial comedy of the period. They reveal the good-natured and easy-going character of the author, though his satire is sometimes pungent. He is said to have been deceived by his wife, from love of him, about her fortune, but to have always treated her with tenderness and indulgence. He died in poverty. A present of twenty guineas from the actor Robert Wilks gave him the means of writing his last play, 'The Beaux' Stratagem', and he lived just long enough to hear of its success.

Fascist (pron. *fashist*), from Italian *fascisti*, which is derived from *fascio* (Latin *fascis*), a sheaf or bundle, used metaphorically in *fascio delle forze* in the sense of union or association of forces. In this sense the word *fascio* was adopted by the Italian socialists at the end of the 19th cent., particularly in Sicily, where certain socialist groups called *Fasci Siciliani* became well known. Early in 1915 a group of Italian revolutionary socialists led by Mussolini and Corridoni separated themselves from the official party and formed a *Fascio interventista*, advocating intervention in the War. This had 'Il Popolo d'Italia' as its organ in the press, and obtained a rapidly increasing membership. In March 1919, Mussolini formed at Milan a small group of young men called *Fascio nazionale di combattimento*, with the object of resisting by every means, including violence, the communist and socialist movements. Its success was due to strong organization and leadership and the fine fighting qualities of the *fascisti*, a large number of whom met their death in conflicts with their political opponents. At the end of 1921, when the government of the day seemed inclined to declare the *Fasci* to be unlawful armed bands, a party was formed (*Partito nazionale fascista*) which absorbed the old *Fascio di combattimento* and took as its symbol the Roman fasces. It was this party that in Oct. 1922 marched on Rome and accomplished the Fascist revolution. See also *Mussolini*.

Fashion, SIR NOVELTY and YOUNG, characters in Vanbrugh's 'The Relapse' (q.v.), who reappear in Sheridan's adaptation ('A Trip to Scarborough').

Fastidious Brisk, a character in Jonson's 'Every Man out of his Humour' (q.v.).

Fastolf, SIR JOHN (1378–1459), a distinguished warrior in the French wars of Henry V, who contributed towards the building of the philosophy schools at Cambridge and bequeathed funds which were devoted to the foundation of Magdalen College, Oxford. The few coincidences between the careers of Fastolf and Shakespeare's Sir John Falstaff are accidental.

Fastrade (764–94), queen of France, fourth wife of Charlemagne. She is mentioned by Longfellow in the 'Golden Legend', vi.

Fat Boy, The, Joe, Mr. Wardle's servant in 'The Pickwick Papers' (q.v.).

Fata Morgana, see *Morgan le Fay.* (The word *fata* in Italian means 'fairy'.)

Fatal Curiosity, The, a tragedy by Lillo (q.v.), published in 1736, based on an old story of a Cornish murder. Old Wilmot, under stress of poverty and urged by his wife, murders a stranger who has deposited a casket with them, only to find that the murdered man is his son, supposed to have been lost in a shipwreck.

The Fatal Curiosity is also another name for the episode in 'Don Quixote' of 'The Curious Impertinent'.

Fatal Dowry, The, a tragedy by Massinger and Field (qq.v.), printed in 1632. The text as we have it is corrupt.

When the play opens, Charalois's father, the distinguished marshal of Charles, duke of Burgundy, has just died in debt, and his creditors refuse to allow his body to be buried. Charalois offers to go to prison if the creditors will release the body. The offer is accepted; Charalois goes to prison with his friend, the blunt soldier Romont. Rochfort, ex-president of the parliament, touched by the piety of Charalois and the honesty of Romont, procures their release, and moreover gives Charalois his daughter, Beaumelle, to wife. She is presently found by Romont exchanging kisses with her former suitor, the mean-spirited fop Novall. Charalois, at first incredulous, presently himself finds Beaumelle and Novall together, and forcing a duel on the latter kills him. He calls upon Rochfort to judge his daughter. The father himself condemns her, and Charalois stabs her. But the father immediately turns on Charalois and upbraids him for his lack of mercy. Charalois is tried for the murder of Novall and Beaumelle, and acquitted, but killed by a friend of Novall, who in turn is killed by Romont.

Rowe's 'Fair Penitent' (q.v.) is founded on this play.

Fatal Marriage, The, or the Innocent Adultery, a tragedy by Southerne (q.v.), produced in 1694.

Biron, having married Isabella against his father's wish, is sent by him to the siege of Candy, and reported killed. His widow is repudiated by the father and brought to misery. During seven years she is courted by Villeroy, and finally, from gratitude for his devotion and urged by Carlos, Biron's younger brother, she marries him. Biron, who has all this time been a captive, now returns and reveals himself to Isabella. Carlos, it now appears, had known that Biron was alive, but had concealed his knowledge, wishing to oust him from the succession. For the same reason he had urged the marriage of Isabella, in order finally to ruin her and her son in his father's estimation. Carlos waylays and mortally wounds Biron. Isabella, already distracted by the situation in which she finds herself, takes her own life. The guilt of Carlos is exposed.

The play is founded on Mrs. Aphra Behn's novel 'The Nun or the Perjur'd Beauty'. Isabella was one of Mrs. Barry's (q.v.) most effective parts. The play was revived (with alterations) by Garrick under the title 'Isabella, or the Fatal Marriage'.

Fates, THE, see *Parcae*.

Father Brown, see *Brown (Father).*

Father O'Flynn, a popular Irish song, by A. P. Graves (q.v.).

Fathers, THE APOSTOLIC, the Fathers of the Church (q.v.) who were contemporary, or nearly contemporary, with the apostles, as Clement, Hermas, Barnabas, Polycarp, Papias, and Ignatius.

Fathers of the Church, the early Christian writers, a term usually applied to those of the first five centuries. Sometimes the Greek and Latin fathers are distinguished, the former including Clement of Alexandria, Origen, Cyprian, Athanasius, Basil the Great, Gregory Nazianzen, and Chrysostom; the latter Tertullian, Jerome, Ambrose, Augustine, Gregory (Pope Gregory I), and Bernard.

Fathom, FERDINAND COUNT, see *Ferdinand.*

Fatima, the daughter of Mohammed (q.v.) and the wife of the Caliph Ali (q.v.). Her descendants, known as the FATIMIDS, include the rulers of Egypt from 959 to 1171. In fiction Fatima is the name of the last wife of Bluebeard (q.v.).

Faulconbridge, ROBERT and PHILIP THE BASTARD, his half-brother, characters in Shakespeare's 'King John' (q.v.).

Faulkland, a character in Sheridan's 'The Rivals' (q.v.).

FAULKNER, WILLIAM (1897–1962), American novelist. He was born in Mississippi, where his family had long been settled, and spent most of his life there, in the town of Oxford. The history and legends of the South, and of his own family, were the material of his greater books. 'Sartoris' (1929), his third novel, was the first of the series in which he described the decline of the Compson and Sartoris families, representative of the Old South, and the rise of the crude and unscrupulous Snopes family. The principal setting of these novels is Jefferson— a composite picture of several Mississippi Towns—in Yoknapatawpha County. In his masterpiece, 'The Sound and the Fury' (1929), Faulkner views the decline of the South through several eyes, most remarkably, those of Benjy, an idiot. The work is an astonishing display of technique and style, written in a sombre and lyrical mood. 'As I Lay Dying' (1930) is equally distinguished, and illustrates Faulkner's comic as well as his tragic vision. He made his name, however, not with these, but with 'Sanctuary' (1931), an inferior work. 'Light in August' (1932) and 'Absalom, Absalom!' (1936) confirmed his reputation as one of the finest of modern novelists. His later work shows a decline, but among his important novels are 'The Wild Palms' (1939), 'The Hamlet' (1940), 'Intruder in the Dust' (1948), 'Requiem for a Nun' (1951), and 'A Fable' (1954). Faulkner also published many excellent short stories, collected in 1950. He was awarded a Nobel Prize in 1949.

Faunus, an ancient Italian nature-god, worshipped as the guardian of herds and patron of rural pursuits; developed from an earlier conception of a number of *Fauni*, spirits of the countryside and assimilated to the *Satyrs* (q.v.) of Greek mythology.

Faust, the subject of the great dramas of Marlowe and Goethe, was a wandering conjurer, who lived in Germany about 1488–1541 (H. G. Meek, 'Johann Faust', 1930) and is mentioned in various documents of the period. (Not to be confused with Johann Fust or Faust the printer, q.v.) For Marlowe's play see *Doctor Faustus*. 'Faust', the drama by Goethe, was begun by him about the year 1770 and not completed till just before his death in 1832. It consists of two parts, the first of which was published in 1808, the second in 1832. It begins with a Prologue in Heaven, in which Mephistopheles obtains permission to try to effect the ruin of the soul of Faust, the Lord being confident that he will fail. The play itself opens with a soliloquy by Faust, disillusioned with the world and despairing. Mephistopheles having presented himself, Faust enters into a compact to become his servant if Faust should exclaim, of any moment of delight procured for him, 'Stay, thou art so fair'. Then follow the attempts of Mephistopheles to satisfy Faust, culminating in the incident of Gretchen (Margaret), whom Faust, at the Devil's instigation, though not without some rebellion by his better self, seduces, bringing about her miserable death. This is the end of Pt. I, Faust being left remorseful and dissatisfied.

The story of Pt. II is extremely complex and its symbolism obscure. It consists in the main of two portions, of which the first is the incident of Helen, originally written as a separate and complete poem. Helen, symbolizing perfect beauty as produced by Greek art, is recalled from Hades and ardently pursued by Faust, but finally reft from him. Euphorion, their son, personifying poetry and the union of the classical and the romantic, and at the end representing Lord Byron, vanishes in a flame. In the second portion (Acts IV and V), the purified Faust, pursuing the service of man, reclaims from the sea, with the help of Mephistopheles, a stretch of submerged land. But Care attacks and blinds him. Finally satisfied in the consciousness of a good work done, he cries to the fleeting moment, 'Ah, stay, thou art so fair', and falls dead. Hell tries to seize his soul, but it is borne away by angels.

Faustus, DOCTOR, see *Doctor Faustus*.

Fauves, LES (wild beasts), a group of French painters, so-called by a critic of the Paris Salon d'Automne of 1905, on account of the violent colours in their paintings. They reduced landscape and other subjects to flat patterns, suggesting form by outline rather than by perspective and chiaroscuro. Henri Matisse (1869–1954) was the principal painter of the group.

Favonius, the Latin name of the zephyr or west wind. Also of a celebrated Derby winner (1871).

Fawn, The, see *Parasitaster*.

Fawnia, see *Pandosto*.

Feast of Fools, a medieval festival originally of the sub-deacons of the cathedral, held about the time of the Feast of the Circumcision (i.e. 1 Jan.), in which the humbler cathedral officials burlesqued the sacred ceremonies. A lord of the feast was elected, styled bishop, cardinal, abbot, etc., according to the locality (cf. *Boy Bishop*). The Feast of Fools had its chief vogue in the French cathedrals, but there are records of it in a few English cathedrals, notably at Lincoln, and at Beverley Minster.

Feathernest, MR., in Peacock's 'Melincourt' (q.v.), a caricature of Southey.

Federal States, the name given to those northern States in the American War of Secession (1861–5) which resisted the attempt of the Southern or Confederate (q.v.) States to secede.

Feeble, in Shakespeare's '2 Henry IV', III. ii, 'most forcible Feeble', 'a woman's tailor', one of the recruits brought up before Falstaff.

Feenix, COUSIN, a character in Dickens's 'Dombey and Son' (q.v.), the nephew of Mrs. Skewton, and cousin of Edith, Dombey's second wife.

Feet of Fines: 'fine' here means the compromise of a collusive suit for the possession of lands, a procedure formerly in use as a mode of conveyance where the ordinary modes were unsuitable (cf. 'Recovery', the process, based on a legal fiction, by which entailed estate was commonly transferred from one party to another. 'A great buyer of land, with . . . his fines, his double vouchers, his recoveries'; Shakespeare, 'Hamlet', v. i. 121–3). The person to whom the land was to be conveyed sued the holder for wrongfully keeping him out of possession; the defendant acknowledged the right of the plaintiff; the compromise was entered on the records of the court; and the particulars of it were set out in a document called 'the foot of the fine', one of the parts of a tripartite indenture, which remained with the court, the other two being retained by the parties. It was at the 'foot' of the undivided parchment, so that its indentation was at the top. [OED.] The collection of feet of fines is continuous from the time of Richard I and almost coeval with the royal court. Conveyance by fine was looked upon with great respect. It was said in parliament in 1291 that 'in this realm there is neither provided nor devised a greater or more solemn assurance, nor one through which a man may have a more secure estate . . . than a fine levied in the court of our lord the king' (Holdsworth, 'History of English Law').

Félibrige, a movement begun in 1854 by a group of French writers (Mistral (q.v.) and others) for the restoration of Provençal (q.v.) as a living language.

Felix, see *Hildesheim.*

Felix Holt the Radical, a novel by G. Eliot (q.v.), published in 1866.

Felix Holt is a noble-minded young reformer, an example of self-sacrifice, with the courage of his political convictions, who deliberately chooses the life of a humble artisan in order to bring home to his fellow workers that the hope of an improvement in their conditions lies in education and learning to think for themselves, and not in this or that legislative programme. With him is contrasted the conventional radical politician, the rich Harold Transome, a decent good-natured fellow, whose political convictions, however, when he stands for parliament, are not incompatible with 'treating' and other demoralizing practices. The heroine, Esther, supposed to be the daughter of old Lyon, the Independent minister, is brought by circumstances to a choice between the two men and the contrasted lives they offer her, and after a struggle chooses Felix and poverty. The story is complicated by the involved legal question of the ownership of the Transome estate, and marred for many readers by melodramatic and improbable elements.

FELL, Dr. JOHN (1625–86), dean of Christ Church, Oxford, and bishop of Oxford, is chiefly to be remembered in a literary connexion as the promoter of the Oxford University Press (q.v.), to the development of which he greatly contributed, procuring for it the matrixes and punches of the best types that could be found (from which the 'Fell types' are still cast), undertaking with three other University men the financial responsibility for the printing work (previously done by craft printers), and arranging every year for the publication of some classical author. Fell was author of a critical edition of Cyprian, and edited with many arbitrary alterations the 'Historia Universitatis Oxoniensis' of Anthony à Wood (q.v.). He built the tower over the principal gateway of Christ Church, to which he transferred the re-cast bell 'Great Tom'.

It is curious that the name of so considerable a benefactor of letters should be principally associated with the widely known jingle,

> I do not love you, Dr. Fell;
> But why I cannot tell;
> But this I know full well,
> I do not love you, Dr. Fell.

a translation of Martial, Epigrams, i. 32, by Thomas Brown (q.v.), one of the undergraduates of his college. 'Doctor Fell' has thus come to be used to describe a type of vaguely unamiable person against whom no precise ground of dislike can be adduced.

FELLTHAM, OWEN (1602?–68), published c. 1620, when 18 years of age, 'Resolves',

a series of moral essays. He contributed to 'Jonsonus Virbius' (see *Jonson*).

Felton, JOHN (1595?–1628), assassin of the duke of Buckingham (1592–1628, q.v.).

Female or FEMININE **Rhymes,** see *Rhymes.*

Female Quixote, The, or *The Adventures of Arabella,* a romance in imitation of 'Don Quixote' by Mrs. Charlotte Lennox (1720–1804), a lady who was flattered and befriended by Dr. Johnson. It was published in 1752.

Fencible, a person capable of making defence, fit and liable to be called on for military service. 'The Fencibles' was the name of bodies of militia raised at various times, and particularly of a force of some 15,000 men raised in 1794 and in subsequent years for service in any part of Great Britain during the war with France. 'Sea-Fencibles' were similarly raised for coast defence.

Fenella or ZARAH, a character in Scott's 'Peveril of the Peak' (q.v.), suggested to the author by Goethe's 'Mignon' (q.v.).

Fenellan, DARTREY and SIMON, characters in Meredith's 'One of our Conquerors' (q.v.).

FÉNELON, FRANÇOIS DE SALIGNAC DE LA MOTHE- (1651–1715), French divine, tutor of the duc de Bourgogne (the son of the Dauphin), and archbishop of Cambrai. He came into conflict with Bossuet (q.v.) by reason of his religious views. 'The apostle of interior inspiration', as opposed to the inflexible dogmatism of Bossuet, he expounded his Quietist (q.v.) doctrine in the 'Maximes des Saints' (1697), of which Bossuet obtained the condemnation by Rome. Fénelon at once submitted. His best-known work is 'Les Aventures de Télémaque' (1699), a graceful narrative in admirable prose of the imaginary adventures of Telemachus, written for the instruction of his pupil, as were also his 'Dialogues des morts' (1700–18) and 'Examen de la conscience d'un roi' (1734). His numerous other writings include a 'Traité de l'éducation des filles' (1687) and some excellent critical works: 'Lettre sur les occupations de l'Académie Française', 'Dialogues sur l'éloquence', etc.

Fenians, originally a semi-mythical, semi-historical military body said to have been raised for the defence of Ireland against Norse raids. Finn (q.v.), in his day, was its chief. The force was exterminated by King Cairbré, it is said, at the end of the 3rd cent. The Fenians of modern times were an association formed among the Irish in the United States and in Ireland in the middle of the 19th cent. for promoting the overthrow of the English government in Ireland. Their activity was greatest between 1865 and 1870, when they attempted invasions of Canada, and caused a disastrous explosion at Clerkenwell, but it continued to the end of the century and a Fenian plot to blow up public buildings in London was discovered in 1883.

Fenrir or the FENRIS-WOLF, in Scandinavian mythology, a monster, the son of Loki (q.v.). He is fettered by Tyr (q.v.) with the chain, Gleipnir, made by the Dwarfs, but breaks loose at Ragnarök (q.v.), helps to defeat the gods, and is slain by Vidar (q.v.).

Fenton, a character in Shakespeare's 'The Merry Wives of Windsor' (q.v.).

Feramorz, in Moore's 'Lalla Rookh' (q.v.), the name assumed by the king of Bucharia.

Ferdinand, (1) in Shakespeare's 'The Tempest' (q.v.), son of the king of Naples; (2) in Shakespeare's 'Love's Labour's Lost' (q.v.), the king of Navarre.

Ferdinand Count Fathom, The Adventures of, a romance by Smollett (q.v.), published in 1753.

This is the story of an unmitigated villain, whose mother was a camp-follower in Marlborough's army, and who took the title of count without any right to it. Endowed with talents and adroitness, but with no spark of honour or decency, he is received and brought up in the family of the German Count Melville, whose benevolence he repays by attempting to beguile his daughter into marriage, and, when he fails, by organizing with his confederate, the daughter's maid, a series of thefts on the family. Fathom passes from fraud to fraud, and seduction to seduction, in repulsive succession. His principal achievement is the betrayal of the honest Renaldo, his benefactor's son, and his attempt to seduce Monimia, the woman whom Renaldo is about to marry, and who only escapes his violence by feigning death. Finally Fathom is detected in his crimes and imprisoned; and Monimia, whom Renaldo had mourned as dead, is restored to her lover. But the author relents and saves Fathom from the fate he has richly merited, by an unconvincing repentance.

FERGUSON, SIR SAMUEL (1810–86), educated at Trinity College, Dublin, deputy-keeper of the records of Ireland. He came into notice as a poet by his 'Forging of the Anchor' contributed to 'Blackwood' in 1832, wrote a fine elegy on Thomas Davis, the nationalist leader, in 1845, and his epic 'Congal' (on the last stand of Irish paganism against Christianity) in 1872. 'Conary' (q.v.), perhaps his finest poem, and 'Deirdre', appeared in 1880. 'Ogham Inscriptions in Ireland, Wales, and Scotland' (1887) is his most important antiquarian work.

FERGUSSON, ROBERT (1750–74), educated at St. Andrews, and subsequently employed in the commissary clerk's and sheriff clerk's offices, published a volume of poems in 1773, which were much praised by Burns and Stevenson. His lyrics are interesting as an anticipation of the manner of Burns, and as giving a vivid and racy picture of the life and amusements of the Edinburgh poor.

Feridun, one of the principal heroes of the 'Shahnameh' of Firdusi (q.v.), a legendary king of Persia, who overthrew and succeeded Zohak, the slayer of Jamshid. He divided his dominions among his three sons, Salm, Tur, and Iraj. Their quarrels represent the frequent wars between the Iranians and Turanians.

Fern seed: before the mode of reproduction of ferns was understood, they were popularly supposed to produce an invisible seed, which was capable of communicating its invisibility to any person who possessed it.

'We have the receipt of fern-seed, we walk invisible.'
   (Shakespeare, '1 Henry IV', II. i. 96.)

Ferney, a village near Geneva, but within the French frontier, where Voltaire (q.v.) spent the last twenty years of his life. He is in consequence frequently referred to as the 'Philosopher of Ferney'.

Ferragus, (1) in the tale of 'Valentine and Orson' (q.v.), the giant from whose power their mother Bellisant is rescued; (2) the giant (also called *Ferracute*) whom Roland fights and slays in Charlemagne's Spanish war. He figures in the 'Orlando Innamorato' and in the 'Orlando Furioso' (qq.v.).

Ferrar, NICHOLAS (1592–1637), educated at, and fellow of, Clare College, Cambridge, was a member of parliament, and active in the affairs of the Virginia Company. In 1625 he retired to Little Gidding, received holy orders, and acted as chaplain there to a small Anglican community, composed of his brother's and brother-in-law's families, who devoted their lives to contemplation and prayer. The community was dispersed and their house and church ransacked by the parliamentary troops in 1646. A record of its activities survives in the 'Little Gidding Story Books', five manuscript volumes bound by Mary Collett, a member of the community, of which a part was printed in 1899, containing romances and pious discourses. An interesting picture of the community is given in 'John Inglesant' (q.v.).

Ferrara, see *Andrea Ferrara.*

Ferrars, WILLIAM PITT, ENDYMION, and MYRA, characters in Disraeli's 'Endymion' (q.v.).

Ferrau or FERRAGUS, in the 'Orlando Innamorato' and in the 'Orlando Furioso' (qq.v.), a Moorish knight of Spain, one of the suitors for the hand of Angelica (q.v.), and the slayer of her brother Argalia. He is killed by Orlando.

Ferrers, GEORGE, see *Mirror for Magistrates.*

Ferrex and Porrex, see *Gorboduc.*

FERRIER, JAMES FREDERICK (1808–64), nephew of Susan Ferrier (q.v.), educated at Edinburgh University and Magdalen College, Oxford, studied German philosophy at Heidelberg, and was successively professor of civil history at Edinburgh (1842–5) and of moral philosophy and political economy at St. Andrews (1845–64).

His idealist philosophy, connected with that of Berkeley, is set forth in 'The Institutes of Metaphysics' (1854) and 'Lectures on Greek Philosophy and other Philosophical Remains' (1866). The principal positions of his philosophy are two: first, that 'Along with whatever any intelligence knows, it must, as the ground or condition of its knowledge, have some cognisance of itself'. Nor can it know itself except in relation with objects. Mind and matter, *per se*, are unknowable. Secondly, that we can be ignorant only of what is capable of being known. From these positions he reaches his ontological conclusion: 'Speculation shows us that the universe . . . is incapable of self-subsistency, that it can exist only *cum alio*, that all true and cogitable and non-contradictory existence is a synthesis of the subjective and the objective; and *then* we are compelled, by the most stringent necessity of thinking, to conceive a supreme intelligence as the ground and essence of the Universal whole. Thus the postulation of the Deity is not only permissible, it is unavoidable.' In substance, Ferrier's conclusions closely resemble those of Hegel (q.v.), though reached independently and from a different starting-point. They are well set out in his 'Introduction to the Philosophy of Consciousness' (1838–9) and in his 'Berkeley and Idealism' (1842). He is a vigorous and stimulating writer.

FERRIER, SUSAN EDMONSTONE (1782–1854), a friend of Sir W. Scott, and the authoress of three good novels of Scottish life, 'Marriage' (q.v., 1818), 'The Inheritance' (q.v., 1824), and 'Destiny' (1831), all marked by a sense of humour and high comedy.

Ferumbras or **Firumbras, Sir**, a Middle English metrical version of the French Charlemagne romance *Fierabras*. Ferumbras is the son of the sultan of Babylon. He captures Rome and removes the holy relics. He is overcome in single combat by Oliver (q.v.) and baptized. His sister Floripas, for love of the Christians, obtains the care of Roland and Oliver, whom the pagans have taken prisoners, and helps them to kill many pagans at a feast. The sultan besieges the Christians. Charlemagne comes to their help and is caught between the gates of the city, but is rescued by Ferumbras. Floripas is baptized and marries Guy of Burgundy. The holy relics are recovered. The same story is told in the 'Sowdone of Babylon', a paraphrase (of about the year 1400) of a lost French poem.

Fescennine Verses, an ancient Italian form of verse, originally embodying rustic banter at harvest festivals, supposed to have the power of averting misfortune. Such verses long continued to be sung at marriages and triumphs. The name is perhaps derived from Fescennium in Etruria.

Fesolè, the modern Fiesole, a hill and small town adjoining Florence.

The moon, whose orb
Through optic glass the Tuscan artist views
At evening from the top of Fesolè,
Or in Valdarno.
(Milton, 'Paradise Lost', i. 228.)

Feste, the fool in Shakespeare's 'Twelfth Night' (q.v.).

Festin de Pierre, Le, see *Don Juan*.

Festus, a poem by P. J. Bailey (q.v.), first published in 1839. Successive editions appeared, and the poem gradually increased in length, until the fiftieth anniversary edition (1893) contained some 40,000 lines. The work was at one time immensely popular. It is written in blank verse, interspersed with couplets and lyrics, and takes the form of dialogues distributed over some fifty scenes.

The story is on the lines of that of Faust. Lucifer receives from God permission to tempt Festus, and accompanies him through life, as does also Festus's guardian angel. But the bulk of the dialogue is carried on, sometimes in speeches of tremendous length, between Festus and Lucifer. Together they perambulate the universe, from the Interstellar Space, Heaven, and Hell, to 'An Apartment in a Mansion' and 'A Garden, and Bower by the Sea'. In the supra-mundane scenes Festus converses with the great spirits of those regions, Luniel, Martiel, etc. In the terrestrial scenes he enjoys the society of a succession of fair ladies and other companions. With one of the ladies designed for Festus's temptation, Elissa, Lucifer has the misfortune himself to fall in love; another, Festus finally marries under pressure from his guardian angel. At the bidding of Festus, Lucifer reveals to him all the mysteries of the universe, and finally makes him lord of the earth; for the aim of Festus, who never wholly yields to Lucifer's temptations, is to unite all peoples in peace and brotherly love. But immediately after this consummation of his desires, the end of the world supervenes, all mankind dies, and Festus likewise; and the long work ends with the Last Judgement and the admission of Festus among the Elect Spirits.

The poem is 'a sketch of world-life and a summary of its combined moral and physical conditions, estimated on a theory of spiritual things opposed as far as possible to that of the . . . sceptic; not only in regard to the creation and government of the world, but in its views as to the origin of moral evil; and in its general positions known as universalist' (Author's preface to the fiftieth anniversary edition). Watts-Dunton claimed for it that it contains 'lovely oases of poetry' among 'wide tracts of ratiocinative writing'.

Festus, PORCIUS, Roman procurator of Judaea *c.* A.D. 60–62, before whom the apostle Paul was brought. He declared that Paul had done nothing worthy of death, but as he had appealed to Caesar, sent him to Rome (Acts xxv and xxvi).

Fetter Lane, from Fleet Street to Holborn, London, probably a corruption of Faitours Lane, from *faitour*, an impostor, vagabond; 'so called of the fewters or idle people lying there' (Stow).

FEUCHTWANGER, LION (1884–1958), German novelist, best known as the author of 'Die hässliche Herzogin' (1923, 'The Ugly Duchess') and 'Jud Süss' (1925, 'Jew Süss'). After being an expatriate in London and France he went to the United States in 1940.

Feuilleton, a portion of French newspapers marked off by a rule and appropriated to light literature, criticism, etc. Also, incorrectly, used in England for a serial or short story in a daily paper.

Fezziwig, MR. and MRS., characters in Dickens's 'A Christmas Carol' (q.v.).

Fiammetta, the name given by Boccaccio (q.v.) to the lady whom he loved, one Maria, illegitimate daughter of Robert, king of Naples, and wife of a Count d'Aquino.

FICHTE, JOHANN GOTTLIEB (1762–1814), German philosopher, a pupil of Kant (q.v.), from whose dualism he subsequently dissented. He became professor of philosophy at Jena in 1794, but was accused of atheism and dismissed. He subsequently taught at the universities of Erlangen and Berlin. Fichte's philosophy is pure idealism. Though his philosophical system grew out of Kant's, it has the distinguishing feature that the thinking self or *ego* is seen as the only reality. This *ego*, in defining and limiting itself, creates the *non-ego*, the world of experience, as its opposite, the medium through which it asserts its freedom. This doctrine he expounded in his principal work, 'Wissenschaftslehre', published in 1794. Influenced by the humiliation of Prussia in 1806–7, he became increasingly interested in the idea of nationhood, and sought reality, not in the *ego*, but in the notion of a divine idea lying at the base of all experience, of which the world of the senses is the manifestation. His 'Reden an die deutsche Nation' (1814) helped to arouse the patriotism of his contemporaries under the Napoleonic occupation.

Fidele, in Shakespeare's 'Cymbeline' (q.v.), the name assumed by Imogen when disguised as a boy.

Fidelio, Beethoven's opera, see *Leonora*.

Fidessa, in Spenser's 'Faerie Queene', I. ii, the name assumed by the fair companion of Sansfoy (q.v.), whom the Red Cross Knight takes under his protection after slaying that 'faithless Sarazin'. She turns out to be the false Duessa (q.v.).

FIELD, EUGENE (1850–95), American journalist and poet, born in Missouri. His 'A Little Book of Western Verse' (1889) had a considerable vogue in England. Among his other works were 'With Trumpet and Drum' (1892) and 'The Love Affairs of a Bibliomaniac' (1896).

FIELD, MICHAEL, the pseudonym of Katharine Bradley (1846–1914) and Edith Cooper (1862–1913). The following are among their joint works: 'Calirrhoe' (1884), 'The Father's Tragedy' (1885), 'Brutus Ultor' (1886), 'Canute the Great' (1887), 'Deirdre' (1918), 'In the Name of Time' (1919).

FIELD, NATHANIEL (1587–1633), actor and dramatist, acted in plays by Shakespeare, Ben Jonson, and Beaumont and Fletcher. His name is made synonymous with 'best actor' in Jonson's 'Bartholomew Fayre'. He wrote two comedies of some merit, the first of which shows the influence of Jonson, 'A Woman's a Weathercock' (1612) and 'Amends for Ladies' (1618). But he is remembered chiefly as having collaborated in Massinger's 'The Fatal Dowry' (q.v.).

Field of the Cloth of Gold, the meeting-place of Henry VIII and François I of France, near Calais, in 1520, so called from the magnificence of the display made by the two monarchs. The meeting was the preliminary to the long struggle between François and the Emperor Charles V, when each was endeavouring to secure the support of Henry VIII.

Field of the Forty Footsteps, The, a story by A. M. Porter (q.v.) embodying a legend about a field behind the present British Museum, at the north-east corner of what is now Upper Montagu Street, where two brothers met in a sanguinary duel at the time of the duke of Monmouth's rebellion. It was believed that no grass would grow where they had trodden.

Fielding, MRS. and MAY, characters in Dickens's 'The Cricket on the Hearth' (q.v.).

FIELDING, HENRY (1707–54), was born at Sharpham Park in Somerset, was educated at Eton (where he was contemporary with the elder Pitt and the elder Fox), and studied law at Leyden. He supported himself in London by writing for the stage, mostly comedies and farces, which contain some spirited songs, but of which the only ones that are remembered are his burlesque of the popular playwrights of the day, 'The Tragedy of Tragedies, or Tom Thumb' (q.v., 1730), and his two political and social satires, 'Pasquin' (1736) and 'The Historical Register for 1736' (1737). He reverted to the study of the law and was called to the bar in 1740. In 1734 he had married Charlotte Cradock, from whom Sophia Western (in 'Tom Jones') and Amelia were drawn. She died in 1744, and in 1747 Fielding married her maid, Mary Daniel. During 1739–41 he conducted the 'Champion' periodical (q.v.). The publication of Richardson's 'Pamela' (q.v.) provoked Fielding to parody it and led to the publication in 1742 of 'The History of the Adventures of Joseph Andrews and his friend Mr. Abraham Adams' (q.v.). Fielding was also perhaps the author of 'Shamela' (1741). In 1743 he published three volumes of 'Miscellanies', including his powerful satire 'Jonathan Wild the Great' (q.v.), and

'A Journey from this World to the Next' (q.v.). He now took up political journalism and by the help of his patron, Lord Lyttelton, was made justice of the peace for Westminster, where he was specially active in suppressing ruffianism. In 1749 appeared his great novel 'Tom Jones' (q.v.), and in 1751 'Amelia'(q.v.). In 1752 he started 'The Covent Garden Journal' (q.v.) under the pseudonym Sir Alexander Drawcansir; this contains some of his best miscellaneous essays. His health now broke down, and in 1754, in an attempt to recover it, he made a voyage to Portugal, of which he has left a pleasant account in his 'Journal of a Voyage to Lisbon', published posthumously. He died at Lisbon. He contributed powerfully to determine the form of the English novel. An essentially honest, manly, and humane character, he poured contempt on hypocrisy, meanness, and vanity.

FIELDING, SARAH (1710–68), sister of Henry Fielding (q.v.), and authoress of romances, including 'The Adventures of David Simple in search of a Faithful Friend' (q.v.), published in 1744. She translated Xenophon's 'Memorabilia' and 'Apologia' (1762).

FIENNES, CELIA (1662–1741), granddaughter of the first Viscount Saye and Sele, was probably born at Newton Toney near Salisbury. Nearly all that is known about her life is to be found in her Journal, of which an incomplete version was published in 1888 under the title 'Through England on a Side Saddle in the Time of William and Mary'. A definitive edition, 'The Journeys of Celia Fiennes', edited by Christopher Morris, was published in 1947. Between 1685 and 1703 Celia Fiennes travelled into every county of England, and her journal provided the first comprehensive survey of the country since Harrison and Camden (qq.v.). She recorded throughout what interested her: enclosures, mining, cloth manufacture, gardens, and domestic architecture; and while living in London she described in detail the coronations of James II, William and Mary, and Anne. Her style is breathless and her spelling erratic, but she communicates a lively enthusiasm.

Fierabras or FIEREBRAS, see *Ferumbras*.

Fiery Cross or FIRE-CROSS, a signal used anciently to summon the clansmen of the Scottish Highlands to a rendezvous on the outbreak of war. It consisted of a cross of wood, burnt at one end and dipped in blood at the other—symbolical of fire and sword—which was handed from clansman to clansman. [OED.]

Fifine at the Fair, a poem by R. Browning (q.v.), published in 1872.

The poet puts into the mouth of a Breton 'Don Juan' a defence of inconstancy in love, on the occasion of a visit to a fair, where he is fascinated with the beauty of the rope-dancer, Fifine. He expatiates on her charms, dis-

cusses her deficiencies, contrasts her with Helen and Cleopatra, avows himself a lover of novelty, and strives to reassure his wife Elvire by proclaiming her superiority to them all. He discourses interminably on the ethics of love, and then leaves Elvire with a lie on his lips—to join Fifine. He finds his punishment in the epilogue.

Fifteen, THE, the Jacobite rising of 1715.

Fifth Monarchy Men, English fanatics of the 17th cent. who believed that the second coming of Christ was at hand, and that it was the duty of Christians to be prepared to assist in establishing his reign by force, and in the meantime to repudiate allegiance to any other government. The Fifth Monarchy is the last of the five great empires referred to in the prophecy of Daniel (Dan. ii. 44), identified by the above with the millennial reign of Christ predicted in the Apocalypse. [OED.]

Fig Sunday, a dialectal name for Palm Sunday (q.v.).

Figaro, the barber in Beaumarchais's 'Barbier de Séville' and the hero of his 'Mariage de Figaro', a witty resourceful fellow, and a rebel against the abuses of the *ancien régime*.

Filer, a canting churl in Dickens's 'The Chimes' (q.v.).

Filioque, the Latin word meaning 'and from the Son' irregularly inserted in the Western version of the Nicene creed to assert the doctrine of the procession of the Holy Ghost from the Son as well as from the Father. More than anything else it prevented the reunion of the Western and Eastern Churches.

Filomena, Santa, a poem by Longfellow, in which the poet celebrated Florence Nightingale. A note to the poem states that 'at Pisa the church of San Francisco contains a chapel added recently to St. Filomena. Over the altar is a picture by Sabatelli representing the saint . . . floating down from heaven . . . and beneath in the foreground the sick and maimed, who are healed by her intercession.'

Filostrato, a poem in *ottava rima* on the story of Troilus and Cressida, by Boccaccio (q.v.), of special interest as the source of Chaucer's 'Troylus and Cryseyde'.

Finch, ANNE, see *Winchilsea (Countess of)*.

Fine and Recovery, see *Feet of Fines*.

Fingal, the name given by Macpherson (q.v.) in his Ossianic poems to the hero Finn (q.v.). He is the son of the giant Comhal, and king of Morven, the land of the north-west Caledonians. In the epic entitled 'Fingal' he crosses to Ireland and aids Cuthullin, vicegerent of the Irish kingdom during Cormac's minority, against Swaran, the Scandinavian king of Lochlin, who invades Ireland. Swaran is defeated and captured by Fingal. The story is continued in the further epic 'Temora' (q.v.). Fingal moreover figures, chiefly as a righter of wrongs and defender of the oppressed, in many of the other Ossianic poems.

It is noteworthy that Macpherson brings together Fingal and Cuthullin (the Irish Cuchulain, q.v.), who according to legend were divided by centuries, and makes the Irish Finn into a Scot.

Fingal's Cave, a vast natural cavern in the island of Staffa, in a stratum of columnar basalt, described by Sir W. Scott in his 'Lord of the Isles' (Canto iv).

FINLAY, GEORGE (1799–1875), studied law at Glasgow and Göttingen, and went to Greece in 1823, where he took part in the war of independence. At the close of this he bought an estate in Attica and died at Athens. His 'History of Greece' covers the period from its conquest by the Romans (146 B.C.) to modern times, thus covering the Byzantine Empire and the long period of Greece's subjugation. It appeared in sections between 1844 and 1861, and was published collectively in 1877. In his later years he wrote from Greece to 'The Times' letters chronicling the political developments of that country.

Finn or FIONN, the principal hero of the southern or later cycle of Irish legends, also called the Fenian or Ossianic cycle. Finn Mac Coul has been thought an historical personage by some modern authorities; others regard him as mythical. He was the son of Cumal (Comhal) and father of Ossian (q.v.), and is supposed to have lived in the 3rd cent. A.D., a contemporary of King Cormac. The king appointed him chief of the *Fianna* (pron. *Fēna*) or Fenians, a military body composed of men of exceptional strength and prowess, of whose heroic or romantic deeds there are endless tales. Finn was chosen their leader not for surpassing physical qualities, but on account of his truth, wisdom, and generosity. He is said to have perished in an affray with mutinous Fenians in A.D. 283.

For the story of Finn, Grainne, and Diarmait, see *Grainne*.

Finnegans Wake, a prose work by James Joyce (q.v.), published in 1939. It is written in a unique and extremely difficult style, making use of puns and portmanteau words, and a very wide range of allusion. The central theme of the work is a cyclical pattern of fall and resurrection. This is presented in the story of H. C. Earwicker, a Dublin tavern keeper, and the book is apparently a dream-sequence representing the stream of his unconscious mind through the course of one night. Other characters are his wife Anna Livia, their sons Shem and Shaun, and their daughter Isabel. In the relationships of these characters all human experience, mythical and historical, is seen to be historically subsumed. In spite of its obscurity it contains passages of great lyrical beauty, and also much humour.

Finnsburh, the name given to a fragment (of 50 lines) of an Old English epic poem, dealing with a portion of the tale of Finn and Hilde-burh sung by the minstrel in the poem 'Beowulf' (q.v.).

Finsbury, a district north of the old city of London, so called from the fen or marsh formed there probably by the interruption of water-courses when the city wall was built. It adjoins Moorgate and Moorfields.

FIONA MACLEOD, see *Sharp (W.)*.

Fionnuala, the subject of one of Moore's 'Irish Melodies', is a daughter of Lêr (q.v.), transformed by supernatural power into a swan and condemned to wander over the waters of Ireland until the coming there of Christianity.

Fir Bolgs, legendary early invaders of Ireland, according to tradition of an Iberian tribe, who were driven into Arran, Islay, and the Hebrides, by the Milesians (q.v.).

FIRBANK, (ARTHUR ANNESLEY) RONALD (1886–1926), novelist, was educated privately before going to Trinity Hall, Cambridge, where he completed only five terms and sat for no examinations. His first published novel was 'Vainglory' (1915), but although this was followed by 'Inclinations' (1916), 'Caprice' (1917), 'Valmouth' (1919), and 'The Flower beneath the Foot' (1923), his work was not widely appreciated until the publication in 1925 of 'Sorrow in Sunlight' (which appeared in New York as 'Prancing Nigger'). His last book, 'The Eccentricities of Cardinel Pirelli', was completed in Egypt in 1925. 'The New Rhythm' (1962) is a collection of extracts from juvenilia plus the extant chapters from 'Lady Appledore's Mésalliance', the novel Firbank was working on just before he died. He was an aesthete whose work reflects a fastidious and sophisticated mind.

FIRDUSI or FIRDAUSI, ABUL KASIM MANSUR (c. 950–1020), Persian poet, and author of the 'Shahnameh', the great epic recounting the deeds of Persian heroes and kings from the earliest times. He is said to have been shabbily treated by the Sultan Mahmud of Ghazni (q.v.), who had promised him a piece of gold for every line of the 'Shahnameh', but gave him silver instead, and repented too late. He is believed to be buried near Meshed. For the subject of the 'Shahnameh' see *Feridun, Isfendiyar, Jamshid, Rustem*.

Fire of London, THE GREAT, in 1666, broke out in a baker's house in Pudding Lane, and in four days (2–6 Sept.) destroyed the buildings on some 400 acres, including St. Paul's and eighty-seven churches, and over 13,000 houses. It extended from the Tower to the Temple and northwards as far as Cripplegate.

Fire-drake, a fiery dragon of Germanic mythology, used in a transferred sense of a person with a fiery nose, as in Shakespeare, 'Henry VIII', v. iv. 46, 'That fire-drake did I hit three times on the head'.

Fire-worshippers, The, see *Lalla Rookh*.

Firmilian, see *Aytoun.*

Firmin, DR. GEORGE BRAND and PHILIP, the principal characters in Thackeray's 'The Adventures of Philip' (q.v.); Dr. Firmin had previously figured in his 'A Shabby Genteel Story'.

Firouz, a Persian prince, the hero of one of the tales in the 'Arabian Nights' (q.v.). An Indian provides him with a magic horse, on which he is transported to Bengal. There he falls in love with a princess and brings her back to Persia. The Indian, being defrauded of the recompense stipulated for the horse, carries her off to Cashmere, where the sultan cuts off his head and proposes to marry the princess himself. She feigns madness and is rescued by Firouz in the guise of a physician.

First Gentleman of Europe, GEORGE IV, so called on account of the gracious manner he could assume, and his deportment in public.

First of June, THE GLORIOUS, the date of a naval battle in which, in 1794, Lord Howe defeated a French fleet some distance out from Ushant.

FIRTH, SIR CHARLES HARDING (1857–1936), historian and literary critic; Regius professor of modern history at Oxford, 1904–25 (and Emeritus professor from 1925); fellow of the British Academy. His writings include 'Oliver Cromwell' (1900); he contributed many articles to the 'Dictionary of National Biography'. A bibliography of his writings was published in 1928.

Firumbras, *Sir,* see *Ferumbras, Sir.*

FISHER, ST. JOHN (1459–1535), was educated at Michaelhouse (absorbed in Trinity College, 1546), Cambridge, of which he was appointed master in 1497. He became chancellor of the university and bishop of Rochester, 1504, and was president of Queens' College, Cambridge, from 1505 to 1508. He was a patron of Erasmus (q.v.) and induced him to lecture on Greek at Cambridge from 1511 to 1514. He wrote three treatises against the Lutheran reformation and was fined for denying the validity of the divorce of Queen Catherine, 1534. He was committed to the Tower for refusing to swear to the Act of Succession, and the pope did not improve his chances of escape from death by sending him a cardinal's hat while he was in prison. Fisher was deprived, attainted, and beheaded, 1535, for refusing to acknowledge the king as supreme head of the Church. His Latin theological works were issued in 1597; vol. i of his collected English works appeared in 1876, and no other has since been published. His English prose style showed a great advance, in point of rhetorical artifice and effect, on that of his predecessors. He was canonized in 1935 and is commemorated on 22 June.

FITZ-BOODLE, GEORGE SAVAGE, a pseudonym assumed by Thackeray (q.v.) in the 'Fitz-Boodle Papers' contributed to 'Fraser's Magazine', 1842–3.

Fitz-Fulke, HEBE, *Duchess of,* a character in Byron's 'Don Juan' (q.v.).

FITZGERALD, EDWARD (1809–83), educated at Bury St. Edmunds and Trinity College, Cambridge, lived a retired life in Suffolk and was a friend of Carlyle, Thackeray, and the Tennysons. His chief work was the English poetic version (from the Persian) of the 'Rubáiyát of Omar Khayyám' (q.v.), published in 1859 anonymously. In 1851 had appeared his 'Euphranor', a dialogue on systems of education set in the scenery of Cambridge. In 1852 he published 'Polonius', a collection of aphorisms, and in 1853 'Six Dramas of Calderon', free translations in blank verse and prose (he subsequently translated two more). He likewise made English versions of the 'Agamemnon' of Aeschylus and of the two 'Oedipus' tragedies of Sophocles. He also wrote a biography of his father-in-law, Bernard Barton, the poet and friend of Charles Lamb, for an edition of some of his poems, and compiled 'Readings from Crabbe' (1879). His charming letters were published in 1889–1901. FitzGerald collected the materials for a Dictionary of the *dramatis personae* of Mme de Sévigne's letters. This Dictionary was edited by his great-niece in 1914 and contains much that is useful to the English reader of the letters.

FITZGERALD, F. SCOTT (1896–1940), American novelist and short story writer, born in Minnesota. He was the typical figure of the 'jazz age', as he called it, the decade of the 'lost generation' following the First World War. He sprang into fame with 'This Side of Paradise' (1920), a novel set in Princeton, where he had been a student, and for several years he enjoyed a deserved success. He published two collections of short stories, 'Flappers and Philosophers' (1920) and 'Tales of the Jazz Age' (1922), and another novel, 'The Beautiful and the Damned' (1922), before 'The Great Gatsby' (1925), the story of the tragic love affair of a shady financier, symbolic of the age, which is his finest work. A further collection of stories, 'All the Sad Young Men' appeared in 1926, and the novel 'Tender is the Night' in 1934, by which time Fitzgerald's work had begun to deteriorate. His last novel, 'The Last Tycoon' (1941), was unfinished.

Fitzpiers, EDRED, a character in Hardy's 'The Woodlanders' (q.v.).

FITZRALPH, RICHARD (*d.* 1360), frequently referred to as 'Armachanus', was chancellor of Oxford (1333) and archbishop of Armagh (1347). He had great repute as a preacher, attacked the friars, and was cited in 1357 to defend his opinions before the pope at Avignon, which he did in his 'Defensio Curatorum'. He also wrote a treatise against the friars' doctrine of obligatory poverty, 'De Pauperie Salvatoris', in which he discussed 'dominion' or 'lordship', expressing the view on this subject that Wycliffe (q.v.) adopted.

FITZROY, VICE-ADMIRAL ROBERT (1805–65), commanded the 'Beagle' in the surveying expedition to Patagonia and the Straits of Magellan (1828–36), having Darwin as naturalist for the last five years. With Darwin he wrote a narrative of the voyage. He became chief of the meteorological department of the Board of Trade in 1854 and is regarded as the founder of meteorological science. He suggested the plan of the Fitzroy barometer and instituted a system of storm warnings, the first weather forecasts.

FITZSTEPHEN, WILLIAM (d. 1190?), author of a life of Thomas à Becket, which contains a valuable account of early London.

Five Nations, The, a collection of poems by Kipling (q.v.) published in 1903. The 'Five Nations' are the chief component parts of the British Empire.

In America the *Five Nations* were a league of five tribes of Iroquois Indians, living in Central New York State, formed in the 16th cent. shortly before the arrival of white settlers. The Tuscarora Indians joined them in 1715, and they then formed the 'League of Six Nations'.

Five Towns, THE, in the novels of Arnold Bennett (q.v.), Tunstall, Burslem, Hanley, Stoke-upon-Trent, and Longton, now forming the federated borough of Stoke-on-Trent. These are represented in the novels by Turnhill, Bursley, Hanbridge, Knype, and Longshaw.

Fizkin, HORATIO, in Dickens's 'The Pickwick Papers' (q.v.), the Buff candidate in the Eatanswill election.

FLACCUS, see *Horace.*

Flagellants, a sect of fanatics that arose in Europe in the 13th cent., and again in 1348 as a consequence of the Black Death, asserting that self-flagellation was necessary to appease the divine anger. They were declared heretics by Clement VI in 1349. In Italy processions of flagellants continued to be held at intervals over the centuries, one being seen as late as 1870.

Flamborough, FARMER and the MISSES, characters in Goldsmith's 'The Vicar of Wakefield' (q.v.).

Flaming Tinman, THE, a character in Borrow's 'Lavengro' (q.v.).

Flaminian Way, THE, the great northern road of Rome. It was constructed in the censorship of Gaius Flaminius (220 B.C.) and ran from Rome northwards across the Apennines to Ariminum (Rimini) on the Adriatic. It was extended thence under the name of the Aemilian Way through the heart of Cisalpine Gaul.

Flanders, MOLL, see *Moll Flanders.*

Flanders Mare: Henry VIII said of Anne of Cleves, his fourth wife, on the day after first meeting her at Rochester, that she was 'no better than a Flanders mare'. He married and divorced her in 1540. T. Fuller (1732) gives as a proverb, 'Like Flanders mares, fairest afar off'.

FLATMAN, THOMAS (1637–88), scholar of Winchester, and scholar and fellow of New College, Oxford, much esteemed as a painter of miniatures. He also wrote poems, 'A Thought of Death', 'Death, a Song', and some hymns ('Poems and Songs', 1674).

FLAUBERT, GUSTAVE (1821–80), French novelist, whose works include, notably, 'Madame Bovary' (1857), one of the great 19th-cent. French novels, a realistic picture of small-town bourgeois life, and 'L'Education sentimentale' (1869), a study of uneventful lives in the Paris of 1848; as well as 'Salammbô' (1862), a novel of ancient Carthage, and the unfinished 'Bouvard et Pécuchet' (1881). He also wrote shorter tales, some elaborately constructed, and one, 'Un Cœur simple', the story of a country servant, a masterpiece of studied simplicity.

Remarkable features of Flaubert's work are his care for form, style, and severe objectivity; also his painstaking documentation.

Flavius, in Shakespeare's 'Timon of Athens' (q.v.), the faithful steward of Timon.

Fleance, in Shakespeare's 'Macbeth' (q.v.), the son of Banquo.

FLECKER, (HERMAN) JAMES ELROY (1884–1915), educated at Uppingham and Trinity College, Oxford, entered the consular service and spent two years at Beirut. But his health broke down and he died of consumption in Switzerland. He published 'The Bridge of Fire' (1907), 'Forty-Two Poems' (1911), 'The Golden Journey to Samarkand' (1913), and 'The Old Ships' (1915). His 'Collected Prose', of less importance, appeared in 1920. His two plays, 'Hassan' and 'Don Juan', were published posthumously in 1922 and 1925. The former has attained celebrity.

FLECKNOE, RICHARD (d. 1678?), said to have been an Irish priest, printed privately several poems and prose works, including 'A Relation of Ten Years' Travel in Europe, Asia, Affrique, and America' (1656) and 'A short Discourse on the English Stage' (1664). He was the subject of a lampoon by Andrew Marvell (1645), which suggested to Dryden his satire on Shadwell, 'Mac Flecknoe' (q.v.).

Fledgeby, in Dickens's 'Our Mutual Friend' (q.v.), a cowardly villain, who conceals his money-lending business under the description 'Pubsey and Co.'

Fleece, GOLDEN, see *Golden Fleece.*

Fleet Prison, THE, stood in the neighbourhood of the present Farringdon Street, London, alongside of the Fleet river. It was built in the time of Richard I, and long afterwards served as a place of imprisonment for persons condemned by the Star Chamber. After the abolition of the latter in 1640, it served mainly as a debtors' prison, until demolished in 1848. As a debtors' prison it figures in Dickens's novels, notably in 'The Pickwick Papers' (q.v.).

In the early part of the 18th cent. the notorious FLEET MARRIAGES were celebrated by accommodating parsons confined in its precincts, without licence or banns, until the practice was stopped by the Marriage Act of 1753. Its evils are depicted in 'The Chaplain of the Fleet' by Besant (q.v.) and Rice.

Fleet Street, now the headquarters of London journalism, takes its name from the old Fleet river, which, running south from Hampstead, along the line of the Farringdon Road, flowed into the Thames at Blackfriars, passing under the Fleet Bridge at what is now Ludgate Circus. In its upper course it appears to have been known as the Hole Bourne (Holborn), or the Turnmill (q.v.) Brook. Boats could ascend the Fleet as far as the Holborn Bridge as late as the 16th cent. (Stow). Wren in his plan for rebuilding London after the Great Fire proposed to canalize it as far as Holborn Bridge.

Fleet Street Eclogues, see *Davidson.*

Fleetwood, THE EARL OF, a character in Meredith's 'The Amazing Marriage' (q.v.).

Fleming, SIR ALEXANDER (1881–1955), bacteriologist, born in Ayrshire. He entered the medical school of St. Mary's Hospital, Paddington, in 1901 and worked in the inoculation department under Almroth Wright. In the First World War he went to France as a lieutenant in the R.A.M.C. to establish a laboratory and research centre at Boulogne, where he worked on the treatment of infected wounds. After the war he continued his research at St. Mary's and in 1928 discovered the properties of a mould that had grown by chance in one of his laboratory dishes. This was *penicillium notatum,* from which the antibiotic, penicillin, was eventually isolated and produced for general use by Dr. Howard Florey and Dr. E. B. Chain at Oxford. Fleming was knighted in 1944 and, with Chain and Florey, was awarded the Nobel Prize for Medicine in 1945.

FLEMING, MARJORY (1803–11), 'Pet Marjorie', the daughter of James Fleming of Kirkcaldy, was a youthful prodigy. She wrote a quaint diary, a poem on Mary Queen of Scots, and other verses, and she was the subject of an essay by Dr. John Brown (q.v.), though his story of the friendship of Sir Walter Scott and Marjory is now believed to be apocryphal.

Fleming, (1) ROSE and AGNES, characters in Dickens's 'Oliver Twist' (q.v.); (2) ARCHDEACON, in Scott's 'The Heart of Midlothian'; (3) LADY MARY, in Scott's 'The Abbot'; (4) SIR MALCOLM, in Scott's 'Castle Dangerous';

(5) PAUL, in Longfellow's 'Hyperion'; (6) FARMER, RHODA, and DAHLIA, in Meredith's 'Rhoda Fleming' (qq.v.).

Flemish painting. Flanders roughly corresponds to modern Belgium and Luxembourg. In the 15th cent. religious subjects and portraits were painted with minute finish and realistic detail by Jan van Eyck, Rogier van der Weyden, and other artists of the Flemish school. In the following century Patenier and Pieter Bruegel developed landscape painting and in the 17th cent. Rubens's religious subjects served the Counter Reformation and his secular paintings the Court, while the genre painters, such as Brouwer and David Teniers, appealed to the middle classes.

Fleshly School of Poetry, The, the title of an article in the 'Contemporary Review' (Oct. 1871), in which Robert Buchanan (q.v.), under the pseudonym of 'Thomas Maitland', attacked the Pre-Raphaelites (q.v.), especially D. G. Rossetti. This attack was the prelude to a long and bitter controversy.

Fleta, a Latin treatise on the common law of England, largely a summary of Bracton (q.v.), published anonymously *c.* 1290.

FLETCHER, GILES, the elder (1549?–1611), educated at Eton and King's College, Cambridge, of which he became a fellow in 1568, was sent as envoy to Russia in 1588. His book on Russia (1591), suppressed, and only partially printed in Hakluyt and Purchas, was published entire in 1856 (ed. Bond). 'Licia, or Poemes of Love' (1593), printed by Grosart, 1871, is of some importance as one of the first collections of sonnets that followed the appearance of Sidney's 'Astrophel and Stella'. He was uncle of John Fletcher (q.v.), the collaborator of Beaumont.

FLETCHER, GILES, the younger (1588?–1623), the younger son of Giles Fletcher the elder (q.v.), was educated at Trinity College, Cambridge. He was rector of Alderton, Suffolk, and a poet of the Spenserian School, who dealt with religious themes allegorically. His 'Christ's Victorie and Triumph in Heaven and Earth' (1610) has been several times reprinted.

FLETCHER, JOHN (1579–1625), was born at Rye in Sussex, of which place his father (who subsequently was chaplain at the execution of Mary Queen of Scots and became bishop of Bristol and of London) was then minister. John Fletcher was nephew of Giles Fletcher the elder (q.v.) and cousin of Giles the younger and Phineas Fletcher (qq.v.). He was educated at Benet College, Cambridge. He died of the plague and was buried at St. Saviour's, Southwark. Fletcher collaborated with Francis Beaumont from about 1606 to 1616 in the production of plays, the exact number of which is not known, but does not exceed fifteen. He was sole author of not less than sixteen plays, and collaborated with Massinger, Rowley, and others in yet other plays.

The principal plays of which Fletcher was author or part author are the following:

Probably by Fletcher alone: 'The Faithful Shepherdess' (q.v.), printed by 1610; 'Wit without Money', a comedy, printed in 1639; 'Valentinian' (q.v.), acted before 1619; 'The Loyal Subject' (q.v.), acted in 1618; 'The Mad Lover', acted before 1619; 'The Humorous Lieutenant' (q.v.), acted in 1619; 'Women Pleased', a comedy, *c.* 1620, printed in 1647; 'The Wild Goose Chase' (q.v.), 1621, printed in 1652; 'The Pilgrim', a comedy, 1621, printed in 1647; 'The Island Princess', 1621, a romantic comedy; 'Monsieur Thomas', 1619, printed in 1639; 'The Woman's Prize, or The Tamer Tamed', a comedy (the taming of Shakespeare's Petruchio), written before 1625, printed in 1647; 'A Wife for a Month', a romantic drama, acted in 1624; 'Rule a Wife and have a Wife' (q.v.), acted in 1624; 'The Chances' (q.v.), 1620, printed in 1647.

Certainly or probably by Beaumont and Fletcher: 'Four Plays in One', four short plays (two founded on Boccaccio, one on Bandello, one an allegory about false and true friends), probably acted *c.* 1608; 'The Knight of the Burning Pestle' (q.v.), 1609, printed in 1613; 'The Scornful Lady', 1610, printed in 1616; 'Philaster' (q.v.), 1611, printed in 1620; 'The Maid's Tragedy' and 'A King and no King' (qq.v.), 1611, printed in 1619; 'The Coxcomb', a romantic comedy, acted in 1612, printed in 1647; 'Cupid's Revenge', a tragedy based on material in the second Book of Sidney's 'Arcadia', acted in 1612, printed in 1615; 'The Captain', a comedy, acted in 1612–13; 'The Honest Man's Fortune', printed in 1647; 'Bonduca' (q.v.), 1614, printed in 1647; 'The Knight of Malta', a tragicomedy, acted before March 1619, printed in 1647; 'Thierry and Theodoret' (q.v.), printed in 1621; 'Love's Cure', printed in 1647.

Probably by Fletcher and some other dramatist: 'Love's Pilgrimage' and 'The Double Marriage', comedies printed in 1647; 'Sir John van Olden Barnavelt' (q.v.), acted in 1619; 'The False One' (a Cleopatra play), 'The Little French Lawyer' (q.v.), 'The Custom of the Country' (q.v.), and 'The Laws of Candy', all printed in 1647; 'The Spanish Curate' (q.v.) and 'The Beggars Bush' (q.v.), acted in 1622. In all the above Fletcher certainly or probably collaborated with Massinger. The romantic drama, 'The Lovers' Progress' (q.v.), produced in 1623 and printed in 1647, was an adaptation by Massinger of an earlier play by Fletcher. 'The Maid in the Mill' was written by Fletcher and Rowley (licensed in 1623). 'The Elder Brother' (q.v.), printed in 1637, is thought to have been written by Fletcher and revised by Massinger. 'The Fair Maid of the Inn', printed in 1647, was probably the result of similar collaboration, with perhaps assistance from Jonson and Rowley. 'The Nice Valour', a comedy, printed in 1647, was probably written by Fletcher and Middleton. It contains the lyric 'Hence all you vain delights', which

suggested 'Il Penseroso' to Milton. In 'The Bloody Brother, or Rollo, Duke of Normandy' (q.v.), Fletcher is supposed to have had the assistance of Jonson (in the astrological scene) and others; this tragedy was probably produced about 1616. It contains the lyric 'Take, oh take those lips away', which occurs with certain changes in Shakespeare's 'Measure for Measure'. 'The Noble Gentleman', a comedy acted in 1626, is by Fletcher with Beaumont, or perhaps Rowley. 'The Two Noble Kinsmen' (q.v.), printed 1634, was probably the work of Fletcher and Shakespeare. It is probable also that Fletcher had a share in the composition of Shakespeare's 'Henry VIII'.

FLETCHER, PHINEAS (1582–1650), the elder son of Giles Fletcher the elder (q.v.), was educated at Eton and King's College, Cambridge, and was rector of Hilgay, Norfolk, 1621–50. Like his brother Giles, he was a poet of the Spenserian School. His chief work, 'The Purple Island', an allegorical poem on the human body, the mind, and the virtues and vices, was published in 1633; 'The Locusts or Apollyonists', an attack on the Jesuits, in 1627; and 'Elisa', an elegy on the death of Sir Antony Irby, in 1633. 'Britain's Ida', 1628, seems to be his.

Fleur and Blanchefleur, see *Flores and Blancheflour.*

Flibbertigibbet, probably in its original form 'flibbergib', which Latimer uses in a sermon for a chattering or gossiping person. Harsnet in his 'Popish Impostures' (1603) gives 'Fliberdigibbet' as the name of a devil or fiend. And Shakespeare in 'King Lear' III. iv has 'Flibbertigibbet', 'the foul fiend' who walks at night, 'gives the web and the pin, squints the eye, and makes the hare-lip'. Scott, in 'Kenilworth' (q.v.), gives the nickname 'Flibbertigibbet' to Dickie Sludge.

Flintwinch, a character in Dickens's 'Little Dorrit' (q.v.). His wife was known as Affery.

Flippanta, a character in Vanbrugh's 'The Confederacy' (q.v.).

Flite, MISS, a character in Dickens's 'Bleak House' (q.v.).

Flodden or FLODDON **Field,** the battle of Flodden, in Northumberland, fought on 9 Sept. 1513, when the earl of Surrey on behalf of Henry VIII (then in France) defeated James IV of Scotland, the latter sovereign being killed on the field. It was made the subject of poems, of rejoicing or lament, on both sides of the border. Skelton's 'Against the Scots' is a rude song of exultation on the English victory, and several English ballads appeared, of which one by Thomas Deloney (q.v.) is printed in Ritson's collection. On the Scottish side there is the beautiful lament, 'The Flowers of the Forest', of which the most popular version is by Jane Elliot (q.v.). The battle is described in the 6th canto of

Scott's 'Marmion, A Tale of Flodden Field' (q.v.).

FLODOARD (894–966), of Rheims in France, left valuable chronicles of the period 919–66, and a 'Historia Remensis Ecclesiae'.

Flora, the goddess of flowers and spring of the ancient Romans.

Florac, COMTE DE, in Thackeray's 'The Virginians' (q.v.), a young French officer who rescues George Warrington from the Indians; in 'The Newcomes' (q.v.) an *émigré* from France. His wife (who had been loved as a girl by Thomas Newcome), son, and daughter-in-law figure in the same novel.

Flordelis, in the 'Orlando Furioso' (q.v.), the devoted wife of Brandimarte, the paladin killed in the great fight with Agramant and Gradasso at Lipadusa.

Flordespina, in the 'Orlando Furioso' (q.v.), a princess who falls in love with Bradamante, being led by her armour to take her for a man.

FLORENCE OF WORCESTER (*d.* 1118), a monk of Worcester who was author of a 'Chronicon ex Chronicis' (based upon the work of Marianus, an Irish monk), extending to 1117, which was continued by other hands till 1295 (Cambridge MS.). It was first printed in 1592, and translated for Bohn (1847) and for Stevenson's 'Church Historians' (1853).

Florent or FLORENTIUS, the subject of a tale in Gower's 'Confessio Amantis' (q.v.), and of 'The Wife of Bath's Tale' in Chaucer's 'The Canterbury Tales' (q.v.).

Flores (pron. Flō'rĕs), the westernmost island of the Azores off which Sir Richard Grenville fought his great sea fight with the Spaniards in 1591, celebrated in Tennyson's 'The Revenge'.

Flores and Blancheflour, a metrical romance of the Middle English period, relating the adventures of Blancheflour, a Christian princess carried off by the Saracens and brought up with the Christian prince Flores. They fall in love and are separated, but Blancheflour gives Flores a ring which will tarnish when she is in danger. Blancheflour is threatened by a false accusation, and Flores, warned by the ring, finds her in a seraglio in Egypt, whither she has been sent as a slave. The lovers are pardoned by the Emir and all ends well. A version of this story forms the subject of Boccaccio's 'Filocolo'.

Florestan, KING, a character in Disraeli's 'Endymion' (q.v.).

Florimell, in Spenser's 'Faerie Queene', Bks. III and IV, the type of chastity and virtue in woman. She is in love with the knight Marinell, who 'sets nought' by her. She takes refuge from her pursuers in the sea and is imprisoned by Proteus. Finally the heart of Marinell is touched by her complaint, and Neptune orders Proteus to release her.

Florin, the English name of a gold coin first

issued at Florence in 1252, so called because it had a flower stamped upon it. The name was applied to two English gold coins (known also as 'leopards' and 'double leopards') of the value of 3s. and 6s., issued by Edward III, of the weight of one and two Florentine florins respectively. The English silver coin worth 2s. called a florin was first minted in 1849.

Florinda, a character in Southey's 'Roderick' (q.v.).

FLORIO, JOHN (1553?–1625), son of an Italian Protestant refugee, was born in London and educated at Magdalen College, Oxford. He was reader in Italian to Anne of Denmark, wife of James I, 1603, and groom of the privy chamber, 1604. His Italian-English dictionary appeared in 1598. He published a translation of Montaigne's 'Essays' in 1603, which had an important influence on English literature and philosophy. It is marked by a certain extravagance and eccentricity of language, but he loved his author and made a vivid work of the translation.

Florisando, see *Amadis of Gaul.*

Florismart, in the Charlemagne romances, one of the paladins, and friend of Roland.

Florizel, a character in Shakespeare's 'The Winter's Tale' (q.v.), the lover of Perdita. 'Florizel' was the name adopted by George IV, when Prince of Wales, in his correspondence with Mary Robinson, the actress, with whose performance as Perdita he had been captivated.

Florizel, PRINCE, the chief character in the 'New Arabian Nights' of R. L. Stevenson (q.v.).

Flosky, MR., a character in Peacock's 'Nightmare Abbey' (q.v.), who illustrates the transcendentalism of Coleridge.

Flower and the Leaf, The, an allegory of 600 lines in rhyme-royal, formerly attributed to Chaucer, in which the poet wandering in a grove sees the white company of knights and ladies of the leaf (Diana, goddess of chastity), and the green company of the flower (Flora), the 'folk that loved idleness' and had delight 'of no businesse, but for to hunt and hauke, and pley in medes', and witnesses their processions and sports.

Linguistic characteristics suggest that this poem is of later date than Chaucer or was extensively re-written. The spirit of the poem is thoroughly Chaucerian.

Flowers of the Forest, see *Elliot (Jane).*

FLUDD, ROBERT (1574–1637), physician and Rosicrucian (q.v.), was as a writer a medical mystic of the school that looked to the Bible for secret clues to science. He vindicated the fraternity of the Rosy Cross in several treatises.

Fluellen, in Shakespeare's 'Henry V' (q.v.), a brave, choleric, and pedantic Welsh officer.

Flute, in Shakespeare's 'A Midsummer Night's Dream' (q.v.), a bellows-mender, who takes the part of Thisbe in the play of 'Pyramus and Thisbe'.

Flutter, SIR FOPLING, a character in Etherege's 'The Man of Mode' (q.v.).

Flying Childers, reputed the fastest race-horse ever bred, the son of Darley Arabian (q.v.), was bred in 1715 by the duke of Devonshire, and died in 1741.

Flying Dutchman, The, a phantom ship, which, in consequence of a murder committed on board, is supposed to haunt the sea in a perpetual endeavour to make Table Bay. It is seen in stormy weather off the Cape of Good Hope, and forebodes disaster. Capt. Marryat's novel 'The Phantom Ship' and a music-drama by R. Wagner (q.v.) are founded on this legend.

Flying Fox, a famous racehorse belonging to the duke of Westminster, which (in 1899) won the 'Triple Crown', that is to say, the Two Thousand Guineas, the Derby, and the St. Leger.

Foedera, Conventiones, et cujuscunque generis Acta Publica, a collection of public records in twenty volumes, by Rymer (q.v.) and Robert Sanderson, published in 1704–35 (vols. xvi-xx were prepared by Sanderson, the first of these chiefly from Rymer's materials). The documents (treaties, conventions, letters, etc. between the kings of England and foreign sovereigns and states) extend down to 1654, and provided for the first time a scientific basis for the writing of history.

FOGAZZARO, ANTONIO (1842–1911), novelist, poet, and essayist, ranks with Verga (q.v.) as the greatest of 19th-cent. Italian novelists after Manzoni (q.v.). His humour (often called 'Dickensian') and his powers of characterization (his greatest asset as a novelist) are at their best in his masterpiece 'Piccolo mondo antico' ('A Little World of Former Time', 1895), a novel set in the Valsolda region north of Lake Lugano during the last ten years of Austrian rule (1850–60). The tense relations between the hero and his wife (Franco is a devout Catholic, but somewhat ineffectual; Luisa, full of active virtue, is an atheist) reflect the author's religious preoccupations and are typical of the ideological and psychological conflicts upon which Fogazzaro based his novels.

Fogg, PHILEAS, the hero of Jules Verne's 'Round the World in Eighty Days'.

Foible, in Congreve's 'The Way of the World' (q.v.), Lady Wishfort's woman.

Foigard, FATHER, in Farquhar's 'The Beaux' Stratagem' (q.v.), a pretended French priest; 'his French shows him to be English, and his English shows him to be Irish'.

Foker, HARRY, a character in Thackeray's 'Pendennis' (q.v.).

FOLENGO, TEOPHILO (1496?–1544), an Italian monk, who wrote, under the pseudonym Merlin Coccai, a long burlesque-heroic poem, 'Opus Macaronicum', in macaronic (q.v.) verse. Its hero is Baldus, who has for followers the giant Fracassus and the cunning Cingar. Rabelais's Panurge (q.v.) is partly modelled on the latter.

Folio, a sheet of paper folded once only, or a volume made up of sheets so folded (consequently of the largest size).

Folios and Quartos, SHAKESPEARIAN. Shakespeare's earliest published plays are referred to as folios or quartos according to the folding of the printed sheets and therefore the size of the book, folios being large tall volumes, and the quartos usually smaller and squarer. Of about 1,200 copies of the 'First Folio' printed by the Jaggards (q.v.) between Feb. 1622 and Nov. 1623, some 230 survive, eighty in the Folger Shakespeare Library and five, the next largest collection, in the British Museum. The Second, Third, and Fourth Folios followed in 1632, 1663, and 1685 respectively. Thirty-six plays, eighteen printed for the first time, were arranged by Heming and Condell (q.v.) into sections of comedies, histories, and tragedies. F1, which was dedicated to William Herbert, earl of Pembroke and Philip Herbert, earl of Montgomery, contains the Droeshout portrait (q.v.), together with commendatory verses by contemporaries including Jonson (q.v.), who may also have written the address to the readers. 'An Epitaph on . . . Shakespeare' by Milton (q.v.), his first printed poem, was added to F2.

The nineteen texts which first appeared as quartos were divided by Pollard (q.v.) into 'bad' (mutilated texts perhaps reconstructed from memory) and 'good' quartos (those based on authoritative manuscripts). The fullest accounts of F1 are by Sir W. W. Greg ('The Shakespeare First Folio', 1955) and C. Hinman ('The Printing and Proof-reading of the First Folio of Shakespeare', 1963).

Folio, TOM, a pedantic bibliophile, the subject of one of Addison's essays.

Folklore, the traditional beliefs, legends, and customs, current among the common people; and the study of them. The term was first introduced by W. J. Thoms in the 'Athenaeum' (1846).

Folliott, THE REVD. DOCTOR, a character in Peacock's 'Crotchet Castle' (q.v.).

Fomors, THE, the sea-giants of Gaelic mythology. They are represented as more ancient than the gods (the *Tuatha Dé Danann*), and as having been ousted by them and destroyed at the battle of Moytura (C. Squire, 'Mythology of the British Islands'). See also *Balor*.

Fondlewife, one of the characters in Congreve's 'The Old Bachelor' (q.v.).

Fontarabia, now FUENTERRABIA, in Spain at the mouth of the Bidassoa. Milton appears to have confused it with Roncesvalles, some forty miles away, where the rout of the rearguard of Charlemagne's army is generally supposed to have occurred:

> When Charlemagne with all his peerage fell
> By Fontarabia.
>
> ('Paradise Lost', i. 587.)

Scott, in 'Marmion', vi. 33, refers to 'Fontarabian echoes' in connexion with the defeat at Roncesvalles.

Fonthill, see *Beckford* (*W.*).

Fool of Quality, The, a novel by H. Brooke (q.v.), published 1766–72.

The 'fool of quality' is Henry, second son of an earl of Moreland, and so called because he appears to his parents of less intelligence than his elder brother. He is banished from their house and brought up by his fostermother and subsequently by his uncle, and develops not only great physical beauty and athletic prowess, but a high degree of virtue and generosity, which he displays in the relief of the poor, sick, and oppressed. The incidents of the story are neither very probable nor very interesting, but they are oddly diversified by discourses on a great variety of subjects (in the latter part of the book on the mystical aspects of Christianity), and by discussions between the author and a 'friend' on passages in the book itself. The work breathes the spirit of Rousseau, the revolt against oppression and suffering, and anticipates the doctrines of Godwin and Paine (qq.v.). It was highly admired by John Wesley, who edited it for Methodist use, and by Charles Kingsley (q.v.), who contributed a laudatory preface to the edition of 1859.

FOOTE, SAMUEL (1720–77), actor and dramatist, was educated at Worcester College, Oxford, where he dissipated a fortune. As an actor he was particularly successful in comic mimicry; acting in his own plays, he caricatured his fellow actors and various well-known persons. He wrote a number of short dramatic sketches of two or three acts, depending largely for their success on topical allusions, of which 'Taste' (1752) was the first. 'The Minor' (1760), a satire directed against the Methodists, in which Foote mimicked George Whitefield ('Dr. Squintum'), was his most powerful work. 'The Liar' (1762) is a lively farce in which Young Wilding is the liar, constantly exposed, and constantly gay and unabashed. 'The Mayor of Garret' (q.v.) appeared in 1764. In 'The Maid of Bath' (1771) Foote pilloried Squire Long, the unscrupulous sexagenarian lover of Miss Elizabeth Linley, the lady who subsequently married Sheridan. 'The Nabob' (1772) was aimed at the directors and servants of the East India Company. One of his plays, 'A Trip to Calais' (1776), involved him in a quarrel with the duchess of Kingston, and was altered to 'The Capuchin' (the offending character of 'Lady Kitty Crocodile' being replaced by another). Foote had a leg amputated in 1766, but this did not quell his spirit. He received as compensation a patent for a theatre, and built the new Haymarket in 1767. He was known to his contemporaries as the English Aristophanes, counsel in a libel action having likened his client to Socrates and Foote to Aristophanes.

Fopling Flutter, SIR, a character in Etherege's 'The Man of Mode' (q.v.).

Foppington, LORD, a character in Vanbrugh's comedy 'The Relapse' (q.v.) and Sheridan's 'A Trip to Scarborough' (q.v.); also in Colley Cibber's 'The Careless Husband' (q.v.).

FORCELLINI, EGIDIO (1688–1768), lexicographer; author, with J. Facciolati, of the famous 'Totius Latinitatis Lexicon' (1771), commonly known as 'Forcellini-Facciolati'.

Ford and **Mrs. Ford**, characters in Shakespeare's 'The Merry Wives of Windsor' (q.v.).

FORD, FORD MADOX (formerly Ford Madox Hueffer, 1873–1939), was the son of Dr. Francis Hueffer, a music critic of 'The Times', and grandson of Ford Madox Brown. In 1908 he founded 'The English Review', a monthly which he edited until the end of 1909 and which published the first stories of D. H. Lawrence and whose contributors included Hardy, Henry James, Galsworthy, and H. G. Wells (qq.v.). He collaborated with Conrad (q.v.) in the novels 'The Inheritors' (1901) and 'Romance' (1903). Of his own large output of novels the best known are 'The Good Soldier' (1915) and the Tietjens sequence, 'Some Do Not' (1924), 'No More Parades' (1925), 'A Man Could Stand Up' (1926), 'The Last Post' (1928), subsequently collected under the title 'Parade's End'. His work includes critical studies, verse, and reminiscences 'Ancient Lights', 1911; 'Thus to Revisit', 1921; 'Return to Yesterday', 1931; 'It was the Nightingale', 1934; 'Mightier than the Sword', 1938). From 1926 onwards he lived partly in America and partly in France.

FORD, JOHN (*fl.* 1639), was born in Devonshire, and was admitted at the Middle Temple in 1602. He probably spent his last years in Devonshire. Some of his plays have perished (four were destroyed by Warburton's cook). Of those which have survived the chief are the 'Lover's Melancholy' (q.v., 1629), 'Love's Sacrifice' (q.v., 1633), ''Tis Pity she 's a Whore' (q.v., 1633), 'The Broken Heart' (q.v., 1633), 'Perkin Warbeck' (q.v., 1634), 'The Ladies Triall' (1638). He collaborated with Dekker and Rowley in 'The Witch of Edmonton' (q.v.). The best edition of his collected works is Dyce's reissue of Gifford's edition (1869). The principal characteristic of his work is the powerful depiction of melancholy, sorrow, and despair. A vivid little portrait of him has been preserved in the couplet, from the 'Time-Poets' ('Choice Drollery', 1656):

> Deep in a dump John Ford was alone got,
> With folded arms and melancholy hat.

FORD, RICHARD (1796–1858), educated at Winchester and Trinity College, Oxford, a contributor to the 'Quarterly', 'Edinburgh', and 'Westminster' Reviews (qq.v.), is remembered as the author of the 'Handbook for Travellers in Spain' (1845), a work agreeable by its charming style and rendered exceptionally interesting by the author's sympathetic knowledge of the people and the frequent references to incidents of the Peninsular War. His 'Gatherings from Spain' (1846) is a no less agreeable work. His 'Letters' have been edited (1905) by Lord Ernle.

Foresight, the foolish old astrologer in Congreve's 'Love for Love' (q.v.).

Forester, SYLVAN, a character in Peacock's 'Melincourt' (q.v.).

Forgers and **Fabricators,** LITERARY, and other **Impostors,** see under *Apollonius of Tyana, Berosus, Bertram (Charles), Cagliostro, Chatterton, Claude, Clement I, Collier (John Payne), Cortese, Croyland History, Decretals, Demetrius (Pseudo-), Dodd, Guerre, Hermes Trismegistus, Ireland (W. H.), Lauder, Lucas (V.), Mandeville, Munchausen, Psalmanazar, Pythagoras, Rougemont, Sanchoniathon, Sanson, Shapira, Smerdis, Steevens, Tichborne, Timothy, Wise.*

There is a remarkable invocation of forgers and impostors in ch. xx of Anatole France's 'M. Bergeret à Paris'.

Forrest, The, a collection of miscellaneous short poems, odes, epistles, and songs, by Jonson (q.v.), printed in the folio of 1616. It includes the beautiful songs: 'Drink to me only with thine eyes', and 'Come, my Celia, let us prove'.

Fors Clavigera, a collection of letters to the workmen and labourers of Great Britain, by Ruskin (q.v.), published in 1871–84.

This remarkable collection deals with a great variety of subjects, though the underlying motive—the redress of poverty and misery—is present throughout. 'For my own part,' he writes, 'I will put up with this state of things not an hour longer. . . . I simply cannot paint, nor read, nor look at minerals nor do anything else that I like . . . because of the misery that I know of, and see signs of where I know it not.' He sets out to show the causes of the evil and the means of remedying it. His practical contribution was the founding of the Guild of St. George (see under *Ruskin, John*). The title of the work is explained by the author: 'Fors Clavigera' is fortune bearing a club, a key, and a nail, symbolizing the deed of Hercules, the patience of Ulysses, and the law of Lycurgus.

FORSTER, EDWARD MORGAN (1879–), novelist, educated at Tonbridge School and King's College, Cambridge. He lived for a time in Italy, the background of 'Where Angels Fear to Tread' (1905) and 'A Room with a View' (1908). 'The Longest Journey' (1907), which has a considerable

element of autobiography, was followed by 'Howards End' (q.v., 1910), which has been considered his best novel, although 'A Passage to India' (q.v., 1924) has attracted much attention, not only for its formal merits, but because of the approach to its subject-matter. Forster's experiences in India, where he went in 1912, and again in 1921 after being in Alexandria during the war, are described in 'The Hill of Devi' (1953). He has also written short stories: 'The Celestial Omnibus' (1914) and 'The Eternal Moment' (1928); essays, collected in 'Abinger Harvest' (1936) and 'Two Cheers for Democracy' (1951); and 'Alexandria: a History and a Guide' (1922). He wrote, with Eric Crozier, the libretto for Benjamin Britten's opera 'Billy Budd' (1951). 'Some Aspects of the Novel' is the title of his Clark lectures at Cambridge (1927).

FORSTER, JOHN (1812–76), educated at Newcastle Grammar School and University College, London, contributed to Lardner's 'Cyclopaedia' 'Lives of the Statesmen of the Commonwealth' (1836–9), that of Sir John Eliot being issued separately in an expanded form in 1864. He edited the 'Foreign Quarterly Review' in 1842–3, the 'Daily News' in 1846, and the 'Examiner' in 1847–55. He was subsequently a lunacy commissioner. Forster wrote a number of biographical works: 'Life and Adventures of Oliver Goldsmith' (1848), lives of his friends Walter Savage Landor (1869) and Charles Dickens (1872–4), and the first volume of a 'Life of Swift' (1876). His other works include 'Historical and Biographical Essays' (1858), 'The Arrest of the Five Members' and 'The Debates on the Grand Remonstrance' (1860).

Forsyte Saga, see *Galsworthy.*

FORTESCUE, SIR JOHN (1394?–1476?), chief justice of the king's bench under Henry VI, and the earliest English constitutional lawyer. He was a Lancastrian during the Wars of the Roses, but, having been captured at Tewkesbury in 1471, was pardoned and made a member of the council on recognizing Edward IV (1471). His principal works were a Latin treatise, 'De Natura Legis Naturae' (1461–3), distinguishing absolute from constitutional monarchy; an English treatise on the same subject ('Monarchia' or 'The Difference between an Absolute and a Limited Monarchy'); a Latin treatise, 'De Laudibus Legum Angliae' (1471); and an English work, 'On the Governance of England'. His recantation of his Lancastrian views is contained in 'A Declaration upon Certain Wrytinges' (1471–3).

FORTESCUE, HON. SIR JOHN (1859–1933), librarian of Windsor Castle, 1905–26, author of a 'History of the British Army' (1899–1929) and other works of military history.

Forties, THE HUNGRY, a term applied to a period of acute distress among the poorer classes of England, resulting from a series of bad harvests beginning in 1837, coupled with the taxation of imported wheat. This distress culminated in 1842, and was marked by the Chartist and Anti-Corn-Law agitations, and a good deal of turbulence and intimidation.

Fortnightly Review, The, was founded in 1865, as the organ of advanced liberalism, and edited successively by G. H. Lewes, John Morley (1867–83), T. H. S. Escott, Frank Harris, Oswald Crawfurd, and W. L. Courtney. It was at first, as its name implies, issued fortnightly, but before long only once a month.

Fortunate Isles, THE, in the belief of the ancient Greeks and Romans, lay west of the Pillars of Hercules in the Atlantic Ocean. They are supposed to be the Canary Islands. They were represented as the seat of the blessed, where the souls of the virtuous were placed after death.

Fortunate Mistress, The, see *Roxana*.

Fortunatus's purse, the subject of a European 15th-cent. romance, translated into many languages and dramatized by Dekker. For the story see *Old Fortunatus*.

Fortune, MR. REGINALD, in H. C. Bailey's detective stories, the adviser of the C.I.D. 'when surgery, medicine, or kindred sciences can elucidate what is or is not crime'.

Fortunes of Nigel, The, a novel by Sir W. Scott (q.v.), published in 1822.

The young Nigel Olifaunt, Lord Glenvarloch, threatened with the loss of his ancestral estate if he is unable promptly to redeem a heavy mortgage, comes to London to endeavour to recover from James I a sum of 40,000 marks advanced to the latter at a crisis in his fortunes by Nigel's father. The king is induced to sign an order on the Scottish treasury for the amount in favour of Nigel. But the estate is coveted by Prince Charles and the duke of Buckingham, and Nigel finds great difficulties opposed to his recovery of the money. Lord Dalgarno, the favourite of Charles and Buckingham, a dissembling villain, lures Nigel into evil ways, keeps him from the court, and spreads false rumours about him. Nigel, discovering his treachery, challenges him in St. James's Park, and strikes him, an offence for which he is liable to lose his right hand. He takes sanctuary in Alsatia (q.v.), the strange and lawless society of which is vividly described. He is subsequently imprisoned in the Tower. Meanwhile Margaret Ramsay, the pretty, petulant daughter of an old clockmaker in the City, has fallen deeply in love with Nigel. She takes secret steps to effect his rescue, and moreover, in the disguise of a page, seeks an interview with James himself, to advance the cause of the man she loves and at the same time to secure reparation for her patroness, Lady Hermione, who has been grievously wronged by her husband Lord Dalgarno. She is successful in her endeavours. Nigel is released, and, touched by the devotion of Margaret,

marries her. He recovers his estate, and Lord Dalgarno is killed by robbers as he proceeds to Scotland in a last attempt to seize the property.

The novel contains a number of interesting characters, including the pedantic freakish James I; Richard Moniplies, Nigel's conceited servant; Dame Ursula Suddlechop, milliner and secret agent; the miser Trapbois and his austere daughter; the rattling Templar, Lowestoffe; and the embittered courtier, Sir Mungo Malagrowther.

Forty Thieves, THE, see *Ali Baba*.

Forty-five, THE, the year 1745, and the Jacobite rebellion in that year.

Forty-niner, in the U.S., one of those who 'rushed' to California during the gold-fever, *c*. 1849.

Foscari, The Two, see *Two Foscari*.

Fosco, COUNT, a character in Wilkie Collins's 'The Woman in White' (q.v.).

Fosse Way, THE, a Roman road running across England from Bath to Lincoln. It intersects Watling Street at High Cross, sometimes called the centre of England.

Foster, ANTHONY, a character in Scott's 'Kenilworth' (q.v.).

Fotheringay, MISS, the stage name of Emily Costigan, a character in Thackeray's 'Pendennis' (q.v.).

Foul Play, a novel by C. Reade (q.v.), published in 1869.

The story turns on the scuttling in the Pacific of a ship, supposed to be carrying a large consignment of gold, by the design of the owner, Arthur Wardlaw, in order to defraud the underwriters. Unfortunately, Arthur's sweetheart, Helen Rolleston, is on board, and also Robert Penfold, who has been transported for a forgery committed by Arthur. The two are thrown together on a Pacific island, and the story, a good example of Reade's narrative power, ends in the exposure of the villain and the marriage of Robert and Helen.

Foulis, ROBERT (1707–76), originally named Faulls, was a barber's apprentice at Glasgow. With his brother Andrew he visited Oxford and France in 1738–40 collecting rare books, and started as bookseller and printer at Glasgow. He printed for the university their first Greek book (1743) and the 'immaculate' Horace (1744). He issued a number of other remarkable books, the fine folio 'Iliad' of 1756, 'Odyssey' (1758), the Olivet Cicero (1749), the small folio Callimachus (1755), the quarto edition of Gray (1768), and 'Paradise Lost' (1770). (See James MacLehose, 'The Glasgow University Press', 1931.)

Fountain of Youth, *fontaine de jouvence,* in the 'Roman d'Alisandre' (see under *Alexander the Great*), a magic fountain (a sidestream of the Euphrates) in which Alexander and his army bathe, and are thereby restored to the prime of life.

The belief in a fountain possessing this magical property was widespread in the Middle Ages. After the discovery of America it was supposed to be situated in the Bahamas, and Juan Ponce de Leon (a companion of Columbus in 1493 and the discoverer of Florida) received in 1512 authority to discover and settle Bimini, a mythical island, in which the Fountain of Youth was supposed to be.

FOUQUÉ, FRIEDRICH, BARON DE LA MOTTE, see *Undine*.

Four Georges, The, a series of lectures on Kings George I–IV and their times, delivered by Thackeray (q.v.) in the United States and London in 1855–6. They were printed in the 'Cornhill Magazine', 1860.

Four Horsemen of the Apocalypse, The, a novel by B. Ibañez (q.v.); it was the basis of one of the earliest spectacular films.

Four Just Men, The, a novel by Edgar Wallace (q.v.), published in 1905. The Four Just Men undertake a crusade for the destruction of noxious members of society.

Four P's, The, see *Interludes*.

Four Sons of Aymon, see *Aymon*.

Four Zoas, The, see *Blake*.

Fourierism, a communistic system for the reorganization of society devised by Charles Fourier (1772–1837) of Besançon, a French author. Under it the population was to be grouped in phalansteries, or socialistic groups of about 1,800 persons, who would live together as one family and hold property in common.

Fourteenth of July, see *Bastille*.

Fourth Estate, THE, the Press. The use of the expression in this sense is attributed by Carlyle to Burke, but not traced in his speeches. A correspondent of 'N. and Q.' (1st Series, xi. 452) attributes it to Brougham.

Fourth of June, an Eton College celebration.

Fourth of July, 'Independence Day', a national holiday in the United States, being the anniversary of the day on which, in 1776, was signed the Declaration of Independence, by which the original thirteen States of the union broke their allegiance to the British crown.

FOWLER, H. W. and **F. G.,** lexicographers and grammarians; joint authors of 'The King's English' (1906), 'The Concise Oxford Dictionary' (1911), and 'The Pocket Oxford Dictionary' (1924). 'A Dictionary of Modern English Usage' (1926; 2nd edition, 1965, ed. Sir E. Gowers) is the work of H. W. Fowler (*d.* 1933). F. G. Fowler *d.* 1918.

FOWLER, KATHERINE, see *Philips (K.)*.

FOX, CHARLES JAMES (1749–1806), third son of the first Lord Holland and 'our first great statesman of the modern school' (Sir G. Trevelyan), was educated at Eton and Hertford College, Oxford. He became M.P. for Midhurst in 1768, making his mark by his speeches against Wilkes in 1769, and was a lord of the Admiralty under Lord North in 1770; but his independent attitude brought him into disfavour with the king, and he was dismissed from the ministry in 1774. Fox took a leading part in opposition to North's American policy, in debates on economical reform, and in support of Roman Catholic relief. In spite of great pecuniary distress he refused to be bribed by the emoluments of office and continued his attacks on the government. In 1782 he was appointed foreign secretary in Lord Rockingham's ministry, but was thwarted by Shelburne and resigned when the latter became premier. In 1783 he formed a coalition with North, becoming joint-secretary of state with him under the duke of Portland, but was dismissed in the same year. He was one of the managers of the proceedings against Warren Hastings, and opened the Benares charge in a speech of nearly five hours. Fox was a constant opponent of the policy of Pitt (during the first long ministry of the latter), on the commercial treaties with Ireland and France, the Eastern question, the French Revolution, etc., and made a three hours' speech in favour of peace in 1803. But when Napoleon obviously threatened invasion and stood forth as a conqueror unabashed, Fox saw how dangerous the situation was; he showed himself a patriot and was willing to serve with Pitt in the 1804 Ministry, but the prejudice of George III excluded him. After Trafalgar he held that the danger was over, and was willing to receive (as foreign secretary under Grenville) overtures from France. But he soon found out Napoleon's duplicity, and his last act was to knit up close relations with Russia against France. Fox was a man of great personal charm, noted for his love of letters and his scholarship; also for his passion for gambling and for the bad influence he exercised over the Prince of Wales.

For the 'Early History of Charles James Fox' see under *Trevelyan (Sir George)*.

FOX, GEORGE (1624–91), son of a Leicestershire weaver, and founder of the Society of Friends (q.v.). His 'Journal', revised by a committee under William Penn's superintendence and published in 1694, is a narrative, in simple and direct style, of his spiritual experiences and of the troubles to which he and his followers were exposed by the persecution of the authorities. A 'Collection of . . . Epistles' was issued in 1698 and his 'Gospel Truth' in 1706.

FOXE, JOHN (1516–87), the martyrologist, was born at Boston, Lincolnshire, and was educated at Oxford, where he became a fellow of Magdalen College, but resigned his fellowship in 1545, being unwilling to conform to the statutes in religious matters. In 1554 he retired to the Continent, and issued at Strasburg his 'Commentarii' (the earliest draft of his 'Actes and Monuments'). From

1555 to 1559 he was employed at Basle as reader of the press by Oporinus (Herbst), who published Foxe's 'Christus Triumphans' in 1556, his appeal to the English nobility on toleration in 1557, and the first issue of his 'Rerum in ecclesia gestarum . . . Commentarii' in 1559. On his return to England he was ordained priest by Grindal in 1560, and in 1564 joined John Day, the printer, who in 1563 had issued the English version of the 'Rerum in ecclesia gestarum . . . Commentarii' as 'Actes and Monuments' (q.v.), popularly known as the 'Book of Martyrs'. He became a canon of Salisbury in 1563, but objected to the use of the surplice and to contributing to the repairs of the cathedral. He preached at Paul's Cross a famous sermon 'On Christ Crucified' in 1570. His 'Reformatio Legum' appeared in 1571. He was buried in St. Giles' Church, Cripplegate. Four editions of the 'Actes and Monuments' (1563, 1570, 1576, and 1583) appeared in the author's lifetime; of the posthumous issues, that of 1641 contains a memoir of Foxe, attributed to his son, but of doubtful authenticity.

Fra Angelico, see *Angelico, Fra*.

Fra Diavolo ('Brother Devil'), the popular name of an Italian brigand, Michele Pezza (1771–1806), who was connected with the political movements in southern Italy for the recovery of Naples from the French at the beginning of the 19th cent. He was leader of a troop of guerrillas, and was arrested and shot. He is the subject of the famous opera by Auber which bears his name.

Fra Lippo Lippi, a poem by R. Browning (q.v.), included in 'Men and Women', published in 1855.

The painter monk (Fra Filippo Lippi, c. 1406?–1469), who has broken out of Cosimo dei Medici's house on a night frolic, with much humour narrates his life: his entry as a half-starved child into a Carmelite convent, where his talent for painting led to his employment to embellish the church; the different views on art of the prior and himself; and his present mode of life, painting under the influence of the prior's doctrine, but breaking bounds at times.

Fra Rupert, see *Andrea of Hungary*.

Fradubio, in Spenser's 'Faerie Queene', I. ii. 32 et seq., 'the doubter', the lover of Fraelissa; he doubts whether her beauty is equal to that of Duessa. Duessa transforms Fraelissa into a tree, obtains Fradubio's love, and when he discovers her deformity, turns him also into a tree.

Frail, MRS., a character in Congreve's 'Love for Love' (q.v.).

Fram, The, the specially constructed steamer in which Nansen (q.v.) attempted to reach the North Pole in 1893–6.

Framley Parsonage, a novel by A. Trollope (q.v.), published in 1861.

This was the fourth of the Barsetshire series. Mark Robarts, a young clergyman, the close friend of Lord Lufton, is appointed to the living of Framley by the widowed Lady Lufton, the latter's mother. He is brought by Lord Lufton into relations with Mr. Sowerby, an unscrupulous spendthrift, and the disreputable duke of Omnium, obtains by their influence a prebendal stall at Barchester, after weakly consenting to back bills for Mr. Sowerby, and generally conducts himself so as to incur the disapproval of his patroness, Lady Lufton. Meanwhile Lord Lufton falls in love with Robarts's sister Lucy, a young lady of insignificant appearance but endowed with much character and vivacity. Lady Lufton vigorously opposes the match, and Lucy tells her lover she will not marry him unless asked to do so by his mother. His pertinacity and Lucy's self-sacrificing character finally win over Lady Lufton, and she complies with Lucy's condition. Meanwhile Robarts is rescued from his grave embarrassments by Lord Lufton, and having learnt his lesson, forswears his dangerous courses. Sowerby, whose estates are heavily mortgaged to the duke of Omnium, endeavours to escape from ruin by proposing to the rich Miss Dunstable, who refuses him and marries Dr. Thorne (q.v.). Bishop and Mrs. Proudie again appear, and also Archdeacon and Mrs. Grantly, whose beautiful daughter Griselda is married to Lord Dumbello, the heir of the marquis of Hartletop. The Revd. Josiah Crawley, the hero of the 'Last Chronicle of Barset' (q.v.), makes his first appearance.

FRANCE, ANATOLE, the pseudonym of FRANÇOIS ANATOLE THIBAULT (1844–1924), French man of letters, the son of a bookseller. His first book of stories 'Jocaste et le chat maigre' appeared in 1879, followed in 1881 by 'Le Crime de Sylvestre Bonnard', which established his reputation as a novelist. He thereafter produced a long series of witty, graceful, and satirical tales, of which the best known are the following: 'Le Livre de mon ami' (1885); 'Thaïs' (an historical novel of which Alexandria in the first century is the scene, 1890); 'L'Étui de nacre' (1892); 'Les Opinions de Jérôme Coignard' (1893); 'La Rôtisserie de la Reine Pédauque' (1893); 'Sur la pierre blanche' (containing the story of Gallio, 1905); the four political satires with the figure of M. Bergeret as the centre, 'L'Orme du Mail' (1897), 'Le Mannequin d'osier' (1897), 'L'Anneau d'améthyste' (1899), 'M. Bergeret à Paris' (1901); 'Crainquebille' (1904); 'L'Île des pingouins' (1908); 'La Révolte des anges' (1914); 'Le Petit Pierre' (1918). 'Les Dieux ont soif' (1912) is a novel of the French Revolution.

France, ILE DE, (1) a region of old France comprising the modern departments of Aisne, Oise, Seine, Seine-et-Oise, Seine-et-Marne, and part of Somme, with Paris as its capital, which was constituted a province in the 15th cent.; (2) the name given by the French to the island of Mauritius, when they occupied it in 1715. The island was taken by the English in 1810, and the old name Mauritius, given to it by its discoverers, the Dutch, in honour of their stadholder Prince Maurice, was restored.

Francesca da Rimini, see *Paolo and Francesca.*

Franceschini, COUNT GUIDO, a character in Browning's 'The Ring and the Book' (q.v.).

Francis, SIR PHILIP (1740–1818), the son of the Philip Francis who was Gibbon's schoolmaster at Esher and tutor of Charles James Fox, was educated at St. Paul's School with Woodfall, subsequently the publisher of the letters of Junius. He became a junior clerk in the office of the secretary of state in 1756, and clerk or amanuensis to General Edward Bligh, Lord Kinnoul, and the elder Pitt. From 1762 to 1772 he was a clerk in the War Office, but retired owing to some disagreement with Lord Barrington, secretary at war. On the latter's recommendation, however, he became one of the four newly appointed councillors of the governor-general of India in 1774. He opposed Warren Hastings, charging him with corruption in the case of Nuncomar, and was wounded in a duel with him. He left India in 1780, became a member of parliament, and assisted Burke to prepare the charges against Hastings. He quarrelled with Fox for refusing to appoint him viceroy. He was intimate with the Prince Regent and was created a K.C.B.

There is strong evidence, but falling short of certainty, for identifying Francis with the author of the letters of 'Junius' (q.v.). It rests upon the acquaintance of 'Junius' with the affairs of the secretary of state's office and the war office, his displeasure at the removal of Francis from the latter, coincidence between the silences of Junius and the absences from London of Francis, private letters to Woodfall the publisher, expert evidence on handwriting, and moral resemblance. Against the identification are adduced the denial of Woodfall, and the malignity of 'Junius' towards some of Francis's friends and benefactors.

Francis of Assisi, ST., GIOVANNI FRANCESCO BERNARDONE (1181?–1226), experienced as a young man a spiritual crisis while on a military expedition, in consequence of which he lived for a time in solitude and prayer and devoted himself to the relief of the poor, the sick, and the lepers. He was joined by disciples, the first of the Franciscan order, for whom he drew up the rule. He preached in Italy, and went to the Holy Land and Spain. The special note of his teaching was joyousness and love of nature (St. Francis preaching to the birds is a favourite subject in art). Two years before his death, after a period of fasting on Mt. Alverno, he is said to have discovered on his body the marks of Christ's crucifixion (the *stigmata*).

The 'Fioretti di San Francisco' ('Little Flowers of St. Francis') is a 14th-cent. Italian narrative, partly legendary, of the doings of St. Francis and his first disciples.

Franciscans, an order of friars founded by St. Francis of Assisi (q.v.) about 1209. Their rules require chastity, poverty, and obedience, and special stress is laid on preaching and ministry to the sick. They came to England about 1220, where they were known as Minors, Minorites, or Greyfriars (from the colour of their dress). See also *Cordeliers, Observants, Capuchins, Recollects.*

Frank Fairleigh, a novel by Smedley (q.v.).

Frankenstein, or the Modern Prometheus, a tale of terror by Mary W. Shelley (q.v.) published in 1818. The preface records the circumstances under which the work was produced. Byron and the Shelleys spent part of a wet summer in Switzerland in reading and writing ghost stories. 'Frankenstein', developed into a long story at her husband's suggestion, was Mrs. Shelley's contribution.

Frankenstein, a Genevan student of natural philosophy, learns the secret of imparting life to inanimate matter. Collecting bones from the charnel-houses he constructs the semblance of a human being and gives it life. The creature, endowed with supernatural size and strength, but revolting in appearance, inspires loathing in whoever sees it. Lonely and miserable, it is filled with hatred for its creator, and murders Frankenstein's brother and his bride. Frankenstein pursues it to the Arctic regions to destroy it, but dies in the pursuit. The monster looks at his dead body and claims him as its last victim, then disappears in order to end its own life.

Frankie and Johnny, or FRANKIE AND ALBERT, the most popular specimen of modern American balladry. It is of Negro origin and is known to exist in more than two hundred variants. The refrain is of the type:

He was her man, but he done her wrong.

Frankie revenged the wrong by shooting her lover.

FRANKLIN, BENJAMIN (1706–90), born in Massachusetts, was the son of a tallow-chandler and largely self-educated. He was apprenticed at the age of 12 to his half-brother, a printer, to whose 'New England Courant' he also contributed. He set up his own press in Philadelphia, published 'The Pennsylvania Gazette' (1729–66), and became prosperous. He acquired a wide reputation by his occasional writings, especially by his 'Poor Richard's Almanac' (1733–58), in which by maxims and proverbs he retailed humour and common sense. He was active as a public figure, devising several schemes for the general good, and founded the American Philosophical Society and the academy that became the University of Pennsylvania. He was an enthusiastic natural philosopher, and his experiment in electricity and lightning with the use of a kite is famous. A stove of his designing bears his name. He travelled to England in 1757 as agent for the colonies and mixed widely in intellectual society. He contributed greatly to the controversies that led to the breach with England. He returned home in 1774 and after helping to draft the Declaration of Independence, travelled to France as ambassador. He was enthusiastically welcomed and proved himself of inestimable service to the American cause. Upon his return in 1785, he served as president of the executive council of Pennsylvania and as a member of the Federal Constitution Convention (1787), signing the Constitution. He was a talented and versatile writer, as his many pieces testify, and his 'Autobiography' reveals his cool, rational, and pragmatic character.

FRANKLIN, SIR JOHN (1786–1847), Arctic explorer, was author of two remarkable 'Narratives' of voyages to the Polar Sea, published in 1823 and 1828. Franklin started on his last voyage of discovery, with the 'Erebus' and 'Terror', in 1845, and never returned. Numerous expeditions to search for his ships were organized, and Sir Leopold McClintock's 'Fox' finally solved the problem (so far as it could be solved) and proved that Franklin had in fact discovered the 'N.W. Passage', but that no use could be made of it.

Franklin's Tale, The, see *Canterbury Tales.*

FRASER, ALEXANDER CAMPBELL (1819–1914), a pupil of Sir William Hamilton (q.v.) at Edinburgh University, succeeded him as professor of logic and metaphysics in 1856, a position which he held until 1891. His first book, 'Essays in Philosophy' (reprints of contributions to the 'North British Review'), appeared in 1856. He is remembered chiefly as the editor of the standard edition of Berkeley (1871) and of Locke's 'Essay concerning Human Understanding' (1894), and as the author of monographs on these two philosophers. Holding a middle position between agnosticism and Hegelian idealism, he insisted on the element of faith which must lie at the basis of all our conclusions, and this is the standpoint of his Gifford lectures on 'The Philosophy of Theism' (1895–6). In 1898 he published a monograph on Thomas Reid (q.v.), and in 1904 'Biographia Philosophica', an interesting retrospect of a long life and a restatement of his philosophical conclusions.

Fraser's Magazine, founded in 1830 by Maginn (q.v.) and Hugh Fraser. Among the notable early contributors to it were Carlyle, Lockhart, Theodore Hook, Hogg, Coleridge, Harrison Ainsworth, Thackeray, Southey, and Barry Cornwall. It was taken over by Longmans in 1863, and ceased to appear in 1882. It was edited by J. A. Froude (q.v.), 1860–74, and by W. Allingham, 1874–9.

Fraternitye of Vacabones, a tract by John Awdeley (*fl.* 1559–77), published in 1561, in two parts, the first dealing with thieves' cant and the devices of beggars to excite compassion; the second with the methods employed by well-dressed impostors.

FRAZER, SIR JAMES GEORGE (1854–1941), fellow of Trinity College, Cambridge, held the chair of social anthropology at Liverpool, 1907–22. His publications include: 'Totemism' (1887), 'The Golden Bough' (q.v.), of which the first volume appeared in 1890 and the twelfth and last in 1915, followed by 'Aftermath, a supplement', in 1936; a translation with commentary of Pausanias's 'Description of Greece' (1898), 'Pausanias and other Greek Sketches' (1900), 'Letters of William Cowper' (1912), and a large number of other works on anthropology and folklore. His 'Fasti of Ovid' (with translation and commentary) appeared in 1929.

Frea, see *Freyja.*

Frederick, the usurping duke in Shakespeare's 'As You Like It' (q.v.).

Frederick Barbarossa, see *Barbarossa.*

Frederick II, Emperor of the Holy Roman Empire (1220–50), grandson of Frederick Barbarossa (q.v.), 'the greatest single human force in the middle ages' (H. A. L. Fisher). A skilful soldier and resourceful statesman, he endeavoured to make Italy and Sicily a single united kingdom within the Empire. In this purpose he was defeated by Popes Gregory IX and Innocent IV. See also *Stupor Mundi.*

Frederick the Great, Friedrich II of Prussia (1712–86), son of Friedrich Wilhelm I and Sophia Dorothea, daughter of George I of England, ascended the throne in 1740. He engaged in prolonged wars with Austria, the dominions of which had passed to Maria Theresa by virtue of the Pragmatic Sanction; and was supported by England, mainly through subsidies, in the Seven Years War (q.v., 1756). By his military talent he raised Prussia to the position of a powerful state, while his intellectual interests were shown by his long intimacy with Voltaire (q.v.). See also *Carlyle (T.).*

Freeman, MRS., the name under which the duchess of Marlborough corresponded with Queen Anne. The latter called herself Mrs. Morley.

FREEMAN, EDWARD AUGUSTUS (1823–92), scholar and probationary fellow of Trinity College, Oxford, and Regius professor of modern history at Oxford from 1884 to 1892, was a regular contributor to the 'Saturday Review' and other periodicals, and an historian of eminence (particularly in regard to the eleventh and twelfth centuries of English history). His principal work was the 'History of the Norman Conquest' (1867–79), in which he maintained the general position that the Norman Conquest produced no fundamental change either in the character of the population of England or in the Germanic type of the country's institutions. Freeman also wrote the 'History and Conquests of the Saracens' (1856), 'Growth of the English Constitution' (1872), 'Historical Geography of Europe' (1881–2), 'The Reign of William Rufus and the Accession of Henry I' (1882), 'Methods of Historical Study' (1886), 'Chief Periods of European History' (1886), a 'History of Sicily to 300 B.C.' (1891–4), and the first volume of a 'History of Federal Government' (1863). This volume, part of a much larger scheme, dealt with the history of federalism in ancient Greece. Freeman, a most voluminous writer, also published, in collaboration with G. W. Cox, 'Poems, Legendary and Historical' in 1850, and was the author of numerous historical and architectural essays (of which four series were published in 1871–92), lectures, and sketches of travel. In his historical works Freeman relied wholly on printed chronicles and knew nothing of manuscripts. Many of his conclusions have in consequence been upset.

FREEMAN, MARY E. WILKINS (1852–1930), American author, born in Massachusetts, distinguished for her realistic stories of New England life. Her best-known books are: 'A Humble Romance and Other Stories' (1887), and 'A New England Nun and Other Stories' (1891).

Freemason, originally a member of a certain class of skilled workers in stone who travelled from place to place, finding employment wherever important buildings were being erected, and had a system of secret signs and passwords by which they could be recognized. The term first occurs in the 14th cent. Early in the 17th cent. the societies of freemasons began to admit honorary members, known as ACCEPTED MASONS, who were admitted to a knowledge of the secret signs and instructed in the legendary history of the craft. In 1717, under the guidance of the physicist, J. T. Desaguliers, four of these societies or 'lodges' in London united to form a 'grand lodge', whose object was mutual help and the promotion of brotherly feeling among its members. The London 'grand lodge' became the parent of other lodges in Great Britain and abroad, and there are now powerful bodies of freemasons, more or less recognizing each other, in most countries of the world. [OED.] MASON'S MARKS, also called 'Banker Marks'—the marks cut by medieval masons upon the dressed stones of a building to identify the stone-cutter who prepared the stone, so-called from the 'Banker' or stone bench at which the stone-cutter worked. In the 17th cent., when others besides working masons were admitted to the lodges of the masonic guilds, they too received identifying banker marks, which were preserved in the register of the lodge. The custom is now obsolete.

Freischütz, DER, in German folklore, a man who has made a compact with the Devil by which he gains possession of a number of bullets which unerringly hit whatever they are aimed at. But the Devil retains control of one of them. The legend is the subject of Weber's opera of this name (1821).

French, INSPECTOR, the detective in Freeman Wills Croft's detective stories, a member of the C.I.D.

French Revolution, THE, is generally regarded as beginning with the meeting of the States General in May 1789. The Bastille was stormed on 14 July 1789, and the royal family was removed from Versailles to Paris in October of the same year. The king's attempted flight from Paris took place in June 1791. The Legislative Assembly sat from Oct. 1791 to Sept. 1792, when, under the menace of the allied advance, it was replaced by the National Convention, and the Republic was proclaimed. The king was brought to trial in Dec. 1792, and executed 21 Jan. 1793. The institution of the Committee of Public Safety and of the Revolutionary Tribunal immediately followed. The Reign of Terror began in Sept. 1793 and lasted until the fall of Robespierre, 27 July (9 Thermidor) 1794. The Convention in Oct. 1795 gave place to the Directory, which in turn gave place to the Consulate in 1799. Napoleon became emperor in May 1804.

French Revolution, Reflections on the, by Edmund Burke, see *Revolution in France.*

French Revolution, The, A History, by T. Carlyle, published in 1837.

The work was written in London. The manuscript of the first volume, while in the keeping of John Stuart Mill, was accidentally destroyed, but the author courageously set to work to rewrite it. The history, beginning with the death of Louis XV in 1774, deals with the reign of Louis XVI, the period which included the assembly of the States General, the fall of the Bastille, the Constituent and Legislative Assemblies, the flight of the king to Varennes, the Convention, the trial and execution of the king and queen, the reign of terror, the fall of Robespierre, and extends to 5 Oct. 1795, when Buonaparte quelled the insurrection of Vendémiaire. The work, said to be a very partial view of the Revolution, may be regarded as the poetic unrolling of a great historical drama, illustrating the nemesis that comes upon the oppression of the poor. It offers in addition a gallery of magnificent portraits (Mirabeau, Lafayette, Danton, Robespierre), and stamps upon the memory such episodes as the march to Versailles, the fall of the Bastille, and the flight to Varennes.

FRENEAU, PHILIP (1752–1832), the 'poet of the American Revolution' and miscellaneous writer, born in New York. He wrote many satires in the cause of freedom. His romantic verse was based largely upon his own experiences, as a resident in the West Indies (1775–8) and as a ship's master (1784–90). He published his first collection of 'Poems' in 1786 and his last in 1815.

FRERE, JOHN HOOKHAM (1769–1846), educated at Eton and Caius College, Cambridge, was a friend of Canning and British envoy at Lisbon (1800–2), at Madrid (1802–4), and with the Junta (1808–9). While at Eton, Frere wrote a translation of 'Brunanburh' (q.v.). He was one of the founders of 'The Microcosm' periodical (1786–7), and contributed to 'The Anti-Jacobin' (q.v.) most of the 'Loves of the Triangles' and parts of 'The Friend of Humanity and the Knife-grinder' and 'The Rovers'. He collaborated in Ellis's 'Specimens of the Early English Poets' (1801) and in Southey's 'Chronicle of the Cid' (1808), and was one of the founders of the 'Quarterly Review' (q.v.). He published metrical versions of Aristophanes' 'Frogs' (1839) and 'Acharnians', 'Knights', and 'Birds' (1840); also 'Theognis Restitutus' (1842). His mock-romantic Arthurian poem, written under the pseudonym 'Whistlecraft', of which four cantos appeared in 1817–18, provided a model for Byron's 'Don Juan' and 'Beppo' (qq.v.).

Freud, SIGMUND (1856–1939), born at Freiberg in Moravia, of a Jewish family, is known as the inventor of psycho-analysis. He studied under the great neurologist Charcot in Paris, and undertook with Dr. Breuer the investigation of hysteria from a psychological standpoint. The study of neurotic ailments led him to various conclusions relating to the normal mind, which are the basis of psychoanalysis, such as the existence of an unconscious element in the mind which influences consciousness, and of conflicts in it between various sets of forces (including repression); also the importance of a child's semi-consciousness of sex as a factor in mental development.

Frey or FREYR, in Scandinavian mythology, one of the Vanir (q.v.), the son of Niörd, and the god of fertility and dispenser of rain and sunshine. He is the husband of Gerda (q.v.), the frozen Earth, and king of the Elves.

Freya or FREYJA, in Scandinavian mythology, one of the Vanir (q.v.), the most beautiful of the goddesses, the northern Venus, the goddess of love and of the night. She is the sister of Frey and wife of Odhir, from whom, however, she is separated. She is sometimes indistinguishable from Frigga (q.v.), the wife of Odin.

Friar Bacon and Friar Bungay, The honorable historie of, a comedy in verse and prose by Greene (q.v.), acted in 1594. The play is based on a prose pamphlet 'The famous history of Friar Bacon', embodying legends relating to Roger Bacon and Thomas Bungay (qq.v.). Bacon with the help of Friar Bungay makes a head of brass, and, conjuring up the Devil, learns how to give it speech. It is to speak within a month, but 'if they heard it not before it had done speaking, all their labour should be lost'. After watching day and night for three weeks, Bacon hands over the duty of watching to his servant Miles and falls asleep. The head speaks two words 'Time is'. Miles, thinking his master would be angry if waked for so little, lets him sleep. The head presently speaks again, 'Time was'; and finally 'Time is past', when it falls down and breaks. Bacon awakes, and heaps curses on Miles's head. The above is diversified with the pleasant story of the loves of Edward Prince of Wales (afterwards Edward I) and Lord Lacy for the fair Margaret, the keeper's daughter of Freshingfield, and the prince's surrender of her to Lacy. There is also an amusing scene where Bacon, Bungay, and a German rival display their respective powers before the German emperor and the kings of England and Castile.

Friar Bungay, see *Bungay (T.)*.

Friar John (JEAN DES ENTOMMEURES), see *Gargantua* and *Thelema*.

Friar Rush, the *Bruder Rausch* of German folklore, a devil disguised as a friar who takes service in a monastery to lead the monks astray. An English translation of the legend was published in 1568 and frequently reprinted. The story is given in W. C. Hazlitt's 'Tales and Legends'. Scott, perhaps misled by Milton's 'L'Allegro' ('by Friar's lantern led'), confuses Friar Rush with the Will-o'-the-Wisp:

> Better we had . . . Been lanthorn-led by
> Friar Rush.
>
> ('Marmion', IV. i.)

Friar Tuck, one of the principal characters in the legend of Robin Hood (q.v.); the fat, jovial, and pugnacious father confessor of the outlaw chief. He figures in Scott's 'Ivanhoe' and in Peacock's 'Maid Marian' (qq.v.).

Friar's or *Frere's* **Tale**, *The*, see *Canterbury Tales*.

Friars Minor, the Franciscans (q.v.).

Friday, MAN, see *Robinson Crusoe*.

Friends, SOCIETY OF, a religious society founded in 1648–50 by George Fox (q.v.), distinguished by peaceful principles and plainness of dress and manners. See *Quakers*.

Frigga, in Scandinavian mythology, the wife of Odin (q.v.), the goddess of married love and of the hearth. Our 'Friday' is named from her. See also *Freya*.

Friscobaldo, ORLANDO, see *Orlando Friscobaldo*.

Frith, MARY, see *Moll Cutpurse*.

Frithiof, the hero of an Icelandic saga assigned to the 14th cent.

Frobisher, SIR MARTIN (1535?–94), navigator, made his first expedition in search of the North-West Passage in 1576, and further expeditions in 1577 and 1578. He commanded the 'Triumph' against the Spanish Armada, and was vice-admiral in Sir John Hawkins's expedition to the Portuguese coast in 1590. He died of a wound received in an expedition sent for the relief of Brest.

FROISSART, JEAN (1337?–*c.* 1410), a French chronicler, of Hainault, who spent most of his life at the courts of princes. He visited England after the peace of Bretigny (1360) and was received at the court of Edward III and Queen Philippa his countrywoman. His travels, in which he untiringly sought information about historical events, extended to Scotland, Italy, and Belgium. His 'Chroniques' cover the period 1325–1400; they deal with the affairs of Flanders, France, Spain, Portugal, and England. Three editions of them were issued at different periods of his life. They are the work of a literary artist rather than a trustworthy historian (he was dependent on oral testimony), but give a faithful picture of the broad features of his period, and are instinct with the spirit of chivalry. They were admirably translated into English by John Bourchier, Lord Berners (q.v.), 1523–5.

Fronde, THE, the name given to the rebellion which took place (1648–52) in France against Mazarin and the Court during the minority of Louis XIV. The word *fronde* means a sling.

FROST, ROBERT (1874–1963), American poet, born in San Francisco, of New England stock. He moved to New England in 1885 and his later poetry is deeply expressive of the region. He spent a year at both Dartmouth College and Harvard, but left to teach and farm and write poetry, unsuccessfully. He farmed in England from 1912 to 1915, where his first 2 vols. of verse, 'A Boy's Will' (1913) and 'North of Boston' (1914), were published, and where he became a friend of Edward Thomas (q.v.). Upon his return to New England he devoted himself to poetry, supporting himself by successive teaching appointments in several colleges. He became one of the most popular of modern American poets, and his verse excellently continues the tradition of Wordsworth and, at home, of Emerson and Emily Dickinson (qq.v.). Ten vols. of his verse were collected in 1949, and his last volume of lyrics, 'In the Clearing', appeared in 1962.

Froth, LORD and LADY, characters in Congreve's 'The Double Dealer' (q.v.).

FROUDE, JAMES ANTHONY (1818–94), was educated at Westminster and Oriel College, Oxford, where, like his brother, R. H. Froude (q.v.), he took part in the Tractarian Movement and came under the influence of Newman; but on the latter's secession he reacted towards scepticism. He became a friend of C. Kingsley, and made the acquaintance of Carlyle in 1849, subsequently becoming his chief disciple. In 1856–70 he published his 'History of England from the Fall of Wolsey to the Defeat of the Spanish Armada', which has been criticized on the score of inaccuracy and prolixity. Froude was editor of 'Fraser's Magazine' from 1860 to 1874, and wrote for various other periodicals,

some of his best essays being republished in 'Short Studies on Great Subjects' (1867–83), dealing with matters of theology, travel, history, and including some good fables. In 1872–4 he published 'The English in Ireland in the Eighteenth Century', which met with severe criticism, from Lecky (q.v.) among others. In 1874–5 he visited South Africa on a mission from the government to ascertain the obstacles to federation among the South African states. From 1881 to 1884 he was engaged, as Carlyle's literary executor, in issuing biographical remains of Carlyle and his wife, the frankness with which he discharged this task provoking much indignation. Froude visited Australia in 1884–5, and published 'Oceana, or England and her Colonies' in 1886; he visited the West Indies in 1886–7, and published 'The English in the West Indies' in 1888. He was appointed Regius professor of modern history at Oxford in 1892. His lectures appeared as 'The Life and Letters of Erasmus' (1894), 'English Seamen in the Sixteenth Century' (1895), and 'The Council of Trent' (1896).

FROUDE, RICHARD HURRELL (1803–36), brother of J. A. Froude (q.v.), was educated at Ottery, Eton, and Oriel College, Oxford, of which he became a fellow. He was intimate with Newman, with whom he wrote the poems contained in 'Lyra Apostolica' (1836), and greatly influenced the Tractarians, contributing three of the 'Tracts for the Times' (see under *Oxford Movement*). His 'Remains' (1838–9), including strictures on the Reformation, helped to rouse public hostility against the Tractarian movement.

Frugal, SIR JOHN and LEEKE, characters in Massinger's 'The City Madam' (q.v.).

FRY, CHRISTOPHER (1907–   ), dramatist. His verse plays owe their success to his skill as a poet and his experience as an actor and producer. Among the best known are: 'A Phoenix too Frequent' (1946), 'The Lady's not for Burning' (1948), 'Venus Observed' (1950), and 'A Sleep of Prisoners' (1951). He has also translated two plays by Anouilh (q.v.): 'L'Invitation au Château' ('Ring Round the Moon', 1950) and 'L'Alouette' ('The Lark', 1955); and 'La Gùerre de Troie n'aura pas lieu' ('Tiger at the Gates', 1955) by Giraudoux (q.v.).

Fry, MRS. ELIZABETH (1780–1845), *née* GURNEY, a Quaker reformer and successful preacher, celebrated for her efforts to improve the state of the prisons, the condition of convicts on their voyage to Australia, and the lot of vagrants in London and Brighton.

FRY, ROGER (1866–1934), painter and art critic. He introduced to the English public the work of the French painters whom he labelled Post-Impressionists (q.v.) by organizing an exhibition of their work in 1910, and by his essays, published in 'Vision and Design', 1921, and 'Transformations', 1926.

Fudge Family in Paris, The, satirical verses by T. Moore (q.v.), published in 1818.

These light verses take the form of letters written by or to various members of the Fudge family when visiting Paris in 1817, shortly after the restoration of the Bourbon dynasty. They include mock letters from and to Castlereagh. In them the author endeavoured to collect the 'concentrated essence of the various forms of cockneyism and nonsense of those groups of ridiculous English who were at that time swarming in all directions throughout Paris'.

Fugger, the name of a German family of merchants and bankers famous in the 16th cent. for their wealth, which they acquired by trade and by lending money to the emperors and other sovereigns. Johann Fugger, the founder of the family, was a master weaver in Augsburg in the 14th cent. The Fuggers played an important part in the election of Charles V to be emperor.

Fugger News-letters, a collection of newsletters, consisting of about 36,000 pages of manuscript, collected at random and copied by professional clerks; they were sent mostly to Count Philip Edward Fugger (1546–1618), son of Count George Fugger and Ursula von Leichtenstein, and a member of the family referred to in the previous entry. The letters cover the period 1568–1605; most of them are in German, but Italian is well represented; French is rarely met with, and Spanish hardly at all. Latin reports, in the worst church- and dog-Latin, are more frequent. Two series of the Letters have been published in English: the first series (1924) being translated from a Vienna edition by P. de Chary, the second (1926), never before published, translated by L. S. R. Byrne.

Fulgens and Lucrece, a 15th-cent. secular play by Henry Medwall (*fl.* 1486); important in dramatic history as the earliest known English secular play. It was edited by F. S. Boas and A. W. Reed in 1926.

FULLER, MARGARET (1810–50), American author, born in Massachusetts, whose name is associated with the New England Transcendentalists, and with the movement for 'women's rights', in which she was a pioneer. She helped to found 'The Dial' (q.v.), which she edited for two years. Later she moved to New York to write for Horace Greeley's (q.v.) 'Tribune', published a volume of critical essays, travelled in Europe, and settled in Italy, where she married the Marquis Ossoli in 1847. Sailing from Leghorn for America in 1850, she and her husband perished when their ship was wrecked just short of its destination.

FULLER, THOMAS (1608–61), was born at Aldwinkle St. Peter's in Northamptonshire and was educated at Queens' and Sidney Sussex Colleges, Cambridge. He became a prebendary of Salisbury in 1631, and rector of Broadwinsor, Dorset, in 1634. Shortly before the Civil War he was made preacher at the Savoy, and followed the war as chaplain to Sir Ralph Hopton. He was a moderate Royalist and an Anglican, but after his return to London, on the surrender of Exeter, was allowed to preach on sufferance. After the Restoration he resumed his canonry and lectureship at the Savoy and became 'chaplain in extraordinary' to the king. He published his 'History of the Holy Warre', viz. the crusades, in 1639; 'The Holy State and the Profane State' (q.v.), 1642; 'A Pisgah-sight of Palestine', 1650; his 'Church History of Britain', and 'History of Cambridge University', 1655. 'The Worthies of England' (q.v.), his best-known and most characteristic work, appeared after his death, in 1662. His 'Good Thoughts in Bad Times' (q.v., 1645), followed by two sequels, contain much 'sound, shrewd good sense, and freedom of intellect' (Coleridge). His writings, which were highly approved by Southey, Coleridge, and Lamb, are marked by humour and a quaint wit, sometimes a little incongruous with the subject.

Fum or FUNG, a fabulous bird, one of the symbols of the imperial dignity in China. T. Moore wrote a poem on 'Fum and Hum, the Two Birds of Royalty', and Byron in 'Don Juan', xi. 77, refers to George IV as 'Fum the fourth.'

Funeral, The, or Grief à-la-Mode, a comedy by R. Steele (q.v.), produced in 1701.

Lord Brumpton has disinherited his son, Lord Hardy, owing to the misrepresentations of his wife, the young man's stepmother; he has left her all his property, as well as two wards, the ladies Sharlot and Harriot. When the play opens Lord Brumpton has, as is generally believed, just died. He has in fact, however, recovered from a 'lethargic slumber', a fact known only to himself and to Trusty, his steward. At Trusty's instance, he remains in concealment, and thus discovers his supposed widow's unseemly rejoicing at her release, her machinations against her stepson, and her unscrupulous design to dispose profitably of Sharlot and Harriot. The widow is exposed. Lord Hardy reinstated, and the ladies bestowed on their true lovers, Lord Hardy and his friend. The devices by which these results are effected are somewhat clumsy; but the play is notable as marking a change of moral tone in the drama after the licentiousness of the Restoration period.

Funeral Oration, The, of Pericles, at the celebration of the Athenians who had fallen in the first year of the Peloponnesian War (431 B.C.). In it Pericles reviews the Athenian character and policy. It is given in Thucydides, ii. 35 et seq.

Fungoso, a character in Jonson's 'Every Man out of his Humour' (q.v.).

Furies, or EUMENIDES, or ERINYES, THE, in Greek mythology, the avenging deities, Allecto, Megaera, and Tisiphonē, who executed the curses pronounced upon criminals, tortured the guilty with the stings of conscience, or inflicted famines and pestilences. 'Eumenides', 'the kindly ones', is a euphemism used with a propitiatory purpose.

FURNIVALL, FREDERICK JAMES (1825–1910), educated at University College, London, and Trinity Hall, Cambridge, was a member of the Philological Society from 1847 and became in 1861 editor of its suggested English Dictionary, which developed into the 'Oxford English Dictionary' (q.v.). He was founder of the Early English Text Society, the Chaucer Society, the Ballad and New Shakespere Societies, and the Shelley, Wiclif, and Browning Societies. He edited Chaucer's works and the 'Percy Ballads'. He was an enthusiastic oarsman, and helped to found the Working Men's College in London (1854).

Furred Law-cats, The (*chats fourrés*), in Rabelais, v. xi et seq., the magistrates, so called from their furred gowns, the embodiment of the administration of the criminal law in France, the object of the author's most ferocious satire.

Fusbos, a character in Rhodes's burlesque 'Bombastes Furioso' (q.v.).

Fust, JOHANN (*d.* 1467), German goldsmith. He financed Gutenberg's (q.v.) experiments in printing, but the partnership between them was dissolved probably in 1455 and Fust carried on with his son-in-law Peter Schöffer. Their Latin Psalter of 1457 is the first to bear a printers' imprint and date. R. Browning wrote a dialogue, 'Fust and his Friends' (in 'Parleyings with certain People').

Futhorc, the Runic alphabet, so named from its first six letters (th = þ; cf. 'ye' a survival of 'þe').

Futurism, a 20th-cent. movement in Italian art, literature, and music, promoted by Marinetti (q.v.) and others. Futurist painting was a development of Cubism (q.v.), designed to represent nature not in a static but a dynamic state, to give in other words a cinematographic effect. It sought to produce this in the case, e.g. of an arm in motion, by painting a number of arms in successive positions. Séverin's 'Bal Tabarin' (1912) is regarded as a good illustration of the method. The movement was so named as being a glorification of youth and the future as against the academic past.

Futurism in Russia was largely a revolt against the mysticism and aestheticism of Symbolism. Futurists were interested in a 'trans-sense' language (*zaumny yazyk*), in abandoning literary traditions and in shocking their readers. The most important Futurists, those who signed the Cubo-Futurist Manifesto of 1912, were Klebnikov, Kruchonykh, Mayakovsky, and Burlyuk. The movement lingered on in Russia until the mid-1920s.

G

G.O.M., the initial letters of 'Grand Old Man', a current journalistic appellation for W. E. Gladstone from 1882, said to have been first applied to him by Lord Rosebery.

Gabble-rachet, see *Gabriel*.

Gabelle, a word of Teutonic origin (cf. OE. *gafol*), meaning a tax. The term was originally applied in France to taxes on all commodities, but was gradually limited to the tax on salt. The tax was first imposed in 1286 and gradually became one of the most hated and grossly unequal of taxes in the country; it was not abolished until 1790.

Gaberlunzie, a wandering mendicant; in Scotland a public almsman or licensed beggar. There is a spirited ballad of 'The Gaberlunzie Man' in Percy's 'Reliques', which is attributed to King James V. It relates the adventure of a Gaberlunzie and a country lass.

GABORIAU, ÉMILE (1835–73), French novelist, a pioneer in the romance of crime and its detection, and the creator of Monsieur Lecoq and Père Tabaret. His best-known works are: 'L'Affaire Lerouge' (1866), 'Le Dossier No. 113' (1867), 'Le Crime d'Orcival' (1868), 'Monsieur Lecoq' (1869), and 'Les Esclaves de Paris' (1869).

Gabriel, the name of one of the archangels (Dan. ix. 21 and Luke i. 19, 26). Also in the Muslim religion one of the four principal angels. Milton makes him 'Chief of the angelic guards' ('Paradise Lost', iv. 550).

GABRIEL-HOUNDS, GABRIEL-RACHET, GABBLE-RACHET, a name applied to wild geese, whose cry is heard as they fly high through the air; hence, perhaps, the technical sporting term, 'a gaggle of geese' (for a flock).

Gabriel Lajeunesse, a character in Longfellow's 'Evangeline' (q.v.).

Gadarene Swine, THE MIRACLE OF THE, related in Mark v, was the subject of a celebrated controversy between Huxley and Gladstone (qq.v.), in the 'Nineteenth Century' (1890–91), echoed in Gladstone's 'Impregnable Rock of Holy Scripture' and Huxley's 'Science and Christian Tradition'.

Gadshill, near Rochester, the scene of Falstaff's famous exploit ('1 Henry IV', II. ii), and also the name of one of Falstaff's companions. Gadshill was the home of Dickens in his later years.

Gael, from old Irish *Gaidel, Goidel,* a Scottish Highlander or Celt. The word in more recent times has also been applied to the Irish branch of the Celtic race.

Gahagan, MAJOR, see *Major Gahagan.*

Gaheris, SIR, in Malory's 'Morte Darthur', son of King Lot and Morgause, sister of Arthur. He was brother of Gawain, Agravain, and Gareth; and was by mishap slain by Sir Launcelot.

Gai saber, a late medieval Provençal term, the gay science, the poetry of the troubadours (q.v.).

Gainsborough, THOMAS (1727–88), painter, was the youngest son of a Sudbury (Suffolk) wool manufacturer. His early paintings are landscapes and conversation pieces, and he continued to paint landscapes all his life, though he became a fashionable portrait painter and rival of Reynolds (q.v.). He settled in Ipswich in 1753, went to Bath in 1759, and to London in 1774.

GAIRDNER, JAMES (1828–1912), an official in the Public Record Office, was associated with J. S. Brewer in the preparation of the voluminous 'Calendar of Letters and Papers of the Reign of King Henry VIII' for the Rolls Series, and completed the work after Brewer's death. He published the standard edition of the Paston Letters (q.v.) in 1904, and lives of Richard III and Henry VII (1878 and 1889). He contributed the volume on the period 1509–59 to Stephens's and Hunt's 'History of the English Church' (1902), and in 1908 began to publish his longest work, 'Lollardy and the Reformation in England', of which vol. iv was issued after his death.

GAIUS (*c.* A.D. 110–180), a celebrated Roman jurist, who flourished in the reigns of Antoninus Pius and Marcus Aurelius and was author of works on Roman Law, including four books of 'Institutiones'.

Galafron or GALAPHRON, in the 'Orlando Innamorato' and 'Orlando Furioso' (qq.v.), the king of Cathay and father of Angelica.

Galahad, SIR, in Malory's 'Morte Darthur', is (by enchantment) the son of Launcelot and Elaine, daughter of King Pelles. He is predestined by his immaculate purity to achieve the quest of the Holy Grail (see *Grail*).

Galahalt or GALAHAULT, SIR, described in Malory's 'Morte Darthur' as the 'haut prince' of Surluse and the Long Isles, is, in the story of the early loves of Launcelot and Guinevere, as told in a 13th-cent. French romance, the knight who introduces Launcelot to the queen. He is the Galeotto of Dante's reference to this story ('Inferno', v. 137).

Galaor, brother of Amadis of Gaul (q.v.), a gay knight, light of love.

Galapas, in Malory's 'Morte Darthur', v. viii, a Roman giant slain by King Arthur. 'He shorted him and smote off both his legs by the knees, saying, Now art thou of a better size to deal with than thou were, and after smote off his head.'

Galaphron, see *Galafron.*

Galatea, (1) a sea-nymph, loved by the Cyclops Polyphemus (q.v.), whom she treated with disdain, while Acis, a Sicilian shepherd, enjoyed her affection. The jealous Cyclops crushed his rival with a rock while in the arms of Galatea; and she, since she could not restore him to life, changed him into a river at the foot of Mt. Etna; (2) also the name given to the statue wrought by Pygmalion (q.v.) and brought to life.

Galathea, a play by Lyly (q.v.).

GALEN or GALENUS, CLAUDIUS (*c.* A.D. 129–199), a celebrated physician, born at Pergamum in Asia Minor, and a friend of Marcus Aurelius. He is said to have written no fewer than 500 treatises. Of these a great part were burnt in the temple of Peace at Rome where they were deposited, but over a hundred survive. He wrote in Greek. Linacre (q.v.) translated six of his works, and there are references to him in Chaucer.

Galeotti, MARTIUS, in Scott's 'Quentin Durward' (q.v.), the astrologer of Louis XI.

Galeotto, see *Galahalt.*

Galerie des Glaces, see *Versailles.*

Galignani, GIOVANNI ANTONIO (*d.* 1821), founded in Paris in 1814 'Galignani's messenger', which had a wide circulation among English residents on the Continent. The paper was carried on by his sons, John Anthony (1796–1873) and William (1798–1882), who were born in London. As publishers in Paris they issued reprints of English books.

GALILEO GALILEI (1564–1642), Italian astronomer and physicist, was born at Pisa of a Florentine family. He made important discoveries (the isochronism of the pendulum, Jupiter's satellites, the libration of the moon) and experiments, proving, e.g., that unequal weights drop with equal velocity, by making the experiment from the leaning tower of Pisa. His observations brought him into conflict with the Inquisition, and in 1633 he was compelled to repudiate the Copernican theory ('eppur si muove', he is said to have muttered after his recantation, 'and yet it [the earth] moves'), and was sent to prison. His principal works were the dialogues 'Delle nuove Scienze' and 'Ai Due Massimi Sistemi'.

Galliambic, the metre of the 'Attis' of Catullus, imitated by Tennyson in his 'Boadicea' and by G. Meredith in his 'Phaethon'. It is so called because it was the metre used by the Galli or priests of Cybele in their songs.

Galligantus, a giant slain by Jack the Giant-killer (q.v.).

Gallio, in Acts xviii, the proconsul of Achaia (and brother of Seneca), who, when Paul was brought before him by the Jews, dismissed the case as 'a question of words and names, and of your law'. Then the Greeks took Sosthenes, the chief ruler of the synagogue, and beat him before the judgement-seat, 'and Gallio cared for none of these things'; hence 'a careless Gallio', a term of reproach in the Puritan literature of the 17th cent.

GALSWORTHY, JOHN (1867–1933), of a Devonshire family, was educated at Harrow and New College, Oxford. His purpose as a novelist was to throw light on the dark places, the evils and abuses, of life, for the guidance of others; and to do so impartially, showing the good at the same time as the bad (see 'A Novelist's Allegory' in 'The Inn of Tranquillity' (1912), and the discussion of this in A. C. Ward, 'Twentieth-century Literature').

Galsworthy's most important work was the series of novels, including 'The Man of Property' (1906), 'In Chancery' (1920), and 'To Let' (1921), collectively entitled 'The Forsyte Saga', of which the main theme is the possessive instinct, embodied to an exaggerated degree in Soames Forsyte, a man with a passion for acquiring all things desirable, and for exercising his proprietary rights to the utmost, even over his reluctant wife. The record of the Forsyte family extends over the later Victorian period, and is resumed in 'A Modern Comedy' (1929), containing 'The White Monkey' (1924), 'The Silver Spoon' (1926), and 'Swan Song' (1928). In these the author depicts a society whose foundations have been shattered by the Great War, left without faith or principles, whose only purpose is 'to have a good time because we don't believe anything can last', but in which the Victorianism of a glum Soames Forsyte here and there survives. The 'Forsyte Saga' includes two 'Interludes': 'Indian Summer of a Forsyte' (1918) and 'Awakening' (1920); and there are two in 'A Modern Comedy': 'A Silent Wooing' (1927) and 'Passers By' (1927). In 1930 appeared a collection of 'apocryphal Forsyte tales' under the title 'On Forsyte Change'. Among Galsworthy's other best-known novels are 'The Island Pharisees' (1904), 'The Country House' (1907), 'Fraternity' (1909), 'The Patrician' (1911).

Of Galsworthy's plays the most notable are: 'The Silver Box', 1909; 'Strife' (an industrial dispute in which reconciliation is occasioned by the death of the wife of the men's leader), 1909; 'Justice' (a criticism of the existing prison system), 1910; 'The Skin Game' (a conflict between a parvenu manufacturer and an old-established aristocrat), 1920; and 'Loyalties', 1922.

GALT, JOHN (1779–1839), born at Irvine in Ayrshire, was employed for some time in the custom-house at Greenock. While travelling on the Continent he made the acquaintance of Byron (of whom he published a life in 1830), and subsequently of Carlyle, by whom he was favourably noticed. In 1824 he visited Canada as secretary of a land company, which obtained no immediate profit, and Galt was presently superseded. Galt did a great amount of miscellaneous writing. His poems, dramas, historical novels, and travels call for no special notice. But he also wrote three admirable studies of country life in Scotland, by which he deserves to be remembered: 'The Ayrshire Legatees' (q.v., 1821), 'Annals of the Parish' (q.v., 1821), and 'The Entail' (q.v., 1823). 'The Provost' (1822) is an amusing picture of life and character in a Scottish municipality.

Galvani, LUIGI (1737–98), of Bologna, the discoverer of electricity produced by chemical action. It is said that his wife first observed the convulsive movement in the muscles of frogs when brought into contact with two different metals. Hence 'galvanic', 'galvanism'

Galway Blazers, a celebrated Irish pack of foxhounds.

Gama, KING, in Tennyson's 'The Princess' (q.v.), the father of Princess Ida.

Gama, VASCO DA (c. 1469–1524), a great Portuguese navigator, who was the first to double the Cape of Good Hope (1497) and sail to India, the hero of the 'Lusiads' of Camoëns (q.v.). He died at Cochin on Christmas Day 1524.

Gamaliel, a Pharisee, 'a doctor of the law, had in reputation among all the people', who dissuaded the Jews from slaying the Apostles. The apostle Paul was 'brought up at his feet' (Acts v. 34 and xxii. 3). He was president of the Sanhedrim.

Game and Playe of the Chesse, The, a translation by Caxton (q.v.) from Vignay's French version of the 'Liber de ludo scacchorum' of Jacobus de Cessolis, probably the second book printed at Caxton's press in Bruges, c. 1475.

Game at Chesse, A, a comedy by T. Middleton (q.v.), produced in 1624 and chiefly interesting in its political connexion.

It deals allegorically with the rivalry of England and Spain (the White House and the Black House), and the project of the 'Spanish Marriage' (1623). It places on the stage the sovereigns of the two countries, Charles, Prince of Wales, Buckingham, and the Spanish Ambassador Gondomar, and represents the discomfiture of the Black House. The play, reflecting the popular aversion to the Spanish Match, was enthusiastically received, but gave great offence to the Spanish Ambassador and to King James. Proceedings were taken against the actors and author, and the performance of the play was prohibited.

Gamelyn, The Tale of, a verse romance of c. 1350, containing some 900 lines. Gamelyn is the youngest of three sons of Sir John de Boundys, who leaves his property to them in equal shares. The eldest brother maltreats Gamelyn and robs him of his property. Gamelyn asserts his rights by force, defeats the champion wrestler, and kills the porter of the castle. He allows himself to be bound to a post, breaks away, and with the help of Adam the 'spencer', belabours the clergy who are at a feast given by his brother and have refused to help him. The sheriff comes to arrest him. Gamelyn and Adam take to the forest and Gamelyn becomes lieutenant and subsequently chief of a band of outlaws. His eldest brother becomes sheriff. Gamelyn comes to the moot hall and is cast in prison. Ote, the second brother, goes bail for him till next gaol delivery. Gamelyn returns to the forest but promises to present himself for trial. At the trial Ote appears in fetters. The hero arrives, releases him, throws the justice over the bar and takes his place. Justice, sheriff, and jurors are hanged. Gamelyn and Ote make their peace with the king, Ote becomes a justice, and Gamelyn Chief Justice of the Free Forest.

The piece is interesting because apparently Chaucer intended to make it his 'Cook's Tale of Gamelyn' in 'The Canterbury Tales' (q.v.); also as providing materials for Shakespeare's 'As You Like It', and as connected with the Robin Hood story.

Gamester, The, a comedy by James Shirley (q.v.), acted in 1633, printed in 1637.

The main plot, somewhat coarse in tone and incident, is that of a story in Margaret of Navarre's 'Heptameron'. Wilding is in love with Penelope, his ward and the relative of his wife, whom he does not scruple to inform of this illicit affection. By the contrivance of Mrs. Wilding, Penelope makes an assignation with Wilding. When the time comes, Wilding, deeply engaged in a gambling bout, sends his friend Hazard in his place, secure that the deception will not be discovered in the darkness. He learns from his wife next day that she has taken Penelope's place. To escape humiliation he persuades Hazard to marry Penelope, only to discover that he has been doubly cheated and that the meeting between Hazard and the lady never took place. There is a romantic underplot concerned with the loves of Violante and Leonore, while young Barnacle, who aspires to be a 'roarer' (see *Roaring Boys*), provides some amusing scenes. The play was adapted by Garrick in his 'Gamesters'.

The Gamester is also the title of a play by Mrs. Centlivre (q.v.), and of a tragedy by Edward Moore (q.v.).

Gammer Gurton's Needle, the second English comedy in verse (the first being 'Ralph Roister Doister', q.v.), was published in 1575, having previously been acted, in 1566, at Christ's College, Cambridge. Its authorship has been attributed to J. Still (q.v.), but the evidence is inconclusive, and an alternative suggestion is that it may have been written by William Stevenson, a fellow

of the College and one of its leading spirits in dramatic activities. It is written in rhymed long doggerel, and deals farcically with the losing and finding of the needle used to mend the garments of Hodge, Gammer Gurton's man. The other characters, besides Hodge and the Gammer, are Tib and Cock, their maid and boy; Diccon the Bedlam; Dame Chat and Doll, her maid; Master Baily and his servant, Spendthrift; Doctor Rat, the curate; and Gib the cat. The mischievous Diccon persuades the Gammer that Dame Chat has taken the needle; a quarrel ensues and Doctor Rat is called in, but gets his head broken. Finally Hodge becomes acutely aware that the needle is in the seat of his breeches. The play includes the famous old drinking-song with the refrain:

> Back and side go bare, go bare,
>   Both foot and hand go cold;
> But Belly, God send thee good ale enough,
>   Whether it be new or old!

Gamp, SARAH, a character in Dickens's 'Martin Chuzzlewit' (q.v.). Her large cotton umbrella has given rise to the expression 'a gamp', for an umbrella, especially an untidy one; also for a midwife.

Gandalin, in Amadis of Gaul (q.v.), the son of a knight of Scotland and squire of Amadis. Don Quixote (I. xx) reminds Sancho that Gandalin 'always spoke to his master cap in hand, his head inclined and his body bent, in the Turkish fashion'.

Gandercleugh, the imaginary place of residence of Jedediah Cleishbotham (q.v.) in Scott's 'Tales of my Landlord'.

Gandersheim, NUN OF, see *Hrotsvitha*.

GANDHI, MOHANDAS KARAMCH-AND (1869–1948), was born in Rajkot, in western India, of Banya (merchant caste) parents. After studying law in England he practised in South Africa, where he devoted himself to the welfare of the Indian settlers, and led them in passive resistance campaigns against discriminatory legislation. He returned to India in 1915 and quickly established his ascendancy over the Indian National Congress party, which he persuaded in 1920 to adopt a policy of non-violent non-co-operation to secure *swaraj* (independence) from Britain. He also devised tactics of civil disobedience, which involved the public breach of unpopular laws and the acceptance of the consequent penalties. These methods won much support for the nationalist movement, though they occasionally led to popular violence, much to his distress. He claimed that they were in harmony with Hindu doctrines of *ahimsa* (non-violence), and that they would have a moral effect both on those who practised them and on those against whom they were directed. He lived an austere life in an *ashram*, or religious community, devoted to truth, non-violence, chastity, and vegetarianism. In his search for spiritual development he was willing to learn from western writers like Tolstoy and Thoreau, as well as from the teachings of Hinduism and other religions—a pragmatic approach indicated by the title of his autobiography, 'The Story of My Experiments with Truth'. The government soon found that imprisonment only added to his prestige as a *mahatma* (great soul) suffering for his ideals. The last months of his life were saddened by the partition of the subcontinent and the communal violence that followed. His pleas for tolerance towards Muslims living in India aroused hostility among certain fanatical groups, and in January 1948 he was assassinated by an Hindu extremist.

Gandish's, in Thackeray's 'The Newcomes' (q.v.), Professor Gandish's 'Academy of Drawing', where young Clive studies art.

Ganelon or GANO, in the Charlemagne romances and the 'Morgante Maggiore' of Pulci: count of Mayence, the villain and traitor who schemes for the defeat of the rearguard at Roncesvalles. He figures in Dante's 'Inferno' (xxxii. 122) and Chaucer's 'Nun's Priest's Tale'.

Ganesh or GANESHA, in Hindu mythology, the god of wisdom and prudence, who is invoked when any important undertaking or written composition is begun. He is the son of Siva, and is represented with the head of an elephant.

Ganlesse, in Scott's 'Peveril of the Peak' (q.v.), a name taken by Edward Christian.

Ganymēdēs or GANYMEDE, a beautiful youth of Phrygia. As he was tending his father's flocks on Mt. Ida he was carried up into heaven by an eagle at the command of Zeus, and became cup-bearer to the gods in place of Hebe. 'Catamite' is a corrupt form of his name.

Garamantes, a people mentioned by Herodotus (iv. 183), whose capital was Garama in Phazania (probably Fezzan in N. Africa), whence was the shortest road to the Lotophagi (Lotus-eaters). In the country of the Garamantes were found the oxen which as they graze walk backwards, because their horns curve outward in front of their heads.

Garamanta in the 'Orlando Innamorato' (q.v.) is a country in Africa whose wizard king prophesies to Agramant the destruction of the Saracen host.

Garamond, CLAUDE (*d.* 1561), French typefounder. His roman types, inspired by one cut for Aldus in 1495, were of great elegance and were widely adopted in France and, for Latin books, in Germany and the Low Countries. He cut a Greek type in three sizes for Francis I, which was used by R. Estienne (q.v.) and now belongs to the French national printing office.

Garcias, PEDRO: in the preface to the 'Gil Blas' (q.v.) of Le Sage there is a story of two students who, on their way to Salamanca, observe a tombstone on which is inscribed: 'Here is enclosed the soul of Pedro Garcias'.

One of the students laughs at the absurdity and goes away. The other lifts the stone and finds a leather purse with a hundred ducats and the direction, 'Be my heir, thou who hast been clever enough to interpret the inscription, and make better use than I did of my money.' The reader of the adventures of Gil Blas is like one or other of the students, as he perceives or not their moral instruction.

GARCILASSO DE LA VEGA (1503–36), Spanish poet and friend of Boscan (q.v.); the names of the two poets are coupled in Byron's 'Don Juan' (i. 95). With Boscan he brought about the renaissance of poetry in Spain, writing in his short and active life (he was a soldier in the armies of Charles V and received his death in battle) sonnets, eclogues, and odes, which won the praise of Cervantes ('Don Quixote', II. lviii).

Garden, The, a poem by Marvell (q.v.).

Garden of Cyrus, a treatise on the merits of the quincunx (:·:), by Sir Thomas Browne (q.v.), published (with 'Urn Burial', q.v.) in 1658.

This is a lighter work than its companion piece, treating quaintly of the Gardens of Antiquity and in particular of those of Cyrus as described by Xenophon, and of the garden of Paradise (with the Tree of Knowledge in the centre). From this the author passes to the use of the quincunx in a multitude of other connexions, such as architecture and military tactics, returning to plantations and certain mysterious properties of the number five.

Gardiner, COLONEL JAMES, a character in Scott's 'Waverley' (q.v.). For the original of the character see under *Doddridge (Philip)*. He was also commemorated in a song by Sir Gilbert Elliot (1722–77).

GARDINER, SAMUEL RAWSON (1829–1902), educated at Christ Church, Oxford, of which he became student in 1850. He settled in London to study the history of the Puritan revolution, supporting himself meanwhile by teaching. In 1872 he became lecturer and subsequently professor of modern history at King's College, London. Gardiner was offered the Regius professorship of history in succession to Froude, but declined it. He was elected a fellow of All Souls in 1884, and of Merton in 1892. As Ford lecturer in 1896 he lectured on 'Cromwell's place in history'. The first instalment of his great 'History' of the first Stuarts and Cromwell appeared in 1863 as the 'History of England from the Accession of James I to the Disgrace of Chief Justice Coke'. Successive instalments followed, and in 1883–4 appeared a second edition of all these, entitled a 'History of England from the Accession of James I to the Outbreak of the Civil War, 1603–42'. The 'History of the Great Civil War' (1886–91) and the 'History of the Commonwealth and Protectorate' (1894–1901) carried the record down to the year 1656 (an additional chapter was published posthumously). Gardiner published many other historical works, including 'The Thirty Years War' (1874) and a 'Student's History of England' (1890–1). His historical writing shows minute accuracy and impartiality, but is, perhaps necessarily, lacking in picturesque quality. He was very proud of his descent from Bridget, daughter of Oliver Cromwell and wife of Henry Ireton.

Gareth, SIR, in Malory's 'Morte Darthur', nicknamed 'Beaumains' by Sir Kay the steward. For his story see under *Gareth and Lynette* below.

Gareth and Lynette, one of Tennyson's 'Idylls of the King' (q.v.), published in 1872.

This idyll shows Arthur's court in its early days of innocence and promise. Gareth, son of Lot, king of Orkney, and Bellicent his wife, obtains his mother's reluctant permission to go to the court on the condition that he will hire himself for a year there as a scullion. He presents himself in disguise and serves as a kitchen knave under Kay the Seneschal, until released from his vow by his mother. Lynette comes to the court to ask that Lancelot may release her sister Lyonors, besieged in her castle by four knights. The kitchen knave claims the adventure and to Lynette's disgust is granted it by the king. On the way she bitterly reviles him, but is gradually won over as he conquers the first three knights. Before his encounter with the fourth, named Death, she even trembles for his safety, and would have Lancelot take his place. But Gareth clings to his task, which, it turns out, has already been accomplished, for the fourth knight proves a mere boy masquerading in hideous armour.

And he that told the tale in older times
Says that Sir Gareth wedded Lyonors,
But he, that told it later, says Lynette.

Gargamelle, in Rabelais's 'Gargantua' (q.v.), the wife of Grandgousier and mother of Gargantua.

Gargantua, originally the name of a beneficent giant of French folklore, connected with the Arthurian cycle. It is probably to this folklore giant that Shakespeare refers in 'As You Like It', III. ii. 239. In the prologue to his 'Pantagruel' Rabelais refers to a chapbook (the 'Grandes Cronicques') embodying the legends about him, which he had himself perhaps written or edited. This probably suggested to him his own story of 'La Vie très horrificque du Grand Gargantua', published in 1534, as a preliminary volume to 'Pantagruel' (q.v.), which had appeared in 1532. In this, Gargantua is presented as a prince of gigantic stature and appetite, the son of Grandgousier and Gargamelle. His education is described first under the scholastic system, and when this proves a failure, under a reformed system advocated by Rabelais. Then follows the war between Grandgousier and Picrochole, an episode suggested by a local quarrel in Touraine over certain water-

rights, in which Rabelais's father was involved. Finally comes the description of the Abbey of Thelema (q.v.), granted to Friar John by Grandgousier to reward him for his prowess in the above war.

So far as the book had a serious purpose, it was to illustrate the trivial causes that might give rise to devastating wars, and the author's views on the reform of education and of the monastic system. Gargantua himself is represented as a mighty eater and drinker, as befits a giant, but also as a studious, athletic, good-humoured, and peace-loving prince.

Gargery, JOE, a character in Dickens's 'Great Expectations' (q.v.).

Garibaldi, GIUSEPPE (1807–82), the celebrated Italian patriot and hero of the Risorgimento (q.v.). Having been exiled from Italy for political reasons he spent the years 1836–48 in S. America, in the service of the republics of Rio Grande do Sul and Uruguay. During 1850–4 he was in the United States, and returned in the latter year to Italy. He commanded a volunteer force on the Sardinian side in the campaign of 1859 against Austria. He organized expeditions by which he made himself master of Sicily, expelled Francis II from Naples, and finally marched (unsuccessfully) against Rome (1860–2). His independent course of action was frequently embarrassing to Cavour, but he was devoted to Victor Emmanuel, whose orders he unquestioningly obeyed. He was enthusiastically received in England in 1864. Garibaldi's campaigns have been narrated by G. M. Trevelyan (q.v.).

Garland, MR. and MRS., characters in Dickens's 'The Old Curiosity Shop' (q.v.).

GARLAND, HAMLIN (1860–1940), American author, best known for his realistic studies of the Middle West. His chief works are: 'Main-Travelled Roads' (1891), 'Prairie Folks' (1893), 'Rose of Dutcher's Coolly' (1895), 'A Son of the Middle Border' (1917), and 'A Daughter of the Middle Border' (1921).

Garm, (1) in Scandinavian mythology, the dog that guards the entrance to Helheim; (2) a bull-terrier, the subject of a story by Kipling (q.v., 'Actions and Reactions').

GARNETT, CONSTANCE (1861–1946), the daughter-in-law of Richard Garnett (q.v.), was a distinguished translator of the Russian classics. Her translations included all the works of Turgenev, Dostoevsky, and Gogol, virtually all of Chekhov, the two great novels of Tolstoy, and the memoirs of Herzen, and it was chiefly thanks to her that Russian literature exerted its influence in England in the first half of the 20th cent.

DAVID GARNETT (1892–), the novelist, is her son.

GARNETT, RICHARD (1835–1906), keeper of printed books in the British Museum, published in 1862 'Relics of

Shelley', and in 1888 'The Twilight of the Gods' (pleasant apologues in Lucian's vein). He also wrote brief biographies of Milton and Carlyle (1877), Emerson (1888), Edward Gibbon Wakefield (1898), Coleridge (1904), and a 'History of Italian Literature' (1897), as well as several volumes of original and translated verse.

Garratt, a village in Surrey near Wandsworth of which the villagers in the latter part of the 18th cent. made a practice of electing a 'mayor' when a general election took place, in reality a chairman of a local body for the defence of their rights. Samuel Foote wrote a farce, 'The Mayor of Garret', produced in 1764, in which Jerry Sneak, a miserable henpecked creature, is elected mayor.

Garraway's, a celebrated coffee-house in Change Alley, Cornhill, founded by one Thomas Garway, a tea, coffee, and tobacco merchant, in the 17th cent. It was a meeting-place of dealers in stocks and shares, notably in the days of the South Sea Bubble, and contained an auction-room (referred to in the 'Tatler', No. 147).

GARRICK, DAVID (1717–79), was S. Johnson's pupil at Edial, and accompanied him when he left Lichfield for London. His mythological burlesque 'Lethe' was performed at Drury Lane in 1740. He first appeared as an actor at Ipswich in 'Oroonoko'in 1741, and in the same year made his reputation in the part of Richard III. He subsequently proved his versatility by many triumphs in both tragic and comic parts. In 1747 he joined Lacy in the management of Drury Lane, where he produced a large number of Shakespeare's dramas. He made his last appearance in 1776 and sold a moiety of his patent to Sheridan and two others for £35,000. He collaborated with Colman in writing 'The Clandestine Marriage' (q.v.), and also wrote a number of lively farces, including 'The Lying Valet' (1741), 'Miss in her Teens' (1747), 'The Irish Widow' (1772), and 'Bon Ton, or High Life above Stairs' (1775). He was a member of Johnson's Literary Club, and his portrait was painted by Reynolds, Hogarth, and Gainsborough. He married in 1749 the dancer, Eve Marie Violetti (1724–1822). He was buried in Westminster Abbey. His interesting correspondence with many of the most distinguished men of his day was published in 1831–2, and, in a greatly enlarged collection, edited by D. M. Little and G. M. Kahrl, in 1963. See also *Lichtenberg*.

Garrick Club, THE, founded in 1831 as a club in which 'actors and men of education and refinement might meet on equal terms'. Its original premises were at 35 King Street. Barham, Count d'Orsay, and Samuel Rogers (qq.v.) were among its first members. It was much frequented by Thackeray, and possesses a famous collection of portraits of actors and actresses.

Garter, ORDER OF THE, the highest order of English knighthood. The institution of the order is attributed on the authority of Froissart to Edward III about the year 1344. By the time of Selden it was traditionally asserted that the garter was that of the countess of Salisbury, which fell off while she danced with the king, who picked it up and tied it on his own leg, saying to those present *Honi soit qui mal y pense*. The Garter as the badge of the order is a ribbon of dark blue velvet, edged and buckled with gold and bearing the above words embroidered in gold, and is worn below the left knee. [OED.]

Garter King of Arms, also known as GARTER, the principal king of arms. The two provincial kings of arms are Clarenceux and Norroy (qq.v.). See *Heralds' College*.

GARTH, SIR SAMUEL (1661–1719), a physician, and a member of the Kit-Cat Club (q.v.), is remembered as the author of 'The Dispensary' (1699), a burlesque poem in which he ridiculed the opposition of the apothecaries to the supply of medicines to out-patients' dispensaries. Pope described him as 'the best good Christian without knowing it'.

GASCOIGNE, GEORGE (1525?–77), a man of a good Bedfordshire family, educated at Trinity College, Cambridge, entered Gray's Inn and represented Bedfordshire in parliament. His 'Supposes', an adaptation of Ariosto's 'Suppositi', our earliest extant comedy in prose, was acted at Gray's Inn in 1566. Gascoigne saw military service in Holland, 1572–5, and was captured by the Spaniards. An unauthorized book of poems by him was published in his absence, and in 1575 he issued 'The Posies of G. Gascoigne, corrected and completed', containing 'Jocasta' (paraphrased from the 'Phoenissae' of Euripides), the second earliest tragedy in English in blank verse. The book also contained 'Certain Notes of Instruction concerning the making of verse', the earliest English critical essay. He published his 'tragicall comedie', the 'Glasse of Government', a 'prodigal son' play, in 1575. His other works include 'The Steele Glas' (q.v.), a satire, published in 1576, 'The Droomme of Doomesday', and the posthumously published 'Tale of Hemetes'. Gascoigne is notable as a pioneer in various branches of literature.

Gascoigne, SIR WILLIAM (1350?–1419), appointed chief justice of the king's bench in 1400, figures in that capacity in Shakespeare's '2 Henry IV'. The story taken by Hall from Sir T. Elyot's 'Governour' of his committing Henry V when Prince of Wales is unfounded.

Gashford, a character in Dickens's 'Barnaby Rudge' (q.v.).

GASKELL, ELIZABETH CLEGHORN (1810–65), daughter of William Stevenson, Unitarian minister and keeper of the Treasury records, was brought up by her aunt at Knutsford in Cheshire, which is the original of Cranford, and of Hollingford (in 'Wives and Daughters'). In 1832 she married William Gaskell, minister at the Cross Street Unitarian chapel in Manchester, with whom her life was one of calm and perfect harmony. In 1848 she published 'Mary Barton' (q.v.), her first novel, based on the industrial troubles of the years 1842–3. This was severely criticized by W. R. Greg and others as hostile to the employers, but was highly popular. It brought her into relations with Dickens, for whose 'Household Words' and 'All the Year Round' she subsequently wrote much. To the former of these (after publishing 'The Moorland Cottage' in 1850) she contributed in 1851–3 the famous series of papers subsequently republished under the title of 'Cranford' (q.v.). In 1853 appeared 'Ruth' (q.v.), also the subject of some controversy (on ethical grounds); followed by 'North and South' (q.v.) in 1855, which reflects the easier industrial conditions that then prevailed. In 1857 Mrs. Gaskell produced her remarkable 'Life of Charlotte Brontë', some of the statements in which gave rise to complaint and were withdrawn. 'My Lady Ludlow' appeared in 'Household Words' in 1858 and was republished in 1859 in the 'Round the Sofa' collection; 'Lois the Witch' (q.v.) in 1859; and 'Sylvia's Lovers' (q.v.) followed in 1863–4. 'Wives and Daughters' (q.v.), like its predecessor, was first printed in the 'Cornhill Magazine', appearing in 1864–6, but Mrs. Gaskell died before the work was completed. The Knutsford edition of her collected works was issued in 1906. Her 'Letters', ed. J. A. V. Chapple and A. Pollard, were published in 1966.

Gaspar, one of the three Magi (q.v.). He is represented as an Ethiopian, king of Tarshish.

GASQUET, FRANCIS AIDAN (1846–1929), cardinal and historian. He was educated at Downside, entered the Benedictine Order in 1866, and was ordained priest in 1874. He taught at Downside and was prior at the monastery until ill health caused him to resign in 1885. He then turned to historical research, in which from 1885 to 1901 he had the close collaboration of Edmund Bishop, the distinguished liturgical scholar, and published his great work on the Reformation in England, 'Henry VIII and the English Monasteries' (2 vols., 1888–9). He was appointed president of the international commission for revising the text of the Vulgate in 1907, and in 1914 was created cardinal, living thereafter in Rome. His other publications include 'Parish Life in Medieval England' (1906), 'Religio Religiosi' (1918), and 'Monastic Life in the Middle Ages' (1922). From 1904 onwards his work was subjected to constant criticism on the grounds of inaccuracy by the historian G. G. Coulton, but this he entirely ignored.

GASSENDI, PIERRE (1592–1655), French mathematician, astronomer, and philosopher, a friend of Galileo and Pascal. He was an opponent of the philosophy of Aristotle

(against whom he wrote 'Paradoxical Exercitations') and of Descartes, revived that of Epicurus, and attempted to reconcile the theory of atoms with Christianity. He wrote lives of Copernicus and Regiomontanus.

Gaster, THE REVD. DR., a character in Peacock's 'Headlong Hall' (q.v.).

Gastrolaters, in Rabelais, IV. lvii, a people visited by Pantagruel, whose god is their belly. They represent greedy monks. They have a ridiculous idol *Manduce*, whose eyes are bigger than its belly. The author gives a formidable list of the flesh and fowl, and 'on the interlarded fish days' of the caviare, botargoes, and the like, that 'these idle lobcocks sacrifice to their gorbellied god'.

Gates of Dreams, see *Dreams.*

GAUDEN, DR. JOHN (1605–62), educated at St. John's College, Oxford, became bishop of Worcester. He claimed to be the author of 'Eikon Basilike' (q.v.).

Gauguin, PAUL (1848–1903), French painter. While working as a stockbroker he painted and exhibited with the Impressionists until in 1883 he gave up his job to devote his time to painting. The latter part of his life he spent in the South Sea Islands and died in poverty in the Maquesas. His exotic figure composition and landscapes, rendered in rich flat colours, were influential in the development of 20th-cent. art.

Gaunt, JOHN OF, see *John of Gaunt.*

Gautama, see *Buddha.*

Gautier, MARGUERITE, heroine of 'La Dame aux Camélias' of Alexandre Dumas *fils* (q.v.).

GAUTIER, THÉOPHILE (1811–72), French poet, novelist, and journalist, an extreme Romantic in youth, in later life an exponent of 'Art for art's sake'. 'Émaux et Camées' (1852) contains his best poetry. His two chief novels are 'Mademoiselle de Maupin' (1835) and the picaresque 'Capitaine Fracasse' (1863). He was, like Mérimée (q.v.), a pioneer of the short story (e.g. 'Jettatura' and 'La Morte amoureuse', a vampire story).

Gavroche, a character in 'Les Misérables' of Victor Hugo (q.v.), whose name has been adopted as typifying the Parisian street-arab.

Gawain (WALWAIN), is associated as a hero with King Arthur in the earliest of the Arthurian legends. He is the perfect knight, courageous, pure, and courteous. In the later developments of the story, however, his character shows deterioration. Gawain is the son of the king's sister Morgause (wife of King Lot of Orkney) and brother of Agravain, Gaheris, and Gareth. In Geoffrey of Monmouth's narrative he is Arthur's ambassador to Rome and bears himself bravely in the ensuing combat. In Malory's 'Morte Darthur' he becomes the bitter enemy of Launcelot because the latter has killed his three brothers. He is killed when Arthur lands at Dover to recover his kingdom from Mordred. It is noteworthy that Gawain's strength increased daily until noon and then declined (Malory, VIII. xviii), the characteristic of a solar deity. For his relation to Gwalchmei, the sun-god of Welsh mythology, see Rhys, 'Arthurian Legend'. The north portal of Modena Cathedral has a sculpture said to be early 12th cent., on which are mounted figures of Artus de Bretani, Galvaginus (i.e. Gawain), and others, so inscribed (R. S. Loomis, 'Celtic Myth and Arthurian Romance'). The principal single adventure of Gawain is perhaps that described in 'Sir Gawain and the Green Knight' (q.v.). See also *Ywain and Gawain*.

Gawain and the Green Knight, *Sir,* an alliterative poem of 2,500 lines of the 14th cent.

On New Year's Day Arthur and his knights sit feasting at Camelot. A giant knight, Bercilak de Hautdesert, comes in clad in green. Gawain accepts his challenge to give him a stroke with the axe and take one in return. Gawain beheads the knight at one blow, but the trunk picks up the head and rides off, appointing Gawain to meet him a year hence at the Green Chapel in North Wales. On the next Christmas Eve, in a dreary forest, Gawain sees a great castle where he is welcomed by the lord and lady. Gawain and the lord agree to exchange what they get by hunting or otherwise. The lady tempts Gawain on three successive nights, but he accepts only kisses and a girdle that makes him invulnerable. Gawain gives the lord the kisses but not the girdle. On New Year's Day Gawain goes to the Green Chapel and meets the Green Knight. He is wounded, and the knight reveals that he is lord of the castle and that he and his wife had agreed to tempt Gawain. As the latter has emerged successfully from the trial, save in the matter of the girdle, he has saved his life but suffered a wound. Gawain tells his story to the court at Camelot and all the knights and ladies agree to wear like girdles of green. The poem may be connected with the creation of the order of the garter (q.v.). The same story, in a later version, is used to account for the foundation of the order of the bath.

Gawries, see *Peter Wilkins*.

GAY, JOHN (1685–1732), born at Barnstaple, was apprenticed for a time to a London mercer. In 1708 he published an indifferent poem 'Wine', denying the possibility of successful authorship to water-drinkers. He was secretary to the duchess of Monmouth during 1712–14. In 1713 he issued 'Rural Sports' on the model of Pope's 'Windsor, Forest', and contributed to Steele's 'Guardian'. His 'Shepherd's Week' (q.v.), the first work that showed his real ability, appeared in 1714. His first play, 'What d'ye Call it', a satirical farce, was produced in 1715, and his 'Trivia' (q.v.) was published in 1716. With Pope and Arbuthnot he wrote 'Three Hours after Marriage', a comedy, which was acted in 1717. He speculated disastrously in South Sea funds with the proceeds of the publication of his poems, and his hopes of advancement under the new king were disappointed. He became an inmate of the household of the duke and duchess of Queensberry, and in 1727 brought out the first series of his 'Fables', which were very popular. His 'Beggar's Opera' (q.v.) met with remarkable success in 1728, and was followed by the publication of its sequel 'Polly' (q.v.). The production of the latter on the stage was forbidden. These two plays contain many of Gay's pleasant ballads, but 'Sweet William's Farewell to Black-eyed Susan' was published separately, and ' 'Twas when the seas were roaring' is from his first play. Some of his 'Eclogues' and the 'Epistles', including 'Mr. Pope's Welcome from Greece' on the completion of Pope's 'Iliad', deserve notice. He wrote the libretto of Handel's 'Acis and Galatea' in 1732, and 'Achilles', an opera produced at Covent Garden in 1733. The second series of his 'Fables' appeared in 1738 after his death. He was buried in Westminster Abbey, and on his monument is inscribed the epitaph written by himself:

Life is a jest, and all things show it;
I thought so once, and now I know it.

Gay, WALTER, a character in Dickens's 'Dombey and Son' (q.v.).

Gayferos, DON, in Spanish romance, a kinsman of Roland (q.v.) and husband of Melisenda, Charlemagne's daughter. The latter is carried off by the Moors and rescued by Gayferos. The legend is referred to in 'Don Quixote', II. xxvi, where it is the subject of a puppet play.

Gaylord, MARCIA, the heroine of W. D. Howells's 'A Modern Instance' (q.v.), and the best of the author's female characters.

Gazette, from the Italian *gazzetta,* apparently so called from the coin of that name, which may have been the sum paid either for the paper itself or for the privilege of reading it. [OED.] The *gazzetta* was a news-sheet first published in Venice about the middle of the 16th cent., and similar news-sheets (see *Coranto*) appeared in England in the 17th cent., giving news from foreign parts.

The OXFORD GAZETTE was the first real newspaper, other than a newsletter, to be published in England. It appeared in Nov. 1665, the court being then at Oxford owing to the great plague, and was started by Henry Muddiman (q.v.) under the direction of Sir Joseph Williamson (q.v.), as a supplement to Muddiman's newsletters. It later became the 'London Gazette', which still survives. The 'London Gazette' is not now a newspaper, but a record of official appointments, notices of bankruptcies, etc., and in war time it is the official register of casualties.

Gazetteer, a geographical index or dictionary. A work of this kind by L. Echard (ed. 2, 1693) bore the title 'The Gazetteer's or Newsman's Interpreter; Being a Geographical Index', intended for the use of 'gazetteers' or journalists.

Gē or **Gaea**, in Greek mythology, the personification of the Earth, a divine being, the wife of Uranus (q.v.), and mother of the Titans (q.v.).

GEBER, an Arabian, thought to have been born at Seville at the end of the 8th cent. Certain Latin works on alchemy are regarded as translations from his Arabic text. Whether they are so, or who their Latin author was, and what were his relations with the Arabian Geber, is uncertain. Burton, in the Preface to the 'Anatomy of Melancholy', speaks of him as 'that first inventor of Algebra', which implies an erroneous derivation of the latter word.

Gebir, an epic poem by W. S. Landor (q.v.), published in 1798.

Gebir, an Iberian prince, invades Egypt, but his conquest is arrested by his love for its young queen Charoba. By the treachery of her nurse, Dalica, he is slain amid the marriage feast, and the city that he is founding is destroyed by magic. Tamar, his shepherd brother, whose only ambition is to win the love of a sea-nymph, is carried away by her beyond the world of mortals.

Parts of the poem were first written in Latin, and the author subsequently published a Latin version, 'Gebirus'. The English poems contains the often-quoted passage on a shell:

Apply
Its polisht lips to your attentive ear;
And it remembers its august abode,
And murmurs as the ocean murmurs there.

Geddes, Jenny, supposed name of the woman who threw a stool at Bishop Lindsay in St. Giles's, Edinburgh, when the new service was introduced, *temp.* Charles I.

Gehazi, the covetous servant of Elisha, who was punished with leprosy for deceitfully obtaining, in his master's name, a present from Naaman (2 Kings v. 20–27).

Gehenna, originally a place-name, *ge ben hinnom*, the valley of the son of Hinnom, near Jerusalem, which was at one time the scene of the idolatrous worship of a god named in the Hebrew text Molek. This worship was abolished in the religious reforms of Josiah, and the valley desecrated (2 Kings xxiii. 10). Thereafter it was used as a place for casting refuse, and the dead bodies of animals and criminals. Fires were kept burning there to prevent infection. Hence the name was used figuratively for hell.

Gelert, see *Bethgelert.*

Gellatley, Davie, in Scott's 'Waverley' (q.v.), the 'innocent' dependant of the Baron Bradwardine, in whose mouth the author places some of his finest lyrics.

GELLIUS, Aulus, a Latin grammarian of the 2nd cent. A.D., author of twenty books of 'Noctes Atticae', so named because they were written in a house near Athens on winter nights. They form a miscellany, important as containing extracts from many lost authors, on many topics, literature, history, philosophy, philology, and natural science.

Gem, *The,* (1) a literary annual, edited by T. Hood (q.v.), 1829–32; (2) a weekly paper for boys, written by C. Hamilton (q.v.) under the pen-name Martin Clifford, 1907–39.

Gemara, the later of the two portions of the Talmud (q.v.), consisting of a commentary on the older part (the Mishna).

Gemini ('the twins'), a constellation, otherwise known as 'Castor and Pollux' (q.v.); also the third sign of the zodiac with which this constellation was anciently identical.

General, Mrs., in Dickens's 'Little Dorrit' (q.v.), the lady companion to Mr. Dorrit's daughters, the inventor of the formula 'prunes and prism' (q.v.).

Genesis, meaning origin, creation, is the first in order of the books of the Bible, containing the account of the creation of the world. The name was given to it by the Greek translators. There is an OE. poetic paraphrase of the book, formerly attributed to Cædmon (q.v.). It contains an interpolated section (usually called 'Genesis B'), which is translated from an Old Saxon original by another author, and deals in a dramatic and vivid manner with the fall of the angels and the temptation.

Genesis and **Exodus,** poems in rhymed couplets, written about the middle of the 13th cent., relating scriptural history down to the death of Moses in popular form, based not on the Bible, but mainly on the 'Historia Scholastica' of Petrus Comestor; and important as the first instance in English of the iambic dimeter frequently used by later poets, e.g. by Coleridge in 'Christabel'.

GENEST, JOHN (1764–1839), educated at Westminster and Trinity College, Cambridge, author of 'Some Account of the English Stage from the Restoration in 1660 to 1830' (1832), an exceptionally trustworthy book of reference.

Geneva, in Switzerland, used allusively for the League of Nations, of which it was the headquarters.

Geneva Bible, see *Bible (The English).*

Geneva gown, a black gown such as was worn by the Calvinist clergy when preaching.

Genevieve, the heroine of S. T. Coleridge's poem 'Love', first published in the 'Morning Post' (1799) and included in the second edition of 'Lyrical Ballads' (q.v.).

Geneviève, St. (*c.* 419–512), the patron saint of Paris, was born at Nanterre and went to Paris, where she lived an austere life. At the time of Attila's invasion (451) she encouraged the panic-stricken inhabitants and urged them to repentance; and Attila turned away from Paris towards Orléans.

Genghis Khan (1162–1227), the great Mongol conqueror, whose empire at his death extended from the shores of the Pacific to the northern shores of the Black Sea.

Genius, in classical pagan belief, the tutelary god or attendant spirit allotted to every person at his birth, to govern his fortunes and determine his character; also the tutelary spirit similarly connected with a place (whence the expression *genius loci*), an institution, etc. A person's *good*, or *evil, genius* are the two mutually opposed spirits by whom every person was supposed to be attended throughout life. [OED.]

Genii, the plural, is also used as a rendering of the Arabic *jinn* (q.v.). A *genie* or *jinnee* is one of the *jinn.*

GENTILIS, ALBERICUS (1552–1608), an Italian, the most learned lawyer of his time, and D.C.L. of Perugia, was obliged to leave Italy on account of heretical opinions. He was appointed Regius professor of civil law at Oxford in 1587 and practised as a barrister in England. He was the author of 'De Legationibus' (1584), a treatise on diplomatic privilege, and 'De Jure Belli' (1588–98). Gentilis was one of the founders of the system of international law, and Grotius (q.v.) owed much to him.

Gentle Art of Making Enemies, The, a collection, published in 1890, of the pungent letters and comments of J. McN. Whistler (q.v.) on criticisms of his works. The first subject dealt with is Whistler's libel action against Ruskin in respect of a passage in 'Fors Clavigera'.

Gentle Shepherd, The, see under *Ramsay* (*A.*).

Gentleman Dancing-Master, The, a comedy by Wycherley (q.v.), produced in 1673.

This is the most entertaining of Wycherley's plays. Hippolita, daughter of Mr. Formal, is about to be married to her cousin, who has just returned from France, affects the French dress and language, and calls himself Monsieur de Paris. She despises him, but has been kept closely pent up by her aunt, Mrs. Caution, and knows no other man. By a trick she induces her cousin to send Gerrard, a young gentleman, to pay her a secret visit, and they fall in love with one another. Her father, just returned from Spain, who affects the Spanish dress and punctilio, and calls himself Don Diego, surprises them together, whereupon Hippolita passes off Gerrard as her dancing-master. There follow a number of diverting scenes in which Gerrard is constantly on the point of being betrayed by his incompetence as a dancing-master, but is saved by the squabble between Mrs. Caution, who sees through the trick, and Don Diego, who cannot conceive that any one should fool him. Finally, in the turmoil caused by Gerrard's ultimate exposure, the lovers avail themselves of the services of the parson who has arrived to marry Hippolita to her cousin.

Gentleman Usher, The, a tragicomedy, by Chapman (q.v.), printed in 1606, and probably acted *c.* 1602.

The Duke Alphonso and his son Vincentio are both in love with Margaret, daughter of Earl Lasso. The daughter loves Vincentio, who is ordered into exile. Margaret in despair disfigures herself with a poisonous unguent. The duke, remorseful, surrenders Margaret, who on account of her disfigurement refuses to marry Vincentio. But the doctor provides a remedy and solves the difficulty. The name of the play is taken from the usher, Bassiolo, a conceited major-domo, somewhat after the kind of Malvolio, who acts as go-between for the lovers and is fooled and made ridiculous.

Gentleman's Journal, a periodical edited by Motteux (q.v.) from 1691 to 1694, containing the news of the month and miscellaneous prose and poetry. It was the germ of the modern magazine.

Gentleman's Magazine, The, a periodical founded in 1731 by Cave (q.v.), under the pseudonym Sylvanus Urban. Its original intention was to reproduce monthly from the journals such news, essays, or other matter as appeared most interesting. Hence the use for the first time of the word 'magazine' in this sense. By Jan. 1739 original matter had largely replaced such extracts; the magazine assumed a more serious character, and included parliamentary reports, maps, music, and a record of publications. The change in the character of the paper was in accordance with suggestions made to the editor by Samuel Johnson (q.v.), who at this time became a regular contributor (until 1744), with considerable influence on its management. He at first edited, and subsequently wrote, the parliamentary reports. The 'Gentleman's Magazine' lasted until 1914.

GEOFFREY CRAYON, see *Crayon.*

GEOFFREY OF MONMOUTH, Gaufridus Monemutensis (1100?–1154), probably a Benedictine monk of Monmouth, studied at Oxford, and was attached to Robert, earl of Gloucester. He is said to have been archdeacon of Llandaff, and he was appointed bishop of St. Asaph in 1152.

In his 'Historia Regum Britanniae' he purports to give an account of 'the kings who dwelt in Britain before the incarnation of Christ' and especially of 'Arthur and the many others who succeeded him after the incarnation'. For this purpose he states that he drew upon a 'most ancient book in the British tongue' handed to him by Walter, archdeacon of Oxford, also known as Walter Calenius (q.v.); but this book is unknown to any chronicler of the time. There is reason to suppose that this alleged work was in the main a mystification; his contemporary, William of Newburgh (q.v.), condemns it as such in strong terms. Geoffrey's veracity was also challenged by Ranulf Higden

('Polychronicon'). Geoffrey drew on Bede and Nennius, on British traditions, perhaps on Welsh documents now lost, and probably for the rest on a romantic imagination. He is the creator of King Arthur as a romantic hero. His 'Historia' was translated into Anglo-Norman by Gaimar and Wace, and into English by Layamon and Robert of Gloucester; it was first printed in 1508 (Paris). There is a good modern translation (1903) by Sebastian Evans. Geoffrey's 'Prophetia Anglicana Merlini Ambrosii Britanni' was first printed in 1603. See also Edmond Faral, 'La Légende arthurienne; des origines à Geoffroy de Monmouth . . .', 3 vols., published in 1929 by Champion.

Geoffry Hamlyn, see *Kingsley (H).*

George I, king of England, 1714–27.

George II, king of England, 1727–60.

George III, king of England, 1760–1820.

George IV, king of England, 1820–30.

George V, king of England, 1910–36.

George VI, king of England, 1936–52.

George, GUILD OF ST., see *Ruskin.*

GEORGE, HENRY (1839–97), American writer on political economy and sociology, author of 'Progress and Poverty' (1879), 'The Irish Land Question' (1881), 'Social Problems' (1884), 'Protection or Free Trade' (1886). George was an advocate of the nationalization of land and of the 'single tax' on its increment value.

George, ST., patron saint of England, Portugal, and formerly of Aragon and the republic of Genoa, is said to have been a native of Cappadocia, who, according to Metaphrastes, the Byzantine hagiologist, rose to high military rank under Diocletian. He was arrested on account of his Christian religion, tortured, and executed at Nicomedia in A.D. 303, his remains being subsequently transferred to Lydda. The legend is open to criticism, but it is probable that there was an officer of his name in the Roman army who suffered martyrdom under Diocletian. Gibbon adopted, it appears wrongly, the view that St. George was identical with a certain Arian bishop of Alexandria, a man of discreditable antecedents as a purveyor of provisions to the army ('Decline and Fall', xxiii). St. George's connexion with the dragon is of much later date and its origin is obscure. The saint is perhaps the inheritor of some local myth, such as that of Perseus (q.v.) who slew at Joppa (near Lydda) the monster that threatened Andromeda. Sir Wallis Budge ('George of Lydda') regards the dragon as merely symbolical of the powers of evil. St. George has been recognized as the patron saint of England from the days of Edward III, perhaps because of having been regarded as the patron of the order of the garter. He is commemorated on 23 April.

George and Vulture, THE, a hostelry in George Yard, Lombard Street. It was the temporary abode of Mr. Pickwick and Sam Weller when the action of Bardell and Pickwick was impending ('Pickwick Papers', ch. xxvi, xxxi, etc.). It is said to have been previously a coffee-house, frequented by Swift, Addison, and Steele, and at a later period by Hogarth and Wilkes.

George Barnwell, The History of, or The London Merchant, a domestic tragedy in prose by Lillo (q.v.), produced in 1731.

In this play, for the first time, everyday commercial life is made the theme of a tragedy. The play was a great success, was translated into French, German, and Dutch, and was highly commended by Diderot (q.v.) and by Lessing (q.v.), who modelled on it his 'Miss Sara Sampson'. The story was parodied in the 'George Barnwell Travestie' of the 'Rejected Addresses' (q.v.), and caricatured by Thackeray in 'George de Barnwell'. It is based on an old ballad of 'George Barnwell', and deals with the seduction of an apprentice by the heartless courtesan Millwood. He becomes so infatuated that he not only robs his employer, Thorowgood, but is even induced by Millwood to murder his uncle, for which crime he and Millwood are brought to execution.

George Play, ST., see *Mummers' Play.*

George-a'-Green, the merry pinner or pinder (pound-keeper) of Wakefield. The story is given in W. C. Hazlitt's 'Tales and Legends'. George-a'-Green wins the pindership by defeating all competitors at quarter-staff, defies the messenger who comes from Prince John (during Richard I's absence) demanding a contribution from Wakefield, and elopes with Justice Grymes's daughter. Maid Marian provokes Robin Hood to challenge him, but George-a'-Green defeats both Robin and his companions.

He is the subject of a play (licensed for publication, 1595; the earliest known edition appears to be that of 1599, in the Bodleian) probably by Robert Greene (q.v.).

George's, ST., HANOVER SQUARE, one of the fifty new churches built after the Fire of London, completed in 1724, frequently referred to as the scene of fashionable weddings, where the duke of Wellington gave away many brides.

Georgian architecture, the English architecture of the 18th cent., especially the simple town house common throughout England, and in some towns developed in planned squares and terraces, e.g. Bath. Palladian (q.v.) principles of classical proportions were adopted to an unpretentious, refined, and discreet style suited to the needs of the rising middle classes.

Georgian Poetry, an anthology of contemporary verse initiated in 1912 by a group consisting of Rupert Brooke, John Drinkwater, Harold Monro, Wilfrid Wilson Gibson, Arundel del Ré, and Edward Marsh, of which five volumes appeared between 1912 and 1922, containing poems by Rupert Brooke, William H. Davies, W. de la Mare, John Drinkwater, D. H. Lawrence, John Masefield, Robert Graves, James Elroy Flecker, and others.

Georgics, The, a didactic poem by Virgil (q.v.) in four books, on agriculture, the care of domestic animals, and the keeping of bees.

Geraint and Enid, one of Tennyson's 'Idylls of the King', originally forming with 'The Marriage of Geraint' a single idyll, 'Enid'. The story is taken from Lady Charlotte Guest's 'Mabinogion' (q.v.) and had been previously treated in Chrétien de Troyes's 'Erec'. It was published in 1859.

In this idyll the baneful influence of the sin of Guinevere is first indicated. Geraint, one of Arthur's knights and a tributary prince of Devon, the husband of Enid, daughter of earl Yniol, fearing the contaminating influence of Guinevere upon his wife, withdraws from the court to his own lands. A word spoken by Enid ('Oh, me! I fear that I am no true wife') and misunderstood by him, confirms this fear and provokes him to senseless suspicion of her fidelity. He now rides out into bandit-haunted lands, making her ride before and forbidding her to speak to him. Her devotion to him in successive encounters, in meeting the dishonourable proposal of Earl Limours, and in the hall of Earl Doorm when he lies wounded, gradually convinces him of her innocence and wins back his love.

Geraldine, THE FAIR, see *Surrey.*

Gerard, the hero of Reade's 'The Cloister and the Hearth' (q.v.).

GERARD, JOHN (1545–1612), a herbalist and superintendent of Burghley's gardens, was author of the celebrated 'Herball or generall Historie of Plantes' (1597), in a large measure adapted from the 'Pemptades' of Rembert Dodoens. A revised edition of the 'Herball' was issued by Thomas Johnson in 1633. The work gives a description of each plant, the localities in which it is found, and its medical virtues (correcting superstitions, e.g. about the mandrake); discusses nomenclature; and contains a large number of beautiful woodcuts, many of which had appeared in an earlier work.

Gerbert of Aquitaine (*c.* 940–1003), Pope Sylvester II from 999 to 1003, the greatest figure in the 10th–11th cents., reckoned a magician for his knowledge, inventor, mathematician, scholar. He was archbishop successively of Rheims and Ravenna before his election to the papal see.

Gerda or GERD, in Scandinavian mythology, the frozen Earth, whom Frey (q.v.) marries.

GERHARDI, WILLIAM ALEXANDER (1895–), author, born of English parents in St. Petersburg and educated there and at Worcester College, Oxford. He served in the First World War, became military attaché to the British Embassy at Petrograd, and went with the British Military Mission to Siberia, 1918–20. His novels ('humorous tragedies' he calls them in 'My Literary Credo', the introduction to the Collected Edition, 1947) were in a manner new to English imaginative literature and had much influence on younger writers. They include 'Futility: a Novel on Russian Themes' (1922), 'The Polyglots' (1925), 'Resurrection' (1934), which he describes as 'an autobiographical novel recording a true experience developed into a passionate argument for the immortality of the soul', and 'Of Mortal Love' (1936). His critical writings include 'Anton Chehov' (1923, a critical and biographical study), 'Memoirs of a Polyglot' (1931, autobiographical), and 'The Romanoffs' (1940, historical biography of the dynasty, substantially a history of Russia).

Germ, The, *Thoughts towards Nature in Poetry, Literature, and Art,* a periodical of which the first number appeared on 1 Jan. 1850. It was the organ of the 'Pre-Raphaelite Brotherhood' (q.v.). The title was changed in the third number to 'Art and Poetry, being Thoughts towards Nature'. Only four numbers in all appeared.

Gernutus, the Jew of Venice, an old ballad included in Percy's 'Reliques', embodying a story (somewhat resembling that in Shakespeare's 'The Merchant of Venice') in which a Jew wagers a pound of his flesh that certain property which he has insured has not been lost.

Géronte, in Molière's comedies, the typical old man whose absurdities are held up to ridicule. In 'Les Fourberies de Scapin' he is a miser, outwitted by Scapin. In 'Le Médecin malgré lui', he is a credulous fool, imposed upon by Sganarelle.

Gerontius, *Dream of,* see *Newman.*

Gertrude, the queen of Denmark in Shakespeare's 'Hamlet' (q.v.).

Gertrude of Wyoming, a poem by T. Campbell (q.v.), in the Spenserian stanza, published in 1809.

The poem centres in the desolation in 1778 of the settlement of Wyoming, in Pennsylvania, by a force of Indians under one Brandt, a Mohawk, and the destruction of the felicity of a home by the death of Gertrude, the newly married wife of Henry Waldegrave, and of her father Albert. Campbell subsequently withdrew the charge of cruelty against Brandt.

Gerusalemme Liberata, see *Jerusalem Delivered.*

Geryon, a monster with three bodies or three heads, who lived in the island of Gades. He owned numerous oxen, guarded by the two-headed dog Orthrus and the giant Eurytion. All three were destroyed by Hercules (q.v.), who carried away the oxen.

In Dante's 'Inferno' (xvii–xviii) he is the symbol of Fraud and guardian of the Eighth

Circle of Hell, the place of punishment of traitors. He has the face of a just man, two hairy arms, and a forked tail.

Geryoneo, in Spenser's 'Faerie Queene', v. x and xi, a giant who represents Philip II of Spain, the Spanish power in the Netherlands, and the Inquisition.

GESNER, JOHANN MATTHIAS (1691–1761), a German pioneer of humanistic studies, author of the 'Novus Linguae et Eruditionis Romanae Thesaurus' (1746–8) and editor of various classics; a precursor of Lessing and Goethe.

Gessler, see *Tell.*

Gesta Francorum, a chronicle in medieval Latin, the first known to have been written by a layman. It gives the story of the First Crusade. Its actual author is unknown. It has been edited with a translation by Rosalind Hill (Nelson's Medieval Texts), 1962.

Gesta Romanorum, a collection of tales in Latin, some of Eastern origin, romances of chivalry, and legends of saints, originally compiled in England in the 14th cent. and first printed about 1472. An English translation was printed by Wynkyn de Worde (q.v.). Though Roman emperors are mentioned in some of these, they are not true narratives of historical events. To each tale a moral is attached. They provided materials for many subsequent authors.

Gestapo, abbreviation of *Geheime Staatspolizei,* the German Secret Police under the Nazi régime.

Gestas, see *Dismas.*

Gettysburg, in southern Pennsylvania, the scene of the defeat in 1863 of the confederate army under Gen. Robert E. Lee by the Federals under Gen. Meade. See *Lincoln(A.).*

Ghebers, see *Guebres.*

Ghibellines, see *Guelphs.*

Ghost of Abel, The, see *Blake.*

Ghost-words, a term used by Skeat (q.v.) to signify words which have no real existence, 'coinages due to the blunders of printers or scribes, or to the perfervid imaginations of ignorant or blundering editors' ('Trans. Philol. Soc.', 1885–7, ii. 350).

Giafar, see *Ja'far.*

Giaffir, in Byron's 'The Bride of Abydos' (q.v.), the father of Zuleika.

Giant Pope, in Bunyan's 'Pilgrim's Progress' (q.v.), a giant by whose power and tyranny many men have in old time been cruelly put to death, but who is grown so crazy and stiff in his joints that he can now do little more than sit in his cave's mouth, grinning at the pilgrims as they go by, and biting his nails because he cannot come at them.

Giants or GIGANTES, THE, according to Greek mythology, were children of Gē (q.v.), of great stature and strength, frequently con-

fused with the Titans (q.v.). They are said to have conspired to dethrone Zeus, and heaped Ossa on Pelion in order to scale the walls of heaven. They were defeated and imprisoned in the earth.

Giaour, The, a poem by Lord Byron (q.v.), published in 1813. Eight editions of the work appeared in the last seven months of that year, increasing in length from 685 lines to 1334.

The word 'giaour' (pron. 'dja-oor') is a term of reproach applied by Turks to non-Moslems, especially Christians. The tale is of a female slave, Leila, who is unfaithful to her Turkish lord, Hassan, and is in consequence bound and thrown into the sea. Her lover, the Giaour, avenges her by killing Hassan. The story is told in fragments, at first by a Turkish fisherman, who witnesses some of the events, and finally in the Giaour's confession to a monk.

Gibbie, GUSE, in Scott's 'Old Mortality' (q.v.), a half-witted lad, of very small stature, who kept Lady Margaret Bellenden's poultry.

GIBBON, EDWARD (1737–94), born at Putney-on-Thames, of a good family, was educated at Westminster and Magdalen College, Oxford, but derived little benefit from either. At the age of 16 he became a Roman Catholic, and was sent by his father to Lausanne, where he was reconverted to Protestantism and read widely. Here he became attached to Suzanne Curchod (afterwards Madame Necker), but in deference to his father broke off the engagement. He returned to England in 1758 and published his 'Essai sur l'étude de la littérature' in 1761, of which an English version appeared in 1764. From 1759 to 1763 he served in the Hampshire militia, and in 1764, during a tour in Italy, while 'musing amid the ruins of the Capitol', formed the plan of his 'History of the Decline and Fall of the Roman Empire' (q.v.). The death of his father, who had wasted his wealth, left him in some embarrassment, but enough remained from the wreck to enable him to settle in London in 1772 and proceed with his great work.

He entered parliament in 1774, voted steadily for Lord North, and was made a commissioner of trade and plantations; but his parliamentary career added nothing to his reputation, though he regarded it as 'a school of civil prudence'. In 1776 appeared the first volume of his 'History', which was very favourably received; but his chapters on the growth of Christianity provoked criticisms, of which the most weighty were those of Lord Hailes and Porson. To his theological critics Gibbon replied in 1779 in 'A Vindication of some Passages in the Fifteenth and Sixteenth Chapters'. The second and third volumes appeared in 1781, but were less warmly received. He retired to Lausanne in 1783, where he completed the work, of which the last three volumes were published in 1788. Gibbon returned to England and passed most of his remaining days under the roof of his friend the earl of Sheffield (John Baker Holroyd). He died in London, and was buried in the church of Fletching (Sussex). His 'Memoirs', put together by Lord Sheffield from various fragments by Gibbon, were published in 1796, together with his 'Miscellaneous Works' (1796–1815). An edition of the 'Decline and Fall' with preface and notes by H. H. Milman was published in 1838–9; another, with notes by Milman, Guizot, and William Smith, in 1854; and a standard edition, by J. B. Bury, in 1909–13.

Gibbons, GRINLING (1648–1721), woodcarver of great virtuosity and sculptor. Evelyn (q.v.) describes in his 'Diary' how he discovered him in 1671 at Deptford and introduced him to Wren (q.v.), who employed him to carve decorative woodwork, principally in his houses and in St. Paul's Cathedral and St. James's, Piccadilly. He modelled bronze statues of Charles II and James II.

Gibbons, ORLANDO (1583–1625), composer, especially of madrigals.

Gibraltar, from *gebel-el-Tarik*, the hill of Tarik, a Saracen commander who, after probably landing there, defeated Roderick, king of the Goths, in 711. It was known to the ancients as Calpe, or, with Abyla on the opposite coast, as the Pillars of Hercules. It was captured by the British under Sir George Rooke in 1704, besieged in 1705–6, assigned to England by the Treaty of Utrecht, again besieged in 1726, and gallantly defended against the French and Spaniards by General Eliott (Lord Heathfield), 1779–83.

Gibson, DR., MRS., and MOLLY, characters in Mrs. Gaskell's 'Wives and Daughters' (q.v.).

GIDE, ANDRÉ (1869–1951), French novelist, dramatist, and critic, author of, notably, 'Les Nourritures terrestres' (1897, verse and prose); a number of short novels which he termed *récits*, e.g. 'L'Immoralistes' (1902), 'La Porte étroite' (1909), 'La Symphonie pastorale' (1919), 'Thésée' (1946), &c.; two longer novels 'Les Caves du Vatican' (1914) and 'Les Faux-Monnayeurs' (1926); dramas, e.g. 'Saül' (written *c.* 1895), 'Œdipe' (produced 1932); collections of essays and criticism, e.g. 'Amyntas', 'Prétextes', and 'Nouveaux Prétextes'; an autobiography of his early years, 'Si le grain ne meurt' (1926) which describes his revolt against his Protestant upbringing; a self-revealing diary which covers more than fifty years from 1895 (1939–51), etc. In 1947 he was awarded the Nobel Prize for literature.

GIFFORD, WILLIAM (1756–1826), the son of a glazier at Ashburton and a shoemaker's apprentice (see under *Apelles and the Cobbler*), was sent by the help of William Cookesley, a surgeon, to Exeter College, Oxford. He published in 1794 and 1795 two satires, 'The Baviad' and 'The Maeviad', against the Della Cruscan (q.v.) school of poets and the contemporary drama. He became editor of 'The Anti-Jacobin' (q.v.) in

1797, and in 1809 first editor of the 'Quarterly Review' (q.v.). Gifford's rigorous adherence, as a literary critic, to the old school in literature and his hatred of radicals, coupled with constant ill health, gave bitterness to his judgements of the rising authors. He translated Juvenal (1802) and Persius (1821), and edited some of the older English dramatists. A short autobiography is prefixed to the translation of Juvenal.

Gifford Lectures, on natural theology without reference to creeds, founded in the universities of Edinburgh, Glasgow, Aberdeen, and St. Andrews by the bequest of £80,000 by Adam, Lord Gifford (1820–87), a Scottish Judge.

Gigadibs, MR., in R. Browning's 'Bishop Blougram's Apology' (q.v.), the bishop's interlocutor.

***Gil Blas of Santillane,** The Adventures of,* a picaresque romance by Le Sage (q.v.), published 1715–35.

Gil Blas, the son of humble parents, at 17 is sent off on a mule, with a few ducats in his pocket and little in the way of scruples or morality, to the University of Salamanca. He never reaches it, but falls in with robbers, by whom he is detained. This is the beginning of a long series of adventures, in the course of which he takes service with Dr. Sangrado (a quack physician) and becomes a physician himself, with the archbishop of Granada (who after inviting Gil Blas's criticism of his sermons, resents it when given), and with a variety of other persons. He finally becomes the secretary and confidant of Olivares, the prime minister of Spain, and attains prosperity, having acquired worldly wisdom, and even some tincture of benevolence and morality, from his experiences. The work gives an admirable and consolatory picture of life with its vicissitudes and recoveries. Pitt, we are told, regarded it as the best of all novels. It was translated into English (or the translation was revised) by Smollett (q.v.) in 1749.

'Gil Blas' is also the title of a comedy by E. Moore (q.v.).

Gil Morrice, the subject of an old Scottish ballad, included in Percy's 'Reliques'. He is the natural son of an earl and Lady Barnard. A message he sends to his mother leads Lord Barnard to think that he is his wife's lover, and to fall on him and slay him. The ballad is the same as that of 'Child Maurice' in the 'Oxford Book of Ballads', where 'Lord Barnard' is 'John Steward'.

GILBERT, SIR HUMPHREY (1539?–83), half-brother of Sir Walter Ralegh, made his first voyage of discovery with the latter in 1578. In 1583 he left Plymouth with five ships for Newfoundland, where he founded the first British colony in North America. On his return journey his ship the 'Squirrel' was lost in a storm off the Azores. Hakluyt (q.v.) gives a striking narrative of his end.

Gilbert was the author of a 'Discourse of a Discoverie for a new passage to Cataia', published in 1576, urging the search for the North-West Passage.

GILBERT, WILLIAM (1540–1603), physician to Queen Elizabeth and James I. He declared the earth to be a magnet in his 'De Magnete' (1600), the first great scientific book to be published in England.

GILBERT, Sir WILLIAM SCHWENCK (1836–1911), after service as an officer in the militia and as a clerk in the Education Department, began his literary career in 1861 as a regular contributor to 'Fun'. He excelled as a writer of humorous verse, and his 'Bab Ballads' (q.v.), originally contributed to 'Fun' and published in volume form in 1869–73, were very popular. His first dramatic work was 'Dulcamara' (1866), a successful burlesque. He wrote a blank-verse fairy comedy 'The Palace of Truth' (1870), 'Pygmalion and Galatea' (1871), and various serious dramas in verse. His very successful comedy 'The Happy Land' (1873) was written in collaboration with Gilbert Arthur à Beckett. He collaborated with Sir Arthur Sullivan for D'Oyly Carte's opera company in a long series of comic operas (see *Gilbert and Sullivan Operas*), with Alfred Cellier in 'The Mountebanks' (1892), and with Edward German in 'Fallen Fairies' (1909). 'The Hooligans', a serious sketch, appeared in 1911.

Gilbert and Sullivan Operas, comic operas, including much social and topical satire, written in collaboration by Sir W. S. Gilbert and Sir A. Sullivan (qq.v.) for Richard D'Oyly Carte (1844–1901). The operas are: 'Trial by Jury' (1875), 'The Sorcerer' (1877), 'H.M.S. Pinafore' (1878), 'The Pirates of Penzance' (produced in New York, 1879, and in London, 1880), 'Patience' (1881), 'Iolanthe' (1882), 'Princess Ida' (1884), 'The Mikado' (1885), 'Ruddigore' (1887), 'The Yeomen of the Guard' (1888), 'The Gondoliers' (1889), 'Utopia, Limited' (1893), and 'The Grand Duke' (1896). They are known as the 'Savoy Operas' because from 'Iolanthe' onwards they were produced at the Savoy Theatre.

Gilbert Markham, in Anne Brontë's 'Wildfell Hall' (q.v.), the narrator of the story, and one of the principal characters.

Gilbert of Sempringham, ST. (1083?–1189), the founder of the Gilbertine order (c. 1135), with headquarters at Sempringham in Lincolnshire, which included both monks and nuns, numbered thirteen houses, and did good educational work. He was held in great regard by Henry II and Queen Eleanor, lived to be over 100, and was canonized by Innocent III.

Gilbertian, a word derived from the name of Sir W. S. Gilbert (q.v.) to signify the kind of humorous absurdity and topsy-turvydom which distinguishes many of the characters and situations in the librettos of the Gilbert and Sullivan operas.

Gilbertines, see *Gilbert of Sempringham.*

GILCHRIST, ALEXANDER (1828–61), author of a 'Life of Etty' (1855) and of a 'Life of Blake'. The latter was finished by his widow, Anne Gilchrist (1828–85), and published in 1863. She also published a 'Life of Mary Lamb' (1883) and essays on Walt Whitman's poetry.

GILDAS, a British historian, who lived in the west of England and wrote in Latin shortly before 547 a sketch of the history of Britain, 'De Excidio et Conquestu Britanniae', followed by a castigation of the degraded princes and clergy of his day. In the historical portion he says nothing of Arthur, but refers to the victory of Mt. Badon (q.v.).

Gilderoy, a famous Scottish highwayman, whose real name was Patrick Macgregor (of the same clan as Rob Roy), who carried on depredations in Perthshire. He was hanged in 1636 at Edinburgh. He is the subject of one of the ballads in Percy's 'Reliques', and of a ballad by T. Campbell (a lament for Gilderoy by his wife).

Gildippe, in Tasso's 'Jerusalem Delivered' (q.v., ix. 71 and xx. 32), a female warrior in the Christian host.

Giles, BROTHER, of Assisi (*d. c.* 1261), convert and friend of St. Francis of Assisi (q.v.). An account of his life is given in 'Blessed Giles of Assisi', by W. W. Seton (1918), and (in verse) by James Rhoades (in 'Little Flowers of St. Francis and Brother Giles', 1925).

Giles (Aegidius), ST. (*fl.* 7th cent.), is said to have been of Athenian parentage and to have gone to France, where, from devotion to spiritual things, he established himself in the wilderness near the mouth of the Rhône, in a dense forest, with a hind for sole companion. After a time he received disciples, and built a monastery. He died early in the 8th cent. with a high repute for sanctity, and came to be regarded as the patron of cripples and lepers. His festival is celebrated on 1 Sept.

Giles' Bowl, ST.: at St. Giles' Hospital in Holborn, the prisoners on the way to execution at Tyburn were presented with a great bowl of ale, 'thereof to drink at their pleasure, as to be their last refreshing in this life' (Stow).

Giles's Fair, ST., at Oxford, is held on the Monday and Tuesday after the first Sunday after St. Giles's day (1 Sept.) in Saint Giles's Street. It is an institution of great antiquity, at one time a mart for the neighbouring Midlands, now degenerated into a mere pleasure fair. There was a St. Giles's Fair at Winchester, which was originally granted by William the Conqueror to the bishop of Winchester and endured until the 19th cent. During the fair, the jurisdiction of the corporation of Winchester was in abeyance and was replaced by that of officials appointed by the bishop, to whom the keys of the city were surrendered. [E.B.]

Gilfil, The Revd. Maynard, see *Scenes of Clerical Life.*

Gill, Eric (1882–1940), sculptor, engraver, and printer. He cut lettering and designed types, among them Perpetua and Gill Sans. In his sculpture and essays he proclaimed the religious basis of art and the validity of craftsmanship in the machine age. He published 'Sculpture: an essay on Stone-Cutting with a preface about God' (1918), 'Art and Love' (1927), 'Christianity and Art' (1928), 'Autobiography' (1940).

Gilles de Retz or Rais (1404–40), a marshal of France, who accompanied Joan of Arc to Orleans and fought by her side. Later in life he engaged in necromancy, kidnapped children and murdered them, was arrested on a charge of heresy and murder, confessed, and was absolved. He had only one wife, Catherine de Thouars, who left him. His name is connected with Blue Beard (q.v.) in the local traditions of Brittany, where he had large estates. Probably the French folklore tale concerning the latter has come to be attached to the name of Gilles de Retz as a perpetrator of atrocities.

Gillray, James (1757–1815), caricaturist. He used his mordant wit and political independence to show up the abuses and vices of parliament and the royal family, and his often vicious caricatures of Napoleon helped to rouse the patriotism of the country on the threat of invasion.

Gills, Solomon, a character in Dickens's 'Dombey and Son' (q.v.).

Gilpin, John, see *John Gilpin.*

GILPIN, WILLIAM (1724–1804), educated at Queen's College, Oxford, subsequently a schoolmaster and vicar of Boldre, is remembered for his series of illustrated picturesque tours ('The Wye and South Wales', 1782; 'The Lakes', 1789; 'Forest Scenery', 1791; 'The West of England and the Isle of Wight', 1798; 'The Highlands', 1800), which were parodied by William Combe (q.v.) in his 'Dr. Syntax'.

Giltspur Street, London, just outside the ancient Newgate, was, according to Stow, 'called Giltspur or Knightriders Street, of knights and others riding that way to Smithfield' (q.v.).

Gines de Passamonte, in 'Don Quixote' (I. xxii), a noted cheat and robber whom Don Quixote releases as he is being conveyed to the galleys.

Ginevra, (1) a character in the 'Orlando Furioso' (q.v.). Her story is that of Hero in Shakespeare's 'Much Ado about Nothing' (q.v.); (2) of the Orsini family, married to Francesco Doria, who on her wedding-day in playful mood hid herself in a trunk, of which

the lid closed with a spring lock. Fifty years later her skeleton was discovered there (Rogers, 'Italy'). Thomas Haynes Bayly treated the same subject in his ballad, 'The Mistletoe Bough'.

Ginn, see *Jinn.*

Ginnungagap, in Scandinavian mythology, the chasm or void between Niflheim and Muspellheim (qq.v.).

Gioconda, La, or La Joconde, names given to the famous portrait of Mona Lisa (q.v.) by Leonardo da Vinci.

Giorgione (*c.* 1477–1510), Venetian painter. Little is known of his short life; few paintings can be definitely attributed to him; and his evocative subjects are difficult to interpret. Nevertheless, the reputation he gained in his lifetime has never been questioned.

Giotto's O: Giotto (1266?–1337) was a Florentine painter mentioned by Dante and famous for having revived the art of painting. Vasari (q.v.) tells how when the Pope sent for an example of his work before commissioning him to paint in St. Peter's he drew a perfect circle with one turn of the hand.

Giovanna of Naples, see *Andrea of Hungary.*

Giovanni, Don, Italian for Don Juan (q.v.).

Gipsy, a corruption of 'Egyptian', a member of a wandering race, by themselves called Romany, of Hindu origin, which first appeared in England about the beginning of the 16th cent. and was then believed to have come from Egypt. Their language is a greatly corrupted dialect of Hindi, with a large admixture of words from various European languages. [OED.] A Gitano is a Spanish gipsy, a Tzigane a Hungarian gipsy.

Giralda, the great tower of the cathedral of Seville, so called from the weather-vane (Sp. *giralda*) in the form of a statue of Faith on its summit. See *Carrasco.*

GIRALDUS DE BARRI, called Cambrensis (1146?–1220?), a native of Pembrokeshire and son of Nesta, a Welsh princess. He studied at Paris before 1176 and again 1177–80. As a churchman he had a stormy career. He was archdeacon of Brecon, and twice (1176 and 1198) a nominee for the see of St. David's, but was rejected, as a Welshman, first by Henry II, then by Archbishop Hubert. He appealed to Rome, sought the support of the Welsh, was outlawed, fled abroad, and was imprisoned at Châtillon. He was finally reconciled to the king and archbishop, and was buried at St. David's. In 1184 he accompanied Prince John to Ireland. From 1196 to 1198 he led a student's life at Lincoln. His works (edited by J. S. Brewer and J. F. Dimock, 1861–77) include 'Topographia Hibernica', 'Expugnatio Hibernica', 'Itinerarium Cambriae', 'Gemma Ecclesiastica', 'De Rebus a se gestis', and lives of St.

Hugh of Lincoln, St. David, and others. The 'Topographia', which he read aloud to the assembled masters at Oxford in 1184 or 1185, is an account of the geography, fauna, marvels, and early history of Ireland; the 'Expugnatio', a narrative of the partial conquest of Ireland (1169–85); the 'Itinerarium' (the most important of his works), a description of the topography of Wales; the 'Gemma' a charge to the clergy of his district, affording interesting information as to the conditions then prevailing. See also *Glastonbury*.

GIRAUDOUX, JEAN (1882–1944), French novelist, essayist, and dramatist. His first novel 'Suzanne et le Pacifique' was published in 1921. In 1928 the novel 'Siegfried et le Limousin' (1922) was successfully adapted for the stage. Thereafter the drama became the most suitable medium for Giraudoux's gifts, among which irony, paradox, and poetic imagery are paramount. His plots are most frequently derived from biblical or classical legend. Between 'Siegfried' and 1939 his plays include 'Amphitryon 38', 'Judith', 'La Guerre de Troie n'aura pas lieu' (tr. 'Tiger at the Gates'), 'Electre'; also 'Intermezzo', a fantasy, and 'Ondine' (from the fairy tale by La Motte Fouqué). 'La Folle de Chaillot' (1945) is a satire of 20th-cent. society.

Girondists, the moderate republican party in the French Legislative Assembly of 1791–2 and the Convention of 1792–5, led mainly by deputies from the Gironde district.

Girton College, a college for women, which owes its existence mainly to the energy of Sarah Emily Davies (1830–1921), a pioneer in the cause of the higher education of women. The college was opened at Hitchin in 1869 and transferred to Cambridge in 1873.

Gisborne, MARIA (1770–1836), *née* James, a friend of Shelley (q.v.). She refused William Godwin, and married John Gisborne in 1800. Shelley's 'Letter to Maria Gisborne' was written in 1820.

Gismond of Salerne, see *Tancred and Gismund.*

GISSING, GEORGE ROBERT (1857–1903), was educated at Owens College, Manchester, but left it, owing to an unfortunate marriage in 1875, for London and subsequently for America, where he experienced the extreme poverty and misery reflected in many of his novels. After a short period at Jena, where he studied philosophy, he returned to London, and in 1880 published his first novel 'Workers in the Dawn', making a precarious livelihood by private tuition, and finding an appreciative employer in Mr. Frederic Harrison. He published 'The Unclassed' in 1884, 'Demos' in 1886, and other novels illustrating the degrading effects of poverty on character. 'A Life's Morning' appeared in 1888, 'The Nether World' in 1889, 'The Emancipated' in 1890, 'New Grub Street' (q.v.) in 1891, 'Born in Exile' in 1892, and 'The Odd Women' in 1893. A visit to

Italy led to the publication in 1901 of impressions and experiences under the title 'By the Ionian Sea', and the preparation during several years of the historical novel 'Veranilda' (of which Italy in the 6th cent. is the scene), which was published posthumously in 1904. On his return to England he wrote 'The Town Traveller' (1898), 'The Crown of Life' (1899), 'Our Friend the Charlatan' (1901), and 'Will Warburton' (1905). Of a different character was 'The Private Papers of Henry Ryecroft' (1903), the imaginary journal of a recluse, who enjoys release from poverty and worry, amid books, memories, and reflection; it represents Gissing's own aspirations. Mention should also be made of his critical study of Charles Dickens, an author by whom Gissing had been deeply influenced, published in 1898. 'Human Odds and Ends', a collection of short stories, appeared in the same year, and a second collection, 'The House of Cobwebs', posthumously in 1906.

Gitano, see *Gipsy.*

Giudecca or JUDECCA, (1) in Dante's 'Inferno' (canto xxxiv), the lowest ring in the ninth circle of Hell, so named after Judas Iscariot, who is confined there, together with Satan himself; (2) an island at Venice, at one time the Jewish quarter.

Gjallar, in Scandinavian mythology, the horn of Heimdal (q.v.), with which he gives warning of anyone approaching the bridge Bifröst (q.v.), and summons the gods to Ragnarök.

Gladsheim, in Scandinavian mythology, the abode of Odin (q.v.).

GLADSTONE, WILLIAM EWART (1809–98), the great Liberal statesman, is principally remembered in literary history for his 'Studies on Homer and the Homeric Age' (1858), a subject further dealt with in his 'Juventus Mundi' (1869) and 'Homeric Synchronism' (1876). 'Translations' by him and Lord Lyttelton appeared in 1863. His political writings include 'The State in its Relations with the Church' (1838), in which he defended the principle of a single state religion, a principle that he was later to abandon; 'Letters to the Earl of Aberdeen' on the Neapolitan Government (1851); 'The Vatican Decrees in their Bearing on Civil Allegiance' (1874); 'Vaticanism' (1875); 'Bulgarian Horrors and the Question of the East' (1876); and 'Lessons in Massacre' (1877). Gladstone's minor political writings and contributions to periodicals were republished as 'Gleanings of Past Years' (7 vols., 1879, with a supplementary volume, 1890). John Morley's 'Life of Gladstone' was published in 1903. There is an interesting description of Gladstone as a young man by Macaulay, in his review of 'The State . . .', in the 'Edinburgh Review', April 1839.

GLANVILL, JOSEPH (1636–80), educated at Exeter College and Lincoln College, Oxford, was rector of the Abbey Church at

Bath, and held other benefices. He attacked the scholastic philosophy in 'The Vanity of Dogmatizing' (1661), a work that contains the story of the 'Scholar-Gipsy' (q.v.). He defended the belief in the pre-existence of souls in 'Lux Orientalis' (1662), and the belief in witchcraft in 'Saducismus Triumphatus' (1681).

GLANVILLE, RANULF DE (*d.* 1190), chief justiciar of England. The authorship of the first great treatise on the laws of England, 'Tractatus de Legibus et Consuetudinibus Angliae', has been doubtfully ascribed to him on the evidence of Roger of Hoveden.

Glasgerion, an old English ballad of a king's son who is a harper and wins the favour of the king's daughter of Normandy. By a trick his page takes his place at an assignation. When the lady learns the deceit she takes her own life, and Glasgerion cuts off the lad's head and kills himself. The ballad is included in Percy's 'Reliques'.

GLASGOW, ELLEN (1874–1945), American novelist, born in Virginia. She took her native region as her subject and attempted to show realistically its social and political conflicts and development. She published the first of her many novels in 1897 but she did not mature until much later. Among her chief works are 'Barren Ground' (1925), 'The Romantic Comedians' (1926), 'Vein of Iron' (1935), and 'In This Our Life' (1941), which was awarded a Pulitzer Prize. She also wrote many short stories.

GLASSE, HANNAH (*fl.* 1747), author of 'The Art of Cookery made Plain and Easy' (1747), 'The Compleat Confectioner' (1770), and 'The Servant's Directory or 'Housekeeper's Companion' (1770). She was habitmaker to the Prince of Wales. The authorship of 'The Art of Cookery' has been erroneously attributed to Dr. John Hill.

Glastonbury, in Somerset, famous as the place where, according to legend, Joseph of Arimathea founded Glastonbury Abbey, and where, according to Giraldus Cambrensis (q.v.), the tomb of Arthur and Guinevere was discovered in the reign of Henry II. (A leaden cross, he states, was found in it, with an inscription relating to 'inclitus rex Arthurus cum Wenneveria uxore sua secunda'.)

The name Glastonbury, according to William of Malmesbury, is derived from one Glasteing, who, searching for his lost sow, came to an apple-tree by the old church, and, liking the spot, settled there with his family. William does not connect the place with Arthur. But Giraldus Cambrensis and Ralph of Coggeshall (*fl.* 1207) identify Glastonbury with Avalon, which they say meant the 'isle of apples'. (For a discussion of the whole question see Sir Edmund Chambers, 'Arthur of Britain'.)

Glatisant, in Malory's 'Morte Darthur' (q.v.), the name of the 'questing beast'.

Glaucé, in Spenser's 'Faerie Queene', III. ii. 30, etc., the nurse of Britomart.

Glaucus: (1) in Greek mythology, a god of the Sea, originally a Boeotian fisherman who became immortal through eating a marvellous herb. 'Glaucus, or the Wonders of the Shore' is the title of a natural history work by C. Kingsley (1855); (2) Glaucus of Potniae in Boeotia, another legendary figure, who was torn to pieces by his own mares; (3) son of Sisyphus and father of Bellerophon (qq.v.); (4) in Homer's 'Iliad', the grandson of Bellerophon, an ally of King Priam. He meets Diomedes in battle, who, on the plea that they are old guest-friends, exchanges his bronze armour with the golden armour of Glaucus, for 'Zeus son of Cronos took from Glaucus his wits'.

Glegg, MR. and MRS., characters in G. Eliot's 'The Mill on the Floss' (q.v.).

GLEIG, GEORGE ROBERT (1796–1888), educated at Glasgow and Balliol College, Oxford, became Chaplain General of the Forces. He served with the 85th in the Peninsula. He is remembered as the author of 'The Subaltern', written for 'Blackwood' in 1826.

Gleipnir, in Scandinavian mythology, the chain made by the Dwarfs to bind Fenrir (q.v.).

Glenallan, EARL OF, a character in Scott's 'The Antiquary' (q.v.).

Glenarvon, see *Lamb* (*Lady C.*).

Glencoe, in Argyllshire, memorable for the massacre of the inhabitants (Macdonalds) in 1692, under the orders of William III, obtained by Sir John Dalrymple, Master of Stair, their enemy. The massacre was carried out by Campbell of Glen Lyon and 120 soldiers, after these had lived for twelve days on friendly terms with the clansmen. The ground for this cruel and treacherous act was the failure of MacIan, chief of the clan, to take the oath of allegiance by the appointed day.

Scott wrote a poem on the subject, published in Thomson's 'Select Melodies' (1814), and Talfourd a play (1840), and there is an echo of it in Campbell's 'Pilgrim of Glencoe'. Aytoun's 'Widow of Glencoe' is also well known.

Glendinning, HALBERT and EDWARD, characters in Scott's 'The Monastery' and 'The Abbot' (qq.v.).

Glendoveer, one of a race of beautiful sprites in Southey's artificial quasi-Hindu mythology ('Curse of Kehama', VI. ii), a word avowedly altered from *Grandouver,* which occurs in Sonnerat, 'Voyage aux Indes' (1782).

Glendower, OWEN (1359?–1416?), the leader of the Welsh rebellion against Henry IV, who figures in Shakespeare's '1 Henry IV'.

Glenmire, LADY, a character in Mrs. Gaskell's 'Cranford' (q.v.).

Glennaquoich, the seat of Fergus Mac-Ivor, in Scott's 'Waverley' (q.v.).

Glenvarloch, LORD, the title borne by Nigel Olifaunt in Scott's 'Fortunes of Nigel' (q.v.).

Globe Theatre, THE, the Burbages' theatre on the Bankside in Southwark, erected in 1599 with materials from the old Theatre on the north side of the river. It was a large circular building, thatched, with the centre open to the sky. The thatch caught fire in 1613, owing to the discharge of a peal of ordnance at an entry of the king in the play of 'Henry VIII', and the whole building was destroyed. It was rebuilt in 1614. Shakespeare had a share in the theatre and acted there.

Gloria, a name for each of several formulae in Christian liturgical worship. (1) GLORIA PATRI, the doxology beginning 'Glory be to the Father'; (2) GLORIA TIBI, the response 'Glory be to thee, O Lord', following the announcement of the Gospel; (3) GLORIA IN EXCELSIS, the hymn 'Glory be to God on high' in the communion service or mass. [OED.]

Gloriana, one of the names under which Queen Elizabeth is indicated in Spenser's 'Faerie Queene'.

Glorious First of June, THE, see *First of June.*

Glorious John, a familiar designation of Dryden (q.v.).

Glossin, GILBERT, a character in Scott's 'Guy Mannering'.

Gloucester, EARL OF, a character in Shakespeare's 'King Lear' (q.v.).

Gloucester, ROBERT, EARL OF, see *Robert Earl of Gloucester.*

GLOVER, RICHARD (1712–85), was M.P. for Weymouth, 1761–8, and an opponent of Walpole. He published much blank verse: 'Leonidas' (1737), in nine books, and 'The Athenaid' in thirty, and produced two plays, 'Boadicea' and 'Medea', in 1753 and 1763 respectively. But he is remembered only as the author of 'Hosier's Ghost', a ballad included in Percy's 'Reliques'. This was a party song, contrasting the fate of Admiral Hosier (sent in 1726 with a fleet to the Spanish West Indies but obliged to remain inactive there till most of his men perished and he himself died of a broken heart) with the successful attack of Admiral Vernon in 1739 on Porto Bello.

Glover, SIMON and CATHARINE, two of the principal characters in Scott's 'Fair Maid of Perth' (q.v.).

Glowry, CHRISTOPHER and SCYTHROP, characters in Peacock's 'Nightmare Abbey' (q.v.).

Glozel, a hamlet near Vichy, in the centre of France, where in 1924 the son of a local farmer, by name Fradin, discovered the remains of an old glass-furnace, and in 1925–6, in association with Dr. Morlet of Vichy, a number of antique tablets inscribed with alphabetical signs, and other objects connecting the tablets with neolithic culture. These discoveries, if genuine, involved a reconsideration of current theories regarding neolithic civilization. But their genuineness was contested and an acrimonious controversy arose on the subject. The French government, in 1927, appointed an international commission to investigate the matter, which reported that the antiquity of the objects discovered at Glozel had not been established.

Glubbdubdrib, in 'Gulliver's Travels' (q.v.), the island of sorcerers, where Homer and Aristotle, Descartes and Gassendi, and many kings and generals are called up at Gulliver's request, and he learns the untrustworthy character of history.

Gluck, CHRISTOPH WILLIBALD (1714–87), a famous operatic composer born in Bavaria, was the son of a gamekeeper. He spent ten years (1754–64) in Vienna as director of the court opera, subsequently went to Paris, and finally retired to Vienna. He visited London in 1745. His first great opera was 'Orfeo' (1762), which was followed by 'Alceste' (1766), 'Iphigénie en Aulide' (1774), 'Armide' (1777), and 'Iphigénie en Tauride' (1779). A celebrated contention arose in Paris in 1776 between his followers and those of Piccini (q.v.), in substance a dispute as to the relative merits of the German and Italian schools of music.

Glumdalclitch, in 'Gulliver's Travels' (q.v.), the farmer's daughter who attended on Gulliver during his visit to Brobdingnag.

Glums, see *Peter Wilkins.*

GLYN, ELINOR (Mrs. Clayton Glyn, 1864–1943), authoress, born in Toronto, Canada. Among her novels were: 'The Visits of Elizabeth' (1900), 'Three Weeks' (1907), 'The Career of Katherine Bush' (1916), 'Six Days' (1924), 'Man and Maid' (1925).

Gnome, from modern Latin *gnomus,* used by Paracelsus, though perhaps not invented by him, to signify beings that have earth for their element, through which they move as fishes through the water. The word as generally used means one of a race of diminutive spirits fabled to inhabit the earth and to be guardians of its treasures.

Gnomic, from Gr. γνώμη, consisting of gnomes or general maxims, sententious.

Gnosticism, from Gr. γνῶσις knowledge, a religious movement of oriental origin which penetrated early Christianity, giving rise to a great variety of sects, prominent in the 2nd cent. A.D., who claimed special knowledge, in particular how the divine element in man, the soul, became detached from the divine world, and how it may be reunited to its proper sphere. They held the material world to be the work, not of the supreme Deity, but of an inferior Demiurge, antagonistic to what was truly spiritual. They divided men into two main classes, 'spiritual' (πνευματικοί) and 'material' (ὑλικοί). Many Gnostic ideas appear in the writings of William Blake (q.v.). It was allied to Manichaeism (q.v.).

Gobbo, LAUNCELOT, the clown in Shakespeare's 'The Merchant of Venice' (q.v.), servant to Shylock; OLD GOBBO is his father.

Gobelin Tapestry, the tapestry made at the 'Gobelins', the State factory of tapestry in Paris, named after Jean Gobelin (d. 1476), head of a family of dyers who settled in Paris about 1450 and made a great reputation by the discovery of a scarlet dye. In the 17th cent. the works were purchased for Louis XIV, and since then (with a short break during the Revolution) have been run as a State concern for the manufacture of upholstery, furniture, and carpets.

Goblin, from French *gobelin*, an obsolete word of uncertain derivation, means a mischievous and ugly demon.

Goblin Market, a poem by C. Rossetti (q.v.), published in 1862.

The poem is a fairy tale, in which some see an allegory. Laura yields to the allurements of the fruits offered for sale by the goblins (worldly pleasures), pines for more of them, which the goblins refuse, falls sick, and nearly dies. Her sister Lizzy, for Laura's sake, braves their temptations and redeems her sister.

God and Mammon, The Triumph of Mammon, the first two parts of a blank verse trilogy (the third was never written) by Davidson (q.v.), published in 1907.

The eldest son of Christian, king of Thule, called Mammon, and expelled from the kingdom because of his atheism and blasphemy, returns, kills the king and his younger brother, appropriates the latter's bride, and triumphantly ascends the throne. The poem is an expression of materialistic idealism.

God from the machine, see *Deus ex machina*.

Godīva, the wife of Leofric, earl of Mercia, one of Edward the Confessor's great earls. According to legend, her husband having imposed a tax on the inhabitants of Coventry, she importuned him to remit it, which he jestingly promised to do if she would ride naked through the streets at noonday. She took him at his word, directed the people to keep within doors and shut their windows, and complied with his condition. Peeping Tom, who looked out, was struck blind.

The story is told by Drayton in his 'Polyolbion' (q.v.), xiii; by Leigh Hunt; and by Tennyson in his 'Godiva'. Lady Godiva figures, as the mother of Hereward, in C. Kingsley's 'Hereward the Wake' (q.v.), and in one of Landor's 'Imaginary Conversations' (q.v.).

GODLEY, ALFRED DENIS (1856–1925), classical scholar and writer of light verse, public orator at the University of Oxford, 1910–25. He edited Tacitus's Histories (1887, 1890), translated the Odes of Horace (1898) and Herodotus (Loeb Series 1921–3), and was joint editor of the 'Classical Review', 1910–20. His verse, much of which deals with University life, appears in 'Verses to Order' (1892), 'Lyra Frivola' (1899), 'Second Strings' (1902), 'The Casual Ward' (1912), 'Echoes from the Oxford Magazine' (1896), 'Reliquiae A. D. Godley' (1926).

Godmer, in Spenser's 'Faerie Queene', II. x. 11, a British giant, son of Albion, slain by Canutus.

Godolphin, a novel by Bulwer Lytton (q.v.).

GODWIN, MRS. MARY WOLLSTONECRAFT (1759–97), née Wollstonecraft, kept a school at Newington Green with her sister Eliza, and subsequently became governess to Lord Kingsborough's children. After this she was employed for five years by Johnson, a London publisher. In Paris she formed a connexion with Gilbert Imlay (1793–5), an American, by whom she had a daughter, Fanny; his infidelity drove her to attempted suicide. She married William Godwin in 1797, and died at the birth of her daughter Mary, the future Mrs. Shelley. Her 'Vindication of the Rights of Woman' (1792) was a courageous attack on the conventions of the day.

GODWIN, WILLIAM (1756–1836), educated at Hoxton Academy, was at first a dissenting minister, but became an atheist and a philosopher of anarchical views. He believed that men acted according to reason, that it was impossible to be rationally persuaded and not act accordingly, that reason taught benevolence, and that therefore rational creatures could live in harmony without laws and institutions. He married Mary Wollstonecraft (see *Godwin, Mrs. M. W.*) in 1797, who died at the birth of her daughter, the future wife of Shelley. Godwin subsequently married Mrs. Clairmont, whose daughter by her first marriage, Claire Clairmont (q.v.), bore a daughter, Allegra, to Lord Byron (q.v.).

Godwin published in 1793 his 'Enquiry concerning Political Justice', in which he exposed his philosophical and political views, in 1794 the 'Adventures of Caleb Williams' (q.v.), and in 1799 'St. Leon', novels designed to propagate these views. This last contains a portrait of Mary Wollstonecraft, of whom he also wrote a remarkable life ('Memoirs of the author of a Vindication of the Rights of Woman', 1798). Godwin produced a 'Life' of Chaucer in 1803.

Goëmot, the name under which Gogmagog (q.v.) figures in Spenser's 'Faerie Queene' (II. x. 10).

Goës, BENEDICT, see *Cathay*.

GOETHE, JOHANN WOLFGANG VON (1749–1832), born at Frankfort-on-the-Main, the son of an Imperial Councillor, was trained for the law against his inclination. In 1775 he was invited by the duke of Weimar to his court, and thereafter spent the greater part of his life in Weimar, occupying positions in the government of increasing importance until 1786. In 1791 he was appointed director of the ducal theatre, a post which he retained for twenty-two years. Throughout his life he devoted much time to the study of painting, for which he had only a mediocre gift. Apart from this, he divided his energies mainly between scientific research and literature. In the former sphere he evolved a new theory of the character of light, which he expounded and defended at length in the 'Farbenlehre' (1810). He also made important discoveries in connexion with plant and animal life.

In the sphere of literature, apart from his great dramatic poem 'Faust' (q.v.), his principal works were (i) 'Goetz von Berlichingen' (1771), a drama dealing with the story of a predatory knight of the German Empire in the 16th cent. The play was translated by Sir Walter Scott in 1799; (ii) 'The Sorrows of Young Werther' (first published 1774), a romance in epistolary form, based on two incidents in the author's life. Werther falls in love with Charlotte, who is betrothed to Albert, and gives himself up to a few weeks' happiness, while Albert is absent. Then he tears himself away. Albert and Charlotte are married, and despair gradually comes over Werther, who finally takes his own life; (iii) 'Egmont', a play dealing with the revolt of the Netherlands against the power of Spain; (iv) 'Iphigenie auf Tauris' (1787), a drama based on the play of Euripides, but differing from it in essential respects, notably in its more humane conception of man; (v) 'Hermann und Dorothea' (1797), a poem founded on the expulsion of the Protestants by the archbishop of Salzburg in 1732, but with the scene shifted to France under the Revolution. It was translated by Thomas Holcroft and others; (vi) 'Die Wahlverwandtschaften' (1808), a romance dealing with the 'elective affinities' of a married couple for two other persons; (vii) 'Der West-östliche Divan' (1819), a collection of poems, many of which are philosophical in character, modelled on the 'Divan' of the Persian poet Hafiz; (viii) 'Dichtung und Wahrheit' ('Poetry and Truth'), completed in 1831, an autobiography in which those experiences are selected which had most influenced the author's development; (ix) 'Wilhelm Meister', written at intervals between 1777 and 1829, the prototype of the German *Bildungsroman*, the first part of which tells the story of a stage-struck youth, who travels about the country with a theatrical company; among its members are Mignon and the Harper, whose songs, particularly 'Kennst du das Land', are well known. To the 'Lehrjahre' Goethe added in the last years of his life the 'Wanderjahre', in which Wilhelm Meister's 'education' is completed. (Part of this was translated by Carlyle.) As a lyric poet Goethe was of unequalled importance in German literature.

Goethe and Schiller came together in 1794, and were much associated until the latter's death in 1805. From 1823 to the end of his life Goethe was attended by Johann Eckermann, whose faithful record of Goethe's conversations has been translated into English. In 1806 he married Christiane Vulpius, who had been his mistress since 1789, and who bore him four children.

Goetz von Berlichingen, see *Goethe.*

Gog and **Magog.** In Gen. x. 2, Magog is a son of Japhet. In Ezek. xxxviii and xxxix, Gog is the chief prince of Meshech and Tubal, who shall come from his 'place out of the north parts'; and the land of Magog is also referred to as his territory. In Rev. xx. 7–9, Gog and Magog represent the nations of the earth that are deceived by Satan.

In the cycle of legends relating to Alexander the Great, Gog and Magog were allies of the Indian king Porus, in his resistance to that conqueror. They were shut off by the great wall built by Alexander in the Caucasus. They were presumably Scythian tribes. (There is a reference to this in c. xviii of the Koran. Sale in his notes thereto says that *Yajuj and Majuj* are the Arabian names of two barbarous tribes descended from Japhet against whom Dhu'lkarnain or Alexander built a rampart.) See also under *Gogmagog.*

Gogh, VINCENT VAN (1853–90), painter, the son of a Dutch pastor, who worked in France from 1886. The emotional quality of his work provided the starting-point for Expressionism (q.v.). Some of his revealing letters have been translated ('The Letters of Vincent van Gogh to His Brother', 1927).

Gogmagog and **Corineus:** Gogmagog (called Goëmagot by Geoffrey of Monmouth and Spenser, 'Faerie Queene', III. ix. 50) was the chief of the giants of Albion whom Brute (q.v.) destroyed. Corineus was one of Brute's companions. He wrestled with Gogmagog and threw him into the sea, and Cornwall was assigned to him as a reward. The statues called Gog and Magog in the Guildhall in London are said to represent Gogmagog and Corineus. The original statues were destroyed in the Great Fire, and were replaced by new ones in 1709. See also under *Gog and Magog.*

Gogmagog Hill, a hill three miles SE. of Cambridge. It is referred to in C. Kingsley's 'Hereward the Wake' (q.v.).

GOGOL, NIKOLAI VASILEVICH (1809–52), Russian writer, born in the Ukraine. He used his homeland, its folklore and language as material for his first major work 'Evenings on a farm near Dikanka' (1831–2). Two collections of stories followed: 'Mirgorod' and 'Arabesques' (1835). Other well-known tales are 'The Nose' (1835) and 'The Greatcoat' (1842). Gogol also wrote several plays, the best known being 'The Inspector-General' (1836). His masterpiece is the novel 'Dead Souls' (first part, 1842), which is noteworthy for a series of brilliant caricatures. It was never finished and Gogol destroyed most of the second part under the influence of the growing morbid religiosity which led to his death. Gogol's writing was a mixture of humour, fantasy, and the horrific, which owed something to Hoffmann and in turn influenced Dostoevsky.

A number of Gogol's works were translated from 1867 ('The Portrait') in 'Blackwood's Edinburgh Magazine') onwards. The most complete translation is by C. Garnett, 'The Works of Nikolay Gogol' (1922–8).

Goidels, according to legend, the first Celtic invaders of Ireland. The name is used to signify the Scoto-Irish or Gaelic branch of the Celtic race, as distinguished from the Brythonic branch, the Britons of Wales, Cornwall, and Brittany.

Golagros and Gawain, an alliterative poem in Middle English, of 105 stanzas of thirteen lines, contained in a pamphlet printed in Scotland in 1508. It deals with incidents on a pilgrimage of Arthur and his knights to the Holy Land. Golagros is lord of a castle on the Rhône, and is defeated in single combat by Gawain.

Golconda, the old name of Hyderabad, formerly celebrated for its diamonds, a synonym for a mine of wealth.

Gold of Tolosa, see *Tolosa*.

Golden Age, THE, the first and best age of the world, in which, according to the Greek and Roman poets, man lived in a state of ideal prosperity and happiness. It was thought to have occurred under the reign of Saturn (q.v.) on earth.

Golden Ass, The, a satire by Apuleius of Madaura in Africa (q.v.). It takes the form of the supposed autobiography of the author, who is transformed into an ass by the mistake of the servant of an enchantress. He passes from master to master, observing the vices and follies of men, and finally recovers human form by the intervention of the goddess Isis. The story includes a number of episodes, of which the best known is the beautiful allegory of 'Cupid and Psyche' (q.v.). The work is imitated from the Λούκιος ἢ ὄνος attributed to Lucian, or from an original common to both. It was translated into English in the 16th cent. by W. Adlington.

Golden Bough, The, a comparative study of the beliefs and institutions of mankind, by Sir J. G. Frazer (q.v.), in 12 vols. published in 1890–1915. His own abridged one-volume edition was published in 1922. 'Aftermath: a supplement' followed in 1936.

This work began with a treatise on the ancient rule of the priesthood or sacred king-

ship of the grove of Nemi or Aricia near Rome, by which a candidate for the priesthood could obtain the office only by slaying the priest, and held it until he was himself slain. The grove was devoted to the worship of Diana Nemorensis. In it grew, according to legend, a tree of which no bough might be broken, save by a runaway slave. If he succeeded, he might fight the priest, and if he slew him, take over his office. The 'Golden Bough' which Aeneas broke off at the bidding of the Sybil before venturing to the nether world (Virgil, 'Aeneid', vi. 136) was believed to be a branch of this tree. The explanation by Frazer of the priest of Aricia as an embodiment of the tree-spirit, slain in his character of incarnate deity, led to the discussion of a vast number of other primitive customs and superstitions, contained in the successive volumes of this monumental work.

Golden Bowl, The, a novel by H. James (q.v.), published in 1904.

Golden Bull, THE, see *Bull*.

Golden Fleece, THE, the name of an order of chivalry instituted by Philip the Good, duke of Burgundy, in 1429. For the Golden Fleece of Greek mythology see under *Argonauts*.

Golden Grove, The, see *Taylor (Jeremy)*.

Golden Hind, The, originally named 'The Pelican', a ship of 100 tons in which Drake circumnavigated the globe.

Golden Horde, a Mongol tribe who possessed the khanate of Kiptchak, and extended their dominion over eastern Russia, and western and central Asia, from the 13th cent. till 1480, when they were overthrown by Ivan III of Russia.

Golden Horn, THE, the harbour of Constantinople, a curved arm of the Bosphorus. The name dates from remote antiquity. The epithet 'golden' 'was expressive of the riches which every wind wafted from the most distant countries into the secure and capacious port' (Gibbon).

Golden Legend, The, a medieval manual of ecclesiastical lore: lives of saints, commentary on the church service, homilies for saints' days, etc. A version of this compilation from various sources was published by Caxton (q.v.) and was his most popular production. One of its sources was the 'Legenda Aurea' of Jacobus a Voragine (Jacopo de' Varazze, 1230–98), archbishop of Genoa.

Golden Legend, The, a poem by Longfellow (q.v.), published in 1852.

Prince Henry of Hoheneck suffers from a leprosy, from which he can be cured only if a maiden will give her life as the price. Elsie, a farmer's daughter, decides to make the sacrifice, and Prince Henry under the advice of Lucifer decides reluctantly to accept it. At the door of the convent of Salerno, where her life is to be surrendered, Henry, struck with remorse, at the last moment saves her, and is himself cured by the relics of St. Matthew. The story is taken from 'Der arme Heinrich' of Hartmann von der Auë, a German minnesinger of the 12th cent.

Golden Treasury of Songs and Lyrics, The, see *Palgrave* (*F. T.*).

Golding, ARTHUR (1536?–1605?), translator of Latin and French works, including Ovid's 'Metamorphoses' (1565–7), Caesar's 'Gallic War' (1565), and Justin's abbreviation of Trogus Pompeius (1570). His translations are clear, faithful, and fluent, and his Ovid was known to Shakespeare.

GOLDONI, CARLO (1707–93), Italian writer of stage comedies, most of whose working life was spent in his native Venice, the social background of which gave him the material of his plays. His significance in the history of Italian literature lies in the new impetus he gave to stage comedy, which, for the generation preceding his own, had been largely the monopoly of the 'Commedia dell'Arte', that loosely conceived form of semi-spontaneous playing which, starting with the fresh impulses and inspirations of its popular origins, had become by the middle of the 18th cent. a worn and decadent form. In 1762 Goldoni settled in Paris, where, after writing two successful plays in French—'L'éventail' ('The Fan') and 'Le Bourru bienfaisant' ('The Beneficent Grumbler')—he died a pauper. The majority of his plays fall into three categories: comedies retaining the masked characters of the 'Commedia dell'Arte', who speak in their traditional dialects, e.g. 'La vedova scaltra' ('The Clever Widow'); Italian comedies of character and manners without the masks, e.g. 'La locandiera' ('The Mistress of the Inn'), 'La bottega di caffè' ('The Coffee-Shop'); and comedies in Venetian dialect, generally considered his best, e.g. 'I rusteghi' ('The Tyrants'), 'La casa nova' ('The New House').

GOLDSMITH, OLIVER (1730?–74), the second son of an Irish clergyman, was born probably at Pallasmore in the county of Longford, or perhaps at Elphin, Roscommon. He entered Trinity College, Dublin, as a sizar in 1744, and ran away to Cork in consequence of 'personal chastisement' from his tutor. He returned, however, and graduated B.A. in 1749. In 1751 he presented himself for ordination but was rejected. He then studied medicine at Edinburgh and at Leyden, and during 1755–6 wandered about France, Switzerland, and Italy, obtaining it is said a medical degree at some foreign university. He reached London in destitution in 1756, and supported himself with difficulty as a physician in Southwark, an usher at Peckham, and a hack-writer on Griffiths's 'Monthly Review'. He failed in 1758 to qualify for a medical appointment in India, and in the same year published, under the pseudonym 'James Willington', his notable translation of 'The

Memoirs of a Protestant, condemned to the Galleys of France for his Religion' (Jean Marteilhe of Bergerac, a victim of the revocation of the Edict of Nantes). He published in 1759 his 'Enquiry into the present State of Polite Learning' (q.v.), and about this time became acquainted with Thomas Percy, afterwards bishop of Dromore. He published during Oct. and Nov. 1759 his little periodical 'The Bee', including the 'Elegy on Mrs. Mary Blaize', 'A City Night-Piece', and 'The Fame Machine'. He contributed to various magazines, writing 'A Reverie in the Boar's Head Tavern' and the 'Adventures of a Strolling Player' for Smollett's 'British Magazine'; he was also employed by John Newbery, the publisher, in whose 'Public Ledger' Goldsmith's 'Chinese Letters' appeared, subsequently republished as 'The Citizen of the World' (q.v.), in 1762.

He made the acquaintance of Samuel Johnson (q.v.) in 1761, and was one of the original members of 'The Club'. The manuscript of his 'Vicar of Wakefield' (q.v.) was sold, probably in 1762, by Johnson for Goldsmith for £60, and the proceeds saved him from arrest for debt. His poem 'The Traveller' (q.v.) appeared in 1764 and was welcomed by the public. It introduced him to his only patron, Lord Clare. In the same year appeared his 'History of England in a Series of Letters'. Goldsmith tried once more in 1765 to set up as a physician, with no success. The 'Vicar of Wakefield', the publication of which had been delayed for unexplained reasons, appeared in 1766. About this time he removed from Islington, where he had been living, to the Temple, first to Garden Court, then to Brick Court. He wrote as hack-work for bricksellers a life of Voltaire (1761), a good memoir of Beau Nash (1762), a 'History of Rome' (1769), lives of Parnell and Bolingbroke (1770), and an English history (1771). His first comedy 'The Good-natur'd Man' (q.v.) was rejected by Garrick, but produced at Covent Garden in 1768. It was a moderate success and brought him £500. His second comedy, 'She Stoops to Conquer' (q.v.), was played at Covent Garden in 1773 with immense success; in this year he adapted as a farce Sedley's adaptation 'The Grumbler'. In 1770 appeared 'The Deserted Village' (q.v.), and in 1771 took place his altercation with Evans, publisher of the 'London Packet', in which was published the letter of 'Tom Tickle' abusing Goldsmith and impertinently alluding to his friend Miss Horneck. Goldsmith's 'Retaliation' (q.v.), his 'History of Greece', and 'Animated Nature' (with 'tygers' in Canada) were his last works (published in 1774). The pleasant light verses entitled 'The Haunch of Venison' appeared posthumously in 1776. Goldsmith was buried in the Temple Church, a monument at the expense of 'The Club' being erected to him in Westminster Abbey. His Latin epitaph (by Johnson) states that he adorned whatever he touched. Boswell's 'Life of Johnson' contains many anecdotes about Goldsmith, which represent him as a ridiculous, blundering, envious and vain creature, but tender-hearted, simple, and generous, with flashes of brilliancy now and then in his conversation. Johnson, who was quite awake to his absurdities, had a high respect for his worth and literary abilities.

The first collected edition (1801) of Goldsmith's works contains the life by Bishop Percy, for which Goldsmith had supplied materials. The best edition is that of J. W. M. Gibbs (1885–6). The best Lives are Forster's (1848) and Prior's (1837). There is a critical edition of Goldsmith's Letters by K. C. Balderston (1928).

Golgotha, the hill of the Crucifixion near Jerusalem, from an Aramaic word meaning 'skull'; it is used to signify a place of interment, and in 18th-cent. university slang, a place where heads of colleges and halls assemble.

Golias or GOLIARDUS, the name found attached in English MSS. of the 12th and 13th cents. to Latin poems of a satirical and profane kind, the most famous of these being the so-called 'Apocalypse of Golias', for which no certain evidence of authorship can be claimed. According to F. J. E. Raby ('A History of Secular Latin Poetry in the Middle Ages'), the conception of Golias as 'Bishop' or 'Arch-poet' (q.v.) is a myth, largely of English creation. The 'Goliards' are, it seems, to be linked with Golias, Goliath of Gath, the symbol of lawlessness and of evil, though the original derivation may have been from 'gula', on account of their gluttony. The famous 'Goliardic' measure or 'Vaganten-strophe' appears to have passed from secular into religious verse.

Goliath, the Philistine giant slain by David, 1 Sam. xvii.

Gomez, DON RUY, see *Hernani*.

GONCOURT, EDMOND and JULES DE (1822–96 and 1830–70), French authors, brothers, who wrote in close collaboration. Their earliest interests were art criticism ('L'Art du dix-huitième siècle', still much read) and French social history. From 1851 they wrote novels, of a closely documented type which evolved into the naturalism of Zola. 'Germinie Lacerteux' (1864), 'Madame Gervaisais' (1869), 'La Fille Éliza' and 'Les Frères Zemganno' (1877 and 1879, by Edmond de Goncourt alone) are examples. Their 'écriture artiste', an impressionistic, highly mannered style, elaborate in syntax and vocabulary, is well exemplified in 'Manette Salomon' (1867), a novel of artist life.

The famous Goncourt Diary, first published in its entirety between 1936 and 1940, is an almost day-to-day record of literary life in Paris. The Académie Goncourt, founded under the will of Edmond de Goncourt, is a body of ten men or women of letters which awards an annual money prize (*Prix Goncourt*) for imaginative prose.

Gondibert, a romantic epic by D'Avenant (q.v.), published in 1651.

This work, which was never finished, consists of some 1,700 quatrains. It is a tale of chivalry, of which the scene is Lombardy and the court of King Aribert. Duke Gondibert loves Birtha, and is therefore impervious to the love of Rhodalind, the king's daughter, who in turn is loved by Prince Oswald. Oswald attempts to destroy Gondibert. But before any issue is reached, the author frankly declares himself bored with his poem.

Gondomar, DON DIEGO SARMIENTO DE ACUÑA, MARQUIS DE, the Spanish Ambassador in the reign of James I. He was the enemy of Sir Walter Ralegh, and caused Middleton to be imprisoned for his play, 'A Game at Chesse' (q.v.).

Gondwanaland, the name given by the geologist Eduard Suess (q.v.) to a supposed ancient continent uniting India, Australia, and Africa. It was so called from the Gondwana geological beds in India. Gondwana is the historical name of a region in India roughly corresponding to the Central Provinces, the home of the Gonds, an aboriginal tribe still inhabiting it. Cf. *Lemuria*.

Goneril and **Regan,** in Shakespeare's 'King Lear' (q.v.), the elder daughters of the king.

Gongorism, an affected type of diction and style introduced into Spanish literature in the 16th cent. by the poet Don Luis de Góngora y Argote (1561–1627), a style akin to Euphuism (q.v.) in England and Marinism (see *Marino*) in Italy. But Góngora was none the less a poet of genius, and both his earlier and his latest verses were simple and unaffected.

Goodfellow, ROBIN, see *Robin Goodfellow*.

Good-natur'd Man, The, a comedy by Goldsmith (q.v.), produced in 1768.

Mr. Honeywood is an open-hearted but foolishly good-natured and credulous young man, who gives away to the importunate what he owes to his creditors. His uncle, Sir William Honeywood, decides to teach him a lesson by having him arrested for debt and letting him see who are his true friends. Young Honeywood is in love with Miss Richland, a lady of fortune, and she with him, but he is too diffident to propose to her. He even recommends to her the suit of Lofty, a government official to whom he believes himself indebted for release from arrest. In fact it is Miss Richland who has secured his release, and the impostor Lofty is amusingly exposed. Honeywood, being cured of his folly by this experience, is by his uncle's intervention united to Miss Richland. The plot is complicated by a subordinate love-affair. Leontine, the son of Croaker, Miss Richland's doleful guardian, is destined by his father to marry Miss Richland. But

Leontine, having been sent to Lyons to fetch his sister, who has been educated there for the last ten years, brings back instead Olivia, a young lady with whom he has fallen in love, and who personates the sister. Leontine, to prevent suspicion, proposes to Miss Richland, expecting to be refused. But she, knowing the truth about Olivia, mischievously accepts him. Whereupon Leontine and Olivia attempt to elope. The attempt is defeated by Sir William, who, however, obtains old Croaker's consent to the match.

Good Thoughts in Bad Times, a collection of reflections by Fuller (q.v.), published in 1645 at Exeter, where Fuller was living as chaplain to Sir Ralph Hopton. It was followed in 1647 by 'Good Thoughts in Worse Times', and in 1660, at the Restoration, by 'Mixt Contemplations in Better Times'. The work consists of meditations on his own shortcomings, observations on passages of scripture, and applications of historical incidents and anecdotes to current events, many of them whimsical and humorous, and most of them pithy and wise.

Goody Two-Shoes, a nursery tale, said to have been written by Goldsmith (q.v.), published by Newbery (q.v.).

GOOGE, BARNABE (1504–94), a member of both universities, was a kinsman of Sir William Cecil, who employed him in Ireland, 1574–85. He published 'Eglogs, Epytaphes, and Sonnetes', 1563 (reprinted, 1871), and translations, including Heresbachius's 'Foure Bookes of Husbandrie', 1577. His eclogues are of interest as being, with those of Barclay (q.v.), the earliest examples of pastorals in English.

Goose, MOTHER, see *Mother Goose's Tales.*

Gorboduc, or *Ferrex and Porrex,* one of the earliest of English tragedies, of which the first three acts are by Thomas Norton (1532–84) and the last two by T. Sackville (q.v.). It was acted in the Inner Temple Hall in 1561. The play is constructed on the model of a Senecan tragedy, and the subject is taken from the legendary chronicles of Britain. Gorboduc and Videna are king and queen, Ferrex and Porrex are their two sons, and the dukes of Cornwall, Albany, Logres, and Cumberland are the other chief characters. Ferrex and Porrex quarrel over the division of the kingdom. Ferrex is killed by Porrex, and Porrex is murdered in revenge by his mother. The duke of Albany tries to seize the kingdom and civil war breaks out. There is no action on the stage, the events being narrated in blank verse.

The legend of Gorboduc is told by Geoffrey of Monmouth, and figures in Spenser's 'Faerie Queene' (II. x. 34 and 35), where Gorboduc is called Gorbogud.

Gordius, the father of Midas (q.v.), a Phrygian peasant who became king, in consequence of an oracle which told the Phrygians, in a time of sedition, that their troubles would cease if they appointed king the first man they met approaching the temple of Jupiter in a wagon. Gordius was the man thus chosen. He dedicated his wagon to Jupiter. The knot with which the yoke was fastened to the pole was so artful that the legend arose that whoever could untie it would gain the empire of Asia. Alexander the Great cut the *Gordian knot* with his sword and applied the legend to himself.

GORDON, ADAM LINDSAY (1833–70), Australian poet, born in the Azores and educated in England. He went to Australia in 1853, where he joined the mounted police. He spent most of his life in Australia among horses, and this is reflected in much of his poetry, for instance in his well-known pieces, 'The Sick Stockrider', 'How we beat the Favourite', 'The Ride from the Wreck', and 'Wolf and Hound'. Much of his best work is collected in 'Sea Spray and Smoke Drift' (1867), 'Bush Ballads and Galloping Rhymes' (1870). Gordon committed suicide.

Gordon, CHARLES GEORGE (1833–85), 'Chinese Gordon', an officer of the Royal Engineers, who commanded the Chinese forces against the Taiping rebels in 1863–4 and put down the rebellion. He was governor of the Egyptian equatorial provinces of Africa, 1874–6, and governor-general of the Sudan, 1877–80, where he put down the slave trade. He was sent by the British government in 1884 to rescue the Egyptian garrisons in the Sudan previous to abandonment, was hemmed in at Khartoum, and there killed, after having sustained a siege of 317 days; he was the only Englishman there after the murder of his companions, Colonel Stewart and Frank Power. His Chinese diaries, Khartoum journals, and several volumes of his letters have been published. See his biography in 'Eminent Victorians' by Lytton Strachey (q.v.).

Gordon Riots, THE, in 1780, led by Lord George Gordon, were intended to compel parliament to repeal the Act of 1778 for the relief of Roman Catholics. They resulted in much tumult and the burning of a number of houses in London; also in the establishment of a regular police force. They figure in Dickens's 'Barnaby Rudge' (q.v.).

GORE, CHARLES (1853–1932), educated at Harrow and Balliol College, Oxford, bishop of Oxford from 1911 to 1919, was editor of, and contributor to, 'Lux Mundi' (q.v.), and published a number of works on religious subjects: 'Epistle to the Ephesians' (1898), 'Epistle to the Romans' (1899), 'Epistle of St. John' (1920), 'The Old Theology and the New Religion' (1908), 'The Religion of the Church' (1916), etc.

GORE, MRS. CATHERINE GRACE FRANCES (1799–1861), *née* Moody, published about seventy works between 1824 and 1862, including the novels 'Mrs. Armytage' (1836) and 'Mothers and Daughters' (1831), which are her best; 'Cecil, or the Adventures of a Coxcomb' (1841); and 'The Banker's Wife' (1843). Of her plays, 'The School for Coquettes' was acted in 1831, and 'Lords and Commons' and 'Quid pro Quo' in 1844. Her novels were parodied by Thackeray in 'Lords and Liveries', one of the 'Novels by Eminent Hands'.

Gorges, Sir Arthur, see *Alcyon*.

Gorgius Midas, Sir, see *Midas (Sir G.).*

Gorgons, The, three sisters, daughters of Phorcys and Ceto, whose names were Stheno, Euryălē, and Medusa. Of these the first two were immortal; Medusa (q.v.) was mortal and is the most celebrated. According to the mythologists, their hair was entwined with serpents, their hands were of brass, their body covered with impenetrable scales, their teeth like a wild boar's tusks, and they turned to stones all on whom they fixed their eyes.

Gorham Case, The, an ecclesiastical lawsuit in 1848 arising out of the refusal of the bishop of Exeter (Henry Phillpotts) to institute the Revd. Cornelius Gorham into the living of Brampton-Speke, on the ground of his alleged unorthodoxy in the matter of infant baptism. The Judicial Committee of the Privy Council decided in favour of Mr. Gorham.

GORKY, MAXIM (ALEXEI MAXIMO-VICH PESHKOV) (1868–1936), Russian novelist. Obliged to work for his living from the age of 8, Gorky roamed all over Russia. He was self-educated and read voraciously. He suffered for his radical views and after taking part in the 1905 Revolution he went abroad to collect funds for the revolutionary movement. After the 1917 Revolution his independent views, his emotional attitude to revolution, and increasing ill-health led, in 1921, to his leaving Russia for Italy. In 1928 he returned to the Soviet Union as an enthusiastic supporter of the government. He was partly responsible for the formulation of the doctrine of Socialist Realism and in 1934 he became President of the Union of Soviet Writers. His first story was 'Makar Chudra' (1892), but it was 'Chelkash' (1895) which established his reputation. His best known works are 'Twenty-six Men and a Girl' (1899), 'Foma Gordeer' (1899), 'The Mother' (1907) (all on the theme of the underprivileged), and his autobiographical masterpiece 'Childhood' (1913–14), 'In the World' (1915–16), 'My Universities' (1923). Then came 'The Artomanovs' Business' (1925) and the unfinished cycle of novels, 'The Life of Klim Samgin' (first part, 1927). Gorky also wrote plays, of which the most famous is 'At the Bottom' (1902; translated by L. Irving in 1910 as 'The Lower Depths'). 'The Orloff Couple and Malva', translated by E. Jakowleff and D. Montefiore, appeared in 1901. Since then there have been many translations covering most of Gorky's works.

Gorlois, in the Arthurian legend, duke of Cornwall and husband of Igraine (q.v.).

GOSSE, Sir EDMUND (1849–1928), the son of Philip H. Gosse, an eminent zoologist and a Plymouth Brother, his relations with whom are described in his 'Father and Son' (first published anonymously in 1907). Gosse was privately educated and entered the British Museum as assistant librarian in 1867. In 1875 he became translator to the board of trade, a post which he held until 1904, when he became librarian to the House of Lords till 1914. He devoted much attention to the northern languages, and published 'Ethical Conditions of Early Scandinavian Peoples' in 1875, and 'Northern Studies' (essays on Danish, Swedish, Norwegian, and Dutch poets) in 1879. He wrote an admirable life of Ibsen in 1908, and in 1911 published a description of 'Two Visits to Denmark', paid many years before. Gosse was Clark lecturer at Trinity College, Cambridge, from 1884 to 1890, and his inaugural course 'From Shakespeare to Pope' (1885) gave rise to some controversy between him and Churton Collins. He published the 'Life and Letters of John Donne' in 1899, lives of Gray (1882), Jeremy Taylor (1904), and Sir Thomas Browne (1905) for the English Men of Letters series; also lives of Congreve (1888) and Swinburne (1917). His collected poems appeared in 1911 and his 'Life and Letters', by the Hon. E. Charteris, in 1931. Gosse had known almost all his literary contemporaries, and was a specially close friend of Swinburne in earlier years, of Stevenson, and of Henry James (qq.v.).

GOSSON, STEPHEN (1554–1624), was educated at Corpus Christi College, Oxford. His plays are not now extant but were ranked by Meres among 'the best for pastorall'. He was converted by Puritan censures and attacked poets and players in his 'Schoole of Abuse' (1579), defended it in 'Ephemerides of Phialo' (1579), and replied to Lodge and 'The Play of Playes' in 'Playes confuted in Fiue Actions' (1582). He evoked, by his unauthorized dedication of his 'Schoole of Abuse' to Sir Philip Sidney, Sidney's 'Apologie for Poetrie' (published 1595). He was rector of Great Wigborough, 1591, and St. Botolph's, Bishopsgate, 1600.

Gotha, Almanach de, a genealogical, diplomatic, and statistical annual, covering all the states of the world, published in French by Justus Perthes of Gotha since 1763.

Gotham, and **Gothamite,** names frequently applied to New York City and its inhabitants.

Gotham, Wise Men of. For some reason, which is not clearly established, a reputation for folly was from very early times attributed to the inhabitants of Gotham, a village in Nottinghamshire. There is reference to such a tradition in the Towneley 'Mysteries' (q.v.). The tradition once established, it seems probable that many new stories of folly were fathered on the village. These were collected in the 'Merrie Tales of the Mad Men of Gotam by A. B.' (perhaps Andrew Borde, physician, *c.* 1490–1549), of which a 1630 edition is extant. A reprint of a copy (prob. 1565) was published in 1965, ed. S. J Kahrl.

The origin of the tradition is perhaps to be found in certain customary law tenures belonging to the place or neighbourhood (Laird's 'Nottinghamshire'). According to Stapleton ('The Merry Tales of Gotham') the explanation most widely accepted is that recorded by Throsby in his 'History of Nottinghamshire' (1797): 'King John, passing through this place towards Nottingham, intending to go over the meadows I have just described, was prevented by the villagers, they apprehending that the ground over which a king passed was for ever after to become a public road. The king, incensed at their proceedings, sent from his court some of his servants to inquire of them the reason for their incivility, that he might punish them. . . . The villagers, hearing of the approach of the king's servants, thought of an expedient to turn away his majesty's displeasure. When the messengers arrived at Gotham, they found some of the inhabitants engaged in endeavouring to drown an eel in a pool of water . . . and some in hedging in a cuckoo which had perched upon an old bush. In short they were all employed in some foolish way or other, which convinced the king's servants that it was a village of fools.'

Gothic, a style of architecture prevalent in Western Europe from the 12th to the 16th cents., and the art of the same period. Its chief characteristics are the pointed arch, the rib-vault supported by buttresses, traceried windows, and clustered pillars. The name, originally a term of abuse, appears to have been taken in the first instance from the French, and employed to denote any style of building that was not classical. The phases of English Gothic are EARLY ENGLISH (*c.* 1150–1250), DECORATED (*c.* 1250–1350; subdivided into GEOMETRIC and CURVILINEAR), and PERPENDICULAR (*c.* 1350–1540). The later French Gothic is called FLAMBOYANT.

GOTHIC or BLACK-LETTER TYPE is that most commonly used for printing German. It is descended from the script used in the later Middle Ages.

Gothic novels, a class of novel dealing with the frightening and supernatural, and chiefly associated with Horace Walpole's 'Castle of Otranto' (q.v., 1764), and the works of Ann Radcliffe, M. G. Lewis, and C. R. Maturin (qq.v.). Walpole, like some later writers, called his novel 'A Gothic [that is, medieval] Story' (on the title-page of the second edition, 1765). The popularity of such works, due in part to their supernatural element, led to the identification of 'Gothic' with 'supernatural', and many works with only a very slight 'medieval' element or none at all thus came to be called 'Gothic'. The Gothic novel specializes in ruins, haunted castles, frightening landscapes, magic. Some of its

elements of atmosphere or characterization have been traced to other and earlier genres, such as Jacobean tragedy and 18th-cent. graveyard poetry. There are Gothic elements, too, in Smollett's novel, 'Ferdinand Count Fathom' (q.v., 1753). The Gothic novel and its readers are satirized in Jane Austen's 'Northanger Abbey' (q.v., 1818). 19th-cent. exponents of the Gothic novel (in one form or another) include Mary Shelley, Poe, and Sheridan Le Fanu (qq.v.); and much of the horror-fiction of our own time may be seen to belong to the tradition.

Gothic Revival, the name given to architecture based on the Gothic style. It applies particularly to English architecture from *c.* 1840 when a scholarly study of Gothic was made, it being considered the only proper style for churches. Earlier exercises in Gothic, e.g. Horace Walpole's house, Strawberry Hill, were usually romantic in aim and used Gothic motifs to adorn buildings of contemporary plan.

Goths, THE, a Germanic tribe, who, in the 3rd, 4th, and 5th cents., invaded both the Eastern and the Western Empires. The Ostrogoths were the Eastern division of the tribe, which founded a kingdom in Italy; the Visigoths were the western division, which founded a kingdom in Spain. The word 'Goth' is applied in a transferred sense to one who behaves like a barbarian, especially in the destruction or neglect of works of art.

Götterdämmerung, 'Twilight of the Gods', the last of Wagner's operas in the series of the 'Ring der Nibelungen' (q.v.). It follows the 'Siegfried' (q.v.).

Siegfried leaves Brynhilde, having given her the Nibelung ring, and comes to the Hall of the Gibichungs. Owing to a magic potion, he forgets Brynhilde and falls in love with Gutrune. In order to obtain her he undertakes to win Brynhilde for Gunther, Gutrune's brother. This he does, taking Gunther's shape with the help of the tarn-helm, and takes from Brynhilde the ring. Later she sees it on his finger, then she comes, as Gunther's bride, to the Gibichung hall, and thus discovers the trick that has been played upon her. She bitterly upbraids Siegfried, and with Hagen and Gunther plots Siegfried's death. Siegfried is treacherously slain by Hagen, who hopes to get the ring. But Brynhilde places it on her finger before she throws herself on Siegfried's pyre. The Rhine rises, envelops the pyre, and the Rhine-maidens recover the ring.

Götz von Berlichingen, see *Goethe.*

GOULD, NATHANIEL (1857–1919), known as Nat Gould, journalist and novelist. His first book, 'The Double Event', published when he was working as a journalist in Australia, achieved immediate success; he subsequently wrote about 130 novels, all concerned with horse-racing. He also wrote two books on Australian life, 'On and Off the

Turf' (1895) and 'Town and Bush' (1896), as well as 'The Magic of Sport: Mainly Autobiographical' (1909).

Gounod, CHARLES FRANÇOIS (1818–93), French musical composer. He wrote a number of operas, of which the best known are 'Faust' (1859) and 'Roméo et Juliette' (1867), church music, and many shorter pieces.

Governour, The, a treatise on politics and education by Elyot (q.v.).

Gow, HENRY, or Henry Smith, a character in Scott's 'The Fair Maid of Perth' (q.v.).

GOWER, JOHN (1330?–1408), of a Kentish family and a man of some wealth, probably lived mostly in London and was well known at court in his later years. He became blind in 1400, died at the priory of St. Mary Overies, Southwark, and was buried in the church (now St. Saviour's), where he is commemorated by a fine tomb and effigy. He was a friend of Chaucer, who called him 'moral Gower'. Of his chief works the 'Speculum Meditantis' (q.v.) or 'Mirour de l'Omme' is written in French, the 'Vox Clamantis' (q.v., c. 1382?) in Latin, and the 'Confessio Amantis' (q.v., 1390) in English. His later works include a series of ballades in French ('Cinkante Ballades'), an English poem 'In Praise of Peace', and a Latin poem in leonine hexameters, 'Cronica Tripertita', relating the events of the last years of Richard II's reign, including his deposition.

Gower, a character in Shakespeare's 'Henry V' (q.v.).

Goya y Lucientes, FRANCISCO (1746–1828), Spanish painter. His position as Court painter did not prevent him from portraying his patrons with cynical realism. He painted the duke of Wellington during the Peninsular War. The series of etchings, 'Los Caprichos' and 'Los Desastres de la Guerra' are bitter comments on the evils of society and war.

Graal, HOLY, see *Grail.*

Grace, LADY, a character in Vanbrugh's and Cibber's 'The Provok'd Husband' (q.v.).

Grace Abounding to the Chief of Sinners, or the brief Relation of the exceeding Mercy of God in Christ to his poor Servant John Bunyan, a homiletic narrative by Bunyan (q.v.), published in 1666.

The author relates his spiritual history, his mean birth, wicked childhood and youth, his escapes from death by various accidents and the perils of military service, and his gradual awakening to religion as a result of reading two works of devotion owned by his wife. He tells how he went to Bedford and there entered a small religious community, and recounts his spiritual experiences, temptations, and final call to the ministry. The book is written with intense fervour and sincerity.

Gracechurch, London, originally Grass Church. 'Then higher in Grasse Streete is

the parish church of Saint Bennet called Grasse Church, of the Herbe market there kept' (Stow).

Graces, THE, called CHĂRĬTĚS by the Greeks, daughters of Zeus; Euphrosyne, Aglaia, and Thalia by name. They were goddesses of beauty and grace, who distributed joy and gentleness.

Gracioso, the buffoon of Spanish comedy.

Gradasso, in the 'Orlando Innamorato' (q.v.), the king of Sericane, who invades Spain, overcomes its king Marsilio, and presses Charlemagne back to Paris. His object is to secure Bayard and Durindana (qq.v.), which he succeeds in doing, but not by his prowess. He is killed with Agramant by Orlando, in the great fight at Lipadusa.

Gradgrind, MR., LOUISA, and TOM, leading characters in Dickens's 'Hard Times' (q.v.).

Graeme or AVENEL, ROLAND, the hero of Scott's 'The Abbot' (q.v.).

Graevius, JOHANN GEORG (GREFFE) (1632–1703), Dutch scholar and antiquary, professor at Utrecht, the foremost Latinist of his day, a friend of Bentley.

Graham of Claverhouse, JOHN (1649?–89), *first Viscount Dundee,* a Royalist officer employed by the Scottish Privy Council in executing the severities of the government in Scotland during the reigns of Charles II and James II. In 1688, when James 'forsook his own cause', Dundee's life was in danger even in Scotland, and he determined to raise the Highlands for James (after the manner of his collateral, Montrose, in 1644) and was killed at the battle of Killiecrankie. He figures prominently in Scott's 'Old Mortality' (q.v.).

GRAHAME, KENNETH (1859–1932), author of 'The Golden Age' (1895), studies of childhood in an English countryside setting, which proved extremely popular. 'Dream Days', a sequel, followed in 1898. Grahame also wrote 'The Wind in the Willows' (1908), a book for children which many of their elders have also enjoyed.

Graiae or PHORCIDS, THE, the three daughters of the sea-god Phorcys, and sisters of the Gorgons (q.v.). They had one tooth and one eye between them.

Grail, THE HOLY. The word 'Grail' in medieval legend signified the vessel used by our Saviour at the Last Supper, in which Joseph of Arimathea received the Saviour's blood at the Cross. Its etymology is commonly referred to a popular Latin form *cratalis* from L. *cratus* altered from L. *crater* a cup. [OED.]

The Grail cycle, as a whole, embodies two distinct legends: (1) that of the quest by Perceval for certain talismans; this is probably the more ancient legend and, in its original form, of a pagan and mythological character (see John Rhys, 'Studies in the Arthurian Legend'). (2) The early history of the Holy Grail (see Alfred Nutt, 'The Legends of the Holy Grail'). See also under *Boron*.

In the earliest English poems dealing with the latter subject ('Joseph of Arimathea' of the 14th cent. and the 'History of the Holy Grail' by Henry Lovelich of the 15th cent.) based on the French prose 'Grand Saint Graal', Joseph of Arimathea goes to Sarras, carrying the dish containing Christ's blood. He tells the story of Christ to Evalak, king of Sarras. Joseph aids him to defeat Tholomer, king of Babylon, by means of prayer to Christ, before a shield marked with a red cross. Evalak and his brother-in-law are baptized by the names of Mordziens and Naciens (who figures in later narratives). Joseph goes on a missionary journey, leaving the Grail in the care of two guardians, and is imprisoned in North Wales. (For another version of the legend see *Titurel*.)

This narrative is in part reproduced and continued in Malory's 'Morte Darthur'. Launcelot is brought to the castle of King Pelles, and by enchantment has intercourse with the king's daughter Elaine, supposing her to be Guinevere. Their son (Galahad) is brought by an old man at Pentecost to the knights seated at the Round Table, and set in the vacant 'Siege Perilous' (see *Round Table*). The knights know him as destined to achieve the adventure of the Grail. In a burst of thunder and light the Holy Grail enters the hall, but none may see it. The knights, led by Gawain, vow to undertake its quest. The hermit Naciens warns them that none can achieve it who is not clean of his sins. Galahad obtains in an abbey a white shield with a red cross, which Joseph of Arimathea had given to King Evalak. Then follow numerous adventures by various knights in the course of their quest. Launcelot has several glimpses of the Grail, but on each occasion is warned to withdraw because of his sins, so that he repents (but only temporarily). Gawain wearies of the quest and gives it up. Finally Galahad, Percival, and Bors, all qualified by their purity for the adventure, come to the castle of Carbonek, see a marvellous vision of the Saviour and partake of his body, receive the Grail from his hands, and convey it to Sarras. Galahad prays that when he shall ask for death he may receive it, and the request is granted him. Galahad becomes king of Sarras, and after a year dies. The Grail is borne up to heaven and never seen again.

For Tennyson's idyll on this subject, see *Holy Grail*.

Grainne, in the legends relating to the Irish hero Finn, the daughter of King Cormac. Finn, though a great warrior and hunter, was unfortunate in love. He sought to marry Grainne, but she fell in love with Finn's nephew Diarmait O'Duibhne and eloped with him. The long story of their flight and Finn's unsuccessful pursuit ends in Finn's temporary acceptance of the situation; but Finn finally caused the death of Diarmait.

Grammar of Assent, The, a philosophical and religious treatise by Newman (q.v.), published in 1870.

The author examines in this work, on lines somewhat similar to those of Coleridge's 'Aids to Reflection' (q.v.), the nature of belief. Assent or belief, he holds, is an act of apprehension, subjective in character, incapable of logical proof, though rational. Logic deals with what is 'notional' or abstract, assent with what is real and concrete. The real universe is not logical, and the premisses of logic are not realities but assumptions. We reach certainties, not through logic, but by intuitive perception (the 'illative' sense), from 'the cumulation of probabilities', 'probabilities too fine to avail separately, too subtle and circuitous to be convertible into syllogisms'. It is the 'living mind' of the individual that determines the process. 'It follows that what to one intellect is a proof is not so to another, and that the certainty of a proposition does properly consist in the certitude of the mind that contemplates it.'

Grammont, see *Gramont*.

Gramont, Mémoires de la Vie du Comte de, an anonymous work published at Cologne in 1713, written by Anthony Hamilton (1646?–1720), third son of Sir George Hamilton and grandson of the earl of Abercorn. Anthony Hamilton was the brother-in-law of the Comte de Gramont, who married Elizabeth Hamilton in 1663. The memoirs were edited (in French) by Horace Walpole and translated into English (with many errors) by Boyer (q.v.) in 1714; and this translation, revised and annotated by Sir W. Scott, was reissued in 1811. A new translation was made in 1930 by Peter Quennell, with an introduction and commentary by C. H. Hartmann.

The first part of the memoirs, dealing with Gramont's life on the Continent down to the time of his banishment from the French court, was probably dictated by Gramont to Hamilton. The second part, relating to the English court, appears to be Hamilton's own work. It is an important source of information, but its trustworthiness on details is doubtful.

Granby, JOHN MANNERS, *Marquis of* (1721–70), commanded the Blues at the battle of Minden (1759), where his advance was stayed by orders of Lord George Sackville. He was afterwards commander-in-chief.

Granby, THE MARQUIS OF, in Dickens's 'Pickwick Papers' (q.v.), the inn at Dorking kept by the second Mrs. Tony Weller.

GRAND, SARAH (pseudonym of Mrs. David C. M'Fall, *née* Frances Elizabeth Clarke) (1862–1943), novelist, best known for her novel 'The Heavenly Twins' (1893). She was six times mayor of Bath.

Grand Cyrus, Le, see *Scudéry*.

Grand Monarque, LE, Louis XIV.

Grand Old Man, see *G.O.M.*

Grand Question Debated, The, a poem by Swift (q.v.), published in 1729.

The question is whether a building belonging to Sir A. Acheson, known as Hamilton's Bawn, shall be turned into a barracks or a malthouse. Sir Arthur urges the profit to be derived from the malthouse, his wife the advantage of military society. Hannah, her maid, emphasizes this in a spirited picture of the arrival of the garrison, with drums and trumpets and the gold-laced captain. The poem is largely a satire on the military ignoramus.

Grand Remonstrance, an indictment drawn up by the House of Commons in the autumn of 1641 of the unconstitutional and unwise acts of Charles I from the beginning of his reign, and a demand for ministers responsible to parliament and for the settlement of Church matters by an assembly of divines selected by parliament.

Grand Siècle, LE, the age of Louis XIV of France, whose reign extended from 1643 to 1715, and was signalized by military conquests (many of which, however, had to be abandoned, and left his kingdom exhausted) and by literary and artistic splendour.

Grandgousier, the father of Gargantua (q.v.).

Grandison, CARDINAL, a character in Disraeli's 'Lothair' (q.v.).

Grandison, SIR CHARLES, see *Sir Charles Grandison*.

Granger, EDITH, in Dickens's 'Dombey and Son' (q.v.), the daughter of the Hon. Mrs. Skewton, and Dombey's second wife.

Grangerize, To, to illustrate a book by the addition of prints, engravings, etc., especially such as have been cut out of other books. In 1769 James Granger (1723–76) published a 'Biographical History of England', with blank pages for the reception of engraved portraits or other pictorial illustrations of the text. The filling up of the 'Granger' became a favourite hobby, and afterwards other books were treated in the same manner. [OED.]

Grania, see *Grainne*.

GRANT, JAMES (1822–87), served for three years in the 62nd Regiment. Of his numerous novels the best are 'The Romance of War' (1845) and 'Adventures of an Aide-de-Camp' (1848). His other works include memoirs of Kirkcaldy of Grange, Sir J. Hepburn, and Montrose; 'British Battles on Land and Sea' (1873, with continuation, 1884); and 'Old and New Edinburgh' (1880).

GRANT DUFF, JAMES, see *Duff*.

Granta, THE, the old name of the river Cam, which it retains above Cambridge.

Granta, The, a Cambridge University undergraduate periodical started in 1889 by Murray Guthrie to replace the 'Gadfly', which came to an end owing to an article of a personal character. The name 'Granta' was appropriated by Guthrie from Oscar Browning, who intended it for a paper that he was about to edit. Guthrie, the first editor, was succeeded by R. C. Lehmann, and the last editor before the First World War was John Norman of Emmanuel College, who was killed at the Dardanelles in 1915. Among distinguished contributors to the 'Granta' have been J. K. Stephen, Owen Seaman, Barry Pain, and 'F. Anstey' (Thomas Anstey Guthrie).

Grantly, ARCHDEACON, a prominent character in A. Trollope's 'The Warden' (q.v.), 'Barchester Towers' (q.v.), and other novels of the Barsetshire series. Mrs. Grantly is the elder daughter of Mr. Harding (the Warden); and Griselda, their beautiful but frigid and astute daughter, marries Lord Dumbello.

Grantorto, in Spenser's 'Faerie Queene', v. xii, the tyrant from whom Sir Artegall rescues Irena (Ireland). He probably represents the spirit of rebellion.

GRANVILLE-BARKER, HARLEY GRANVILLE (1877–1946), actor and dramatist, author of 'The Marrying of Ann Leete' (1901), 'The Voysey Inheritance' (1905), 'Waste' (1907), 'The Madras House' (1910), 'The Secret Life' (1923), and a number of other plays and publications, including four interesting series of Prefaces to plays of Shakespeare (1927, 1930, 1937, 1945). As a theatrical producer Granville-Barker was especially known for his remarkable productions of Shakespeare's 'The Winter's Tale', 'A Midsummer Night's Dream', and 'Twelfth Night', at the Savoy Theatre in 1912–14.

Gratiano, a character in Shakespeare's 'The Merchant of Venice' (q.v.).

Graustark, a romantic novel of 'love behind the throne' in the imaginary kingdom of Graustark, by George Barr M'Cutcheon, published in 1901. The novel enjoyed such popularity that a sequel was demanded, and provided in 'Beverly of Graustark' (1904).

Grave Poem, a fragment of 24 lines in Old English, probably of the 12th cent., describing in gloomy and poignant terms the fate of the body committed to the grave, and beginning:

For thee was a house built ere thou wast born.

The translation by Longfellow is widely known.

For another poem on 'The Grave' see *Blair*.

Graveairs, LADY, a character in Cibber's 'The Careless Husband' (q.v.).

GRAVES, ALFRED PERCEVAL (1846–1931), born in Dublin, an inspector of schools, 1875–1910, published many volumes of Irish songs and ballads, and an autobiography, 'To Return to All That' (1930). He composed the popular 'Father O'Flynn', written in 1875, first published in the 'Spectator'.

GRAVES, RICHARD (1715–1804), educated at Pembroke College, Oxford, and a fellow of All Souls, was for many years rector of Claverton near Bath. At Pembroke he was contemporary with Whitefield, whom he satirizes in 'The Spiritual Quixote'; and became intimate with Shenstone, whom he depicts in the same work and in 'Columella', and of whom he published a 'Recollection' in 1788. His principal novels appeared as follows: 'The Spiritual Quixote' (q.v., 1772); 'Columella, the Distressed Anchoret' (1776); 'Eugenius or Anecdotes of the Golden Vale' (1785); 'Plexippus or the Aspiring Plebeian' (1790); interesting less for their plots than for the picture they give of the social conditions of the time.

GRAVES, ROBERT RANKE (1895–), poet and novelist, son of A. P. Graves (q.v.). His first poetry appeared while he was serving in the First World War—'Over the Brazier' (1916), 'Fairies and Fusiliers' (1917) —and he has continued to publish poetry over the years, steadily increasing his reputation. As a prose writer he has always shown energy and versatility, and is probably best known for the historical novels, 'I, Claudius' (1934), 'Claudius the God' (1934), and 'Count Belisarius' (1938). 'Good-bye to All That' (1929) is an autobiography as well as a reflection of the post-war disillusionment of his generation. His critical work includes 'A Survey of Modernist Poetry' (with Laura Riding, 1927) and 'The Common Asphodel' (1949), collected essays on poetry, 1922–49. 'The White Goddess: a historical grammar of poetic myth' (1948; amended and enlarged, 1952 and 1961) is considered his most important work of poetical theory. He was professor of poetry at Oxford from 1961 to 1966.

Graveyard School, the imitators of Robert Blair and Edward Young (qq.v.).

Gray, GIDEON, the surgeon in Scott's 'The Surgeon's Daughter' (q.v.). His daughter is JANET.

GRAY, THOMAS (1716–71), was born in London, and educated at Eton with Horace Walpole, and at Peterhouse, Cambridge. He accompanied Horace Walpole on a tour on the Continent in 1739–41, but they quarrelled in 1741 and returned home separately. Their friendship was renewed in 1744. Gray then resided at Cambridge, removing from Peterhouse to Pembroke College in 1756 in consequence of a practical joke by undergraduates. He refused the laureateship in 1757, and was appointed professor of history and modern languages at Cambridge in 1768. He was buried at Stoke Poges in Bucks., a village with which the 'Elegy in a Country Churchyard' was perhaps identified. Here some of his relations lived and his mother was buried.

His work as an English poet began in 1742, when he wrote his odes 'On Spring', 'On a Distant Prospect of Eton College', and 'On Adversity', and the 'Sonnet on the Death of West' (his friend Richard West, to whose

memory he also indited some fine lines in his Latin poem 'De Principiis Cogitandi'). About the same year he began the 'Elegy in a Country Churchyard' (q.v.), which was finished in 1750. The 'Ode on the Death of a favourite Cat' (Walpole's) was written about 1747. In 1754 Gray finished his Pindaric ode on 'The Progress of Poesy' (q.v.) and in 1757 a second Pindaric ode 'The Bard' (q.v.). These were published by Walpole in 1757. The popularity of his 'Elegy' led to the general recognition of Gray as the foremost poet of the day and to the offer of the laureateship on the death of Colley Cibber. In his later years he devoted attention to Icelandic and Celtic verse and in imitation of this wrote the lays 'The Fatal Sisters' and 'The Descent of Odin' (1761). Gray's poems were republished in 1768 by Dodsley and by Foulis. In 1769 he wrote his fine ode on the installation of the duke of Grafton as chancellor of the University of Cambridge and took a journey among the English Lakes, which is commemorated in the 'Journal' published in 1775, his most finished prose work. His letters (3 vols., ed. P. Toynbee and L. Whibley, 1935) are among the best in the language; they reveal his character and humorous spirit.

Gray's Inn, Holborn, one of the old inns of court. The manor on which it stands was granted to Reginald de Grey, Justiciar of Chester, 1294, who let part of it as a *hospitium* for law students (G. R. Stirling Taylor). In its hall Shakespeare's 'Comedy of Errors' was acted in Dec. 1594. Laud, Francis Bacon, and Southey were students there, and Tonson (qq.v.) lived there.

Great Captain, THE, see *Cordova*.

Great Cham, see *Cham*.

Great Commoner, THE, a name sometimes given to William Pitt the elder (q.v.).

Great Duke of Florence, The, a romantic comedy by Massinger (q.v.), acted in 1627 and printed in 1636; one of Massinger's best plays.

Giovanni, nephew of the widowed duke of Florence, has for three years been entrusted to a tutor, Charomonte, at whose house he has fallen in love with Charomonte's daughter, Lidia, when he is recalled to his uncle's court. The messenger who goes to fetch him brings to the duke so fervent an account of Lidia's beauty, that the duke sends his favourite, Sanazarro, to report upon her, with the idea of making her his second wife. Sanazarro is himself so struck with Lidia's beauty that for his own ends he conceals it from the duke, and persuades Giovanni also to dispraise her. Perplexed by these contradictory reports, the duke goes to Charomonte's house to see for himself. Giovanni sends warning to Lidia, and an attempt is made to keep up the deception, Lidia's maid impersonating her before the duke. But Charomonte has not been made a party to the scheme and unwittingly reveals it. However, in the end, the duke remembers his vow never to remarry, and Giovanni and Lidia obtain their pardon.

Great Eastern, The, a steamship, the largest of its day, designed by I. K. Brunel (q.v.) and launched in 1858. It was 692 ft. long and had a displacement of 12,000 tons. It was designed for the Atlantic passenger service, but was mostly employed in cable-laying and was broken up in 1886.

Great Elector, THE, Frederick William, Elector of Brandenburg (1620–88).

Great Expectations, a novel by Dickens (q.v.), which first appeared in 'All the Year Round' in 1860–1, and was published in book form in the latter year.

It is the story of the development of the character of Philip Pirrip, commonly known as 'Pip', a village boy brought up by his termagant sister, the wife of the gentle, humorous, kindly blacksmith Joe Gargery. He is introduced to the house of Miss Havisham, a lady half-crazed by the desertion of her lover on her bridal night, who, in a spirit of revenge, has brought up the girl Estella to use her beauty as a means of torturing men. Pip falls in love with Estella, and aspires to become a gentleman. Money and expectations of more wealth come to him from a mysterious source, which he believes to be Miss Havisham. He goes to London, and in his new mode of life meanly abandons the devoted Joe Gargery, a humble connexion of whom he is now ashamed. Misfortunes come upon him. His unknown benefactor proves to be an escaped convict, Abel Magwitch, to whom he, as a boy, had rendered a service; his great expectations fade away and he is penniless. Estella marries his sulky enemy, Bentley Drummle, by whom she is cruelly ill-treated. Taught by adversity, Pip returns to Joe Gargery and honest labour, and is finally reunited to Estella who has also learnt her lesson. Other notable characters in the book are Joe's uncle, the impudent old impostor Pumblechook; Jaggers, the skilful Old Bailey lawyer, and his good-hearted clerk Wemmick; and Pip's friend in London, Herbert Pocket.

It appears from Forster's 'Life' of Dickens that the author originally devised a less happy ending to the story, which he altered in deference to the advice of Lytton.

Great Harry, The, or Henry Grâce à Dieu, a great ship of Henry VIII's navy, of 1,000 tons burden. Refitted in 1515, she carried a crew of 700 men, and 50 large and 200 small guns. She was burnt in 1553.

Great-heart, in Bunyan's 'The Pilgrim's Progress' (q.v.), the escort of Christiana and her children on their pilgrimage.

Great Nassau, William III.

Greats, in the University of Oxford, the colloquial name for the final examination for the degree of B.A., especially the examination for Honours in Literae Humaniores. It was formerly known as GREAT GO.

Greaves, SIR LAUNCELOT, the hero of a novel of that name by Smollett (q.v.).

Grecian Coffee-house, THE, stood in Devereux Court, Essex Street, Strand, and was frequented by Addison, Steele, and Goldsmith. It was announced in No. 1 of the 'Tatler' that all learned articles would proceed from the Grecian.

Grecian Fire, see *Greek Fire*.

Grecian Urn, Ode on a, see *Keats*.

Greco, EL, the name given to DOMENIKOS THEOTOKOPOULOS (1541–1614). He was born in Crete, probably studied under Titian, and settled in Toledo by 1577. He painted chiefly religious works and portraits in a mannerist but intensely personal style, using distortion of form and livid colour for mystical and dramatic effect.

Greek Calends, a humorous expression for 'never', for the Greeks had no Calends, which were the first day of each month in the Roman calendar.

Greek Church, THE, see *Orthodox Church*.

Greek Fire, a combustible composition for setting fire to an enemy's ships or works, so called from being used by the Greeks of Constantinople. The components were naphtha, nitre, and sulphur, and it was discharged through tubes or carried by means of arrows. Bury (Gibbon, vi. 9, 10, and 540) says there was more than one kind of mixture and that it was propelled through the tubes by *true gunpowder*: if the Greeks had used this powder to propel solid missiles they would have revolutionized warfare. But the secret was lost, and it was one of the three things, said the Emperor Constantine Porphyrogenitus, 'that must never be given to the barbarians'.

Greeley, HORACE (1811–72), founder of the 'New York Tribune' (1841), and one of the prominent figures in the history of American journalism, who did much to raise its political and literary standards.

GREEN, HENRY, the pseudonym of HENRY VINCENT YORKE (1905–), novelist, whose works include 'Living' (1929), 'Caught' (1943), 'Loving' (1945), 'Back' (1946), and 'Doting' (1952). 'Pack My Bag' (1940) is a self-portrait.

GREEN, JOHN RICHARD (1837–83), educated at Magdalen College School and Jesus College, Oxford, was a frequent contributor to the 'Saturday Review', but is best known by his 'Short History of the English People', published in 1874. This work owed its great popularity to its simple style and generous outlook, for the author shows his interest in the life of the humbler classes of the population, and includes in the scope of his work all the aspects, social, political, economic, and intellectual, of the national history. It was enlarged in 'The History of the English People' (1877–80). 'The Making of England' and 'The Conquest of England', in which he developed more fully certain parts of the 'History', appeared in 1881 and 1883. Some of Green's contributions to the 'Saturday Review' were republished as 'Studies from England and Italy' in 1876.

GREEN, Mrs. MARY ANNE EVERETT (1818–95), was author of 'Letters of Royal Ladies of Great Britain' (published in 1846 under her maiden name of Wood), 'Lives of Princesses of Great Britain' (1849–55), and 'Life and Letters of Henrietta Maria' (1857). She edited at the Public Record Office forty-one volumes of Calendars of Domestic State Papers.

GREEN, MATTHEW (1696–1737), author of 'The Spleen', a poem in praise of the simple contemplative life, as a cure for boredom, written in witty, fluent, octosyllabic verse.

GREEN, THOMAS HILL (1836–82), educated at Rugby and Balliol College, Oxford, was appointed White's professor of moral philosophy in 1878. He was the 'Mr. Gray' of 'Robert Elsmere' (q.v.). Green's philosophical publications began with a criticism of Locke, Hume, and Berkeley in the form of two very full introductions to a new edition of Hume's 'Treatise' (1874). His philosophical views as set forth in his 'Prolegomena to Ethics' (1883) and in his collected 'Works' (1885–8) show a qualified acceptance of the doctrines of Hegel (q.v.) as speculatively true but requiring to be supplemented for practical purposes. He holds that Reality as known is a system of relations, presupposing the synthetic activity of the self. 'We believe that these questions cannot be worked out without leading to the conclusion that the real world is essentially a spiritual world, which forms one interrelated whole because related throughout to a single subject. . . . But when we have satisfied ourselves that the world in its truth or full reality is spiritual . . . we may still have to confess that a knowledge of it in its spiritual reality . . . is impossible to us.' From the freedom of man to seek his satisfaction where alone he can find it, in 'a complete realisation of what he has it in him to be', he deduces the existence of God and the personal immortality of man.

Green, VERDANT, the hero of a novel of that name (1853–7) by E. Bradley (q.v.) ('Cuthbert Bede'). It is a humorous account of the adventures of an innocent undergraduate.

Green Knight, see *Gawain and the Green Knight.*

Green Mountain Boys, THE, an irregular force of some 300 men, led by Ethan Allen (q.v.), originally organized to defend the independence of the 'New Hampshire Grants' against the interference of the New York land-jobbers.

GREENAWAY, KATE (1846–1901), illustrator of children's books, such as 'Kate Greenaway's Birthday Book' and 'Mother Goose', for which she often supplied the text. Her children, quaintly dressed in the costume of the early 19th cent., captured the public taste.

Green-sleeves, the name of an inconstant lady-love, who is the subject of a ballad published in 1580. This, and the tune to which it was sung, became very popular, and both are mentioned by Shakespeare ('The Merry Wives of Windsor', II. i and v. v). The ballad is included in the 'Roxburghe Ballads' (ed. J. P. Collier, 1847).

GREENE, GRAHAM (1904–   ), novelist and dramatist. He was a sub-editor on 'The Times' from 1926 to 1930 and literary editor of the 'Spectator' in 1940. From 1941 to 1944 he worked at the Foreign Office. He early became a Roman Catholic convert and his religious views are reflected in most of his novels. These novels include 'Brighton Rock' (1938), 'The Power and the Glory' (1940), 'The Heart of the Matter' (1948), 'The End of the Affair' (1951), 'The Quiet American' (1956), and 'A Burnt-out Case' (1961). Others, described as 'entertainments', include 'Stamboul Train' (1932), 'A Gun for Sale' (1936), 'The Confidential Agent' (1939), and 'Loser Takes All' (1955). 'The Fallen Idol', 'The Third Man' and 'Our Man in Havana' have been made into films; 'The Living Room' and 'The Potting Shed' are plays. He has also published essays and short stories.

GREENE, ROBERT (1560?–92), was educated at St. John's College and Clare Hall, Cambridge, and was incorporated at Oxford in 1588. He appears from his own writings and the attacks of Gabriel Harvey (q.v.) to have been a witty Bohemian, of good intentions but poor performance, who drifted to a miserable end, and is said to have died after an illness brought on by a surfeit of pickled herrings and Rhenish wine. He was assailed by Harvey in 'Foure Letters' as 'The Ape of Euphues', and defended by Nashe (q.v.) in 'Strange Newes'. He probably had some share in the authorship of the original 'Henry VI' plays, which Shakespeare revised or re-wrote. Among his thirty-eight publications were pamphlets, romances, and five (posthumous) plays, including 'The Honorable Historie of Friar Bacon and Friar Bungay' (q.v.), acted in 1594. Of the romances, 'Menaphon' (q.v., 1589), reprinted as 'Greene's Arcadia' (1599, etc.), 'Pandosto, or Dorastus and Fawnia' (q.v., 1588), 'Philomela' (q.v., 1592), and 'Perimedes the Blacksmith' (1588), contain lyrical passages of great charm. One of the best known of these is Sephestia's song in 'Menaphon', 'Weepe not, my wanton'. His numerous pamphlets include 'Euphues, his Censure of Philautus' (a continuation of Lyly's work, 1587), 'Greene's Mourning Garment' (1590), 'Never Too Late' (1590), 'Farewell to Folly' (1591), 'A Quip for an Upstart Courtier' (1592, an account of a dispute between a spendthrift courtier and a tradesman, containing an interesting review of various trades), and the autobiographical 'A Groatsworth of Wit bought with a Million of Repentance' (q.v., 1592), in which occurs the attack on Shakespeare. His autobiographical sketches, and his tracts on 'Conny-catching' (1591 and 1592), in which he describes the methods of London rogues and swindlers, male and female, throw light on the low life of the times. His plays and poems were edited by Dyce, 1831, his complete works by Grosart, 1881–6, and his plays and poems by Churton Collins, 1905.

Greenwich Hospital stands beside the Thames on the site of a Tudor palace where Henry VIII and his daughters, Mary and Elizabeth, were born. The Queen's House (now the Royal Naval Museum) was built by Inigo Jones (1618–35) higher up the hill. A new palace was planned by Charles II, but only King Charles's Block was built by John Webb. This was incorporated into the hospital for disabled seamen established by Queen Mary and built by Wren. Hawksmoor and Vanbrugh also contributed to the design. The life in Greenwich Hospital is described in Marryat's 'Poor Jack' (1840).

Greenwich Observatory was erected by Charles II at the instance of Sir Jonas Moore, the mathematician, and Sir Christopher Wren, and here John Flamsteed, the first astronomer-royal, took up his residence in 1676. The meridian of Greenwich was adopted as the universal meridian at an international conference in Washington in 1884. (The work of the Observatory is now carried out at Herstmonceux Castle in Sussex.)

GREENWICH TIME is the mean time of the meridian of Greenwich.

GREG, SIR WALTER WILSON (1875–1959), bibliographer, general editor of the Malone Society's publications from 1906 to 1939. His writings include, besides much editorial work on Shakespeare and on other Elizabethan texts, 'The Calculus of Variants' (1927), 'Principles of Emendation in Shakespeare' (1928), and 'Dramatic Documents from the Elizabethan Playhouses' (1931). His 'English Literary Autographs, 1550–1650' was published in three parts and supplement (1925–32).

Gregorian Calendar, see *Calendar*.

Gregorian chant, music, etc., the ancient system of ritual music, otherwise known as plain-chant or plain-song (where 'plain' has the sense of even, level), characterized by free rhythm and a limited scale. It is founded on the *Antiphonarium*, of which Pope Gregory I is presumed to have been the compiler.

GREGORY I, ST., 'The Great', Pope 590–604, one of the greatest of the early occupants of the see, a zealous propagator of Christianity and reformer of clerical and monastic discipline (see also *Gregorian chant*). It was he who sent Augustine (q.v.) to England. He

was the author of the 'Cura Pastoralis' (see *Alfred*), 'Dialogues', 'Letters', homilies, etc. It is told of him that, seeing Anglo-Saxon boys offered for sale in the slave-market at Rome, he remarked: 'Not *Angli* but *Angeli*, if they were Christians.'

Gregory VII, see *Hildebrand*.

GREGORY, AUGUSTA, LADY (1852–1932), née Persse, married in 1881 Sir William Gregory, formerly M.P. for co. Galway and governor of Ceylon. She co-operated with W. B. Yeats (q.v.) in the creation of the Irish National Theatre, for which she wrote many plays. Her publications include: 'Cuchulain of Muirthemne' (1902); 'Gods and Fighting Men' (1904); 'Seven Short Plays' (1909, 'Spreading the News', 'Hyacinth Halvey', 'The Rising of the Moon', 'The Jackdaw', 'The Workhouse Ward', 'The Travelling Man', 'The Gaol Gate'); 'The Kiltartan History Book' (1909); 'Irish Folk History Plays' (1912, 'Kincora', 'The White Cockade', 'Dervorgilla', 'The Canavans', 'The Deliverer', 'Grania'); 'New Comedies' (1913, 'Coats', 'The Full Moon', 'The Bogie Man', 'Damer's Gold', 'McDonough's Wife'); 'The Kiltartan Poetry Book' (1919); 'Three Wonder Plays' (1922); 'The Story brought by Brigit' (1924); 'Three Last Plays' (1928); 'My First Play' (1930); 'Coole' (1931); and adaptations of Molière.

Gregory of Tours (c. 540–94), bishop of Tours, our chief authority for the early Merovingian period of French history (translation, O. M. Dalton, 1927).

Grendel, see *Beowulf*.

GRENFELL, JULIAN HENRY (1888–1915), son of William Henry Grenfell, afterwards first baron Desborough, was educated at Eton and Balliol College, Oxford, obtained a commission in the army in 1910, and was killed early in the First World War. He is the author of the fine poem 'Into Battle'. The few other poems left by Grenfell are in lighter vein.

Grenville, SIR RICHARD (1541?–91), the naval commander who, when his ship the 'Revenge' was isolated off Flores, fought fifteen Spanish ships for fifteen hours, and was mortally wounded. The exploit is celebrated in Tennyson's poem 'The Revenge'; and Grenville figures in Kingsley's 'Westward Ho!' A curiously antagonistic interpretation of him occurs in Stevenson's essay, 'The English Admirals'.

Gresham, FRANK, one of the principal characters in Trollope's 'Dr. Thorne' (q.v.).

Gresham, SIR THOMAS (1519?–79), a celebrated financier and financial agent of the Crown, and an intimate friend of Cecil. He was the son of Sir Richard Gresham (1485?–1549), lord mayor of London, who initiated the design of the Royal Exchange (q.v.). This was built at the expense of Sir Thomas Gresham, who also founded Gresham College. The foolish story that he was a foundling, and adopted his well-known crest because his life was saved by the chirping of a grasshopper, is disproved by the fact that the crest was used by his ancestor, James Gresham, in the 15th cent.

Gresham's Law, that in a bimetallic currency the dearer metal will drive out the cheaper; where *dearer metal* is that which is undervalued by the law at home, but in another country is dearer in terms of the commodities it will buy there; and *cheaper metal* is the converse; in other words 'bad money drives out good'. The law is attributed to Sir T. Gresham in allusion to the beginning of his letter of 1558 to Queen Elizabeth 'touching the fall of the exchange'. (See Lord Aldenham's 'Colloquy on Currency'.)

Gretchen, diminutive in German of Margaret, the principal female character in Pt. I of Goethe's 'Faust' (q.v.).

Gretna Green, a few miles NW. of Carlisle and just across the border, a spot celebrated for runaway marriages; for under Scottish law a declaration by the parties before witnesses of intention to marry constitutes a legal marriage. The declarations were in the latter part of the 18th cent. received by Joseph Paisley, known as a blacksmith. The practice was in 1856 made illegal unless one of the parties had lived in Scotland for 21 days.

Grettla Saga, see *Saga.*

Greuze, JEAN-BAPTISTE (1725–1805), French painter of sentimental and moral scenes.

Grève, PLACE DE, the open space in front of the present Hôtel de Ville in Paris, where, under the *ancien régime*, executions used to take place.

GREVILLE, CHARLES CAVENDISH FULKE (1794–1865), was clerk to the council from 1821 to 1859, and intimate with statesmen of both political parties, especially Wellington (to whom his brother Algernon Frederick was private secretary, 1827–42) and Palmerston. This, and his remarkable insight into character, give exceptional interest to the three series of 'Greville Memoirs', of which the first, covering the reigns of George IV and William IV, was published in 1874. The second, dealing with the years 1837–52, and the third with the years 1852–60, appeared, with some suppressions by the editor, Henry Reeve, in 1885 and 1887. A complete edition with the suppressed passages restored appeared in 1938. Greville published anonymously in 1845 'The Past and Present Policy of England to Ireland', advocating a liberal treatment in the matter of religious endowments.

GREVILLE, SIR FULKE, *first Baron Brooke* (1554–1628), educated at Jesus College, Cambridge, came to court with Sir Philip Sidney, and became a favourite of Elizabeth. He was a member of Gabriel Harvey's 'Areopagus', a member of parliament, and held various important offices. He

was created a peer in 1621 and granted Warwick Castle and Knowle Park by James I. He befriended Bacon, Camden, Coke, Daniel, and D'Avenant. His end was tragic, for he was murdered by his servant Haywood, who thought himself omitted from his master's will. His epitaph reads: 'Servant to Queen Elizabeth, Counceller to King James, Frend to Sir Philip Sidney, Trophaeum Peccati.'

Except the tragedy of 'Mustapha' (1609) and one or two poems in 'The Phoenix Nest' and 'England's Helicon', Greville's works appeared only after his death. A collection of works 'written in his youth' was printed in 1633, his 'Life of Sidney' in 1652, and his 'Remains' in 1670. His complete works were reprinted by Grosart in 1870. Of these the principal are the tragedies of 'Mustapha' and 'Alaham' (qq.v.), which Charles Lamb described as 'political treatises, not plays', but which contain some impressive choruses and striking phrases; and 'Caelica', a collection of 'sonnets' and songs, some of them love poems, others of a religious or philosophical cast. His life of Sir Philip Sidney gives vivid portraits of Queen Elizabeth, William of Orange, and Sidney. The latter's pastoral, 'Join, mates, in mirth with me', is addressed to Greville and Sir Edward Dyer (q.v.).

Grewgious, MR., a character in Dickens's 'Edwin Drood' (q.v.).

GREY, SIR GEORGE (1812–98), an eminent colonial governor, educated at Sandhurst, governor of South Australia (1841–5), New Zealand (1845–53), both of which colonies he raised from disorder to comparative prosperity, Cape Colony (1853–61), and again New Zealand (1861–7). He published 'Polynesian Mythology' (1855) and other works on the history, geography, and language of Australia and New Zealand.

GREY OF FALL'ODON, EDWARD GREY, *Viscount* (1862–1933), educated at Winchester and Balliol College, Oxford, foreign secretary, 1905–16; chancellor of Oxford University, 1928–33; author of 'Fly-Fishing' (1899), 'The Charm of Birds' (1927), 'Twenty-Five Years' (memoirs, 1925).

Grey Friars, Franciscans (q.v.).

Gride, ARTHUR, a character in Dickens's 'Nicholas Nickleby' (q.v.).

Grieux, CHEVALIER DES, the hero of the Abbé Prévost's 'Manon Lescaut' (q.v.).

GRIEVE, CHRISTOPHER MURRAY (1892–), poet and critic, was one of the founders of the Scottish Nationalist Party. Under the pseudonym 'Hugh McDiarmid' he became a leader of the Scottish literary renaissance, using Lowland Scots ('Lallans') in his poetry and seeking to revive the tradition of Henryson, Dunbar, and Burns (qq.v.) and the Scottish ballads. His poems include 'Sangschaw' (1925), 'A Drunk Man Looks at a Thistle' (1926), 'First Hymn to Lenin' (1932), and 'Second Hymn to Lenin' (1935).

His 'Collected Poems' were published in 1962. Among his critical works are 'Contemporary Scottish Studies' (1924), 'Albyn, or Scotland and the Future' (1927), and 'At the Sign of the Thistle' (1934). His autobiography, 'Lucky Poet' (1943), expresses his passionate Anglophobia and desire for Scottish independence, and, as an idiosyncratic Communist, his aim of establishing Workers' Republics in Scotland, Ireland, Wales, and Cornwall—'a sort of Celtic Union of Socialist Soviet Republics in the British Isles'.

GRIFFIN, GERALD (1803–40), Irish dramatist and novelist, remembered for his novel 'The Collegians' (q.v., 1829), which Boucicault made the basis of his play 'Colleen Bawn' (q.v.). Griffin's play 'Gisippus' was produced at Drury Lane in 1842.

Griffin, GRIFFON, GRYPHON, a fabulous animal usually represented with the head and wings of an eagle and the body and hindquarters of a lion. By the Greeks the griffins were believed to inhabit Scythia and to keep guard over the gold of that country (see *Arimaspians*).

Griffith Gaunt, or Jealousy, a novel by C. Reade (q.v.), published in 1866.

The story is set in the 18th cent. Griffith Gaunt, a Cumberland gentleman of no fortune, marries Kate Peyton, a Roman Catholic heiress, a woman of incalculable pride and temper. The harmony of the household is gradually broken by Kate's spiritual director, Father Leonard, an eloquent young priest who falls in love with Kate. Griffith, whose suspicions have been aroused by a designing maid-servant, finds them together under equivocal circumstances, and after a violent scene leaves his wife intending never to return. He is nursed through a severe illness by Mercy Vint, an innkeeper's daughter, and bigamously marries her under the name of Thomas Leicester, his illegitimate half-brother, who resembles him in appearance. He returns to his old home to recover a sum of money, accidentally meets Kate, is reconciled to her, and determines to break off with Mercy Vint. Before he effects the separation his crime is discovered by his wife, who furiously upbraids and threatens him. Griffith leaves the house, a pistol-shot and a cry of murder are heard, and he disappears. Some days later a disfigured body, believed to be his, is found in a neighbouring mere. Kate is tried for the murder of her husband, and is in danger of conviction, when Mercy intervenes and proves that the body is that of Tom Leicester. Griffith and Kate are once more reconciled, and Mercy marries Sir George Neville, a former suitor of Kate. The work, when it appeared, was severely criticized as immoral.

Grim, the fisherman in the story of 'Havelok the Dane' (q.v.), and the legendary founder of Grimsby.

GRIMALD, GRIMALDE, or GRIMVALD, NICHOLAS (1519–62), of Christ's College, Cambridge, chaplain to Bishop Ridley, contributed to, and assisted in the compilation of, 'Tottel's Miscellany' (see *Tottel*). He published translations from Virgil and Cicero, and two Latin dramas.

Grimaldi, JOSEPH (1779–1837), a celebrated clown and pantomimist, who first appeared as an infant dancer at Sadler's Wells, and acted there and at Drury Lane for many years. He had a son of the same name who succeeded him as pantomimist and died in 1863. Grimaldi's 'Memoirs' were edited by Dickens (2 vols. 1838).

Grimalkin, probably from *grey* and *malkin*, a name given to a cat, especially an old she-cat, and contemptuously applied to a jealous or imperious old woman.

Grimbald, or GRIMBOLD, or GRYMBOLD, ST. (820?–903), a native of Flanders and a monk of St. Bertin's. Alfred, when king, summoned him to England for the promotion of learning, and appointed him abbot of the New Minster at Winchester. According to the entirely mythical history of Oxford, Grimbald was sent there to direct the recently established schools, but owing to the jealousy of the masters was obliged to withdraw. He is commemorated on 8 July.

Grimbert or GRYMBERT, the badger in 'Reynard the Fox' (q.v.).

Grimes, PETER, the subject of Letter xxii in Crabbe's 'The Borough' (q.v.). He was a villainous fellow who 'fish'd by water and filch'd by land', and killed his apprentices by ill-treatment, until, becoming suspect and forbidden to keep apprentices, he lived in solitude. Under the sting of guilty conscience he became insane, and died after undergoing awful terrors. B. Britten's opera 'Peter Grimes' was produced in 1945.

Grimes, THOMAS, chimney-sweep, Tom's employer in C. Kingsley's 'The Water Babies' (q.v.).

GRIMM, FRIEDRICH MELCHIOR (1723–1807), born at Ratisbon, author during 1753–73 of the greater part of a 'Correspondance littéraire', letters to German sovereigns containing a survey of French literary and artistic activities during that period. The 'Correspondance' was continued to 1790 by J. H. Meister.

GRIMM, JACOB LUDWIG CARL (1785–1863), and **WILHELM CARL** (1786–1859), brothers and Germans, were authors of works on German philology, law, mythology, and folklore, which served to put the study of the German past, including the language, on a more scientific basis. They are chiefly known in England by their fairy tales ('Kinder- und Hausmärchen', 1812–15), of which an English translation, illustrated by George Cruikshank, was published in 1823 under the title 'German Popular Stories'. There have been many later editions and selections in this country.

Jacob Grimm in his 'Deutsche Grammatik'

formulated *Grimm's Law* of the mutations of the consonants in the several Aryan languages.

GRIMMELSHAUSEN, JOHANNES JACOB CHRISTOFFEL von (*c.* 1621–76), German writer, author of the picaresque novel 'Simplicissimus' (q.v.) and, amongst other things, of a novel from which Brecht (q.v.) took the story of his 'Mother Courage'.

Grimwig, MR., a character in Dickens's 'Oliver Twist' (q.v.).

Gringolet, Gawain's horse (e.g. in the story of 'Sir Gawain and the Green Knight', q.v.); French *Gringalet*, a word of unknown etymology, which appears in the 12th cent., signifying a kind of horse (Hatzfeld and Darmesteter). It has been said (by Prof. I. Gollancz) that the name belonged originally to the boat of the mythical hero Wade (q.v.); but it is found some centuries earlier as the name of Gawain's horse. The earliest authority for 'Gringalet' as the name of Wade's boat is Speght (in his edition of Chaucer, 1598).

Grip, in Dickens's 'Barnaby Rudge' (q.v.), Barnaby's raven.

Gripe, one of the chief characters in Vanbrugh's 'The Confederacy' (q.v.).

Gripe, SIR FRANCIS, a character in Mrs. Centlivre's 'The Busybody' (q.v.).

Grippy, and LEDDY GRIPPY, Claud Walkinshaw and his wife, characters in Galt's 'The Entail' (q.v.).

Griselda, the type of long-suffering fortitude; see *Patient Grissil.*

Groat, a silver coin first issued in England by Edward I, and more permanently by Edward III, worth fourpence. None were struck after the time of Charles II, until the fourpenny piece was revived by William IV and continued to be issued until 1856. The word is taken from the Dutch *groot*, meaning great, in the sense of thick (i.e. a thick penny).

Groatsettar, THE MISSES, characters in Scott's 'The Pirate' (q.v.).

Groatsworth of Wit bought with a Million of Repentance, A, an autobiographical prose tract by R. Greene (q.v.), published in 1592. It begins with the death of the miser Gorinius, who leaves the bulk of his large fortune to his elder son, and only 'an old Groate' to the younger, Roberto (i.e. the author), 'wherewith I wish him to buy a groatsworth of wit'. Roberto conspires with a courtesan to fleece his brother, Lucanio, but the courtesan betrays him to the latter, subsequently ruining Lucanio for her sole profit. The gradual degradation of Roberto is then narrated, and the tract ends with the curious 'Address' to his fellow playwrights, Marlowe, Lodge, and Peele, urging them to spend their wits to better purpose than the making of plays. It contains the well-known passage about the 'Crow, beautified with our Feathers',

the 'Johannes Factotum', who 'is in his owne conceit the only Shake-scene in a Countrey', probably referring to Shakespeare, whose earliest plays were adaptations of works by his predecessors.

Grobian (German *Grobheit*, rudeness), the name of an imaginary personage, often referred to by writers of the 15th and 16th cents. in Germany as a type of boorishness. Sebastian Brant in his 'Narrenschiff' (see *Ship of Fools*) invented St. Grobianus as typical of ill-mannered and indecent behaviour. In 1549 F. Dedekind, a German student, wrote a poem in Latin elegiacs, 'Grobianus, De Morum Simplicitate', a burlesque of the generally uncivilized social conditions then prevailing in Germany, in the form of ironical advice on conduct given to a gallant. This was translated into German by Kaspar Scheidt, and into English, and suggested to Dekker his 'Guls Hornebooke' (q.v.).

Grocyn, WILLIAM (1446?–1519), educated at Winchester and New College, Oxford, held various ecclesiastical preferments. He studied in Italy with Linacre (q.v.) under Poliziano and Chalcondyles, and was instrumental in introducing the study of Greek at Oxford.

Grongar Hill, see *Dyer* (*J.*).

GRONOVIUS, JOHANN FRIEDRICH (1611–71), a Dutch scholar and editor of Greek and Roman classics. His son, JAKOB GRONOVIUS (1645–1716), was professor of Greek at Leyden, and, like his father, an editor of classical authors.

GROSART, ALEXANDER BALLOCH (1827–1899), author and editor. His claim to remembrance rests on his reprints of rare Elizabethan and Jacobean literature. Between 1868 and 1886 he edited more than 130 volumes. He also published several original devotional works, and contributed to literary and theological periodicals.

GROSE, FRANCIS (1731?–91), antiquary and draughtsman, author of a 'Classical Dictionary of the Vulgar Tongue' (1785), reissued as 'Lexicon Balatronicum' (1811).

GROSSETESTE, ROBERT (*d.* 1253), bishop of Lincoln, and the first chancellor of the University of Oxford. He was the author of translations from the Greek, including Aristotle's Nichomachean Ethics and the works of Pseudo Dionysius Ariopagita (see *Dionysius the Areopagite*); of works on philosophy, theology, and husbandry; and of an allegorical poem on the Virgin and Son, the 'Château d'Amour', in French (edited by R. F. Weymouth, 1864). 'He gave a powerful impulse to almost every department of intellectual activity' in England [F. S. Stevenson], and earned the commendation of Roger Bacon in the field of science, of Matthew Paris, of Wycliffe, and of Gower. Also he stood up to Popes (especially Innocent IV) against their encroachments on the Church in England.

Grosvenor Gallery, THE, Bond Street,

London, for the exhibition of pictures of the modern school, erected by Sir Coutts Lindsay in 1876 (Haydn). It was especially associated for a time with the 'aesthetic movement' (q.v.). Bunthorne in Gilbert and Sullivan's 'Patience' describes himself as:

A pallid and thin young man,
A haggard and lank young man,
A greenery-yallery, Grosvenor Gallery,
Foot-in-the-grave young man.

The Gallery is now closed.

GROTE, GEORGE (1794–1871), banker, educated at Charterhouse, was M.P. for the City of London from 1832 to 1841 and took an active part in favour of the reform movement, publishing a pamphlet on the subject in 1820 and another in 1831. He retired from parliament in order to devote himself to historical work. His famous 'History of Greece' in eight volumes, on which he had been intermittently at work since 1823, was published in 1846–56 and achieved immediate success. It has been translated into French and German. Grote also published works on the philosophies of Plato and Aristotle ('Plato and the other Companions of Socrates', 1865; 'Aristotle', 1872), and 'Fragments on Ethical Subjects' (1876). He was buried in Westminster Abbey.

Grotesque, from Italian *grottesca*, apparently from *grotte*, grottoes, the popular name in Rome for the chambers of ancient buildings which had been revealed by excavations and which contained those mural paintings which were typical examples of the 'grotesque' style; hence a kind of decorative painting or sculpture, consisting of representations of portions of human and animal forms, fantastically combined and interwoven with foliage and flowers. [OED.]

GROTIUS, HUGO (1583–1645), Dutch statesman and jurist, was born at Delft, studied law at Orleans and Leyden, and became the leader of the bar at The Hague. He wrote in 1601 a sacred drama in Latin, 'Adamus Exsul', with which Milton was probably familiar when he wrote 'Paradise Lost'. Grotius was Dutch ambassador in London in 1613, but his intimacy with Barneveld (who was executed in 1619 for conspiracy against the State) led to his condemnation to imprisonment for life. From this he escaped in a large box in which books were sent to him for the purpose of study, and took refuge in Paris. He became the ambassador of Queen Christina of Sweden at the French Court, and died, after shipwreck, in her service. He wrote a large number of works, including a Latin history of the revolt of the Netherlands. But his principal title to fame is his great treatise of international law, the 'De jure Belli et Pacis', published in 1625. In the midst of the Thirty Years War (1618–48) he asserted in this work the principle of a rule of law binding upon nations in their relations with one another.

GROVE, Sir GEORGE (1820–1900), a writer on a great variety of subjects, is especially notable as having projected and edited the 'Dictionary of Music and Musicians' (4 vols. 1878–89, and later editions).

Growth of Love, The, a sonnet-sequence by R. Bridges (q.v.).

Grub Street, London, according to Samuel Johnson was 'originally the name of a street near Moorfields in London, much inhabited by writers of small histories, dictionaries, and temporary poems, whence any mean production is called *grubstreet*' ('Dictionary'). The name of the street was changed in the 19th cent. to Milton Street (Cripplegate). 'Grub Street' is current in modern usage as an epithet meaning 'of the nature of literary hack-work'.

According to Stow (1598), Grub Street was 'of late years inhabited for the most part by Bowyers, Fletchers, Bowstring makers, and such like', but in his time given up to bowling alleys and dicing houses. Neanias, in Randolph's 'Hey for Honesty' (IV. iii) says of Anus: 'Her eyes are Cupid's Grub Street: the blind archer makes his love-arrows there.'

Grub Street Journal, The, which appeared during 1730–8, vigorously attacked Pope's adversaries in the 'Dunciad' controversy. Pope probably had some part in its production.

Grubbinol, a shepherd in Gay's 'Shepherd's Week' (q.v.).

Grueby, JOHN, a character in Dickens's 'Barnaby Rudge' (q.v.), servant to Lord George Gordon.

Grundy, MRS., the symbol of conventional propriety. For the origin of the expression see *Speed the Plough*.

Gryll, in Spenser's 'Faerie Queene', II. xii. 86, the hog in the Bower of Acrasia who repined greatly at being changed back into a man. The incident is taken from a dialogue of Plutarch, in which Gryllus is one of the Greeks transformed into swine by Circe (see also *Gryll Grange*).

Gryll Grange, the last novel of Peacock (q.v.), published in 1860 or early in 1861.

In it we have the house party that is the usual feature of most of his books, diversified by the addition of an eccentric young gentleman, Algernon Falconer, who lives in a tower, attended by seven 'Vestals', as beautiful and accomplished as they are virtuous. Mr. Gryll of Gryll Grange believes himself descended from Circe's Gryllus (see under *Gryll*), though he finds it difficult to establish the pedigree. The Revd. Dr. Opimian, 'a man of purple cheer, A rosy man right plump to see', an agreeable gourmet who combines much learning with conservative views, is the most notable of the characters. These discourse on many subjects, from the Greek theatre and ancient music to cooking and card-playing, with much display of curious learning and apt quotation. The slender thread of the plot, concerned with the love affairs of Mr. Falconer and Lord Curryfin, ends in a prodigious marriage, at which nine brides are wedded to nine bridegrooms.

Gryphon, see *Griffin*.

Guanhamara, see *Guinevere*.

Guardian, The, (1) a periodical started by Steele (q.v.) in March 1713. It professed at the outset to abstain from political questions, and Addison contributed fifty-one papers to it. It included also among its contributors Berkeley, Pope, and Gay. But Steele soon launched into political controversy, falling foul of the Tory 'Examiner' (q.v.). Owing to some disagreement with Tonson, the publisher, the 'Guardian' came to an abrupt end in Oct. 1713 and was succeeded by the 'Englishman'; (2) a national daily paper originally published as 'The Manchester Guardian' (q.v.).

GUARINI, GIOVANNI BATTISTA (1538–1612), an Italian poet, born at Ferrara, author of the pastoral drama, 'Il Pastor Fido' (1589), which had considerable vogue in England in the 17th cent. It was repeatedly translated into English, and also acted in a Latin version at Cambridge. Guarini also wrote an influential defence of tragicomedy: the 'Compendio della poesia tragicomica' (1601).

Gubbins or GUBBINGS, a contemptuous name formerly given to the inhabitants of a district near Brent Tor on the edge of Dartmoor (described as 'a Scythia within England' by Fuller), who are said to have been absolute savages. The 'King of the Gubbings' appears in C. Kingsley's 'Westward Ho!' (q.v.).

Gudrun, (1) the subject of a German national epic of the 13th cent., composed in Austria. She is the daughter of King Hetel, and betrothed to Herwig of Seeland. She is carried off by Hartmut of Normandy, and because she refuses to be his wife is set to do menial work. After thirteen years she is rescued, and marries Herwig [E.B. 11th ed.]; (2) in the 'Volsunga Saga' and in W. Morris's 'Sigurd the Volsung' (q.v.), the daughter of the king of the Niblungs; (3) the heroine of the Laxdaela Saga (see *Gudrun, The Lovers of*).

Gudrun, The Lovers of, one of the wanderers' tales in W. Morris's 'The Earthly Paradise' (q.v.), a translation of the Laxdaela Saga (see *Saga*).

It is the story of Gudrun, daughter of Oswif, a great lord in Iceland, and of the many men who loved her, but in particular of Kiartan and his bosom friend and cousin Bodli. Gudrun passionately returns the love of Kiartan, who excels all in manly deeds and is kindly in disposition, but Kiartan, before he will marry her, goes with Bodli to Norway in search of fame, and there spends some years at the court of Olaf Trygvesson. Bodli returns to Iceland and, yielding to the temp-

tation of his passion for Gudrun, tells her that Kiartan now loves Ingibiorg, the sister of King Olaf, and will marry her. Brokenhearted, but at last convinced of Kiartan's unfaithfulness, Gudrun marries Bodli. Then Kiartan returns to claim his bride. Gudrun curses the miserable Bodli, and Kiartan, likewise broken-hearted, half contemptuously spares him. Bodli, driven by despair and the taunts of those about him, joins in an ambush prepared by Kiartan's enemies, and slays his friend, to be slain later by Kiartan's brothers. Gudrun later marries again.

Guebres (pron. Gē'bers), adherents of the ancient Persian religion, fire-worshippers, Zoroastrians. The name is more or less obsolete.

GUEDALLA, PHILIP (1889–1944), historian and biographer. After ten years as a barrister of the Inner Temple he retired to devote himself to writing. His works include 'The Partition of Europe 1715–1815' (1914), 'Supers and Supermen' (1920), 'The Second Empire' (1922), 'Masters and Men' (1923), 'Palmerston' (1926), 'The Duke' (biography of Wellington, 1931), 'Mr. Churchill' (1941).

Guelphs and the **Ghibellines, THE,** the two great parties in medieval Italian politics, supporting respectively the popes and the emperors. GUELPH is the name of the princely family represented in modern times by the ducal house of Brunswick, and WELF is said to have been used at the battle of Weinsberg in 1140 as a war-cry by the partisans of the duke of Bavaria, who belonged to this family and fought against the Emperor Conrad III. GHIBELLINE is said to be a corruption of *Waiblinghi*, the name of an estate belonging to the Hohenstaufen family, used as a war-cry by the partisans of the emperor at the same battle. [OED.]

Guendolen, in Scott's 'Bridal of Triermain' (q.v.), a fay who beguiles King Arthur into loving her, and becomes the mother of Gyneth. See also *Gwendolen*.

Guerre, MARTIN, a Gascon gentleman of the 16th cent., who after ten years of married life disappeared from the country. Subsequently, a certain Arnaud du Thil, bearing a close resemblance to Guerre, presented himself as the missing man, of whose circumstances he had made a careful study. He was recognized by Martin Guerre's wife as her husband, and lived with her until a soldier published the fact that the true Martin Guerre was living in Flanders. After a long trial, which excited the greatest interest, and the final reappearance of Guerre himself, du Thil was sentenced and executed in 1560.

Guest, STEPHEN, a character in G. Eliot's 'The Mill on the Floss' (q.v.).

Gueux, meaning 'beggars', a name first given in contempt to the Protestant nobles who opposed Margaret of Parma (Regent of the Netherlands, on behalf of Philip II of

Spain), and afterwards adopted by various bodies of Dutch and Flemish partisans in the wars with the Spaniards in the 16th cent.

GUICCIARDINI, FRANCESCO (1483–1540), Florentine historian and statesman, employed by the Medici and the Papacy. He was commissioner general for the papal army at the time of the Sack of Rome (1527). His best-known works were: the 'Storia d' Italia', a history of Italy from 1492 to 1534, which was translated into English (from a French version) by Fenton, and is of lasting significance; and the 'Ricordi', a collection of aphorisms, which also had a wide diffusion.

Guiderius, in Shakespeare's 'Cymbeline' (q.v.), the elder son of the king.

GUIDO DA COLONNA, or DELLE COLONNE, a 13th-cent. Sicilian writer of Latin romances, author of a 'Historia Trojana' which was in fact a prose version of a poem of Benoît de Sainte-Maure (q.v.), though Guido did not acknowledge this. His romance was translated in poems attributed to Barbour and Huchoun, and by Lydgate in his 'Troy Book'. The story of 'Troilus and Cressida', taken by Guido from Benoît de Sainte-Maure, was in turn developed by Boccaccio, Chaucer, Henryson, and Shakespeare (qq.v.).

Guido Franceschini, COUNT, one of the principal characters in R. Browning's 'The Ring and the Book' (q.v.).

Guignol, the chief character in the popular French puppet-show of that name, similar to our 'Punch and Judy'. The word is also used for the theatre where the show is performed. GRAND GUIGNOL is a term applied to a theatre presenting plays of a gruesome character (resembling in this respect the play of 'Punch and Judy', q.v.).

Guild of St. George, see *Ruskin*.

Guildenstern, a character in Shakespeare's 'Hamlet' (q.v.).

GUILDFORD, JOHN OF, and NICHOLAS OF, see *Owl and the Nightingale*.

Guildhall, THE, the town hall of the city of London. The name signifies a hall where a trade guild met, but from its use as a meeting-place for the corporation was often synonymous with town hall. [OED.] According to another view the name is derived from the peace guilds or frith guilds of Athelstane (see Lethaby, 'London before the Conquest'). The present Guildhall was built early in the 15th cent., replacing an earlier hall in Aldermanbury. The interior of the hall was burnt out in the Great Fire of 1666, and was restored. It was severely damaged in an air-raid in Dec. 1940 but the main hall and crypt have been restored.

GUILLAUME DE LORRIS, see *Roman de la Rose*.

Guillotin, JOSEPH IGNACE (1738–1814), a French physician, member of the Constituent Assembly, who, from humanitarian motives, proposed that decapitation should be the sole form of capital punishment. His proposal was adopted and the machine constructed and brought into use in April 1792 was eventually named 'guillotine'.

Guinea, the name of an English gold coin. In 1663 the newly issued 'gold 20s. piece commanded a premium, and was ere long generally taken for 21s. or 22s. By a curious freak of chance the Guinea gold money, struck from the intake from the African Company, was so prevalent at this time, that the coin which official documents still called a pound was usually nicknamed a "guinea", and the name stuck to it till 1813', when the last guineas were coined (in spite of the existence of paper currency in Great Britain) to supply Wellington's army in the Pyrenees. By that time the gold guinea was worth 27s. in bank-notes. In 1816, when monometallism was adopted, the gold £1 was substituted for the 21s. guinea. (See Oman, 'Coinage of England' (1931), from which the above quotation is taken.)

Guinea, Chrysal, or the Adventures of a, see *Adventures of a Guinea*.

Guinevere, the wife of King Arthur (q.v.) in the Arthurian legend. The name figures in various forms in the early romances. In Geoffrey of Monmouth she is *Guanhamara*, of a noble Roman family, brought up in the household of Cador, duke of Cornwall. In Layamon's 'Brut' she is *Wenhaver*, a relative of Cador of Cornwall. In 'Arthour and Merlin' (13th cent.) she is *Gvenour*, daughter of Leodegran, king of Carohaise. For her story see *Arthur* and *Launcelot*. A more subtle and favourable view of her character than is found in the old romances is given in W. Morris's 'Defence of Guenevere' (1858) and in Tennyson's idyll 'Guinevere' (1859, q.v.). See also *Awntyrs of Arthure at the Terne Wathelyne*.

Guinevere, one of Tennyson's 'Idylls of the King' (q.v.), published in 1859.

The poem describes how Guinevere, under the growing stress of conscience and fear of exposure, bids Lancelot leave her and withdraw to his own lands. They meet for the last time, when the voice of the spying Modred is heard. Lancelot rushes out and hurls him headlong; then bids the queen fly with him to 'his castle overseas'. But she, declaring that she is shamed for ever, betakes herself to the nunnery at Almesbury. There, after a period of sorrowful meditation, she is visited by Arthur, and falls prostrate at his feet. He denounces the evil that she has wrought in the wreck of his high hopes, and finally forgives her and bids her farewell. Heart-broken and contrite, she remains with the nuns, becomes their abbess, and after three years dies.

Guiscardo, see *Sigismonda*.

Guise, the name of a branch of the princely house of Lorraine, especially prominent in the campaigns of violence and intrigue directed in the 16th cent. against the Huguenots. The best-known member of the family is Henri de Guise, *le Balafré* (q.v., 1550–88). Mary of Guise (his aunt, 1515–60), was the queen of James V of Scotland and mother of Mary Stuart.

GUIZOT, FRANÇOIS (1787–1874), French statesman and historian, a minister under Louis Philippe, to the failure of whose conservative policy is attributed the revolution of 1848. He was a Protestant. Among his historical works were the 'Histoire de la révolution d'Angleterre', 'Histoire de la civilisation en Europe', 'Essais sur l'histoire de France', etc.

Gulbeyaz, in Byron's 'Don Juan' (q.v.), the sultana to whom the hero is sold as a slave.

Gulistan, 'the rose garden', the name of the principal poem of the Persian poet Sadi (q.v.), a work of edification in which moral instruction is mingled with tales and other lighter matter.

Gulliver's Travels, a satire by Swift (q.v.), published in 1726.

Swift probably got the idea of a satire in the form of a narrative of travels at the meetings of the Scriblerus Club (q.v.), and intended it to form part of the 'Memoirs of Scriblerus'; Scriblerus indeed is described in the 'Memoirs' as visiting the same countries as Gulliver. Swift appears to have worked at the book from as early as 1720.

In the first part Lemuel Gulliver, a surgeon on a merchant ship, relates his shipwreck on the island of *Lilliput*, the inhabitants of which are six inches high, everything on the island being in proportion of one inch to one foot as compared with things as we know them. Owing to this diminutive scale, the pomp of the emperor, the civil feuds of the inhabitants, the war with their neighbours across the channel, are made to look ridiculous. The English political parties and religious dissensions are satirized in the description of the wearers of high heels and low heels, and of the controversy on the question whether eggs should be broken at the big or small end.

In the second part Gulliver is accidentally left ashore on *Brobdingnag*, where the inhabitants are as tall as steeples, and everything else is in proportion. Here the king, after inquiring into the manners, government, and learning of Europe, sums up his impression of what Gulliver tells him as follows: 'By what I have gathered from your own relation . . . I cannot but conclude the bulk of your natives to be the most pernicious race of little odious vermin that nature ever suffered to crawl upon the surface of the earth.'

The third part is occupied with a visit to the flying island of *Laputa*, and its neighbouring continent and capital *Lagado*. Here the satire is directed against philosophers, men of science, historians, and projectors, with special reference to the South Sea Bubble. In Laputa Gulliver finds the wise men so wrapped up in their speculations as to be utter dotards

in practical affairs. At Lagado he visits the Academy of Projectors, where professors are engaged in extracting sunshine from cucumbers and similar absurd enterprises. In the Island of Sorcerers he is enabled to call up the great men of old, and discovers, from their answers to his questions, the deceptions of history. The *Struldbrugs*, a race endowed with immortality, so far from finding this a boon, turn out to be the most miserable of mankind.

The bitterness and misanthropy of Swift, of which there are indications in the second and third parts of the 'Travels', are accentuated in the fourth, describing the country of the *Houyhnhnms*, or horses endowed with reason. Here the simplicity and virtues of the horses are contrasted with the disgusting brutality of the *Yahoos*, beasts in the shape of men.

The whole work, with the exception of certain passages, has the rare merit of appealing to both old and young, as a powerful satire on man and human institutions, and as a fascinating tale of travels in wonderland.

Gulnare, a character in Byron's 'The Corsair' (q.v.).

Guls Hornebooke, The, a satirical book of manners, by Dekker (q.v.), published in 1609. It is an attack on the fops and gallants of the day under the guise of ironical instructions how they may make themselves conspicuous in places of public resort by their offensive conduct. The occupations of a young man of leisure are described; his dressing, his walk in 'Paul's' (q.v.), his meal at the 'ordinary', the visit to the playhouse, etc.

Gummidge, MRS., a character in Dickens's 'David Copperfield' (q.v.), a 'lone lorn creetur'.

Gunnar, in the 'Volsunga Saga' and W. Morris's 'Sigurd the Volsung' (q.v.), the king of the Niblungs and the husband of Brynhild.

Gunner's Daughter, the gun to which seamen were lashed to be flogged.

Gunning, MARIA (1733–60) and ELIZABETH (1734–90), daughters of James Gunning of Castlecoote, Roscommon, famous beauties. Maria became countess of Coventry; Elizabeth, duchess of Hamilton and of Argyll.

GUNNING, MRS. SUSANNAH (1740?–1800), *née* Minifie, of Fairwater, Somersetshire, married John Gunning (the brother of Maria and Elizabeth Gunning, q.v.), a man of dissolute life, from whom she separated. Before her marriage, and after her separation, she wrote a number of novels of a harmless description, and without much plot. These include 'The Histories of Lady Frances S— and Lady Caroline S—' (with her sister Margaret, 1763); 'Barford Abbey' (1768); the 'Count de Poland' (1780); 'Memoirs of Mary' (1793), etc.

Gunpowder Plot, the plot of a few Roman Catholics to blow up the Houses of Parliament on 5 Nov. 1605, while king, lords, and commons were assembled there. The plot was devised by Robert Catesby, and Guy Fawkes was chosen to put it into execution. But it was betrayed, and Fawkes arrested on 4 Nov. The conspirators who were taken alive were executed; Catesby was killed while resisting arrest.

Gunther, in the Nibelungenlied (q.v.), the brother of Kriemhild.

Guppy, a character in Dickens's 'Bleak House' (q.v.).

GURNEY, THOMAS (1705–70), appointed shorthand-writer at the Old Bailey, 1737 (?1748), the first shorthand-writer to hold an official appointment. His 'Brachygraphy' (1750), originally an improvement of W. Mason's 'Shorthand', has been frequently reissued and improved. It is his grandson, William Brodie Gurney, shorthand-writer to the Houses of Parliament (1813), who is referred to by Byron in 'Don Juan', i. 189.

Gurth, the Saxon swineherd in Scott's 'Ivanhoe' (q.v.).

Gushtasp, one of the later legendary kings of Persia whose story is told in the Shahnameh of Firdusi (q.v.). He was the father of Isfendiyar (q.v.).

Gustavus Adolphus (1594–1632), king of Sweden (1611–32). In 1630 he invaded Germany, and carried out his celebrated campaign, in which he defeated Tilly at Breitenfeld near Leipzig and Wallenstein at Lützen, but fell in the latter battle.

Gustavus Vasa liberated the Swedes in 1521 from the Danish yoke and ascended the throne of Sweden in 1523. A tragedy on the subject was written by H. Brooke (q.v.).

Guster, a character in Dickens's 'Bleak House' (q.v.).

Gutenberg, JOHANN (c. 1400–1468?), the inventor of printing with movable types. Born at Mainz, he went to Strasbourg in 1428 and there began experimenting with the use of cast letters and a press for printing. He went back to Mainz c. 1445, and developed his invention in partnership with Johann Fust (q.v.) who provided the capital. Fust dissolved the partnership in 1455 and took possession of the implements and stock. Gutenberg died in 1467 or 1468, leaving an equipment for printing. No work printed by him can be identified, though the 42-line Bible and others of the earliest books have been attributed to him on grounds of probability.

Guthlac, ST. (d. 714), a young nobleman of Mercia who became a hermit at Crowland or Croyland in Lincolnshire. Æthelbald, king of Mercia, built a church over his tomb, which later became the Abbey of Crowland. His life is the subject of an Anglo-Saxon poem in the 'Exeter Book' (q.v.) There are frequent references to St. Guthlac and the abbey in C. Kingsley's 'Hereward the Wake' (q.v.).

GUTHRIE, THOMAS ANSTEY, see *Anstey* (*F.*)

Gutter Lane, in the city of London, formerly Guthuron's Lane or Gudrun's Lane, was probably named after Guthrum the Dane (Lethaby), who defeated Alfred, and subsequently ceded London to him. It was the street of the goldsmiths before Stow's time, when they were for the most part removed to the Cheap. Stow speaks of 'fine silver, of such as . . . was commonly called silver of Guthuron's lane'.

Guy, THOMAS (1645?–1724), the founder of Guy's Hospital, set up as a bookseller in London in 1668 and was one of the Oxford University printers, 1679–92. He greatly increased his fortune by selling his South Sea stock. He lived a penurious life but was liberal in benefactions, erecting the hospital that bears his name at a cost of some £18,000 and leaving £200,000 for its endowment, besides other charitable bequests.

Guy Fawkes, see *Gunpowder Plot*.

Guy Livingstone, or Thorough, a novel by G. A. Lawrence (q.v.), published in 1857.

This novel shows a revolt against the moral and domestic conventions of the period. The hero is an officer of the Life Guards, very wealthy, of colossal size and strength, and a great sportsman, who beats prize-fighters and performs other exploits, but whose lack of principle involves him in amatory difficulties. He becomes engaged to Constance Brandon, but is discovered by her kissing Flora Bellasys, and Constance presently dies of a broken heart. Contrasted with Guy is Bruce, who doesn't hunt, is a muff with a gun, and is generally despicable. He is engaged to Guy's cousin Isabel, but Guy's friend Forrester elopes with Isabel a month before the intended wedding, and they live happily until Bruce meets Forrester and kills him, to be subsequently tracked down by Guy. The latter, whose truculence has been somewhat softened by his experiences, dies from a fall in the hunting field.

This crude piece of melodrama was parodied by Bret Harte in his 'Guy Heavystone'.

Guy Mannering, a novel by Sir W. Scott (q.v.), published in 1815.

The story, laid in the 18th cent., centres in the fortunes of young Harry Bertram, son of the laird of Ellangowan in the county of Dumfries, who is kidnapped by smugglers when a child, and carried to Holland. This is done at the instigation of a rascally lawyer, Glossin, who has hopes of acquiring on easy terms the Ellangowan estate, in default of an heir male. Bertram, ignorant of his parentage, and bearing the name of Brown, goes to India, joins the army, and serves with distinction under Colonel Guy Mannering. Bertram (or Brown) is suspected by Mannering of paying attentions to his wife, and is wounded by him in a duel and left for dead. In reality Bertram is in love with Julia, Mannering's daughter. Recovering from his wound, he follows her to England and the neighbourhood of Ellangowan. Glossin, now in possession of the Ellangowan estate, is alarmed by the return of Bertram and the possibility that he may learn the secret of his parentage. He plots with Dirk Hatteraick, the smuggler who had originally kidnapped the child, to carry him off once more and make away with him. But an old gipsy, Meg Merrilies, also recognizes Harry for whom she still retained her affection since his childhood and devotes all her energies to secure his restoration. She frustrates the plot with the help of Bertram and Dandie Dinmont, a sturdy Lowland farmer, but at the sacrifice of her own life. Hatteraick and Glossin are captured, and Hatteraick, after murdering Glossin in prison as the author of his misfortunes, takes his own life. Bertram is acknowledged and restored to his property and to Mannering's favour, and marries Julia. The novel not only includes the notable characters of Meg Merrilies and Dandie Dinmont but also that of Dominie Sampson, the uncouth simple-minded tutor of the little Harry Bertram.

Guy of Gisborne, in a ballad included in Percy's 'Reliques', a yeoman sworn to take Robin Hood. He meets the outlaw in the forest and, after a contest in archery, is slain by him.

Guy of Warwick, a popular verse romance, containing some 7,000 lines, of the early 14th cent. Guy is the son of Siward, steward of Rohand, earl of Warwick. The poem recounts his exploits undertaken in order to win the hand of Felice, daughter of the earl. He rescues the daughter of the emperor of Germany, fights against the Saracens, and slays the Soldan. Having returned to England, where he is honourably received by King Æthelstan, he marries Felice, but before long returns to the Holy Land and performs many notable exploits. He comes once more to England, where he encounters the Danish giant Colbrand (the account of this combat is famous), slays the dun cow of Dunsmore, and a winged dragon in Northumberland. He then turns hermit, receiving his bread daily from Felice, his wife, who knows him not, until, when dying, he sends her his ring.

The legend was accepted as authentic by the chroniclers and versified by Lydgate about 1450, and the Beauchamp earls assumed descent from Guy. The story of the encounter between Guy and Colbrand is also told in Drayton's 'Polyolbion', xii. 130 et seq., and other feats of Guy in xiii. 327 et seq.

Guyon, SIR, in Spenser's 'Faerie Queene', the knight of Temperance. His various exploits, the conquest of Pyrochles, the visit to the cave of Mammon, the capture of Acrasia,

and the destruction of her Bower of Bliss, are related in Bk. II. v–xii.

Guzman de Alfarache, a Spanish picaresque romance, the second of its kind (the successor of 'Lazarillo de Tormes', q.v.), by Mateo Aleman (1547–c. 1614). It was translated into English (as 'The Rogue') in 1622 and published with an introductory poem by Ben Jonson. Guzman is by turns scullion, thief, gentleman, beggar, soldier, page to a cardinal and to a French ambassador, and his career gives occasion for 'sketches of character and humorous descriptions to which it would be difficult to produce anything superior' (Hazlitt).

Gwawl, see *Mabinogion.*

Gwendolen or GUENDOLENE, the legendary wife of King Locrine, who threw Estrildis and Sabrina into the Severn (see *Estrildis*). See also *Guendolen.*

Gwendolen Harleth, the heroine of G. Eliot's 'Daniel Deronda' (q.v.).

Gwyn, ELEANOR (1650–87), generally known as Nell Gwyn, orange-girl, actress, and mistress of Charles II. One of her sons was created duke of St. Albans in 1684. She was illiterate, but good in comedy, prologues, and epilogues. There is a story that she induced King Charles to found Chelsea Hospital. Charles's dying request to his brother, according to Burnet and Evelyn, was 'Don't let poor Nelly starve'. She figures in Scott's 'Peveril of the Peak' (q.v.).

Gwynedd or GWYNETH, North Wales.

Gyges, a Lydian shepherd, who, according to Plato ('Republic', ii. 359), descended into a chasm of the earth, where he found a brazen horse. Opening its side he saw within it the body of a man of unusual size. From his finger Gyges took a brazen ring, which, when he wore it, made him invisible. By means of this he introduced himself to the queen, murdered her husband, married her, and usurped the crown of Lydia.

According to Herodotus (i. 7 et seq.), the king, Candaules, boasted of his wife's beauty to Gyges, and allowed him to see her unveiled. She thereupon persuaded Gyges to murder her husband.

Gymnosophists (from Gr. γυμνός naked), a sect of ancient Hindu philosophers of ascetic habits (known to the Greeks through the reports of the companions of Alexander) who wore little or no clothing, ate no flesh, and gave themselves to mystical contemplation.

Gyneth, in Scott's 'Bridal of Triermain' (q.v.), the daughter of King Arthur and Guendolen (q.v.).

H

Habakkuk Mucklewrath, a crazy covenanting preacher in Scott's 'Old Mortality' (q.v.).

Habeas Corpus, a writ requiring the production in court of the body of a person who has been imprisoned, in order that the lawfulness of the imprisonment may be investigated. The right to sue for such a writ was an old common-law right, gradually built up by lawyers, who professed that it was based on Magna Carta. The HABEAS CORPUS ACT is the name commonly given to the Act of 1679 by which the granting and enforcement of this writ were much facilitated.

HABINGTON, WILLIAM (1605–64), educated at St. Omer and Paris, married Lucy Herbert, daughter of the first Baron Powis, and celebrated her in 'Castara', a collection of love poems, first published (anonymously) in 1634. A later edition (1635) contained in addition some elegies on a friend, and the final edition of 1640 a number of sacred poems. In the latter year Habington also published a tragicomedy, 'The Queene of Arragon'.

Habitant, a native of Canada (also of Louisiana) of French descent.

Habsburg, see *Hapsburg*.

Hackney, the London suburb, was probably Hacon's Ey, the island of Hacon, a Danish name. The Knights Templars had an estate there, which, at the dissolution, was granted to the 6th earl of Northumberland, who as Lord Percy was to have married Anne Boleyn [Loftie].

A HACKNEY horse is from the old French *haquenée*, an ambling horse or mare. The word came to be used for horses kept for hire, whence HACK, HACKNEY-COACH, etc.

Hadēs or PLUTO, in Greek mythology, the god of the nether world, the son of Cronos and Rhea, and brother of Zeus and Poseidon. He received, as his share of his father's empire, the kingdom of the infernal regions. He desired to marry Proserpine (q.v.), a virgin goddess of great beauty, and in order to defeat the reluctance of her mother Demeter (Ceres) carried her off as she was gathering flowers in the plain of Enna in Sicily, so that she became queen of the nether world.

The name 'Hades' was transferred to this kingdom, a gloomy sunless abode, where, according to Homer, the ghosts of the dead flit about like bats. Its approach was barred by the rivers Styx, Acheron, Cocytus, and Phlegethon (see *Styx*). Tartarus was the region of Hades in which the most impious of men suffered retribution. The asphodel meadows were reserved for those who deserved neither bliss nor extreme punishment.

The shades of the blessed were conveyed elsewhere (see *Elysium, Fortunate Isles*), but Virgil places Elysium in Hades.

Hadith, in the Muslim religion, the tradition relating to the life of Mohammed, handed down by the companions of the prophet. It came to be regarded as an independent revelation comparable for sanctity with the Koran. The traditions were collected and sifted in the 3rd cent. of the Muslim era.

Hadrian (PUBLIUS AELIUS HADRIANUS) (A.D. 76–138) was Roman emperor from 117 to 138. He was a patron of art and learning. He visited Britain and caused the wall to be built between the Solway and the mouth of the Tyne, known as HADRIAN'S WALL.

Haemony, in Milton's 'Comus', a herb 'more medicinal than moly' (q.v.) and potent against 'enchantments, mildew, blast, or damp, Or ghastly Furies' apparition'.

Haemus, a lofty range of mountains forming the northern boundary of Thrace, the true Balkan range.

Hafed, the hero of 'The Fire-Worshippers', one of the tales of Moore's 'Lalla Rookh' (q.v.).

HAFIZ, SHAMS-ED-DIN MUHAMMAD (*d. c.* 1390), a famous Persian poet and philosopher, born at Shiraz. He sang of love and flowers and nightingales, and the mutability of life, and is said by his enemies to have been given to dissipation. His tomb is still visited by pilgrims. His principal work is the 'Diwan', a collection of short pieces, called 'ghazals', of anacreontic character, in which some commentators see a mystic meaning. Hafiz and Sadi (q.v.) were buried near one another at Shiraz.

Hafnia, in imprints, Copenhagen.

Haga Comitum, in imprints, The Hague.

Hagarene, a reputed descendant of Hagar, the mother of Ishmael: an Arab, a Saracen.

Hagen, a character in the 'Nibelungenlied' (q.v.).

Hagenbach, ARCHIBALD OF, a character in Scott's 'Anne of Geierstein' (q.v.).

Haggadah, a legend, anecdote, or the like, introduced into the Talmud (q.v.) to illustrate a point of the law; hence the legendary element of the Talmud, as distinguished from the HALACHAH, the legal teaching.

HAGGARD, SIR HENRY RIDER (1856–1925), author of many popular romances, including 'King Solomon's Mines' (1886), 'She' (1887), 'Allan Quatermain' (1887), 'Ayesha, or the Return of She' (1905). He collaborated with Andrew Lang (q.v.) in 'The World's Desire' (1891).

Haidée, a character in Byron's 'Don Juan' (q.v.).

Hail, Columbia!, an American patriotic song written in 1798 by Joseph Hopkinson (1770–1842), an eminent American lawyer, to the tune of 'The President's March', for the benefit performance of an actor, Gilbert Fox.

Haj or HAJJ, the pilgrimage to Mecca, imposed as a moral obligation on all Muslims. HAJJI is a title conferred on those who have performed the pilgrimage.

Hajji Baba of Ispahan, The Adventures of, see *Morier.*

Hăki'm in Muslim countries and India means a physician; whereas HĀKI'M (from a different root) means a judge, ruler, or governor. In Browning's 'Return of the Druses' (q.v.), HAKIM is the vanished chief of the Druses.

HAKLUYT, RICHARD (1553?–1616), of a Herefordshire family, was educated at Westminster and Christ Church, Oxford. He was chaplain to Sir Edward Stafford, ambassador at Paris, 1583–8. Here he learnt much of the maritime enterprises of other nations, and found that the English were reputed for 'their sluggish security'. He accordingly decided to devote himself to collecting and publishing the accounts of English explorations, and to this purpose he gave the remainder of his life. He had already been amassing material, for in 1582 he published 'Divers Voyages touching the Discovery of America'. In 1587 he published in Paris a revised edition of the 'De Orbe Novo' of Peter Martyr of Anghiera (subsequently translated into English by Michael Lok), and in the same year appeared his 'Notable History, containing four Voyages made by certain French Captains into Florida'. His 'Principall Navigations, Voiages, and Discoveries of the English Nation' was issued in 1589, and, much enlarged, in three volumes, 1598–1600. He therein gave to the world some account of the voyages of the Cabots, and narratives of Sir Hugh Willoughby's voyage to the N.E. in search of Cathay, Sir John Hawkins's voyage to Guinea and the West Indies, Drake's voyages of 1570–2 and his circumnavigation, Sir Humphrey Gilbert's last voyage in which he perished, Martin Frobisher's search for the N.W. Passage, John Davy's Arctic voyages, and the voyages of Ralegh, James Lancaster, and others. He thus brought to light the hitherto obscure achievements of English navigators, and gave a great impetus to discovery and colonization. Hakluyt was rector of Wetheringsett in 1590, and archdeacon of Westminster in 1603. He is buried in Westminster Abbey. He left unpublished a number of papers which came into the hands of Purchas (q.v.).

Halachah, see *Haggadah.*

Halagaver Court, according to a Cornish

pro erb (quoted by W. C. Hazlitt from Ray's 'Collection'), a jocular imaginary court for judging people who go slovenly in their attire.

Halcombe, MARIAN, a character in Wilkie Collins's 'The Woman in White' (q.v.).

Halcro, CLAUD, a character in Scott's 'The Pirate' (q.v.).

Halcyŏnē or ALCYONE, a daughter of Aeolus and the wife of Ceyx. Her husband perished in a shipwreck. Halcyone was warned in a dream of her husband's fate, and when she found, on the morrow, his body on the shore, she threw herself into the sea. Halcyone and Ceyx were changed into birds, which are fabled to keep the waters calm while they are nesting. Hence the expression 'Halcyon days'.

HALDANE, JOHN BURDON SANDERSON (1892–1964), biologist. He was elected Fellow of the Royal Society in 1932, and was professor of Genetics in London University in 1933 and professor of Biometry from 1937 to 1957. He was chairman of the editorial board of the 'Daily Worker' from 1940 to 1949. His works include 'Daedalus, or, Science and the Future' (1924), 'Possible Worlds' (1927), 'Animal Biology' (with J. S. Huxley, 1927), 'Science and Ethics' (1928), 'The Inequality of Man' (1932), 'The Marxist Philosophy and the Sciences' (1938), 'Science in Peace and War' (1940), and 'The Biochemistry of Genetics' (1954).

HALDANE, RICHARD BURDON, *Viscount* (1856–1928), educated at Edinburgh and Göttingen Universities; secretary of state for war, 1905–12; lord chancellor, 1912–15 and 1924; author of a 'Life of Adam Smith' (1887), 'Pathway to Reality' (Gifford Lecture, 1903), 'Reign of Relativity' (1921), 'Philosophy of Humanism' (1922), 'Human Experience' (1926). With J. Kemp he translated Schopenhauer's 'World as Will and Idea' (1883–6).

Hale, MR., MRS., MARGARET, and FREDERICK, characters in Mrs. Gaskell's 'North and South' (q.v.).

HALE, SIR MATTHEW (1609–76), educated at Magdalen Hall, Oxford, became lord chief justice, and was a voluminous writer on many subjects; but much of his best work was left in manuscript, and published long after his death. His principal legal works were a 'History of the Common Law of England' (1713) and a 'Historia Placitorum Coronae' (1736). He was the subject of a biography by G. Burnet (q.v.).

Hale, NATHAN (1755–76), American hero of the War of Independence, who was hanged as a spy, and whose dying utterance—'I regret that I have but one life to give for my country'—is among the famous 'last words' of history.

HALES, ALEXANDER OF, see *Alexander of Hales.*

HALÉVY, ÉLIE (1870–1937), French social

and political historian, author of 'Histoire du peuple anglais au XIXe siècle' (1912–23 and 1926–32), a study of political, economic, and religious evolution in England after 1815. The English translation (1924–48, by E. I. Watkin and D. A. Barker) includes some sections completed from the author's notes.

HALIBURTON, THOMAS CHANDLER (1796–1865), born at Windsor, Nova Scotia, became a judge of the supreme court of the province. Of the shrewd sayings of the Yankee clock-maker 'Sam Slick', the literary work by which he is best known, the first series appeared in 1837, the second in 1838, and the third in 1840, subsequently republished in one volume. Under its humorous disguise, the work is in reality a piece of political propaganda, designed to stimulate reform in the author's native province. 'The Attaché, or Sam Slick in England' was published in 1843–4; 'The Old Judge, or Life in a Colony', in 1849; 'Traits of American Humour', in 1852; 'Sam Slick's Wise Saws', in 1853; and 'Nature and Human Nature' in 1855.

HALIFAX, MARQUESS OF, see *Savile.*

Halkett, COLONEL and CECILIA, characters in Meredith's 'Beauchamp's Career' (q.v.).

HALL, EDWARD (*d.* 1547), educated at Eton and King's College, Cambridge, was the author of a chronicle entitled 'The Union of the Noble and Illustre Families of Lancastre and York', which was prohibited by Queen Mary, and which is interesting for the account it gives of the times of Henry VIII and the vivid description of his court and of the Field of the Cloth of Gold.

HALL, JOSEPH (1574–1656), was educated at Ashby-de-la-Zouch and Emmanuel College, Cambridge, and was bishop of Exeter 1627–41, and Norwich 1641–7. He was impeached in 1641 in the course of the attack of that year on episcopacy, and imprisoned in 1642, his episcopal revenues were sequestrated in 1643, and his cathedral desecrated. He was expelled from his palace about 1647. He published his 'Virgidemiarum Sex Libri' (q.v.), vol. i in 1597, and vol. ii in 1598 (ed. A. B. Grosart, 1879). His 'Characters of Virtues and Vices' (1608) are sketches on the model of Theophrastus (q.v.), designed with an educative and moral purpose. Besides satires and controversial works against Brownists and Presbyterians, he published poems (ed. Singer, 1824, Grosart, 1879), meditations, devotional works, and autobiographical tracts, also 'Observations of some Specialities of Divine Providence', 'Hard Measure' (1647), and 'The Shaking of the Olive Tree' (posthumous, 1660); collective editions were issued, 1808, 1837, and 1863. Hall claimed to be the first of English satirists, and although Lodge and Donne may in some respects have anticipated him, he certainly introduced the Juvenalian satire in English.

HALLAM, ARTHUR HENRY (1811–33), educated at Eton and Trinity College, Cambridge, the close friend of Lord Tennyson, died suddenly at Vienna at an early age. He is chiefly remembered as the subject of Tennyson's 'In Memoriam' (q.v.). His own 'Remains' (in verse and prose) appeared in 1834.

HALLAM, HENRY (1777–1859), historian, was educated at Eton and Christ Church, Oxford. He spent some ten years on the preparation of his first published work, 'A View of the State of Europe during the Middle Ages' (1818), a survey of the process of formation of the principal European States. Hallam's best-known work, his 'Constitutional History of England' to the death of George II, appeared in 1827. It is essentially the story of the conflict of the British principles of law with the claims of royal prerogative. The work was subsequently continued by Sir T. E. May (q.v.). Hallam's last great work was an 'Introduction to the Literature of Europe during the Fifteenth, Sixteenth, and Seventeenth Centuries' (1837–9).

Byron, in 'English Bards and Scotch Reviewers' (q.v.), sneers at 'classic Hallam much renowned for Greek'. A note explains that Hallam reviewed Payne Knight in the 'Edinburgh Review' and condemned certain Greek verses, not knowing that they were by Pindar. The article was probably not by Hallam.

Hallel, a hymn of praise, consisting of Psalms cxiii–cxviii, sung at the Jewish feasts of the Passover, Pentecost, Dedication, and Tabernacles, and in shortened form at other feasts.

Hallelujah, from two Hebrew words meaning 'praise Jehovah'. HALLELUJAH-LASS was a popular name for a female member of the Salvation Army.

Halley, EDMUND (1656–1742), the astronomer, was educated at St. Paul's School and Queen's College, Oxford. He originated by his suggestions Newton's 'Principia', which he introduced to the Royal Society and published at his own expense. Among the great mass of his valuable astronomical work may be mentioned his accurate prediction of the return in 1758 of the comet (named after him) of 1531, 1607, and 1682. He became astronomer-royal in 1721.

HALLIWELL, afterwards HALLIWELL-PHILLIPPS, JAMES ORCHARD (1820–89), was a noted Shakespearian scholar. His published works include: 'Life of Shakespeare' (1848), 'Shakespearean Forgeries at Bridgewater House' (1853), 'Curiosities of Modern Shakespearean Criticism' (1853), 'Dictionary of Old English Plays' (1860), 'Outlines of the Life of Shakespeare' (1881; 7th ed., 1887), and numerous notes on the separate plays and on Shakespeariana in general.

Hallow-e'en, see *All-Hallows' Day.*

Hals, FRANS (*c.* 1580–1666), Dutch portrait-painter. With brilliant technique he caught the fleeting expressions of his sitters, even in the group portraits of Dutch burghers at which he excelled.

Hamadryads, see *Dryads.*

Hambledon Club, THE, a famous cricket club of the early days of the game. It flourished about 1750–91, being supported by wealthy patrons of cricket, and played its matches on Broadhalfpenny and Windmill Downs in Hampshire. Its historian was John Nyren (q.v.).

Hamel, the cow in 'Reynard the Fox' (q.v.).

Hamelin, or *Hameln,* see *Pied Piper of Hamelin.*

Hamet Ben Engeli, CID, see *Cid Hamet Ben Engeli.*

HAMILTON, ANTHONY, see *Gramont.*

HAMILTON, CHARLES (1875–1961), author, under many pseudonyms, of boys' weekly papers, of which the most famous were 'The Gem' (1907–39), written under the name MARTIN CLIFFORD, and 'The Magnet' (1908–40), under the name FRANK RICHARDS. 'The Magnet' introduced Billy Bunter of Greyfriars School.

Hamilton, EMMA, LADY (1761?–1815), *née* Lyon, went to London in 1778, probably as nursemaid to the family of Dr. Richard Budd, and is said to have been the 'Goddess of Health' in the 'Temple of Health' opened by the quack doctor, James Graham, in the Adelphi about 1780. After living, as Emily Hart, under the protection of various men, and coming under the refining influence of Romney, who painted her many times, she married Sir William Hamilton (1730–1803), British ambassador at Naples, in 1791. She first saw Nelson in 1793, and became intimate with him in 1798. She gave birth to her daughter Horatia in 1801. She claimed to have rendered important political services at Naples, but these claims, though endorsed by Nelson, were ignored by the British Government. Owing to her extravagance, she died in obscurity and poverty, in spite of legacies from Nelson and Hamilton.

HAMILTON, WILLIAM, OF BANGOUR (1704–54), author of the melodious 'Braes of Yarrow', published in Ramsay's 'Miscellany' (1724–32), and of the Jacobite 'Ode to the Battle of Gladsmuir'. He made the earliest Homeric translation into English blank verse.

HAMILTON, SIR WILLIAM (1788–1856), the philosopher, was educated at Glasgow and Balliol College, Oxford. His philosophical reputation was made by a number of articles which appeared in the 'Edinburgh Review' from 1829 to 1836 (republished in 1852 as 'Discussions on Philosophy and Literature, Education and University Reform'), of which the most important were those on 'the Philosophy of the Unconditioned', 'the Philosophy of Perception', and 'Logic'. He was elected to the chair of logic and metaphysics at Edinburgh in 1836. His 'Lectures on Metaphysics

and Logic' appeared in 1859–60, after his death.

A man of great philosophical erudition rather than a great philosophical thinker, Hamilton represents the influence of Kant upon the common-sense philosophy of the Scottish school as set forth by Reid. He maintained, like the latter, our immediate consciousness of a perceiving subject and an external reality, and distinguished between the primary and objectively real qualities, and the secondary or subjective qualities; he also expounded the doctrine of the phenomenal and relative quality of all knowledge, according to which we must remain ignorant of ultimate reality, since knowledge, whether of mind or matter, must be conditioned by the knowing mind and cannot therefore be knowledge of the thing-in-itself. If we attempt to know the unconditioned, we are faced by two contradictory propositions, both inconceivable, and one of which must be true: the unconditioned is either the Absolute (i.e. limited) or the Infinite. We cannot conceive time or space, for instance, as either limited or infinite.

In Logic, Hamilton introduced a modification of the traditional doctrine, known as the 'Quantification of the Predicate', which has been further elaborated by mathematicians. Hamilton's philosophical views were vigorously attacked by J. S. Mill (q.v.) in his 'Examination of Sir W. Hamilton's Philosophy' (q.v.).

Hamilton, WILLIAM GERARD, see *Single-speech Hamilton.*

HAMILTON, SIR WILLIAM ROWAN (1805–65), educated at Trinity College, Dublin, showed extraordinary precocity of mathematical genius, detecting at 16 an error in Laplace's 'Mécanique céleste', and in his undergraduate days predicting conical refraction from mathematical analysis. He was appointed Andrews professor of astronomy in 1827, and royal astronomer of Ireland. His fame rests principally on his discovery of the science of quaternions, a higher branch of the calculus ('Lectures on Quaternions', 1853; 'Elements of Quaternions', 1866). The first volume of his 'Mathematical Papers', edited by A. W. Conway and J. L. Synge, was published in 1931. Hamilton had considerable poetical gifts, and was a close friend of Wordsworth.

Hamlet, a tragedy by Shakespeare (q.v.), probably produced before 1603–4, published imperfectly in quarto in 1603, and fully in quarto in 1604, and with some omissions in the first folio. The story is in Saxo Grammaticus and was accessible in Belleforest's 'Histoires Tragiques'. There was also an earlier play on the subject, not now extant.

A noble king of Denmark has been murdered by his brother Claudius, after Claudius had seduced Gertrude, the king's wife. Claudius has supplanted on the throne the dead man's son, Hamlet, and married with indecent haste the dead man's widow. Hamlet meets the ghost of his dead father, who relates the circumstances of the murder and demands vengeance. Hamlet vows obedience; but his melancholy, introspective, and scrupulous nature makes him irresolute and dilatory in action. He counterfeits madness to escape the suspicion that he is threatening danger to the king. His behaviour is attributed to love for Ophelia (daughter of Polonius, the lord chamberlain), whom he has previously courted but now treats rudely. He tests the ghost's story by having a play acted before the king reproducing the circumstances of the murder, and the king betrays himself. A scene follows in which Hamlet violently upbraids the queen. Thinking he hears the king listening behind the arras, he draws his sword and kills instead Polonius. The king now determines to destroy Hamlet. He sends him on a mission to England, with intent to have him killed there. But pirates capture Hamlet and send him back to Denmark. He arrives to find that Ophelia, crazed with grief, has perished by drowning. Her brother Laertes, a strong contrast to the character of Hamlet, has hurried home to take vengeance for the death of his father Polonius. The king contrives a fencing match between Hamlet and Laertes, in which the latter uses a poisoned sword, and kills Hamlet; but not before Hamlet has mortally wounded Laertes and stabbed the king; while Gertrude has drunk a poisoned cup intended for her son.

Hamley, MR., MRS., OSBORNE, and ROGER, characters in Mrs. Gaskell's 'Wives and Daughters' (q.v.).

HAMMETT, DASHIELL (1894–1961), American writer of detective stories, born in Maryland. His best-known books are 'The Glass Key' (1931) and 'The Thin Man' (1932).

Hampden, JOHN (1594–1643), educated at Magdalen College, Oxford, and M.P. for Grampound, Wendover, and subsequently Buckinghamshire, is famous as the leader of the resistance to the imposition of ship-money (q.v.). He was impeached in 1642, but escaped the king's attempt to arrest him. He was mortally wounded in a skirmish at Chalgrove Field, near Oxford.

Hampton Court, on the Thames, some twelve miles W. of the centre of London, was built by Cardinal Wolsey on land that had formerly belonged to the knights of St. John, and was ceded by him to Henry VIII. For two centuries it was a favourite residence of the English sovereigns. In William III's reign part of it was rebuilt by Wren.

Hampton Court Conference, a conference held in 1604 to settle points of dispute between the Church party and the Puritans, out of which arose the preparation of the Authorized Version of the Bible. See *Bible, The English.*

Hanaud, the detective in A. E. W. Mason's stories, 'At the Villa Rose', 'The House of the Arrow', and 'The Prisoner in the Opal'.

Hand of Ethelberta, The, a novel by Hardy (q.v.), published in 1876. As the author states in the preface, this is a 'somewhat frivolous narrative' and one in which the drawing-room is 'sketched in many cases from the point of view of the servants' hall'.

Ethelberta is one of a numerous family, sons and daughters of a butler, Chickerel by name. An ambitious and masterful young woman, she marries the son of the house where she is a governess, and is soon left a widow of one-and-twenty. The story is occupied with her spirited endeavour to maintain the social position she has acquired, while concealing her relationship with the butler, and yet actively helping her brothers and sisters. After humiliating experiences, she finally secures a wicked old peer for a husband, and rules him with a firm hand. Christopher Julian, the musician, her faithful admirer whom she has alternately encouraged and snubbed, is in the end left to marry her pink-cheeked sister Picotee.

Handel, originally HAENDEL, GEORGE FREDERICK (1685–1759), born in Saxony, came to England in 1710, after composing some of his operas and oratorios. His opera 'Rinaldo' was produced with great success at the Queen's Theatre, Haymarket, in 1711. He settled permanently in England in 1712. He was organist for the duke of Chandos at Canons Whitchurch, near Edgware (1718–20). It was here that he composed 'Esther', his first English oratorio (performed 1720), and 'Acis and Galatea' (performed 1720 or 1721). From 1720 to 1728 he was director of a speculative operatic venture known as the Royal Academy of Music. About this time a rivalry sprang up between Handel and the musician Buononcini, which divided the music-loving public and occasioned the epigram, variously attributed to Pope, Swift, and Byron:

> Strange all this difference should be
> 'Twixt Tweedledum and Tweedledee.

Handel was appointed court composer in 1727 and produced a number of operas at Covent Garden and Lincoln's Inn Fields, also musical settings for Dryden's 'Ode on St. Cecilia's Day' and 'Alexander's Feast'. His oratorio 'Israel in Egypt' was composed in 1738; the 'Messiah' was first heard (in Dublin) in 1741; his last oratorio 'Jephthah' was produced at Covent Garden in 1752. Handel was buried in Westminster Abbey. He carried choral music to its highest point, but in instrumental did not advance beyond his contemporaries.

Handlyng Synne, a translation, in eight-syllabled verse, of the 'Manuel des Pechiez' of William of Wadington, by Robert Mannyng (1288–1338) of Brunne (Bourne in Lincolnshire), a Gilbertine monk, written between 1303 and 1338. The author sets forth, with illustrative stories, first the ten commandments, then the seven deadly sins, then the sin of sacrilege, then the seven sacraments, dealing finally with shrift. Mannyng is a good story-teller, and his work throws much light on the manners of the time, notably on the tyranny and rapacity of the lords and knights. See *Colbek*.

Handy Andy, a novel by Lover (q.v.).

Hanging Gardens of Babylon, see *Babylon*.

Hans Carvel, a *fabliau* by Matthew Prior (q.v.). The subject of it, a coarse jest on the method of retaining a wife's fidelity, has been treated in the *Facetiae* of Poggio, by Rabelais (III. xxviii), and other writers.

Hansard, the official reports of the proceedings of the Houses of Parliament, colloquially so called because they were for a long period compiled by Messrs. Hansard. Luke Hansard (1752–1828) commenced printing the 'House of Commons' Journals' in 1774. 'Hansard' is now no more than an established familiar title. The name disappeared from the title-page of the Reports from 1892 onwards; the Reports were published by Reuter's Telegram Company in 1892, Eyre & Spottiswoode, 1893–4, and subsequently by a number of other firms in succession; they are now a regular publication of H.M. Stationery Office.

Hanse, THE, from a MHG. word meaning association, merchants' guild, was the name of a famous political and commercial league, also called the HANSEATIC LEAGUE, of Germanic towns, signed in 1241. The Hanse towns and their confederates numbered about one hundred in the 14th cent., their commercial object being to carry on trade between the east and west of Northern Europe. They had their own fleet and army, and waged war with Denmark. But their strength decayed during the Thirty Years War (1618–48) and finally only Lübeck, Hamburg, and Bremen remained in the League. This endured until the 19th cent., when its remaining property was sold and the three cities entered the North German Confederation. The Hanse had a house in London (*Guildhalla Teutonicorum*; see also *Steelyard*) and enjoyed certain privileges (withdrawn in 1567), together with the obligation of maintaining Bishopsgate.

The word 'hanse' was also used in English for an association of merchants trading with foreign parts, for the merchant guild of a town, and for the monopolies and privileges possessed by it.

Hansom, JOSEPH ALOYSIUS (1803–82), an architect who erected the Birmingham town hall, and in 1834 registered his invention of a 'Patent Safety Cab', from which the hansom cab, although differing in many respects, took its name. The latter is a low-hung two-wheeled cabriolet holding two persons inside, the driver being mounted on a dickey behind and the reins going over the roof.

Hapsburg or HABSBURG, HOUSE OF, the family to which the Imperial dynasty of Austria traced its descent. Rodolph, count of

Hapsburg, was chosen 'Holy Roman' emperor in 1273. Charles VI, the last ruler of Austria of the male Hapsburg line, died in 1740. His daughter Maria Theresa became queen of Hungary, and from her and her husband, Francis, duke of Lorraine, the modern Hapsburgs are descended. The last of this line, the emperor Charles I, abdicated in 1918 (when Austria and Hungary were proclaimed separate republics); he died in 1922. The Spanish Hapsburgs are descended from Philip II of Spain (*d.* 1598), son of Charles V of Austria. The title Hapsburg is derived from the castle of Habsburg, near Aarau in Switzerland, built by Werner, bishop of Strasburg, in the 11th cent.

Harapha, in Milton's 'Samson Agonistes', the giant of Gath who comes to mock the blind Samson in prison.

Hard Cash, a novel by C. Reade (q.v.), published in 1863, a sequel to 'Love me little, love me long'; it was perhaps the best known of the author's propagandist novels and was designed to expose the abuses prevailing in lunatic asylums. It gave rise to lively protests in certain quarters.

The first part of the story is chiefly occupied with the voyage from India of David Dodd, a sea-captain, who is bringing home the 'hard cash', the accumulated savings which he destines for his family's support. The narrative of his encounters with pirates, and of the storm, shipwrecks, and other adventures that follow, is vividly told. Dodd entrusts his fortune to the scoundrelly banker, Richard Hardie, in ignorance that he is bankrupt; and the discovery of the loss of his hard-earned savings deprives him of his reason. Hardie, to prevent his son Alfred, who is engaged to Dodd's daughter, from revealing his appropriation of Dodd's money, has Alfred confined as a lunatic. The second portion of the book is devoted to the exposure of the horrors of the private asylum in which Dodd and young Hardie are confined; to the subsequent life of Dodd as an ordinary seaman, after his escape from the asylum; and to the exposure of old Hardie and the recovery of Dodd's fortune.

Hard Times, a novel by Dickens (q.v.), published in 1854.

Thomas Gradgrind, a citizen of Coketown, an industrial centre, is an 'eminently practical man', who believes in facts and statistics, and nothing else, and brings up his children, Louisa and young Tom, accordingly, ruthlessly repressing the imaginative and spiritual sides of their nature. He marries Louisa to Josiah Bounderby, a manufacturer, humbug, and curmudgeon, thirty years older than herself. Louisa consents partly from the indifference and cynicism engendered by her father's treatment, partly from a desire to help her brother, who is employed by Bounderby and who is the only person she loves. James Harthouse, a young politician, without heart or principles, comes to Coketown, is thrown into contact with her, and, taking advantage of her unhappy life with Bounderby, attempts to seduce her. The better side of her nature is awakened by this experience, and at the crisis she flees for protection to her father, who in turn is awakened to the folly of his system. He shelters her from Bounderby and the couple are permanently separated. But further trouble is in store for Gradgrind. His son, young Tom, has robbed the bank of his employer, and though he contrives for a time to throw the suspicion on a blameless artisan, Stephen Blackpool, is finally detected and hustled out of the country. Among the notable minor characters are Sleary, the proprietor of a circus; Cissy Jupe, whose father had been a performer in his troupe; and Mrs. Sparsit, Mr. Bounderby's housekeeper.

Hardcastle, SQUIRE, MRS., and MISS, characters in Goldsmith's 'She Stoops to Conquer' (q.v.).

HARDENBERG, FRIEDRICH LEOPOLD VON (1772–1801), German romantic poet and novelist, author of poems religious, mystic, and secular, including 'Hymns of Night', laments on the death of his lovely Sophie von Kühn, and the novels 'Heinrich von Ofterdingen' and 'Die Lehrlinge zu Sais' ('The Disciples at Sais'). He wrote under the pseudonym 'Novalis'.

Hardicanute, king of England, 1040–2, son of Canute. He divided the kingdom with Harold I on Canute's death in 1035, but did not come to England until Harold's death in 1040.

Harding, THE REVD. SEPTIMUS, the principal character in A. Trollope's 'The Warden' (q.v.), who also takes a prominent part in its sequel 'Barchester Towers' (q.v.). His death occurs in 'The Last Chronicle of Barset'.

Hardy, MR. and LETITIA, characters in Mrs. Cowley's 'The Belle's Stratagem' (q.v.).

HARDY, THOMAS (1840–1928), born at Upper Bockhampton, near Dorchester, was the son of a builder. In early life he practised architecture. The underlying theme of much of Hardy's writing, of many of the novels, the short poems, and the great epic-drama 'The Dynasts', is the struggle of man against the force, neutral and indifferent to his sufferings as Hardy conceives it, that rules the world; or, in another aspect, the ironies and disappointments of life and love. His strong sense of humour is seen principally in his rustic characters. Hardy's novels, according to his own classification, divide themselves into three groups; the chief of them are dealt with separately under their titles.

I. *Novels of Character and Environment*—'Under the Greenwood Tree' (1872); 'Far from the Madding Crowd' (1874); 'The Return of the Native' (1878); 'The Mayor of Casterbridge' (1886); 'The Woodlanders' (1887); 'Wessex Tales' (1888); 'Tess of the D'Urbervilles' (1891); 'Life's Little Ironies' (1894); 'Jude the Obscure' (1896, in the edition of the 'Works' of that year).

II. *Romances and Fantasies*—'A Pair of Blue Eyes' (1873); 'The Trumpet-Major' (1880); 'Two on a Tower' (1882); 'A Group of Noble Dames' (1891); 'The Well-Beloved', published serially in 1892, revised and reissued in 1897.

III. *Novels of Ingenuity*—'Desperate Remedies' (1871); 'The Hand of Ethelberta' (1876); 'A Laodicean' (1881). 'A Changed Man, The Waiting Supper, and other Tales' (1913) is a reprint of 'a dozen minor novels' belonging to the various groups. For the topography of the novels see Hermann Lea's 'Thomas Hardy's Wessex', written with the novelist's help.

Seven volumes of Hardy's lyrics were published at various dates from 1898 to 1928; these were subsequently included in his 'Collected Poems'. His great epic-drama 'The Dynasts' (q.v.) was published in three parts; Pt. I, 1904, Pt. II, 1906, Pt. III, 1908. His Arthurian drama, 'The Famous Tragedy of the Queen of Cornwall' (q.v.), was produced in 1923.

Hardy, SIR THOMAS MASTERMAN (1769–1839), Nelson's flag-captain in various ships and finally in the 'Victory'. Nelson died in his arms.

HARE, JULIUS CHARLES (1795–1855), educated at Charterhouse and Trinity College, Cambridge, was rector of Hurstmonceux and subsequently archdeacon of Lewes. He was joint author with his brother Augustus of 'Guesses at Truth' (1827), a collection of observations on philosophy, religion, literature, and many other subjects, supplemented in the edition of 1837 by longer essays. He also collaborated with Connop Thirlwall (q.v.) in a translation of the 'Roman History' of Niebuhr (q.v.), published in 1828–32. The first volume having been attacked in the 'Quarterly Review', the translators published in 1829 a 'Vindication of Niebuhr's History'. He also wrote 'The Victory of Faith' (1840), 'The Mission of the Comforter' (1846), and 'Miscellaneous Pamphlets on Church Questions' (1855).

Hare, WILLIAM, the accomplice of the murderer William Burke (q.v.). He was set at liberty from the Tolbooth, the law officers having decided that he could not legally be put on his trial.

Haredale, GEOFFREY and EMMA, characters in Dickens's 'Barnaby Rudge' (q.v.).

Harington, the name currently given to the copper farthing when first issued in the reign of James I, a patent for the issue having been given to Lord Harington of Exton.

HARINGTON or HARRINGTON, JAMES (1611–77), educated at Trinity College, Oxford, was for some time in the service of the Elector Palatine, and attended Charles I in his captivity in spite of his republican principles. He published in 1656 'The Commonwealth of Oceana' (q.v.), a political romance, and several tracts in defence of it. Harington was founder of the

Rota Club (q.v., 1659–60). He was imprisoned after the Restoration.

HARINGTON, Sir JOHN (1561–1612), godson of Queen Elizabeth, was educated at Eton and Christ's College, Cambridge. He translated Ariosto's 'Orlando Furioso' (q.v.), by Queen Elizabeth's direction. His Rabelaisian 'Metamorphosis of Ajax' ('a jakes', 1596) and other satires led to his banishment from the court. He accompanied Essex to Ireland, and was deputed to appease the Queen's anger against him, unsuccessfully. His letters and miscellaneous writings, in 'Nugae Antiquae', appeared in 1769.

Harkness, EDWARD STEPHEN, see *Pilgrim Trust.*

HARLAND, HENRY (1861–1905), American author, born in St. Petersburg, Russia, educated at Harvard University. He became editor of the 'Yellow Book' in 1894, thereby figuring prominently in the literary life of London. He published several romances, the most charming and successful being 'The Cardinal's Snuff-Box' (1900).

Harleian MSS., THE, were collected by Robert and Edward Harley, the first and second earls of Oxford (1661–1724, 1689–1741), and are now in the British Museum, having been purchased for the nation under an act of 1754.

Harleian Miscellany, a reprint of a selection of tracts from the library of Edward Harley, 2nd earl of Oxford, edited by William Oldys, his secretary, and Samuel Johnson, published in 1744–6 by Thomas Osborne.

Harleian Society, THE, was founded in 1869 for the publication of heraldic visitations, pedigrees, etc.

Harlequin, from the Italian *arlecchino,* originally a character in Italian comedy, a mixture of childlike ignorance, wit, and grace, always in love, always in trouble, easily despairing, easily consoled; in English pantomime a mute character supposed to be invisible to the clown and the pantaloon, the rival of the clown in the affections of Columbine. The Italian word is possibly the same as the old French *Hellequin, Hennequin,* one of a troop of demon horsemen riding by night. [OED.]

Harleth, GWENDOLEN, the heroine of G. Eliot's 'Daniel Deronda' (q.v.).

Harley, the principal character in 'The Man of Feeling' of H. Mackenzie (q.v.).

Harley, ADRIAN, in Meredith's 'The Ordeal of Richard Feverel' (q.v.), the cynical 'wise youth' and tutor of Richard, drawn from Meredith's friend Maurice Fitz-Gerald.

Harley Street, used allusively of medical specialists, from the fact that many medical specialists live in or near this street, which is in the West End of London.

Harlowe, CLARISSA, see *Clarissa Harlowe.*

Harmattan, a parching land-wind, which blows from the NE. during Dec., Jan., and Feb. in the Sahara and W. Sudan, very occasionally reaching even the Guinea coast.

Harmodius and **Aristogeiton**: when the brothers Hippias and Hipparchus, the sons of Peisistratus, were tyrants of Athens (527–514 B.C.), Hipparchus, disappointed in a disreputable love-affair, avenged himself ·by a public insult to the family of the person concerned, Harmodius. The latter, his friend Aristogeiton, and some others, joined in a conspiracy to slay the tyrants at the festival of the Panathenaea. Owing to an error, Hipparchus was killed before Hippias arrived, Harmodius was immediately struck down by the guards, and Aristogeiton tortured in vain before death to make him reveal the names of the conspirators. Subsequently Hippias was expelled, and Harmodius and Aristogeiton, though they had been engaged in an act of private vengeance, came to be highly honoured as patriots and liberators of the State.

Harmon, JOHN, *alias* JOHN ROKESMITH, *alias* JULIUS HANDFORD, the hero of Dickens's 'Our Mutual Friend' (q.v.).

Harmonia, a daughter of Ares and Aphrodite, who married Cadmus (q.v.). Cadmus gave her the famous necklace which he had received from Hephaestus (or from Europa) and which became fatal to all who possessed it.

Harmonious Blacksmith, The, an air in a harpsichord suite written (1720) by Handel (q.v.) for his pupils, the daughters of the Prince of Wales.

Harold, an historical drama by A. Tennyson (q.v.), published in 1876. It presents in dramatic form the events dealt with in Bulwer Lytton's romance of the same name (see below).

Harold, the Last of the Saxon Kings, an historical romance by Bulwer Lytton (q.v.), published in 1848.

The story deals with the latter years of the reign of Edward the Confessor and the short reign of Harold, from the visit of Harold to William, duke of Normandy, to his death at Senlac. With this is woven the romance of Harold's love for Edith the Fair, whom, owing to their relationship, he is forbidden by the Church to marry. For political reasons, and at Edith's behest, he marries Aldyth, sister of the northern earls Eadwine and Morkere. But when he lies dead on the field of Senlac, Edith seeks him out and dies beside him, thus fulfilling the saying of Hilda, the Saxon prophetess, that they should be united.

Harold, Childe, see *Childe Harold.*

Harold I, son of Canute, king of England, 1035–1040.

Harold II, son of Godwine, king of England in 1066, killed in that year at the battle of Hastings or Senlac. See *Harold, the Last of the Saxon Kings.*

Harold the Dauntless, a poem by Sir W. Scott, published in 1817. Harold is the son of Witikind, a Danish Viking, converted to Christianity by St. Cuthbert and granted lands between the Wear and the Tyne. Harold, like his father a fierce warrior, comes to England to claim these lands, which have been resumed at his father's death. A probation is imposed on him, that he shall spend a night in a lonely castle. In the course of this he sees visions, which lead to his conversion.

Haroun-al-Raschid (763–809), caliph of Baghdad, who figures in many tales of the 'Arabian Nights' (q.v.), together with Ja'far, his vizier, and Mesrour his executioner. He was the most powerful and vigorous of the Abbasid Caliphs, his rule extending from India to Africa. He entertained friendly relations with Charlemagne, who was almost his exact contemporary.

Harpagon, a character in Molière's 'L'Avare' (q.v.), the typical miser, whose avarice causes him to be surrounded by persons who deceive him. See *Euclio.*

Harper's New Monthly Magazine, founded in 1850 by Messrs. Harper & Brothers of New York, originally for the avowed purpose of reproducing in America the work of distinguished English contributors to magazines (such as Dickens and Bulwer Lytton). It subsequently became truly American in character.

Harpier, in Shakespeare's 'Macbeth', IV. i. 3 ('Harpier cries, 'tis time, 'tis time'), apparently an error for Harpy. [OED.]

Harpies, THE, in Greek HARPYIAE, winged monsters, by name Aello, Ocўpētē, and Celaeno, who were supposed to carry off persons or things. They plundered Aeneas during his voyage to Italy. See also under *Phineus.*

Harpocrătēs, the Roman equivalent of the Egyptian *Horus* (q.v.), who was called 'Harpechrat' in his character of the youthful sun, born afresh every morning, and represented sitting with his finger in his mouth, an attitude symbolical of childhood. From a misunderstanding of this attitude, he came to be regarded by the Greeks and Romans as the god of silence.

HARPUR, CHARLES (1817–68), Australian poet, published a number of volumes of verse ('Thoughts: a series of sonnets', 1845; 'A Poet's Home', 1862; 'The Tower of the Dream', 1865, etc.), many of which give a good presentment of the scenery and life of the Australian bush. His best poem is 'The Creek of the Four Graves'. A collected edition of his poems was issued in 1883.

Harriet Byron, the heroine of Richardson's 'Sir Charles Grandison' (q.v.).

Harriet Smith, a character in Jane Austen's 'Emma' (q.v.).

Harrington, see *Harington.*

Harris, MRS., in Dickens's 'Martin Chuzzlewit' (q.v.), the mythical friend of Mrs. Gamp.

HARRIS, FRANK (1856–1931), successively editor of the 'Fortnightly Review', the 'Saturday Review', and 'Vanity Fair'; founder and editor of the 'Candid Friend'. His books include: 'The Man Shakespeare' (1909), 'The Women of Shakespeare' (1911), 'Oscar Wilde' (1918); his plays are: 'Mr. and Mrs. Daventry' (1900), 'Shakespeare and his Love' (1910).

HARRIS, JOEL CHANDLER (1848–1908), American author, was born at Eatonton, Georgia, and devoted from childhood to English literature. To this taste he added an extraordinary knowledge of Negro myth and custom and of Negro dialect and idiom, which he reproduced in his famous 'Uncle Remus' series. These contain a great number of folk-lore tales, relating to a variety of animals, with the rabbit as hero and the fox next in importance, told by a Negro to a little boy and interspersed with comments on many other subjects. The principal volumes of this series were 'Uncle Remus, his Songs and Sayings' (1880), 'Uncle Remus and his Friends' (1892), 'Mr. Rabbit at Home' (1895), 'The Tar-Baby' (1904), 'Told by Uncle Remus' (1905), 'Uncle Remus and Brer Rabbit' (1906), 'Uncle Remus and the Little Boy' (1910).

Harrison, DR., a character in Fielding's 'Amelia' (q.v.).

HARRISON, FREDERIC (1831–1923), educated at King's College, London, and Wadham College, Oxford, was professor of jurisprudence and international law to the Inns of Court from 1877 to 1889, and from 1880 to 1905 president of the English Positivist Committee, formed to represent in this country the philosophic doctrines of Auguste Comte (q.v.). He was author of many works, including: 'The Meaning of History' (1862, enlarged 1894), 'Order and Progress' (1875), 'The Choice of Books' (1886), 'Oliver Cromwell' (1888), 'Introduction to Comte's Positive Philosophy' (1896), 'Victorian Literature' (1895), 'William the Silent' (1897), 'Byzantine History in the Early Middle Ages' (1900), 'Ruskin' (1902), 'Chatham' (1905), 'The Philosophy of Common Sense' (1907), 'Among my Books' (1912), 'The Positive Evolution of Religion' (1912).

HARRISON, WILLIAM (1534–93), born in London and educated at Westminster School, Cambridge, and Oxford, was rector of Radwinter and canon of Windsor. He was the author of the admirable 'Description of England' included in the 'Chronicles' of Holinshed (q.v.), and translator of Bellenden's Scottish version of Boece's 'Description of Scotland', also included in the same.

Harrow School, at Harrow-on-the-Hill, Middlesex, founded and endowed by John Lyon (c. 1514–91), of Preston, under Letters Patent and a Charter granted by Queen Elizabeth. Rodney was the first of the many great men educated at Harrow, a list which includes Samuel Parr, Bryan Waller Procter ('Barry Cornwall'), Theodore Hook, James Morier, Lord Byron (qq.v.), besides several prime ministers (Perceval, Sir Robert Peel, Lord Aberdeen, Lord Palmerston, Mr. Baldwin, and Sir Winston Churchill). The founder made special provision for the encouragement of archery at the school, and Sir Gilbert Talbot in 1684 presented a silver arrow to be shot for annually. Arrow shooting was regarded as peculiarly characteristic of the school (Sir John Fischer Williams, 'Harrow').

Harrowing of Hell, The, a poem of some 250 lines in octosyllabic couplets of the late 13th or 14th cent. It consists of a narrative introduction, followed by speeches, as in a drama, assigned to Christ, Satan, the Door-Keeper, and persons in Hell (Adam, Eve, Abraham, David, John, Moses). Christ reproves Satan and claims Adam. Satan retorts with a threat to seduce a man for each soul that Christ releases. Christ breaks in the door, binds Satan, and frees his servants.

HARRY THE MINSTREL, or BLIND HARRY, see *Henry the Minstrel.*

Harry Richmond, The Adventures of, a novel by G. Meredith (q.v.), published in 1871.

The father of Harry Richmond is the son of an actress and of a royal personage. Obsessed with the idea of the royal blood in his veins, a man of florid imagination, amusing gifts, little scruple, and a lunatic's cleverness in the pursuit of his monomania, his one object in life is to obtain an exalted position for his son. As a teacher of singing he has entered the house of the wealthy Squire Beltham, has fascinated both his daughters, carried off and married one of them, driven her crazy and to an early grave, and incurred the deep hatred of the bluff old squire, who strives to attach his grandson to himself and save him from his father. The conflict between the two makes the comedy of the story. The dominating influence in the early life of Harry Richmond is an intense love for this fascinating buffoon, which develops, as understanding comes, into loyalty and compassion. The father leads a life of semi-regal splendour, interrupted by periods in a debtor's prison and by wanderings among the courts of petty German princes, to which his audacity and talents gain him admission. At one of these Harry Richmond and the romantic Princess Ottilia, daughter of the reigning duke, fall in love; and the masterly if unscrupulous manœuvres of Harry's father to overcome the obstacles to so absurd a match, and the humiliations to which Harry is in consequence exposed, make the central feature of the story. On the other side we have the squire's attempts to marry his grandson to the typical if somewhat commonplace English girl, Janet Ilchester. Finally the father's crazy schemes and illusions are shattered, and the squire's designs, after his death, are realized.

HARTE, FRANCIS BRET (1836–1902), born at Albany, New York, was taken to California when 18, where he saw something of mining life. He worked on various newspapers and periodicals in San Francisco, to which he contributed some excellent writing including the short stories which made him famous. Notable among these were 'The Luck of Roaring Camp' (1868), and 'Tennessee's Partner' and 'The Outcasts of Poker Flat', which were included in 'The Luck of Roaring Camp and Other Sketches' (1870). His humorous-pathetic verse includes: 'Jim', 'Her Letter', and 'Plain Language from Truthful James'. Bret Harte was American consul at Crefeld in Germany (1878–80) and at Glasgow (1880–5), after which he lived in England.

Hartford (*or* **Connecticut**) **Wits, The**, a group of writers who flourished during the last two decades of the 18th cent. at Hartford and New Haven, Connecticut, U.S.A., now chiefly remembered for their vigorous political verse satires. Chief among them were Timothy Dwight, Joel Barlow, John Trumbull, David Humphreys, Richard Alsop, Lemuel Hopkins, and Theodore Dwight. They were all either graduates of Yale or associated with that college.

Harthacnut, see *Hardicanute.*

Harthouse, JAMES, a character in Dickens's 'Hard Times' (q.v.).

Hartley, ADAM, a character in Scott's 'The Surgeon's Daughter' (q.v.).

HARTLEY, DAVID (1705–57), philosopher, was educated at Bradford Grammar School and Jesus College, Cambridge, and practised as a physician. In his 'Observations on Man, his Frame, Duty, and Expectations', published in 1749, he repudiated the view of Shaftesbury and Hutcheson that 'moral sense' is instinctively innate in us, and attributed it to the association of ideas, i.e. the tendency of ideas which have occurred together, or in immediate succession, to recall one another. From this association of the ideas of pain and pleasure with certain actions, he traces the evolution of the higher pleasures out of the lower, until the mind is carried to 'the pure love of God, as our highest and ultimate perfection'. With this psychological doctrine he combined a physical theory of 'vibrations' or 'vibratiuncles' in the 'medullary substance' of the brain.

Harun-al-Rashid, see *Haroun-al-Raschid.*

Harût and Marût, in the Koran (c. ii), two angels sent to tempt men and teach them sorcery. According to another version of the legend (Sale), they were sent to administer justice on earth. Zohara (or the planet Venus) came before them, and complained of her husband. They both fell in love with her and were diverted from their duty, and now suffer punishment in Babel. See also *Loves of the Angels.*

Harvard, JOHN (1607–38), of humble origin, M.A. of Emmanuel College, Cambridge, settled in Charlestown, Massachusetts, and bequeathed half his estate and all his books to the newly founded educational institution at Cambridge, Massachusetts, known in memory of him as HARVARD COLLEGE. He is commemorated also by the Harvard Chapel in St. Saviour's, Southwark, where he was baptized.

HARVEY, GABRIEL (1545?–1630), son of a rope-maker at Saffron Walden, was educated at Christ's College, Cambridge. As fellow of Pembroke Hall he became acquainted with Spenser, over whom he exercised some literary influence, not always for the best. He published satirical verses in 1579 which gave offence at court; attacked Robert Greene in 'Foure Letters' in 1592; wrote 'Pierce's Supererogation' and the 'Trimming of Thomas Nashe' (1593 and 1597) against Nashe, both disputants being silenced by authority. His English works (he also wrote in Latin on rhetoric), including correspondence with Spenser, were edited by Dr. Grosart. Harvey tried, with others, to introduce the classical metres into English, and claimed to be the father of the English hexameter. His literary judgement may be further gauged by his condemnation of the 'Faerie Queene'.

HARVEY, WILLIAM (1578–1657), educated at King's School, Canterbury, Caius College, Cambridge, and at Padua, expounded his theory of the circulation of the blood to the College of Physicians in 1616. But his treatise on the subject, 'Exercitatio Anatomica de Motu Cordis et Sanguinis in Animalibus', was not published until 1628. His second great work, 'Exercitationes de Generatione Animalium', appeared in 1651. His collected Latin works were edited by Dr. Lawrence in 1766. An English edition (Sydenham Society) appeared in 1847. Harvey was physician to Charles I and was present with him at the battle of Edgehill (1642).

Hasan-i-Sabbah, the Old Man of the Mountain, see *Assassins* and *Nizam-ul-Mulk.*

Hashim, the ancestor of Mohammed (q.v.), whose descendants include not only the prophet and his family, but his relatives the Alids and Abbasides (qq.v.). The contests of the HASHIMITES with the Umayyads (q.v.) for the caliphate occupy the early period of Muslim history.

Hastings, a character in Goldsmith's 'She Stoops to Conquer' (q.v.).

Hastings, WARREN (1732–1818), the first governor-general of British India, was educated at Westminster School and went to India in 1750. He was appointed governor of Bengal in 1772, and in 1778 threw himself energetically into the struggle with the Mahrattas, obtaining money for the purpose by despotic methods. In 1780 he wounded in a duel Sir P. Francis (q.v.), his chief opponent

in the council; and in the same year drove Hyder Ali from the Carnatic. He left India in 1785, was impeached on the ground of corruption and cruelty in his administration, and acquitted after a trial of 145 days, extending, with long intervals, from 1788 to 1795. Burke and Fox were among the prosecutors.

Hatchway, LIEUTENANT, a character in Smollett's 'Peregrine Pickle'-(q.v.).

Hathaway, ANNE (1557?–1623), the wife of Shakespeare (q.v.).

Hatter, THE MAD, in Lewis Carroll's 'Alice in Wonderland' (q.v.). 'In that direction,' the Cheshire Cat said, 'lives a Hatter: and in that direction lives a March Hare. Visit either you like: they are both mad.' The illustration of the Mad Hatter is said (by those who remember him) to have been taken from an upholsterer in Oxford High Street, by name Carter. For the proverb, 'Mad as a hatter', the earliest quotation given in OED. is from Haliburton's 'Clockmaker' (1837–40). W. C. Hazlitt ('English Proverbs') refers to the dedication to the 'Hospital for Incurable Fools' (1600), from which it appears that there was living at that time an eccentric character known as John Hodgson, *alias* John Hatter, who was possibly the origin of the expression.

Hatteraick, DIRK, the smuggler captain in Scott's 'Guy Mannering' (q.v.).

Hatto, see *Bishop Hatto.*

HATTON, SIR CHRISTOPHER (1540–91), is said to have attracted the attention of Queen Elizabeth by his graceful dancing (alluded to by Sheridan, 'The Critic', II. i), became her favourite, and received grants of offices and estates (including Ely Place, see *Holborn*). Hatton was lord chancellor, 1587–91, and chancellor of Oxford University, 1588. He was the friend and patron of Spenser and Churchyard, and wrote Act IV of 'Tancred and Gismund' (q.v.).

Hatton Garden, see *Holborn.*

Haunch of Venison, *The,* a poetical epistle to Lord Clare, by Goldsmith (q.v.), written about 1770.

Haunted Man and the Ghost's Bargain, *The,* a Christmas book by Dickens (q.v.) published in 1848.

Redlaw, a learned man in chemistry, is haunted by the memories of a life blighted by sorrow and wrong. His Evil Genius tempts him to think that these memories are his curse, and makes a bargain with him by which he shall forget them; but on condition that he communicates this power of oblivion to all with whom he comes in contact. He discovers with horror that with remembrance of the past he blots out from his own life and the lives of those about him (in particular the delightful Tetterbys), gratitude, repentance, compassion, and forbearance. He prays to be released from his bargain, which is effected by the influence of the good angel, Milly Swidger.

HAUPTMANN, GERHART (1862–1946), German dramatist. His early plays ('Vor Sonnenaufgang', 1889, 'Das Friedensfest', 1890, 'Einsame Menschen', 1891, 'Die Weber', 1892) are important documents of German Naturalism. With 'Hanneles Himmelfahrt' (1893) he began to move towards a new romanticism and symbolism ('Die versunkene Glocke', 1896, 'Und Pippa tanzt', 1906), returning, however, from time to time to more realistic drama ('Rose Bernd', 1903). His narrative works are of considerable literary importance in Germany ('Bahnwärter Thiel', 1888, 'Der Narr in Christo Emanuel Quint', 1910, 'Der Ketzer von Soana', 1918). As a whole his output is characterized by its variety of styles.

Haussmann, GEORGES EUGÈNE, BARON (1809–91), French administrator, who as prefect of the Seine in 1853 directed the modernization of the streets of Paris.

Haut-ton, SIR ORAN, the orang-outang in Peacock's 'Melincourt' (q.v.).

Havelok the Dane, The Lay of, one of the oldest verse romances in English, dating from the early 14th cent. and containing 3,000 lines. It tells the story of Havelok, son of Birkabeyne, king of Denmark, and of Goldborough, daughter of Æthelwold, king of England. These are excluded from their rights by their respective guardians, Godard and Godrich. Godard hands Havelok over to a fisherman, Grim, to drown; but the latter, warned by a mystic light about the boy's head, escapes with him to England and lands at the future Grimsby. Havelock, taking service as scullion in Earl Godrich's household, and distinguishing himself by his strength and athletic skill, is chosen by Godrich as husband for Goldborough, whom Godrich seeks to degrade. The mystic flame reveals to her the identity of her husband. Havelok, with Grim, returns to Denmark, where, with the help of the Earl Ubbe, he defeats Godard and becomes king. Godard is hanged and Godrich burnt at the stake.

The name Havelok (Abloyc) is said [E.B. 11th ed.] to correspond in Welsh to Anlaf or Olaf, and Havelok as scullion bore the name Cuaran. The historical Anlaf Curan was son of a Viking chief Sihtric, king of Northumbria in 925. Anlaf, being driven into exile, took refuge in Scotland and married the daughter of Constantine III. He was defeated with Constantine at Brunanburh.

Havisham, MISS, a character in Dickens's 'Great Expectations' (q.v.).

Hawcubites, a band of dissolute young men who infested the streets of London in the beginning of the 18th cent., street-bullies.

HAWES, STEPHEN (*d.* 1523?), a poet of the school of Chaucer and Lydgate, was groom of the chamber to Henry VII. His 'Passetyme of Pleasure, or History of Graunde Amoure and la Bel Pucel' (q.v.) was first printed by Wynkyn de Worde, 1509. His 'Example of Virtue', a poem in the seven-line Chaucerian stanza, an allegory of life spent in the pursuit of purity, much after the manner of the 'Passetyme of Pleasure', was also printed by Wynkyn de Worde, in 1512.

Hawk, SIR MULBERRY, a character in Dickens's 'Nicholas Nickleby' (q.v.).

HAWKER, ROBERT STEPHEN (1803–75), educated at Pembroke College, Oxford, was vicar of Morwenstow in Cornwall. As a poet he is remembered principally for his 'Song of the Western Men' (rewritten from an old Cornish ballad, with the refrain 'And shall Trelawny die?'). But he wrote other fine poems, 'Queen Gwennivar's Round' and 'The Silent Tower of Bottreaux' among them. In 1864 he published part of a long poem, 'The Quest of the Sangraal'. (See Baring-Gould's 'Vicar of Morwenstow'.)

Hawkesworth, JOHN, see *Adventurer.*

Hawkeye, the name under which Natty Bumppo (q.v.) appears in J. F. Cooper's 'The Last of the Mohicans'.

Hawkins, MR., the fighting naval chaplain in Marryat's 'Mr. Midshipman Easy' (q.v.).

HAWKINS, SIR ANTHONY HOPE (1863–1933), author (as 'Anthony Hope') of 'The Prisoner of Zenda' (q.v., 1894), 'Rupert of Hentzau' (1898), 'The Dolly Dialogues' (q.v., 1894), and other novels and plays.

Hawkins, JIM, the narrator and hero of R. L. Stevenson's 'Treasure Island' (q.v.).

HAWKINS, SIR JOHN (1532–95), naval commander, led expeditions in 1562, 1564, and 1567 to the W. African and Spanish-American coasts, slave-trading, and fighting the Spaniards; these expeditions, together with the actions of Drake, contributed to bring about the breach with Spain. He published 'A True Declaration of the Troublesome voyage of Mr. John Hawkins to Guinea and the West Indies in . . . 1567 and 1568' (1569). He commanded an expedition sent to the Portuguese coast in 1590, and died at sea while serving with Drake's expedition to the West Indies.

His son, SIR RICHARD HAWKINS (1562?–1622), also a famous naval commander, published in 1622 'Observations . . . in his voiage into the South Sea; A.D. 1593'.

HAWKINS, SIR JOHN (1719–89), a lawyer and magistrate who devoted much of his time to music and literature. His 'History of Music', published in 5 vols. in 1776, is of particular antiquarian interest. He was a friend of Dr. Johnson and wrote his 'Life' in 1787.

Hawksmoor or HAWKESMORE, NICHOLAS (1661 or 1666–1736), architect. He was employed by Wren from the age of 18 and later by Vanbrugh; his contribution to the works of both has been underestimated. He designed six London churches under the 1711 act and the west front of Westminster Abbey.

Hawkwood, SIR JOHN (*d.* 1394), the famous condottiere, figures in Froissart as 'Haccoude'. Machiavelli calls him 'Giovanni Acuto'. He was the leader of the body of English mercenaries known as the White Company and fought for one Italian city or another, and for pope or prince, from 1360 to 1390. He was finally commander-in-chief of the Florentine forces, died at Florence, and was buried in the Duomo (his body was subsequently removed to England). He is said to have started life as a tailor's apprentice.

HAWTHORNE, NATHANIEL (1804–64), born at Salem, Massachusetts, was a descendant of Major William Hathorne, one of the Puritan settlers in America, the 'grave, bearded, sable-cloaked and steeple-crowned progenitor' whose portrait we have in the Introduction to 'The Scarlet Letter'. He was educated at Bowdoin College (Brunswick, Maine). He received an appointment in the custom house of his native town in 1846, and in 1853 was American Consul at Liverpool. He subsequently visited Italy, where he wrote the romance 'Transformation' or 'The Marble Faun' (q.v., 1860). But he is best known as the author of 'The Scarlet Letter' (q.v., 1850) and 'The House of the Seven Gables (q.v., 1851). His other principal works were 'The Blithedale Romance' (1852), and several volumes of short stories, 'Twice-Told Tales' (1837–42), 'Mosses from an Old Manse' (1846), 'The Snow Image' (1852), and 'A Wonder Book' and 'Tanglewood Tales' (1852 and 1853, stories from Greek mythology for children).

Hawthorne was a moralist and allegorist, much occupied with the mystery of sin, the paradox of its occasionally regenerative power, and the compensation for unmerited suffering and for crime. The optimistic answers of Emerson (q.v.) to these problems left him unconvinced. And with one or other aspect of them he deals in his three principal romances, against a background (except in 'The Marble Faun') of Puritan New England. The subject of 'The Blithedale Romance' (a satire on the Brook Farm experiment of the New England transcendentalists) is somewhat different. It illustrates the dangers of philanthropy adopted as a profession; for Hollingsworth, the ardent social reformer, in the pursuit of his ideal, deadens his own heart and ruins the lives of those near him.

Haydn, FRANZ JOSEF (1732–1809), the composer, was born in Austria, the son of a wheelwright who was also organist of his village church. In 1760 he became Capellmeister to Prince Paul, and subsequently to his brother Prince Nicholas, Esterhazy, and thus obtained an assured position. He has been described as 'the father of modern instrumental music', and it may be noted that Beethoven received lessons from him. He twice visited England, and received an honorary degree at Oxford. He composed three oratorios, a number of masses, cantatas, and songs, more than 100 symphonies, and many concertos, quartets, etc.

HAYDON, BENJAMIN ROBERT (1786–1846), painter, author of 'Lectures on Painting and Design' (1846), and an autobiography (ed. T. Taylor, 1853) which reveals his vehement nature and the pathos of his unsuccessful struggle to establish himself as an historical painter. Severe strictures were passed on him by Ruskin in 'Modern Painters' (q.v.), he was the object of Keats's youthful enthusiasm, and Wordsworth wrote a sonnet on him. He recognized the quality of the Elgin Marbles and campaigned for their purchase by the British Museum. He quarrelled with his patrons, was imprisoned for debt, and finally committed suicide.

HAYLEY, WILLIAM (1745–1820), poet, of Eton and Trinity Hall, Cambridge; friend of Cowper, Blake, Romney, and Southey; author of lives of Milton, Cowper, and Romney, and of an amusing autobiography.

Haymarket, THE, London, so called from the Hay Market established there in 1664, and maintained until 1830. Her Majesty's Theatre, Haymarket (called also the Opera House), was the first opera house in London (1705). The first performances in England of Handel's operas were given there. The present Her Majesty's Theatre occupies half the original site, the rest of the site being occupied by the Carlton Hotel. The Haymarket Theatre, on the opposite side of the street, was also built at the beginning of the 18th cent., and was Foote's theatre from 1747, and later that of the Bancrofts.

Hayraddin, the Maugrabin or gipsy, a character in Scott's 'Quentin Durward' (q.v.).

Hayston, FRANK, the laird of Bucklaw, a character in Scott's 'The Bride of Lammermoor' (q.v.).

HAYWARD, ABRAHAM (1801–84), is chiefly remembered as the author of 'The Art of Dining' (1852) and of many essays and contributions to periodicals, republished in three series of 'Essays' (1858, 1873, 1874), which include a vigorous attack on the theory of those who would identify 'Junius' with Sir Philip Francis. He was a focus of socialliterary intercourse in the thirties, forties, and fifties of the last century ['London Mercury', Jan.–Feb. 1932].

HAYWARD, SIR JOHN (1564?–1627), educated at Pembroke College, Cambridge, was the author of various historical works, in which he emulated the style of the great Roman historians. His 'First Part of the Life and Raigne of Henrie the IIII' (1599), dedicated to Essex, gave offence to Elizabeth and led to his imprisonment. His other chief works were the 'Lives of the III Normans, Kings of England' (1613), the 'Life and Raigne of King Edward the Sixt' (1630), and 'The Beginning of the Reign of Elizabeth' (1636), the last two printed posthumously.

HAYWOOD, Mrs. ELIZA (1693?–1756), *née* Fowler, after writing plays and libellous memoirs, issued in 1744–6 the periodical 'The Female Spectator', followed by 'The Parrot' (1747), and subsequently produced two lively novels, 'The History of Betsy Thoughtless' (1751) and 'The History of Jemmy and Jenny Jessamy' (1753).

Hazard, a character in Shirley's 'The Gamester' (q.v.).

Hazard of New Fortunes, A, a novel by W. D. Howells (q.v.).

HAZLITT, WILLIAM (1778–1830), born at Maidstone, the son of a Unitarian minister of strong liberal views, spent most of his youth at the secluded village of Wem near Shrewsbury. His early relations with S. T. Coleridge and Wordsworth are described in his essay 'My First Acquaintance with Poets'. He was a quarrelsome and unamiable man, of a curiously divided nature, almost as much an artist as a thinker and writer. At first he showed an inclination for painting, but he soon gave this up for literature. In London he became the friend of Lamb and other literary men, and in 1808 married Sarah Stoddart, a friend of Mary Lamb, from whom he was divorced in 1822. In 1824 he married Mrs. Bridgewater. From 1812 onwards he wrote abundantly for various periodicals, including the 'Edinburgh Review', on the Liberal side. His chief writings divide themselves into three classes: (1) those on art and the drama, including the pleasant 'Notes on a Journey through France and Italy' (1826), written after his second marriage; the 'Conversations of James Northcote' (1830), republished with an introductory essay by E. Gosse in 1894); and 'A View of the English Stage' (1818–21). (2) The essays on miscellaneous subjects, which contain some of his best work (e.g. 'The Feeling of Immortality in Youth', 'Going a Journey', 'Going to a Fight'). (3) The essays in literary criticism, which in the opinion of some are his chief title to fame. The best of these are included in his 'Characters of Shakespeare's Plays' (1817–18), 'Lectures on the English Poets' (1818–19), 'English Comic Writers' (1819), 'Dramatic Literature of the Age of Elizabeth' (1820), and 'Table Talk, or Original Essays on Men and Manners' (1821–2); while 'The Spirit of the Age' (1825) contains interesting appreciations of his contemporaries. Mention should be made of the posthumous 'Winterslow' and 'Sketches and Essays', which contain some of his best essays; also of his 'Characteristics', containing some notable aphorisms, and of the 'Liber Amoris' (1823), the record of a miserable love-affair. Of his ability in controversy his famous 'Letter to William Gifford' (1819) is an example. His 'Life of Napoleon' and a philosophical work, 'The Principles of Human Action', are of less importance.

HAZLITT, WILLIAM CAREW (1834–

1913), bibliographer, grandson of William Hazlitt (q.v.), was author of a 'Handbook to the Popular, Political, and Dramatic Literature of Great Britain . . . to the Restoration' (1867), and of three series of 'Bibliographical Collections and Notes' (1876–89). His 'Confessions of a Collector' appeared in 1897.

Headlong Hall, a novel by Peacock (q.v.), published in 1816.

It contains hardly any plot, but much discourse between Mr. Foster, the optimist, Mr. Escot, the pessimist, Mr. Jenkinson, the 'statu-quo-ite', Dr. Gaster, a gluttonous cleric, and other characters, enlivened by burlesque incident, and a number of good songs.

Headrigg, CUDDIE, in Scott's 'Old Mortality' (q.v.), ploughman to Lady Margaret Bellenden, and MAUSE, his old covenanting mother.

Headstone, BRADLEY, a character in Dickens's 'Our Mutual Friend' (q.v.).

HEARN, LAFCADIO (1850–1904), was born in Santa Maura (otherwise known as Lefcas or Lefcada or Leucas), one of the Ionian Islands, his father, an Irishman, being surgeon of a British regiment quartered there, and his mother a Greek. He was educated at Ushaw College. He worked as a journalist in America, and resided for a time at St. Pierre, Martinique, an experience recorded in his 'Two Years in the French West Indies' (1890). In 1891 he moved to Japan, where he married a Japanese wife. He was lecturer on English Literature in the Imperial University, Tokyo, 1896–1903; and a subject of the Japanese Empire under the name of Yakumo Koizumi. His power of communicating impressions is shown in his remarkable 'Glimpses of Unfamiliar Japan' (1894). His 'Japan: an attempt at interpretation' (1904) was less successful. 'Karma', and other short stories, appeared in 1921. Hearn died in Japan.

HEARNE, THOMAS (1678–1735), historical antiquary, author of 'Reliquiae Bodleianae' (1703), and editor of a valuable collection of early English chronicles, of Leland's 'Itinerary', Camden's 'Annales', and other works. He was the 'Wormius' of Pope's 'Dunciad'. He might have held high office in Oxford University but for his staunch Jacobitism: he refused to take the oath of allegiance to George I. He was for a time second librarian of the Bodleian.

Heart of Midlothian, The, a novel by Sir W. Scott (q.v.), published in 1818, as the second series of 'Tales of My Landlord'.

The novel takes its name from the old Edinburgh Tolbooth or prison, known as the 'Heart of Midlothian', and opens with the story of the Porteous riot of 1736. Captain John Porteous, commander of the City Guard, had, without sufficient justification, caused the death of a number of citizens by ordering his force to fire, and had himself fired, on the crowd on the occasion of the hanging of a convicted robber, by name Wilson. He had been sentenced to death but been reprieved; whereupon a body of the incensed citizens, headed by one Robertson, the associate of Wilson, broke into the Tolbooth, carried Porteous out, and hanged him. With these substantially historical events, Scott links the story of Jeanie and Effie Deans, which also has some basis in fact. Robertson, whose real name is George Staunton, a reckless young man of good family, is the lover of Effie Deans, who is imprisoned in the Tolbooth on a charge of child-murder, and the attack on the Tolbooth is partly designed by him with a view to the flight of Effie. But Effie refuses to escape. She is tried, and as her devoted half-sister Jeanie, in a poignant scene, refuses to give the false evidence which would secure her acquittal, is sentenced to death. Thereupon Jeanie sets out on foot for London, and through the influence of the duke of Argyle obtains an interview with Queen Caroline, and by her moving and dignified pleading obtains her sister's pardon. By the duke's favour, she is also enabled to marry her lover, the Presbyterian minister Reuben Butler; and her stern Cameronian father, 'Douce Davie Deans', is placed on a comfortable farm on the duke's estate, under the rule of the duke's agent, the Captain of Knockdunder. Effie marries her lover, and becomes Lady Staunton, and it comes to light that her child, whom she was accused of having murdered, is in fact alive. He had been sold to a vagrant woman by Meg Murdockson (who had charge of Effie during her confinement) presumably in revenge against Robertson (alias Staunton) for having seduced her daughter 'Madge Wildfire'. Staunton, in his efforts to recover his son, encounters a band of ruffians and is killed by a boy who turns out to be his own son.

Among the notable minor characters of the story may be mentioned the officious Bartoline Saddletree, the law-loving harness-maker; and the Laird of Dumbiedikes, Jeanie's taciturn suitor. Reference may also be made to the beautiful lyrics placed in the mouth of Madge Wildfire, in particular to 'Proud Maisie', which she sings on her death-bed.

Heartbreak House, a play by G. B. Shaw (q.v.).

Heartfree, a character in Vanbrugh's 'The Provok'd Wife' (q.v.).

Heartwell, the 'Old Bachelor' (q.v.) in Congreve's comedy of that name.

Heathcliff, the central figure in Emily Brontë's 'Wuthering Heights' (q.v.).

Heathen Chinee, THE, in Bret Harte's humorous poem, 'Plain Language from Truthful James' ('That for ways that are dark, and for tricks that are vain, the Heathen Chinee is peculiar').

Heaven, THE SEVENTH. In the cosmographies based on the Ptolemaic system, the realms of space round the earth were divided into successive spheres or heavens, in which the sun, moon, and planets severally revolved. Their number varied in different computations from seven to eleven. The Jews (at least in later times) recognized seven heavens, the highest being the abode of God and the most exalted angels. According to the Koran also there are seven heavens. These conceptions have given rise to the expression *in the seventh heaven*, signifying 'supremely happy'.

Heaven and Earth, a drama by Lord Byron, published in the second number of 'The Liberal' (1822). It deals with the biblical legend of the marriage between angels and the daughters of men. The principal characters are the seraph Samiasa and Aholibamah, the granddaughter of Cain.

Heavenly Twins, THE, Castor and Pollux (q.v.). Also the title of a novel by Sarah Grand (q.v.).

Hēbē, the daughter of Zeus and Hera, and the goddess of youth. She attended on Hera and filled the cups of the gods.

HEBER, REGINALD (1783–1826), educated at Brasenose College, Oxford, became incumbent of the living of Hodnet and in 1822 bishop of Calcutta. He wrote some well-known hymns and other verses and a pleasant 'Narrative of a Journey' in India (1824, 1844).

HEBER, RICHARD (1773–1833), half-brother of Reginald Heber (q.v.), travelled widely to collect his library of 150,000 volumes and edited Persius and other classical authors. He is the 'Atticus' of 'Bibliomania' by T. F. Dibdin (q.v.), and Sir W. Scott in the introduction to the 6th canto of 'Marmion' exhorts him, at Christmas time, to

Cease, then, my friend! a moment cease,
And leave these classic tomes in peace.

Hebrew Melodies, a collection of short poems by Lord Byron (q.v.), published in 1815. They were written in the autumn of 1814, when Byron was engaged to marry Miss Milbanke, and were set by I. Nathan to favourite airs sung in the religious services of the Jews. Most of them deal with scriptural subjects, but they include some love-songs, such as

She walks in Beauty, like the night
Of cloudless climes and starry skies.

Hebrides, The Journal of a Tour to the, see Journal of a Tour to the Hebrides. See also Journey to the Western Islands of Scotland.

Hĕcătē, a Greek goddess associated with the lower world and with night, a queen of ghosts and magic, the protectress of enchanters and witches. In statues she was often represented in triple form, perhaps looking down three roads which met where her statue stood.

Hector, a son of Priam (q.v.) and Hecuba, the most valiant of the Trojans who fought against the Greeks. He married Andromache (q.v.), and was father of Astyanax. He was slain by Achilles (q.v.), in revenge for the death of Patroclus, whom Hector had killed; and his body was tied to the chariot of Achilles and dragged to the Greek ships. In medieval romance he is the great hero of the Trojan War.

Hector de Mares, see *Ector de Maris.*

Hĕcŭba, the wife of Priam, king of Troy, and mother of Hector, Paris, and Cassandra (qq.v.) among other children. After the capture of Troy she fell to the lot of Odysseus and embarked with the conquerors for Greece. At the Thracian Chersonese, where they landed, her daughter Polyxena was sacrificed at the instance of the ghost of Achilles, and Hecuba had the further grief of seeing the body of her son Polydorus washed up by the sea; he had been treacherously murdered by his host Polymestor, a Thracian king, on whom Hecuba now took vengeance. She was finally metamorphosed into a dog. She is the subject of a tragedy by Euripides.

Hedonism, from the Greek word meaning pleasure, the doctrine of ethics in which pleasure is regarded as the chief good, or the proper end of action. This was, in a certain sense, the doctrine of the Cyrenaic school (see *Aristippus*).

Heenan, JOHN C., the American pugilist, see *Benicia Boy.*

Heep, URIAH, a character in Dickens's 'David Copperfield' (q.v.).

HEGEL, GEORG WILHELM FRIEDRICH (1770–1831), born at Stuttgart, was rector at Nuremberg gymnasium, 1808–16, and subsequently professor of philosophy at Heidelberg and at Berlin. His first important work was the 'Phaenomenology of Spirit' (1807), followed by his 'Logic' (1812–16), and later by the 'Philosophy of Right' (1820), embodying his political views.

Kant (q.v.) had left an essential dualism in his philosophy, nature opposed to spirit, object opposed to subject, the outer world composed of isolated unrelated substances whose nature is beyond the reach of knowledge. Hegel endeavours to bridge the gulf, and reduce duality to unity. He shows that all difference presupposes a unity, that a definite thought cannot be separated from its opposite, that the idea of fullness, e.g., cannot be separated from that of emptiness, that they are identical in difference. Duality and unity are blended in consciousness and the boundaries between mind and matter set aside. Hegel's central idea is the dialectic of thesis—antithesis—synthesis which he applied to the problem of historical evolution. He did this in a very abstract way, utilizing the concept of *Weltgeist*, and in such a manner incidentally that the use of Prussia was seen as the consummation of the process.

Hegira, see *Hijra.*

Heidelberg, a beautiful town of romantic associations in southern Germany. Its university (founded in 1386) is a famous resort of foreign students.

Heidelberg, MRS., a character in Colman and Garrick's 'Clandestine Marriage' (q.v.). Her illiteracy and mispronunciation of words bring her into some sort of kinship with Mrs. Malaprop (q.v.).

Heimdal, in Scandinavian mythology, one of the Vanir (q.v.), the warder of the gods, who guards the bridge Bifröst (q.v.). He is described as the son of nine mothers. He and Loki (q.v.) slay one another.

Heimskringla, a history of Norse kings from mythical times to 1177 by Snorri Sturlason (q.v.), containing graphic pictures of the domestic and adventurous life of the Vikings, and especially of King Olaf, of whose last fight on his ship, the 'Long Serpent', and death, there is a memorable account. It has a bearing on English history, covering as it does the reigns of the Danish kings, Sweyn, Canute, Harold, and Hardicanute. It describes the expedition of Olaf in aid of Æthelred, and the fight at London Bridge. The title ('the round world') is taken from the first words in the manuscript.

HEINE, HEINRICH (1797–1856), the German poet, was born of Jewish parents in Düsseldorf. Disappointed of his hopes of a Liberal régime in Germany as a sequence to the expulsion of Napoleon, and a sufferer from ill-health which culminated in almost complete paralysis during the last eight years of his life, he migrated to Paris after the revolution of 1830 and there spent his remaining days. He was baptized a Christian in 1835. His political works show him a radical and a cosmopolitan (he wrote both in German and French and many of his prose works exist in both languages). He was an acute critic of philosophy. But he was most famous as a lyrical poet, pre-eminent in wit and raillery, and the Romantic movement in Germany was in part checked by his irony. His chief works include the poems in the 'Buch der Lieder' (1827), one of the most widely read and influential books of poetry in Germany, combining strongly Romantic features with Heine's characteristic irony; the travel sketches in his 'Reisbilder' (1826–31); 'Zur Geschichte der Religion und Philosophie in Deutschland' (1834) and 'Die Romantische Schule' (1836); and among his later writings two collections of poems, 'Atta Troll' (1847), and 'Romanzero' (1851). There is an essay on him by M. Arnold ('Essays in Criticism', 1st Series).

HEINSIUS, DANIEL (1580–1655), Dutch scholar, editor of Aristotle's 'Poetics', and author of a Latin work on tragedy. His son NICOLAAS HEINSIUS (1620–81), also a famous scholar, published critical editions of Roman poets, and travelled in England; his Virgil is most famous.

Heir-at-Law, The, a comedy by G. Colman the younger (q.v.).

Heir of Linne, THE, the subject of a ballad in Percy's 'Reliques', a spendthrift who sells his estate to John o' Scales, wastes the proceeds, and goes to hang himself in a lonesome lodge which he has reserved by his father's direction. But the ceiling breaks with his weight, and reveals three chests full of treasure. He goes to John o' Scales, who refuses him a loan of forty pence, but offers to sell him back his estate for a hundred marks less than he gave for it, and is much disconcerted at being taken at his word.

Heir of Redclyffe, The, a novel by Miss Yonge (q.v.) published in 1853.

In this simple romance, Sir Guy Morville, the generous young heir of Redclyffe, falls in love with Amy, his guardian's daughter, but is suspected of gambling by his malevolent and conceited cousin Philip. In fact, he has paid the debts of a disreputable uncle, but rather than betray the latter, sacrifices his own character. He is banished from his guardian's household, until his gallant rescue of some shipwrecked sailors, and his uncle's intervention, rehabilitate him. Guy and Amy are now married, and on their honeymoon in Italy find Philip severely ill with fever. Guy forgives the injury done him by Philip, nurses him through his illness, catches the fever himself, and dies; and Philip, reduced to contrition by his adversary's generosity, inherits Redclyffe.

Heiress, The, a comedy by Burgoyne (q.v.).

Hejira, see *Hijra.*

Hel, see *Hell.*

Helen, according to Greek legend, the most beautiful woman of her age, was daughter of Zeus and Leda (q.v.). When still a child she was carried off by Theseus (q.v.), but was recovered by her brothers. She selected Menelaus (q.v.), king of Sparta, for her husband, after her many suitors had bound themselves by an oath to defend her. She was subsequently seduced by Paris, son of Priam, king of Troy, and carried off to Troy. To get her back, Menelaus assembled the Greek princes who had been her suitors, and these resolved to make war on Troy for her recovery. After the fall of Troy she was reconciled with Menelaus and lived with him at Sparta.

Helen Huntingdon, or GRAHAM, the heroine of A. Brontë's 'The Tenant of Wildfell Hall' (q.v.).

Helen of Kirkconnell, the subject of an old ballad (included in Scott's 'Border Minstrelsy' and the 'Golden Treasury'), who throws herself before her lover when his rival fires at him, and dies to save him. The story is also the subject of Wordsworth's 'Ellen Irwin'.

Helena, (1) the heroine of Shakespeare's 'All's Well that Ends Well' (q.v.); (2) a character in his 'A Midsummer Night's Dream' (q.v.); (3) Helen of Troy in Goethe's 'Faust' (q.v.).

Helena, ST., the mother of the Emperor Constantine, converted to Christianity by her son. The legend that she was British has no contemporary authority. It is said that she discovered the True Cross, having instituted a search for it in consequence of the Emperor Constantine's vision of the sign of a cross in the sky, with the inscription 'In hoc signo vinces'. This is the *Invention of the Cross,* commemorated on 3 May. St. Helena is the 'Elene' of Cynewulf (q.v.).

The ISLAND OF SAINT HELENA in the S. Atlantic was discovered by the Portuguese on St. Helena's day, 21 May 1502. It was the place of Napoleon's captivity from 1815 until his death in 1821.

Helenore, see *Ross (A.).*

Helenus, a son of Priam and Hecuba, and a soothsayer, who revealed to the Greeks that they could not capture Troy without the help of Philoctetes (q.v.). After the capture of Troy he fell to the lot of Neoptolemus, and after the latter's death married Andromache, the widow of his brother Hector. Aeneas found him ruling in Epirus and was hospitably received by him.

Heliand, The, an Old Saxon paraphrase of the N.T., dating from the 9th cent. Fragments also survive of a paraphrase of the O.T. by the author of the 'Heliand'.

Helias, see *Knight of the Swan.*

Helicon, a mountain of Boeotia sacred to the Muses, who had a temple there. The fountains Hippocrene and Aganippe flowed from this mountain.

Helinore, see *Hellenore.*

HELIODORUS, see *Aethiopica.*

Heliogabălus, see *Elagabalus.*

Hēlios, the Greek name of the sun-god, the son of (and sometimes identified with) Hyperion, and father of Phaethon (qq.v.).

Hell, a word derived from Old Norse *Hel,* 'the coverer up or hider', the Proserpine of northern mythology, the goddess of the infernal regions. Hel was the daughter of Loki (q.v.) and was cast by the Father of the Gods, who feared her evil influence, into Niflheim (q.v.), and given power over nine worlds, among which she distributed the dead. The word Hell is used in the authorized version of the N.T. as a rendering of the Greek words *Hades, Gehenna,* and *Tartarus* (qq.v.). In modern use the word has the sense of (1) the abode of the dead; (2) the place or state of punishment of the wicked after death; (3) something resembling hell, e.g. a place or state of wickedness or suffering; (4) a gaming-house.

For Dante's 'Hell' see *Divina Commedia.*

Hell-fire Clubs, associations of reckless and profligate young ruffians who were a nuisance to London chiefly in the early 18th cent. There was a later and more famous Hell-fire

378

Club, founded about 1745, for which see *Medmenham Abbey*.

Hellas, the name used by the Greeks to signify the abode of the HELLENES, which the Romans called GRAECIA, and we call Greece. Hellas was originally a small district in Thessaly. The name was attributed to a mythical ancestor HELLĒN, son of Deucalion and Pyrrha (qq.v.), and father of Aeolus, Xuthus, and Dorus, ancestors of the Aeolians, Ionians, and Dorians.

Hellas, a lyrical drama by P. B. Shelley (q.v.) composed at Pisa in 1821 and published in 1822. It was inspired by the Greek proclamation of independence, followed by the war of liberation from the Turkish yoke. In form it follows the 'Persae' of Aeschylus. The principal character is the Sultan Mahmud, who learns from successive messengers of the revolt in various parts of his dominions, and to whom the old Jew Ahasuerus calls up a vision of the fall of Stamboul. The poet puts some of his finest lyrics in the mouths of the chorus of Greek captive women.

Hellēn, HELLENES, see *Hellas.*

Hellenistic, a term applied to the civilization, language, and literature, Greek in its general character, but pervading people not exclusively Greek, current in Asia Minor, Egypt, Syria, and other countries after the time of Alexander the Great. The HELLENISTIC AGE OF GREEK LITERATURE is that which extended, with Alexandria as its chief centre, from Alexander's death (323 B.C.) to the end of the Ptolemaic dynasty and the complete Roman subjugation of the Mediterranean world in the latter part of the 1st cent. B.C.

Hellenore, in Spenser's 'Faerie Queene', III. x, the wife of Malbecco, who elopes with Paridel (qq.v.).

Hellespont, see *Argonauts.*

Héloïse, see *Abélard.*

Helot, a class of serf in ancient Sparta. The expression DRUNKEN HELOT is an allusion to a statement by Plutarch that Helots were, on certain occasions, compelled to appear in a state of intoxication, in order to excite in the Spartan youth repugnance to drunken habits.

HELPS, SIR ARTHUR (1813–75), educated at Eton and Trinity College, Cambridge, became clerk of the privy council in 1860. Besides revising (at Queen Victoria's request) Prince Albert's speeches, published in 1862, and preparing for the press the Queen's 'Leaves from the Journal of Our Life in the Highlands' (1868), he acquired popularity by his 'Friends in Council' (four series, 1847–59), dialogues on ethical and aesthetic questions. His 'Conquerors of the New World' appeared in 1848, and 'The Spanish Conquest in America' in 1855–61. Helps also wrote dramas, 'Realmah' (a novel, 1868), and 'Brevia' (short essays, 1871).

Helvetia, Switzerland, the country formerly of the HELVETII, a people of the ancient *Gallia Lugdunensis.*

HELVÉTIUS, CLAUDE ARIEN (1715–71), see *Philosophes.*

HEMANS, MRS. FELICIA DOROTHEA (1793–1835), *née* Browne, married Captain Alfred Hemans in 1812, but separated from him in 1818. Her writings were highly popular in America, and she was the 'Egeria' of Maria Jane Jewsbury's 'Three Histories'. Her collected works (issued in 1839) include 'Translations from Camoens and other Poets', 'Lays of Many Lands', 'The Forest Sanctuary', and 'Songs of the Affections'. She is perhaps chiefly remembered as the author of 'Casabianca' ('The boy stood on the burning deck'), 'The Landing of the Pilgrim Fathers', 'England's Dead', and 'The Better Land'.

Heming or HEMINGES, JOHN (d. 1630) and **Condell,** HENRY (d. 1627), fellow actors of Shakespeare and joint editors of the first folio of his plays (1623). Heming is said to have been the first actor of Falstaff.

HEMINGWAY, ERNEST (1898–1961), American short story writer and novelist, born in Illinois. After serving with an ambulance unit in 1918 on the Italian Front, he worked as a journalist on the Toronto 'Star', until settling in Paris among the American expatriate literary group. He published his first collection of short stories, 'In Our Time', in 1925, a satirical novel, 'The Torrents of Spring', in 1926, and, in the same year, 'The Sun Also Rises', the novel with which he made his name. He succeeded exactly in catching the post-war mood of disillusion, and made a great impression with the economy of his style and characterization, and the stoicism—the 'toughness'—of his attitude of mind. 'A Farewell to Arms' (1925), the story of a love affair between an American lieutenant and an English nurse during the war on the Italian Front, confirmed his position as one of the most influential writers of the time. He was a finer writer of short stories than a novelist, and his collections, 'Men Without Women' (1927) and 'Winner Take Nothing' (1933), are especially notable. His growing dissatisfaction with contemporary culture was shown by his deliberate cultivation of the brutal and the primitive; he celebrated bull-fighting in 'Death in the Afternoon' (1932) and big game hunting in 'The Green Hills of Africa' (1935). He actively supported the Republicans during the Spanish Civil War, and his powerful novel 'For Whom the Bell Tolls' (1940) is set against its background. He was a war correspondent in Europe in the Second World War. His later work declined, but the failure of his novel 'Across the River and into the Trees' (1950) was to some extent redeemed by the success of his long short story 'The Old Man and the Sea' (1952). He was awarded a Nobel Prize in 1954.

Hemistich, half of a line of verse.

Henchard, MICHAEL, the principal character in Hardy's 'The Mayor of Casterbridge' (q.v.).

Hendecasyllabic, a verse of eleven syllables, a metre used by Catullus (–––∪∪–∪–∪––) and imitated by Tennyson:

O you chorus of indolent reviewers.

Hendiadys, from the Greek words meaning 'one by means of two', a figure of speech by which a single complex idea is expressed by two words joined by a conjunction, e.g. 'Such as sit in darkness and in the shadow of death, being fast bound in misery and iron' (Ps. cvii. 10).

Hengist and **Horsa,** the traditional leaders of the Jutes who landed at Ebbsfleet in or about 449, and were given by Vortigern the Isle of Thanet for a dwelling-place. The names signify 'horse' and 'mare', and may be those of real warriors.

HENLEY, JOHN (1692–1756), generally known as 'Orator Henley', educated at St. John's College, Cambridge, and a contributor to the 'Spectator' as 'Dr. Quir', claimed to be a restorer of church oratory. He published works on oratory, theology, and grammar. He was caricatured by Hogarth and ridiculed by Pope:

> Still break the benches, Henley, with thy strain,
> While Sherlock, Hare, and Gibson preach in vain.
>
> ('Dunciad', iii. 203.)

HENLEY, WILLIAM ERNEST (1849–1903), born at Gloucester and a pupil there of T. E. Brown (q.v.), was a cripple from boyhood. He did a great deal of miscellaneous literary work, as editor at various times of the 'Magazine of Art', the 'National Observer', the 'New Review', etc. He was a friend of R. L. Stevenson (q.v.), with whom he collaborated in the plays 'Deacon Brodie', 'Beau Austin', 'Admiral Guinea', and 'Macaire' (1892). He compiled 'Lyra Heroica' (1891), a book of verse for boys, and was joint compiler of the 'Slang Dictionary' (1894–1904). His poetical work includes the 'Book of Verses' (1888), 'The Song of the Sword' (1892, revised 1893), 'London Voluntaries' (1893), 'Hawthorn and Lavender' (1899), and the remarkable volume entitled 'In Hospital' (1903), written in an Edinburgh infirmary. His collected works were published in 1908. Among his best-known pieces are 'Invictus' ('Out of the night that covers me'), the ballad with the refrain

> I was a king in Babylon
> And you were a Christian slave,

and 'England, my England'. Henley is portrayed as 'Burly' in R. L. Stevenson's essay, 'Talk and Talkers'.

Henri IV, king of France, 1589–1610. He had been king of Navarre since 1570 and had married Marguerite de Valois, sister of Charles IX. He figures in Macaulay's lay, 'Ivry'.

Henriade, La, a poem in ten cantos by Voltaire (q.v.), exalting Henri IV, published in 1723.

Henrietta Temple, a novel by Disraeli (q.v.), published in 1837.

Ferdinand Armine, the son of noble but impoverished parents , a brilliant and impetuous youth, enters the army, gets into debt, and being disappointed of his grandfather's heritage, which was counted on to redress the family fortunes, proposes to his wealthy cousin, Katherine Grandison, and is accepted. But his own heart is not engaged, and, the wedding being postponed until a year after his grandfather's recent death, Ferdinand falls desperately in love with the beautiful but penniless Henrietta Temple, and, carried away by his passion, becomes engaged to her also. When his previous entanglement is revealed, Henrietta, shocked by his perfidy, falls seriously ill and leaves the country, while Ferdinand nearly succumbs to brain fever. Henrietta meets in Italy the admirable Lord Montfort, and under pressure from her father consents to marry him. Before the wedding is celebrated, she again meets Ferdinand, is touched by his sufferings, and discovers that her heart is still his. Katherine, who has forgiven and released Ferdinand, and the latter's resourceful friend Count Mirabel, set to work to straighten out the imbroglio, with the result that Lord Montfort renounces Henrietta, who has unexpectedly become a rich heiress, and marries Katherine; while Ferdinand, released from the sponging-house to which his debts have brought him, marries Henrietta.

Henry I, king of England, 1100–35.

Henry II, king of England, 1154–89. This was a period of (Latin) literary eminence: see *Glanville, Dialogus de Scaccario, Map, Giraldus Cambrensis.*

Henry III, king of England, 1216–72.

Henry IV, king of England, 1399–1413.

Henry IV, King, Parts I and II, an historical drama by Shakespeare (q.v.), produced about 1597, and printed in quarto, Pt. I in 1598, and Pt. II in 1600.

The subject of Pt. I is the rebellion of the Percys, assisted by Douglas, and in concert with Mortimer and Glendower; and its defeat by the king and the Prince of Wales at Shrewsbury (1403). Falstaff (q.v.) first appears in this play. The Prince of Wales associates with him and his boon companions, Poins, Bardolph, and Peto, in their riotous life. Poins and the prince contrive that the others shall set on some travellers at Gadshill and rob them, and be robbed in their turn by themselves. The plot succeeds, and leads to Falstaff's well-known fabrication to explain the loss of the booty, and his exposure. At the battle of Shrewsbury, Falstaff finds the body of the lately slain Hotspur, and pretends to have killed him.

Pt. II deals with the rebellion of Archbishop Scroop, Mowbray, and Hastings; while in the comic under-plot, the story of Falstaff's doings is continued, with those of the prince, Pistol (q.v.), Poins, Mistress Quickly (q.v.), and Doll Tearsheet. Falstaff, summoned to the army for the repression of the rebellion, falls in with Justices Shallow and Silence (qq.v.) in the course of his recruiting, makes a butt of them, and extracts a thousand pounds from the former. Henry IV dies, and Falstaff conceives that the Prince's accession to the throne will make himself all-powerful. He is rudely disabused when he encounters the new king, is banished from his presence, and thrown into prison.

The play is notable, among other things, for the memories of Shakespeare's early life in Warwickshire interwoven in the story.

Henry V, king of England, 1413–22.

Henry V, King, an historical drama by Shakespeare (q.v.), performed in 1599, an imperfect draft being printed in 1600, the corrected text appearing in the first folio (1623).

The play deals with the arrest of Lord Scroop, Sir Thomas Grey, and the earl of Cambridge for treason; the invasion of France and siege and capture of Harfleur; the battle of Agincourt (1415); and Henry's wooing of Katharine of France. The knaves Nym and Bardolph and the braggart Pistol, who is made to eat the leek by the choleric Welshman Fluellen, provide relief from the more serious theme. The death of Falstaff is related by Mistress Quickly (II. iii).

Henry VI, king of England, 1422–61, restored for six months, 1470–1, and then murdered in the Tower of London in 1471.

Henry VI, King, Parts I, II, and III, an historical drama ascribed to Shakespeare (q.v.). The extent to which it was actually written or revised by him is uncertain. The three parts were acted about 1592; the first part was published in 1623, the second part anonymously in 1594 as 'The first part of the contention betwixt the two famous houses of Yorke and Lancaster', and the third part in 1595, as 'The True Tragedie of Richard, Duke of Yorke, and the death of good King Henrie the Sixt'. The second and third parts (with modifications of the text) appeared, together with the first part, in the folio of 1623. Various commentators have found the hands of Marlowe, Kyd, Peele, Greene, Lodge, and Nash, as well as Shakespeare, in different passages of the play, but the question of authorship remains undecided. The play probably evoked Greene's famous censure of Shakespeare in his 'A Groatsworth of Wit bought with a Million of Repentance' (q.v.).

Pt. I deals with the wars in France during the early years of Henry VI, the relief of Orleans by the French and the gradual expulsion of the English from a large part of France. The French are guided and inspired by Joan of Arc, who in accordance with the ideas of the time is represented as a 'minister of hell' and a wanton. On the English side, the commanding figure of Talbot, until his death near Bordeaux, throws the other leaders into the shade. At home, the play deals with the dissensions between the nobles, and the beginning of the strife of York and Lancaster.

Pt. II presents the marriage of Henry to Margaret of Anjou, the intrigues of the Yorkist faction, and the other chief historical events, including Jack Cade's rebellion, down to the battle of St. Albans (1455) and the death of Somerset.

Pt. III takes us from Henry's surrender of the succession to the crown to the duke of York, and Queen Margaret's revolt against the disinheriting of her son, to the battle of Tewkesbury in 1471, concluding with the murder of Henry VI by Richard, duke of Gloucester, whose ambitious and unscrupulous character (as subsequently developed in 'King Richard III') is here first indicated.

Henry VII, king of England, 1485–1509. His life was written by Francis Bacon (q.v.).

Henry VIII, king of England, 1509–47. His life was written by Lord Herbert of Cherbury (q.v.). His book, 'A defence of the Seven Sacraments', directed against Luther's teaching, was printed in 1521 and presented to Leo X, who thereupon conferred on Henry the title 'Defender of the Faith'.

Henry VIII, an historical drama by Shakespeare (q.v.), with parts perhaps written by a collaborator, probably Fletcher. It was acted in 1613 and included in the folio of 1623.

It deals with the accusation and execution of the duke of Buckingham; the question of the royal divorce (vividly depicting the dignity and resignation of Queen Katharine); the pride and fall of Cardinal Wolsey and his death; the advancement and coronation of Anne Boleyn: the triumph of Cranmer over his enemies; and the christening of the Princess Elizabeth. The firing of the cannon at the end of Act I caused the burning of the Globe Theatre in 1613.

For another Elizabethan play on the subject of Henry VIII, see *Rowley (S.).*

Henry and Emma, see *Prior.*

Henry Grâce à Dieu, The, see *Great Harry.*

Henry of Hoheneck, PRINCE, the subject of the story of Longfellow's 'Golden Legend' (q.v.).

HENRY OF HUNTINGDON (1084?–1155), archdeacon of Huntingdon, compiled at the request of Bishop Alexander of Lincoln a 'Historia Anglorum', which in its latest form extends to 1154.

HENRY THE MINSTREL, or BLIND HARRY or HARY (*fl.* 1470–92), Scottish poet; probably a native of Lothian. He wrote a spirited poem on the life of Sir William Wallace, containing some 12,000 lines in heroic couplets, which purports to be based on a work by John Blair, Wallace's chaplain. It is inspired by violent animosity against the English. Its chronology and general accuracy have been questioned, but in some instances corroborated. The best printed editions are those of Jamieson (1820) and Moir (Scottish Text Society, 1884–9); William Hamilton of Gilbertfield's modern version (1722) became more familiar than the original.

HENRY, O., pseudonym of WILLIAM SYDNEY PORTER (1862–1910), American short story writer, born in North Carolina. He had a chequered early career, which included a term in prison for embezzlement (1896). He began to write short stories in prison, based on his observations of life, and published the first of his many collections, 'Cabbages and Kings', in 1904. He was prolific, humorous, and highly ingenious, especially in his use of coincidence, and became the most famous writer of his kind of the day.

HENRYSON or HENDERSON, ROBERT (1430?–1506), a Scottish poet of the school of Chaucer. He was probably a clerical schoolmaster attached to Dunfermline Abbey. His 'Tale of Orpheus' was first printed in 1508. His 'Testament of Cresseid' (q.v.) was attributed to Chaucer till 1721, though printed as his own in 1593. His 'Morall Fables of Esope the Phrygian' were printed in 1621. 'The Poems of Robert Henryson' were edited by G. Gregory Smith for the Scottish Text Society, 3 vols., 1906–14.

Henslowe, PHILIP (d. 1616), a theatrical manager who rebuilt and managed till 1603 the Rose playhouse on Bankside, and subsequently managed other theatres. He employed a number of the minor Elizabethan dramatists, including Munday, Chettle, Day, Samuel Rowley, and Drayton, and his diary contains valuable information as to their works.

HENTY, GEORGE ALFRED (1832–1902), writer for boys, who also published some twelve orthodox novels, including 'Dr. Thorndyke's Secret' (1898).

Heorot, in 'Beowulf' (q.v.), the palace of Hrothgar.

Hepburn, PHILIP, a character in Mrs. Gaskell's 'Sylvia's Lovers' (q.v.).

Hephaestus, the Greek god of fire, called by the Romans Vulcan (q.v.).

Hepplewhite, GEORGE (d. 1786), cabinet-maker, in business in St. Giles', Cripplegate. His designs, published in 'The Cabinet Maker and Upholsterer's Guide', 1788, include the 'shield back' chair.

Heptameron, The, a collection of tales of love (depicted not as vulgar gallantry, but as a serious and sometimes a tragic passion), linked by the fiction that the narrators are travellers detained in an inn by a flood, and composed, according to the explicit statement of Brantôme, by Marguerite, sister of Francis I and queen of Navarre (1492–1549). The

name 'Heptameron', meaning 'seven days' (on the analogy of Boccaccio's 'Decameron'), was given by a later editor to what were originally called the 'Contes de la Reine de Navarre'.

Heptarchy, THE, the seven kingdoms reckoned to have been established in Britain by the Angles and Saxons (5th–9th cents.). The term appears to have been introduced by 16th-cent. historians, in accordance with their notion that there were seven Angle and Saxon kingdoms so related that one of their rulers had always the supreme position. The correctness of the designation has often been called in question. [OED.]

Hera, known as JUNO by the Romans, was the daughter of Cronos and Rhea and the sister and wife of Zeus or Jupiter. She is represented in mythology as pursuing with inexorable jealousy the mistresses of Zeus and their children, Ino, Semele, Hercules, etc. She was mother of Ares (Mars), Hebe, and Hephaestus (Vulcan). She was worshipped as the queen of the heavens, the goddess representative of women, especially of wives, and protectress of marriage. The peacock among birds was specially sacred to her. Her worship was widespread, but particularly developed in Argos.

Hĕrăclēs, see *Hercules.*

HERACLITUS, of Ephesus, a philosopher who wrote, about 500 B.C., a work 'Concerning Nature' (περὶ φύσεως), in which he maintained that all things are in a state of flux, coming into existence and passing away, and that fire, the type of this constant change, is their origin. From the passing impressions of experience, the mind derives, according to Heraclitus, a false idea of the permanence of the external world, which is really in a harmonious process of constant change. The melancholy view of Heraclitus as to the changing and fleeting character of life led to his being known as the 'weeping philosopher'.

Heralds' College or COLLEGE OF ARMS, a royal corporation, founded in 1483, exercising jurisdiction in matters armorial, and now recording proved pedigrees, and granting armorial bearings. The officers of the College are as follows: three kings of arms: Garter, Clarenceux, and Norroy and Ulster; six heralds: Windsor, Somerset, Lancaster, York, Chester, and Richmond; four pursuivants: Bluemantle, Portcullis, Rouge Croix, and Rouge Dragon. In Scotland the Lord Lyon king of arms is head of the office of arms.

Herball or general historie of Plantes, see *Gerard (J.).*

HERBERT, EDWARD, *first Baron Herbert of Cherbury* (1583–1648), philosopher, historian, poet, and diplomatist, was the elder brother of the poet, G. Herbert (q.v.). He was educated at University College, Oxford, and had a career full of incident as a diplomatist (he was ambassador to France, 1619–24), traveller, and soldier (on the Royalist side, until he submitted to parliament and received a pension). His 'Autobiography' (which extends only to 1624) was first printed by Horace Walpole in 1764 and edited by Sir Sidney Lee in 1886. His 'De Veritate' in Latin (published in Paris in 1624, in London 1625), the chief of his philosophical works, is the first purely metaphysical work by an Englishman, and important as advancing a theory of knowledge substantially the same as that of the Cambridge Platonists (see *Cudworth*). He is known as the 'Father of Deism', for he maintained that among the 'common notions' apprehended by instinct are the existence of God, the duty of worship and repentance, and future rewards and punishment. This 'natural religion', he held, had been vitiated by superstition and dogma. His 'Life of Henry VIII' was published in 1649. His poems, which show grace and freshness, were edited by Churton Collins in 1881 and by G. C. Moore-Smith in 1923. They are noteworthy for his use of the metre subsequently adopted by Tennyson in his 'In Memoriam'.

HERBERT, GEORGE (1593–1633), was younger brother of Lord Herbert of Cherbury (q.v.), and was educated at Westminster and Trinity College, Cambridge, where he was public orator from 1619 to 1627. He took orders and accepted in 1630 the living of Bemerton, where he died. His verse is almost entirely included in 'The Temple', a collection of 160 poems of a religious character, marked by quaint and ingenious imagery rather than exaltation, and occasionally marred by extravagant conceits and bathos. This work was published in 1633. His chief prose work 'A Priest to the Temple', described by Izaak Walton (q.v.) as containing 'plain, prudent, useful rules for the country parson', set forth with fervent piety, was first printed in his 'Remains', 1652. His complete works were edited by Dr. Grosart, 1874. I. Walton wrote a life of George Herbert, which appeared in 1670.

Herbert, MARY, see *Pembroke*.

Hercules, or in Greek HĒRĂCLĒS, was the son of Zeus and Alcmena (see *Amphitryon*). Hera's jealousy of Alcmena extended to her son. She sought to destroy the infant by sending two serpents to devour him, but he seized and crushed them in his hands. He was instructed in the various arts of war and music, and became the most valiant and accomplished of men. In his youth occurred the incident of the 'CHOICE OF HERCULES', described by Socrates in Xenophon's 'Memorabilia', II. i. 21–33. He sat in a lonely place in doubt which course of life to follow. Virtue and Pleasure appeared to him, and offered him, one a life of toil and glory, the other a life of ease and enjoyment. Hercules chose the former. After various exploits he married Megara, the daughter of Creon, but being driven mad by Hera, killed his children. By

direction of an oracle he submitted himself to the authority of Eurystheus, king of Argos and Mycenae, and at the order of the latter undertook a number of enterprises, known as the twelve 'LABOURS OF HERCULES'. These were as follows: (1) the destruction of the lion of Nemea, which Hercules strangled, and whose skin he afterwards wore; (2) the destruction of the Lernaean hydra, a creature with many heads, each of which when cut off gave place to two new ones; (3) the capture of an incredibly swift stag; (4) the capture of a destructive wild boar; (5) the cleansing of the stables of Augeas (q.v.); (6) the destruction of the carnivorous birds near lake Stymphalus; (7) the capture of the Cretan wild bull; (8) the capture of the mares of Diomedes, which fed on human flesh; (9) the obtaining of the girdle of the queen of the Amazons; (10) the destruction of the monster Geryon, king of Gades, and the capture of his flocks; (11) the obtaining of apples from the garden of the Hesperides (q.v.); (12) the bringing from hell of the three-headed dog, Cerberus (q.v.). Many other achievements are credited to him. He was again the victim of an attack of insanity, killed Iphitus (brother of Iolē, with whom Hercules had fallen in love), and was sold as a slave to Omphale (q.v.). For his destruction by the cloak of Nessus, see under *Deianira*. After his death he obtained divine honours, having devoted the labours of his life to the benefit of mankind. See *Ex pede Herculem*.

Hercules, PILLARS or COLUMNS OF, a name given to two mountains opposite one another at the entrance of the Mediterranean, called Calpe (Gibraltar) and Abyla, supposed to have been parted by the arm of Hercules.

Hercynian Forest, the Roman name for an ill-defined tract of wooded mountains in southern and central Germany.

HERDER, JOHANN GOTTFRIED (1744–1803), German philosopher and critic, who decisively influenced Goethe (q.v.) during the latter's early Storm and Stress period. He was an ardent student and collector of folk-song (essay on 'Volkslieder', 1779), an investigator of problems of language ('Über den Ursprung der Sprache', 1772), a critic of Shakespeare (essay in 'Von deutscher Art und Kunst', 1773) and a philosopher of history ('Auch eine Philosophie der Geschichte zur Bildung der Menschheit', 1774, 'Ideen zur Philosophie der Geschichte der Menschheit', 1784–91). As a philosopher Herder's great contribution lay in his recognition of historical evolution, which helped to bridge the gap between the Enlightenment and Romanticism.

Hereward the Wake (*fl.* 1070), an outlaw, a legendary account of whose wanderings is given by the 15th-cent. forger who called himself Ingulf of Croyland in his 'Gesta Herewardi'. He headed a rising of English against William the Conqueror at Ely in 1070, and with the assistance of the Danish fleet plundered Peterborough in the same year. He was joined by Morcar and other refugees, and escaped when his allies surrendered to William. He is said to have subsequently been pardoned by William, and, according to Geoffrey Gaimar, to have been slain by Normans in Maine.

The last of the completed novels of C. Kingsley (q.v.) bears this name, and was published in 1865. It is based on the legends of Hereward's exploits and extraordinary strength. The earlier and more attractive part of the book deals with his youth (Kingsley makes him the son of Leofric of Mercia and the Lady Godiva), his outlawry for robbing a monastery, his numerous exploits in England and Flanders, and his marriage with the learned and noble-hearted Torfrida. Then comes the Conquest, and Hereward's gallant efforts to save England from the Normans, but the story becomes involved in the political details of the subjugation of the country. The love of Hereward for the faithful Torfrida gives way to the wiles and attractions of a rival, and hero and heroine end their lives in sorrow. See also *Swallow*.

HERGESHEIMER, JOSEPH (1880–1954), American writer, born at Philadelphia. His best-known books are 'The Three Black Pennys' (1917), 'Java Head' (1919), and 'Linda Condon' (1919).

Hergest, RED BOOK OF, a Welsh manuscript of the 14th–15th cents. containing the 'Mabinogion' (q.v.), the 'Triads' (q.v.), Welsh translations of British chronicles, etc.

Hermae, quadrangular pillars surmounted by a bust of the god Hermes (q.v.). These were extremely numerous in ancient Athens, where they were erected at street corners, before houses, and on the high roads. Just before the sailing of the Sicilian expedition (415 B.C.) Athens was thrown into perturbation by the mutilation in a single night of all the Hermae in the city. The outrage was attributed by public opinion to Alcibiades, but the mystery was never explained.

Hermandad, a Spanish word meaning 'brotherhood', originally the name in Spain of popular combinations formed chiefly to resist the exactions of the nobles, to which were subsequently given general police functions. Isabella of Castile in 1476 converted this popular institution into an organized constabulary, the SANTA HERMANDAD, the 'Holy Brotherhood' in English translations of 'Don Quixote'.

Hermann und Dorothea, see *Goethe*.

Hermaphrŏdĭtus, a son of Hermes and Aphrodite, was beloved by Salmacis, the nymph of a fountain in which he bathed. As he continued deaf to her entreaties, she closely embraced him and prayed the gods to make the twain one body, which they did. Hence 'Hermaphrodite', a name for a being combining both sexes in a single body.

Hermegyld, in Chaucer's 'Man of Law's Tale' (see *Canterbury Tales*), the wife of the constable of Northumberland, to whose coast Constance is borne when set adrift on the sea.

Hermensul, see *Irminsul*.

Hermes, called MERCURY by the Romans, was the son of Zeus and Maia, the inventor of the lyre (he placed strings across the shell of a tortoise), and the messenger and herald of the gods. He was regarded as the god of luck and wealth, the patron of travellers and merchants, and of thieves. It was he who conducted the souls of the dead to the infernal regions. He is generally represented as equipped with the *cadŭcĕus*, a rod entwined by two serpents, the *pĕtăsus* or broad-brimmed hat, and *talăria* or winged sandals.

Hermes Trismegistus, the 'thrice great Hermes' of Milton's 'Il Penseroso', the name given by the Neoplatonists and the devotees of mysticism and alchemy to the Egyptian god THOTH, regarded as more or less identical with the Grecian Hermes, and as the author of all mystical doctrines. From the 3rd cent. onwards the name was applied to the author of various Neoplatonic writings, some of which have survived, notably the Ποιμάνδρης, a word of uncertain derivation, used to signify the Divine Intelligence. Hence HERMETIC PHILOSOPHY, alchemy; HERMETIC BOOKS, the philosophical, theosophical, and other writings ascribed to Hermes Trismegistus.

Hermia, a character in Shakespeare's 'A Midsummer Night's Dream' (q.v.).

Hermĭŏnē, (1) daughter of Menelaus and Helen, and the wife, first of Neoptolemus, then of Orestes; (2) in Shakespeare's 'The Winter's Tale' (q.v.), the wife of Leontes. For the Hermione mentioned in Milton's 'Paradise Lost', ix. 506, see *Harmonia*.

Hermit, The, a poem by T. Parnell (q.v.).

Hermit, The, or *Edwin and Angelina*, a ballad by Goldsmith (q.v.), written in 1764, and included in 'The Vicar of Wakefield' (q.v.). Angelina, benighted in the wilderness, and sorrowing for her lost Edwin, whom she believes dead, is welcomed to the Hermit's cell and in answer to his questions reveals the cause of her sorrow. Whereupon the Hermit acknowledges himself to be Edwin.

Hermit of Hampole, THE, Richard Rolle (q.v.).

Hermitage, THE, a museum in Leningrad containing a splendid gallery of paintings, and collections of ancient sculpture and other antiquities.

Hermod or HERMODR, in Scandinavian mythology, one of the Æsir (q.v.), a son of Odin. It is he who undertakes the voyage to hell to bring back the dead Balder to the upper world (see *Balder Dead*).

Hermsprong, or Man as he is not, see *Bage*.

Hernani, a tragedy (1830) by V. Hugo (q.v.), in which Count Hernani, in love with Elvira and about to marry her, takes his own life at the blast of a horn sounded by his enemy, Don Ruy Gomez, to fulfil the pledge that he has given to do so. Verdi's opera 'Ernani' is founded on Hugo's drama.

Herne the Hunter, a spectral hunter of medieval legend, said to have been originally a keeper in Windsor Forest, who figures in Shakespeare's 'The Merry Wives of Windsor', IV. iv, and in Harrison Ainsworth's 'Windsor Castle'.

Hero, (1) a beautiful priestess of Aphrodite at Sestos on the European shore of the Hellespont, beloved of Leander, a youth of Abȳdos on the opposite shore. Leander at night used to swim across to Hero, who directed his course by holding up a lighted torch. One tempestuous night Leander was drowned, and Hero in despair threw herself into the sea; (2) the heroine of Shakespeare's 'Much Ado about Nothing' (q.v.).

Hero and Leander, see above under *Hero* (1). The story has been made the subject of poems by Marlowe and T. Hood (qq.v.), and of a burlesque by T. Nashe (q.v.) in his 'Prayse of Red Herring'.

Herod, To OUT-HEROD, to outdo Herod (represented in the old miracle plays as a blustering tyrant) in violence; to outdo in any excess of evil or extravagance—a Shakespearian expression ('Hamlet', III. ii) which has come into current use.

Herod Agrippa I (*d.* A.D. 44), MARCUS JULIUS AGRIPPA, grandson of Herod the Great (q.v.), ruler of the tetrarchies of north-eastern Palestine. He persecuted the Christians and died a horrible death (Acts xii). It was before his son, Agrippa II (*c.* A.D. 27–100), that Paul was brought (Acts xxv; the Bernice there referred to was his sister).

Herod the Great, of Idumaean origin, king of Judaea, 40–4 B.C. His father Antipater had been appointed by Julius Caesar procurator of Judaea in 47 B.C., and Herod himself had been governor of Galilee. In 40 Herod was named by the Roman senate king of Judaea. His rule was a cruel despotism. In a fit of jealousy he put to death his wife Mariamne and his sons by her, Alexander and Aristobulus, and other murders are attributed to him. According to Matt. ii, he ordered the slaughter of all the children in Bethlehem, from two years old and under, in order that the infant Jesus should be destroyed.

HERODAS or HERONDAS, a Greek writer of mimes (q.v.) of the 3rd cent. B.C. Seven of these, recovered in an Egyptian papyrus, were published by Dr. Kenyon in 1891 (there is an edition by W. Headlam, 1922).

Herodias, the sister of Herod Agrippa I, granddaughter of Herod the Great, the wife of Herod Philip (son of Herod the Great) and afterwards of his half-brother Herod Antipas, whom she caused to imprison and execute John the Baptist. She was the mother of Salome (q.v.).

HERODŎTUS (*c.* 480–*c.* 425 B.C.), a Greek historian, born at Halicarnassus, at that time a city under Persian rule. He is known as 'the father of history', for he was the first to collect his materials systematically, test their accuracy so far as he was able, and arrange them agreeably. His work, the first masterpiece of Greek prose, is divided into nine books, each called after one of the Muses, but the division was probably made by Alexandrian editors. He travelled widely in Europe, Asia, and Africa. The main theme of his work is the enmity between Asia and Europe. He traces it from mythical times, through the reign of Croesus in Lydia, the rise of the Persian monarchy, the expedition of Cambyses into Egypt (with details of Egyptian history), that of Darius against the Scythians, the Ionian revolt, and the struggle between Persia and Greece.

Heroes and Hero-Worship, see *Carlyle* (*T.*).

Heroic poetry, the same as *Epic* (q.v.).

Heroic verse, that used in epic poetry: in Greek and Latin poetry, the hexameter; in English, the iambic of five feet or ten syllables; in French, the alexandrine of twelve syllables.

Herostrătus, an Ephesian who set the temple of Artemis at Ephesus on fire in 356 B.C., according to his own confession in order to immortalize himself. On the night that he did this Alexander the Great was born.

HERRICK, ROBERT (1591–1674), was born in London, and was apprenticed for ten years to his uncle, a goldsmith. He then went to St. John's College, Cambridge, but graduated from Trinity Hall in 1617. He was incumbent of Dean Prior, in Devonshire, from 1629 to 1647, when he was ejected; after which he lived in Westminster, until restored to his living in 1662. He was a devoted admirer of Ben Jonson. His chief work is the 'Hesperides' (1648), a collection of some 1,200 poems, mostly written in Devonshire, as the title suggests, the best of which are aptly described in his own lines:

> I sing of brooks, of blossoms, birds, and
> bowers,
> Of April, May, of June, and July flowers;
> I sing of maypoles, hock-carts, wassails,
> wakes,
> Of bridegrooms, brides, and of their bridal-
> cakes.

His 'Noble Numbers' (published in one book with 'Hesperides', but bearing on its separate title-page the date 1647) is a collection of short poems dealing with sacred subjects. His poems show great diversity of form, from imitations of Horace and Catullus, epistles, eclogues, and epigrams, to love-poetry and simple folk-songs. Complete editions have been published by T. Maitland (1823), E. Walford (1859), W. C. Hazlitt (1869), and Dr. Grosart (1876). The most recent complete edition is in the Oxford English Texts, edited by L. C. Martin (1956). Several of his pieces were set to music by Henry Lawes and others.

HERRICK, ROBERT (1868–1938), American novelist, born in Massachusetts. Among his best-known novels are 'The Master of the Inn' (1908), 'Together' (1908), 'One Woman's Life' (1913), and 'Clark's Field' (1914).

Herschel, SIR JOHN FREDERICK WILLIAM (1792–1871), astronomer, son of Sir W. Herschel (q.v.). He was senior wrangler, and subsequently fellow of St. John's College, Cambridge. He was secretary to the Royal Society, 1824–7, president of the Astronomical Society, 1827–32, and master of the Mint, 1850–5. He discovered a great number of double stars and nebulae, and did a vast amount of work in connexion with these and other branches of astronomical science.

Herschel, SIR WILLIAM (1738–1822), astronomer, born at Hanover, was sent to England by his parents in 1757 and became organist at Halifax, and subsequently at the Octagon Chapel, Bath. He began to construct optical instruments in 1773 and to observe stars. He discovered Uranus in 1781, and in 1782 exhibited his telescope to George III, by whom he was appointed court astronomer. His great forty-foot reflector was begun in 1785 and finished in 1811. He discovered many stars and nebulae, and contributed greatly to the knowledge of astronomy. He was the first president of the Astronomical Society.

Hertha or NERTHUS, according to Tacitus, a goddess of some ancient Germanic tribes, representing the earth or fertility.

'Hertha' is the title of one of Swinburne's 'Songs before Sunrise' (q.v.); the author rated it 'highest as a single piece, finding in it the most of lyric force and music combined with the most of condensed and clarified thought'. In it he gives voice to his religious unorthodoxy, and sings of the emancipation of the soul under the influence of Hertha, the earth-goddess, the spirit of life.

Hervé Riel, the subject of a poem by R. Browning (q.v.), a Breton sailor who piloted a French squadron to safety in St. Malo harbour after the defeat of the fleet at La Hogue in 1692. As a reward he asked for a whole day's holiday, nothing more. (In fact, he appears to have asked for an absolute discharge—Nicoll and Wise, 'Literary Anecdotes'.)

HERVEY, JAMES (1714–58), educated at Lincoln College, Oxford, was rector of Collingtree and Weston Favell in Northamptonshire, and was prominent in the early Methodist movement. His 'Meditations among the Tombs', 'Reflections in a Flower Garden', and 'Contemplations on the Night', published in 1746–7, were extremely popular, but are marked by a pompous and affected style.

HERVEY, JOHN, *Baron Hervey of Ickworth* (1696–1743), as vice-chamberlain exercised great influence over Queen Caroline. He was a close friend of Lady Mary Wortley Montagu (q.v.) and engaged in controversy with Pope, by whom he was attacked in 'The Dunciad' and 'Bathos' as 'Lord Fanny', and as the 'Sporus' of the 'Epistle to Arbuthnot'. His 'Memoirs of the Reign of George II' give a vivid satirical picture of the court. They were edited by J. W. Croker in 1848. A new edition in 3 vols., by R. Sedgwick, was published in 1931.

HERZEN (GERTSEN), ALEXANDER IVANOVICH (1812–70), leading Russian revolutionary thinker. In 1852 he settled in England and, with Ogaryov, published a Russian newspaper 'The Bell' (1857–65 in London, later in Geneva) which was smuggled into Russia where it had considerable influence. German idealist philosophy and French utopian socialism were early influences on Herzen's thought. He was well acquainted with such revolutionaries as Garibaldi, Bakunin, and Proudhon, and had contacts in English radical circles. However, the failure of the 1848 revolution led him to embrace a more nationalistic and agrarian kind of socialism. His works include one novel, 'Who is to blame?' (1841–6), a collection of political articles, 'From the Other Shore' (1847–50), and his memoirs, 'My Past and Thoughts' (1885), which have been translated by C. Garnett (1924–7).

HESIOD (8th cent. B.C.?), one of the earliest of Greek poets, was born at Ascra in Boeotia, where he tended his father's sheep on the slopes of Mt. Helicon. He was author of 'Works and Days', a poem addressed to his brother Perses, urging him to toil, and descriptive of agricultural life in Boeotia; probably of the 'Theogony', containing a mythical account of the origin of the world and the genealogy of the gods, differing in many details from that of Homer; and of a 'Catalogue of Women', who, being beloved by the gods, had become mothers of heroes. Of this last work only fragments survive. Legend says that Hesiod was murdered at Oenoe in Locris.

Hesiŏnĕ, daughter of Laomedon, king of Troy, and sister of Priam. She was chained by her father on a rock to be devoured by a monster in order to appease the anger of Apollo and Poseidon, whom he had cheated of their pay for building the walls of Troy. Hercules promised to deliver her, for a reward of six horses, and killed the monster. But Laomedon then refused to surrender the horses. Hercules, incensed at his treachery, besieged Troy, slew Laomedon, and gave Hesione to his friend Telamon, by whom she became the mother of Teucer.

Hesperia, the western land, for the Greek poets was Italy. The Roman poets similarly gave the name to Spain, as lying west of Italy.

Hespĕrīdes, nymphs appointed to guard the golden apples that Gē gave to Hera on the day of her nuptials with Zeus. ·They grew in a garden beyond the sea protected by a fearful dragon. One of the labours of Hercules was to secure these apples, which he did after slaying the dragon; or, according to another account, with the help of Atlas, whom he for the purpose relieved of the burden of the heavens.

Hesperides, the title of the collection of secular poems written by Herrick (q.v.).

Hesperus, the Evening Star, the planet Venus.

Hester Rose, a character in Mrs. Gaskell's 'Sylvia's Lovers' (q.v.).

Hestia, the Greek goddess of the hearth, daughter of Cronos and Rhea, akin to the Roman Vesta (q.v.).

Hetty Sorrel, a character in George Eliot's 'Adam Bede' (q.v.).

HEWLETT, MAURICE (1861–1923), novelist, poet, and essayist, became known by his romantic novel of the Middle Ages, 'The Forest Lovers' (1898). He subsequently wrote historical novels ('The Life and Death of Richard Yea-and-Nay'—i.e. Richard Cœur de Lion—1900, 'The Queen's Quair', q.v., 1904, etc.); three books, 'Halfway House' (1908), 'The Open Country' (1909), 'Rest Harrow' (1910), of which the imaginary gipsy-scholar, John Maxwell Senhouse, is the central figure; 'Song of the Plow' (1916), a long poem in which the history of the 'governed race' in England and particularly of Hodge, the agricultural labourer, from the Norman Conquest, is made the subject of pungent comments; some volumes of essays written in the retirement of a Wiltshire village ('In a Green Shade' (1920), 'Wiltshire Essays' (1921), 'Extemporary Essays' (1922), 'Last Essays' (1924)); and a number of other volumes of fiction, poetry, and essays.

Hexameter (see *Metre*), a verse of six metrical feet, which in the typical form consists of five dactyls and a trochee or spondee; for any of the dactyls a spondee may be substituted, except in the fifth foot, where a spondee is rare. The hexameter is the Greek and Latin heroic metre. Longfellow's 'Evangeline' and Clough's 'Bothie' are examples of English hexameter poems.

Hexapla, see *Bible*.

Hexenhammer, see *Malleus Maleficarum.*

Hey for Honesty, Down with Knavery, a comedy by T. Randolph (q.v.), printed in 1651.

'Chremylus, an honest decayed gentleman, willing to become rich, repaireth to the oracle of Apollo, to inquire how he might compass his design. The oracle enjoineth him to follow that man whom he first met with, and never part from his company. The man whom he met is the old blind God of Wealth

disguised. After this Chremylus calleth his poor (but honest) neighbours to partake of his happiness. The honest party rejoice at the news; rascals only and vicious persons are discontented. Plutus is led to the temple of Esculapius and recovers his eyesight. At this knaves are even mad, they murmur and complain exceedingly. Nay the Pope himself is even starved. Lastly to vex them more, the God of Wealth is introduced, married to Honesty' (Argument prefixed to the play). The play is a free adaptation of Aristophanes' 'Plutus', and contains interesting allusions to current events and recent plays, including mentions of Falstaff, Hamlet's ghost, and Shakespeare himself.

HEYLYN, PETER (1600–62), educated at Magdalen College, Oxford, was a notable controversial writer, chiefly on ecclesiastical history. His chief works were 'Ecclesia Restaurata, or History of the Reformation' (1661), 'Cyprianus Anglicus' (i.e. Archbishop Laud) (1668), and 'Aerius Redivivus, or History of Presbyterianism' (1670). He was also author of 'Microcosmus: a little Description of the Great World', reissued in an enlarged form in 1652 as 'Cosmographie', a compilation of descriptions of the various countries of the world.

HEYWOOD, JOHN (1497?–1580?), was probably born in London. He married Elizabeth Rastell, niece of Sir T. More. Under Henry VIII he was a singer and player on the virginals. He was much favoured by Queen Mary, and on her death withdrew to Malines, and afterwards to Antwerp and Louvain. He published interludes, substituting the human comedy of contemporary types for the allegory and instructive purpose of the morality; but he did this in the form of narrative and debate rather than of plot and action. His principal works were 'The Four P's' (see *Interludes*), first printed in 1545(?), the 'Play of the Wether' (1533), in which Jupiter takes the conflicting opinions of various persons regarding the kind of weather to be supplied, and 'A Play of Love' (1534). He may also have been the author of 'The Pardoner and the Frere' and 'Johan the husbande Johan Tyb the wife & syr Jhān the preest', comedies of a wider scope. Heywood also wrote 'A Dialogue concerning Witty and Witless', and collections of proverbs and epigrams.

HEYWOOD, THOMAS (1574?–1641), dramatist, a Lincolnshire man, a student at Cambridge, and perhaps a fellow of Peterhouse. He was a member of the lord admiral's company in 1598, and later one of the queen's players, and a retainer of the earl of Southampton and the earl of Worcester. He wrote a large number of plays, many of which are lost; his chief strength lay in the domestic drama. His best plays are 'A Woman Kilde with Kindnesse' (q.v., acted 1603, printed 1607), 'The Fair Maid of the West' (q.v., printed 1631), and 'The English

Traveller' (q.v., printed 1633). His other chief plays were 'The Four Prentices of London' (produced c. 1600, published 1615), ridiculed in Fletcher's 'Knight of the Burning Pestle'; 'Edward IV' (two parts, 1599); 'The Rape of Lucrece' (1608); 'The Captives' (1624); 'The Royal King and the Loyal Subject' (1637); and perhaps 'The Fayre Mayde of the Exchange' (printed 1607) and 'The Wise Woman of Hogsdon' (1638), though the attribution of these has been questioned. He also published 'An Apology for Actors' (1612), and poems (including 'Hierarchy of the Blessed Angels', 1635), translations, and compilations.

Hiawatha, a poem in trochaic dimeters by H. W. Longfellow (q.v.), published in 1855, reproducing American Indian stories which centre in the life and death of Hiawatha, son of the beautiful Wenonah and the West Wind, who marries Minnehaha ('laughing water'), the Dacota maiden.

The original legendary Hiawatha (Haion 'hwa 'tha) was a Mohawk chief, statesman, and reformer, the advocate of a League of Nations among the Indians.

Hibernia, one of the Latin names for Ireland, Ptolemy's Ἰουερνία, a corruption of *Iverna*, the equivalent of an old Celtic word, whence 'Erin' is derived. Claudian used the form 'Iernē'.

Hickathrift, TOM, see *Tom Hickathrift*.

HICKEY, WILLIAM (1749?–1830), son of the Joseph Hickey who figures in Goldsmith's 'Retaliation', was the author of entertaining 'Memoirs', 1749–1809 (first published 1913–25), in which he describes his numerous voyages to India and other parts of the world, his chequered career as an attorney, and, with great frankness, his weaknesses for women and claret.

HIERŎCLĒS, the name of several philosophers and writers of the early centuries of our era, among them the author, probably in the 4th cent., of facetious moral verses, a translation of which was absurdly attributed to Dr. Johnson.

Hieroglyphics, the characters used in writing by the ancient Egyptians, consisting of figures of objects representing (directly or figuratively) words or parts of words. They were first interpreted by Champollion (q.v.). The term is also used of the picture-writing of other peoples.

Hieronimo, the principal character in Kyd's 'The Spanish Tragedy' (q.v.).

Hieronymus, see *Jerome* (*St.*).

Higden, MRS. BETTY, a character in Dickens's 'Our Mutual Friend' (q.v.).

HIGDEN, RANULF (d. 1364), a Benedictine of St. Werburg's, Chester. He wrote the 'Polychronicon', a universal history down to his own days, in Latin prose. A translation of this by John Trevisa (q.v.), dated 1387,

was printed by Caxton, 1482, Wynkyn de Worde, 1495, and Peter Treveris, 1527. Another translation was made in the 15th cent.; the original Latin was issued in the Rolls Series, with both English versions and continuation.

HIGGINS, MATTHEW JAMES (1810–68), known as 'Jacob Omnium' from the title of his first published article, a prominent journalist and contributor to 'The Times', 'Punch', the 'Cornhill Magazine', etc. His 'Essays on Social Subjects' was edited in 1875.

High Heels and **Low Heels,** in Swift's 'Gulliver's Travels' (q.v.), the name of two political parties in Lilliput.

High Life above Stairs, the sub-title of 'Bon Ton', a farce by Garrick (q.v.).

High Life below Stairs, a comedy by the Revd. James Townley (1714–78), produced in 1759.

Lovel, a rich young West Indian, receives warning that he is being outrageously robbed by his servants. He pretends to go to Devonshire, but returns, assumes the character of a country lad who seeks to be trained as a servant, and obtains employment under his own butler. We are presented with the gay doings below stairs, in which the servants ape the vices and follies of their masters, until, the iniquities of most of his staff having been revealed to him, Lovel discovers himself and packs them off.

Highland Widow, The, a short tragic tale, by Sir W. Scott (q.v.), one of the stories in the 'Chronicles of the Canongate', published in 1827.

The story, which purports to be communicated by Mrs. Bethune Baliol to Chrystal Croftangry, is that of the widow of MacTavish Mhor, one of the last of the Highland caterans, killed by 'red soldiers' after the '45. She lives a lonely life in the mountains with her infant son, and when he grows to manhood, being quite unconscious of the change in the times, expects to see him revive the feats and mode of life of his cateran father. The son, who adds common sense and some knowledge of the world to a brave heart, enlists instead for active service in a regiment going to America. At first incredulous, then indignant at what she considers a base surrender, the widow contrives by a sleeping potion to make him outstay his leave, and then goads him by taunts into killing the Cameron sergeant who comes to arrest him. He is shot as a deserter and a murderer, and the mother, a melancholy survival of a departed age, spends her remaining years in misery and remorse, and disappears to die, like a wild beast, where none may see her.

Hijra or HEGIRA or HEJIRA, the flight of Mohammed from Mecca to Medina in A.D. 622, from which the Muslim era is reckoned.

Hildebrand (c. 1020–85), Pope Gregory VII,

Benedictine monk of obscure 'Lombard-Tuscan' origin, became archdeacon of Rome in 1059 and from that time exercised great influence on the policy of the Papal see, whose temporal power he endeavoured consistently to magnify. He was elected pope in 1073, and in 1076 summoned the Emperor Henry IV to Rome to answer various charges. As a result of the conflict that ensued, Henry did penance at Canossa. But the struggle was resumed; the pope was besieged in the castle of Sant' Angelo, and died in exile.

Hildebrandslied, a fragment of an alliterative German poem of about the year 800, containing a dialogue between Hildebrand, a follower of King Theodoric, who is returning home after many years' absence, and a young knight, who challenges him. Hildebrand tries to avert the fight but fails. The knight turns out to be his own son Hadubrand. At this point the fragment breaks off.

Hildesheim, a town of Hanover. According to legend a monk of Hildesheim, reading St. Augustine's statement that to God a thousand years could be as one day, said, 'I believe, O God, what I read, but I do not understand.' He thereupon heard a white bird singing, and listened to its song with delight. On returning to his convent, he found that a hundred years had passed. Longfellow introduces the story in his 'Golden Legend' (q.v.), calling the monk Felix.

HILL, AARON (1685–1750), dramatist, satirized by Pope, whom he attacked in his 'Progress of Wit' (1730). He wrote the words of Handel's 'Rinaldo' (1711).

HILL, GEORGE BIRKBECK NORMAN (1835–1903), educated at Pembroke College, Oxford, editor of Boswell's 'Life of Johnson' (6 vols., 1887) and other Johnsoniana.

Hill, SIR ROWLAND (1795–1879), originator of penny postage and other postal reforms.

Hind and the Panther, The, a poem by Dryden (q.v.), published in 1687.

Dryden was converted to Roman Catholicism in 1685, and this poem is an outcome of his change of view. It is divided into three parts. The first is occupied with a description of the various religious sects under the guise of the different beasts, and particularly the church of Rome (the 'milk-white Hind, immortal and unchanged') and the church of England (the fierce and inexorable Panther). The second part is occupied with the arguments between the two churches. The third passes from theological controversy to a satirical discussion of temporal and political matters. It contains the well-known fable of the swallows refusing to cross the sea, told by the Panther; and the retort of the Hind, in the fable of the doves, in which Gilbert Burnet (q.v.) is caricatured as the buzzard.

Hinda, a character in T. Moore's 'The Fireworshippers' (see *Lallah Rookh*).

Hindenburg Line, known to the Germans as the SIEGFRIED LINE, the line to which, in the First World War, the German forces retreated in Feb.–Mar. 1917, the line of the Somme having proved hardly tenable in the fighting of the previous Sept. The new German position extended from the Vimy Ridge to the Chemin des Dames, passing through or near Cambrai, St. Quentin, and La Fère. The name 'Siegfried Line' properly applied only to the section between Cambrai and La Fère.

Hindi, the great Aryan vernacular language of Northern India. See *Urdu*.

Hindustani, see *Urdu*.

Hinemoa, the subject of a Maori legend, a beautiful maiden, the daughter of a chieftain of Rotorua in New Zealand, who fell in love with Tutanekai, the illegitimate son of Rangi-Uru, the wife of another chief, and preferred him to his three half-brothers. Guided by the sound of the music that he played in the night, she swam across the lake of Rotorua and joined him, and became his wife. (Sir G. Grey, 'Polynesian Mythology'.)

Hippo, THE BISHOP OF, St. Augustine (q.v.).

Hippocampus, a sea-horse having two fore-feet and a dolphin's tail, represented as drawing the car of Neptune. The name is given to a genus of small sea-fishes, having heads something like that of a horse.

Hippocleides, the subject of an amusing anecdote in Herodotus (vi. 128). He was the chosen suitor of the hand of the daughter of the great tyrant Cleisthenes. At the wedding-feast he ordered the flute-player to play a dance, and 'he danced, probably, so as to please himself', and wound up by standing on his head and gesticulating with his legs, to the grave displeasure of his intended father-in-law, who remarked, 'Son of Tisander, you have danced away your marriage.' 'No matter to Hippocleides', was the rejoinder.

HIPPOCRĀTĒS (*c.* 460–357 B.C.), born in the island of Cos, one of the Cyclades, the most celebrated physician of antiquity. Of the 'Corpus Hippocraticum' or collection of Greek medical works of various dates which have come down to us, only a small portion can be attributed to Hippocrates himself. One of the most interesting parts of it is the so-called 'Hippocratic Oath', expressing the ethical doctrine of the medical profession. (It is given on p. 213 of 'The Legacy of Greece', Clarendon Press, 1921.)

Hippocrene, a fountain on Mt. Helicon in Boeotia, sacred to the Muses. It rose from the ground when struck by the hoof of the horse Pegasus (q.v.).

Hippodămīa, (1) the wife of Peirithous (see *Centaurs*); (2) the daughter of Oenomaus (see *Pelops*).

Hippogriff, a fabulous animal, the front part like a winged griffin, the hind part like a horse; not, according to Ariosto, the product of magic, but a natural creature, though uncommon, found in mountainous regions of the north. It is on a beast of this kind that Rogero rescues Angelica from the Orc, and that Astolpho visits the moon (see *Orlando Furioso*).

Hippŏlўta, a queen of the Amazons (q.v.), given in marriage to Theseus (q.v.) by Hercules, who had conquered her and taken away her girdle, the achievement being one of his twelve labours. She had a son by Theseus called Hippolytus (q.v.). According to another version she was slain by Hercules, and it was her sister Antiope that was the wife of Theseus. She figures as one of the characters in Shakespeare's 'A Midsummer Night's Dream' (q.v.).

Hippŏlўtus, a son of Theseus and Hippolyta (qq.v.), famous for his virtue and misfortunes. His stepmother Phaedra fell in love with him, and, when he repulsed her advances, accused him to her husband Theseus of having offered her violence. Hippolytus fled from his father's resentment, and as he went along the sea-shore, his horses took fright at a sea-monster sent there by Poseidon at the prayer of Theseus, so that they ran away, the chariot was broken among the rocks, and Hippolytus was killed. He is the subject of a play by Euripides and of Racine's 'Phèdre'. (See also Browning's 'Artemis Prologizes'.)

Hippŏměnēs, see *Atalanta*.

Hippŏtădēs, Aeolus (q.v.), the son of Hippotes, and ruler of the winds.

Hiren, a corruption of Irene, the name of a female character in Peele's lost play 'The Turkish Mahamet and Hyren the fair Greek' (*c.* 1594), used allusively by Shakespeare ('2 Henry IV', II. iv) and early 17th-cent. writers for a seductive woman, a harlot.

Hispalis, in imprints, Seville.

Historia Britonum, see *Nennius*.

Historia Ecclesiastica Gentis Anglorum, by Bede (q.v.), was completed in 731.

It is a Latin history of the English people, in five books, from the invasion of Julius Caesar to the year 731, beginning with a description of Britain and ending with an account of the state of the country in 731. The author draws on Pliny and other Latin authors, and on Gildas (q.v.) and probably the 'Historia Britonum' of Nennius (q.v.). In the second book, in connexion with the consultation between Edwin of Northumbria and his nobles whether they shall accept the gospel as preached by Paulinus, occurs the famous simile of the sparrow flying out of the night into the lighted hall, and out again into the night. There is a version of this in Wordsworth's 'Ecclesiastical Sonnets', entitled 'Persuasion'.

Historic Doubts on : . . Richard III, see *Walpole* (*Horace*).

Historical Society, THE ROYAL, was founded towards the end of the year 1868, to deal with biographical and chronological investigations of historical subjects, such as do not fall within the province of archaeological societies, and yet present difficulties for private inquirers.

Histriomastix, see *Prynne*.

HITLER, ADOLF (1889–1945), an Austrian by birth. He became leader of the German National Socialist (Nazi) Party after the First World War, was appointed chancellor of the Reich by Hindenburg in 1933 and succeeded him as president the following year. As dictator (*Führer*) of Germany he pursued the policy outlined in his political manifesto 'Mein Kampf' ('My Struggle') of flouting the Versailles Treaty and rearming, of national economic self-sufficiency, suppression of trade unions, and persecution of the Jews.

He seized Austria by force in 1938 and Czechoslovakia in March 1939 (see *Munich*), and finally by attacking Poland on 1 Sept. 1939 caused the outbreak of the war with Britain and France. After overrunning France in 1940 and Greece in 1941, he attacked Russia. He took over the supreme military command in 1942, escaped a plot to kill him in 1944, and is believed to have perished during the Russian attack on Berlin of 30 April 1945.

Hitopadesa, the name of one version of the famous collection of Hindu tales, known in its earliest form as the *Panchatantra* (q.v.), and in a later form as the 'Fables of Bidpai' (q.v.) or 'Pilpay'. It dates from about the 13th cent., and was translated by Sir W. Jones (q.v.).

HOADLY, DR. BENJAMIN (1706–57), son of Benjamin Hoadly (q.v.). He was a physician and (with his brother) the author of one comedy, 'The Suspicious Husband' (1747, q.v.).

Hoadly, BENJAMIN (1676–1761), bishop successively of Bangor, Hereford, Salisbury, and Winchester, famous as the initiator of the 'Bangorian Controversy' (q.v.). He was high in the favour of Queen Caroline.

Hobbema, MEINDERT (1638–1709), Dutch landscape-painter, best known in England by his picture in the National Gallery, 'The Avenue, Middelharnis'.

'Hobbema, my dear Hobbema, how I have loved you': the dying words of Crome (q.v.).

HOBBES, JOHN OLIVER, pseudonym of Mrs. P. M. T. Craigie (1867–1906), novelist and playwright. Among her novels were 'The Sinner's Comedy' (1892), 'The Serious Wooing' (1901), 'Robert Orange' (1900); and among her plays, 'The Ambassador' (1892) and 'A Repentance' (1899).

HOBBES, THOMAS (1588–1679), philosopher, was born at Malmesbury and educated at Magdalen Hall, Oxford. For a great part of his life he was in the service of the Cavendish family, and in 1647 was appointed mathematical tutor to the Prince of Wales.

At some time (probably between 1621 and 1626) he was in relation with Bacon, translated some of his essays into Latin and took down his thoughts from his dictation. On three occasions he travelled on the Continent with a pupil, and met Galileo, Gassendi, Descartes, and Mersenne (the French mathematician). On his return to England in 1652 he submitted to the Council of State, and was pensioned after the Restoration. He was intimate with Harvey, Ben Jonson, Cowley, and Sidney Godolphin.

As a philosopher Hobbes resembles Bacon in the practical or utilitarian importance that he attaches to knowledge. Nature and man are the objects of his inquiry. With the supernatural world he is little concerned. But he does not share Bacon's enthusiasm for the inductive method; he regards science as essentially deductive, and the geometrical method of demonstration as the true scientific method. Hobbes has been generally described as a nominalist, owing to the importance that he attaches to the definition of the meaning of terms. But he does not deny the reality of the common element entitling things to the same name (Seth, 'English Philosophers'). The basis of all knowledge, according to him, is sensation, and the causes of all sensations are the 'several motions of matter, by which it presseth on our organs diversely'. Motion is the one universal cause, and our appetites are our reactions, in the direction of self-preservation, to external motions. Accordingly man is essentially a selfish unit. Upon this theory Hobbes bases the political philosophy which is expounded in his 'Leviathan' (q.v.), published in 1651. This brought him into general disfavour both on political and religious grounds; and, indeed, the Royalists had some reason to regard it as designed to induce Cromwell to take the crown.

Hobbes's philosophical works, founded on a comprehensive plan in which matter, human nature, and society were successively to be dealt with, further include the 'De Cive' (Latin text 1642, English 1651), 'Human Nature' (1650), 'De Corpore Politico' (originally 'Elements of Law' and subsequently worked up in the 'Leviathan'), 'De Corpore' (Latin text 1655, English 1656), 'De Homine' (1658). He published a translation of Thucydides in 1629, and of Homer in quatrains (1674–5); also a sketch of the Civil Wars, 'Behemoth, or the Long Parliament' (1680), which was suppressed. His complete works were edited by Sir William Molesworth (1839–45). Hobbes was a master of English prose. Without Bacon's profusion of imagery, his style, by its economy and invariable choice of the right and striking word, is most vivid and effective.

Hobbididance, the name of a malevolent sprite or fiend, one of those introduced into the morris-dance, and one of the five fiends that pestered Poor Tom in Shakespeare's 'King Lear', IV. i.

Hobbinol, in Edmund Spenser's writings, was the poet's friend G. Harvey (q.v.).

Hobgoblin, a mischievous tricksy imp or sprite, another name for Puck or Robin Goodfellow. Figuratively, an object that inspires superstitious dread.

HOBHOUSE, JOHN CAM (1786–1869), politician and friend of Byron. Author of the notes to the 4th Canto of 'Childe Harold', which is dedicated to him. Byron's executor.

Hobson, a Cambridge carrier, who 'sickened in the time of his vacancy, being forbidden to go to London by reason of the plague'. He died in Jan. 1630–1. Milton wrote two epitaphs on him, and his name survives in 'Hobson's choice', which refers to his custom of letting out his horses in rotation, and not allowing his customers to choose among them. (See 'Spectator', No. 509.)

Hobson-Jobson, the well-known dictionary of Anglo-Indian colloquial words and phrases by Sir H. Yule (q.v.) and Arthur Coke Burnell, first published in 1886. The title is an Anglo-Indian vernacular term for a native festal excitement, and was chosen by the authors as an alternative characteristic title.

HOBY, SIR THOMAS (1530–66), translator of the 'Cortegiano' of Castiglione (q.v.).

HOCCLEVE, see *Occleve.*

HOCKLEY, WILLIAM BROWNE (1792–1860), author of some good Anglo-Indian stories, of which the best known is 'Tales of the Zenana, or a Nawab's Leisure Hours' (1827). He also wrote 'Pandurang Hari, or Memoirs of a Hindoo' (1826), 'The Vizier's Son' (1831), 'Memoirs of a Brahmin' (1843), etc.

Hockley in the Hole, the birthplace of Jonathan Wild (q.v.), adjoined Clerkenwell. The 'Hole' was the hollow in which the Holebourne (Holborn) flowed, and a place of more or less disreputable gatherings.

Hocktide, Hock Monday and Tuesday, the second Monday and Tuesday after Easter, on which, in pre-Reformation times, money was collected for church and parish expenses, with various festive and sportive customs.

Hock-Tuesday Play, an early English mimetic performance, perhaps of ritual origin, representing the defeat of the Danes by the English. It was revived during the festival given to Queen Elizabeth at Kenilworth, and our knowledge of it is chiefly based on descriptions of this. See *Hocktide.*

Hocus-pocus, originally, it appears, the assumed name of a 17th-cent. conjurer, derived from the sham Latin formula employed by him. The notion that this is a corruption of *hoc est corpus*, the words used in the Eucharist, rests merely on a conjecture thrown out by Tillotson. [OED.]

Hodge, a familiar adaptation of Roger, used as a typical name for the English rustic. Also the name of Dr. Johnson's cat.

HODGSON, RALPH (1871–1962), poet, whose chief works are 'The Bull', 'A Song of Honour', 'Eve' (all 1913).

HODGSON, SHADWORTH HOLLWAY (1832–1912), educated at Rugby and Corpus Christi College, Oxford, devoted his life, after the death of his wife and child in 1858, to the study of philosophy. He was the first president and leading spirit of the Aristotelian Society, whose proceedings contain many addresses by him.

Hodgson regarded himself as continuing and improving on the work of Hume and Kant. He refused to accept the distinction of subject and object, the analysis of experience showing the true distinction to be between consciousness and its content. But while he rejects the traditional assumption of mind and matter, analysis leads to the conclusion that this distinction is necessary. Hodgson's chief publications were 'Time and Space: a Metaphysical Essay' (1865), 'The Theory of Practice' (1870), 'The Philosophy of Reflection' (1878), and 'The Metaphysic of Experience' (1898), the last fully expounding his philosophy.

Hödur or HÖDR, in Scandinavian mythology, one of the Æsir (q.v.), a son of Odin, a blind god, who by the machination of Loki (q.v.) kills his twin brother Balder (q.v.). He is the god of night.

HOEL, see *Howell*.

Hofer, ANDREAS (1767–1810), the son of a Tyrolese innkeeper, was a leader of the insurrection of his compatriots against Bavarian rule, when by the Treaty of Pressburg in 1805 the Tyrol was transferred from Austria to Bavaria. Encouraged by the emperor of Austria, he twice liberated the Tyrol, but was each time deserted by Austria and the country ceded afresh to Bavaria. A further attempt to renew the revolt led to the capture of Hofer by Italian troops. He was executed at Mantua in 1810, it was said by Napoleon's order, but Napoleon denied this.

HOFFMANN, ERNST THEODOR AMADEUS (originally Wilhelm), (1776–1822), German romantic writer and music critic. His works include: 'Phantasiestücke' (1814–15), 'Elixire des Teufels' (1815–16), 'Serapionsbrüder' (1819–21), 'Kater Murr' (1820–2). His stories provided the inspiration for Offenbach's 'Les Contes d'Hoffmann'.

HOFFMAN, HEINRICH (1809–74), German physician, author of the immortal 'Struwwelpeter'('Shock-headed Peter', 1847), written for the amusement of his children, and translated into several languages.

HOFMANNSTHAL, HUGO VON (1874–1929), Austrian poet, dramatist, and essayist. Among his earlier plays are 'Gestern' (1891), 'Der Tod des Tizian' (1892), 'Oedipus und die Sphinx' (1906). 'Jedermann' (1912), a modernization of the old morality play destined to become a regular feature (originally in Max Reinhardt's production) of the Salzburg Festival (which Hofmannsthal helped to found), prefigures 'Das Salzburger Grosse Welttheater' (1922) and inaugurated Hofmannsthal's increasing tendency towards a religious art with strongly Roman Catholic associations. He wrote the libretti for Strauss's operas 'Der Rosenkavalier' (1911). 'Ariadne auf Naxos' (1912), and 'Arabella', and his correspondence with Strauss is of both literary and musical interest. His last play 'Der Turm', influenced (like some of his other works) by Calderón (q.v.), completed Hofmannsthal's development away from the aestheticism of the *fin de siècle* to the idea of literature as carrying a social and religious message.

HOGARTH, DAVID GEORGE (1862–1927), archaeologist and authority on Near Eastern affairs. His publications include: 'A Wandering Scholar in the Levant' (1896), 'The Penetration of Arabia' (1904), 'Accidents of an Antiquary's Life' (1910), 'The Life of C. M. Doughty' (1928).

Hogarth, WILLIAM (1697–1764), painter and engraver. He was apprenticed to a goldsmith and began engraving *c.* 1720. He engraved illustrations for Butler's 'Hudibras' (1726). His earliest paintings were conversation pieces, and he also painted portraits. The 'Harlot's Progress' (1732) was the first of his series of engravings on moral subjects; it was followed by the 'Rake's Progress', 'Marriage à la Mode', the 'Election', the 'Apprentice' series, and other social and political caricatures. For many of these he first painted pictures in oils. His success was such that his work was pirated and he was instrumental in obtaining the passage of 'Hogarth's Act' (1735), protecting the copyright of engravers. He published a work on aesthetics, 'The Analysis of Beauty' (1753).

Hogen Mogen, a popular corruption of the Dutch *Hoogmogendheiden* 'High Mightinesses', the title of the States General, used contemptuously for the Dutch or a Dutchman, or for any high and mighty person.

HOGG, JAMES (1770–1835), the 'Ettrick Shepherd', was born in Ettrick Forest, and early became a shepherd. His poetical gift was discovered by Scott, to whom he furnished material for the 'Border Minstrelsy'. His early ballads were published by Constable as 'The Mountain Bard' in 1807, but he lost in farming the money that he received from this publication. He came to Edinburgh in 1810 and obtained poetical reputation by 'The Queen's Wake' (q.v., 1813), making the acquaintance of Byron, Wordsworth, Southey, Prof. John Wilson, and John Murray. The duke of Buccleuch, in 1816, granted him the farm of Altrive in Yarrow at a nominal rent, and here he mainly resided for the rest of his life, combining agriculture with literary work. He published the 'Forest Minstrel' in 1810, 'Pilgrims of the Sun' in 1815, 'Queen Hynde' in 1826, but is remembered as a poet chiefly on account of 'The Queen's Wake' and particularly the verse tale of 'Kilmeny' included therein; also for a few of his songs and 'The Jacobite Relics of Scotland' (with music), published in 1819. His prose works include 'The Three Perils of Man' (1822), 'The Confessions of a Justified Sinner' (1824), and 'Domestic manners and private life of Sir Walter Scott' (1834). With William Motherwell he published an edition of Burns in 1834–5. Hogg was a contributor to 'Blackwood's Magazine' (q.v.), and is impersonated as the 'Ettrick Shepherd' in its 'Noctes Ambrosianae' (q.v.).

HOGG, THOMAS JEFFERSON (1792–1862), educated at University College, Oxford, with Shelley (q.v.), and sent down on the publication of the latter's 'Necessity of Atheism'. He was the friend and biographer of the poet, publishing two volumes of his life in 1858. He had in 1832 contributed reminiscences of Shelley at Oxford to Bulwer's 'New Monthly Magazine'. An edition of his letters was published in 1943.

Hoggarty Diamond, The Great, a novel by Thackeray (q.v.), published in 'Fraser's Magazine' in 1841.

It is the story of the struggles and misfortunes of Mr. Samuel Titmarsh. The Hoggarty Diamond given him by his stingy old aunt is the means of bringing him temporary prosperity. But he falls into the hands of the swindling Mr. Brough and the West Diddlesex Association. The unfortunate career of this Association as an insurance office brings Samuel to prison, whence he is rescued by the efforts of his excellent young wife.

Hoggins, MR., a character in Mrs. Gaskell's 'Cranford' (q.v.).

Hogmanay, the name given in Scotland and some parts of the north of England to the last day of the year, also called 'Cake-Day'; also to the gift of an oatmeal cake or the like, which children expect, and in some parts systematically solicit on that day. The word corresponds exactly in sense and use to the Old French *aguillanneuf* (Norman form, *hoguinané*), from which it is no doubt derived. The origin of the French word is obscure. Cotgrave's explanation 'Au gui l'an neuf' ('to the mistletoe the new year') is now rejected. The Spanish word 'aguilando', a handsel, Christmas-box, is found before 1600. [OED.]

Hohenlinden, in Bavaria, the scene of a great battle in 1800, in which the French revolutionary general, Moreau, defeated the Austrians; celebrated by T. Campbell (q.v.) in his 'Battle of Hohenlinden'.

HOLBACH, PAUL HENRI, *Baron d'* (1723–89), see *Philosophes*.

Holbein, HANS, (1497/8–1543), the Younger, son and pupil of Hans Holbein the Elder (*c.* 1465–1524), an Augsburg painter. He settled in Basle, painting and illustrating books. In 1526 he visited Sir Thomas More in London, with an introduction from Erasmus.

By 1532 he was again in England, working for the German merchants of the Steelyard, and he became Court painter to Henry VIII *c.* 1536, painting portraits, often from drawings, and designing architectural decorations and goldsmith's work.

Holborn, a district of London whose name is derived from the *Holeburne*, 'the burn in the hollow'. This was probably the stream known in its lower course as the Fleet (see *Fleet Street*). In this district the bishops of Ely had from the 13th cent. a splendid palace (Ely Place) with a great garden, referred to in Shakespeare's 'King Richard III', III. iv:

> My lord of Ely, when I was last in Holborn,
> I saw good strawberries in your garden there.

The garden was made over to Sir Christopher Hatton, the favourite of Elizabeth, during a vacancy in the see (1581), and its site now bears his name (Hatton Garden). Matthew Wren, the uncle of Sir Christopher and bishop of Ely, made prolonged efforts, but without success, to recover it from Hatton's widow, who married Sir Edward Coke. Hatton Garden is now the centre of the diamond trade.

HOLCROFT, THOMAS (1745–1809), successively stable-boy, shoemaker, tutor, actor, and author, and a friend and associate of Thomas Paine and William Godwin (qq.v.), wrote an entertaining autobiography ('Memoirs', edited and completed by Hazlitt, after his death, 1816) and a number of sentimental plays, of which the best known is 'The Road to Ruin' (1792). In this, Harry Dornton, whose spendthrift habits have imperilled his father's bank, is prepared to sacrifice himself by marrying the odious rich widow Mrs. Warren in place of the girl he loves, a sacrifice rendered unnecessary by the fidelity of the bank's head clerk, the grim old Mr. Sulky. Holcroft also wrote some novels, including 'Alwyn, or the Gentleman Comedian' (1780), based on his own odd experiences, 'Anna St. Ives' (1792), and 'Hugh Trevor' (1794), written in the spirit of Godwin's 'Caleb Williams' in defence of revolutionary ideas. He also translated Goethe's 'Hermann und Dorothea' (1801) and other works.

HOLE, SAMUEL REYNOLDS (1819–1904), educated at Brasenose College, Oxford, became dean of Rochester in 1887. He was an enthusiastic huntsman, sportsman, and gardener, and a close friend of John Leech, who introduced him to Thackeray. He was an early contributor to 'Punch'. His 'Book about Roses' (1869) helped to popularize horticulture. He published 'Hints to Freshmen' (1847), 'A Little Tour in Ireland' (illustrated by Leech) (1859), 'The Six of Spades' (a gardeners' club) (1872); 'Memories' (1892), 'More Memories' (1894), and 'Then and Now' (1901). His humorous and charming 'Letters' were edited with a memoir by G. A. B. Dewar in 1907.

Holger Danske, the tutelary hero of Denmark, who is supposed to be sleeping under the Kronenborg at Elsinore, his long beard grown into the table, waiting to arise in the hour of Denmark's peril. He is the subject of one of Hans Andersen's Tales. See *Ogier the Dane*.

Holiday House, a very popular story for children, by Catherine Sinclair, published in 1839.

HOLINSHED, RAPHAEL (*d.* 1580?), was of a Cheshire family and is said by Anthony à Wood to have been a 'minister of God's word'. He came to London early in the reign of Elizabeth, and was employed as a translator by Reginald Wolfe, the printer and publisher. While in his employ he planned the 'Chronicles' (1577) which are known by his name and are by several hands. The 'Historie of England' was written by Holinshed himself. The 'Description of England', a vivid account, not devoid of humour, of English towns, villages, crops, customs, etc., of the day, was written by William Harrison (q.v.). The 'History and Description of Scotland' and the 'History of Ireland' were translations or adaptations, and the 'Description of Ireland' was written by Richard Stanyhurst and Edward Campion. A few passages in the 'History of Ireland' offended the Queen and her ministers, and were expunged. A copy containing the expunged passages is in the Grenville collection in the British Museum. The 'Chronicle' was reissued, with continuation, edited by John Hooker, *alias* Vowell, in 1586, and politically offensive passages again taken out; it was utilized by Shakespeare and other dramatists.

HOLLAND, PHILEMON (1552–1637), educated at Trinity College, Cambridge, and a doctor of medicine, was master of the free school at Coventry from 1628, and received a pension from that city in 1632. He is celebrated for his translations of Livy (1600), Pliny's 'Natural History' (1601), Plutarch's 'Moralia' (1603), Suetonius (1606), Ammianus Marcellinus (1609), Camden's 'Britannia' (1610), and Xenophon's 'Cyropaedia' (1632). His knowledge of Greek and Latin was accurate and profound, and his renderings are made in a vivid, familiar, and somewhat ornamented English.

Holland House, Kensington, built at the beginning of the 17th cent. for Sir Walter Cope, passed by marriage into the possession of Henry Rich (son of Penelope Rich, q.v.), 1st earl of Holland, who took his title from the 'parts of Holland' in Lincolnshire, and was executed in 1649. In 1767 it was acquired by Henry Fox, 1st baron Holland, who entertained Horace Walpole and George Selwyn there. In the time of his grandson, the 3rd baron Holland (1773–1840), Holland House became a great political, literary, and artistic centre, and many eminent authors, such as Sheridan, Moore, Thomas Campbell, Macaulay, Grote, and Dickens, were among the

guests received there. Jospeh Addison, who had married the widow of one of the earls of Warwick and Holland, died at Holland House in 1719.

HOLME, CONSTANCE (1881–1955), novelist, author of 'The Lonely Plough' (1914), 'The Splendid Fairing' (1919), 'The Trumpet in the Dust' (1921), etc.

HOLMES, OLIVER WENDELL (1809–94), born at Cambridge, Massachusetts, was professor of anatomy and physiology at Harvard University from 1847 to 1882. His 'Autocrat of the Breakfast-Table' appeared in the 'Atlantic Monthly' in 1857–8, 'The Professor at the Breakfast-Table' in 1860, 'The Poet at the Breakfast-Table' in 1872, and 'Over the Tea-Cups' in 1891. He also wrote novels, 'Elsie Venner' (1861) and 'The Guardian Angel' (1867), some volumes of poems and essays, and memoirs of R. W. Emerson and J. L. Motley. His essays in the 'Breakfast-Table' series are notable for their kindly humour and general sagacity; they take the form of discourses by the author, the other characters being listeners, who interpose occasional remarks. His poems include a few good lyrics and familiar verses, such as 'The Chambered Nautilus', 'Homesick in Heaven', 'The Last Leaf', 'Dorothy Q', and 'The Deacon's Masterpiece; or The Wonderful One-Hoss Shay'.

Holmes, SHERLOCK, the famous private detective who figures in a number of works by Sir A. Conan Doyle (q.v.). The character was in part suggested by an eminent Edinburgh surgeon, Dr. Joseph Bell (1837–1911), under whom Doyle studied medicine. Sherlock Holmes was familiarized to the public by his eccentricities and mannerisms, his nonchalance alternating with energy, his dressing-gown and hypodermic syringe, as well as his amazing mental powers. His assistant and foil is Dr. Watson (q.v.), his great enemy Prof. Moriarty.

Holofernes, (1) Nebuchadnezzar's general, who was killed by Judith (Judith iv. 1, etc.); (2) the great doctor in theology (Thubal Holoferne) who instructed the youthful Gargantua (Rabelais, 1, xiv); (3) the pedantic schoolmaster in Shakespeare's 'Love's Labour's Lost'. This character has been thought to represent John Florio (q.v.), 'Holofernes' being a partial anagram of his name.

Holt, FATHER, in Thackeray's 'Esmond' (q.v.), a Jesuit priest and Jacobite intriguer.

Holy Alliance, THE, an alliance formed in 1815, after the fall of Napoleon, between the sovereigns of Russia, Austria, and Prussia, with the professed object of uniting their governments in a Christian brotherhood. Great Britain refused to be a party; and Castlereagh called it 'a piece of sublime mysticism and nonsense'. It virtually came to an end in 1822, and entirely in 1825.

Holy Bottle, THE ORACLE OF THE, see *Pantagruel*.

Holy Cross Day, the festival of the exaltation of the Cross, 14 Sept., on which the Jews in Rome were obliged formerly to go to church and hear a sermon. It is the subject of a satirical poem by R. Browning, in which the Rabbi Ben Ezra on his death-bed in a prayer to Christ sets forth the degradation of the Jews and appeals against Christ's so-called followers.

Holy Grail, THE, see *Grail.*

Holy Grail, The, one of Tennyson's 'Idylls of the King' (q.v.), published in 1869.

Sir Percivale, having left the court of Arthur for the cowl, recounts to a fellow monk the story of the quest of the Holy Grail (q.v.) and the success of Sir Galahad. Percivale has not, like Galahad, 'lost himself to save himself' and, though approaching near the sacred vessel, fails. The honest Bors has the vision of the Grail, but no more. Gawain fails utterly. Lancelot, after a fierce struggle to pluck asunder the noble elements from the one sin in his soul, fails also.

Holy Living and *Holy Dying,* see *Taylor (Jeremy).*

Holy Mountain, see *Athos.*

Holy Office, THE, see *Inquisition.*

Holy Roman Empire, the name given to the realm of the sovereign who claimed to inherit the authority of the ancient Roman emperors in the West. It comprised, in general, the German-speaking States of Central Europe. Its creation may be traced to the need felt by the popes in the 8th cent. for temporal support, which led Leo III to invoke the aid of Charlemagne and finally to crown him emperor on Christmas Day, 800. The empire degenerated under his successors, but was revived by Otto the Great in 962. After the successive falls of the Saxon, Salian, and Swabian dynasties, and an interregnum of nineteen years, it passed by election to the Hapsburgs. These came into prominence with Maximilian I in 1493, and their line was all but continuous until the abdication of Francis II in 1806. The epithet 'Holy', adopted by Frederick Barbarossa, was significative of the supposed divine institution of the empire and of its union with the Church. The emperor was elected by seven electors, the archbishops of Trèves, Mayence, and Cologne, the king of Bohemia, the count Palatine of the Rhine, the duke of Saxony, and the margrave of Brandenburg. Bavaria was added to the electorate in 1648 and Hanover in 1699. For the classic work on the Holy Roman Empire, see under *Bryce (J.).*

Holy State and Profane State, The, a series of characters and essays, by Fuller (q.v.), published in 1642.

This is one of Fuller's most popular works. The author describes with much good sense and humour a number of good and evil characters, such as 'The Good Widow', 'The Good Merchant', 'The True Gentleman', 'The Liar'; and adds essays on various subjects, among the best of which are those 'Of Building' and 'Of Recreations'.

Holy War, The, an allegory by Bunyan (q.v.), published in 1682.

The author narrates how Diabolus gets possession by his wiles of the city Mansoul (i.e. soul of man), the metropolis of the universe. Thereupon King Shaddai, the builder of the city, sends Boanerges and three other captains to recover it, and finally his own son Emmanuel to lead the besieging army. The vicissitudes of the siege are recounted with much spirit. The city falls to the assault conducted by Emmanuel, after much parley between the defenders ('Diabolonians') and the besiegers. But when the power of the king has been re-established, the city presently relapses into evil ways. Diabolus recaptures the city but cannot take the citadel, and is presently defeated by Emmanuel. Bunyan in this allegory evidently drew upon his experience as a soldier in the parliamentary war.

Holy Willie's Prayer, a poem by Burns (q.v.).

Holyroodhouse, Edinburgh, a royal palace of the Kings of Scotland and the United Kingdom. King David I founded the abbey of Holyrood in 1128; Robert the Bruce and subsequent Scottish kings held parliament there, and in the 15th cent. it became a royal residence. James IV built a palace beside the abbey, 1498–1503; both were destroyed by the English in 1544 and 1547, but the palace was repaired for Mary Queen of Scots in 1561. It was burnt by Cromwell's troops, rebuilt by Cromwell in 1651–8, and again by Charles II in 1671–9.

Holywell Street, London, a street that ran parallel to the Strand between the churches of St. Clement Danes and St. Mary le Strand, where second-hand booksellers congregated. It was demolished towards the end of the 19th cent. Holywell is mentioned by William Fitzstephen (q.v.) in the introduction to his life of Thomas à Becket, among 'the excellent springs in the outskirts [of London], with sweet wholesome and clear water that flows rippling over the bright stones' (quoted by G. R. Stirling Taylor, 'Historical Guide to London').

HOME, DANIEL DUNGLAS (1833–86), a spiritualistic medium, whose seances in England in 1855 and subsequent years were attended by well-known people, many of whom, including Sir William Crookes, were convinced of the genuineness of the phenomena. Browning, who witnessed them, remained sceptical (see his 'Mr. Sludge "The Medium" '). Home was expelled from Rome in 1864 as a sorcerer. He published 'Incidents of my Life' (1863 and 1872).

HOME, HENRY, LORD KAMES (1696–1782), a Scottish judge and psychologist. His 'Introduction to the Art of Thinking' (1761) and 'Elements of Criticism' (1762) were widely read in his day.

HOME, JOHN (1722–1808), a Scottish minister and, after his resignation from the ministry, secretary to Lord Bute and tutor to the Prince of Wales, and a friend of Hume, Robertson, and Collins. He was the author of a tragedy 'Douglas' (q.v.), produced in 1756, which enjoyed much popularity. He subsequently wrote other tragedies which were less successful. Home was a friend of Macpherson (q.v.) and a firm believer in 'Ossian'.

Home Rule, the name given to the movement, begun about 1870, to obtain for Ireland self-government through the agency of a national parliament. The phrase 'Home Rule' had been used incidentally in 1860. But at the meeting for the local autonomy of Ireland held on 19 May 1870, the phrase 'Home Government' was adopted, though 'Home Rule' is said to have been suggested and became immediately popular. [OED.]

Home, Sweet Home, a song by J. H. Payne (q.v.), an American dramatist and songwriter. It formed part originally of the opera 'Clari'. The music is by Sir Henry Rowley Bishop (1786–1855), musical composer.

HOMER, the great Greek epic poet, who was regarded by the ancients (though the belief has in modern times been contested) as the author of the 'Iliad' and the 'Odyssey' (qq.v.). There is doubt as to both his birthplace and his date, the latter being variously placed between 1050 and 850 B.C. The seven cities that claimed to be his birthplace were 'Smyrna, Rhodus, Colophon, Salamis, Chios, Argos, Athenae'. Tradition represents him as blind and poor in his old age. The origin of the epics, whether by the enlargement and remodelling of earlier material by one or more hands or as a direct composition from traditional material, is disputed. Recent scholarship tends to recur to the view of 'One Homer'.

The HOMERIC HYMNS, of unknown authorship and various dates, are preludes to epic poems, addressed to various deities, and recounting legends relating to them.

Homilies, BOOKS OF, a title applied in the Church of England to two books of Homilies, published in 1547 and 1563, appointed to be read in the Churches. The second Book of Homilies is mentioned in Article 35 of the Thirty-nine Articles in the Book of Common Prayer.

Homonym, the same name or word used to denote different things; or a person or thing having the same name as another, a namesake. Cf. *Synonym*.

Homophone, a word having the same sound as another, but a different meaning. Cf. *Synonym*.

HONE, WILLIAM (1780–1842), author and bookseller, who published political satires on the government illustrated by Cruikshank and was prosecuted for his 'Political Litany'

(1817). He published his 'Every-Day Book' (dedicated to Lamb and praised by Scott and Southey) in 1826–7, and his 'Table-Book' in 1827–8.

Honest Whore, The, a play by Dekker (q.v.) in two parts, of which the first was printed in 1604 and the second in 1630. It appears from Henslowe's diary that Middleton collaborated in writing the first part.

In Pt. I Count Hippolito, making the acquaintance of Bellafront, and discovering that she is a harlot, upbraids her bitterly for her mode of life and converts her to honesty. She falls in love with Hippolito, who repels her and marries Infelice, daughter of the duke of Milan. Bellafront is married to Matheo, who had caused her downfall.

In Pt. II we find the converted Bellafront as the devoted wife of the worthless Matheo, who, to get money for his vices, is prepared to see her return to her old way of life. Hippolito, now falling in love with her, tries to seduce her. She stoutly resists temptation, and is finally rescued from misery by her father, Orlando Friscobaldo. The painful character of the play, one of the great dramas of the age, heightened by Dekker's powerful treatment and by scenes in Bedlam and Bridewell, is somewhat alleviated by the admirable character, Orlando Friscobaldo, and by the comic underplot, dealing with the eccentricities of the patient husband, Candido the linen-draper.

Honeycomb, WILL, in Addison's 'Spectator' (q.v.), one of the members of the club by which that periodical is described as being conducted.

Honeyman, CHARLES, in Thackeray's 'The Newcomes' (q.v.), brother-in-law of Colonel Newcome, a self-indulgent clergyman, incumbent of Lady Whittlesea's fashionable chapel. His worthy sister, MARTHA HONEYMAN, keeps lodgings at Brighton.

Honeythunder, LUKE, a character in Dickens's 'Edwin Drood' (q.v.).

Honeywood, MR. and SIR WILLIAM, characters in Goldsmith's 'The Good-Natur'd Man' (q.v.).

Honi soit qui mal y pense, see *Garter*.

Honorable Peter Stirling, The, see *Ford* (*P. L.*).

Honoria, see *Theodore and Honoria*.

Honorificabilitudinitatibus, the long word in Shakespeare's 'Love's Labour's Lost' (v. i), in which Baconians see a cryptogram indicating that Bacon was the author of the works attributed to Shakespeare.

Hood, ROBIN, see *Robin Hood*.

HOOD, THOMAS (1799–1845), born in London, the son of a bookseller, became subeditor of the 'London Magazine', 1821–3, and made the acquaintance of Lamb, Hazlitt, and De Quincey. He edited various periodicals at different times: the 'Gem' (1829), in which his 'Eugene Aram' appeared; the 'Comic Annual' (1830); the 'New Monthly Magazine' (1841–3); and 'Hood's Magazine' (1843). In addition to the humorous work for which he is perhaps chiefly remembered (including 'Miss Kilmansegg', q.v., which appeared in the 'New Monthly Magazine'), Hood wrote a number of serious poems: the popular 'Song of the Shirt' (published anonymously in 'Punch' in 1843) and 'The Bridge of Sighs', 'The Haunted House', 'The Elm Tree', 'The Plea of the Midsummer Fairies', and shorter pieces such as 'The Death-bed'. Among his prose writings may be mentioned a humorous comedy called 'York and Lancaster', and the 'Literary Reminiscences' in 'Hood's Own' (1839), which include the notable account of an assembly at Charles Lamb's. Hood received a civil list pension not long before his death.

HOOD, THOMAS, the younger (1835–74), known as Tom Hood, was the son of Thomas Hood (q.v.). He was editor of a comic paper 'Fun' (1865), and in 1867 began 'Tom Hood's Comic Annual', which was continued after his death. His works, which are mainly humorous, include 'Pen and Pencil Pictures' (1857) and 'Captain Master's Children' (1865). A collection of his verse, 'Favourite Poems', was published in 1877.

Hoodoo, see *Voodoo*.

Hook, CAPTAIN, the pirate captain in Barrie's 'Peter Pan' (q.v.).

HOOK, THEODORE EDWARD (1788–1841), is remembered as a wit, a writer of light verses, a successful editor (chiefly of the Tory 'John Bull'), and a novelist. But his novels, 'Sayings and Doings' (1826–9), 'Maxwell' (1830), 'Gilbert Gurney' (1836), 'Jack Brag' (1837), 'Gurney Married' (1838), etc., full of the crude fun of the period and popular as they once were, have now lost their interest. He went to Mauritius as accountant general in 1813, but was recalled owing to a deficiency of £12,000 in his accounts—or, as he put it, 'on account of a disorder in his chest'.

HOOKER, RICHARD (1554?–1600), theologian, was born at Exeter of poor parents, and by Bishop Jewel's patronage sent to Corpus Christi College, Oxford, where he remained till 1579, becoming a fellow and deputy professor of Hebrew. He was appointed to the living of Drayton-Beauchamp in 1584, master of the Temple 1585, rector of Boscombe in Wiltshire, and of Bishopsbourne in Kent, where he died and where the inscription on his monument first called him 'Judicious'. Of his great prose classic, the defence of the Church of England as established in Queen Elizabeth's reign, entitled 'Of the Laws of Ecclesiastical Politie' (q.v.), four books appeared in 1594, the fifth in 1597. Other works by Hooker were issued at Oxford in 1613. A pleasant biography of Hooker was written by Izaak Walton and published with the 1665 edition of his 'Ecclesiastical Politie'.

There is some reason to credit Hooker with the first steps towards making known in England the theory of 'original contract' as a basis of sovereignty.

HOOKER, SIR JOSEPH DALTON (1817–1911), the son of Sir William Jackson Hooker (1785–1865) and, like him, a botanist and traveller, and director of Kew. Sir Joseph became a friend of Darwin and collaborated with him in researches into the origin of species. He went on scientific expeditions in various parts of the world, and published many botanical works.

Hookey Walker, see *Walker*.

Hooligan, a member of a gang of street roughs. 'The original *Hooligans* were a spirited Irish family of that name whose proceedings enlivened the drab monotony of life in Southwark towards the end of the 19th cent.' (Ernest Weekley, 'Romance of Words').

Hoosier Schoolmaster, The, see *Eggleston*.

Hop-o'-my-thumb, a name applied generically to a dwarf or pygmy, occurring as early as the 16th cent. See also below.

Hop o' my Thumb, Little Thumb, a fairy tale, from the French of Perrault (q.v.), translated by Robert Samber (1729?).

Hop o' my Thumb (*petit Poucet*) is the youngest of seven children of a woodman and his wife, who are forced by poverty to rid themselves of the children by losing them in the forest. Hop o' my Thumb, having overheard this decision, fills his pocket with white pebbles, which he drops along the way, and by means of these leads his brothers home again. The parents once more lose them, Hop o' my Thumb this time using bread-crumbs to mark the way. But the birds eat up the bread-crumbs, and the children arrive at the house of an ogre, who is deluded by Hop o' my Thumb into killing his own children instead of the woodman's. Hop o' my Thumb moreover steals his seven-league boots, and with the help of these obtains enough wealth to set his parents at ease. Andrew Lang in his 'Perrault's Popular Tales' discusses the origins of this story.

HOPE, ANTHONY, see *Hawkins* (*A. H.*)

HOPE, THOMAS (1770?–1831), a man of great wealth, a traveller, and a virtuoso, was the author of the once popular novel 'Anastasius' (q.v.), published in 1819.

Hope Theatre, THE, on Bankside, Southwark, built in 1613 by Henslowe (q.v.) as a bear-garden, with a movable stage on which plays could be performed. Jonson's 'Bartholomew Fayre' was acted there in 1614.

HOPKINS, GERARD MANLEY (1844–89), was educated at Highgate School and Balliol College, Oxford. He was the pupil of Jowett and Pater, numbered Bridges and Dolben (and later in life Coventry Patmore) among his friends, and was a disciple of Pusey and Liddon, and, after his conversion in 1866 to the Church of Rome, of Newman. He entered the Jesuit novitiate in 1868, and in 1884 was appointed to the chair of Greek at Dublin University. He was a poet of much originality and a skilful innovator in rhythm. His poems, none of which were published in his lifetime, were collected by Robert Bridges, who published a small selection in Miles's 'Poets and Poetry of the Century'. The first edition of the poems, edited by Bridges, appeared in 1918 and a substantially enlarged new edition, edited by W. H. Gardner and N. H. Mackenzie, was published in 1967. His Letters to Bridges, Dixon and Patmore have been edited by C. C. Abbott (1935-8, 1955-6); his 'Notebooks and Papers' by H. House (1937, 1959).

HOPKINS, MATTHEW (*d.* 1647), the witch-finder, said to have been a lawyer at Ipswich and Manningtree. He made journeys for the discovery of witches in the eastern counties in 1644-7, and procured a special judicial commission under which sixty women were hanged in Essex in one year, and many in Norfolk and Huntingdonshire. He published his 'Discovery of Witches' in 1647. He was exposed and hanged as a sorcerer. He is referred to in Butler's 'Hudibras'.

HOPKINSON, JOSEPH, see *Hail, Columbia.*

HORACE, (QUINTUS HORATIUS FLACCUS, 65-8 B.C.), the Roman poet, was born at Venusia in Apulia, educated at the school of Orbilius (q.v.) and at Athens. He was present on the losing side at the battle of Philippi, but obtained his pardon and returned to Rome; here he became the friend of Maecenas (q.v.), who bestowed on him a Sabine farm. His poems include the 'Satires', 'Odes' and 'Epodes', 'Epistles', and the 'Ars Poetica'.

Horae, in classical mythology, originally the goddesses of the seasons, generally three in number. According to Homer they control the weather and grant the rain. According to Hesiod they are daughters of Zeus and Themis, and give laws, justice, and peace.

Horatii and the Curiatii, THE, three Roman brothers and three Alban brothers, a battle between whom, according to legend, decided the struggle between Alba and Rome in the reign of Tullus Hostilius. This story, and the love of one of the Curiatii for the sister of the Horatii, form the subject of William Whitehead's successful play 'The Roman Father' (1750) and of a tragedy by P. Corneille.

Horatio, in Shakespeare's 'Hamlet' (q.v.), the friend of Hamlet.

Horatius Cocles, see *Cocles.*

Horizon, a literary magazine founded by Cyril Connolly in 1939 to provide a medium for contemporary literature in war-time, and edited by him until it ceased publication in 1950.

HORMAN, WILLIAM (*d.* 1535), fellow of New College, Oxford, and vice-provost of

Eton, author of 'Vulgaria' or 'Vulgaria Puerorum', Latin aphorisms for boys to learn. It was printed by Pynson (1519), Wynkyn de Worde (1540), and for the Roxburghe Club (edited by M. R. James, 1926); a most remarkable book.

Horn, CAPE, the southernmost point of America, on the last island of the Fuegian archipelago, was discovered by the Dutch navigator Schouten in 1616, and named after Hoorn, his birthplace.

Horn, King, see *King Horn.*

Horn Childe, a verse romance of the early part of the 14th cent., containing some 1,100 lines. The general plot is similar to that of 'King Horn' (q.v.), but is different in details. Horn is the son of Hatheolf of the North of England. Arlaund, the instructor of Horn and his eight companions, flees with them to Honlac, a king in the South of England, whose daughter Rimnild falls in love with Horn. Arlaund substitutes Hatherof, one of the companions, for Horn when Rimnild summons him to her chamber. Two of Horn's companions, Wiard and Wikel, betray Horn and Rimnild to the king. Horn goes to Wales, taking Rimnild's magic ring and promising seven years' fidelity, and to Ireland, where he drives out the pagan invaders of King Finlac's realm. He returns to England and in a tournament overcomes the suitor of Rimnild, slays Wiard, blinds Wikel, and marries Rimnild. The poem is inferior to 'King Horn', and is one of those referred to by Chaucer in his 'Tale of Sir Thopas', see *Canterbury Tales* (19).

Horn-book, a leaf of paper containing the alphabet (often with the addition of the ten digits, some elements of spelling, and the Lord's Prayer) protected by a thin plate of translucent horn, and mounted on a tablet of wood with a projecting piece for a handle, used for teaching children to read. A simpler and later form of this, consisting of the tablet without the horn covering, or a piece of stiff cardboard varnished, was also called a battledore. For an exhaustive account see A. W. Tuer, 'History of the Hornbook' (1896).

Hornbook, DR., see *Death and Dr. Hornbook.*

HORNE, JOHN, see *Tooke (J. H.).*

HORNE, RICHARD HENRY or HENGIST (1803-84), educated at Sandhurst, served in the Mexican navy in the Mexican war of independence, and led an adventurous life until he was thirty, when he took up literature. He is remembered chiefly as the author of the epic 'Orion' (q.v.), which he published in 1843 at a farthing 'to mark the public contempt into which epic poetry had fallen'. He published 'Cosmo de' Medici' and 'The Death of Marlowe' in 1837, and other tragedies ('Gregory VII' in 1840, 'Judas Iscariot' in 1848); also 'Ballad Romances' in 1846 and 'The Poor Artist' in 1850. Then, abandoning poetry, he went to Australia from 1852 to 1869, where he was a commissioner for crown lands, commanded the gold escort from Ballarat to Melbourne, taught gymnastics and swimming, etc. He published in 1859 his entertaining 'Australian Facts and Prospects', with his 'Australian Autobiography' as preface, in which he gives a stirring account of his experiences. Horne was granted a civil list pension in 1874. He had much correspondence with E. B. Browning, and published two volumes of her letters to him. She collaborated with him in his 'A New Spirit of the Age' (1844).

Horner, a character in Wycherley's 'The Country Wife' (q.v.).

Horner, JACK, see *Jack Horner*.

Horniman, ANNIE ELIZABETH FREDERICKA (1860–1937), a pioneer supporter of the modern English drama, founder of 'Miss Horniman's Company' of actors, and of the Manchester Repertory Theatre, for the purposes of which she acquired the Gaiety Theatre in that town in 1908. By her generous assistance the Irish National Theatre Society was provided with a permanent home in the Abbey Theatre, Dublin (q.v.).

Horse, THE TROJAN or WOODEN, the artifice by which the Greeks got possession of Troy. They constructed a large wooden horse and filled it with armed men, and then withdrew their forces from the neighbourhood of Troy as if to return home. Sinon, son of Sisyphus (q.v.), allowed himself to be taken prisoner by the Trojans, pretending to have been maltreated by the Greeks, and persuaded Priam to have the horse drawn into the city, on the ground that it was an offering to Athene and would render Troy impregnable. When the horse was within the walls, Sinon at dead of night released the armed men, who made themselves masters of the city.

Horse, THE WHITE, see *White Horse*.

Horsel, the Hörselberg in Thuringia, see *Tannhäuser*. The legend is the subject of Swinburne's 'Laus Veneris'.

Horses, FAMOUS, see *Arion, Bayard, Black Bess, Borak, Brigliadoro, Bucephalus, Carbine, Cid* (for *Babieca*), *Copenhagen, Darley Arabian, Eclipse, Favonius, Flying Childers, Flying Fox, Gringolet, Hrimfaxi, Ladas, Marocco, Pegasus, Rosinante, Sejan horse, Sleipnir, Swallow, White Surrey, Xanthus.*

HORT, FENTON JOHN ANTHONY (1828–92), theological scholar, famous for his recension, jointly with B. F. Westcott, of the Greek text of the New Testament (1871). His Hulsean lectures of 1871 were published in 1893 under the title, 'The Way, The Truth, The Life'.

Hortensio, a character in Shakespeare's 'The Taming of the Shrew' (q.v.).

Horus, the Egyptian god of light, the son of Osiris and Isis (qq.v.), who avenges the death of Osiris by defeating the evil deity Typhon and wages war with the powers of darkness. He was regarded as the rising sun, born afresh daily, the symbol of renewed life. See also *Harpocrates*.

Hosier's Ghost, Admiral, see *Glover (R.)*.

Hospitallers of St. John of Jerusalem, KNIGHTS, also called KNIGHTS OF ST. JOHN, KNIGHTS OF RHODES, and KNIGHTS OF MALTA, a military religious order, originally an association that provided a hostel at Jerusalem for the reception of pilgrims. The military order was founded about 1099 on the earlier (1070) foundation of a hospital for sick pilgrims by a citizen of Amalfi. A branch was established in England in the 12th cent., and had its house at Clerkenwell, where their church of St. John, much rebuilt, still exists. Their badge was a white cross of eight points on a black ground. The Knights of St. John defended Acre in 1290, took Rhodes in 1310 and defended it against the Saracens until 1525; then retired to Candia and Sicily, and finally in 1530 were given Malta by the Emperor Charles V. This they were obliged to surrender to Buonaparte in 1798; it was taken by the British in 1800 and ceded by the Treaty of Paris of 1814.

The original order survives on the Continent. It was suppressed in England in the 16th cent. The modern British order was formed in the 19th cent., receiving a charter of incorporation in 1888, for the purpose of ambulance and other charitable work.

Hotspur, SIR HENRY PERCY (1364–1403), called 'Hotspur', eldest son of the first earl of Northumberland, figures in Shakespeare's 'King Henry IV' (q.v.), a gallant fiery character.

HOUGHTON, LORD, see *Milnes (R. M.)*.

HOUGHTON, WILLIAM STANLEY (1881–1913), the son of a Manchester merchant, devoted from early life to the drama. He wrote a number of plays of Lancashire life, strongly influenced by the Ibsen tradition. The first of these was 'The Dear Departed', produced in 1908 by the Manchester Repertory Theatre; followed by 'Independent Means' (1909), 'The Younger Generation' and 'The Master of the House' (1910), 'Fancy-Free' (1911), and 'Hindle Wakes', his most successful work (1912). In 1913 Houghton migrated to Paris, but died within a few months.

Hound of Heaven, The, see *Thompson (F.)*.

Houndsditch, a district in London, largely inhabited by Jewish shopkeepers, originally part of the ditch outside the city walls.

Hours, see *Horae*.

Hours, Book of, a book containing the prayers or offices of the Roman Catholic Church to be said at the seven times of the day appointed for prayer.

Hous of Fame, The, a poem by Chaucer of 1,080 lines composed probably between 1372 and 1386. In a dream the poet visits the Temple of Venus, where he sees graven the story of the flight of Aeneas after the fall of Troy, and of his reception by, and betrayal of, Dido. He is then carried by an eagle to the House of Fame, full of a great company of aspirants for renown and adorned with the statues of historians and poets; and sees the queen, Fame, distributing fame and slander. He is then taken to the House of Rumour, crowded with shipmen, pilgrims, and pardoners, and other bearers of false tidings. The poem is unfinished.

House, ASTROLOGICAL, a twelfth part of the heavens as divided by great circles through the north and south points of the horizon. A special signification was attached to each house. They were numbered eastwards beginning with the HOUSE OF THE ASCENDANT. THE ASCENDANT was the degree of the zodiac which at any moment, e.g. that of the birth of a child, is rising above the eastern horizon. The 'house of the ascendant' included five degrees of the zodiac above this point and twenty-five degrees below it. THE LORD OF THE ASCENDANT was any planet within the house of the ascendant. The ascendant and its lord were supposed to exercise a special influence on the life of a child born at the moment.

House, THE, a familiar name for (1) the House of Commons; (2) Christ Church, Oxford; (3) the Stock Exchange; (4) the workhouse.

House of Life, The, a sonnet-sequence by D. G. Rossetti (q.v.), published partly in 1870, partly in 1881. The sonnets are records of the poet's spiritual experience, inspired by love of his wife and sorrow for her death, and permeated with mysticism.

House of the Seven Gables, The, a novel by N. Hawthorne (q.v.), published in 1851.

In this tale the author presents the problem of unmerited misfortune and prosperous and unrequited crime. Hepzibah Pyncheon is a poor grotesque old spinster, inhabiting the paternal mansion of a decayed New England family, which has suffered from generation to generation the curse of old Maule, the dispossessed owner of the property. Under stress of poverty she is obliged to do violence to her family pride by opening a small shop. At this moment, to add to Hepzibah's perplexities, her brother Clifford Pyncheon, an amiable Epicurean bachelor of enfeebled intellect, who has spent long years in prison for a crime of which he has been unjustly convicted by the machinations of his cousin Judge Pyncheon, returns to his home. On the other hand, a fresh little country cousin, Phoebe Pyncheon, arrives to lighten the gloom of the old house. Judge Pyncheon, the bland prosperous hypocrite, diffusing a 'sultry' benevolence, continues his persecution of Clifford; but this is arrested by the Judge's sudden death, and with the help of Holgrave, a young daguerreotypist and descendant of old Maule, a typical modern American, independent and self-reliant, who falls in love with and marries Phoebe, Clifford is rehabilitated, and a belated happiness brightens the declining years of the poor old brother and sister.

House of Usher, The Fall of the, one of the 'Tales of Mystery and Imagination' of Poe (q.v.).

House that Jack Built, The, a nursery accumulative tale of great antiquity, probably based on an old Hebrew original, a hymn in Sepher Haggadah, beginning 'A kid my father bought for two pieces of money'; 'then came the cat and ate the kid, etc.'; 'then came the dog and bit the cat, etc.'; ending with the Angel of Death who killed the butcher who slew the ox, etc.; and the Holy One who slew the Angel of Death. That the English version is an early one is indicated by the reference to the 'priest, all shaven and shorn'. There is also a Danish version (Halliwell).

House with the Green Shutters, The, a novel by G. D. Brown (q.v.), written under the name GEORGE DOUGLAS and published in 1901.

Household Words, a weekly periodical started in 1850 by Dickens (q.v.), from which politics were ostensibly excluded and which was adapted to a more popular standard of taste than such magazines as 'Blackwood'. It received contributions from such noted writers (besides Dickens himself) as Bulwer Lytton, Lever, Wilkie Collins, and Mrs. Gaskell.

HOUSMAN, ALFRED EDWARD (1859–1936), a distinguished classical scholar, professor of Latin at Cambridge University, was the author of two volumes of lyrics, remarkable for economy of words and simplicity, 'A Shropshire Lad' (1896) and 'Last Poems' (1922). He published an edition of Manilius (q.v., 5 vols., 1903–30).

HOUSMAN, LAURENCE (1865–1959), brother of the above, author and artist. His best-known works are: 'Prunella' (1906), 'Angels and Ministers' (1921), 'Little Plays of St. Francis' (1922), 'Palace Plays' (1930); also satirical novels, 'The Duke of Flamborough' (1928), 'Trimblerigg' (1924). He was the author of 'An Englishwoman's Love-letters', published anonymously in 1900.

Houyhnhnms, the talking horses in 'Gulliver's Travels' (q.v.).

HOVEDEN or HOWDEN, ROGER OF (*d.* 1201?), a Yorkshireman and a chronicler who lived in the reign of Henry II. He was the author of both the main chronicles of the reigns of Henry II and Richard I, the 'Gesta Regis Henrici', that long went under the name of Benedict of Peterborough, and the 'Chronica'.

How they brought the Good News from Ghent to Aix, a poem by R. Browning (q.v.), included in 'Dramatic Romances', published in 'Bells and Pomegranates' (1842–5).

This, one of the most popular of the author's poems, is a vivid imaginary tale of three horsemen galloping to save their town, one horse falling dead on the way, the second within sight of the town, the third reaching the market-place, where the town's last measure of wine is poured down its throat.

Howard, HENRY, see *Surrey.*

Howards End, a novel by E. M. Forster (q.v.), published in 1910, deals with personal relationships and conflicting values. On the one hand are the Schlegel sisters, Margaret and Helen, and their brother Tibby, who care about civilized living, music, literature, and conversation with their friends; on the other, the Wilcoxes, Henry and his children, Charles, Paul, and Evie, who are concerned with the business side of life and distrust emotions and imagination. Helen Schlegel is drawn to the Wilcox family, falls briefly in and out of love with Paul Wilcox, and there-after reacts away from them. Margaret becomes more deeply involved. She is stimulated by the very differences of their way of life and acknowledges the debt of the intellectuals to the men of affairs who guarantee stability, whose virtues of 'neatness, decision and obedience . . . keep the soul from becoming sloppy'. She marries Henry Wilcox, to the consternation of both families, and her love and steadiness of purpose are tested by the ensuing strains and misunderstandings. Her marriage cracks but does not break. In the end, torn between her sister and her husband, she succeeds in bridging the mistrust that divides them. Howards End, where the story begins and ends, is the house that belonged to Henry Wilcox's first wife, and is a symbol of human dignity and endurance.

HOWE, JULIA WARD, see *Battle Hymn of the Republic.*

Howe, MISS, a character in Richardson's 'Clarissa Harlowe' (q.v.).

Howell or HOEL, in the Arthurian legend, duke of Brittany and cousin of King Arthur.

HOWELL, JAMES (1594?–1666), educated at Jesus College, Oxford, held diplomatic and administrative posts under Charles I, and was imprisoned in the Fleet as a Royalist from 1643 to 1651. He wrote a number of historical and political pamphlets, but is chiefly remembered for his 'Epistolae Ho-elianae: Familiar Letters', mostly written in the Fleet and generally to imaginary correspondents (collected in 1650, and edited by Joseph Jacobs in 1890–2). Some of these are political or historical and deal with various countries, others are essays on literary and social topics. In 1649 he wrote his satirical 'Perfect Description of the Country of Scotland', which was reprinted by Wilkes in No. 31 of the 'North Briton'. In 1642 he issued his entertaining 'Instructions for Forreine Travel' (enlarged in 1650), and in 1657 his 'Londinopolis; an Historical Discourse or Perlustration of the City of London'.

HOWELLS, WILLIAM DEAN (1837–1920), American novelist, was born in Ohio, and began life as a printer and journalist. He was American consul at Venice, 1861 to 1865, an experience reflected in his 'Venetian Life' (1866) and 'Italian Journeys' (1867). He was sub-editor of the 'Atlantic Monthly' (q.v.), 1866–71, and chief editor, 1871–81, and was associate editor of 'Harper's Magazine' (q.v.), 1886–91, to which periodicals he contributed many articles on literary subjects. His numerous romances include 'Their Wedding Journey' (1872), 'A Chance Acquaintance' (1873), 'A Foregone Conclusion' (1875), 'The Lady of the Aroostook' (q.v., 1879), 'The Undiscovered Country' (1880), 'A Fearful Responsibility' (1881), 'A Modern Instance' (1881), 'The Rise of Silas Lapham' (q.v., his greatest work, 1885), 'Indian Summer' (another charming book, 1886), 'A Hazard of New Fortunes' (1890), which shows the effect of his political and critical moves towards socialism and social realism, 'The Landlord at Lion's Head'(1897). His works of criticism and reminiscence include 'Criticism and Fiction' (1891), 'My Literary Passions' (1895), 'Literary Friends and Acquaintances' (1900), 'Literature and Life' (1902). He also wrote several dramas. His industry and his influence made him the leading American man-of-letters of his age.

Howleglass, see *Eulenspiegel.*

Hoyden, MISS, a character in Vanbrugh's 'The Relapse' (q.v.), and in Sheridan's 'A Trip to Scarborough' (q.v.).

HOYLE, EDMOND (1672–1769), author of a 'Short Treatise on Whist' (1742 and later editions). Hoyle's 'Laws' of 1760 ruled Whist till 1864.

Hrimfaxi ('dewy-mane'), in Scandinavian mythology, the horse of Night.

Hrothgar, the Danish king in 'Beowulf' (q.v.).

Hrotsvitha or ROSWITHA, a Benedictine abbess, in the 10th cent., of Gandersheim in Saxony, who adapted the comedies of Terence for the use of her convent, an example of the survival of classical influence in the Middle Ages.

Hubbard, MOTHER, see *Mother Hubbard* and *Mother Hubberd's Tale.*

Hubert, ST., the patron saint of the chase, is said to have been son of Bertrand, duke of Aquitaine, and to have lived in the 7th cent. He was passionately devoted to hunting, for which he neglected his religious duties. One day a stag appeared before him, with a crucifix between his horns, and threatened him with eternal punishment if he did not repent of his sins. He thereupon took holy orders and later became bishop of Liège and Maestricht. He is commemorated on 3 Nov.

HUCHOUN (*fl.* 14th cent.), Scottish author of romances in alliterative verse. Among the poems attributed to him, with various degrees of probability, are the alliterative 'Morte Arthure', 'The Awntyrs of Arthure', 'Sir Gawain and the Green Knight', 'The Pistyl of Susan', 'Patience', 'Pearl', and 'Cleanness' (qq.v.). He is perhaps to be identified with Sir Hugh of Eglintoun, a statesman of the reigns of David II and Robert II.

Huckleberry Finn, a novel by S. L. Clemens (q.v.), published in 1884 as a sequel to 'Tom Sawyer' (q.v.), under the pseudonym MARK TWAIN. It is accepted as his masterpiece and one of the greatest works of American fiction. Huck Finn, the hero, recounts his adventures after being taken away from the Widow Douglas's by his drunken and roguish father. He escapes from his father and joins up with a runaway slave, Jim, and together they make their way down the Mississippi on a raft. The picaresque device of a journey serves to introduce a number of adventures and a variety of characters: Huck becomes a witness of the bloodfeud between the Granger and Shepherdson families; he and Jim are joined by two villainous confidence men, the 'Duke' and the 'Dauphin'; these scoundrels sell Jim into captivity again but at the end of the book Tom Sawyer reappears in time to help Huck to rescue him (unnecessarily, as it turns out, for Jim has been earlier and unknowingly given his freedom): but the story is also a myth and a moral commentary bearing directly on the nature of the 'American experience'. Huck tells his tale in the vernacular, and the telling is a triumph of style.

Hudibras or HUDDIBRAS, in Spenser's 'Faerie Queene', II. ii. 17, the lover of Elissa,

An hardy man,
Yet not so good of deeds as great of name
Which he by many rash adventures wan.

Another Huddibras in II. x. 25 of the same poem is a legendary king of Britain.

Hudibras, a satire in octosyllabic couplets, and in three parts, each containing three cantos, by S. Butler (1612–80, q.v.), published, Pt. I in 1663, Pt. II in 1664, and Pt. III in 1678.

The satire takes the form of a mock-heroic poem, in which the hypocrisy and self-seeking of the Presbyterians and Independents are held up to ridicule. It is externally modelled on 'Don Quixote', while there are Rabelaisian touches, and the influence of Scarron on the style has been pointed out. The name 'Hudibras' is taken from the 'Faerie Queene' (see above). The character has been thought to represent the Puritan Sir S. Luke. He is pictured as a pedantic Presbyterian, setting forth 'a-colonelling', a grotesque figure on a miserable horse, with rusty arms but ample provisions. He is accompanied by his squire Ralpho, an Independent, and the satire is largely occupied with their sectarian squabbles. The pair light upon a crowd intent on bear-baiting, a popular sport vigorously condemned by the Puritans. A battle ensues in which the bear-baiters are at first defeated, and their leader, the one-legged fiddler Crowdero, is put in the stocks. But the bear-baiters rally their forces, Hudibras and Ralpho replace Crowdero in the stocks, and there they resume their sectarian disputes.

In Pt. II a widow, with whose 'jointure-land' Hudibras is in love, visits him in the stocks, exposes his self-seeking and requires him (after the model of 'Don Quixote') to submit to a whipping in order to win her favour. This gives an opportunity of exposing the casuistry of the Puritans; for Hudibras wishes to escape from his promise, and his squire suggests a whipping by proxy. To this Hudibras readily assents and orders Ralpho to be the substitute, whence a furious quarrel. They then consult Sidrophel (q.v.), an astrologer, on Hudibras's prospects with the widow. The astrologer is discovered to be a humbug, is beaten and left for dead by Hudibras, who escapes (after emptying the astrologer's pockets), intending that Ralpho shall bear the charge of murder.

In Pt. III Hudibras goes alone to the widow and gives her an account of his pretended sufferings on her behalf; but he has been forestalled by Ralpho, and is accordingly exposed. His cowardice is revealed when fierce knocking is heard at the gate. He attributes this to the astrologer's supernatural agents, hides under a table, is drawn out and cudgelled, and confesses his iniquities. He next consults a lawyer, who counsels him to write love-letters to the widow, in order to inveigle her in her replies. The second Canto of Pt. III has no connexion with the adventures of Hudibras, but is an account of the principles and proceedings of the republicans prior to the Restoration (it includes an admirable character of Anthony Ashley Cooper).

It is probable that Butler intended to complete the story in a fourth part.

Hudibrastic, in the metre or after the manner of Butler's 'Hudibras' (q.v.), burlesque-heroic.

Hudson, JEFFERY or GEOFFREY (1619–82), a dwarf who was served up in a pie to Charles I and entered the service of Queen Henrietta Maria. He was a captain of horse in the civil wars, was captured by pirates while on his way to France and carried to Barbary, escaped and returned to England, and was imprisoned for supposed complicity in the 'Popish Plot'. He figures in Scott's 'Peveril of the Peak' (q.v.).

Hudson, RODERICK, hero of Henry James's novel of that name (q.v.).

HUDSON, WILLIAM HENRY (1841–1922), born of American parents near Buenos Aires, came to England in 1869, where he at first, and indeed till nearly the end of his life, suffered much from poverty and loneliness. He was naturalized a British subject in 1900. He has left an admirable picture of his early life in the Argentine in 'Far Away and Long

Ago' (1918). From his youngest days he was an intense observer of nature, and a large proportion of his writings was devoted to birds (e.g. 'The Naturalist in La Plata', 1892; 'Birds in London', 1898; 'Birds and Man', 1901; 'Adventures among Birds', 1913). His most remarkable work is probably 'A Shepherd's Life' (1910), in which he depicts the humble folk of the Wiltshire downs, their dogs, their sheep, and the wild life of the region, with Caleb Bawcombe, a shepherd, as the principal figure. He also wrote a striking romance of the S. American forest, 'Green Mansions' (1904), of which the central figure 'Rima', the semi-human embodiment of the spirit of the forest, has been made familiar by Epstein's sculpture. His other writings include: 'The Purple Land' (1885), 'Nature in Downland' (1900), 'El Ombu' (1902), 'Hampshire Days' (1903), 'A Crystal Age' (1906), 'Afoot in England' (1909), 'A Traveller in Little Things' (1921), 'A Hind in Richmond Park' (1922).

Hudson's Bay Company: the 'governor and company of adventurers of England trading into Hudson's Bay' received a charter from Charles II in 1670, for trade and 'to discover a passage leading to the Pacific Ocean'. Prince Rupert was the company's first governor. On the expiration of the charter in 1869, the bulk of their territories was transferred, against compensation, to the Dominion of Canada. Hudson Bay is named after Henry Hudson, the explorer, who was turned adrift there with his son and some companions by a mutinous crew, and perished in 1611.

Hugh, in Dickens's 'Barnaby Rudge' (q.v.), the ostler of the Maypole Inn.

Hugh of Lincoln, St. (?1246–55), a child supposed to have been crucified by a Jew named Copin or Joppin at Lincoln, after having been starved and tortured. The body is said to have been discovered in a well and buried near that of Grosseteste in the cathedral, and to have been the cause of several miracles. The story, a frequent theme for poets, is referred to by Chaucer ('Prioress's Tale') and by Marlowe in 'The Jew of Malta'. See also the ballad of 'The Jew's Daughter' in Percy's 'Reliques'. Cf. *William of Norwich*.

HUGHES, RICHARD (ARTHUR WARREN (1900–), writer, of Welsh descent. While up at Oxford he published a one-act play, 'The Sisters' Tragedy', and a volume of poems, 'Gipsy Night' (1922). 'Confessio Juvenis' (collected poems) appeared in 1926. He spent some time in the U.S.A., Canada, and the West Indies, and published the novels, 'A High Wind in Jamaica' (1929) and 'In Hazard' (1938). 'A Moment of Time' (1926), 'The Spider's Palace' (1931), and 'Don't Blame Me' (1940) are books of short stories, the last two being for children. 'The Fox in the Attic' (1961) is the first volume of a long historical novel of his own times culminating in the Second World War.

HUGHES, THOMAS (1822–96), educated at Rugby and Oriel College, Oxford, was a follower of Frederick Denison Maurice (q.v.). He published in 1857, over the signature 'An Old Boy', his chief work, 'Tom Brown's Schooldays', the story of an ordinary schoolboy at Rugby under Dr. Arnold's headmastership. In this he depicted, with a didactic purpose, schoolboy cruelties and loyalties, and considerably influenced English ideas on public schools. The sequel, 'Tom Brown at Oxford' (1861), has less merit. Hughes also published 'The Scouring of the White Horse' (1859), a 'Memoir of a Brother' (his brother George, 1873, containing George Hughes's fine poem on the Oxford and Cambridge boat race of 1868), and various biographies.

Hugin and Munin, see *Odin*.

HUGO, VICTOR-MARIE (1802–85), French poet and novelist, the leader of the French Romantic movement. He entered political life after the revolution of 1848 and showed himself an eloquent defender of liberty. He spent the years 1851–70 in exile, the greater part of the time in Guernsey. His poetical creed was expounded in the preface to his long drama 'Cromwell' (1827), while the production of his 'Hernani' (q.v.) on the stage in 1830 was one of the principal events of the literary revolution. Hugo introduced flexibility, sonority, and melody into the rigid verse that had prevailed during many generations. His other important plays were: 'Marion de Lorme' (1831), 'Le Roi s'amuse' (1832), and 'Ruy Blas' (1838). His poetry includes the earlier 'Odes' (1822), 'Odes et Ballades' (1826), 'Les Orientales' (1829), 'Feuilles d'Automne' (1831), 'Chants du Crépuscule' (1835), 'Voix intérieures' (1837), 'Les Rayons et les Ombres' (1840), followed after a long interval by 'Les Châtiments' (1853, a violent satire against Louis Napoleon, written in exile), 'Les Contemplations' (1856), 'La Légende des Siècles' (some of his finest work, 1859, 1877, 1883), 'Chansons des Rues et des Bois' (1865), 'Les Quatre Vents de l'Esprit' (1881). Two posthumous fragments 'La Fin de Satan' and 'Dieu' (1886 and 1891), intended as part of 'La Légende des Siècles', should also be mentioned. His most famous novels are 'Notre Dame de Paris' (1831), 'Les Misérables' (1862), 'Les Travailleurs de la Mer' (1866, the scene is Guernsey), and 'Quatre-vingt-treize' (1873, Royalist insurrections in Brittany during the French Revolution).

Huguenot, a member of the Reformed or Calvinistic communion of France in the 16th and 17th cents. The name, according to Hatzfeldt and Darmesteter, is a corruption, under the influence of the proper name Hugues, of the German *Eidgenossen*, confederates.

Huitzilopochtli, the supreme deity and war-god of the ancient Mexicans, regarded as a bloodthirsty deity, to whom vast numbers of human beings were sacrificed. He was also known as *Mextli*.

Hulde, in Teutonic mythology, the goddess of marriage.

HULME, THOMAS ERNEST (1883–1917), an anti-romantic whose advocacy of the 'hard dry image' in poetry influenced Imagism (q.v.). He published a series of articles on Bergson (q.v.) in 1911 in the 'New Age', a political and literary weekly edited by A. R. Orage, which also published five short poems called 'The Complete Poetical Works of T. E. Hulme'. Hulme also published translations of works by Bergson and Georges Sorel, and was full of plans for further work when he was killed in action. His 'Speculations: essays on humanism and the philosophy of art' were published in 1924 (ed. Herbert Read).

Hulse, JOHN (1708–90), educated at St. John's College, Cambridge, bequeathed his estates to the University of Cambridge for the advancement of religious learning, by the payment of a lecturer and the institution of a Christian advocate. The HULSEAN PROFESSOR of divinity was substituted for the latter in 1860. The HULSEAN LECTURES are delivered annually.

Human Nature, Treatise of, see *Treatise of Human Nature*.

Humber, according to Geoffrey of Monmouth, a king of the Huns who invaded Britain in the reign of Locrine, and was defeated near the river Abus. He was driven into the river, which thereafter was named after him. (See Spenser's 'Faerie Queene', II. x. 15 and 16.)

HUMBOLDT, (FRIEDRICH HEINRICH) ALEXANDER VON (1769–1859), German traveller and scientist, published a series of works embodying the results of a scientific expedition to South America and Mexico, which were translated into English (1814–21). His greatest work was the 'Cosmos' (published in German, 1845–62), a physical description of the universe, passing from celestial phenomena to the earth and its atmosphere, and finally to organic life.

HUME, DAVID (1711–76), born of Berwickshire parents at Edinburgh, developed early in life a passion for philosophy. He spent three years (1734–7) with the Jesuits at La Flèche, and in 1739 published anonymously his 'Treatise of Human Nature' (q.v.) in two volumes, a third volume appearing in 1740. The work aroused little interest, but his 'Essays Moral and Political' (1741–2) were more successful. He accompanied General St. Clair as judge-advocate in the expedition to Port L'Orient in 1747 and on a mission to Vienna and Turin in 1748. His 'Enquiry concerning Human Understanding' (originally entitled 'Philosophical Essays') appeared in 1748 and his 'Enquiry concerning the Principles of Morals' in 1751 (for these two works see *Treatise of Human Nature*). In

1752 he published his 'Political Discourses', which was translated into French and made Hume famous on the Continent. In the same year he was appointed keeper of the Advocates' Library in Edinburgh. In 1754 appeared the first volume of his 'History of Great Britain' (see below), followed by further volumes in 1757, 1759, and 1761. The first two volumes were translated into French. From 1763 to 1765 Hume was secretary to the Embassy in Paris, where he was well received by the court and by literary society. He brought back Rousseau to England and befriended him, but Rousseau's suspicious nature presently led to a quarrel. Hume was under-secretary of state in 1767–8, and after this finally settled in Edinburgh. After his death, his friend Adam Smith (q.v.) published his autobiography (1777). Hume's 'Dialogues concerning Natural Religion' (q.v.) were published in 1779 by his nephew. A complete edition of Hume's Letters, edited by J. Y. T. Greig, appeared in 1932.

Hume's philosophical works are dealt with under the heading 'Treatise of Human Nature'. His views on religion are contained, (*a*) in the essay 'Of Miracles' (included in the 'Enquiry concerning Human Understanding'), in which he argues that the evidence for miracles is necessarily inferior to the evidence for the 'laws of nature' established by uniform experience of which they are a violation; (*b*) in the dissertation entitled 'The Natural History of Religion' (included in 'Four Dissertations', 1757), in which he investigates its origin in human nature, attributing it to a 'concern with regard to the events of life', to the 'incessant hopes and fears which actuate the human mind', and traces its development from polytheism to monotheism and its inevitable degeneration; (*c*) in the 'Dialogues concerning Natural Religion' (q.v.), of which the conclusion is that there is evidence of design in the universe, but that while it is possible to infer from design the intelligence of God, it is impossible to infer his goodness. We thus have an 'attenuated theism' (Prof. Campbell Fraser), the view 'that the cause or causes of order in the universe probably bear some remote analogy to human intelligence'.

Hume's political opinions as expressed in his various writings show a process of development. He appears to have abandoned the view that men are naturally equal and that society is established by contract. He finally seems to have regarded political society as evolved from the family and existing for the purpose of administering justice ('Of the Origin of Government', 1777); and in contrast to his Tory attitude in the 'History' (see below), in his later essays he regards liberty as an ideal limiting the sphere of authority of government.

As a political economist Hume attacked the mercantile system, and in general anticipated the views of later economists (including Adam Smith). He insisted on the distinction between money and wealth; he held that a low rate of interest does not result from an abundance of money but from the increase in the industry and frugality of the people; he thought that the best taxes were those on consumption and denied that all taxes ultimately fall on land.

Hume's Enquiry concerning Human Understanding, see *Treatise of Human Nature.*

Hume's History of Great Britain (see *Hume*), containing the reigns of the Stuarts, was published in 1754–7. Two further volumes on the Tudor reigns appeared in 1759, and two on the period from Julius Caesar to Henry VII in 1761.

Hume's object was to trace the steps by which the nation had arrived at its present system of government, and he started with the reign of James I as the period in which the revolt against the prerogative of the crown commenced. The work is criticized as superficial and as containing many misstatements, and the author is said to show Tory prejudice. But it was the first great English history, and, however imperfect, a fine conception. It was not a mere chronicle of political events, but includes periodical reviews of the material and intellectual state of the nation. The first volume was coldly received, but the work subsequently became popular, and for long was regarded as a standard history.

Humgudgeon, CORPORAL GRACE-BE-HERE, a character in Scott's 'Woodstock'.

Humorous Lieutenant, The, a comedy by J. Fletcher (q.v.), produced about 1620.

Prince Demetrius is in love with Celia, a captive. His father, Antigonus, king of Syria, also falls in love with her, and during his son's absence at the wars, tries to inveigle Celia, but she remains faithful to her younger lover. On Demetrius's return from victory, Antigonus informs him that Celia is dead, and while Demetrius shuts himself up in despair, tries to obtain her affection by a love-philtre. But the plot miscarries, and finally Celia's virtue and loyalty prevail on the king to surrender her to his son.

The name of the play is taken from an eccentric lieutenant, suffering from an infirmity which stimulates him to wonderful deeds of courage in war. When cured, his courage fails him; and it comes again when he is deluded into thinking himself sick once more. By accident he drinks the love-philtre intended for Celia, and in consequence falls grotesquely in love with the king.

Humours, COMEDY OF, a term applied especially to the type of comic drama written by Ben Jonson (q.v.), where a 'humour' is the embodiment in one of the characters of some individual passion or propensity.

Humphrey, DUKE OF GLOUCESTER (1391–1447), youngest son of Henry IV, 'the Good Duke Humphrey', was perhaps educated at Balliol College, Oxford. He was appointed Protector on the death of Henry V. He owed the epithet 'Good' only to his patronage of men of letters (including Lydgate and Capgrave). He read Latin and Italian literature, collected books from his youth, and gave the first books for a library at Oxford. His original library, built in the 15th cent., forms the oldest part of the Bodleian. He was the husband of Eleanor Cobham, who was imprisoned for witchcraft.

Humphrey, To DINE WITH DUKE, to go dinnerless. The origin of the phrase is not clear. In the 17th cent. it was associated with old St. Paul's, London, and said of those who, while others were dining, passed their time walking in that place. According to Stow, the monument of Sir John Beauchamp there was 'by ignorant people misnamed to be' that of Humphrey, duke of Gloucester, son of Henry IV (who was really buried at St. Albans). Nares says an (adjacent) part of the church was termed 'Duke Humphrey's Walk'. The equivalent expression in Edinburgh appears to have been 'to dine with St. Giles and the Earl of Murray' (who was buried in St. Giles's). [OED.]

Humphrey's Clock, Master, see *Master Humphrey's Clock.*

Humphry Clinker, The Expedition of, a novel by Smollett (q.v.), published in 1771.

This is the last and the pleasantest of Smollett's novels. It relates, in the form of letters, the adventures of Mr. Matthew Bramble's family party as they travel through England and Scotland. The party consists of Bramble himself, an outwardly misanthropical but really kind-hearted old valetudinarian bachelor; his sister Tabitha, a virago bent on matrimony; his nephew Jery, an amiable young spark, and his sister Lydia; Mrs. Winifred Jenkins, the maid; and Humphry Clinker, a ragged ostler whom they pick up *en route* as postilion, and who turns out a creature of much resource and devotion. Their wanderings, which take them to Bath, London, Harrogate, Edinburgh, and the Highlands, are made the occasion for many amusing adventures and episodes, for conveying much interesting information about contemporary manners, and for many discussions on matters political and other. The thread of narrative is slender. There is the love-affair of Lydia with a good-looking young actor, who turns out to be a gentleman of good family. Humphry becomes a Methodist and suffers a short imprisonment on a false charge of robbery. At Durham the party is joined by an eccentric Scottish soldier, Lieutenant Obadiah Lismahago, no less proud than he is needy. He wins the heart and hand of Miss Tabitha. Finally Humphry himself turns out to be the natural son of Matthew Bramble, and is united to Winifred Jenkins.

Humpty-Dumpty, a short, dumpy, humpshouldered person. In the well-known nursery rhyme or riddle the name is commonly explained as signifying an egg. The riddle is found in one form or another in many parts of Europe (Halliwell). The name is thence allusively applied to any thing or person which when shattered cannot be restored. 'Humpty-Dumpty' occurs in 1698 as the name of a liquor; according to Disraeli ('Venetia'), ale boiled with brandy. [OED.]

Huncamunca, in Fielding's 'Tom Thumb, a Tragedy' (q.v.), the daughter of King Arthur and the wife of Tom Thumb.

Hundred Days, THE, the period in 1815 between Napoleon's arrival in Paris after his escape from Elba and the restoration of Louis XVIII after Waterloo.

Hundreth good pointes of husbandrie, see *Tusser (T.).*

Hungarian Brothers, The, a novel by A. M. Porter (q.v.).

Hungry Forties, see *Forties.*

Huniades, see *Hunyadi.*

Huns, an Asiatic race of warlike nomads who invaded Europe *c.* A.D. 375. They perhaps also invaded Hindustan: the Rajputs are believed to be of Hun stock. In the middle of the 5th cent. under their king, Attila (q.v.), they overran and ravaged a great part of Europe. The name is believed to represent the native name of the people, who were known to the Chinese as *Hiong-nu* and also *Han.* It is used in a transferred sense (like 'Vandal') of uncultured devastators, especially of the Germans. The immediate source of the latter application was a speech delivered by Wilhelm II on 27 July 1900 to the German troops about to embark for China, urging ruthless treatment of the enemy, like that of Attila and the Huns. [OED.]

HUNT, JAMES HENRY LEIGH (1784–1859), was educated at Christ's Hospital. He began to edit the 'Examiner' in 1808 and the 'Reflector' in 1810, and was sentenced with his brother to a fine and two years' imprisonment in 1813 for reflections in the former paper on the Prince Regent. He continued editing the 'Examiner' while in jail, where he was visited by Byron, Moore, Bentham, and Lamb. Subsequently he brought about the meeting of Keats and Shelley, and introduced the two poets to the public in the 'Examiner'. He published his chief poetical work 'The Story of Rimini' (based on the story of Paolo and Francesca, q.v.) in 1816 (it was subsequently revised), and 'Hero and Leander' in 1819. He joined Byron at Pisa in 1822 and there for a time carried on with him 'The Liberal' magazine (see under *Byron*). In 1847 he received a civil list pension. His poetical work, which was far less extensive than his prose writings, includes, besides the two poems mentioned above, 'Captain Sword and Captain Pen' (1835, depicting the horrors of war and foretelling the ultimate discomfiture of military power), the lines entitled 'Abou Ben Adhem' (q.v.) and 'Jenny kissed me', the apologue 'The Fish, the Man, and

the Spirit', and a translation of Redi's 'Bacchus in Tuscany' (1825). His play 'A Legend of Florence' was successfully produced at Covent Garden in 1840. In addition to the two periodicals already mentioned, Leigh Hunt at various times conducted and largely wrote the 'Indicator' (1819–21), the 'Companion' (1828), a new 'Tatler' (1830–2), and 'Leigh Hunt's London Journal' (1834–5). Other works of his are 'Imagination and Fancy' (1844), 'Wit and Humour' and 'Stories from Italian Poets' (1846), 'Men, Women, and Books' (1847), 'A Jar of Honey from Mount Hybla' (1848), 'The Town' (1848), an 'Autobiography' (1850, enlarged edition 1860), 'Table Talk' (1851), 'The Old Court Suburb' (1855), and an edition of Beaumont and Fletcher in the same year.

The importance of Leigh Hunt lies chiefly in his development of the light miscellaneous essay, in his recognition of the genius of Shelley and Keats, and in the wide range of his critical work. He was depicted by Dickens as Skimpole (in 'Bleak House', q.v.), at any rate as regards 'the light externals of character', that is to say a certain vagueness and irresponsibility.

Hunt, THE REVD. TUFTON, the blackmailing parson in Thackeray's 'The Adventures of Philip' (q.v.). He had previously figured in his 'A Shabby Genteel Story'.

HUNTER, JOHN (1728–93), surgeon and anatomist, contributed very greatly by his writings, discoveries, and collections to the advance of surgical science. His MUSEUM was bought by the nation and transferred to the Royal College of Surgeons. He is commemorated in the annual HUNTERIAN ORATION.

Hunter, WILLIAM (1718–83), elder brother of John Hunter (above), was, like him, a distinguished anatomist, and first professor of anatomy at the Royal Academy. His museum was acquired by Glasgow University.

HUNTER, SIR WILLIAM WILSON (1840–1900), a distinguished Indian civilian and a man of wide culture, was appointed by Lord Mayo to compile a statistical survey of the Indian Empire, which he condensed in 'The Imperial Gazetteer of India' (1881). He published 'Annals of Rural Bengal' (1868), 'Orissa' (1872), 'A Brief History of the Indian Peoples' (1882), 'The Life of Brian Houghton Hodgson' (1896), and two charming lighter works, 'The Old Missionary' (1890) and 'The Thackerays in India' (1897). Of his 'History of British India' (1899) only two volumes had been completed at his death. He was editor of the series 'Rulers of India'.

Hunting of the Snark, The, a mock-heroic nonsense poem by Lewis Carroll (see *Dodgson*) published in 1876. The Snark is an imaginary animal of elusive character. On this occasion, it turns out to be a Boojum, a highly dangerous variety.

Hunting the Fox, see *Willoughby de Broke.*

Huntingdon, ARTHUR and HELEN, leading characters in Anne Brontë's 'The Tenant of Wildfell Hall' (q.v.).

Huntingdon, HENRY OF, see *Henry of Huntingdon.*

Huntingdon, ROBERT, EARL OF, see *Robin Hood.*

Huntingdon's Connection, *The Countess of,* see *Whitefield.*

Huntinglen, EARL OF, a character in Scott's 'The Fortunes of Nigel' (q.v.).

Hunyadi or HUNIADES, JANOS (1387–1456), a great Hungarian captain, who served under Ladislaus, king of Hungary and Poland. Owing to his military skill and valour the invading Turks suffered two signal defeats in 1443 and were obliged to make peace. He was regent of Hungary after the death of Ladislaus I in 1444, and father of Matthias Corvinus, the great king of Hungary.

Huon of Bordeaux, the hero of a French 13th-cent. *chanson de geste.* He has the misfortune to kill Charlot, son of the Emperor Charlemagne, in an affray, not knowing who his assailant is. He is thereupon condemned to death by the emperor, but reprieved on condition that he will go to the court of Gaudisse, amir of Babylon, bring back a handful of his hair and four of his teeth, kill his doughtiest knight, and kiss Esclarmonde his daughter. By the help of the fairy Oberon, Huon achieves the adventure. The work was translated by Lord Berners (q.v.) and printed by Wynkyn de Worde in 1534. Huon's adventure is the theme of Gluck's opera 'Oberon'.

HURD, RICHARD (1720–1808), son of a Staffordshire farmer, was educated at Cambridge and became bishop successively of Lichfield and Worcester. He produced editions of Horace's 'Ars Poetica' (1749) and 'Epistola ad Augustum' (1751), and his own writings include 'The Polite Arts: or, a dissertation on poetry, painting, music, etc.' (1749), 'Letters on Chivalry and Romance' (1762), and 'An Introduction to the Study of Prophecies concerning the Christian Church' (1772).

HURDIS, JAMES (1763–1801), minor poet of the school of Cowper. He wrote 'The Village Curate and other Poems' (1788) and was professor of poetry at Oxford in 1793.

Hurlothrumbo, a popular burlesque (1729) by Samuel Johnson (1691–1773), a Manchester dancing-master.

Husbandrie, (*Five*) *Hundreth good pointes of,* see *Tusser* (*T.*).

Husband's Message, The, an OE. poem included in the 'Exeter Book' (q.v.). It takes the form of a message to a woman from her husband, who has had to leave his home owing to a vendetta, telling her that he has obtained wealth and position on another land, and asking her to sail and join him when spring comes.

Hussars, from a Hungarian word meaning originally 'free-booter' (Latin *cursarius,* a pirate), the name in the 15th cent. of an organized body of light horsemen in the Hungarian army and extended to similar bodies of light cavalry in other armies.

The BLACK HUSSARS were the 'Black Brunswickers' (a force raised by the duke of Brunswick during the Napoleonic wars, so called from the colour of their uniform), who neither gave nor received quarter. Scott in a letter to Ballantyne wrote, 'I belong to the Black Hussars of Literature, who neither give nor receive criticism.' The letter and the incident which occasioned it are interesting (Lockhart, ch. xxxvii).

Hussites, followers of John Huss (1373–1415), the Bohemian preacher of the Reformation, who was convicted of heresy by the Council of Constance (1414–18) and burnt alive. The Hussites after his death took up arms under Zisca (q.v.), and inflicted many defeats on the Imperialists.

HUTCHESON, FRANCIS (1694–1746), a Scotsman born in Ulster and educated at Glasgow University, was professor of moral philosophy at Glasgow from 1729 until his death. Before this he had published two volumes, 'An Inquiry into the Original of our Ideas of Beauty and Virtue' (1725) and 'An Essay on the Nature and Conduct of the Passions and Affections' (1726). These were followed by textbooks on philosophical subjects, and in 1755, after his death, was published his 'System of Moral Philosophy'.

Hutcheson, in his ethical system, developed the ideas of Shaftesbury (q.v.). He elaborated the theory of the moral sense, giving it greater prominence than did his predecessor. While Shaftesbury made virtue reasonable as well as beautiful, Hutcheson sees it solely in its aesthetic aspect. The Author of Nature has 'made Virtue a lovely Form, that we might easily distinguish it from its contrary and be made happy in pursuit of it'. We have a 'moral sense of beauty in actions and affections'. At the same time he identifies virtue with general benevolence, and finds that action best which procures the greatest general happiness, in this respect anticipating the utilitarians.

Hutchinson, JOHN (1615–64), of Peterhouse, Cambridge, and Lincoln's Inn, held Nottingham for parliament as governor, signed the king's death-warrant, and was a member of the first two councils of state, but retired in 1653. He was saved from death and confiscation at the Restoration by the influence of kinsmen, but was imprisoned. See *Hutchinson (Mrs. L.).*

HUTCHINSON, MRS. LUCY (*b.* 1620), daughter of Sir Allen Apsley, and wife of John Hutchinson (q.v.). She was author of

'The Memoirs of the Life of Colonel Hutchinson', her husband, published in 1806, and of a fragment of a 'Life' of herself. The 'Memoirs' give an interesting picture, from the Puritan standpoint, of the state of the country at the outbreak of the civil war and of the conflict in the vicinity of Nottingham.

Hutchinsonians, followers of Mrs. Anne Hutchinson (1591–1643), *née* Marbury, who followed John Cotton to Massachusetts, and there founded an Antinomian (q.v.) sect. She was murdered by Indians at Hell Gate, New York county.

HUTH, HENRY (1815–78), merchant banker and bibliophile. He collected narratives of voyages, Shakespearian and early English literature, and early Spanish and German books. He printed 'Ancient Ballads and Broadsides', 1867; 'Inedited Poetical Miscellanies (1584–1700)', 1870; 'Prefaces, Dedications, and Epistles (1540–1701)', 1874; 'Fugitive Tracts (1493–1700)', 1875.

HUTTEN, ULRICH VON, see *Epistolae Obscurorum Virorum.*

HUTTON, RICHARD HOLT (1826–97), educated at University College School and University College, London, studied at Heidelberg and Berlin and prepared at Manchester New College for the Unitarian ministry. He was principal of University Hall, London, and edited the Unitarian magazine 'The Enquirer' from 1851 to 1853. With Walter Bagehot (q.v.) he was joint editor of the 'National Review' from 1855 to 1864. He was also assistant editor of the 'Economist' (1858–60), and joint editor of the 'Spectator' (1861–97). His works, mainly of literary and theological criticism, include, besides a volume on Cardinal Newman, 'Essays, Theological and Literary' (1871; revised, 1877), 'Essays on some Modern Guides of English Thought' (1887), 'Criticisms on Contemporary Thought and Thinkers' (1894), and 'Aspects of Religious and Scientific Thought' (1899).

HUXLEY, ALDOUS (LEONARD) (1894–1963), novelist and essayist, educated at Eton and Balliol College, Oxford. His best-known books are: 'Crome Yellow' (1921), 'Antic Hay' (1923), 'Those Barren Leaves' (1925), 'Point Counter Point' (1928), 'Brave New World' (q.v., 1932), 'Eyeless in Gaza' (1936), 'After Many a Summer' (1939), 'Time Must Have a Stop' (1944), 'The Genius and the Goddess' (1955), 'Island' (1962), all novels. Also 'Leda' (1920), a poem; and 'On the Margin' (1923), 'Jesting Pilate' (1926), 'Beyond the Mexique Bay' (1934), 'The Olive Tree' (1936), 'Ape and Essence' (1948), 'Heaven and Hell' (1956), essays.

HUXLEY, SIR JULIAN, F.R.S. (1887–), biologist and writer, educated at Eton and Balliol. He won the Newdigate Prize for Poetry in 1908. He has held many posts and appointments and was particularly influential as senior demonstrator in zoology at Oxford University, 1919–25, professor of zoology at King's College, London, 1925–7, professor of physiology in the Royal Institution, 1926–9, and secretary of the Zoological Society of London, 1935–42. His works include 'Essays of a Biologist' (1923), 'Animal Biology' (with J. B. S. Haldane, 1927), 'The Science of Life' (with H. G. and G. P. Wells, 1929), 'The Captive Shrew and other poems' (1932), 'Evolution, the Modern Synthesis' (1942), 'Soviet Genetics and World Science' (1949), and 'Towards a New Humanism' (1957).

HUXLEY, THOMAS HENRY (1825–95), studied at Charing Cross Hospital and from 1846 to 1850 was assistant surgeon on H.M.S. 'Rattlesnake'. Apart from a large number of papers on technical subjects, he influenced English thought by many addresses and publications on philosophical and religious subjects. Among these may be mentioned 'Man's Place in Nature' (1863), 'The Physical Basis of Life' (1868), 'Lay Sermons, Addresses and Reviews' (1870), 'Critiques and Addresses' (1873), a monograph on Hume (1879), 'Science and Morals' (1886), in which he defines the relation of science to philosophical and religious speculation, 'Essays upon some Controverted Questions' (1892), and his Romanes Lecture, 'Ethics and Evolution' (1893). In this last he refuses to see in the struggle of evolution a basis for morality, of which the criterion is to be sought elsewhere. Huxley coined the word 'agnostic' to express his own philosophical attitude. Huxley's 'Collected Essays' were published in 1894, and his 'Scientific Memoirs' in 1898–1901. His 'Life and Letters' were edited by his son (1900). He was a powerful but discriminating supporter of Darwinism, and a vigorous disputant. A controversy between him and Gladstone, carried on in the magazines, on the subject of the Gadarene swine, is celebrated.

Hvergelmir, in Scandinavian mythology, the spring in Niflheim (q.v.) from which twelve rivers issued, the largest of which was *Elivagar* (the cold stormy waters).

Hyacinthus, a son of Amyclas, a king of Sparta, beloved by Apollo and Zephyrus. He returned the love of the former, and Zephyrus, incensed at his preference of his rival, resolved to punish him. As Apollo was playing at quoits with Hyacinthus, Zephyrus blew the quoit thrown by Apollo so that it struck the boy and killed him. Apollo changed his blood into the flower that bears his name.

Hyacinthus de Archangelis, DOMINUS, in R. Browning's 'The Ring and the Book' (q.v.), Count Guido's counsel.

Hyades, daughters of Atlas (q.v.), who were so disconsolate at the death of their brother Hyas, killed by a wild boar, that they pined away and died, and were placed among the stars (cf. *Pleiades*). Their names were Ambrosia, Eudora, Pedīlē, Corōnis, Polyxo, Phyto, and Diōnē. The rising of the group of stars simultaneously with the sun was supposed to indicate rainy weather, whence probably its name (from ὕειν, to rain).

Hybla, a town in Sicily, on the slope of Mt. Etna, where thyme and odoriferous herbs grew in abundance, famous for its honey.

HYDE, DOUGLAS (1860–1949), Irish writer, 'An Craoibhin' according to his Gaelic designation, was a pioneer of the movement for the revival of the Irish language and literature. He founded the Gaelic League in 1893 and was its president until 1915. He was also one of the founders of the Abbey Theatre (q.v.). He wrote a 'Literary History of Ireland' (1899) and the 'Love Songs of Connacht' (1894), among many publications. He was the first president of Eire, holding office from 1938 to 1945.

Hyde Park, London, the ancient manor of Hyde, part of the property of the old Abbey of Westminster, passed into the possession of the Crown at the dissolution of the monasteries. Races were held there in Stuart times (see below). The Serpentine lake was formed in 1733, by Queen Caroline's direction, from the waters of the Westbourne stream. The corner near the Marble Arch is the favourite pitch of HYDE PARK ORATORS, popular exponents of various causes, social, political, and religious.

Hyde Park, a comedy by Shirley (q.v.), acted in 1632 on the occasion of the opening of Hyde Park to the public. It was printed in 1637. Several of the scenes are in the park, and in the fourth act races take place; when Pepys saw the play, horses were led across the stage, causing much excitement. The plot is very slight, and the chief interest is in the representation of contemporary manners.

Hydra, a many-headed monster that infested the neighbourhood of the lake Lerna in the Peloponnese. It was one of the labours of Hercules to destroy it, but as soon as one head was struck off, two arose in its place. This difficulty was overcome with the help of Iolaus, who applied a burning brand to the wound as each head fell. Hercules dipped his arrows in the Hydra's blood, so that the wounds they gave were incurable.

Hydriotaphia, see *Urn Burial*.

Hye Way to the Spyttel House, The, a tract printed and probably composed by Robert Copland (*fl.* 1508–47), describing the beggars and other types of the poorer classes who visit the hospital, in the form of a dialogue between the author and the porter of the hospital. It throws a vivid light on the poverty prevailing in the early 16th cent.

Hygiëa, the goddess of health, and daughter of Aesculapius (q.v.).

Hyksos, THE, or Shepherd Kings of Egypt, foreign rulers who conquered Egypt in the second millennium B.C., and ruled it, according to Manetho, for 510 years. But his figures are untrustworthy. The word 'Hyksos' is the

Egyptian *hek-shasu*, 'chief of the Bedouins' or 'shepherds'.

Hylas, a beautiful youth beloved by Hercules, and his companion on board the ship 'Argo'. On the Asiatic coast, the Argonauts (q.v.) landed to take a fresh supply of water, when Hylas fell into the fountain and was drowned, or according to the poets was carried away by the nymphs for love of his beauty. Hercules, disconsolate, abandoned the Argonautic expedition.

Hyleg, in astrology, the ruling planet of a nativity. See *House* (*Astrological*).

Hymen, in Greek and Roman mythology, the god of marriage, represented as a young man carrying a torch and veil.

Hymettus, a mountain in Attica celebrated for its honey and for its marble.

Hymir, in Scandinavian mythology, one of the sea-giants. He was destroyed by the gods under Woden, and from his body the earth was made.

Hymn to the Naiads, a poem by Akenside (q.v.), written in 1746 and published in 1758 in Dodsley's 'Collection of Poems'.

The poet traces the mythological origin of the Naiads, and considers them successively as producing the brooks and breezes, nourishing verdure, yielding health, and so forth. Finally he treats of their union with the Muses and the true inspiration that temperance alone can give.

Hymns Ancient and Modern, a collection promoted and edited by the Revd. Sir H. W. Baker (1821–77), vicar of Monkland, near Leominster, who contributed to it many original hymns and translations from the Latin. The collection first appeared in 1861. Supplements were added in 1889 and 1916, edited respectively by C. Steggall and S. H. Nicholson. A revised edition appeared in 1950.

Hypallăgē, from a Greek word meaning 'exchange', a transference of epithet, as 'Sansfoy's dead dowry' for 'dead Sansfoy's dowry' (Spenser).

Hypatia, or New Foes with an Old Face, an historical novel by C. Kingsley (q.v.), published in 'Fraser's Magazine' in 1851 and in book form in 1853.

The time of the story is the 5th cent., when the Western Empire was rapidly succumbing before the Teutonic advance. The scene is Alexandria, and the book presents a striking and crowded picture of the turbulent city, scarcely controlled by the shifty prefect Orestes and his legionaries; the vigorous aggressive church under the patriarch Cyril; the lawless intruding Goths; and the subtle influence of the ancient Greek philosophy, in the person of the beautiful Hypatia, its noble expounder. Philammon, a young Christian monk from the Egyptian desert, comes to Alexandria, and in the turmoil of sensations awakened by his first experience of the city is swept from his faith. He is fascinated by Hypatia and the temperance and sanity of her doctrine; he is repelled by the violence and fanaticism of the Alexandrian monks. He sees Hypatia torn to pieces by a mob of infuriated Christians. And finally he returns to the solitude of the desert cliffs, having learnt tolerance to all men.

The historical Hypatia was daughter of the Alexandrian mathematician Theon; she was a Neoplatonic philosopher, and perished as described in the novel.

Hyperbŏlē, the use of exaggerated terms not in order to deceive but to emphasize the importance or extent of something. Cf. *Meiosis*.

Hyperboreans, THE, in Greek legends connected with the worship of Apollo, a happy and peaceful people, worshippers of that god, who lived in a land of perpetual sunshine and plenty. This came to be conceived as lying in the extreme north, 'beyond the influence of the north wind', perhaps from the derivation of their name, now generally rejected, from ὑπὲρ Βορέας (Smith's 'Classical Dictionary').

Hyperion, a son of Uranus and Gē, one of the Titans. He married Thea, by whom he was father of Aurora, the Sun, and the Moon. Hyperion is often taken by the poets for the Sun itself. In Greek the word was pronounced Hyperīon, but Shakespeare and most English poets accent it Hyper′ion. The phrase 'Hyperion to a satyr' is in 'Hamlet', I. ii.

Hyperion, a poem by Keats (q.v.), written in 1818–19.

Keats wrote two versions of the poem and each remains an uncompleted fragment. In the first the story of Hyperion is told in simple narrative; in the other in the form of an allegorical vision granted to the poet. In the former, Saturn is presented mourning his fallen realm, and debating with the Titans how he may recover it. They look in vain to Hyperion, the sun-god, who is still unde-

posed, to help them. Then the young Apollo is introduced, the god of music, poetry, and knowledge. At this point the fragment ends.

In the other form of the poem, the poet in a dream passes through a garden towards a shrine, of which the approach is granted to none

But those to whom the miseries of the
    world
Are misery, and will not let them rest.

Then the fate of Hyperion, the last of the Titans, who is dethroned by Apollo, is revealed to him by Moneta, the mournful goddess of the 'wither'd race' of Saturn; but the tale is uncompleted.

Hyperion, a prose romance by Longfellow (q.v.).

Hypermnestra, see *Danaides*.

Hypocorism, a childish or pet name, used endearingly or euphemistically.

Hypsĭpўlē, daughter of Thoas, king of Lemnos. When the women of the island, being neglected by their husbands, decided to kill all the men, she saved her father. On the occasion of the visit of the Argonauts (q.v.) to the island, she wedded Jason and bore him twin sons. The Lemnian women discovered that she had saved Thoas, and drove her from the island.

Hyrcania, a region of the ancient Persian Empire adjoining the Caspian or Hyrcanian sea. It was reputed to abound in wild beasts, serpents, etc.

Hystĕron Protĕron, in grammar and rhetoric, a figure of speech in which the word or phrase that should properly come last is put first; in general, 'putting the cart before the horse'.

Hythloday, RAPHAEL, in More's 'Utopia' (q.v.), the traveller in whose mouth the author places the criticisms of English institutions, and the description of the 'wise and godly ordinances' of the Utopians.

I

IHS, representing the Greek *IHΣ*, an abbreviation of *IH(ΣOY)Σ*, Jesus. The Romanized form of the abbreviation would be IES, but from the retention of the Greek form in Latin manuscripts and subsequent forgetfulness of its origin, it has often been looked upon as a Latin abbreviation or contraction, and explained as meaning I*esus* H*ominum* S*alvator*, Jesus Saviour of men, or I*n* H*oc* S*igno* [*vinces*], in this sign (thou shalt conquer), or I*n* H*ac* S*alus*, in this (cross) is salvation. [OED.]

I.N.R.I., I*esus* N*azarenus* R*ex* I*udaeorum*, Jesus of Nazareth king of the Jews; the title on the Cross.

Iachimo, a character in Shakespeare's 'Cymbeline' (q.v.).

Iago, a character in Shakespeare's 'Othello' (q.v.).

Iambic, verse consisting of, or based on, iambuses, that is feet consisting of a short followed by a long syllable (see *Metre*). The IAMBIC TRIMETER is a verse of six iambuses, the first, third, and fifth of which may be replaced by a tribrach or a spondee or a dactyl. This was the principal metre of the Greek drama. In modern use, an iambic verse of six feet is known as an *Alexandrine* (q.v.).

Iamblĭchus (*d. c.* A.D. 330), born at Calchis in Coele-Syria, a Neoplatonic philosopher, who was author of a work, part of which survives, on the Pythagorean philosophy.

Ianthe, (1) the heroine of D'Avenant's 'The Siege of Rhodes' (q.v.); (2) the young lady to whom Byron dedicated his 'Childe Harold's Pilgrimage', Lady Charlotte Mary Harley (1801–80), who married Captain Anthony Bacon; (3) the lady whom Landor addressed in a series of poems, Sophia Jane Swifte, an Irishwoman, who became Countess de Molandé; (4) the name of the daughter of Shelley and his wife Harriet; (5) in Shelley's 'Queen Mab' (q.v.), the maiden to whom the fairy grants a vision of the world.

Iăpĕtus, one of the Titans (q.v.) and the father of Atlas, Prometheus, and Epimetheus, and the grandfather of Deucalion (qq.v.). He was thus regarded by the ancient Greeks as the progenitor of the human race.

IBÁÑEZ, VICENTE BLASCO (1867– 1928), Spanish novelist, whose best-known works (translated into English) are: 'La Catedral' (1903, 'The Shadow of the Cathedral'), 'Sangre y Arena' (1908, 'Blood and Sand'), 'Los Cuatro Jinetes del Apocalipsis' (1916, 'The Four Horsemen of the Apocalypse'), 'Mare Nostrum' (1918, 'Our Sea').

Iberia, a Greek and Latin name for Spain, from the river *Iberus*, the Ebro.

Iberians, a name applied to the neolithic inhabitants of Britain.

Iblis, see *Eblis*.

Ibn Batuta, see *Cathay*.

IBSEN, HENRIK (1828–1906), Norwegian dramatist, whose satirical problem-plays, directed to social reforms, obtained wide fame and exerted a powerful influence. Ibsen's early work consisted of historical romantic dramas, 'Fru Inger at Osterrad', 'The Banquet at Solhaug', 'The Warriors at Helgeland' and 'Kongsemnerne' ('Royal Candidates', 1862). These were followed by 'Love's Comedy' (1863), the first of his satirical dramas, of which the theme is the destructive effect on love of the prosaic and official aspects of courtship and matrimony. Sooner than see their love thus blighted, Falk and Swanhild decide to part while it is still in its perfect bloom.

Then, in a moment of pecuniary distress, and embittered by disappointment at the attitude taken by his country in the Dano-German war, Ibsen gave vent to his despondency in his two great lyrical dramas 'Brand' and 'Peer Gynt' (qq.v., 1866 and 1867). After these came 'The Young Men's League' (1869), a satire on Norwegian politics, and 'Emperor and Galilean' (1873), a double play on Julian the Apostate and his relations

with Christianity and Paganism. Then followed the series of problem plays, of which the general subject is the relation of the individual to his social environment, the shams and conventions that hinder his self-expression and especially the case of woman in the state of marriage. These plays were: 'Pillars of Society' (1877), 'A Doll's House' (1879), 'Ghosts' (1881), 'An Enemy of the People' (1882), 'The Wild Duck' (1884), 'Rosmersholm' (1886), 'The Lady from the Sea' (1888), 'Hedda Gabler' (1890), 'The Master Builder' (1892), 'Little Eyolf' (1894), 'John Gabriel Borkman' (1896), and 'When we Dead awake' (1900). These have been very differently judged. Saintsbury goes so far as to call Ibsen parochial, and attributes his success (apart from the measure of genius that he allows to the author) to the prevailing lack of sense of humour and the revolt against the classical and conventional. But other competent judges, supported by the wide influence of Ibsen's work, profoundly disagree.

Icarius, an Athenian who, having hospitably received Dionysus when he came to Attica, was taught by him the cultivation of the vine. He gave wine to some peasants who became intoxicated, slew Icarius and threw his body into a well. His daughter Erigone discovered it by the help of her dog Maera. Erigone in despair hanged herself, and was changed into the constellation Virgo, and her father into the star Boötes.

Icărus, see *Daedalus*.

Icĕlus, in classical mythology, the son of Somnus (sleep) and brother of Morpheus, a god who took the form of birds, beasts, and serpents in the dreams of men. But men, says Ovid (Met. xi. 640), call this god *Phobetor* 'the terrifier'.

Ichabod, 'inglorious', the name that the wife of Phinehas gave to her child, saying, 'The glory is departed from Israel', because of the tidings that the ark of God was taken, the sons of Eli (Hophni and Phinehas) slain by the Philistines, and Eli himself dead at the news. (1 Sam. iv. 21.)

Ichor, in Greek mythology, the ethereal fluid supposed to flow like blood in the veins of the gods.

Ichthys, the Greek word for 'fish', used in early Christian times as a symbol of Christ, as being composed of the initials of the words *Iesous CHristos THeou Uios Soter*, Jesus Christ, son of God, Saviour.

Icknield Way, an ancient road dating probably from pre-Roman times, crossing England in a wide curve from Norfolk (the country of the *Iceni*, from whom the name is perhaps derived) to Cornwall.

Icon Basilike, see *Eikon Basilike*.

Ictus, Latin 'beat', the stress on particular syllables that marks the rhythm of a verse.

Ida, the name of a mountain in Phrygia near

Troy, where the Simoïs and Scamander had their sources. From its summit the gods watched the Trojan War. It was the scene of the rape of Ganymede (q.v.) and the home of Paris and Oenone (qq.v.). There was another Mt. Ida in Crete; in a cave on this mountain Zeus (q.v.) was said to have been brought up. A cave on the Cretan Mt. Ida has been excavated and has yielded a great quantity of votive offerings of the classical Greek period. The IDAEAN MOTHER was Cybele (q.v.), whose worship was universal in Phrygia and who was particularly connected with Mt. Ida in Crete and the Phrygian Ida (Smith, 'Classical Dictionary').

Ida, PRINCESS, the heroine of Tennyson's 'The Princess' (q.v.), which is the basis of the Gilbert and Sullivan opera 'Princess Ida'.

Idalia, a name sometimes given to Venus, from *Idalium*, a mountain-city in Cyprus, sacred to her worship.

Idea, the Shepheards Garland, nine pastorals by M. Drayton (q.v.), issued, 1st ed. 1593, 3rd revision (entitled 'Pastorals') 1619.

Ideal of a Christian Church, The, see *Ward* (W. G.) and *Oxford Movement.*

Idealism, in philosophy, any system of thought in which the object of external perception is held to consist, either in itself, or as perceived, of ideas, whether of the perceiving mind or of the universal mind; or in which no independent reality is held to underlie our ideas of external objects. The principal exponents of idealistic philosophies include Kant, Fichte, Schelling, and Hegel (qq.v.). In common use the word means the representation of things in an ideal form, or as they might be; the imaginative treatment of a subject in art or literature.

Iden, ALEXANDER, in Shakespeare's '2 Henry VI', a Kentish gentleman, who slew Jack Cade.

Ides, in the ancient Roman calendar, the 15th of March, May, July, and Oct., and the 13th of all the other months. The *Ides of March* was the day on which Julius Caesar was assassinated. See Shakespeare, 'Julius Caesar', I. ii and III. i.

Idler, The, a series of papers contributed by S. Johnson (q.v.) to the 'Universal Chronicle, or Weekly Gazette', between 15 April 1758 and 5 April 1760. These papers are shorter and lighter than those of the 'Rambler' (q.v.), but their general character is the same. They include the well-known sketches of Dick Minim, the critic, of Mr. Sober (the author himself), Jack Whirler, and Tom Restless.

Also the title of a monthly journal edited by Jerome K. Jerome and Robert Barr, 1892–1911.

Idols of the Tribe, etc., see *Novum Organum.*

Idŏmĕnēūs, king of Crete, an ally of the Greeks in the Trojan War. While returning, he vowed, if saved from a tempest that threatened his ship, to sacrifice to Poseidon whatever he first met on his arrival. This proved to be his own son, whom Idomeneus accordingly sacrificed. For his inhumanity the Cretans expelled him from his kingdom.

Idun or IDUNA, in Scandinavian mythology, the goddess who had in her keeping in Asgard the apples that restored the youth of the gods. She was the wife of Bragi (q.v.), and appears to personify the fruitful season of the year.

Idyll, from a Greek word meaning a little picture, a short poem, descriptive of some picturesque scene or incident, chiefly in rustic life; e.g. the 'Idylls' of Theocritus (q.v.).

Idylls of the King, The, a series of connected poems by A. Tennyson (q.v.), of which the first fragment, 'The Morte d'Arthur', subsequently incorporated in 'The Passing of Arthur', was published in 1842. In 1859 appeared 'Enid', 'Vivien', 'Elaine', and 'Guinevere'. In 1869 were added 'The Coming of Arthur', 'The Holy Grail', 'Pelleas and Ettarre', and 'The Passing of Arthur'. 'The Last Tournament' appeared in 1871, 'Gareth and Lynette' in 1872, 'Balin and Balan' in 1885; and finally 'Enid' was divided into two parts, 'The Marriage of Geraint' and 'Geraint and Enid'.

These poems form parts in a general presentment of the story of Arthur, of his noble design of the Round Table, and of its failure under the ever-widening influence of evil, in the shape of the sin of Lancelot and Guinevere. It is a story of bright hope (in 'The Coming of Arthur' and 'Gareth and Lynette'), followed by growing disillusionment, of which the protagonists are the melancholy characters of Arthur and Guinevere, Lancelot and Elaine. The chief criticism passed on it relates to the shadowy and unreal, almost symbolical, character of Arthur himself. Summaries of the several parts are given herein under their respective titles.

Ierne, IVERNA, see *Hibernia.*

Igdrasil, see *Yggdrasil.*

Igerne, see *Igraine.*

IGNATIUS, ST. (*c.* 50–?107 or 116), bishop of Antioch, said to have been appointed to his see by St. Peter, and martyred under the Emperor Trajan. He is the author of epistles from which we derive the little that is known about him. He was called Theophorus, whence has arisen the romantic tradition that he was the child whom Christ took in his arms, as described in Mark ix. 35.

Ignatius Loyola, see *Loyola.*

Ignis Fatuus, meaning 'foolish fire', is a phosphorescent light seen hovering or flitting over marshy ground, and supposed to be due to the spontaneous combustion of an inflammable gas derived from decaying vegetable matter, popularly called Will-o'-the-wisp, Jack-o'-lantern, etc. It seems to have been formerly a common phenomenon. When approached, the *ignis fatuus* appeared to recede and finally to vanish, sometimes reappearing in another direction. This led to the notion that it was the work of a mischievous sprite, intentionally leading benighted travellers astray. Hence the term is often used allusively for any delusive hope, aim, etc. [OED.]

Ignoge (three syllables), according to Geoffrey of Monmouth, a Greek princess, the wife of Brute (q.v.), and the mother of Locrine, Albanact, and Camber. Spenser calls her Inogene of Italy ('Faerie Queene', II. x. 13).

Ignorāmus, a famous university farcical play by George Ruggle (1575–1622), a fellow of Clare College, Cambridge, produced in 1615 before James I, an adaptation of an Italian comedy by Della Porta. The title part is a burlesque of the recorder of Cambridge, Brackyn, who is subjected to various humiliations; he falls in love with the heroine Rosabella, but is fobbed off with the virago Polla, belaboured, thought to be possessed by evil spirits, subjected to exorcism, and finally carried off to a monastery for treatment. Brackyn had already been held up to ridicule in the last part of the 'Parnassus' plays (q.v.).

Ignoratio elenchi, a logical fallacy which consists in apparently refuting an opponent while actually disproving some statement other than that advanced by him.

Igraine, or IGERNE, or YGERNE, in the Arthurian legend, the wife of Gorlois of Cornwall, whom Uther Pendragon, assuming the likeness of her husband by the help of Merlin's magic, won for his wife. Of their union Arthur (q.v.) was born.

Il Penseroso, see *Penseroso.*

Ilchester, JANET, one of the principal characters in Meredith's 'Harry Richmond' (q.v.).

Iliad, The, a Greek epic poem attributed to Homer (q.v.), describing the war waged by Achaean princes against Troy for the purpose of recovering Helen, wife of Menelaus, whom Paris, son of Priam, king of Troy, had carried away. In particular it deals with the wrath of Achilles, the special hero of the poem, at the slight put upon him by Agamemnon, leader of the host, and his final return to the field and slaying of Hector. See *Achilles.*

Ilissus, a river of Attica, flowing east and south of Athens and joining the Cephissus.

Ilium, see *Troy.*

Ilk, in Scottish, means 'same', *of that ilk,* of the same place, designation, or name; e.g. *Guthrie of that ilk,* Guthrie of Guthrie.

Illuminati, a name applied to, or assumed by, various societies or sects because of their claim to special enlightenment in religious or intellectual matters. It is used also to render the German *Illuminaten,* the name of a celebrated secret society founded at Ingolstadt in Bavaria in 1776 by Prof. Adam Weishaupt,

holding deistic and republican principles, and having an organization akin to freemasonry. It obtained Goethe and Herder among its recruits. It was attacked by the Rosicrucians, and became an object of political suspicion to the Bavarian government, and its activities were prohibited in 1785. The Jacobins of the French Revolution were supposed to be connected with the Illuminati. The name is also applied generally, often in a satirical sense, to persons claiming special knowledge on any subject.

Ilmarinen, one of the principal heroes of the 'Kalevala' (q.v.), the metal-worker who makes the magic mill, the Sampo (q.v.).

Imaginary Conversations, by Landor (q.v.), published 1824–9, followed by 'Imaginary Conversations of Greeks and Romans', published in 1853.

These represent, particularly if 'Pericles and Aspasia' (q.v.) and the 'The Pentameron' (q.v.) are included, the bulk of Landor's prose work. The conversations are between characters of all the ages, from classical to recent times; some are dramatic, some idyllic, some satirical, while others treat of political, social, or literary questions; action and incidents are occasionally interposed, which add to their variety. There are some 150 of these dialogues. Their form is admirable, but the matter is unequal; for Landor made use of them to express his personal views, which were sometimes ill-judged, on a multitude of subjects. The following are some of the best known: 'Dante and Beatrice', 'Princess Mary and Princess Elizabeth', 'Louis XIV and Père La Chaise', 'Aesop and Rhodope', 'Romilly and Wilberforce', 'Fra Filippo Lippi and Pope Eugenius IV', and 'Calvin and Melanchthon'.

Imagism, a movement of English and American poets in revolt from romanticism, seeking clarity of expression through the use of precise images. It flourished from 1910 to 1918 and its first anthology, 'Des Imagistes' published in 1914 with Pound as editor, had eleven contributors: Richard Aldington, 'H. D.' (Hilda Doolittle), F. S. Flint, Skipwith Cannell, Amy Lowell, William Carlos James, James Joyce, Ezra Pound, Ford Madox Hueffer (Ford), Allen Upward, and John Cournos. The principles of the Imagist manifesto were laid down by Pound in 1913, but the official credo was not prepared until the 1915 anthology, 'Some Imagist Poets', edited by Amy Lowell.

Imāus, a great mountain range of Asia, mentioned by the ancient geographers.

Imitation of Christ, or *De Imitatione Christi,* see *Thomas à Kempis.*

Imitations of Horace, see *Pope (A.).*

Imlac, a character in Johnson's 'Rasselas' (q.v.).

Immortals, THE (LES IMMORTELS), the forty members of the French Academy, so called because of their enduring fame, with side reference to the fact that their number is always filled up. The name was also given in ancient times to a body of 10,000 Persian infantry, the flower of the army, whose number was kept constantly full.

Imogen, in Shakespeare's 'Cymbeline' (q.v.), the wife of Posthumus.

Imoinda, a character in Mrs. Behn's 'Oroonoko' (q.v.) and Southerne's tragedy of the same name.

Imp, originally a young shoot of a plant or tree; hence a scion, especially of a noble house (e.g. in the epitaph of Lord Denbigh in the Beauchamp Chapel at Warwick, 'Heere resteth the body of the noble Impe Robert of Dudley'). It came to be used specifically of a child of the devil; a little devil, an evil spirit; a mischievous child, a young urchin.

Impertinent, The Curious, see *Curious Impertinent.*

Imposture, The, a comedy by James Shirley (q.v.), produced in 1640.

Flaviano, the favourite of the duke of Mantua, hopes to win the hand of the duke's daughter, Fioretta. The prince of Ferrara comes to proffer his suit for her. The 'imposture' consists in the passing off, for the young duchess, of the favourite's cast-off mistress, Juliana, and is for a time successful; but all is put right in the end.

Impressionism, the name given in derision (from a painting by Monet called '*Impression, soleil levant*') to the work of a group of French painters who held their first exhibition in 1874. Their aim was to render the effects of light on objects rather than the objects themselves. They painted out of doors, using a high key and bright colours. Claude Monet (1840–1926), Alfred Sisley (1839–99), and Camille Pissarro (1831–1903) carried out their aims most completely; Auguste Renoir (1841–1919), Edgar Degas, and Cézanne (qq.v.) were also associated with the Movement. The term is used by transference in literature and music.

Imprimātur, meaning 'let it be printed', the formula signed by an official licenser authorizing the printing of a book.

In commendam, from the Latin *dare in commendam,* to give in trust, used of the tenure of a benefice given in charge to some person until a proper incumbent was found for it, especially used of a benefice which a bishop or other dignitary was allowed to hold along with his own preferment (abolished in England by statute in 1836).

In Memoriam A. H. H., a poem by A. Tennyson (q.v.) written between 1833 and 1850, and published in the latter year. The poem was written in memory of Arthur H. Hallam, the son of Henry Hallam, the historian, a young man of extraordinary promise and an intimate friend of Tennyson, who died

in 1833 at Vienna when 22 years old. It is written in stanzas of four octosyllabic lines rhyming a b b a.

'In Memoriam' is not so much a single elegy as a series of poems written at different times, inspired by the changing moods of the author's regret for his dead friend. The series describes, broadly speaking, the 'Way of the Soul', as Tennyson sometimes called it, in presence of a great loss, the gradual transformation of the regret felt by the living for the dead and of the longing for his bodily presence, into a sense of spiritual contact and possession, and a wider love of God and humanity. (See A. C. Bradley, 'A Commentary on Tennyson's "In Memoriam" '.)

The epilogue is a marriage-song on the occasion of the wedding of the poet's sister, Cecilia, to Edward Lushington, and gives a cheerful ending to the whole work.

In petto, Italian, in one's own breast or private intention, in contemplation, undisclosed; used, in the phraseology of the Roman Curia, for the nomination of a cardinal, which nomination is not yet to be disclosed.

In principio, Latin, in the beginning; the first words of Genesis and of St. John's Gospel in the Vulgate. Hence, the short name for the first fourteen verses of St. John, which were supposed to have extraordinary virtues. Chaucer says of the Friar in 'The Canterbury Tales' (q.v.):

> He was the beste beggar in al his house,
> For though a widdewe hadde but oo schoo,
> So plesaunt was his *In principio,*
> Yet wolde he have a ferthing or he wente.
> ('Prologue', 252.)

In the Midst of Life, a collection of short stories by Ambrose Bierce (q.v.), originally entitled 'Tales of Soldiers and Civilians'.

Inca, the title of the emperor or king of Peru before its conquest by the Spaniards; also one of the royal race of Peru, descended from Manco Capac (q.v.) and Mama Ocollo.

INCHBALD, MRS. ELIZABETH (1753–1821), *née* Simpson, was a novelist, dramatist, and actress. She is chiefly remembered for her two prose romances 'A Simple Story' (1791) and 'Nature and Art' (1796), (qq.v.). Her most successful comedy was 'I'll tell you what', produced in 1785. She edited 'The British Theatre', a collection of old plays, in 1806–9.

Inchcape Rock, THE, a rock in the North Sea, off the Firth of Tay, dangerous to mariners, near which the abbot of Arbroath or Aberbrothock fixed a warning bell on a float. In Southey's ballad on the subject, Sir Ralph the Rover, to plague the abbot, cuts the bell from the float, and later, on his homeward way, is wrecked on the rock.

Incunabula, a Latin word meaning swaddling-clothes, is used to signify books produced in the infancy of the art of printing, especially those printed before 1500.

Indamora, a character in Dryden's 'Aureng-Zebe' (q.v.).

Independence Day, 4 July, see *Fourth of July*.

Index Expurgatorius, strictly, an authoritative specification of the passages to be expunged or altered in works otherwise permitted to be read by Roman Catholics. The term is frequently used in England to cover the 'Index Librorum Prohibitorum', or list of forbidden books (not authors, as sometimes thought). Rules for the formation of this list and of the 'Index Expurgatorius' were drawn up by the Council of Trent, and successive editions of the former have been published from time to time. [OED.] The 'Index Expurgatorius' and the 'Index Librorum Prohibitorum' were abrogated in 1966.

Indian Summer, the name given to a period of the autumn in the United States when the atmosphere is dry and hazy, the sky cloudless, and the temperature mild. It corresponds to what is known in England as St. Luke's Summer.

Indian Summer, a novel by W. D. Howells (q.v.), published in 1886.

Indicator, The, a periodical conducted by Leigh Hunt (q.v.), 1819–21.

Indo-European, the name applied to the great family of cognate languages (also called Indo-Germanic and Aryan) spoken over the greater part of Europe and extending into Asia as far as northern India; also applied to the race, or its divisions, using one or other of these languages. [OED.]

Indra, in Vedic theology, the chief god of the air, the rain-giver, the type of beneficent heroic power, struggling against evil demons; later subordinated to the triad Brahma, Vishnu, and Siva.

Iñez, DONNA, in Byron's 'Don Juan' (q.v.), the mother of the hero.

Iñez de Castro, the daughter of a Castilian nobleman, attached to the court of Alphonso IV of Portugal. Prince Pedro married her secretly, and lived with her in happy seclusion. When the marriage was discovered, the king authorized the murder of Iñez. On the accession (1357) of Pedro, who had been reduced to despair by the death of his wife, his first measure was to take vengeance on her murderers. The subject has been treated by various poets and dramatists, including Camoëns, Landor, and, more recently, the French author Henri de Montherlant.

Infangthief (Infangenetheof) and **Outfangthief**, the ancient right of the lord of the manor to hang, respectively, his own man (one of his feudal tenants or serfs) if caught in the act of crime, and someone else's man, if caught in the act of crime within his jurisdiction. The two stone balls that decorate the gateways of many old manor-houses are said to have originally represented the heads of two malefactors, symbols of the lord's jurisdiction.

Infernal Marriage, The, a short burlesque tale published by B. Disraeli in 1834, describing the 'runaway match' of Pluto and Proserpine and what ensued, and introducing some political banter.

Inferno, The, of Dante, see *Divina Commedia*.

Infralapsarian, see *Sublapsarian*.

INGE, THE VERY REVD. WILLIAM RALPH (1860–1954), dean of St. Paul's Cathedral, London, 1911–34. He published many works of a philosophical character. On account of his outlook on modern life he was jocularly called 'The Gloomy Dean'. His 'Outspoken Essays' were published in two series, 1919 and 1922.

INGELOW, JEAN (1820–97), poetess, born at Boston in Lincolnshire. Her works include three series of poems (1871, 1876, and 1885) and stories for children. Her most remarkable poems are 'Divided' and 'The High Tide on the Coast of Lincolnshire, 1571' (1863), and 'A Story of Doom' (1867).

Ingoldsby Legends, The, see *Barham*.

Ingres, JEAN AUGUSTE DOMINIQUE (1780–1867), French painter of portraits, history pieces, and oriental scenes. An exquisite draughtsman, for him 'drawing is the probity of art', and he was opposed to the Romantic Movement (q.v.).

Ingres, VIOLIN OF (*Violon d'Ingres*): Ingres (see previous entry), besides being a great painter, was a moderate performer on the violin. It is said that he was less flattered by compliments on his painting (in which he knew himself a master) than by compliments on his fiddling. The expression is used of a secondary occupation or hobby, a subject of pride or vanity to the person concerned.

Ingulf, see *Croyland History*.

Inheritance, The, a novel by S. E. Ferrier (q.v.), published in 1824.

It deals with the fortunes of Gertrude St. Clair, granddaughter of the earl of Rossville and heiress presumptive of his estate. On the death of her father, who had been repudiated by the earl as having married beneath him, she and her mother are admitted to Rossville Castle and the countenance of the earl, a pompous self-conceited tyrant. Contrary to his wishes, Gertrude falls in love with her fascinating profligate cousin, Colonel Delmour, and after the earl's death becomes engaged to him, to the despair of those who know his real character. Among these is another cousin, Edward Lyndsay, who loves Gertrude with self-effacing humility. A low-bred American now comes forward and claims to be Gertrude's father. It comes to light that the ambitious Mrs. St. Clair, despairing of issue, has adopted the daughter of a servant and passed her off as her own child. The reaction of the two cousins to this catastrophe is characteristic. Gertrude having lost title and fortunes is abandoned by Colonel Delmour, while Edward Lyndsay is faithful to her and gradually wins her love. Miss Pratt, the garrulous and eccentric spinster, is an amusing character in the story.

Inkle and Yarico, a romantic comedy by G. Colman (q.v.) the younger, performed in 1787, in which the young Londoner Inkle, saved from death on a voyage to Barbados by the beautiful savage Yarico, has to decide between fidelity to her and a wealthy marriage to Narcissa, the governor's daughter; he chooses the latter, and is punished for his ingratitude. The story occurs in Addison's 'Spectator' (No. 11), and is taken from Ligon's 'History of Barbados'.

Inn Album, The, a poem by R. Browning (q.v.), published in 1875.

The poem is a tragedy, in eight scenic divisions, of a motherless girl seduced by an elderly adventurer, driven to marry an old, poor, and narrow-minded clergyman, and finally to suicide by the threat of her seducer to reveal her secret to her husband. The 'inn-album' is used as the means of conveying this threat to her. A young man, who had honourably loved the woman and had come under the pernicious influence of the adventurer, not knowing that he was the woman's seducer, reappears at the crisis of the story, and, learning the elder man's infamy, strangles him. The story in its main outlines was founded on fact. (See Nicoll and Wise, 'Literary Anecdotes', i. 533.)

Innes, FRANK, a character in R. L. Stevenson's 'Weir of Hermiston' (q.v.).

Innisfail, a poetical name for Ireland.

Innocents Abroad, The, an autobiographical account by S. L. Clemens (q.v.), published under the pseudonym MARK TWAIN, of a cruise to the Mediterranean with a company of Americans in 1867. The fun consists in seeing Europe, its scenes and customs, viewed through the irreverent eyes of an American 'innocent'. The work was a great success on both sides of the Atlantic upon its publication in 1869, and won Clemens his reputation as the leading American humorist.

Inns of Court and of **Chancery** were the earliest settled places of residence, resembling colleges, of associations of law students in London, and date from the 13th and 14th cents. The Inns of Court are the four sets of buildings belonging to the four legal societies that have the exclusive right of admitting persons to practise at the bar. They are: Lincoln's Inn, Inner Temple, Middle Temple, and Gray's Inn. Each of the societies comprises benchers, barristers, and students. The first are the senior members and managers of the society. The Inns were the frequent scene of masques and revels in the 16th and 17th cents. The Inns of Chancery were formerly attached to one or other of the Inns of Court.

They have ceased to exist as corporate bodies. The buildings of some of them (e.g. Furnivall's Inn or Clifford's Inn) have been destroyed. But those of others (e.g. Staple Inn or Barnard's Inn) survive in private ownership.

Ino, a daughter of Cadmus and Harmonia (qq.v.) and wife of Athamas, king of Thebes. Athamas had previously, by order of Hera, married Nephele, and by her had become father of Phrixus and Helle. Ino conceived a bitter hatred of her stepchildren, who escaped from her on a golden ram (see under *Argonauts*). Ino's own children were Learchus and Melicertes. Hera, angered with Ino, drove Athamas mad, so that he killed Learchus. Ino fled from him and threw herself into the sea with Melicertes in her arms. They became deities of the sea, under the names Leucothea and Palaemon. It was Ino who saved Odysseus when his raft was wrecked, lending her scarf to support him.

Inogene, see *Ignoge.*

Inquisition, THE, in the Roman Catholic Church, an ecclesiastical tribunal (officially styled the Holy Office) directed to the suppression of heresy and punishment of heretics. At first it was in the hands of the Dominican Friars, and early in the 13th cent. was entrusted by Innocent III with the extirpation of heresy in southern France. Soon there grew up a central governing body at Rome called the Congregation of the Holy Office, whose activities were gradually extended over France, the Netherlands, Spain, Portugal, and the Spanish and Portuguese colonies. It was abolished in France in 1772, and finally in Spain in 1834. The Congregation of the Holy Office still exists, but is chiefly concerned with heretical literature.

Instauratio Magna, the title of Francis Bacon's (q.v.) great projected work, of which his 'Novum Organum' is the second part.

Institutes of Justinian, The, an elementary treatise on Roman Law compiled by order of the Emperor Justinian in A.D. 533, and intended as an introduction to the Pandects (q.v.).

Instructions to a Painter, Last, see *Marvell.* 'Instructions to a Painter' or 'Advice to a Painter' was the title adopted (with minor modifications) for a number of political satires (by Denham and others) published in the latter half of the 17th cent. The original 'Instructions' were those of Waller for the celebration of the duke of York's victories over the Dutch.

Intelligencer, The, see *L'Estrange.*

Interim of Augsburg, see *Augsburg.* Three 'Interims', or provisional arrangements for the adjustment of religious differences between the German Protestants and the Roman Catholic Church, were promulgated, that of Ratisbon in 1541, which proved ineffective, and those of Augsburg and Leipzig in 1548.

The Protestants finally obtained toleration in 1552 as a result of the Peace of Passau between the Elector of Saxony and the emperor Charles V.

Interludes were plays performed at Court, in the halls of the nobles, at the Inns of Court, and in colleges, generally but not exclusively by professional actors, dealing with a short episode and involving a limited number of characters. That interludes were sometimes performed by villagers we know from 'Pyramus and Thisbe' in 'A Midsummer Night's Dream' (q.v.). Their vogue was chiefly in the 15th and 16th cents. They succeeded 'moralities' (q.v.) in the history of the drama, and are not always clearly distinguishable from them. The characters are still frequently allegorical, but the comic or farcical element is more prevalent. The versification tends to doggerel, and they are shorter than the moralities. A notable producer of interludes was J. Heywood (q.v.), author of 'The Four P's', in which a Palmer, a Pardoner, and a 'Pothecary contend as to the merits of their respective callings. A Pedlar comes in and offers to decide which shows the greatest capacity as a liar, and the Palmer wins the prize by asserting that 'he never saw or never knew Any woman out of patience'. This follows a humorous description by the Pardoner of his visit to hell to rescue the soul of the shrewish Margery Coorson. 'Thersites', another interlude (c. 1537), perhaps by Heywood, is a farcical treatment of boasting, in which the braggart Thersites, having had arms made for him by Mulciber, successfully encounters a snail, but runs away behind his mother when threatened by Miles, a knight.

The origin of the name is obscure. The OED. speaks of interludes as 'commonly introduced between the acts of long mystery-plays or moralities'; Ward finds the probable origin in the fact that interludes were 'occasionally performed in the intervals of banquets and entertainments'. E. K. Chambers gives reasons for questioning both these explanations. He is inclined to interpret *interludium* not as a *ludus* in the intervals of something else, but as a *ludus* carried on between two or more performers, and as primarily applicable to any kind of dramatic performance.

Invalides, HÔTEL DES, an institution founded in Paris by Louis XIV in 1670 for superannuated or disabled soldiers. The tomb of Napoleon I is in its church.

Invention of the Cross, THE, see *Helena* (*St.*).

Invincible Doctor, THE, Ockham (q.v.).

Io, a daughter of Inachus, king of Argos, who was loved by Zeus. To escape the jealousy of Hera, Zeus changed his mistress into a beautiful heifer. Hera, who discovered the fraud, obtained the animal from her husband and set Argos (q.v.) to watch it. Zeus caused Hermes to destroy Argos and set Io at liberty. Hera then sent a gadfly to torment Io, so that she wandered over the face of the earth, swimming the Bosporus (i.e. passage of the ox), and reaching the banks of the Nile, where she recovered her human shape and bore a son named Epaphus. According to Herodotus, Io was carried off by Phoenician merchants, who wished to make reprisals for the theft of Europa (q.v.).

Iŏlāus, the friend of Hercules (q.v.). He helped Hercules to destroy the Hydra, and aided the sons of Hercules, after their father's death, against Eurystheus.

Iona or ICOLMKILL, an island of the Inner Hebrides, where St. Columba (q.v.) founded a monastery about 563, an important centre of Celtic missions. Adamnan, in his life of St. Columba, wrote the name *Ioua*, which has been erroneously converted into *Iona*. Shakespeare, in 'Macbeth', II. iv, calls it 'Colmekill'. 'I-colm-kill' means 'island of St. Columb's chapel'.

Ionian Mode, (1) one of the modes of ancient Greek music, characterized as soft and effeminate; (2) the last of the 'authentic' ecclesiastical modes corresponding to the modern major diatonic scale. [OED.]

Ionic Dialect, the most important branch of ancient Greek, the language of that part of the Hellenic race which occupied Attica and the northern coast of the Peloponnese, and founded colonies in Italy, Sicily, and especially Asia Minor. Attic was a development of Ionic.

Ionic Order, one of the orders of classical architecture, characterized by a capital with volutes.

Ionica, see *Cory.*

Iphĭgĕnīa, a daughter of Agamemnon and Clytemnestra (qq.v.). When the Greeks on their way to the Trojan War were detained by contrary winds at Aulis, they were told that Iphigenia must be sacrificed to appease the wrath of Diana, whose stag Agamemnon had killed. Agamemnon reluctantly consented, but, as the priest was about to strike the fatal blow, Iphigenia disappeared and a deer was found in her place. The goddess, moved by Iphigenia's innocence, had borne her away to Tauris and entrusted her with the care of her temple. Here Iphigenia was obliged to sacrifice all strangers who came to the country. When Orestes (q.v.) and Pylades came to Tauris, Iphigenia discovered that one of the strangers she was about to immolate was her brother. Thereupon she conspired with them to escape and to carry away the statue of the goddess, as the oracle had directed; and this they accomplished.

The story of Iphigenia was made the subject of plays by Aeschylus and Sophocles (not extant), and notably by Euripides; also in modern times by Racine and Goethe.

Iphigenie auf Tauris, see *Goethe.*

Ipomedon, a romance of the Middle English period, taken from the French of Huon de

Rotelande. There are versions both in rhyme and prose.

Ipomedon, prince of Apulia, having by knightly exploits won the favour of the queen of Calabria without revealing who he is, leaves her; but returns on hearing that a tournament is to be held at which her hand will be the prize. He disclaims the intention of competing and sets out hunting, but returns disguised on the successive days in different coloured armour and defeats the other suitors. Other adventures follow before the lovers are united. Ipomedon, who appears to have a passion for disguises, to the confusion of his mistress, assumes that of a fool, and finally slays a hideous Indian, Lyoline, who is besieging her.

Iqbal, SIR MUHAMMAD (1875–1938), poet and philosopher, was born in the Punjab, where his education began. He continued his studies in England, where he was called to the Bar, and in Germany, before returning home to practise as a lawyer. Writing in Persian as well as Urdu, he soon became a leader of Islamic modernism not only in India but elsewhere in the Islamic world. He emphasized the international character of Islam, but eventually concluded that it could only find expression, in the modern world, in the free association of Muslim states. As President of the Muslim League in 1930 he advocated the creation of a separate Muslim state in N.W. India, and he subsequently helped to convert Jinnah to the idea of Pakistan.

Iran, the Persian name for Persia. IRANIAN in Comparative Philology is used to designate one of the two Asiatic families of Indo-European languages, comprising Zend and Old Persian and their modern descendants or cognates. IRAN is opposed to TURAN, the name used by Firdusi (q.v.) for the realm beyond the Oxus; and TURANIAN is applied to languages of Asiatic origin that are neither Aryan nor Semitic.

Iras, in Shakespeare's 'Antony and Cleopatra' (q.v.), one of Cleopatra's attendants. Her name is in Plutarch's 'Life of Antony'.

Ireland, JOHN (1761–1842), the son of an Ashburton butcher, bible-clerk at Oriel College, Oxford, became dean of Westminster, and founded a professorship of exegesis and the IRELAND SCHOLARSHIP for classics at Oxford.

Ireland, WILLIAM HENRY (1777–1835), son of Samuel Ireland the engraver, is remembered as a forger of Shakespeare manuscripts. He had access to Elizabethan parchments in the lawyer's chambers where he was employed, and in 1794–5 forged deeds and signatures of, or relating to, Shakespeare. He also fabricated in forged handwriting the pseudo-Shakespearian plays 'Vortigern and Rowena' and 'Henry II', which deceived many experts and men of letters. The former was produced unsuccessfully by Sheridan at Drury Lane in 1796. Ireland subsequently made an avowal of his fraud.

Ireland Scholarship, THE see *Ireland (J.)*.

Irena, in Spenser's 'Faerie Queene' (Bk. v), personifies Ireland, oppressed by Grantorto (q.v.), and righted by Sir Artegall (q.v.).

Irenaeus, ST., a Greek Father of the Church, of the 2nd cent., born in Asia Minor, who became bishop of Lyons. He suffered martyrdom about A.D. 200. A Latin translation ('Contra Hereticos') survives of a Greek work by him.

Irene, a tragedy by S. Johnson (q.v.).

Irene Iddesleigh, title of a novel by Amanda M'Kittrick Ros, published in 1897.

Iris, according to mythology, the messenger of the gods, and particularly of Zeus and Hera. The rainbow was the path by which she travelled between the gods and men.

Irish National Theatre, see *Abbey Theatre*.

Irish R. M., Experiences of an, see *Somerville (E. Œ.)*.

Irminsul or ERMENSUL, in the ancient Saxon religion, a mysterious tree or wooden pillar, venerated as the support of the world. Frankish annals relate that Charlemagne in 772 destroyed near Eresburg (Stadtberg) a centre of this worship called 'Ermensul'.

Iron Crown, THE, of the Lombard kingdom, generally assumed by the 'Holy Roman' emperors, was kept at Pavia. Napoleon assumed it when he crowned himself king of Italy in 1805. See also *Luke's Iron Crown*.

Iron Duke, a popular name for the duke of Wellington (1769–1852).

Iron Mask, THE MAN IN THE, a state prisoner in the reign of Louis XIV, confined at Pignerol, in the island of St. Marguerite, and finally in the Bastille, whose name was concealed and who wore a mask covered with black velvet. He was probably Count Mattioli, an Italian agent, but his identity has never been established, and various other suggestions were made, such as that the prisoner was a son of Louis XIV and Mlle de la Vallière, the twin (younger) brother of Louis XIV, or Monmouth (supposed to have survived his execution in 1685).

IRON, RALPH, pseudonym of OLIVE SCHREINER (q.v.).

Ironside, IRONSIDES, a name given, in allusion to their hardihood or bravery, to Edmund, king of England (1016), and Oliver Cromwell. In the case of the latter, the appellation was a nickname of Royalist origin. 'Ironsides' was also applied to Cromwell's troopers in the Civil War, perhaps originally as a possessive, *Ironside's Men*.

Iroquois, a confederacy of North American Indians, known in English as the 'Five Nations' (q.v.). They sided with the English against the French, and subsequently against the American colonists.

Irredentist, from (*Italia*) *irredenta*. unredeemed, in Italian politics (from 1878) a member of the party that advocated the recovery and union to Italy of Italian-speaking districts still subject to other countries. Hence the general application.

Irrefragable Doctor, THE, Alexander of Hales (q.v.).

Irus, in Homer's 'Odyssey', a beggar who executed commissions for Penelope's suitors. On Odysseus' return, Irus tried to drive him from the house, and, a boxing match between them having been arranged, Irus was struck down and thrown out by the hero.

Irving, EDWARD, see *Irvingites*.

Irving, SIR HENRY (1838–1905), whose original name was JOHN HENRY BRODRIBB, first appeared as an actor as Gaston in Bulwer Lytton's 'Richelieu' at Sunderland in 1856. His first Shakespearian character was Hamlet, in 1864. He became famous by his acting in the melodrama 'The Bells' (1871–2), and afterwards scored successes in a large number of Shakespearian and other parts, his impersonation of Tennyson's 'Becket' being one of his chief triumphs. His managership of the Lyceum Theatre in association with Miss Ellen Terry from 1878 to 1902 was a notable incident in the history of the English theatre. Irving revived popular interest in Shakespeare. He was pre-eminently a romantic actor, highly intellectual, of magnetic personality and originality of conception, but of mannered elocution and gait.

IRVING, WASHINGTON (1783–1859), born at New York, the son of an Englishman, first came into literary repute by his humorous 'History of New York to the end of the Dutch Dynasty, by Diedrich Knickerbocker' (1809). He was attached to the American Legation in Spain in 1826, was secretary of legation in London in 1829, and minister in Spain in 1842. His writings include 'The Sketch-Book' (1820), 'Bracebridge Hall' (1822), 'Tales of a Traveller' (1824), 'Life and Voyages of Christopher Columbus' (1828), 'The Companions of Columbus' (1831), 'The Conquest of Granada' (1829), 'Legends of the Alhambra' (1832), 'Astoria' (1836), an account of John Jacob Astor's development of the fur-trade, 'Adventures of Captain Benneville' (1837), 'Oliver Goldsmith' (1849), and 'Life of George Washington' (1855–9). This last is his greatest work; but he is perhaps best known by his pleasant collections of essays and tales, 'The Sketch-Book' (which includes 'Rip van Winkle' (q.v.) and 'The Legend of Sleepy Hollow'), and the later volume 'Bracebridge Hall', in which figures Squire Bracebridge, a sort of 19th-cent. Sir Roger de Coverley. Irving was the first American man of letters to be internationally celebrated, and deserved his fame.

Irvingites, a religious body founded about 1835 on the basis of principles promulgated by Edward Irving (1792–1834), a minister of the Church of Scotland, excommunicated in

1833. Ritualism, symbolism, and mystery are prominent features in its worship. The name is not accepted by the body itself, which assumes the title Catholic Apostolic Church. Edward Irving, the son of a tanner of Annan, was a friend and encourager of Carlyle; both Carlyle and Hazlitt have left us descriptions of him.

Irwine, THE REVD. ADOLPHUS, the rector in George Eliot's 'Adam Bede' (q.v.).

Isaac, a character in Sheridan's 'The Duenna' (q.v.).

Isaac Comnenus, a novel by Sir Henry Taylor (q.v.).

Isaac of York, in Scott's 'Ivanhoe' (q.v.), the father of Rebecca.

Isabella, in the 'Orlando Furioso' (q.v.), daughter of a Saracen king of Spain, with whom the Scottish prince Zerbino (q.v.) fell in love. After his death, while on her way, broken-hearted, with a hermit to a convent near Marseille, she fell into the power of Rodomont, and to protect her honour caused him by guile to slay her.

Isabella, a character in (1) Kyd's 'The Spanish Tragedy' (q.v.); (2) Shakespeare's 'Measure for Measure' (q.v.); (3) Southerne's 'The Fatal Marriage' (q.v.).

Isabella, or the Pot of Basil, a poem by Keats (q.v.), published in 'Lamia . . . and other Poems' in 1820.

The poem is based on Boccaccio's 'Decameron', IV. v. The proud brothers of Isabella, a Florentine lady, having discovered the love of Lorenzo and their sister, decoy Lorenzo away, murder him, and bury his body in a forest. Isabella, apprised by a vision, finds his body, places the head in a flower-pot, and sets a plant of basil over it. Her brothers, observing how she cherishes the basil, steal the pot, discover the head, and fly conscience-stricken; and Isabella pines and dies. See *Basil*.

Isaiah, the greatest of the prophets of the O.T. He prophesied in Judah during the reigns of Uzziah, Jotham, Ahaz, and Hezekiah (the latter part of the 8th cent. B.C.). The chapters of the Book of Isaiah from xl onwards appear to be by other hands and of much later date. The author of xl–lv is an exile in Babylon.

Isegrym or ISENGRIN, the wolf in 'Reynard the Fox' (q.v.).

Isenbras, Sir, see *Isumbras*.

Iseult (ISOUD, YSOLDE, or YSOUDE), LA BEALE, in the Arthurian legend, is the sister or daughter of the king of Ireland. For her story see *Tristram*.

Iseult (ISOUD, YSOLDE, or YSOUDE), LA BLANCHE MAINS, in the Arthurian legend, is the daughter of the duke of Brittany and the wife of Tristram (q.v.).

Isfendiyar or ASFANDIYAR, after Rustem

(q.v.) the principal hero of the 'Shahnameh' of Firdusi (q.v.). He is the son of Gushtasp, king of Persia, achieves great conquests and spreads the Zoroastrian faith. But his father's mind is poisoned against him and he is thrown into prison. Later, under stress of the victorious advance of his enemy Arjasp, Gushtasp releases Isfendiyar, who, like Rustem, performs seven superhuman feats, rescues his sisters who have been captured by Arjasp, and kills the latter. His father, still suspicious of him, orders Isfendiyar to bring Rustem to him in fetters. Isfendiyar forces Rustem to fight with him, and after the first day's inconclusive fighting, is killed by Rustem with a magic arrow that pierces his eyes.

ISHERWOOD, CHRISTOPHER WILLIAM BRADSHAW (1904–   ), novelist, since 1946 an American citizen. His novels include 'The Memorial' (1932), 'Mr. Norris Changes Trains' (1935), 'Goodbye to Berlin' (1939), 'Prater Violet' (1945), 'The World in the Evening' (1954), and 'Down There on a Visit' (1962). The earlier books give an interesting picture of Berlin on the eve of Hitler's rise. He also wrote plays in collaboration with W. H. Auden (q.v.): 'The Dog Beneath the Skin' (1935), 'The Ascent of F 6' (1937), and 'On the Frontier' (1938). Since living in America he has become interested in Indian religious philosophy.

Ishmael, the son of Abraham by Hagar, hence allusively an outcast, one 'whose hand is against every man, and every man's hand against him' (Gen. xvi. 12). ISHMAELITE is used in the same sense.

Ishtar, see *Astarte.*

ISIDORE OF SEVILLE (*c.* 560–636), bishop of Seville, an encyclopaedic writer esteemed in the Middle Ages, author of 'Originum seu Etymologiarum libri xx', etc.

Isidorian Decretals, see *Decretals.*

Isis, one of the great Egyptian deities, the sister and wife of Osiris (q.v.), and mother of Horus (q.v.). She came to be looked upon as the great nature-goddess, and her worship spread to Western Asia and Southern Europe (including Rome), where she was identified with various local deities.

Isis, the river: see *Thames.*

Iskanderbeg, see *Scanderbeg.*

Islam, an Arabic word meaning 'resignation', signifies the religion revealed through the Prophet Mohammed (q.v.), or the Muslim world.

Island, The, a poem by Lord Byron (q.v.), published in 1823.

The poem is based on the narrative of the mutiny on H.M.S. 'Bounty' (q.v.), and the life of the mutineers on Tahiti, with which a pleasant love-idyll is interwoven.

Isle of Saints, a medieval name for Ireland, from the welcome it gave to Christianity.

Ismēnē, the sister of Antigone (q.v.), who,

when the latter was ordered to be buried alive, demanded to share her punishment.

Isocrătēs (436–338 B.C.), an Attic orator and teacher of rhetoric, who took his own life after the defeat of the Greeks by Philip of Macedon at the battle of Chaeronea. He is 'that old man eloquent' referred to by Milton in the sonnet to the Lady Margaret Ley.

Israfel, in the Muslim religion, the angel of music, who is to sound the trumpet at the day of resurrection. Poe (q.v.) wrote his poem 'Israfel' on the text, 'the angel Israfel, whose heartstrings are a lute and who has the sweetest voice of all God's creatures'.

Istakhar, the capital of the Persian Empire under the Sasanian (q.v.) dynasty, and the centre of priestly learning. It adjoined Persepolis, the earlier capital.

Isthmian Games, one of the four great national festivals of the ancient Greeks, held in the Isthmus of Corinth. It included all sorts of athletic contests, horse and chariot races, and musical and poetical competitions. Victory at these games was celebrated in odes, of which Pindar has left examples.

Isumbras, or *Isenbras, Sir,* a popular verse tale of the 14th cent. Isumbras is strong, handsome, and prosperous, but proud and arrogant. A bird sent by God gives him the choice between suffering in youth or in old age. He chooses the former. Extreme misfortunes befall him, which he bears patiently. He loses wife, children, and possessions, and for twenty-one years suffers among the Saracens, doing deeds of prowess; after which an angel announces that his sins are forgiven, and he is restored to his family and happiness.

Millais's picture 'Sir Isumbras at the Ford' was painted in 1857.

It is Never too Late to Mend, a novel by Reade (q.v.), published in 1856. Reade had previously written a play, 'Gold!' on the same subject.

The novel combines, rather loosely, two distinct stories: first, that of a young farmer who emigrates to Australia to earn the £1,000 necessary to win the father's consent to marry his sweetheart, a purpose which he achieves in spite of the machinations of the money-lending villain Meadows. This gives an opportunity for a description of the perils of an Australian miner's life during the gold rush. Secondly, that of a thief sentenced to jail and transportation, in the course of which the author exposes the brutalities and abuses of the English prison system.

Itala, the name given to an old Latin version of the Bible (q.v.) on which, after Jerome's recension of it, the Vulgate came to be founded.

Italic type, a compact sloping type based on an Italian 15th-cent. style of cursive writing, introduced by Aldus Manutius (q.v.) in 1501 for use in his small editions of the classics.

Italy, a collection of tales in verse by S. Rogers (q.v.).

Ithaca, the kingdom of Odysseus (q.v.), a small island in the Ionian sea.

Ithuriel, in Milton's 'Paradise Lost', IV. 788 et seq., one of the Cherubim, a 'strong and subtle spirit', charged by Gabriel to search for Satan in Paradise. Touched by Ithuriel's spear, which 'no falsehood can endure', the Fiend starts up in his own shape.

Itinerary of Antoninus, an official list of the roads in the Roman Empire, with the distances between stations, probably an early 3rd-cent. compilation embodying a good deal of material from the 2nd cent. Nothing is known of the author.

Ĭtўlus, the son of Aēdon, who was wife of Zethus, king of Thebes. According to legend, Aedon, jealous of Niobe, the wife of her brother, who had six sons and six daughters, determined to kill one of these sons, but by mistake killed Itylus. She was changed by Zeus into a nightingale, whose song is Aedon's lament for her son. Swinburne (q.v.) wrote a poem on this subject ('Itylus' in 'Poems and Ballads', First Series).

Itys, see *Philomela.*

Ivanhoe, a novel by Sir W. Scott (q.v.), published in 1819. This was the first of the author's novels in which he adopted a purely English subject. Freeman ('Hist. of the Norman Conquest', vol. v, appx.) has criticized, as unsupported by the evidence of contemporary records, the enmity of Saxon and Norman, represented as persisting in the days of Richard I, which forms the basis of the story.

Wilfred of Ivanhoe, son of Cedric, of noble Saxon birth, loves his father's ward, the lady Rowena, who traces her descent to King Alfred, and who returns his love. For this reason Cedric, who is passionately devoted to the cause of the restoration of the Saxon line to the throne of England and sees the best chance of effecting this in the marriage of Rowena to Athelstane of Coningsburgh, also of the Saxon blood royal, has in anger banished his son. Ivanhoe has joined Richard Cœur de Lion at the crusade and there won the king's affection. In Richard's absence, his brother John has found support among the lawless and dissolute Norman nobles for his design of ousting Richard from the throne, a design favoured by Richard's imprisonment in Austria on his return from Palestine.

The story centres in two chief events: a great tournament at Ashby-de-la-Zouche, where Ivanhoe aided by Richard, who unknown to all has returned to England with Ivanhoe, defeats all the knights of John's party, including the fierce Templar, Sir Brian de Bois-Guilbert, and Sir Reginald Front-de-Bœuf; and the siege of Front-de-Bœuf's castle of Torquilstone, whither Cedric and Rowena, with the wounded Ivanhoe, Athelstane, the Jew Isaac, and his beautiful and courageous daughter Rebecca, have been carried captives by the Norman nobles. After an exciting fight, the castle is carried by a force of outlaws and Saxons, led by Locksley (otherwise Robin Hood) and King Richard himself. The prisoners are rescued, with the exception of Rebecca, of whom the Templar has become passionately enamoured, and whom he carries off to the Preceptory of Templestowe. Here the unexpected arrival of the Grand Master of the order, while relieving Rebecca from the dishonourable advances of Bois-Guilbert, exposes her to the charge of witchcraft, and she escapes sentence of death only by demanding trial by combat. Ivanhoe, whose gratitude she has earned by nursing him when wounded at the tournament of Ashby, appears as her champion, and in the encounter between him and Bois-Guilbert (on whom has been thrust the unwelcome duty of appearing as the accuser), the latter falls dead, untouched by his opponent's lance, the victim of his own contending passions. Ivanhoe and Rowena, by the intervention of Richard, are united; the more interesting Rebecca, suppressing her love for Ivanhoe, leaves England with her father.

Among the many characters in the story, besides Robin Hood and Friar Tuck, mention may be made of the poor fool Wamba, who imperils his life to save that of his master Cedric; Gurth, the swineherd; and Isaac the Jew, divided between love of his shekels and love of his daughter. Thackeray's 'Rebecca and Rowena' (q.v.) is an amusing sequel to, and critical reinterpretation of, Scott's tale.

Ivory Gate see *Dreams.*

Ivory Tower, The, an unfinished story, by H. James (q.v.).

Ivry, in the department of the Eure, France, the scene of a famous battle in which Henri IV of France defeated the Leaguers under the duke of Mayenne (1590). 'Ivry' is the subject of a lay by T. B. Macaulay (q.v.), published in 1824.

Ixīon, a Thessalian, who married Dia, daughter of Deïoneus. When the latter came to fetch the bride-price, Ixion contrived that he should fall into a pit containing burning coals. As a consequence of this treachery Ixion was shunned by men and refused purification of his murder. He took refuge with Zeus, who consented to purify him. With gross ingratitude Ixion tried to seduce Hera. Thereupon Zeus formed a cloud, Nephelē, to resemble Hera, and by her Ixion became father of the Centaurs (q.v.). As a punishment for his crimes Ixion in the underworld was bound on a burning wheel, which turned for ever. R. Browning wrote a poem on this subject ('Ixion' in 'Jocoseria', 1883) and Disraeli a short burlesque, 'Ixion in Heaven'.

Ixion in Heaven, a short burlesque tale published by B. Disraeli in 1833, describing amusingly the visit of Ixion to Olympus as the guest of Jove.

J

Jabberwock, a fictitious monster, the subject of the poem 'Jabberwocky' in Lewis Carroll's 'Through the Looking-Glass' (q.v.). The story, told in an invented vocabulary, begins: ''Twas brillig, and the slithy toves'.

J'accuse, see *Dreyfus.*

Jachin and **Boaz,** the names of the two pillars of the porch of the Temple of Solomon (1 Kings vii. 21).

Jacintha, the heroine of Hoadly's 'The Suspicious Husband' (q.v.).

Jack, COLONEL, see *Colonel Jack.*

Jack-a-Lent, a figure of a man, set up to be pelted: an ancient form of the sport of 'Aunt Sally' practised during Lent. Hence figuratively a butt for everyone to throw at (Shakespeare, 'The Merry Wives of Windsor', v. v. 137).

Jack and Jill, a nursery rhyme, involving perhaps originally some political allusion now lost. Lord Houghton is quoted by Sir M. Grant Duff ('Notes from a Diary', 7 June 1878) as thinking that Jack and Jill were Empson and Dudley, notorious for their fiscal exactions in Henry VII's reign and executed for constructive treason soon after Henry VIII came to the throne, to the great satisfaction of the Londoners. Baring-Gould ('Curious Myths') finds the origin of Jack and Jill in the Hjuki and Bil of Scandinavian mythology, two children who had been drawing water and were stolen by the moon.

Jack and the Bean-stalk, a nursery tale based on a world-wide myth, found e.g. among the North American Indians and the native tribes of S. Africa. The bean-stalk is said to be derived from the ash, the world-tree of northern mythology (see *Yggdrasil*).

Jack, the son of a poor widow, exchanges his mother's cow for a hatful of beans. His mother in anger throws the beans out of the window. The next morning a bean-stalk has grown up into the clouds. Jack climbs up and finds himself in a strange country, where a fairy directs him to the house of a giant who has killed his father. He robs the giant of a hen that lays golden eggs, a self-playing harp, and bags of diamonds, and is finally discovered by the giant and pursued down the bean-stalk. Jack reaching the ground first, cuts the bean-stalk with an axe, and the giant falls and is killed.

Jack Brag, a vulgar pretentious snob, a term derived from the novel of that name by Hook (q.v.).

Jack Drum's Entertainment, see *Drum's Entertainment.*

Jack Horner, the subject of a nursery rhyme ('Little Jack Horner sat in a corner', etc.), which occurs in an 18th-cent. chapbook, 'The Pleasant History of Jack Horner, containing his witty Tricks, etc.' The rhyme is also referred to by Carey (q.v.) about 1720. The origin of the rhyme is attributed to a Jack Horner who was steward to the abbot of Glastonbury in the reign of Henry VIII and by a trick acquired the deeds of the manor of Mells at the dissolution of the monasteries, took them to the king, and was handsomely rewarded: the family still holds the manor.

Jack-in-office, a consequential petty official.

Jack in the Green, a feature in the chimney-sweepers' celebration of the May-day festival: 'a large hollow cone of hoops and basket-work, so completely covered with ivy, holly, flowers, and ribbons that the person carrying it is altogether hidden except his feet' (Soane, 'New Curiosities of Literature', i. 262).

Jack of Dover, in the Prologue to Chaucer's 'Cook's Tale',

And many a Jakk of Dover hastow sold
That hath be twyes hoot and twyes cold,

is probably some sort of pie.

In 'Jack of Dover, his quest of Inquirie' (1604), given in W. C. Hazlitt's 'Shakespearean Jest-books', Jack travels in search of a greater fool than himself, and fails to find him.

Jack of Newbery or NEWBURY, John Winchcombe, *alias* Smalwoode (*d.* 1520), a clothier of Newbury, whose wealth inspired the authors of numerous chapbook stories. According to a legend he led 100 or 250 men, equipped at his own expense, at the battle of Flodden Field. See *Delony (T).*

Jack-o'-Lantern or JACK-A-LANTERN, see *Ignis Fatuus.*

Jack-pudding, a clown or buffoon. 'A set of merry Drolls . . . whom every nation calls by the name of that Dish of Meat which it loves best. In Holland they are termed Pickled Herrings; in France, Jean Pottages; in Italy, Maccaronies; and in Great Britain, Jack Puddings.' (Addison, 'Spectator', No. 47.)

Jack Robinson, 'before one can say Jack Robinson', i.e. very quickly, a phrase whose origin is unknown. The earliest quotation given for it in the OED. is from Miss Burney's 'Evelina' (II. xxxvii).

Jack Sprat, of the nursery rhyme, who 'would eat no fat', figures in a rhyme given by James Howell, in the collection of proverbs annexed to his 'Tetraglotton' (1659), as 'Archdeacon Pratt', who had the same aversion:

> Archdeacon Pratt would eat no fatt,
> His wife would eat no lean.
> Twixt Archdeacon Pratt and Joan his wife,
> The meat was eat up clean.

Jack Straw, the leader of a party of insurgents from Essex in the Peasants' Rising of 1381. There have been inns called 'Jack Straw's Castle' at Islington, Highbury, and Hampstead Heath, but there does not appear to be any historical connexion between them and the above.

Jack the Giant-killer, a nursery tale of Northern origin, known in England from very early times.

Jack was the son of a Cornish farmer, and lived in the days of King Arthur. His first achievement was the destruction of the giant of Mount Cornwall, which he effected by digging a pit, covering it with branches and earth, and luring the giant into it. He subsequently acquired from another giant by his ingenuity a coat that made him invisible, shoes that gave him extraordinary speed, and a sword of magic potency. With the help of these, he destroyed all the giants in the land.

Jack the Ripper, the name assumed by an unknown man who claimed to be the perpetrator of a series of murders, characterized by the same revolting features, in the East end of London in 1888–9.

Jackanapes, a word which, so far as yet found, first appears as an opprobrious nickname of William de la Pole, duke of Suffolk (murdered 1450), whose badge was a clog and chain, such as was attached to a tame ape. Hence he is referred to as *Jack Napes*, this being inferentially already a quasi-proper name for a tame ape. But of *Jack Napes* and its relation to *an ape* or *apes*, no certain explanation can be offered. The word is used to signify a tame ape or monkey, or one who is like a monkey in tricks, air, or behaviour. [OED.]

Jackanapes, a story by Juliana Horatia Ewing (q.v.), published in 1884.

Jackdaw of Rheims, The, one of the best known of Barham's 'Ingoldsby Legends' (see *Barham*) which tells how a jackdaw stole the ring of the cardinal archbishop of Rheims. The archbishop's terrible curse on the thief reduced the jackdaw to a pitiable state. He showed where he had hidden the ring, the curse was removed, the bird recovered his sleekness, became devout, and on his death was canonized by the name of Jim Crow.

Jacke Wilton, The Life of, see *Unfortunate Traveller.*

Jacob and **Esau,** the twin sons of Isaac and Rebecca. Esau, the elder, was a hunter, Jacob a dweller in tents. Esau, coming in faint from the field, sold his birthright to Jacob for a mess of pottage (Gen. xxv). Jacob, personating Esau, obtained Isaac's death-bed blessing (Gen. xxvii). The name Jacob means 'supplanter'.

Jacob Faithful, a novel by Marryat (q.v.), published in 1834.

Jacob Faithful is born on a Thames lighter and spends his early years there, until his mother, a heavy drinker of gin, dies of spontaneous combustion, and his father, scared out of his wits, jumps overboard and is drowned. Jacob fortunately finds kind friends, gets a good education, and shows natural talent fitting him for a much higher station. But he has a mistaken notion of the value of 'independence', and a pride that makes him vindictively resent an injury unwittingly done him by the protector who is trying to further his career. So he sticks to the river as lighterman and wherryman, and meets with various adventures and entertaining characters, until he is pressed on a frigate and carried to sea. From this life he is soon rescued by the inheritance of a fortune from an old gentleman who has befriended him and whom he has saved from drowning.

Among the amusing characters in the book are honest Domine Dobbs, Jacob's schoolmaster, old Tom Beazley, the loss of whose legs has not impaired his cheeriness, and his mischievous son, young Tom.

Jacob Omnium, see *Higgins.*

Jacob's Ladder, the ladder that Jacob saw in a dream, at the place that he named Bethel, set up on earth and reaching to heaven, with the angels of God ascending and descending on it (Gen. xxviii. 12). The name is given to the garden plant *Polemonium caeruleum* and also popularly or locally to the plant Solomon's Seal.

Jacob's Staff, a pilgrim's staff, derived from St. James (*Jacobus*), whose symbols in religious art are a staff and a scallop shell (see Spenser, 'Faerie Queene', I. vi); perhaps also derived from Gen. xxxii. 10, 'with my staff I passed over this Jordan'.

Jacobin, originally a name of the French friars of the order of St. Dominic, so called because the church of St. Jacques in Paris was given to them and they built their first convent near it. From them the name was transferred to the members of a French political club established in 1789, in Paris, in the old convent of the Jacobins, to maintain the principles of extreme democracy and absolute equality. It was applied in a transferred sense to sympathizers with their principles, and about 1800 was a nickname for any political reformer.

Jacobite, a partisan of the Stuarts after the revolution of 1688, from *Jacobus*, Latin for James.

JACOBS, WILLIAM WYMARK (1863–1943), writer of short stories, principally of two kinds: those of macabre invention, of which 'The Monkey's Paw' is the best known, and those of a humorous nature, particularly concerning seafaring men and the famous 'Night-watchman'; they have been collected, e.g., in 'Many Cargoes' (1896), 'The Skipper's Wooing' (1897), 'A Master of Craft' (1900), 'Night Watches' (1914). 'The Monkey's Paw' and others of his stories (such as 'Beauty and the Barge') have been dramatized.

Jacōbus, the unofficial name of a gold coin struck in the reign of James I, worth 20–24*s*.

Jacobus a Voragine, see *Golden Legend*.

Jacquerie, LA, a bloody insurrection of the peasantry of northern France in 1358, occasioned by their sufferings in consequence of the English invasion. The name is derived from JACQUES BONHOMME, a nickname given to the peasants at this time.

Jaffar the Barmecide (Ja'far al Barmeki), in the 'Arabian Nights' (q.v.), the vizier of Haroun-al-Raschid, who, with the executioner Mesrour, accompanied him when, disguised as a merchant, he walked at night about the streets of Baghdad. See *Barmecide*.

Jaffier, one of the principal characters in Otway's 'Venice Preserv'd' (q.v.).

Jaggard, WILLIAM (*fl.* 1594–1623), and ISAAC (*fl.* 1613–27), London printers and principal publishers of the Shakespeare First Folio (see *Folios and Quartos, Shakespearian*).

Jaggers, MR., a character in Dickens's 'Great Expectations' (q.v.).

JAGO, RICHARD (1715–81), born in Warwickshire and the holder of three livings in that county, was the author of 'Edge-Hill', a poem in four books describing, with many moral and other digressions, the views seen at morning, noon, afternoon, and evening, as he looks from that famous spot over his favourite county.

Jahangir, or JEHANGIR, the son of Akbar, reigned as Mogul Emperor, 1605–27.

Jahvistic, see *Elohim*.

Jakin, BOB, a character in G. Eliot's 'The Mill on the Floss' (q.v.).

JAMES I (1394–1437), king of Scotland, was captured while on his way to France by an English ship, probably in 1406. He was detained in England for nineteen years and well educated. While in England he composed his poem, 'The Kingis Quair' (q.v.). In 1424 he married Lady Jane Beaufort, daughter of the earl of Somerset and granddaughter of John of Gaunt, the heroine of the above poem. James I was assassinated at Perth. One or two other poems, 'The Ballad of Good Counsel', 'Christ's Kirk on the Green', 'Peblis to the Play', have been doubtfully attributed to him. He is the subject of D. G. Rossetti's 'The King's Tragedy' (included in 'Sonnets and Ballads', 1881).

JAMES I (James VI of Scotland), king of England, 1603–25. He is reputed the author of 'True Law of Free Monarchies' (1603), a

reply to the argument of G. Buchanan (q.v.) in his 'De Jure Regni' that the king is elected by, and is responsible to, the people. He also wrote 'Basilikon Doron' (1599, precepts on the art of government, addressed to his son); 'A Counterblaste to Tobacco' (1604), in which the alleged virtues of the plant are refuted; and a good many mainly theological works. James I figures in Scott's 'The Fortunes of Nigel' (q.v.).

James II, king of England, 1685–8. In 1688 he was driven out by an aristocratic revolution and threw the Great Seal into the Thames. He was succeeded in 1689 by William and Mary, the throne being declared vacant. He lived until 1701.

JAMES, GEORGE PAYNE RAINSFORD (1799–1860), wrote, besides historical novels ('Richelieu', 1829, 'Philip Augustus', 1831, and others), 'Memoirs of the Great Commanders' (1832), 'Life of the Black Prince' (1836), and other popular historical works and poems. The style of his romances was parodied by Thackeray in 'Novels by Eminent Hands' ('Barbazure').

JAMES, HENRY (1843–1916), was born in New York of ancestry originally both Irish and Scottish. His father, Henry James, sen., was a remarkable writer on questions of theology and a follower of Swedenborg. His elder brother, William James (q.v.), was a distinguished philosopher. After a desultory education in New York, London, Paris, and Geneva, Henry James entered the law school at Harvard in 1862. He settled in Europe in 1875. From 1865 he was a regular contributor of reviews and short stories to American periodicals, and owed much to his friendship with the novelist Howells (q.v.). His first considerable piece of fiction, 'Watch and Ward', appeared serially in 1871, followed by 'Transatlantic Sketches' and 'A Passionate Pilgrim' in 1875, and his first important novel 'Roderick Hudson' (q.v.) in 1876 (in the 'Atlantic Monthly', 1875). For more than twenty years he lived in London, and in 1898 moved to Lamb House, Rye, where his later novels were written. He at first chiefly concerned himself with the impact of the older civilization of Europe upon American life, and to this period belong his more popular novels: 'Roderick Hudson' (1875), 'The American' (1877), 'Daisy Miller' (1879), and the exquisite 'Portrait of a Lady' (q.v., 1881). He next turned to a more exclusively English stage' in 'The Tragic Muse' (1890), 'The Spoils of Poynton' (1897), and 'The Awkward Age' (1899), in which he analysed English character with extreme subtlety, verging at times on obscurity. 'What Maisie Knew' appeared in 1897. In his last three great novels, 'The Wings of the Dove' (1902), 'The Ambassadors' (q.v., 1903), and 'The Golden Bowl' (1904), he returned to the 'international' theme of the contrast of American and European character. In 1914 he began work on two novels, 'The Ivory Tower' and 'The Sense of the Past', which remained unfinished at his death and were published as fragments in 1917. For the revised collection of his fiction, of which the issue began in 1907, James wrote a series of critical prefaces of high interest.

Besides nearly a hundred short stories (including the well-known ghost-story, 'The Turn of the Screw',1898), James wrote several volumes of sketches of travel ('Portraits of Places', 1883; 'A Little Tour in France', 1884) and literary criticism; a number of plays, of which the few that were acted were not successful; a life of Nathaniel Hawthorne for the English Men of Letters series; and, in 'The American Scene' (1906), a record of the impressions produced on him by a visit to America after an absence of nearly twenty years. 'A Small Boy and Others' (1913) and 'Notes of a Son and a Brother' (1914) are evocations of his early days in New York and Europe. A short story called 'The Middle Years' appeared in the volume 'Terminations' in 1895. The autobiographical work of the same title is a fragment (published posthumously in 1917) 'representing all that James lived to write of a volume of autobiographical reminiscences to which he had given the name of one of his own short stories' (from the prefatory note to the autobiographical fragment). Two volumes of his letters were published in 1920. Under the influence of an ardent sympathy for the British cause in the War, Henry James was in 1915 naturalized a British subject. His portrait by J. S. Sargent is in the National Portrait Gallery.

In addition to the works referred to above, the following may be mentioned: 'Madonna of the Future' (1879), 'Washington Square' (1881), 'The Siege of London' (1883), 'The Bostonians' (1886), 'The Princess Casamassima' (1886), 'The Reverberator' (1888), 'The Aspern Papers' (1888), 'The Real Thing' (1893), 'Embarrassments' (1896), 'The Other House' (1896), 'In the Cage' (1898), 'The Two Magics' (1898), 'The Better Sort' (1903).

JAMES, MONTAGUE RHODES (1862–1936), medievalist, provost of Eton from 1918. As well as editing a great number of bibliographical and palaeographical works he edited and translated 'The Apocryphal New Testament' (1924). His ghost stories are well known and have been collected in one volume (1931) which includes 'Ghost Stories of an Antiquary'.

JAMES, WILLIAM (1842–1910), American philosopher, the son of Henry James, sen. (a Swedenborgian philosopher), and elder brother of Henry James (q.v.), was at first a student of art and then a teacher of physiology, but turned his attention to psychology. His views are embodied in his 'Principles of Psychology' (1890), and show a tendency to subordinate logical proof to intuitional conviction. He was a vigorous antagonist of the idealistic school of Kant and Hegel, and an empiricist who made empiricism more radical by treating pure experience as the very sub-

stance of the world. Yet he was not a monist but a pluralist, 'willing to believe that there may ultimately never be an all-form at all, that the substance of reality may never get totally collected . . . and that a distributive form of reality, the each-form, is as acceptable as the all-form' ('Pluralistic Universe', p. 34). Pragmatism was his method of approach to metaphysics: abstract ideas are true if 'they work', if they harmonize with our other experience and accepted ideas. James's principal works were, besides the 'Principles of Psychology' above mentioned, 'Varieties of Religious Experience' (1902), 'Pragmatism' (1907), 'The Meaning of Truth' (1909), 'A Pluralistic Universe' (1909), 'Essays in Radical Empiricism' (1912). The conclusions of his 'Varieties of Religious Experience' are notable: 'the visible world is part of a more spiritual universe from which it draws its chief significance; union with the higher universe is our true end; spiritual energy flows in and produces effects within the phenomenal world'.

JAMESON, ANNA BROWNELL (1794–1860), author. Of her many critical works on art and literature the best known is 'Shakespeare's Heroines' (formerly entitled 'Characteristics of Women', 1832).

Jameson Raid: the discontent of the 'Uitlander' (mainly British) population of the Transvaal with the government of the South African Republic became acute in 1895, and a 'reform committee' in Johannesburg in the autumn of that year was making plans for its forcible overthrow. It was supported by Cecil Rhodes, and to L. S. Jameson (1853–1917), administrator of what was later to become Southern Rhodesia, was allotted the task of raising a mounted force in Rhodesia and of holding it in readiness on the border of the Transvaal, to be used if events in Johannesburg should make it necessary. Jameson decided to take the initiative, and on 29 Dec., in spite of messages calling upon him to stay his hand, he marched his force, under the military command of Sir John Willoughby, across the Transvaal frontier. The force which Jameson expected to be sent from Johannesburg to meet him was not sent, he was surrounded by the Boers, and his little band was forced to surrender to P. A. Cronje, the Boer commandant, on 2 Jan. 1896.

JAMIESON, JOHN (1759–1838), antiquary and philologist, a friend of Scott. His 'Etymological Dictionary of the Scottish Language' first appeared in 1808.

Jamieson, THE HON. MRS., a character in Mrs. Gaskell's 'Cranford' (q.v.).

JAMMES, FRANCIS (1868–1938), French author of poetry inspired by nature and religion: 'De l'angélus de l'aube à l'angélus du soir' (1898), 'Le Deuil des Primevères' (1901), 'Les Georgiques chrétiennes' (1911), etc.; also of prose tales, e.g. 'Le Roman du Lièvre' (1903).

Jamshid or JEMSHID, an early legendary king of Persia, celebrated in the 'Shahnameh' of Firdusi (q.v.). He was the reputed inventor of the arts of medicine, weaving, iron-working, navigation, etc. His reign was a period of prosperity and magnificence. But Jamshid waxed arrogant and, incurring the wrath of heaven, was reduced to utter wretchedness and degradation, became a wanderer and was put to a miserable death by Zohak (Dahak), the usurper of his throne. He is mentioned in the 'Rubáiyát' of Omar Khayyám (q.v.), 'The Courts where Jamshyd gloried and drank deep'.

Jane, a small silver coin of Genoa (Fr. *Gênes*) introduced into England towards the end of the 14th cent. The word is used by Chaucer ('Sir Thopas') and Spenser ('Faerie Queene', III. vii).

Jane Eyre, a novel by C. Brontë (q.v.), published in 1847.

The heroine, a penniless orphan, has been left to the care of her aunt, Mrs. Reed. Harsh and unsympathetic treatment rouses the spirit of the child, and a passionate outbreak leads to her consignment to Lowood Asylum, a charitable institution, where after some miserable years she becomes a teacher. Thence she passes to be a governess at Thornfield Hall to a little girl, the natural daughter of Mr. Rochester, a man of grim aspect and sardonic temper. In spite of Jane Eyre's plainness, Rochester is fascinated by her elfish wit and courageous spirit, and falls in love with her, and she with him. Their marriage is prevented at the last moment by the revelation that he has a wife living, a raving lunatic, kept in seclusion at Thornfield Hall. Jane flees from the Hall, and after nearly perishing on the moors is taken in and cared for by the Revd. St. John Rivers and his sisters. Under the influence of the strong personality of Rivers, she nearly consents (in spite of her undiminished love for Rochester) to marry him and accompany him to India. She is prevented by a telepathic appeal from Rochester, and sets out for Thornfield Hall, to learn that the place has been burnt down, and that Rochester, in vainly trying to save his wife from the flames, has been blinded and maimed. She finds him in utter dejection, becomes his wife, and restores him to happiness.

In Lowood Asylum Miss Brontë depicted the school at Cowan Bridge where she spent some unhappy years, and where her sisters Maria (portrayed in Helen Burns) and Elizabeth contracted the consumption of which they died.

Jane Shore, see *Shore.*

Janet's Repentance, see *Scenes of Clerical Life.*

Janice Meredith, novel by P. L. Ford (q.v.).

Janissaries or JANIZARIES, a body of Turkish infantry, first organized in the 14th cent., and constituting the sultan's guard. It was recruited mainly from the children of *rayahs*

or Christian subjects of the Turks. The force became powerful and turbulent, and after a revolt deliberately provoked by the Sultan Mahmud II, many thousands of Janissaries were massacred, and the organization abolished (1826).

Jansenism, the doctrine of a school that developed in the Roman Catholic Church holding the doctrines of Cornelius Jansen (1585–1638), bishop of Ypres in Flanders, who maintained after St. Augustine the perverseness and inability for good of the natural human will. The capacity for the love of God, he held, could be obtained only by 'conversion', and God converts whom He pleases. His doctrine thus approximated to that of predestination and was closely analogous to Calvinism. But Jansen repudiated justification by faith and maintained that the personal relation of the human soul with God was possible only through the Roman Church. His doctrine was developed in France by Antoine Arnauld. The Jansenists were a powerful body in the 17th cent., but were strongly opposed by the Jesuits, and their doctrines were condemned by several popes, especially by Clement X in his Bull *Unigenitus.* The headquarters of Jansenism was Port-Royal (q.v.). There is said to be still a Jansenist Church in Holland. See also *Pascal.*

Januarius, ST., a bishop of Benevento, who was martyred under Diocletian. His head and some of his blood are preserved as relics at Naples; the blood is said to have the miraculous power of liquefying on certain days in each year. He is commemorated on 19 Sept.

January and May, the title of a version by Pope of Chaucer's 'Merchant's Tale' (see *Canterbury Tales*).

Janus, an ancient Italian deity, the god of the doorway (*janua*). He was guardian both of private doors and of the city gates, and presided over the year, his own special month being named January. He is most famous as the guardian of the state during war, when the gates of his temple were left open (being closed in peace time). He is represented in statues with two heads, facing opposite ways, perhaps suggestive of vigilance, looking both before and behind.

Japhetic, a name sometimes applied to the Indo-European family, as supposed to be descended from Japhet, one of the sons of Noah.

Jaquenetta, in Shakespeare's 'Love's Labour's Lost' (q.v.), a country maid with whom Armado is in love.

Jaques, a character in Shakespeare's 'As You Like It' (q.v.).

Jarley, MRS., in Dickens's 'Old Curiosity Shop' (q.v.), the proprietor of a travelling wax-works show.

Jarnac, COUP DE: in a duel fought in 1547

before Henri II and the French court by two young nobles, Jarnac and La Châtaigneraie, Jarnac by an unexpected blow hamstrung his opponent. The *coup de Jarnac* became proverbial for an unforeseen and decisive stroke.

Jarndyce, JOHN, a character in Dickens's 'Bleak House' (q.v.).

Jarvey, a hackney-coachman, a by-form of *Jarvis* or *Jervis*, personal name; according to Serjeant Ballantine, 'a compliment paid to the class in consequence of one of them named Jarvis having been hanged'.

Jarvie, BAILIE NICOL, a character in Scott's 'Rob Roy' (q.v.).

Jason, a celebrated hero of antiquity, son of Aeson, king of Iolcos. When his father's kingdom was usurped by his uncle Pelias, he was entrusted to the care of Cheiron the centaur (q.v.), by whom he was educated. Returning to Iolcos by the direction of the oracle, he boldly demanded from Pelias the restoration of the kingdom, and to obtain it undertook the expedition to Colchis to recover the Golden Fleece (see under *Argonauts*). This he accomplished successfully with the help of Medea (q.v.), whom he married, but subsequently abandoned in order to marry Glaucē or Creūsa (q.v.).

Jason, The Life and Death of, a poem in heroic couplets by W. Morris (q.v.), published in 1867.

The story is that of Jason and Medea, the Argonauts and the Golden Fleece (see under *Jason, supra*), permeated with a spirit of romance and pathos, and ending on a melancholy note, as Jason dies 'of love, of honour, and of joy bereft'.

Jasper Packlemerton, 'of atrocious memory', in Dickens's 'Old Curiosity Shop' (q.v.), a notable figure in Mrs. Jarley's wax-works, who had murdered fourteen wives.

Javan, according to Gen. x. 2, a son of Japhet; mentioned also in Ezekiel xxvii. 13 as trading with the Tyrians, and here signifying the Ionians of Asia Minor, in which sense Milton uses the expressions 'Javan's issue', in 'Paradise Lost', i. 508, and 'bound for the isles of Javan and Gadire' in 'Samson Agonistes', 716.

Jeames de la Pluche, The Diary of, a short story by Thackeray (q.v.), published in 'Punch' in 1845–6, reprinted in 'Miscellanies', 1856.

James Plush, a footman, makes a fortune by railway speculation, changes his name, and takes up his abode in the Albany. Lord Bareacres proposes to marry his daughter, Lady Angelina, to Jeames. But the latter wakes up one day to find that Lady Angelina has eloped with someone else, and that his fortune has likewise disappeared with a collapse of the market. He takes a public-house and marries Mary Ann Hoggins. See also *Yellowplush*.

JEAN DE MEUN(G), see *Roman de la Rose.*

Jean Jacques, a current abbreviation of the name of Jean Jacques Rousseau (q.v.).

Jean Paul, a frequent abbreviation of the name of J. P. F. Richter (q.v.).

JEANS, SIR JAMES HOPWOOD (1877–1946), astronomer and writer on cosmogony and stellar physics. His popular work 'The Mysterious Universe' appeared in 1930.

JEBB, SIR RICHARD CLAVERHOUSE (1841–1905), educated at Charterhouse and Trinity College, Cambridge, was professor of Greek at Glasgow in 1875, and at Cambridge in 1889. He was M.P. for the University during the later years of his life. He is remembered for his critical editions and translations of Sophocles (1883–96) and Bacchylides (1905), his translation of Theophrastus (1870), 'The Attic Orators from Antiphon to Isaeus' (1876–80), and other works on classical subjects. He also wrote a life of Bentley for the English Men of Letters series (1882).

Jebusites, in Dryden's 'Absalom and Achitophel' (q.v.), and generally in the 17th cent., the Roman Catholics.

Jedburgh, the capital of Roxburghshire, Scotland, famous in the annals of Border warfare. JEDBURGH, JEDWOOD, or JEDDART JUSTICE was proverbial for its summary character, the suspected culprit being hanged first and tried afterwards.

Jeeves, in many of P. G. Wodehouse's stories, the omniscient and resourceful valet.

JEFFERIES, RICHARD (1848–87), the son of a Wiltshire farmer, and a writer with a remarkable power of observing nature and representing it in combination with a strain of poetry and philosophy. He first attracted notice by his 'Gamekeeper at Home' (1878), reprinted from the 'Pall Mall Gazette'. There followed 'Wild Life in a Southern County' (1879), 'Hodge and his Master' (1880), 'Round about a Great Estate' (1880), 'Wood Magic' (1881), 'Bevis' (1882), 'The Life of the Fields' (1884); also his remarkable spiritual autobiography, 'The Story of my Heart' (1883). His novels were less successful.

JEFFERS, ROBINSON (1887–1962), American poet, born in Pennsylvania. He made his name with a narrative poem, based on the biblical story of Tamar, 'Tamar and Other Poems' (1924). Among his other volumes are 'Roan Stallion, Tamar and Other Poems' (1925), 'Cawdor and Other Poems' (1928), and 'Thurso's Landing and Other Poems' (1932). His adaptation of Euripedes' 'Medea' was produced in 1946.

Jefferson, THOMAS (1743–1826), born in Virginia, third president of the United States, holding the presidency for two terms (1801–9). He drafted the Declaration of Independence (1776), and is noted for his liberal policy and the educational and humanitarian reforms that he advocated.

JEFFREY, FRANCIS, *Lord Jeffrey* (1773–1850), educated at Edinburgh High School and at Glasgow and Edinburgh Universities, became a Scottish judge. He is principally remembered as the founder, with Sydney Smith, of the 'Edinburgh Review' (q.v.), as its editor until 1829, and for his unsparing criticism of the authors (notably the Lake school) of whom he disapproved. His article on Wordsworth's 'Excursion' (1814), beginning with 'This will never do', contains his chief objections. On the other hand, he would have made appreciation of Keats the touchstone of aptitude for poetry.

Jeffreys, GEORGE, *first Baron Jeffreys* (1644–89), educated at St. Paul's School, at Westminster, and at Trinity College, Cambridge, was lord thief justice, 1682. He presided at the trial of Titus Oates, and is chiefly notorious for his brutality and as the judge who held the 'Bloody Assizes' (q.v.). He was arrested in 1688 and died in the Tower after petitioning for a pardon.

Jehovah, the English representation of the Hebrew principal and personal name of God in the O.T., which was considered by the Jews too sacred for utterance. It has been held that the original name was YAHWEH, generally understood to mean 'he that exists', 'the self-existent'.

Jehovistic, see *Elohim*.

Jehu, a fast and furious driver; a coachman; in humorous allusion to 2 Kings ix. 20.

Jekyll and Mr. Hyde, *The Strange Case of Dr.*, a novel by R. L. Stevenson published in 1886.

Dr. Jekyll, a physician conscious of the duality, the mixed good and evil, in his own nature, and fascinated by the idea of the advantage that would arise if these two elements could be clothed in different personalities, discovers a drug by means of which he can create for himself a separate personality that absorbs all his evil instincts. This personality, repulsive in appearance, he assumes from time to time and calls Mr. Hyde, and in it he gives rein to his evil impulses. The personality of Hyde is pure evil. It gradually gains a greater ascendancy, and Hyde commits a horrible murder. Jekyll now finds himself from time to time involuntarily transformed into Hyde, while the drug loses its efficacy in restoring his original form and character. On the point of discovery and arrest, he takes his own life.

Jellyby, MRS., a character in Dickens's 'Bleak House' (q.v.).

Jemmy Dawson, see *Dawson* (*J.*).

Jemmy Twitcher, see *Twitcher*.

Jemshid, see *Jamshid*.

Jenghis Khan, see *Genghis Khan*.

Jenkins, HENRY (*d.* 1670), called the 'Modern Methuselah', was a native of Ellerton-upon-Swale in Yorkshire. He claimed to have been born about 1501, and when 10–12 years old to have been sent at the time of the battle of Flodden with a horse-load of arrows for the army at Northallerton; also to have been butler to Lord Conyers, abbot of Fountains, and to have witnessed the dissolution of the monasteries. He was buried at Bolton, where he is commemorated by an obelisk, but his extreme old age rests only on his own statements, which are in some respects contradictory.

Jenkins, MRS. WINIFRED, a character in Smollett's 'Humphry Clinker' (q.v.).

Jenkins's Ear, an allusion to a political incident of 1738, which precipitated the war with Spain of 1739. Robert Jenkins, a master mariner, produced to a committee of the House of Commons what he declared to be his ear, cut off by the Spanish captain Frandino at Havana in the exercise of the right of search which the Spaniards claimed in order to prevent English trade with Spanish America. There was some truth in the story; but it was a pirate captain who had cut off the ear, and the Spanish governor had punished the pirate.

Jenkinson, EPHRAIM, in Goldsmith's 'Vicar of Wakefield' (q.v.), an old swindler who imposed on Dr. Primrose and his son Moses.

Jenkinson, MRS. MOUNTSTUART, a character in Meredith's 'The Egoist' (q.v.).

Jenkyns, DEBORAH, MATILDA, and PETER, characters in Mrs. Gaskell's 'Cranford' (q.v.).

Jennings, MRS., (1) a character in Jane Austen's 'Sense and Sensibility' (q.v.); (2) the mother of John Keats (q.v.), as she became by her second marriage.

Jenny Wren, see *Wren*.

JENYNS, SOAME (1704–87), educated at St. John's College, Cambridge, was M.P. for Cambridgeshire and for Dunwich, 1742–80, and author of 'Poems' (1752) and of 'A Free Enquiry into the Nature and Origin of Evil' (1757). The latter was vigorously criticized by Johnson in the 'Literary Magazine'. Jenyns also wrote a 'View of the Internal Evidence of the Christian Religion' (1776), which had considerable vogue.

Jephthah's daughter, see Judges xi. 30 et seq. When Jephthah went out against the Ammonites he vowed to sacrifice, if victorious, whatever came forth from his house to meet him. This proved to be his daughter, and he 'did with her according to his vow'. She figures in Tennyson's 'Dream of Fair Women'. (Cf. the story of *Idomeneus*.)

The ballad in Percy's 'Reliques' entitled 'Jephthah Judge of Israel' is that which Hamlet quotes in Shakespeare's play (II. ii).

Jeremiad, a doleful complaint, in allusion to the *Lamentations of Jeremiah* in the O.T.

Jeremy, a character in Congreve's 'Love for Love' (q.v.).

Jeremy Diddler, see *Diddler*.

Jeroboam, a very large wine-bottle, equivalent to six standard bottles (Saintsbury) so called in allusion to Jeroboam, 'a mighty man of valour' (1 Kings xi. 28) 'who made Israel to sin' (xiv. 16) by setting up other sanctuaries besides the Temple.

JEROME, JEROME KLAPKA (1859–1927), novelist and playwright, whose 'Idle Thoughts of an Idle Fellow' and 'Three Men in a Boat' appeared in 1889, and by their blending of humour and sentiment proved very popular; the latter work has been translated into many languages. Jerome's 'The Passing of the Third Floor Back' (1908) brought him fame as a dramatist. With others he founded in 1892 'The Idler', a successful monthly magazine.

JEROME, ST. (HIERONYMUS) (c. 342–420), was born at Strido, on the borders of Dalmatia, of Christian parents, educated at Rome, and baptized in 360. He visited Gaul and Asia Minor, and after a period of dissipation devoted himself to the practice of asceticism. He lived as a hermit near Chalcis (SE. of Antioch), spent the years 382–5 at Rome, where he was the spiritual counsellor of a group of noble Roman ladies, and in 386 settled at Bethlehem, where he died in 420. His principal works were a translation and continuation of the chronicles of Eusebius and the Latin version of the Scriptures which came to be known as the Vulgate. He is commemorated on 30 Sept.

Jeronimo or HIERONIMO, the chief character in Kyd's 'The Spanish Tragedy' (q.v.).

JERROLD, DOUGLAS WILLIAM (1803–57), is chiefly remembered as the contributor to 'Punch' of 'Mrs. Caudle's Curtain Lectures' (q.v.), which added greatly to that periodical's popularity and appeared in book form in 1846. He was also author of the successful plays 'Black-ey'd Susan' (1829) and 'The Bride of Ludgate' (1831). Other amusing comedies by Jerrold were 'The Prisoner of War' (1842), 'Time works Wonders' (1845), and 'The Catspaw' (1850). He wrote in 'Punch', over the signature 'Q', a number of social and political satires of a liberal tendency. He published 'The Story of a Feather' in 1844 and several novels. From 1852 till his death he edited 'Lloyd's Weekly Newspaper'.

Jerry Cruncher, see *Cruncher*.

Jerry Hawthorn, a character in Pierce Egan's 'Life in London' (see *Egan*).

Jerusalem: for the poem of that name by William Blake, see *Blake*.

Jerusalem Chamber, THE, the old abbot's parlour in the monastic buildings of Westminster Abbey, the scene of the conspiracy against Henry IV and of his death. Its name was probably derived from tapestries representing the history of Jerusalem. It became the chapter-house of the abbey at an uncertain date, probably as early as the 16th cent.

Jerusalem Delivered (*Gerusalemme Liberata*), a poem by Tasso (q.v.), published without his consent in 1580 and in authorized form in 1581. (Tasso later rewrote the poem, giving it a more 'regular' structure and a more austere moral tone, and changing the title to 'Gerusalemme Conquistata'. The new work, published in 1593, was inferior to the original.)

The poem is the epic of a crusade, with the addition of romantic and fabulous elements. By the side of Godfrey of Bouillon, the leader of the Christian host besieging Jerusalem, and other historical characters, we have the romantic figures of Sophronia and her lover Olindo, who are prepared to face martyrdom to save the Christians in the beleaguered city; the Amazon Clorinda who is beloved by Tancred the Norman, and killed by him unwittingly; and Armida, the niece of the wizard king of Damascus, who lures away the Christian knights her enchanted gardens. Rinaldo, prince of Este (an imaginary personage, introduced as a way of extolling the author's patron), rescues the prisoners of Armida, and Armida falls in love with him. By her enchantments they live happily together till Rinaldo is summoned away to help the army. He takes the chief part in the capture of Jerusalem.

The poem was translated into English in 1594 by R. Carew, and by Edward Fairfax in 1600 (under the title 'Godfrey of Bulloigne'). Spenser's description of Acrasia's Bower of Bliss ('Faerie Queene', II. xii) was modelled on the gardens of Armida.

Jerusalem, THE NEW, the celestial city (Rev. xxi. 2).

JESPERSEN, JENS OTTO HARRY (1860–1943), Danish philologist, educated at Copenhagen, where he became professor of English in 1893. He wrote many philological books, the most important perhaps being the Modern English Grammar' (four parts, 1909–31), and invented the artificial language Novial.

Jessamy Bride, THE, the name given by Goldsmith (q.v.) to the younger Miss Horneck, with whom he is supposed to have been in love.

Jesse, a genealogical tree representing the genealogy of Christ from 'the root of Jesse' (the father of David, 1 Sam. xvi; cf. Isa. xi. 1), used in churches in the Middle Ages as a decoration of windows, walls, etc., or in the form of a large branched candlestick. Sometimes the tree is represented as rising from the body of Jesse, who is shown recumbent.

Jessica, Shylock's daughter in Shakespeare's 'The Merchant of Venice' (q.v.).

Jessica's First Prayer, a story of a girl waif's awakening to the meaning of religion; written by Hesba Stretton (i.e. Sarah Smith, 1832–1911); first published in 1866, in 'The Sunday at Home', issued in book form in 1867. The work had a sale of over one and a half million copies, and has been translated into every European language, and into most Asiatic and African tongues.

Jesuits, see *Loyola*.

Jew, THE WANDERING, see *Wandering Jew*.

Jew of Malta, *The*, a drama in blank verse by Marlowe (q.v.), produced about 1592 but not published until 1633.

The Grand Seignior of Turkey having demanded the tribute of Malta, the governor of Malta decides that it shall be paid by the Jews of the island. Barabas, a rich Jew, who resists the edict, has all his wealth impounded and his house turned into a nunnery. In revenge he indulges in an orgy of slaughter, procuring the death of his daughter Abigail's lover among others, and poisoning Abigail herself. Malta being besieged by the Turks, he betrays the fortress to them, and, as a reward, is made its governor. He now plots the destruction of the Turkish commander and his force at a banquet by means of a collapsible floor; but is himself betrayed and hurled through this same floor into a cauldron, where he dies.

JEWETT, SARAH ORNE (1849–1909), American author, born in Maine, known for her stories of New England life, and particularly for 'The Country of the Pointed Firs' (1896). Among her other books are: 'Deephaven' (1877), 'A White Heron' (1886), 'The Tory Lover' (1901).

JEWSBURY, GERALDINE ENDSOR (1812–80), novelist and intimate friend of the Carlyles. She was the author of 'Zoe' (1845), 'The Half-Sisters' (1848), 'Marian Withers' (1851), and 'Right or Wrong' (1859). Her sister MARIA JANE JEWSBURY (afterwards Mrs. Fletcher) published 'Phantasmagoria' (1824), 'The Three Histories' (1830),and other works.

Jezebel, the proud and infamous wife of Ahab, king of Israel (1 Kings xvi. 31, xix, and 2 Kings ix), hence used allusively of a wicked, impudent, or abandoned woman; also of a painted woman (2 Kings ix. 30).

Jihad or JEHAD, a religious war of Muslims against unbelievers in Islam, inculcated as a duty by the Koran and by traditions.

Jingle, ALFRED, a character in Dickens's 'The Pickwick Papers' (q.v.).

Jingo. The word appears first about 1670 as a piece of conjurer's gibberish, usually *hey* or *high jingo!*, probably a mere piece of sonorous nonsense. In 1694 *by jingo* occurs in Motteux's translation of Rabelais, where the French has 'par Dieu'. This may be presumed (though not proved) to be the same as the conjurer's word, substituted for a sacred name (cf. 'by Gosh', etc.). A recent conjecture that *jingo* is from the Basque word for God (*Jinko, Jainko*), caught up from Basque sailors, is not impossible, but is, as yet unsupported by evidence.

The word was adopted as a nickname for those who supported the policy of Lord Beaconsfield in sending a British fleet into Turkish waters to resist the advance of Russia in 1878, from the refrain of a music-hall song of the period ('We don't want to fight, but by Jingo if we do'). It is extended to advocates in general of bellicose nationalism in dealing with foreign powers. [OED.]

Jiniwin, MRS., in Dickens's 'Old Curiosity Shop' (q.v.), the mother of Mrs. Quilp.

Jinn or DJINN, in Muslim demonology, an intermediate order of beings between angels and men, created out of fire, said to have the power of assuming human or animal forms, and to have a supernatural influence over men. There are good and evil jinn. See also under *Genius*.

Jo, the crossing-sweeper in Dickens's 'Bleak House' (q.v.).

Joan of Arc, ST. (1412–31), JEANNE D'ARC, or more correctly JEANNE DARC, as it was spelt in all contemporary documents (Littré), the daughter of Jacques Darc, an agriculturist of Domremy in the valley of the Meuse, an illiterate girl who contributed powerfully to liberate France from the English in the reign of Charles VII. Her mission was a double one, (1) to raise the siege of Orléans; (2) to conduct Charles to his coronation at Rheims. She accomplished both these tasks and then wished to return home; but she yielded to the demands of the French patriots and was taken prisoner by the Burgundians, who handed her over to the English. But it was a French court of ecclesiastics (with the help of the Inquisition) who sentenced her as a witch, and the English who burned her at Rouen. She was at last canonized in 1920. She is the subject of Voltaire's 'La Pucelle', of a tragedy by Schiller, of a poem by Southey, and of dramas by G. B. Shaw and Anouilh.

Joan, POPE, a mythical female pope, supposed to have intervened as John VIII between Leo IV and Benedict III in the 9th cent. She was described as of English descent, though born in Germany. After fleeing, disguised as a man, to Greece with her lover, a Benedictine monk, she was said to have removed to Rome and there risen to be a cardinal and ultimately to the papacy, and to have died in childbirth during a procession. From a simple mention (probably a later interpolation) in the chronicle of the contemporary Anastasius Bibliothecarius that Joanna, a woman, succeeded Leo as pope in 854, the story was developed by the addition of the above details. Its truth has repeatedly been contested, and it was finally shown to be unfounded by Döllinger ('Papstfabeln des Mittelalters', Engl. tr. 1872). The name of the Pope-Joan card game is perhaps a corruption of *nain jaune*, its name in French.

Job, the hero of the O.T. book that bears his name, a wealthy and prosperous man suddenly overtaken by dire calamities. These give rise to discussions between Job and the friends who come to visit him (*Job's comforters*) as to the connexion between suffering and sin, the friends assuming that Job's misfortunes are a punishment, while Job maintains his innocence. Job is the typical example of patience under misfortune.

Job Thornberry, see *John Bull*.

Job Trotter, a character in Dickens's 'The Pickwick Papers' (q.v.).

Joblillies, see *Panjandrum*.

Jocasta, see *Oedipus*.

Jocasta, a tragedy in blank verse, translated from an Italian adaptation of the 'Phoenissae' of Euripides, by George Gascoigne (q.v.) and F. Kinwelmarshe, included in Gascoigne's 'Posies', published in 1575.

JOCELIN DE BRAKELOND (*fl.* 1200), a monk of Bury St. Edmunds, whose chronicle of his abbey (1173–1202) inspired Carlyle's 'Past and Present'.

Jocelyn, ROSE, a character in Meredith's 'Evan Harrington' (q.v.).

Jock o' Hazeldean, a ballad, of which one stanza is ancient, the rest by Sir W. Scott. The lady is to marry young Frank, chief of Errington, but she weeps for Jock. On her wedding-day she is found to have eloped with him over the Border.

Jockey Club, THE, founded in 1750 or 1751 to administer racing at Newmarket, now controls racing throughout England, grants licences to jockeys, settles disputes, etc.

Jockey of Norfolk, in the lines:

Jockey of Norfolk, be not so bold,
For Dickon thy master is bought and sold
(Shakespeare, Richard III, v. iii. 305–6.)

was Sir John Howard, first duke of Norfolk, who commanded Richard's vanguard at the battle of Bosworth, and was slain.

Joe, 'the fat boy' in Dickens's 'The Pickwick Papers' (q.v.).

Joe Gargery, a character in Dickens's 'Great Expectations' (q.v.).

Joe Manton, ' a name given to fowling-pieces made by Joseph Manton, a celebrated London gunsmith' (1766?–1835) (Farmer, 'Slang').

Joe Miller's Jests, a jest-book by John Mottley (q.v.), published in 1739. The name is taken from Joseph Miller (1684–1738), an actor in the Drury Lane company and reputed humorist. A 'Joe Miller' is a stale jest.

Johannes Factotum, 'John Do-everything', a Jack of all trades, a would-be universal genius. The phrase, as also *Dominus Factotum, Magister Factotum,* and the corresponding Italian *fa il tutto,* is found in the 16th cent. It occurs in Greene's famous attack on Shakespeare in 'A Groatsworth of Wit bought with a Million of Repentance' (q.v.):

'Being an absolute *Johannes fac totum,* is in his owne conceit the only Shake-scene in a countrey.'

John, king of England, 1199–1216.

JOHN, AUGUSTUS EDWIN, O.M. (1878–1961), painter, born at Tenby and trained at the Slade School. His portraits and drawings show great technical virtuosity. His autobiography, 'Chiaroscuro' (1952), contains much good gossip about writers whom he met or knew as friends, such as Oscar Wilde, Yeats, Shaw, James Joyce, Wyndham Lewis, and T. E. Lawrence.

John, DON, a character in Shakespeare's 'Much Ado about Nothing' (q.v.).

John, FRIAR, Frère Jean des Entommeures, see *Gargantua* and *Thelema*.

John, LITTLE, one of the companions of Robin Hood (q.v.).

John, PRESTER, see *Prester John*.

John Anderson, my Jo, a lyric by Burns (q.v.), suggested to him by an older song.

John Barleycorn, see *Barleycorn*.

John Brown's body lies a-mouldering in the grave, a famous marching song of the American Civil War. See *Brown (John, 'of Osawatomie')*.

John Bull, The History of, a collection of pamphlets by Arbuthnot (q.v.), issued in 1712, and rearranged and republished in Pope and Swift's 'Miscellanies' of 1727.

The pamphlets, of which the first appeared on 6 Mar. 1712, were designed to advocate, in the form of humorous allegories, the cessation of the war with France, the various parties concerned being designated under the names of John Bull, Nicholas Frog (the Dutch), Lord Strutt (Philip of Spain), Lewis Baboon (the French king). Bull and Frog are engaged in a law-suit with Baboon, and their case is put in the hands of Humphrey Hocus, an attorney (the duke of Marlborough), and won. John Bull, however, discovers an intrigue between Hocus and Mrs. Bull, his first wife (the Whig parliament), and trouble follows. Mrs. Bull dies and John marries again (the Tory parliament), but is much disturbed at the cost of the litigation. The second and subsequent pamphlets are conceived on the same lines, satirizing the Whigs, and dealing with various current political topics.

John Bull himself is described as 'an honest plain-dealing fellow, choleric, bold, and of a very inconstant temper ... very apt to quarrel with his best friends, especially if they pretended to govern him. ... John's temper depended very much upon the air; his spirits rose and fell with the weather-glass. John was quick and understood his business very well ... a boon companion, loving his bottle and his diversion'.

'John Bull' is also the title of a play by George Colman the younger, acted in 1803, and containing the well-known character, Job Thornberry, an honest tradesman, generous and kindhearted, but irascible under a sense of injustice, supposed to typify the national character.

John Buncle, Esq., The Life of, a work of fiction by Amory (q.v.), published in two volumes in 1756–66.

This strange book takes the form of an autobiography, and the hero, in the words of the 'illustrious Miss Noel', his first love, is 'an odd compound of a man'. Like the author himself, he is a Unitarian, a man of learning and serious tastes, amorous but virtuous in a way. He marries seven wives in succession, each of them dying within a couple of years, and each of them surpassingly beautiful and clever. Statia's 'bright victorious eyes flash celestial fire', and she says 'two or three good things on the beauty of the morning'. Miss Spence has 'the head of Aristotle, the heart of a primitive Christian, and the form of Venus de Medicis', and discusses the differential calculus after supper. Miss Turner dies with a Latin quotation on her lips. After the death of each—he is not a believer in a long period of mourning—he sets out to see if he can find 'another good country girl for a wife and get a little more money'. The story of his matrimonial ventures is varied with digressions on religious, literary, and scientific subjects, descriptions of scenery, algebra and trigonometry, and a good deal of eating and drinking.

John Company, see *East India Company.*

John de Reeve, the subject of an old ballad, containing a comic element. He is a sturdy independent 'villein', who rides to court with pitchfork and sword, and is knighted.

John Doe and **Richard Roe,** legal fictions in old actions of ejectment, adopted to simplify the old procedure under which a number of irrelevant matters had to be proved. The fictitious John Doe was stated to have entered under a lease granted by the plaintiff, and to have been ejected by the fictitious Richard Roe, who made no defence and was allowed to be replaced by the true defendant, the tenant in possession. All that was thus left to the court to decide was the real point at issue, whether the plaintiff or defendant had the better title. (See Holdsworth, 'History of English Law'.) All this was swept away by the Common Law Procedure Act, 1852.

John Gilpin, The Diverting History of, a poem by Cowper (q.v.), first published anonymously in the 'Public Advertiser', reprinted in chapbook form, and included in the same volume as 'The Task' in 1785. The story of John Gilpin was told to Cowper by Lady Austen to divert him from melancholy. He laughed over it during the night and next day had turned it into a ballad.

John Gilpin, a 'linen-draper bold' of Cheapside, and his wife, decide to celebrate their twentieth wedding-day by a trip to the Bell at Edmonton, he on a borrowed horse, she, her sister, and the children in a chaise and pair. But when John's horse begins to trot John loses control; and the poem describes his headlong career to Edmonton, and ten miles beyond it to Ware, and then back again.

Nor stopped till where he had got up
He did again get down.

It appears that John Gilpin was the name of a real citizen of London, owning land near Olney, where Cowper was living in 1785.

John Halifax, Gentleman, a novel by Dinah Mulock (q.v.), published in 1857.

This is the plain domestic tale of a poor but honest and hard-working boy, left an orphan in childhood, who by his own exertions and with the help of Phineas Fletcher, the son of one of his employers, improves his education, achieves a good position, and marries the heroine, Ursula March. The story is intended to illustrate the doctrine that the character of a true gentleman resides in integrity and nobility of purpose, rather than in birth and wealth.

John Inglesant, an historical novel by Shorthouse (q.v.), published in 1881 (privately printed in 1880).

The story is set in the time of Charles I and the Commonwealth. John Inglesant, a high-souled gentleman, of a serious and mystical cast of mind, is brought in his early years under the influence of a Jesuit emissary and becomes the tool of the Jesuit body in the political intrigues that attended the later years of Charles I. He comes into close contact with the community of Little Gidding (see under *Ferrar, Nicholas*), and falls in love with Mary Collet, a member of the community. He joins the court of Charles I and is employed by him in the dangerous negotiations for bringing an Irish army into England. When these are discovered, he is repudiated by the king, and his loyal refusal to betray his master nearly costs him his head. After the death of Charles I he passes to Italy, partly for the purpose of discovering and taking vengeance on an Italian ruffian who has murdered his brother. The story presents a picture of the Italian life of the period, and of the religious factions and political intrigues, culminating in the long-drawn-out election of a pope on the death of Innocent X. The reaction of the hero's character to various temptations and influences (including that of Molinos, the founder of the Quietists, q.v.) is described, the climax being reached when his brother's murderer finally falls into his power, and he renounces his own vengeance and leaves him to that of God. The style of the 17th cent. is admirably imitated. But it has recently been discovered that Shorthouse drew certain passages from 17th-cent. books.

John of Gaunt (1340–99), Duke of Lancaster, fourth son of Edward III, born at Ghent ('Gaunt'), a notable figure in political history, a patron of Wycliffe and Chaucer, and a character in Shakespeare's 'Richard II'.

John o' Groat's House, at the extreme NE. point of the Scottish mainland, is the reputed site of an octagonal house said to have been built in the 16th cent. by a Dutchman, John Groot, who migrated thither and was followed by other members of the Groot family. Disputes arose among them as to precedence at the annual feasts, and to settle these John Groot built his house with eight doors, so that each claimant could enter by his own door and sit at his own table.

JOHN OF SALISBURY (*d.* 1180) was born at Salisbury and studied at Paris under Abélard (q.v.) and at Chartres. He returned to England about 1150, residing mainly at Canterbury, where he was secretary to Archbishop Theobald and was sent on missions to Rome. He fell into disfavour with Henry II and retired to Rheims, where he composed his 'Historia Pontificalis'. He was present in Canterbury Cathedral when Becket was murdered, wrote his life, and urged his canonization. He also wrote a life of Anselm with a view to his canonization. He became bishop of Chartres in 1176. He was not only an able politician and ecclesiastic but the most learned classical writer of his time; he may be called the fine flower of the first (primitive) Renaissance. His works include the 'Policraticus' or 'De Nugis Curialium', on the vanities of the court and miscellaneous questions of philosophy and learning; the 'Metalogicon', a treatise on logic and an account of Aristotle's treatment of the subject; and the 'Entheticus', an elegiac poem in praise of Becket. There is a 'Life' of John of Salisbury (1932) by C. C. J. Webb, who made splendid editions of the 'Policraticus' and 'Metalogicon'.

John o' Scales, see *Heir of Linne.*

John of the Cross, ST. (1549–91), a Spanish mystical poet and a friar of the Carmelite order. He was canonized in 1726.

John Silence, a novel by Algernon Blackwood, published in 1908. John Silence is a 'psychic doctor' and the book is a collection of narratives of uncanny psychic experiences.

John Thomson's man or JOHN TAMSON'S MAN, a Scottish proverbial appellation for a man who is governed by his wife (Scott, 'Old Mortality', xxxviii). The origin of the expression is unknown. W. C. Hazlitt states that it occurs in the works of Dunbar (q.v.).

John-a-Nokes, a fictitious name for one of the parties in a legal action, usually coupled with JOHN-A-STILES as the name of the other.

Johnson, Anecdotes of the late Samuel, by Mrs. Piozzi (see *Thrale),* published in 1786.

Johnson, ESTHER, Swift's 'Stella', see *Swift.*

JOHNSON, LIONEL PIGOT (1867–1902), educated at Winchester and New College, Oxford, a scholar-poet and critic. He became a Roman Catholic. His chief works are 'Postliminium' (essays and critical papers, 1912), 'The Art of Thomas Hardy' (1896), and two books of verse, 'Poems' (1895) and 'Ireland' (1897). He contributed to the 'Spectator', 'Academy', 'Athenaeum', 'Daily Chronicle', etc.

JOHNSON, RICHARD (1573–1659?), was a freeman of London, and author of the

'Famous Historie of the Seven Champions of Christendom' (q.v., *c.* 1597), 'The Nine Worthies of London' (1592), 'The Crowne Garland of Golden Roses' (1612, reprinted by the Percy Society), and 'Pleasant Conceites of Old Hobson' (1607, reprinted 1843).

Johnson, THE REVD. SAMUEL (1649–1703), a Whig divine who was imprisoned, pilloried, fined, and whipped for his Protestant pamphlets. He received a pension and bounty from William III. He figures in 'Absalom and Achitophel' (q.v.) as 'Ben-Jochanan'.

JOHNSON, SAMUEL (1709–84), born at Lichfield, the son of a bookseller of that town. When 3 years old he was brought to London to be touched for the king's evil by Queen Anne. He was educated at Lichfield Grammar School and at Pembroke College, Oxford, where he spent fourteen months in 1728–9, but took no degree. His father died in 1731 and left his family in poverty, and Johnson's career for a time is not clearly known. He worked as an usher at Market Bosworth and lived for a time at Birmingham, where he contributed essays to the 'Birmingham Journal'. In 1735 he published anonymously a condensed translation of a French version of Father Lobo's 'Voyage to Abyssinia'. In the same year he married Mrs. Elizabeth Porter, a widow considerably older than himself, and started a private school at Edial, near Lichfield. This was not successful, and in 1737, accompanied by one of his pupils, David Garrick (q.v.), he set out for London, which was henceforth to be his home. He entered the service of Edward Cave, the printer (1691–1754), who had founded 'The Gentleman's Magazine' (q.v.) in 1731. To this he contributed essays, poems (notably 'Friendship, an Ode'), Latin verses, biographies, and reports of parliamentary debates. The latter were in reality discussions in Johnson's own language of the current political questions, for which the speeches actually made in parliament furnished merely a basis. In 1738 he published his poem 'London' (q.v.). In 1744 appeared his notable 'Life of Mr. Richard Savage', subsequently included in the 'Lives of the Poets', the affectionate record of a friend with whom he had shared extreme poverty (see under *Savage, Richard).* In 1747 he issued the 'Plan' of his 'Dictionary' (see *Johnson's Dictionary),* addressed to Lord Chesterfield, with results referred to under the name of that nobleman. In 1749 he published 'The Vanity of Human Wishes' (q.v.), his longest and best poem, and in the same year Garrick produced his tragedy 'Irene', which Johnson had written in 1736 at Edial, and which is little but a series of dialogues on moral themes between Mahomet, emperor of the Turks, his attendants, and various Greek captives. By this act of kindness of Garrick's, Johnson made nearly £300. In 1750 he started the 'Rambler' (q.v.), a periodical written almost entirely by himself, which ran until 1752 (when his wife died), appearing twice a week. From March 1753 to March 1754 Johnson contributed regularly to Hawkesworth's 'Adventurer'. His lives of Cheynel and Cave were contributed, the first to 'The Student' in 1751, the second to 'The Gentleman's Magazine' in 1754. The 'Dictionary' was published in 1755, and an abridgement in 1756. In the same year he contributed to Smart's 'Universal Visiter' and during this year and the next edited the 'Literary Magazine', which published a number of his political articles and reviews, including his essay on tea, and his criticism of Soame Jenyns's 'Free Enquiry into the Nature and Origin of Evil'. In 1757 he also contributed the introduction to the 'Morning Chronicle'. He wrote the life of Sir T. Browne which is prefixed to his edition of that author's 'Christian Morals' (1756), and the life of Ascham in J. Bennet's edition of his Works (1761). During 1758–60 he contributed the 'Idler' (q.v.) series of papers to the 'Universal Chronicle'. In 1759 appeared his 'Rasselas, Prince of Abyssinia' (q.v.). In 1762 Johnson received, on Wedderburn's application, a pension of £300 a year from Lord Bute, and in 1763 made the acquaintance of James Boswell (q.v.), his biographer. It was in the next year (1764) that 'The Club', later known as the 'Literary Club', was founded, including, besides Johnson, among its original members Reynolds, Burke, and Goldsmith, to whom Garrick, C. J. Fox, and Boswell were shortly added. The Club held its meetings at the Turk's Head in Gerrard Street. Besides a number of writings of minor importance, including an exposure of the Cock Lane ghost, he worked at his edition of Shakespeare, which after much delay was published in 1765; although superseded by later scholarship, it contained valuable notes and some emendations that have been maintained. He was introduced to the Thrales (q.v.) in 1764, in whose town and country houses he was hospitably received. In 1773 Johnson undertook a journey with Boswell to the Scottish Highlands and Hebrides, recorded in his 'Journey to the Western Islands of Scotland' (1775) and in Boswell's 'Journal of a Tour to the Hebrides' (1785). Johnson's diary of his tour with the Thrales in 1774 to north Wales was printed in 1816. In 1777 he undertook, at the request of a number of booksellers, to write the 'Lives of the Poets' (q.v.), published in 1779–81. In 1783 the death of his faithful old dependant, Robert Levett, elicited his beautiful little elegy, 'His virtues walked their narrow round', and in 1784, after two melancholy years, further saddened by the death of his friend Thrale and his quarrel with Mrs. Thrale, he died at his house in Bolt Court and was buried in Westminster Abbey. A monument was erected to him in St. Paul's. Johnson's literary output bears no proportion to his reputation. The latter is due in great measure to the fortunate accident by which an ideal biographer was found in Boswell to record for us the humour, wit, and sturdy common sense of his

conversation, and a kindness of heart sometimes concealed under a gruff exterior.

Apart from Boswell's 'Life', much information about Johnson is to be found in Mrs. Piozzi's (Mrs. Thrale's) 'Anecdotes of the late Samuel Johnson' (1786) and in his 'Life' by Sir John Hawkins (1787). Besides those of Johnson's works above referred to, mention may be made of the following: translation into Latin verse of Pope's 'Messiah' (1731), written while Johnson was at college, and commended by Pope himself; 'Marmor Norfolciense: or an Essay on an ancient Prophetical Inscription' (1739), a political pamphlet in ironical disguise; 'A Compleat Vindication of the Licensers of the Stage' (1739), an ironical attack on them for refusing Brooke's 'Gustavus Vasa'; the 'Proposals' for printing the catalogue of the Harleian Library, and the 'Account' of it (1742–4); the 'Proposals' for, and the introduction to, the 'Harleian Miscellany' (q.v.), published in 1744, and the latter reprinted separately as an 'Essay on the Origin and Importance of Small Tracts and Fugitive Pieces'; 'Miscellaneous Observations on the Tragedy of Macbeth' (1745), an anticipation of the edition of Shakespeare; an apologue of human life entitled 'The Vision of Theodore, the Hermit of Teneriffe', contributed in 1748 to 'The Preceptor' (a work on education published by Dodsley), which Johnson described to Percy as the best thing he ever wrote; dedications to Mrs. Lennox's 'Female Quixote' (1753) and 'Shakespeare Illustrated' (1754), and many other dedications, prologues, etc.; 'An Account of an Attempt to ascertain the Longitude at Sea' (1755), written for Zachariah Williams; three letters in the 'Gazetteer' on the plans for Blackfriars bridge (1759); reviews in the 'Critical Review' of Goldsmith's 'Traveller' and of two other works (1763–4); 'Considerations on the Corn Laws' written in 1766 for 'single speech' Hamilton, and printed in Hamilton's 'Parliamentary Logick' (1808); four political pamphlets, 'The False Alarm' (1770), 'Thoughts . . . respecting Falkland's Islands' (1771), 'The Patriot' (1774), and 'Taxation no Tyranny' (1775); 'Occasional Papers by the late William Dodd, D.D.' (by Johnson, except Dodd's 'Account of Himself', suppressed but published in 1785). Johnson's remarkable 'Prayers and Meditations' were published in 1785, also two volumes of sermons (1788–9). His 'Poems' (ed. D. N. Smith and E. L. McAdam) were published in 1941; his 'letters' (ed. R. W. Chapman) in 1952.

Johnson, The Life of Samuel, by Boswell (q.v.), published in 1791.

Boswell informed Johnson in 1772 of his intention to write his life, and had collected materials for the purpose ever since he first met him in 1763. After Johnson's death in 1784 he set to work arranging and adding to the 'prodigious multiplicity of materials', a task which, he writes in 1789, involved him in great labour, perplexity, and vexation. The final edition, after Boswell's death, was revised by Edmund Malone. The standard edition, that of G. B. Hill, has been revised by Dr. L. F. Powell (1934–50; 1964).

Johnson's Dictionary, *A Dictionary of the English Language*, by S. Johnson (q.v.), published in 1755.

The prospectus of the Dictionary was issued in 1747 (for the incident with Lord Chesterfield to which it gave rise see under *Chesterfield, earl of*). Johnson's object was to produce 'a dictionary by which the pronunciation of our language may be fixed, and its attainment facilitated; by which its purity may be preserved, its use ascertained, and its duration lengthened'. In his collection of words he does not go back further than the works of Sidney, holding that 'from the authors which rose in the time of Elizabeth a speech might be formed adequate to all the purposes of use or elegance'. As regards words imported from other languages he 'warned others against the folly of naturalizing useless foreigners to the injury of the natives'. His derivations suffer from the scantiness of etymological knowledge in his day. But the dictionary is principally remarkable for the definitions of the meanings of words, and for the quotations in illustration of their use. Five editions of the Dictionary were published in Johnson's lifetime.

Johnson's 'Dixonary' was Miss Pinkerton's invariable present to departing scholars. Becky Sharp threw her copy into the garden as the coach drove off ('Vanity Fair', ch. i).

JOHNSTONE, CHARLES, see *Adventures of a Guinea*.

JOINVILLE, JEAN DE (1244–1317), seneschal of Champagne, and a witness of the events of the disastrous crusade of Louis IX, wrote a vivid account of the latter in his 'Histoire de Saint Louis'.

Jolly Beggars, *The*, a cantata by Burns (q.v.), written in 1785.

A company of vagrants meet and carouse in a hedge ale-house. There is a maimed soldier, a fiddler, a strolling player, a ballad-singer, with their female companions. Each sings a song in character, and the songs are connected by vivid descriptions of the various rogues.

Jolly Roger, the pirates' black flag.

Jonah, A, a bearer of ill-luck, an allusion to the O.T. story. When Jonah was ordered to prophesy against Nineveh, he sailed instead for Tarshish. A tempest arising, the sailors threw lots to know for whose cause it was sent, and the lot fell upon Jonah, whom they accordingly cast into the sea. He was swallowed by 'a great fish' and thrown up again upon the land.

Jonathan, see *David and Jonathan*.

Jonathan, BROTHER, see *Brother Jonathan*.

Jonathan Wild the Great, *The Life of*, a satirical romance by H. Fielding (q.v.), published in his 'Miscellanies' in 1743. See also *Wild*.

The author's purpose is to expose the true meaning and reward of 'greatness' as distinct from 'goodness', when the 'greatness' is not obscured by worldly eminence. He relates the career of a consummate rogue, from his birth and his baptism by Titus Oates, to his arrival at the 'tree of glory', the gallows. The hero, having shown at school his disposition for iniquity, enters on his career of crime under the auspices of Mr. Snap, keeper of a sponging-house, and shows dexterity as a pickpocket. He becomes the chief of a gang of robbers, contriving their exploits, taking the largest share of the booty, keeping himself out of the clutches of the law, and maintaining discipline by denouncing any of the gang who contest his authority. He marries Snap's daughter, Letitia, who is as worthless as himself, and whose assumption of virtue provides some amusing scenes. His principal undertaking is his attempt to ruin the fortunes and domestic happiness of his old schoolfellow, the virtuous jeweller Heartfree. He robs him and gets him locked up as a bankrupt, induces Heartfree's wife by a trick to leave England, accuses Heartfree of having made away with her, and brings him within an ace of execution. But his trickery is fortunately exposed, and he meets his end with the 'greatness' that has distinguished him throughout.

Jonathan's, a coffee-house in Change Alley, Cornhill, referred to in the 'Tatler' (No. 38) and the 'Spectator' (No. 1) as a mart for stock-jobbers.

JONES, DAVID (1895–   ), writer and artist. 'In Parenthesis' (1937), based on his experiences in the First World War, is experimental in form, being written partly in prose and partly in free verse. 'Anathemata' (1952) is a religious poem which combines references to the Catholic Mass with images from the author's personal and racial past.

JONES, HENRY ARTHUR (1851–1929), dramatist, of a Welsh dissenting family, was for a time a shop assistant. Among his successful plays were: 'A Clerical Error' (1879, a one-act comedy in which the author himself acted), 'The Silver King' (1882, in which Henry Herman in a small degree collaborated, and which enjoyed great popularity), 'Saints and Sinners' (1884), 'The Middleman' (1889), 'The Dancing Girl' (1891). In 'The Crusaders' (1891), 'The Masqueraders' (1894), 'The Case of Rebellious Susan' (1894), 'The Triumph of the Philistines' (1895), and 'Dolly Reforming Herself' (1908), Jones showed an increased command of the art of comedy, and reached his masterpiece in 1897 in 'The Liars', acted by Charles Wyndham and Mary Moore. 'Michael and his Lost Angel', which Jones believed his best play, proved a failure on the stage in 1896. Jones wrote in all some sixty plays, and also 'The Renascence of the English Drama' (1896), 'Foundations of a

National Drama' (1913), and 'The Theatre of Ideas, A Burlesque Allegory' (1914). His 'Life' by his daughter appeared in 1930.

Jones, INIGO (1573–1652), architect, who introduced into England the fully realized Renaissance style based on Palladio and Roman antiquities, which he had studied in Italy. He designed settings for court masques by Ben Jonson and others, introducing the proscenium arch and movable scenery. He quarrelled with Ben Jonson, who satirized him as 'In-and-In Medlay' in 'A Tale of a Tub' (q.v.). In 1615 he was made royal surveyor and designed the Queen's House at Greenwich and the Banqueting House, Whitehall. He built a classical façade to old St. Paul's, and worked on the layout of Covent Garden piazza and Lincoln's Inn Fields.

Jones, JOHN PAUL (1747–92), naval adventurer, was the son of a Kircudbrightshire gardener named Paul. After some years spent in the slave trade, smuggling, and trading to the W. Indies, he entered the American navy in 1775. While in command of the 'Ranger' he took the fort at Whitehaven and captured the 'Drake' off Carrickfergus (1778), and in the following year in the 'Bonhomme Richard', accompanied by three French ships and one American, threatened Edinburgh and captured the 'Serapis'. Jones afterwards served in the French navy.

JONES, SIR WILLIAM (1746–94), educated at Harrow and at University College, Oxford, a distinguished orientalist and jurist, was judge of the high court at Calcutta from 1783 till his death. He published his 'Essay on Bailments' in 1781, but is best known for his works on oriental languages: 'Poeseos Asiaticae Commentariorum Libri Sex' (1774), his version of the Arabic 'Moallakat' (1783), his translations of the 'Hitopadesa' and 'Sakuntala,' and his 'Persian Grammar' (1771). He also began 'The Institutes of Hindu Law, or Ordinances of Manu'. Jones mastered Sanskrit and was a pioneer in the science of comparative philology. His collected works were edited by Lord Teignmouth (1799).

JONSON, BENJAMIN (1572–1637) ('Ben Jonson'), was of Border descent, but born probably in Westminster. He was educated at Westminster School under William Camden, and was for a time in the business of his stepfather, a bricklayer. His occupation from 1591/2 to 1597 is uncertain, but included some voluntary military service in Flanders. In 1597 he began to work for Henslowe's company as player and playwright. He killed a fellow actor in a duel, but escaped death by benefit of clergy, 1598; became a Roman Catholic during imprisonment, but abjured twelve years later. His 'Every Man in his Humour' (q.v.), with Shakespeare in the cast, was performed by the lord chamberlain's company at the Curtain, 1598, and 'Every Man out of his Humour' (q.v.) at the Globe, 1599; his 'Cynthia's Revels' (q.v.), 1600, and 'The Poetaster' (q.v., attacking Dekker and

Marston), 1601, were performed by the children of the Queen's Chapel. In 1600–1 he was writing additions to Kyd's 'Spanish Tragedy' (q.v.). His first extant tragedy, 'Sejanus' (q.v.) was given at the Globe by Shakespeare's company, 1603; his first court masque 'of Blacknesse' (with scenery by Inigo Jones, q.v.) was given on Twelfth Night, 1605. He was temporarily imprisoned for his share in 'Eastward hoe' (q.v.), a play reflecting on the Scots. His 'Volpone' (q.v.) was acted at both the Globe and the two universities in 1606. 'Epicœne, or the Silent Woman' (q.v.) followed in 1609; 'The Alchemist' (q.v.) in 1610; 'Bartholomew Fayre' (q.v.) in 1614; and 'The Devil is an Ass' (q.v.) in 1616. Though not formally appointed the first poet laureate, the essentials of the position were conferred on him in 1616, when a pension was granted to him by James I. In 1618 he went to Scotland, where he was entertained by Drummond of Hawthornden (q.v.), who recorded their conversation. He produced 'The Staple of News' (q.v.), his last great play, in 1625. He was elected chronologer of London in 1628. 'The New Inn', a comedy, which shows decline in his powers, and proved a failure, was produced in 1629. From 1605 onwards he was constantly producing masques (q.v.) for the court, a form of entertainment that reached its highest elaboration in Jonson's hands. He introduced into it the 'antimasque', sometimes a foil to the principal masque, sometimes a dramatic scene, frequently of Aristophanic comedy. We have instances of this in the 'Masque of Queens' (1609), 'Love Restored' (1612), 'Mercury vindicated from the Alchemists' (1615), 'Pleasure reconciled to Vertue' (1618, which gave Milton his idea for 'Comus'), and 'Newes from the New World' (1621). Jonson quarrelled with Inigo Jones after production of the masque 'Chloridia', 1630, and lost court patronage. He produced 'The Magnetic Lady', 1632, and 'A Tale of a Tub', 1633 (comedies, qq.v.); his last masques were produced in 1633–4. He was buried in Westminster Abbey and celebrated in a collection of elegies entitled 'Jonsonus Virbius' (1637–8). His friends included Bacon, Selden, Chapman, Beaumont, Fletcher, Donne, and Shakespeare, and of the younger writers (his 'sons') Cartwright, Herrick, Suckling, Sir Kenelm Digby, and Lord Falkland. Among his patrons were the Sidneys, the earl of Pembroke, and the duke and duchess of Newcastle. His poems include 'Epigrammes' (containing the epitaph on Salathiel Pavy, the boy actor) and 'The Forrest' (q.v.), printed in the folio of 1616, 'Underwoods' (q.v.), printed in 1640 and translations. His chief prose work is 'Timber; or Discoveries made upon Men and Matter' (q.v.), 1640. His works have been edited by William Gifford (1816) and Colonel Cunningham (1875); the standard edition by C. H. Herford and P. and E. Simpson in 11 vols. was published between 1925 and 1951.

As a man Jonson was arrogant and quarrelsome, but fearless, warm-hearted, and intellectually honest. The estimate of him formed by his contemporaries is summed up in the inscription of one of these upon his tomb, 'O rare Ben Jonson', which has been adopted as his epitaph.

Jonsonus Virbius, see *Jonson.*

Jordan, DOROTHY (1761–1816), actress, *née* Phillips, made her first stage appearance in 1779 in Dublin under the name of Miss Francis. She came to England and adopted the name of Mrs. Jordan, under which she appeared as Calista at Leeds in 1782. She made her début at Drury Lane as Peggy in 'The Country Girl' in 1785, and took many parts there, at the Haymarket, and at Covent Garden, Lady Teazle being one of her finest roles. Her last London performance was in 1814 and her final stage appearance at Margate in 1815. She was much praised by Hazlitt, Lamb, Leigh Hunt, etc. She was for long mistress of the duke of Clarence (William IV), and bore him ten children. She went to France in 1815 and died at St. Cloud.

Jorkins, see *Spenlow and Jorkins.*

Jörmungander, in Scandinavian mythology a monstrous serpent, the offspring of Loki (q.v.). Odin threw it into the ocean, where it grew till it encircled the whole earth, finally swallowing its own tail. It was also known as the *Midgard Serpent.*

Jorrocks, JOHN, 'a great city grocer of the old school' and a natural born sportsman whose lot was cast behind the counter instead of in the country, is, with Mr. Sponge and Mr. Facey Romford, among the celebrated characters of the novels of R. S. Surtees (q.v.). He first appears in 'Jorrocks' Jaunts and Jollities' (published in periodical form in 1831–4, and as a book in 1838), and later in 'Handley Cross', etc., becoming master of the Handley Cross foxhounds.

Josaphat, see *Barlaam and Josaphat.*

José, DON, the father of the hero in Byron's 'Don Juan' (q.v.).

Joseph, a long cloak, buttoned down the front, with a small cape, worn chiefly by women in the 18th cent. when riding, so called in allusion to the upper coat which Joseph left behind him (Genesis xxxix).

A pea-green Joseph was her favourite dress.
  (Crabbe, 'Parish Register', III).

Joseph and his brethren, an allusion to the story, in Gen. xxxvi et seq., of Joseph the son of Jacob, the jealousy of his brethren, his sale to Ishmaelites who took him to Egypt and sold him to Potiphar, and his reception of his brethren, when he had been advanced to be ruler over Egypt and they came there to buy corn at a time of famine. 'Joseph and his Brethren' is the title of a drama by Charles Jeremiah Wells (1799?–1879), published under a pseudonym in 1823–4.

Joseph Andrews and his Friend Mr. Abraham Adams, The History of the Adventures of, a novel by H. Fielding (q.v.), published in 1742.

This was the first of Fielding's novels and was begun as a skit on Richardson's 'Pamela' (q.v.). As the latter had related the efforts of Pamela Andrews, the serving-maid, to escape the attentions of her master, so here her brother Joseph, also in service is exposed to, attacks on his virtue. Mr. B. of 'Pamela' becomes young Squire Booby, and mild fun is made of Pamela herself. But presently the satire is in the main dropped, Joseph sinks rather into the background, and the hero of the remainder of the novel is Parson Adams, the simple, good-hearted, slightly ridiculous but lovable curate in Sir Thomas Booby's family.

Joseph Andrews having been dismissed from service in that family for repelling the advances of Lady Booby and her amorous attendant, Mrs. Slipslop, sets out on foot for the village, where his sweetheart, Fanny, lives. He is knocked down and stripped by robbers and carried to an inn, where he is found by Parson Adams. After this the pair travel together and meet with many ridiculous adventures, until the story brings Joseph and Fanny, Parson Adams, Lady Booby, and Mrs. Slipslop all together in the parish of Lady Booby's country seat. Lady Booby's malevolence pursues the unfortunate Joseph, but the timely arrival of young Squire Booby, who has now married Pamela, effects his brother-in-law's rescue from her persecution. Joseph presently turns out to be not Pamela's brother at all, but the son of persons of much greater consequence, and the story ends with his marriage to Fanny. Among the other amusing characters in this comedy are Mrs. Tow-wouse, the shrewish hostess of the inn, Peter Pounce, the rascally steward, and Trulliber, the boorish farmer-parson. The character of Parson Adams was drawn from William Young, with whom Fielding collaborated in the translation of the 'Plutus' of Aristophanes.

Joseph of Arimathea. For the legend of Joseph and the Holy Grail, see *Grail.* According to fable, St. Philip sent twelve disciples into Britain to preach Christianity, of whom Joseph of Arimathea was the leader. They founded at Glastonbury the first primitive church, which subsequently was developed into Glastonbury Abbey. Here Joseph was buried. His staff, planted in the ground, became the famous Glastonbury Thorn, which flowered at Christmas (William of Malmesbury, 'De Antiquitate Glastoniensis Ecclesiae').

Joseph Vance, a novel by De Morgan (q.v.), published in 1906.

JOSEPHUS, FLAVIUS (A.D. 37–c. 98), a celebrated Jew, who proved his military abilities by supporting against Vespasian a siege of forty-seven days in a small town of

Judaea. He obtained the esteem of Vespasian by foretelling that he would one day become ruler of the Roman Empire. He was present at the siege of Jerusalem by Titus, and received from the conqueror the gift of certain sacred books that it contained, besides an estate in Judaea. He came to Rome with Titus, was honoured with Roman citizenship, and devoted himself to study. He wrote in Greek a 'History of the Jewish War', and 'Jewish Antiquities', which is a history of the Jews down to A.D. 66.

JOSH BILLINGS, see *Shaw (H. W.).*

Josian, the wife of Bevis of Hampton (q.v.).

Jötun, the giants of Scandinavian mythology, the enemies of the Æsir (q.v.) or gods. Their abode was called *Jötunheim.*

Jourdain, MONSIEUR, in Molière's 'Le Bourgeois Gentilhomme', a wealthy bourgeois obsessed with the desire to pass for a perfect gentleman. He apes people of quality, and is exploited in consequence. His surprise at learning, in the course of his education, that he has been talking prose all his life is proverbial.

Journal of a Tour to the Hebrides, The. by Boswell (q.v.), published in 1785. It is a narrative of the journey taken by Boswell and Dr. Johnson in Scotland and the Hebrides in 1773. Boswell's manuscript, which Johnson and others read, was discovered at Malahide Castle with other manuscripts and private papers and was published in 1936, edited by F. A. Pottle and C. H. Bennett; it is longer by about a third than the earlier publication.

Journal of the Plague Year, A, see *Plague Year.*

Journey from this World to the Next, A, a Lucianic (see *Lucian*) narrative by H. Fielding (q.v.), included in his 'Miscellanies' published in 1743.

After a lively satirical account by the author of his spirit's journey in a stage-coach, in company with the spirits of other recently dead persons, to Elysium, and of the judgement by Minos of the spirits seeking admittance there, we have a long discourse by the spirit of Julian the Apostate, describing its adventures in its successive embodiments. This is followed by a fragment containing a similar narrative by the spirit of Anne Boleyn.

Journey to London, The, see *Provok'd Husband.*

Journey to the Western Islands of Scotland, A, by S. Johnson (q.v.), published in 1775. It is a narrative of the tour undertaken by Johnson and Boswell in 1773 in Scotland and the Hebrides.

Jove, a poetical equivalent of Jupiter (q.v.).

Joviall Crew, A, or The Merry Beggars, a romantic comedy by Brome (q.v.) produced in 1641.

Oldrents, a rich and kindly country squire, has been thrown into melancholy by a gipsy's prediction that his two daughters must be beggars. Springlove, an honest vagabond, whom Oldrents has tried to reclaim to a settled life by making him his steward, is seized each spring with a desire to return to his wandering life, and rejoins a party of beggars, whom Oldrents from kindness of heart entertains in his barn. Oldrents's daughters, wearied with their father's melancholy, decide to join the beggars for a frolic, with their two lovers. They thus give effect to the gipsy's prediction, but their begging exposes them to unforeseen dangers. Meanwhile Justice Clack's niece has run away with the Justice's clerk, and they too fall in with the beggars. The search for the runaways, and the apprehension of the beggars, give occasion for amusing scenes, and all ends well.

The play, Brome's masterpiece, is highly original in more than one respect, notably in the picture of Oldrents's compassion for the poor, and of Springlove's bent for vagabondage and response to the call of the spring.

JOWETT, BENJAMIN (1817–93), educated at St. Paul's School and Balliol College, Oxford, became fellow of Balliol in 1838, Regius professor of Greek at Oxford in 1855, and master of Balliol in 1870. He contributed to 'Essays and Reviews' (q.v.) an essay on 'The Interpretation of Scripture' (1860), and published translations of Plato (1871), Thucydides (1881), and Aristotle's 'Politics' (1885). He also published in 1855 a commentary on St. Paul's Epistles to the Thessalonians, Galatians, and Romans, notable for the freedom and freshness of its treatment, the orthodoxy of which was criticized. Jowett was an Oxford figure and the subject of innumerable stories.

JOYCE, JAMES AUGUSTINE ALOYSIUS (1882–1941), novelist, born at Rathgar, Dublin, and educated at the Jesuit schools, Clongowes Wood College and Belvedere College, and at University College, Dublin. Dissatisfied with the narrowness and bigotry of Irish Catholicism, as he saw it, he went for a year to Paris in 1902 and after returning to Dublin for a short time left Ireland for good. He spent the rest of his life abroad, chiefly in Trieste, Zürich, and Paris, supporting himself by teaching English, contending for many years with poverty, and suffering latterly from severe eye trouble. His first published work was a volume of verse, 'Chamber Music' (1907), followed by 'Dubliners' (short stories, 1914), 'Exiles' (a play, 1918), 'A Portrait of the Artist as a Young Man' (a largely autobiographical work, first published serially in the 'Egoist' (q.v.), 1914–15), and 'Pomes Penyeach' (verse, 1917). His famous novel 'Ulysses' (q.v.) was first published in Paris in 1922, and 'Finnegans Wake' (q.v.), extracts of which had already appeared as 'Work in Progress', was published in its complete form in 1939. These last two works revolutionized the form and structure of the novel in the development of the stream of consciousness technique, and in 'Finnegans Wake', especially, language was pushed to the extreme limits of communication.

JOYCE, PATRICK WESTON (1827–1914), was author of 'Irish Names of Places' (1869) and a 'Grammar of Irish' (1881), and contributed Irish folk-songs to Petrie's 'Ancient Music of Ireland'. He also wrote a 'Social History of Ireland' (1903), and his 'Old Celtic Romances' was the source from which Tennyson drew the subject of his 'Voyage of Maeldune'.

Joyous Gard, Launcelot's castle in the Arthurian legend. Malory says that 'some men say it was Anwick, and some men say it was Bamborow'. The latter is near Berwick-on-Tweed.

Juan, DON, see *Don Juan.*

Juan Fernandez, an island off the coast of Chile, discovered by Juan Fernandez, a Spaniard, about 1565. See *Robinson Crusoe.*

Juba, a character in Addison's 'Cato' (q.v.).

Jubal, a son of Lamech and Adah, and the 'father of all such as handle the harp and organ' (Gen. iv. 19–21). He is the subject of a poem by G. Eliot (1874).

Judas Iscariot (i.e. 'man of Kerioth' in Judaea), the disciple who betrayed Christ (Matt. xxvi. 14–15) for thirty pieces of silver. He repented, brought back the thirty pieces, and hanged himself (Matt. xxvii. 3). The legend that he is once a year, on Christmas eve, allowed to cool himself for a day on an iceberg is treated by M. Arnold (q.v.) in his 'Saint Brandan', and by Sebastian Evans (q.v.) in his 'Judas Iscariot's Paradise'.

Judas Maccabaeus (*d.* 160 B.C.), the third son of Mattathias the Hasmonean, and after the death of his father, leader of the Jews in their revolt against Antiochus Epiphanes (see *Maccabees*).

Jude the Obscure, a novel by Hardy (q.v.), reprinted in revised form from 'Harper's Magazine' in the 1895 edition of his 'Works'.

It is a story, in the author's words, 'of a deadly war waged with old Apostolic desperation between flesh and spirit', and tells how the intellectual aspirations of Jude Fawley, a South Wessex villager, are thwarted by a sensuous temperament, lack of character, and the play of circumstances. Early in life, while he is supporting his passion for learning by work as a stonemason, he is entangled in a love-affair with Arabella Donn, a 'mere female animal', and entrapped into marrying her. She presently deserts him and he resumes his studies, and aims at becoming a priest. But he falls in love with his cousin, Sue Bridehead, a vivacious intelligent young school-teacher. She marries an elderly schoolmaster, Phillotson. Though Jude tries to suppress his passion for Sue, he hovers about her, and presently Sue, driven by physical repulsion, leaves Phillotson and flies to Jude, and their guilty connexion debars Jude from hope of the priesthood. Though they become free to marry as a result of divorce from their respective spouses, Sue shrinks from this step. Social disapproval makes itself felt, and the couple go downhill. Their children perish by a tragic fate, and Sue in an agony of remorse and self-abasement returns to Phillotson. Jude takes to drink, is inveigled back by Arabella, and dies miserably. The horrors of his own creation in this, the last of his stories, perhaps turned Hardy away from novel-writing to poetry.

Judecca, see *Giudecca.*

Judith, the heroine of the book of the Apocrypha that bears her name, a widow of Bethulia who, when the army of Nebuchadnezzar was threatening her town, adventured herself in the camp and tent of Holofernes, the enemy general, and cut off his head. She figures in Lascelles Abercrombie's (q.v.) 'Emblems of Love'. The story was dramatized by E. A. Bennett (q.v.).

Judith, a fragment of 350 lines of a poem in Old English. It relates the deeds of Judith of the Apocrypha. The extant cantos, x, xi, and xii, describe the banquet in the Assyrian camp, the bringing of Judith to Holofernes' tent, the slaying of Holofernes, the escape of Judith, the attack on the Assyrians, and their flight.

Judy, a familiar pet-form of the name JUDITH, the name of the wife of Punch in the puppet-show 'Punch and Judy' (q.v.).

Juggernaut or JAGANNĀTH, in Hindu mythology, a title of Krishna, the eighth avatar of Vishnu; also specifically the uncouth idol of this deity at Pūrī in Orissa, annually dragged in procession on an enormous car, under the wheels of which many devotees are said formerly to have thrown themselves to be crushed. Hence JUGGERNAUT CAR is used of practices, institutions, etc., to which persons blindly sacrifice themselves. [OED.]

Julia, a character in Shakespeare's 'Two Gentlemen of Verona' (q.v.).

Julia de Roubigné, see *Mackenzie (H.).*

Julia, DONNA, in Byron's 'Don Juan' (q.v.), a lady of Seville, whose love for the hero is the first incident in his career.

Julia Melville, a character in Sheridan's 'The Rivals' (q.v.).

Julian, COUNT, a character in Southey's 'Roderick' (q.v.).

Julian and Maddalo, A Conversation, a poem by P. B. Shelley (q.v.), written on the occasion of his visit to Venice in 1818.

The poem takes the form of a conversation between Julian (the author) and Maddalo (Lord Byron) on the power of man over his mind, followed by a visit to a Venetian madhouse, where a maniac, whose mind has been unhinged by unfortunate love, recounts his story.

Julian the Apostate, Roman emperor A.D. 361–3, was brought up compulsorily as a Christian, and on attaining the throne proclaimed himself a pagan. He made a great effort to revive the worship of the old gods. He was killed in a valiant attack on the Persians near the Tigris. The story that he was murdered by a Christian and died exclaiming 'Vicisti, Galilaee' ('Galilean, you have conquered') is unfounded.

JULIANA OF NORWICH (1343–1443), anchoret; she wrote 'XVI Revelations of Divine Love', two manuscript copies of which are in the British Museum.

Julie, the heroine of the 'Nouvelle Héloïse' of Rousseau (q.v.), loved by Saint-Preux.

Julie de Mortemar, the heroine of Bulwer Lytton's 'Richelieu' (q.v.).

Juliet, the heroine of Shakespeare's 'Romeo and Juliet' (q.v.).

Julius Caesar, a Roman tragedy by Shakespeare (q.v.), probably produced in 1599, and printed in the 1623 folio. The plot is taken from North's translation of Plutarch's Lives, and deals with the events of the year 44 B.C., after Caesar, already endowed with the dictatorship, had returned to Rome from a successful campaign in Spain.

Distrust of Caesar's ambition gives rise to a conspiracy against him among Roman lovers of freedom, notably Cassius and Casca; they win over to their cause Brutus, who reluctantly joins them from a sense of duty to the republic. Caesar is slain by the conspirators in the Senate-house. Antony, Caesar's friend, stirs the people to fury against the conspirators by a skilful speech at Caesar's funeral. Octavius, nephew of Julius Caesar, Antony, and Lepidus, united as triumvirs, oppose the forces raised by Brutus and Cassius. The quarrel and reconciliation of Brutus and Cassius, with the news of the death of Portia, wife of Brutus, provide one of the finest scenes in the play. Brutus and Cassius are defeated at the battle of Philippi (42 B.C.), and kill themselves.

Jumping Frog of Calaveras County, The Celebrated, one of Mark Twain's (see *Clemens*) most famous humorous stories.

JUNG, CARL GUSTAVE (1875–1961), Swiss psychiatrist, whose early work on the psychology of mental disorder began at the Burghölzli Hospital in Zürich. He was a pioneer in word association tests and in applying psychoanalytic concepts to the study of schizophrenia. His 'The Psychology of Dementia Praecox' appeared in 1906 and 'Studies in Word Association' in 1916. The terms 'extravert' and 'introvert' which he introduced into his study of psychological types have become part of everyday language. In his later work Jung developed his theory of the 'collective unconscious', based upon the evidence provided by mythology and by the dreams and phantasies of his patients, which seemed to derive from the common experience of primitive society rather than from the personal experience of the individual.

Jungle, The, a novel by Upton Sinclair (q.v.), published in 1906, which exposed the life and evil practices of the Chicago stockyards. Its effect was so great that many Americans refused for a time to eat meat from Chicago, and an investigation of the yards was instituted by the U.S. government.

Jungle Book, The, and *The Second Jungle Book,* stories by Kipling (q.v.), published in 1894 and 1895 respectively, which tell how the child Mowgli was brought up by wolves and was taught by Baloo, the bear, and by Bagheera, the black panther, the law and business of the jungle.

JUNIUS, the pseudonym of the author of a series of letters that appeared in the 'Public Advertiser' (q.v.) from 1769 to 1771, attacking with bitter scorn and invective, among others, the duke of Grafton, the duke of Bedford, Lord North, and Lord Mansfield in his judicial capacity, while George III is not spared the irony of the writer. Junius also takes an active part on behalf of Wilkes. Both before 1769 and after 1771 political letters under other pseudonyms, which have been traced to the same hand, appeared in the public press. In the former the writer attacks the ministry of Lord Chatham; in the latter he violently abuses Lord Barrington, secretary at war. Though personal invective is the chief weapon of Junius, his political arguments, written from the Whig standpoint, are shrewd and lucidly expressed. The identity of Junius, which he concealed with great skill, has never been definitely established; but there are strong reasons for attributing the letters to Sir Philip Francis (q.v.). Lord Temple has also been claimed as the author. An authorized edition of the 'Letters of Junius' appeared in 1772.

JUNIUS, FRANCIS, or DU JON, FRANÇOIS (1589–1677), philologist and antiquary, born at Heidelberg. He was librarian to Thomas Howard, second earl of Arundel, and tutor to his son, and a friend of Milton. He presented Anglo-Saxon manuscripts and philological collections to the Bodleian Library, and published 'De Pictura Veterum' in 1637, an edition of Cædmon (q.v.) in 1655, and other works. His 'Etymologicum Anglicanum' (first printed in 1743) was largely used by Dr. Johnson. He took an active interest in the Oxford University Press (q.v.) and presented it with materials for Gothic, Runic, Anglo-Saxon, and Roman printing.

Juno, see *Hera*.

Jupe, CISSY, a character in Dickens's 'Hard Times' (q.v.).

Jupiter, originally the elemental god of the Romans, came to be identified with the Greek Zeus (q.v.), the myths concerning whom were transferred to Jupiter. The name signifies 'father of the bright heaven'.

Justified Sinner, Confessions of a, see *Hogg* (*J*).

Justinian I, emperor of Constantinople 527–65, famous for his successful wars (Belisarius, q.v., and Narses were his generals), and for the code of Roman law that he caused to be drawn up, known as the *Corpus Juris Civilis*, and consisting of (1) the Institutes (q.v.); (2) the Digesta or Pandects (opinions of jurists); (3) the Codex Justinianus; and (4) the Novellae (collection of ordinances). Famous also for building St. Sophia at Constantinople.

Jutes, a Low German tribe that invaded Great Britain (according to tradition under Hengist and Horsa, at the invitation of the Britons to help them against the Picts) in the 5th cent. Their connexion with Jutland is disputed.

Jutland, BATTLE OF, a naval engagement between the British Grand Fleet under Admiral Sir J. R. Jellicoe and the German High Seas Fleet under Admiral Reinhard Scheer, fought in the North Sea on 31 May 1916. Admiral Scheer had sent out Admiral Hipper with a scouting force with the idea of luring out the British Fleet, and himself followed with the High Seas Fleet. The British Fleet, which had received warning of extensive German operations, had put to sea on the evening of the 30th.

The battle began with an engagement between the British battle-cruisers under Admiral Beatty and Hipper's force, in which the British ships suffered heavily. The main engagement followed, but the evening was so still and misty that the biggest ships were within (long-distance) range of each other for barely half an hour. Scheer avoided envelopment by the British fleet, refusing action, and manœuvring so as to return safely to his base. The British lost 3 battle-cruisers, 3 cruisers, and 8 torpedo craft; the Germans 1 battleship, 1 battle-cruiser, 4 light cruisers, and 5 torpedo craft. After this engagement the High Seas Fleet did not again put out to sea.

JUVENAL, Decimus Junius Juvenalis (*c.* A.D. 60–*c.* 130), the great Roman satirical poet, born probably at Aquinum. His extant works consist of sixteen satires, depicting contemporary society and denouncing its vices, which have served as models to many English poets.

The references to 'The English Juvenal' in Scott's 'Waverley' (q.v.) and 'The British Juvenal' in his 'The Heart of Midlothian' (q.v.) are to George Crabbe (q.v.). The title 'English Juvenal' has also been applied to John Oldham (q.v.).

K

Kaaba, THE, in the ancient temple enclosure at Mecca, the 'Holy of Holies' of Islam, a roughly cubical, windowless, stone structure, 30–40 ft. in length, height, and breadth, said to have been erected by Abraham and Ishmael. In its SE. corner is the celebrated black stone, of which legend tells that it fell from Paradise with Adam and was given by the angel Gabriel to Abraham when he was building the Kaaba. It was originally white but became black from the kisses of sinful but believing lips.

Kabbalah, THE, see *Cabbala.*

Kabir, an Indian mystic, who lived at Benares in the 15th cent., and taught a monotheistic religion designed apparently to reconcile Hindus and Muslims.

Kâf or KAFF, in Muslim mythology, a mountain which encircles the earth, the abode of the Jinn (q.v.). A name also used to signify the Caucasus.

KAFKA, FRANZ (1883–1924), German novelist (of Czech origin). He made little or no mark during his lifetime, but has since achieved a position and influence of outstanding importance. He is the author of three novels ('The Trial', 'The Castle', and 'America') and also of a large number of short stories, of which 'The Transformation' and 'The Judgment' are among the best known.

He also wrote many very short prose-pieces, often suggestive of parables, and the fragmentary philosophic items in his published notebooks are of very great interest. Characteristic of Kafka's work is the portrayal of an enigmatic reality, in which the individual is seen as lonely, perplexed, and threatened, and guilt is one of his major themes. His work is difficult because it resists any single interpretation and allows various simultaneous possibilities. Much of his work was published posthumously.

Kaikhosru, see *Khusrau I.*

Kaikobad, known to history as Qubad I, the father of Khusrau I (q.v.), figures in the 'Shahnameh' of Firdusi (q.v.) as one of the descendants of Feridun, and king of Iran, who carries on the war with Afrasiab, king of Turan. He is mentioned in the 'Rubáiyát' of Omar Khayyám (q.v.).

Kailyal, a character in Southey's 'Curse of Kehama' (q.v.).

Kailyard School, from 'Kail-yard', a cabbage patch such as is commonly attached to a small cottage, a term applied to writers of a class of romantic fiction affecting to describe, with much use of the vernacular, common life in Scotland, e.g. J. M. Barrie (q.v.), 'Ian Maclaren' (John Watson, 1850–1907), and S. R. Crockett (1860–1914).

KAISER, GEORG (1878–1945), German dramatist, who died in exile, author of 'The Burghers of Calais' (1912), 'From Morning till Midnight' (1916), and 'Gas' (1918–20), all leading examples of the German Expressionist theatre. He was a prolific and highly inventive writer, author in all of some sixty plays.

Kalends, see *Calends.*

Kalevala ('Land of Heroes'), the national epic poem of Finland, compiled from popular lays transmitted orally until the 19th cent., when a collection was published by Zacharias Topelius (1822). They were arranged in a connected form by Elias Lönnrott, who in 1835 published a version of 12,000 lines, and in 1849 a longer version of 23,000 lines in alliterative eight-syllabled trochaic verse (the metre of 'Hiawatha'). The poem is concerned with the myths of Finland, centring in Wainamoinen, the god of music and poetry, his brother Ilmarinen the smith, who makes the magic mill (the Sampo), and the conflicts of the Finns with the Lapps. The myths are of great antiquity, perhaps dating, according to internal evidence, from the time when Finns and Hungarians were still one people. The poem was translated into English by W. M. Crawford in 1887.

Kali, in Hindu mythology, a form of *Durga,* the bloodthirsty wife of Siva, represented in idols with a black body, a necklace of human heads, and a protruding blood-stained tongue.

KALIDASA, a great Indian poet and dramatist, best known by his play 'Sakuntala' (q.v.), of which we have a translation by Sir W. Jones (q.v.). Monier-Williams thinks that he lived at the beginning of the 3rd cent. A.D., but there is diversity of opinion on the point.

Kalmucks, a race of Mongol nomads, ranging from parts of China to south-eastern Russia, whose religion is a form of Buddhism.

Kalpa, in Hindu cosmology, a great age of the world, a thousand yugas (q.v.), 4,320,000,000 years, a day of Brahma.

Kama or KAMADEVA, in Hindu mythology, the god of love, the Indian Cupid, represented as riding on a sparrow and armed with bow and arrows. His wife is Rati (pleasure).

KAMES, LORD, see *Home* (H.).

Kanaka, a word meaning 'man', a native of the South Sea Islands, especially one employed in Queensland on the sugar plantations.

KANT, IMMANUEL (1724–1804), second son of a leather-worker of Königsberg in Prussia (of Scottish descent), was educated at the university of that town, and supported himself as a tutor. He published his first considerable work, 'A General Natural History and Theory of the Heavens', in 1755, and in that year became a lecturer at Königsberg, an unsalaried post in which he remained for fifteen years, during which he published a number of minor philosophical treatises. In

1770 he became professor of logic and metaphysics at Königsberg, retaining the appointment until his death. He remained unmarried. His 'Critique of Pure Reason' appeared in 1781, 'Prolegomena to every future Metaphysic of Ethic' in 1783, 'Foundation for the Metaphysic of Ethic' in 1785, 'Metaphysical Rudiments of Natural Philosophy' in 1786, the second edition of the 'Critique of Pure Reason' in 1787, the 'Critique of Practical Reason' in 1788, and the 'Critique of Judgement' in 1790. His 'Religion within the Boundaries of Pure Reason' (1793) called down on him the censure of the government.

The following are some of the leading ideas of Kant's philosophy. Knowledge is the outcome of two factors, the senses and the understanding. Sensations are the starting-point of knowledge. Space and time are essential conditions of our sensuous perception, the forms under which our sensations are translated into consciousness. Therefore knowledge has space and time for its essential conditions. Nor have space and time any existence except as forms of our consciousness. These forms, continuous and infinite, provide the possibility of unifying our individual perceptions, and the unification is effected by the understanding. This act of synthesis Kant analyses into twelve principles or 'categories', or laws of thought. The categories are to the understanding very much what time and space are to the consciousness. They include such notions as quality, quantity, and, notably, causation. The external world is thus the product of sensations conditioned by the forms of consciousness and linked by thought according to its own laws. It consists of appearances, 'phenomena'; but the causes of these appearances, 'noumena', things in themselves, lie beyond the limits of knowledge, nor can we, by the aid of reason alone, apart from appearances, arrive at absolute truth, for reason leads to certain insoluble contradictions, or 'antinomies', such as the impossibility of conceiving either limited or unlimited space.

But where metaphysics fails us, practical reason comes to our aid. The moral consciousness assents to certain 'categorical imperatives', such as 'do not lie'. From this follow the conviction that man is in a certain sense free, the belief in immortality (because self-realization within any finite period is impossible), and the belief in God. We are driven by the nature of our minds to see design in nature, and man as the centre of that design. Though the advantages resulting from the obedience to particular moral laws can be shown, the moral obligation itself is a categorical imperative, something that we feel but cannot explain. Interpreted as a practical rule of conduct, the moral law bids you 'act as if the principle by which you act were about to be turned into a universal law of nature', and do all in your power to promote the highest good of all human beings. This highest good is not realizable unless the course of the world is itself guided by moral law, that is to say by a moral Master of the universe, whose existence we are driven to assume. But metaphysics places religion and morality outside the province of knowledge, and in the region of faith.

Kant's philosophy was developed and profoundly modified by Fichte, Schelling, and Hegel (qq.v.).

Karma, in Buddhism, the sum of a person's actions in one of his successive states of existence, regarded as determining his fate in the next; hence necessary fate or destiny. [OED.]

Karmathians, a Shia sect of Muslims in Eastern Arabia founded in the 9th cent., 'pantheistic in theory and socialist in practice' [E.B.], called after Karmat, their founder.

Karttikeya, see *Skanda*.

Kastril, one of the characters in Jonson's 'The Alchemist' (q.v.).

Kate, CRAZY, see *Crazy Kate*.

Kate Barlass, see *King's Tragedy*.

Katharina, a character in Shakespeare's 'The Taming of the Shrew' (q.v.).

Katharine of Aragon, QUEEN, the wife of Henry VIII, whose divorce is one of the principal incidents in Shakespeare's 'Henry VIII'.

Katharine, (1) a character in Shakespeare's 'Love's Labour's Lost' (q.v.); (2) in his 'Henry V' (q.v.), the daughter of the king of France.

Katinka, in Byron's 'Don Juan' (canto VI), one of the beauties of the harem.

Katmer, KRATIM, or KRATIMER, the dog of the Seven Sleepers (q.v.), in the Muslim version of the tale. Sale says that the Muslims have great respect for this dog, allow him a place in Paradise, and write his name on their letters which go far or cross the sea, as a kind of talisman to prevent them from miscarriage.

Katterfelto, GUSTAVUS, a quack, notorious in the latter part of the 18th cent. He appeared in London during the influenza epidemic of 1782, exhibiting 'philosophical apparatus' in Spring Gardens, and giving microscopic and magnetic demonstrations. He was the subject of a novel by Whyte-Melville (q.v., 1875).

KAVANAGH, JULIA (1824–77), author of a number of tales of French life, notable for their faithful rendering of French character. Her 'Natalie' appeared in 1851, 'Adèle' in 1858, 'French Women of Letters' in 1861, 'English Women of Letters' in 1862.

Kay, SIR, in Malory's 'Morte Darthur' (q.v.), King Arthur's seneschal, a brave but disagreeable, spiteful knight. He was son of Sir Ector (q.v.). He figures in the Modena sculpture (see *Gawain*).

KAZANTZAKIS, NIKOS (1883–1957), Greek novelist and poet, born in Crete and educated in Athens and Paris. His 'Odyssey', a philosophical epic, describes the author's spiritual journey through life. His novels, 'Alexis Zorbas', 'Christ Recrucified', 'Freedom and Death', 'The Poor Man of God', and 'The Last Temptation', have been translated into many European languages. He also published philosophic essays (the most important of which is the 'Salvatores Dei'), tragedies, and travel books, and translated into modern Greek certain western classics, notably Dante's 'Divine Comedy' and Goethe's 'Faust'. His writings are rich in humanity, but there is also a deep trend of pessimism which occasionally borders on nihilism.

Kean, CHARLES JOHN (1811?–68), actor, second son of Edmund Kean (q.v.), educated at Eton, appeared in 1827 as Young Norval, in 'Douglas', and subsequently sustained many parts, but excelled only as Hamlet and Louis XI.

Kean, EDMUND (1789–1833), the son of an itinerant actress, deserted by his mother, was an unrivalled tragic actor. After an adventurous boyhood and the performance of subordinate parts, he made a triumphant appearance in 1814 as Shylock. His numerous successes included Richard III, Hamlet, Othello, Iago, Macbeth, and Lear.

Kearney, CAPTAIN, a character in Marryat's 'Peter Simple' (q.v.).

KEATS, JOHN (1795–1821), the son of a livery-stable keeper in Moorfields, London, acquired a knowledge of Latin and history, and some French, but no Greek. He was apprenticed to an apothecary, but his indentures were cancelled that he might qualify for a surgeon. He passed his examinations, but abandoned surgery owing to his passion for literature. He became intimate with Hazlitt and Leigh Hunt, who printed a sonnet for him in the 'Examiner' in May 1816, and in whose house he met Shelley. His sonnet on Chapman's 'Homer' was printed in the 'Examiner' in Dec. 1816. With the help of Shelley he published in 1817 'Poems by John Keats', which were financially a failure. They include 'Sleep and Poetry', an expression of the author's own poetic aspirations. In the course of 1818 Keats wrote 'Endymion' (q.v.), which was savagely criticized in 'Blackwood's Magazine' and the 'Quarterly'; and commenced 'Hyperion' (q.v.). In the same year he nursed his brother Tom until his death. He began 'The Eve of St. Agnes' (q.v.) early in 1819, and wrote 'La Belle Dame sans Merci' (q.v.) and the unfinished 'Eve of St. Mark', another poem on a young girl and the legend of a saint's day. About the same time he wrote his great odes 'On a Grecian Urn', 'To a Nightingale', and 'To Autumn'; and those 'On Melancholy', 'On Indolence', and 'To Psyche'. His dramatic experiments, 'Otho the Great' and 'King Stephen', also belong to 1819, and a little after them the burlesque poem 'Cap and Bells'. He had meanwhile fallen deeply in love with Fanny Brawne. His 'Lamia (q.v.) and other Poems', including

'The Eve of St. Agnes' and 'Isabella, or the Pot of Basil' (q.v.), appeared in 1820 and was praised by Jeffrey (q.v.) in the 'Edinburgh Review'. Keats was by now seriously ill with consumption. He sailed for Italy in Sept. 1820, reached Rome in Nov., and died there, desiring that there should be engraved on his tomb the words, 'Here lies one whose name was writ in water'. He was lamented by Shelley in 'Adonais' (q.v.). Of Keats's letters, which throw a valuable light on his poetical development, there have been several editions; the most complete is that of H. E. Rollins, 1958.

KEBLE, JOHN (1792–1866), educated at Corpus Christi College, Oxford, became fellow and tutor of Oriel College (where Newman and Pusey were also fellows), and professor of poetry at Oxford. By his sermon on national apostasy in 1833 he initiated the Oxford Movement (q.v.), which he also supported by seven of the 'Tracts for the Times' (q.v.), by his translation of Irenaeus, and by his 'Life' and 'Works' of Bishop Thomas Wilson. He also edited Hooker's works (1836) and helped Newman with R. H. Froude's 'Remains'. Keble was eminent as a writer of sacred verse. His poetical work is contained in 'The Christian Year' (1827), which obtained immense popularity, 'Lyra Innocentium' (1846), and 'Miscellaneous Poems' (1869). His Latin 'Praelections' as professor of poetry, 'De Poeticae Vi Medicâ' (1844), have been translated by E. K. Francis (1912).

Keble College, Oxford, was founded in 1870 as a memorial to John Keble.

Kedar, a son of Ishmael (Gen. xxv. 13), whose reputed descendants were a tribe of nomadic Arabs. 'Woe is me, that I am constrained . . . to have my habitation among the tents of Kedar' is in Ps. cxx. 4 (Prayer Book version).

Kehama, The Curse of, see *Curse of Kehama.*

Kells, Book of, an 8th- to 9th-cent. manuscript of the four Gospels, with Prefaces, Summaries, and Canon Tables; seven charters of the abbey of Kells have been added on blank pages. It is written in Irish majuscule and has magnificent illustrations consisting of intricate patterns made up of abstract and animal forms. It was probably written at Kells in County Meath, the headquarters of the Columban community after the sack of Iona in 806. It was collated by James Ussher (q.v.) in 1621 and presented to Trinity College, Dublin, after the Restoration.

Kelly, a name applied to the series of directories published by Kelly's Directories Ltd. and including Kelly's Post Office London Directory, the county, town, and trades directories, and the Handbook to the titled, landed, and official classes. The Post Office directory was first published in 1799.

KELLY, HUGH (1739–77), an Irishman who came to London in 1760, edited the 'Court Magazine' and the 'Ladies' Museum',

and afterwards the 'Public Ledger'. He wrote three comedies, 'False Delicacy' (produced by Garrick in 1768), 'A Word for the Wise' (1770), and 'The School for Wives' (1773).

Kelmscott Press, see *Morris (W).*

Kelpie or KELPY, the Lowland Scottish name of a fabled water-spirit or demon assuming various shapes, but usually that of a horse; it is reputed to haunt lakes and rivers and to delight in, or even to bring about, the drowning of travellers and others. [OED.]

KELVIN, LORD, see *Thomson (Sir W.).*

Kemble, CHARLES (1775–1854), an actor of great range and pre-eminent in comic parts, younger brother of John Philip Kemble and Mrs. Siddons (qq.v.). Among the characters he impersonated were Charles Surface, Falstaff, Mercutio, Macbeth, and Romeo. He was the father of Fanny Kemble and John Mitchell Kemble (qq.v.).

KEMBLE, FRANCES ANNE, afterwards MRS. BUTLER, generally known as FANNY KEMBLE (1809–93), daughter of Charles Kemble (q.v.), an actress who appeared with great success as Juliet to her father's Mercutio, and subsequently as Lady Macbeth, Portia, Beatrice, Queen Katharine, and in many other parts. She published a volume of 'Poems' in 1844, and 'Records of Later Life' (1882). She gave Shakespearian readings on which Longfellow wrote a sonnet. An appreciation of her may be found in Henry James's 'Essays in London'.

KEMBLE, JOHN MITCHELL (1807–57), elder son of Charles Kemble (q.v.), historian and philologist, was educated at Trinity College, Cambridge, and was a pupil and friend of Jacob Grimm (q.v.). He edited the poems of Beowulf (1833–7) and did good work on the early history of England: 'Codex Diplomaticus Aevi Saxonici' (1839–48), 'The Saxons in England' (1849, ed. Birch 1876). He also issued a collection of 'State Papers' illustrating the period 1688–1714 (1857).

Kemble, JOHN PHILIP (1757–1823), an eminent actor, elder brother of Charles Kemble and Mrs. Siddons (q.v.), played with great success a large number of parts, beginning with Hamlet, and including Iago, Romeo, Prospero, Petruchio, and Wolsey.

Kemp, WILLIAM (*fl.* 1600), a comic actor and dancer, who acted in plays by Shakespeare and Jonson. He danced a morris-dance from London to Norwich, of which an account, 'Kemps Nine Daies Wonder', written by himself (1600), has been twice reprinted.

Kemp Owyne, an old ballad in Child's collection, from an Icelandic source. Isabel, who has been transformed into a monster by a wicked stepmother, is released from the enchantment by three kisses of her lover, Kemp Owyne. In modern versions of the ballad he is 'Kempion'.

KEMPE, MARGERY (*b. c.* 1373), a mystic,

daughter of John Brunham of Lynn, married John Kempe, also of Lynn, *c.* 1393. 'The Book of Margery Kempe' (which she dictated, being illiterate) is a narrative of her spiritual history, in the course of which she undertook extensive travels (to Italy, Jerusalem, Compostella, and Germany). The only extant manuscript (which is not the original one) of the work dates probably from the middle of the 15th cent. Extracts from it were printed by Wynkyn de Worde in 1501. It has been published by the E.E.T.S. (1940).

Kempenfelt, RICHARD (1718–82), the son of a Swede in the service of James II, served as naval officer, and was present at a number of actions in the West and East Indies rising to be rear-admiral. He was flying his flag on the Royal George when his ship went down at Spithead, as commemorated in Cowper's poem.

KEMPIS, THOMAS À, see *Thomas à Kempis.*

KEN, THOMAS (1637–1711), fellow of Winchester and New College, Oxford, became bishop of Bath and Wells. He was a writer of devotional prose and verse; his works include 'Ichabod' (1663), the 'Practice of Divine Love' (1685–6), a 'Manual of Prayers for Winchester Scholars' (1695), and some well-known hymns. His works were collected by W. Hawkins in 1721.

KENDALL, HENRY CLARENCE (1841– 82), Australian poet, published several volumes of verse, of which the most notable are: 'Poems and Songs' (1862), 'Leaves from Australian Forests' (1869), and 'Songs from the Mountains' (1880).

Kenelm Chillingly, a novel by Bulwer Lytton (q.v.), published in 1873.

The work contains, in the opinions and doings of the hero, a good deal of the author's criticism on contemporary society. Kenelm Chillingly, a young man of good family, generous and high-minded, but cynical and disgusted with the shams by which he feels himself surrounded, and in his own estimation a woman-hater, goes out into the world, a sort of knight-errant in humble garb, to seek adventures. By his strength and pugilistic skill he knocks out the ferocious farrier Tom Bowles, who is pressing distasteful attentions on a village maiden; unites the latter to her cripple lover; and awakens the latent nobility in Tom Bowles's character. In accordance with his views on women, he refuses to be led into a marriage with the amiable Cecilia Travers, but presently finds himself desperately in love with Lily, a young girl of natural charm, but uneducated and the daughter of a felon. Lily, though devoted to him, is forced by a sense of gratitude to promise her hand to the guardian who has protected her in childhood, but, broken-hearted, dies before her marriage. After an interval, Kenelm, who has now experienced the love and sorrow of romance, decides to turn his thoughts to

practical life and to become 'a soldier in the ranks', in the service of some honoured cause.

Kenilworth, a novel by Sir W. Scott (q.v.), published in 1821.

The novel is based on the tradition of the tragic fate, in the reign of Elizabeth, of the beautiful Amy Robsart, daughter of Sir John Robsart (called Sir Hugh in the novel). She has been enticed, by the designs of the villainous Richard Varney, into a secret marriage with his patron, the earl of Leicester, Elizabeth's favourite, rejecting the suit of the worthy Edmund Tressilian, a Cornish gentleman and an adherent of Leicester's rival, the earl of Sussex. This marriage Leicester is forced to conceal, on pain of incurring the displeasure of the jealous queen. Amy is accordingly mewed up in Cumnor Place, an old country house near Oxford, and is believed by Tressilian to be living there as the paramour of Varney, Leicester's connexion with her not being suspected. Tressilian, after vainly attempting to induce her to return to her father, lays before the queen a charge of seduction against Varney, who, to shield Leicester, declares Amy to be his wife. Elizabeth thereupon orders that Amy shall appear before her at Kenilworth, whither the queen is shortly going as the guest of Leicester. Varney, who has evil designs on Amy, persuades Leicester, in order to prevent the discovery of the true facts, to direct Amy to present herself at Kenilworth in the character of Varney's wife. Amy, indignant at the order, goes secretly to Kenilworth, aided by Tressilian, determined to demand recognition as Leicester's countess. She obtains admission to the castle, unknown to Leicester, and is discovered by the queen. Amy's strange behaviour arouses Elizabeth's jealous suspicions and she finally extorts from Leicester a confession of his marriage. But Varney, by misrepresenting the relations of Amy and Tressilian, has already induced Leicester to believe her guilty of infidelity to him and in a passion Leicester has ordered Varney to remove Amy to Cumnor Place and kill her. Leicester learns too late that Varney's accusations are false and Tressilian arrives at Cumnor only to find that Amy, by Varney's machinations, has fallen through a trap-door and perished.

Among the many interesting features in the novel are the glimpses of the court of Elizabeth, where the young Walter Ralegh is just coming into favour; the descriptions of the revels at Kenilworth; and the adaptations of the legend of Wayland Smith (q.v.), the skilful farrier and physician, who aids Tressilian in his attempts to recover the unfortunate Amy. Dickie Sludge, or Flibbertigibbet, the impish friend of Wayland Smith, also deserves mention.

KENNEDY, JOHN PENDLETON (1795– 1870), American author and statesman, born at Baltimore, Maryland; his writing was much influenced by Washington Irving, whose friend and admirer he was. His best-known books are 'Swallow Barn' (1832), a kind of Virginia 'Bracebridge Hall'; and 'Horse-Shoe Robinson' (1835), a tale of the American Revolution, laid in the Carolinas.

KENNEDY, MARGARET (1896–), novelist, author of 'The Constant Nymph' (1924) and its sequel, 'The Fool of the Family' (1930).

KENNEDY, WALTER (1460?–1508?), Scottish poet, the rival of William Dunbar (q.v.), in 'The Flyting of Dunbar and Kennedie' (1508), of whom only a few, not very interesting, poems survive.

Kenneth, SIR, or the KNIGHT OF THE LEOPARD, the hero of Scott's 'The Talisman' (q.v.).

Kensington Gardens, originally the gardens of Kensington Palace (q.v.), thrown open to the public in the 18th cent. They were the subject of a poem by Tickell (q.v.), published in 1722, in which he imagines the gardens, recently laid out, as peopled by Oberon and his fairies, and the scene of many adventures. Cf. also 'Peter Pan in Kensington Gardens', by Sir J. M. Barrie (q.v.).

Kensington Palace was built about 1610 by Heneage Finch, earl of Nottingham, and bought by William III and enlarged by Wren, 1689–1721. It was a royal residence until the death of George II, after which it was assigned to various members of the royal family. Queen Victoria was born there. The London Museum is now housed in the state apartments.

Kensington Square became fashionable in the days of William III. Thackeray (who lived near by in Young Street) placed the residence of Lady Castlewood (see *Esmond*) there. It is associated with the names of Steele, Addison, J. S. Mill, and J. R. Green.

Kent, THE NUN or MAID OF, see *Barton* (E.).

Kent, EARL OF, a character in Shakespeare's 'King Lear' (q.v.).

Kentigern, ST., or ST. MUNGO (518?–603), a grandson of Loth, a British prince, after whom the Lothians are named. St. Kentigern was brought up in the monastic school of Culross under the discipline of St. Serf, from whom he received the name of MUNGO (Celtic for 'my dear one'). He became a missionary and was chosen bishop for the Strathclyde Britons, whose centre was Cathures (now Glasgow). He was driven by persecution to Wales, and is said to have stayed on his way to convert the inhabitants of Cumberland. In Wales he founded the monastery of Llanelwy (afterwards St. Asaph's). He was recalled to Strathclyde, and after reclaiming the Picts of Galloway from idolatry, settled at Glasgow, and was buried in the crypt of Glasgow Cathedral, called after him St. Mungo's. He is commemorated on 13 Jan. Some of his miracles, including the resuscitation of St. Serf's favourite robin-redbreast and of a meritorious cook, are celebrated in a canticle formerly sung as part of his office (quoted by J. H. Burton, 'The Book-hunter'):

> Garrit ales pernecatus,
> Cocus est resuscitatus,
> Salit vervex trucidatus
> Amputato capite.

Kentish Fire, a prolonged and ordered salvo of applause, or demonstration of impatience and dissent, said to have originated in reference to meetings held in Kent in 1828–9 in opposition to the Catholic Emancipation Bill.

Kenwigs, MR. and MRS., a genteel couple in Dickens's 'Nicholas Nickleby' (q.v.).

Kepler, JOHANN (1571–1630), of Würtemberg, the celebrated German astronomer, whose three laws of planetary motion provided the basis for much of Newton's work.

KER, WILLIAM PATON (1855–1923), fellow of All Souls College, Oxford, professor of poetry at Oxford, and Quain professor of English literature in London; author of many learned critical books on English, Scottish, and Scandinavian literature ('Epic and Romance' (1897), 'The Dark Ages' (1904), 'Essays on Medieval Literature' (1905), etc.).

Kester, the old farm servant in Mrs. Gaskell's 'Sylvia's Lovers' (q.v.).

Ketch, JACK (d. 1686), executioner, probably from 1663. He executed Lord Russell in 1683 and Monmouth in 1685. He was notorious for his excessive barbarity (or perhaps clumsiness, as in the killing of Russell and of Monmouth). The name is used allusively for an official executioner.

Kettle, CAPTAIN, the hero of many adventures in stories by C. J. Cutcliffe Wright Hyne (1865–1944). The stories were published in book form from 1898 to 1932.

Kettledrummle, THE REVD. MR., in Scott's 'Old Mortality' (q.v.), a fanatical covenanting divine.

Kew, COUNTESS OF, a character in Thackeray's 'The Newcomes' (q.v.).

Kew Gardens, Richmond, since 1841 the Royal Botanic Gardens, are the principal national botanical gardens. Originally the gardens of Kew House and Richmond Lodge, they were laid out as a botanic garden by the mother of George III. See also *Hooker* (W.J.).

KEY, FRANCIS SCOTT (1779–1843), American lawyer and poet, born at Frederick, Maryland, author of the national anthem, 'The Star-Spangled Banner' (q.v.).

KEYES, SIDNEY (1922–43), a poet of originality and promise, killed in the Second World War. 'The Iron Laurel' was published in 1942, 'The Cruel Solstice' in 1943, and his 'Collected Poems' in 1946.

Keyne, WELL OF ST., see *Well of St. Keyne*.

KEYNES, JOHN MAYNARD, *first Baron* (1883–1946), a distinguished economist and man of wide cultural interests, author of 'The

Economic Consequences of the Peace' (1919),
'A General Theory of Employment, Interest,
and Money' (1936), etc. A memoir, 'My Early
Beliefs', was published in 1949. He founded
and endowed the Arts Theatre at Cambridge
and was chairman of C.E.M.A. (Council for
the Encouragement of Music and the Arts) in
1942 and the first chairman when it became
the Arts Council of Great Britain in 1945.

Keys or HOUSE OF KEYS, a body of twenty-
four members forming the elective branch of
the legislature of the Isle of Man. The origin
of the name is unknown.

Khadijah, a noble and rich widow, who became the first wife of Mohammed (q.v.).

Khartoum, a city at the junction of the Blue
and White Niles, opposite Omdurman,
founded in 1822 and adopted by Mehemet
Ali in 1830 as the capital of the Egyptian
Sudan. It was captured by the troops of the
Mahdi in 1885, after a gallent defence by
General Gordon (q.v.). It was reconquered
by the British in 1898.

Khorassan, The Veiled Prophet of, one of
the tales in Moore's 'Lalla Rookh' (q.v.).

Khusrau I (CHOSROES, KAIKHOSRU), king of
Iran, A.D. 531–79, who took the name of ANU-
SHIRVAN, and extended the Persian dominions
from the Indus to the Red Sea. Within them,
during his reign, Mohammed was born. He
caused a number of Sanskrit, Greek, and Latin
works to be translated into Persian, including
the book known as 'Kalila and Dimna',
containing the fables of Bidpai (q.v.). Under
the name of Kaikhosru he is mentioned
in the 'Rubáiyát' of Omar Khayyám (q.v.).

Kiblah, the point (the temple at Mecca) towards which Muslims turn at prayer.

KID, THOMAS, see *Kyd.*

Kidd, WILLIAM (*d.* 1701), pirate; lived at
Boston, Massachusetts; captain of the 'Adventure' privateer; imprisoned for piracy,
1699; sent to England under arrest, 1700;
hanged, 1701.

Kidnapped and *Catriona* (Gaelic for
Catherine and pronounced *Catree'na*), a
novel and its sequel by R. L. Stevenson (q.v.),
published in 1886 and 1893.

The central incident in the story is the
murder of Colin Campbell, the 'Red Fox' of
Glenure, the king's factor on the forfeited
estate of Ardshiel. This is an historical event.
The young David Balfour, whose uncle
Ebenezer unlawfully detains his estate, being
left in poverty on the death of his father,
goes to Ebenezer for assistance. Ebenezer, a
miserly old villain, having failed to effect the
death of David, has him kidnapped on a ship
to be carried off to the Carolinas. On the
voyage Alan Breck is picked up from a sinking
boat. He is 'one of those honest gentlemen
that were in trouble about the years forty-five
and six', a Jacobite who 'wearies for the
heather and the deer'. The ship is wrecked on
the coast of Mull, and David and Alan journey

together. They are witnesses of the murder of
Colin Campbell, and suspicion falls on them.
After a perilous journey across the Highlands,
they escape across the Forth, and the first
novel ends with the discomfiture of Ebenezer
and David's recovery of his rights.

'Catriona' is principally occupied with the
unsuccessful attempt of David Balfour to
secure, at the risk of his own life and freedom,
the acquittal of James Stewart of the Glens,
who is falsely accused, from political motives,
of the murder of Colin Campbell; with the
escape of Alan Breck to the Continent; and
with David's love-affair with Catriona Drummond, the daughter of the renegade James
More.

KIERKEGAARD, SØREN AABYE (1813–
55), Danish philosopher and theologian. His
life was tortured and unhappy, but within
its short span he managed to write a very large
number of books on a wide variety of topics.
Thus, although he is now chiefly remembered
and referred to as having initiated much that
is characteristic of existentialist trends in modern philosophy (e.g. in 'Concluding Unscien-
tific Postscript', trans. W. Lowrie and D. F.
Swenson, 1941), he was also the author of
works whose themes were primarily religious,
psychological, or literary (e.g. 'The Concept
of Dread' and 'Fear and Trembling', both
trans. W. Lowrie, 1944); moreover, his satirical gifts made him a formidable social critic,
witness his essay on 'The Present Age' (trans.
A. Dru, 1962) (reminiscent in some respects
of Carlyle's polemics). Yet, for all their
diversity of subject, his writings have certain
distinctive common features: a distrust of
abstract dogma and a correlative emphasis
upon the particular case or concrete example;
an acute and imaginative concern with the
forms under which human character and
motivation may manifest themselves; and
a passionate belief in the value of individual
choice and judgement as contrasted with tame
acquiescence in established opinions and
norms. It was precisely his insistence upon
the importance of personal decision, direct
and unmediated by artificial ratiocination,
that lay at the root of his rejection of Hegel.
For he saw in Hegelianism a philosophy
which tended to obliterate, in the name of
pretended metaphysical demonstrations, the
element of subjective commitment and 'risk'
implicit in every valid act of faith, and which
sought to submerge the unique and unassimil-
able consciousness of the individual beneath
a welter of universal categories. To all such
speculative attempts to conceal or explain
away what is central to human existence as
genuinely understood and known, Kierkegaard opposed the conception of authentic
choice, the explicit self-commitment of a person who stakes his whole being and future
upon a belief which he cannot prove but
which he maintains in the face of all intellectual doubt and uncertainty. This idea
finds forceful exemplification in the religious

sphere, but it also applies within other domains of experience, e.g. the ethical. Some of Kierkegaard's most penetrating psychological observations occur in his descriptions of the 'leap of faith' and in his analyses of the state of 'dread' (*Angst*) which precedes and accompanies it; in such passages, too, one is made aware of the peculiar significance he attached to the notion of freedom. The stress upon freedom in his sense, as an inescapable condition of life and action and as something which both fascinates and repels the choosing individual, represents perhaps the clearest link between his philosophical ideas and the doctrines of his existentialist successors.

Kilhwch (or *Kulhwch*) **and Olwen,** one of the stories included in Lady C. Guest's translation of 'The 'Mabinogion' (q.v.). Besides being an excellent fairy-tale, the work is important for its reference to King Arthur (q.v.). Lady Guest's translation is from the text in the 'Red Book of Hergest' (q.v.); but the story is assigned to the 10th cent. And its author, as Matthew Arnold pointed out, is dealing with materials taken from a far older architecture.

Kilhwch (pron. 'Keelhookh') is doomed to have no wife at all unless he can secure Olwen, daughter of Hawthorn, chief of the giants (Yspaddadeu Penkawr). He goes to Arthur, who is his cousin, for assistance in his attempt to secure the lady. Arthur orders Kay and Bedivere and Gawain (Gwalchemi), and other knights to attend him, and they visit Hawthorn, who demands an exorbitant bride-price for his daughter, in the shape of thirteen 'treasures' involving almost impossible quests. These are successfully achieved by the various members of the party. There is a great catalogue of the members of Arthur's court, interlarded with amusing notes on their peculiarities.

Kilkenny Cats, To FIGHT LIKE. According to 'N. and Q.', III Series, v. 433, the origin of the allusion is as follows: During the rebellion of 1798 (or it may be of 1803) Kilkenny was garrisoned by a regiment of Hessian soldiers whose custom it was to tie together two cats by their tails and throw them across a clothes-line. The cats naturally fought until one or both died. The officers, apprised of these acts of cruelty, resolved to stop them and made inspections for the purpose. On one occasion an officer was heard approaching while a pair of cats were fighting. One of the troopers with a sword cut their tails and the cats escaped. The presence of the cats' tails on the line was explained to the officer by the statement that two cats had been fighting so desperately that they had devoured each other, with the exception of their tails.

KILLIGREW, HENRY (1613–1700), brother of T. Killigrew (q.v.), the elder, educated at Christ Church, Oxford, master of the Savoy in 1663, was the author of one play, 'The Conspiracy', published in 1638,

and re-written as 'Pallantus and Eudora' in 1653. He was the father of Anne Killigrew (1660–85; see *Dryden*).

Killigrew, Mrs. Anne, Ode to the Memory of, see *Dryden*.

KILLIGREW, THOMAS, the elder (1612–83), was page to Charles I, and groom of the bedchamber and a favourite companion of Charles II. With D'Avenant (q.v.) he held the monopoly of acting in Restoration London. He built a playhouse on the site of the present Drury Lane Theatre, London, in 1663, and was master of the revels in 1679. His most popular play, 'The Parson's Wedding', a comedy whose coarseness is not redeemed by any notable wit or humour, was played between 1637 and 1642, and printed in 1664. Among his other plays are 'The Prisoners', 'Claracilla', and 'The Princess', romantic tragicomedies, acted before the closing of the theatres. His 'Cecilia and Clorinda', a tragicomedy, the subject of which is partly taken from 'Le Grand Cyrus', is of later date.

KILLIGREW, THOMAS, the younger (1657–1719), son of T. Killigrew the elder (q.v.), and gentleman of the bedchamber to George II when Prince of Wales. He was author of 'Chit Chat', a comedy, acted in 1719.

KILLIGREW, SIR WILLIAM (1606?–1695), brother of T. Killigrew the elder (q.v.), and author of 'Selindra', 'Ormasdes, or Love and Friendship', tragicomedies, and 'Pandora', a comedy, published in 1664; and of 'The Siege of Urbin', a tragicomedy, said to be a pleasant play, published in 1666. 'Pandora' and 'Selindra' were acted, and there is reason to think [T.L.S. 18 Oct. 1928] that 'The Siege of Urbin' was also acted.

Killing No Murder, a pamphlet advocating the assassination of Oliver Cromwell, printed in Holland in 1657, when it was believed that Cromwell would accept the crown. It was written by Edward Sexby (*d.* 1658), who had been one of Cromwell's troopers, and revised by Capt. Silas Titus. The name on the title-page, however, is that of William Allen, who had also been one of Cromwell's Ironsides.

Killingworth, Birds of, one of Longfellow's (q.v.) 'Tales of a Wayside Inn'.

Kilmansegg, see *Miss Kilmansegg and her precious Leg*.

Kilmeny, the subject of the thirteenth bard's song in 'The Queen's Wake' of James Hogg (q.v.), and Hogg's chief title to fame as a poet. Kilmeny goes up the glen to hear the birds sing and to pluck berries, does not return, and is mourned for dead. At last she comes back. She has been carried away from the snares of men to the land of spirits, of glory and light, whence she has had a vision of the world below, and of war and sin. She has asked to return to tell her friends what she has seen, and comes transformed and sanctified, with a mysterious influence on all about her; but after a month disappears and passes again to the land of thought.

KILVERT, ROBERT FRANCIS (1840–79), was a curate at Clyro in Radnorshire for seven years and later vicar of Bredwardine on the Wye. His Diary (1870–9) gives a lively picture of contemporary rural life in his several parishes, and of a young clergyman diligent in his parochial duties, sensitive to suffering and distress, and at the same time keenly enjoying the beauties of nature and the pleasant diversions of social intercourse. A selection from his notebooks (ed. W. Plomer) was published in 3 vols. in 1938–40.

Kim, a novel by Kipling (q.v.), published in 1901.

Kim, by his proper name Kimball O'Hara, the orphaned son of a sergeant in an Irish regiment, spends his childhood as a vagabond in Lahore, until he meets an old lama from Tibet, and accompanies him in his travels. He falls into the hands of his father's old regiment, is adopted, and sent to school, resuming his wanderings in his holidays. Colonel Creighton of the Ethnological Survey remarks his aptitude for secret service, and on this he embarks under the direction of the native agent, Hurree Babu. While still a lad he distinguishes himself by capturing the papers of a couple of Russian spies in the Himalayas. The book presents a vivid picture of India, its teeming populations, religions and superstitions, and the life of the bazaars and the road.

Kinde Hart's Dream, a pamphlet by Chettle (q.v.), licensed in 1592(?), noteworthy for its allusion to Shakespeare.

King, see *Catholic king, Christian king, Defender of the Faith.*

King, EDWARD (1612–37), friend of Milton (q.v.); commemorated in 'Lycidas' (q.v.).

KING, HENRY (1592–1669), educated at Westminster and Christ Church, Oxford, became bishop of Chichester and was the friend of Izaak Walton, Donne, and Jonson. He published verses sacred and profane, including the pleasant piece, 'Tell me no more how fair she is'.

KING, WILLIAM (1650–1729), archbishop of Dublin, author of 'State of the Protestants in Ireland under the late King James's Government' (1691) and 'De Origine Mali' (1702).

KING, WILLIAM (1663–1712), educated at Westminster School and Christ Church, Oxford, an advocate at Doctors' Commons, the holder of various minor posts in England and Ireland, and a clever and amusing writer. His 'Dialogue concerning the way to Modern Preferment' was published in 1690, and his 'Dialogues of the Dead', in which (with Charles Boyle) he joined in the attack on Bentley (see *Battle of the Books*), in 1699. He wrote a number of other burlesques and light pieces, some of the best of which are included in 'Miscellanies in Prose and Verse', dedicated

to the members of the Beef-Steak Club (q.v.), 1709, and 'Useful Miscellanies' (1712). His 'Art of Cookery, in imitation of Horace's Art of Poetry' was published in 1708, and his 'Useful Transactions in Philosophy', a skit on Sloane's 'Philosophical Transactions', in 1709.

King Alisaunder, see *Alisaunder.*

King and no King, A, a romantic drama by Beaumont and Fletcher (see *Fletcher, J.*), acted in 1611, printed 1619.

Arbaces, king of Iberia, defeats Tigranes, king of Armenia, in single combat, thus bringing to an end a long war. Arbaces offers his prisoner freedom if he will marry his sister Panthea, who has grown up to womanhood during his long absence. Tigranes loves Spaconia, an Armenian lady, declines the offer, and sends Spaconia to engage Panthea to oppose the match. But when Tigranes, Arbaces, and Panthea meet, not only is Tigranes shaken in his fidelity by the sight of Panthea's beauty, but Arbaces is smitten with a guilty passion for her, which he in vain endeavours to check. An interview with Panthea reveals that she shares his love. Gobrias, who has been Lord Protector of the kingdom since the late king's death, now confesses that Arbaces is his son, adopted secretly by the queen-mother and passed off as her son when she despaired of issue, Panthea being born six years later. Panthea is thus queen of Iberia, Arbaces is unrelated to her, and the lovers can be united. Tigranes, repenting his infidelity, takes Spaconia as his queen, and is released from captivity. Bessus, a cowardly braggart captain in Arbaces' army, provides comic relief.

King Charles's Head, in Mr. Dick's memorial, see *David Copperfield.*

King Horn, the earliest of the extant English verse romances, dating from the late 13th cent. and containing some 1,500 lines. Horn is a beautiful child, the son of King Murray and Queen Godhild of Suddene (Isle of Man). A host of invading Saracens slay the inhabitants, including the king. Horn's beauty saves him from the sword, and he is turned adrift in a boat with his companions, Athulf and Fikenhild. They reach the coast of Westernesse, where King Almair's daughter, Rymenhild, falls in love with Horn. The steward Athelbrus brings Athulf to her chamber in place of Horn, to the indignation of the princess when she discovers the trick. Fikenhild betrays the lovers to the king. Horn is banished and goes to Ireland, and enters the service of the king under the name of Cutberd. He slays the champion of the Saracens, who are attacking the country. The king offers his realm and daughter to Horn, who postpones acceptance. Meanwhile Rymenhild sends word that she is sought in marriage by a powerful suitor. Horn arrives disguised as a palmer and makes himself known to Rymenhild by means of the ring she had given him. With the help of Athulf he slays the rival suitor. He now reveals his birth to the king, and returns to Suddene to recover his kingdom, leaving Rymenhild with her father. He presently learns that Rymenhild is wedded to Fikenhild. Disguised as a harper he makes his way into the castle and slays Fikenhild, thereafter living happily with Rymenhild in Suddene.

See also *Horn Childe*.

King John, an historical play by Shakespeare (q.v.), adapted by him before 1598 from an earlier work, 'The Troublesome Raigne of King John', and not printed until the folio of 1623.

The play, with some departures from historical accuracy, deals with various events in King John's reign, and principally with the tragedy of young Arthur. It ends with the death of John at Swinstead abbey. It is significant that no mention of Magna Carta appears in it. The tragic quality of the play, the poignant grief of Constance, Arthur's mother, and the political complications depicted, are relieved by the wit, humour, and gallantry of the Bastard of Faulconbridge.

King John, an historical drama (*c.* 1547) by Bale (q.v.).

King Lear, a tragedy by Shakespeare (q.v.), was performed in 1606 and two slightly different versions of it were printed in 1608. For the origin of the name 'Lear' see *Llyr*. The story of Lear and his daughters is given by Geoffrey of Monmouth and by Holinshed. 'King Lear' resembles in certain respects an older play 'Leir', which had been 'lately acted' in 1605.

Lear, king of Britain, a petulant and unwise old man, has three daughters: Goneril, wife of the duke of Albany; Regan, wife of the duke of Cornwall; and Cordelia, for whom the king of France and duke of Burgundy are suitors. Intending to divide his kingdom among his daughters according to their affection for him, he bids them say which loves him most. Goneril and Regan make profession of extreme affection, and each receives one-third of the kingdom. Cordelia, self-willed, and disgusted with their hollow flattery, says she loves him according to her duty, not more nor less. Infuriated with this reply, Lear divides her portion between his other daughters, with the condition that himself with a hundred knights shall be maintained by each daughter in turn. Burgundy withdraws his suit for Cordelia, and the king of France accepts her without dowry. The earl of Kent, taking her part, is banished. Goneril and Regan reveal their heartless character by grudging their father the maintenance that he had stipulated for, and finally turning him out of doors in a storm. The earl of Gloucester shows pity for the old king, and is suspected of complicity with the French, who have landed in England. His eyes are put out by Cornwall, who receives a death-wound·in the affray. Gloucester's son Edgar, who has been traduced to his father by his bastard brother Edmund, takes the disguise of a lunatic beggar, and tends his

father till the latter's death. Lear, whom rage and ill-treatment have deprived of his wits, is conveyed to Dover by the faithful Kent in disguise, where Cordelia receives him. Meanwhile Goneril and Regan have both turned their affections to Edmund. Embittered by this rivalry, Goneril poisons Regan, and takes her own life. The English forces under Edmund and Albany defeat the French, and Lear and Cordelia are imprisoned; by Edmund's order Cordelia is hanged, and Lear dies from grief. The treachery of Edmund is proved on him by his brother Edgar. Albany, who has not abetted Goneril in her cruel treatment of Lear, takes over the·kingdom.

King Log and King Stork, in the fable of the frogs who asked for a king. Jupiter sent them a log, and they complained of its inertness. He then sent them a stork, which devoured them.

King of Bath, R. Nash (q.v.).

King of Misrule, see *Misrule*.

King of the Bean, see *Twelfth Day*.

King Philip's War, the conflict (1675–6) between New England colonists and Philip, chief of the Wampanoag Indians.

Kingis Quair, The, a poem of some 200 stanzas, in rhyme-royal, by James I of Scotland (q.v.), written in 1423 and 1424 while he was a prisoner in England and about the time of his marriage with Lady Jane Beaufort, the heroine of the poem. It was discovered and printed by Lord Woodhouselee in 1783. The poem shows the influence of Chaucer. The royal prisoner, lamenting his fortune, sees a beautiful lady walking in the garden below, and is smitten with love. He visits the Empire of Venus and the Palace of Minerva, goddess of Wisdom, has speech with the goddess of Fortune, and finally receives a message from Venus promising the success of his suit. Rossetti quotes from the poem in 'The King's Tragedy' (q.v.). There is an important article on it by Sir W. A. Craigie in 'Essays and Studies by members of the English Association', vol. xxv.

The word 'Quair' means 'quire' or 'book'.

KINGLAKE, ALEXANDER WILLIAM (1809–91), educated at Eton and Trinity College, Cambridge, published in 1844 'Eōthen', a charming narrative of his travels in the Near East. Having followed the British expedition to the Crimea, Kinglake undertook, at the request of Lady Raglan, the history of the Crimean War to the death of Lord Raglan. The first two volumes of this long and exhaustive work appeared in 1863, and the remaining six volumes at intervals down to 1887.

King-maker, THE, Richard Neville, earl of Warwick (1428–71), so named for his influence on the fortunes of Henry VI and Edward IV.

King's or **Queen's Bench,** THE, the King's or Queen's Bench division of the High Court of Justice. 'Bench' in this expression is the seat where judges sit in court; hence the place where justice is administered. The COURT OF KING'S BENCH was originally that in which the sovereign presided, and which followed him in his movements.

King's Bench Prison, a jail in Southwark which was appropriated to debtors and criminals confined by order of the supreme courts. It is mentioned by Stow as of unknown antiquity. The RULES OF THE KING'S BENCH were a defined area outside the prison within which certain prisoners, especially debtors, could live on giving security.

King's College, Cambridge, founded in 1441 by Henry VI and completed by Henry VII and Henry VIII. Its great Chapel is famous as a fine example of ornate Perpendicular. Giles Fletcher, Sir W. Temple, E. Waller, and Horace Walpole (qq.v.) were educated at this college.

King's Evil, or THE EVIL, scrofula, which the king was popularly supposed to be able to cure by touching the diseased person. Anne was the last sovereign who 'touched' for it.

King's Friends, THE, the so-called 'corrupt' members of parliament who under the administrations of Lord Bute and Lord North voted subserviently as George III required, in expectation of offices, pensions, and honours. So named in allusion to 1 Maccabees ii. 18.

King's or **Queen's Printer,** the printer of royal proclamations, etc., appointed under royal patent. The earliest known patent was granted to Thomas Berthelet (or Bartlet) in 1530. At the present day the controller of the Stationery Office (under Letters Patent) is the Queen's Printer of Acts of Parliament, and in him is vested the copyright in all government publications. Messrs. Eyre & Spottiswoode are also termed the Queen's Printers; their privilege is the printing of the Bible and Prayer Book, a privilege shared with the University Presses of Oxford and Cambridge.

King's Tragedy, The, a poem by D. G. Rossetti (q.v.), included in 'Ballads and Sonnets', published in 1881.

It is the story, which purports to be told by Catherine Douglas ('Kate Barlass'), of the ominous incidents which preceded the attack on the life of King James I of Scotland, and of her attempt to save him by barring the door with her arm against his murderers.

Kings of Cologne, THE THREE, see *Cologne.*

KINGSLEY, CHARLES (1819–75), born at Holne in Devonshire, where his father was vicar, was educated at King's College, London, and Magdalene College, Cambridge. He became curate and subsequently, in 1844, rector of Eversley in Hampshire and held the living for the remainder of his life. He was professor of modern history at Cambridge from 1860 to 1869, and after this held canonries at Chester and Westminster. He came much under the influence of F. D. Maurice and the writings of Carlyle, and took a vigor-

ous interest in the movement for social reform of the middle of the century, though disapproving of the violent policy of the Chartists. He contributed, over the signature 'Parson Lot', to the 'Politics of the People' in 1848, and to the 'Christian Socialist' in 1850–1. His literary activities were large and varied. In 'The Heroes' (1856) he tells for young readers the stories of Perseus, Theseus, and the Argonauts. His poetry included 'The Saint's Tragedy' (1848), a drama concerning St. Elizabeth of Hungary, the wife of Lewis, Landgrave of Thuringia, torn between her natural affections and her religious duties as enforced by a domineering monk; 'Andromeda' (1859), dealing with the classical myth; and many pleasant songs and ballads. His principal novels were 'Yeast' (q.v.), published in 'Fraser's Magazine' in 1848 and separately in 1850, and 'Alton Locke' (q.v., 1850), showing his sympathy with the sufferings of the working classes; 'Hypatia' (q.v., 1853); 'Westward Ho!' (q.v., 1855); 'Two Years Ago' (q.v., 1857); 'The Water Babies' (q.v., 1863); and 'Hereward the Wake' (q.v., 1865). His enthusiasm for natural history was shown by 'Glaucus; or the Wonders of the Shore' (1855). In 'Macmillan's Magazine', Jan. 1864, he published a review of Froude's 'History of England', vols. vii and viii, which led him into controversy with J. H. Newman (q.v.) and furnished the occasion for the latter's 'Apologia'. In the same year he published a course of lectures entitled 'The Roman and the Teuton'. 'At Last' (1871) is the record of a long-desired visit to the West Indies. His beautiful 'Prose Idylls' (1873) are among his last works. Kingsley published several volumes of sermons, many of them remarkable for their style, their interesting subjects, and the broad spirit of humanity they display.

KINGSLEY, HENRY (1830–76), younger brother of C. Kingsley (q.v.), was educated at King's College School and Worcester College, Oxford. At the latter his exuberance led him into some sort of trouble, as a result of which he went, without a degree, to Australia, where he spent five years (1853–8), and was for a time a trooper in the Sydney mounted police. His experiences with bushrangers while in this force are reflected in some of his novels. On his return he published 'Geoffry Hamlyn' (1859), a somewhat melodramatic story of the life of early settlers in Australia, in which bush-fires, attacks of bushrangers, etc., provide exciting incidents. This was followed by 'Ravenshoe' (q.v., 1862); 'Austin Elliott' (1863); 'The Hillyars and the Burtons' (1865), a second Australian story; 'Leighton Court' (1866); 'Silcote of Silcotes' (1867), and a number of less-known novels. During the Franco-Prussian war Henry Kingsley was a newspaper correspondent with the German army.

KINGSTON, WILLIAM HENRY GILES (1814–80), writer of boys' stories: 'Peter the

Whaler' (1851), 'The Three Midshipmen' (1862), and many others.

Kinmont Willie, see *Armstrong (W.).*

Kinraid, CHARLEY, a character in Mrs. Gaskell's 'Sylvia's Lovers' (q.v.).

Kiomi, the gipsy girl in Meredith's 'The Adventures of Harry Richmond' (q.v.).

KIPLING, RUDYARD (1865–1936), son of John Lockwood Kipling, the illustrator of 'Beast and Man in India', was born in Bombay and educated at the United Services College, Westward Ho! He was engaged in journalistic work in India from 1882 to 1889. His fame rests principally on his short stories, dealing with India, the sea, the jungle and its beasts, the army, the navy, and a multitude of other subjects; and in a less degree on his verse, which is variously judged, and as diversified in subject as his tales. His publications include: 'Departmental Ditties' (1886); 'Plain Tales from the Hills', 'Soldiers Three' (1888); 'In Black and White', 'The Story of the Gadsbys', 'Under the Deodars', 'The Phantom 'Rickshaw', 'Wee Willie Winkie' (1889); 'The City of Dreadful Night', 'The Light that Failed' (1890); 'Life's Handicap', 'Letters of Marque', 'The Smith Administration' (1891); 'Barrack-room Ballads', 'The Naulahka' (1892); 'Many Inventions' (1893); 'The Jungle Book' (q.v., 1894); 'The Second Jungle Book' (1895); 'The Seven Seas' (1896); 'Captains Courageous' (1897); 'The Day's Work' (1898); 'Stalky & Co.' (1899); 'Kim' (q.v., 1901); 'Just So Stories' (1902); 'The Five Nations' (1903); 'Traffics and Discoveries' (1904); 'Puck of Pook's Hill' (1906); 'Actions and Reactions' (1909); 'Rewards and Fairies' (1910); 'The New Army in Training' (1914); 'France at War', 'The Fringes of the Fleet' (1915); 'Sea Warfare' (1916); 'A Diversity of Creatures' (1917); 'The Years Between' (1919); 'Letters of Travel, 1892–1913' (1920); 'Land and Sea Tales for Scouts and Guides' (1923); 'Debits and Credits' (1926); 'A Book of Words' (1928); 'Thy Servant a Dog' (1930). Kipling edited 'The Irish Guards in the Great War' (1923). He was awarded a Nobel Prize in 1907.

Kipps, a novel by H. G. Wells (q.v.), published in 1905.

Arthur Kipps is a little, vulgar, uneducated draper's assistant at Folkestone, who unexpectedly inherits twelve hundred a year. After the first days of delirious joy, he finds his troubles begin. He becomes engaged to a young lady of the superior classes, but impecunious, who had previously been a distant star in his firmament. She has ambitions of her own, and sets firmly about Kipps's social education. The problems of correct eating and dressing, and generally of living up to his new position and his future bride, prove too much for Kipps's fortitude, and at last, driven desperate, he bolts, and hastily marries Ann, his boyhood's love, now in domestic service. But even then he is not out of his troubles;

for his wealth, with its trail of social obligations, follows him into married life, and threatens his happiness. So that the loss of nearly the whole of it—by the embezzlement of a solicitor—comes soon to be felt as a positive relief, and real happiness begins only when he starts life again as a shopkeeper. The description of Kipps's early life as a draper's apprentice is interesting for its autobiographical character.

KIRKE, EDWARD (1553–1613), a friend of Edmund Spenser, educated at Pembroke Hall and Caius College, Cambridge. He wrote the preface, the arguments, and a verbal commentary to Spenser's 'Shepheards Calender', under the initials 'E. K.' (1579). Modern critics have, on insufficient grounds, sought to prove that 'E. K.' was Spenser himself.

Kirke, PERCY (1646?–91), colonel of KIRKE'S LAMBS, the old Tangier regiment, the badge of which was a Paschal Lamb. He was present at Sedgemoor in 1685 and notorious for his cruelty to the rebels.

Kirkrapine, in Spenser's 'Faerie Queene', I. iii, 'a stout and sturdy thief' of the church, who was destroyed by Una's lion.

Kirstie Elliott, a character in R. L. Stevenson's 'Weir of Hermiston' (q.v.).

Kismet, a Turkish word meaning fate, destiny (from the Arabic *qisma(t)*, 'lot' or 'portion').

Kit Nubbles, a character in Dickens's 'The Old Curiosity Shop' (q.v.).

Kit-Cat Club, founded in the early part of the 18th cent. by leading Whigs, including (according to Pope) Steele, Addison, Congreve, Garth, and Vanbrugh (qq.v.). Jacob Tonson (q.v.), the publisher, was for many years its secretary and moving spirit. It met at the house of Christopher Katt, a pastrycook, in Shire Lane (which ran north from Temple Bar). Katt's mutton-pies were called *Kit-cats*, hence the name of the club ('Spectator', No. ix). The club subsequently met at Tonson's house at Barn Elms. The portraits of the members (painted by Sir Godfrey Kneller and now in the possession of the National Portrait Gallery) had to be less than half-length because the dining-room was too low for half-size portraits. The word 'kit-cat' is in consequence still used for portraits of this size.

Kite, SERGEANT, one of the chief characters in Farquhar's 'The Recruiting Officer' (q.v.). One of his songs is the well-known 'Over the hills and far away'.

Kitely, a character in Jonson's 'Every Man in his Humour' (q.v.).

Klaboterman, see *Carmilhan.*

Klephts (M.Gk. κλέφτης, thief), the Greeks who refused to submit to the Turks after the conquest of Greece in the 15th cent., and maintained their independence in the mountains. After the war of independence (1821–8) those who continued this existence became mere brigands. Hence the word is used for brigands, bandits.

Klingsor, in the version of the legend of the Grail (q.v.) adopted by Wagner in his opera 'Parsifal', the magician who, with the help of the enchantress, Kundry, and the flower maidens, strives to lure away the knights of Titurel (q.v.), until overcome by Parsifal.

KLOPSTOCK, FRIEDRICH GOTT-LIEB (1724–1803), German poet, famous for his patriotic odes and his great religious epic 'Messias' ('The Messiah'), inspired by Milton's 'Paradise Lost', of which the first three cantos were published in 1748 and the last in 1773, and which is characterized by its pietistic delight in sentiment and its disregard for action.

Knag, MISS, in Dickens's 'Nicholas Nickleby' (q.v.), Madame Mantalini's forewoman.

KNICKERBOCKER, DIEDRICH, the pseudonym under which W. Irving (q.v.) wrote his 'History of New York', and 'Rip van Winkle' and 'The Legend of Sleepy Hollow' (in 'The Sketch-Book'). The name 'Knickerbocker' became synonymous with a descendant of the original Dutch settlers of the New Netherlands in America. The word as used for loose-fitting breeches is said to have been given to these because of their resemblance to the knee-breeches of the Dutchmen in Cruikshank's illustrations to W. Irving's 'History of New York'. [OED.]

The KNICKERBOCKER CLUB is one of the oldest clubs in New York, founded in 1871.

Knickerbocker Magazine, The, founded in New York City, 1 Jan. 1833, under the editorship of Charles Fenno Hoffman. From that date until it was discontinued in 1865, the *Knickerbocker* numbered many of the foremost American writers among its contributors, including Washington Irving, H. W. Longfellow, W. C. Bryant, O. W. Holmes, J. R. Lowell, Horace Greeley, and J. F. Cooper.

KNIGHT, CHARLES (1791–1873), editor and publisher, produced the 'Penny Magazine' (1832–45), the 'Penny Cyclopaedia' (1833–44), and other cheap series designed to popularize knowledge.

Knight Hospitaller, see *Hospitallers of St. John of Jerusalem.*

Knight of the Burning Pestle, The, a comedy by Beaumont and Fletcher (see *Fletcher, J.*), printed in 1613. It is probably in the main the work of Beaumont.

The play is at once a burlesque of knight-errantry and of T. Heywood's (q.v.) 'The Four Prentices of London'—and thus the first of English parody plays—and a comedy of manners. The plot is very slight. A grocer and his wife in the audience insist that their apprentice, Ralph, shall have a part in the play. He therefore becomes a Grocer Errant, with a Burning Pestle portrayed on his shield, and undertakes various absurd adventures,

including the release of the patients held captive by a barber (Barbaroso). These are interspersed in the real plot, in which Jasper, a merchant's apprentice, is in love with his master's daughter Luce. He carries her off when she is about to be married to his rival, Humphrey, who is favoured by her father. The father and Humphrey recover her, and she is locked up. Jasper, feigning death, has himself conveyed to her in a coffin, frightens her father by assuming the character of his own ghost, and finally obtains his consent to the match.

Knight of the Leopard, Sir Kenneth of Scotland, the earl of Huntingdon, hero of Scott's 'The Talisman' (q.v.).

Knight of the Rueful Countenance, Don Quixote (q.v.).

Knight of the Swan, THE, Lohengrin (q.v.). In early forms of the legend he is called HELIAS. There is an Icelandic saga in which Helis, Knight of the Swan, is represented as a son of Julius Caesar. See also *Rudiger,* a ballad by R. Southey.

Knight's Tale, The, see *Canterbury Tales.*

Knights of Malta, see *Hospitallers of St. John of Jerusalem.*

Knights of Rhodes, see *Hospitallers of St. John of Jerusalem.*

Knights of the Bath, see *Bath (Order of the).*

Knights of the Garter, see *Garter.*

Knights of the Golden Fleece, see *Golden Fleece.*

Knights of the Post, notorious perjurers, who got their living by giving false evidence; perhaps for 'knights of the whipping-post' or pillory. [OED.]

Knights of the Round Table, see *Round Table.*

Knights of Windsor, a small body of military officers who have pensions and apartments in Windsor Castle.

Knights Templar, see *Templars.*

Knightley, GEORGE, the bachelor owner of Donwell Abbey, and JOHN, his brother, characters in Jane Austen's 'Emma' (q.v.).

Knightriders Street, see *Giltspur Street.*

Knightsbridge, in the West End of London, at the end of the 17th cent. was a place of some notoriety, with two taverns of questionable reputation, the Swan and the World's End, referred to in Congreve's 'Love for Love' (q.v.).

Knipperdolling, an adherent of Bernhard Knipperdolling, a leader of the Münster Anabaptists (q.v.) in 1533–5; an Anabaptist; hence a religious fanatic.

Knockdunder, THE CAPTAIN OF, in Scott's 'The Heart of Midlothian' (q.v.), the duke of Argyle's agent.

KNOLLES, RICHARD (1550?–1610),

author of a 'General Historie of the Turkes' (1603), not only valuable as a contribution to contemporary knowledge of the East, but interesting for the influence which Byron acknowledges that it had upon himself.

Knossos, see under *Minoan*.

Knowell, a character in Jonson's 'Every Man in his Humour' (q.v.).

KNOWLES, JAMES SHERIDAN (1784–1862), after trying the army, medicine, the stage, and teaching, as professions, became an author. His best plays were the tragedies of 'Caius Gracchus' (produced 1815), 'Virginius' (produced 1820), 'William Tell' (1825), and 'The Wife' (1833); and his comedies, 'The Beggar's Daughter of Bethnal Green' (1828), 'The Hunchback' (1832), and 'The Love Chase' (1837).

Knowles, SIR JAMES THOMAS (1831–1908), editor of the 'Contemporary Review', 1870–7; and founder of the 'Nineteenth Century' and the Metaphysical Society (qq.v.).

Knox, FLURRY, the M.F.H. in the 'Experiences of an Irish R.M.' by E. Œ. Somerville (q.v.) and Martin Ross.

KNOX, JOHN (1505–72), was educated at Haddington School and Glasgow University. He was called to the ministry and began preaching for the reformed religion in 1547. He went abroad at the accession of Mary Tudor, wrote his 'Epistle on Justification by Faith' in 1548, met Calvin at Geneva in 1554, was pastor of the English congregation at Frankfort-on-the-Main, 1554–5, and from 1556 to 1558 lived at Geneva. Thence he addressed epistles to his brethren in England suffering under the rule of Mary Tudor, and in Scotland under the regency of Mary of Lorraine. It was this situation which led to the publication of his 'First Blast of the Trumpet against the Monstrous Regiment of Women' (1558), of which the title, Saintsbury remarks, was the best part. In 1559 appeared the 'First Book of Discipline', of which Knox was part-author, advocating a national system of education ranging from a school in every parish to the three universities. His 'Treatise on Predestination' was published in 1560. In 1572 he was appointed minister at Edinburgh, where he died. His 'History of the Reformation of Religion within the realm of Scotland' was first printed in 1587 (the best edition of this is in the first two vols. of Laing's edition of Knox's 'Works', 1846–8). It contains, in its fourth book, the notable account of the return of Mary Stuart to Scotland, of Knox's interviews with her, and his fierce denunciations from the pulpit of St. Giles.

KNOX, THE RT. REVD. MONSIGNOR RONALD ARBUTHNOTT (1888–1957), educated at Eton and Balliol College, Oxford, and fellow of Trinity from 1910 to 1917, when he was received into the Church of Rome. He was Catholic chaplain at the University of Oxford from 1926 to 1939. He published a new translation of the Bible, based on the Vulgate text; the New Testament in 1945 and the Old Testament in 2 vols. in 1949. His works include 'Some Loose Stones' (1913), 'A Spiritual Aeneid' (1918), (autobiographical), 'The Belief of Catholics' (1927), 'Essays in Satire' (1928), 'Broadcast Minds' (1932), 'Barchester Pilgrimage' (1935), 'Let Dons Delight' (1939), 'God and the Atom' (1945), 'Enthusiasm' (1950), 'A Retreat for Lay People' (1955), 'Bridegroom and Bride' (1957), 'On Translation' (Romanes Lecture, 1957). He also wrote six detective stories. Among his posthumous publications are 'Literary Distractions' (1958) and 'In Three Tongues' (1959).

KNOX, VICESIMUS (1752–1821), educated at St. John's College, Oxford, is remembered as the compiler of 'Elegant Extracts' (1789). He was author of 'Essays Moral and Literary' (1778).

KNYVETT, SIR HENRY (*d.* 1598), of Charlton, near Malmesbury, a valiant soldier in Elizabeth's wars, wrote 'The Defence of the Realme' (1596); it was published in the 'Tudor and Stuart Library' in 1906. It advocates universal training for military service.

Knyvett, THOMAS (1596–1658), born at Ashwellthorpe in Norfolk, and educated at Emmanuel College, Cambridge, was a landowner in the eastern counties, and a Royalist in sympathy during the Civil War. His letters to his wife, which have been preserved, throw an interesting light on the life of the period. They have been edited by B. Schofield (1949).

Kobold, in German folk-lore, a familiar spirit haunting houses and rendering services to the inmates, but often of a tricksy disposition; also an underground spirit haunting mines and caves.

KOESTLER, ARTHUR (1905–), author, born in Budapest and educated at the University of Vienna. He worked as a foreign correspondent in the Middle East, Paris, and Berlin, and was imprisoned by Franco during the Spanish Civil War. He served in the French Foreign Legion (1939–40) and settled in England in 1940. His publications include 'Spanish Testament' (1938), 'The Gladiators' (1939), 'Darkness at Noon' (1940), 'Arrival and Departure' (1943), 'Thieves in the Night' (1946), 'The Age of Longing' (1951), 'The Trail of the Dinosaur and other essays' (1955), 'Reflections on Hanging' (1956), 'The Sleepwalkers: a history of man's changing view of the universe' (1959), and 'The Act of Creation: a study in the history of scientific discovery and an essay in the analysis of literary and artistic creation' (1964). 'Scum of the Earth' (1941) and 'Arrow in the Blue' (1952) are autobiographical.

Koh-i-noor, an Indian diamond, famous for its size and history, extending, it is said, to 2,000 years, which became one of the British crown jewels on the annexation of the Punjab in 1849. It belonged in the past to Aurungzebe, and subsequently to Nadir Shah and to Runjeet Singh.

Königsberg, a seaport on the Baltic, the capital of East Prussia, a town associated with the life of Kant (q.v.). 'Königsberg' was also the name of a German light cruiser, engaged in commerce destruction in the early part of the First World War, blockaded in the Rufiji river in Nov. 1914, and destroyed in July 1915.

Koppenberg, see *Pied Piper of Hamelin.*

Koran or QURÂN, THE, from the Arabic verb signifying 'to read', the sacred book of the Muslims, consisting of revelations orally delivered from time to time by Mohammed, some at Mecca, others at Medina, taken down by scribes, and collected and put in order after his death by Abu Bakr (q.v.). The Koran teaches the unity of God, which it attests by examples of the punishments inflicted on those who maltreated his messengers, and supplements with directions and admonitions. The four chief duties that it enjoins are prayer (to be preceded by ablution), the giving of alms, fasting, and the pilgrimage to Mecca. The Koran is written in a very pure Arabic, the standard language.

Koraysh or QURAYSH, the Arabian tribe to which Mohammed belonged. It included the rival families of the Hashimites and the Umayyads (qq.v.).

Kosciusko, TADEUS (1746–1817), Polish patriot and general, who led the Polish insurrection of 1794.

Kottabos, a Trinity College, Dublin, magazine started by R. Y. Tyrrell, an eminent classical scholar, translator, and conversationalist, in 1868. It ran for some twenty years in all, in two periods, and excelled in light verse and parodies. Its contributors included Edward Dowden, Oscar Wilde, Standish O'Grady, and John Todhunter. (κότταβος was a game introduced into Greece from Sicily, which depended on skill in throwing wine from a goblet, at a certain distance, into a metal basin.)

KOTZEBUE, AUGUST VON (1761–1819), a German dramatist, author of a large number of sentimental plays which had considerable vogue in their day and influenced the English stage. His 'Menschenhass und Reue' enjoyed great popularity here as 'The Stranger', brought out by Sheridan in 1798, the story of a wife duped and erring, her husband in consequence turned misanthropical, the wife's repentance, the reconciliation, and the husband's return to sanity. 'Lovers' Vows' (q.v.), made famous by Jane Austen's 'Mansfield Park', was adapted from Kotzebue's 'Das Kind der Liebe'. Sheridan adapted 'Die Spanier in Peru' in 'Pizarro'.

Kraken, a mythical sea-monster of enormous size, said to have been seen at times off the coast of Norway. The name was first brought to general notice by the description (1752) of Pontoppidan (q.v.). Tennyson wrote a short poem about the Kraken.

Kratim or KRATIMER, see *Katmer.*

Kremlin, the ancient citadel of Moscow, containing a palace and many curious churches; now the seat of the Soviet government.

Kreutzer Sonata, The, a famous sonata for piano and violin by Beethoven (q.v.), dedicated by him to Rodolphe Kreutzer (1766–1831), a French violinist and composer. Also the title of a work by Tolstoy.

Kriemhild, see *Nibelungenlied.*

Krishna, a great deity or deified hero of later Hinduism, worshipped as an incarnation of Vishnu (q.v.), the god of fire, lightning, and storm; in the myths a brave, crafty, invincible hero, the destroyer of the tyrannical King Kansa, and the lover of Radha.

Kronos, see *Cronos.*

Krook, a character in Dickens's 'Bleak House' (q.v.).

Kshatriya, the second of the great Hindu castes, the military caste.

Ku-Klux-Klan, a widespread secret society (κύκλος), which arose in the Southern States of North America after the civil war of 1861–5, beginning with an effort to overawe the Negro population by whipping and arson, and developing into a system of political outrage and murder. Though suppressed in 1871 by an act of Congress, a kindred organization still survives.

Kubla Khan, a Vision in a Dream, a poem by S. T. Coleridge (q.v.), published in 1816.

The poet, in 1797, living at a lonely farmhouse on the confines of Somerset and Devon, fell asleep in his chair when reading a passage in 'Purchas his Pilgrimage' relating to the Khan Kubla and the palace that he commanded to be built. On awaking he was conscious of having composed in his sleep two or three hundred lines on this theme, and immediately set down the lines that form this fragment. He was then unfortunately interrupted, and, on returning to his task an hour later, found that the remainder of the poem had passed from his memory. All that remains to us is the vision of the scene amid which Kubla's palace was built. See *Xanadu.*

Kufic, see *Cufic.*

Kulhwch and Olwen, see *Kilhwch and Olwen.*

Kulturkampf, the struggle between Bismarck and the Vatican, which began in 1873, concerning the relations of Church and State.

Kundry, see *Klingsor.*

Kvasir, see *Odhaerir.*

KYD or KID, THOMAS (1558?–94?), dramatist, was educated at Merchant Taylors' School, London, and was by profession a scrivener. His 'The Spanish Tragedy' (q.v.) was printed in 1594 (?), and 'Pompey the Great, his faire Corneliaes Tragedy' (q.v.) in 1595. 'The First Part of Ieronimo', published in 1605, a fore-piece to 'The Spanish Tragedy', is frequently attributed to Kyd, but was probably not by him, though some other such fore-piece by him probably at one time existed. It is also uncertain whether he was the author of 'The Tragedy of Solyman and Perseda' (printed in 1599). He was perhaps the author of a pre-Shakespearian play (now lost) on the subject of Hamlet. He was one of the best-known tragic poets of his time, and his work shows an advance in the construction of plot and development of character.

Kýrie Eléison, Greek words meaning 'Lord,

have mercy', a short petition used in various offices of the Eastern and Roman churches; also a musical setting of these words. An English version is part of the Communion service.

Kyrle, JOHN, the MAN OF ROSS (1637–1724), educated at Ross Grammar School and Balliol College, Oxford, lived very simply on his estates at Ross and devoted his surplus income to works of charity. He was celebrated by Pope in the 'Moral Essays' (q.v.), Epistle III, and the Kyrle Society (for brightening the lot and improving the taste of the poorer classes) was inaugurated in 1877 as a memorial of him.

Kywert, see *Coart.*

L

L. E. L., see *Landon (L. E.).*

La Balue, CARDINAL (1421–91), a minister of Louis XI, who was for many years imprisoned in an iron cage for treason. He figures in Scott's 'Quentin Durward' (q.v.).

La Belle Dame sans Merci, see *Belle Dame sans Merci.*

La Belle Sauvage, see *Belle Sauvage Inn.*

LA BOÉTIE, ÉTIENNE DE (1530–63), French writer and humanist, the intimate friend of Montaigne (q.v.). His most famous work was the 'Discours sur la servitude volontaire' or 'Contr'un'.

LA BRUYÈRE, JEAN DE (1645–96), French ethical writer, author of 'Caractères' on the model of Theophrastus.

LA CALPRENÈDE, GAUTHIER DE COSTES DE (1614–63), a Gascon by birth, author of several very lengthy heroic romances, which were much admired by contemporaries, but are found intolerably tedious today. These were: 'Cassandre' (ten vols., 1644–50), which has for its heroine the daughter of Darius whom Alexander the Great married; 'Cléopâtre' (ten vols., 1647–56), of which the heroine is not Antony's Cleopatra, but a supposed daughter of their marriage, and one of the characters is a certain Artaban, who became proverbial for pride; 'Pharamond' (twelve vols., 1661–70, the last five vols. by a continuator), which deals with the early legendary history of France, in particular the love of the first of the French kings for Rosemonde, daughter of the king of the Cimbrians. All these romances were translated into English and other languages.

La Chaise, PÈRE, see *Père La Chaise.*

La Creevy, MISS, the cheerful little miniature-painter in Dickens's 'Nicholas Nickleby' (q.v.).

LA FAYETTE, MME DE (1634–93), French writer, author of 'La Princesse de Clèves' (q.v.).

LA FONTAINE, JEAN DE (1621–95), a French poet of great versatility, who wrote dramas, satires, and light verse, but is chiefly famous for his 'Contes et Nouvelles' (1664–74), successive collections of verse-tales in which he recast the popular *fabliaux* of Europe; and still more for his 'Fables' (1668, 1678–9, and 1694). These were taken from Eastern, Greek, Roman, and modern sources, and while in their more serious aspect presenting a somewhat hard and sceptical view of life, are told with an inimitable naïveté and a semi-pagan sentiment for nature that make La Fontaine the greatest fabulist of all time.

La Mancha, an ancient province of Spain, from which Don Quixote (q.v.) took his title.

La Palisse (more correctly LA PALICE), JACQUES DE CHABANNES, *Seigneur de* (c. 1470–1525), Marshal of France under Charles VIII–Francis I, killed at the battle of Pavia. He was unjustly ridiculed in a famous song written in the 18th cent., embodying a number of incontestable truths, known as 'vérités de La Palisse', e.g.

> Il mourut le vendredi,
> Le dernier jour de son âge,
> S'il fût mort le samedi,
> Il eût vécu davantage.

LA ROCHEFOUCAULD, FRANÇOIS DE MARSILLAC, *Duc de* (1613–80), author of interesting 'Mémoires', but chiefly famous for his 'Réflexions, Sentences, et Maximes Morales' (1665), pithy maxims of extreme concision and finish, embodying a somewhat cynical philosophy that finds in self-love the prime motive of all action.

La Saisiaz, a poem by R. Browning (q.v.), written in 1877 under the influence of the sudden death of a friend who had been spending the summer of that year with Browning and his sister at the villa 'La Saisiaz' near Geneva. In it the poet examines afresh the basis of his faith in a future life.

Lăbărum, the imperial standard adopted by Constantine the Great (q.v.), being the Roman military standard of the late empire modified by the addition of Christian symbols.

Labour and Life of the People, see *Booth* (*C.*).

Labyrinth of Crete, THE, a maze constructed by Daedalus (q.v.) for Minos (q.v.), king of Crete. In it the Minotaur (q.v.) was confined. The word 'labyrinth' is of uncertain origin, perhaps from λάβρυς, a Lydian or Carian word meaning double-headed axe, a symbol of religious signification, such as is found frequently incised on stones and pillars in Cretan excavations of the Minoan period.

Lachesis, see *Parcae.*

LACHMANN, KARL KONRAD FRIEDRICH WILHELM (1793–1851), a German philologist, distinguished both in the German and classical spheres. By a careful study of Old German and Middle High German literature he determined its metrical principles. He published editions of the Greek New Testament, of Lucretius, Propertius, and Tibullus; and critical works on Homer, &c. His 'Lucretius' was his greatest work, and a landmark in the history of textual criticism. He was the first scholar to break away from the *textus receptus* ('Received Text') of the Greek New Testament.

Laconic, following the Laconian (i.e. Spartan, q.v.) manner especially in speech and writing; brief, concise, sententious.

Ladas, a celebrated courier of Alexander the Great, who won a crown at Olympia. Ladas was the name of Lord Rosebery's Derby winner in 1894.

Ladislaw, WILL, a character in G. Eliot's 'Middlemarch' (q.v.).

Ladon, the dragon that guarded the apples of the Hesperides (q.v.), and was slain by Hercules.

Ladrones (Spanish, 'robbers'), a chain of fifteen islands in the North Pacific, discovered by Magellan and occupied by Spain in the 17th cent.; so called by Magellan because the islanders stole some of his goods.

Ladurlad, a character in Southey's 'Curse of Kehama' (q.v.).

Lady Bountiful, in Farquhar's 'The Beaux' Stratagem' (q.v.) a 'country gentlewoman, that cures all her neighbours of their distempers' and lays out half her income in charitable uses.

Lady Day, a day kept in celebration of some event in the life of the Virgin Mary; now used only of 25 March, the Feast of the Annunciation; formerly also 8 Dec. (the Conception of the Virgin), 8 Sept. (the Nativity), and 15 Aug. (the Assumption).

Lady Margaret foundations at Oxford and Cambridge were instituted by Margaret Beaufort, daughter of John duke of Somerset, wife of Edmund Tudor, and mother of Henry VII. She was an early patron of Caxton and Wynkyn de Worde.

Lady of Christ's, Milton's nickname at Cambridge.

Lady of Lyons, The, or Love and Pride, a romantic comedy by Bulwer Lytton (q.v.), produced in 1838.

The time of the play is 1795–8. Pauline Deschapelles, the proud daughter of a merchant of Lyons, rejects various suitors, including a *ci-devant* marquis, Beauséant. Young Claude Melnotte, son of the Deschapelles' old gardener, self-educated and accomplished, loves her humbly. Beauséant, in order to be avenged on Pauline, persuades Claude to personate a foreign prince and to court her in that disguise. The fraud is completely successful, the pair are married, and Claude carries his wife off to his mother's humble cottage. Then he is filled with remorse and seeks to make atonement by restoring Pauline to her father and facilitating the annulment of the marriage. Pauline's heart is won by this proof of his real love. Claude joins the army of Buonaparte, greatly distinguishes himself under an assumed name, and returns to Lyons two years later, rich and a colonel, to find that Pauline is on the point of marrying Beauséant to save her father from bankruptcy. Pauline not recognizing him, but believing him to be the friend of Claude, sends to her former husband a final message of her undying love for him. Claude reveals himself, is rapturously received, and Beauséant departs, raving at his discomfiture.

Lady of Shalott, The, a poem by A. Tennyson (q.v.), published in 1852, of which the story finds fuller development in the author's 'Lancelot and Elaine' (q.v.), one of the 'Idylls of the King'.

Lady of the Aroostook, The, a novel by W. D. Howells (q.v.), published in 1879, which relates the fortunes of Lydia Blood, a young New England school-teacher who finds herself set down in the midst of fashionable and sophisticated Venice.

Lady of the Idle Lake, see *Phaedria.*

Lady of the Lake, THE, in the Arthurian legends, a somewhat indistinct supernatural character. In Malory's 'Morte Darthur', she first appears as giving Arthur the sword Excalibur, and when she comes to claim Balin's head as her reward, is killed by Balin (II. iii). But Nimue is spoken of later in the same work as the Lady of the Lake. Nimue befriends Arthur and rescues him in peril, and marries Pelleas. Merlin falls into a dotage on her, and Nimue, to get rid of him, inveigles him under a rock and buries him under a great stone. She is one of the three queens in the ship in which Arthur is borne away to be healed of his wounds. These, as Professor Rhys points out ('Arthurian Legend'), 'may all be taken as different aspects of one mythic figure, the lake lady Morgen', who appears also as Morgan le Fay (q.v.), at one time a benevolent, at another a malicious being. He traces her to the Rhiannon of British mythology, the wife of Pwyll (see under *Mabinogion*), the names 'Nimue' and 'Vivien' arising from miscopyings by successive scribes.

Lady of the Lake, The, a poem in six cantos by Sir W. Scott (q.v.), published in 1810.

A knight, who gives his name as James Fitz-James, receives hospitality in the home of Roderick Dhu, the fierce Highland chief, on Loch Katrine, where he falls in love with Ellen, daughter of the outlawed Lord James of Douglas. Roderick himself and the young Malcolm Graeme are also suitors for her hand, and Ellen loves the latter. Under threat of an attack by the royal forces, Roderick summons his clans. Douglas, regarding himself as the cause of the attack, sets out for Stirling to surrender himself to the king. Meanwhile James Fitz-James returns and proposes to carry Ellen off to safety. She refuses, confessing her love for another. Fitz-James generously withdraws, giving her a signet-ring which will enable her to obtain from the king any boon she may ask. On his way back to Stirling he falls in with Roderick. A fierce quarrel springs up between them and they fight. Fitz-James's skill prevails, and the wounded Roderick is carried prisoner to Stirling. Ellen appears at the king's court, presents her signet-ring, asks for her father's pardon, and discovers that Fitz-James is the king himself. The king and Douglas are reconciled, Roderick dies of his wounds, and Ellen marries Malcolm Graeme. The poem includes the beautiful *coronach* 'He is gone on the mountain', and Ellen's song 'Soldier, rest, thy warfare o'er'. The king is as much drawn from James V as from anyone.

Lady of the Lamp, The, a name given to Florence Nightingale (q.v.) in allusion to her visits at night to the hospital wards during the Crimean War.

Lady or the Tiger, The, a famous short story by Frank Stockton (q.v.), published in 1882.

Laelaps, see *Cephalus*.

Laertes, (1) the father of Odysseus (q.v.); (2) in Shakespeare's 'Hamlet' (q.v.) the brother of Ophelia.

Laestrygŏnes, in Homer's 'Odyssey' (Bk. x), a race of giants who inhabited Sicily and fed on human flesh. They sank eleven of the twelve ships of Odysseus and devoured his companions.

Lafeu, a character in Shakespeare's 'All's Well that Ends Well' (q.v.).

Lagado, see *Gulliver's Travels*.

Laïs, a celebrated Greek courtesan, a Sicilian, carried to Corinth at the time of the Athenian expedition to Sicily.

Lake Poets, LAKE SCHOOL, THE, terms applied to the three poets Coleridge, Southey, and Wordsworth, who resided in the neighbourhood of the English Lakes. 'Lake School' first appears in this sense in the 'Edinburgh Review', Aug. 1817.

Lake Regillus, near Rome, memorable for the victory of the Romans over the Latins and Tarquin c. 496 B.C., celebrated by T. B. Macaulay (q.v.) in his lay, 'The Battle of Lake Regillus'.

Lakshmi or SRI, in Hindu mythology, the wife of Vishnu (q.v.), the goddess of prosperity. She is represented in the 'Ramayana' (q.v.) as produced from the foam of the sea, when the gods and the demons churned the ocean in order to obtain the *Amrita* (q.v.) or water of life.

Lalla Rookh, a series of oriental tales in verse, connected together by a story in prose, by T. Moore (q.v.), published in 1817.

The prose story relates the journey of Lalla Rookh, the daughter of the Emperor Aurungzebe, from Delhi to Cashmere, to be married to the young king of Bucharia. On the way, she and her train are diverted by four tales told by Feramorz, a young Cashmerian poet, with whom she falls in love, and who turns out, on her arrival at her destination, to be the king of Bucharia himself. An element of humour is introduced by the self-important chamberlain, Fadladeen. A series of accidents on the way has thrown him into a bad temper, which he vents in pungent criticisms on the young man's verses (in the style of the 'Edinburgh' reviewers), and he is correspondingly discomfited on discovering the latter's identity. The four tales are as follows.

The Veiled Prophet of Khorassan. The beautiful Zelica, half demented by the loss of Azim, her lover, supposed dead, is lured into the haram of Mokanna, a repulsive impostor who poses as a prophet, on the promise of admission to Paradise. Azim, returning from the wars, finds Zelica wedded to Mokanna, and joins the army of the Caliph, on its way to punish the blasphemy of Mokanna. The latter is defeated, throws himself into a vat of corrosive poison, and dies. Zelica, seeking death, puts on his veil, and being mistaken for the prophet, is killed by Azim and dies in his arms.

Paradise and the Peri. A Peri, one of 'those beautiful spirits of the air who live on perfumes', offspring of fallen angels, is promised admission to Paradise if she will bring to the gate the gift that is most dear to Heaven. She brings first a drop of the blood of a youthful warrior who dies to free India from the tyrant Mahmoud of Gazna, but it fails to open the gate. Then the expiring sigh of an Egyptian maiden who dies from grief at the loss of her plague-stricken lover; this is equally unavailing. Lastly, the repentant tear wrung from a criminal by his child's prayer to God, and this opens the gate.

The Fire-Worshippers, a tale of the Ghebers or Persians of the old religion, who maintained their resistance against the conquering Muslims. Hafed, a young Gheber, falls in love with Hinda, daughter of the Emir Al Hassan, who has been sent from Arabia to quell this resistance. Hafed scales the rocks on which her bower stands, and wins her love. Presently Hinda is captured by the Ghebers and discovers that her lover is their chief. The Ghebers are betrayed to Al Hassan, and Hafed throws himself on a funeral pyre. Hinda leaps from the boat on which she is being carried back to her father and is drowned.

The Light of the Haram, a story of Nourmahal, the beloved wife of Selim, son of the Great Akbar. The Feast of Roses is being celebrated in the Vale of Cashmere, but Nourmahal has quarrelled with her husband. Namouna, the enchantress, teaches her a magic song, which Nourmahal sings, masked, at Selim's banquet, and thus wins back his love.

The first of the tales is written in heroic couplets, the others in stanzas of varied metre, mostly octosyllabic. Lady Holland said to Moore at her own table, 'Mr. Moore, I have not read your Larry O'Rourke; I don't like Irish stories.'

Lallans, the vernacular speech of the Lowlands of Scotland. Its use for literary purposes has been revived by C. M. Grieve, Tom Scott, S. Goodsir Smith, and others.

L'Allegro, see *Allegro.*

Lamachus, an Athenian general, colleague of Alcibiades and Nicias in the Sicilian expedition of 415 B.C. His plan for the capture of Syracuse, and immediate attack, was the boldest, but he was overborne by his colleagues.

LAMARCK, JEAN BAPTISTE, *Chevalier de* (1744–1829), French biologist and botanist. He advanced the view that species were not unalterable, and that the higher and more complex forms of life were derived from lower and simpler forms; that environment and new needs created new organs, and that these were transmitted to descendants. Darwin adopted from Lamarck the theory of the transmissibility of acquired characteristics, but in other respects their views were not in harmony.

LAMARTINE, ALPHONSE DE (1790–1869), one of the chief poets of the early Romantic Movement in France, and a diplomat by profession till about 1830, best known by his 'Méditations poétiques' (1820), meditative poems of a religious and mystical cast, followed by 'Nouvelles Méditations poétiques' (1823), and 'Harmonies poétiques et religieuses' (1830). He also wrote two long narrative poems, 'Jocelyn' (1836) and 'La Chute

d'un ange' (1838). He turned to politics in 1833 (winning fame as an orator), and for a brief period he was in 1848 head of the provisional government. His 'Histoire des Girondins' (1847), a work of great emotional fervour, contributed powerfully to the Revolution of 1848. After his retirement he published two series of 'Confidences' (1849–51), and some novels and further poems.

LAMB, LADY CAROLINE (1785–1828), daughter of the third earl of Bessborough, married William Lamb, afterwards second Viscount Melbourne. She became passionately infatuated with Byron. Her first novel 'Glenarvon', published anonymously in 1816, after his rupture with her (republished as 'The Fatal Passion', 1865), contained a caricature portrait of him. She published 'Graham Hamilton' in 1822, and 'Ada Reis, a Tale' in 1823. Her accidental meeting with Byron's funeral procession on its way to Newstead in 1824 permanently affected her mind.

LAMB, CHARLES (1775–1834), was born in London. His father, the Lovel of the 'Essays of Elia' ('The Old Benchers of the Inner Temple'), was the clerk and confidential attendant of Samuel Salt, a lawyer, whose house in Crown Office Row was Lamb's birthplace and his home during his youth. His grandmother, Mrs. Field, was housekeeper at Blakesware (near Ware), described in the 'Blakesmoor' essay and in 'Mrs. Leicester's School'. Lamb was educated at Christ's Hospital, where he formed an enduring friendship with S. T. Coleridge. After a few months' employment at the South Sea House, he obtained at 17 an appointment in the East India House, where he remained from 1792 to 1825. In 1796 his mother was killed by his sister Mary in a fit of insanity. Lamb undertook the charge of his sister, who remained subject to periodic seizures, and she repaid him with her sympathy and affection. He himself was for a short time (1795–6) mentally deranged, and the curse of madness acted as a shadow on his life. A volume of poems by S. T. Coleridge published in 1796 contains four sonnets by Lamb, and in 1798 appeared 'Blank Verse' by Charles Lloyd and Charles Lamb, which includes 'The Old Familiar Faces'. In the same year appeared 'The Tale of Rosamund Gray and Old Blind Margaret', a simple tragic tale of a young girl, the victim of an undeserved misfortune. In 1802 Lamb published 'John Woodvil' (first called 'Pride's Cure'), a tragedy in the Elizabethan style; in 1806 his farce 'Mr. H——' proved a failure at Drury Lane. With his sister he wrote 'Tales from Shakespear' (1807), designed to make Shakespeare familiar to the young; also 'Mrs. Leicester's School' (1809), a collection of ten stories, reminiscences of childhood supposed to be told by the pupils at a Hertfordshire school, containing autobiographic details of the authors. 'The Adventures of Ulysses' (1808) is a successful attempt by Lamb to do for the 'Odyssey' what with his sister he had done for Shakespeare.

In 1808 he also published his 'Specimens of English Dramatic Poets contemporary with Shakespeare, with Notes'. Between 1810 and 1820 his literary output was small. It includes the essays on 'The Tragedies of Shakespeare' and 'On the Genius and Character of Hogarth' (1811). He wrote for Leigh Hunt's 'Reflector' and for the 'Examiner', and in 1814 contributed to the 'Quarterly Review' an article (much altered editorially) on Wordsworth's 'Excursion'. A collection of his miscellaneous writings in prose and verse appeared in 1818. From 1820 to 1823 Lamb was a regular contributor to the 'London Magazine', in which appeared the first series of miscellaneous essays known as the 'Essays of Elia' (q.v.), published in a separate volume in 1823. The second series was published in 1833. His correspondence was first published by Sir Thomas Talfourd in 1834; an enlarged collection was issued by Canon Ainger in 1899–1900. Of his poems the best known are 'The Old Familiar Faces' (referred to above), the lyrical ballad 'Hester' (1803), and the elegy 'On an Infant dying as soon as born' (1827); but 'Album Verses', published in 1830, also includes many charming lyrics and sonnets. From 1797 to 1823 Lamb lived with his sister in London (at Pentonville, Southampton Buildings, The Temple, and Covent Garden); in 1823 they moved to Islington, in 1827 to Enfield, and thence in 1833 to Edmonton, where Lamb died and was buried. His sister survived him for thirteen years. The standard life of Lamb was written, and the most complete collection of his letters edited, by E. V. Lucas (1905, 5th ed. 1921, 'Letters', 1935).

LAMB, MARY ANN (1764–1847), the sister of Charles Lamb (q.v.), under whose name the chief facts of her life will be found. Besides 'The Tales from Shakespear' there referred to (her share in which was the comedies), she wrote the greater part of 'Mrs. Leicester's School' (1809), to which her brother contributed three tales.

Lambert, GENERAL, MRS., THEO, and HETTY, characters in Thackeray's 'The Virginians' (q.v.).

Lambeth, from very early times the property of the see of Rochester, was in 1197 acquired by the archbishop of Canterbury. Of the palace an important part was built by Hubert Walter, who was archbishop in 1193–1205, and other parts were added at various times. The Lollards' Tower (15th cent.) was used during the Interregnum as a prison for Royalists, as it had been for Lollards 250 years before. The archbishops, notably Bancroft, collected a great library at Lambeth. This was saved with difficulty at the Great Rebellion. It was transferred to the University of Cambridge under a provision of Bancroft's will. Many books were lost, but a good proportion returned to Lambeth, being claimed by Archbishop Juxon at the restoration, and were housed in the fine hall that Juxon built.

The palace is on the Thames, 1½ miles southwest of St. Paul's Cathedral.

Lamela, AMBROSE, see *Don Raphael.*

Lamia, a poem by Keats (q.v.), written in 1819.

The story was taken by Keats from Burton ('Anatomy of Melancholy', III. ii. 1. 1), who quotes it from Philostratus ('De Vita Apollonii'). Lamia, a witch, is transformed by Hermes from a serpent into a beautiful maiden. She loves the young Corinthian Lycius, and he, spellbound by her beauty, takes her secretly to his house. Not content with his happiness, he makes a bridal feast and summons his friends. Among them comes the sage Apollonius, who pierces through Lamia's disguise, and calls her by her name, whereupon with a frightful scream she vanishes.

'Lamia' was the Latin name for a witch who was supposed to suck children's blood, a sorceress.

Lammas, from OE. *hlafmæsse*, loaf-mass, 1 Aug., in the early English Church observed as a harvest festival, at which loaves of bread were consecrated, made from the first ripe corn. In Scotland one of the quarter-days.

Lammle, ALFRED and SOPHRONIA, in Dickens's 'Our Mutual Friend' (q.v.), unscrupulous social adventurers.

Lamorak de Galis, SIR, in the 'Morte Darthur' (q.v.), son of Sir Pellinore and brother of Sir Percival, 'the biggest knight that ever I met withal, but if it were Sir Launcelot', said Sir Tristram. He was slain by Gawaine, Agravaine, Gaheris, and Mordred, Mordred giving him his death-wound treacherously at his back. This they did because of Sir Lamorak's adultery with their mother, King Lot's wife.

LA MOTTE FOUQUÉ, FRIEDRICH BARON DE, see *Undine.*

Lamourette, ADRIEN (1742–94), bishop of Lyons and member of the Legislative Assembly (in the French Revolution), where he brought about a temporary reconciliation between the parties which was soon forgotten. Whence a *baiser Lamourette* or 'Lamourette kiss' signifies an ephemeral reconciliation.

Lamplighter, The, a novel by the American authoress Maria Susanna Cummins (1827–66), published in 1854.

LAMPMAN, ARCHIBALD (1861–99), Canadian poet, born in Ontario; one of the group of poets who came to maturity after the Confederation and expressed the developing national consciousness. He published two volumes of verse, 'Among the Millet' (1888) and 'Lyrics of Earth' (1896). A third volume 'Alcyone' was in preparation when he died. It contained one of his finest works 'The City of the End of Things', a sombre allegory of human life. But Lampman's strength lay in his observation and description of nature, and he has given many vivid pictures of the Canadian landscape.

Lampoon, a virulent or scurrilous satire, according to French etymologists derived from *lampons*, let us drink, a drunken song.

LANCASTER, JOSEPH (1778–1838), the founder of a system of education, based 'on general Christian principles' (i.e. undenominational), in schools organized 'on the monitorial or mutual system', described in 'Improvements in Education' (1803). The proposal gave rise to heated controversy, of which the outcome was the 'voluntary system' of elementary schools that endured until 1870.

LANCASTER, WILLIAM, see *Warren* (*J. B. L.*).

Lancelot, see *Launcelot of the Lake.*

Lancelot and Elaine, one of A. Tennyson's 'Idylls of the King' (q.v.), published in 1859.

In this idyll we see the beginning of the retribution for the sin of Lancelot and Guinevere. Lancelot, the guilty lover of the queen, leaves the court so as to attend the 'diamond jousts' unknown, and goes to the castle of Astolat. The events that follow, ending with the death of Elaine, 'the lily maid of Astolat', and Lancelot's remorse, are given under *Launcelot of the Lake.*

Lancelot Bogle, The Rhyme of Sir, see *Bon Gaultier Ballads.*

Lancelot du Lake, Sir, a ballad included in Percy's 'Reliques', recounting the adventure of Lancelot with Tarquin, who had in prison threescore of Arthur's knights. Lancelot kills him and liberates the knights. Falstaff sings a snatch from this ballad in Shakespeare's '2 Henry IV', II. iv.

Land League, an association of Irish tenant farmers and others organized in 1879 by Charles Stewart Parnell and suppressed by the government in 1881, having primarily for its object the reduction of rent and ultimately the substitution of peasant proprietors for landlords.

Land of Cakes, THE, i.e. the land of oaten bread or oat-cake, Scotland.

Land o' the Leal, The (the land of the blessed departed), the title of a song by Lady Nairne (q.v.).

Landfall, a New Zealand quarterly review, established in 1947 and edited by Charles Brasch.

Landless, NEVILLE and HELENA, characters in Dickens's 'Edwin Drood' (q.v.).

Landlord at Lion's Head, The, a novel by W. D. Howells (q.v.), published in 1897.

LANDON, LETITIA ELIZABETH (1802–38), afterwards Mrs. Maclean, wrote under the initials L. E. L. She published between 1824 and her death a number of poems, collected editions of which appeared in 1850 and 1873. She also wrote novels, of which the best is 'Ethel Churchill', published in

1837. She died mysteriously, probably from an accidental overdose of prussic acid, in West Africa shortly after her marriage.

LANDOR, ROBERT EYRES (1781–1869), youngest brother of Walter Savage Landor (q.v.), was author of a tragedy, 'The Count of Arezzi' (1823), which was attributed to Byron, of a poem 'The Impious Feast' (of Belshazzar, 1828), of a fantastic prose story 'The Fawn of Sertorius' (1846), and of 'The Fountain of Arethusa' (1848), dialogues between a certain Antony Lugwardine and Aristotle, Cicero, and other famous men of ancient times.

LANDOR, WALTER SAVAGE (1775–1864), of a Warwickshire family, was educated at Rugby and at Trinity College, Oxford, whence he was rusticated, an intractable temper frequently involving him in trouble throughout his life. He married in 1811 Julia Thuillier, with whom he quarrelled in 1835, lived in Italy (Como, Pisa, and Florence) from 1815 to 1835, at Bath from 1838 to 1858, and the last part of his life in Florence. His principal prose work took the form of 'Imaginary Conversations' (q.v.), published 1824–9. The 'Citation and Examination of William Shakespeare touching deer-stealing' appeared in 1834, his 'Pericles and Aspasia' (q.v.) in 1836, and 'The Pentameron' in 1837. These show an elaborate and finished style of great charm. Landor's verse was spread over most of his life, and includes 'Gebir' (q.v.), published in 1798; 'Count Julian' (q.v.), a tragedy (1812); 'Andrea of Hungary' (q.v.), 'Giovanna of Naples', and 'Fra Rupert', an historical trilogy (1839); 'The Hellenics' (1846–7), short tales or dialogues in verse on Greek mythical or idyllic subjects; and among shorter pieces the various verses addressed to 'Ianthe' (q.v.), the beautiful 'Dirce', 'Rose Aylmer' (q.v.), and 'The Three Roses'. Boythorn, in Dickens's 'Bleak House' (q.v.), is a genial caricature of some peculiarities of Landor.

Landseer, SIR EDWIN HENRY (1802–73), animal-painter. He visited Sir W. Scott at Abbotsford in 1824 and drew the poet and his dogs. He had enormous popular success and enjoyed the favour of Queen Victoria and the Prince Consort. He modelled the lions for the Nelson monument in Trafalgar Square.

LANE, EDWARD WILLIAM (1801–76), Arabic scholar, published in 1836 his 'Account of the Manners and Customs of the Modern Egyptians', and in 1838–41 a translation of the 'Thousand and One Nights'. He compiled an exhaustive thesaurus of the Arabic language from native lexicons, which was published at intervals during 1863–92.

Lanfranc (1005 ?–89), archbishop of Canterbury from 1070, a man educated in the secular learning of the time and in Greek, reputed as a teacher, prior of Bec in Normandy from 1045. As archbishop he worked in accord with William the Conqueror. He rebuilt Canterbury Cathedral after the fire of 1067.

LANG, ANDREW (1844–1912), born at Selkirk, was educated at Selkirk Grammar School, Edinburgh Academy, St. Andrews University, and Balliol College, Oxford, and became a fellow of Merton. In 1875 he settled down in London to a life of journalism and letters.

Lang's first book was of verse, 'Ballads and Lyrics of Old France' (1872); followed by 'Ballades in Blue China' (1880 and 1881); 'Helen of Troy' (1882), a more ambitious narrative poem in six books; 'Rhymes à la Mode' (1884), 'Grass of Parnassus' (1892), 'Ban and Arrière Ban' (1894), and 'New Collected Rhymes' (1905). Many of his poems were written in the old French forms of ballade, rondeau, triolet, virelai, etc. Among the best of them are the sonnets, 'The Odyssey' and 'Colonel Burnaby'. His 'Collected Poems' were published in 1923.

Lang valued himself most as an anthropologist. His first book on folklore, 'Custom and Myth', did not appear until 1884, but contained papers written and printed much earlier. 'Myth, Ritual, and Religion', dealing chiefly with totemism, was published in 1887, and 'The Making of Religion' in 1898, the second edition of 'Myth, Ritual, and Religion' in 1899 being drastically rehandled to harmonize with his more developed views. These books involved him in much controversy, but he 'conferred', in the words of M. Salomon Reinach, 'a benefit on the world of learning' in proving that folklore is not the debris of a higher or literary mythology, but the foundation on which that mythology rests. Mention should be made in this connexion of Lang's 'Perrault's Popular Tales' (1888, see *Perrault*), in which he discusses the origins of many of our nursery tales.

Lang, as a Greek scholar, devoted himself to Homer. He was one of the joint authors (with S. H. Butcher) of the admirable prose versions of the 'Odyssey' (preceded by his best sonnet, 1879) and (with W. Leaf and E. Myers) of the 'Iliad' (1883), and also published translations of Theocritus (1880), the 'Homeric Hymns' (1899), and three books on the Homeric question, 'Homer and the Epic' (1893), 'Homer and his Age' (1906), and 'The World of Homer' (1910).

His chief work as an historian is the 'History of Scotland from the Roman Occupation to the Suppression of the last Jacobite Rising' (1900–7). He also wrote a number of historical monographs: 'Pickle the Spy' (1897) and 'The Companions of Pickle' (1898), on the identity of the Jacobite spy hinted at in the Introduction to Scott's 'Redgauntlet'; 'Prince Charles Edward' (1900); 'The Mystery of Mary Stuart' (1901); 'James VI and the Gowrie Conspiracy' (1902); 'John Knox and the Reformation' (1905); the 'Life of Sir George Mackenzie' (1909); and 'The Maid of France' (1908), on Joan of Arc. His last published work was a 'History of English Literature' (1912). He also wrote biographies of Sir Stafford Northcote (1890) and J. G.

Lockhart (1896), the latter one of the best works of this kind of the century.

Lang's novels, with the exception of 'The Mark of Cain' (1886) and 'The Disentanglers' (1902), were less remarkable. In his 'Shakespeare, Bacon, and the Great Unknown' (1912) he took part, in defence of Shakespearian authorship, in the Shakespeare–Bacon controversy. Mention should be made of his two pleasant bibliographical works, 'The Library' (1881) and 'Books and Bookmen' (1887); and of his preface to his translation of Theocritus, his 'Letters to Dead Authors' (1886), 'In the Wrong Paradise', 'Old Friends', and 'Essays in Little', as some of his most delightful works. He collaborated with H. R. Haggard (q.v.) in 'The World's Desire' (1891), and with A. E. W. Mason in 'Parson Kelly' (1899). His collections of Fairy Tales, each volume named after a different colour, are well known.

LANGLAND, WILLIAM (1330?–1400?), poet, details of whose life are chiefly supplied from the work generally attributed to him, 'The Vision concerning Piers the Plowman' (q.v.). He was a native of the western Midlands, was probably educated at the monastery of Great Malvern, went to London, and was engaged on his great work, which appeared in three versions (in 1362, 1377, and 1392). But recent critical discussion of these three versions has left the question of their authorship undecided. Langland was possibly the author of 'Richard the Redeless' (see *Mum, Sothsegger*).

Langtry, MRS. EMILY CHARLOTTE (1853–1929), a famous beauty, 'the Jersey Lily', daughter of the Very Revd. W. C. le Breton, Dean of Jersey. She married Edward Langtry in 1874, and after his death Sir Hugo de Bathe.

Langue d'oïl, the language of the north of France during the medieval period, so called to distinguish it from the langue d'oc (see *Provençal*), the distinction being based on the particle of affirmation; L. Latin 'hoc ille' for 'yes' became 'o il' in the North and 'oc' in the South. The distinction of language corresponded to a difference of culture and literature, the langue d'oïl being the literary medium of the trouvères (q.v.), the langue d'oc or Provençal that of the troubadours (q.v.). The dialects of the langue d'oïl, particularly Norman, Picard, and Francien (the language of the Paris region), each had some literary independence during the 12th and 13th cents., but Francien gradually became the standard language, and is the ancestor of modern standard French.

Languish, LYDIA, the heroine of Sheridan's 'The Rivals' (q.v.).

LANIER, SIDNEY (1842–81), American poet and critic, born in Georgia. After serving in the Confederate Army during the Civil War, he devoted himself to poetry, in spite of ill health and poverty. He published his

'Poems' in 1877; a complete 'Poems' appeared in 1884, with further additions in subsequent editions. His lyrical verse is strongly influenced by his knowledge and practice of music. He became a lecturer in English at Johns Hopkins University in 1879, and among his critical writings are 'The Science of English Verse' (1880) and 'The English Novel' (1883).

Lantern-land, in Rabelais's 'Pantagruel', v. xxxiii, the country of learning, visited by Pantagruel and his companions on their way to the oracle of Bacbuc. The lanterns are the philosophers and poets.

Laocoön, according to legend a Trojan priest of Apollo, who, when he was offering a sacrifice to Poseidon, saw two serpents issue from the sea and attack his sons. He rushed to their defence, but the serpents wreathed themselves about him and crushed him. This was said to be a punishment for his temerity in dissuading the Trojans from admitting the wooden horse into Troy.

For Lessing's essay see *Laokoon*.

Laodămīa, the wife of Protěsīlăus, who was slain by Hector before Troy. Visited by the spectre of her dead husband, she could not bear to part with it, and followed it to the shades. Wordsworth wrote a poem on her.

Laodicean, one who has the fault for which the Church of Laodicea is reproached in Rev. iii. 15, 16; lukewarm, indifferent in religion or politics.

Laodicean, A, a novel by Hardy (q.v.), published in 1881.

The Laodicean is Miss Paula Power, the daughter of a successful railway contractor, a vacillating lukewarm character. She is first presented in a striking scene, faced with the ordeal of being baptized according to the rites of the Baptist persuasion to which her father belonged, and unable to take the plunge. We then see her vacillating between her love for George Somerset, a young architect of no particular position, and the offer of marriage of Captain De Stancy, the heir of an ancient family which once owned the castle in which she now lives. Her romantic inclinations make her accept the latter, but she is arrested at the eleventh hour by the discovery of a plot hatched by Willy Dare, an odious little villain, De Stancy's illegitimate son, to blacken George Somerset's character in her eyes. She marries her prosaic lover, her romantic castle is burnt to the ground, but she remains a Laodicean to the end.

Laokoon, an essay in literary and artistic criticism by Lessing (q.v.), published in 1766. It takes its title from the celebrated group of statuary disinterred at Rome in the 16th cent. representing Laocoön (q.v.) and his sons in the coils of a serpent. Adopting this group and the Horatian formula 'ut pictura poesis' ('poetry resembles painting') as the initial subject of discussion, Lessing examines the grounds for the divergence in the treatment

of the scene by the artist and by Virgil who described it, and develops the essential differences between the art of poetry and the plastic arts. The work was left unfinished.

Laŏmĕdon, see *Hesione*.

Laon and Cythna, see *Revolt of Islam*.

Lao-tzu, see *Taoism*.

Lapham, SILAS, hero of W. D. Howells's (q.v.) novel, 'The Rise of Silas Lapham'.

Lăpĭthae, a race inhabiting Thessaly, chiefly famous in mythology for their fight with the Centaurs (q.v.) on the occasion of the marriage of Peirĭthŏus, king of the Lapithae, with Hippodămia.

Laputa, see *Gulliver's Travels*.

Lara, a poem in heroic couplets by Lord Byron (q.v.), published in 1814.

'The Reader', says the publisher's advertisement, 'may probably regard ["Lara"] as a sequel to the "Corsair" ' (q.v.). Lara is in fact Conrad, the pirate chief, returned to his domains in Spain, accompanied by his page, Kaled, who is Gulnare in disguise. He lives aloof and a mystery hangs over him. He is recognized, and involved in a feud in which he is finally killed, dying in the arms of Kaled. But the interest of the poem lies not in the story but in the character of Lara, in which one may see the author's conception of himself.

Lārēs, Roman tutelary deities of the home. They are generally linked in Latin literature with the *Penates*, from whom they are scarcely distinguishable. Besides these private gods, there were *Lares Compitales* or *Viales*, worshipped by the community. Similarly there were both private and public Penates.

LAROUSSE, PIERRE ATHANASE (1817–75), French lexicographer, compiler of the 'Grand Dictionnaire universel du xixe siècle', a vast encyclopaedia (1866–76). The present series of 'Dictionnaires Larousse' are independent works and are produced under the direction of Claude Augé.

Larrikin, the Australian equivalent of the hooligan, or street rough. The name arose in Melbourne not long before 1870, but its origin is uncertain; perhaps from *Larry*, the nickname for Lawrence.

Lars, a praenomen of Etruscan origin, in Etruscan usually the prefix of the first-born, while a younger son was called Aruns; an honorary appellation, equivalent to the English 'lord' (Lewis and Short). Thus, 'Lars Porsena', in Macaulay's lay of 'Horatius'.

Larynx, THE REVD. MR., a character in Peacock's 'Nightmare Abbey' (q.v.).

LAS CASAS, BARTOLOMÉ DE (1474?–1566), Spanish historian and bishop of Chaipa (Mexico), famous for his protest against the ill treatment by his countrymen of the Indians of America, in his 'Very Brief Account of the Ruin of the Indies' (1542). He also wrote in his old age a general 'History of the Indies'.

Lassalle, FERDINAND, see *Tragic Comedians.*

Last Chronicle of Barset, The, a novel by
A. Trollope (q.v.), published in 1866-7.

This is the last of the Barsetshire series and
the principal characters had already appeared
in earlier works. It is chiefly occupied with
the tribulations of the Revd. Josiah Crawley,
the cross-grained perpetual curate of Hoggle-
stock. Mr. Soames, agent to Lord Lufton,
has lost a pocket-book containing a cheque
for £20, and believes that he dropped it in
Mr. Crawley's house. Subsequently Mr.
Crawley has cashed this cheque and applied
the proceeds to pay his bills. Called upon to
explain whence he got it, he first states erroneously that he received it from Soames in payment of his stipend; then that it was part of a
gift from Dean Arabin, which the latter (who
is on a journey to Jerusalem) denies. Brought
before the magistrates, Mr. Crawley is committed for trial but allowed bail. Then follows
a period of persecution, principally instigated
by Mrs. Proudie, wife of the bishop, which
finally leads to Mr. Crawley's surrender of his
incumbency. Meanwhile Major Grantly, son
of the archdeacon, who is in love with Grace,
Mr. Crawley's daughter, has insisted on engaging himself to her, thereby bringing about
a breach with his father. When matters reach
a crisis, the mystery of the origin of the cheque
finds a simple explanation. It had been given
to Crawley by Mrs. Arabin, being slipped into
the envelope containing the dean's gift without the latter's knowledge. The cheque had
been previously stolen from Soames by a servant and paid to Mrs. Arabin as money due
to her. Mr. Crawley's innocence having been
established, he is appointed to the living of St.
Ewold's, vacant by the death of old Mr. Harding, and Grace is married to Major Grantly.

Of other characters in the Barsetshire
drama we hear a good deal. John Eames continues unavailingly his suit of Lily Dale and
becomes entangled in a dangerous flirtation
with the intriguing Madalina Demolines;
Mrs. Proudie dies, too soon to witness the
rehabilitation of Mr. Crawley; and Lady
Lufton, Mr. Robarts, the Greshams, and the
Thornes also figure in the story.

Last Days of Pompeii, The, a novel by
Bulwer Lytton (q.v.), published in 1834.

The scene is laid at Pompeii, shortly before
its destruction, and deals with the love of two
young Greeks, Glaucus and Ione, and the
villainous designs of Arbaces, the girl's guardian, who is enamoured of his ward. When
the city is overwhelmed, the blind girl Nydia,
who cherishes a hopeless passion for Glaucus,
saves the lovers by leading them through the
darkness to the sea. The work gives an interesting picture of Roman life at the time of
the catastrophe (A.D. 79).

Last Man, The, the title of poems by T. Campbell and by T. Hood (qq.v.).

Last of the Barons, The, an historical novel
by Bulwer Lytton (q.v.), published in 1843.

The 'Last of the Barons' is Warwick the
king-maker, and the historical events described in the novel occurred between 1467
and the death of Warwick at the battle of
Barnet in 1471, that is to say in the last years
of the feudal period. These events include
the quarrel between Warwick and Edward IV
over the marriage of Edward's sister, Margaret; their reconciliation and final dissension,
this last attributed by the author to an attempt
by Edward on the honour of Warwick's
daughter Anne; the short-lived restoration of
Henry VI, and the battle of Tewkesbury, fatal
to Warwick and the Lancastrians. With these
historical events is woven the tragic story of
a poor philosopher and mechanical inventor,
Adam Warner, and his beautiful daughter,
Sibyll, beloved but deserted by the great Lord
Hastings. After many vicissitudes, they meet
their death as the result of popular prejudice
and superstition, personified in the character
of the astrologer, Friar Bungey.

Last of the Mohicans, The, a novel by J. F.
Cooper (q.v.).

Last of the Tribunes, The, see *Rienzi.*

Last Ride Together, The, a short poem by
R. Browning (q.v.), included in 'Dramatic
Romances', published in 'Men and Women'
(1855).

Last Tournament, The, one of A. Tennyson's 'Idylls of the King' (q.v.), privately
printed in 1871, and included in the published
volume of 1889.

At the last tournament held at Arthur's
court, the 'Tournament of the Dead Innocence', held on a wet and windy day, and
presided over by the weary and disillusioned
Lancelot, Tristram, late returned from Brittany, wins the prize, a carcanet (necklace) of
rubies. Disloyal to his wife, Iseult of Brittany,
he carries this to his paramour, Iseult, the
wife of Mark. He finds her alone at Tintagel,
and, as he clasps it round her neck,

Behind him rose a shadow and a shriek—
'Mark's way', said Mark, and clove him
   through the brain.

Arthur returns 'in the death-dumb autumn-
dripping gloom' to find his home empty and
Guinevere fled. A notable feature in the idyll
is the moral uprightness of Dagonet the jester,
who does not spare Tristram his scarcely
veiled reproaches.

Latchfords, a name applied to spurs, from
a well-known maker.

Lateran, a locality in Rome, originally the
site of the palace of the family of the Plautii
Laterani, afterwards of the palace of the popes
and the cathedral church known as St. John
Lateran. The LATERAN COUNCILS were five
general councils of the Western Church held
in the church of St. John Lateran (1123, 1139,
1179, 1215, 1512-17).

LATHAM, SIMON (*fl.* 1618), the chief

17th-cent. authority on falconry, published 'Latham's Falconry' in 1615–18.

Latimer, DARSIE, in Scott's 'Redgauntlet' (q.v.), the name born by the hero, Sir Arthur Darsie Redgauntlet.

LATIMER, HUGH (1485?–1555), was educated at Cambridge, took priest's orders, and became known as a preacher. He was accused of heresy, brought before convocation, and absolved on making a complete submission, in 1532. He was appointed bishop of Worcester in 1535, but resigned his bishopric and was kept in custody for a year, because he could not support the Act of the Six Articles (q.v.), 1539. His famous sermon 'of the plough' was preached in 1548. Latimer was committed to the Tower on Mary's accession, 1553; was sent to Oxford with Ridley and Cranmer to defend his views before the leading divines of the University, 1554; and was condemned as a heretic and burnt at Oxford with Ridley on 16 Oct. 1555. His extant writings were edited for the Parker Society in 1844–5. They are notable for a simple vernacular style and for their graphic and vivid illustrations.

Latin Quarter, in Paris, on the left bank of the Seine, the quarter where students live and the principal university buildings are situated.

Latīnus, the legendary king of the ancient inhabitants of Latium, who, after at first opposing Aeneas when he landed, was reconciled with him and gave him his daughter Lavinia in marriage.

Latitudinarians, a name applied to those divines of the English Church in the 17th cent. who, while attached to episcopal government and forms of worship, regarded them as things indifferent. Hence applied to those who, though not sceptics, are indifferent to particular creeds and forms of worship.

Latōna, known to the Greeks as LETO, was the daughter of a Titan, and beloved by Zeus. Hera, jealous of her, sent the serpent Python to persecute her during her pregnancy. She wandered about the earth, unable to find a place to rest, until Zeus fastened the floating island of Delos to the bottom of the sea, as a resting-place for her, where she gave birth to Apollo and Artemis.

Latter-Day Pamphlets, see *Carlyle* (*T.*).

Latter-day Saints, see *Mormons.*

LAUD, WILLIAM (1573–1645), educated at St. John's College, Oxford, became predominant in the Church of England at Charles I's accession, being at the time bishop of St. David's. He was promoted successively to the sees of Bath and Wells and London, and became archbishop of Canterbury (1633). He supported the king in his struggle with the Commons and adopted the policy of enforcing uniformity in the Church of England. He was impeached of high treason by the Long Parliament in 1640, committed to the Tower in 1641, tried in 1644, condemned and beheaded in 1645. A few of his sermons were published in 1651, and a collected edition of his works in 1695–1700. In these he shows himself a sturdy defender of the Anglican Church as a national institution, resisting the claim of the Church of Rome to universality and infallibility, and equally resisting the claims of Puritanism. Laud gave some 1,300 manuscripts in eighteen different languages, and his collection of coins, to the Bodleian Library.

Lauder, WILLIAM (*d.* 1771), literary forger, a good classical scholar, was proved to have interpolated in the works of Masenius and Staphorstius (17th-cent. Latin poets) extracts from a Latin verse rendering of 'Paradise Lost'. Incidentally he proved that Milton had deeply studied the works of modern Latin poets.

Laughing Philosopher, THE, see *Democritus.*

Launce, a character in Shakespeare's 'The Two Gentlemen of Verona' (q.v.).

Launcelot Gobbo, in Shakespeare's 'The Merchant of Venice' (q.v.), a clown, servant to Shylock.

Launcelot of the Lake, appears only late in the series of English Arthurian romances, though he is the subject of a great French prose-work, 'Lancelot', of the 13th cent. He is the son of King Ban of Brittany, stolen in childhood by Vivien, the Lady of the Lake, and brought by her, when he reached manhood, to Arthur's court. His story is first dealt with at length in English in the 14th-cent. poem 'Le Morte Arthur' (not Malory's). In this, Launcelot, a knight of the Round Table, is the lover of Queen Guinevere. King Arthur having proclaimed a tournament at Winchester, Launcelot goes secretly to the jousts. He is welcomed by the lord of Ascolot (Astolat, Guildford in Surrey). The daughter of the lord, Elaine the Fair Maid of Astolat, falls in love with him; though remaining faithful to the queen, he consents to wear the maid's sleeve at the tournament. There he takes the weaker side and is wounded by his kinsman, Sir Ector de Maris. He is carried to Ascolot and gives his own armour as a keepsake to Elaine. Gawain comes to Ascolot and the maid tells him that she is Launcelot's love, which Gawain reports to Arthur and his court, to Guinevere's distress. Launcelot returns, and being reproached by the queen, leaves the court in anger. The Maid of Ascolot is brought dead in a barge to Arthur's palace, a letter in her purse declaring that she has died for love of Launcelot. Launcelot and the queen are reconciled. Agravain (brother of Gawain) betrays them to the king, and with twelve knights surprises the lovers. Launcelot slays all except Modred (q.v.), escapes and carries off the queen, who is sentenced to the stake. Arthur and Gawain besiege Launcelot and the queen in Launcelot's castle Joyous Gard (q.v.). Launcelot restores the queen to

Arthur and retires to Brittany, where Arthur and Gawain pursue him. Launcelot wounds Gawain. Modred seizes Arthur's kingdom, and tries to get possession of Guinevere. Arthur, returning, lands at Dover, where Gawain is slain. After several battles, Modred retreats to Cornwall. In the final battle all the knights are slain except Arthur, Modred, and two others. Arthur and Modred mortally wound each other, the sword Excalibur is thrown into the river, and Arthur is borne off to Avalon. Launcelot arrives to aid Arthur, and, finding him dead, seeks the queen, but finds that she has taken the veil. Launcelot becomes a priest and helps to guard Arthur's grave. On his death he is carried to Joyous Gard, and visions indicate that he has been received into heaven. The queen is buried with Arthur, and the abbey of Glastonbury rises over their graves.

The story as told in Malory's 'Morte Darthur' is substantially similar, but fuller, and more exploits are attributed to Launcelot. He is the first of the knights of the Round Table and takes part in the quest of the Holy Grail, of which he has glimpses but no more, being hindered by his sins. He is the father of Galahad by Elaine, daughter of King Pelleas. Gawain becomes Launcelot's bitter enemy, because Launcelot has slain his brothers, Agravain, Gaheris, and Gareth. He prevents Arthur from making peace with Launcelot, when Arthur pursues the latter to Brittany.

Launfal, Sir, a poem by Thomas Chestre (*fl.* 1430). Sir Launfal, a Knight of the Round Table (q.v.), leaves the court, offended by the reputed misconduct of Queen Guinevere. He lives in poverty at Caerleon. Tryamour, the daughter of the fairy king of Olyroun, declares her love for him, gives him wealth, a horse, and a page, and promises to come to him unseen when he summons her, on condition that he does not reveal their love. He returns to Arthur's court, where Guinevere declares her love for him. He rejects her advances, saying that he loves a lady whose very maids are more beautiful than the queen. In consequence of this indiscreet speech, Launfal's horse and page and wealth disappear; the queen accuses him of trying to seduce her. At the trial he is required to produce within a certain period the lady of whose beauty he has boasted. After the expiration of the period Tryamour appears, justifies the knight, and breathing on the queen's eyes, blinds her. Tryamour and Launfal thereafter live in the Isle of Olyroun.

The story occurs in the *lais* of Marie de France (12th cent.). J. R. Lowell (q.v.) in his 'Vision of Sir Launfal' makes him one of those who sought the Holy Grail.

Laura, (1) see *Petrarch*; (2) the wife of Beppo, in Byron's poem 'Beppo' (q.v.).

Laura Bell, the heroine of Thackeray's 'Pendennis' (q.v.).

Laurence, FRIAR, a character in Shakespeare's 'Romeo and Juliet' (q.v.).

Laurence, ST., an early Christian martyr who, according to a tradition, was roasted alive at Rome in the 3rd cent.

Laurentian Library, THE, had its origin in the private collections of Cosimo and Lorenzo de' Medici (q.v.) in the 15th cent. On the expulsion of the Medici from Florence, the collection passed to the monks of S. Marco in Florence and was subsequently purchased from them by Leo X (q.v.), taken to Rome, and enlarged by him, with the intention that it should ultimately be returned to Florence. This intention was carried out by Clement VII (also a Medici).

Laurie, ANNIE (1682–1764), the subject of the famous Scottish song that bears her name. She was the daughter of Sir Robert Laurie of Maxwelton, Dumfriesshire, and married Alexander Ferguson. The song was written by her rejected lover, William Douglas. It was revised and set to music by Lady John Scott in 1835.

Laus Veneris, see *Swinburne (A. C.)* and *Tannhäuser.*

LAVATER, JOHANN KASPAR (1741–1801), a Swiss divine and poet, chiefly remembered as the inventor of the so-called science of phrenology (or physiognomy, as he called it).

Lavengro, the Scholar—the Gypsy—the Priest, a novel by Borrow (q.v.), published in 1851. 'Lavengro', in gipsy language, means 'philologist'. The name was applied to Borrow in his youth by Ambrose Smith, the Norfolk gipsy, who figures in this work as Jasper Petulengro.

In this book, as in 'The Romany Rye' and 'The Bible in Spain', autobiography is inextricably mingled with fiction. It purports to be the story, told by himself, of the son of a military officer, a wanderer from his birth, at first accompanying his father from station to station, and later under the impulse of his own restless spirit. In the course of his wanderings he makes the acquaintance of a family of gipsies, with whom he becomes intimate, and of many other strange characters, an Armenian, an old apple-woman, a tinker (the Flaming Tinman with whom he has a memorable fight), pickpockets and sharpers, and the like. In London he experiences the hardships of the life of a literary hack. He is much given to the comparative study of languages, of which the reader is told a good deal, and he shows his aversion to the Roman Catholic Church. The book closes in the midst of the romantic episode of Belle Berners, the sturdy wandering lass, which is resumed in the sequel, 'The Romany Rye' (q.v.).

Lavinia, (1) the daughter of King Latinus (q.v.), who, though betrothed to Turnus, was given in marriage to Aeneas; (2) a character in Shakespeare's 'Titus Andronicus' (q.v.).

Lavinia and **Palemon,** characters in an episode, resembling the story of Ruth and Boaz, in Thomson's 'Seasons' ('Autumn') (q.v.).

Law, JOHN (1671–1729), educated at Edinburgh, escaped from prison after being sentenced to death for killing 'Beau' Wilson in a duel, and fled to France. With the support of the Regent he established in 1716 the first French bank, a sucessful venture on sound principles, and in 1717 a company to exploit the territories of Louisiana and later to trade also with the East Indies. In 1719, in return for the valuable privilege of farming the taxes, the company undertook to convert the French national debt, which bore interest at about 4%, into a debt to itself at 3%. Law was appointed controller-general of French finances in 1720. The conversion was mismanaged. Speculation on a vast scale in the shares of the company led to their gross overvaluation followed by the inevitable reaction. The scheme failed, involving widespread ruin. Law fled from France, and died a few years later in poverty at Venice.

LAW, WILLIAM (1686–1761), born at King's Cliffe near Stamford, was elected a fellow of Emmanuel College, Cambridge, but, declining to take the oath of allegiance to George I, lost his fellowship. Edward Gibbon made him the tutor of his son, the father of the historian, in 1728, and he remained as the honoured friend of the family until 1740, when he returned to King's Cliffe and became the centre of a small spiritual community.

Law's earlier writings are of a controversial character; he replied to bishop Benjamin Hoadly's latitudinarian doctrine in his 'Three Letters to the Bishop of Bangor', 1717–19 (see *Bangorian Controversy*); he wrote his 'Remarks on the Fable of the Bees' in 1723 in answer to Mandeville's satire of that name (q.v.); and to the deists he replied in 'The Case for Reason' (1731). But his chief claim to be remembered rests on his treatises of practical morality, 'A Practical Treatise on Christian Perfection' (1726), and more particularly his 'Serious Call to a Devout and Holy Life', 1729, of which Wesley admitted that it sowed the seed of Methodism and said that it 'will hardly be excelled, if it be equalled, in the English tongue, either for beauty of expression or for justice and depth of thought'. Dr. Johnson attributed to his reading of it his first attention to religion. The work contains admirable portraits of typical characters, such as the man of affairs and the woman of fashion.

In his later life Law's writing assumed a mystical character. He was strongly influenced by Jacob Boehme (q.v.), and his treatises, 'An Appeal to all that Doubt' (1740) and 'The Way to Divine Knowledge' (1752), are in harmony with Boehme's teaching. See also *Byrom*.

Law is a Bottomless Pit, see *Arbuthnot.*

LAWLESS, EMILY (1845–1913), daughter of Lord Cloncurry, was author of the successful Irish novels 'Hurrish' (1886) and 'Grania' (1892). Among her other works may be mentioned 'With Essex in Ireland' (1890) and 'With the Wild Geese' (poems, 1902). The 'Wild Geese' are the exiles who left Ireland after the surrender of Limerick in 1691.

LAWRENCE, DAVID HERBERT (1885–1930), one of the great English novelists of the century. He was the son of a Nottinghamshire miner, was educated at University College, Nottingham, and was for a time a schoolmaster before turning to writing as a profession. Apart from the years in England during the First World War, he and his wife, Frieda, lived mostly abroad, in Italy, Australia, and New Mexico. He died in Vence, near Nice. Among his best-known novels are 'The White Peacock' (1911), 'Sons and Lovers' (1913), 'The Rainbow' (1915), 'Women in Love' (1920), 'Aaron's Rod' (1922), 'Kangaroo' (1923), 'The Plumed Serpent' (1926), 'Lady Chatterley's Lover' (expurgated edition 1928; unabridged, Paris, 1929; first published in full in England, 1960: see Appendix I, section 3). His short stories include 'The Prussian Officer' (1914), 'England, My England' (1922), and 'The Woman who Rode Away' (1928). His essay, 'Fantasia of the Unconscious', appeared in 1922. Lawrence published several volumes of poems, of which a collected edition appeared in 1928.

LAWRENCE, GEORGE ALFRED (1827–76), educated at Rugby and Balliol College, Oxford, was the author of 'Guy Livingstone' (q.v., 1857), a novel that enjoyed great popularity, but was denounced in some quarters for its exaltation of the muscular blackguard. His other novels included 'Sword and Gown' (1859), 'Barren Honour', 'Sans Merci', etc.

Lawrence, SIR THOMAS (1769–1830), painter. He was an infant prodigy, drawing likenesses at the age of 4 or 5. His portraits are distinguished for their courtliness and social elegance. He painted portraits for the Waterloo Chamber at Windsor of persons who took part in the defeat of Napoleon.

LAWRENCE, THOMAS EDWARD (1888–1935), was educated at Jesus College, Oxford, became an archaeologist, and travelled and excavated in Syria. In the First World War he was one of the British officers sent from Egypt to help the Sherif of Mecca in his revolt against the Turks. He gained a position of great influence with the Arabs, performed many daring exploits, and entered Damascus in 1918 with the leading Arab forces. His narrative of these experiences, 'Seven Pillars of Wisdom', was printed for private circulation in a limited edition in 1926 (published 1935); a shortened version, 'Revolt in the Desert', was published in 1927. After the War he joined the Royal Air Force as an aircraftman, changing his name to Shaw by deed-poll in 1927.

Laws of Ecclesiastical Politie, Of the, by Hooker (q.v.), a philosophical and theological treatise of which four books appeared in 1594, the fifth in 1597. The last three books, as we have them, were not published until after Hooker's death, and do not represent work prepared by him for the press. The sixth and eighth appeared in 1648, the seventh was first included in Gauden's edition of 1662. The whole was reissued with a life of Hooker by Izaak Walton in 1666.

The work is a defence, written in a dignified and harmonious prose, of the position of the Anglican Church against the attacks of the Puritans. The first book is a philosophical discussion of the origin and nature of law in general, as governing the universe and human society, and of the distinction between laws of a permanent and of a temporary character. The second, third, and fourth books deal with the assertion of the Puritan party that Scripture is the sole guide in determining the actions of a Christian and the form of Church polity, and that the Anglican Church is corrupted with popish rites and ceremonies. The fifth book is a defence of the Book of Common Prayer. According to Hooker's scheme, the last three books were to deal with Church discipline, the power of jurisdiction (whether of the bishops, or lay elders), and the nature of the king's supreme authority. The principal characteristics of the work are its breadth of outlook and tolerant spirit, and its advocacy of intellectual liberty against the dogmatism of Calvin and the ecclesiastical despotism recommended in the 'Admonition to Parliament', a statement of the Puritan case by John Field and Thomas Wilcox (1572).

Laxdaela Saga, see *Saga*.

Lay, a short lyric or narrative poem intended to be sung; originally applied specifically to the poems, usually dealing with matter of history or romantic adventure, which were sung by minstrels.

Lay of the Last Minstrel, The, a poem in six cantos by Sir W. Scott (q.v.), published in 1805. It is in irregular stanzas of lines of four accents and seven to twelve syllables. This was Scott's first important original work. It is a metrical romance, put in the mouth of an ancient minstrel, the last of his race. It is based on an old Border legend of the goblin Gilpin Horner. The period of the tale is the middle of the 16th cent.

The lady of Branksome Hall, the seat of the Buccleuchs, has lost her husband in an affray in which Lord Cranstoun was one of his opponents. Lord Cranstoun and Margaret, the lady's daughter, are in love, but the feud renders their passion hopeless. The lady commissions Sir William Deloraine to recover from the tomb of the wizard Michael Scott in Melrose Abbey the magic book which is to help her in her vengeance. As Deloraine returns, he encounters Lord Cranstoun and is wounded by him. At Lord Cranstoun's bidding, his elfin page carries the wounded man to Branksome Hall, and, impelled by the spirit of mischief, lures away the lady's little son, the heir of the house, who falls into the hands of her English enemy, Lord Dacre. The latter, with Lord William Howard, intends to storm Branksome, alleging Deloraine's misdeeds as a Border thief. The Scots army is on its way to relieve Branksome. A single combat is suggested between Sir William Deloraine, now lying wounded, and Sir Richard Musgrave, whose lands Deloraine has harried; the lady's little son to be the prize. The challenge is accepted and Musgrave defeated. It is discovered that the victor is Lord Cranstoun, who with his page's assistance has assumed the form and arms of Deloraine. The service rendered to the house of Buccleuch heals the feud, and Lord Cranstoun marries Margaret. The poem includes some notable ballads, such as that of Albert Graeme and the touching 'Rosabelle'; also a version of the Latin hymn 'Dies Irae'.

LAYAMON or **LAWEMON** (meaning Lawman) (*fl.* 1200), according to his own statement a priest of Ernley (Arley Regis, Worcester), author of a 'Brut' or history of England from the arrival of the legendary Brutus to Cadwalader (A.D. 689), based directly or indirectly on Wace's French version of the 'Historia Regum Britanniae' of Geoffrey of Monmouth (q.v.), with additions from Breton or Norman sources. It is especially interesting as giving for the first time in English not only the story of Arthur, but also that of Lear and Cymbeline and other personages dealt with in later English literature. It is the first considerable work in Middle English and shows no little literary power. It is written in the Old English alliterative line of two short sections, but the alliteration is frequently abandoned and rhyme is occasionally introduced. The standard text is that of Sir F. Madden, 1847. Vol. I of the E.E.T.S. edition appeared in 1963.

LAYARD, Sir AUSTEN HENRY (1817–94), the excavator of Nineveh, and in later life under-secretary for foreign affairs and British minister successively at Madrid and Constantinople. He published his 'Nineveh and its Remains' in 1848–9, his 'Popular Account of Discoveries at Nineveh' in 1851, 'Nineveh and Babylon' in 1853, and 'Early Adventures in Persia, Susiana, and Babylonia' in 1887.

Lays of Ancient Rome, by Macaulay (q.v.), published in 1842.

These are attempts to reconstruct, in English form, the lost ballad-poetry of Rome out of which its traditional history was thought to have grown. The lays are: 'Horatius', dealing with the valiant defence by Horatius Cocles of the bridge leading to Rome against the Tuscan bands; 'The Battle of Lake Regillus', in which the Romans, aided by the gods Castor and Pollux, defeated the Latins; 'Virginia', the story of the slaying of a young Roman maiden by her father Virginius, to save her from the lust of the patrician Appius

Claudius; and 'The Prophecy of Capys' the blind seer, who foretells to Romulus the great future of the Roman race.

In the edition of 1848 there were added: 'Ivry', a ballad of the victory of the Huguenots under Henry of Navarre at that place in 1590; and the fragment 'The Armada', describing the scenes in England on the arrival of the news that the Spanish fleet was coming.

Lays of the Scottish Cavaliers, a collection of ballads by Aytoun (q.v.), of which the first, the 'Burial March of Dundee', appeared in 'Blackwood's Magazine' in April 1843, and the whole were published in 1849.

They are ballad-romances, in the style of those of Scott, dealing with such subjects as the pilgrimage of Sir James Douglas to the Holy Land to bury there the heart of Bruce, and—the best of them—'The Island of the Scots', an exploit of the company of old officers of Dundee's army serving the French king against the Germans.

Lazarillo de Tormes, the first of the Spanish picaresque (q.v.) romances, of uncertain authorship, printed in 1553. It is the autobiography of the son of a miller, who lived on the banks of the Tormes, near Salamanca. The boy begins his career of wit and fraud as a blind man's guide, whose money and victuals he steals. He passes into the service of various poverty-stricken or rascally employers, and ultimately reaches the position of town-crier of Toledo. His career provides occasion for many satirical portraits of Spanish types.

Le Corbusier (1888–1965), the name by which the Swiss-born French architect C.-E. Jeanneret was known. His books, such as 'Vers une Architecture' (1923, translated by F. Etchells, 1927), and his buildings, such as the 'Unité d'Habitation' at Marseilles (1952), have profoundly influenced architecture.

LE FANU, JOSEPH SHERIDAN (1814–73), great-grand-nephew of R. B. Sheridan (q.v.), was educated at Trinity College, Dublin. His principal novels and stories, in which he successfully introduced the element of the mysterious and the terrible, include 'Uncle Silas' (q.v., 1864), 'The House by the Churchyard' (1863), and 'In a Glass Darkly' (1872, containing 'The Watcher', 'The Room in the Dragon Volant', etc.). Le Fanu also wrote a drama 'Beatrice', and some good Irish ballads ('Shamus O'Brien', 1837, is the best known) and other poems.

Le Fevre, the hero of an episode in Sterne's 'Tristram Shandy' (q.v., vol. vi).

LE GALLIENNE, RICHARD (1866–1947), poet and essayist, born in Liverpool, of Channel Island descent. He went to live in the U.S. in 1898 and finally settled on the Riviera. 'The Romantic Nineties' (1926, new ed. 1951) is a first-hand account of the literary and artistic group of which Beardsley, Symons,

and Wilde (qq.v.) were the chief figures. 'The Lonely Dancer' (1913) is a book of verse.

LE SAGE, ALAIN RENÉ (1668–1747), a French novelist and dramatist, whose first important work was 'Le Diable Boiteux' (q.v., 1707), followed in 1709 by 'Turcaret', a comedy satirizing the plutocratic basis of society; and in 1715–35 by the famous picaresque romance 'Gil Blas' (q.v.), which gives a wonderful picture of Spanish life, though the author's knowledge of Spain was solely derived from Spanish writers.

Leabhar Gabhala, 'Book of Invasions', a Celtic record of legendary invasions of Ireland. The earliest copy of it is in the 'Book of Leinster', a 12th-cent. manuscript.

LEACOCK, STEPHEN BUTLER (1869–1944), political economist, but better known as a writer of humorous stories, among which are 'Nonsense Novels' (1911), 'Sunshine Sketches of a Little Town' (1912), 'Frenzied Fiction' (1917), 'Winsome Winnie' (1920).

Leadenhall Market, London, which takes its name from the hall with lead roof which stood at the corner of Gracechurch Street, lies at the crossing of the two main thoroughfares, north and south, and east and west, which traversed the Roman city. Remains of an important Roman building have been found there, and the spot has probably been devoted to public service ever since.

Leadenhall Street, a street in the City of London in which stood the offices of the old East India Company. The name was frequently used to designate the Company.

Leader, The, a weekly periodical started in 1850 by Lewes (q.v.) and Thornton Leigh Hunt, with a staff that included Spencer (q.v.) and Kinglake (q.v.). It ran until 1866.

League of Nations, a league of the principal nations of the world (exclusive of the United States) and many of the smaller nations 'to promote international co-operation and to achieve international peace and security', set up by a Covenant which forms the first 26 articles of the Treaty of Versailles of 1919. The League worked through an assembly and a council, with a permanent secretariat, and had its headquarters at Geneva. Its closing session was held in April 1946.

Leander, see *Hero.*

Leander Club, THE, the oldest of the English open rowing clubs, dating from early in the 19th cent. It was originally a club of London oarsmen, but was reorganized and made an open club in 1862, and is now mainly composed of university men.

LEAR, EDWARD (1812–88), artist and traveller, as well as author, wrote 'The Book of Nonsense' (1846) for the grandchildren of his patron, the earl of Derby, which did much to popularize the 'Limerick' (q.v.); 'Nonsense Songs, Stories, and Botany' (1870); and accounts (illustrated by his own drawings) of his travels in Greece and southern Italy. The last drew from Tennyson the poem to 'E. L.', 'Illyrian woodlands, echoing falls'.

Lear, KING, see *King Lear* and *Llyr*.

Learoyd, JOHN, with Terence Mulvaney and Stanley Ortheris, the three privates in Rudyard Kipling's 'Soldiers Three'.

Leasowes, see *Shenstone*.

Leatherstocking, a nickname of Natty Bumppo, the hero of the five novels of American frontier life by J. F. Cooper (q.v.), which are in consequence called the 'Leatherstocking' novels.

Leatherwood God, The, a novel by W. D. Howells (q.v.), published in 1916, concerned with a charlatan who proclaims himself a god.

LEAVIS, FRANK RAYMOND (1895–), critic, and fellow of Downing College, Cambridge. He was editor and co-founder of 'Scrutiny' (1932–53), a critical quarterly review. His publications include 'Mass Civilization and Minority Culture' (1930), 'New Bearings in English Poetry' (1932; a study of Hopkins, Eliot, and Pound), 'Tradition and Development in English Poetry' (1936), 'The Great Tradition: George Eliot, James, and Conrad' (1948), 'The Common Pursuit' (1952), and 'D. H. Lawrence, Novelist' (1955).

His wife, MRS. Q. D. LEAVIS, published a study of the development of popular reading habits, 'Fiction and the Reading Public' (1932).

LECKY, WILLIAM EDWARD HART-POLE (1838–1903), educated at Cheltenham and Trinity College, Dublin, published anonymously in 1860 'The Religious Tendencies of the Age', and in 1862 'Leaders of Public Opinion in Ireland', which at the time met with little success. After travelling in Spain and Italy he published an essay on 'The Declining Sense of the Miraculous' (1863), which subsequently formed the first two chapters of his 'History of Rationalism' (1865). In this he traced the progress of the spirit of rationalism and tolerance as opposed to theological dogmatism. The work first brought him into fame. In 1869 he published his 'History of European Morals from Augustus to Charlemagne', describing man's changing estimate of the various virtues and its effect on happiness. Lecky next set himself to collect materials for his 'History of England in the Eighteenth Century', of which the first two volumes appeared in 1878, and the others at various dates to 1890. It is concerned primarily with the history of political ideas and institutions, and social and economic history; while biographical, party, and military matters are accorded less space. The last volumes are devoted to the history of Ireland and designed to refute Froude's misstatements. Lecky's later works were: 'Democracy and Liberty', a study of social and political questions in England, France, Germany, and America (1896; a revised edition of 1899 gave an admirable estimate of Gladstone's work and character); 'The Map of Life' (1899), and 'Historical and Political Essays' (1908). Lecky was M.P. for Dublin University from 1895 to 1902.

Lecoq, the professional detective in Gaboriau's stories of crime. See *Tabaret*.

Leda, a daughter of Thestius, and wife of Tyndareus, king of Sparta. She was seen bathing in the river Eurotas by Zeus, who became enamoured of her and took the form of a swan in order to approach her. Of their union were born Castor and Pollux, and Helèn (qq.v.).

Lee, SIR HENRY, COLONEL ALBERT, and ALICE, characters in Scott's 'Woodstock' (q.v.).

LEE, NATHANIEL (1653?–92), was educated at Westminster School and Trinity College, Cambridge. He failed as an actor and became a playwright, producing 'Nero' in 1675, and 'Gloriana' and 'Sophonisba', in heroics, in 1676. His best-known tragedy 'The Rival Queens; or The Death of Alexander the Great' (q.v.), in blank verse, appeared in 1677, 'Mithridates' in 1678, 'Theodosius', which enjoyed a long popularity, in 1680, and 'Lucius Junius Brutus' in 1681. He collaborated with Dryden in 'Oedipus' (1679) and 'The Duke of Guise' (1682). He lost his reason and was confined in Bedlam from 1684 to 1689. He produced 'The Massacre of Paris' in 1690, and went mad once more, escaped from his keepers, and perished. His plays, which are marked by rant and extravagance, were long popular.

LEE, SIR SIDNEY (1859–1926), educated at City of London School and Balliol College, Oxford, a member of the editorial staff of the 'D.N.B.' from the beginning, joint editor in 1890, and sole editor from 1891. His publications include 'Stratford-on-Avon from the Earliest Times to the Death of Shakespeare' (1885, new edition 1906), 'Life of William Shakespeare' (1898, revised edition, 1915), 'Life of Queen Victoria' (1902), 'Great Englishmen of the 16th Century' (1904), 'Elizabethan Sonnets' (1904), 'Shakespeare and the Modern Stage' (1906), 'The French Renaissance in England' (1910), 'Principles of Biography' (1911), 'Shakespeare and the Italian Renaissance' (1915), 'Life of King Edward VII' (1925–7).

LEE, VERNON, pseudonym of VIOLET PAGET (1856–1935), English essayist and novelist.

Leech, JOHN (1817–64). humorous draughtsman. His lifelong friendship with Thackeray began at Charterhouse. From 1841 till his death he contributed to 'Punch' political cartoons and scenes of everyday middle-class life. He drew for a number of magazines and illustrated books by Surtees.

LEFROY, EDWARD CRACROFT (1855–

91), author of some remarkable sonnets, 'Echoes from Theocritus, and other Sonnets', published in 1885.

Legend, SIR SAMPSON, a character in Congreve's 'Love for Love' (q.v.).

Legend of Good Women, The, written by Chaucer (q.v.) probably between 1372 and 1386, was his first experiment in the heroic couplet.

The poem begins with an allegorical prologue (of which there are two versions extant) in which the god of love rebukes the poet for the reflections on the fidelity of women contained in the 'Romaunt of the Rose' and 'Troylus and Cryseyde'. Alceste, his queen, defends the poet, but directs that he shall write henceforth in praise of women. The poet accordingly narrates nine stories of good women, classical heroines: Cleopatra, Thisbe, Dido, Hypsipyle and Medea, Lucrece, Ariadne, Philomela, Phyllis, and Hypermnestra. The matter is taken from the *Heroides* of Ovid, and various authors.

Tennyson refers to the poem in 'A Dream of Fair Women':

'The Legend of Good Women', long ago
Sung by the morning star of song, who made
His music heard below.

Legend of Montrose, A, a novel by Sir W. Scott (q.v.), published in 1819, in the third series of 'Tales of My Landlord'.

It is the story of the campaign of 1644, in which the Highland clans, having risen in favour of Charles I and against the Covenanters of their own country, inflicted a succession of defeats on their opponents, thanks in great measure to the skilful generalship of their great commander, the earl of Montrose, whose character the author strongly contrasts with that of his rival, the marquess of Argyle.

With this for historical background, the author tells the tale, which also has some basis of fact, of a barbarous murder committed by a small clan of Highland bandits, the Children of the Mist, and of the tragic events following thereon. Allan M'Aulay, the nephew of the murdered man, obsessed with the thirst for vengeance, grows up moody and violent, and passionately loves Annot Lyle, a young girl whom in one of his forays against his uncle's murderers he has rescued from them. She, however, returns the love of the gallant young earl of Menteith. Both Allan and Menteith are prevented from pressing their suit by the obscurity in which the birth of Annot Lyle is involved. When the leader of the caterans reveals on his death-bed that Annot is the daughter of Sir Duncan Campbell, her marriage with Menteith becomes possible, but is interrupted by Allan, who furiously attacks and stabs his rival, and then disappears.

The gloom of the story is relieved by the character of Captain Dugald Dalgetty, a mixture of the loquacious pedant, who makes great show of the knowledge gained at the Marischal College of Aberdeen, and the brave but self-seeking soldier of fortune; he has served indifferently under Gustavus and Wallenstein, and is prepared to do so under King Charles or the Covenanters according to the prospects offered by each.

Legenda Aurea, see *Golden Legend.*

Legion of Honour, an order instituted in 1802 by Buonaparte, when First Consul, to reward civil and military services.

LEHMANN, JOHN FREDERICK (1907–), poet and essayist, is best known as the editor of 'New Writing' (q.v.) and 'The London Magazine'(from its foundation in 1954 to 1961). He has published several anthologies of modern stories and poetry, as well as critical essays. 'The Age of the Dragon'(1951) is a collection of his own poems. His autobiography, 'The Whispering Gallery' (vol. i, 1951) and 'I am my Brother' (vol. ii, 1960), describes the birth and development of 'New Writing' and his work with Virginia and Leonard Woolf at the Hogarth Press from 1931 to 1946.

LEIBNIZ, GOTTFRIED WILHELM (1646–1716), German philosopher and mathematician, born at Leipzig, was the founder of the Society (later Academy) of Sciences at Berlin. He discovered the infinitesimal calculus at about the same time as Newton, but by a different method. As a philosopher he was inspired by Descartes, Spinoza, and Hobbes (qq.v.), but broke away from Descartes's mechanical conception of the universe. Matter he regarded as a multitude of monads, each a nucleus of force and a microcosm or concentration of the universe. Admitting that the interaction of spirit and matter is inexplicable, he assumed a 'preestablished harmony' between them: the spirit is modified by final causes, bodies by efficient causes; the two series are brought together, like two clocks ticking in unison (the simile is Voltaire's), by a harmony established from all time by God, the supreme monad and perfect exemplar of the human soul. His system is embodied in his 'Theodicée' (1710) and 'Monadologie' (1714), written in French. Leibniz was one of the chief forces in the German Enlightenment movement.

Leicester, ROBERT DUDLEY, EARL OF, the favourite of Queen Elizabeth, figures in Scott's 'Kenilworth' (q.v.) as the husband of the unfortunate Amy Robsart.

Leicester Fields, now Leicester Square, London, was so named from a residence built there early in the 17th cent. by the earl of Leicester (the nephew of Robert Dudley, Elizabeth's favourite). Many eminent persons lived there at various times, among others Swift, Hogarth, Reynolds, and Mrs. Inchbald.

Leif Eriksson, Icelandic discoverer of America, *c.* A.D. 1000. See *Vinland.*

Leigh, AMYAS, the hero of C. Kingsley's 'Westward Ho!' (q.v.).

Leigh, AUGUSTA, half-sister of Lord Byron (q.v.), being the daughter of his father by the latter's earlier marriage with Lady Conyers. Her relations with Lord Byron were the object of Lady Byron's jealousy and occasioned their separation.

Leila, (1) in Byron's 'Don Juan' (q.v.), the Moslem child whom Juan rescues at the siege of Ismail; (2) in Byron's 'The Giaour' (q.v.), the unfortunate heroine.

Leinster, *Book of,* an Irish MS. of the 12th cent., containing stories of Gaelic mythology, in particular the feats of Cuchulain (q.v.).

LELAND, CHARLES GODFREY (1824–1903), American author, remembered as the writer of the humorous dialect verses, 'Hans Breitmann's Ballads' (1857, final edition 1914).

LELAND or LEYLAND, JOHN (1506?–52), the earliest of modern English antiquaries, was educated at St. Paul's School, London, and Christ's College, Cambridge. He studied at Paris, took holy orders, became library-keeper to Henry VIII before 1530, and king's antiquary, 1533. He made an antiquarian tour through England, 1534–43, intending his researches to be the basis of a great work on the 'History and Antiquities of this Nation', but he left in fact merely a mass of undigested notes. In 'A New Year's Gift' (1545) he described to the king the manner and aims of his researches. He became insane in 1550. 'Leland's Itinerary' was first published at Oxford in nine volumes (1710), and his 'Collectanea' in six (1715). Leland claimed to have 'conserved many good authors, the which otherwise had been like to have perished', in the dissolution of the religious houses. There is a good edition of the 'Itinerary' by Lucy Toulmin Smith (1906–7).

Lemnos, one of the largest islands in the Aegean. Hephaestus (Vulcan) is said to have fallen there when hurled from Olympus by Zeus. The Argonauts (q.v.) visited it and found it peopled by women, who had killed their husbands (see *Hypsipyle*). On this account and because of the murder by the later Pelasgian occupants of the island of the Attic women they had brought with them and their children, 'Lemnian deeds' became proverbial in Greece for atrocious deeds. See also *Terra Sigillata*.

LEMON, MARK (1809–70), is remembered as one of the founders and first joint-editors, and subsequently sole editor, of 'Punch' (q.v.). He also published farces, melodramas, and operas, and besides contributing to 'Household Words' and other periodicals, was editor of the 'Family Herald' and 'Once a Week'.

LEMPRIÈRE, JOHN (*d.* 1824), classical scholar; author of 'Bibliotheca Classica' (Classical Dictionary), 1788, which has become a standard work of reference and has been revised and enlarged from time to time.

Lĕmŭres, the name given by the Romans to the spirits of the dead, regarded as maleficent, who were supposed to rove at night, haunting houses and frightening the occupants. The LEMURIA was a festival designed to propitiate them.

Lemuria, the name proposed by Philip Lutley Sclater, the zoologist, for the supposed lost continent between Madagascar and Malaya, which would account for the peculiar geographical distribution of the lemur, a small mammal akin to the monkey. Cf. *Gondwana*.

Lenclos, ANNE, known as NINON DE LENCLOS (1620–1705), a Frenchwoman noted for her beauty and wit, which she retained to a very advanced age, depicted by Mlle Scudéry as 'Clarisse' in her 'Clélie'. She had many celebrities for her lovers, and her *salon* was frequented by St. Évremond, Molière, the youthful Voltaire, etc.

LENIN (real name UL'YANOV), VLADIMIR IL'ICH (1870–1924), born in the Volga area, son of a schools inspector. A lawyer by training, he soon stopped practising and in 1893 became a professional revolutionary. He was active for the Marxists in polemics against the Populists, rivals in the socialist movement, and in 1895 led the St. Petersburg Union of Struggle for the Liberation of the Working Class. Arrested that year, he spent two years in prison and three in Siberia, publishing 'The Development of Capitalism in Russia' (1899). Upon release Lenin set out, with the help of an informal organization inside the party called 'The Spark', to gain control of the Social-Democratic Labour Party (founded in 1898). In the pamphlet 'What Is To Be Done?' (1902) he laid down his views on political strategy, tactics, and organization, the basis of Communist practice ever since. From 1900 to 1917 (except during the 1905–7 revolution) he was an *émigré* in Western Europe, whence he tried to direct the activities in Russia of the Social-Democratic Party, which was torn by factional strife, largely due to his uncompromising attitude towards opponents. He constantly insisted on Marxist orthodoxy (though his interpretation of Marxism was challenged by other leaders) and on the priority of the political struggle against the government over the workers' struggle against the employers for better conditions.

During the First World War Lenin took up a 'defeatist' stand, and argued that workers in each country should aim at a defeat of their own government so as to facilitate a proletarian revolution. After the fall of the monarchy in March 1917, he returned and led his supporters, now organized in a separate Bolshevik Party (later renamed Communist), towards the seizure of power from the democratically minded, half-socialist Provisional Government, arguing (in 'Imperialism as the

Last Stage of Capitalism') that Russia was ripe for a socialist revolution and (in 'State and Revolution') that such a revolution should bring about a 'dictatorship of the proletariat'. The régime established after the *coup* in Nov. 1917 was in fact a dictatorship of the Party, which was regarded as the *avant-garde* of the working class but actually remained a self-perpetuating body. The Communist government headed by Lenin confiscated privately owned land, distributing it among the peasants, and most industry, dispersed the Constituent Assembly (where the Communists were a minority), concluded a separate peace treaty with Germany and won the Civil War (1918–20), during which a policy of 'War Communism' included nationalization of all industry, suppression of private trade, wages in kind, compulsory food deliveries by the peasants and labour service. In 1921 Lenin inaugurated the 'New Economic Policy' of concessions to the peasants and the permitting of some private trade and industry, though at the same time he suppressed the socialist parties, and rival factions within the Communist party. Lenin became paralysed in 1922 and thereafter took a much less active part in public affairs.

LENNOX, Mrs. CHARLOTTE (1720–1804), daughter of Colonel James Ramsay, lieutenant-governor of New York, where she was born, was author of a novel, 'The Female Quixote' (1752), and a 'Shakespeare Illustrated', to both of which Dr. Johnson wrote dedications. She also wrote a comedy, 'The Sister', acted in 1769.

Lenore, the heroine of a celebrated ballad by Gottfried August Bürger (1747–94), a German poet. Lenore is carried off on horseback by the spectre of her lover after his death and married to him at the grave's side. Sir W. Scott's translation or imitation of the ballad was one of his first poetical works; it appeared as 'William and Helen' in 'The Chase and William and Helen', published anonymously in 1796.

Leo, the 5th sign of the zodiac; also a constellation, which, according to mythology, was originally the Nemean lion killed by Hercules (q.v.).

Leo Hunter, Mrs., a character in Dickens's 'The Pickwick Papers' (q.v.).

Leo X, Giovanni de' Medici, Pope 1513–21, a patron of literature and art, notably of Raphael (q.v.). It fell to him to deal with the theses of Luther, whom he excommunicated in 1520. It was he who gave Henry VIII the title of 'Defender of the Faith'. See also *Laurentian Library*.

LEO, JOHANNES, generally known as Leo Africanus (*c.* 1494–1552), a Moor born in Spain, who travelled widely in Africa (the Sudan, the Sahara, the Niger basin, Egypt). He was captured by pirates while returning by sea from Egypt, and given as a slave to

Leo X, who induced him to become a Christian, and gave him his own names Johannes and Leo. Leo Africanus was author of a 'Description of Africa', of which the Italian text survives (1526).

Leo the Isaurian or **Iconoclast,** Byzantine emperor, 718–41, famous for his edict proscribing the veneration of images, which was repudiated by Pope Gregory II (726–31).

Leodegrance, in Malory's 'Morte Darthur' king of Cameliard, and father of Guinevere.

LEON, FRAY LUIS PONCE DE (*c.* 1528–91), a Spanish Augustinian monk, celebrated as a mystic poet. A life of him by James Fitzmaurice-Kelly was published in 1921.

Leonarda, Dame, in Le Sage's 'Gil Blas' (q.v.), the old cook in the robber's cave.

LEONARDO DA VINCI (1452–1519), Florentine painter, sculptor, and engineer, the illegitimate son of a lawyer, who brought him up. In his painting he developed greater significance and complexity in composition, chiaroscuro, and psychological insight than had been achieved before, but few of his works were completed, and some, such as the 'Last Supper' in Sta Maria delle Grazie, Milan, suffered as a result of his unsuccessful experiments in technique. He was in Milan in 1483, in the employ of Ludovico Sforza, until 1499, then in Florence, Rome, and Milan again, and he finally went to France in *c.* 1516–17, where he died. The range of Leonardo's genius is revealed in his notebooks and drawings, which include studies of clouds, water, and other physical phenomena, engineering projects and inventions, such as aeroplanes and weapons, and anatomical research, as well as studies for unfinished works of art, now lost. He made notes for a treatise on painting which were first published in 1651 as 'Trattato della Pittura'. See also *Mona Lisa*.

Leonato, in Shakespeare's 'Much Ado about Nothing' (q.v.), the father of Hero and uncle of Beatrice.

Leonidas, king of Sparta (491–480 B.C.), the hero of the defence of the pass of Thermopylae in 480 B.C. against the invading army of Xerxes.

Leonine City, the part of Rome in which the Vatican stands, walled and fortified by Leo IV because of the Saracen invasions.

Leonine verse, a kind of Latin verse much used in the Middle Ages, consisting of hexameters, or alternate hexameters and pentameters, in which the last word rhymes with that preceding the caesura; for instance:

His replicans clare tres causas explico quare
More Leonino dicere metra sino.

The term is applied to English verse of which the middle and last syllables rhyme. It is derived, according to Du Cange, from the name of a certain poet Leo, who lived about the time of Louis VII of France (1137–80) or his successor Philippe-Auguste (1180–1223).

Leonora, (1) 'the unfortunate jilt', an episode in Fielding's 'Joseph Andrews' (q.v.); (2) the original name of Beethoven's one opera, based on a libretto by Bouilly, and produced as 'Fidelio' in 1805. Fidelio is the name assumed by Leonora when, disguised as a boy, she rescues from captivity her husband Florestan, a state prisoner; (3) Bürger's ballad, see *Lenore*.

Leonora d'Este, sister of Alfonso II, duke of Ferrara, with whom (according to a story now declared untrue) the poet Torquato Tasso (q.v.) fell in love, and was in consequence imprisoned in a madhouse. The legend is the foundation of Byron's 'The Lament of Tasso'.

Leontes, in Shakespeare's 'The Winter's Tale' (q.v.), the husband of Hermione.

Leontius, a character in Fletcher's 'The Humorous Lieutenant' (q.v.).

LEOPARDI, GIACOMO (1798–1837), Italian poet and scholar, an invalid from his youth, the author of some of the finest poetry in modern Italian literature, imbued with melancholy and pessimism. His works, small in total bulk, include patriotic odes ('To Italy', 'On the Monument of Dante', 1819) and a score or two of short poems, and essays, dialogues, etc., in prose, showing a wide scholarship ('Operette morali').

Leporello, the valet of Don Giovanni in Mozart's opera of that name, and of Don Juan in Shadwell's 'The Libertine'. (In Molière's comedy 'Le Festin de Pierre', Don Juan's valet is Sganarelle.)

Leprechaun, a fabulous creature of Irish folklore, who makes shoes for the fairies and knows where treasures lie hidden.

Lêr, in Gaelic mythology, the sea-god, one of the *Tuatha Dé Danann* (q.v.); perhaps to be identified with Llyr (q.v.) the British sea-god. He was the father of Manannán (q.v.).

According to the story of 'The Children of Lêr', one of the 'three sorrowful tales of Erin', Lêr had one daughter, Fionnuala (q.v.), and three sons. These were changed into swans by their jealous stepmother Aeife, and condemned to spend 900 years on the seas and lakes of Ireland. Before the end of this period, St. Patrick arrived, the old gods were swept away, and the swans were able to return to their home. They were converted to Christianity and restored to human shape; but were now old people and soon died.

LERMONTOV, MIKHAIL YURIEVICH (1814–41), Russian Romantic poet and novelist. Descended from a 17th-cent. Scottish mercenary, Lermontov was himself an army officer. Strongly influenced by Byron, he wrote much lyrical and narrative poetry on themes of disillusionment, rebellion, and personal freedom. He was killed in a duel in 1841. Lermontov's best-known poems are 'The Angel' and 'The Sail' (1832), 'The Death of a Poet' and 'The Song of the Merchant

Kalashnikov' (1837), 'The Demon' (1839), 'Mtsyri' (1840). His prose masterpiece, the novel 'A Hero of Our Times' (1840), was first translated in 1854 and has been translated many times since. Other works may be found in anthologies of translated verse.

Lesbia, the name under which the poet Catullus celebrated the lady whom he loved. She was the beautiful but infamous Clodia, sister of Publius Clodius, and wife of Metellus Celer.

Lesbos, an island in the Aegean, famous, in a literary connexion, as the birthplace of Terpander, Alcaeus, Sappho, and Arion (qq.v.). Hence 'Lesbian' is sometimes used to signify 'pertaining to or resembling Sappho' in the perverted character attributed to her.

Lesly, LUDOVIC, 'le Balafré', a character in Scott's 'Quentin Durward' (q.v.).

LESSING, GOTTHOLD EPHRAIM (1729–81), German critic and dramatist. He was educated at Leipzig University, was the critic of the National Theatre at Hamburg (1765–9), and in 1770 became librarian to the duke of Brunswick at Wolfenbüttel, where he died. As a dramatist his principal works were: the serious comedy 'Minna von Barnhelm' (1767); 'Emilia Galotti' (1772), a tragedy on a social theme; and 'Nathan der Weise' (1779), a plea for religious tolerance. Lessing was, in the words of Macaulay, 'beyond all dispute, the first critic in Europe', who emancipated German literature from the narrow conventions of the French classical school, and one of the principal figures of the 'Aufklärung' or 'Enlightenment'. His chief critical works were the 'Briefe die neueste Litteratur betreffend' (1759–65), the 'Laokoon' (q.v., 1766) on the limits of the several arts, and the 'Hamburgische Dramaturgie' (1767–9).

Lester, MADELINE, the heroine of Bulwer Lytton's 'Eugene Aram' (q.v.).

L'ESTRANGE, SIR ROGER (1616–1704), of a good Norfolk family, probably studied at Cambridge and was one of the earliest of English journalists and writers of political pamphlets. He was an active Royalist and was obliged to flee the country during the parliamentary wars. He wrote a number of pamphlets in favour of the monarchy and against the army leaders and Presbyterians. After the Restoration, in 1663, he was appointed surveyor of printing presses and licenser of the press. He issued the 'Intelligencer' and 'The News' during 1663–6, but these were ousted by the 'London Gazette' of Henry Muddiman (q.v.). He also perhaps projected the 'City Mercury' in 1675. His political activities in connexion with the Popish Plot again obliged him to leave the country for a while in 1680. In his periodical 'The Observator' (1681–7) he attacked the Whigs, Titus Oates, and the dissenters. He was knighted in 1685. At the revolution he was deprived of his office and repeatedly imprisoned. He was an accomplished linguist and produced many translations, notably of the 'Colloquies' of Erasmus (1680 and 1689), of Aesop's 'Fables' (1692 and 1699), of the 'Visions' of Quevedo (1668), and of the works of Josephus (1702).

Lestrigonians, see *Laestrygones.*

Lēthē, a Greek word meaning 'oblivion', the name of one of the rivers of Hades, of which the souls of the dead about to be reincarnated were supposed to drink. It had the power of making them forget their past lives.

Letitia Hardy, the heroine of Mrs. Cowley's 'The Belle's Stratagem' (q.v.).

Leto, see *Latona.*

Letter to a Noble Lord on the attacks made upon him and his pension in the House of Lords by the Duke of Bedford and the Earl of Lauderdale, by E. Burke (q.v.), published in 1796.

Burke retired from parliament in 1794 and received a pension from the government of Pitt. This grant was criticized in the House of Lords, principally by the peers above named, as excessive in amount and inconsistent with Burke's own principles of economical reform. Burke replied in one of the greatest masterpieces of irony and feeling in the English language, comparing his own services to the State with those rendered by the duke of Bedford and his house, which had been the recipient of enormous grants from the Crown.

Letter to Sir William Windham, A, written in 1717 by Viscount Bolingbroke (q.v.) while in exile, was his first important contribution to political literature. It was not published until 1753. It is intended to vindicate his conduct during the period 1710–15, and to persuade the Tories to renounce all idea of a Jacobite restoration. To that end he recounts his relations with Harley and the Tories, his fall from power and attainder, his relations with the Pretender, and in particular detail the disastrous failure of the Jacobite rising of 1715 and his own dismissal by the Pretender. The facts are misrepresented, but the 'Letter' is a brilliant and effective piece of writing, notably in the invective against Harley and the sarcastic description of the Pretender's court in 1715.

Letter to the Sheriffs of Bristol, A, by E. Burke (q.v.), published in 1777.

The American War had at this time followed its disastrous course for two years. The letter begins with a protest against certain acts of parliament subjecting the rebels to exceptional legal disabilities, treating them in fact as traitors, and passes to a review of the present humiliating situation. Burke goes on to defend the course that he has taken. Asserting his zeal for the supremacy of parliament, he defines the problem which the exercise of this supremacy involves: 'to conform our government to the character and circumstances of the several people who compose this mighty and strangely diversified' empire. The scheme of taxing America is

incompatible with this conception of imperial policy, and Burke has consequently voted for the pacification of 1766, and even for the surrender of the whole right of taxation.

Letters on a Regicide Peace, see *Regicide Peace.*

Letters to Archdeacon Singleton, by Sydney Smith (q.v.), published in 1837.

In these three letters the author argues against the attempts of the Reformed Government (through the Ecclesiastical Commission) to interfere with the incomes of the clergy.

Lettres persanes, see *Montesquieu.*

Leucadia, an island in the Ionian Sea (*Luceas, Santa Maura*), on the southern promontory of which stood a temple of Apollo. At the annual festival of the god, it was the custom to throw a criminal into the sea, as an expiatory rite. This gave rise to the story that unhappy lovers threw themselves from 'Leucadia's Rock' (Byron, 'Don Juan', ii. 205), and that Sappho leapt from it in despair at her unrequitted love for Phaon.

Leucothĕa, the name of the sea-goddess into whom Ino (q.v.) was changed.

LEVER, CHARLES JAMES (1806–72), was educated at Trinity College, Dublin, and practised medicine. He contributed much of his early work to the 'Dublin University Magazine', which he edited during 1842–5. His 'Harry Lorrequer' appeared there in 1837, 'Charles O'Malley' in 1840, 'Jack Hinton the Guardsman' in 1843, 'Tom Burke of Ours' and 'Arthur O'Leary' in 1844, 'The O'Donoghue' in 1845, and 'The Knight of Gwynne' in 1847. He then settled at Florence, where he wrote 'Con Cregan' (1849), 'Roland Cashel' (1850), 'Maurice Tiernay' (1852), and 'The Dodd Family Abroad' (1853–4). His last works included 'A Day's Ride' (1863), 'Cornelius O'Dowd' (1864), 'Luttrell of Arran' (1865), and 'Lord Kilgobbin' (1872). His vivid rollicking pictures of military life and of the hard-drinking fox-hunting Irish society of his days were very popular. There is an amusing parody of Lever in Thackeray's 'Novels by Eminent Hands'.

Leviathan, a Hebrew word of uncertain origin, the name of some aquatic animal (real or imaginary) frequently mentioned in Hebrew poetry. It is used in English in this and various figurative senses, e.g. a ship of great size, a man of formidable power, etc.

Leviathan, The, or the Matter, Form, and Power of a Commonwealth, Ecclesiastical and Civil, a treatise of political philosophy by Hobbes (q.v.), published in 1651.

By 'The Leviathan' the author signified sovereign power. The basis of his political philosophy is that man is not, as Aristotle held, naturally a social being, recognizing the claims of the community upon him and sharing in its prosperity, but a purely selfish creature, seeking only his own advantage and resisting the competing claims of others. The result is 'contention, enmity, and war'. The 'state of nature' is one of general war, and 'the notions of right and wrong, justice and injustice, have there no place'. There is 'continual fear; and the life of man is solitary, poor, nasty, brutish and short'. To escape from these intolerable conditions man has adopted certain 'articles of peace', those 'Laws of Nature' 'by which a man is forbidden to do that which is destructive of his life' and of which the science is 'true moral philosophy'. Virtue is 'the means of peaceable, sociable, comfortable living'. The first law of nature is 'that every man ought to endeavour peace'. The second is 'that a man be willing, when others are so too, to lay down his right to all things; and be contented with so much liberty against other men, as he would allow other men against himself'. The third is 'that men perform their covenants made'.

To enforce these covenants it is necessary to establish an external power, which shall punish their infraction; accordingly all individuals must enter into a contract 'to confer all their power and strength upon one man, or upon an assembly of men'. 'This done, the multitude so united in one person, is called a commonwealth.' This representative person is sovereign, and his power is inalienable. The contract is not between the subjects and the sovereign, but only between the subjects. The sovereign power is indivisible; it cannot for instance be divided between king and parliament. Hobbes is careful to repudiate the rival claim of the Church to control over the citizen, which involves either a division of sovereign power, or the absorption of the State in the Church. He accordingly makes the Church subordinate to the State.

The absolute power thus given to the sovereign is, however, subject to certain limits. There is liberty to refuse obedience if the command of the sovereign frustrates the end for which the sovereignty was ordained, i.e. the preservation of the life of the individual. Moreover, the obligation of subjects to the sovereign is understood to last so long as, and no longer than, 'the power lasteth, by which he is able to protect them'. The sovereign finally is responsible to God, if not to his subjects, for the proper discharge of his office.

Levin, CONSTANTINE, a character in Tolstoy's 'Anna Karenina'.

LEWES, GEORGE HENRY (1817–78), a versatile writer, was the author of a popular 'Biographical History of Philosophy' (1845–6), a 'Life of Goethe' (1855), 'Seaside Studies' (1858), 'Physiology of Common Life' (1859), 'Studies of Animal Life' (1862), and 'Problems of Life and Mind' (1873–9), this last a philosophical work of considerable importance. Lewes collaborated with Thornton Leigh Hunt in the 'Leader' in 1850 and edited the 'Fortnightly Review' in 1865–6. He made the acquaintance in 1851 of Mary Ann Evans ('George Eliot', q.v.) and in 1854 formed a lifelong union with her.

Lewesdon Hill, a descriptive poem, somewhat in the style of Thomson and Cowper, by William Crowe (1745–1829), of Winchester and New College, Oxford, at one time public orator at Oxford, published in 1788.

LEWIS, ALUN (1915–44), a promising poet of the Second World War, who died in the Burma campaign. His work includes 'Raider's Dawn' (1942), 'Ha! Ha! Amongst the Trumpets' (1945), and 'In the Green Tree' (1948).

LEWIS, CECIL DAY, see *Day-Lewis*.

LEWIS, CLIVE STAPLES (1898–1963), literary scholar and critic, professor of Medieval and Renaissance English at Cambridge, 1954–63. His critical works include 'The Allegory of Love' (1936) and 'English Literature in the Sixteenth Century' (vol. 3 in the Oxford History of English Literature, 1954), and he is also known for his religious and moral writings such as 'The Pilgrim's Regress' (1933), 'The Problem of Pain' (1940), 'The Screwtape Letters' (1942), and 'The Four Loves' (1960). 'Out of the Silent Planet' (1938) is science fiction with a strong moral flavour. He has also written a number of children's books. 'Surprised by Joy' (1955) is autobiographical.

LEWIS, SIR GEORGE CORNEWALL (1806–63), educated at Eton and Christ Church, Oxford, was editor of the 'Edinburgh Review' (q.v.), 1852–5. He wrote an essay 'On the Influence of Authority in Matters of Opinion' (1849), an 'Enquiry into the Credibility of Ancient Roman History' (1855), 'The Astronomy of the Ancients' (1862), and translated Boeckh's 'Public Economy of Athens' (1828). He also wrote treatises entitled 'The Government of Dependencies' and 'The Best Form of Government'. He was M.P. for Radnor Burghs, and was chancellor of the exchequer (1855–8), home secretary (1859–61), and secretary for war (1861–3).

LEWIS, MATTHEW GREGORY (1775–1818), educated at Westminster and Christ Church, Oxford, is remembered as the author of the novel 'The Monk' (q.v., 1796). He wrote numerous dramas, and his verses (of which 'Alonzo the Brave and the Fair Imogine' is perhaps the best) had a considerable influence on Scott's earlier poetry.

LEWIS, PERCY WYNDHAM (1884–1957), artist, novelist, and critic. He was born in the U.S.A., but came to England as a child and studied at the Slade School of Art. He was a leader of the Vorticist movement, and, with Ezra Pound, edited 'Blast, the Review of the Great English Vortex' (1914–15). His writing, which is mainly satirical, includes the novels 'Tarr' (1918), 'The Childermass', Book I (1928) of a trilogy entitled 'The Human Age', of which Books II and III, 'Monstre Gai' and 'Malign Fiesta' were published in 1955 (a projected fourth Book, 'The Trial of Man', was not completed), 'The Apes of God' (1930), 'Self Condemned' (1954), 'The Red Priest' (1956); short stories: 'Rotting Hill' (1951); essays and criticism: 'The Art of Being Ruled' (1926), 'Time and Western Man' (1927), 'The Writer and the Absolute' (1952), and verse: 'One Way Song' (1933). 'Blasting and Bombardiering' (1937) and 'Rude Assignment' (1950) are autobiographies.

LEWIS, SINCLAIR (1885–1951), American novelist and journalist, born in Minnesota. After graduating from Yale he spent some years in journalism. He wrote several novels, but none was of much importance until 'Main Street', which scored an enormous success upon its appearance in 1920. In it, he described with realism and satire the dullness of life in a small mid-western town, called Gopher Prairie. He strengthened his reputation as the most widely read and controversial of American writers with 'Babbitt' (q.v., 1922) and 'Arrowsmith' (1925), which describes the career of a bacteriologist and is based, like all of Lewis's later novels, upon considerable research. 'Elmer Gantry' (1927), whose theme is mid-western religious evangelism, was followed by 'The Man Who Knew Coolidge' (1928) and 'Dodsworth' (1929), a better novel, which describes the marital relations of a middle-aged American industrialist and his adventures in Europe. Lewis was awarded a Nobel Prize in 1930, the first American writer to be so honoured. His later novels lack the strength and originality of those with which he made his reputation. Among them are 'Ann Vickers' (1933), 'It Can't Happen Here' (1935), which is concerned with the setting up of a Fascist dictatorship in the U.S., 'Cass Tamberlane' (1945), and 'Kingsblood Royal' (1949).

Lewis and Short, the well-known Latin-English dictionary, the work of Charlton T. Lewis and Charles Short, published in 1879.

Lewis Baboon, in Arbuthnot's 'The History of John Bull', represents Louis XIV of France.

Lewknor's Lane, now Charles Street, Drury Lane, so named after Sir Lewis Lewknor, of the time of James I, who resided in Drury Lane, is frequently mentioned in 17th- and 18th-cent. literature as a disreputable haunt.

LEYDEN, JOHN (1775–1811), physician, poet, and orientalist, assisted Scott (q.v.) in the preparation of the earlier volumes of the 'Border Minstrelsy', published an essay on the Indo-Persian, etc., languages (1807), and translated the 'Malay Annals' (1821) and the 'Commentaries of Baber' (1826).

Li Beaus Desconus (= le bel inconnu), a 14th-cent. verse romance attributed to Thomas Chestre, the author of 'Sir Launfal' (q.v.). Gingelein, the bastard son of Gawain, demands knighthood of Arthur. As his name is unknown, he is knighted as *Li Beaus Desconus*. The poem recounts his adventures in rescuing the imprisoned lady of Sinadoune. This is one of the romances referred to by Chaucer in 'Sir Thopas' (see under *Canterbury Tales* (19)).

Libel of English Policy, The, a political poem written c. 1436, in which the author exhorts his countrymen to regard the sea as the source of the national strength, discusses commercial relations with other countries, and urges the importance of retaining Calais, Ireland, and Wales. The poem was included by Hakluyt, and is in Political Poems II, Rolls Series. It is perhaps the work of Adam Moleyns or Molyneux, clerk of the king's council. See the Introduction by Sir F. G. Warner (Oxford, 1926). 'Libel' in the title means 'a little book'.

Liber Albus, see *Carpenter (J.).*

Liber Amoris, see *Hazlitt (W.).*

Liberal, The, magazine, see *Byron (Lord).*

Liberty or LIBERTIES of a city, the district extending beyond the bounds of a city, which is subject to the control of the municipal authority. The 'Liberties' of a prison (especially the Fleet and the Marshalsea) were the limits, outside the prison, within which prisoners were sometimes permitted to reside.

Liberty, On, an essay by J. S. Mill (q.v.), published in 1859.

In this work Mill examines from the standpoint of Utilitarian philosophy the proper relations of society to the individual, and criticizes the tyranny of the custom-ridden majority that is concealed under such expressions as 'self-government' and 'the power of the people over themselves'. In his view 'the sole end for which mankind are warranted, individually or collectively, in interfering with the liberty of action of any of their number, is self-protection'. The only part of the conduct of anyone, for which he is amenable to society, is that which concerns others. A man's own good, either physical or moral, is not a sufficient warrant for the interference of society. 'Mankind are greater gainers by suffering each other to live as seems good to themselves, than by compelling each to live as seems good to the rest.' But Mill is careful to point out that this doctrine is reconcilable with the State's interference in trade and industry.

Liberty Hall, a place where one may do as one likes. 'This is Liberty Hall, gentlemen,' says Squire Hardcastle (in 'She Stoops to Conquer') to Marlow and Hastings, who have mistaken his house for an inn.

Liberty of Prophesying, see *Taylor (Jeremy).*

Libĭtīna, an ancient Italian divinity, originally, it appears, a goddess of the earth, who came to be regarded as goddess of the dead, and is sometimes identified with Proserpine.

Libra or THE BALANCE, one of the zodiacal constellations; also the seventh sign of the zodiac into which the sun enters at the autumnal equinox. (The sign and constellation owing to the precession of the equinoxes no longer correspond.)

Library, The, a magazine of bibliography and literature, published from 1889 to 1898 as the organ of the Library Association, and from 1899 to 1918 as an independent journal. In 1920 it was merged with the 'Transactions' of the Bibliographical Society (q.v.), though retaining its original title.

Libri, THE BOOK THIEF, whose full name was Guglielmus Brutus Icilius Timoleon, Count Libri-Carucci dalla Somaja (1803–69), belonged to an old Florentine family and was a distinguished mathematician, and author of a number of learned works, especially a history of the mathematical sciences in Italy (1837–41). Being implicated in a conspiracy, he migrated to France in 1830, where he obtained professional posts, was highly esteemed by Guizot, and was appointed to inspect libraries and archives. His visits to these were found to be followed by the disappearance of valuable books and manuscripts, but the police reports on the subject were suppressed by his friend Guizot, the prime minister. On the fall of Louis Philippe, Libri, receiving anonymous warning, fled to England, where he protested his innocence, but sold books and manuscripts purloined from French and Italian libraries, and acquired thereby a fortune. Many of these were unwittingly bought by Lord Ashburnham, and some were repurchased by the French government.

Libya, the ancient Greek name for the continent of Africa.

Lichas, the servant of Hercules (q.v.) who brought him the poisoned cloak of Nessus. Hercules hurled him into the sea, where the gods turned him into a rock.

LICHTENBERG, GEORG CHRISTOPH (1742–99), born in Hessen, was educated and later a professor at Göttingen, thus becoming a subject of George III, of whose Hanoverian dominions Göttingen formed part. A distinguished scientist, but interested also in philosophy (a disciple of Kant), he twice visited England, in 1770 and 1774–5, and was a guest at Kew of George III. He was an ardent admirer of English institutions and literature and a keen dramatic critic. His letters from England to his friends in Germany ('Lichtenberg's Visits to England', Clarendon Press, 1938) contain shrewd comments on the acting of Garrick, Macklin, etc., and throw an interesting light on contemporary English manners. He also published (1794–9) in Germany explanations of Hogarth's engravings.

Licia, or Poems of Love, see Fletcher (G., the elder).

LIDDELL, HENRY GEORGE (1811–98),

educated at Charterhouse and Christ Church, Oxford, was headmaster of Westminster School 1846–55, and dean of Christ Church 1855–91. He is remembered as the author, with Robert Scott (1811–87), of the famous 'Greek-English Lexicon'.

It was for Alice Liddell (afterwards Mrs. Reginald Hargreaves), daughter of Dean Liddell, that Dodgson (q.v.) wrote 'Alice in Wonderland'.

LIDDON, HENRY PARRY (1829–90), educated at King's College School, London, and Christ Church, Oxford, a disciple of Pusey and Keble, became canon of St. Paul's (1870), where his sermons for twenty years were an important factor in London life. His Bampton Lectures of 1866 on 'The Divinity of our Lord and Saviour Jesus Christ' were published in 1867. Many volumes of his sermons were published, and he left at his death a 'Life of Pusey' ready for publication (1893–7).

Lien Chi Altangi, in Goldsmith's 'Citizen of the World' (q.v.), the Chinaman who studies English customs.

Life and Death of Jason, The, see Jason (Life and Death of).

Life and Labour of the People in London, see Booth(C.).

Life in London, see Egan (P., the elder).

Life on the Mississippi, by Mark Twain (see Clemens, S. L.), published in 1883, an autobiographical account of the author's early years as a river pilot.

Ligēa, one of the Nymphs (q.v.), mentioned by Milton in 'Comus' (l. 880).

Light of Asia, or The Great Renunciation, a poem in eight books of blank verse, by Sir E. Arnold (q.v.), published in 1879.

In it the author, to use his own words, seeks 'by the medium of an imaginary Buddhist votary to depict the life and character and indicate the philosophy of that noble hero and reformer, Prince Gautama of India, founder of Buddhism'.

Light of the Haram, The, see Lalla Rookh.

LIGHTFOOT, JOSEPH BARBER (1828–89), bishop of Durham, published many valuable works of biblical criticism and on early Christian history and literature, notably commentaries on St. Paul's Epistles (1865, 1868, 1875).

Ligurian Republic, THE, the republic of Genoa formed in 1797 after Napoleon's victorious Italian campaign. It was annexed to France in 1805, and subsequently merged in the kingdom of Italy.

Lilburne, JOHN (1614?–57), known as 'Freeborn John', a political agitator and pamphleteer, supporter of the parliament, repeatedly imprisoned, proverbial for his quarrelsome disposition.

Lili, celebrated by Goethe (q.v.) in his lyrics,

was Anne Elizabeth Schönemann, to whom Goethe was for a time engaged. She married the Baron von Türkheim.

Lilith, an Assyrian demon, associated with the night, a vampire. The name occurs in Isa. xxxiv. 14, where it is translated 'screech-owl' (Revised Version, 'night-monster'). In Rabbinical literature Lilith was the first wife of Adam, and was dispossessed by Eve. D. G. Rossetti, in his 'Eden Bower', tells of Lilith's vengeance on Adam and Eve. Lilith also makes a brief appearance in the Walpurgis-night scene of Goethe's 'Faust'.

Lilli-Burlēro Bullen-a-la! These 'are said to have been the words of distinction used among the Irish Papists at the time of their massacre of the Protestants in 1641' (Percy). They were made the refrain of a song, written by Lord Wharton, satirizing the earl of Tyrconnel on the occasion of his going to Ireland in Jan. 1686–7 as James II's papist lieutenant. The song is given in Percy's 'Reliques'. Burnet (q.v.) wrote as follows regarding it:

'A foolish ballad was made at the time, treating the Papists, and chiefly the Irish, in a very ridiculous manner, which had a burden said to be Irish words, "Lero, lero, lilli-burlero", that made an impression on the army, that cannot be imagined by those that saw it not. The whole army, and at last the people, both in city and country, were singing it perpetually. And perhaps never had so slight a thing so great an effect.'

According to Chappell's 'Popular Music of the Olden Time', the tune of 'Lilliburlero' was included, in 1689, in the second part of 'Music's Handmaid' as 'a new Irish Tune' by 'Mr. Purcell', but it occurs in 'The Delightful Companion' of 1686.

Lilliput, see *Gulliver's Travels.*

Lilliput Levēe, a book of verse for children, with illustrations by J. E. Millais and G. J. Pinwell, by W. B. Rands (q.v.), published in 1864. The same author published 'Lilliput Lectures' (mostly prose) in 1871, and 'Lilliput Legends' in 1872. All three appeared anonymously.

LILLO, GEORGE (1693–1739), was the author of the famous prose domestic tragedy 'The London Merchant, or the History of George Barnwell' (q.v.), produced in 1731. Very little is known about him. He was very possibly the descendant of Flemish refugees, and is said to have carried on the trade of jeweller in London. His other plays include 'The Christian Hero', produced in 1735, 'Fatal Curiosity' (q.v.), 1736, and 'Elmerick, or Justice Triumphant', produced in 1740 after his death. He also wrote a tragedy on the subject of 'Arden of Feversham', published posthumously. Lillo is important as a pioneer, and his introduction of domestic tragedy had an influence which extended beyond English literature.

LILLY, WILLIAM (1602–81), a noted

astrologer, who published almanacs yearly from 1644 until his death, and pamphlets of prophecy. While ostensibly serving the parliament, he endeavoured to aid Charles I. He published also a 'True History of King James I and King Charles I' (1651).

Lillyvick, MR., a character in Dickens's 'Nicholas Nickleby' (q.v.).

LILY, WILLIAM (1468?–1522), was the first high-master of St. Paul's School. He contributed a short Latin syntax, with the rules in English, under the title 'Grammatices Rudimenta', to Colet's 'Aeditio' (1527).

Limbo (from Latin *limbus*, an edge), a region supposed to exist on the border of hell as the abode of the just who died before Christ's coming, and of unbaptized infants. Also referred to as *limbo patrum* and *limbo infantum*. (See also *Paradise of Fools*.) The word came to be used to mean prison, confinement; and later for a place of rubbish and forgetfulness.

Limehouse, used of virulent political abuse, in allusion to a celebrated speech at Limehouse, London, by Lloyd George (30 July 1909), directed against territorial and financial magnates.

Limerick, a form of facetious jingle, of which the first instances occur in 'Anecdotes and Adventures of Fifteen Young Ladies' and the 'History of Sixteen Wonderful Old Women' (1820), subsequently popularized by Edward Lear (q.v.) in his 'Book of Nonsense'. (The name is said to be derived from a custom at convivial parties, according to which each member sang an extemporized 'nonsense-verse', which was followed by a chorus containing the words 'Will you come up to Limerick?' [OED.]) Limericks have been composed on a great variety of subjects, even to express philosophic doctrines. The following, for instance, ridicules English pronunciation of French:

There was an old man of Boolong,
Who frightened the birds with his song.
    It wasn't the words
    That frightened the birds,
But the horrible *dooble ong-tong.*

LINACRE, THOMAS (1460?–1524), physician and classical scholar, was educated at Oxford and was a fellow of All Souls College. He was M.D. of Padua, and became one of Henry VIII's physicians. Later he was Latin tutor to the Princess Mary, for whom he composed a Latin grammar, 'Rudimenta Grammatices'. He was mainly instrumental in founding the College of Physicians in 1518. He wrote grammatical and medical works, and translated from the Greek, mainly from Galen.

LINCOLN, ABRAHAM (1809–65), was president of the United States, 1861–5, and political leader of the Northern States in the American Civil War. He was assassinated in 1865. In a literary connexion he is remarkable as an interpreter of the American theory of democracy and as a framer of political aphorisms. His great inaugural and other orations show a direct, pregnant, non-rhetorical style, and a strong sense of rhythm. Notable among these was his 'Gettysburg Address', given in Nov. 1863 at the dedication of the national cemetery of Gettysburg, soon after the battle at that place. John Drinkwater (q.v.) made Abraham Lincoln the subject of a successful drama.

Lincoln Green, a bright green stuff made at Lincoln, used for woodmen's jackets and the like.

Lincoln's Inn, off Chancery Lane, said to be named after Henry de Lacy, third earl of Lincoln, who had a mansion there in Edward I's reign. It became an Inn of Court in 1310. LINCOLN'S INN FIELDS were laid out by Inigo Jones, who designed Lindsay House (Nos. 57–60). The house of Mr. Tulkinghorn in Dickens's 'Bleak House' (q.v.) is No. 58.

Lind, JOHANNA MARIA, known as JENNY LIND (1820–87), the 'Swedish Nightingale', born at Stockholm, was remarkable for the combination of the histrionic gift with a magnificent voice and great musical talent. She first appeared in England in 1847 at Her Majesty's Theatre with immense success. She gave up the stage in 1849 and thereafter confined herself to singing in concerts and oratorios. In Sept. 1850 she began an American tour under the management of Barnum. She married Otto Goldschmidt (her conductor during the second year of her American tour) in 1852 and during the latter part of her life settled in England.

Linda'bridēs, the daughter of the emperor Alicandro in the 'Mirror of Knighthood', a romance of Spanish origin translated into English by Richard Percival at the end of the 16th cent. The name is used (e.g. in Scott's 'Kenilworth') to signify a lady-love, a mistress.

Lindisfarne, Holy Island, off the coast of Northumberland. See *Cuthbert (St.).*

Lindisfarne Gospels, a manuscript of the four Gospels in the Vulgate text, probably written in honour of the canonization of St. Cuthbert (698; q.v.). The script is Anglo-Saxon majuscule and there are magnificent illuminations and decorative capitals. An Anglo-Saxon gloss was added in the 10th cent. with a colophon stating that the text was written by Eadfrith, Bishop of Lindisfarne, 698–721, and naming the binder, the goldsmith who ornamented the binding, and the translator. The manuscript is in the Cottonian collection in the British Museum.

Lindor, a conventional poetical name for a shepherd lover.

LINDSAY, LADY ANNE (1750–1825), daughter of the fifth earl of Balcarres, wrote in 1771 the popular ballad 'Auld Robin Gray'. She became by marriage Lady Anne Barnard, and accompanied her husband to S. Africa.

'Lady Anne Barnard at the Cape, 1797–1802', edited by Miss D. Fairbridge (Oxford, 1924), is an important authority for the events during the first British occupation of Capetown.

LINDSAY or **LYNDSAY, SIR DAVID** (1490–1555), Scottish poet and Lyon king-of-arms; usher to Prince James (afterwards James V). His first poem, 'The Dreme', written in 1528, but not printed till after his death, is an allegorical lament on the misgovernment of the realm, followed by a vigorous exhortation to the king. In 1529 he wrote the 'Complaynt to the King', in octosyllabic couplets, commenting on the improved social condition of the realm except as regards the Church, lamenting that others have been preferred before him at court, and requesting the king that 'thy Grace will uther geve, or lend me' 'of gold ane thousand pound, or tway'. The 'Testament and Complaynt of our Soverane Lordis Papyngo' (finished in 1530, printed in 1538) combines advice to the king, put in the mouth of his parrot, with a warning to courtiers drawn from the examples of Scottish history, and with a satire on ecclesiastics in the form of a conference between the dying parrot and its 'holy executors'. Lindsay's principal poem, 'Ane Pleasant Satyre of the Thrie Estaitis' (q.v.), a morality, was produced in 1540 before the king and court. Other poems by Lindsay include 'The Monarchie (Ane dialog betwix Experience and ane Courtier of the miserabill estait of the World)' (1554) and the 'History of Squire Meldrum' (first published in 1582), a spirited verse romance on the career and exploits of a Scottish laird.

LINDSAY, ROBERT (1500?–65?), of Pitscottie, author of 'The Historie and Cronicles of Scotland' from the reign of James II, one of Sir W. Scott's principal sources for the period.

LINDSAY, [NICHOLAS] VACHEL (1879–1931), American poet. Among his best-known poems are 'General William Booth enters into Heaven' (1913) and 'The Congo' (1914).

Linet, in the 'Morte Darthur', the sister of dame Lyones (q.v.). She marries Sir Gaheris. See also *Gareth and Lynette.*

LINGARD, JOHN (1771–1851), educated at Douai, and ordained a Roman Catholic priest, was the author of a 'History of England' (published 1819–30) which remains a principal authority from the point of view of enlightened Roman Catholicism. Lingard also wrote 'The Antiquities of the Anglo-Saxon Church', published in 1806.

Lingua, see *Tomkis.*

Lingua franca, a mixed language or jargon used in the Levant, consisting largely of Italian words deprived of their inflexions. The term is extended to any mixed jargon formed as a medium of intercourse between people speaking different languages.

Linkinwater, TIM, in Dickens's 'Nicholas Nickleby' (q.v.), clerk to the brothers Cheeryble.

Linne, THE HEIR OF, see *Heir of Linne.*

Linnean Society, THE, was founded in 1788 by Sir James Edward Smith, in honour of Linnaeus (Carl von Linné, 1707–78), the great Swedish naturalist and founder of modern botany, whose collections Smith purchased. The Linnean Society publishes journals and transactions on matters of natural history.

Linton, EDGAR, ISABELLA, and CATHERINE, characters in E. Brontë's 'Wuthering Heights' (q.v.).

Lintot, BARNABY BERNARD (1675–1736), published many poems and plays by Pope, Gay, Farquhar, Steele, and Rowe. His uncouth appearance was compared by Pope, in the 'Dunciad', ii. 63, to that of a dabchick.

Linus, in Greek mythology, a hero whose untimely death was celebrated in a dirge, the 'Song of Linus', sung annually, from Homeric days, at harvest time. He was perhaps originally a harvest deity.

Lion, THE BRITISH, the lion as the national emblem of Great Britain, used figuratively for the British nation, perhaps derived from the royal arms. The first mention of the British Lion quoted by the OED. is in Dryden's 'The Hind and the Panther' (1687).

Lion of Cotswold, a sheep.

Lion of the North, Gustavus Adolphus (q.v.).

Liones, or LYONES(SE), in the 'Morte Darthur' (q.v.), Linet's sister, whom Beaumains (Gareth) rescued from the castle where she was imprisoned, and married.

Lionesse, see *Lyonesse.*

Lipsia, in imprints, Leipzig.

LIPSIUS, JUSTUS, or JOEST LIPS (1547–1606), a Flemish humanist, who adopted the Protestant faith and was professor at Jena and subsequently at the University of Leyden, where he was succeeded by Scaliger. His principal work was a learned edition of Tacitus.

Lismahago, LIEUTENANT OBADIAH, a character in Smollett's 'Humpry Clinker' (q.v.).

Lister, JOSEPH, *first Baron Lister* (1827–1912), the founder of modern surgery by his discovery of the antiseptic treatment of wounds.

Lisuarte, see *Amadis of Gaul.*

Literary Anecdotes of the Eighteenth Century, see *Nichols (J.).*

Literary Club, THE, see *Johnson (S.).*

Literary Magazine, *The, or Universal Review,* a periodical started in 1756 and edited in 1756–7 by Samuel Johnson (q.v.), to which he contributed many articles, notably his Essay on Tea, and his review of Soame Jenyns's (q.v.) 'Free Enquiry into the Nature and Origin of Evil'.

Literature, THE ROYAL SOCIETY OF, was founded in 1823 at the suggestion of Thomas Burgess, bishop of St. David's, and under the patronage of George IV, who assigned the sum of 1,100 guineas to be applied in pensions of 100 guineas to each of ten Royal Associates, and in a premium of 100 guineas for a prize dissertation. The Associates were elected by the council of the Society (Malthus and S. T. Coleridge were among the first ten). The Society has published Transactions and a certain number of separate works.

Litōtēs, a figure of speech in which an affirmative is expressed by the negative of the contrary, e.g. 'a citizen of no mean city'; an ironical under-statement.

Littimer, in Dickens's 'David Copperfield' (q.v.), Steerforth's hypocritical valet.

LITTLE, THOMAS, see *Moore (T.).*

Little Billee, a humorous ballad of three sailors of Bristol, of whom Little Billee is the youngest. When provisions fail he narrowly escapes being eaten by the other two. Thackeray wrote a version of the ballad. Du Maurier uses 'Little Billee' as the nickname of the hero of 'Trilby' (q.v.).

Little Britain, near Aldersgate Street, in the City of London. It was formerly known as Britten or Briton Street, from the dukes of Brittany who are supposed to have had a mansion in it. Many bookstalls were located there in the 17th cent.

Little Dorrit, a novel by Dickens (q.v.), published in monthly parts, 1855–7.

William Dorrit has been so long in the Marshalsea prison for debtors that he has become the 'Father of the Marshalsea'. He has had the misfortune to be responsible for an uncompleted contract with the Circumlocution Office (a satirical presentment of the government departments of the day, with their incompetent and obstructive officials, typified in the Barnacles). His lot is alleviated by the devotion of Amy, his youngest daughter, 'Little Dorrit', born in the Marshalsea, whose diminutive stature is compensated by the greatness of her heart. Amy has a snobbish sister Fanny, a theatrical dancer, and a scapegrace brother, Tip. Old Dorrit and Amy are befriended by Arthur Clennam, the middle-aged hero, for whom Little Dorrit conceives a deep passion, at first unrequited. The unexpected discovery that William Dorrit is heir to a fortune raises the family to affluence. Except Little Dorrit, they become arrogant and purse-proud. Clennam, on the other hand, owing to an unfortunate speculation, is brought in turn to the debtors' prison, and is found in the Marshalsea, sick and despairing, by Little Dorrit, who tenderly nurses and consoles him. He has meanwhile learnt the value of her love, but her fortune stands in the way of his asking her hand. The loss of this makes their union possible, on Clennam's release.

With this main theme is wound the thread of an elaborate mystery. Clennam has long suspected that his mother, a grim old puritanical paralysed woman, living in a gloomy house with a former attendant and present partner, Flintwinch, has done some wrong to Little Dorrit. Through the agency of a stagy villain, Rigaud *alias* Blandois, this is brought to light, and it appears that Mrs. Clennam is not Arthur's mother, and that her religious principles have not prevented her from suppressing a codicil in a will that benefited the Dorrit family.

There are a host of minor characters in the work, of whom the most notable are the worthy Pancks, rent-collector to the humbug Casby; Casby's voluble daughter Flora, the early love of Arthur Clennam; her eccentric relative 'Mr. F's Aunt'; Merdle, the swindling financier, and Mrs. Merdle, who 'piques herself on being society'; Affery, the villain Flintwinch's wife; 'Young John' Chivery, the son of the Marshalsea warder; and the Meagles and Gowan households. The Marshalsea scenes have more reality than the rest of the story, for Dickens's father had been immured in that prison.

Little-endians, see *Gulliver's Travels.* The Little-endians were the orthodox party on the question at which end an egg should be broken.

Little Englander, one who desires to restrict the dimensions and responsibilities of the Empire. It was a current term of opprobrium during the Boer War of 1899–1901.

Little French Lawyer, The, a comedy probably by J. Fletcher (q.v.) and Massinger (q.v.), though Dyce attributed it to Beaumont and Fletcher. It was produced between 1619 and 1622.

Lamira marries Champernel, a lame but gallant old gentleman, throwing over Dinant, who conceived himself the favoured suitor. Dinant and his friend Cleremont insult the bride and bridegroom as they return from church. The play deals with the befooling of Dinant and Cleremont by Lamira, the revenge taken by them upon her, and the humiliation of La-Writ, the brawling little French lawyer.

Little Gidding Community and *Little Gidding Story Books,* see *Ferrar* (N.).

Little-go, the popular name at Cambridge for the matriculation examination, and at the University of Dublin for the final Freshman examination taken at the end of the second year.

Little John, one of the companions of Robin Hood in the legends relating to that outlaw. He was a sturdy yeoman and a skilled archer, originally called John Little. He figures in Sir W. Scott's 'Ivanhoe' (q.v.).

'Littlejohn', HUGH, John Hugh Lockhart, the grandson of Sir W. Scott, to whom the 'Tales of a Grandfather' are dedicated.

Little Lord Fauntleroy, see *Burnett (F. E. H.).*

Little Musgrave and Lady Barnard, an ancient ballad, given in Percy's 'Reliques' (III. i. 11), which tells how Lady Barnard, loving Little Musgrave, invited him to pass the night with her in her bower at Bucklesford-Buty. A little foot-page overhears the assignation, and tells Lord Barnard. He finds the lovers together, fights with Musgrave and kills him, then kills his wife, and is afterwards filled with remorse.

Musgrave is referred to in Beaumont and Fletcher's 'The Knight of the Burning Pestle' (q.v.), Act V, and in D'Avenant's 'The Wits', III. iii.

Little Nell (TRENT), the heroine of Dickens's 'Old Curiosity Shop' (q.v.).

Little Peterkin, in Southey's poem, 'The Battle of Blenheim', old Kaspar's grandson, who finds a skull and questions him about the battle.

Little Red Ridinghood, see *Red Ridinghood.*

Little Women, one of the most popular juvenile books ever written, by L. M. Alcott (q.v.), published in 1868. The story is concerned with the daily lives of four girls— Jo, Meg, Beth, and Amy March—in a New England family of the mid-nineteenth cent. For her portrayal of this family the author drew upon her own memories of home.

LITTLETON, SIR THOMAS (1422–81), judge and legal author. His fame rests on his treatise on 'Tenures', written in law-French; and his text, with Sir Edward Coke's comments, long remained the principal authority on English real property law. The *editio princeps* was published in London without date or title.

LITTRÉ, MAXIMILIEN PAUL ÉMILE (1801–81), French scholar, philosopher, and lexicographer, began his great dictionary of the French language in 1844. It was published in 4 vols. (1863–72) with a supplementary volume in 1877. The whole work was reprinted in 1950. He was a supporter of the philosophy of Comte (q.v.), on whom he published in 1863 'Auguste Comte et la philosophie positive'. He also published editions of the works of Hippocrates and Pliny.

Lityerses, son of Midas, king of Phrygia. It was said that he required all who passed his fields to help in the harvest, and if they did not surpass his activity in reaping the corn, put them to death, until a mightier hero (some say Hercules) arrived and killed him.

LIUTPRAND (*d.* 972) of Cremona, perhaps the most picturesque chronicler of the Dark Ages, and distinguished for having written worse Latin than anyone else; a good illustration of the darkness of the 10th cent.

Livery Companies, the London City companies, descended from the old City Guilds, so called because they formerly had distinctive costumes for special occasions. A LIVERY-MAN is a freeman of the City of London who is entitled to wear the 'livery' of the company to which he belongs. The word 'livery' is derived (through French) from the Latin *liberare*, and meant originally the dispensing of food or clothing to retainers or servants, or the food or clothing so dispensed.

Lives of the Poets, The, a biographical and critical work by S. Johnson (q.v.), published in 1779–81.

   Johnson was invited in 1777 by a deputation of London booksellers to undertake the preparation of biographical notices for an edition of the English poets that they were contemplating. When the work was completed, these notices were issued without the texts, under the above title. It had originally been intended to include all important poets from Chaucer onwards, but the scheme was curtailed and Cowley was taken as the point of departure. Fifty-two poets were included and it is significant of the taste of the age that Herrick and Marvell are not among them. The facts of each life are given and the character of the man brought out; and then Johnson passes to an estimate of his poems. In this respect the work is now considered unequal. The severe strictures, for instance, on Milton's 'Lycidas' and Gray's 'Odes' would not be endorsed at the present day. There is a good edition of the 'Lives' by G. Birkbeck Hill (Oxford, 1905).

LIVINGSTONE, DAVID (1813–73), the great African missionary and explorer. He educated himself while working at a cotton factory near Glasgow, and embarked for the Cape of Good Hope in 1840. He made a number of journeys into the interior in the following years, discovered Lake Ngami in 1849, and the Zambesi in the interior of the continent in 1851. Livingstone published 'Missionary Travels in S. Africa' in 1857, and 'The Zambesi and its Tributaries' in 1865. In that year he started on an expedition to discover the sources of the Nile, returned almost dying to Ujiji, where he was rescued by H. M. Stanley (q.v.), resumed his explorations, and finally died at a village in the country of Ilala. He was buried in Westminster Abbey. Livingstone's 'Last Journals in Central Africa, 1865 to his death' were published posthumously (1874).

LIVY (TITUS LIVIUS) (59 B.C.–A.D. 17), the Roman historian, born at Patavium (Padua). He was a friend of the Emperor Augustus though he showed a preference for republican institutions. His great work was the history of Rome from the foundation of the city to the death of Drusus (9 B.C.). Of the 142 books in which it was contained

we have 35, and epitomes of the greater part of the rest. See *Patavinity*.

Lizzie Hexam, a character in Dickens's 'Our Mutual Friend' (q.v.).

Lleu Llaw Gyffes, in British mythology, a sun-god, son of Gwydion and Arianrod. See *Mabinogion.*

Lloyd's, an association in London of shipowners, merchants, and underwriters, which had its origin in a coffee-house kept by Edward Lloyd in Lombard Street early in the 18th cent. It subsequently moved to rooms in the new Royal Exchange, to a new building in Leadenhall Street in 1928, and to Lime Street in 1957. It is principally concerned with marine insurance and the collection of shipping intelligence.

Lludd or NUDD, one of the chief gods of the ancient Britons, who survived in later times as the mythical King Lud, and perhaps as the Arthurian King Lot (qq.v.). See C. Squire, 'Mythology of the British Islands'.

Llyr, the sea-god of the ancient Britons, perhaps to be identified with the Lêr (q.v.) of Gaelic mythology. He figures in the 'Mabinogion' (q.v.) and his name survived as that of a British king in Shakespeare's 'King Lear'. The town of Leicester is said to have been originally Llyr-cestre (C. Squire, 'Mythology of the British Islands').

Lob's Pound, also COB'S POUND, HOB'S POUND, a jail or lock-up. 'Lob' means a country bumpkin, a clown; also a fairy of the Puck variety.

Lochiel, the title of the chief of the clan Cameron. T. Campbell (q.v.) wrote a poem called 'Lochiel's Warning'.

Lochinvar, the hero of a ballad included in the fifth canto of Scott's 'Marmion'. His fair Ellen is about to be married to 'a laggard in love and a dastard in war', when the brave Lochinvar arrives at the bridal feast, claims a dance with her, and, as they reach the hall door, swings the lady on to his horse, and rides off with her.

LOCKE, JOHN (1632–1704), born at Wrington in Somerset, was educated at Westminster and Christ Church, Oxford. He held various academic posts at that university, and became physician to Anthony Ashley Cooper (first earl of Shaftesbury) and settled in his house in 1667. He held official positions and subsequently resided at Oxford until expelled for supposed complicity in Shaftesbury's plots in 1684. He then lived in Holland, where he became known to the Prince of Orange. He was commissioner of appeals and member of the council of trade under William III. He died and was buried at High Laver, Essex. His portrait was painted by Kneller.

   His principal philosophical work is the 'Essay concerning Human Understanding' (q.v.), published in 1690, which led John Stuart Mill to call him the 'unquestioned founder of the analytic philosophy of mind'. He was a strong advocate of religious liberty. He wrote a 'Letter concerning Toleration' in 1689, a second letter on Toleration in 1690, and a third in 1692; a fourth was left unpublished at his death. He published an essay on the 'Reasonableness of Christianity' in 1695, maintaining that, as our understanding is not commensurate with reality, knowledge must be supplemented by religious faith.

Locke published in 1690 two 'Treatises of Government' designed to combat the theory of the divine right of kings and to justify the Revolution. He finds the origin of the civil State in a contract. The 'legislative', or government, 'being only a fiduciary power to act for certain ends, there remains still in the people the supreme power to remove or alter the legislative when they find the legislative act contrary to the trust reposed in them'. Throughout, Locke in his theory of the 'Original Contract' is the opponent of Hobbes's 'Leviathan' (q.v.; though he seems to be more actively criticizing Sir Robert Filmer's 'Patriarcha' than Hobbes). He published treatises 'On Education' in 1693, and on the rate of interest and the value of money in 1691 and 1695. The 1st edition of his collected works appeared in 1714.

LOCKE, WILLIAM JOHN (1863–1930), born in Barbados, educated at Queen's Royal College, Trinidad, and St. John's College, Cambridge, and from 1897 to 1907 secretary to the Royal Institute of British Architects, was a successful writer of fiction. His 'Morals of Marcus Ordeyne' (1905), and still more 'The Beloved Vagabond' (1906), enjoyed a very wide popularity. Locke also wrote a few plays.

Locke on the Human Understanding, see *Essay concerning Human Understanding.*

LOCKER, FREDERICK (1821–95), who took the name of LOCKER-LAMPSON in 1885, was a clerk in Somerset House and the Admiralty, but left the government service *c.* 1850. He published in 1857 a volume of light verse entitled 'London Lyrics', followed in 1867 by 'Lyra Elegantiarum', an anthology of verse of the same character, and in 1879 'Patchwork', a miscellany of verse and prose. 'My Confidences', in prose, appeared posthumously in 1896.

Locket, LUCY, see *Lucy Locket.*

Locket's, a fashionable ordinary or tavern in Charing Cross, frequently alluded to in the drama of the 17th–18th cents., so named from Adam Locket, the landlord.

LOCKHART, JOHN GIBSON (1794–1854), born at Cambusnethan, was educated at the high school and University of Glasgow, and at Balliol College, Oxford. He was called to the Scottish bar, and became one of the chief contributors to 'Blackwood's Magazine' (q.v.) in 1817. His fierceness as a critic earned him the nickname of 'The Scorpion'.

In 1820 he married Sir W. Scott's elder daughter Sophia, and from 1825 to 1853 was editor of the 'Quarterly Review' (q.v.). He published his 'Life of Burns' in 1828, and his famous 'Life of Scott' in 1837–8. He wrote several novels, of which the most notable is 'Some Passages in the Life of Adam Blair' (1822), the tragic story of the sin of a Scottish minister, and its expiation. His 'Valerius' (1821) is a story of Rome under Trajan. The other two novels are 'Reginald Dalton' (1823) and 'Matthew Wald' (1824). His 'Peter's Letters to his Kinsfolk', containing lively sketches of the Edinburgh and Glasgow of the day, appeared in 1819. His poetry is seen at its best in his adaptations of 'Ancient Spanish Ballads' (1823). Lockhart, it may be noted, was an early admirer of Wordsworth and Coleridge, though he condemned Keats and Shelley.

Lockit, and his daughter LUCY, characters in Gay's 'Beggar's Opera' (q.v.).

Locksley, the name under which Robin Hood figures in Scott's 'Ivanhoe' (q.v.). Ritson (q.v.) states that Robin Hood was born at Locksley in Nottinghamshire.

Locksley Hall, a poem by A. Tennyson (q.v.), published in 1842.

It takes the form of a monologue, in which the speaker, revisiting Locksley Hall, the home of his youth, recalls his love for his cousin Amy, 'shallow-hearted', who abandoned him in deference to her parents for a worldly marriage. This leads him to conjure up again his youthful vision of the progress of the world, in which he finally expresses his confidence.

A sequel, 'Locksley Hall Sixty Years After', appeared in 1886.

Locrine or LOGRIN, according to the legend told by Geoffrey of Monmouth and reproduced by Spenser ('Faerie Queene', II. x), was the eldest son of Brute (q.v.), and succeeded him as king of Loegria or England. He was the father of Sabrina (see *Estrildis*).

Swinburne wrote a play on the subject ('Locrine', 1887).

Locrine, The Lamentable Tragedie of, a play published in 1595, and included in the third Shakespeare folio. The authorship is unknown; modern opinion is inclined to attribute it to Peele (q.v.). The play deals with the legend of Locrine, king of England, his queen, Gwendolen, and Estrildis (see *Estrildis*).

Locusta or LUCUSTA, a skilful poisoner employed by Agrippina to poison Claudius, and by Nero to poison Britannicus. She was executed in the reign of Galba.

Lodbrog, or LODBROK, RAGNAR, see *Ragnar Lodbrog.*

LODGE, SIR OLIVER (1851–1940), physicist. In addition to numerous scientific papers he wrote: 'Conductors and Lightning Guards', 'Signalling without Wires', and 'The Ether of Space'; 'Relativity' (1925),

LODGE LOHENGRIN

'Ether and Reality' (1925). After 1910 he became known as a leader in psychic research, and among his writings dealing with this subject are: 'The Survival of Man' (1909), 'Reason and Belief' (3rd ed., 1911), 'Raymond, or Life and Death' (1916), and 'The Reality of a Spiritual World' (1930).

LODGE, THOMAS (1558?–1625), was son of Sir Thomas Lodge, lord mayor of London; born in Lincolnshire and educated at Merchant Taylors' School, London, and Trinity College, Oxford. He was a student of Lincoln's Inn in 1578. He abandoned law for literature, and published 'A Defence of Plays', a reply to the 'School of Abuse' of S. Gosson (q.v.), in 1580; and in 1584 'An Alarum against Usurers', depicting the dangers that money-lenders present for young spendthrifts.

His first romance, 'The Delectable Historie of Forbonius and Priscilla', appeared in 1584, and 'Scillaes Metamorphosis' in 1589 (reissued in 1610 as 'Glaucus and Scilla'). This work is interesting as the first romantic treatment in verse of a classical subject, the prototype of Shakespeare's 'Venus and Adonis'. Lodge sailed on a freebooting expedition to the islands of Terceras and the Canaries in 1588, and to South America in 1591. In the course of the former voyage he wrote his second and best-known romance, 'Rosalynde. Euphues Golden Legacie' (q.v.), which appeared in 1590. His chief volume of verse, 'Phillis', a cycle of amorous sonnets, largely translations or imitations of French and Italian poems, with songs and lyrics, was issued in 1593. He published 'A Fig for Momus', containing satires and epistles in verse on the Horatian model, in 1595. During his voyage to South America, amid the winter storms of the Straits of Magellan, he wrote 'A Margarite of America', a romance dealing with the tragical love of Arsadachas, son of the emperor of Cusco, for Margarita, daughter of the king of Muscovy, which appeared in 1596; as did also his 'Wits Miserie and Worlds Madnesse'. He was converted to Roman Catholicism and studied medicine, becoming M.D. at Oxford, 1603. He published a laborious volume, 'The Famous and Memorable Workes of Josephus' (1602), 'A Treatise of the Plague' (1603), and 'The Workes, both Morrall and Natural, of Lucius Annaeus Seneca' (1614). His last literary undertaking, 'A learned Summary upon the famous Poeme of William of Saluste, lord of Bartas, translated out of the French', was published in 1625. Lodge excelled as a lyric poet and was the best of the imitators of the style of 'Euphues'.

Loeb, JAMES (1867–1933), an American banker, educated at Harvard, a member until 1900 of the firm of Kuhn, Loeb & Co. He founded in 1912 the well-known Loeb Classical Library of Greek and Latin authors, which gives the original text and the translation on opposite pages.

Loegria, according to Geoffrey of Monmouth, the part of Britain assigned to King Locrine (q.v.); England. Spenser calls it *Logris* ('Faerie Queene', II. x. 14).

Logic, *A System of, ratiocinative and inductive,* a treatise by J. S. Mill (q.v.), published in 1843, revised and enlarged in the editions of 1850 and 1872.

The importance of Mill's 'Logic' lies in the fact that it supplied, to use the author's own words ('Autobiography'), 'a text-book of the opposite doctrine [to the *a priori* view of human knowledge put forward by the German school]—that which derives all knowledge from experience, and all moral and intellectual qualities principally from the direction given to the associations'. In this work Mill formulated the inductive procedure of modern science, while, unlike Bacon, giving its proper share to deduction. He lays down methods for investigating the causal relations of phenomena, assuming the causal principle, in defence of which he can only say that 'the belief we entertain in the universality, throughout nature, of the law of cause and effect, is itself an instance of induction', constantly verified by experience, and to which, if there were an exception, we should probably have discovered it.

In attributing to experience and association our belief in mathematical and physical laws, he came into conflict with the intuitional philosophers, and gave his own explanation 'of that peculiar character of what are called necessary truths, which is adduced as proof that their evidence must come from a deeper source than experience'. This peculiar certainty, he holds, is 'an illusion, in order to sustain which it is necessary to suppose that those truths relate to, and express the properties of purely imaginary objects', as in the laws of geometry, which are only approximately true in the real world. Geometry being built on hypotheses, 'it owes to this alone the peculiar certainty supposed to distinguish it'. This conflict with the intuitional school is further developed in Mill's 'Examination of Sir William Hamilton's Philosophy' (q.v.).

Logistilla, in the 'Orlando Furioso' (q.v.), a beneficent witch, who defends Rogero against Alcina (qq.v.) and gives Astolfo (q.v.) his magic horn and book.

Logrin, see *Locrine.*

Logris, or LOGRES, see *Loegria.*

Lohengrin, the son of Percival (q.v.), first mentioned, as Loherangrin, in the 'Parzival' of Wolfram of Eschenbach (q.v.). According to legend he is summoned from the temple of the Grail at Montsalvatch (which is perhaps Montserrat in Catalonia) and borne in a swan-boat to Antwerp, where he defends the Princess Elsa of Brabant against Frederick of Telramund, who claims to marry her. He overcomes Frederick and consents to marry Elsa on condition that he shall not ask his race. But she fails to abide by this condition, and the swan-boat comes and carries Lohengrin back to the castle of the Grail. Lohen-

485

grin is mentioned in 'Titurel' (q.v.), and the legend is repeated in other early poems. It forms the subject of Wagner's music-drama 'Lohengrin', produced in 1850.

A similar tale is told of Helias, the legendary grandfather of Godfrey de Bouillon (see Baring-Gould, 'Curious Myths').

Lois the Witch, a novel by Mrs. Gaskell (q.v.), published in 1859, telling how the fanatical frenzy of the people of New England caused an innocent English girl to be hanged as a witch.

Loki, in Norse mythology, one of the Æsir (q.v.), the spirit of evil and mischief, the father of Hel, Jörmungander, and the Fenriswolf (qq.v.). It is he who contrives the death of Balder (q.v.).

Lokman or LUQMÂN, a mythical person to whom has been attributed a collection of fables in Arabic, in consequence of a passage in the 31st Surah of the Koran, which says, 'We gave to Luqmân wisdom'. The fables, which are drawn from various sources, some of them Greek, date, in the form in which we have them, from the 13th cent. They are not mentioned by Arabic writers.

Lola Montez, the stage name of Marie Dolores Eliza Rosanna Gilbert (1818–61), the daughter of a military officer, an adventuress, who appeared in London as a dancer in 1843, and was highly successful on the Continent. She became the mistress of Ludwig I of Bavaria and exercised full control over the government of that country, until banished by Austrian and Jesuit influence. She died in New York.

Lolah, one of the beauties of the harem in Byron's 'Don Juan' (q.v.), vi.

Lollards, from a Dutch word meaning 'mumbler', a name of contempt given in the 14th cent. to certain heretics, who were either followers of Wycliffe (q.v.) or held opinions similar to his. Their activities were the occasion of the statute 'De haeretico comburendo' (1401). See also *Oldcastle*.

LOLLIUS, an unknown author mentioned by Chaucer twice in 'Troylus and Cryseyde' (i. 394 and vi. 1667), and once in 'The Hous of Fame' (iii. 378). The problem of his identity is increased by the fact that the first mention in 'Troylus and Cryseyde' relates to the love-song of Troilus, which is a translation from Petrarch; while the second points, from its context, to Boccaccio. In 'The Hous of Fame' he is one of six authors of the story of Troy, the others being Homer, Dares, Tytus (? Dictys), Guido da Colonna, and Geoffrey of Monmouth.

LOMBARD, PETER, see *Peter Lombard*.

Lombard Street, London, 'so called of the Longobards and other Merchants, strangers of divers nations, assembling there twice a day' (Stow), a financial centre of the city, as indicated in the expression, 'All Lombard

Street to a China orange'. Lombard merchants came to England as early as the 13th cent., and were employed to help in collecting the dues payable to the popes, notably Gregory IX, in the reign of Henry III. Our word 'lumber' is derived from the pawnbroking establishments of the Lombards.

London : the name *Londinium* is first mentioned by Tacitus ('Annals', 14. 33, A.D. 61) as that of a place notable for its concourse of merchants; but the earlier existence of the town is proved by coins (of Cunobelin) and other Celtic objects found on the site. The origin of the name is uncertain. Geoffrey of Monmouth connects it with King Lud who built walls round the city founded by Brute and enlarged by Belinus, and called it Cær Lud. According to Loftie, it is from the Celtic *Llyn-din*, the lake fort, a name that would be explained by the much wider spread in ancient times of the estuary of the Thames, with its creeks and tributaries, round the original settlement. Ekwall ('Oxford Dictionary of English Place-names') connects it with a stem, found in OIr. *lond*, meaning 'wild, bold'. After evacuation by the Romans, conquest by the Saxons, and plundering by the Danes in the 9th cent., London was resettled by Alfred in 886.

LONDON, JACK (1876–1916), American novelist, born in California. He grew up in poverty, served as a common sailor, and took part in the Klondike gold rush (1897). All these experiences were the material of his very popular books, and led him to socialism. 'The Son of the Wolf' (1900), the first of his many collections of tales, is based upon life in the Far North, as are 'The Call of the Wild' (1903), 'The Sea-Wolf' (1904), and 'White Fang' (1906). He travelled widely and his knowledge of the South Seas in particular is shown in 'South Sea Tales' (1911). 'Martin Eden' (1909) and 'John Barleycorn' (1913) are both semi-autobiographical novels, and among the novels dealing with social themes are 'The Iron Heel' (1907), which prophesied a fascist revolution, and 'The Valley of the Moon' (1913).

London, Survey of, see *Stow*.

London, a poem by S. Johnson (q.v.), published in 1738, in imitation of the Third Satire of Juvenal.

Thalēs (perhaps Richard Savage, q.v.), disgusted with London and its vices, leaves it for the fields of Wales, and as he does so utters his indignant reflections on the degeneracy of the times, the oppression of the poor and the arrogance of wealth, the prevalence of French fashions (the 'supple Gaul' takes the place of the 'Graeculus esuriens' of Juvenal), and the dangers to which the Londoner is exposed from roisterers and criminals.

London Bridge. There is evidence in Dio Cassius of the existence of a bridge at London in A.D. 43, confirmed by the finds of Roman coins and the iron shoes of oaken piles in the bed of the river. No further mention of a bridge is found until the 10th cent. One was certainly in existence in the reign of Æthelred (979–1016), when Cnut found it an obstruction to the advance of his ships up the river. The 'Heimskringla' (q.v.) gives a spirited description of an attack on it by Olaf's fleet in the last year of Sweyn. The wooden bridge that existed in 1136 was burnt down in that year. The great medieval stone bridge was begun in 1176 by Peter the Bridge Master and curate of St. Mary Colechurch (d. 1205) and finished in 1209. It consisted of twenty openings about 28 ft. wide, and twenty piers about 20 ft. wide. One great pier near the centre was over 34 ft. wide and carried a two-story chapel dedicated to St. Thomas of Canterbury. The bridge itself was 20 ft. wide, with a 12 ft. roadway, and houses on either side, projecting over the river, supported by struts. The seventh opening from the Southwark end was spanned by a drawbridge. A gate stood just north of this; and another gate stood nearer the Southwark shore. On the first of these, until its demolition, the heads of traitors were exposed; after 1577 they were exposed on the Southwark Gate. The confinement of the river by the massive piers caused a dangerously violent current (with a fall at times of as much as 5 ft.) through the arches, and accidents were frequent, although 'shooting the Bridge' was a well-known pastime in the 17th cent. The houses on the bridge were demolished in 1758–62, and the old bridge itself was taken down in 1831. See Gordon Home, 'Old London Bridge'. There is a good description of the bridge in its last phase in 'Lavengro', ch. xxxi.

London Cuckolds, The, a rollicking farce by Edward Ravenscroft (*fl.* 1671–97), which was produced in 1682 and annually revived on Lord Mayor's Day for nearly a century.

London Gazette, see *Gazette.*

London Labour and the London Poor, see *Mayhew (H.).*

London Library, THE, was founded in 1840, largely at the instance of T. Carlyle (q.v.), and opened in 1841 (in two rooms of a house at 49 Pall Mall). It was moved to its present premises in St. James's Square in 1866. Its present membership exceeds 4,000.

London Lickpenny, see *Lydgate.*

London Magazine, The, a periodical which ran from 1732 to 1785, founded in opposition to the 'Gentleman's Magazine' (q.v.).

A magazine bearing the same name had a distinguished career from 1820 to 1829, in opposition to 'Blackwood's' (q.v.), with Lamb, Hazlitt, De Quincey, Hood, and Miss Mitford on its staff. It published Lamb's 'Dissertation on Roast Pig' and De Quincey's 'Opium Eater'. The tragic outcome of the hostility between the 'London Magazine' and 'Blackwood's' was a duel, in which John Scott, first editor of the 'London', was killed.

A new 'London Magazine' was founded in 1954 with John Lehmann (q.v.) as editor.

London Merchant, The, or The History of George Barnwell, see *George Barnwell.*

London Prodigal, The, a comedy published in 1605, attributed to Shakespeare in the title of the quarto edition of that year and included in the 3rd and 4th folios, but undoubtedly by some other hand.

The play is a comedy of London manners, and deals with the reclaiming of the prodigal young Flowerdale by the fidelity of his wife.

London Spy, The, see *Ward (E.).*

London Stone, of which a fragment survives (now in the wall of St. Swithin's Church, near its original site), was perhaps a military or Roman milestone, but was thought by Wren 'by reason of the large foundation' to be 'rather some more considerable monument' ('Parentalia', quoted by Lethaby). Later it became associated with the house of the first mayor of London (Fitz Aylwin, 1189), and appears to have had some institutional character. It was against this stone that Jack Cade is said to have struck his sword and said, 'Now is Mortimer lord of this city' (Shakespeare, '2 Henry VI', IV. vi).

Long John Silver, a character in Stevenson's 'Treasure Island' (q.v.).

Long Meg, see *Meg of Westminster.*

Long Melford, in Borrow's 'Lavengro' (q.v.), the expression that Belle Berners uses for Lavengro's long right arm (Belle was born in the workhouse at Long Melford). It was with a blow from 'Long Melford' that Lavengro knocked out the Flaming Tinman.

Long Parliament, THE, the second of the two parliaments summoned by Charles I in 1640. It passed a Triennial Bill, impeached Strafford, and adopted a number of constitutional reforms by which the personal government of the sovereign was terminated. In 1642 hostilities broke out between this parliament and the king. In 1648 those members who were favourable to the latter were expelled by a body of soldiers under Colonel Pride, an act of violence known as *Pride's Purge*. The Long Parliament was dissolved by Cromwell in 1653. In 1659 forty-two members of the Rump—as the portion which had continued to sit until 1653 was called—returned to Westminster; and when the survivors of those excluded in 1648 returned, early in 1660, the Rump, under pressure from Monk, voted its own dissolution.

Longaville, in Shakespeare's 'Love's Labour's Lost' (q.v.), one of the three lords attending on the king of Navarre.

LONGFELLOW, HENRY WADS-WORTH (1807–82), American poet, born in Maine and educated at Bowdoin (where he was the class-mate of Hawthorne, q.v.) and at Harvard, became professor of modern languages at Bowdoin and in 1836 at Harvard.

From that time Cambridge (U.S.A.) became his home. He travelled in France, Spain, Italy, and Germany after leaving college, and again went to Europe (Sweden, Denmark, and Holland) before taking up his professorship at Harvard. Longfellow was twice 'married, his first wife dying while he was in Holland, and the second being burnt to death in 1861.

Longfellow's prose romance, 'Hyperion', appeared in 1839, a product of his first bereavement, the tale of a young man who seeks to forget sorrow in travel, a thread on which are hung philosophical discourses, poems, and legends. In the same year was published 'Voices of the Night', including his didactic pieces, 'The Psalm of Life', 'Footsteps of the Angels', and 'The Reaper and the Flowers'. In 1841 appeared 'Ballads and other Poems', containing 'The Wreck of the Hesperus', 'Excelsior', and 'The Village Blacksmith'. Longfellow visited London in 1842, and was the guest of Dickens. On the return voyage he wrote his 'Poems on Slavery'. In 1845 appeared 'The Belfry of Bruges and other Poems'; in 1847, 'Evangeline' (q.v.); in 1849, 'Kavanagh', a tale in prose, and 'The Seaside and the Fireside', containing 'The Building of the Ship' and 'Resignation'; in 1855, 'Hiawatha' (q.v.); in 1858, 'The Courtship of Miles Standish' (q.v.); in 1863, the first series of 'Tales of a Wayside Inn', including 'Paul Revere's Ride' and 'The Saga of King Olaf'; in 1867, his translation of Dante's 'Divine Comedy'. In 1872 appeared his 'Christus', a trilogy which Longfellow regarded as his greatest achievement. The three parts of it had appeared earlier: (1) 'The Divine Tragedy', in 1871; (2) 'The Golden Legend' (q.v.), in 1851; (3) 'New England Tragedies', in 1868. In 1872 he also published 'Three Books of Song', including further 'Tales of a Wayside Inn', the third instalment of these appearing in 'Aftermath' (1874). The 'Masque of Pandora' (1875) includes the fine ode 'Morituri Salutamus' and some notable sonnets. Longfellow's last volumes were 'Ultima Thule' (1880) and 'In the Harbor', published in 1882 after his death.

LONGINUS, CASSIUS, a Greek philosopher and critic of the 3rd cent. A.D., the instructor and counsellor of Zenobia. The author, conventionally called Longinus, of the remarkable treatise of literary criticism, 'On the Sublime', was probably of earlier date.

Longinus or LONGIUS, the traditional name of the Roman soldier who pierced with his spear the side of our Lord at the crucifixion. His spear figures in certain versions of the Grail legend, and is mentioned in Malory's 'Morte Darthur', II. xvi. It was dug up in a church at Antioch during the First Crusade, and enabled the Crusaders to overcome a vast host of Muslims.

Longomontanus, CHRISTIAN SEVERIN (1562–1647), of Longberg (of which Longo-

montanus is the latinized form), a Danish astronomer, assistant of Tycho Brahe (q.v.).

LONGUS, the reputed author of 'Daphnis and Chloe' (q.v.), of whom nothing is known.

Looking Backward, a Utopian novel by Edward Bellamy (q.v.), published in 1888.

LOPE DE VEGA, see *Vega.*

Lorbrulgrud, in 'Gulliver's Travels' (q.v.), the capital of Brobdingnag.

LORCA, FEDERICO GARCÍA (1899–1936), poet and dramatist, born in Andalusia. His most famous work was 'Romancero Gitano' (1928), a collection of eighteen ballads about gipsies and the simple people of his own countryside. The themes are based on the primitive and deep-rooted passions which he considered unchanging elements in Spanish life. Among his successful plays are 'Bodas de Sangre', 'Yerma', and 'La Casa de Bernarda'. He was assassinated in 1936 at the beginning of the Civil War.

Lord of Burleigh, The, a poem by A. Tennyson (q.v.), of which the story (of a country girl who marries a landscape-painter and discovers that he is a wealthy noble) is founded on the marriage of Henry, marquess of Exeter (1754–1804), in 1791, with Sarah Hoggins of Bolas in Shropshire.

Lord of the Ascendant, see *House (Astrological).*

Lord of the Isles, The, a poem in six cantos by Sir W. Scott (q.v.), published in 1815.

The poem, founded on the chronicles of the Bruce, deals with the return of Robert Bruce in 1307 to Scotland, whence he had been driven after the murder of the Red Comyn, and the period of his subsequent struggle against the English, culminating in the battle of Bannockburn. With this is woven the story of the love of Edith of Lorn for Lord Ronald, the Lord of the Isles. She is his affianced bride, but his heart is given to Isabel, Bruce's sister. His marriage to Edith is prevented by the return of Bruce. Edith, in the disguise of a mute page, follows Bruce and Ronald, and, at the risk of her life, saves them from destruction. Her devotion finally wins Lord Ronald's heart.

Lord Ormont and his Aminta, a novel by G. Meredith (q.v.), published in 1894.

Major-general the earl of Ormont, a distinguished cavalry commander, who has retired from the service with a grievance against the East India Company and the British public, has met the young and beautiful Aminta Farrell on a trip to Spain, and, in spite of her inferior birth and her dreadful aunt, Mrs. Pagnell, and his own sixty years, has married her at the embassy at Madrid. On her side Aminta has been led to the step by intense hero-worship. Lord Ormont contemplates a life of travel on the Continent, and when Aminta tires of this and they return to London, he does not introduce her to society or publicly recognize her as his wife, but leaves her in an equivocal position and to the companionship of a shady and highly emancipated set. Matthew (Matie) Weyburn, another young admirer of Lord Ormont's military prowess, is appointed his secretary, and discovers in the countess the 'Browny' of his schooldays and the object of a boyish passion. In spite of honourable restraint on both sides, circumstances revive their mutual affection. Lord Ormont's treatment and Mrs. Pagnell's mischievous interference expose Aminta to the persecution of the profligate Morsfield, from which Weyburn helps to rescue her. Lord Ormont finally repents of his course and prepares to give Aminta her pròper position. But it is too late, and Aminta leaves him for ever. Matie and Browny, ·both great swimmers, meet one morning in the sea, and the meeting decides their fate. They defy conventions and go off together to keep a school in Switzerland. Some years later, before Lord Ormont's death, they receive his forgiveness.

Lord Strutt, in Arbuthnot's 'History of John Bull' (q.v.), represents King Philip of Spain.

Lord Ullin's Daughter, a ballad by T. Campbell (q.v.).

Lords and Liveries, in Thackeray's 'Novels by Eminent Hands', is a parody of the novels of Mrs. C. G. F. Gore (q.v.).

Lorel, the swineherd in Jonson's 'The Sad Shepherd' (q.v.).

Lorelei, a cliff on the Rhine, where, according to German legend, dwelt a siren of the same name, who lured boatmen to destruction by her song. It is the subject of a poem by Heine.

Lorenzo, a character in Shakespeare's 'The Merchant of Venice' (q.v.).

Loretto or LORETO, a small town near Ancona in Italy, where in a church stands the SANTA CASA ('Holy House'), reputed to be the veritable house of the Holy Family miraculously transported there from Nazareth in 1294.

Lorna Doone, a novel by R. D. Blackmore (q.v.), published in 1869. The story is set in the times of Charles II and James II, and has a slight historical background, for Monmouth's rebellion and Judge Jeffreys figure in it, and John Ridd and the highwayman Tom Faggus have some traditional foundation.

John Ridd is a young Exmoor yeoman of herculean strength and stature. His father has been· killed by the Doones, a clan of robbers and murderers who inhabit a neighbouring valley. The vengeance which John and his neighbours finally exact from the Doones for their numerous crimes, complicated by John's love for Lorna Doone, provides the main theme of the book and the occasion for many thrilling and romantic adventures. John rescues Lorna from her

villainous associates, and the chief impediment to their marriage is the fact that her reputed father was the murderer of John's father. It turns out that Lorna is really the daughter of a Scottish noble, stolen from her parents by the Doones, and the difficulty now lies in the disparity in the social positions of Lorna and John. But this is overcome by Lorna's fidelity and by the services that John renders to an old kinsman of Lorna and to the king.

Lorraine, MRS., a character in Disraeli's 'Vivian Grey' (q.v.).

LORRIS, GUILLAUME DE, see *Roman de la Rose.*

Lorry, JARVIS, a character in Dickens's 'A Tale of Two Cities' (q.v.).

Los, a character in the mystical books of Blake (q.v.).

Lost Leader, The, a poem by R. Browning (q.v.), a lament on the desertion by a poet (Wordsworth?) of the cause of liberty and progress.

Lot or Loth, in the Arthurian legend, is king of Orkney and the husband of Arthur's sister, Margawse or Morgause, and the father of Gawain and, in the earlier version, of Modred. He is perhaps, in origin, the Lludd of British mythology.

LOT, PARSON, the pseudonym of C. Kingsley (q.v.).

Lothair, a novel by Disraeli (q.v.), published in 1870. This is one of Disraeli's last two novels, written while out of office, and, though containing many references to politics, has no political purpose.

Lothair is a young nobleman of immense wealth, an orphan left to the guardianship of Lord Culloden, a Scottish noble, and of a clergyman of shining talent, who, after his appointment as guardian, enters the Church of Rome and becomes Cardinal Grandison. Lothair, after a strictly Protestant education in Scotland, comes of age about the time (1866) when the Garibaldian forces were threatening the papal government. The plot of the novel consists principally of the efforts of Cardinal Grandison, assisted by his attendant Monsignor Catesby, and supported by the ascendancy of the beautiful and devout Catholic, Clare Arundel, to secure for the Roman Church the influence and wealth of Lothair. The forces opposed to his conversion are Lord Culloden, Lady Corisande (whom from his Oxford days Lothair has wished to marry), and the heroic Theodora, the enthusiastic supporter of Italian liberty. Lothair joins in the campaign against the papal forces, in the course of which Theodora is killed, obtaining from Lothair on her death-bed a promise that he will never enter the Roman Church. Lothair himself is wounded at Mentana, and the struggle to secure him is renewed by the Roman ecclesiastics. Their efforts are related with genial humour, and there is a capital passage where the cardinal blandly attempts to persuade Lothair that his belief that he fought at Mentana is a delusion comparable to that of George IV that he commanded at Waterloo. Lothair with difficulty escapes from the cardinal's vigilance, and finally returns to England to marry Lady Corisande. Among the delightful characters in the book is that of Lord St. Aldegonde, the red republican opposed to all privileges, except those of dukes, and in favour of the equal division of all property, except land.

Lothario, (1) the heartless libertine (proverbial as 'the Gay Lothario') in Nicholas Rowe's 'The Fair Penitent' (q.v.); (2) a character in the episode of 'The Curious Impertinent' (q.v.) in 'Don Quixote'; (3) a character in Goethe's 'Wilhelm Meister'.

LOTI, PIERRE, pseudonym of JULIEN VIAUD (1850–1923), French naval officer and author. Loti was an impressionist writer, with a remarkable gift for depicting exotic scenery and the melancholy aspects of nature, especially of the sea. He is seen at his best in some of his earlier works, such as 'Mon Frère Yves' (1883), 'Pêcheur d'Islande' (1886), and 'Le Marriage de Loti' (1880).

Lotophăgi or LOTUS-EATERS, according to the 'Odyssey', a people inhabiting a coast visited by Odysseus, who fed on a fruit called the lotus. Those who ate it lost all desire to return to their native country. 'The Lotoseaters' is the subject of one of Tennyson's best-known poems, founded on the Homeric story, in Spenserian stanzas followed by a choric ode of the sailors.

Lotte, the heroine of Goethe's 'The Sorrows of Werther' (see *Goethe*). Lotte was drawn from Lotte Buff, with whom Goethe fell in love at Wetzlar, and who married Goethe's friend Kestner.

Lotus-eaters, see *Lotophagi*.

Louis XI, king of France (1461–83), figures in Scott's 'Quentin Durward' and 'Anne of Geierstein' (qq.v.).

Louisa, the heroine of Sheridan's 'The Duenna' (q.v.).

Louisiana Purchase, THE, the transaction, completed in 1803, whereby the United States purchased from Napoleon, for $15,000,000, a vast tract of land west of the Mississippi, containing 828,000 square miles, or an area greater than that of all the thirteen original States. 'The bargain was a great one for America. It not only precluded all possibility of a foreign power getting a foothold on the lower Mississippi; it also secured control of the great river. . . .' [H. W. Elson.]

Lourdes, a town on the Gave de Pau in the Hautes-Pyrénées, France, one of the chief centres of Roman Catholic pilgrimage. The principal object visited is a grotto in which the Virgin is said to have appeared in 1858 and revealed the miraculous properties of a local spring. Lourdes is the subject of Zola's (q.v.) novel of that name (1894).

Lousiad, *The*, a mock-heroic poem by Wolcot (q.v.), published in 1785.

Its subject is the appearance of a louse in a dish of peas served to George III, which led to an order that all the servants in the king's kitchen should have their heads shaved.

Louvre, THE, the ancient palace of the kings of France in Paris, dating according to tradition from King Dagobert (628–38), who is said to have had a hunting-seat there (*Louvre* is from the late Latin *lupara*, which appears to mean a place or equipment for hunting wolves). It was entirely rebuilt in the reign of Philip II, and enlarged by Francis I and his successors down to Napoleon III. See also *Louvre* (*Musée du*).

Louvre, MUSÉE DU, housed in the former royal palace (see above), the principal art museum in France, containing a number of collections, of which the most important are those of pictures and of sculpture. The private collections of the kings of France form the nucleus of the former, which dates from the Renaissance, and particularly from Francis I, who imported a number of paintings from Italy (including Leonardo's 'Mona Lisa'). Louis XIV added largely to it, and it was immensely increased by the spoils of conquest during the wars of the Revolution and the Empire (after the fall of Napoleon, the Allies caused 5,000 works of art to be restored to their former owners). Since then it has been added to by purchase and bequests. The sculptures, like the pictures, come in part from royal collections; many are the fruit of archaeological missions.

Love à la Mode, a comedy by Macklin (q.v.), produced in 1759.

Four suitors, an Englishman, an Irishman, a Scot, and a Jew, are rivals for the hand of the heroine. Their quality is tested by the pretence that she has lost her fortune. The play is famous for the characters of Sir Archy MacSarcasm and Sir Callaghan O'Brallaghan.

Love for Love, a comedy by Congreve (q.v.), produced in 1695.

Valentine has fallen under the displeasure of his father by his extravagance, and is besieged by duns. His father, Sir Sampson Legend, offers him £4,000 (only enough to pay his debts) if he will sign a bond engaging to make over his right to his inheritance to his younger brother Ben. Valentine, to escape from his embarrassment, signs the bond. He is in love with Angelica, who possesses a fortune of her own, but she has hitherto not yielded to his suit. Sir Sampson has arranged a match between Ben, who is at sea, and Miss Prue, an awkward country girl, the daughter of Foresight, a superstitious old fool who claims to be an astrologer. Valentine, realizing the ruin entailed by the signature of the bond, tries to move his father by submission, and fails; then pretends to be mad and unable to sign the final deed of conveyance to his brother. Finally Angelica intervenes. She induces Sir Sampson to propose marriage to her, pretends to accept, and gets possession of Valentine's bond. When Valentine, in despair at finding that Angelica is about to marry his father, declares himself ready to sign the conveyance, she reveals the plot, tears up the bond, and declares her love for Valentine.

The comedy is enlivened by its witty dialogue and its humorous characters. Among these are Jeremy, Valentine's resourceful servant; Sir Sampson, with his 'blunt vivacity'; Ben, the rough young sea-dog, who intends to marry whom he chooses; Miss Prue, only too ready to learn the lessons in love given her by Tattle, the vain, half-witted beau, who finds himself married to Mrs. Frail, the lady of easy virtue, when he thinks he has captured Angelica; and Foresight, the gullible old astrologer.

Love in a Tub, see *Comical Revenge.*

Love Rune, see *Luve Ron.*

Love's Cruelty, a tragedy by James Shirley (q.v.), produced in 1631, printed in 1640.

Hippolito refuses to meet Clariana, the wife of his friend Bellamente, for fear that her beauty may tempt him to disloyalty to her husband. Clariana, piqued at his refusal, visits Hippolito, concealing her identity, with consequences disastrous to all three.

Love's Labour's Lost, a comedy by Shakespeare (q.v.), on internal evidence one of his earliest works, probably produced about 1595, printed in quarto in 1598.

The king of Navarre and three of his lords have sworn for three years to keep from the sight of woman and to live studying and fasting. The arrival of the princess of France on an embassy, with her attendant ladies, obliges them 'of mere necessity' to disregard their vows. The king is soon in love with the princess, his lords with her ladies, and the courting proceeds amidst disguises and merriment, to which the other characters contribute, viz. Don Adriano de Armado, the Spaniard, a master of extravagant language, Holofernes the schoolmaster, Dull the constable, Sir Nathaniel the curate, and Costard the clown. News of the death of the princess's father interrupts the wooing, and the ladies impose a year's ordeal on their lovers. The play ends with the beautiful owl and cuckoo-song, 'When icicles hang by the wall'.

Love's Sacrifice, a tragedy by J. Ford (q.v.), printed in 1633.

Fernando, favourite of the duke of Pavia, falls in love with Bianca, the duchess. He declares his love, but is repulsed. Presently, however, the duchess, in whom he has awakened a strong passion, comes to his room and offers herself to him, but warns him that she will not survive her shame, but take her own life before morning. Fernando masters his passion and determines to remain her distant lover. Fiormonda, the duke's sister,

who has vainly importuned Fernando with her love for him, discovers his affection for Bianca, and pursues her vengeance. With the help of D'Avolos, the duke's base secretary, she stirs up the duke's jealousy, and a trap is laid for Fernando and Bianca. The duke finds them together, and kills Bianca. Convinced too late, by Fernando's declarations and Bianca's manner of meeting her death, of her innocence, he stabs himself, and Fernando takes poison in Bianca's tomb.

Loveday, JOHN and BOB, the sons of Miller Loveday, in Hardy's 'The Trumpet-Major' (q.v.).

Lovel, (1) the name assumed by the hero in Scott's 'The Antiquary' (q.v.); (2) the principal character in Townley's 'High Life below Stairs' (q.v.).

Lovel the dog, see *Rat, the Cat,* etc.

Lovel the Widower, a short story by Thackeray (q.v.), published in 1860 in the 'Cornhill Magazine'. The principal characters are Lovel, the well-to-do widower; his odious mother-in-law Lady Baker, who makes his home intolerable; and Miss Prior, the governess in his family, a young woman who has learnt diplomacy in the school of adversity. It comes to light that she once danced at a theatre, and Lady Baker indignantly orders her to leave. But Lovel asks her to remain, as his wife, and Lady Baker is routed.

LOVELACE, RICHARD (1618–58), educated at Charterhouse School and Gloucester Hall, Oxford, was the heir to great estates in Kent. Wealthy, handsome, and of graceful manners, he had a romantic career. He was a courtier and served in the Scottish expeditions of 1639. Having presented a 'Kentish Petition' to the House of Commons in 1642, he was thrown into the Gatehouse prison, where he wrote the song, 'To Althea'. He rejoined Charles I in 1645 and served with the French king in 1646. It being reported that he was killed, his betrothed Lucy Sacheverell — 'Lucasta' — married another man. He was again imprisoned in 1648, and in prison prepared for the press his 'Lucasta; Epodes, Odes, Sonnets, Songs, etc.', which includes the beautiful lyric 'On going to the wars'. He died in extreme want. After his death his brother published his remaining verses ('Lucasta: Posthume Poems'). He wrote two plays, which have perished, and is remembered only by his lyrics, which are of unequal quality. His works have been edited by C. H. Wilkinson (2 vols., Oxford, 1925).

Lovelace, ROBERT, a character in Richardson's 'Clarissa Harlowe' (q.v.).

Loveless, a character in Vanbrugh's 'The Relapse' and Sheridan's 'A Trip to Scarborough' (qq.v.).

Lovell, LORD, a character in Massinger's 'A New Way to pay Old Debts' (q.v.).

LOVER, SAMUEL (1797–1868), Irish

novelist and song-writer, is remembered for his ballad, and the novel developed out of it, 'Rory O'More' (1836), which deal with the tragic events in Ireland in 1798; also for his novel 'Handy Andy' (1842), in which he depicts the whimsical aspects of Irish character. Andy Rooney, known as 'Handy Andy', is the servant of Squire Egan, and has an unrivalled faculty of 'doing everything the wrong way'. The rivalry of Squire Egan and Squire O'Grady and the blunders of Andy give rise to many amusing incidents, ending in the discovery that Andy is an Irish peer, Lord Scatterbrain. Lover published his 'Songs and Ballads' in 1839.

Lover's Melancholy, The, a romantic comedy by J. Ford (q.v.), acted in 1628.

Palador, prince of Cyprus, has been betrothed to Eroclea, daughter of Meleander, an old lord; but, to escape the evil designs of Palador's father, she has been conveyed away to Greece, where she has remained disguised as a boy. Meleander has been accused of treason, imprisoned, and driven to madness. Palador, after his father's death, is left in a state of hopeless melancholy. Eroclea returns to Cyprus as the page of Menaphon. Thamasta, cousin of the prince, falls in love with her in this disguise, and to escape her attentions Eroclea is obliged to reveal her identity. She is then restored to Palador; Meleander is released and cured; Thamasta marries Menaphon; and all ends happily. The play contains a version of Strada's contest of the lute-player and the nightingale, which is also dealt with by Crashaw (q.v.).

Lovers of Gudrun, The, see *Gudrun (The Lovers of).*

Lovers' Progress, The, a romantic drama by J. Fletcher (q.v.), revised by Massinger (q.v.), produced in 1623 and printed in 1647.

Lidian and Clarangè, devoted friends, are both in love with Olinda. Clarangè lets it be believed that he is dead, and finally turns friar, in order to surrender Olinda to Lidian. The plot is complicated with another illustration of the conflict of love and friendship. Lisander loves the virtuous Calista, wife of his friend Cleander. Cleander is killed by a servant. The imprudent but not criminal conduct of Lisander and Calista throws grave suspicion on them, and they narrowly escape condemnation for the murder.

Lovers' Vows, a play by Mrs. Inchbald (q.v.), adapted from 'Das Kind der Liebe' of Kotzebue (q.v.), acted in 1798.

Baron Wildenhaim has in his youth seduced and deserted Agatha Friburg, a chambermaid, and married another woman. Agatha, when the play opens, is reduced to destitution, in which state she is found by her son, Frederic, a young soldier, who now for the first time learns the story of his birth. To relieve his mother's needs, he goes out to beg, and chances upon his unknown father, and attempts to rob him. He is arrested, dis-

covers who the baron is, reveals his own identity and his mother's, and finally, with the aid of the good pastor Anhalt, persuades the baron to marry Agatha. The baron consents also to the marriage of his daughter Amelia with Anhalt, abandoning the projected marriage with Count Cassell which he had at heart.

The play would be of little interest but for the place it occupies in the story of Jane Austen's 'Mansfield Park' (q.v.).

Loves of the Angels, The, a poem by T. Moore, published in 1823. This was Moore's last long poem, and it had a very wide vogue. It was translated into several languages.

The poem recounts the loves of three fallen angels for mortal women, being founded on the eastern tale of 'Harût and Marût' (q.v.) and certain rabbinical fictions. In the poet's intention it represents emblematically the decline of the soul from purity. The first angel loved Lea, and taught her the spell-word which opens the gate of heaven. At once she uttered it and rose to the stars. The second loved Lilis; he came to her in his full celestial glory, and she was burnt to death. The third, Zaraph, loved Nama; they were condemned to live in imperfect happiness among mortals, but would ultimately be admitted to immortality.

Loves of the Plants, The, see *Darwin (E.).*

Loves of the Triangles, The, a parody by Canning and J. H. Frere in the 'Anti-Jacobin' (q.v.) of E. Darwin's (q.v.) 'The Loves of the Plants'. The authors claim to have enlightened by illustration 'the arid truths of Euclid and Algebra', and, 'as it were, to have strewed the Asses' Bridge with flowers'.

Lovewell, one of the principal characters in Colman and Garrick's 'The Clandestine Marriage' (q.v.).

LOWELL, AMY (1874–1925), American poet, born in Massachusetts. She was an Imagist and so active in the movement that Ezra Pound (q.v.) spoke of 'Amy-gism'. Among her collections of verse are 'Men, Women, and Ghosts' (1916) and 'Can Grande's Castle' (1918). She also published several books of critical prose, among them a notable life of John Keats (1925).

LOWELL, JAMES RUSSELL (1819–91), born in Massachusetts, and educated at Harvard, succeeded Longfellow as professor of belles-lettres at Harvard in 1855, and was American minister in Spain, 1877–80, and in England, 1880–5. He was editor of the 'Atlantic Monthly' magazine (q.v.) in 1857, and subsequently (1864), with C. E. Norton, of the 'North American Review' (q.v.). His works include several volumes of verse, the satirical 'Biglow Papers' (1848 and 1867), and memorial odes after the Civil War; and prose essays, 'Conversations on some of the old Poets' (1845), 'Fireside Travels' (1864), 'Among my Books' (1870 and 1876), 'My

Study Windows' (1871), 'Democracy' (1884), and 'Political Essays' (1888). His 'Letters', edited by C. E. Norton, appeared in 1894.

Low-heels and **High-heels,** in 'Gulliver's Travels' (q.v.), two factions in Lilliput.

LOWNDES, WILLIAM THOMAS (d. 1843), author of 'The Bibliographer's Manual of English Literature' (1834) and 'The British Librarian' (1839), early bibliographical works of importance. The former was revised and enlarged (1857–8) by H. G. Bohn (q.v.).

LOWRY, CLARENCE MALCOLM (1909–57), novelist. After publishing his first novel, 'Ultramarine' (1933), he went to France and then to the U.S., where the next three novels he wrote were rejected—including the first draft of 'Under the Volcano', which was finally published in England and America in 1947. At the time of his death he was putting the finishing touches to 'Hear Us O Lord from Heaven Thy Dwelling-place' (1962).

Loyal Subject, The, a drama by J. Fletcher (q.v.), produced in 1618.

The subject is the jealousy shown by the duke of Muscovy of his late father's loyal general, Archas, whom he dismisses and replaces by an incompetent flatterer Boroskie. The young Archas, son of the general, disguised as a girl (Alinda) is placed in the service of Olympia, the duke's sister, wins her affection, and attracts the duke's love. On an invasion of the Tartars, Boroskie feigns sickness, Archas is recalled and conquers. But Boroskie inflames the duke's suspicion of Archas. On signs of the disaffection of the troops, who are devoted to Archas, Archas is carried off to torture. The infuriated troops attack the palace, and then march away to join the Tartars, but are brought back to submission by Archas, fresh from the rack. The repentant duke marries Honora, daughter of Archas. The identity of Alinda, who has been dismissed by Olympia on suspicion of yielding to the duke's advances, is now declared, and the young Archas is married to Olympia.

Loyola, ST. IGNATIUS (1491–1556), a page to Ferdinand V of Aragon, and subsequently an officer in the Spanish army, was wounded in both legs at the siege of Pampeluna (1521), and thereafter devoted himself to religion. He constituted himself the Knight of the Blessed Virgin, went on a pilgrimage to the Holy Land, and on his return in 1534 founded in Paris the society of the Jesuits, bound by vows of chastity, poverty, obedience, and submission to the holy see, and authorized by papal bull in 1540. Its principal activities were preaching, instruction, and confession, and it formed a spiritual army bound to obedience. The object of the society was to support the Roman church in its conflict with the 16th-cent. reformers and to propagate its faith among the heathen. Francis Xavier and other missionaries carried on the latter work in the most distant parts of the world. The

secret power of the organization brought it into collision with the civil authorities even in Roman Catholic countries, whence its members have at times been expelled. Loyola's 'Exercitia' ('Spiritual Exercises'), a manual of devotion and of rules for meditation and prayer, was finished in 1548.

Luath, in the Ossianic poems of Macpherson (q.v.), Cuthullin's dog. The name was adopted by Burns for the ploughman's collie in his poem 'The Twa Dogs' (q.v.).

LUBBOCK, SIR JOHN, *first Baron Avebury* (1834–1913), educated at Eton, and head of the banking house of Robarts, Lubbock & Co., was elected M.P. for Maidstone in 1870 and subsequently sat for London University; in 1871 he secured the passing of the Bank Holidays Act, and in 1882 the Act for the Preservation of Ancient Monuments. From early days he devoted his leisure to natural science and was a pioneer in the study of the life histories of insects. His scientific works include the following: 'Prehistoric Times' (1865), 'The Origin of Civilization' (1870), 'On the Origin and Metamorphoses of Insects' (1874), 'Ants, Bees, and Wasps' (1882), 'On the Senses, Instincts, and Intelligence of Animals' (1888), 'A Contribution to our Knowledge of Seedlings' (1892), 'The Scenery of Switzerland' (1896), 'On Buds and Stipules' (1899), and 'Marriage, Totemism, and Religion' (1911). He wrote other works which enjoyed much popularity: the list of the 'Hundred Best Books', 'The Pleasures of Life' (1887–9), 'The Beauties of Nature' (1892), 'The Use of Life' (1894), and 'Peace and Happiness' (1909).

LUBBOCK, PERCY (1879–1965), historian and biographer. He published a study of Pepys in 1909, and an analysis of great novels in 'The Craft of Fiction' in 1921. His other works include 'Roman Pictures' (1923), 'Shades of Eton' (1929), and 'Portrait of Edith Wharton' (1947).

LUCAN, Marcus Annaeus Lucanus (A.D. 39–65), a Roman poet born at Corduba (Cordova) in Spain. His success as a poet aroused the jealousy of Nero, who forbade him to recite in public. In consequence Lucan joined in the conspiracy of Piso, and was compelled to take his own life. His chief work is the 'Pharsalia', a heroic poem describing the struggle between Caesar and Pompey.

LUCAS, EDWARD VERRALL (1868–1938), educated at London University, an essayist of remarkable charm, at one time assistant editor of 'Punch', published, among numerous works, a standard life of Charles Lamb (1905, 5th ed., 1921), editions of the works and letters of Charles and Mary Lamb (1903–35), and two pleasant anthologies, 'The Open Road' (1899, revised 1905) and 'The Friendly Town' (1905). Among the best of his discursive 'entertainments', a blend of the novel and the essay, are 'Over Bemerton's' (1908) and 'Listener's Lure' (1911).

Lucas, VRAIN- (*b. c.* 1818?), French forger, born at Châteaudun. His forgeries consisted of over 27,000 letters alleged to be from historical personages, among them being Abélard, Alcuin, Alexander the Great, Attila, Julius Caesar, Cervantes, Cicero, Cleopatra, Galileo, Herod, Joan of Arc, Judas Iscariot, Pascal, Pontius Pilate, Vercingetorix. The letters were written in French (except Galileo's, which was in Italian), and were on contemporary paper. They were sold over a period of about nine years (1861–9) to Michel Chasles (1793–1880), the eminent French geometrician and member of the Académie des Sciences. Chasles, being an old man and a fellow provincial of Lucas, seems to have entirely believed in him, and to have had no suspicion of imposture, notwithstanding the remarkable range of the letters, and, as afterwards appeared, the glaring errors of chronology. Over 140,000 frs. were paid by him for the various letters. Lucas represented that the letters had come from a collection made by the Comte de Boisjardin, who, he alleged, had emigrated to America in 1791, was shipwrecked and drowned. The letters, however, were saved, a few pieces being damaged by water.

In 1867 Chasles gave various letters to the Académie, including some from Pascal to Boyle and Newton. These were designed to show that Pascal had preceded Newton in establishing the law of gravitation, but it was later shown that at the date of the alleged letters Newton was only 10½ years old. The publication of these letters immediately raised doubts of their authenticity. They were exposed in 1868 by P. Faugère in his 'Défense de B. Pascal, et accessoirement de Newton, Galilée', etc., which contains facsimiles of some of the forged documents as well as genuine letters. Vrain-Lucas was tried in 1870, and was sentenced to a heavy fine and two years' imprisonment. On his release he again tried to pass off further forgeries and was sentenced to a further three years' imprisonment.

Lucasta, see *Lovelace.*

Lucca, THE HOLY FACE (*Volto Santo*) or SACRED COUNTENANCE OF, is a crucifix of cedar-wood in the Cathedral of St. Martin at Lucca, reputed to have been carved by Nicodemus and to give a true likeness of the Saviour. Alban Butler in his 'Lives of the Saints' (s.v. 'Anselm') states that 'by the holy face of Lucca' was the 'usual oath' of William Rufus.

Lucentio, a character in Shakespeare's 'The Taming of the Shrew' (q.v.).

Lucia, a character in Addison's 'Cato' (q.v.).

LUCIAN (*c.* A.D. 115–*c.* 200), a Greek writer born at Samosata on the banks of the Euphrates, author of 'Dialogues of the Gods' and 'Dialogues of the Dead' in which mythology, philosophers, and the society of the time are satirized with much humour and vivacity

(though some of the dialogues are melancholy, or despairing under a veil of cynical levity). The 'Dialogues' have been translated by H. W. and F. G. Fowler (1905). In his 'Auction of Philosophers', Socrates, Aristotle, and other great thinkers are offered by the gods to the highest bidder. His 'Veracious History' is a narrative of imaginary travels, the prototype of Gulliver. 'Lucius, or the Ass', a different version of the tale of the 'Golden Ass' (q.v.) of Apuleius, is doubtfully attributed to Lucian.

Lucifer, the morning star; the Phosphorus of the Greeks, the planet Venus when it appears in the sky before sunrise. The application of the name to Satan, the rebel archangel who was hurled from heaven, arises from a mistaken interpretation of Isa. xiv. 12, 'How art thou fallen from heaven, O Lucifer, son of the morning'.

Lucifera, in Spenser's 'Faerie Queene', I. iv. 12, the symbol of baseless pride and worldliness.

Lucilius, GAIUS (180–102 B.C.), Roman satirist.

Lucīna, 'She who brings to light', the Roman goddess who presided over childbirth. She was identified with Juno.

Lucina, in the 'Orlando Innamorato' and 'Orlando Furioso' (qq.v.), a lady in the power of a cruel monster called an orc, released by Mandricardo and Gradasso.

Lucinda, see *Cardenio.*

Lucius, (1) a mythical king of Britain, supposed to have been the first to receive Christianity. See Spenser, 'Faerie Queene', II. x. 53; (2) in the legend of Arthur (q.v.) Lucius is the Roman emperor against whom Arthur wages war; (3) Brutus's page in Shakespeare's 'Julius Caesar' (q.v.); (4) a character in his 'Timon of Athens' (q.v.); (5) a character in his 'Titus Andronicus' (q.v.); (6) in his 'Cymbeline' (q.v.), Caius Lucius is 'General of the Roman Forces'.

Luck of Eden Hall, a goblet of enamelled glass long kept at Eden Hall in Cumberland. The luck of the Musgrave family was traditionally held to depend on its safe preservation. It is the subject of a ballad by Uhland, translated by Longfellow.

Luck of Roaring Camp, The, title of a collection of stories by Bret Harte (q.v.).

Lucrece or LUCRETIA, a celebrated Roman lady, daughter of Lucretius, and wife of Tarquinius Collatinus, whose beauty inflamed the passion of Sextus (son of Tarquin, king of Rome), which he used threats and violence to satisfy. Lucretia, after informing her father and husband of what had passed, and entreating them to avenge her indignities, took her own life. The outrage committed by Sextus, coupled with the oppression of the king, led to the expulsion of the Tarquins from Rome, and the introduction of republican government.

Lucrece, The Play of, see *Fulgens and Lucrece.*

Lucrece, The Rape of, a poem in seven-lined stanzas by Shakespeare (q.v.), published in 1594 and dedicated to Henry Wriothesley, earl of Southampton. For the subject of the poem see *Lucrece,* above.

LUCRETIUS, Titus Lucretius Carus, the Roman poet, lived during the 1st cent. B.C., probably *c.* 99–55 B.C. It is said that he was driven mad by a love-potion administered by his wife Lucilia, and that he took his own life in his 44th year. His chief work is a philosophical poem in hexameters, in six books, 'De Rerum Naturâ'. He adopts the atomic theory of the universe of Epicurus (q.v.), and seeks to show that the course of the world can be explained without resorting to divine intervention, his object being to free mankind from terror of the gods. The work is marked by passages of great poetical beauty.

Lucretius, a dramatic monologue by A. Tennyson (q.v.), published in 1868.

This, perhaps the greatest of Tennyson's poems on classical subjects, presents the philosopher, his mind distraught, and his 'settled, sweet, Epicurean life' deranged, by the love-potion that Lucilia has administered, mingling visions of atoms and of gods, lamenting his subjugation to 'some unseen monster', and finally taking his own life.

Lucrezia Borgia, see *Borgia* (L.).

Lucullus, LUCIUS LICINIUS (*b. c.* 110 B.C.), Sulla's quaestor and subsequently consul, who for eight years (74–67) carried on the war with Mithridates. After his return to Rome, having amassed much wealth, he became famous for his magnificence and luxury, spending vast sums on a single dinner. He was also a patron of literature.

Lucy, in the episode of Amidas and Bracidas in Spenser's 'Faerie Queene', v. iv, the dowerless maid abandoned by Amidas and married by Bracidas.

Lucy, the subject of several poems by Wordsworth (q.v.) written about 1799, has been taken for a real person and was made the heroine of a story by the Baroness von Stockhausen. But nothing is known to suggest that she really existed. Coleridge surmised that one of the poems, 'A slumber did my spirit steal', referred to Dorothy Wordsworth. See, however, H. W. Garrod, 'Wordsworth's Lucy' in his 'Profession of Poetry' (1929).

Lucy Locket and **Kitty Fisher** (in the nursery rhyme about Lucy Locket losing her pocket) were, according to Halliwell, celebrated courtesans in the time of Charles II. A Kitty Fisher (*d.* 1767), described under the name of Kitty Willis in Mrs. Cowley's 'Belle's Stratagem', was several times painted by Sir J. Reynolds.

For LUCY LOCKIT see *Beggar's Opera.*

Lud, a mythical king of Britain, originally a god of the ancient Britons. According to Geoffrey of Monmouth (q.v.), he built walls round the city founded by Brute, which subsequently was known as London, and called it *Caer Lud.* See also *Ludgate.*

Luddites, English mechanics, who, under the pressure of the economic disturbance caused by the introduction of machinery to replace handicraft in the period 1811–16, set themselves to destroy machinery in the midlands and north of England. Their name is said to be taken from one Ned Ludd, a person of weak intellect, who lived in a Leicestershire village about 1779, and in a fit of insane fury broke up two frames in a stockinger's house. The Luddites figure in C. Brontë's 'Shirley' (q.v.). Byron's 'Song for·the Luddites' was written in 1816 and published in 1830.

Ludgate, the name of one of the ancient gates of London, traditionally connected with King Lud, but now believed to be a corruption of the OE. *ludgeat,* a postern. The gatehouse became a prison for debtors of the better sort (others being sent to the Fleet).

LUDLOW, EDMUND (1617?–92), Puritan general and regicide, author of famous 'Memoirs', first printed in 1698–9.

Lugdunum, in imprints, Lyons.

Lugdunum Batavorum, in imprints, Leyden.

Luggnagg, a kingdom visited by Gulliver in his third voyage (see *Guilliver's Travels*). It was here that the Struldbrugs (q.v.) lived.

Lugh, see *Tuatha Dé Danann.*

Luke, ST., the evangelist, by tradition a physician (Col. iv. 14) and a painter, and the patron saint of these crafts. His festival is kept on 18 Oct., whence a period of fine weather about that day is called 'St. Luke's Summer'.

Luke's iron crown, in the well-known lines in Goldsmith's 'The Traveller', is an allusion to the Hungarian peasant revolt in 1514 against the oppressive Magyar rule, led by György Dosza. Dosza was finally routed at Temesvar and condemned to sit on a red-hot iron throne, with a red-hot crown on his head. Goldsmith wrote 'Luke' in error for George.

Lulli or LULLY, JEAN BAPTISTE (1633–87), a Florentine by birth, composer and director of the opera in Paris under Louis XIV; the founder of the French grand opera.

LULLY, RAYMOND (*Raimon Lull*) (*c.* 1235–1315), a Catalan born in Majorca, who, after visions of Christ crucified, became a Franciscan, a mystic, a philosopher, a missionary to the Arabs, an author of controversial treatises, and a poet. He urged on the Council of Vienne (1311) the establishment of schools for missionary languages and obtained a decree for the foundation of chairs of Hebrew, Greek, Chaldee, and Arabic at various universities (including Oxford; Rashdall, ii. 459). He died of wounds received in a missionary crusade in North Africa, undertaken in his 80th year, after he had been twice expelled from Barbary.

Lumpkin, TONY, a character in Goldsmith's 'She Stoops to Conquer' (q.v.).

Lunsford, SIR THOMAS (1610?–53?), a royalist colonel and a man of violent temper, who was removed from the lieutenancy of the Tower on the petition of the Commons. He is referred to in Butler's 'Hudibras', iii. 2, 1111.

Lupercal, a cave on the Palatine hill in ancient Rome, sacred to LUPERCUS, or Faunus in the form of a wolf-deity. The story of Romulus and Remus having been suckled by a wolf is connected with this deity. The 'Lupercalia' was the annual festival of Lupercus, when the priests (*Luperci*) ran about the city striking the women whom they met, a ceremony supposed to make them fruitful [Lewis and Short].

Lupin, ARSÈNE, the hero of Maurice Leblanc's novels of crime, at once a criminal and a detective. In some of Leblanc's short stories he is brought amusingly into conflict with Sherlock Holmes.

Luqmân, see *Lokman.*

Luria, a poetical drama by R. Browning (q.v.), published in 1846.

The play deals with an episode of the struggle between Florence and Pisa in the 15th cent. Luria is a heroic Moor, the hired commander of the Florentine forces, whom, however, the Signoria distrust and plot to overthrow when he shall have achieved victory. Braccio is set to watch him and to gather materials for his trial. The Pisan general Tiburzio brings to Luria an intercepted letter from Braccio to the Signoria, but the loyal Luria refuses to read it. After the battle he learns with indignation what is being contrived against him. He has Florence and Pisa at his mercy, but refuses to avail himself of his power, takes poison, and dies.

Lusiads, The, see *Camoëns.*

Lusitania, (1) the Roman name of Portugal and western Spain; (2) the name of the Cunard liner that was sunk by a German submarine in the Atlantic on 7 May 1915, with the loss of over a thousand lives.

Lutetia or LUTETIA PARISIORUM, the modern Paris, on an island in the Sequana (Seine), was the capital of the Parisii, a Gallic tribe. Two wooden bridges connected it with the banks of the river, and it became a place of importance during the Roman Empire.

'Lutetia', in imprints, stands for Paris.

LUTHER, MARTIN (1483–1546), the leader of the Reformation in Germany, was born of humble parents at Eisleben, and entered the Augustinian order. As a monk he visited Rome, and his experience of the corruption in high ecclesiastical places influenced his future career. He attacked the principle of papal indulgences by nailing his famous *Theses* to the door of the church at Wittenberg, and as a consequence the papal ban was pronounced on him (1521) at the Diet of Worms. He left the monastic order and married, and devoted himself to forming the League of Protestantism. His chief literary work, apart from polemical treatises, was his translation into German of the Old and New Testaments, known as the Lutheran Bible (1534; portions had appeared earlier). He also composed Hymns of great popularity in Germany, notably 'Ein' feste Burg'.

Luther's power lay in these hymns of joy and strength and in his revival of the doctrine of justification by the faith of the individual, implying religious liberty and attacking the scandal of indulgences.

Lutine Bell. H.M.S. 'Lutine', a 32-gun frigate, previously of the French navy but captured by Admiral Duncan, sank in a heavy gale off the mouth of the Zuyder Zee in October 1799. She was carrying a large amount of coin and bullion, the property of merchants, and this entailed a heavy loss to the underwriters. In the course of salvage operations in 1857–8 the bell and rudder of the ship were recovered and taken to Lloyd's. There the bell now hangs; it is sounded on the occasion of important announcements.

LUTTRELL, HENRY (1765?–1851), author of an admirable light verse poem, 'Advice to Julia' (1820).

LUTTRELL, NARCISSUS (1657–1732), annalist and bibliographer, compiled 'A Brief Historical Relation of State Affairs, 1678–1714' (Oxford, 1857).

Luve Ron, or *Love Rune,* a mystic love-poem by Thomas de Hales, written probably between 1216 and 1240, in eight-lined stanzas. It deals with the theme of the love of Christ and of the joy of mystic union with Him.

Lux Mundi, a collection of essays on the Christian faith, by various hands, edited by C. Gore (q.v.), at that time principal of Pusey House, published in 1889.

The collection is an attempt to present the central ideas and principles of the Catholic faith in the light of contemporary thought and current problems. It was written by a group of Oxford men engaged in university tuition. The several essays and their contributors were as follows: 'Faith' (Rev. Henry Scott Holland); 'The Christian Doctrine of God' (Rev. Aubrey Moore); 'The Problem of Pain' and 'The Incarnation in Relation to Development' (Rev. J. R. Illingworth); 'The Preparation in History for Christ' (Rev. E. S. Talbot); 'The Incarnation as the Basis of Dogma' (Rev. R. C. Moberly); 'The Atonement' (Rev. and Hon. Arthur Lyttelton); 'The Holy Spirit and Inspiration' (Rev. C. Gore); 'The Church' (Rev. W. Lock); 'Sacraments' (Rev. F. Paget); 'Christianity and Politics' (Rev. W. J. H. Campion); 'Christian Ethics' (Rev. R. L. Ottley).

LXX, the Septuagint (q.v.).

LYALL, EDNA, the pseudonym of Ada Ellen Bayly (1857–1903), novelist and ardent supporter of women's emancipation and of all political liberal movements. Her best-known novels were 'Donovan' (1882, admired by Gladstone), its sequel 'We Two' (1884), and 'In the Golden Days' (1885).

LYALL, SIR ALFRED COMYN (1835–1911), educated at Eton and Haileybury, joined the Indian Civil Service in 1856, and served actively in the mutiny. He had a distinguished career, becoming lieutenant-governor of the North-West Provinces and member of the India Council in London. He was author of 'Asiatic Studies' (1882; second series, 1899), treating principally of the Hindu religion; 'The Rise and Expansion of the British Dominion in India'·(1893); lives of Warren Hastings (1889), Tennyson (1902), and Lord Dufferin (1905); and 'Studies in Literature and History' (1915). He also published a volume of remarkable 'Verses written in India' (1889), including the beautiful piece 'The Land of Regrets', 'Siva, or Mors Janua Vitae', 'The Old Pindaree', 'Retrospection', and 'Theology in Extremis' (the imaginary soliloquy of an Englishman in the mutiny who is offered his life if he will profess Mohammedanism. His biography was written by Sir H. M. Durand (1913).

Lycaon, an impious king of Arcadia, to punish whom Zeus visited the earth. To test the divinity of Zeus, Lycaon set before him a dish of human flesh. The god rejected it and slew Lycaon and his wicked sons, or turned them into wolves. Lycaon was the father also of Callisto (q.v.). See *Werewolf*.

Lyceum, THE, a gymnasium outside the city of Athens, on the banks of the Ilissus, sacred to Apollo Lyceus, where Aristotle taught philosophy.

Lyceum Theatre, THE, in London, at first known as the English Opera House, was originally built in 1794, and rebuilt, after being destroyed by fire, in 1834. It is especially associated with the name of Sir Henry Irving, who was lessee and manager for many years from 1878.

Lycidas, a poem by Milton (q.v.), written in 1637, while at Horton.
It is an elegy, in pastoral form, on the death of Edward King, a fellow of Christ's College, Cambridge, who had been a student there at the same time as Milton. King was drowned while crossing from Chester Bay to Dublin, his ship having struck a rock and foundered in calm weather.

LYCOPHRON (*b. c.* 325 B.C.), a Greek tragic poet, native of Euboea, who lived at Alexandria. His only extant poem is the 'Alexandra', in which Cassandra prophesies the fall of Troy and the fate of the Trojans and Greeks and their descendants.

Lycurgus, the legendary legislator of Sparta, of whom nothing certain is known. According to tradition he was the son of Eunomus, king of Sparta. After travelling in Crete and eastern lands, he returned to his country, then in a state of anarchy, and was acclaimed by all parties. He remodelled the constitution and obtained from the people a promise that they would not alter his laws until his return. He then went into voluntary exile, that the people's oath might be binding on them for ever, or according to Plutarch took his own life.

Lydford law, like 'Jedburgh justice' (q.v.), execution first, trial afterwards. Lydford is a town in Devon where a Stannaries court was formerly held.

LYDGATE, JOHN (1370?–1451?), probably of the Suffolk village of which he bears the name, and a monk of Bury St. Edmunds. He enjoyed the patronage of Duke Humphrey of Gloucester (q.v.). He was a most voluminous writer of verse. His chief poems are: 'Troy Book' (q.v.), written between 1412 and 1420, first printed in 1513; 'The Story of Thebes', written *c.* 1420, first printed *c.* 1500; 'Falls of Princes', founded on Boccaccio's 'De Casibus Virorum Illustrium', some 36,000 lines in rhyme-royal, written between 1430 and 1438, first printed in 1494; 'The Pilgrimage of Man', a very prolix 'Pilgrim's Progress', translated from Guillaume de Deguileville. A minor poem, 'London Lickpenny' (edited for the Percy Society by Halliwell), gives a vivid description of contemporary manners in London and Westminster (Howell says, 'Some call London a Lickpenny, as Paris is called a pick-purse, because of feastings and other occasions of expense'). This poem was long ascribed to Lydgate, but was excluded by H. N. McCracken from the list of his works (see the preface to 'Minor Poems', ed. 1910). Lydgate wrote also devotional, philosophical, scientific, historical, and occasional poems, besides allegories, fables, and moral romances. One prose work, 'The Damage and Destruccyon in Realmes', written in 1400, is assigned to him.

Lydia, a part of Asia Minor, adjoining the Aegean Sea; its capital was Sardis. The first historical kings of Lydia were of the Mermnadae dynasty (*c.* 685–546 B.C.), which included Gyges and Croesus (qq.v.), and was overthrown by Cyrus of Persia. Previously an active and industrious people, the Lydians gained under the Persian rule a reputation for effeminate luxury.

Lydian mode, one of the three principal modes of ancient Greek music, a minor scale appropriate to soft pathos.

LYELL, SIR CHARLES (1797–1875), geologist, was a pupil of William Buckland (author of 'Reliquiae Diluvianae', 1823). He travelled extensively, studying geology, and published his famous works 'The Principles of Geology' in 1830–3, 'The Elements of Geology' in 1838, and (after the appearance of Darwin's 'Origin of Species') 'The Antiquity of Man' in 1863. A record of his 'Travels in North

America' appeared in 1845, and of a 'Second Visit' in 1849. Lyell was professor of geology at King's College, London, 1831–3, and president of the Geological Society 1835–6 and 1849–50. He completely revolutionized the prevailing ideas of the age of the earth, and substituted for the old conception of 'catastrophic' change the gradual process of natural laws.

Lyle, ANNOT, a character in Scott's 'A Legend of Montrose' (q.v.).

LYLY, JOHN (1554?–1606), was educated at Magdalen College, Oxford, and studied also at Cambridge. He was M.P. successively for Hindon, Aylesbury, and Appleby (1589–1601), and supported the cause of the bishops in the Martin Marprelate controversy in a worthless pamphlet, 'Pappe with an Hatchet', in 1589. The first part of his 'Euphues' (q.v.), 'The Anatomy of Wit', appeared in 1578, and the second part, 'Euphues and his England', in 1580. Its peculiar style (see *Euphues*) received the name 'Euphuism'. Lyly's best plays are 'Alexander and Campaspe' (1584, see *Campaspe*), 'Endimion' (q.v., 1591), 'Midas' (q.v., 1592), and 'The Woman in the Moone' (q.v., 1597). His 'Sapho and Phao' was acted in 1584. For his 'Mother Bombie' see *Bumby*. The plays contain attractive lyrics, which were first printed in Blount's collected edition of the plays (1632). Lyly as a dramatist is important as the first English writer of what is essentially high comedy, and as having adopted prose as the medium for its expression.

Lynceus, (1) one of the Argonauts (q.v.), noted, like the lynx, for his keen sight. He was killed by Pollux; (2) the husband of Hypermnestra (see *Danaides*).

Lynch law, the practice of inflicting summary punishment on an offender, irrespective of trial by a properly constituted court. The origin of the term is uncertain. It is often asserted to have arisen from the proceedings of Charles Lynch, a justice of the peace in Virginia, who in 1782 was indemnified by an act of the Virginia Assembly for having illegally fined and imprisoned certain Tories in 1780. Some have conjectured that the term is derived from Lynch's creek in South Carolina, a meeting-place in 1768 of the 'Regulators', a band of men who professed to supply the want of a regular administration of criminal justice in the Carolinas. [OED.]

LYNDSAY, SIR DAVID, see *Lindsay (Sir D.)*.

Lynette, see *Gareth and Lynette*.

Lyon King-of-Arms, the title of the chief herald in Scotland, so named from the lion on the royal shield.

Lyones or LYONESSE, in Malory's 'Morte Darthur' (q.v.), the lady of the castle Perilous, whom Sir Gareth rescues and marries.

Lyonesse, LIONES, or LYONAS, in the Arthurian legends, the country of Tristram's

birth, is supposed to be a tract between the Land's End and the Scilly Isles, now submerged.

Lyonors, see *Gareth and Lynette*.

Lyons Mail, *The*, originally 'The Courier of Lyons', a melodrama by C. Reade (q.v.), produced in 1854. It kept the stage and furnished one of Sir H. Irving's successful parts.

Lyra Apostolica, a collection of sacred poems contributed originally to the 'British Magazine' by Keble, Newman, R. H. Froude, Wilberforce, and I. Williams (qq.v.), and reprinted in a separate volume in 1836.

Lyrical Ballads, a collection of poems by Wordsworth and S. T. Coleridge (qq.v.), of which the first edition appeared in 1798, the second with new poems and a preface in 1800, and a third in 1802.

Coleridge in his 'Biographia Literaria' (q.v.), ch. xiv, describes how Wordsworth and he decided to divide the field between them: 'it was agreed that my endeavours should be directed to persons and characters supernatural or at least romantic. . . . Mr. Wordsworth, on the other hand, was to propose to himself as his object, to give the charm of novelty to things of every day. . . .' Coleridge's contributions to the first edition were three, increased in the second to five ('The Ancient Mariner', 'The Foster-Mother's Tale', 'The Nightingale', 'The Dungeon', and 'Love'). Wordsworth contributed such simple tales as 'Goody Blake and Harry Gill' and 'Simon Lee the Old Huntsman'. His fine meditative poem 'Lines composed above Tintern Abbey' was also included.

The 'Lyrical Ballads', with their sudden revolt from the artificial literature of the day to the utmost simplicity of subject and diction, were unfavourably received; and the hostility of the critics was even increased by the appearance in the second edition of a preface in which Wordsworth expounded his poetical principles, and by his additional essay on 'Poetical Diction'.

Lysander, (1) a famous Spartan commander, who captured the Athenian fleet off Aegospotami in 405 B.C., and fell at the battle of Haliartus, 395 B.C.; (2) a character in Shakespeare's 'A Midsummer Night's Dream' (q.v.).

Lysias (*b. c.* 450 B.C.), Greek rhetorician and pleader, son of Cephalus, a wealthy Syracusan who settled at Athens and figures in Plato's 'Republic'.

Lysippus (4th cent. B.C.), Greek sculptor. His figures express emotion and his poses are effective from all angles.

LYTTELTON, GEORGE, *first Baron Lyttelton* (1709–73), educated at Eton and Christ Church, Oxford, a political opponent of Walpole and for a short time chancellor of the exchequer (1756), was a friend of Pope and Fielding and a liberal patron of literature. It is he whom James Thomson addresses in

The Seasons' (q.v.) and who procured the poet a pension. He published, among numerous works, 'Dialogues of the Dead' (1760) and 'The History of the Life of Henry the Second' (1767–71). Of the 'Dialogues', Mrs. Montagu (q.v.) was the author of the last three.

LYTTON, EDWARD GEORGE EARLE LYTTON BULWER-, *first Baron Lytton* (1803–73), son of General Bulwer, educated at Trinity College and Trinity Hall, Cambridge, became M.P. for St. Ives and later for Lincoln, supporting himself by literary labour. He was secretary for the colonies in 1858–9, and was created Baron Lytton of Knebworth in 1866. The principal novels of this versatile writer were published at the following dates: 'Falkland' (1827), 'Pelham' (q.v., 1828), 'The Disowned' (q.v.) and 'Devereux' (1829), 'Paul Clifford' (q.v., 1830), 'Eugene Aram' (q.v., 1832), 'Godolphin' (1833), 'The Last Days of Pompeii' (q.v., 1834), 'Rienzi' (q.v., 1835), 'Ernest Maltravers' (q.v., 1837), 'Zanoni' (1842), 'The Last of the Barons'(q.v., 1843), 'Harold' (q.v., 1848), 'The Caxtons' (q.v., 1849), 'My Novel' (q.v., 1853), 'What Will He Do with It?' (1858), 'The Coming Race' (q.v., 1871), 'Kenelm Chillingly' (q.v.) and 'The Parisians' (q.v.,

reprinted from 'Blackwood', 1873). In addition Lytton produced three plays: 'The Lady of Lyons' and 'Richelieu' (qq.v., 1838), and 'Money' (q.v., 1840). Among notable shorter stories were his 'The Haunted and the Haunters' (1859), and 'A Strange Story' (1862), in which he successfully introduces occult powers. His poem 'The New Timon' (1846) contained an incidental sarcasm on Tennyson, to which the latter replied in verse. Lytton's poem 'King Arthur' appeared in 1849 (revised, 1870).

LYTTON, EDWARD ROBERT BULWER, *first earl of Lytton* (1831–91), son of Edward Bulwer-Lytton, first Baron Lytton (q.v.), was educated at Harrow and Bonn, and after a career in the diplomatic service became viceroy of India (1876–80), where his 'Forward' policy was the subject of much opposition. He published a number of volumes of verse, at first under the pseudonym 'Owen Meredith'. His poetry in general is marred by prolixity, but some good lyrics are included in the 'Wanderer' (1857) and 'Marah' (1892), while the fantastic epic 'King Poppy' (1892) is generally considered his best work. 'Lucile' (1860) and 'Glenaveril' (1885) are long verse-romances.

M

Mab, QUEEN, see *Queen Mab.*

MABBE, JAMES (1572–1642?), educated at, and fellow of, Magdalen College, Oxford, became a lay prebendary of Wells. He is remembered for his translations of Fernando de Rojas's 'Celestina' (q.v.) and of 'The Spanish Ladye', one of Cervantes's 'Exemplary Novels'. Mabbe hispaniolized his name as *Puedeser* (may-be).

MABILLON, JEAN (1632–1707), a Benedictine monk of St. Maur (see *Maurists*), who worked at St. Germain-des-Prés. He was author of 'De re diplomatica' (1681, with supplement 1704), in which he created the science of Latin palaeography and laid down the principles for the critical study of medieval archives. He also wrote in 1691 a 'Traité des études monastiques', and was author or editor of many Maurist publications.

Mabinogion, The, a collection of Welsh tales (*mabinogi* = instruction for young bards). Four 'Mabinogi' are contained in the 'Red Book of Hergest', compiled in the 14th and 15th cents. They deal with old Celtic legends and mythology, in which the supernatural and magical play the chief part. They are, said Matthew Arnold, the *'detritus* of something far older'. The four Mabinogi are

concerned respectively with: (1) Pwyll, prince of Dyved; (2) Branwen, daughter of Llyr; (3) Manawyddan, son of Llyr; and (4) Math, son of Mathonwy; and they are to some extent interconnected.

The first tells how Pwyll, prince of Dyved (Pembrokeshire), temporarily exchanged shapes with the king of Annwyn (Hades), became known as *Pen Annwyn* or 'Head of Hades', and got Rhiannon to wife though she was promised to Gwawl (whose name, meaning 'light', suggests that he was a sun-god). He did this by luring Gwawl into a bag and releasing him only on condition that he gave up all claim to Rhiannon. The son of Pwyll and Rhiannon was Pryderi, who mysteriously vanished soon after his birth (Rhiannon was accused of having devoured him) and was restored some years later.

In the second tale, Matholwch, king of Ireland, comes to Wales and is married to Branwen, sister of Bran and daughter of Llyr (q.v., the sea-god of British mythology). During his visit a gross insult is put upon him by the mischief-making Evnissyen; and although Bran offers compensation, Branwen is in consequence ill-treated at her husband's court, war ensues, the Irish force and almost all the British are destroyed, and Bran himself is wounded in the foot with a poisoned arrow. In his agony he orders his head to be cut off, carried to the White Mount in London, and buried there with the face towards France. Branwen dies of grief and is buried in Anglesey. (The White Mount is explained to mean the Tower of London. The head was a kind of palladium, and, so long as it remained interred, no invasion of England could take place. See Lethaby, 'London before the Conquest'.)

The third tale tells of the association of Manawyddan, the last surviving child of Llyr, with Pryderi, and of the evils that came upon them in vengeance for the outrageous treatment of Gwawl, as told in the first tale.

The fourth tells how Gilvaethwy, son of Don, and Gwydion his brother, nephews of Math, the wizard, tricked Pryderi, son of Pwyll and Rhiannon, out of the pigs sent him by the Arawn, the king of Hades, by giving in exchange some attractive-looking horses, greyhounds and shields, in reality made of fungus; and how war ensued in which Pryderi was killed; also of the birth of Llew Llaw Gyffes, and of his marriage with Blodenwedd, a maiden composed of the blossoms of the oak, the broom, and the meadowsweet; of her treachery to her husband, and of her transformation into an owl.

For the position of these various characters in the ancient British pantheon, see J. Rhys, 'Hibbert Lectures', and C. Squire, 'Mythology of the British Islands'. Lady Charlotte Guest published in 1838–49 a collection of eleven Welsh tales, with translation and notes, including the above Mabinogi, under the title of 'Mabinogion'. The above abstract is based upon her book.

There is no mention of Arthur in the four Mabinogi, but among Lady Charlotte Guest's other seven Welsh tales from the 'Red Book of Hergest' there are five that deal with him. Three of them are drawn from French originals ('The Lady of the Fountain', 'Geraint, Son of Erbin', and 'Peredur, Son of Evrawc'). Two are of British origin, 'Kilhwch and Olwen' (q.v.) and 'The Dream of Rhonabwy'. In the first and more important of these two Arthur is represented, not as a hero of chivalry, but as a fairy king, surrounded by superhuman warriors, and able by his magic powers to overcome monsters.

Macabre, DANSE, see *Dance of Death*.

McAdam, JOHN LOUDON (1756–1836), the 'macadamizer' of roads.

Macaire, ROBERT, a character in 'L'Auberge des Adrets', a French melodrama of 1823, the type of clever and audacious rogue.

Macaroni, an exquisite of a class which arose in England about 1760 and consisted of young men who had travelled and affected the tastes and fashions prevalent in continental society. [OED.] Horace Walpole refers to the Macaroni Club, 'which is composed of all the travelled young men who wear long curls and spying-glasses'.

Macaronic verse, a term used to designate a burlesque form of verse in which vernacular words are introduced into a Latin context with Latin terminations and in Latin constructions . . . and *loosely* to any form of verse in which two or more languages are mingled together. [OED.] The chief writer of macaronic verse was the Italian, Folengo (q.v.).

M'Aulay, ANGUS and ALLAN, characters in Scott's 'Legend of Montrose' (q.v.).

MACAULAY, DAME ROSE (1881–1958), novelist, whose works include: 'Potterism' (1920), 'Told by an Idiot' (1923), 'Orphan Island' (1924), 'Going Abroad' (1934), 'The World My Wilderness' (1950), and 'The Towers of Trebizond' (1956). She wrote a study of Milton in 1933.

MACAULAY, THOMAS BABINGTON, *first Baron Macaulay* (1800–59), son of Zachary Macaulay, the philanthropist, was educated at Trinity College, Cambridge. His first article (on Milton) was published in 1825 in the 'Edinburgh Review' (q.v.), of which he became a mainstay. He became liberal M.P. for Calne in 1830 and for Leeds in 1831, and was a member of the supreme council of India from 1834 to 1838. There he exerted his influence in favour of the choice of an English, instead of an oriental, type of education in India. He returned to London and engaged in literature and politics, being M.P. for Edinburgh in 1839–47 and 1852–6; he was secretary of war in 1839–41, and paymaster of the forces in 1846–7. He published his 'Lays of Ancient Rome' (q.v.) in 1842, and a collection of his 'Essays' (q.v.) in 1843 (enlarged in later editions). Volumes i and ii of his 'History of England' (q.v.) appeared in 1849, iii and iv in 1855. He also contributed to the 'Encyclopaedia Britannica' a remarkable series of articles on Atterbury, Bunyan, Goldsmith, Johnson, and the younger Pitt. He was buried in Westminster Abbey. A life of Macaulay by his nephew, Sir George Trevelyan, appeared in 1876.

Macaulay's History of England *from the Accession of James II*, by T. B. Macaulay (q.v.), in five volumes, published in 1849–61 (vol. v was posthumous; edited by his sister, Lady Trevelyan, in 1861).

Macaulay had hoped to write the history of England from the reign of James II to the time of Sir Robert Walpole; but the work does not go beyond the death of William III, and, as regards the reign of the latter king, is incomplete. The 'History' is written on a vast scale, involving immense research, and presents a detailed and vivid picture of the age. The hero is William III, and the work, written from a Whig and Protestant point of view, is criticized as showing partiality. Nevertheless, it was, and remains, extremely popular, and is one of the great literary works of the 19th cent.

Macaulay's New Zealander, whom the author imagines, in the distant future, visiting London when it is a ruined city (Essay on Von Ranke's 'History of the Popes' and elsewhere).

Macaulay's Schoolboy: Macaulay was apt to attribute to schoolboys a range of historical and literary knowledge not usually found among them. Taking exception, for instance, to a statement on a more or less abstruse historical point in a book under review, he would assert that 'any schoolboy of fourteen' knew better. (See e.g. the essays on Croker's 'Boswell' and on Sir William Temple.)

Macbeth, a tragedy by Shakespeare (q.v.), founded on Holinshed's 'Chronicle of Scottish History', and probably finished in 1606; it was no doubt designed as a tribute to King James I. First printed in the folio of 1623.

Macbeth and Banquo, generals of Duncan, king of Scotland, returning from a victorious campaign against rebels, encounter the three weird sisters, or witches, upon a heath, who prophesy that Macbeth shall be thane of Cawdor, and king hereafter, and that Banquo shall beget kings though he be none. Immediately afterwards comes the news that the king has created Macbeth thane of Cawdor. Stimulated by the prophecy, and spurred on by Lady Macbeth, Macbeth murders Duncan, who is on a visit to his castle. Duncan's sons, Malcolm and Donalbain, escape, and Macbeth assumes the crown. To defeat the prophecy of the witches regarding Banquo, he contrives the murder of Banquo and his son Fleance, but the latter escapes. Haunted by the ghost of Banquo, Macbeth consults the weird sisters, and is told to beware of Macduff, the thane of Fife; that none born of woman has power to harm Macbeth; and that he never will be vanquished till Birnam Wood shall come to Dunsinane. Learning that Macduff has joined Malcolm, who is gathering an army in England, he surprises the castle of Macduff and causes Lady Macduff and her children to be slaughtered. Lady Macbeth loses her reason and dies. The army of Malcolm and Macduff attacks Macbeth; passing through Birnam Wood every man cuts a bough and under this 'leavy screen' marches on Dunsinane. Macduff, who was 'from his mother's womb untimely ripped', kills Macbeth. Malcolm is hailed king of Scotland.

Maccabaeus, JUDAS, see *Judas Maccabaeus.*

Maccabees, THE, originally known as the Hasmoneans, a family of Jews, consisting of Mattathias and his five sons, Jochanan, Simon, Judas (surnamed Maccabi, 'the hammer', his father's successor in the command), Eleazar, and Jonathan, who led the revolt of their compatriots against the oppression of the Syrian king, Antiochus Epiphanes (175–164 B.C.). They afterwards established a dynasty of priest-kings who ruled until the time of Herod (40 B.C.). Two 'Books of the Maccabees' are included in the 'Apocrypha'. The first deals mainly with the struggle of the Jews for independence during the period 168–135 B.C. The second is not a continuation of the first, but covers a somewhat longer period, beginning about 185 B.C.

Mac Callum, or MAC CALAIN, **More,** the Gaelic title of the earls, marquises, and dukes of Argyll, chiefs of the clan of Campbell (q.v.).

McCARTHY, JUSTIN (1830–1912), Irish politician, historian, and novelist, author of the 'History of Our Own Times' which covers the period from the accession of Queen Victoria to the accession of Edward VII (published in several editions from 1879 to 1907). His best-known novels are: 'Dear Lady Disdain' (1875) and 'Miss Misanthrope' (1878).

McClure, SIR ROBERT JOHN LE MESURIER (1807–73), commander in the search for Sir John Franklin, 1850–4. He found the North West Passage, but had to abandon his ship.

McDIARMID, HUGH, see *Grieve (C. M.).*

Macdonald, FLORA (1722–90), a Jacobite heroine, daughter of a farmer at South Uist (Hebrides), who helped Prince Charles Edward to escape after Culloden (q.v.) by disguising him as her female servant. She was committed to custody and released under the Act of Indemnity (1747).

MACDONALD, GEORGE (1824–1905), poet and novelist, author of 'Within and Without' (1855, a narrative poem admired by Tennyson); 'Phantastes: a faerie romance' (1858, prose and verse); 'David Elginbrod' (1863), 'Alec Forbes' (1865), and 'Robert Falconer', prose fiction, the first mystical in character, the others descriptive of Scottish humble life.

Macduff and **Lady Macduff,** characters in Shakespeare's 'Macbeth' (q.v.).

Mac Flecknoe, *or A Satyr upon the True-Blew-Protestant Poet, T. S.,* a satire directed against Shadwell (q.v.) by Dryden (q.v.), published in 1682.

Shadwell had replied to Dryden's 'Medal' (q.v.) by the 'Medal of John Bayes', and moreover had called Dryden an atheist. Dryden thereupon dealt with the political character of Shadwell in the second part of 'Absalom and Achitophel' (q.v.), and with his literary character in this work. Flecknoe, an Irish writer of verse (some of it fine), is represented as passing on to Shadwell his pre-eminence in the realm of dullness (it is not clear why Dryden thus pilloried Flecknoe). Shadwell is accordingly crowned in the Barbican suburb, and his claims to distinction on the score of stupidity are enumerated.

The rest to some faint meaning make pretence,
But Shadwell never deviates into sense.

McGill University, THE, in Canada, commemorates James McGill (1744–1813), who left £30,000 for the foundation of a university. A charter was granted in 1821, but it was not until the middle of the century that the institution became prosperous. It has its headquarters at Montreal, with affiliated colleges in certain other centres.

Macgregor, ROB ROY and HELEN, see *Rob Roy*.

Macham, ROBERT, see *Machin*.

Machāon, a son of Asclepius (Aesculapius, q.v.), and one of the two surgeons of the Greek army in the Trojan War (Podaleirius, his brother, was the other).

MACHAUT or **MACHAULT, GUILLAUME DE** (c. 1300–77), of Machaut in the Ardennes, French poet. He was secretary to the king of Bohemia killed at Crécy, and afterwards at the court of John the Good, who became king of France. He was author of ballades and of several long poems, of interest because of their influence, which has been variously estimated, on Chaucer, notably in his 'The Boke of the Duchesse' (q.v.) (see T. R. Lounsbury, 'Studies in Chaucer', ii. 212 et seq.).

Macheath, CAPTAIN, the hero of Gay's 'Beggar's Opera' (q.v.).

MACHEN, ARTHUR (1863–1947), a writer of tales, mystical, romantic, and macabre. His chief works are: 'The House of Souls' (1906), 'Hieroglyphics' (1902), 'The Great Return' (1915), 'Things Near and Far' (1923), 'The Shining Pyramid' (1924). A collected edition was published in 1923.

MACHIAVELLI, NICCOLÒ (1469–1527), a Florentine statesman and political theorist. After holding office in the restored Florentine republic and discharging various missions abroad, he was exiled on suspicion of conspiracy against the Medici, but was subsequently restored to some degree of favour. He then turned his experience to advantage in his writings on history and statecraft. Among these are his 'Art of war' (written between 1517 and 1520 and translated into English in 1560–2) and his 'Florentine History' (1520–5, translated in 1595). His best-known work was the 'Prince' (written in 1513), a treatise on statecraft by an acute observer of the contemporary political scene with an idealistic vision of an Italian saviour who should expel all foreign usurpers. He teaches that the lessons of the past (of Roman history in particular) should be applied to the present, and that the acquisition and effective use of power may necessitate unethical methods not in themselves desirable. Although manuscript English versions of the work were circulating earlier, the first published translation was that of Edward Dacres in 1640. It is none the less repeatedly referred to in the Elizabethan drama, and influenced the policy of Thomas Cromwell, Cecil, and Leicester. Selected maxims from the 'Prince' were translated into French, and

attacked by Gentillet, the French Huguenot, in 1576; and this treatise in turn was translated into English in 1602. It is from Gentillet's work that the Elizabethans derived their idea of, and hostility to, Machiavelli. There is a sketch of his character in George Eliot's 'Romola' (q.v.). Machiavelli's 'Mandragola' (probably written in 1518) is the most powerful comedy of the Italian Renaissance.

'The New Machiavelli' is a novel (1911) by H. G. Wells (q.v.).

Machin or MACHAM, ROBERT (*fl.* 1344), the legendary discoverer of the island of Madeira. He is supposed to have fled from England with Anna Dorset, daughter of an English noble, and landed on an island at a port which he called Machico. His ship was driven out to sea while he was ashore, and Anne died of grief on board. He and his companions made their way to the mainland and home to England. Madeira was discovered by Genoese sailors in the Portuguese service prior to the date of Machin's voyage.

M'Ian, IAN EACHIN, otherwise CONACHAR, in Scott's 'The Fair Maid of Perth' (q.v.), Simon Glover's Highland apprentice.

M'Intyre, CAPTAIN HECTOR and MARIA, in Scott's 'The Antiquary' (q.v.), nephew and niece of Jonathan Oldbuck.

Mac-Ivor, FERGUS, of Glennaquoich, otherwise known as VICH IAN VOHR, a character in Scott's 'Waverley' (q.v.).

MACKENZIE, SIR COMPTON (1883–), educated at St. Paul's School and Magdalen College, Oxford, author. Among his chief works are: 'Carnival' (1912), 'Sinister Street' (two volumes, 1913–14), 'Guy and Pauline' (1915), 'Vestal Fire' (1927), 'Extraordinary Women' (1928), 'Our Street' (1931), 'The Four Winds of Love' (6 vols., 1937–45), 'Whisky Galore' (1947), all novels; 'Gallipoli Memories' (1929), 'First Athenian Memories' (1931), 'My Life and Times. Octave 1, 1883–1891; Octave 2. 1891–1900' (1963); 'Octave 3. 1900–1907' (1964); 'Octave 4. 1907–1915' (1965); 'Octave 5. 1915–1923' (1966), autobiography.

MACKENZIE, HENRY (1745–1831), who held the position of comptroller of the taxes for Scotland, was the author of 'The Man of Feeling' (1771), in which the hero is presented in a series of sentimental sketches loosely woven together, somewhat after the manner of Addison's Sir Roger. This book was one of Burns's 'bosom favourites'. It was followed in 1773 by 'The Man of the World', in which the hero, this time, is a villain and a seducer; and in 1777 by 'Julia de Roubigné', a novel after the manner of Richardson's 'Clarissa' (q.v.). Mackenzie also wrote a play, 'The Prince of Tunis' (1773), was chairman of the committee that investigated Macpherson's (q.v.) 'Ossian', and edited two forgotten periodicals, the 'Mirror' (1770) and the 'Lounger' (1785–6). Sometimes spoken of as the 'Addison of the North'.

Mackenzie, MRS. and ROSEY, characters in Thackeray's 'The Newcomes' (q.v.).

McKERROW, RONALD BRUNLEES (1872–1940), bibliographer and Elizabethan scholar. Joint secretary of the Bibliographical Society (q.v.); editor of the 'Review of English Studies'. His 'Introduction to Bibliography for Students' was published in 1927, his 'Prolegomena for the Oxford Shakespeare' in 1939.

MACKINTOSH, SIR JAMES (1765–1832), educated at Aberdeen University and subsequently a student of medicine, was the author of 'Vindiciae Gallicae' (1791), a reasoned defence of the French Revolution and an answer to Burke's 'Reflections on the Revolution in France'. Mackintosh subsequently recanted, and finally summed up in 1815 in his 'On the State of France'. He published in 1830 a much-discussed 'Dissertation on the Progress of Ethical Philosophy', which provoked James Mill's 'Fragment on Mackintosh'. He also wrote the first three volumes of a 'History of England' (1830–1) for Lardner's 'Cabinet Cyclopaedia', and an unfinished 'History of the Revolution in England in 1688' (1834), the subject of one of Macaulay's 'Essays' (q.v.).

MACKLIN, CHARLES (1697?–1797), an actor who made his reputation by his impersonation of Shylock. He was author of the excellent comedy 'The Man of the World' (q.v.), produced in 1781, and of 'Love à la Mode' (q.v.), produced in 1759.

MACLEISH, ARCHIBALD (1892–), American poet and dramatist, born in Illinois. He was one of the American expatriates in Paris in the 1920s, and was strongly influenced by T. S. Eliot and Ezra Pound (qq.v.). Among his early volumes of verse are 'The Pot of Earth' (1924) and 'The Hamlet of A. MacLeish' (1928). His 'Collected Poems 1917–1952' appeared in 1953. Among his verse dramas are 'Panic' (1935), 'The Fall of the City' (1937), and the successfully staged 'J. B.' (1958).

Macmillan's Magazine was started by David Masson (q.v.) in 1859, and edited by him till 1867. Among notable early contributors were Henry and Charles Kingsley, and Matthew Arnold. It came to an end in 1907.

Macmorris, CAPTAIN, in Shakespeare's 'Henry V' (q.v.), the only Irishman presented in Shakespeare's plays.

Macmurray, JOHN, see *Murray (John)*.

MACNEICE, LOUIS (1907–63), poet, was born in Belfast, the son of the bishop of Down, Connor, and Dromore, and educated at Marlborough and Merton College, Oxford. He lectured in Classics at Birmingham University and Bedford College, London. In 1941 he joined the staff of the B.B.C. and wrote many radio scripts and features. During the 1930s MacNeice was associated as a poet with Auden and Spender but was more detached politically than they. His skill

in metrical control has often distracted critics from the wry and often moving quality of his poetry. His work includes 'Poems' (1935), 'The Earth Compels' (1938), 'Autumn Journal' (1939), 'Plant and Phantom' (1941), and other volumes of verse, as well as translations of Aeschylus' 'Agamemnon' and Goethe's 'Faust'. He also wrote a study of Yeats, 'The Poetry of W. B. Yeats' (1941). His collected poems appeared in 1949.

MACPHERSON, JAMES (1736–96), born near Kingussie, the son of a farmer, was educated at Aberdeen and Edinburgh Universities. He was a man of considerable literary ability, with some knowledge of Gaelic poetry, which was popular in the district of his birth. In 1760 he published 'Fragments of Ancient Poetry collected in the Highlands of Scotland, and translated from the Gaelic or Erse language'. Then with the assistance of 'several gentlemen in the Highlands' he produced in 1762 'Fingal, an ancient epic poem in six books' (see under *Fingal*), and in 1763 'Temora' (q.v.), another epic, in eight books, purporting to be translations from the Gaelic of a poet called Ossian (q.v.). They were much admired (by Goethe among others) for their romantic spirit and rhythm, but their authenticity was challenged, notably by Dr. Johnson. Called upon to produce his originals, Macpherson was obliged to fabricate them. A committee appointed after his death to investigate the Ossianic poems reported that Macpherson had liberally edited traditional Gaelic poems and inserted passages of his own, and subsequent investigation supports this view. Macpherson published in 1775 a 'History of Great Britain from the Restoration till the Accession of George I', and was M.P. for Camelford from 1780 to 1786. He was buried in Westminster Abbey, by his own desire.

Macready, WILLIAM CHARLES (1793–1873), educated at Rugby, first achieved eminence as an actor by his impersonation of Richard III (1819), and subsequently of King Lear. He was manager of Covent Garden Theatre in 1837–9, and of Drury Lane in 1841–3. Tennyson wrote a sonnet on his retirement from the stage in 1851.

MacSarcasm, SIR ARCHY, a character in Macklin's 'Love à la Mode' (q.v.).

MacStinger, MRS., in Dickens's 'Dombey and Son' (q.v.), Captain Cuttle's termagant landlady.

MacSycophant, SIR PERTINAX, a character in Macklin's 'The Man of the World' (q.v.).

McTAGGART, JOHN McTAGGART ELLIS (1866–1925), philosopher, fellow of Trinity College, Cambridge, and lecturer in moral sciences, 1897–1923. He was an exponent of Hegel's 'Logic' and published 'Studies in the Hegelian Dialectic' (1896), 'Studies in Hegelian Cosmology' (1901), and 'Commentary on Hegel's Logic' (1910). He rejected theism, on grounds set out in

'Some Dogmas of Religion' (1906), but sought to prove his belief in human immortality. His massive treatise, 'The Nature of Existence' was published in 2 vols. (1921–7).

MacTurk, CAPTAIN, a character in Scott's 'St. Ronan's Well' (q.v.).

Macwheeble, BAILIE DUNCAN, a character in Scott's 'Waverley' (q.v.).

Mad Hatter, THE, see *Hatter.*

Madame Bovary, the chief work of Gustave Flaubert (q.v.).

Madame Tussaud's, see *Tussaud.*

MADDEN, DODGSON HAMILTON (1840–1928), judge of the High Court of Justice of Ireland, attorney-general for Ireland, 1889–92. He was author of 'The Diary of William Silence', a Study of Shakespeare and Elizabethan Sport' (1897).

Madge Wildfire, see *Murdockson.*

Madoc, a poem by Southey (q.v.), published in 1805.

Madoc is the youngest son of Owen Gwyneth, king of Wales (*d.* 1169). He has left Wales and sailed to a western land across the ocean where he has founded a settlement and defeated the Aztecas. He returns to Wales for a fresh supply of adventurers, and tells his tale. After arriving once more at the settlement in Aztlan, war breaks out again with the Aztecas. Madoc is ambushed and captured, chained by the foot to the stone of human sacrifice, and required to fight in succession six Azteca champions. He slays the first, Ocellopan, and engages Tlalala 'the Tiger'. Then Cadwallon comes to the rescue, and after much fighting the Aztecas are finally defeated and migrate to another country. Among the Aztecas figures Coatel, the daughter of Aculhua, a priest; she assists the white men, and thus brings herself, her husband, and her father to a tragic end.

MADVIG, JOHANN NICOLAI (1804–86), Danish scholar and philologist, professor at Copenhagen of Latin, and later of classical philology, and author of a celebrated Latin grammar (1841).

Maeander, a river of Phrygia, remarkable for its many windings; the origin of our verb 'to meander'.

Maecēnas, GAIUS CILNIUS (*c.* 70–8 B.C.), a Roman knight who became celebrated for his patronage of learning and letters in the time of Augustus, of whom he was the friend and adviser. He was the protector and benefactor of Virgil and Horace.

Maeldune or MAILDUN, the hero of an ancient Irish legend, who sets out in a ship to avenge his father, slain by plunderers shortly before his birth. He disregards a wizard's advice to take only seventeen companions, for he also takes his three foster-brothers, and it is only after the loss or death of these, and

visiting many lands, that he is persuaded by a holy man to forgive his enemy, as God has forgiven him. Maeldune finds his enemy and they are reconciled. The legend was translated by P. W. Joyce (q.v.) in his 'Old Celtic Romances', and forms the subject of Tennyson's 'The Voyage of Maeldune'.

Maelstrom, from Dutch words meaning 'whirling stream', a famous whirlpool in the Arctic Ocean off the west coast of Norway, formerly supposed to suck in and destroy vessels within a long radius. Poe (q.v.) wrote an imaginative description of 'A Descent into the Maelström'.

Maenads, a name of the Bacchantes (q.v.) or priestesses of Bacchus.

Maeonia, an early name for Lydia (q.v.). The epithet *Maeonian* and the name *Maeonides* are sometimes applied to Homer, who was supposed to be a native of this region.

He [Aristotle] steered securely, and discovered far,
Led by the light of the Maeonian star.
(Pope, 'Essay on Criticism', l. 648.)

Maeōtis, the ancient name of the sea of Azov.

MAETERLINCK, MAURICE (1862–1949) Belgian poetic-dramatist and essayist. His Symbolist dramas include: 'La Princesse Maleine' (1889), 'Pelléas et Mélisande' (1892), 'Alladine et Palomides' (1894), 'Monna Vanna' (1902). 'L'Oiseau bleu' (1909) is a fairy play. His essays, of a philosophical character, include 'Le Trésor des humbles' (1896), 'Sagesse et destinée', 'La Vie des abeilles', 'Le Double Jardin', 'L'Intelligence des fleurs', 'La Mort'. He received the Nobel Prize for literature in 1911. His early works show a more sombre imagination than his later essays: death and love and dark mysteries governing men's lives.

Maeviad, The, see *Gifford.*

Maffick, To, to indulge in extravagant demonstrations of exultation on occasions of national rejoicing. A word originally used to designate the behaviour of the crowds in London and other towns on the occasion of the relief of Mafeking (17 May 1900).

Mafia, in Sicily, the spirit of hostility to the law and its ministers prevailing among a part of the population; also the body of those who share in this spirit; not, as often supposed, an organized secret society.

Maga, see *Blackwood's Edinburgh Magazine.*

Magazine, originally a place where goods are laid up, has come also to mean a periodical publication containing articles by different authors. Thus the 'Gentleman's Magazine' in the introduction to its first number (1731) described itself as 'a Monthly Collection to store up, as in a Magazine, the most remarkable Pieces on the Subjects above-mentioned'. But the word had been used before this for a storehouse of information.

Magdalen, MAGDALENE (pron. 'Maudlen' in

the names of Magdalen College, Oxford, and Magdalene College, Cambridge), the appellation (signifying a woman of Magdala) of a disciple of Christ named Mary, 'out of whom went seven devils' (Luke viii. 2). She has commonly been supposed to be identical with the unnamed 'sinner' of Luke vii. 37, and therefore appears in western hagiology as a harlot restored to purity and transmuted to sanctity by repentance and faith. The word is used to signify one whose history resembles that of the Magdalene; also as short for MAGDALEN HOSPITAL, a home for refuge and reformation of prostitutes. [OED.]

Magdalen (pron. 'Maudlen') **College**, Oxford, was founded in 1458 by William Waynflete (1395–1486), provost of Eton, bishop of Winchester, and lord chancellor of England. Among famous members of the college have been Cardinal Wolsey, Prince Rupert, Henry, Prince of Wales, son of James I, and the present Duke of Windsor. Its beautiful tower is celebrated. On the morning of 1 May at 5 a.m. (6 a.m. Summer Time) the Magdalen choristers sing a hymn on the top of this tower. See also *Oxford University*.

Magdalenian, the name given to a culture (of the palaeolithic age) that followed the Aurignacian (see *Aurignac*), so called from the rock-shelter of La Madeleine in the Dordogne, France. The Magdalenian industry is characterized by weapons and tools of horn and bone, which reached a high quality before the close of the period (Peake and Fleure, 'Hunters and Artists').

Magdeburg, CENTURIATORS OF, a number of Protestant divines who in the 16th cent. compiled a Church History in thirteen volumes, one for each century (called the *Centuries of Magdeburg*).

Magellan, the English form of the name of the Portuguese navigator Fernão de Magalhães (?1470–1521), the first European to pass through the straits that bear his name.

Maggie, the mare to which Burns's 'The Auld Farmer's New Year Salutation' is addressed.

Maggie Lauder, (1) the subject of an old Scottish song doubtfully attributed to Francis Semple of Beltrees, who is said to have written it in 1642; (2) the heroine of 'Anster Fair', by W. Tennant (q.v.).

Magi, the ancient Persian priestly caste, the priests of Zoroastrianism. Hence, in a wider sense, persons skilled in oriental magic and astrology, ancient magicians or sorcerers.

THE (THREE) MAGI, the three wise men who came from the East, bearing offerings to the infant Christ, named according to tradition Gaspar, Melchior, and Balthazar. They are also known as the 'Three Kings of Cologne' (see *Cologne*).

Magic Flute, *The*, 'Die Zauberflöte', a famous opera by Mozart (q.v.); also a book by C. Lowes Dickinson (1920).

MAGINN, WILLIAM (1793–1842), educated at Trinity College, Dublin, was one of the principal early contributors to 'Blackwood's Edinburgh Magazine' (q.v.) under the pseudonym of Ensign O'Doherty, and was perhaps the originator of the 'Noctes Ambrosianae' (q.v.). He settled in London in 1823, wrote for various periodicals, and established 'Fraser's Magazine' (q.v.), in which he published his 'Homeric Ballads' and his 'Illustrious Literary Characters'. But his best work is contained in his shorter stories and verses, which are marked by humour, wit, and pathos. He was the original of Captain Shandon in Thackeray's 'Pendennis' (q.v.).

Maginot Line, a strong system of defences constructed by the French, chiefly during the period 1929–36, along the frontier between their country and Germany (a distance of about 200 miles). It consisted in the main of powerful and elaborate forts so echeloned as to bring the maximum fire-power on an advancing enemy. The system was extended, but on a far weaker scale, northwards along the Belgian frontier. It was through this extension, near Sedan and Malmédy, that the Germans penetrated in May 1940. The line takes its name from André Maginot, minister of war in a number of French governments from 1922.

Magliabechi, ANTONIO (1633–1714), a Florentine bibliophile, librarian to Cosimo III, grand duke of Tuscany, and noted for his great and varied learning. He bequeathed to the grand duke his large collection of books and manuscripts, which is now included in the *Biblioteca Nazionale*.

Magna Carta, the Great Charter of the liberties of England, granted by John under pressure from the Barons, at Runnymede in Surrey, on 15 June 1215. Its chief provisions were that no freeman should be imprisoned, banished, or in any way destroyed except by the law of the land; and that supplies (except aids imposed on tenants-in-chief on certain specified occasions) should not be demanded without the consent of the Common Council of the realm.

Magnano, in Butler's 'Hudibras' (q.v.), one of the characters in the bear-baiting episode, is Simon Wait (*mañana* is Spanish for 'tomorrow, by and by'), a tinker and a noted Independent preacher.

Magnet, *The*, a weekly paper for boys written by C. Hamilton (q.v.) under the penname Frank Richards, 1908–40.

Magnetic Lady, *The, or Humours Reconciled*, a comedy by Jonson (q.v.), produced in 1632.

Lady Loadstone, the 'Magnetic Lady', who 'draws unto her guests of all sorts', has a niece Placentia, of age to be married, whose dower is detained by her uncle, Sir Moth Interest. The bride and dowry are the object of various intrigues, until it is found, first that Placentia is already with child, and secondly that she is not the true niece but a changeling.

Magnus, Mr. Peter, a character in Dickens's 'Pickwick Papers' (q.v.).

Magog, see *Gog.*

Magog Wrath and **Bully Bluck,** in Disraeli's 'Coningsby' (q.v.), the hired leaders of the two political parties in the Darlford constituency.

Magwitch, Abel, a character in Dickens's 'Great Expectations' (q.v.).

Mahābhārata, The, one of the two great epics (the other being the 'Rāmāyana') of the Hindus. They are believed to have been composed before 500 B.C., but, in the form in which we have it, the 'Mahābhārata' probably dates from 200 B.C.

MAHAFFY, Sir JOHN PENTLAND (1839–1919), provost of Trinity College, Dublin, and author of numerous works on Greek literature and history.

Mahatma, Sanskrit *mahātman,* meaning 'great-souled'; in 'esoteric Buddhism', one of a class of persons with preternatural powers imagined to exist in India and Tibet. [OED.] The word is also used by Theosophists.

Mahdi, a spiritual and temporal leader expected by the Muslims. The title has been claimed by various insurrectionary leaders in the Sudan, but is especially applied to Mohammed Ahmed (1843–85), who destroyed General Hicks's army in 1883, besieged Gordon (q.v.) in Khartoum, and overthrew the Egyptian power in the Sudan.

Mahmud of Ghazni or THE GREAT, son of Sabuktegin, and Turkish ruler of the Persian Empire, 998–1030. He was a great conqueror, who extended his dominions from the Tigris to the Ganges and the Oxus, and made Ghazni in Afghanistan his capital. He besieged and captured Somnath in Gujerat, obtaining there an immense treasure and carrying off its gates. (These, or others mistaken for them, were restored to India in 1842.) Mahmud was a patron of Persian literature. For his treatment of Firdusi see under the latter.

Mahomet, see *Mohammed.* 'Mahomet' is the title of a drama by Voltaire (q.v.).

MAHONY, FRANCIS SYLVESTER (1804–66), best known by his pseudonym of Father Prout, a Jesuit (dismissed from the order in 1830) and author of many entertaining papers and poems contributed to 'Fraser's Magazine' and 'Bentley's Miscellany'. These included translations from Horace, Béranger, Victor Hugo, etc., and, interspersed among them, mystifications in the shape of invented 'originals' in French, Latin, and Greek for some of Moore's songs, etc. The contributions to 'Fraser' were collected in 1836 as 'The Reliques of Father Prout'. He is best remembered for his 'Bells of Shandon'.

Mahound, the 'false prophet' Mohammed; in the Middle Ages often vaguely imagined to be worshipped as a god.

Mahrattas, a warlike Hindu race, Brahman in religion, inhabiting western and central India. They rose to power in the latter part of the 17th cent. and formed a confederacy of States under their rule. They were from time to time in conflict with the British in the 18th cent., and were reduced to submission in 1803 (Wellesley's victories at Assaye and Argaum, and Lake's at Aligurh and Laswaree), and to complete dependency in 1817–18.

Mahu, the fiend of stealing, one of the five that pestered 'poor Tom' in Shakespeare's 'King Lear' (IV. i).

Maia, a daughter of Atlas, one of the Pleiades, and the mother by Zeus of Hermes. There was also an old Italian goddess of the same name, also known as Bona Dea.

Maid Marian, a female personage in the May-game and Morris-dance. In the later forms of the story of Robin Hood she appears as the companion of the outlaw, the association having probably been suggested by the fact that the two were both represented in the May-day pageants. [OED.] According to one version of the legend she was Matilda, the daughter of Lord Fitzwater.

Maid Marian, a novel by Peacock (q.v.), published in 1822. It is a gay parody of medieval romance, based on the story of Robin Hood, adopting the version that the outlaw was Robert, earl of Huntingdon, and Maid Marian was Matilda Fitzwater. It contains some excellent songs.

Maid of Athens, THE, in Byron's poem is said to have been the daughter of Theodore Macri, who was a consul at Athens.

Maid of Bath, The, see *Foote.*

Maid of Honour, The, a romantic drama, by Massinger (q.v.), published in 1632.

Bertoldo, natural brother of the king of Sicily and a knight of Malta, is in love with Camiola. Departing on an expedition to aid the duke of Urbino against the duchess of Sienna, he asks for her hand, but she refuses on the ground of the disparity of their station and his oath as a knight of Malta not to marry. Bertoldo is taken prisoner by the Siennese, cast into prison and held to ransom for a large sum, which the king of Sicily, being incensed against Bertoldo, forbids anyone to pay. Camiola directs her follower Adorni, who is passionately devoted to her, to carry the ransom (which she provides from her own estate) to Bertoldo, and to require of him a contract to marry her. Adorni, though it means the defeat of his own hopes, faithfully discharges his mission; Bertoldo is released and signs the contract. But the duchess of Sienna falls in love with him, and he yields to her wooing. They are on the point of being married when Camiola interposes and pleads her cause with spirit, so that all, including the duchess, condemn the ingratitude of Bertoldo, and the marriage is broken off. Camiola, 'the Maid of Honour', takes the veil, and the humiliated and repentant Bertoldo resumes his vocation as a knight of Malta. Camiola is Massinger's best female character, and the play contains some of his finest scenes.

Maid of Kent, see *Barton* (*Elizabeth*).

Maid of Norway, MARGARET (1283–90), daughter of King Erik of Norway and granddaughter of Alexander III of Scotland, recognized as queen of Scotland on the latter's death in 1285. She was betrothed to Edward, Prince of Wales, but died on her way to Scotland in 1290.

Maid of Orleans, Joan of Arc (q.v.).

Maid of Saragoza, THE, Augustina, whose bravery in the defence of Saragossa (a town on the Ebro in Spain) against the French in 1808–9 was celebrated by Byron in his 'Childe Harold' (I. liv-lvi).

Maid's Tragedy, *The,* a tragedy by Beaumont and Fletcher (see *Fletcher, J.*) published in 1619, generally accounted the best of their dramas.

Amintor, a gentleman of Rhodes, engaged to marry Aspatia, daughter of Calianax, the lord chamberlain, at the order of the king breaks off the match and marries Evadne, sister of his friend Melantius. Evadne on the wedding night declares herself the king's mistress and denies Amintor her bed. Amintor's loyalty makes him conceal the position, but Melantius learns the cause of his melancholy, terrifies Evadne into murdering the king, and obtains from Calianax possession of the citadel. Meanwhile Aspatia, brokenhearted, disguising herself as her brother, forces Amintor to fight a duel with her and kill her. Evadne comes to Amintor after the murder of the king, expecting now to be pardoned by him, and being rejected commits suicide. Melantius, holding the citadel, secures pardon for himself and his associates.

The last act of the play was re-written by Edmund Waller (q.v.). The king is not murdered, but Evadne is got out of the way, Melantius is pardoned, Aspatia is prevented from committing suicide and is married to Amintor.

Maiden, THE, the instrument, similar to the guillotine, formerly used in Scotland for beheading criminals; said to have been introduced by the regent Morton (d. 1581) and to have been used for his execution.

Maigret, LE COMMISSAIRE, the detective-superintendent in the crime stories of G. Simenon (q.v.).

Maildun, see *Maeldune.*

MAIMONIDES (1135–1204), a Jew of Cordova, who, on the expulsion of the Jews from Spain, went to Fez and Cairo. He was a rationalist and anti-mystic philosopher. His chief work was 'The Guide for the Perplexed',

of which there are English, French, and German translations.

Main Street, a novel by S. Lewis (q.v.), published in 1920.

MAINE, SIR HENRY JAMES SUMNER (1822–88), educated at Christ's Hospital, London, and Pembroke College, Cambridge, became fellow of Trinity Hall, Cambridge, of which he died master. He was appointed Regius professor of civil law in 1847, but exchanged this post for a readership at the Inns of Court. He was legal member of the council of India, 1862–9, and Corpus professor of jurisprudence at Oxford, 1869–78. Besides reviews, Maine wrote many works on the philosophy of law, history, and politics, marked by scholarship and a fine style, the best known of which are his 'Ancient Law' (1861), 'Village Communities' (1871), 'Early History of Institutions' (1875), and 'Dissertations on Early Law and Custom' (1883). He also wrote a criticism of democratic institutions entitled 'Popular Government' (1885).

Mainotes, inhabitants of *Maina,* a mountainous district in the southern Morea, a sturdy and independent people who were never subdued by the Turks.

Maintenon, FRANÇOISE D'AUBIGNÉ, MARQUISE DE (1635–1719), the wife of the French burlesque poet Scarron (q.v.). After her husband's death she was charged with the education of the children of Louis XIV and Mme de Montespan. She obtained a great ascendancy over the king, who secretly married her in 1684.

Main–Travelled Roads, stories of the American middle west, by H. Garland (q.v.), published in 1891.

MAITLAND, FREDERIC WILLIAM (1850–1906), educated at Eton and Trinity College, Cambridge, was called to the bar in 1876 and after eight years' practice became reader in English law at Cambridge and, from 1888 until his death, Downing professor. In 1887 he founded the Selden Society for encouraging the study of English law, and edited several of its publications. His first important work was 'Bracton's Note-Book' (1887), followed by the 'History of English Law before the time of Edward I' (1895), the standard authority on the subject, which he wrote in collaboration with Sir Frederick Pollock. He traced Roman influence on English law in the 13th cent. in his 'Bracton and Azo' (the famous doctor of canon law of Bologna, d. 1200), which appeared in 1895, and in 'Roman Canon Law in the Church of England' (1898). His Essays on 'Domesday Book and Beyond' (1897), his Ford lectures on 'Township and Borough' (1898), his Rede lecture on 'English Law and the Renaissance' (1901), were other notable productions. The lectures delivered by him in 1887 on 'The Constitutional History of England' from the death of Edward I to the present time were posthumously published under that title in 1908. His

'Year Books of Edward II' (text and translation) for 1307–10 were published in 1903–5. His collected papers were edited in 1911 by H. A. L. Fisher, who also published a memoir of Maitland in 1910. A. L. Smith's memoir of Maitland appeared in 1908.

Maitland Club, a club founded at Glasgow in 1828 for the publication of works on the literature and antiquities of Scotland.

MAJOR or **MAIR, JOHN** (1469–1550), born in Haddingtonshire, has been called 'the last of the schoolmen'. He studied at Cambridge and Paris, where he became doctor of theology. He lectured on scholastic logic and theology at Glasgow and St. Andrews from 1518 to 1525, and then returned to Paris, where he was regarded as the most eminent exponent of medieval learning. He published between 1509 and 1517 a Latin 'Commentary on the Sentences of Peter Lombard', and in 1521 a Latin 'History of Greater Britain, both England and Scotland', in which he showed himself in advance of his times by advocating the union of the two kingdoms.

According to Rabelais (II. vii), among the books found by Pantagruel in the library of St. Victor was a treatise by Major 'De modo faciendi boudinos' ('On the art of making black-puddings').

Major Gahagan, Some Passages in the Life of, and *Historical Recollections by*, an early work by Thackeray (q.v.), published in the 'New Monthly Magazine' in 1838–9. Major Goliah O'Grady Gahagan, of the Indian Irregular Horse, relates his Munchausen-like military adventures in India and Spain.

Majuscule, a large letter or script, used in palaeography to denote the scripts of Greek and Roman antiquity, uncial (q.v.) or capital.

Malagigi, in the 'Orlando Innamorato' (q.v.), a cousin of Rinaldo, possessed of magic lore, who detects the wiles of Angelica and attempts to slay her, but is taken prisoner and carried to Cathay. He is released on condition that he shall lure Rinaldo to her.

MALAGROWTHER, MALACHI, the pseudonym under which Sir W. Scott addressed three letters in 1826, on the question of the Scottish paper currency, to the 'Edinburgh Weekly Journal'.

Malagrowther, Sir Mungo, a character in Scott's 'Fortunes of Nigel' (q.v.).

Malambruno, in 'Don Quixote', II. xxxix, the giant necromancer who transforms Antonomasia into a monkey of brass and Don Clavijo into a metal crocodile, and is appeased by Don Quixote.

Malaprop, Mrs., in Sheridan's 'The Rivals' (q.v.), the aunt and guardian of Lydia Languish, noted for her aptitude for misapplying long words, e.g. 'as headstrong as an allegory on the banks of the Nile'.

Malbecco, in Spenser's 'Faerie Queene' (III. ix, x), a 'cancred crabbed carle', jealous and avaricious, married to the lovely Hellenore. Paridell elopes with her, and Malbecco, unable to escape from his jealous thoughts, throws himself from a rock. But his 'aery spright' lives for ever, under the name of Jealousy.

Malbrouk s'en va–t–en guerre, the first line of an old French song, perhaps, but not very probably, referring to the campaigns of the duke of Marlborough. Malbrouk goes off to war; he may return at Easter or at the Trinity. His lady mounts to the top of the tower, sees his page returning, and learns that her lord is dead. The song was sung as a lullaby by a nurse to one of Marie Antoinette's children, took the queen's fancy, and became popular. Beaumarchais introduced the tune, which resembles that of 'We won't go home till morning', into his 'Mariage de Figaro'.

Maldon, Battle of, a poem in Old English, perhaps of the 10th century, dealing with the raid of the Northmen under Anlaf, at Maldon in Essex, in 991. The Northmen are drawn up on the shore of the Blackwater. The ealdorman Byrhtnoth, the friend of Ælfric, exhorts his men to stand firm. An offer by the herald of the Northmen that their attack shall be bought off by payment of tribute is scornfully rejected. The fight is delayed by the rising tide which separates the two armies. Then Byrhtnoth is slain with a poisoned spear and some of his men flee. A fresh attack is led by Ælfwine, son of Ælfric. Godric falls. The end of the poem is lost.

Maldon, Jack, in Dickens's 'David Copperfield' (q.v.), the scapegrace cousin of Mrs. Strong.

Male or Masculine **Rhymes,** see *Rhymes*.

Male Règle, La, see *Occleve*.

Malebolge, the name given by Dante to his eighth circle in Hell, consisting of ten circular trenches, designated *bolge*. The word is chiefly used in English in allusion to the pool of filth in the second *bolgia*, or to the boiling pitch in the fifth *bolgia* ('Inferno', xviii and xxi).

Malecasta, 'unchaste', in Spenser's 'Faerie Queene', III. i, the lady of Castle Joyeous.

Maleger, in Spenser's 'Faerie Queene', II. xi, the captain of twelve troops, the seven deadly sins and the evil passions that assail the five senses. He is lean and ghostlike, and Prince Arthur's sword has no effect on him. Finally, remembering that earth is his mother and that he draws his strength from her, Arthur lifts him up and squeezes the life out of him. (Cf. the legend of *Antaeus*.)

Malengin, in Spenser's 'Faerie Queene', v. ix, the personification of guile. Sought out by Sir Arthur and Artegall, he runs away assuming various disguises, but is destroyed by Talus.

Malibran, Mme Maria Felicita Garcia (1808–36), a famous opera singer, born in Paris. She had a contralto voice and sang with increasing success in Paris, London, and other cities until her early death. Alfred de Musset's 'Stances à la Malibran' are famous.

Mall, THE, a walk sheltered by trees along the N. side of St. James's Park, London, originally a 'mall' where the game of 'pall mall' (q.v.) was played. It was a fashionable promenade in the 17th–18th cents.

MALLARMÉ, STÉPHANE (1842–98), French poet, the leader of the Symbolist movement at its height. 'Poésies' (1887) and 'Vers et prose' (1893), the two collections published in his lifetime, contain sonnets and longer poems famous for their musical and evocative beauty but also in some cases for an obscurity which makes them the province of a few. His poem 'L'Après-midi d'un faune' inspired a well-known prelude by Debussy.

MALLET (or MALLOCH), DAVID (1705?–65), author of the well-known ballad of 'William and Margaret' (q.v.). He collaborated with J. Thomson (1700–48, q.v.) in the masque of 'Alfred', which contains 'Rule, Britannia'; but that song is generally attributed to Thomson. Mallet was the literary executor of Bolingbroke (q.v.).

Malleus Maleficarum, or *Hexenhammer,* the 'Hammer of Witches', published in 1484 by Jakob Sprenger, the Dominican inquisitor of Cologne, and Heinrich Krämer, Prior of Cologne. It was the textbook of the day on witchcraft, setting forth how it may be discovered and how it should be punished.

MALLOCH, DAVID, see *Mallet.*

MALLOCK, WILLIAM HURRELL (1849–1923), educated at Balliol College, Oxford, is best known as author of 'The New Republic' (1877), a lively satire on English society and ideas, in which Ruskin figures as Mr. Herbert, and Jowett, Matthew Arnold, Pater, Huxley, Tyndall, etc., figure under thin disguises among the other characters. Mallock's other works include 'The New Paul and Virginia' (1878), 'Memoirs of Life and Literature' (1920), and various studies of social and economic science directed against the doctrines of socialism.

Malmesbury, THE SAGE OF, Hobbes (q.v.).

Malmesbury, WILLIAM OF, see *William of Malmesbury.*

MALONE, EDMOND (1741–1812), literary critic and Shakespearian scholar. He published in 1778 his 'Attempt to ascertain the Order in which the Plays of Shakespeare were written', and an edition of the works in 1790; the revised edition, 1821, was the best to that date. A member of The Club and a friend of Boswell, he revised the 'Tour to the Hebrides', 1785, while it was going through the press, and gave great assistance with 'The Life of Johnson', 1791, of which he edited the third to sixth editions.

Malone Society, THE, was founded in 1906 for the purpose of making accessible materials for the study of early English drama, by printing dramatic texts and documents. Its name is taken from Edmond Malone (q.v.).

MALORY, SIR THOMAS (*d.* 1471), author of 'Le Morte Darthur' (q.v.), is identified by E. Vinaver with Sir Thomas Malory, Knight of Newbold Revel (Warwicks.) and Winwick (Northants.) who succeeded to his estates in 1433 or 1434. In 1450 he was charged with attempted murder, and he later suffered terms of imprisonment for various major crimes. He sat for his shire in Parliament in 1456, with the Earl of Warwick followed Edward IV to Northumberland, and, probably with Warwick, joined the Lancastrians, for he is excluded by name from two pardons granted them by Edward. Three 'prayers for deliverance' occurring in his manuscript suggest that he wrote most of it to occupy himself while in prison, attracted by the adventurous content of the French Arthurian material.

Malperdy (*Malpertuis*), the castle of 'Reynard the Fox' (q.v.).

MALRAUX, ANDRÉ (1901–), French novelist, essayist, and art-historian, whose outstanding works include: 'La Condition humaine' (1933), a novel of early Communism in China; 'L'Espoir' (1937), a more documentary novel, about the Spanish Civil War of 1936; 'Psychologie de l'art' (1948–50, 3 vols.), art history. Phases in this author's career have been his early sympathy with Communist ideals, anti-Nazi and Resistance activities, and, under the Fifth Republic, ministerial responsibility for the furtherance of culture.

Malta, KNIGHTS OF, see *Hospitallers of St. John of Jerusalem.*

MALTHUS, THOMAS ROBERT (1766–1834), educated at Jesus College, Cambridge, became curate of Albury in Surrey in 1798. In that year he published 'An Essay on the Principle of Population', in which he argued that population would soon increase beyond the means of subsistence and that checks on this increase are necessary. The 'Essay' was recast in the second edition (1803); in this the author somewhat modifies his conclusions, recognizing a slackening in the pressure of population, and the influence of morality among the checks on its increase. The work aroused a storm of controversy and exerted a powerful influence on social thought in the 19th cent. The economic writings of Malthus included 'An Inquiry into the Nature and Progress of Rent' (1815) and a treatise on 'Principles of Political Economy' (1820).

Malvina, in Macpherson's (q.v.) Ossianic poems, a daughter of Toscar, betrothed to Oscar the son of Ossian. Oscar is killed by Cairbar (q.v.) just before their intended marriage. Ossian addresses several of his poems to her.

Malvolio, a character in Shakespeare's 'Twelfth Night' (q.v.).

Mamamouchi, the mock-Turkish title pretended to have been conferred by the Sultan upon M. Jourdain (q.v.), in Molière's 'Le Bourgeois Gentilhomme'.

Mambrino, in the 'Orlando Furioso' (q.v.) a pagan king whose magic helmet is acquired by Rinaldo. In 'Don Quixote' (q.v., Part I) there is frequent mention of Mambrino's helmet. Don Quixote, seeing a barber riding with his brass basin upon his head, takes this for the golden helmet of Mambrino, and gets possession of it.

Mamelukes, a military body, originally composed of Caucasian slaves of the Sultan of Egypt. They seized the government of Egypt in 1254 and made one of their number sultan. The Mameluke sultans reigned from 1254 to 1517, when the Ottoman sultan Selim I assumed the sovereignty. Subsequently Egypt was governed, under the nominal rule of a Turkish viceroy, by twenty-four Mameluke beys. In 1811 the remaining Mamelukes were massacred by Mohammed Ali, pasha of Egypt.

Mammet or MAUMET, a corruption of Mahomet, a false god, an idol, a doll.

Mammon, the Aramaic word for 'riches', occurring in the Greek text of Matt. vi. 24, and Luke xvi. 9–13. Owing to the quasi-personification in these passages, the name was taken by medieval writers as the proper name of the devil of covetousness. This use was revived by Milton in 'Paradise Lost', i. 678 and ii. 228.

Mammon, *The Triumph of,* see *God and Mammon.*

Mammon, THE CAVE OF, described in Spenser's 'Faerie Queene', II. vii, is the treasure-house of the god of wealth, visited by Sir Guyon.

Mammon, SIR EPICURE, in Jonson's 'The Alchemist' (q.v.), an arrogant, avaricious, voluptuous knight. Charles Lamb in his 'Specimens' says of him: 'It is just such a swaggerer as contemporaries have described old Ben to be'.

Man and Superman, a comedy by G. B. Shaw (q.v.), published in 1903; 'a stage projection of the tragi-comic love chase of the man by the woman', in which 'Don Juan is the quarry instead of the huntsman' (Author's Epistle Dedicatory).

Man in Black, THE, (1) a character in Goldsmith's 'Citizen of the World' (q.v.), a humorist, a man generous to profusion, who wishes to be thought a prodigy of parsimony; (2) the Jesuit priest in Borrow's 'Romany Rye' (q.v.).

Man in the Iron Mask, THE, see *Iron Mask.*

Man in the Moon, THE, a fancied figure, with a bundle of sticks on his back, made by the shadows on the moon. The nursery tale is that he is a man banished to the moon for gathering sticks on the Sabbath (an allusion to Num. xv. 32 et seq.). The myth that the moon is inhabited by a sabbath-breaker is found with variations in several countries. In England it is at least as old as Henryson, who refers to it in the 'Testament of Cresseid' (l. 260), and there are references to it in Shakespeare's 'A Midsummer Night's Dream' (III. i) and 'The Tempest' (II. ii). In Dante, 'Inferno' xx. 126 and 'Paradiso' ii. 49–51, 'the old popular belief that the Man in the Moon was Cain with a bundle of thorns (probably with reference to his unacceptable offering)' is alluded to (Toynbee).

Man in the Street, THE, the ordinary man, as distinguished from the expert or the man who has special opportunities of knowledge. The earliest use of the expression quoted by OED. is 1831, when Greville ('Memoirs', 22 Mar.) writes, 'knowing, as "the man in the street" (as we call him at Newmarket) always does, the greatest secrets of kings'.

Man of Blood, THE, David, King of Israel (2 Sam. xvi. 7, R.V.); also, Charles I, so called by the Puritans.

Man of Brass, see *Talus.*

Man of December, THE, Napoleon III, with reference to his *coup d'état* in Dec. 1851.

Man of Destiny, Napoleon I.

Man of Feeling, *The,* a novel by H. Mackenzie (q.v.).

Man of Law's Tale, *The,* see *Canterbury Tales.*

Man of Mode, *The,* or *Sir Fopling Flutter,* a comedy by Etherege (q.v.), produced in 1676. The play has no plot. It is a picture of a society living exclusively for pleasure, a slight web of love-affairs providing the occasion for brilliant dialogue and character-drawing. We have Dorimant, a portrait of Lord Rochester; Sir Fopling Flutter, the prince of fops, the perfect product of Parisian taste of the day; Young Bellair, the portrait of the poet; and so on.

Man of Ross, see *Kyrle.*

Man of Sin, THE, see *Antichrist.*

Man of Straw, (*a*) a person or thing compared to a straw image, a dummy; (*b*) an imaginary adversary or invented adverse argument, adduced in order to be defeated; (*c*) a person of no substance, especially one who undertakes a pecuniary responsibility without having the means to discharge it; (*d*) a fictitious or irresponsible person fraudulently put forward as a surety or as a party in an action. [OED.]

Man of the World, *The,* a novel by H. Mackenzie (q.v.).

Man of the World, *The,* a comedy by Macklin (q.v.), produced in 1781.

This amusing play satirizes the peculiarities

of a Scottish politician, Sir Pertinax Mac-Sycophant, who, having started life as a 'beggarly clerk in Sawney Gordon's compting house', has, by the judicious application of his doctrine of pliability, risen to parliamentary eminence. In order to gain the control of three parliamentary boroughs, he proposes to marry his eldest son, Egerton, to the daughter, Lady Rodolpha, of another servile but needy politician, Lord Lambercourt, who gets some hard cash by the arrangement. Unfortunately Egerton is devoted to his father's poor ward Constantia, and Lady Rodolpha to Egerton's younger brother. The parents dictatorially insist, and the young people are summarily set to their courting, in view of a marriage the next day. There follows an amusing scene, in which Lady Rodolpha, finding her proposed lover speechless from embarrassment, dutifully makes the first advances in broad Scotch. Each, however, presently discovers that the other's affections are already otherwise engaged and they combine to defeat their parents' purposes. Egerton secretly marries Constantia, and Sir Pertinax, momentarily defeated, recovers the lost ground by proposing a marriage between Lady Rodolpha and his second son, on the same financial terms. This of course is welcome to the lady, while her father doesn't 'care a pinch of snuff if she concorporates with the Cham of Tartary', provided he gets his cash.

Man of Wrath, THE, the husband in 'Elizabeth and her German Garden' (q.v.).

Man that Corrupted Hadleyburg, The, a story by Mark Twain (see *Clemens, S. L.*), published in 1899, which displays the destructive effects of greed within the circle of a small town.

Manannán, the son of Lêr (q.v.), a highly popular god of the old Gaelic pantheon, the subject of many legends and the patron of sailors and merchants. The Isle of Man was his favourite abode, and is said to take its name from him. There he has degenerated into a traditionary giant, with three legs (seen revolving in the coat of arms of the island).

Manasseh, the firstborn son of Joseph, to whom Jacob, in his death-bed blessing, preferred Manasseh's younger brother Ephraim (Gen. xlviii. 19).

Manawyddan, in British mythology, a son of Llyr (q.v.) and a king of the nether world. See *Mabinogion.*

Manchester Guardian, The, founded in 1821 as a weekly, and in 1855 as a daily, paper; the principal liberal organ outside London, edited 1872–99 by Charles Prestwich Scott (1846–1932). Its title was changed to 'The Guardian' in 1959.

Manchester Massacre, THE, see *Peterloo.*

Manchester School, the name first applied by Disraeli to the political party, led by Cobden and Bright, who advocated the principles of free trade. It was afterwards extended to the party who supported those leaders on other questions of policy. 'Manchester policy' was used derisively to signify a policy of laissez-faire and self-interest.

Manciple's Tale, The, see *Canterbury Tales.*

Manco Capac, the legendary founder of the Inca monarchy of Peru. He is represented as a child of the sun, sent to civilize the Indians, but was probably a real person, the chief of an Indian tribe in the 13th cent.

Mancus, an old English money of account worth thirty pence [OED.]. Offa, king of Mercia in the 8th cent., struck a gold coin closely imitated from an Arabic gold dinar of the Caliph Al Mansur, of which a single specimen, found near Rome, survives. This coin may have been one of the 365 gold 'mancuses' of which Offa had promised an annual gift to Pope Adrian I (Oman, 'Coinage of England', 1931). See *Peter's Pence.*

Mandaeans, known also as NASORAEANS or SABIANS, or (owing to a misunderstanding) CHRISTIANS OF ST. JOHN, a body of pagan gnostics of whom a small community survives in Lower Mesopotamia. They date perhaps from about the beginning of the Christian era. Their sacred writings (in a special form of Aramaic) survive. The name 'Mandaean' means 'Gnostic' (q.v.). Their doctrines appear to have been formed from contact with Jews, Christians, and Manichaeans, and have developed into a monotheistic worship of the 'Light King', while 'Manda d'Hayye', 'Knowledge of Life' personified, plays in their religion the part of an incarnate Saviour. They revere John the Baptist, and practise frequent baptism, but are hostile to Christianity. [EB.]

Mandane, the daughter of Astyages, king of Persia. She was married to Cambyses, a man of humble birth, because it had been foretold to Astyages that his daughter's son would dethrone him. Her son Cyrus was exposed as soon as born, but was saved by a shepherdess and survived to carry out the prophecy.

MANDEVILLE, BERNARD DE (1670–1733), born in Holland, settled in London and became a physician. He was author of a satire in octosyllabic verse, entitled 'The Grumbling Hive, or Knaves turned Honest' (1705), reissued with a prose commentary as 'The Fable of the Bees, or Private Vices, Public Benefits' (1714), designed to illustrate the essential vileness of human nature. Society, like a hive of bees, thrives on a system of mutual rapacities. The paradox was widely controverted, among others by W. Law (q.v.), and by Berkeley in his 'Alciphron' (q.v.). Mandeville figures in R. Browning's 'Parleyings with some Persons of Importance'.

MANDEVILLE, SIR JOHN, was the ostensible author of a book of travels bearing his name, composed soon after the middle of the 14th cent., purporting to be an account of his own journeys in the East, but really a mere compilation, especially from William of Boldensele and Friar Odoric of Pordenone, and from the 'Speculum' of Vincent de Beauvais. The work was written originally in French, from which English, Latin, German, and other translations were made.

The writer of this remarkable literary forgery remains unknown, but probability points to a certain Jean d'Outremeuse, a writer of histories and fables, who lived at Liège at the time in question. According to him, Sir John Mandeville, who had assumed the name of Jehan de Bourgogne, or Jean à la Barbe, died in 1372 and was buried in the church of the Guillemins at Liège.

The 'Voiage of Sir John Maundevile' purports to be a guide to pilgrims to the Holy Land, but carries the reader a good deal further, to Turkey, Tartary, Persia, Egypt, and India. It is an entertaining work combining geography and natural history with romance and marvels, such as the fountain of youth and ant-hills of gold-dust.

Mandricardo, in the 'Orlando Furioso' (q.v.), the son of Agrican, king of Tartary. He wears the armour of Hector, and comes to Europe to secure Hector's sword, Durindana, now in the possession of Orlando, and to avenge his father's death. He carries off Doralis, who is betrothed to Rodomont, meets Orlando and fights with him (but the fight is broken off), gets Durindana after Orlando in his madness has thrown it away, and is finally killed by Rogero.

Manduce, see *Gastrolaters*.

Mānĕs (Latin, the good beings), the deified souls of the departed, the ghosts of shades of the dead, whom the ancient Romans thought it desirable to propitiate.

MA'NĔTHO, an Egyptian priest who lived in the reign of Ptolemy Philadelphus (285–246 B.C.) and wrote chronicles of his country, of which only fragments survive.

Manette, DR. and LUCIE, characters in Dickens's 'A Tale of Two Cities' (q.v.).

Manfred, a dramatic poem by Lord Byron (q.v.), published in 1817.

Manfred, guilty of some inexpiable and mysterious crime, living among the Alps an outcast from society, is tortured by remorse. He calls up the spirits of the universe; they offer him everything but the one thing he seeks—oblivion. In vain he tries to throw himself from a high peak, and invokes the Witch of the Alps. He visits the Hall of Arimanes (Ahriman), resolutely refuses submission to the spirits of evil, bids them call up the dead, and has a vision of Astarte, the woman whom he has loved. In answer to his invocation, she foretells his death on the morrow, but will say no more. At the appointed time, demons appear to summon him. He denies their power over him; they disappear, and Manfred expires.

Mani, in Scandinavian mythology, the Moon.

Mani or MANES, see *Manichaeism*.

Manichaeism, a religious system widely accepted from the 3rd to the 5th cent. Like Mithraism, which it replaced, it was of Iranian origin, and was composed of Gnostic, Christian, Mazdean, and pagan elements. It was founded by Mani (Manes or Manichaeus), a Persian of Ecbatana, who lived in the 3rd cent. after Christ. He proclaimed the new religion at the court of Shapur I and became its travelling prophet. He was opposed by the fanatical Magians and crucified in the year A.D. 274 (?) under Bahram I. He wrote many works, most of which are lost; his doctrines are chiefly known from the 'Acta Archelai'.

The essential feature of the system is its dualistic theology, of which the principal elements are light and darkness, God and Satan, the soul and the body. Man was created by Satan in his image, but contains portions of light. Eve, the type of sensual seduction, was given him by Satan. A conflict is in progress between the demons and the angels of light for the possession of mankind. The angels send prophets to the world to impart true knowledge, by which alone man can be liberated. Of these prophets Mani is the last. Ultimately, when all the particles of captive light and the souls of the just have been set free, the end of the world will come in a general conflagration.

Manichaeism is essentially ascetic, and reprehends all forms of uncleanness. It spread both eastward to China and westward to Europe, where it was especially prevalent in Bulgaria and southern France (see Bridges, 'The Testament of Beauty', iii. 680 et seq.). Manichaean views were held by the Albigenses (q.v.) and exposed them to the terrible persecution (1207) of Innocent III. Augustine in his younger days was a Manichaean, but later wrote against the religion.

Manila ship, see *Acapulco ship*.

MANILIUS, the name given to the author of 'Astronomica', a Latin poem in five books on astrology and astronomy, written in the time of Augustus and Tiberius. Nothing is known of the author beyond his name, found variously spelt in some of the manuscripts. An edition of the poem was published by A. E. Housman (5 vols., 1903–30).

Manitou, one of the American Indian deities or spirits, both good and bad, which dominate nature.

MANLEY, MRS. MARY DE LA RIVIÈRE (1663–1724), having been drawn into a false marriage by her cousin John Manley, who was already married, fell into disreputable courses, and avenged herself on society for an unhappy life by her 'New Atalantis' (1709), in which Whigs and persons of note were slandered. She was arrested but escaped punishment. She wrote other scandalous memoirs and several plays, and succeeded Swift as editor of the 'Examiner' in 1711.

Manlius Capitolīnus, MARCUS, Roman consul in 392 B.C., was in the Capitol when the Gauls attempted to surprise it. Awakened, it is said, by the cackling of the geese, he hastily collected a few men and repelled the attack. Subsequently he befriended the poorer classes of Romans; he was accused of aiming to make himself tyrant and was sentenced to be thrown from the Tarpeian rock.

Manlius Torquātus, TITUS, Roman dictator in 363 B.C., who was celebrated for slaying in single combat, in 361, a gigantic Gaul. He took from him a chain (*torques*) which he placed round his own neck, whence his surname Torquatus. When consul in 340, he caused his own son to be executed for engaging in single combat, contrary to his orders, and slaying a Tusculan noble who had provoked him.

Manly, (1) a character in Wycherley's 'The Plain Dealer' (q.v.); (2) a character in Vanbrugh and Cibber's 'The Provok'd Husband' (q.v.).

MANN, HEINRICH (1871–1950), German novelist, brother of Thomas Mann (q.v.). His early work includes some notable satirical novels directed against the life and institutions of Wilhelminian Germany ('Professor Unrat', 1905, 'Der Untertan', 1918, for example). Of his later works the most important is the novel 'Die Vollendung des Königs Henri Quatre' (1938). More politically engaged than his brother in the period before 1918, and standing more to the left, he provided the model for the type of 'Zivilisationsliterat' with whom his brother polemically took issue in his 'Betrachtungen eines Unpolitischen' (1918). Like his brother, he emigrated from Nazi Germany.

Mann, SIR HORACE (1701–86), British envoy at Florence, 1740–86, where the Young Pretender was residing. He is chiefly remembered as Horace Walpole's friend and correspondent.

MANN, THOMAS (1875–1955), German novelist and essayist. Born in Lübeck, he went into emigration (most of the time in America) in the Nazi period. 'Buddenbrooks', a novel on the theme of the decay of a family, with strongly autobiographical features, appeared in 1901 and quickly made him famous. 'Tonio Kröger' (1903), one of his most celebrated stories, is, like so many of his works, about the nature of the artist. 'Der Tod in Venedig' (1912), influenced particularly by the thought of Schopenhauer (q.v.) and Nietzsche (q.v.), presents the artist and artistic creation in a highly ironic and critical light. Originally a man of rather conservative sympathies ('Betrachtungen eines Unpolitischen', 1918), he caused surprise by quickly lending his public support to the Weimar Republic. 'Der Zauberberg' appeared in 1924, the Joseph novels (in four parts) in 1933–43, during which time he

published also his novel about Goethe ('Lotte in Weimar'). Constantly concerned with the role and character of the artist, he linked up this theme with the problem of Nazism in his novel 'Dr. Faustus' (1947), and elaborated the subject in a book about this novel 'Die Entstehung des Dr. Faustus' (1949). His last full-length novel derived from the picaresque tradition ('Die Bekenntnisse des Hochstaplers Felix Krull', 1954). He was awarded the Nobel Prize in 1929.

Mannerism, the style of Italian art of *c.* 1520 to 1600, between the High Renaissance and the Baroque. A strident effect is achieved by distorted figures, with strained and exaggerated gestures and expressions, harsh colour, and violent perspective. The beginning of the style can be seen in the late work of Michelangelo and Raphael; it was developed by their followers, particularly Vasari and Giulio Romano, and justified by the genius of Tintoretto and El Greco.

MANNING, HENRY EDWARD (1808–92), educated at Balliol College, Oxford, and fellow of Merton. He became archdeacon of Chichester in 1840. In 1851 he joined the Roman Catholic church, and became archbishop of Westminster in 1865 and cardinal in 1875. He published many religious and polemical works, including: 'The Vatican Decrees' (1875) in reply to W. E. Gladstone. He was a great preacher and ecclesiastical statesman, of ascetic temper, and a subtle controversialist.

Manny or MAUNY, SIR WALTER DE, afterwards *Baron de Manny* (d. 1372), a native of Hainault and esquire to Queen Philippa, won great distinction as a military commander under Edward III. He founded the Charterhouse in London (1371). Drayton ('Polyolbion', xviii. 227) relates a legend about his forming a band of warriors who 'closed their left eyes up' until they had performed 'some high adventurous deed'.

Mannyng, ROBERT, of Brunne, see *Handlyng Synne*.

Manoa, see *El Dorado*.

Manon Lescaut, *Histoire du Chevalier des Grieux et de,* a famous novel by the Abbé Prévost (Antoine François Prévost d'Exiles, 1697–1763), published in 1731.

It is the story of a young man who is led into evil courses by his passionate attachment to a courtesan. She is finally transported to America, whither her lover follows her, and where she dies, her character transformed by love and suffering.

MANSEL, HENRY LONGUEVILLE (1820–71), educated at Merchant Taylors' School and St. John's College, Oxford, was professor of ecclesiastical history at Oxford, 1866–8, and dean of St. Paul's for the last three years of his life. He contributed to the 'Encyclopaedia Britannica' an exposition of the Hamiltonian philosophy, subsequently pub-

lished (1860) as 'Metaphysics'. In his 'Artis
Logicae Rudimenta' (1849) and 'Prolegomena
Logica' (1851) he had already shown himself
a follower of Sir W. Hamilton (q.v.). But his
fame rests chiefly on his Bampton Lectures
(1858), 'The Limits of Religious Thought', in
which he applied the Hamiltonian 'philosophy
of the conditioned' to theology. Mansel's
position is that human knowledge is limited
to the finite, and that a conception of the
Deity, in His absolute existence, involves a
contradiction; for conception itself is a limitation, and conception of the absolute Deity is
a limitation of the illimitable. Theology is
properly 'regulative' not speculative. We
have 'regulative ideas of the Deity, which are
sufficient to guide our practice, but not to
satisfy our intellect, which tell us, not what
God is in Himself, but how he wills that we
should think of Him'. Mansel published in
1850 'Phrontisterion', a satire on the University Commission, in the form of an excellent
Aristophanic parody.

MANSFIELD, KATHERINE, pen-name
of KATHLEEN MANSFIELD BEAUCHAMP (1888–
1923), short story writer, born in Wellington,
New Zealand, and educated there and in
London, whither she went in 1903. Apart
from a stay in New Zealand from 1906 to
1908, she spent the rest of her life in Europe,
writing stories and continually seeking higher
standards in her art, while at the same time
battling with persistent ill health. Her work
includes 'Bliss and Other Stories' (1920),
'The Garden Party' (1922), and 'The Dove's
Nest' (1923), and her 'Collected Stories' were
published in 1945. Her 'Journal' (1927) and
'Letters' (1928) were edited by her husband,
John Middleton Murry (q.v.).

Mansfield Park, a novel by J. Austen (q.v.),
begun in 1812 and published in 1814.

Sir Thomas Bertram of Mansfield Park, a
stern but good-hearted baronet, has two sons,
Tom and Edmund, and two daughters, Maria
and Julia. His wife, a selfish, indolent woman,
has two sisters: the widow Mrs. Norris, selfish
and spiteful, a near neighbour, and Mrs. Price,
wife of an impecunious officer of marines,
with a large family of young children. In
order to assist the latter, the Bertrams undertake the charge of Fanny Price, a girl of nine.
In spite of her humble situation and the constant bullying of Mrs. Norris, Fanny, by her
honesty and modest disposition, gradually
becomes an indispensable part of the household. Her sterling character is especially
shown during Sir Thomas's absence in the
West Indies, when the family discipline is
relaxed, private theatricals are indulged in,
and there is some unseemly flirtation between
Maria Bertram, who is engaged to marry Mr.
Rushworth, 'a heavy young man, with not
more than common sense', and Henry Crawford, the attractive but unprincipled brother-
in-law of the parson of Mansfield. Against all
this, Fanny resolutely sets her face. Loving her
cousin Edmund, she grieves to see him fasci-

nated by the worldly-minded Mary Crawford,
Henry's sister. Maria having become Mrs.
Rushworth, Henry Crawford turns his attention to Fanny, falls in love with her, and
proposes. Fanny unhesitatingly rejects him,
incurring the grave displeasure of Sir Thomas
by what he regards as a piece of ungrateful
perversity. During a visit paid by Fanny to
her own home, matters come to a crisis.
Henry, accidentally thrown again into contact with Mrs. Rushworth, runs away with
her; and Julia elopes with an ineligible suitor,
Mr. Yates. Mary Crawford's failure to reprobate her brother's conduct, coupled with
her aversion to marrying a clergyman (Edmund has now taken orders), finally opens
Edmund's eyes to her lack of principle. He
turns for comfort to Fanny, falls in love with
her, and marries her.

Mansie Wauch, see *Moir.*

Mansoul, see *Holy War.* Also the title of a
poem by Doughty (q.v.).

Mantalini, MADAME, in Dickens's 'Nicholas
Nickleby' (q.v.), a fashionable dressmaker.
Her husband, Mr. Mantalini, a selfish, affected
fop, lives on her earnings and ruins her.

Manto, see *Tiresias.*

Manton, JOE, see *Joe Manton.*

Mantua Carpetanorum, in imprints,
Madrid.

MANTUAN or **MANTUANUS** (1448–
1516), Johannes Baptista Spagnolo, a Carmelite of Mantua who wrote Latin eclogues.
These had a considerable vogue in England
and influenced the pastorals of Barclay and
Spenser.

Mantuan Poet, THE, Virgil (q.v.).

Manu, in Hindu mythology, the progenitor
of the human race, an emanation of Brahma.
To him are traditionally attributed the LAWS
OF MANU, sacred laws forming part of the
Veda (q.v.).

Manutius, ALDUS, see *Aldus Manutius.*

MANZONI, ALESSANDRO (1785–1873),
Italian novelist, dramatist, and poet, wrote
the greatest of Italian historical novels, 'I
promessi sposi' ('The Betrothed'), published in a first version in 1825–7, and in its
final form in 1840–2. Hero and heroine of the
novel—which is remarkable both for its
powerful characterization and as an example
of historical reconstruction—are poor silk-
weavers, and the events take place in Lombardy in 1628–31, during the period of
Spanish administration. Manzoni also wrote
two historical tragedies, 'Il conte di Carma-
gnola' (1820) and 'Aldechi (1822), in both of
which he broke with neo-classical conventions by disregarding the unities of time and
place. He and Sir W. Scott admired each
other's novels.

MAO TSE-TUNG (1893–   ), revolutionary
leader, Marxist theoretician, and head of the

Chinese Communist Party since 1936. After many years of fighting, both against the Kuomintang and against the Japanese invaders, he defeated Chiang Kai-shek and became Chairman of the People's Republic of China from its inception in 1949. The son of a Hunan farmer, he based his revolutionary strategy on the peasants, and his voluminous theoretical writings have inspired a distinctive Chinese version of Marxist theory.

MAP or **MAPES, WALTER** (*fl.* 1200), a Welshman, archdeacon of Oxford under Henry II, author of a satirical miscellany 'De nugis curialium', which included the 'Dissuasio Valerii ad Rufinum de non ducenda uxore', formerly attributed to St. Augustine (Chaucer refers to this in the Prologue of the Wife of Bath). Satirical poems on Bishop Golias (see *Golias*) have been doubtfully attributed to him; also a lost Latin original of the prose romance of 'Lancelot du Lac' (see the volume of 'Poems attributed to Walter Mapes', Camden Society).

Mar's Year, 1715, so called from the earl of Mar, who in that year led the rebellion in favour of the Old Pretender.

Maramoline, see *Miramolin.*

MARANA, GIOVANNI PAOLO, see *Turkish Spy.*

Maranatha, an Aramaic phrase occurring in 1 Cor. xvi. 22, meaning 'Our Lord has come' or 'O our Lord, come thou!', often erroneously regarded as forming, with the word 'anathema' which precedes it, a formula of imprecation.

Marathon, a plain near the east coast of Attica, the scene of the defeat of the Persian army by Miltiades in 490 B.C.

Marathon Race, see *Pheidippides.*

Maravedi, from *Almoravides* ('the hermits'), the name of a Moorish dynasty which reigned at Cordova 1087–1147, a former Spanish copper coin valued at about ⅛ of a penny.

Marble Faun, *The,* a novel by Hawthorne (q.v.), published in 1860 (under the title in England of 'Transformation').

The scene is laid in Rome, and the title is taken from the resemblance of one of the principal characters, Count Donatello, to the Marble Faun of Praxiteles. The story is mainly concerned with the development of the innocent, morally unconscious, character of Donatello under the pressure of a great tragedy. Donatello loves the art student Miriam, who is dogged and persecuted by another man. Roused to sudden fury, on encountering him when with her on a moonlight expedition, Donatello kills the intruder. From a faunlike creature, Donatello becomes a conscious remorseful man, and finally surrenders himself to justice.

Marcel, a character in Proust's novel, 'À la recherche du temps perdu' (q.v.).

Marcelia, the heroine of Massinger's 'The Duke of Milan' (q.v.).

Marchioness, THE, a character in Dickens's 'The Old Curiosity Shop' (q.v.).

Marcia, a character in Addison's 'Cato' (q.v.).

MARCIAN, see *Martianus Capella.*

Marcionites, a sect founded at Rome in the 2nd cent. by Marcion of Sinope. He accepted as sacred a garbled form of the Gospel of St. Luke and ten of St. Paul's Epistles, but regarded the creation of the material world and the revelation of the O.T. as the work of an imperfect god, whose authority is abrogated by the manifestation of the supreme god in Jesus Christ. He inculcated a rigorous asceticism. [OED.]

MARCO POLO, see *Polo.*

Marconi, GUGLIELMO (1874–1937), born at Bologna, the son of an Italian father and an Irish mother, is famous for establishing wireless telegraphy on a commercial basis, by means of electro-magnetic waves, the existence of which had been foreseen by Clerk-Maxwell in 1864. Marconi began to experiment in 1895. His first patent was taken out in 1896, and the system was soon after tested between Penarth and Weston and installed between the East Goodwin lightship and the South Foreland lighthouse. Communication across the English Channel was established in 1899, and across the Atlantic in 1902.

MARCONIGRAM, for a message transmitted by this system, is derived from his name.

MARCUS AURELIUS ANTONINUS (A.D. 121–180), Roman emperor A.D. 161–180 and religious philosopher, was author of twelve books of 'Meditations' in Greek, imbued with a Stoic philosophy. Man's duty is to obey the divine law that resides in his reason, superior to pains and pleasures; to forgive injuries and regard all men as brothers; to await death with equanimity. The 'Meditations' were first printed in 1550 from a manuscript now lost.

Mardi, an allegorical South Sea romance by Herman Melville (q.v.), published in 1849.

Marfisa, in the 'Orlando Innamorato' and the 'Orlando Furioso' (qq.v.), the sister of Rogero (q.v.). Brought up by an African magician, she becomes queen of India, and leads an army to the relief of Angelica (q.v.) besieged in Albracca. Later, discovering her own Christian parentage, Marfisa joins Charlemagne and is baptized. She falls in love with Rogero before discovering that he is her brother.

Marforio, see *Pasquil.*

Margaret, (1) in Shakespeare's 'Much Ado about Nothing' (q.v.), the gentlewoman attending on Hero; (2) in Goethe's 'Faust' (q.v.), the principal female character ('Gretchen') of Pt. I, a girl of humble station, simple, confiding, and affectionate.

Margaret, LADY, see *Lady Margaret.*

Margaret, Queen and Saint of Scotland (*d.* 1093). She was a granddaughter of Edmund Ironside, and brought the West Saxon blood back to the Royal (Norman) House of England by the marriage of her daughter with Henry I.

Margaret of Anjou (1430–82), 'the she-wolf of Anjou', queen consort of Henry VI of England; she played a prominent part in the Wars of the Roses. She figures in Shakespeare's 'Henry VI' (q.v.) and in Scott's 'Anne of Geierstein' (q.v.).

Margaret of Navarre, see *Heptameron.*

Margaret's Ghost, see *William and Margaret.*

Margarita, the heroine of Fletcher's 'Rule a Wife and Have a Wife' (q.v.).

Margītēs, 'The Booby', the name of a lost Greek comic poem, perhaps of about 700 B.C., regarded by Aristotle as the germ of comedy. It dealt with a foolish jack-of-all-trades 'who knew many things, but knew them all badly' (Jebb).

Marguerite of Navarre, see *Heptameron.*

Margutte, a character in Pulci's 'Morgante Maggiore' (q.v.), a cunning companion of Morgante. Rabelais's Panurge (q.v.) is in part modelled on him.

Maria, (1) a character in Shakespeare's 'Twelfth Night' (q.v.); (2) a character in Sterne's 'Tristram Shandy' (vol. vii) and 'A Sentimental Journey' (qq.v.); (3) a character in Sheridan's 'School for Scandal' (q.v.).

Mariamne, the wife of Herod the Great, executed by him in a fit of jealousy, the subject of tragedies by Voltaire and other authors.

Marian, MAID, see *Maid Marian.*

Mariana, in Shakespeare's 'Measure for Measure' (q.v.), the lady betrothed to Angelo and cast off by him, who lives, dejected, at the moated grange.

Mariana and *Mariana in the South,* two poems by A. Tennyson, suggested by the Mariana of 'the moated grange' (see preceding entry) in Shakespeare's 'Measure for Measure'.

MARIANA, JUAN DE (1532–1624), born at Talavera, a Jesuit, who taught theology at Rome and Paris, and then settled at Toledo, and wrote a long and remarkable history of Spain. He also wrote a notable Latin treatise 'de Rege et Regis Institutione' (Toledo, 1598), in which he spoke with approval of the assassination of Henri III of France by Jacques Clément and defined the circumstances in which it was legitimate to get rid, even by violence, of a tyrannical prince. This book was condemned in Paris to be burnt by the public executioner immediately after the

assassination of Henri IV by Ravaillac in 1610. See *Marianne.*

Marianne, a familiar name given to the government of the French Republic. A secret society formed about 1852, with the object of establishing the Republic and effecting other reforms, had taken the name of *Marianne.* Some of its members were prosecuted in 1854 and sentenced to imprisonment. The name of *Marianne* was then transferred from the society to its republican ideal, and in the language of the partisans of the Empire, *Marianne* was used to designate the Republic. For a Frenchman, *Marianne* still signifies the republican form of government, and not France. By foreigners, it is used more and more as a name for France, as John Bull for England.

The I.D.C. contains many inquiries and notes as to the ulterior origin of the symbolical use of the name 'Marianne'. They are inconclusive. They only show that 'Marianne' figured in the sign and countersign of the secret society of 1852, and that the name was a symbol of republican institutions probably as early as the first Revolution. The most interesting suggestion (unsupported by evidence) connects it with Juan de Mariana (q.v.).

Marie Celeste, see *Mary Celeste.*

MARIE DE FRANCE, a late 12th cent. French poetess, of whom little that is certain is known. She appears to have been born in France and to have done much or all of her literary work in England. She was a woman of culture, who knew Latin and English as well as French. She wrote 'Lays', tales of love and adventure, in some of which Arthur and Tristram figure; a collection of Aesopic fables, to which she gave the name 'Isopet'; and a French version of the Latin legend of the Purgatory of St. Patrick (q.v.).

Marie Roget, The Mystery of, a detective story by Poe (q.v.).

Maries, THE QUEEN'S, see *Queen's Maries.*

Marina, (1) in Shakespeare's 'Pericles' (q.v.), the daughter of Pericles; (2) in Byron's 'The Two Foscari' (q.v.), the wife of Jacopo Foscari.

Marinell, see *Florimell.*

Mariner's Mirror, The, the quarterly journal of the Society for Nautical Research, founded in 1910. The name is taken from an old Elizabethan book.

MARINETTI, FILIPPO TOMMASO (1876–1944), Italian dramatist, novelist, and poet, who launched the Futurist movement in 1909. In his poems he anticipated the Dadaist technique of juxtaposing words without syntactical links. In his plays he abandoned verisimilitude and traditional methods of characterization and plot development. His innovations include: the use of robots; the simultaneous staging of unrelated actions; the 'drama of objects', in which human interlocutors play no significant part.

MARINO, GIAMBATTISTA (1569–1625), Neapolitan poet, best known for his 'Adone' (1623), a long poem on the love of Venus and Adonis. The term *marinismo* denotes the flamboyant style of Marino and his 17th-cent. imitators, with its extravagant imagery, excessive ornamentation, and verbal ingenuity (or 'conceits').

Marino Faliero, Doge of Venice, an historical tragedy by Lord Byron (q.v.) published in 1821, and produced in the same year at Drury Lane (against Byron's wish).

Marino Faliero was elected Doge of Venice in 1354. Michele Steno, a gentleman of poor estate, having been affronted by the doge, a haughty and choleric man, wrote on the latter's chair of state a gross lampoon on the doge and his wife. He was tried by the Council of Forty and sentenced to a punishment which the doge considered utterly inadequate. The doge thereupon entered into a conspiracy with a number of discontented men to overturn the Venetian constitution and take vengeance on the senators. The plot was revealed and defeated, and Faliero decapitated.

The conspiracy of the doge was likewise the subject of a tragedy, 'Marino Faliero', by Swinburne (q.v.), published in 1885.

Mariolatry, the idolatrous worship of the Virgin Mary attributed by opponents to Roman Catholics. [OED.]

Marischal College, ABERDEEN, was founded in 1593 by George Keith, fifth Earl Marischal (1553?–1623), a Scottish statesman who took an active part in affairs under James VI.

MARITAIN, JAQUES (1882–　). French neo-Thomist philosopher, a convert to Roman Catholicism, author also of works on poetry and aesthetics: 'Art et Scolastique' (1920), 'Situation de la poésie' (1938). He has been much translated and has also written directly in English.

Maritornes, the chambermaid at the inn that Don Quixote (q.v.) took for a castle.

Marius among the ruins of Carthage, an allusion to an incident in the life of Gaius Marius, the great Roman general (157–86 B.C.), who had conquered Jugurtha in Africa and destroyed the Cimbri. Overcome by his rival Sulla, he fled in 88 to Africa and landed at Carthage. The Roman governor sent to bid him leave the country. His only reply was, 'Tell the praetor you have seen Gaius Marius a fugitive sitting among the ruins of Carthage.'

Marius the Epicurean, a philosophical romance by Pater (q.v.), published in 1885.

This is the story of the life, in the time of the Antonines, of a grave young Roman, his childhood on his family's Etruscan farm, his education at Pisa, and his maturer years in Rome. Against a background of the customs and modes of thought of that fortunate period, the author traces the reactions of Marius to the various spiritual influences to which he is from time to time subjected, from his first reading of the 'Golden Book' of Apuleius and the philosophies of Heraclitus and Aristippus the Cyrenaic, to the stoicism of Marcus Aurelius, the beauties of the ancient Roman religion, and the horrors of the Roman amphitheatre. Finally the quiet courage and enthusiasm of the young Christian community make a growing impression on his receptive mind, and his end comes as a result of an act of self-sacrifice undertaken in order to save a Christian friend. One of the pleasantest passages of the book is the version of the fable of 'Cupid and Psyche' (q.v.) from Apuleius.

MARIVAUX, PIERRE CARLET DE CHAMBLAIN DE (1688–1763), French author of prose comedies and romances, marked by a delicate analysis of sentiment, and a subtle affected style which has given rise to the term *Marivaudage.*

Mark, a money of account, originally representing the value of a mark weight (usually regarded as equivalent to 8 oz.) of silver. In England, after the Conquest, the ratio of twenty sterling pennies to the ounce was the basis of computation; hence the value of the mark became fixed at 160 pence = 13s. 4d. or $\frac{2}{3}$ of the £ sterling. In Scotland the value of the mark was lowered proportionately with that of the shilling and the penny, so that it represented 13s. 4d. Scots = 13$\frac{1}{3}$d. English.

Mark, KING, in the Arthurian legend king of Cornwall, and husband of La Beale Isoud (see *Tristram*). He is held up to ridicule as a treacherous coward. According to Rhys ('Hibbert Lectures') his origin is perhaps to be found in a deformed deity of the underworld common to Gaelic and British mythology.

Mark, ST., the evangelist, represented in art accompanied by a winged lion, and commemorated on 25 Apr. Keats left, unfinished, a poem on the Eve of St. Mark, with which day certain superstitions were connected.

MARK RUTHERFORD, see *White (W..H.).*

Mark Tapley, in Dickens's 'Martin Chuzzlewit' (q.v.), servant at the Dragon Inn, who leaves it to find some position in which it will be a credit to show his indomitable good humour. He becomes the devoted attendant of Martin during his American tour, and finally marries the hostess of the Dragon.

MARK TWAIN, see *Clemens.*

Mark's, ST., a famous Byzantine basilica built in 830 at Venice to receive the relics of the evangelist, which were brought from Alexandria. The church was rebuilt in 976 and 1052.

MARKHAM, MRS., pseudonym of Mrs. Elizabeth Penrose (1780–1837), *née* Cartwright, who wrote well-known school histories of England (1823) and France (1828).

MARKHAM, GERVASE (1568–1637), after

a military career of some years in the Netherlands, became a writer on country pursuits,
on the art of war, but especially on horsemanship and the veterinary art. He also wrote
plays and poems. His principal works on
horses are 'A Discourse of Horsemanshippe'
(1593), 'Cavelarice, or the English Horseman',
1607 (in which there is mention of 'Bankes his
Curtall', the wonderful performing horse
Marocco, referred to in Shakespeare's 'Love's
Labour's Lost'), 'Markham's Method, or
Epitome' (1616), 'The Faithful Farrier' (1635).
His chief work on country occupations has
the title 'A Way to get Wealth' (1631–8), containing treatises on 'Cheap and Good Husbandry' (the management of domestic
animals); 'Country Contentments' (hunting,
hawking, fishing), with a section on the
'English Huswife' (cookery, dairying, physic);
and agriculture and horticulture. (These
treatises had been separately published at
earlier dates.) His other principal works were
'The most Honourable Tragedie of Sir Richard
Grinvile, Knight' (1595), 'The English Arcadia' (1607), 'The Soldier's Accidence'
(1625). Markham is said to have been the
first to import an Arab horse into England.

Markleham, MRS., in Dickens's 'David
Copperfield' (q.v.), familiarly known as the
'Old Soldier', was the mother-in-law of
Copperfield's old schoolmaster at Canterbury, Dr. Strong. Her nickname was due to
the 'skill with which she marshalled great
forces of relations against the Doctor.'

Marley, in Dickens's 'A Christmas Carol'
(q.v.), Scrooge's late partner, whose ghost
appears.

Marlow, SIR CHARLES, and his son, characters in Goldsmith's 'She Stoops to Conquer'
(q.v.).

MARLOWE, CHRISTOPHER (1564–93),
son of a Canterbury shoemaker, was educated
at King's School, Canterbury, and Corpus
Christi College, Cambridge. He attached
himself to the earl of Nottingham's theatrical
company, which produced most of his plays.
He was acquainted with the leading men of
letters, including Ralegh. He wrote not later
than 1587 'Tamburlaine' (q.v.), which was
published in 1590 and gave a new development to blank verse. His 'Tragedy of Dr.
Faustus' (q.v.) was first entered on the
'Stationers' Register' in 1601, but not apparently published till 1604. At some date
after 1588 he wrote 'The Jew of Malta' (q.v.),
which was first published in 1633; and about
1593 his best play, 'Edward II' (q.v., first
published in 1594); also two inferior pieces,
the 'Massacre at Paris' (probably published
in 1600) and 'Tragedy of Dido' (joint work of
Marlowe and Nash), published in 1594. It
has been suggested from internal evidence
that he was part author of Shakespeare's
'Titus Andronicus'. He perhaps also wrote
parts of 'Henry VI', which Shakespeare
revised and completed, and of 'Edward III'

(qq.v.). He translated Ovid's 'Amores' (published with Sir John Davies's 'Epigrammes
and Elegies', c. 1597); paraphrased part of
Musaeus's 'Hero and Leander' (completed by
George Chapman and published 1598); translated 'The First Book of Lucan['s Pharsalia]'
(published 1600); and wrote the song 'Come
live with me and be my love' (published in
'The Passionate Pilgrim', 1599, and in
'England's Helicon'). Marlowe held and pro-
pagated atheistical opinions, and a warrant
was issued for his arrest in 1593, but later
researches have suggested that he was a
government agent, and that his murder had a
political complexion. He was killed, as Dr.
Leslie Hotson has shown, by one Ingram
Frisar, at a tavern in Deptford where the pair
had supped, and, according to the inquiry
held at the time, as the result of a quarrel
about the score. Marlowe was spoken of with
affection by Edward Blount, Nashe, and
Chapman, and Jonson referred to his 'mighty
line'. He was quoted and apostrophized by
Shakespeare in 'As You Like It', and praised
by Drayton ('To Henery Reynolds, Esq., of
Poets and Poems') in the fine lines beginning:

> Next Marlow, bathed in the Thespian
>   Springs,
> Had in him those brave translunary things
> That the poets had.

Marmion, *A Tale of Flodden Field,* a poem
in six cantos by Sir W. Scott (q.v.), published
in 1808.

The story relates to the year 1513. Lord
Marmion, a fictitious character, a favourite of
King Henry VIII and a compound of villainy
and noble qualities, having tired of Constance
de Beverley, a perjured nun who has followed
him disguised as a page, seeks to marry the
wealthy Lady Clare, who is affianced to Sir
Ralph de Wilton. To effect his purpose he
accuses de Wilton of treason, and proves it by
a forged letter. In this he is assisted by Constance, who hopes to recover her hold over
Marmion by her knowledge of his perfidy.
She is, however, betrayed to her convent and
walled up alive. Meanwhile, Marmion and
de Wilton have fought in the lists, and the
latter has been defeated and left for dead. The
Lady Clare betakes herself to a convent to
escape Marmion. Marmion in the course of an
embassy to Scotland is unknowingly thrown
into contact with de Wilton, who has survived
and is now disguised as a Palmer; while de
Wilton meets with the Abbess of St. Hilda,
who has received from Constance the proofs
of Marmion's crime, and with Clare in attendance on the Abbess. The Abbess entrusts
these proofs to the Palmer, who reveals himself to Clare and escapes to the English camp,
where he is rehabilitated. Marmion, with
Clare in his train, joins the English forces at
the battle of Flodden, where he is killed. De
Wilton and Clare are finally united. The poem
contains the two well-known songs, 'Where
shall the lover rest', and 'Lochinvar', and
beautiful introductions to each canto.

MARMION, SHACKERLEY (1603–39), educated at Wadham College, Oxford, was the author of several plays, of which the best is 'The Antiquary' (published in 1641), and of a poem in heroic couplets 'Cupid and Psyche' (q.v.). He contributed verse to the 'Annalia Dubrensia' (see *Cotswold Games*).

Marne, BATTLE OF THE, in September 1914, one of the decisive battles of the war of 1914–18. On 4 Sept. the advance of Von Kluck and the German First Army was diverted from the direction of Paris towards the south-east. He had then reached the line of the Ourcq, and at this point on the 5th the retirement of the French and British forces ceased. On the 6th the battle of the Marne opened with a general offensive of the Allies. Von Kluck's plan was to march across the front of Maunoury's 6th Army and of the British, in order to attack D'Espérey's 5th Army. He under-estimated the resilience of the forces he had been driving before him. By the 9th the British and D'Espérey had reached the Marne, while Maunoury had carried the Ourcq. On the 10th the Germans retreated further, and took up a line on the northern bank of the Aisne from near Compiègne towards the Meuse.

The SECOND BATTLE OF THE MARNE (July–August 1918) was the turning-point of the last year of the War. The last German offensive near Rheims was checked on 15 July, and followed by a counter-offensive of the reserve group of armies, the reoccupation of the south bank of the Marne by the centre group, the advance of both groups, leading to the battle of Tardenois, the recapture of Soissons, and the German retirement to the Vesle. The allied movement was under Pétain's direction.

Maro, the family name of the Roman poet Virgil (q.v.).

Marocco, the wonderful performing horse trained by Bankes, the Scottish showman (*fl.* 1588–1637). Its power of counting is referred to in Shakespeare's 'Love's Labour's Lost' (1. ii), and by other authors of the day. See also *Markham* (*G.*).

Maronites, a sect of Syrian Christians, inhabiting Lebanon and Anti-Lebanon, named after their founder Maron, who lived probably in the 4th cent.

MAROT, CLÉMENT (1496–1544), French Protestant poet, whose sonnets and pastorals and translations of the Psalms had some influence on the contemporary school of English poetry. He figures in R. Browning's poem, 'The Glove'.

Marplot, a character in Mrs. Centlivre's 'The Busybody' (q.v.).

Marprelate Controversy, see *Martin Marprelate*.

Marquis of Granby, THE, in Dickens's 'Pickwick Papers' (q.v.), the inn at Dorking kept by the second Mrs. Tony Weller.

Marriage, a novel by S. E. Ferrier (q.v.), published in 1818.

Lady Juliana, the daughter of the earl of Courtland, from romantic notions elopes with the penniless younger officer Henry Douglas, who takes her to his Highland home, a gaunt, lonely house where she is greeted by 'three long-chinn'd spinsters' and 'five awkward purple girls'. The dismay of the worldly Lady Juliana at her new surroundings, and the characters of the members of the household and of the neighbouring gentry, are excellently depicted. Lady Juliana gives birth to twin daughters, the climax of her misfortunes. The couple move to London and get into debt. Henry is imprisoned; on his release he joins a regiment in India, and is permanently separated from his wife. Of the children, one is brought up in Scotland, and grows up plain and virtuous; the other accompanies her mother to Lord Courtland's house, and grows up beautiful and heartless. Their story is told as far as their respectively happy and unhappy marriages.

Marriage-à-la Mode, a comedy by Dryden (q.v.), produced in 1672.

The theme of the principal plot is expressed in the first lines of the lyric with which the play opens:

> Why should a foolish marriage vow,
>   Which long ago was made,
> Oblige us to each other now,
>   When passion is decayed?

This is the view of Rhodophil and his wife, Doralia, who, having been married two years, find that the first glamour of marriage has worn off. Rhodophil's friend, Palamede, returns from his travels, having been ordered by his father on pain of disinheritance to marry Melantha, whose delight is in the latest fashions and in newly imported French words. But Palamede has seen and fallen in love with Doralia, not knowing her to be his friend's wife, and views Melantha's affectations with disgust. And Rhodophil has begun to court Melantha, not knowing that she is the destined bride of Palamede. The two amorous intrigues go on, with amusing incidents, until the friends, each discovering that the other is in love with the woman on whom he himself has a claim, conclude that there must be some undiscovered charm in her, become jealous, quarrel, and finally decide not to trespass on each other's property.

Marrow of Modern Divinity, The, the title of a book advocating Calvinistic views, written by E. F. (Edward Fisher) in 1645, the condemnation of which (in 1718) by the general assembly of the Church of Scotland led to a prolonged controversy, known as the MARROW CONTROVERSY.

MARRYAT, FREDERICK (1792–1848), a captain in the Royal Navy, in which he served with distinction, was the author of a series of novels of sea-life, of which the best known are 'Frank Mildmay' (1829), 'Peter Simple' (q.v., 1834), 'Jacob Faithful' (q.v., 1834), and 'Mr. Midshipman Easy' (q.v., 1836). 'Japhet in Search of a Father' (1836), another of his most successful books, is not a story of the sea, but the autobiography of a foundling, who reaches fortune after a multitude of escapades. Mention should also be made of 'Snarleyyow' (1837), the story of a mysterious and indestructible cur, 'The Pacha of Many Tales' (1836), 'The Phantom Ship' (1839), and 'Poor Jack' (1840). 'Masterman Ready' (1841), 'The Settlers in Canada' (1844), and others, were specially intended by the author for boys. Marryat spent the years 1837–9 in the U.S. and Canada, and in 1839 published his 'Diary in America' containing an unflattering account of American manners.

Mars, the god of war of the ancient Romans, identified by them with the *Ares* (q.v.) of the Greeks.

Mars is the name of the fourth planet in the order of distance from the sun, revolving in an orbit lying between that of the earth and Jupiter. Its proximity to the earth has enabled its surface to be carefully mapped, and the existence on it of what appear to be canals (discovered by Schiaparelli) and cultivated areas has given rise to conjectures that Mars is inhabited by intelligent beings (for a fanciful account of these, see *Martians*).

Mars, MLLE, stage name of Anne Boutet (1779–1847), a famous French actress. ' "Did you ever see the Mars, Miss Fotheringay?" "There was two Mahers in Crow Street," remarked Miss Emily, "Fanny was well enough, but Biddy was no great things." "Sure, the Major means the god of war," interposed the parent.' (Thackeray, 'Pendennis', ch. xi.)

Marseillaise, The, the French national anthem, was composed by a young French engineer officer, Rouget de Lisle, at Strasbourg in 1792, on the declaration of war against Austria. It was shortly afterwards sung at a banquet at Marseilles, and adopted by a Marseilles battalion that was starting for Paris. There it became popular, being known as the 'Chant des Marseillais'. It was suppressed by Napoleon and at the restoration of the Bourbons.

MARSH, SIR EDWARD (1872–1953), was editor of 'Georgian Poetry' (q.v.) and a friend and biographer of Rupert Brooke (q.v.). He translated the fables of La Fontaine (completed in 1931).

MARSH, NGAIO (pronounced 'Ny-o') EDITH (1899–), writer of detective stories, born at Christchurch, New Zealand. Her hero is Chief Detective Inspector Alleyn and her titles include 'A Man Lay Dead' (1934), 'Died in the Wool' (1945), and 'Spinsters in Jeopardy' (1954).

Marshalsea, a prison in Southwark, under the control of the knight-marshal, used latterly for debtors. It was abolished in the 19th cent. See *Little Dorrit*.

MARSTON, JOHN (1575 ?–1634), the dramatist, was born probably at Coventry, where he was educated, subsequently going to Brasenose College, Oxford. His mother was Italian. He renounced the drama in 1607 and took orders; he was incumbent of Christchurch, Hampshire, from 1616 to 1631. He figures as 'Kinsayder' in 'The Returne from Pernassus', (see *Parnassus Plays*). He quarrelled with Ben Jonson, who attacked him in 'Every Man out of his Humour', 'Cynthia's Revels', and 'The Poetaster', where he is presented as Crispinus. But the pair made friends again. Marston published 'The Metamorphosis of Pigmalion's Image' (an erotic poem) 'and certain Satyres' in 1598, and further satires under the title 'The Scourge of Villanie' in the same year. Some of these were studies in social vices and others were directed against literary rivals, including Bishop Hall (q.v.). His dramatic works were printed as follows: the 'History of Antonio and Mellida' (q.v.), a tragedy, in 1602 ('Antonios Revenge' is the second part of this play); 'The Malcontent', a comedy, with additions by Webster, in 1604; 'Eastward hoe' (q.v.), a comedy, written with Jonson and Chapman, for which they were imprisoned in 1605; 'The Dutch Courtezan' (q.v.), in the same year; 'The Parasitaster' (a comedy), in 1606; 'Sophonisba' (a tragedy) in the same year; 'What you Will' (a comedy) in 1607; and 'The Insatiate Countess' (a tragedy) in 1613—the last is sometimes assigned to William Barksteed. The works of Marston were edited by A. H. Bullen in 1887; the plays, by H. Harvey Wood, in 1934–9; and the poems, by Arnold Davenport, in 1961.

MARSTON, JOHN WESTLAND (1819–90), was author of some notable dramas: 'The Patrician's Daughter' (1842), 'Strathmore' (1849), 'Marie de Méranie' (1850), 'A Life's Ransom' (1857), and 'Life for Life' (1869). His most successful comedy was 'The Favourite of Fortune' (1866).

MARSTON, PHILIP BOURKE (1850–87), son of John Westland Marston (q.v.), a blind poet, author of some beautiful sonnets. He published 'Song-tide and other Poems' (1871), 'All in All' (1875), and 'Wind Voices' (1883). Three volumes appeared posthumously: 'For a Song's Sake' (short stories) 1887, 'Garden Secrets' (1887), and 'A Last Harvest' (1891).

Marsўas, in Greek mythology, a celebrated player on the pipe, of Celaena in Phrygia, who had the imprudence to challenge Apollo to a musical contest, it being agreed that the victor should treat the loser as he wished. The victory having with difficulty been adjudged to Apollo by the Muses, Apollo tied Marsyas to a tree and flayed him alive. It is said by some that Marsyas had picked up the flute of Athene, which the goddess had thrown away after observing the distortion of the face of the person who played on it; she had invoked a melancholy death on him who found it.

Martello Tower, a small circular fort with

massive walls. The name is a corruption of Cape Murtella in Corsica, where there was a tower of this kind which the English fleet captured in 1794. Many Martello towers were erected on the south and east coasts of England as a defensive measure about 1804.

Martext, SIR OLIVER, the vicar in Shakespeare's 'As You Like It' (q.v.).

MARTIAL, Marcus Valerius Martialis (*c.* A.D. 40–104), born at Bilbilis in Spain. He came to Rome in 64, and lived there for thirty-five years and then returned to Spain. He left a collection of short poems or epigrams, 1,500 in number, witty but frequently coarse, which throw a valuable light on Roman life and manners.

Martians, in H. G. Wells's 'The War of the Worlds', inhabitants of Mars, who, driven by the progressive cooling of their planet to seek a warmer world, invade the earth. They are described as round bodies, about 4 ft. in diameter, each body containing a huge brain, and having in front of it a face, with very large dark eyes, a kind of fleshy beak, sixteen slender tentacles, no nostrils, and an oily brown skin. They live by the injection into themselves of the fresh living blood of other creatures, mostly human beings. They rely on highly developed machinery for locomotion, warfare, etc. They devastate England by means of a terrible heat-ray and an asphyxiating gas; but soon fall victims to diseases caused by the bacteria against which they have no power of resistance.

MARTIANUS CAPELLA, or MARCIAN, a N. African writer celebrated in the Middle Ages who lived in the 5th cent. He was author of 'De Nuptiis Philologiae et Mercurii' in prose and verse, in nine books, of which the first two deal with the wooing of Philology (in a wide sense) by Mercury, while the last seven are an allegorical encyclopaedia of the arts of the trivium and quadrivium. In one of these he anticipates the doctrine that the planets do not revolve about the earth. Marcian is referred to by Chaucer in 'The Merchant's Tale', ll. 488 et seq., and in 'The Hous of Fame', l. 985.

Martin, in 'Reynard the Fox' (q.v.), the ape. His wife is Dame Rukenawe.

Martin, in Dryden's 'The Hind and the Panther' (q.v.), symbolizes the Lutheran party; and in Swift's 'A Tale of a Tub' (q.v.) the Anglican Church, the allusion being to Martin Luther.

Martin, ST., bishop of Tours about 371, the patron saint of tavern-keepers. Legend represents him as a Roman soldier who once divided his cloak in two to clothe a beggar. He is commemorated on 11 Nov., known as MARTINMAS or MARTLEMAS, which was formerly the usual time in England for hiring servants and for slaughtering cattle to be salted for winter provision. ST. MARTIN'S

SUMMER is a period of fine mild weather sometimes occurring about this date.

MARTIN, SIR THEODORE (1816–1909), educated at Edinburgh High School and University, practised as a solicitor at Edinburgh, and migrated to London in 1846. He contributed, under the pseudonym 'Bon Gaultier', humorous pieces to 'Tait's' and 'Fraser's' magazines, some of which attracted the attention of W. E. Aytoun (q.v.). Martin and Aytoun formed 'a kind of Beaumont and Fletcher partnership' until 1844, and collaborated in the 'Bon Gaultier Ballads' (q.v.) (published 1845), parodying verse of the day. Martin was also a translator of Danish and German dramas, and of Horace. His 'Faust' appeared, Pt. I in 1865, and Pt. II in 1886, and 'Heine's Poems' in 1878. His 'Biography of the Prince Consort' was published in 1875–80; his 'Life of Lord Lyndhurst' in 1883.

Martin Chuzzlewit, *The Life and Adventures of,* a novel by Dickens (q.v.), published in 1843–4.

Martin, the hero, is the grandson of old Martin Chuzzlewit, a wealthy gentleman who has been rendered misanthropical by the greed of the members of his family. The old man has bred up Mary Graham, a young orphan, to tend him, and regards her as his daughter. Young Chuzzlewit is in love with Mary; but the grandfather, distrusting his selfish character, repudiates him and gets him dismissed from his position as pupil to his cousin, Mr. Pecksniff, an architect and an arch-hypocrite. Thrown nearly penniless on the world, young Martin, accompanied by the indomitably cheerful Mark Tapley as his servant, sails for America to try his fortunes. He goes as an architect to the settlement of the Eden Land Corporation, a fraudulent affair, where he loses his money and nearly dies of fever. (This part gave great offence in the United States.) Martin then returns to England, purged by his experiences of his earlier selfishness. Meanwhile his grandfather has established himself and Mary in Pecksniff's household, and pretends to place himself under the latter's direction. By this means he becomes satisfied of Pecksniff's meanness and treachery (Pecksniff tries to inveigle and bully Mary into marrying him), exposes the hypocrite, restores his grandson to favour, and gives him the hand of Mary.

A second plot runs through the book, concerned with the doings of Jonas Chuzzlewit, the son of Anthony, old Martin's brother, a character of almost incredible villainy. He murders his father (in intention if not in fact); marries Mercy, one of Pecksniff's daughters, and treats her with the utmost brutality; murders the director of a bogus insurance company, by whom he has been inveigled and blackmailed; is detected; and finally poisons himself.

Besides the finished portraits of Pecksniff and Mark Tapley, the book contains many pleasant characters: Tom Pinch, Pecksniff's gentle loyal assistant, and his sister Ruth; Charity and Mercy (Cherry and Merry), Pecksniff's daughters; and Mrs. Gamp, the disreputable old nurse; while in 'Todgers's' the author depicts the humours of a London boarding-house.

MARTIN DUGARD, ROGER (1881–1958), French novelist, best known by 'Les Thibault' a long novel in seven parts (10 vols., 1922–40). It is the story of two brothers and their reaction to the Pharisaical standards of their bourgeois upbringing. The background is the era ended (like their lives) by the 1914–18 war. An earlier novel by this author, 'Jean Barois' (1913), depicts French intellectual circles towards the end of the 19th cent.

MARTIN MARPRELATE, the name assumed by the author of a number of anonymous pamphlets (seven are extant) issued in 1588–9 from a secret press, containing attacks in a railing rollicking style on the bishops and defending the Presbyterian system of discipline. They were occasioned by the decree issued in 1586 by Archbishop Whitgift and the Star Chamber, with the object of checking the flow of Puritan pamphlets, requiring the previous approval of the ecclesiastical authorities to every publication.

The importance of the Marprelate tracts lies in the fact that they are the best prose satires of the Elizabethan age. Their titles (in their abbreviated form) are: 'The Epistle', 'The Epitome', 'The Minerall Conclusions', 'Hay any work for Cooper' (a familiar street-cry with allusion to the name of Thomas Cooper, bishop of Winchester), 'Martin Junior', 'Martin Senior', and 'The Protestation'. They called forth replies from such noted writers as Lyly and Nash, and Gabriel and Richard Harvey were presently involved in the controversy. But the replies show less literary ability than the original tracts.

The suspected authors of these, a Welshman named Penry and a clergyman named Udall, were arrested. The latter died in prison, the former was executed. Their collaborator, Job Throckmorton, probably the real author, denied his complicity at the trial of Penry, and escaped punishment.

MARTINEAU, HARRIET (1802–76), the daughter of a Norwich manufacturer, and sister of J. Martineau (q.v.). She was a Unitarian, and began her literary career as a writer on religious subjects. But she was chiefly successful in stories designed to popularize economic subjects, which show her as an ardent advocate of social reform: 'Illustrations of Political Economy' (1832–4), 'Poor Law and Paupers Illustrated' (1833), and 'Illustrations of Taxation' (1834). She visited America and wrote 'Society in America' (1837) and 'Retrospect of Western Travel' (1838). She published a novel, 'Deerbrook', in 1839; an historical romance, 'The Hour and the Man', in 1841; also a series of stories

for young people, 'The Playfellow' (including 'The Settlers at Home' and 'Feats on the Fiord'), in 1841. She was also an active journalist, contributing to the 'Daily News' and 'Edinburgh Review'. Her later writings display anti-theological views. She issued a condensed translation of Comte's 'Philosophie positive' in 1853. Her 'History of Thirty Years Peace, 1815–45', prejudiced on the Whig side, but otherwise sound, was published in 1849. Miss Martineau wrote an 'Autobiographical Memoir', published posthumously, which contains interesting comments on the great literary figures of her day.

MARTINEAU, JAMES (1805–1900), Unitarian divine and brother of Harriet Martineau (q.v.), was professor of mental and moral philosophy at Manchester New College for many years. His philosophical works, published very late in his life, show a religious and conservatively spiritual attitude and hostility to materialism and naturalism. They include 'Ideal Substitutes for God' (1879), 'Study of Spinoza' (1882), 'Types of Ethical Theory' (1885), 'A Study of Religion' (1888), 'The Seat of Authority in Religion' (1890). Martineau contributed much to the 'National Review', and was joint-editor of the 'Prospective Review' (1845–54).

Martinus Scriblerus, Memoirs of, a satirical work, directed against 'false tastes in learning', initiated by the Scriblerus Club (q.v.), and written mainly if not entirely by Arbuthnot (q.v.). It was printed in the second volume of Pope's prose works in 1741. Martinus is the son of Cornelius, an antiquary of Münster in Germany. His birth, christening, and education are described, all conducted in the light of the teaching of the ancients. He becomes a critic, a physician, and a philosopher, and sets out on travels, the sketch of which corresponds with the travels of Gulliver. The work is incomplete, and we have only the first book of it.

The name 'Martinus Scriblerus' was occasionally used by Pope as a pseudonym; and under it George Crabbe wrote some of his earlier poems.

MARTYN, EDWARD (1859–1924), born in Co. Galway, and educated at Beaumont College, Windsor, and Christ Church, Oxford, was one of the founders of the Irish Literary Theatre (see Yeats). He also founded the Palestrina Choir in Dublin for the reform of liturgical music, and was the promoter of various movements for the improvement of education in Ireland. His best-known plays are 'The Heather Field' and 'Maeve'. He is one of the central figures in G. Moore's (q.v.) 'Hail and Farewell'.

MARTYR, PETER, see *Peter Martyr.*

MARVELL, ANDREW (1621–78), was born at Winestead near Hull, and educated at Hull Grammar School and Trinity College, Cambridge. He spent four years on the Continent, part of the time at Rome, and in

1650 became tutor to the daughter of Lord Fairfax, at Nun Appleton in Yorkshire. Here he wrote poems in praise of gardens and country life, including 'The Hill and Grove at Billborow' and 'Appleton House'. These tastes are again shown in his well-known poem 'The Garden'. Another poem of this period, 'The Bermudas', is a beautiful song of praise and thanksgiving by a party of exiles on approaching those islands. In 1653 he became tutor to Cromwell's ward, William Dutton, and in 1657 Milton's assistant in the Latin secretaryship to the council. He wrote several poems in the Protector's honour, including the 'Horatian Ode upon Cromwell's Return from Ireland' (1650) and the elegy upon his death. After the Restoration he entered parliament and became a violent politician and wrote satires and pamphlets, attacking first the ministers, but afterwards Charles II himself. His principal verse satire is the 'Last Instructions to a Painter' (q.v.), on the subject of the Dutch War. The painter is to represent the corruption of the court, the State without a fleet, 'our ships unrigg'd, our forts unmanned', contrasting with the activity of the Dutch. Marvell vigorously defended Milton, and wrote lines in praise of 'Paradise Lost', which were included with the second edition of that poem. From 1660 to 1678 he wrote a series of newsletters to his constituents at Hull, which are of historical importance. The bulk of his poems were not published until 1681, the satires not until 1689, after the revolution.

Marvellous Boy, The, a name given by Wordsworth to Chatterton (q.v.).

Marwood, Mrs., a character in Congreve's 'The Way of the World' (q.v.).

MARX, KARL (1818–83), born in Rhenish Prussia, of Jewish descent, was editor of the 'Rheinische Zeitung' at Cologne in 1842. His extreme radical views led to the suppression of the paper, and Marx went to Paris, where he came into touch with Friedrich Engels and collaborated with him in works of political philosophy. He was expelled from Paris, moved to Brussels, and at the time of the revolutionary movement of 1848 returned to Cologne, where, with Engels, he again conducted a newspaper, the 'Neue Rheinische Zeitung'. His revolutionary and communistic views caused him to be once more expelled, and he finally settled in London. In 1867 appeared the first volume of his treatise 'Das Kapital', in which he propounded his theory of political economy. This was completed by Engels after the death of Marx from his papers. It is a criticism of the capitalistic system under which, according to Marx, a diminishing number of capitalists appropriate the benefits of improved industrial methods, while the labouring class are left in increasing dependency and misery. Marx holds the view that the price of a commodity should be the remuneration of the labour required to produce it, and that it fails to be this because capital exacts a share of the price, while competition among the workers obliges them to accept less than their proper due. The remedy for this state of things Marx finds in the total abolition of private property, to be effected by the class war. When the community has acquired possession of all property and the means of production, it will distribute work to each individual and provide him with the means of sustenance: 'From everyone according to his faculties, to everyone according to his needs.'

Marx was the principal creator of the First International Working Men's Council.

Mary, in Dickens's 'Pickwick Papers' (q.v.), Mr. Nupkins's pretty housemaid, who marries Sam Weller.

Mary I, queen of England, 1553–8. She married Philip of Spain in 1554. Tennyson made her the subject of a drama.

Mary II, eldest child of James II, queen of England, 1689–94, and consort of William III, whom she married in 1677. Her little-known 'Memoirs' were edited by R. Doebner in 1886.

Mary Barton, *a Tale of Manchester Life,* a novel by Mrs. Gaskell (q.v.), published in 1848. It was written soon after, and under the influence of, the death of her infant son.

The background of the story is Manchester in the 'hungry forties' of the last century, a period of acute distress in the industrial districts. John Barton, a steady, thoughtful workman, is one of the sufferers, and various circumstances have rendered him an active and embittered trade unionist. A group of workmen, driven to desperation, decide to kill one of the employers, young Henry Carson, as a warning to the class, and the lot falls on Barton to do the deed. Meanwhile Barton's daughter, Mary, has attracted the admiration of Henry Carson; she has been flattered by his attentions and the hope of a grand marriage, and has repulsed in his favour her lover in her own class, a brave young engineer, Jem Wilson. But she has come to her senses, discovered that her real love is for the latter, and endeavoured to break with Carson. At this moment Carson is shot dead by some person unknown, and circumstances point strongly to Jem Wilson, his rival, as the murderer, while Mary discovers that in fact it is her father who has done the deed. Jem is tried for his life and is saved by Mary's desperate and finally successful efforts to prove his innocence, while not betraying her father. The latter, brought by mental anguish to the verge of death, finally confesses his crime to the fiercely vindictive old father of Henry Carson, and wins his forgiveness as he dies.

The author's emphasis on the lack of sympathy shown by the employers for their workers provoked much criticism as being unjust, but the literary merits of the work were fully recognized.

Mary Celeste, The, an American brig bound from New York to Genoa, picked up in the North Atlantic by a British barque on 5 Dec. 1872, derelict but in perfect condition. The ship's boats were missing and the fate of the crew is unknown; it is one of the unsolved 'mysteries of the sea'.

Mary Graham, a character in Dickens's 'Martin Chuzzlewit' (q.v.).

Mary Magdalene, ST., see *Magdalen*.

Mary Magdalene, *Play of,* the single surviving English drama of the late ME. period that is based on the legend of a saint (see *Miracle Plays*). It presents events in the saint's life both before the Resurrection and during her subsequent legendary residence in Provence.

Mary Morison, of Burns's song, was possibly Alison Begbie, an early love of the poet.

Mary Queen of Scots (MARY STUART) (1542–87), daughter of James V of Scotland, married to Francis II of France (1558), to Lord Darnley (1565), and to Bothwell (1567). She was imprisoned by Elizabeth and finally beheaded on a charge of conspiring against the latter's life. She figures in Scott's 'The Abbot' (q.v.), and is the subject of a tragedy by Schiller (q.v.), of a trilogy of plays by Swinburne (q.v.), and of the novel 'The Queen's Quair' (q.v.) by Maurice Hewlett; she also figures in Maurice Baring's 'In My End is My Beginning' (1931).

Marylebone, a district of London, north of Oxford Street. The old church of St. John's, Tyburn (q.v.), stood in a lonely spot on the Tyburn Road, now Oxford Street, and was in the 15th cent. replaced by the church of St. Mary, nearer Tyburn village. This village thenceforth took the name of St. Mary le Bourne. The greater part of the old manor was acquired by the duke of Newcastle; it passed by marriage to the second earl of Oxford, from whom Oxford Street (q.v.) is named.

Marys, THE QUEEN'S, see *Queen's Maries*.

Marys, THE THREE, AT THE CROSS, were Mary the mother of Jesus, Mary the wife of Cleophas (a disciple), and Mary Magdalene (John xix. 25).

Mas John or MESS JOHN, a term applied jocularly or contemptuously to a Scottish Presbyterian clergyman (shortened from Master John).

Masaccio (1401–27/9), Florentine painter, whose real name was TOMMASO DI GIOVANNI. He was the first painter to express the ideas of the Renaissance in the grandeur of his figures, and in the rendering of space and solidity of form.

Masaniello (TOMMASO ANIELLO), a Neapolitan fisherman, who in 1647 led a revolt of the inhabitants of Naples against their Spanish rulers. He was assassinated after the tem-

porary success of the revolt. He is the subject of an opera by Auber.

Mascarille, a type of clever impudent valet, occurring in three of Molière's comedies, 'L'Étourdi', 'Le Dépit amoureux', and 'Les Précieuses ridicules'. In this last it is he who, in the character of a marquis and in the clothes of his master, makes love to the *précieuses*, in order to render them ridiculous.

MASEFIELD, JOHN, O.M. (1878–1967), ran away to sea early in life (an experience of which there are reminiscences in his narrative poem 'Dauber', 1913), went to America, where he undertook various humble occupations, and on his return to England became a journalist on the staff of the 'Manchester Guardian'. He then settled in London and during the first ten years of this century wrote poems ('Salt-Water Ballads', 1902, containing the well-known 'I must go down to the sea again', 'Ballads and Poems', 1910); collections of short stories ('A Mainsail Haul', 1905; 'A Tarpaulin Muster', 1907); plays ('The Tragedy of Nan', 1909; 'The Tragedy of Pompey the Great', 1910); and essays. In 1911 appeared his remarkable poem 'The Everlasting Mercy', the realistic story of the conversion of the ruffianly Saul Kane, followed by 'The Widow in the Bye Street' (1912), 'Dauber' and 'The Daffodil Fields' (1913), and 'Reynard the Fox' (1919). His later plays include 'The Faithful' (1915), 'Good Friday' (1916), and 'The Coming of Christ' (1928). Among his other works may be mentioned the novels, 'Captain Margaret' (1908), 'Multitude and Solitude' (1909), 'Lost Endeavour' (1910), 'Sard Harker' (1924), 'Odtaa' (1926), 'The Hawbucks' (1929), 'The Bird of Dawning' (1933); the poems, 'Lollingdon Downs' (1917), 'A Tale of Troy' (1932), 'A Letter from Pontus' (1936), 'Land Workers' (1942), and 'Collected Poems' (1946); his edition of the 'Chronicles of the Pilgrim Fathers' (1910); also the account of the evacuation of Dunkirk, 'The Nine Days Wonder' (1941), and 'So Long to Learn' (1952), which is autobiographical. He was appointed poet laureate in 1930.

Masks or MASQUES, dramatic entertainments, involving dances and disguises, in which the spectacular and musical elements predominated over plot and character. They were acted by amateurs, and were popular at court and among the nobility. They were perhaps of Italian origin, but assumed a distinctive character in England in the 16th and 17th cents. Many of the great dramatic writers, Beaumont, Middleton, Chapman, wrote masques, and they reached their highest degree of elaboration in the hands of Ben Jonson (q.v.), who introduced the 'antimasque' and an element of Aristophanic comedy. The great architect, Inigo Jones (q.v.), designed the machinery and decorations for some of them. Ben Jonson's 'The Sad Shepherd' (q.v.), Fletcher's 'The Faithful Shepherdess' (q.v.), Randolph's 'Amyntas' (q.v.), and Milton's 'Comus' (q.v.), though sometimes described as masques, are strictly pastoral dramas.

Masks and Faces, see *Peg Woffington.*

Maskwell, the 'Double Dealer' in Congreve's comedy of that name (q.v.), 'a sedate, thinking villain, whose black blood runs temperately bad'.

MASON, ALFRED EDWARD WOODLEY (1865–1948), author of many novels, including 'The Four Feathers', 'At the Villa Rose', 'The House of the Arrow', 'No other Tiger', 'Running Water'.

Mason and Dixon Line, THE, the boundary established in 1763–7 between Virginia and Pennsylvania by Charles Mason and Jeremiah Dixon, English astronomers, employed by William Penn and Lord Baltimore for the purpose. The line was of special interest at a later date as separating the slave States from the free States (see also *Dixie*).

Mason and Slidell, see *Trent Case.*

Masons' Marks, see *Freemasons.*

Masora(h) or MASSORA(H), the body of traditional information relating to the text of the Hebrew Bible, compiled by Jewish scholars in the tenth and preceding centuries; or the collection of critical notes in which this information is preserved. Also occasionally used as a collective name for the scholars (*Masoretes*) whose opinions are embodied in the *Masora*, and to whom is ascribed the constitution of the present Hebrew text and the addition of the vowel points, etc.

Masques, see *Masks.*

Massacre of St. Bartholomew, see *Bartholomew (Massacre of St.).*

Massey, BARTLE, a character in George Eliot's 'Adam Bede' (q.v.).

Massillon, JEAN BAPTISTE (1663–1742), a celebrated French divine and court preacher in the reign of Louis XIV.

MASSINGER, PHILIP (1583–1640), was born at Salisbury, and educated at St. Alban Hall, Oxford. His father had been in the service of the Herbert family, to members of which the poet addressed various dedications and other pieces. He soon became a famous playwright, collaborating frequently with Fletcher, and also with Nathaniel Field and Dekker. He was buried at St. Saviour's, Southwark.

The principal surviving plays entirely written by him are 'The Duke of Milan' (q.v., 1623), 'The Bondman' (1624), 'The Renegado' (1630), 'The Unnatural Combat' (1639), 'The Parliament of Love' (licensed, 1624), 'The Roman Actor' (q.v., 1629), 'The Maid of Honour' (q.v., 1632), 'The Picture' (1630), 'The Emperor of the East' (1632), 'A New Way to pay Old Debts' (q.v., 1633), 'The Great Duke of Florence' (q.v., 1636), 'Believe as you list' ('Stationers' Register',

1653), 'The Guardian' and 'The Bashful Lover' (1655), 'The City Madam' (q.v., 1658). In collaboration with Fletcher he wrote 'The False One', 'The Elder Brother', and 'The Custom of the Country'. Some see his hand also in portions of 'Henry VIII' and of 'Two Noble Kinsmen' (q.v., 1634), in both of which a share is attributed to Shakespeare. In collaboration with Dekker he wrote 'The Virgin Martyr' (q.v., 1622); and with Field 'The Fatal Dowry' (q.v., 1632). His principal field was the romantic drama, of which his best examples are perhaps 'The Duke of Milan', 'The Great Duke of Florence', and 'The Fatal Dowry' (qq.v.). His best-known work is the fine comedy 'A New Way to pay Old Debts' (q.v.). His political views in favour of the popular party, and his religious views in sympathy with the Church of Rome, are freely indicated in his plays; in 'The Bondman' he denounced Buckingham under the guise of Gisco.

MASSON, DAVID (1822–1907), educated at Aberdeen University, was professor of rhetoric and English literature at Edinburgh University, 1865–95. His most important published work was his standard 'Life of Milton' (1859–80). He started 'Macmillan's Magazine' in 1859 and edited it till 1867. His voluminous writings include biographies of Drummond of Hawthornden (1873) and De Quincey (1878), and editions of Milton, Goldsmith, and De Quincey.

Massorah, MASSORETE, see *Masorah.*

Master Humphrey's Clock, the framework, soon abandoned, in which Dickens set his novels 'The Old Curiosity Shop' and 'Barnaby Rudge' (qq.v.).

Master of Ballantrae, The, a novel by R. L. Stevenson (q.v.), published in 1889.

It is the story of the lifelong feud between the Master of Ballantrae, violent and unscrupulous, and his younger brother Henry, at the outset a quiet, honest fellow. The Master joins Prince Charles Edward in the '45, disappears after Culloden, and is believed dead. After many adventures the Master returns, with a price on his head, to find that Henry has succeeded to his place and to the woman whom he was to have married. Embittered by misfortune, he enters on a course of persecution, first in Scotland, then America, which finally drives Henry mad, and brings both brothers to an untimely grave.

Master of the Sentences, Peter Lombard (q.v.).

MASTERS, EDGAR LEE (1869–1950), American poet and novelist. His best-known work is 'The Spoon River Anthology' (1916), a series of confessions and revelations from beyond the grave by the former inhabitants of a Middle Western village.

Matamoro (Spanish, 'slayer of Moors'), the Bobadil of Spanish comedy.

Matchless Orinda, THE, see *Philips (K.).*

Materialism, in philosophy, the opinion that nothing exists except matter and its movements and modifications; also, in a more limited sense, the opinion that the phenomena of consciousness and will are wholly due to the operation of material agencies.

MATHER, COTTON (1663–1728), Presbyterian divine of Boston, America, a narrow, self-righteous minister and voluminous writer, one of the best-known examples of the tyrannical Puritan ministers of his time in New England. He was noted for the part he played in the Salem witchcraft trials of 1692, on which he commented in his best-known work, 'Magnalia Christi Americana' (1702).

Mathias, the chief character in 'The Bells' (q.v.).

MATHIAS, THOMAS JAMES (1754?– 1835), educated at Trinity College, Cambridge, became librarian at Buckingham Palace. In 1794 he published his 'Pursuits of Literature', a vigorous satire on contemporary authors, which went through sixteen editions and provoked many replies.

Matisse, HENRI, see *Fauves (Les)*.

Matsya, in Hindu mythology, the incarnation of Vishnu (q.v.) as a fish.

MATTHEW PARIS, see *Paris (M.)*.

Matthew's Bible, see *Bible (The English)*.

Matthews, MISS, a character in Fielding's 'Amelia' (q.v.).

Matty Jenkyns, MISS, the principal character in Mrs. Gaskell's 'Cranford' (q.v.).

MATURIN, CHARLES ROBERT (1782– 1824), educated at Trinity College, Dublin, took orders and for a time kept a school. He was one of the principal writers of the terror or mystery novels called 'Gothic novels' (q.v.). He published 'The Fatal Revenge, or the Family of Montorio' in 1807, 'The Wild Irish Boy' in 1808, and 'The Milesian Chief' in 1811. In 1816 his tragedy 'Bertram' was produced by Kean at Drury Lane, on the recommendation of Scott and Byron, with great success. He then returned to novels, publishing 'Women, or Pour et Contre' (a powerful story, turning on the rivalry of a mother and daughter for the love of the same man) in 1818, and his masterpiece, 'Melmoth the Wanderer' (q.v.), in 1820. His last novel, 'The Albigenses', was published in 1824. Maturin's other tragedies, 'Manuel' (1817) and 'Fredolfo' (1819), were failures.

Maud, a poem by A. Tennyson (q.v.), published in 1855.

The poem is a monodrama in sections of different metres, in which the narrator, a man of morbid and unbalanced temperament, gives voice to his feelings at various stages of the story: first lamenting the mysterious death of his father, and his family's ruin by the contrivance of the old lord of the Hall; then expressing the gradual development of his love for Maud, the old lord's daughter, in spite of the scorn of her brother and the rivalry of a 'new-made lord', 'first of his noble line'; his triumph at winning the love of Maud; the fatal encounter with the brother; his own flight abroad and the madness that follows the blighting of his hopes; and his final reawakening to life in the service of his country. The poem contains several of Tennyson's best love-lyrics ('I have led her home', 'Come into the garden, Maud', etc.); but some of the opinions expressed or implied in it, notably the approval of war in certain circumstances, were distasteful to many.

MAUGHAM, WILLIAM SOMERSET (1874–1965), author, among whose chief works are: 'Liza of Lambeth' (1897), 'Of Human Bondage' (1915), 'The Moon and Sixpence' (1919), 'The Painted Veil' (1925), 'Cakes and Ale' (1930), 'The Razor's Edge' (1944), all novels; 'A Man of Honour' (1904), 'Lady Frederick' (1907), 'Home and Beauty' (1919), 'The Circle' (1921), 'East of Suez' (1922), 'Our Betters' (1923), 'The Constant Wife' (1927), 'For Services Rendered' (1932), 'Sheppey' (1933), plays; 'The Trembling of a Leaf' (1921), 'On a Chinese Screen' (1923), 'Ashenden' (1928), short stories. Several of his short stories have been dramatized.

Maugis, a hero of the Charlemagne romances, the French equivalent of Malagigi (q.v.), a wizard who aids the emperor's cause.

Maugrabin, HAYRADDIN, a character in Scott's 'Quentin Durward' (q.v.). *Maugrabin* is an Arabic word meaning 'man of the West', an African Moor.

Maul, in Pt. II of Bunyan's 'Pilgrim's Progress' (q.v.), a giant slain by Mr. Greatheart.

Maule, MATTHEW, a character in Hawthorne's 'House of the Seven Gables' (q.v.).

Maumet, see *Mammet*.

Maundy, from Latin *mandatum*, a commandment, the ceremony of washing the feet of a number of poor people, performed by royal or other eminent persons, or ecclesiastics, on the Thursday before Easter, and commonly followed by the distribution of clothing, food, or money. It was instituted in commemoration of Christ's washing the Apostles' feet at the Last Supper.

MAUPASSANT, GUY DE (1850–93), French novelist of the naturalistic school, a master of the short story, and a disciple of Gustave Flaubert (q.v.). His most remarkable work is the short story 'Boule de Suif', an audacious tale of an episode in the Franco-German war. 'La Maison Tellier', 'Mademoiselle Fifi', 'Miss Harriet', 'Monsieur Parent' are other familiar titles. Besides several collections of short stories he wrote six novels; the best, 'Pierre et Jean' (1888), is a study of the havoc wrought by jealousy. 'Une Vie' (1883) and 'Bel Ami' (1885) are also notable.

Mauretania, in ancient geography, the western part of North Africa, having Numidia on the east and Gaetulia on the south; the country of the *Mauri* or Moors. It became a Roman province in A.D. 40.

MAURIAC, FRANÇOIS (1885–   ), French novelist, dramatist, and critic, author of: 'Thérèse Desqueyroux' (1927) and other short psychological tales set usually in the 'Landes' country round Bordeaux; 'Le Noeud de Vipères' (1932) and 'Le Mystère Fontenac' (1933), longer studies of family life; 'Asmodée' (1938) and 'Les Mal Aimés' (1945), dramas, etc. His characters are fettered by prosperous bourgeois convention and by religion and human frailty.

MAURICE, JOHN FREDERICK DENISON (1805–72), the son of a Unitarian minister, and educated at Trinity Hall, Cambridge. He took orders in the Church of England and felt himself called to the pursuit of religious unity. The basis of his theological belief was the infinite love of God for all his creatures, and he attacked any theological doctrines that appeared to him to conflict with this. He declared himself a Christian socialist, believing that 'a true socialism is the necessary result of a sound Christianity'. He was chaplain at Guy's Hospital, London, 1836–46, and subsequently held other incumbencies. He was professor of English literature and history at King's College, London, 1840–53, and was dismissed in the latter year because of his unorthodoxy on the subject of Eternal Punishment. He was appointed professor of moral philosophy at Cambridge in 1866. His religious views are principally contained in his 'The Religions of the World' (1847) and 'Theological Essays' (1853). A treatise by him on 'Moral and Metaphysical Philosophy', in the main an historical account of early thought, appeared in 1847 in the 'Encyclopaedia Metropolitana'. One of his most popular works, 'The Kingdom of Christ', a plea for religious unity, appeared in 1838. Tennyson's lyric to him is well known.

Maurists, a congregation of French Benedictine monks, named after St. Maurus, the legendary founder of the Benedictine rule in France. The Maurist congregation was established in 1618 with a view to the reform of the Benedictine order. But it became famous for the learning and literary industry of its members even more than for their monastic zeal. Under the impulse of its first superior-general, Dom Tarisse, it carried out an immense amount of historical and critical work, in connexion with patristic and biblical literature, monastic and ecclesiastical history, collections of documents, palaeography, and other branches of technical erudition. Its chief house was at St. Germain-des-Prés near Paris.

MAUROIS, ANDRÉ (1885–   ), French author of biography: 'Ariel' (Shelley, 1923), 'Disraëli' (1927), 'Byron' (1930), 'À la recherche de Marcel Proust' (1949), 'Lélia'

(i.e. George Sand, 1952), etc.; histories of England (1937) and the United States (1948); novels: 'Climats' (1929), 'Le Cercle de famille' (1932), etc.; also of the early 'Silences du Colonel Bramble' (1918), sketches of an English officers' mess.

Mause Headrigg, in Scott's 'Old Mortality' (q.v.), the zealous covenanting mother of Cuddie, the ploughman.

Mausōlus, a king of Caria (377–353 B.C.) and husband of Artemisia (q.v.), who erected to his memory a magnificent monument called the MAUSOLEUM at Halicarnassus, *c.* 350 B.C., one of the seven wonders of the world.

MAVOR, O. H., see *Bridie (J.).*

Mawworm, see *Bickerstaffe.*

MAX MÜLLER, FRIEDRICH (1823–1900), son of the German poet Wilhelm Müller, was born at Dessau and educated at Leipzig. He was naturalized a British subject under the name of Frederick Max-Müller. He came to England in 1846 and was commissioned by the directors of the East India Company to bring out an edition of the Sanskrit 'Rigveda' (see *Veda*), which was published in 1849–73. He settled at Oxford in 1848 and was Taylorian professor of modern European languages from 1854 to 1868, and one of the curators of the Bodleian Library, 1856–63 and 1881–94. Max Müller delivered two remarkable courses of lectures on 'The Science of Languages' at the Royal Institution in 1861–4, and was professor of comparative philology at Oxford from 1868 till his death, though he retired from the active duties of the chair in 1875. He devoted much attention to comparative mythology and the comparative study of religions. He edited, from 1875, the 'Sacred Books of the East', a series of English translations of the oriental religious classics. A collected edition of Max Müller's essays, entitled 'Chips from a German Workshop', appeared in 1867–75. A full edition of his works, which dealt with the great variety of subjects indicated above, and others, was published in 1903.

Maximin, a character in Dryden's 'Tyrannic Love' (q.v.).

MAXWELL, JAMES CLERK-, see *Clerk-Maxwell.*

MAY, THOMAS (1595–1650), educated at Sidney Sussex College, Cambridge, adopted the parliamentary cause and was secretary for the parliament (1646). He was author of two narrative poems on the reigns of Edward III and Henry II, and of a 'History of the Long Parliament' (1647). He also wrote translations of the 'Georgics' and of Lucan's 'Pharsalia' (which were praised by Ben Jonson), two comedies, 'The Heir' and 'The Old Couple' (*c.* 1620), and tragedies on classical subjects ('Antigone'; 'Cleopatra', 1626; 'Julia Agrippina', 1628). Marvell speaks of his 'most servile wit and mercenary pen'.

MAY, Sir THOMAS ERSKINE, *first Baron Farnborough* (1815–86), clerk of the House of Commons, 1871–86, was author of the standard work, 'The Rules, Orders and Proceedings of the House of Commons' (1854), and of 'The Constitutional History of England since the accession of George III' (1861–3), a continuation of Hallam's treatise.

May Day, the 1st of May, celebrated with garlands and dancing, the choice of a queen of the May (gaily dressed and crowned with flowers), the erection of a Maypole (painted with spiral stripes and decked with flowers) to dance round, and so forth. Perhaps derived from the Roman *Floralia*. The MAY-GAME was a set performance in the May-day festivities, in which Robin Hood and Maid Marian figured. May Day was adopted in 1889 as the international Labour holiday.

Maya, the name of an ancient race of Mexican and Central American Indians, noted for their architecture, stone-carving, pottery, and textiles. A feature of their architecture was the stepped pyramidal mound; the arch was unknown to them. The Maya had pictographic records of their history. Their art, which is of uncertain date, came to an end with the Spanish conquest.

MAYAKOVSKY, VLADIMIR VLADIMIROVICH (1893–1930), Russian Futurist poet. He joined the Bolshevik Party at the age of 14, and political and social themes are prominent in his work. In 1912 he signed the Cubo-Futurist Manifesto, rejecting the language and literature of the past. In 1923 he attempted to found a Soviet school of Futurism ('Left Front') but with little success. In 1930 he committed suicide. Mayakovsky was a linguistic and metric innovator; his verse was violent and sometimes coarse, full of extravagant conceits and original metaphors, often satirical and propagandistic. His best-known poems are 'A Cloud in Trousers' (1915), '150,000,000' (1922), 'About This' (1923). He also wrote plays, the best known being 'The Bedbug' (1928). The first translations of Mayakovsky appeared in 1929. The most complete translation is by H. Marshall (1942). 'The Bedbug' was translated in 1961 by M. Hayward and G. Reavey.

Mayfair, a district north of Piccadilly, London, so called from an annual fair held there in the month of May from Stuart times until the reign of George III (temporarily suppressed in 1708). Mayfair was, from about 1800 to 1914, the 'smart' quarter of London. It has now lost its exclusive character, and business premises are to be seen in its greatest squares.

Mayflower, *The,* the ship in which the Pilgrim Fathers sailed from Plymouth in 1620 to Cape Cod, Massachusetts, where they founded New Plymouth.

May-game, see *May Day.*

MAYHEW, HENRY (1812–87), a London

solicitor's son who turned from a legal apprenticeship to play-writing and popular journalism. He was one of the original proprietors of 'Punch' (q.v.) and co-editor with Mark Lemon during its first year. His great sociological study, 'London Labour and the London Poor' (4 vols., 1861–2), which began with a series of articles (1849–50) for 'The Morning Chronicle' (q.v.), is a record of his investigations into the life and work of the poor and underprivileged, often told in the words of the people he talked to. A volume of selections from 'London Labour and the London Poor', chosen by J. L. Bradley, was published in 1965.

Maylie, Mrs. and Harry, characters in Dickens's 'Oliver Twist' (q.v.).

Mayor of Casterbridge, The, a novel by Hardy (q.v.), published in 1886.

Michael Henchard, a hay-tresser, when drunk at a fair, sells his wife and child for five guineas to a sailor, Newson. Returning to his senses he takes a solemn vow not to touch intoxicants for twenty years. By his energy he becomes rich, respected, and the mayor of Casterbridge (Dorchester). After eighteen years his wife returns, Newson being then supposed dead, and is reunited to her husband; she brings with her her daughter, Elizabeth-Jane, and Henchard is led to believe that Elizabeth-Jane is his child, whereas she is Newson's. Trouble soon comes, owing to the wrong-headedness of Henchard. He quarrels with his capable assistant in his corn business, Donald Farfrae. Mrs. Henchard dies, and Henchard learns the truth about the girl. Farfrae becomes Henchard's successful rival in business and in love and marries the woman that Henchard had hoped to win. Henchard is ruined, the story of the sale of his wife is revealed, and he takes to drink. His stepdaughter is his only comfort, and Newson returns and claims her. Henchard becomes lonelier and more desolate, and dies wretchedly in a hut on Egdon Heath.

Mayor of Garratt, see *Garratt.*

Mayor of London, Lord: the first mayor of London on record is Henry FitzAylwin (1189), the appointment replacing that of sheriff or portreeve, whom Henry I had allowed the citizens to elect. But the mayor was still occasionally appointed by the king, for instance Richard Whittington by Richard II. The title of 'Lord Mayor' became current in Richard III's reign [Loftie].

Mayor of the Palace, the title borne by the steward of the royal household and principal political agent of the Merovingian (q.v.) kings of France. The mayors of the palace gradually became the real rulers of the country, and finally, in the person of Pepin the Short, ascended the throne.

Maypole in the Strand, The, stood near the present church of St. Mary le Strand. Aubrey says that at the restoration maypoles were set up at every crossway, 'the most prodigious one for height' 'at the Strand near Drury Lane'. It was broken by a high wind in 1672. Strype says it was taken down and removed to Wansted in Essex, where it served the Rev. Mr. Pound for raising a telescope.

Mazarin, JULES (1602–61), of an ancient Sicilian family, was sent as papal legate to Paris in 1634, attracted the notice of Richelieu, entered the French service, and was made a cardinal in 1641. He succeeded Richelieu as prime minister, was retained in that office by the queen regent (Anne of Austria) on the death of Louis XIII, and governed France during the minority of Louis XIV. His internal administration provoked the civil wars of the Fronde (q.v.). He founded a splendid library in Paris, the *Bibliothèque Mazarine*.

Mazarin Bible, THE, the first printed bible, and probably the first book to be printed with movable type, *c.* 1455, attributed to Gutenberg (q.v.) but perhaps by Fust (q.v.) and Schöffer. The first known copy was discovered in the Mazarine Library (see preceding entry) in Paris. It is also known as the 'forty-two line Bible' from the number of lines to the column.

Mazdeism or MAZDAISM, the ancient Persian religion as taught in the Avesta; Zoroastrianism (q.v.).

Mazeppa, a poem by Lord Byron (q.v.), published in 1819.

The poem is founded on a passage in Voltaire's 'Charles XII'. Ivan Stepanovich Mazeppa, a Polish nobleman, born about 1645, became in later life hetman (military commander) of the Eastern Ukraine. He abandoned his allegiance to Peter the Great and fought on the side of Charles XII of Sweden at the battle of Pultowa (1709). While the king and his band rest under an oak after their defeat, Mazeppa tells a tale of his early life, when he was a page to Casimir V, king of Poland. Being detected in an intrigue with the wife of a local magnate, he had been bound naked on the back of a wild horse of the Ukraine, which was then loosed and lashed into madness. The horse galloped off, through forest and river, carrying his torn and fainting rider, never stopping till he reached the plains of the Ukraine, where he fell dead. Mazeppa, himself at the point of death, was rescued by peasants.

Mazzini, GIUSEPPE (1805?–72), Italian patriot and revolutionary agitator, born at Genoa, was imprisoned in 1830 on a charge of political conspiracy, and subsequently resided in France and later in London, where he actively plotted for the liberation of Italy and its union under a republican government. He returned to Rome during the revolutionary movement in 1848, but was once more driven into exile. He fomented risings in Italian cities, but his activities impeded rather than assisted the policy of Cavour (q.v.) and contributed little directly to the

liberation. Mazzini remained a republican and refused allegiance to Victor Emmanuel.

M.B. Waistcoat, THE: '[the undivided clerical waistcoat] was deemed so distinctly Popish, that it acquired the nickname of "The Mark of the Beast" and ... among the tailors ... was familiarly known as "the M.B. waistcoat" ' (W. E. Gladstone in 'Contemporary Review', Oct. 1874).

Meagles, MR., MRS., and their daughter PET, characters in Dickens's 'Little Dorrit' (q.v.).

Meal-tub Plot, THE, the pretended conspiracy of the duke of Monmouth in 1679, the papers of which were said to be kept in a meal-tub.

Meander, see *Maeander*.

Meanjin Quarterly, a review of literature and art in Australia, founded in 1940 and edited by C. B. Christesen. The title (pronounced Me-an'-jin) is taken from the aboriginal name for Brisbane, where the magazine was first published.

Measure for Measure, a comedy by Shakespeare (q.v.), probably first acted in 1604, but not printed till the folio of 1623. The plot is taken from Cinthio (q.v.) (translated by Whetstone (q.v.)).

The duke of Vienna, on the pretext of a journey to Poland, hands over the government to Angelo, that he may escape the odium of enforcing laws against unchastity that have long been disregarded. Angelo at once sentences to death Claudio as guilty of seduction. Claudio sends word of his position to his sister Isabella, a novice, and begs her to intercede with Angelo. Isabella's prayers fail to win her brother's pardon, but her beauty awakens Angelo's passion, and, at a second interview, he offers her her brother's life if she will sacrifice to him her honour. Isabella indignantly refuses; and there follows the famous scene in the prison, when Isabella tells her brother of Angelo's offer, and he, momentarily weakening, pleads with her for his life. Meanwhile the duke, who has not left Vienna, but assumed the disguise of a friar, and thus learnt the infamous conduct of Angelo, contrives the saving of Claudio as follows. He bids Isabella consent to go to Angelo's house at midnight, and obtains that Mariana, who had been betrothed to Angelo and loves him, but had been cast off by him, shall go there in Isabella's place. The ruse is successful; but none the less Angelo orders Claudio's execution at dawn. The provost of the prison disobeys. The duke, laying aside his friar's robes and simulating an unexpected return to Vienna, hears the complaint of Isabella and the suit of Mariana, and confutes Angelo, who denies their stories. Angelo is pardoned at the instance of Mariana and Isabella, and married to the former; and the duke reveals his love for Isabella. The play contains the beautiful song, 'Take, O take those lips away'.

Meaux, The Bishop of, Bossuet (q.v.).

Mecca, in Arabia, the birthplace of Mohammed (q.v.), and the chief place of pilgrimage of the Muslims.

Mechitarists, see *Mekhitarists.*

Medal, The, a satirical poem by Dryden (q.v.), published in 1682.

The grand jury of Middlesex having thrown out the bill for high treason against the earl of Shaftesbury in 1681, the triumph of the Whigs was celebrated by the striking of a medal with the legend 'Laetamur'. Thereupon Dryden wrote this poem. It is a bitter attack on Shaftesbury, but contains none of the scurrilities to be found in 'Absalom and Achitophel' (q.v.). Instead it ridicules the policy of demagogic appeal to the people. It was prefaced by a prose 'Epistle to the Whigs'.

These attacks called forth a number of replies, including the 'Medal of John Bayes' by Shadwell (q.v.) and 'The Medal Revers'd' by Samuel Pordage.

Medea, in Greek mythology, a magician, daughter of Aeētes, king of Colchis. When Jason (q.v.) came to Colchis in quest of the golden fleece, he and Medea fell in love. After Jason had with her help overcome all the difficulties placed by Aeētes in his way, Jason and Medea embarked to return to Greece; and to delay the pursuit of her father, Medea tore to pieces her brother Absyrtus and left his mangled limbs on the way that Aeētes would pass. On their arrival at Iolcos, Medea restored Jason's father Aeson to youth by boiling him in a cauldron with magic herbs. The daughters of Pelias, king of Iolcos, were also desirous to see their father rejuvenated, and encouraged by Medea, who wished to revenge the injuries that her husband's family had suffered from Pelias, they killed Pelias and boiled his flesh in a cauldron; but Medea refused to restore him. Driven in consequence from Iolcos, Jason and Medea fled to Corinth, where Jason deserted her for Glaucē, the daughter of the king. Medea avenged herself by killing the two children she had had by Jason and destroying Glaucē. She then married Aegeus, the father of Theseus, plotted to poison the latter for fear of his influence, and finally escaped to Asia. One of the tragedies of Euripides has Medea for its subject.

Medes, The, the earliest Iranian inhabitants of Persia. The *Law of the Medes and Persians* is proverbially immutable (Dan. vi. 8).

Medici, The, the family that were rulers of Florence from 1434 and grand dukes of Tuscany from 1569 to 1737. The earlier Medici were great patrons of art and literature, chief among them Cosimo (1389–1464) and Lorenzo 'The Magnificent' (*c.* 1449–92), founders of the Medicean or Laurentian Library (q.v.). The latter, himself a poet, was father of Pope Leo X (q.v.). Clement VII

also belonged to this family. Catherine de Médicis (as she is known in France, 1519–89), daughter of the grandson of Lorenzo the Magnificent, was consort of Henry II of France, and regent during the minority of Charles IX. Marie de Médicis (1573–1642), niece of the grand duke of Tuscany, was consort of Henry IV of France from 1600, and regent 1610–17.

Medina, in Arabia, the second great city of the Muslims, to which Mohammed went at the Flight or *Hijra* (q.v.), and where he died and was buried.

Medina, in Spenser's 'Faerie Queene', II. ii, represents the golden mean, her sisters Elissa and Perissa representing the extremes, of sensibility.

Mediolanum, in imprints, Milan.

Medmenham Abbey, a ruined Cistercian abbey on the bank of the Thames near Marlow, rebuilt as a residence and notorious in the 18th cent. as the meeting-place of a convivial club known as the Franciscans or the Hell-fire Club. This was founded by Sir Francis Dashwood, and Wilkes and Bubb Dodington were among its members. Its motto 'Fay ce que voudras' was adopted from that of Rabelais's Abbey of Thelema (q.v.). There is a good deal about it in Johnstone's 'Chrysal, or the Adventures of a Guinea' (III. ii, chs. 17 et seq.).

Medora, a character in Byron's 'The Corsair' (q.v.).

Medoro, in the 'Orlando Furioso' (q.v.), a young Moor of humble birth, with whom Angelica (q.v.) falls in love and whom she marries, thereby causing the despair and madness of Orlando.

Medūsa, one of the three Gorgons (q.v.), and the only one that was mortal. According to Ovid, she incurred the resentment of Athene by granting her favours to Poseidon in the temple of the goddess, who changed the locks that Poseidon admired into serpents. For her destruction by Perseus, see under the name of the latter. See also *Pegasus.*

MEDWALL, HENRY, see *Fulgens and Lucrece.*

Meg Dods, see *Dods.*

Meg Merrilies, see *Merrilies.*

Meg Murdockson, see *Murdockson.*

Meg of Westminster, Long, the subject of ballads and pamphlets that appeared in 1582, 1590, and 1594, and referred to in Middleton and Dekker's 'Roaring Girl' (q.v.), and by Nash, Harvey, and other authors of the period. Her biography appeared in 1635. She was a Lancashire girl who came to London, served in an alehouse, included among her acquaintance Will Sommers, Henry VIII's fool, and Skelton, assumed man's clothes and went to the wars, married a soldier and set up a public house at Islington.

Megaera, one of the Furies (q.v.).

Megaric, the name of a school of philosophy founded about 400 B.C. by Eucleides of Megara, a disciple of Socrates, noted for its study of dialectics and its invention of logical fallacies or puzzles (Jebb).

Megatherium, THE, a club mentioned in several of Thackeray's novels, e.g. 'The Newcomes' (v), 'Philip' (v, ix), etc.

Mein Kampf, see *Hitler.*

MEINHOLD, JOHANN WILHELM (1797–1851), German theologian and writer, a pastor in various parishes of Pomerania, author of 'Maria Schweidler die Bernstein-hexe' (1843), translated into English by Lady Duff Gordon as 'The Amber Witch' (q.v.); and of 'Sidonia von Bork, die Klosterhexe', translated into English by Lady Wilde as 'Sidonia the Sorceress'.

Meiōsis, an under-statement, sometimes ironical or humorous and intended to emphasize the size, importance, etc., of what is belittled. Except in *litotes* (q.v.), which is a form of meiosis, the use of meiosis is chiefly colloquial; e.g. the use of 'rather' as a strong affirmative, 'I should rather think so'.

Meistersinger, a title taken in the 15th cent. by certain professional German poets of high skill and culture, to distinguish themselves from the wandering gleemen. They were often craftsmen in their ordinary avocations —smiths, weavers, and the like. They represent a phase of the development of German verse from the minnesang (see *Minnesingers*). The Meistersang and singer were governed by an elaborate set of rules and organization, which are depicted in Wagner's opera on the subject, 'Die Meistersinger von Nürnberg', produced in 1868.

Mekhitarists, a congregation of Armenian monks of the Roman Catholic Church, originally founded at Constantinople in 1701 by Mekhitar, an Armenian, and by him finally established in 1717 in the island of San Lazzaro, south of Venice. They have devoted themselves to literary work and published ancient manuscripts relating to the Armenians.

Mel, THE GREAT, see *Evan Harrington.*

Melampus, the son of Amythaon, was regarded by the ancients as the first mortal to receive prophetic powers and to practise medicine, and as the founder of the worship of Dionysus in Greece. He took care of some young serpents whose parents had been killed by his servants, and these one day licked his ears as he was sleeping. On awakening he found that he understood the language of birds and could predict the future. His brother Bias sought the hand of Pero, daughter of Neleus, but the latter would give her only to the man who brought him the oxen of Iphiclus. Melampus obtained them for Bias, by the services he rendered to Iphiclus

through his prophetic powers. He cured the women of Argos of an epidemic of frenzy, and obtained in consequence a share of that kingdom.

Melampus is the subject of a poem by G. Meredith (q.v.).

Melanchthon, the graecized name of PHILIP SCHWARTZERD (1497–1560), German humanist who was professor of Greek at Wittenberg University; one of the principal advocates of the Reformation.

Melantius, a character in Beaumont and Fletcher's 'The Maid's Tragedy' (q.v.).

Melba, DAME NELLIE, the great singer, whose original name was Helen Porter Mitchell (1859–1931), was born near Melbourne of Scottish parents settled in Australia. Her first appearance on the operatic stage took place in 1887 at Brussels in the part of Gilda in 'Rigoletto'. In England she first appeared in 1888 in 'Lucia di Lammermoor'. The wonderful purity of her voice and her engaging personality won her immense fame and popularity.

Melbury, GRACE, a character in Thomas Hardy's 'The Woodlanders' (q.v.).

Melchior, one of the three Magi (q.v.) or 'Wise men of the East'. He is represented as a king of Nubia.

Melchizedek, in Gen. xiv. 18, king of Salem and the priest of the most high God, who blessed Abraham and to whom Abraham gave tithes of all. He is sometimes quoted as the type of self-originating power, with reference to the words concerning him in Heb. vii. 3–4: 'Without father, without mother, without descent, having neither beginning of days nor end of life. . . . Now consider how great this man was, unto whom even the patriarch Abraham gave a tenth of the spoils.'

Mĕlĕăger, son of Oeneus, king of Calydon, and Althaea. The Parcae were present at his birth: Clotho said that he would be courageous, Lachesis that he would be strong, Atropos that he would live as long as the brand that was on the fire was not consumed. Althaea snatched the brand from the fire and kept it with jealous care. Meleager took part in the expedition of the Argonauts (q.v.) and subsequently in the hunt of the Calydonian boar that was ravaging his father's country. He slew the boar and gave the head to Atalanta (q.v.), who had first wounded it. This partiality angered the brothers of Althaea and they endeavoured to rob Atalanta of the prize. Meleager defended her and slew his uncles. As Althaea was going to the temple to give thanks for her son's victory over the boar, she learnt that he had killed her brothers, and in the moment of resentment threw into the fire the fatal brand, and as soon as it was consumed Meleager died.

Melesĭgĕnĕs, an ancient epithet of Homer, indicating that he was born near the Meles, the name of a stream that flowed through

Smyrna, and bearing out the view that connects him with that city.

Meliadus, see *Meliodas*.

Meliagraunce, SIR, in Malory's 'Morte Darthur' (xix. ii), the knight who captures Queen Guinevere and carries her off to his castle. He is perhaps to be identified with Melwas, a god of the darkness in British mythology (Rhys, 'Arthurian Legend').

Melian Dialogue, THE, in Thucydides, v. 84 et seq., the discussion between the Athenian envoys and the magistrates of Melos, an island colonized by the Lacedaemonians which had refused to surrender to Athens and which consequently the Athenians were proposing to subdue (416 B.C.). It is an exposition of the *realpolitik* and jingoism of Athens.

Melibeus, The Tale of, see *Canterbury Tales* (19).

Meliboea, an ancient town on the coast of Thessaly, celebrated for its purple dye.

Melicertes, see *Ino*.

Melincourt, or Sir Oran Haut-ton, a novel by Peacock (q.v.), published in 1817.

The plot is, as usual in Peacock's novels, slight and unimportant, and is concerned with the attempts of various suitors to win the hand of the rich Anthelia Melincourt, attempts which bring together the usual collection of odd characters and give occasion for much discussion of slavery in the West Indies, rotten boroughs, the Lake poets, etc. A prominent feature in the story is Sir Oran Haut-ton (see under *Monboddo, Lord*), an orang-outang whom Mr. Sylvan Forester, a rich young philosopher, has educated to everything except speech, and for whom he has bought a baronetcy and a seat in parliament. He is an amiable and chivalrous gentleman, and plays delightfully on the flute. The book includes a virulent and unjustified attack on Southey (Mr. Feathernest), while Gifford (Mr. Vamp), Coleridge (Mr. Mystic), and Wordsworth (Mr. Paperstamp) come in for a share of the author's satire. Mr. Simon Sarcastic appears to represent the author himself. The book contains long discussions on social and economic questions between Mr. Forester and Mr. Fax (in whom some have seen a caricature of Malthus).

Meliodas or MELIADUS, in Malory's 'Morte Darthur' (q.v.), king of Lyonesse and father of Tristram.

Melisande or MELISINDA, a name sometimes apparently confused with *Melusina* (q.v.). The historical Melisinda was daughter of Baldwin II, king of Jerusalem, and wife of Fulk, who succeeded him. In Spanish romance, Melisenda or Melisendra is the daughter of Charlemagne (see under *Gayferos*). 'Pelléas et Mélisande' is one of the earlier plays of Maeterlinck (q.v.).

Melisendra, see preceding entry.

Melissa, in the 'Orlando Furioso' (q.v.), the beneficent witch who releases Rogero from the power of Alcina (qq.v.).

Mělĭta, the ancient name of Malta.

Mell, MR., in Dickens's 'David Copperfield' (q.v.), the poor usher at Creakle's school.

Mellefont, a character in Congreve's 'The Double Dealer' (q.v.).

Mellifluous Doctor, THE, St. Bernard.

Melmoth the Wanderer, a novel by Maturin (q.v.), published in 1820.

This is one of the most powerful of the tales of mystery and terror of which a number were produced in the early part of the 19th cent. The theme is the sale of a soul to the devil in return for prolonged life, the bargain being transferable if anyone else can be persuaded to take it over. The original transaction in the story took place in the 17th cent., and Melmoth the Wanderer is still alive. The novel is a succession of different tales, the chief character in each of which, at the climax of his or her sufferings, is offered by Melmoth relief from distress on the condition indicated. But they all—Stanton imprisoned in a lunatic's cell, Monçada in the grip of the Inquisition, Walberg, who sees his children perishing from hunger, Elinor Mortimer, and Isidora, Melmoth's wife—reject the proposed compact.

About 1898 Oscar Wilde (q.v.) adopted the name Sebastian Melmoth—Melmoth from the romance of Maturin, a connexion of his mother, Lady Wilde; Sebastian suggested by the arrows on his prison dress. He had contributed some information to the 1892 edition of 'Melmoth the Wanderer'.

Melnotte, CLAUDE, a character in Bulwer Lytton's 'The Lady of Lyons' (q.v.).

Melodrama, in early 19th-cent. use, a stage play (usually romantic and sensational in plot and incident) in which songs and music were interspersed. In later use the musical element gradually ceased to be an essential feature, and the name now denotes a dramatic piece characterized by sensational incident and violent appeals to the emotions, but with a happy ending. [OED.]

Melpŏměnē, the Muse (q.v.) of tragedy.

Melton Mowbray, in Leicestershire, the centre of a celebrated hunting district, and famous for its pies.

Melusĭna, a fairy of French folklore, the water-sprite of the fountain of Lusignan in Poitou, and the legendary ancestress and tutelary spirit of the house of that name. She consented to marry Raymond of Poitiers on condition that he should never see her on a Saturday, on which day she reverted to her mermaid-like condition. Her husband broke the compact, whereupon she fled. She was supposed to give warning by shrieks when misfortune menaced a member of the family. The story was written by Jean d'Arras in his 'Chronique de la Princesse' (*c.* 1387), translated by A. K. Donald for the E.E.T.S. It resembles in certain features those of Undine and Lohengrin (qq.v.) and the legend of the Banshee. Baring-Gould ('Curious Myths') traces the origin of Melusina to the oriental goddess Mylitta.

Melvil, Sir John, a character in Colman and Garrick's 'The Clandestine Marriage' (q.v.).

MELVILLE, HERMAN (1819–91), American writer, born in New York. After the bankruptcy and early death of his father he was a clerk for a time and later a schoolmaster, and shipped as a cabin boy to Liverpool in 1839. In 1841 he sailed in the whaler 'Acushnet' for the South Seas. He jumped ship at the Marquesas, lived for a time with the savages, and eventually made his way home as an ordinary seaman on the ·U.S. frigate 'United States', being discharged in 1843. These experiences were the basis of his early and popular books. 'Typee' (q.v., 1846) described his life among the savages, 'Omoo' (q.v., 1847) continued the story of his wanderings among the islands, 'Redburn' (1849) was based upon his earlier voyage to Liverpool, and 'White Jacket' (1850) was a remarkable account of life on the naval frigate. He used his experience of whaling in his masterpiece 'Moby Dick' (q.v., 1851), the story of the hunting of the demoniac white whale. He began to lose his popularity with 'Moby Dick', whose metaphysics and allegorical method had been foreshadowed in his earlier work—especially in 'Mardi' (1849), a discursive novel of the South Seas—and the process was hastened by his novel 'Pierre, or, The Ambiguities' (1852), which did not suit the public taste. Neither his historical romance 'Israel Potter' (1855), nor his collection of short stories 'The Piazza Tales' (1856), in spite of containing such works as 'Bartleby the Scrivener' and 'Benito Cereno', helped him to recover ground, and his satire 'The Confidence Man' (1857) was disregarded. He took a post as customs inspector, and, with the exception of his long short story 'Billy Budd' (q.v.), completed just before his death, wrote only verse, his most important poem being 'Clarel' (1876). He died in obscurity, and not until the 1920s was his extraordinary genius recognized for what it is.

Memling, Hans (active 1465–94), Flemish painter. He settled in Bruges and a number of his works, including the 'Reliquary of St. Ursula', are in the Hospital of St. John there.

Memnon, the son of Tithonus (q.v.) and Eōs (Aurora). He is referred to in the 'Odyssey' as the handsomest of mortals. In the post-Homeric legends he was a prince of the Ethiopians who came to the Trojan War in support of his uncle Priam and was slain by Achilles. According to tradition, a colossal statue near Thebes (in reality that of Amenophis) was supposed to represent Memnon. It gave forth a musical note when struck by the rays of the rising sun, explained in modern times as due to currents of air created in the fissures of the statue by the change of temperature. The reference in Milton's 'Il Penseroso' to 'Prince Memnon's sister' is obscure; there is a reference to such a character in the History of the Trojan War of Dictys Cretensis.

Memoirs of a Cavalier, an historical romance attributed with good reason to Defoe (q.v.), published in 1724.

The pretended author, 'Col. Andrew Newport', a young English gentleman born in 1608, travels on the Continent, starting in 1630, goes to Vienna and accompanies the army of the emperor, being present at the siege and sack of Magdeburg, which is vividly presented. He then joins the army of Gustavus Adolphus, remaining with it until the death of that king, and taking part in a number of engagements which he describes in detail. After his return to England he joins the king's army, first against the Scots, then against the forces of parliament, being present at the battle of Edgehill, which he fully describes, the relief of York, and the battle of Naseby.

Memoirs of Captain Carleton, a narrative published in 1728, whose authorship has been contested, and attributed by some to Defoe (q.v.), by others to Swift (q.v.). Captain Carleton, who unquestionably existed, is the subject of an attractive story of soldierly adventure. Sir W. Scott, who regarded the 'Memoirs' as Carleton's own work, brought out a new edition in 1808.

Carleton volunteers on board the 'London' on the declaration of war with the Dutch in 1672. In 1674 he enters the service of the Prince of Orange, remaining there until the peace of Nimwegen. Returning to England, he receives a commission from James II and serves in Scotland, and then in Flanders until the peace of Ryswick. The most interesting part of the memoirs follows. Carleton embarks with Lord Peterborough for Spain in 1705, and gives a stirring narrative of the siege and capture, and subsequent relief, of Barcelona, and of the campaign by which Peterborough, with scanty resources, temporarily placed the Archduke Charles on the throne of Spain. This is followed by some account of various parts of Spain visited by the author as a prisoner of war.

Memoirs of several Ladies of Great Britain, see *Amory*.

Men and Women, a collection of poems by R. Browning (q.v.), published in 1855. These were redistributed in the collection of 1868, and only thirteen (most of them dramatic monologues) of the original fifty pieces were retained under the heading of 'Men and Women'. The original issue contained many of Browning's finest love-poems, e.g. 'Love among the Ruins', 'A Woman's Last Word', 'Any Wife to Any Husband', and 'One Word More'. It also included 'Bishop Blougram's

Apology' (q.v.), 'Fra Lippo Lippi' (q.v.), 'Cleon', and 'Andrea del Sarto' (q.v.).

Menaechmi, a celebrated comedy by Plautus (q.v.), turning on the mistakes that result from the resemblance of twin brothers. It probably suggested Shakespeare's 'Comedy of Errors'.

MÉNAGE, GILLES DE (1613–92), French philologist, author of the four volumes of 'Menagiana', containing some interesting literary anecdotes. He was a member of the circle of the Hôtel de Rambouillet (q.v.).

MENANDER (c. 342–292 B.C.), an Athenian dramatic poet, was the most distinguished writer of New Comedy, which, with its trend towards realistic fiction based on contemporary life, gave a pattern for much light drama from the Renaissance onwards, making its influence felt through Latin adaptations by Plautus and Terence (qq.v.), at least eight from Menander himself. No play survived the Dark Ages; but 'Dyskolos' (or 'Misanthrope'), a light-hearted early play, and large parts of others have been recovered from papyri in the 20th cent.; they show at first hand something of the blend of amusement and perceptive human sympathy which earned Menander his reputation.

Menaphon, a prose romance, with interludes of verse, written by Greene (q.v.) and published in 1589; it was reprinted as 'Greene's Arcadia' in 1599. It tells the adventures of the Princess Sephestia, shipwrecked on the coast of Arcadia, where the shepherd Menaphon falls in love with her; and of her restoration to her husband and son. Among other pleasant lyrics, it contains the charming cradle-song, 'Weepe not, my wanton, smile upon my knee'.

MENCKEN, HENRY LOUIS (1880–1956), American journalist, born at Baltimore. He was a satirist of the 'cruder' manifestations of American civilization, and held strong views about European 'patronage' of America. He had a considerable influence on his contemporaries. He published many works and among the chief are 'George Bernard Shaw—His Plays' (1905), 'Prejudices' (6 series, 1919–27), and especially his scholarly 'The American Language' (1919). See also *Nathan (G. J.)*.

Mendelism, the law or theory of heredity worked out by Gregor Johann Mendel (1822–84), abbot of Brünn, from his experiments on the cross-fertilization of sweet peas.

Mendelssohn-Bartholdy, FELIX (1809–47) the composer, was born at Hamburg, the son of a Jewish banker, and the grandson of a philosopher. Besides being a composer he was an eminent pianist, organist, and conductor. His works include oratorios and cantatas, the music to 'A Midsummer Night's Dream' and other dramas, four symphonies, a quantity of chamber and pianoforte music, etc.

Mendoza Codex, an Aztec manuscript setting forth in pictures the history of the Mexican people from 1324 to 1502, with a description of the customs of the country. An explanation in the Mexican language is added and a translation into Spanish. It was obtained by the Spanish Governor of Mexico, Mendoza, and sent to Charles V, but was captured by a French man-of-war, together with the ship that carried it. Hakluyt bought it from André Thevet, the French king's geographer, and it passed to Purchas, who published it in the 'Pilgrimages' (iii. 1066 of the folio). The manuscript is now in the Bodleian.

Měnělāus, king of Sparta, son of Atreus (q.v.), and brother of Agamemnon (q.v.). He was the successful suitor of Helen (q.v.), but was robbed of her by Paris, the son of Priam. Thereupon he assembled the princes who had been suitors of Helen and had bound themselves to defend her, and the expedition against Troy was undertaken. During the war Menelaus behaved with spirit and would have slain Paris but for the interposition of Venus to protect her favourite. After the fall of Troy he was reunited to Helen.

Ménippée, Satire, see *Satire Ménippée.*

Menteith, EARL OF, a character in Scott's 'A Legend of Montrose' (q.v.).

Mentor, a faithful friend of Odysseus, whose form Athene assumes when she accompanies Telemachus (q.v.) as guide and adviser in his search for his father. Hence 'a mentor' is frequently used for 'an adviser'.

Mephistopheles, a word of unknown origin, which appears first in the German 'Faustbuch' of 1587 as 'Mephostophiles'. It is the name of the evil spirit to whom Faust (q.v.) was said in the German legend to have sold his soul. Shakespeare in 'The Merry Wives of Windsor' (1. i) mentions 'Mephostophilus'.

Mercantile System, DOCTRINE, or THEORY, a term used by Adam Smith (q.v.) and later political economists for the system of economic doctrine and legislative policy based on the principle that money alone constituted wealth.

Mercator, GERARDUS, the latinized form of the name of Gerhard Kremer (1512–94), a Flemish geographer who devised the form of map known as 'MERCATOR'S PROJECTION', in which the meridians of longitude are at right angles to the parallels of latitude, while it gives the navigator the correct compass bearing of his course from one point to another.

Mercator, a trade journal edited by Defoe (q.v.). It succeeded the 'Review' (q.v.) in 1713 and continued till the following year.

Merchant Adventurers, THE, originally

merchants engaged independently in oversea trade, who combined in guilds in different areas (Germany, the Netherlands, Scandinavia) in the 15th cent. They are first heard of as infringing the privileges in the Baltic trade of the Hanseatic League in the reign of Henry IV; and they also to some extent infringed those of the 'Merchants of the Staple' (English wool exporters). Henry VII gave their first official 'patent', but not a regular charter. Then they were incorporated as a single company in 1564. Throughout the reign of Elizabeth this enjoyed a monopoly of the trade carried on by English subjects with the Low Countries and Germany, controlling not only the importation of most of the articles of foreign manufacture used in England, but also the exportation of the leading manufactures of England, especially its woollen cloth. It furnished the main agency for the taxation of foreign trade, and at certain periods it advanced money to the government on the security of that taxation; it also served as the machinery for the discharge of international debts. It thus became the greatest financial power in the country. It attacked the Hanse (q.v.) and finally drove it from England, and invaded the territory of the Hanse itself, contributing largely to its ultimate dissolution. Its headquarters on the Continent at various times were Antwerp, Emden, and Hamburg. (See G. Unwin, 'Studies in Economic History'.)

Merchant of Venice, The, a comedy by Shakespeare (q.v.), probably written about 1596, printed in quarto in 1600. It is based on material in Giovanni Fiorentino's collection of Italian novels, 'Il Pecorone', and the 'Gesta Romanorum', and perhaps on works in which this material was rehandled.

Bassanio, a noble but poor Venetian, asks Antonio, his friend, a rich merchant, for three thousand ducats to enable him to prosecute fittingly his suit of the rich heiress Portia. Antonio, whose money is all employed in foreign ventures, undertakes to borrow the sum from Shylock, a Jewish usurer, whom he has been wont to upbraid for his extortions. Shylock consents to lend the money against a bond by which, in case the sum is not repaid at the appointed day, Antonio shall forfeit a pound of flesh. Bassanio prospers in his suit. By her father's will Portia is to marry that suitor who selects of three caskets (one of gold, one of silver, one of lead) that which contains her portrait. He makes the right choice—the leaden casket—and is wedded to Portia, and his friend Gratiano to her maid Nerissa. News comes that Antonio's ships have been wrecked, that the debt has not been repaid when due, and that Shylock claims his pound of flesh. The matter is brought before the duke. Portia disguises herself as an advocate, and Nerissa as her clerk, and they come to the court to defend Antonio, unknown to their husbands. Failing in her appeal to Shylock for mercy, Portia admits the validity of his claim, but warns him that his life is forfeit if he spills one drop of blood, since his bond gives him right to nothing beyond the flesh. Pursuing her advantage, she argues that Shylock's life is forfeit for having conspired against the life of a Venetian citizen. The duke grants Shylock his life, but gives half his wealth to Antonio, half to the State. Antonio surrenders his claim if Shylock will turn Christian and make over his property on his death to his daughter, Jessica, who has run away and married a Christian and been disinherited; to which Shylock agrees. Portia and Nerissa ask as rewards from Bassanio and Gratiano the rings that their wives have given them, which they have promised never to part with. Reluctantly they give them up, and are taken to task accordingly on their return home. The play ends with news of the safe arrival of Antonio's ships.

Merchant's Tale, The, see *Canterbury Tales*.

Mercia, a kingdom founded in the 6th cent. by the Anglian invaders known as Mercians (i.e. men of the mark or borderland), between Wessex, Northumbria, and Wales. At the treaty of Wedmore (878) the eastern half became part of the Danelaw, Alfred retaining the western. Under Canute and his successors until the Norman Conquest, Mercia was an earldom.

Mercia, LADY OF, see *Æthelflæd*.

Mercilla, in Spenser's 'Faerie Queene', v. viii, 'a mayden Queene of high renowne' (Queen Elizabeth), whose crown the Soldan seeks to subvert.

Mercurius Librarius, or a Faithful Account of all Books and Pamphlets, the first English literary periodical, published in 1680. It was a weekly or fortnightly catalogue of books issued.

Mercury, see *Hermes*.

Mercutio, a character in Shakespeare's 'Romeo and Juliet' (q.v.).

Mercy, in Bunyan's 'The Pilgrim's Progress' (q.v.), a companion of Christiana.

Merdle and **Mrs. Merdle**, characters in Dickens's 'Little Dorrit' (q.v.).

MEREDITH, GEORGE (1828–1909), was grandson of Melchizedek Meredith, a prosperous tailor and naval outfitter of Portsmouth (a circumstance reflected in his novel 'Evan Harrington'). He was privately educated at Portsmouth and Southsea and at the Moravian school at Neuwied. In London, after being articled to a solicitor, he turned to journalism, contributing to 'Household Words' and 'Chambers's Journal', and in 1849 married Mary Ellen Nicolls, a widowed daughter of Thomas Love Peacock (q.v.). In 1858 he was deserted by his wife, who had borne him a son and who died in 1861. Meanwhile he had published 'Poems' (dedicated to Peacock) in 1851, and the burlesque fantasies 'The Shaving of Shagpat: an Arabian Entertainment' (q.v., 1856) and 'Farina, a Legend of Cologne' (1857). His first great novel, 'The Ordeal of Richard Feverel' (q.v.), appeared in 1859, and he became acquainted with Swinburne, Rossetti and the Pre-Raphaelite group, and other notable people. But his book did not sell well and for long his means were scanty and precarious. He contributed to periodicals, and more especially to the 'Fortnightly Review', in which much of his later work was first published. 'Evan Harrington' (q.v.) appeared serially during 1860. During 1861–2 he lodged for a time with Swinburne and Rossetti in Chelsea, and in the latter year published his chief tragic poem, 'Modern Love' (q.v.). At the same time he became reader for Messrs. Chapman & Hall, a position which he retained until 1894. In 1864 appeared 'Emilia in England' (subsequently renamed 'Sandra Belloni', q.v.). He married in Sept. 1864 his second wife, Marie Vulliamy, who died in 1885. With her he settled for life at Flint Cottage, facing Box Hill, in 1867. He published 'Rhoda Fleming' (q.v.) in 1865, 'Vittoria' (q.v.) in 1866, 'The Adventures of Harry Richmond' (q.v., in the 'Cornhill' in 1870, separately in 1871), 'Beauchamp's Career' (q.v., in the 'Fortnightly' in 1875, separately in 1876), and 'The Tale of Chloe' and 'The Egoist' (qq.v.) in 1879. He delivered in 1877 a characteristic lecture on 'The Idea of Comedy and the Uses of the Comic Spirit' (separately published in 1897). He published 'The Tragic Comedians' (q.v.), embodying the love-story of Ferdinand Lassalle, the German socialist, in 1880, and 'Poems and Lyrics of the Joy of Earth' in 1883. Meredith obtained general popularity for his work for the first time by 'Diana of the Crossways' (q.v., 1885). This was followed by 'Ballads and Poems of Tragic Life' (1887), containing the ode 'France, December 1870'; 'A Reading of Earth' (1888), including 'A Faith on Trial'; 'Odes in Contribution to the Song of French History' (1898), and 'A Reading of Life' (1901); some of his most characteristic volumes of verse. His last three novels were 'One of our Conquerors' (q.v., 1891), 'Lord Ormont and his Aminta' (q.v., 1894), and 'The Amazing Marriage' (q.v., 1895). 'Last Poems' appeared in 1909, and 'Celt and Saxon', an unfinished story, appeared in 1910 after his death. 'The Sentimentalists', a conversational comedy, was produced also in the same year. An edition de luxe of his collected works appeared in 1896–1911 and a memorial edition in 1909–11. There is a portrait of Meredith by Watts in the National Portrait Gallery.

MEREDITH, OWEN, the pseudonym under which E. R. B. Lytton (q.v.), first earl of Lytton, published some of his earlier works.

MERES, FRANCIS (1565–1647), educated at Pembroke College, Cambridge, and rector and schoolmaster at Wing, was author of 'Palladis Tamia, Wit's Treasury' (1598), containing quotations and maxims from various writers. In this, Meres reviewed all literary effort from the time of Chaucer to his own day, contrasting each English author with a writer of like character in Latin, Greek, or Italian. He thus commemorates 125 Englishmen; and his list of Shakespeare's works with his commendation of the dramatist's 'fine filed phrase', and his account of Marlowe's death, are notable elements in English literary history.

MÉRIMÉE, PROSPER (1803–70), French novelist and dramatist, a member of the court of Napoleon III, was the author of admirable novels and short stories ('Colomba', 'La Vénus d'Ille', 1841; 'Carmen', which inspired Bizet's opera, 1852), of plays ('Théâtre de Clara Gazul', 1825), of 'La Jacquerie' (feudal scenes in dialogue form), and of the historical novel, 'Chronique de Charles IX' (1829). His well-known 'Lettres à une Inconnue' display his ironic and critical temperament. He was a strong supporter of the innocence of 'Libri the book-thief' (q.v.).

Merion, DIANA, the heroine of Meredith's 'Diana of the Crossways' (q.v.).

MERIVALE, CHARLES (1808–93), educated at Harrow and St. John's College, Cambridge, became dean of Ely, and published his 'History of the Romans under the Empire' in 1850–64, his 'Conversion of the Roman Empire' in 1864, and 'Conversion of the Northern Nations' in 1866. 'The Fall of the Roman Republic', an epitome by him of the early part of the first of the above works, appeared in 1853.

MERIVALE, HERMAN (1806–74), brother of Charles Merivale (q.v.), educated at Harrow and Oxford, became under-secretary for India, and published works on historical, colonial, and Indian subjects.

MERIVALE, HERMAN CHARLES (1839–1906), son of Herman Merivale (q.v.), educated at Harrow and Balliol College, Oxford, was a skilful playwright. He collaborated in 'All for Her' (1875) and 'Forget me not' (1879), successful plays, and wrote 'The White Pilgrim' (1883), a poetic drama, and 'Florien', a tragedy (1884). His farces and burlesques include 'The Butler' (1886) and 'The Don' (1888). He published a novel, 'Faucit of Balliol', in 1882, and a children's fairy tale, 'Binko's Blues', in 1884. He wrote some pleasant lyrics and sonnets, including 'Thaisa's Dirge'. He collaborated with F. T. Marzials in a short life of Thackeray (1891).

Merle, MADAME, a character in H. James's 'Portrait of a Lady' (q.v.).

Merlin. The germ of the story of Merlin is found in Nennius's 'Historia Britonum'. The British king, Vortigern, is building a citadel against Hengist and the Saxons, but the foundations are swallowed up as they are laid. Ambrosius, a boy without mortal sire, explains that beneath the site of the citadel there live two dragons, one red and one white. The dragons are found, they fight, and the white dragon is defeated. The boy interprets this as an omen that the Saxons will be expelled by the Britons.

Geoffrey of Monmouth identifies this Ambrosius with Merlin and recounts the same story. He makes Merlin assist Uther in the deceit by which he becomes the husband of Igraine and father of Arthur (q.v.), and it is by Merlin's help that the great stones are brought to Stonehenge from Naas in Ireland. In 'Arthour and Merlin', a poem of the late 13th cent., the story is developed. Merlin's birth is narrated (the devil is his father) and he aids Arthur to defeat his foes by his counsel and magic. Reference is made to the beguiling of Merlin by Nimiane (Nimue or Vivien, see *Lady of the Lake*). According to Spenser's 'Faerie Queene' (III. iii) his mother was a nun, Matilda, daughter of Pubidius, king of Mathraval. In Malory's 'Morte Darthur' it is Merlin who makes the Round Table for Uther Pendragon. He dotes upon Nimue, who, to get rid of him, inveigles him under a great stone. Tennyson in his 'Idylls' makes Vivien induce Merlin to take refuge from a storm in an old oak-tree and leave him there spell-bound.

In Welsh vernacular literature there is a group of poems of a patriotic character attributed to a bard Merlin (Myrddhin), alluded to in Shakespeare ('1 Henry IV', III. i. 150, and 'King Lear', III. ii. 95); and the Welsh 'Dialogue between Merlin and Taliessin' (a brother bard, who lived about 550) may have some basis in genuine tradition. There is perhaps some connexion between this bard and the Merlin of the Arthurian legend. The bard, in turn, was perhaps originally a god of British mythology, especially worshipped at Stonehenge (Rhys, 'Hibbert Lectures').

In a trilogy composed by the French poet Robert de Boron (q.v.) in the late 12th or early 13th cent., Merlin, with his knowledge of the past and the future, forms the connecting link between the early history of the Grail (q.v.) and the days of King Arthur.

Merlin and Vivien, one of Tennyson's 'Idylls of the King' (q.v.), published in 1859.

Vivien, the wily and malignant daughter of a man killed fighting against King Arthur, filled with hatred for the king, leaves the court of Mark to go to that of Arthur and there sow suspicion. She sets herself to win the aged enchanter Merlin, accompanies him to Broceliande, and there extracts from him the knowledge of a charm, which she immediately uses to leave him shut up for ever in an old oak.

Mermaid Tavern, THE, a tavern that stood in Bread Street (with an entrance in Friday Street), London. One of the earliest of English clubs, the Friday Street Club, started by Sir Walter Ralegh, met there, and was frequented by Shakespeare, Selden, Donne, Beaumont, and Fletcher. It is celebrated by Beaumont in the fine lines ('Master Francis Beaumont to Ben Jonson'):

> What things have we seen
> Done at the Mermaid! heard words that have been
> So nimble, and so full of subtle flame,
> As if that every one from whence they came
> Had meant to put his whole wit in a.jest,
> And had resolved to live a fool the rest
> Of his dull life.

Keats also wrote 'Lines on the Mermaid Tavern' beginning: 'Souls of poets dead and gone'.

Merŏpē, (1) one of the daughters of Atlas, the wife of Sisyphus (q.v.), and one of the Pleiades (q.v.); (2) the daughter of Cypselus, wife of Cresphontes and mother of Aepytus.

Matthew Arnold's tragedy 'Merope' is concerned with the latter. It deals with the revenge of Aepytus on Polyphontes, who has killed Cresphontes, king of Messenia, the father of Aepytus, and has, for reasons of state, proposed marriage to Merope, the widowed mother of Aepytus.

Merovingian, the name of the first dynasty of Frankish kings, derived from Merwig or Merovaeus, its legendary founder in the 5th cent. It rose to importance under Clovis I (481–511), but declined owing to family feuds and the growing power of the Mayors of the Palace (q.v.), until the Merovingians were finally ousted by Pepin the Short in 751.

Merrilies, MEG, the old gipsy woman in Scott's 'Guy Mannering' (q.v.). She is the subject of a poem by Keats, 'Old Meg she was a gipsy'.

MERRIMAN, HENRY SETON, pseudonym of Hugh Stowell Scott (1862–1903), novelist, author of 'Young Mistley' (published anonymously, 1888), 'The Slave of the Lamp' (1892), 'With Edged Tools' (1894), 'The Sowers' (1896), 'In Kedar's Tents' (1897), 'Barlasch of the Guard' (1902), etc.

Merry, ROBERT, see *Della Crusca*.

Merry Devil of Edmonton, The, a romantic comedy published in 1608, whose authorship is unknown. Charles Lamb, who praised it highly, suggested Drayton as the possible author. It was included in a volume in Charles II's library entitled 'Shakespeare', but there is no evidence in support of this attribution.

The prologue presents Peter Fabel of Edmonton, a magician, who has made a compact with the devil. The period of it has run out, and the fiend comes to claim Fabel. He is, however, tricked into sitting down in a necromantic chair, where he is held fast and is obliged to give a respite. The play itself, in which the magical element is practically absent, deals with the attempt of Sir Arthur Clare and his wife to break off the match between their daughter Millicent and Raymond Mounchensey, and its defeat by the elopement of the young couple, aided by the kindly magician Fabel.

Merry Monarch, The, Charles II.

Merry Mount, the name given by Thomas Morton, a British trader and adventurer, to his settlement near Plymouth, Mass., which was established about 1625. Having come into conflict with the Plymouth settlers, Morton was captured and sent to England in 1628 and the settlement suppressed. He returned to Plymouth in the following year and made an abortive attempt to re-establish his colony.

Merry Wives of Windsor, The, a comedy by Shakespeare (q.v.), probably of 1600–1. An imperfect text was printed in 1602, the corrected text in the folio of 1623. It is said by Dennis to have been written by command of Queen Elizabeth to show Sir John Falstaff in love.

Falstaff (q.v.), who is 'out at heels', determines to make love to the wives of Ford and Page, two gentlemen dwelling at Windsor, because they have the rule of their husband's purses. Nym and Pistol, the discarded followers of Falstaff, warn the husbands. Falstaff sends identical love-letters to Mrs. Ford and Mrs. Page, who contrive the discomfiture of the knight. At a first assignation at Ford's house, on the arrival of the husband, they hide Falstaff in a basket, cover him with foul linen, and have him tipped into a muddy ditch. At a second assignation, they disguise him as the 'fat woman of Brentford', in which character he is soundly beaten by Ford. The jealous husband having also been twice befooled, the plot is now revealed to him, and a final assignation is given to Falstaff in Windsor Forest, where he is beset and pinched by mock fairies and finally seized and exposed by Ford and Page.

The underplot is concerned with the wooing of Anne, the daughter of Page, by three suitors: Doctor Caius, a French physician, Slender, the foolish cousin of Justice Shallow, and Fenton, a wild young gentleman, whom Anne loves. Mistress Quickly, servant to Dr. Caius, acts as go-between for all three suitors, and encourages them all impartially. Sir Hugh Evans, a Welsh parson, interferes on behalf of Slender and incurs the enmity of, and receives a challenge from, the irascible Dr. Caius, but hostilities are confined to the 'hacking' of the English tongue. At the final assignation with Falstaff in the forest, Page, who favours Slender, arranges that the latter shall carry off his daughter, who is to be dressed in white; while Mrs. Page, who favours Dr. Caius, arranges that he shall carry her off dressed in green. In the event both of these find themselves fobbed off with a boy in disguise, while Fenton has run away with and married the true Anne.

Merry-Andrew, one who entertains people by antics and buffoonery, a clown. The OED. observes that Hearne's statement, in the preface to his edition of Benedictus Abbas (1735),

that 'Merry Andrew' was originally applied to Dr. Andrew Borde (*d.* 1549) has neither evidence nor intrinsic probability, though Borde had a reputation for buffoonery.

Merton College, Oxford, was founded in 1264 by Walter de Merton, chancellor of England and bishop of Rochester (*d.* 1277). It is generally regarded as the first society on the present collegiate model. Roger Bacon, Duns Scotus, and Wycliffe (qq.v.) are traditionally connected with it. Anthony Wood (q.v.) was educated there.

Mertoun, BASIL and MORDAUNT, characters in Scott's 'The Pirate' (q.v.).

Merygreek, MATTHEW, a character in Udall's 'Ralph Roister Doister' (q.v.).

Mesmer, FRIEDRICH ANTON (1733–1815), an Austrian physician, who popularized the doctrine or system known as *Mesmerism,* according to which a hypnotic state can be induced by an influence exercised by the operator over the will and nervous system of the patient.

Mesopotamia, THAT BLESSED WORD: a contributor to 'N. and Q.' (XIth Ser., i. 458) connects the phrase with the famous Methodist preacher George Whitefield, as the explanation 'commonly current in religious circles'. He says, 'The genesis of the story was indicated several years ago by Mr. Francis Jacox. Garrick, who greatly admired Whitefield's preaching, was it seems responsible for its introduction in religious literature. Whitefield's voice was so wonderfully modulated that Garrick said "he could make men either laugh or cry by pronouncing the word Mesopotamia".' No reference is given to Garrick's writings.

According to Brewer, the allusion is to the story of an old woman who told her pastor that she 'found great support in that blessed word Mesopotamia'. Cf. Cowper's 'Selkirk',

> Religion, what treasure untold
> Resides in that heavenly word!

Mesrour, in the 'Arabian Nights' (q.v.), the executioner of the Caliph Haroun-al-Rashid, who with the vizier Jaffar used to accompany him when he walked at night disguised about the streets of Baghdad.

Mess John, see *Mas John.*

Messalina, the wife of the Roman emperor Claudius, proverbial for her profligacy. She was put to death in A.D. 48.

Messiah, the Hebrew title (meaning 'anointed') applied in the O.T. prophetic writings to a promised deliverer of the Jewish nation, and hence applied to Jesus of Nazareth as the fulfilment of that promise. Hence, in a transferred sense, an expected liberator of an oppressed people or country. [OED.]

Messiah, The, (1) a sacred eclogue by Pope (q.v.), published in 'The Spectator' in May 1712, embodying in verse the Messianic prophecies of Isaiah; (2) a famous oratorio by

Handel (q.v.); (3) a religious epic ('Messias') by Klopstock (q.v.).

Mesty, a character in Marryat's 'Midshipman Easy' (q.v.).

Metalogicus, see *John of Salisbury*.

Metamorphōses, a series of mythological tales in verse by the Roman poet Ovid (q.v.), parts of which have been translated by various English poets, and which provide the material for many literary allusions.

Metaphor, the transfer of a name or descriptive term to an object different from, but analogous to, that to which it is properly applicable, e.g. 'abysmal ignorance'. MIXED METAPHOR is the application of two inconsistent metaphors to one object.

Metaphysical Poets, a term invented by Dryden and adopted by Johnson as the designation of certain 17th-cent. poets (chief of whom were Donne and Cowley) addicted to 'witty conceits' and far-fetched imagery (Johnson, 'Lives of the Poets', 'Cowley'). But modern opinion does not wholly endorse Johnson's condemnation of these poets.

Metaphysical Society, THE, was founded in 1869 by Sir J. T. Knowles (q.v.). It lasted until 1881 and brought together most of the leaders of English thought of the period, of all shades of opinion.

METASTASIO, or, according to his original name, PIETRO TRAPASSI (1698–1782), one of the most representative of Italian Arcadian poets, was called to Vienna as court poet in 1730 and remained there until his death. His many operas include 'Didone abbandonata' (1724), 'Attilio Regolo' (1733), the 'Olimpiade' (1733), and the 'Clemenza di Tito' (1734).

Metathĕsis, the transposition of letters or sounds in a word. When the transposition is between the letters or sounds of two words, it is popularly known as a 'Spoonerism', of which a well-known specimen (attributed to the Rev. W. A. Spooner (1844–1930), Warden of New College, Oxford) is 'Kinquering congs their titles take'.

Methodism, a movement of reaction against the apathy of the Church of England that prevailed in the early part of the 18th cent. Its leaders were J. and C. Wesley and Whitefield (qq.v.). John Wesley came under the influence of the Moravians while Whitefield adopted Calvinistic views; their followers consequently separated, those of Whitefield becoming Calvinistic Methodists, sometimes called Lady Huntingdon's Connexion.

The name 'Methodist' was originally applied to the members of a religious society established at Oxford in 1729 by the Wesleys and other members of the University, having for its object the promotion of piety and morality. It was subsequently extended to those who took part in or sympathized with the movement above described.

Methuselah, proverbial for the extremely long life attributed to him in Gen. v. 27.

Metre, from Gk. μέτρον measure, any specific form of poetic rhythm, determined by the number and character of the feet which it contains. In the compounds DIMETER, TRIMETER, etc., it is the unit which is repeated a certain number of times in a line of verse. This unit consists of two iambuses, trochees, or anapaests, or of one dactyl (qq.v.). Thus an iambic dimeter consists of four iambuses, a hexameter (q.v.) of six dactyls (or equivalents). In English (accentual) verse stressed syllables replace the long syllables, and unstressed syllables the short syllables, of Greek and Latin (quantitative) verse.

Meudon, CURÉ DE (parish priest of), a title by which Rabelais (q.v.) is sometimes designated.

MEUN(G), JEAN DE, see *Roman de la Rose*.

Mews, THE (meaning originally cages for hawks while mewing or moulting), stood on the site of Trafalgar Square; the king's falcons were kept there. The Mews were converted into stables for the royal horses in the reigns of Edward VI and Mary (Stow).

Mextli or **Mexitl,** see *Huitzilopochtli*.

Meyerbeer, GIACOMO (originally JAKOB) (1791–1864), born in Berlin of Jewish descent, a famous composer of operas, of which the most successful were: 'Robert le Diable' (1831), 'Les Huguenots' (1836), 'Le Prophète' (1842), 'L'Africaine' (1865).

MEYNELL, ALICE (1847–1922), poet, essayist, and critic. Her rare gifts, both in prose and poetry, may be seen in her volumes of essays: 'The Rhythm of Life' (1893), 'The Colour of Life' (1896), 'The Children' (1896), 'The Spirit of Peace' (1898), 'Ceres' Runaway' (1910), 'The Second Person Singular' (1921); and in her early volume of 'Preludes' (1875), 'Poems' (1893), 'Later Poems' (1901), 'A Father of Women' (1918), and 'Last Poems' (1923). A complete edition of her poems was published in 1923. See also *Thompson (F.)*.

Micawber, WILKINS and MRS., characters in Dickens's 'David Copperfield' (q.v.).

Michael, a pastoral poem by W. Wordsworth (q.v.), published in 1800.

Michael, ST., the archangel, mentioned as the leader of the angels against the dragon and his host in Rev. xii. 7, and described by Milton ('Paradise Lost', vi. 44) as 'of celestial armies prince'. He is one of the four principal angels enumerated in the Koran, the champion of the faith. His feast is celebrated on 29 Sept., known as MICHAELMAS (q.v.).

MICHAEL ANGELO BUONARROTI, see *Michelangelo Buonarroti*.

MICHAEL ANGELO TITMARSH, the pseudonym adopted by Thackeray (q.v.) in 'The Paris Sketch-Book', 'The Great Hoggarty Diamond' (q.v.), 'The Irish Sketch-Book', 'Bluebeard's Ghost', 'A Legend of the Rhine', 'Rebecca and Rowena', 'Mrs. Perkins's Ball', etc.

Michael's Mount, ST., on the coast of Cornwall. See *Namancos*.

Michaelmas, the feast of St. Michael (q.v.), 29 Sept., one of the four quarter-days of the English business year, a date on which servants used to be hired, and from which leases frequently run, etc. There is an old proverb that 'Who eats goose on Michael's day, Shan't money lack his debts to pay' ('British Apollo', ed. 3, 1726, II. 648).

Michaelmas Terme, a comedy by T. Middleton (q.v.), printed in 1607.

Quomodo, a usurer, with his attendants, Shortyard and Falselight, as confederates, tries to effect the ruin of Easy, a simple country gentleman. He succeeds in getting from him bonds for his estate in Essex and is overjoyed at becoming a landed proprietor. Wishing to see how his wife and son will conduct themselves in their new dignity, he feigns death. He is dismayed to find that his wife promptly marries Easy, with whom she is in love, and that his son shows no particular respect for his late father. He is then tricked into signing a document releasing Easy from his obligations.

Michal, in Dryden's 'Absalom and Achitophel' (q.v.), is the queen of Charles II, Catharine of Portugal, accused by Oates of conspiracy against the king's life. For the biblical Michal see 1 Sam. xviii. 20.

MICHELANGELO BUONARROTI (1475–1564), Italian painter, sculptor, architect, and poet. His early works (e.g. the 'David', 1504, and the 'Bathers', a cartoon for a battle scene to decorate the Florence Town Hall, 1505), express the humanistic ideals of the High Renaissance through the portrayal of the nude, depicting the beauty, strength, and rich diversity of movement and expression of which the human body is capable. His unfinished figures of slaves for the tomb of Julius II show his method of working, as though the figures were latent within the marble, awaiting his chisel to be released. His later work, such as the 'Last Judgement' in the Sistine Chapel, reveals a disillusionment which echoes the instability of Church and State after the Reformation and the Sack of Rome. From youth Michelangelo was acclaimed a great artist, and did much to raise the status of the artist from that of a craftsman to the equal of scholars and the friend of patrons. His first patron was Lorenzo de' Medici, and he worked for the Medici family for much of his life, designing the Medici chapel attached to S. Lorenzo, Florence, with its tombs of Giuliano and Lorenzo crowned by the figures of 'Day' and 'Night', 'Dawn' and 'Evening'. Pope Julius II first commissioned him to carve his tomb and then interrupted the work by requiring him to paint the

ceiling of the Sistine Chapel. In 1546 he became Chief Architect to St. Peter's and designed the dome. He wrote a number of sonnets and madrigals, some addressed to his friend Vittoria Colonna (q.v.). 'He belongs to the genus of deep, violent, colossal, passionately striving natures' (J. A. Symonds).

MICHELET, JULES (1798–1874), French historian, whose principal work, the 'Histoire de France' (1833–67), is remarkable for its luminous and eloquent style and for the part that the author attributes to physical circumstances, such as the health or heredity of the principal actors, in determining political events. Michelet wrote a number of monographs, 'Des Jésuites', 'Du Prêtre', 'La Sorcière', etc., on subjects allied to history in his broad conception of it.

Miching malicho, a phrase of uncertain meaning occurring in Shakespeare's 'Hamlet', III. ii. 148. 'Miching' is probably the participle of the late Middle English verb 'to miche' (surviving in 'to mike'), meaning to pilfer, skulk, play truant. 'Malicho' perhaps represents the Spanish *malhecho*, misdeed. This yields a fairly satisfactory sense, but there is no evidence that the Spanish word was familiar in English. [OED.] Lord Miching Malicho in Peacock's 'Gryll Grange' (q.v.) represents Lord John Russell.

Micomicona, the princess whom Don Quixote (q.v.) thinks that he is rescuing when he attacks the wine-bags.

Microcosm of London, The, see *Ackermann*.

Microcosmographie, a collection of character sketches on the model of Theophrastus (q.v.), chiefly by John Earle (1601?–65), bishop of Salisbury, published in 1628. The author analyses inconspicuous types, such as the plain country fellow, a modest man, and a poor man. The sketches are interesting in the evolution of the English essay.

Micromégas, a philosophical tale written by Voltaire (q.v.) in imitation of 'Gulliver's Travels'.

Midas, a semi-legendary king of Phrygia, who, having hospitably entertained Silenus, the tutor of Dionysus, when he had lost his way, was permitted by the god to choose his recompense. He asked that whatever he touched might be turned to gold. His prayer was granted, but when he found that the very meat he attempted to eat became gold in his mouth, he entreated Dionysus to relieve him of the gift. He was ordered to wash himself in the river Pactōlus, whose sands thereafter contained gold. On another occasion Midas had the imprudence to declare that Pan was a superior flute-player to Apollo, whereupon the offended god changed his ears to those of an ass, to indicate his stupidity. This Midas attempted to conceal; but his barber saw the length of his ears, and, unable to keep the secret, and afraid to reveal it, whispered the fact to some reeds, and these, whenever agitated by the wind, repeated to the world that Midas had the ears of an ass.

Midas, a prose play by Lyly (q.v.), published in 1592, on the legend of Midas, king of Phrygia (see above).

Midas, SIR GORGIUS and LADY, types of ostentatious wealth, depicted in some of Du Maurier's (q.v.) drawings in 'Punch'.

Middle Ages, THE, the period of time from the Roman decadence (5th cent. A.D.) to the Renaissance (about 1500). The notion is that of an interval between two periods of advancing knowledge (cf. Bacon, 'Novum Organum' 1, § 78). The earliest use of *Middle Age*, in this sense, yet discovered is in one of Donne's sermons (1621), but the corresponding Latin terms, *media aetas, medium aevum*, etc., are found at various dates in the 16th cent. The term is no longer used in a pejorative sense and may include only the 11th–15th cents., the earlier period being called the Dark Ages. (See an article on this subject by George Gordon in S.P.E. Tract XIX.)

Middle English, see *English.*

Middlemarch, *a Study of Provincial Life,* a novel by G. Eliot (q.v.), published in 1871–2.

The scene is laid in the provincial town of Middlemarch in the first half of the 19th cent. The story is concerned principally with Dorothea Brooke, a St. Theresa, ardent, puritanical, with a high ideal of life. She marries the elderly pedant Mr. Casaubon, possessed of an archangelical manner, for whom she feels 'the reverence of a neophyte entering on a higher grade of initiation'. The marriage is intensely unhappy. Mr. Casaubon spends the honeymoon in research into what his cousin, young Will Ladislaw, irreverently calls his 'mouldy futilities', and alienates Dorothea by his lack of sympathy. There supervenes a suspicion in his mind of his wife's preference for the said Will Ladislaw, and before he dies, which he shortly does, he adds with characteristic meanness a codicil to his will by which Dorothea forfeits her fortune if she marries Ladislaw. Nevertheless, in the end, Dorothea and Ladislaw are brought together. Parallel with this plot runs the story of the unhappy marriage of Tertius Lydgate, an ambitious young doctor, animated by hopes of scientific discoveries and medical reform, with the beautiful but commonplace Rosamond Vincy, whose materialism brings about the failure of his hopes.

The canvas is a broad one, and contains many good characters, including the humorous Mrs. Cadwallader, the rector's wife; the conventional English gentleman, Sir James Chettam; Dorothea's uncle, Mr. Brooke, a man 'of acquiescent temper, miscellaneous opinions, and uncertain vote'; and Mr. Bulstrode, the religious humbug.

Middlemas, RICHARD, a character in Scott's 'The Surgeon's Daughter' (q.v.).

Middleton, CLARA and DR., characters in Meredith's 'The Egoist' (q.v.).

MIDDLETON, CONYERS (1683–1750), educated at Trinity College, Cambridge, and subsequently fellow of the college, was involved in the disputes with Bentley, the master. He was protobibliothecarius of the university library (1721). His chief works were his 'Life of Cicero' (1741) and a latitudinarian 'Free Inquiry into Miracles' (1748). His conclusion that post-apostolic miracles were unreal aroused much controversy.

Middleton, SIR HUGH, see *Myddelton.*

MIDDLETON, THOMAS (1570?–1627), dramatist, was the son of parents settled in London. He wrote satirical comedies of contemporary manners, and later, under the influence of W. Rowley, romantic comedies. Much of his work was done in collaboration with Dekker, Rowley, Munday, and others. He also wrote pageants and masques for city ceremonials, and was appointed city chronologer in 1620. In 1624 he wrote a political drama 'A Game at Chesse' (q.v.), for which he and the actors were summoned before the Privy Council. His other plays (which were very popular) include 'The Mayor of Quinborough' (1661) and possibly 'The Old Law' (1656, in collaboration with Massinger and Rowley), 'Michaelmas Terme' (q.v., 1607), 'A Trick to catch the Old-One' (1608), 'The Familie of Love' (1608), 'A Mad World, my Masters' (1608), 'The Roaring Girle' (q.v., 1611, with Dekker), 'A Faire Quarrell' (q.v., 1617, with Rowley), 'The Changeling' (q.v., 1623, with Rowley), 'The Spanish Gipsy' (q.v., 1623, with Rowley), 'More Dissemblers besides Women' (1657), 'A Chaste Maid in Cheapside' (q.v., 1630), 'No Wit, no Help like a Woman's' (1657), 'Women beware Women' (q.v., 1657), 'The Witch' (q.v., not published until 1778), 'Anything for a Quiet Life' (1662), 'The Widow' (1652, with Ben Jonson and Fletcher). His pageants and masques include 'The Triumphs of Truth' (1613), 'Civitatis Amor' (1616), 'The Triumphs of Honor and Industry' (1617), 'The Inner Temple Masque' (1619), 'The Triumphs of Love and Antiquity' (1619), 'The World Tost at Tennis' (1620), 'The Triumphs of Honor and Virtue' (1622), 'The Triumphs of Integrity' (1623), 'The Triumphs of Health and Prosperity' (1626). He is supposed to have also written some miscellaneous verse and prose.

Midgard, in early Scandinavian cosmography, the region, encircled by the sea, in which men live, the earth.

Midgard Serpent, THE, see *Jörmungander.*

Midshipman Easy, Mr., a novel by Marryat (q.v.), published in 1836.

Jack Easy is the son of Mr. Nicodemus Easy, a rich country gentleman with a bee in his bonnet, who believes all men are equal, and instils these ideas into his son. When Jack Easy goes to sea as a midshipman his insistence on these ideas, and his argumentative disposition, bring him into conflict with naval discipline. But as he has the good fortune to meet with a kindly and sensible captain, and is moreover a plucky and straightforward youth, and heir to eight thousand a year, he gets well out of his scrapes. His adventurous disposition leads him into a number of exciting incidents; their fortunate outcome is largely due to the devotion of the resourceful Ashantee, Mesty, and of his fellow midshipman, Edward Gascoigne. Among the many amusing naval characters in the book may be mentioned the bellicose chaplain, Hawkins, Mr. Biggs, the boatswain ('Duty before decency'), and Mr. Pottyfar, the lieutenant who kills himself with his own universal medicine.

Midsummer Night's Dream, A, a comedy by Shakespeare (q.v.), probably written in 1595 or 1596, and printed in 1600.

Hermia, ordered by her father, Egeus, to marry Demetrius, refuses, because she loves Lysander, while Demetrius has formerly professed love for her friend Helena, and Helena loves Demetrius. Under the law of Athens, Theseus, the duke, gives Hermia four days in which to obey her father; else she must suffer death or enter a nunnery. Hermia and Lysander agree to leave Athens secretly in order to be married where the Athenian law cannot pursue them, and to meet in a wood a few miles from the city. Hermia tells Helena of the project, and the latter tells Demetrius. Demetrius pursues Hermia to the wood, and Helena Demetrius, so that all four are that night in the wood. This wood is the favourite haunt of the fairies.

Oberon and Titania, king and queen of the fairies, have quarrelled, because Titania refuses to give up to him a little changeling boy for a page. Oberon tells Puck, a mischievous sprite, to fetch him a certain magic flower, of which he will press the juice on the eyes of Titania while she sleeps, so that she may fall in love with what she first sees when she wakes. Overhearing Demetrius in the wood reproaching Helena for following him, and desirous to reconcile them, Oberon orders Puck to place some of the love-juice on Demetrius's eyes, but so that Helena shall be near him when he does it. Puck, mistaking Lysander for Demetrius, applies the love-charm to him, and it chances that Helena is the first person that Lysander sees, to whom he at once makes love, enraging her because she thinks she is made a jest of. Oberon discovering Puck's mistake, now places some of the juice on Demetrius's eyes, and he on waking first sees Helena, so that both Lysander and Demetrius are now making love to Helena. The ladies fall to high words and the men go off to fight for Helena.

Meanwhile Oberon has placed the love-juice on Titania's eyelids, who wakes to find Bottom the weaver near her, wearing an ass's head (Bottom and a company of Athenian tradesmen are in the wood to rehearse a play for the Duke's wedding, and Puck has put an ass's head on Bottom); Titania at once becomes enamoured of him, and toys with his 'amiable cheeks' and 'fair large ears'. Oberon, finding them together, reproaches Titania for bestowing her love on an ass, and again demands the changeling boy, whom she in her confusion surrenders; whereupon Oberon releases her from the charm. Puck at Oberon's orders throws a thick fog about the human lovers, and brings them all together, unknown to one another, and they fall asleep. He applies a remedy to their eyes, so that when they awake they return to their former loves. Theseus and Egeus appear on the scene, the runaways are forgiven, and the couples married. The play ends with the scene of 'Pyramus and Thisbe', comically acted by Bottom and his fellow tradesmen, to grace these nuptials and those of Theseus and Hippolyta.

Miggs, MISS, in Dickens's 'Barnaby Rudge' (q.v.), the shrewish maidservant of Mrs. Varden.

Migne, JACQUES PAUL (1800–75), French priest and publisher, who issued a large number of theological works, especially the great 'Patrologiae Cursus Completus', a collection of patristic writings (Latin series, 1844–55; Greek series, 1856–61) numbering over 300 volumes.

Mignon, in the 'Wilhelm Meister's Apprenticeship' of Goethe (q.v.), a fairy-like child rescued by Wilhelm from a troupe of rope-dancers. She becomes passionately attached to him, and from hopeless love and longing for her Italian home pines away and dies. She is the prototype of Fenella in Scott's 'Peveril of the Peak' (q.v.). Goethe puts in her mouth the famous song 'Kennst du das Land', for which Beethoven wrote the music. Ambroise Thomas wrote the opera 'Mignon', founded on the above.

Mikado, THE, meaning the 'august door', the title of the Emperor of Japan. (Cf. *Sublime Porte*.) For the comic opera, 'The Mikado', see *Gilbert and Sullivan Operas*.

Mikli-gard, the name applied by the Norsemen to Constantinople in the 10th and 11th cents.

Milan Decree, THE, an edict of Napoleon issued at Milan 17 Dec. 1807, prohibiting all continental intercourse with Great Britain, and declaring the forfeiture of all vessels bound to or from British ports. See *Orders in Council*.

Milanion, see *Atalanta*.

Mildendo, in 'Gulliver's Travels' (q.v.), the capital of Lilliput.

Miles Standish, The Courtship of, a poem in hexameters by Longfellow, published in 1858.

Miles Standish is the blunt old Puritan captain of Plymouth in the land of the Pilgrim Fathers. Having lost his wife, he sends his friend John Alden to make an offer of marriage on his behalf to the fair Priscilla. She indignantly replies that if she is worth winning she is worth wooing, and, when John woos for his friend, exclaims, 'Why don't you speak for yourself, John?' But John Alden, though loving her, is faithful to his trust. He tells Miles Standish the result of his mission, and the latter departs in anger. At last news comes of his death in battle, after which John and Priscilla are married. On the completion of their wedding, Standish reappears, repentant, and is reconciled to his friend.

Milesian Tales, a collection of short Greek stories of love and adventure, of a generally licentious character, by Aristides of Miletus of the 2nd cent. B.C., now lost.

Milesians, the people of Miledh, a fabulous Spanish king, whose sons are said to have invaded Ireland about 1300 B.C. They represent probably the first Gaelic invaders of the country. See *Fir Bolgs.*

MILL, JAMES (1773-1836), born near Montrose, the son of a farmer, was educated for the ministry, but came to London in 1802 and took up journalism. He published in 1818 a 'History of British India', which obtained him a high post in the East India Company's service. He was closely associated with Bentham and Ricardo (qq.v.), whose views in philosophy and political economy, respectively, he adopted. He published his 'Elements of Political Economy' in 1821, his 'Analysis of the Human Mind' in 1829, and his 'Fragment on Mackintosh' in 1835. In the 'Analysis' he provided, by his theory of association, a psychological basis for Bentham's utilitarianism. Associations may become inseparable and transform what had merely been means into ends sought on their own account, thus explaining disinterested conduct by the egoistic individual. He also endeavoured to found on the association of ultimate sensations a theory of knowledge and reality. The 'Fragment on Mackintosh' is a rejoinder to the attack on the utilitarians contained in the 'Dissertation on the Progress of Ethical Philosophy' of Mackintosh (q.v.). Mill helped to found, and contributed to, the 'Westminster Review' (q.v.).

An interesting picture of James Mill's rather grim personality is given in the 'Autobiography' of his son J. S. Mill (q.v.).

MILL, JOHN STUART (1806-73), son of James Mill (q.v.), by whom he was educated and by whose influence he obtained a clerkship in the India House. He formed the Utilitarian Society, which met during 1823-6 to read essays and discuss them, and in 1825 edited Bentham's 'Treatise upon Evidence'. But he gradually departed in some degree from the utilitarian doctrine expounded by Bentham, as is shown by his essay on that philosopher published in the 'London and Westminster Review' in 1832, and later in his 'Utilitarianism' (q.v.), published in 1861. In 1843 he published his chief work, the 'System of Logic' (q.v.), and his 'Principles of Political Economy' in 1848. In 1859 appeared his essay on 'Liberty' (q.v.), and two volumes of 'Dissertations and Discussions', and in 1865 his 'Examination of Sir William Hamilton's Philosophy' (q.v.). Among minor works may be mentioned the 'Thoughts on Parliamentary Reform' (1859), 'Representative Government' (1861), 'Auguste Comte and Positivism' (1865), his 'Inaugural Address' on being installed lord rector of the University of St. Andrews in 1867, an important discussion of the functions of a university, and 'The Subjection of Women' (1869). His interesting 'Autobiography' appeared in 1873.

On the dissolution of the East India Company in 1858 he retired with a pension, and was M.P. for Westminster, 1865-8. He passed most of the remainder of his life in France, and died at Avignon.

***Mill on the Floss,** The,* a novel by G. Eliot (q.v.), published in 1860.

Tom and Maggie, the principal characters in the story, are the children of the honest but ignorant and obstinate Mr. Tulliver, the miller of Dorlcote Mill on the Floss. Tom is a prosaic youth, narrow of imagination and intellect, animated by conscious rectitude of purpose, and a disposition to exercise control over others. Maggie is of a far nobler type, highly strung and intelligent, of intense sensibility, and artistic and poetic tastes. From this conflict of temperaments and the incongruity of Maggie's character with her surroundings spring much unhappiness for the girl and ultimate tragedy. Maggie's love for her brother is thwarted by his lack of understanding, and the intellectual and emotional sides of her nature are starved. She finds in Philip Wakem, the deformed son of a neighbouring lawyer, a temperament like her own, and they are mutually attracted. Unfortunately lawyer Wakem is the object of Mr. Tulliver's suspicion and dislike, which develop into intense hatred when Tulliver is made bankrupt as a result of litigation in which Wakem is on the other side. Tom, loyal to his father, discovers the relations of affectionate friendship secretly maintained between Maggie and Philip, and the first deep dissension between brother and sister ensues; but Maggie yields to her brother's authority and ceases to see Philip. After Mr. Tulliver's death, accelerated by a scene of violence in which he thrashes the lawyer, Maggie leaves the Mill for a visit at St. Ogg's to her cousin Lucy Deane, who is to marry the cultivated and agreeable Stephen Guest. Stephen, though loyal in intention to Lucy, is attracted by Maggie's beauty; she, though similarly loyal to Philip, is drawn to Stephen. A boating expedition on the tidal river leads, partly by Stephen's design, partly by accident, to

Maggie's being innocently but irremediably compromised. Her brother turns her out of his house; the society of St. Ogg's ostracizes her. Only Lucy and Philip, whose hopes of happiness she has ruined, show more understanding. The situation appears without issue. A great flood descends upon the town, in the course of which Maggie, whose first thought in danger is for her brother, courageously rescues Tom from the mill. There comes a moment of revelation to the spirit of the awe-struck Tom before the boat is overwhelmed, and brother and sister, reconciled at last, are drowned.

The tragedy of the story is somewhat relieved by a number of entertaining characters, notably Mrs. Tulliver's sisters, the strong-minded Mrs. Glegg and the melancholy Mrs. Pullet, with their respective spouses, and the ingenious packman Bob Jakin.

Millais, SIR JOHN EVERETT (1829–96), a precocious and brilliant painter. He was a member of the Pre-Raphaelite Brotherhood (q.v.), painting romantic and literary subjects, e.g. 'Isabella' (from Keats), and illustrating magazine stories. After *c.* 1860 he became a fashionable painter of portraits and genre scenes.

Millamant, the heroine of Congreve's 'The Way of the World' (q.v.), a witty coquette, a Beatrice who is at the same time a lady of fashion, the author's most vivid creation.

MILLAY, EDNA ST. VINCENT (1892–1950), American poet, born in Maine. Her works include 'Renascence and other Poems' (1917), 'The Harp-Weaver and Other Poems' (1923), and the play 'The Princess Marries the Page' (1932). Her 'Collected Sonnets' appeared in 1941 and her 'Collected Lyrics' in 1943.

Millbank, MR., OSWALD, and EDITH, characters in Disraeli's 'Coningsby' (q.v.).

MILLER, ARTHUR (1915–   ), American dramatist, born in New York. He made his name with 'All My Sons' (1947), and established himself as a leading dramatist with 'Death of a Salesman' (1949), in which a travelling salesman, Willie Loman, is brought to disaster by accepting the false values of contemporary society. He took the Salem Witchcraft Trials of 1692 as the subject for 'The Crucible' (1953). Another important play is 'A View from the Bridge' (1955).

MILLER, HUGH (1802–56), by trade a stonemason, was author of geological and other works, including 'The Old Red Sandstone' (contributed to the 'Witness', the organ of the non-intrusionists (q.v.), of which Miller was the editor, 1841); 'Footprints of the Creator' (1847); the pleasant autobiography, 'My Schools and Schoolmasters' (1854); and 'The Testimony of the Rocks' (1857).

MILLER, JOAQUIN (CINCINNATUS HEINE) (1841?–1913), American poet, author of 'Songs of the Sierras' (1871), which won

him a reputation in England as a 'frontier' poet.

Miller, JOE, see *Joe Miller's Jests.*

Miller of Mansfield, THE, the subject of a ballad included in Percy's 'Reliques', who entertains Henry II unawares and is knighted by him.

Miller of the Dee, the subject of a song in the comic opera 'Love in a Village' by Bickerstaffe (q.v.).

Miller of Trumpington, THE, the miller in 'The Reeve's Tale' in Chaucer's 'Canterbury Tales' (q.v.).

Miller's Tale, The, see *Canterbury Tales.*

Mills, MISS, in Dickens's 'David Copperfield' (q.v.), Dora's friend.

Millwood, see *George Barnwell.*

Milly Swidger, the good angel in Dickens's 'The Haunted Man' (q.v.).

MILMAN, HENRY HART (1791–1868), educated at Eton and Brasenose College, Oxford, became incumbent of St. Mary's, Reading, then professor of poetry at Oxford (1821–31), and dean of St. Paul's (1849). He wrote a number of dramas, of which 'Fazio' (1815), a tragedy placed in Italy, proved successful on the stage. But Milman is chiefly remembered for his historical writings: his 'History of the Jews' (1830), 'History of Christianity from the Birth of Christ . . .' (1840), and his principal work, 'The History of Latin Christianity' (1854–5), which gave him high fame as an historian. His 'Annals of St. Paul's Cathedral' were published in 1868.

MILNE, ALAN ALEXANDER (1882–1956), journalist and playwright, author of books of children's stories and verse, 'Winnie-the-Pooh', 'When We Were Very Young', etc., which enjoyed great popularity; and also of plays including 'Mr. Pim Passes By' and 'The Truth about Blayds'.

MILNES, RICHARD MONCKTON (1809–85), *first Baron Houghton,* was educated at Trinity College, Cambridge, where he was intimate with Tennyson, Hallam, and Thackeray. He became an active politician. Of his songs and other poems ('Poetical Works', 1876), those best known are 'The Brookside' and 'Strangers Yet'. He also wrote on political and critical subjects ('Monographs', 1873), and edited and wrote a Life of Keats (1848); in fact he was the first open champion of Keats as a poet of the first rank.

Milo, a celebrated athlete of Crotona in Italy, who attained immense strength, was six times victor in wrestling at the Olympic games and is said to have led the army of Crotona against Sybaris in 511 B.C. He fell a prey to wolves in the end, his hands caught in the trunk of a tree which he was trying to split open.

Milton, for the poem of that name by Blake, see *Blake.*

MILTON, JOHN (1608–74), was born in Bread Street, Cheapside, at the Sign of the Spread Eagle, the house of his father, John Milton the elder, a scrivener and composer of music. He was educated at St. Paul's School and Christ's College, Cambridge, becoming B.A. in 1629 and M.A. in 1632. While at Cambridge he wrote the poems 'On the Death of a Fair Infant' and 'At a Vacation Exercise', in his 17th and 19th year respectively, and some Latin elegies and epigrams; but he first struck a distinctive note in the stately ode 'On the Morning of Christ's Nativity' (1629), the fragmentary 'Passion', and the poem 'On Shakespeare' (1630). The two pieces on Hobson, the university carrier, belong to the same period, also the 'Epitaph on the Marchioness of Winchester', and probably the Italian poems. After leaving Cambridge, Milton took up no profession, but lived at Horton in Bucks. with his father, reading the classics and preparing himself for his vocation as a poet, from 1632 to 1637. Here he composed 'L'Allegro' and 'Il Penseroso' (qq.v.) in 1632, and at the invitation of Henry Lawes (who wrote the music for them) the 'Arcades' (part of a masque, 1633?) and 'Comus' (q.v., 1634, published 1637). In 1637 he wrote 'Lycidas' (q.v.). During the twenty years that elapsed between this and his composition of 'Paradise Lost', Milton wrote no poetry, apart from some Latin and Italian pieces, but sonnets, of which the most notable are those 'On the late Massacre in Piedmont', on his blindness, on his deceased wife, the addresses to Cromwell, Fairfax, and Vane, and those to Lawrence, Lawes, and Cyriack Skinner. From 1637 to 1639 Milton travelled abroad, chiefly in Italy, and visited Grotius and Galileo (the latter in prison). On his return he became tutor to his nephews, Edward and John Philips, and other pupils. In 1641 he published a series of pamphlets against episcopacy, engaging in controversy with Bishop Hall. These were followed in 1642 by his 'Apology against a pamphlet . . . against Smectymnuus' (see *Smectymnuus*), containing some interesting autobiographical details. Milton married Mary Powell, daughter of Royalist parents, probably in June 1642 (not 1643 as has been generally supposed: see B. A. Wright in 'Modern Language Review', Oct. 1931 and Jan. 1932). Within six weeks he consented to her going home to her parents on condition that she returned by Michaelmas. She did not do so, perhaps for reasons connected with the outbreak of the Civil War. Milton published in 1643 his pamphlet on the 'doctrine and discipline of divorce' which made him notorious. In 1644–5 he published three further pamphlets on divorce (including 'Tetrachordon', q.v.), his 'Tractate of Education', and the 'Areopagitica' (q.v.) on the liberty of the press. His wife rejoined him in 1645, and in 1647 he gave up teaching pupils, his circumstances having become easier on the death of his father in 1646. After the execu-

tion of Charles I he published the 'Tenure of Kings and Magistrates' (1649), and was appointed Latin secretary to the newly formed Council of State. He replied officially to 'Eikon Basilike' (q.v.) in 'Eikonoclastes' (i.e. Image-breaker, 1649), and to Salmasius (q.v.) in 'Pro Populo Anglicano Defensio' (1651), and also to Du Moulin's 'Clamor' (which he attributed to Morus, or More) in 'Defensio Secunda' (1654), containing some autobiographical passages (the two 'Defensiones' were in Latin). Having become blind, he assisted in his secretarial duties successively by G. R. Weckherlin, Philip Meadows, and Marvell (q.v.). His first wife died in 1652, leaving three daughters, and in 1656 he married Catharine Woodcock, who died in 1658. He retained his post as Latin secretary until the Restoration, having lived while holding it chiefly in a house in Petty France, Westminster. At the Restoration he was arrested and fined, but released; he lost the greater part of his fortune. On the discomfiture of his principles and aspirations, he returned to poetry and set about the composition of 'Paradise Lost' (q.v.), the first sketch of which can be dated as early as 1642. He married his third wife, Elizabeth Minshull (who survived him), in 1662, and moved to what is now Bunhill Row, where he spent the remaining years of his life. The 'Paradise Lost' is said by Aubrey to have been finished in 1663, but the agreement for his copyright was not signed till 1667. His last poems, 'Paradise Regained' (q.v.) and 'Samson Agonistes' (q.v.), were published together in 1671. He published his Latin grammar and 'History of Britain' (from legendary times to the Norman Conquest) in 1669 and 1670 respectively; a compendium of Ramus's 'Logic', 1672; a tract on 'True Religion', 1673; 'Familiar Letters', 1674; and 'College Exercises', 1674. His 'Brief History of Moscovia', containing a curious account of the country, drawn from the Hakluyt and Purchas collections, appeared in 1682.

Of Milton's Latin poems, the finest is the 'Epitaphium Damonis', written in 1639, on the death of his friend Charles Diodati (q.v.); while the epistle 'Ad Patrem' and the address to 'Mansus' (Giovanni Battista Manso, the intimate friend of Tasso and Marini) have great interest.

The 'State Papers' that he wrote as Latin secretary are mostly concerned with the routine work of diplomacy, but include an interesting series of dispatches, from 1655 to 1658, on the subject of the expulsion and massacre of the Protestant Vaudois by the orders of the Prince of Savoy, which breathe the same indignation that found more unrestrained expression in his sonnet 'Avenge, O Lord, thy slaughtered saints'. The Latin prose writings include his 'De Doctrina Christiana', printed in 1825, which served as the occasion for Macaulay's essay on Milton.

Milton died from 'gout struck in', and was buried beside his father, in St. Giles',

Cripplegate, London. His most important biography is David Masson's 'Life of Milton, narrated in connection with the Political, Ecclesiastical, and Literary History of his Time' (1859–80).

Milward, RICHARD (1609–80), amanuensis to Selden (q.v.), whose 'Table Talk' he compiled.

Mime, a kind of simple farcical drama among the Greeks and Romans, characterized by mimicry and the ludicrous representation of familiar types of character; or a dialogue written for recital in a performance of this kind. The term is also occasionally applied to similar performances or compositions in modern times. [OED.] But in the modern usage the word generally means dumb acting.

Miming, in northern mythology, a magical sword forged by Völundr (Wieland, see *Wayland the Smith*). This sword, in the hands of Hödur, was, according to one form of the legend, the means of slaying Balder (q.v.).

Mimir or MIMER, in Scandinavian mythology, a giant water-demon who dwelt at the root of Yggdrasil (q.v.) guarding the waters of the well of wisdom.

Mincing Lane, in the City of London, originally, according to Stow, *Mincheon Lane*, from *minchen*, a nun, so called from the nuns of the priory of St. Helen's in Bishopsgate, which owned the lane. It is now the chief centre of the trade in tea, sugar, and other colonial produce. In Stow's day it was occupied by 'galley-men' from Genoa, who brought up wines and other merchandize, which they landed in Thames Street.

Mind, a quarterly review of psychology and philosophy, founded in 1876 by A. Bain (q.v.).

Minerva, the Roman goddess of wisdom and of arts and trades, subsequently identified with the Greek Athene (q.v.), which led to her being regarded also as the goddess of war. She was further held to have invented musical instruments.

Minerva, Jahrbuch der gelehrten Welt, a reference book of the universities, colleges, libraries, museums, learned societies, scientific institutions, etc., of the whole world, published by Walter de Gruyter & Co., Berlin and Leipzig.

Minerva Press, a printing press formerly existing in Leadenhall Street, London; hence the series of ultra-sentimental novels issued with the imprint of this press about 1800.

Ming, the dynasty that ruled in China from 1368 until ousted by the Manchu (Tsing) dynasty in 1643. The porcelain of this period is highly esteemed.

Minifie, SUSANNAH, see *Gunning (Mrs. S.).*

Minim, a friar belonging to the mendicant order (*Ordo Minimorum Eremitarum*) founded by St. Francis of Paola (*c.* 1416–1507).

Minim, DICK, a character sketched in

Johnson's 'Idler' (q.v.). Inheriting a fortune, he turns man of wit and humour and sets up as a critic. He has his own seat in a coffee-house and heads a party in the pit, where he prudently spares the authors whose reputation is well established and censures those who are unknown.

Minnehaha, see *Hiawatha.*

Minnesingers, German lyrical poets and singers of the 12th, 13th, and 14th cents., so called because love (*minne*) was the chief theme of their songs. They corresponded to the French *troubadours*. The best-known name among these poets of the old chivalry is that of Walther von der Vogelweide (*fl.* 1200).

Minoan, the name given by Sir A. Evans (q.v.) to the civilization revealed by his excavations at the Palace of Minos at Knossos in Crete, so called after the legendary King Minos (q.v.). Of this civilization (represented by products of arts and crafts, with hazy political inferences therefrom) he recognized three main phases, Early, Middle, and Late Minoan, and he subdivided each phase into three sub-periods, of advance, acme, and decline, I, II, and III. The earliest Minoan dates from the last part of the Neolithic Age, It has been found possible to relate this civilization to the history of Egypt, Early Minoan being roughly synchronous with the first ten Egyptian dynasties (3400–2100 B.C.), Middle Minoan with the 11th–17th Egyptian dynasties (2100–1600 B.C.), and Late Minoan with the 18th and 19th Egyptian dynasties (1600–1200 B.C.). Knossos was, in classical tradition, the seat of King Minos and the abode of the Minotaur.

Minories, a street leading from Aldgate to the Tower of London, which derives its name from the *Minoresses*, nuns of the second order of St. Francis, known as Poor Clares, whose house stood outside Aldgate.

Minorites, Franciscan friars.

Minos, a legendary king of Crete, son of Zeus and Europa (q.v.), who gave laws to his subjects and displayed so much justice and moderation that he was rewarded after death by being made supreme judge in the infernal regions. Attic legend, on the other hand, represented him as a cruel tyrant who imposed on Athens a yearly tribute of seven youths and seven maidens to be devoured by the Minotaur (q.v.). He caused Daedalus (q.v.), the constructor of the Labyrinth, to be imprisoned, and when Daedalus escaped, pursued him to Sicily, and was there slain by Cocalus, the king.

MINOT, LAURENCE, probably a soldier, the author, about 1352, of war-songs in various metres, on Halidon Hill, the Capture of Berwick, the battle of Crécy, the siege of Calais, and similar historical subjects. Though not of a high poetical order, the songs are spirited, giving a vivid idea of medieval warfare, and marked by keen patriotism and loyalty to the king.

Minotaur, THE, a Cretan monster. Minos (q.v.) refused to sacrifice to Neptune a white bull which the god had given him for that purpose. The god to punish him caused his wife Pasiphaë to become enamoured of the bull, and she gave birth to this monster. Minos confined it in the labyrinth made by Daedalus (q.v.), where it consumed the youths and maidens paid by the conquered Athenians as a tribute, until Theseus (q.v.) delivered his country and destroyed the monster. Representations of a sport of bull-leaping or baiting (perhaps ritual or cere-monial) are frequent in Cretan art of the Minoan period.

Minstrel, The, see *Beattie.*

Minuscule, a small letter or script, a term used in palaeography to denote the scripts developed in the early Middle Ages. The best known is Caroline minuscule, the ancestor of 'Roman' type.

Miölnir or MJÖLNIR, in Scandinavian mythology, the hammer of Thor (q.v.).

Mirabeau, GABRIEL HONORÉ RIQUETTI, COMTE DE (1749–91), a member, and in 1791 president, of the Constituent Assembly in the French Revolution; a man of fervid temperament and fiery eloquence, yet a cool politician, who played an important part in the early stage of the Revolution.

Mirabeau, VICTOR DE RIQUETTI, *Marquis de,* father of the preceding, see *Physiocrats.*

Mirabell, (1) the hero of J. Fletcher's 'Wild Goose Chase' (q.v.); (2) in Congreve's 'The Way of the World' (q.v.), the lover of Milla-mant.

Mirabilia Urbis Romae, a medieval guide-book to Rome. Its first form probably dates from the 12th cent., and it was perhaps 'kept up to date' till the 15th. There is a translation by F. Nichols (1889).

Miracle Plays, medieval dramatic repre-sentations based on sacred history or on legends of the saints. Whether they were evolved from alternating songs sung in church (e.g. at the service on Easter Eve, be-tween the three women approaching the grave and the Angel who guards it), or were spontaneous expressions of the dramatic instinct, is a point on which the authorities are not agreed. What is perhaps the earliest English miracle play, 'The Harrowing of Hell' (q.v.), is of the late 13th or 14th cent., though such plays existed in France much earlier. They reached their fullest develop-ment in the 15th and 16th cents. The four great collections of extant English 'miracles' or 'mysteries' are known by the names of the towns where they were, or are supposed to have been, performed, York, Chester, Coven-try, and Wakefield (the last being also known as the 'Towneley' plays). Their performance was supervised by the corporation of the town, the several episodes being generally distributed among the guilds of handicrafts, and acted on wheeled stages moved pro-cessionally from one open place to another, or only in one place. The scenes varied in length from 180 to 800 lines, and were written in different metres, sometimes rhymed, sometimes alliterative, sometimes both. They were played principally on festivals, Corpus Christi day, Christmas, Whitsuntide, Easter. See also *Mary Magda-lene (Play of).*

Not only is there no dearth of humour in these plays, but they are notable in the history of the drama for the introduction of comic by-play and episode. A good instance of this is afforded by the 'Second Shepherd's Play' in the Towneley cycle. The shepherds are watching their sheep by night, when Mak the sheep-stealer makes his appearance. He succeeds in stealing a sheep and takes it to his home, where he and his wife put it in a cradle. When the shepherds search his house, Mak pretends that there is a new-born baby in the cradle; but the fraud is discovered and gives rise to much hilarity. They toss Mak in a blanket till they are tired; then lie down and sleep. They are awakened by an angel who tells them that the Redeemer is born and they must go to Bethlehem.

Sir E. K. Chambers's 'The Mediaeval Stage' is the classic work on this subject.

Miramolin (written *Maramoline* by R. Browning in 'Sordello'), a Spanish word, corruption of the Arabic *Amir ul Muminin,* 'Commander of the Faithful', the European designation in the Middle Ages of the emperor of Morocco.

Miranda, in Shakespeare's 'The Tempest' (q.v.), the daughter of Prospero.

Mirobolant, MONSIEUR, in Thackeray's 'Pendennis' (q.v.), the French cook at Clavering Park.

Mirror for Magistrates, A, a work planned by George Ferrers, Master of the King's Pastimes in the reign of Henry VIII, and William Baldwin of Oxford, in which divers illustrious men, most of them characters in English history, recount in verse their down-fall, after the manner of Lydgate's version of Boccaccio's 'Fall of Princes'. It was licensed for publication in 1559, and contained twenty tragedies by various authors. Thomas Sack-ville contributed the 'Induction' (in which Sorrow leads the poet to the realms of the dead) and 'The Complaint of Buckingham' (q.v.) to the enlarged edition of 1563. Further editions were published in 1574, 1578, 1587, and 1610. Sackville's contribution is the only part having literary merit.

Mirror of Fools, 'Speculum Stultorum', see *Wireker.*

Mirvan, CAPTAIN and MRS., and their daughter Maria, characters in Fanny Bur-ney's 'Evelina' (q.v.).

Mirza, The Vision of, see *Vision of Mirza.*

Misanthrope, Le, one of the greatest comedies of Molière (q.v.), produced in 1666, in which he represents the conflict between the noble but cross-grained Alceste, exasperated by the corruption of society, and the worldly coquettish Célimène whom he loves.

Miserrimus, the sole inscription on a tombstone in the cloisters of Worcester Cathedral. The tomb is said to be that of the Rev. Thomas Morris, a minor canon, who refused to take the oaths to William III, was deprived of his preferment, and died destitute. Wordsworth takes a more mysterious view in his sonnet on 'A Gravestone', beginning:

'*Miserrimus*', and neither name nor date.

'Miserrimus, a Tale', by Frederic Mansel Reynolds (*d.* 1850), was published in 1833.

Misfortunes of Elphin, The, a novel by Peacock (q.v.), published in 1829.

It is an entertaining parody of the Arthurian legends. Elphin is king of Caredigion in southern Wales, but the bulk of his territory has been engulfed by the sea, owing to the drunkenness of Prince Seithenyn, who was charged with the duty of maintaining the embankment to keep out the waves. Elphin himself, during the greater part of the story, is imprisoned by a more powerful neighbour for refusing to recognize that the latter's wife is more chaste and beautiful than his own. The young bard Taliesin effects his rescue by enlisting the aid of King Arthur. This he obtains by restoring to him Guinevere, who has been abducted by King Melvas. The book includes the celebrated 'War-Song of Dinas Vawr'.

Mishnah, the collection of binding precepts or *halakhoth* (see 'Halachah' under *Haggadah*) which forms the basis of the Talmud (q.v.) and embodies the contents of the oral law of the Jews.

Misrule, KING, LORD, or ABBOT OF, at the end of the 15th and beginning of the 16th cents., an officer appointed at court to superintend the Christmas revels. At the Scottish court he was called the 'Abbot of Unreason'. Lords of Misrule were also appointed in some of the university colleges and inns of court.

Miss Kilmansegg and her precious Leg, A Golden Legend, a tragi-comic poem by T. Hood (q.v.), published in the 'New Monthly Magazine' (1841–3).

Miss Kilmansegg, the daughter of the wealthy Sir Jacob, is born and brought up in the midst of gold. Her horse runs away with her and falls, and she has to lose her leg. It is replaced by one made of gold, and becomes famous. The heiress has many suitors, but marries a sinister foreign count, who breaks her heart, and finally her head, this last with the golden leg itself, and the jury bring in a verdict of *felo de se*, 'Because her own leg had killed her'.

Mr. Clutterbuck's Election, a novel by H. Belloc (q.v.).

'**Mr. F's Aunt**', an eccentric character in Dickens's 'Little Dorrit' (q.v.).

Mr. Gilfil's Love-Story, see *Scenes of Clerical Life.*

Mr. Polly, The History of, a novel by H. G. Wells (q.v.), published in 1910.

Alfred Polly, when the story opens, is a dyspeptic inefficient shopkeeper with a literary turn, who, after a career as salesman to various employers, a small legacy, and an injudicious marriage, has bought an unprofitable little shop in a small seaside town. After fifteen years of passive endurance he finds bankruptcy approaching and prepares for suicide. Instead, he sets his shop on fire and bolts. He chances upon a perfect situation as man of all work at the Potwell Inn— perfect but for the landlady's ferocious nephew, who terrorizes and persecutes his aunt and threatens destruction to Polly if he doesn't clear out. Polly, nobly conquering his innate timidity, in three murderous encounters defeats and finally ousts the villain, and is left completely happy, having in the course of the story entirely gained the reader's affection.

Mr. Sludge, the 'Medium', a poem by R. Browning (q.v.) included in 'Dramatis Personae', published in 1864.

The poet puts into the mouth of Sludge, the detected cheat, a confession and defence of his profession of fraudulent medium. Browning distrusted mediums, and was strongly antagonistic to the American spiritualist, Daniel D. Home (q.v.). But here he allows Sludge to make the best of his case and to place a fair share of the blame on the folly of his audiences.

Mistletoe (from old English *mistel*, (1) basil (q.v.) or (2) mistletoe, and *tan*, twig), a parasitic plant growing on various trees. The mistletoe of the oak was regarded by the Druids as a sacred plant. The cutting of it by the Druids with a golden sickle at the beginning of the year and with attendant sacrifice is described by Pliny (xvi. 44). A trace of this practice is to be found in our use of mistletoe in Christmas decorations. Shakespeare ('Titus Andronicus', II. iii) speaks of it as the 'baleful mistletoe'. According to Scandinavian mythology, Balder (q.v.) was slain with a sprig of mistletoe, the only thing that could harm him.

Mistletoe Bough, The, see *Ginevra.*

MISTRAL, FRÉDÉRIC (1830–1914), a French poet of Provence, who revived the glory of Provençal literature. His best-known works are the pastoral epic 'Mirèio' (1859), 'Calendau' (1867), 'Lis Isclo d'or' (1875), 'Nerto' (1884), 'La Rèino Jano' (1890). These were accompanied by a French translation.

Mrs. Caudle's Curtain Lectures, by D.W. Jerrold (q.v.), appeared in 'Punch' during the year 1845, and greatly added to that periodical's popularity.

Mr. Caudle is a 'toyman and doll-merchant' and his wife is a voluble and jealous scold. The lectures, addressed to him when he wants to go to sleep, are reproofs for his mildly convivial habits, exhortations to take the family to the seaside, or disquisitions on similar domestic subjects.

Mrs. Lirriper's Lodgings, and *Mrs. Lirriper's Legacy,* Christmas stories by Dickens (q.v.), which appeared in 'All the Year Round', 1863 and 1864. Mrs. Lirriper lets lodgings in Norfolk Street, Strand, and her lodgers and past lodgers tell their stories.

Mistress of Phil'Arete, Fair Virtue, the, a pastoral poem by G. Wither (q.v., 1622).

Mrs. Perkins's Ball, one of Thackeray's (q.v.) 'Christmas Books' (1847).

Mrs. Warren's Profession, a play by G. B. Shaw (q.v.), included in 'Plays Pleasant and Unpleasant' (q.v.).

MITCHEL, JOHN (1818–75), an Irish nationalist, educated at Trinity College, Dublin, and a solicitor. He wrote for, and was editor of, the 'Nation', and was tried for sedition and transported to serve a sentence of fourteen years in 1848. He has left in his 'Jail Journal, or Five Years in British Prisons' (1856) a vivid account of his experiences. He escaped to America, where he engaged in journalistic work. His writings also include a 'Life of Aodh O'Neill', earl of Tyrone (1845), and a 'History of Ireland' (1869).

MITFORD, MARY RUSSELL (1787–1855), is remembered for her charming collection of essays, 'Our Village, sketches of rural life, character, and scenery', begun in 'The Lady's Magazine' (1819) and published separately, 1824–32. The scene of these is Three Mile Cross near Reading. She also published 'Belford Regis, sketches of a country town' (Reading) in 1835, 'Country Stories' in 1837, a novel, 'Atherton', in 1854, various plays, and 'Recollections of a Literary Life' (1852), which is of value for its chapters on some of her contemporaries.

MITFORD, WILLIAM (1744–1827), educated at Queen's College, Oxford, was the author of a 'History of Greece' (1785–1810), down to the death of Alexander, written at the suggestion of Gibbon, which enjoyed great popularity. It was the work of a pioneer and was superseded by the histories of Grote and Thirlwall (qq.v.).

Mithraism, the religion of the worshippers of Mithras, one of the chief gods of the ancient Persians, in later times often identified with the sun. His worship was introduced among the Romans under the Empire, and spread over most of northern and western Europe during the first three centuries A.D., the principal rival of Christianity.

Mithridate, a composition of many ingredients in the form of an electuary (a paste made with honey or syrup) regarded as a universal antidote against poison and infec-tious disease, so called from Mithridates VI, king of Pontus (131–63 B.C.), who was said to have rendered himself proof against poisons by the constant use of poisons as antidotes.

Mitre Tavern, THE, frequented by Dr. Johnson, stood in Mitre Court, Fleet Street, over against Fetter Lane, not to be confused with the Mitre in Fleet Street of the days of Shakespeare and Jonson, which stood farther west (Wheatley and Cunningham, 'London Past and Present').

Mnemŏsўnĕ, the mother, by Zeus, of the nine Muses (q.v.). The name signifies 'Memory'.

Moabite Stone, THE, a monument erected by Mesha, king of Moab, about 850 B.C., which furnishes the earliest-known inscription in the Phoenician alphabet. It is now in the Louvre in Paris, restored after having been broken in pieces by Arabs.

Moby Dick, a romance of the sea, by H. Melville (q.v.), published in 1851.

Moby Dick is the name of a particularly cunning and ferocious whale, known to many whalers by the peculiarities of its appearance, which has been the cause of so many disasters to its pursuers that it has become an object of fear and superstition. It has bereft Captain Ahab of his leg, and he has vowed revenge, and the story is that of the voyage of the ship 'Pequod' in pursuit of it. The author gives a mass of detailed information concerning the varieties of whales, their habits, anatomy, and commercial value, and the methods of killing them. He also paints a vivid gallery of pictures of the strange characters aboard the 'Pequod', and, strangest of all, of the monomaniac Ahab. From a story of whale-fishing, the work becomes the epic of Ahab's attempted vengeance on his personal enemy. After a search round three-quarters of the globe, Moby Dick is found, and a thrilling contest, drawn out through three days, ends in its triumphant victory. It breaks Ahab's neck, crunches up or swamps all the boats, and finally sinks the 'Pequod' herself, with all hands, save one survivor.

Modern Instance, A, one of W. D. Howells's (q.v.) best-known novels, published in 1881.

Modern Love, a series of fifty connected poems, each of sixteen lines, by G. Meredith (q.v.), published in 1862. It is the tragic tale, somewhat obscurely indicated in monodramatic form, of passionate married love giving place to discord, jealousy, and intense unhappiness, and ending in the separation and ruin of two ill-mated lives, and the death by poison of the wife.

Modern Painters, a treatise by Ruskin (q.v.), of which vol. i was published in 1843, vol. ii in 1846, vols. iii and iv in 1856, and vol. v in 1860.

The first volume, written when the author was only four-and-twenty, was conceived in a mood of indignation at the artistic ignorance of England, and written in particular to defend Turner against the attacks on his paintings. It expounds the author's views of the principles of true art, points out the faults of such painters as Claude, Gaspar Poussin, and Salvator Rosa, and explains the merits of Turner's work.

Vol. ii, in the author's words, 'expresses the first and fundamental law respecting human contemplation of the natural phenomena under whose influence we exist—that they can only be seen with their properly belonging joy and interpreted up to the measure of proper human intelligence, when they are accepted as the work and the gift of a Living Spirit greater than our own'. The latter part is chiefly concerned with the function of imagination in art. This volume expresses the author's admiration for Tintoretto.

The third volume, after an essay on the Grand Style and a discussion of Idealism, passes to a history of the appreciation of landscape through the ages, from Homer onwards. It winds up, oddly, with an excursus on the Crimean War.

The fourth volume contains the famous passage on the tower of Calais church, and chapters on colour and illumination; followed, in this and the last volume, by a study of natural landscape in its various details, such as leaves and clouds. There is a notable digression (part v, ch. xix) on the peasantry of the Valais mountains.

The fifth volume proceeds to discuss the four orders of landscape painters—Heroic (Titian), Classical (Poussin), Pastoral (Cuyp), Contemplative (Turner); Dürer and Salvator Rosa; Wouvermans and Angelico. In the chapter on 'The Two Boyhoods', Ruskin describes the Venice of Giorgione and the London of Turner, and the work closes with a final passionate lament for the latter painter.

Modest Proposal, A, see *Swift.*

Modish, LADY BETTY, the coquette in Colley Cibber's 'The Careless Husband' (q.v.).

Modo, in Shakespeare's 'King Lear' (q.v.), IV. i, the fiend of murder, one of the five that possess 'poor Tom'.

Modred or MORDRED, in the earliest Arthurian legends is the nephew of King Arthur, being the son of Lot, king of Norway, and Arthur's sister. In Geoffrey of Monmouth he is the son of Arthur and his sister Morgawse. He traitorously seized the kingdom and Guinevere during Arthur's absence, and was killed by Arthur in the final battle in Cornwall. Modred may be identified with the Medrawt of British mythology, a god of darkness (see Rhys, 'Arthurian Legend').

Moeliades, in the pastoral elegy, 'Tears on the death of Moeliades', by Drummond of Hawthornden (q.v.), was Prince Henry, son of James I.

Mogul, from the Persian and Arabic *Mughal,* a mispronunciation of the native name *Mongol,* is the name applied to the Muslim Mongol empire in Hindustan. This was founded by Baber (a descendant of Tamerlane) in 1526. It reached its height under Akbar, Jehangir, Shah Jehan, and Aurungzebe, was broken up after the death of the last named, and finally disappeared in 1857. The GREAT MOGUL was the common designation among Europeans of the Mogul emperor.

'Moguls', in the middle of the 19th cent., was the name given to the best quality of playing-cards, from a fancy picture of the Great Mogul on the wrapper.

Moguntia or MOGUNTIACUM, in imprints, Mainz.

Mohammed or MAHOMET, the name of the founder of the Muslim religion, born at Mecca about A.D. 570, died in 632.

After marrying his first wife, Khadijah, he declared himself a prophet about 611, and sought to turn his fellow-countrymen from their idolatry and to restore the ancient monotheistic religion of Adam, Noah, Abraham, etc. He fled to Medina (the *Hijra*) in 622. He imparted from time to time to his disciples the revelations that he claimed to receive, known as the Koran. His favourite wife was Ayesha (q.v.), his favourite daughter Fatima.

Legend records that Mohammed, invited to show his miraculous powers, summoned Mt. Safa to come to him. He attributed its failure to do so to the mercy of Allah, for if it had come it would have overwhelmed him and the bystanders. Therefore, said Mohammed, he must go to the mountain, a proverbial example of bowing to the inevitable. Another legend tells of his miraculous conveyance on the horse Al Borak from Mecca to Jerusalem, and of his journey thence with the angel Gabriel through the seven heavens, to within two bow-shots of the throne. He was touched by the hand of God, returned to Jerusalem, and was carried back to Mecca. The story that Mohammed's iron coffin floated in mid-air at Mecca attracted by loadstones is said by Gibbon to have been invented by Greeks and Latins. Mohammed was buried at Medina and his tomb has been a regular object of pilgrimage.

See also under *Abbasides, Ali, Ayesha, Borak, Fatima, Hashim, Khadijah, Koran, Shi'ites, Sunnites, Umayyads.*

Mohican (pron. Mohēcan), the name of a warlike tribe of North American Indians of the Algonquin stock, formerly occupying both banks of the Upper Hudson River, nearly as far as Lake Champlain, and extending into Massachusetts.

For 'The Last of the Mohicans' see *Cooper (J. F.).*

Mohock, one of a class of aristocratic ruffians who infested the streets of London at night in the early years of the 18th cent. The word is taken from *Mohawk*, the name of a North American Indian tribe, formerly supposed to be cannibals. There are references to the Mohocks in Swift's 'Journal to Stella' (8 Mar. 1711/12), in Gay's 'Trivia' (iii. 326), and in the 'Spectator' (No. 324).

Mohun (Mōōn), CHARLES, *fifth Baron* (1675?–1712), was a noted duellist. He fought his first recorded duel in 1692, and was tried in the following year for being concerned in the death of William Mountfort, a player, but was acquitted. He distinguished himself in the army, and, after another duel, engaged in a dispute with the 4th duke of Hamilton. In the encounter that followed, both combatants were mortally wounded. Lord Mohun figures prominently in Thackeray's 'Esmond' (q.v.).

Moidore, a gold coin of Portugal current in England in the first half of the 18th cent., from *moeda d'ouro*, money of gold. It was worth about 27s. 6d. In later use the word survived as a name for the sum of 27s.

MOIR, DAVID MACBETH (1798–1851), physician, wrote for 'Blackwood's' 'The Life of Mansie Wauch, Tailor in Dalkeith' (reprinted 1828), an amusing study of life and character in a small Scottish town, as seen through the eyes of the simple tailor, and depicted in racy language and with much humour. He used the pseudonym 'Delta'.

Mokanna, the 'Veiled Prophet of Khorassan' in Moore's 'Lalla Rookh' (q.v.).

MOLIÈRE, the name assumed by JEAN BAPTISTE POQUELIN (1622–73), French comic dramatist, the son of an upholsterer attached to the court. He began his career as groom-upholsterer to the king, but soon turned to the stage, became an actor and subsequently manager of a perambulating company, for which he composed some of his minor comedies and farces 'L'Étourdi' (1655), 'Le Dépit amoureux' (1656). His real genius is first shown in 'Les Précieuses ridicules', acted in Paris in 1659. In this, abandoning imitations of Plautus and Terence, he introduced the ridicule of actual French society, with its various types of folly, oddity, pedantry, or vice, as the subject of French comedy. His most famous plays were, besides that above mentioned: 'Sganarelle' (1660), 'L'École des maris' (1661), 'L'École des femmes' (1662), 'Le Tartuffe' (1664), 'Le Festin de Pierre' (Don Juan) (1665), 'Le Misanthrope' and 'Le Médecin malgré lui' (1666), 'Amphitryon' (q.v., 1668), 'George Dandin' (1668), 'L'Avare' (q.v., 1668), 'Le Bourgeois gentilhomme' (1670), 'Les Femmes savantes' and 'Le Malade imaginaire' (1673).

Molina, LUIS (1535–1600), a Spanish Jesuit who propounded the doctrine that the efficacy of grace depends simply on the will which freely accepts it. The term MOLINISM is applied both to this doctrine and to the Quietism of Miguel Molinos (q.v.).

MOLINA, TIRSO DA, see *Tellez*.

MOLINOS, MIGUEL (1640–96), a Spanish priest, founder of the Quietist (q.v.) sect. His work, 'The Spiritual Guide', was published in 1675.

Moll Cutpurse, Mary Frith, a notorious thief, fortune-teller, and forger, who lived about 1584–1659. She did penance at St. Paul's Cross in 1612. She is the heroine of Middleton and Dekker's 'The Roaring Girle' (q.v.).

Moll Flanders, The Fortunes and Misfortunes of the famous, a romance by Defoe (q.v.), published in 1722.

This purports to be the autobiography of the daughter of a woman who had been transported to Virginia for theft soon after her child's birth. The child, abandoned in England, is brought up in the house of the compassionate mayor of Colchester. The story relates her seduction, her subsequent marriages and liaisons, and her visit to Virginia, where she finds her mother and discovers that she has unwittingly married her own brother. After leaving him and returning to England, she is presently reduced to destitution. She becomes an extremely successful pickpocket and thief, but is presently detected and transported to Virginia, in company with one of her former husbands, a highwayman. With the funds that each has amassed, they set up as planters, and Moll moreover finds that she has inherited a plantation from her mother. She and her husband spend their declining years in an atmosphere of penitence and prosperity.

Molly Bawn, or *The Shooting of his Dear*, a traditional ballad (in Jamieson's 'Popular Ballads', 1806, Child's collection, etc.).

Molly Maguires, members of a secret society formed in Ireland in 1843 for the purpose of resisting the payment of rent. They 'were generally stout active young men, dressed up in women's clothes' (W. S. Trench, 'Realities of Irish Life').

Molly Mog, or the Fair Maid of the Inn, a ballad probably by John Gay, and it has been suggested that Pope and Swift were part authors. It first appeared in 'Mist's Weekly Journal', with a note to the effect that 'it was writ by two or three men of wit, upon the occasion of their lying at a certain Inn at Ockingham, where the daughter of the House was remarkably pretty, and whose name was Molly Mog'.

Moloch or MOLECH, the name of a Canaanite idol, to whom children were sacrificed as burnt-offerings (Lev. xviii. 21 and 2 Kings xxiii. 10), represented by Milton ('Paradise Lost', i. 392) as one of the chief of the fallen angels. Hence applied to an object to which horrible sacrifices are made.

Moly, a fabulous herb endowed with magic properties, said by Homer to have been given by Hermes to Odysseus as a charm against the sorceries of Circe ('Odyssey', x).

MOMMSEN, THEODOR (1817–1903), a great German historian and archaeologist, was from 1857 professor of ancient history at Berlin. He published his celebrated 'Roman History' in 1854–6, and other treatises and articles relating to Roman chronology, coins, law, etc. He edited Cassiodorus and was also editor of the great 'Corpus Inscriptionum Latinarum' for the Berlin Academy. Mommsen took an active part in politics and was a member of the Prussian House of Delegates.

Momus, the god of fault-finding among the ancients, who criticized whatever the gods did. For instance he blamed Vulcan because, in the human form that he had made of clay, he had not placed a window in the breast by which its secret thoughts might be brought to light.

Mona, an island between Britain and Ireland, anciently inhabited by Druids, supposed by some to be Anglesey, by others the Isle of Man.

Mona Lisa, ('La Joconde', 'La Gioconda'), portrait by Leonardo da Vinci (q.v.) of the wife of Francesco del Giocondo. It was taken to France by François I and is now in the Louvre. It is famous for its technical virtuosity and its enigmatic smile.

Monastery, The, a novel by Sir W. Scott (q.v.), published in 1820.

The story centres in the monastery of Kennaquhair, of which the prototype is Melrose Abbey on the Tweed, and the period chosen is the reign of Elizabeth, when the reformed doctrines were first making their way in Scotland and raising up troubles for the religious community that gives its title to the work. The plot is slight. Halbert and Edward, sons of a tenant of the monastery, Simon Glendinning, are brought up with Mary Avenel, orphan daughter of a noble house, whose misfortunes have brought her to the hospitable roof of the Glendinnings. Both lads fall in love with Mary, on whose affections the gallant Halbert gains a stronger hold than the more studious and contemplative Edward. An English knight, Sir Piercie Shafton, takes refuge in Scotland from the pursuit to which his intrigues in the Catholic interest have exposed him, and is lodged by the abbot of Kennaquhair at the home of the Glendinnings. His arrogance, vanity, and ridiculous euphuistic manner of speech incense Halbert, and a duel ensues in which the knight is left for dead. Halbert flees, enters the service of the earl of Murray, whose favour he wins by his gallant demeanour, and who finally bestows on him the hand of Mary Avenel. Edward, disappointed of Mary, becomes a monk.

The author makes use in this novel of supernatural machinery, in the form of the White Lady of Avenel, a spirit or sylph, to restore Sir Piercie Shafton to life after being mortally wounded, and to work other marvels.

More interesting are the characters of the easy-going abbot Boniface; of his energetic subprior, Father Eustace; and of the stern reformer, Henry Warden. See also *Abbot, (The).*

Monasticon Anglicanum, see *Dugdale.*

MONBODDO, JAMES BURNETT, LORD (1714–99), a Scottish judge and a pioneer in anthropology, who published 'Of the Origin and Progress of Language' (1773–92) and 'Antient Metaphysics' (1779–99). He is perhaps chiefly remembered for his orang-outang, who figures in both these works as an example of 'the infantine state of our species', who could play the flute but 'never learned to speak', and who suggested to Peacock the character of Sir Oran Haut-ton in his 'Melincourt' (q.v.).

Monçada, a character in Maturin's 'Melmoth the Wanderer' (q.v.).

Monēta, JUNO, 'Juno the admonisher', a goddess in whose temple at Rome money was coined; the origin of our word 'money'.

Money, a comedy by Bulwer Lytton (q.v.), produced in 1840.

Alfred Evelyn, private secretary to the wordly-wise Sir John Vesey, loves Clara Douglas, as poor as himself. She refuses him, not wishing to involve him in her own poverty. Evelyn comes into a large fortune, and, stung by Clara's refusal, which he attributes to the wrong motive, proposes to the worldly Georgina, daughter of Sir John; but soon has reason to regret the step. To test her affection and her father's loyalty, he pretends to be ruined by gambling and the breaking of a bank. Thereupon Georgina promptly transfers the promise of her hand to a rival suitor, while Clara comes forward to help Evelyn. Thus released, and earlier misconceptions removed, Evelyn marries Clara.

Monica, ST. (332–87), the mother of St. Augustine (q.v.).

Monimia, (1) the heroine of Otway's 'The Orphan' (q.v.); (2) a character in Smollett's 'Ferdinand Count Fathom' (q.v.).

Moniplies, RICHIE, a character in Scott's 'Fortunes of Nigel' (q.v.).

Monism, in philosophy, a general name for those theories which deny the duality (i.e. the existence as two ultimate kinds of substance) of matter and mind; opposed to dualism or pluralism.

Monitor, The, a weekly political paper founded in 1755 by Richard Beckford, a London merchant, and edited by John Entick, in the Whig interest. Wilkes contributed to it, and it was prosecuted for its attacks on Lord Bute's government.

Monk, The, a novel by M. G. Lewis (q.v.), published in 1796.

Ambrosio, the saintly superior of the Capuchins of Madrid, falls to the temptations of Matilda de Villanegas, a fiend-inspired wanton, who, disguised as a boy, has entered his monastery as a novice. Now utterly depraved, he becomes enamoured of one of his penitents, pursues his object with the help of magic and murder, and finally kills the girl herself in an attempt to escape detection. He is discovered, tortured by the Inquisition, and sentenced to death, finally compounding with the Devil for escape from the *auto-da-fé*, only to be hurled by him to destruction in another form.

The mixture of the supernatural, the horrible, and the indecent makes the book unreadable today. But it has power, contains some notable verses ('Alonzo the Brave and the Fair Imogine'), and attained a considerable vogue.

'Monk Lewis', soubriquet of M. G. Lewis (q.v.), author of 'The Monk' (q.v.).

Monks, a character in Dickens's 'Oliver Twist' (q.v.).

Monk's Tale, *The,* see *Canterbury Tales.*

Monkbarns, LAIRD OF, Jonathan Oldbuck, the principal character in Sir W. Scott's 'The Antiquary' (q.v.).

Monmouth Street, named after the duke of Monmouth, the son of Charles II, now forms part of Shaftesbury Avenue. It was at one time noted for its numerous old-clothes shops.

Monomotapa, an ancient African kingdom on the Zambezi, celebrated by old Portuguese writers for its gold-mines.

Monophysites, Christians who believe that there is only one nature in the person of Jesus Christ. They include at the present day the Coptic, Armenian, Abyssinian, and Jacobite churches. The dispute as to the single or dual nature of Christ began before the middle of the 5th cent. and lasted for more than 200 years; it did much towards the separation of the Eastern and Western Churches. The intellectuals in the East were on the whole Monophysites; the mob in the East and nearly everyone in the West were for the 'two Natures'. The dispute finally merged in that whether Christ had two 'wills' or one (Monothelite heresy).

Monotheists, those who believe that there is only one God.

MONRO, HAROLD (1879–1932), poet, born in Brussels and educated at Radley and Caius College, Cambridge. He wrote several volumes of poetry (his 'Collected Poems' were published in 1933, with an introduction by T. S. Eliot), but is chiefly remembered as the founder of the 'Poetry Review' in 1912 and the Poetry Bookshop which he opened in London in 1913 and ran until the end of his life. The Bookshop became a centre for anyone who was interested in poetry and a place where poetry readings could be given.

Monroe Doctrine, a political doctrine derived from the annual message of the President (in this instance President Monroe) to the United States Congress in 1823, when interference in Spanish America by the powers of the Holy Alliance was anticipated. The President stated that interposition by any European power in the affairs of the Spanish-American republics would be regarded as an act unfriendly to the United States, and that the American continents were no longer open to European colonial settlement.

Mons Meg, a great 15th-cent. gun in Edinburgh Castle, so called perhaps from having been cast at Mons in Flanders; but Maitland ('History of Edinburgh') calls it 'Mounts-Megg'. It was removed to the Tower of London after the campaign of 1745, and restored to Edinburgh (at Sir W. Scott's instance) in 1829.

Monsieur D'Olive, a comedy by Chapman (q.v.), published in 1606 and acted a few years before. The plot is of little interest, but the play is enlivened by the remarkable character, D'Olive, 'the perfect model of an impudent upstart', fluent, self-confident, good-humoured, witty, 'a mongrel of a gull and a villain'.

MONTAGU, BASIL (1770–1851), legal and miscellaneous writer, educated at Charterhouse and Christ's College, Cambridge, where he was intimate with Coleridge and Wordsworth. He published 'Essays' and edited Bacon (1825–37).

MONTAGU, MRS. ELIZABETH (1720–1800), *née* Robinson, married Edward Montagu, grandson of the first earl of Sandwich, and became well known as one of the leaders of the Blue Stocking (q.v.) circles. She combined beauty with wit and learning, and her conversation was highly praised by Dr. Johnson. She was author of the last three of the dialogues included in Lord Lyttelton's 'Dialogues of the Dead' (1760), and of an 'Essay on the Writings and Genius of Shakespeare' (1769), in which she defended the poet against the strictures of Voltaire.

MONTAGU, LADY MARY WORTLEY (1689–1762), daughter of the fifth earl and the first duke of Kingston, and wife of Edward Wortley Montagu, ambassador to Constantinople in 1716. She wrote from there some charming 'Turkish Letters' (published in 1763 after her death), and introduced into England the practice of inoculation against the small-pox. In 1716 Curll piratically published some of her 'Town Eclogues' and 'Court Poems by a Lady of Quality'. The 'Eclogues' were republished in 1747. They are lively pictures of contemporary manners. In 1743 she settled on the Lago d'Iseo, and during her residence there wrote many letters, most of them to her daughter, Lady Bute, published in 1763–7. She is also remembered for her quarrels with Pope, who attacked her outrageously in his verse. Her 'Letters and Works' were edited by Lord Wharncliffe (1837, enlarged in 1861 and 1893); her 'Complete Letters' by R. Halsband (1965–6).

MONTAGUE, CHARLES EDWARD (1867–1928), educated at the City of London School and Balliol College, Oxford. In 1890 he joined the staff of the 'Manchester Guardian' and later became assistant editor. He wrote novels, of which 'Right Off the Map' (1927) is probably the best known, short stories, and literary criticism. 'Disenchantment' (1922) is an account of the First World War, written with bitterness and restraint.

Montagues, THE, in Shakespeare's 'Romeo and Juliet' (q.v.), the Montecchi, a noble house of Verona, to which Romeo belongs, enemies of the Capulets (Cappelletti).

MONTAIGNE, MICHEL EYQUEM DE (1533–92), born in Périgord, and educated at Bordeaux, where he had among other teachers George Buchanan (q.v.), was the author of the famous 'Essais', of which Bks. I and II appeared in 1580, an enlarged edition with Book III in 1588, and a posthumous edition in 1595. The first English translations were those of John Florio (q.v., 1603) and Charles Cotton (q.v., 1685). The essays reveal the author as a man of insatiable intellectual curiosity, kindly and sagacious, condemning pedantry and lying, but tolerant of an easy morality. After the premature death of his friend La Boétie, he is much preoccupied with the subject of death. The general conclusion of the essays, embodied in his famous question, 'Que sais-je?', is the recognition of the fallibility of human reason and the relativity of human science.

Montalban, in the 'Orlando Innamorato', the home of Rinaldo (q.v.), and the scene of a great battle, in which the Christians under Charlemagne are driven back by the Saracens under Marsilio.

Montargis, DOG OF: Aubry de Montdidier, a courtier of Charles V of France, was murdered in 1371 in the forest of Montargis (in the Loiret) by Richard de Macaire. The murderer was discovered by the persistency with which Aubry's dog showed its enmity to Richard. The king ordered a judicial combat between dog and man. The latter was pulled down by the dog and confessed his crime.

Monte Carlo, one of the three communes of Monaco, a principality on the Mediterranean coast of France, under the protection (since 1861) of France. Monte Carlo is a fashionable pleasure resort. The gambling tables there were made a popular attraction by François Blanc of Homburg, who obtained in 1861 a fifty-year concession, since transferred to a company and extended.

Monte Cristo, Count of, a novel by Dumas (q.v.) the elder, published in 1844–5. Edmond Dantès, falsely denounced by a personal enemy as a Bonapartist conspirator in 1815, is imprisoned in the Château d'If for many years, escapes, recovers a concealed treasure in the Island of Monte Cristo, and devotes years to the pursuit of his revenge under various names, including that of Count of Monte Cristo.

Montem, from the Latin *ad montem*, 'to the hill', a festival formerly celebrated every third year on Whit-Tuesday by the scholars of Eton, who in fancy costumes went in procession to 'Salt Hill', a mound near Slough, and there collected money from the bystanders. The money collected (known as 'salt') was applied to defray the expenses of the senior colleger (the 'Captain of Montem') at King's College, Cambridge. The last celebration was in 1844. [OED.] There is a description of Montem in Disraeli's 'Coningsby' (q.v.).

MONTEMAYOR, JORGE DE (c. 1521–61), a Portuguese poet, who wrote in Spanish. His chief work is his prose pastoral, interspersed with verses, the 'Diana Enamorada', in which he transferred Arcadia to the heart of Spain. It was extremely popular and was translated into English, German, and French. The English translation was made by Bartholomew Young (1598), and was perhaps used by Shakespeare in his 'Two Gentlemen of Verona'. The scene is laid at the foot of the mountains of Leon and the pastoral is occupied with the misfortunes of Sereno and Sylvanus, two shepherd lovers of the fair Diana, a shepherdess; and the loves, transferences of affection, and disguises of various other shepherds and shepherdesses. Happiness is finally restored by the agency of enchanted potions. (This was one of the few books spared from the holocaust of Don Quixote's library carried out by the curate and the barber, but parts of it were expunged.)

Montesinos, a character of medieval romance, who retired to a cave in La Mancha and lived there. Don Quixote visited the cave, and had a vision of Montesinos and other heroes (II. xxii, xxiii).

MONTESQUIEU, CHARLES LOUIS DE SECONDAT DE (1689–1755), French political philosopher, best known for his 'Lettres persanes' (1721), in which, through the medium of an imaginary Persian visitor, the author criticized French legal and political institutions; and his greatest work, 'De l'Esprit des lois' (1748), in which he analysed the various kinds of political constitutions, denounced the abuses of the French monarchical system, and advocated a liberal and beneficent (yet monarchical) type of government.

Montez, LOLA, see *Lola Montez*.

Montezuma (1466–1520), the ruler of Mexico at the time of the Spanish conquest. He was seized by Cortez and held as a hostage. The Aztecs rose and attacked the Spaniards' quarters, and Montezuma, who at the request of Cortez attempted to dissuade them, was mortally wounded. W. H. Prescott's 'Conquest of Mexico' may be consulted. Dryden's play 'The Indian Emperor' has Montezuma for its subject.

MONTFAUCON, BERNARD DE (1655–1741), served as a soldier under Turenne in Germany, and subsequently entered the Maurist (q.v.) community of Benedictines, working in various abbeys and at Rome on the study of manuscripts. His chief publication is 'Palaeographia Graeca' (1708), which did for the science of Greek palaeography what the 'De re diplomatica' of Mabillon (q.v.) had done for Latin palaeography. His other writings include editions of Athanasius (1698) and Chrysostom (1738), 'L'Antiquité expliquée et représentée en figures' (1719), and 'Les Monuments de la monarchie française' (unfinished, 1729–33).

MONTGOMERIE, ALEXANDER (1556?–1610?), a Scottish poet, who held office in the Scottish court in 1577 and became laureate of the court, but got into trouble and was dismissed. His principal work is 'The Cherry and the Slae', a long allegorical poem in quatorzains, on the contrast between the cherry growing high up and valued, and the sloe growing close at hand and despised, in which Hope, Experience, Cupid, etc., take part in the conversation. This was published in 1597. He also wrote a 'Flyting betwixt Montgomery and Polwart', published in 1621, and sonnets and miscellaneous poems.

MONTGOMERY, ROBERT (1807–55), poetaster, author of religious poems ('The Omnipresence of the Deity', 1828, and 'Satan', 1830) which were extravagantly praised in the press, and severely criticized by Macaulay in the 'Edinburgh Review' (q.v.), 1830.

Monthly Review, The, founded in 1749 by the bookseller Ralph Griffiths. Oliver Goldsmith contributed to it articles of literary criticism in 1757. It was conducted by Griffiths until 1803, by his son until 1825, and expired in 1845. It was a rival to the 'Critical Review' (q.v.).

Mont-Joie-Saint Denis, the medieval warcry of the French. St. Denis (q.v.) is the patron saint of France.

Montmartre, a district in the north of Paris, a centre of literary and artistic cabarets. The name is perhaps derived from *Mons Martyrum*, the hill where St. Denis (q.v.) and his companions suffered martyrdom.

Montrose, JAMES GRAHAM, *first marquess and fifth earl of* (1612–50), the great general and rival of the marquess of Argyle, took a prominent part in Scottish history on the royalist side in the period immediately preceding the downfall of Charles I. He is the principal figure in Scott's 'A Legend of Montrose' (q.v.). An admirable 'Life of Montrose' was published by J. Buchan (q.v.) in 1913, revised and enlarged 1928.

Mont-Saint-Jean, a hamlet near Waterloo, whose name is sometimes used to signify the battle of Waterloo.

Monument, THE, London, was erected by Wren in 1671–7 to commemorate the Fire of London, which broke out in Pudding Lane, near by. On its plinth there was formerly an inscription attributing the fire to the Roman Catholics. To this Pope refers in the lines:

Where London's column, pointing to the skies,
Like a tall bully, lifts its head, and lies.

Monumenta Germaniae Historica, a great series of the medieval texts bearing on the history of Germany, begun in 1816 and still continuing. Its editors have included many famous scholars, such as G. H. Pertz, G. Waitz, T. Mommsen (q.v.), and L. Traube (q.v.). There is a full history of the enterprise by H. Bresslau, Hanover, 1921.

Monumentum Ancyranum, a famous inscription in Latin and Greek in the temple of Augustus at Ancyra (modern Angora), a copy of the record of the chief events of the life of Augustus, which in accordance with his wish was after his death engraved on bronze tablets in Rome.

Moody and Sankey, Dwight Lyman Moody (1837–99) and Ira David Sankey (1840–1908), American evangelists. After undergoing 'conversion' as a young man, Moody began his evangelizing activities by starting a Sunday-school in Chicago. He devoted himself to missionary work there and among soldiers during the American Civil War. With Sankey as singer and organist, they carried on a revival campaign in America and England. The compilation of the well-known 'Sacred Songs and Solos' was due to Sankey.

Moon, MAN IN THE, see *Man in the Moon.*

Moonraker, a native of Wiltshire, so called according to Grose (1787) because 'some Wiltshire rustics seeing the figure of the moon in a pond attempted to rake it out'. In Wiltshire it is said that they were raking a pond for kegs of smuggled brandy, and put off the revenue men by pretending folly.

Moonstone, The, a novel by Wilkie Collins (q.v.), published in 1868.
The moonstone is an enormous diamond that had once been set in the forehead of an image of the Indian moon-god. At the siege of Seringapatam it had come into the possession of an English officer, John Herncastle, who had killed its three Brahmin guards. It proved a dangerous acquisition, for other Brahmins set to work, with the utmost determination, to recover it. The moonstone is handed to Miss Verinder, in accordance with a testamentary disposition, on her eighteenth birthday, and mysteriously disappears the same night. Suspicion falls on three Indian jugglers who have been seen in the neighbourhood of the house. It has in fact been taken from Miss Verinder's cabinet, unconsciously, by her lover Franklin Blake, while under the influence of opium, and he has been seen to take it by Miss Verinder,

who consequently breaks off relations with him, though determined to screen him from detection. From Franklin Blake, while still unconscious, the villain Godfrey Ablewhite, Franklin's rival for the hand of Miss Verinder, has obtained it; and the story is occupied with the contest of cunning between Godfrey and the three Indians, ending in the murder of the former, the recovery of the diamond by the latter, and the revelation of the mystery. Sergeant Cuff, one of the first detectives in English fiction, figures in the story.

MOORE, EDWARD (1712–57), author of the lively comedy of intrigue 'Gil Blas' (1751), and of the tragedy 'The Gamester' (1753), an exposure of the vice of gambling, through which the weak creature Beverley is lured to ruin and death by the villain Stukeley.

The plot of the former play is taken from 'Gil Blas of Santillane', IV. iii et seq., where a lady masquerades as a student in order to get acquainted with a young man who has taken her fancy, maintains by a series of quick changes the dual role of the lady and the student, and achieves her object of winning the young man's heart.

MOORE, GEORGE (1852–1933), Anglo-Irish novelist, dramatist, and short-story writer. He studied painting in Paris from 1872 to 1882 and the knowledge of French writing he gained there stood him in good stead when, returning to England, he set about revitalizing the Victorian novel with naturalistic and, later, realistic techniques borrowed from Zola, Flaubert, the Goncourts, and, chiefly, Balzac (qq.v.). His first novel was 'A Modern Lover' (1883), followed by 'A Mummer's Wife' (1885), 'Esther Waters' (q.v., 1894), 'Evelyn Innes' (1898) and its sequel 'Sister Teresa' (1901). In his later novels, e.g. 'The Brook Kerith' (1916) and 'Ulick and Soracha' (1924), he aimed at epic effect. His 'Untilled Field' (1903), a group of short stories of outstanding merit, is strongly evocative of Turgenev and Dostoevsky (qq.v.). 'Confessions of a Young Man' (1888), 'Memoirs of my Dead Life' (1906), and 'Hail and Farewell' ('Ave', 1911, 'Salve', 1912, 'Vale', 1914), are all auto-biographical. The last-named is an important, though unreliable, source for the Irish literary movement associated with Yeats, 'AE', Lady Gregory (qq.v.), and others. He collaborated in the planning of the Irish National Theatre (see *Abbey Theatre*), a work which, in the words of Yeats, 'could not have been done at all without Moore's knowledge of the stage'.

MOORE, GEORGE EDWARD (1873–1958), educated at Dulwich College and Trinity College, Cambridge, professor of philosophy in the University of Cambridge (1925–39). His first book 'Principia Ethica' (1903) inaugurated a new era in British moral philosophy and also had great influence outside academic philosophy, particularly on the Bloomsbury group (q.v.). His other writings,

which include 'Philosophical Studies' (1922) and 'Some Main Problems of Philosophy' (1953), have had great, but more narrowly confined, influence.

Moore, HENRY (1898–   ), sculptor, son of a Yorkshire miner. His figures and groups show, on the one hand, a deep humanity and, on the other, an interest in the forms and rhythms of natural objects.

MOORE, DR. JOHN (1729–1802), studied medicine at Glasgow, and accompanied the young duke of Hamilton in his travels abroad from 1773 to 1778. He published 'A View of Society and Manners in France, Switzerland, and Germany' in 1779, with a continuation relating to Italy two years later. His most popular novel, 'Zeluco' (q.v.), appeared in 1786, 'Edward' in 1796, and 'Mordaunt' in 1800. He went with Lord Lauderdale to France in 1792, and his 'Journal during a Residence in France' was published during the next two years. He was father of General Sir John Moore (q.v.).

Moore, SIR JOHN (1761–1809), lieutenant-general, son of the above, became commander-in-chief in the Peninsula on the recall of Sir Harry Burrard (1808). He led the historic retreat to Coruña during the winter of 1808–9 and began the embarkation of the British force on 13 Jan. The French, who now appeared, were repulsed, but Moore was mortally wounded, and buried at midnight of 16 Jan. 1809, in the citadel of Coruña. For the poem on this subject see *Wolfe*.

Moore, JOHN, the 'author of the celebrated worm powder', an apothecary to whom Pope addressed the 'Lines to Mr. John Moore', ending:

O learned friend of Abchurch Lane
Who sett'st our entrails free,
Vain is thy art, thy powder vain,
Since worms shall eat ev'n thee.

MOORE, MARIANNE (1887–   ), American poet, born in Missouri. Among the few volumes of poetry, which have brought her great reputation, are 'Observations' (1924), 'Selected Poems' (1935), and 'Collected Poems' (1951). She has also translated the fables of La Fontaine (1954). She was editor of 'The Dial' (q.v.) from 1925 to 1929, and contributed greatly to its achievement.

MOORE, THOMAS (1779–1852), born in Dublin, the son of a grocer, was educated at Trinity College, Dublin, and entered at the Middle Temple. In 1801 he issued a volume of 'Poetical Works' under the pseudonym of 'Thomas Little', by which Byron refers to him in 'English Bards and Scotch Reviewers'. In 1803 he received the appointment of admiralty registrar at Bermuda, which he transferred to a deputy. He became the national lyrist of Ireland (Moore was a musician as well as a poet) by the publication of his 'Irish Melodies' (1807–35). In 1813 he issued 'The Twopenny Post Bag', a collection of satires directed against the Regent. He acquired a European reputation by his 'Lalla Rookh' (q.v.), published in 1817. Owing to the defalcation of his deputy in Bermuda he became responsible for a debt of £6,000, and left England, returning in 1822, when the debt had been paid. His 'Loves of the Angels' (q.v.), published in 1823, excited much reprobation. He received in 1835 a literary pension, to which a civil list pension was added in 1850. Among his other works may be mentioned his novel, 'The Epicurean' (q.v.), published in 1827; his 'History of Ireland', which was not a success (1846); 'The Fudge Family in Paris' (q.v.), 1818; 'The Fudges in England', 1835, and his lives of Sheridan (1825), Lord Edward Fitzgerald (1831), 'and Lord Byron (1830). Of the last Moore was an intimate friend and Byron left him his memoirs (these were destroyed by Moore). Moore's own 'Memoirs' were edited by Lord John Russell, 1853–6.

Moorfields, see *Moorgate*.

Moorgate, one of the gates in the old walls of the City of London, opening on Moorfields, 'the great fen or moor' on the north side of the city, caused perhaps by the damming up, by the walls, of the streams flowing towards the Thames. Stow relates the attempts repeatedly made to drain this marshy area.

Mopsa, a character in Sidney's 'Arcadia' (q.v.).

Moral and Political Philosophy, Principles of, by Paley (q.v.), published in 1785.

This exposition of theological utilitarianism is largely based on the doctrine of Abraham Tucker (q.v.), to which it gives method and clarity. The happiness of the individual is always the motive of his conduct. It is brought into conformity with the general happiness by the incentives and sanctions provided by the Christian religion. The virtuous or vicious character of our actions, their conformity to or variance from God's will (which is for the general happiness of his creatures), can be determined by their consequences on mankind. An act of prudence is distinguished from an act of virtue in that 'in the one case, we consider what we shall gain or lose in the present world; in the other case, we consider also what we shall gain or lose in the world to come'. In other words, posthumous rewards and penalties are an essential part of Paley's ethical system; and the evidence for these is marshalled in his later works.

Moral Essays, four ethical poems by Pope (q.v.), published 1731–5.

They were inspired by Lord Bolingbroke (q.v.) and take the form of four Epistles. Epistle I, addressed to Viscount Cobham, deals with the knowledge and characters of men; it sets forth the difficulties in judging a man's character and finds their solution in the discovery of the ruling passion, which 'clue once found unravels all the rest'. Epistle II, addressed to Martha Blount,

deals with the characters of women, the most interesting of these being Atossa, intended for Sarah, duchess of Marlborough, Chloe for Lady Suffolk, Philomedé for Henrietta, duchess of Marlborough. It was said, but never proved, that Pope received £1,000 for suppressing the character of Atossa. These three characters were withheld until Warburton's edition of 1751. Epistle III, to Lord Bathurst, deals with the use of riches, which is understood by few, neither the avaricious nor the prodigal deriving happiness from them. The Epistle contains the famous characters of the 'Man of Ross' (see *Kyrle*) and 'Sir Balaam' (q.v.). Epistle IV, to Lord Burlington, treats of the same subject as Epistle III, giving instances of the tasteless use of wealth, particularly in architecture and gardening, where nature should be followed. The epistle ends with advice on the proper use of wealth.

Moral Ode, see *Poema Morale*.

Moral Sentiments, Theory of, see *Theory of Moral Sentiments*.

Moralities, medieval dramatic pieces in verse, in which the biblical personages of the Miracle Plays (q.v.) gave place to personified abstractions, such as the vices and virtues. The action was simple and the purpose edifying. They belong mainly to the 15th cent., developing alongside of the 'Miracles'. They perhaps reached their greatest elaboration in Sir David Lindsay's 'Ane Pleasant Satyre of the Thrie Estaitis' (q.v.). Other well-known moralities were 'Everyman' (q.v.), 'Lusty Juventus' (the punishment of extravagance and debauchery), 'The Cradle of Security' (on the vices of kings), 'Respublica' (acted in 1553, under Queen Mary, directed against those who had enriched themselves out of Church property), and 'Magnificence' (this last by Skelton).

Morat, in the canton of Fribourg, Switzerland, the scene of the famous victory of the Swiss over Charles the Bold of Burgundy in 1476.

MORAVIA, ALBERTO (A. PINCHERLE) (1907–   ), the most widely known and influential Italian novelist of the period immediately following the Second World War, played a major part in shaping the new realism dominant in post-war Italian fiction. His first and most important novel, 'Gli indifferenti' ('Indifference', 1929), portrayed an upper-middle-class society sick with moral and spiritual inertia. Subsequent novels continued to anatomize to the point of nausea various aspects of human weakness, viciousness, apathy, and cynicism. The later full-length novels have never quite equalled his first, and the best of his subsequent writing is in his short stories and in the two short psychological novels 'Agostino' and 'La disubbidienza' ('Disobedience').

Moravians, the 'Unity of Moravian brethren', a Protestant sect founded early in the

18th cent. in Saxony by emigrants from Moravia, and continuing the tradition of the *Unitas Fratrum*, a body holding Hussite doctrines. Its virtual founder was Count Zinzendorf, and it obtained many adherents in England and the American colonies. They strongly influenced John Wesley (q.v.).

Morddure, in Spenser's 'Faerie Queene', II. viii. 20–21, the name of the sword made by Merlin for Prince Arthur. Its more general name is 'Excalibur'.

Mordecai, in the book of Esther, a Jew of the tribe of Benjamin, the foster-father of Esther, who, when Ahasuerus (the Persian king Xerxes) made Esther his queen, sat in the king's gate and frustrated the design of the chamberlains to lay hands on the king, and also the machinations of Haman. Hence 'A Mordecai at the gate'.

Mordrains or MORDRIENS, in the legend of the Grail (q.v.), the name under which King Evalak was baptized.

Mordred, see *Modred.*

Mordure, see *Morddure.*

MORE, HANNAH (1745–1833), was educated at her sisters' boarding-school at Bristol, where she acquired Italian, Spanish, and Latin. In 1773 she published 'The Search after Happiness', a pastoral play for schools. She was engaged to a Mr. Turner, but the match was broken off. She came to London in 1774, where she became intimate with Garrick and his wife, and obtained the friendship of Burke, Horace Walpole, Reynolds, Dr. Johnson, Mrs. Montagu, and the other ladies of the Blue Stocking (q.v.) coterie. Her tragedy 'Percy' was successfully produced by Garrick in 1777. It deals, in the light of 18th-cent. social ethics, with the conflict, supposed to occur in the 12th cent., between a woman's passion for her lover and her duty to the husband whom she has been forced to marry. This was followed by another tragedy, 'The Fatal Falsehood', in 1779. After Garrick's death, Hannah More turned her attention to other subjects, and published tracts for the reformation of the poor, 'Village Politics' and 'Repository Tracts' (of which the best known was 'The Shepherd of Salisbury Plain'), which proved very successful and led to the foundation of the Religious Tract Society. Her 'Thoughts on the Importance of the Manners of the Great' (1788) also met with great success. In 1809 she published a popular novel, 'Cœlebs in Search of a Wife' (q.v.). The later part of her life was devoted to philanthropic objects. She was an excellent letter-writer, and gives a vivid picture of the intellectual world which she frequented. Samuel Wilberforce and Zachary Macaulay were among her later correspondents. Her letters were published in 1834.

MORE, HENRY (1614–87), educated at Eton and Christ's College, Cambridge, and a fellow of his college, was one of the leaders of the Platonist movement at Cambridge. He received holy orders but refused all preferment, including two bishoprics. His voluminous works include 'Ψυχωδία Platonica, or a Platonical Song of the Soul' (1642), reprinted in 'Philosophicall Poems'(1647), 'An Antidote against Atheism' (1653), 'Conjectura Cabbalistica' (1653), 'Enthusiasmus Triumphatus' (1656, an exposure of the prevalent claim to inspiration in the interpretation of the Scriptures), 'The Immortality of the Soul' (1659), 'An Explanation of the Grand Mystery of Godliness' (1660), 'The Mystery of Iniquity' (1664), 'Enchiridion Ethicum' (1667), and 'Divine Dialogues' (1668), his best-known work. In his earlier writings More's object was to combat scepticism by calling pagan philosophy and contemporary science to the support of Christianity, though later (in his 'Enchiridion Metaphysicum' (1668)) he renounced Cartesianism.

For the chief characteristics of the philosophy of the Cambridge Platonists, see *Cudworth.*

MORE, SIR THOMAS (ST.) (1478–1535), son of Sir John More, a judge, was educated at St. Anthony's School, Threadneedle Street, London, and at Canterbury Hall, Oxford, where he was the pupil of Linacre and Grocyn. He was for a time in youth in the household of Cardinal Morton, and it was probably from Morton's information that he derived his knowledge of Richard III's murder of the Princes, etc. He was called to the bar, where he was brilliantly successful. He devoted his leisure to literature, becoming intimate (1497) with Colet, Lily, and Erasmus, who afterwards stayed frequently at his house. He entered parliament in 1504. During an absence as envoy to Flanders he sketched his description (in Latin) of the imaginary island of 'Utopia' (q.v.), which he completed and published in 1516. He became master of requests and privy councillor in 1518, being treated by Henry VIII with exceptional courtesy during his residence at court. He was present at the Field of the Cloth of Gold, 1520, where he met William Budé, or Budaeus, the greatest Greek scholar of the age. He completed his 'Dialogue', his first controversial book in English (directed mainly against Tyndale's writings), in 1528. He succeeded Wolsey as lord chancellor in 1529, but resigned the post in 1532 and lived for some time in retirement, mainly engaged in controversy with Tyndale and Frith.

Although willing to swear fidelity to the new Act of Succession, More refused to take any oath that should impugn the pope's authority, or assume the justice of the king's divorce from Queen Catherine, 1534; he was therefore committed to the Tower of London with John Fisher (q.v.), bishop of Rochester, who had assumed a like attitude. During the first days of his imprisonment he prepared a 'Dialogue of Comfort against Tribulation' and treatises on Christ's passion. He was indicted of high treason, found guilty, and beheaded in 1535. His body was buried in St. Peter's in the Tower and his head exhibited on London Bridge. See also *Roper*.

More was a critic and a patron of art, and Holbein is said to have stayed three years in his house at Chelsea, and painted portraits of More and his family. More's other chief English works are his 'Life of John Picus, Earl of Mirandula' (printed by Wynkyn de Worde, 1510), his 'History of Richard III' (printed imperfectly in Grafton's 'Chronicle', 1543, used by Hall, and printed fully by Rastell in 1557), 'Supplycacyon of Soulys' (1529), 'Confutacyon of Tyndale's Answere' (1532), and 'An Apologye of Syr Thomas More' (1533). His English works were collected in 1557. His Latin publications (collected 1563, etc.) included, besides the 'Utopia', four dialogues of Lucian, epigrams, and controversial tracts in divinity. There is a pleasant description of More in his Chelsea home in the epistle of Erasmus to Ulrich Hutten, 23 July 1519 (No. 999 in P. S. and H. M. Allen's edition, translation in Froude's 'Erasmus').

More, Sir Thomas, a play written *c*. 1595–6 by Munday, Chettle, and probably Heywood, and further revised *c*. 1600–1 by a professional scribe (Hand C), Dekker, and Shakespeare (qq.v.). It was not performed. The three pages in which More's oratory quells the mob are the only known examples of Shakespeare's original composition, his addition forming part of MS. Harley 7368 in the British Museum. R. C. Bold surveys discussion on the manuscript in 'Shakespeare Survey 2' (1949).

The play is based on some of the chief events in the life of More, as recorded in Hall's Chronicle: his rise to favour as a result of his successful handling of an insurrection in London, his friendship with Erasmus, his refusal to support Henry VIII's policy, and his consequent imprisonment and execution.

More of More Hall, see *Dragon of Wantley*.

MORÉRI, LOUIS (1643–80), a French priest, author of a 'Grand dictionnaire historique' (1674), a pioneer work of its kind.

Moresque, the Moorish Arabesque style of decoration (see *Arabesque*).

MORGAN, CHARLES LANGBRIDGE (1894–1958), dramatic critic and author of the following novels: 'Portrait in a Mirror' (1929), 'The Fountain' (1932), 'Sparkenbroke' (1936), 'A Voyage' (1940), 'The Empty Room' (1941), 'The Judge's Story' (1947), and 'The River Line' (1949; adapted as a play 1952).

MORGAN, LADY (1783?–1859), *née* Sydney Owenson, the wife of Sir Thomas Charles Morgan, made her reputation as a writer by her romance of Irish life, 'The Wild Irish Girl' (1806). Her best works were 'O'Donnel' (1814) and 'The O'Briens and the O'Flahertys' (1827). Her book 'France' (1817) was popular; 'Italy' followed in 1821.

MORGAN, WILLIAM DE, see *De Morgan*.

Morgan, in Thackeray's 'Pendennis' (q.v.), Major Pendennis's valet.

Morgan, MR., a character in Smollett's 'Roderick Random' (q.v.).

Morgan le Fay, one of King Arthur's sisters, possessing magic powers, who married King Uriens. According to one version of the legend, she reveals to Arthur the intrigue of Launcelot and Guinevere. In the 'Morte Darthur' of Malory she endeavours to kill Arthur, by means of Sir Accolon, her paramour, to whom she sends Arthur's sword Excalibur; and also tries to kill her husband, but the latter is saved by Sir Uwaine, her son. She is one of the three queens in the ship in which Arthur is carried off to be healed of his wounds. See also *Lady of the Lake*.

As MORGANA she figures in the 'Orlando Innamorato' and in the 'Orlando Furioso' (qq.v.). She lives at the bottom of a lake and dispenses the treasures of the earth. Orlando penetrates to her residence and forces her, in the name of Demogorgon her master, to release the knights whom she detains. The term *Fata Morgana* is given in Sicily to a mirage occasionally seen at sea on the Calabrian coast (there are various legends about Arthur in Sicily, perhaps imported by Norman conquerors; see E. K. Chambers, 'Arthur of Britain').

In the romance of Ogier the Dane (q.v.) the fairy Morgan rejuvenates Ogier, when over a hundred years old, and marries him.

Morgana and **Fata Morgana,** see *Morgan le Fay*.

MORGANN, MAURICE (1726–1802), secretary to the embassy for peace with America in 1782, is remembered as the author of an 'Essay on the Dramatic Character of Sir John Falstaff', a vindication of Falstaff's courage (1777).

Morgante Maggiore, a poem by Pulci (q.v.) which recast, with humorous additions and alterations, the popular epic 'Orlando'. Orlando (Roland) encounters three giants. He slays two and subdues the third, Morgante, converts him, and makes him his brother in arms. Byron translated the first canto.

Morgawse or MARGAWSE, in Malory's 'Morte Darthur' (q.v.), sister of King Arthur, wife of King Lot, and mother of Mordred, Gawaine, Agravaine, Gaheris, and Gareth. She is called *Anna* by Geoffrey of Monmouth.

Morgiana, a character in the story of 'Ali Baba and the Forty Thieves' (q.v.).

Morglay, the name of the sword of Bevis of Hampton (q.v.). It is sometimes used allusively for a sword in general.

MORIER, JAMES JUSTINIAN (1780?–1849), born at Smyrna, entered the diplomatic service in 1807, being attached to Sir Harford Jones's mission to Persia, and became secretary of embassy. He published two books of travel, 'A Journey through Persia ... in 1808 and 1809' (1812) and 'A Second Journey through Persia' (1818), which provided valuable information about a country then little known. He also published a number of oriental romances, of which the best is 'The Adventures of Hajji Baba of Ispahan' (1824), which, in the form of a picaresque story (the hero, successively barber, doctor, assistant-executioner, and rogue generally, undergoes amusing vicissitudes), gives an accurate picture of Persian life and manners, and is said to have provoked a remonstrance from the Persian minister in London. This was printed in Morier's introduction to the sequel, a book in which Hajji Baba is transferred to England, whose customs are seen through the astonished eyes of the Persian.

Morland, CATHERINE, the heroine of Jane Austen's 'Northanger Abbey' (q.v.).

Morland, GEORGE (1763–1804), genre painter, son of a painter, Henry Robert Morland (1716–97). He first exhibited at the Royal Academy at the age of 10. His vast output of country scenes, popular but superficial, failed to keep him out of debt and he died in a sponging-house, his own epitaph on himself being 'Here lies a drunken dog'.

MORLEY, CHRISTOPHER (1890–1957), American novelist and journalist, born in Pennsylvania, and a Rhodes scholar at Oxford. His chief works are: 'Where the Blue Begins' (1922), 'Parsons' Pleasure' (1923), 'Thunder on the Left' (1925), 'Kitty Foyle' (1939).

MORLEY, JOHN, *first Viscount Morley of Blackburn* (1838–1923), educated at Cheltenham College and Lincoln College, Oxford, was twice chief secretary for Ireland (1886 and 1892–5), secretary of state for India (1905–10), and Lord President of the Council (1910–14). His chief publications were: 'Edmund Burke; an historical Study' (1867), 'Critical Miscellanies' (1871, second series, 1877), 'Voltaire' (1872), 'Rousseau' (1873), 'The Struggle for National Education' (1873), 'On Compromise' (1874), 'Diderot and the Encyclopaedists' (1878), 'Burke' (biography) (1879), 'The Life of Richard Cobden' (1881), 'Studies in Literature' (1891), 'Oliver Cromwell' (1900), 'Life of Gladstone' (1903), 'Politics and History' (1914), 'Recollections' (1917). He chose 'Machiavelli' for the subject of his Romanes Lecture of 1897. Morley was editor of the 'Fortnightly Review' from 1867 to 1882, and of the 'Pall Mall Gazette' from 1881 to 1883. He was also editor of the English Men of Letters series.

Morley, MRS., the name under which Queen Anne corresponded with the duchess of Marlborough (Mrs. Freeman).

Mormons, the popular name for 'The Church of Jesus Christ of Latter-day Saints', founded at Manchester, New York, in 1830 by Joseph Smith (1805–44). The 'Book of Mormon', it is claimed, was revealed to him in 1827 as a 'parallel volume' to the Bible. Its doctrines are in general harmony with those of the Bible. An additional revelation in favour of polygamy, which Smith claimed to have received in 1843, aroused general hostility to the sect. Under the leadership of Brigham Young (q.v.), who succeeded Smith as president of the Mormon church in 1844, they made a remarkable pilgrimage to Utah, where they founded Salt Lake City in 1847. The 'Book of Mormon' establishes government of the community by a complicated hierarchy, including a president, two counsellors, a patriarch and twelve apostles, elders, priests, deacons, etc. Polygamy was prohibited by the constitution of Utah in 1896.

Morning Advertiser, The, one of the oldest of London newspapers with a continuous history, having been founded in 1794. It was devoted primarily to the defence of trade interests, having been founded by the Society of Licensed Victuallers of London, whose organ it remains.

Morning Chronicle, The, a Whig journal founded by William Woodfall (1746–1803), the printer, in 1769, and successfully conducted by him for twenty years. It rose to importance when James Perry became chief proprietor and editor in 1789. Its staff then included Sheridan, C. Lamb, Thomas Campbell, Sir James Mackintosh, Henry Brougham, Thomas Moore, and David Ricardo. Perry was followed by John Black in 1821, a most successful editor. Among his contributors were James and John Stuart Mill; Charles Dickens was among his reporters, and Thackeray his art critic. 'The Morning Chronicle' came to an end in 1862.

Morning Herald, The, a London newspaper that ran from 1780 to 1869, having at one time a very large circulation. One of its special features for a time was a selection of reports of police cases, illustrated by George Cruikshank.

Morning Post, The, a London daily newspaper founded in 1772. Under the management of Stuart (q.v.), Sir J. Mackintosh and S. T. Coleridge were enlisted in its service at the end of the 18th cent., and Southey, Wordsworth, and Arthur Young also wrote for it. It fell on evil days about 1850, but recovered its position under the direction of Peter Borthwick and his son Algernon Borthwick (Lord Glenesk, 1830–1908). It was amalgamated with 'The Daily Telegraph' in 1937.

Morning Star of the Reformation, THE, Wycliffe (q.v.), so named by Daniel Neal in his 'History of the Puritans' (1732).

Morocco: for Bankes's famous performing horse see *Marocco*.

Morose, the principal character in Jonson's 'Epicœne' (q.v.).

Morpheūs, the son of the god of sleep, and himself the god of dreams.

Morrice, GIL, see *Gil Morrice*.

Morris, DINAH, a character in G. Eliot's 'Adam Bede' (q.v.).

MORRIS, SIR LEWIS (1833–1907), born at Carmarthen and educated at Jesus College, Oxford, contributed actively to the establishment of the University of Wales. His principal poetical works were the 'Songs of Two Worlds' (1871) and the 'Epic of Hades' (q.v., 1876–7). His simplicity of expression, melodious verse, cheerful optimism, and occasional exaltation made his work extremely popular, in spite of its poetic mediocrity. Morris wrote many later poems ('Gwen, a Drama in Monologue' (1879), 'Songs Unsung' (1883), 'Gycia, a tragedy' (1886), 'A Vision of Saints' (1890)), of which a collection was published in 1907. 'A Vision of Saints' is a Christian counterpart of the 'Epic of Hades', in which eminent Christian characters (including Elizabeth Fry and Father Damien) take the place of the figures of Greek mythology. Morris also published a volume of essays, 'The New Rambler' (1905).

MORRIS, WILLIAM (1834–96), educated at Marlborough School and Exeter College, Oxford, was distinguished not only as a poet and artist, but also as a decorator, manufacturer and printer, and as a socialist. He was articled to the architect G. E. Street, and in 1858 he worked with Rossetti, Burne-Jones (qq.v.), and others on the frescoes in the Oxford Union. He was one of the originators of the 'Oxford and Cambridge Magazine', to which he contributed poems, essays, and tales. In 1858 he published his 'Defence of Guenevere, and other Poems'. The Red House, Bexley, designed for him by Philip Webb, was an important turning-point in the development of domestic architecture. Failing to find suitable furniture for it, Morris and a number of artists, including Rossetti, Burne-Jones, Madox Brown, and Webb, founded the firm of Morris, Marshall, Faulkner & Co. in 1861, which produced furniture, printed textiles, tapestries, wallpapers, and stained glass; his and his colleagues' designs brought about a complete revolution in the taste of the English public. In 1867 he published the 'Life and Death of Jason' (q.v.), and in 1868–70 the 'Earthly Paradise' (q.v.). 'Love is enough' (a morality) appeared in 1872, a verse translation of the 'Aeneids of Virgil' in 1875, 'Three Northern Love Songs' in the same year, and the epic 'Sigurd the Volsung' (q.v.), perhaps his finest work, in 1876. He founded in 1877 the Society for the Protection of Ancient Buildings (the 'Antiscrape Society'), in protest against the destruction being caused by the restorers, and in 1883 joined the Social Democratic Federation, the doctrine of which, largely under his leadership, developed into socialism. On its disruption in 1884 he became head of the seceders, who organized themselves as the Socialist League. The verse tale, 'The Pilgrims of Hope', appeared in the magazine 'The Commonweal' in 1885. In 1887 he published a verse translation of the 'Odyssey'. His later works, with the exception of 'Poems by the Way' (ballads and lyrics), published in 1891, were mainly in prose. Two of them, 'The Dream of John Ball' (mixed prose and verse, 1888) and 'News from Nowhere' (1891), were romances of socialist propaganda. The others were pure romances, of which 'The House of the Wolfings' (1889), 'The Roots of the Mountains' (1890), and 'The Story of the Glittering Plain' (1890) have their scene in the remote northern regions of Europe. These were followed by 'The Wood beyond the World' (1894), 'Child Christopher' (1895), 'The Well at the World's End' (1896), 'The Water of the Wondrous Isles' (posthumous, 1897), and 'The Story of the Sundering Flood' (1898). Morris started in 1890, at Hammersmith, the Kelmscott Press, for which he designed founts of type and ornamental letters and borders, and from which were issued fifty-three books, comprising (1) Morris's own works, (2) reprints of English classics, and (3) various smaller books.

Morris twice visited Iceland, and the influence of the Sagas (many of which he translated in collaboration with Magnusson), as well as that of Chaucer, is apparent in his writings.

Morris-dance, a grotesque dance performed by persons in fancy costume, usually representing characters in the Robin Hood legend, especially Maid Marian and Friar Tuck. Maid Marian sometimes appears as Queen of May. The dance is referred to as early as the 15th cent. See also *Revesby Play*.

Morte Arthur, *Le*, a late 14th-cent. poem of 3,800 lines, in eight-lined rhyming stanzas, dealing with the loves of Launcelot and the Maid of Astolat, with Launcelot's love for Queen Guinevere, and with the last battles of Arthur and his bearing away to Avalon. See *Arthur* and *Launcelot*.

Morte Arthure, a 14th-cent. poem of 4,300 alliterative lines, dealing with the later history of King Arthur, and similar in essentials to the narrative given in the 'Historia' of Geoffrey of Monmouth and Layamon's 'Brut' (see *Arthur*), but with some details from other sources or the poet's own imagination, and with allusions to contemporary history. The poem was written in northern England or southern Scotland, and has been attributed by some to the Scottish poet Huchoun (q.v.). It shows pathos and humour, and includes vivid scenes, such as the description of the sea-fight between Arthur and Modred.

Morte Darthur, *Le*, a prose translation made from the French, with adaptations from other sources, by Malory (q.v.), in twenty-one books, and finished between Mar. 1469 and

Mar. 1470. It was edited and printed by Caxton in 1485. The work is a skilful selection and blending of materials taken from the mass of Arthurian legends. The central story consists of two main elements: the reign of King Arthur ending in catastrophe and the dissolution of the Round Table; and the quest of the Holy Grail, in which Launcelot fails by reason of his sin, and Galahad succeeds. See under *Grail* and the names of the various characters in the book.

A MS. contemporary with Caxton and considerably fuller than his text was found in Winchester College Library in 1934. It was edited by E. Vinaver and published under the title 'The Works of Sir Thomas Malory', 3 vols., 1947.

Morte d'Arthur, The, a poem by A. Tennyson (q.v.), published in 1842 and subsequently incorporated in 'The Passing of Arthur' (q.v.), one of the 'Idylls of the King'.

Morton, HENRY, OF MILNWOOD, the hero of Scott's 'Old Mortality' (q.v.).

MORTON, JOHN MADDISON (1811–91), son of the dramatist Thomas Morton (see below), educated in France, wrote farces and showed a special gift for adaptations from the French. His most successful piece was 'Box and Cox' (q.v., 1847); 'Done on both Sides' appeared in the same year.

MORTON, THOMAS (1764?–1838), who entered Lincoln's Inn in 1784, was the author of the successful comedies, 'The Way to get Married' (1796), 'A Cure for Heartache' (1797), and 'Speed the Plough' (q.v., 1798), which contain some humorous situations. The last of these introduced the name of 'Mrs. Grundy' into England.

Morton's Fork, the dilemma that Cardinal Morton, Henry VII's chancellor, proposed to merchants and others whom he invited to contribute to benevolences. Either their handsome way of life manifested their opulence; or, if their course of living was less sumptuous, they must have grown rich by their economy.

Morven, in the Ossianic poems of Macpherson (q.v.), the kingdom of Fingal, situated in the north-west of Scotland.

Mosca, a character in Jonson's 'Volpone' (q.v.).

MOSCHUS (*fl. c.* 150 B.C.), a pastoral poet of Syracuse. The beautiful 'Lament for Bion', doubtfully attributed to Moschus, is a dirge for the author's friend and teacher. There is an echo of it in Milton's Latin 'Epitaphium Damonis', in his 'Lycidas', in Shelley's 'Adonais', and in M. Arnold's 'Thyrsis'.

Mosses from an Old Manse, published in 1846, is a collection of tales and sketches by Nathaniel Hawthorne (q.v.). The Old Manse itself is the author's Concord home, and best known among the book's contents are:

'Young Goodman Brown', 'Rappaccini's Daughter', and 'Roger Malvin's Burial'.

Moth, (1) in Shakespeare's 'Love's Labour's Lost' (q.v.), Armado's page, connected by Sir S. Lee with La Mothe, the French ambassador long popular in London; (2) a fairy in 'A Midsummer Night's Dream' (q.v.).

Mother Bumby, Mother Bunch, Mother Shipton, see under those names.

Mother Goose's Tales, and *Mother Goose's Melody,* nursery tales and verses published by Newbery (q.v.). The name is taken from the 'Contes de ma mère l'Oye' by Perrault (q.v.), though 'Mother Goose' probably had a traditional existence much earlier. Scott in his 'Journal' (ed. Douglas), 2 [?5] Jan. 1832, tells how he came across an early Italian edition in Naples, but A. Lang notes in the Appendix that this was probably a translation of the French.

Mother Hubbard, the subject of a nursery rhyme written by Sarah Catherine Martin (1768–1826) and published in 1805.

Mother Hubberd's Tale, or *Prosopopoia,* a satire in rhymed couplets, by Spenser (q.v.), included in the volume of 'Complaints' published in 1590. The ape and the fox, 'disliking of their hard estate', determine to seek their fortunes abroad, and assume the disguises first of an old soldier and his dog, then of a parish priest and his clerk, then of a courtier and his groom; their knaveries in these characters are recounted. Finally they steal the lion's crown and sceptre and abuse the regal power, until Jove intervenes and exposes them. The poem is a satire on abuses of the church and the evils of the court.

Mothering Sunday, Mid-Lent Sunday, so called from an old custom of visiting parents on that day and giving or receiving presents. See also the Epistle for the Fourth Sunday in Lent.

MOTHERWELL, WILLIAM (1797–1835), a native of Glasgow, became editor of the 'Paisley Advertiser' and 'Glasgow Courier'. In 1827 he published his 'Minstrelsy, Ancient and Modern', a collection of ballads, and in 1832 his 'Poems, Narrative and Lyrical', of which the best known and least characteristic is 'Jeanie Morrison'. With Hogg (q.v.) he issued an edition of Burns's works in 1834–5.

Motion, the name given to puppet-plays in the 16th and 17th cents. These dealt originally with scriptural subjects, but their scope was afterwards extended. Shakespeare in 'The Winter's Tale' (IV. ii) refers to a 'motion of the Prodigal Son', and we have references to 'motions' in Jonson's 'Bartholomew Fayre', 'A Tale of a Tub', and 'Every Man out of his Humour'.

MOTLEY, JOHN LOTHROP (1814–77), was born in Massachusetts, and educated at Harvard, Göttingen, and Berlin (where he formed a life-long friendship with Count Bismarck). He was American minister to

Austria, 1861–7, and to Great Britain, 1869–70, and from that time until his death lived in England. His principal works are 'The Rise of the Dutch Republic' (1856), 'History of the United Netherlands' (1860–7), and 'The Life and Death of John Barneveld' (1874).

MOTTEUX, PETER ANTHONY (1660–1718), was born at Rouen and came to England in 1685. He edited the 'Gentleman's Journal' (q.v.), and completed Sir T. Urquhart's translation of Rabelais (1693–4). He published a free translation of 'Don Quixote' in 1700–3.

MOTTLEY, JOHN (1692–1750), author of two dull pseudo-classical tragedies, a few comedies and lives of Peter the Great and Catharine I, is remembered as having published 'Joe Miller's Jest-book' in 1739.

Mouldy, RALPH, in Shakespeare's '2 Henry IV' (q.v.), III. ii, one of Falstaff's recruits.

Mount Zion or SION, the hill on which Jerusalem was built, used sometimes figuratively for the Christian Church, or (e.g. in 'The Pilgrim's Progress') for heaven. The name has often been given to dissenting chapels, as in R. Browning's 'Christmas Eve'.

Mountain, THE, the extreme democratic party led at first by Danton and afterwards by Robespierre in the first French Revolution, so called from the fact that it occupied the highest benches in the hall of the National Convention.

Mountain, THE OLD MAN OF THE, see *Assassins.*

Mourning Bride, The, a tragedy by Congreve (q.v.), produced in 1697. This was the author's only attempt at tragedy, and was received with enthusiasm.

Almeria, daughter of Manuel, king of Granada, has been secretly married to Alphonso, prince of the enemy state of Valencia. Circumstances place him a captive in the power of Manuel. The discovery of his marriage to Almeria infuriates the king, who orders the immediate murder of Alphonso, and further to punish his daughter determines to personate the captive in his cell, so that when she comes to save him, he may mock her disappointment. As a result he is by mistake killed instead, and decapitated. Zara, a Moorish queen, a fellow captive in love with Alphonso, but repulsed by him, finding the headless body of, as she supposes, Alphonso, takes poison in despair. A revolt against Manuel releases the true Alphonso, and he and Almeria are reunited.

The play contains lines that are widely known, such as the first in the play:

Music has charms to soothe a savage breast,

and those which close the third act:

Heaven has no rage, like love to hatred turned,
Nor hell a fury, like a woman scorned.

Mouse Tower, see *Bishop Hatto.*

Mousterian, a name applied by archaeologists to an early form of palaeolithic industry, in which flints were mainly worked on one side only. It is associated with Neanderthal (q.v.) man. The name is derived from Le Moustier, a rock shelter near Les Eyzies, in the Dordogne, France.

Mowbray, CLARA and her brother JOHN, characters in Scott's 'St. Ronan's Well' (q.v.).

Mowcher, MISS, in Dickens's 'David Copperfield' (q.v.), a humorous and good-hearted dwarf, a hairdresser and manicure.

Mowgli, the child in Rudyard Kipling's 'The Jungle Book' (q.v.).

MOXON, EDWARD (1801–58), publisher and verse-writer, came to London from Wakefield in 1817 and entered the service of Messrs. Longman. He set up as a publisher in 1830, his first publication being Lamb's 'Album Verses'. He married Lamb's adopted daughter Emma Isola. He published illustrated editions of Southey, Wordsworth, Tennyson, Browning, Landor, and other well-known authors. Moxon published two volumes of his own sonnets, 1826 and 1837.

Moxon, JOSEPH (1627–91), maker of globes and mathematical instruments, printer and typefounder. He wrote 'Mechanick Exercises, or the Doctrine of Handy-Works' (1683–4), the first manual of printing and typefounding in any language and probably the first book to be published in parts serially.

Mozart, WOLFGANG AMADEUS (1756–91), was born at Salzburg, and showed extraordinary precocity as a musician and composer. He composed his first oratorio in 1767 (when eleven years old), and his first opera was produced in 1769. His work met with great success, but he was improvident, experienced much poverty during his brief life, and died in destitution. His principal operas were 'Le Nozze di Figaro', 'Don Giovanni', 'Così fan tutte', and 'Die Zauberflöte'. Besides these, he wrote church music, songs, forty-one symphonies, concertos, pianoforte sonatas, and much chamber music.

Mucedorus, The Comedie of, a play, published in 1598, of uncertain authorship included in a volume with the title of 'Shakespeare' in Charles II's library (but not by Shakespeare).

Mucedorus, prince of Valencia, in order to discover the virtues of Amadine, the daughter of the king of Arragon, assumes the disguise of a shepherd, saves her from a bear, and falls in love with her. Banished from her father's court, he next appears as a hermit, saves Amadine from a 'wild man', reveals his identity to her father, and is now successful in his suit.

Much, in the Robin Hood legend, a miller's son, one of the outlaw's companions. He figures in 'A Lytell Geste of Robyn Hode' (Ritson's collection of ballads).

Much Ado about Nothing, a comedy by Shakespeare (q.v.), probably produced in the winter of 1598–9, and printed in 1600. The trick played by Borachio is in Bandello and Ariosto.

The Prince of Arragon, with Cláudio and Benedick in his suite, visits Leonato, duke of Messina, father of Hero and uncle of Beatrice. Claudio falls in love with Hero and their marriage is arranged. Beatrice, a mirthful, teasing creature, and the wild and witty Benedick are ever engaged in wordy warfare. A plot is devised to make them fall in love. It is contrived that Benedick shall overhear the Prince and Claudio speak of the secret love of Beatrice for him; and Beatrice is made to overhear a like account of Benedick's love for her. The scheme is successful and they are brought to a mutual liking.

Don John, the soured and malignant brother of the prince, in order to wreck Claudio's marriage, contrives with a follower, Borachio, that Claudio shall be brought to doubt of Hero's honour. Borachio converses at midnight with Margaret, Hero's maid, dressed as Hero, at Hero's window, and the prince and Claudio, who have been posted near, are deceived by the trick.

At the wedding ceremony, Claudio and the prince denounce Hero, who falls in a swoon. By the advice of the Friar, who is sure of Hero's innocence, Leonato gives out that she is dead. Benedick, at the instance of Beatrice, challenges Claudio for slandering her cousin. At this moment Borachio, overheard boasting of his exploit, is arrested and confesses. Claudio offers to make Leonato any amends in his power, and is required to marry a cousin of Hero in her place. This lady when unmasked turns out to be Hero herself. Benedick asks to be married at the same time, and Beatrice, 'on great persuasion, and partly to save your life, because I was told you were in a consumption', consents.

Mucklebackit, ELSPETH, STEENIE, etc., characters in Scott's 'The Antiquary' (q.v.).

Mucklewrath, HABAKKUK, a fanatical preacher in Scott's 'Old Mortality' (q.v.).

MUDDIMAN, HENRY (*b.* 1629), a pensioner at St. John's College, Cambridge, was authorized as a journalist by the Rump Parliament at the request of General Monck, in 1659, in which year he started 'The Parliamentary Intelligencer' and 'Mercurius Publicus'. He became the most famous of 17th-cent. journalists, and his newsletters in manuscript, sent twice a week to subscribers all over the kingdom, were an important political feature of the day. One of his principal rivals was L'Estrange (q.v.), whose papers, however, he drove from the field. In 1665, under the direction of his patron, Sir J. Williamson (q.v.), he started the 'Oxford Gazette' (the predecessor of the 'London Gazette'), the court being then at Oxford on account of the Great Plague.

Mug, MATTHEW, a character in Foote's 'Mayor of Garret', said to be a caricature of the duke of Newcastle.

Muggleton v. Dingley Dell, the cricket-match in ch. vii of 'The Pickwick Papers'(q.v.).

Muggletonians, a sect founded about 1651 by Lodowicke Muggleton and John Reeve. The belief of the sect rested on the personal inspiration of the founders, who claimed to be the 'two witnesses' of Rev. xi. 3–6. Muggleton (1609–98) was a journeyman tailor, and was imprisoned and fined for blasphemy. Reeve and Muggleton's 'Transcendent Spirituall Treatise' was published in 1652.

Mugwump, from an American Indian word meaning 'great chief', the name applied in the United States in 1884 to the Republicans who refused to support the nominee (Blaine) of their party for the presidency. It is used to signify one who stands aloof from party politics, professing disinterested and superior views. [OED.]

Muhajirs, the companions of Mohammed in his migration from Mecca to Medina (the Hijra, 622).

MUIR, EDWIN (1887–1959), novelist, poet, and critic, born and educated in Orkney. He was director of the British Institute at Rome in 1949, and professor of poetry at Harvard University, 1955–6. His novels are 'The Marionette' (1927), 'The Three Brothers' (1931), and 'Poor Tom' (1932). His poetry includes 'First Poems' (1925), 'The Chorus of the Newly Dead' (1926), 'Variations on a Time Theme' (1934), and 'The Voyage' (1946); 'Collected Poems, 1921–51' was published in 1952. He published a number of critical works, including 'Transition: essays on contemporary literature' (1926) and 'Scott and Scotland' (1936), and a life of John Knox (1929). With his wife, Willa, he translated Kafka's 'The Castle' and 'The Trial'. 'The Story and the Fable' (1940) is the first part of an autobiography completed in 1954.

MULCASTER, RICHARD (1530?–1611), educated at Eton and Christ Church, was headmaster of Merchant Taylors' School and high-master of St. Paul's School. He was author of two books on the education of children of the middle classes, 'The Positions' and 'The Elementarie', published in 1581 and 1582.

Mulciber, a name of Vulcan (q.v.), meaning 'the smelter' of metals.

MULGRAVE, EARL OF, see *Sheffield.*

Mulla, frequently referred to in Spenser's poems, is the river Mulla or Awbeg, a tributary of the Blackwater in Ireland, near which stood Kilcolman Castle, his residence when he composed 'The Faerie Queene'.

Mullah, THE MAD, a fanatical Muslim teacher, of Surat on the Indian frontier, who incited risings in 1897–8. A 'Mad Mullah' also led risings in Somaliland in 1899–1910.

'Mullah' is a corrupt pronunciation of an Arabic word meaning one learned in the sacred law.

MÜLLER, FRIEDRICH MAX, see *Max Müller.*

Mulliner, MR., (1) in Mrs. Gaskell's 'Cranford' (q.v.), the Hon. Mrs. Jamieson's butler; (2) the teller of some of the stories by P. G. Wodehouse (q.v.).

MULOCK, DINAH MARIA (Mrs. Craik) (1826–87), author of 'John Halifax, Gentleman' (q.v.).

Mulvaney, TERENCE, with Stanley Ortheris and John Learoyd, the three privates in Rudyard Kipling's 'Soldiers Three'.

Mum, Sothsegger, 'Hush, Truthteller', the title of an alliterative poem of the time of 'Piers Plowman' (q.v.). The title has long been known. The identification of the poem with a fragment which occurs in one of the manuscripts of the B-text of 'Piers Plowman', named 'Richard the Redeless' by Skeat, has been rendered possible by the discovery of a manuscript published by the E.E.T.S. in 1936. The fragment, which deals with the misrule of Richard II, was ascribed by Skeat and Jusserand to the author of 'Piers Plowman', but internal evidence makes the ascription doubtful.

Mumbo Jumbo, a grotesque idol said to have been worshipped by certain Negro tribes in Africa. According to the descriptions given by Moore and Mungo Park, it was a bugbear used by husbands to terrify their wives and keep them in order. The term is used in English to signify an object of unintelligent veneration and the ceremonies connected with it.

Mummers' Play, THE, or ST. GEORGE PLAY, a folk-play evolved from the sword-dance (q.v.), widely spread through England, Scotland, Ireland, and Wales. The play, in its characters and detailed action, varies in different localities, but the main lines are as follows. The principal characters are St. George (Sir George, King George, Prince George), the Turkish knight, Captain Slasher, and the Doctor. By the side of these are minor personages, bearing, according to the different versions, a great variety of names. After a brief prologue, the several fighting characters advance and introduce themselves, or are introduced, in vaunting rhymes. A duel or several duels follow, and one or other of the combatants is killed. The Doctor then enters, boasts his skill, and resuscitates the slain. Supernumerary grotesque characters are then presented, and a collection is made. The central incident of the play is doubtless connected with the celebration of the death of the year and its resurrection in the spring. The subject is treated in E. K. Chambers's 'The English Folk-Play' (1933).

Mumpsimus, used as a vague term of contempt, an 'old fogey'; also a traditional custom or notion obstinately adhered to, however unreasonable it is shown to be. The term originates from the story (in R. Pace, 'De Fructu', 1517) of an illiterate English priest, who when corrected for reading 'quod in ore mumpsimus' in the Mass, replied, 'I will not change my old mumpsimus for your new sumpsimus'. [OED.]

MUNBY, ARTHUR JOSEPH (1828–1910), educated at Trinity College, Cambridge, published various poems: 'Benoni' (1852), 'Verses New and Old' (1865), and 'Dorothy' (1880). His later works include 'Poems, Chiefly Lyric and Elegiac' (1901) and 'Relicta' (1909). Munby was secretly and happily married to his servant, who refused to quit her station. The fact explains some of the allusions in his poems.

Munchausen, Baron, Narrative of his Marvellous Travels, by Rudolph Erich Raspe, published in 1785.

The original Baron Münchausen is said to have lived in 1720–97, to have served in the Russian army against the Turks, and to have been in the habit of grossly exaggerating his experiences. Raspe (1737–94) was a Hanoverian who, when librarian at Cassel, stole gems from the Landgraf's collection, fled to England to escape the consequences, and added to his resources by publishing in English a version of the Baron's narratives. They include such stories as that of the horse who was cut in two, drank of a fountain, and was sewn up again; of the stag that the Baron shot with a cherry-stone, and afterwards found with a cherry-tree growing out of his forehead; and so forth.

MUNDAY, ANTHONY (1553–1633), wrote or collaborated in a number of plays, and was ridiculed by Ben Jonson as Antonio Balladino in 'The Case is Altered' (q.v.). Among his plays are 'John a Kent and John a Cumber' (acted *c.* 1594, dealing with a conflict between two wizards of those names) and 'The Downfall of Robert, Earle of Huntington' (printed 1601), followed by 'The Death' of the same, of which the subject is the legend of Robin Hood, with whom the earl is identified. Munday wrote ballads, which are lost, unless the charming 'Beauty sat bathing by a spring' in 'England's Helicon' (q.v.) is his, as it appears to be. He also translated popular romances, including 'Palladino of England' (1588) and 'Amadis of Gaule' (q.v., 1590?), and wrote City pageants.

Mundungus (from Spanish *mondongo*, tripe, black-pudding), bad-smelling tobacco. Under the name of Mundungus, Sterne, in the 'Sentimental Journey' (q.v.), satirized Dr. S. Sharp, author of 'Letters from Italy' (1766).

Munera, THE LADY, in Spenser's 'Faerie Queene', v. ii, the daughter of the Saracen Pollente, the personification of ill-gotten wealth, whom Sir Artegall besieges and whom Talus drowns in the moat of her castle after chopping off her golden hands and feet.

Munera Pulveris, chapters by Ruskin (q.v.) of an unfinished treatise on political economy contributed to 'Fraser's Magazine' in 1862–3, the remainder of which was suppressed by popular clamour. The work was published in book form in 1872.

It purports to be an 'accurate analysis of the laws of Political Economy', and begins with a series of definitions, of which the most important, being the key to the subsequent treatment of the subject, is that of Wealth. Wealth consists of things essentially valuable, intrinsic value being the life-giving power of anything. A cluster of flowers, for instance, has a fixed power of enlivening or animating the senses and heart. This intrinsic value is not affected by men's contempt for it, and is thus distinguished from exchange value.

Mungo, ST., see *Kentigern.*

Munich, the capital of Bavaria, a stronghold of the Nazi party from its early days. At Munich took place in 1938, after the German absorption of Austria, the negotiations between Neville Chamberlain and Hitler as a result of which the subjugation of Czechoslovakia was postponed but not averted. An informal peace pact was also signed by Chamberlain and Hitler. The name is sometimes used as a symbol of the policy of 'appeasement', of compromise or surrender in the face of threats.

Munin, see *Odin.*

MUNRO, HECTOR HUGH (1870–1916), writer of fiction, began his literary career as a political satirist for the 'Westminster Gazette', and during 1902–8 was correspondent in Russia and subsequently in Paris of 'The Morning Post'. 'Reginald', his first characteristic collection of short stories, was published under the pseudonym 'Saki' in 1904, and was followed by 'Reginald in Russia' (1910), 'The Chronicles of Clovis' (1911), and 'Beasts and Superbeasts' (1914). 'The Unbearable Bassington', a novel, appeared in 1912.

MUNRO, HUGH ANDREW JOHNSTONE (1819–85), educated at Shrewsbury School and Trinity College, Cambridge, one of the foremost of English latinists, produced a famous critical edition of Lucretius, with a translation into English prose, in 1864. His 'Criticisms and Elucidations of Catullus' appeared in 1878. His 'Translations into Latin and Greek Verse' was privately printed in 1884.

Murdockson, MEG, and her daughter MAGDALEN, called 'Madge Wildfire', characters in Scott's 'The Heart of Midlothian' (q.v.).

Murdstone, EDWARD and JANE, characters in Dickens's 'David Copperfield' (q.v.).

Murillo, BARTOLOMÉ ESTEBAN (1617–82), Spanish painter, chiefly of devotional subjects, such as the 'Immaculate Conception', and genre scenes of street arabs.

MURPHY, ARTHUR (1727–1805), a playwright of the Garrick era, of more industry than originality. He wrote comedies, some of them adapted from Molière, tragedies ('The Grecian Daughter' and 'Zenobia'), and farces, which met with some success. Among his best comedies are 'Three Weeks after Marriage' (q.v.), produced in 1764; and 'The Way to Keep Him' (1760), on the duty of wives to be bright and amiable, and of husbands to be faithful.

MURRAY, GEORGE GILBERT AIMÉ (1866–1957), classical scholar, born at Sydney, N.S.W., Regius professor of Greek at Oxford 1908–36. A distinguished interpreter of Greek ideas, both by his editions and translations of the Greek dramatists, and special studies like 'The Rise of the Greek Epic' (1907), 'Euripides and his Age' (1913), 'Aristophanes: a Study' (1933), 'Aeschylus, the Creator of Tragedy' (1940), and 'Greek Studies' (1946). In 1952 he became President of the Society of Australian Writers. He was buried in Westminster Abbey.

MURRAY, SIR JAMES AUGUSTUS HENRY (1837–1915), the son of a clothier of Hawick, was educated at Cavers school, near his native village of Denholm, and at Minto school. He became a schoolmaster and showed great activity in the study of languages and antiquities. In 1879 he was appointed editor of the 'Oxford English Dictionary' (q.v.), of which work he laid down the lines and with which his name is principally associated. He had previously to this established his reputation as a philologist by his article on the English language in the 'Encyclopaedia Britannica'. He was also author of a treatise on the 'Dialect of the Southern Counties of Scotland' (1873), and sent many contributions to the 'Athenaeum'.

MURRAY, JOHN (1745–93), the first of the famous publishing house of that name, changed his name to Murray from Macmurray. In 1768 he bought the publishing business of William Sandby in London. He was succeeded by his son JOHN MURRAY (1778–1843), who started the 'Quarterly Review' (q.v.) in 1809. The latter moved to Albemarle Street in 1812 and became acquainted with Byron, whose works he published. He also published for Jane Austen, Crabbe, Borrow, and many others. In 1820 he published Mrs. Mariana Starke's 'Guide for Travellers on the Continent', which led to the series of Murray's guide-books, several of these being written by his son JOHN MURRAY (1808–92), who succeeded his father in the business. Among the third John Murray's publications were works of Layard, Grote, Milman, Darwin, and Dean Stanley.

MURRAY, LINDLEY (1745–1826), grammarian, born in Pennsylvania, settled in England in 1784. He published an 'English Grammar' (1795), 'Reader' (1799), and 'Spelling Book' (1804), which were used in schools to the exclusion of all others. He has been called the 'father of English grammar'.

MURRY, JOHN MIDDLETON (1889–1957), a critic who worked on the staff of the 'Westminster Gazette' and later of the 'Nation'. He met Katherine Mansfield (q.v.) in 1913 and later married her, and his writing was influenced both by her and by their friend D. H. Lawrence (q.v.). After the First World War he became editor of the 'Athenaeum' (1919–21), and in 1923 he founded the 'Adelphi' (1923–48). His works of literary criticism include 'Countries of the Mind' (1922, 1931), 'The Problem of Style' (1922), 'Keats and Shakespeare' (1925), 'Son of Woman, the Story of D. H. Lawrence' (1931), 'The Life of Katherine Mansfield' (1933), 'William Blake' (1933), and 'Swift' (1954). He also wrote a number of religious books including 'To the Unknown God' (1924) and 'The Life of Jesus' (1926).

MUSAEUS, (1) a legendary Greek poet, said to have been a pupil of Orpheus (q.v.); (2) a Greek poet, who perhaps lived about A.D. 500, the author of a poem on the story of Hero and Leander (q.v.), which provided the groundwork for Marlowe's poem.

Muse's Looking-Glasse, The, a defence of the drama, in the form of a play, by Randolph (q.v.), printed in 1638.

The scene lies in the play-house at Blackfriars. Bird and Mistress Flowerdew, two Puritans, who serve the theatre with feathers and other small wares, enter; they express their abhorrence of play-houses; Roscius joins them; he prevails on them to see the representation of the play; Roscius explains the drift of it to them as it proceeds. This play has no plot; the object of it is to show that all virtues, and every commendable passion, proceed from mediocrity or a just medium between two extremes. At the conclusion [Bird and Mistress Flowerdew] agree that a play may be productive of moral good' (Genest). Dodsley remarks of 'The Muse's Looking-Glass' that 'it has always been esteemed an excellent commonplace book for authors, to instruct them in the art of drawing characters'. The scenes between the personages representing the extremes, e.g. Colax, the flatterer, and Dyscolus, the churl, are spirited and entertaining.

Muses, THE, the nine daughters of Zeus and Mnemŏsÿnē, born in Pieria at the foot of Mt. Olympus, who presided over the various kinds of poetry, arts, and sciences. Their names were Clīo, Euterpē, Thalīa, Melpŏmĕnē, Terpsĭchŏrē, Ĕrăto, Pŏlÿhymnĭa, Urania, and Calliŏpē (qq.v.). Helicon was sacred to them, and Parnassus, with its Castalian spring, was one of their chief seats.

Musgrave, LITTLE, see *Little Musgrave and Lady Barnard.*

Musgrave, SIR RICHARD, a character in Scott's 'The Lay of the Last Minstrel' (q.v.).

Musgrove, MR. and **MRS.,** their son **CHARLES** and his wife **MARY** (*née* **ELLIOT**), and their daughters **HENRIETTA** and **LOUISA,** characters in Jane Austen's 'Persuasion' (q.v.).

Musidōra, see *Damon and Musidora.*

Musidōrus, a character in Sidney's 'Arcadia' (q.v.).

Musophilus, or Defence of all Learning, a poem in six- and eight-lined stanzas by S. Daniel (q.v.), published in 1599. It takes the form of a discussion between Musophilus and Philocosmus, in which the former defends the merits of knowledge and virtue against the more worldly unlettered arts, and it shows Daniel's gift for moral reflection at its best. It contains the notable prophetic lines:

And who, in time, knowes whither we may vent
The treasure of our tongue, to what strange shores
The gaine of our best glory shall be sent,
T'inrich unknowing Nations with our stores?
What worlds in th'yet unformed Occident
May come refin'd with th'accents that are ours?

Muspellheim, in Scandinavian mythology, the home of Muspell or elemental fire, a region separated from Niflheim (q.v.) by the chasm Ginnungagap (q.v.). It is the sons of Muspell who, under Surtur their leader, destroy the world at Ragnarök (q.v.).

MUSSET, ALFRED DE (1810–57), French poet of the romantic school. 'Les Nuits' (1835–7, four poems) and 'Souvenir' (1841) are the finest examples of his passionate, lyrical verse. He was also a dramatist, author of poetically written comedies and *proverbes* (short dramatic sketches intended to illustrate their proverb-titles) which include: 'On ne saurait penser à tout', 'On ne badine pas avec l'amour', 'Le Chandelier', etc., and of a fine historical drama 'Lorenzaccio' (5 acts, prose). His long novel 'La Confession d'un enfant du siècle' (1836) is partly autobiographical. The episode of his journey to Italy with George Sand in 1833–4 and their rupture, with its literary reverberations, had considerable notoriety.

Mussolini, BENITO (1883–1945), was the leader (*Il Duce*) of Fascism (q.v) in Italy. After the 'march on Rome' in October 1922 Mussolini became prime minister of a coalition government and, in 1925, dictator, with the Fascist party as the sole official instrument of political power. He pursued a policy of economic self-sufficiency and rearmament together with colonial aggrandizement as manifested in the Italian conquest of Abyssinia, 1935–6. He allied himself with Hitler in 1936 in the 'Berlin–Rome Axis'. After the fall of France in 1940 he entered the war as Germany's ally, but was forced to resign in 1943 and was executed by Italian partisans in 1945.

Mustapha, a tragedy by Sir F. Greville (q.v.), published in 1609. Rossa, the wife of the Turkish Emperor Solyman, persuades her husband that Mustapha, his son by a former marriage, seeks his life; she endeavours thereby to advance the prospects of her own children. Camena, the virtuous daughter of Rossa, defends the innocence of Mustapha, in vain. Mustapha refuses to seek safety in the destruction of Rossa and her faction, and is presently executed.

Mustapha, a heroic play (1665) by R. Boyle (q.v.), based on the 'Ibrahim' of G. de Scudéry.

My Mind to me a Kingdom is, the first line of a philosophical song which appears to have been popular in the 16th cent. It is referred to by Jonson in his 'Every Man out of his Humour', I. i. The text is given in Percy's 'Reliques'. Bartlett ('Familiar Quotations') attributes it to Edward Dyer (q.v.), with alternative versions by other authors.

My Novel, or Varieties in English Life, a novel by Bulwer Lytton (q.v.), published in 1853.

The main story is that of the career of Leonard Fairfield, a self-taught poet, who spends his infancy in a peasant household, suffers poverty and hardship, and turns out to be the son of Audley Egerton, a distinguished politician. With this is woven the tale of Dr. Riccabocca, an Italian refugee, who ultimately recovers his rights as duke of Salerno; of Harley, Lord L'Estrange, who has been ousted by his friend, Audley Egerton, from the affections of Nora Avenel, Leonard Fairfield's mother; and of the complicated intrigue by which the villains of the plot, the ambitious young Randal Leslie and Levy the money-lender, endeavour to effect the ruin of Audley Egerton, Frank Hazeldean (the squire's son), and Violante, the daughter of the Italian exile.

Myddelton or MIDDLETON, SIR HUGH (1560?–1631), a banker, goldsmith, and clothmaker, remembered as having carried out the New River scheme, whereby a supply of pure water from the Chadswell Springs in Hertfordshire was brought to London by a canal forty miles long. He is mentioned in Lamb's 'Amicus Redivivus'.

MYERS, FREDERIC WILLIAM HENRY (1843–1901), educated at Cheltenham and Trinity College, Cambridge, became an inspector under the education department. He published several volumes of poems, including 'St. Paul' (1867), and 'Essays Classical and Modern' (1883). He wrote a monograph on Wordsworth (1881) for the English Men of Letters series, and also on Shelley for Ward's 'English Poets'. He gave much attention to phenomena of mesmerism and spiritualism and was one of the founders of the Society for Psychical Research. He was joint-author of 'Phantasms of the Living' (1886), which embodied the first considerable results of the society's labours.

MYERS, LEOPOLD HAMILTON (1881–1944), novelist, the son of F. W. H. Myers (q.v.). His novels are concerned with social and ethical problems and the conflict between material and spiritual values. Apart from 'The Orissers' (1922), 'The "Clio"' (1925), and 'Strange Glory' (1936), the novels are set in 16th-cent. India and were published as follows: 'The Near and the Far' (1929), 'Prince Jali' (1931), 'The Root and the Flower' (1935), and 'The Pool of Vishnu' (1940); all collected under the title 'The Near and the Far' (1943).

Myrmidons, the name borne by a people on the southern borders of Thessaly who accompanied Achilles to the Trojan War, and were named after a legendary ancestor, Myrmidon, son of Zeus. According to another legend, a pestilence having destroyed all the subjects of Aeacus, king of Aegina, he entreated Zeus to repeople his kingdom. In consequence all the ants that were in an old oak were changed into men and called by Aeacus *myrmidons* from μύρμηξ, an ant.

Myron (active *c.* 480–445 B.C.), Greek sculptor. Working chiefly in bronze, he introduced variety of pose and movement into his figures, e.g. the 'Discobolus'.

Myrrha, the daughter of Cinyras, king of Cyprus, who became by him mother of Adonis (q.v.). When apprized of the incest that he had committed he attempted to stab her, and she, fleeing into Arabia, was changed into the plant called myrrh.

'Myrrha' is also the name of a character in Byron's 'Sardanapalus' (q.v.).

Mysie Happer, the miller's daughter in Scott's 'The Monastery' (q.v.), who marries Sir Piercie Shafton.

Mysteries, a term used by modern writers as a name for 'Miracle Plays' (q.v.). A. W. Ward in 'English Dramatic Literature', i. 23, draws a distinction between 'Mysteries' as dealing with Gospel events only, and 'Miracle Plays' as concerned with legends of the saints. But this is not generally accepted. [OED.]

Mysteries of Udolpho, The, a novel by Mrs. Radcliffe (q.v.), published in 1794, which attained a wide fame.

The period of the story is the end of the 16th cent. Emily de St. Aubert, the beautiful daughter of a Gascon family, loses her mother and her father, and comes under the despotic guardianship of an aunt, Madame Cheron. An affection has sprung up between Emily and Valancourt, a young man of good family but moderate means. The aunt, who has more ambitious views, and has herself married a sinister Italian, Signor Montoni, carries off Emily to the sombre castle of Udolpho in the Apennines, the home of Montoni. Here, with all the apparatus of sliding panels, secret passages, abductions, and a suggestion of the supernatural, dark dealings are carried on. Emily escapes, returns to Languedoc, meets

Valancourt again, and after further vicissitudes is finally united to him. Montoni, who proves to be the chief of a robber band, is captured and suffers the penalty of his crimes.

Mysterious Mother, The, a tragedy by H. Walpole (q.v.), published in 1768.

It deals with the remorse of a mother (the countess of Narbonne) for an act of incest committed many years before. Under the calamity of the marriage of her son, who had been the unwitting participant in her crime, with the girl born of their union, she takes her own life.

Mysterious Stranger, The, written by Mark Twain (see *Clemens, S. L.*) in 1898, and posthumously published in 1916, the tale of a visit of Satan to a medieval village.

Mystic, MR., a character in Peacock's 'Melincourt', a caricature of Coleridge.

N

N.E.D., the 'New English Dictionary', more generally known now as the 'Oxford English Dictionary' (q.v.).

N or M, the first answer in the Catechism of the English Church. The most probable explanation is that N stood for *nomen* (name), and that *nomen vel nomina* (name or names) was expressed by 𝔑 *vel* 𝔑𝔑, the double *N* being afterwards corrupted into 𝔐 (J. H. Blunt, 'Annotated Book of Common Prayer', 1890).

n.d., in bibliographies, booksellers' catalogues, etc., 'no date'.

Nabob, The, a play by Foote (q.v.), produced in 1772.

NABOKOV, VLADIMIR (1899–), Russian emigré novelist, poet, and critic, sometimes using the pseudonym 'Vladimir Sirin'. He was born in St. Petersburg, studied in Cambridge, where he took his degree in 1922, and then lived mostly in France and Germany until 1940, when he settled in the United States. Nabokov's early work was written in Russian. Much of it has been translated, often by the author himself. It includes 'Grozd'' (1923), 'Zashchita Luzhina' (1929), 'Camera Obscura' (1933), 'Otchayaniye' (1934), and 'Priglashenie na kazn'' (1938). Later work, in English, includes 'The Real Life of Sebastian Knight' (1941), 'Bend Sinister' (1947), 'Conclusive Evidence' (1951), 'Lolita' (1955), 'Pnin' (1957), 'Pale Fire' (1962). Nabokov also wrote a study of Pushkin's 'Eugene Onegin' (1964), with translation and notes, and translations of poems by Pushkin, Lermontov, and Tyutchev.

Nabonassar, ERA OF, an era used in the chronology of the Chaldeans and other ancient writers, reckoned from the accession of Nabonassar, king of Babylonia, 747 B.C.

Naboth's Vineyard, the vineyard of Naboth the Jezreelite, coveted by Ahab. Jezebel caused Naboth to be put to death that Ahab might have it (1 Kings xxi).

Naciens, in the legend of the Grail (q.v.), the brother-in-law of King Evalak of Sarras. In the 'Morte Darthur', NACIEN is the hermit who tells how the quest of the Grail should be made.

Nagifar, in Scandinavian mythology, the ship that the giants will embark in at Ragnarök (q.v.).

Nag's Head Tavern, a tavern that stood in Friday Street, Cheapside. It was alleged by unscrupulous controversialists at the end of the 16th cent. that Archbishop Parker and others had, in 1559, after the Reformation, been irregularly and irreverently admitted bishops in this tavern, by Scory (formerly bishop of Chichester). As a matter of fact Parker was regularly consecrated by four bishops in the chapel of Lambeth Palace.

Naiads, see *Nymphs*.

Naiads, *Hymn to the,* see *Hymn to the Naiads*.

NAIRNE, CAROLINA, BARONESS, *née* Oliphant (1766–1845), was the author of some spirited Jacobite songs, of which the best-known are 'Will ye no come back again?', 'Charlie is my Darling', and 'He's o'er the Hills that I lo'e weel'; also of humorous and pathetic ballads, such as 'The Laird of Cockpen' (suggested by an older song) and 'The Land o' the Leal'. Her poems, anonymous in her lifetime, were collected and published as 'Lays from Strathearn' in 1846.

Nala and Damayanti, one of the 'Indian Idylls' of Sir E. Arnold (q.v.), taken from the 'Mahābhārata' (q.v.). Prince Nala and Damayanti, daughter of the king of Vidarbha, fall in love. The four gods, Indra, Varuna, Yama, and Agni, hearing of her beauty, send Nala to her to bid her choose one of them for her husband. She rejects them all and adheres to her choice of Nala, and wins their approval of her action. They confer gifts on Nala, but later he loses his kingdom and all he has by gambling, and the pair are separated, to be united after many adventures.

Namancos, in Milton's 'Lycidas', 'Where the great vision of the guarded mount Looks toward Namancos ánd Bayona's hold', is a place in Galicia, near Cape Finisterre, shown in Mercator's Atlas of 1623. The Castle of Bayona is shown near it. A line from the 'guarded mount' (St. Michael's Mount in Cornwall) to Finisterre passes clear of Ushant.

Namby-Pamby, see *Philips (A.).*

Nancy, in Dickens's 'Oliver Twist' (q.v.), the companion of Bill Sikes.

Nancy Lammeter, a character in G. Eliot's 'Silas Marner' (q.v.).

Nandy, JOHN EDWARD, in Dickens's 'Little Dorrit' (q.v.), the father of Mrs. Plornish.

Nanna, in Scandinavian mythology, the wife of Balder (q.v.). After his death she died of grief and was burnt on his funeral pyre.

Nannetae, in imprints, Nantes.

NANSEN, FRIDTJOF (1861–1930), Norwegian explorer and statesman. His 'The First Crossing of Greenland' appeared in 1892. He sailed in the 'Fram' in 1893 with Johansen for the Arctic regions and reached on foot 86° 14′ N., a voyage recorded in his 'Farthest North' (1897).

Nantes, EDICT OF, see *Edict of Nantes.*

NAPIER or **NEPER,** JOHN (1550–1617), laird of Merchiston, near Edinburgh, was educated at St. Andrews. He devoted himself for a time to the invention of instruments of warfare (including a prototype of the modern 'tank') and of a hydraulic screw for pumping out coal-pits. He then set himself to facilitate arithmetical operations, and devised logarithms, the nature of which he explained in his 'Mirifici Logarithmorum Canonis Descriptio', published in 1614 (the 'Constructio' followed in 1619). His 'Rabdologia', published in 1615, explains the use of numerating rods, commonly called 'Napier's bones', and metal plates for effecting multiplications and divisions—the earliest form of calculating machine. He also invented the present notation of decimal fractions.

NAPIER, SIR WILLIAM FRANCIS PATRICK (1785–1860), served in Sir John Moore's campaign in Spain (1808), and in the subsequent war in the Peninsula. He published in 1828–40 his 'History of the Peninsular War', recounting events of which he had been in part an eyewitness. It earned a handsome commendation from the duke of Wellington in spite of the author's Radical outlook, and placed him high among historical writers; it was translated into many languages. He subsequently (1844–6) published a history of the conquest of Scinde (a defence of his brother Charles). He was promoted to Major-General in 1841 and to General in 1859.

Napoleon I, NAPOLEON BONAPARTE (BUONA-PARTE) (1769–1821), of a Corsican family, first came into prominence as an artillery officer at the recapture of Toulon from the English in 1793. He was general-in-chief of the French army of Italy 1796–7, and was then sent to conquer Egypt, whence he returned in 1799. By a *coup d'état* at the end of that year he became master of the government and was named First Consul. Then followed the series of his European conquests. In 1804 he proclaimed himself emperor. The tide turned against him with the disastrous Russian campaign of 1812, followed by the defeat at Leipzig and by Wellington's victories. In 1814 Napoleon abdicated and was sent to Elba. He returned in 1815 and was in that year finally defeated at Waterloo. He died at St. Helena. He married in 1795 Joséphine, widow of the Comte de Beauharnais, divorced her, and married in 1810 Marie Louise, daughter of the Austrian Emperor Francis II, by whom he had a son, the duke of Reichstadt (*d.* 1832).

Napoleon III, (CHARLES) LOUIS NAPOLEON BONAPARTE (1808–73), was the nephew of Napoleon I (q.v.). In 1836 and 1840, while living in exile, he made two unsuccessful attempts, at Strasburg and Boulogne, to stir up Bonapartist risings. After the second of these he was imprisoned at Ham in France, whence he escaped in 1846. In December 1848, after the fall of Louis Philippe, he was elected president of the French Republic, became, as a result of a *coup d'état*, president for ten years in 1851, and was proclaimed emperor in 1852. Under him, France was Britain's ally in the Crimean War, and played an important part in the liberation of Italy by fighting with Sardinia against Austria in 1859. In the Franco-Prussian War of 1870–1 he was taken prisoner at Sedan in September 1870, and, after a period of captivity, spent the remainder of his life at Chiselhurst. He married in 1853 Eugénie de Montijo (the Empress Eugénie).

Narcissa, in Pope's 'Moral Essays' is Anne Oldfield (q.v.). For the 'Narcissa' of Young's 'Night Thoughts', see under the name of that poem.

Narcissus, a beautiful youth, son of the river god Cephissus and the nymph Līriopē. He saw his image reflected in a fountain and became enamoured of it, thinking it to be the nymph of the place. His fruitless attempts to approach this beautiful object drove him to despair and death. He was changed into the flower which bears his name.

Narrenschiff, see *Ship of Fools.*

Nash, JOHN (1752–1835), architect. Patronized by the Prince Regent, he designed Regent's Park and Regent Street, Buckingham Palace (q.v.), and the Royal Pavilion, Brighton.

Nash, RICHARD, 'Beau Nash' (1674–1762), born at Swansea, was educated at Carmarthen Grammar School and for a time at Jesus College, Oxford. He supported himself in

London as a gamester, and went to Bath in 1705, where he established the Assembly Rooms, drew up a code of etiquette and dress, and became unquestioned autocrat of society. He assisted in founding the mineral-water hospital for poor patients. The gambling laws of 1740–5 deprived him of his source of income, and his popularity waned after 1745. In 1758 he was allowed £10 a month by the corporation of Bath. A biography of Nash was written by Oliver Goldsmith (q.v.).

NASH or NASHE, THOMAS (1567–1601), was a sizar of St. John's College, Cambridge. He made a hasty tour through France and Italy, and before 1588 settled in London. His first publication was an acrid review of recent literature (prefixed to Greene's 'Menaphon', 1589), which he discussed at greater length in the 'Anatomie of Absurditie' (1589). He was attracted to the Martin Marprelate controversy (q.v.) by his hatred of Puritanism. Under the pseudonym of 'Pasquil' he wrote 'A Countercuffe given to Martin Junior' (1598), 'The Returne of the renouned Cavaliero Pasquil of England' (1589), and 'The First Parte of Pasquils Apologie' (1590). He was possibly the author of other attacks on the Martinists. Nash replied in 1591 to the savage denunciations of Richard Harvey, the astrologer and brother of Gabriel Harvey (q.v.), with 'A wonderful, strange, and miraculous Astrologicall Prognostication', and in 1592 wrote 'Pierce Pennilesse his Supplication to the Divell' (q.v.). This was translated into French, and the second edition was called 'The Apologie of Pierce Pennilesse'. Nash avenged Gabriel Harvey's attack on Greene (q.v.) with 'Strange Newes of the Intercepting certaine Letters' (1593). Being subsequently troubled with religious doubts, he published his repentant reflections under the title 'Christes Teares over Jerusalem' (q.v.) in 1593. 'The Terrors of the Night', notable for the praise of Daniel's 'Delia', appeared in 1594, and in the same year 'The Unfortunate Traveller, or the Life of Jacke Wilton' (q.v.), a spirited romance of adventure. Nash further satirized Harvey in 'Haue with you to Saffron-Walden' (1596), to which Harvey replied, the government subsequently ordering the two authors to desist. He attacked so many current abuses in the State in his lost comedy 'The Isle of Dogs' (1597) that he was sent to the Fleet prison for some months. He published in 1599 'Lenten Stuffe', a burlesque panegyric of the red herring, written to repay hospitality enjoyed at Yarmouth, and a comedy still extant, called 'Summers Last Will', 1600. Nash's original personality gives him a unique place in Elizabethan literature, and his writings have something of the fascination of Rabelais. His romance of 'Jacke Wilton' inaugurated the novel of adventure in England.

NASO, see *Ovid*. The word means 'nose', to which Holofernes alludes in Shakespeare's 'Love's Labour's Lost' (q.v.), IV. ii.

Nasr-ed-Din, KHOJA, a Turk born in the latter part of the 14th cent., the author of a celebrated collection of humorous and satirical tales.

Naströnd, in Scandinavian mythology, a place of torment for the wicked in hell.

NATHAN, GEORGE JEAN (1882–1958), American essayist and critic, born in Indiana, co-founder with H. L. Mencken (q.v.) of 'The American Mercury', of which he remained an editor until 1930. Among his chief works are: 'The Popular Theatre' (1918), 'The American Credo' (with H. L. Mencken) (1920), 'The Critic and the Drama' (1922), 'The Autobiography of an Attitude' (1925).

Nathan the Wise, see *Lessing.*

Nathaniel, SIR, in Shakespeare's 'Love's Labour's Lost' (q.v.), a curate.

National Anthem, THE. The first recorded public performance of 'God save the King' took place at Drury Lane Theatre on 28 September 1745, during the excitement and alarm caused by the Jacobite invasion of that year. It was an unannounced addition by the actors to the ordinary programme of the day and a manifestation of their loyal zeal. The score used on this occasion was prepared by Thomas Augustine Arne (1710–78), leader of the orchestra at the theatre and composer of 'Rule, Britannia' (q.v.). The example set at Drury Lane was followed at other theatres and the song was soon very popular. It became customary about 1747 or 1748 to greet the king with it when he entered a place of public entertainment. In George III's reign it figured as a political battle-song in connexion with the Regency troubles and later during the dissensions aroused by the French Revolution. It was sung at the coronation banquet of George IV and the description of it as National Anthem appears to have been adopted early in the 19th cent. Variant versions, imitations, and parodies have been very numerous; among the imitations may be mentioned the 'New National Anthem' written by Shelley in 1819 after Peterloo, and the 'New National Anthem' of Ebenezer Elliott (q.v.), the Corn-law Rhymer (1830).

The remoter origin of 'God save the King' is obscure. Before being sung at Drury Lane in 1745, words and tune, with slight differences, had appeared in 'Thesaurus Musicus', a song collection published in 1744. The opening words in the Drury Lane version were

> God bless our noble King,
> God save great George our King,
> God save the King.

In the 'Thesaurus Musicus' they were

> God save our Lord the King,
> Long live our noble King,

which might apply equally to a Stuart or a Hanoverian monarch. There is good evidence that the song was originally written in favour of James II in 1688 (when the invasion by the

Prince of Orange was threatening) or possibly of Charles II in 1681; but the author is unknown. As regards the melody, various 17th-cent. tunes of the same rhythm more or less resemble that of 'God save the King'. The closest resemblance is that of a galliard composed by Dr. John Bull (q.v.) in the early 17th cent. But this may be the keyboard setting of some folk tune or other well-known air of the time, and the tune of 'God save the King' may have been drawn directly from that original. The tune has been adopted by a number of continental countries for their national anthems.

For a fuller treatment of the subject see Percy Scholes, 'God save the King' (Oxford, 1942), on which the above article is based.

For the national anthem of the United States see *Star-spangled Banner*.

National Biography, Dictionary of, designed and published by George Smith (q.v.), was begun in 1882 with Sir Leslie Stephen (q.v.) as editor. It included in its original form biographies of all national notabilities from earliest times to 1900. The work has been continued by the publishing of decennial supplements. Sir Leslie Stephen was succeeded in the editorship by Sir Sidney Lee. Their names appear jointly on the title-pages of vols. xxii–xxvi (1890), and Lee's name appeared alone from vol. xxvii till 1913. In 1917 the Dictionary was transferred to the Oxford University Press. The 1912–21 volume was edited by H. W. C. Davis and J. R. H. Weaver; 1922–30 by J. R. H. Weaver; 1931–40 by L. G. Wickam Legg; 1941–50 by L. G. Wickam Legg and E. T. Williams. The 'Concise D.N.B.' is in two parts: Part 1, epitome of the D.N.B. from earliest times to 1900, and Part 2, epitome of the supplements, 1901–50.

National Gallery, The, built by William Wilkins, and opened in 1838. The nucleus of the collection was the Angerstein collection, purchased in 1824, the pictures given by Sir George Beaumont, who was largely responsible for the foundation of the gallery, and those bequeathed by the Rev. W. H. Carr in 1831.

National Library of Scotland, see *Advocates' Library*.

Nationalist, an advocate of national rights, a term used specifically of one who advocated the claims of Ireland to be an independent nation. The earliest quotation given by the OED for the latter use of the word is from the 'Daily News' of 20 May 1869.

Natty Bumppo, the hero of the 'Leatherstocking' novels of J. F. Cooper (q.v.).

Natural Religion, Dialogues on, see *Dialogues on Natural Religion*.

Nature, a periodical founded in 1869, with Norman Lockyer as editor, for the purpose of providing the public with information on scientific matters. Charles Darwin, Huxley,

Tyndall, and Lubbock were among its distinguished early supporters.

Nature and Art, a romance by Mrs. Inchbald (q.v.), published in 1796. It is the story of two contrasted brothers, William and Henry, and their sons. William, worldly and ambitious, becomes a dean. His son, a capable villain, becomes a judge, and hangs the victim of his own seduction. Henry, the good brother, a fiddler, marries beneath him, loses his wife, and goes to Africa. He is wrecked on Socotra with his infant son, and some years later sends home this boy, the younger Henry, to be educated by his uncle William. Young Henry, who has lived far from the conventions of the civilized world and retained his natural simplicity, makes pungent comments on what he sees in England, meets with various misfortunes, but eventually attains happiness, while the younger William becomes the prey of remorse and ends wretchedly.

Nausicaa, in Homer's 'Odyssey', daughter of Alcinous, king of Phaeacia. She finds Odysseus (q.v.) shipwrecked on the coast, feeds and clothes him, and brings him to her father's court. Samuel ('Erewhon') Butler (q.v.) argued that she was the authoress of the 'Odyssey'.

Navarino, a bay in the south-west of the Peloponnese where in 1827 the British fleet under Admiral Codrington, with the French and Russian squadrons, defeated the combined Turkish and Egyptian fleets and rendered possible the liberation of Greece from the Turkish dominion.

In the same bay, then known as the Bay of Pylos, the Athenian fleet had in 425 B.C. defeated that of Sparta and cut off the Spartan hoplites on the island of Sphacteria.

Nazarene, (1) a native of Nazareth; (2) a follower of Jesus of Nazareth, a Christian (so called especially by Jews and Muslims); (3) in the plural, an early Jewish Christian sect, who accepted the divinity of Christ while conforming to the Mosaic law; (4) the name given to a group of German religious painters who settled in Rome in 1810.

Nazarites, the name given among the Hebrews to such as had taken certain vows of abstinence (see Num. vi).

Nazis, abbreviation of German *nationale Sozialisten*, the German National-Socialist party or its members.

Neaëra, a conventional name among the Roman poets for a lady-love, and referred to as such in Milton's 'Lycidas' (q.v.).

NEALE, JOHN MASON (1818–66), educated at Trinity College, Cambridge, a man of much versatility, was the founder of the Cambridge Camden Society (q.v.). He was author of a 'History of the Holy Eastern Church' (1847–50) and of many well-known hymns, including 'Jerusalem the Golden', 'The day is past and over', 'Art thou weary, art thou languid', 'Brief life is here our portion', several of them translated from the 'Rhythm' of Bernard of Morlaix (q.v.), others from hymns of the Eastern Church. He also wrote an historical novel, 'Theodora Phranza', on the subject of the fall of Constantinople, reprinted in 1857 from the 'Churchman's Companion' of 1853–4.

Neanderthal, near Düsseldorf in Germany, gives its name to an early type of the human race, from a skull-cap and certain other bones found there in deposits of the Middle Pleistocene period. Neanderthal man, who is associated with what is known as the Mousterian (q.v.) industry, is believed to have arrived in Europe from the East, probably from northern Asia. He spread over the greater part of Europe, but died out, and modern man is not descended from him. He was succeeded by Aurignacian man (see *Aurignac*). (Peake and Fleure, 'Apes and Men', 'Hunters and Artists'.)

Nebuchadnezzar, the king of Babylonia 605–562 B.C., who built the walls of Babylon (q.v.), and perhaps the famous 'Hanging Gardens'. His insanity is related in Dan. iv.

Necker, MADAME (SUSANNE CURCHOD) (1739–94), a Swiss woman, at one time engaged to Gibbon the historian (q.v.); she became the wife of Jacques Necker, the French financier and statesman. She was prominent in French literary circles of the period preceding the Revolution. Her daughter was the celebrated Mme de Staël (q.v.).

Neckett, MR., the sheriff's officer in Dickens's 'Bleak House' (q.v.), generally referred to as COAVINSES, the name of the sponging-house which he keeps. He has three children, Tom, Emma, and Charlotte (known as 'Charley', who becomes Esther Summerson's maid).

Nectabanus, the dwarf in Scott's 'The Talisman' (q.v.).

Nectanabus, in the fabulous history of Alexander the Great (q.v.), is an Egyptian king and magician, who goes to Macedonia, falls in love with Olympias, and becomes by her father of Alexander (not, however, in the great 'Roman d'Alexandre'), supervises Alexander's education, and is ultimately killed by him.

Ned Bratts, the subject and title of one of the 'Dramatic Idyls' of R. Browning (q.v.).

The poem is an adaptation of the episode of 'old Tod' in Bunyan's 'Mr. Badman' (q.v.), the 'veriest rogue that breathes upon earth', who is converted, confesses his felonies, and is hanged.

Needy Knife-grinder, The, see *Anti-Jacobin.*

Negus, (1) the title of the ruler of Abyssinia; (2) a mixture of wine, hot water, and sugar called *Negus,* so named after its inventor, Colonel Francis Negus (*d.* 1732).

NEHRU, JAWAHARLAL (1889–1964), Indian statesman, was born at Allahabad, the son of Motilal Nehru, an eminent lawyer. He was educated in England, at Harrow and Trinity College, Cambridge, and was called to the Bar before returning to Allahabad to practise there. He joined the non-co-operation movement under Gandhi in 1920, was imprisoned several times and soon attained a leading position in the Indian National Congress party. He became the first prime minister of independent India, remaining in office until his death. He wanted India to be a secular state, based on parliamentary government and a socialistic economy, with a foreign policy of 'neutralism', or independence of both the Western and Communist blocs. His policy of friendship with China was discredited by the Chinese invasion of India in 1962. His 'Autobiography' (1936) gives some insight into the development of his ideas. His 'Glimpses of World History' (1939) paid more attention to Asia than was usual in universal histories, and his 'Discovery of India' (1946) revealed his sympathy with India's traditions.

Nekayah, in Johnson's 'Rasselas' (q.v.), the sister of the hero.

Nell Trent, 'Little Nell', heroine of Dickens's 'The Old Curiosity Shop' (q.v.).

Nelson, HORATIO, VISCOUNT (1758–1805), born at Burnham-Thorpe, Norfolk, entered the navy in 1770. He lost his right eye at Calvi in Corsica in 1794, took a prominent part in the battle of Cape St. Vincent in 1797, and lost his right arm at Santa Cruz in the same year. In 1798 he destroyed the French fleet in Abukir Bay (Battle of the Nile). He commanded the attack on Copenhagen in 1801, and was killed at Trafalgar in 1805. He was made duke of Bronté (in Sicily). See also *Hamilton (Emma, Lady).*

Nelson's last words, 'Thank God, I have done my duty', or, according to another account, 'Kiss me, Hardy'.

Nĕmĕa, a town in Argolis, the neighbourhood of which was infested by the famous Nemean lion, killed by Hercules (q.v.). The scene also of ancient panhellenic games.

Nemesis, according to Hesiod a child of Night, was in early Greek thought a personification of the gods' resentment at, and consequent punishment of, insolence (*hubris*) towards themselves.

Nemo, the law-writer in Dickens's 'Bleak House' (q.v.).

Nemo, CAPTAIN, the hero of Jules Verne's 'Twenty Thousand Leagues under the Sea', in which the author anticipated the development of the submarine.

NENNIUS (*fl.* 796), the traditional author, but probably only the reviser, of the 'Historia Britonum', lived on the borders of Mercia, in Brecknock or Radnor, and was a pupil of Elbod, bishop of Bangor (*d. c.* 811). There are several versions of the 'Historia', the North-Welsh, the South-Welsh, the Irish, and the English. It is a collection of notes, drawn from various sources, on the history and geography of Britain, and is chiefly interesting for the account it purports to give of the historical Arthur, who, as *dux bellorum*, after Hengist's death led the Britons against the Saxons in twelve battles, which Nennius enumerates (including Mount Badon).

It is one of the sources on which Geoffrey of Monmouth (q.v.) drew for his 'Historia Regum Britanniae'. The 'Historia Britonum' was first printed by Gall, 1691, in 'Scriptores Quindecim'.

Neo-Impressionism, the style of painting developed by Georges Seurat (1859–91), who tried to work out a scientific basis to the Impressionists' ideas on the rendering of light. The movement is sometimes called Pointillism or Divisionism, for the pigment was applied in dots of pure colour which appear to fuse when seen from a distance, giving the effect of blended colour without loss of brilliance.

Neoplatonism, a philosophical and religious system, combining Platonic ideas with oriental mysticism, which originated at Alexandria in the 3rd cent., and is especially represented in the writings of Plotinus, Porphyry, and Proclus. The works of St. Augustine show its influence. One of the best-known exponents of Neoplatonism was Hypatia (murdered by the Alexandrian mob in A.D. 415), whose noble figure is depicted in C. Kingsley's novel called by her name (q.v.).

Neoptŏlĕmus, the son of Achilles (q.v.), also called PYRRHUS on account of his yellow hair. It was he who killed Priam. When the Trojan captives were distributed, Andromache (q.v.) fell to his portion. He subsequently married Hermione, daughter of Menelaus, and was slain by Orestes, to whom Hermione had been betrothed.

Nepenthe, a drug supposed to banish sorrow (see *Thone*). 'Nepenthe' is the title of a beautiful poem by G. Darley (q.v.).

Nephelococcygia, 'cloud-cuckoo-land', in the 'Birds' of Aristophanes, an imaginary city built in the air by the birds.

Nepomuk, ST. JOHN, the patron saint of Bohemia, born at Pomuk in that country, an ecclesiastic whom King Wenceslaus in 1393 caused to be drowned in the river Moldau at Prague.

NEPOS, CORNELIUS (*c.* 99–*c.* 24 B.C.), Roman historian, a friend of Atticus and Catullus. His chief work was 'De Viris Illustribus', of which part survives.

Neptune, the Roman god of the sea, identified with the Poseidon (q.v.) of the Greeks.

The planet NEPTUNE was discovered in 1846, as a result of the mathematical calculations of J. C. Adams in England and Leverrier in France.

Nēreïds, THE, in Greek mythology, the daughters of Nereus, a deity of the sea; the nymphs (q.v.) of the Mediterranean.

Neri, see *Bianchi and Neri*.

Nerissa, in Shakespeare's 'The Merchant of Venice' (q.v.), Portia's waiting-maid.

Nero, a Roman emperor (A.D. 54–68), the last of the Julio-Claudian dynasty, proverbial for his tyranny and brutality. He was an artist and actor of some merit, and started well under the tuition of Seneca and Burrus. Some ancient authors assert that the burning of Rome in 64 was due to his order and that he fiddled while it burnt. His subjects revolted against his oppression in 68, and Nero took his own life. 'Qualis artifex pereo!' ('What an artist dies with me!') are said to have been his dying words.

Nerthus, see *Hertha*.

NESBIT, EDITH (MRS. HUBERT BLAND, later MRS. BLAND-TUCKER) (1858–1924), aspired to be a poet but achieved fame in writing books for children. As a young girl she enjoyed the society of her sister Mary's friends, who included Swinburne, the Rossettis, and William Morris, and she and her husband, Hubert Bland, were founder members of the Fabian Society (q.v.). Although for many years she wrote pot-boilers for various journals, her gift as a writer of children's stories did not appear until the publication of 'The Treasure Seekers' in 1899. Of the thirty or so that followed, the best known are: 'The Wouldbegoods' (1901), 'The Phoenix and the Carpet' (1904), 'The Enchanted Castle' (1907), 'The Railway Children' (1908), and 'The Magic City' (1910). The stories, with their direct appeal to the imagination of children, were at once immensely popular and have continued to be read by children of succeeding generations.

Nessus, see *Deianira*.

Nestor, king of Pylos in the Peloponnese, and a grandson of Poseidon, led his subjects to the Trojan War, where he distinguished himself among the Grecian chiefs, in his old age, by his wisdom, justice, and eloquence.

Nestorians, followers of Nestorius, sometime a disciple of St. Chrysostom and patriarch of Constantinople in A.D. 428, who held that Christ had distinct human and divine persons (the doctrine opposite to that of the Monophysites, q.v.). Nestorius was condemned by the Councils of Ephesus in 431 and Chalcedon in 451, his fiercest opponent being Cyril of Alexandria. The missionaries of the sect penetrated to Central Asia. A remnant of Nestorian Christians survives in the mountains of E. Anatolia and Kurdistan (driven into Iraq during the war of 1914–18). See *Prester John*.

Neville, MISS, a character in Goldsmith's 'She Stoops to Conquer' (q.v.).

New Atalantis, see *Manley*.

New Atlantis, The, a treatise of political philosophy in the form of a fable, by Francis Bacon (q.v.). The work, which was left unfinished, was published in 1626.

It is an account of a visit to an imaginary island of Bensalem in the Pacific and of the social conditions prevailing there; and also of 'Solomon's House', a college of natural philosophy 'dedicated to the study of the works and creatures of God'.

New Bath Guide, see *Anstey (C.)*.

New England Nun and Other Stories, A, by Mary E. Wilkins Freeman (q.v.).

New English Dictionary, The, more generally known now as the 'Oxford English Dictionary' (q.v.).

New Grub Street, a novel by Gissing (q.v.), published in 1891.

In this work Gissing depicts the struggle for life, the jealousies and intrigues, of the literary world of his time, and the blighting effect of poverty on artistic endeavour. The main theme is the contrast of the career of Jasper Milvain, the facile, clever, selfish, and unscrupulous writer of reviews (who accepts the materialistic conditions of literary success), with those of more artistic temperaments. Among these are Edwin Reardon, the author of two fine works, who is hampered by poverty and by the lack of sympathy of his worldly-minded wife, and the generous Harold Biffen, a poor scholar, the author of a work of 'absolute realism in the sphere of the ignobly decent'. The literary world is presented in a multitude of characters, of which one of the best is the learned pedant Alfred Yule, rendered rancorous and sardonic by constant disappointment. Jasper is attracted to Yule's daughter and assistant, Marian, who passionately loves him; but he proposes to her only when she inherits a legacy of £5,000. When this legacy proves not to be forthcoming, he shabbily withdraws, and marries Amy Reardon, the young widow of Edwin, whom failure and his wife's desertion have driven to an early grave. The sombre story ends with Jasper's success, the triumph of self-advertisement over artistic conscience.

New Holland, a former name of Australia. The Dutch were among the first discoverers of the continent (1606), and their navigators surveyed some part of its coasts between 1618 and 1627. The West coast was probably known to the Portuguese earlier.

New Inne, The, a comedy by Jonson (q.v.), first acted in 1629, when it was a complete failure, not being heard to the conclusion.

Frances, the young Lady Frampul, invites some lords and gentlemen to make merry at the New Inn at Barnet. One of the guests, Lord Beaufort, falls in love with, and is promptly married to, the son of the innkeeper, who has been dressed up as a lady, while Frances falls in love with Lovel, a melancholy gentleman staying at the inn. Finally the host turns out to be the lost father of Frances, and his son to be not a boy, but Laetitia, sister of Frances.

New Model Army, THE, was organized by the parliament in 1645, after the passing of the 'Self-denying Ordinance', the dispersal of Waller's army, and the indecisive second battle of Newbury. It was composed solely with a view to military efficiency, was regularly paid, and was composed largely of Puritans, the officers being mostly Independents. Sir Thomas Fairfax was its general.

New Monthly Magazine, The, a periodical founded in 1814, and continued, with various changes in its sub-title, until 1871, when it was continued without sub-title till 1881, and then until 1884 as 'The New Monthly'. It had as editors, at various periods, Thomas Campbell, Bulwer Lytton, Theodore Hook, Thomas Hood, and W. H. Ainsworth.

New Order, the term used to denote the political, economic, and social system, involving German domination over Europe and the annexation of vast eastern territories for German settlement, which the Nazis hoped to establish. The project was renounced in November 1944.

New Republic, The, see *Mallock*.

New Statesman, The, a weekly journal of politics, art, letters, and science, originally planned as an organ of Fabianism (q.v.), socialist in standing but independent of party. It was first published in 1913 with Clifford Sharp as editor, J. C. Squire as literary editor, and the Webbs and G. B. Shaw as regular contributors. From that time and under the editorships of Kingsley Martin (1931–60), John Freeman (1961–5), and Paul Johnson (1965–) it has maintained its policy 'of dissent, of scepticism, of inquiry, of nonconformity'. Among other writers connected with the journal have been J. M. Keynes, G. D. H. Cole, Raymond Mortimer, and J. B. Priestley.

New Survey of London Life and Labour, see *Booth (C.)*.

New Timon, The, a satirical poem by Bulwer Lytton (q.v.), published in 1846, in which he sketches various celebrities of the day.

New Way to pay Old Debts, A, a comedy by Massinger (q.v.), published in 1633, perhaps the best known of his works.

The play deals with the discomfiture of Sir Giles Overreach, a character modelled on the notorious extortioner, Sir Giles Mompesson (1584–1651?), who was fined and imprisoned for his proceedings. The cruel and rapacious Overreach, having got possession of the property of his prodigal nephew Frank Wellborn, who is reduced to utter poverty, treats him with contumely. Lady Allworth, a rich widow, to whose husband

Wellborn had rendered important services, consents to help him by giving ground for the belief that she is about to marry him. Overreach, deceived, changes his attitude, and gives Wellborn assistance. Tom Allworth, Lady Allworth's stepson, and page to Lord Lovell, is in love with Overreach's daughter Margaret, who returns his love. Overreach is consumed with a desire that his daughter shall marry Lord Lovell and become 'right honourable'. Lord Lovell consents to help Allworth to win Margaret, and a trick is played on Overreach by which he facilitates the marriage, thinking that Lord Lovell is to be the bridegroom. Overreach becomes crazy on discovering the deceit and on finding that, by the device of one of his satellites, his claim to Wellborn's property cannot be maintained; he is sent to Bedlam. Wellborn receives a company in Lord Lovell's regiment, and Lord Lovell marries Lady Allworth.

New Writing, a book-periodical edited by John Lehmann (q.v.), first published in 1936 and afterwards at approximately half-yearly intervals until 1940. It published imaginative writing, mainly by young authors, and particularly those whose work was too unorthodox for the established magazines. New contributors were recruited from many parts of Europe, India, New Zealand, South Africa, China, and Russia. In 1940 it came out as 'Folios of New Writing', which became 'New Writing and Daylight' in 1942 and lasted until 1946. Meanwhile 'Penguin New Writing' appeared in 1940, first as a monthly paperback and then in 1942 as a quarterly. It reprinted some work from 'New Writing', but relied more and more on new material. A series of articles based on personal experience of the upheavals of war, 'The Way We Live Now', was especially notable.

New Yorker, The, an American weekly established in 1925 by Harold Ross. It is sophisticated, satirical, and cultivated, and is distinguished for its short stories, articles, and cartoons.

Newbery, JOHN (1713–67), a publisher and bookseller, who established himself in 1744 in St. Paul's Churchyard, London, and originated the publication of children's books. Goldsmith (q.v.) was among those who worked for him, probably writing 'Goody Two Shoes'. Newbery figures in 'The Vicar of Wakefield' (q.v.).

NEWBOLT, SIR HENRY (JOHN) (1862–1938), barrister, author, and poet. Among his poems are 'Admirals All and Other Verses' (1897), which includes 'Drake's Drum'; 'Songs of the Sea' (1904); Songs of the Fleet' (1910). His 'Naval History of the War, 1914–18' appeared in 1920.

NEWCASTLE, MARGARET, DUCHESS OF (1624?–74), daughter of Sir Thomas Lucas, was the second wife of William Cavendish, duke of Newcastle. She wrote a multitude of verses, essays, and plays (1653–68), and a biography of her husband. She is principally remembered for Pepys's condemnation of her as 'a mad, conceited, ridiculous woman', and on the other hand for Charles Lamb's encomium of her, 'that princely woman, the thrice noble Margaret of Newcastle'.

Newcomen, THOMAS (1663–1729), an ironmonger or blacksmith of Dartmouth, inventor of the atmospheric steam-engine.

Newcomes, The, a novel by Thackeray (q.v.), published serially in 1853–5.

The story, which purports to be told by Pendennis (q.v.), centres round the career of young Clive Newcome, a youth of generous instincts and human failings, the son of Colonel Thomas Newcome, an officer of the Indian army, in whom Thackeray has drawn an admirable portrait of a simple-minded gentleman, guided through life solely by the sentiments of duty and honour. Clive Newcome falls in love with his cousin, Ethel Newcome, daughter of the wealthy banker Sir Brian Newcome. But she is destined for a more exalted match by her grandmother, the countess of Kew, a worldly, cynical old woman, and by her other relatives. The most vigorous opponent of Clive's suit is Ethel's brother, Barnes Newcome, a mean, venomous little snob, in whom Thackeray has almost overdrawn the character of a villain. Ethel, a fine and honourable girl, though capricious and at times influenced by ambition and her worldly surroundings, yields to these so far as to engage herself first to her cousin, Lord Kew, and then to a worthless puppy, Lord Farintosh; but both these matches she breaks off. Meanwhile Clive, despairing of Ethel, allows himself to be married to a pretty nonentity, Rosey Mackenzie, the daughter of a scheming widow. The marriage turns out miserably. Moreover, Colonel Newcome loses his fortune; and his household, including Clive and his wife and Mrs. Mackenzie, the 'campaigner', are reduced to dire poverty. This brings out the worst qualities of Mrs. Mackenzie. A virago and a harpy, she subjects the Colonel to a long martyrdom by her taunts and reproaches, until he takes refuge in the Greyfriars [Charterhouse] almshouses. The pathos of the story reaches its climax with the scene of the Colonel's death-bed, where 'he, whose heart was as that of a little child, had answered to his name, and stood in the presence of The Master'. Rosey having meanwhile died, we are left to infer that Clive and Ethel are finally united.

Newdigate, SIR ROGER (1719–1806), educated at Westminster School and University College, Oxford, M.P. successively for Middlesex and Oxford University, was founder of the NEWDIGATE PRIZE at Oxford for English verse (1805).

Newgate, the principal west gate of the ancient city of London, so called probably because it was the reconstruction of an earlier gate dating from Roman times, at the point where Watling Street (q.v.) reached London (roughly along the line of Oxford Street and Holborn). Its gate-house was a prison from the 12th cent. This prison was enlarged, reconstructed, and improved out of funds left by Sir Richard Whittington. Attention was drawn to its insanitary condition by John Howard, the prison reformer (1726–90) (two Lord Mayors died of jail fever caught at the sessions), and in 1780 it was burnt down by the Gordon rioters. It was then rebuilt, and finally demolished in 1902, when the Central Criminal Court was built on its site.

Newgate Calendar, The, or Malefactors' *Bloody Register*, was published (the original series) about 1774, and dealt with notorious crimes from 1700 to that date. Later series ('The Newgate Calendar, comprising interesting memoirs of the most notorious characters' and 'The New Newgate Calendar') were issued about 1826 by Andrew Knapp and William Baldwin.

Borrow's 'Lavengro' (q.v.) compiled the 'Chronicles of Newgate' (ch. xxxvi).

Newland, ABRAHAM (1730–1807), chief cashier of the Bank of England from 1782. Bank-notes were long known as 'Abraham Newlands' from bearing his signature. See *Abraham-man*.

NEWMAN, JOHN HENRY (1801–90), educated privately at Ealing and at Trinity College, Oxford, became a fellow of Oriel, where he came in contact with his brother-fellows Keble and Pusey, and later with R. H. Froude (qq.v.). In 1828 he was presented to the vicarage of St. Mary's, Oxford. In 1832 he went to the south of Europe with R. H. Froude, and with him wrote in Rome much of the 'Lyra Apostolica' (1836), sacred poems contributed in the first instance to 'The British Magazine'. In 1833 he composed the hymn 'Lead, kindly Light', during a passage from Palermo to Marseilles. In the same year he resolved with William Palmer, R. H. Froude, and A. P. Perceval to fight for the doctrine of apostolical succession and the integrity of the Prayer-book, and began 'Tracts for the Times' (see *Oxford Movement*), in which he found a supporter in Dr. Pusey (q.v.). In 1837–8 he published a number of treatises in defence of the Anglo-Catholic view, including the 'Lectures on the Prophetical Office of the Church', and in 1841 his famous Tract XC, on the compatibility of the Articles with Catholic theology; this tract brought the Tractarians under the official ban. He retired to Littlemore in 1842, wrote his 'Essay on Miracles' in that year, resigned the living of St. Mary's in 1843, and joined the Church of Rome in 1845. He went to Rome in 1846, where he was ordained priest and created D.D., and became an Oratorian. He returned to England in 1847 and established the Oratory at Birmingham. His 'Essay on the Development of Christian Doctrine' was written at the time of his transition and published in 1845. In 1851 appeared his 'Lectures on the

Present Position of the Roman Catholics', a fiercely contemptuous reply to the No-Popery agitation of the moment. In 1854 he was appointed rector of the new Catholic University of Dublin, and in 1852, previous to his formal appointment, delivered his lectures on 'The Scope and Nature of University Education'. 'Lectures on Universities' appeared in 1859. The third edition (1873) of 'The Idea of a University Defined' contains both series of lectures. In these Newman, opposing the popular doctrines of the day, maintained that the duty of a university is instruction rather than research, and to train the mind rather than to diffuse useful knowledge; and defended theological teaching and tutorial supervision as parts of the university system. Newman found the Irish clergy and the 'New Catholic University' quite intractable and soon gave up his appointment.

In 1864 appeared his 'Apologia pro Vita sua', in answer to Charles Kingsley, who in 'Macmillan's Magazine', misrepresenting Newman, had remarked that Newman did not consider truth as a necessary virtue. The 'Apologia' came out serially, and when it was published as a book much of the controversial matter was omitted. It is an exposition, written with the utmost simplicity and sincerity, and in a style of limpid clearness, of his spiritual history, and has obtained recognition as a literary masterpiece. In 1866 appeared his poem, 'The Dream of Gerontius', a dramatic monologue of a just soul leaving the body at death, which made a wide appeal to religious minds. In 1868 was published his 'Verses on Various Occasions', containing many poems of tender beauty. In 1870 Newman published 'The Grammar of Assent' (q.v.), and at various times volumes of sermons preached at St. Mary's, Oxford, and elsewhere. Mention should also be made of his religious novels, 'Loss and Gain' (1848), containing a celebrated account of an Oxford tutor's breakfast party, and 'Callista' (1856). In 1877 he was made an honorary fellow of Trinity College, Oxford, and in 1879 was created Cardinal of St. George in Velabro.

Newnes, GEORGE (1851–1910), publisher and magazine proprietor. He founded in particular 'The Strand Magazine' (in which Conan Doyle's 'Adventures of Sherlock Holmes' first appeared) and 'Tit-Bits'.

Newnham College, a college for women at Cambridge, opened in 1876, developed from an earlier house of residence for women students, of which Sidgwick (q.v.) was one of the chief promoters, and Anne Jemima Clough (1820–92) the first principal.

News, The, see *L'Estrange*.

Newsbooks, or DIURNALLS, the successors of the 'Corantos' (q.v.) in the evolution of the newspaper. Newsbooks, consisting of one printed sheet (8 pages) or later of two printed sheets (16 pages), and containing domestic intelligence and the principal features of the modern newspaper, were issued, by various journalists and under various titles, during the period 1641–65. They then gave place to the 'Oxford' (later 'London') 'Gazette' (see *Gazette*).

Newsletters, a term specially applied to the manuscript records of parliamentary and court news, sent twice a week to subscribers from the London office of Muddiman (q.v.) in the second half of the 17th cent. A survival of these may be seen in the 'London Letter' which still appears in many provincial journals, as well as in contemporary 'newsletters'.

Newsome, MRS. and CHAD, leading characters in H. James's 'The Ambassadors' (q.v.).

NEWTON, SIR ISAAC (1642–1727), the philosopher, was born at Woolsthorpe near Grantham, and educated at Grantham Grammar School and Trinity College, Cambridge. He made his first communication to the Royal Society on his theory of light and colours in 1672. His researches on this subject were summed up in his 'Optics', published in 1704, to which was appended his 'Method of Fluxions', his great mathematical discovery, and the source of a bitter quarrel with Leibniz as to the priority of the invention. The first book of his 'Philosophiae Naturalis Principia Mathematica', embodying his laws of motion and the idea of universal gravitation, was exhibited at the Royal Society in 1686, and the whole published in 1687. Newton was elected president of the Royal Society in 1703, and was annually re-elected for 25 years. He was knighted in 1705, became master of the Mint in 1699, and presented reports on the coinage in 1717 and 1718. He was buried in Westminster Abbey. But it is his statue in the ante-chapel of Trinity College, Cambridge, that is his best-known memorial, perhaps because of Wordsworth's glorious lines on it (in 'The Prelude'):

The marble index of a mind for ever
Voyaging through strange seas of Thought
    alone.

Newton's works (incomplete) were edited by Samuel Horsley in 1779–85.

NEWTON, JOHN (1725–1807), clergyman and friend of Cowper (q.v.), with whom he published the 'Olney Hymns' in 1779. 'An Authentic Narrative', first published anonymously in 1764, is an account of his early adventurous life at sea (including slave-trading) and his religious conversion.

Niamh, in the second or southern cycle of Irish mythology, the daughter of Manannán, the sea-god. She fell in love with Ossian, the son of Finn (q.v.), carried him off over the sea, and kept him with her for three hundred years. She then let him return to his own country, mounted on a magic steed, but on condition that he should not set foot on earth. Ossian disregarded the caution, immediately lost his youth, and became a blind, decrepit old man.

Nibelung (NIBLUNG, NIEBELUNG), in the Norse sagas and German 'Nibelungenlied' (q.v.), a mythical king of a race of dwarfs, the Nibelungs, who dwelt in Norway. The Nibelung kings and people also figure in W. Morris's 'Sigurd the Volsung' (q.v.).

Nibelungen, *Ring des,* see *Ring des Nibelungen.*

Nibelungenlied, a German poem of the 13th cent. embodying a story found in primitive shape in both forms of the Edda (q.v.). In these the story is substantially as told by William Morris in his 'Sigurd the Volsung' (q.v.), Sigurd being the Siegfried of the German poem.

In the 'Nibelungenlied' the story is somewhat different. Siegfried, son of Siegmund and Sieglind, king and queen of the Netherlands, having got possession of the Nibelung hoard guarded by Alberich, rides to woo Kriemhild, a Burgundian princess, sister of Gunther, Gernot, and Giselher. Hagen, their grim retainer, warns them against Siegfried, but the match is arranged, and the hoard is given to Kriemhild as marriage portion. Siegfried undertakes to help Gunther to win Brunhild, queen of Issland, by defeating her in trials of skill and strength, which he succeeds in doing. The double marriage takes place, but Brunhild remains suspicious and ill-humoured, and Siegfried, called in by Gunther to subdue her, does so in Gunther's semblance and takes away her ring and girdle, which he gives to Kriemhild. The two queens quarrel, and Kriemhild reveals to Brunhild the trick that has been played on her. Hagen, who thinks his master's honour injured by Siegfried, treacherously kills the latter at a hunt.

Kriemhild later marries Etzel (Attila), king of the Huns, and in order to avenge her husband and secure the hoard, which her brothers have seized and sunk in the Rhine, persuades them to visit Etzel's court. There they are set upon and overcome, but refuse to betray the hiding-place of the hoard, and are slain. Hagen, the last survivor of the party who knows the secret, is killed by Kriemhild with Siegfried's sword; and Kriemhild herself is slain by Hildebrand, a knight of Dietrich of Bern.

Nice, SIR COURTLY, see *Sir Courtly Nice.*

Nice Valour, *The,* or *The Passionate Madman,* see *Fletcher (J.).*

Nicholas, ST., said to have been bishop of Myra in Asia Minor about A.D. 300, is the patron saint of Russia, and of children, scholars, sailors, virgins, and thieves, in consequence of various legends relating to benefits conferred by him on these. His festival is 6 Dec. See also *Santa Claus* and *Nicholas's Clerk.*

Nicholas's Clerk, ST., a highwayman, thief. So used in Shakespeare's '1 Henry IV' (q.v.), II. i, and in Scott's 'Ivanhoe' (q.v.). It was also used to signify a poor scholar, St. Nicholas being the patron saint of scholars.

Nicholas Nickleby, a novel by Dickens (q.v.), published in 1838-9.

Nicholas, a generous, high-spirited lad of nineteen, his mother, and his gentle sister Kate are left penniless on the death of his father. They appeal for assistance to his uncle, Ralph Nickleby, a griping usurer, of whom Nicholas at once makes an enemy by his independent bearing. He is sent as usher to Dotheboys Hall, where Wackford Squeers starves and maltreats forty urchins under pretence of education. His special cruelty is expended on Smike, a half-witted lad left on his hands and employed as a drudge. Nicholas, infuriated by what he witnesses, thrashes Squeers and escapes with Smike, who becomes his devoted friend. For a time he supports himself and Smike as an actor in the provincial company of Vincent Crummles; he then enters the service of the brothers Cheeryble, whose benevolence and good humour spread happiness around them. Meanwhile Kate, apprenticed to Madame Mantalini, dressmaker, is by her uncle's designs exposed to the gross insults of Sir Mulberry Hawk, one of his associates. From this persecution she is released by Nicholas, who breaks Sir Mulberry's head and makes a home for his mother and sister. Nicholas himself falls in love with Madeline Bray, the support of a selfish father and the object of a conspiracy of Ralph Nickleby and another revolting old usurer, Gride, to marry her to the latter. Ralph, whose hatred for Nicholas has been intensified by the failure of his plans, knowing Nicholas's affection for Smike, conspires to remove the latter from him; but Smike succumbs to failing health and terror of his enemies. All Ralph's plots are baffled by the help of Newman Noggs, his eccentric clerk. Confronted with ruin and exposure, and finally shattered by the discovery that Smike was his own son, Ralph hangs himself. Nicholas, befriended by the Cheerybles, marries Madeline, and Kate marries the Cheerybles' nephew, Frank. Squeers is transported, and Gride is murdered.

NICHOLS, JOHN (1745-1826), printer and author, apprenticed to William Bowyer the younger (1699-1777, 'the learned printer'), joined David Henry in the management of the 'Gentleman's Magazine' (q.v) in 1778, and was sole manager from 1792 to 1826. He published his 'Royal Wills' in 1780, a 'Collection of Miscellaneous Poems' (1780-2), his 'Bibliotheca Topographica' (1780-90), and 'Biographical Anecdotes of Hogarth' (1781). His most important work, 'The History and Antiquities of Leicester', appeared between 1795 and 1815, and in 1801 his edition of Swift's works (19 vols.). In 1812-15 appeared the 'Literary Anecdotes of the Eighteenth Century', an invaluable bibliographical and biographical storehouse of information in nine

volumes; six volumes of a supplementary work, 'Illustrations of the Literary History of the Eighteenth Century', appeared between 1817 and 1831, two being published posthumously, and John Bowyer Nichols (his son, 1779-1863) added two more volumes in 1848 and 1858. John Nichols's collection of newspapers is now in the Bodleian Library.

Nicias, an Athenian general during the Peloponnesian War, a man of upright character, and an advocate of peace. He was in command (with Alcibiades and Lamachus, and later with Demosthenes) of the disastrous Syracusan expedition, and on the surrender of the Athenian force was put to death by the Syracusans (413 B.C.).

Nick, OLD, see Old Nick.

Nicolette, see Aucassin and Nicolette.

Nidhöggr, in Scandinavian mythology, a monstrous serpent which gnaws at the root of Yggdrasil (q.v.).

Niebelung, see Nibelung.

NIEBUHR, BARTHOLD GEORG (1776-1831), the son of a distinguished German traveller, was educated at Kiel, and studied physical science at Edinburgh in 1798. His great 'History of Rome', which originally took the form of lectures delivered at Berlin in 1810-12, appeared in 1827-8. Niebuhr was the first historian to deal with the subject in a scientific spirit, discussing critically the early Roman legends and paying more attention to the development of institutions and to social characteristics than to individuals and incidents. The 'History' was translated into English by J. C. Hare and Bishop Thirlwall in 1828-42.

NIETZSCHE, FRIEDRICH WILHELM (1844-1900), German philosopher and poet, educated at the ancient grammar school of Schulpforta and appointed very young to a professorship of classical philology at Basel. He resigned because of ill health and in 1889 suffered a mental breakdown from which he never properly recovered. His first work 'Die Geburt der Tragödie' (1872) was of revolutionary importance, challenging the accepted tradition of classical scholarship; it argued against the 'Apolline' views associated with Winckelmann (q.v.) in favour of a 'Dionysiac' interpretation which allowed for pessimism and passion as central features. His other main works include the 'Unzeitgemässe Betrachtungen' (1873-6), in which he heavily criticized the complacency of German culture in the age of Bismarck, 'Morgenröte' (1881) and 'Die fröhliche Wissenschaft' (1882). For his general philosophic position, his most important works were 'Also sprach Zarathustra' (1883-92), 'Jenseits von Gut und Böse' (1886) and 'Der Wille zur Macht' (published posthumously from fragments). His basic ideas are the affirmation of the Superman, the rejection of Christian morality, the doctrine of power, and the 'revision of all values'. Nietzsche began as a disciple of Schopenhauer (q.v.), but later rejected his pessimism and quietism. For some time he was an admirer of Wagner (q.v.), but was eventually unable to accept the Schopenhauerian elements in Wagner's outlook, and the breach with Wagner was one of the main episodes in Nietzsche's career. His influence on modern German literature has been enormous.

Niflheim, in Scandinavian mythology, an underworld of cold and darkness, the abode of the dead, who were distributed among its nine regions. It was ruled over by Hel (see *Hell*). It was separated by Ginnungagap (q.v.) from Muspellheim (q.v.), and Yggdrasil (q.v.) had its roots there.

Night Thoughts on Life, Death, and Immortality, The Complaint or, a didactic poem of some 10,000 lines of blank verse, in nine books, by E. Young (q.v.), published in 1742–5.

The first book is occupied with the poet's reflections on life's vicissitudes, death, and immortality. The next seven form a soliloquy, partly argumentative, partly reflective, addressed to a certain worldly infidel, named Lorenzo, who is exhorted to turn to faith and virtue. The ninth book, entitled 'The Consolation', contains a vision of the last day and of eternity, a survey of the wonders of the firmament at night, a final exhortation to Lorenzo, and an invocation to the Deity.

The poem for a time enjoyed great popularity. It contains a few autobiographical allusions. Narcissa and Philander have not been identified, but may have been his stepdaughter and her husband, Mr. Temple. Mrs. Temple died of consumption at Lyons in 1736; but she was not buried surreptitiously, as told in the poem.

Nightingale, FLORENCE (1820–1910), the founder of the modern nursing profession, famous for her services during the Crimean War and the reforms that she brought about in Army hospitals.

Nightingale, Ode to a, see *Keats.*

Nightingale and the Lute-player, The, see *Lover's Melancholy* and *Crashaw.*

Nightmare Abbey, a novel by Peacock (q.v.), published in 1818.

The book is an entertaining satire on Byronism, Coleridgian transcendentalism, and pessimism in general. There is, as usual in Peacock's novels, little plot, but the houseparty of amusing characters brings together Mr. Glowry, his son Scythrop, and Mr. Toobad, pessimists of various shades; Mr. Flosky, a caricature of Coleridge, and Mr. Cypress, of Byron; Mr. Larynx, the versatile and accommodating clergyman; and Mr. Hilary, 'a very cheerful and elastic gentleman'. Scythrop, in his inability to fix his affections on one or other of two charmers, resembles Shelley. It is characteristic of Shelley's

sweetness of temper that he did not in the least resent his friend's caricature of him.

Nihilism (Latin *nihil*, nothing), originally a movement in Russia repudiating the customary social institutions, such as marriage and parental authority. The term was introduced by the novelist Turgenev (q.v.). It was extended to a secret revolutionary movement, social and political, which developed in the middle of the 19th cent.

Nile, BATTLE OF THE, fought on 1 Aug. 1798, in which Nelson destroyed in Abukir Bay the French fleet that had conveyed Buonaparte to Egypt, and by cutting off the latter's army from France, defeated his project of creating a French empire in the East.

Nimrod, 'the mighty hunter before the Lord' (Gen. x. 9), of whom Milton says (basing himself on the Targum) 'and men not beasts shall be his game' ('Paradise Lost', xii. 30). He is represented in Genesis as the ruler of Shinar (Sumeria) and builder of Nineveh, but the monuments of Assyria and Babylonia are silent about him.

Nimrod, see *Apperley.*

Nimue, NIMIANE, or VIVIEN, see *Lady of the Lake,* and *Merlin and Vivien.*

Nine Worthies, The, see *Worthies of the World.*

Nineteen Eighty-four, a novel by George Orwell (q.v.), published in 1949. It is a nightmare story of totalitarianism of the future and one man's hopeless struggle against it and final defeat by acceptance. Winston Smith, the hero, has no heroic qualities, only a wistful longing for truth and decency. But in a social system where there is no privacy and to have unorthodox ideas incurs the death penalty he knows that there is no hope for him. His brief love affair ends in arrest by the Thought Police, and when, after months of torture and brain-washing, he is released, he makes his final submission of his own accord. The book is a warning of the possibilities of the police state brought to perfection, where power is the only thing that counts, where the past is constantly being modified to fit the present, and where the official language, 'Newspeak', progressively narrows the range of ideas and independent thought.

Nineteenth Century, The, a monthly review founded in 1877 by Sir J. T. Knowles (q.v.), who was its first editor. It was more impartial in its attitude than the 'Fortnightly' (q.v.), bringing together in its pages the most eminent advocates of conflicting views. When the said century ended, the Review added to its old title 'And After'.

Ninian, ST. (*d.* 432?), a native of Britain, who in youth made a pilgrimage to Rome and was educated there. He was sent on a mission to convert the pagans in the northern parts of Britain. Ninian was consecrated bishop and his see was established in Galloway at Whithorn, where he built a stone church, known as *Candida Casa*, dedicated to St. Martin of Tours. He evangelized the Southern Picts. St. Ninian is commemorated on 16 Sept. He is also called St. Ringan (see e.g. Scott's 'The Pirate'), and is frequently invoked as St. Treignan in Rabelais.

Ninon de Lenclos, see *Lenclos.*

Ninus, see *Semiramis.*

Niŏbē, a daughter of Tantalus and wife of Amphion (qq.v.). She was the mother of six sons and six daughters, and this so increased her pride that she boasted herself superior to Latona, the mother of Apollo and Artemis. For this arrogance the sons of Niobe were immediately slain by the darts of Apollo, and the daughters (except one, Chloris) by Artemis; and Niobe herself was changed into stone, and still wept for her children in streams that trickled down the rock; so that the group was a favourite one for a fountain. Hence also 'Niobe all tears' (Shakespeare, 'Hamlet', I. ii. 149).

Niörd, or NJÖRDHR, in Scandinavian mythology, one of the Vanir (q.v.), a god of the waters, the father of Frey and Freya.

Niphates, a mountain-chain in Armenia. Milton makes Satan light on it when he first comes to the earth ('Paradise Lost', iii. 742).

Nipper, SUSAN, a character in Dickens's 'Dombey and Son' (q.v.).

Nirvana, in Buddhist theology, the extinction of individual existence and the absorption of the soul in the supreme spirit, or the extinction of all desires and passions and the attainment of perfect beatitude. [OED.]

Nisroch, an Assyrian deity, in whose temple at Nineveh Sennacherib was slain (2 Kings xix. 37). Milton calls him 'of Principalities the prime' in the council of Satan ('Paradise Lost', vi. 446).

Nīsus, a Trojan, who accompanied Aeneas to Italy, and signalized himself by his valour against the Rutulians. He was united in closest friendship to Euryǎlus, another Trojan, and together at night they penetrated the enemy camp. After slaying many of the Rutulians, they were returning, when Euryalus fell into the enemies' hands. Nisus in endeavouring to rescue his friend perished with him, and their great friendship has become proverbial.

Nitouche, SAINTE, a French term for a person who affects an air of excessive innocence, a facetious adaptation of 'n'y touche'.

Nixie, a female water-elf (from German and Scandinavian folk-lore).

Nizam-ul-Mulk, the vizier of Alp Arslan the son, and of Malik Shah the grandson, of Toghrul Beg (the founder of the Seljuk dynasty). FitzGerald in his introduction to the 'Rubáiyát' of Omar Khayyám (q.v.) quotes Nizam-ul-Mulk's story (difficult to reconcile

with the dates) of his studying at Naishapur under a doctor of law with Omar Khayyám and Hasan-ben-Sabbah (the 'Old Man of the Mountain'—see under *Assassins*), and of the pledge of the three friends to help each other in after-life. Nizam-ul-Mulk, when he became vizier, granted Omar a pension. He was himself ultimately murdered by the order of Hasan-ben-Sabbah.

Njala Saga, see *Saga.*

Njördhr, see *Niördr.*

No Cross, No Crown, a dissertation by Penn (q.v., 1669).

Nobel Prizes, THE, were established under the will of Alfred Bernhard Nobel (1833–96), a Swedish chemist distinguished in the development of explosives, by which the interest on the greater part of his large fortune is distributed in annual prizes for the most important discoveries in physics, chemistry, and physiology or medicine respectively, to the author of the most important literary work of an idealist tendency, and to the person who shall have most promoted the fraternity of nations.

Noble, in 'Reynard the Fox' (q.v.), the name of the lion.

Noble, a former English gold coin, first minted by Edward III, issued as the equivalent of 6s. 8d. silver. It was a handsome coin, showing on the obverse the king in armour in a ship, and bearing the inscription: IHC: TRANSIENS : PER : MEDIUM : ILLORUM : IBAT : from Luke iv. 30, perhaps used as a charm against theft.

The ANGEL, called more fully at first the ANGEL-NOBLE, being originally a new issue of the Noble, had as its device the archangel Michael standing upon, and piercing, the dragon. It was first coined by Edward IV in 1465, when its value was 6s. 8d. Under Edward VI it was 10s. It was last coined by Charles I. This was the coin always presented to a patient 'touched' for the king's evil. When it ceased to be coined, small medals having the same device were substituted for it.

The ROSE-NOBLE or RYAL was a gold coin first issued by Edward IV, as the equivalent of 10s. silver. The general design of the king in his ship was retained, but a very large Yorkist rose covered part of the hull of the ship.

Noble Numbers, the title of the collection of religious poems written by Herrick (q.v.).

Nobs, Dr. Dove's horse in Southey's 'The Doctor' (q.v.).

Noctes Ambrosianae, a series of papers that appeared in 'Blackwood's Magazine' (q.v.) from 1822 to 1835. They were by several hands, Prof. John Wilson's, Lockhart's, Hogg's, and Maginn's (qq.v.); but of the 71, 41 were by the first of these, Wilson ('Christopher North'), and have been reprinted in his works. The 'Noctes' take the form of imaginary conversations, of a boisterous, convivial kind, at Ambrose's (q.v.), between the Ettrick Shepherd, Christopher North, and a few others, on a great variety of topics, from literary and political criticism to the rearing of poultry. The impersonation of the Ettrick Shepherd (Hogg) is particularly brilliant, and the novelty, wit, and humour of the conversations added greatly to the popularity of the magazine.

NOEL, RODEN BERKELEY WRIOTHESLEY (1834–94), educated at Trinity College, Cambridge, was author of several volumes of verse, including 'Livingstone in Africa' (1874), 'A Little Child's Monument' (1881), and 'Songs of the Heights and Deeps' (1885). A selection of his poems was edited by P. Addleshaw in 1897, and his collected works were issued in 1902.

Noetics, THE, a group of fellows of Oriel College, Oxford, who in the first quarter of the 19th cent. were noted for their free criticism of current theology. Chief among them was Whately (q.v.). The name is derived from Gr. νόησις, intelligence.

Noggs, NEWMAN, in Dickens's 'Nicholas Nickleby' (q.v.), Ralph Nickleby's clerk, who has seen better days.

Noh or Nō Plays, THE, a form of traditional, ceremonial, or ritualistic drama peculiar to Japan, symbolical and spiritual in character. It was evolved from religious rites of Shinto worship, was perfected in the 15th cent. and flourished during the Tokugawa period (1652–1868). It has since been revived. The plays are short (one or two acts), in prose and verse, and a chorus contributes poetical comments. They were formerly acted as a rule only at the Shogun's court, five or six in succession, presenting a complete life drama, beginning with a play of the divine age, then a battle piece, a 'play of women', a psychological piece (dealing with the sins and struggles of mortals), a morality, and finally a congratulatory piece, praising the lords and the reign. The text was helped out by symbolic gestures and chanting. About two hundred Noh Plays are extant. Of these the most interesting are the psychological pieces, in which some type of human character or some intense emotion is taken as the subject. In various respects the Noh Plays are comparable with the early Greek drama (see 'Noh, or Accomplishment', by Ernest Fenollosa and Ezra Pound).

Noli me tangĕre, Latin, 'Touch me not', a phrase occurring in the Vulgate, John xx. 17, applied to paintings representing the appearance of Christ to the Magdalen at the sepulchre; also used generally as a warning against interference.

Noll or OLD NOLL, a nickname of Oliver Cromwell.

Nomentānus, L. CASSIUS, frequently mentioned by Horace in his Satires, and proverbial for riotous living.

Nominalism, the view of those schoolmen and later philosophers who regard universals or abstract conceptions as mere names without corresponding reality. See *Ockham*, the father of this school.

Nonce-word, a term employed in the OED. to describe a word which is apparently used only for the nonce, coined for the occasion.

Nones, in the ancient Roman calendar, the 7th of March, May, July, and October, and the 5th of all the other months.

Non-Intrusionists, in the Church of Scotland, those who, in the 19th cent., resisted the intrusion by patrons of unacceptable ministers upon resisting congregations (see *Miller, H.*).

Nonjurors, the beneficed clergy who refused in 1689 to take the oath of allegiance to William and Mary.

Nore, THE, a sandbank in the mouth of the Thames off Sheerness. A mutiny broke out in 1797 in the fleet stationed there, occasioned by the inadequate pay and bad food of the sailors. Its leader, Parker, was hanged.

Norimberga, in imprints, Nuremberg.

Norman, the style of Romanesque (q.v.) architecture used in England from the mid-10th to the end of the 12th cent. The reorganization of dioceses and development of monasticism after the Conquest provided the opportunity for the building of large churches for which the Norman builders supplied the technical ability and the native love of ornament engendered the rich decoration.

Norna of the Fitful-head, Ulla Troil, a character in Scott's 'The Pirate' (q.v.).

Norns, in Scandinavian mythology, the three fates, Urd, Verdandi, and Skuld, who live at the summit of the rainbow (Bifröst), under the branches of Yggdrasil (q.v.), by the fountain Urda.

Norris, MRS., a character in Jane Austen's 'Mansfield Park' (q.v.).

NORRIS, FRANK (1870–1902), American novelist, born in Chicago. He was deeply influenced by Zola and naturalism, as shown in his finest works, 'McTeague' (1899), a story of lower class life in San Francisco, and especially in the masterly first two volumes of his unfinished trilogy, an 'Epic of the Wheat': 'The Octopus' (1901) and 'The Pit' (1903).

NORRIS, JOHN (1657–1711), philosopher and poet, educated at Winchester College and Exeter College, Oxford, and a fellow of All Souls, became rector of Bemerton. The work for which he is best known is 'An Essay towards the Theory of an Ideal and Intelligible World' (1701–4), in which he shows himself a supporter of Malebranche's spiritual development of Cartesianism (q.v.). His poems include 'The Passion of the Virgin Mother' which appears in Palgrave's 'Treasury of Sacred Song'.

Norroy and Ulster, the title of the third king-of-arms, whose jurisdiction lies north of the Trent. See *Clarenceux.*

North, CHRISTOPHER, a pseudonym used by J. Wilson (1785–1854, q.v.).

NORTH, ROGER (1653–1734), educated at Jesus College, Cambridge, and a lawyer, was the author of interesting biographies, published in 1742–4, of his brothers, Francis North, Lord Guilford, Keeper of the Great Seal; Dudley North, the great Turkey merchant; and John North, master of Trinity College, Cambridge. His own 'Autobiography' was published in 1887. His 'Discourse of Fish and Fish Ponds' appeared in 1683, and in 1740 his 'Examen' or criticism of Kennett's volume of the 'Compleat History of England' (1706).

NORTH, SIR THOMAS (1535?–1601?), son of Edward North, first baron North, perhaps studied at Peterhouse, Cambridge. He entered Lincoln's Inn, was knighted in 1591, and pensioned by Queen Elizabeth in 1601. He is famous for his translations, which include the 'Diall of Princes' (1557) from Guevara's 'El Relox de Principes', 'The Morall Philosophie of Doni', from the Italian (1570), and Plutarch's 'Lives' from the French of Amyot (1579), to which he made additions from other authors (1595). His Plutarch, written in a noble and vivid English, formed Shakespeare's chief storehouse of classical learning, and exerted a powerful influence on Elizabethan prose.

North American Review, The (1815–1940), a quarterly and later a monthly review of the old solid type and one of the most distinguished of American journals.

North and South, a novel by Mrs. Gaskell (q.v.), published in 'Household Words' in 1854–5. The book, as its title suggests, is a study in the contrast between the inhabitants of the North and of the South of England. It is also a study of the relations of employers and men in industry.

Circumstances bring Margaret Hale from a luxurious life in London and a quiet parsonage in the New Forest, imbued with prejudices against trade of every sort, to a humble home in a murky, cotton-spinning town. Here she is brought into contact with the workers and with the employers, at a time of conflict between them, and particularly with John Thornton, a stubborn, hard-headed leader of the masters. In spite of her unpalatable advocacy of a more sympathetic attitude towards the men, he is fascinated by her beauty and proud bearing. The courage with which she exposes herself to protect him from a dangerous mob of strikers leads him, from a misunderstanding of her motives, to propose to her, and he is deeply hurt by her contemptuous rejection. An incident occurs to increase the estrangement. Thornton sees Margaret under equivocal circumstances

with an unknown man (in fact her brother), and her denial (for the purpose of screening her brother, who is in danger of arrest) intensifies Thornton's suspicions. Margaret now discovers, from her unhappiness at being degraded in Thornton's estimation, that she loves him. It is only after much suffering on both sides, when misfortunes have come on Thornton and he has learnt the need of more humane relations between masters and men, that the misunderstanding is cleared up, and the two are brought together.

North Briton, The, a weekly political periodical founded in 1762 by Wilkes (q.v.), in opposition to 'The Briton', which Smollett was conducting in the interests of Lord Bute. In this venture Wilkes was assisted by Charles Churchill (q.v.), the author of 'The Rosciad'. 'The North Briton' purports ironically to be edited by a Scotsman, who rejoices in Lord Bute's success and the ousting of the English from power. Wilkes's attacks on the government grew bolder, and in No. 45 of 'The North Briton', in an article on the speech from the throne, he exposed himself to prosecution for libel. Though Wilkes was discharged on the ground of privilege, 'The North Briton' was suppressed. It was revived later, but was no longer of importance.

Northanger Abbey, a novel by J. Austen (q.v.), begun in 1798, prepared for the press in 1803, but not published until 1818, when it appeared with 'Persuasion'. The origin of the story is the desire to ridicule tales of romance and terror such as Mrs. Radcliffe's 'Mysteries of Udolpho' and to contrast with these life as it really is.

Catherine Morland, the daughter of a well-to-do clergyman, is taken to Bath for the season by her friends, Mr. and Mrs. Allen. Here she makes the acquaintance of Henry Tilney, the son of the eccentric General Tilney, and his pleasant sister Eleanor. Catherine falls in love with Henry, and has the good fortune to obtain his father's approval, founded upon an exaggerated report of her parents' wealth given him by the crazy young fop, John Thorpe, brother of Catherine's friend, Isabella. Catherine is invited to Northanger Abbey, the medieval seat of the Tilneys. Somewhat unbalanced by assiduous reading of Mrs. Radcliffe's novels, Catherine here conjures up a gruesome mystery in which she persuades herself that General Tilney is criminally involved, and suffers severe humiliation when her suspicions are discovered. Presently General Tilney, having received from John Thorpe a report as misleading as the first, representing Catherine's parents as in an extremely humble situation, packs her off back to her family, and forbids Henry to have any further thought of her. Henry, disobeying his father, follows Catherine to her home, proposes, and is accepted. General Tilney's consent is before long obtained, when he discovers the true situation of Catherine's family and is put in good humour by the marriage of his own daughter to a peer.

The main plot is complicated by a flirtation between Captain Tilney, Henry's elder brother, and the vulgar Isabella Thorpe, who is engaged to marry Catherine's brother; the consequent rupture of the engagement and of the friendship between Catherine and Isabella; and the latter's failure to secure Captain Tilney, who has formed a just estimate of Isabella's character, and pays his attentions in a spirit of mischief.

NORTHCLIFFE, ALFRED CHARLES WILLIAM HARMSWORTH, *Viscount* (1865–1922), born in Dublin, his father belonging to a Hampshire family, laid the foundation of his career as a newspaper proprietor by starting in 1888 'Answers to Correspondents', which, as 'Answers', and with other weekly periodicals owned by him and his brother Harold (first Viscount Rothermere), became extremely popular. In 1894 the brothers acquired the 'Evening News', and in 1896 Alfred started the 'Daily Mail', a half-penny morning paper, the pioneer of a new phase of journalism, which was followed in 1903 by the illustrated 'Daily Mirror'. In 1905 Alfred Harmsworth was raised to the peerage, and in 1908 acquired the control of 'The Times', which he retained for some years. Through the influence which his newspapers exerted, Northcliffe took an important part in the war of 1914–18; and in 1918 was appointed to have charge of propaganda in foreign countries.

Northern Farmer, The ('Old Style' and 'New Style'), two poems in Lincolnshire dialect by A. Tennyson (q.v.).

Northern Lass, The, a comedy by Brome (q.v.), printed in 1632.

This is the earliest of Brome's extant plays, and was very popular. Sir Philip Luckless is about to marry the rich city widow, Fitchow, when he receives a letter from Constance, the 'northern lass', reminding him of her love for him. Mistaking the writer for another Constance of a less reputable character, he disregards the letter and marries the widow, only to discover his mistake too late. The play is occupied with the devices by which the widow is induced to agree to a divorce, while her foolish brother, whom she tries to marry to Constance, is fobbed off with an inferior substitute, and Luckless and the true Constance are united.

Northward Hoe, a comedy by Webster and Dekker (qq.v.), printed in 1607.

Greenshield, having failed to seduce Mayberry's wife, but having obtained by force her ring, to avenge himself produces the ring to her husband as evidence of her infidelity. The husband, assisted by the little old poet Bellamont, a genial caricature of Chapman, becomes convinced of her innocence, and obtains an appropriate revenge on Greenshield and his confederate Featherstone.

The play was a good-humoured retort to the 'Eastward Hoe' (q.v.) of Chapman, Jonson, and Marston. Like 'Westward Hoe' (q.v.) it presents a curious picture of the manners of the day.

North-West Passage, a passage for ships round the north coast of the American continent from the Atlantic to the Pacific, which it was long the object of Arctic explorers to discover. When found, as the result of the explorations of Franklin, Parry, and McClure, it proved of no practical utility.

It was first navigated by Roald Amundsen in 1903–5, and for the first time from west to east by the 'St. Roch', a Canadian Mounted Police patrol ship of eighty tons, commanded by Sergeant Henry Larsen, in 1940–2.

Norton, CHARLES ELIOT (1827–1908), professor of Fine Arts at Harvard University, made only small contributions to literature, but was an intellectual leader of great influence in America. His aim was, in his own words, to arouse in his countrymen 'the sense of connection with the past and gratitude for the effort and labours of other nations and former generations'. Norton was joint-editor of the 'North American Review' (q.v.), 1864–8.

Norton, THE HON. MRS., see *Diana of the Crossways*.

Norumbega, a region on the Atlantic coast of North America, variously shown in 16th-and 17th-cent. maps. It is mentioned, with 'the Samoed shore', by Milton, 'Paradise Lost', x. 696.

Norval, see *Douglas* (the tragedy).

Norway, MAID OF, see *Maid of Norway*.

Norwich School, a group of landscape painters living in Norwich, founded by Crome (q.v.) in 1803.

Nosey, a nickname applied to Oliver Cromwell, the Duke of Wellington, and others.

Nostradamus (1503–66), a Provençal astrologer, whose prophecies, published under the name of 'Centuries', had an extensive vogue. Catherine de Médicis brought him to her court, and he was physician to Charles IX. There is an allusion to him in the opening scene of Goethe's 'Faust'.

Notes and Queries, a periodical founded in 1849 by Thoms (q.v.), designed to furnish a means for the interchange of thought and information among those engaged in literature, art, and science, and a medium of communication with each other. Its motto was (until 1923) Captain Cuttle's 'When found, make a note of'.

Notions of the Americans, by J. F. Cooper (q.v.), published in 1828, was an attempt by the author to explain his countrymen to Europeans.

Notre Dame de Paris, the cathedral church of Paris. Also the title of a romance by Victor

Hugo, in which he depicts the Paris of the time of Louis XI.

Notre Dame des Amours, a name given by Horace Walpole to Ninon de Lenclos (see *Lenclos*).

Notus, the classic name for the south wind, synonymous with Auster.

Noureddin, see *Nur-ed-Din*.

Nourjahad, the subject of a romance by Mrs. F. Sheridan (q.v.), a sleeper who awakes every fifty years.

Nourmahal, (1) the empress in Dryden's 'Aureng-Zebe' (q.v.); (2) the wife of the emperor Selim, in 'The Light of the Haram', one of the tales in Moore's 'Lalla Rookh' (q.v.).

Nouronihar, a character in Beckford's 'Vathek' (q.v.).

Nous avons changé tout cela, see *Sganarelle*.

Nouvelle Héloïse, La, see *Rousseau*.

Nova Scotia, see *Acadia*.

Nova Solyma, *the ideal city; or, Jerusalem Regained*: an anonymous Latin romance written in the time of Charles I. It contains a notable scheme of education, and has been attributed to Milton, but is probably by Samuel Gott.

NOVALIS, pseudonym of Hardenberg (q.v.).

Novels by Eminent Hands, see *Prize Novelists*.

Novum Organum, a philosophical treatise in Latin by Francis Bacon (q.v.), published in 1620.

The ambition of Bacon was to extend to the utmost the dominion of man over nature by means of knowledge. The 'Novum Organum' describes, in a series of aphorisms, the *method* by which knowledge was to be universalized. It may be very briefly summarized as follows.

Experience is the source, and induction is the method, of knowledge. The syllogism, the instrument of the deductive method, based on abstractions which may be hasty or confused, 'is no match for the subtlety of nature'. The rational processes of the mind must be applied to the fruits of experience by the method of induction. But the mind is subject to defects, which Bacon picturesquely classifies under four heads or 'Idols', that is false images of the mind, which vitiate knowledge. (1) *Idols of the Tribe* (*Idola tribus*), which have their origin in human nature itself, e.g. the tendency to observe instances favourable to a preconceived opinion. (2) *Idols of the Cave* (*Idola specus*), originating in the peculiar constitution and circumstances of the individual. (3) *Idols of the Market-place* (*Idola fori*), verbal fictions and confusions which have crept into the understanding as a result of the association of men with one another. (4) *Idols of the Theatre* (*Idola theatri*),

received into the mind from philosophical systems, which like so many stage-plays represent worlds of their own creation after an unreal and scenic fashion. This analysis of the sources of error leads to the 'just and methodical process' of interpreting nature by three inductive methods, which correspond, in some sort, to Mill's methods of *Agreement*, of *Difference*, and of *Concomitant Variations*.

This procedure of investigation is to be applied to the facts of nature. Bacon claimed only to have provided the 'machine'. Like an image at a cross-roads 'he points the way but cannot go it'. But although his method was defective owing to his neglect of hypothesis and rejection of the deductive method, and in practice useless for purposes of scientific discovery, his principles of investigation were correct, and gave a great impulse to experimental science.

An important part in Bacon's system is played by his doctrine of 'Forms'. 'Of a given nature to discover the form . . . is the work and aim of human knowledge.' The 'form' is what differentiates one thing from another, its essential being, the very thing itself, differing from it only as the real differs from the apparent. These 'forms' constitute the 'alphabet of nature', out of the manifold combinations of whose letters all the variety of its phenomena may be explained. Bacon here shows how incompletely he had broken with Scholasticism. 'The position of Bacon', Fowler remarks, is 'midway between Scholasticism, on the one side, and Modern Philosophy and Science, on the other.'

The title 'Novum Organum', meaning 'new instrument', is taken from the Greek word 'organon', which was applied to the logical treatises of Aristotle.

Noyau, a liqueur made of brandy flavoured with the kernel of certain fruits.

> This cherry-bounce, this loved Noyau,
>   My drink for ever be.
>   (Canning, 'The Rovers'.)

NOYES, ALFRED (1880–1958), a poet whose favourite topics were the sea and fairyland. He was professor of modern English literature at Princeton University from 1914 to 1923. His best-known works are 'Drake' (1908), a sea epic, 'Tales of the Mermaid Tavern' (1913), and 'The Torchbearers' (1922–30). His collected poems were published in 1950.

Nubbles, MRS. and KIT, characters in Dickens's 'The Old Curiosity Shop' (q.v.).

Numa, the legendary second king of Rome, successor to Romulus, and revered as the founder of the Roman religious system. See also *Egeria*.

Number of the Beast, see *Beast*.

Nun of Gandersheim, see *Hrotsvitha*.

Nun of Kent, see *Barton*.

Nun's Priest's Tale, see *Canterbury Tales*.

Nupkins, MR., a character in Dickens's 'The Pickwick Papers' (q.v.).

Nur-ed-Din and **Shems-ed-Din,** in the 'Arabian Nights' (q.v.) were two brothers, sons of a vizier of the sultan of Cairo. The son of Nur-ed-Din, Hasan Bedr-ed-Din, was, by the interposition of a jinn, married to Sitt-el-Hosn, the daughter of Shems-ed-Din, in place of an ugly hunchback, her destined bridegroom, and then miraculously borne away to Damascus, where he was ultimately found plying the trade of pastry-cook, and restored to his bride. He was discovered owing to his skill in making a confection of pomegranate grains (or according to another version cream-tarts without pepper in them).

There was a real Nur-ed-Din, sultan of Aleppo and later of Damascus (1154), the most politic and dangerous enemy of the Christian kingdom of Jerusalem before Saladin. He died in 1174.

Nut–Brown Maid, *The,* a 15th-cent. poem in praise of woman's fidelity. The lover, to prove the Maid, tells her that he must to the greenwood go, 'alone, a banyshed man' and live the life of an outlaw. She declares her intention of accompanying him, nor can be dissuaded by the prospect of hardships and humiliations. The lover finally reveals his deceit and that he is an earl's son 'and not a banyshed man'. The poem is included in Percy's 'Reliques'. It is the foundation of Prior's 'Henry and Emma' (see *Prior*).

Nym, in Shakespeare's 'The Merry Wives of Windsor' and 'Henry V' (qq.v.), a follower of Falstaff, a corporal and an amusing rogue and thief.

Nymphidia, a fairy poem by Drayton (q.v.), which appeared in 1627.

Nymphidia, a fairy attendant on Queen Mab, reports to the poet the doings at the fairy court. It appears that Pigwiggin has fallen in love with Mab and made an assignation to meet her in a cowslip. The queen in her snail-shell coach, and the maids of honour hurrying after her on a grasshopper and shrouded with a spider's web, set off for the cowslip. King Oberon, roused to frenzy by the loss of his queen, and armed with an acorn cup, goes in pursuit, belabouring whomsoever he finds, and meeting with mortifying adventures. He comes upon the faithful Puck (or Hobgoblin) and sends him to continue the search. Meanwhile Pigwiggin sends a challenge to Oberon, and a combat ensues between the two, mounted on earwigs. Proserpina, goddess of fairyland, intervenes, with mist and Lethe water, and restores harmony.

Nymphs, in Greek mythology, female personifications of various natural objects, mountains, springs, rivers, and trees. The water nymphs were the OCEANIDES (the daughters of Oceanus, nymphs of the Ocean), NEREIDS (nymphs of the Mediterranean Sea), and NAIADS (nymphs of lakes, rivers, and fountains). The OREADS were nymphs of the mountains. The DRYADS and HAMADRYADS were nymphs of trees. They possessed some divine gifts, such as that of prophecy, and were long-lived, but not immortal. They had no temples, but were honoured with gifts of milk, honey, fruit, etc.

NYREN, JOHN (1764–1837), a famous early cricketer and cricket chronicler. He belonged to the Hambledon Club (q.v.), and was a left-handed batsman of average ability and a fine field at point and mid-wicket. His recollections were published in 'The Young Cricketer's Tutor' (edited by Charles Cowden Clark, 1833, and E. V. Lucas, 1907). Andrew Lang (in the 'Badminton Library') described him as the 'delightful Herodotus of the Early Historic Period of cricket'.

O

O, GIOTTO's, see *Giotto's O.*

O. HENRY, see *Henry* (*O.*).

O.P., 'opposite the prompter's side' of the stage in a theatre; that is, the right-hand side (when facing the auditorium).

O.P. Club, 'Old Playgoers' Club'.

O.P. ('old prices') **Riots,** the demonstrations at Covent Garden Theatre, London, in 1809, against the proposed new tariff of prices.

o.p., in booksellers' catalogues, 'out of print'.

O's of Advent, the seven Advent anthems sung on the days next preceding Christmas Eve, each containing a separate invocation to Christ beginning with O.

Oak, GABRIEL, a character in Thomas Hardy's 'Far from the Madding Crowd' (q.v.).

Oak-apple Day, 29 May, the anniversary of the restoration of Charles II, when oak-apples or oak-leaves are worn in memory of his hiding in the oak at Boscobel (q.v.) on 6 Sept. 1651.

Oannes, in Babylonian mythology, a god with the head of a man and the body of a fish, who appeared from the Persian Gulf and gave the Babylonians their civilization.

Oates, TITUS (1649–1705), the fabricator of the Popish Plot (1678), figures in Scott's 'Peveril of the Peak' (q.v.). He is the 'Corah' of Dryden's 'Absalom and Achitophel' (q.v.).

Obadiah, in the O.T. is (1) the minister of Ahab who protected the prophets of the Lord (1 Kings xviii), and (2) the author of the prophetic book which bears his name; (3) in Sterne's 'Tristram Shandy' (q.v.), a servant of Mr. Walter Shandy.

Obadiah Prim, a character in Mrs. Centlivre's 'A Bold Stroke for a Wife' (q.v.). The word *Obadiah* is sometimes used as slang for a Quaker.

Obeah or OBI, a pretended sorcery practised by the Negroes in Africa and formerly in the West Indies. The word is West African and signifies a thing put into the ground to act as a charm, producing sickness or death.

Obelisk or OBELUS, a straight horizontal stroke, either simple or with a dot above and below, used in ancient manuscripts to indicate a spurious or corrupt word or passage. Hence to *obelize*. In modern use the word *obelisk* is applied to the mark † used in printing for reference to footnotes, etc. It is derived from the diminutive of Gr. ὀβελός, a spit, and is used also of the tapering shafts of stone which are a characteristic monument of ancient Egypt.

Oberammergau, a village in Upper Bavaria, noted for the performances there, every tenth year, of the Passion Play. These performances are said to have had their origin in a vow taken by the villagers in 1633 in order to stay an epidemic of the plague. The text of the play was probably written by the monks of the neighbouring monastery of Ettal.

Obermann, a psychological romance in letter form by Étienne Pivert de Senancour (1770–1846), French novelist, describing the sentimental speculations and aspirations of a melancholy egoist. Matthew Arnold (q.v.), in his 'Stanzas in Memory' of its author, compares its message with that of Wordsworth and Goethe. See also M. Arnold's 'Obermann once more', the last of his published poems.

Oberon, in Shakespeare's 'A Midsummer Night's Dream' (q.v.), the king of the Fairies and husband of Titania; also the hero of Weber's opera of that name.

Obi, see *Obeah*.

Obidicut, in Shakespeare's 'King Lear' (q.v), v. i, the fiend of lust, one of the five that harassed 'poor Tom'.

Obol, OBOLUS, a small coin of ancient Greece, worth about 1½d. (see *Charon*). In the Middle Ages there were *oboli* of gold, silver, and copper, current in Europe.

O'Brallaghan, SIR CALLAGHAN, a character in 'Love à la Mode' by Macklin (q.v.).

O'Brien, TERENCE, a character in Marryat's 'Peter Simple' (q.v.).

Obscurorum Virorum, Epistolae, see *Epistolae Obscurorum Virorum*.

Observants or OBSERVANTINES, Franciscan friars of the strict rule, as restored at the beginning of the 15th cent.

Observations on Man, his Frame, Duty, and Expectations, see *Hartley*.

Observations on the Present State of the Nation, see *Present State of the Nation*.

Observations upon Lord Orrery's Remarks on the Life and Writings of Dr. Jonathan Swift, a series of letters to his lordship published in 1754. These letters, signed 'J. R.', were written by Dr. Patrick Delany in an attempt to correct what he describes as 'the very mistaken and erroneous accounts [of Swift] that have been published'.

Observator, The, see *L'Estrange*. The title was also adopted in 1702 by John Tutchin for his Whig periodical.

Observer, The, a Sunday paper founded in 1792 by William Clement. It added greatly to its popularity by the early adoption of wood engraving to illustrate sensational incidents. A London paper, still in existence.

O'CASEY, SEAN (1884–1964), Irish playwright, educated, according to himself, in the streets of Dublin. His plays are informed with his own experience of poverty and violence, and show a strong sense of tragic irony as well as humour. His best-known plays are 'The Shadow of a Gunman' (1925), 'Juno and the Paycock' (1925), 'The Plough and the Stars' (1926), 'The Silver Tassie' (1928), 'Red Roses for Me' (1942), 'Cock-a-Doodle Dandy' (1949), and 'The Bishop's Bonfire' (1955). He wrote an autobiography in six volumes (1939–54).

OCCAM, and OCCAM'S RAZOR, see *Ockham*.

OCCLEVE or HOCCLEVE, THOMAS (1370?–1450?), was for many years a clerk in the office of the Privy Seal. His principal work, 'De Regimine Principum', written c. 1411–12, edited by Thomas Wright, 1860, is an English version in rhyme-royal of a Latin treatise by Aegidius (a disciple of St. Thomas Aquinas) on the duty of a ruler, addressed to Henry, Prince of Wales. The proem of 2,000 lines contains a eulogy of Chaucer and other interesting material. In 1406 he wrote a curious autobiographical poem 'La Male Règle', in which he petitions for payment of his salary, and confesses to various mean vices. He also wrote two versestories from the 'Gesta Romanorum', a manly 'Ars Sciendi Mori', a 'Complaint' and a 'Dialogue' containing autobiographical matter, and some shorter poems.

Oceana, see *Froude (J. A.)*.

Oceana, The Commonwealth of, a political romance by James Harington (q.v.), published in 1656.

The work depicts the author's conception of an ideal government, 'Oceana' being England. At the head of the State is a prince or Archon, elected like all the other magistrates by the people, who live in a condition of freedom and equality, and detestation of war. Property in land is limited, 'so that no one man or number of men . . . can come to overpower the whole people'. The senate debate and propose, the people resolve, the magistracy execute. None the less there is room for a prince as leader, and for a gentry. The scheme is in contrast to that of Hobbes's 'Leviathan', published a few years previously.

Oceanus, in early Greek cosmology, the river supposed to encircle the plain of the Earth. Also personified as one of the Titans (q.v.), the progenitor (with his consort Tethys) of the gods, and the father of the rivers and water-nymphs.

Ochiltree, EDIE, a character in Scott's 'The Antiquary' (q.v.).

OCKHAM or OCCAM, WILLIAM (d. 1349?), 'Doctor invincibilis', studied at Oxford, became a Franciscan, and graduated in Paris. He entered into the Franciscan controversy concerning poverty, and defended against Pope John XXII the doctrine of 'Evangelical poverty'. He was imprisoned at Avignon on a charge of heresy (1328), but escaped and spent the remainder of his life at the Franciscan house at Munich, where he died and was buried.

His principal importance lies in his philosophical work. He condemned the doctrine of Realism without accepting the extravagances of Nominalism. The real is always individual, not universal. The realists had abstracted the common or universal element from individual things, and attributed to it a higher degree of reality than to those individual things. But this universal is *quoddam fictum*, a 'term' or 'sign', not a 'thing', and 'entities must not be unnecessarily multiplied' (a principle known as *Occam's razor*). This concept nevertheless has importance, and the duty of science is to investigate the real likenesses between individual things. He thus approaches the point of view of Roger Bacon. Instead of reasoning from universal premisses, received from authority, we must generalize from experience of the natural order, the doctrine which we find advocated later by F. Bacon, Hobbes, and Berkeley.

Ocnus, in Roman fable, a man remarkable for his industry, who had a wife remarkable for her prodigality. He is represented as twisting a rope, which an ass standing by eats up as fast as he makes it; whence the CORD OF OCNUS, proverbial for wasted labour.

O'CONNOR, FRANK, the pseudonym of MICHAEL O'DONOVAN (1903–66), who was born and educated in Cork. His work includes novels, plays, and criticism, but he is best known for his short stories, such as 'Bones of Contention' (1936), 'Crab-Apple Jelly' (1944), 'The Common Chord' (1947), and 'Traveller's Samples' (1950). 'Kings, Lords, and Commons' (1961) is an anthology of translations from the Irish.

O'CONNOR, RT. HON. THOMAS POWER (1848–1929), M.P. and founder and first editor of 'The Star', 'The Sun', etc.; author of a life of Beaconsfield, etc.

Octavia, the sister of Octavian (Augustus) and Mark Antony's wife, figures in Shakespeare's 'Antony and Cleopatra' and Dryden's 'All for Love' (qq.v.).

Octavo, a book in which the sheets are so folded that each leaf is one-eighth of a whole sheet.

October Club, THE, a club of Tory members of parliament of Queen Anne's time, who met at the Bell (afterwards the Crown) in King Street, Westminster, to drink October ale, 'consult affairs and drive things on to extremes against the Whigs' (Swift, Letter of 10 Feb. 1710–11).

Octosyllabic, consisting of eight syllables, usually applied to the eight-syllabled rhyming iambic metre of, e.g., 'The Lady of the Lake'.

Od or ODYL, a hypothetical force, held by Baron von Reichenbach (1788–1869) to pervade all nature, manifesting itself in certain persons of sensitive temperament (streaming from their finger-tips) and exhibited especially by magnets, heat, light, etc. It has been held to explain the phenomena of mesmerism and animal magnetism. [OED.]

Ode, in ancient literature, a poem intended or adapted to be sung; in modern use, a rhymed (rarely unrhymed) lyric, often in the form of an address, generally dignified or exalted in subject, feeling and style, but sometimes (in earlier use) simple and familiar (though less so than a *song*). [OED.]

Ode on a Grecian Urn, see *Keats*.

Ode to Evening, see *Collins (William)*.

Ode to the West Wind, see *Shelley*.

ODETS, CLIFFORD (1906–63), American dramatist, born in Pennsylvania. He was a leading figure in the Group Theatre, which followed the naturalistic methods of the Moscow Arts Theatre, and his first plays, dealing with social conflicts, are his best: 'Waiting for Lefty' (1935) and 'Awake and Sing' (1935).

Odhaerir or ODHROERIR, in Scandinavian mythology, a golden mead, symbolizing poetry, a gift of Odin to gods and men, made from the blood of Kvasir, a wise man killed by the dwarfs.

Odin, the Norse form of the Old English *Woden* (whence our 'Wednesday'), in northern mythology the supreme god and creator; also the god of the atmosphere, of the infernal regions, of wisdom, and of eloquence. He is the son of Bör, the husband of Frigga, and the father of Thor, Balder, and Hödr (qq.v.). He obtained wisdom by drinking from the well of Mimir (q.v.), sacrificing an eye for the purpose. He has a horse called SLEIPNIR, a magic ring called DRAUPNIR, his abode is GLADS-HEIM, and he is attended by two black ravens HUGIN and MUNIN (thought and memory). See the first of Carlyle's 'Lectures of Heroes', 'The Hero as Divinity'.

Odoric, FRIAR, see *Cathay.*

O'Dowd, MAJOR, MRS., and GLORVINA, characters in Thackeray's 'Vanity Fair' (q.v.).

Odyl, see *Od.*

Odysseus, or, according to his Latin name, ULYSSES, son of Laertes and Anticlea (daughter of Autolycus), and king of the island of Ithaca. He became one of the suitors of Helen, but despairing of success married Penelope (qq.v.). It was by his advice that Tyndareus, father of Helen, bound her suitors by an oath to join in protecting her if she were exposed to violence. When she was carried off to Troy, Odysseus joined the other Greek princes in the expedition to recover her, after having failed to evade his obligation by simulating madness (see *Pala-medes*). During the Trojan War he was distinguished for his prudence and sagacity no less than for his valour, and was awarded the arms of Achilles, after the death of that hero, in preference to Ajax. After the war he embarked to return home, but met on the way with a series of adventures recounted in Homer's 'Odyssey'. He was thrown upon the coast of Africa and visited the country of the Lotus-eaters; narrowly escaped destruction by the Cyclops, Polyphemus (q.v.); received a bag of winds from Aeolus (q.v.); lost eleven of his twelve ships at the hands of the Laestrygones (q.v.); was detained a year by Circe (q.v.), and for seven years by Calypso (q.v.); was cast on the island of the Phaeacians, where he was kindly entertained by Nausicaa and her father Alcinous; and finally after an absence of twenty years reached Ithaca, where with the assistance of his son, Tele-machus, and the swineherd, Eumaeus (qq.v.), he destroyed the importunate suitors of Penelope. He lived some sixteen years after his return. Then Telegonus, his son by Circe, who had come to Ithaca to make himself known to his father, was shipwrecked on the island, and, being destitute, plundered some of the inhabitants. In the ensuing quarrel, Telegonus killed Odysseus, not knowing who he was.

In a dramatic monologue, Tennyson presents Odysseus, in his last years, setting out 'to sail beyond the sunset', 'to follow know-ledge like a sinking star'. The episode is not in Homer, but in Dante ('Inferno', xxvi).

Odyssey, *The,* a Greek epic poem attributed to Homer (q.v.), describing the adventures of Odysseus (q.v.) in the course of his return from the Trojan War to his kingdom of Ithaca.

Oedipus, son of Laius, king of Thebes, and Jocasta. His father was informed by an oracle that he must perish at his son's hands, and consequently ordered the destruction of the child. Oedipus was exposed, hung to a tree by a twig passed through his feet (whence his name, 'swollen-foot'), but was rescued by a shepherd. In ignorance of his parentage, Oedipus later slew Laius his father, and went on to Thebes, which was then plagued by the Sphinx (q.v.). Creon, brother of Jocasta and regent of Thebes, offered the kingdom and his sister's hand to whoever should rid the country of this pest. Oedipus, having solved the Sphinx's riddle, thus obtained the king-dom and Jocasta, his mother, for his wife, by whom he had two sons, Polyneices and Eteocles, and two daughters, Ismene and Antigone. Having discovered the facts of his parentage, Oedipus, in horror at his crimes, put out his own eyes, while Jocasta hanged herself. He retired, led by his daughter Antigone, to Colonus in Attica, where he died. The story of Oedipus is the theme of tragedies by Sophocles (q.v.). For 'Davus sum, non Oedipus' see *Davus.*

Oedipus complex, in the psycho-analysis of Freud (q.v.), a manifestation of infantile sexuality in the relations of the child to its parents.

Œil-de-bœuf (bull's-eye), an antechamber in the palace of Versailles, adjoining the king's bedroom, so named from a small oval window in one of the walls; here the courtiers awaited the king's appearance, intrigued, and discussed the news.

Oenomăus, see *Pelops.*

Oenōnē, a nymph of Mt. Ida, who became enamoured of the youthful shepherd, Paris (q.v.), before he was known to be the son of Priam, and lived with him in great happiness. Having the gift of prophecy, she foretold to him the disasters which would ensue from his voyage into Greece, and that he should have recourse to her knowledge of medicine at the hour of death. When Paris had received his fatal wound, he had recourse to Oenone, whom he had scurvily abandoned, and sought her help to cure him. She refused, but later, when she learnt that he was dead, took her own life from remorse. The story of Oenone is the theme of 'The Death of Paris' in Morris's 'The Earthly Paradise' (q.v.), and of two poems by A. Tennyson, 'Oenone' and 'The Death of Oenone'.

Oeta, MT., a branch of Mt. Pindus in Thessaly, on which Hercules erected his own funeral pyre. Spenser calls Hercules 'that great Œtean knight' ('Faerie Queene', VIII. ii. 4).

Oexmelin, see *Esquemeling.*

Offa's Dyke, an entrenchment running from

near the mouth of the Wye to near the mouth of the Dee, built (or repaired) by Offa, king of Mercia (757–95), for defence against the Welsh. This line is still roughly the border line between England and Wales.

Offenbach, JACQUES (1819–80), born at Cologne, the son of a Jew, the 'creator of French burlesque opera', a composer of sprightly humorous music which has enjoyed great popularity. His best-known operas are 'Orphée aux enfers' and 'The Tales of Hoffmann'.

Office, THE HOLY, see *Inquisition*.

O'FLAHERTY, LIAM (1897–), novelist and master of the short story, born in the Aran Islands. His novels include 'The Informer' (1925), 'The Puritan' (1931), and 'Famine', an historical novel (1937), and he has published many volumes of short stories, as 'Spring Sowing' (1926), 'The Mountain Tavern' (1929), 'The Wild Swan' (1932), and 'Two Lovely Beasts' (1948). 'Shame the Devil' (1934) is an autobiography.

Og, in Dryden's 'Absalom and Achitophel' (q.v.), represents Thomas Shadwell (q.v.), in allusion to his stoutness (Deut. iii. 11).

Ogham or OGAM, an alphabet of twenty characters used by the ancient British and Irish, and consisting of strokes upright or sloping, and dots, in various numbers; adapted to, and only used for, inscriptions on stone or wood. The alphabet is traditionally attributed to a mythical inventor OGMA. There was a Gaulish deity OGMIOS, who presided over language and eloquence.

Ogier the Dane, a hero of the Charlemagne cycle of legends, identified with a Frankish warrior Autgarius who fought against Charlemagne and then submitted to him. According to the Charlemagne romances he is hostage for his father Gaufrey of 'Dannemarch' at Charlemagne's court. He gains the emperor's favour by his exploits in Italy. His son having been killed by the son of Charlemagne in a quarrel, Ogier in a fury kills the queen's nephew, and would have killed the king himself but for the intervention of his knights. Ogier flies and is besieged, and at last imprisoned. He is released to fight the Saracen chiefs, and recovers favour by his success. He marries an English princess and receives from Charlemagne the fiefs of Hainaut and Brabant. When over a hundred years old, according to another legend, he was rejuvenated by the fairy Morgana, who retained him in her palace of oblivion for two hundred years, after which he reappeared for a time at the court of France; but, when on the point of marrying the widowed queen of that country, was snatched away again by Morgana. Ogier is included in some of the lists of Charlemagne's paladins (q.v.). It is doubtful whether he had anything to do with Denmark, 'Dannemarch' signifying perhaps the marches of the Ardennes. None the less, as Holger Danske, he became the subject of

Danish folk-song and a Danish national hero, who fought with the German Dietrich of Bern (q.v.).

OGILBY, JOHN (1600–76), author and printer, published verse translations of Virgil, 'Aesop's Fables', and Homer, with plates by Hollar; and 'Road Books of England and Wales', constantly re-edited till they faded into Mogg's 'Road Books'.

Ogre, a man-eating monster of fairy-tale, usually represented as a hideous giant. The origin of the word is unknown. It is said [OED.] to be first used by Perrault (q.v.) in his 'Contes', but Hatzfeld and Darmesteter give a quotation of 1527 containing the word.

Ogȳgia, in the 'Odyssey', the mythical island of Calypso. It is represented as being far away to the westward, beyond Scheria, the land of the Phaeacians.

O'HARA, JOHN (1905–), American novelist, born in Pennsylvania. The first of his many novels, 'Appointment in Samarra' (1934), brought him fame. Other titles are 'Butterfield 8' (1935), 'A Rage to Live' (1949), and 'From the Terrace' (1958).

Oisin, the legendary Gaelic warrior, son of Finn, also known as Ossian (q.v.). His wanderings are the subject of a poem by Yeats (q.v.).

Okba, the magician in Southey's 'Thalaba' (q.v.).

O'KEEFE or O'KEEFFE, JOHN (1747–1833), actor and dramatist, produced his 'Tony Lumpkin in Town' in 1778, after which he wrote some fifty comic and musical pieces. Of these the best known are 'Wild Oats' (1791) and 'The Castle of Andalusia' (1782). He was the author of the famous song 'I am a Friar of Orders Grey' (in his opera 'Merry Sherwood').

Olaf, ST., son of King Harald Grenske, was king of Norway, 1015–28. In his youth he is said to have gone to England as an ally of Æthelred. The 'Heimskringla' (q.v.) relates how his fleet, sailing up the Thames, was stopped by a bridge, between London and Southwark, which the Norsemen attacked and pulled down. Like his cousin and predecessor, Olaf Tryggvesson, St. Olaf was active in the diffusion of Christianity in his kingdom. He was expelled from Norway by Canute in 1028, and, returning in 1030, met the rebels at Stiklestad, where he fell mortally wounded. Among the churches in London dedicated to St. Olave, that in Tooley Street, Southwark, is probably a survival of a Danish settlement (G. R. Stirling Taylor). Tooley Street itself preserves, in a corrupt form, Olaf's name.

Olaf Tryggvesson, king of Norway, 995–1000, not to be confused with Olaf Haraldson (St. Olaf, q.v.). He invaded England, and with Svend (or Sweyn) of Denmark attacked London in 994. According to the 'Heimskringla' (q.v.) he harried the coast from

Northumberland to Scilly, where he was converted to Christianity. He deposed Hakon the Bad and became king of Norway in his stead in 995, and introduced Christianity into his realm by forcible methods. He was defeated and killed in 1000 by the kings of Denmark and Sweden, aided by his disaffected subjects. The story of his last great sea-fight, of the capture of his ship the 'Long Serpent', and of his leap to death in the sea, makes one of the most stirring narratives in the 'Heimskringla'. He is described as a man of surpassing strength and nimbleness, who could walk outboard along the oars of the 'Serpent' while his men were rowing.

OLAUS MAGNUS (1490–1558), Swedish ecclesiastic and historian, was archbishop of Upsala. After the triumph of the Reformed Faith in Sweden, he settled at Rome in 1527, where he lived most of the remainder of his life. His 'Historia de Gentibus Septentrionalibus' (1555) contains interesting information on the early Norsemen.

Olcott, COLONEL H. S., see *Theosophy*.

Old Bachelor, The, the first comedy of Congreve, produced in 1693.

The 'Old Bachelor' is Heartwell, 'a surly old pretended woman-hater', who falls in love with Silvia, not knowing her to be the forsaken mistress of Vainlove, and is inveigled into marrying her, only discovering her true character afterwards, from the gibes of his acquaintances. The parson who has been brought in to marry them, however, is in fact Vainlove's friend Belmour, who has assumed the disguise for the purpose of an intrigue with Laetitia, the young wife of an uxorious old banker, Fondlewife; and Heartwell is relieved to discover that the marriage was a pretence. The comedy includes the amusing characters of Sir Joseph Wittol, a foolish knight, who allows himself to be really married to Silvia, under the impression that she is the wealthy Araminta; and his companion, the cowardly bully, Captain Bluffe, who under the same delusion is married to Silvia's maid. The success of the play was in part due to the acting of Betterton and Mrs. Bracegirdle (qq.v.).

Old Buccaneer, THE, Captain John Peter Kirby, a character in Meredith's 'The Amazing Marriage' (q.v.).

Old Cloak, The, an anonymous poem ('Oxford Book of Sixteenth-Century Verse', No. 99).

Old Curiosity Shop, The, a novel by Dickens (q.v.), published as a separate volume in 1841. It was originally intended to be fitted into the framework of 'Master Humphrey's Clock' (1840–1), and Master Humphrey is, in fact, the narrator of the first few chapters. But this idea was soon abandoned.

Little Nell (Trent) lives in the gloomy atmosphere of the old curiosity shop kept by her grandfather, whom she tends with devotion. Reduced to poverty by a spendthrift son-in-law, and his remaining means drained by Nell's profligate brother Fred, he has borrowed money from Daniel Quilp, a hideous dwarf and a monster of iniquity, and this money he secretly expends in gambling, in the vain hope of retrieving his fortunes, for Little Nell's sake. Quilp, who believes him a rich miser, at last discovers where the borrowed money has gone, and seizes the shop. The old man and the child flee and wander about the country, suffering great hardships, and haunted by the fear of being discovered by Quilp, who pursues them with unremitting hatred. They at last find a haven in a cottage by a country church, which they are appointed to look after. The grandfather's brother, returning from abroad, and anxious to relieve their needs, has great difficulty in tracing them. At last he finds them, but Nell, worn out with her troubles, has just died, and the grandfather soon follows her.

The novel contains a number of well-known characters. Besides the loathsome and grotesque Quilp (who is drowned when on the point of being arrested for felony), there are his associates, the attorney Sampson Brass and his grim sister Sally; the honest lad Kit Nubbles, devoted to Little Nell, who incurs the hatred of Quilp, and is nearly transported through his machinations; Mr. and Mrs. Garland, the kindly old couple who befriend Kit; Dick Swiveller, the disreputable facetious friend of Fred Trent, placed by Quilp for his own purposes as clerk to Brass; 'the Marchioness', the half-starved drudge in the Brass household (she marries Dick in the end); Codlin and Short, the Punch and Judy men, whom Little Nell and her grandfather accompany for a time in their wanderings; and Mrs. Jarley, of the wax-works.

Old English, see *English*.

Old English Baron, The, see *Reeve*.

Old Fortunatus, a comedy by Dekker (q.v.), published in 1600, based on a story contained in the German 'Volksbuch' of 1509 and dramatized by Hans Sachs in 1553.

The beggar Fortunatus, encountering Fortune, is offered the choice between wisdom, strength, health, beauty, long life, and riches, and chooses the last. He receives a purse from which he can at any time draw ten pieces of gold. He goes on his travels, in the course of which he secures the marvellous hat of the Soldan of Turkey, which transports the wearer wherever he wishes to go. But at the height of his success Fortune steps in and puts an end to his life. His son Andelocia, refusing to take warning by his father's fate, and equipped with the purse and hat, goes through a series of adventures at the court of Athelstane, is finally deprived of his talismans and meets a miserable death.

The character of Orleans, the 'frantic lover' of Athelstane's daughter, has been much praised by Charles Lamb.

Old Glory, the flag of the United States.

Old Hickory, a nickname of Andrew Jackson, president of the United States 1829–37, from his toughness of character.

Old Lady of Threadneedle Street, THE, see *Threadneedle Street.*

Old Man Eloquent, THAT, Isocrates (q.v.), so called by Milton in his sonnet to the Lady Margaret Ley.

Old Man of the Mountain, see *Assassins.*

Old Man of the Sea, see *Sindbad.*

OLD MOORE, Francis Moore (1657–1715), physician, astrologer, and schoolmaster, who in 1699 published an almanac containing weather predictions in order to promote the sale of his pills. In 1700 appeared his 'Vox Stellarum, an Almanac for 1701 with Astrological Observations'. There are now several almanacs called 'Old Moore', and the predictions range far beyond the weather.

Old Mortality, a novel by Sir W. Scott (q.v.), published in 1816 (in the first series of the 'Tales of My Landlord').

The title is taken from the nickname of a certain Robert Paterson, who towards the end of the 18th cent. wandered about Scotland cleaning and repairing the tombs of the Cameronians, a sect of strict Covenanters who took up arms for their religious opinions in the reign of Charles II. The story, by a fiction of Scott, is said to be based on the anecdotes told by this supporter of their cause, and covers the period from the military operations undertaken against them in 1679, under the command of John Grahame of Claverhouse, to the more peaceful days of religious toleration introduced by William III. It is particularly concerned with the fortunes of Henry Morton of Milnwood, a young man of courage and high character, and a moderate Presbyterian, who, at the outset of the tale, is arrested by the dragoons of Claverhouse for having harboured an old friend of his father, the fanatical Covenanter, John Balfour of Burley, not knowing that this man had just taken part in the assassination of the archbishop of St. Andrews. Morton narrowly escapes immediate execution, and this act of oppression, coupled with a sense of his countrymen's sufferings, induces him to throw in his lot with the Covenanters, who have taken up arms for the cause of religious freedom, little as he shares their extreme religious opinions. He accordingly becomes one of their leaders. This brings him into violent antagonism with Lady Margaret Bellenden, the Royalist owner of Tillietudlem Castle, with whose granddaughter Edith he is in love. It is to the latter's intervention with Lord Evandale, one of Claverhouse's officers and Morton's rival for the hand of Edith, that Morton owes his life when first brought before Claverhouse. This act of generosity on Evandale's part is repaid by Morton at the skirmish of Drumclog, and

again when the rebel forces under Burley have almost reduced Tillietudlem to surrender and have captured Evandale himself. Morton thus retains his place in Edith's heart. But the final defeat of the Covenanters at Bothwell Bridge, and his own capture and banishment, sever him for years from Edith, who believes him dead; and she is on the point of yielding to the patient suit of Evandale, when Morton, after the accession of William III, returns to England, and his arrival puts an end to the preparations for Edith's marriage. Evandale, in spite of the efforts of Morton to save him, is killed in a skirmish with a few fanatics, and Morton marries Edith. The story includes an interesting study of the character of Claverhouse and a vivid picture of the follies to which religious enthusiasm carried the Covenanters.

Old Nick, the Devil, where Nick is probably the familiar abbreviation of Nicholas, though the reason for the appellation is obscure. The earliest occurrence of the expression quoted in the OED. is 1643. Brewer suggests as origin *Nickel,* the German mischievous demon of the mines.

Old Parr, see *Parr (T.).*

Old Pretender, THE, James Francis Edward Stuart (1688–1766), son of James II and Mary of Modena. He was popularly, but erroneously, believed to be a supposititious child. He served with the French army and distinguished himself at Oudenarde (1708) and Malplaquet (1709). He took a part in the unsuccessful rising in Scotland of 1715, and gave money for the rising of 1745. He is buried in St. Peter's, Rome.

Old Q, the nickname of William Douglas, third Earl of March and fourth duke of Queensberry (1724–1810), a friend of the Prince of Wales, notorious for his escapades and dissolute life, much interested in horse-racing. He was satirized by Burns, and is the 'degenerate Douglas' of Wordsworth's sonnet.

Old Rowley, see *Rowley (Old).*

Old Style, see *Calendar.*

Old Uncle Tom Cobbleigh, and all, see *Widdicome Fair.*

Old Vic, THE, a theatre in the Waterloo Bridge Road, London, opened in 1818 as the 'Royal Coburg', shortly after the building of Waterloo Bridge. The foundation-stone was laid by the Prince of Saxe-Coburg, the husband of Princess Charlotte, daughter of the Regent. It was renamed the 'Victoria' in 1833. Before long it declined into a music-hall with a promenade. It was started afresh in 1880 on more respectable lines. Miss Lilian Baylis became manager in 1912, and made it famous by her notable productions of Shakespeare plays.

Old Wives' Tale, The, a play in prose by Peele (q.v.), published in 1595.

The play is a satire on the romantic dramas

of the time, the first English work of this kind. Two brothers are searching for their sister Delia, who is held captive by the magician Sacrapant. The brothers also fall into his hands. They are all rescued by the knight Eumenides aided by Jack's Ghost, who is impelled by motives of gratitude, because the knight had borne the expense of Jack's funeral.

Old Wives' Tale, The, a novel by E. A. Bennett (q.v.), published in 1908.

It is the long chronicle of the lives of two sisters, Constance and Sophia Baines, daughters of a draper of Bursley (Burslem, one of the 'Five Towns', q.v.), from their ardent girlhood, through disillusionment, to death. The drab life of the draper's shop, its trivial incidents, are made interesting and important. Constance, a staid and sensible young woman, marries the estimable and superficially insignificant Samuel Povey, the chief assistant in the shop, and spends all her life in Bursley. The more passionate and imaginative Sophia elopes with the fascinating Gerald Scales, a commercial traveller who has come into a fortune. He is an unprincipled blackguard, has to be forced to marry her, carries her to Paris, where she is exposed to indignities, and finally deserts her. She struggles to success as a lodging-house keeper in Paris, where she lives through the siege of 1870. The sisters are reunited, and spend their last years together in Bursley.

Oldbuck, JONATHAN, *Laird of Monkbarns*, the principal character in Sir W. Scott's 'The Antiquary' (q.v.). MISS GRISELDA ('GRIZZY') OLDBUCK is his sister.

Oldcastle, SIR JOHN (*d.* 1417), Lord Cobham in right of his wife, a leader of the Lollards (q.v.), after heterodox declarations of faith, was declared a heretic in 1414 and imprisoned in the Tower. He escaped, was outlawed, captured near Welshpool, and 'hung and burnt hanging' in St. Giles's Fields.

Oldcastle, The First Part of Sir John, a play published in 1600, of unknown authorship, included in the 3rd and 4th Shakespeare folios, but certainly not by him.

It deals with the proceedings in Henry V's reign against Sir John Oldcastle (q.v.), as the chief supporter of the Lollards.

Oldfield, ANNE (1683-1730), an actress who excelled both in tragedy and comedy. She first made her mark as Lady Betty Modish in Colley Cibber's 'The Careless Husband' (q.v.), but her best parts are said to have been Cleopatra, Calista (in Rowe's 'Fair Penitent', q.v.), and Lady Townly (in Cibber's 'The Provok'd Husband', q.v.). She was buried in Westminster Abbey, beneath Congreve's monument. She is the 'Narcissa' of Pope's 'Moral Essays'.

OLDHAM, JOHN (1653-83), educated at St. Edmund Hall, Oxford, published several Pindaric odes, but is chiefly remem-

bered for his ironical 'Satire against Virtue' and 'Satires against the Jesuits' (1681). He also wrote imitations of Horace, Bion, Moschus, and Boileau. His 'Poems and Translations' were collected in 1683. He has been called the 'English Juvenal'. Dryden addressed some beautiful lines to his memory.

OLDMIXON, JOHN (1673-1742), a Whig historian and pamphleteer, published 'The British Empire in America' (1708), 'The Secret History of Europe' (1712-15), and histories of England during the Stuart reigns (1729) and those of William III, Anne, and George I (1735-9). By his 'Essay on Criticism', prefixed to the third edition (1727) of his 'Critical History of England' (1724-6), he incurred the hostility of Pope, who pilloried him in the 'Dunciad' and the 'Art of Sinking in Poetry'.

OLDYS, WILLIAM (1696-1761), antiquary, and editor of the 'Harleian Miscellany' (q.v.). He wrote a 'Life of Sir Walter Ralegh' and contributed many biographies to the 'Biographia Britannica'. He was also author of one well-known poem, 'Busy, curious, thirsty fly!' ('Oxford Book of English Verse', No. 438). He was relieved from poverty and the Fleet prison by being appointed Norroy king-of-arms.

Olindo, the lover of Sophronia in Tasso's 'Jerusalem Delivered' (q.v.).

OLIPHANT, LAURENCE (1829-88), was born at Cape Town of Scottish descent, and after a desultory education and extensive travels with his parents, became a barrister in Ceylon, where his father was chief justice. He published a 'Journey to Khatmandu' (in Nepal) in 1852, and 'The Russian Shores of the Black Sea' in 1853. In 1853-4 he was secretary to Lord Elgin at Washington and in Canada, and then accompanied Lord Stratford de Redcliffe to the Crimea. He acted as correspondent to 'The Times' in Circassia during the war. He next accompanied Lord Elgin to China as private secretary, and in 1859 published a 'Narrative of a Mission to China in 1857-8-9'. He is then heard of as plotting with Garibaldi in Italy, as secretary of legation in Japan, and in other parts of the world. He was 'Times' correspondent during the Franco-German War. His satirical novel, 'Piccadilly', which had appeared in 'Blackwood' in 1865, was republished in 1870. In 1867 he had come under the subjection of the American 'prophet', Thomas Lake Harris, to whom he surrendered his property at Brocton, and by whom he was commercially employed in America, an experience which led to the publication, in 1876, of 'The Autobiography of a Joint-Stock Company', exposing the methods of American financiers. Oliphant had married Miss L'Estrange in 1872, and with her wrote the strange 'Sympneumata' (1885), a work which they believed to have been dictated by a spirit. He wrote his novel 'Altiora Peto' (1883) and several mystical works at Haifa in Palestine, where, with his second wife, he founded a community of Jewish immigrants. His many experiences provided materials for 'Episodes of a Life of Adventure' which appeared in 1887, not long before his death. His 'Life' was written by Margaret Oliphant (q.v.).

OLIPHANT, MARGARET OLIPHANT (1828–97), *née* Wilson, married her cousin, Francis William Oliphant, a painter and designer of stained glass. She published many novels, of which the best known are the 'Chronicles of Carlingford', issued anonymously between 1863 and 1876, including 'Salem Chapel', 'The Perpetual Curate', 'The Rector', 'Miss Marjoribanks', and 'Phoebe Junior'. Of these the best are 'Miss Marjoribanks' (the story of the social ambitions of a young lady, told with genial humour) and 'Salem Chapel' (which depicts the narrow and intolerant piety of a dissenting community). In 'A Beleaguered City' (1880) and 'A Little Pilgrim of the Unseen' (1882), Mrs. Oliphant introduces a supernatural element. She wrote a number of stories of which Scotland is the scene, beginning with 'Passages in the Life of Mrs. Maitland' (1849) and including 'Kirsteen' (1890). She also published lives of Edward Irving (1862) and Laurence Oliphant (1892), 'Makers of Florence' (1888), and 'Makers of Venice' (1889). Her 'Annals of a Publishing House: William Blackwood and his Sons' appeared in 1897. Her 'Autobiography' (1899) describes her efforts, by her voluminous writings, to provide for the maintenance and education of her own and her brother's children.

Olivant, the ivory horn (from *Oliphaunt*) of Orlando.

Oliver, in the Charlemagne cycle of legends, one of Charlemagne's paladins (q.v.). He is the close friend of Roland, with whom he has a prolonged and undecided single combat (the origin of their comradeship, see *Roland for an Oliver*), and his equal in bravery, but more prudent. At the battle of Roncevaux (see *Roland*) he urges Roland to summon help by sounding his horn, but Roland postpones doing so till too late. Oliver's sister Aude is betrothed to Roland.

Oliver, a character in Shakespeare's 'As You Like It' (q.v.).

Oliver Dain (OLIVIER LE DAIN), barber and counsellor of Louis XI; he figures in Scott's 'Quentin Durward' (q.v.).

Oliver Twist, a novel by Dickens (q.v.), published in 1837–8.

Oliver Twist is the name given to a child of unknown parentage born in a workhouse and brought up under the cruel conditions to which pauper children were formerly exposed, the tyrant at whose hands he especially suffers being Bumble, the parish beadle. After experience of an unhappy apprenticeship, he runs away, reaches London, and falls into the hands of a gang of thieves, at the head of which is the old Jew Fagin, and whose other chief members are the burglar, Bill Sikes, his companion Nancy, and 'the Artful Dodger', an impudent young pickpocket. Every effort is made to convert Oliver into a thief. He is temporarily rescued by the benevolent Mr. Brownlow, but kidnapped by the gang, whose interest in his retention has been increased by the offers of a sinister person named Monks, who has a special interest, presently disclosed, in Oliver's perversion. Oliver is now made to accompany Bill Sikes on a burgling expedition, in the course of which he receives a gunshot wound, and comes into the hands of Mrs. Maylie and her protégée Rose, by whom he is kindly treated and brought up. After a time, Nancy, who develops some redeeming traits, reveals to Rose that Monks is aware of Oliver's parentage, and wishes all proof of it destroyed; also that there is some relationship between Oliver and Rose herself. Inquiry is set on foot. In the course of it Nancy's action is discovered by the gang, and she is brutally murdered by Bill Sikes. A hue and cry is raised; Sikes, trying to escape, accidentally hangs himself, and the rest of the gang are secured and Fagin executed. Monks, found and threatened with exposure, confesses what remains unknown. He is the half-brother of Oliver, and has pursued his ruin, animated by hatred and the desire to retain the whole of his father's property. Rose is the sister of Oliver's unfortunate mother. Oliver is adopted by Mr. Brownlow. Monks emigrates and dies in prison. Bumble ends his career in the workhouse over which he formerly ruled.

Olivia, (1) one of the principal characters in Shakespeare's 'Twelfth Night' (q.v.); (2) a character in Wycherley's 'The Plain Dealer' (q.v.); (3) the elder daughter of Dr. Primrose, in Goldsmith's 'The Vicar of Wakefield' (q.v.).

Olney Hymns, see *Cowper*.

Olor Iscanus, a collection of poems by Vaughan (q.v.), published in 1651, but written some years earlier. The poem which gives its title to the book is in praise of the river Usk.

Olympia, a small plain in Elis in the northwest of the Peloponnese, where the Olympic Games (q.v.) were celebrated. It contained a sacred precinct, in which were temples of Zeus and Hera. Here stood the famous statue of the Olympian Zeus by Phidias (see under *Zeus*), and here was found the statue of Hermes by Praxiteles, now in the museum of Olympia.

Olympiad, see *Olympic Games*.

Olympian Odes, THE, of Pindar were written to celebrate victories at the Olympic Games (q.v.), while the Pythian Odes were written in honour of victories at the Pythian Games held at Delphi. The other two books of Pindar's odes were the Nemeans and the Isthmians, for the Nemean Games (at Nemea) and the Isthmian Games (at the Isthmus of Corinth). They were written to the order of any victor who would pay for them. The four groups of odes are known together as the 'Epinicia'.

Olympian Zeus, THE STATUE OF, see *Zeus.*

Olympic Games, THE, were held every fourth year at Olympia in Elis in the Peloponnese. Their origin is lost in antiquity, but legend attributes it to Hercules. The intervals of four years between the successive celebrations were known as *Olympiads* and were reckoned in Greek chronology from the year 776 B.C., when Coroebus won the foot-race. The games included foot-races, wrestling, boxing, the *pancratium* (a mixture of boxing and wrestling), the chariot-race, and the horse-race. The Olympic Games were revived in 1896, on an international basis, at the suggestion of Baron Pierre de Coubertin.

Other important periodic games were the Pythian Games of the Boeotians, the Nemean Games of the Argives, and the Isthmian Games of the Corinthians.

Olympus, a lofty mountain standing at the eastern extremity of the range that divided Greece from Macedonia, on the Thermaic Gulf. It was regarded in Greek mythology as the home of the gods, who met in conclave on the summit.

The MYSIAN OLYMPUS was a lofty chain of mountains in the north-west of Asia Minor.

Olyssipo, in imprints, Lisbon.

Om, a mystic and holy word in Hindu religious literature, regarded as summing up all truth. It is also the first word in the Buddhist formula *om mani padme hum,* regarded as of special sanctity and potency, and variously translated.

Omai, a native of Tahiti (Otaheite) who was brought to England by Captain Cook, and returned with him on the latter's last voyage.

Omar, the second caliph, who succeeded Abu Bakr (q.v.) in 634.

Omar, MOSQUE OF, or 'Dome of the Rock', a famous mosque on the platform of the Temple at Jerusalem. It was originally a Byzantine church (much altered) and contains the rock on which, according to legend, Abraham prepared to sacrifice Isaac.

Omar Khayyám, The Rubáiyát of, a translation of the *rubais* or quatrains of the Persian poet of that name, by Edward FitzGerald (q.v.), first published anonymously in 1859 (75 quatrains), remodelled and enlarged (110 quatrains) in 1868, and further modified and reduced (101 quatrains) in 1872 and 1879.

Omar Khayyám ('Khayyám' means 'tent-maker'), an astronomer and poet, was born at Naishapur in Khorassan in the latter half of the 11th cent. and died in 1123. For the story of his relations with Nizam-ul-Mulk and Hasan-ben-Sabbah (the 'Old Man of the Mountain'), see *Nizam-ul-Mulk.* The original 'rubáiyát' or quatrains are independent stanzas, of which the form is reproduced in the translation; but the translator has woven them together in a connected train of thought. The stanzas contain the poet's meditations and speculations on the mysteries of existence, and his counsel to drink and make merry while life lasts.

Ombre (from Spanish *hombre,* man), a card game played by three persons with forty cards, the 'ombre' being the player who undertakes to win the pool. The game was very popular in the 17th and 18th cents., until superseded by quadrille. It figures prominently in Pope's 'The Rape of the Lock' (q.v.).

Ommiades, see *Umayyads.*

Omnium, DUKE OF, a character in A. Trollope's 'Dr. Thorne' and 'Framley Parsonage' (qq.v.). His successor in the title, Plantagenet Palliser, figures in the 'Phineas Finn' (q.v.) series of Trollope's novels.

OMNIUM, JACOB, see *Higgins.*

Omoo, a Narrative of Adventures in the South Seas, a romance by Melville (q.v.), published in 1847.

'Omoo' is a continuation of the adventures begun in 'Typee' (q.v.). The narrator is taken off (from the island of Nukahura) by a whaler, the crew mostly desperadoes, and the conditions on board abominable. At Papeetee in Tahiti he and some other malcontents are put ashore and sent to the 'calabooza', where they spend some weeks in the custody of an old native, 'Captain Bob'. The narrator and a humorous companion, 'Doctor Long Ghost', escape and live a wandering life, the story of their experiences furnishing vivid pictures of the manners and customs of the superficially converted Polynesians, and including a visit to the court of Queen Pomare.

Omphălē, a queen of Lydia. When Hercules (q.v.) in a fit of insanity murdered Iphitus, the oracle required him to go into slavery for three years. He was accordingly sold to Omphale and set to women's work, while his mistress assumed his lion's skin and club.

On, the Hebrew name of Heliopolis in Egypt, the chief seat of the Egyptian worship of the sun.

One of our Conquerors, a novel by G. Meredith (q.v.), published in 1891.

Victor Radnor has, as a young man, married a rich elderly widow and then fallen in love with her young companion Natalia Dreighton. Victor and Natalia have defied convention and united their lives. They have a daughter, Nesta Victoria, attractive and courageous, who presently becomes aware of the stain on her birth. The novel is a study of the resulting situation: Victor's wife prolonging her life interminably; a constant threat of social exposure to the young couple; Victor optimistic, energetic, and financially prosperous; Natalia timid and shrinking under the cloud and anxiety; Nesta growing up, with several suitors around her, the most eligible being the Hon. Dudley Sowerby, heir to an earldom. The discovery of the fact of Nesta's illegitimate birth damps his ardour for a time. Her determined befriending of Mrs. Marsett, the frail and notorious but not depraved mistress of a young officer, is the final blow to their projected union, as it is the source of deep affliction to her mother. Harrassed by her anxieties and cares, Natalia at this crisis dies, Victor's wife surviving her by a few hours. Victor, driven insane by grief, lives a few years longer. Nesta marries Dartrey Fenellan, a man with a juster perception than Sowerby of the girl's noble qualities. Daniel Skepsey, Victor's pugilistic little clerk, is an amusing figure in the story.

Oneida Community, a religious society also called PERFECTIONISTS, founded in 1848 by John H. Noyes, at Oneida Creek, New York State. Its principles were thoroughly communistic until, in 1879, in deference to public opinion, marriage was introduced.

O'NEILL, EUGENE GLADSTONE (1888–1953), American dramatist, born in New York. The son of a well-known actor, he had a varied career before associating himself (1916) with the famous Provincetown Players. After writing several one-act plays, he scored his first big success with 'Beyond the Horizon' (1920). His reputation as America's leading and most original dramatist, however influenced by Ibsen and Strindberg, was confirmed with the production of the expressionistic 'Emperor Jones' (1920), which describes the rise and tragic fall of the Negro 'emperor' of a West Indian island, and 'Anna Christie' (1921), a naturalistic study of a prostitute of the New York waterfront and her redemption. Among other important plays of this period were 'The Hairy Ape' (1922), 'All God's Chillun Got Wings' (1924), and 'Desire Under the Elms' (1924). O'Neill's criticism of contemporary materialistic values was powerfully and poetically expressed in 'The Fountain' (1925), 'The Great God Brown' (1926), 'Lazarus Laughed' (1927), and 'Marco Millions' (1927). He experimented with the stream-of-consciousness in 'Strange Interlude' (1928), and adapted a Greek theme to the aftermath of the American Civil War in 'Mourning Becomes Electra' (1931). Among his later plays was 'The Iceman Cometh' (1946). He was awarded a Nobel Prize in 1936.

Oneiza, in Southey's 'Thalaba' (q.v.), the wife of Thalaba.

Onesti, NASTAGIO DEGLI, see *Theodore and Honoria.*

Only Way, The, a play adapted by F. Wills from Dickens's 'A Tale of Two Cities' (1890).

Onomatopoeia, the formation of a word by an imitation of the sound associated with the object or action designated; as 'hurlyburly'.

Open, Sesamè!, the magic formula in 'Ali Baba and the Forty Thieves' (q.v.).

Opera, a dramatic performance in which music forms an essential part, consisting of recitatives, arias, and choruses, with orchestral accompaniment and scenery. [OED.] It was first adopted in Italy. The first English work that may be called an opera was D'Avenant's 'Siege of Rhodes' (q.v.).

Opera Bouffe, comic opera, especially of a farcical character.

Ophelia, in Shakespeare's 'Hamlet' (q.v.), the daughter of Polonius.

Ophir, in O.T. geography, the place from which the ships of King Solomon brought gold and precious stones (1 Kings x. 11). It has been variously identified, and was probably in south-eastern Arabia, where the tribes trace their descent to Joktan (cf. Gen. x. 29; Sayce, 'Races of the O.T.', c. iii); perhaps Dhufar (see B. Thomas, 'Arabia Felix', 1932).

Ophiuchus, 'the Serpent-bearer', a northern constellation in ancient astronomy. In modern astronomy it extends north and south of the equinoctial near the Scorpion.

OPIE, MRS. AMELIA (1769–1853), *née* Alderson, wife of John Opie the painter. She was a novelist and poet, and intimate with Sydney Smith, Sheridan, and Mme de Staël. Her writings include: 'Adeline Mowbray' (suggested by the story of Mary Wollstonecraft, 1804), 'Simple Tales' (1806), 'Lays for the Dead' (1833). She wrote a memoir of her husband (1809).

Opimian, THE REV. DR. THEOPHILUS, a character in Peacock's 'Gryll Grange' (q.v.). (*Opimianum* was a celebrated wine of the vintage of A.U.C. 633 = B.C. 121, when Opimius was consul. Lewis and Short.)

Opium Eater, *Confessions of an English*, see *Confessions of an English Opium Eater.*

Oppidan, from the Latin *oppidum*, a town; at Eton College, a student not on the foundation (who boards in the town or at one of the assistant masters' houses), distinguished from a *Colleger*. Formerly also at other great schools.

Ops, a Roman goddess of fertility and agriculture, regarded as the wife of Saturnus.

Oran Haut-ton, SIR, the amiable orangoutang, a character in Peacock's 'Melincourt' (q.v.).

Orange, a name applied to the ultra-Protestant party in Ireland, in reference to the secret Association of Orangemen formed in 1795. The exact origin of this use of 'Orange' is somewhat obscure, but it is supposed to be due to the fact that two members (by name Cope) of the 'Orange Lodge' of Freemasons existing in Belfast in 1795 were active in organizing the Protestant party, who were in consequence styled 'Orange boys'. The name of this 'Orange Lodge' probably had reference to William of Orange, or to the use of orange badges at the anniversaries at which his memory was celebrated. William of Orange derived his title from the small town and principality of that name on the Rhône, which passed to the House of Nassau in 1530. The name of this town is derived from its ancient Latin name *Arausio*, and has no connexion with the name of the fruit, which comes through Spanish from the Arabic *naranj*. [OED.]

Oranges and Lemons: what the bells of St. Clement's say, in the old rhyme that accompanies a nursery game. The rhyme begins:

> Gay go up and gay go down
> To ring the bells of London town,

and a couplet follows for each church, St. Clement's, St. Martin's, etc., ending with 'the great bell at Bow'. The text is in Halliwell, 'Nursery Rhymes'.

Orator Henley, see *Henley (J.)*.

Orator Hunt, HENRY HUNT (1773–1835), an active radical politician and agitator, who presided at the meeting in St. Peter's Fields, Manchester (the 'Peterloo Massacre'); a violent and stentorian but impressive speaker. He published memoirs in 1820.

Oratorians, an order founded at Rome by St. Philip Neri (Filippo de' Neri, 1515–95) an Italian priest. Its members are priests under no vows. Newman (q.v.) attached himself to the order and founded the Oratory at Birmingham in 1847 and in London in 1850.

Orbaneja, the painter of Ubeda referred to in 'Don Quixote' (II. i. 3), who, when asked what he was painting, replied 'As it may turn out'.

Orbilius, the schoolmaster of Horace, a flogger:

> Delendaque carmina Livî, . . . memini quae plagosum mihi parvo Orbilium dictare.
>   (Horace, Ep. II. i. 69.)

Orc, in the mystical poems of Blake (q.v.), the symbol of rebellious anarchy, the opponent of Urizen.

Orcades, the Orkney Islands.

Orcus, a Roman name for the god of the Lower World, the abode of the dead.

Ordeal of Richard Feverel, The, a novel by G. Meredith (q.v.), published in 1859.

Richard is the son of Sir Austin Feverel, a wealthy baronet, who has been deserted by his wife and left with the boy to bring up. Sir Austin prides himself on his wisdom, which is less than he supposes, and has a 'system' of education, which consists in keeping him at home, for he thinks schools corrupt, and in trusting to parental vigilance. The breakdown of the system at adolescence is the underlying theme of the book. Richard, a spirited youth, and Lucy Desborough, a neighbouring farmer's niece, fall in love at first sight. An idyllic courtship ends in their discovery. She has every charm that nature can give, but not the birth that Sir Austin demands for his son's bride. Attempts to break the attachment result in their secret marriage and the anger of Sir Austin, who cruelly secures the separation of the young couple by working on his son's love for him. Richard, ordered to await his father's pleasure in London, sets about the redemption of an erring beautiful woman, and falls instead momentarily a victim to her lures. These have been spread at the instance of Lord Mountfalcon, who has designs on the innocent Lucy. Overwhelmed with shame at his infidelity to his wife, Richard prolongs his absence from her until he learns that he is a father and that Lucy and Sir Austin are reconciled. At the moment of returning to her, when the way to happiness seems at last open, he learns of the designs of Lord Mountfalcon, challenges him to a duel, and is seriously wounded. The shock is too severe for Lucy, who becomes crazy and dies.

Order, in classical architecture, the unit of composition, consisting of entablature, column, and base. The five orders are Doric, Ionic, and Corinthian (qq.v.), of which there are Greek and Roman forms, and Composite and Tuscan (qq.v.), which are Roman. No example of Roman Tuscan exists, but the form, based on Vitruvius, was much used by Renaissance and later architects, as were the other Roman orders; Greek orders were little used until the neo-classical revival.

An ATTIC ORDER has a square column of any of the five above orders.

An ATTIC is originally a decorative structure consisting of a small order placed above another order of much greater height constituting the main façade. This was usually an Attic order, whence the name. From this the term is applied to the top storey of the building, under the beams of the roof, when there are more than two storeys above ground.

ORDERICUS VITALIS (1075–1143?), a Norman born in England, and a monk of St. Évroul in Normandy. He wrote an 'Ecclesiastical History' in Latin extending from the beginning of the Christian era down to 1141, one of the standard authorities for the Norman period.

Orders, MONASTIC, see *Benedictines, Capuchins, Cordeliers, Dominicans, Franciscans, Observants, Oratorians, Recollects*, etc.

Orders in Council, THE, of 1807, declared the ports of France and her allies in a state of blockade, and all neutral ships that attempted to enter them liable to seizure unless they had first called at a British port. These Orders in Council were provoked by Napoleon's Berlin Decree excluding British commerce from European ports and declaring the blockade of British ports. They were answered by Napoleon's Milan Decree making neutral vessels liable to seizure if they called at a

British port. They resulted in the war of 1812–14 with the United States.

Oreads, nymphs (q.v.) of the mountains.

Oregon Trail, The, 'Sketches of the Prairie and Rocky-Mountain Life' (1849), by Francis Parkman (q.v.).

Orellana, an early name for the river Amazon, from Francisco de Orellana (*fl.* 1540), who served with Pizarro and first explored it. In the course of his voyage he heard from Indians of the existence of a tribe of Amazons or female warriors, and asserted that he had encountered them. Hence the present name of the river.

Orestes, son of Agamemnon and Clytemnestra (qq.v.). When his father was murdered by Clytemnestra and Aegisthus, the life of the young Orestes was saved and he was educated by his uncle Strophius with his son Pylades. Between Orestes and Pylades the closest friendship sprang up. When Orestes reached manhood he avenged his father's death by assassinating Aegisthus and Clytemnestra. To obtain purification from this murder Orestes was directed by the oracle at Delphi to bring to Greece a statue of Artemis from the Tauric Chersonese. Orestes and Pylades undertook the enterprise, and, having reached the Chersonese, were seized and ordered to be sacrificed, in accordance with the custom of the country. Iphigenia (q.v.) was then priestess of the temple of Artemis and it was her office to immolate these strangers. Having discovered that one of them was her brother, she resolved to fly with them from the Chersonese, carrying away the statue of Artemis. This they accomplished. Subsequently, after his return, Orestes carried off Hermione, daughter of Menelaus, who had been betrothed to him, but had married Neoptolemus.

Orfeo, Sir, a metrical romance of the Middle English period, in which the classical story of Orpheus and Eurydice (see *Orpheus*) is reproduced in Celtic guise. Queen Heurodys is carried off to fairyland, and pursued by King Orfeo, as a minstrel, whose melodious lays succeed in bringing her back to the world of men. On this was founded the ballad 'King Orfeo' (in Child's collection).

Orgilus, a character in Ford's 'The Broken Heart' (q.v.).

Orgoglio (Ital., signifying haughtiness), in Spenser's 'Faerie Queene', I. vii. 9 and 10, captures the Red Cross Knight, and is slain by Prince Arthur.

Orgon, the credulous dupe in Molière's 'Le Tartuffe' (q.v.).

Oriana, see under *Amadis of Gaul.* Oriana is (1) a name frequently applied by the Elizabethan poets to Queen Elizabeth; (2) the heroine of Fletcher's 'The Wild-Goose Chase' (q.v.); (3) the subject of a ballad by Tennyson.

Oriflamme, said to be derived from *aurea*

flamma, 'golden flame', a small red silk three-pointed banner of the abbots of Saint-Denis, which, when the abbey passed into the hands of the kings of France, became the French royal banner. The French armies fought under it from 1124 to 1415. The kings 'took it' from the altar of Saint-Denis before each campaign.

ORIGEN (*c.* 185–*c.* 253), the second great Christian thinker and scholar of the Alexandrian school (Clement was the first). He combined with his orthodox Christianity personal speculations which were rejected by the Church. He was author of many theological works, and compiler of the famous *Hexapla* versions of the Old Testament (see *Bible*).

Origin of Species, The, the great work of C. Darwin (q.v.), of which the full title was 'On the Origin of Species by means of Natural Selection, or the Preservation of Favoured Races in the Struggle for Life', was published in 1859.

Original, The, see *Walker* (T.).

Original Poems for Infant Minds, see *Taylor* (*Jane and Anne*).

Orinda, THE MATCHLESS, see *Philips* (K.).

Orīon, a giant and hunter of Boeotia, the subject of various legends, according to which he was deprived of sight by Dionysus, or killed by Artemis, or died of the sting of a scorpion, after boasting that he would clear the earth of all wild beasts. After his death he was placed among the stars. His constellation used to set about November, whence it was associated with storms and rain.

Orion, an allegorical poem by R. H. Horne (q.v.), published in 1843 at one farthing, as a satirical comment on the current estimation of poetry.

The poem is based on the myth of Orion (q.v. above), and is 'an attempt to re-establish the union which had existed in ancient times between philosophy and poetry' (Gosse). Orion here is 'the worker, the builder-up of things and of himself', 'a type of the struggle of man with himself, the contest between the intellect and the senses'. He is taken into the train of the goddess Artemis, 'the Queen of maiden immortality', who guides him in his duties and instils knowledge into his mind. But presently Orion is led astray by love of the beautiful Merope and loses his sight. He devotes himself to the service of mankind, and strives to admit the light of dawn to the temple of Artemis, by hewing down the trees and destroying the poisonous Harpies that obstruct it. But Artemis slays him. Orion is contrasted with Akinetos, his brother giant, the 'Great Unmoved' or Apathy, who discourages all effort as useless and fatal to the agent. Nevertheless Orion, after his death, is raised to the sky to continue his beneficent and stimulating work.

Orlando, (1) the Italian form of Roland (q.v.), a hero of the Charlemagne romances (see also *Orlando Furioso* and *Orlando Inna-morato*); (2) in Shakespeare's 'As You Like It' (q.v.), the lover of Rosalind; (3) the title of a novel by V. Woolf (q.v.).

Orlando Friscobaldo, in Dekker's 'The Honest Whore' (q.v.), the father of Bellafront.

Orlando Furioso, a poem by Ariosto (q.v.), published in its complete form in 1532, designed to exalt the house of Este and its legendary ancestor Rogero (Ruggiero) and to continue the story of Orlando's love for Angelica begun by Boiardo in the 'Orlando Innamorato' (q.v.).

The main theme of the poem is this: Saracens and Christians, in the days of Charlemagne, are at war for the possession of Europe. The Saracens under Agramante, king of Africa, are besieging Charlemagne in Paris with the help of Marsilio, the Moorish king of Spain, and two mighty warriors, Rodomont and Mandricardo (qq.v.). Christendom is imperilled. Angelica, who at the end of Boiardo's poem had been consigned by Charlemagne to the care of Namo, escapes. Orlando, chief of the paladins, a perfect knight, invincible and invulnerable, is lured by her beauty to forget his duty and pursue her. Angelica meets with various adventures, finally coming upon the wounded Moorish youth Medoro, whom she tends, falls in love with, and marries. A charming description follows of their honeymoon in the woods. Orlando, arriving there by chance, and learning their story, is seized with a furious and grotesque madness, runs naked through the country, destroying everything in his path, and at last returns to Charlemagne's camp, where he is finally cured of his madness and his love, and in a great conclusive battle kills Agramante.

Although the madness of Orlando gives the poem its name, a not less important theme in it is the love of Rogero (q.v.) for Bradamant, a maiden warrior, sister of Rinaldo (q.v.), and the many adventures and vicissitudes that interrupt the course of true love. Other notable episodes in the work are the voyage of Astolfo (q.v.) on the hippogriff to the moon, whence he brings back the lost wits of Orlando; and the self-immolation of Isabella, the widow of the Scottish prince Zerbino (qq.v.), to escape the attentions of the pagan king, Rodomont. Orlando's horse is Brigliadoro; his sword Durindana.

The best translation of the 'Orlando Furioso' into English is that of Sir John Harington (q.v.). Unfortunately the book is rare. That of Hoole is more accessible, but less inspired. There are some well-told 'Tales from Ariosto' by J. Shield Nicholson.

Orlando Innamorato, a poem by Boiardo (q.v.), published in 1487, on the subject of the falling in love of Orlando (the Roland of the Charlemagne cycle) with Angelica, daughter of Galafron, the king of Cathay. She arrives at the court of Charlemagne, with her brother Argalia, under false pretences,

to carry off the Christian knights to her father's country. Several knights attempt to win her, the chief of them being Astolfo, Ferragus, Rinaldo, and Orlando (qq.v.). Argalia is slain and Angelica flees, but, drinking of an enchanted fountain, falls in love with Rinaldo, who, drinking of another enchanted fountain, conceives a violent aversion to her. He runs away pursued by her, and they reach her father's country, where she is besieged in the capital, Albracca, by Agrican king of Tartary, to whom her hand had been promised (an incident referred to by Milton, 'Paradise Regained', iii. 337–43). Orlando comes to Angelica's rescue, slays Agrican, and carries off Angelica to France whither he has been summoned to assist Charlemagne against Agramante, king of the Moors. Owing once more to enchanted waters, Rinaldo this time falls in love with Angelica, and Angelica into hatred of him. A fierce combat ensues between Orlando and Rinaldo, suppressed by Charlemagne, who entrusts Angelica to Namo, duke of Bavaria.

The poem, which was left unfinished, was refashioned by Berni. Its sequel is in the 'Orlando Furioso' (q.v.) of Ariosto.

Orley Farm, a novel by A. Trollope (q.v.), published in 1862.

Sir Joseph Mason, having remarried late in life, is found on his death to have left by codicil Orley Farm, an estate forming part of his property, to his baby son Lucius. The validity of the codicil is disputed by the eldest son, but affirmed after a trial, and the widow and Lucius remain in possession for twenty years. Then Mr. Dockwrath, an attorney of questionable character, a tenant of part of Orley Farm, is given notice to quit, and, exasperated by what he considers unjust treatment, seeks vengeance in a revival of the question of the codicil. He discovers that there is another document that purports to have been signed by Sir Joseph on the same day as the codicil and witnessed by the same witnesses, whereas the witnesses declare that they attested only one document. The inference is that the codicil with its signatures is a forgery. The story deals with the gradual growth of the belief that Lady Mason has forged the codicil, her increasing anguish and final confession of the fact to Sir Peregrine Orme, her aged lover, her trial and acquittal, thanks to the dialectical skill of Mr. Chaffanbrass (see 'The Three Clerks'), her surrender of the property, and the influence of these events on the love-affairs and fortunes of the various minor characters in the novel.

Ormandine, in R. Johnson's 'The Seven Champions of Christendom' (q.v.), the necromancer in whose enchanted garden St. David slept for seven years, being at last released by St. George.

Ormazd or ORMUZD (AHURA MAZDA), in the Avesta or Zoroastrian religion, the god of goodness and light, in perpetual conflict with Ahriman, the spirit of evil.

ORME, ROBERT (1728–1801), born in India and a successful Anglo-Indian official, was author of the important 'History of the Military Transactions of the British Nation in Indostan' (1763–78), and of 'Historical Fragments of the Mogul Empire' (1782).

Ormond, a novel by M. Edgeworth (q.v.), published in 1817.

This is a tale of life in Ireland, and in a minor degree in fashionable Paris society in the 18th cent. The principal characters are Harry Ormond, an orphan; his fascinating but unprincipled and designing guardian, Sir Ulick O'Shane; the kind-hearted eccentric Cornelius O'Shane, the 'king of the Black Islands'; and his daughter Dora, who has been plighted, before her birth, to one or other of the twin sons of Cornelius's boon companion, Connal, with disastrous results.

Ormulum, The, a poem of some 10,000 lines in the vernacular, written in the first half of the 13th cent., by one Orm or Ormin, an Augustinian monk who probably lived in the east of England. It consists of paraphrases of the gospels for the year as arranged in the mass book, supplemented by a homily on each; but the scheme was not completed. It is orthodox and conservative in matter. It is composed of lines of fifteen syllables without rhyme or alliteration. The author has his own system of spelling and his work is important for the light it throws on the evolution of the English language and literary form.

Ormuz or HORMUZ, an ancient city on an island at the mouth of the Persian Gulf, an important centre of commerce in the Middle Ages; referred to by Milton, 'Paradise Lost', II. 2. The Portuguese were the first Europeans to take it. In 1622 the Persian 'Sultan' invoked the aid of the East India Company, and captured it (after a gallant resistance) with English vessels.

Oroonoko, or the History of the Royal Slave, a novel by Aphra Behn (q.v.), published about 1678. (For the tragedy by Southerne, see below.)

Oroonoko, grandson and heir of an African king, obtains the love of the beautiful Imoinda, daughter of the king's general, of whom the king himself is enamoured. Infuriated at learning this, the king orders Imoinda to be sold out of the country as a slave. Oroonoko himself is presently entrapped by the captain of an English slave-trading ship, and carried off to Surinam, an English colony in the West Indies. There he discovers Imoinda and is reunited to her. He presently stirs up the other slaves to escape from their miserable condition. They are pursued and induced to surrender on promise from the deputy-governor, Byam, of a pardon. Nevertheless, Oroonoko, when once in the governor's hands, is cruelly whipped. Oroonoko, determined to avenge himself on Byam, but not expecting to survive the attempt, and fearing to leave Imoinda a prey to the enraged slave-drivers, de-

cides to kill her. Imoinda welcomes her fate and meets death smiling. Oroonoko is found near her dead body, attempts to take his own life, but is prevented and cruelly executed.

The novel is remarkable as the first expression in English literature of sympathy for the oppressed Negroes. It no doubt reflects the authoress's memories of her early days in Surinam. It was made the subject of a tragedy by Southerne (q.v.), 'Oroonoko: A Tragedy', which was produced in 1695, and kept the stage for a considerable time. The play follows the broad lines of the novel, except that the deputy-governor's passion for Imoinda is one of the chief motives of action. The play is further enlivened by a comic underplot.

OROSIUS, a priest of Tarragona in Spain, *fl.* A.D. 500, disciple of St. Augustine and friend of St. Jerome, author of the 'Historia adversus Paganos', a universal history and geography, which King Alfred translated.

Orphan, The, a tragedy in blank verse by Otway (q.v.), produced in 1680.

Castalio and Polydore are the twin sons of Acasto. Monimia, the orphan daughter of a friend of Acasto's, has been brought up with them. Castalio and Polydore, loyally devoted to one another, have both fallen in love with Monimia, who returns the love of Castalio. But the latter, out of mistaken consideration for his brother, feigns indifference for Monimia. Chamont, an honest but rough and tactless soldier, brother of Monimia, comes as a guest to Acasto's house; he suspects that Monimia has been wronged by one of the young men, and annoys her with his questions. Castalio and Monimia thereupon are secretly married. Polydore, ignorant of this, and overhearing them arranging for a meeting in the night, takes Castalio's place in the darkness, and is not detected. Castalio, coming later, is shut out, and curses his wife for what he supposes to be her heartless and rebellious conduct. The truth being discovered through Charmont, the brothers fall into despair. Both kill themselves, and Monimia takes poison.

The play proved a great success, and was frequently revived. Monimia was one of Mrs. Barry's (q.v.) most celebrated parts.

Orpheus, a legendary pre-Homeric poet, said to be son of the muse Calliope, and a follower of Dionysus (q.v.). He was so skilled a player on the lyre that the wild beasts were spellbound by his music. He took part in the expedition of the Argonauts (q.v.) and helped them by his song to resist the lure of the Sirens (q.v.). He passionately loved his wife Eurydice, and, when she died of the bite of a serpent, determined to recover her. He entered the infernal regions and charmed Pluto and Persephone with his music. They consented to restore Eurydice to him on condition that he forbore to look behind him until he had emerged from Hades.

Orpheus was already in sight of the upper regions when he forgot the condition and turned back to look at Eurydice. She instantly vanished from his sight, and his attempts to rejoin her were vain. He now separated himself from the society of mankind, and the Thracian women, whom he had offended by his coldness, tore him in pieces and threw his head, which still uttered the name 'Eurydice', into the river Hebrus. Poems ascribed to Orpheus were current in Greece in the 6th and 5th cents. B.C. and were known to Plato. They embodied the doctrines of the mystical religion known as Orphicism (q.v.). The poems now extant that bear the name of Orpheus are Neoplatonist forgeries. Orpheus, in the eyes of the ancients, was the founder of religious mysteries, 'sacer interpresque deorum' in the words of Horace. There are echoes of the story of Orpheus in Milton's 'Paradise Lost', vii. 30 et seq.; 'Lycidas', 58–63; and 'L'Allegro', 145 et seq.

Orphicism, a mystic religion of ancient Greece, of which Orpheus (q.v.) was the centre. Its origins are obscure, but it appears to have developed in the 6th cent. B.C., when there was an abundant Orphic literature, little of which has survived. It sank to the level of a sectarian superstition in the 5th cent., but the profound thoughts which underlay it affected Pindar and Plato. In the Orphic doctrine, the abstract principle Time stood at the origin of all things. Time formed an egg, from which the gods proceeded. Zeus and Persephone had a son, Dionysos-Zagreus, who was torn in pieces by the Titans. They ate his limbs, but his heart was saved by Athena and brought to Zeus, and from it was afterwards born the new Dionysos. The Titans were reduced to ashes by the lightning of Zeus, and from those ashes man was formed. He thus contains something of the divine, derived from Zeus, and something of his enemies, the Titans. The Orphics taught the transmigration of souls, retribution in a future life, and final liberation from man's Titanic inheritance by the observation of strict purity (M. P. Nilsson, 'A History of Greek Religion', 1925).

Orrery, EARLS OF, see *Boyle*.

Orsino, in Shakespeare's 'Twelfth Night' (q.v.), the duke of Illyria.

Orson, see *Valentine and Orson*.

ORTEGA Y GASSET, JOSÉ (1883–1955), Spanish writer and philosopher, born in Madrid. He studied philosophy in Germany and was professor of Metaphysics in Madrid University from 1910 to 1936. He was a bitter opponent of the dictator, Primo de Rivera, and was elected to the Constituent Cortes of the Second Republic. During the Civil War he went into voluntary exile, finally returning to Spain in 1945. He was a prolific and versatile writer of essays on philosophy, literature, and politics; his newspaper articles and his journal, 'Revista de Occidente' (1923–35), were influential in introducing European writers to Spain. His publications include 'El Tema de Nuestra Tiempo' (1923, tr. 'The Modern Theme', 1933), 'España Invertebrada' (1921, tr. 'Invertebrate Spain', 1937), and 'La Rebelión de las Masas' (1930, tr. 'The Revolt of the Masses', 1932).

Ortelius, ABRAHAM (1527–98), a geographer of Antwerp, who came to England and became familiar with Camden (q.v.). He published his atlas, 'Theatrum Orbis Terrarum', in 1570.

Ortheris, STANLEY, with Terence Mulvaney and John Learoyd, the three privates in Rudyard Kipling's 'Soldiers Three'.

Orthodox Church or GREEK CHURCH, THE, the Eastern Church which recognizes the headship of the Patriarch of Constantinople, together with the national churches of Russia, Rumania, etc., which hold the same 'orthodox' creed. It repudiates the papal claim to supremacy and the celibacy of the clergy, and holds the doctrine that the Holy Ghost proceeds from the Father through the Son. It rejects the *filioque* clause of the Nicene Creed as being unauthorized by the Universal Church. In most other respects it agrees with the Roman Catholic Church. The epithet 'orthodox' was originally assumed to distinguish it from the various divisions of the Eastern Church (e.g. the Monophysite, Nestorian, etc.), which separated on points of doctrine and have not accepted all the decrees of successive general councils. [OED.] The final severance of the Orthodox Church from the Roman Church occurred in 1054, when Pope and Patriarch mutually excommunicated each other's churches. Owing to the non-acceptance by the Orthodox Church of the Gregorian calendar (q.v.), Easter Day (q.v.) falls to be observed in that Church, in most years, on a later date than in the other churches.

Orthrus, see *Geryon*.

Orton, ARTHUR, see *Tichborne Case*.

Orville, LORD, the hero of Fanny Burney's 'Evelina' (q.v.).

ORWELL, GEORGE, the pen-name of ERIC BLAIR (1903–50), who was born in Bengal, brought to England at an early age and educated at Eton. He served with the Indian Imperial Police in Burma from 1922 to 1927 and his experiences are reflected in his first novel, 'Burmese Days' (1934). Later he came back to Europe and worked in Paris and London in a series of ill-paid jobs (see 'Down and Out in Paris and London', 1933). 'Homage to Catalonia' (1938) is an autobiographical record of the Spanish Civil War, in which he fought for the Republicans and was wounded. He considered himself a democratic socialist, but he hated totalitarianism and became more and more disillusioned with the aims and methods of

Communism. His political satires, 'Animal Farm' (1945) and 'Nineteen Eighty Four' (1949) (qq.v.) were immensely popular. His other writings include the novels, 'Keep the Aspidistra Flying' (1936) and 'Coming Up for Air' (1939), and essays and studies such as 'The Road to Wigan Pier' (1937), an account of unemployment, 'Inside the Whale' (1940), 'Critical Essays' (1946), and 'Shooting an Elephant' (1950).

Osbaldeston, GEORGE (1787–1866), a famous sportsman, who was master of hounds while at Brasenose College, Oxford. He was master of the Quorn hounds, 1817–21 and 1823–8, and afterwards of the Pytchley. In 1831 he rode 200 miles in less than nine consecutive hours.

Osbaldistone, MR., FRANCIS, RASHLEIGH, and SIR HILDEBRAND, characters in Scott's 'Rob Roy' (q.v.).

Osborne, DOROTHY (1627–95), married Sir W. Temple (q.v.) in 1655. Her letters to him during the period 1652–4 were published in 1888. A new edition by G. C. Moore Smith appeared in 1928.

OSBORNE, JOHN JAMES (1929–), playwright, whose play 'Look Back in Anger' (1957) helped to give currency to the phrase 'angry young man' in reference to certain writers of the 50s. ('Angry Young Man' was the title of a work by Leslie Paul, 1951.) Other plays by Osborne include 'The Entertainer' (1957), 'Epitaph for George Dillon' (with A. Creighton, 1958), 'The World of Paul Slickey' (1959), and 'Luther' (1961).

Osborne, MR., GEORGE, his son, and MARIA and JANE, his daughters, characters in Thackeray's 'Vanity Fair' (q.v.).

Osborne, THOMAS (d. 1767), bookseller, remembered as having issued Richardson's 'Pamela' (q.v.), and published the 'Harleian Miscellany' (q.v.). He was beaten by Dr. Johnson for impertinence and ridiculed by Pope.

Oscan Fables, see *Atellan Fables*.

Oscar, the son of Ossian (q.v.), figures in many of the Ossianic poems of Macpherson.

Oscar of Alva, a poem by Lord Byron (q.v.), included in 'Hours of Idleness' (1807).

The poem shows the influence of the ballad poets and of Macpherson's 'Ossian'. Oscar the heroic, and Allan the smooth-tongued, are two brothers of the Alva clan. Oscar is to marry Mora, but disappears on the wedding-day and is not heard of for three years. Then Allan is to marry Mora in his stead. At the wedding feast, Oscar's wraith appears in the guise of a stranger chief and bids the assembled guests drink to the memory of the lost Oscar. Allan betrays himself by his terror, and is declared by the apparition his brother's murderer.

O'Shane, SIR ULICK and CORNELIUS, characters in Maria Edgeworth's 'Ormond' (q.v.).

O'SHAUGHNESSY, ARTHUR WIL-LIAM EDGAR (1844–81), poet and friend of D. G. Rossetti (q.v.), was born in London and educated privately. His books of poetry include 'An Epic of Women' (1870), 'Lays of France' (1872), and 'Music and Moonlight' (1874). His best-known poem, 'Ode', begins:
We are the music makers,
And we are the dreamers of dreams.

Osīris, a great deity of the ancient Egyptians. As king of Egypt he civilized and educated his people. He then resolved to spread civilization to other regions of the earth, and left the kingdom in the charge of his wife Isis. On his return he found his subjects disturbed by the sedition of his brother Set, and was by him murdered and his body cut into pieces. Isis, with her son Horus, defeated Set and his partisans, and revenged her husband's death. She recovered the mangled remains of his body, and had statues of him distributed over Egypt and divine honours paid to him. Osiris is sometimes identified with the sun and Isis with the moon; and the ox was taken as the symbol of the former, the cow of the latter. Osiris was regarded as the god of the dead, and his son Horus as the god of renewed life. By the Greeks Osiris was identified with Dionysus, and Set, the god of evil, with Typhon (q.v.).

OSLER, SIR WILLIAM (1849–1919), born in Canada, a great physician, Regius professor of medicine in the University of Oxford. His valuable medical library is now at McGill University, Montreal. His great 'Principles and Practice of Medicine' appeared in 1891; his essays and addresses have been collected in, e.g., 'Aequanimitas' (1904), 'An Alabama Student' (1908), and 'A Way of Life' (1913). He edited Sir T. Browne's 'Religio Medici' and William MacMichael's 'The Gold-headed Cane' (biographies of five 18th-cent. physicians). 'Too old at forty' has been attributed to him.

Osney, a wealthy priory (afterwards abbey) founded in 1129 by Robert d'Oilgi II (a Norman baron) on a branch of the Thames near Oxford, where his wife had noticed the noise of 'chattering pyes', explained by her confessor as complaints of souls in purgatory. It no longer exists.

Osorius, JEROME (d. 1580), a Portuguese, an associate of Loyola (q.v.), noted for his knowledge of Hebrew and theology, professor of theology at Coimbra, and a bishop. In 1562 he wrote an attack on the English Reformation, which was answered by Haddon, Master of Requests to Elizabeth, and by John Foxe (1577, English translation 1581). His library was seized on the occasion of Essex's expedition of 1596 and subsequently given to the newly founded Bodleian.

Ossa, a lofty mountain in Thessaly, which the Giants (q.v.) heaped on Pelion in their endeavour to reach heaven.

Ossian, the name commonly given to *Oisin,*

a legendary Gaelic warrior and bard, the son of Finn (Fingal), supposed to have lived in the 3rd cent. For the poems attributed to him, see under *Macpherson*. They deal with tales of Finn (q.v.) and his fellow warriors, which (according to Alfred Nutt) are Gaelic variants of legends common to the Celtic and other 'Aryan' races. Both Ireland and Scotland, as inhabited by Gaels, have claim to them. So far as historical facts are embodied in them against a mythical background, those facts are Irish. See also *Finn* and *Niamh*.

Oswald, ST. (*d.* 992), was nephew of Archbishop Odo (*d.* 959). He became a Benedictine monk in the abbey of Fleury, and accompanied Oskitel, archbishop of York, to Rome. On St. Dunstan's initiative he was appointed bishop of Worcester in 961, and co-operated with him and with St. Ethelwold (q.v.) in the revival of religion and learning in the land, bringing scholars from the Continent, among them the distinguished Abbo of Fleury. He founded monasteries at Westbury, Worcester, Winchcombe, and in the Isle of Ramsey. In 972 he was promoted archbishop of York, but retained the government of the see of Worcester, for which he had a special affection. St. Oswald was buried in the church of St. Mary at Worcester. He is commemorated on 28 February.

Othello, The Moor of Venice, a tragedy by Shakespeare (q.v.) acted in 1604, printed in quarto in 1622. The story is drawn from Cinthio (q.v.).

Desdemona, daughter of the Venetian senator, Brabantio, has secretly married the Moor, Othello, a gallant general in the service of the Venetian state, who has won her love by the tale of his adventures and encounters. Haled before the duke, Othello is accused by Brabantio of carrying off his daughter; simultaneously comes news of an impending attack on Cyprus by the Turks, against whom Othello is needed to lead the Venetian forces. Othello explains by what simple means he has won Desdemona, who confirms his story. Brabantio reluctantly hands his daughter over to the Moor, who at once sets out with Desdemona for Cyprus.

Othello had lately promoted to the lieutenancy Cassio, a young Florentine whom he trusted. By this promotion he had deeply offended Iago, an older soldier who thought he had a better claim, and who now plots his revenge. By a device he first discredits Cassio, as a soldier, with Othello, so that Cassio is deprived of his lieutenancy. He instigates the latter to ask Desdemona to plead in his favour with Othello, which Desdemona warmly does. At the same time he craftily instils in Othello's mind suspicion of his wife's fidelity, and jealousy of Cassio. Finally by a trick he arranges that a handkerchief given by Othello to Desdemona shall be found on Cassio. He stirs Othello to such a frenzy of jealousy that the Moor smothers Desdemona in her bed. Shortly afterwards Cassio,

whom Iago had set Roderigo, one of his associates and dupes, to assassinate, is brought in wounded. But Roderigo has failed in his purpose, and has been killed by Iago to prevent discovery of the plot; on him are found letters revealing the guilt of Iago and the innocence of Cassio. Othello, thunderstruck by the discovery that he has murdered Desdemona without cause, kills himself from remorse.

Otho the Great, a play written by Keats (q.v.) in 1819 in collaboration with his friend Charles Armitage Brown (1786-1842), who planned its construction. The plot is based on the history of the rebellion against Otho, during his Hungarian wars, by his son Ludolf and the Red Duke Conrad of Lorraine.

O'Trigger, SIR LUCIUS, a character in Sheridan's 'The Rivals' (q.v.).

Ottava rima, an Italian stanza of eight eleven-syllabled lines, rhyming a b a b a b c c, employed by Tasso, Ariosto, etc. The English adaptation, as used by Byron, has English heroic lines of ten syllables.

Otter, CAPTAIN, a character in Jonson's 'Epicœne' (q.v.).

Otterbourne, The Battle of, one of the earliest of English ballads, included in Percy's 'Reliques'.

The Scots in 1388, returning from a raid into England, attacked the castle of Otterburn in Northumberland, and after an unsuccessful assault were surprised in their camp by Henry Hotspur, Lord Percy. In the ensuing engagement James, earl of Douglas, commanding the Scottish force, was killed, and Percy taken prisoner. These events are the subject of the ballad.

Ottilia, PRINCESS OF EPPENWELZEN-SARKELD, a character in Meredith's 'Harry Richmond' (q.v.).

Ottoman Empire, the Turkish Empire, so called from its founder Othman or Osman (whence *Osmanli*), who flourished *c.* 1300.

Otuel, SIR, a pagan knight, miraculously converted, who became one of Charlemagne's paladins.

OTWAY, THOMAS (1652-85), born at Milland near Trotton in Sussex, was educated at Winchester and Christ Church, Oxford. He appeared unsuccessfully on the stage, being given a part by the kindness of Mrs. Aphra Behn (q.v.). He for many years cherished an unrequited passion for Mrs. Barry (q.v.), the actress. In 1678 he enlisted in the army in Holland and received a commission, but soon returned. He died in destitution at the early age of 33.

Of his three great tragedies, 'Don Carlos' (q.v.), in rhymed verse, was produced in 1676; 'The Orphan' (q.v.), in blank verse, in 1680; 'Venice Preserv'd' (q.v.), also in blank verse, in 1682. Of his other plays, 'Alcibiades', a tragedy, was produced in 1675 (and provided Mrs. Barry with her first successful part); 'Titus and Berenice', adapted from a tragedy by Racine, and 'The Cheats of Scapin' from a comedy by Molière, in 1677; 'Friendship in Fashion', a comedy, in 1678; 'The Soldier's Fortune', a comedy, in 1681; 'The Atheist', a comedy, in 1684. He also wrote prologues, epilogues, and a few poems. The complete works of Otway, edited by J. C. Ghose, were published in 1932.

OUIDA (MARIE LOUISE DE LA RAMÉE) (1839–1908), was born at Bury St. Edmunds, the daughter of Louis Ramé, a teacher of French. Her pseudonym, 'Ouida', was a childish mispronunciation of her name Louise. She first became known by the publication in 'Bentley's Miscellany' in 1859–60 of a number of short tales. Her forty-five novels deal chiefly with fashionable life and show a spirit of rebellion against the moral ideals reflected in much of the fiction of the time. She incurred a good deal of ridicule on account of the languid guardsmen, miracles of strength, courage, and beauty, whom she frequently presented as her heroes, and of her amusing mistakes in matters of men's sports and occupations. But these faults were redeemed by her gift for stirring narrative and other merits. Her novels include 'Under Two Flags' (1867), 'Tricotrin' (1869), 'Puck' (1870), 'Folle Farine' (1871), 'Two Little Wooden Shoes' (1874), 'Moths' (1880), 'In Maremma' (1882), and 'Bimbi, Stories for Children' (1882). She wrote some good animal stories, of which 'A Dog of Flanders' (1872) is the best. Her novel 'A Village Commune' (1881) was highly praised by Ruskin as a faithful picture of peasant life.

Oulton, THE OLD MAN OF: Borrow (q.v.).

Our Mutual Friend, a novel by Dickens (q.v.), published in monthly parts between May 1864 and Nov. 1865.

John Harmon returns from the exile to which he has been sent by a harsh father, a rich dust-contractor; he expects to receive the inheritance to which his father has attached the condition that he shall marry a certain girl, Bella Wilfer. Bella is unknown to him, and he confides to a mate of the ship which is bringing him home his intention of concealing his identity until he has formed some judgement of his allotted wife. The mate lures him to a riverside haunt, attempts to murder him, throws his body into the river, and is in turn murdered and his body likewise thrown into the river. Harmon recovers and escapes; the mate's body is found after some days, and, owing to Harmon's papers found upon it, it is taken to be that of Harmon. Harmon's intention of remaining unknown is thus facilitated, and he assumes the name of John Rokesmith, and becomes the secretary of the kindly, disinterested Mr. Boffin, old Harmon's foreman, who, in default of young Harmon, inherits the property. He is thrown into close contact with Bella, a flighty minx, who is adopted by Boffin, and who is turned by her first taste of wealth into an arrogant mercenary

jade. Rokesmith nevertheless falls in love with her and is contemptuously rejected. Harmon's identity is now discovered by the amiable Mrs. Boffin, and the Boffins, devoted to their old master's son and convinced of Bella's soundness of heart, contrive a plot to prove her. Boffin pretends to be transformed by his wealth into a hard and griping miser, and heaps indignities on Harmon, who is finally dismissed with contumely. Bella, awakened to the evils of wealth and to the merits of Rokesmith, flies from the Boffins and marries her suitor. His identity presently comes to light, and with his assistance the scheme of the one-legged old villain, Silas Wegg, to blackmail Boffin is exposed.

Concurrently with this main theme we have the story of the love of Eugene Wrayburn, a careless insolent young barrister, for Lizzy Hexam, daughter of a disreputable boatman. His rival for her affections, Bradley Headstone, a schoolmaster, attempts to murder Wrayburn. The latter is saved by Lizzy and marries her. Among the notable characters in the book are the Veneerings, types of social parvenus; the good Jew Riah; the blackmailing waterside villain, Rogue Riderhood; Jenny Wren, the dolls' dressmaker; Bella Wilfer's grotesque father, mother, and sister; and the spirited Betty Higden, an old woman with a haunting dread of the workhouse.

OVERBURY, SIR THOMAS (1581–1613), of a Warwickshire family, was educated at Queen's College, Oxford, and went to the Middle Temple. He opposed the marriage of his patron, Robert Carr (afterwards earl of Somerset), with the divorced countess of Essex, and on the pretext of his refusal of diplomatic employment was sent to the Tower, where he was slowly poisoned by agents of Lady Essex. Four of these were hanged; Somerset and his wife were convicted and pardoned. The prosecution was conducted by F. Bacon (q.v.). The whole business is an historical mystery. Overbury's poem 'A Wife' was published in 1614. But he is chiefly remembered for his 'Characters', on the model of those of Theophrastus (q.v.)—not all of which, however, were written by Overbury himself—including such types as 'The fayre and happy Milkmaid', 'The Mere Fellow of a College', etc. The first edition of these appeared in 1614. His 'Miscellaneous Works in Verse and Prose' were edited by E. F. Rimbault in 1856.

Overdo, JUSTICE, a character in Jonson's 'Bartholomew Fayre' (q.v.).

Overreach, SIR GILES, a character in Massinger's 'A New Way to pay Old Debts' (q.v.).

OVID (PUBLIUS OVIDIUS NASO) (43 B.C.–A.D. 18), the Roman poet, was banished from Rome by Augustus in A.D. 8 to Tomi (Kustendje) near the mouths of the Danube for reasons connected with his 'Ars Amatoria' and some scandal affecting the imperial family, and there died. His 'Tristia' and 'Epistulae ex Ponto' contain a pathetic account of his sufferings in exile. His works include (in rough chronological order) the 'Amores', 'Heroides', 'Ars Amatoria', 'Remedia Amoris', 'Metamorphoses', 'Fasti', 'Tristia', and 'Epistulae ex Ponto'. Ovid wrote in elegiacs (q.v.), and was the favourite Latin poet of the Middle Ages.

Owain, SIR, see *Patrick's Purgatory.*

OWEN, JOHN (1563?–1622), educated at Winchester College and New College, Oxford, was the author of several volumes of Latin epigrams, mostly elegiac couplets, marked by great neatness and wit, which have been compared to those of Martial. They deal with a wide range of subjects, institutions such as Oxford University, literary works, imaginary personages, and familiar types. They were translated into several languages and frequently reprinted down to the 19th cent.

OWEN, SIR RICHARD (1804–92), educated at Lancaster School with Whewell (q.v.), became conservator of the Hunterian museum and first Hunterian professor of comparative anatomy and physiology. He did much to advance the science of animal structure. His great feat was to reconstruct the extinct New Zealand moa, a giant wingless bird, from its femur (1839). His chief works include 'Lectures on the Comparative Anatomy and Physiology of the Invertebrate Animals' (1843–6), 'A History of British Fossil Mammals and Birds' (1846), 'A History of British Fossil Reptiles' (1849–84), 'Geology and Inhabitants of the Ancient World' (1854), etc. He opposed Darwin's views on evolution and was a very fierce controversialist.

OWEN, ROBERT (1771–1858), socialist and philanthropist, was a successful owner of cotton-spinning mills in Manchester. He became famous for his 'institution for the formation of character' (New Lanark), including infant schools and schools of two other grades (opened in 1816), and for other proposals of social reform. His example was largely instrumental in bringing about the Factory Act of 1819. Owen was the pioneer of co-operation between labour and consumption. His head was perhaps a little turned by the adulation he received, and at last he became mainly a dreamer of noble (but unpractical) dreams. He published 'A New View of Society' in 1813, 'Revolution in Mind and Practice' in 1849, and his autobiography in 1857–8.

OWEN, WILFRED (1893–1918), poet of the First World War, killed just before the Armistice and before he was able to complete the book of poetry he had planned, of which he said in the preface 'the subject of it is War and the pity of War'. His Collected Poems were published in 1920 by his friend Siegfried Sassoon, a new edition appeared in 1931 by Edmund Blunden, and a third in 1963 by C. Day Lewis, with a memoir by Blunden.

Owl and the Nightingale, The, a poem of some 2,000 lines, in octosyllabic couplets, probably of the early 13th cent. It is a debate between the grave Owl and the gay Nightingale as to the benefits they confer on man, symbolizing perhaps respectively the religious poet and the poet of love. It is marked by a sense of the charm of nature in its milder aspects, the coming of spring and the golden autumn. The poem is attributed to one Nicholas de Guildford (*fl.* 1250), who is stated in the poem to have lived at Portisham in Dorset; but John of Guildford (probably *fl.* 1225), who is known to have written verse about this time, is also possibly the author.

Owlglass, see *Eulenspiegel.*

Ox, THE DUMB, see *Aquinas.*

Oxford and Cambridge Magazine, The, a periodical of the year 1856, of which twelve monthly numbers appeared, financed mainly by William Morris (q.v.). Among its contributors were Morris and Burne-Jones (of Oxford), Lushington (of Cambridge), and by invitation D. G. Rossetti, whose 'Burden of Nineveh' appeared in its pages.

Oxford, JOHN, EARL OF, figuring as the merchant Philipson, a character in Scott's 'Anne of Geierstein' (q.v.).

Oxford English Dictionary, The. The scheme of 'a completely new English Dictionary' was conceived in 1858, and Herbert Coleridge (1830–61), and after him Dr. F. J. Furnivall (1825–1910), were the first editors. Their work, which covered twenty years, consisted only in the collection of materials, and it was not until Dr. J. A. H. Murray (q.v.) took the matter up in 1878 that the preparation of the Dictionary began to take active form. The first part was published in 1884, at which time Dr. Murray estimated that the whole might be completed in another twelve years. It was not in fact finished until 1928, seventy years from the inception of the undertaking. Dr. (afterwards Sir James) Murray, who laid down the lines of the work, did not live to see it completed, but more than half was produced under his personal editorship. He was succeeded by Dr. H. Bradley (q.v.), Dr. (later Sir) William Alexander Craigie (1867–1957), and Dr. Charles Talbot Onions (1873–1965). The essential feature of the Dictionary is its historical method, by which the meaning and form of the words are traced from their earliest appearance on the basis of an immense number of quotations, collected by more than 800 voluntary workers. The Dictionary contains a record of 414,825 words, whose history is illustrated by 1,827,306 quotations. An important supplement appeared in 1933. A reissue of the main work has also been published. The original title of the work was 'A New English Dictionary on Historical Principles' (abbreviated as NED.). The title

'The Oxford English Dictionary' first appeared in the reprint of 1933.

Oxford Gazette, The, see *Gazette.*

Oxford Movement or TRACTARIAN MOVEMENT, THE, a movement initiated in 1833 in revival of a higher conception than was generally prevalent of the position and functions of the Church, as 'more than a merely human institution' and as possessing 'privileges, sacraments, a ministry, ordained by Christ'. The movement began with a sermon preached in July 1833 at Oxford by Keble (q.v.) before the judges of assize, on national apostasy, directed against the Latitudinarian and Erastian tendencies of the day. This was followed by concerted action among the men who shared his views, and in September of the same year appeared the first of the 'Tracts for the Times' (q.v.). The principal leaders of the movement were, besides Keble, Newman, R. H. Froude, and Pusey (qq.v.). It was Pusey, already Regius professor of Hebrew, and a man of real learning (he joined the party in 1835), who first gave the movement cohesion, fame, and a name; its adherents soon came to be called 'Puseyites'. Other leaders were J. W. Bowden, W. Palmer, A. P. Perceval, and Isaac Williams. In course of time, with new recruits, including W. G. Ward (q.v.), new forces came into play, which had a disruptive effect on the movement, while public feeling was roused against it by the issue of the first volumes of the 'Literary Remains of Richard Hurrell Froude' (1838), with its strictures on the Reformation. Newman's famous Tract XC on the compatibility of the Thirty-nine Articles with Roman Catholic theology intensified the general hostility. Newman's own confidence in his position was presently shaken by an article by Dr. Wiseman. In 1843 he resigned his living and in 1845 he joined the Church of Rome. In the latter year W. G. Ward's book, 'The Ideal of the Christian Church', was condemned by Oxford Convocation. From this time the movement in its original form was broken up.

A remarkable history of the Oxford Movement was written by Dean Church (1891), while much light is also thrown on it by the 'Autobiography' of I. Williams (q.v.) and Newman's 'Apologia'.

Oxford Sausage, The, see *Warton (T.).*

Oxford Street took its name early in the 18th cent. from Edward Harley, 2nd earl of Oxford, the collector of the Harleian MSS., who obtained by marriage the Marylebone estate of John Holles, duke of Newcastle. It was the old Tyburn (q.v.) Road. This, in turn, probably followed approximately the line of the ancient Roman road from east to west, the Here Street, which crossed Watling Street where the Marble Arch now stands.

Oxford University was organized as a *studium generale* soon after 1167, perhaps as a result of a migration of students from Paris.

A Legatine Ordinance of 1214 mentions its Chancellor. Roger Bacon and Duns Scotus testify to its importance in the 13th cent. University College, the first of its colleges, was founded in 1249, Balliol about 1263, Merton in 1264. Oxford was the home of Wycliffism in the 14th cent. Erasmus lectured there, and Grocyn, Colet, and More (qq.v.) were among its famous scholars in the 15th–16th cents. The University was incorporated by Act of 1571. It sided with the king in the Civil War. Under James II it opposed the king's attempt to open the University to Roman Catholics, a quarrel which culminated in the king's endeavour to impose his nominee as president of Magdalen (1687). See also *Oxford Movement, All Souls, Balliol, Christ Church, Magdalen, Merton.*

Oxford University Press, THE, a publishing and printing business owned by the University and directed by its Delegates of the Press, of whom the Vice-Chancellor is *ex officio* chairman. Its aims are to produce books of religious, scholarly, and educational value, and its surplus profits are devoted to financing the editing and production of unremunerative works of this kind.

Printing in Oxford by independent craftsmen began in the 15th cent. (see University Presses), and in 1584 one of these was appointed 'Printer to the University'. This title was borne by a succession of printers in the 17th cent. and was revived in 1925 for the head of the printing department of the Press. One press at Oxford was excepted from the prohibition of printing outside London by a decree of the Star Chamber in 1586, and in 1632 a royal charter allowed the University three presses and to print and sell 'all manner of books'. Archbishop Laud in 1634 bound the University to provide itself with a printing house; but a press under its immediate control did not come into being until 1690. In the meantime John Fell (q.v.) had won an international reputation for Oxford books by his exercise of the University's privilege of printing, let to him in 1672. By his bequest his unsold books and printing equipment became the property of the University in 1690.

Under the management of the Delegates since then the Press has produced such famous books as Clarendon's 'History' (1702), Blackstone's 'Commentaries' (1769), Kennicott's Hebrew Bible (1780), Clerk Maxwell's 'Treatise on Electricity and Magnetism' (1873), the Revised Version of the English Bible (1885), and 'The Oxford English Dictionary', completed in 1928, besides many millions of Bibles and prayer books and, in recent times, of standard classical and modern texts and school books.

The copyright in Lord Clarendon's works, once very profitable, is secured to the University in perpetuity, and in his honour the building to which the Press moved in 1829 was named 'The Clarendon Press'. This address is the imprint given to learned books whose production is supervised by the Secretary to the Delegates at Oxford. Distribution of these and other books produced at Oxford together with the publication of a larger class of books with the imprint of 'The Oxford University Press, London' has been undertaken since 1880 by the Delegates' London office.

Oxonian, of or belonging to the University of Oxford.

Oxymōron, from two Greek words meaning 'sharp', 'dull', a rhetorical figure by which two incongruous or contradictory terms are united in an expression so as to give it point; e.g. 'Faith unfaithful kept him falsely true.'

Oyer and terminer, COMMISSION OF, a commission 'to hear and determine', granted to judges on circuit, directing them to hold courts for the trial of offences.

Ozymandias of Egypt, a sonnet by P. B. Shelley (q.v.). The Ramesseum (of Rameses II) at Thebes is called by Diodorus Siculus (i. 47 et seq.) the tomb of Ozymandias.

P

P.E.N., an international association of Poets, Playwrights, Editors, Essayists, and Novelists founded in 1921 by Mrs. Dawson Scott, under the presidency of J. Galsworthy, to promote co-operation between writers all over the world in the interests of literature, freedom of expression, and international goodwill.

Pacha of Many Tales, The, a novel (1835) by Marryat (q.v.).

Pacific Ocean, THE, said to have been so named by the Portuguese explorer Magellan, who was the first to navigate it (1520), on account of the calm weather he experienced there.

Pacolet, in the tale of 'Valentine and Orson' (q.v.), a dwarf in the service of the Lady Clerimond. He possessed a winged horse, who bore off Valentine, Orson, and Clerimond from the castle of the giant Ferragus.

'Pacolet' is the name of Mr. Bickerstaff's 'familiar' in Steele's 'The Tatler' (No. 15), and of Norna's dwarf in Scott's 'The Pirate' (q.v.).

Pactōlus, a river in Lydia, rising in Mt. Tmolus, and falling into the Hermus after watering the city of Sardes. It was in this river that Midas (q.v.) washed himself when his touch converted everything to gold. Its sands were in consequence turned into gold.

PACUVIUS, Roman tragic poet, born about 220 B.C. Only fragments of his work survive.

Padishah, a Persian title, meaning 'lord King', equivalent to 'Great King' or 'Emperor', applied in Persia to the Shah, in Europe (in former days) usually to the Sultan of Turkey, in India to the Great Mógul.

Padlock, The, a comic opera by Bickerstaffe (q.v.), produced in 1768 and very successful.

The elderly Don Diego is the temporary guardian of the young Leonora and is about to make her his wife. But, in spite of a large padlock on the door, Leander, a young lover, presents himself during Diego's absence, cajoles the duenna and Mungo, the negro servant, and gains admission to the lady. Diego returns unexpectedly, but sensibly accepts the situation and handsomely endows Leonora. The story is taken from one of Cervantes's novels.

Prior (q.v.) wrote a short poem called 'An English Padlock', containing advice to the jealous husband of a young wife. It contains the well-known lines:

> Be to her virtues very kind;
> Be to her faults a little blind;
> Let all her ways be unconfin'd,
> And clasp a padlock on her mind.

Paean, in Greek antiquity an invocation or thanksgiving addressed to Apollo (later to other gods also), so called from its refrain 'Iē Paiōn'; especially a song of triumph after victory. The word is now used for a song of praise or thanksgiving, or a shout or song of triumph.

Paeon, a metrical foot of four syllables, one long and three short, named, according to the position of the long syllable, a first, second, third, or fourth paeon.

Paeonia, the ancient name of a country lying north of Macedonia and east of Illyria, on the upper course of what is now the Vardar.

Paetus, CAECĪNA, was sentenced to death in A.D. 42 on a charge of conspiring against the emperor Claudius. When he hesitated to take his own life in accordance with the sentence, his wife Arria stabbed herself and handed him the dagger, saying, 'Paetus, it does not hurt' (Plin. Ep. iii. 16).

PAGAN, ISOBEL (*Tibby*) (*d.* 1821), hostess of an Ayrshire inn, the reputed author of the songs 'Ca' the Yowes to the Knowes' and 'The Crook and Plaid', in which there is an anticipation of the genius of Burns.

Paganini, Nicolo (1782–1840), a famous Italian violinist, whose playing produced an extraordinary effect on his hearers. 'With the first notes his audience was spell-bound; there was certainly in him . . . a daemonic element which irresistibly took hold of those that came within his sphere' (Grove).

Page, Mrs. Page, and Anne Page, their daughter, characters in Shakespeare's 'The Merry Wives of Windsor' (q.v.).

Pagett, M.P., the subject of one of Kipling's poems, an arrogant M.P. who goes to India on a short visit to 'study the East', but is cured of his arrogance by a taste of Indian hot weather, and flees from the country before his time is up.

Pahlavi or Pehlevi, the name given by the followers of Zoroaster to the character in which are written the ancient translations of their sacred books; also the name for Middle Persian speech (the language transitional from Old Persian to Modern Persian) written in Aramaic script. The word is used in this sense in FitzGerald's translation of Omar Khayyám.

PAIN, BARRY ERIC ODELL (1864–1928), British novelist, author of 'The One Before' (1902), 'Eliza' (1900), 'Eliza Getting On' (1911), 'Exit Eliza' (1912), 'Eliza's Son' (1913), etc.

PAINE, THOMAS (1737–1809), son of a staymaker and small farmer of Thetford. After following various humble avocations he became an excise officer, but was dismissed from the service in 1772 in connexion with an agitation for an increase of excisemen's pay. He sailed for America, where he published in 1776 his pamphlet, 'Common Sense', a history of the transactions that had led to the war with England, and in 1776–83 a series of pamphlets 'The Crisis', encouraging resistance to England. He held various posts under the American government until 1787, when he returned to England. In 1791 he published the first part of his 'Rights of Man' (q.v.) in reply to Burke's 'Reflections on the Revolution in France' (q.v.), and the second part in 1792. He fled to France to avoid prosecution, and was there warmly received and elected a member of the Convention. He opposed the execution of Louis XVI and narrowly escaped the guillotine. He published in 1793 'The Age of Reason', a defence of Deism against Christianity and Atheism, written in a tone of arrogance and coarse violence. This work increased the odium in which he was held in England. He returned to America in 1802, where his 'Age of Reason' and his opposition to Washington and the federalists made him unpopular. He died at New York. His connexion with the American struggle and afterwards with the French Revolution gave him a unique position, and his writings, which show him a shrewd political thinker, became a sort of textbook for the extreme radical party in England.

PAINTER, WILLIAM, see *Palace of Pleasure.*

Pair of Blue Eyes, A, a novel by Hardy (q.v.), published in 1873.

The scene of the story is the northern coast of Cornwall. Stephen Smith, a young architect, having come to Endelstow to restore a church tower, falls in love with Elfride Swancourt, the blue-eyed daughter of the vicar. It comes to light that he is the son of humble parents, and the vicar is highly incensed at the idea of his daughter's marrying him. Stephen and Elfride run away together to be married, but the project is frustrated by the girl's vacillation, and Stephen, hoping for better luck when he has made a fortune, accepts a post in India. While he is there, his place as Elfride's wooer is taken by Henry Knight, a man of letters, formerly Stephen's friend and patron. Elfride saves his life on a cliff, and they are engaged. But Knight is rather a stern character. He has never kissed a woman in his life, and expects the same inexperience in his bride. Elfride's escapade with Stephen has been witnessed by a woman who, having a motive for revenge on Elfride, reveals what she knows to Knight, putting the worst aspect on the matter. Knight harshly breaks off the engagement and leaves Elfride heart-stricken. After a time he and Stephen meet; Stephen learns that Elfride is still unmarried, Knight learns the true facts of her escapade. They both rush down to Cornwall, only to find that the train which carries them also carries her corpse.

There is, incidentally, some admirable Shakespearian dialogue among the workmen preparing the vault of the Luxellian family for a burial.

Palace of Pleasure, a collection of translations into English of 'pleasant histories and excellent novels' 'out of divers good and commendable authors', made by William Painter (1540?–94), master of Sevenoaks school in Kent, published in 1566 and 1567. It served as a storehouse from which the Elizabethan dramatists drew many of their plots. Many of the translations are from Boccaccio and Bandello, but the compiler draws also on Herodotus and Livy.

Palace of Westminster, see *Westminster Palace.*

Paladins, The, in the cycle of Charlemagne legends, were the twelve peers who accompanied the king. The origin of the conception is seen in the 'Chanson de Roland' (see *Roland*), where the twelve peers are merely an association of particularly brave warriors, under the leadership of Roland and Oliver, who all perish at Roncevaux. From the Spanish war the idea was transported by later writers to other parts of the cycle, and Charlemagne is found always surrounded by twelve peers. In England the word 'douceper' (see *Douzepers*) in the singular was even adopted to signify a paladin. The names of the twelve are differently stated by different authors, most of the original names given by the 'Chanson de Roland' being forgotten by them; but Roland and Oliver figure in all the enumerations. Among the best known are Fierabras or Ferumbras and Ogier the Dane. In the early 13th (and probably in the late 12th) cents. there were in fact 'Twelve Peers of France', forming a 'Court of Peers', six ecclesiastical and six lay. This court in 1202 declared King John deprived of his fiefs in France.

Palaemon, see *Ino*.

Palaeologi, a Byzantine dynasty which furnished rulers of the Eastern empire from 1261 (Michael Palaeologus) to the fall of Constantinople (1453).

Palafox, in Wordsworth's sonnet ('Sonnets to Liberty', 1810), was José de Palafox y Melzi, a Spanish general, who defended Saragossa against the French in 1808.

Pălămēdēs, a Grecian chief, son of Nauplius king of Euboea, sent by the Greek princes to oblige Odysseus to join the expedition to Troy. Odysseus, reluctant to leave his wife Penelope, feigned madness, but Palamedes exposed the deceit. Odysseus in consequence conceived a bitter enmity against him, and forged a letter supposed to be written by King Priam to Palamedes treating of the delivery of the Greek army into Trojan hands. He also had a large sum of money concealed in a hole in Palamedes' tent, and by these means caused him to be convicted of treason and stoned to death. Palamedes is credited with much learning and ingenuity, the addition of certain letters to the alphabet of Cadmus, and the invention of various games and devices.

Palamides, Sir, in the Arthurian legend, a Saracen. He falls in love with La Beale Isoud in Ireland, and comes into conflict with Tristram (q.v.), who defeats him and makes him be baptized. His constant occupation is the pursuit of the 'Questing Beast'.

Palamon and Arcite, the subject of 'The Knight's Tale' in Chaucer's 'The Canterbury Tales' (q.v.). This tale was paraphrased in heroic couplets by Dryden (q.v.) under the title 'Palamon and Arcite'. It is also the subject of Fletcher's 'The Two Noble Kinsmen' (q.v.), and of a play, no longer extant, but praised by Meres, by Richard Edwards (q.v.).

Palatine, see *County Palatine, Elector Palatine*.

Pale, THE ENGLISH, also simply THE PALE, in Ireland, that part of Ireland (varying in extent at different times) over which English jurisdiction was established. The term appears to have been first used (in respect of Ireland) in a statute of Edward IV, which orders it to be fortified with a double ditch and palisade. The Statute of Kilkenny (1367) had recognized some such condition, viz. that the inhabitants of that part of Ireland

where the king's writ ran were not to have intercourse with the wild Irishry outside it. The term was also applied to the territory of Calais.

Palemon, see *Lavinia and Palemon*.

Palēs, in Roman religion, a rustic spirit, supposed to protect shepherds and their flocks.

Palestrina, GIOVANNI PIERLUIGI DA (1524?–94), born at Palestrina near Rome, the great composer of sacred music for the Roman Catholic Church. He composed a large number of masses, litanies, hymns, and chants, and was hailed as the 'saviour of music' on account of his 'Missa papae Marcelli' (of which the story is told in 'N. & Q.', III. vi. 84). His 'Improperia' are still sung every Good Friday in the Sistine Chapel.

PALEY, WILLIAM (1743–1805), educated at Christ's College, Cambridge, of which he became fellow. He was senior wrangler in 1763. Paley was one of the principal exponents of theological utilitarianism, of which his 'Moral and Political Philosophy' (q.v.), published in 1785, is the textbook. In his 'Horae Paulinae' (1790), 'Evidences of Christianity' (1794), and 'Natural Theology' (1802) he finds proof of the existence of God in the design apparent in natural phenomena, and particularly in the human body, and controverts the theory of the adaptation of the organism to its circumstances by use, taking up a position that has been weakened by subsequent evolutionary discoveries. For his utilitarian theory of morality see *Moral and Political Philosophy*.

PALGRAVE, SIR FRANCIS (1788–1861), the son of Meyer Cohen, a Jew, was the author of 'The Rise and Progress of the English Commonwealth' (1832) and of 'The History of Normandy and England' (1851–64); also of an 'Essay on the Original Authority of the King's Council' (1834) and of 'Truth and Fictions of the Middle Ages: the Merchant and the Friar' (1837). He was deputy-keeper of the records, 1838–61, and rendered great service in promoting the critical study in England of medieval history.

PALGRAVE, FRANCIS TURNER (1824–97), son of Sir F. Palgrave (q.v.), was educated at Charterhouse and Balliol College, Oxford, and was a close friend of Tennyson. He was an official in the education department from 1855 to 1884. From 1885 to 1895 he was professor of poetry at Oxford. He is chiefly remembered for his anthology, 'The Golden Treasury of Songs and Lyrics' (1861; second series, 1896), but was also himself a poet, and published several volumes of lyrics, etc. 'The Visions of England' (1881) is perhaps his best work.

PALGRAVE, WILLIAM GIFFORD (1826–88), son of Sir F. Palgrave (q.v.), educated at Charterhouse and Trinity College, Oxford, became a Jesuit missionary in Syria and Arabia. He published in 1865 his 'Narrative of a Year's Journey through Central and Eastern Arabia'. Some doubt has been cast on the accuracy of his reminiscences. He severed his connexion with the Jesuits in 1865 and entered the diplomatic service. His pleasant romance 'Hermann Agha', somewhat after the style of Hope's 'Anastasius' (q.v.), appeared in 1872.

Palimpsest, from πάλιν 'again', and ψηστός 'rubbed smooth', a manuscript in which a later writing is written over an effaced earlier writing. Of frequent occurrence in the early Middle Ages because of the cost of parchment.

Palindrome, from παλίνδρομος, 'running back again', a word, verse, or sentence that reads the same forwards or backwards, e.g.:

Lewd did I live & evil I did dwel

(Phillips, 1706),

and the Latin line descriptive of moths:

In girum imus noctes et consumimur igni.

Palinode, from παλινῳδία, 'singing over again', a recantation. 'Palinode' is the name of the Catholic shepherd in the fifth eclogue of Spenser's 'The Shepheards Calender' (q.v.).

Palinūrus, the pilot of Aeneas, who 'nodded at the helm', fell into the sea, and after reaching the shore was murdered by the inhabitants of the place.

Palisse, LA, see *La Palisse*.

Palissy, BERNARD (1510–89), a celebrated French potter, who discovered the secret of Italian enamels. He was a Huguenot and died in the Bastille for his faith.

Pall Mall, London, from the obsolete French *pallemaille*, literally 'ball-mallet', the name of a game introduced into England in the 17th cent., in which a wooden ball was driven through an iron ring suspended at some height above the ground in a long alley. [OED.]. The present street was developed from one of these alleys. Nell Gwyn lived there in the latter part of the 17th cent., and a century later Gainsborough and Cosway.

Pall Mall Gazette, The, was founded in 1865 by Frederick Greenwood (1830–1909), to combine the features of a newspaper with the literary features of the 'Spectator' and 'Saturday Review'. Its name was taken from Thackeray's 'Pendennis' (q.v.), where Captain Shandon in the Marshalsea prepares the prospectus of 'The Pall Mall Gazette', 'written by gentlemen for gentlemen'. Its early contributors included Sir Henry Maine, Anthony Trollope, and Sir James Fitzjames Stephen. In 1880, 'The Pall Mall Gazette' having been bought by a Radical, Greenwood was superseded by John Morley as editor, with W. T. Stead as his lieutenant; and Greenwood produced instead the newly founded Conservative 'St. James's Gazette'.

Palladian architecture, 18th-cent. English architecture based on the study of Palladio (q.v.). The style is illustrated in Colen Campbell's 'Vitruvius Brittanicus' (published in three volumes, 1715, 1717, and 1725, containing designs of contemporary architecture).

Palladio, ANDREA (1518–80), Italian architect. The refinement of his classical detail and originality of his domestic architecture made his work particularly attractive to English architects, from Inigo Jones, who possessed a copy of his 'I quattro libri dell' architettura' (1570) in which he made copious notes (now in Worcester College, Oxford), to Lord Burlington and his associates who developed the Palladian style based on a study of his Venetian villas.

Palladis Tamia, see *Meres*.

Palladium, a statue of Pallas Athene, which was supposed to confer security on the town that contained it and was accordingly kept hidden. The most celebrated statue of this kind was that supposed to have fallen from heaven when Ilus was building Troy, where it was retained until carried off by Odysseus and Diomedes, or, according to another version, by Aeneas.

Pallas, a name of *Athene* (q.v.).

Palliser, PLANTAGENET, and his wife **LADY GLENCORA,** characters appearing in several of A. Trollope's (q.v.) novels ('The Small House at Allington', 'Can You Forgive Her?', 'Phineas Finn', 'The Prime Minister', and 'The Duke's Children'). He is the nephew and heir of the duke of Omnium and becomes prime minister, 'a very noble gentleman—such a one as justifies to the nation the seeming anomaly of an hereditary peerage and of primogeniture', wrote the author himself. He looked upon his presentation of Palliser and his wife in these novels as the best work of his life.

Palm Sunday, the Sunday next before Easter Day, observed, in commemoration of Jesus Christ's triumphal entry into Jerusalem, by processions in which branches of palm, or, in northern regions, of other trees, are carried.

Palmerin of England (*Palmeirim de Inglaterra*), a chivalric romance of uncertain authorship, attributed to the Portuguese Francisco de Moraes (*c.* 1500–72) or the Spaniard, Luis Hurtado (1530–79?).

The 'Palmerines' consist of eight books dealing with exploits and loves of Palmerin de Oliva, emperor of Constantinople, and his various descendants, of which Palmerin of England is the subject of the sixth. The daughter of Palmerin de Oliva, Flerida by name, married Don Duardos, son of Fadrique, king of Great Britain, and became the mother of Palmerin of England and his brother, Floriano of the Desert. Duardos having been imprisoned in the castle of the giant Dramusiando by Eutropa, a magician, a savage carries off the young children (Palmerin and Floriano) intending them as food for his hunting lions, but his wife insists on bringing them up. Palmerin is taken to Constantinople and appointed to wait on his cousin Polinarda, with whom he falls in love; while Floriano is taken to London and appointed to wait on Flerida. Palmerin and Floriano undertake the quest of Don Duardos, and the former is successful. Thereafter the identity of the brothers is revealed and Palmerin marries Polinarda. Then the Soldan advances against the Christians and demands the surrender of Polinarda as a condition of peace. Finally the Turks attack Constantinople; all the Turks and most of the Christians perish, but Palmerin survives. Southey (q.v.) published a revised translation of this romance (1807).

'Palmerin of England' and 'Amadis of Gaul' were two romances of chivalry specially excepted from the holocaust of such works carried out by the curate and the barber in 'Don Quixote' (q.v.).

Palmȳra or TADMOR, the capital of a country situated east of Syria, once the seat of the famous Zenobia (q.v.), now in ruins.

PALTOCK, ROBERT (1697–1767), author of 'Peter Wilkins' (q.v.). He was an attorney of Clement's Inn.

Pam, (1) a familiar abbreviation of Palmerston (Henry John Temple, third Viscount Palmerston, 1784–1865, the statesman); (2) the knave of clubs, ranking as the highest trump in 'five-card loo', apparently an abbreviation of French *pamphile*, the name of a card game, and of the knave of clubs in it.

Pamēla, a character in Sidney's 'Arcadia' (q.v.).

Pam'ela, or Virtue Rewarded, a novel by Richardson (q.v.), published in 1740.

This was the author's first work of fiction, and the first example of what may be called the modern English novel of character. The story is told in a series of letters from the heroine, Pamela Andrews, a young maidservant, whose mistress has just died when the story opens. The lady's son, Mr. B., becomes enamoured of Pamela, and, taking a dishonourable advantage of her position, pursues her with his advances. She indignantly repels them, leaves the house, is pursued by B., and shows considerable astuteness in defending herself. Finally B., being much in love with her, comes to terms and decides to marry her.

The second part of the book (published in 1741), which is less interesting, presents Pamela married, suffering with dignity and sweetness the burden of a profligate husband.

The novel was translated into French and Dutch and made the object of several skits. The most famous of these were 'An Apology for the Life of Mrs. Shamela Andrews' (1741), of which the authorship is uncertain (it was perhaps by Fielding), and Fielding's 'Joseph Andrews' (q.v.).

Pamphlet, a small unbound treatise, especially on a subject of current interest. The word is apparently a generalized use of *Pamphilet*, a familiar name of the 12th-century Latin amatory poem or comedy called 'Pamphilus, seu de Amore', a highly popular opuscule in the 13th cent. [OED.]

Pan, the god of shepherds and huntsmen, represented as a monster, with two small horns on his head, flat nose, ruddy complexion, and the legs and feet of a goat. He is said by some authors to have been the son of Hermes and to have been carried to heaven by his father, where the oddity of his appearance greatly delighted the gods, and in particular Bacchus. Pan invented the flute with seven reeds, which he called *syrinx* in honour of the beautiful nymph of that name. Shelley's 'Hymn of Pan' is an echo of a story that Pan once engaged in a musical contest with Apollo (see *Midas*). His worship was widespread and particularly established in Arcadia. Plutarch mentions that in the reign of Tiberius a ship with passengers was driven near the coast of the Isles of Paxi. A loud voice was heard calling to one Thamus that the great god Pan was dead. The emperor ordered an inquiry, but the astrologers were unable to explain the meaning of this supernatural announcement. The incident in Christian legend is associated with the birth of Christ. According to M. Salomon Reinach the explanation may be found in the lament of the worshippers of the god Thamuz (q.v.), 'θαμμοῦζ ὁ πάμμεγας τεθνῆκε', overheard and misunderstood by the passengers of a ship while his annual obsequies were being celebrated.

PANIC FEAR is the fear that seizes people without obvious cause: Pan was thought responsible for the alarms felt by people, especially travellers in remote and desolate places.

Panchatantra, a Sanskrit collection of fables, from which are derived the 'Fables of Bidpai' (q.v.) and many more or less direct European versions.

Pancks, a character in Dickens's 'Little Dorrit' (q.v.).

Pandărus, son of Lycaon, leader in the Trojan war of the Trojans who lived about the foot of Mt. Ida. The part which he played in the tale of Troilus and Cressida (q.v.) has no foundation in classical antiquity. In Chaucer's 'Troylus and Cryseyde' and in Shakespeare's 'Troilus and Cressida' he is the uncle of Cressida and the go-between in her relations with Troilus; hence our word 'pander'.

Pandects, The, or *Digest*, of Justinian, a compendium in fifty books of Roman civil law, made by order of the Emperor Justinian in the sixth cent., systematizing opinions of eminent jurists, to which the emperor gave the force of law.

Pandemonium, the abode of all the demons; a place represented by Milton ('Paradise

Lost', i. 756) as the capital of Hell, containing the council-chamber of the Evil Spirits.

Pandēmus, meaning 'common to all the people', a surname of the goddess Aphrodite (see *Venus*) in her character of Worldly or Profane Love, as distinguished from the Uranian Aphrodite, Heavenly or Sacred Love.

Pandīon, the father of Philomela (q.v.) and Procne.

Pandōra, according to Hesiod, the first woman that ever lived. She was made of clay by Hephaestus at the request of Zeus, who wished to be revenged on Prometheus for his championship of mankind. When this woman of clay had received life, she was endowed by the gods with every gift, and Zeus gave her a box, which she was directed to present to the man who married her. Hermes then conducted her, not to Prometheus, who was too sagacious to accept her, but to Epimetheus, his brother. The latter, less prudent, married her and opened the box, whereupon there issued from it all the evils and distempers that have since afflicted the human race. Hope alone remained at the bottom of the box to assuage the lot of man. The fable is charmingly turned (to the advantage of Epimetheus) in Kingsley's 'Water Babies'.

Pandosto, or *Dorastus and Fawnia,* a prose romance by Greene (q.v.) published in 1588, is chiefly memorable as the basis of Shakespeare's 'The Winter's Tale' (q.v.). In certain details the story is treated less effectively by Greene. In 'Pandosto' for instance the queen Bellaria (Shakespeare's Hermione) actually dies on hearing of the death of her son, so that her final restoration to her husband does not occur. The escape of Dorastus and Fawnia (Florizel and Perdita), and the final identification of the latter, are less pleasantly contrived by Greene than by Shakespeare. Characters corresponding to Antigonus, Paulina, Autolycus, and the Clown are not found in Greene's version.

Pandours, the name borne by a local force organized in 1741 by Baron Trenck on his estates in Croatia, to clear the country near the Turkish frontier of bands of robbers. The Pandours were subsequently enrolled as a regiment in the Austrian army, where their rapacity and brutality caused them to be dreaded over Germany, and made *Pandour* synonymous with 'brutal Croatian soldier'. The word is derived from medieval Latin *banderius,* originally 'a follower of a standard or banner'.

Panem et circenses, 'bread doles and circus-shows', the only things that, according to Juvenal (x. 78–81), the degenerate Roman populace cared about:

nam qui dabat olim
Imperium fasces legiones omnia, nunc se
Continet atque duas tantum res anxius
  optat,
Panem et circenses.

And those who once, with unresisted sway,
Gave armies, empires, every thing away,
For two poor claims have long renounced
  the whole,
And only ask—the Circus and the Dole.
      (Gifford's translation.)

Pangloss, Dr., in the 'Candide' of Voltaire (q.v.), an optimistic philosopher who holds that all is for the best in the best of all possible worlds, in spite of a series of most distressing adventures (including unsuccessful hanging by the Inquisition and subsequent dissection). He is brought, however, to recognize that, to be happy, man must work and must 'cultivate his garden'. The intended object of the satire was Leibniz (q.v.).

Pangloss, Dr., in 'The Heir-at-Law' of Colman (q.v.) the younger, a pompous avaricious pedant.

Panjandrum: 'and there were present the Picninnies, and the Joblillies, and the Garyulies, and the Grand Panjandrum himself, with the little round button at top', part of the farrago of nonsense composed by Foote to test the memory of Macklin (qq.v.), who asserted that he could repeat anything after once hearing it. Hence 'Panjandrum' is used as a mock title for an imaginary personage of much power, or a personage of great pretensions. [OED.]

Panŏpē, one of the Nereids (q.v.), whom mariners invoked in a storm.

Pantagruel, the second book (in chronological order of the narrative) of Rabelais's great work, but the first to be written and published (1532). The name had been given in 15th-cent. French mysteries to a demon who provoked thirst, and its primitive sense appears to have been 'suffocation'. Rabelais uses it to mean 'the all-thirsty one'. Pantagruel is presented as the son of Gargantua (q.v.) and Badebec, daughter of the king of the Amaurotes of Utopia (a reference to Sir Thomas More's work). The book tells of his birth and education, satirizing the ancient learning and mingling serious and pious advice with burlesque. It then introduces Panurge (q.v.), and describes the ridiculous dispute by signs between Panurge and the English philosopher Thaumast. A war with the invading Dipsodes ('Thirsty People') follows, involving the interesting voyage to Utopia round the Cape of Good Hope, and the notable account of Epistemon's visit to the nether world. In the Third, Fourth, and Fifth Books (for their dates and the question of the authenticity of the Fifth Book, see *Rabelais*), Panurge becomes the principal figure, Pantagruel retires into the background as a kindly, serious, courteous prince, and the fantastic giant element disappears. The question arises whether Panurge shall marry. It is debated with the help of an old poet (Raminagrobis), an astrologer (Trippa), a physician (Rondibilis), a philosopher (Trouillogan), and the fool (Triboulet). The episode of Justice

Bridlegoose (who decides all cases by throw of dice) is here introduced. No conclusion being reached, Panurge, Pantagruel, and the rest of the party set out on a voyage to Cathay to consult the oracle of the Bottle (Bacbuc). On the account of this voyage, in the course of which they visit a number of different countries, recent researches have thrown an interesting light. It is evidently based on the narratives of contemporary explorers in their search for the North-West Passage. The travellers finally reach the oracle, whose advice is summed up in the one word 'Trinch' (drink). Whether this was intended by Rabelais as the conclusion of the whole story, or indeed was written by him, is doubtful. At the end of the Second Book Rabelais had promised to tell how Panurge was married and what came of it, and how Pantagruel married the daughter of Prester John, but this the work never does. The narrative provides occasion for abundant satire directed against monks and schoolmen, the Papacy (especially in the episode of the Papimanes and Bishop Homenas), and the magistrature (in the ferocious description of the Chats Fourrés or Furred Law-cats).

Pantagruelion, THE HERB, in Rabelais, III. xlix et seq., is hemp.

Pantagruelism, defined by Rabelais in the prologue to his Fourth Book as 'a certain gaiety of spirit steeped in disregard of things fortuitous'.

Pantaloon, adapted from the Italian *pantalone*, 'a kind of mask on the Italian stage, representing the Venetian', of whom *Pantalone* was a nickname, supposed to be derived from *San Pantaleone*, formerly a favourite saint of the Venetians. The Venetian character in Italian comedy was represented as a lean and foolish old man, wearing slippers, pantaloons, and spectacles. In modern pantomime or harlequinade he is represented as a foolish and vicious old man, the butt of the clown's jokes, and his abettor in his tricks. [OED.]

Panthēa, in Xenophon's 'Cyropaedia', the wife of Abradatus, king of Susa. She was taken prisoner by Cyrus, who refused to visit her, lest he should be ensnared by her charms. She killed herself on the body of her husband, who had been slain in battle. Panthea is also the name of the heroine of Beaumont and Fletcher's 'A King and no King' (q.v.).

Pantheism, (1) the doctrine that God and the universe are identical, that God is everything, and everything is God (implying a denial of the personality and transcendence of God); (2) the heathen worship of all the gods.

Pantheon, originally a temple dedicated to all the gods, especially that at Rome built by Agrippa *c.* 25 B.C., and transformed in A.D. 609 into a Christian church. The name is now used of a building serving to honour the illustrious dead of a nation. The Panthéon at Paris, which is devoted to this purpose, was

formerly the church of Ste Geneviève, and was named the Panthéon at the Revolution.

Pantheon, THE, Oxford Street, London, originally a theatre and public promenade, with a rotunda like that at Ranelagh (but Johnson and Boswell thought it inferior to the latter). There are references to it in Walpole's letters and in Goldsmith's 'She Stoops to Conquer'. It was famous for its masquerades, to which Gibbon at one time subscribed (letter to Holroyd, 1774). The Pantheon was burnt down in 1792 and rebuilt, but never recovered its former glory (Wheatley and Cunningham).

Pantisocracy, see *Coleridge (S. T.).*

Pantomime, (1) originally a Roman actor, who performed in dumb show, representing by mimicry various characters and scenes; (2) an English dramatic performance, originally consisting of action without speech, but in its further development consisting of a dramatized traditional fairy-tale, with singing, dancing, acrobatics, clowning, topical jokes, a transformation scene, and certain stock roles, especially the 'principal boy' (i.e. hero) acted by a woman and the 'dame' acted by a man.

Panurge, one of the principal characters in Rabelais's 'Pantagruel' (q.v.), a cunning, voluble, witty, and in the later books cowardly buffoon, 'and a very dissolute and debauched fellow, if there were any in Paris: otherwise and in all matters else, the best and most virtuous man in the world; and he was still contriving some plot, and devising mischief against the serjeants and the watch'.

Panza, SANCHO, see *Don Quixote.*

Paolo and Francesca: Francesca, daughter of Giovanni da Polenta, count of Ravenna, was given in marriage by him to Giovanni (Sciancato, the Lame) Malatesta, of Rimini, an ill-favoured man, in return for his military services. She fell in love with Paolo, her husband's handsome brother, and, their relations being discovered, the two lovers were put to death in 1289. Dante, at the end of the fifth canto of his 'Inferno', relates his conversation with Francesca, who told him how her fall was occasioned by the reading of the tale of Launcelot and Guinevere. The Galeotto mentioned by Dante is Galahault, the prince who, in the story of the early loves of Launcelot and Guinevere, not included in Malory, introduces Launcelot to the queen.

The story of Paolo and Francesca was made by Leigh Hunt (q.v.) the subject of his poem 'The Story of Rimini'; it was also the subject of a play that had a temporary vogue, by Stephen Phillips (1866–1915).

Paperstamp, MR., in Peacock's 'Melincourt' (q.v.), a caricature of Wordsworth.

Paphos, a city of Cyprus sacred to Aphrodite. Hence PAPHIAN, a courtesan.

Papimany, in Rabelais's 'Pantagruel', IV. xlviii et seq., an island visited by Pantagruel and his companions. Its inhabitants, the Papimanes, carry their blind zeal for the pope and the Decretals (q.v.) to the point of absurdity. Their bishop was Homenas. When this satire was written Henry II of France was in acute conflict with Pope Julius III.

Pappe with an hatchet, the title of a tract contributed in 1589 by Lyly (q.v.) to the Marprelate controversy (see *Martin Marprelate*) on the side of the bishops. The sense of the expression appears to be 'the administration of punishment under the ironical style of a kindness or benefit' [OED.]. Lyly's pamphlet is a worthless mixture of abuse and ribaldry.

Paracelsus, PHILIPPUS AUREOLUS THEOPHRASTUS BOMBASTUS AB HOHENHEIM (1493–1541), born at Einsiedeln near Zürich in Switzerland, the son of a doctor of medicine. He wandered from country to country, practising magic, alchemy, and astrology, and visiting the universities of Germany, France, and Italy. He returned to Germany, effected there many remarkable cures, and was appointed to a chair of physic and surgery at Basel. He publicly burnt the works of Galen and Avicenna, boasting himself their superior. He was, however, presently pronounced a quack, fled from Basel, resumed his wanderings, and died at Salzburg in the Hospital of St. Sebastian. He initiated modern. chemistry

Paracelsus, a dramatic poem by R. Browning (q.v.), published in 1835.

It is based on the actual life of Paracelsus, summarized above. Paracelsus is presented as a man possessed from childhood with an aspiration to discover the secret of the world, and a conviction that he is chosen to conquer that knowledge. He sets out to seek it in strange places, in spite of the dissuasion of his common-sense friend, Festus, and the gentle, loving Michael. Pt. II shows him at Constantinople, having learnt much, but despondent, for the ultimate secret has escaped him. He meets Aprile the poet, who unconsciously reveals to him the error he has made in pursuing knowledge to the exclusion of love—'the worth of love in man's estate and what proportion love should hold with power'. We next find Paracelsus at Basel, at first admired, then dismissed as a charlatan; and finally dying at Salzburg, where he makes the last proclamation of his faith. He has failed because, in spite of his learning, he has lacked sympathy with mankind; has failed to appreciate

> their half-reasons, faint aspirings, dim
> Struggles for truth, their poorest fallacies,
> Their prejudice and fears and cares and
>   doubts;
> All with a touch of nobleness, upward
>   tending.

Meanwhile he has 'done well, though not all well', and will 'emerge one day'.

Paraclete, THE, from a Greek word meaning

advocate, intercessor, a title of the Holy Spirit, used frequently in the sense of 'the Comforter' (John xiv. 16, etc.).

Paradise, derived from an Old Persian word meaning enclosure or park, was used in its Greek form by the Septuagint translators for the Garden of Eden; and in the N.T. for the abode of the blessed, which is the earliest sense recorded in English [OED.]. It is now used (1) in the sense of the Garden of Eden; (2) by some theologians, as used in Luke xxiii. 43, in the sense of an intermediate state or place where the souls of the righteous await the Last Judgement; (3) in that of Heaven, the final abode of the righteous; and (4) also figuratively as a place of surpassing delight or bliss. It was also used for a pleasure-garden in general, e.g. the garden of a convent, in which sense it sometimes survives in the street nomenclature of old towns (e.g. 'Paradise Square', Oxford). In slang it was used for the gallery of a theatre, where the 'gods' sit. See also *Paradise of Fools.*

Paradise, THE EARTHLY: the belief in the existence of a terrestrial paradise was widespread in the Middle Ages, and references to it are found in manuscripts and maps of the time, e.g. in the legend of the navigation of St. Brendan (q.v.). It is sometimes regarded as the old Garden of Eden, in the extreme east of the world.

For W. Morris's poem of this name see *Earthly Paradise (The).*

Paradise and the Peri, see *Lalla Rookh.*

Paradise Lost, an epic poem by Milton (q.v.), originally in ten books, subsequently rearranged in twelve, first printed in 1667.

Milton formed the intention of writing a great epic poem, as he tells us, as early as 1639. A list of possible subjects, some of them scriptural, some from British history, written in his own hand about 1640–1, still exists, with drafts of the scheme of a poem on Paradise Lost. The work was not, however, begun in earnest until 1658, and it was finished, according to Aubrey, in 1663. It was licensed for publication by the Rev. Thomas Tomkyns, chaplain to the archbishop of Canterbury. Milton entered into an agreement for the copyright with Samuel Simmons by which he received £5 down, and a further £5 when the first impression of 1,300 copies was exhausted. His widow subsequently parted with all further claims for the sum of £8.

Book I. The general subject is briefly stated: man's disobedience and the loss thereupon of Paradise, with its prime cause, Satan, who, having revolted from God, has been driven out of heaven. Satan is presented, with his angels, lying on the burning lake of hell. He awakens his legions, comforts them, and summons a council. Pandemonium, the palace of Satan, is built.

Book II. The council debates whether another battle for the recovery of Heaven shall be hazarded, but decides to examine the report that a new world, with new creatures in it, has been created. Satan undertakes alone the search. He passes through Hell-gates, guarded by Sin and Death, and passes upward through the realm of Chaos.

Book III. God sees Satan flying towards our world, and foretells his success and the fall and punishment of Man. The Son of God offers himself a ransom for Man, is accepted, and exalted. Satan alights on the outer convex of our universe, the future Paradise of Fools (q.v.). He finds the stairs leading up to Heaven, descends to the Sun, and is directed by Uriel to this Earth, alighting on Mount Niphates.

Book IV. The Garden of Eden is described, where Satan first sees Adam and Eve, and overhears their discourse regarding the Tree of Knowledge, of which they are forbidden to eat the fruit. He decides to found his enterprise upon this, and proceeds to tempt Eve in a dream; but is discovered by Gabriel and Ithuriel, and ejected from the garden.

Book V. Eve relates her disquieting dream to Adam. Raphael, sent by God, comes to Paradise, warns Adam of his enemy, and enjoins obedience. At Adam's request he relates how and why Satan incited his legions to revolt.

Book VI. Raphael continues his narrative, how Michael and Gabriel were sent to fight against Satan. After indecisive battles the Son of God himself, causing his legions to stand still, alone attacked the hosts of Satan, and, driving them to the edge of Heaven, forced them to leap down into the deep.

Book VII. Raphael relates how thereafter God decided on the creation of another world with new creatures to dwell therein, and sent his son to perform the creation in six days.

Book VIII. Adam inquires concerning the motions of the heavenly bodies, and is answered ambiguously. [The controversy regarding the Ptolemaic and Copernican systems was at its height when the 'Paradise Lost' was written, and Milton was unable to decide between them, as seen in Bk. X, 668 et seq.] Adam relates what he remembers since his own creation, and discourses with the angel regarding the relations of man with woman. Raphael departs.

Book IX. Satan enters into the serpent, and in this form finds Eve alone. He persuades her to eat of the Tree of Knowledge. Eve relates to Adam what has passed and brings him of the fruit. Adam, perceiving that she is lost, from extreme love for her, resolves to perish with her, and eats of the fruit. This robs them of their innocence: they cover their nakedness, and fall to recriminations.

Book X. God sends his Son to judge the transgressors. He passes sentence on the man and on the woman. Sin and Death resolve to come to this world and make a broad highway thither from Hell. Satan returns to Hell and relates his success; he and his angels are temporarily transformed into serpents. Adam

and Eve confer how to evade the curse upon their offspring, and finally approach the Son of God with repentance and supplication.

Book XI. The Son of God intercedes for Adam and Eve. God decides on their expulsion from Paradise. Michael comes down to carry out the decree. Eve laments, Adam pleads but submits. The angel leads him to a high hill and shows him in a series of visions the future misery of man and what shall happen till the Flood.

Book XII. Michael relates what shall follow, and explains the future coming of the Messiah, his incarnation, death, resurrection, and ascension, and foretells the corrupt state of the Church till his second coming. Adam and Eve, submissive, are led out of Paradise.

Paradise of Dainty Devices, see *Paradyse of Daynty Devises.*

Paradise of Fools: Milton in 'Paradise Lost', III. 448 et seq., describes, on the outer edge of our universe, a 'Limbo large and broad, since called the Paradise of Fools', to which are consigned 'all who in vain things Built their fond hopes of glory or lasting fame' (see *Limbo*).

Paradise Regained, an epic poem in four books by Milton (q.v.), published in 1671. See *Ellwood.*

It is a sequel to 'Paradise Lost', and deals exclusively with the temptation of Christ in the wilderness. According to the poet's conception, whereas Paradise was lost by the yielding of Adam and Eve to Satan's temptation, so it was regained by the resistance of the Son of God to the temptation of the same spirit. Satan is here represented not in the majestic lineaments that we find in 'Paradise Lost', but as a cunning, smooth, and dissembling creature, a 'Spirit unfortunate', as he describes himself. There is a comparative scarcity of similes and ornament, and only a vivid and ingenious expansion of the Biblical texts.

Book I relates the baptism of Christ by John at Bethabara, and the proclamation from Heaven that he is the Son of God. Satan, alarmed, summons a council of his peers, and undertakes his temptation. Christ is led into the wilderness, where, after forty days, Satan in the guise of 'an aged man in rural weeds' approaches him and suggests that he, being now hungry, should prove his divine character by turning the stones around him into bread. Christ, seeing through his guile, sternly replies. Night falls on the desert.

Books II and III. Meanwhile Andrew and Simon seek Christ, and Mary is troubled at his absence. Satan confers again with his council. He once more tries the hunger temptation, placing before the eyes of Christ a 'table richly spread', which is contemptuously rejected. He then makes appeal to the higher appetites for wealth and power, and a disputation follows as to the real value of earthly glory. Satan, confuted, next reminds Christ that the kingdom of David is now under the Roman yoke, and suggests that he should free it. He takes Christ to a high mountain and shows him the kingdoms of the earth. A description follows (iii. 251–346) of the contemporary state of the eastern world, divided between the powers of Rome and of the Parthians, as seen in this vision. Satan offers an alliance with, or conquest of, the Parthians, and the liberation of the Jews then in captivity.

Book IV. Christ remaining unmoved by Satan's 'politic maxims', the tempter, turning to the western side, draws his attention to Rome and proposes the expulsion of the wicked emperor Tiberius; and finally, pointing out Athens, urges the attractions of her poets, orators, and philosophers. All these failing, Satan brings Christ back to the wilderness, and the second night falls. On the third morning, confessing Christ proof against all temptation, Satan carries him to the highest pinnacle of the temple and bids him cast himself down, 'to know what more he is than man', only to receive the well-known answer. Satan falls dismayed, and angels bear Christ away.

Paradiso, Il, of Dante, see *Divina Commedia.*

Paradyse of Daynty Devises, The, a collection of works by poets of the second rank who wrote in the early part of the 16th cent. (Lord Vaux, Lord Oxford, Kinwelmersh, Hunnis). It was compiled by Richard Edwards (q.v.) and published after his death, in 1576.

Parasitaster, The, or *The Fawn,* a comedy by J. Marston (q.v.), published in 1606.

Hercules, the widowed duke of Ferrara, wishes his son Tiberio to marry Dulcimel, daughter of a neighbouring prince, and, in order to defeat his unwillingness, declares that he will marry Dulcimel himself, and sends Tiberio to negotiate the marriage. Hercules, under the name of Faunus, follows in disguise to watch the issue. Dulcimel falls in love with Tiberio, and, being a woman of wit and resource, manages to win him.

Parcae or FATES, THE, the MOIRAE of the Greeks, goddesses who presided over the birth and life of men. They were sisters, three in number, Clotho, Lachesis, and Atropos. Clotho, the youngest, presided over the moment of man's birth and held a distaff in her hands. Lachesis with her spindle spun out the events and actions of his life. Atropos, the eldest, cut the thread of human life with her shears. They were held to be inexorable, and the gods could not alter their decrees.

Pardiggle, MRS., in Dickens's 'Bleak House' (q.v.), a lady 'distinguished for rapacious benevolence'.

Pardoner's Tale, The, see *Canterbury Tales.*

Parian Chronicle, THE, one of the Arundel Marbles (q.v.), a marble inscription in which are recorded the chief events of Greek history from the reign of the mythical Cecrops to 354 B.C. It was first deciphered by John Selden (q.v.).

Paridell, in Spenser's 'Faerie Queene', a false and libertine knight (Bks. III. viii, ix, and x, and IV. i) who consorts with Duessa (q.v.) and elopes with Hellenore, the wife of Malbecco (q.v.).

Paris, also known as ALEXANDER, was a son of Priam, king of Troy, and of Hecuba. He was exposed as a child because of a prophecy that he should bring destruction on Troy, but was brought up by shepherds on Mt. Ida. Here he won the favour of the nymph Oenone, with whom he lived happily until appointed by the gods to adjudge the prize of beauty among the three goddesses, Hera, Aphrodite, and Athene. Each tried by promises to influence his judgement; Aphrodite offered him the fairest woman in the world for wife, and to her he awarded the prize. At an athletic contest held at Priam's court, Paris was recognized as Priam's son, and soon after visited Sparta, where he persuaded Helen, the wife of Menelaus, the fairest woman of her age, to elope with him. This brought about the expedition of the Greek princes against Troy. In the course of the ensuing war Paris was mortally wounded by an arrow shot by Philoctetes, and sought Oenone's help in vain (see under the name of the latter).

Paris, COUNT, a character in Shakespeare's 'Romeo and Juliet' (q.v.).

PARIS, MATTHEW (d. 1259), historian and monk, entered the monastery of St. Albans in 1217, and became an expert in writing, in drawing and painting, and in working gold and silver. He succeeded Roger of Wendover in his office of chronicler to the monastery, 1236, and carried on the 'Chronica Majora' from the summer of 1235. He expanded the scope of the chronicle, introducing narratives and accounts of events in foreign countries as well as in England, which he obtained from kings and all manner of great persons who came to St. Albans. He was a favourite with Henry III, and visited Norway in 1248 on a mission from Innocent IV. He carried his greater chronicle down to May 1259, where he ends abruptly, and certainly died about that time. In vigour and brightness of expression he stands before every other English chronicler; and his writing possesses peculiar historic value. Besides the great chronicle he wrote a summary of the chief events between 1200 and 1250, which is known as the 'Historia Minor', or 'Historia Anglorum'. The Cotton manuscripts include 'Vitae duae Offarum', which are attributed to Matthew Paris, though probably spurious. These lives are followed by 'Vitae Abbatum S. Albani', being the lives of the first twenty-three abbots to 1255, of which all were certainly compiled, and the last two or three composed, by him. They were incorporated, with some alterations, by Thomas Walsingham in his 'Gesta Abbatum'. The whole of his writings are discussed by Luard in the prefaces to his edition of the 'Chronica Majora'. Paris describes himself in the manuscripts as 'Matheus Parisiensis'; whether from birth or residence in Paris, or because Paris was his family name, is uncertain. Leland and Pits favour the latter view, which is borne out by the numerous instances of persons of that name living in England (particularly in Lincolnshire) in the 13th cent. On the other hand he perhaps spent some time in Paris, for he knew French (Madden).

Paris Garden, a place for bull- and bear-baiting on Bankside, Southwark, referred to in Shakespeare's 'Henry VIII', v. iv.

Paris Sketch Book, The, a collection of six short stories, with essays and criticisms, by Thackeray (q.v.), published in 1840.

Parish Register, The, a poem by Crabbe (q.v.), published in 1807.

A country parson relates the memories awakened in him as he looks through the entries in his registers of births, marriages, and deaths. It includes the well-known pathetic tale of Phoebe Dawson, which pleased Fox and Sir Walter Scott.

Parisian Massacre or WEDDING, THE, the massacre of St. Bartholomew in Paris (1572), when many Huguenots were slain during the festivities in celebration of the marriage of Henry of Navarre with Margaret of France.

Parisians, The, a novel (unfinished) by Bulwer Lytton (q.v.), published in 1873.

Lytton here depicts the corrupt Parisian society of the last days of the second Empire, and the revolutionary forces that sprang up to overthrow it. The main elements in the story are two. Graham Vane, an Englishman of good family, has been left a fortune by his uncle, Richard King, with the request that he shall seek out the daughter of the wife who many years before deserted King and disappeared, and, if she survives, bestow the bulk of the fortune upon her or marry her. The search brings him in contact with various circles of French society. The second is the story of the efforts of a ruined French nobleman, Alain de Rochebriant, to rehabilitate his fortunes, efforts which make him the pawn of rival financiers and moneylenders.

Parisi'na, a poem by Lord Byron (q.v.), published in 1816.

The poem is founded on the following passage in Gibbon's 'Antiquities of the House of Brunswick' ('Miscellaneous Works', iii. 470): 'Under the reign of Nicholas III [A.D. 1425] Ferra was polluted by a domestic tragedy. By the testimony of a maid, and his own observation, the marquis of Este discovered the incestuous loves of his wife Parisina and Hugo his bastard son, a beautiful and valiant youth. They were beheaded in the castle by the sentence of a father and husband, who published his shame, and survived their execution.'

PARK, MUNGO (1771–1806), born near Selkirk, was educated at Edinburgh University and became a surgeon in the mercantile marine. He explored the course of the Niger and became famous by his 'Travels in the Interior of Africa', published in 1799. He returned to the Niger in 1805, and perished at Boussa in a conflict with the natives. He was a friend of Sir W. Scott.

PARKER, MATTHEW (1504–75), educated at St. Mary's Hostel, Cambridge, and Corpus Christi College, Cambridge, was licensed to preach by Cranmer in 1533, and in 1535 appointed chaplain to Anne Boleyn and dean of Stoke-by-Clare, where he spent much of the next ten years. He was in 1544 elected Master of Corpus Christi College, Cambridge, where he reformed the library. He subsequently bequeathed to the college his fine collection of manuscripts. He was made dean of Lincoln in 1552, espoused the cause of Lady Jane Grey, was deprived of his preferments by Queen Mary, and fled to Frankfort-on-the-Main during the persecution. He reluctantly accepted the archbishopric of Canterbury on Elizabeth's accession and was consecrated at Lambeth (see *Nag's Head Tavern*) in 1559. He identified himself with the party (afterwards known as the Anglican party) which sought to establish a *via media* between Romanism and Puritanism. From 1563 to 1568 he was occupied with the production of the 'Bishops' Bible' (see *Bible, the English*), his most distinguished service to the theological studies of the day. With respect to this he informed Cecil that he contemplated undertaking, besides the prefaces, Genesis, Exodus, Matthew, Mark, and the Pauline Epistles, except Romans and 1 Corinthians. In his later years he retired more and more from society, being conscious of the strength of the opposing current, headed by Leicester. He was buried in his private chapel at Lambeth. In 1648 his remains were disinterred and buried under a dunghill, but after the Restoration they were restored to their original resting-place. He was a great benefactor to his college and to the University of Cambridge, where he constructed a handsome new street, which he named University Street, leading from the schools to Great St. Mary's. To his efforts we are indebted for the earliest editions of Gildas, Asser, Ælfric, the 'Flores Historiarum', Matthew Paris, and other early chroniclers (an important manuscript of the 'Anglo-Saxon Chronicle' (q.v.), given by him to Corpus Christi College, Cambridge, is known as the 'Parker Chronicle'). In spite of Queen Elizabeth's dislike of clerical matrimony, he was married, and left one son. His 'De Antiquitate Ecclesiae et Privilegiis Ecclesiae Cantuariensis cum Archiepiscopis ejusdem 70' (1572) is said to be the first book privately printed in England.

PARKINSON, JOHN (1567–1650), king's herbarist, author of 'Paradisi in sole Paradisus terrestris, or a garden of all sorts of pleasant flowers which our English ayre will permitt to be noursed up . . .' (1629), with woodcuts; also of a great herbal, 'Theatrum botanicum' (1640).

PARKMAN, FRANCIS (1823–93), American historian, born in Boston. After graduating from Harvard, he travelled in Europe and then journeyed out to Wyoming to study the Indians, giving an account of this journey in 'The Oregon Trail' (1849). His history of the struggle of the English and French for dominion in North America was published in a series of studies under the following titles: 'History of the Conspiracy of Pontiac' (1851), 'Pioneers of France in the New World' (1865), 'The Jesuits in North America in the Seventeenth Century' (1867), 'La Salle and the Discovery of the Great West' (1869), 'The Old Régime in Canada' (1874), 'Count Frontenac and New France under Louis XIV' (1877), 'Montcalm and Wolfe' (1884), and 'A Half-Century of Conflict' (1892).

Parlement of Briddes, see *Parlement of Foules.*

Parlement of Foules, The, or *The Parlement of Briddes,* a poem of 700 lines in rhyme-royal by Chaucer, probably written between 1372 and 1386. In a vision the poet sees the Court of Nature on St. Valentine's day, 'when every fowl cometh there to choose his mate'. Three tiercel eagles advance their claims to a beautiful 'formel' (female), and a debate of the fowls follows. Nature decides that the formel shall make election, and the formel asks for a year's respite 'to advise' her. The poem probably refers to some lady sought by royal lovers, perhaps Anne of Bohemia, and is noteworthy, *inter alia,* for its fine opening lines:

> The lyf so short, the crafte so long to lerne,
> Thassay so harde, so sharpe the conquerynge,

and its descriptive catalogues of trees and birds.

Parliament, HOUSES OF: before the erection of the present Houses of Parliament, the House of Commons sat in the chapel of St. Stephen, and the House of Lords in the Painted Chamber, in the ancient palace of Westminster, originally built by Edward the Confessor, and rebuilt by Henry III. These were destroyed by fire in 1834. The present houses were built from the designs of Sir Charles Barry.

Parliament of Bees, The, a dramatic allegory or masque by J. Day (*fl.* 1606, q.v.), published, it appears, in 1607, though the earliest extant copy is of the year 1641.

It consists first of the opening of the parliament, with the viceroy's, 'Mr. Bee's', opening address; then of a series of 'characters' of different bees with their virtues and vices: the hospitable bee, the reveller, the neglected soldier, the neglected poet, the 'usuring' bee,

the quacksalver, the thrifty bee, the passionate bee. Finally we have Oberon's Starchamber, with the pronouncement of penalties on offenders, the wasp, the drone, and the humble-bee.

Parmĕnĭdēs (*b. c.* 513 B.C.), of Elea in Italy, the founder of the Eleatic school of philosophy. He rejected the views of Heraclitus (q.v.), and regarded the universe as a single, continuous, unchanging, indivisible whole; what is mutable, and phenomena such as motion, are in his view illusions.

Parmenides, MY FATHER: in Plato's dialogue 'The Sophist', the Eleatic Stranger speaks of laying hands on his father Parmenides (q.v.) in the sense of criticizing the doctrines in which he has been brought up.

Parmĕnĭon, one of the generals of Alexander the Great (q.v.). When Darius, king of Persia, offered Alexander his daughter Statira in marriage, with the territories west of the Euphrates and a large sum of money, Parmenion observed that he would accept the offer if he were Alexander. Alexander replied, 'So should I, if I were Parmenion'.

Parnassian School, THE, the name given to a group of French poets of the latter half of the 19th cent. who reflected the scientific spirit of the age. They diverged from the earlier romantics in the importance they attached to restraint and form and to a severely objective quality in descriptive poetry which they called 'impassibility'. The name is taken from the title, 'Le Parnasse contemporain', of three collections of their poems published in 1866–76. Leconte de Lisle (1818–94) was their leader. Others were Heredia, Catulle Mendès, Sully Prudhomme, etc. Gautier and to some extent Baudelaire count as precursors.

Parnassus, a mountain in Greece, a few miles north of Delphi, sacred to the Muses. One of its peaks was sacred to Apollo; the other, as George Saintsbury reminds us, to Dionysus.

Parnassus Plays, The, the name given to a trilogy, produced about the year 1600 by the students of St. John's College, Cambridge, consisting of 'The Pilgrimage to Pernassus' and 'The Returne from Pernassus', the latter in two parts, with 'The Scourge for Simony' as sub-title of the second. They have been attributed to J. Day (*fl.* 1606, q.v.), but their authorship is doubtful.

The 'Pilgrimage' deals allegorically with the journey of Philomusus and his cousin Studioso to Parnassus by way of the *Trivium,* and the regions of Rhetoric and Philosophy; and their encounters with Madido, the votary of wine, Amoretto, the voluptuary, and Ingenioso, who has given up the voyage and burnt his books. But the travellers resist their counsels and struggle on to their goal.

In the 'Return', where the tone becomes satirical, the students are seen on their way back to London, learning how to catch a patron or cheat a tradesman; and following menial occupations, as sexton and private tutor, as fiddlers, and so forth; and finally, in utter discouragement, as simple shepherds.

The second part of the 'Return' contains an interesting review of the merits of certain contemporary poets, including Shakespeare and Jonson; and introduces Kemp and Burbage. Some of the scenes deal with the feud between town and gown at Cambridge, and hold up to obloquy Brackyn, the recorder of Cambridge, who figures again in 'Ignoramus' (q.v.).

Parnell, CHARLES STEWART (1846–91), born at Avondale, co. Wicklow, and educated at Magdalene College, Cambridge. He entered parliament as M.P. for Meath in 1875 and by his extreme attitude won the confidence of the Fenians and obtained an alliance with the Clan-na-Gael or new Fenians, who had hitherto despised parliamentary agitation. He was elected chairman of the Home Rule party in the House of Commons in 1880 and, in spite of his being a Protestant, exerted an extraordinary sway over his supporters and enormous influence outside the house. He was arrested for his incendiary speeches in 1881 and imprisoned in Kilmainham jail, gaining thereby great popularity and the appellation of 'the uncrowned king of Ireland'. With the help of the Liberal party he overthrew the Tory government in 1886, and converted Gladstone to his home-rule scheme. He vindicated himself in 1888–9 of the charge of connivance with outrage and crime brought in the articles on 'Parnellism and Crime' which were published in 'The Times' in 1887. His career was ruined by his appearance as co-respondent in a suit for divorce by Capt. O'Shea against his wife in 1890. His influence may be estimated by the fact that within eleven years of his entering public life he had induced a majority of one of the great English political parties to regard home rule for Ireland, hitherto viewed as an impracticable dream, as an urgent necessity.

PARNELL, THOMAS (1679–1718), born in Dublin and educated at Trinity College, Dublin, was archdeacon of Clogher and a friend of Swift and Pope (to whose 'Iliad' he contributed an introductory essay). His works, which were published posthumously by Pope, include 'The Night Piece on Death', 'The Hymn to Contentment', and 'The Hermit', the two first being octosyllabic odes of great fluency, and the last a narrative poem in heroic couplets. Parnell's life was written by Goldsmith. His 'Elegy to an Old Beauty' includes the couplet:

And all that's madly wild, or oddly gay
We call it only pretty Fanny's way.

'Pretty Fanny's way' has become proverbial for some perverse or annoying habit regarded with toleration by the friends of the person guilty of it. Parnell's 'Homer's Battle of the Frogs and Mice with the Remarks of Zoilus',

satirizing Theobald and Dennis, was published in 1717.

Parolles, a character in Shakespeare's 'All's Well that Ends Well' (q.v.).

Paronomasia, a play on words, a pun:

As we curtail the already cur-tailed cur
(You catch the paronomasia, play 'po' words?).
　　　Calverley, 'The Cock and the Bull'
　　　　(parody of Browning).

PARR, SAMUEL (1747–1825), educated at Harrow and Emmanuel College, Cambridge, was headmaster of three schools, and then settled at Hatton in Warwickshire as perpetual curate, where he built up a library containing 10,000 volumes. He engaged in political controversy as a strong Whig, and in numerous literary quarrels. He was a fine Latin scholar, and excelled as a writer of Latin epitaphs (he wrote that on Samuel Johnson in St. Paul's). He was regarded as the Whig Johnson, but his conversation was apparently far inferior to that of his model. His works, which contain little of permanent value, and are marked by verbosity and mannerism, were collected in eight volumes in 1828. His reputation was severely handled by De Quincey in an essay, 'Dr. Samuel Parr, or Whiggism in relation to Literature'.

Parr, THOMAS (1483?–1635), OLD PARR, a native of Alderbury, near Shrewsbury, whose longevity was celebrated by Taylor, the waterpoet (q.v.). He was sent to court in 1635 by the earl of Arundel, where the change in his mode of life killed him. Sir G. Cornewall Lewis and W. J. Thoms regard the story of his extraordinary age as unsupported by any trustworthy evidence.

Parrhăsius (late 5th cent. B.C.), Greek painter from Ephesus, famed for the subtlety of his outline and the expressiveness of his faces. He wrote on painting. He is said to have excelled Zeuxis (q.v.) in illusionistic painting; in a trial of skill Zeuxis mistook Parrhăsius' painting of a curtain for reality, attempting to draw it aside to discover the painting he supposed to be beneath it.

PARRY, SIR WILLIAM EDWARD (1790–1855), Arctic explorer, was author of four narratives of voyages to the Polar Sea, published in 1821–4, 1824, 1826, and 1828.

Parsees, descendants of those Persians who fled to India in the 7th and 8th cents. to escape Muslim persecution, and who still retain their religion (Zoroastrianism, q.v.). They are also known as Guebres.

Parsifal, the title of a music-drama by R. Wagner (q.v.). See *Parzival* and *Perceval.*

PARSON LOT, see *Kingsley (C.).*

Parson's Tale, see *Canterbury Tales.*

Parthenissa, see *Boyle (R.).*

Parthenon, THE, a temple at Athens sacred to Athene. It was destroyed by the Persians and rebuilt in a more splendid manner by Pericles. The statue in it of the goddess, made of gold and ivory, passed for one of the masterpieces of Phidias. The temple was turned into a Christian church probably in the reign of Justinian I, into a mosque soon after 1453, and was almost destroyed in 1687 by an explosion of gunpowder during the siege of Athens by the Venetians.

Parthenopean Republic, the short-lived republic established by the French at Naples in 1799. Parthenope was the name of a Greek settlement from Cumae on the site where Naples now stands, derived from the association of the locality with the siren of that name.

Parthenophil and Parthenope, a collection of sonnets by B. Barnes (q.v.), issued in 1593, notable as one of the first of such collections to appear after Sidney's 'Astrophel and Stella'.

Parthians, THE, a people of Scythian origin who lived SE. of the Caspian Sea and came into conflict with the Romans. They were celebrated as mounted archers, who spread round the enemy, poured in a shower of arrows, and then fled, avoiding close contact, and still shooting their arrows as they retreated. Whence the expression 'a Parthian shaft'.

Particularism, in theology, the dogma that Divine Grace is provided for or offered to a selected part, not the whole, of the human race.

Partington, MRS., referred to by Sydney Smith (q.v.) in his speech at Taunton in Oct. 1831 on the rejection of the Reform Bill. He compares the attempts of the House of Lords to stop the progress of reform to the efforts of Mrs. Partington, who lived close to the beach at Sidmouth, to keep out the Atlantic with a mop when a great storm in 1824 caused a flood in that town.

Benjamin Penhallow Shillaber (1814–90), American humorist, published in 1854 the 'Life and Sayings of Mrs. Partington', a benevolent village gossip, an American variety of Mrs. Malaprop.

Partlet or PERTELOTE, the hen in 'Reynard the Fox' (q.v.) and in Chaucer's 'Nun's Priest's Tale' (see *Canterbury Tales*). 'Sister Partlet with her hooded head' in Dryden's 'The Hind and the Panther' (q.v.) stands for the Roman Catholic nuns.

Partridge, a character in Fielding's 'Tom Jones' (q.v.).

Partridge, JOHN, the victim of a mystification by Swift. See *Bickerstaff*.

Parzival, an epic by Wolfram von Eschenbach (q.v.), composed early in the 13th cent. on the subject of the legend of Perceval (q.v.) and the Holy Grail. See also *Titurel*.

PASCAL, BLAISE (1623–62), French mathematician, physicist, and moralist, came early under the influence of Jansenism (q.v.). His first important ethical work was the 'Lettres à un Provincial' (1656–7), polemical letters directed against the casuistry of the Jesuits. His famous 'Pensées' (issued posthumously in 1670) were fragments of an uncompleted Defence of the Christian Religion, directed principally against the free-thinkers. A contemporary of Descartes (q.v.), he contested that philosopher's view of the supremacy of human reason, and showed its inability to deal with ultimate metaphysical problems. He finds room in his own philosophy for the teaching of the Scriptures, and for intuition alongside of reason. Pascal showed his mathematical and scientific aptitudes by a juvenile treatise on conic sections, by inventing a calculating machine, and by proving experimentally the weight of air.

PASCOLI, GIOVANNI (1855–1912), major Italian poet. A socialist sympathizer, he was imprisoned for some months for participating in demonstrations in 1879. In 1905 he succeeded Carducci (q.v.) in the Chair of Italian Literature at Bologna. Nature and the simple things of everyday life provide the themes of much of his poetry, whose prevailing mood is one of sad resignation before the mystery of human existence. In form and diction it breaks with the classic Italian tradition. Its musicality and suggestiveness, its power of evoking the mysterious and the evanescent, are qualities which it shares with French Symbolism. In his treatment of refrains Pascoli resembles Edgar Allan Poe (q.v.), whose poem 'The Raven' he translated into Italian verse. The essential Pascoli is in 'Myricae' (1891–1905) and 'Canti di Castelvecchio' (1903).

Pasha, a title borne in Turkey by officers of high rank, e.g. military commanders and governors of provinces. There were three grades of pashas, distinguished by the number of horse-tails displayed as a symbol in war; the highest grade (of three tails) corresponding to a commanding general, admiral, or governor of equivalent rank.

Pasht, a cat-headed goddess of the ancient Egyptians, especially worshipped at Bubastis.

Pasiphaë, see *Minotaur*.

Pasquil, PASQUIN. *Pasquino* or *Pasquillo* was the name popularly given to a mutilated statue disinterred at Rome in 1501, and set up by Cardinal Caraffa at the corner of his palace near the Piazza Navona. It became the custom to salute Pasquin on St. Mark's day in Latin verses. In process of time these *pasquinate* or pasquinades tended to become satirical, and the term began to be applied, not only in Rome but in other countries, to satirical compositions and lampoons, political, ecclesiastical, or personal. According to Mazocchi, the name Pasquino originated in that of a schoolmaster who lived opposite the spot where the statue was found; a later tradition made Pasquino a caustic tailor or shoemaker; another calls him a barber. [OED.] Replies to the pasquinades used to be attached to the *Marforio*, an ancient statue of a river-god, thought to be of Mars.

PASQUIN, ANTHONY, see *Williams (J)*.

Passage to India, A, a novel by E. M. Forster (q.v.), published in 1924. It is a picture of society in India under the British Raj, of the clash between East and West, and of the prejudices and misunderstandings that foredoomed goodwill. Criticized at first for anti-British and possibly inaccurate bias, it has been praised as a superb character study of the people of one race by a writer of another. The story is told in three parts, *I, Mosque, II, Caves, III, Temple*, and concerns Aziz, a young Muslim doctor, whose friendliness and enthusiasm for the British turn to bitterness and disillusionment when his pride is injured. A sympathy springs up between him and the elderly Mrs. Moore, who has come to visit her son, the City Magistrate. Accompanying her is Adela Quested, young, earnest, and charmless, who longs to know the 'real' India and tries to disregard the taboos and snobberies of the British circle. Aziz organizes an expedition for the visitors to the famous Caves of Marabar, where an unforeseen development plunges him into disgrace and rouses deep antagonism between the two races. Adela accuses him of insulting her in the Caves, he is committed to prison and stands trial. Adela withdraws her charge, but Aziz turns furiously away from the British, towards a Hindu–Muslim *entente*. In the third part of the book he has moved to a post in a native state, and is bringing up his family in peace, writing poetry and reading Persian. He is visited by his friend Mr. Fielding, the former Principal of the Government College, an intelligent, hard-bitten man. They discuss the future of India and Aziz prophesies that only when the British are driven out can he and Fielding really be friends. Among the many characters is Professor Godbole, the detached and saintly Brahman who is the innocent cause of the contretemps, and who makes his final appearance in supreme tranquillity at the festival of the Hindu temple.

Passetyme of Pleasure, or the Historie of Graunde Amoure and La Belle Pucel, an allegorical poem in rhyme-royal and deca-syllabic couplets by Hawes (q.v.), written about 1506 and first printed by Wynkyn de Worde in 1509 (edited by Southey, 1831, and by Wright for the Percy Society, 1845). It describes the education of a certain Graunde Amour in the accomplishments required to make a knight perfect and worthy of the love of La Belle Pucel, and narrates his encounters with giants (representing the vices), his marriage, and his death; the whole constituting an allegory of life in the form of a romance of chivalry. It contains a well-known couplet in perhaps its original form:

For though the day be never so longe,
At last the belles ringeth to evensonge.

Passing of Arthur, The, one of Tennyson's

'Idylls of the King' (q.v.), published in 1869.

Sir Bedivere, the last surviving of Arthur's knights, relates the final scenes of the king's life, the coming of the ghost of Gawain with its warning of the impending end; the pressing back of Modred's forces to the western bound of Lyonesse; the great battle when all but Arthur, Bedivere, and Modred are killed; the slaying of Modred by Arthur and his own mortal wound; the throwing of Excalibur into the mere; and the coming of the black barge with the three queens, who bear off Arthur.

The poem incorporates the 'Morte d'Arthur', the earlier fragment published in 1842.

Passion, THE, the sufferings of Jesus Christ on the Cross (also often including the Agony in Gethsemane). A CROSS OF THE PASSION is a term of Heraldry, used of a cross not crossed in the middle but somewhat below the top. PASSION WEEK was, until the middle of the 19th cent., generally used to signify the week immediately before Easter. Since then this period has been designated *Holy Week*, and the term *Passion Week* has been applied by some to the week beginning with Passion Sunday, i.e. the fifth week in Lent.

Passion Play, a miracle play (q.v.) representing the Passion of Christ. See also *Oberammergau*.

Passionate Pilgrim, A, a story by H. James (q.v.), written in 1870 and published in 1875.

Passionate Pilgrim, The, an unauthorized anthology of poems by various authors, published by William Jaggard in 1599, and attributed on the title-page to William Shakespeare.

Passover, THE, the name of a Jewish feast, held on the evening of the 14th day of the month Nisan, commemorative of the 'passing over' of the houses of the Israelites whose doorposts were marked with the blood of the lamb, when the Egyptians were smitten with the death of their first-born (Exod. xii). It is extended to include the seven following days.

PASTERNAK, BORIS LEONIDOVICH (1890–1960) was born in Moscow and brought up in a household devoted to art and music. He originally intended to be a composer, but at the age of 18 turned to writing poetry and published 'My Sister Life' in 1922 and 'Themes and Variations' in 1923. Although an admirer of Mayakovsky's early work, he was not a Futurist or a partisan of particular causes, but a poet of the whole movement for liberation and a new life. He is best known outside Russia for his novel, 'Dr. Zhivago' (1958), for which he was awarded, but declined, the Nobel Prize. He regarded the novel as his most important work, for which the poems were preparatory steps (see his 'Essay in Autobiography', 1959). Pasternak was also the author of several fine translations of Shakespeare's plays.

Pasteur, LOUIS (1822–95), a famous French

chemist and biologist, the founder of the science of bacteriology, the author of many works on bacteria and the preventive treatment of disease, and the discoverer of the method of inoculation for hydrophobia.

Pastiche, a literary composition made up from various authors or sources, or in imitation of the style of another author; or a picture made up of fragments pieced together or copied with modification from an original, or in professed imitation of the style of another artist.

Paston Letters, a collection of letters preserved by the Pastons, a well-to-do Norfolk family, written between *c.* 1420 and 1503.

They concern three generations of the family and most were written under the reigns of Henry VI, Edward IV, and Richard III. They are unique as materials for history, and interesting as showing the violence and anarchy that prevailed in the land, and the domestic conditions in which a family of this class lived. The history of the manuscripts is curious. The second earl of Yarmouth (1652–1732), the head of the Paston family, sold some of his family papers to Peter Le Neve, the antiquary. They passed through various hands into those of John Fenn, who published two volumes of selected letters in 1787. These attracted the interest of the king, and Fenn presented to the Royal Library the manuscript of the letters which he had published, and was knighted in acknowledgement. Two further volumes of letters were published in 1789, and a fifth in 1823. The originals of these volumes were all for a time lost. Those of the fifth volume were found in 1865, those of the third and fourth in 1875; but it was not until 1889 that the originals of the first two volumes were discovered in the library of Orwell Hall, where they had come with the papers of Bishop Tomline. The whole collection, with many additional documents, was re-edited by Dr. J. Gairdner in 1901 and 1904.

Pastor Fido, Il, see *Guarini.*

Pastoral poetry was, in its origin, distinctively Dorian and especially Sicilian. Theocritus (q.v.) was its principal Greek representative. Pastoral romances and plays were developed in England in the 16th and 17th cents. from Italian and Spanish works, notably from the 'Diana' of Jorge de Montemayor (printed *c.* 1560, and translated into English by Bartholomew Young, 1598), which inspired Sidney's 'Arcadia' (q.v.); also from Tasso's 'Aminta' (1581) and 'Il Pastor Fido' of Guarini (1590), translated in 1596 and 1602 respectively, the latter of which served as a model for Fletcher's 'Faithful Shepherdess' (q.v.). The essence of the pastoral is simplicity of thought and action in a rustic setting. The most important examples of this kind of composition in English include, besides the two works above mentioned, Lodge's 'Rosalynde' (q.v.), Shakespeare's 'As

You Like It' (q.v.), Jonson's 'Sad Shepherd' (q.v.), and Milton's 'Comus' (q.v.).

Pastorella, in Spenser's 'Faerie Queene', VI. ix–xii, a shepherdess, loved by Coridon the shepherd and by Sir Calidore, believed to be the daughter of Meliboe. She is carried off by brigands, rescued by Sir Calidore, and discovered to be the daughter of Sir Bellamoure and the Lady Claribell.

Patavinity, provincialism in style. The word originally means the dialectal peculiarities of Patavium (Padua), as shown in the writings of Livy (q.v.); hence provincialism in style.

Patavium, in imprints, Padua.

Patch, originally the name or nickname of Cardinal Wolsey's domestic fool (perhaps an anglicized form of the Italian *pazzo*, fool), hence a synonym for fool (whence 'cross-patch').

Patelin, see *Pathelin.*

PATER, WALTER HORATIO (1839–94), educated at King's School, Canterbury, and Queen's College, Oxford, and a fellow of Brasenose, became associated with the Pre-Raphaelities, particularly with Swinburne, whom perhaps he never met, and began his literary career by contributing in 1867 to the 'Westminster Review' an essay on 'Winckelmann', subsequently embodied in his volume of 'Studies in the History of the Renaissance' (1873). This work first made Pater's fame. It was followed in 1885 by 'Marius the Epicurean' (q.v.), a philosophic romance; 'Imaginary Portraits' (1887), 'Appreciations' (1889) containing his judgements of Shakespeare, Wordsworth, and other English writers; 'Plato and Platonism' (1893), and 'The Child in the House' (1894). 'Greek Studies' (1895) and 'Gaston de Latour' (1896) were published posthumously. 'Gaston', which remained unfinished, is a story of the France of Charles IX, containing a portrait of Montaigne, and introducing Ronsard and Giordano Bruno.

PATERCULUS, GAIUS VELLEIUS (*c.* 19 B.C.–A.D. 31), Roman historian, who served in Germany under Tiberius; author of a succinct history of Greece and Rome to his own time, contrasting with Tacitus and Suetonius in its praise of Tiberius.

Paternoster, from the L. *pater noster,* 'Our Father', the first two words of the Lord's Prayer in Latin, used to signify that prayer, especially in the Latin version. It is sometimes extended to any form of words repeated or muttered by way of prayer, imprecation, or charm, e.g. *Devil's Paternoster,* a muttered imprecation; also to a special bead in a rosary indicating that a paternoster is to be said; and to the whole rosary.

Paternoster Row, London, adjoining St. Paul's Cathedral, was perhaps so called from the makers of rosaries or paternosters. Stow records that 'Pater noster makers of olde time, or beade makers, and text writers are gone out of Pater noster Rowe'. Or it may have been here that processions going to St. Paul's began their *pater noster* (cf. Amen Corner, Ave Maria Lane, etc., in the vicinity).

Path to Rome, The, see *Belloc.*

Pathelin or *Patelin, Maître Pierre*, the most famous of early French farces, probably of the 15th cent., of unknown authorship.

Pathelin, the lawyer, tricks the close-fisted Joceaume, the draper, out of a piece of cloth. Joceaume presently discovers that he is being defrauded by his shepherd Aignelet, whom he hales before the judge. Aignelet consults Pathelin as to his defence. Joceaume, confused at seeing the rascal Pathelin in court, mixes up his two complaints, against the lawyer and against the shepherd, and is recalled to the business of the moment by the judge in the famous phrase, 'Revenons à ces moutons'. Aignelet, who to every question replies, in accordance with Pathelin's advice, by merely bleating, is discharged as an idiot. But the tables are turned on Pathelin when, in reply to his demand for his promised fee, Aignelet merely bleats.

Among modern editions of this amusing piece may be mentioned those of E. Fournier, 1872, and of R. T. Holbrook (*Classiques français du moyen âge*), 1924.

Pathfinder, The, one of the 'Leatherstocking' novels of J. F. Cooper (q.v.), and a nickname of the hero, Natty Bumppo.

Patience, an alliterative poem of 500 lines, of the later 14th cent., of which the story of Jonah is the subject. It is attributed to the same author as 'Pearl' and 'Cleanness' (qq.v.).

Patience, an opera by Gilbert and Sullivan (q.v.), produced in 1881, ridiculing the aesthetic movement (q.v.).

Patient Grissil, a comedy by Dekker (q.v.) in collaboration with Chettle and Haughton, printed in 1603.

The marquess of Saluzzo, smitten with the beauty of Grissil, the virtuous daughter of a poor basket-maker, makes her his bride. Wishing to try her patience, he subjects her to a series of humiliations and cruelties, robbing her of her children and making her believe them dead, and finally pretending to take another wife, and making her attend upon the new bride. All these trials she bears submissively. The new bride is revealed to be Grissil's daughter, and Grissil is restored to honour. The play contains the beautiful song: 'Art thou poor, yet hast thou golden slumbers, O sweet content.'

The same subject is treated in Chaucer's 'Clerk's Tale' (see *Canterbury Tales*). It was taken originally from the 'Decameron' (x. x).

PATMORE, COVENTRY KERSEY DIGHTON (1823–96), was an assistant in the printed book department of the British Museum. He was a friend of Tennyson and Ruskin, and made the acquaintance of the Pre-Raphaelite (q.v.) group, to whose organ, 'The Germ', he contributed. In 1854 he issued 'The Betrothal'; in 1856 'The Espousals'; in 1860 'Faithful for Ever'; and in 1862 'The Victories of Love'—four poems forming part of 'The Angel in the House', a long work designed to be the apotheosis of married love. Felix courts and weds Honoria, a dean's daughter, and the poet traces the progress of a deep pure love amid the incidents of a commonplace life, giving the subject in the end a mystical turn. Patmore became a Roman Catholic in 1864. In 1877 he published 'The Unknown Eros', odes on high themes very different from the domesticity of his previous poems; and 'Amelia' in 1878. His collected poetical works were published, with an appendix on English metrical law, in 1886. Articles contributed mostly to the 'St. James's Gazette' were subsequently issued under the titles of 'Principle in Art' (1889) and 'Religio Poetae' (1893). His 'Rod, Root, and Flower', chiefly meditations on religious subjects, appeared in 1895.

Patmos, the island in the Aegean Sea, one of the Sporades, where, according to legend, St. John saw the visions of the Apocalypse.

Patrick, St. (373?–463?), the patron saint of Ireland, originally named Sucat, and apparently of mixed Roman and British parentage, was born probably in Ailclyde (now Dumbarton). He was captured in a raid of Picts and Scots in 389 and sold to Miliuc, a chieftain of Antrim. After six years of bondage, he went to Gaul and studied under Martin of Tours. He then returned to Britain and, feeling a supernatural call to preach to the heathen Irish, landed in Wicklow in 405 (432?), proceeding thence to Strangford Lough, where he converted all the Ulstermen. He subsequently journeyed through Ireland and founded his first mission settlement near Armagh, where, according to St. Bernard, he was buried. Some 'epistles' of St. Patrick, believed to be genuine, are extant. His festival is on 17 Mar. His life has been written by J. B. Bury (1805).

Patrick's, The Dean of St., Swift (q.v.).

Patrick's Purgatory, St., a cave on an island on Lough Derg in the west of Ireland, where, according to legend, an entrance to purgatory was revealed to St. Patrick, that he might overcome the obstinacy of those whom he was trying to convert. Henry of Saltrey (*fl.* 1150), a Cistercian of Saltrey in Huntingdonshire, who had the story from Gilbert of Louth, wrote an account of the visit of Sir Owain, a knight of King Stephen, to St. Patrick's Purgatory, undertaken by way of penance for his sins. This was translated into other languages, and the cave has been a place of pilgrimage since at least the 13th cent. Calderón (q.v.), the Spanish dramatist, has a play on this subject, translated (1853, and again 1873) by D. F. MacCarthy.

Patrick Spens, Sir, an early Scottish ballad. According to Andrew Lang 'it is a confused echo of the Scotch expedition which should have brought the Maid of Norway to Scotland, about 1285'. Sir Patrick's ship is wrecked off Aberdour (in Aberdeenshire) on the return journey with the king's daughter aboard. The ballad is included in Percy's 'Reliques'.

Patriot King, The Idea of a, a political treatise by Viscount Bolingbroke (q.v.), written in 1738, and published in 1749.

The institution of monarchy, the author declares, has been degraded by the spirit of tyranny, ambition, and vanity, aided by the adulation of interested men. Monarchy should be limited so far as to preserve liberty. Liberty without government becomes licence; government without liberty becomes tyranny. The role of the patriot king is to maintain the constitution. Only he can save a country whose ruin is so far advanced as that of England. He must begin to govern as soon as he begins to reign, and call into the administration such men as will serve on the same principles as he intends to follow, dismissing the adventurers previously in power. He will espouse no party, but govern like the common father of the people, aiming to subdue faction. The proper personal conduct of the patriot king is illustrated from the example of Elizabeth and of various rulers of antiquity.

This treatise is generally accounted the best, as it was practically the last, of Bolingbroke's political writings.

Patro'clus, one of the Grecian warriors during the Trojan War, and the close friend of Achilles (q.v.). When the latter retired to his tent, Patroclus followed his example, until Nestor, in consequence of the many defeats of the Greeks, prevailed upon him to return to the field. To this Achilles consented, and lent Patroclus his armour. In the ensuing battle Patroclus was slain by Hector with the aid of Apollo. Achilles now left his seclusion and set about avenging the death of his friend. He slew Hector, who had increased his wrath by appearing in the armour taken from the body of Patroclus.

Patrologiae, see *Migne.*

Patterne, SIR WILLOUGHBY, ELEANOR and ISABEL, LIEUTENANT, and CROSSJAY, characters in Meredith's 'The Egoist' (q.v.).

Patti, ADELINA (1843–1919), a famous soprano opera-singer, born at Madrid, who first appeared at New York in 1859 and in London in 1861, and became one of the most popular singers of her time.

Pattieson, PETER, a schoolmaster, the imaginary author of the 'Tales of My Landlord' of Sir W. Scott (q.v.).

PATTISON, MARK (1813–84), educated at Oriel College, Oxford, and a fellow and tutor of Lincoln College, Oxford, was for a time an ardent follower of Newman, but when the latter entered the Roman Church, gradually separated himself from the high church party, and contributed to 'Essays and Reviews' (q.v.) a valuable paper on the 'Tendencies of Religious Thought in England, 1688 to 1750'. In 1851 he failed to be elected rector of Lincoln College, a disappointment that seems to have permanently embittered him. He threw up his tutorship in 1855 and wrote principally on educational subjects. In 1861 he became rector of Lincoln College, continuing his literary activity in a wider field. He wrote a life of Isaac Casaubon (1875), and for the English Men of Letters series a life of Milton (1879); contributed to the E.B. articles on Erasmus, More, and Grotius, and edited certain works of Milton and Pope. He also collected materials for a life of Joseph Scaliger (q.v.). He dictated in 1883 his interesting 'Memoirs' to the year 1860 (published posthumously). His collected 'Essays' appeared in 1889.

It is probable that Pattison was the model for Mr. Casaubon in 'Middlemarch' (q.v.).

Paul Clifford, a novel by Bulwer Lytton (q.v.), published in 1830. The work was written with the object of securing an improvement of English penal discipline and penal law, a cause in which Romilly, Mackintosh, and others were working. It is interesting as one of the first novels of philanthropic purpose.

Paul Clifford, whose parents are unknown, is brought up by an innkeeper among undesirable companions, is arrested for a theft of which he is guiltless, and is imprisoned among hardened criminals. Escaping, he becomes the leader of a band of highwaymen. While residing at Bath under the name of Captain Clifford, he falls in love with, and wins the affection of, Lucy Brandon, an heiress and niece of Sir William Brandon, an ambitious and hard-hearted judge. Realizing the impossibility of their marriage, he takes leave of her, hinting at the nature of the obstacle in its way. He presently rescues two of his associates who have been captured in the course of a robbery, but is himself wounded and taken prisoner. Sir William Brandon is the judge before whom he is tried. Just as Brandon is about to pronounce sentence of death on Clifford, a piece of paper reaches him intimating that the prisoner is his son, stolen from him in infancy. Brandon nevertheless pronounces sentence, but is shortly afterwards found dead in his carriage. The paper on him reveals the facts, and Clifford's sentence is commuted to transportation. Clifford escapes, with Lucy, to America, where his remaining days are devoted to philanthropic work.

Paul Emanuel, MONSIEUR, one of the principal characters in C. Brontë's 'Villette' (q.v.).

Paul et Virginie, a romance by Bernardin de St. Pierre (q.v.), published in 1787.

It is a simple tale of a boy and a girl, children of two mothers who have sought refuge from their troubles in the Île de France (Mauritius). Brought up together far from the civilization and conventions of Europe, they fall deeply in love. Virginie is summoned to France for a few years by a rich relative and her return is awaited by Paul, with intense longing. The ship arrives, but is wrecked by a hurricane within sight of the shore, and Paul's efforts to reach it fail. Virginie is seen on the poop. A naked sailor approaches and entreats her to take off her clothes and allow herself to be saved, but she refuses and perishes—an excess of delicacy which probably appeared less singular when the book was written than it may today. Paul shortly after dies of grief.

Paul Ferroll, a novel by Mrs. Clive (q.v.), published in 1855.

Paul Ferroll, a man of wealth, culture, and ability, murders his wife, a woman of violent and domineering character, who by a stratagem has prevented him from marrying the woman that he loved. He escapes suspicion, but will not allow any innocent person to suffer for his crime, even though this attitude, after eighteen years of happy life with his second wife, the woman of his heart, entails his voluntary confession, the death from shock of his wife, and the ruin of his daughter.

This remarkable novel was followed by a less powerful sequel, 'Why Paul Ferroll Killed his Wife'.

Paul Pry, the title of a farce by Poole (q.v.), produced in 1825.

Paul Pry is an inquisitive, meddlesome fellow, said to be drawn from one Thomas Hill, who turned his inquisitiveness to account by writing for the press.

PAUL THE DEACON (PAULUS DIACONUS), a Lombard of the 8th cent., and at one time inmate of the Benedictine house at Monte Cassino, where he made the acquaintance of Charlemagne; one of the best chroniclers of the Dark Ages, author of the 'Historia Longobardorum' included in the 'Monumenta Germaniae Historica' (q.v.).

PAUL THE SILENTIARY (PAULUS SILENTIARIUS), one of the *silentiarii* or secretaries of the Emperor Justinian, was a Greek elegiac poet, author of a description of the church of St. Sophia at Constantinople.

Paul's, CHILDREN OF, a company of boy actors, recruited from the choristers of St. Paul's Cathedral, whose performances enjoyed great popularity at the end of the 16th and beginning of the 17th cents. The CHILDREN OF THE CHAPEL, recruited from the choristers of the Chapel Royal, was another company enjoying popular favour at the same time. Their rivalry with men actors is alluded to in 'Hamlet', II. ii.

Paul's, ST., Covent Garden, built about 1635 by Inigo Jones, and after destruction by fire in 1795 rebuilt according to the original design. It contains the burial-places of

Samuel Butler (the author of 'Hudibras'), Wycherley, Mrs. Centlivre, Dr. Arne, and Grinling Gibbons (qq.v.).

Paul's Cathedral, ST., was founded early in the 7th cent. by Mellitus (or according to Bede by King Æthelbert for Mellitus), who was sent to England from Rome in 601 and consecrated bishop of London by St. Augustine in 604. Erkenwald, son of Offa, was a notable early successor (675–93) of Mellitus. Miracles were associated with him, and his shrine, says Lethaby ('London before the Conquest'), was the palladium of the city until the Reformation. The cathedral that preceded the present edifice, now spoken of as old St. Paul's, was begun in the 11th cent. after the great fire of 1087, and not finished until 1314. It had a tall wooden spire (destroyed by lightning in 1561), and Inigo Jones added an Ionic façade to it. It lost much of its sacred character. As early as the days of Bishop Braybrook (end of the 14th cent.) we hear of its being used as a market. There are frequent references in the 16th and 17th cents. to the secular uses to which it was put. Its central aisle, known as 'Paul's Walk', is mentioned as a promenade, place of business and assignation, and an exchange of gossip. Whence the term 'Paul's man'. Thus the scene of Jonson's 'Every Man out of his Humour', III. i, is laid there. It was a place where servants were hired: Falstaff says of Bardolph, 'I bought him in Paul's and he'll buy me a horse in Smithfield' ('2 Henry IV', I. ii). Earle, in his 'Microcosmographie' (q.v.), gives a full account of 'Paul's Walk' (ch. 52). In the course of this he says: 'The principal inhabitants and possessors are stall knights, captains out of service, men of long rapiers and breeches, which after all turn merchants here, and traffic for news.' (Cf. A. J. C. Hare, 'Walks in London', i. III (ed. 1894), and Milman, 'Annals of St. Paul's', pp. 284 et seq.)

Old St. Paul's was destroyed in the Fire of London (1666), and the cathedral as we know it was built by Sir C. Wren (q.v.). Besides the tombs of naval and military heroes, it contains those of Wren himself, Reynolds, and Turner, and a monument to Dr. Johnson. Among the eminent persons buried in old St. Paul's may be mentioned Sir P. Sidney, Colet, and Donne (qq.v.).

Paul's Cross, ST.: 'about the middest of this churchyard (St. Paul's) is a Pulpit Crosse of timber, mounted upon steppes of stone and covered with leade, in which are sermons preached by learned Divines every Sundaye in the fornoone' (Stow). The Cross was demolished in 1643. Another cross now occupies its place.

Paul's Letters to his Kinsfolk, a series of letters by Sir W. Scott (q.v.), published in 1816, describing a visit by the author to Brussels, Waterloo, and Paris a few weeks after the battle of Waterloo. The account of the battle is interesting for the details it contains, some of them obtained from Napoleon's Belgian guide.

Paul's Man, see *Paul's Cathedral*.

Paul's School, St., was founded in 1512 by Colet (q.v.). Lily (q.v.) was its first master. The school was removed from St. Paul's Churchyard to Hammersmith in 1884. Among its many distinguished scholars may be mentioned Milton, Samuel Pepys, and Sir Philip Francis (qq.v.).

Paul's Walk, see *Paul's Cathedral*.

Paulicians, a religious sect that arose in Armenia about the 7th cent., holding modified Manichaean opinions. They asserted that all matter is evil and that Christ's body was ethereal, and rejected the authority of the O.T. They probably derive their name from Paul of Samosata, patriarch of Antioch, 260–72. They spread to Europe and Syria, becoming very numerous by the time of the Crusades.

Paulina, a character in Shakespeare's 'The Winter's Tale' (q.v.).

Pauline, the first published poem of R. Browning (q.v.). It appeared anonymously in 1833, when the author was only twenty, and was subsequently an object of aversion to him. It is an obscure and incoherent confession of the young poet's sentiments, largely it would seem of admiration for Shelley, made to a very shadowy Pauline.

Pauline Deschapelles, the heroine of Bulwer Lytton's 'Lady of Lyons' (q.v.).

PAUSANIAS, traveller and geographer, perhaps a native of Lydia, wrote in the reign of Marcus Aurelius his 'Periegesis' (Itinerary) of Greece, in which he describes the legends and objects of antiquity connected with the places that he visited. A very important writer, for he saw the monuments of ancient Greece before any serious destruction had taken place. The first Renaissance edition of him was printed at Venice in 1510.

PAVESE, CESARE (1908–50), Italian writer, born in Piedmont, whose reputation rests on his nine short novels. His last, 'La luna e i falò' ('The Moon and the Bonfires', 1950), is also his finest. Realism and myth, reminiscence and the observation of contemporary reality, combine to form the highly individual texture of his lyrical prose, which expresses the heart-searchings of a solitary man with a restless social conscience. Pavese also wrote poems and short stories, and made many translations from the English and American authors (Joyce, Faulkner, etc.) who influenced him.

Pavia, a town of N. Italy, the old capital of the Lombard kingdom; the Iron Crown (q.v.) was kept there. Under its walls was fought in 1525 the battle in which Francis I of France was defeated and captured by the army of the Emperor Charles V.

Paxarett, Sir Telegraph, a character in Peacock's 'Melincourt' (q.v.).

PAYN, JAMES (1830–98), went as a boy to Eton, Woolwich Academy (for a year), and Trinity College, Cambridge, but can hardly be said to have been educated there, for, according to Leslie Stephen's memoir, he refused to be moulded by them and developed unconventionally. He began early in life to contribute to 'Household Words' (q.v.) (he had a strong admiration for its editor, Dickens) and to 'Chambers's Journal', of which he became co-editor in 1858 and sole editor from 1859 to 1874. From 1883 to 1896 he was editor of 'The Cornhill Magazine' (q.v.). He published a volume of 'Poems' in 1853, 'Some Private Views' in 1882, 'Some Literary Recollections' in 1884, and 'Gleams of Memory' in 1894. 'The Backwater of Life' and other essays appeared posthumously in 1899. Payn was the author of a large number of novels, including 'Lost Sir Massingberd' (1864), 'By Proxy' (1878), 'The Luck of the Darrells' (1885).

PAYNE, JOHN HOWARD (1791–1852), American actor and playwright, born in New York City, famous as author of the popular song, 'Home, Sweet Home' (q.v.).

Peace with honour: the gain that Lord Beaconsfield, in his speech of 16 July 1878, claimed to have brought back from the Congress of Berlin. The expression occurs in Shakespeare's 'Coriolanus' (q.v.), III. ii.

PEACHAM, HENRY (1576?–1643?), educated at Trinity College, Cambridge, an author and a man of very varied talents. He published in 1606 'Graphice', a practical treatise on art, issued in many subsequent editions under the title 'The Gentleman's Exercise'. He published 'The Compleat Gentleman', the work by which he is best known, in 1622. From the last edition of this (1661) Johnson drew all the heraldic definitions in his dictionary.

Peachum, and his daughter Polly, characters in Gay's 'Beggar's Opera' (q.v.).

PEACOCK, THOMAS LOVE (1785–1866), novelist and poet, was the son of a London merchant. He found mercantile occupation uncongenial, and for a time lived on his private means, producing some verse, and his satirical romances, 'Headlong Hall' (1816), 'Melincourt' (1817), and 'Nightmare Abbey' (1818). He entered the East India Company's service in 1819, published another satirical novel, 'Crotchet Castle', in 1831, and late in life, in 1860 or 1861, the last of these, 'Gryll Grange'. The above works (noticed under their respective titles) are a curious mixture of satire (personal, social, and political) and romance, and are written in a piquant and attractive style. They are diversified by some capital songs. The general scheme is the same in all of them, the gathering of a miscellaneous party of odd characters in a country house, followed by diverting dialogue and absurd incidents.

In Peacock's other novels, 'Maid Marian' (q.v., 1822) and 'The Misfortunes of Elphin' (q.v., 1829), the satire is veiled under a more simply romantic form. Peacock also published two or three volumes of verse, which are of less interest. Peacock married Jane Gryffydh, the 'White Snowdonian antelope' of Shelley's 'Letter to Maria Gisborne', and was the father of George Meredith's first wife. He was an intimate friend of Shelley, and his executor. His 'Memorials of Shelley' were edited by H. Brett Smith (1909). There is a life of Peacock by Carl van Doren (1911).

Pearl, an alliterative poem in twelve-lined octosyllabic stanzas, of the period 1350–80. The author is unknown. The two poems 'Patience' and 'Cleanness' (qq.v.) are attributed to the same author, and also 'Gawain and the Green Knight' (q.v.).

Pearl is the author's daughter, an only child, whom he has lost when she was less than two years old. Wandering disconsolate in the garden where she is buried, he has a vision of a river beyond which lies Paradise. Here he sees a maiden seated, in whom he recognizes his daughter grown to maturity. She upbraids him for his excessive grief, and explains her blessed state. He strives to join her and plunges into the river, and awakes from his trance, comforted and resigned to his lot.

PEARSON, JOHN (1613–86), a fellow of King's College, Cambridge, a Royalist chaplain during the Civil War, and after the Restoration Master of Jesus College, and subsequently of Trinity College, Cambridge. He became bishop of Chester in 1673. In 1654 he preached at St. Clement's, Eastcheap, London, the series of sermons which he published in 1659 as an 'Exposition of the Creed'. This work, on which his reputation still mainly rests, has long been a standard book in English divinity. The notes of the 'Exposition'—a rich mine of patristic and general learning—are at least as remarkable as the text, and form a complete catena of the best authorities upon doctrinal points. He was probably the ablest scholar and best systematic theologian among Englishmen of the 17th cent.

Peau de Chagrin, La, the title of a novel by Balzac (q.v.). The 'peau de chagrin' (shagreen or ass's skin) has the magic property of giving its owner his every wish, but shrinks with every wish thus gratified, till it entirely disappears, and the owner dies.

Pecksniff, MR., a character in Dickens's 'Martin Chuzzlewit' (q.v.).

PECOCK, REGINALD (1395?–1460?), a Welshman by birth and bishop successively of St. Asaph and Chichester. He distinguished himself by his writings against the Lollards, notably by his 'Repressor of over much Blaming of the Clergy' (1455), a monument of 15th-cent. English, clear and pointed, if voluminous, in style. His 'Book of Faith',

also in English, was issued in 1456. In his 'Donet' he sought to find a minimum of religious belief acceptable by all, asserting that the Apostles' Creed was named after them, not drawn up by them. He alienated by his writings every section of theological opinion in England, was cited before the archbishop of Canterbury, and obliged to resign his bishopric and make public abjuration (1458). He was sent to Thorney Abbey, where he probably lived in seclusion. His 'Repressor' and 'Book of Faith' have been printed, and a collection of excerpts from his works included in Foxe's 'Commentarii Rerum in Ecclesia Gestarum' (1554). His work is important from a literary standpoint for its development of the English vocabulary, and from a theological standpoint for his advocacy of converting the Lollards by argument instead of by burning them.

Peculiar People, a name applied to the Jews as God's chosen people; also to a religious sect founded in 1838 and most numerous about London, who have no preachers, creed, or church organization, and rely on prayer for the cure of disease, rejecting medical aid. [OED.]

Pecunia, LADY, an allegorical character in Jonson's 'The Staple of News' (q.v.).

Pedro, DON, the Prince of Aragon in Shakespeare's 'Much Ado about Nothing' (q.v.).

Peebles, PETER, a character in Scott's 'Redgauntlet' (q.v.).

Peel, JOHN, the hero of the well-known hunting song, 'D'ye ken John Peel?', was born at Caldbeck, Cumberland, in 1776, and for over 40 years ran the famous pack of hounds that bore his name. He died in 1854. The words of the song were composed by his friend John Woodcock Graves. The tune is based on that of an old rant called 'Bonnie Annie', and is the regimental march of the Border Regiment. ('The Times', 19 Oct. 1929.)

PEELE, GEORGE (1558?–97?), son of a London citizen and salter, was educated at Christ's Hospital, London, and Broadgates Hall (Pembroke College) and Christ Church, Oxford. He led a dissipated life, and in 1579 was turned out of his father's dwelling, within the precincts of Christ's Hospital, by the governors of the institution. He was almost certainly a successful player as well as playwright, and his lyrics were popular in literary circles. His works, which are very numerous, fall under three heads: plays, pageants, and 'gratulatory' and miscellaneous verse. Among his plays may be mentioned 'The Arraignment of Paris' (q.v., c. 1581), 'The Battle of Alcazar' (q.v., printed in 1594), 'The Old Wives' Tale' (q.v., 1595), and 'David and Bethsabe' (q.v., 1599). Among his miscellaneous verse were 'Polyhymnia' (q.v., 1590) and 'The Honour of the Garter' (1593), a gratulatory poem to the earl of Northumberland on his being created a knight of that order. The lyrics in Peele's plays are particularly attractive.

Peelers, a nickname first given to the Irish constabulary instituted in 1814 by Sir Robert Peel, and extended to the police in England (cf. *Bobby*).

Peep of Day Boys, a Protestant organization in the north of Ireland (*c.* 1784–95), whose members visited the houses of their Roman Catholic opponents at daybreak in search of arms.

Peeping Tom, see *Godiva*.

Peer Gynt, a lyrical drama by Ibsen (q.v.), published in 1867. Peer Gynt was intended by the author as the embodiment of certain aspects in the character of his countrymen at the end of the romantic period, and the work is an indictment of the half-heartedness, lack of character, and egoism that Ibsen reproved.

The hero is a Norwegian peasant, indolent and dissipated, a dreamer and a braggart, though possessed of fascination and plentiful capacities for good. His good angel is the virtuous maiden, Solvejg, but effort and perseverance are required to win her, and to the difficulties involved Peer Gynt is unequal. Instead he carries off Ingrid, the destined bride of another, and becomes an outlaw. The poem presents through a multitude of episodes his gradual degradation, his association with the trolls, Solvejg's fruitless efforts to reclaim him, and the wonderful scene of the death of his mother, Aase. In the 4th and 5th acts, we see him a selfish worldling who has made a fortune dealing in Negro slaves, posing as a prophet in Africa, flirting with the Arab damsel Anitra, and finally returning, an old disillusioned man, to Norway, to find the button-moulder waiting to melt him up, as waste, into raw material. But he finds redemption in the pure love of Solvejg, who has waited faithfully for him during many years.

Peerybingle, JOHN and DOT, characters in Dickens's 'The Cricket on the Hearth' (q.v.).

Peg Woffington, a novel by Reade (q.v.), published in 1853 and based on the successful play 'Masks and Faces' (1852), composed by him jointly with Tom Taylor.

It deals with an episode in the life of the famous Irish actress, Margaret Woffington (q.v.), who makes a conquest of a wealthy gentleman, Ernest Vane, not knowing him to be recently married. She cuts out the face from a portrait of herself by a poor scene-painter and substitutes her own, to fool a party of critics who have come to abuse the portrait. She then plays the same trick on Mabel Vane, with the result that she hears the young wife's touching prayer, that the actress shall not steal her husband's heart. Peg is moved by the prayer and a tear on her face reveals the deception. She effects the reconciliation of the young couple, and the story ends with her retirement to a life of piety and good deeds.

Peg-a-Ramsey, the heroine of an old song popular in Shakespeare's day. He refers to her in 'Twelfth Night', II. iii.

Pegăsus, a winged horse sprung from the blood of Medusa, when Perseus cut off her head. By striking Mt. Helicon with his foot, Pegasus gave rise to the fountain Hippocrene. He became the favourite of the Muses, and, being tamed by Neptune or Minerva, was given to Bellerophon (q.v.) to enable him to conquer the Chimaera. Some authors have supposed that Bellerophon attempted to fly to heaven upon Pegasus, and that this act of temerity was punished by Jupiter, who sent an insect to torment Pegasus and caused the fall of the rider.

Peggotty, DANIEL, CLARA, and HAM, characters in Dickens's 'David Copperfield' (q.v.).

Pegler, MRS., in Dickens's 'Hard Times' (q.v.), Bounderby's mother.

Pehlevi, see *Pahlevi*.

Peirēnē, a fountain at Corinth, where Bellerophon, according to one form of his legend, is supposed to have caught the horse Pegasus (qq.v.).

Peirithŏus, see *Theseus* and *Centaurs*.

Peisistrătus (*d.* 527 B.C.) became tyrant of Athens in 560 B.C., was twice expelled, but returned to power. He endowed Athens with many splendid buildings, including the temple of the Olympian Zeus, which was not completed until the days of the Emperor Hadrian. He also encouraged literature. It was probably under his auspices that dramatic contests were introduced at Athens, and he is said to have commissioned some learned men, among them the poet Onomacritus, to collect the poems of Homer.

Pelagian, derived from *Pelagius*, the latinized form of the name of a British monk, Morgan, of the 4th and 5th cents., whose doctrines were fiercely combated by Germanus, bishop of Auxerre, and by St. Augustine, and condemned by Pope Zosimus in 418. The Pelagians, his followers, denied the Catholic doctrine of original sin, asserting that Adam's fall did not involve his posterity, and maintained that the human will is of itself capable of good without the assistance of divine grace. They did not admit the doctrine of the eternal punishment of un-baptized infants.

Pelayo, a character in Southey's 'Roderick' (q.v.).

Pelēus, son of Aeacus, king of Phthia in Thessaly. Being guilty of some murder, he went to Iolcos, where Acastus, the king, purified him. Hippolyte, wife of Acastus, fell in love with him, but being repulsed denounced him to her husband. Acastus tried to have him killed by wild beasts on Mt. Pelion, but with the help of Cheiron (q.v.) Peleus was able to overcome these. He courted Thetis, a Nereid (q.v.), who tried in vain to escape him by assuming various shapes. Of their union was born Achilles (q.v.). All the goddesses were invited to the nuptials, except Eris or Discord, who to avenge herself threw among the guests an apple inscribed 'To the fairest', which was claimed by Hera, Aphrodite, and Athene (see *Paris*).

Pelham, or The Adventures of a Gentleman, a novel by Bulwer Lytton (q.v.), published in 1828.

This was Lytton's second novel, and is generally considered his best. Henry Pelham, a young dandy, wit, and zealous politician, falls in love with the accomplished Ellen, sister of his old friend Sir Reginald Glanville. The latter is suspected of the murder of Sir John Tirrell, against whom he has had grave cause of complaint, and the circumstantial evidence against him appears overwhelming. Glanville tells his story to Pelham and asserts his innocence. With the assistance of the disreputable Job Jonson, Pelham unearths the real murderer, Thornton, who is convicted on the testimony of a confederate. The character of Thornton was drawn from the well-known murderer, Thurtell. The story is enlivened with amusing scenes of social and political life. Thackeray made some of his best fun of Bulwer Lytton about this novel in his 'Diary of Jeames de la Pluche'.

Pelias, a king of Iolcos, whom his daughters put to death and boiled at the instigation of Medea (q.v.), in order to restore him to youth. Alcestis (q.v.) was one of his daughters.

Pelican, The, see *Golden Hind.*

Pelican's Piety, more correctly *Pelican in her Piety*, an heraldic term signifying a pelican represented as vulning (i.e. wounding) her breast in order to feed her young with her blood.

Pelion, a mountain in Thessaly, on which the Giants (q.v.) in their war with the gods heaped Mt. Ossa, in order to scale the heights of heaven. The spear of Achilles (q.v.) was made from a tree cut on this mountain.

Pell, SOLOMON, in Dickens's 'The Pickwick Papers (q.v)', an attorney in the Insolvent Court.

Pella, in Macedonia, the capital of the Macedonian kings and the birthplace of Alexander the Great. It stood near the modern town of Yenidje (Yanitsa), west of the lower course of the Vardar. Little trace of it remains.

Pelleas, SIR, in the Arthurian legend, the lover of Ettard or Ettarre (see below, *Pelleas and Ettarre*). He may, like Pelles (q.v.), have been developed from the Pwyll of British mythology. It is noteworthy that after Ettard's death he marries (Malory, IV. xxiii) the damsel of the lake, Nimue, who is thought to be identical with Rhiannon, the wife of Pwyll (see Rhys, 'Arthurian Legend').

Pelleas and Ettarre, one of Tennyson's 'Idylls of the King' (q.v.), published in 1869.

The youth Pelleas, strong and guileless, on his way to Arthur's court to seek knighthood falls in with the vain and heartless Ettarre, and is smitten with love for her. She, thinking that Pelleas may win the prize at the forthcoming tournament, encourages his love. Pelleas wins the prize and gives it to her. Her object gained, she now becomes ungracious to him. He follows her to her castle, from which he is excluded, and day by day sits on his horse outside it. She sends her three knights to kill him, but he defeats them. Finally Gawain, the 'light-of-love', appears, and, on the pretext of furthering the suit of Pelleas, borrows his armour, claims to have killed him, and gains admission to the castle. Pelleas, distrustful, presently follows, and discovers Gawain's perfidy. Riding away distraught, he comes upon Percivale, and learns from him that not Gawain alone is faithless, but Lancelot and Guinevere, and the knights generally. He presently meets Lancelot, declares himself 'a scourge to lash the treasons of the Table Round', fights with him, and is defeated; but his life is spared, and the two knights return to the hall. Then fear falls upon the queen and her lover, and each foresees 'the dolorous day to be'. The poem closes under the shadow of impending calamity.

Pelles, KING, in Malory's 'Morte Darthur', 'cousin nigh unto Joseph of Arimathie', and intimately connected with the story of the Holy Grail. He was father of Elaine, who becomes the mother of Galahad by Sir Launcelot. He is thought by Prof. Rhys ('Arthurian Legend') to have had his origin in the Pwyll of British mythology (see *Mabinogion* and *Pelleas*).

Pellinore, KING, in Malory's 'Morte Darthur', the father of Sir Lamorak, Sir Percival, and Sir Tor.

Peloponnesian War, THE, between Athens and Sparta and their respective allies, 431–404 B.C. It ended in the surrender of Athens and the brief transfer of the leadership of Greece to Sparta.

Pelops, the son of Tantalus (q.v.) and founder of the Pelopid dynasty from which the Peloponnese took its name. According to legend his father, having invited the gods to a repast, killed his son and set the flesh before them to eat. But they knew what it was and ordered Hermes to restore Pelops to life. Demeter, however, distracted by grief for the loss of Persephone, had consumed the shoulder, and its place was supplied by one made of ivory. Pelops won Hippodamia, daughter of King Oenomaus, for his wife by defeating her father in a chariot race. To effect this he bribed Myrtilus, the charioteer of Oenomaus, and subsequently threw him into the sea when he claimed his reward. This murder was the origin of the curse that fell upon the house of Pelops. By Hippodamia Pelops was father of Atreus (q.v.) and Thyestes.

Pelōrus, the north-east point of Sicily, Capo del Faro.

Pembroke, MARY HERBERT, COUNTESS OF (1561–1621), Sir Philip Sidney's sister. She is referred to as 'Sidney's sister, Pembroke's mother' in her epitaph by W. Browne (q.v.). She suggested the composition of her brother's 'Arcadia' (q.v.), which she revised and added to. She was a patron of Samuel Daniel, Nicholas Breton, Jonson, and other poets.

Penātēs, see *Lares*.

Pendennis, *The History of*, a novel by Thackeray (q.v.), published serially in 1848–50.

Arthur is the son of John Pendennis, a gentleman of old family, formerly an apothecary and surgeon, and Helen his wife, a woman of saintly character. Leaving school at 16 on the death of his father, Arthur falls in love with an actress, Emily Costigan (Miss Fotheringay), the daughter of Captain Costigan, a wild tipsy Irishman, who persuades himself that Arthur is the heir to a fine estate, and when undeceived by Major Pendennis, Arthur's tactful uncle, is very angry and breaks off the engagement. Arthur, a frank but selfish and conceited young fellow, goes to the university, where he is idle and extravagant, and involves himself and his mother in financial difficulties from which they are rescued by Laura Bell, an amiable girl, the daughter of a former unfortunate lover of Helen, whom she has adopted. Laura also enables Arthur to start on a literary career in London. Here he shares chambers with George Warrington (a descendant of the Warringtons of 'The Virginians', q.v.), a fine character, one of the good influences in Arthur's life. Helen's hope is that Arthur shall marry Laura, but their relations are those of affectionate brother and sister, and when Arthur in deference to his mother's wish proposes half-heartedly to Laura, not concealing his motive for doing so, she indignantly refuses him. Arthur's second entanglement is with Blanche Amory, daughter of Lady Clavering by her first husband. Blanche, though outwardly pretty and accomplished, is in reality a selfish little shrew. Old Major Pendennis, Arthur's uncle, is so actuated by worldly ambition on his nephew's behalf as to lose all sense of rectitude, and strongly favours the match, although aware that Blanche's father, an escaped convict, is, unknown to Lady Clavering, still alive. The story is much concerned with the doings of this convict, who masquerades as Col. Altamont, and blackmails Sir Francis Clavering, a despicable creature.

After a flirtation with Fanny Bolton, the porter's daughter of Shepherd's Inn, and a period during which Laura is in love with Warrington (who in fact has had his life ruined by an imprudent early marriage), Laura and Arthur are finally united. But this occurs only after the latter has narrowly escaped from marriage with Blanche Amory. For, under the influence of his uncle's advice and his own cynicism, he accepts a loveless match with her for the sake of the wealth and position it promises. At this point comes the exposure of the whole affair of Blanche's convict father. Arthur feels it his duty to be faithful to Blanche in her troubles and goes to tell her so, but finds himself supplanted by his friend Harry Foker, who has just inherited the great fortune of his father, proprietor of 'Foker's Entire'.

Among the many amusing characters in the story may be mentioned Captain Shandon, the first editor of the 'Pall Mall Gazette', of which he drafts the prospectus in the Fleet; the rival publishers Bungay and Bacon; the jovial adventurer Capt. Strong, Clavering's factotum; the vulgar but amiable 'Begum', Lady Clavering; and Morgan, the Major's blackmailing servant.

Pendragon, a title given to an ancient British or Welsh chief holding or claiming supreme power. In English chiefly known as the title of Uther Pendragon, father of Arthur. The word means 'chief dragon', the dragon being the war standard.

Pendrell or PENDEREL, the name of the five brothers, tenants on the demesnes of Boscobel (q.v.) and White Ladies, who helped to conceal Charles II after the battle of Worcester (1651). By patent dated 24 July 1676, certain fee farm rents were settled on them and their heirs for ever, with benefit of survivorship to the others on failure of heirs of any one of the beneficiaries. ('Boscobel Tracts', edited by J. Hughes.) On 26 Nov. 1931 'The Times' reported that the Penderell Pension was being drawn by Mr. George Penderell, of Brooklyn, U.S.A., a retired laundryman.

Penĕlŏpē, daughter of Icarius, wife of Odysseus, and mother of Telemachus. When, at the close of the Trojan War, her husband did not return to Ithaca, and she received no news of him, she was beset by importunate suitors. She received their addresses coldly; but, being without power to get rid of them, she flattered them with hopes and declared that she would make choice of one of them when she had completed the piece of tapestry on which she was engaged. To prolong the period she undid at night the work that she had done during the day, whence the proverb of *Penelope's web* for a labour that is never ended. The return of Odysseus after twenty years delivered her from the suitors.

Penelophon, the name of the beggar maid loved by King Cophetua, in the ballad included in Percy's 'Reliques'. Shakespeare ('Love's Labour's Lost (q.v)', IV. i) gives it as 'Zenelophon'.

Penfeather, LADY PENELOPE, a character in Scott's 'St. Ronan's Well' (q.v.).

Penguin New Writing, see *New Writing*.

Penia, poverty; according to Motteux's translation of Rabelais, IV. lvii, the mother of 'the ninety-nine Muses'.

PENN, WILLIAM (1644–1718), a Quaker and the founder of Pennsylvania, son of Sir William Penn, the admiral. He was committed to the Tower of London in 1668 for publishing his once celebrated 'The Sandy Foundation Shaken' (an attack on the Athanasian doctrine of the Trinity, the Anselmian theory of the atonement, and the Calvinistic theory of justification), and there wrote 'No Cross, no Crown' (1669), an eloquent and learned dissertation on the Christian duty of self-sacrifice. He suffered frequent persecutions and imprisonments, and turned his thoughts to America as a refuge for his co-religionists. In 1682 he obtained grants of East New Jersey and Pennsylvania, and framed, in concert with Algernon Sydney, a constitution for the colony, by which religious toleration was secured. In the same year he sailed for America. He returned to England in 1684, hoping much from the accession of James II, whom he believed to be a sincere advocate of toleration. Penn obtained in 1693 a formal expression of William III's goodwill towards him, and was in Pennsylvania again, 1699–1701, but spent the remaining years of his life in England. His 'Some Fruits of Solitude', a collection of aphorisms praised by R. L. Stevenson, was published anonymously in 1693.

PENNANT, THOMAS (1726–98), naturalist, antiquarian, and traveller, published his 'Tour in Scotland' in 1771, 'A Tour in Wales' in 1778–81, 'A Tour in Scotland and Voyage to the Hebrides' in 1774–6, and 'The Journey from Chester to London' in 1782. He also wrote 'British Zoology' (1768–70), and a 'History of Quadrupeds' (1781), which long remained classical works. He figures in Gilbert White's (q.v.) 'Selborne' as one of the author's correspondents.

Penseroso, *Il*, a poem by Milton (q.v.), written at Horton in 1632 with its companion piece 'L'Allegro' (q.v.).

The title suggests, as Dean Church pointed out, that Milton at this time had not attained full proficiency in the Italian tongue; the word, which is intended to mean 'contemplative', should be 'pensieroso'. The poem is an invocation to the goddess Melancholy, bidding her bring Peace and Quiet, and Leisure and Contemplation. It describes the pleasures of the studious, meditative life, of tragedy, epic poetry, and music.

Pentameron, *The*, one of the longer prose works of Landor (q.v.), published in 1837. 'The Pentameron' is an expression of Landor's enthusiastic admiration of Boccaccio (q.v.), and was written at the Villa Gherardesca, at Fiesole, near Florence, where Boccaccio had in part laid the scene of his 'Decameron'.

It consists of imaginary conversations between Petrarch and Boccaccio, the latter lying ill at his villa near Certaldo, and Petrarch being supposed to visit him on five successive days (whence the name of the work). They discourse mainly of Dante's 'Divina Commedia', but also of other matters. In particular Petrarch reproves Boccaccio for the licentious character of some of his tales. Whatever may be thought of the criticisms of Dante that the author puts into the mouths of the interlocutors, there can be nothing but praise for the form of the dialogue, the pleasant picture of the two old friends, the humorous scene of the dignified *canonico* struggling to saddle his palfrey, the little maid Assuntina, and Ser Biagio, the village priest.

Pentameter, in Greek and Latin prosody, a form of dactylic verse of which each half consists of two feet and a long syllable. In English literature, a line of verse of five feet, e.g. the English 'heroic' or iambic verse of ten syllables, as used for instance in 'Paradise Lost', or in the rhymed couplets of Dryden (an exception to the rule given under *Metre*, q.v.).

Pentapolin, see *Alifanfaron*.

Pentateuch, THE (Greek πέντε five, τεῦχος implement or vessel), the first five books of the Old Testament (Genesis, Exodus, Leviticus, Numbers, and Deuteronomy) taken together as a connected group, and traditionally ascribed to Moses.

Pentecost, from the Greek word meaning fiftieth [day], a name for the Jewish harvest festival observed on the fiftieth day of the Omer, i.e. at the conclusion of seven weeks from the offering of the wave-sheaf, on the second day of Passover (q.v.). Also a festival of the Christian Church, observed on the seventh Sunday after Easter, Whit-Sunday, in commemoration of the descent of the Holy Spirit upon the disciples on the day of Pentecost.

Penthea, a character in Ford's 'The Broken Heart' (q.v.).

Penthĕsĭlĕa, a daughter of Ares and queen of the Amazons. She came to the aid of the Trojans after the death of Hector, and was slain by Achilles, who, moved by her youth and beauty, mourned over her. Thersites (q.v.) mocked at the grief of Achilles and was thereupon slain by him.

Penthēus, a king of Thebes, who resisted the introduction of the worship of Dionysus into his kingdom. He was driven mad by the god, his palace destroyed, and himself torn to pieces by the Bacchanals, among whom were his mother and two sisters.

Pentonville, the name applied originally to the houses built about 1773 on the land in Clerkenwell of one Henry Penton (*d.* 1812). The Pentonville Prison, in Caledonian Road, Islington, is at some distance from Pentonville. It was built in 1840–2 as part of the scheme for abolishing the system of transportation.

PEPYS, SAMUEL (1633–1703) (pron. Peeps or Pĕpȳs), son of John Pepys, a London tailor, was educated at St. Paul's School, London, and at Trinity Hall and Magdalene College, Cambridge. In 1655, when 22, he married Elizabeth St. Michel, a girl of 15, the daughter of a French father and English mother. He entered the household of Sir Edward Montagu (afterwards first earl of Sandwich), his father's first cousin, in 1656; and his subsequent successful career was largely due to Montagu's patronage. His famous 'Diary' opens on 1 Jan. 1660, when Pepys was living in Axe Yard, Westminster, and was very poor. Soon after this he was appointed 'clerk of the King's ships' and clerk of the privy seal, with a salary of £350 (supplemented by fees). In 1665 he became surveyor-general of the victualling office, in which capacity he showed himself an energetic official and a zealous reformer of abuses. Owing to failing eyesight he closed his diary on 31 May 1669, and in the same year his wife died. In 1672 he was appointed secretary to the Admiralty. He was committed to the Tower on a charge of complicity in the 'Popish Plot' in 1679 and deprived of his office, but was soon set free. In 1683 he was sent to Tangier with Lord Dartmouth and wrote an interesting diary while there. In 1684 he was reappointed secretary to the Admiralty, a post which he held until the revolution, labouring hard to provide the country with an efficient fleet. At the revolution he was deprived of his appointment and afterwards lived in retirement, principally at Clapham. His 'Diary' remained in cipher (a system of shorthand) at Magdalene College, Cambridge, until 1825, when it was deciphered by John Smith and edited by Lord Braybrooke. An enlarged edition by Mynors Bright appeared in 1875–9, and the whole, except a few passages, was published by Henry B. Wheatley in 1893–6. It is a document of extraordinary interest, on account both of the light that its sincere narrative throws on the author's own lovable character, and of the vivid picture that it gives of contemporary everyday life, of the administration of the navy, and of the ways of the court. Pepys's 'Memoirs of the Navy, 1690' were edited by J. R. Tanner, 1906, who also published 'Mr. Pepys: an Introduction to the Diary' in 1925.

Perceforest, a vast French prose romance of the 14th cent., in which the author seeks to link the legends of Alexander and Arthur. Alexander, after the conquest of India, is driven by a storm on the coast of England, and makes one of his followers (called Perceforest because he has killed a magician in an impenetrable forest) king of the land. Under the latter's grandson the Grail (q.v.) is brought to England.

Perceval. The legend of Perceval, of great antiquity as a folk-tale, is first found in poetical form in the French 'Perceval' of Chrétien de Troyes (q.v.) and in the German 'Parzival' of Wolfram von Eschenbach (q.v.). In English it was treated in 'Sir Percyvelle of Galles' and by Malory. The former, a 15th-cent. verse romance, is a narrative of the childhood of Perceval and the adventures that led to his being knighted by King Arthur; it contains no mention of the Holy Grail. Malory's 'Morte Darthur' makes Percivale a son of King Pellinore, and narrates his adventures in the course of his quest of the Grail (q.v.), and his final admission, with Galahad and Bors, to its presence. He may be identified with the Peredur of Welsh mythology, the hero of the tale of 'Peredur, Son of Evrawc' in Lady C. Guest's 'Mabinogion' (q.v.), an early form of the Grail story.

PERCY, THOMAS (1729–1811), educated at Christ Church, Oxford, became bishop of Dromore in 1782. He published in 1765 his 'Reliques of Ancient English Poetry' (see *Percy's 'Reliques'*). This work did much to promote the revival of interest in the older English poetry. In 1763, stimulated by the success of the Ossianic publications, Percy issued 'Five Pieces of Runic Poetry', from the Icelandic, including the 'Incantation of Hervor' and the 'Death-Song of Ragnar Lodbrog'.

Percy, a tragedy by H. More (q.v.).

Percy Folio, THE, a manuscript in mid-17th-cent. handwriting, which belonged to Humphrey Pitt of Shifnal, the most important source of our ballad literature and the basis of Child's collection. From it T. Percy (q.v.) drew the ballads included in Percy's 'Reliques' (q.v.). It also contains the 14th-cent. alliterative allegorical poem 'Death and Liffe' (modelled on 'Piers the Plowman') and 'Scottish Feilde' (mainly on the battle of Flodden). The Percy Folio was printed in its entirety by Hales and Furnivall in 1867–8. It is now in the British Museum.

Percy Society, THE, was founded in 1840 by Thomas Wright, Thomas Crofton Croker, Alexander Dyce, J. O. Halliwell(-Phillipps), and John Payne Collier, for the purpose of publishing old English lyrics and ballads. It was so named in honour of T. Percy (q.v.).

Percy's 'Reliques' of Ancient English Poetry, a collection of ballads, sonnets, historical songs, and metrical romances, published in 1765 by T. Percy (q.v.). The majority of them were extracted from the Percy Folio (q.v.) and were edited and 'restored' by Percy. They were of very different periods, some of great antiquity, others as recent as the reign of Charles I. Ancient poems drawn from other sources and a few of more modern date were added by the editor. The editions of 1767, 1775, and 1794 each contained new matter.

Perdiccas, a favourite general of Alexander the Great, who received the ring of Alexander from the hand of the dying monarch. On this he based his claim to succeed him; but his ambitious schemes were opposed by Antipater, Antigonus, and Ptolemy. He was murdered while attacking Egypt.

Perdita, a character in Shakespeare's 'The Winter's Tale' (q.v.). 'Perdita' was a name given to the actress Mary Robinson (1758–1800), who took the part. She attracted the attention of the Prince of Wales (afterwards George IV) and became his mistress for a short time.

Père Goriot, Le, the title of one of the greatest of Balzac's (q.v.) novels.

Père-Lachaise, the most important cemetery of Paris, named after the Jesuit confessor of Louis XIV, who figures in one of Landor's 'Imaginary Conversations' (q.v.). The cemetery was established on the site of a house belonging to his order, where he frequently resided.

Peredur, the Welsh name of one of the chief heroes of Arthur's court, and the subject of the tale of 'Peredur, Son of Evrawc' in Lady C. Guest's 'Mabinogion' (q.v.), where he is identifiable with the Perceval of the Grail legend.

Peregrine Pickle, The Adventures of, a novel by Smollett (q.v.), published in 1751.

The hero is a scoundrel and a swash-buckler, with little to his credit except wit and courage; and the book is mainly occupied with his adventures in England and on the Continent, many of them of an amatory character. In the course of these he visits Paris, fights a duel with a mousquetaire, is imprisoned in the Bastille, visits the Netherlands, hoaxes the physicians of Bath, sets up as a magician, endeavours to enter parliament, is confined in the Fleet and released on inheriting his father's property, finally marrying Emily Gauntlet, a young lady whom he has, from the outset of the story, intermittently pursued with his attentions (even attempting to achieve his ends by drugging her).

The principal attraction of the work lies in the amusing characters that it includes: Peregrine's father, the phlegmatic Gamaliel, and his aunt Grizzle; and, chief of all, the old sea-dog Commodore Hawser Trunnion, the ferocity of whose language is equalled only by the kindness of his heart. His house is called 'the garrison', and is run like a fortress, with the assistance of Lieut. Hatchway, 'a very brave man and a great joker', who has had one leg shot away; and the boatswain, Tom Pipes, who becomes the devoted companion of Peregrine Pickle on his foreign travels. A famous episode in the story is the ridiculous dinner in the manner of the ancients; and the last part of the book contains much satire on the social, literary, and political conditions of the day. The course of the narrative is interrupted by the long and offensive 'Memoirs of

a Lady of Quality' (contributed by Viscountess Vane, 1713–88, a woman notorious for gambling and profligacy).

Perfectibilism, the doctrine that man, individual and social, is capable of progressing indefinitely towards physical, mental, and moral perfection. Mr. Foster in Peacock's 'Headlong Hall' (q.v.) was a 'perfectibilian'.

Perfectionists, see *Oneida Community.*

Peri, in Persian mythology, one of a class of superhuman beings, originally represented as of malevolent character, but subsequently as good genii or fairies, endowed with grace and beauty. According to the Koran, they were under the sway of Eblis, and Mohammed undertook their conversion. For 'Paradise and the Peri' see *Lalla Rookh.*

Periander, son of Cypselus and tyrant of Corinth (*c.* 625–*c.* 585 B.C.). The first years of his rule were mild and popular until he consulted Thrasybulus, the tyrant of Miletus, as to the best means of securing himself on the throne. The latter returned no answer to the messenger, but walked about a field of corn, plucking the ears that seemed to tower above the rest. Periander understood what was signified and put to death the richest and most powerful citizens of Corinth. (Cf. the story of Tarquinius Superbus, under *Tarquins.*) Though cruel, Periander was a patron of learning and the arts (see *Arion*).

Peri-Banou, THE FAIRY, see *Ahmed.*

Pericles, the great Athenian statesman and military commander, who controlled the affairs of the State from 460 B.C. until his death in 429 B.C., including the earlier period of the Peloponnesian War. During his administration Athens reached the summit of her power, and the Parthenon and Propylaea were built. See also *Aspasia, Pericles and Aspasia,* and *Funeral Oration.*

Pericles, MR., a character in Meredith's 'Sandra Belloni' and 'Vittoria' (qq.v.).

Pericles, Prince of Tyre, a romantic drama by Shakespeare (q.v.), produced probably about 1608, and first printed (in a mangled form) in 1609, and in the third folio of 1664. Internal evidence suggests that the play was not written entirely by Shakespeare. The story is drawn from the 'Apollonius of Tyre' in Gower's 'Confessio Amantis' (q.v.). Gower himself appears as Chorus.

Pericles, prince of Tyre, having guessed the secret infamy of Antiochus, emperor of Greece, and his life being threatened in consequence, leaves his government in the hands of his honest minister, Helicanus, and sails from Tyre. His ship is wrecked on the coast of Pentapolis, Pericles alone being saved. Here he defeats in the lists the other suitors for the hand of Thaisa, daughter of King Simonides, whom he weds. Shortly after, Helicanus makes known to him that Antiochus is dead and the people are clamouring to make him (Helicanus) king. Pericles and Thaisa set off for Tyre, but, a storm arising, Thaisa falls in travail with fear, and gives birth to a daughter. A deep swoon gives the impression that Thaisa is dead, and she is committed to the waves in a chest. The chest is cast ashore near Ephesus, where Cerimon, a physician, opens it and restores Thaisa to life. She, thinking her husband drowned, becomes a priestess in the temple of Diana. Pericles carries his daughter Marina to Tarsus, where he leaves her with Cleon, the governor, and his wife, Dionyza. When the child grows up, Dionyza, jealous of her superior accomplishments, designs to kill her; but Marina is carried off by pirates and sold in Mitylene into a brothel, where her purity and piety win the admiration of Lysimachus, the governor of Mitylene, and the respect of even the brothel-keeper's brutal servant, and secure her release. Pericles, mourning the supposed death of his daughter, comes to Mitylene, where he discovers her, to his intense joy. A dream directs him to go to the temple of Diana at Ephesus and there recount the story of his life. This he does, with the result that the priestess Thaisa, his lost wife, recognizes him, and is reunited to her husband and daughter. Marina is married to Lysimachus. Cleon and Dionyza are burnt as a penalty for their intended crime.

Pericles and Aspasia, one of the longer prose works of Landor (q.v.), published in 1836.

It consists of imaginary letters relating to the period of the union of Pericles and Aspasia (qq.v.). The majority of them are from Aspasia to the friend Cleone whom she has left at Miletus, and Cleone's replies. Others are addressed by Pericles to Aspasia, or by her to him; while others again are from or to noted personages of the time, such as Anaxagoras and Alcibiades. They include discussions of artistic, literary, religious, philosophical, and political subjects, and contain passages of great beauty. The letters terminate with the death of Pericles.

Perigot, a character in Fletcher's 'The Faithful Shepherdess' (q.v.).

Perillus, see *Phalaris.*

Perilous Chair, THE, the 'Siege Perilous' at the Round Table (q.v.).

Peripatetics, see *Aristotle.*

Perissa, in Spenser's 'Faerie Queene', see *Medina.*

Periphrasis, a roundabout form of statement, a circumlocution.

Perker, MR., in Dickens's 'Pickwick Papers' (q.v.), Mr. Pickwick's attorney.

Perkin Warbeck, an historical play by J. Ford (q.v.), published in 1634.

The play deals with the arrival of Warbeck at the court of King James IV of Scotland, and his marriage at the king's instance and against her father's wish to Lady Katherine

Gordon; the treason of Sir William Stanley and his execution; the expedition of James IV with Warbeck into England; the desertion of Warbeck's cause by James; Warbeck's landing in Cornwall, his defeat, capture, and execution. The portrait of Warbeck is a sympathetic one, and the devotion of Lady Katherine to him is touchingly drawn. The play is entirely unlike Ford's other work, and is a good historical drama.

For the facts and dates of Perkin Warbeck's history, see *Warbeck.*

PERRAULT, CHARLES (1628–1703), a French poet, critic, and member of the Academy, chiefly known in England for the fairy tales published by him under the title 'Histoires et Contes du Tems Passé' (1697) with the legend on the frontispiece, 'Contes de Ma Mère l'Oye' ('Mother Goose's Tales'). They were translated into English by Robert Samber (1729?), and were doubtless French popular tales collected from various sources. Andrew Lang, in his 'Perrault's Popular Tales' (1888), discusses their origins and analogies in the fables current in different times and among different peoples. The tales are the following: *La Belle au bois dormant* ('Sleeping Beauty', q.v.), *Le Petit Chaperon rouge* ('Red Riding Hood', q.v.), *La Barbe bleue* ('Blue Beard', q.v.), *Le Maistre Chat, ou le Chat botté* ('Puss in Boots', q.v.), *Les Fées* ('The Fairy'), *Cendrillon ou la petite pantoufle de verre* ('Cinderella', q.v.), *Riquet à la houppe* ('Riquet with the Tuft', q.v.), *Petit Poucet* ('Hop o' My Thumb, Little Thumb', q.v.).

To each story is attached a moral; though, as Lang points out, it is not very obvious in the story of the success of that 'unscrupulous adventurer', Puss in Boots.

Perrette, in the fables of La Fontaine (q.v.), the milkmaid who, carried away by dreams of the profits to be made from the milk she is carrying on her head, lets it drop. Cf. *Alnaschar.*

Persant of Inde, SIR, in Malory's 'Morte Darthur', one of the knights who kept the approach to Castle Perilous, overthrown by Sir Gareth (see *Gareth and Lynette*).

Persĕphŏnē, see *Proserpine.*

Persĕpŏlis, the capital of the Persian empire, not far from the modern Shiraz, laid in ruins by Alexander after the conquest of Darius, some say at the instigation of the courtesan Thais, after a bout of drinking.

Persēus, the son of Zeus and Danae. His early story will be found under *Danae.* Polydectes, having received the mother and child, became enamoured of Danae. Wishing to get rid of Perseus, Polydectes sent him to fetch the head of the Medusa (q.v.), thinking that he would be destroyed. But the gods favoured Perseus. Pluto lent him a helmet that would make him invisible, Athene a buckler resplendent as a mirror (so that he did not need to look directly at the Medusa), and Hermes the *talaria* or wings for the feet. He was thus enabled to escape the eyes of the Gorgons (which turned what they gazed on to stone) and cut off the Medusa's head. Continuing his flight, he came to the palace of Atlas (q.v.), who received him inhospitably. Thereupon Perseus showed him the Medusa's head, and Atlas was changed into a mountain. In his further course, Perseus discovered Andromeda (q.v.) exposed on a rock to a dragon that was about to devour her. Having obtained from Cepheus, her father, the promise of her hand, Perseus slew the dragon. But Phineus, another suitor, attempted to carry away the bride, and, with his attendants, was changed into stones by the Medusa's head. Perseus then returned to Seriphos, just in time to save Danae from the violence of Polydectes, whom he likewise destroyed. Perseus now placed the Medusa's head on the aegis of Athene, where it is usually represented, and embarked to return to his native country. At Larissa he took part in some funeral games that were proceeding and, when throwing the quoit, had the misfortune to kill a man in the throng who turned out to be Acrisius, his grandfather, thus fulfilling the prophecy concerning Danae's son. He refused to ascend the throne of Argos to which he became heir by this calamity, but exchanged this kingdom for another and founded the new city of Mycenae, or withdrew to Asia, where his son Perses became king of the Persians, supposed to be named after him.

PERSIUS (AULUS PERSIUS FLAC-CUS) (A.D. 34–62), Roman satirist, author of six satires, which show the influence of Horace and of the Stoic philosophy.

Persuasion, a novel by Jane Austen (q.v.), finished in 1816 and published in 1818.

Sir Walter Elliot, a foolish spendthrift baronet and a widower, with an overweening sense of his social importance and personal elegance, is obliged to retrench, and lets his seat, Kellynch Hall, to Admiral and Mrs. Croft. His eldest daughter Elizabeth, haughty and unmarried, is now 29; the second, Anne, pretty, intelligent, and of an amiable disposition, had some years before been engaged to a young naval officer, Frederick Wentworth, the brother of Mrs. Croft, but had been persuaded by her trusted friend, Lady Russell, to break off the engagement on the ground of his lack of fortune and from a misunderstanding of his sanguine temper. The breach had produced deep unhappiness in Anne and intense indignation in Wentworth. Anne is now 27 and the bloom of her beauty gone. The youngest daughter of Sir Walter, Mary, is married to Charles Musgrove, the heir of a neighbouring landed proprietor. Capt. Wentworth, who has had a successful career and is become rich, is now thrown again into Anne's society by the letting of Kellynch to the Crofts; and the story is concerned with the gradual revival of Wentworth's passion for Anne. The

course of the reconciliation is, however, hindered by various impediments. Charles Musgrove has two sisters, Louisa and Henrietta. Wentworth at first is attracted by them both, and presently becomes entangled with Louisa, though no explicit declaration passes. A crisis arrives during a visit of the party to Lyme Regis, when Louisa, being 'jumped down' from the Cobb by Capt. Wentworth, falls to the ground and is dangerously injured. Wentworth's partial responsibility for the accident makes him feel an increased obligation to Louisa at the very time that his heart is being drawn back to Anne. Fortunately, during her convalescence and Wentworth's absence, Louisa becomes engaged to Capt. Benwick, a brother naval officer of Wentworth's, and the latter is free to proceed with his courtship. He goes accordingly to Bath, where Sir Walter is now established with his two elder daughters and Elizabeth's companion, Mrs. Clay, an artful woman with matrimonial designs on Sir Walter. But at Bath Wentworth finds the field occupied by another suitor for Anne's hand, in her cousin William Elliot, the heir presumptive to the Kellynch estate, who is paying assiduous attention to Anne and at the same time carrying on an intrigue with Mrs. Clay, so as to detach her from Sir Walter. Anne, however, becomes awakened to the duplicity and cunning of Mr. Elliot, and indeed her affection for Wentworth has remained unshaken. Being accidentally made aware of Anne's constancy, Wentworth takes courage to renew his offer of marriage and is accepted.

In this, Miss Austen's last work, satire and ridicule take a milder form, the tone is graver and tenderer, and the interest lies in a more subtle interplay of the characters: indeed, it is a matter of tradition that a love-story of her own life is reflected in Anne Elliot's.

Pertelote, the hen in Chaucer's 'Nun's Priest's Tale' (see *Canterbury Tales*); also the wife of Chanticleer in *Reynard the Fox* (q.v.). The word in Old French was a female proper name. Its later equivalent, used as the proper name of a hen, is Partlet.

Perugino (active 1469–1523), PIETRO VAN-NUCCI, Italian painter and master of Raphael.

Pervigilium Veneris, the name of a short Latin poem by an unknown author, perhaps of the 2nd cent. A.D. It is a hymn to love and springtime, with the refrain, 'Cras amet qui nunquam amavit, quique amavit cras amet'.

Pet Marjorie, see *Fleming.*

Pétaud, KING, the king formerly elected by the community of beggars in France, so named facetiously from the Latin *peto*, I beg. His authority over his subjects was slight, and the 'court of King Pétaud' was proverbial for an assembly where every one wishes to command or speak at once.

Peter ad Vincula, ST., see *Tower of London.*

Peter Bell, a poem by Wordsworth (q.v.),

published in 1819 with dedication to Southey, but written long before at Alfoxden, in 1798, the year of the 'Lyrical Ballads'.

Peter Bell is a potter, a lawless man insensible to the beauties of nature. Coming to the edge of the Swale, he espies a solitary ass and thinks to steal it. The ass is gazing into the water at something, which turns out to be the dead body of its owner. Peter mounts the ass to seek the cottage of the drowned man and tell his widow. His spiritual experiences on this ride make him a reformed man.

The ludicrous character of parts of the poem diverted attention from its merits, and it was received with much hilarity and made the subject of many parodies (among others one by Shelley). A stanza that occurred in the first two editions but was subsequently suppressed was the following (Peter Bell is staring at the object floating in the river):

Is it a party in a parlour?
Cramm'd just as they on earth are cramm'd—
Some sipping punch, some sipping tea,
But as you by their faces see,
All silent and all damn'd!

PETER LOMBARD (*c.* 1100–*c.* 1160), *Magister Sententiarum*, or master of the sentences, born of an obscure family at Novara, and educated at Bologna. He came to France and became professor of theology, and subsequently in 1159 bishop of Paris. He wrote his 'Sententiae' between 1145 and 1150. They are a collection of opinions of the Fathers, dealing with God, the creation, redemption, and (their most important feature) the nature of the sacraments. The work was very popular and became a theological textbook. It was the subject of many commentaries both abroad and in England.

Peter Martyr, PIETRO VERMIGLI (1500–62), born in Florence, an Augustinian monk, who accepted the Reformed faith, fled from Italy in 1542 to Switzerland, and subsequently to England, and became Regius professor of divinity at Oxford (1548). He helped Cranmer in the preparation of the second Prayer Book. In 1553 he escaped to Strasburg and died at Zürich. His wife is buried in Christ Church Cathedral, Oxford.

PETER MARTYR of Anghiera in the state of Milan (*fl.* 1510), the author of a history of the early Spanish explorations, entitled 'De Orbe Novo', of which the first 'Decade' appeared in 1511. The work was translated into English by Richard Eden ('The Decades of the Newe Worlde or West India', 1555) and re-edited by Hakluyt in 1587. It helped to stimulate the Elizabethan explorers and contributed to their knowledge of the science of navigation.

Peter Pan, *or the Boy who wouldn't grow up*, a dramatic fantasy by Barrie (q.v.), produced in 1904. The story of the play was published in 1911 under the title 'Peter and Wendy'.

It is a story of the three children of Mr. and Mrs. Darling, Wendy, John, and Michael, the nurse Nana (who is a Newfoundland dog), and the motherless Peter Pan, who, with the fairy Tinker Bell, takes the children off to Never-Never Land, where they encounter Redskins and pirates, including the notable Capt. Hook and the agreeable Smee.

PETER PARLEY, the pseudonym of Samuel Griswold Goodrich (1793–1860), an American author, who produced a series of books for the young which enjoyed much popularity. The name was appropriated by various publishers for works by other authors.

Peter Peebles, a character in Scott's 'Redgauntlet' (q.v.).

PETER PINDAR, see *Wolcot*.

Peter Plymley, *Letters of*, see *Plymley*.

PETER PORCUPINE, see *Cobbett*.

Peter Simple, a novel by Marryat (q.v.), published in 1834, generally considered his masterpiece.

The hero is sent to sea as the 'fool of the family', and his simplicity at first exposes him to several ludicrous adventures. But he soon shows himself a gallant and capable officer, sees many exciting naval actions, is taken prisoner and escapes, rises in the service, and wins a charming wife. Of the many entertaining characters in the book, the best is Chucks the boatswain, who aspires to be a gentleman and emerges in the end as the Danish Count Shucksen; he begins his reproofs with an elegant courtesy, but winds them up with a volley of expletives. Mention may also be made of Swinburne, the quartermaster; Terence O'Brien, the plucky and very human Irishman; Capt. Kearney, the incorrigible liar; and that fine seaman, Capt. Savage.

Peter the Great (1672–1725) became Tsar jointly with his half-brother Ivan in 1682. He was colossal in stature, a heavy drinker, magnanimous but capable of barbarous cruelty, deeply interested in science, fond of manual labour, especially ship-building. He founded St. Petersburg, created the Russian fleet, and modernized Russia. He acquired Esthonia and Livonia from Charles XII of Sweden, whom he utterly defeated at Pultowa (1709). He visited England in 1698.

Peter the Hermit, PETER OF AMIENS (*c.* 1050–1115), a gentleman of Picardy, who first followed the career of arms and then became a monk. He preached the first crusade, and led a multitude of followers into Asia Minor (1096). Nearly all these died or were killed by the Turkish garrison of Nicaea before the real 'Crusaders' arrived. Peter, however, survived and accompanied these Crusaders eastwards in 1097. He was certainly present at the siege and counter-siege of Antioch in 1098, but there were other 'holy men' called Peter among the Crusaders, and his later history is uncertain.

Peter Wilkins, *The Life and Adventures of*,

a romance by Paltock (q.v.), published in 1751.

This is a tale after the manner of 'Robinson Crusoe', but not written with the convincing touch of Defoe. Wilkins is shipwrecked in the Antarctic region and reaches a land inhabited by a strange winged race of 'Glums' and 'Gawries', enveloped in an outer silk-like skin which can be spread and enables them to fly. One of these, the beautiful Youwarkee, falls by accident outside his hut. He takes her up, tends her, and marries her, and presently becomes a person of importance in the kingdom.

Southey's 'Glendoveers' in his 'Curse of Kehama' (q.v.) were suggested by the 'Gawries'.

Peter's, ST., Eaton Square, a church built in 1824–6, frequently mentioned in connexion with fashionable ceremonies.

Peter's, ST., Rome, the metropolitan church of the Roman see. The original basilica was said to have been built by Constantine near the site of St. Peter's martyrdom; it was the most venerated church in Christendom and an object of pilgrimage from all parts of Europe. The present church was begun by Pope Julius II in 1506 to the designs of Bramante. Little was done after his death in 1514 until 1547 when Michelangelo made a new plan and work continued under Popes Paul III and Julius III. The dome follows Michelangelo's designs. In the early 17th cent. Maderno added the nave and façade. The church was dedicated in 1627, and Bernini designed the elliptical colonnade surrounding the piazza in 1667. Recent excavations have revealed what is claimed to be the tomb of St. Peter.

Peter's Letters to his Kinsfolk, see *Lockhart*.

Peter's Pence, an annual tax or tribute of a penny from each householder having land of a certain value, paid before the Reformation to the papal see at Rome. It is traditionally ascribed to Offa (see *Mancus*) and was called in Anglo-Saxon times the Romescot. The term Peter's Pence is now used of voluntary contributions by Roman Catholics to the papal treasury.

Peterborough Chronicle, The, a version of the 'Anglo-Saxon Chronicle' (q.v.), written at Peterborough and including annals up to 1154.

Peterloo, the name (a burlesque adaptation of Waterloo) given to a charge of cavalry and yeomanry on the Manchester reform meeting held in St. Peter's Field, Manchester, on 16 Aug. 1819, as a result of which 11 persons are said (the figures are doubtful) to have been killed and about 600 injured.

Petition of Right, a demand put forward by the Commons in 1628 that there should be no imprisonment without cause shown, no forced loans or taxes imposed without par-liamentary grant, no martial law or enforced billeting. The Petition was reluctantly accepted by Charles I and became law. The point of proceeding by the method of a 'Petition of Right' instead of a 'Bill' was that the Crown had to give an immediate answer instead of waiting for the end of the session.

Peto, a character in Shakespeare's '1 and 2 Henry IV' (q.v.).

Petowker, HENRIETTA, a character in Dickens's 'Nicholas Nickleby' (q.v.). She marries Mr. Lillyvick.

PETRARCH (FRANCESCO PETRARCA) (1304–74), Italian poet and humanist, was born at Arezzo, the son of a notary, named Petracco, who was expelled from Florence (in the same year as Dante) by the Black Guelfs and migrated to Avignon in 1312. Here in 1327 Petrarch first saw the woman who inspired his love-poetry. He calls her Laura; her true identity is unknown. Until 1353 Petrarch's life was centred in Provence (Avignon and his beloved retreat at Vaucluse), but he made extended visits to Italy, on the first of which, in 1341, he was crowned Poet Laureate in Rome, for him the most memorable episode of his life. From 1353 onwards he resided in Italy, first at Milan, later at Padua, Venice, and Pavia, and finally at Arquà in the Euganean Hills, but he never lived for long in one place, and he travelled extensively on his own account and at the instance of princely patrons, his missions taking him as far afield as Paris and Prague. He died in Arquà.

Today Petrarch is most famous for the 'Rime sparse', the collection of Italian lyrics which includes the long series of love-poems in praise of Laura; but to his contemporaries and the generations that immediately succeeded him, he was best known as a devoted student of classical antiquity. This enthusiasm he shared with his friend Boccaccio on the several occasions on which Boccaccio stayed under his roof, and at other times by correspondence. The encouragement which Petrarch gave to Cola di Rienzo in 1347, at the time of the restitution of the Roman republic, may be seen as an expression of the humanist spirit with which he was imbued, and in accordance with which he wrote the majority of his works in Latin. These include: a large number of letters and treatises ('De vita solitaria', 'De remediis utriusque fortuna', etc.); a Latin epic, 'Africa', on the struggle between Rome and Carthage; and the 'Secretum', a self-analysis in the form of a dialogue between himself and St. Augustine.

Petrarch is justly regarded as the father of Italian humanism, the initiator of the revived study of Greek and Latin literature.

PETRONIUS, GAIUS, one of the emperor Nero's companions, and director of the pleasures of the imperial court (*arbiter elegantiae*). He had been proconsul in Bithynia. He was the author of 'Petronii Arbitri Satyricon', a prose satirical romance interspersed with verse, which has survived in a fragmentary state. The 'Cena Trimalchionis', the most important episode in this, describes the sumptuous dinner at which the rich, vulgar upstart Trimalchio entertains Encolpius, the hero of the romance. Tacitus mentions that Petronius committed suicide (about A.D. 65) to avoid being killed by Nero.

Petruchio, in Shakespeare's 'Taming of the Shrew' (q.v.), the husband of the termagant Katharina.

PETTY, SIR WILLIAM (1623–87), political economist, studied on the Continent and became the friend of Hobbes. He executed for the Commonwealth the 'Down Survey' of forfeited lands in Ireland, the first attempt on a large scale at carrying out a survey scientifically. Petty acquiesced in the Restoration, and was knighted and made an original member of the Royal Society in 1662. He published economic treatises, the principal of which was entitled 'Political Arithmetic', 1690, a term signifying that which we now call statistics. In this he examined, by the quantitative method, the current allegations of national decay. He rejected the old 'prohibitory' system, and showed the error of the supporters of the 'mercantile' system in regarding the abundance of the precious metals as the standard of prosperity. He traced the sources of wealth to labour and land.

Petulengro, JASPER, the principal gipsy character in Borrow's 'Lavengro' and 'The Romany Rye' (qq.v.), founded upon the Norfolk gipsy, Ambrose Smith, with whom Borrow was acquainted in his youth. 'Petulengro' means 'shoeing smith'.

Peutinger, KONRAD (1465–1547), a German antiquary, who has given his name to an ancient map of the roads of the Roman empire which he discovered. This is one of our few sources of knowledge of this road-system. It is said to be a 12th-cent. copy of a set of maps dating from about A.D. 365–6 when Theodosius the elder was fighting on the frontiers. The best edition is that of Desjardins, Paris, 1869.

Peveril of the Peak, a novel by Sir W. Scott (q.v.), published in 1823.

The story is in the main concerned with the times of the pretended Popish Plot (1678), though it is only in the 14th chapter that the principal theme is reached. Sir Geoffrey Peveril, an old Cavalier, and Major Bridgenorth, a fanatical Puritan, are neighbouring landowners in Derbyshire, and though of widely different opinions and modes of life, have been connected by ties of reciprocal kindness in the days of the Civil War. Julian, son of Sir Geoffrey, and Alice, the daughter of Bridgenorth, are deeply in love. The recrudescence of bitter political feeling during the period of the 'Popish Plot' brings the parents into acute conflict. Julian, who has spent some years in the household of the countess of Derby, goes to England on her service. He arrives at the moment when popular suspicion of the Catholics has reached its greatest intensity, finds his father under arrest by Bridgenorth as a suspected Papist, attempts to liberate him, is himself arrested, is rescued by tenants and friends, and finally reaches London. Meanwhile the fate of Alice Bridgenorth is gravely imperilled. Edward Christian, Bridgenorth's brother-in-law, to whom Alice has been entrusted by her father, contrives with Chiffinch, the minister of Charles II's pleasures, to bring her to the king's notice, with a view to her becoming his mistress. In order to avenge his brother, the victim of a judicial murder carried out in the Isle of Man under Lady Derby's authority, he has, moreover, placed in the latter's service Fenella, his daughter by a Moorish woman. This creature, gifted with strange beauty and grace, has maintained for years the character of a deaf-mute, in order to worm herself into her employer's secrets. In the events that ensue she plays an important part. Alice Bridgenorth falls into the hands of the licentious Buckingham, and is rescued by Fenella's agency. Julian Peveril, with whom Fenella has fallen in love, is by her action brought to the notice of the king and Buckingham, incurs the hostility of the latter, and is imprisoned and involved, with his father, in an accusation of participation in the 'Plot'. They are acquitted on trial, thanks to the intervention of the king, who shows some sense of obligation to the old Cavalier; and all ends well.

The author draws elaborate portraits of Charles II and Buckingham, and gives glimpses of such historical characters as Titus Oates, Colonel Blood (the impudent revolutionary who tried to steal the crown jewels from the Tower), and Sir Geoffrey Hudson (Henrietta Maria's dwarf).

Pew, the blind buccaneer in Stevenson's 'Treasure Island' (q.v.).

Pfefferkorn, an apostate Jew, the associate of the Dominicans in their controversy with Reuchlin (q.v.) regarding the proposed destruction of works of Jewish literature and philosophy. See *Epistolae Obscurorum Virorum*.

Phaeacians, THE, in the 'Odyssey', the inhabitants of the island *Scheria*, in the extreme western part of the earth, where Odysseus landed after leaving Ogygia, the island of Calypso. They were famous sailors. Alcinous was king of the Phaeacians, and Nausicaa was his daughter.

Phaedra, a daughter of Minos (q.v.) and Pasiphae, and wife of Theseus (q.v.). She became enamoured of Hippolytus (q.v.), the son of Theseus by the amazon Hippolyta. Her advances being rejected, she accused Hippolytus to Theseus of attempts upon her virtue and caused his death. This story is the subject of tragedies by Euripides, Seneca, and Racine.

Phaedria, in Spenser's 'Faerie Queene', II. vi, the Lady of the Idle Lake, symbolizing immodest mirth.

PHAEDRUS, a Thracian slave who came to Rome and became a freedman in the household of Augustus. He was author of a collection of Latin fables, based on those attributed to Aesop (q.v.).

Phăĕton or PHAETHON, a son of Phoebus, the sun, by Clymene, daughter of Minyas of Orchomenus in Boeotia. He became proud and aspiring, and begged his father to allow him to drive the chariot of the sun. He soon betrayed his incapacity and the horses departed from their usual course, threatening the earth with a conflagration. Zeus, perceiving the disorder, hurled a thunderbolt and struck Phaeton, who fell into the river Eridanus (Po), mourned by his sisters till they turned into trees from which amber is distilled. 'Phaethon' is the title of a poem by G. Meredith (q.v.), written in galliambics.

The name *Phaeton* is given to a four-wheeled open carriage of light construction, usually drawn by a pair of horses, with one or two seats facing forward; but also applied to carriages variously modified and distinguished as ,Stanhope, Mail, Park, etc.

Phaistos Disc, a clay disc inscribed on both sides with uninterpreted hieroglyphic characters arranged spirally; thought not to be Cretan but possibly of SW. Asia Minor. It was found by Italian archaeologists in the excavation of Phaistos, Crete.

Phalaris, a tyrant of Agrigentum in Sicily, probably in the first half of the 6th cent. B.C., said to have been a cruel ruler. Perillus made him a brazen bull, in which criminals were put to death by a fire lit under the beast's belly, so that their cries were like the bellowing of a bull. Phalaris made the first experiment of it on the person of its inventor. The people of Agrigentum revolted c. 554 B.C. and put Phalaris to death.

For the 'Phalaris controversy' see *Phalaris (Epistles of)*.

Phalaris, *Epistles of*, certain letters attributed to Phalaris (q.v.), which were praised by Sir William Temple (q.v.) and edited by Charles Boyle (q.v.) in 1695. Richard Bentley (q.v.) was able to show that they were spurious, for towns were mentioned in them that did not exist in the days of Phalaris, the dialect was Attic not Dorian, etc. There is an echo of the controversy in Swift's 'Battle of the Books' (q.v.).

Phantasmion, see *Coleridge (Sara)*.

Phantom Ship, THE, see *Flying Dutchman*.

Phaon, a boatman of Mitylene in Lesbos. It is said that, when old and ugly, he carried Venus, who presented herself in the guise of an old woman, over to Asia without accepting payment, and the goddess in consequence bestowed on him youth and beauty. Sappho (q.v.), a legend relates, fell in love with him,

and when he received her advances coldly, threw herself into the sea. Lyly (q.v.) wrote a play on the subject, 'Sapho and Phao'.

PHAON, in Spenser's 'Faerie Queene', II. iv, is the unfortunate squire who, deceived by Philemon and under the influence of Furor (mad rage), slays Claribel and poisons Philemon.

Pharamond, the legendary first king of the Franks, the subject of a heroic novel by La Calprenède (q.v.). Pharamond is also the name of a character in (1) Beaumont and Fletcher's 'Philaster' (q.v.), and (2) W. Morris's 'Love is Enough'.

Pharaoh, from an Egyptian word meaning 'great house', the generic appellation of the ancient Egyptian kings, especially used of those of the time of Joseph and the Exodus. Rameses II, the great builder of temples, may have been the Pharaoh of the Oppression; his son Meneptah, the Pharaoh of the Exodus In Dryden's 'Absalom and Achitophel' 'Pharaoh' stands for the king of France.

Pharisees, from a Hebrew word meaning 'separated', an ancient Jewish sect distinguished for their strict observance of the law, and by their pretensions to superior sanctity. The word is applied to self-righteous or hypocritical persons.

Pharonnida, see *Chamberlayne (W.)*.

Pharos, a small island in the bay of Alexandria, which was joined to the Egyptian shore by a causeway built by order of Alexander the Great. On it was erected in the reign of Ptolemy Philadelphus (285–246 B.C.) a tower which was accounted one of the seven wonders of the world. It stood about 400 feet high and on the top fires were kept burning to direct sailors. Hence the word is often used as a synonym for a lighthouse (pharos, faro, phare).

Pharsālia, the epic poem of Lucan (q.v.) on the civil war between Pompey and Caesar; so named from the battle of Pharsālus (48 B.C.), in which the latter was victorious.

Phebe, a shepherdess in Shakespeare's 'As You Like It' (q.v.).

Pheidippĭdēs, the best runner in Greece, was sent from Athens to Sparta to announce the arrival of the invading Persians in 490 B.C. and beg for help. He covered the distance between the two cities, 150 miles, in two days. But the Spartans were unwilling to send help until the time of the full moon. On his return journey, Pheidippides had a vision of the god Pan, who spoke words of encouragement for the Athenian cause. Browning in one of his 'Dramatic Idyls' makes Pheidippides fight at Marathon, and, though now released from service as a messenger, run once more to Athens (a distance of 22 miles) to announce the victory, and fall dead after doing so. The basis of this story is in Plutarch ('de Gloria Atheniensium' 347 C), who tells it of a different messenger. The exploit has in recent times been commemorated in the 'Marathon Race' of the modern Olympic Games.

Phi Beta Kappa, an honour society in some universities and colleges in the United States, membership of which is conferred in recognition of academic attainment, primarily in the arts and pure sciences. It is considered an honour for a university or college to be granted a charter to establish a Phi Beta Kappa chapter. The Society was founded at the College of William and Mary, Williamsburg, Virginia, in 1776, and now has chapters at not quite 200 of the more than 1,200 American colleges and universities. The name is taken from the initial letters of its motto Φιλοσοφία Βίον Κυβερνήτης, 'Philosophy, the guide of life'. Election for membership depends, on high academic qualification in one of three groups: undergraduates in the liberal arts programme; graduates (usually reading for Ph.D. degrees); and distinguished alumni and faculty members. Its quarterly publication, 'The American Scholar', takes its name from Emerson's famous oration delivered before the ΦBK chapter at Harvard in 1837.

Phidias (c. 490–c. 448 B.C.), Greek sculptor. His bronze Athena Promachos (460–450), some 30 ft. high, stood on the Acropolis at Athens. He was commissioned by Pericles to design the sculptures of the Parthenon (447–432) and he made the chryselephantine statues of Athena Parthenos for the Parthenon and Zeus for Olympia. He fell a victim to the enemies of Pericles and went into exile.

Phigalia, see *Bassae.*

Philander, To, to play the Philander or trifling and even promiscuous lover. Philander, in an old ballad, was the lover of Phillis; and in Beaumont and Fletcher's 'Laws of Candy', the lover of Erota.

Philaster, or *Love lies a-bleeding,* a romantic drama by Beaumont and Fletcher (see *Fletcher, J.*), produced in 1611 and printed in 1620.

The king of Calabria has usurped the crown of Sicily. The rightful heir, Philaster, loves, and is loved by, Arethusa daughter of the usurper, but the latter designs to marry her to Pharamond, prince of Spain. To secure communication with her, Philaster places his page, Bellario, in her service. Arethusa reveals to the king an amour between Pharamond and Megra, a lady of the court, who in revenge accuses Arethusa of misconduct with Bellario. Philaster bids farewell to the princess, being assured that the accusation is true, and dismisses Bellario. The events that follow lead to the discovery that Bellario is the daughter of a Sicilian lord, who, having fallen in love with Philaster, has assumed the disguise of a page in order to serve him.

Philêmon and **Baucis,** an aged couple who lived in a poor cottage in Phrygia when Zeus and Hermes travelled in disguise over Asia. They entertained the gods hospitably, and Zeus transformed their dwelling into a splendid temple, of which the old couple were made the priest and priestess. Having lived to extreme old age, they died in the same hour, according to their request, and were changed into trees, whose boughs intertwined. They are the subject of a poem by Swift (q.v.).

Philip, *The Adventures of,* the last complete novel of Thackeray (q.v.), published in 'The Cornhill Magazine' (q.v.) in 1861–2.

The story is told by Arthur Pendennis (q.v.), who, with his wife Laura, figures slightly in the incidents. Philip is the son of Dr. George Firmin, a fashionable and prosperous London physician, but under the surface an unprincipled and heartless scoundrel. As told in 'A Shabby Genteel Story' (contributed by Thackeray to 'Fraser' in 1840), Dr. Firmin, when a young man, has, under the name of Brandon, gone through a form of marriage with the daughter, Caroline, of a Margate lodging-house keeper, has then cruelly deserted her, and has married Philip's mother while Caroline was alive. The parson who performed the ceremony, a disreputable villain named Hunt, uses his knowledge of the incident to blackmail Dr. Firmin; and when the latter revolts and confesses the story to his son, endeavours to ruin them by revealing the marriage, which he declares a genuine one, to Twysden, Dr. Firmin's brother-in-law, who will benefit largely if Philip is proved illegitimate. But Caroline has a heart of gold and refuses the testimony required to prove the case. She has become a sick-nurse (the 'Little Sister'), has nursed Philip through scarlet fever, has become devoted to him, and will do nothing to injure him. But, though this plot is defeated, misfortune awaits Philip, for his father presently bolts to America, ruined by speculations which have engulfed not only his own means but Philip's fortune, carelessly entrusted to Dr. Firmin by his co-trustee General Baynes. Philip forgoes his claim on Baynes, and becomes a struggling journalist. He falls in love with and marries Baynes's daughter, Charlotte, in spite of her virago of a mother; and, as Dr. Firmin continues to sponge on him, barely keeps his head above water. He is saved in the end by a *deus ex machina* device, the 'machine' in this case being an old post chariot of Lord Ringwood, Philip's great-uncle, in the pocket of which is found a will leaving Philip a handsome legacy.

Philip drunk to Philip sober, APPEAL FROM: Valerius Maximus (vi. 2) relates that a foreign woman undeservedly condemned by Philip of Macedon (who reigned 359–336 B.C., father of Alexander the Great) in his cups, declared that she would appeal to Philip, 'sed sobrium', 'but when he was sober'.

Philip Quarll, *Adventures of,* the story of a pseudo-Robinson Crusoe, attributed to one Edward Dorrington, published in 1727, and frequently adapted for children.

Philip Sparrow, see *Phylyp Sparowe.*

Philip van Artevelde, an historical drama in two parts, in blank verse, by Sir H. Taylor (q.v.), published in 1834.

The historical events described in the play occurred in 1381–2. It Pt. I the Flemish town of Ghent is in rebellion against the count of Flanders and at enmity with his capital, Bruges. Ghent is torn with dissension between the war party and the peace party of its citizens. Its only hope of salvation is to appoint a leader whom all will accept, and the choice falls on the hitherto peaceful, meditative Philip van Artevelde, who is recommended by the memory of his great father, Jacques van Artevelde (the 'Brewer of Ghent', president of Flanders about 1337, ally of Edward III). As soon as elected, Philip develops unexpected qualities of determination and valour, quells sedition with a stern hand, defeats the count of Flanders, captures Bruges, and becomes Regent of Flanders.

In Pt. II of the play Philip is seen declining from the zenith of his power, and at war with the French and the duke of Burgundy, the heir presumptive of the count of Flanders. The drama closes with the defeat of the Flemish forces at Rosebecque and the death of van Artevelde at the hands of the perfidious Sir Fleuréant of Heurlée.

With these historical events is woven the story, in the first part, of the love of van Artevelde for Adriana van Merestyn, whom he marries; and in the second part, after the death of his wife, of his less hallowed union with the Italian Elena della Torre.

Philip Wakem, a character in George Eliot's 'The Mill on the Floss' (q.v.).

Philippi, a town in Macedonia founded by Philip of Macedon, famous as the site of the battle in 42 B.C. in which Octavianus and Antony defeated Brutus and Cassius. This defeat figures in Shakespeare's 'Julius Caesar' (q.v.).

Philippics, see *Demosthenes* and *Cicero.*

PHILIPS, AMBROSE (1675?–1749), poet, and fellow of St. John's College, Cambridge, is principally remembered on account of a quarrel between him and Pope about the relative merits of their pastorals. Pope drew, in the 'Guardian', 'a comparison of Philips's performance with his own, in which, with an unexampled and unequalled artifice of irony, though he has himself always the advantage, he gives the preference to Philips' (Johnson, 'Lives of the Poets'). Philips's adulatory verses, in a seven-syllabled measure, addressed 'to all ages and characters, from Walpole *steerer of the realm,* to miss Pulteney in the nursery', earned him the nickname of 'Namby-Pamby', though, as Johnson says, they are his pleasantest pieces.

PHILIPS, JOHN (1676–1709), educated at Christ Church, Oxford, and author of 'The Splendid Shilling' (q.v.), published in 1705,

and 'Cyder' (q.v.), published in 1708. He was employed by Harley and Bolingbroke to write verses on the battle of Blenheim as a Tory counterpart to Addison's 'Campaign'.

PHILIPS, KATHERINE (1631–64), the 'Matchless Orinda', was daughter of John Fowler, a London merchant. She married in 1647 James Philips of Cardigan and instituted a 'Society of Friendship', a literary salon for the discussion of poetry, religion, and similar topics, in which she assumed the pseudonym 'Orinda', to which her contemporaries added the epithet 'Matchless'. Her earliest verses were prefixed (1651) to the 'Poems' of Henry Vaughan (q.v.). Her translation of Corneille's 'Pompée' was acted in Dublin with great success. Her collected verses appeared in 1667. Jeremy Taylor (q.v.) dedicated to her his 'Discourse on the Nature of Friendship', and Cowley (q.v.) mourned her death in an elegy.

Philipson, the assumed name used by the earl of Oxford and his son Arthur de Vere in Scott's 'Anne of Geierstein' (q.v.).

Philistine, the name of an alien warlike people who occupied the southern sea-coast of Palestine, and in early times constantly harassed the Israelites. The name is applied, (1) humorously or otherwise, to persons regarded as 'the enemy' into whose hands one may fall, bailiffs, literary critics, etc.; (2) to persons deficient in liberal culture and enlightenment, from *philister,* the term applied by German students to one who is not a student at the university, a townsman. In sense (2) the word was introduced into English by Matthew Arnold ('Essays in Criticism', 'Heine'). *Philister* is said to have originated at Jena in 1693 in a sermon preached at the funeral of a student killed in a 'town and gown' quarrel, from the text 'The Philistines be upon thee, Samson!' [OED.]

Phillipps Library, THE, a collection of manuscripts and books made by Sir Thomas Phillipps, first baronet (1792–1872, educated at Rugby and University College, Oxford). The collection was rich in classical, historical, and topographical manuscripts. Phillipps established a private printing-press at his residence at Broadway, Worcestershire, where he printed visitations, extracts from registers, cartularies, etc. The story of the collection is told by A. N. L. Munby in 'Phillipps Studies'.

PHILLIPS, EDWARD (1630–96?), elder nephew of Milton, by whom he was educated. He was a hack-writer in London, and tutor (1663) to the son of John Evelyn (q.v.) and (1665) to Philip Herbert, afterwards seventh earl of Pembroke. His 'New World of Words' (1658), a philological dictionary, was very popular.

PHILLIPS, JOHN (1631–1706), younger nephew of Milton, by whom he was brought up, wrote a scathing attack on Puritanism in 1655 in his 'Satyr against Hypocrites'. He was employed as a translator and hack-writer.

He translated La Calprenède's 'Pharamond' and Madeleine de Scudéry's 'Almahide', and wrote a travesty of 'Don Quixote'. He also wrote in support of Titus Oates and edited a serious periodical, 'The Present State of Europe', from 1690 till his death.

Philoclea, a character in Sidney's 'Arcadia' (q.v.).

Philoctētēs, one of the Greek heroes of the Trojan War, who had inherited the bow and arrows of Heracles. He brought warriors from Methone and other places to the war in seven ships, but was left by his companions in the island of Lemnos, at the instance of Odysseus, owing to a noisome wound in his foot. But in the tenth year of the war, a seer having revealed that only with the bow of Philoctetes could Troy be taken, Odysseus and Diomedes came to fetch him to Troy, where he slew Paris. He was the subject of a play by Sophocles.

Philŏmēla, a daughter of Pandion, king of Athens. Her sister Procne, having married Tereus, king of Thrace, pined for the company of Philomela. Tereus obtained Pandion's permission to conduct Philomela to her sister, but became enamoured of her, and after having offered violence to her, cut off her tongue that she might not be able to discover his ill-usage, and hid her in a lonely place. He then told Procne that her sister was dead. But Philomela during her captivity depicted her misfortunes on a piece of tapestry and privately conveyed this to Procne, who delivered her and concerted with her how they should be avenged on Tereus. Procne accordingly murdered her son Itys and served up his flesh to Tereus. Tereus drew his sword to punish Procne and Philomela, but at that moment he was changed into a hoopoe, Philomela into a nightingale, and Procne into a swallow.

Philosophes, LES, a name given in France to a group of 18th-cent. authors, sceptical in religion, materialist in philosophy, and hedonist in ethics, of whom the principal were Diderot, D'Alembert, the Baron d'Holbach, Helvétius, and Condorcet. The 'Encyclopédie' (q.v.) embodied their ideas.

Philosophical Enquiry into the Origin of our Ideas of the Sublime and Beautiful, A, see *Sublime and Beautiful.*

Philosophical Essays concerning Human Understanding, see *Hume.*

Philotas, a Senecan tragedy in blank verse by Samuel Daniel (q.v.), published in 1605.

Philotas, a gallant and bountiful soldier, held in high estimation among the Macedonians, incurs the suspicion of Alexander by his boasts, and, having concealed his knowledge of a conspiracy against the king, is accused and tortured, and, having confessed, is stoned to death.

The author had subsequently to defend himself against the charge of covertly defending, by this play, the rebellion of Essex.

Philotimē, in Spenser's 'Faerie Queene', II. vii. 48, 49, the daughter of Mammon, symbolizes ambition.

Philtra, in Spenser's 'Faerie Queene', v. iv, a self-seeking damsel in the episode of Amidas and Bracidas.

Phineas Finn, Phineas Redux, The Prime Minister, and ***The Duke's Children,*** novels of parliamentary life by A. Trollope (q.v.), published respectively in 1869, 1873, 1875, and 1880.

These novels form a series. The first presents Phineas, an irresistible but penniless young Irishman, who enters parliament and comes to London, leaving behind him an Irish sweetheart, Mary Flood-Jones. In London he falls more or less in love with Violet Effingham, Lady Laura Standish, and the wealthy widow, Madame Max Goesler. He becomes under-secretary for the colonies, but quarrels with the government, resigns, bids adieu to his ladyloves, and returns to marry Miss Flood-Jones and accept a modest post at Cork.

Phineas Redux comes back, a widower, to London and parliamentary life, almost gets a seat in the cabinet, again receives the love or friendship of ladies of position, is accused of the murder of a political enemy, narrowly escapes the gallows, and marries Madame Goesler, who has been instrumental in saving him.

The 'Prime Minister' and 'The Duke's Children' are principally occupied with the affairs, domestic and political, of Plantagenet Palliser and Lady Glencora (now duke and duchess of Omnium), who have figured in the earlier novels. Phineas Finn occasionally reappears.

The series contains some capital parliamentary and hunting scenes, and good characters: Phineas himself, somewhat of a philanderer, weak, but on the whole honest and attractive; the high-spirited Violet Effingham; while Trollope himself regarded the characters of Plantagenet Palliser (q.v.) and Lady Glencora as his chief titles to fame.

Phineūs, son of Agenor and king of Thrace, a soothsayer blinded by the gods on account of his cruelty to his sons, whose eyes he had put out on a false accusation by their stepmother. He was constantly harassed by the Harpies, who carried off the food that was put before him. When the Argonauts (q.v.) visited Thrace, he was delivered from these pests by Zetes and Călăis, the brothers of his first wife, and in return instructed them regarding their way to Colchis.

Phiz, see *Browne (H. K.).*

Phlĕgĕthon or PYRIPHLEGETHON, a river of Hades, whose waters were flames. The name means 'blazing'. See *Styx.*

Phlegraean Plain, the volcanic region on

the coast of Italy between Cumae and Capua. It was fabled that the giants had been buried beneath it by the gods.

Phobētor, see *Icelus.*

Phocaean, an epithet sometimes applied to Marseilles, in accordance with a legend that this town was founded by emigrants from Phocaea, a Greek colony in Ionia between Smyrna and Cyme. Landor has a long blank-verse poem called 'The Phocaeans'.

Phoebe and **Phoebus,** names given respectively to Diana (the moon) and Apollo (the sun), signifying bright, radiant.

Phoebe Dawson, the heroine of one of the tales in Crabbe's 'The Parish Register', II (q.v.).

Phoebus, MR., a character in Disraeli's 'Lothair' (q.v.), the most successful painter of his age, gallant, brilliant, and boastful.

Phoenix, a fabulous bird, of golden and red plumage, which, according to a tale reported by Herodotus (ii. 73), came to Heliopolis every 500 years, on the death of his father, and there buried his body in the temple of the sun. According to another version, the phoenix, after living 500 years, built himself a funeral pile and died upon it. From his remains a fresh phoenix arose.

'The Phoenix and the Turtle', a poem attributed to Shakespeare, was included in 1601 in Robert Chester's 'Love's Martyr'.

Phoenix, THE, a theatre that stood in the parish of St. Giles-in-the-Fields, London, in the 16th and 17th cents. It was adapted from a cockpit.

Phoenix Nest, *The,* a poetical miscellany published in 1593, containing, amongst others, poems by Lodge and Breton (qq.v.).

Phonetic Spelling, a system of spelling in which each letter represents invariably the same spoken sound, e.g. the system proposed for the reform of English spelling, as opposed to the traditional (historical or etymological) system.

Phorcids, THE, see *Graiae.*

Phorcys, a sea deity, father of the Gorgons, the Graiae (qq.v.), and other monsters.

Phosphorus, 'the light-bringer', the morning star of the Greeks, corresponding to the Lucifer of the Romans. It is the planet Venus, which also figures as Hesperus, the evening star. 'Sweet Hesper-Phosphor, double name' occurs in Tennyson's 'In Memoriam' (q.v.).

Phrygian bonnet, see *Cap of Liberty.*

Phrygian mode, one of the three modes of ancient Greek music, a minor scale appropriate to passion (Jebb).

Phrynē, a celebrated Greek courtesan, said to have been the model of the Cnidian Venus of Praxiteles and of the Venus Anadyomene of Apelles.

Phunky, MR., in Dickens's 'Pickwick Papers'

(q.v.), Serjeant Snubbin's junior in the case of Bardell *v.* Pickwick.

Phylyp Sparowe, a poem by Skelton (q.v.).

Physiocrat, one of a school of political economists founded by François Quesnay (1694–1774) in France in the 18th cent. They maintained that society should be governed according to an inherent natural order, that the soil is the sole source of wealth and the only proper object of taxation, and that security of property and freedom of industry and exchange are essential. [OED.] The other principal exponents of the physiocrat doctrines were Jacques Turgot (1727–81), an able financier, whose dismissal in 1776 from the post of controller-general of the finances was the prelude of the French national bankruptcy; and Victor de Riquetti, Marquis de Mirabeau (1715–89), the author of 'L'Ami des hommes' and father of the revolutionary statesman. Adam Smith, though no physiocrat in the technical sense of the word, was strongly influenced by the sounder doctrines of the school.

Physiologus, see *Bestiaries.*

Piastre, from the Italian *piastra,* short for *piastra d'argento,* 'plate of silver', a name applied to the Spanish *peso,* or piece of eight or dollar (q.v.); in modern usage, the small Turkish coin, $\frac{1}{100}$ of a Turkish pound.

Picardil, a stiff collar attached to the coat, worn in the early 17th cent., 'generally understood to be the origin of the name Pickadilly Hall, given before 1622 to a house in the parish of St. Martin's in the Fields, London, and now perpetuated in the street called Piccadilly'. [OED.]

Picaresque, from the Spanish *picaro,* a rogue, a term applied to a class of romances that deal with rogues and knaves, of which the earliest important examples, such as 'Lazarillo de Tormes' and 'Guzman de Alfarache' (qq.v.), were written in Spanish. 'Gil Blas' (q.v.) is the most famous picaresque story in French.

Picasso, PABLO RUIZ Y (1881–), Spanish painter. He settled in Paris in 1901 and first painted the characters of the Paris slums with a predominantly blue palette, then actors and clowns in warmer colours. In 1907 Picasso and Braque developed Cubism (q.v.). In 1917 he designed ballets for Diaghilev; then came the period of monumental nudes which developed in the 1930s into terrifyingly distorted forms (Guernica, 1936). Latterly he has designed ceramics. A brilliant draughtsman, Picasso has produced an enormous number of etchings and lithographs, and has illustrated books.

Piccadilly, see *Picardil.*

Piccadilly Weepers were a fashion of drooping whiskers affected by men in the sixties of the 19th century.

Piccini or PICCINNI, NICOLO (1728–1800),

an Italian composer of opera. He went to Paris in 1776 and became the subject of a celebrated dispute between his followers and those of Gluck (q.v.).

Pickering, WILLIAM (1796–1854), publisher, commenced business in London in 1820, and did much to raise the standard of design in printing. He published the 'Diamond Classics' 1821–31, and in 1830 adopted the trade-mark of the Aldine press (see *Aldus Manutius*). He increased his reputation by his Aldine edition of the English poets in fifty-three volumes.

Pickle the Spy, ALASTAIR RUADH MACDONELL (1725?–61), chief of Glengarry. He was employed by the Highland chiefs on a secret mission to Prince Charles Edward in 1745, was captured by the English, and imprisoned in the Tower. Under the pseudonym of 'Pickle', he acted as a spy on Prince Charles Edward, 1749–54. He is the subject of a book by A. Lang (q.v.).

Pickle-herring, a clown or buffoon. This application of the term originated in Germany, where it was the name of a humorous character in an early 17th-cent. play, and of the chief actor in a series of 'Pickelhäringsspiele'.

Pickwick Papers, *The* (*The Posthumous Papers of the Pickwick Club*), a novel by Dickens (q.v.), first issued in twenty monthly parts from April 1836 to Nov. 1837, and as a volume in 1837 (when Dickens was only 25 years old).

Mr. Samuel Pickwick, general chairman of the Pickwick Club which he has founded, Messrs. Tracy Tupman, Augustus Snodgrass, and Nathaniel Winkle, members of the club, are constituted a Corresponding Society of the Club to report to it their journeys and adventures, and observations of character and manners. This is the basis on which the novel is constructed, and the Club serves as a connecting link for a series of detached incidents and changing characters, without elaborate plot. The entertaining adventures with which Mr. Pickwick and his associates meet are interspersed with incidental tales contributed by various characters. The principal elements in the story are: (1) the visit of Pickwick and his friends to Rochester, where they fall in with the specious rascal, Jingle, who gets Winkle involved in the prospect of a duel (fortunately averted). (2) The visit to Dingley Dell, the home of the hospitable Mr. Wardle; the elopement of Jingle with Wardle's sister, their pursuit by Wardle and Pickwick, and the recovery of the lady; followed by the engagement of Sam Weller as Pickwick's servant. (3) The visit to Eatanswill, where a parliamentary election is in progress, and Mr. Pickwick makes the acquaintance of Pott, editor of a political newspaper, and Mrs. Leo Hunter. (4) The visit to Bury St. Edmunds, where Mr. Pickwick and Sam Weller are fooled by Jingle and

his servant, Job Trotter. (5) The pursuit of Jingle to Ipswich, where Mr. Pickwick inadvertently enters the bedroom of a middle-aged lady at night; is in consequence involved in a quarrel with Mr. Peter Magnus, her admirer; is brought before Mr. Nupkins, the magistrate, on a charge of intending to fight a duel; and obtains his release on exposing the nefarious designs of Jingle on Nupkins's daughter. (6) The Christmas festivities at Dingley Dell. (7) The misapprehension of Mrs. Bardell, Mr. Pickwick's landlady, regarding her lodger's intentions, which leads to the famous action of Bardell *v.* Pickwick for breach of promise of marriage, in which judgement is given for the plaintiff, with damages £750. (8) The visit to Bath, in which Winkle figures prominently, first in the adventure with the blustering Dowler, and secondly in his courtship of Arabella Allen. (9) The period of Mr. Pickwick's imprisonment in the Fleet in consequence of his refusal to pay the damages and costs of his action; and the discovery of Jingle and Job Trotter in that prison, and their relief by Mr. Pickwick. (10) The affairs of Tony Weller (Sam's father) and the second Mrs. Weller, ending in the death of the latter and the discomfiture of the pious humbug and greedy drunkard Stiggins, deputy shepherd in the Ebenezer Temperance Association. (11) The affairs of Bob Sawyer and Benjamin Allen, medical students and subsequently struggling practitioners. The novel ends with the happy marriage of Allen's sister, Arabella, to Winkle.

Pickwickian sense, IN A, applied to uncomplimentary language which in the circumstances is not to be interpreted in its strictly literal meaning; from the scene in ch. i of 'Pickwick Papers', where the Chairman calls upon Mr. Blotton to say whether he had used the word 'humbug' of Mr. Pickwick in a common sense. Mr. Blotton 'had no hesitation in saying that he had not—he had used the word in its Pickwickian sense'.

PICO DELLA MIRANDOLA, GIOVANNI (1463–94), an Italian humanist and philosopher, born at Mirandola, of which his family were the lords. He spent part of his short life at Florence in the circle of Lorenzo de' Medici. In 1486 he published 900 theses, offering to maintain them at Rome, but some of his propositions were pronounced heretical, and the public debate did not take place. The famous oration 'De dignitate hominis', with which he intended to introduce the debate, is one of the most important philosophical works of the 15th cent. Pico was a daring syncretist, who vainly tried to make a synthesis of Christianity, Platonism, Aristotelianism, and the Jewish Cabbala. As a pioneer in the study of Hebrew philosophy he influenced Reuchlin (q.v.). His life ('Life of John Picus, Erle of Myrandula, Greate Lorde of Italy'), and some of his pious writings, were translated by Sir Thomas

More. John Colet (q.v.) was influenced by Pico's writings.

Picrochole, see *Gargantua.*

Pict-hatch, a notorious resort of disreputable characters in Clerkenwell, frequently referred to by the Elizabethan dramatists.

Picumnus and **Pilumnus,** two Roman divinities, probably gods of agriculture, regarded also as protectors of women in childbed. Pilumnus was thought to be the inventor of the pestle (*pilum*) for grinding corn.

Pidgin, a Chinese corruption of the English word 'business'. Hence PIDGIN-ENGLISH, the jargon, consisting chiefly of English words, often corrupted in pronunciation, and arranged according to Chinese idiom, used for intercommunication between Chinese and Europeans in China, the Straits Settlements, etc. [OED.]

Piece of Eight, see *Dollar.*

Pied Piper of Hamelin, The, A Child's Story, a poem by R. Browning (q.v.), included in 'Dramatic Romances', published in 1845, based on an old legend.

The town of Hamelin in Brunswick is overrun by rats, and the mayor and corporation are at their wits' end. The Pied Piper offers to get rid of the pest by a secret charm, and is promised a thousand guilders if he does so. He goes along the street playing on his pipe, and all the rats come out and follow him down to the river Weser, where they are drowned. The Piper claims his reward, which the mayor and corporation refuse. Thereupon the Piper again walks down the street piping, and all the children run out and follow him to a hill called the Koppenberg, where 'a wondrous portal opens wide', and the Piper and the children enter, and the door shuts fast. The last words of the poem indicate that the children emerged in Transylvania, where their descendants are still to be found. Another version had been written by Browning's father.

The event was long regarded as historical and is supposed to have occurred in 1284. The piper's name was Bunting. Baring-Gould ('Curious Myths') discusses the origin of the legend, which is told, with variations, of other places. The story is commonly held to be connected with the 'Children's Crusade' of 1212, when, at a moment of crusading enthusiasm, a child named Nicolas, of Cologne, is said to have gathered 20,000 young crusaders, many of whom perished.

Piepowder Court, from French *pieds poudreux* ('dusty feet'), a court of justice formerly held at fairs to determine disputes between persons resorting to them. There is a reference to these courts in Ben Jonson's 'Bartholomew Fayre' (q.v.), II. i.

Pierce Pennilesse, His Supplication to the Divell, a fantastic prose satire by T. Nash (q.v.), published in 1592. The author, in the form of a humorous complaint to the Devil,

discourses on the vices of the day, throwing interesting light on the customs of his time. One of the best passages is that relating to the recently developed practice of excessive drinking, 'a sinne, that ever since we have mixt ourselves with the Low-Countries, is counted honourable', and containing a description of the various types of drunkards, drawn with a coarse Rabelaisian humour and vigour. The work is directed in part against Richard Harvey the astrologer (brother of Gabriel Harvey) and the Martinists (see *Martin Marprelate*). It ends with a discussion of the nature of spirits.

Pierian, PIERIDES, names applied to the Muses (q.v.), from Pieria near Mt. Olympus, where they were worshipped.

Pierides is also a name of the nine daughters of Pierus, king of Emathia, who challenged the Muses in a contest of song, and, being defeated, were changed into magpies.

Piero della Francesca (active 1439–92), Umbrian painter. The ordered composition of his paintings reflects his interest in mathematics; he wrote books on geometry and perspective.

Pierre, a character in Otway's 'Venice Preserv'd' (q.v.).

Pierre, or, The Ambiguities, by H. Melville (q.v.), published in 1852.

Pierrot, a typical character in French pantomime; now, in English, applied to a buffoon or itinerant minstrel, having, like the stage Pierrot, a whitened face and loose white fancy dress.

Piers Plowman, The Vision concerning, the most important work in Middle English with the exception of Chaucer's 'Canterbury Tales', is an alliterative poem of which the three versions, of very different length (2,500 to 7,300 lines), are attributed to William Langland, 'Long Will' as he calls himself. He seems to have been an educated man, and to have lived near Malvern, and in later life in London. He is supposed to have written them between 1360 and 1399. But recent critical discussion has left the question of the authorship of the three versions (known as the A, the B, and the C texts), and of the component parts of the A text, undecided. As to the details regarding the life of the author, drawn from the poem itself, modern criticism has thrown doubt on their validity, and the whole subject remains involved in obscurity.

Taking first the A text, the work may be very briefly summarized as follows:

Wandering on the Malvern Hills, the poet sees a vision of a high tower (Truth), a deep dungeon (Wrong), and a 'fair field full of folk' (the earth) between, with the people going about their various avocations, beggars, friars, priests, lawyers, labourers idle or hardworking, hermits and nuns, cooks crying 'hot pies, hot', and taverners, 'White wine of Osey'. There follows a vision in which Lady Meed (reward, but more particularly in a bad sense, bribery), Reason, Conscience, and other abstractions are confronted. Then we have Conscience preaching to the people, and Repentance moving their hearts, the confession of the seven deadly sins (which includes a vivid description of a tavern scene), and 'a thousand of men' moved to seek St. Truth. But the way is difficult to find, and here Piers Plowman makes his appearance, and offers to guide the pilgrims if they will help him plough his half-acre. Some help him, but some are shirkers. Then follows a discussion of the labour problem of the day. Able-bodied beggars must be severely dealt with. Labourers must not be dainty in their food and extravagant in their demands.

This takes us to the end of *passus VIII*. With *passus IX* (where according to some authorities the work of a continuator begins) the poem passes to a search for 'Do-well', 'Do-bet', and 'Do-best', who are vainly looked for among the friars, the priests, and in Scripture, with the help of Thought, Wit, and Study.

The additions contained in the B and C texts, though characterized by sincerity and power of impression, are too incoherent to be easily summarized. Their author is specially concerned with the corruption in the Church, with the merits of poverty, and the supreme virtue of love. The seven new visions include a long disquisition by 'Ymaginatif' on wealth and learning; a theological discussion between Reason, Conscience, Clergy, and a doctor of divinity; a conversation between Patience and 'Activa-Vita', the humble worker, who receives his reward hereafter; narratives of Christ's life in which Christ and Piers Plowman blend one into the other; and finally the attack of Antichrist and Pride upon the house 'Unity', and of Death upon Mankind.

Pierston, JOCELYN, the lover in Hardy's 'The Well-Beloved' (q.v.).

Pigwiggin, a character in Drayton's 'Nymphidia' (q.v.).

Pilate's Question, 'What is truth?' (John xviii. 38).

Pilatus, MT., a mountain south-west of Lucerne in Switzerland, so named from a tradition that the corpse of Pontius Pilate found its final resting-place there (or that Pilate was banished, or committed suicide, there). The name is perhaps a corruption of 'pileatus', i.e. 'capped' with clouds.

Pilgarlic, originally applied to a 'peeled' or bald head, ludicrously likened to a peeled head of garlic; then to a bald-headed man; and from the 17th cent. used in a ludicrously contemptuous or mock-pitiful way, a 'poor creature'. [OED.]

Pilgrim Fathers, THE, the English Puritans who in 1620 set out from Delft Haven and Plymouth in the 'Mayflower', and who founded the colony of Plymouth in New England.

Governor Bradford in 1630 wrote of his company as 'pilgrims' in the spiritual sense. The same phraseology was repeated by Cotton Mather, and others, and became familiar in New England. Later, anniversary feasts were held of the 'Sons' or 'Heirs' of the 'Pilgrims', and thus the expression 'Pilgrim Fathers' naturally arose, first as a rhetorical phrase, and finally as an historical designation. [OED.] Mention may be made of the poems by Mrs. Hemans, 'The Landing of the Pilgrim Fathers', and by O. W. Holmes, 'The Pilgrim's Vision'.

Pilgrim Trust, THE, a sum of some £2,000,000 placed in September 1930 by Mr. Edward Stephen Harkness (1874–1940), the American railway magnate and philanthropist, in the hands of trustees to be spent for the benefit of Great Britain. Mr. Harkness, who was born at Cleveland, Ohio, and educated at Yale, made other generous gifts for British purposes, as also did his mother, Mrs. Stephen Harkness (1838?–1926).

Pilgrim's Progress, *The, from this World to that which is to come,* an allegory by Bunyan (q.v.), published in 1678 (a second edition with additions appeared in the same year, and a third in 1679).

The allegory takes the form of a dream by the author. In this he sees Christian, with a burden on his back, and reading in a book, from which he learns that the city in which he and his family dwell will be burned with fire. On the advice of Evangelist, Christian flees from the City of Destruction, having failed to persuade his wife and children to accompany him. Pt. I describes his pilgrimage through the Slough of Despond, the Interpreter's House, the Palace Beautiful, the Valley of Humiliation, the Valley of the Shadow of Death, Vanity Fair, Doubting Castle, the Delectable Mountains, the country of Beulah, to the Celestial City. On the way he encounters various allegorical personages, among them Mr. Worldly Wiseman, Faithful (who accompanies Christian on his way but is put to death in Vanity Fair), Hopeful (who next joins Christian), Giant Despair, the foul fiend Apollyon, and many others.

Pt. II relates how Christian's wife, Christiana, moved by a vision, sets out with her children on the same pilgrimage, accompanied by her neighbour Mercy, despite the objections of Mrs. Timorous and others. They are escorted by Great-heart, who overcomes Giant Despair and other monsters, and brings them to their destination.

The work is remarkable for the beauty and simplicity of its language (Bunyan was permeated with the English of the Bible), the vividness and reality of the impersonations, and the author's sense of humour and feeling for the world of nature. The extraordinary appeal which it makes to the human mind is shown by the fact that it has been translated into no fewer than one hundred and eight different languages and dialects [C.H.E.L.].

Pilgrimage of Grace, THE, a rising in Yorkshire in 1536 in protest against the dissolution of the monasteries. It was at the same time North versus South, the old nobility against the new. The insurgents, headed by Robert Aske, and carrying a banner on which were depicted the five wounds of Christ, adopted this name, and became so numerous that the duke of Norfolk, sent to disperse them, made terms. These were not kept, and the leaders were seized and executed.

Pilgrimage of Man, The, see *Lydgate.*

Pilgrimage to Pernassus, see *Parnassus Plays.*

Pillars of Hercules, see *Hercules (Pillars of).*

Pilot that weathered the storm, THE, William Pitt the younger, in a song by George Canning (q.v.).
    For 'Dropping the Pilot', see *Tenniel.*

Pilpay, see *Bidpai.*

Piltdown, a down near Lewes, in Sussex, where prehistoric remains of a human skull and ape-like lower jaw and of worked flints and bone implements were discovered in 1912; they were claimed as belonging to the early pleistocene period, but scientific tests made in 1953 proved them to be forgeries.

Pilumnus, see *Picumnus.*

Pimlyco, or Runne Red-Cap, a satirical pamphlet, published in 1609, of unknown authorship, in which the poet describes a crowd of persons of all classes of society, from courtiers to 'greasie lownes', pressing towards Hogsden to drink Pimlico ale.
    The origin of the name 'Pimlico' is obscure, and has been the subject of much discussion in 'N. and Q.', especially series XI and XII. The name first appears in a tract, 'News from Hogsdon', of 1598, where 'Ben Pimlico's nut-browne' is referred to. The derivations are discussed also in E. Walford, 'Old and New London' (1892, v. 39), in which Hogsdon's Pimlico is referred to Hoxton, where there is still a Pimlico Walk. It appears that 'pim-lico' is the natives' name for a wading bird in the West Indies, and that some of the West Indian islets are named after them. The word, as the name of a bird, first appears in 1614. How it came to be applied to a district in the SW. of London has not been ascertained.

Pinch, a schoolmaster in Shakespeare's 'A Comedy of Errors' (q.v.).

Pinch, TOM and RUTH, characters in Dickens's 'Martin Chuzzlewit' (q.v.).

Pinchbeck, CHRISTOPHER (d. 1732), a watch- and toy-maker in Fleet Street, inventor of an alloy of five parts of copper with one of zinc, resembling gold, used in cheap jewellery and named after him.

Pinchwife, a character in Wycherley's 'The Country Wife' (q.v.).

PINDAR (c. 522–442 B.C.), the great Greek lyric poet, was born at or near Thebes. He acquired fame at an early age and was employed by many winners at the Games to celebrate their victories. The only complete poems of his that are extant are his 'Epinicia' or triumphal odes (see *Olympian Odes*); but he wrote many kinds of verse, hymns, paeans, processional odes, etc., enumerated by Horace in Od. iv. 2, and fragments of these survive. He exercised a great influence on Latin poetry (especially Horace). The English *Ode* (e.g. Dryden's 'Alexander's Feast') is written in imitation of the odes of Pindar. It is characterized by the irregularity in the number of feet in the different lines and the arbitrary disposition of the rhymes.

PINDAR, PETER, see *Wolcot.*

Pindus, a range of mountains in northern Greece, separating Thessaly from Epirus.

PINERO, SIR ARTHUR WING (1855–1934), the son of a solicitor and intended for his father's profession, took to the stage at 19, but in 1882 gave this up for dramatic writing. His first notable play, 'The Money Spinner', was produced in 1881, and was followed by three successful farces, 'The Magistrate' (1885), 'The Schoolmistress' (1886), and 'Dandy Dick' (1887). He then turned to more serious dramatic works, of which the most important were 'Sweet Lavender' (1888), 'The Second Mrs. Tanqueray' (1893), and 'Trelawny of the Wells' (1898). His numerous other plays include: 'Lady Bountiful' (1891), 'The Cabinet Minister' (1892), 'The Weaker Sex' (1894), 'The Amazons' (1895), 'The Notorious Mrs. Ebbsmith' (1895), 'The Princess and the Butterfly' (1898), 'The Gay Lord Quex' (1899), 'Iris' (1901), 'His House in Order' (1906), 'The Thunderbolt' (1908), 'Mid-Channel' (1909), 'The Widow of Wasdale Head' (1912), 'Playgoers' (1913).

Pinkerton, THE MISSES, managers of an academy for young ladies, on Chiswick Mall, in Thackeray's 'Vanity Fair' (q.v.).

Pinner of Wakefield, THE, see *George-a'-Green.*

PINTO, FERNÃO MENDES (1509?–83), a Portuguese traveller in the East, who left a narrative of his voyages ('Peregrinação', 1614), marked by a vivid imagination. Cervantes calls him the 'Prince of Liars' and Congreve in 'Love for Love' cites him as a typical liar.

Piozzi, MRS., see *Thrale.*

Pip, in Dickens's 'Great Expectations' (q.v.), the name by which the hero, Philip Pirrip, is commonly known.

Pipchin, MRS., in Dickens's 'Dombey and Son' (q.v.), a boarding-house keeper at Brighton.

Pipe Rolls, see *Rolls.*

Pipes, Tom, a character in Smollett's 'Peregrine Pickle' (q.v.).

Pippa Passes, a dramatic poem by R. Browning (q.v.), published in 1841 (the first of the series entitled 'Bells and Pomegranates').

It is Pippa's yearly holiday, and she wanders through the town singing and wondering which of four happy and beloved persons she would rather be, Ottima, Phene, Luigi, or the Bishop. She decides for the last, because he has God's love.

Now, Ottima and her lover Sebald have just murdered Ottima's husband. Pippa's song ('God's in His heaven') as she passes fills Sebald with remorse.

Phene is the newly married bride of Jules, the French sculptor. Jules finds that he has been tricked off with an ignorant girl, and is about to dismiss her. Pippa's song ('Give her but a least excuse to love me') awakens better feelings in him, and he decides to retain and save Phene.

Luigi, the patriot, has resolved to kill the Austrian emperor. His loving mother almost succeeds in dissuading him. Pippa's song ('A King lived long ago') rouses him to action, and he rushes away, thereby escaping the pursuit of the police.

The Bishop is planning with his intendant the destruction of Pippa herself; for she is the daughter of the Bishop's murdered brother, whose riches he has appropriated. Pippa's song ('Suddenly God took me') awakens his conscience. Pippa goes home at sunset, all unconscious of what her songs have effected.

PIRANDELLO, LUIGI (1867–1936), Italian dramatist, novelist, and short-story writer. His best-known works are: 'Cosí è (se vi pare)' (1917), 'Sei personaggi in cerca di autore' ('Six Characters in Search of an Author') (1921), 'Enrico IV' (1922), plays; 'Il fu Mattia Pascal' (1904), novel. His typical plays are built upon the theoretical presuppositions that truth is relative and that the personality of the individual is not single and unchanging, but multiform and fluid.

Pirate, The, a novel by Sir W. Scott (q.v.), published in 1821. Lockhart refers to 'the wild freshness' of its atmosphere. Scott absorbed the 'local colour' on a voyage of the Scottish Lighthouse Commissioners (on which he was an invited guest) with R. L. Stevenson's grandfather.

The scene is laid principally in Zetland (or Shetland) in the 17th cent. In a remote part of the island live a misanthropical recluse, Basil Mertoun, of whose antecedents nothing is known, and his son, Mordaunt, a gallant attractive youth. Mertoun is tenant of Magnus Troil, a rich Zetlander of noble Norse ancestry, the father of two daughters, Minna, high-minded and imaginative, and Brenda, of a cheerful and more homely temperament. Mordaunt is their constant guest, and friend of the girls. Their pleasant relations are interrupted by the arrival of Clement Cleveland, a buccaneer captain, shipwrecked on the coast,

and rescued from the sea by Mordaunt. Between these two a bitter enmity springs up. Minna, ignorant of the true character of a pirate's life, falls in love with Cleveland and he with her. Mordaunt, on the other hand, finds himself excluded from the friendship of the Troils, owing to false reports about him which have reached Magnus, but Brenda remains faithful to him and attracts thereby his love. A half-crazy relative of Magnus, Ulla Troil, known as Norna of the Fitful-head, who believes herself endowed with supernatural powers, has an interest in the destinies of the principal characters, thinking herself to be the mother of Mordaunt. She contrives to bring them all to Orkney, in which island the denouement takes place. In Kirkwall Cleveland is recognized by his old comrades and compelled to rejoin them. The pirates are eventually captured by a government frigate on information supplied by Norna, who discovers too late that Cleveland is her son by Basil Mertoun and that Mordaunt is his son by another woman. Minna and Cleveland are separated for ever; Brenda and Mordaunt are united.

There are some entertaining minor characters, in the persons of Triptolemus Yellowley, a farmer in the Mearns, sent to introduce an improved agriculture among the backward islanders, and his shrewish sister, Barbara; Claud Halcro, poet and bard, and worshipper of John Dryden; Bryce Snailsfoot, the pedlar; and Jack Bunce, the actor-pirate.

Pirene, see _Peirene._

Pirithous, see _Peirithous._

Pisa, The Leaning Tower of, the campanile of Pisa cathedral, built in 1173. It is 179 feet high and leans 13 feet from the perpendicular. It is circular and decorated with tiers of marble arcades.

Pisistratus, see _Peisistratus._ Pisistratus Caxton is a character in B. Lytton's 'The Caxtons' (q.v.).

Piso's Justice: Seneca ('Dial'. III. 18) relates this story of Gnaeus Piso, a man who took obstinacy for firmness. He had sentenced a soldier to death for murder, but when the execution was about to take place the man supposed to have been murdered appeared. The centurion stopped the execution and reported the matter to Piso. Piso thereupon condemned all three to death, the first as having already been sentenced, the centurion for disobeying orders, and the man who was supposed to have been murdered for being the cause of the death of the other two.

Pistol, Ancient, in Shakespeare's '2 Henry IV', 'Henry V', and 'The Merry Wives of Windsor' (qq.v.), one of Falstaff's associates, a braggart with a fine command of bombastic language.

Pistole, a name applied specifically from _c._ 1600 to a Spanish gold coin equivalent to four silver *pieces of eight* (see *Dollar*) and worth from 16s. 6d. to 18s.; also applied (after the French) to the louis d'or of Louis XIII issued in 1640. The name, apparently shortened from *pistolet*, is ultimately derived from Pistoia, a town in Tuscany which still manufactures iron and steel, and especially guns. But the history of the word, and the connexion of the coin with the weapon, are obscure.

Pistyl of Susan, The, an alliterative poem of the 14th cent., which relates the story of Susannah and Daniel. It is attributed by some to Huchoun (q.v.). 'Pistyl' = Epistle.

Pit, The, a novel by Frank Norris (q.v.).

Pities, THE, see *Dynasts.*

PITMAN, SIR ISAAC (1813–97), the inventor of phonography. He published at fourpence in 1837 'Stenographic Sound-Hand', substituting phonographic for the mainly orthographic methods adopted by former shorthand authors. A penny plate entitled 'Phonography' was published by him in 1840, and fuller explanations of the system followed in that and subsequent years. His system, which has been adapted to several foreign languages, has, to a large extent, superseded all others.

PITT, CHRISTOPHER (1699–1748), minor poet. He translated Virgil's 'Aeneid' (1740). He is included in Johnson's 'Lives of the Poets' (q.v.).

Pitt, THOMAS, known as DIAMOND PITT (1653–1726), East India merchant and governor of Madras, who obtained the great Pitt diamond from an Indian merchant. He sold it to the French regent for £135,000 and it is still among the State jewels of France. Thomas Pitt was grandfather of the earl of Chatham.

Pitt, WILLIAM, *first earl of Chatham* (1708–78), educated at Eton and Trinity College, Oxford, a great Whig statesman and orator. He entered parliament in 1735, was admitted to office in Pelham's administration, and was dismissed in 1755 owing to his attacks on Sir Thomas Robinson (leader of the House of Commons) and even Newcastle the premier. He was secretary of state in 1756–7, but his fame as a great administrator rests chiefly on the period that immediately followed, when Pitt and Newcastle were the chief ministers in coalition and when, thanks to Pitt's choice of able commanders for the prosecution of the Seven Years War and the new spirit and courage that he breathed into the services, 'the wind, from whatever quarter it blew, carried to England tidings of battles won, fortresses taken, provinces added to the empire' (Macaulay). Pitt resigned in 1761, having failed to convince the cabinet of the necessity of war with Spain. He formed an administration in 1766 and accepted an earldom, but ill health forced his resignation in 1768. He strenuously opposed from 1774

onwards the harsh measures taken against the American colonies, though unwilling to recognize their independence. His speeches were marked by lofty and impassioned eloquence, and, judged by their effect on their hearers, place him among the greatest orators. But only fragments have survived.

Pitt, WILLIAM (1759–1806), second son of the first earl of Chatham, educated at Pembroke Hall, Cambridge. He became chancellor of the exchequer in his twenty-second, and prime minister in 1783 in his twenty-fifth year, and retained the position until 1801, during the troubled years which followed the outbreak of the French Revolution, forming the great European coalitions that opposed French military aggression. He returned to office in 1804, formed the third coalition, and died in January 1806, shortly after the battle of Austerlitz, his last words being, 'Oh, my country! How I leave my country!'

Pitt Diamond, see *Pitt (T.).*

Pittacus (7th–6th cent. B.C.), of Mitylene, where he was chosen to be ruler, was one of the so-called 'Seven Sages of Greece' (q.v.). Two maxims were attributed to him: χαλεπὸν ἐσθλὸν ἔμμεναι (eminence is difficult), and καιρὸν γνῶθι (know the opportunity).

Pius II, see *Aeneas Silvius.*

Pizarro, a tragedy by Sheridan (q.v.). FRANCISCO PIZARRO, the Spanish conqueror of Peru, was born about 1471 and died in 1541.

Place-Name Society, THE, see *English Place-Name Society.*

Placēbo, Latin, 'I shall be pleasing', occurring in Ps. cxiv. 9 (*Placebo Domino in regione vivorum*), is used allusively in such phrases as 'sing placebo' to signify 'play the sycophant'. Chaucer uses Placebo in 'The Merchant's Tale' as a proper name for a flatterer, one of the brothers of old January.

Placidas, in Spenser's 'Faerie Queene', see *Poeana.*

Plagiary, SIR FRETFUL, a character in Sheridan's 'The Critic' (q.v.), a caricature of Richard Cumberland (q.v.).

Plague of London, THE GREAT, the epidemic of bubonic plague that visited London in 1665.

Plague Year, A Journal of the, an historical fiction by Defoe (q.v.), published in 1722.

It purports to be the narrative of a resident in London during 1664–5, the year of the Great Plague. It describes the gradual spread of the plague, and the growing terror of the inhabitants. It relates the public measures taken by the authorities, such as the sequestration of the sick, the closing of infected houses, and the prohibition of assemblies, with their effect on the minds of the people. The symptoms of the disease, the circulation of the dead-carts, the burials in great pits, and the lamentable scenes witnessed by the supposed narrator are described with extraordinary vividness. The general effects of the epidemic, notably in the cessation of many trades, and the exodus from the city, are also set forth, and an estimate made of the total number of deaths from the disease.

The 'Journal' no doubt embodies much information that Defoe received from one source or another, including official documents. Some scenes, it has been pointed out, appear to be borrowed from Dekker's 'Wonderful Year 1603'. Sir Walter Scott observes that even if Defoe had not been the author of 'Robinson Crusoe', he would have deserved immortality for the genius displayed in this work.

Plain, THE, the name applied to the more moderate (or perhaps the more timid) party in the French national convention at the time of the Revolution, from the fact that they sat on the floor of the hall. (Cf. *Mountain.*) They were also called the 'Marais' or 'crapauds du Marais'. It was their junction with the rump of the Dantonists that overthrew Robespierre (q.v.) on the 9th Thermidor.

Plain Dealer, The, a comedy by Wycherley (q.v.), produced in 1677.

This, perhaps the best of Wycherley's plays, a remote adaptation of Molière's 'Le Misanthrope', shows the author at his fiercest as a satirist. The 'plain dealer' is Manly, an honest misanthropic sea-captain, who has lost confidence in everyone save his one trusty friend Vernish, and his love, Olivia, to whom he has confided his money. The plot turns on the perfidy of Vernish and Olivia. On his return from fighting the Dutch, Manly finds that Olivia scorns him, has married another, and makes pretexts for not returning his money. Fidelia, a young lady who cherishes a secret passion for Manly and has followed him to sea in man's clothes, continues to attend him in spite of his rebuffs, and her disguise is not suspected. Manly, still hoping to win Olivia's favour, sends Fidelia to plead for him. Olivia becomes enamoured of the disguised Fidelia, who, by Manly's direction, makes an assignation with Olivia, to which Manly, under cover of darkness, also comes, intending to expose Olivia's perfidy. Olivia's husband, who has helped to appropriate Manly's money, and who now turns out to be the trusted Vernish, finds Olivia with Manly and Fidelia, and rushes at Manly to kill him. Fidelia saves Manly and is herself wounded in the scuffle; her disguise is discovered. Manly, cured of his infatuation for Olivia, and touched by Fidelia's devotion, gives her his heart.

Among other amusing characters is the widow Blackacre, a litigious creature thoroughly at home in the courts and in legal jargon, who trains up her son to follow in her footsteps, and thereby overreaches herself. The son, Jerry Blackacre, is the literary ancestor of Tony Lumpkin.

Plan of Campaign, THE, a method of conducting operations against landlords in Ireland who refused to reduce rents, entered upon in 1886–7. The tenants in a body were to pay what they considered the fair rent into the hands of a political leader, charged to retain it until the landlord should accept the sum offered, less any amount expended in maintaining the struggle. [OED.]

PLANCHÉ, JAMES ROBINSON (1796–1880), English playwright of Huguenot descent. He was a versatile and prolific writer, mainly of burlesques and extravaganzas (e.g. 'Success; or, A Hit if you like it,' 1825, and 'High, Low, Jack, and the Game; or The Card Party', 1833), which enjoyed great popularity and may be considered as forerunners of the Gilbert and Sullivan Operas (q.v.). He also wrote the libretto for Weber's 'Oberon' and the English versions of 'William Tell' and 'The Magic Flute'. His 'History of British Costumes' (1834) was for long a standard work, and he also published an edition of Strutt's 'Regal and Ecclesiastical Antiquities of England' (1842). He was appointed Somerset Herald in 1866.

Plancus, L., Roman consul in 42 B.C.: 'in the consulship of Plancus', 'when I was young'; from Horace, 'Odes', III. xvi.

Plantin, CHRISTOPHE (c 1520–89), printer, born near Tours; he settled at Antwerp and began printing in 1555. His press was carried on by his widow and son-in-law, Moretus. His house is now a museum.

PLATO (c. 427–348 B.C.), the great Greek philosopher, was the son of an Athenian of ancient family. He became a pupil and devoted admirer of Socrates, and after his death in 399 retired to Megara, and subsequently paid three visits to the courts of Dionysius I and Dionysius II at Syracuse. After the first of these, about 386, he began teaching philosophy in the Academy, an olive-grove near Athens, whence his school derives its name. He twice made some attempt to enter political life, but was repelled by the iniquities he encountered. The remainder of his life was mainly occupied with instruction and the composition of the Dialogues in which he embodied his views, and in which Socrates figures as conducting the discussions. All these Dialogues are extant. They are based on the teaching of Socrates (q.v.) and show the influence of the Pythagoreans (q.v.), but are not altogether self-consistent, and indicate an evolution of Plato's thought. Much of their charm lies in their dramatic setting, the description of the scenes in which they take place, the amusing and interesting characters that he stages, and the genial irony of Socrates.

One of Plato's principal contributions to philosophical thought is his 'Theory of Ideas'. The *idea* or *form* of a thing, in this theory, is somewhat of the nature of our abstract conception of that thing, but having a real existence outside the world of sense; it is the unchanging reality behind the changing appearance. The supreme *idea* is that of the Good. With Plato, as with Socrates, virtue is knowledge, knowledge of this supreme *idea*, which implies the effort to realize it. This perfect virtue is given to very few. Ordinary practical virtue consists in conduct in accordance with man's true nature, developed by education, which represents the constraint of the State's laws.

Plato's principal Dialogues were the 'Protagoras', 'Gorgias', 'Phaedo', 'Symposium', 'Republic', 'Phaedrus', 'Parmenides', 'Theaetetus', 'Sophist', 'Philebus', 'Timaeus', 'Laws', and the 'Apology' (a reproduction of Socrates' defence at his trial). Jowett's (q.v.) classic translation of the Dialogues appeared in 1871.

Platonic love, love of a purely spiritual character, free from sensual desire. *Amor Platonicus* was used by the Florentine Marsilio Ficino (1433–99), synonymously with *Amor Socraticus*, to denote the kind of interest in young men which was imputed to Socrates; cf. the last few pages of Plato's 'Symposium'. As thus originally used it had no reference to women. [OED.]

Platonic year, a cycle imagined by some ancient astronomers, in which the heavenly bodies were to return to their original relative positions (after which, according to some, all events would recur in the same order as before); sometimes identified with the period of the revolution of the equinoxes (about 25,800 years).

Platonists, THE CAMBRIDGE, a group of philosophers, whose headquarters were Cambridge University, and who flourished in the middle of the 17th cent. For the chief features of their philosophy see *Cudworth*. The principal members of the group, besides Cudworth, were Henry More, John Smith (1618–52), and Culverwel (qq.v.).

PLAUTUS, TITUS MACCIUS (c. 254–184 B.C.), the celebrated Roman comic poet, was born in a village of Umbria. He was poor when he came to Rome and accepted humble employments, at one time turning a hand-mill for a baker. We possess twenty of his comedies, some of them imitations of Menander's plays: 'Amphitruo', 'Asinaria', 'Aulularia', 'Bacchides', 'Captivi', 'Casina', 'Cistellaria', 'Curculio', 'Epidicus', 'Menaechmi', 'Mercator', 'Miles', 'Mostellaria', 'Persa', 'Poenulus', 'Pseudolus', Rudens', 'Stichus', 'Trinummus', 'Truculentus'. Several of his plays have been imitated by Molière, Shakespeare, and other modern writers.

Playboy of the Western World, The, a comedy by Synge (q.v.), published in 1907.

Christy Mahon, 'a slight young man, very tired and frightened', arrives at a village in Mayo. He gives out that he is a fugitive from justice, who in a quarrel has killed his bullying father, splitting him to the chine with a single blow. He is hospitably entertained, and his character as a dare-devil gives him a great advantage with the women over the milder-spirited lads of the place. But admiration gives place to angry contempt when the father himself arrives in pursuit of the fugitive, who has merely given him a crack on the head and run away.

Plays for Puritans, a collection of three plays by G. B. Shaw (q.v.), published in 1901. The plays are 'The Devil's Disciple', 'Caesar and Cleopatra', and 'Captain Brassbound's Conversion'.

Plays, Pleasant and Unpleasant, a collection of seven plays (in two volumes) by G. B. Shaw (q.v.), published in 1898. The plays are (pleasant): 'Arms and the Man', 'Candida', 'The Man of Destiny', and 'You Never Can Tell'; (unpleasant): 'Widowers' Houses', 'The Philanderer', 'Mrs. Warren's Profession'.

Pleasant Satyre of the Thrie Estaitis in Commendatioun of Vertew and Vituperatioun of Vyce, Ane, a morality play by Sir D. Lindsay (q.v.), produced in 1540.

Pt. I represents the temptation of Rex Humanitas by Sensuality, Wantonness, Solace, and other evil companions, while Good Counsel is hustled away, Verity is put in the stocks, and Chastity is warned off. An interlude follows in which are described the adventures of Chastity among humbler folks, a tailor, a soutar, and their wives. Then Chastity is put in the stocks. But the arrival of Correction alters the situation. Verity, Good Counsel, and Chastity are admitted to the king, and Sensuality is banished.

After an interlude in which an impoverished farmer exposes his sufferings at the hands of the ecclesiastics, and a pardoner's trade is ridiculed, Pt. II presents the Three Estates summoned before the king, and their misdeeds denounced by John the Common Weal. The Lords and Commons repent, but the clergy remain impenitent, are exposed, and the malefactors brought to the scaffold.

The play, which is extremely long, is written in various metres, eight- and six-lined stanzas and couplets. It is, as a dramatic representation, in advance of all contemporary English plays, and gives an interesting picture of the Scottish life of the time.

Pleasures of Hope, The, a poem by T. Campbell (q.v.), published in 1799.

In Pt. I the poet considers the consolation and inspiration of Hope in various circumstances, its effects on the individual and on the community, and by contrast the hard fate of a people deprived of it (the well-known passage on the downfall of Poland). In Pt. II he passes to the consideration of Love in combination with Hope, and to the blessings of the belief in a future life. The poem contains single lines that have become proverbial, such as

'Tis distance lends enchantment to the view,

and

Like angel-visits, few and far between.

Pleasures of Imagination, The, a didactic poem by Akenside (q.v.), published in 1744; it was completely re-written and issued as 'The Pleasures of the Imagination' in 1757.

The object of the poet, in his own words, is

To pierce divine Philosophy's retreats,
And teach the Muse her lore.

He examines the pleasures of imagination, dividing them into (a) primary pleasures connected with the sublime, the wonderful, and the beautiful, whose connexion with the moral faculties he traces; and (b) secondary pleasures, such as those of sense and all the passions of men's hearts, finding delight even in 'ennobling sorrows'. In the third of the three books composing the poem, he considers the origin of vice, the nature of ridicule, the pleasures of memory and association of ideas, and the nature of taste.

Akenside is indebted to Addison, Shaftesbury, and Hutcheson for the philosophical groundwork of his poem.

Pleasures of Memory, The, see *Rogers (S.)*.

Pléiade, La, a group of French poets of the latter part of the 16th cent., consisting of Pierre de Ronsard (q.v.), Joachim du Bellay, Pontus de Thiard, Jodelle, Belleau, Baïf, and Dorat (or, according to other authorities, Peletier), animated by a common veneration for the writers of antiquity, and a desire to improve the quality of French verse. Their inauguration in France of the sonnet stimulated the interest in England in this form of verse. The title was taken ultimately from the Pleiades (q.v.), and was first given to a group of seven Hellenist poets of the reign of Ptolemy Philadelphus, including Theocritus, Lycophron, and Aratus.

Pleĭădes, seven daughters of Atlas, who after their death were placed in heaven and form a group of stars. Their names were Alcўŏnē, Mĕrŏpē, Maia, Electra, Taўgĕtē, Stĕrŏpē, and Celaeno. Of these Merope married Sisyphus (q.v.), the others had gods for their lovers. Therefore Merope is dimmer than her sister stars. The rising of the constellation was in May and its setting in November. Hence the connexion of the Pleiades with the beneficent showers of spring, the autumn seed-time, and autumn storms.

Pleydell, Mr. Counsellor Paulus, a character in Scott's 'Guy Mannering' (q.v.).

Pliable, in Bunyan's 'Pilgrim's Progress' (q.v.), one of Christian's companions, who turns back at the Slough of Despond.

Pliant, Dame, a character in Jonson's 'The Alchemist' (q.v.).

Pliant, Sir Paul, see *Plyant*.

PLINY THE ELDER, GAIUS PLINIUS SECUNDUS (A.D. 23–79), the author of the 'Historia Naturalis', and the intimate friend of Vespasian. He perished while observing the eruption of Vesuvius that destroyed Herculaneum and Pompeii.

PLINY THE YOUNGER, GAIUS PLINIUS CAECILIUS SECUNDUS (*b.* A.D. 61), nephew of the above, an advocate who held many public offices, was author of a 'Panegyricus' of Trajan, and of a number of interesting letters ('Epistolae') throwing much light on Pliny's time and contemporaries. As proconsul in Bithynia he gives (in one of his letters to Trajan) one of the earliest authentic references to the sect of 'Christians'.

Plornish, Mr. and Mrs., in Dickens's 'Little Dorrit' (q.v.), a plasterer and his wife who lived in Bleeding Heart Yard. Mrs. Plornish was a notable interpreter of the Italian language.

PLOTINUS (*c.* A.D. 203–62), born at Lycopolis in Egypt, was the chief exponent of the Neoplatonic philosophy. After studying at Alexandria, he opened his school at Rome. He is generally described as a 'mystic', who developed Plato's teaching, and appears to have had some knowledge of oriental philosophies. His aim was the conversion of his disciples to the highest and most spiritual mode of life. The 'Enneads' are the six divisions of Porphyry's collections of Plotinus' works, each of which contains nine books (translated by S. McKenna and B. S. Page, 1917-30). Plotinus has been elucidated, and his influence on Christianity discussed, by Dean Inge in the Gifford Lectures of 1918.

Plough-Monday, the first Monday after Epiphany, on which, especially in the north and east of England, the commencement of the ploughing season was celebrated by a procession of disguised ploughmen and boys drawing a plough from door to door. See *Plough Monday Play*.

Plough Monday Play, a folk-drama of the East Midlands. In the version from Cropwell in Nottinghamshire the characters are Tom the Fool, a Recruiting Sergeant, a Ribboner or Recruit, three farm-servants, a Doctor, and Beelzebub; and two women, a Young Lady and old Dame Jane. The Ribboner's suit is rejected by the Young Lady and he enlists; Tom Fool consoles the Lady. The farm-servants describe their several occupations. Dame Jane claims Tom Fool as father of her child. Beelzebub strikes her with his club and kills her. The Doctor, after vaunting his abilities, declares that she is only in a trance and revives her. The play concludes with dance and songs and a collection. The other extant version, from Lincolnshire, is in its main features similar. Like the St. George play, the Plough Monday play probably symbolizes, in its central incident, the death and resurrection of the year. The subject is treated in E. K. Chambers, 'The Medieval Stage', on which the above is based. (For the Cropwell version, Chambers refers to Mrs. Chaworth Musters, 'A Cavalier Stronghold'.)

Plumdamas, PETER, a character in Scott's 'The Heart of Midlothian' (q.v.).

Plume, CAPTAIN, a character in Farquhar's 'The Recruiting Officer' (q.v.).

Plumian Professorship, THE, of Astronomy and Experimental Philosophy at Cambridge, owes its name to Thomas Plume (1630–1704), of Christ's College, Cambridge, archdeacon of Rochester, who left sums of money for the erection of an observatory and the maintenance of this professorship.

Plummer, CALEB and BERTHA, characters in Dickens's 'The Cricket on the Hearth' (q.v.).

PLUTARCH, the biographer and moral philosopher, was born at Chaeronea in Boeotia; the date of his birth is unknown, but according to his own statement he was studying philosophy in A.D. 66. His most famous work is the 'Parallel Lives' of twenty-three Greeks and twenty-three Romans, arranged in pairs. These biographies are the source of the plots of many of our dramas, including some of Shakespeare's.

Sir Thomas North's version of them (1579) is a translation, not of the original Greek, but of the French rendering of Jacques Amyot. It is not a strictly accurate version, but is embellished by North's vivid English. Another important translation of the 'Lives' is that of John and William Langhorne (1770). Plutarch also wrote lives of Artaxerxes II, Aratus, Galba, and Otho, and a collection of Essays known as 'Moralia', some of them ethical, some on historical subjects; these were translated by Philemon Holland in 1603.

Pluto, another name of the god Hades (q.v.).

Plutus, the son of Demeter (q.v.), and the god of wealth. The Greeks represented him as blind, because he distributed riches indiscriminately; as lame, because riches come slowly; and with wings, because riches disappear more quickly than they come.

Plyant, SIR PAUL, in Congreve's 'The Double Dealer' (q.v.), 'an uxorious foolish old knight'.

Plymley, Peter, Letters of, by S. Smith (q.v.), published in 1807–8.

The letters purport to be written by one Peter Plymley to his brother in the country, the Rev. Abraham Plymley, in favour of Catholic Emancipation. The supposed arguments of the Rev. Abraham for maintaining the disabilities of the Roman Catholics are taken one by one, and demolished with an abundance of good sense, wit, and humour; while at the same time the author ridicules what he calls the 'nonsense' of the Roman Catholic religion.

Plymouth Brethren, a religious body that arose at Plymouth, c. 1830. They have no formal creed (though believing in Christ) or official order of ministers.

Pocahontas or MATOAKA (1595–1617), an American-Indian princess, the daughter of Powhattan, an Indian chief in Virginia. According to the untrustworthy account of Capt. John Smith (q.v.), one of the Virginia colonists who had been taken prisoner by the Indians, he was rescued by her when her father was about to slay him in 1607 (she was then only 12). In 1612 she was seized as a hostage by the Colonists for the good behaviour of the Indian tribes (or for the restitution of English captives), became a Christian, was named Rebecca, and married a colonist, John Rolfe. She was brought to England in 1616, where she at first attracted considerable attention, but died neglected and in poverty in 1617. Those who claim descent from her are legion. She is introduced by Ben Jonson in his 'The Staple of News' (q.v.), II. i. George Warrington, in Thackeray's 'The Virginians', composes a tragedy on her.

Pocket, HERBERT, a character in Dickens's 'Great Expectations' (q.v.).

Podsnap, MR., a character in Dickens's 'Our Mutual Friend' (q.v.), a type of self-satisfaction and self-importance.

POE, EDGAR ALLAN (1809–49), born at Boston, Mass., of actor parents, became an orphan in early childhood, and was brought up and protected by John Allan, a tobacco exporter of Richmond, who appears to have reaped little satisfaction or gratitude from Poe for his kindness. Poe was brought to England and sent to school at Stoke Newington (see his 'William Wilson'), and was subsequently at the university of Virginia for a year. His first publication, 'Tamerlane, and other Poems', belongs to the year 1827. In 1828 he enlisted in the U.S. army. His discharge was procured and he entered the Military Academy at West Point, but was dismissed in 1831. Meanwhile his poems had met with no success and he turned to journalism. He became editor of various periodicals, including the 'Southern Literary Messenger', in which he published some of his best stories. His 'Tales of the Grotesque and Arabesque' appeared in 1839; 'The Murders in the Rue Morgue' in 1841; 'The Gold Bug', dealing with the solution of a cryptogram, in 1843; 'The Raven', the first poem that brought him wide popularity, in 1845. But he had already written some notable verse, 'To Helen', 'Israfel', 'The City in the Sea', 'The Haunted Palace', and 'Dream Land', between 1831 and 1844. His 'Ulalume' appeared in 1847; 'For Annie', 'Annabel Lee', and 'The Bells', in 1849. Among his other remarkable tales may be mentioned 'The House of Usher', 1839; 'A Descent into the Maelstrom', 1841; 'The Masque of the Red Death' and 'The Mystery of Marie Roget', 1842; and 'The Cask of Amontillado', 1846. Poe also wrote much literary criticism.

Poeana, in Spenser's 'Faerie Queene', IV.

viii. 49 et seq., the daughter of the giant Corflambo (q.v.). She falls in love with Amyas, the 'Squire of low degree', whom her father has taken prisoner. But Amyas loves Aemylia. His friend Placidas, who closely resembles him, goes to him in his captivity and is mistaken for him by Poeana, but escapes from her. Amyas is released by Prince Arthur.

Poema Morale, or *Moral Ode,* a poem in English of the period 1200–50, chiefly interesting for its metrical form, rhymed couplets of fourteen syllables. It is a disquisition on the shortness of life, the failure of wisdom to increase with age, the coming of Judgement, and the joys of Heaven.

Poems and Ballads, see *Swinburne (A. C.).*

Poet Laureate, the title given to a poet who receives a stipend as an officer of the Royal Household, his duty (no longer enforced) being to write court-odes, etc. The title formerly was sometimes conferred by certain universities.

The first poet laureate in the modern sense was Ben Jonson, but the title seems to have been first officially given to Dryden. The other laureates in chronological order are as follows: Shadwell, Tate, Rowe, Eusden, Cibber, Whitehead, T. Warton, Pye, Southey, Wordsworth, A. Tennyson, A. Austin, Bridges, Masefield (qq.v.). See E. K. Broadus, 'The Laureateship' (1921).

Poets' Corner, part of the south transept of Westminster Abbey containing the tombs or monuments of Chaucer, Spenser, Shakespeare, Ben Jonson, Milton, Drayton, Samuel Butler, and many later distinguished poets and authors. It is called in the 'Spectator' (1711) 'the poetical Quarter'.

Poetaster, The, a satirical comedy by Jonson (q.v.), produced in 1601. The scene is the court of Caesar Augustus, but the play deals with the quarrels and rivalries of the poets of Jonson's own day, though many of the incidents alluded to are now lost to us. The principal characters, besides the emperor, are Horace, representing Jonson himself, Virgil, perhaps representing Shakespeare, Crispinus, who stands for Marston, and Demetrius, who is described as 'a dresser of plays about the town', for Dekker. Another notable character is Tucca, a foul-mouthed bully and coward, copied from a certain Capt. Hannam, a notorious parasite of the day. The plot, so far as there is one, consists in a conspiracy of Crispinus and Demetrius, instigated by Tucca, to defame Horace. The matter is tried before Caesar. The arraignments, in ridiculous verse, are read, Horace is acquitted, and a 'light vomit' is administered to Crispinus to rid him of his long words. The incident of Ovid's banishment by Augustus is also introduced.

To the attack on Marston and Dekker the latter replied in 'Satiromastix' (q.v.).

Poetical Rapsody, A, a collection of Elizabethan verse, published by F. Davison (q.v.) and his brother Walter in 1602, and edited by Bullen in Arber's 'English Scholar's Library'. It includes 'The Lie', attributed to Sir Walter Ralegh; the song 'In praise of a Beggar's Life', quoted by Izaak Walton in 'The Compleat Angler'; and poems by Greene, Wotton, Sidney, Spenser, Donne, and others.

Poetry Bookshop, see *Monro (H.).*

POGGIO BRACCIOLINI, GIAN FRANCESCO (1380–1459), Italian humanist, who recovered many lost works of Roman literature.

Poilu (French 'hairy'), a familiar name for the French private soldier of 1914–18, who frequently wore a beard.

Poins, in Shakespeare's '1 and 2 Henry IV' (q.v.), one of Falstaff's companions.

Pointillism, see *Neo-Impressionism.*

Poirot, HERCULE, the Belgian detective in Agatha Christie's stories of crime.

Polack, an obsolete name for a Pole, used by Shakespeare in 'Hamlet', I. i, and four times in other places in the same play.

Pole, WILFRID, a character in Meredith's 'Sandra Belloni' and 'Vittoria' (qq.v.).

Policraticus, see *John of Salisbury.*

Polinarda, a character in 'Palmerin of England' (q.v.).

Polite Learning, An Enquiry into the Present State of, see *Enquiry into the Present State of Polite Learning.*

POLITIAN, see *Poliziano.*

Political Arithmetic, see *Petty.*

Political Eclogues, see *Rolliad.*

Political Register, The, a weekly newspaper founded in 1802 by Cobbett (q.v.), which he continued to issue even when in prison. It obtained a large circulation and gave Cobbett a strong hold on public opinion. It survived until 1835.

Politick Would-be, SIR and LADY, characters in Jonson's 'Volpone' (q.v.).

Polixenes, a character in Shakespeare's 'The Winter's Tale' (q.v.).

POLIZIANO, ANGELO (in English POLITIAN) (1454–94), the name assumed (from his birthplace Montepulciano) by AGNOLO AMBROGINI, Italian humanist and friend of Lorenzo the Magnificent. He was professor of Greek and Latin in the University of Florence, and wrote poetry in both these languages. His Italian works include the 'Stanze per la giostra' and 'Orfeo', the first secular drama in Italian. His philological acumen, seen at its best in two collections of studies of textual problems (the first and second 'Miscellaneorum anturia') make him one of the founders of modern textual criticism.

POLLARD, ALFRED WILLIAM (1859–1944), bibliographer and scholar, joint-secretary of the Bibliographical Society (q.v.) and fellow of the British Academy (q.v.). He wrote many bibliographical works, was editor of the 'Globe' Chaucer, and made important contributions to Shakespearian scholarship.

Pollentë, in Spenser's 'Faerie Queene', v. ii, the 'cruel sarazin' who holds a bridge and despoils those who pass over it, the father of Munera (q.v.). He is slain by Sir Artegall.

Pollexfen, SIR HARGRAVE, the villain in Richardson's 'Sir Charles Grandison' (q.v.).

POLLOCK, SIR FREDERICK (1845–1937), educated at Eton and Trinity College, Cambridge, was professor of jurisprudence at Oxford, 1883–1903. His numerous publications on legal subjects include: 'The Principles of Contract' (1876), 'Essays in Jurisprudence and Ethics' (1882), 'The Law of Torts' (1887), 'History of English Law before the time of Edward I' (with F. W. Maitland, 1895), 'The Expansion of the Common Law' (1904). He also wrote 'Spinoza, his Life and Philosophy' (1880, 1899, 1912) and with E. F. Maitland published 'The Etchingham Letters' in 1899.

Pollux, see *Castor.*

Polly, a musical play by J. Gay (q.v.), published in 1729. Its production on the stage was prohibited by the lord chamberlain. The play is a sequel to 'The Beggar's Opera' (q.v.).

The principal characters are the Macheath and Polly Peachum of the earlier play. Macheath has been transported to the West Indies, has run away from the plantation, and is thought dead, but is in fact disguised as Morano, chief of the pirates. Polly comes to the West Indies to seek him, is entrapped into the household of Ducat, a planter, from whose amorous intentions she escapes owing to an attack of the pirates on the settlement. Disguised as a man she joins the loyal Indians, helps to beat off the attack, takes Morano prisoner, learns his identity too late to save him from execution, and marries an Indian prince.

Thanks to the advertisement which the play received by its prohibition, it brought in £1,200 to the author.

Polly, *The History of Mr.,* see *Mr. Polly.*

POLO, MARCO (1254–1324), a member of a patrician family of Venice, accompanied his father and uncle in 1271 on an embassy from the Pope to Kublai, Grand Khan of Tartary. They travelled through Armenia, Iraq, Khorasan, and the Pamir, to Kashgar; thence to Khoten, across the desert of Lop and into Chinese territory, where they were well received by the emperor and where Marco was employed on services of importance. After seventeen years in the territories of the Grand Khan, the Polos obtained permission to return home, which they did by sea to the Persian Gulf, eventually reaching Venice

after an absence of twenty-four years. Marco Polo's account of his travels was written while imprisoned by the Genoese, by whom he had been captured in a sea-fight with the Venetians. The original text appears to have been in French. The existence of other and wilder romances of Eastern travel (such as Mandeville, etc.) tended to make Polo 'suspect', at least in places; but there is no reason for any such suspicion. The work became very popular and was translated into many languages. It was englished by John Frampton in 1579; but the first serious English translation was by W. Marsden early in the 19th cent. The classical one is by Sir Henry Yule, with full notes, which first appeared in 1871 (there are subsequent editions). A standard edition of the Italian text, with new materials, by L. F. Benedetto was published in Florence in 1928.

Polonius, a character in Shakespeare's 'Hamlet' (q.v.).

Poltergeist (from the German *polter*, noise, *geist*, spirit), a spirit that makes its presence known by noises.

Polton, in the detective stories of Austin Freeman, the laboratory assistant of Dr. Thorndyke (q.v.).

POLYBIUS (*c.* 204–122 B.C.), born at Megalopolis in Arcadia, and brought to Rome as a hostage in 167, became the friend of P. Cornelius Scipio Africanus Minor. He was enabled through his patronage to obtain access to materials for his great historical work (written in Greek). This consisted of forty books, of which five, besides passages from the others, are extant. It begins at 264 B.C. with the Punic Wars, and extends to 146 B.C. There is a good translation by E. S. Shuckburgh (2 vols., 1889).

Polychronicon, *The,* see *Higden.*

Polyclëtus (active 452–405 B.C.), Greek sculptor from Argos. He made statues of Olympic victors and embodied in his 'Doryphorus', or 'Spear-bearer', the 'Canon' or rule of ideal proportions, on which he wrote a treatise.

Polycratës, a tyrant of Samos, who acquired great riches by his piratical enterprises. Amāsis, king of Egypt (572–528 B.C.), his ally, alarmed, according to Herodotus, by the unfailing good fortune of Polycrates, advised him to throw away something that he valued highly, so as to avert the disaster that must sooner or later overtake him. Polycrates thereupon threw into the sea a ring of extraordinary beauty. But shortly afterwards the ring was found in the belly of a fish that a fisherman had presented to Polycrates. Polycrates was finally captured by Oroetes, satrap of Sardis, and crucified.

Polydore, (1) in Shakespeare's 'Cymbeline' (q.v.), the name borne by Guiderius while in the Welsh forest; (2) a character in Otway's

'The Orphan' (q.v.); (3) a character in Fletcher's 'The Mad Lover'.

POLYDORE VERGIL, see *Vergil (P.).*

Polyglot Bible, THE, edited in 1654–7 by Brian Walton (1600?–61), bishop of Chester, with the help of many scholars. It contains various oriental texts of the Bible with Latin translations, and a critical apparatus.

Polyhymnia or POLYMNIA, the Muse (q.v.) of sacred song.

Polyhymnia, a poem by Peele (q.v.) written in 1590, commemorating the retirement of Sir Henry Lee from the office of queen's champion, and describing the ceremonies that took place on this occasion. It contains at the end the beautiful song 'His golden locks time hath to silver turned . . .' made widely known by Thackeray's quotation of it in 'The Newcomes'.

Polyneices, see *Eteocles.*

Poly-Olbion, The (this is the spelling of the 1st edition), the principal work of Drayton (q.v.). It was written between 1613 and 1622 and consists of thirty 'Songs' each of 300–500 lines, in hexameter couplets, in which the author endeavours to awaken his readers to the beauties and glories of their country. Travelling from the SW. to Chester, down through the Midlands to London, up the eastern counties to Lincoln, and then through Lancashire and Yorkshire to Northumberland and Westmorland, he describes, or at least enumerates, the principal topographical features of the country, but chiefly the rivers and rivulets, interspersing in the appropriate places legends, fragments of history, catalogues of British saints and hermits, of great discoverers, of birds, fishes, and plants with their properties. The first eighteen songs were annotated by John Selden (q.v.). The word 'poly-olbion' (from the Greek) means 'having many blessings'.

Polyphēmus, one of the Cyclopes (q.v.), a son of Poseidon (q.v.). He kept his flocks on the coast of Sicily when Odysseus, returning from the Trojan War, was driven there. Odysseus and twelve companions were seized by Polyphemus, who confined them in his cave, blocked the entrance with a huge stone, and daily devoured two of them. Odysseus would have shared this fate, had he not intoxicated the Cyclops, put out his eye with a firebrand while he slept, and escaped from the cave by concealing himself in the wool under the belly of one of the rams of Polyphemus as they were let out to feed. Polyphemus loved the nymph Galatea (q.v.) and crushed his rival Acis with a rock.

Polyxěna, a daughter of Priam (q.v.) and Hecuba, who was loved by Achilles. When the Greeks were returning from the siege of Troy, the ghost of Achilles appeared to them and demanded her. Polyxena was accordingly sacrificed by Neoptolemus on the tomb of Achilles.

Pomare (pron. Pō-mā-rē), the name of a succession of native rulers of Tahiti (Otaheite), one of the Society Islands in the Pacific. The best known is Queen Pomare IV, who reigned from 1827 to 1877. She figures in Herman Melville's 'Omoo' (q.v.).

POMFRET, JOHN (1667–1702), chiefly remembered as the author of a poem, 'The Choice' (1700), which for a time enjoyed great popularity and secured for Pomfret inclusion in Johnson's 'Lives of the Poets'. It describes the kind of life and modest competence that the author would choose.

Pomōna, an Italian goddess of gardens and fruit-trees. She was loved by Vertumnus (q.v.).

Pompadour, MARQUISE DE (1721–64), mistress of Louis XV of France, an intelligent patroness of art and literature, but her political influence was less fortunate. It was she who said, 'Après nous le déluge!' The name 'pompadour' is applied to fashions, colours, etc., popular in her day.

Pompeii, The Last Days of, see *Last Days of Pompeii.*

Pompey, naval slang for Portsmouth.

Pompey (GNAEUS POMPEIUS) (106–48 B.C.), surnamed 'The Great', a famous Roman general, who joined forces with Sulla and showed great military ability in the campaigns against the Marians. He aided in finishing the Servile War in 71, cleared the western Mediterranean of pirates in 67, and brought to an end the war with Mithridates. He formed with Julius Caesar and Crassus the first triumvirate in 60; but Caesar's increasing power in the ensuing years made a struggle between him and Pompey inevitable, and the death of Pompey's wife Julia (Caesar's daughter) in 54 severed one of the links between them. Pompey became the leader of the aristocracy and conservative party, and began the civil war with Caesar in 49. He was defeated at Pharsalus in 48, and sailed for Egypt. While landing from a small boat, he was stabbed in the back and killed by Septimus, formerly one of his centurions.

Pompey the Great, his faire Corneliaes Tragedy, a Senecan tragedy in blank verse by Kyd (q.v.), published in 1595. An anonymous text entitled 'Cornelia' had appeared in the preceding year. The work is a translation from the French of Garnier, and deals with the story of Cornelia, daughter of Metellus Scipio, and wife of Pompey the Great. The latter, after the battle of Pharsalus, is killed on the way to Egypt. Scipio, Cornelia's father, then assembles new forces, but is defeated by Caesar at Thapsus in Africa, and ultimately takes his own life. The play consists, in great part, of Cornelia's lamentations for her misfortunes.

'The Tragedy of Pompey the Great' is the title of a play by Masefield (q.v.).

Pompey the Little, *The History of,* see *Coventry (F.).*

Pompey's Pillar, a Corinthian column of red granite, erected at Alexandria in A.D. 302 in honour of the Emperor Diocletian. It has no connexion with Pompey.

Pompilia, in R. Browning's 'The Ring and the Book' (q.v.), the murdered wife of Count Guido Franceschini.

Pomponius Ego, the sporting journalist in 'Handley Cross', by R. S. Surtees (q.v.).

Pons Asinorum (Latin, the bridge of asses), a name humorously given to the fifth proposition of the first book of Euclid, owing to the difficulty that beginners or dull-witted persons find in 'getting over' it.

PONTOPPIDAN, ERIK (1698–1764), a Danish author and bishop of Bergen in Norway. His principal works are the 'Gesta et vestigia Danorum extra Daniam' (1740), and a 'Natural History of Norway' (1755), frequently mentioned on account of its description of the kraken or sea-serpent.

Pooh-Bah, a character in Gilbert and Sullivan's opera 'The Mikado', who has been described as 'the essence of cultivated diplomacy behind which lurks the basest of motives'.

POOLE, JOHN (1786?–1872), dramatist, remembered chiefly as the author of the successful farces 'Paul Pry' (1825), ' 'Twixt the Cup and the Lip' (1827), and 'Lodgings for Single Gentlemen' (1829).

Poor Richard's Almanack, a series of almanacs, with maxims, issued by B. Franklin (q.v.), 1732–57. They contain much proverbial philosophy and some good fooling, in ridicule of the prophecies of almanac-makers. They attained remarkable popularity and were translated into many languages.

Poor Robin, the name of a facetious almanac, first published in 1661 or 1662.

Poor Tom, a name assumed by an 'Abraham man' (q.v.), who feigns madness, in the 'Fraternitye of Vacabones' (q.v.); also by Edgar in Shakespeare's 'King Lear' (q.v.), III. iv.

Pooter, CHARLES, see *Diary of a Nobody.*

POPE, ALEXANDER (1688–1744), was the son of a Roman Catholic linen-draper of London. His health was ruined and his figure distorted by a severe illness at the age of 12, brought on by 'perpetual application'. He lived with his parents at Binfield in Windsor Forest and was largely self-educated. He showed his precocious metrical skill in his 'Pastorals', written, according to himself, when he was 16, and published in Tonson's 'Miscellany' (vol. vi) in 1709. (For Pope's quarrel with Ambrose Philips on this subject see under *Philips, A.*) He became intimate with Wycherley (q.v.), who introduced him to London life. His 'Essay on Criticism' (q.v.), 1711, made him known to Addison's circle, and his 'Messiah' (q.v.) was published in the

'Spectator' in 1712. His 'Rape of the Lock' (q.v.) appeared in Lintot's 'Miscellanies' in the same year and was republished, enlarged, in 1714. His 'Ode for Music on St. Cecilia's Day', published in 1713, one of his rare attempts at lyric, shows that his gifts did not lie in this direction. In 1713 he also published 'Windsor Forest' (q.v.), which appealed to the Tories by its references to the Peace of Utrecht, and won him the friendship of Swift (q.v.). He drifted away from Addison's 'little senate' and became a member of the 'Scriblerus Club', an association that included Swift, Gay, Arbuthnot, Atterbury (qq.v.), and others. He issued in 1715 the first volume of his translation in heroic couplets of Homer's 'Iliad'. This work, completed in 1720, though not an accurate version of the original, is one of the great poems of the age. It was supplemented in 1725–6 by a translation of the 'Odyssey', in which he was assisted by William Broome and Elijah Fenton. The two translations added considerably to his fortune. He bought in 1719 the lease of a house at Twickenham, where he spent the remainder of his life.

In 1717 had appeared a collection of his works including two poems of importance, not only on account of some beautiful passages, but also as dealing, alone among his writings, with the passion of love. They are the 'Verses to the Memory of an Unfortunate Lady', an impassioned elegy on a lady who has taken her life to escape the torture of hopeless love, and 'Eloisa to Abelard', a longer poem expressing the conflict in the soul of a woman who loves and has renounced love for the service of God. About this time he became strongly attached to Martha Blount, with whom his intimacy continued throughout his life, and to Lady Mary Wortley Montagu, whom in later years he assailed with bitterness.

Pope assisted Gay in writing the comedy 'Three Hours after Marriage' (1717), but made no other attempt at drama. In 1723, four years after Addison's death, appeared (in a miscellany called 'Cythera') Pope's portrait of Atticus, a satire on Addison, probably written some years earlier. An extended version of this appeared as 'A Fragment of a Satire' in a 1727 volume of the 'Miscellanies' (by Pope, Swift, Arbuthnot, and Gay), and it took its final form in 'An Epistle to Dr. Arbuthnot' (1735). In the same 'Miscellanies' volume Pope published his 'Martinus Scriblerus ΠΕΡΙ ΒΆΘΟΥΣ, or the Art of Sinking in Poetry', ridiculing among others Ambrose Philips, Theobald, and J. Dennis (qq.v.). In 1725 Pope published an edition of Shakespeare, the errors in which were pointed out in a pamphlet by Theobald (q.v.). This led to the selection of Theobald by Pope as the hero of his 'Dunciad' (q.v.), a satire on Dullness, in three books, on which he had been at work for some time and of which the first edition appeared anonymously in 1728. A further enlarged edition was published in 1729. An additional book, 'The New Dunciad', was published in 1742, perhaps at the suggestion of his friend William Warburton; and the complete 'Dunciad' in four books appeared in 1743. In this Cibber replaces Theobald as the hero. Influenced by the philosophy of his friend Bolingbroke, Pope published a series of moral and philosophical poems, 'An Essay on Man' (q.v.), 1733–4, consisting of four Epistles; and 'Moral Essays' (q.v.), four in number: 'Of the Knowledge and Characters of Men', 'Of the Characters of Women', and two on the subject 'Of the Use of Riches' (1731–5). A fifth epistle was added, addressed to Addison, occasioned by his dialogue on Medals. This was originally written in Addison's lifetime in 1715. In 1733 Pope published the first of his miscellaneous satires, 'Imitations of Horace', entitled 'Satire I', a paraphrase of the first satire of the second book of Horace, in the form of a dialogue between the poet and William Fortescue, the lawyer. In it Pope defends himself against the charge of malignity, and professes to be inspired only by love of virtue. He inserts, however, a gross attack on his former friend Lady Mary Wortley Montagu. He followed this up with his 'Imitations' of Horace's Satires II, ii and I, ii ('Sober Advice from Horace'), in 1734, and of Epistles I, vi; II, ii; II, i, and I, i, in 1737. Horace's Epistle I, vii and the latter part of Sat. II, vi, 'imitated in the manner of Dr. Swift', appeared in 1738. The year 1735 saw the appearance of the 'Epistle to Dr. Arbuthnot' (above referred to), the prologue to the above Satires, one of Pope's most brilliant pieces of irony and invective, mingled with autobiography. It contains the famous portraits of Addison (ll. 193–214) and Lord Hervey (q.v.), and lashes his minor critics, Dennis, Colley Cibber, Curll, Theobald, etc. In 1738 appeared 'One Thousand Seven Hundred and Thirty Eight', two satirical dialogues. These satires, and the 'Satires (II and IV) of Dr. Donne Versified' (1735), with the 'New Dunciad', previously mentioned, closed his literary career.

He was partly occupied during his later years with the publication of his earlier correspondence, which he edited and amended in such a manner as to misrepresent the literary history of the time. He also employed discreditable artifices to make it appear that it was published against his wish. Thus he procured the publication by Curll (q.v.) of his 'Literary Correspondence' in 1735, and then endeavoured to disavow him. He appears to have taken advantage of Swift's failing powers to saddle him with the responsibility for a similar publication in 1741.

Minor works by Pope that deserve mention are:

Verse: the Epistles 'To a Young Lady [Miss Blount] with the works of Voiture' (1712), to the same 'On her leaving the town after the Coronation' (1717), 'To Mr. Jervas with Dryden's translation of Fresnoy's Art of Painting' (1716), and 'To Robert, Earl of Oxford and Earl Mortimer' (1721); 'Vertumnus and Pomona', 'Sappho to Phaon', and 'The Fable of Dryope', translations from Ovid (1712); 'January and May', 'The Wife of Bath, her Prologue', and 'The Temple of Fame', from Chaucer (1709, 1714, 1715).

Prose: 'The Narrative of Dr. Robert Norris' (1713), a satirical attack on J. Dennis, (q.v.); 'A full and true Account of a horrid and barbarous Revenge by poison, on . . . Mr. Edmund Curll' (1716), an attack on Curll the publisher.

Pope was buried in Twickenham church. The first collective edition of his 'Works' appeared in 1751. The standard edition is that edited by Whitwell Elwin and W. J. Courthope, and published between 1871 and 1889.

Pope, GIANT, see *Giant Pope*.

Pope-figs, in Rabelais, IV. xlv, the inhabitants of an island visited by Pantagruel, representing the Calvinists or Lutherans, so named because they said, 'a fig for the pope's image'.

Pope Joan, see *Joan (Pope)*.

Popish Plot, THE, a plot fabricated in 1678 by Titus Oates. He deposed before the Middlesex magistrate Sir Edmond Berry Godfrey that it was intended to murder Charles II, place James on the throne, and suppress Protestantism. Godfrey was found murdered the next morning. The existence of the plot was widely believed and great excitement prevailed. Many persons were falsely accused and executed. J. Pollock ('The Popish Plot', 1903) has written a careful study of the story. He inclines to think that the Jesuits had some plot afoot, not necessarily anything so extensive as Oates pretended, but not stopping short of assassination if necessary.

Porch, THE, a name given to the Stoic school of Greek philosophy (see *Stoics*).

PORDAGE, SAMUEL (1633–91?), author of 'Azaria and Hushai' (1682), a feeble reply to Dryden's 'Absalom and Achitophel' (q.v.), and of 'The Medal Revers'd' (1682).

Porphyrion, in Greek mythology, one of the giants who made war against the gods. He was overcome by Zeus and Hercules.

PORPHYRIUS (233–c. 301), a Neoplatonic philosopher and opponent of Christianity, author of the PORPHYRIAN TREE, a kind of genealogical table or tree, furnishing a definition of *man*. It starts with the *summum genus* 'substance', and arrives at man by a process of dichotomy.

Porphyrogenite, originally one born of the imperial family at Constantinople, and (as is said) in a chamber called the *Porphyra* (purple). Hence, a child born after his father's accession to the throne; and, in a more general sense, one 'born in the purple'. Constantine VII (911–59) called himself or was called 'Porphyrogenitus'. He was a man of letters and wrote a book about the administration of the Empire.

Porrex, see *Gorboduc.*

Porsenna or PORSENA, LARS (6th cent. B.C.), a king of Etruria, who according to legend declared war against the Romans because they refused to restore Tarquin (q.v.) to the throne. He would have entered Rome but for the bravery of Horatius Cocles (q.v.) at the bridge. This legend conceals an invasion of Rome by the Etruscans for purpose of conquest.

PORSON, RICHARD (1759–1808), son of the parish clerk at East Ruston, near North Walsham, showed extraordinary memory when a boy, and by the help of various protectors was educated at Eton and Trinity College, Cambridge. He was elected Regius professor of Greek at Cambridge in 1792. He edited four plays of Euripides, the 'Hecuba' in 1797, 'Orestes' in 1798, 'Phoenissae' in 1799, and 'Medea' in 1801. 'His finest single piece of criticism' (Jebb) was his supplement to the preface to his 'Hecuba', in which he states and illustrates certain rules of iambic and trochaic verse, in opposition to the views of Hermann. Some of his best English writing is to be seen in his 'Letters to Archdeacon Travis' (1788–9) on the authenticity of the text of 1 John v. 7 ('For there are three that bear record in heaven'); the letters also show his spirit of mischievous humour. His literary remains were published after his death, between 1812 and 1834. His correspondence appeared in 1867. He advanced Greek scholarship by his elucidation of Greek idiom and usage, by his knowledge of Greek prosody, and by his emendation of texts. He was also famous as a lover of wine.

Porte, THE SUBLIME, a translation of the Turkish *bab-i-ali,* the high or sublime gate, the official title of the central office of the Ottoman government under the rule of the Sultans. 'Gate' is supposed to refer to the ancient place of audience, etc., at the gate of the tent or the king's gate. The attribute 'high' is not literal but honorific.

Porteous, CAPTAIN JOHN, see *Heart of Midlothian.*

PORTER, ANNA MARIA (1780–1832), sister of J. Porter (q.v.), and authoress of 'The Hungarian Brothers' (1807), a tale of the French revolutionary war, and other novels.

Porter, ENDYMION (1587–1649), was brought up in Spain, and on his return obtained a place in Buckingham's household. He became groom of the bed-chamber to Prince Charles and accompanied him and Buckingham on the visit to Spain in 1623. He was the friend and patron of poets, including Jonson, Herrick, D'Avenant, and Dekker (qq.v.), and the subject of their encomiums. He sat in the Long Parliament, but was expelled, lived abroad in poverty, and compounded with the parliament for a small fine in 1649.

PORTER, JANE (1776–1850), authoress of two successful novels, 'Thaddeus of Warsaw' (q.v.), published in 1803, and 'The Scottish Chiefs' (q.v.), published in 1810. The latter was translated into German and Russian. She attempted plays with less success. She was sister of A. M. Porter (q.v.).

PORTER, KATHERINE ANNE (1890–), distinguished American short story writer, born in Texas. Her collections include 'Flowering Judas' (1930), 'Pale Horse, Pale Rider' (1939), and 'The Leaning Tower' (1944). Her powerful novel, 'Ship of Fools', appeared in 1962.

PORTER, WILLIAM SYDNEY, see *Henry (O.).*

Porthos, see *Three Musketeers.*

Portia, (1) the heroine of Shakespeare's 'The Merchant of Venice' (q.v.); (2) in his 'Julius Caesar' (q.v.), the wife of Brutus.

Portland Club, THE, a London card-playing club, the recognized authority on the game of bridge, as formerly on whist.

Portland Vase, also known as the BARBERINI VASE, a celebrated urn found in a sarcophagus near Rome, and purchased by Sir William Hamilton in 1770, from whom it passed into the possession of the Portland family. It is of dark blue transparent glass ornamented with cameos of opaque white glass, representing probably scenes from the legend of Peleus and Thetis. It was broken to pieces by a lunatic in 1845, and mended.

Portpipe, MR., a convivial cleric in Peacock's 'Melincourt' (q.v.).

Portrait of a Lady, *The,* a novel by H. James (q.v.), published in 1881.

This is one of the best of James's early works, in which he presents various types of American character transplanted into a European environment. The story centres in Isabel Archer, the 'Lady', an attractive American girl, whom circumstances have brought to Europe. Around her we have the placid old American banker, Mr. Touchett; his hard repellent wife; his ugly, invalid, witty, charming son Ralph, whom England has thoroughly assimilated; and the crude, brilliant, indomitably American Henrietta Stackpole, the journalist. Isabel refuses the offer of marriage of a typical English peer, the excellent Lord Warburton, and of a bulldog-like New Englander, Caspar Goodwood, to fall a victim, under the influence of the slightly sinister Madame Merle (another cosmopolitan American), to a worthless and spiteful dilettante, Gilbert Osmond, who marries her for her fortune and ruins her life; but to whom she remains loyal in spite of her realization of his vileness.

Port-Royal, originally a Cistercian nunnery near Chevreuse (Seine-et-Oise, France), became in 1636 a place of retreat for pious and learned men holding the Jansenist (q.v.) doctrine, where they devoted themselves to prayer, study, and manual employments. It became the headquarters of Jansenism and the centre of a system of education, and exercised a wide influence, notably on Pascal and Racine. The institution was persecuted by the Jesuits, and finally destroyed by Louis XIV in 1710. A history of Port-Royal was published by Sainte-Beuve (q.v.) in 1840–8.

Poseidon, called NEPTUNE by the Romans, was according to Greek mythology a son of Cronos and Rhea, and brother of Zeus and Hades. He shared with these his father's empire, receiving as his portion the kingdom of the sea. He was the husband of Amphitrite, the builder (with Apollo) of the walls of Troy for Laomedon, and the implacable enemy of the Trojans because Laomedon refused to give the gods the reward stipulated for this service.

Positivist Philosophy, see *Comte*.

Posthumus Leonatus, a character in Shakespeare's 'Cymbeline' (q.v.).

Post-Impressionism, a term invented by Roger Fry (q.v.) to cover the work of painters, particularly Cézanne, Gauguin, and van Gogh (qq.v.), who were opposed to the aims of Impressionism (q.v.).

Postumus, a friend of Horace, to whom the poet addressed his Ode, II. xiv, 'Eheu fugaces, Postume, Postume'.

Pot of Basil, The, see *Isabella, or the Pot of Basil*.

Potiphar's Wife, who tempted Joseph (Gen. xxxix), 'some call her Raïl, but the name by which she is best known is Zoleikha' (Sale's notes to the Koran).

Potŏ'mac, THE ARMY OF THE, the principal federal (Northern) army in the American Civil War.

Pott, MR., in Dickens's 'Pickwick Papers' (q.v.), the editor of the 'Eatanswill Gazette'.

POTTER, BEATRIX (MRS. WILLIAM HEELIS) (1866–1943), wrote and illustrated little story books for children, which became known as the 'Peter Rabbit' series. 'The Tale of Peter Rabbit' began with a letter to a little boy in 1893, was privately printed and sold in 1900, and published in its present form in 1902. It was followed by 'The Tailor of Gloucester' (her own favourite) in 1903, 'The Tale of Squirrel Nutkin', 'The Tale of Benjamin Bunny', and many others. The stories are the result of Beatrix Potter's love and knowledge of the countryside, combined with fantasy and humour. The animal characters are drawn sympathetically and shrewdly, never sentimentally. The illustrations, which usually interleave the text, are perfectly matched to the stories and owe their delicacy and precision to the discipline

of observation and drawing practised from childhood onwards. The books have been translated into French, German, Spanish, and Welsh.

Pottyfar, MR., a character in Marryat's 'Midshipman Easy' (q.v.).

Potwalloper, a popular alteration of *pot-waller*, i.e. pot-boiler, the term applied in some English boroughs, before the Reform Act of 1832, to a man qualified for the parliamentary vote as a householder, the test of which was his having a separate fireplace, on which his own pot was boiled.

Poulter's measure, a fanciful name for a metre consisting of lines of 12 and 14 syllables alternately. Poulter = poulterer.
  'Poulter's measure, which giveth xii for one dozen, and xiiij for another.'
                    (Gascoigne, 'Steele Glas')

Pounce, PETER, a character in Fielding's 'Joseph Andrews' (q.v.).

POUND, EZRA (1885–), American poet born in Idaho. He taught languages for a short period in Indiana, but was asked to resign. He came to Europe in 1908 and published his first volume of poems, 'A Lume Spento', in Italy. He then settled in London, where he became prominent in literary circles. He published several other volumes of verse including 'Personae' (1909), 'Canzoni' (1911), and 'Ripostes' (1912). Together with Richard Aldington and H. D. (Hilda Doolittle), he founded the so-called Imagist school of poets, advocating the use of free rhythms and concreteness and concision of language and imagery. Pound also championed the work of *avant-garde* writers and artists like Joyce and Eliot and Wyndham Lewis (qq.v.), whom he was always ready to assist critically and materially. Further volumes included the Chinese translations, 'Cathay' (1916), and 'Hugh Selwyn Mauberley' (1920). In 1920 he left England for Paris, and subsequently settled in Italy at Rapallo. There he worked on his long poem, the 'Cantos', of which the first thirty appeared between 1925 and 1930, and which by 1960 had almost completed its projected span. He became increasingly preoccupied with economics, embraced Social Credit theories, and was persuaded that usura, or credit capitalism, lay at the root of all social and spiritual evils. His own interpretations of these theories led him into anti-Semitism, and at least partial support for Mussolini's social programme in Italy. During the Second World War he broadcast over the Italian Radio: after giving himself up to American troops in 1945 he was charged with treason, but was found unfit to plead and confined to a mental institution. He was released in 1961 and returned to Italy. His critical writings are collected in 'Literary Essays of Ezra Pound' (1954). His Letters were published in 1951.

Poundtext, THE REV. PETER, in Scott's 'Old

Mortality', a Presbyterian divine, the 'indulged' pastor of Milnwood's parish.

Poussin, NICHOLAS (1593/4–1665), French painter. He spent most of his working life in Rome and was the exemplary classical painter.

Povey, SAMUEL, a character in Bennett's 'The Old Wives' Tale' (q.v.).

POWELL, ANTHONY DYMOKE (1905–   ), novelist. Much of his work is satirical, especially the early novels, 'Afternoon Men' (1931), 'Venusberg' (1932), 'From a View to a Death' (1933), 'What's Become of Waring?' (1939). After the war he embarked on a novel sequence entitled 'The Music of Time', the first titles being 'A Question of Upbringing' (1951), 'A Buyer's Market' (1952), 'The Acceptance World' (1955), 'At Lady Molly's' (1957), 'Casanova's Chinese Restaurant' (1960), 'The Kindly Ones' (1962), and 'The Valley of Bones' (1964).

Powis, MERTHYR, a character in Meredith's 'Sandra Belloni' and 'Vittoria' (qq.v.).

POWYS, JOHN COWPER (1872–1963), author and poet, the brother of Llewelyn and Theodore Francis (qq.v.). He was educated at Sherborne School and Corpus Christi College, Cambridge. His writing expresses an individualistic philosophy, which interprets the meaning of life through ancient myths and elemental forces. His epic novel, 'A Glastonbury Romance' (1933), gives the legend of the Grail a modern context. His other works include the novels 'Wood and Stone' (1915), 'Ducdame' (1925), and 'Wolf Solent' (1929); critical and philosophical essays: 'The Meaning of Culture' (1930), 'In Defence of Sensuality' (1930), 'The Pleasures of Literature' (1938), and 'The Art of Growing Old' (1943); poetry: 'Wolfsbane Rhymes' (1916), 'Mandragora' (1917), and 'Samphire' (1922). His 'Autobiography' was published in 1934.

POWYS, LLEWELYN (1884–1939), essayist and novelist, brother of John Cowper and Theodore Francis (qq.v.). He was educated at Sherborne School and Corpus Christi College, Cambridge, visited the U.S., E. Africa, and Palestine, and spent his last years in Switzerland. His essays and stories include 'Confessions of Two Brothers' (with J. C. Powys, 1916), 'Thirteen Worthies' (1923), 'Black Laughter' (1924), 'Ebony and Ivory' (1925), 'The Pathetic Fallacy' (a study of Christianity, 1928), 'A Pagan's Pilgrimage' (1931), and 'Dorset Essays' (1935). 'Apples be Ripe' (1930) and 'Love and Death' (1939) are novels.

POWYS, THEODORE FRANCIS (1875–1953), novelist, brother of John Cowper and Llewelyn (qq.v.). He was educated at Dorchester Grammar School and in 1905 settled for life in Dorset, the rural background of his allegorical stories of love and death, God and evil. His novels include 'Mr.

Tasker's Gods' (1925), 'Mr. Weston's Good Wine' (1927), and 'Unclay' (1931). He also wrote short stories: 'The Left Leg' (1923), 'Fables' (1929, reprinted under the title 'No Painted Plumage', 1934), and 'The Only Penitent' (1931), among many others.

Poyser, MARTIN and MRS., characters in G. Eliot's 'Adam Bede' (q.v.).

PRAED, WINTHROP MACKWORTH (1802–39), was educated at Eton, where he founded the 'Etonian', and at Trinity College, Cambridge. He went to the bar and then into parliament, and was appointed secretary to the Board of Control in 1834. He is remembered principally as a humorous poet, though like Hood, with whom he is naturally compared, he sometimes uses humour to clothe a grim subject, as in 'The Red Fisherman'. Of his lighter verse, social and political, 'The County Ball', 'The Letter of Advice', 'Goodnight to the Season', 'Stanzas on seeing the Speaker asleep', 'Molly Mog', 'The Vicar', 'Twenty-Eight and Twenty-Nine', are among the best examples. In purely serious poetry, Praed fell far short of Hood at his best; in this kind, 'Time's Song' and 'Arminius' are perhaps Praed's most notable works.

Praeterita, *Outlines of scenes and thoughts perhaps worthy of memory in my past life,* an uncompleted autobiography by Ruskin (q.v.), published at intervals during 1885–9.

It tells of the influence on Ruskin of Copley Fielding (1787–1855) and Turner, of his childhood, of his first visit to the 'Gates of the Hills' (the Alps), of his travels in France and Italy, and of his friends, Dr. John Brown and Charles Eliot Norton.

Praetorian Guard, THE, at Rome, originally the *praetoria cohors* or select troops which attended the person of the praetor or general of the army; subsequently the force instituted by Augustus for the protection of Italy (where no legion was stationed). Their number was increased in the reign of Vitellius to 16,000 men, and they acquired great political power, often, especially in the 3rd cent., deposing and elevating emperors.

Pragmatic sanction, a rendering of the late juridical Latin *pragmatica sanctio,* 'an imperial decree relating to the affairs of a community', the technical name given to some imperial and royal ordinances issued as fundamental laws. It was applied first to edicts of the Eastern emperors; subsequently to certain decrees of Western sovereigns, as the Pragmatic sanction attributed to St. Louis of France, 1268, containing articles directed against the assumptions of the papacy. In more recent history it is applied particularly to the ordinance of the Emperor Charles VI in 1724, settling the succession to the territories of the House of Hapsburg. [OED.]

Pragmatism, in philosophy, the doctrine

that the test of the value of any assertion lies in its practical consequences, i.e. in its practical bearing upon human interests and purposes. See *James (W.)*.

Prajapati ('lord of creatures'), in Hindu theology of the Vedic period, a name applied to various gods in their character of protectors of the human race. In later speculation the Prajapatis are the offspring of Manu (q.v.) and progenitors of living creatures.

Prasutagus, king of the Iceni (a British tribe), husband of Boadicea, died A.D. 61.

Pratt, MISS, a character in Miss Ferrier's 'The Inheritance' (q.v.).

PRATT, EDWIN JOHN (1883–   ), poet, born in Newfoundland. The most distinguished of recent Canadian poets, Pratt has published several narrative poems of considerable interest and power. Chief among them are 'The Roosevelt and the Antinoe' (1930), a story of a rescue at sea, 'The Titanic' (1935), 'Brébeuf and his Brethren' (1940), a retelling of the martyrdom of the Jesuit missionaries, and 'Towards the Last Spike' (1952), an account of the building of the Canadian Pacific Railway.

Praxitĕlēs (4th cent. B.C.), Greek sculptor. His 'Hermes with the infant Dionysus', at Olympia, appears to be the original work; his 'Aphrodite of Cnidos' is known only from copies.

Prayer, THE BOOK OF COMMON, see *Common Prayer*.

Pre-adamite, an appellation given by Isaac de la Peyrère in his 'Prae-adamitae', 1655, to a race of men, the progenitors of the Gentile peoples, supposed by him to have existed long before Adam, whom he held to be the first parent of the Jews only.

For the PRE-ADAMITE SULTANS see *Vathek*.

Précieuse, the French equivalent of our Blue Stocking (q.v.). See *Rambouillet*.

Prelude, The, an autobiographical poem, in fourteen books, by Wordsworth (q.v.), commenced in 1799 and completed in 1805, but not published until 1850, after the author's death.

In his preface to the 'Excursion', Wordsworth explains that, having retired to his native mountains with the hope of writing a literary work that might live, he thought it reasonable to take a review of his own mind, and record in verse the origin and progress of his own powers. This record we have in the 'Prelude'. It is addressed to his friend Coleridge (q.v.). Wordsworth successively recalls his childhood, schooldays, his years at Cambridge, his first impressions of London, his first visit to France and the Alps, his residence in France during the Revolution (but not his connexion with Annette), and his reaction to those various experiences; showing the development of his love for humankind and for

the unassuming things that hold
A silent station in this beauteous world.

The full text, showing the work of Wordsworth on it in his later years, was published by E. de Sélincourt (Oxford, 1926). The early versions (1805–6 and 1817–19), which were much altered in the 1850 standard text, are there printed for the first time.

Premium, MR., the name taken by Sir Oliver Surface in Sheridan's 'School for Scandal' (q.v.), when he assumes the character of a money-lender.

Premonstratensians, a Roman Catholic order of regular canons founded early in the 12th cent. by St. Norbert at Prémontré, near Laon in France, so called because the site of their original house is said to have been prophetically pointed out to St. Norbert. They were known in England, where they had many monasteries (and still have one at Storringtom, Sussex), as the White Canons.

Pre-Raphaelite Brotherhood, a group of artists and critics—William Holman Hunt, John Everett Millais, Dante Gabriel Rossetti, William Michael Rossetti, Thomas Woolner, Frederick George Stephens, and James Collinson—who sought to infuse art with moral qualities through a scrupulous study of nature and the depiction of uplifting subjects. They published their doctrines in 'The Germ' (q.v.). The name indicated that they considered that art from Raphael onwards was degenerate. D. G. Rossetti first used the initials PRB in his signature on a painting exhibited in 1849.

Presbyterianism, a system of church government (the National Church of Scotland) in which no higher order than that of presbyter or elder is recognized, and all elders are ecclesiastically of equal rank. Each congregation is governed by its session of elders; these are subordinate to provincial Presbyteries, and these again are subordinate to the General Assembly of the Church.

PRESCOTT, WILLIAM HICKLING (1796–1859), born at Salem, Massachusetts, and educated at Harvard, had his sight affected by an accident while at college, but nevertheless devoted himself, with the help of a reader, to the study of ancient and modern literatures. His first work, 'The History of Ferdinand and Isabella', appeared in 1838. It was followed by the 'History of the Conquest of Mexico' (1843) and the 'History of the Conquest of Peru' (1847). The first two volumes of his unfinished 'History of Philip II, King of Spain' appeared in 1855, the third in 1858.

Present Discontents, Thoughts on the cause of the, a political treatise by E. Burke (q.v.), published in 1770.

The occasion of this work was the turbulence that had attended and followed the expulsion of Wilkes from parliament after his election for Middlesex, and in it Burke expounds for the first time his constitutional creed. He attributes the convulsions in the country to the control of parliament by the cabal known as the 'King's friends', a system of favouritism essentially at variance with the constitution. Burke considers in detail the Wilkes case, of which the importance lies in its being a test whether the favour of the people or of the court is the surer road to positions of trust. He dismisses various remedies that have been proposed, as endangering the constitution, which 'stands on a nice equipoise'. He thinks the first requirement is the restoration of the right of free election, and looks for further safeguards in the 'interposition of the body of the people itself' to secure decent attention to public interests, and in the restoration of party government.

Present State of Europe, The, see *Phillips* (*J.*).

Present State of the Nation, Observations on a late publication intituled the, a political treatise by E. Burke (q.v.), published in 1769.

This was Burke's first controversial publication on political matters. It is a reply to an anonymous pamphlet attributed to George Grenville, in which the decision of the Grenville administration to tax America was defended on the ground that the charges left by the war had made this course necessary. Burke reviews the economic condition of England and France, and defends the repeal of the Stamp Act by the Rockingham administration for the reason that 'politics should be adjusted, not to human reasonings, but to human nature', and that 'people must be governed in a manner agreeable to their temper and disposition'.

Prester John, i.e. 'Priest John', the name given in the Middle Ages to an alleged Christian priest and king, originally supposed to reign in the extreme Orient, beyond Persia and Armenia, but from the 15th cent. generally identified with the king of Ethiopia or Abyssinia. Baring-Gould('Curious Myths') thinks it probable that the origin of the legend lies in the reports which reached Europe of the success of the Nestorian (q.v.) religion in the East. Marco Polo identifies Prester John with a certain Un-Khan, an historical person (*d.* 1203), who received tribute from the Tartars and was overcome and slain by Genghis Khan.

PRESTON, GEORGE F., see *Warren* (*J. B. L.*).

PRESTON, THOMAS (1537–98), dramatist. He was a fellow of King's College, Cambridge, master of Trinity Hall, Cambridge, 1584–98, and vice-chancellor of Cambridge University, 1589–90. He wrote 'A Lamentable Tragedy mixed full of Mirth conteyning the Life of Cambises, King of Percia' (1569), which illustrates the transition from the morality play to historical drama.

The bombastic grandiloquence of the piece became proverbial.

Pretenders: THE OLD, James Francis Edward Stuart (1688–1766), son of James II; THE YOUNG, Charles Edward Stuart (1720–88), son of the Old Pretender. 'Pretender' here means one who makes pretensions, a claimant.

Pretenders, The, an early play by Ibsen (q.v.).

Pretty Fanny's Way, see *Parnell* (*T.*).

Pretty-man, PRINCE, in Buckingham's 'The Rehearsal' (q.v.), 'sometimes a fisher's son, sometimes a prince', falls asleep while making love to Cloris, his mistress.

PRÉVOST D'EXILES, ANTOINE FRANÇOIS (1697–1763), generally known as the ABBÉ PRÉVOST, at one time a soldier, at another a Benedictine monk, was an industrious writer principally remembered for his novel, 'Histoire du Chevalier des Grieux et de Manon Lescaut' (q.v., 1731). Among Prévost's translations from the English are those of Richardson's (q.v.) three novels.

Priam, the last king of Troy, was son of Laomedon, husband of Hecuba, and father of many sons (fifty according to Homer) and daughters, of whom the most famous were Hector, Paris, and Cassandra (qq.v.). Many of his sons were killed during the siege of Troy, and he himself was slain by Neoptolemus, son of Achilles, at the taking of the city.

Priăpus, a god of fertility whose cult spread from the East to Greece and Italy. He was said to be the son of Aphrodite and Dionysus or some other god. In his statues, often placed in gardens or at the doors of houses, he was represented as a grotesque deformed creature; and it was customary to inscribe short humorous poems or epigrams on these statues.

Price, FANNY, the heroine of Jane Austen's 'Mansfield Park' (q.v.).

PRICE, RICHARD (1723–91), a native of Glamorgan, was a Unitarian minister in London. He published in 1756 his best-known work, a 'Review of the Principal Questions in Morals', directed against Hutcheson's doctrine of the 'moral sense' and Hume's development thereof. He agrees with the views of J. Butler (q.v.) concerning conscience, self-love, and benevolence, and regards right and wrong as self-evident ideas, belonging to the nature of things, incapable of proof, but apprehended by the understanding. Price subsequently became known as a writer on financial and political questions, advocating the reduction of the national debt, 1771, and attacking the justice and policy of the American War, 1776. He was the intimate friend of Franklin, and in 1778 was invited by Congress to transfer himself to America. He was denounced by Burke (q.v.) for his approbation of the French Revolution.

Pride and Prejudice, a novel by J. Austen (q.v.). It was begun in 1796, and in its early form entitled 'First Impressions'. It was offered to Cadell, the publisher, in 1797 and refused. In its revised form it was published in 1813.

Mr. and Mrs. Bennet live with their five daughters at Longbourn in Hertfordshire. In the absence of a male heir, the property will pass by entail to a cousin, William Collins (q.v.), who, by the patronage of the haughty and insolent Lady Catherine de Bourgh, has been presented to a rectory in the immediate vicinity of her seat, Rosings, near Westerham in Kent. Charles Bingley, a rich bachelor, takes Netherfield, a house near Longbourn, and brings there his two sisters and his friend, Fitzwilliam Darcy, nephew of Lady Catherine. Bingley and Jane, the eldest Bennet girl, fall mutually in love. Darcy, though attracted to her next sister, the lively Elizabeth, offends her by his supercilious behaviour at a ball. The dislike is increased by the (false) account given to her by George Wickham, a young militia officer, and son of the late steward of the Darcy property, of the unjust treatment he has met with at Darcy's hands. The aversion is still further intensified when Darcy and Bingley's sisters, disgusted with the impropriety of Mrs. Bennet and her younger daughters, effect the separation of Bingley and Jane.

Meanwhile Mr. Collins, urged to marry by Lady Catherine, for whom he shows the most obsequious respect, and thinking to remedy in part the hardship caused to the Bennet girls by the entail, proposes to Elizabeth and is rejected. He promptly transfers his affections to Charlotte Lucas, a friend of the latter, who accepts him. Staying with the newly married couple at the parsonage, Elizabeth is again thrown into contact with Darcy, who is visiting Lady Catherine. Captivated by her in spite of himself, Darcy proposes to her in terms which do not conceal the violence that the proposal does to his pride. Elizabeth indignantly rejects him, adducing as reasons the part he has played in separating Jane from Bingley, and his alleged treatment of Wickham. Much mortified, Darcy in a letter justifies the former action and proves the baselessness of the latter charge, Wickham being in fact an unprincipled adventurer.

On a trip to the north of England with her uncle and aunt, Mr. and Mrs. Gardiner, Elizabeth visits Pemberley, Darcy's place in Derbyshire, thinking Darcy himself absent. Darcy appears on the scene, welcomes the visitors, and introduces them to his sister, showing greatly improved manners. At this point news reaches Elizabeth that her sister Lydia has eloped with Wickham. By Darcy's help the fugitives are traced, their marriage is brought about, and they are suitably provided for. The attachment between Bingley and Jane is renewed and leads to their engagement. In spite, and indeed in consequence, of the insolent intervention of Lady Catherine, Darcy and Elizabeth also become engaged. The story ends with the marriages of Jane and Elizabeth, an indication of their subsequent happiness, and the eventual reconciliation of Lady Catherine.

Pride's Purge, see *Long Parliament.*

PRIESTLEY, JOHN BOYNTON (1894–), novelist, dramatist, and critic; educated at Trinity Hall, Cambridge. His best-known novels are 'The Good Companions' (1929) and 'Angel Pavement' (1930), and his plays include 'Dangerous Corner' (1932), 'Time and the Conways' and 'I Have Been Here Before' (1937), and 'The Linden Tree' (1947). He contributed a Life of George Meredith to the English Men of Letters series in 1926.

PRIESTLEY, JOSEPH (1733–1804), the son of a Yorkshire cloth-dresser, was educated at Batley Grammar School and Heckmondwike, and at Daventry academy. He became Presbyterian (Unitarian) minister at Nantwich and other places. He published in 1768 his 'Essay on the First Principles of Government', advocating the view that the happiness of the majority is 'the great standard by which everything relating to' social life 'must finally be determined', the theory taken up and developed by Bentham. His celebration of the fall of the Bastille led to a riot in which his house was wrecked. As a psychologist he was a materialist, but was influenced by Hartley (q.v.), of whose work he published a simplification, omitting the theory of vibrations. In 1774 he published his 'Examination of Scottish Philosophy'.

Priestley was also a chemist. He was the discoverer of oxygen ('dephlogisticated air'), and author of 'The History and present State of Electricity' (1767) and of other works recording valuable investigations. Finding life in England uncomfortable, owing to his opinions, he emigrated in 1794 to America, where he died.

Prig, BETSEY, a character in Dickens's 'Martin Chuzzlewit' (q.v.), who nurses in partnership with Mrs. Gamp, until her remark concerning the apocryphal Mrs. Harris, 'I don't believe there's no sich person', causes a difference between them.

Primas, the name given to Hugh of Orleans, a 12th-cent. poet who excelled in the writing of Latin lyrics which reveal both his scholarship and his love of wine, women, and gambling. Although he taught in Paris and Orleans, and was admired by his contemporaries, his career was erratic and failed to bring a permanent position of honour. Cf. *Archpoet.*

Prime Minister, The, a novel by A. Trollope, see *Phineas Finn.*

Primer, originally a name for prayer-books or devotional manuals for the use of the laity, used in England before, and for some time after, the Reformation. The medieval Primer was mainly a copy or translation of different parts of the Breviary and Manual. The name was also given in the 16th cent. to books similar in character, partly based upon the 'Sarum Horae', whether put out by private persons or by royal authority (the 'King's Primer' of 1545 and successive recensions issued in the reigns of Henry VIII, Edward VI, and Elizabeth). After the Reformation, *primer* was also applied to books in which the offices for daily prayers were based upon the orders contained in the Book of Common Prayer. Later forms of this appeared at various times down to 1783. [OED.] From this sense was gradually developed that of an elementary school-book. Johnson defines *Primer* as 'a small prayer-book in which children are taught to read'.

Primrose, Dr., the hero of Goldsmith's 'Vicar of Wakefield' (q.v.). The other principal members of the family are: DEBORAH his wife; GEORGE their eldest son, who wanders about the Continent, much as Goldsmith himself did, seeking his fortune, then returns home, becomes a captain, and finally marries Miss Wilmot, an heiress; MOSES, the second son, a simpleton and a pedant, who, when sent to the fair to sell a horse, comes home with a gross of green spectacles in exchange; OLIVIA, the elder daughter, sprightly and commanding, who wishes for many lovers; and SOPHIA, her sister, 'soft, modest, and alluring', who wishes to secure one. All four children are 'equally generous, credulous, simple, and inoffensive'.

Primrose League, THE, was formed in 1883, in memory of Lord Beaconsfield (whose favourite flower is said to have been the primrose), for the maintenance of Conservative principles. It is said to have included at one time over 1,000,000 members, and is still active. The anniversary of Lord Beaconsfield's death (19 April) is celebrated as 'Primrose Day'.

Primrose path, way to destruction; probably from two phrases of Shakespeare: 'primrose path of dalliance', 'Hamlet', I. iii. 47, and 'primrose way to the everlasting bonfire', 'Macbeth', II. iii. 22.

Primum Mobile (Latin, 'first moving thing'), the supposed outermost sphere (at first reckoned the ninth, later the tenth), added in the Middle Ages to the Ptolemaic system of astronomy, and supposed to revolve round the earth from east to west in twenty-four hours, carrying with it the contained spheres. Hence, a prime source of motion.

Prince Hohenstiel-Schwangau, a poem by R. Browning (q.v.), published in 1871.

It takes the form of a monologue by Louis Napoleon, emperor of the French, under the above pseudonym; in which he defends the policy of expediency, of making the best of things as they are instead of endeavouring to reform them; and in particular his course of action in some of the principal conjunctures of his career.

Prince Imperial, THE, Napoléon Eugène Louis Jean Joseph (1856–79), son of Napoléon III, educated at the Military Academy, Woolwich. He asked permission to join the British forces in the Zulu War of 1879, and was allowed to go as a guest. He was killed on a reconnoitring party on 1 June 1879.

Prince of the Peace, Manuel de Godoy (Marquis of Alcudia) (1767–1851), who as prime minister of Spain negotiated peace between that country and France in 1795. He was the queen's paramour, incurred popular hatred, and in 1808 was obliged to flee from the country. His 'Memoirs' were translated by J. B. D'Esménard in 1836.

Prince of the Power of the Air, Satan (Eph. ii. 2).

Princes in the Tower, THE, Edward V and Richard, duke of York, his brother. They were lodged in the Tower in 1483 and were there secretly murdered in the same year, probably by order of their uncle, Richard III, Edward being then 13 years old. The story is told by Sir Thomas More in his 'History of King Richard III'. The discovery in the reign of Charles II of two skeletons buried at the foot of a staircase in the Tower (being those of boys of the age of the two princes) makes More's story almost a certainty.

Prince's Progress, The, an allegorical poem by C. Rossetti (q.v.), published in 1866.

The princess waits in her tower for her appointed bridegroom. The prince sets out, strong and light-hearted, to seek his waiting bride. But the way is long and arduous, and the prince tarries, yielding first to one allurement, then another. When at last he arrives he is too late, and his bride is dead.

Princess, The, A Medley, a poem by A. Tennyson (q.v.), published in 1847. The beautiful lyrics enshrined in it were added in the third edition, 1853. The poem purports to be a tale of fancy composed by some young people on a summer's day, based on a text in an old chronicle. Gilbert and Sullivan's opera 'Princess Ida' is founded on it.

A prince has been betrothed in childhood to the Princess Ida, daughter of the neighbouring King Gama. But the princess becomes a devotee of the rights of women, abjures marriage, and founds a university to promote her ideal. The prince and two companions, Cyril and Florian, gain admission to the university in the disguise of girl students. They are detected by the two tutors, the amiable Lady Psyche, Florian's sister, and the sour duenna, Lady Blanche, who from different motives are induced temporarily to conceal their knowledge. The deceit is, however, presently detected by Princess Ida, but not before the prince has had occasion to save her from drowning. This, however, does not avail to shake her determination, and the three comrades are in peril of their lives, when the arrival of the prince's father with his army is announced. To decide the matter, a combat is arranged between fifty warriors led by the prince, and fifty led by King Gama's mighty son Arak. The latter are victorious, and the three comrades are laid wounded on the field. What neither force nor wooing could effect is now achieved by womanly pity. The university is turned into a hospital, the wounded are kindly tended, and the princess's heart is won.

Princesse de Clèves, La, a French romance by Mme de La Fayette (1633–93), published in 1678. It initiated a new era in the history of the romance, and may be regarded as one of the first examples of the novel of character. The scene is laid at the court of Henry II of France and the story is that of the passion of the Duc de Nemours for the virtuous wife of the Prince de Clèves, a passion which she returns; but she is faithful to her husband, to whom she avows the situation, hoping to be fortified in her virtue. His life is now embittered by jealousy and he dies of a broken heart, and the princess retires to a convent.

Princeton University, founded as a college for the middle American colonies (corresponding to Harvard and Yale for New England) under a charter of 1746, first at Elizabeth N.J., transferred to Princeton in 1754.

Principall Navigations, Voiages and Discoveries of the English Nation, The, see Hakluyt.

Principia Mathematica, Philosophiae Naturalis, see Newton (I).

Principles of Moral and Political Philosophy, by Paley, see Moral and Political Philosophy.

Principles of Morals, Enquiry concerning the, by Hume, see Treatise of Human Nature.

Principles of Morals and Legislation, An Introduction to the, see Bentham.

PRINGLE, THOMAS (1789–1834), born near Kelso, the son of a farmer, studied at Edinburgh University, made a friend of Sir Walter Scott (q.v.), and became editor of the 'Edinburgh Monthly Magazine'. In 1819, the year in which his first volume of poems was published, he emigrated to South Africa, and is remembered chiefly as a poet of that country. His 'Ephemerides' (1828) and 'African Sketches' (1834) contain many striking pieces revealing his interest in the native races and wild life of Africa. In 1835, after Pringle's death, appeared his prose 'Narrative of a Residence in South Africa'.

Printing House Square, London, now the office of 'The Times' newspaper, is so named as the place where formerly the King's Printers had their premises.

PRIOR, MATTHEW (1664–1721), the son of a joiner of Wimborne, Dorset, was sent to Westminster School under the patronage of Lord Dorset, and went thence to St. John's

College, Cambridge. He was appointed secretary to the ambassador at The Hague and employed in the negotiations for the treaty of Ryswick. He joined the Tories and in 1711 was sent to Paris as a secret agent at the time of the peace negotiations, the subsequent treaty of Utrecht (1713) being popularly known as 'Matt's Peace'. He was recalled on Queen Anne's death and imprisoned for two years. A folio edition of his poems was brought out by his admirers after his release, by which he gained four thousand guineas, and Lord Harley gave him £4,000 for the purchase of Down Hall in Essex. He was buried in Westminster Abbey. He was one of the neatest of English epigrammatists, and in occasional pieces and familiar verse he had no rival in English. Among his longer poems may be mentioned 'Henry and Emma', a paraphrase (or travesty) in classical style of the old ballad 'The Nut-Brown Maid' (q.v.); 'Alma or the Progress of the Mind', a dialogue, in three cantos, in the metre and manner of 'Hudibras', nominally on the progress of the soul upwards from the legs in childhood to the head in maturity, in fact on the vanity of worldly concerns; 'Solomon on the Vanity of the World' (1718), a long soliloquy, in three books, in heroic couplets, on the same theme; 'Down-Hall, a Ballad' (1723), the lively account of a trip to Essex; 'Carmen Saeculare' (1700), celebrating the arrival of William III from Holland; and 'The Secretary', a pleasant piece of reminiscence of his early diplomatic days. He joined with Charles Montagu (Halifax) in writing 'The Hind and the Panther Transvers'd to the Story of the Country and City Mouse' (1687), a satire, after the manner of Buckingham's 'The Rehearsal' (q.v.), on Dryden's 'The Hind and the Panther' (q.v.). His more important prose works include an 'Essay upon Learning', an 'Essay upon Opinion' and 'Four Dialogues of the Dead' (q.v.).

Prioress's Tale, The, see Canterbury Tales.

Priscian, a Roman grammarian, born at Caesarea in Mauretania, who taught at Constantinople under the Emperor Anastasius (A.D. 491–518). He was the favourite grammarian of the Middle Ages. To BREAK PRISCIAN'S HEAD is to violate the rules of grammar.

Priscilla, the heroine of Longfellow's 'The Courtship of Miles Standish' (see Miles Standish).

Priscillian, a Spanish heretic executed in A.D. 385, to whom is attributed the composition of the verse 1 John v. 7, 'For there are three that bear record in heaven'.

Prisoner of Chillon, The, a poem by Lord Byron (q.v.), published in 1816.

The poem deals with the imprisonment of Bonnivard in the castle of Chillon, on the Lake of Geneva. François de Bonnivard was born in 1496, became prior of the monastery of St. Victor near Geneva, and conspired with a band of ardent patriots of that city to throw off the yoke of the duke of Savoy and establish a free republic. For this he was twice imprisoned by the duke; his second imprisonment was in the castle of Chillon and lasted from 1530 to 1536, when he was released by the Bernese. He lived a long time after this, received a house and pension in Geneva, and was married no less than four times. He is said to have died in 1570.

Prisoner of Zenda, The, and its sequel, 'Rupert of Hentzau', successful novels by Anthony Hope (see *Hawkins*), published in 1894 and 1898.

They deal with the perilous and romantic adventures of Rudolf Rassendyll, an English gentleman, in Ruritania, where, by personating the king at his coronation, he defeats a plot to oust him from the throne. He falls in love with the Princess Flavia and she with him, releases the imprisoned king, and surrenders Flavia to him. In the sequel he defeats a plot of the villain Rupert of Hentzau against Flavia, now the unhappy wife of the king, and has another chance of taking the throne, this time permanently, and of marrying Flavia. But he is assassinated before his decision is known.

PRITCHETT, VICTOR SAWDON (1900–   ), author and critic, director of the 'New Statesman and Nation'. His stories show a shrewd understanding of the quirks of human behaviour and his criticism is fresh and stimulating. His novels include 'Clare Drummer' (1929), 'Dead Man Leading' (1937), and 'Mr. Beluncle' (1951). His short stories were published in a collected edition in 1956. 'In My Good Books' (1942) and 'The Living Novel' (1946) are works of criticism.

Private Presses are distinguished by aims that are aesthetic rather than commercial and by printing for the gratification of their owners rather than to order. Many such have been set up since the 17th cent. by amateurs of books or printing: that of Horace Walpole (q.v.) at Strawberry Hill (1757–97) is a well-known example. At the end of the 19th cent. presses of the kind were intended as a protest against the low artistic standards and degradation of labour in the printing trade. William Morris (q.v.) set up the Kelmscott Press with this object in 1891; and others, notably C. H. St. John Hornby (the Ashendene Press, 1895), Charles Ricketts (the Vale Press, 1896), and T. J. Cobden-Sanderson and Emery Walker (the Doves Press, 1839), followed him. In the present century the expression 'private press' had been applied, perhaps unjustifiably, to businesses specializing in producing books in the tradition of craftsmanship established by Morris.

Prize Novelists, Mr. Punch's, by Thackeray (q.v.), published in 'Punch' in 1847, and reissued as 'Novels by Eminent Hands' in 'Miscellanies' (1856), are parodies of Disraeli,

Lever, Lytton, Mrs. Gore, G. P. R. James, and Fenimore Cooper (qq.v.).

Probationary Odes for the laureateship, see *Rolliad*.

Procne, see *Philomela*.

Procris, see *Cephalus*.

Procrustes, meaning 'the Stretcher', or DAMASTES, a famous robber of Attica, who was killed by Theseus. He tied travellers on a bed, and if their length exceeded that of the bed, he cut short their limbs; but if the bed proved longer, he stretched them to make their length equal to it.

PROCTER, ADELAIDE ANNE (1825–64), daughter of B. W. Procter (q.v.), was author of 'Legends and Lyrics' (1858–61, including 'A Lost Chord'), 'A Chaplet of Verses' (1862), and 'The Message' (1892). Her complete works were issued in 1905.

PROCTER, BRYAN WALLER (1787–1874), was educated at Harrow, practised as a solicitor in London, and was made a commissioner in lunacy. He was intimate with Leigh Hunt, Charles Lamb, Hazlitt, and Dickens (qq.v.), and had a considerable reputation as a writer, under the pseudonym of 'Barry Cornwall', of pretty songs, of which, however, not many are remembered today. In 1821 he produced a successful tragedy, 'Mirandola', at Covent Garden Theatre. His 'Dramatic Scenes' (1819) were praised by Charles Lamb, of whom, as well as of Edmund Kean, Procter wrote a biography.

Prodigal Son, THE, the general subject of a group of plays written about 1540–75, showing the influence of the continental neoclassic writers of the period on the early Tudor dramatists. The chief of these are 'Misogonus', written about 1560 (author unknown), and Gascoigne's 'Glasse of Government' (1575). The parable of the Prodigal Son is in Luke xv. 11–32.

Prodigious! the favourite exclamation of Dominie Sampson, in Scott's 'Guy Mannering' (q.v.).

Professor, The, a novel by C. Brontë (q.v.), written in 1846 (before 'Jane Eyre' and 'Shirley'), but not published until 1857.

The story, based on the authoress's experiences in Brussels, is in subject the same as that more successfully told in 'Villette' (q.v.), with the two principal characters transposed. Instead of a girl, we have a young man, William Crimsworth, going to seek his fortune as a schoolmaster in Brussels. At the girls' school where he teaches English he falls in love with an Anglo-Swiss pupil-teacher, over whom he exercises the same sort of influence that M. Paul Emanuel exercised over the heroine of 'Villette'.

Progress of Poetry, a Pindaric ode by Gray (q.v.), written in 1754 and published in 1759.

The poet describes the sources of poetry and its progress, now smooth and majestic, now headlong and impetuous. It can calm the frantic passions of the soul or give graceful motion to the body. It can charm away the ills of life, and has power over the most uncivilized nations. It came from Greece to Italy and England, where Shakespeare, Milton, and Dryden have been great poets, but no one equals them today.

Projectors, The, see *Wilson* (*J.*, 1627–96).

Promētheūs, a son of the Titan Iăpĕtus and Themis or Clymene, and brother of Epimetheus (qq.v.). He made mankind out of clay, and when Zeus oppressed them and deprived them of fire, he stole fire for them from heaven and taught them many arts. Zeus, to avenge himself, sent Pandora (q.v.) and her box to earth, and Epimetheus, in spite of the warning of Prometheus, married her. Zeus, moreover, caused Prometheus to be chained to a rock on Mt. Caucasus, where during the daytime a vulture fed on his liver, which was restored each succeeding night. From this torture Prometheus was delivered by Hercules.

The name PROMETHEAN was given to a contrivance used, before the introduction of lucifer matches, for obtaining fire; it consisted in bringing concentrated sulphuric acid into contact with an inflammable mixture.

PROMETHEAN FIRE, the divine spark; often so used in literature; as where Berowne in 'Love's Labour's Lost', IV. iii, says:

> From women's eyes this doctrine I derive:
> They are the ground, the books, the academes,
> From whence doth spring the true Promethean fire.

But cf. Shakespeare's use of 'Promethean heat' in 'Othello', v. ii. 12.

Prometheus Bound, a tragedy by Aeschylus, translated by E. B. Browning (q.v.).

Prometheus the Firegiver, a poem by Bridges (q.v.).

Prometheus Unbound, a lyrical drama in four acts, by P. B. Shelley (q.v.), published in 1820.

Prometheus, the champion of mankind, is chained to a rock and subjected to perpetual torture. Characterized by 'courage, majesty, and a firm and patient opposition to omnipotent force, and exempt from the taints of ambition, envy, and revenge', instinct also with the spirit of love, he remains unyielding to the threats of Jupiter (Zeus) the spirit of evil and hate. He is supported by Earth, his mother, and the thought of Asia, his bride, the spirit of Nature. At the appointed hour, Demogorgon, the Primal Power of the world, drives Jupiter from his throne, and Prometheus is released by Hercules, typifying strength. The reign of love follows, when 'Thrones, altars, judgement-seats, and prisons' are things of the past and 'Man remains

> Sceptreless, free, uncircumscribed, but man

> Equal, unclassed, tribeless, and nationless,
> Exempt from awe, worship, degree, the king
> Over himself; just, gentle, wise, but man'.

Promos and Cassandra, see *Whetstone*.

Propaganda, THE, the *Congregatio de propaganda fide*, a committee of cardinals of the Roman Catholic Church having the care and oversight of foreign missions, founded in 1622 by Pope Gregory XV. Hence any association, scheme, or concerted movement for the propagation of a doctrine or practice.

PROPERTIUS, SEXTUS (*c.* 50–*c.* 16 B.C.), Roman elegiac poet, whose four extant books are concerned mainly with the successive phases of ecstasy, disenchantment, weariness, and disgust of the poet's irregular union with a certain 'Cynthia', identified, according to tradition, with Hostia, a lady of good position.

Prophecy of Famine, The, see *Churchill* (*C.*).

Proserpine, or, according to her Greek name, PERSĔPHŎNĒ, was a daughter of Zeus and Demeter. Legend tells that she was carried off by Pluto (Hades) while gathering flowers in the vale of Enna in Sicily, and made queen in the lower world. Demeter wandered over the earth seeking her, and at her prayer Zeus consented to the return of Persephone on condition that she had eaten nothing in the infernal regions. But she had eaten some pomegranate seeds there, as was revealed by Ascalaphus, son of Acheron (who was turned into an owl for his betrayal). Finally, to appease the resentment of Demeter, Zeus allowed Persephone to spend six months of the year on earth and the remainder with Pluto, a myth symbolical of the burying of the seed in the ground and the growth of the corn. The story has been treated by Tennyson in his 'Demeter and Persephone', and by Robert Bridges in his masque 'Demeter'. See also the allusion in Milton, P.L. iv. 268–72. Swinburne's 'Hymn to Proserpine' is included in 'Poems and Ballads'.

Prosopopoia, the sub-title of Spenser's 'Mother Hubberd's Tale' (q.v.).

Prospero, in Shakespeare's 'Tempest' (q.v.), the duke of Milan and father of Miranda.

Proteūs, an old man of the sea, who tended the flocks of Poseidon. He had received the gift of prophecy from the god, but those who wished to consult him found him difficult of access. For he, on being questioned, assumed different shapes, and eluded their grasp. Among his daughters was Eidothea, who taught Menelaus how to obtain the information he desired from her father. Homer places the residence of Proteus in the island of Pharos, off the Egyptian coast, Virgil in Carpathos, between Crete and Rhodes, whence Milton ('Comus') speaks of him as the 'Carpathian wizard'.

Proteus, one of the 'Two Gentlemen of

Verona' (q.v.) in Shakespeare's play of that name.

Prothalamion, a 'spousal verse' written by Spenser (q.v.), published in 1596, in celebration of the double marriage of the Lady Elizabeth and the Lady Katherine Somerset, daughters of the earl of Worcester. The name was invented by Spenser on the model of 'Epithalamion' (q.v.).

Protomartyr, the first (Christian) martyr, St. Stephen.

Proudfute, OLIVER, the bonnet-maker in Scott's 'The Fair Maid of Perth' (q.v.).

Proudie, DR. and MRS., characters in A. Trollope's Barsetshire series of novels (see in particular *Barchester Towers*).

PROUST, MARCEL (1871–1922), French novelist, author of the famous novel 'À la recherche du temps perdu' (q.v.), was born, lived, and died in Paris. From boyhood he was an asthmatic, finally a martyr to the disease, fighting against death to consolidate and complete his work. He was hypersensitive and neurotic, with abnormal tendencies which probably explain the long studies of similar characters in 'À la recherche . . .'. In earlier life, before anyone took him very seriously as an author, he published collections of essays and short stories as well as translations of Ruskin's 'Bible of Amiens' and 'Sesame and Lilies'. Fragments of a novel, 'Jean Santeuil', which contains much of 'À la recherche . . .' in embryo, and other fragments, mainly criticism ('Contre Sainte-Beuve'), were found and published after his death (1952 and 1954).

Prout, FATHER, see *Mahony*.

Provençal or LANGUE D'OC, the language of the southern part of France (cf. *Langue d'oïl*), and the literary medium of the troubadours. Their language was a *koiné*, a class language avoiding marked regional features; it was known as *lemosi* (limousin), probably because some of the most famous troubadours came from that region. Provençal declined as a literary language after the defeat of the south in the Albigensian War, and the attempt to revive it made by the municipal authorities of Toulouse in the 14th cent., when they instituted the literary competitions known as the *Jeux Floraux*, was unsuccessful. A more successful revival made in the 19th cent. by Mistral and the *félibrige* (q.v.) has led to a continuous production of literature in Provençal into the 20th cent., but the modern literary language is not unified, and is based on peasant, not aristocratic usage. The language is now generally called *occitan*, though the terms *provençal* and *langue d'oc* are still in use.

Provençal literature in the medieval period consisted chiefly of the lyric poetry composed by the troubadours (q.v.) for the feudal courts of the Midi, northern Italy and Spain. The *canso*, the love song in the courtly style which was the troubadours' special achieve-ment, was known all over western Europe, and gave rise to the courtly poetry of northern France, the Minnesang of Germany, and the Petrarchan poetry of Italy. The *sirventés*, the satirical poem mostly on political or moral themes, was also much cultivated by the troubadours. There is little literature of an epic kind, or of literature in prose, extant in Old Provençal, and Provençal was considered the language *par excellence* of lyric poetry, courtly in content and very elaborate in style. This poetic flowering came to an end with the decline, after the Albigensian crusade, of the aristocratic society which had produced it.

Proverbial Philosophy, see *Tupper*.

Proverbs of Alfred, a poem dating, in the form which has reached us, from the 13th cent., though much older in substance. It begins by giving some account of King Alfred, and proceeds to a number of stanzas each beginning 'Thus quad Alfred', and containing instruction of various kinds, precepts as to conduct, shrewd proverbs of popular origin, and religious teaching. The connexion of the proverbs with King Alfred is more than doubtful.

Provok'd Husband, The, or a Journey to London, a comedy written by Vanbrugh (q.v.) and finished by Cibber (q.v.), produced in 1728.

The 'provok'd husband' is Lord Townly, a man of regular life, who is driven to desperation by the extravagance and dissipation of his wife, and decides to separate from her and let the cause be known. This sentence (according to Cibber's ending) brings Lady Townly to her senses and contrition, and a reconciliation follows, promoted by Manly, Lord Townly's sensible friend, the successful suitor of Lady Grace, Lord Townly's exemplary sister. A second element in the plot is the visit to London of Sir Francis Wronghead, a simple country gentleman, with his wife, a foolish woman who wants to be a fine lady and seeks to achieve her end by extravagance, and their son and daughter. They are the intended prey of Count Basset, an unprincipled gamester, who, under cover of making love to Lady Wronghead, designs to entice her daughter into a secret marriage, and to effect a match between her son and his own cast-off mistress. The plot nearly succeeds, but is discovered and frustrated by Manly.

Provok'd Wife, The, a comedy by Vanbrugh (q.v.), produced in 1697.

Sir John Brute, a churlish man of quality, ill-uses his wife, and is a coward to boot. She is courted by Constant, but has remained faithful to her husband. Constant's friend, Heartfree, who prides himself on his cynical indifference to women, falls in love with her niece Belinda. The two ladies, for a frolic, invite Constant and Heartfree to meet them in Spring Garden. Here Lady Brute's virtue is on the point of yielding to the ardent addresses of Constant, when they are interrupted by the jealous Lady Fancyfull. The two couples return to Lady Brute's house and sit down to cards, confident that Sir John will not return from a drinking-bout for some hours. Sir John, however, having been arrested by the watch for brawling in the streets disguised in a parson's gown, has been dismissed by the magistrate after an amusing scene. (Vanbrugh rewrote scenes i and iii of act IV for the 1725/6 revival and had Sir John put on 'a light lady's short cloak and wrapping goun' and call himself 'Bonduca, Queen of the Welchmen' when arrested, but 'Lady Brute' before the justice.) He comes home unexpectedly early, finds the two men concealed in a closet, but has no stomach for the duel offered him by Constant. The presence of the men is attributed to the proposed marriage of Heartfree and Belinda, and, in spite of the attempts of Lady Fancyfull to make mischief, all ends happily.

Prue: 'dear Prue' was Steele's (q.v.) familiar name for his second wife, Mary Scurlock (see Steele's 'Correspondence').

Prue, MISS, a character in Congreve's 'Love for Love' (q.v.).

Prunes and prism: 'Father is rather vulgar . . . Papa . . . gives a pretty form to the lips. Papa, potatoes, poultry, prunes, and prism, are all very good for the lips, especially prunes and prism.' (Dickens's 'Little Dorrit', II. v and vii.)

Prussian Blue, a deep blue pigment of great body, so called from being accidentally discovered by Diesbach, a colour-maker in Berlin, in 1704. In Dickens (where Sam Weller calls his father 'My Prooshan Blue') probably a variant or intensive of 'true blue' [OED.], or with reference to a public-house sign common after the battle of Waterloo, the 'King of Prussia' in a blue uniform.

Prussianism, the national spirit or political system of Prussia, with reference to the arrogant and overbearing character attributed to the former, and to the militarism of the latter.

Pryderi, see *Mabinogion*.

Prynne, HESTER, the heroine of Hawthorne's 'The Scarlet Letter' (q.v.).

PRYNNE, WILLIAM (1600–69), Puritan pamphleteer, was educated at Bath grammar school and Oriel College, Oxford, and was a barrister of Lincoln's Inn. He wrote against Arminianism from 1627, and endeavoured to reform the manners of his age. He published 'Histriomastix', an enormous work directed against stage-plays, in 1632. For a supposed aspersion on Charles I and his queen in 'Histriomastix' he was sentenced by the Star Chamber, in 1634, to be imprisoned during life, to be fined £5,000, and to lose both his ears in the pillory. He continued to write in the Tower of London, and (1637) was again fined £5,000, deprived of the remainder of

his ears, and branded on the cheeks with the letters S. L. (seditious libeller) which Prynne, with humour, asserted to mean 'Stigmata Laudis' (i.e. of Archbishop Laud). He was released by the Long Parliament, and his sentences declared illegal in November 1640. He continued an active paper warfare, attacking Laud, then the independents, then the army (1647), then, after being arrested by Pride, the government. In 1660 he asserted the rights of Charles II, and was thanked by him. He was M.P. for Bath in the Convention Parliament and was appointed keeper of the records in the Tower of London. He published his most valuable work, 'Brevia Parliamentaria Rediviva', in 1662. He published altogether about two hundred books and pamphlets.

PSALMANAZAR, GEORGE (1679?–1763), a literary impostor, was a native of the south of France. His real name is unknown, his usual designation being fashioned by himself from the biblical character, Shalmaneser. He was educated at a Dominican convent and commenced life as a mendicant in the character of a native Japanese Christian, but afterwards represented himself as still a pagan, living on raw flesh, roots, and herbs, and invented an elaborate alphabet and grammar and a worship of his own. He enlisted in a regiment of the duke of Mecklenburg, and attracted the attention of William Innes, chaplain to the Scottish regiment at Sluys, who became a confederate in the imposture, baptized Psalmanazar as a Protestant convert, and for security persuaded him to remove his birthplace to the obscurity of Formosa. He came to London at the end of 1703 and became a centre of interest, presenting Bishop Compton with the catechism in 'Formosan' (his invented language), and talking volubly in Latin to Archbishop Tillotson. He published in 1704 a 'Description' of Formosa, with an introductory autobiography. After the withdrawal of his mentor Innes, who was rewarded for his zeal in converting Psalmanazar by being appointed chaplain-general to the forces in Portugal (c. 1707), he was unable to sustain the imposture unaided, and passed from ridicule to obscurity, although he still found patrons. He renounced his past life after a serious illness in 1728, became an accomplished hebraist, wrote 'A General History of Printing', and contributed to the 'Universal History'. Psalmanazar was regarded with veneration by Dr. Johnson, who used to sit with him at an alehouse in Old Street, London. In 1764 appeared posthumously his autobiographical 'Memoirs', containing an account of the imposture.

Psalms, The, the Book of Psalms, one of the books of the Old Testament, forming the hymn-book of the Jewish Church, often called *the Psalms of David*, in accordance with the belief that they, or part of them, were composed by David, king of Israel. (In 2 Sam. xxii, Psalm xviii is attributed to David.) The

Psalms were the basis of the medieval church services, probably the only book in the Bible on the use of which, by the laity, the medieval church imposed no veto at all. For our own Prayer Book version of them, one of our greatest literary inheritances, see *Coverdale*. A *Metrical Version* of the Psalms was begun by Sternhold (q.v.) and Hopkins (2nd ed., 1551), and continued at Geneva during Mary's reign by Protestant refugees. The complete *Old Version* (metrical) was published in 1562. The *New Version* by Dr. Nicholas Brady and Nahum Tate (q.v.) appeared in 1696. The word *psalm* is from the Greek ψάλλειν, to twitch (the strings of the harp).

Psapho's birds: Psapho was a Libyan who kept a number of birds in captivity and taught them to say 'Psapho is a god'. He then liberated them. The Africans in consequence paid divine honours to Psapho. The story is attributed in Lemprière to Aelian. Other dictionaries give no reference. It is given by Erasmus ('Adagia', 1. ii. 99), who merely says, 'Narrant in Lybia fuisse quendam Psaphonem', etc.

Pseudodoxia Epidemica, see *Vulgar Errors*.

Psȳchē, see *Cupid and Psyche*.

Ptah, the Vulcan of Egyptian mythology, the deity regarded as a creative force, the builder of the world and vivifying power. He was worshipped in particular at Memphis.

PTOLEMY (CLAUDIUS PTOLEMAE-US), who lived at Alexandria in the 2nd cent. A.D., was a celebrated mathematician, astronomer, and geographer. He devised the system of astronomy (according to which the sun, planets, and stars revolved round the earth) which was generally accepted until displaced by that of Copernicus. His work on this subject is generally known by its Arabic name of 'Almagest'. His great geographical treatise remained a textbook until superseded by the discoveries of the 15th cent. Ptolemy compiled a map of the world in which both the parallels and meridians are curved. Though defective in details, it had a great influence on map-making in the 15th cent. His underestimate of the circumference of the earth is said to have encouraged Columbus to undertake his voyage to the west.

Ptolemy Philadelphus (309–246 B.C.), king of Egypt, the son of Ptolemy Soter (the first king of the Ptolemaic dynasty, 323–285), is important in a literary connexion as a patron of learning. In his reign Alexandria was the resort of the most distinguished men of letters of the time, and the celebrated Alexandrian Library, begun by his father, was increased. Manetho (q.v.) wrote during his reign, and according to tradition the Septuagint (q.v.) version of the Scriptures was made at his request.

Public Advertiser, The, originally 'The London Daily Post and General Advertiser', was started in 1752 and expired in 1798, being then amalgamated with 'The Public Ledger' (q.v.). From 1758 to 1793 it was edited by Henry Sampson Woodfall, and published the famous 'Letters' of 'Junius' (q.v.). It contained home and foreign intelligence, and correspondence, mainly political, from writers of all shades of opinion. Wilkes and Tooke (qq.v.) carried on a dispute in its columns. The notable pamphlets of 'Candor' against Lord Mansfield (1764) also appeared originally as letters to 'The Public Advertiser'. The author of these is unknown.

Public Ledger, The, a commercial periodical founded in 1759 by Newbery (q.v.), to which Goldsmith (q.v.) contributed his 'Chinese Letters'. It absorbed 'The Public Advertiser' (q.v.) in 1798.

Puccini, GIACOMO (1858–1924), a popular opera composer, born at Lucca. His most successful works were 'Manon Lescaut' (1893), 'La Bohème' (1896), 'La Tosca' (1899), 'Madama Butterfly' (1904), 'La Fanciulla del West' (1910).

Pucelle, La ('The Maid', i.e. Joan of Arc), a burlesque epic by Voltaire (q.v.) on the subject of Joan of Arc (q.v.), published in 1755. Joan is called 'la Pucelle' in Shakespeare's '1 King Henry VI' (q.v.).

Puck, originally an evil or malicious spirit or demon of popular superstition; from the 16th cent. the name of a fancied mischievous or tricksy goblin or sprite, called also Robin Goodfellow and Hobgoblin. In this character he figures in Shakespeare's 'A Midsummer Night's Dream' (II. i. 40) and Drayton's 'Nymphidia' (xxxvi) (qq.v.).

Puddingfield, a character in 'The Rovers' (see *Anti-Jacobin*).

Puff, a character in Sheridan's 'The Critic' (q.v.).

Pugilistica, a work on British boxing by Henry Downes Miles, published in 1906. It carries on the story of the prize-ring begun in the 'Boxiana' of Egan (q.v.).

Pugin, AUGUSTUS WELBY NORTHMORE (1812–52), architect, protagonist of the Gothic Revival. He designed the decoration of Barry's Houses of Parliament. His designs for churches were based on a deep study of Gothic architecture. He developed his thesis that Gothic was the only proper Christian architecture in 'Contrasts: or, a Parallel between the noble Edifices of the Middle Ages, and Corresponding Buildings of the present Day; shewing the Decline of Taste' (1846), 'The True Principles of Pointed or Christian Architecture' (1841), and 'Apology for the Revival of Christian Architecture in England' (1843).

PULCI, LUIGI (1432–84), Florentine poet of the circle of Lorenzo de' Medici. His poem 'Morgante Maggiore' (q.v.) was the first romantic epic to be written by an Italian *letterato*.

Pulitzer Prizes, annual prizes established under the will of Joseph Pulitzer (1847–1911), an American newspaper-proprietor of Hungarian birth, who used sensational journalism for the correction of social abuses. The prizes, which are confined to American citizens, are offered in the interest of letters (American history and biography, poetry, drama, and novel-writing), music, and good newspaper work. A fund of $500,000 was set aside for the prizes, which are controlled by the School of Journalism (also founded under the terms of Pulitzer's will) at Columbia University.

PULLEN, THE REVD. HENRY WILLIAM (1836–1903), remembered as the author of the allegorical pamphlet, 'The Fight in Dame Europa's School' (1870), accusing England of cowardice and selfishness in observing neutrality in the Franco-Prussian War.

Pullet, MR. and MRS., characters in George Eliot's 'The Mill on the Floss' (q.v.).

Pumblechook, MR., a character in Dickens's 'Great Expectations' (q.v.).

Pumpernickel, the name under which Thackeray genially satirizes the minor German principalities, particularly in 'Vanity Fair', where the description of Pumpernickel is based on his recollections of Weimar in 1831. The word in German means a kind of dark brown bread made from coarsely ground unbolted rye.

Punch, probably short for *Punchinello*, apparently adapted from Neapolitan dialectal *polecenella*, equivalent to Italian *pulcinella*. The latter word is the diminutive of *pulcina*, chicken; and *polecenella* is diminutive of *polecena*, the young of the turkey-cock, to the hooked bill of which the nose of Punch's mask bears a resemblance. [OED.] See further under *Punch and Judy*.

Punch, *or the London Charivari*, an illustrated weekly comic periodical, founded in 1841; at first a rather strongly Radical paper, but gradually coming round to its present attitude.

The circumstances of the birth of this famous paper have been variously stated. One or two illustrated comic papers had already appeared in London, notably Gilbert Abbott à Beckett's 'Figaro in London' (1831) and 'Punchinello' (1832) illustrated by Cruikshank. It appears that the idea of starting in London a comic paper somewhat on the lines of Philippon's Paris 'Charivari' first occurred to Ebenezer Landells, draughtsman and wood-engraver, who submitted it to Henry Mayhew (q.v.). Mayhew took up the proposal, and enlisted the support of Lemon (q.v.) and Joseph Stirling Coyne (1803–68), these three being the first joint-editors. The first number was issued on 17 July 1841. Joseph Last was the first printer, and Landells the first engraver. À Beckett (q.v.) and Jerrold (q.v.) were among the

original staff, soon joined by Thackeray, Hood, Leech, and Tenniel (qq.v.) among others. Shirley Brooks (1816–74) became editor in 1870, Tom Taylor (q.v.) in 1874, and Burnand (q.v.) in 1880. Sir Owen Seaman was editor from 1906 to 1932. Among other famous draughtsmen may be mentioned Charles Keene (1823–91), whose first drawing in 'Punch' appeared in 1851 and who joined the staff in 1860; and Du Maurier (q.v.), who contributed drawings from 1860 and joined the staff in 1864. The most famous drawing for the cover, by Richard Doyle (q.v.), was used from 1849 to 1956, when it was replaced by a full-colour design, different each week. The Punch figure and the dog, Toby, usually appear in the design, and the frieze from the original Doyle drawing is reproduced weekly at the head of the Charivari page.

Punch and Judy, a puppet-show drama probably introduced into England from the Continent towards the end of the 17th cent. The character of *Pulcinella* (see *Punch*) is stated by Italian authors to have been invented by Silvio Fiorillo, a comedian, about the year 1600, for the Neapolitan impromptu comedies, to imitate the peasants of Acerra, a town near Naples. But the origin is uncertain.

The plot of the drama and the dialogue have varied in different presentations, but the main outline is as follows. Punch is a hump-backed, long-nosed creature, dissipated, violent, and cunning. In a fit of anger he kills his child. His wife Judy, discovering the murder, attacks him with a bludgeon, but he wrests the weapon from her and kills her. The dog Toby seizes him by the nose, and he kills it. He is visited by a doctor when ill, kicks him, and when the doctor retaliates, bludgeons him to death. He is arrested and sentenced to death. He beguiles the hangman into putting his own head in the noose and promptly hangs him. Finally he is visited by the devil, whom he likewise vanquishes. (Much information is contained in J. Payne Collier's 'Punch and Judy', 1870. The character of Punch may be in part derived from the Vice of the old Moralities.)

Punch's Prize Novelists, *Mr.*, see *Prize Novelists*.

Punic Faith, faithlessness. The Carthaginians were proverbial among the Romans for perfidy; as, no doubt, the Romans were among the Carthaginians. (For the derivation of *Punic*, see under *Carthage*.)

Puntarvolo, in Jonson's 'Every Man out of his Humour' (q.v.), a vainglorious knight.

Puppet-play, see *Motion*.

Purānas, THE, sacred mythological works in Sanskrit containing the mythology of the Hindus. They are of comparatively recent date, none of them being thought to be more ancient than the 8th cent. A.D. They divide themselves into three groups, relating respectively to Brahma, Vishnu, and Siva (qq.v.).

Purcell, HENRY (1658?–95), one of the greatest of English composers. His father and uncle were both musicians, the former being master of the choristers of Westminster Abbey. Purcell became, when six years old, a chorister of the Chapel Royal, and in 1680, when 22, was appointed organist of Westminster Abbey. About 1690 he produced the music of 'Dido and Aeneas' (Nahum Tate (q.v.) composing the words), his best-known work, including the great song, 'When I am laid in earth'. He wrote the incidental music for many plays and much church music. He is buried beneath the organ in Westminster Abbey.

PURCHAS, SAMUEL (1575?–1626), was born at Thaxted in Essex, and educated at St. John's College, Cambridge. He was rector of St. Martin's, Ludgate, London, 1614–26. In 1613 he published 'Purchas his Pilgrimage, or Relations of the World and the Religions observed in all Ages'; in 1619 'Purchas his Pilgrim, Microcosmus or the Histories of Man'; and in 1625 'Hakluytus Posthumus, or Purchas his Pilgrimes, contayning a History of the World in Sea Voyages and Land Travell by Englishmen and others'. This last is in part based on manuscripts left by Hakluyt (q.v.) and is a continuation of the latter's work (Purchas appears to have assisted Hakluyt to arrange papers which were unpublished at the latter's death). It consists of two divisions, each of ten books. In the first division, after an introductory book, are set forth narratives of voyages to India, China, Japan, Africa, and the Mediterranean. The second division deals with attempts to discover the North-West Passage, the Muscovy expeditions, and explorations of the West Indies and Florida. Among the best narratives are William Adam's description of his voyage to Japan and residence there, and William Hawkins's account of his visit to the court of the Great Mogul at Agra. The works of Purchas were not reprinted until the Glasgow edition of 1905–7.

Pure, SIMON, see *Simon Pure.*

Purgatorio, *The,* of Dante, see *Divina Commedia.*

Purgatory, ST. PATRICK'S, see *Patrick's Purgatory.*

Puritan, a member of that party of English Protestants who regarded the reformation of the Church under Elizabeth as incomplete, and called for its further 'purification' from what they considered to be unscriptural and corrupt forms and ceremonies retained from the unreformed Church. The term appears in early use as one of reproach by opponents, and was applied to the Presbyterians, Independents, or Baptists, and consequently to the typical 'Roundheads' of the Commonwealth period, whose Puritanism was sometimes little more than political. In later times the term has become historical, without opprobrious connotation; but is also often used of one who affects extreme strictness in morals.

Puritan, *The, or the Widow of Watling-Street,* a comedy published in 1607 as 'written by W. S.' and included in the 3rd and 4th Shakespeare folios, but certainly by some other hand, perhaps John Marston (q.v.).

The play is a farcical comedy of London manners, and sets forth the tricks played on the widow and her daughter .by Capt. Idle and George Pye-boord in order to win their hands, with scenes in the Marshalsea.

Puritans, *Plays for,* see *Plays for Puritans.*

Purley, *The Diversions of,* see *Tooke.*

Purple Island, *The,* a philosophical poem on the human body by P. Fletcher (q.v.).

Pursuits of Literature, see *Mathias.*

PUSEY, EDWARD BOUVERIE (1800–82), educated at Eton and Christ Church, Oxford, was elected in 1822 a fellow of Oriel College, Oxford, where Keble and Newman (qq.v.) were also fellows. In 1828 he was appointed Regius professor of Hebrew. Becoming alarmed by the spread of rationalism in the Church of England and convinced that it could only be checked by a wider sense of her divine institution, he joined Newman and Keble in the production of 'Tracts for the Times' (1833, see *Oxford Movement*), contributing Tracts on baptism (1835) and the holy eucharist (1837). He supported Newman's explanation of the Thirty-nine Articles in the famous 'Tract XC', and in 1843 was suspended from the office of university preacher for heresy. He continued to maintain high Anglican views, publishing in 1856 his learned 'Doctrine of the Real Presence', while endeavouring to hinder secessions to the Church of Rome among his supporters. Later he attempted to bring about the union of the English and Roman churches, and of the English Church with the Wesleyans and Eastern Church. PUSEY HOUSE at Oxford, founded in memory of him, was opened in 1884. A 'Life of Pusey' by Liddon (q.v.) was published in 1893–7.

PUSHKIN, ALEXANDER SERGEYEVICH (1799–1837), the national poet of Russia. A liberal aristocrat, he was exiled for some time from St. Petersburg for his political and atheistic writings, and was in sympathy with the Decembrist revolt of 1825. He was fatally wounded in a duel in 1837. Though Pushkin's style reflects his classical education his themes are largely Romantic, containing Byronic and folklore elements. His work consists of a large amount of lyric poetry; long narrative poems in various styles: 'Ruslan and Lyndmila' (1820), 'The Prisoner of the Caucasus' (1821), 'The Gypsies' (1827), 'Poltava' (1829), 'The Bronze Horseman' (1833); one 'novel in verse', 'Eugenii Onegin' (1823–31) (his greatest work); one blank-verse historical drama, 'Boris Godunov' (1825). After 1830 Pushkin turned more to prose writing: 'The Tales of Belkin' (1830), 'The Queen of Spades' (1834), 'The Captain's Daughter' (1836), and 'The History of the Pugachov Rebellion' (1834).

Most of Pushkin's work may be read in English, the earliest translations being those of G. Borrow (St. Petersburg, 1835). 'The Works of Alexander Pushkin' (Nonesuch Press, 1936) contains translations by various hands of all the major works.

Puss in Boots, a popular tale, from the French of Perrault (q.v.), translated by Robert Samber (1729?).

A miller bequeathes to his three sons respectively, his mill, his ass, and his cat. The youngest, who inherits the cat, laments his ill-fortune. But the resourceful cat, by a series of unscrupulous ruses, in which he represents his master to the king as the wealthy marquis of Carabas, secures for him the hand of the king's daughter.

Andrew Lang (q.v.), in his 'Perrault's Popular Tales', discusses the origin of the story, which is found, in various forms, in several countries.

Pussyfoot, the nickname of William Eugene Johnson (1862–1945), an American prohibition propagandist, earned by his catlike policies in pursuing law-breakers in the Indian Territories.

PUTTENHAM, RICHARD (1520?–1601?), author of 'The Arte of English Poesie', a critical discussion of English poetry, chiefly in its formal aspect, published anonymously in 1589. The work is sometimes assigned to his brother George.

Pwyll, in British mythology, prince of Dyfed and 'Head of Hades'; see *Mabinogion*. The stories of Pelles and of Pelleas in the 'Morte Darthur' are perhaps connected with his myth (see Rhys, 'Arthurian Legend').

Pyannet Sneakup, Mrs., a character in Brome's 'The City Witt' (q.v.).

PYE, HENRY JAMES (1745–1813), became poet laureate in 1790, and was the constant butt of contemporary ridicule.

Pygmalion, a king of Cyprus and a sculptor. He became enamoured of a beautiful statue that he had made of a woman, and at his prayer Aphrodite gave it life. The story is told in Ovid's 'Metamorphoses', in Marston's erotic poem, 'The Metamorphosis of Pigmalion's Image' (1598), in William Morris's 'Earthly Paradise' (q.v.), and is the subject of a comedy by W. S. Gilbert ('Pygmalion and Galatea'). 'Pygmalion' is also the title of a play by G. B. Shaw (q.v.).

Pygmies, a race of men of very small size, mentioned by ancient writers as inhabiting parts of Africa. In the last quarter of the 19th cent. dwarf races were ascertained to exist in equatorial Africa, who may be the 'pygmies' of Homer and Herodotus. According to ancient fable, the cranes came annually from Scythia and made war on them.

Pyke and **Pluck,** in Dickens's 'Nicholas Nickleby' (q.v.), the toadies of Sir Mulberry Hawk.

Pylădēs, see *Orestes*.

Pyncheon, HEPHZIBAH, a character in N. Hawthorne's 'The House of the Seven Gables' (q.v.).

Pyracmon, see *Cyclopes*.

Pyramids of stone or brick containing burial chambers were the principal structures of the tomb complexes erected by pharaohs *c.* 2800–1700 B.C. The earliest is the 'Step Pyramid' at Sakkara, built by Zoser, and the largest are three at Giza, built by the IVth Dynasty pharaohs, Cheops (the Great Pyramid), Chephren, and Mycerinus.

Pyramus, a youth of Babylon, who became enamoured of Thisbe. The two lovers, whom their parents forbade to marry, exchanged their vows through a chink in the wall which separated their two houses. They agreed to meet at the tomb of Ninus, outside the walls of Babylon, under a white mulberry tree. Thisbe came first to the appointed place, but being frightened by a lioness fled into a cave, dropping her veil, which the lioness covered with blood. Pyramus, arriving, found the bloody veil, and, concluding that Thisbe had been devoured, stabbed himself with his sword. Thisbe, emerging from the cave, distraught at the sight of the dying Pyramus, fell upon his sword. This tragic scene occurred under the mulberry tree, which thereafter bore only red fruit. The story, of Asiatic origin, is the subject of the 'tedious brief scene' played by Bottom and his friends in 'A Midsummer Night's Dream' (q.v.).

Pyrgopolynīcēs, a braggart, the hero of the 'Miles Gloriosus' of Plautus (q.v.). The name is a combination of 'fortress' and 'much victory'.

Pyriphlĕgĕthon, see *Phlegethon*.

Pyrochles, in Spenser's 'Faerie Queene', symbolizes rage. He is the brother of Cymochles (q.v.), the son of 'old Acrates and Despight' (II. iv. 41). On his shield is a flaming fire, with the words 'Burnt I do burn'. He is overcome by Sir Guyon (II. v), and tries to drown himself in a lake to quench his flames. He is rescued and healed by Archimago (II. vi. 42–51), and finally killed by Prince Arthur (II. viii).

Pyrocles, one of the chief characters in Sidney's 'Arcadia' (q.v.).

Pyrrha, the wife of Deucalion (q.v.).

Pyrrhic, in ancient Greek and Latin verse, a foot consisting of two short syllables. In modern accentual verse, the term is sometimes applied to a group of two unstressed syllables.

Pyrrhic dance, the war-dance of the ancient Greeks, in which the motions of warfare were gone through in armour, to a musical accompaniment. It is said to have been so named from Pyrrhicus, the inventor.

Pyrrhic victory, a victory gained at too great a cost; in allusion to the exclamation attributed to Pyrrhus (q.v.) after the battle of Asculum (in which he routed the Romans but with the loss of the flower of his army), 'One more such victory and we are lost.'

Pyrrho, a native of Elis in the Peloponnese, who lived in the time of Alexander the Great and joined his expedition. He was the founder of the Sceptical or PYRRHONIAN school of philosophy, and maintained that certain knowledge on any matter was unattainable, and that suspension of judgement was true wisdom and the source of happiness.

Pyrrhus, (1) see *Neoptolemus*; (2) king of Epirus (318–272 B.C.), a great military adventurer, who carried on a series of campaigns against Rome and in Sicily, 280–275.

Pytchley ('Py' pronounced as 'pie'), THE, a famous pack of fox-hounds, whose country lies between Rugby and Northampton. It was much associated with the Spencer family in the 18th cent. The name is said to be derived from that of an Elizabethan house, now demolished. But Charles Clarke is quoted, in the Badminton Library volume on 'Hunting', as having traced it back to one William of Pightesley who hunted 'wolves, foxes, and other vermin' in Henry III's reign.

Pythagoras, the Greek philosopher, a native of Samos, lived in the 6th cent. B.C. He settled at Crotona in Italy, where he founded a brotherhood who followed his ascetic practices (especially in the matter of food) and studied his philosophical teaching. The brotherhood incurred political suspicion, and was suppressed, but the Pythagorean doctrines survived. Pythagoras assigned a mathematical basis to the universe, and musical principles were also prominent in his system. The heavenly bodies he supposed to be divided by intervals according to the law of musical harmony, whence arose the idea of the harmony of the spheres. He discovered the rotation of the earth on its own axis, and found in this the cause of day and night. He adopted the Orphic doctrine of metempsychosis or the transmigration of souls from man to man, or man to animal, or animal to man, in a process of purification or punishment. He himself, it is said, claimed to remember having assisted the Greeks in the Trojan War in the character of Euphorbus. There are references to this Pythagorean doctrine in the dialogue between Feste and Malvolio ('Twelfth Night', IV. ii), in 'The Merchant of Venice', IV. i, and in 'As You Like It', iii. 2.

As a mathematician Pythagoras is credited with the discovery of the proof of the 47th proposition of the 1st book of Euclid, that the square on the hypotenuse of a right-angled triangle is equal to the sum of the squares on the other two sides, hence called the PYTHAGOREAN THEOREM. The PYTHAGOREAN LETTER is the Greek *Y*, used by Pythagoras as a symbol of the divergent paths of vice and virtue. None of his writings is extant.

Pytheas, a Greek of Marseilles, contemporary with Alexander the Great, who made a courageous voyage up the W. coast of Europe to Britain, Jutland, and the Orkneys and Shetlands. His narrative is lost, but was used by Strabo.

Pythia, the priestess of Apollo at Delphi (q.v.).

Pythian Games, see *Python* and *Delphi*.

Pythias, see *Damon and Pythias*.

Python, a serpent that rose from the mud left by the deluge of Deucalion. It lived in a cave on Mt. Parnassus and was slain by Apollo, who established the Pythian Games to celebrate the event.

Q

Q, the initial of German *Quelle*, 'source', is the symbol used, in the comparative study of the synoptic Gospels, to designate a supposed Greek translation of a collection attributed to Matthew of the *logia* of Christ, from which the parts common to the Gospels of Matthew and Luke, but omitted from Mark, are derived. It is supposed to have contained certain narrative parts, but not the Passion.

'Q', see *Jerrold* and *Quiller-Couch*. See also *Old Q*.

Quackleben, DR., a character in Scott's 'St. Ronan's Well' (q.v.).

Quadrilateral, THE, the region lying between, and defended by, the four fortresses of Mantua, Verona, Peschiera, and Legnano. It was of special importance in the wars of the Risorgimento in Italy.

Quadrille, a card game played by four persons with forty cards (the eights, nines, and tens being discarded). It replaced ombre (q.v.) as the fashionable game about 1726, and was in turn superseded by whist. The square dance called *quadrille* is of French origin. The first mention of it quoted in the OED. is dated 1773.

Quadrivium, in the Middle Ages, the higher division of the seven liberal arts, comprising the mathematical sciences (arithmetic, geometry, astronomy, and music); see *Trivium.*

Quai d'Orsay, sometimes used as a synonym for the French Ministry of Foreign Affairs, which stands on this quay (on the left bank of the Seine in the centre of Paris).

Quakers, members of the religious society (the Society of Friends, q.v.) founded by George Fox in 1648–50. According to Fox, the name was first given to himself and his followers by Justice Bennet at Derby in 1650 'because I bid them, Tremble at the word of the Lord'. It appears, however, that the name had previously been applied to some foreign religious sect. [OED.]

QUARITCH, BERNARD (1819–99), bookseller and author of the valuable bibliographical work, 'A General Catalogue of Old Books and MSS.' (1887–9; index, 1892); he was the leading second-hand bookseller in London.

QUARLES, FRANCIS (1592–1644), born near Romford in Essex, was educated at Christ's College, Cambridge, and at Lincoln's Inn. He went abroad in the suite of the Princess Elizabeth on her marriage with the Elector Palatine. He wrote pamphlets in defence of Charles I, which led to the sequestration of his property and the destruction of his manuscripts. He published in 1620 his 'Feast for Wormes', a paraphrase of the book of Jonah; but is chiefly remembered for his 'Emblems' (q.v.), published in 1635. He was appointed chronologer to the City of London in 1639. A complete collection of his works was edited by Grosart in 1874 for the 'Chertsey Worthies Library'.

Quarll, *Adventures of Philip*, see *Philip Quarll.*

Quarterly Review, *The*, was founded in Feb. 1809 by J. Murray (q.v.), as a Tory rival to 'The Edinburgh Review' (q.v.). The liberal, conciliatory, and impartial lines on which it should be run were indicated by Sir W. Scott, an ardent promoter of the venture, in a letter to Gifford (q.v.), the first editor. Gifford was succeeded by Sir J. T. Coleridge (nephew of the poet) and Lockhart (q.v.). Among famous contributors to it have been Sir W. Scott, Canning, Southey, Rogers, Lord Salisbury, and Gladstone. Sir J. Barrow (q.v.) was a pillar of the Review during the years 1809–48. Special interest attaches to Scott's favourable review in it of Jane Austen's 'Emma', in which he speaks of the 'spirit and originality of her sketches', the first encouragement from high quarters received by the young writer; and to Scott's review (Jan. 1817) of his own 'Tales of My Landlord', written to defend himself against Dr. McCrie's suggestion of an anti-covenanting bias in 'Old Mortality' and for fun (the review criticized the 'flimsiness and incoherent texture' of the narrative, and the insipidity of the heroes); also to Croker's article (in 1818) on Keats's 'Endymion', which was supposed to have hastened the poet's death in 1821.

> Who killed John Keats?
> 'I' says the Quarterly,
> So cruel and Tartarly,
> ' 'Twas one of my feats.'
>
> (Byron.)

Quarto, a volume in which the sheets are folded twice, so that each leaf is a quarter of the sheet. Twenty of the plays of Shakespeare were printed separately in quarto during his lifetime or before the Restoration.

Quasimodo Sunday, the first Sunday after Easter, so called from the first two words of the *Introit* of the mass of that day.

QUASIMODO is the name of the deformed bell-ringer of Notre Dame in Victor Hugo's 'Notre Dame de Paris'.

Queen Anne's Bounty, a fund formed out of the first-fruits and tenths of clerical livings, payable before the Reformation to the papal see, transferred to the Crown by Henry VIII, and vested by Queen Anne in trustees for the augmentation of poor livings.

Queen Mab, in Shakespeare's 'Romeo and Juliet' (q.v.), i. iv, 'the fairies' midwife', who brings to birth men's secret hopes in the form of dreams, by driving 'athwart their noses' in her chariot as they lie asleep. In Drayton's 'Nymphidia' (q.v.) she is Oberon's wife and queen of the fairies. For Shelley's poem 'Queen Mab', see below. 'Mab' is perhaps from the Irish 'Medb', a legendary queen of Connaught, or from the Welsh 'Mab', a child.

Queen Mab, a poem by P. B. Shelley (q.v.), surreptitiously published in 1813.

This poem was written by Shelley when he was eighteen, and, whatever promise it may show, is a crude and juvenile production. The fairy Queen Mab carries off in her celestial chariot the spirit of the maiden Ianthe, and shows her the past history of the world and expounds to her the causes of its miserable state. The poet inveighs through her mouth against 'kings, priests, and statesmen', human institutions such as marriage and commerce, and the Christian religion. The fairy finally reveals the future state of a regenerate world when 'all things are re-created, and the flame of consentaneous love inspires all life'.

Queen Mary, an historical drama by A. Tennyson (q.v.), published in 1875.

The play presents the principal events of the reign of Mary Tudor, Wyatt's rebellion, the marriage with Philip, the submission of England to Cardinal Pole as the Pope's legate, the death of Cranmer at the stake, the loss of Calais, and the death of the unhappy and disappointed Mary.

Queen Mother, *The*, a play on Catherine de' Medici (1861), by A. C. Swinburne (q.v.).

Queen of Cornwall, The Famous Tragedy of the, a drama by Hardy (q.v.) on the story of King Mark, the two Iseults, and Tristram, produced in 1923.

Queen of Hearts, THE, figures prominently in Lewis Carroll's 'Alice's Adventures in Wonderland' (q.v.); also an endearing name for Elizabeth (1596–1662), eldest daughter of James I, wife of Frederick, Elector Palatine and king of Bohemia in 1619–20. She was mother of Prince Rupert and of Sophia (the mother of George I).

Queen of the May, see *May Day*.

Queen's Maries or MARYS, THE, the four ladies named Mary attendant on Mary Queen of Scots. The list is variously given, including: Mary Seton, Mary Beaton, Mary Livingstone, Mary Fleming, Mary Hamilton, and Mary Carmichael. They are frequently mentioned in Scottish ballads.

Queen's Quair, The, an historical romance by Hewlett (q.v.), published in 1904. It deals with the life of Mary Queen of Scots from the time of the death of her first husband, Francis II of France, to her marriage with Bothwell and his flight. (Quair = quire, little book.)

Queen's Wake, The, a poem by Hogg (q.v.), published in 1813.

Queen Mary of Scotland holds her 'wake' at Holyrood, during which seventeen bards, including Rizzio, sing their songs in competition. These are a number of verse-tales in various styles, martial, comic, horrible, or mystical. The best of these, according to modern opinion, is the beautiful tale of 'Kilmeny' (q.v.). But 'The Witch of Fife' is also a fine work, humorous and fantastic.

Queenhithe, previously, according to Stow, called Edredshithe, one of the early quays pertaining to the city of London. The queen commemorated in the name is, according to Lethaby, Matilda, wife of Henry I. There was a drawbridge in old London Bridge which allowed ships to pass through to Queenhithe.

Queensberry Rules, THE, for boxing, were drawn up in 1867 under the supervision of Sir John Sholto-Douglas, 8th marquess of Queensberry (1844–1900).

Quentin Durward, a novel by Sir W. Scott (q.v.), published in 1823.

The scene is laid in the 15th cent. and the principal character is Louis XI of France, crafty, cruel, and superstitious, yet prudent and capable. With him is contrasted his vassal and enemy, the violent and impetuous Charles the Bold of Burgundy. The story is concerned with the intrigues by which Louis attempts to procure, with the assistance of William de la Marck, the Wild Boar of the Ardennes, the revolt of Liege against Charles; with the murder of the bishop of Liege; and with the famous visit of Louis to Charles at Peronne and their temporary reconciliation.

The romance of Quentin Durward is subordinate to these. He is a young Scot of good family who engages himself in the corps of the Scottish Archers of the Guard of Louis. He is sent to conduct the young Countess Isabelle de Croye, a Burgundian heiress who has fled from a threatened marriage with the odious Campo-Basso, to the protection of the bishop of Liege; saves her from many perils; and finally wins her hand by compassing the destruction of William de la Marck. Among the interesting secondary characters may be mentioned: Tristan l'Hermite, Louis's provost marshal; Oliver le Dain, his counsellor and whilom barber; Martius Galeotti, his astrologer; the Cardinal La Balue (q.v.), and Philippe de Commines (q.v., called Philip des Comines in the novel). The well-known lyric 'County Guy' occurs in ch. iv.

Querno, in Pope's 'Dunciad', ii. 15 ('Rome in her capitol saw Querno sit'), was an Apulian poet to whom the author compares Cibber. According to Paulus Jovius (quoted in Elwin and Courthope's notes on the 'Dunciad'), Querno, hearing that Pope Leo X patronized literature, set out for Rome, where he recited some 20,000 lines of his 'Alexias', and was made poet laureate as a joke. He was introduced to the pope as a buffoon, and frequented his table.

Questing Beast, THE, in Malory's 'Morte Darthur' (q.v.), pursued by Palamedes the Saracen.

QUEVEDO, FRANCISCO GOMEZ DE (1580–1645), Spanish writer, author of the picaresque romance 'Pablo de Segovia' (the 'Great Sharper') and of 'Visions' of various vicious and rascally types, which last were translated into English by L'Estrange (q.v.); also of much satirical poetry.

Quickly, MISTRESS NELL, in Shakespeare's '2 Henry IV' and 'Henry V' (qq.v.), hostess of the Boar's Head Tavern in Eastcheap.

Quickly, MISTRESS, in Shakespeare's 'The Merry Wives of Windsor' (q.v.), the servant of Dr. Caius.

Quietism, a form of religious mysticism (originated prior to 1675 by Molinos, q.v., a Spanish priest), consisting in passive devotional contemplation, with extinction of the will and withdrawal from all things of the senses. [OED.] One of the best-known exponents of Quietist doctrines was Fénelon (q.v.), archbishop of Cambrai, whose 'Maximes des Saints', embodying his opinions, was condemned by Rome. Another noted Quietist was Mme Guyon (1648–1717). There is a good deal about the Quietists in Shorthouse's novel, 'John Inglesant' (q.v.).

Qui-hi, from Urdū *koī hai*, 'Is any one there?', a call used in India to summon a servant, a nickname for an Anglo-Indian.

QUILLER-COUCH, SIR ARTHUR THOMAS (1863–1944), a Cornishman, educated at Newton Abbot College, Clifton

College, and Trinity College, Oxford, became professor of English literature at Cambridge in 1912. His publications (most of them under the pseudonym 'Q') include: 'Dead Man's Rock' (1887), 'Troy Town' (1888), 'The Splendid Spur' (1889), 'Noughts and Crosses' (1891), 'The Ship of Stars' (1899), 'The Oxford Book of English Verse' (1900, 1939), 'The Oxford Book of Ballads' (1910), 'The Oxford Book of Victorian Verse' (1912), 'On the Art of Writing' (1916), 'Studies in Literature' (1918, 1922), 'On the Art of Reading' (1920), 'The Oxford Book of English Prose' (1925). He wrote the conclusion of Stevenson's unfinished 'St. Ives' (chs. 31 to the end) in 1899. His collected poems were published in 1929.

Quilp, DANIEL and MRS., characters in Dickens's 'The Old Curiosity Shop' (q.v.).

Quin, JAMES (1693–1766), an actor who first came into note by his impersonation of Bajazet in Rowe's 'Tamerlane' (q.v.). He took leading parts in tragedy at Drury Lane, Lincoln's Inn Fields, and Covent Garden. He was the last of the old school of actors, which gave place to that of Garrick. Smollett introduces him in 'Humphry Clinker' (q.v.).

Quinapalus, a character invented by the clown in Shakespeare's 'Twelfth Night' (q.v.) (I. v), as authority for a saying of his own.

Quince, PETER, in Shakespeare's 'A Midsummer Night's Dream' (q.v.), a carpenter, the stage-manager of the interlude 'Pyramus and Thisbe'.

QUINTILIAN (MARCUS FABIUS QUINTILIANUS) (c. A.D. 35–c. 100), a great Roman rhetorician. Pliny the younger was among his pupils, and he was given the title of consul by Domitian. His great work was the 'De Institutione Oratoria', the tenth book of which contains a history of Greek and Roman literature. Milton in one of his sonnets

refers to 'Those rugged names ... that would have made Quintilian stare and gasp'.

Quinze Joyes de Mariage, Les, a famous 15th-cent. French satire on women, doubtfully attributed to Antoine de la Salle (1388–c. 1470), translated into English as the 'Fifteen Comforts of Matrimony' (1682).

Quirīnus, originally the local deity (perhaps the war god) of the Sabine community settled on the Quirinal hill. He became one of the state gods of Rome and was later identified with Romulus, the founder of the city. The derivation from Cures, the name of a Sabine town (Lewis and Short), is now questioned.

Quirk, Gammon, and Snap, a firm of scoundrelly solicitors in Warren's 'Ten Thousand a Year' (see *Warren, S.*).

Quisling, VIDKUN, leader of the Norwegian Nazi party, formed on 9 April 1940, under German direction, a puppet Government of Norway. He was sentenced to death in Sept. 1945. The name *quisling* has been popularly adopted to signify a traitor to the cause of his country's freedom.

Quiteria, see *Camacho.*

Quixote, see *Don Quixote.*

Quorum (Latin, 'of whom'), originally certain justices of the peace, usually of eminent learning or ability, whose presence is necessary to constitute a bench. 'Justice of the peace and *coram*', Slender calls Shallow in Shakespeare's 'The Merry Wives of Windsor' (q.v.) (I. i). Hence a fixed number of any body whose presence is necessary for the valid transaction of business.

Quos ego—, from Virgil's 'Aeneid', i. 139, where Neptune is threatening the rebellious winds with punishment, but breaks off at the words 'Whom I—', in an eloquent aposiopesis. The words are proverbial for a threat of punishment.

Quraysh, see *Koraysh.*

R

Ra, in Egyptian mythology, the sun-god and supreme deity, often identified with Horus, and generally represented as a hawk. The ancient kings of Egypt, at least from the time of the 5th dynasty (c. 2750 B.C.), were regarded as his sons. His cult was in a measure superseded by that of Ammon, under the Theban Pharaohs, to be temporarily restored to supremacy under Amenhotep IV (Akhnaton).

Rab and his Friends, see *Brown (Dr. J.).*

Rabbi Ben Ezra, a poem by R. Browning (q.v.) included in 'Dramatis Personae' (q.v.).

It is an exposition of the author's religious philosophy through the mouth of a learned Jew. The soul is immortal; life is but the fashioning of the pot for the Master's hand.

RABELAIS, FRANÇOIS (1494?–1553), French humanist, satirist, and physician, was born near Chinon in Touraine, where his father was a well-to-do lawyer. He was a Franciscan friar at Fontenay-le-Comte in Poitou in 1520 and probably earlier, but, being persecuted there for his addiction to the study of Greek, became a monk at the Benedictine abbey of Maillezais, also in Poitou.

This he left, visited various provincial universities, and studied medicine at Paris, giving up the Benedictine dress. He took his medical degrees at Montpellier, and practised and lectured on medicine at Lyons, at that time a great intellectual centre. He thrice visited Rome as physician to his friend and protector, Cardinal Jean du Bellay (1534, 1535–6, and 1548–50), and was at Turin in 1540–1 with the cardinal's brother, Guillaume. In the course of his second visit to Rome he obtained from Paul III absolution for his 'apostasy'. In 1550 he was appointed to two livings, Meudon near Paris and Jambet near Le Mans, but appears to have discharged personally the duties of neither. He published 'Pantagruel' (q.v.) in 1532, 'Gargantua' (q.v.) in 1534, the 'Third Book' in 1546, part of the 'Fourth Book' in 1548, and the whole in 1552. The authenticity of the 'Fifth Book' is questionable; it certainly contains work by other hands and is not in a form which Rabelais intended for publication. The first sixteen chapters of it, under the title of 'L'Isle sonnante', appeared in 1562, after his death; the whole book in 1564.

Rabelais was held in high regard in his own day as an eminent physician, as a pioneer of humanism and enlightenment, and as the author of an entertaining book. His courageous attacks on obscurantism brought on him the enmity of the Sorbonne and the Paris Parliament, and, in spite of the protection of Francis I, he was obliged repeatedly to withdraw from France (to Rome, as stated above, and in 1546–7 to Metz).

The first three books of his chief work were translated into English by Urquhart (q.v., two being published in 1653, the third in 1693); the last two by Motteux (q.v.) in 1693–4. There is a modern translation with useful notes by W. F. Smith (1893, 1934). The whole five books are generally numbered consecutively, 'Gargantua' being reckoned the first, 'Pantagruel' the second.

Rachel (ÉLISA FÉLIX) (1821–58), a celebrated French actress, of Jewish descent, whose finest parts were in the tragedies of Racine and Corneille. There is a poem by M. Arnold (q.v.) on her last illness.

RACINE, JEAN (1639–99), French dramatic poet, spent some years of his youth among the Jansenists of Port-Royal (with whom he subsequently quarrelled); then was introduced to the fashionable world of the Paris of Louis XIV, and acquired the friendship of Molière, La Fontaine, and Boileau. As a tragedian, he presented his characters in a more human and natural form than did Corneille; they are governed more by their passions, less by their wills. He gave them classical names, but what he depicted were the loves, the failings, and the intrigues of the society around him. His tragedies divide themselves into three groups, those whose subjects are taken from Euripides: 'Andromaque' (1667), 'Iphigénie' (1674), and

'Phèdre' (1677); from history: 'Britannicus' (1669), 'Bérénice' (1670), 'Mithridate' (1673); from the Scriptures: 'Esther' (1689) and 'Athalie '(1691). 'Phèdre' and 'Athalie' were his greatest works. Racine also wrote one comedy, 'Les Plaideurs' (1668).

Radcliffe, JOHN (1650–1714), physician, who attended William III, Queen Mary, and Queen Anne. He left property from which the Radcliffe Library, Infirmary, and Observatory at Oxford were built.

RADCLIFFE, MRS. ANN (1764–1823), *née* Ward, a novelist whose fame rests on her 'Romance of the Forest'(1791), 'The Mysteries of Udolpho' (q.v., 1794), and 'The Italian' (1797, a romance of the Inquisition). She also wrote 'A Sicilian Romance' (1790) and 'An Italian Romance'(1791). Mrs. Radcliffe's method, which found a number of imitators, was to arouse terror and curiosity by events apparently supernatural, but afterwards explained by natural means.

'Radical Jack', the first earl of Durham (1792–1840). See *Durham Report*.

Radigund, in Spenser's 'Faerie Queene', v. iv–vii, a queen of the Amazons, who subdues Artegall, and forces him to spin flax and tow until he is rescued by Britomart.

Radnor, VICTOR, NATALIA, and NESTA VICTORIA, characters in Meredith's 'One of our Conquerors' (q.v.).

Raeburn, SIR HENRY (1756–1823), a Scottish portrait-painter, sometimes called the 'Scottish Reynolds', who settled in Edinburgh in 1787 and during thirty years painted portraits of a large number of his contemporaries. In the estimation of many good critics, the greatest portrait-painter Britain ever produced.

Rag Fair, see *Rosemary Lane*.

Rages, RHAGES or RHAGAE (modern *Rayy*), a great city of Media, on the southern slope of the hills bordering the southern shore of the Caspian Sea. It was more than once destroyed, first by earthquake, then in the Parthian wars, and finally by the Tartars (1221). It is mentioned in the Book of Tobit (q.v.). RHAGES POTTERY is fine glazed Persian pottery of the 10th–12th cents., datable by the occurrence of examples in the ruins of Rhages.

Ragman Roll, see *Roll*.

Ragnar Lodbrog, The Death-Song of, an old Icelandic poem translated by T. Percy (q.v.), in his 'Five Pieces of Runic Poetry'. Its publication exerted a great literary influence and stimulated the study in England of ancient Norse writings. The hero was a Norse viking who, according to legend, invaded England in the 8th cent.

Ragnarök, in Scandinavian mythology, the day of the great battle between the gods and the powers of evil, when both are destroyed and the old order and most of the old gods disappear, to be replaced by another and a happier scheme of things. Vidar and Vali survive, and Balder and Hödr return from the nether world.

Ragnel, a devil in medieval mystery plays.

Rahere (*d.* 1144), born in the reign of William the Conqueror, followed a church career and became prebendary of St. Paul's in 1111. Legend attributes to him the position of King's jester to Henry I, before his conversion to clerical life. He made a pilgrimage to Rome, where, while convalescent from a fever, he made a vow to build a hospital and church in honour of St. Bartholomew. He began to build St. Bartholomew's Hospital in London in 1123 on land granted for the purpose by Henry I. He is also said to have founded St. Bartholomew's Church, Smithfield, in which a fine monument to him is still to be seen.

Rahu, in Hindu mythology, the demon who pursues the sun and moon, occasionally catches them, and causes their eclipses.

Raikes, JACK, a character in Meredith's 'Evan Harrington' (q.v.).

Rakshas or RAKSHASAS, in Hindu belief, evil demons, who in hideous shape haunt cemeteries and devour men, or ensnare them by assuming beautiful forms.

RALEGH, SIR WALTER (1552?–1618), son of a Devonshire gentleman, was born at Hayes Barton in South Devon, and educated at Oriel College, Oxford. He served in the Huguenot army at Jarnac and Moncontour (1569), and was engaged in various voyages of discovery and expeditions to the American continent, and in the plantation of Munster. He obtained the favour of Queen Elizabeth, but forfeited it and was committed to the Tower (1592) on account of his relations with Elizabeth Throgmorton, whom he subsequently married. After a most unfair trial he was condemned to death, respited, and again sent to the Tower in 1603 on a charge of conspiring against James I. He lived there with his wife and son until 1616, when he was permitted to undertake an expedition to the Orinoco in search of gold, in the course of which the Spanish settlement of San Tomás was burnt. On the failure of the expedition, and at the demand of the Spanish ambassador, Ralegh was arrested, and executed at Westminster on 29 Oct. 1618; his remains were buried in St. Margaret's, Westminster. Much of his poetry is lost. About thirty short pieces survive, the principal of which is a fragment of a long elegy entitled 'Cynthia, the Lady of the Sea', expressing devotion to Elizabeth. Another notable poem is his introductory sonnet to the 'Faerie Queene'—'Methought I saw the grave where Laura lay'. The well-known short pieces 'The Lie' and 'The Pilgrimage' were probably written during his imprisonments, and the lines found in his Bible in the Gate-house at Westminster,

beginning 'Even such is time', on the night before his execution. In prose he published 'A Report of the Truth of the Fight about the Isles of the Azores' (1591), which contains a narrative of the famous encounter of Sir Richard Grenville with the Spanish fleet; and 'The Discovery of the Empyre of Guiana' (1596), giving an account of his first expedition to those parts in 1595. His 'History of the World' (1614) was designed for Prince Henry, who showed sympathy with Ralegh and visited him in the Tower. One passage from it is famous as a specimen of English prose ('Oxford Book of English Prose', No. 88). The first volume, which alone was completed, deals with the history of the Jews, early Egyptian history and Greek mythology, and Greek and Roman times down to 130 B.C. His object, according to his preface, is to show God's judgement on the wicked. In addition he wrote many essays on political subjects, some of which were published after his death. Though Ralegh spelt his name in several different ways, he never used the common modern form 'Raleigh'. After 1584 he used only the form 'Ralegh'. His pronunciation of the name is shown by the fact that in early life he often wrote it 'Rauley'. [C.H.E.L.] Ralegh figures as the 'Shepheard of the Sea' in Spenser's 'Colin Clouts come home againe' (q.v.). He is introduced in Scott's 'Kenilworth' (q.v.), where is told the story of his laying down his cloak in a muddy spot at Greenwich for the queen to step on.

RALEIGH, SIR WALTER (1861–1922), professor of English literature at Oxford from 1904. Among his works are lives of Milton (1900), Wordsworth (1903), Shakespeare (1907); 'Six Essays on Johnson' (1910), 'Some Authors' (posthumous, 1923), and the first volume of the official 'War in the Air' (1922).

Ralph Roister Doister, the earliest known English comedy, by Udall (q.v.), probably written about 1553 and printed about 1567, and perhaps played by Westminster boys while Udall was headmaster of that school. The play, in short rhymed doggerel, represents the courting of the widow Christian Custance, who is betrothed to Gawin Goodluck, an absent merchant, by Roister, a swaggering simpleton, instigated thereto by the mischievous Matthew Merygreek. Roister is repulsed and beaten by Custance and her maids; and Goodluck, after being deceived by false reports, is reconciled to her. The play shows similarity to the comedies of Plautus and Terence.

Ralph the Rover, see *Inchcape Rock*.

Ralpho, the squire in Butler's 'Hudibras' (q.v.).

Ram, THE, or ARIES, one of the zodiacal constellations, and the zodiacal sign entered by the sun on 21 March. According to mythology the constellation represents the ram which carried Phrixus and Helle on its back and whose golden fleece was carried off by the Argonauts (q.v.) from Colchis.

Ram Alley, now Mitre Court, Fleet Street (Wheatley and Cunningham), was noted for its cooks' shops and public-houses, and 'a place of no great reputation' (Strype). Its cooks' shops are referred to in Massinger's 'A New Way to pay Old Debts', Ben Jonson's 'The Staple of News' (qq.v.), etc.

Rāma, see *Rāmāyana*.

Ramadan, one of the months of the Arabian year, during which Muslims, according to the precept of the Koran, fast from sunrise to sunset.

Rāmāyana, The, one of the two great Hindu epic poems, the other being the 'Mahābhārata' (q.v.), originally composed, it is thought, not later than 500 B.C.: the 'Rāmāyana' as we have it dates probably from about 300 B.C. Its main subject is the war waged by Rama, the son of King Dasaratha of Ayodha and an impersonation of Vishnu (q.v.), against the Giant Rāvan, the fierce king of Lanka or Ceylon and the dread enemy of gods and men, who carries off Rama's wife, Sita, and whom Rama slays.

Rambler, The, a periodical in 208 numbers issued by S. Johnson (q.v.) from 20 Mar. 1749/50 to 14 Mar. 1751/52.

The contents are essays on all kinds of subjects, character-studies, allegories, criticism, etc., and were, with the exception of five, all written by Johnson himself. Their object was the instruction of his readers in wisdom or piety, and at the same time the refinement of the English language. The contributors of the remaining numbers were Richardson (q.v.), Elizabeth Carter (q.v.), Mrs. Chapone (q.v.), and Catherine Talbot (1720–70).

'The Rambler' was also the name of a 19th-cent. periodical directed successively by J. H. Newman and Lord Acton (qq.v.), and converted under the latter's management into 'The Home and Foreign Review' (see *Acton*).

Rambouillet, CATHERINE DE VIVONNE-PISANI, *Marquise de* (1588–1665), a distinguished Frenchwoman who presided over a salon in her house, the Hôtel de Rambouillet, near the Louvre, in which the most eminent writers and wits of her day met and conversed. Among these were La Rochefoucauld, Mlle de Scudéry, Saint-Évremond, Corneille, and Mme de Sévigné. The delicacy of thought and expression aimed at in this and similar assemblies developed into a spirit of pedantry and affectation, which was ridiculed by Molière in 'Les Précieuses ridicules'. Nevertheless, the Hôtel de Rambouillet helped to purify the language and introduce greater refinement in manners.

Ramillie or RAMILLIES **Wig,** a wig having a long plait behind with a bow at top and bottom, from Ramillies in Belgium, the scene of Marlborough's victory in 1706.

Raminagrobis, an old French word meaning 'big purring cat'. Rabelais applied it satirically to an ancient French poet, probably Jean le Maire de Belges (15th cent.), whom Panurge consults on the subject of his proposed marriage. La Fontaine uses it ('Fables', vii. 16) as the name of the cat who, being chosen as an umpire between the rabbit and the weasel, eats them both.

Ramorny, SIR JOHN, a character in Scott's 'The Fair Maid of Perth' (q.v.).

RAMSAY, ALLAN (1686–1758), a Scottish poet, and an Edinburgh wig-maker and subsequently bookseller by trade. He wrote elegies, partly pathetic, partly humorous, and satires, and published a collection of these in 1721. In 1724–32 he issued the 'Tea-table Miscellany', and in 1724 'The Evergreen', collections of old Scottish and English songs, with some by himself and contemporary poets, important as contributing to the revival of vernacular Scottish poetry. Ramsay's pastoral drama, 'The Gentle Shepherd', his principal work, appeared in 1725. He also composed two additional cantos to 'Christis Kirk on the Green' (q.v.).

Ramsay, MARGARET, a character in Scott's 'The Fortunes of Nigel' (q.v.).

RAMUS, PETRUS, latinized form of Pierre la Ramée (1515–72), a French logician and holder of a royal professorship in 1551, was famous as an opponent of the Aristotelian logic. The Ramist doctrine, as expounded in his 'Dialectica', was introduced into England in the latter part of the 16th cent. by Andrew Melville and William Temple, and obtained a wide currency in the universities, notably at Cambridge. Ramus fell a victim to the massacre of St. Bartholomew.

Ran, in Scandinavian mythology, the wife of Aegir, the cruel goddess of the sea, the cause of shipwrecks and the dread of mariners.

Randolph, LORD, a character in Home's 'Douglas' (q.v.).

RANDOLPH, THOMAS (1605–35,) was educated at Westminster School and Trinity College, Cambridge, and became a fellow of Trinity. He made the acquaintance of Ben Jonson and, after becoming famous in Cambridge as a writer of English and Latin verse, went to London in 1632. His 'Aristippus, or the Joviall Philosopher', an early dramatic sketch, is an amusing debate on the rival merits of ale and sack (printed in 1630). His principal plays are 'Amyntas', a pastoral comedy, and 'The Muse's Looking-Glasse' (q.v.), printed in 1638; and 'Hey for Honesty' (q.v.), printed in 1651. He was also the author of a pleasant eclogue included in 'Annalia Dubrensia', verses in celebration of Captain Dover's 'Cotswold Games' (q.v.). His plays and poems were edited by W. C. Hazlitt in 1875.

RANDS, WILLIAM BRIGHTY (1823–82), 'the laureate of the nursery', who wrote sometimes under the pseudonymns Henry Holbeach and Matthew Browne. After much struggle with poverty he became a reporter in the House of Commons. He was especially esteemed for his poems and fairy tales for children. See *Lilliput Levée*.

Ranelagh Gardens, Chelsea, a place of public amusement opened in 1742 in the grounds of the earl of Ranelagh. It had a famous Rotunda, 150 feet in diameter, with an orchestra in the centre and boxes round it, where people promenaded. The gardens were closed in 1804. They now form part of Chelsea Hospital Gardens, between Church Row and the river, to the east of the hospital (Wheatley and Cunningham). The modern 'Ranelagh' is at Barn Elms, a club where polo and other games are played.

Ranger, (1) a rakish man of fashion in 'Love in a Wood' by Wycherley (q.v.); (2) a character in Hoadly's 'The Suspicious Husband' (q.v.).

RANKE, LEOPOLD VON (1795–1886), a celebrated German historian. His history of 'The Popes of Rome' (1834–6) is, among his numerous works, that best known in England. He began writing a 'History of the World' when he was over 80 and got down to the 12th cent. A.D. before his death.

Ranks of Tuscany, in Macaulay's 'Lays of Ancient Rome' ('Horatius', lx), the opposing side moved to applause:

> And even the ranks of Tuscany
> Could scarce forbear to cheer.

Ranz-des-vaches, the melodies peculiar to Swiss herdsmen, usually played on an Alpine horn. The origin and meaning of the word *ranz* (Swiss dialect of Fribourg) is uncertain.

Rape of the Lock, The, a poem by Pope (q.v.), in two cantos, published in Lintot's 'Miscellany' in 1712; subsequently enlarged to five cantos and thus published in 1714.

Lord Petre having forcibly cut off a lock of Miss Arabella Fermor's hair, the incident gave rise to a quarrel between the families. With the idea of allaying this, Pope treated the subject in a playful mock-heroic poem, on the model of Boileau's 'Le Lutrin'. He presents Belinda at her toilet, a game of ombre, the snipping of the lock while Belinda sips her coffee, the wrath of Belinda and her demand that the lock be restored, the final wafting of the lock, as a new star, to adorn the skies. The poem was published in its original form with Miss Fermor's permission. Pope then expanded the sketch by introducing the machinery of sylphs and gnomes, and its renewed publication gave offence to the lady, who thought that her affairs had been sufficiently brought before the public.

Raphael, one of the archangels (see *Angel*). In the 'Book of Tobit' (q.v.) he accompanies and instructs Tobias on his journey. Milton makes him the seraph, 'the sociable Spirit', also (alas!) 'the affable Archangel', sent to Paradise to converse with Adam ('Paradise Lost' (q.v.), v. 221, vi. 41).

Raphael (1483–1520), Italian painter. RAFFAELLO SANZIO, son of the painter Giovanni Santi, was born at Urbino. He worked in Perugino's studio and then in Florence. In 1509 he was painting the Stanze in the Vatican; the 'School of Athens' and the 'Disputà' in the Stanza della Segnatura exemplify to perfection the art of the High Renaissance. He succeeded Bramante as architect of St. Peter's. Seven of his cartoons for tapestries for the Sistine Chapel were bought by Charles I (now on loan to the Victoria and Albert Museum). He employed assistants to cope with the great number of commissions he received, among them the decoration of the Farnesina, Rome, and many portraits and Madonnas.

Raphael, DON, see *Don Raphael and Ambrose Lamela*.

RASHDALL, THE VERY REVD. HASTINGS (1858–1924), philosopher, theologian, and historian, educated at Harrow and New College, Oxford. His philosophical works include: 'The Theory of Good and Evil' (1907) and 'The Idea of Atonement in Christian Theology' (1919). 'The Universities of Europe in the Middle Ages' (1895, a new edition, ed. Powicke and Emden, 1935) is a standard work.

RASPE, RUDOLPH ERICH, see *Munchausen*.

Rasselas, Prince of Abissinia, The History of, a didactic romance by S. Johnson (q.v.), published in 1759.

It was composed in the evenings of a week to defray the expenses of the funeral of Johnson's mother and to pay her debts. It is an essay on the 'choice of life' and consists mainly of dissertations strung on a thin thread of story. Rasselas, a son of the emperor of Abyssinia, weary of the joys of the 'happy valley', where the inhabitants know only 'the soft vicissitudes of pleasure and repose', escapes to Egypt, accompanied by his sister Nekayah and the much-travelled old philosopher Imlac. Here they study the various conditions of men's lives, and, after a few incidents of no great interest, return to Abyssinia. The charm of the work lies in the wisdom, humanity, and melancholy of the episodes and disquisitions, enlivened with a few gleams of humour. Rasselas thinks that 'surely happiness is somewhere to be found'; but he finds it nowhere. The teachers of philosophy are unable to support their own misfortunes. The hermit admits that the solitary life will be certainly miserable, but not certainly devout. The prosperous man lives in terror of the Bashaw, and the Bashaw of the Sultan. The Sultan is subject to the torments of suspicion. Virtue can afford only quietness of conscience and a steady prospect of a happier state. The monks of St. Antony alone endure without complaint a life, not of uniform delight, but of uniform hardship.

Rastignac, EUGÈNE DE, one of the principal characters drawn by Balzac (q.v.). He figures intermittently throughout the series of the 'Scènes de la Vie Parisienne', but is especially analysed in 'Le Père Goriot'. He starts as a humble student, and with the help of his female admirers achieves success in the corrupt society of the Paris of the day.

Rat, the Cat, and Lovel the dog, THE, in the political rhyme:

The Rat, the Cat, and Lovel the dog
Rule all England under the Hog,

refers to three adherents of Richard III: Sir Richard Ratcliffe (killed at Bosworth, 1485), Sir John Catesby (d. 1486), and Francis, first Viscount Lovell (1454–88?; his skeleton was found in a vault, where he had evidently starved to death). The Hog is a reference to the boar that figured as one of the supporters of the royal arms.

Ratcliffe, JAMES, a character in Scott's 'The Heart of Midlothian' (q.v.); a notorious thief who ingratiates himself with the magistrates and becomes a warder in the Tolbooth.

Ratcliffe Highway, see *Wapping*.

Ratsey, GAMALIEL, a Northamptonshire highwayman, hanged at Bedford in 1605, and frequently mentioned in 17th-cent. literature.

Rattlin, JACK, a character in Smollett's 'Roderick Random' (q.v.).

Rattlin the Reefer, a novel of the sea by Edward Howard (d. 1841)—according to Prof. Elton ('Survey') the Hon. Edward George Greville Howard—a shipmate of Capt. Marryat, published in 1836. The book was announced as edited by the author of 'Peter Simple' and was in consequence wrongly attributed to Marryat.

The story resembles the sea-yarns of Marryat, but without his high spirits. We have the bullying captain; the adventures, hoaxes, and horse-play; and some good fighting in the West Indies. But the general atmosphere is more serious.

Rauf Coilyear, a rhymed poem of the Charlemagne cycle, in stanzas of thirteen lines, of which a copy survives, printed in Scotland in 1572.

The poem, which is quaint and humorous, recounts how Charles, lost and benighted, takes refuge in the hut of Rauf, a plain-spoken and self-willed charcoal-burner, who treats him hospitably but with excessive freedom.

Ravaillac, FRANÇOIS (c. 1578–1610), the assassin of Henry IV of France.

Ravel, MAURICE (1875–1937), one of the most prominent French composers of his time.

The Raven, a poem by Poe (q.v.).

Ravenshoe, a novel by H. Kingsley (q.v.), published in 1861.

The Ravenshoes are a wealthy Roman Catholic family, but Charles, the second son of Densil Ravenshoe and a Protestant mother, is brought up in his mother's religion. On Densil's death, Father Mackworth, the confessor of the family, produces evidence that Charles is not Densil's son, as had been supposed, but the son of Densil's illegitimate half-brother, the keeper, the children having been exchanged when babies. But the Jesuit keeps back what he also knows, that this half-brother was not illegitimate and that Charles is the true heir of the estate. Other blows fall on Charles; for his old school-friend, Lord Welter, runs off with the woman whom Charles loves; and it is discovered that Welter has also seduced Ellen, the keeper's daughter, Charles's sister. Disinherited, disgraced, and broken-hearted, Charles hides himself from the world and enlists. One of the few survivors of Balaclava, he returns to England, shattered in mind and body, and is on the point of suicide when he is discovered by his friends. The true facts have now come to light, the death of Charles's elder brother solves the difficulties of the succession, and Charles is tardily restored to his rightful position.

Ravenswood, EDGAR, MASTER OF, the hero of Scott's 'The Bride of Lammermoor' (q.v.).

RAWLINSON, GEORGE (1812–1902), educated at Trinity College, Oxford, and a fellow of Exeter College, was Camden professor of ancient history, 1861–89. He was author of 'The History of Herodotus' (1858–60), a translation accompanied by valuable historical and ethnological notes, for which the discoveries of his brother, Sir Henry Rawlinson, the Assyriologist, provided much material. He also published histories of the seven great monarchies of the Eastern world (1862–76), and other kindred works. He wrote a life of his brother, which appeared in 1908.

Rawlinson, SIR HENRY CRESWICKE (1810–95), who held various important positions in the service of the East India Company, is remembered chiefly as an Assyriologist. He deciphered the great Behistun Inscription (q.v.) in 1846.

Rawlinson, THOMAS (1681–1725), educated at Eton and St. John's College, Oxford, a book-collector, whose manuscripts are in the Bodleian Library. He was satirized by Addison in the 'Tatler' (No. 158) as 'Tom Folio'.

RAY, JOHN (1627–1705), one of England's greatest naturalists. He was pre-eminently a botanist (he originated the division of plants into monocotyledons and dicotyledons), but also took up the unfinished zoological work of his friend Francis Willughby. In later life he devoted himself especially to the study of insects. His 'Historia Plantarum' was published in 1686–1704. His work was not limited to these fields: he published 'A Collection of English Proverbs' in 1670, and was keenly interested in philology.

READ, SIR HERBERT (1893–   ), poet and critic of art and literature, born in Yorkshire and educated at Halifax and Leeds University. After distinguished war service he was Assistant Keeper at the Victoria and Albert Museum, 1922–31, and professor of fine art at Edinburgh, 1931–3. His poetry includes 'Naked Warriors' (1919; a collection of war poems), 'Collected Poems 1913–25' (1926), 'The End of a War' (1933), 'Poems 1914–34' (1935), and 'Collected Poems' (1946, 2nd ed. 1953). 'In Retreat' (1925) and 'Ambush' (1930) are prose records of trench warfare. His critical writing includes 'English Prose Style' (1928), 'Form in Modern Poetry' (1932), 'Art and Industry' (1934), 'Education through Art' (1943), and 'The True Voice of Feeling' (1953). 'The Innocent Eye' (1933) and 'Annals of Innocence and Experience' (1940; enlarged edn., including 'The Innocent Eye' and 'In Retreat', 1946) are autobiographical. He has also written an allegorical novel, 'The Green Child' (1935).

READE, CHARLES (1814–84), born at Ipsden in Oxfordshire, a demy[1] and subsequently a fellow of Magdalen College, Oxford, and entered Lincoln's Inn. He was an ardent reformer of abuses, but appears to have been cantankerous and perverse. He began his literary career as a dramatist, his most successful play 'Masks and Faces' appearing at the Haymarket in 1852. This he turned into a novel with the title 'Peg Woffington' (q.v.), published in 1853. The pleasant romance 'Christie Johnstone' and the propagandist novel 'It is Never too Late to Mend' (qq.v.) appeared also in 1853, and were followed by 'The Course of True Love never did run Smooth' (1857), 'The Autobiography of a Thief' and 'Jack of all Trades' (1858), stories of strange avocations, in the manner of Defoe; 'Love me Little, Love me Long' (1859); 'The Cloister and the Hearth' (q.v., 1861), Reade's greatest work; 'Hard Cash' (q.v., 1863), 'Griffith Gaunt' (q.v., 1866), 'Foul Play' (q.v., 1869); 'Put Yourself in his Place' (1870), dealing with the form of terrorism organized by trade unions known as 'rattening'; 'A Terrible Temptation' (q.v., 1871), 'The Wandering Heir', suggested by the Tichborne trial (published in 'The Graphic', 1872), 'A Hero and a Martyr' (1874), 'A Woman Hater' (1874). Reade also wrote 'The Courier of Lyons' (1854), the well-known melodrama frequently produced by Sir H. Irving under the name of 'The Lyons Mail'. His play 'Drink' (1879) was based on Zola's 'L'Assommoir'.

Reade was an admirable story-teller. He relied greatly on documentary information, which he accumulated in great ledgers in his well-known house in Albert Terrace (immediately opposite Sloane Street). There is a description of his methods in 'A Terrible Temptation'.

[1] *Demy*, a foundation scholar at Magdalen College, Oxford, so called because a demy's allowance or 'commons' was formerly half that of a fellow.

READE, WILLIAM WINWOOD (1838–75), traveller, novelist, and controversialist, nephew of Charles Reade (q.v.). He made exploratory voyages in West and South-West Africa in 1861 and 1869, and was special correspondent of 'The Times' in the Ashanti War. He published 'Savage Africa' in 1863 and 'The African Sketch-book' in 1873. 'The Martyrdom of Man' (1872 and many subsequent editions) contains his criticism of religious beliefs.

Ready-to-Halt, MR., in Bunyan's 'Pilgrim's Progress', a pilgrim who follows Mr. Greatheart, though upon crutches. When he comes to the land of Beulah and is about to cross the river, he bequeaths his crutches to his son, for he sees chariots and horses ready to carry him into the City.

Realism, in scholastic philosophy, the doctrine that attributes objective or absolute existence to universals, of which Thomas Aquinas (q.v.) was the chief exponent. Duns Scotus (q.v.) also maintained realism in an extreme form. Also in the arts a loosely used term meaning truth to the observed facts of life (especially when they are gloomy).

Reason, GODDESS OF, a divinity invented by the National Convention during the French Revolution, personated by Mlle Candeille of the Opera, who was borne in procession to Notre Dame and there made the object of a mock-worship (1793). There were other 'Goddesses of Reason' (including Mme Momoro) and the worship was conducted at several churches.

Reasonableness of Christianity, see *Essay concerning Human Understanding.*

Rebecca, (1) the name given (in allusion to Gen. xxiv. 60) to the leader, in woman's attire, of the rioters who demolished toll-gates in S. Wales in 1843–4; (2) a character in Scott's 'Ivanhoe' (q.v.).

Rebecca and Rowena, *a Romance upon Romance, by Mr. Michael Angelo Titmarsh,* a humorous sequel to Scott's 'Ivanhoe' (q.v.), by Thackeray (q.v.), published in 1850.

Ivanhoe soon wearies of life with his wife, the Lady Rowena, who rules the roost and bores everybody with stories of Edward the Confessor; he goes off to join King Richard in France. He is present when the latter is killed at the siege of Chalus, and is himself left for dead on the field. Wamba rather precipitately carries home the news to Rowena, who promptly marries Athelstane, in whom she finds a congenial mate. Ivanhoe recovers, returns to find Rowena besieged in her castle, and Athelstane dead in the siege. Rowena dies, making Ivanhoe promise he will 'never marry a Jewess'. After many adventures Ivanhoe rescues Rebecca, who has turned Christian and been imprisoned by old Isaac, and marries her.

Récamier, MME (1777–1849), a French-woman famous for her beauty and wit, whose salon during the Restoration was frequented by the most brilliant society of the day, including Chateaubriand.

Rechabite, one of a Jewish family descended from Jonadab, son of Rechab, who refused to drink wine or live in houses (see Jer. xxxv). Hence one who abstains from intoxicating liquors, and specifically a member of the Independent Order of Rechabites, a benefit society founded in 1835; or a dweller in tents. [OED.]

Recluse, The, see *Excursion.*

Recollect or RECOLLET, a member of the Observantine (q.v.) branch of the Franciscan (q.v.) order, which originated in Spain in the end of the 15th cent. and was so named 'from the detachment from creatures and recollection in God which the founders aimed at' (Catholic Dictionary).

Record Office, PUBLIC: before the construction of the present office in Fetter Lane, the national records were kept in the Tower of London and Rolls House (q.v.). Among important keepers of the records may be mentioned Selden and Prynne (qq.v.), Samuel Lysons the antiquary (1803), and Sir F. Palgrave (q.v.).

Recovery, see *Feet of Fines.*

Recruiting Officer, The, a comedy by Farquhar (q.v.), produced in 1706.

It deals with the humours of recruiting in a country town, with a vividness suggesting that the author drew on his own experience. The plot is slender; it presents Capt. Plume making love to the women in order to secure their followers as recruits; Kite, his resourceful sergeant, employing his wiles and assuming the character of an astrologer, for the same purpose; while Sylvia, daughter of Justice Ballance, who is in love with Plume, but has promised not to marry him without her father's consent, runs away from home disguised as a man, gets herself arrested for scandalous conduct, is brought before her father, and by him delivered over to Capt. Plume, as a recruit. Capt. Brazen, a rival recruiting officer, who boasts of battles and friends in every quarter of the globe, endeavours to marry the rich Melinda, but finds himself fobbed off with her maid.

Red Badge of Courage, The, by Stephen Crane (q.v.), published in 1895, is the author's best-known work and won him immediate recognition in England as well as America. It is a study of an inexperienced soldier's reactions to the ordeal of battle during the American Civil War. Determined to be a hero, he suddenly turns coward; then recovers himself and behaves as the fighter he had wished to be.

Red Book of Hergest, a Welsh manuscript of the end of the 14th cent., containing the 'Mabinogion' (q.v.), chronicles, and poems.

Red Chamber Dream, The, the *Hung-lou*

Mêng (formerly *Shih-t'ou Chi*), an 18th-cent. Chinese novel by Ts'ao Chan. The reputation of the book, which still enjoys the highest popularity in China, may be judged from a song current among Peking literati in the late 19th cent.

> If one can't open his talk with a theme
> Culled from the Red Chamber Dream,
> Though versed in books of *Odes*,
>   *History* and all the rest
> He can arouse nobody's interest.

It has been used in Western universities as an important text for teaching Chinese, and has been translated into English, French, Italian, German, and Russian, the last being the only complete version of the whole novel. A critical study by Wu Shih-Ch'ang of two annotated manuscripts of the 18th cent., 'On the Red Chamber Dream', was published in 1961.

Red Cotton Night-Cap Country, or, Turf and Towers, a poem by R. Browning (q.v.), published in 1873.

The story is based on a series of dramatic incidents that occurred in France shortly before the poem was written (see Nicoll and Wise, 'Literary Anecdotes', i. 516), and describes the spiritual experiences of Leonce Miranda, a wealthy Spaniard resident in France and devotedly united to Clara Mulhausen, the wife of another man. He makes repeated attempts at suicide under the influence of his conscience, provoked successively by his mother's rebuke, by her death, and by the desire to test the miraculous powers of Christianity. For this last purpose he throws himself from a tower and is killed.

The title of the book arose out of a meeting with Miss Annie Thackeray, to whom it is dedicated, at St. Aubin, which she had nick-named 'White Cotton Night-Cap Country' from its sleepy appearance and the white caps of the women. The change to '*Red* Cotton Night-Cap' is symbolical of the contrast of this with the tale of blood.

Red Cross, THE, the badge (adapted from the Swiss national flag under the Geneva Convention of 1864) of military ambulance and hospital services.

A red cross was the mark made on the doors of infected houses during the London plagues of the 17th cent.

Red Cross Knight, THE, in Bk. 1 of Spenser's 'Faerie Queene' is Saint George, the patron saint of England. He is the 'patron' or champion of Holiness, and represents the Anglican Church. He is separated from Una (the true religion) by the wiles of Archimago (hypocrisy), and is led away by Duessa (the Roman Catholic religion) to the House of Pride. He drinks of an enchanted stream, loses his strength, and is made captive by the giant Orgoglio (pride). Orgoglio is slain by Prince Arthur, and Una leads her knight to the House of Holiness, to learn repentance and be healed. The Knight and Una are finally united.

Red Riding Hood, Little, a popular tale translated from the French of Perrault (q.v.) by Robert Samber (1729?).

Little Red Riding Hood is sent by her mother to take a cake and a pot of butter to her sick grandmother. She loiters on the way, and gets into conversation with a wolf, who learns her errand. He hurries on, eats up the grandmother, takes her place in the bed, and personates her when Red Riding Hood arrives, finally devouring the child. In the German variant the child is resuscitated. Andrew Lang, in his 'Perrault's Popular Tales', discusses the analogies of the story in other legends.

Redbreasts, according to Dickens ('Letters', 18 Apr. 1862), a nickname for the old Bow Street 'runners' or police officers, because they wore red waistcoats.

Redburn, by H. Melville (q.v.), published in 1849, a narrative based on the author's voyage as a cabin boy to Liverpool in 1837.

Redgauntlet, a novel by Sir W. Scott (q.v.), published in 1824.

The story is concerned with an apocryphal return of Prince Charles Edward to England some years after 1745, to try once more his fortunes, an attempt that meets with inglorious failure. Mr. Redgauntlet, otherwise known as Herries of Birrenswork, a fanatical Jacobite, is the leader of the movement, and, to promote its success, kidnaps his young nephew, Darsie Latimer (whose true name is Sir Arthur Darsie Redgauntlet), the head of his house, in order that he may get the support of his followers. Darsie's experiences, and those of his young friend Alan Fairford, who sets out to rescue him, make up the substance of the novel; which also contains the notable characters of Joshua Geddes, the Quaker, the hypocrite Thomas Trumbull, Nanty Ewart the sea-captain, and the blind fiddler 'Wandering Willie'; together with some amusing pictures of old legal Edinburgh (including the grotesque-pathetic figure of Peter Peebles, the crazy litigant). Though not generally accounted one of the three or four greatest Waverley novels, 'Redgauntlet' (written in the last years of Scott's prosperity) contains some of his finest writing, notably in 'Wandering Willie's Tale', a perfect example of the short story.

REDI, FRANCESCO (1626–98), physician to the grand duke of Tuscany and author of a spirited dithyrambic poem, 'Bacco in Toscana' ('Bacchus in Tuscany'), which Leigh Hunt (q.v.) translated. It may have helped to inspire Dryden's 'Alexander's Feast'.

Redlaw, a character in Dickens's 'The Haunted Man' (q.v.).

Redmond O'Neale, a character in Scott's 'Rokeby' (q.v.).

Redworth, THOMAS, a character in G. Meredith's 'Diana of the Crossways' (q.v.).

REEVE, CLARA (1729–1807), a disciple of Horace Walpole as a novelist, published 'The Champion of Virtue, a Gothic Story', her best-known work, in 1777. The title was changed to 'The Old English Baron' in the second edition. It is a romance of the 15th cent., in which a slight element of the supernatural is introduced, in the shape of the ghost of a murdered baron. Clara Reeve also wrote 'The Progress of Romance through Times, Centuries, and Manners' (1785).

Reeve's Tale, The, see *Canterbury Tales.*

Reflections on the Revolution in France, see *Revolution in France.*

Reform Bill, a bill for widening the parliamentary franchise and removing inequalities and abuses in the system of representation, introduced by Lord John Russell (a member of Lord Grey's government) in 1831 and carried after an acute struggle in 1832. The second Reform Bill, giving a more democratic representation, was carried in 1867; the third in 1884. Several more were needed to produce the present state of things.

Reformation, THE, the great religious movement of the 16th cent., having for its object the reform of the doctrines and practices of the Church of Rome, and ending in the establishment of the various Reformed or Protestant churches of central and northwestern Europe. Its principal leaders were Luther in Germany, Calvin in France and Geneva, Zwingli in Switzerland, and Knox in Scotland. The principal points contended for by the reformers were the general use and authority of the Scriptures and the need of justification by faith; while they repudiated the doctrine of transubstantiation, the worship of the Virgin Mary, and the supremacy of the pope.

Reformation, History of the, see *Knox (J.).*

Regan, in Shakespeare's 'King Lear' (q.v.), the second of Lear's daughters.

Regency, THE, in English history, the period (1811–20) during which George, Prince of Wales, acted as Regent, owing to the insanity of George III. The term is used for the neo-classical style of architecture and furniture prevailing from the Regency to the accession of Victoria. In French history it is the period (1715–23) during which Philip, duke of Orleans, acted as Regent, owing to the minority of Louis XV.

Regent Street, London, designed and carried out by John Nash (q.v.) to connect the Regent's residence, Carlton House, with Regent's Park, as authorized by an Act of 1813. It was completely rebuilt in 1922–6.

Regent's Park was laid out, on royal property, in 1814 by John Nash, and named in honour of the Prince Regent. It contains the Zoological Gardens (q.v.), and until recently contained the gardens of the Royal Botanic Society.

Regicide Peace, Letters on a, by E. Burke (q.v.), the first two published in 1796, the third in 1797, the fourth posthumously in the collected works.

By the end of 1796 France had reached a dominating position on the Continent. Her only serious enemies during that year had been England, Austria, and Sardinia, and the Austrian and Sardinian armies had been defeated by Buonaparte in Italy. In Oct. 1796 Pitt sent Lord Malmesbury to Paris to negotiate a peace, but his proposals were scornfully rejected. It was in these circumstances that Burke wrote these letters, which purport to be addressed to a member of parliament. Their theme is the necessity for stamping out the Jacobin government of France, that 'vast tremendous unformed spectre'; the futile and humiliating character of the negotiations undertaken; and the ability of England from an economic standpoint to carry on the struggle. Burke defines Jacobinism as the revolt of the enterprising talents of a country against its property, and their association for the destruction of its pre-existing laws and institutions.

Regillus, Lake, see *Lake Regillus*.

Regiomontanus, JOHANN MÜLLER (1436–76), of Königsberg, from which place he took his Latin name, a German mathematician and astronomer, and bishop of Ratisbon. He was the author of 'Ephemerides', a navigators' almanac, published in 1474, and calculated for the years 1474–1506. His alleged prediction of political convulsions in 1588 (the year of the Armada) is referred to by Bacon in Essay xxxv.

Regiomontium, in imprints, Königsberg.

Regius professorships were first founded by Henry VIII in 1540 at Cambridge (divinity, civil law, physic, Hebrew, and Greek). In 1546 five further Regius professorships were founded at Oxford (divinity, medicine, civil law, Hebrew, and Greek). Regius professorships of modern history at Cambridge, and of ecclesiastical history, modern history, and moral and pastoral theology at Oxford, have since been added.

Regulus, MARCUS ATILIUS, Roman consul in 267 and 256 B.C. He is quoted as an instance of heroic constancy in misfortune. It is related that, having been taken prisoner by the Carthaginians, and kept in captivity for five years, he was allowed to accompany an embassy to Rome on condition that he should return if the Carthaginian proposals were not accepted; that he advised the senate not to consent to peace, and that when, through his influence, the terms proposed were refused, he returned to Carthage and was put to death with torture. (See Horace, 'Odes', III. v, 'Atqui sciebat quae sibi barbarus Tortor pararet'.)

Rehearsal, The, a farcical comedy attributed to George Villiers, 2nd duke of Buckingham, but probably written by him in collaboration with others, among whom are mentioned S. Butler (q.v.) and Martin Clifford, Master of the Charterhouse. It was printed in 1672.

The play is designed to satirize the heroic tragedies of the day, and consists of a series of parodies of passages from these, strung together in an absurd heroic plot. The author of the mock play is evidently a laureate (hence his name 'Bayes'), and D'Avenant (q.v.) was probably intended; but there are also hits at Dryden (q.v.) (particularly his 'Conquest of Granada') and his brothers-in-law, Edward and Robert Howard. Bayes takes two friends, Smith and Johnson, to see the rehearsal of his play, and the absurdity of this work (which includes the two kings of Brentford, entering hand in hand), coupled with the comments of Bayes, his instructions to the actors, and the remarks of Smith and Johnson, makes excellent reading. Prince Prettyman and Prince Volscius are among the characters.

Rehoboam, a name given to a wine-bottle of the largest size, equivalent to eight standard bottles (Saintsbury). C. Brontë in 'Shirley' (q.v., chs. 1 and 17) applies the name to a shovel hat.

REID, FORREST (1875–1947), novelist, educated at Belfast and Christ's College, Cambridge. His works include 'The Brackwells' (1911) and the trilogy 'Uncle Stephen' (1931), 'The Retreat' (1936), and 'Young Tom' (1944).

REID, THOMAS (1710–96), was educated at Marischal College, Aberdeen, where he became professor of moral philosophy in 1751. He was appointed to a similar post at Glasgow University in 1764. He published his 'Inquiry into the Human Mind' in 1764, his essay on the 'Intellectual Powers' in 1785, and that on the 'Active Powers' in 1788. He is the leading representative of the school of common sense, by which phrase he meant not vulgar opinion, but the beliefs common to rational beings as such. His most important doctrine was that belief in an external world is intuitive or immediate. He contested the view of Locke, Berkeley, and Hume (qq.v.) that the objects of knowledge are 'ideas', maintaining that the object of perception, not the unrelated idea, is that which exists.

REID, THOMAS MAYNE (1818–83), novelist; author of 'The Rifle Rangers' (1850), 'The Scalp-Hunters' (1851), 'The Headless Horseman' (1866), etc.

Reign of Terror, THE, or THE TERROR, that period of the first French Revolution from March (or according to another view June) 1793 to July 1794 when the ruling faction ruthlessly executed persons of both sexes and all ages and conditions whom they regarded as obnoxious. It was terminated by the fall of Robespierre. The RED TERROR is the term applied to the last six weeks before 27 July

1794, when 1,366 people were guillotined in Paris alone.

Reim-kennar, one skilled in magic rhymes, a name apparently invented by Scott in his 'The Pirate' (q.v.).

Rejected Addresses, a collection of parodies by James and Horace Smith (q.v.), published in 1812.

On the occasion of the opening of the present Drury Lane Theatre, which replaced Sheridan's building destroyed by fire, the committee in charge advertised for a suitable address to be spoken at the opening. The addresses submitted proved unsatisfactory, and the task of preparing a prologue was finally entrusted to Byron. It was suggested to the two Smiths that they should avail themselves of this opportunity, which they did by composing the imaginary addresses submitted by a number of the popular poets of the day, parodying their style. These include Wordsworth, Byron, Moore, Southey, Coleridge, Crabbe, and Sir Walter Scott. Not least is the parody in prose of Cobbett called 'The Hampshire Farmer's Address'. The remarkable appositeness and humour of the parodies made them extremely popular.

Relapse, The, or Virtue in Danger, a comedy by Vanbrugh (q.v.), produced in 1696.

This was Vanbrugh's first play and was very well received. It is an avowed continuation of 'Love's Last Shift' by Colley Cibber (q.v.), the characters being retained, though more effectively presented. It contains two plots, very slenderly related to each other. Loveless, a reformed libertine, living in the country in mutual affection with his wife, Amanda, is obliged to go with her to London, where he suffers a relapse under the temptation of the beautiful Berinthia, an unscrupulous young widow. Worthy, a former lover of Berinthia, prevails on her to favour Loveless's suit and to persuade Amanda of the infidelity of her husband, in order to promote his own chances of seducing Amanda. But Amanda, though bitterly resenting her husband's faithlessness, remains firm in her virtue.

The second plot is more entertaining. Sir Novelty Fashion, the perfect beau, who has just become (by purchase) Lord Foppington, is about to marry Miss Hoyden, daughter of Sir Tunbelly Clumsey, a country squire, neither father nor daughter having yet seen him. Foppington's younger brother, Young Fashion, having outrun his allowance, appeals to Foppington for assistance, but is repulsed with contumely. To revenge himself and rehabilitate his fortunes, he decides to go down to Sir Tunbelly's house, personate his brother, and marry the heiress. The plot is at first quite successful. Sir Tunbelly welcomes him unsuspectingly, and Miss Hoyden is only too ready to marry him next morning; but Sir Tunbelly will not hear of the marriage for a week. In view of the danger of delay, Fashion bribes the nurse and parson, and a secret marriage is at once celebrated. No

sooner is this done than Foppington arrives, is treated as an impostor, and subjected to indignities, until a neighbour vouches for his identity. Meanwhile young Fashion escapes. Hoyden, the parson, and the nurse decide to say nothing of the former marriage, and Hoyden is now married to Foppington, who immediately brings his wife to London. Here young Fashion claims his bride, the nurse and parson are bullied and cajoled into admitting the earlier marriage, and Hoyden is reconciled to her lot on learning that Fashion is Lord Foppington's brother.

The play was adapted by Sheridan and produced as 'A Trip to Scarborough'.

Relations, a name applied to printed newspamphlets of the early part of the 17th cent., recording domestic events.

Relativity, a theory of the physical universe evolved by A. Einstein (q.v.).

Religio Laici, a poem by Dryden (q.v.), published in 1682.

The poet argues for the credibility of the Christian religion and against Deism, and (perhaps with less conviction) for the Anglican Church against that of Rome. See *Hind and the Panther (The).*

Religio Medici, a work by Sir T. Browne (q.v.), first printed without his sanction in 1642, reissued with his approval in 1643. It was written about 1635, at Shipden Hall, near Halifax, before the author settled at Norwich. He states, in the 1643 edition, that it was not intended for publication but was 'composed at leisurable hours for his private exercise and satisfaction', but, having been printed without his knowledge and consent, he felt bound to issue a 'full and intended copy'.

It is a confession of Christian faith (qualified by an eclectic and generally sceptical attitude), and a collection of opinions on a vast number of subjects more or less connected with religion, expressed with a wealth of fancy and wide erudition. The headings of a few of the sections will suggest the variety of matters dealt with: 'Nature doeth nothing in vain', 'of miracles', 'of witchcraft', 'of guardian and attendant spirits', 'of marriage and harmony', 'of sleep', 'avarice a ridiculous vice'. The work contains two beautiful prayers in verse.

Reliques of Ancient Poetry, see *Percy (T.).*

Remarks on the Life and Writings of Dr. Jonathan Swift, see *Boyle (J.).*

REMARQUE, ERICH MARIA (1898–), German novelist, author of 'Im Westen nichts Neues' ('All Quiet on the Western Front', 1929) and 'Der Weg zurück' ('The Road Back', 1931).

Rembrandt van Ryn (1606–69), Dutch painter and etcher. He was born in Leyden, the son of a miller, and spent most of his life in Amsterdam. After an early success and prosperity his uncompromising character offended his patrons and he died in poverty. His output was enormous: paintings, including many portraits and self-portraits; etchings of biblical subjects, landscapes, portraits, and genre subjects; and drawings; all searching studies of character and form, infused with profound feeling.

Remora, the sucking-fish (*Echeneis remora*), believed by the ancients to have the power of staying the course of any ship to which it attached itself. It attaches itself to the belly of the shark or other large fish.

Remorse, a blank verse tragedy by S. T. Coleridge (q.v.), produced at Drury Lane in 1813.

Renaissance, THE, the great flowering of art and letters, under the influence of classical models, which began in Italy in the 15th cent., culminating in the High Renaissance at the end of the century and spreading to northern Europe in the 16th and 17th cents. Among writers who have dealt with the subject may be mentioned Symonds, Pater (qq.v.), and the German, Burckhardt.

RENAN, ERNEST (1823–92), a Breton by birth, and a learned French writer, philologist, and historian. The result of his studies of Christianity is embodied in the famous series 'Origines du Christianisme', in which he applied the method of the historian to the Biblical narrative: 'Vie de Jésus' (1863), 'Les Apôtres' (1866), 'St. Paul' (1869), 'L'Antéchrist' (1873), 'Les Évangiles' (1877), 'L'Église chrétienne' (1879), 'Marc Aurèle' (1881). His other best-known works, all of them remarkable for the beauty of their style, were his 'Histoire du Peuple d'Israël' (1887–93), 'Drames philosophiques' (1878–86), and the autobiographical 'Souvenirs d'enfance et de jeunesse' (1883). Renan also wrote an important 'Histoire des langues sémitiques' (1855), a life of Averroës (1852), and studies of the 'Book of Job' (1858) and the 'Song of Solomon' (1860).

Renascence of Wonder, The, see *Watts-Dunton* (*W. T.*).

Renaud, in the *chansons de geste* (q.v.) a rebel against Charlemagne, better known under the Italian name of Rinaldo (q.v.).

Renault, a character in Otway's 'Venice Preserv'd' (q.v.).

René, a romance by Chateaubriand (q.v.).

René of Provence (1408–80), known as 'le bon Roi René', son of Louis II, duke of Anjou, was titular king of Naples, the two Sicilies, and Jerusalem, 'whose large style agrees not with the leanness of his purse' (Shakespeare, '2 Henry VI', I. i). His daughter, Margaret of Anjou, was wife of Henry VI. As Count of Provence, he gave free play to his love of music and poetry, tilting and hunting, minstrels and knight-errants, and showed indifference to political affairs. There is a picture of his court in Scott's 'Anne of

Geierstein' (q.v.). He figures in Shakespeare's 'Henry VI' as 'Reignier'. He left some prose and verse romances, pastorals, and allegories.

Renée de Croisnel, afterwards *Marquise de Rouaillout,* a character in Meredith's 'Beauchamp's Career' (q.v.).

Representative Men, by Emerson (q.v.), a series of studies of Plato, Swedenborg, Montaigne, Napoleon, Goethe (1850).

Repressor of over much Blaming of the Clergy, see *Pecock.*

Republic, The, one of the dialogues of Plato (q.v.), in which Socrates is represented as eliciting, in the course of a discussion on justice, the ideal type of state. In this the perfect forms of goodness, truth, and beauty are cultivated, and everything repugnant to them excluded. The famous apologue of the men who live bound in a cavern, so that they can see only the shadows of real objects projected by a bright fire on its inner wall, occurs in Bk. VII.

Republic of Letters, THE, the collective body of those engaged in literary pursuits. The expression occurs first in Addison's 'Dialogues upon Ancient Medals', i. 19.

RERESBY, SIR JOHN (1634–89), travelled during the Commonwealth in France, Italy, Germany, and the Netherlands. His interesting 'Memoirs' were published in 1734, and his 'Travels and Memoirs' in 1813.

Restoration, THE, the re-establishment of monarchy in England with the return of Charles II (1660); also the period marked by this event, of which the chief literary figures are Dryden, Etherege, Wycherley, Congreve, Vanbrugh, Farquhar, Rochester, Bunyan, Pepys, and Locke (qq.v.).

Resurrection man, or RESURRECTIONIST, one who made a trade of exhuming bodies in order to sell them to anatomists (as Jerry Cruncher did in Dickens's 'Tale of Two Cities', q.v.). The term came into use towards the end of the 18th cent.

Retaliation, an unfinished poem by Goldsmith (q.v.), published in 1774, consisting of a string of humorous and critical epitaphs on David Garrick, Reynolds, Burke, and other friends, in reply to their similar efforts directed against himself. Of the latter Garrick's is the best known:

> Here lies Nolly Goldsmith, for shortness called Noll,
> Who wrote like an angel, but talked like poor Poll.

Retort courteous, THE, the first of Touchstone's seven causes of quarrel (Shakespeare's 'As You Like It', v. iv); followed by the 'quip modest', the 'reply churlish', the 'reproof valiant', the 'counatercheck quarrelsome', the 'lie circumstantial', and the 'lie direct'.

Returne from Pernassus, The, see *Parnassus Plays.*

Return of the Druses, The, a tragedy in blank verse by R. Browning (q.v.), published in 1843.

The Druses (q.v.) are living in exile on a small island in the Aegean, the victims of the tyranny of the prefect of the Knights of Rhodes. Djabal, the son of the last Emir, who has taken refuge in Europe, plans to return and murder the oppressor. On his return he falls in love with Anael, a Druse girl, who will marry none but the deliverer of her race. He now determines to assume the character of an incarnation of the Hakeem, the divine founder of the religion. But presently conscience is too strong for him, and he resolves on flight after he shall have killed the tyrant. In this assassination Anael anticipates him; whereupon Djabal confesses his imposture. Anael falls dead, and Djabal kills himself on her body.

Return of the Native, The, a novel by Hardy (q.v.), published in 1878.

The scene is the sombre Egdon Heath, typical of the country near Wareham and Poole in Dorset. Damon Wildeve, engineer turned publican, after playing fast and loose with two women by whom he is loved—the gentle, unselfish Thomasin Yeobright and the selfish, capricious Eustacia Vye—marries the former to spite the latter; while Thomasin rejects her humble adorer, the reddleman, Diggory Venn. Her cousin, Clym Yeobright, a diamond merchant in Paris, disgusted with the vanity and uselessness of his occupation, returns to Egdon with the intention of becoming a schoolmaster in his native county. He falls in love with Eustacia, and she in a brief infatuation marries him, in the hope of inducing him to return to Paris. His sight fails and he becomes a furze-cutter on the heath, to Eustacia's despair. She is the cause of estrangement between Clym and his mother, and unintentionally of her death. This, and the discovery that Eustacia's relations with Wildeve have not ceased, lead to a violent scene between Clym and his wife, and ultimately to Eustacia's flight with Wildeve, in the course of which both are drowned. Clym, attributing to himself some responsibility for the death of his mother and his wife, becomes an itinerant preacher. Thomasin marries Diggory Venn.

REUCHLIN, JOHANN (1455–1522), born at Pforzheim, a celebrated humanist and the foremost oriental scholar of his day. Braving the powerful Dominicans, he published in 1494 his 'De Verbo Mirifico', defending Jewish literature and philosophy, and became the centre of an acute controversy in which he was opposed by Pfefferkorn (q.v.) and which was the occasion of the publication of the 'Epistolae Obscurorum Virorum' (q.v.). Reuchlin was author of the first Hebrew grammar.

Revels, MASTER OF, an officer appointed to superintend masques and other entertainments at court. He is first mentioned in the reign of Henry VII. The first permanent Master of the Revels was Sir Thomas Cawarden, appointed in 1545.

Revenge, The, (1) the name of Sir R. Grenville's (q.v.) ship; (2) the title and subject of a ballad by A. Tennyson (q.v.); (3) a tragedy by E. Young (q.v.), of which the plot is akin to that of Shakespeare's 'Othello' (q.v.). Zanga, the captive of Don Alonzo, devises a revenge on the conqueror who has humiliated him. He throws suspicion on Leonora, Alonzo's wife, and Don Carlos, Alonzo's friend, and succeeds in bringing all three to an untimely end.

Revenge of Bussy D'Ambois, The, see Bussy d'Ambois (The Revenge of).

Revenger's Tragedy, The, see Tourneur.

Revere, PAUL (1735–1818), Boston silversmith, printer, and patriot; remembered for his famous midnight ride from Charlestown to Lexington (18–19 April 1775) to give warning of the approach of British troops from Boston—the subject of Longfellow's poem in 'Tales of a Wayside Inn'.

Revesby Play, THE, a folk-drama acted by morris-dancers at Revesby in Lincolnshire at the end of the 18th cent. The characters are the Fool and his sons—Pickle Herring, Blue Breeches, Pepper Breeches, Ginger Breeches —and Mr. Allspice and Cicely. The Fool fights with a hobby-horse and a dragon. The sons decide to kill the Fool; he kneels down, the swords of the dancers are locked around his neck, and he is slain. He revives when Pickle Herring stamps his foot. Sword-dances and the wooing of Cicely by the Fool and his sons conclude the play. The central incident no doubt symbolizes the death of the year and its resuscitation in the spring. The text is given by T. F. Ordish in the 'Folk-Lore Journal', vii. 338. See also E. K. Chambers, 'The Mediaeval Stage'.

Review, The, a periodical started by Defoe (q.v.) in 1704, under the title, originally, of 'A Review of the Affairs of France: and of all Europe'. It continued until 1713, as a nonpartisan paper, an organ of the commercial interests of the nation. It appeared thrice a week and was written, practically in its entirety, by Defoe himself, who expressed in it his opinions on all current political topics, thus initiating the political leading article. It contains much valuable information on home and foreign affairs of the period.

Review of English Studies, The, a quarterly journal devoted to English scholarship, started in 1925.

Revised Version, THE, see Bible (The English).

Revival of Letters, THE, the Renaissance (q.v.) in its literary aspect.

Revolt of Islam, The, originally entitled Laon and Cythna, a poem by P. B. Shelley (q.v.) in Spenserian stanzas, published in 1818.

This poem was written in 1817, at a time when the reaction that followed the fall of Napoleon had brought much misery among the poorer classes, and had stirred Shelley's revolutionary instincts. It is a symbolic tale, in some respects obscure, 'illustrating', in Shelley's own words, 'the growth and progress of individual mind aspiring after excellence and devoted to the love of mankind', and 'its impatience at all the oppressions that are done under the sun'. Cythna, a heroic maiden devoted to the liberation of her sex, united with Laon in a common ideal, rouses the spirit of revolt among the people of Islam against their tyrants. The revolt is temporarily successful, but the tyrants return with increased forces, and in revenge lay the land desolate. Famine and plague descend upon it. To avert these Laon and Cythna are burnt at the stake, at the instigation of a priest. But the poem closes with an indication of the 'transient nature of error' and of 'the eternity of genius and virtue'.

Revolution in France, *Reflections on the,* by Burke (q.v.), published in 1790.

This treatise was provoked by a sermon preached by Dr. Richard Price, a nonconformist minister, in Nov. 1789, in which he exulted in the French Revolution and asserted that the king of England owes his throne to the choice of the people, who are at liberty to cashier him for misconduct. Burke repudiates this constitutional doctrine, showing that under the Declaration of Right the system of hereditary succession was carefully asserted, and that nothing done at the Revolution of 1689 gives countenance to Price's doctrine. He contrasts the inherited rights of which the English are tenacious with the 'rights of man' of the French revolutionaries, based on 'extravagant and presumptuous speculations', inconsistent with an ordered society and leading to poverty and chaos. He examines the character of the men who made the French Revolution, and the proceedings of their National Assembly, a 'profane burlesque of that sacred institute'. The well-known eloquent passage on the downfall of Marie Antoinette leads to the lament that 'the age of chivalry is gone. . . . All the decent drapery of life is to be rudely torn off' in deference to 'the new conquering empire of light and reason'. His general conclusion is that the defective institutions of the old régime should have been reformed, not destroyed. No doubt the work led to the breach between Burke and Fox and the splitting of the Whig party.

Reynard the Fox, the hero of various popular satirical fables or 'bestiaries' (q.v.) which were collected in France under the title of 'Roman de Renart'. The first part of this was written about 1200 and was followed by other parts during the 13th cent. There is a Latin text ('Isengrimus') of the 12th cent., and German texts of somewhat later date, and a ver-

sion of about 1250 by a Fleming named Willem. It is probable that the development of the legend is due to many unknown authors. A Flemish version no longer extant was translated and printed by Caxton in 1481. Goethe wrote a free translation, called 'Reinecke Fuchs' in 1794. The fox in these fables is used to symbolize the man who, under various characters, preys upon and deludes society, is brought to judgement, but escapes by his cunning. We have an example of this type of fable in Chaucer's 'Nun's Priest's Tale' (see *Canterbury Tales,* 21). But it was principally developed in France. The popularity of this group of works gave 'renard' to the French language as the ordinary word for a fox, in place of the older 'goupil'. 'Renard' is from OHG. 'regin-hart', strong in counsel.

The principal characters in Caxton's version are, besides Reynard, King Noble the lion, Isegrym the wolf, Courtoys the hound, Bruin the bear, Tybert the cat, Grymbert the badger, Coart or Cuwaert the hare, Bellyn the ram, Martin and Dame Rukenawe the apes, Chanticleer the cock, and Partlet the hen. Ermeline is Reynard's wife, and Malperdy (*Malpertuis*) his castle.

REYNOLDS, JOHN HAMILTON (1796–1852), poet, educated at St. Paul's School, London. His work includes two volumes of verse published in 1814 and 'Garden of Florence and Other Poems' (1821). He was a friend and correspondent of Keats (q.v.).

REYNOLDS, Sir JOSHUA (1723–92), portrait painter, born at Plympton, Devon, the son of a schoolmaster. He was one of the founders of 'The Club' (see *Johnson, Samuel*), and did much to raise the social and intellectual status of the painter. He was the first President of the Royal Academy, and in his 'Fifteen Discourses', delivered to the students between 1769 and 1790, he sought to encourage history painting as the most noble form of art. But portraits remained his chief and most successful works. 'The Life and Times of Sir J. Reynolds', by C. R. Leslie and Tom Taylor, appeared in 1865.

Rhadamanthus, a son of Zeus and Europa, and brother of Minos, king of Crete. He showed so much justice and wisdom in his lifetime that he became after death one of the judges in the infernal regions.

Rhampsinĩtus, Rameses III, king of Egypt. Herodotus tells a romantic story (II. 121) of two brothers, whose father, architect of this king's treasury, left a movable stone in the wall thereof. The sons, by means of this, were able to purloin a great quantity of treasure. The king, finding the seals unbroken but the treasure diminished, set a man-trap, in which one of the brothers was caught. He immediately called to his brother and bade him cut off his head, to avoid detection, which was done. A similar story is told of Agamedes and Trophonius (q.v.).

Rhapsody, originally an epic poem or part

of one, sung by a 'rhapsode' or 'rhapsodist' (meaning a stitcher together of song). It is applied also to an exalted or exaggeratedly enthusiastic expression of sentiment, or a speech, letter, or poem marked by extravagance of idea and expression. [OED.]

RHASIS or RHAZES (ABU BAKR MUHAMMAD IBN ZAKARIA EL RAZI), a Persian physician of the 10th cent., who practised at Baghdad and wrote encyclopaedic treatises on medicine.

Rhea, an ancient Greek nature-goddess, commonly identified with the Asiatic CYBĒLĒ (q.v.), the wife of Cronos (Saturn) and the mother of Zeus, Poseidon (Neptune), Pluto, Demeter (Ceres), Hera, etc.

Rheims, The Jackdaw of, see Jackdaw of Rheims.

Rhiannon, in British mythology, the wife of Pwyll (q.v.), and subsequently of Manawyddan. (See Mabinogion.) She had three birds, who could sing the dead to life, and the living to death.

Rhine Gold, THE, the hoard of the Nibelungs (see under Nibelungenlied) of which Siegfried got possession and which, after Siegfried's death, the brothers of Kriemhild concealed by sinking it in the Rhine. It is the subject, though the story is differently dealt with, of Wagner's opera, 'Das Rheingold' in the 'Ring' series. In this opera Alberich, the king of the Nibelungs, steals the gold of the Rhine Maidens and forges from it the magic ring that is to make him master of the world. This ring Wotan, with the help of Loge, takes from him by force; but Alberich sets his curse upon it. Wotan is in turn forced to surrender it to the giant Fafner as a ransom for Freia, whom he has promised to give to the giants as a reward for the building of Walhalla. For the continuation see Valkyrie.

Rhoda Fleming, a novel by G. Meredith (q.v.), published in 1865.

Rhoda and Dahlia Fleming are daughters of a Kentish yeoman farmer. Robert Eccles, his assistant, ex-soldier, reformed drunkard, a strong, determined, good-hearted fellow, is also of the yeoman class. The gentle Dahlia is seduced by Edward Blancove, the cynical bookish son of a rich banker. After a few months Edward shabbily deserts her; and Robert, who loves the proud and untamed Rhoda, sets out to see her sister righted. At first he tries violence, but in this he is worsted by Edward, who hires a scoundrel, Sedgett, to waylay Robert and knock him on the head. Robert at last succeeds in discovering Dahlia's hiding-place. But Edward has meanwhile been base enough to bribe Sedgett to marry her, and the sick and broken-hearted Dahlia has consented, for her family's sake, to be made in this way 'an honest woman'. Robert is too late to prevent the ceremony, but Dahlia is carried off from her husband at the church door, and Robert succeeds in

keeping him away by main force long enough to permit of the discovery that Sedgett is already married to another wife. Edward has by now repented and seeks to atone for his crime. But Dahlia, terrified at the thought of falling into Sedgett's hands, has taken poison, and, though her life is saved, she is changed by the trial through which she has passed, and marriage with Edward is now for her impossible. Rhoda, tamed at last by trouble, marries Robert.

Rhodes, CECIL JOHN (1853–1902), was educated at Bishop Stortford Grammar School, and, owing to failure of health, went to S. Africa and worked a moderately prosperous claim in the newly discovered diamond fields of the Orange Free State. Meanwhile he matriculated at Oriel College, Oxford (1873), and revisited Oxford at intervals until he succeeded in graduating as a passman B.A. in 1881. During this period he increased his holdings in the Kimberley diamond fields, and subsequently succeeded in amalgamating these under his own control. He formed the aspiration of federating South Africa under British rule with the assent of the Cape Dutch; and towards this end he worked in the Cape legislature, to which he was elected in 1880. He helped to secure a great part of Bechuanaland for the Cape government. The British South Africa Company was incorporated by royal charter in 1889 to administer the territory north of Bechuanaland, and this territory was named Rhodesia after the projector of the scheme. Rhodes directed the war with the Matabeles in 1893–4, whereby he greatly extended the territory of Rhodesia, of which Dr. L. S. Jameson had become administrator in 1890. From 1890 to 1896 Rhodes was also prime minister at the Cape. In 1895 he secretly encouraged the Uitlander population of the Transvaal to look to an armed insurrection for the redress of their grievances, and, after the catastrophe of the Jameson Raid (q.v.), he was pronounced (as the result of inquiries by the Cape parliament and British House of Commons) guilty of grave breaches of duty. Thereupon he resigned the office of premier and devoted himself to the development of Rhodesia. During the S. African War he was besieged in Kimberley. He died after long suffering from heart disease and was buried in the Matoppo Hills. By his will he left about £6,000,000 to the public service, endowing some 170 scholarships at Oxford for students from various parts of the Empire, from the United States, and from Germany; £100,000 was left to his old college, Oriel.

Rhodes, COLOSSUS OF, see Colossus.

Rhodes, KNIGHTS OF, see Hospitallers of St. John of Jerusalem.

Rhodes Scholars, see Rhodes (C. J.).

Rhodolinda, the heroine of D'Avenant's tragedy 'Albovine' (q.v.).

Rhodōpē or RHODŌPIS, a Greek courtesan,

said to have been a fellow-slave of Aesop (q.v.) and to have been taken to Naucratis in Egypt. Aelian relates that one day, while Rhodope was bathing, an eagle carried off her sandal and dropped it near Psammetichus, king of Egypt. The king was struck with the beauty of the sandal, had search made for the owner, and, when discovered, married her—a curious parallel to the story of Cinderella. There was a story (rejected by Herodotus) that she built the third Pyramid; to this Tennyson alludes in 'The Princess', ii:

> The Rhodope that built the pyramid.

Rhopalic verse (from the Greek ῥόπαλον, a cudgel thicker towards one end), verse of which each word contains one more syllable than the last, e.g. (Ausonius):

> Spes Deus aeternae stationis conciliator.

Rhyme: MALE or MASCULINE rhymes or endings are those having a final accented syllable, as distinguished from FEMALE or FEMININE rhymes or endings in which the last syllable is unaccented.

Rhyme-royal, the seven-lined decasyllabic stanza, rhymed a b a b b c c. Its first appearance in English is in Chaucer's 'Complaint unto Pity'. Its name derives probably from the French *chant royal*, not from its adoption by James I in 'The Kingis Quair' (q.v.). It was used by Shakespeare in 'The Rape of Lucrece' (q.v.).

Rhymer, THOMAS THE, see *Erceldoune*.

Rhyming Poem, The, included in the 'Exeter Book' (q.v.) and therefore of not later date than the 10th cent., is important as being arranged in rhymed couplets, with rhymes in the verses. It is a disquisition on the vicissitudes of life, contrasting the misfortunes of a fallen king with the days of his past glory. It has been suggested that it is a paraphrase of Job xxix and xxx.

Riah, the Jew in Dickens's 'Our Mutual Friend' (q.v.).

Rialto, THE (the 'Ponte di Rivo Alto' or 'bridge of the deep stream', on which Venice was founded), a beautiful single-span marble bridge across the Grand Canal in Venice, built at the end of the 16th cent. It was in the centre of the mercantile quarter of old Venice, and it is to this that Shylock refers as the Rialto in Shakespeare's 'The Merchant of Venice', I. iii.

Ribbon Society, a Roman Catholic secret society formed in the north and north-west of Ireland early in the 19th cent. to counteract the Protestant influence, and associated with agrarian disorders. The doings of the Ribbonmen figure in some of the 'Traits and Stories of the Irish Peasantry' by William Carleton (q.v.), and in his 'Fardorougha the Miser' (q.v.).

RICARDO, DAVID (1772–1823), the son of a Dutch Jew, who made a fortune on the London Stock Exchange, and then devoted himself to the study of economics. Encouraged by James Mill (q.v.), he published in 1817 his chief work, 'Principles of Political Economy and Taxation', which is mainly occupied with the causes determining the distribution of wealth. In this his famous theory of rent played an important part.

Riccabocca, DR., a character in Bulwer Lytton's 'My Novel' (q.v.).

RICE, ELMER (1892–   ), American dramatist, born in New York. Among his many plays are: 'The Adding Machine' (1923) and 'Street Scene' (1929). He has also written several novels.

RICE, JAMES (1843–82), educated at Queens' College, Cambridge, is remembered for his collaboration in a number of novels with Besant (q.v.).

RICH, BARNABE (1540?–1617), fought in Queen Mary's war with France (1557–8) and in the Low Countries, rose to the rank of Captain, and from 1574 onwards devoted himself to the production of romances in the style of Lyly's 'Euphues' (q.v.), pamphlets, and reminiscences. Notable among these are his 'Farewell to the Military Profession' (1581, which includes 'Apolonius and Silla', the source of the plot of Shakespeare's 'Twelfth Night') and 'The Honesty of this Age'.

Rich, JOHN (1682?–1761), theatrical producer. He opened the New Theatre at Lincoln's Inn Fields in 1714, and the theatre at Covent Garden in 1732. In 1728 he produced Gay's 'Beggar's Opera' with such success that the play was said popularly to have 'made Rich gay and Gay rich'. See also *Beef Steaks*.

Rich, PENELOPE (1562?–1607), daughter of Walter Devereux, the first earl of Essex. Her charms were celebrated by Sir P. Sidney (q.v.) in his 'Astrophel and Stella' sonnets. She married Lord Rich, was divorced by him, and married Lord Mountjoy, with whom she had lived, and who had now become earl of Devonshire.

Richard I, 'Cœur de Lion', king of England, 1189–99. He is introduced in two of Scott's novels, 'The Talisman' and 'Ivanhoe' (qq.v.); and is also the hero of Hewlett's (q.v.) 'Richard Yea-and-Nay'.

Richard Cœur de Lion, a spirited verse romance of the 14th cent. The author is unknown. It is a patriotic tale exalting the haughty valorous Richard, and pouring contempt on Philip and the French. The course of the crusade is related, with the discomfiture of the Saracens, until a truce is arranged for three years, at which point the poem ends. Quotations from it are to be found in the notes to Sir W. Scott's 'The Talisman' (q.v.), referring to the cooking and eating of the Saracen's head, and of the heads served to the Paynim ambassadors.

Richard II, king of England, 1377–99.

Richard II, King, an historical tragedy by Shakespeare (q.v.), produced probably about 1595, printed in 1597, and based on Holinshed. The play shows the influence of Marlowe, and is comparable with the latter's 'Edward II' (q.v.).

It deals with the arbitrary exile of Henry Bolingbroke and the duke of Norfolk by King Richard; the death of John of Gaunt and the confiscation of his property by the king; the invasion of England by Bolingbroke during the king's absence in Ireland; the king's return and withdrawal to Flint Castle; his surrender to Bolingbroke; the latter's triumphal progress through London with Richard in his train; Richard's removal to Pomfret and his murder. The contrast of the characters of Richard and Bolingbroke is a notable feature. The play contains practically no comic element.

Richard III, king of England, 1483–5.

Richard III, King, an historical tragedy by Shakespeare (q.v.), produced probably in 1594, printed in 1597, and based on Holinshed. Shakespeare perhaps had before him an earlier play, 'The True Tragedie of Richard III'.

The play centres in the character of Richard of Gloucester, afterwards King Richard III, ambitious and sanguinary, bold and subtle, treacherous, yet brave in battle, a murderer and usurper of the crown. The principal incidents of the play are the imprisonment and murder of Clarence procured by his brother Richard; the wooing of Anne, widow of Edward, Prince of Wales, by Richard as she accompanies the bier of her dead father-in-law; the death of Edward IV and the machinations of Richard to get the crown; the execution of Hastings, Rivers, and Grey; the accession of Richard; the murder of the princes in the Tower; Richard's project of marrying his niece, Elizabeth of York; Buckingham's rebellion in support of the earl of Richmond, his capture and execution; Richmond's invasion, and the defeat and death of Richard at Bosworth (1485).

Richard the Thirde, *The History of*, a work first printed in 1534 and questionably attributed to Sir T. More and to Cardinal Morton. It is distinguished from earlier English chronicles by its unity of scheme and dramatic effectiveness.

Richard Carstone, one of the two wards in Chancery in Dickens's 'Bleak House' (q.v.).

RICHARD DE BURY, see *Bury*.

Richard Feverel, see *Ordeal of Richard Feverel*

Richard Roe, see *John Doe*.

Richard the Redeless, see *Mum, Sothsegger*.

RICHARDS, IVOR ARMSTRONG (1893–), critic and authority on semantics. He was the founder with C. K. Ogden of Basic English. Among his writings 'The Meaning of Meaning' (with C. K. Ogden, 1923) and

'Practical Criticism' (1929) are the best known.

RICHARDSON, DOROTHY MILLER (1873–1957), novelist, was a pioneer of the 'stream-of-consciousness' method in the novel. Her novels, written between 1915 and 1938, form a single sequence entitled 'Pilgrimage'.

RICHARDSON, HENRY HANDEL, pen-name of ETHEL FLORENCE RICHARDSON (MRS. J. G. ROBERTSON) (1870–1946), novelist, who was born in Melbourne, studied music at the Leipzig Conservatorium, and settled in London after her marriage. Her novels include 'Maurice Guest' (1908), 'The Getting of Wisdom' (1910), 'The Fortunes of Richard Mahoney' (a trilogy consisting of 'Australia Felix' (1917), 'The Way Home' (1925), and 'Ultima Thule' (1929)), and 'The Young Cosima' (1939). Her autobiography, 'Myself When Young', was unfinished at her death.

RICHARDSON, SAMUEL (1689–1761), the son of a joiner, received little education, and was apprenticed to a printer. He set up a printing business, first in Fleet Street, London, then in Salisbury Court, London, where he lived for the rest of his life. He was employed as printer to the House of Commons. At the request of two other printers he prepared 'a little volume of letters, in a common style, on such subjects as might be of use to country readers who are unable to indite for themselves'. This appeared in 1741 and provided, in addition, directions 'how to think and act justly and prudently in the common Concerns of Human Life'. Out of this arose Richardson's first novel, 'Pamela' (q.v.), of which two volumes appeared in 1740 and two in 1741. This was followed by 'Clarissa Harlowe' (q.v., 1747–8), which surpassed the success of 'Pamela', and won Richardson European fame. His 'Sir Charles Grandison' (q.v., 1753–4), though it never held so high a position as 'Clarissa', was received also with enthusiasm. The three works had a marked influence on subsequent writers of fiction, both in England and abroad.

Richelieu, ARMAND JEAN DU PLESSIS, *Cardinal* and *Duc de* (1585–1642), one of the greatest of French statesmen, first came into prominence as bishop of Luçon, and became prime minister of Louis XIII in 1624. He reduced the nobles to discipline by a series of executions, destroyed the political importance of the Protestants by the siege and capture of La Rochelle (1628), and intervened successfully in the Thirty Years War. He was the founder of the French Academy, and built the Palais-Royal in Paris (originally called Palais-Cardinal). He figures in 'The Three Musketeers' of Dumas (q.v.).

Richelieu, *or The Conspiracy*, an historical play in blank verse by Bulwer Lytton (q.v.), produced in 1839.

The play deals with the attempts made in

France during the period 1630–42 by the Duc d'Orléans, the Duc de Bouillon, Cinq-Mars, and others, to overthrow Cardinal Richelieu, the events being adapted to dramatic purposes. The cardinal, by his adroitness, courage, and skilful use of spies, defeats the attempts to assassinate him and to effect an alliance with Spain, and triumphs over the conspirators. A love element is introduced in the person of Julie de Mortemar, the cardinal's ward, who is honourably loved by the Chevalier de Mauprat, and dishonourably pursued by the king.

Richland, MISS, the heroine of Goldsmith's 'The Good-Natur'd Man' (q.v.).

Richmond, 'another Richmond in the field' (Henry, earl of Richmond, afterwards Henry VII), i.e. a fresh adversary, in allusion to Shakespeare's 'King Richard III', v. iv:

> I think there be six Richmonds in the field:
> Five have I slain to-day instead of him.

RICHMOND, SIR BRUCE, educated at Winchester and New College, Oxford, editor of the 'Times Literary Supplement' (q.v.) from its first production until 1938.

RICHMOND, LEGH, see *Dairyman's Daughter*.

RICHTER, JOHANN PAUL FRIEDRICH (1763–1825), German romantic novelist, who wrote under the name 'Jean Paul'. Reared in humble village surroundings, he was at his best in idyllic representations of the life he knew. He had also a certain gift of humour, which earned the enthusiastic praise of Carlyle. His best-known works are: 'Hesperus' (1795), 'Quintus Fixlein' (1796), 'Siebenkäs' (1796), 'Titan' (1800–3), 'Flegeljahre' (1804–5), and 'Die Vorschule der Ästhetik' (1804).

Ridd, JOHN, see *Lorna Doone*.

Riddle of the Sands, *The*, a novel by Erskine Childers, published in 1903. It deals with the discovery of a threatened invasion of England by a continental power.

Riderhood, ROGUE, a character in Dickens's 'Our Mutual Friend' (q.v.).

RIDLEY, NICHOLAS (1500?–55), successively bishop of Rochester and London, was a fellow of Pembroke Hall, Cambridge. He became one of Cranmer's chaplains and began gradually to reject many Roman doctrines. If any hand beside that of Cranmer can be detected in the two Prayer Books of Edward VI, it is believed to be Ridley's. As bishop of London he exerted himself to propagate reformed opinions. On Edward VI's death he denounced Queen Mary and Elizabeth as illegitimate at St. Paul's Cross, London. He was sent to the Tower in June 1553 and deprived of his bishopric. In September 1555 he was condemned on the charge of heresy and burnt alive with Latimer (q.v.) at Oxford, 16 Oct. He wrote several theological treatises, which appeared after his death.

In 1841 the 'Works of Nicholas Ridley' were edited for the Parker Society by Henry Christmas.

Ridolfi or RIDOLFO, ROBERTO DI (1531–1612), a Florentine banker who settled in London in Mary's reign. In Elizabeth's reign he intrigued with the French and Spanish ambassadors, was privy to the Northern rebellion of 1569, and was arrested but not proved guilty. In 1570 he engaged in a fresh conspiracy, in which Norfolk was implicated, to overthrow the government of Elizabeth with the aid of a Spanish army. His confederates were arrested, and Ridolfi himself, who was absent at Brussels, retired to Italy. This latter was the real 'Ridolfi Plot'.

Ridotto, an Italian word, meant originally, like the French *réduit*, a retreat or withdrawing-place. Florio defines it as 'a home or retiring place. Also a gaming house, an ordinary or tabling house or other place where good company doth meet.' It was used in English to mean an entertainment or social assembly consisting of music and dancing; introduced into England 'in the year 1722, at the Opera House in the Haymarket' (Busby, 'Dictionary of Music') and a marked feature of London social life during the 18th cent. [OED.]

Rience, see *Ryence*.

Rienzi, or The Last of the Tribunes, a novel by Bulwer Lytton (q.v.), published in 1835.

The story is based on the career of Cola di Rienzi, tribune of the people at Rome, who in 1347 established a republic, and after seven months was excommunicated and obliged to abdicate. For seven years he was in exile, then returned in 1354, was made a senator, but was assassinated a few months later. The novel follows closely the historical facts, and depicts not only the political situation and the mode of living of the times, but also the consummate ability of Rienzi himself, marred by arrogance and love of display. The other chief characters are his gentle sister Irene, loved by the enlightened Adrian Colonna; his ambitious wife Nina; the unscrupulous but heroic condottiere Walter de Montreal; and the stout smith Cecco del Vecchio.

Rigadoon, a lively and somewhat complicated dance for two persons, formerly in vogue. The word is adapted from the French *rigaudon*, of doubtful origin. Rousseau states ('Dict. de la Musique') that he had heard a dancing-master attribute it to the name of its inventor Rigaud; and Mistral says that Rigaud was a celebrated dancing-master at Marseilles.

Rigaud, a character in Dickens's 'Little Dorrit' (q.v.).

Rigby, MR., a character in Disraeli's 'Coningsby' (q.v.).

Rigdum-Funnidos, see *Chrononhotonthologos*.

Rights, BILL OF, a measure adopted by the Convention Parliament of 1689 condemning the interference by the Crown with civil liberty and the execution of the law, and restoring the monarchy to its constitutional position.

Rights of Man, The, a political treatise by Paine (q.v.), in two parts, published in 1791 and 1792.

Pt. I is in the main a reply to Burke's 'Reflections on the Revolution in France' (q.v.). Condemning its unhistorical and unbalanced violence, Paine repudiates Burke's doctrine of prescription and denies that one generation can bind another as regards the form of government. The constitution of a country is an act of the people constituting the government, and in the absence of such a written constitution, government is tyranny. Thus Paine justifies the French Revolution, of which he traces the incidents to the adoption of the Declaration of the Rights of Man by the National Assembly.

In Pt. II Paine touches on Burke's 'Appeal from the New to the Old Whigs', but soon passes to a comparison of the principles of the new French and American constitutions with those of British institutions, to the disadvantage of the latter. The most interesting part of the work, however, consists in Paine's constructive proposals for 'improving the condition of Europe' and particularly of England. Notable among these are: a large reduction of administrative expenditure and taxation; provision for the aged poor; family allowances; allowances for the education of the poor; maternity grants; funeral grants; a graduated income tax; and limitation of armaments by treaty.

Rights of Woman, Vindication of the, see Godwin (Mrs. M. W.).

Rig-Veda, see Veda.

RILKE, RAINER MARIA (1875–1926), German lyric poet. His early collections were not particularly interesting or distinguished. Of decisive importance were his two visits to Russia which, deepening his religious experience, led to 'The Book of Hours' (1905), in which death is the central theme, handled in a highly individual way. The subjective emotionalism of the early poetry began to give way to poetry of a more objective type, the transition to which is seen in 'The Book of Pictures' (1902) and which finds its mature expression in the 'New Poems' (1907–8). The latter was greatly influenced by the French sculptor Rodin, whose secretary Rilke was for a time. In 1910 appeared a full-scale prose work, 'Sketches of Malte Laurids Brigge', in which Rilke explored the relationship between a sensitive poet and a threatening environment. The 'Duino Elegies', begun shortly before the First World War and completed not long afterwards, arose from Rilke's endeavour to discover for himself as a poet a satisfactory spiritual position amid the decay of reality; and the 'Sonnets to Orpheus'

(1923), written in a sudden frenzy of inspiration, are the jubilant outcome of that endeavour. His extensive correspondence is of great literary interest. He is the most important lyric poet of 20th-cent. Germany, and his poetry has been translated into many languages—various collections have appeared in English translated by J. B. Leishmann, sometimes in collaboration with Stephen Spender.

Rima, see Hudson (W. H.).

RIMBAUD, ARTHUR (1854–91), French poet, a precocious genius of violent and vagabond character. He began writing at 15, ran away from home to Paris (for the first time) at 16, had composed his famous poem 'Le Bateau ivre' before he was 17, and by 20 or at most 25 had abandoned literature. By this time he had also written the prose and verse fragments 'Une saison en enfer' and the prose poems 'Les Illuminations'. His later years were spent as a trader and explorer, with a period when he trafficked in arms, in what is now Abyssinia. He died in hospital in France. His collected works were first published in 1898. There is also a Pléiade edition (1946). His remarkable visionary and evocative writing has been one of the great influences on modern poetry.

Rimini, FRANCESCA DA, see Paolo and Francesca.

Rimini, The Story of, see Hunt (J. H. L.).

Rimmon, an Assyrian divinity, mentioned in 2 Kings v. 18. Milton makes Rimmon one of the fallen angels ('Paradise Lost', i. 467).

Rinaldo or RENAUD first figures under the latter name in the Charlemagne cycle of legends, as the eldest of the four sons of Aymon, count of Dordogne, against whom the emperor makes war for their insubordination. They are beleaguered in Montfort, and when driven thence, in Montauban, a fortress that they build near the confluence of the Dordogne and Gironde. They carry on the war until Charlemagne is prevailed on by his paladins to make terms, under which the sons of Aymon are pardoned on condition that Renaud goes to Palestine to fight against the Saracens and surrenders his famous steed Bayard. Bayard, however, refuses to allow any one to mount him, and, when thrown by the emperor's orders into the river, weighted with stones, disengages himself and escapes. Renaud goes to Palestine, where he performs further exploits and becomes a hermit.

As Rinaldo, the hero figures in the 'Orlando Innamorato' and 'Orlando Furioso' (qq.v.). There he is the cousin of Orlando, the lord of Montalban, and one of the suitors for the hand of Angelica. But, drinking of the fountain of hate, his love for her is turned to aversion, while she, drinking of the fountain of love, becomes enamoured of him. Later their dispositions to one another are reversed, again by the magic fountains. He is the brother of Bradamante (q.v.).

In the 'Jerusalem Delivered' (q.v.), Rinaldo is the Prince of Este and the lover of Armida, and in the final battle for Jerusalem his prowess decides the day.

Ring and the Book, The, a poem by R. Browning (q.v.), published in 1868–9.

The poem is based on the story of a Roman murder-case related in an old parchment-covered volume that Browning picked up one day in a Florentine market stall. This is the 'Book' of the title. As the goldsmith, to make a ring from pure gold, mixes alloy with it, moulds the ring, then disengages the alloy; so the author, to the pure gold of this old volume, has added something of himself, and so arrived at the absolute elusive truth. Hence the 'Ring' of the title. The book contained the pleadings and depositions of the case, the 'Definitive Verdict' and some manuscript letters. These provided the raw material of the story, which is briefly as follows.

Count Guido Franceschini, an impoverished nobleman of Arezzo, marries Pompilia Comparini, a young girl of obscure family, but possessed of some slight wealth, of which he has received an exaggerated estimate. Disaster follows. Violante Comparini, Pompilia's supposed mother, confesses that Pompilia is not really her daughter, but a supposititious child procured to defraud the Comparinis' rightful heirs. Guido thereupon determines to get rid of his base-born wife, accuses her of infidelity with a certain Canon Giuseppe Caponsacchi, and so harasses her that she persuades the Canon to carry her off from her husband's house at Arezzo to her old home. Guido pursues them and has them arrested. Pompilia is tried for adultery, which she denies, and is sent to a convent; Caponsacchi is banished for three years. Pompilia, being about to become a mother, is moved from the convent to her old home, where, after giving birth to a son, she is one night murdered, together with her putative parents, by her husband, assisted by four ruffians. Guido is arrested, tried, and on the Pope's final decision executed.

The poem, after the preface, is occupied first with the opinion on the case of 'Half-Rome', then with the opinion of 'The Other Half-Rome', and then of 'Tertium Quid', who takes an impartial attitude. Count Guido next tells his story, which is followed by that of Caponsacchi; then come the pleadings of the advocates on the question of the justifiability of Guido's crime. After these we have the Pope's reflections as he considers his sentence, and Guido's scornful and ferocious defiance, collapsing into abject cowardice when he finally knows his fate. The last section of the poem completes the story with an account of the execution, the attempt of the convent to appropriate Pompilia's property, and its defeat by the Pope's 'Instrument' pronouncing her innocence.

Ring des Nibelungen, Der, the series of four musical dramas by Richard Wagner (q.v.), 'Das Rheingold', 'Die Walküre', 'Siegfried', and 'Götterdämmerung', based on the Norse legends of the Nibelungs (see *Nibelungenlied*), and composed in 1853–70 (produced 1869–76).

Ringan, ST., see *Ninian*.

Rintherout, JENNY, in Scott's 'The Antiquary' (q.v.), servant to Jonathan Oldbuck.

Rip Van Winkle, a story by W. Irving (q.v.) attributed to 'Diedrich Knickerbocker' (q.v.) and included in 'The Sketch Book' (1820).

Rip Van Winkle, taking refuge from a termagant wife in a solitary ramble in the Catskill mountains, falls asleep, and awakens after twenty years, to find his wife dead, his house in ruins, and the world completely changed.

Riquet with the Tuft, one of the fairy tales of Perrault (q.v.), 'Riquet à la houppe'. He was an ugly prince who had the power of conferring wit on the person he loved best. He married a beautiful but stupid princess, who had the corresponding power of conferring beauty.

Rise of Silas Lapham, The, the best known of W. D. Howells's (q.v.) novels, published in 1885. Lapham, who has risen from a Vermont farm to fortune, is typical of the self-made New Englander; and the story is mainly occupied with his, and his family's, adjustments to the Boston society in which they find themselves.

Risingham, BERTRAM, a character in Scott's 'Rokeby' (q.v.).

Risorgimento, an Italian word meaning resurrection', a name given to the movement for the union and liberation of Italy which took place in the middle of the 19th cent. The principal names associated with it are those of Mazzini, Cavour, Victor Emmanuel (king of Sardinia), and Garibaldi. In 1847 Cavour founded a newspaper called 'Risorgimento'. An insurrection in Lombardy and Venice, in 1848, supported by the king of Sardinia (Charles Albert, Victor Emmanuel's father), was suppressed by Austria in 1849, the king being defeated at Novara and abdicating in favour of his son. The movement gathered way in 1859, in which year Napoleon III in alliance with the Italians defeated the Austrians at Magenta. Victor Emmanuel was declared king of Italy in 1860, and the kingdom of Italy, with Florence as its first capital, was recognized by foreign States in 1861. Venetia was ceded to Victor Emmanuel in 1866, and the union of Italy was completed when Italian troops entered Rome in 1870 and the temporal power of the papacy came to an end. See also *Cavour, Garibaldi, Mazzini*.

Ristori, ADELAIDE (1821–1906), a famous Italian tragic actress.

RITCHIE, ANNE ISABELLA THACKERAY, *Lady* (1837–1919), elder daughter of Thackeray (q.v.), author of a number of novels, of which the best known are 'The Village on the Cliff' (1867) and 'Old Kensington' (1873); and of some volumes of essays, including 'The Blackstick Papers' (1908) and 'From the Porch' (1913). She contributed the life of Elizabeth Barrett Browning to the D.N.B.

Ritho, see *Ryence.*

RITSON, JOSEPH (1752–1803), literary antiquary, a zealous student of English literature, attacked (1782) the 'History of English Poetry' of Thomas Warton (q.v.), and also Johnson and Steevens's edition of Shakespeare. In 1783 he published a 'Select Collection of English Songs' containing strictures on Percy's 'Reliques'. He detected the forgeries in Pinkerton's 'Select Scottish Ballads' (1784), and the Ireland (q.v.) forgeries in 1795. He produced in 1802 a useful 'Bibliographia Poetica', a catalogue of English poets from the 12th to the 16th cents.

Rival Queens, The, a tragedy by N. Lee (q.v.), produced in 1677, and founded on the 'Cassandre' of La Calprenède (q.v.).

Statira, daughter of Darius and married to Alexander the Great, learning that Alexander in the course of his campaign has again fallen a victim to the charms of Roxana, daughter of Oxyartes, his first wife, whom he had promised Statira to discard, vows never to see him more. Alexander, returning, and passionately loving Statira, is deeply disturbed by her decision. Roxana, meeting Statira, taunts her and goads her to fury, so that Statira revokes her vow and pardons Alexander, who banishes Roxana. Roxana obtains admission to Statira's chamber and stabs her to death. Alexander is poisoned by the conspirator Cassander.

Rivals, The, a comedy by R. B. Sheridan (q.v.), produced in 1775. This was the first of Sheridan's plays, and he was only 23 when he wrote it. The play was not a success on the first night, owing to the indifferent performance of the part of Sir Lucius O'Trigger.

Captain Absolute, son of Sir Anthony Absolute, a warm-hearted but choleric old gentleman who requires absolute docility from his son, is in love with Lydia Languish, the niece of Mrs. Malaprop (q.v.). As the romantic Lydia prefers a half-pay lieutenant to the heir of a baronet of three thousand a year, he has assumed at Bath (the scene of the play) the character of Ensign Beverley, in order to pay his court, which has been favourably received. But Lydia loses half her fortune if she marries without her aunt's consent, and Mrs. Malaprop will have nothing to say to a beggarly ensign.

Sir Anthony arrives at Bath, ignorant of his son's proceedings, to propose a match between the said son and Lydia Languish, a proposal welcomed by Mrs. Malaprop. An amusing situation results, for Capt. Absolute is afraid of revealing his deception to Lydia;

while he has a rival in Bob Acres, who has heard of Ensign Beverley's courtship, and at the instigation of the fire-eating Sir Lucius O'Trigger asks Capt. Absolute to carry a challenge to Beverley. Sir Lucius himself, who has been deluded into thinking that some amatory letters received by him from Mrs. Malaprop are from Lydia, likewise finds Capt. Absolute in his way and challenges him. But when Acres finds that Beverley is his friend Absolute (his courage had already been 'oozing out at the palms of his hands') he declines to fight and resigns all claim to Lydia. Sir Lucius is disabused by the arrival of Mrs. Malaprop, and Lydia, after a pretty quarrel with her lover for shattering her hopes of an elopement, finally forgives him. A subsidiary element in the play is the love-affair of the perverse and jealous Faulkland and Lydia's friend, Julia Melville.

Rizpah, a poem by A. Tennyson (q.v.), included in 'Ballads and other Poems' (1880).

The poem, which is founded on fact, is the monologue of the mother of a lad who had been hanged for mail-robbery. Night after night she visits the gallows and collects his bones as they fall, to bury them in consecrated ground. The title is an allusion to 2 Sam. xxi. 8–10.

Road-Books, see *Ogilby.*

Road to Ruin, The, see *Holcroft.*

Roaring Boys, a cant term used in the 16th to 18th cents. for riotous, quarrelsome blades, who abounded in London and took pleasure in annoying its quieter inhabitants.

Roaring Girle, The, or *Moll Cut-Purse,* a comedy by T. Middleton and Dekker (qq.v.), produced in 1611.

In this play Moll Cutpurse (q.v.), a notorious thief in real life, takes on for the nonce the character of an honest girl, who helps lovers in distress and defends her virtue with her sword. Sebastian Wentgrave is in love with and betrothed to Mary Fitzallard, but his covetous father forbids the match. To bring him to terms, Sebastian now pretends to have fallen desperately in love with Moll Cutpurse, and to be about to marry her; and Moll good-naturedly lends herself to the deception. Old Wentgrave, distracted at the prospect, is only too glad to give his blessing when the real bride turns out to be Mary Fitz-allard. There are some pleasant bustling scenes in which the life of the London streets is vividly presented, shopkeepers selling tobacco and feathers, their wives intriguing with gallants, and Moll talking thieves' cant and discomfiting overbold admirers.

Rob Roy, a novel by Sir W. Scott (q.v.), published in 1817.

The period of the story is that immediately preceding the Jacobite rising of 1715. Francis Osbaldistone, the son of a rich London merchant, on refusing to adopt his father's profession, is banished by the latter to Osbaldistone

Hall in the north of England, the home of his fox-hunting, hard-drinking uncle, Sir Hildebrand Osbaldistone. Here he is brought into contact with Sir Hildebrand's five boorish sons, a sixth son, Rashleigh (a malignant plotter who has been selected to occupy the place of Francis in the London counting-house), and Sir Hildebrand's niece, the high-spirited Diana Vernon. Rashleigh is deeply involved in Jacobite intrigues, has evil designs on Diana, and becomes the bitter enemy of Francis, who falls in love with Diana and is received by her with favour. The story is occupied with the attempts of Rashleigh to destroy Francis, and to rob and ruin Francis's father, attempts that are defeated partly by Diana, and partly by the singular Scotsman, Rob Roy Macgregor, from whom the novel takes its title. This historical character, a member of a proscribed clan, was once an honest drover; but misfortune and injustice have embittered him and he is now a powerful and dangerous outlaw, the ruthless and cunning opponent of the government's agents, but capable of acts of justice and even generosity. At the instance of Diana, he supports the cause of Francis against Rashleigh. To avert the ruin which threatens his father as a result of Rashleigh's machinations, Francis, accompanied by a delightful character, Bailie Nicol Jarvie of Glasgow, goes to seek Rob Roy in the Highlands, and is the unwilling witness of an encounter between the clansmen and the royal troops, and of the extraordinary escape of Rob Roy himself from their hands. In the outcome, Rashleigh is forced to surrender the funds that he has misappropriated, and is ultimately killed by Rob Roy after having betrayed his Jacobite associates to the government. Francis is restored to his father's favour, becomes the owner of Osbaldistone Hall, and marries Diana. His rascally servant, Andrew Fairservice (q.v.), is one of Scott's great characters.

Robarts, THE REV. MARK, his wife, and LUCY, characters in Trollope's 'Framley Parsonage' (q.v.).

Robbery under Arms, a novel by R. Boldrewood; see *Browne* (*T. A.*).

Robbia, LUCA DELLA (1400–82), Florentine sculptor. He perfected a method of colouring and glazing terracotta sculpture which he and his nephew ANDREA, and the latter's sons, used, especially for architectural decoration.

Robert, Earl of Gloucester (*d.* 1147), a natural son of Henry I, and the chief supporter of Matilda against Stephen. He was a patron of literature, in particular of William of Malmesbury, Henry of Huntingdon, and Geoffrey of Monmouth (qq.v.). Geoffrey's 'History' is dedicated to him.

Robert Elsmere, see *Ward* (*M. A.*).

Robert Macaire, see *Macaire.*

ROBERT OF GLOUCESTER (*fl.* 1260–1300), the reputed author of a metrical chronicle from earliest times down to 1272, illustrated in the later years by personal reminiscences, and written in long lines, running to fourteen syllables and more. It is not the work of a single hand, though probably the whole was composed in the abbey of Gloucester. It contains among passages of special interest the account of a town and gown riot at Oxford in 1263, and a famous description of the death of Simon de Montfort at the battle of Evesham.

Robert the Devil, sixth duke of Normandy, and father of William the Conqueror, a personage about whom many legends gathered, in consequence of his violence and cruelty. In the verse-tale of 'The Life of Robert the Devil', Robert is represented as having been devoted soul and body to Satan by his mother, who had long been childless and prayed to the Devil to give her a son; but as finally repenting of his misdeeds and marrying the emperor's daughter (and, in fact, he died on a pilgrimage to Palestine). This verse-tale is a translation from the French of 1496 and was printed by Wynkyn de Worde. Thomas Lodge (q.v.) wrote a drama on the same subject.

ROBERTS, SIR CHARLES G. D. (1860–1943), Canadian poet, born in New Brunswick; one of the group of poets that came to maturity after the Confederation and expressed the developing national consciousness. He published 'Orion and Other Poems' in 1880, and among other volumes are 'In Divers Tones' (1887), 'Songs of the Common Day' (1893), and 'Collected Poems' (1900). He also wrote novels and Tales.

ROBERTS, MICHAEL (WILLIAM EDWARD) (1902–48), poet and critic. He edited 'New Signatures: poems by several hands' (1932) and the influential 'Faber Book of Modern Verse' (1936). His 'The Recovery of the West' (1941) is a study of the ills of Western civilization and their remedies.

ROBERTSON, FREDERICK WILLIAM (1816–53), educated at Edinburgh University and Balliol College, Oxford. He became incumbent of Trinity Chapel, Brighton, in 1847, and died six years later. He acquired during his short life great influence among all ecclesiastical parties, and his sermons (five series), published at various dates, posthumously, have had a wide circle of readers. His 'Life and Letters' by A. Stopford Brooke appeared in 1865.

ROBERTSON, THOMAS WILLIAM (1829–71), began life as an actor, but retired from the stage and became a dramatist. His plays, 'Society' (1865), 'Ours' (1866), 'Caste' (1867), 'Play' (1868), 'School' (1869), and 'M.P.' (1870), introduced a new and more natural type of comedy to the English stage than had been seen during the first half of the century. His earlier drama, 'David Garrick' (1864), was also well received and is still popular. Marie Wilton (Lady Bancroft) was the great exponent of Robertson's best female characters.

ROBERTSON, WILLIAM (1721–93), born in Midlothian and educated at Edinburgh University, a Presbyterian minister, came into fame by the publication in 1759 of his 'History of Scotland during the Reigns of Queen Mary and of James VI'. This was followed in 1769 by his 'History of Charles V', which brought him the large sum of £4,500 and European reputation, and was translated into French. His 'History of America' was published in 1777 (the third volume, uncompleted, in 1796), and his 'Disquisition concerning the Knowledge which the Ancients had of India' in 1791. Robertson was appointed principal of Edinburgh University in 1762, moderator of the General Assembly and historiographer of Scotland in 1763. His work, in style and method, shows a resemblance to that of Hume (q.v.), but is somewhat more animated and popular, and is based on more careful investigation.

Robespierre, ISIDORE MAXIMILIEN DE (1758–94), one of the most prominent figures in the French Revolution, a leader of the 'Mountain' or extreme party. He was among the promoters of the reign of Terror and finally exercised a kind of dictatorship, but was overthrown in July 1794 and executed. See also *Sea-green Incorruptible.*

Robin and Makyne, an old Scottish pastoral by Henryson (q.v.), included in Percy's 'Reliques'. Robin is a shepherd, and Makyne (a form of 'Malkin') loves him, but Robin rejects her advances, and Makyne goes sadly home. Then Robin's heart is touched, and he in turn pleads with her. But her reply is

Robin, thou hast heard sung and say,
  In gests and storys auld,
The man that will not when he may,
  Sall have nocht when he wald.

Robin Goodfellow, a 'shrewd and knavish sprite' (Shakespeare, 'A Midsummer Night's Dream', II. i), Puck or Hobgoblin, at times a domestic spirit who renders services to the family (as in Milton's 'L'Allegro', ll. 105–10), at others a mischievous elf.

Robin Gray, AULD, see *Lindsay (Lady A.).*

Robin Hood, a legendary outlaw. The name is part of the designation of places and plants in every part of England. The facts behind the legend are uncertain. In the portion of the Pipe Roll of 1230 relating to Yorkshire there is mention of a 'Robertus Hood fugitivus'. Robin Hood is referred to in 'Piers Plowman' (q.v.). As an historical character he appears in Wyntoun's 'Chronicle of Scotland' (c. 1420), and is referred to as a ballad hero by Bower, Major, and Stow. The first detailed history, 'Lytell Geste of Robyn Hoode' (printed, c. 1495), locates him in south-west Yorkshire; later writers place him in Sherwood and Plumpton Park (Cumberland), and finally make him earl of Hunting-

don. Ritson, who collected all the ancient songs and ballads about Robin Hood, says definitely that he was born at Locksley in Nottinghamshire about 1160, that his true name was Robert Fitz-Ooth, and that he was commonly reputed to have been earl of Huntingdon. There is a pleasant account of the activities of his band in Drayton's 'Polyolbion', song 26. According to Stow, there were about the year 1190 many robbers and outlaws, among whom were Robin Hood and Little John, who abode in the woods, robbing the rich, but killing none but such as would invade them, suffering no woman to be molested, and sparing poor men's goods. A date for his death (18 Nov. 1247) was given by Martin Parker ('True Tale', c. 1632) and by Thoresby, and his pedigree was supplied by Stukeley. Legend says that he was bled to death by a treacherous nun at Kirklees in Yorkshire. According to Joseph Hunter (antiquary, 1783–1861), with support from the court rolls of the manor of Wakefield in Yorkshire, he was a contemporary of Edward II (1307–27) and adherent of Thomas of Lancaster. He is the centre of a whole cycle of ballads, one of the best of which is 'Robin Hood and Guy of Gisborne' (q.v.), printed in Percy's 'Reliques', and his legend shows affinity with Chaucer's 'Cook's Tale of Gamelyn' (see *Canterbury Tales*) and with the tales of other legendary outlaws such as Clym of the Clough and Adam Bell (q.v.). Popular plays embodying the legend appear to have been developed out of the village May game, the king and queen of the May giving place to Robin and Maid Marian. Plays dealing with the same theme were written by Munday, Chettle, Tennyson, and others. The 'True Tale of Robin Hood' (verse) was published in 1632, 'Robin Hood's Garland' in 1670, and a prose narrative in 1678. He figures in Scott's 'Ivanhoe' (q.v.) as Locksley.

Robin Hood, *A Tale of,* sub-title of Jonson's 'The Sad Shepherd' (q.v.).

Robin Hood and Guy of Gisborne, one of the best known of the ballads of the Robin Hood cycle. Robin Hood and Little John having gone on their separate ways in the forest, the latter is arrested by the sheriff of Nottingham and tied to a tree. Meanwhile Robin Hood meets with Guy of Gisborne, who has sworn to take Robin; they fight and Guy is slain. Robin puts on the horse-hide with which Guy was clad, takes his arms, and blows a blast on his horn. The Sheriff mistakes him for Guy, thinks he has killed Robin, and gives him permission, as a reward, to kill Little John. Robin releases Little John, gives him Guy's bow, and the sheriff and his company take to their heels.

Robin Oig M'Combich, the Highland drover in Scott's 'The Two Drovers' (q.v.).

ROBINSON, EDWIN ARLINGTON (1869–1935), American poet, born at Head Tide, Maine. The following are among his works: 'The Torrent and the Night Before' (1896), 'The Children of the Night' (1897), 'Captain Craig' (1902), 'The Town Down the River' (1910), 'The Man Against the Sky' (1916), 'Merlin' (1917), 'The Three Taverns' (1920), 'Lancelot' (1920), 'Avon's Harvest' (1921), 'Collected Poems' (1921), 'Roman Bartholow' (1923), 'The Man Who Died Twice' (1924), 'Tristram' (1927), 'Cavender's House' (1929), 'The Glory of the Nightingales' (1930), 'Matthias at the Door' (1931).

ROBINSON, (ESMÉ STUART) LENNOX (1886–1958), Irish dramatist. He was manager of the Abbey Theatre from 1910 to 1923, when he became director. Among his best-known plays are 'The Clancy Name' (1908), 'The Lost Leader' (1918), 'The White-headed Boy' (1920), 'The Round Table' (1924), 'Crabbed Youth and Age' (1924), 'The White Blackbird' (1926), and 'The Far-off Hills' (1928). He also edited 'The Golden Treasury of Irish Verse' (1925), 'The Little Anthology of Irish Verse' (1929), and 'The Oxford Book of Irish Verse' (with Donagh MacDonagh, 1958).

ROBINSON, HENRY CRABB (1775–1867), after spending some years in a solicitor's office in London, travelled in Germany, where he met Goethe and Schiller, and studied at Jena University. He became a foreign correspondent (in 1807, one of the first of the class), and subsequently foreign editor of 'The Times', and its special correspondent in the Peninsula in 1808–9. He was afterwards a barrister. He was acquainted with many notable people of his day and was one of the founders of the Athenaeum Club and of University College, London. Part of his famous diary and correspondence, throwing light on many literary characters, such as Wordsworth, Coleridge, Lamb, and Hazlitt, was published in 1869 (ed. T. Sadler); new editions of his letters were published by Edith J. Morley under the titles 'The Correspondence of Crabb Robinson with the Wordsworth Circle' (2 vols., 1927) and 'Henry Crabb Robinson in Germany' (1929); 'Henry Crabb Robinson on Books and Their Writers' (3 vols., 1938) is compiled from his diary, travel journals, and reminiscences.

Robinson Crusoe, The Life and strange surprising Adventures of, a romance by Defoe (q.v.), published in 1719.

In 1704 Alexander Selkirk (q.v.), son of a shoemaker of Largo, who had run away to sea and joined a privateering expedition under Capt. William Dampier, was, at his own request, put ashore on the uninhabited island of Juan Fernandez. He was rescued in 1709 by Woodes Rogers (q.v.). Defoe embellished the narrative of his residence on the island with many incidents of his imagination and presented it as a true story. The extraordinarily convincing account of the shipwrecked Crusoe's successful efforts to make himself a tolerable existence in his solitude first revealed Defoe's genius for vivid fiction. Defoe was nearly sixty when he wrote it.

The author tells in minute detail the methods by which, with the help of a few stores and utensils saved from the wreck and the exercise of infinite ingenuity, Crusoe built himself a house, domesticated goats, and made himself a boat. He describes the perturbation of his mind caused by the visit of cannibal savages to his island, and his rescue of the poor savage Friday from death; and finally the coming of an English ship, whose crew are in a state of mutiny, the subduing of the mutineers, and Crusoe's rescue.

The book had immediate and permanent success, was translated into many languages, and inspired many imitations. It was followed, also in 1719, by Defoe's 'The Farther Adventures of Robinson Crusoe', in which, with Friday, he revisits his island, is attacked by a fleet of canoes on his departure, and loses Friday in the encounter. 'The Serious Reflections . . . of Robinson Crusoe', 'with his vision of the Angelick World', appeared in 1720.

Robot, derived from a Slav word meaning 'work', well known in 18th-cent. Austria-Hungary, where it was applied to servile labour. Both Maria Theresa and Joseph II granted *robot-patente,* limiting the amount of work that the feudal lords might exact from their serfs. It was adopted about 1923 to designate certain mechanical contrivances so ingenious as to resemble human beings in their ability to perform particular actions, reply to questions, etc. It was popularized by a play 'R.U.R.' (Rossum's Universal Robots) written by the Czech dramatist, Karel Čapek, in which society is represented as dependent on these mechanical men. The latter revolt against their employers and destroy them.

Robsart, AMY, daughter of Sir John Robsart, married to Sir Robert Dudley, afterwards earl of Leicester, in 1549, she figures in Scott's 'Kenilworth' (q.v.).

Robson, DANIEL, MRS., and SYLVIA, characters in Mrs. Gaskell's 'Sylvia's Lovers' (q.v.).

Robyne and Makyne, see *Robin and Makyne.*

Roc, a mythical bird of Eastern legend, imagined as being of enormous size and strength. In the 'Arabian Nights' story of Sindbad the Sailor, the Roc carries Sindbad out of the valley of diamonds.

Roche, SIR BOYLE (1743–1807), a baronet and Irish M.P., celebrated as a perpetrator of 'bulls'. That attributed to him about being in two places at once 'like a bird' is said by J. H. Burton (q.v., in 'The Book-hunter') to occur, much earlier, in the letters of the Jacobite, Robertson of Struan.

ROCHESTER, JOHN WILMOT, *second earl of* (1648–80), born at Ditchley, near Woodstock, and educated at Wadham College,

Oxford, a poet of genius and a notorious libertine. He fought at sea in the Dutch War, and showed conspicuous gallantry. Rochester was attractive in person and manners and a favourite of Charles II, who frequently banished him from the court and as frequently pardoned him. He was a patron of Elizabeth Barry (q.v.) and temporarily of several poets, including Dryden, whom, however, he caused to be waylaid and beaten on account of a passage in Mulgrave's anonymous 'Essay on Satire', which he attributed to Dryden. His repentant deathbed scene was described by G. Burnet (q.v.) in a pamphlet which became extremely popular. His best literary work was satirical, notably in 'A Satire against Mankind' (1675), and among his amorous lyrics there are some marked with sincerity and feeling, as well as wit and finish.

Rochester, MR., the hero of Charlotte Brontë's 'Jane Eyre' (q.v.).

Rock day, the day after Twelfth Day, so called because on that day women resumed their spinning (cf. *Plough Monday*). 'Rock' here means a distaff.

Rockefeller, JOHN DAVISON (1839–1937), started life as an accountant, and, having saved a little capital, went into partnership in an oil-refining business. He organized the Standard Oil Co. in 1870, substituting combination for the previous competition among the American oil companies, and became immensely rich. From 1890 he undertook the philanthropic distribution of his fortune, and by the end of 1927 is said to have bestowed some £100,000,000 on such purposes. The principal institutions that he set up were the 'Rockefeller Institute for Medical Research'; the 'Rockefeller Foundation' for medical education and the control of certain diseases; and the 'General Education Board' and 'International Education Board' for the development of teaching and research in the U.S.A. and the rest of the world respectively. His son (1874–1960), who bore the same names, continued to give large sums for education, research, and kindred purposes, including $2,000,000 for an Archaeological Museum in Palestine. [E.B.]

Rococo, apparently a fanciful formation on the stem of *rocaille*, shell- or pebble-work. The term is used for the style of interior decoration introduced into France in the first half of the 18th cent. The effect was of lightness and gaiety, achieved by the use of intricate gilded carving framing mirrors or against a light background, refined in detail and asymmetrical in design. It spread to Germany and Austria but was too frivolous for English taste.

Roderick, *the last of the Goths*, a poem by Southey (q.v.), published in 1814.

Roderick, the last king of the Visigoths, has dishonoured Florinda, daughter of Count Julian. The latter, in revenge, calls the Moors into Spain, and Roderick is driven from his throne. In penitence for his crime, Roderick consecrates his life to God and assumes the garb of a monk. A spark of revolt against the Moors is kindled in the devastated country, and Roderick, under the name of Father Maccabee, goes to the Moorish camp, where Pelayo, his cousin, is held as a hostage. He persuades Pelayo to escape and place himself at the head of the Christian forces. Pelayo is acclaimed king, and leads his army against Moors at the battle of Covadonga. In the heat of the battle, Roderick, who, unrecognized as a monk, has received the confession of Florinda (which partly absolves him) and has made his peace with his mother and Count Julian, leaps on his old war-horse, reveals himself to the Christian army, and leads it to victory. He then disappears, and it is only generations later that, in a hermitage, a tomb bearing his name is discovered. Pelayo becomes the founder of the Spanish royal line.

The subject is also treated by W. S. Landor (q.v.) in his 'Count Julian'.

Roderick, *Vision of Don*, a poem by Sir W. Scott (q.v.), published in 1811.

Roderick, the last Gothic king of Spain, in order to learn the future, has the temerity to enter a magic vault which has been denounced as fatal to the Spanish monarchy. He there sees a vision of his own defeat by the Moors and their occupation of the country; next, of the peninsula when Spanish and Portuguese conquests have raised it to the height of its power, sullied, however, by superstition; lastly, of the usurpation of the Spanish crown by Buonaparte, and the arrival of British succour.

Roderick Dhu, a character in Sir W. Scott's 'Lady of the Lake' (q.v.).

Roderick Hudson, the first novel of H. James (q.v.), published in book form in 1876. It is the story of a young man transplanted from a lawyer's office in a Massachusetts town to a sculptor's studio in Rome. Incapable of adjustment to his environment, he fails both in art and love, and meets a tragic end in Switzerland.

Roderick Random, *The Adventures of,* a picaresque novel by Smollett (q.v.), published in 1748.

This was the first important work by Smollett. It is modelled on Le Sage's 'Gil Blas', and is a series of episodes, told with infinite vigour and vividness, strung together on the life of the selfish and unprincipled hero, who relates them. Its chief interest is in the picture that it gives, drawn from personal experience, of the British navy and the British sailor of the day. But much of the story is repulsive.

Roderick, left penniless by his grandfather (his father has been disinherited and has left the country), is befriended by his uncle, Lieut. Tom Bowling of the navy. Accompanied by an old schoolfellow, Strap, he goes to London, meets with many adventures at the hands of rogues of various kinds, and qualifies as a surgeon's mate in the navy. He is pressed as a common sailor on board the man-of-war 'Thunder', becomes mate to the Welsh surgeon, Morgan, is present at the siege of Cartagena (1741), and after suffering much misery and ill-treatment returns to England. Here he meets with further adventures, falls in love with Narcissa, and is carried by smugglers to France, where he finds and relieves his uncle Tom Bowling. He joins the French army and fights at Dettingen. His fortunes are rehabilitated by his generous friend Strap, who even undertakes to serve Roderick as his valet, and he sets out to marry a lady of fortune. He makes love to Miss Melinda Goosetrap, but does not impose upon her mother; and other matrimonial enterprises are not more successful. Having lost all his money at play, he embarks as surgeon on a ship commanded by Tom Bowling, and in the course of the voyage meets Don Roderigo, a wealthy trader, who turns out to be Roderick's father. They return to England, Roderick is married to Narcissa, and Strap to her maid, Miss Williams.

Roderigo, a character in Shakespeare's 'Othello' (q.v.).

Rodin, AUGUSTE (1840–1917), French sculptor. A replica of his 'Burghers of Calais' stands near the Houses of Parliament. He presented a number of his works to the Victoria and Albert Museum.

Rodney Stone, a novel by Sir A. Conan Doyle (q.v.).

Rodomont, in the 'Orlando Innamorato' and the 'Orlando Furioso' (qq.v.), the king of Sarza, arrogant and valiant, the doughtiest of the followers of Agramant (q.v.). His boastfulness gave rise to the word *rodomontade*. He leads the first Saracen invasion into France. Doralis, princess of Granada, is betrothed to him, but falls into the power of Mandricardo (q.v.). After an indecisive duel between the two Saracen heroes, the conflict is referred to the princess herself, who, to Rodomont's surprise, expresses her preference for Mandricardo. Rodomont retires in disgust to the south of France. Here Isabella (q.v.) falls into his power and, preferring death, by guile causes him to slay her. In remorse, in order to commemorate her, he builds a bridge and takes toll of all who pass that way. Orlando, coming in his madness to the bridge, throws Rodomont into the river. Rodomont is also defeated by Bradamant (q.v.). Thus humiliated he temporarily retires from arms, emerges once more, and is finally killed by Rogero (q.v.).

Roger, THE JOLLY, the pirates' black flag.

Roger, the name of the Cook in Chaucer's 'The Canterbury Tales' (q.v.).

Roger Bontemps, see *Bontemps*.

Roger de Coverley, SIR, see *Coverley*.

Rogero or RUGGIERO, the legendary ancestor of the house of Este, extolled in the 'Orlando Furioso' (q.v.). He is the son of a Christian knight and a Saracen lady of royal birth, brought up in Africa, and taken by Agramant (q.v.) on the expedition against Charlemagne, where he falls in love with the warrior maiden Bradamant (q.v.) and she with him. He falls into the power of Alcina (q.v.) and is released by Melissa (q.v.). He then, mounted on the hippogriff, rescues Angelica from the Orc. Bradamant has also an active rival in Marfisa, a lady fighting on the Moorish side, who is smitten with love for Rogero, but eventually turns out to be his sister. Finally, after the retreat of Agramant, Rogero joins Charlemagne and is baptized. He now hopes to marry Bradamant, but her ambitious parents vigorously oppose the match. Bradamant, to secure her lover without openly opposing her parents, declares, with Charlemagne's approval, that she will marry no one who has not withstood her in battle for a whole day. This Rogero alone does, and after many vicissitudes the lovers are united. In a final duel Rogero slays Rodomont (q.v.).

Rogero, SONG BY, a song in 'The Rovers' (see *Anti-Jacobin*).

Rogers, BRUCE (1870–1957), born in the United States, an eminent designer of books, printing adviser to the Cambridge University Press, 1918–19, and subsequently to the Harvard University Press.

ROGERS, JAMES EDWIN THOROLD (1823–90), educated at King's College, London, and Magdalen Hall, Oxford, was professor of political economy at Oxford in 1862–7 and again in 1888. He had been a strong Tractarian till about 1860, but put off his orders and swung right round, being the first clergyman to take advantage of the Clerical Disabilities Relief Act of 1870. He was Radical M.P. for Southwark, 1880–6. His best-known works are the 'History of Agriculture and Prices in England from 1259 to 1793' (1866–87) and 'Six Centuries of Work and Wages' (1884 and 1886). He wrote a number of other treatises of political and economic history, including 'A Complete Collection of the Protests of the Lords' (1875), and edited Adam Smith's 'Wealth of Nations' (1869).

ROGERS, SAMUEL (1763–1855), born at Stoke Newington, the son of a banker and a man of wealth, published in 1792 his 'The Pleasures of Memory', a piece of agreeable verse, which achieved popularity. He attained a high position among men of letters, at a time when the poetical standard was not high, and in 1810 published a fragmentary epic, 'Columbus', in 1814 'Jacqueline', and in 1822–8 'Italy', a collection of verse tales, which also obtained a certain degree of fame. He was offered, but declined, the laureateship in 1850. His 'Recollections', dealing with a long life and a wide acquaintance, were published in 1859. 'Recollections of the Table Talk of Samuel Rogers' (ed. Dyce) was issued in 1856.

ROGERS, WOODES (*d.* 1732), commander of a privateering expedition (1708–11) in which William Dampier (q.v.) was pilot, and in the course of which Alexander Selkirk (q.v.) was discovered on the island of Juan Fernandez and rescued, the town of Guayaquil was taken and held to ransom, and a Manila ship captured. These incidents are described in Rogers's entertaining journal, 'A Cruizing Voyage round the World' (1712). He was twice (1718–21 and 1729–32) governor of the Bahamas, and most successful in putting down piracy.

Roi d'Yvetot, LE, the subject and title of a song by Béranger (q.v.), the type of easy-going, pleasure-loving monarch, the ruler of a very small but peaceful and contented territory. The song appeared in 1813 when France was wearying of the sacrifices entailed by Napoleon's campaigns. There is an excellent rendering by Thackeray.

Roi Soliel, LE, the name given to the French king Louis XIV.

Rois Fainéants, LES, the 'do-nothing kings', a name given to the later Merovingian kings of France, who were mere figureheads, under the domination of the Mayors of the Palace (q.v.).

ROJAS, FERNANDO DE (*c.* 1465–1541), a Spanish author born at Puebla de Montalbán, near Toledo, his family being *conversos*, or Jews converted to Christianity. He studied law at the University of Salamanca and, in spite of difficulties owing to his racial origin, rose to the position of *alcalde mayor* of Talavera. He is remembered for his masterpiece, 'Celestina' (q.v.), but there is no record of any other work by his hand.

Rokeby, a poem in six cantos by Sir W. Scott (q.v.), published in 1813.

The scene is laid chiefly at Rokeby near Greta Bridge in Yorkshire, and the time is immediately after the battle of Marston Moor (1644). The complicated plot is concerned with the conspiracy of Oswald Wycliffe, lord of Barnard Castle, with the sturdy ruffian, Bertram Risingham, to murder the latter's patron, Philip of Mortham, in order to obtain his lands and the treasure which had been obtained by him on the Spanish main. Mortham is shot and left for dead, but recovers. An attack on Rokeby Castle to secure the treasure is defeated, largely by the prowess of young Redmond O'Neale, Lord Rokeby's page. Meanwhile Oswald, to whom Lord Rokeby has been entrusted as a prisoner after Marston Moor, threatens to execute his prisoner unless Rokeby's daughter, Matilda, consents to marry Oswald's son, Wilfrid, a gentle poetic youth, who refuses to avail himself of Matilda's reluctant consent. Just as Lord Rokeby is about to be executed, Bertram, struck with remorse, rides in and kills Oswald,

and is himself slain. Redmond O'Neale is discovered to be the lost son of Mortham, and marries Matilda.

The poem includes the beautiful songs, 'A weary lot is thine, fair maid', and 'Brignal Banks'. It is interesting for the fact that Scott (in spite of the good first reception of the poem) recognized his own comparative failure as a poet, and thereupon turned to his true vocation as a romantic novelist.

Rokesmith, JOHN, in Dickens's 'Our Mutual Friend' (q.v.), the name assumed by John Harmon.

Roland, the most famous of the paladins (q.v.) of Charlemagne. According to the chronicler Eginhard, his legend has the following basis of fact. In August 778 the rear-guard of the French army of Charlemagne was returning through the Pyrenees from a successful expedition in the north of Spain, when it was surprised in the valley of Roncevaux by the Basque inhabitants of the mountains; the baggage was looted and all the rear-guard killed, including Hrodland, count of the Breton marches. The story of this disaster was developed by the imagination of numerous poets. For the Basques were substituted the Saracens. Roland becomes the commander of the rear-guard, appointed to the post at the instance of the traitor Ganelon, who is in league with the Saracen king, Marsile. Oliver is introduced, Roland's companion in arms, the brother of Aude, Roland's betrothed. Oliver thrice urges Roland to summon aid by sounding his horn, but Roland from excess of pride defers doing so till too late. Charlemagne returns and destroys the pagan army. Ganelon is tried and executed.

The legend has been handed down in three principal forms: in the fabricated Latin chronicle of the 12th cent. erroneously attributed to Archbishop Turpin (*d. c.* 800); in the 'Carmen de proditione Guenonis' of the same epoch; and in the 'Chanson de Roland', in medieval French, also of the early 12th cent. It is a well-known tradition that Taillefer, a *jongleur* in the army of William the Conqueror, sang a poem on Roncevaux at the battle of Hastings (1066), possibly an earlier version of the extant 'Chanson'.

Roland, as Orlando, is the hero of Boiardo's 'Orlando Innamorato' and Ariosto's 'Orlando Furioso' (qq.v.). Roland's sword was called 'Durandal' or 'Durindana', and his horn 'Olivant'. See also *Oliver*.

Roland for an Oliver, A, tit for tat, with reference to the evenly matched combat between Roland and Oliver. See *Oliver*.

Roland, *Childe*, see *Childe Roland*.

Roland, MME JEANNE (1754–93), the daughter of Gatien Phlipon, an engraver, and wife of Jean Marie Roland de la Platière, French economist and politician, was the Egeria (and a most unfortunate and dangerous one) of the Girondists (q.v.) in the French

Revolution and was executed in 1793. When mounting the scaffold she uttered the famous words, 'O liberté! que de crimes on commet en ton nom.' Her husband killed himself on learning her fate.

Roland de Vaux, (1) the baron of Triermain, in Scott's 'Bridal of Triermain' (q.v.); (2) also in Coleridge's 'Christabel' (q.v.), the name of the estranged friend of Christabel's father.

ROLFE, FREDERICK WILLIAM (1860–1913), who liked to call himself 'Baron Corvo', was by turns schoolmaster, painter, and writer. He was a convert to Roman Catholicism and an unsuccessful candidate for the priesthood, and his most outstanding work, 'Hadrian the Seventh' (1904), appears to be a dramatized autobiography—a self-justification and a dream of wish-fulfilment. His other writings include 'Stories Toto Told Me' (published in 1898 after first appearing in 'The Yellow Book' (q.v.)), 'Chronicles of the House of Borgia' (1901), and 'The Desire and Pursuit of the Whole' (written in 1909, but considered too libellous at the time and not published till 1934). The story of Rolfe's frustrated life and unhappy death is told by A. J. A. Symons in 'The Quest for Corvo' (1934).

Roll, RAGMAN, a set of rolls in the Public Record Office, in which are recorded the instruments of homage made to Edward I by the Scottish king (Balliol), nobles, etc., at the Parliament of Berwick in 1296; so called apparently from the pendent seals attached.

ROLLAND, ROMAIN (1866–1944), French historian and critic of music, novelist, biographer, and dramatist; author of 'Jean Christophe' (1905–12, a series of novels in ten volumes, about a musical genius), 'Beethoven' (1903, biography), 'Michel Ange' (1907, biography), and works on Indian religious thought.

ROLLE OF HAMPOLE, RICHARD (c. 1300–49), born at Thornton in the North Riding of Yorkshire, is said to have left Oxford in his 19th year and to have become a hermit. He lived at various places in Yorkshire, finally at Hampole, where he died, near a Cistercian nunnery in which he had disciples. Among these was Margaret Kirkeby, who became an anchoress and was enclosed in his neighbourhood. Rolle wrote a number of scriptural commentaries, meditations, and other religious works, in Latin and English. Their bibliography and the materials relating to the life of Rolle are discussed by H. E. Allen in 'Writings ascribed to Richard Rolle' (1927).

Rolliad, Criticisms on the, a collection of Whig political satires directed against William Pitt and his followers after their success at the election of 1784, first published in the 'Morning Herald' and 'Daily Advertiser' during that year. The authors, members of the 'Esto Perpetua' club (q.v.), are not known with certainty, but among them were Dr.

French Laurence, who became Regius professor of civil law at Oxford; George Ellis, the antiquary; General Richard Fitzpatrick; and Lord John Townshend. The satires originally took the form of reviews of an imaginary epic, 'The Rolliad', which took its name from John Rolle, M.P., one of Pitt's supporters, and dealt with the adventures of a mythical Norman duke, Rollo, his ancestor. These were followed by 'Political Eclogues', 'Probationary Odes' for the vacant laureateship, and 'Political Miscellanies', all directed to the same purpose, the ridicule of the Tories. A complete collection was published in 1791.

Rollright Stones, THE, a circle of stones perhaps of pre-Celtic origin, near Chipping Norton, on the confines of Oxfordshire and Warwickshire. Drayton ('Polyolbion', xiii. 414) alludes to a legend that they are a witness of a victory over Rollo and the Danes.

Rolls, CLOSE, the rolls in which close-writs (grants given to private persons under the great seal), private indentures, and recognizances are recorded.

Rolls, PIPE, the Great Rolls of the Exchequer, comprising the various 'pipes', or enrolled accounts, of sheriffs and others for a financial year. The origin of this use of 'pipe' is doubtful; some would explain it from the pipe-like form of a thin roll or (?) from its being transmitted in a cylindrical case. Bacon saw in it a metaphor, 'because the whole receipt is finally conveyed into it [the Exchequer] by means of divers small pipes or quills'. The complete series of Pipe Rolls dates from the reign of Henry II, but there is an isolated one (of the highest importance) of the year 1130.

Rolls House in Chancery Lane, formerly a house of maintenance for converted Jews, founded by Henry III, was annexed by Edward III to the office of the Master of the Rolls, who had his official residence there. The rolls and records of the Court of Chancery were kept there until the erection of the Record Office in Fetter Lane. The chapel, greatly altered and disfigured, survived (Wheatley and Cunningham).

Rolls Series, otherwise 'Chronicles and Memorials of Great Britain and Ireland from the Invasion of the Romans to the Reign of Henry VIII'. Their publication was authorized by government in 1857 on the suggestion of Joseph Stevenson, the archivist, and the recommendation of Sir John Romilly, master of the rolls. Before 1914, ninety-nine chronicles, etc., had appeared in the series, most of them edited by the greatest historical scholars of the time.

Romaic, the modern Greek language.

ROMAINS, JULES (1885–   ), French novelist. His best-known work 'Les Hommes de bonne volonté' (1932–47), a series of twenty-seven novels, connected but not continuous, forms a panorama of French life and thought in Paris and the provinces and in various sections of society between 1908 and 1933. It has been translated ('Men of Good Will').

Roman Actor, The, a tragedy by Massinger (q.v.), printed in 1629. The play is based on the life of the Emperor Domitian as told by Suetonius and Dio Cassius.

The cruel and licentious emperor forcibly takes from Aelius Lamia, a Roman senator, his wife Domitia, makes her empress, and dotes on her. Domitia falls in love with Paris the actor. So well does he act before her a scene in which, as Iphis scorned by Anaxarete, he threatens to take his life, that she betrays herself. The emperor, his suspicions inflamed by enemies of Domitia, finds her and Paris together, kills Paris with his own hand (making him act the part of a false servant and himself taking the part of the injured lord), but cannot find heart to punish Domitia. She, incensed at the death of Paris and presuming on her power over the emperor, rails at and taunts him. Unable to kill her with his own hand, he writes down her name in the list of those condemned to death. This list Domitia finds while he sleeps. Hastily conspiring with others whose names are in the list, they lure him away from his guards and kill him.

Roman d'Alexandre, see *Alexander the Great.*

Roman de Brut and Roman de Rou, see *Wace.*

Roman de la Rose. The first 4,058 lines of this allegorical romance were written *c.* 1240 by Guillaume de Lorris to expound the 'whole Art of Love'; the last 18,000 lines were composed about forty years later by Jean de Meung, as a refutation of courtly doctrines within a philosophical framework. The story in Guillaume de Lorris's part of the poem is an allegorical presentation of courtly love, substantially as presented in 'The Romaunt of the Rose' (q.v.); the allegorical figures mainly embody various aspects of the lady whom the lover (the narrator) meets in his endeavours to reach the rose, which symbolizes the lady's love; the story is set in a walled garden, the dream world of *courtoisie,* the unpleasant realities of life being shown as painted on the walls outside. In the second part, Jean de Meung shows love in the real world, gives a naturalistic and cynical view of the relationship between the sexes, and links it to an exposition of the new rationalist philosophy of the 13th cent. The difference between the two parts of the poem is best shown in the use of the allegorical figure of Reason; a minor figure for Guillaume, she represents the common sense which tries to dissuade a man from the extravagances of courtly love; for Jean a major character, she is the reasoning faculty of man, and it is through her mouth that he expounds his philosophical views. The Roman, in its allegorical dream form, in its presentation of both the courtly

and the realist conceptions of love, and by its clear exposition of philosophical ideas for the layman, remained a powerful influence all through the later Middle Ages, both inside and outside France.

Roman de Renart, see *Reynard the Fox.*

Roman Empire, THE HOLY, see *Holy Roman Empire.*

Roman Father, THE, see *Horatii and the Curiatii.*

Roman Question, THE, the dispute between the papacy and the Italian state after 1870 on the territorial claims of the pope, settled by Pius XI and Mussolini in 1929.

Roman type, the form normally used today, developed by early printers from humanist script, itself deriving from the capitals of Roman monumental inscriptions and the small letters of 9th-cent. (Carolingian) script, which Italian scholars of the 15th cent. preferred for classical texts.

Roman Wall, THE, see *Hadrian* and *Severus.*

Romance languages, generally used as the collective name for the group of languages descended from Latin, the chief of which are French, Italian, Spanish, and Provençal.

Romanes Lectures, lectures founded at Oxford in 1891 by George John Romanes (1848–94), a scientist born at Kingston, Canada, author of 'Darwin and after Darwin' (1892). He was educated at Gonville and Caius College, Cambridge, was a friend of Darwin and a professor at Edinburgh and at the Royal Institution, and was noted for his studies in physiology and zoology. The lectures are on subjects approved by the vice-chancellor, relating to science, art, or literature.

Romanesque, the style of architecture, based on Roman methods of building (i.e. using the round arch), used in Europe from, very roughly, A.D. 600 to 1150. The form used in England from the 11th cent. is called Norman (q.v.).

Romantic, a word for which, in connexion with literature, there is no generally accepted definition. The OED. says 'Characterized ... by, invested ... with, romance or imaginative appeal', where romance appears to mean 'redolence or suggestion of, association with, the adventurous and chivalrous', something remote from the scenes and incidents of ordinary life.

Romantic Movement, THE, began in the late 18th cent. (though there are earlier isolated examples of the romantic spirit) and lasted into the 19th cent. In literature and art the classical, intellectual attitude gave way to a wider outlook, which recognized the claims of passion and emotion, and in which the critical was replaced by the imaginative spirit, and wit by humour and pathos.

Romany or ROMMANY, a gipsy (q.v.) word meaning a gipsy, or the gipsy language.

Romany Rye, The, a novel by Borrow (q.v.), published in 1857. 'Romany Rye', in gipsy (q.v.) language, means 'Gipsy Gentleman', a name applied to Borrow in his youth by Ambrose Smith, the Norfolk gipsy. This book is a sequel to 'Lavengro' (q.v.), and continues in the same style the story of the author's wanderings and adventures.

Romaunt of the Rose, The, a poem of 7,700 lines in short couplets, attributed to Chaucer, but of which part only was probably written by him. It is a translation, with amplifications, of so much of the French 'Roman de la Rose' (q.v.) as was written by Guillaume de Lorris, and of parts of the continuation by Jean de Meung. The story is put into the form of a dream in which the poet visits the Garden of Mirth, being invited to enter by Idleness. Here he sees various allegorical personages, the God of Love, Gladness, Courtesy, and so on, disporting themselves. In the water of the fountain of Narcissus he sees mirrored a rose-tree and falls in love with a rose-bud. His attempts to cull this are aided or obstructed by various allegorical personages, Bialacoil (Bel-Accueil, Welcome), Danger, False-Semblant, Reason, Shame, Jealousy. The God of Love shoots arrows at the poet and makes him yield himself his servant. He lays his commands upon him, and instructs him in the means by which the lover achieves his ends (not omitting largesse to the maid). Finally Jealousy builds a castle about the rose. The latter part of the poem, which is fragmentary, contains a version of about one-sixth of Jean de Meung's continuation; it is a vigorous satire on religion, women, and the social order.

Rome, King of, the title given to the son of Napoleon Buonaparte and the Empress Marie Louise, at his birth in 1811. The title was a deliberate parallel to, or imitation of, the medieval title of 'King of the Romans', which was commonly given to the destined successor of the 'Holy Roman Emperor'.

Romeo and Juliet, the first romantic tragedy of Shakespeare (q.v.), based on an Italian romance by Bandello frequently translated into English. Shakespeare's play was probably written in 1595, first printed in corrupt form in 1597 (authentic second quarto, 1599).

The Montagues and the Capulets, the two chief families of Verona, are at bitter enmity. Romeo, son of old Lord Montague, attends, disguised by a mask, a feast given by old Lord Capulet. He sees and falls in love with Juliet, daughter of Capulet, and she with him. After the feast he overhears, under her window, Juliet's confession of her love for him, and wins her consent to a secret marriage. With the help of Friar Laurence, they are wedded next day. Mercutio, a friend of Romeo, meets Tybalt, of the Capulet family, who is infuriated by his discovery of Romeo's presence at the feast, and they quarrel. Romeo comes on the scene, and attempts to reason with Tybalt, but Tybalt and Mercutio fight, and Mercutio falls. Then Romeo draws and Tybalt is killed. The duke with Montague and Capulet come up, and Romeo is sentenced to banishment. Early next day, after passing the night with Juliet, he leaves Verona for Mantua, counselled by the friar, who intends to publish Romeo's marriage at an opportune moment. Capulet proposes to marry Juliet to Count Paris, and when she seeks excuses to avoid this, peremptorily insists. Juliet consults the friar, who bids her consent to the match, but on the night before the wedding drink a potion which will render her apparently lifeless for 40 hours. He will warn Romeo, who will rescue her from the vault on her awakening and carry her to Mantua. Juliet does his bidding. The friar's message to Romeo miscarries, and Romeo hears that Juliet is dead. Buying poison, he comes to the vault to have a last sight of Juliet. He chances upon Count Paris outside the vault; they fight and Paris is killed. Then Romeo, after a last kiss on Juliet's lips, drinks the poison and dies. Juliet awakes and finds Romeo dead by her side, and the cup still in his hand. Guessing what has happened, she stabs herself and dies. The story is unfolded by the friar and Count Paris's page, and Montague and Capulet, faced by the tragic results of their enmity, are reconciled.

Romford, MR. FACEY, see *Surtees* (R. S.).

Romfrey, THE HON. EVERARD, afterwards *earl of,* a character in Meredith's 'Beauchamp's Career' (q.v.).

Romney, GEORGE (1734–1802), portrait painter, born in Lancashire. After visiting Rome in 1773–5 he aspired to the Grand Style, often achieving a compromise between history painting and portrait in, for instance, some of his many portraits of Lady Hamilton (e.g. 'Lady Hamilton as Cassandra'). He is the subject of Tennyson's poem 'Romney's Remorse'.

Romola, a novel by G. Eliot (q.v.), published in 1863.

The background of the novel is Florence at the end of the 15th cent., the troubled period, following the expulsion of the Medici, of the expedition of Charles VIII, of distracted counsels in the city, of the excitement caused by the preaching of Savonarola, and of acute division between the popular party and the supporters of the Medici. The various historical figures, including Charles VIII, Machiavelli, and Savonarola himself, are drawn with great care, as well as the whole picturesque complexion of the city. The story is that of the purification by trials of the noble-natured Romola, devoted daughter of an old blind scholar. Into their lives comes the clever, adaptable, young Greek, Tito Melema, whose self-indulgence develops into utter perfidy. He robs, and abandons in imprisonment, the benefactor of his childhood, Baldassare. He cruelly goes through a mock marriage ceremony with the innocent little contadina Tessa. After marrying Romola he wounds her deepest feelings by betraying her father's solemn trust. He plays a double game in the political intrigues of the day. Nemesis pursues and at last overtakes him in the person of old Baldassare, who escapes from imprisonment crazed with sorrow and suffering. Romola, with her love for her husband turned to contempt, and her trust in Savonarola destroyed by his falling away from his high prophetic mission, is left in utter isolation, from which she is rescued by the discovery of her duty in self-sacrifice. Concurrently with this termination the author relates the undermining of Savonarola's influence over the city, his trial, condemnation, and execution.

Romulus, the legendary founder of Rome, a son of Mars and Ilia, the daughter of Numitor, king of Alba. Remus was his twin-brother. These two children were thrown into the Tiber, by order of Amulius, who had usurped the throne of his brother Numitor. But they were preserved and suckled by a she-wolf. In due course they put Amulius to death and restored Numitor to the throne. They afterwards undertook to build a city, the future Rome, and the omens having given the preference to Romulus, he began to lay the foundations. But Remus, in ridicule, leapt over them. This angered Romulus, who slew his brother. He gathered fugitives and criminals in his city, and conquered the Sabines, who then came to live in Rome; and their king, Tatius, shared the sovereignty with Romulus. The latter was deified and identified with Quirinus (q.v.).

Roncesvalles or RONCEVAUX, a valley in the western Pyrenees, celebrated as the scene of the defeat of the rear-guard of Charlemagne's army and the death of Roland (q.v.) in 778 (see also *Fontarabia*).

Rondeau, a poem consisting of ten (or, in stricter sense, of thirteen) lines, having only two rhymes throughout, and with the opening words used twice as a refrain.

Rondel, a RONDEAU (q.v.), or a special form of this.

Rondibilis, in Rabelais, III. xxxi et seq., the physician whom Panurge consults on the subject of his marriage.

RONSARD, PIERRE DE (1524–85), French lyric poet, the principal figure in the 'Pléiade' (q.v.). A page at the court of France, he was transferred to that of James V of Scotland, where he remained till the latter's marriage with Marie de Guise, the mother of Queen Mary Stuart, to whom he later addressed some of his poems. He was subsequently in the service of Charles IX of France. As a poet he was regarded by his contemporaries with intense admiration. He contributed powerfully to the reform of French literature, creating a new poetic language, and exercised considerable influence on the English sonnet-

writers of the 16th cent. He is seen at his best and most original in his lighter verse.

Röntgen Rays or X-RAYS, electro-magnetic waves of shorter length than the ultra-violet, possessing the power of passing through certain opaque substances. They were discovered by Prof. Wilhelm Konrad Röntgen (1845–1923), a German physicist, in the course of experiments in electric discharge through rarefied gas. Being uncertain as to their nature, he called them X-rays.

Roosevelt, FRANKLIN DELANO (1882–1945), President of the United States, a distant cousin of President Theodore Roosevelt, and a man of remarkable vision, keen feeling for suffering humanity, democratic principles, and vigour in action. After service in the administration of President Wilson, and two terms as Governor of New York, he was elected President in 1932. He took office at a moment of profound economic depression in America, and averted a panic only by the confidence and vigour with which he applied himself to reform. In 1938–9, during his second term of office, he strove for the maintenance of peace in Europe, but when it proved impossible to curb the aggressive policy of Hitler, he gave unstinted support to Britain, adopting the generous and far-sighted measure known as Lease-Lend, and stimulating to the utmost the production of war supplies in America. It was during his third term of office that the Japanese attack on Peal Harbour (1941) led to declarations of war by the United States against the three Axis countries. Overcoming the handicap of physical infirmity (due to an attack of polio-myelitis in 1921) Roosevelt was the first President to leave national territory in war time, visiting Canada, Casablanca, Cairo, Teheran, and the Crimea to confer with the heads of allied governments. He died on 12 April 1945, a few months after entering on his fourth term of office, and only a few weeks before the surrender of Germany which he had so powerfully contributed to bring about.

Root-and-Branch, the name given to a bill supported by a majority of the House of Commons in 1641 for the abolition of episcopacy and the transfer of the bishops' powers to committees of laymen in each diocese. It was rejected by the Lords, and not reintroduced until the summer of 1643.

Roper, MARGARET (1505–44), daughter of Sir T. More (q.v.). According to Stapleton (1535–98) she purchased the head of her dead father a month after it had been exposed on London Bridge and preserved it in spices till her death. It is believed that it was buried with her. Tennyson alludes to this:

Her, who clasped in her last trance
Her murdered father's head.
　　　　　('Dream of Fair Women.')

Rosa Bud, a character in Dickens's 'Edwin Drood' (q.v.).

Rosa Bunion, see *Bunion*.

Rosa Dartle, a character in Dickens's 'David Copperfield' (q.v.).

Rosalind, (1) in Spenser's 'Shepheards Calender' and 'Colin Clouts come home againe' (qq.v.), an unknown lady celebrated by the poet as his love; (2) a character in Shakespeare's 'As You Like It' (q.v.).

Rosaline, (1) in Shakespeare's 'Love's Labour's Lost' (q.v.), a lady attendant on the Princess of France; (2) in Shakespeare's 'Romeo and Juliet' (q.v.), a Capulet, with whom Romeo was in love before he first saw Juliet.

Rosalynde. Euphues Golden Legacie, a pastoral romance in the style of Lyly's 'Euphues' (q.v.), diversified with sonnets and eclogues, written by Lodge (q.v.) during his voyage to the Canaries ('every line wet with a surge'), and published in 1590. The story is borrowed in part from 'The Tale of Gamelyn' (q.v.) and was dramatized with little alteration by Shakespeare in his 'As You Like It' (q.v.). Lodge's Rosader is Shakespeare's Orlando; Saladyne is Oliver; Alinda, Celia; and Rosalind is common to both. The ill-treatment of Rosader (Orlando) by his elder brother is more developed by Lodge, and the restoration of the rightful duke to his dukedom is effected by arms instead of persuasion. The characters of Jaques and Touchstone, and the humour that enriches 'As You Like It', are found only in Shakespeare's work. Lodge's romance includes the pleasant and well-known madrigal,

> Love in my bosome like a Bee
> Doth suck his sweet.

Rosamond, FAIR, Rosamond Clifford (*d.* 1176?), daughter of Walter de Clifford, probably acknowledged as mistress of Henry II in 1174. She was buried in the choir of Godstow Abbey, but her remains were removed to the Chapter House, *c.* 1191.

These are the known facts on which the popular legend was based. As told by Stow (q.v.) following Higden (q.v.) the legend related that 'Rosamond the fayre daughter of Walter Lord Clifford, concubine to Henry II (poisoned by Queen Elianor as some thought) dyed at Woodstocke where King Henry had made for her a house of wonderful working, so that no man or woman might come to her but he that was instructed by the King. This house after some was named Labyrinthus, or Dedalus worke, wrought like unto a knot in a garden, called a maze; but it was commonly said that lastly the queene came to her by a clue of thridde or silke, and so dealt with her that she lived not long after: but when she was dead, she was buried at Godstow in an house of nunnes, beside Oxford, with these verses upon her tombe:

> Hic jacet in tumba Rosa mundi, non rosa munda:
> Non redolet, sed olet, quae redolere solet.'

The story is told in a ballad by Deloney (q.v.) included in Percy's 'Reliques'; and S. Daniel (q.v.) published in 1592 'The Complaint of Rosamond', a poem in rhyme-royal; Addison wrote an opera 'Rosamond' (1707).

Rosamond Vincy, a character in G. Eliot's 'Middlemarch' (q.v.).

Rosamund, Queen of the Lombards, a play by Swinburne (q.v.), published in 1861.

Rosary, The, a novel by Florence Louisa Barclay (1909).

Rosciad, The, see *Churchill* (*C.*).

Roscius, whose full name was QUINTUS ROSCIUS GALLUS (*d.* 62 B.C.), the most celebrated of Roman comic actors. Cicero's oration 'Pro Q. Roscio Comoedo' relates to a claim against him for 50,000 sesterces.

Roscius, The Young, see *Betty* (*W. H. W.*).

ROSCOE, WILLIAM (1753–1831), author of a successful 'Life of Lorenzo de' Medici' (1795), and of the 'Life and Pontificate of Leo the Tenth' (1805). He also wrote some volumes of verse, including 'The Butterfly's Ball and the Grasshopper's Feast' (1807), which became a children's classic.

ROSCOMMON, EARL OF, see *Dillon*.

Rose, Romaunt of the, see *Romaunt of the Rose* and *Roman de la Rose*.

Rose Alley Ambuscade, see *Dryden*.

Rose and the Ring, The, a humorous fairy-tale by Thackeray (q.v.), published in 1855.

It turns on the possession of a magic rose and a magic ring, which have the property of making their owners appear beautiful, and deals with the adventures of Prince Giglio, who has been ousted from the throne by his uncle; his rivalry for the hand, first of the princess Angelica, then of her maid Betsinda (who turns out to be the princess Rosalba), with the ridiculous Prince Bulbo, and the misfortunes of the latter; and his entanglement with Countess Gruffanuff, Angelica's ugly governess. Gruffanuff's husband has been head footman at the palace, and for his rudeness has been turned into a door-knocker by the fairy Blackstick. He is restored to life by the fairy just in time to prevent Giglio from having to marry his supposed widow. Giglio marries Rosalba, and Bulbo marries Angelica.

Rose Aylmer, an elegy by W. S. Landor (q.v.) on the daughter of Lord Aylmer. She was an early love of Landor's, but on her mother's second marriage was sent out to her aunt at Calcutta, where she died, aged twenty.

Rose Fleming, a character in Dickens's 'Oliver Twist' (q.v.).

Rose Jocelyn, a character in Meredith's 'Evan Harrington' (q.v.).

Rose Mary, a poem by D. G. Rossetti (q.v.), included in 'Ballads and Sonnets', published in 1881.

Rose Mary, looking into a magic beryl, in which only the pure can see the truth, sees, as she thinks, the peril to which her lover is exposed, and he is warned. But Rose Mary has sinned and her sin has admitted into the beryl evil spirits, who have concealed the truth from her. Her lover is faithless and is killed. She takes her father's sword and breaks the beryl, thus releasing her soul from destruction.

Rosemary Lane, Whitechapel, now called Royal Mint Street, formerly noted for its old clothes market, known as 'Rag Fair' (mentioned by Pope in 'The Dunciad'). A sort of 'Rag Fair' still survives in the street.

Rose Noble, see *Noble*.

Rose Tavern, THE, in Russell Street, Covent Garden, was a favourite place of resort in the latter part of the 17th and early 18th cents. It is frequently referred to in the literature of the period, e.g. by Pepys (18 May 1668), and by Farquhar ('The Recruiting Officer').

Rose Theatre, THE, on Bankside, Southwark, opened in 1592 and was managed by P. Henslowe (q.v.). Shakespeare acted there.

ROSEBERY, ARCHIBALD PHILIP PRIMROSE, *fifth earl of* (1847–1929), foreign secretary in the Gladstone governments of 1886 and 1892, prime minister in 1894–5, an eloquent and witty speaker. He was author of the works: 'Pitt' (1891), 'Sir Robert Peel' (1899), 'Napoleon—the Last Phase' (1900), 'Cromwell' (1900). He three times won the Derby, with Ladas in 1894, Sir Visto in 1895, and Cicero in 1905.

'Rose-red city—half as old as time', in Dean J. W. Burgon's poem, 'Petra', the ancient capital of Arabia Petraea, now in ruins, discovered by Burckhardt in 1812.

ROSENBERG, ISAAC (1890–1918), a poet of promise, killed in the First World War. His work was experimental in character, strongly influenced by his Jewish background, and his best-known poems deal with his experiences in the trenches. His collected works were published in 1937.

Rosencrantz and **Guildenstern,** characters in Shakespeare's 'Hamlet' (q.v.).

Rosetta Stone, a piece of black basalt found by Napoleon's soldiers near the Rosetta mouth of the Nile, bearing an inscription in Egyptian hieroglyphics, demotic characters, and Greek, which proved the key to the interpretation of hieroglyphics. It is now in the British Museum.

Rosey Mackenzie, a character in Thackeray's 'The Newcomes' (q.v).

Rosicrucian, a member of a supposed society or order, reputedly founded by one Christian Rosenkreuz in 1484, but first mentioned in 1614, whose members were said to claim various forms of secret and magic knowledge, such as the transmutation of metals, the prolongation of life, and power over the elements and elemental spirits. [OED.] No Rosicrucian society appears to have actually existed. The Rosicrucians of the early 17th cent. seem to have been moral and religious reformers, who covered their views under a cloak of mysticism and alchemy. There is a good deal on the subject in Shorthouse's 'John Inglesant' (q.v.).

Rosinante or ROZINANTE, the horse of Don Quixote (q.v.).

ROSS, ALEXANDER (1699–1784), educated at Aberdeen University, became a Forfarshire schoolmaster, and was the author of the long pastoral narrative 'Helenore, or the Fortunate Shepherdess', and of a number of witty and spirited songs, including 'Woo'd and Married and a' '.

ROSS, SIR JAMES CLARK (1800–62), Arctic and Antarctic explorer, was author of 'A Voyage in the Southern and Antarctic Regions (1839–43)', published in 1847. Ross commanded the first expedition for the relief of Sir J. Franklin (q.v.) in 1848–9.

ROSS, SIR JOHN (1777–1856), uncle of the above, Arctic explorer, was author of two narratives of voyages in search of the North-West Passage, published in 1819 and 1835.

Ross, THE MAN OF, see *Kyrle*.

Ross, MARTIN, see under *Somerville* (E. Œ.).

Ross, MOTHER, see *Davies* (C.).

ROSSETTI, CHRISTINA GEORGINA (1830–94), the sister of D. G. Rossetti (q.v.), contributed to 'The Germ' (q.v.) under the pseudonym 'Ellen Alleyne', and published her first work in book form, 'Goblin Market [q.v.] and other Poems', in 1862. 'The Prince's Progress' (q.v.) appeared in 1866, 'Sing-Song' in 1872, and 'A Pageant and other Poems' in 1881. Notable among her contributions to 'The Germ' is the lyric entitled 'The Dream'. A volume of 'New Poems' appeared in 1896 after her death. 'Time Flies, a Reading Diary', with some poem or thought for each day, was published in 1883. Her work ranged from poems of fantasy and verses for the young to religious poetry, which constituted the greater part of her writings. They are in general pervaded by a spiritual and melancholy cast, and marked by a high degree of technical perfection. Her 'Monna Innominata' is a series of sonnets of unhappy love.

ROSSETTI, DANTE GABRIEL (1828–82), whose full Christian name was Gabriel Charles Dante (but the form which he gave it has become inveterate), the son of Gabriele Rossetti, an Italian patriot who came to England in 1824, was educated at King's College, London. He studied painting under Millais and Holman Hunt and in 1848, with them and four other artists, founded the Pre-Raphaelite Brotherhood (q.v.). For many years he was known only as a painter, though he began to write poetry very early (from

1847). 'The Blessed Damozel' (q.v.), one of his earliest works, subsequently more than once revised, appeared in 'The Germ' (q.v.). In 1860 he married Miss Eleanor Siddal, and in 1861 he published his first volume, 'The Early Italian Poets', a collection of scrupulous translations from Dante (including the 'Vita Nuova' and the sonnets) and his predecessors and contemporaries. His wife died in 1862 and a manuscript containing a number of his poems was buried with her. These were subsequently disinterred and published in 'Poems by D. G. Rossetti' in 1870. They include 'Sister Helen', 'Eden Bower' (qq.v.), 'The Stream's Secret', and 'Love's Nocturn'. 'Ballads and Sonnets' appeared in 1881, completing the sequence of love-sonnets called 'The House of Life', of which part had appeared in the earlier volume, and including such notable poems as 'Rose Mary' (q.v.), 'The White Ship' (q.v.), and 'The King's Tragedy' (q.v.). Mention should be made of Rossetti's translations, not only from the Italian, but also from the French and German, and particularly from Villon (q.v.). Many of his poems were written as commentaries on his pictures.

In 1871 Rossetti was attacked by Robert Buchanan under the pseudonym 'Thomas Maitland' in an article entitled 'The Fleshly School', to which Rossetti published a convincing reply.

ROSSETTI, WILLIAM MICHAEL (1829–1919), brother of D. G. Rossetti (q.v.), educated at King's College School, London, was a man of letters and art-critic, and an official in the Inland Revenue Department. He was one of the seven Pre-Raphaelite 'brothers', edited 'The Germ' (q.v.), and wrote the sonnet that was printed on its cover. He wrote art-criticisms for the 'Spectator', republished under the title 'Fine Art, chiefly contemporary' (1867). His other works include a blank-verse translation of Dante's 'Inferno' (1865), 'Lives of famous Poets' (1878), a 'Life of Keats' (1887), a 'Memoir, with Family Letters' of his brother (1895), a 'Memoir' (1904) and 'Family Letters' (1904) of his sister Christina, and a study of 'Dante and his Convito' (1910).

Rossini, GIOACHINO ANTONIO (1792–1868), Italian operatic composer. He visited London in 1823 and then Paris, where he was for a time director of the Théâtre Italien. His best-known operas are 'The Barber of Seville' (1816, based on the comedy by Beaumarchais) and 'William Tell' (his greatest work, 1829).

Rossville, LORD, a character in S. E. Ferrier's 'The Inheritance' (q.v.).

ROSTAND, EDMOND (1868–1918), French dramatist, whose best-known works are 'Cyrano de Bergerac' (1898, see *Bergerac*), 'L'Aiglon' (1900), and 'Chantecler' (1910).

Roswitha, see *Hrotsvitha*.

Rota, THE, (1) a political club founded in

1659 by James Harington (q.v.), which advocated rotation in the offices of government, and other republican ideas; (2) in the Roman Catholic Church, the supreme court for ecclesiastical and secular cases.

Rothomagus, in imprints, Rouen.

Rothsay, DUKE OF, eldest son of Robert III of Scotland, figures in Scott's 'The Fair Maid of Perth' (q.v.).

Rothschild, the name of a famous Jewish banking-house founded at Frankfort-on-the-Main towards the end of the 18th cent. by Mayer Anselm Rothschild. It is said to be derived from the sign of the house, 'zum rothen Schilde', 'at the red shield'. It is also said that the fortune of the house was in part founded on the securing of early news about the battle of Waterloo.

Rotten Row, a road in Hyde Park, extending from Apsley Gate to Kensington Gardens, a fashionable resort for riders. The name was formerly applied to various streets in different towns, and its origin is obscure. The OED. does not recognize the popular derivation from *route du roi*, and remarks that the older form in the north of England and Scotland, *ratton raw*, is apparently of different origin. The obvious derivation is probably the right one, a row or road of rotten earth, suitable material for a riding-track.

Rouge Croix, Rouge Dragon, two of the pursuivants of the English College of Arms, so called from their badges (see *Heralds' College*).

Rouge et le Noir, Le, a novel by Stendhal (q.v.).

ROUGEMONT, LOUIS DE, the name assumed by an adventurer, Grin, a Swiss by birth, and at one time servant to Fanny Kemble, who, after spending many years in Australia, contributed in 1898 to the 'Wide World Magazine' articles relating a number of fantastic adventures, mostly imaginary, among the Australian aborigines (see Sitwell and Barton, 'Sober Truth'). He is said to have betrayed himself by writing of a 'flight of wombats'.

ROUGET DE L'ISLE, CLAUDE JOSEPH (1760–1836), an engineer officer in the French army, who in 1792 composed the 'Marseillaise' (words and music), the French national hymn. M. Loth in 'Le Chant de la Marseillaise' (Paris, 1886) suggests that Rouget got the air from a march in an oratorio called 'Esther' by one Grisons, choirmaster at Saint-Omer, 1787.

ROUND, JOHN HORACE (1854–1928), historian, the grandson of Horace (Horatio) Smith (q.v.), was educated at Balliol, where he learnt from his tutor, William Stubbs (q.v.), the value of genealogy in historical research. Round early became one of the foremost students of the Domesday Survey and also took a special interest in the Pipe Rolls Society, for printing the early rolls of the Exchequer, which was started in 1884. In 1892 he established his reputation with 'Geoffrey de Mandeville: a Study of Anarchy'. His other works include 'Feudal England: Historical Studies in the 11th and 12th Centuries' (1895), 'Studies in Peerage and Family History' (1901), and 'Peerage and Pedigree' (1910). He was a fierce controversialist and attacked E. A. Freeman's (q.v.) 'History of the Norman Conquest'. He also helped launch the 'Victoria History of the Counties of England'.

Round Table, THE, in the Arthurian legend, was made (according to one version by Merlin) for Uther Pendragon and given by him to King Leodegrance of Cameliard. The latter gave it as a wedding gift, with 100 knights, to Arthur when he married Guinevere, his daughter. It would seat 150 knights, and all places round it were equal. The 'Siege Perilous' was reserved for the knight who should achieve the quest of the Grail (q.v.). In Layamon's 'Brut', however, the table was made for Arthur by a crafty workman. It is first mentioned by Wace (q.v.).

Round Table, The, a Collection of Essays on Literature, Men, and Manners, consists of forty essays by William Hazlitt and twelve by Leigh Hunt, published in 2 vols., 1817.

Round Table, The, a quarterly review of the politics of the British Empire, founded in 1910.

Roundabout Papers, The, a series of discursive essays by W. M. Thackeray (q.v.), published in 'The Cornhill Magazine', 1860–3.

Roundheads, members or adherents of the parliamentary party in the Civil War of the 17th cent., so called from the Puritan custom of wearing the hair cut close, while the Cavaliers usually wore theirs in long locks. The name appears to have arisen towards the end of the year 1641. [OED.] There is a pamphlet called 'The unloveliness of love-locks' somewhat earlier than this.

ROUSSEAU, JEAN-JACQUES (1712–78), was born at Geneva, son of a watchmaker. Lacking in stability of character and moral principle, he led a wretched erratic life, sometimes taken up and protected by benefactors whose kindness he ill repaid, sometimes occupying humble situations, as footman or music-master, living for twenty-five years with a kitchen-maid, Thérèse Le Vasseur, and depositing their five babies at the Foundling Hospital. This life he has described in his masterpiece, the 'Confessions' (published after his death).

He came early into notice by the works in which he expounded his revolt against the existing social order. The first of these was a 'Discourse on the Influence of Learning and Art' (1750), followed by a 'Discourse on the

Origin of Inequality' (1754). 'La Nouvelle Héloïse', a novel in which the question of the return to nature was discussed in its relation to the sexes and the family, appeared in 1761. 'Du Contrat social', setting forth his political philosophy, was published in 1762, and 'Émile', his views on education, in the same year. The 'Contrat Social' had a profound influence on French thought, especially after 1789. After the appearance of 'Émile' Rousseau was the object of persecution, and went into exile, first to Geneva and then to England (under the protection of Hume), until 1767.

Rousseau attributed evil, not to sin, but to society, as a departure from the natural state, in which man is both good and happy. To revert to these desirable conditions, we must banish from life its artificial elements. Instead of attending to the doctrines of the philosophers, we should listen to our own intuitions, which tell us that there is a benevolent divine spirit, who rewards virtue and punishes crime, and that the human soul is free and immortal. In political philosophy Rousseau held the view that society is founded on a contract, and that the head of the State is the people's mandatary, not their master. In education he developed the useful theory that instruction should proceed by an appeal to the child's curiosity, by stimulating his intelligence, rather than by imposing cut-and-dried notions upon it.

ROUTH, MARTIN JOSEPH (1755–1854), president of Magdalen College, Oxford, for sixty-three years, edited the 'Gorgias' and 'Euthydemus' of Plato, and 'Reliquiae Sacrae' (1814–43), a collection of writings of ecclesiastical authors of the 2nd and 3rd cents. Routh was a man of immense learning, and a strong, old-fashioned 'High Churchman'. He was also, perhaps, the last man in England who always wore a wig. His long life (he died in his hundredth year) and literary experience lend weight to his famous utterance: 'I think, Sir, you will find it a very good practice *always to verify your references.*' A life of Routh by R. D. Middleton was published in 1938.

Rover, The, or the Banished Cavaliers, see *Behn.*

Rovers, The, see *Anti-Jacobin.*

ROWE, NICHOLAS (1674–1718), was educated at Westminster School, and became a barrister of the Middle Temple; but abandoned the legal profession for that of playwright, and made the acquaintance of Pope and Addison. He produced at Lincoln's Inn Fields his tragedies, 'The Ambitious Stepmother' (1700), 'Tamerlane' (q.v., 1702), and 'The Fair Penitent' (q.v., adapted from Massinger's 'Fatal Dowry', 1703). His 'Ulysses' was staged in 1706, his 'Royal Convert' at the Haymarket in 1707, and 'Jane Shore' and 'Lady Jane Grey' in 1714 and 1715 respectively, at Drury Lane. He produced an unsuccessful comedy, 'The Biter', at Lincoln's Inn Fields, in 1704. The moral tone of his plays is in strong contrast to the licentiousness of the drama of the preceding fifty years. His 'Fair Penitent' and 'Jane Shore' provided two of Mrs. Siddons's most successful parts. Rowe became poet laureate in 1715, and was buried in Westminster Abbey. His portrait was twice painted by Kneller. His poetical works include a famous translation of Lucan (1718), 'one of the greatest productions of English poetry', said Johnson. His collected works appeared in 1727. Rowe did some useful work as editor of Shakespeare's plays (1709), dividing them into acts and scenes, supplying stage directions, and generally making the text more intelligible.

Rowena, (1) the legendary daughter of Hengist, who married the British chief Vortigern (see *Vortigern and Rowena*); (2) a character in Scott's 'Ivanhoe' (q.v.; see also *Rebecca and Rowena*).

Rowland, *Childe,* see *Childe Roland.*

ROWLANDS, SAMUEL (1570?–1630?), a writer mainly of satirical tracts in prose and verse. He began his literary career with a religious poem, 'The Betraying of Christ' (1598), followed by a satire on the manners of Londoners, 'The Letting of Humours Blood in the Head-Vaine' (1600). In 1602 appeared his 'Tis Merrie when Gossips meete', a vivid and dramatic character-sketch of a widow, a wife, and a maid who meet in a tavern and converse. His 'Greene's Ghost', on the subject of 'coney-catchers' (cheats, swindlers), belongs to the same year. He published 'Hell's Broke Loose' (1605), 'Democritus, or Doctor Merryman his Medicines against Melancholy Humors' (1607), 'Humors Looking Glasse' (1608), 'Martin Mark-all' (an account of the habits and language of thieves, 1610), and 'The Melancholie Knight' (1615).

Rowlandson, THOMAS (1756–1827), caricaturist and painter of humorous low life subjects. Among his illustrations were those for 'Dr. Syntax' (see *Combe*); Ackermann (q.v.) published many of his prints.

Rowley, in Sheridan's 'School for Scandal' (q.v.), the old servant of the Surfaces.

Rowley, OLD, a nickname of Charles II, derived from the name of a horse in the royal stud, renowned for the number and beauty of its offspring (notes in John Hayward's edition of the works of Rochester).

ROWLEY, SAMUEL (d. 1633?), an actor in the Admiral's company and a playwright employed by Henslowe (q.v.). His principal extant play is, 'When you see me, You know me. Or the famous Chronicle Historie of King Henry VIII', acted in 1603.

ROWLEY, WILLIAM (1585?–1642?), dramatist and actor. He played in Queen Anne's company before 1610, and under Henslowe's management at the 'Hope'. His best dramatic work was done in collaboration with T.

Middleton (q.v.). He wrote, unassisted, 'A New Wonder' (1632), 'All's Lost by Lust' (q.v., 1633), 'A Match at Midnight' (1633), and 'A Shoomaker a Gentleman' (1638). He collaborated in 'A Fair Quarrel' (q.v., 1617), 'The Changeling' (q.v., performed 1621), and other plays, with Middleton; in 'Fortune by Land and Sea' (printed 1655) with Heywood; in 'The Thracian Wonder' (printed 1661) with Webster; and in other pieces with Ford, Massinger, and Dekker (qq.v.). He was probably author or reviser of 'The Birth of Merlin' (printed 1662).

Rowley Poems, see *Chatterton.*

Rowley Powley, THE REV., in Byron's 'Don Juan', xi. 57, was Croly (q.v.).

Rowton Houses, named after Montague William Lowry-Corry, Baron Rowton (1838–1903), who studied working-class conditions and designed a 'poor man's hotel' with better conditions than those offered by the common lodging-houses. The first Rowton House was opened in Vauxhall in 1892. It proved very successful, and a company was formed in 1894 to extend their use.

Roxāna, the daughter of a Persian satrap, who was taken captive by Alexander the Great, and became his wife. Later, Alexander took a second wife, Barsinē, daughter of Darius and Statira. On this has been based the story of the jealousy of Roxana and her vengeance on her rival. It forms the basis of Nathaniel Lee's tragedy, 'The Rival Queens' (q.v.), where the second wife is called Statira.

Roxana, *or the Fortunate Mistress,* a romance by Defoe (q.v.), published in 1724.

This purports to be the autobiography of Mlle Beleau, the beautiful daughter of French Protestant refugees, brought up in England, and married to a London brewer, who, having wasted his property, deserts her and her five children. She enters upon a career of prosperous wickedness, passing from one protector to another in England, France, and Holland, amassing much wealth, and receiving the name Roxana by accident, in consequence of a dance that she performs. She is accompanied in her adventures by a faithful maid, Amy, a very human figure. She finally marries a Dutch merchant and lives as a person of consequence in Holland, until he discovers the deceit that has been put upon him. He shortly afterwards dies, leaving her only a small sum of money. She is imprisoned for debt, and dies in a state of penitence.

Roxburghe, JOHN KER, *third duke of* (1740–1804), an ardent bibliophile, who secured an unrivalled collection of books from Caxton's press. His splendid library, housed in St. James's Square, was dispersed in 1812. Valdarfer's edition of Boccaccio (1471), for which the second duke of Roxburghe had paid one hundred guineas, was then sold to the marquis of Blandford for £2,260. To celebrate this event the chief bibliophiles of the day dined together at St. Alban's Tavern, St. Alban's Street, under the presidency of Lord Spencer, and there inaugurated the ROXBURGHE CLUB, the first of the book-clubs, consisting of twenty-four members, with T. F. Dibdin as its first secretary. The Club, at first rather convivial in character, began its valuable literary work with the printing of the metrical romance of Havelok the Dane (1828). Each member is expected once in his career to present (and pay for a limited edition of) a volume of some rarity.

Roxburghe Club, see *Roxburghe (J. K.).*

Royal Academy, THE, see *Academy.*

Royal Exchange, THE, see *Exchange (The Royal).*

Royal Historical Society, see *Historical Society.*

Royal Martyr, THE, (1) Charles I; (2) see *Tyrannic Love.*

Royal Society, THE, originated in the Philosophical Society, which was founded in 1645. The operations of the latter were in great measure interrupted by the Civil War. Its meetings in London were resumed at the Restoration, and it received its charter as the Royal Society in 1662. Among its principal projectors were Abraham Cowley (q.v.) and Robert Boyle the chemist (see under *Boyle Lectures*). Its 'Philosophical Transactions' were first issued in 1665. The remarkable feature of the Royal Society among scientific academies was that it took the whole field of knowledge for its province and included among its early members such men of letters as Dryden, Waller, Evelyn, and Aubrey. Its first historian was Bishop Sprat (q.v.), who describes its aims. Among these was the improvement of English prose. It exacted from all its members 'a close, naked, natural way of speaking; positive expressions; clear senses; a native easiness'.

Royal Society of Literature, see *Literature.*

Rozinante, see *Rosinante.*

Rubáiyát of Omar Khayyám, The, see *Omar Khayyám.*

Rubens, PETER PAUL (1577–1640), Flemish painter, the chief northern exponent of the baroque. Studying first under Flemish masters, he went to Italy in 1600 and became court painter to the duke of Mantua. He returned to Antwerp in 1608, became court painter to the Spanish ruler of Flanders, and set up a large workshop with numerous assistants, from which poured religious, decorative, historical, and mythological paintings, as well as portraits and landscapes. His control and organization of the work ensured its quality. In addition he served on various diplomatic missions, visiting Spain in 1628, when he became a friend of Velasquez (q.v.), and England in 1629, where he was knighted and commissioned to paint the ceiling of the Banqueting House, Whitehall.

Rubens was an enormously prolific and vital painter, robust and rich. His style was based on the great Italian masters, but in later life he painted for his own pleasure landscapes with a new feeling for the country.

Rubicon, a small river rising in the Apennines and flowing into the Adriatic; it separated Italy from Cisalpine Gaul. By crossing it with an army and thus overstepping the boundaries of his province, Julius Caesar committed himself to war against the Senate and Pompey (49 B.C.).

Rudabah, in the 'Shahnameh' of Firdusi (q.v.), the wife of Zâl and mother of Rustem (q.v.). The story of the love of Zâl for Rudabah is one of the most romantic portions of the work.

Rüdiger, a character in the 'Nibelungenlied' (q.v.). He is a follower of Etzel, who, when Gunther and his brothers visit Etzel's court after the death of Siegfried and Kriemhild's marriage to Etzel, entertains them hospitably. In the affray between the Huns and the Burgundians, Rüdiger and Gernot, Gunther's brother, slay one another.

Rudiger, a ballad by R. Southey (q.v.), of a stranger knight borne to Waldhurst on the Rhine in a boat drawn by a swan. Later the boat returns and carries away Rudiger, his wife Margaret, and their child. They come to a cavern where two giant arms emerge, seize Rudiger, and draw him into the earth.

Rudolphine Tables, a series of astronomical calculations published by Kepler in 1627, and named after his patron, the emperor Rudolph II.

Rudra, in Vedic mythology, the storm-god. His arrows carry destruction, but he is also the giver of remedial herbs.

Ruff's Guide to the Turf, an annual publication devoted to horse-racing; originated in 1842 by William Ruff (1801–56).

Rugby, JACK, in Shakespeare's 'The Merry Wives of Windsor' (q.v.), servant to Dr. Caius.

Rugby Chapel, a poem by M. Arnold (q.v.).

Rugby School, founded by Laurence Sheriff in 1567. T. Arnold (q.v.) was its headmaster from 1828 to 1842. A vivid picture of school-life at Rugby in his days is given in 'Tom Brown's Schooldays' by Hughes (q.v.). Here originated the game of Rugby football; a tablet in Rugby School close commemorates William Webb Ellis 'who, with a fine disregard of the rules of football as played in his time, first took the ball in his arms and ran with it' in 1823.

Ruggiero, see *Rogero.*

Ruggle, GEORGE, see *Ignoramus.*

Ruin, The, an Old English poem of some thirty-five lines included in the 'Exeter Book' (q.v.), describing the result of the devastation by the Saxons of a Roman settlement (perhaps Bath), and showing, with deep feeling, the contrast of past splendour with present desolation.

Ruined Cottage, The, or *The Story of Margaret*, a poem by Wordsworth (q.v.), written in 1797, and subsequently embodied in Bk. I of 'The Excursion' (q.v.).

It is a harrowing tale of misfortune befalling a cottager and his wife. The husband leaves his home and joins a troop of soldiers going to a distant land. The wife stays on, pining for his return, in increasing wretchedness, till she dies and the cottage falls into ruin.

Ruines of Time, The, a poem by Spenser (q.v.), included in the 'Complaints' published in 1591. It is an allegorical elegy on the death of Sir P. Sidney (q.v.), which had also been the occasion of his earlier elegy 'Astrophel' (q.v.). The poet passes to a lament on the neglect of letters, with allusion to his own case. The poem is dedicated to the countess of Pembroke, Sidney's sister.

Rukenaw, DAME, the ape's wife in 'Reynard the Fox' (q.v.).

Rule a Wife and Have a Wife, a comedy by J. Fletcher (q.v.), produced in 1624.

Margarita, a rich heiress of Seville, desires to marry, but only to obtain liberty for her amorous proclivities; she must therefore marry a fool. Altea, her companion, plots to win her for her brother Leon, who assumes a character of utter simplicity, promises subservience, and is accepted by Margarita. After the marriage, Margarita prepares to receive her admirers; Leon now reveals himself in his true colours, and asserts his authority over his wife in presence of her guests, notably the Duke of Medina. The duke and Margarita attempt various stratagems, but Leon defeats them, and Margarita is finally won over to his side, and joins him in fooling the duke, who at last is reconciled to Leon.

In the under-plot, Estefania, Margarita's servant, beguiles the conceited copper-captain, Michael Perez, into marrying her by posing as the owner of the absent Margarita's house. On Margarita's return, Estefania pretends that Margarita wants to borrow the house in order to play the same trick that Estefania has played on Perez. When her deceit is finally discovered, she braves it out, and wins Perez's forgiveness by cheating the vile Cacafogo out of a thousand ducats.

Rule, Britannia: for the words see *Thomson, James* (1700–48); the air was composed by Thomas Augustine Arne (1710–78) for Thomson and Mallet's mask, 'Alfred'.

Rules, see *King's Bench Prison*. There were Rules also outside the Fleet prison.

Rumpelstiltzkin, the subject of one of Grimm's fairy tales, a little manikin who taught the miller's daughter how to spin straw into gold, so that she became the king's wife. She was required to guess the goblin's

name, and overheard him say it. When he found that she had discovered it, in a fury he stamped his foot into the ground up to his waist, and then tore himself in two.

Rumwold, ST. (*c.* 650), the son of one of the kings of Northumbria (perhaps Alchfrid, son of Oswy), honoured as a saint on account of the following prodigy. It is related that immediately after his baptism in infancy he began to speak and professed the Christian faith by a recital of the creed. He is commemorated on 28 August.

Rune, a letter or character of the earliest Teutonic alphabet, which was most extensively used (in various forms) by the Scandinavians and Anglo-Saxons (cf. the story by M. R. James, 'The Passing of the Runes'). Also a similar character or mark having magical or mysterious powers attributed to it. The earliest runic alphabet dates from at least the 2nd or 3rd cent., and was formed by modifying the letters of the Roman or Greek alphabet so as to facilitate cutting them upon wood or stone. The name is also applied to a Finnish poem or division of a poem, especially to one of the separate songs of the 'Kalevala' (q.v.). The word *runic* is used of such poetry as might be written in runes; belonging to the people or the age which made use of runes; also of ancient Scottish poetry. Also of ornament of the interlacing type, characteristic of rune-bearing monuments. [OED.]

Runnymede, on the right bank of the Thames in Surrey, where on 15 June 1215 the barons forced John to confirm *Magna Carta* (q.v.).

Rupert of debate, THE, Edward Stanley, fourteenth earl of Derby (1799–1869), statesman and brilliant parliamentary speaker, so named by Lord Lytton in the 'New Timon', in allusion to Prince Rupert, the celebrated cavalry leader in the Civil War. In Monypenny and Buckle's 'Life of Lord Beaconsfield' (ii. 237) the nickname is mentioned as having been given by Disraeli in 1844 with these words, 'in his charge he is resistless, but when he returns from the pursuit he always finds his camp in the possession of the enemy'.

Rupert of Hentzau, a novel by Anthony Hope, a sequel to his 'The Prisoner of Zenda' (q.v.).

Rupert's drops, PRINCE, pear-shaped pieces of glass, made by dropping molten glass into water, which burst into fragments if the slender tail is broken. They were introduced into England from Germany by Prince Rupert.

Rural Rides, by Cobbett (q.v.), collected in 1830, descriptive of various parts of England, with agricultural and political comments. A committee in 1821 had proposed certain remedies for the agricultural distress that followed the war. Cobbett disapproved of these and 'made up his mind to see for himself, and to enforce by actual observation of rural conditions, the statements he had made in answer to the arguments of the landlords before the Agricultural Committee'. The standard edition is that by G. D. H. and Margaret Cole (3 vols., 1930).

Ruritania, an imaginary kingdom in central Europe, the scene of Anthony Hope's 'Prisoner of Zenda' (q.v.) and its sequel, 'Rupert of Hentzau'. The name connotes, more generally, make-believe romance, chivalry, intrigue, at a royal court in a modern European setting.

Rush, FRIAR, see *Friar Rush.*

RUSKIN, JOHN (1819–1900), the son of John James Ruskin, a partner in a wine business, who while sending his son to no school gave him plentiful opportunities of early travel. John Ruskin went to Christ Church, Oxford, in 1836, won the Newdigate prize in 1839, and in 1843 published anonymously the first volume of the famous 'Modern Painters' (q.v.), of which five volumes in all were issued over a period of seventeen years (his name first appeared on the title-page of the edition of 1851). His first published writings, however, were articles in Loudon's 'Magazine of Natural History' (1834) and verses contributed to 'Friendship's Offering'. The early prose pieces were reprinted in 1892 under the title 'The Poetry of Architecture', and embody principles subsequently developed in Ruskin's later works. He made the acquaintance of Turner in 1840 and of Millais in 1851. In 1849 he published his 'Seven Lamps of Architecture' (q.v.), and 'Stones of Venice' (q.v.) in 1851–3. As 'Modern Painters' was begun in defence of Turner, so in 1851 he wrote letters to 'The Times' and pamphlets conscientiously defending the Pre-Raphaelites (q.v.). From 1855 to 1859 he issued annual 'Notes on the Royal Academy', and treatises on drawing and perspective. His lectures 'On Architecture and Painting' were delivered at Edinburgh in 1853, those on 'The Political Economy of Art' at Manchester in 1857. His 'Two Paths', lectures on the part that organic nature should play as a guide to art, appeared in 1859. His mind was now turning to economics, and some essays which he published on this subject in 'The Cornhill Magazine' in 1860 and in 'Fraser's Magazine' in 1862–3 aroused strong opposition by their heterodoxy. They were subsequently republished as 'Unto this Last' (q.v., 1862) and 'Munera Pulveris' (q.v., 1872). These and other treatises and pamphlets advocated a system of national education, the organization of labour, and other social reforms. He attacked the policy of non-interference by the State, and the validity of a science of political economy based on the conception of the 'economic man', actuated by no motive other than profit. Wealth, in the ordinary sense of the term, he never ceased to insist, is not the only thing worth having. His interest in social reform is again shown in his most popular work 'Sesame and Lilies' (q.v., 1865), and in 'The Crown of Wild Olive' (q.v., 1866). 'The Ethics of the Dust' (elementary lectures on crystallography) appeared in 1866, and further letters on social subjects in 'Time and Tide, by Weare and Tyne' (q.v.) in 1867. In 1871 he settled at Coniston, and in that year began his monthly letters in 'Fors Clavigera' (q.v.), 'to the workmen and labourers of Great Britain'. In the same year he founded the guild of St. George on the principles that 'food can only be got out of the ground and happiness out of honesty', and that 'the highest wisdom and the highest treasure need not be costly or exclusive'. The members of the guild were to give a tithe of their fortunes to philanthropic purposes, and to these Ruskin contributed generously from his own purse. He also engaged in several industrial experiments, including the revival of the hand-made linen industry in Langdale. He was Slade professor of art at Oxford in 1870–9 and 1883–4, and published eight volumes of lectures. His 'Praeterita' (q.v.), an autobiography which was never completed, was published at intervals during 1885–9. Ruskin was buried at Coniston. He inherited from his father a large fortune, all of which was dispersed, chiefly on philanthropic objects, before his death. There is a life of Ruskin by Alice Meynell in the 'Modern English Writers' series, on which the notices herein of his separate works are in part based. His Diaries were published in 1956–9 (3 vols., ed. Joan Evans and J. H. Whitehouse).

RUSSELL, BERTRAND ARTHUR WILLIAM, *third Earl Russell* (1872–   ), educated privately and at Trinity College, Cambridge, fellow of Trinity College, Cambridge. He has written voluminously on philosophy, logic, education, economics, and politics. While much of this writing was relatively practical and ephemeral in intent, his work in some of the most technical fields of philosophy and logic is of lasting importance. 'The Principles of Mathematics' (1903) and 'Principia Mathematica' (the latter in collaboration with A. N. Whitehead, 1910) are already classics of mathematical logic. Other important philosophical works include 'The Analysis of Mind' (1921), 'An Inquiry into Meaning and Truth' (1940), and 'Human Knowledge, its Scope and Limits' (1948).

RUSSELL, GEORGE WILLIAM (1867–1935), an Irish poet and artist, widely known under his pseudonym 'Æ', 'AE', or 'A.E.' (Russell had once signed an article 'Æon', and the compositor's difficulty in making out the word had suggested the use of the diphthong alone, for which the other more convenient forms were generally substituted). He was educated at Rathmines School and about 1899 was appointed organizer to Sir Horace Plunkett's 'Agricultural Association'. His poems, the work of a mystic, are 'the most delicate and subtle that any Irishman of our time has written' (W. B. Yeats). The production of his drama 'Deirdre' by an amateur company in 1902 was one of the early steps towards the formation of the Irish National Theatre. Russell was editor of 'The Irish Statesman' from 1923 to 1930. His other works include: 'The Divine Vision' (1904), 'New Poems' (1904), 'By Still Waters' (1906), 'The Hero in Man' (1909), 'The Renewal of Youth' (1911), 'Gods of War' (1915), 'Imaginations and Reveries' (1915), 'The Candle of Vision' (1918), 'The Interpreters' (1922), 'Midsummer Eve' (1928), 'Enchantment, and other poems' (1930).

RUSSELL, LORD JOHN, *first Earl Russell* (1792–1878), third son of the sixth duke of Bedford, was educated at Westminster and Edinburgh University. He entered parliament in 1813, and was a strenuous advocate of parliamentary reform until the adoption in 1832 of the Reform Bill introduced by him. He supported the repeal of the Corn Laws by Peel in 1845 and was prime minister 1846–52. He was foreign secretary in Aberdeen's ministry in 1852–3, and again under Palmerston, 1859–65, and in that capacity advocated 'Italy for the Italians'. On the death of Palmerston, Russell once more became prime minister, 1865–6. He published a 'Life of William, Lord Russell' (1819), 'Memoirs of Affairs of Europe' (1824–9), 'Memoirs of Thomas Moore' (1853–6), 'Life and Times of Charles James Fox' (1859–60), and other works. He was a very small and somewhat quaint figure, which made him a godsend to the cartoonists of 'Punch'.

RUSSELL, WILLIAM CLARK (1844–1911), was in the British merchant service from 1858 to 1866. He wrote some sixty tales of nautical adventure, of which the chief are 'John Holdsworth, Chief Mate' (1875) and 'The Wreck of the Grosvenor' (1877). Some of his contributions to 'The Daily Telegraph' on sea topics were republished in 'My Watch Below' (1882) and 'Round the Galley Fire' (1883). His writings led to improved conditions in the merchant service. Russell also wrote lives of Dampier (1889), Nelson (1890), and Collingwood (1891).

RUSSELL, SIR WILLIAM HOWARD (1820–1907), the distinguished war correspondent, served in that capacity in the Crimea (where he applied the phrase 'the thin red streak'—usually misquoted as 'the thin red line'—to the British Infantry at Balaclava, called attention to the sufferings of the troops, and inspired the work of Florence Nightingale); in the Indian Mutiny, 1858; in the American Civil War, 1861–2; at the battle of Königgrätz in 1866; in the Franco-German War of 1870; and in the Zulu War of 1879. Russell also published accounts of his travels in Canada (1863–5) and the United States (1882).

Russell, LADY, a character in Jane Austen's 'Persuasion' (q.v.).

Russell Square, London, was built in the early 19th cent. on land of the dukes of Bedford. It figures as the residence of wealthy citizens in the novels of Thackeray, e.g. of the Osbornes in 'Vanity Fair' (q.v.).

Rustem or RUSTUM, the principal figure in the 'Shahnameh' of Firdusi (q.v.), is the great Persian national hero, the son of Zâl. He is represented as living during several centuries, a constant conqueror until killed by treachery in the reign of Gushtasp. A celebrated incident is his fight with Isfendiyar (q.v.), the son of Gushtasp, which lasts for two days, and ends in the death of Isfendiyar. He also fights with and defeats Afrasiab, the Turanian hero, overcomes dragons and demons, and unwittingly fights with and kills his son Sohrab. This last episode is the subject of M. Arnold's 'Sohrab and Rustum' (q.v.).

Ruth, the principal character of the Book of Ruth of the O.T. Ruth was a Moabitess, the widowed daughter-in-law of Naomi of Bethlehem, who gleaned in the fields of the wealthy Boaz, and became his wife and the ancestress of King David.

Ruth, a novel by Mrs. Gaskell (q.v.), published in 1853.

Ruth Hilton, an orphan and a dressmaker's assistant, is seduced and heartlessly deserted by Henry Bellingham. In her distress she is taken by Thurston Benson, a dissenting minister, and his sister, into their home. The story sets forth the redemption of Ruth by her love for her child, and the gradual elevation of her character, until she succumbs to a fever caught while nursing her worthless lover. Their story is complicated by the treatment of another ethical problem. Benson, at his sister's instance, and in order to lighten Ruth's burden, advises her to pass as a widow, and in that character obtains for her employment as a governess in the house of the pharisaical and tyrannical Mr. Bradshaw. The deceit brings grievous punishment. For when Bradshaw learns Ruth's past history he brutally dismisses her, publishes the facts abroad, and renders miserable the lives of Ruth and her son.

Rutherford, ERNEST, *first Baron* (1871–1937), born at Nelson, New Zealand, was regarded as the greatest experimental physicist of his generation. He was professor at McGill University, Montreal, from 1898 to 1907, and at Manchester from 1907 to 1919, when he became professor at the Cavendish Laboratory, Cambridge. He led the study of radioactivity and established the conception of the nuclear atom, which prepared the way for the discovery of nuclear fission and atomic energy. Accounts of his researches were published in 'Radioactivity' (1904) and 'Radiations from Radioactive Substances' (1930).

RUTHERFORD, MARK, see *White (W. H.).*

Ruthwell Cross, a stone monument in Dumfriesshire, dating perhaps from the 8th cent., on which are inscribed, in runes, extracts from 'The Dream of the Rood' (q.v.). It was thrown down by the Presbyterians in 1642 and the inscriptions partly effaced. It is now housed in the parish church of Dalton, near Ecclefechan, Dumfriesshire.

Ruy Diaz, see *Cid.*

RUY LOPEZ DE SEGURA, a Spanish writer on chess (1561), at the time when the game took its final development by the introduction of castling.

Rye House Plot, THE, a conspiracy in 1683 among some of the more violent followers of Shaftesbury to seize Charles II and his brother on their return from Newmarket at the Rye House in Hertfordshire. The plot failed, but its discovery brought to light a combination of parliamentary Whigs, who, while perhaps intending no personal violence against the king, contemplated compelling him to summon a parliament. Lord William Russell and Algernon Sidney were implicated in this, and were executed.

Ryecroft Papers, see *Gissing.*

Ryence, RIENCE, or RYONS, KING, in Malory's 'Morte Darthur', a king of north Wales, who sent a message to King Arthur that he had overcome eleven kings and trimmed his mantle with their beards, and that he lacked one beard and demanded that of King Arthur; to which Arthur made a suitable reply. Ryence was overcome and taken prisoner by Balin and Balan. The story is the subject of a ballad in Percy's 'Reliques', which was sung before Queen Elizabeth at the great entertainment at Kenilworth in 1575. Ryence is perhaps to be identified with

Urien, a British god of the underworld (Rhys, 'Arthurian Legend').

Geoffrey of Monmouth (x. 3) has a story of the giant Ritho, upon Mount Aravius, who challenged Arthur to fight, and demanded the king's beard to trim his mantle.

RYLE, GILBERT (1900–   ), educated at Brighton College and the Queen's College, Oxford; Waynflete professor of metaphysical philosophy in the University of Oxford (1945–   ). The author of numerous articles on a wide variety of philosophical topics, he is best known for his attack on the traditional metaphysical dualism of mind and body, which he calls the 'dogma of the ghost in the machine'. His best-known book is 'The Concept of Mind' (1949). A general account of his view of philosophical problems is contained in 'Dilemmas' (1954).

Rymenhild, see *King Horn.*

RYMER, THOMAS (1641–1713), educated at Sidney Sussex College, Cambridge, is chiefly remembered for his valuable collection of historical records, 'Foedera' (q.v., 1704–35). He wrote a play in rhymed verse, 'Edgar, or the English Monarch' (1678), but is better known for his 'Tragedies of the last age considered' (1678), in which he discussed some of Beaumont and Fletcher's plays, and for his 'Short View of Tragedy' (1692), in which he condemned 'Othello'.

Ryswick, THE TREATY OF, brought to an end in 1697 the war between the Grand Alliance (England, Holland, Austria, and Spain) and France, which had lasted since 1689. Louis XIV abandoned the Stuart cause, recognized William III as king of England, and restored his conquests, except in Alsace. It was no more than a truce, for the question of the Spanish succession loomed very near, and both sides were aware of the danger involved therein; both therefore had to take breath.

S

S.F., abbreviation of Science Fiction (q.v.).

S.P.C.K., the Society for Promoting Christian Knowledge, was founded in 1698. One of its primary objects was the setting up of charitable schools for the instruction of poor children in reading, writing, and the catechism, with the addition of arithmetic for boys and sewing for girls. The Society was also a publishing agency for the dissemination of works of a Christian character.

S.P.E., the Society for Pure English (q.v.).

S.P.Q.R., initial letters of *Senatus Populus-Que Romanus,* 'the Senate and People of Rome'.

SS, COLLAR OF, an ornamental chain consisting of a series of S's, originally worn as a badge by adherents of the House of Lancaster. It still forms part of the official dress of certain officers. It is mentioned in the Order of the Coronation in Shakespeare's 'Henry VIII' (IV. i). OED. quotes (1407), 'A collar of gold worked with the motto *Soveignez* [Remember] and the letter S.'

Sabaeans, the ancient name of the people of Yemen, in south-western Arabia; from L. *Sabaei* for Hebrew *Sheba,* used in Job i. 15 of Arabian marauders.

Sabaoth, a Hebrew word meaning 'armies',

'hosts', left untranslated in the English N.T. (A.V. and R.V.) in the phrase 'the Lord of Sabaoth'; translated as 'Lord of Hosts' in the New English Bible.

Sabbath, from the Hebrew *Shābath*, to rest; in the original use the seventh day of the week (Saturday) considered as the day of religious rest enjoined on the Israelites by the 4th commandment. Since the Reformation it is often applied to 'the Lord's day', i.e. the first day of the week (Sunday), observed by Christians in commemoration of the resurrection of Christ.

Sabbath, WITCHES', a midnight meeting of demons, sorcerers, and witches, presided over by the Devil, supposed in medieval times to have been held annually as an orgy or festival.

Sabbath day's journey, the distance (2,000 *ammōth* = 1,125 yards) which (according to Rabbinical prescription in the time of Christ) was the utmost limit of permitted travel on the Sabbath.

Sabbatical river, THE, an imaginary river, celebrated in Jewish legend, which was said to observe the Sabbath, resting (or, according to another version, flowing only) on that day.

Sabbatical Year, the seventh year, which according to Mosaic law was to be observed as a 'Sabbath' (q.v.), the land remaining untilled, and all debtors and Israelitish slaves being released.

Sabellianism, the doctrine concerning the coequality and consubstantiality of the Trinity held by the followers of Sabellius, a heresiarch of Ptolemais who lived in the 3rd cent. His chief tenet was that the Father, Son, and Holy Spirit are one person, in three manifestations. Sabellianism came to be used as a term covering such of the unitarian doctrines as recognize the divinity of Christ.

Sabians, see *Mandaeans*.

Sabines, THE, an ancient people of Italy, whose lands were in the neighbourhood of Rome. They are celebrated in legend as having taken up arms against the Romans, to avenge the carrying off of their women by the latter at a spectacle to which they had been invited. Subsequently they are said to have made peace and migrated to Rome, where they settled with their new allies.

Sabra, in Richard Johnson's 'The Seven Champions of Christendom' (q.v.), the daughter of a king of Egypt, whom St. George rescued from the dragon and married.

Sabreur, LE BEAU, Joachim Murat (1767–1815), the son of an inn-keeper and a great cavalry commander, who became one of Napoleon's marshals and king of Naples, and married Napoleon's sister, Caroline. He was captured in 1815 in an attempt to recover his throne and was executed.

Sabrīna, a poetic name for the river Severn

(see under *Estrildis*). In Milton's 'Comus' (q.v.), which was presented at Ludlow Castle, Sabrina is the nymph of the Severn.

MISS SABRINA is the new schoolmistress in Galt's 'Annals of the Parish' (q.v.). 'Old Mr. Hookie, her father, had, from the time he read his Virgil, maintained a sort of intromission with the Nine Muses, by which he was led to baptize her Sabrina, after a name mentioned by John Milton in one of his works.'

Sacharissa, see *Waller*.

SACHS, HANS (1494–1576), shoemaker of Nuremberg, and author of a vast quantity of verse, including meistersongs and some 200 plays. He figures in Wagner's opera 'Die Meistersinger von Nürnberg'.

Sack, adapted from the French *vin sec*, 'dry wine', i.e. wine 'free from sweetness and fruity flavour'. This derivation, however, involves some difficulty, for sack was often described as a sweet wine. 'It is possible that before the recorded history of the name begins it had already been extended from the "dry" wines of a certain class to the whole class.' [OED.] The word was used as a general name for a class of white wines imported from Spain and the Canaries. It is sometimes coupled with a name indicating the place of production, e.g. Sherry-sack, (or Sherris-sack), Canary-sack. Sack was the favourite drink of Falstaff (Shakespeare, '2 Henry IV', IV. iii).

Sackerson, a famous bear kept at Paris Garden (q.v.) in Shakespeare's time. Slender tells Anne Page that he has seen him loose twenty times, and taken him by the chain ('The Merry Wives of Windsor', I. i).

SACKVILLE, CHARLES, *Lord Buckhurst*, and later *sixth earl of Dorset* (1638–1706), a man dissipated in his youth but successful in public affairs in his maturity, was a friend and patron of poets, and was himself eulogized as a poet by Dryden and Prior. His poems include some pleasant songs (the best known is the ballad 'To all you Ladies now at Land') and mordant satires. They appeared with Sedley's (q.v.) in 1701.

SACKVILLE, THOMAS, *first earl of Dorset* and *Baron Buckhurst* (1536–1608), was son of Sir Richard Sackville. He was perhaps educated at Hart Hall, Oxford, and St. John's College, Cambridge. He was a barrister of the Inner Temple. He entered parliament in 1558, was raised to the peerage in 1567, and held a number of high official positions, including those of lord treasurer and chancellor of Oxford University. He wrote the 'Induction' and 'The Complaint of Buckingham' for 'A Mirror for Magistrates' (q.v.), and collaborated (probably writing only the last two acts) with Thomas Norton in the tragedy 'Gorboduc' (q.v.). His poetical works were collected in 1859.

Sacred Band, THE, a force of 300 young

Theban nobles, formed to fight against Sparta in the wars that followed the rising of 379 B.C. It was specially prominent at the victories of Leuctra (371) and Mantinea (362), and was destroyed by Philip at Chaeronea (338).

Sacred College, the college of Cardinals, who form the pope's council, and elect to the papacy from their own number.

Sacred Nine, THE, the Muses (q.v.).

Sacred Wars, THE, in Greek history wars conducted by the Amphictionic Council (q.v.). The first was waged early in the 6th cent. B.C. to release Delphi from the inhabitants of the neighbouring Crisa, who levied dues on pilgrims; another, in the middle of the 4th cent. B.C., to oust Phocis from the control it had obtained over Delphi.

Sacripant, in the 'Orlando Innamorato' and the 'Orlando Furioso' (qq.v.), the king of Circassia and a lover of Angelica. He catches Rinaldo's horse, Bayard, and rides away on it, and Rinaldo calls him a horse-thief. In Tasso's 'Secchia Rapita' ('The Rape of the Bucket'), he is a hectoring braggart. SACRA-PANT figures as a magician in Peele's 'The Old Wives' Tale' (q.v.). In modern French *sacripant* is a rascal or blackguard.

Sad Shepherd, *The, or, A Tale of Robin Hood,* the last and unfinished play of Jonson (q.v.), a pastoral drama, first published in the folio of 1641.

Robin Hood invites the shepherds and shepherdesses of the Vale of Belvoir to a feast in the forest of Sherwood, but the feast is marred by the arts of the witch Maudlin. Æglamour, the Sad Shepherd, relates the loss of his beloved Earine, whom he believes drowned in the Trent. In reality Maudlin has stripped her of her garments to adorn her daughter, and shut her up in a tree as a prey for her son, the uncouth swineherd Lorel. The witch assumes the form of Maid Marian, sends away the venison prepared for the feast, abuses Robin Hood, and throws the guests into confusion. Lorel tries to win Earine but fails. The wiles of Maudlin are detected, and the huntsmen pursue her.

Saddletree, BARTOLINE, a character in Scott's 'The Heart of Midlothian' (q.v.).

Sadducees, one of the three sects (the others being the Pharisees and the Essenes, qq.v.) into which the Jews were divided in the time of Christ. According to the N.T. and Josephus, they denied the resurrection of the dead, the existence of angels, and the obligation of the traditional unwritten law. The name is apparently derived from Zadok, the high-priest of David's time.

SADE, DONATIEN ALPHONSE, *Count* (generally known as *Marquis*) *de* (1740–1814), a French author whose licentious writings have given his name to SADISM, a form of sexual perversion marked by a love of cruelty.

SADI, a celebrated Persian poet, born at Shiraz, said to have lived *c.* 1200, whose real name was Muslihu-'d-Din. He was a devout Muslim and is honoured as a saint. His principal works were the collections of verse known as the *Gulistan* or 'Rose-Garden', and the *Bustan* or 'Tree-Garden'.

Sadler's Wells, in north London, originally a hydropathic establishment at a mineral spring, developed by a Mr. Sadler in 1683. A place of entertainment was added, and in 1765 a theatre was opened. Here the pantomimist, Joseph Grimaldi (q.v.), gave his earliest performances. From 1844 to 1859 it was under the management of Mrs. Warner and Mrs. Phelps, whose Shakespeare productions are historic. The theatre was rebuilt, to a large extent by means of a grant from the Carnegie Trust, and reopened in 1931, to be for North London what the 'Old Vic' (q.v.) is for South London—a theatre where good plays can be seen at 'popular prices'.

Sæhrimnir, in Scandinavian mythology, the boar that is eaten every night by the gods in Valhalla and is every night miraculously renewed.

Saemund (11th cent.), an Icelandic scholar, erroneously supposed at one time to be the compiler of the 'Elder' or 'Poetic Edda' (see *Edda*).

Saga, an old Norse word meaning 'story', applied to the narrative compositions in prose that were written in Iceland or Norway during the Middle Ages. In English use it is often applied specially to those which embody the traditional history of the Icelandic families or of the kings of Norway. The Icelandic sagas are highly national and insular, in respect of the physical character of the country, the types of men and women, the conditions of life, law, and morality, which they depict. They divide themselves into two groups, the more historical, of which the 'Heimskringla' (q.v.) of Snorri Sturlason and the 'Sturlunga Saga' of Sturla (q.v.) are the principal examples; and the less historical, of which the chief are: the 'Laxdaela', the story of the fascinating Gudrun and her lovers (of which we have a version in W. Morris's 'Earthly Paradise', q.v.); the 'Eyrbyggya', legends, without central plot, relating to an entire district; the 'Egla', dealing with the exploits (at Brunanburh among other places) of Egil, son of Skallagrim, the friend of Æthelstan and enemy of Eric Bloodaxe; the 'Njala', the story of the calamities brought about by the wickedness of Hallgerd, wife of Gunnar, culminating in the burning of Njal, the lawyer, and most of his family; and the 'Grettla', or the story of Grettir the Strong, a generous scapegrace, marred by a quarrelsome and unamiable temper, whose slayings and blood-feuds make him an outcast. He overcomes the ghost of the shepherd Glam, but as a result of the ghost's curse becomes haunted and unlucky, lives for many years a hunted life in remote corners of the island, still known as 'Grettir's lairs', and finally dies a miserable death. The 'Grettla' saga has been translated by William Morris and Eirikr Magnusson, the 'Njala' by Sir George Dasent.

Sagittarius, the zodiacal constellation of the *Archer*, according to myth the centaur Cheiron (q.v.); the ninth sign of the zodiac, which the sun enters about 22 November.

Sagittary, the centaur who, according to medieval romance, fought in the Trojan army against the Greeks. In Shakespeare's 'Othello', I. i, 'Lead to the Sagittary the raised search', the name is probably that of an inn. (Cf. 'Centaur' as the name of an imaginary inn at Ephesus in 'The Comedy of Errors', I. ii.) [OED.]

Sailor William, William IV, who served in the navy from 1779 (when he was 14) to 1790.

Saint: for names with this prefix see, with the following exceptions, the names themselves.

St. Aldegonde, LORD, a character in Disraeli's 'Lothair' (q.v.).

St. Clair, MRS., a character in S. E. Ferrier's 'The Inheritance' (q.v.), of which her supposed daughter, Gertrude, is the heroine.

Saint-Cyr, a village near Versailles, France, where Louis XIV, at the instigation of Mme de Maintenon, founded a convent school for young ladies of the French nobility. This in 1808 was transformed into a military school, the French Sandhurst.

St. Dunstan's, an institution for the care of British soldiers, sailors, and airmen blinded in the war of 1914–18 (or subsequent operations), founded in 1915 by Sir Arthur Pearson (himself blind). It had its commencement in St. Dunstan's Lodge, a house in Regent's Park, lent for the period of the war by the American financier, Otto Kahn.

SAINT-ÉVREMOND, CHARLES DE MARGUETEL DE SAINT-DENIS DE (1616–1703), a French author, who was exiled from his own country for political reasons, and came to England, where he spent the years 1662–5 and from 1670 to his death. He was on intimate terms with the wits and courtiers of the day, and wrote essays on a variety of literary, philosophic, and other subjects, including one on English comedy (1685). Some of these were translated into English from time to time (with a character of St.-Évremond by Dryden in a collection of 1692). His 'Works', with a 'Life' by Des Maizeaux, appeared in an English translation in 1714.

Saint-Germain-en-Laye, a town on the Seine, a few miles north-west of Paris, at the château of which James II held his court after his deposition.

St. Irvyne, *or the Rosicrucian,* see *Shelley* (*P. B.*).

St. James's Palace was built by Henry VIII on the site of an ancient hospital of St. James for leprous women. The lepers were pensioned off, and the site surrendered to Henry VIII, who built there 'a goodly manor'. Here slept Charles I on the night before his execution. After Stuart times it superseded Whitehall as the principal royal residence in London, and gave the official title to the 'Court of St. James'.

St. James's Park is mentioned by Stow as serving the two palaces of St. James's and Whitehall. From fields it was developed by Charles II in the fashion of the Dutch gardens he had seen in exile, but was remodelled on its present lines by John Nash for George IV. It is much referred to by Pepys, Evelyn, and Goldsmith. The piece of water in the Park is a relic of the course of the Tyburn stream which flowed into the Thames at Westminster.

St. James's Square was constructed soon after the restoration of Charles II on fields that were the leasehold property of the earl of St. Albans. It at once became a fashionable centre. It was at first called the Piazza, and had a large pond in the centre (Loftie).

ST. JOHN, HENRY, *first Viscount Bolingbroke,* see *Bolingbroke* (*Visc.*).

St. Martin's-le-Grand, a street in the east central district of London, where the General Post Office long stood. It formerly enjoyed rights of sanctuary, originating from the exclusive jurisdiction granted by charter of William I to the dean and secular canons of St. Martin within the precincts of their college, one of the oldest monasteries in the kingdom. The premises were demolished in the 16th cent., but the sanctuary survived until the reign of James I. The bell of St. Martin's, by ordinance of Edward I, tolled the curfew in London. The parish was formerly noted as the resort of dealers in imitation jewellery.

SAINT-PIERRE, JACQUES HENRI BERNARDIN DE (1737–1814), a French writer and follower of Rousseau (q.v.), chiefly known as the author of 'Paul et Virginie' (q.v., 1787), a poetic romance of naïve and virtuous love, which obtained immense popularity. But the principal work of Bernardin was his 'Études de la Nature' (1784), the work of a poetical moralist who seeks to trace in the various phenomena of nature the hand of a beneficent Providence.

Saint-Preux, the lover of Julie in the 'Nouvelle Héloïse' of Rousseau (q.v.).

St. Ronan's Well, a novel by Sir W. Scott (q.v.), published in 1823.

In this work the author for once chose a scene of contemporary life, in the Scottish spa of St. Ronan's Well, whose idle fashionable society is satirically described: Lady Penelope Penfeather, Sir Bingo Binks, Capt. MacTurk, and so on. Against this background we have the story of two half-brothers, sons of the late earl of Etherington, who had married, first secretly abroad, and then publicly at home. The younger son bears the title, though not entitled to it, and is at bitter enmity with his elder half-brother, Francis Tyrrel. For he had basely intervened in a love-affair between Francis and Clara Mowbray, the daughter of the laird of St. Ronan's, and has actually personated his brother at a midnight marriage with Clara, so that Clara finds herself wedded to a man whom she fears and detests. (Scott had intended that Francis should seduce Clara, but altered the plot in deference to James Ballantyne.) The brothers make a compact to leave Clara undisturbed and still bearing her maiden name, both undertaking never to return to Scotland; and the whole affair remains a secret. But Etherington, menaced with dispossession of the earldom by Francis, and finding that an unexpected accession of fortune will accrue to him if his marriage with Clara is acknowledged, breaks the compact and comes to St. Ronan's to demand the hand of Clara in more regular fashion. For this purpose he cunningly avails himself of the gambling vice of Clara's brother, now the laird, and puts such pressure on him that Mowbray actually menaces his sister with death if she does not accept Etherington's suit. Meanwhile Francis has been active to defend Clara, and the plotter has been counterplotted and is finally exposed by the intrigue-loving old nabob, Mr. Touchwood, but too late. For the unfortunate Clara, whose mind has already been unhinged by her misfortunes, succumbs to her fresh terrors before these can be dissipated.

One of the best characters in the book is Meg Dods, the sturdy refractory landlady of the old inn at St. Ronan's.

SAINT-SIMON, CLAUDE HENRI, *Comte de* (1760–1825), a distant relation of the Duc de Saint-Simon (q.v. below), social philosopher, author of various projects for social and political reform and of many books and articles out of which his followers (Saint-Simonians) developed the system known as Saint-Simonism. He sought to promote international peace by creating a sort of League of Nations of Europe, and to reorganize society on a socialist basis and by a better organization of industry and labour.

SAINT-SIMON, LOUIS DE ROUVROY, *Duc de* (1675–1755), author of 'Mémoires' (first authentic edition in 21 vols., 1829–30), famous for their picture of the courts of Louis XIV and the Régent d'Orléans, and for their brilliant character sketches. There are modern, more correct editions in the 'Collection des Grands Ecrivains de France' and the 'Bibliothèque de la Pléiade'.

St. Stephen's Chapel, Westminster, was originally erected by King Stephen, and rebuilt by Edward III. In the reign of Edward VI it was assigned to the use of parliament, and the House of Commons continued to sit there until the building was destroyed by fire in 1834.

Saint's Everlasting Rest, The, see *Baxter.*

Saint's Tragedy, The, see *Kingsley* (C.).

SAINTE-BEUVE, CHARLES AUGUSTIN (1804–69), the first great French critic to break away from the dogmas of the classical school. His famous articles in various periodicals extend from the 'Portraits littéraires' begun in 1829, through the series of 'Causeries du lundi' (from 1850), to the 'Nouveaux lundis' of 1863–70. His two long literary and biographical studies are the important 'Port-Royal' (q.v., 1840–8) and 'Chateaubriand et son groupe littéraire' (1861). Some of his early criticisms, notably the 'Tableau ... de la poésie française ... au XVIᵉ siècle' (1828), did much to promote the Romantic movement in France by the attention he drew to the poetry of the 16th cent., though his own sympathy with the Romantics did not last. He wrote some poetry: 'Joseph Delorme' (1829) and 'Les Consolations' (1830), which reflects his feeling for the English Lake poets. His introspective novel 'Volupté' (1834) is partly autobiographical.

SAINTE-MAURE, BENOÎT DE, see *Benoît.*

SAINTSBURY, GEORGE EDWARD BATEMAN (1845–1933), educated at King's College School, London, and Merton College, Oxford, was a distinguished literary critic and historian, and professor of rhetoric and English literature at Edinburgh University, 1895–1915. He was the author of a large number of works on English and European literature, including a 'Short History of English Literature' (1898), 'Elizabethan Literature' (1887), 'Nineteenth-Century Literature' (1896), a 'History of Criticism' (1900–4), a 'History of English Prosody' (1906–10), a 'Short History of French Literature' (1882), and lives of Dryden, Sir Walter Scott, and Matthew Arnold. He was general editor of 'Periods of European Literature' (1897–1907), to which he contributed the sections on 'The Earlier Renaissance', 'The Flourishing of Romance', and 'The Later Nineteenth Century'. He also wrote interesting and entertaining 'Notes on a Cellar Book' (1920), 'A Letter Book' and 'A Scrap Book' (1922), etc.

SAKI, see *Munro* (H. H.).

Sakuntala, a celebrated Sanskrit drama by Kalidasa (q.v.).

King Dushyanta while hunting in the forest sees the maiden Sakuntala and contracts with her a summary marriage, giving her a royal ring as pledge when he leaves her. Later she sets forth to join him, but loses the ring while bathing in a pool. This has the unfortunate effect that the king does not recognize her, and she returns to the forest, where she gives birth to Bharata, the founder of a glorious race. Presently a fisherman catches a fish which has swallowed the royal ring. This is taken to the king, the spell from which he suffered is removed, and he now remembers Sakuntala, and goes to seek her.

The drama was translated by Sir W. Jones (q.v.).

Sakyamuni, one of the names of Gautama Buddha, who belonged to the Sakhya tribe.

SALA, GEORGE AUGUSTUS (1828–96), journalist, began his literary career as editor of 'Chat' in 1848, and after writing regularly for 'Household Words' (1851–6), joined the staff of 'The Daily Telegraph' in 1857. He was special correspondent of the 'Telegraph' in the American Civil War (1863) and afterwards in various countries. He published novels and books of travel.

Saladin (SALA-ED-DIN YUSUF IBN AYUB, Joseph the son of Jacob, Honour of the Faith) (1137–1193), a Kurd by birth, became Sultan of Egypt about 1174, invaded Palestine, defeated the Christians, and captured Jerusalem. He was attacked by the Crusaders under Richard Cœur-de-Lion and Philip II of France and forced to conclude a truce. He appears to have been chivalrous, loyal, and magnanimous, no fanatic Muslim, nor a man of deep piety. He figures prominently in Scott's 'The Talisman' (q.v.).

Salamander, see *Sylph.*

Salanio and **Salarino,** characters in Shakespeare's 'The Merchant of Venice' (q.v.).

Salathiel, see *Croly.*

Saldar de Sancorvo, LOUISA, *countess of,* one of the principal characters in Meredith's 'Evan Harrington' (q.v.).

Salerno, in Italy, the seat of a medical school famous in the Middle Ages. It produced the maxim:

Si tibi deficiant medici, medici tibi fiant
Haec tria: mens hilaris, requies, moderata
      dieta.

The metrical 'Regimen Sanitatis Salerni', dedicated to Robert of Normandy as 'King of the English' (he had gone there to be cured of a wound after the crusade of 1099), was edited by Sir A. Croke in 1830.

Salic Law, originally a code of law of the Salian Franks, written in Latin, and extant in five recensions of Merovingian and Carolingian (qq.v.) date. It contains a passage to the effect that a woman can have no portion of the inheritance of 'Salic land', a term the meaning of which is disputed. In early use, and still in popular language, the Salic Law is the alleged fundamental law of the French monarchy by which females were excluded from succession to the crown. The claim of Edward III to the French throne was opposed on the ground of this law and the above-mentioned ancient text adduced. [OED.] Cf. Shakespeare, 'Henry V', I. i.

Sallee-man or SALLEE ROVER, a Moorish pirate-ship, from *Salee,* the name of a Moroccan port formerly of piratical repute.

SALLUST (GAIUS SALLUSTIUS CRISPUS) (86–35 B.C.), a Roman historian and an ad-

herent of Caesar in the civil war. The latter made him quaestor, and after the African war governor of Numidia, where Sallust acquired great riches. He wrote a history of the conspiracy of Catiline; 'Bellum Jugurthinum', a history of the Roman war against Jugurtha (111–106 B.C.); and 'Histories' covering the period 78–67 B.C. Of the last very little survives.

Sally in our Alley, a ballad by Carey (q.v.).

Sally Lunn, a kind of tea-cake. According to Hone ('Every-Day Book') the cakes were so called from a young woman of that name who used to cry them at Bath, at the end of the 18th cent. Dalmer, a respectable baker and musician, bought her business and made a song about her.

Salmacis, see *Hermaphroditus.*

Salmagundy, a dish of chopped meat, anchovies, eggs, onions, etc. The word is from the French *salmigondis,* of obscure origin (Rabelais has *salmiguondin*). 'Salmagundi' was the title of a periodical edited by W. Irving (q.v.) early in his career.

Salmantica, in imprints, Salamanca.

SALMASIUS (CLAUDE DE SAUMAISE) (1588–1653), an eminent French scholar, professor at Leyden University in 1649, when Charles II was living at The Hague. He was commissioned by Charles to draw up a defence of his father and an indictment of the regicide government. This took the form of the Latin 'Defensio Regia', which reached England at the end of 1649. Milton (q.v.) was ordered by the Council in 1650 to prepare a reply to it, and in 1651 issued his 'Pro Populo Anglicano Defensio', also in Latin. In this, instead of defending the people of England, as he purports to do, he merely heaps invective on his adversary. To this Salmasius rejoined in his 'Responsio', which is similarly composed mainly of personal abuse. See also *Anthology (The Greek).*

Salmōnéus, a son of Aeolus and brother of Sisyphus (qq.v.). His arrogance was such that he caused sacrifices to be offered to himself and imitated the thunder of Zeus, who killed him with a thunderbolt and placed him in Tartarus.

Salmonia, see *Davy (Sir H.).*

Salō´mĕ, the daughter of Herodias (q.v.) by her first husband Herod Philip. Herod Antipas, her stepfather, enchanted by her dancing, offered her a reward 'unto the half of my kingdom'. Instructed by Herodias, Salome asked for the head of John the Baptist in a charger (see Matt. xiv). The story is the subject of a drama by Wilde (q.v.), 'Salomé' (1893), written in French, a marvel of mimetic power. The licenser of plays in the summer of 1893 refused to sanction the performance of this. It was translated into English by Wilde's friend, Lord Alfred Douglas, in 1893 (with ten pictures by Aubrey

Beardsley), and afterwards formed the libretto of an opera by Richard Strauss. The original version was produced in Paris in 1896. The ban on the public performance in England was removed in 1931, and the play was produced at the Savoy Theatre, London, on 5 Oct. 1931.

Salsabil, a fountain in the Muslim paradise, mentioned in the Koran, c. lxxvi.

Salt and **Salt Hill,** see *Montem.*

Saltero's Coffee-house, see *Don Saltero.*

Saluzzo, The Marquis of, Wautier of Saluces in Chaucer's 'Clerkes Tale', is the husband of Griselda (see *Patient Grissil*).

Salvagge or Salvatsch, Mount, see *Titurel.*

Salvation Army, The, was started as the 'Christian Mission' in Whitechapel in 1865 by William Booth (q.v.). It was converted into the 'Salvation Army' in 1878, as a consequence of Booth's accidental use of a metaphor, and reorganized on a quasi-military basis. It became a world-wide engine of revivalism, addressing itself mainly to the depressed and outcasts and setting up numerous centres for the relief of the unfortunate, not only in Great Britain, but notably in the United States, Canada, Australia, India, and Japan.

Salvation Yeo, a character in C. Kingsley's 'Westward Ho!' (q.v.).

Sam, Uncle, see *Uncle Sam.*

Sam Slick, see *Haliburton.*

Samael or Sammael, in rabbinical legend, the personification of evil, the devil.

Samaritan, Good, an allusion to Luke x. 33.

Sambenite, see *Sanbenito.*

Samian letter, another name for the *Pythagorean letter* (see *Pythagoras*), so called from Samos (q.v.), the birthplace of Pythagoras.

Samian ware, originally pottery made of Samian earth; extended to a fine kind of pottery found extensively on Roman sites.

Samiasa, in Byron's 'Heaven and Earth' (q.v.), the seraph-lover of Aholibamah.

Samiel, the Turkish name for the Simoom, a hot, dry, suffocating wind that blows across the African and Asiatic deserts at times in spring and summer.

Samient, in Spenser's 'Faerie Queene', v. viii, the lady sent by Queen Mercilla to Adicia, the wife of the Souldan, received by her with contumely, and rescued by Sir Artegall.

Samos, a large island in the Aegean, the birthplace of Pythagoras; a strong naval power under Polycrates (q.v.) in the 6th cent. B.C.

Samosata, an ancient town in Syria, the birthplace of Lucian (q.v.).

Samothrace, Winged Victory of, a colossal statue, made about 200 B.C., representing Victory alighting on the bow of a war-galley. It was found in fragments on the island of Samothrace in 1863 (a few more pieces were found in 1950), and is now in the Louvre.

Samoyed, the name of a Mongolian race inhabiting Siberia. Milton ('Paradise Lost', x. 696) refers to 'Norumbega and the Samoed shore'.

Sampo, The, in the 'Kalevala' (q.v.), the magic mill made by Ilmarinen (q.v.), which grinds out flour, salt, and money, and is the object of contention between the Finns and the Lapps.

Sampson, Dominie, a character in Scott's 'Guy Mannering' (q.v.). His favourite expression of astonishment is 'Prodigious!'

Samson Agonistes, a tragedy by Milton (q.v.), published in 1671 in the same volume as 'Paradise Regained' (q.v.). In form it is modelled on Greek tragedies. 'Samson Agonistes' (i.e. Samson the Athlete or Wrestler) deals with the last phase of the life of the Samson of the Book of Judges (xvi), when he is a prisoner of the Philistines and blind, a phase which presents a certain pathetic similarity to the circumstances of the poet himself when he wrote the play.

Samson, in the prison at Gaza, is visited by friends of his tribe, who form the Chorus, and seek to comfort him; then by his old father Manoa, who holds out hope of securing his release; then by his wife Dalila, who seeks pardon and reconciliation, but being repudiated shows herself 'a manifest serpent in the end'; then by Harapha, a strong man of Gath, who taunts Samson. He is finally summoned to provide amusement by feats of strength for the Philistine lords, who are celebrating a feast to Dagon. He goes, and presently a messenger brings news of their destruction and the death of Samson, by his pulling down of the pillars supporting the roof of the place wherein they were.

Samuel, a Hebrew prophet, the son of Elkanah, a Levite, and Hannah, brought up to the priesthood under Eli at Shiloh. After the defeat of the Israelites by the Philistines, he rallied the people, and became their ruler. But, in his old age, owing to the misgovernment of his sons, whom he had made Judges, the Israelites demanded a king, and Samuel reluctantly anointed Saul. The two books of the O.T. called after him were not written by him, but cover the history of Israel from his birth to the end of the reign of David.

Sanbenito or Sambenite, under the Spanish Inquisition, a penitential garment of yellow cloth, resembling a scapular in shape, ornamented with a red St. Andrew's cross before and behind, worn by a confessed and penitent heretic. Also a similar garment of a black colour ornamented with flames, demons, and other devices, worn by an impenitent confessed heretic at an *auto-da-fé* (also called a *Samarra*). So called from its resemblance in shape to the scapular introduced by St. Benedict. [OED.]

Sancho Panza, the squire of Don Quixote (q.v.), who accompanies him in his adventures and shares some of their unpleasant consequences. The duke who entertains the pair, in the second part of the work, appoints Sancho Panza for a few days governor of Barataria. Sancho Panza's conversation is full of common sense and pithy proverbs.

SANCHONIATHON, an ancient Phoenician writer upon whom Philo of Byblos (in the Lebanon, *fl. c.* A.D. 100) claimed to have drawn for the purpose of his Phoenician history, of which there are extracts in Eusebius. It is probable that no such person as Sanchoniathon ever existed, but that he was invented by Philo.

SAND, GEORGE, the pseudonym of ARMANDINE AURORE LUCILE DUPIN, *Baronne Dudevant* (1804–76), French novelist. She was married young, and after some years separated from her husband. She subsequently had relations with Alfred de Musset (1833–5, see her 'Elle et Lui', 1859, and 'Lui et Elle', 1860, by Paul de Musset) and the composer Chopin, which influenced her work. Her novels divide themselves into three periods: the first (1831–4) includes 'Indiana', 'Lélia', 'Jacques', marked by freshness and a spirit of revolt against the institution of marriage; the second (1837–44) includes 'Spiridion', 'Consuelo', 'La Comtesse de Rudolstadt', 'Les Sept Cordes de la Lyre', etc., the product of her study of philosophy and politics and intercourse with great minds; and third, which began shortly before she retired to her country home at Nohant, includes her charming rustic idylls, 'La Petite Fadette', 'La Mare au Diable', etc., and also her 'Histoire de ma Vie' (1854–5).

Sandabar, see *Syntipas*.

Sandalphon, in Jewish legend, one of the three angels who receive the prayers of the Jews and weave them into garlands; the subject of a poem by Longfellow.

SANDBURG, CARL (1878–1967), American poet, born in Illinois. He challenged contemporary taste by his use of colloquialisms and free verse, and became the principal among the authors writing in Chicago during and after the First World War. He also 'Chicago Poems' (1916), 'Cornhuskers' (1918), 'Smoke and Steel' (1920), 'Slabs of the Sunburnt West' (1922), 'Good Morning America' (1928), and 'Complete Poems' (1950). He also compiled a collection of folk-songs, 'The American Songbag' (1927). The most important of his many prose works is his monumental life of Abraham Lincoln (6 vols., 1926–39).

Sandford and Merton, The History of, a children's tale by Thomas Day (q.v.), of which vol. i appeared in 1783, vol. ii in 1787, and vol. iii in 1789.

It consists of a succession of episodes in which the rich and objectionable Tommy Merton is contrasted with the virtuous Harry Sandford, a farmer's son, and the moral is drawn by the Rev. Mr. Barlow, their tutor. Its most human incident is the fight between Harry Sandford and Master Mash. It is written, without the least sense of humour, to illustrate the author's doctrine that virtue pays and that man may be made good by instruction and by appeal to his humanity and reason—the system advocated by Miss Edgeworth's father. It was translated into French before the end of the 18th cent.

A parody, 'The New History of Sandford and Merton', by F. C. Burnand, illustrated by Linley Sambourne, was published in 1872.

Sandra Belloni, originally entitled *Emilia in England,* a novel by Meredith (q.v.), published in 1864.

Emilia Sandra Belloni, a simple ardent nature, daughter of a disreputable Italian musician, and the possessor of a fine but untrained voice, leaves her wretched home and becomes the protégée of the Pole family—a city merchant, his three aspiring daughters, and his son Wilfrid, a young man of weak character inclined to 'diplomacy' in conduct of his affairs. Mr. Pericles, a rich Greek, the business ally and fellow speculator of old Pole, has a mania for discovering and developing beautiful voices, and tries to lure and bully Emilia into accepting musical training in Italy under his direction. But Emilia falls desperately in love with Wilfrid, and he with her. Old Pole, deeply involved by Pericles in speculation, is brought by him to the verge of ruin, and tries to save himself by various expedients. His daughters are to make successful matches. His son is to marry Lady Charlotte Chillingworth. He himself tampers with the money of Mrs. Chump, a rich vulgar Irish widow, whose trustee he is, and with whom he becomes moreover entangled in a project of marriage. Wilfrid, torn between his passion for Emilia and his attraction to Lady Charlotte with her worldly position and 'victorious aplomb', cuts a sorry figure, is exposed by Lady Charlotte to Emilia, and nearly breaks the latter's heart. Emilia temporarily loses her voice and is befriended by Merthyr Powys and his sister. To save the Poles from ruin, she extracts a large sum from Pericles by consenting to go to the *conservatorio* at Milan for training. Finally awakened to the inconstancy of Wilfrid, she holds out to Powys hopes that she will marry him after her training. The sequel of the story is in the author's 'Vittoria' (q.v.).

SANDYS, GEORGE (1578–1644), educated at St. Mary Hall, Oxford, a traveller in Italy, Turkey, Egypt, and Palestine. In 1621 he went to America as treasurer of the Virginia Company and remained there till about 1626. His chief works were a verse translation of Ovid's 'Metamorphoses' (1621–6), a verse 'Paraphrase upon the Psalmes' (1636), and

'Christ's Passion, a Tragedy', a verse translation from the Latin of Grotius (1640). He is of some importance in the history of English verse.

Sanger, JOHN (1816–89), the celebrated circus proprietor, began with his brother George conjuring exhibitions at Birmingham in 1845. They then started a circus entertainment at Lynn, and afterwards acquired the Agricultural Hall at Islington and in 1871 Astley's Amphitheatre in London. The brothers subsequently dissolved their partnership, each continuing independently. In his later years John Sanger was known as Lord John Sanger.

Sanglier, SIR, in Spenser's 'Faerie Queene', v. i, the wicked knight who has cut off his lady's head, and is forced by Sir Artegall to bear the head before him, in token of his shame. He is thought to represent Shane O'Neill, second earl of Tyrone (1530?–67), a leader of the Irish, who invaded the Pale in 1566. *Sanglier* in French means 'wild boar'.

Sangrado, DR., a quack physician in 'Gil Blas' (q.v.), the whole of whose science consisted in bleeding his patients and making them drink hot water.

Sangreal, SANCGREAL, the Holy Grail, see *Grail.*

Sanhedrim, more correctly SANHEDRIN, a late Hebrew word adapted from the Greek συνέδριον, 'sitting together'; 'the name applied to the highest court of justice and supreme council at Jerusalem, and in a wider sense also to lower courts of justice' (Hastings's 'Dictionary of the Bible'). The Great Sanhedrin is said to have consisted of seventy-one members.

SANNAZAR (JACOPO SANNAZZARO) (1458–1530), Neapolitan author and rediscoverer of the charms of nature and the rustic life, was author of a pastoral, in prose and verse, the 'Arcadia' (q.v.), and of Latin eclogues and other poems.

Sansculotte, in the French Revolution, a republican of the poorer classes in Paris. Usually explained as one who wore trousers (*pantalon*) instead of knee-breeches (*culotte*), but the origin is disputed.

Sansculottide, derived from the preceding word, one of the five (in leap-years six) complementary days added at the end of the month *Fructidor* in the Republican Calendar. These with the twelve months, each of thirty days, made up the 365 (or 366) days of the year.

Sansfoy, Sansjoy, and **Sansloy,** three brothers in Spenser's 'Faerie Queene', I. ii. 25 et seq. Sansfoy ('faithless') is slain by the Red Cross Knight, who also defeats Sansjoy ('joyless'), but the latter is saved from death by Duessa. Sansloy ('lawless') carries off Una and kills her lion (I. iii). This incident is supposed to refer to the suppression of the

Protestant religion in the reign of Queen Mary.

Sanskrit, the ancient and sacred language of India, the oldest member of the Indo-European family of languages. The extensive Hindu literature from the Vedas downward is composed in it.

Sanson, CHARLES (1740–93), executioner of the city of Paris, who put to death Louis XVI. His son and successor Henri (1767–1840) was the executioner of Marie Antoinette. Fabricated memoirs of the family were published in 1862.

Santa Casa, see *Loretto.*

Santa Claus, a contraction of St. Nicholas, who is supposed to come, on the night before Christmas Day, to bring presents for children. St. Nicholas was the patron saint of children, and authorities quoted by Brand ('Popular Antiquities') state that it was in many places the custom for parents on the eve of his festival (6 Dec.) to convey secretly presents to their children and pretend that they were brought by St. Nicholas. The transference of this custom to Christmas was perhaps due to a spirit of economy.

SANTAYANA, GEORGE (1863–1952), a Spaniard brought up in Boston and educated at Harvard, where he became professor of philosophy in 1889. He came to Europe in 1912, living in France and England and later in Italy, where he died. He was an eminent speculative philosopher, of a naturalist tendency and opposed to German idealism, whose views are embodied in his 'Life of Reason' (1905–6). He holds that the human mind is an effect of physical growth and organization; but that our ideas, though of bodily origin, stand on a higher and non-material plane; that the true function of reason is not in idealistic dreams but in a logical activity that takes account of facts. He analyses our religious and other institutions, distinguishing the ideal element from its material embodiment. Thus the wisdom embodied in the ritual and dogmas of religion is not truth about existence, but about the ideals on which mental strength and serenity are founded. He later modified and supplemented his philosophy in a series of five books, collectively entitled 'The Realms of Being' (1923–40). The most notable among his other writings are 'Soliloquies in England' (1922), essays on the English character, and 'Character and Opinion in the United States' (1920), one of several studies of American life. He also examined the American tradition in his only novel, 'The Last Puritan' (1935). His complex personality and admirable style can be seen to advantage in his memoirs, 'Persons and Places' (3 vols., 1944–53).

SAPPER, the pen-name of H. C. McNEILE (1888–1937), author of the popular 'Bulldog Drummond' stories about the British ex-army officer who foils the activities of Carl Peterson, the international crook.

SAPPHO, a Greek lyric poetess, born in Lesbos probably about the middle of the 7th cent. B.C. Like her fellow-countryman and contemporary Alcaeus (q.v.), she appears to have left Lesbos in consequence of political troubles, to have gone to Sicily, and to have died there. The story of her throwing herself into the sea in despair at her unrequited love for Phaon (q.v.) is mere romance. Only fragments of her work survive, including one complete ode and four stanzas of a second. The principal subject of her poems was love, expressed always with natural simplicity, sometimes with tenderness, sometimes with passionate fire. The SAPPHIC STANZA (used by Horace with some modification of its rules) is only one of the many metres that Sappho employed. It consists of ‿–‿–‿‿–‿–‿ thrice repeated, and followed by –‿‿–‿. Such fragments of her poems as survive have been edited by E. Lobel (Oxford, 1925).

Sapsea, MR., in Dickens's 'Edwin Drood' (q.v.), an auctioneer and mayor of Cloisterham.

Saracen, a name whose ultimate etymology is obscure. The derivation from the Arabic *sharqi,* 'eastern', is not well founded. In medieval times the name was often associated with Sarah, the wife of Abraham. St. Jerome identifies the Saracens with the Hagarenes, descendants of Hagar. Among the later Greeks and Romans the name was applied to the nomadic tribes of the Syro-Arabian desert. Hence it was used for an Arab, and by extension a Muslim, especially with reference to the Crusades. [OED.] In the 9th and 10th cents. it was always used for Muslim pirates who ravaged the coasts of Italy and southern France.

Saragossa or SARAGOZA, THE MAID OF, see *Maid of Saragoza.*

Saratoga, near the Hudson River, the scene of the decisive victory of the American army under Gates over the British army under Burgoyne in 1777, in the American War of Independence, and of the surrender of Burgoyne and his army.

A SARATOGA is a trunk of large dimensions 'much used by ladies'. [OED.]

Sarcastic, MR. SIMON, a character in Peacock's 'Melincourt' (q.v.).

Sardănăpālus, the last king of Assyria, notorious according to legend for his luxury and effeminacy. Arbaces the Mede and Belesis the Chaldean conspired against him and collected a numerous force to dethrone him. Sardanapalus thereupon quitted his effeminate pursuits, appeared at the head of his army, and defeated the rebels in three successive battles. He was at last overcome and besieged for two years in the city of Ninus. Despairing of success, he burnt himself in his palace with his concubines,

eunuchs, and treasures, and the empire of Assyria was divided among the conspirators. The real Sardanapalus was Assur-bani-pal (probably the Asnapper of Ezra iv. 10), who about the years 670–650 B.C. made two successful expeditions against Egypt, but subsequently lost his empire and perished in Nineveh, which was destroyed.

Sardanapalus, a tragedy by Lord Byron (q.v.), published in 1821.

It was written at Ravenna and the materials were taken from the 'Bibliotheca Historica' of Diodorus Siculus, but freely treated. Sardanapalus (see above) is represented as a luxurious but courageous monarch, cynically humorous and amiable, if not estimable. When Beleses, a Chaldaean soothsayer, and Arbaces, governor of Media, lead a revolt against him, he shakes off his sloth, and, stimulated by Myrrha, his favourite Greek slave, fights bravely in the van of his troops. Defeated, he makes provision for the safe withdrawal of his queen, Zarina, and his supporters, prepares a funeral pyre round his throne, and perishes in it with Myrrha.

Sargasso Sea, a region in the N. Atlantic, south of the 35th parallel, so named from the prevalence in it of the weed *Sargassum bacciferum* (from the Portuguese *sargaço*).

SARGESON, FRANK (1903–), New Zealand novelist, author of 'A Man and His Wife' (1940), which is included in a collection of short stories entitled 'That Summer' (1946), and the novel, 'I Saw in my Dream' (1949), the first part of which appeared as 'When the Wind Blows' in 'Penguin New Writing' (see *New Writing*).

Sarmatia, used occasionally by English poets to signify Poland, though in ancient geography it extended from the Vistula to the Volga.

Sarpēdon, a Lycian prince, son, according to one story, of Zeus and Laodamia, an ally of the Trojans in the Trojan War, who was slain by Patroclus.

Sarpego, a comical pedant in Brome's 'The City Witt' (q.v.), a character modelled on Clove in Jonson's 'Every Man out of his Humour' (q.v.).

Sarra, the city of Tyre in Phoenicia, celebrated for its purple dye, referred to by Milton, 'Paradise Lost', xi. 240.

Sarras, in the legend of the Grail (q.v.), the country to which Joseph of Arimathea fled from Jerusalem.

Sartor Resartus: The Life and Opinions of Herr Teufelsdröckh, by T. Carlyle (q.v.), originally published in 'Fraser's Magazine' in 1833–4, and as a separate volume, at Boston, Mass. in 1836; first English edition, 1838.

This work was written under the influence of the German romantic school and particularly of Jean Paul Richter (q.v.). It consists of two parts: a discourse on the philosophy of clothes (*sartor resartus* means 'the tailor re-patched') based on the speculations of an imaginary Professor Teufelsdröckh, and leading to the conclusion that all symbols, forms, and human institutions are properly clothes, and as such temporary; and a biography of Teufelsdröckh himself, which is in some measure the author's autobiography, particularly in the description of the village of Entepfuhl and of the German university (suggested by Ecclefechan and Edinburgh), and still more in the notable chapters on 'The Everlasting No', 'Centre of Indifference', and 'The Everlasting Yea', which depict a spiritual crisis such as Carlyle himself had experienced.

SARTRE, JEAN-PAUL (1905–), French existentialist philosopher and critic (see *Existentialism*). He has also, as novelist and dramatist, conveyed his philosophical ideas to a wide public in France and other countries. The novels include 'La Nausée' (1938) and three volumes (1945–9) of 'Les Chemins de la liberté', a contemplated series of four. His plays include 'Les Mouches' (1942) and 'Huis Clos' (1944), followed by 'Les Mains sales', 'Le Diable et le bon Dieu', 'Les Séquestrés d'Altona', and others. His works have been translated.

Sarum Use, the order of divine service used in the diocese of Salisbury, especially from the 13th cent. until the Reformation. The 'Sarum Missal' is a 13th-cent. compilation.

Sasanian, the name of the dynasty that ruled the Persian Empire from A.D. 226 to 651, so named from Sasan, grandson of Ardashir Babagan (q.v.), who founded the dynasty.

Sassenach, representing the Gaelic *sasunnach*, the name given by the Gaelic inhabitants of Great Britain and Ireland to their 'Saxon' or English neighbours.

SASSOON, SIEGFRIED (1886–), was educated at Marlborough and Clare College, Cambridge. He enlisted at the outbreak of the First World War and was awarded the M.C. His war poetry is vivid and often satirical, expressing his bitterness towards hypocrisy and romanticism. His published works include 'The Old Huntsman' (1917), 'Counterattack' (1918), 'Satirical Poems' (1926), 'The Heart's Journey' (1928), 'Vigils' (1935), 'Collected Poems' (1947); the semi-autobiographical fiction, 'Memoirs of a Fox-Hunting Man' (1928), 'Memoirs of an Infantry Officer' (1930), and 'Sherston's Progress' (1936); and a biography of George Meredith (1948).

Sastri, TINA, a character in George Eliot's 'Mr. Gilfil's Love-Story' (see *Scenes of Clerical Life*).

Satan, from a Hebrew word *sātān*, meaning adversary, one who plots against another. In the O.T. the Hebrew word ordinarily denotes a human adversary, but in certain passages it designates an angelic being who torments, belittles, or provokes man, sometimes with the cognizance or direct authority of Jehovah (see e.g. Job i. 6–12; ii. 1–6). It is commonly used as the proper name of the supreme evil spirit, the Devil.

Satanic School, THE, Southey's designation (in the Preface to the 'Vision of Judgment', q.v.) of Byron, Shelley, and their imitators.

Satire, from the Latin *satira*, a later form of *satura*, which means 'medley', being elliptical for *lanx satura*, 'a full dish, a hotch-potch'. The word has no connexion with *satyr*, as was formerly often supposed. A *satire* is a poem, or in modern use sometimes a prose composition, in which prevailing vices or follies are held up to ridicule. [OED.]

Satire Ménippée, a bold and original French satire, published in 1594, directed against the Catholic League (headed by the Guises and having as its object the overthrow of the heretical Henry IV). It was written by seven men, otherwise undistinguished, Leroy, Gillot, Passerat, Rapin, Chrestien, Pithou, and Durant; and takes the form of a burlesque account of the opening of the assembly of the estates at Paris, referring sarcastically to private and public actions of the leaders of the league. The title is taken from the name of Menippus, the cynic philosopher, author of satires, celebrated by Lucian.

Satiromastix, or The Untrussing of the Humorous Poet, a comedy by Dekker (q.v.), printed in 1602.

Jonson in his 'Poetaster' (q.v.) had satirized Dekker and Marston, under the names of Crispinus and Demetrius, while he himself figured as Horace. Dekker here retorts, bringing the same Horace, Crispinus, and Demetrius on the stage once more. Horace is discovered sitting in a study laboriously composing an Epithalamium, and at a loss for a rhyme. Crispinus and Demetrius enter and reprove him gravely for his querulousness. Presently Capt. Tucca (of the 'Poetaster') enters, and turns effectively on Horace the flow of his profanity. Horace's peculiarities of dress and appearance, his vanity and bitterness, are ridiculed; and he is finally untrussed and crowned with nettles.

The satirical part of the play is set in a somewhat inappropriate romantic setting—the wedding of Sir Walter Terill at the court of William Rufus, and the drinking of poison (as she thinks) by his wife, Caelestina, but really of a sleeping-potion, to escape the king's attentions.

Saturday Review, The, a weekly periodical started in the Liberal interest in 1855. Among the many brilliant contributors of its early days were Sir H. Maine, Sir J. F. Stephen, J. R. Green, Freeman, and later Hardy, G. B. Shaw, and Max Beerbohm (qq.v.).

Saturn, an ancient Italian god of agriculture, subsequently identified with the Cronos (q.v.)

of Greek mythology. He was thought to have been an early king of Rome, where he civilized the people and taught them agriculture. His reign was so mild and beneficent that it was regarded as the Golden Age.

Saturnalia, an ancient Roman festival held in December in honour of Saturn and (originally) to celebrate the sowing of the crops. It was a period of general festivity, licence for slaves, giving of presents, lighting of candles, the prototype, if not the origin, of our Christmas festivities.

Saturnian Age, the Golden Age, the *Saturnia regna* of the Roman poets. See *Saturn.*

Saturnian metre, the metre used in early Roman poetry, before the introduction of the Greek metres. It depended on the arrangement of accented syllables, but what this arrangement was is still disputed, though a considerable number of Saturnian lines have been preserved.

Satyr, in Greek mythology, one of a class of woodland spirits, in form partly human, partly bestial, supposed to be the companions of Dionysus (q.v.). In Greek art of the pre-Roman period the satyr was represented with the tail and ears of a horse. Roman sculptors assimilated it in some degree to the faun of their native mythology, giving it the ears, tail, and legs of a goat, and budding horns. Cf. the two mentions of satyrs in Isaiah, 'owls shall dwell there, and satyrs shall dance there' (xiii. 21), and 'the satyr shall cry to his fellow' (xxxiv. 14). The Hebrew word in these passages means a 'he-goat', perhaps some demon of popular superstition believed to have goat-like form.

The chorus of the Greek satyric drama (q.v.) was composed of satyrs. The confusion between *satyric* and *satiric* (see *Satire*) occasioned in the 16th–17th cents. the frequent attribution to the satyrs of censoriousness as a characteristic quality. [OED.]

Satyrane, Sir, in Spenser's 'Faerie Queene' (I. vi), a knight, 'plain, faithful, true, and enemy of shame', son of a satyr and the nymph Thyamis. He rescues Una from the satyrs, perhaps symbolizing the liberation of the true religion by Luther.

Satyric Drama, the fourth play in the tetralogy of the ancient Greeks, a semi-serious, semi-mocking presentation of a legendary theme. The 'Cyclops' of Euripides (q.v.) is the only complete extant satyric drama.

Satyricon, see *Petronius.*

Saul, (1) the first king of Israel (1 Samuel x, in verse 11 of which occurs the question, 'Is Saul also among the prophets?'); (2) Saul of Tarsus, afterwards St. Paul (Acts vii. 58 and the following chapters).

Saul, DEAD MARCH IN, the celebrated Dead March included in Handel's oratorio, 'Saul', produced in London in 1739.

Saunderson, MRS., see *Betterton (Mrs.).*

Savage, CAPTAIN, a character in Marryat's 'Peter Simple' (q.v.), the first captain under whom the hero serves.

SAVAGE, RICHARD (d. 1743), probably of humble birth, claimed to be the illegitimate son of the fourth Earl Rivers and of the wife of the second earl of Macclesfield. The romantic story of his birth and ill-treatment as given in Samuel Johnson's long and interesting life of him is now generally disbelieved. He wrote several second-rate comedies and poems, including 'The Wanderer' (q.v., 1729) and 'The Bastard' (1728), a censure on his supposed mother, the first part of which, at any rate, is vigorous and effective, and contains the often-quoted line, 'No tenth transmitter of a foolish face'. He applied unsuccessfully for the post of poet laureate, but obtained a pension from Queen Caroline on condition of celebrating her birthday annually in an ode. He was condemned to death in 1727 for killing a gentleman in a tavern brawl, but was pardoned. He died in great poverty.

SAVIGNY, FRIEDRICH KARL VON (1779–1861), professor of Roman law at Berlin, was author of the great 'Geschichte des römischen Rechts im Mittelalter' (1815–31), a work that has had an important influence on the study of the history of law, and among others on F. W. Maitland (q.v.), who began, but did not complete, a translation of it.

SAVILE, GEORGE, *marquess of Halifax* (1633–95), one of the first writers of political pamphlets, is chiefly remembered for his 'Character of a Trimmer' (1688), a brilliant piece of writing, in which he urged Charles II to free himself from the influence of his brother. His political tracts (which include his subtle piece of argument, 'The Anatomy of an Equivalent', 1688) were reprinted in 1898. He also wrote some pleasant essays under the title of 'A Lady's Gift, or Advice to a Daughter' (1688). His other works include 'A Letter to a Dissenter upon Occasion of His Majesties late Gracious Declaration of Indulgence' (1686), and 'A Character of King Charles II' (printed with 'Political, Moral, and Miscellaneous Reflexions' in 1750). He saved the throne in 1679–81 by his resolute opposition to the Exclusion Bill. He is the 'Jotham' of Dryden's 'Absalom and Achitophel' (q.v.).

SAVILE, Sir HENRY (1549–1622), educated at Brasenose College, Oxford, and a fellow and subsequently warden of Merton College and provost of Eton. He was secretary of the Latin tongue to Queen Elizabeth, and one of the scholars commissioned to prepare the authorized translation of the Bible. He translated the 'Histories' of Tacitus (1591) and published an edition of St. Chrysostom (1610–13) and of Xenophon's 'Cyropaedia' (1613). Savile assisted Bodley in founding his library and established the SAVILIAN PROFESSORSHIPS of geometry and astronomy at Oxford. He left a collection of manuscripts, now in the Bodleian Library.

Saviour's Church, ST., Southwark, originally the church of the priory of St. Mary Overy, is interesting in a literary connexion as containing the effigy of Gower and the burial-places of Fletcher and Massinger (qq.v.). The Harvard chapel commemorates John Harvard (q.v.), from whom Harvard University takes its name. The church is now the cathedral of the diocese of Southwark.

Savonaro'la, FRA GIROLAMO (1452–98), Dominican monk, an eloquent preacher whose sermons at Florence gave expression to the religious reaction against the artistic licence and social corruption of the Renaissance. Savonarola was leader of the democratic party in Florence after the expulsion of the Medici, and aroused the hostility of Pope Alexander VI by his political attitude in favour of Charles VIII of France. His influence was gradually undermined, and he was tried, condemned, and executed as a heretic. There is a careful study of his character in G. Eliot's 'Romola' (q.v.).

Savoy, THE, a precinct between the Strand, London, and the river, so called from having been given by Henry III in 1246 to Peter of Savoy, his wife's uncle, who built a palace there. Here King John of France resided when a prisoner in England (1357). The palace was destroyed by fire in Wat Tyler's insurrection, and was restored as a hospital of St. John the Baptist in Henry VII's reign. The manor, after passing through various hands, reverted to the Crown. The hospital was dissolved in 1702, and a military prison installed in its place. The buildings (with the exception of the ancient chapel) were finally demolished early in the 19th cent., when Waterloo Bridge was constructed.

Savoy Operas, see *Gilbert and Sullivan.*

Savoyard, (1) a native or inhabitant of Savoy (Savoyards were formerly well known in other countries as musicians itinerating with hurdy-gurdy and monkey); (2) a member of the D'Oyly Carte Company which originally performed the Gilbert and Sullivan operas at the Savoy Theatre.

Sawney, a Scottish local variant of Sandy, short for Alexander, a derisive nickname for a Scotsman.

Sawyer, BOB, a character in Dickens's 'Pickwick Papers' (q.v.).

SAXO GRAMMATICUS, a Danish historian (13th cent.), author of 'Gesta Danorum', a history of the Danes in Latin, partly mythical. This contains the legend of Hamlet.

Saxon, the name of a Germanic people which in the early centuries of the Christian era dwelt in a region near the mouth of the Elbe, and of which one portion, distinguished as ANGLO-SAXONS, conquered and occupied certain parts of south Britain in the 5th and 6th cents., while the other, the OLD SAXONS,

remained in Germany. It has been conjectured that the name may have been derived from *sahso*, the name of the weapon used by the Saxons. The name *Anglo-Saxon* (q.v.) was extended to the entire Old English people and language before the Norman Conquest. [OED.]

Saxon shore, THE, the eastern and southern coasts of England from the Wash to Shoreham (or, according to some, only to the South Foreland) which in the 4th cent. were exposed to the attacks of Saxon raiders and were governed by a military officer known as the *Comes* or Count of the Saxon shore.

SAYERS, DOROTHY LEIGH(1893–1957), author of 'The Nine Tailors' (1934) and other detective stories; also plays on religious themes, such as 'The Man Born to be King' (1942). She made translations of Dante's 'Inferno' (1949) and 'Purgatorio' (1955).

Sayers, TOM (1826–65), the pugilist, was a bricklayer by profession. He began his pugilistic career in 1849, when he beat Crouch at Greenhithe. He won the champion's belt in 1857. His last fight was with the American, John C. Heenan (the Benicia Boy, q.v.), at Farnborough in 1860, declared a draw.

Scaevŏla, GAIUS MUCIUS, a legendary Roman famous for his courage and firmness. When Porsenna was besieging Rome, Scaevola introduced himself into the enemy's camp with a view to assassinating the king. Being seized and threatened with death, he laid his hand on an altar of burning coal to prove his fortitude, and told the king that there were 300 Roman youths prepared to take his life. Porsenna, amazed at Scaevola's courage, released him, and in fear for his own life withdrew his army and made proposals of peace.

Scala, CANE GRANDE DELLA, usually known as CAN GRANDE (1291–1329), prince of Verona, famous as the patron of Dante (q.v.).

Scald, see *Skald.*

Scales, GERALD, a character in Bennett's 'The Old Wives' Tale' (q.v.).

SCALIGER, JOSEPH JUSTUS (1540–1609), the son of Julius Caesar Scaliger (q.v.), was the greatest scholar of the Renaissance; he has been described as 'the founder of historical criticism'. His edition of Manilius (1579) and his 'De Emendatione Temporum' revolutionized ancient chronology by insisting on the recognition of the historical material relating to the Jews, the Persians, the Babylonians, and the Egyptians. He reconstructed the lost chronicle of Eusebius in his 'Thesaurus Temporum'. He also issued critical editions of many classical authors. He incurred the enmity of the Jesuits and retired from France to Lausanne in 1572, and subsequently to Leyden. He was attacked in his old age by Gaspar Scioppius on behalf of the Jesuits, who contested the claim of the Scaligers to belong to the Della Scala family.

SCALIGER, JULIUS CAESAR (1484–1558), born at Riva on the Lago di Garda, settled at Agen in France as a physician. Besides polemical works directed against Erasmus (1531), he wrote a long Latin treatise on poetics, scientific commentaries on botanical works, and a philosophical treatise ('Exercitationes' on the 'De Subtilitate' of Cardan). These show encyclopaedic knowledge and acute observation, marred by arrogance and vanity. He claimed to belong to the princely family of Della Scala.

Scallop-shell, the badge of the pilgrim. Pilgrims returning from the shrine of St. James at Compostella were accustomed to wear a scallop-shell found on the Galician shore; hence this shell (in ecclesiastical symbolism used as the emblem of the apostle) is often referred to as the distinctive badge of the pilgrim.

Scamander, a river of Asia Minor, flowing into the sea near Troy. Homer calls it Xanthos (yellow), and in the 'Iliad' (xxi) describes the great fight of Achilles with the river, in which the hero would have been overcome had not Hephaestus sent fire and driven the river back.

Scandalum magnatum, medieval Latin, meaning 'Scandal of magnates'; the utterance of a malicious report against any person holding a position of dignity. The term was suggested by the wording of the statute of 2 Richard II (repealed in 1887) which provided penalties for the offence.

Scanderbeg, the Turkish appellation of George Castriot (1403–67), the son of the hereditary prince of a district in Albania. He was brought up as a hostage at the court of the Sultan Amurath (Murad II), and became the successful champion of Albanian independence, and for many years resisted the forces of the Ottoman Empire.

Scandinavia, a geographical term including Norway, Sweden, and Denmark. The name, which appears in the existing text of Pliny, is a mistake for *Scadinavia*, an adaptation of the Teutonic *Skadinauja*, the name of the southern extremity of Sweden. The terminal element is *auja*, island.

Scapegoat, a word apparently invented by Tindale (1530) to express what he believed to be the literal meaning of the Hebrew '*azāzēl* in Lev. XVI. 8, 10, 26, an interpretation now regarded as inadmissible. The word does not appear in the Revised Version of 1884, which has 'Azazel' as a proper name and 'dismissal' in the margin as an alternative reading. The word is used for that one of two goats which, in the Mosaic ritual of the Day of Atonement, was chosen by lot to be sent alive into the wilderness, the sins of the people having been symbolically laid upon it, while the other was appointed to be sacrificed. [OED.]

Scapin, in the 'Fourberies de Scapin' of Molière (q.v.), the type of rascally resourceful servant who gets out of difficulties by his audacious lies. One of these gives the occasion for a much quoted phrase. In order to extract a sum of money needed by his young master from his avaricious father, he tells the latter a cock-and-bull story of the son's having gone on board a Turkish galley, been carried to sea, and held to ransom. The father, gradually convinced by Scapin's eloquence that he will have to produce the ransom, constantly reverts to the question, 'Mais que diable allait-il faire dans cette galère?' The phrase and the scene were taken by Molière from 'Le Pédant Joué' (II. iv) of Cyrano de Bergerac (q.v.).

Scaramouch, adaptation of the Italian *scaramuccia* meaning 'skirmish', a stock character in Italian farce, a cowardly and foolish boaster, who is constantly cudgelled by Harlequin. The character was intended in ridicule of the Spanish don, and was dressed in Spanish costume, usually black. The clever impersonation of the part by Tiberio Fiurelli, who brought his company of Italian players to London in 1673, rendered the word very popular in England during the last quarter of the 17th cent. [OED.] A comedy entitled 'Scaramouch', by Edward Ravenscroft, was produced in 1677.

Scarborough warning, very short notice, or no notice at all. The origin of the phrase is unknown. The statement of Fuller, that it is an allusion to the surprise of Scarborough by Thomas Stafford in 1557, is disproved by its occurrence in John Heywood's 'Proverbs' (1546).

Scarlet, or SCADLOCK, or SCATHELOCKE, WILL, one of the companions of Robin Hood (q.v.).

Scarlet Letter, The, a novel by Hawthorne (q.v.), published in 1850.

The scene of the story is Boston, in the Puritan New England of the 17th cent. To this place an aged and learned Englishman has sent his young wife, intending to follow her, but captivity among the Indians has delayed him for two years. He arrives to find her, Hester Prynne, in the pillory, with a babe in her arms. She has refused to name her lover, and has been sentenced to this ordeal and to wear for the remainder of her life the red letter A, signifying adulteress, upon her bosom. The husband assumes the name of Roger Chillingworth and obtains from Hester an oath that she will conceal his identity. Hester takes up her abode on the outskirts of the town, an object of contempt and insult, with her child, Pearl. Her ostracism opens for her a broader view of life, she devotes herself to works of mercy, and gradually wins the respect of the townsfolk. Roger Chillingworth, in the character of a physician, applies himself to the discovery of her paramour. Hester's lover is, in fact, the Rev. Arthur Dimmesdale, a young and highly revered minister whose lack of courage has prevented him from declaring his guilt and sharing Hester's punishment. The author traces the steps by which Chillingworth discovers him, the cruelty with which he fastens on and tortures him, and at the same time the moral degradation that this process involves for Chillingworth himself. When Dimmesdale at the end of seven years is reduced to the verge of lunacy and death, Hester, emancipated by her experience, proposes to him that they shall flee to Europe, and for a moment he dallies with the idea. But he puts it from him as a temptation of the Evil One, makes public confession on the pillory which had been the scene of Hester's shame, and dies in her arms.

Scarlet Pimpernel, The, a romantic novel by Baroness Orczy (Mrs. Montagu Barstow, 1865–1947), published in 1905. It is the story of the leader of the League of the Scarlet Pimpernel, a band of young Englishmen pledged to rescue the innocent victims of the Reign of Terror in Paris. The hero, Sir Percy Blakeney, outwits his opponents—in particular the wily Chauvelin—by means of his courage and ingenious disguises, at the same time concealing his identity from his friends in England, including, for a time, his beautiful wife. The book was immensely popular, was dramatized, and had several sequels.

Scarlet Woman, THE, an abusive term applied to the Roman Catholic Church in allusion to Rev. xvii. 1–5.

SCARRON, PAUL (1610–60), a French burlesque dramatist and novelist, deformed and paralysed in his lower limbs, who in 1652 married Françoise d'Aubigné, later the celebrated Mme de Maintenon (q.v.).

Scatcherd, ROGER, LOUIS, and MARY, characters in Trollope's 'Dr. Thorne' (q.v.).

Scavenger's Daughter, see *Skeffington's Daughter.*

Scazon, from a Greek word which means limping, halting, a modification of the iambic trimeter in which a spondee or trochee is substituted for the final iambus. It is also called *Choliamb.*

Scenario, a sketch or outline of the plot of a play or film, giving particulars of the scenes, situations, etc.

Scenes of Clerical Life, a series of three tales by George Eliot (q.v.), published in two volumes in 1858, after having appeared in 'Blackwood's Magazine' in the previous year.

The first of these is 'The Sad Fortunes of the Rev. Amos Barton', the sketch of a commonplace clergyman, the curate of Shepperton, without learning, tact, or charm, underpaid, unpopular with his parishioners, who earns their affection by his misfortune—the loss from overwork and general wretchedness of his beautiful gentle wife, Milly.

The second is 'Mr. Gilfil's Love-Story', the tale of a man whose nature has been warped by a tragic love experience. Maynard Gilfil was parson at Shepperton before the days of Amos Barton. He had been the ward of Sir Christopher Cheverel and his domestic chaplain, and had fallen deeply in love with Caterina Sastri (Tina), the daughter of an unlucky Italian singer, whom the Cheverels had adopted. But Capt. Anthony Wybrow, the heir of Sir Christopher, a shallow selfish fellow, had made love to Tina and won her heart. On his part it was little more than a flirtation, and at his uncle's bidding he had thrown her over for the rich Miss Assher. The strain of this and various aggravating circumstances brought Tina's passionate nature to the verge of lunacy. All this Gilfil had watched with sorrow and unabated love. Tina rallied for a time under his devoted care and finally married him, but died in a few months, leaving Gilfil like a tree lopped of its best branches.

The third tale is 'Janet's Repentance', the story of a conflict between religion and irreligion, and of the influence of a sympathetic human soul. The Rev. Edgar Tryan, an earnest evangelical clergyman, comes to the neighbourhood of Milby, an industrial town sunk in religious apathy, which the scanty ministrations of the avaricious old curate, Mr. Crewe, do nothing to stir. His endeavour to remedy this condition is opposed with the utmost vigour and bitterness by a group of inhabitants led by Dempster, a hectoring drunken brute of a lawyer, who beats and bullies his long-suffering wife, Janet, until he drives her to seek solace in drink. She shares her husband's prejudices against the methodistical innovator, until she discovers in him a sympathetic fellow sufferer. Her husband's ill-treatment, which culminates in an act of gross brutality, causes her to appeal to Tryan for help, and under his guidance her struggle against the craving for drink begins. Dempster dies of *delirium tremens*, and Janet gradually achieves self-conquest. The death of Tryan from consumption leaves her bereaved, but strengthened for a life of service.

Sceptic, in philosophy, originally a follower of the school of Pyrrho (q.v.); popularly applied to one who maintains a doubting attitude with reference to some particular question or to assertions of apparent fact.

Schamir, in Rabbinical and medieval myth, the impersonation of a mysterious force which enabled Solomon to build his temple without the use of iron. It is sometimes represented as a worm. It can shatter stones, paralyse, or restore to life. Baring-Gould ('Curious Myths') thinks that in its various forms it represents the lightning.

Scheherazade or SHAHRAZAD, in the 'Arabian Nights' (q.v.), the daughter of the vizir of King Shahriyar, who married the king, and escaped the death that was the usual fate of his wives by telling him the tales which compose that work, interrupting them at an interesting point, and postponing the continuation till the next night.

SCHELLING, FRIEDRICH WILHELM JOSEPH VON (1775–1854), German philosopher, a professor of philosophy at Jena, Wurzburg, Munich, and Berlin. He was a disciple at first of Fichte (q.v.), but soon departed from his doctrine. Unlike Fichte, Schelling makes the universe rather than the *ego* the element of reality. Nature, obedient to the laws of human intelligence, is a single living organism working towards self-consciousness, a faculty dormant in inanimate objects and fully awake only in man, whose being consists in 'intellectual intuition' of the world he creates. Schelling's numerous works include 'Ideen zu einer Philosophie der Natur' (1797), 'Von der Weltseele' (1798), and 'System des transcendentalen Idealismus' (1800). In his later writings his philosophy took a more religious tinge.

SCHILLER, JOHANN CHRISTOPH FRIEDRICH VON (1759–1805), German dramatist and lyric poet, the son of an army surgeon, and the chief figure of the 'Sturm und Drang' (q.v.) period of German literature. Schiller first came into prominence and struck the note of revolt in his prose drama, 'Die Räuber' ('The Robbers', 1781), in which Karl von Moor the heroic robber, who takes to the woods to redress the evils of his father's court, is contrasted with the stage villain, his wicked brother, in a series of extravagant incidents. The crudities which marred this play disappear in great measure in Schiller's next great dramatic work, the blank-verse 'Don Carlos' (1787); but he reached the summit of his dramatic power in the long historical tragedy 'Wallenstein' (1799), composed of three parts: 'Wallenstein's Camp', 'The Piccolomini', and 'Wallenstein's Death' (translated into English verse by S. T. Coleridge in 1800). This treats of the treasonable attempt of Wallenstein (the Emperor's great general and opponent of Gustavus Adolphus) to overthrow the Emperor, an attempt that is defeated by the murder of the traitor. 'Wallenstein' was followed by 'Maria Stuart' in 1800, 'Die Jungfrau von Orleans' (Joan of Arc) in 1801, 'Die Braut von Messina' (on the theme of the passion of two brothers for the same woman) in 1803, and 'Wilhelm Tell' in 1804.

Schiller was no less great as a writer of reflective and lyrical poems and of ballads, and his best work of this kind belongs to the period of his intimacy with Goethe, dating from 1794. Among the more notable of these poems are 'Das Ideal und das Leben', 'Der Taucher', 'Die Klage der Ceres', and 'Die Glocke', a work immensely popular in Germany, in which the process of casting a bell forms the symbolic centre in the presentment of the chequered life of man. Mention should also be made of the earlier 'Die Künstler', a poem on the humanizing influence of art.

Schiller was also author of philosophical and historical works, of which the most important are the 'Philosophische Briefe' (1786), and histories of the Revolt in the Netherlands (1788) and the Thirty Years War (1789–93). Schiller was appointed professor of history at Jena in 1789.

Schism, THE GREAT, the state of divided allegiance in the Western Church due to the election of rival Italian and French popes (Urban VI and Clement VII) in 1378. It was ended in 1417 by the Council of Constance, but other schisms followed till 1448.

SCHLEGEL, AUGUST WILHELM VON (1767–1845), a German Romanticist, chiefly known in England for his translation into the German language, with the assistance of his wife and others, of the plays of Shakespeare.

SCHLEGEL, FRIEDRICH VON (1772–1829), younger brother of August Wilhelm von Schlegel (q.v.), notable for his studies of the history of literature ('Geschichte der griechischen Poesie' and 'Geschichte der alten und neuen Litteratur'), and especially for his recognition of the importance of the ancient Hindu poetry ('Sprache und Weisheit der Indier', 1808).

Schlemihl, PETER, in the story or allegory by Chamisso (q.v.), the impecunious young man who surrendered his shadow to the devil, a thin elderly gentleman in a grey coat, in exchange for a purse of Fortunatus. The lack of shadow exposes Peter to disagreeable remark, and in spite of his wealth he finds himself an outcast from human society.

Schliemann, HEINRICH (1822–90), born in Mecklenburg-Schwerin, the celebrated German archaeologist who excavated Troy, Tiryns, and Mycenae. He was engaged during the early part of his life in commerce, mainly in Russia, and did not begin archaeological work until nearly fifty years of age. His excavation of Troy was carried out in the years 1870–3.

Scholar-Gipsy, The, a poem by M. Arnold (q.v.), published in 1853.

The poem, pastoral in setting, is based on an old legend, narrated by Glanvill (q.v.) in his 'The Vanity of Dogmatizing', of an 'Oxford scholar poor' who, tired of seeking preferment, joined the gipsies to learn their lore, roamed the world with them, and still haunts the Oxford countryside. With this is woven a wonderful evocation of that landscape, and reflections on the contrast between the concentration and faith of the scholar-gipsy and

this strange disease of modern life,
With its sick hurry, and divided aims.

Scholasticism, or the doctrines of the Schoolmen (q.v.), the predominant theological and philosophical teaching of the period 1100–1500, in the main an attempt to reconcile Aristotle with the Scriptures, reason with faith. In the 14th cent., after Ockham, scholasticism, as an intellectual movement, had exhausted itself. It degenerated into an endless discussion of logical futilities, completely divorced from the realities of life. The term is also used of a narrow and unenlightened insistence on traditional doctrines and forms of exposition.

Scholemaster, The, see *Ascham.*

School for Scandal, The, a comedy by R. B. Sheridan (q.v.), produced in 1777.

In this play, his masterpiece, the author contrasts two brothers, Joseph Surface the hypocrite, and Charles Surface the good-natured reckless spendthrift. Charles is in love with Maria, Sir Peter Teazle's ward, and his affection is returned; and Joseph is courting her for her fortune, while at the same time making love to Lady Teazle. Sir Peter, an old man who has married a young wife six months before, is made miserable by her frivolity. The scandal-mongers, Sir Benjamin Backbite, Lady Sneerwell, and Mrs. Candour, who 'strike a character dead at every word', provide the background and give occasion for Sir Peter's classic remark, on leaving their company, 'Your ladyship must excuse me. . . . But I leave my character behind me.' Sir Oliver Surface, the rich uncle of Joseph and Charles, returns unexpectedly from India and decides to test the characters of his nephews before revealing himself. He visits Charles in the character of a moneylender, and Charles light-heartedly sells him the family pictures, but refuses to sell at any price the portrait of 'the ill-looking little fellow over the settee', who is Sir Oliver himself, and thus wins the old man's heart. Meanwhile Joseph receives a visit from Lady Teazle in his library and insidiously attempts to seduce her. The sudden arrival of Sir Peter obliges Lady Teazle to hide behind a screen, where she is put to shame by hearing proof of Sir Peter's generosity to her, though he suspects an attachment between her and Charles. The arrival of Charles sends Sir Peter in turn to cover. Sir Peter detects the presence of a woman behind the screen, but is told by Joseph that it is a little French milliner, and takes refuge in a cupboard. The conversation between Joseph and Charles proves to Sir Peter that his suspicion of Charles was unfounded, and the throwing down of the screen reveals Lady Teazle. Scarcely is this revelation of Joseph's hypocrisy accomplished when Sir Oliver visits him in the character of a needy but deserving relative applying for assistance, which Joseph refuses on the plea of the stinginess of his uncle. This completes the exposure of Joseph. Charles is united to Maria, and Sir Peter is reconciled to Lady Teazle.

Schoole of Abuse, see *Gosson.*

Schoolmen, the succession of writers, from about the 11th to the 15th cent., who treat of logic, metaphysics, and theology, as taught in the 'schools' or universities of Italy, France, Germany, and England, that is to say on the basis of Aristotle and the Christian

Fathers, whom the schoolmen endeavoured to harmonize. Among the great Schoolmen were Peter Lombard, Abélard, Albertus Magnus, Aquinas, Duns Scotus, and Ockham (qq.v.).

Schoolmistress, The, see **Shenstone.**

SCHOPENHAUER, ARTHUR (1788–1860), was the author of a pessimistic philosophy embodied in his 'Die Welt als Wille und Vorstellung' (1819, 'The World as Will and Representation'). According to this, Will, of which we have direct intuition, is the 'thing-in-itself', the only reality. Will, which is self-conscious in man, finds its equivalent in the unconscious forces of nature. Will, then, it is that creates the world; and the world is not only an illusion but a malignant thing, which inveigles us into reproducing and perpetuating life. Asceticism, and primarily chastity, are the duty of man, with a view to terminating the evil. Egoism, which manifests itself principally in the 'will to live', must be overcome. Its opposite is compassion, the moral law, based on the intuition of the essential identity of all beings. God, free-will, and the immortality of the soul, are illusions.

SCHREINER, OLIVE EMILIE ALBERTINA (1855–1920), born in Cape Colony, came to England in 1881 and published under the pseudonym 'Ralph Iron' in 1883 the most successful of her works, 'The Story of an African Farm'. Her 'Women and Labour' appeared in 1911, and an uncompleted novel 'From Man to Man' posthumously in 1926. She married in 1894 a South African politician, Samuel Cron Cronwright, who wrote an introduction to this last work.

Schubert, FRANZ PETER (1797–1828), the Austrian composer, who in his short life produced several operas, ten symphonies, and much other music. He was one of the greatest of song-writers and composed more than 500 songs ('Erlkönig', 'The Trout', 'The Wanderer', etc.).

Science Fiction is the current name for a class of prose narrative which assumes an imaginary technological or scientific advance, or depends upon an imaginary and spectacular change in human environment. Although examples exist from the time of Lucian (q.v.), it was not until the end of the 19th cent. that the form emerged as we know it today. The works of Jules Verne (q.v.) have always been popular in this country, but the first successful English author was H. G. Wells (q.v.), whose stories include several of the themes later dominant: invasion from outer space ('The War of the Worlds', 1898), biological change or catastrophe ('The Food of the Gods', 1904), time travel ('The Time Machine', 1895), and air warfare ('The War in the Air', 1908).

Since the Second World War scientific developments and their possible consequences have been reflected in fictional form by motifs such as interplanetary travel, robots or mechanical brains, and atomic hand-weapons; and the destruction of the world as a result of its own technological achievements has been a favourite theme. But the scientific element is often ancillary to an inquiry into the nature of man and his behaviour.

Scipio Africanus Major, PUBLIUS CORNELIUS (236/5–c. 183 B.C.), the conqueror of Spain, and of Hannibal at the battle of Zama (202 B.C.), and one of the greatest of the Romans. When accused of peculation and brought to trial in 185 he proudly reminded the people that it was the anniversary of the battle of Zama and triumphantly brushed aside the charge. It is recorded of him that he refused to see a beautiful Spanish princess who had fallen into his hands after the taking of Carthago Nova, and not only restored her to her parents but added presents for the person to whom she was betrothed.

How he surnamed of Africa dismissed,
In his prime youth, the fair Iberian maid.
(Milton, 'Paradise Regained', II. 199.)

Sciron, a legendary robber in Attica, who waylaid travellers, compelled them to wash his feet, robbed them, and finally threw them down from the 'Scironian rocks' (near Megara) into the sea. He was destroyed by Theseus.

SCOGAN, HENRY (1361?–1407), a poet and a correspondent of Chaucer, to whom the latter addressed an 'envoy' or verse epistle. He was tutor to four sons of Henry IV. He is referred to by Leland as a man given to all sorts of jocoseness and wit, by Shakespeare in '2 Henry IV', III. ii, and by Jonson in 'The Fortunate Isles'.

Scogan, JOHN, a celebrated jester of Edward IV, whose exploits, real or imagined, are recorded in 'The Geystes of Skoggan' (1565–6).

Scone stone, a stone supposed to have been brought to Scone in Scotland from Tara in Ireland, and used as the coronation stone of the Scottish kings. Edward I had it removed to Westminster Abbey, where it was placed under the coronation chair, and still remains. In Irish legend the stone of Tara is said to be that on which Jacob rested his head at Bethel.

Scot, MICHAEL and REGINALD, see *Scott*.

Scotist, a follower or disciple of Duns Scotus (q.v.), whose system was in many respects opposed to that of Thomas Aquinas. The followers of the latter were known as 'Thomists'.

Scotland Yard, in Whitehall, near Charing Cross, London, where formerly stood 'great buildings for receipt of the kings of Scotland and other estates of that country', and where Margaret queen of Scots, sister of Henry VIII, 'had her abiding' (Stow) when she paid a visit to London before her marriage with the earl of Angus. It was the headquarters of the

Metropolitan Police *c.* 1842–90. These were moved to New Scotland Yard, near Westminster Bridge, in 1890, and to Broadway, Westminster, in 1967.

Scots Musical Museum, a collection of Scots songs published by James Johnson (*d.* 1811) in five volumes, 1787–1803. Burns (q.v.) took an important part in the editing, and contributed two songs to vol. i. Lady Anne Lindsay's 'Auld Robin Gray' appeared in it; also songs by Joanna Baillie, Dr. Blacklock, James Tytler, and Sir Alexander Boswell.

SCOTT or SCOT, MICHAEL (1175?–1234?), a scholar of Scottish birth, who studied at Oxford and on the Continent, and was attached to the court of the Emperor Frederick II, probably in the capacity of official astrologer. He was sent by Frederick II, about 1230, to the universities of Europe to communicate to them versions of Aristotle made by Michael and others. Legends of his magical power have served as a theme to many great writers from Dante ('Inferno', c. xx, 116) to Sir W. Scott ('Lay of the Last Minstrel'). His printed works include 'Liber Physiognomiae' (1477), a translation of Aristotle's 'De Animalibus' (1496), and 'Quaestio Curiosa de Natura Solis et Lunae' (1622). Works of his on astronomy and alchemy, and various translations, still remain in manuscript.

SCOTT, MICHAEL (1789–1835), author of 'Tom Cringle's Log', which was published in 'Blackwood's Magazine' in 1829–33. It gives vivid and amusing pictures of life in Jamaica and the islands of the Caribbean Sea in the early days of the 19th cent. Scott contributed 'The Cruise of the Midge' to the same periodical in 1834–5. Both works were republished in 1836.

SCOTT or SCOT, REGINALD (1538?–99), educated at Hart Hall, Oxford, and M.P. for New Romney, 1588–9, was author of 'The Discoverie of Witchcraft' (1584). This was written with the aim of preventing the persecution of poor, aged, and simple persons who were popularly believed to be witches, by exposing the impostures on the one hand, and the credulity on the other, that supported the belief in sorcery.

SCOTT, ROBERT FALCON (1868–1912), captain R.N., Antarctic explorer, was author of 'The Voyage of the Discovery' (1905), a record of the first National Antarctic Expedition (1901–4); and of the notable journal, published as 'Scott's Last Expedition', in 1913, kept during the second Antarctic expedition (1910–12), the last entry in which was made as the writer was dying, stormbound by a blizzard on his return from the South Pole.

SCOTT, SIR WALTER (1771–1832), son of Walter Scott, a writer to the signet, was born in College Wynd, Edinburgh, was educated at Edinburgh High School and University, and was apprenticed to his father. He was called to the bar in 1792. His interest in the old Border tales and ballads had early been awakened, and was stimulated by Percy's 'Reliques', and by the study of the old romantic poetry of France and Italy and of the modern German poets. He devoted much of his leisure to the exploration of the Border country. In 1796 he published, anonymously, a translation of Bürger's 'Lenore' and 'Der Wilde Jäger', and in 1799 a translation of Goethe's 'Goetz von Berlichingen'. In 1797 he married Margaret Charlotte Charpentier (or Carpenter), daughter of Jean Charpentier of Lyon in France, and was appointed sheriff-depute of Selkirkshire in 1799. In 1802–3 appeared the three volumes of Scott's 'Minstrelsy of the Scottish Border' (a collection of ballads, historical, traditional, and romantic, with imitations in a separate section); and in 1805 his first considerable original work, the romantic poem, 'The Lay of the Last Minstrel' (q.v.). He then became a partner in James Ballantyne's printing business, published 'Marmion' (q.v.) in 1808, and in the same year his edition of Dryden's works, with a 'Life' of the poet. This was followed by 'The Lady of the Lake' (q.v.) in 1810, 'Rokeby' and 'The Bridal of Triermain' (qq.v.) in 1813, 'The Lord of the Isles' (q.v.) in 1815, and 'Harold the Dauntless', his last long poem, in 1817. In 1809 he had entered into partnership with John Ballantyne in the bookselling business known as 'John Ballantyne & Co.', and in 1811 he had purchased Abbotsford on the Tweed, where he built himself a residence. Scott promoted the foundation in 1809 of the Tory 'Quarterly Review' (q.v.), having previously been a contributor to the 'Edinburgh Review' (q.v.), but seceded from it owing to its Whig attitude. In 1813 he refused the offer of the laureateship, and recommended Southey for the honour. In 1814 he issued his edition of Swift. Eclipsed in a measure by Byron as a poet, in spite of the great popularity of his verse romances, he now turned his attention to the novel as a means of giving play to his wide erudition, his humour, and his sympathies. His novels appeared anonymously in the following order: 'Waverley' (q.v.), 1814; 'Guy Mannering' (q.v.), 1815; 'The Antiquary' (q.v.) in 1816; 'The Black Dwarf' and 'Old Mortality' (qq.v.) together in 1816 as the first series of 'Tales of My Landlord'; 'Rob Roy' (q.v.) in 1817; 'The Heart of Midlothian' (q.v.), second series of 'Tales of My Landlord', in 1818; 'The Bride of Lammermoor' and 'A Legend of Montrose' (qq.v.), the third series of 'Tales of My Landlord', in 1819; 'Ivanhoe' (q.v.), 1819; 'The Monastery' (q.v.), 1820; 'The Abbot' (q.v.), 1820; 'Kenilworth' (q.v.), 1821; 'The Pirate' (q.v.), 1821; 'The Fortunes of Nigel' (q.v.), 1822; 'Peveril of the Peak' (q.v.), 1823; 'Quentin Durward' (q.v.), 1823; 'St. Ronan's Well' (q.v.), 1823; 'Redgauntlet' (q.v.), 1824; 'The Betrothed' and 'The Talisman' (qq.v.) together as

'Tales of the Crusaders' in 1825; 'Woodstock' (q.v.), 1826; 'Chronicles of the Canongate' (containing 'The Highland Widow', 'The Two Drovers', and 'The Surgeon's Daughter' (qq.v.)), 1827; 'Chronicles of the Canongate' (second series): 'St. Valentine's Day, or The Fair Maid of Perth' (q.v.), 1828; 'Anne of Geierstein' (q.v.), 1829; 'Tales of My Landlord' (fourth series): 'Count Robert of Paris' (q.v.) and 'Castle Dangerous' (q.v.), in 1831. Scott was created a baronet in 1820, and avowed the authorship of the novels in 1827. In 1826 James Ballantyne & Co. became involved in the bankruptcy of Constable & Co., and Scott, as a partner of the former, found himself liable for a debt of about £114,000. He shouldered the whole burden himself and henceforth worked heroically, shortening his own life by strenuous efforts, to pay off the creditors who received full payment after his death.

Scott's dramatic work, in which he did not excel, includes 'Halidon Hill' (1822), 'Macduff's Cross' (1823), 'The Doom of Devorgoil, a Melo-drama'; 'Auchindrane' or, the Ayrshire Tragedy' (1830). Of these 'Auchindrane' is the best. It is founded on the case of Mure of Auchindrane in Pitcairn's 'Ancient Criminal Trials'. Mention must also be made of the important historical, literary, and antiquarian works written by Scott or issued under his editorship: 'The Works of Dryden' with a life (1808); 'The Works of Swift' with a life (1814); 'Provincial Antiquities of Scotland' (1819–26); an abstract of the 'Eyrbiggia Saga' in 'Northern Antiquities' (1814); 'Description of the Regalia of Scotland' (1819); 'Lives of the Novelists' prefixed to Ballantyne's Novelist's Library (1821–4); Essays on Chivalry (1818), the Drama (1819) and Romance (1824) contributed to the 'Encyclopaedia Britannica'; 'The Life of Napoleon Buonaparte' (1827); 'Tales of a Grandfather' (q.v., 1827–30); 'History of Scotland' (1829–30); 'Letters on Demonology and Witchcraft' (1830); 'Original Memoirs written during the Great Civil War' of Sir H. Slingsby and Captain Hodgson (1806); the 'Memoirs of Captain George Carleton' (1808); the 'State Papers of Sir Ralph Sadler' (1809); the 'Secret History of James I' (1811); and 'Memorie of the Somervilles' (1815). 'Paul's Letters to his Kinsfolk' (q.v.) appeared in 1816. Scott founded the Bannatyne Club (q.v.) in 1823. In 1826 he addressed to the 'Edinburgh Weekly Journal' three letters 'from Malachi Malagrowther', 'Thoughts on the proposed Change of Currency', defending the rights of Scotland.

Scott's 'Life' by John Gibson Lockhart (q.v.), published in 1837–8, is one of the great biographies of English literature. A short Life of Scott was published in 1932 by John Buchan (q.v.). Scott's 'Journal' was published in 1890 and again in 1939–46, in 3 vols., edited by J. G. Tait. An edition of his letters in 12 vols. was published by Sir H. J. C. Grierson (1932–7).

SCOTT, WILLIAM BELL (1811–90), poet and artist, a friend of Swinburne and Rossetti. He published five volumes of verse, the best of which is of a mystical and metaphysical character.

Scottish Chiefs, The, an historical novel by Jane Porter (q.v.), published in 1810. It was extremely successful and was translated into German and Russian.

The story is a romance based on the historical events in the life of William Wallace, and opens with the murder of Wallace's wife in 1296 by Heselrigge, the English governor of Lanark, for refusing to divulge her husband's hiding-place. The vicissitudes of Wallace's career are followed to his execution, and the story closes with the battle of Bannockburn.

Scottish Text Society, THE, founded in 1882 for the purpose of printing and editing texts illustrative of the Scottish language and literature, has issued editions of many works of general literary interest, such as 'The Kingis Quair', Barbour's 'Bruce', and the 'Basilikon Doron', and the poems of W. Dunbar, R. Henryson, Drummond of Hawthornden, and Sir D. Lyndsay (qq.v.).

SCOTUS or **ERIGENA, JOHN** (*fl.* 850), of Irish origin, was employed as teacher at the court of King Charles the Bald, afterwards emperor, *c.* 847. He is often confused with one John who came to England with Grimbald (q.v.) at Alfred's request and was established at Malmesbury. All the known works of Scotus, which include a series of commentaries on Dionysius the Areopagite, and translations, were collected by H. J. Floss in Migne's 'Patrologia Latina', cxxii (1853); two other works claiming his authorship have since come to light. The leading principle of his philosophy, as expounded in his great work, 'De Divisione Naturae', is that of the unity of nature, proceeding from (1) God, the first and only real being; through (2) the creative ideas to (3) the sensible universe, which ultimately is resolved into (4) its first Cause. He was thus one of the originators of the mystical thought of the Middle Ages, and he prepared the way for the scholastic philosophy.

SCOTUS, JOANNES DUNS, see *Duns Scotus.*

Scourers or SCOWRERS, in the 17th–18th cents., a set of men who made a practice of roistering through the streets at night, beating the watch, breaking windows, etc. They are frequently referred to in the literature of the period (Wycherley, Gay, 'The Spectator', etc.).

Scourge of God, see *Attila.*

Scriblerus Club, an association of which Pope, Swift, Arbuthnot, Gay, Parnell, Congreve, Lord Oxford, and Atterbury were members, formed about 1713. They undertook the production of the 'Memoirs of Martinus Scriblerus' (see *Martinus Scrib-*

lerus), designed to ridicule 'all the false tastes in learning, under the character of a man of capacity enough, that had dipped into every art and science, but injudiciously in each'.

Scrooge, a character in Dickens's 'A Christmas Carol' (q.v.).

Scrub, man-of-all-work to Lady Bountiful's household in Farquhar's 'The Beaux' Stratagem' (q.v.).

Scrutiny, a quarterly review aimed at raising the critical standards for English literature and culture, which ran from 1932 to 1953 with F. R. Leavis (q.v.) as its chief editor. Among others, the editorial board included L. C. Knights and D. W. Harding. The complete series was reissued in 20 vols. in 1963.

Scudamour, SIR, in Spenser's 'Faerie Queene', Bk. IV, the lover of Amoret, who is reft from him on his wedding-day by the enchanter Busyrane.

SCUDÉRY, MADELEINE DE (1607–1701), one of the most voluminous writers of French heroic romances. Her principal work was 'Artamène, ou le Grand Cyrus' (ten volumes, 1649–53), which deals with the love of the youthful Cyrus, grandson of the king of Media, travelling incognito under the name of Artamenes, for Mandane, daughter of Cyaxares, his uncle, and the rivalry of the kings of Pontus and Assyria for her hand, resulting in sieges, abductions, pursuits, incredible adventures, and the final union of hero and heroine. The characters are portraits of notable persons of the author's day. A play founded on the romance was brought out by John Banks in 1696. Madeleine de Scudéry also wrote 'Clélie' (1656–60), on the subject of the Clelia who escaped from the power of Porsenna by swimming the Tiber; and 'Almahide' (1660), a story of the Moors in Spain, from which Dryden took the name of the heroine of his 'Conquest of Granada'. All these romances were translated into English and enjoyed for a time great popularity; Pepys had to check his wife for her long stories out of the 'Grand Cyrus' ('Diary', 12 May 1666). The brother of Madeleine de Scudéry, George, a dramatic poet, gave some assistance in the composition of her earlier romances. They were vigorously satirized by Boileau (q.v.).

Scylla, a nymph loved by Poseidon, or according to Ovid by Glaucus, one of the deities of the sea. Amphitrite (or Circe) from jealousy of Scylla placed magic herbs in the fountain where she bathed. By these Scylla was changed into a monster, which thenceforth became a terror to mariners, seizing and devouring them as they sailed past its cave, situated according to tradition in the Straits of Messina, opposite the whirlpool of Charybdis (q.v.). The passage of the straits is the theme of part of the twelfth book of the 'Odyssey', and the story of Scylla is referred to by Keats in 'Endymion' (iii).

Scythrop, a character in Peacock's 'Nightmare Abbey' (q.v.).

Seafarer, The, an Old English poem of some 120 lines, included in the Exeter Book (q.v.), discussing the miseries and attractions of life at sea, and passing to a comparison of earthly pleasures and heavenly rewards. An early critic suggested that it represents a dialogue between an old seaman and a young man who wishes to follow the sea; recent interpretations have attempted to relate it to the practice of penitential pilgrimage, or (with 'The Wanderer' (q.v.)) to the Christian tradition of man as an exile from Paradise, wandering as a pilgrim on the earth.

Sea-green Incorruptible, a name applied to Robespierre (q.v.) by T. Carlyle in his 'French Revolution'. According to H. Belloc's introduction to this work in Everyman's Library, 1906, ' "Sea Green" is based on *one* phrase of Mme de Staël's misread. What Mme de Staël said was that the prominent veins in Robespierre's forehead showed greenish-blue against his fair and somewhat pale skin. But his complexion was healthy and his expression, if anything, winning.'

Seagrim, MOLLY, a character in Fielding's 'Tom Jones' (q.v.).

Seasons, The, a poem in blank verse, in four books, one for each season, and a final 'Hymn', by James Thomson (1700–48, q.v.), published in 1726–30.

'Winter' was the first of the four 'Seasons', written and published in 1726. It describes the rain, wind, and snow; the visit of the redbreast; a man perishing in the snowdrift while his family anxiously await him; wolves descending from the mountains; a winter evening as spent by a student, or in a village, or a city; frost and skating; and the Arctic circle.

Next came 'Summer' (1727), which sets forth the progress of a summer's day, with such scenes as haymaking, sheep-shearing, and bathing, followed by a panegyric of Great Britain. It also includes a picture of the torrid zone and two narrative episodes (of the lover Celadon whose Amelia is struck by lightning, and of Damon who beholds Musidora bathing).

'Spring' appeared in 1728. The poet describes the influence of the season on inanimate objects, on vegetables, brute beasts, and lastly man, with a final panegyric on nuptial love. In the charming picture of the angler, the poet returns to the earlier manner exemplified in 'Winter'.

'Autumn' followed in 1730. The poet gives a vivid picture of shooting and hunting, and condemns these sports for their barbarity. He describes the reaping of the fruits of the earth, the coming of fogs, the migration of birds, and the mirth of the country after the harvest is gathered in. This part includes the episode of Palemon who falls in love with

Lavinia, a gleaner in his fields (the story of Boaz and Ruth).

The poem is completed by the 'Hymn' to Nature (1730).

Seaton, THOMAS (1684–1741), fellow of Clare College, Cambridge, founded by legacy the SEATONIAN PRIZE at Cambridge for sacred poetry. This is referred to in Byron's 'English Bards and Scotch Reviewers'.

Sebastian (1554–78), king of Portugal, killed at the battle of Alcazar in the course of an expedition against Morocco. There was a widespread popular belief that he was not dead but would reappear, and various impostors came forward who claimed the crown in his name. Dryden's play, 'Don Sebastian' (q.v.), refers to this monarch.

Sebastian, (1) in Shakespeare's 'The Tempest' (q.v.), brother to the king of Naples; (2) in his 'Twelfth Night' (q.v.), brother to Viola.

Sebastian, ST., a Roman soldier and Christian martyr. He was born at Narbonne, and shot to death with arrows in Rome, about A.D. 288, under Diocletian. He is commemorated on 20 January.

Second Nun's Tale, The, see *Canterbury Tales*.

Sedan, the scene of the defeat of the army of Napoleon III by the Germans on 2 Sept. 1870, and of the French emperor's surrender; the central incident of Zola's 'La Débâcle'.

Sedgemoor, in Somerset, the scene of the battle of 6 July 1685 in which Monmouth, who had landed at Lyme Regis as the champion of the Protestant party, was defeated by the Royal troops.

Sedley, MR., MRS., JOSEPH, and AMELIA, characters in Thackeray's 'Vanity Fair' (q.v.).

SEDLEY, SIR CHARLES (1639?–1701), educated at Wadham College, Oxford, famous for his wit and urbanity and notorious as a fashionable profligate, was the author of two indifferent tragedies and three comedies. Of these the best are 'Bellamira' (q.v.), produced in 1687, and 'The Mulberry Garden', partly based on Molière's 'L'École des Maris', produced in 1668. Sedley also wrote some pleasant songs: 'Phillis is my only joy', 'Hears not my Phillis how the birds', etc. He figures in Dryden's 'Essay of Dramatick Poesie' (q.v.) as Lisideius, who defends the imitation of French comedy in English.

SEELEY, SIR JOHN ROBERT (1834–95), educated at the City of London School and Christ's College, Cambridge, was professor of Latin at University College, London, from 1863, and of modern history at Cambridge from 1869 until his death. In 1865 he published anonymously his 'Ecce Homo', a survey of the life of Christ as one of the great religious reformers, and a defence of Christian ethics. His historical works, designed to promote a practical object, the training of statesmen, include: 'The Expansion of England in the Eighteenth Century' (1883), which reviews the growth of the Empire as an inevitable process, and infers the imperial mission of Britain from the lessons of the past, a work which met with great success; 'The Life and Times of Stein, or Germany and Prussia in the Napoleonic Age' (1878); and 'The Growth of British Policy' (1895), tracing the development of British foreign policy from the time of Elizabeth.

Sejan horse, THE, *equus Sejanus*, the horse of a certain Gnaeus Sejus, which brought misfortune to him (put to death by Mark Antony) and all subsequent possessors.

Sejanus, his Fall, a Roman tragedy by Jonson (q.v.), first acted in 1603, Shakespeare and Burbage having parts in the cast.

The play deals with the rise of the historical Sejanus, the confidant of the emperor Tiberius, his machinations with a view to securing the imperial throne, his fall and execution.

Selborne, *Natural History and Antiquities of,* see *White* (G.).

SELDEN, JOHN (1584–1654), the son of a Sussex yeoman, was educated at Chichester and Hart Hall, Oxford, and became an eminent lawyer and bencher of the Inner Temple. He was keeper of the records in 1643. His 'History of Tythes', published in 1618, which gave offence to the clergy, was suppressed by public authority. In parliament he took an active part against the Crown until 1649, after which he withdrew from public affairs. He won fame as an orientalist by his treatise 'De Diis Syris' (1617), and subsequently made a valuable collection of oriental manuscripts, most of which passed at his death into the Bodleian Library. His work in this direction consisted chiefly in the exposition of rabbinical law. His 'Table Talk', containing reports of his utterances from time to time during the last twenty years of his life, composed by his secretary, Richard Milward, appeared in 1689. His works include 'Titles of Honour' (1614), an edition of Eadmer (1623), 'Marmora Arundelliana' (1624), 'De Successionibus' (1631), 'Mare Clausum' (in which he maintained against Grotius that the sea is capable of sovereignty, 1635), 'De Jure Naturali' (1640), 'Judicature in Parliament' (1640), 'Privileges of Baronage' (1642), 'Fleta' (1647), and 'On the Nativity of Christ' (1661). He wrote 'Illustrations' to the first eighteen 'songs' of Drayton's 'Polyolbion' (q.v.). His works were collected by Dr. David Wilkins (1726).

Selden Society, THE, was founded in 1887 by Maitland (q.v.), for the publication of ancient legal records.

Select Society, THE, an association of educated Scotsmen formed in 1754, whose members met in Edinburgh to discuss philosophical questions. Hume and Robertson were among its prominent members.

Selēnē, in Greek mythology, the goddess of the moon, the Luna of the Romans, the sister of Helios (Sol, the sun) and of Eos (Aurora, the dawn). In later myths she is identified with Artemis (Diana).

Seleucids, THE, the dynasty founded by Seleucus Nicator (one of the generals of Alexander the Great), which reigned over Syria from 312 to 65 B.C. and subjected a great part of western Asia.

Self-Help, a work by Smiles (q.v.), published in 1864, which enjoyed great popularity and was translated into many other languages. It inculcates, by examples of the lives and characters of authors, artists, inventors, missionaries, etc., the doctrine that the spirit of self-help is the root of all genuine growth in the individual.

Selim, the hero of Byron's 'Bride of Abydos' (q.v.).

Selima, Horace Walpole's cat, whose death by drowning in a bowl of goldfish was lamented in a poem by Gray.

Seljuk, the name of certain Turkish dynasties that ruled over large parts of Asia from the 11th to the 13th cents., so called from the name of their reputed ancestor. Hence used to designate that branch of the Turkish people to whom these dynasties belonged, in contradistinction to the Osmanli or Ottoman Turks. The dynasties began with Togrul Beg, grandson of Seljuk, who made himself a sort of mayor of the palace to the caliph of Baghdad (c. 1060). The Seljuk 'Turks' were the men whom the Crusaders of the 11th and 12th cents. had to fight; they had recently burst the frontier of the Eastern Empire and smashed the Greek army at Manzikert (1071), and all Asia Minor was in their hands in 1090.

Selkirk, ALEXANDER (1676–1721), the son of John Selcraig, shoemaker of Largo, ran away to sea, and joined the privateering expedition of Capt. William Dampier (q.v.), in 1703. Having quarrelled with his captain, Thomas Stradling, he was, at his own request, put ashore on the uninhabited island of Juan Fernandez in 1704, and remained there until 1709, when he was rescued by Capt. W. Rogers (q.v.). His experiences there formed the basis of Defoe's 'Robinson Crusoe' (q.v.).

Semēlē, a daughter of Cadmus (q.v.) and Harmonia, was beloved by Zeus. At the instigation of the jealous Hera she prayed Zeus to visit her in all the splendour of a god. This rash request was acceded to by Zeus, who came accordingly attended by lightning and thunderbolts, by which Semele was instantly consumed. Her child, however, was saved from the flames, and was known as Dionysus (q.v.).

Semirămis, a mythical queen of Assyria, supposed to be the daughter of the fish-goddess Derceto. She married Onnes, an Assyrian general, and accompanied him to the siege of Bactra, where her prudent advice hastened the fall of the city. She subsequently married Ninus, king of Assyria, the reputed founder of Nineveh, and succeeded him on the throne (having according to one form of the story contrived his death). She built many cities, and some of the great works of the East are by tradition ascribed to her.

Semiramis of the North, a term sometimes applied to (1) Margaret (1353–1412), daughter of Valdemar IV of Denmark and wife of Haakon VI of Norway, who became in 1381 regent of Norway and Denmark, and in 1388 ruler of Sweden; and (2) Catharine II of Russia (1729–96), originally a princess of Anhalt-Zerbst, and empress of Russia from 1762 (in which year her husband, Peter III, was deposed) until her death.

Semitic, meaning originally 'of or pertaining to the Semites', the descendants of Shem the son of Noah (in recent use, often specifically equivalent to Jewish), is used in a linguistic sense to designate that family of languages of which Hebrew, Aramaic, Arabic, Ethiopic, and ancient Assyrian are the principal members.

Sempronius, (1) in Shakespeare's 'Timon of Athens' (q.v.), one of the false friends of Timon; (2) a character in Addison's 'Cato' (q.v.).

Senae, in imprints, Sienna.

SENECA, LUCIUS ANNAEUS (d. A.D. 65), the philosopher, was born at Corduba in Spain a few years before the Christian era. He was tutor to the young Nero, and when the latter became emperor was one of his chief advisers, and exerted himself to check his vices. But he condoned Nero's crimes and grew wealthy at his court. He was accused of participating in the conspiracy of Piso and was ordered to take his own life, which he did with stoic courage. His writings include works on moral philosophy (he was an illustrious representative of the Stoic school) and nine tragedies in a rhetorical style; whence 'Senecan' tragedy.

Senhouse, JOHN MAXWELL, see *Hewlett.*

SENIOR, NASSAU WILLIAM (1790–1864), educated at Eton and Magdalen College, Oxford, was professor of political economy at Oxford, 1825–30 and 1847–52. Besides important political articles contributed to the 'Edinburgh Review' after 1840, he wrote 'An Outline of the Science of Political Economy' (1836), 'Conversations with M. Thiers, M. Guizot, and other distinguished persons during the Second Empire' (1878), 'Correspondence and Conversations of A. de Tocqueville' (1872), 'Biographical Sketches' (1863), and 'Journals'—'Kept in Turkey and Greece' (1859), 'Relating to Ireland' (1868), and 'Kept in France and Italy' (1871). He also wrote a notable series of reviews of the Waverley Novels: 'Essays on Fiction' (1864).

Sennacherib, the subject of Byron's poem, 'The Destruction of Sennacherib', was king of Assyria 705–681 B.C. He invaded Palestine in the reign of Hezekiah, and was obliged to retire by a pestilence that broke out in his army. The poem is based on the narrative of his discomfiture in 2 Chron. xxxii.

Sense and Sensibility, a novel by Jane Austen (q.v.), begun in 1797 and published in 1811. A first sketch of the story, read by the author to her family in 1795, was entitled 'Elinor and Marianne'.

Mrs. Henry Dashwood and her daughters, Elinor and Marianne, and the still younger Margaret, are left in straitened circumstances, for the estate of which her husband had the life interest has passed to her stepson, John Dashwood. Henry Dashwood, before his death, has urgently recommended to John the interest of his step-mother and sisters. But John's selfishness, encouraged (in a discussion which is one of Jane Austen's most perfect pieces of satire) by his wife, the daughter of the arrogant Mrs. Ferrars, defeats his father's wish. Mrs. Henry Dashwood and her daughters accordingly retire to a cottage in Devonshire, but not before Elinor and Edward Ferrars, brother of Mrs. John Dashwood, have become mutually attracted, though Edward shows uneasiness in his relations with Elinor. In Devonshire Marianne is thrown into the company of John Willoughby, an attractive but impecunious and unprincipled young man, with whom she falls desperately in love, Willoughby likewise showing signs of strong affection for her. Willoughby suddenly departs for London, leaving Marianne in acute distress at the separation. Presently Elinor and Marianne also go to London, on the invitation of their friend, Mrs. Jennings. Here Willoughby shows complete indifference to Marianne, and finally, in an insolent letter, informs her of his approaching marriage to a rich heiress. Marianne, whose sensibility is extreme, makes no effort to control the outward symptoms of her grief. Meanwhile Elinor has learnt under pledge of secrecy from Lucy Steele, a sly, self-seeking young woman, niece of a former tutor of Edward Ferrars, that she and Edward have been secretly engaged for four years. Elinor, whose sense and self-control are in strong contrast to Marianne's weakness, conceals her distress. Edward's engagement, which was kept secret owing to his dependence on his mother, now becomes known to the latter. In her fury at Edward's refusal to give up Lucy, she dismisses him from her sight, and settles on his younger brother, Robert, the property that would otherwise have gone to Edward. At this conjuncture a small living is offered to Edward, and the way seems open for his early marriage with Lucy. But now Robert, his brother, a foolish young fop, falls in love with Lucy, who, finding her interest in a marriage with the more wealthy brother, throws over Edward and marries Robert. Edward, delighted to be released from an engagement that he has long regretted, at once proposes to Elinor and is accepted. Marianne, gradually recovering from the despair that had followed her abandonment by Willoughby, is finally won by her old admirer, Colonel Brandon, a quiet serious man of five-and-thirty, whose modest attractions had been completely eclipsed by his brilliant rival.

The cheerful, vulgar Mrs. Jennings, her silly daughter, and Mr. Palmer, her ill-mannered son-in-law, are among the amusing characters in the story.

Sensitive Plant, The, a poem by P. B. Shelley (q.v.) written in 1820.

The poet's spirit is represented as a 'sensitive plant', or mimosa, in the midst of a lovely garden tended by a lady, the ideal of beauty. The lady dies, and death and corruption settle on the garden. This awakens in the author the question whether, seeing that beauty is permanent, it is not life that is unreal.

Sentences, MASTER OF THE, Peter Lombard (q.v.).

Sentimental Comedy, a type of sentimental drama introduced by Steele (q.v.), a reaction from the comedy of the Restoration.

Sentimental Journey through France and Italy, A, by Mr. Yorick, a narrative by Sterne (q.v.) of his adventures in France in 1765–6, published in 1768. It has been translated into many languages.

The work was to consist of four volumes, of which only two were finished. In it, the humour of 'Tristram Shandy' gives place to sentiment as the predominant element. The author travels to Calais, Rouen, Paris, through the Bourbonnais (where he finds the Maria of vol. vii of 'Tristram Shandy'), and nearly to Lyons, where the book abruptly ends. At every turn he meets with a sentimental adventure, and finds pleasure in everything, in contrast to Smelfungus (Smollett) who saw every object distorted by his spleen, and Mundungus (Dr. S. Sharp) who travelled across Europe 'without one generous connection or pleasurable anecdote to tell of'.

Sentry, CAPTAIN, see *Spectator*.

Sephardim, the Spanish and Portuguese Jews, so called from *Sepharad*, the name of a country mentioned in Obad. xx, and identified by the Rabbins with Spain. The Sephardim regard themselves as the aristocracy of the race, as opposed to the *Ashkenazim*, the Jews of Central and Eastern Europe (Ashchenaz is mentioned as a descendant of Japhet in 1 Chron. i. 6).

Sepher Yezirah, see *Cabbala*.

Sephiroth, in the philosophy of the Cabbala (q.v.) the attributes or emanations by which the infinite enters into relation with the finite.

September Massacre, THE, the massacre of political prisoners, including the Princesse de Lamballe, in Paris on 2–5 Sept. 1792. The massacres dwindled in number after the 5th, but went on occasionally to the 9th.

Septuagint, The (commonly designated LXX), the Greek version of the O.T. which derives its name from the story that it was made by seventy-two Palestinian Jews at the request of Ptolemy Philadelphus (q.v.) and completed by them in seclusion on the island of Pharos, in seventy-two days [OED.]; or it may have been so called because it was authorized by the seventy members of the Jewish sanhedrin (Jebb).

Seraph, a word perhaps identical with the Hebrew *saraph* meaning a 'fiery serpent', is, in Biblical use (Isa. vi. 2), the name of the creatures with six wings seen in Isaiah's vision as hovering over the throne of God. By Christian interpreters the Seraphim were from an early period supposed to be a class of angels, and the name associated with that of the Cherubim was introduced into the Eucharistic preface and the 'Te Deum'. In the system of the Pseudo-Dionysius, the chief source of later angelology, the Seraphim are the highest, and the Cherubim the second, of the nine orders of angels (q.v.). [OED.]

Serāpis, a god invented and introduced into Egypt by Ptolemy I to unite Greeks and Egyptians in a common worship, combining the Egyptian Osiris (q.v.) with attributes of Zeus, Hades, and Aesculapius.

Serbonian Bog or LAKE, a great morass near the coast of Lower Egypt.

'Betwixt Damiata and Mount Casius old,
Where armies whole have sunk'.
(Milton, 'Paradise Lost', ii. 593.)

Serendipity, from *Serendip*, a former name for Ceylon, a word coined by Horace Walpole, who says (letter to Mann, 28 Jan. 1754) that he had formed it on the title of the fairy-tale 'The Three Princes of Serendip', to signify the faculty of making happy discoveries by accident, which these princes possessed.

Serious Call to a Devout and Holy Life, see under *Law (W.)*.

Serpentine verse, a metrical line beginning and ending with the same word, in allusion to the representation of a serpent with its tail in its mouth.

SERVĒTUS, MICHAEL (MIGUEL SER-VETO) (1511–53), a Spanish physician and theologian, who graduated in medicine in Paris and lectured there on geometry and astrology, and subsequently practised medicine at various places in France. He published in 1531 'De trinitatis erroribus' directed against the doctrine of the Trinity, and in 1553 'Christianismi restitutio', in consequence of which he was arrested at Lyons by the Inquisition. He escaped to Geneva, but was arrested and burnt by order of Calvin.

Sesame, see *Ali Baba*.

Sesame and Lilies, two lectures by Ruskin (q.v.), published in 1865, to which a third was added in the revised edition.

The first lecture, 'Sesame: of Kings'

Treasuries', deals principally with the questions what to read and how to read, passing to the necessity for the diffusion of literature as 'conferring the purest kingship that can exist among men'. The second, 'Lilies: of Queen's Gardens', treats of the sphere, education, and duties of women of the privileged classes. The third lecture, delivered in 1868, is on 'The Mystery of Life and its Arts', the mystery that 'the most splendid genius in the arts might be permitted to labour and perish uselessly', and the mystery of man's indifference to religion and the purpose of life.

Of the first two lectures Ruskin wrote in 1882 that 'if read in connection with "Unto this Last", [they contain] the chief truths I have endeavoured through all my past life to display'.

Sesha, in Hindu mythology, the king of the serpents, who supports the world on his head.

Sesostris, the name given by the Greeks to Rameses II, the great king of the 19th Egyptian dynasty, who overran Syria and defeated the Hittites.

Session of the Poets, see *Suckling.*

Sestina, a poem of six six-line stanzas (with an envoy) in which the line-endings of the first stanza are repeated, but in different order, in the other five. [OED.]

Sestos, on the European shore of the Hellespont, at its narrowest part, famous as the residence of Hero (q.v.). Here Xerxes built a bridge of boats when he invaded Europe.

Set, in Egyptian mythology, the god of evil, the brother, or the son, of Osiris, and his constant enemy. He is identified with the Typhon (q.v.) of the Greeks.

Setebos, a god of the Patagonians, worshipped by Caliban's mother, Sycorax (in Shakespeare's 'The Tempest'). His purpose in creating the world is worked out by Caliban in R. Browning's 'Caliban upon Setebos' (q.v.).

Pigafetta's description of Patagonia had been translated, and Drake and Cavendish had visited the country, when Shakespeare wrote 'The Tempest'.

SETTLE, ELKANAH (1648–1724), educated at Trinity College, Oxford, was the author of a series of bombastic dramas which endangered at court Dryden's popularity as a dramatist. Settle's heroic play, 'The Empress of Morocco', in particular, had considerable vogue, and Dryden, with Crowne and Shadwell, wrote a pamphlet of criticism on the play. Settle retorted with an attack on Dryden's 'Almanzor and Almahide' (q.v.). Dryden vented his resentment by satirizing Settle as Doeg in the second part of 'Absalom and Achitophel' (q.v.). Settle published 'Absalom Senior, or Achitophel Transpros'd' in 1682, and 'Reflections on several of Mr. Dryden's Plays' in 1687. He was appointed

city poet in 1691, and found employment after the revolution in writing drolls for Bartholomew Fair. He died in the Charterhouse.

Seven against Thebes, The, a tragedy by Aeschylus (q.v.); see *Eteocles.*

Seven Bishops, THE: Sancroft, archbishop of Canterbury, and six other bishops (Ken of Bath and Wells, White of Peterborough, Lloyd of St. Asaph's, Trelawny of Bristol, Lake of Chichester, and Turner of Ely), who in 1688 signed a petition asking that the clergy should be excused from reading in their churches James II's second 'Declaration of Indulgence' (q.v.). James regarded this as an act of rebellion; the bishops were tried for seditious libel and found not guilty, to the intense joy of the nation.

Seven Champions of Christendom, The Famous Historie of the, a romance by R. Johnson (q.v.), printed about 1597. It relates legends of St. George of England, who releases from enchantment the other six knights, St. Denis of France, St. James of Spain, St. Anthony of Italy, St. Andrew of Scotland, St. Patrick of Ireland, and St. David of Wales; and adds legends concerning these. The book, the contents of which are inspired by the old romances of chivalry, was widely read, and influenced Spenser.

Seven Cities, THE ISLAND OF THE, or ANTILIA, a fabulous island believed in the 14th and 15th cents. to exist in the Atlantic. It was said that seven bishops and their followers, driven from Spain in the 8th cent. by the Moors, had founded seven cities on it. It appears in some 15th-cent. maps. It is uncertain whether it represents some actual discovery (e.g. of the Azores) or a form of the legend of the Fortunate Isles (q.v.), or Atlantis (q.v.), or perhaps even Brazil, which is occasionally called 'The Island of Brasilia'.

Seven Deadly Sins, THE, usually given as Pride, Lechery, Envy, Anger, Covetousness, Gluttony, Sloth; frequently personified in medieval literature, e.g. in 'Piers Plowman' Passus V (B), Chaucer's 'Parson's Tale', and Spenser's 'Faerie Queene', I. iv.

Seven Dials, an open space in the parish of St. Giles-in-the-Fields, London, from which seven streets radiated. It was designed by Thomas Neale, master of the royal mint and a great 'projector' in the 17th cent., whose name is preserved in Neal Street. In the centre stood a column, on the summit of which were, it is said, seven sun-dials facing the several streets. The column, which was in fact hexagonal, was taken down in 1773 and removed to Addlestone, and thence to Weybridge (Wheatley and Cunningham). The district, which was formerly one of narrow and squalid streets, has been much improved by the opening up of Charing Cross Road and Shaftesbury Avenue.

Seven Lamps of Architecture, The, a treatise by Ruskin (q.v.), published in 1849.

This was an incidental work, composed while 'Modern Painters' (q.v.) was being written. It deals, as its title indicates, with the leading principles of architecture. The 'Seven Lamps' are those of Sacrifice, Truth, Power, Beauty, Life, Memory, and Obedience. In the 'Lamp of Sacrifice' the author suggests the distinction between sacrifice (work that carries on visible ornament into partial concealment) and useless work. The 'Lamp of Power' deals largely with shadow and its uses; 'The Lamp of Life', with 'the expression of vital energy in organic things' and the 'subjection to such energy of things naturally passive and powerless'; the 'Lamp of Memory', with the application of architectural features to appropriate or inappropriate circumstances; the 'Lamp of Obedience', with the choice of a style of architecture. The other two 'Lamps' explain themselves. As a whole, the work is a defence of Gothic, as the noblest style of architecture.

Seven Names of God, The, El, Elohim (q.v.), Adonai, Yahweh (see *Jehovah*), Ehyeh-Asher-Ehyeh, Shaddai, and Zaba'ot ('Jewish Encyclopaedia').

Seven Psalms, the seven Penitential Psalms, vi, xxxii, xxxviii, li, cii, cxxx, cxliii.

Seven Sages of Greece, The. The list of these commonly given is: Thales (q.v.) of Miletus, Solon (q.v.) of Athens, Bias of Priene (the reputed author of the saying Φιλεῖν ὡς μισήσοντας), Chilo of Sparta, Cleobūlus of Lindus in Rhodes, Periander (q.v.) of Corinth, and Pittacus (q.v.) of Mitylene.

Seven Sages of Rome, The, a metrical romance of the early 14th cent. It is an English version (through Latin and French) of short Eastern tales, interesting as one of the earliest instances in English of the form of short verse-story subsequently adopted by Chaucer in 'The Canterbury Tales'. Diocletian has his son educated by seven sages. His stepmother, jealous of him, accuses him to the emperor of attempting to seduce her. The boy is silent for seven days (under the influence of his stepmother's magic) and is ordered to execution. Then follow seven tales by the queen on each of seven nights, designed to show the emperor the danger of the heir's supplanting him, and seven tales by the sages, on each of the following mornings, designed to show the danger of trusting women. The emperor is alternately convinced by the queen and the sages. The seven days being passed, the youth speaks, the queen's malice is exposed, and she is burnt at the stake. See *Syntipas*.

Seven Seas, The, the Arctic, Antarctic, North and South Pacific, North and South Atlantic, and Indian Oceans. 'The Seven Seas' is the title of a collection of poems by Kipling (q.v.) published in 1896.

Seven Sisters, or Seven Stars, The, the Pleiades (q.v.).

Seven Sleepers of Ephesus, The, seven noble Christian youths of Ephesus who, fleeing from the persecution of Decius (A.D. 250), concealed themselves in a cavern in a neighbouring mountain. They were ordered by the emperor to be walled up therein, and fell into a deep slumber, which was miraculously prolonged for 187 years. At the end of that time the slaves of one Adolius, to whom the inheritance of the mountain had descended, removed for some purpose the stones with which the cavern had been walled up, and the seven sleepers were permitted to awake. Under the impression that they had slept a few hours, one of them proceeded to the city for food, but was unable to recognize the once familiar aspect of the place. His singular dress and obsolete speech (or, in some versions, the fact that he tried to buy food with obsolete money) caused him to be brought before a magistrate, whereupon the miracle that had occurred was brought to light. The people, headed by the bishop, hastened to visit the cavern of the sleepers, 'who bestowed their benediction, related their story, and at the same instant expired' (Gibbon, 'Decline and Fall', xxxiii). The legend was translated from the Syriac by Gregory of Tours, and is also given by other authors. It is included in the Koran, c. xviii, among Mohammed's revelations. See also *Katmer*.

Seven Weeks War, the war of 1866 between Austria and Prussia, as a result of which Prussia became the predominant power in Germany.

Seven Wise Masters, The, see *Syntipas*.

Seven Wonders of the World, The, the seven structures regarded as the most remarkable monuments of antiquity, viz. the Egyptian Pyramids (q.v.), the Mausoleum at Halicarnassus (see *Mausolus*), the Hanging Gardens of Babylon (see *Babylon*), the temple of Artemis at Ephesus, the statue of Zeus by Phidias (q.v.) at Olympia, the Colossus (q.v.) at Rhodes, and the Pharos (q.v.) at Alexandria, or, according to another list, the walls of Babylon.

Seven Years War, The, or Third Silesian War, the war waged by France, Austria, and Russia against Frederick the Great (q.v.) of Prussia, who was assisted by Hanoverian troops and subsidies from England. It lasted from 1756 to 1763 and was terminated by the treaty of Hubertusburg, by which Frederick, though he had been hard pressed, retained all his dominions. Simultaneous and closely connected with this war was the struggle between the English and French which ended in the Peace of Paris of 1763, leaving England predominant in America and India.

Seventh Heaven, The, see *Heaven*.

Severn, Joseph (1793–1879), painter, a friend of Keats (q.v.); he accompanied Keats to Italy in 1820 and attended him at his death.

Severus, WALL OF, a reconstruction in stone by the emperor Septimius Severus, about the year 208, of the Wall of Hadrian (q.v.).

SÉVIGNÉ, MARIE DE RABUTIN-CHANTAL, *Marquise de* (1626–96), was left a widow at 25 years of age with two children. Of these, Françoise, Mme de Grignan, became the principal recipient of the letters for which her mother is famous. Written with wit and charm, they give a vivid picture of the life of the nobility in the time of Louis XIV. See also under *FitzGerald*.

Sèvres, a town adjacent to Paris on the south-west, famous for its costly porcelain, the manufacture of which was removed from Vincennes to Sèvres in 1756 and subsequently acquired by the State.

SEWARD, ANNA (1747–1809), the 'Swan of Lichfield', bequeathed her poetical works to Sir W. Scott, who published them with a memoir in 1810. Six volumes of her letters appeared in 1811. She frequently met Dr. Johnson and supplied Boswell with particulars concerning him.

SEWELL, ANNA (1820–78), remembered as the author of 'Black Beauty', the 'autobiography' of a horse, published in 1877.

Seyton, CATHERINE, a character in Scott's 'The Abbot' (q.v.).

Sforza, FRANCESCO I, FRANCESCO II, and LUDOVICO, dukes of Milan in the 15th and 16th cents. The first of them was a condottiere in the service of the older line of dukes, the Visconti, ousted them, and took the duchy. Ludovico was the foolish duke who called Charles VIII of France into Italy; he is the hero of Massinger's tragedy, 'The Duke of Milan' (q.v.).

Sganarelle, the name of characters in several of Molière's comedies, notably of Don Juan's pusillanimous servant in 'Le Festin de Pierre', and of the hero of 'Le Médecin malgré lui'. It is this last who, in the character of the pseudo-doctor, declares that 'Nous avons changé tout cela', when someone suggests that the heart is usually on the left side of the body, and not on the right as Sganarelle supposes.

Shabby Genteel Story, A, see *Philip* (*The Adventures of*).

Shades, THE, a name for wine or beer vaults with a drinking-bar, either underground or sheltered by an arcade. The name, now rare, is said to have originated at Brighton.

Shadow, SIMON, in Shakespeare's '2 Henry IV', III. ii, one of Falstaff's recruits.

SHADWELL, THOMAS (1642?–92), dramatist and poet, was educated at Caius College, Cambridge, and entered the Middle Temple. He produced the 'Sullen Lovers', based on Molière's 'Les Fâcheux', at Lincoln's Inn Fields, London, in 1668. His dramatic pieces include an opera, the 'Enchanted Island' (from Shakespeare's 'The Tempest', 1673), 'Timon of Athens' (1678), the 'Squire of Alsatia' (1688), 'Epsom Wells' (1673), and 'Bury Fair' (1689). The last two give interesting pictures of contemporary manners, watering-places, and amusements; and Scott and Macaulay drew on the 'Squire of Alsatia' for information regarding the locality. Shadwell was at open feud with Dryden from 1682, the quarrel arising out of some qualified praise bestowed by the latter on Ben Jonson, of whom Shadwell claimed to be the special votary. The two poets repeatedly attacked one another in satires, among which were Dryden's 'The Medal' and 'Mac Flecknoe' (qq.v.), and Shadwell's 'The Medal of John Bayes' (1682) and a translation of the 'Tenth Satire of Juvenal' (1687). Shadwell superseded Dryden as poet laureate and historiographer at the revolution, but his claims to the position were not high. Lord Dorset, to whom the appointment was due, remarked, 'I do not pretend to say how great a poet Shadwell may be, but I am sure he is an honest man.'

Shafalus, see *Cephalus*.

Shaftesbury, ANTHONY ASHLEY COOPER, *first Baron Ashley* and *first earl of Shaftesbury* (1621–83), a statesman prominent on the king's side in the Parliamentary War, as leader of the parliamentary opposition to Cromwell, after the Restoration as a member of the Cabal and chancellor. After his dismissal he was leader of the opposition, a fomenter of the belief in the 'Popish Plot', a promoter of the Exclusion Bill, and a supporter of Monmouth. He was satirized as Achitophel in Dryden's 'Absalom and Achitophel' (q.v.).

SHAFTESBURY, ANTHONY ASHLEY COOPER, *third earl of* (1671–1713), excluded by ill-health from active politics, devoted himself to intellectual pursuits, and in particular to moral philosophy. His principal writings are embodied in his 'Characteristics of Men, Manners, Opinions, Times', published in 1711 (revised in 1713), which included various treatises previously published (notably his 'Enquiry concerning Virtue' of 1699). Shaftesbury was influenced by Deism; he was at once a Platonist and a churchman, an opponent of the selfish theory of conduct advocated by Hobbes (q.v.). Man has 'affections', Shaftesbury held, not only for himself but for the creatures about him. 'To have one's affections right and entire, not only in respect of oneself, but of society and the public: this is rectitude, integrity, or virtue.' And there is no conflict between the self-regarding and social affections; for the individual's own good is included in the good of society. Moreover, man has a capacity for distinguishing right and wrong, the beauty or ugliness of actions and affections, and this he calls the 'moral sense'. To be truly virtuous, a man must have a *disinterested* affection for what he perceives to be right.

Shaftesbury, ANTHONY ASHLEY COOPER, *seventh earl of Shaftesbury* (1801–85), philanthropist, active in many movements for the protection of the working classes and the benefit of the poor. He is commemorated by the 'Eros' (q.v.) statue in Piccadilly Circus.

Shafton, SIR PIERCIE, a character in Scott's 'The Monastery' (q.v.).

Shagpat, The Shaving of, see *Shaving of Shagpat.*

Shahnameh, see *Firdusi.*

Shahrazad, see *Scheherazade.*

Shakers, an American religious sect (calling itself 'The Society of Believers in Christ's Second Appearing'), which exists in the form of mixed communities of men and women living in celibacy. The first of these communities was founded by Ann Lee (1736–84), a factory hand and afterwards a cook in Manchester, who in 1758 joined a band of seceders from the Society of Friends, nicknamed the 'Shaking Quakers' or 'Shakers'. She discovered celibacy to be the holy state, and was in time acknowledged by the Shakers as their spiritual head. In 1774 she emigrated to America, where she founded the first American Shaker Society in 1776. The name, according to Dickens, 'American Notes', xv, was given to the sect from their peculiar form of adoration, consisting of a dance by men and women arranged in opposite parties. Artemus Ward (see *Browne, C. F.*) made fun of them.

SHAKESPEARE,WILLIAM(1564–1616), eldest son and third child of John Shakespeare and Mary, daughter of Robert Arden (a well-to-do farmer of Wilmcote), was born at Stratford-on-Avon, and baptized on 26 Apr. 1564. Shakespeare's father was a husbandman (also variously described as a yeoman, a glover, a butcher, and a wool-dealer) at Stratford and held various municipal offices. Shakespeare was educated at the free grammar school at Stratford. He married in 1582 Anne, daughter of Richard Hathaway of Shottery and his third child, Susannah, was baptized the next year. He left Stratford about 1585, having spent, it has been suggested, some time as a schoolmaster, and is next heard of in London where he became acquainted with Lord Southampton, his principal patron. He was probably engaged in some subordinate capacity at one of the two theatres (The Theatre or The Curtain) then existing in London, and afterwards became a member of the Lord Chamberlain's (after the accession of James I, the King's) company of players, which acted at the Theatre, the Curtain, the Globe (qq.v.), and from *c.* 1609 at the Blackfriars Theatre (q.v.). It is established that by September 1592 Shakespeare was both an actor and a playwright. He took part in the original performances of Jonson's 'Every Man in his Humour' (1598) and 'Sejanus' (1603), after which he drops out of the actor-lists and may have acted little. By

1598 he was sufficiently prominent in the company to share with the Burbages (qq.v.) and other notable players in the establishment of the new Globe Theatre on the Bankside; it was built in 1599. His earliest work as a dramatist, the three parts of 'Henry VI', dates from 1590–1. This, and Shakespeare's other plays and poems, are the subject of separate articles in the present book. The order and dates assigned to them below are those which Sir E. K. Chambers thinks most probable, though there is much conjecture about the dates, and even about the order. 'Henry VI' was followed by 'Richard III' and 'The Comedy of Errors' in the theatrical season of 1592–3, and by 'Titus Andronicus' and 'The Taming of the Shrew' in 1593–4. Some critics, including the Arden editor, suspect Peele's hand in Act I of 'Titus'. Shakespeare published the poems 'Venus and Adonis' and 'Lucrece' respectively in 1593 and 1594, each with a dedication to Henry Wriothesley, earl of Southampton, with whom, in the latter year, he was, it seems, on terms of intimate friendship. The 'Sonnets' (q.v.) were printed in 1609, but the bulk of them appear to have been written between 1593 and 1596, and the remainder at intervals down to 1600. 'The Two Gentlemen of Verona', 'Love's Labour's Lost', and 'Romeo and Juliet' (Shakespeare's first tragedy) are assigned to 1594–5; 'Richard II' and 'A Midsummer Night's Dream' to 1595–6. In 1596 Shakespeare applied for a grant of arms in his father's name, and in 1599 the Shakespeares were given the right to impale the arms of Arden, his mother's family. He purchased 'New Place', the second largest house in Stratford, in 1597, but does not appear to have settled permanently there till 1611 when he had by further purchases built up an estate at Stratford. 'King John' and 'The Merchant of Venice' are assigned to 1596–7, the two parts of 'Henry IV' to 1597–8. Shakespeare's most perfect essays in comedy, 'Much Ado about Nothing', 'As You Like It', and 'Twelfth Night', belong to the years 1598–1600, together with 'Henry V' and 'Julius Caesar'. 'Hamlet' and 'The Merry Wives of Windsor' (the latter, according to tradition, written by order of the Queen) are assigned to 1600–1, 'Troilus and Cressida' and 'All's Well that Ends Well' to the next two theatrical seasons. Then came the accession of James I, who (according to Ben Jonson), no less than Elizabeth held Shakespeare in high esteem. A period of gloom in the author's life appears to have occurred about this time, manifested in the great tragedies, and succeeded, about 1608, by a new outlook in the final romances. The probable order and dates of the plays of the reign of James are given as follows by Sir E. Chambers: 'Measure for Measure' and 'Othello', 1604–5; 'King Lear' and 'Macbeth', 1605–6; 'Antony and Cleopatra', 1606–7; 'Coriolanus' and 'Timon of Athens', 1607–8. 'Pericles', 'Cymbeline', and 'The Winter's Tale' are assigned to the next three seasons;

and 'The Tempest', probably the last drama that Shakespeare completed, to 1611–12. 'Two Noble Kinsmen' (q.v.) and 'Henry VIII', in which Fletcher is often thought to have collaborated, were written in 1612–13.

Meanwhile his name was applied by unprincipled publishers to such writings of obscure men as 'The Tragedie of Locrine' (q.v., 1595), 'The Puritaine, or the Widdow of Watling-streete' (q.v., 1607), 'The True Chronicle Historie of Thomas, Lord Cromwell' (1602), 'The Life of Oldcastle' (1600), 'The London Prodigall' (q.v., 1605), 'A Yorkshire Tragedy' (1608), and an old play on the subject of King John (1611). Only two sonnets and three poems from 'Love's Labour's Lost' appeared in 'The Passionate Pilgrim, by W. Shakespeare' (1599), the bulk of the volume being by others. Shakespeare's name was also appended to 'a poetical essaie on the Turtle and the Phœnix', which was published in Robert Chester's 'Love's Martyr', a collection of poems by Marston, Chapman, Jonson, and others, 1601. Shakespeare may have had some part in the authorship of the historical play 'Edward III' (q.v.), published in 1596, and he is generally agreed to have written an act of 'Sir Thomas More' (q.v.) which, besides the six signatures, is the only known example of his handwriting.

Shakespeare now abandoned dramatic composition. He spent the concluding years of his life (1611–16) mainly at Stratford, but paid frequent visits to London till 1614, and continued his relations with actors and poets till the end. He purchased a house in Blackfriars in 1613. He drafted his will in January 1616, and completed it in March. He died 23 Apr. (o.s., i.e. 3 May), and was buried in Stratford Church, where before 1623 a monument, with a bust by a London sculptor, Gerard Johnson, was erected. His wife died in 1623, and Elizabeth (d. 1670), daughter of Susannah, his elder daughter, and of John Hall, was his last surviving descendant. His younger daughter Judith (Quiney) had children, but the last died in 1639. His only son, Hamnet, Judith's twin, died in 1596.

Two portraits of Shakespeare may be regarded as authenticated, the bust in Stratford Church, and the frontispiece to the folio of 1623, engraved by Martin Droeshout. But Droeshout is unlikely to have had personal knowledge of the poet. Shakespeare appears to have written his name usually 'Shakspere', sometimes in abbreviated form, but the main signature to the poet's will is 'Shakspeare'. The form generally accepted is 'Shakespeare', being that in which the name appears in most of the contemporary editions of his plays and in the dedicatory epistles to the authorized editions of 'Venus and Adonis' and 'Lucrece'.

Shakespeare's plays were first collected in 1623, when a folio edition was published containing all the canonical plays excepting 'Pericles', which was added in the second impression of F3, 1664. The printer William Jaggard's attempt at a collection in 1619 had been frustrated by the King's Players, after nine quartos, some with falsely dated title pages, had been published. Further folio editions appeared in 1632, 1663, 1664, and 1685. The first attempt to produce a critical edition of Shakespeare was that of Rowe (q.v., 1709), who provided lists of dramatis personae and a systematic division into acts and scenes. Pope's edition followed (1725) and the valuable emendations of Theobald (q.v.). Johnson's edition appeared in 1765. Capell (1768), Steevens (q.v., 1773), and Malone (q.v., 1790) also contributed important editions, Malone's third Variorum edition of 1821 edited by Boswell (son of the biographer) being a permanently useful monument to earlier scholarship. The Cambridge Shakespeare in 1863–6 (2nd ed. by Aldis Wright in 1891–3) formed the basis of Wright's 1874 Globe edition, which provides the standard line numbering. The Variorum edition, edited by H. H. Furness and others from 1871, is an important source of information. The edition of separate plays by Quiller-Couch and J. D. Wilson (Cambridge, 1921–62) deals fully with textual problems; other important modern editions are the Arden (1899–1924; revised 1950) and the Oxford Old-spelling edition, undertaken by Dr. Alice Walker. Sir E. K. Chambers's 'William Shakespeare, a Study of Facts and Problems' (1930) is the standard life.

Shakespeare-Bacon Controversy, see *Baconian Theory.*

Shakuntala, see *Sakuntala.*

Shallow, in Shakespeare's '2 Henry IV', a foolish country justice. He appears again in 'The Merry Wives of Windsor', upbraiding Falstaff for beating his men and killing his deer. Shallow perhaps represents Sir Thomas Lucy of Charlecote (he is identified by his coat of arms bearing 'luces', 'Merry Wives', I. i), and the mention of the killing of his deer perhaps has reference to a poaching incident in Shakespeare's early days. But much doubt has been thrown on the story and its application to the Lucys of Charlecote. L. Hotson ('Shakespeare versus Shallow', 1961) suggests that Shakespeare was satirizing William Gardiner the Surrey magistrate with whom he had quarrelled; his arms impaled three luces.

Shalott, THE LADY OF, Elaine, the fair maid of Astolat (see *Launcelot of the Lake*), the subject and title of a poem by Tennyson.

Shamanism, the primitive religion of the Ural-Altaic peoples of Siberia, in which all the good and evil of life are thought to be brought about by spirits who can be influenced only by *shamans*, priests or priest-doctors. The word Shamanism is now extended to other similar religions, especially of North-West American Indians. [OED.]

Shamela Andrews, *An Apology for the Life of Mrs.,* see *Pamela.*

Shamrock, THE, adopted as the national

emblem of Ireland because (according to a late tradition) it was used by St. Patrick to illustrate the doctrine of the Trinity.

Shan Van Vocht, The, the title of an Irish revolutionary song of 1798, meaning 'the poor old woman', i.e. Ireland. The refrain is:

Yes! Ireland shall be free
From the centre to the sea!
Then Hurra! for Liberty!
Says the Shan Van Vocht.

Shandean, having the characteristics of 'Tristram Shandy' (q.v.) or of the Shandy family there portrayed. Sterne himself describes 'Tristram Shandy' as a 'civil, non-sensical, good-humoured Shandean book, which will do all your hearts good'.

Shandon, CAPTAIN, a character in Thackeray's 'Pendennis' (q.v.).

Shandy, TRISTRAM, WALTER, and MRS., and CAPTAIN TOBIAS, see *Tristram Shandy.*

Shapira, M. W. (1830–84), of Jerusalem, noted forger. His frauds included alleged pottery objects from Moab (1872) and a manuscript of part of the Old Testament (Deuteronomy) of very ancient date. The manuscript was actually written on treated sheepskin some 300 years old. On the exposure of this latter fraud Shapira shot himself in 1884.

Sharp, JAMES (1618–79), was appointed archbishop of St. Andrews in 1661 as a reward for his assistance in restoring episcopacy in Scotland. His treachery to the Presbyterian cause made him obnoxious to the Covenanters, a party of whom murdered him on Magus Muir in 1679. Oliver Cromwell had already nicknamed him 'Sharp of that ilk'. The incident of his murder figures in Scott's 'Old Mortality' (q.v.).

Sharp, REBECCA ('BECKY'), the principal character in Thackeray's 'Vanity Fair' (q.v.).

SHARP, WILLIAM ('FIONA MACLEOD'), (1855–1905), educated at Glasgow Academy and University, wrote under his own name lives of D. G. Rossetti (1882), Shelley (1887), Heine (1888), and Browning (1890); volumes of poems, including 'Romantic Ballads and Poems of Phantasy' (1888); and romances, 'The Children of To-morrow' (1889), 'Sospiri di Roma' (1891), 'The Gypsy Christ' (1895), and 'Wives in Exile' (1896). He began to write mystical prose and verse under the pseudonym 'Fiona Macleod' in 1893: 'Pharais' (1894), 'The Mountain Lovers' (1895), 'The Sin Eater' (Celtic tales, 1895), and plays including 'The House of Usna' (1900), 'The Immortal Hour' (1900). Sharp's identity with 'Fiona Macleod' was not known till his death.

Shavian, having the characteristic humour of G. B. Shaw (q.v.), a word coined from his name.

Shaving of Shagpat, The, an Arabian

Entertainment, a story by Meredith (q.v.), published in 1856.

The author adopts the form and style of the oriental story-tellers. Shagpat is an enchanter and holds the whole of a city and the king thereof in enchantment by means of one hair of his head, 'The Identical'. It is ordained that Shibli Bagarag, nephew to the renowned Baba Mustapha, chief barber to the court of Persia, shall shave Shagpat and break the spell. And this by the help of his betrothed, Noorna bin Noorka, and much magic, and in spite of thwackings and counter-magic, he at last succeeds in doing.

Shaw, CAPTAIN (afterwards SIR EYRE MASSEY), the chief of the London Fire Brigade, mentioned in the Queen's song, 'Oh, foolish fay', in Gilbert's 'Iolanthe' (see *Gilbert and Sullivan*). He was present at the opening performance.

SHAW, GEORGE BERNARD (1856–1950), born in Dublin, came to London in 1876 and became a member of the Fabian Society (q.v.), for which he wrote political and economic tracts. He also applied himself to public speaking, and in 1885 took to journalism, writing for 'The Pall Mall Gazette', 'The World', musical criticism for 'The Star' (1888), and dramatic criticism for 'The Saturday Review' (1895). He had meanwhile begun to write for the stage, and at once showed his unorthodox turn of mind and distrust of conventions and accepted institutions. 'Widowers' Houses' (begun in collaboration with William Archer) was produced in 1892, and subsequently included in the collection of 'Plays: Pleasant and Unpleasant' (1898). These were followed by 'Three Plays for Puritans' (1901) and 'Man and Superman' (1903). The latter, described as 'A Comedy and a Philosophy', introduces Shaw's conception of the 'Life Force', a power that seeks to raise mankind, with their co-operation, to a higher and better existence. The same doctrine appears in 'Heartbreak House' (1917) and in 'Back to Methuselah' (1921), in which the causes of the failure of our civilization, as demonstrated by the Great War, are examined. The best known of Shaw's other plays are the following: the powerful and effective historical drama 'Saint Joan' (1924); 'Arms and the Man', 'Candida', 'Mrs. Warren's Profession', and 'You Never can Tell' (in 'Plays: Pleasant and Unpleasant'); 'Caesar and Cleopatra' (in 'Three Plays for Puritans') and 'John Bull's other Island' and 'Major Barbara' (1907); 'Fanny's First Play' (1911); 'Pygmalion' (1912); and 'The Apple Cart' (1929). Among his other writings should be mentioned the important Prefaces to the plays, the novel 'Cashel Byron's Profession' (1886), 'The Quintessence of Ibsenism' (1891), 'The Perfect Wagnerite' (1898), 'The Intelligent Woman's Guide to Socialism and Capitalism' (1928), and 'Adventures of a Black Girl in search of God' (1932).

SHAW, HENRY WHEELER (1818–85),

who wrote under the pseudonym 'Josh Billings', an American comic essayist and witty philosopher, who ridiculed humbug of all kinds. He first popularized his work by adopting a special phonetic spelling of his own.

She Stoops to Conquer, *or The Mistakes of a Night*, a comedy by Goldsmith (q.v.), produced in 1773.

The principal characters are Hardcastle, who loves 'everything that's old; old friends, old times, old manners, old books, old wine'; Mrs. Hardcastle, and Miss Hardcastle their daughter; Mrs. Hardcastle's son by a former marriage, Tony Lumpkin, a frequenter of the 'Three Jolly Pigeons', idle and ignorant, but cunning and mischievous, and doted on by his mother; and young Marlow, 'one of the most bashful and reserved young fellows in the world', except with barmaids and servant-girls. His father, Sir Charles Marlow, has proposed a match between young Marlow and Miss Hardcastle, and the young man and his friend, Hastings, accordingly travel down to pay the Hardcastles a visit. Losing their way they arrive at night at the 'Three Jolly Pigeons', where Tony Lumpkin directs them to a neighbouring inn, which is in reality the Hardcastles' house. The fun of the play arises largely from the resulting misunderstanding, Marlow treating Hardcastle as the landlord of the supposed inn, and making violent love to Miss Hardcastle, whom he takes for one of the servants. This contrasts with his bashful attitude when presented to her in her real character. The arrival of Sir Charles Marlow clears up the misconception and all ends well, including a subsidiary love-affair between Hastings and Miss Hardcastle's cousin, Miss Neville, whom Mrs. Hardcastle destines for Tony Lumpkin.

The mistaking of a private residence for an inn is said to have been founded on an actual incident in Goldsmith's boyhood.

She would if she could, the second of the comedies by Etherege (q.v.), produced in 1668.

Sir Oliver Cockwood and his wife, Sir Joslin Jolley and his young kinswomen, Ariana and Gatty, come up from the country to London to divert themselves, Sir Oliver and Sir Joslin with dissipation, Lady Cockwood, in spite of her virtuous professions, with a discreditable intrigue, and the two sprightly young ladies with innocent flirtations. They take lodgings at the 'Black Posts' in St. James Street. Lady Cockwood pursues Mr. Courtal, a gentleman of the town, with her unwelcome attentions. Mr. Courtal and his friend, Mr. Freeman, strike up acquaintance with the young ladies, and take them and Lady Cockwood to the Bear in Drury Lane for a dance, where Sir Joslin and Sir Oliver arrive, bent on less innocent pleasures. Sir Oliver gets drunk, dances with his wife, supposing her to be someone quite different, and confusion ensues. The ladies go home. Freeman arrives to console Lady Cockwood. Courtal arrives, and Freeman is concealed in a cupboard. Sir Oliver arrives, and Courtal is hidden under the table. Sir Oliver drops a 'China orange', which rolls under the table. The two men are discovered, the young ladies are awarded to them, and Lady Cockwood resolves to 'give over the great business of the town' and confine herself hereafter to the affairs of her own family.

Sheba, THE QUEEN OF, see *Balkis*.

Sheer Thursday, the Thursday in Holy Week, Maundy Thursday, so named with allusion to the purification of the soul by confession (cf. *Shrove Thursday*, another name for this day), and perhaps also to the practice of washing the altars on that day. (*Sheer* is related to a Scandinavian word meaning 'to purify'.) [OED.]

SHEFFIELD, JOHN, *third earl of Mulgrave*, and afterwards *first duke of Buckingham and Normanby* (1648–1721), a patron of Dryden and friend of Pope, and a statesman who held high offices but was 'neither esteemed nor beloved'. He is remembered as the author of the 'Essay on Satire', published anonymously, which cost Dryden (q.v.) a beating by Rochester's bravoes. He also wrote an 'Essay upon Poetry', of no great value, and some fluent verses. He erected the monument to Dryden in Westminster Abbey.

Shekinah, the visible manifestation of the Divine Majesty, especially when resting between the Cherubim over the mercy-seat (Exod. xxvi. 17) or in the temple of Solomon. In the Targums the word is used as a periphrasis to designate God. [OED.]

Sheldon, GILBERT (1598–1677), educated at Trinity College, Oxford, was warden of All Souls College, Oxford, 1626–48, and archbishop of Canterbury from 1663 till his death. As chancellor of Oxford he built and endowed, at his own expense, in 1669, the Sheldonian Theatre, where, in accordance with his intention, much of the printing work of the University was conducted until the Clarendon Building was erected in 1713.

SHELLEY,MARY WOLLSTONECRAFT (1797–1851), the daughter of W. Godwin (q.v.) and second wife of P. B. Shelley (q.v.). She was author of 'Frankenstein, or the Modern Prometheus' (q.v., 1818), 'The Last Man' (1826, the story of the gradual destruction of the human race, with the exception of one man, by an epidemic), 'Valperga' (1823, a romance of Italy in the Middle Ages), and the autobiographical 'Lodore' (1835).

SHELLEY, PERCY BYSSHE (1792–1822), born at Field Place, Sussex, was educated at Eton and University College, Oxford, publishing, while at the former, 'Zastrozzi', and in 1810 'St. Irvyne', romances in the style of 'Monk' Lewis. In 1810 also appeared 'Original Poetry' 'by Victor and Cazire', P. B. and Elizabeth Shelley. From Oxford he was sent down in 1811 after circulating a pamphlet on 'The Necessity of Atheism'. In the same year he married Harriet Westbrook, who was aged sixteen, and from whom he separated after three years of a wandering life, during which he wrote 'Queen Mab' (q.v., piratically published in 1821). Some portions of this were subsequently remodelled as 'The Daemon of the World'. He left England in 1814 with Mary Godwin (see preceding entry), to whom he was married after the unhappy Harriet had, in 1816, drowned herself in the Serpentine; and Claire Clairmont, Mary's step-sister, accompanied them. Shelley's 'Alastor' (q.v.) was written near Windsor and published in 1816. In the same year began his friendship with Byron, with whom Shelley and Mary spent the summer in Switzerland. To this period belong the 'Hymn to Intellectual Beauty' and 'Mont Blanc'. The winter of 1816–17 he spent at Marlow, and wrote, among other poems, 'Laon and Cythna', subsequently renamed 'The Revolt of Islam' (q.v., 1818), and the fragment, 'Prince Athanase'. In 1818 Shelley left England for Italy, translated Plato's 'Symposium', finished 'Rosalind and Helen' at Lucca, and in the summer, at Byron's villa near Este, composed the 'Lines written in the Euganean Hills'. He visited Byron at Venice, where he wrote 'Julian and Maddalo' (q.v.), and at the end of the same year the 'Stanzas written in dejection, near Naples'. Early in 1819 he was at Rome. Here, stirred to indignation by the political events at home, and in particular by the Peterloo affair, he wrote the 'Masque of Anarchy', an indictment of Castlereagh's administration. He also published 'Peter Bell the Third', a satire on Wordsworth. The same year, 1819, saw the publication of 'The Cenci' (q.v.) and the composition of his great lyrical drama, 'Prometheus Unbound' (q.v.), published in 1820. At the end of 1819 the Shelleys moved to Pisa, and it was now that he wrote some of his finest lyrics, including the 'Ode to the West Wind', 'To a Skylark', and 'The Cloud'. His 'Oedipus Tyrannus, or Swellfoot the Tyrant', a dramatic satire on George IV's matrimonial affairs, appeared in 1820. To this period also belong the apologue of 'The Sensitive Plant' (q.v.); the 'Letter to Maria Gisborne' (the outcome of an intellectual friendship); the Odes 'to Naples' and 'to Liberty'; the notable 'Defence of Poetry' (1821), a vindication of the elements of imagination and love in poetry against the strictures of his great friend, T. L. Peacock, in 'The Four Ages of Poetry'; 'Adonais' (q.v., 1821); and 'Epipsychidion' (q.v., 1821).

Shelley removed in April 1821 to Lerici on the shores of the bay of Spezia, and completed his lyrical drama, 'Hellas' (1822), inspired by the struggle of Greece for freedom. He had also been at work on the drama, 'Charles I', which remained unfinished. On 8 July 1822 he was drowned, in his 30th year, while sailing near Spezia. He was at the time engaged on his uncompleted poem, 'The Triumph of Life' (q.v.). The last period also saw the production of some of his most beautiful lyrics, 'O, world! O, life! O, time', 'When the lamp is shattered', and the love poems inspired by Jane Williams. Shelley's ashes were buried in the Protestant cemetery at Rome. His 'Posthumous Poems', including 'Julian and Maddalo' and 'The Witch of Atlas', were published in 1824. But no perfect collection of his works was issued till that of Mrs. Shelley (1847). His prose works, besides those mentioned above, include: a 'Letter to Lord Ellenborough' (1812); 'A Vindication of Natural Diet' (1813); 'A Refutation of Deism' (1814); a series of unfinished philosophical essays of the year 1815 'On Life', 'On a Future State', etc.; and a 'History of a Six Weeks' Tour' (written with Mrs. Shelley, 1817). T. L. Peacock's 'Memoirs of Shelley' are in Peacock's 'Works' (1875); also edited by H. F. B. Brett-Smith (1909). E. J. Trelawney's 'Recollections of the Last Days of Shelley and Byron' appeared in 1858, his 'Records of Shelley, Byron, and the Author' in 1878. Shelley's 'Letters', ed. F. L. Jones, were published in 1964.

Shelta, a cryptic language used by tinkers, composed partly of Irish or Gaelic words, mostly disguised by inversion or alteration of initial consonants.

SHENSTONE, WILLIAM (1714–63), a contemporary of S. Johnson (q.v.) at Pembroke College, Oxford. As a poet much of his work is criticized for an artificial prettiness similar to that which he pursued in adorning his estate at the Leasowes, near Halesowen. Of this, his 'Pastoral Ballad' (1755) is an example. His best-known work is 'The Schoolmistress' (1742). He wrote miscellaneous verse (including 'I have found out a gift for my fair'), elegies, odes, songs, and ballads (including 'Jemmy Dawson', q.v.); and prose, 'Essays on Men and Manners'. The correspondence of Shenstone and a circle of friends (see C.H.E.L. x. xi, 'The Warwickshire Coterie') was much valued at the time and is still of interest. There is a sketch of Shenston and the Leasowes in Graves's 'The Spiritual Quixote' (q.v., IX. vii).

Sheol, a word frequently occurring in the Revised Version of the O.T., where in the Authorized Version it was translated hell, grave, or pit; the abode of the dead, conceived by the Hebrews as a subterranean region clothed in thick darkness. [OED.]

Shepheards Calender, The, was the earliest important work of Spenser (q.v.), published in 1579. It consists of twelve eclogues, one for each month of the year, written in different metres, and modelled on the eclogues of Theocritus, Virgil, and more modern writers, such as Baptist Mantuan and Marot. They take the form of dialogues among shepherds, except the first and last, which are complaints by 'Colin Cloute', the author himself. Four of them deal with love, one is in praise of Elysa (Queen Elizabeth), one a lament for a 'mayden of greate bloud', four deal allegorically with matters of religion or conduct, one describes a singing-match, and one laments the contempt in which poetry is held.

Shepherd, LORD CLIFFORD, THE, Henry de Clifford, *fourteenth Baron Clifford* (1455?–1523), celebrated in Wordsworth's 'Brougham Castle' and 'The White Doe of Rylstone'. His father was attainted and his estates forfeited in 1461. Henry de Clifford was brought up as a shepherd, and restored to his estates and title on the accession of Henry VII.

Shepherd, THE ETTRICK, see *Hogg.*

Shepherd of Salisbury Plain, THE, see under *More (Hannah).*

Shepherd's Calendar, *The,* a volume of verse by J. Clare (q.v.).

Shepherd's Hunting, *The,* pastorals written by Wither (q.v.) in the Marshalsea.

Shepherd's Week, *The,* a series of six pastorals by J. Gay (q.v.), published in 1714.

They are eclogues in the mock-classical style, presenting shepherds and milkmaids, not of the golden age, but of the poet's day, in their grotesque reality. They were designed to parody those of Ambrose ('Namby-Pamby') Philips, but they have survived on their own merits, for their drollery and humour.

Sheppard, JOHN (1702–24): 'Jack Sheppard', the son of a carpenter, and brought up in Bishopsgate workhouse, became a thief and highwayman, and, after repeated escapes from prison, was hanged at Tyburn. He was the subject of tracts by Defoe, of many plays and ballads, and of a novel by W. H. Ainsworth.

SHERATON, THOMAS (1751–1806), furniture designer. His book of designs, 'The Cabinet-Maker and Upholsterer's Drawing Book' (1791), 'The Cabinet Dictionary' (1802–3), and 'Cabinet-Maker, Upholsterer and General Artist's Encyclopaedia' (1804), were immensely popular and influential.

SHERIDAN, MRS. FRANCES (1724–66), the mother of Richard Brinsley Sheridan, was author of the 'Memoirs of Miss Sidney Bidulph' (1761–7, a novel after the manner of 'Pamela'), of the 'History of Nourjahad' (1767), and of 'The Discovery', a comedy successfully produced by Garrick in 1763.

SHERIDAN, RICHARD BRINSLEY (1751–1816), the son of Thomas Sheridan (an actor and author), was educated at Harrow. He married Elizabeth Ann Linley in 1773, after escorting her from Bath to France and fighting two duels with Major Mathews, her persecutor. His comedy, 'The Rivals' (q.v., written when the author was only 23), was acted at Covent Garden in 1775. 'St. Patrick's Day' and 'The Duenna' (q.v.) were played in the same year. He acquired Garrick's share in Drury Lane Theatre in 1776, and in 1777 produced there 'A Trip to

Scarborough' (q.v.) and 'The School for Scandal' (q.v.). His famous farce, 'The Critic' (q.v.), was given in 1779, and 'Pizarro' (adapted from Kotzebue's 'The Spaniards in Peru' and showing a great decline in style) in 1799. His new theatre was opened in 1794, but destroyed by fire in 1809. He was returned to parliament in 1780 as a supporter of Fox, and thereafter devoted himself to public affairs. In 1787 he made his great speech of nearly six hours in moving the adoption of the Oude charge against Warren Hastings, and again made a celebrated speech in 1788 as manager of the impeachment. He was treasurer of the navy in the ministry 'of all the talents', 1806–7. He was arrested for debt in 1813, and in his last years suffered from brain disease. He received a great public funeral. There are several portraits of him by Reynolds.

Sheriffs of Bristol, *A Letter to the,* see *Letter to the Sheriffs of Bristol.*

SHERLOCK, THOMAS (1678–1761), son of W. Sherlock (q.v.), educated at Eton, became a fellow and subsequently master of St. Catharine's Hall, Cambridge. As master of the Temple (1704–53) he obtained reputation as a preacher, and rose successively to the sees of Bangor, Salisbury, and London (1748–61). He took part in the Bangorian controversy (q.v.), and published, among other works, 'A Tryal of the Witnesses of the Resurrection of Jesus' (1729), a defence of the historical occurrence of miracles in the singular form of the trial and acquittal of the Apostles in the Inns of Court on the charge of giving false evidence.

SHERLOCK, WILLIAM (1641?–1707), educated at Eton and Peterhouse, Cambridge, became master of the Temple and dean of St. Paul's. He was author of 'A Practical Discourse concerning Death' (1689) and 'A Practical Discourse concerning a Future Judgment' (1692), besides numerous controversial treatises; and was regarded in his time as a great preacher. Macaulay says of him ('History of England') that though there were more brilliant men among the contemporary clergy, none spoke more precisely the sense of the Anglican priesthood, without taint of Latitudinarianism, Puritanism, or Popery. He was a non-juror and was suspended, but was converted and took the oaths in 1691. This created an uproar and made him the object of attacks, vindications, and pasquinades.

Sherlock Holmes, see *Holmes (Sherlock).*

SHERRIFF, ROBERT CEDRIC (1896–), playwright and novelist. His best-known play 'Journey's End', based on his letters written from the front in the First World War, was produced in 1929 and was followed by others of less outstanding success, such as 'Badger's Green' (1930), 'Miss Mabel' (1948), 'Home at Seven' (1950), and 'The Long Sunset' (1955). He has written several novels, the first, 'A Fortnight in September' (1931), being the best known; also a number of screen-plays which include 'The Invisible Man' (1933), 'Good-bye Mr. Chips' (1936), and 'The Dam Busters' (1955).

SHERWOOD, Mrs. MARY MARTHA (1775–1851), *née* Butt, was author of numerous popular books for children and young people, including 'Susan Gray' (1802), 'Little Henry and his Bearer' (1815, the outcome of a period spent in India), and, best known of all, 'The History of the Fairchild Family' (3 parts, 1818–47), which has frequently been reprinted. Mrs. Sherwood's 'Life, chiefly autobiographical', ed. S. Kelly (1854), is lively and interesting.

Shi'a or SHI'ITES, the Muslim sect that regards Ali (q.v.) and his descendants as the rightful Caliphs. The Persians are the chief representatives of the Shi'ites.

Shibboleth, the Hebrew word used by Jephthah as a test-word by which to distinguish the fleeing Ephraimites (who could not pronounce the *sh*) from his own men, the Gileadites (Judges xii. 4–6). Hence a word or formula used as a test by which the adherents of a party, etc., may be distinguished from others. In the above passage the word probably means 'stream in flood'. [OED.]

Shillibeer, GEORGE (1797–1866), the pioneer in London of omnibuses, which were familiarly known by his name.

Shimei, in Dryden's 'Absalom and Achitophel' (q.v.), Slingsby Bethel, the sheriff of London and Middlesex, whose taking of the oaths in order to qualify for office was the subject of several pamphlets. The reference in the name is to 1 Kings ii. 37 et seq.

Shinto, the native religious system of Japan, the central belief of which was that the Mikado (q.v.) was the descendant of the sun-goddess, and that implicit obedience was due to him.

Ship of Fools, The, an adaptation of the famous 'Narrenschiff' of Sebastian Brandt. The 'Narrenschiff' was written in the dialect of Swabia and first published in 1494. It became extremely popular and was translated into many languages. Its theme is the shipping off of fools of all kinds from their native land to the Land of Fools. The fools are introduced by classes and reproved for their folly. The popularity of the book was largely due to the spirited illustrations, which show a sense of humour that the text lacks.

It was translated into English 'out of Latin, French, and Doche' by Alexander Barclay (q.v.), and published in England in 1509; the translation is not literal but is an adaptation to English conditions, and gives a picture of contemporary English life. It starts with the fool who has great plenty of books,

But fewe I rede and fewer understande,

and the fool 'that new garments loves and devises', and passes to a condemnation of the various evils of the time, notably the misdeeds of officials and the corruption of the courts. The work is interesting as an early collection of satirical types. Its influence is seen in 'Cocke Lorell's Bote' (q.v.).

Shipman's Tale, The, see *Canterbury Tales.*

Ship-money, an ancient tax levied in time of war on the ports and maritime towns and counties of England to provide ships for the king's service. It was revived by Charles I (with an extended application to inland counties); his first two writs of ship-money provoked grumbling, the third led to Hampden's case in the Exchequer Chamber; it was finally declared illegal by statute of 1641. The imposition was one of the causes that led to the Civil War. But ship-money *was* spent on the navy; one of the finest ships ever built, 'The Sovereign of the Seas', Pett's masterpiece, was built with ship-money. The real danger was that, if acquiesced in, it might lead to 'soldier-money' too.

Ships, FAMOUS, see *Alabama, Argonauts* (for *Argo*), *Ark, Beagle, Bellerophon, Bounty, Cutty Sark, Dreadnought, Endeavour, Erebus and Terror, Fram, Golden Hind, Great Eastern, Great Harry, Lusitania, Mary Celeste, Mayflower, Revenge, Ship-money* (for *Sovereign of the Seas*), *Skidbladnir, Titanic, Victory, Vittoria.*

Shipton, MOTHER, according to tradition, a witch and prophetess who lived near Knaresborough in Yorkshire at the end of the 15th cent. (her maiden name being Ursula Southill or Southiel), and married one Tobias Shipton, a builder of York. She is said to have produced prophecies relating to persons of importance at the court of Henry VIII, and to have foretold the Great Fire of London, and other notable events. Her history is not supported by serious authority.

Shipwreck, The, see *Falconer* (W.).

Shirburne Ballads, The, edited in 1907 by Andrew Clark from a manuscript of 1600–16 (a few pieces are later) at Shirburne Castle, Oxfordshire, belonging to the earl of Macclesfield. The collection contains ballads not found elsewhere, dealing with political events, with legends and fairy tales, or with stories of domestic life. Some of them are homilies.

Shirley, a novel by C. Brontë (q.v.), published in 1849.

The scene of the story is Yorkshire and the period the latter part of the Napoleonic wars, the time of the Luddite riots, when the wool industry of the country was suffering from the almost complete cessation of exports. In spite of these conditions Robert Gérard Moore, half English, half Belgian by birth, a mill-owner of determined character, persists in introducing the latest labour-saving machinery, undeterred by the opposition of the workers, which culminates in an attempt first to destroy his mill, and finally to take his life. To overcome the financial difficulties that hamper his plans he proposes to Shirley Keeldar, a young lady of wealth and high spirit, though he loves, not her, but the gentle and retiring Caroline Helstone, who is pining away for love of him in the oppressive atmosphere of her uncle's rectory. Robert is contemptuously rejected by Shirley, and, when the end of the war releases him from his embarrassments, marries the faithful Caroline. Meanwhile Shirley and Robert's brother, Louis, another strong, proud character, occupying the humble position of tutor in her family, successfully overcome the difficulties in the way of their mutual love. In Shirley Keeldar, Charlotte Brontë depicted the character of her sister Emily, as she saw it.

SHIRLEY, JAMES (1596–1666), was born in London and educated at Merchant Taylors' School, St. John's College, Oxford, and St. Catharine's Hall, Cambridge. He took orders, but was presently converted to the Church of Rome and became a schoolmaster. He followed the earl of Newcastle in the Civil Wars, after which he returned to the profession of schoolmaster. His graceful poem, 'Narcissus', on the efforts of an enamoured maiden to awaken love in a cold youth (after the manner of Shakespeare's 'Venus and Adonis'), was published as 'Eccho' in 1618. He made an attack on Prynne (q.v.), then in prison, for his condemnation of the stage, in the dedication of 'A Bird in a Cage', printed in 1633. He was in Dublin from 1636 to 1640. He died as a result of terror and exposure on the occasion of the Great Fire of London.

Shirley wrote some forty dramas, of which the greater number are extant. The tragedies include: 'The Maid's Revenge' (1626, printed 1639), 'The Traitor' (q.v., 1631, printed 1635), 'Love's Cruelty' (q.v., 1631, printed 1640), and 'The Cardinall' (q.v., 1641, printed 1653). He also wrote comedies of manners and romantic comedies, including: 'Changes, or Love in a Maze' (1632, the interchanges of affection between three pairs of lovers), 'Hyde Park' (q.v., 1632, printed 1637), 'The Gamester' (q.v., 1633, adapted by Garrick and others), 'The Coronation' (1635, printed 1640, the transference of a crown, owing to the discovery, successively, of two brothers of a queen), 'The Lady of Pleasure' (1635, the cure of a wife's desire for a life of fashionable folly by her husband's feigning to engage in gambling and intrigue), 'The Imposture' (q.v., 1640, printed 1652), 'The Sisters' (q.v., 1642, printed 1652). Shirley also wrote 'The Contention of Ajax and Ulysses' (1659) for the armour of the dead Achilles, a dramatic entertainment ending with the famous dirge

The glories of our blood and state
Are shadows, not substantial things,

'the fine song which old Bowman used to sing to King Charles' and which is said to have terrified Oliver Cromwell. He was disparaged by Dryden ('Mac Flecknoe'), but his reputation was revived by Charles Lamb. Shirley's works were edited by Alexander Dyce in 1833.

SHIRLEY, JOHN (1366?–1456), said to have been a traveller in various lands, and described by Skeat as an amateur rather than a professional scribe. He was buried in St. Bartholomew's the Less. He translated from the French and Latin and transcribed the works of Chaucer, Lydgate, and others. His collections of their poems are extant, and it is on his authority that various poems are attributed to Chaucer.

Shiva, see *Siva*.

Shoemaker's Holiday, The, or A pleasant comedy of the Gentle Craft, a comedy by Dekker (q.v.), published in 1600.

Rowland Lacy, a kinsman of the earl of Lincoln, loves Rose, the daughter of the lord mayor of London. To prevent the match, the earl sends him to France in command of a company of men. Lacy resigns his place to a friend, and, disguised as a Dutch shoemaker, takes service with Simon Eyre, who supplies the family of the lord mayor with shoes. Here he successfully pursues his suit, is married in spite of the efforts of the earl and the lord mayor to prevent it, and is pardoned by the king. The most entertaining character in the play is that of Simon Eyre, the cheery, eccentric master-shoemaker, who becomes lord mayor of London. See also *Deloney* (*T.*).

Shogun, THE, the hereditary commander-in-chief of the Japanese army, also called *Tycoon*. By successive usurpations of power the Shogun became the real ruler of Japan, though nominally the subject of the Mikado and acting in his name. In 1867, with the abolition of the feudal system, the Mikado assumed the actual sovereignty, and the reign of the Shoguns came to an end.

Shore, JANE (*d.* 1527?), mistress of Edward IV. She was the daughter of a Cheapside mercer and wife of a Lombard Street goldsmith, and exercised great influence over Edward IV by her beauty and wit. She was afterwards mistress of Thomas Grey, first marquess of Dorset. She was accused by Richard III of sorcery, imprisoned, and made to do public penance in 1483, and died in poverty. There are two portraits of her at Eton, which foundation she is said to have saved from confiscation at the hands of the Yorkist king, her lover.

She is the subject of a ballad included in Percy's 'Reliques', of a remarkable passage in Sir Thomas More's history of Richard III, and of a descriptive note by Drayton ('England's Heroical Epistles'). The last two passages are quoted in Percy's 'Reliques'. Her adversities are the subject of a tragedy by Rowe (q.v.).

Shoreditch, a district in London named, according to legend, from Jane Shore (q.v.), the mistress of Edward IV, who is supposed to have died there in a ditch. But the name dates from before her time. Stow calls it Soersditch or Soerditch, and says that it had borne the name for 400 years.

Short, CODLIN AND, see *Codlin.*

Short Parliament, THE, the first of the two parliaments summoned by Charles I in 1640. It resolved to ask for a redress of the nation's grievances before granting supply, and prepared to demand the abandonment of the war with Scotland. In fact it was disposed to go as far as the Long Parliament did. It was dissolved after it had sat for three weeks.

Short-Title Catalogue, see *Bibliographical Society.*

Short View of the Immorality and Profaneness of the English Stage, see *Collier.*

Shortest Way with the Dissenters, see *Defoe.*

SHORTHOUSE, JOSEPH HENRY (1834–1903), author of 'John Inglesant' (q.v.), published in 1881 (privately printed in 1880), and other novels of less importance.

Shropshire Lad, A, see *Housman* (*A. E.*).

Shrove-tide, the period immediately preceding Lent, so called from the practice of being shriven preparatory to the fast. It was formerly marked by a final indulgence in merry-making, eating, and drinking.

Shylock, the Jewish usurer in Shakespeare's 'The Merchant of Venice' (q.v.), said to have been drawn from Roderigo Lopez, the queen's Jewish physician, hanged in 1594 on a charge of conspiring to murder her.

Siamese Twins, two male natives of Siam, Chang and Eng (1814–74), who were united by a tubular band in the region of the waist. They were exhibited in 1829 and again in 1869. They married sisters.

Sibylline Books, THE, see *Sibyls.*

Sibylline Leaves, a volume of poems by S. T. Coleridge (q.v.).

Sibyls, THE, certain inspired women said to have lived in various parts of the ancient world, at Cumae, Delphi, Erythrae in Ionia, etc. The best known is the Cumaean (sometimes identified with the Erythraean) sibyl, Herophïlë by name, who was beloved by Apollo. He offered to give her whatever she wished. She asked to live as many years as she had grains of sand in her hand, but omitted to demand health and youth as well. She had already lived 700 years when Aeneas came to Italy. It was usual for the sibyl to write her prophecies on leaves which she placed at the entrance of her cave, and those who consulted her had to be careful to take these up before the wind dispersed them. She instructed Aeneas how to find his father in the infernal regions. According to another legend, she came to the palace of Tarquin II with nine volumes (the *Sibylline Books*), which she offered at a high price. The monarch refused them. The sibyl burnt three, and offered the remainder at the same price; and when Tarquin refused to buy them, burnt three more and again offered the

remainder at the same price. Whereupon Tarquin bought the last three books. These were probably written in Greek, and were kept, under the custody of special officers, in the temple of Jupiter Capitolinus. They were consulted in times of national calamity in order to discover how to avert the anger of the gods. When the temple of Jupiter was burnt down in 83 B.C., the books were destroyed. Thereupon a fresh collection of sibylline prophecies was made in Asia Minor and the Greek cities of Italy and Sicily. These were re-copied in the time of Augustus, and, it is said, other fabricated prophecies added to them. They continued to be consulted occasionally for several centuries.

There are representations of five of the sibyls in Michelangelo's painted ceiling of the Sistine Chapel.

Sicilian Bull, THE, see *Phalaris.*

Sicilian Vespers, THE, a general massacre of the French in Sicily in 1282, of which the signal was the tolling of the bell for vespers. The cruelties of the Angevin rulers of Sicily provoked the massacre, and the crown passed to the rival House of Aragon.

Sick Man of Europe, THE, a term frequently applied during the latter part of the 19th cent. to Turkey. It was first so applied by Nicholas I, Tsar of Russia, in conversation with the British ambassador in 1853.

Sickert, WALTER RICHARD (1860–1942), painter, one of the leading figures in the English Impressionist movement. Before studying painting he spent three years on the stage. After living at Dieppe from 1900 to 1905 he settled in London and in 1911 founded the Camden Town Group. His subjects include music-hall scenes and drab interiors and views of Dieppe and Venice.

Siddartha, see *Buddha.*

Siddons, MRS. SARAH (1755–1831), the sister of J. Kemble (q.v.), the actor, probably the one great tragedy queen that Britain ever produced. She first attracted attention in the part of Belvidera in Otway's 'Venice Preserv'd' (q.v.), and was subsequently famous in her impersonation of Lady Macbeth and other Shakespearian characters. One of her most effective parts was that of the heroine in Rowe's 'Jane Shore'. She married William Siddons, an actor. A picture of her by Reynolds as 'The Tragic Muse' is at Dulwich, and her portrait by Gainsborough is in the National Portrait Gallery.

SIDGWICK, HENRY (1838–1900), educated at Rugby and Trinity College, Cambridge, was from 1883 professor of moral philosophy at that university. A follower in economics and politics of John Stuart Mill, his attitude on the question of our knowledge of the external world resembles that of Reid (q.v.). But his most important work as a philosophical writer relates to ethics, and his reputation rests on his 'Methods of Ethics', published in 1874. Here his doctrine combines an intuitional notion of duty, certain 'axioms of the practical reason' (prudence, benevolence, and justice), with an empirical discovery of the nature of goodness. The ultimate conflict between prudence and benevolence remains unresolved, and in this duality Sidgwick finds the argument for a divine government of the world. But Sidgwick was seen at his best in analysis and criticism, rather than in construction. His other works include: 'Ethics of Conformity and Subscription' (1871), 'Principles of Political Economy' (1883), 'The Scope and Method of Economic Science' (1885), 'Outlines of the History of Ethics' (1886), and 'Elements of Politics' (1891).

Sídhe (pron. 'shē') or AES SÍDHE, the 'People of the Hills', the name used by the Irish peasantry for the fairies.

SIDNEY, ALGERNON (1622–83), the grand-nephew of Sir Philip Sidney, and younger brother of Waller's 'Sacharissa' (see *Waller*), took up arms against Charles I and was wounded at Marston Moor. He was employed on government service until the Restoration, but his firm republicanism was the source of hostility to Cromwell. At the Restoration he refused to give pledges to Charles II, and lived abroad in poverty and exile until 1677. He was sent to the Tower of London after the discovery of the Rye House Plot, tried before Jeffreys, and condemned without adequate evidence, though there was little doubt of his guilt. He was executed on Tower Hill. He wrote 'Discourses concerning Government', first printed in 1698, and a treatise on 'Love', published in 1884.

SIDNEY, SIR PHILIP (1554–86), son of Sir Henry Sidney (who was thrice lord-deputy of Ireland) and of Leicester's sister, was educated at Shrewsbury and Christ Church, Oxford. He became intimate with Sir F. Greville (q.v., Lord Brooke) and Camden (q.v.), and was favoured by Sir William Cecil (Lord Burghley). He visited France, Austria, Venice (meeting Tintoretto and Paolo Veronese), Genoa, and Padua, between 1572 and 1575. In 1583 he married Frances, daughter of Sir Francis Walsingham. In 1576 he became acquainted with Walter Devereux, first earl of Essex, and his daughter Penelope, to whom he addressed the famous series of sonnets known as 'Astrophel and Stella' (q.v.), written during 1580–4. He saw much of Spenser at Leicester House, and received the dedication of his 'Shepheards Calender'. He became a member of the Areopagus (a club formed chiefly for the purpose of naturalizing the classical metres in English verse, which included Spenser, Fulke Greville, Harvey, Dyer, and others). In 1584 he was appointed governor of Flushing; with Prince Maurice he surprised Axel in 1586, and in the same year joined as a volunteer the attack on a Spanish convoy for the relief of Zutphen. Here, on 22 Sept., he

received a fatal wound in the thigh. As he lay dying, he passed a cup of water to another wounded man, saying, 'Thy necessity is greater than mine'. He was buried in St. Paul's Cathedral, and his death evoked elegies by Spenser ('Astrophel'), Matthew Roydon (included after 'Astrophel' in Spenser's Works), James VI, Breton, Drayton, and others. There are portraits of him at Penshurst and elsewhere. He is the subject of a poem by Swinburne.

Sidney exercised an extraordinary influence on the poets of his own and the following generations, heightened, perhaps, by the romantic character of his personal history. None of his works appeared in his lifetime; the 'Arcadia' (q.v.) was first published in 1590; the 3rd edition (1598) included his 'Apologie for Poetrie' (q.v.) and 'Astrophel and Stella' (q.v.), of which an unauthorized edition had appeared in 1591. Sidney's version of the Psalms was published in 1823 and reprinted as 'Rock Honeycomb' in Ruskin's 'Bibliotheca Pastorum'. His collective poetical works were edited by Dr. Grosart in 1873.

Sidney Bidulph, The Memoirs of Miss, see under *Sheridan* (*Mrs. F.*).

'Sidney's sister, Pembroke's mother', see *Pembroke*.

Sidonia, a character in Disraeli's 'Coningsby' and 'Tancred' (qq.v.), a wealthy and powerful Jewish banker, a man of profound learning, devoid of human affections.

Sidonia the Sorceress, see *Meinhold*.

SIDONIUS APOLLINĀRIS (*c.* A.D. 431–84), the foremost representative of Latin literature of his time, author of letters on the model of those of the younger Pliny, and of poems. He was bishop of Auvergne.

Sidrophel, the astrologer in Butler's 'Hudibras' (q.v., II. iii). He is supposed to represent Sir Paul Neal, a conceited member of the Royal Society, who thought he had discovered an elephant in the moon, in fact a mouse in his telescope.

Siege of Corinth, The, a poem by Lord Byron (q.v.), published in 1816.
It is founded on the story of the siege by the Turks, in 1715, of Corinth, then held by the Venetians. The Turks, guided by the renegade Alp, who loves the daughter of the Venetian governor, Minotti, make their way into the fortress. Minotti fires the magazine, and destroys victors and defenders, including himself.

Siege of Rhodes, The, the first attempt at English opera, by D'Avenant (q.v.), performed in 1656.
Dramatic performances having been suppressed by the Commonwealth government, D'Avenant obtained authority in 1656 to produce at Rutland House an 'Entertainment after the manner of the ancients', in which Diogenes and Aristophanes argue against and for public amusements, and a Londoner and

Parisian compare the merits of their two cities; this was accompanied by vocal and instrumental music, composed by Henry Lawes. Immediately after this prologue was given 'The Siege of Rhodes' (at first in one, but in 1662 in two parts), a heroic play, the 'story sung in recitative music', which was composed by Dr. Charles Coleman and George Hudson. The play deals with the siege of Rhodes by Solyman the Magnificent, and the devotion by which Ianthe, wife of the Sicilian Duke Alphonso, saves her husband and the defenders of the island.

Siege of Urbin, The, see *Killigrew (Sir W.)*.

Siege Perilous, see *Round Table*.

Siegfried, the hero of the first part of the 'Nibelungenlied' (q.v.).

In Wagner's opera, 'Siegfried', the hero, son of Siegmund and Sieglinde (see *Valkyrie*), brought up by the Nibelung smith, Mime, forges the Nothung sword from the fragments of the sword of his father. With this he slays Fafner, the giant snake who guards the stolen Rhine-gold, and obtains the magic ring and the 'tarn-helm' which enables him to assume any shape he pleases. He passes through the flames that surround Brynhilde and awakens her, and they plight their troth. For the end of the story see *Götterdämmerung*.

Sieglind, in the 'Nibelungenlied' (q.v.), the mother of Siegfried.

Siegmund, in the 'Nibelungenlied' (q.v.), the father of Siegfried.

Sigismonda (Ghismonda), in Boccaccio's 'Decameron' (iv. i), daughter of Tancred, prince of Salerno. Her father, having discovered her love for his squire Guiscardo, slew the latter and sent his heart in a golden cup to Sigismonda, who took poison and died. The father, repenting his cruelty, caused the pair to be buried in the same tomb. The story is the subject of Dryden's 'Sigismunda and Guiscardo', and of Robert Wilmot's 'Tancred and Gismund'(q.v.). James Thomson's 'Tancred and Sigismunda' (1745) deals with a different story (see *Tancred and Sigismunda*).

Sigmund, in the 'Volsunga Saga' (q.v.) and in W. Morris's 'Sigurd the Volsung' (q.v.), the son of King Volsung and the father of Sigurd.

Signy, in the 'Volsunga Saga' and in W. Morris's 'Sigurd the Volsung' (q.v.), the daughter of King Volsung and the sister of Sigmund.

Siguna, in Norse mythology, the wife of Loki (q.v.).

Sigurd the Volsung and the Fall of the Niblungs, The Story of, an epic in four books, in anapaestic couplets, by W. Morris (q.v.), founded upon the 'Volsunga Saga', and published in 1876.

The first book of this, Morris's most important work, recounts the grim tale of Sigmund, the father of Sigurd, and the three

other books deal with the story of Sigurd himself. Signy, daughter of King Volsung, is married to Siggeir, the dastardly king of the Goths. Hatred springs up between Siggeir and Sigmund, son of Volsung and brother of Signy. Siggeir treacherously causes the death of Volsung and of all his sons except Sigmund, whose great strength enables him to escape. He and Signy devise revenge, and this is effected by the help of Sinfiotli, a son born to Signy of Sigmund. Siggeir is burnt in his palace, Signy voluntarily sharing his fate. Sigmund recovers his kingdom; Sinfiotli is poisoned, and Sigmund is killed in battle.

Sigurd, the son of Sigmund by Hiordis, having learnt the lore of Regin, the dwarf-smith, and acquired Greyfell, the brave horse of Gripir, and the sword that was the gift of Odin, slays Fafnir, the serpent enemy of the gods that guards the elf-gold, and takes the treasure. He finds the beautiful and all-wise Brynhild sleeping in the midst of the wild-fire, awakes her, and is betrothed to her. He then joins the Niblungs, and as the result of a magic draught given him by Grimhild, their queen, forgets Brynhild, and is married to Gudrun, the Niblung king's daughter. He woos Brynhild for Gunnar, Gudrun's brother, assuming his semblance, and wins her, but lays his sword between himself and her as they lie together. Brynhild is wedded to Gunnar. Strife arises between her and Gudrun, and Brynhild learns the trick that has been played upon her. Deeply incensed, she provokes Gunnar to have Sigurd slain, and kills herself that she may join her beloved. Gudrun, in her exceeding grief for Sigurd, withdraws into the wilds.

The last book narrates the fall of the Niblungs. Atli (Attila), 'a king of the outlands', false and avaricious, attracted by the Niblung treasure, seeks the hand of Gudrun, and obtains it, for Gudrun meditates vengeance for the death of Sigurd. Then Atli lures Gunnar and his kinsfolk to his city, and causes them to be slain. Gudrun kills Atli and takes her own life. There is some historical basis for the legend from the point where Attila comes into the story.

Sikes, BILL, a character in Dickens's 'Oliver Twist' (q.v.).

Silas Lapham, see *Rise of Silas Lapham*.

Silas Marner, a novel by George Eliot (q.v.), published in 1861.

Silas Marner, a linen-weaver, has been driven out of the small religious community to which he belongs by a false charge of theft, and has taken refuge in the agricultural village of Raveloe. His only consolation in his loneliness is his growing pile of gold. This is stolen from his cottage by the squire's reprobate son, Dunstan Cass, who disappears. Dunstan's elder brother, Godfrey, is in love with Nancy Lammeter, but is secretly and unhappily married to a woman of low class in a neighbouring town. Meditating revenge for

Godfrey's refusal to acknowledge her, this woman carries her child one New Year's Eve to Raveloe, intending to force her way into the Casses' house; but dies in the snow. Her child, Eppie, finds her way into Silas's cottage, is adopted by him, and restores to him the happiness which he has lost with his gold. After many years, the draining of a pond near Silas's door reveals the body of Dunstan with the gold. Moved by this revelation, Godfrey, now married to Nancy, acknowledges himself the father of Eppie and claims her, but she refuses to leave Silas. The solemnity of the story is relieved by the humour of the rustic revellers at the Rainbow Inn, and the genial motherliness of Dolly Winthrop, who befriends Silas.

Silence, in Shakespeare's '2 Henry IV' (q.v.), a country justice.

Silēni, a name given of old to apothecaries' boxes ornamented with grotesque figures of, amongst others, Silenus (q.v.), and containing perfumes and spices. Alcibiades, in Plato's 'Symposium', compares Socrates to one of these. They figure in the prologue to Rabelais's 'Gargantua'.

Silent Woman, The, see *Epicœne.*

Silēnus, in Greek mythology a satyr (q.v.), the foster-father and attendant of Dionysus (q.v.). He is generally represented as a fat and jolly old man, riding on an ass, intoxicated and crowned with flowers. He once lost his way in Phrygia and was brought by peasants to King Midas, who entertained him kindly. In reward for this, Midas was given the power of turning to gold whatever he touched (see *Midas*). He is the subject of a poem by Thomas Woolner (1825–92).

Silhouette, a portrait obtained by tracing the outline of a profile, head, or figure, by means of its shadow, and filling in the whole outline with black; or cut out of black paper. The word is derived from Étienne de Silhouette (1709–67), controller-general of finances in France for eight months in 1759. According to the usual account it was intended to ridicule the petty economies introduced by Silhouette while holding the appointment; but Hatzfeldt and Darmesteter take the expression 'à la silhouette' to refer to his brief tenure of office, 'appliqué plaisamment à tout ce qui paraissait éphémère'. Littré, however, also quotes a statement that Silhouette himself decorated the walls of his château at Bry-sur-Marne with outline portraits.

SILIUS ITALICUS, TIBERIUS CATIUS (A.D. 25–101), Roman poet, author of a long epic, the 'Punica', on the wars with Hannibal.

Silurians, an ancient British tribe that inhabited the south-east part of Wales.

Silurist, THE, see *Vaughan.*

SILVA, FELICIANO DA, a 16th-cent. Spanish romance writer, who composed sequels to 'Amadis of Gaul' and to 'Celestina' (qq.v.), and was ridiculed in 'Don Quixote'.

Silver-fork, a term used to designate a school of novelists about 1830 (Mrs. Gore (q.v.) and others), distinguished by an affectation of gentility.

Silvia, a character in Shakespeare's 'Two Gentlemen of Verona' (q.v.). See also *Sylvia.*

SIMENON, GEORGES (1903–), Belgian-born novelist, a prolific, widely read and widely translated author of crime fiction. His stories create their effect by atmosphere and psychological intuition rather than by intricacies of plot. His detective-superintendent Maigret, who dominates many volumes, has become one of the famous crime-investigators of modern fiction.

Simile, an object, scene, or action, introduced by way of comparison for explanatory, illustrative, or merely ornamental purpose.

SIMMS, WILLIAM GILMORE (1806–70), prolific American writer, author of some fifty volumes in prose and verse, born in Charleston, South Carolina. His poetry was highly esteemed by contemporary critics, and among romantic novelists he was Cooper's closest rival. His works include: 'Atlantis, A Story of the Sea' (1832), 'Martin Faber' (1833), 'Guy Rivers' (1834), 'The Yemassee' (1835), 'The Partisan' (1835), 'Mellichampe' (1836), 'The Kinsman' (1841), 'Donna Florida' (1843), 'Katherine Walton' (1851), 'The Sword and the Distaff' (1853), 'The Cassique of Kiawah' (1859). His literary labours also include biographies of Chevalier Bayard, Captain John Smith, Nathaniel Greene, and Francis Marion, and popular histories of South Carolina.

Simnel, LAMBERT (*fl.* 1475–1525), of humble parentage, was educated by Richard Simon, a priest, taken by him to Ireland, and persuaded to give himself out as Edward, earl of Warwick, son of the duke of Clarence (there seems to have been some hesitation whether he should personate Warwick or Richard, duke of York). He was joined by Lord Lovell and the earl of Lincoln, was crowned at Dublin as Edward VI (1487), and crossed to England, where the force that he brought with him from Ireland was utterly defeated by Henry VII at Stoke-on-Trent. Simnel was pardoned and employed as a turnspit in the royal kitchen. Long afterwards Henry VII invited some reconciled Irish peers to dine with him and made Simnel wait on them. They did not appreciate the joke.

Simon Eyre (*d.* 1459), according to Stow, a draper who became mayor of London, was a generous benefactor of the city, and built Leadenhall as a public granary and market. He figures in Dekker's 'The Shoemaker's Holiday' (q.v.).

Simon Magus, the sorcerer of Samaria referred to in Acts viii. 9–13 as converted by Philip. His attempts to purchase miraculous powers by offering the Apostles money (Acts viii. 18–19) is alluded to in our word *Simony*. According to other accounts, he claimed divine attributes and was the founder of an early Christian sect known as the Simonians, regarded as heretical.

Simon Pure, a character in Mrs. Centlivre's 'A Bold Stroke for a Wife' (q.v.).

SIMONĬDĒS (*c.* 556–*c.* 468 B.C.), of the Ionian island of Ceos, the first great lyric poet of Greece as a whole (Jebb). His most distinctive work was in his epigrams, notable for their simplicity and power, especially a famous epitaph on the Three Hundred who fell at Thermopylae. Some fragments of his poetry survive, as also of the iambic poet SIMONIDES (or SEMONIDES) OF AMORGOS (*c.* 640 B.C.).

Simorg, see *Simurgh.*

Simple Simon, the subject of various nursery rhymes, used generally to indicate a silly gullible person.

Simple Story, *A,* a romance by Mrs. Inchbald (q.v.), published in 1791.

Miss Milner, a gay flirt, falls in love with her guardian, Dorriforth, who is a priest, and he with her, but both conceal their feelings. Dorriforth becomes Lord Elmwood, and is dispensed by Rome from his vows, and the pair marry. In the second part of the story, Lady Elmwood, led astray by Sir Frederick Lawnley, a former suitor, has been banished with her daughter from her husband's house, and it is only after her death, when her daughter, Matilda, has been carried off by a brutal ravisher, that Lord Elmwood relents and rescues Matilda, and restores her to her proper position. A second priest, the arrogant Sandford, plays an important part in directing the course of events. The author's purpose, she states at the end, is to show the value of 'a proper education'.

Simplicissimus, the name of a well-known German comic paper.

Simplicissimus, *The Adventurous,* the English title of 'Der Abentheurliche Simplicissimus Teutsch' (1669), by J. J. C. von Grimmelshausen (q.v.): a description of the life of a strange vagabond named Melchior Sternfels von Fuchshaim. The work was first translated into English (with an account of the author) in 1912; its chief interest lies in the fact that it is one of the few existing contemporary records of the life of the people during the Thirty Years War.

Simurgh or SIMORG, a monstrous bird of Persian legend, imagined as rational, having the power of speech, and of great age. [OED.] In the 'Shahnameh' of Firdusi (q.v.) a Simurgh nourishes the infant Zâl (q.v.) and afterwards befriends him. One of the feats of Isfendiyar (q.v.) is the slaying of a Simurgh.

Sinadoune, see *Li Beaus Desconus.*

Sinbad, see *Sindbad.*

SINCLAIR, CATHERINE (1800–64), author of 'Holiday House' (1839), a popular book for children, and other books of the same kind, besides many novels.

SINCLAIR, UPTON (1878–   ), American novelist and journalist, born in Baltimore. Sinclair is a novelist with a strong sociological bias, and most of his books have been written definitely in protest against abuses due (according to Sinclair) to the industrial system. Some notable novels among his over a hundred books are 'The Jungle' (q.v., 1906), 'King Coal' (1917), 'The Brass Check' (1919), 'Oil' (1927), 'Boston' (1928), and 'Dragon's Teeth' (1942).

Sindabar or SANDABAR, see *Syntipas.*

Sindbad of the Sea, or *Sindbad the Sailor,* one of the tales in the 'Arabian Nights' (q.v.).

Sindbad, a rich young man of Baghdad, having wasted much of his wealth in prodigal living, undertakes a number of sea-voyages as a merchant and meets with various marvellous adventures. The best known are those of the Roc, a huge bird that could lift elephants in its claws, and of the Old Man of the Sea. The latter persuades Sindbad to carry him on his shoulders, whereupon he twines his legs round Sindbad, so that Sindbad cannot dislodge him and remains his captive, until at last he intoxicates the Old Man with wine, succeeds in dislodging him, and kills him.

Sindibad, see *Syntipas.*

Sinfiotli, in W. Morris's 'Sigurd the Volsung' (q.v.), the son of Sigmund and Signy. He appears in 'Beowulf' (q.v.) as Fitela.

Single-speech Hamilton: William Gerard Hamilton (1729–96), who as M.P. for Petersfield made a celebrated maiden speech. He was chief secretary for Ireland (1761–4) and chancellor of the Irish exchequer (1763–84). He spoke ably in the Irish parliament and his conversational powers were praised by Dr. Johnson. The 'Letters of Junius' were attributed to him by some of his contemporaries. His works were published after his death by Malone under the title of 'Parliamentary Logick'.

Singleton, *Adventures of Captain,* a romance of adventure by Defoe (q.v.), published in 1720. Singleton, who is the narrator of his own story, having been kidnapped in his infancy is sent to sea. Having 'no sense of virtue or religion', he takes part in a mutiny and is put ashore in Madagascar with his comrades; he reaches the continent of Africa and crosses it from east to west, encountering many adventures and obtaining much gold, which he dissipates on his return to England. He takes once more to the sea, becomes a pirate, carrying on his depredations in the West Indies, Indian Ocean, and China Seas, acquires great wealth, which he brings home, and finally marries the sister of a shipmate.

Sinis, a legendary robber who haunted the isthmus of Corinth and killed his victims by tying them to the tops of two pine-trees, which he bent down and then allowed to fly up. He was destroyed by Theseus.

Sinn Fein (pron. *Shin Fane*), 'ourselves', the policy of the Irish Republican party, formulated in 1902; also used for the party itself.

Sinon, see *Horse (The Trojan)*.

Sion College, London, on the site of the ancient Elsynge Spital (a hospital founded in the 14th cent. by William Elsynge, a mercer, and converted by him into an Augustinian priory), was established by Dr. Thomas White in 1623 as a guild of the clergy of London and its suburbs, with an almshouse for twenty persons. It contains a valuable library of theological works.

Sir Charles Grandison, The History of, a novel by Richardson (q.v.), published in 1754.

As in Richardson's previous novels, the story is told by means of letters. The beautiful and accomplished Harriet Byron comes to London, where she attracts many admirers. Among these, Sir Hargrave Pollexfen, rich, arrogant, and unscrupulous, presses his court and offers marriage with insolent persistence. Infuriated by Harriet's refusal, he has her carried off from a masquerade, attempts by outrageous pressure to carry through a secret marriage ceremony, and being foiled, forcibly removes her in a coach to the country. The coach is fortunately stopped by that of Sir Charles Grandison, a gentleman of high character and fine appearance, by whom Harriet is rescued. Sir Charles and Harriet fall in love, but the former is precluded from offering marriage by certain obligations. When living in Italy, he has rendered great services to the noble family of the Porrettas, and a quasi-engagement has been formed between him and Clementina Porretta, in which her heart is more engaged than his. The difference of their religion has hitherto made it impossible to arrive at an agreement with the parents, and Clementina's mind becomes deranged by her unhappiness. Grandison is summoned to Italy, the parents being now prepared to accept any conditions which will ensure their daughter's recovery. As she gets better, however, she decides that she cannot marry a heretic. Sir Charles is released, and is united to Harriet Byron.

Sir Courtly Nice, or It cannot be, a comedy by Crowne (q.v.), produced in 1685.

This is the best of Crowne's plays and is founded on a comedy by the Spanish dramatist, Moreto. Leonora is in love with Farewel, a young man of quality. But her brother Lord Bellguard, owing to a feud between the families, is determined she shall not marry him. Bellguard keeps Leonora under watch by her aunt, 'an old amorous envious maid', and a pair of spies, Hothead and Fanatick, who hold violently opposed views on religious matters and quarrel amusingly in consequence. Thanks to the resourcefulness of Crack, who introduces himself in an assumed

character into Lord Bellguard's house, Farewel is enabled to carry off and marry Leonora; while her rival suitor, favoured by Lord Bellguard, Sir Courtly Nice, a fop whose 'linen is all made in Holland by neat women that dip their fingers in rosewater', is fobbed off with the aunt; and Surly, the rough ill-mannered cynic, gets no wife at all.

Sir Launcelot Greaves, The Adventures of, a novel by Smollett (q.v.).

Sirat, see *Al Sirat*.

Sirens, THE, fabulous creatures, two (or three) in number, who had the power of luring men to destruction by their song. Their names (variously given) were, according to one version, Parthenope, Ligeia, and Leucosia, and they lived in an island off the SW. coast of Italy. Odysseus, informed of the power of their voices by Circe, when passing by this point stopped the ears of his companions with wax and caused himself to be tied to the mast of the ship, and so passed them in safety ('Odyssey', xii). They also attempted to beguile the Argonauts, but Orpheus surpassed them in song. In Plato's 'Republic' (followed by Milton in 'Blest pair of Sirens') they have a good character and supply the music of the spheres. According to later legend the Sirens drowned themselves from annoyance at the escape of Odysseus, and the body of Parthenope was washed ashore at the site of the future Naples (see *Parthenopean Republic*).

Sirius, see *Dog-star*.

Sirmio, a promontory on the southern shore of the Lago di Garda (*Lacus Benacus*), on which Catullus (q.v.) had a villa.

Peninsularum, Sirmio, insularumque Ocelle.

(Catullus, xxxii. 1.)

Sirvente, a form of poem or lay, usually satirical, employed by the troubadours. Apparently from Fr. *servir*, to serve, but the connexion is not clear. [OED.]

SISMONDI, LÉONARD SIMOND DE (1773–1842), French historian of Italian descent, who lived mainly in Geneva. His famous work was 'L'Histoire des Républiques italiennes du Moyen-Âge' (1809–18). He had many friends, including Mme de Staël's circle and the Duchess of Albany, widow of the Young Pretender, and he was an interesting letter-writer.

Sister Anne, see *Blue Beard*.

Sister Helen, a poem by D. G. Rossetti (q.v.), published in 1870.

The poem presents in semi-dramatic form the story of a woman who destroys her unfaithful lover by melting his waxen image, and thereby loses her own soul.

Sisters, The, a comedy by James Shirley (q.v.), produced in 1642.

The theme is the contrast of two sisters, Paulina and Angellina, the one arrogant, the other modest. Paulina is fooled by Frapolo, a chief of bandits, masquerading first as a fortune-teller who prophesies her marriage with a prince; then as Prince of Parma, in which character she marries him. The true prince supervenes and falls in love with Angellina. Frapolo's fraud is exposed, and moreover Paulina is discovered to be a peasant's daughter and a changeling.

Sisters, The, a tragedy in prose by Swinburne (q.v.).

Sistine Chapel, THE, built by Pope Sixtus IV in 1473 in the Vatican. The side walls are painted with scenes from the life of Moses and of Christ by Botticelli, Ghirlandaio, Cosimo Rosselli, and Perugino. In 1508–12, under Julius II, Michelangelo painted the ceiling with scenes from the Creation and with prophets and sibyls; he painted the Last Judgement on the altar wall in 1536–41, under Paul III.

Sistine Madonna, a famous painting by Raphael (1518) now in the museum at Dresden. It is named after the church of San Sisto, Piacenza, whose patron saint, Pope Sixtus II, is seen praying to the Virgin.

Sisyphus, a legendary king of Corinth, famous for his cunning, who outwitted Autolycus (q.v.). When the latter stole his neighbours' cattle, Sisyphus, who mistrusted him, was able to pick out his own, having marked them under the feet. After his death, Sisyphus, on account of misdeeds variously related, was condemned in hell to roll to the top of a hill a large stone, which when it reached the summit rolled back to the plain, so that his punishment was eternal.

Sita, in the 'Rāmāyana' (q.v.), the wife of Rama.

SITWELL, DAME EDITH (1887–1964), poet and critic. She was the daughter of Sir George and Lady Ida Sitwell and spent her childhood at the family seat at Renishaw, Yorkshire. From 1916 to 1921 she edited 'Wheels', an annual anthology of modern verse. During the 1920s she published a number of volumes of verse in which she exploited the musical qualities of language, sometimes at the expense of any clear meaning. Her recital of some of these poems, under the title 'Façade', to music by William Walton at the Aeolian Hall in 1923 caused something approaching a riot. Her first volume of 'Collected Poems' appeared in 1930. She also published biographical studies, notably 'Alexander Pope' (1930) and 'The English Eccentrics' (1933). Her later verse developed a graver tone, in 'Street Songs' (1943), 'Green Song' (1944), and 'Song of the Cold' (1945). Further volumes of 'Collected Poems' appeared in 1954 and 1957. She was made a D.B.E. in 1954.

SITWELL, SIR OSBERT (1892–   ), brother of Edith and Sacheverell Sitwell. He has published a number of volumes of verse, mostly light and satirical in character, short stories, including 'Triple Fugue' (1924), and novels, of which 'Before the Bombardment' (1926) is considered the best. His autobiography (5 vols., 1944–50) is especially remarkable for the account of the eccentric and dominating personality of his father, Sir George.

SITWELL, SACHEVERELL (1897–   ), brother of Edith and Osbert Sitwell. His 'Selected Poems' were published in 1948. His poetry has affinities with that of his sister, but is technically more traditional. He is chiefly known for his essays and criticism of the arts, including 'A Life of Liszt' (1936), 'La Vie Parisienne' (1937), and 'Sacred and Profane Love' (1940), and for his travel writings.

Siva or SHIVA, the third god of the great Hindu triad, of which Brahma and Vishnu are the other two members. He is regarded as a development of the Vedic *Rudra*. He is the god of destruction, and of the regeneration which follows it, and is generally worshipped under a phallic symbol. He shares with Vishnu the principal worship of the Hindus. He is represented with three eyes, a necklace of skulls, and a serpent wound about him. His wife is *Durga* (who has also other names, *Devi*, *Uma*, etc.). He is especially worshipped at Benares.

Six Articles, THE, a statute passed in 1539 declaring in favour of the 'real presence' in the Lord's Supper, clerical celibacy, auricular confession, etc. Whoever spoke against the first was to be burnt; whoever spoke against the others was to suffer loss of goods and imprisonment, and to be hanged for a repetition of the offence. The Act marked the return of Henry VIII, after Cromwell's loss of influence, to 'Catholicism without the Pope'. The Protestants called it the 'Whip with six strings'. It was repealed in 1547.

Six Nations, THE, see *Five Nations*.

Sixteen-string Jack, a noted highwayman, John Rann, hanged in 1774, remarkable for his foppery and for wearing a bunch of sixteen strings at the knees of his breeches. He is referred to in Boswell's 'Johnson' (11 Apr. 1776).

Skadi or SKADHI, in Scandinavian mythology, the wife of the sea-god Njörd. The gods, having killed her father, allowed her to choose a husband from among them, but by seeing only their feet.

Skald, an ancient Scandinavian poet, a term usually applied to the poets of the Viking period. The skaldic verse is extraordinarily elaborate in metre and alliteration.

Skanda, in Hindu mythology, a son of Siva, commander of the armies of the gods against the evil demons, the god of war. He is also called KARTTIKEYA.

Skanderbeg, see *Scanderbeg*.

SKEAT, WALTER WILLIAM (1835–1912), educated at King's College School, Highgate School, and Christ's College, Cambridge, was appointed to a mathematical lectureship at his college in 1864, and devoted his leisure to the study of Early English, with the result that in 1878 he was appointed professor of Anglo-Saxon at Cambridge. He edited 'Lancelot of the Laik' for the Early English Text Society in 1864, and began his great edition of 'Piers Plowman' in 1866. The first part of his edition of John Barbour's 'The Bruce' appeared in 1870, and his two standard works in Early English, the 'Anglo-Saxon Gospels', in 1871–87, and Aelfric's 'Lives of the Saints', in 1881–1900. His seven-volume edition of Chaucer appeared in 1894–7. Skeat founded the English Dialect Society in 1873, which prepared the way for the 'English Dialect Dictionary' (edited by Joseph Wright, 1896–1905). Skeat's 'Etymological Dictionary' (1879–82, revised and enlarged, 1910) was begun with the object of collecting and sifting material for the New English Dictionary. In addition to these major works, he wrote many textbooks for schools and universities, and did much to popularize philology and old authors. He also, in his later years, led the way in the systematic study of place-names. In 1871 he edited Chatterton.

SKEFFINGTON, SIR LUMLEY ST. GEORGE (1771–1850), a fop and playwright who belonged to the Carlton House circle. He was caricatured by Gillray and satirized by Byron ('English Bards and Scotch Reviewers', 599) and Moore. His 'The Word of Honour', 'The High Road to Marriage', and 'The Sleeping Beauty' were produced 1802–5.

Skeffington's Daughter, or SKEVINGTON'S, or SCAVENGER'S DAUGHTER, an instrument of torture in which the body was doubled up until the head and feet were drawn together, reputed to have been devised by Leonard Skeffington, associated with his father, Sir William Skeffington, in the Lieutenancy of the Tower in the 16th cent.

Skeggs, CAROLINA WILHELMINA AMELIA, in Goldsmith's 'Vicar of Wakefield' (q.v.), one of the fine ladies introduced to the Primroses by Squire Thornhill.

SKELTON, JOHN (1460?–1529), was created 'poet-laureate' by both universities of Oxford and Cambridge, an academical distinction. He became tutor to Prince Henry (Henry VIII), and enjoyed court favour despite his outspokenness. He was admitted to holy orders in 1498 and became parson of Diss in Norfolk. His principal works include: 'The Bowge of Court' (q.v., a satire on the court of Henry VII), printed by Wynkyn de Worde; the 'Garlande of Laurell' (a self-laudatory allegorical poem, describing the crowning of the author among the great poets of the world); 'Phylyp Sparowe' (a lamenta-

tion put into the mouth of Jane Scroupe, a young lady whose sparrow has been killed by a cat, followed by a eulogy of her by Skelton, and a defence of himself and the poem); 'Colyn Cloute' (a complaint by a vagabond of the misdeeds of ecclesiastics), which gave suggestions to Spenser. Not only this last poem, but also his satires 'Speke, Parrot', and 'Why come ye nat to courte', contained attacks on Cardinal Wolsey, setting forth the evil consequences of his dominating position. As a result Skelton was obliged to take sanctuary at Westminster, where he died. His most vigorous poem was 'The Tunning of Elynour Rumming' (q.v.). His play of 'Magnyfycence' is an example of the Morality (q.v.). In this allegory, Magnificence, symbolizing a generous prince, is ruined by mistaken liberality and bad counsellors, but restored by Goodhope, Perseverance, and other similar figures. Skelton's 'Ballade of the Scottysshe Kynge' is a spirited celebration of the victory of Flodden. A number of Skelton's poems were printed and reprinted in the sixteenth century, most of the extant copies being, though undated, evidently later than the poet's death; in 1568 appeared a fairly full collected edition in one volume. The standard modern edition is by Dyce, 1843. Anecdotes of Skelton appeared in the popular 'Merie Tales' (1566) and similar collections.

His favourite metre was a 'headlong voluble breathless doggerel, which, rattling and clashing on through quick recurring rhymes', 'has taken from its author the title of Skeltonical verse' (Churton Collins). As he himself said ('Colyn Cloute', ii. 53–8):

> For though my ryme be ragged,
> Tattered and iagged,
> Rudely rayne beaten,
> Rusty and mothe eaten;
> If ye take well therwith,
> It hath in it some pyth.

Skepsey, DANIEL, a character in Meredith's 'One of our Conquerors' (q.v.).

Sketches by Boz, a collection of sketches of life and manners, by Dickens (q.v.), first published in various periodicals, and in book form in 1836–7 (in one volume, 1839). These are some of Dickens's earliest literary work.

Skevington's Daughter, see *Skeffington's Daughter.*

Skewton, THE HON. MRS., in Dickens's 'Dombey and Son' (q.v.), the mother of Edith, Dombey's second wife. See also *Cleopatra.*

Skidbladnir, in Scandinavian mythology, the magic ship of Freyr, made by the Dwarfs. It was large enough to carry all the gods, but could be folded up and carried in the pocket.

Skimmington. It was an ancient custom in the rural parts of England and Scotland to expose and ridicule marital quarrels, and particularly nagging, bullying, and infidelity, by forming a ludicrous procession, with figures carried on a pole, symbolical of the circumstances. This was called 'riding Skimmington' or 'riding the stang'. The origin of the word 'Skimmington' is unknown. It is perhaps from 'skimming', for a frontispiece to 'Divers Crabtree Lectures' (1639) entitled 'Skimmington and her Husband' represents a woman beating her husband with a skimming-ladle. There is a description of a 'Skimmington' in Hardy's 'The Mayor of Casterbridge' (q.v.).

Skimpole, HAROLD, a character in Dickens's 'Bleak House' (q.v.).

Skinfaxi (shining-mane), in Scandinavian mythology, the horse of the sun.

SKINNER, JOHN (1721-1807), an Aberdeenshire minister, and the author of 'Tullochgorum', pronounced by Burns 'the best Scotch song Scotland ever saw'. 'Ewie wi' the Crockit Horn', 'Tune your Fiddle', and 'Old Age' are among other favourite songs written by Skinner.

Skinners, marauders who committed depredations on the neutral ground between the British and American lines during the War of Independence.

Skionar, MR., a character in Peacock's 'Crotchet Castle' (q.v.), perhaps a caricature of Coleridge.

Skoggan, see *Scogan (J.)*

Slawkenbergius, HAFEN, in Sterne's 'Tristram Shandy' (q.v.), the German author of a Latin treatise on noses, one of whose Rabelaisian tales is given at the beginning of vol. iv.

Slay-good, in Pt. II of Bunyan's 'The Pilgrim's Progress' (q.v.), a giant whom Mr. Greatheart killed, rescuing Mr. Feeble-mind from his clutches.

Sleary, the circus proprietor in Dickens's 'Hard Times' (q.v.).

Sleeping Beauty, *The,* a fairy tale, translated from the French of Perrault (q.v.) by Robert Samber (1729?).

Seven fairies are invited to attend the baptism of the daughter of a king and are received with great honour. An old fairy has been overlooked and comes unbidden. Six of the first fairies bestow on the child every imaginable perfection. The old fairy spitefully pronounces that she shall wound herself with a spindle and die. The seventh fairy, who has purposely kept in the background, amends this fate, converting the death into a sleep of a hundred years, from which the princess will be awakened by a king's son. And so it falls out, and the fairy puts every one in the castle also to sleep so that the princess may not wake up all alone, and makes an impenetrable hedge of trees and briars to grow up round the castle. In due course the prince comes and wakens the sleepers.

For analogous legends see Andrew Lang,

'Perrault's Popular Tales'. It is suggested that the Sleeping Beauty represents the earth awakened from her winter sleep by the kiss of the sun.

Sleepy Hollow, *The Legend of,* a story by W. Irving (q.v.), included in 'The Sketch Book'. Ichabod Crane is a schoolmaster and suitor for the hand of Katrina van Tassel. He meets his death, or, according to another report, leaves the neighbourhood, in consequence of being pursued at night by a headless horseman, an incident for which his rival Brom Bones is suspected to have been responsible.

Sleipnir, the horse of Odin (q.v.).

Slender, a character in Shakespeare's 'The Merry Wives of Windsor' (q.v.).

Slick, SAM, see *Haliburton.*

Slidell and **Mason,** see *Trent Case.*

Slingsby, a youthful character in one of the nonsense tales of E. Lear (q.v.).

Slipslop, MRS., a character in Fielding's 'Joseph Andrews' (q.v.).

SLOANE, SIR HANS (1660-1753), a physician, secretary to the Royal Society, 1693-1712, and president of the Royal College of Physicians, 1719-35. He purchased the manor of Chelsea and founded there the Botanic Garden. He published (1696) a Latin catalogue of the plants of Jamaica (where he had been physician to the governor, 1687-9) and a 'Voyage' to the West Indies (1707-25). His collections (including a large number of books and manuscripts) were purchased by the nation and placed in Montague House (afterwards the British Museum). Sloane Square and Hans Place are named after him.

Slop, DR., in Sterne's 'Tristram Shandy' (q.v.), a bigoted and clumsy physician, 'a little, squat, uncourtly figure'. The name was scurrilously applied to Sir John Stoddart (1773-1856) during his editorship of 'The New Times'. Stoddart had been a leader-writer on 'The Times', but, in consequence of a difference with it in 1817, started 'The New Times' as a rival. This paper survived until 1828.

Slope, THE REVD. OBADIAH, a character in Trollope's 'Barchester Towers' (q.v.).

Slough of Despond, THE, in Bunyan's 'The Pilgrim's Progress' (q.v.), a miry place on the way from the City of Destruction to the wicket-gate. 'As the sinner is awakened about his lost condition, there arise in his soul many fears and doubts, and discouraging apprehensions, which all of them get together, and settle in this place.'

Slowboy, TILLY, a character in Dickens's 'The Cricket on the Hearth' (q.v.).

Sludge, DICKY, or 'Flibbertigibbet', a character in Scott's 'Kenilworth' (q.v.).

Sludge, 'the Medium', see *Mr. Sludge.*

Slumkey, THE HONOURABLE SAMUEL, in Dickens's 'The Pickwick Papers' (q.v.), the Blue candidate in the Eatanswill election.

Sly, CHRISTOPHER, see *Taming of the Shrew*.

Small House at Allington, The, a novel by A. Trollope (q.v.), published in 1864.

This, though not in the Barsetshire series of novels as named by Trollope, deals with some of the same characters. Squire Dale, an embittered old bachelor, lives at the 'Great House'; his sister-in-law, with her two daughters, Bell and Lily Dale, at the adjacent 'Small House'. Adolphus Crosbie, a rising government official, well-looking but mean and selfish, wins the love of the warm-hearted but penniless Lily, and becomes engaged to her. Learning that the squire will not provide her with a fortune, his determination to marry her wavers. This reluctance is increased by the aristocratic atmosphere of Courcy Castle, where he goes on a visit, and he yields to the temptation to propose to Lady Alexandrina de Courcy, who accepts him. The jilting of Lily, which nearly breaks her heart, brings condign punishment on his head; he receives a thrashing from Johnny Eames, a humble government clerk, the lifelong adorer of Lily, and is thoroughly unhappy in his married life with Lady Alexandrina, which is soon terminated by their separation. Johnny Eames, who obtains the friendship and support of Earl De Guest, now proposes to Lily, who, though fond of Johnny, still loves Crosbie and considers herself bound for life to him, and consequently refuses Eames. Meanwhile Bell, by refusing Bernard, her cousin, defeats a cherished scheme of their uncle, Squire Dale, and brings about temporary estrangement between the 'Small House' and the 'Great House'. But reconciliation follows, Bell marries the honest Dr. Crofts, and both daughters receive fortunes from the Squire.

We hear a good deal of the heartless and astute Lady Dumbello (the Griselda Grantly of the earlier novels), and of Sir Raffle Buffle, the bullying head of a government department.

SMART, CHRISTOPHER (1722–71), educated at Durham School and Cambridge, was author of two volumes of 'Poems' (1752 and 1763); the 'Hilliad' (1753), a satire on John Hill, the quack doctor; a paraphrase of the Psalms; and translations of Phaedrus and Horace. But he is chiefly remembered for his 'Song to David' (1763), a song of praise of King David as the great poet and author of the Psalms, containing splendid imagery. Smart declined into insanity and debt, and died within the rules of the King's Bench.

Smec, LEGION, see *Smectymnuus*.

Smectymnuus, the name under which five Presbyterian divines, Stephen Marshal, Edmund Calamy, Thomas Young, Matthew Newcomen, and William Spurstow, published a pamphlet attacking episcopacy. The name is a combination of the initials of the

five authors. It was answered by Bishop Hall, and defended by Milton (who was already engaged in the controversy) in his 'Animadversions upon the Remonstrant's Defence against Smectymnuus' (1641), and his 'Apology against a Pamphlet . . . against Smectymnuus' (1642), which contains an interesting account of Milton's early studies. From 'Smectymnuus' is derived 'Legion Smec' in Hudibras, II. ii, signifying the Presbyterians:

> New modell'd the Army and cashier'd
> All that to Legion Smec adher'd.

SMEDLEY, FRANCIS EDWARD (1818–64), a cripple from childhood, was author of some pleasant novels, blending romance with sport and adventure. The most popular of these, 'Frank Fairleigh' (1850), was originally contributed anonymously to the 'London Magazine'. 'Lewis Arundel' appeared in 1852, and 'Harry Coverdale's Courtship' in 1855.

Smee, a character in Barrie's 'Peter Pan' (q.v.).

Smelfungus, see *Sentimental Journey*.

Smerdis, according to Herodotus (iii. 30, 61, etc.) a son of Cyrus, king of Persia. He was murdered by order of his brother, Cambyses, and the murder was kept secret. A Magian, Patizithes, who knew the fact, and was weary of the mad tyranny of Cambyses, had a brother who resembled Smerdis in person. He proclaimed this man king, as the younger son of Cyrus, and the false Smerdis reigned for seven months, until the imposture was discovered by one of his wives. The name of the false Smerdis, according to the Behistun inscription, was Gomata.

Smike, a character in Dickens's 'Nicholas Nickleby' (q.v.).

SMILES, SAMUEL (1812–1904), educated at Haddington Grammar School and Edinburgh University, devoted the leisure of a varied career to the advocacy of political and social reform on the lines of the Manchester School, and to the biography of industrial leaders and humble self-taught students. He published the 'Life of George Stephenson' in 1857, 'Lives of the Engineers' in 1861–2, and many similar works. He achieved great popular success with 'Self-help' in 1859, 'Character' (1871), 'Thrift' (1875), 'Duty' (1880), and 'Life and Labour' (1887).

SMITH, ADAM (1723–90), born at Kirkcaldy, studied at Glasgow University and as a Snell exhibitioner at Balliol College, Oxford. He was appointed professor of logic at Glasgow in 1751, and in 1752 of moral philosophy. He became the friend of Hume (q.v.). In 1759 he published his 'Theory of the Moral Sentiments' (q.v.), which brought him into prominence. In 1764 he resigned his professorship and accompanied the young duke of Buccleuch as tutor on a visit to France, where he saw Voltaire, and was admitted into the society of the 'physiocrats' (q.v.). After his return he settled down at Kirkcaldy and devoted himself to the preparation of his great work, 'An Enquiry into the Nature and Causes of the Wealth of Nations' (q.v.), published in 1776. This revolutionized the economic theories of the day. Its appearance at the actual date of the 'Declaration of Independence' of the American rebels was of importance if only for the prophecy in Bk. IV, 'They will be one of the foremost nations of the world'. To obviate the danger he proposed the representation of the colonies in the British parliament. Smith edited the autobiography of Hume in 1777, and was elected rector of Glasgow University in 1787. He was a member of the Literary Club (see *Johnson, S.*).

SMITH, ALEXANDER (1830–67), by occupation a lace-pattern designer in Glasgow, published in 1853 'A Life Drama' and other poems, which were received at first with enthusiasm, and were satirized by Aytoun (q.v.) in 'Firmilian'. He published sonnets on the Crimean War in 1855 jointly with S. T. Dobell (q.v.); 'City Poems' in 1857, containing 'Glasgow', his finest work in verse, giving a sombre picture of the city; and some pleasant prose essays under the title of 'Dreamthorp' in 1863. But his best prose is to be seen in 'A Summer in Skye' (1865), a charming description of the country and its inhabitants. 'Last Leaves', another group of essays, appeared posthumously.

SMITH, EDMUND (1672–1710), poet. He translated Racine's 'Phèdre' ('Phaedra and Hippolitus', 1706).

Smith, GEORGE (1824–1901), joined in 1838 the firm of Smith & Elder, publishers and East India agents, of 65 Cornhill, London, which his father had founded in partnership with Alexander Elder in 1816, soon after coming in youth to London from his native town of Elgin. In 1843 Smith took charge of some of the firm's publishing operations, and on his father's death in 1846 became sole head of the firm. Under his control the business quickly grew in both the India agency and publishing directions. The chief authors whose works he published in his early career were John Ruskin, Charlotte Brontë, whose 'Jane Eyre' he issued in 1848, and W. M. Thackeray, whose 'Esmond' he brought out in 1851. In 1853 he took a partner, H. S. King, and, after weathering the storm of the Indian Mutiny, started in 1859 'The Cornhill Magazine', with Thackeray as editor, and numerous leading authors and artists as contributors. In 1865 Smith (with Frederick Greenwood) founded 'The Pall Mall Gazette', a London evening newspaper of independent character and literary quality, which remained his property till 1880. In 1868 he dissolved partnership with King, leaving him to carry on the India agency branch of the old firm's business, and himself taking over the publishing branch, which he thenceforth conducted at 15 Waterloo Place, London. His

chief authors now included Robert Browning, Matthew Arnold, (Sir) Leslie Stephen, and Miss Thackeray (Lady Ritchie), all of whom were intimate personal friends. He was founder (1882) and proprietor of the 'Dictionary of National Biography' (q.v.).

SMITH, GOLDWIN (1823–1910), educated at Eton and Christ Church, Oxford, was Regius professor of modern history at Oxford, 1858–66, and subsequently professor of history at Cornell University in America, finally settling at Toronto in 1871. He was an active journalist and vigorous controversialist, supporting the cause of the North in the American Civil War, and the sentiment of national independence in Canada. His published works include: 'The Empire' (1863), indicating his distrust of imperialism; 'Irish History and Irish Character' (1862); lectures on 'Three English Statesmen' (Pym, Cromwell, and Pitt, 1867); 'Lectures and Essays' (1881); 'Essays on Questions of the Day' (1893); 'The United States: an Outline of Political History' (1893); 'The United Kingdom: a Political History' (1899); and 'Irish History and the Irish Question' (1906), which showed him faithful to the Unionist policy.

Smith or Gow, Henry, the hero of Scott's 'Fair Maid of Perth' (q.v.).

SMITH, HORATIO (HORACE) (1779–1849), brother of James Smith (q.v.), became famous as the joint-author, with him, of 'Rejected Addresses' (1812, q.v.) and of 'Horace in London' (1813). He subsequently wrote novels, of which the best is 'Brambletye House' (1826), an imitation of Sir Walter Scott, the story of a young Cavalier in the days of Cromwell and Charles II.

SMITH, JAMES (1775–1839), elder brother of H. Smith (q.v.), was solicitor to the Board of Ordnance, and produced with his brother 'Rejected Addresses' (q.v., 1812) and 'Horace in London' (1813).

SMITH, CAPTAIN JOHN (1580–1631), set out with the Virginia colonists in 1606 and is said to have been rescued by Pocahontas (q.v.) when taken prisoner by the Indians. He became head of the colony and explored the coasts of the Chesapeake. He was author of 'The General History of Virginia, New England, and the Summer Isles' (1624), and of a 'Sea Grammar' for young seamen (1626–7).

SMITH, JOHN (1618–52), educated at Emmanuel College, Cambridge, was one of the Cambridge Platonists (see *Platonists*). His 'Select Discourses' were published in 1660.

SMITH, JOHN THOMAS (1766–1833), keeper of drawings and prints at the British Museum, was author of a life of the sculptor Nollekens ('Nollekens and his Times', 1828) remarkable for its singular candour, and of 'A Book for a Rainy Day or Recollections of the Events of the Years 1766–1833', an entertaining picture of the artistic and literary life of the period, published in 1845.

SMITH, LOGAN PEARSALL (1865–1946), born in Philadelphia, spent most of his life in England, devoting himself chiefly to the study of the English language. His works include 'Words and Idioms' (1925), three volumes of 'Trivia' (1918, 1921, 1933), 'Reperusals and Re-collections' (1936), 'Unforgotten Years' (autobiography, 1938).

Smith, MARY, the narrator of the story in Mrs. Gaskell's 'Cranford' (q.v.).

SMITH, ROBERT PERCY, '*Bobus Smith*' (1770–1845), elder brother of Sydney Smith (q.v.), of Eton and King's College, Cambridge. He was advocate-general of Bengal and returned home rich in 1810. He was M.P. for Grantham and later for Lincoln. Famous for his wit and his Latin verses.

SMITH, SYDNEY (1771–1845), educated at Winchester and New College, Oxford, resided for a time, as tutor of Michael Hicks Beach, at Edinburgh, where he was intimate with Jeffrey, Brougham, and Horner, and with the first two of these founded 'The Edinburgh Review' in 1802. He came to London in 1803, lectured on moral philosophy at the Royal Institution, and shone among the Whigs at Holland House. In 1807 he published the 'Letters of Peter Plymley' (q.v.) in defence of Catholic emancipation. He held the livings, first of Foston in Yorkshire, then of Combe-Florey in Somerset, and in 1831 was made a canon of St. Paul's. He was noted for his exuberant drollery and wit, which were principally displayed in his conversation, but are also seen in his numerous reviews and letters.

SMITH, THOMAS (*b.* 1790), master of the Hambledon Hounds in 1825, of the Craven in 1829, and subsequently of the Pytchley, was author of 'The Life of a Fox, written by himself' (1843), and of 'The Diary of a Huntsman' (1838). He had an extraordinary knowledge of the habits of foxes and understanding of their nature. He is not to be confused with THOMAS ASSHETON SMITH (1776–1858), master of the Quorn (1806–16) and of other packs, who was acclaimed the first fox-hunter of the day.

Smith, WAYLAND, see *Wayland the Smith*.

SMITH, SIR WILLIAM (1813–93), educated at University College, London, is remembered as the editor and part author of the 'Dictionary of Greek and Roman Antiquities' (1842), of a 'Dictionary of Greek and Roman Biography and Mythology' (1844–9), of a 'Dictionary of the Bible' (1860–3), of dictionaries of Christian antiquities (1875–80) and Christian biography (1877–87), and of other educational works. He was editor of 'The Quarterly Review', 1867–93.

SMITH, WILLIAM ROBERTSON (1846–94), theologian and Semitic scholar, was educated at Aberdeen, Edinburgh (New College), and Bonn. He became professor of Old Testament exegesis at the Free Church

College, Aberdeen, but was dismissed (1881, perhaps the last victim of a 'heresy-hunt' in Britain) from his chair for the advanced character of his biblical articles in the 'Encyclopaedia Britannica' (9th ed.), of which work he became co-editor in 1881. He was professor of Arabic at Cambridge from 1883. His published works include: 'The Old Testament in the Jewish Church' (1881) and 'The Prophets of Israel' (1882).

Smithfield, WEST, i.e. 'smooth field', was an open space outside the north-west walls of the City of London. Stow writes of the encroachments 'whereby remaineth but a small portion for the old uses, to wit, for markets of horses and cattle, neither for military exercises, as Justings, Turnings, and great triumphs which have been there performed before the princes and nobility both of this Realm and forraigne countries', of which he gives many curious instances. Here Richard II met Wat Tyler, and here the latter was killed. Here also, in the 16th cent., heretics were burnt.

Smith's Prizes, at Cambridge, for mathematics and natural philosophy, were founded by Robert Smith (1689–1768), educated at Trinity College, Cambridge, who became Plumian professor of astronomy and master of Trinity College, Cambridge. He left large sums for university and college purposes, besides pictures and sculptures.

Smithsonian Institution, THE, in Washington, was founded by James Smithson, known in early life as James Lewis Macie (1765–1829), an illegitimate son of Hugh Smithson Percy, duke of Northumberland. He was a distinguished mineralogist and chemist, and spent much time abroad, among his correspondents being many eminent men of science. His politics appear to have been republican, and by his will he left over £100,000 to the United States of America to found the Smithsonian Institution, an establishment for the increase and diffusion of knowledge. The institution was inaugurated in 1846, and the buildings now comprise a national museum (mainly zoological and ethnological) and an astrophysical observatory. His own scientific papers nearly all perished in a fire at the institution in 1865.

SMOLLETT, TOBIAS GEORGE (1721–71), born in Dunbartonshire, the grandson of Sir James Smollett. He was educated at Glasgow University, but left without means of support. He sailed as surgeon's mate on the 'Chichester' in Ogle's West India squadron (1741), was present at the attack on Cartagena, and remained some time in Jamaica, where he married. In 1744 he returned to London, practised as a surgeon, and wrote his novels, which appeared as follows: 'Roderick Random' (q.v.) in 1748, 'Peregrine Pickle' (q.v.) in 1751 (revised edition, 1758), 'Ferdinand Count Fathom' (q.v.) in 1753, 'Sir Launcelot Greaves' (the story of an 18th-cent. Don Quixote) in 1760–2, and 'Humphry Clinker' (q.v.) in 1771. In 1746 Culloden drew from him the poem 'The Tears of Scotland'. In 1753 he had settled at Chelsea, translating 'Don Quixote' in 1755, editing the new 'Critical Review' in 1756, and bringing out a large 'History of England' and also a farce, 'The Reprisal', in 1757. For a libel in the 'Critical Review' he was fined and imprisoned in 1759. In 1762 he conducted, with little success, 'The Briton', a weekly periodical supporting Lord Bute. Ill health sent him abroad in 1763, and in 1766 he published his entertaining but ill-tempered 'Travels in France and Italy', which procured for him, from Sterne, the nickname of 'Smelfungus'. In 1769 appeared his coarse and vigorous sàtire on public affairs entitled 'The Adventures of an Atom' (q.v.). He revisited Scotland and Bath in 1766, but finally left England in 1769 and died at Monte Nero near Leghorn. See also *Covent Garden Journal.*

Smorltork, COUNT, in Dickens's 'The Pickwick Papers' (q.v.), 'the famous foreigner' at Mrs. Leo Hunter's party, 'a well-whiskered individual in a foreign uniform', who is 'gathering materials for his great work on England'.

SMUTS, FIELD MARSHAL THE RT. HON. JAN CHRISTIAN (1870–1950), educated in S. Africa and at Christ's College, Cambridge, practised as a lawyer in Cape Colony and became State Attorney of the S. African Republic. He served in the Boer War, having supreme command of the republican troops in Cape Colony from 1901. In the war of 1914–18 he was in command of the imperial forces in E. Africa and subsequently S. African representative in the Imperial War Cabinet in 1917–18 and at the Peace Conference in 1919. He was prime minister of S. Africa in 1919–24 and from 1939. He was author of 'Holism and Evolution' (1926), 'Africa and some World Problems' (1930). He was Rhodes Memorial Lecturer at Oxford, 1929–30.

Snagsby, MR. and MRS., characters in Dickens's 'Bleak House' (q.v.).

Snailsfoot, BRYCE, the pedlar in Scott's 'The Pirate' (q.v.).

Snake, a character in Sheridan's 'The School for Scandal' (q.v.).

Snark, The, see *Hunting of the Snark.*

Sneak, JERRY, a henpecked husband in Foote's 'The Mayor of Garret'. See *Garratt.*

Sneerwell, LADY, one of the scandal-mongers in Sheridan's 'The School for Scandal' (q.v.).

Snell, HANNAH (1723–92), a female soldier, stated in a chap-book history of her adventures, issued in 1750, to have enlisted in 1745, to have served in the fleet, and to have received a pension for wounds received at Pondicherry. The facts were much embellished, but there was probably a kernel of truth as in the cases of Christian Davies, Mary Anne Talbot (qq.v.), and Phoebe Hessel (1713–1821). Hannah, who was thrice married, died in Bedlam.

Snevellicci, MR., MRS., and MISS, in Dickens's 'Nicholas Nickleby' (q.v.), actors in Crummles's company.

Snobs of England, The, by one of themselves, a collection of papers by Thackeray (q.v.), published in 'Punch' in 1846–7, descriptions of the various types of English snobs. The papers were republished as 'The Book of Snobs' (1848).

Snodgrass, AUGUSTUS, in Dickens's 'The Pickwick Papers' (q.v.), one of the members of the Corresponding Society of the Pickwick Club.

SNORRI STURLASON (1178–1241), an Icelandic historian, author of the 'Heimskringla' (q.v.) or history of the kings of Norway, and of the prose 'Edda' (q.v.). He was also an active and ambitious politician who played a questionable role in his country's relations with Norway, and was finally assassinated by the order of King Hakon. Snorri was uncle of Sturla Thordsson, author of the 'Sturlunga Saga'.

Snout, TOM, in Shakespeare's 'A Midsummer Night's Dream' (q.v.), a tinker. He is cast for the part of Pyramus's father in the play of 'Pyramus and Thisbe', which gives him nothing to say.

SNOW, SIR CHARLES PERCY (1905–), novelist, was a professional scientist in his early career. His first novel was a detective story, 'Death under Sail' (1932), followed by 'New Lives for Old' (1933), and 'The Search' (1934). Since then he has undertaken a novel sequence entitled 'Strangers and Brothers' (the title of the first volume, 1940). Succeeding novels in the series are 'The Light and the Dark' (1947), 'Time of Hope' (1949), 'The Masters' (1951), 'The New Men' (1954), 'Homecomings' (1956), 'The Conscience of the Rich' (1958), 'The Affair' (1959), and 'Corridors of Power' (1963), and have a setting largely academic and scientific—the 'Two Cultures' of his Rede Lecture at Cambridge, 1959.

Snubbin, MR. SERJEANT, in Dickens's 'The Pickwick Papers' (q.v.), counsel for the defendant in Bardell *v.* Pickwick.

Snuffy Davie, or DAVIE WILSON, in Scott's 'The Antiquary' (q.v.), the hero of a favourite story of Monkbarns, the bibliomaniac who bought Caxton's 'The Game at Chess', 1474, for two groschen at a stall in Holland.

Snug, in Shakespeare's 'A Midsummer Night's Dream' (q.v.), a joiner, who takes the part of the lion in 'Pyramus and Thisbe'.

Soane, SIR JOHN (1753–1837), architect, the son of a bricklayer. In 1788 he became surveyor of the Bank of England, which he rebuilt. He gave his house in Lincoln's Inn Fields, with its collection of paintings, prints, sculpture, and architectural drawings, to the nation. He published a number of books on architecture.

Soapy Sam, a nickname of Samuel Wilberforce (1805–73), successively bishop of Oxford and of Winchester, in allusion to his unctuous and ingratiating manners.

Social Contract, The, the English title of 'Du Contrat Social', by J. J. Rousseau (q.v.).

Socialism, a theory or policy of social organization that aims at the control of the means of production, capital, land, property, etc., by the community as a whole, and their administration or distribution in the interests of all. The early history of the word is obscure. It is said [E.B.] to have originated in 1835 in the discussions of a society founded by Richard Owen. It is found in 1833 in the sense of Owenism. G. B. Shaw (q.v.) published in 1928 'The Intelligent Woman's Guide to Socialism and Capitalism'.

Society for Pure English, THE, or S.P.E., was founded in 1913, the original committee consisting of H. Bradley, R. Bridges, Sir Walter Raleigh, and Logan Pearsall Smith (qq.v.). Its proceedings were suspended during the war of 1914–18, and its first Tract, containing a reprint of the original prospectus, is dated October 1919. The object of the promoters was to guide popular taste and the educational authorities in matters connected with the use and development of the English language. The S.P.E. has issued many Tracts, on questions of grammar, pronunciation, etymology, handwriting, etc.

Society of Antiquaries, see *Antiquaries.*

Socinianism, the doctrine of Lelio Sozzini (Socinus) and his nephew Fausto Sozzini (1539–1604) that Jesus was not God but a divine prophet of God's word, and that the sacraments had no supernatural quality. The doctrine was set forth in the Confession of Rakow (1605).

SOCRATES (469–399 B.C.), the great Greek philosopher, born near Athens, was the son of Sophroniscus, a sculptor. He was a man of uncouth appearance. He served with credit in the army, saving the life of Alcibiades at Potidaea (432 B.C.). Late in life he held public office and showed great moral courage in resisting illegalities. He was married to Xanthippe, who had the reputation of a scold. He conceived himself as having a religious mission, receiving guidance from a supernatural voice (his 'daemon'). He occupied his life with oral instruction, frequenting public places and conversing with all and sundry, seeking the truth, and the exposure of pride and error. In consequence he incurred the malevolence of those who pretended to wisdom, was attacked by Aristophanes in the 'Clouds', and finally accused of impiety by

one Meletus, a leather-seller, condemned by a narrow majority of the judges, and sentenced to death (by drinking hemlock). Socrates wrote nothing, but the general method and tendency of his teaching are preserved in the Dialogues of Plato (q.v.); though precisely what contribution to the history of thought is to be attributed to Socrates has been a subject of discussion. A more homely account of him is to be found in Xenophon's 'Memorabilia'. The following appear to have been prominent features in his teaching: (1) the view that it is the duty of philosophy to investigate not physical phenomena, but ethical questions, how men should live and act; (2) the view that virtue is knowledge: no one is willingly wicked, for happiness lies in virtue; if a man is wicked, it is from ignorance. Socrates' concern was therefore to discover what the good is. The question of moral intention was with him secondary. He inclined to the view that the soul is immortal and will meet with judgement and retribution hereafter.

The SOCRATIC METHOD of instruction was by questions aptly proposed so as to arrive at the conclusion he wished to convey.

Sodom and **Gomorrah,** the 'cities of the plain' of Jordan (now covered by the Dead Sea), destroyed, on account of their wickedness, in the days of Lot and Abraham (Gen. xiii, xviii, and xix).

Sofa, The, the name of Bk. I of Cowper's 'The Task' (q.v.). Also the name of a licentious oriental romance by Crébillon the younger (published in 1740): a courtier of the Sultan Shahbahan relates the experiences of a sofa into which his soul has passed in the course of its transmigrations. In the early days of its use in the West the word was always spelt 'sopha'. It is from the Arabic *suffah*, a bench.

Sofronia or **SOPHRONIA,** a character in Tasso's 'Jerusalem Delivered' (q.v.).

Soho, a district of London, the centre of an Italian and French colony. The origin of the name is unknown. The traditional derivations are recorded in E. Walford, 'Old and New London' (1891, iii. 174). It was once a fashionable quarter. James, duke of Monmouth, had a house there, and gave 'Soho' as the watchword on the night before Sedgemoor. Dryden, Evelyn, Burnet, and alderman Beckford resided there.

Sohrab and Rustum, a poem by M. Arnold (q.v.), published in 1853.

Sohrab was a son of the Persian hero, Rustum (see *Rustem*). Unknown to his father (who had been told that his child was a girl), Sohrab has joined the Tartar forces of Afrasiab, and gained great renown for his prowess. The Tartar host is attacking the Persians, and Sohrab challenges the bravest of the Persian lords to meet him in single combat. Rustum, now an old man, but still their greatest warrior, answers the challenge, but he does not know that Sohrab is his son, nor does Sohrab know that he is fighting with his father, until the old man, at a crisis of the struggle, shouts 'Rustum'. His son recoils at the name, and is struck down. Before dying, he reveals to Rustum that he has killed his son.

Soldan, THE, from the Arabic *sulṭān,* the supreme ruler of one of the great Muslim powers or countries of the Middle Ages, especially the Sultan of Egypt. The name Sultan first appears in the sense of 'Captain of the Bodyguard' of the caliph of Baghdad about 1050.

The *Soldan* or *Souldan* in Spenser's 'Faerie Queene', v. viii, represents Philip II of Spain. He is encountered by Prince Arthur and Sir Artegall with a bold defiance from Queen Mercilla (Elizabeth), and the combat is undecided until the prince unveils his shield and terrifies the Soldan's horses, so that they overturn his chariot and the Soldan is torn 'all to rags'. The unveiling of the shield signifies divine interposition.

Solecism, an impropriety or irregularity in speech, diction, or manners; from a Greek word meaning barbarous, stated by ancient writers to refer to the corruption of the Attic dialect among the Athenian colonists of Soloi in Cilicia.

Solemn League and Covenant, see *Covenant.*

Solifidian, one who holds that faith alone, without works, is sufficient for justification.

Solomon, a great and wealthy king of Israel (10th cent. B.C.), son of David and Bathsheba, famous as the builder of the Temple and for his wisdom, illustrated by his judgement in the dispute about the child (1 Kings iii. 16–28). He is credited in oriental legend with power over the jinn.

Solomon Daisy, in Dickens's 'Barnaby Rudge' (q.v.), the parish clerk and bell-ringer at Chigwell.

Solomon Eagle, a crazy fanatic in Ainsworth's 'Old St. Paul's'.

Solomon Pell, in Dickens's 'The Pickwick Papers' (q.v.), an attorney occupied with affairs of the Insolvent Court.

Solomon's carpet, see *Carpet.*

Solomon's House, see *New Atlantis.*

SOLOMONS, IKEY, JUNIOR, the pseudonym under which Thackeray wrote 'Catherine' (q.v.).

Solon (*c.* 638–558 B.C.), the great Athenian legislator, celebrated for his wisdom. He was appointed archon in 594 B.C., and relieved the prevalent distress by his famous ordinance cancelling outstanding debts (σεισάχθεια). He reformed the constitution, introducing some democratic features. The constitution that he set up was overthrown by Peisistratus. Solon was also a successful poet, who used elegy to stir the Athenians to war and also to convey moral instruction. See also *Croesus.*

Solvejg, in Ibsen's 'Peer Gynt' (q.v.), the hero's good angel.

***Solyman and Perseda,** The Tragedye of,* see *Kyd.*

Solymean, of or belonging to Jerusalem. 'Solymean rout' is used in Dryden's 'Absalom and Achitophel' (q.v.) for the London mob.

Soma, in Vedic mythology, the intoxicating juice of a plant, supposed to be *Asclepias Acida,* and the god who dwells in it, the Hindu Bacchus.

Somerset House, London, takes its name from the palace built on the same site by the duke of Somerset, the lord protector (1506?–52). This reverted to the Crown when Somerset was beheaded, and, after being enlarged and improved by Inigo Jones, became the palace of a succession of queens. It was demolished at the end of the 18th cent. and replaced by the present building (designed by Sir William Chambers, 1726–96), in which are housed the offices of the Revenue Department, the principal Probate Registry, and the registrar-general of Births, Marriages, and Deaths.

SOMERVILLE, EDITH ŒNONE (1858–1949), Irish novelist, who collaborated with her cousin Violet Martin ('Martin Ross') (1862–1915) in a series of admirable tales of Irish life, some humorous, some tragic, beginning with 'Some Experiences of an Irish R.M.' (1890), followed by 'Further Experiences' (1908), 'Some Irish Yesterdays' (1906), etc.

SOMERVILLE, WILLIAM (1675–1742), educated at Winchester and New College, Oxford, of which he became a fellow, was author of 'The Chace' (1735), a poem consisting of four books of Miltonic blank verse, which treats of hounds and kennels, hare-hunting, fox-hunting, and otter-hunting, with literary digressions on oriental methods of the chase. In 1742 appeared his 'Field Sports', a short poem on hawking; and in 1740 'Hobbinol', a mock-heroic account of rural games in Gloucestershire.

Somnium Scipionis, from Bk. VI of Cicero's 'de Republica', preserved for us in the commentary of Macrobius (Cicero's text is lost), is a narrative placed in the mouth of the younger Scipio Africanus. He relates a visit to the court of Masinissa, on which occasion there was much talk of the first great Scipio. When the younger Scipio retired to rest, the shade of the elder appeared to him in a dream, foretold the future of his life, and exhorted him to virtue, patriotism, and the disregard of human fame, as the path leading to reward in a future life, the nature of which is indicated.

The 'Somnium Scipionis' is largely based on the fable of Er, the son of Arminius, in Plato's 'Republic'. A poetical summary of it occurs in Chaucer's 'Parlement of Fowles', and it is referred to by him in other passages.

Sompnour's or *Summoner's Tale, The,* see *Canterbury Tales.*

Song of Solomon, The, otherwise 'The Song of Songs', one of the poetical books of the O.T., at one time attributed to the authorship of King Solomon, now considered, on linguistic grounds, to be of later date, perhaps of the 4th or 3rd cent. B.C.

The allegorical interpretation of the poem is now generally abandoned, and it is regarded as a love drama, in which three characters are presented, the woman constant to her beloved, the beloved, and the king.

Song of the Shirt, The, a poem by T. Hood (q.v.), published in the Christmas number of 'Punch' for the year 1843; one of Hood's best-known poems, presenting a picture of the overworked and underpaid sempstress.

Song of the Three Holy Children, The, a portion of the Book of Daniel regarded as apocryphal, purporting to be the prayer and song sung by the three Jews in Nebuchadnezzar's fiery furnace. The latter part figures as the 'Benedicite' in the order for Morning Prayer of the Anglican Church.

Song to David, see *Smart.*

Songs before Sunrise, see *Swinburne.*

Songs of Experience, and *of Innocence,* see *Blake.*

Sonnet, a poem consisting of fourteen lines (of eleven syllables in Italian, generally twelve in French, and ten in English), with rhymes arranged according to one or other of certain definite schemes, of which the Petrarchan and the Elizabethan are the principal, viz.: (1) a b b a a b b a, followed by two, or three, other rhymes in the remaining six lines, with a pause in the thought after the octave (not always observed by English imitators, of whom Milton and Wordsworth are prominent examples); (2) a b a b c d c d e f e f g g. The sonnets of Shakespeare are in the latter form.

Sonnets from the Portuguese, a series of sonnets by E. B. Browning (q.v.), published in 1850, inspired by passionate devotion to her husband. The Portuguese prototypes were probably Camoëns' sonnets to Catarina, one of which is alluded to in Mrs. Browning's poem 'Catarina to Camoëns'. The so-called Reading edition, 1847, has been shown (Carter and Pollard, 'An Enquiry into the Nature of certain Nineteenth Century Pamphlets', 1934) to be spurious.

Sonnets of Shakespeare, The, were printed in 1609, but were probably written, the bulk of them between 1593 and 1596, the remainder before 1600. Most of them trace the course of the writer's affection for a young patron of rank and beauty, and may be addressed to William Lord Herbert, afterwards earl of Pembroke, or Henry Wriothesley, earl of Southampton. The publisher, Thomas Thorpe, issued the 'Sonnets' in 1609 with a dedication to 'Mr. W. H., the onlie begetter of these ensuing sonnets' (who, if he was not one of the persons above-named, was perhaps some friend of Thorpe, through whose good offices the manuscript had reached his hands, 'begetter' being used in the sense of 'getter' or 'procurer'). Other characters are alluded to who evidently played a real part in Shakespeare's life, a stolen mistress (40–42), a rival poet (83–86), a dark beauty loved by the author (127 et seq.).

For the form of these poems see *Sonnet.*

Sophia, St., the name of the principal church of Constantinople, built by the Emperor Justinian (532–7), in place of an earlier church built by Constantine and destroyed by fire. The architect was Anthemius of Tralles. Justinian worked at it in a mason's apron with his own hands, and when it was finished in five years exclaimed, 'I have beaten Solomon!' It was dedicated to HAGIA SOPHIA, the Divine Wisdom. On the capture of Constantinople by the Turks (1453) it was converted into a mosque.

Sophia Western, the heroine of Fielding's 'Tom Jones' (q.v.).

Sophism, a specious but fallacious argument, used either deliberately to mislead or to display ingenuity in reasoning.

Sophist, in ancient Greece, one who undertook to give instruction in intellectual and ethical matters in return for payment; contrasted with 'philosopher', and frequently used as a term of disparagement.

SOPHOCLES (496–406 B.C.), one of the three great Attic tragedians, was born at Colonus near Athens. His first victory as a tragic poet was in 468 B.C., when he won the prize against Aeschylus. After this he was the favourite poet of the Athenians. He was the first to increase the number of actors from two to three. His tragedies are more human, less heroic, than those of Aeschylus. He is 'pre-eminently the dramatist of human character' (Jebb); but he differed from Euripides, to use his own words, in representing men as they ought to be, while Euripides exhibited them as they are. He is the most effective of the three poets as a dramatist, both by his use of tragic contrast in his situations and by his gift of depicting character. His extant plays are: 'Oedipus the King', 'Oedipus at Colonus', 'Antigone', 'Electra', 'Trachiniae' (on the death of Hercules), 'Ajax', and 'Philoctetes'. M. Arnold describes him as one 'who saw life steadily and saw it whole'. Shelley had a volume of Sophocles in his pocket when he was drowned.

Sophonisba, daughter of Hasdrubal, a Carthaginian general. She was betrothed in early life to Masinissa, the Nubian prince; but her father, in order to gain the alliance of Syphax, married her to the latter. Masinissa, fighting in alliance with the Romans under Scipio, defeated Syphax and captured his capital, Cirta, with Sophonisba. Masinissa decided now to marry Sophonisba, but was ordered by Scipio (who dreaded her pro-Carthaginian influence on Masinissa) to surrender her. Masinissa, to save her from captivity, sent her a bowl of poison, which she voluntarily drank, and died.

The story has been made the subject of various plays, notably by Marston (q.v.) in his 'Sophonisba' (printed in 1606), where, however, considerable liberties are taken with the facts; also by Lee (1676) and Thomson (1730); and by Corneille.

The line 'Oh! Sophonisba, Sophonisba, Oh!' is from 'The Tragedy of Sophonisba', 1730 (III. ii), by James Thomson (q.v., 1700–48). The line, 'Oh, Sophonisba, I am wholly thine', was substituted some time after 1738. The earlier text was parodied by Fielding in his 'Tom Thumb'—'O Huncamunca, Huncamunca O!' Johnson ('Lives of the Poets') quotes the burlesque 'O Jemmy Thomson! Jemmy Thomson, O!'

Sophronia, see *Sofronia*.

Sophy, THE, a former title of the supreme ruler of Persia. It was the surname of the ruling dynasty from *c.* 1500 to 1736, derived from an Arabic epithet meaning 'purity of religion'.

Sophy Crewler, in Dickens's 'David Copperfield' (q.v.), 'the dearest girl in the world', whom Traddles marries.

Soracte, a mountain of Etruria, visible from Rome, sacred to Apollo. 'Vides ut alta stet nive candidum Soracte'. Horace, 'Odes', I. ix.

Sorbonne, THE, a theological college in Paris founded by Robert de Sorbon about 1257. The name was applied later to the faculty of theology in the old University of Paris, of great importance down to the 17th cent. The Sorbonne is now the seat of the University of Paris and of the faculties of science, literature, and the *hautes études*.

SORDELLO, a Provençal poet, born near Mantua about 1180, who became in popular tradition a hero of romance. Dante mentions him repeatedly in his 'Purgatorio'.

Sordello, a poem by R. Browning (q.v.), published in 1840.

The action takes place at the time of conflicts of the Guelphs and Ghibellines (*c.* 1200). Eccelino, lord of Vicenza, has been exiled from his city. In the affray on this occasion his wife, Adelaide, has been saved with her infant son by the archer, Elcorte. Retrude, wife of Eccelino's ally, Salinguerra, is also saved, but dies after giving birth to Sordello. Adelaide, to prevent his future rivalry with her son, passes Sordello off as the son of Elcorte and brings him up as her page, in the castle of Goito. He is gifted with an imaginative nature and devotes himself to a poetic, unreal life. His mental powers display themselves in his triumph as a poet over the

troubadour, Eglamor. At a crisis in the political struggle, his identity as the son of Salinguerra is revealed, and power and eminence come within his grasp. But he has a higher spiritual ideal and cannot bring himself, in spite of the love of the beautiful Palma, Eccelino's daughter, and the urging of Salinguerra, to accept the lower, practical course of action. In the struggle of decision, he dies.

But while the outline of the narrative is simple enough, 'Sordello', the story of the 'development of a soul', is in its details and allusions one of the most difficult of Browning's works to interpret.

SOREL, ALBERT (1842–1906), French historian, author of 'L'Europe et la Révolution française' (1885–1911), 'Histoire diplomatique de la guerre franco-allemande' (1875), 'Montesquieu' (1887), 'Madame de Staël' (1890), 'Bonaparte et Hoche en 1797' (1896), 'Essais d'histoire et de critique' (1894, 1898), and other works.

Sorrel, HETTY, a character in George Eliot's 'Adam Bede' (q.v.).

Sorrows of Werther, see *Goethe*.

Sortes Virgilianae, the attempt to foretell the future by opening a volume of Virgil at hazard and reading the first passage lit on.

Dr. Edward Lake's Diary (Camden Miscellany, vol. i) under date 29 Jan. 1677–8, records an instance of Charles I's having recourse to the *Sortes Virgilianae* and lighting on Dido's curse on Aeneas when he left her. The *Sortes* were also resorted to by Panurge (Rabelais, III. x) to decide whether he should marry or not. Many instances are there quoted of *Sortes Virgilianae* and *Homericae*. Vambéry mentions that the Persians use Hafiz (q.v.) for the same purpose; as do uneducated Christians the Bible.

Sosia, a character in Dryden's 'Amphitryon' (q.v.).

Sotadic, a satire after the manner of Sotades, an ancient Greek poet noted for the coarseness and scurrility of his writings. The word is also used of a line capable of being read in the reverse order, like a palindrome (q.v.).

Sotheby's, New Bond Street, London, saleroom for books, paintings, objets d'art, etc.

Sothic cycle or CANICULAR PERIOD, a period of 1,460 full years, containing 1,461 of the ancient Egyptian years of 365 days, which were computed from one heliacal rising of Sirius to the next. The term *Sothic* is derived from *Sothis*, an Egyptian name of *Sirius*, the Dog-star.

Soul's Tragedy, A, a drama by R. Browning (q.v.), in two parts, published in 1846; the first part in verse, the second in prose.

The drama treats humorously the 'tragedy' of the degradation of the soul of Chiappino, a citizen of Faenza in the 16th cent. He has been agitating against the tyrannical provost of the town and is sentenced to exile and confiscation of his property. His generous friend, Luitolfo, has struck the provost and thinks that he has killed him, and that he is pursued by the provost's forces. Chiappino, who has been ungenerously courting the woman that Luitolfo is to marry, shamed by his friend's devotion, seizes the latter's bloody cloak and goes out to face the pursuers and claim the deed as his own, only to find that the throng consists of the citizens of Faenza who acclaim him as their saviour. Here the tragedy of his soul begins, for he fails to undeceive the populace. It continues in the second part, when the pope's legate, arriving at Faenza, lures Chiappino on with the hope that he will be made provost, and finally exposes him.

Sousa's Band, a band organized in 1892 by John Philip Sousa (1854–1932), American composer and bandmaster of the U.S. Marine Corps. Sousa's band visited Europe in 1900–5 and became celebrated.

South, MARTY, a female character in Hardy's 'The Woodlanders' (q.v.).

SOUTH, ROBERT (1634–1716) educated at Christ Church, Oxford, a great court preacher favoured by Charles II. He was homely, pithy, and often very humorous in the pulpit. His 'Animadversions' (1690) contain a crushing attack on W. Sherlock (q.v.).

South Kensington Museum, see *Victoria and Albert Museum.*

South Sea Company, THE, was formed in 1711 by Harley (later earl of Oxford) to trade with Spanish America under the expected treaty with Spain. An exaggerated idea prevailed of the wealth to be acquired from the trading privileges granted by the Treaty of Utrecht and the Asiento Treaty, and money was readily invested in the Company. A bill was passed in 1720 by which persons to whom the nation owed money were enabled to convert their claims into shares in the Company, and the shares rose in value from £100 to £1,000. The Company shortly afterwards failed. But the scheme meanwhile had given rise to a fever of speculation, of which many unprincipled persons took advantage to obtain subscriptions from the public for the most impossible projects. The collapse of these and of the South Sea scheme caused widespread ruin. The whole affair was known as the SOUTH SEA BUBBLE. But the original idea of the South Sea Company was a sound one for perfectly honest trade.

The SOUTH-SEA HOUSE, where the Company had its offices, is the subject of one of Lamb's 'Essays of Elia' (q.v.).

Southcott, JOANNA (1750–1814), a religious fanatic, was a Devonshire farmer's daughter, who was for many years in domestic service. In 1792 she began to write doggerel prophecies and to claim supernatural gifts, and in time attracted a very large number of followers. In 1802 she affirmed that she would be de-livered of a spiritual being, called Shiloh. She died of brain disease, leaving a sealed box with directions that it should be opened at a time of national crisis in the presence of the assembled bishops. It was opened in 1927, one bishop being present, and was found to contain nothing of interest.

Southdown, COUNTESS OF, a character in Thackeray's 'Vanity Fair' (q.v.).

SOUTHERNE or **SOUTHERN, THOMAS** (1659–1746), of Irish parentage, was educated at Trinity College, Dublin, but spent his life in London, where he was the friend of Dryden, for several of whose plays he wrote prologues and epilogues. He wrote several comedies, but is chiefly remembered for his two tragedies, 'The Fatal Marriage' (q.v., 1694) and 'Oroonoko' (q.v., 1695), both founded on novels by Mrs. Behn (q.v.).

SOUTHEY, ROBERT (1774–1843), was the son of a Bristol linen-draper, of a respectable Somerset family. He was expelled from Westminster School for a precocious essay against flogging, and proceeded to Balliol College, Oxford. He made the acquaintance of S. T. Coleridge and joined in his scheme for a 'pantisocratic' settlement. He married Edith Fricker (d. 1837), whose sister became the wife of Coleridge, in 1795. He went to Portugal in the same year, and to Spain in 1800. He published 'Thalaba' (q.v.) in 1801, 'Madoc' (q.v.) in 1805, 'The Curse of Kehama' (q.v.) in 1810, 'Roderick, the Last of the Goths' (q.v.) in 1814, 'A Tale of Paraguay' in 1825, and 'All for Love' (q.v.) in 1829. He settled at Keswick, with the help of an annuity given him by his friend, Charles Wynn, which he relinquished on receiving in 1807 a government pension of about the same amount. He worked at translations from the Spanish, and in 1808 became a regular contributor to 'The Quarterly Review'. His 'Life of Nelson' was expanded from an article in 1813. In the same year he accepted the laureateship, which had been offered to Scott. His 'Wat Tyler', a short drama 'written in three days at Oxford' in 1794, was surreptitiously published in 1817, and in consequence of its crude political sentiments, Southey was attacked as 'a renegado' in the House of Commons. Southey's 'Life of Wesley' appeared in 1820 and his 'A Vision of Judgment' (q.v., parodied by Byron) in 1821. His miscellanies, 'Omniana' and 'The Doctor' (q.v.), were published in 1812 and 1834–47, and his standard 'Life' and edition of Cowper in 1833–7. In 1839 he contracted a second marriage with Caroline Bowles. From 1835 he enjoyed a pension of £300, granted by Peel.

Southey wrote an immense amount both of verse and prose. His longer poems are little read now, but were praised by contemporaries so diverse as Scott, Fox, and Macaulay, and admired even by Byron, who hated the author. He is now best known by some of his shorter pieces, such as 'My days among the dead are past', 'The Battle of

Blenheim', 'The Holly Tree,' and 'The Inchcape Rock'. He was successful in the lighter, comic, or supernatural grotesque style, e.g. in 'St. Michael's Chair', 'The Well of St. Keyne', and 'The Devil's Thoughts' (q.v.). Of his prose works, besides those above mentioned, the principal are his 'Lives of the British Admirals' (1833–40); the long and valuable 'History of Brazil' (1810–19), and the 'History of the Peninsular War' (1823–32), which proved less successful than that of Napier; his ecclesiastical writings, 'The Book of the Church' (1824) and 'Vindiciae Ecclesiae Anglicanae' (1826); his 'Sir Thomas More, Colloquies on the progress and prospects of Society' (1829), in which the author converses with the ghost of More; and 'Essays Moral and Political' (1832). The 'Letters of Espriella', a book of a lighter character, purporting to be the letters written from England by a young Spaniard at the beginning of the 19th cent. and giving a good picture of the times, was published in 1807. Southey did valuable work in revising the old translations of Amadis of Gaul (1803) and 'Palmerin of England' (1807), in translating the 'Chronicle of the Cid' (1808), and in editing Malory (1817). Excessive mental work, as well as domestic misfortunes, at last affected Southey's intellect, and he died of softening of the brain. He was an excellent letter-writer, and three editions of his voluminous correspondence, none of them complete, have been published, by his son in 1849–50, by his son-in-law in 1856, and by E. Dowden in 1881.

Southwark, the 'south work' or bridgehead at the south end of London Bridge, was at one time a royal 'burh' or citadel for the defence of London (hence Southwark is known as 'The Borough'). It certainly existed in Æthelred's time, and probably much earlier. It attracted traders by its privileges and became the great 'cheaping town' mentioned in the 'Heimskringla' (q.v.). It is specially famous in literary history on account of its ancient inns and theatres. The Tabard and the White Hart (qq.v.) inns were there, Burbage's 'Globe' theatre, and Henslowe's 'The Hope' and 'The Rose' (qq.v.). Gower lived within the precincts of the priory of Southwark and is buried in its church (see *Saviour's Church, St.*). In 1550 Edward VI granted the borough to the commonalty of London, and Southwark became a 'ward without' of the City.

SOUTHWELL, ROBERT (1561?–95), a member of an old Catholic family, was educated at Douai and Rome. He took Roman orders and came to England in 1586 with Henry Garnett (who was subsequently executed for complicity in the Gunpowder Plot). He became in 1589 domestic chaplain to the countess of Arundel, was captured when going to celebrate mass in 1592, repeatedly tortured, and executed after three years' imprisonment. His poems were mainly written in prison. Of these it was his object to make

spiritual love, instead of 'unworthy affections', the subject. His chief work was 'St. Peter's Complaint', published in 1595, a long narrative of the closing events of the life of Christ in the mouth of the repentant Peter, in which the spiritual is contrasted with the material by numerous comparisons and antitheses. He also wrote a 'Fourefould Meditation of the foure last things' (1606), and many shorter devotional poems (some of them collected under the title 'Maeoniae', 1595) of a high order, notably 'The Burning Babe', praised by Ben Jonson.

Sowdone of Babylon, see *Ferumbras.*

Sowerberry, in Dickens's 'Oliver Twist' (q.v.), an undertaker, to whom Oliver is apprenticed when he leaves the workhouse.

Sowerby, MR., a character in A. Trollope's 'Framley Parsonage' (q.v.).

Sowerby, THE HON. DUDLEY, a character in Meredith's 'One of our Conquerors' (q.v.).

Spagyric, a term used and probably invented by Paracelsus (q.v.), the science of alchemy or chemistry; also, an alchemist.

SPALDING, JOHN (*fl.* 1650), of Aberdeen, a Scottish historian, author of the valuable 'Memorials of the Troubles in Scotland and England' from 1624 to 1645 (first published in 1792). He is commemorated in the Spalding Club, devoted to the historical literature of northern Scotland.

Spanish Bawd, The, see *Celestina.*

Spanish Curate, The, a comedy by J. Fletcher (q.v.) and probably Massinger (q.v.), composed and produced in 1622.

The main plot deals with the intrigues of Don Henrique's mistress, Violante, the failure of which leads to the reconciliation of Don Henrique with his divorced wife, Jacinta, and his brother, Don Jamie; while Violante is consigned to a nunnery. In the underplot, from which the play takes its name, Leandro, a rich young gentleman, plays on the cupidity of a priest and his sexton, and, with their help, on that of the lawyer Bartolus, the jealous husband of a beautiful wife, Amaranta, to get facilities for an intrigue with the latter.

Spanish Fryar, The, a comedy by Dryden (q.v.).

Spanish Gipsy, The, a romantic comedy by T. Middleton and W. Rowley (qq.v.), acted in 1623 and printed in 1653. It is based on two novels by Cervantes.

Of the two interwoven plots, that from which the play takes its name presents the romance of Pretiosa, daughter of the corregidor of Madrid, who has been carried away as a child by Alvarez, a fugitive from justice and brother-in-law of the corregidor, to live with his friends a gipsy life. The gipsies come to Madrid, where the beauty of Pretiosa attracts admiration. Her lover joins the gipsies, and these act a play at the house of the corregidor. Their identity is discovered, and Pretiosa is restored to her father and married to her lover. Longfellow, in one of his dramas, 'The Spanish Student', adapted much of this, including the name Pretiosa.

Spanish Gipsy, The, a dramatic poem by G. Eliot (q.v.), published in 1868.

Spanish Main, THE, the mainland of America adjacent to the Caribbean Sea, especially that portion of the coast stretching from the Isthmus of Panama to the mouth of the Orinoco. In later use, also, the sea contiguous to this, or the route traversed by the Spanish register ships (i.e. Spanish ships licensed to trade with the Spanish possessions in America).

Spanish Tragedy, The, a tragedy in blank verse by Kyd (q.v.), acted 1592, printed 1594.

The political background of the play is the victory of Spain over Portugal in 1580. Lorenzo and Bel-imperia are son and daughter of Don Cyprian, Duke of Castile (brother of the king of Spain); Hieronimo is marshal of Spain, and Horatio his son. Balthazar is son of the viceroy of Portugal and has been taken prisoner by Lorenzo and Horatio in the war. He courts Bel-imperia, and his suit is favoured by Lorenzo, and by the king of Spain for political reasons. Lorenzo and Balthazar discover that Bel-imperia loves Horatio, and come upon them at night in Hieronimo's arbour, where they kill Horatio and hang him to a tree. Hieronimo coming out and finding his son dead is frantic with grief. He discovers who the murderers are and plots with Bel-imperia their destruction. For this purpose he engages them to act with Bel-imperia and him, before the court, a play that suits his revengeful purpose. In the course of this Lorenzo and Balthazar are killed, Bel-imperia stabs herself, and Hieronimo takes his own life.

Interpolations were made in the play as originally written, probably by Ben Jonson, and the play as revised was very popular, though ridiculed by writers of the time. Charles Lamb declared that certain of these interpolations were the 'very salt of the old play'. He thought that nothing written by Jonson warranted us in attributing them to him; 'I should suspect the agency of some more potent spirit. Webster might have furnished them.' The interpolations in question are given in Lamb's 'Specimens of English Dramatic Writers'.

Sparkish, a character in Wycherley's 'The Country Wife' (q.v.).

Sparkler, EDMUND, a character in Dickens's 'Little Dorrit' (q.v.), who marries Fanny, Little Dorrit's sister.

Sparsit, MRS., a character in Dickens's 'Hard Times' (q.v.), Bounderby's intriguing housekeeper.

Spartan, an inhabitant of Sparta, the capital of the ancient Doric state of Laconia in the Peloponnesus. The Spartan characteristics, to which the adjective in modern use refers, were simplicity, frugality, fortitude, discipline, and brevity of speech. Cf. 'Laconic'.

SPARTAN DOG, a kind of bloodhound (cf. Shakespeare, 'A Midsummer Night's Dream', IV. i. 116).

Spasmodic School, a term applied by Aytoun (q.v.) to a group of poets chiefly represented by P. J. Bailey, Dobell, and Alexander Smith (qq.v.).

Spectator, The, a periodical conducted by R. Steele (q.v.) and Addison (q.v.) from 1 Mar. 1711 to 6 Dec. 1712. It was revived by Addison in 1714, when eighty numbers were issued. 'The Spectator' was the successor of 'The Tatler' (q.v.). It appeared daily. Addison and Steele were the principal contributors, in about equal proportions. Other contributors were Pope, Tickell, Eustace Budgell, Ambrose Philips, and Eusden (qq.v.).

It purported to be conducted (see the first two numbers) by a small club, including Sir Roger de Coverley, who represents the country gentry; Sir Andrew Freeport, Capt. Sentry, and Will Honeycomb, representing respectively commerce, the army, and the town. Mr. Spectator himself, who writes the papers, is a man of travel and learning, who frequents London as an observer, but keeps clear of political strife. The papers are mainly concerned with manners, morals, and literature. Their object is 'to enliven morality with wit, and to temper wit with morality'. Among their pleasantest features are the character sketches, notably in the Coverley papers, and the short stories or episodes, which frequently take the form of letters purporting to be addressed to the editor. Readers of 'Esmond' will remember the faked 'Spectator' which appeared on Beatrix's breakfast-table.

Spectator, The, a weekly periodical started in 1828 by Robert Stephen Rintoul, with funds provided by Joseph Hume and others, as an organ of 'educated radicalism'. It supported Lord John Russell's reform bill of 1831 with a demand for 'the Bill, the whole Bill, and nothing but the Bill'. R. H. Hutton (q.v.) was joint-editor, 1861–97.

Speculum Meditantis or **Mirour de l'Omme,** a didactic poem of 30,000 lines in French by Gower (q.v.).

It relates the contest for the possession of man between the seven vices (with their offspring, such as arrogance and hypocrisy) and the seven virtues, all described at great length. To ascertain who has gained the victory, the author reviews every estate of man, and all are found corrupt. Man must therefore have recourse to the mercy of the Virgin, who will intercede for him. The poem concludes with the Gospel narrative. The description of the estates of man presents a valuable picture of contemporary society.

SPEDDING, JAMES (1808–81), educated at Bury St. Edmunds and Trinity College,

Cambridge, published an edition of Bacon's 'Works' in 1857–9, followed by his 'Life and Letters' (1861–74). His 'Evenings with a Reviewer, or Macaulay and Bacon' (1848) was a refutation, subsequently developed in the greater work, of Macaulay's 'Essay' on Bacon.

SPEED, JOHN (1552?–1629), historian and cartographer, was brought up as a tailor by his father. He settled in Moorfields, London, and obtained a post in the custom-house in 1598. He made various maps of English counties, and was encouraged by Camden, Cotton, and others to write his 'Historie of Great Britaine' (1611). The maps were far more valuable than the history; they began about 1607 and an atlas of them appeared in 1611. There were several later editions of this (called 'The Theatre of the Empire of Great Britain') and the maps are now constantly detached and sold separately.

Speed the Plough, a play by T. Morton (q.v.), produced in 1798.

Sir Philip Blandford, finding that his brother has supplanted him in the affections of the woman he was about to marry, stabs the brother, leaves him for dead, quits the country, and ruins himself by gambling. The brother's child, Henry, the hero of the play, brought up in ignorance of his parentage by a neighbouring farmer, Ashfield, is the object of Sir Philip's hatred. But on the latter's return home, twenty years later, his daughter Emma falls in love with this Henry, who moreover saves her life when the house is burnt down. And Henry's father, who has in fact survived full of remorse, now reveals himself as the restorer of his brother's fortunes. So reconciliation follows and all ends well.

Sir Abel Handy with his shrewish wife and breezy son, and the Ashfield couple, provide some amusement. Mrs. Grundy, who has since become the symbol of the British idea of propriety, is a neighbour and obsession of Dame Ashfield, who constantly refers to her, wondering what Mrs. Grundy will think or say. But Mrs. Grundy herself, a sort of Mrs. Harris, never appears.

Speenhamland System, a system of poor relief adopted by the magistrates of Berkshire at a meeting held on 6 May 1795 at Speenhamland (now part of Newbury), to improve the miserable condition of labourers, the result of the insufficiency of agricultural wages. By this system, which was widely adopted by other counties, an allowance was granted 'for the relief of all poor and industrious men and their families' who endeavoured to the satisfaction of the Justices of their parish to support themselves, this allowance being calculated according to the price of flour, so that the man should have, from his wages and the allowance, the equivalent of three gallon loaves a week, and his wife and each child the equivalent of one and a half. The effect was to pauperize the labouring population, and to relieve the employer at the expense of the rates (see J. L. and Barbara Hammond, 'The Village Labourer').

SPEKE, JOHN HANNING (1827–64), explorer, set out under (Sir) Richard Burton (q.v.) in 1856 to investigate Lake Nyasa, and discovered Lake Tanganyika and Victoria Nyanza. He published in 1863 his 'Journal of the Discovery of the Source of the Nile'. He furnished information to (Sir) Samuel Baker (q.v.), which enabled him to discover the third lake, Albert Nyanza.

Spence's Anecdotes, the reminiscences of Joseph Spence (1699–1768), Pope's friend, which although not published until 1820 were well known and widely quoted during the 18th cent.

SPENCER, HERBERT (1820–1903), trained as an engineer, gave up this profession early and devoted himself to philosophical study and writing. He published 'Social Statics' in 1851, 'Principles of Psychology' in 1855, and in 1860 his 'Programme of a System of Synthetic Philosophy', to the elaboration of which he consecrated the remainder of his life. 'First Principles' appeared in 1862, 'Principles of Biology' (1864–7), 'Principles of Psychology' (a recast of the earlier work, 1870–2), 'Principles of Sociology' (1876–96), and 'Principles of Ethics' (1879–93). Among his other works were 'Education' (1861, see below), 'The Classification of the Sciences' (1864), 'The Study of Sociology' (1873), 'The Man versus The State' (1884), and 'Factors of Organic Evolution' (1887). His 'Autobiography' was published in 1904.

Spencer was the founder of evolutionary philosophy, pursuing the unification of all knowledge on the basis of a single all-pervading principle, that of evolution. All our notions are derived from experiences of Force, a persistent inscrutable power behind phenomena. From the persistence of force are deducible various principles, such as the transformation and equivalence of all forces whether physical or mental, and finally the Law of Evolution, which can also be obtained inductively from phenomena, and to which all phenomena are subject. This law he defines as follows: 'an integration of matter and concomitant dissipation of emotion; during which matter passes from an indefinite incoherent homogeneity to a definite coherent heterogeneity; and during which the retained motion undergoes a parallel transformation'. The process continues until equilibrium is reached, after which the action of the environment will in time bring about disintegration. The law holds good of the visible universe as well as of smaller aggregates, suggesting the conception of past and future evolutions, such as that which is now proceeding. But Spencer recognized the insolubility of the ultimate riddle of the universe.

This theory of a physical system leads up to Spencer's ethical system, to which in his mind all else was subordinated. But here he is less successful in producing a self-consistent whole. For Spencer was essentially an individualist, and his first ethical principle is the equal right of every individual to act as he likes, so long as he does not interfere with the similar liberty of other individuals. His effort is to reconcile utilitarian with evolutionary ethics, and in his 'Data of Ethics' (the first part of his 'Sociology') we have morality treated in its biological and evolutionary aspect, and the conciliation of altruism with egoism explained. But Spencer had to confess that for the purpose of deducing ethical principles 'the Doctrine of Evolution has not furnished guidance to the extent I had hoped'.

Special reference must be made to his 'Education, Intellectual, Moral, and Physical' (1861), a collection of articles previously published in magazines, in which Spencer showed a frank contempt for the humanities, and urged that science should be made the principal instrument of education. Parts of the work proved valuable and have influenced subsequent practice. It had a wide vogue a'.d was translated into many languages.

Spencer has been diversely judged. Carlyle called him 'the most immeasurable ass in Christendom'.

SPENDER, STEPHEN (1909–   ), poet and critic. His father, E. H. Spender, was a distinguished liberal journalist, and on his mother's side he was partly of German–Jewish descent. He was educated at University College, Oxford. After leaving Oxford he lived in Germany for a period and during the Spanish Civil War did propaganda work in Spain for the Republican side. During the Second World War he was a member of the National Fire Service. Since the war he has lectured in America and is joint editor of the magazine 'Encounter'. His work includes 'Collected Poems' (1954), a verse play, 'Trial of a Judge' (1938), political and literary studies such as 'Forward from Liberalism' (1937), 'Life and the Poet' (1942), 'The Destructive Element' (1935), 'The Creative Element' (1953), 'The Struggle of the Modern' (1963), and an autobiography, 'World within World' (1951).

Spenlow, DORA, in Dickens's 'David Copperfield' (q.v.), the hero's 'child-wife'.

Spenlow and Jorkins, in Dickens's 'David Copperfield' (q.v.), a firm of proctors in Doctors' Commons, to whom Copperfield is articled. Jorkins is a gentle, retiring man who seldom appears, but Spenlow makes his supposed intractable character the ground for refusing any inconvenient request.

Spens, *Sir Patrick,* the title of an old Scottish ballad, on the subject of the dispatch of Sir Patrick to sea, on a mission for the king, in winter; of his foreboding of disaster; and of his destruction with his ship's company. The ballad is in Percy's 'Reliques'. Scott, in his version, makes the object of the mission the

bringing to Scotland of the Maid of Norway (q.v.).

SPENSER, EDMUND (1552?–99), was the elder son of John Spenser, who was probably related to the Spencers of Althorp, and was described as a gentleman and journeyman in the art of cloth-making. Edmund Spenser was born probably in East Smithfield, London, and was educated at Merchant Taylors' School and Pembroke Hall, Cambridge. While still at Cambridge, he contributed in 1569 a number of 'Visions' and sonnets (from Petrarch and Du Bellay) to an edifying 'Theatre for Worldlings'. To his 'green youth' also belong the 'Hymnes in honour of Love and Beautie' (not published till 1596), which reflect the Platonic influence, being the adaptation of ideas drawn from the 'Symposium'. Spenser obtained in 1578, through his college friend, G. Harvey (q.v.), a place in Leicester's household, and became, through Leicester, acquainted with Sir Philip Sidney (q.v.). With Sidney, Dyer, and others, he formed a literary club styled the 'Areopagus'. In 1579 he began 'The Faerie Queene' (q.v.). and published his 'The Shepheards Calender' (q.v.), which was enthusiastically received. In 1580 he was appointed secretary to Lord Grey de Wilton, then going to Ireland as lord deputy. In 1586 he became one of the 'undertakers' for the settlement of Munster, and acquired Kilcolman Castle in county Cork. Here he settled and occupied himself with literary work, writing his elegy 'Astrophel' (q.v.) on Sir Philip Sidney, and preparing 'The Faerie Queene' for the press, three books of this work being entrusted to the printer on the poet's visit to London in 1589. He reluctantly returned to Kilcolman, which he regarded as a place of exile, in 1591, and penned 'Colin Clouts come home againe' (q.v., printed 1595). The reputation of 'The Faerie Queene' led the printer, Ponsonby, to issue in 1591 his minor verse and *juvenilia*, in part re-written as 'Complaints, containing sundrie small poems of the worlds vanitie'. This includes 'The Ruines of Time', which is in fact a further elegy on Sir Philip Sidney, dedicated to his sister, the countess of Pembroke. In 1591 appeared his 'Daphnaïda', an elegy on Douglas Howard, the daughter of Lord Byndon and wife of Sir Arthur Gorges (see *Alcyon*). In 1594 Spenser married Elizabeth Boyle, whom he had wooed in his 'Amoretti', and possibly celebrated the marriage in his splendid 'Epithalamion' (the two were printed together in 1595). He published the second instalment of three books of 'The Faerie Queene' and 'Foure Hymnes' in 1596, being in London for the purpose at the house of his friend, the earl of Essex, where he wrote his 'Prothalamion' (q.v.), and also his well-informed, though one-sided, prose 'View of the Present State of Ireland'. He returned to Kilcolman, depressed both in mind and health, in 1597. His castle of Kilcolman was burnt. October 1598, in a sudden insurrection of the natives, chiefly O'Neills, under the earl of Desmond; on which, with his wife and four children, he was compelled to flee for refuge to Cork. Lost books of 'The Faerie Queene' were probably burnt in the castle. He died in London in distress, if not actual destitution, at a lodging in King Street, Westminster, and was buried near his favourite Chaucer in Westminster Abbey, the expenses of the funeral being borne by the earl of Essex.

Spenserian stanza, the stanza invented by Edmund Spenser (q.v.), in which he wrote 'The Faerie Queene'. It consists of eight five-foot iambic lines, followed by an iambic line of six feet, rhyming a b a b b c b c c.

Sphinx, THE, in Greek legend, a monster represented generally with a woman's bust on a lion's body. It frequented the neighbourhood of Thebes, propounded enigmas and devoured the inhabitants if these were unable to explain them. The Thebans were told by an oracle that the Sphinx would destroy herself as soon as one of her riddles was explained. The Sphinx now asked what animal walked on four legs in the morning, two at noon, and three in the evening. Creon, regent of Thebes, promised the kingdom and his sister Jocasta in marriage to whoever should solve the riddle. This was done by Oedipus (q.v.), who observed that man walked on all fours when a child, erect in the noon of life, and supported by a stick in old age. The Sphinx on hearing this answer killed herself in disgust.

The legend appears to have come from Egypt, where, however, the Sphinx is a male creature, representing the god Horus. The most famous figure of the Sphinx is near the Great Pyramid at Ghizeh, Egypt.

Spider, BRUCE AND THE, see *Bruce and the Spider.*

SPINOZA, BENEDICT (BARUCH) DE (1632–77), a Jew of Portuguese origin, born at Amsterdam, who lived there and at The Hague. He was expelled from the Jewish community on account of his criticism of the Scriptures. The principal source of his philosophy was the doctrine of Descartes, transformed by a mind steeped in the Jewish Scriptures. Spinoza rejected the Cartesian dualism of spirit and matter, and saw only 'one infinite substance, of which finite existences are modes or limitations'. The universe must be viewed 'sub specie aeternitatis', and the errors of sense and the illusions of the finite eliminated. God for him is the immanent cause of the universe, not a ruler outside it. 'By the government of God, I understand the fixed and unalterable order of nature and the interconnection of natural things.' His system is thus in a sense pantheistic. Among his conclusions are determinism, a denial of the transcendent distinction between good and evil, and a denial of personal immortality.

Spinoza's famous 'Ethics', finished about 1665, was not published until 1677, after his death. His morality is founded on the 'intellectual love' of God. Man is moved by his instinct to develop and perfect himself, and to seek this development in the knowledge and love of God. And the love of God involves the love of our fellow creatures. It is by goodness and piety that man reaches perfect happiness: virtue is its own reward.

Spinoza founds his political doctrine on man's natural rights. Man, in order to obtain security, has surrendered part of his rights to the State. But the State exists to give liberty, not to hold in slavery. The sovereign in his own interest must rule with justice and wisdom, nor must the State interfere with freedom of thought. Spinoza's 'Tractatus Theologico-politicus' was published in 1670; his unfinished 'Tractatus Politicus' in 1677.

Spirit of Patriotism, A Letter on the, a political treatise by Viscount Bolingbroke (q.v.), written in 1736 and addressed to Lord Lyttelton. It was published in 1749.

Written in retirement at Chanteloup, it represents Bolingbroke's final attitude in political affairs. The author attributes the misfortunes of the country to the servility of the opposition, which has made possible the spread of corruption and the tyranny of the Whig ministry. The opposition should address itself to the reform of the State, not merely to the reform of the administration, so as to secure that government shall not become absolute.

Spiritual Exercises, see *Loyola.*

Spiritual Quixote, The, or the Summer's Ramble of Mr. Geoffry Wildgoose, a novel by Richard Graves (q.v.), published in 1772.

Geoffry Wildgoose, a young man of good position in the Cotswold country, having imbibed the doctrines of the Methodists, sets forth, accompanied by his Sancho Panza, Jerry Tugwell, the village cobbler, to preach those doctrines about the Midlands. Their undertaking involves them in ludicrous incidents and gives occasion for episodic tales, and for much satire of Whitefield, and in a milder degree of the Methodists in general. The book throws light on the life of the roads and inns in the 18th cent. And there is a pleasant sketch of Shenstone (q.v) and the Leasowes.

Spital sermon or SPITTLE SERMON, one of the sermons formerly preached on Easter Monday and Tuesday from a special pulpit at St. Mary Spital outside Bishopsgate (afterwards at other churches).

Spitalfields, London, a district that takes its name from having been the property of the Priory and Hospital of St. Mary, founded by Walter Brune and Rosia his wife for Canons regular in 1197. This hospital, when surrendered to Henry VIII, contained 180 beds, well furnished; 'for it was an Hospitall of great relief' (Stow). French Protestant silk-weavers settled in this district after the revocation of the Edict of Nantes, and really founded our silk industry, which has now lost much of its importance. Among the ironies of religious history ·is that the white silk cassock of the popes continued to be woven by these Protestants till the last quarter of the 19th cent.

Spleen, *The,* see *Green (Matthew).*

Splendid Shilling, *The,* a burlesque poem by J. Philips (q.v.), published in 1705.

The poet sings in Miltonic verse, with much show of classical learning, the contrast between the happy possessor of the splendid shilling, who

> nor hears with pain
> New oysters cry'd, nor sighs for chearful
>   ale

and the penurious poet in his garret, hungry and thirsty, smoking 'Mundungus, ill-perfuming scent', inditing mournful verse of

> desp'rate lady near a purling stream
> Or lover pendent on a willow tree,

and threatened by creditors and catchpoles.

Spondee, a metrical foot composed of two long syllables.

Sponge, MR., the hero of 'Mr. Sponge's Sporting Tour' by R. S. Surtees (q.v.), published in 1853, with pictures by Leech, one of the best of the author's hunting novels.

Spoonerism, see *Metathesis.*

Sports, THE BOOK OF DECLARATION OF, an order issued by James I in 1617 defining for the use of Lancashire the recreations that were permissible on Sunday. These included archery and dancing, but not bear- and bull-baiting, nor bowls. An attempt to extend the order to the whole kingdom in 1618 proved ineffectual. Charles I directed, in 1633, that it should be read in all pulpits, and this was a gratuitous insult to the Puritans. Many clergy, whose austerity was opposed to any games on Sunday, were deprived in consequence.

Sporus, the name under which Pope (q.v.) satirizes Lord Hervey (q.v.) in his 'Epistle to Dr. Arbuthnot' (ll. 305 et seq.). The original Sporus was an effeminate favourite of the Emperor Nero.

Sprat, JACK, see *Jack Sprat.*

SPRAT, THOMAS (1635–1713), educated at Wadham College, Oxford, was bishop of Rochester and dean of Westminster. He sat on James II's objectionable Ecclesiastical Commission in 1686 and allowed the Declaration of Indulgence to be read (amid deep murmurs of disapproval) in the abbey—in short, he was inclined to be a 'Vicar of Bray'. He is remembered for his history of the Royal Society (q.v.), of which he was one of the first fellows. He wrote well, and is

thought to have had a share in Buckingham's 'Rehearsal' (q.v.).

Spring Gardens, at the NE. corner of St. James's Park, adjoining what is now Trafalgar Square, was a fashionable place of amusement in the days of the Stuarts. Spring Gardens were gradually replaced by the New Spring Gardens at Vauxhall (q.v.) in the middle of the 17th cent., though Pepys still refers to them as a popular promenade.

SPURGEON, CHARLES HADDON (1834–92), a Baptist preacher so popular that Exeter Hall could not contain all his would-be hearers. The Metropolitan Tabernacle in Newington, London, having been opened in 1861, to hold 6,000 people, he ministered there until his death. He was a convinced Calvinist, and his resentment at the trend of modern biblical criticism led to his leaving the Baptist Union in 1887. His sermons, of which a large number were published, are marked by a strong vein of homely humour.

Spurs, BATTLE OF THE, see *Battle of the Spurs.*

Spy, *The,* a novel of the American Revolution by J. F. Cooper (q.v.), published in 1821. The action of the tale revolves around the mysterious pedlar, Harvey Birch, who serves Washington as a spy, and shows extraordinary ubiquity, elusiveness, and foreknowledge of military operations. Washington himself figures in the novel under the name of Mr. Harper.

Square, in Fielding's 'Tom Jones' (q.v.), an inmate of Mr. Allworthy's household, deeply read in the ancients, who in morals was a professed Platonist and in religion inclined to be an Aristotelian; but in fact a hypocrite.

Squeers, WACKFORD, in Dickens's 'Nicholas Nickleby' (q.v.), the headmaster of Dotheboys Hall. He has a heartless wife, who joins him in bullying his miserable pupils, a spiteful daughter in MISS FANNY SQUEERS, and a spoilt son in MASTER WACKFORD SQUEERS.

Squintum, DR., the character under which Foote (q.v.) ridiculed George Whitefield in 'The Minor'.

Squire Meldrum, *The History of,* see *Lindsay (Sir D.).*

Squire of Alsatia, *The,* a play by Shadwell (q.v.). ·

Squire of Dames, a humorous character in Spenser's 'Faerie Queene', III. vii. He had been ordered by his lady to 'do service unto gentle dames' and at the end of twelve months to report progress. At the end of the year he was able to bring pledges of three hundred conquests. Thereupon his lady ordered him not to return to her till he had found an equal number of dames who rejected his advances. After three years he had only found three, a courtesan because he would not pay her enough, a nun because she could not trust his discretion, and a Damzell of low degree 'in a country cottage found by chance'.

Squire of Low Degree, a metrical romance of the early 14th cent., opening with the distich

It was a squire of low degree
That loved the King's daughter of Hungary.

The squire tells his love to the princess, who consents to wed him when he becomes a distinguished knight. But the meeting is seen by an interfering steward, who reports to the king and gets killed by the squire for his pains. The squire is imprisoned by the king and is mourned as dead by the princess for seven years, in spite of the king's offer of a variety of delights. The king is at length forced to relent, the squire is released, goes forth on a knightly quest, and finally marries the princess.

Squire of Low Degree, THE, in Spenser's 'Faerie Queene', is Amyas. See *Poeana*.

Squire's Tale, The, see *Canterbury Tales*.

Sri, see *Lakshmi*.

Stabat Mater, a sequence composed by Jacobus de Benedictis (Jacopone da Todi) in the 13th cent., in commemoration of the sorrows of the Blessed Virgin Mary, so called from its opening words, *Stabat mater dolorosa*, 'Stood the mother, full of grief'. There are various musical settings of the sequence.

STAËL, ANNE LOUISE GERMAINE DE (1766–1817), the daughter of Jacques Necker, the French minister of finance famous in the days of the Revolution, and of Suzanne Curchod, the 'first and only love' of Gibbon. She married (1785) but was later separated from the Baron de Staël-Holstein, Swedish ambassador in Paris. A woman of remarkable intellectual gifts and openness of mind, she received in her Paris salon, on the eve of the Revolution, the most progressive elements in French society. Her most important writings were, in the political sphere, her 'Considérations sur la Révolution française' (published posthumously, 1818), and in the sphere of literary criticism, 'De la Littérature dans ses rapports avec les institutions sociales' (1800), in which she developed the theory of the progress of the human reason in conformity with the progress of the national organism. She rendered her greatest service to literature in 'De l'Allemagne' (1810–13), in which she introduced to the French the great literary and philosophic movement that had been proceeding in Germany during the previous half-century. The work proved distasteful to Napoleon: the first impression (1810) was destroyed, the author was exiled, and the work was ultimately published in England (1813). Mme de Staël's many other works include memoirs and two novels ('Delphine', 1802, in letter form, and 'Corinne', 1807) which reflect the frustrations and conflicts of her own life. She had many passionate friendships, notably with Benjamin Constant (q.v.).

Stafford blue, 'to clothe in Stafford blue' is to beat black and blue, with a play on 'staff'.

Stagirite or STAGYRITE, THE, Aristotle, born at Stageira in Macedon.

Stagirius, a young monk to whom St. Chrysostom addressed three books. M. Arnold (q.v.), in the poem 'Stagirius', places in his mouth a litany.

Stalin (real name DZHUGASHVILI), IOSIF VISSARIOVICH (1879–1953), dictator of Russia and of the world Communist movement. A minor member of the Leninist wing of the Russian Social-Democratic Party before 1917, he became General Secretary of the Central Committee in 1922 and used this key position to oust his rivals after Lenin's death. From 1934 onwards he ruled Russia by terror. His main policies included the forced collectivization of agriculture, rapid expansion of heavy industries, mass terror (including a vast system of concentration camps), patriotism in official propaganda instead of the earlier Communist internationalism, and, in his last years, xenophobia and anti-Semitism. Under his rule literature and the arts were reduced to a constant reiteration of the official fiction of Stalin as the source of wisdom and benevolence and as the object of the love and devotion of a happy and prosperous Soviet people.

Stalky & Co., tales of schoolboy life, by Kipling (q.v.), published in 1899.

Stamboul, the Turkish name for Constantinople, derived from the Greek εἰς τὴν πόλιν, 'at the city'.

Standard, BATTLE OF THE, the battle of Luton Moor, near Northallerton, in 1138 between the English and the Scottish armies. Richard of Hexham, a contemporary writer, describes the 'standard' there used as the mast of a ship, with banners at the top (of the three great churches of St. Peter of York, St. John of Beverley, and St. Wilfrid of Ripon), mounted in the middle of a machine which was brought into the field. This sort of standard was also used (and called the *carroccio*) in the wars of the Emperor Frederick Barbarossa with the Lombard League.

Standard in Cheap, Standard in Cornhill, THE, a lofty erection of timber or stone, containing a vertical conduit pipe with taps, for the supply of water to the public, frequently referred to in the 16th–17th cents. The 'Standard in Cornhill' continued as the name of a point from which distances were measured, long after the 'standard' had disappeared.

Standish, MILES, see *Miles Standish*.

Stanhope, LADY HESTER LUCY (1776–1839), was the niece of William Pitt and kept house for him from 1803 till his death in 1806, gaining a reputation as a brilliant political hostess. In 1810 she withdrew from Europe for good, and in 1814 established herself for the rest of her life in a ruined convent at Djoun in the Lebanon. Here she lived with a semi-oriental retinue which she ruled despotically; for several years her high rank and imperious character made her a real political power in Syria and the neighbouring desert. In later years her debts accumulated, her eccentricity increased, and she sought to replace her waning political prestige by an undefined spiritual authority based on claims to be an inspired prophetess and mistress of occult sciences. She became a legendary figure in her lifetime and was visited by many distinguished European travellers. Celebrated accounts of their visits to her were written by Lamartine in 'Voyages en Orient' and Kinglake in 'Eothen'.

STANHOPE, PHILIP HENRY, *fifth earl* (1805–75), nephew of Pitt's niece, Lady Hester Stanhope (q.v.), educated at Christ Church, Oxford, rendered important services by procuring the passage of the Copyright Act of 1842, and the foundation of the National Portrait Gallery (1856) and of the Historical MSS. Commission (1869). He was author of the following historical works: 'The History of the War of the Succession in Spain' (1832), 'The History of England from the Peace of Utrecht to the Peace of Versailles' (1836–63), 'The Life of William Pitt' (1861–2), 'The History of England comprising the reign of Anne until the Peace of Utrecht' (1870); also of two series of 'Miscellanies' (1863–72), and other essays.

Stanhope Press, an iron printing-press invented by Charles, third earl Stanhope (1753–1816), the husband of Lady Hester, sister of the younger William Pitt. He also devised a stereotyping process, and a microscopic lens which bears his name.

STANLEY, ARTHUR PENRHYN (1815–81), son of Edward Stanley (who became bishop of Norwich), was educated at Rugby under Arnold (by whom he was much influenced) and at Balliol College, Oxford, and became professor of ecclesiastical history at Oxford in 1856, and dean of Westminster, 1864–81. He applied himself to the history of the Eastern Church and the geography of Palestine, publishing his 'Sinai and Palestine' in 1856, 'Lectures on the History of the Eastern Church' in 1861, and 'Lectures on the History of the Jewish Church' in 1863, 1865, and 1876. His 'Life of Dr. Arnold' appeared in 1844, 'Memorials of Canterbury' in 1854, 'Memorials of Westminster Abbey' in 1868, 'Lectures on the Church of Scotland' in 1872, and 'Essays, chiefly on Questions of Church and State' in 1870. He was a leader of the Broad Church Movement and a courageous champion of religious toleration. His wife, Lady Augusta (a Bruce of the Elgin family), was a great friend of Queen Victoria.

STANLEY, Sir HENRY MORTON (1841–1904), was sent in 1869 by Gordon Bennett, proprietor of 'The New York Herald', to find David Livingstone (q.v.), who was believed to be lost in Central Africa. Stanley found him at Ujiji, and published his adventures in 'How I found Livingstone' (1872). 'Through the Dark Continent' (1878) relates his experiences while crossing equatorial Africa in 1874–7, when he opened up for the first time the heart of the continent. In 1890 he married Dorothy Tennant, who edited his 'Autobiography' (1909).

Stanley, Sir HUBERT, *Approbation from, is praise indeed*: from 'A Cure for the Heartache', v. ii, by T. Morton (q.v.).

STANLEY, THOMAS (1625–78), a descendant of Edward Stanley, third earl of Derby, educated at Pembroke Hall, Cambridge, was author of a 'History of Philosophy' (1655–62), of an edition of Aeschylus (1663), and of translations from Theocritus, Bion, Moschus, Marino, Gongora, and others, besides original poems.

Staple Inn, Holborn, one of the old Inns (q.v.) of Chancery. It was originally called the 'Stapled hall', and this may have meant no more than a wholesale warehouse (Kingsford's notes on Stow), or it was perhaps originally the property of a guild in some way connected with the wool trade (G. R. Stirling Taylor).

Staple of News, The, a comedy by Jonson (q.v.), first acted in 1625, in which on the one hand he satirizes the credulity of the age, and on the other illustrates the use and abuse of riches. The 'Staple of News' is a new office set up for the collection, sorting, and dissemination of news and gossip, 'authentical and apocryphal'. The scanty plot is concerned with the relations of the Lady Pecunia, an allegorical personage representing riches, with Pennyboy, a young spendthrift; her uncle the usurer; and the master of the Staple.

Star-chamber, THE, an apartment in the royal palace of Westminster in which during the 14th and 15th cents. the chancellor, treasurer, justices, and other members of the king's council sat to exercise jurisdiction, so called according to Stow, 'because the roof thereof is decked with the likeness of Stars gilt'.

The COURT OF STAR-CHAMBER, whose procedure in the reigns of James I and Charles I made it a proverbial type of an arbitrary and oppressive tribunal, was developed from the above judicial sittings in the 15th cent. It was abolished in 1641. In its original (Tudor) capacity, it was essentially the 'poor man's court', to do justice against great lords. See on its history J. F. Baldwin, 'The King's Council in the Middle Ages' (1913).

Stareleigh, MR. JUSTICE, in Dickens's 'The Pickwick Papers' (q.v.), the judge in the case of Bardell v. Pickwick.

Stars and Stripes, THE, the popular name of the flag of the United States. In the early stages of the American Revolution each State had its own flag. The 'Stars and Stripes' was introduced after the Declaration of Independence, and was based on the arms of the Washington family. When adopted by Congress (1777), it contained 13 stripes (alternately red and white) and 13 stars, representing the 13 States of the Union. But it was not at first stated whether there should be seven red and six white stripes or vice versa. Finally seven red and six white stripes were decided on. The flag now contains 13 stripes and a star for each State of the Union (the admission of Hawaii brought the number to 50 in 1959).

Star-spangled Banner, The, the American national anthem since 1931, is said to have its origin partly in the air of 'To Anacreon in Heaven', a convivial song of the Anacreontic Society of London, published in 1771. To this tune Francis Scott Key, an American, set the words of a patriotic hymn on the occasion of the British attack on Fort McHenry in 1814.

Starveling, in Shakespeare's 'A Midsummer Night's Dream' (q.v.), a tailor, who is cast for the part of 'Thisby's mother' in the play of 'Pyramus and Thisbe'. He has nothing to do or say.

State Trials, a collection of reports of trials relating to offences against the state or otherwise illustrative of the law relating to state officers of high rank. The first collection was made by Thomas Salmon (1679–1767) and published in 1719, and was repeatedly enlarged. 'Cobbett's Complete Collection of State Trials', edited by T. B. Howell and subsequently by his son T. J. Howell, and published by William Cobbett, appeared in 1809–26. A new series, superintended by a committee appointed by the Lord Chancellor, was begun in 1888.

Statesman, The, by Sir Henry Taylor (q.v., 1836), an ironical exposition of the arts of succeeding as a civil servant.

Stationers' Company, THE, was incorporated by royal charter in 1557. No one, not a member of the Company, might print anything for sale in the kingdom unless authorized by special privilege or patent. Moreover, by the rules of the Company, every member was required to enter in the register of the Company the name of any book that he desired to print, so that these registers furnish valuable information regarding printed matter during the latter part of the 16th cent. The Company's control of the printing trade waned during the 17th cent., to be revived, in a modified form, under the Copyright Act of 1709. See Appendix II.

Statira, see *The Rival Queens.*

STATIUS, PUBLIUS PAPINIUS (*c.* A.D. 40–*c.* 96), a Roman poet born at Neapolis,

author of a 'Thebaid' in twelve books (on the expedition of the 'Seven against Thebes') and of a collection of poems called 'Silvae'. Dante ('Purgatorio', xxii. 89) refers to his alleged conversion to Christianity. Pope and Gray translated portions of the 'Thebaid'.

Statue and the Bust, The, a poem by R. Browning (q.v.), published in 1855.

In the Piazza dell' Annunziata in Florence stands an equestrian statue of Ferdinando dei Medici, looking in the direction of the Palazzo Riccardi. According to tradition, he loved a lady whose husband from jealousy kept her a prisoner in that palace, and whom he could see only at her window. The duke placed his statue where its eyes could always rest upon her.

Browning makes the love mutual. The lovers decide to fly together, but circumstances cause them to postpone their flight. Every day as the duke passes on his horse they exchange glances, and every day their love grows cooler, till they realize that it was a dream. He places his statue and she her bust where they can look on each other—an ironical conclusion designed as a criticism of infirmity of purpose.

Staunton, SIR GEORGE, *alias* GEORGE ROBERTSON, in Scott's 'The Heart of Midlothian' (q.v.), the lover, and subsequently husband, of Effie Deans.

STEAD, WILLIAM THOMAS (1849–1912), was assistant editor (John Morley being editor) of 'The Pall Mall Gazette', 1880–3, and editor, 1883–8, in which capacity he initiated many social and political movements. He founded 'The Review of Reviews' in 1890, and from 1893 to 1897 edited 'Borderland', a periodical devoted to psychical matters. Stead was drowned in the disaster of the 'Titanic' (q.v.)

STEEL, FLORA ANNIE (1847–1929), an inspector of schools in India, published in 1896 a successful study of the Indian Mutiny, 'On the Face of the Waters'. She wrote a number of other novels, most of them about India.

STEELE, SIR RICHARD (1672–1729), was born at Dublin, in the same year as Addison (q.v.), and was educated with him at the Charterhouse. He was subsequently at Merton College, Oxford, whence he entered the army as a cadet in the Life Guards. As a result of a poem on Queen Mary's funeral dedicated to Lord Cutts, colonel of the Coldstream Guards, he became his secretary and obtained the rank of captain. He published 'The Christian Hero' (q.v.) in 1701, in which he first displayed his missionary and reforming spirit. In the same year he produced his first comedy, 'The Funeral' (q.v.), in which, breaking away from the conventions of the Restoration drama, he tried to present virtue and vice in their true aspects. Neither this nor his two next comedies, 'The Lying Lover' (1703) and 'The Tender Husband' (1705), proved very successful. In 1706 he was appointed gentleman waiter to Prince George of Denmark, and in 1707 gazetteer; and in the same year was married to Mary Scurlock ('dear Prue'), his second wife. In 1709 he started 'The Tatler' (q.v.), which he carried on with the help of Addison till January 1711. He was made a commissioner of stamps in 1710, but lost the gazetteership after the accession of the Tories. In conjunction with Addison he carried on 'The Spectator' (q.v.) during 1711–12. This was followed by 'The Guardian', to which Addison, Berkeley, and Pope contributed, and which was attacked by the Tory 'Examiner' (q.v.). Steele next conducted 'The Englishman' (1713–14), a more political paper. In 1713 he was elected M.P. for Stockbridge. In 1714 he published 'The Crisis', a pamphlet in favour of the Hanoverian succession, which was answered by Swift (q.v.), and led to Steele's expulsion from the House on 18 Mar. 1714. In October of that year he issued his 'Apology for Himself and his Writings', and during the same year conducted 'The Lover', a paper in the manner of 'The Spectator'. The tide turned in his favour with the accession of George I. He was appointed supervisor of Drury Lane Theatre, and to other posts, and was knighted in 1715. In 1718 he denounced in the 'Plebeian' Lord Sunderland's Peerage Bill, and was answered by Addison in the 'Old Whig'. This incident led to the revocation of Steele's Drury Lane patent, and to an estrangement from Addison. He established the 'Theatre', a bi-weekly paper, which continued until 1720, in which year he issued pamphlets against the South Sea mania. His last comedy, 'The Conscious Lovers' (q.v.), based on the 'Andria' of Terence and embodying some of his views on social questions, was produced in 1722. Money difficulties forced him to leave London in 1724, and he died at Carmarthen. His letters to his wife, Mary Scurlock, were printed in 1787.

Steele Glas, *The*, a satire in verse by Gascoigne (q.v.), published in 1576.

The poet's 'steele glas' reveals abuses and how things should be, whereas the common looking-glass only 'shewes a seemely shew', i.e. shows the thing much better than it is. Looking into his 'steele glas' the author sees himself with his faults, and then successively the faults of kings; covetous lords and knights; greedy, braggart, and drunken soldiers; false judges; merchants; and lastly priests. Finally the plowman is held up as a model:

Behold him (priests) and though he stink of sweat,
Disdaine him not, for shall I tel you what,
Such clime to heaven before the shaven crowns.

Steelyard, THE, the place on the north bank of the Thames above London Bridge where the merchants of the Hanse (q.v.) had their establishment. The name is a mistranslation of the MLG. *stålhof*, from *stål*, sample, and *hof*, courtyard. [OED.]

Steenie, James I's nickname for his favourite, George Villiers, first duke of Buckingham, in allusion to the words regarding St. Stephen in Acts vi. 15.

Steenkirk cravats, fashionable after the battle of Steenkirk (1692), where the Allies under William III were defeated by the French. They were arranged to imitate the hasty carelessness with which the French officers had dressed themselves to rush into battle.

Steenson, WILLIE, 'Wandering Willie', the blind fiddler in Scott's 'Redgauntlet' (q.v.).

Steerforth, JAMES, a character in Dickens's 'David Copperfield' (q.v.).

STEEVENS, GEORGE (1736–1800), a well-known Shakespeare commentator. In 1766 he issued, in four volumes, 'Twenty of the Plays of Shakespeare, being the whole number printed in quarto during his lifetime, or before the Restoration', and in 1773 a complete annotated edition (including notes by Dr. Johnson) in ten volumes, to which a supplementary volume of the Poems, together with seven plays ascribed to Shakespeare, was added in 1780. He assisted Dr. Johnson in his 'Lives of the Poets', and was a member of 'The Club'. He constantly quarrelled with his literary associates and was called by Gifford 'the Puck of commentators'. He assisted Tyrwhitt (q.v.) in his edition of the 'Rowley Poems', but declared his disbelief in them. He attacked W. H. Ireland (q.v.), and satirized literary crazes. He forged a letter of George Peele describing a meeting with Shakespeare. See also *Upas*.

STEIN, GERTRUDE (1874–1946), American writer and critic, born in Pennsylvania. She studied psychology and medicine at Radcliffe College and at Johns Hopkins University, but left the United States in 1902 and spent her life in France, writing and encouraging writers. She was deeply interested in style and her experiments influenced many of her contemporaries. She wrote poetry, short stories, novels, criticism—both of literature and art—and autobiography, and was one of the leading and most stimulating figures of her time. Among her many books are 'Three Lives' (1908) and 'The Making of Americans' (1925), fiction; 'Tender Buttons' (1914), poetry; 'Composition and Explanation' (1926) and 'Narration' (1935), criticism; and 'Picasso' (1938). Her autobiography, 'The Autobiography of Alice B. Toklas' (1933), is written as if by her confidant and secretary.

STEINBECK, JOHN (1902–   ), American novelist, born in California. He took his native State as the background for his early short stories and novels, and described the life of those working on the land with realism and understanding. 'Tortilla Flat'

(1935) was his first success, and 'In Dubious Battle' (1936) and, especially, 'Of Mice and Men' (1937), an extraordinary story of two farm labourers, one of huge strength and weak mind, exploited and protected by the other, established him as one of the most interesting writers of the day. His master-piece, 'The Grapes of Wrath' (1940), is an epic account of the efforts of an emigrant farming family from the dust bowl of the West to reach the 'promised land' of Cali-fornia. Among his later novels, which are often marred by sentimentality and un-certainty of purpose, are 'East of Eden' (1952) and 'Winter of Our Discontent' (1961). He was awarded a Nobel Prize in 1962.

Stella, the name under which Sir P. Sidney (q.v.) celebrated Penelope Devereux in his sonnets. She was daughter of the first earl of Essex, and when a girl was destined by her father to be Sidney's wife. The project was abandoned and she married Robert, the second Lord Rich, and after being divorced by him Charles Blount, Lord Mountjoy, afterwards earl of Devonshire.

Stella, in Waller's (q.v.) poems, is Lady Dorothy Sidney, daughter of Robert Dudley, earl of Leicester.

Stella, Swift's name for Esther Johnson, see *Swift*, and in particular the account there of the 'Journal to Stella'.

STENDHAL, pseudonym of HENRI BEYLE (1783–1842), one of the greatest of French novelists. As a young man Beyle served in Napoleon's armies, and was present at the burning of Moscow. After the Restoration he lived much of his life in Italy. He died while on a visit to Paris. His definite gift to fiction was the objective, dispassionate analysis of complicated states of conscience. It is seen in the two great novels 'Le Rouge et le Noir' (1830, France of the Restoration period) and 'La Chartreuse de Parme' (1839, life at a small Italian court) to which modern critics have accorded a place in fiction equal to that of Balzac. His other novels include 'L'Abbesse de Castro' (1839) and the un-finished 'Lucien Leuwen' (posth.). He also wrote much occasional journalism, as well as travel sketches and critical and biographical works, e.g. 'De l'amour' (1822), 'Racine et Shakespeare' (1823, 1825, two pamphlets on Classicism versus Romanticism), 'Vie de Rossini' (1823). The definitive edition of his works (Paris, 1927–37) includes the 'Journal' (of 1801–18) and two other autobiographical fragments, 'La vie de Henri Brûlard' and 'Souvenirs d'Égotisme'.

Stentor, the name of a Greek warrior in the Trojan War ('Iliad', v. 785) 'whose voice was as powerful as fifty voices of other men'.

Stepan Arcadyevitch, in Tolstoy's 'Anna Karenina', the brother of Anna.

Stephano, a drunken butler in Shakespeare's 'The Tempest' (q.v.).

Stephanus, see *Estienne*.

STEPHEN, JAMES KENNETH (1859–92), known as 'J. K. S.', educated at Eton and King's College, Cambridge, was the author of some brilliant light verse, collected in 'Lapsus Calami' and 'Quo Musa Tendis' (1891) and republished in 1896.

Stephen of Blois, king of England, 1135–54.

Stephen, ST., the first Christian martyr, one of the 'seven men of honest report' chosen as a deacon at Jerusalem, accused of blasphemy, and stoned to death (Acts vi and vii).

Stephen, ST., Stephen I, king and patron saint of Hungary, previously the heathen king Waik, who took the name of Stephen at his baptism A.D. 1000. He died in 1038, having during his reign promoted the spread of Christianity. The CROWN OF ST. STEPHEN is the crown of Hungary.

STEPHEN, SIR JAMES (1789–1859), the father of Sir J. F. Stephen and Sir L. Stephen (qq.v.), and himself under-secretary for the colonies (1836–47), professor of modern his-tory at Cambridge (1849–59), and author of 'Essays in Ecclesiastical Biography' (1849) and 'Lectures on the History of France' (1852).

STEPHEN, SIR JAMES FITZJAMES (1829–94), son of Sir J. Stephen and brother of Sir L. Stephen (qq.v.), educated at Eton, King's College, London, and Trinity College, Cambridge, was a barrister of the Inner Temple and counsel for Rowland Williams in the 'Essays and Reviews' (q.v.) case. He rose to be legal member of the Governor-General's council in India (1869–72) and a judge of the high court (1879–91). He contri-buted to 'Fraser's' and the 'Cornhill' maga-zines and to 'The Pall Mall Gazette', and many of these contributions are collected in 'Essays by a Barrister' (1862) and the three series of 'Horae Sabbaticae' (1862, etc.). His chief works were a 'General View of the Criminal Law of England' (1863, 1890), a 'History of the Criminal Law' (1883), and 'The Story of Nuncomar and Sir Elijah Impey' (1885). In his 'Liberty, Equality, Fraternity' (1873) he severely criticized Mill's utilitarian position in the latter's essay 'On Liberty'.

STEPHEN, SIR LESLIE (1832–1904), son of Sir J. Stephen and brother of Sir J. F. Stephen (qq.v.), was educated at Eton, King's College, London, and Trinity Hall, Cam-bridge, where he became tutor, having taken orders. He was a noted athlete and moun-taineer, and in 1868–71 edited the 'Alpine Journal'. His accounts of Alpine ascents were collected in 1871 as 'The Playground of Europe'.

Stephen's reading of Mill, Combe, and Kant inclined him to scepticism and he re-linquished orders after the Act of 1870. In 1864 he came to London for a literary career and contributed critical studies to various periodicals, which were collected in 'Hours in a Library' (1874-6-9). In 1873 he published his 'Essays on Free Thinking and Plain Speaking', defining his agnostic position, and his 'Agnostic's Apology' appeared in the 'Fortnightly' for June 1876. In the latter year there appeared also his 'History of English Thought in the 18th century', reviewing the position of the chief writers in the great deist controversy of that age, and of the intuitional and utilitarian schools of philosophy, followed in 1900 by a further instalment on the same subject in 'The English Utilitarians'. His 'Science of Ethics' appeared in 1882. He contributed a number of biographies to the two series of 'English Men of Letters', Johnson (1878), Pope (1880), Swift (1882), George Eliot (1902), Hobbes (1904), and also wrote lives of Henry Fawcett (1885) and of his brother, Sir James Fitzjames Stephen (1895). After having been from 1871 to 1882 editor of 'The Cornhill Magazine', he accepted in the latter year the editorship of the 'Dictionary of National Biography' (q.v.), himself contributing many of the most important notices, especially of the 18th- and 19th-cent. worthies. As editor he saw completed the first twenty-six volumes of the work, and continued to contribute to it subsequently. His 'Social Rights and Duties' appeared in 1896, 'Studies of a Biographer' in 1898–1902, and 'English Literature and Society in the 18th century' in 1904.

Leslie Stephen was the model from which Meredith drew Vernon Whitford, 'a Phoebus Apollo turned fasting friar', in his 'The Egoist' (q.v.). His first wife was Harriet Marian, Thackeray's younger daughter. Virginia Woolf (q.v.) was his daughter.

Stephen Guest, a character in G. Eliot's 'The Mill on the Floss' (q.v.).

STEPHENS, JAMES (1882–1950), Irish poet and story-writer, whose best-known work is the prose fantasy, 'The Crock of Gold' (1912).

STEPNEY, GEORGE (1663–1701), poet. He contributed to Dryden's 'Miscellany Poems'.

STERLING, JOHN (1806–44), educated at Trinity College and Trinity Hall, Cambridge, contributed to various periodicals, but is chiefly remembered as the centre of a literary group known after him as the STERLING CLUB (founded 1838), which included such men as Carlyle, Tennyson, John Stuart Mill, Lord Houghton, and Sir Francis Palgrave, together with many others more or less eminent in literature. His 'Life' by Carlyle was published in 1851.

STERNE, LAURENCE (1713–68), the son of a subaltern in the army, was born at Clonmel, and after some years of wandering from garrison to garrison spent eight years at school at Halifax. He was left penniless and was sent by his cousin as a sizar to Jesus College, Cambridge. He took orders and became vicar of Sutton-in-the-Forest in 1738, where he remained till 1759, marrying Mias Elizabeth Lumley in 1741. His 'small,

quiet attentions' to various ladies disturbed his conjugal life, and his wife became insane in 1758. He began 'Tristram Shandy' (q.v.) in 1759, volumes i and ii being published in 1760. He carried on a sentimental correspondence with Miss Catherine de Fourmantelle (a young French lady, living at York with her mother), the 'dear, dear Jenny' referred to in 'Tristram Shandy'. He came to London and was well received in society, and in 1760 published the first volumes of his 'Sermons of Mr. Yorick'. But 'Tristram Shandy', of which four more volumes appeared in 1761, was denounced by Dr. Johnson, Richardson, Horace Walpole, Goldsmith, and others, on moral and literary grounds. In 1760 he received the perpetual curacy of Coxwold, and called his house there 'Shandy Hall'. Ill health sent him abroad in 1762 and he lived at Toulouse with his wife and daughter until 1764. Volumes vii and viii of 'Tristram Shandy' appeared in 1765, in which year began his seven months' tour in France and Italy, of which the French part is described in his 'A Sentimental Journey' (q.v., published in 1768). Volume ix of 'Tristram Shandy' appeared in 1767, also volumes iii and iv of his 'Sermons'. He met in London Mrs. Eliza Draper, for whom he kept the journal addressed to her ('The Bramine's Journal') from April to August 1767, after her departure for India. A permanent separation from his wife was arranged in that year, but Sterne parted reluctantly from his daughter. He died of pleurisy in his Old Bond Street lodgings, insolvent, and his wife and daughter were relieved through subscriptions collected by his friend John Hall-Stevenson and by Mrs. Draper, and by the publication (1769) of three more volumes of sermons. The publication of the 'Letters of Yorick to Eliza' was authorized by Mrs. Draper in 1775. The 'Letters from Eliza to Yorick' (1775) and 'Letters supposed to have been written by Yorick and Eliza' (1779) are forgeries.

Among fraudulent imitations of Sterne's writings were John Carr's third volume of 'Tristram Shandy' (1760), J. Hall-Stevenson's continuation of the 'Sentimental Journey' (1769), and Richard Griffith's 'Posthumous Works of a late celebrated Genius' (1770, included in the first collected edition, which appeared, without letters, in 1779). The best early edition of the collected works (with letters and Hogarth's plates) appeared in 1780.

Sternhold and Hopkins, THOMAS STERNHOLD (d. 1549) and JOHN HOPKINS (d. 1570), joint versifiers of the Psalms. A collection of forty-four of these versified psalms appeared in 1549. In 1562 'The Whole Book of Psalms', by Sternhold, Hopkins, Norton, and others, was added to the Prayer Book. This version is ridiculed by Dryden in 'Absalom and Achitophel', II. 403, and it drew the following epigram from Rochester:

Sternhold and Hopkins had great qualms
When they translated David's psalms,

To make the heart right glad:
But had it been King David's fate
To hear thee sing and them translate,
By God 'twould set him mad

(quoted in R. E. Prothero's 'The Psalms in Human Life').

STEUART, SIR JAMES, who assumed the surname of DENHAM (1712–80), a member of the Faculty of Advocates, was author of an 'Inquiry into the Principles of Political Economy' (1767), written from the standpoint of the mercantile system.

STEVENSON, JOHN HALL- (1718–85), the friend of Sterne (q.v.) and the original of the Eugenius of 'Tristram Shandy'. He was author of 'Crazy Tales' (1762), adaptations or imitations of coarse French *fabliaux*, and some indifferent political pamphlets in verse. He wrote a continuation of 'The Sentimental Journey' (q.v.), published in 1769.

STEVENSON, ROBERT LOUIS (1850–94), son of Thomas Stevenson, joint-engineer to the Board of Northern Lighthouses, was born in Edinburgh. He entered Edinburgh University in 1867 and studied engineering, but soon abandoned this for the law and was admitted advocate in 1875. He composed an essay on the 'Pentland Rising of 1666' in his sixteenth year (printed 1866) and contributed to the 'Edinburgh University Magazine' in 1871 and the 'Portfolio' in 1873. An affection of the lungs led to his frequent journeys in search of health. His 'Inland Voyage', describing a canoe tour in Belgium and France, was published in 1878, and his 'Travels with a Donkey in the Cevennes', the description of a tour taken in 1878, in the following year. In 1879 he travelled to California by emigrant ship and train, and married Mrs. Osbourne in America in 1880. After a stay at Calistoga (recorded in 'The Silverado Squatters', 1883) he returned to England. Meanwhile, though very ill with tuberculosis, he contributed to various periodicals and wrote a number of essays, short stories, and fragments of travel and autobiography, collected in 'Virginibus Puerisque' (1881), 'Familiar Studies of Men and Books' (1882), and 'The New Arabian Nights' (1882), including 'The Pavilion on the Links'. To the same categories belong 'Prince Otto' (1885), 'The Merry Men' (1887, including 'Markheim' and 'Thrawn Janet'), 'Memories and Portraits' (1887), 'Across the Plains' (1892), 'Island Nights' Entertainments' (1893), 'In the South Seas' (1896), and 'The Amateur Emigrant' (included in vol. iii of the Edinburgh edition of his collected works). Long before this Stevenson had become famous by the publication in book form in 1883 of 'Treasure Island' (q.v.). This was followed by 'The Strange Case of Dr. Jekyll and Mr. Hyde' (q.v., 1886) and a series of romances: 'Kidnapped' (q.v., 1886) and 'Catriona', its sequel (1893), 'The Black Arrow' (1888), 'The Master of Ballantrae' (q.v., 1889), the

unfinished masterpeice, 'Weir of Hermiston' (q.v., 1896), and 'St. Ives' (published in New York, 1897, and in London, 1898), also unfinished, but completed by Sir A. T. Quiller-Couch. In collaboration with Lloyd Osbourne, Stevenson wrote 'The Wrong Box' (1889), 'The Wrecker' (1892), and 'The Ebb-Tide' (1894). In 1888 Stevenson had set out for the South Seas and settled in Samoa, where he bought the 'Vailima' property and temporarily recovered his health. There he died suddenly from rupture of a blood-vessel in the brain, and there he was buried. He had interested himself greatly in the affairs of the Pacific Islands, and on them wrote 'A Footnote to History' in 1892.

Stevenson wrote some remarkable poetry, collected in 'A 'Child's Garden of Verses' (1885) and 'Underwoods' (1887). He collaborated with W. E. Henley in a few dramas: 'Deacon Brodie' (1880), 'Beau Austin' (1892), and 'Admiral Guinea' (1897). He was a delightful letter-writer, and his 'Vailima Letters' were published in 1895, followed in 1911 by 'The Letters of R. L. S.', edited by Sir Sidney Colvin. The Edinburgh edition of his collected works (edited by Colvin) appeared in 1894–8, the Pentland edition in 1906–7, and the Swanston edition in 1911–12. A 'Life' of Stevenson by Graham Balfour was published in 1901, and there have been several later biographies and studies of his work.

Stewart, ALEXANDER, earl of Buchan and lord of Badenoch, called the 'Wolf of Badenoch' (1343?–1405?), fourth son of King Robert II of Scotland. His quarrels with the bishop of Moray probably led him to burn the town of Forres, and to destroy the hospital, houses of the clergy, and the cathedral of Elgin. These excesses earned for him the above popular designation.

STEWART, DUGALD (1753–1828), educated at Edinburgh High School and at Edinburgh and Glasgow Universities, was professor of moral philosophy at Edinburgh from 1785 to 1810, in which post he exercised a powerful influence on Scottish thought. He was a disciple of Thomas Reid (q.v.). His works, collected by Sir William Hamilton, 1854–60 (11 vols.), include: 'Elements of the Philosophy of the Human Mind' (1792, 1814, 1827), 'Outlines of Moral Philosophy' (1793), 'Lectures on Political Economy' (delivered 1800), and an 'Account of the Life and Writings of Thomas Reid' (1802).

Stewart, FRANCIS, *alias* SERGEANT BOTH-WELL, a character in Scott's 'Old Mortality' (q.v.).

STEWART, JOHN (1749–1822), 'Walking Stewart', described as 'refractory' at Harrow and Charterhouse Schools, went to India in 1763, was a general under Hyder Ali, and prime minister to the Nabob of Arcot. He travelled in Persia, Ethiopia, and Abyssinia, and came to Europe through the Arabian desert, walking through France and Spain in 1783. He also walked from Calais to Vienna in 1784 and in the United States. He made the acquaintance of De Quincey, who, in his 'London Reminiscences', speaks of him as a most interesting man, but 'crazy beyond all reach of hellebore'. He wrote many discursive philosophical works.

Stewart of the Glens, JAMES, a character in R. L. Stevenson's 'Kidnapped' (q.v.) and 'Catriona'; a real character too, who was executed for a murder which he did not commit, after trial by a jury of Campbells (the foes of his clan).

Steyne, MARQUIS OF, a character in Thackeray's 'Vanity Fair' (q.v.), said to have been suggested by the second and third marquises of Hertford.

Stichomythia, in the classical Greek drama, dialogue in alternate lines of verse, employed in sharp disputation. The form is sometimes imitated in modern drama, e.g. in the dialogue between Richard III and Elizabeth in Shakespeare's 'Richard III', IV. iv.

Stiggins, MR., a character in Dickens's 'The Pickwick Papers' (q.v.).

STILL, JOHN (1543–1608), bishop of Bath and Wells; fellow of Christ's College, Cambridge, c. 1562, and master of St. John's, 1574. He has been supposed to have been the author of 'Gammer Gurton's Needle' (q.v.).

STILLINGFLEET, EDWARD (1635–99), fellow of St. John's College, Cambridge, and bishop of Worcester from 1689, was a popular preacher and author of 'The Irenicum' (1659), suggesting a compromise with the Presbyterians. His erudition was displayed in 'Origines Sacrae' (1662) and 'Origines Britannicae' (1685).

Stinkomalee, the name under which Theodore Hook ridiculed London University at the time of its foundation (1828).

STIRLING, EARL OF, see *Alexander (Sir W.)*.

STIRLING, JAMES HUTCHISON (1820–1909), educated at Glasgow University to be a physician, abandoned medicine for philosophy, which he studied in Germany and France. He published in 1865 'The Secret of Hegel', containing a translation and commentary, which was his greatest work. His 'Analysis of Sir William Hamilton's Philosophy' appeared in the same year, and a 'Text Book of Kant' in 1881.

Stiver, a small coin (originally silver) of the Low Countries; in present use applied to the nickel piece of 5 cents of the Netherlands.

Stock Exchange, THE, see *Exchange*.

STOCKTON, FRANK R. (1834–1902), American writer of humorous fiction, remembered as the author of 'Rudder Grange' (1879), 'The Lady or the Tiger' (1882), 'The Casting away of Mrs. Lecks and Mrs. Ale-

shine' (1886), and many other tales and novels.

Stoddart, SIR JOHN, see *Slop*.

Stoics, a school of Greek philosophers, founded by Zeno (q.v.) of Citium about 310 B.C., which derives its name from the fact that Zeno taught under the 'Stoa Poikile' or 'Painted Portico' of Athens. Though the stoic doctrine embraced a complete philosophical system, its chief importance lies on the moral side. It held that happiness consists in liberation from the bondage of the passions and appetites, and in approximation to God by obeying his will; that virtue is thus the highest good, and suffering a matter of indifference. Among the illustrious Stoics of antiquity were Epictetus, Seneca, and Marcus Aurelius (qq.v.).

Stonehenge, a prehistoric stone circle on Salisbury Plain. There are at least three building periods: I, the circular ditch and bank surrounding the whole, and the Heel Stone, 1900–1700 B.C.; II, a double circle of bluestones from Presely Mountain, Wales, and the Avenue, 1700–1600 B.C.; III, the Sarsen circle surrounding a horseshoe of trilithons, c. 1500 B.C. The bluestones were re-erected within the Sarsen circle, c. 1400 B.C. The earliest earthworks may be late neolithic, the bluestone circles belong to the 'Beaker' culture, and the Sarsen stones to the Early Bronze Age Wessex culture.

Stones of Venice, The, a treatise in three volumes by Ruskin (q.v.), published in 1851–3.

It was written while the production of 'Modern Painters' (q.v.) was still proceeding. Its purpose is to glorify Gothic and expose 'the pestilent art of the Renaissance' by attacking it in its central stronghold, Venice. 'Destroy its claims to admiration there, and it can assert them nowhere else.' The author also traces the relation of the rise and fall of Gothic art to the moral temper of the State. He places the division between the 900 years of the rise of Venice and the 500 years of her decline at about the year 1310, the date of the 'Serrar del Consiglio', the establishment of the Council of Ten, 'the final and absolute distinction of the nobles from the commonalty'. He explains the principles of Byzantine architecture exemplified in St. Mark's, and the union of Gothic and Renaissance in the Ducal Palace, 'the central building of the world'. He passes to the minor corruptions of early Renaissance, redeemed by its noble use of inlaid marbles, the more serious faults of the central Renaissance, and the final degradation of grotesque Renaissance.

Stonewall Jackson, a nickname of General Thomas Jonathan Jackson (1824–63), a brilliant general on the Confederate side in the American Civil War. At a critical moment of the battle of Bull Run (1861), another officer remarked of him, 'See, there is

Jackson standing like a stone wall.' He was killed at the battle of Chancellorsville, and Lee said, 'I have lost my right arm'.

Story of an African Farm, The, a novel by Olive Schreiner (q.v.).

Story of Rimini, The, see *Hunt* (*J. H. L.*).

Story of Thebes, The, see *Lydgate.*

STOW, JOHN (1525?–1605), chronicler and antiquary, followed at first the trade of a tailor and was admitted a freeman of the Merchant Taylors' Company in 1547. He occupied himself from 1560 in collecting and transcribing manuscripts, and in producing original historical works. Becoming suspected of partiality for the old faith, he was charged in 1568, 1569, and 1570 with being in possession of popish and dangerous writings, was examined before the ecclesiastical commission, but escaped without punishment. He spent all his fortune on his literary pursuits, and existed for some time upon charitable contributions. A fine effigy of Stow, erected by his wife, still exists in the church of St. Andrew Undershaft, Leadenhall Street, London. He was the most accurate and businesslike of the historians of his century. His chief productions are: 'The Woorkes of Geffrey Chaucer', 1561 (his further notes on Chaucer being subsequently printed by Thomas Speght, 1598); 'Summarie of Englyshe Chronicles', 1565 (an original historical work); Matthew of Westminster's 'Flores Historiarum', 1567; Matthew Paris's 'Chronicle', 1571; Thomas Walsingham's 'Chronicle', 1574; 'The Chronicles of England', 1580 (in subsequent editions styled 'The Annales of England'); the second edition of Holinshed's 'Chronicle', 1585–7; and lastly 'A Survey of London', 1598 and 1603, a book invaluable for the detailed information it gives about the ancient city and its customs. It was brought down to his day by J. Strype (q.v.) in 1720, and modernized and annotated editions have since been published (C. L. Kingsford, 1908).

STOWE, MRS. HARRIET ELIZABETH BEECHER (1811–96), born in Connecticut, sister of Henry Ward Beecher (1813–87, divine and religious author and journalist), was a school-teacher before her marriage in 1836. Her famous anti-slavery novel, 'Uncle Tom's Cabin', appeared in the 'National Era' in 1851–2, and in book form in 1852. She wrote a number of other less well-known works, 'Dred' (1856), 'The Minister's Wooing' (1859), etc. She aroused great opposition by charging Byron with incestuous relations with his half-sister, in 'Lady Byron Vindicated' (1870). 'Uncle Tom's Cabin', by its presentment of the sufferings entailed on the Negroes by the system of slavery, the separation of husbands from wives, and mothers from their children, and the brutality of some of the slave-owners, did much to hasten the American Civil War. It was in Mrs. Stowe's own words 'a collection and arrangement of real incidents . . . grouped

together with reference to a general result'. It was translated into twenty-three languages.

STRABO (*b. c.* 63 B.C.), a native of Amasia in Pontus, author of a history, continuing that of Polybius, which is lost, and of an important historical geography of the Roman Empire in seventeen books, which is extant almost in its entirety.

STRACHEY, GILES LYTTON (1880–1932), educated at Trinity College, Cambridge, the author of a work of literary criticism, 'Landmarks in French Literature' (1912), became widely known in 1918 by his 'Eminent Victorians', biographies of Cardinal Manning, Florence Nightingale, Dr. Arnold, and General Gordon. The preface to 'Eminent Victorians' expounded Strachey's method, avoiding 'scrupulous narration' and attacking 'his subject in unexpected places', shooting 'a sudden revealing searchlight into obscure recesses, hitherto undivined'. This book was followed by a life of Queen Victoria in 1921, 'Books and Characters' in 1922, 'Elizabeth and Essex' in 1928, and 'Portraits in Miniature' in 1931.

Stradivarius, the latinized form of the name of Antonio Stradivari (1644?–1737), a famous maker of stringed musical instruments, born at Cremona, a pupil of Nicolo Amati. The name is also applied to violins of his making. Stradivarius is the subject of a poem by G. Eliot (q.v.).

Strafford, SIR THOMAS WENTWORTH, *first earl of* (1593–1641), educated at St. John's College, Cambridge, at first showed himself in parliament a moderate but firm opponent of the policy of Charles I. He was taken into court favour and made president of the council of the north in 1628, and lord-deputy of Ireland in 1632, where he set himself vigorously to restoring the king's authority. He became informally Charles's chief adviser in 1638, and urged the invasion of Scotland, promising in 1639, it was reported, the assistance of Irish troops against both Scottish and English rebels. He took command in 1640 of Charles I's force in Yorkshire against the invading Scots army. Strafford attended the Long Parliament on the king's personal guarantee of his safety, and urged that the parliamentary leaders should be sent to the Tower. He was impeached by the Commons in 1640, but as it was manifestly impossible to convict him of high treason, a bill of attainder was substituted in 1641, and assented to by Charles in fear of mob violence. He was executed on Tower Hill in May 1641. He was nicknamed 'Black Tom Tyrant'.

Strafford, a tragedy by R. Browning (q.v.), produced in 1837 at Covent Garden, with Macready in the title-role and Helen Faucit as Lady Carlisle. The play was not successful on the stage and ran for only a few nights.

The tragedy deals with the close of Strafford's career. Pym, who loves Strafford, relentlessly pursues his death from patriotic motives; Strafford, whose unshakeable devotion to Charles has ,caused his downfall, is abandoned by the weak and irresolute king; Lady Carlisle (the theme of many poems by Herrick, Carew, and other Cavalier lyrists), after in vain warning Strafford of his danger, devises a plan for his escape from the Tower, which fails; Strafford, after appealing to Pym to save him, and foreseeing the king's own fate, suffers on the scaffold, thanking God that he dies first.

STRANGFORD, PERCY CLINTON SYDNEY SMYTHE, *sixth viscount* (1780–1855), educated at Trinity College, Dublin, a diplomatist, published 'Poems from the Portuguese of Camoëns' in 1803. He is referred to as 'Hibernian Strangford' in Byron's 'English Bards and Scotch Reviewers' (q.v.).

Strap, HUGH, a character in Smollett's 'Roderick Random' (q.v.).

STRAPAROLA, GIOVAN FRANCESCO (*fl.* end of 15th cent.), Italian author of *novelle* entitled 'Piacevoli Notti' ('Pleasant Nights'), which enjoyed much popularity. Painter, in his 'Palace of Pleasure' (q.v.), drew on Straparola among others.

Straw, JACK, see *Jack Straw.*

Strawberry Hill, near Twickenham, about ten miles W. of the centre of London. Horace Walpole (q.v.) settled there in 1747, making it into 'a little Gothic castle', housing in it his collection of articles of virtu, and establishing a private printing-press. 'Strawberry Hill Gothic' is a common term for any example of romantic gothicized architecture of the period.

Strephon, the shepherd whose lament for his lost Urania forms the opening of Sidney's 'Arcadia' (q.v.). 'Strephon' has been adopted as a conventional name for a rustic lover.

Strether, LEWIS LAMBERT, a character in H. James's 'The Ambassadors' (q.v.).

STRICKLAND, AGNES (1796–1874), was author (in collaboration with her elder sister, Elizabeth) of the successful 'Lives of the Queens of England' (1840–8), and 'Lives of the Queens of Scotland and English Princesses' (1850–9). She wrote other historical biographies, and a novel, 'How Will it End?' (1865).

STRINDBERG, AUGUST (1849–1912). Swedish dramatist and novelist, a misogynist, and a disciple of Nietzsche; author, among other works, of the three plays, 'The Father', 'Miss Julia', and 'The Creditors', and of the novels 'Tschandala' and 'By the Open Sea'.

Strode, RALPH (*fl.* 1350–1400), scholastic philosopher and logician, fellow of Merton College, Oxford, where John Wycliffe was his colleague. He entered into controversy with Wycliffe, and Chaucer dedicated to him and to Gower his 'Troylus and Cryseyde'.

Strong, CAPTAIN or CHEVALIER, a character in Thackeray's 'Pendennis' (q.v.).

Strong, DR., in Dickens's 'David Copperfield' (q.v.), an amiable old schoolmaster, who dotes on his young wife, Annie, and supports her worthless cousin, Jack Maldon.

Stro'phe, from the Greek word meaning 'turn', part of a Greek choral ode sung as the chorus proceeded in one direction, followed by the *anti'strophe*, when they turned and proceeded in the opposite direction (see *Alcman*).

Struldbrugs, see *Gulliver's Travels.*

STRUTT, JOSEPH (1749–1802), author, artist, engraver, and antiquary, was author of many works valuable for their research and engravings, including a 'Chronicle of England' (1777–8), 'Dresses and Habits of the English People' (1796–9), and 'Sports and Pastimes of the People of England' (1801). An unfinished novel by Strutt was completed by Sir W. Scott ('Queenhoo Hall'), and suggested to him the publication of his own 'Waverley'.

Struwwelpeter, see *Hoffman (H.).*

STRYPE, JOHN (1643–1737), ecclesiastical historian, educated at St. Paul's School, Jesus College and St. Catharine's Hall, Cambridge, formed a magnificent collection of original documents, mostly of the Tudor period, now in the Harleian and Lansdowne MSS. He published lives of Cranmer (1694), Sir John Cheke (1705), Grindal (1710), Matthew Parker (1711), and Whitgift (1718). He corrected and enlarged Stow's 'Survey of London' (1720).

STUART, DANIEL (1766–1846), journalist, is remembered as having purchased 'The Morning Post' in 1795 and 'The Courier' in 1796, and raised both papers to importance by his management. There is a pleasant sketch of him as 'one of the finest of editors . . . frank, plain, and English all over' in C. Lamb's 'Newspapers Thirty-five Years Ago'.

STUBBES or **STUBBS, PHILIP** (*fl.* 1583–91), a Puritan pamphleteer, author of 'The Anatomie of Abuses' (1583), a denunciation of evil customs of the time which, in the author's opinion, needed abolition. It contains a section on stage plays and is one of the principal sources of information on the social and economic conditions of the period. It was answered by Nashe in the 'Anatomie of Absurditie'.

STUBBS, WILLIAM (1825–1901), educated at Ripon Grammar School and (as a servitor) at Christ Church, Oxford. He became a fellow of Trinity College and was for seventeen years rector of Navestock in Essex (where for a short time he had Swinburne as a pupil). He was much interested in the publication of the Rolls series, to which, in 1857, he contributed his 'Registrum Sacrum Anglicanum', exhibiting by tables the course of ecclesiastical succession in England. He succeeded Goldwin Smith as Regius professor of history at Oxford in 1866. He now published a large number of volumes of the Rolls series, beginning with the 'Chronicles and Memorials of Richard I' in 1864-5, and ending with the 'Historia Novella' of William of Malmesbury in 1885. In 1871-8 he edited, jointly with A. W. Haddan, 'The Councils and Ecclesiastical Documents of Great Britain'. But the works by which he is most widely known are his contributions to English constitutional history: the edition of the 'Select Charters and other Illustrations of English Constitutional History', published in 1870, and 'The Constitutional History of England in its Origin and Development', published in 1874-8, in which the author traces the development of our political institutions from Saxon times to the period of the Tudors. His shorter works, besides lectures, include a book on 'The Early Plantagenets' (1876). Stubbs was appointed bishop of Chester in 1884, and of Oxford in 1888.

Study and Use of History, Letters on the, see under *Bolingbroke*.

Stukeley, a character in George Peele's 'Battle of Alcazar' (q.v.). The real Thomas Stucley or Stukeley (1525?-78) was said to be a natural son of Henry VIII. He was an adventurer, who entered the service of the French king, was sent on a spying expedition to England, and betrayed his employer to Cecil. He next entered the service of Charles V; then embarked on a privateering expedition, for which Queen Elizabeth provided one of his ships, till the remonstrances of foreign powers led to his arrest. He proceeded to Ireland, where his ambitious schemes were distrusted and discountenanced by Elizabeth. He escaped to Spain, having been in treasonable correspondence with Philip II. He joined the king of Portugal's expedition against Morocco and was killed at the battle of Alcazar. Fuller in his 'Worthies' gives an amusing account of a conversation between him and Queen Elizabeth: 'So confident was his ambition that he blushed not to tell Queen Elizabeth that he preferred rather to be soveraign of a mole-hill than the highest subject to the greatest King in Christendome; adding moreover that he was assured he should be a prince before his death. I hope (said Queen Elizabeth) I shall hear from you, when you are stated in your principality. I will write unto you (quoth Stukeley). In what language? (said the Queen). He returned, In the stile of Princes: *To our dear Sister.*'

STUKELEY, WILLIAM (1687-1765), antiquary, educated at Bennet (Corpus Christi) College, Cambridge, was secretary of the Society of Antiquaries, which he shared in founding (1718). He published, among other writings, 'Itinerarium Curiosum' (1724) and 'Stonehenge' (1740), and was specially interested in Druidism. He published in 1757 as a genuine work of Richard of Ciren-cester, Charles Bertram's forgery, 'De Situ Britanniae'.

Stupor Mundi et immutator mirabilis, a term applied to the Emperor Frederick II (q.v., *d.* 1250), expressing contemporary opinion of his versatility. He was highly cultured, and his interests extended to mathematics, natural history, medicine, and other branches of intellectual activity. Frederick's tolerance of Muslims in his service led the papal party to accuse him of being the author of (an imaginary work) 'De Tribus Impostoribus'—Moses, Jesus, and Mohammed.

STURLA THORDSSON (*c.* 1214-84), nephew of Snorri Sturlason (q.v.), Icelandic historian, author of the 'Sturlunga Saga' or contemporary history of the house of Sturla, a vivid picture of old Icelandic life.

Sturm und Drang (storm and stress), the name (taken from the title of an absurd romantic drama of the American War of Independence by the German, Klinger, 1775) given to a period of literary ferment which prevailed in Germany during the latter part of the 18th cent., inspired by Rousseau's fervent idealism, revolt against conventional trammels, and recall to nature. The principal figures of the movement were Schiller, Goethe, and Herder (qq.v.).

Stutly, WILL, one of the legendary companions of Robin Hood (q.v.).

Stylite or STYLĪTĒS, an ascetic who lived on the top of a pillar. The best known of these ascetics was Simeon, a Syrian, who is said to have spent thirty years on a pillar near Antioch before his death in A.D. 459. He had several imitators, and is celebrated in Tennyson's poem, 'St. Simeon Stylites'.

Styx, connected with the Greek στυγεῖν to hate, στυγνός hateful, gloomy, a river of Hades or the lower world, over which the shades of the departed were ferried by Charon, and by which the gods swore their most solemn oaths. In the 'Odyssey' (x. 515) the Acheron is the principal river of Hades, of which the Pyriphlegethon, and the Cocytus, a branch of the Styx, are tributaries:

four infernal rivers that disgorge
Into the burning lake their baleful streams—
Abhorrèd Styx, the flood of deadly hate;
Sad Acheron of sorrow, black and deep;
Cocytus named of lamentation loud
Heard on the rueful stream; fierce Phlegeton
Whose waves of torrent fire inflame with rage.
(Milton, 'Paradise Lost', ii. 575-81.)

Sublapsarian or INFRALAPSARIAN, a Calvinist holding the view that God's election of some to everlasting life was made *after* He had permitted or foreseen the fall of Adam. Cf. *Supralapsarian.*

Sublime, On the, see *Longinus*.

Sublime and Beautiful, *A Philosophical Enquiry into the Origin of our Ideas of the,* a philosophical treatise by E. Burke (q.v.), published in 1756.

This is one of the earliest of Burke's publications. He finds that anything capable of exciting the idea of pain and danger is a source of the sublime; that beauty is the property which causes love (as distinct from desire); and that it consists in relative smallness, smoothness, absence of angularity, and brightness of colour (thus very much narrowing the sense of the word). The treatise contains interesting sections on the effect upon us of the distresses of others as the source of pleasure in terrible sights such as a conflagration, or in tragedies; and on the pleasurable effects of words and poetry.

Sublime Porte, THE, see *Porte*.

Subtle, 'The Alchemist', in Jonson's comedy of that name (q.v.).

Subtle Doctor, THE, *Duns Scotus* (q.v.).

Subura or SUBURRA, à district in ancient Rome, between the Esquiline, Viminal, and Quirinal hills. It contained many shops and houses of ill repute.

> Dum tu forsitan inquietus erras
> Clamosa, Juvenalis, in Suburra.
> (Martial, Epig. xii. 18.)

SUCKLING, SIR JOHN (1609–42), of an old Norfolk family, was educated at Trinity College, Cambridge. He inherited large estates, travelled in France and Italy, and was knighted on his return in 1630. He is said to have fought under Gustavus Adolphus and to have taken part in the defeat of Tilly before Breitenfeld (1631). He returned to London in 1632 and lived at court in a style of great profusion. He became a leader of the Royalist party in the early troubles; then fled to France and is said by Aubrey to have committed suicide in Paris. His chief works are included in 'Fragmenta Aurea' (1646), and consist of poems, plays, letters, and tracts, among them the famous 'Ballad upon a Wedding'. His 'Session of the Poets', in which the various writers of the day, including Ben Jonson, Carew, and D'Avenant, contend for the laurel, appeared in 1637; it is interesting as an expression of contemporary opinion on these writers. Suckling's play, 'Aglaura' (with two fifth acts, one tragic, the other not), appeared in the same year. It contains the famous lyric, 'Why so pale and wan, fond lover?' 'The Goblins', his best play, was acted in 1638. The goblins are thieves who disguise themselves as devils and behave somewhat after the manner of Robin Hood and his men. His 'Brennoralt' (1646), an expansion of the 'Discontented Colonell' (1640), a tragedy, reflecting on the disloyalty of the Scots (in the guise of Lithuanians), is interesting for the light which the melancholy colonel throws on the character of the author himself. The plays, however, are

chiefly valuable for their good lyrics. D'Avenant speaks of Suckling's sparkling wit, describing him further as the greatest gallant and gamester of his day. He invented the game of cribbage.

Suddlechop, BENJAMIN and DAME URSULA, characters in Scott's 'The Fortunes of Nigel' (q.v.).

SUDERMANN, HERMANN (1857–1928), born in East Prussia, dramatist and novelist, chiefly famous for his dramas, of which the best known are 'Magda' ('Heimat', 1892), in which the chief part has been played by Bernhardt, Duse and Mrs. Patrick Campbell; and 'Die Ehre' (1880).

Sudra, the lowest of the four great Hindu castes, the artisans and labourers.

SUE, EUGÈNE (1804–57), French novelist, a prolific writer of sensational novels of the Parisian underworld. The best known are 'Les Mystères de Paris' (1842–3) and 'Le Juif errant' (1844–5).

SUESS, EDUARD (1831–1914), born in London and educated at Prague and Vienna, became professor of geology at Vienna and one of the greatest of recent geologists. His principal work is 'Das Antlitz der Erde' (1885–1909), which was translated as 'The Face of the Earth' (1904–25) by H. B. C. Sollas.

SUETONIUS (GAIUS SUETONIUS TRANQUILLUS) (c. A.D. 70–c. 160), Roman historian, friend of the younger Pliny, author of 'Lives of the Caesars' (from Julius Caesar to Domitian) and of 'De Viris Illustribus' (including lives of Terence, Horace, and Lucan). But much of his writing is lost. An English version of what survives was made by Philemon Holland (q.v.).

Sufi, the name of a sect of Muslim ascetic mystics. There are references to them in the 'Rubáiyát' of Omar Khayyám.

Sullen, SQUIRE and MRS., characters in Farquhar's 'The Beaux' Stratagem' (q.v.).

Sullivan, SIR ARTHUR SEYMOUR (1842–1900), the son of a bandmaster at the Royal Military College, Sandhurst, studied at the Royal Academy of Music and at the Conservatorium, Leipzig, and from 1861 was organist at St. Michael's, Chester Square, and subsequently at St. Peter's, Cranley Gardens, London. He composed in 1866 the comic opera, 'Cox and Box', and in 1871 'Thespis', the libretto of which was by W. S. Gilbert (q.v.), the beginning of a collaboration which produced the famous Gilbert and Sullivan operas (q.v.). He composed a setting for Longfellow's 'Golden Legend' (1886) and a serious opera, 'Ivanhoe' (1891); also cantatas, oratorios, and a great deal of sacred music.

Sumer is icumen in, the first line of what is believed to be the earliest extant English lyric. It was probably written in the first half of the 13th cent.; the author is unknown. The music to which it was sung still survives.

Summa, see *Aquinas.*

Summers, WILL, Henry VIII's jester.

Summerson, ESTHER, a character in Dickens's 'Bleak House' (q.v.), and one of the narrators of the tale.

Summoner's Tale, The, see *Canterbury Tales.*

SUN YAT-SEN (1866–1925), 'The Father of the Chinese Republic', was the son of a Kwangtung farmer. At the age of 13 he joined his brother who was living in Honolulu and came into contact with Western ideas and influences. He later went to Hong Kong. There he became a Christian and studied medicine. He was in practice for a time but then decided to devote his life to political revolution and social reform. His first organized attempts to overthrow the corrupt Manchu government failed and he went abroad for many years, visiting Europe, America, and Japan to study socialist literature and find support for the revolution. Eventually, after further abortive revolts, a successful outbreak at Hankow led to the inauguration of a republic. Sun Yat-Sen was president briefly in 1912, but for the next decade most of the country remained in the hands of reactionary militarists, while the progressive forces held a precarious foothold in the Canton area. Towards the end of his life he reorganized his party, the Kuomintang, on Russian Communist lines, but died a year too soon to see its forces under Chiang Kai-shek finally overthrow the northern militarists.

Sun Yat-Sen's principal work consists of the San Min Chu I (Three People's Principles), delivered in lectures and published after his death, the three principles being nationalism, democracy, and the livelihood of the people.

Sunium, the ancient name of Cape Colonna, at the south-eastern extremity of Attica, in Greece. It was crowned by a marble temple to Athene, of which some columns still remain. It is celebrated in the last stanza of Byron's 'The Isles of Greece' ('Don Juan', III), 'Place me on Sunium's marbled steep'.

Sunna, the body of traditional sayings and customs attributed to Mohammed and supplementing the Koran.

Sunnites, as opposed to the Shi'ites (see *Shi'a*), the orthodox Muslims, who admit the caliphate of Abu Bakr and his immediate successors, but reject the claims of Ali's descendants.

Supernaculum, a modern Latin rendering of the German *auf den Nagel*, on the nail, in the phrase *auf den Nagel trinken*, to drink off liquor to the last drop; used as an adverb in reference to the practice of turning up the emptied cup or glass on one's left thumb-nail, to show that all the liquor has been drunk. Hence, as a substantive, a liquor to be drunk to the last drop, a wine of the highest quality. Hence, anything excellent of its kind. [OED.]

Supralapsarian, a name applied to those Calvinists who held the view that, in the divine decrees, the predestination of some to eternal life and of others to eternal death was antecedent to the Creation and the Fall. [OED.] Cf. *Sublapsarian.*

Supremacy, ACT OF: the first Act of Supremacy was passed in Henry VIII's reign (1534); it declared the King to be the Supreme Head on earth of the Church of England, and made it treasonable to deny this. By the second Act of Supremacy (1559), in Elizabeth's reign, the above title was abandoned, but an oath was imposed on persons holding office or taking a university degree acknowledging the Queen to be supreme governor of the realm in spiritual and ecclesiastical matters.

Sura, a chapter or section of the Koran (q.v.).

Surface, JOSEPH and CHARLES, in Sheridan's 'School for Scandal' (q.v.), two brothers presenting 'a contrast between shameless hypocrisy and reckless good-nature' (Hazlitt).

Surgeon's Daughter, The, a novel by Sir W. Scott (q.v.), published in 1827 as one of the stories in 'Chronicles of Canongate'.

It is the story of Richard Middlemas, an illegitimate child left in the care of Gideon Gray, surgeon of the village of Middlemas, and brought up in his home, where he and the surgeon's daughter Menie fall in love. On coming of age, Richard, being of an ambitious as well as violent and ill-balanced disposition, leaves the doctor's home to push his fortunes in India. Here he falls under the influence of an adventuress, the Begum Mootee Mahal, otherwise Mme Montreville, and has the unspeakable baseness to fall in with her plan to lure Menies out to India with a view to handing her over to Tippoo Sahib. The plot is defeated by Adam Hartley, Richard's fellow pupil at Dr. Gray's, an unsuccessful suitor for Menie's hand. He secures the interposition of Hyder Ali, who orders the release of Menie. By his order also Richard Middlemas is crushed to death by an elephant.

Surly, a character in Jonson's 'The Alchemist' (q.v.).

Surrealism, a movement in literature and art which began in Paris *c.* 1924. It was an attempt to express the subconscious without the restraint of reason, e.g. by automatic writing and the juxtaposition of incongruous ideas or objects.

SURREY, HENRY HOWARD, (by courtesy) *earl of* (1517?–47), the poet, was son of Thomas Howard (afterwards third duke of Norfolk). He married Frances Vere in 1532. He was with the army during the war with France (1544–6), being wounded before Montreuil, and was commander of Boulogne, 1545–6. He was condemned and executed on a frivolous charge of treasonably quartering the royal arms and advising his sister to become the king's mistress. He was then barely 30 years old.

His works consist of sonnets and miscellaneous poems in various metres, notable for their grace and finish. Like Wyatt (q.v.) he studied Italian models, especially Petrarch, and shared with Wyatt the merit of bringing the sonnet from Italy into England. He had the perhaps even greater merit of introducing, in his translation of the 'Aeneid' (Bks. II and IV), the use of blank verse. The subject of many of his love-poems was 'The fair Geraldine', Elizabeth, daughter of the ninth earl of Kildare. Forty of his poems were printed in Tottel's 'Miscellany', 1557 (reprinted 1867 and 1870). The poems, with those of Wyatt, were edited by Dr. G. F. Nott, 1815–16, and others, and for the Aldine poets by James Yeowell, 1866.

SURTEES, ROBERT (1779–1834), educated at Christ Church, Oxford, an antiquary and topographer. He spent his life in collecting materials for his 'History of Durham' county (1816–40). He is commemorated in the Surtees Society, a book-club dealing with the literature of the region constituting the old kingdom of Northumberland. Scott included in his 'Border Minstrelsy' a spurious and spirited ballad by him, 'The Death of Featherstonhaugh'. 'Barthram's Dirge' in the same collection is suspected of being also by Surtees (Burton, 'The Book-hunter').

SURTEES, ROBERT SMITH (1805–64), author of a number of humorous sporting novels. With Rudolph Ackermann the younger, he started in 1831 'The New Sporting Magazine', to which he contributed the sketches of Mr. Jorrocks, the sporting grocer, subsequently republished as 'Jorrocks's Jaunts and Jollities' (1838). This was followed by 'Handley Cross' (1843), 'Hillingdon Hall' (1845, about Jorrocks in his old age), 'Hawbuck Grange' (1847), 'Mr. Sponge's Sporting Tour' (1853), 'Ask Mamma' (1858), 'Plain or Ringlets' (1860), 'Mr. Facey Romford's Hounds' (1865). John Leech's illustrations to most of these books add greatly to their interest. Surtees also wrote in 'Bell's Life in London' a series of papers, some of which were reprinted, with illustrations by Alken, as 'The Analysis of the Hunting Field' (1846).

Surtur, in Scandinavian mythology, the ruler of Muspellheim (q.v.), the fire-god.

Survey of London, A, see *Stow*.

Surya, in Vedic theology, the sun-god, invoked by every devout Brahman when he rises.

Susanna, THE HISTORY OF, one of the apocryphal books of the O.T., detached from the beginning of the book of Daniel. Susanna was the wife of Joakim, a rich man dwelling in Babylon. She was accused of unchastity by two elders, because she had repelled their advances. Daniel exposed the plot by examining the elders separately; their evidence conflicted and they were put to death.

Suspicious Husband, The, a comedy by Dr. Benjamin Hoadly (q.v.) and his brother, produced in 1747 at Covent Garden, Garrick taking the part of Ranger.

Strictland, the suspicious husband of a young wife, is guardian of the wealthy Jacintha. She and Bellamy are in love with one another, but Strictland will not hear of the match. So Jacintha, a young lady of spirit, determines to run away with her lover, who provides a rope ladder for the purpose. Clarinda, a sprightly young friend of Mrs. Strictland, is staying in her house. Frankly, a friend of Bellamy, who has fallen in love with her at Bath, pursues her to London. Frankly and Bellamy meet outside the house at night, just when Jacintha is about to escape and when Clarinda, after a late whist party, is coming home. A general imbroglio ensues. Bellamy suspects Frankly of an intrigue with Jacintha; Strictland, discovering the latter's attempted flight, goes off in pursuit. Meanwhile Ranger, a frolicsome rattlepate, and friend of Bellamy and Frankly, happening to pass and seeing a rope-ladder hanging from the window, climbs up in search of adventure, and makes his way to the bedroom of Mrs. Strictland, whom he has never seen before. The return of Strictland with the captured Jacintha puts him to flight, but he drops his hat in Mrs. Strictland's room, where it is discovered by her husband, who is now convinced that his suspicions were well founded, and sentences his wife to banishment to the country. While this is going on, Ranger, who has taken refuge in another room, discovers Jacintha, and enables her to escape, this time successfully. On the morrow there is a general confrontation and explanation, and all ends happily.

Sutra, in Sanskrit literature, a short mnemonic rule in grammar, law, or philosophy, requiring expansion by means of a commentary.

Svengali, see *Trilby*.

SVEVO, ITALO (ETTORE SCHMITZ) (1861–1928), Italian novelist, born in Trieste of a German father and an Italian mother. He became friendly with James Joyce (q.v.) in Trieste in 1903. The originality of his analytical, introspective technique passed unnoticed until the publication of his third novel 'La cosciénza di Zeno' ('Confessions of Zeno', 1923), the style of which is not unlike Joyce's. It was partly due to Joyce himself that it became accepted as a significant masterpiece.

Swaddler, a nickname originally for a Methodist, especially a Methodist preacher, in Ireland; later for Protestants in general. The explanation commonly accepted (but challenged) is that indicated by C. Wesley in his journal (10 Sept. 1747): 'It seems we are beholden to Mr. Cennick for it, who abounds in such-like expressions as "I curse and blaspheme all the gods in heaven, but the babe that lay in the manger, the babe that lay in Mary's lap, the babe that lay in swaddling clouts". Hence they nicknamed him "Swaddler". And the name sticks to us all, not excepting the clergy.'

Swallow, the mare of Hereward the Wake (q.v.); according to the chronicles the ugliest as well as the swiftest of her time.

Swan, THE MANTUAN, Virgil (q.v.).

Swan of Avon, THE, Shakespeare, so called by Jonson.

Swan of Lichfield, see *Seward*.

Swanhild, according to the Volsunga Saga (q.v.), the daughter of Sigurd. King Jormunrek desires to marry her and sends Randver, his son, to sue for her hand. On his return with Swanhild, Randver is falsely accused to the king of having seduced her. He is ordered to execution, and on the way plucks the feathers from his hawk, and sends it to the king, as a symbol that his honour is taken from him. The king repents, but it is too late, for Randver has been put to death. Swanhild, as the cause of the king's grief, is bound in the gate, and is trodden to death under horses' feet.

Swaran, in the Ossianic poem 'Fingal' (q.v.), the Scandinavian king of Lochlin, who invades Ireland.

Swastika, from Sanskrit *svasti*, meaning 'good fortune', a primitive symbol or ornament consisting of a cross with equal arms having a limb of the same length projecting at right angles from the extremity of each arm, all in the same direction (usually clockwise); adopted by the Nazis as the symbol of Germany (referred to in a speech by Hitler as early as 13 April 1923).

Sweating sickness, the name given to a febrile disease of which highly and rapidly fatal epidemics occurred in the 15th and 16th cents. The principal epidemic in London occurred in 1517.

SWEDENBORG (SWEDBERG), EMANUEL (1688–1772), Swedish philosopher, scientist, and mystic, was the son of a professor of theology at Upsala. He devoted the earlier part of his life to scientific study and engineering, and was ahead of his contemporaries in many branches of scientific discovery. He was gradually led to seek a scientific explanation of the universe, publishing in 1734 his 'Opera philosophica et mineralia', and in the same year his 'Prodromus Philosophiae ratiocinantis de infinito' on the relation of the soul to the body and the finite to the infinite.

After middle age he applied himself to psychical and spiritual subjects. He enjoyed visions culminating in 1745 in a revelation, and thereafter devoted his life to the interpretation of the Scriptures. According to his theosophic system, God, as Divine Man, is infinite love and infinite wisdom, from whom emanate the two worlds of nature and spirit, distinct but closely related. The end of creation is the approximation of man to God. This end having been endangered by evil spirits, Jehovah descended into nature, restored the connexion between God and man, and left the Scriptures as His testimony, of which Swedenborg was the appointed interpreter. The Swedenborgians or followers of Swedenborg were organized in London in 1778 as the 'New Church'.

Sweedlepipe, PAUL or POLL, in Dickens's 'Martin Chuzzlewit' (q.v.), bird-fancier and barber, Mrs. Gamp's landlord.

SWEET, HENRY (1845–1912), philologist, educated at King's College School, London, Heidelberg university, and Balliol College, Oxford, did much foundational work in Anglo-Saxon, phonetics, etc. His publications included the 'History of English Sounds' (1874, 1888), the 'Anglo-Saxon Reader' (1876), 'A New English Grammar' (1892, 1898), 'The History of Language' (1900), 'The Sounds of English: an Introduction to Phonetics' (1908).

Swidger, PHILIP, WILLIAM, and MILLY, characters in Dickens's 'The Haunted Man' (q.v.).

SWIFT, JONATHAN (1667–1745), was born at Dublin after his father's death. He was son of Jonathan Swift by Abigail (Erick) of Leicester, and grandson of Thomas Swift, the well-known Royalist vicar of Goodrich, descended from a Yorkshire family. He was a cousin of Dryden (q.v.). He was educated at Kilkenny Grammar School, having Congreve (q.v.) for schoolfellow. Thence he went to Trinity College, Dublin, where he was censured for offences against discipline, obtaining his degree only by 'special grace'. He was admitted (1689) to the household of Sir W. Temple (q.v.), and there acted as secretary. He was sent by Temple to William III to convince him of the necessity of triennial parliaments, but his mission was not successful. He wrote pindarics, one of which, printed in the 'Athenian Mercury' (1692), provoked, according to Dr. Johnson, Dryden's remark, 'Cousin Swift, you will never be a poet.' Chafing at his position of dependence, and indignant at Temple's delay in getting him preferment, he returned to Ireland, was ordained (1694), and received the small prebend of Kilroot. He returned to Temple at Moor Park in 1696, where he edited Temple's correspondence, and in 1697 wrote 'The Battle of the Books' (q.v.), which was published in 1704, together with 'A Tale of a Tub' (q.v.), his celebrated satire on 'corruptions in religion and learning'. At Moor Park he first met Esther Johnson ('Stella'), the daughter of a servant or companion of Temple's sister, of whom more presently. On the death of Temple in 1699, Swift went again to Ireland, was given a prebend in St. Patrick's, Dublin, and the living of Laracor. He wrote his 'Discourse of the Contests and Dissensions in Athens and Rome' with reference to the impeachment of the Whig lords, in 1701. In the course of numerous visits to London he became acquainted with Addison, Steele, Congreve, and Halifax. He was entrusted in 1707 with a mission to obtain the grant of Queen Anne's Bounty for Ireland, and in 1708 began a series of pamphlets on church questions with his ironical 'Argument against abolishing Christianity', followed in the same year by his 'Letter concerning the Sacramental Test', an attack on the Irish Presbyterians, which injured him with the Whigs. Amid these serious occupations, he diverted himself with the series of squibs upon the astrologer John Partridge (1708–9, see under *Bickerstaff*), which have become famous, and his 'Description of a City Shower' and 'Description of the Morning', poems depicting scenes of London life, which were published in 'The Tatler' (1709). Disgusted at the Whig alliance with dissent, he went over to the Tories in 1710, joined the 'Brothers' Club' (q.v.), attacked the Whig ministers in 'The Examiner' (q.v.), which he edited, and in 1711 wrote 'The Conduct of the Allies' and 'Some Remarks on the Barrier Treaty', pamphlets written to dispose the mind of the nation to peace. He became dean of St. Patrick's in 1713. He had already begun his 'Journal to Stella' (letters 1 and 41–65 published in Hawkesworth's edition of Swift's works in 1766; letters 2–40 in Deane Swift's edition, 1768; the complete 'Journal', edited by Harold Williams, was published in 1948. It is a series of intimate letters (1710–13) to Esther Johnson and her companion Rebecca Dingley partly written in baby-language, recounting the details of his daily life while in London, where he was in close touch with the Tory ministers. Swift's relations with Stella have remained somewhat obscure; she was his worshipper, and he respected her and returned her affection. Whether he ultimately married her is uncertain. Stella died in 1728. Another woman, Esther Vanhomrigh (pron. 'Vanummery'), entered into his life in 1708; she fell deeply in love with him, received some measure of encouragement, and his final rupture with her about 1723 led to her death. The story of their love-affair is related in Swift's poem, 'Cadenus and Vanessa' (q.v.), 'Cadenus' being an anagram of 'Decanus', and 'Vanessa' being the pet name by which Swift knew her.

Swift wrote various political pamphlets, notably 'The Importance of the Guardian considered' (1713) and 'The Public Spirit of the Whigs' (1714), in reply to Steele's 'Crisis'; and about the time of the queen's death in 1714 and the fall of the Tory ministry, several papers (published much later) in defence of the latter. In the same year he joined Pope, Arbuthnot, Gay, and others in the celebrated Scriblerus Club (q.v.). He returned to Ireland in August 1714 and occupied himself with Irish affairs, being led by his resentment of the policy of the Whigs to acquire a sense of their unfair treatment of Ireland. By his famous 'Drapier's Letters' (q.v., 1724) he prevented the introduction of 'Wood's Half-pence' into Ireland. He came to England in 1726, visited Pope and Gay, and dined with Sir Robert Walpole, to whom he addressed a letter of remonstrance on Irish affairs with no result. He published 'Gulliver's Travels' (q.v.) in the same year, and paid a last visit to England in 1727, when the death of George I created for a moment hopes of dislodging Walpole. He wrote some of his most famous tracts and characteristic poems during his last years in Ireland, 'The Grand Question Debated' (q.v., 1729); 'Verses on his own Death' (1731), in which with mingled pathos and humour he posthumously reviews his own life and work; 'A Complete Collection of Polite and Ingenious Conversation' (?1738, q.v. under *Conversation*); and the ironical 'Directions to Servants' (written about 1731 and published after his death). He kept up his correspondence with Bolingbroke, Pope, Gay, and Arbuthnot, attracted to himself a small circle of friends, and was adored by the people. He set up a monument to Schomberg (William III's general, killed at the Boyne) in the cathedral at his own expense, spent a third of his income on charities, and saved up another third to found a charitable institution at his death, St. Patrick's Hospital for Imbeciles (opened 1757). The symptoms of the illness from which he appears to have suffered all his life (a form of vertigo) became very marked *c.* 1738, and for a time before his death he was insane. He was buried by the side of Stella, in St. Patrick's, Dublin, his own famous epitaph, 'ubi sæva indignatio ulterius cor lacerare nequit', being inscribed on his tomb. Dr. Johnson, Macaulay, and Thackeray, among many other writers, were alienated by his ferocity, which was, however, the result of noble qualities soured by hard experience. His indignation at oppression and unfairness was genuine. His writing was sometimes coarse, but never lewd. His political works are founded on common sense, pure and simple, and he had no party bias. Nearly all his works were published anonymously, and for only one, 'Gulliver's Travels', did he receive any payment (£200).

Among earlier biographies of Swift may be mentioned the earl of Orrery's (1751, see *Boyle (J.)*; followed by P. Delany's 'Observations upon Lord Orrery's Remarks', 1754, q.v.) Deane Swift's (1755), and T. Sheridan's (1784). There is a memoir by Sir W. Scott prefixed to his edition of Swift's works (1814), and Lives by John Forster (1875), by Henry Craik (1882), and by Leslie Stephen in the English Men of Letters series (1882). Johnson's criticisms in his 'Lives of the Poets' show an underlying antipathy.

Swift published a great number of works. Besides the more important, referred to above, mention may be made of the following:

Political writings: 'The Virtues of Sid Hamet the Magician's Rod' (1710), an attack on Godolphin; 'The W—ds—r Prophecy' (1711), attacking the duchess of Somerset; 'A short Character of T[homas] E[arl] of W[harton]' (1711); 'The Fable of Midas' (1711); 'Some Advice humbly offered to the Members of the October Club', the extreme Tories (1712); 'Some Free Thoughts upon the present state of affairs' (1714); 'Traulus' (1730), attacking Lord Allen; and the 'History of the Four Last Years of the Queen' [Anne] (1758).

Pamphlets relating to Ireland: 'A Proposal for the Universal Use of Irish Manufacture' (1720); 'The Swearer's-Bank' (1720); 'The Story of the Injured Lady' (?1746); 'A Short View of the State of Ireland' (1728); 'A Modest Proposal for preventing the Children of Poor People from being a Burden to their Parents or the Country'—by using them as food for the rich (1729); 'An Examination of certain Abuses, Corruptions and Enormities in the City of Dublin' (1732); 'The Legion Club' (the Irish parliament, 1736).

Pamphlets on Church questions: 'The Sentiments of a Church of England Man with respect to Religion and Government' (1708); 'A Project for the Advancement of Religion and the Reformation of Manners' (1709); 'A Preface to the B—p of S—r—m's Introduction', an attack on Bishop Burnett (1713); 'Mr. C—ns's Discourse on Free Thinking', a satire on Collins, the deist (1713); 'A Letter to a Young Gentleman, lately entered into Holy Orders' (1721). Mention may here be made of Swift's 'Sermons' (of which four were published in 1744), marked by the author's usual characteristics of vigour and common sense.

Miscellaneous verses and other writings: the 'Petition of Mrs. Frances Harris', a servant who has lost her purse, an amusing burlesque (1709); 'Baucis and Philemon' (1709); 'On Mrs. Biddy Floyd' (1709); 'A Meditation upon a Broom-Stick' (1710); 'A Proposal for Correcting, Improving and Ascertaining the English Tongue' (1712); imitations of the Seventh Epistle of the First Book of Horace, of the First Ode of the Second Book of Horace (1713), and of the Sixth Satire of the Second Book of Horace (1738); 'A Letter of Advice to a Young Poet' (1721); a 'Letter to a very young Lady on her Marriage' (1727); the 'Journal of a Modern Lady' (1729); 'The Lady's Dressing-Room' (1732); 'The Beasts Confession to the Priest' (1732), a satire

on 'the universal folly of mankind in mistaking their talents'; 'A serious and useful scheme to make an Hospital for Incurables'—whether the incurable disease were knavery, folly, lying, or infidelity (1733); 'On Poetry, a Rhapsody' (1733), satirical advice to a poet; 'A Beautiful Young Nymph Going to Bed'; and 'Strephon and Chloe' (1734). His poems were edited by Harold Williams (1937 and 1958).

The principal editions of Swift's works are: John Hawkesworth's (1766), Deane Swift's (1768), Thomas Sheridan's (1784), J. Nichols's (1801–3–8), Sir W. Scott's (1814 and 1824), Temple Scott's (1897–1908), and Herbert Davis's (1939–64). His correspondence, edited by Harold Williams, was published in 1963–5.

Swinburne, the quartermaster in Marryat's 'Peter Simple' (q.v.).

SWINBURNE, ALGERNON CHARLES (1837–1909), was educated at Eton and Balliol College, Oxford, and was early united by ties of friendship with Rossetti and his circle. His first published volume 'The Queen Mother. Rosamond. Two Plays' (1861) attracted no attention, but 'Atalanta in Calydon' (1865), a drama in the classical Greek form, with choruses (notably the hymn to Artemis) that revealed Swinburne's unsurpassed mastery of melodious verse, brought him celebrity. In the same year appeared 'Chastelard', the first of his three romantic dramas on the subject of Mary Queen of Scots. In 1866 followed the first series of 'Poems and Ballads' (containing 'Laus Veneris', 'Dolores', and 'A Litany', among other notable poems), which, by its outspoken repudiation of conventions and its pagan spirit, incurred no little censure. 'A Song of Italy' (1867) and 'Songs before Sunrise' (1871), written during the struggle for Italian independence, show Swinburne's detestation of kings and priests. 'Bothwell, a Tragedy', the second drama in the trilogy of Mary Queen of Scots, appeared in 1874, and 'Erectheus', a second drama in the Greek form, in 1876. The second series of 'Poems and Ballads', more subdued in tone and subject than the first, was published in 1878. It contains 'A Forsaken Garden', the laments for Baudelaire and Théophile Gautier, and translations of the 'Ballades' of Villon (q.v.). 'Songs of the Springtides' and 'Studies in Song' (1880) are marked by the author's passion for the sea. 'Mary Stuart', the third drama of the trilogy, appeared in 1881, and 'Tristram of Lyonesse', a romantic poem in rhymed couplets, considered by many Swinburne's most perfect work, in 1882. The volume containing the latter also included 'Athens, an Ode' (comparing the victory of Salamis with the defeat of the Armada), and other poems, among them a notable series of sonnets on the Elizabethan dramatists. The tragedy of 'Marino Faliero' (q.v.), in which he rehandled a theme previously treated by Byron, was published in 1885, and 'Locrine', another drama, in 1887, followed by a third series of 'Poems and Ballads' in 1889. His last volumes of poems, 'Astrophel' (1894), 'A Tale of Balen' (1896), and 'A Channel Passage' (1904), and his last plays, 'The Sisters', in prose (1892), and 'Rosamund, Queen of the Lombards' (1899), show some decline of power. 'The Duke of Gandia' (1908) was his last work.

Of Swinburne's prose works of literary criticism, the most notable were his 'Essays and Studies' (1875), 'Miscellanies' (1886), and his monographs on Shakespeare (1880), Victor Hugo (1886), Ben Jonson (1889), George Chapman (1875), and other Elizabethan dramatists. He also wrote acute and interesting criticisms of many more modern writers, from Blake to the Brontës and Charles Dickens; and produced the articles on Mary Stuart, Congreve, Keats, Landor, and Hugo for the 'Encyclopaedia Britannica'. His letters were edited by Cecil Y. Lang (6 vols., 1959–62). See also *Watts-Dunton*.

Swing, CAPTAIN, an imaginary person to whom about 1830–3 were attributed a number of outrages against farmers who had adopted the use of agricultural machinery.

Swiss Family Robinson, The, the romance of a family wrecked on a desert island, written in German by Johann Rudolf Wyss (1781–1830), a Swiss author, professor of philosophy at Bern. It was published in two parts in Zürich in 1812–13 and the first English translation was a year later.

Swithin or SWITHUN, ST. (*d.* 863), a priest of the church of Winchester, who was appointed by King Egbert tutor of his son Ethelwulf. On the latter's accession Swithin was consecrated bishop of Winchester, and was one of the king's chief counsellors in ecclesiastical matters. His body was buried by his own wish outside the north wall of Winchester Minster, 'where the rains of heaven might fall on him and he be trodden under foot by those who entered the church' (Stanton, 'Menology'). His remains were translated within the cathedral in 970, when numerous miracles occurred, and Swithin was canonized in popular tradition. His shrine is said to have been destroyed by Henry VIII. He is commemorated on 15 July. There is a legend that if it rains on this day there will be rain for the next forty days.

Swiveller, DICK, a character in Dickens's 'The Old Curiosity Shop' (q.v.).

Sword-dance, a medieval folk custom, of ritual origin, probably symbolizing the death and resurrection of the year. The stock characters were the fool, dressed in the skin of an animal, and the 'Bessy', a man dressed in woman's clothes. In many of the extant dances one of the characters is surrounded with the swords of the other dancers or slain. The characters were introduced in rhymed speeches. The sword-dance is one of the origins of the Mummers' play (q.v.) and so of English drama. See also *Revesby Play*.

Sybaris, an ancient Greek town in southern Italy, an Achaean colony and perhaps the earliest colony in Magna Graecia. Its inhabitants were so notorious for their luxury and love of pleasure, that the name *Sybarite* became proverbial for a voluptuary.

Sybil, or The Two Nations, an historical novel by Disraeli (q.v.), published in 1845.

Having in 'Coningsby' (q.v.) 'called attention to the state of our political parties; their origin, their history, their present position', the author proceeds in this work to 'draw public thought to the state of the People whom those parties for two centuries have governed'. He depicts the conditions prevailing among the working classes in the early years of Queen Victoria's reign, the overcrowding in miserable tenements, the inadequate wages, the 'truck' system, and the selfishness of many of the landlords and employers; and relates the agitation against them that led up to the Chartist riots. The 'Two Nations' of the title are the rich and the poor. With this exposition is woven the story of the love of the generous and enlightened Charles Egremont, younger brother of Lord Marney, one of the meanest of the landlord class, for Sybil, the daughter of Gerard, one of the Chartist leaders. The dramatic force of the situation is heightened by making Sybil belong to the family of the last abbot of Marney, whose lands had been plundered under Henry VIII.

Sybil Warner, a character in Lytton's 'The Last of the Barons' (q.v.).

Sycorax, in Shakespeare's 'The Tempest' (q.v.), a witch, the mother of Caliban.

Syllepsis, a figure of speech by which a word, or a particular form or inflexion of a word, is made to refer to two or more other words in the same sentence, while properly applying to or agreeing with only one of them, or applying to them in different senses; e.g. 'Miss Bolo went home in a flood of tears and a sedan chair'. Cf. *Zeugma*.

Sylph, one of a race of beings or spirits supposed to inhabit the air, originally in the system of Paracelsus (q.v.), who similarly imagined gnomes inhabiting the earth, nymphs the water, and salamanders fire.

Sylva, a book on arboriculture by Evelyn (q.v.).

Sylvander, the name under which Burns corresponded with Clarinda (q.v.), Mrs. Maclehose.

SYLVANUS URBAN, the pseudonym of E. CAVE (q.v.).

Sylvester II, POPE, see *Gerbert*.

Sylvia, a character in Farquhar's 'The Recruiting Officer' (q.v.). See also *Silvia* and below.

Sylvia, or the May Queen, a poetic fantasy by G. Darley (q.v.).

Sylvia's Lovers, a novel by Mrs. Gaskell (q.v.), published in 1863.

Sylvia is the daughter of Daniel Robson, a farmer near Monkshaven (Whitby) on the Yorkshire coast, at the end of the 18th cent., a man who has been sailor and smuggler. He has his grudge against the press-gang, of whose terrors in the days of the naval wars a graphic description opens the story. Sylvia is deeply loved by her plain, pedantic, Quaker cousin, Philip Hepburn, whose honesty and diligence as assistant in the big draper's shop of Monkshaven win him a partnership at 23. But Sylvia falls passionately in love with the gallant sailor, Charley Kinraid, and they plight their troth, to Philip's distress, who knows Charley's reputation as a light-of-love. Philip is sent on a mission to London, and as he walks along a lonely part of the coast, he sees his hated rival (who is simultaneously starting for his whaling-ship) seized by the press-gang. As Charley lies overpowered in their boat, he shouts to Philip a farewell message to Sylvia, which the latter has no opportunity of immediately delivering. On his return from London two months later, he finds Sylvia mourning the missing Charley, whose hat has been found by the shore and who is believed drowned. The temptation is too strong for Philip, and he conceals what he knows. Some time later Farmer Robson takes a leading part in a riotous attack on the press-gang, and is hanged in consequence, and Sylvia and her mother are thrown upon the world. Philip presses the advantage that their distress gives him and persuades Sylvia, still mourning for Charley, to enter into a loveless marriage with him. Then after a year Charley returns, Philip's treachery is revealed, and under the fierce denunciation of his wife he flees from the town and enlists, while Charley also disappears. The two men meet again at the siege of Acre, where Philip saves Charley's life and is himself grievously wounded. A beggar and disfigured, he returns to Monkshaven, drawn by his love for Sylvia and his child. Meanwhile her heart has softened towards him, and she has learnt that Charley, within a few weeks of leaving her, had married another woman. Philip and she are at last brought together, but he is now on his death-bed, and they have time only for mutual forgiveness before he dies. Among the many fine characters in the book may be mentioned the sturdy old servant, Kester, and Hester Rose, the Quakeress, whose self-denying love for Philip remains steadfast and unrequited to the end.

Symbolism, a movement in French poetry which began about 1880, when the poems of Mallarmé and Verlaine (qq.v.) were becoming known, and reached its height about 1890. The poetry aimed to evoke rather than describe, and its matter was impressions, intuitions, sensations.

Symbolism in Russia was the leading literary movement from 1894 to about 1910. Though partly derived from French sources it had peculiarly Russian roots, in particular the work of the philosopher V. Solovyov. Major Russian symbolists were V. Bryusov, A. Blok, A. Bely, K. Balmont, V. Ivanov.

Symkyn, SYMOND, the miller of Trumpington in Chaucer's 'The Reeve's Tale' (see *Canterbury Tales*).

SYMONDS, JOHN ADDINGTON (1840–93), educated at Harrow and Balliol College, Oxford, where he won the Newdigate prize and became a fellow of Magdalen. Symonds suffered long from ill health and spent much of his life in Italy, writing under difficulties. His largest work, a 'History of the Renaissance in Italy' (1875–86), containing much valuable information, is a series of picturesque sketches rather than a continuous treatise. He published his translation of the 'Autobiography of Benvenuto Cellini' in 1888. His other works include 'Studies of the Greek Poets' (1873), 'Sketches in Italy and Greece' (1874), short volumes on Ben Jonson, Sidney, and Shelley, and several volumes of verse (among others, 'Many Moods', 1878; 'New and Old', 1880; 'Animi Figura', 1882). Symonds excelled as a translator, and his versions from the Greek poets, and of the sonnets of Michelangelo and Campanella (1878), are especially praised.

SYMONS, ARTHUR (1865–1945), poet and critic. He was a prolific writer, and his early verse, published between 1889 and 1899, was typical of the literary fashions of the nineties. His critical work covers a wide diversity of subjects, including 'An Introduction to the Study of Browning' (1886) and 'The Symbolist Movement in Literature' (1899).

Symplegädes, see *Cyanean Rocks.*

Symposium, The, or *The Banquet,* the title of a dialogue by Plato in which Socrates, Aristophanes, Alcibiades, and others, at the house of the poet Agathon, discuss the nature of love. It is also the title of a dialogue by Xenophon, in which Socrates and others are the speakers.

Synaeresis, the sounding of two separate vowels as a diphthong, as when *aerial* is pron. *airial*; the opposite of *diaeresis.*

Syndicalism, from the French *chambre syndicale,* a trade union, a movement among industrial workers having as its object the transfer of the means of production and distribution from their present owners to unions of workers for the benefit of the workers. [OED.] The word apparently first occurs in 1907.

Synecdoche (pron. 'sinekdoki'), a figure of speech by which a more comprehensive term is used for a less comprehensive or vice versa, as whole for part or part for whole, e.g. 'There were six guns out on the moor' where 'guns' stands for shooters; and 'Oxford won the match', where 'Oxford' stands for 'the Oxford eleven'.

SYNGE, JOHN MILLINGTON (1871–1909), educated at Trinity College, Dublin, spent his early manhood in Paris. There in 1899 he met W. B.Yeats (q.v.), who persuaded him to apply his talents to the description of Irish peasant life. He visited the Aran Isles annually from 1898 to 1902 and published 'The Aran Islands' in 1907. His remarkable dramas followed in quick succession: 'The Shadow of the Glen' was performed in 1903, 'Riders to the Sea' in 1904, 'The Well of the Saints', 1905, 'The Playboy of the Western World' (q.v.), 1907, and 'The Tinker's Wedding', 1907. 'The Shadow of the Glen' was at first unfavourably received owing to the episode contained in it of the infidelity of an Irish wife to her husband. The suggestion contained in 'The Playboy' that an Irish peasant would condone a murder and harbour the murderer gave rise to much fiercer resentment. But the play is now recognized as one of Synge's best. The unfinished verse drama, 'Deirdre of the Sorrows', was written when Synge was dying, and published in 1910. His 'Works', which also include the descriptive essays 'In Wicklow' and 'In West Kerry' (contributed to 'The Manchester Guardian'), were published in 1910 and his 'Collected Works' (ed. R. Skelton *et al.*) began to be published in 1962.

Synonym, strictly a word having the same meaning as another; but more usually one of two or more words having the same general sense, but possessing each of them meanings or shades of meaning or implications not shared by the other or others; e.g. kill, slay, slaughter.

Synoptic Gospels, THE, those of Matthew, Mark, and Luke, so called as giving an account of the events from the same point of view, or under the same general aspect.

Syntax, DR., see *Combe.*

Syntipas, the Greek form of the name *Sindabar, Sandabar,* or *Sindibad,* an Indian philosopher, said to have lived about 100 B.C., the supposed author of a collection of tales generally known as 'The Seven Wise Masters'. Their main outline is the same as that of 'The Seven Sages of Rome' (q.v.), though details of the several stories vary. 'Syntipas' was translated from Greek into Latin (under the title 'Dolopathos') in the 12th cent., and thence into French. The names *Syntipas, Sindabar,* etc., are probably corruptions of the original Sanskrit word from which *Bidpai* (q.v.) and *Pilpay* are derived.

Syphax, see *Sophonisba.* Also a character in Addison's 'Cato' (q.v.).

Syrinx, in Greek mythology, an Arcadian damsel, who, being pursued by Pan, threw herself into the river Ladon, where she was changed into a reed. Of this Pan made his pipe. In Spenser's 'Shepheards Calender' (April), Syrinx represents Anne Boleyn.

T

T. P., the Rt. Hon. T. P. O'CONNOR (q.v.).

Tabard Inn, THE, in Southwark, the scene of the assembling of the pilgrims in Chaucer's 'The Canterbury Tales' (q.v.). The inn survived until 1875.

A tabard was a short surcoat open at the sides and having short sleeves or none, worn by a knight over his armour, and emblazoned with his armorial bearings; or by a herald and emblazoned with the royal arms.

Tabaret, PÈRE, the amateur detective in Gaboriau's novels of crime (see also *Lecoq*).

Tabley, BARON DE, see *Warren (J. B. L.).*

TACITUS, GAIUS(?) CORNELIUS (*c.* A.D. 55–*c.* 117), the Roman historian, of whose works the following survive in whole or in part: (1) 'Dialogus de Oratoribus'; (2) 'Vita Agricolae', especially interesting for its account of the Roman conquest of Britain; (3) 'Germania', a description of the Germanic peoples and

their institutions; (4) 'Historiae', comprising the period A.D. 68–96, of which we have only a portion; and (5) 'Annales', comprising the period from the death of Augustus to the death of Nero in A.D. 68, of which again the extant portion is incomplete. Tacitus was the son-in-law of Agricola and the intimate friend of the younger Pliny (q.v.), some of whose extant letters are addressed to him. 'Tacitean' prose is incisive, polished, and epigrammatic; it contrasts with the ample periods of the Ciceronian style.

Tackleton, a character in Dickens's 'The Cricket on the Hearth' (q.v.).

Tadmor, see *Palmyra.*

Tadpole and **Taper,** in Disraeli's 'Coningsby' and 'Sybil' (qq.v.), typical party wirepullers. 'Tadpole worshipped registration; Taper adored a Cry.'

Taë-ping, see *Tai-ping.*

Taglioni, Maria (1804–84), the celebrated ballet-dancer, daughter of Filippo Taglioni, an Italian ballet-master. She appeared in London in 1829, retired from the stage in 1847, and died in straitened circumstances at Marseilles. Thackeray's Pendennis was one of her admirers.

A kind of overcoat in use in the early part of the 19th cent. (mentioned by Scott, Thackeray, and in the 'Ingoldsby Legends') was called a *taglioni*.

TAGORE, Sir Rabindranath (1861–1941), Indian poet, was born at Calcutta. Of his works, which are marked by deep religious feeling, a strong sense of the beauty of earth and sky in his native land, and love of child-hood (especially in 'The Crescent Moon'), many have been translated into English. These include 'Gitanjali', 'The Crescent Moon', and 'The Gardener', published in 1913; the three plays, 'Chitra', 'The King of the Dark Chamber', and 'The Post Office' (the last two of which have been performed in London); 'Sadhana' (addresses on life and its realization, 1913), 'Fruit-gathering' (1916), 'My Reminiscences' (1917), an introductory essay to the 'Sakuntala' (1920), and 'Red Oleanders' (a play, 1925). Tagore also wrote many short stories, of which only a few have been translated ('Hungry Stones' 1916; 'Broken Ties', 1925). Tagore wrote mainly in Bengali, but he also wrote in English and translated into English some of his Indian writings.

Taillefer, a minstrel in the army of William the Conqueror, who, at the battle of Hastings, is said to have encouraged the Normans by singing of the deeds of Roland.

Tail-rhyme stanza, a stanza with a tail, tag, or additional short line, unrhymed or rhyming with another tag further on.

Tailors of Tooley Street, The, three tailors of Tooley Street, Southwark, who are said to have begun a petition to the House of Commons with the words: 'We, the people of England'. Canning and also O'Connell are said to have alluded to them, but an inquiry in 'N. & Q.' (10th Ser., ii. 168) failed to elicit a precise reference. A contributor in 'N. & Q.', 7th Ser., v. 55, gave the names of the sup-posed originals, local politicans, and busy-bodies, who, according to him, prepared a petition at the time of the Catholic Emancipa-tion movement. But this was challenged in 7th Ser., v. 114.

Tain-Bo-Cuailgne, the chief epic of the Ulster cycle of Irish mythology, the story of the raid of Queen Maeve of Connaught to secure the Brown Bull of Cuailgne (pron. 'Cooley'), and the defeat of the raid by Cuchulain (q.v.).

TAINE, HIPPOLYTE (1828–93), French philosopher, critic, and historian, whose theories of 'la race, le milieu et le moment' were concerned with the influence of en-vironment and heredity on the development of human character. These can be found notably in 'De l'intelligence' (1870, 2 vols.), in the introduction to his well-known 'Histoire de la littérature anglaise' (1863, 3 vols.) and in essays, philosophical and critical. His historical study, 'Origines de la France contemporaine' (1875–94), treats of the 'ancien régime', the Revolution, and 'Le Régime moderne' (the last incomplete). His other works include the travel sketches 'Voyage aux Pyrénées (1855), 'Voyage en Italie' (1866), etc.

Tai-ping or Taë-ping, the name given to the adherents of a great rebellion that arose in southern China in 1850, under the leader-ship of Hung-sin-tsuen, styled Tai-ping-wang, Prince of Great Peace, who claimed a divine commission to overthrow the Manchu dynasty and establish one of native origin. The rebellion was quelled in 1864 with the help of General Gordon (q.v.).

Taj Mahal, the marble mausoleum at Agra, India, built by the Mogul emperor Shah Jahan for his wife Mumtaz Mahal (*d.* 1632).

Talbot, a variety of hound, formerly used for tracking and hunting, now merely an heraldic animal. The name is understood to be derived from the ancient English family name of *Talbot* [OED.], and this is referred to in Scott's 'Waverley', lxxi.

Talbot, Mary Anne (1778–1808), the 'British Amazon', served as a drummer-boy in Flan-ders, 1792, and as cabin-boy in the 'Le Sage', and afterwards in the 'Brunswick'. She was wounded on board of the latter ship in the great battle of 1 June 1794. After subsequent adventures she became a servant and received a small pension. Her history was embodied by her employer, Robert S. Kirby, in his 'Wonderful Museum', second volume, 1804.

***Tale of a Tub,* A,** a comedy by Jonson (q.v.), licensed in 1633, the last play that the author put on the stage.

It deals with the attempts, in the course of a St. Valentine's Day, of various suitors to marry Awdrey, the daughter of Tobie Turfe, high constable of Kentish Town. Her father wishes to marry her to John Clay, tile-maker, and he and the wedding-party set off for the church. But his intention is defeated by Squire Tub and Canon Hugh the vicar, by means of a bogus story of a highway robbery, of which John Clay is accused. Squire Tub's desire to marry Awdrey is in turn frustrated by Justice Preamble, who conspires with Hugh the vicar to get her for himself. Tub warns Tobie Turfe, who recovers his daughter. But she is presently lured away from him again (together with £100) by the Justice, is intercepted by Tub, and finally carried off and married out of hand by Pol Martin, usher to Tub's mother, 'a groom was never dreamt of'.

Tale of a Tub, A, a satire in prose by Swift (q.v.), written, according to his own statement, about 1696, but not published until 1704.

The author explains in a preface that it is the practice of seamen when they meet a whale to throw him out an empty tub to divert him from attacking the ship. Hence the title of the satire, which is intended to divert Hobbes's 'Leviathan' and the wits of the age from picking holes in the weak sides of religion and government. The author proceeds to tell the story of a father who leaves as a legacy to his three sons, Peter, Martin, and Jack, a coat apiece, with directions that on no account are the coats to be altered. Peter symbolizes the Roman Church, Martin (from Martin Luther) the Anglican, Jack (from John Calvin) the dissenters. The sons gradually disobey the injunction, finding excuses for adding shoulder-knots or gold lace according to the prevailing fashion. Finally Martin and Jack quarrel with the arrogant Peter, and then with each other, and separate. The satire is directed with especial vigour against Peter, his bulls and dispensations, and the doctrine of transubstantiation. But Jack is also treated with contempt. Martin, as representing the church to which Swift himself belonged, is spared, though not very reverently dealt with. The narrative is freely interspersed with digressions, on critics, on the prevailing dispute as to ancient and modern learning, and on madness—this last an early example of Swift's love of paradox and of his misanthropy.

Tale of Chloe, The, a short novel by G. Meredith (q.v.), published in 1879.

This tragic little tale is described by the author as an episode in the history of 'Beau Beamish', the king of Bath. Chloe is a young lady, the soul of generosity, who has stripped herself of her fortune to redeem from prison an unprincipled fellow, Caseldy, whom she loves. But he deserts her and leaves Bath, where she lives uncorrupted, enjoying the favour and esteem of Beau Beamish, and faithful to Caseldy. An old duke who has married a beautiful young dairymaid, Susan Barley, entrusts her for a month to the care of Beamish and he, in turn, to the care of Chloe. Caseldy now returns, not to Chloe, but for the sake of Susan, the 'Duchess of Dewlap', as Beamish christens her. He seduces her from her allegiance, and Chloe, heartbroken, watches the process, determined to save the duchess even at the cost of her own life. And this she finally does by hanging herself on the door through which the duchess is about to make a midnight elopement with Caseldy.

Tale of Genji, The, a classic Japanese novel written c. A.D. 1001–1015 by Lady Murasaki (978?–1031?) and translated by A. Waley (q.v.) in 6 vols. (1925–33): I, 'The Tale of Genji', II, 'The Sacred Tree', III, 'A Wreath of Cloud', IV, Blue Trousers', V, 'The Lady of the Boat', VI, 'The Bridge of Dreams'. Prince Genji is an illegitimate son of the Emperor, living about the time of the authoress's childhood, and vols. I–IV are mainly concerned with the rivalry between the various women whom he loved. Between vols. IV and V there is a gap in the narrative of eight years, during which time Genji has died, and the last two volumes deal with the rivalry in love between Kaoru, Genji's supposed son, and Niou, the Emperor's son and Genji's grandson.

The authoress, who became lady-in-waiting to the Empress c. 1005 and spent a certain amount of her time at court, was nicknamed 'Murasaki' in allusion to the heroine of her book: her real name remains unknown.

Tale of Two Cities, A, a novel by Dickens (q.v.), published in 1859.

The 'two cities' are Paris, in the time of the French Revolution, and London. Dr. Manette, a French physician, having been called in to attend a young peasant and his sister in circumstances that made him aware that the girl had been outrageously treated and the boy mortally wounded by the Marquis de St. Évremonde and his brother, has been confined for eighteen years in the Bastille to secure his silence. He has just been released, demented, when the story opens; he is brought to England, where he gradually recovers his sanity. Charles Darnay, who conceals under that name the fact that he is a nephew of the marquis, has left France and renounced his heritage from detestation of the cruel practices of the old French nobility; he falls in love with Lucie, Dr. Manette's daughter, and they are happily married. During the Terror he goes to Paris to try to save a faithful servant, who is accused of having served the emigrant nobility. He is himself arrested, condemned to death, and is saved only at the last moment by Sydney Carton, a reckless wastrel of an English barrister, whose character is redeemed by his generous devotion to Lucie. Carton, who strikingly resembles Darnay in appearance, smuggles the latter out of prison, and takes his place on the scaffold.

The book gives a vivid picture (modelled on Carlyle's 'The French Revolution') of Paris at this period, and the opening scene of the coach-drive to Dover is one of the finest things in Dickens. Among the typical English characters is Jerry Cruncher, an odd-job man by day, who carries on the trade of body-snatcher by night. The novel was dramatized by F. Wills under the title 'The Only Way' (1890).

Tales in Verse, a collection of poems by Crabbe (q.v.), published in 1812.

Tales of a Grandfather, The, a history of Scotland to the close of the Rebellion of 1745–6, by Sir W. Scott (q.v.), published in 1827–9. A later series (1831) deals with the history of France.

The 'Tales' were designed in the first instance for the author's grandson, John Hugh Lockhart ('Hugh Littlejohn'). After a prefatory chapter on the period of the Roman occupation, the tales proceed to the period of Macbeth, and thence through Wallace and Bruce right through the history of Scotland down to the '45.

Tales of My Landlord, four series of novels by Sir W. Scott (q.v.): 'The Black Dwarf', 'Old Mortality' (1st Series); 'The Heart of Midlothian' (2nd Series); 'The Bride of Lammermoor', 'A Legend of Montrose' (3rd Series); 'Count Robert of Paris', 'Castle Dangerous' (4th Series). Jedediah Cleishbotham, schoolmaster and parish clerk of Gandercleugh, by a fiction of Scott, sold these tales to a publisher. They were supposed to be compiled by his assistant Peter Pattieson. The title of the series is a misnomer as Scott himself admitted, for the tales were not told by the landlord; nor did the landlord have any hand in them at all.

Tales of Soldiers and Civilians, a collection of short stories by Ambrose Bierce (q.v.), subsequently entitled 'In the Midst of Life'.

Tales of the Crusaders, two novels by Sir W. Scott (q.v.), 'The Betrothed' and 'The Talisman' (qq.v.).

Tales of the Hall, a collection of poems by Crabbe (q.v.), published in 1819.

TALFOURD, Sir THOMAS NOON (1795–1854), judge and author, is principally remembered as the friend of C. Lamb, whose 'Letters' and 'Memorials' he published in 1837 and 1848 respectively, and for his 'Ion' (1835), a tragedy conceived in the Greek spirit.

Talgol, in Butler's 'Hudibras' (q.v.), one of the characters in the bear-baiting episode; according to Sir Roger L'Estrange a butcher in Newgate Market.

Taliesin (*fl.* 550), a British bard, perhaps a mythic personage, first mentioned in the 'Saxon Genealogies' appended to the 'Historia Britonum' *c.* 690. A mass of poetry, probably of later date, has been ascribed to him, and the 'Book of Taliesin' (14th cent.) is a collection of poems by different authors and of different dates. The village of Taliesin in Cardiganshire has sprung up near the supposed site of his grave. Taliesin figures prominently in Peacock's 'The Misfortunes of Elphin' (q.v.), and he is mentioned in Tennyson's 'Idylls of the King' as one of the Round Table.

Talisman, The, a novel by Sir W. Scott (q.v.), published in 1825, forming part of the 'Tales of the Crusaders'.

The story presents the forces of the Crusaders, led by Richard I of England, encamped in the Holy Land, and torn by the dissensions and jealousies of the leaders, including, besides Cœur de Lion himself, Philip of France, the duke of Austria, the marquis of Montferrat, and the Grand Master of the Templars. The consequent impotence of the army is accentuated by the illness of Richard. A poor but doughty Scottish crusader, known as Sir Kenneth or the Knight of the Leopard, on a mission far from the camp encounters a Saracen emir, with whom, after an inconclusive combat, he enters into prolonged conversation, and mutual esteem springs up between them. This emir proves subsequently to be Saladin himself, and he presently appears in the Christian camp in the disguise of a physician sent by the Soldan to Richard, whom he quickly cures. Meanwhile the Knight of the Leopard, set to guard during the night the banner of England, is lured from his post by Queen Berengaria, Richard's wife, who in a frolic sends him an urgent message purporting to come from Edith Plantagenet, between whom and the knight there exists a romantic attachment. During his brief absence, his faithful hound is wounded, and the English flag torn down. Sir Kenneth, thus dishonoured, narrowly escapes execution at Richard's order by the intervention of the Moorish physician, who receives him as his slave. Kindly and honourably treated by Saladin, he is sent, in the disguise of a black mute attendant, to Richard, whom he saves from assassination. Richard pierces through Sir Kenneth's disguise and gives him the opportunity he desires of discovering the hand that wounded the hound and tore down the standard. As the Christian princes and their forces defile past the re-erected standard, the hound springs on Conrade of Montferrat and tears him from his horse. A trial by combat is arranged, in which Sir Kenneth defeats and wounds Montferrat, and is revealed to be Prince David of Scotland. The obstacle which his supposed lowly birth presented to his union with Edith Plantagenet is thus removed.

The Talisman from which the novel takes its title is the amulet by which Saladin effects the cure of Richard and which he presents to the Scottish knight. The incident has some historical basis in the amulet, known as the Lee-penny, obtained by Sir Simon Lockhart in a crusade, and long preserved (perhaps still) in the ancient family of the Lockharts of the Lee in Lanarkshire.

Talmud, THE, in the wide sense, the body of Jewish civil and ceremonial traditionary law, consisting of the *Mishnah* or binding precepts of the elders, additional to and developed from the Pentateuch, and the later *Gemara* or commentary upon these. The term was originally applied to the Gemara, of which two recensions exist, known respectively as the Jerusalem (Palestinian) and the Babylonian Talmud. The precepts of the Mishnah were codified about A.D. 200; the redaction of the Jerusalem Talmud had reached almost its present form by A.D. 408, that of the Babylonian Talmud extended from A.D. 400 to 500. [OED.]

Talus, in Greek mythology, a man of brass, made by Hephaestus. He was given to Minos, king of Crete, and protected the island by making himself red-hot and embracing any strangers that landed. He figures in the story of the Argonauts (q.v.) as having received them with a shower of rocks.

Another Talus, a nephew of Daedalus (q.v.), was a mythical person to whom was attributed the invention of the saw, the compasses, and other industrial devices. Daedalus, jealous of his skill, threw him down from the Acropolis of Athens.

Talus, a character in Spenser's 'Faerie Queene'. When Astraea left the world and returned to heaven, she

> left her groome,
> An yron man, which did on her attend
> Always to execute her steadfast doome.
>   (Bk. v. i. 12.)

He thus represents the executive power of government. He attends on Artegall (q.v.), wielding an iron flail, with which he dispatches criminals.

Tam Lin, the subject of an old ballad. Janet wins back to mortal life her elfin lover, Tam Lin, from the queen of the fairies, who has captured him.

Tam o'Shanter, a poem by Burns (q.v.).

Tam o' Shanter, a farmer, returning from Ayr late one night, well primed with liquor, passes the Kirk of Alloway. Seeing it lighted up, he stops and looks in and sees warlocks and witches dancing to the sound of the bagpipes played by Old Nick. Impelled by the sight of one 'winsome wench' among the beldams, Tam shouts, 'Weel done, Cutty Sark!' At once the lights go out, and the witches make for Tam like so many bees. Tam spurs his grey mare Meg, and just reaches the middle of the bridge over the Doon before the 'Cutty Sark' reaches him. There he is out of her power, but the mare's tail is still within the witches' jurisdiction, and this the 'Cutty Sark' pulls off. (A 'sark' is a chemise:

> Her cutty sark, o' Paisley harn . . .
> In longitude tho' sorely scanty.)

Tamberlane, see *Timur*.

Tamburlaine the Great, a drama in blank verse by Marlowe (q.v.), written not later than 1587 and published in 1590. It showed an immense advance on the blank verse of 'Gorboduc' (q.v.) and was received with much popular approval. The material for it was taken by the author from Pedro Maxia's Spanish life of Timur, of which an English translation had appeared in 1571.

Pt. I of the drama deals with the first rise to power of the Scythian shepherd-robber

Tamburlaine; he allies himself with Cosroe in the latter's rebellion against his brother, the king of Persia, and then challenges him for the crown and defeats him. Tamburlaine's unbounded ambition and ruthless cruelty carry all before him. He conquers the Turkish emperor, Bajazet, and leads him about, a prisoner in a cage, goading him and his empress, Zabina, with cruel taunts till they dash out their brains against the bars of the cage. His ferocity is softened only by his love for his captive, Zenocrate, the daughter of the Soldan of Egypt, whose life he spares in deference to the pleadings of Zenocrate when he captures Damascus.

Pt. II deals with the continuation of his conquests, which extend to Babylon, whither he is dragged in a chariot drawn by the kings of Trebizond and Soria, with the kings of Anatolia and Jerusalem as relay, 'pampered jades of Asia' (a phrase quoted by Pistol in Shakespeare, '2 Henry IV', II. iv); it ends with the death of Zenocrate, and of Tamburlaine himself. See *Timurlane*.

Tamerlane, a tragedy by Rowe (q.v.) produced in 1702, of some historical interest because under the name of Tamerlane the author intended to characterize William III, while under that of Bajazet he held up Louis XIV to detestation. The play was, for more than a hundred years, annually revived on 5 Nov., the date of William III's landing. See *Timurlane*.

Taming of the Shrew, The, a comedy by Shakespeare (q.v.) with perhaps a collaborator, was probably written about 1594, partly adapted from a play, 'The Taming of a Shrew', which had appeared in 1594, and partly based on the 'Supposes' of Gascoigne (q.v.). It was first printed in the folio of 1623.

The play is introduced by an 'induction' in which Christopher Sly, a drunken tinker picked up by a lord and his huntsmen on a heath, is brought to the castle, sumptuously treated, and in spite of his protestations that he is only 'old Sly's son of Burton-heath. . . . Ask Marian Hacket the fat ale-wife of Wincot', is assured that he is a lord who has been out of his mind, and is set down to hear the following play, performed for his sole benefit by strolling players.

Petruchio, a gentleman of Verona, of shrewd wit and imperturbable temper, determines to marry Katharina, the notorious termagant elder daughter of Baptista, a rich gentleman of Padua. He carries his courtship through with a high hand, undeterred by her rude rebuffs, but affecting to find her courteous and gentle. Then the taming begins. He humiliates Katharina by keeping her waiting on the wedding-day, and at last appearing clad like a scarecrow. He cuffs the priest, refuses to attend the bridal feast, and hurries his wife off, on a sorry horse, to his home. On arrival, he refuses to let her eat or sleep, on the pretext that the food and bed prepared are not good enough for her, and distresses her by other mad pranks. Finally he takes her back to her father's house, which she reaches completely tamed. Meanwhile Bianca, Katharina's younger sister, has been won by Lucentio, who has made love to her while masquerading as a schoolmaster. Hortensio, the disappointed suitor of Bianca, has married a widow. At the feast which follows there is a wager among the bridegrooms which wife shall prove the most docile; Petruchio wins triumphantly.

Tammany, the name of a Delaware Indian from whom William Penn obtained grants of land. It means 'the Affable'. The name was adopted by a society founded for benevolent purposes in New York in 1789, which before long took an active part in politics and built the original Tammany Hall in New York. This, and the building which replaced it in 1867, became the headquarters of a local political (democratic) party, which by its highly developed organization (and, it is said, by the use of corruption) has from time to time exercised a complete control over the municipal administration of the city.

Tamora, a character in Shakespeare's 'Titus Andronicus' (q.v.).

Tanagra, an ancient town of Boeotia, Greece. In its necropolis were discovered in the last quarter of the 19th cent. the beautiful terracotta figurines with which the name of Tanagra is now principally connected. Tanagra was the birthplace of Corinna (q.v.). Landor in 'Pericles and Aspasia', xliv, includes a poem which purports to be an ode of this poetess to her birthplace.

Tanais, the ancient name for the river Don and a city at its estuary.

Tanaquil, in Roman legend, the wife of Tarquinius Priscus, the first of the Tarquin (Etruscan) kings of Rome. Spenser uses the name to signify Queen Elizabeth in the introduction to Book I of 'The Faerie Queene'.

Tancred, one of the Norman heroes of the first Crusade, figures in Tasso's 'Jerusalem Delivered' (q.v.) as one of the principal knights serving under Godfrey de Bouillon.

Tancred, or The New Crusade, a novel by Disraeli (q.v.), published in 1847.

This was a companion work to Disraeli's two principal political novels, 'Coningsby' and 'Sybil', and in it he breaks new ground. It combines an earnest vindication of the claims and destinies of the Jewish race with a humorous presentment of the aspirations of a visionary young English nobleman to regenerate the world.

Tancred, Lord Montacute, is the son of the highly respectable, and in every way orthodox, duke and duchess of Bellamont. On coming of age, having meditated much on the social and religious conditions of the day, he horrifies his parents by refusing a seat in parliament and announcing his intention of going to the Holy Land to elucidate the great 'Asian Mystery' and to seek a direct communication from God as to His purpose. All attempts to dissuade him having failed, Tancred goes to Jerusalem and thence to Sinai, where, in a trance, he receives the desired communication, directing him to promote the doctrine of 'theocratic equality'. Meanwhile, however, he has become involved in the intrigues of the Druses and Maronites of the Lebanon, and has become a pawn in the game of the amiable arch-intriguer Fakredeen. Some stirring adventures result, which leave Tancred disillusioned but violently in love with a beautiful Jewess, to whom he offers his hand and heart. At the moment that he does this, the arrival of the duke and duchess at Jerusalem is announced.

Tancred and Gismund, or *Gismond of Salerne,* a play by R. Wilmot (q.v.) and others, published in 1591. Act II is by Henry Noel, Act IV by Hatton (q.v.). The play is founded on a tale by Boccaccio (see *Sigismonda*).

Tancred and **Sigismonda:** for Dryden's poem on these, see *Sigismonda*.

Tancred and Sigismunda, a tragedy by J. Thomson (1700–48, q.v.), published in 1745, produced (with Garrick as Tancred) in 1752.

It is based on the story inserted in 'Gil Blas', IV. iv, in which Tancred, the heir to the kingdom of Sicily, is lured by the cunning Siffredi into accepting with the throne a bride, Constantia, whom he does not love, and abandoning Siffredi's daughter, Sigismunda, whom he does. The latter, in despair at her desertion, consents to marry Osmond, her father's choice. But Tancred does not give up his lady-love so easily. He kills Osmond, but not before the latter has fatally stabbed Sigismunda.

Tanglewood Tales, see *Hawthorne*.

Tanner of Tamworth, THE, the hero of an old ballad included in Percy's 'Reliques', who, meeting King Edward IV out riding, takes him for a thief, changes horses with him, is thrown, disabused of his mistake, and instead of being hanged, as he expects, receives Plumpton-park as a gift from the good-humoured king.

Tannhäuser (pron. 'Tanhoizer'), a German minnesinger (q.v.) of the 13th cent., the subject of a legend embodied in a 16th-cent. ballad. According to this, as he rode by the Hörselberg in Thuringia, he was attracted by the figure of a beautiful woman, in whom he recognized Venus. She beckoned him into a cave, where he spent seven years in revelry. Smitten by his conscience he then left the 'Venusberg' and went to Rome to seek absolution from the pope. His Holiness replied that it was as impossible for Tannhäuser to be forgiven as for his dry staff to burgeon, and Tannhäuser departed in despair. But after three days the staff broke into blossom. The pope sent hurriedly for Tannhäuser, but he was nowhere to be found. He had returned to Venus.

The story is the subject of an opera by Wagner and of Swinburne's 'Laus Veneris'.

Tanqueray, The Second Mrs., a successful play by Pinero (q.v.).

Tantălus, in Greek mythology, the father of Pelops and Niobe (qq.v.). He is represented as punished in hell with an intense thirst and placed up to the chin in a pool of water which recedes when he attempts to drink it, while a bough laden with fruit hangs above his head but withdraws from his hand. The reason for this punishment is variously related. Some say that he revealed the secrets of the gods, or stole their nectar and ambrosia and gave these to mortals; others that he killed his son Pelops and offered his flesh to the gods to try them.

Tantivy, a nickname given to the post-Restoration high-churchmen and Tories, especially in the reigns of Charles II and James II. It arose in 1680–1, when a caricature was published in which a number of high-church clergymen were represented as mounted upon the Church of England and 'riding tantivy' to Rome, behind the duke of York. To 'ride tantivy' is to ride at a rapid gallop. The origin of the word 'tantivy' is obscure; perhaps echoic, representing the sound of a horse's feet. [OED.]

Tantony, a shortened form of St. Anthony, chiefly used in reference to the attributes with which the saint was represented, as TANTONY POUCH, TANTONY BELL (a small church bell), TANTONY PIG (the smallest pig of the litter, St. Anthony (of Egypt) being the patron saint of swineherds, and represented as accompanied by a pig).

Taoism. One of the so-called 'Three Teachings' of China, the other two being Confucianism and Buddhism (qq.v.). In opposition to the ethical principles of Confucianism, Taoism maintained that all moral judgements were relative, and idealized a time of primitive bliss unmarred by intellectual evaluations. The Taoist aim was a return to the state of pure experience and an unthinking conformity with the Tao or 'Way' of Nature; and mystical practices were used to attain its goal. Unlike Confucianism, Taoism suited the private contemplative life; it inspired poets and artists, and strongly influenced Ch'an (Zen) Buddhism.

In later centuries Taoism deteriorated into a polytheistic religion, but its great works continued to be admired. They are the 'Chuang-tzu', a masterpiece of intellectual power, poetic imagination, and literary skill dating from about 300 B.C., and the much-translated 'Tao te ching' ('Classic of the Way and its Power'), a pithy and difficult work written at about the same time, but attributed to a legendary figure called Lao-tzu.

Tapley, MARK, see *Mark Tapley*.

Tappertit, SIMON, in Dickens's 'Barnaby Rudge' (q.v.), Gabriel Varden's apprentice.

Taprobane, an ancient name for Ceylon. It is referred to by Sir John Mandeville as containing hills of gold, guarded by gigantic pismires. Arthur Tilley in 'Studies in the French Renaissance' (p. 33) makes Taprobane = Sumatra.

Tar-water, see *Berkeley*.

Tara, THE HILL OF, in county Meath, Ireland, celebrated in Irish tradition as the capital of the Fir Bolgs and of the Tuatha Dè Danann (qq.v.). It was in early times the residence of the high kings of Ireland and the meeting-place of the national legislative assembly. Relics of its importance, in the form of earthworks, still remain.

'The harp that once through Tara's halls The soul of music shed' are the first lines of one of Moore's best-known 'Irish Melodies'.

Targum, a word meaning 'interpretation', the name given to several Aramaic translations, interpretations, or paraphrases of the various divisions of the O.T., made after the Babylonian captivity, at first preserved by oral transmission, and committed to writing from A.D. 100 onwards. [OED.]

TARKINGTON, [NEWTON] BOOTH (1869–1946), American novelist and dramatist, chiefly remembered for his novels 'The Gentleman from Indiana' (1899), 'Monsieur Beaucaire' (1900, dramatized 1901), and 'The Magnificent Andersons' (1918).

Tarlton, RICHARD (d. 1588), actor, a man of humble origin and imperfect education, who attracted attention by his 'happy unhappy answers' and was introduced to Queen Elizabeth through the earl of Leicester. He became one of the Queen's players in 1583, and attained an immense popularity by his jests, comic acting, and improvisations of doggerel verse. He led a dissipated life and died in poverty. He is perhaps to be identified with Spenser's 'Pleasant Willy' (see *Tears of the Muses*) and Shakespeare's Yorick. Many fictitious anecdotes connected with him were published, notably 'Tarlton's Jests' (1592?–1611?) in three parts.

Tarn Wathelyne, see *Awntyrs of Arthure at the Terne Wathelyne*.

Tarot Cards, a set of playing-cards first used in Italy in the 14th cent.; from *tarocchi*, a word of unknown origin. 'Play at Ombre and Taroc, a game with seventy-two cards all painted with suns and moons, devils and monks' (Gray, letter to R. West, 1739).

Tarpa, SPURIUS MAECIUS, a literary critic who was employed by Pompey, and also by Augustus, as censor of plays and poems for public reading or performance.

Tarpeia, in Roman legend, the daughter of Tarpeius, governor of the citadel of Rome.

She promised to open the gates of the city to the Sabines if they would give her their bracelets, or as she expressed it, what they carried on their left arms. Tatius, the king of the Sabines, consented, and as he entered the city, to punish her perfidy, threw not only his bracelet but his shield upon Tarpeia; and, his followers imitating his example, Tarpeia was crushed under the weight of their bucklers. The place was called the Tarpeian rock in consequence, and criminals were thrown from it. There are variants of the legend.

Tarquins, THE, Tarquinius Priscus and Tarquinius Superbus (6th cent. B.C.), the fifth and seventh legendary kings of Rome, of Etruscan origin. The former reigned with moderation and popularity, increased the military power of Rome, and drained the city. The second, his son, was noted for his tyranny and arrogance, and the Romans, provoked by his oppression, when they saw the virtuous Lucretia (q.v.) stab herself after her ravishment by Sextus, son of their king, rose in rebellion and expelled the Tarquins from Rome. It was Tarquinius Superbus who bought the books of the Sibyl (q.v.). And it was he who, when his son Sextus, to whom the people of Gabii had entrusted the command of their armies, sent to consult his father as to his conduct, returned no answer to the messenger, but cut off with a stick the tallest poppies in his garden. His son, taking the hint, put to death the most powerful citizens of Gabii (cf. the story of Periander, q.v.).

Tartar, MR., a character in Dickens's 'Edwin Drood' (q.v.).

Tartarin, in certain novels of A. Daudet (q.v.), a Frenchman of fervid southern temperament, who combines the power of self-deception and enthusiasm for adventure of Don Quixote with the timidity of Sancho Panza. He goes lion-hunting, etc., with absurd results.

Tartars, more properly TATARS, a Mongol tribe that overran eastern Europe in the 13th cent., and called forth the joke of St. Louis, 'Either they will send us to Heaven, or we will send them to Tartarus.'

Tartărus, one of the regions of Hades where the most impious and guilty among mankind were supposed to be punished. According to Virgil it was surrounded by three impenetrable walls and the burning waters of the river Phlegethon.

Tartuffe,[1] LE, in Molière's comedy of that name, an odious hypocrite, who, under an assumption of piety, introduces himself into the household of the credulous Orgon, attempts to seduce his wife, and, being repulsed, endeavours to ruin the family.

[1] So Molière spelt it. The officially recognized spelling is *Tartufe*.

Task, The, a poem in six books by Cowper (q.v.), published in 1785.

Cowper's friend, Lady Austen, having suggested to him the sofa in his room as the subject of a poem in blank verse, the poet set about the task. Its six books are entitled, 'The Sofa', 'The Time-piece', 'The Garden', 'The Winter Evening', 'The Winter Morning Walk', and 'The Winter Walk at Noon'. Starting with a mock-Miltonic narrative of the evolution of the sofa, Cowper soon turns to himself and his delight in rural scenes and sounds, which he describes minutely and exactly. Similarly the later books give a detailed account of the pleasures of gardening and the joys of domestic life in the country, with vignettes of the postman, the wagoner in the snow, the woodman and his dog, and many others. There are interspersed many long didactic passages, condemning the evils of the day, the failings of the clergy, the mischiefs of profusion, the cruelty of certain sports, and the disadvantages of town life in general.

Tasman, ABEL JANZOON (1602–59), a Dutch navigator, who commanded in 1642 an exploring expedition sent to the South Seas by Van Diemen, governor of the Dutch East Indies. He discovered Tasmania (which he named Van Diemen's Land), New Zealand, and some of the Friendly Islands.

TASSO, TORQUATO (1544–95), son of Bernardo Tasso (author of an epic on Amadis of Gaul), was born at Sorrento, and spent many years at the court of Ferrara. He was from early life in constant terror of persecution and adverse criticism, and his conduct at Ferrara was such as to make it necessary for the duke, Alphonso II of Este, to lock him up as mad from 1579 to 1586. (The legend of his passion for Leonora d'Este, the duke's discovery of it, and his consequent imprisonment, is now declared untrue.) He was released on condition of his leaving Ferrara; and after wandering from court to court, he died at Rome. His chief works were the 'Jerusalem Delivered' (q.v.), published in authorized form in 1581; a romantic epic, 'Rinaldo'; a pastoral play, 'Aminta'; and a tragedy, 'Torrismondo'.

Byron's 'The Lament of Tasso' is founded on the above-mentioned legend of Tasso's love for Leonora, and Goethe wrote his 'Torquato Tasso' in 1790.

TATE, NAHUM (1652–1715), educated at Trinity College, Dublin, wrote an adaptation of 'King Lear' (in which Cordelia survives and marries Edgar), which held the stage for many years; and with Dryden's assistance the second part of 'Absalom and Achitophel' (q.v.); also the libretto of Purcell's opera 'Dido and Aeneas'. With Nicholas Brady he published in 1696 the well-known metrical version of the Psalms that bears their name. He was appointed poet laureate in 1692. His chief original poem was 'Panacea—a

Poem on Tea' (1700). He was pilloried in the 'Dunciad' (q.v.).

Tate and Brady, see *Tate* (*N.*).

Tate Gallery, THE, London, commemorates the name of Sir Henry Tate (1819–99), a sugar merchant who gave £80,000 for the construction of the gallery. It was opened in 1897 as the national gallery of British art and modern art of all countries.

Tatler, The, a periodical started by R. Steele (q.v.) in Apr. 1709. It appeared thrice a week until Jan. 1711.

According to No. 1, it was to include 'Accounts of Gallantry, Pleasure, and Entertainment . . . under the article of White's Chocolate House'; poetry under that of Will's Coffee-house; foreign and domestic news from St. James's coffee-house; and so on. Gradually it adopted a higher mission. The evils of duelling and gambling are denounced in some of the earlier numbers, and presently all questions of good manners are discussed from the standpoint of a humaner civilization, and a new standard of good taste is set up. The ideal of a gentleman is examined and its essence is found to lie in forbearance. The author assumes the character of Bickerstaff (q.v.), the marriage of whose sister, Jenny Distaff, with Tranquillus gives occasion for treating of happy married life. The rake and the coquette are shown in their true light, and virtue is held up to admiration in the person of Lady Elizabeth Hastings—'to love her is a liberal education'. Episodes and short stories illustrate the principles advanced.

From an early stage in the history of 'The Tatler' Steele had the collaboration of Addison (q.v.), who besides notes and suggestions contributed a number of complete papers.

Tattersall's, an auction-room for horses founded near Hyde Park Corner in 1766 by Richard Tattersall (1724–95), stud-groom to the second duke of Kingston. His honesty and business-like precision brought him the highest patronage, and the establishment became famous, and survives in premises at Brompton.

Tattle, a character in Congreve's 'Love for Love' (q.v.).

Tattycoram, in Dickens's 'Little Dorrit' (q.v.), a foundling brought up in the Meagles household.

Tauchnitz, CHRISTIAN BERNHARD VON (1816–95), the founder of a publishing house at Leipzig which in 1841 (there being at that time no international agreement on copyright) began the issue of a 'Collection of British and American Authors' for sale on the Continent, followed by a collection of English translations of German authors.

Taurinum, in imprints, Turin.

Taurus, the Bull, the second of the zodiacal constellations, containing the groups of the

Pleiades and the Hyades, and the great star Aldebaran. The sun enters the zodiacal sign Taurus on 21 April.

Taverner's Bible, see *Bible* (*The English*).

Tawdry, see *Audrey.*

TAYLOR, BAYARD (1825–78), American traveller and author, published a large number of books of travel, novels, poems, and a translation of Goethe's 'Faust'.

TAYLOR, EDWARD (1645?–1729), American poet and divine, born in England, emigrating to Boston in 1668. His devotional poems remained in manuscript and were not published until 1937, when their importance to the history of early American letters was at once recognized. He belongs to the metaphysical tradition of George Herbert and Francis Quarles (qq.v.).

TAYLOR, SIR HENRY (1800–86), held an appointment in the Colonial Office from 1824 to 1872, during which time he published a number of plays in verse, 'Isaac Comnenus' (1827), 'Philip van Artevelde' (1834), 'Edwin the Fair' (1842), 'A Sicilian Summer' and 'St. Clement's Eve' (1862). 'The Eve of Conquest' and other poems appeared in 1847, 'The Statesman' (q.v.) in 1836. 'Philip van Artevelde' (q.v.), his masterpiece, is remarkable as a study of character, and also displays his lyrical faculty. There is an interesting critical introduction to the play. His 'Autobiography' appeared in 1885.

TAYLOR, JANE (1783–1824) and ANN (1782–1866), authors of books for the young, published 'Original Poems for Infant Minds' (including contributions by Adelaide O'Keeffe, 1766–1855?) in 1804, which attained immense popularity, and 'Rhymes for the Nursery' (1806), which included 'Twinkle twinkle, little star'; also 'Hymns for Infant Minds' (1810). Jane Taylor also wrote 'Display, a Tale for Young People' (1815) and 'Contributions of Q.Q.' (1824).

TAYLOR, JEREMY (1613–67), was born at Cambridge, and was the son of a barber. He was educated at Gonville and Caius College, Cambridge. Having attracted Laud's attention as a preacher, he was sent by him to Oxford and became a fellow of All Souls College. He was chaplain to Laud and Charles I, and was .appointed rector of Uppingham in 1638. He was taken prisoner in the Royalist defeat before Cardigan Castle in 1645, and retired to Golden Grove, Carmarthenshire, where he wrote most of his greater works. After the Restoration he was made bishop of Down and Connor, and subsequently of Dromore. He died at Lisburn and was buried in his cathedral of Dromore. His fame rests on the combined simplicity and splendour of his style, of which his 'Holy Living' and 'Holy Dying' (1650–1) are perhaps the best examples. Among his other works, the 'Liberty of Prophesying', an argument for toleration, appeared in 1646; his

'Eniautos' or series of sermons for the Christian Year, in 1653; 'The Golden Grove', a manual of daily prayers, in 1655; the 'Ductor Dubitantium', 'a general instrument of moral theology' for determining cases of conscience, in 1660; and his 'The Worthy Communicant' in the same year.

TAYLOR, JOHN (1580–1653), the 'water-poet', born of humble parentage at Glouces-ter, was sent to Gloucester Grammar School; but becoming 'mired' in his Latin accidence was apprenticed to a waterman, pressed for the navy, and was present at the siege of Cadiz. He then became a Thames waterman, and collector of the Lieutenant of the Tower's perquisite of wine. He increased his earnings by rhyming, and showed a marked talent for expressing himself in rollicking verse and prose. He obtained the patronage of Jonson and other men of genius, and diverted both court and city. He went on foot from London to Braemar, visited the Continent, and the queen of Bohemia at Prague, started from London to Queenborough in a brown-paper boat and narrowly escaped drowning, and accomplished other journeys, each one re-sulting in a booklet with an odd title. He was lodged in Oriel College, Oxford, during the plague of 1625. He finally took the 'Crown' public-house in Hanover Court, Long Acre. He published in 1630 a collective edition of his works, 'All the Workes of John Taylor, the Water Poet' (reprinted with other pieces by the Spenser Society, 1868–78).

TAYLOR, JOHN (1703–72), commonly known as the 'Chevalier', an itinerant oculist, who possessed much skill as an operator, but advertised himself like a charlatan. He was the author of treatises on the eye and of a bombastic autobiography, and was the subject of many satires.

TAYLOR, PHILIP MEADOWS (1808–76), an Indian officer and 'Times' correspon-dent in India from 1840 to 1853, was author of 'The Confessions of a Thug' (1839), a very successful book. After his retirement in 1860 Taylor wrote a number of brilliant stories delineating epochs of Indian history, notably the trilogy, 'Tara: a Mahratta Tale' (1863), 'Ralph Darnell' (1865), and 'Seeta' (1873). 'The Story of my Life', edited by his daughter, appeared in 1877.

TAYLOR, THOMAS (1768–1835), mathe-matician and Platonist. He was the first to embark on a systematic translation and exposition of Orphic, Platonic, and other ancient literatures. He also devoted himself to the attempt to discover a metaphysic of mathematics.

TAYLOR, TOM (1817–80), educated at Glasgow University and Trinity College, Cambridge, of which he became fellow, wrote for various newspapers and was editor of 'Punch' from 1874 to 1880. He produced a number of successful plays (some in col-laboration with Charles Reade and others),

taking the plots as a rule from previous writers. The plays include 'To Parents and Guardians' (1845), 'Still Waters Run Deep' (1855), 'Our American Cousin' (1858). He edited Haydon's autobiography in 1853, and C. R. Leslie's 'Autobiographical Recollections' after the author's death (1860).

Tchaikovsky, PETER ILITCH (1840–93), an eminent Russian composer, whose works are marked by the national spirit and the power of portraying every variety of emotion. They include several operas, six symphonies (of which the last three are the best known), pianoforte concertos, etc.

TCHEHOV, ANTON PAVLOVICH, see *Chekhov.*

Te Deum, an ancient Latin psalm of praise, so called from its opening words. The authorship is traditionally ascribed to St. Ambrose (c. 340–97, bishop of Milan), and is connected with the conversion by him of St. Augustine; but modern scholars are inclined to attribute the authorship to Ambrose's younger contemporary, Niceta of Remesiana.

Te igitur, the first prayer in the canon of the mass in the Roman liturgy; hence extended to the liturgical book itself, so called from the opening words of the prayer.

Teague, a nickname for an Irishman, the anglicized spelling of the Irish name *Tadhg.*

Tears of the Muses, The, a poem by Spenser (q.v.), included in the 'Complaints' published in 1590. In this the poet deplores, through the mouth of the several Muses, the decay of literature and learning. It contains, in the lament of Thalia, an interesting passage ('Our pleasant Willy, ah! is dead of late') which has been thought by some to refer to Shakespeare ('dead' being used in the sense of silent) or Tarlton (q.v.), but probably refers to Lyly.

Tearsheet, DOLL, a character in Shake-speare's '2 Henry IV' (q.v.).

Teazle, SIR PETER and LADY, characters in Sheridan's 'The School for Scandal' (q.v.).

Teian Muse, THE, Anacreon (q.v.).

Teiresias, see *Tiresias.*

Telamon (plur. TELAMONES), a figure of a man used as a column to support an entablature or other structure. From the name of Telamon, the father of Ajax (q.v.). Cf. *Caryatids.*

Telegraph Paxarett, SIR, in Peacock's 'Melincourt' (q.v.), one of the suitors of Anthelia.

Tel-el-Amarna Tablets, a series of clay tablets with cuneiform inscriptions found in 1887 in the ruins of the palace of Amen-hotep IV (Akhnaton) at Tel-el-Amarna in Middle Egypt. They contain the diplomatic correspondence of the kings of Babylonia and Assyria with the king of Egypt.

Telĕmăchus, a son of Odysseus and Penelope (qq.v.), who was still a child when his father went to the Trojan War. At the end of the war, when his father did not return, Telemachus went to seek him, accompanied by Athene in the guise of Mentor, and visited Nestor and Menelaus to obtain information. On his return to Ithaca, where the suitors of his mother had conspired to slay him, his father, who had just returned, was revealed to him by Athene. Together they concerted, with the help of Eumaeus (q.v.), the destruction of the suitors.

Télémaque, see *Fénelon.*

Telephus, see *Achilles' spear.*

Telford, THOMAS (1757–1834), civil engineer and architect. He built over 1,000 miles of road, including the London to Holyhead road, including 1,200 bridges, including the Menai Suspension Bridge, churches, docks, and canals, notably the Caledonian Canal. He was a friend of Campbell and Southey, and described in a journal a journey through Scotland which he made with the latter.

Tell, WILLIAM, a legendary hero of the liberation of Switzerland from Austrian oppression. The stories concerning him differ in details, but in its generally accepted form the legend represents him as a skilled Swiss marksman who refused to do honour to the hat of Gessler, the Austrian bailiff of Uri, placed on a pole, and was in consequence arrested and required to hit with an arrow an apple placed on the head of his little son. This he successfully did, and with a second arrow shot Gessler, subsequently stirring up a rebellion against the oppressors. Another version relates how Tell, being carried a prisoner across the lake to Gessler's castle, was given the rudder, on account of his strength, when a storm arose. He steered the boat on to a ledge of rock, subsequently called Tell's Platte, sprang ashore, and shot the bailiff. These events are placed in the 14th cent. But Swiss historians have shown that there is no evidence for the existence of a real William Tell. The story is first found in writings of the 15th century. William Tell is the subject of a play by Schiller and an opera by Rossini (qq.v.).

Similar legends of marksmen shooting at an object placed on the head of a man or child are of widespread occurrence, e.g. in Norway and England (Egil, Clym of the Clough, William of Cloudesley).

TELLEZ, GABRIEL (1570–1648), who wrote under the pseudonym TIRSO DA MOLINA, a Spanish dramatist, famous outside Spain principally as the creator of the prototype of Don Juan in his play 'El Burlador de Sevilla' ('The Seville Deceiver' or 'Jester').

Tellus, the name under which the Earth was worshipped at Rome, corresponding to the Greek Gĕ.

Temora, one of the chief epics among the

Ossianic poems of Macpherson (q.v.). 'Temora' is the name of the palace of the kings of Ulster. Cormac, the young king, has been murdered by Cairbar of Connaught, who has usurped the throne (as told in 'The Death of Cuthullin'). Fingal comes over to Ireland to re-establish the ousted dynasty. In the battle that ensues Cairbar and Oscan (the son of Ossian and grandson of Fingal) fall by each other's hand; Fillan, a son of Fingal, is also slain; and finally Fingal kills Cathmor, the brother of Cairbar and leader of the rebel host.

Tempē, a valley in Thessaly, between Mt. Olympus on the north and Mt. Ossa on the south, through which the river Penēus flows to the sea. It was celebrated for its beauty, cool shades, and warbling birds: 'Zephyris agitata Tempe' (Horace, 'Odes', III. i).

Tempest, The, a romantic drama by Shakespeare (q.v.), was probably written in 1611 and the latest of his completed works. It was not printed till the folio of 1623. The story of the exiled magician and his daughter had figured in a recent German play, and other literary sources have been suggested. Shakespeare has worked into the play details of the shipwreck on Bermuda of Sir G. Somers's ship the 'Sea-Venture' in 1609. He may have got the name of the god Setebos from Richard Eden's 'History of Travaile' (1577).

Prospero, duke of Milan, ousted from his throne by his brother Antonio, and turned adrift on the sea with his child Miranda, has been cast upon a lonely island. This had been the place of banishment of the witch Sycorax. Prospero, by his knowledge of magic, has released various spirits (including Ariel) formerly imprisoned by the witch, and these now obey his orders. He also keeps in service the witch's son Caliban, a misshapen monster, the sole inhabitant of the island. After Prospero and Miranda have lived thus for twelve years, a ship carrying the usurper, his confederate, the king of Naples, and the latter's son Ferdinand is by the art of Prospero wrecked on the island. The passengers are saved, but Ferdinand is thought by the rest to be drowned, and Ferdinand thinks the rest are drowned. Ferdinand and Miranda are thrown together, fall in love, and plight their troth. Ariel, by Prospero's order, subjects Antonio and the king of Naples to various terrors. Antonio is cowed; the king repents his cruelty, is reconciled with Prospero, and his son Ferdinand is restored to him. All ends happily, for the ship is magically restored and Prospero and the others prepare to leave the island, after Prospero has renounced his magical faculties. Caliban, whose intercourse with Stephano, a drunken butler, and Trinculo the jester has provided some excellent fooling, is left, as before, the island's sole inhabitant.

Templars, KNIGHTS, an order founded about 1118, consisting originally of nine knights whose profession was to safeguard pilgrims to Jerusalem, and who were granted by Baldwin, king of Jerusalem, a dwelling-place in his palace near the temple. Many noblemen from all parts of Christendom joined the order, and it acquired great wealth and influence in France, England, and other countries. Active always in the field, they were really a source of weakness to the Christian king of Jerusalem from their direct dependence on the pope and their constant violation of treaties with the Muslim powers. After the battle of 1187 Saladin made an example of the Templars and the (much less guilty) Hospitallers who became his prisoners, and beheaded them all, about 200 in number, while sparing nearly all his other prisoners. The knights were organized in commanderies, under a preceptor in each province, and a grand master at the head of the order. From a state of poverty and humility (their seal represents two of them riding on the same horse) they became so insolent that the order was suppressed. They were accused of blasphemy, sorcery, and other crimes. The order was crushed by the kings of Europe in their various dominions with circumstances, especially in France, of great cruelty. It was also officially suppressed by the pope and the Council of Vienne (1312). Browning's poem, 'The Heretic's Tragedy', alludes to the burning of Jacques du Bourg-Molay, the grand master, in 1314. See also under *Temple* (*The*, of London).

Temple, Miss, in Charlotte Brontë's 'Jane Eyre' (q.v.), the kindly manager of the Lowood Asylum.

Temple, The, of the Jews at Jerusalem, was first built by Solomon, on the summit of Mt. Moriah, 'the threshingfloor of Ornan' (2 Chron. iii). It was destroyed by Nebuchadnezzar in 586 B.C.; rebuilt under Ezra and Nehemiah; partly destroyed by Antiochus Epiphanes, 167 B.C.; splendidly restored by Herod the Great; and finally destroyed by Titus in A.D. 70. The site is now occupied by the Mosque of Omar (q.v.).

Temple, The, a district of London lying between Fleet Street and the Thames, took its name from the Knights Templars (q.v.), who owned it from about 1160 until their suppression. Their church, built on the model of the church of the Holy Sepulchre at Jerusalem and known as the Round Church, was consecrated in 1185, and forms part of the present Temple Church. The Temple was leased to law students and converted into Inns of Court (the Inner and Middle Temple) in the 14th cent.

The Temple Garden is the scene, in Shakespeare's '1 Henry VI' (II. iv), of the plucking of the white and red roses of York and Lancaster; and in '1 Henry IV', III. iii, the prince makes an appointment with Falstaff in the Temple Hall (an anachronism, Loftie points out).

TEMPLE, Sir WILLIAM (1628–99), educated at Emmanuel College, Cambridge, was envoy at Brussels in 1666, and visited The Hague, where he effected the triple alliance between England, Holland, and Sweden, aiming at the protection of Spain from French ambition (1668). He went again to The Hague in 1674, where he brought about the marriage between William of Orange and Mary. He married in 1655 Dorothy Osborne, whose letters to him were published in 1888, and again in a better edition in 1928. He settled first at Sheen and later at Moor Park, near Farnham, where he was much occupied with gardening, and where Swift (q.v.) was an inmate of his household. His principal works are an 'Essay upon the Present State of Ireland' (1668), 'Observations upon . . . the Netherlands' (1672), an essay upon 'The Advancement of Trade in Ireland' (1673), and three volumes of 'Miscellanea' (1680, 1692, and 1701). The second of these contains his best-known essay, 'Of Ancient and Modern Learning', which, by its uncritical praise of the spurious epistles of Phalaris (q.v.), exposed the author to the censure of Bentley (q.v.) and led to a vigorous controversy. The 'Miscellanea' also include the essays 'Upon the Original and Nature of Government' (written about 1671), 'Upon the Gardens of Epicurus', 'Upon Health and Long Life', 'Of Heroic Virtue', and 'Of Poetry'. Temple's Letters were published by Swift in 1701, after Temple's death. His 'Memoirs', relating to the period 1672–9, published in 1692, are an agreeable blend of public affairs with a record of private life.

Temple Bar, like Holborn Bar and other bars on the chief roads leading out of London, marked the limit of the common lands or 'liberties' that surrounded the medieval city. It was rebuilt by Sir C. Wren (1672–3) and removed in 1878. It is now at Theobalds Park, Cheshunt.

Ten Days that Shook the World was written by John Reed, a correspondent of the American Socialist press, and first published in England by the British Communist Party in 1926, with an introduction by Lenin. Reed records the rise of the Bolsheviki, and his story, as he explains in his preface, dated 1 Jan. 1919, is 'what happened in Petrograd in November, 1917, the spirit which animated the people, and how the leaders looked, talked, and acted.' What took place in 'Red Petrograd'—the capital and heart of the insurrection—was almost duplicated at different intervals of time all over Russia. The material comes from Reed's own notes, and from Russian, English, and French newspapers and the *Bulletin de la Presse* issued daily by the French Information Bureau. The chronicle records the triumph of the Bolsheviki—the representatives of the proletarian masses—over the Provisional Government of Kerensky and the Mensheviki—the moderate socialists—which began on 7 Nov. 1917, with Trotsky's declaration, in the name of the Military Revolutionary Committee, that the Provisional Government no longer existed. Reed gives a vivid, almost hour-by-hour account of the violent and decisive ten days that followed, the meetings he attended, impassioned speeches and arguments he heard, proclamations and counter-proclamations he read, and the surrender of Kerensky. After the surrender of the Kremlin to the Bolsheviki on 14 Nov. Reed visited Moscow and attended the funeral of 500 revolutionary dead—'Martyrs of the Beginning of World Social Revolution'—in the Red Square.

As the news of Kerensky's defeat spread, Lenin issued proclamations all over Russia, explaining the Revolution and urging the people to take the power into their own hands. The President of the new Government of the All-Russian Congress of Soviets was Lenin: the People's Commissar for Foreign Affairs, Trotsky.

Ten Thousand a Year, see *Warren* (*S.*).

Tenant of Wildfell Hall, The, see *Wildfell.*

Teniers, DAVID, the Younger (1610–90), Flemish painter, chiefly of genre scenes of peasants and topers. His father David Teniers the Elder (1582–1649), painted chiefly religious subjects, and his son, David (1638–85), was also a painter, often imitating his father.

TENNANT, WILLIAM (1784–1848), educated at St. Andrews University, a parish schoolmaster (at Anstruther in Fife) learned in oriental languages, of which he became professor at St. Andrews. He is remembered in a literary connexion for his poem in six cantos, 'Anster Fair', published in 1812, a mock-heroic description of the humours of the fair (in James V's reign) and of the courting, with fairy interposition, of Maggie Lauder by Rob the Ranter.

Tenniel, SIR JOHN (1820–1914), illustrator. He worked for 'Punch' from 1850, and from 1864 succeeded Leech as its chief cartoonist. 'Dropping the Pilot' (1890), referring to Bismarck's resignation, is one of his best-known cartoons. His illustrations for 'Alice in Wonderland' (1865) and 'Through the Looking Glass' (1871) are perfect examples of the integration of illustration with text.

Tennis Court Oath: on 29 June 1789 the Third Estate of France (self-styled 'National Assembly') met in the Tennis Court (*Jeu de Paume*) at Versailles, in defiance of the royal orders, and its members took an oath not to separate until they had made a constitution.

TENNYSON, ALFRED, *first Baron Tennyson* (1809–92), was born at Somersby, of which place his father was rector, and educated by his father and at Trinity College, Cambridge, where he became acquainted with A. H. Hallam (q.v.). He won the chancellor's medal for English verse in 1829

with a poem, 'Timbuctoo'. 'Poems, by Two Brothers' (1827) contains some of his earlier and unimportant verse. In 1830 he published 'Poems, chiefly Lyrical' (including 'Claribel' and 'Mariana'), which were unfavourably reviewed by Lockhart and Wilson, and in 1832 travelled with Hallam on the Continent. Hallam died in 1833, and in that year Tennyson began his 'In Memoriam' (q.v.) expressive of his grief for his lost friend. He became engaged to Emily Sellwood, to whom, however, he was not married until 1850. In 1833 he published a further volume of 'Poems', containing 'The Two Voices', 'Œnone' (q.v.), 'The Lotos-Eaters' (q.v.), 'A Dream of Fair Women' ('Tithonus', q.v., published in 1860, belongs also to this period); and in 1842 an edition of his poems in two volumes, which included some of his finest work: the 'Morte d'Arthur' (the germ of the 'Idylls'), 'Locksley Hall' (q.v.), 'Ulysses' (q.v.), 'St. Simeon Stylites', etc. He received from Peel a pension of £200. In 1847 he published 'The Princess' (q.v.) and in 1850 'In Memoriam', and was appointed poet laureate in succession to Wordsworth in the latter year. He wrote the 'Ode' on the death of Wellington and 'The Charge of the Light Brigade' in 1854, having at this date taken up his residence at Farringford, in the Isle of Wight. He published 'Maud' (q.v.) in 1855, and in 1859 four 'Idylls of the King' (q.v., Enid, Vivien, Elaine, Guinevere), which finally established his fame and popularity. 'Enoch Arden' (q.v.) appeared in 1864 (the volume included his popular dialect poem, 'The Northern Farmer: Old Style'); 'Lucretius' (q.v.), privately printed in 1868; 'The Holy Grail' (q.v.) in 1869; 'The Last Tournament' (q.v.), privately printed in 1871, and 'Gareth and Lynette' (q.v.) in 1872. Tennyson began building his second residence, Aldworth, near Haslemere, in 1868. His dramas, 'Queen Mary' (q.v.) and 'Harold' (q.v.), appeared in 1875 and 1876, 'The Falcon' (privately printed) in 1879, 'The Cup' (privately printed) in 1881, 'The Promise of May' in 1882, and 'Becket' (q.v.) in 1884, in which year he was made a peer. In 1880 appeared 'Ballads and other poems', which includes, besides 'The Voyage of Maeldune' and 'Rizpah' (qq.v.), the fine war ballads 'The Revenge' (q.v.) and 'The Defence of Lucknow'. Tennyson published 'Tiresias, and other poems' in 1885, 'Locksley Hall, sixty years after' in 1886, and 'Demeter, and other poems' (including 'Merlin and the Gleam', the lines 'To Virgil', and 'Crossing the Bar') in 1889. The 'Death of Œnone, and other poems' and 'The Foresters' appeared in 1892. Tennyson was buried in Westminster Abbey. A life of him by his son was published in 1897.

TENNYSON, FREDERICK (1807–98), elder brother of A. Tennyson (q.v.), contributed to the 'Poems by Two Brothers' (1827), and published 'Days and Hours'

(1854), 'The Isles of Greece' (1890), and other volumes of verse.

TENNYSON TURNER, CHARLES (1808–79), elder brother of A. Tennyson (q.v.), contributed to 'Poems by Two Brothers' (1827) and published from time to time volumes of sonnets (1830–80), simple and restrained in manner, some of them depicting the rustic aspects of the wolds.

Tensons or TENÇONS, dialogues in verse sung in contest between two troubadours.

Teraphim, a kind of idols or images, apparently household gods, an object of reverence and means of divination among the ancient Hebrews and kindred peoples, mentioned, e.g., in Judges xvii. 5; perhaps something like the Tanagra figurines of Greece, or the Lares and Penates of Rome (if statues were made, as they probably were, of these family godlets).

TERENCE, (PUBLIUS TERENTIUS AFER) (*c.* 190–159 B.C.), the Roman comic poet, was born at Carthage and came when young to Rome, as the slave of P. Terentius Lucanus, by whom he was freed. He visited Greece late in his short life and never returned. He wrote six plays, most of them based on comedies by Menander: 'Andria', 'Hecȳra' ('The Mother-in-Law'), 'Heautontimorumenos' ('The Self-punisher'), 'Eunūchus', 'Phormio', 'Adelphoe'.

Teresa, ST., see *Theresa.*

Tereūs, see *Philomela.*

Terill, SIR WALTER, a character in Dekker's 'Satiromastix' (q.v.).

Termagant, the name of an imaginary deity held in medieval Christendom to be worshipped by the Muslims: in the mystery plays represented as a violent overbearing personage; hence 'a bully', and later 'a virago'. From Old French *Tervagant,* Italian *Trivigante,* probably for *Trivagante,* the moon, wandering under three names, Selene (or Luna) in heaven, Artemis (or Diana) on earth, Persephone (Proserpina) in the lower world.

Terpander, the father of Greek music, a native of Lesbos, who probably flourished in the first half of the 7th cent. B.C. He is said to have made of the lyre (which previously had only four strings) a seven-stringed instrument, and to have founded at Sparta the first Greek school of music.

Terpsichŏrē, the Muse (q.v.) who presided over dancing.

Terra sigillata, 'sealed earth', a medicinal earth from the island of Lemnos, so called because cakes of it were sealed or stamped, in antiquity, with the head of Artemis, in later times with the seal of the Grand Signior. It was esteemed an antidote against poisons and was famous during the Renaissance.

Terrae filius, Latin, a 'son of the earth', a man of unknown origin; formerly, at Oxford University, an orator privileged to make humorous and satirical strictures in a speech at the public 'act'. [OED.]

Terrible Temptation, A, a novel by Reade, published in 1871.

It is the story of the persistent warfare waged on Sir Charles Bassett by his unscrupulous cousin Richard Bassett, who considers himself defrauded of his inheritance. This inheritance he is determined to recover either for himself or his children. In pursuit of this purpose he tries by a base device to frustrate his cousin's marriage, and finally gets him locked up in a madhouse—a part of the story designed to show the unsatisfactory state of the law with regard to the certification of lunatics (cf. Reade's *Hard Cash*). His schemes are frustrated by the devotion of Sir Charles's wife, and a reconciliation is in the end effected. The novel possesses a special interest in the description of the methods by which the author (in the character of the lawyer Rolfe) accumulated the documents which served as the basis of his narratives.

Terror, THE, see *Reign of Terror.*

Tertium quid, 'some third thing', something indefinite, related in some way to two definite or known things, but distinct from both. In Browning's 'The Ring and the Book' (q.v.), after the two halves of Rome have given their opinions on the story of Pompilia, comes the impartial opinion of 'Tertium Quid'.

TERTULLIAN (*b. c.* A.D. 150), one of the greatest of the early Christian writers in Latin; author of 'Apologeticus' (197), an eloquent appeal to Roman governors on behalf of the Christians, and of many treatises on the Christian mode of life.

Terza rima, the measure adopted by Dante in the 'Divina Commedia', consisting of lines of five iambic feet with an extra syllable, in sets of three lines, the middle line of each rhyming with the first and third lines of the next set (a b a, b c b, c d c, etc.).

Tess of the D'Urbervilles, A Pure Woman, a novel by Hardy (q.v.), published in 1891.

Tess Durbeyfield is the daughter of a poor, foolish villager of Blackmoor Vale, whose head is turned by learning that he is a descendant of the ancient family of the D'Urbervilles. Tess is seduced by Alec, a young man of means whose parents bear the surname D'Urberville with doubtful right to it. Tess gives birth to a child, which dies in infancy, after an improvised midnight baptism by its mother. Some time later, while working as a dairymaid on a large farm, Tess becomes engaged to Angel Clare, a clergyman's son. On their wedding-night she confesses to him the affair of Alec; and Angel, himself a sinner while Tess has been a victim, abandons her. Misfortune and hardship come upon her and her family, and accident throws her once more in the path of Alec D'Urberville. He has become a preacher, but his temporary religious mania does not prevent him from pressing his attentions upon her. After some pathetic appeals to her husband, she is driven to accept the protection of Alec. Clare, returning from Brazil repentant of his harshness, finds her in this situation. Maddened by this second wrong that has been done her by Alec, she murders him to liberate herself. After a brief period of concealment with Clare in the New Forest, Tess is arrested, tried, and hanged. ' "Justice" was done, and the President of the Immortals (in Aeschylean phrase) had ended his sport with Tess.'

Tessa, a character in George Eliot's 'Romola' (q.v.).

Test, The, and *The Con-test,* political periodicals founded in 1756, in favour of Henry Fox and Pitt respectively.

Testament of a Man Forbid, and other 'Testaments', see *Davidson.*

Testament of Beauty, The, see *Bridges.*

Testament of Cresseid, The, see *Cresseid.*

Testament of Love, The, see *Usk.*

Tester, apparently a corruption or perversion of *teston,* a name for the *teston* or *testoon* (shilling) of Henry VIII, especially as debased and depreciated; subsequently a colloquial or slang term for sixpence. Hence also perhaps the slang 'tizzy'.
    TESTON was originally the French name of a silver coin struck at Milan by Galeazzo Maria Sforza (1468–76), bearing a portrait or head of the duke. In England the name was first applied to the shilling of Henry VII, the first English coin with a true portrait; also to those of Henry VIII and early pieces of Edward VI. It was declared in 1543 to be equal to 12 pence, but was debased in 1545, no less than half of copper being put into it, and sank to 10*d.,* 9*d.,* and 6*d.*; it was recalled in 1548.

Tethys, in Greek mythology, one of the deities of the sea, daughter of Uranus and Gē, and wife of Oceanus. She was regarded as the mother of the chief rivers of the earth, and her daughters were known as the Oceanides.

Tethys, in geology, a S. European ocean, so named by Suess (q.v.), at some time connected with the Atlantic, of which the Mediterranean is a much reduced remnant.

Tetrachordon, the third of Milton's pamphlets on divorce, dealing (whence its name) with four sets of passages from Genesis, Deuteronomy, the Gospel of St. Matthew, and the First Epistle to the Corinthians. Milton also wrote two sonnets on the subject of this pamphlet.

Tetragrammaton, from the Greek, 'the word of four letters', referring specifically to the Hebrew word written YHWH or JHVH (vocalized as *Yahweh* or *Jehovah*). 'Tetragrammaton' is often substituted for that word (regarded as ineffable) and treated as a mysterious symbol of the name of God. The pronunciation of the original word was supposed to be kept hidden, for fear of blasphemy.

Tetterbys, THE, characters in Dickens's 'The Haunted Man' (q.v.).

Teubner, BENEDICT GOTTHELF (1784–1856), the founder of a publishing and book-selling business in Leipzig, famous for the 'Bibliotheca Scriptorum Graecorum et Romanorum Teubneriana', begun in 1849, which attained high renown as containing the best available texts of the ancient classics.

Teucer, a son of Telamon and half-brother of Ajax (q.v.), and the best archer in the Greek army before Troy. On his return to Salamis after the war, Telamon refused to receive him, because he had failed to avenge on Odysseus the death of Ajax. Teucer thereupon sailed to Cyprus, where he established himself.

Teufelsdröckh, HERR, see *Sartor Resartus.*

Thackeray, ANNE ISABELLA, see *Ritchie.*

THACKERAY, WILLIAM MAKEPEACE (1811–63), of a Yorkshire yeoman family, was born in Calcutta, where his father held office as collector. He was sent to England in 1817, and educated at Walpole House, Chiswick, at Charterhouse, and at Trinity College, Cambridge. Here he studied little, and left in June 1830 without a degree, after making friends with Edward FitzGerald, Tennyson, and others. He then travelled abroad and met Goethe at Weimar. In 1831 he entered the Middle Temple, sharing rooms in Crown Office Row with Tom Taylor, but soon gave up the legal profession. In 1833 he became proprietor of 'The National Standard', for which he wrote and drew. It had a short existence, and Thackeray settled in Paris to study drawing. In 1836 he published eight caricatures of ballet-dancers entitled 'Flore et Zéphyr' under the pseudonym 'Théophile Wagstaff', and became Paris correspondent of 'The Constitutional', which failed. In the same year he married Isabella Shawe. He returned to England in 1837 and contributed to 'Fraser's Magazine' 'The Yellowplush Correspondence' (in which Mr. Yellowplush (q.v.), an illiterate footman, relates his social experiences) and wrote reviews for 'The Times' and other papers. 'Some Passages in the Life of Major Gahagan' (q.v.) appeared in 'The New Monthly Magazine' in 1838–9, and 'Catherine' (q.v.), narrated by 'Ikey Solomons, junior' in 'Fraser' in 1839–40, the latter being an attempt to ridicule the exaltation of crime in fiction. In 1840

Thackeray was parted from his wife owing to her insanity, a calamity that had a marked effect upon his writing, in which the element of pathos becomes more pronounced. 'A Shabby Genteel Story' (q.v.) appeared in 'Fraser' in 1840, 'The Paris Sketch-Book, by Mr. Titmarsh' in the same year, and 'The Great Hoggarty Diamond' (q.v.) in 1841. In these last two works Thackeray assumed the pseudonym of Michael Angelo Titmarsh. In the character of George Savage Fitz-Boodle he contributed to 'Fraser' in 1842–3 the 'Fitz-Boodle Papers', the confessions of an elderly clubman of the flames inspired in his susceptible heart by various German maidens. Fitz-Boodle reappears in 'Men's Wives', a series printed in 'Fraser' in 1843, which contains the diverting portraits of the adventurer Captain Howard Walker and the composer Sir George Thrum. 'Bluebeard's Ghost' and 'The Irish Sketch-book' by M. A. Titmarsh were published in the same year; and in 1844 Thackeray, in the character again of Fitz-Boodle as editor, contributed to 'Fraser' 'The Luck of Barry Lyndon' (q.v.). 'Notes of a Journey from Cornhill to Grand Cairo by Mr. M. A. Titmarsh', a long 'sketch-book', appeared in 1846. Thackeray began his contributions to 'Punch' in 1842; of these the best known are 'Jeames's Diary' (1845), 'Mr. Punch's Prize Novelists' (q.v., 1847) and 'The Snobs of England' (1847, afterwards published as 'The Book of Snobs)', a denunciation of social pretentiousness. Even before the 'Snobs' were completed, the serial numbers of 'Vanity Fair' (q.v.) had begun to appear, followed by those of 'Pendennis' (q.v.) in November 1848, 'Esmond' (q.v.) in 1852, and 'The Newcomes' (q.v.) in 1853–5. Meanwhile Thackeray had begun to publish the tales ('Mrs. Perkins's Ball', 'Our Street', 'The Rose and the Ring', q.v., etc.) reprinted in 'Christmas Books' (1857). In these, and in the burlesque 'Legend of the Rhine' (1845), 'The Kickleburys on the Rhine', and 'Rebecca and Rowena' (1850), Michael Angelo Titmarsh reappears as author. Thackeray lectured on 'The English Humourists of the Eighteenth Century' in 1851 (published in 1853) and on 'The Four Georges' in 1855–6 (published in 1860). In 1852 he went on a lecturing tour to America, and the result was the sequel to 'Esmond', 'The Virginians' (q.v.), published in serial numbers in 1857–9. In 1857 Thackeray had unsuccessfully stood for parliament at Oxford. He had retired from 'Punch' in 1854 and became editor of the 'Cornhill' in 1860. He contributed to it 'Lovel the Widower' (1860), 'The Adventures of Philip' (1861–2, in which the characters of 'The Shabby Genteel Story' reappear), the unfinished 'Denis Duval' (q.v.), and 'The Roundabout Papers'. Mention should be made of Thackeray's ballads and other rhymes, written at various periods of his life, and in various moods. The best known perhaps are the 'Ballad of Bouillabaisse' (q.v.), 'The Mahogany Tree', and the two

on Catherine Hayes, the murderess, and Catherine Hayes, the Irish singer.

There is a biography of Thackeray by A. Trollope in the English Men of Letters series (1879), and Lewis Melville published another, in two volumes, in 1910. Sir William Wilson Hunter's 'The Thackerays in India' (1877) contains an interesting account of Thackeray's ancestors in that country. Anne Thackeray Ritchie, Thackeray's daughter, published 'Chapters from Some Memoirs' in 1894.

Thaddeus of Warsaw, an historical novel by J. Porter (q.v.), published in 1803.

Thaddeus, a young nobleman of the family of the famous John Sobieski, king of Poland, accompanies his grandfather, the count palatine, to join the army of King Stanislaus, which Prince Poniatowski and General Kosciuszko are leading against the invading Russians. The old count is killed, the Polish forces defeated, the Sobieski castle burnt, and Thaddeus driven into exile. He comes to England, where, after suffering hardships, he is discovered to be the son of an English gentleman, and happily married.

The work is of some interest as an early example of the historical novel.

Thaïs, (i) an Athenian courtesan who, according to legend, accompanied Alexander on his Asiatic conquests and caused him to burn the royal palace of Persepolis. The incident is treated in Dryden's ode, 'Alexander's Feast;' (2) an Egyptian courtesan, the subject of a novel by Anatole France (q.v.).

Thaisa, in Shakespeare's 'Pericles' (q.v.), the wife of Pericles.

Thalaba the Destroyer, a poem by Southey (q.v.), published in 1801.

The young Thalaba, a Muslim, is the appointed one to destroy the race of magicians who have their seminary in Domdaniel (q.v.), a palace 'under the roots of the sea'. Abdaldar, one of the magicians, seeks to kill him, but is blasted by the simoom. Thalaba, taking Abdaldar's magic ring from his finger, learns through it that his father, Hodeirah, was slain by Okba, the magician, and vows vengeance. He sets out on his quest, learns that the talisman by which he shall accomplish it is faith, and, protected by the ring from the attacks of the magicians, finally makes his way to Domdaniel and destroys it and the sorcerers. He sacrifices his life in doing so, and is reunited in Paradise to his beloved Oneiza, the wife whom death had taken from him on their bridal night.

Thalassa!, 'The sea!', in Xenophon's 'Anabasis', iv. 7, the cry of the Ten Thousand when from the summit of Mt. Theches they first saw the Euxine after their wanderings in Asia Minor.

Thaler, see *Dollar.*

Thalēs (b. c. 624 B.C.), of Miletus in Ionia, one of the seven wise men of Greece. It is said that he travelled in quest of knowledge, and from the priests of Memphis learnt geometry, astronomy, and philosophy, and predicted a solar eclipse. He may be considered the founder of Greek philosophy, being the first to seek in science, instead of mythology, the interpretation of the world. He held that all things had their origin in water.

Thalestris, a queen of the Amazons, who is said to have been attracted by the fame of Alexander the Great, and travelled from her country to see him.

Thalīa, the Muse (q.v.) of comedy and pastoral poetry.

Thames, Old English *Temese,* Latin *Tamesis* or *Tamesa,* the name of the river on which London stands. It is called the Isis from its source to its junction with the Thame, below Oxford, owing to a false etymology of *Tamesis* or *Tamisis* as *Tam + Isis* (Henry Bradley). The meaning of the word, which is perhaps Celtic in origin, is uncertain (cf. the river names Tame, Tamar.)

To set the Thames on fire, to do something marvellous, to work wonders, a phrase always used negatively, 'he will never set the Thames on fire'. It has its parallel in other countries in respect of their rivers, e.g. the Rhine. The conjecture that *Thames* here was originally *temse,* a sieve, which might be set on fire by force of friction, has no basis of fact. [OED.]

Thamuz or **THAMMUZ,** a Syrian god. See under *Adonis* and *Pan.* The relation of Thammuz to Adonis is referred to in Milton, 'Paradise Lost', i. 446–52.

ThamЎris, a Thracian musician, mentioned by Homer ('Iliad', ii. 594). He challenged the Muses to a contest of skill, and, being defeated by them, was deprived of his eyesight and his melodious voice, and his lyre was broken. 'Blind Thamyris and blind Mæonides', Milton, 'Paradise Lost', iii. 35.

Thatched House Club, THE, at the lower end of St. James's Street, London, was originally a tavern much frequented by politicians and men of fashion. The tavern was demolished in 1814.

Thaumast, in Rabelais, II. xix, an English philosopher who carried on a learned discussion with Panurge solely by signs.

Theagenēs, see *Aethiopica.*

Theagēs, THE BRIDLE OF: ill health. Theages was a follower of Socrates. In the sixth book of Plato's 'Republic' Socrates is considering how rare are the worthy disciples of philosophy, a gifted few condemned to exile or who despise politics or the arts; 'Moreover, the bridle which curbs our friend Theages may be equally efficacious in other instances. For Theages is kept in check by ill-health, which excludes him from a public life, though in all other respects he has every inducement to desert philosophy' (tr. Davies and Vaughan).

Thealma and Clearchus, see *Chalkhill.*

Theatre, THE, see *Burbage (James).*

Theban Band, THE, see *Sacred Band.*

Thebes, the capital of Boeotia in Greece, supposed to have been founded by Cadmus (q.v.), and the scene of the legend of Oedipus (q.v.). It was the birthplace of Pindar. For the war of THE SEVEN AGAINST THEBES, see under *Eteocles.* This war was the subject of a long epic poem, 'The Thebaid', by the Roman poet Statius (q.v.).

Thebes, the Greek name for an ancient Egyptian city (*Tapē*), situated on the right bank of the Nile where Luxor now stands. It rose to great importance as the capital of Egypt during the reigns of the kings of the XVIII–XXth dynasties, except for the brief period of Akhnaton's migration to Tel-el-Amarna.

Thebes, The Story of, see *Lydgate.*

Theism, which in its general sense means belief in a deity, or deities, as opposed to *atheism,* or in one deity as opposed to *polytheism* or *pantheism,* is especially used in the sense of belief in one God as Creator and Ruler of the universe, without denial of revelation. In this use it is distinguished from *deism,* which is belief in the existence of a Supreme Being as the source of finite existence, with rejection of revelation and the supernatural doctrines of Christianity. [OED.]

Thel, The Book of, see *Blake.*

Thelema, ABBEY OF, in Rabelais, I. lii et seq., was built and endowed by Gargantua (q.v.) to reward the bold Friar John (Jean des Entommeures) for his prowess in the war with Picrochole. It was to be in every way the opposite of ordinary monasteries and convents. Only men and women favourably endowed by nature were to be admitted to it; it was not to be walled in; it was to contain a magnificent library filled with the works of the humanists. The only rule was to be 'Fay ce que vouldras' ('Do what you like'); because persons who are free, well born, well educated, and associate with honourable companions, are naturally virtuous and averse from vice. See *Medmenham.*

Thellusson Act, the Accumulations Act of 1800, passed in consequence of the eccentric will of Peter Thellusson (1737–97), a rich merchant, by which, after leaving £100 000 to his wife and children, he directed that the remainder of his fortune, valued at £600,000 or £800,000, should accumulate during the lives of his sons, of his sons' sons, and of their issue existing at the time of his death. As it was calculated that the accumulation might reach 140 millions and might be a source of danger, the Accumulations Act prohibited such schemes of bequest.

Themis, in Greek mythology, a Titaness and the mother of Prometheus (q.v.); later the personification of justice.

Thenot, a shepherd in Spenser's 'Shepheards Calender' (q.v.). Also a character in Fletcher's 'The Faithful Shepherdess' (q.v.).

THEOBALD, LEWIS (1688–1744), author of poems, essays, and dramatic works, published in 1726 his 'Shakespeare Restored', exposing the incapacity as a critic shown by Pope in his edition of Shakespeare. Pope, infuriated, made Theobald the hero of his 'Dunciad' (q.v.). But we owe to Theobald's edition of Shakespeare (1734) many valuable restorations and conjectural emendations of the text, among others the admirable touch in the death of Falstaff, 'a' babbled of green fields' ('Henry V', II. iii).

THEOCRITUS, a great Greek pastoral poet, a native of Syracuse, lived in the 3rd cent. B.C. He visited Cos and Alexandria, where he appears to have known Callimachus and to have attracted the attention of Ptolemy Philadelphus. His 'Idylls', short dramatic poems of great charm, in some of which he depicts the rustic life of Sicily, were the first examples of pastoral poetry in the literature of Greece, and were imitated by Virgil in Roman literature. His 'Lament for Daphnis' ('Id.' i) is the prototype of such elegies as Milton's 'Lycidas'.

Theodora Campian, a character in Disraeli's 'Lothair' (q.v.).

THEODORE (602?–90), archbishop of Canterbury, a native of Tarsus in Cilicia, studied at Athens, and was well versed in Greek and Latin literature. He was consecrated archbishop of Canterbury by Pope Vitalius in 668. He imposed the Roman order and was the first archbishop to whom (according to Bede) the whole English church agreed in submitting. He founded a school of learning at Canterbury, and created many new bishoprics. Theodore was a great organizer, the effects of his work surviving to the present day; and was author, at least in part, of the 'Penitential', of considerable ecclesiastical and historical interest.

Theodore and Honoria, one of the 'Fables' of Dryden (q.v.). Theodore, a young gentleman of Ravenna, loves the haughty Honoria, but is disdained by her and meditates taking his own life. In a vision he sees a woman pursued and torn by two mastiffs whom a horseman on a coal-black steed urges on. He interposes to save her, and learns that the horseman is Guido Cavalcanti, who took his own life for hopeless love of a proud maid. Both were in consequence doomed to hell and she to die daily at the hands of her lover. Theodore contrives that Honoria shall also see the vision, by which she is cured of her haughtiness.

The story is from the 'Decameron' (v. viii), where it is told of one Nastagio degli Onesti.

Theodoric, see *Dietrich of Bern.*

THEOGNIS, a Greek elegiac poet, a noble of Megara, who lived about 540 B.C. A long fragment of a poem by him survives, reflecting the political strife of his times.

Theon's tooth, in Horace ('Ep.' I. xviii. 82), the sting of satire.

THEOPHRASTUS (*d. c.* 287 B.C.), a Greek philosopher, native of Lesbos, and pupil of Aristotle. He was the author of two botanical works, but his interest in connexion with English literature lies in his 'Characters', brief but graphic descriptions of various types of human failings, illustrated by typical actions. They served as a model to J. Hall (q.v.), to Overbury (q.v.), to Earle in his 'Microcosmographie' (q.v.), and others, and contributed in some degree towards the evolution of the English essay.

Theophrastus Such, *The Impressions of,* see *Eliot (G.).*

Theory of Moral Sentiments, a philosophical work by Adam Smith (q.v.), published in 1759, and originally delivered in the form of lectures at Glasgow.

The author advances the view that all moral sentiments arise from sympathy, the principle which 'leads us to enter into the situations of other men and to partake with them in the passions which those situations have a tendency to excite', this sympathy giving rise to our notions of the merit or demerit of the agent. Sympathy is thus the basis of the fabric of society, and morality has an essentially social character.

Theosophy, from a Greek word meaning wisdom concerning God or things divine, a term applied in the 17th cent. to a kind of speculation, such as is found in the Jewish Cabbala (q.v.), which sought to derive from the knowledge of God contained in secret books, or traditions mystically interpreted, a profounder knowledge and control of nature than could be obtained by the current philosophical methods. It was often applied specifically to the system of Jacob Boehme (q.v.).

In more recent times it has been adopted by the THEOSOPHICAL SOCIETY, an association founded at New York in 1875 by Col. H. S. Olcott, Madame Blavatsky, and W. Q. Judge, its professed objects being: (1) to form the nucleus of a universal brotherhood; (2) to promote the study of Aryan and other Eastern literature, religions, and sciences; (3) to investigate the unfamiliar laws of nature and the faculties latent in man. [OED.]

Theramĕnēs, a supple statesman, one of the oligarchy of the Four Hundred at Athens (411 B.C.), who was chosen one of the Thirty Tyrants, but endeavoured to check their tyrannical proceedings. He was accused as a traitor and put to death. He appears to have been in favour of a moderate oligarchy, and being placed between two extreme factions acquired the reputation of a trimmer and was nicknamed COTHURNUS (a stage boot which could be worn on either foot).

THERESA or TERESA, ST. (1515–82), a Spanish saint and author, who entered the Carmelite sisterhood and became famous for her mystic visions. Her works include 'El Camino de la Perfección' and 'El Castillo interior'. She was great not only as a mystic, but as an energetic reformer of the Carmelite Order and a foundress of new convents. Her 'Book of the Foundations' narrates her ceaseless journeys for this purpose and the continually growing labour of organization. She is commemorated on 15 Oct.

Thermidor, the eleventh month of the French republican calendar (see *Calendar*). On 9 Thermidor of the second republican year (27 July 1794) occurred the events which brought about the fall of Robespierre and the end of the Terror.

Thermopylae, a narrow pass between mountain and sea leading from Thessaly into Locris and Phocis, celebrated for the battle fought there in 480 B.C., when 6,000 Greeks including 300 Spartans under Leonidas, for three successive days, resisted the vast army of the Persians under Xerxes.

Theron, the faithful dog of Roderick, in Southey's poem of that name (q.v.).

Thersites, the most querulous and ill favoured of the Greek host in the Trojan War. He was killed by Achilles (q.v.) for laughing at the latter's grief over the death of Penthesilea, the queen of the Amazons. He figures in Shakespeare's 'Troilus and Cressida' (q.v.).

Thersites, see *Interludes.*

Thesaurus Linguae Latinae, the great German dictionary of the Latin language, begun in 1900 and still in course of publication.

Theseūs, a son of Poseidon, or, according to a later legend, of Aegeus, king of Athens, by Aethra, daughter of Pittheus, king of Troezen, in whose house he was brought up. When he reached years of maturity he travelled to Athens to make himself known to his father, destroying many robbers and monsters on the way. At Athens, Medea (q.v.), who had taken refuge with Aegeus, attempted to destroy him by poison before he was recognized by Aegeus, but failed. Aegeus knew him to be his son by a sword that he bore. Theseus now achieved many great feats, among others the destruction of the Minotaur (q.v.) with the help of Ariadne, daughter of Minos, whom he carried off and subsequently deserted in Naxos. His return to Athens occasioned the death of Aegeus, who threw himself into the sea when he saw his son's ship approaching, with black sails, hoisted in error, the signal of ill success. Theseus then ascended the throne of Athens, overcame the Amazons, and carried off their queen,

Antiope. He became the close friend of Peirithous, king of the Lapithae, and at the nuptials of the latter with Hippodamia helped to defend her and her attendants against the Centaurs (q.v.). With Peirithous he descended to the infernal regions to carry away Proserpine, but Pluto defeated their attempt. Peirithous was placed on the wheel of Ixion (q.v.), his father, and Theseus suffered a long imprisonment in Hades, until released by Hercules. Theseus was also husband of Phaedra (q.v.) and father of Hippolytus (q.v.).

Theseus, the duke of Athens in Shakespeare's 'A Midsummer Night's Dream' (q.v.).

Thespian, an epithet applied to tragedy or the dramatic art, from Thespis (q.v.).

THESPIS, a Greek poet of Attica, who lived in the 6th cent. B.C. He is important in the history of tragedy, for he gave it a dramatic character by introducing an actor, who replied to the leader of the chorus (or *coryphaeus*). Horace ('Ars Poetica', 276) records a tradition that Thespis was a strolling player who travelled about with a wagon as temporary stage.

Thetis, one of the sea deities, daughter of Nereus and Doris, who became the wife of Peleus (q.v.). It was foretold that her child would be greater than his father, a prophecy that was fulfilled by the birth of her son Achilles (q.v.).

THIBAULT, FRANÇOIS ANATOLE, see *France (A.).*

Thierry and Theodoret, a tragedy by J. Fletcher (q.v.), with perhaps the collaboration of Beaumont and Massinger, published in 1621.

Theodoret, king of Austrasia, reproves his mother, Brunhalt, for her licentious mode of life. To revenge herself, she attempts to sow enmity between him and his younger brother Thierry, king of Burgundy, but fails. With the assistance of her paramour and a physician, specialist in poisons, she first contrives to destroy the happiness of Thierry and his young bride Ordella, then has Theodoret assassinated, then attempts to procure the death of Ordella, and finally poisons Thierry. There is a touching scene in which Thierry on his death-bed is reunited to Ordella, whom he believed dead. Vengeance falls upon Brunhalt and her accomplices.

The play has an historical basis in the tragic story of Brunehaut, the imperious queen of Austrasia, and her grandsons Theodebert and Thierry. There are incidents in it which may be allusions to the queen-regent of France, Marie de Médicis, and her favourite, Concini (murdered in 1617).

Third Estate, THE, the third of the orders or classes of the community regarded as parts of the body politic and participating in the government. The number of 'Estates' in the nations of Christendom has usually been three (exceptionally four, as in Sweden and Aragon), but their enumeration has varied. In England the 'Estates' as represented in parliament were originally: (1) Clergy; (2) Barons and Knights; (3) Commons. After various fluctuations the final arrangement was: (1) Lords Spiritual; (2) Lords Temporal; (3) Commons. In France the three estates were: (1) Clergy; (2) Nobles; (3) Commoners (called 'Tiers État').

THIRLWALL, CONNOP (1797–1875), educated at Charterhouse and Trinity College, Cambridge, became bishop of St. David's. He published in 1828, with Julius Hare, a translation of Niebuhr's 'Roman History', a vindication of Niebuhr in 1829, and in 1835–47 his principal work, the 'History of Greece', which is generally thought more dispassionate, if less vivid, than Grote's (the two works appeared at about the same time). Thirlwall was buried in Westminster Abbey in the same grave with Grote.

Thirty Tyrants, THE, an Athenian oligarchy of thirty magistrates imposed by Sparta upon the Athenians at the close of the Peloponnesian War (403 B.C.).

Thirty Years War, THE, the religious wars of 1618–48, fought chiefly on German soil, between Catholics and Protestants. It is celebrated for the campaigns of Wallenstein and Gustavus Adolphus of Sweden. It was concluded by the Peace of Westphalia, and left Germany a desert.

Thirty-nine Articles, THE, see *Articles of Religion.*

Thisbe, see *Pyramus.*

Thistlewood, ARTHUR (1770–1820), the promoter of the Cato Street Conspiracy (q.v., 1820). He had developed revolutionary sympathies as a result of reading Paine's works and of visits to France and America. He organized a mutiny in 1816, and was imprisoned in 1818 for sending a challenge to Lord Sidmouth. After the Cato Street Conspiracy he was convicted of high treason and hanged

Tholosa, in imprints, Toulouse.

Thomas, DOUBTING, an allusion to John xx. 25, 'Except I shall see in his hands the print of the nails . . . I will not believe.'

THOMAS, DYLAN (1914–53), poet, born in Swansea. He came to London, where he did journalistic work and later film script writing and broadcasting. His poetry, which is full of vitality and, especially in his earlier work, powerful but often obscure imagery, has had a tremendous influence on the younger poets of his generation, and has also roused profound controversy among the critics. He died during a lecture tour of the United States, by which time he was already something of a legend for his poetry readings, his talk, and his Bohemianism. His volumes of poetry include 'Eighteen Poems' (1934), 'Twenty-five Poems' (1936), 'The Map of Love' (1939), 'Deaths and Entrances' (1946), and 'Collected Poems' (1952). His prose includes 'Portrait of the Artist as a Young Dog' (1940) and 'Adventures in the Skin Trade' (1955), both semi-autobiographical. 'Under Milk Wood', a play for voices, had its first public hearing in May 1953, at Cambridge, Mass., when he read it himself in a still unfinished version. He completed it later and it was published the following year.

THOMAS, EDWARD (1878–1917), wrote biographical and topographical works and, when he was over 30, began to compose verse at the suggestion of his friend Robert Frost (q.v.). He enlisted in the Artists' Rifles during the First World War, and was killed in Flanders. His verse shows a loving and accurate observation of the English pastoral scene. His 'Collected Poems' appeared in 1920.

Thomas, ST., one of the twelve apostles. An ancient Syriac work, the 'Acta Thomae', describes him as having laboured as a missionary in India and having suffered martyrdom there. The shrine (rebuilt by the Portuguese in 1547) commemorating his death still stands near Madras. The ancient churches of Southern India are often known as 'Christians of St. Thomas'.

Thomas à Becket, ST. (1118?–70), son of Gilbert Becket, of a Norman family of knights, was educated in London and Paris and subsequently studied canon law at Bologna and Auxerre. Henry II appointed him chancellor, and made him his intimate friend and companion. In 1162 Thomas reluctantly became archbishop of Canterbury, and thereafter opposed the king's measures against the excessive privileges of the Church. As a result of a prolonged and bitter struggle, he was driven into exile and resided on the Continent for seven years. He then returned to England, a reconciliation with the king having been effected. But the peace between them was of short duration, and the king in a passion made use of hasty words which led four knights to start for Canterbury and slay the prelate, who met his death with splendid courage in his own cathedral on 29 Dec. 1170. His shrine became the most famous in Christendom and Henry II did penance at his tomb. Thomas à Becket was canonized in 1173 and his festival is observed on 7 July. He is the subject of dramas by G. Darley, A. Tennyson, and T. S. Eliot (qq.v.).

THOMAS À KEMPIS (THOMAS HÄMMERLEIN or HÄMMERKEN) (1380–1471), born of humble parents at Kempen near Cologne. He became an Augustinian monk and wrote Christian mystical works, among which is probably to be included the famous 'De Imitatione Christi', which has been translated from the Latin into many languages (into English in the middle of the 15th cent.). This work was at one time attributed to Jean Charlier de Gerson, a French theologian. It traces in four books the gradual progress of the soul to Christian perfection, its detachment from the world and its union with God; and obtained wide popularity by its simplicity and sincerity and the universal quality of its religious teaching.

Thomas the Rhymer, see *Erceldoune.*

Thomason, GEORGE (*d.* 1666), a London bookseller and publisher and friend of Milton and Prynne (qq.v.). His collection of political tracts and broadsides published between the outbreak of the Civil War and the Restoration was presented to the British Museum in 1762. These tracts were catalogued in 1908 by the keeper, George Fortescue.

Thomist (pron. 'Tomist'), a follower of the scholastic philosopher, Aquinas (q.v.). Cf. *Scotist.*

THOMPSON, FRANCIS (1859–1907), educated at Ushaw College, studied medicine without success at Owens College, Manchester, and lived a life of ill health and, for a time, of extreme poverty, from which he was rescued by Alice Meynell (q.v.) and her husband. His first volume of 'Poems' (1893) included his famous 'Hound of Heaven' (describing the poet's flight from God, the pursuit, and the overtaking), which shows the influence of Crashaw (q.v.). This was followed by 'Sister Songs' in 1895, and 'New Poems' in 1897. He contributed literary criticism to the 'Academy' and 'Athenaeum'. His prose work includes 'Health and Holiness' (1905) and an 'Essay on Shelley' (1909).

THOMS, WILLIAM JOHN (1803–85), author and editor of a number of works of antiquarian interest including 'The Book of the Court' (1838) and an edition of 'Reynard the Fox' (1844). He was secretary to the Camden Society, 1838–73, and clerk, and subsequently deputy-librarian, to the House of Lords. He started 'Notes and Queries' (q.v.) in 1849.

THOMSON, JAMES (1700–48), born at Ednam on the Scottish border, the son of a minister, was educated at Edinburgh University. He began early to write verse that showed his fondness for rustic scenes. He came to London in 1725 and under stress of poverty wrote 'Winter', the first of his 'Seasons' (q.v.), which appeared successively in 1726–30. He made the acquaintance of Arbuthnot, Gay, and Pope, found patrons, and eventually, through the influence of Lord Lyttelton, received a sinecure. He travelled in France and Italy as tutor to Charles Richard Talbot, son of the solicitor-general, and in 1734–6 published his long poem 'Liberty', in which Liberty herself narrates the vicissitudes of her progress through the ages in Greece, Rome, and Britain. He produced a series of tragedies, 'Sophonisba' (q.v., 1730), 'Agamemnon' (1738), 'Edward and Eleanora' (1739, of which the plot has some points of resemblance to that of Scott's 'The Talisman'); 'Tancred and Sigismunda' (q.v., published in 1745), and 'Coriolanus' (1749) were produced after his death. In 1740 was performed the masque of 'Alfred' by Thomson and David Mallet (q.v.) containing 'Rule, Britannia', which was probably written by the former. Thomson published in 1748 'The Castle of Indolence' (q.v.). This contains a portrait of himself as an inmate of the castle ('A bard here dwelt'), contributed by Lord Lyttelton (the first line by Armstrong). Thomson was buried in Richmond church. His 'Seasons' first challenged the artificiality of English poetry, and inaugurated a new era by their sentiment for nature.

THOMSON, JAMES (1834–82), the child of poor parents, was educated at the Royal Caledonian Asylum, and became an army schoolmaster, but was discharged for a breach of discipline in 1862. He made friends with Charles Bradlaugh (q.v.), wrote for the 'National Reformer', and took an active part in the propaganda of free thought. He lived a sad and isolated life in London, aggravated by insomnia and addiction to drink, and died in University College Hospital. His chief poem, 'The City of Dreadful Night', a powerful and sincere expression of an atheistic and despairing creed, was contributed to the 'National Reformer' in 1874. It was republished with other poems in 1880. 'Vane's Story and other Poems' appeared in 1881. These collections show that Thomson could also write in other and happier moods, though he reverts to gloom and terror in 'Insomnia' (1882). His prose papers are collected in 'Satires and Profanities', posthumously published (1884). He wrote under the initials B. V. (for Bysshe Vanolis).

THOMSON, SIR WILLIAM, *first Baron Kelvin* (1824–1907), was educated at Glasgow University, where he became professor of natural philosophy, and at Peterhouse, Cambridge, where he was second wrangler and a famous sculler. He advanced the science of thermodynamics and electricity, and evolved the theory of electric oscillations, which forms the basis of wireless telegraphy. He succeeded in laying a transatlantic cable in 1866, improved the system of electrical units, and invented much useful scientific apparatus. His 'Mathematical and Physical Papers' were published in 1882–1911. Prof. Silvanus P. Thompson wrote his 'Life' (1910).

Thonē, in Milton's 'Comus', 675:

> Not that nepenthes which the wife of Thone
> In Egypt gave to Jove-born Helena,

a reference to Homer's 'Odyssey', iv. 228, where Helen, to divert Menelaus and Telemachus from their gloomy thoughts, casts a drug into their wine, which Polydamna, wife of Thon, a woman of Egypt, had given her, 'a drug to lull all pain and anger, and bring forgetfulness of every sorrow' (Butcher and Lang).

Thopas, The Tale of Sir, see *Canterbury Tales*.

Thor, in northern mythology, the god of thunder, son of Odin (q.v.), and one of the three great gods (Odin, Thor, and Frigga) of the Scandinavians. He was the god of the home, and presided over the weather and crops. He married Sif, a peasant woman, typifying the earth; his hammer was called 'Miölnir', typifying thunder. His name is perpetuated in our 'Thursday'.

THOREAU, HENRY DAVID (1817–62), born in Massachusetts, and educated at Harvard, devoted himself to a literary life, supporting himself by school-teaching and, later, by surveying. He was a friend and disciple of Emerson (q.v.) and, in his own words, 'a mystic, a transcendentalist, and a natural philosopher to boot'. He rebelled against the Puritanism of New England, and against the State in the matter of slavery and the Mexican War, refusing to pay his poll-tax, and going to prison for a day in consequence. He also rebelled against the materialistic values of modern society and in search of the simple life built himself a cabin by Walden Pond, where he lived on an expenditure of a few dollars for more than two years. He was an ardent lover and observer of nature, as well as a scholar and fine stylist, and his 'Walden, or Life in the Woods' (1854), the account of his residence at the Pond, is admirable for his descriptions of natural phenomena, in addition to his independence of thought. His other works include 'A Week on the Concord and Merrimac Rivers' (1849), 'Civil Disobedience', an essay (1849), 'Excursions in Field and Forest' (with a memoir by Emerson, 1863), 'The Maine Woods' (1864), and 'Cape Cod' (1865). His interesting and important 'Journal' was printed in 14 vols. in 1906 (reprinted 1963).

Thornberry, JOB, in 'John Bull' by Colman the younger (q.v.), an honest, kindly English tradesman, supposed to typify the national character.

Thorndyke, DR., in the detective stories of Richard Austin Freeman (1862–1943), 'a barrister and doctor of medicine', 'probably the greatest criminal lawyer of our time' and 'the leading authority on poisons and crimes connected with them' ('As a Thief in the Night'). His companion and foil is Dr. Jervis; his laboratory assistant, Polton.

Thornhill, SIR WILLIAM and **SQUIRE,** characters in Goldsmith's 'Vicar of Wakefield' (q.v.).

Thornton, a character in Bulwer Lytton's

'Pelham' (q.v.), drawn from Thurtell, the murderer.

Thornton, JOHN, a character in Mrs. Gaskell's 'North and South' (q.v.).

Thorough, the motto adopted by Sir Thomas Wentworth, earl of Strafford (q.v.), and applied to his policy as lord deputy of Ireland, 'by which he meant a "thorough" devotion to the service of the King and the State, without regard for private interests' (S. R. Gardiner). It first occurs, apparently, in a letter from Laud to Strafford, c. 1634.

Thorpe, JOHN and **ISABELLA,** characters in Jane Austen's 'Northanger Abbey' (q.v.).

Thoth, an ancient Egyptian god, identified by the Greeks with their Hermes. He was the god of wisdom and science, the inventor of speech and letters, represented as a human figure with the head of an ibis.

Thousand and One Nights, The, the 'Arabian Nights' Entertainments' (q.v.).

THRALE, HESTER LYNCH, MRS. (1741–1821), the friend of Dr. Johnson, was the only child of John Salusbury of Bachycraig, Flintshire, and was married against her inclinations to Henry Thrale, the son of a wealthy brewer. Her intimacy with Dr. Johnson became famous, Johnson at one time being almost domesticated at Thrale's house at Streatham Park. After Thrale's death she married Gabriel Piozzi, an Italian Roman Catholic musician. In 1786 she published her 'Anecdotes of the late Samuel Johnson', which give a lively picture of the Doctor, and in 1788 her correspondence with him.

Thraso, a braggart soldier in Terence's 'Eunuchus'.

Threadneedle Street, THE OLD LADY OF, a familiar expression, dating from the 18th cent., for the Bank of England, which stands in the street. The name of the street appears in Stow's 'Survey' (1598) as 'Three needle Street' ('beginning at the Well with two buckets'). Its origin is uncertain. Loftie ('History of London') says that the guild of the tailors seems 'to have had a hall in Cordwainers ward, and then to have bought the ground on which Merchant Taylors' Hall still stands, in the lane which their trade endued with its nickname, now long become permanent, of Threadneedle Street'.

Three Clerks, The, a novel by A. Trollope (q.v.) published in 1858, which gives some glimpses of the author's youth.

The story is concerned with the careers of three government clerks: Harry Norman, a steady, hard-working fellow, the cleverer but unprincipled Alaric Tudor, and the latter's cousin, Charley, a weak but good-hearted youth; and the three daughters, Gertrude, Linda, and Katie, of Mrs. Woodward, a cousin of Norman. Norman falls in love with Gertrude, but she marries Alaric Tudor, whom he has introduced to the Woodward family. Not only does Alaric thus defeat Norman's hopes, but he rapidly outdistances him in the public service. Presently, however, Alaric falls into the hands of the Hon. Undecimus Scott, an unscrupulous adventurer, who induces him first to accept a bribe offered him in virtue of his official political position, then to speculate in shares, and finally to appropriate funds of which he is trustee. The inevitable catastrophe follows. Alaric is tried and found guilty of misappropriation and sentenced to imprisonment. Norman consoles himself with Linda, and unexpectedly comes into the family property. Charley, the course of whose love has been impeded by his debts and general unsatisfactoriness as a suitor, reforms, becomes a steady official and a successful author, and marries the gentle Katie. Mr. Chaffanbrass, Alaric's counsel in his trial, is a well-drawn type of bullying cross-examiner.

Three Men in a Boat, see *Jerome (Jerome K.).*

Three Musketeers, The ('Les Trois Mousquetaires'), one of the most popular of the romances of Dumas (q.v.) the elder, published in 1844.

With its sequels 'Twenty Years After' and 'The Vicomte de Bragelonne' it deals with the life of a poor Gascon gentleman, d'Artagnan, who comes to Paris in the reign of Louis XIII to join the king's musketeers, gets involved in duels with three valiant members of that force, Athos, Porthos, and Aramis, and thereafter becomes their friend and shares their fortunes and their many heroic adventures. 'The Three Musketeers' is more particularly concerned with the love of Anne of Austria and Buckingham, and the life of Miladi at whose instigation Felton stabs the Duke.

The original d'Artagnan was a Gascon gentleman born *c.* 1611 and killed at the siege of Maestricht as captain of the king's musketeers.

Three Weeks after Marriage, a comedy by Murphy (q.v.), produced in 1764. The subject is the disillusionment of Mr. Drugget, a rich retired tradesman, who has married his eldest daughter to Sir Charles Rackett, and proposes to marry his second daughter, Nancy, to another penniless man of fashion, Lovelace, in spite of the fact that she is in love with Woodley, a rival suitor. The result of his experience with the recently wedded couple is to make him abjure all dealings with men of fashion.

Thresher, A, a member of an Irish political organization instituted in 1806 and directed against the Orangemen (q.v.), which issued manifestoes signed 'Captain Thresher'.

Thrie Estaitis, Satyre of the, see *Lindsay (Sir D.).*

Through the Looking-Glass, a book for children by Lewis Carroll (see *Dodgson*), published in 1872.

Alice (see *Alice's Adventures in Wonderland*) walks in a dream through the looking-glass into Looking-Glass House, where she finds that the chessmen, particularly the red and white queens, are alive; meets with Tweedledum and Tweedledee and Humpty-Dumpty; and so forth. The story ends with Alice, who has the red queen in her arms, 'shaking her into a kitten' (for she had gone to sleep playing with the black and white kittens). The well-known verses about the Jabberwock, and the Walrus and the Carpenter, occur in the course of the story.

THUCYDĬDĒS, the great Athenian historian, was born about 460 B.C. and died in about the end of the 5th cent. Owing to failure as a naval commander in 424, he went into exile for twenty years and spent much time in the Peloponnese. His history, which deals with the great war between Athens and Sparta down to the year 411 B.C., is concise sometimes to the point of obscurity, but is marked by scrupulous accuracy and also by a gift for expressing the sadness of a tragic story. It is noteworthy, moreover, as the first work of the kind in which events are traced to their cause and their political lessons brought out. A translation by Thomas Hobbes was published in 1629, and one by Benjamin Jowett in 1881.

Thulē, an island in the northern seas, first mentioned by Pytheas, a Greek navigator of the 4th cent. B.C., where the day and night each lasted for six months, and the sea was thick and impenetrable to rowers. It may have been Iceland, or Norway, or the Shetlands. ULTIMA THULE, 'farthest Thule', is used figuratively for the uttermost point attainable.

Thumb, TOM, see *Tom Thumb.*

Thunderer, The, a nickname given to 'The Times' newspaper in the middle of the 19th cent., in allusion to the style of writing of Edward Sterling (1773–1847), a member of its staff, and father of John Sterling (q.v.). Trollope similarly alludes in some of his novels to 'The Times' as 'The Jupiter' (from Jupiter Tonans).

THURBER, JAMES (1894–1961), American short story writer, humorist, and illustrator, born in Ohio. He was a staff writer on, and later a frequent contributor to, 'The New Yorker' (q.v.). He had a delightful vein of fantasy and comedy, which appeared in both his prose and drawings, and a sharp but kind eye for human follies. Among his many books are: 'The Owl in the Attic and Other Perplexities' (1931), 'The Seal in the Bedroom and Other Predicaments' (1932), 'The Last Flower' (1939), 'My World—and Welcome to It' (1942), 'Men, Women, and Dogs' (1943), 'The Thurber Carnival' (1945), and 'Thurber Country' (1953).

Thurio, a character in Shakespeare's 'The Two Gentlemen of Verona' (q.v.).

THURLOW, EDWARD, *second Baron Thurlow* (1781–1892), minor romantic poet. His 'Poems on Several Occasions' was published in 1813.

Thus spake Zarathustra, English title of 'Also sprach Zarathustra' by Nietzsche (q.v.).

Thwackum, in Fielding's 'Tom Jones' (q.v.), the tutor of Tom and Blifil, a divine with a reputation for learning, religion, and sobriety of manners, but in fact a narrow-minded pedant.

Thyestes, see *Atreus.* Thyestes was the subject of a play by Crowne (q.v.).

Thyrsis, A Monody, to commemorate the author's friend, Arthur Hugh Clough, who died at Florence 1861, by M. Arnold (q.v.), published in 1867.

The poem, pastoral in form, and containing frequent reference to 'The Scholar-Gipsy' (q.v.), combines a lament for the dead friend with an exquisite description of the Oxford country, similar to that found in the earlier poem.

Thyrsus, a staff or spear tipped with a pine-cone, and sometimes wreathed with ivy or vine branches, carried by Dionysus (Bacchus) and his votaries.

Tib's Eve, ST., a remote date, perhaps never (cf. 'Greek calends'). 'Saint Tibb's evening, the evening of the last day or day of judgement; he will pay you on St. Tibb's eve (Irish)', Grose, 'Dictionary of the Vulgar Tongue' (1785). *Tib* is perhaps a shortened form of *Isabel.* A St. Tibba is mentioned in the late Peterborough recension of the Anglo-Saxon Chronicle, under the year 963.

Tibbs, BEAU, see *Beau Tibbs.*

Tibert, the cat in 'Reynard the Fox' (q.v.). The name is the same as Tybalt (see the dialogue between Mercutio and Tybalt in Shakespeare, 'Romeo and Juliet', III. i).

TIBULLUS, ALBIUS (*c.* 60–19 B.C.), a Roman poet, a contemporary of Virgil and Horace. Of the three books of elegies that bear his name, only two were published in his lifetime. The third, published posthumously, includes pieces by other hands. His poems are marked by quiet charm and tenderness, and their theme is love, peace, and rural simplicity.

Tichborne Case, THE: Roger Charles Tichborne (1829–54), heir presumptive to the Tichborne estates, sailed from Rio de Janeiro in 1854 in a ship that was lost at sea. Arthur Orton's claim to be Roger Tichborne gave rise to a famous trial, which was decided against the claimant in 1872. Orton was tried for perjury and sentenced to imprisonment.

TICKELL, THOMAS (1686–1740), edu-

cated at Queen's College, Oxford, contributed verse to the 'Guardian', 'Spectator', and other publications, and was author of a poem 'On the Prospect of Peace' (1712). He enjoyed the patronage of Addison and is chiefly remembered as having occasioned the quarrel between Pope and Addison by publishing a translation of the first book of the 'Iliad' at the same time as Pope, at Addison's instigation as Pope supposed. He edited Addison's works, publishing in the first volume his celebrated elegy on Addison's death. Tickell was also author of a ballad, 'Colin and Lucy', which was declared by Gray and Goldsmith to be one of the best in the language.

Tickler, TIMOTHY, see *Timothy Tickler.*

TICKNOR, GEORGE (1791–1871), professor of Belles Lettres and French and Spanish at Harvard University from 1819 to 1835. He travelled extensively in Europe and is remembered for his 'History of Spanish Literature' (1849).

Tiger, THE, a nickname of Georges Clemenceau (1841–1929), the French Prime Minister during the latter part of the war of 1914–18 and the peace negotiations that followed it.

Tiger! Tiger! burning bright, see *Blake.*

Tigg, MONTAGUE, a character in Dickens's 'Martin Chuzzlewit' (q.v.).

Tilburina, the heroine of Mr. Puff's tragedy 'The Spanish Armada' in Sheridan's 'The Critic' (q.v.). It is she who observes that even an oyster may be crossed in love.

Tilde, the diacritic mark ∼ placed in Spanish above the letter n to indicate the palatalized sound (nʸ), as in *señor* (senʸor).

Till Eulenspiegel, see *Eulenspiegel.*

Tillietudlem, in Scott's 'Old Mortality' (q.v.), the castle of Lady Margaret Bellenden.

Tillotson, JOHN (1630–94), educated at Clare Hall, Cambridge, a 'latitudinarian' who became archbishop of Canterbury. His sermons, marked by lucidity of style, were very popular, and earned the approval of Dryden.

Tilney, GENERAL, and his sons and daughter, characters in Jane Austen's 'Northanger Abbey' (q.v.).

Timber, or Discoveries made upon Men and Matters, by Jonson (q.v.), printed in the folio of 1640, a collection of notes, extracts, and reflections on miscellaneous subjects, made in the course of the author's wide reading, varying in length from a single sentence to short essays. They are, for the greater part, adapted from Latin writers.

Time and Tide, by Weare and Tyne, twenty-five letters by Ruskin (q.v.) on the laws of work, addressed to a working man of Sunderland, published in 1867. They are in effect essays on social reconstruction, expressions of Ruskin's aspirations for a happier world and the disappearance of luxury and poverty, greed and suffering.

Times, The, was founded under the name of 'The Daily Universal Register' on 1 Jan. 1785 by John Walter, the name being changed to 'The Times' in 1788. The founder and his son, also named John Walter, introduced great improvements both in the mechanism of newspaper printing and in the collection of intelligence. Among the famous editors of 'The Times' have been Thomas Barnes (1817–41) and John Thaddeus Delane (1841–77). The latter was followed by Thomas Chenery, and in 1884 by G. E. Buckle. 'The Times' was one of the first papers to employ special foreign correspondents (Henry Crabb Robinson, q.v., was sent out to North Germany in this capacity in 1807) and war correspondents (W. H. Russell, q.v., in the Crimea). Among notable men of letters who contributed to 'The Times' in early days were George Borrow (from Spain), Leigh Hunt, and Disraeli ('Runnymede Letters').

Times Literary Supplement, The, was first published on 17 Jan. 1902 under the editorship of Mr. (later Sir) Bruce Richmond, and has since then appeared weekly. It is important among English literary periodicals by reason of its articles and reviews, of the correspondence on bibliographical and other subjects that appears in its columns, and of its record of current literary publications.

Timias, in Spenser's 'Faerie Queene', Prince Arthur's squire, represents Sir Walter Ralegh. When wounded (III. v), he is healed by Belphoebe (q.v.). The incident of Timias and Amoret (q.v.), in IV. vii. 35 and 36, refers to Ralegh's relations with Elizabeth Throgmorton (see *Ralegh*).

Timmins, FITZROY, in Thackeray's 'A Little Dinner at Timmins's' (1848), an easygoing barrister, induced by his wife, Rosa, to give a dinner-party beyond their means.

Timoleon (*d.* 336 B.C.), a Corinthian noble who liberated Syracuse and the other Sicilian cities from their tyrants. It is said that when his brother Timophanes aspired to become tyrant of his own city, Timoleon endeavoured to dissuade him, and, failing in this, stood by while two of his friends stabbed him to death; an incident referred to by Thomson in his 'Seasons' ('Winter'). Timoleon is also the subject of a tragedy (1730) by Benjamin Martyn, 'not to be despised' (Prof. Elton).

Timon, a misanthropical citizen of Athens who lived about the time of the Peloponnesian War, the subject (1) of one of Lucian's finest Dialogues; (2) of Shakespeare's 'Timon of Athens' (q.v.).

Pope's Timon, in 'Moral Epistles', iv. 98 et seq., an example of ostentatious wealth without sense or taste, was perhaps drawn from the duke of Chandos.

Timon of Athens, a drama by Shakespeare

(q.v.) written probably about 1607, perhaps left unfinished or written in collaboration with another dramatist; not printed until the first folio.

The material of the play is in Plutarch's 'Antony', Lucian's 'Misanthropos', and an anonymous play 'Timon' in the Dyce MS. Timon, a rich and noble Athenian of good and gracious nature, having ruined himself by his prodigal liberality to friends, flatterers, and parasites, turns to the richest of his friends for assistance in his difficulties, and is denied it and deserted by all who had previously frequented him. He surprises these by inviting them once more to a banquet; but when the covers are removed from the dishes (Timon crying, 'Uncover, dogs, and lap!'), they are found to contain warm water, which with imprecations he throws in his guests' faces. Cursing the city, he betakes himself to a cave, where he lives solitary and misanthropical. While digging for roots he finds a hoard of gold, which has now no value for him. His embittered spirit is manifested in his talk with the exiled Alcibiades, the churlish philosopher Apemantus, the thieves and flatterers attracted by the gold, and his faithful steward Flavius. When the senators of Athens, hard pressed by the attack of Alcibiades, come to entreat him to return to the city and help them, he offers them his fig-tree, on which to hang themselves as a refuge from affliction. Soon his tomb is found by the sea-shore, with an epitaph expressing his hatred of mankind.

TIMOTHĒUS (447–357 B.C.), of Miletus, a celebrated musician and poet, mentioned by Dryden (q.v.) in his 'Alexander's Feast'.

Timothy, the tortoise of Gilbert White (q.v.). See in particular his letter to Hester Mulso (afterwards Mrs. Chapone), 31 Aug. 1784, besides various references in his 'Selborne'.

Timothy and **Titus**, companions of the apostle Paul, to whom the Pastoral Epistles in the N.T. are addressed. It is held by some that these epistles were by an author who, 'believing himself to be in accord with St. Paul's teaching and possessing some remains of his correspondence, expanded such into these letters in order to combat erroneous speculations in the church. . . . He probably lived at a time when ecclesiastical organization was growing in importance. Timothy and Titus are thus representative figures, standing for those whom the writer wished to admonish and instruct' (G. W. Wade, 'New Testament History').

Timothy Tickler, in the 'Noctes Ambrosianae' (q.v.), was Robert Sym (1750–1844), writer to the signet, uncle to John Wilson (1785–1854, q.v.).

Timur or *Timur-Leng* ('Timur the Lame'), corrupted to *Tamerlane* or *Tamberlane* (*d.* 1405), said to have been a descendant in the female line from Genghis Khan (q.v.), established himself in Samarkand and extended his rule by terror and desolation over parts of Turkestan, Siberia, Persia, and India, assuming the title of the Great Khan. He captured Delhi and founded the Mogul dynasty in India.

Tina Sastri, a character in George Eliot's 'Mr. Gilfil's Love-Story' (see *Scenes of Clerical Life*).

TINDAL, WILLIAM (*d.* 1536), see *Tyndale*.

Tinta'gel, a castle on the north coast of Cornwall, of which ruins remain. It figures in Malory's 'Morte Darthur' as the castle where Uther Pendragon (q.v.) was wedded to Igraine, and subsequently as the home of King Mark of Cornwall.

Tinto, DICK, a poor artist and sign-painter, who, by a fiction of Scott, supplied notes out of which Peter Pattieson compiled 'The Bride of Lammermoor' (q.v.).

Tintoretto (1518–94), JACOPO ROBUSTI, Venetian painter, the son of a dyer, hence his nickname ('little dyer'). He was said to aim at combining the drawing of Michelangelo with the colouring of Titian. Ruskin glorifies him in vol. ii of 'Modern Painters' (q.v.).

Tiphys, the pilot of the ship of the Argonauts (q.v.).

> Alter erit tum Tiphys et altera quae vehat
>   Argo
> Delectos heroas.
>
> (Virgil, 'Ecl.' iv. 34.)

Tippoo Sahib (1749–99), son of Hyder Ali, and Sultan of Mysore, who was engaged in repeated wars with the British. He figures in Scott's 'The Surgeon's Daughter' (q.v.). He was killed in the gate of his own city, Seringapatam, when it was stormed by General Harris in 1799.

Tiresias or TEIRESIAS, a Theban soothsayer, who was struck with blindness in his youth for reasons variously given, one that he had seen Athene bathing. As some compensation, he was given the power of prophecy, and a staff which guided his footsteps. He advised the Thebans in the wars of the Seven against Thebes and the Epigoni. He lived to a great age. His daughter Manto was also a prophetess. She was captured by the victorious Argives and sent to Delphi as a priestess of Apollo.

The legend of Tiresias is the subject of a poem by T. Woolner (q.v.), and of a dramatic monologue by Lord Tennyson, in which the seer recounts his blinding by Athene:

> Henceforth be blind, for thou hast seen too
>   much,
> And speak the truth that no man may
>   believe,

and laments his impotence for good and the approaching fall of Thebes. Swinburne has a poem on the same subject.

Tironian notes, a system of shorthand in use in ancient Rome, said to have been invented by Tiro, Cicero's freedman.

Tirynthian, an epithet sometimes applied to Hercules, because legend associates him with Tiryns, a city of Argolis, in Greece; though he is also claimed by Thebes.

'Tis Pity She's a Whore, a tragedy by J. Ford (q.v.), published in 1633.

The play deals with the guilty passion of Giovanni and his sister Annabella for each other. Being with child, Annabella marries one of her suitors, Soranzo, who discovers her condition. She refuses to name her lover, though threatened with death by Soranzo. On the advice of Varques, his faithful servant, Soranzo feigns forgiveness, Varques undertaking to discover the truth, which he does. Soranzo invites Annabella's father and the magnificoes of the city, with Giovanni, to a sumptuous feast, intending to execute his vengeance. Although warned of Soranzo's intentions, Giovanni boldly comes. He has a last meeting with Annabella just before the feast, and to forestall Soranzo's vengeance stabs her himself. He then enters the banqueting-room, defiantly tells what he has done, fights with and kills Soranzo, and is himself killed by Varques.

Tisïphŏnē, one of the Furies (q.v.).

Titania, in Shakespeare's 'A Midsummer Night's Dream' (q.v.), the queen of the fairies, and wife of Oberon.

The name is given by Ovid in the 'Metamorphoses' to Latona, Pyrrha, Diana, and Circe, as descendants of the Titans.

Titanic, The, a passenger steamer of the White Star line, the largest ship of her day, sunk on 15 Apr. 1912, on her maiden voyage from Southampton to New York, owing to collision with an iceberg, with the loss of over 1,500 lives.

Titans, THE, sons and daughters of Uranus and Gē (qq.v.). They included Cronos (Saturn), Rhea, Oceanus, Tethys, and Hyperion. The legend says that Uranus had thrown his elder sons (Briareus, Cottys, and Gyes, the hundred-handed ones, and the Cyclopes) into Tartarus, and that Gē incited the Titans to rise against him. This they did, deposed Uranus, and raised Cronos to the throne. Subsequently Zeus (q.v.) revolted in turn against Cronos and the other Titans, and with the help of thunder and lightning hurled them from heaven. (This contest is sometimes confused by the poets with the rising of the Giants (q.v.) against Zeus and the later gods.)

Tithōnus, a son of Laomedon, king of Troy. He was so beautiful that Aurora (q.v.) became enamoured of him. The goddess granted him immortality at his request; but he omitted to ask at the same time for perpetual youth, and soon became old and decrepit.

('Longa Tithonum minuit senectus', Horace, 'Od.', II. xvi). As life became insupportable to him, he prayed Aurora to remove him from this world, and she changed him into a grasshopper.

Tennyson presents him, in a dramatic monologue, lamenting his unhappy fate.

Titian, (*c.* 1487/90–1576), TIZIANO VECELLI, Venetian painter. He worked when young with Giorgione (q.v.) and developed the truly painterly style which the latter introduced, using colour rather than line to suggest form.

Titivil or TUTIVILLUS, a medieval word of unknown origin, the name of a devil said to collect fragments of words dropped, skipped, or mumbled in the recitation of divine service, and to carry them to hell to be registered against the offender. Hence it became a name for a devil in the mystery plays, and hence again it passed into popular speech as a term of reprobation, a scoundrel, villain. 'Tilley-valley, Mr. Lovel—which, by the way, one commentator derives from *tittivili-tium*, and another from *talley-ho*' (Scott, 'The Antiquary', ch. vi).

Titivil was evidently in origin a creation of monastic wit. The earliest mention of the name and function occurs apparently in a Latin sermon attributed to the Dominican Petrus de Palude, a Burgundian student at Paris, who became patriarch of Jerusalem and died in 1342. [OED.]

Titmarsh, MICHAEL ANGELO, see *Michael Angelo Titmarsh.*

Titmarsh, SAMUEL, the hero of Thackeray's 'The Great Hoggarty Diamond' (q.v.).

Tito Melema, a character in G. Eliot's 'Romola' (q.v.).

Titurel, a German romance of the Holy Grail (q.v.) of the 13th cent., of which Wolfram von Eschenbach wrote fragments. According to one version of the Grail legend, the Grail was preserved in heaven until the coming on earth of a race of heroes fitted to be its guardians. The chief of this race was Perillus or Parille of Cappadocia. Titurel is the son of Titurisone and Eligabel, and grandson of Parille. Angels announce that he is to be the defender of the Grail, and he is conducted to Mount Salvagge (Montsalvatsch), where he builds a chapel and organizes a band of defenders for the holy vessel. He marries Richonde of Spain, and is great-grandfather of Parzival.

Titus Andronicus, a tragedy attributed to Shakespeare (q.v.), acted and printed in 1594. The extent of Shakespeare's share in the authorship is uncertain.

It deals with the revenge exacted by Titus Andronicus, a Roman general under the Empire, for the revolting atrocities committed against Lavinia his daughter, his sons, and himself, and for the murder of his daughter's lover, by Tamora the captive queen of the Goths, her sons, and her paramour, Aaron

the Moor. ('Andronicus' in the play is accentuated on the second syllable; in Latin it is 'Andronīcus'.)

TITUS LIVIUS FOROJULIENSIS, an Italian in the service of Duke Humphrey of Gloucester, who wrote, about 1440, a chronicle of the reign of Henry V.

For TITUS LIVIUS, the Roman historian, see *Livy.*

Tityre-tu or TITTYRY, one of an association of well-to-do roughs who infested the London streets in the 17th cent. The name is taken from the first words of Virgil's first Eclogue, 'Tityre, tu patulae recubans sub tegmine fagi.'

Tityus, a giant of Greek mythology, who attempted to do violence to Leto (Latona), but was killed by the arrows of Apollo and Artemis, her children. He was placed in Hades, where a serpent (or vultures) continually devoured his liver.

Tiu, TIW, TYR, an ancient Teutonic deity, a war-god identified with the Roman Mars. In Norse legend Tyr is the son of the giant Hymir, and helps the gods to fetter Fenrir (q.v.), losing his hand in doing so. Tiu is commemorated in our 'Tuesday'.

Tobit, The Book of, a romance of the Jewish captivity, forming part of the Apocrypha. Tobit, a Jew who has been carried captive to Nineveh, is deprived of his property by Sennacherib, and in his distress bethinks him of ten talents of silver he has left in deposit at Rages in Media. He sends his son Tobias to fetch them. The angel Raphael, in the guise of a fellow countryman, accompanies the young man. They catch a fish in the Tigris, and by burning its heart and liver drive off the evil spirit Asmodæus, who has destroyed the seven successive bridegrooms of Sarah, the daughter of Raguel, Tobit's kinsman. Tobias marries Sarah and acquires half Raguel's goods. The gall of the fish serves to remove the blindness with which Tobit is afflicted. The angel also recovers Tobit's deposit. He then reveals himself and exhorts Tobit and Tobias to bless God for his mercies. The dog in Tobit, which accompanies Raphael and Tobias, is probably the eponym of 'Dog Toby' of 'Punch and Judy'.

Toboso, DULCINEA DEL, see *Dulcinea del Toboso.*

Toby, the dog in the puppet-show drama of 'Punch and Judy' (q.v.). See also *Tobit.*

Toby, MY UNCLE, Captain Shandy, uncle of the nominal hero of Sterne's 'Tristram Shandy' (q.v.).

Toby ('TROTTY') **Veck,** a character in Dickens's 'The Chimes' (q.v.).

TOCQUEVILLE, ALEXIS DE (1805–59), French writer on political history, was author of the famous 'La Démocratie en Amérique' (1835–40) and of 'L'Ancien Régime et la

Révolution' (1856). He left interesting 'Souvenirs' (1893), also correspondence, much of it with English friends including John Stuart Mill.

Todgers, Mrs., in Dickens's 'Martin Chuzzlewit' (q.v.), mistress of a boarding-house.

Toffana or Tofana, Aqua, see *Aqua Toffana.*

Toga, in Roman antiquity, the white outer garment of a Roman citizen in time of peace. The *toga praetexta,* with a broad purple border, was worn by children, magistrates, persons engaged in sacred rites, and later by emperors. The *toga virilis* was the toga of manhood, as opposed to the preceding, and was white throughout; the term is hence used figuratively: 'During this period Mr. Clive assumed the *toga virilis*' (Thackeray, 'The Newcomes', xvii).

Tolbooth, originally a booth or stall where customs were collected, came to mean a town hall or town prison (formerly consisting of cells under the town hall). The Tolbooth at Edinburgh figures prominently in Scott's 'The Heart of Midlothian' (q.v.).

Toledo, a city in Spain, long famous for its manufacture of finely tempered sword-blades. Hence a sword made at Toledo.

Toletan Tables, see *Alphonsine Tables.*

TOLKIEN, JOHN RONALD REUEL (1892–   ), Merton professor of English language and literature, 1945–59. He has published a number of philological and critical studies as well as novels based on a mythology of his own: 'The Hobbit' (1937); and 'The Fellowship of the Ring', a sequence in 3 vols.: 'The Lord of the Rings' (1954), 'The Two Towers' (1954), and 'The Return of the King' (1955).

TOLLER, ERNST (1893–1939), German revolutionary poet and dramatist, author of (according to their English titles) 'The Machine Wreckers' (1923), 'Masses and Man' (1923), 'The Swallow Book' (1924).

Tolōsa, Gold of, gold plundered by the Roman consul, Quintus Servilius Caepio, in 106 B.C. from sacred deposits at Tolosa (now Toulouse), a town which had revolted to the Cimbri. Shortly afterwards Quintus Servilius was defeated by the Cimbri and lost, it is said, 80,000 men, a disaster that was regarded as a punishment for his sacrilege. The phrase is used to signify ill-gotten gains.

Tolpuddle Martyrs. The outburst of trade-unionism which occurred in 1833–4, in great measure under the inspiration of the reformer Robert Owen (1771–1858), was met by the Government with a series of prosecutions. These culminated in the trial of six Dorsetshire labourers, natives of Tolpuddle, who had sought to obtain by combination an increase of their wages (then seven shillings a week). They were charged with the offence of taking an oath to their trade union and sentenced to seven years' transportation in 1834. In spite of widespread protests, it was not till 1836 that the men were pardoned and brought back from Australia.

TOLSTOY, Count LEO NIKOLAE-VICH (1828–1910), Russian writer. He was of noble birth and heir to large estates, but his intense sincerity of thought gradually led him to abandon his normal career. He arrived eventually at intellectual conclusions which involved non-resistance to evil, the abolition of governments and nationality, of churches and dogmas, but involved also belief in God and love of men. He made attempts, more or less successful, to renounce his own property. His chief importance rose from his amazing power, which entered into his books, whether they were discussions, novels, plays, or exhortations. This power raised him to a point of reputation and greatness in his own lifetime such that the Imperial Government did not dare to interfere with him, though his writings were, of course, censored. It spread his influence far beyond Russia, and made him something like a prophet to many minds in the West. His chief novels are: 'War and Peace' (1865–72, an epic tale of the Napoleonic invasion), 'Anna Karenina' (1875–6), 'The Death of Ivan Ilyitch' (1884), 'The Kreutzer Sonata' (1890), 'Resurrection' (1899).

Of his other books, 'What is Art?' (1898) is a profound analysis of the nature of art, 'in which', Bernard Shaw has said, 'we hear the voice of the master'; 'Confession' (1882) is an autobiographical description of the great spiritual crisis of his life; 'What then must we do?' (1886) is a study of economic conditions. Besides these, there are essays and short stories, all full of the same power and intensity, and the plays, of which 'The Power of Darkness' (1886) is the greatest.

'The Cossacks', one of the best of his early works, written *c.* 1852 and published in a revised form in 1863, was translated in 1878 and was followed by a large number of translations in the 1880s. Tolstoy's collected works were published in an English translation in 1899–1902.

The union of a great moral conviction and realistic details, and an immense imaginative vision, combine to make him one of the great European writers.

Tom's, a coffee-house famous in the 18th cent., named from Thomas West, its landlord. It was situated in Russell Street, Covent Garden, and was frequented by the best company after the play.

There was another 'Tom's Coffee-house' in Birchin Lane, Cornhill.

Tom and **Jerry,** names of the two chief characters in Egan's 'Life in London' (see *Egan*); hence used in various allusive senses, e.g. of riotous behaviour.

Tom a Lincoln, a romance by R. Johnson

(q.v.), the author of 'The Seven Champions of Christendom'. Tom a Lincoln is the son of King Arthur and Angelica, daughter of the earl of London, and is born in a monastery at Lincoln. He becomes a knight of the Round Table, conquers the Portingales, visits Fairyland, marries Anglitora, the daughter of Prester John, but is overtaken by misfortune and murdered.

Tom Brown's Schooldays, see *Hughes.*

Tom Cringle's Log, see *Scott (M., 1739–1835).*

Tom Folio, see *Rawlinson (T.).*

Tom Fool, a quasi-proper name applied to a man mentally deficient, or to one who acts the part of a fool in a drama, a buffoon. 'More know Tom Fool than Tom Fool knows' (proverb).

Tom Hickathrift or HICKIFRIC, according to an old popular romance, was the son of a labourer in the Isle of Ely before the Norman Conquest. He was endowed with such prodigious strength that he was able to kill a giant with the axle-tree and wheel of a wagon, and, with the help of Henry Nonsuch, an equally stout tinker, to suppress an insurrection in the Isle of Ely; for which exploit he was knighted by the king.

Tom Jones, a Foundling, a novel by H. Fielding (q.v.), published in 1749, consisting of eighteen 'books', each preceded by an introductory chapter in the nature of an essay on some theme more or less connected with the story, in the manner subsequently adopted by Thackeray and George Eliot. These essays contain some of Fielding's best prose.

The plot of this, which is generally regarded as Fielding's greatest work, is briefly as follows. Tom Jones is a foundling, mysteriously discovered one night in the bed of the wealthy, virtuous, and benevolent Mr. Allworthy, who gives him a home and educates him, but presently repudiates him. The causes which lead to Tom's dismissal are several. In the first place Tom, a generous and manly, but too human, youth, has incurred his benefactor's displeasure by his amour with Molly Seagrim, the keeper's daughter. Then he has fallen in love with the beautiful Sophia (daughter of the bluff irascible foxhunter, Squire Western), who is destined for another. He has incurred the enmity of his tutor, the pedantic divine, Thwackum, and, in a less degree, of his colleague, the hypocritical philosopher, Square. And lastly he is the victim of the cunning misrepresentations of young Blifil, a mean sneak, who expects to marry Sophia himself, and hates Tom. Tom sets out on his travels, accompanied by the schoolmaster, Partridge, a simple lovable creature, and meets with many adventures, some of them of an amorous description, notably that with Lady Bellaston, which has been much criticized.

Lady Bellaston falls in love with Tom, who does not show himself recalcitrant, and supports him in London out of her liberality. Meanwhile Sophia, who is in love with Tom and determined to escape from the marriage with Blifil to which her despotic father has condemned her, runs away from home, with Mrs. Honour, her maid, to a relative in London. Here she escapes a wicked design of Lady Bellaston to place her in the power of Lord Fellamar, thanks to the opportune arrival of Squire Western in pursuit of her. Finally Tom is discovered to be the son of Allworthy's sister, the machinations of Blifil are exposed, Sophia forgives Tom his infidelities, and all ends happily.

Tom-noddy, a foolish or stupid person. NODDY, of obscure origin, means a simpleton.

Tom o' Bedlam, a wandering beggar. After the dissolution of the religious houses, where the poor used to be relieved, there was for long no settled provision for them. In consequence they wandered over the country, many assuming disguises calculated to obtain them charity. Among other disguises some affected madness, and were called Bedlam Beggars (so in 'Gammer Gurton's Needle', 'Diccon the Bedlam'). Edgar, in 'King Lear', II. iii, adopts this disguise:

Of Bedlam beggars, who, with roaring voices,
Strike in their numb'd and mortified bare arms
Pins, wooden pricks, nailes, sprigs of rosemary.

In Dekker's 'Bellman of London' (1616) 'Tom of Bedlam's band of mad caps' are enumerated among the species of beggars. Some of these Bedlam beggars sang mad songs, examples of which are given in Percy's 'Reliques'. They were also called 'Abraham-men', from the name, it is said (Brewer), of one of the wards in Bedlam.

Tom of Lincoln, 'an extraordinary great bell, hanging in one of the towers of Lincoln Minster' (Ray, quoted by W. C. Hazlitt). See also *Tom a Lincoln.*

Tom of Oxford, GREAT, the great bell of Christ Church, Oxford; it hangs in TOM TOWER (q.v.), and the great quadrangle of the college, TOM QUAD, is called after it.

Tom Sawyer, a novel by Mark Twain (see *Clemens, S. L.*), published in 1876. Tom Sawyer lives with his brother Sid and his Aunt Polly in St. Petersburg, Missouri. He is both mischievous and ingenious, and brave and generous. In the course of his pranks he sees Injun Joe stab the village doctor to death and is able to absolve Muff Potter of the crime when he is mistakenly charged with it and tried. He and his sweetheart Becky Thatcher wander away on a school picnic and become lost in the caves where Injun Joe has also been trapped and has died. This leads to the finding of Joe's treasure, which Tom shares with his companion Huck Finn, the hero of the later classic, 'Huckleberry Finn' (q.v.).

Tom Thumb, an old nursery tale, of which there are several Northern versions.

According to the English tale, Tom was the son of a ploughman in the days of King Arthur, and he was as tall as the ploughman's thumb. His diminutive size was the occasion of many absurd adventures, as when he was swallowed by a cow, was carried off by a raven, and was swallowed by Giant Grumbo.

GENERAL TOM THUMB was the name given to Charles Sherwood Stratton (1838–83), an American midget exhibited in England by Barnum in 1844 and 1857. Stratton married Lavinia Warren, also a midget, in 1863.

Tom Thumb, a Tragedy, a burlesque of contemporary playwrights by H. Fielding (q.v.), first acted in 1730; reissued, enlarged, in 1731 as 'The Tragedy of Tragedies; or the Life and Death of Tom Thumb the Great'.

Tom Tiddler's Ground or TOM TITTLER'S GROUND, the name of a children's game, in which one of the players is Tom Tiddler, his territory being marked by a line drawn across the ground; over this the other players run, crying, 'Here we're on Tom Tiddler's ground, picking up gold and silver.' They are chased by Tom Tiddler, and the player caught takes his place. 'Tom Tiddler's Ground' is used for a 'debatable territory, a no man's land between two states' (Slang Dictionary).

Tom Tiler or TYLER, a hen-pecked husband (the ἐνπεπεγμένος of a line in an epigram by the Rev. W. W. Merry, Τὴν ἐνπεκοῦσαν καὶ τὸν ἐνπεπεγμένον).

Tom Tower, over the gate of TOM QUAD, Christ Church, Oxford, was built by Wren.

TOMASI DI LAMPEDUSA, GIUSEPPE (1896–1957), a Sicilian aristocrat, prince of Lampedusa, was the author of a remarkable historical novel, 'Il gattopardo' ('The Leopard', written in 1955–6 and published posthumously in 1958), which deals with the reactions of a noble Sicilian family to the political and social changes that followed Garibaldi's annexation of Sicily in 1860.

TOMKIS, THOMAS (fl. 1604–15), fellow of Trinity College, Cambridge, author of 'Albumazar' (q.v.), a comedy acted before James I, and probably of another comedy, 'Lingua, or the Combat of the Tongue and the five Senses for Superiority' (1607).

Tomkyns, MRS. PONSONBY DE, a type of vulgar parvenue caricatured by Du Maurier (q.v.) in 'Punch'.

TOMLINSON, HENRY MAJOR (1873–1958), novelist, journalist, and traveller, among whose best-known works are 'The Sea and the Jungle' (1912), 'Old Junk' (1918), 'London River' (1921), 'Gallions Reach' (1927), 'All Our Yesterdays' (1930).

Tommy and Grizel, a novel by Barrie (q.v.), a sequel to his 'Sentimental Tommy', published in 1900, the tragic story of an erratic, inconstant, fascinating genius, and a patient constant woman whose life is blighted by her love for him.

Tommy Atkins, a familiar name for the typical private soldier in the British Army; arising out of the casual use of this name in the specimen forms given in the official Army regulations from 1815 onwards, to show how such forms should be filled up, with the name of the soldier concerned, etc.

Tŏmўris, queen of the Massăgĕtae (a tribe which dwelt south of the Jaxartes), by whom Cyrus, who had invaded her territory, was slain in battle in 529 B.C.

Tono-Bungay, see *Wells (H. G.)*.

Tonson, JACOB (1656–1736), publisher. He purchased the copyright of 'Paradise Lost', and published many works by Dryden and Addison, besides Rowe's 'Shakespeare' and an edition of Beaumont and Fletcher. The six parts of his 'Miscellany', edited by Dryden, and including poems by Pope, Swift, and Ambrose Philips, appeared from 1684 to 1708. He was secretary to the Kit-Cat Club (q.v.). His publishing business was continued by his nephew and great-nephew, who bore the same name as he. Pope (adapting Dryden) mentions Tonson in the 'Dunciad' as 'left-legged Jacob', but his other references to him are more kindly.

Tontine, a financial scheme by which the subscribers to a fund receive each an annuity, which increases as their number is diminished by death, until the last survivor enjoys the whole income; so named from Lorenzo Tonti, a Neapolitan banker who initiated the system in France c. 1653. [OED.]

A tontine forms the basis of R. L. Stevenson and Lloyd Osbourne's 'The Wrong Box' (1889), in which the prize comes to lie between two brothers, Joseph and Masterman Finsbury.

Tony Lumpkin, a character in Goldsmith's 'She Stoops to Conquer' (q.v.).

Toodle, POLLY and ROBIN ('Rob the Grinder'), her son, characters in Dickens's 'Dombey and Son' (q.v.). Polly was Paul Dombey's foster-mother.

TOOKE, JOHN HORNE (1736–1812), the son of a poulterer named Horne, who added the name of his friend William Tooke to his own in 1782. He vigorously supported Wilkes (q.v.) in connexion with the Middlesex election, but subsequently quarrelled with him, the dispute being conducted in the columns of 'The Public Advertiser' (q.v.). He published in 1786 and 1798 "Ἔπεα πτερόεντα, or the Diversions of Purley', a philological work emphasizing the necessity of studying Gothic and Anglo-Saxon, which established his reputation as a philologist. He was more than once in conflict with the authorities, was fined and imprisoned for sedition, and was tried for high treason and acquitted.

Tooley Street, see *Olaf (St.)*. See also *Tailors of Tooley Street*.

Toots, MR., a character in Dickens's 'Dombey and Son' (q.v.).

Tophet or TOPHETH, a place near Gehenna or the Valley of Hinnom, to the south of Jerusalem, where the Jews, according to 2 Kings xxiii. 10 and Jer. xix. 4, made human sacrifices to strange gods. Later it was used as a place for the deposit of rubbish, where bonfires were kept burning, and became symbolic of the torments of hell.

TOPLADY, AUGUSTUS MONTAGUE (1740–78), educated at Westminster and Trinity College, Dublin, incumbent of Broad Hembury, is remembered as the author of the hymn 'Rock of Ages', published in the 'Gospel Magazine' in 1775. He engaged in violent controversy with John Wesley.

Topsy, in Mrs. Beecher Stowe's 'Uncle Tom's Cabin' (see under *Stowe, Mrs. H. B.*), a little slave girl who asserted that she had neither father nor mother, and being asked who made her, replied 'I spect I grow'd'.

Tor, SIR, in Malory's 'Morte Darthur', the son of King Pellinore and the milkmaid, a knight of the Round Table. See also *Torre*.

Torah, THE, the teaching or instruction, and judicial decisions, given by the ancient Hebrew priests as a revelation of the divine will; the Mosaic or Jewish law; hence a name for the first five books of the law, the Pentateuch. [OED.]

Torfrida, in C. Kingsley's novel, 'Hereward the Wake' (q.v.), the wife of Hereward.

Torquatus, T. MANLIUS, see *Manlius Torquatus*.

Torquemada, TOMÁS DE (1420–98), a Spanish Dominican monk, appointed in 1483 the first inquisitor-general by Ferdinand and Isabella. He was famous for the untiring energy with which the work of the Inquisition in Spain was carried on under his direction. Hence his name became a synonym for a cruel persecutor. But Torquemada's code of instructions for the application of torture was relatively moderate. It was twisted and extended by his successors.

Torquil of the Oak, a character in Scott's 'The Fair Maid of Perth' (q.v.).

Torre, SIR, in Tennyson's 'Lancelot and Elaine' (q.v.), is son of the Lord of Astolat and one of Elaine's two brothers, the other being Lavaine.

TORRENS, WILLIAM McCULLAGH (1813–94), a successful barrister, M.P. for several constituencies (first in 1847), was author of a good life of Melbourne (1878), and

lives of R. L. Sheil (1855), Sir James Graham (1863), and Lord Wellesley (1880), besides some notable works on political subjects ('Industrial History of Free Nations', 1846; 'Twenty Years in Parliament', 1893).

Torres Vedras, LINES OF, three lines of earthworks constructed by Wellington across the peninsula that lies between the Tagus and the sea. They were defended by him against Masséna in 1810–11 with English and Portuguese troops, leaving the French armies to exist in a country that had been entirely stripped of food.

Torricelli (1608–47), an Italian physicist, who by the *Torricellian Experiment* proved in 1643 that the column of mercury in an inverted closed tube is supported by the pressure of the atmosphere. TORRICELLIAN TUBE was an early name for the mercurial barometer.

Torrigiano, PIETRO (1472–1528), Florentine sculptor who, as he recounted to Benvenuto Cellini, when young broke Michelangelo's nose. He worked in England, modelling the bronze effigies of Margaret Beaufort and of Henry VII and Elizabeth of York in Westminster Abbey. He died in Seville, starving himself to death when imprisoned by the Inquisition.

Tory, from an Irish word meaning 'pursuer', was a name applied in the 17th cent. to the dispossessed Irish, who became outlaws, subsisting by killing and plundering the English settlers and soldiers. In 1679–80 it was applied as a nickname by the Exclusionists to those who opposed the exclusion of the Roman Catholic James, duke of York, from the succession to the Crown. Hence, from 1689, it became the name of one of the two great political parties in England, that which sprang from the 17th-cent. Royalists or Cavaliers, whose members were more or less identical with the Anti-Exclusionists mentioned above. For some years after 1689 the Tories leant more or less decidedly towards the dethroned House of Stuart. But from the accession of George III they abandoned this attitude, retaining the principle of strenuously upholding the constituted authority and order in Church and State, and of opposing concessions in the direction of greater religious liberty. Opposition to the growing demands of Liberalism, a consistent antagonism to measures for widening the basis of parliamentary representation, etc., became their most marked characteristic. But this has in course of time undergone many modifications. As a formal name 'Tory' was superseded by 'Conservative' about 1830, a term introduced by Croker. [OED.]

Toscar, in the Ossianic poems, the father of Malvina, betrothed to Oscar the son of Ossian.

TOTTEL, RICHARD (d. 1594), a publisher who carried on business at 'The Hand

and Star' within Temple Bar from 1553 to 1594, is chiefly known as the compiler (with Grimald, q.v.) of 'Songs and Sonnets', known as 'Tottel's Miscellany' (1557), comprising the chief works of Wyatt and Surrey (q.v.). He also published, besides law-books, More's 'Dialogue of Comfort' (1553), Lydgate's 'Fall of Princes' (1554), and Surrey's 'Aeneid' (1557).

Slender, in Shakespeare's 'The Merry Wives of Windsor' (q.v.), had 'rather than forty shillings' he had Tottel's 'Book of Songs and Sonnets' with him when courting Anne Page; and the grave-digger in 'Hamlet' mumbles a song from the same collection.

Touchett, MR., MRS., and RALPH, characters in H. James's 'Portrait of a Lady' (q.v.).

Touchstone, a clown in Shakespeare's 'As You Like It' (q.v.).

Touchwood, LORD, a character in Congreve's 'The Double Dealer' (q.v.).

Touchwood, MR. SCROGIE, a character in Scott's 'St. Ronan's Well' (q.v.).

Touchwood, SIR GEORGE and LADY FRANCES, characters in Mrs. Cowley's 'The Belle's Stratagem' (q.v.).

TOURGUENIEF, see *Turgenieff.*

TOURNEUR, TURNOUR, or TURNER, CYRIL (1575?–1626), dramatist. Practically nothing is known of his life. Of his two plays (assuming that they are both his, which is contested), 'The Revenger's Tragedy' was published in 1607. It deals with the revenge of Vendice for the murder of his betrothed lady by the licentious duke, and for the attempt of the duke's son, Lussorioso, to seduce Vendice's sister, the chaste Castiza. It is a gloomy work, relieved by the poetic beauty of several passages and the tragic intensity of the plot. 'The Atheist's Tragedy' (q.v.) appeared in 1611. (The dates and order of the two plays, however, are disputed.) 'The Transformed Metamorphosis', published in 1600, is a lament, in allegorical form, on the political conditions of the day, the corruption of the Roman Church, and the dangerous state of Ireland, ending with hope for happier times. Tourneur's 'Plays and Poems' were edited by John Churton Collins in 1878, and by Prof. A. Nicoll in 1929.

Toussaint L'Ouverture (1743–1803), to whom Wordsworth addressed a sonnet, was a Negro revolutionist who made himself master of the French colony of San Domingo (Haiti) when the decree of 1791 freeing the Negroes was revoked. For some years he administered the island with great success, but he was overcome by a military expedition sent by Buonaparte, and transported to France, where he died.

Tower Hill, adjacent to the Tower of London, was probably a site of military importance from pre-Conquest days, and traces of Roman buildings have been

found there (Lethaby). According to Stow (1598) a scaffold was erected there for the execution of traitors, and Sir Thomas More, the earl of Surrey (the poet), Strafford, Laud, Algernon Sidney, and many others, perished on Tower Hill.

Tower of London, THE, the ancient fortress-palace of London, an irregular agglomeration of buildings surrounded by wall and moat, standing on the bank of the Thames at the SE. angle of the old walled city. It was constructed by William the Conqueror (who built what is now called the White Tower) and his successors, principally Henry III. The foundation of the White Tower (rebuilt in 1638) overlies that of a 'great and solid bastion' (Loftie) perhaps of Roman construction. The Tower of London has been used as a prison for kings and queens and other eminent persons, captive foreign sovereigns (e.g. John Balliol, nominal king of Scotland), prisoners awaiting trial (e.g. Sir W. Ralegh), and others swiftly destined to the scaffold (e.g. Anne Boleyn). Of the church of St. Peter in the Tower (Ad Vincula), Macaulay wrote: 'Thither have been carried through successive ages, by the rude hands of gaolers, without one mourner following, the bleeding relics of men who had been captains of armies, the leaders of parties, the oracles of senates, and the ornaments of courts' ('History of England', ch. v).

For the 'Lions in the Tower' see under *Zoological Garden.*

Town and Gown, at Oxford and Cambridge, the body of citizens or townsmen on the one hand, and the members of the university on the other. Frequent riots took place between these 'factions' from the 13th to the 19th cents.—in the last period generally on the fifth of November. One of the most considerable of these riots was the 'Great Slaughter' of St. Scholastica's Day (10 Feb.) 1354 at Oxford, for which the mayor and citizens long did annual penance.

Town Mouse and Country Mouse, a fable told by Horace ('Sat.' II. vi) and by La Fontaine (though the latter substitutes rats for mice). The city mouse, contemptuous of the country mouse's cave and humble fare, invites it to a sumptuous supper in its palace. But the feast is disturbed by an alarm, and the mice scurry away. The country mouse concludes that it prefers its wood and cave free from surprises, and its homely tares.

M. Prior (q.v.) was at least part-author of 'The Hind and Panther transvers'd to the tale of the Town Mouse and the Country Mouse'.

Towneley, a character in Sheridan's 'A Trip to Scarborough' (q.v.).

Towneley Mysteries, see *Mysteries.*

Townly, LORD, 'The Provok'd Husband' in Vanbrugh and Cibber's play of that name (q.v.).

TOWNSHEND, AURELIAN (*fl.* 1601–43),

was sent to Paris in 1600 and later to Italy by Sir Robert Cecil to be trained for service with his son William, although there is no evidence that he was later so employed. Early in 1632 he appears as a writer of court masques and seems to have collaborated with Inigo Jones (q.v.) in the 'invention' of the king's masque of 'Albion's Triumph', and to have contributed verses for the queen's masque of 'Tempe Restored'. He enjoyed favour at the court of Charles I and his lyric 'On his hearing Her Majesty sing' records this privilege. His poems seem not to have been collected in his life time, but are found in various miscellanies. A poem addressed to Lady Salisbury and another addressed to his daughter, 'Let not thy Beauty make thee proud', were printed with musical settings in 1652. An edition of his 'Poems and Masques' was published by E. K. Chambers in 1912.

Townshend, CHARLES, *second Viscount Townshend* (1674–1738), a distinguished statesman of the reign of George I. He carried on at Rainham agricultural experiments which earned him his nickname of 'Turnip Townshend'. Pope('Imitations of Horace', Ep. II. ii. 273) refers to Townshend's turnips, and in a footnote states that 'that kind of rural improvement which arises from turnips' was 'the favourite subject of Townshend's conversation'.

Tow-wouse, MR. and MRS., characters in H. Fielding's 'Joseph Andrews' (q.v.).

TOYNBEE, ARNOLD JOSEPH (1889–), historian. He was professor of Byzantine and Modern Greek language, literature, and history at London University, 1919–24, and then director of studies at the Royal Institute of International Affairs and research professor of international history until he retired in 1955. His great work, 'A Study of History', published in 10 vols. between 1934 and 1954, is a survey of the chief civilizations of the world. Among his other publications are: 'Nationality and the War' (1915), 'Civilization on Trial' (1948), 'War and Civilization' (1951), and 'The World and the West' (1953).

Toxophilus, see *Ascham.*

Tractarian Movement, see *Oxford Movement.*

Tracts for the Times, a series of tracts on religious subjects, of which the principal authors were Newman, Keble, R. H. Froude, and Pusey (qq.v.), published from 1833 to 1841.
They were issued 'with the object of contributing something towards the revival of doctrines which, although held by the great divines of our Church, at present have become obsolete with the majority of her members. . . . The Apostolic succession and the Holy Catholic Church were principles of action in the minds of our predecessors of the 17th century. . . . Nothing but these neglected

doctrines faithfully preached . . . will repress the extension of Popery'. The first tract was by Newman, 'Thoughts on the Ministerial Commission, respectfully addressed to the Clergy', and the most famous, 'Tract XC', was also by him. See *Oxford Movement.*

Traddles, a character in Dickens's 'David Copperfield' (q.v.).

Tradescant, JOHN (*d.* 1637?), traveller, naturalist, and gardener, probably author of 'A voiag of ambasad' (1618) describing a voyage under Sir Dudley Digges to Archangel, containing the earliest account extant of Russian plants. From the expedition (1620) against the Algerine pirates he brought back the 'Algier apricot'. He established a physic garden at Lambeth. His son, JOHN TRADESCANT (1608–62), was likewise a traveller and gardener. He published 'Museum Tradescantianum' in 1656, and gave his collection to Elias Ashmole, who presented it to the University of Oxford. Both this Tradescant and his father held the appointment of gardener to Charles I.

Trafalgar (Trafalgār', usually pron. Trafal'gar), BATTLE OF, fought on 21 Oct. 1805. Nelson had 27 ships of the line and 4 frigates; the French and Spanish fleets, under Villeneuve, numbered 33 ships of the line and 5 frigates. The British fleet attacked in two lines towards the centre of the enemy so as to break his line in two. The enemy fleet was almost entirely captured or destroyed, but, owing to the stormy weather that followed, only four of their ships were brought into harbour. Nelson was killed in the course of the battle. Villeneuve was taken prisoner, was soon exchanged and repatriated, but committed suicide at Rennes shortly after his landing in France.

Trafalgar Square, London, where formerly were the Royal Mews (q.v.) and 'The Bermudas' (q.v.), was laid out in 1829 and the following years, and finished according to plans prepared by Sir Charles Barry. It is named after the last victory of Nelson, whose statue stands on a lofty column in the square.

Tragedy, a word derived from the Greek τραγῳδία, apparently meaning 'goat-song'. As to the reason of the name many theories have been advanced, some even disputing the connexion with goat. It is applied to a play or other literary work of a serious or sorrowful character with a fatal or disastrous conclusion; also to that branch of dramatic art which treats of sorrowful or terrible events in a serious and dignified style. [OED.]

Tragedy of Tragedies, see *Tom Thumb, a Tragedy.*

Tragic Comedians, *The,* a novel by G. Meredith (q.v.), published in 1880.
It is based on the account given by Helene von Dönniges of her tragic love-affair with Ferdinand Lassalle, the German Socialist. Helene figures in the novel as Clotilde, the

daughter of a noble house, who falls in love with Alvan (Lassalle) and is prepared to defy her family and marry him. But he insists that she shall go back to them and obtain their free consent to the match. So Clotilde returns, and is bullied and deceived into accepting another suitor in her own world, Marko. Alvan, infuriated, writes an insulting letter to Clotilde's father. Marko fights with him and kills him, and marries Clotilde.

TRAHERNE, THOMAS (1637–74), a writer of religious works, both in prose and verse, 'Christian Ethics' (1675), 'Poems' (1903), and 'Centuries of Meditation' (1908), marked by originality of thought and by a remarkably musical quality.

TRAILL, HENRY DUFF (1842–1900). by profession a journalist, wrote two volumes of light satiric verse, 'Recaptured Rhymes' (1882) and 'Saturday Songs' (1890), and other poems; 'The New Lucian' (new dialogues of the dead, 1884), 'Number Twenty, fables and fantasies' (1892). He was the first editor of 'Literature' (1897 till his death), and wrote a life of Sir John Franklin (1896). He also edited in six vols. (1893–7) 'Social England', a history by various contributors, and wrote for the 'Twelve English Statesmen' series a good life of William III.

Traitor, The, a tragedy by James Shirley (q.v.), produced in 1631 and printed in 1635. It has some historical foundation in the assassination of Duke Alessandro de' Medici.

Lorenzo plots against his kinsman, the duke of Florence, and for this purpose furthers the duke's desire to seduce Amidea, sister of Sciarrha, a Florentine noble. At the same time he inflames Sciarrha against the duke's tyranny, so that Sciarrha determines to kill him. Finally Sciarrha kills Amidea to save her from dishonour, and lays her corpse on a bed, where the duke finds her. In his amazement he calls for Lorenzo, who enters and stabs him to death, and is in turn killed by Sciarrha. The latter is himself wounded in the affray and dies.

Traitor's Gate, the river gate of the Tower of London, by which traitors, and state prisoners generally, were committed to the Tower.

Trajan (MARCUS ULPIUS TRAIĀNUS), Roman emperor, A.D. 98–117, of Spanish birth, a great soldier, simple and unassuming. His victories are commemorated on TRAJAN'S COLUMN in Rome, a circular marble column bearing reliefs ascending in a spiral and representing the emperor's campaigns, set up in the Forum which bears his name in A.D. 113. The inscription on the column has been used as a model for lettering; 'Trajan' or 'architects' lettering' is a regular term for a modern style of roman capitals. There is a specimen from Trajan's Column in Pl. I of 'The Art of Lettering and its Use in Divers Crafts and Trades', the report of a Special Committee of the British Institute of Industrial Art, 1931.

The FORUM OF TRAJAN lies below the north-eastern slope of the Capitol Hill at Rome; and there are two marble ARCHES OF TRAJAN, one at Benevento over the Appian Way, and one at Ancona.

Trajectum ad Rhenum, also *Ultrajectum,* in imprints, Utrecht.

Transcendental, a word that signifies, in the philosophy of Kant (q.v.), not derived from experience but concerned with the pre-suppositions of experience; pertaining to the general theory of the nature of experience or knowledge. The term is also used of any philosophy which resembles Kant's in being based upon the recognition of an *a priori* element in experience. [OED.]

For American Transcendentalism see *Transcendental Club* and *Emerson.*

Transcendental Club, a group of American intellectuals who met informally for philosophical discussion at Emerson's (q.v.) house and elsewhere during some years from 1836, the embodiment of a movement of thought, philosophical, religious, social, and economic, produced in New England between 1830 and 1850 by the spirit of revolutionary Europe, German philosophy, and Wordsworth, Coleridge, and Carlyle (qq.v.). The philosophical views of this Transcendentalism may be gathered from Emerson's short treatise, 'Nature' (1836). Its literary organ was 'The Dial' (q.v.).

Its social and economic aspects took form in the 'Brook Farm Institute' (1841–7) of George Ripley, a self-supporting group of men and women, who shared in manual labour and intellectual pursuits.

Transformation, see *Marble Faun.*

Transformed Metamorphosis, The, see *Tourneur.*

Transmontane, dwelling or situated beyond the mountains; from the Italian point of view, north of the Alps. Cf. *Ultramontane.* The word 'Tramontana' signifies a cold north wind.

Transome, HAROLD, a character in George Eliot's 'Felix Holt' (q.v.).

Trapbois, and his daughter MARTHA, characters in Scott's 'The Fortunes of Nigel' (q.v.).

Trappist, a monk of the Cistercian order observing the reformed rule established in 1664 by De Rancé, abbot of La Trappe in Normandy. The observance of almost constant silence is a special feature of the rule, which is in other respects also extremely austere.

Traveller, The, a poem by Goldsmith (q.v.), published in 1764, his earliest production under his own name. It is dedicated and addressed to his brother, a country clergyman. The author, in the character of a traveller, places himself on the summit of the Alps, and compares social and political conditions in the countries that he sees, noting the inconveniences of each, and endeavouring to show that there may be equal happiness in other States though differently governed from our own. Johnson contributed nine lines to the poem, ll. 420, 429–34, 437–8.

Travels in France, a record of travel in that country during the years 1787–90, by A. Young (q.v.), published in 1792. The first journey takes him through the south-west (Berri, Poitou, Languedoc), the second through Brittany and Anjou, the third through Alsace-Lorraine, the Jura, Burgundy, and Provence. Visiting France shortly before and during the Revolution, Young draws attention to the defective social and economic conditions of the *ancien régime*. The work was translated into various languages and has always been highly valued in France. It contains the famous phrase, 'The magic of property turns sand into gold'. There is a good modern edition by Miss Betham-Edwards, with a Memoir (1 vol., 1892).

Travels with a Donkey, see *Stevenson* (R. L.).

Treasure Island, a romance by R. L. Stevenson (q.v.) published in book form in 1883. It had previously appeared as a serial in 'Young Folks' from late in 1881 under the title 'The Sea Cook or Treasure Island'.

The narrator is the lad, Jim Hawkins, whose mother keeps the 'Admiral Benbow' somewhere on the coast in the west of England, in the 18th cent. An old buccaneer takes up his quarters at the inn. He has in his chest information, in the shape of a manuscript map, as to the whereabouts of Capt. Flint's treasure. Of this his former confederates are determined to obtain possession, and a body of them, led by the sinister blind pirate, Pew, make a descent on the inn. But Jim Hawkins outwits them, secures the map, and delivers it to Squire Trelawney. The Squire and his friend Dr. Livesey set off for Treasure Island in the 'Hispaniola' schooner, taking Jim with them. Some of the crew are the squire's faithful dependants, but the majority are old buccaneers recruited by the plausible one-legged villain, Long John Silver. Their design to seize the ship and kill the squire's party is discovered by Jim, and after a series of thrilling fights and adventures is completely thwarted; and the squire, with the help of the marooned pirate, Ben Gunn, secures the treasure.

Treatise of Human Nature, A, a philosophical work by Hume (q.v.), published in 1739–40.

It is convenient to consider this work, composed before the author was five-and-twenty, together with the 'Enquiry concerning Human Understanding' (1748) and the 'Enquiry concerning the Principles of Morals' (1751), which are recastings of the earlier treatise in the light of a maturer judgement. Hume's purpose in these is to correct and complete the philosophy of Locke and Berkeley as set forth in the 'Essay concerning Human Understanding' (q.v.), and in the earlier works of Berkeley (q.v.). Whereas his predecessors had maintained a distinction between reason on the one hand and the effects of sensation and experience on the other, Hume endeavours to show that our 'rational' judgements are simply impressions associated by custom, expectations resulting from experience. The problem of knowledge, in his treatment, becomes the problem of causation, instead of the problem of substance. He arrives at the conclusion, with regard to our notion of causation, that 'reason can never show us the connexion of one object with another, tho' aided by experience, and the observation of their constant conjunction in all past instances. When the mind, therefore, passes from the idea or impression of one object to the idea or belief of another, it is not determined by reason, but by certain principles, which associate together the ideas of these objects and unite them in the imagination.' 'Objects have no discoverable connexion together; nor is it from any other principle but custom operating on the imagination, that we can draw any inference from the appearance of one to the existence of another.' He summarizes the position in the statement 'that objects bear to each other the relations of contiguity and succession; that like objects may be observed in several instances to have like relations; and that all this is independent of, and antecedent to, the operations of the understanding'. The repetition of the same impressions in the same relation produces 'a new impression, and by that means the idea' of causation; 'for after a frequent repetition, I find, that upon the appearance of one of the objects, the mind is *determined* by custom to consider its usual attendant, and to consider it in a stronger light upon account of its relation to the first object. 'Tis this impression, then, or *determination*, which affords me the idea of necessity.' The seat of the necessary connexion is in the mind, not in the objects.

As regards the problem of substance, he concludes that the continued existence of objects distinct from perception is an illusion. Berkeley's belief in a spiritual substance is as untenable as Locke's belief in a material substance. For we have no single permanent impression of self, but only a succession of particular ever-changing impressions. Men may call themselves persons, but 'are nothing but a bundle or collection of different perceptions'. A variable interrupted existence is mistaken by the imagination for an invariable uninterrupted existence.

The weakness of this position was, however, admitted by Hume in the Appendix to the 'Treatise'; he confesses that he 'cannot discover any theory which gives him satisfaction on this head'. And he omitted the whole discussion from the later 'Enquiry'.

The general sceptical argument Hume confines to our knowledge of matters of fact, and excludes from it our knowledge of the relations of ideas, as exemplified in 'the sciences of Geometry, Algebra, and Arithmetic'. (This at least is the view propounded in the 'Enquiry', but in the 'Treatise' he attaches less certainty to the science of geometry, owing to the empirical basis of our idea of space. The subject was also discussed by J. S. Mill; see *Logic*.)

The second and third books of the 'Treatise' are occupied with an examination of the passions, and with morals. As regards the latter, he rejects the view that the distinction between right and wrong is one of reason. It derives from a sentiment of approval or disapproval of an action which arises in one's breast. 'It lies in yourself, not in the object.' But while in the 'Treatise' Hume makes moral approval or disapproval a matter of regard for our own happiness, in the 'Enquiry' morality is the outcome of a 'moral sense' (the view already expressed by Hutcheson), a disinterested preference for what is morally good; benevolence, or disinterested regard for the general happiness, becomes the supreme end, and social utility the sole source or inseparable accompaniment of all the social virtues. At the same time Hume comes finally to the conclusion that the happiness of others and the happiness of oneself are not discordant but harmonious aims.

Trecento, the 14th-cent. as a period in Italian art and literature. To this period belonged Dante, Petrarch, and Boccaccio.

Trelawny, of the ballad, see *Hawker*.

TRELAWNY, EDWARD JOHN (1792–1881), Shelley's friend, who was present at Leghorn when Shelley was drowned, was author of the remarkable 'Adventures of a Younger Son' (q.v., 1831), and of 'Records of Shelley, Byron, and the Author' (1858).

TRENCH, RICHARD CHENEVIX (1807–86), educated at Harrow and Trinity College, Cambridge, afterwards dean of Westminster and archbishop of Dublin. He was the author of works dealing with history and literature, poetry, divinity, and philology. As a philologist, and notably by his 'The Study of Words', published in 1851, he popularized the scientific study of language. The scheme of the 'Oxford English Dictionary' originated in a resolution passed, at his suggestion, in 1857 by the Philological Society. His 'Notes on the Parables of our Lord' appeared in 1841, and 'Notes on the Miracles of our Lord' in 1846. His sonnets, lyrics, and hymns show much poetic ability. His 'Sacred Latin Poetry, chiefly Lyrical' (1849) drew attention to the masterpieces of Latin hymnody.

Trent, the detective in E. C. Bentley's 'Trent's Last Case' (1913).

Trent, FRED, a character in Dickens's 'Old Curiosity Shop' (q.v.). His sister is 'Little Nell'.

Trent Case, THE: James Murray Mason and John Slidell, commissioners of the American Confederate States, were in 1861, during the American Civil War, seized on the British ship 'Trent' by the Federal captain, Wilkes. His action was disavowed by the Federal government.

Trent, COUNCIL OF, see *Council of Trent*.

Tressilian, EDMUND, a character in Scott's 'Kenilworth' (q.v.).

TREVELYAN, GEORGE MACAULAY (1876–1962), son of Sir G. O. Trevelyan (q.v.), was educated at Harrow and Trinity College, Cambridge, and appointed Regius professor of modern history at Cambridge in 1927 and Master of Trinity in 1940. He was author of three remarkable works on Garibaldi, 'Garibaldi's Defence of the Roman Republic' (1907), 'Garibaldi and the Thousand' (1909), and 'Garibaldi and the Making of Italy' (1911); of a 'Life of John Bright' (1913); of a 'History of England' (1926); of 'England under Queen Anne' (1930); and of 'English Social History' (1944).

TREVELYAN, SIR GEORGE OTTO (1838–1928), the nephew of Lord Macaulay (q.v.), was educated at Harrow and Trinity College, Cambridge. He entered parliament in 1865 and held at various times important offices. Some of his early humorous writings, including 'Horace at the University of Athens' and 'The Ladies in Parliament', were collected and published in 1869. A year spent in India led to the publication of 'The Dawk Bungalow', a comedy, in 1863; the 'Letters of a Competition Wallah', which gives a vivid picture of the Indian Civil Service, in 1864; and 'Cawnpore', a clear and moving account of the Mutiny tragedy, in 1865. The first of his great works, 'The Life and Letters of Lord Macaulay', appeared in 1876; the second, 'The Early History of Charles James Fox', in 1880. The latter was the first instalment of what the author intended to be a complete life of the great Whig statesman. But the sequel did not take precisely this form. 'The American Revolution' followed in 1909, in which Fox is not the dominant figure. In 1912–14 appeared the two volumes of 'George III and Charles Fox'. Of the series, the most brilliant and stimulating part is the 'Early History', which gives a striking picture of social and political England in the later part of the 18th century.

TREVI'SA, JOHN DE (1326–1412), fellow of Exeter (1362–9) and Queen's (1369–79) Colleges, Oxford. He was expelled 'for unworthiness' in 1379, and became vicar of Berkeley. He translated Higden's 'Polychronicon' (see *Higden*) in 1387, adding an introduction and short continuation, and other Latin works. The translation of the 'Polychronicon' is one of the early examples of English prose, and is written in a vigorous and colloquial style. Trevisa also translated (1398) the 'De Proprietatibus Rerum' of Bartholomaeus Anglicus, and there is evidence that he made a translation of the Bible, though this is lost.

Triads, in ancient Welsh literature, verses celebrating famous subjects of tradition; a form of composition characterized by an arrangement of subjects or statements in groups of three. There are satirical allusions to these 'triads' in Peacock's 'The Misfortunes of Elphin' (q.v.).

Triamond, in Spenser's 'Faerie Queene', iv. iii and iv, the Knight of Friendship. After an inconclusive fight with Cambello in the contest to decide to which of her suitors Canace is to be awarded, Triamond and Cambello swear eternal friendship. In the tournament arranged by Satyrane, Triamond, though wounded, returns to rescue Cambello. He marries Canace, Cambello's sister.

Trianon, see *Versailles*.

Tribes of Israel. The twelve tribes of Israel are regarded as being descended from the sons of Jacob: *Reuben, Simeon, Levi, Judah, Zebulun, Issachar, Dan, Gad, Asher, Naphthali, Joseph,* and *Benjamin.* See Gen. xlix; also the article *Tribes of Israel* in 'The Dictionary of the Bible' (Hastings, rev. Grant and Rowley, 1963).

Tribrach, a foot consisting of three short syllables.

Tribulation Wholesome, a character in Jonson's 'The Alchemist' (q.v.).

Tricolour, having three colours, especially used of the national flag of France, adopted at the Revolution, which has equal vertical stripes of blue, white, and red.

Tricoteuses, from the French *tricoter,* to knit, the women who, during the French Revolution, plied their knitting-needles while attending the sittings of the political assemblies and also while watching the guillotining of aristos on the Place de la Concorde and elsewhere.

Tridentum, in imprints, Trent.

Trifaldi, THE COUNTESS OF, in ' Don Quixote' (q.v.), the 'Afflicted Duenna', whose adventure Don Quixote undertakes (Pt. II, chs. xxxvi-xli).

Trilby, a novel by Du Maurier (q.v.), published in 1894.
    It is the tragic story of Trilby O'Ferrall, an amiable artist's model in Paris, with whom various young English art-students fall in love. She becomes a famous singer under the

mesmeric influence of Svengali, a German-Polish musician, but loses her voice when the latter dies, and herself languishes and dies soon after. 'Trilby hat' became a popular name for a soft felt hat with indented crown.

Trilogy, in Greek antiquities, a series of three tragedies (originally connected in subject) performed at Athens at the festival of Dionysus. Hence any series of three related dramatic or other literary works.

Trim, CORPORAL, one of the principal characters in Sterne's 'Tristram Shandy' (q.v.).

Trimalchio, a type of ostentatious extravagance and gluttony; see *Petronius.*

Trimeter, see *Metre* and *Iambic.*

Trimmer, originally applied to one who trims between opposing parties in politics; hence, one who inclines as his interest dictates. But Lord Halifax in his 'Character of a Trimmer' (1682) accepted the nickname in the sense of 'one who keeps even the ship of state'.

TRIMMER, MRS. SARAH (1741–1810), *née* Kirby, Calverley's 'good Mrs. Trimmer', was author of the popular children's book, 'The History of the Robins', originally entitled 'Fabulous Histories' (1786), and of a number of exemplary tales and educational works. She is referred to in Byron's 'Don Juan', Canto I.

Trimurti, in Hindu theology, the triad of the three supreme gods, Brahma, Vishnu, and Siva (qq.v.).

Trinacria, an ancient name for Sicily, meaning 'with three promontories'.

Trinculo, a jester in Shakespeare's 'The Tempest' (q.v.).

Trinity College, Cambridge, the largest college of Cambridge University, founded by Henry VIII in 1546, in place of several older foundations. The library was built by Sir C. Wren (q.v.). Among the distinguished men of letters educated there may be mentioned F. Bacon, Herbert, Cowley, Dryden, Newton, Porson, Byron, Macaulay, Thackeray, and Tennyson. Bentley and Whewell (qq.v.) were Masters of Trinity.

Trinity House, Tower Hill, London, the hall of the 'Guild, Fraternity, or Brotherhood of the Most Glorious and Undividable Trinity', founded by Sir Thomas Spert in 1512 (incorporated in 1514) for the benefit and protection of the shipping industry. This corporation is charged with the licensing of pilots, and the maintenance of lighthouses, beacons, and buoys. In spite of an Act of Elizabeth I (which charges it with the duty of doing its best to increase the Navy in ships and men), it is now wholly international in its operations, and refuses to distinguish, in time of war, between friend and foe. It is governed by 'Elder Brethren'.

Trinovantes, see *Brute.*

Triolet, a poem of eight lines, with two rhymes, in which the first line is repeated as the fourth and seventh, and the second as the eighth.

Trip to Scarborough, A, a comedy by R. B. Sheridan (q.v.) produced in 1777.

The plot is that of Vanbrugh's 'The Relapse' (q.v.) with some modifications. Berinthia is no longer an unscrupulous adventuress, but tempts Loveless in order to punish Towneley (the Worthy of the earlier play) for deserting her in favour of Amanda, Loveless's wife. And it is shame, not exposure, that restores Loveless to Amanda.

Triple Entente, THE, the political understanding between Great Britain, France, and Russia (an extension of the *Entente Cordiale,* q.v., between Great Britain and France) concluded in 1907 by means of conventions settling differences between Great Britain and Russia in Persia, Afghanistan, and Tibet. It constituted a balance of power with the Triple Alliance of Germany, Austria, and Italy during the period which preceded the war of 1914–18.

Triplet, three successive lines of verse rhyming together, occasionally introduced among heroic couplets, e.g. by Dryden.

Tripos, at Cambridge University, formerly (*a*) a bachelor of arts appointed to dispute, in a humorous or satirical style, with candidates for degrees at 'Commencement' (corresponding to the *Terrae filius* at Oxford); so called from the three-legged stool on which he sat. (*b*) A set of humorous verses, originally composed by the 'Tripos', and (until 1894) published at Commencement after his office was abolished. (*c*) The list of candidates qualified for the honours degree in mathematics, originally printed on the back of the paper containing these verses. Hence, in current use, the final honours examination in any subject for the B.A. degree. [OED.]

Triptŏ′lĕmus, in Greek mythology, a hero worshipped at Eleusis, the son of Celĕus, king of Eleusis. Celeus hospitably entertained Demeter (q.v.) when she was wandering in search of her daughter, and the goddess in return gave Triptolemus a winged chariot, wherein he travelled over the world teaching men the arts of agriculture, which he had learnt from the goddess.

Triptolemus Yellowley, and his sister BARBARA, characters in Scott's 'The Pirate'.

Trismegistus, see *Hermes Trismegistus.*

Tristan und Isolde, a music-drama by R. Wagner (q.v.).

Tristan l'Hermite, a character in Scott's 'Quentin Durward' (q.v.).

Tristram. The story of Tristram and his love for Iseult is much older than the parallel tale of Launcelot and Guinevere, and in its earlier form was not connected with the Arthurian cycle. Before Malory's 'Morte Darthur' it figures in English only in 'Sir Tristrem', one of the earliest romances in the vernacular, probably dating from before 1300. This was drawn from earlier French sources, and was possibly composed by Thomas of Erceldoune (q.v.). According to this poem Tristrem is the son of Rouland of Erminia and Blanchefleur, sister of King Mark of England. He slays Moraunt, king of Ireland, but is himself wounded and is tended by Ysoude, sister of Moraunt. Tristrem returns to England and tells King Mark of Ysoude. Mark sends Tristrem to request Ysoude in marriage. The remainder of the story is in essentials similar to that of Tristram as given by Malory (see below), except that Ganhardin (brother of Ysoude with the White Hand), who does not figure in the latter, falls in love with Brangwain, Ysoude of Ireland's maid.

In Malory's 'Morte Darthur', Tristram is son of Meliodas, king of Lyonesse (q.v.), and Elizabeth sister of King Mark of Cornwall. Meliodas is led away by enchantment and made prisoner. Elizabeth distracted seeks him in the forest, when she is seized with the pangs of travail. She dies after having given birth to a son, whom she calls Tristram, 'that is as much to say as a sorrowful birth'. Tristram escapes poisoning by his stepmother and begs her life when she is condemned to the stake. He becomes a skilful hunter and harper. He fights and defeats Sir Marhaus, who comes on behalf of the king of Ireland to claim the 'truage' of Cornwall, but is wounded himself. Marhaus dies, and Tristram is sent to Ireland to be cured of his wound. Owing to his skill with the harp he is received with favour by the king and is placed in the care of his daughter, La Beale Isoud. Tristram and she fall in love. The queen discovers that their guest is the knight who slew Sir Marhaus, her brother, and Tristram leaves the court after exchanging vows of fidelity with Isoud, and returns to Cornwall. After a time King Mark, being jealous of Tristram and desirous to destroy him, sends him to Ireland to ask the hand of La Beale Isoud, whose praises he has heard from Tristram. Tristram, having rendered an important service to the king of Ireland, asks as reward the hand of Isoud for King Mark. Isoud and Bragwaine, her attendant, set off with Tristram. Bragwaine has received from Isoud's mother a love potion to be given to King Mark. On the ship Tristram and Isoud find the flask and in ignorance drink its contents, with the result that they love each other for the rest of their lives. Mark and Isoud are married, but the relations between Tristram and Isoud continue, till the lovers are betrayed to Mark. (According to another version Bragwaine or Brengwaine takes Isoud's place on the wedding night; after which Isoud ungratefully plots to murder her.) Tristram leaves the court of

Mark and fighting for King Howel of Brittany falls in love with Isoud la Blanche Mains and marries her, 'almost forsaking' Isoud of Ireland. However, on the invitation of the latter he returns privily to Cornwall. He is banished thence and is welcomed at Arthur's court, where he shows his prowess in many contests. Finally it is stated that Mark slew Tristram as he sat harping before La Beale Isoud.

But a more romantic ending is given in one of the manuscripts and has been adopted and developed by later poets. Tristram, in Brittany, is wounded by a poisoned arrow. Feeling that he is dying, he sends a messenger for Isoud of Ireland. If she comes, the ship that brings her is to set a white sail, if not, a black. Isoud of Brittany overhears, and when the ship returns tells Tristram the sail is black. Tristram in despair turns his face to the wall and dies (cf. the story of Theseus, q.v., and Aegeus). Isoud of Ireland finds her lover dead, lies down beside him, and dies.

Tristram and Iseult, a poem by M. Arnold (q.v.), published in 1852.

The subject is the death of Tristram (q.v.) in Brittany. As he lies on his bed of sickness, while Iseult of Brittany watches by him, he dreams in his fever of the happy days of his prime and pines for Iseult of Ireland. She comes, and after a brief passionate dialogue between them, Tristram dies.

Tristram of Lyonesse, a romance in couplets by Swinburne (q.v.), published in 1882.

It tells the tale of Tristram (q.v.), his first visit to the court of the king of Ireland, his subsequent mission to fetch Iseult to be Mark's bride, the love of Tristram and Queen Iseult, their separation and the marriage of Tristram with Iseult of Brittany, the sending for Queen Iseult when Tristram lies dying, and Tristram's death under the blow of the false cry that the sail of the returning ship is black.

Tristram Shandy, *The Life and Opinions of,* a novel by Sterne (q.v.), of which vols. i and ii appeared in 1760, vols. iii to vi in 1761–2, vols. vii and viii in 1765, and vol. ix in 1767. It was translated into French and German.

In spite of the title, the book gives us very little of the life, and nothing of the opinions, of the nominal hero, who gets born only in vol. iv, and breeched in vol. vi, and then disappears from the story. Instead we have a group of humorous figures: Walter Shandy of Shandy Hall, Tristram's father, peevish but frank and generous, full of paradoxical notions, which he defends with great show of learning; 'my Uncle Toby', his brother, wounded in the groin at the siege of Namur, whose hobby is the science of attacking fortified towns, which he studies by means of miniature scarps, ravelins, and bastions on his bowling-green, a man 'of unparalleled modesty' and amiability; Corporal Trim, his servant, wounded in the knee at Landen,

devoted to his master and sharing his enthusiasm for the military art, voluble but respectful. Behind these three major figures, the minor characters, Yorick the parson, Dr. Slop, Mrs. Shandy, and the widow Wadman, play a more elusive part.

The book, which is chiefly occupied with exposing the author's own personality and whimsical imaginations, presents very few incidents. The first three volumes are concerned, amid many digressions (including the great curse of Ernulphus, bishop of Rochester), with the circumstances attending the hero's birth; after which the author finds time to write his preface. Vol. iv begins with the story of Slawkenbergius, the author of a treatise on noses; followed by the naming of the infant 'Tristram' by mistake for 'Trismegistus'. Vol. v contains the notable discourse of Corporal Trim on mortality; vol. vi the affecting episode of Le Fevre, and the delightful dialogue between Mr. and Mrs. Shandy on the breeching of Tristram. Vols. vii and viii abandon the narrative to give an account of the author's travels in France and the story of the king of Bohemia; and vol. ix is concerned mainly with the love-affair of Uncle Toby and the widow Wadman.

Triton, a sea deity, son of Poseidon (Neptune) and Amphitrite. He is generally represented as blowing on a shell, his body above the waist being that of a man, below it of a dolphin.

Triumph of Life, *The,* an uncompleted poem by P. B. Shelley (q.v.), in *terza rima,* published after his death.

The poem, on which Shelley was engaged at the time of his death, is an allegory of which the sense is obscure. The poet sees a vision of the human multitude, and in the midst of it the Triumph passes, the chariot of Life the Conqueror, trampling on youth and dragging others in chains. Rousseau interprets the vision to the poet and tells him that those chained to the car are 'the wise, the great, the unforgotten', vanquished by the mystery of Life. He shows him, among the captives, Napoleon, Plato, Aristotle, Alexander. The vision passes to the allegory of a single life, which after a youth of aspirations, succumbs to the same mystery.

Triumph of Mammon, see *God and Mammon.*

Trivia, or *The Art of Walking the Streets of London,* a poem by J. Gay (q.v.), in three books, published in 1716.

In this entertaining work, on the model of Swift's 'City Shower', the author takes the reader through the streets of London, first by day and then by night, instructing him in a mock-serious style about the coats and boots he should wear, the signs of the weather, and the dangers to be avoided, notably pickpockets, mischievous boys who pull off wigs, the splashing mud below and the spouting rain above. 'Safety first' among the side-headings has a familiar sound. The reader's attention is drawn to the various characters he will meet: ballad-singers, chairmen, footmen, bullies, and the like. The poem is a mine of information on 18th-cent. manners.

Trivium, in the Middle Ages, the lower division of the seven liberal arts, comprising grammar, logic, and rhetoric. Cf. *Quadrivium.*

Trochee, a metrical foot consisting of a long followed by a short syllable; in accentual verse, of an accented followed by an unaccented syllable.

Trochilus, a small Egyptian bird (not certainly identified) said by the ancients to enter the crocodile's mouth and pick its teeth.

Troglodyte, from the Greek τρώγλη, hole, and δύειν, to get into, a cave-dweller. The ancients (Pliny, Strabo, etc.) mention races of Troglodytes in Aethiopia and elsewhere.

Troil, MAGNUS, MINNA, BRENDA, and ULLA (NORNA), characters in Scott's 'The Pirate' (q.v.).

Troilus and Cressida. This story, which has no basis in classical antiquity but has its origin in the 'Roman de Troie' of Benoît de Sainte-Maure (q.v.), itself based on the pretended records of Dares Phrygius and Dictys Cretensis (qq.v.), has also been dealt with by Guido da Colonna in the 'Historia Trojana', by Boccaccio in 'Filostrato', by Chaucer, by Lydgate in his 'Troy-Book', by Henryson, by Shakespeare, and by Dryden.

The first of these makes *Briseida* (Homer's Briseis) the daughter of Calchas (the seer who advised the restoration of Chryseis to her father; see *Briseis* and *Chryseis*), and Troilus and Diomede her successive lovers. *Briseida* was changed to *Griseida* by Boccaccio, and to *Cryseyde* by Chaucer. The story is that of the love of Troilus, a son of Priam, king of Troy, for Cressida, daughter of Calchas the priest, who, foreknowing the fall of Troy, has fled to the Greeks but left his daughter in Troy. Cressida returns the love of Troilus, and Pandarus acts as go-between. But an exchange of prisoners is arranged and Cressida is sent to the Greek camp, where Diomede urges his suit and is finally preferred to Troilus. Troilus and Diomede meet in the field but neither kills the other. Troilus is at last killed by Achilles.

Chaucer's poem, 'Troylus and Cryseyde', probably written between 1372 and 1386, contains some 8,200 lines of rhyme-royal (annotated text by R. K. Root, 1926); in it the poet enriched the story as he got it from Boccaccio by the vivid and humorous figure of Pandarus and by the development of the character of Cressida, 'a grave, sober, considerate personage, who has an alternate eye to her character, her interest, and her pleasure'.

Shakespeare's Cressida, on the other hand, is 'a giddy girl, an unpractised jilt, who falls in love with Troilus, as she afterwards deserts

him, from mere levity and thoughtlessness of temper'. His Pandarus, again, instead of being a friendly, officious go-between, 'has "a stamp exclusive and professional": he wears the badge of his trade; he is a regular knight of the game'. (The above quotations are from Hazlitt.) Shakespeare's play, produced probably in 1602, and printed in 1609, presents, as background to the story, the principal characters of the 'Iliad': Agamemnon, Ajax, Ulysses, Nestor, Achilles sulking in his tent, the railer Thersites; and on the Trojan side, Priam, Aeneas, Hector and Andromache, Paris, and Helen. The death of Hector at the hands of Achilles is summarily dealt with.

For Henryson's pathetic treatment of the latter days of Cressida see *Cresseid.* Dryden in 1679 published a play, 'Troilus and Cressida', which Saintsbury, in his life of Dryden (English Men of Letters), calls a 'pot boiler', 'which might much better have been left unattempted'.

Trojan Horse, THE, see *Horse (The Trojan).*

Trojan War, see *Troy.*

Troll, in Scandinavian mythology, one of a race of supernatural beings formerly conceived as giants, now in Denmark and Sweden as dwarfs or imps supposed to inhabit caves or subterranean dwellings. [OED.]

TROLLOPE, ANTHONY (1815–82), was born in London. He has described in his 'Autobiography' the miserable conditions under which, owing to the poverty of his family, induced by the misfortunes or mismanagement of his father, he went, first to Harrow, then to Winchester, then again to Harrow; and how, when his father's debts obliged the family to take refuge in Belgium, his mother supported them by her writings. Anthony Trollope entered the General Post Office as a clerk in 1834 and in time proved himself an active and valuable public servant. His first novels were: 'The Macdermots of Ballycloran' (1847) and 'The Kellys and the O'Kellys' (1848). 'The Warden' (q.v., 1855), the first of the Barsetshire series, was a moderate success. But from this point his popularity as a novelist steadily increased. His output was considerable, having regard to the fact that his official work was arduous and that he also found time to hunt twice a week; it was achieved by a mechanical regularity in his writing which he has himself described. His chief remaining novels were: 'Barchester Towers' (q.v., 1857), 'The Three Clerks' (q.v., 1858), 'Doctor Thorne' (q.v., 1858), 'Framley Parsonage' (q.v., 1861), 'Orley Farm' (q.v., 1862), 'The Small House at Allington' (q.v., 1864), 'The Belton Estate' (q.v., 1865), 'The Claverings' (q.v., 1867), 'The Last Chronicle of Barset' (q.v., 1867), 'Phineas Finn' (q.v., 1869), 'The Eustace Diamonds' (q.v., 1873), 'Phineas Redux' (1874), 'The Prime Minister' (1876), 'The American Senator' (1877), 'Is he Popenjoy?'

(1878), 'The Duke's Children' (1880), 'Ayala's Angel' (q.v., 1881), 'Dr. Wortle's School' (q.v., 1881). Trollope also published various books of travel, on the West Indies and Spanish Main (1859), North America (1862), Australia (1873), and South Africa (1878); also a monograph on Thackeray (1879). His interesting 'Autobiography' appeared in 1883. According to this his publications, down to 1879, had brought him in some £70,000.

TROLLOPE, FRANCES (1780–1863), *née* Milton, the mother of A. Trollope (q.v.). When her family were reduced to poverty she supported them by writing novels, of which the best known is 'The Widow Barnaby' (1838), the story of an unscrupulous and astute widow, whose schemes to make a rich marriage prove unsuccessful. She is finally imprisoned for debt, and marries a fellow prisoner, the Revd. Patrick O'Donagough, who turns out a gambler and drinker; while her niece, Agnes, whom she has cruelly ill-treated, makes a happy match. Mrs. Trollope's 'The Vicar of Wrexhill' (1837) is a more sombre if more powerful story, the picture of a cold, evil-minded, cruel clergyman. Her 'Domestic Manners of the Americans' (1832), written after a visit to America, gave great offence, of much the same kind as did parts of Dickens's 'Martin Chuzzlewit'.

Trompart, in Spenser's 'Faerie Queene', II. iii,

wylie witted and grown old
In cunning sleights and practick knavery,

attends Braggadochio (q.v.) as his squire, and with him is finally exposed and beaten out of court.

Trophee, an unknown writer mentioned by Chaucer in the Monk's Tale (l. 127):

At bothe the worldes endes, seith Trophee,
In stide of boundes he [Hercules] a pileer sette.

A marginal note in the Ellesmere and Hengwrt MSS. says, 'Ille vates Chaldeorum Tropheus'. Lydgate states that Chaucer in his youth made a translation of a book called in the Lombard tongue *Trophe*, and that he later named it 'Troilus and Cressida'. No such book as 'Trophe' is known.

Trophonius, son of Erginus, king of Orchomenos in Boeotia, and brother of Agamedes. The two brothers built a temple of Apollo at Delphi, and a treasury for Hyrieus, king of Hyria, in Boeotia. About this treasury a story is told similar to that of the treasury of King Rhampsinitus (q.v.). The two brothers robbed the treasury by means of a movable stone in the wall, and when Agamedes was caught in a trap, Trophonius cut off his head to avoid detection. Trophonius was subsequently swallowed up by the earth, or, according to another story, was granted death by Apollo, as the best reward for men. At Lebadeia in Boeotia, Trophonius after his death was consulted

as an oracle in a cave. The suppliant always emerged from this *Cave of Trophonius* pale and dejected, and it became proverbial to say of a melancholy man that he had consulted the oracle of Trophonius.

Trotcosey, in Scott's 'The Antiquary' (q.v.), a favourite subject of reference by Jonathan Oldbuck; the house of Monkbarns stood on the lands of the ancient abbey of Trotcosey. Scott prepared in his later years 'Reliquiae Trottcosienses', a *catalogue raisonné* of the most curious articles in the library and museum at Abbotsford.

Trotsky (real name BRONSTEIN), LEV DAVIDOVICH (1879–1940), Russian politician. Having joined the Social-Democratic Party in early youth and at first supported Lenin, from 1903 to 1917 he opposed Lenin's dictatorial methods within the party. He joined the Bolshevik party in 1917, however, when Lenin substantially accepted his idea of 'permanent revolution', i.e. of making a 'socialist' revolution immediately follow the 'bourgeois' one of March 1917. He took the leading part in the Bolshevik seizure of power and in the ensuing civil war directed the Red Army, whose success owed much to his leadership. In the struggle among the party leaders after Lenin's death, he was defeated by Stalin and expelled from the Soviet Union. He was murdered in Mexico by Stalin's agents. As a Communist leader, Trotsky advocated a comparatively liberal cultural policy, and maintained that a writer should be free in his work if he accepted the Bolshevik revolution.

Trotter, JOB, in Dickens's 'Pickwick Papers' (q.v.), Jingle's servant.

Trotwood, BETSEY, a character in Dickens's 'David Copperfield' (q.v.).

Troubadours, poets composing and singing in Old Provençal during the 12th and 13th cents. They were famous for their mastery of verse forms in the lyric, and for the conception of courtly love (q.v.) which is first found in their poetry. William Count of Poitiers and Duke of Aquitaine is the first known troubadour; Jaufre Rudel invented the theme of the 'distant love' which suggested the 'Princesse lointaine' to Rostand (q.v.); Bernart de Ventadour was in his own time, as he is now, acknowledged as the most truly lyric in inspiration, while Arnaut Daniel was praised by Dante as the finest craftsman among the troubadours, and his ornate and difficult style pleased in modern times Ezra Pound, who translated some of his poems and imitated his verse forms. The troubadours flourished in the courts of Spain and Italy as well as in the south of France, and poetry in Provençal in the courtly style was being written and cultivated in Italy in the late 13th cent., when it was disappearing in the Midi as a result of the Albigensian War.

Trouillogan, in Rabelais, III. xxxv et seq., the philosopher whom Panurge consults on the subject of his marriage.

Trouvères, poets composing narrative, dramatic, satiric, lyric, and comic verse in the north of France during the Old French period. They may be professional entertainers, *clercs* or, when courtly society develops, feudal lords composing the fashionable courtly lyrics. Chrétien de Troyes (q.v.) was a *clerc*; Conon de Béthune was a courtly poet, a noble of Picardy who took a prominent part in the Fourth Crusade; Colin Muset appears to have been a poor minstrel, Rutebeuf possibly a *clerc* who turned to secular verse to earn his living, while Thibaut de Champagne was a great lord, count of Champagne and king of Navarre.

Trows or DROWS, in the mythology of the Orkneys and Shetland, supernatural beings, dwarfs, or imps, inhabiting caves and the sea. They figure in Scott's 'The Pirate' (q.v.). The word is a survival from the *Troll* (q.v.) of Norse mythology.

Troy or ILIUM, a city that stood near the Hellespont and the river Scamander in the NW. of Asia Minor. Its ruins have been discovered near the modern Hissarlik. The opinion now is that several cities have been buried, one on the top of the other, at the site of Hissarlik, which must always have been important as commanding the passage from Europe to Asia. According to legend, as related by Homer in his 'Iliad', Troy was the capital of King Priam, and was for ten years besieged by the Greeks in their endeavour to recover Helen, wife of Menelaus, king of Sparta, who had been carried off by Paris, son of Priam. See *Agamemnon, Menelaus, Helen, Paris, Achilles, Horse (The Trojan),* etc.

Troy, SERGEANT, a character in Hardy's 'Far from the Madding Crowd' (q.v.).

Troy-book, a poem in five books, in tensyllable couplets, written by Lydgate (q.v.), at the request of Prince Henry, afterwards Henry V. It was begun in 1412 and finished in 1420. It tells the 'noble storye' of Troy, following the Latin history of Guido da Colonna (which had drawn largely on the apocryphal tales of Dictys Cretensis and Dares Phrygius, qq.v.), and serves in some sort as an introduction to the story of the Trojan settlement of England by Brutus, greatgrandson of Aeneas, told by Geoffrey of Monmouth and Wace. In the third book, in connexion with the story of Troilus and Cressida, he introduces a tribute to his 'maister Chaucer'.

Troynovant, see *Brute.*

Truce of God, 'Treuga Dei', also 'Pax Dei', a suspension of hostilities between armies, or of private feuds, ordered by the Church during certain days and seasons in medieval times. The general acceptance of it seems to have been about 1033 (a thousand years from the Passion). The close days of the week were from Wednesday evening to Monday morning. Urban II proclaimed a universal 'Treuga Dei' when urging the First Crusade at Clermont (Auvergne) in 1095.

True Law of Free Monarchies, The, a political treatise attributed to James I, published in 1603, and written to combat the Calvinistic theory of government advocated by George Buchanan in his 'De-Jure Regni' (1579). It sets forth the doctrine of the divine right of kings, and of the king's responsibility to God alone.

Trulla, a virago, one of the bear-baiters in Butler's 'Hudibras' (q.v.).

Trulliber, PARSON, a character in Fielding's 'Joseph Andrews' (q.v.).

Trumpet-Major, The, a novel by Hardy (q.v.), published in 1880.

This is one of Hardy's simplest and pleasantest tales, with hardly a trace of irony or bitterness. It is set in the time of the Napoleonic wars, and deals with the wooing of Anne Garland, whose mother is the tenant of part of Overcombe Mill, where the dragoons come down from the camp to water their horses. One of these dragoons is John Loveday, the trumpet-major, the gentle unselfish son of the miller, and he is one of Anne's suitors. Another is his brother Bob, a cheery light-hearted sailor. The third is the braggart boorish yeoman, Festus Derriman. The story ends in the exposure and discomfiture of Festus and the success of Bob while John marches off into the night, 'to blow his trumpet till silenced for ever upon one of the bloody battle-fields of Spain'.

Trumpington, THE MILLER OF, the miller in 'The Reeve's Tale' in Chaucer's 'The Canterbury Tales' (q.v.).

Trunnion, COMMODORE HAWSER, see *Peregrine Pickle.*

Tryamour, see *Launfal.*

Tryan, THE REVD. EDGAR, a character in George Eliot's 'Janet's Repentance' (see *Scenes of Clerical Life*).

Tschaikovsky, see *Tchaikovsky.*

Tuatha Dé Danann, in Gaelic mythology, the gods, the 'Folk of the goddess Danu', the enemies of the Fomors (q.v.). They are represented as invaders of Ireland, subsequent to the Fomors and the Fir Bolgs. They rout the Fomors at the battle of Moytura, and are ousted in their turn by the Milesians (q.v.). Conspicuous among the Tuatha Dé Danann are Lugh, the Gaelic sun-god, their leader; and Lêr (q.v.), the god of the sea.

Tubal-cain, according to Gen. iv. 22, the 'instructer of every artificer in brass and iron'.

Tuck, FRIAR, see *Friar Tuck*.

TUCKER, ABRAHAM (1705–74), a country gentleman and one of the first writers of the utilitarian school of philosophy. In his great work, 'The Light of Nature pursued', of which three volumes were published in 1768 and three after his death in 1778, he rejects the moral sense theory of Shaftesbury and Hutcheson (qq.v.), and finds the criterion of moral conduct in general happiness, and the motive of the individual in his own happiness. The coincidence of these two is almost, but not quite, complete. There comes a point where virtue requires a self-sacrifice that prudential motives do not justify. Here Tucker finds the place for religion and its promise of a future life, where 'the accounts of all are to be set even', and the sacrifice of personal happiness required by virtue is to be made good.

Tucker's writings are diffuse and unmethodical, but marked by humour and quaint illustration and comment. His theories were systematized by Paley (q.v.).

Tugwell, JEREMIAH, in Graves's 'Spiritual Quixote' (q.v.), Geoffry Wildgoose's Sancho Panza.

Tuileries, THE, in Paris, a royal palace adjoining the Louvre, built by Catherine de Médicis on the site of a *tuilerie* or brickyard. It was destroyed at the time of the Commune (1871).

Tuirenn, *The Fate of the Sons of,* one of the 'three sorrowful tales of Erin', a mythological tale in which the three sons of Tuirenn are punished for killing Cian, the father of the hero-god Lugh, by being required, by way of fine, to achieve a number of quests, in the last of which they perish.

Tulchan bishops, a term applied derisively to the titular Scottish bishops appointed after the Reformation, on the understanding that they should not receive the revenues of their sees, which had been confiscated in 1560 and had mostly gone to the lay barons; a *tulchan* is a calf's skin stuffed with straw, placed under a cow to induce her to give her milk.

Tulkinghorn, MR., a character in Dickens's 'Bleak House' (q.v.).

Tulliver, MR. and MRS., and TOM and MAGGIE, the principal characters in G. Eliot's 'The Mill on the Floss' (q.v.).

Tullochgorum, see *Skinner*.

Tully, see *Cicero*.

Tully-Veolan, in Scott's 'Waverley' (q.v.), the castle of the Baron of Bradwardine.

Tunning of Elynour Rumming, *The,* a poem by Skelton (q.v.), is a vigorous Hogarthian description of contemporary low life. Elynour Rumming is an alewife who dwells beside Leatherhead and brews 'noppy ale' for 'travellers and tynkers, for sweters and swynkers, and all good ale drynkers', and the poem, coarse but full of humour and life, describes the mixed company who throng to drink it.

TUNSTALL, CUTHBERT (1474–1559), studied both at Oxford and Cambridge, and also at Padua, and became learned in Greek, Hebrew, mathematics, and civil law. He was appointed master of the rolls and bishop successively of London and Durham, and was employed in the diplomatic service of Henry VIII. He was Wolsey's agent at the Diet of Worms. During the ecclesiastical revolution he remained faithful to the Roman Catholic dogma, but obeyed passively the civil power. He was the author of religious works and of an arithmetical treatise, 'De arte supputandi'. Rabelais refers to this in 'Gargantua', xxiii.

Tupman, TRACY, in Dickens's 'The Pickwick Papers' (q.v.), one of the members of the Corresponding Society of the Pickwick Club.

TUPPER, MARTIN FARQUHAR (1810–89), of an old Huguenot family, was educated at Christ Church, Oxford. He published in 1838–42 his 'Proverbial Philosophy', commonplace maxims and reflections couched in a rhythmical form, which achieved extraordinary popularity. He published numerous other works, including 'The Crock of Gold' (1844, a book of poems) and a naïve 'Autobiography' (1886).

Turan, see *Iran*.

TURBERVILLE or **TURBERVILE,** GEORGE (1540?–1610?), scholar of Winchester and fellow of New College, Oxford, published 'Epitaphs, Epigrams, Songs, and Sonets' (1567), 'Poems describing . . . Russia' (1568), 'The Booke of Faulconrie' (1575), and various translations from Ovid and modern Italians. 'The Noble Art of Venerie or Hunting' is also attributed to him (1575, reprinted, Oxford, 1908). He familiarized the employment of Italian models and shows the influence of Surrey and Wyatt (qq.v.).

Turcaret, see *Le Sage*.

TURGENEV, IVAN SERGEYEVICH (1818–83), leading Russian novelist. After early attempts at poetry he turned to novels and stories. His novels examine, in personal terms, social and political problems of 19th-cent. Russia, though Turgenev himself avoided association with particular schools of thought. He lived much abroad, was more 'Western' in spirit than most major Russian writers and received a correspondingly more immediate recognition outside Russia. His first important work was 'Sketches of a Sportsman' (1847–51, tr. by J. D. Meiklejohn, 1855). His novels are 'Rudin' (1856), 'A Nest of Gentlefolk' (1859), 'On the Eve' (1860), 'Fathers and Sons' (1862), 'Smoke' (1867), 'Virgin Soil' (1877). All Turgenev's major work was translated into English before 1890. The most complete translation is by C. Garnett, 'Turgenev—The Novels and Tales' (1894–99)..

Turgot, ANNE ROBERT JACQUES, see *Physiocrats.*

Turk Gregory, in Shakespeare's '1 Henry IV', v. iii, where Falstaff compares his deeds in arms with those of 'Turk Gregory', is a facetious combination of the characters of 'terrible Turk' and militant pope (Gregory VII).

Turkish Spy, Letters written by a, eight vols. published in 1687?–94. The first is a translation of 'L'Espion du Grand Seigneur' by Giovanni Paolo Marana, a Genoese residing in Paris, published in French in 1684–86, partly itself a translation from an Italian version. The work inaugurated a new *genre* in European literature, the pseudo-foreign letter, of which the 'Lettres persanes' of Montesquieu (q.v.) is the chief example.

Mahmut, a Turkish spy, employed by the Porte to report on the Christian courts, writes letters from Paris, between 1637 and 1682, addressed to various members of his government and to relations and friends. In these he discusses the political, historical, and social affairs of France, Spain, England, and Italy, and a variety of other subjects, scientific and religious, and also his personal concerns and those of his own country.

A continuation to the 'Letters', probably by Defoe, was published in England in 1718.

Turks, THE YOUNG, the party of reform in the former Ottoman Empire, who came into prominence about the year 1907, deposed the Sultan Abdul Hamid, and endeavoured to introduce modern methods into the administration of the country

Turn of the Screw, The, a masterpiece of supernatural fiction by H. James (q.v.), published in 1898.

Turnbull Street, see *Turnmill Street.*

TURNER, CHARLES TENNYSON, see *Tennyson Turner.*

Turner, JOSEPH MALLORD WILLIAM (1775–1851), landscape painter, son of a London barber. His talent was precocious; he exhibited in the Royal Academy from 1791, becoming an Academician in 1802. He worked first as a topographical draughtsman and painted water-colours for engravings in topographical books. After studying the Dutch landscape painters and Claude, he developed an interest in romantic subjects, such as storms at sea and mountains, often appending to his paintings quotations from a poem, apparently his own, 'The Fallacies of Hope'. In his later work his rendering of light transforms both oils and water-colours. The first volume of Ruskin's 'Modern Painters' (q.v.) was written to defend Turner against criticism, and it assured his reputation. Turner left most of his work to the nation. He is buried in St. Paul's Cathedral.

TURNER, SHARON (1768–1847), a student of Icelandic and Anglo-Saxon literature, whose 'History of the Anglo-Saxons from the earliest period to the Norman Conquest' (1799–1805), subsequently extended to the death of Elizabeth, initiated an entirely new treatment of the origins of English history.

TURNER, WALTER JAMES REDFERN (1889–1946), poet, novelist, and music critic. He was born in Melbourne and came to London at the age of 17. After serving in the First World War he became music critic of 'The New Statesman', dramatic critic of 'The London Mercury', and from 1942 literary editor of 'The Spectator'. His poetry, which has a strong exotic strain, includes, 'The Dark Fire' (1918), 'Pursuit of Psyche' (1931), and 'Songs and Incantations' (1936). 'Blow for Balloons' (1935), a novel in the form of a biography with fantastic and philosophical digressions, is obviously more than a little autobiographical. He also wrote a play, 'The Man who ate the Popomak' (1922), and a number of books on music.

'Turnip Townshend', see *Townshend.*

Turnmill or TURNBULL **Street,** Clerkenwell, London, frequently mentioned by the Elizabethan dramatists (e.g. Shakespeare, '2 Henry IV', III. ii), took its name from the Turnmill brook, probably identical with the upper course of the Fleet (q.v.) stream. The street was notorious for its low haunts.

Turnus, a king of the Rutuli, and a brave warrior, who fought against Aeneas, because Latinus proposed to give the latter his daughter Lavinia, who had been betrothed to Turnus. He was killed by Aeneas in single combat (Bk. XII of the 'Aeneid').

Turonum or TURONIUM, in imprints, Tours.

Turpin (*d. c.* 800), archbishop of Rheims in the days of Charlemagne, to whom is erroneously attributed the Latin chronicle, 'De Vita et Gestis Caroli Magni', the source from which Boiardo and other authors drew some of their romantic tales. According to one version of the story he died among the last of the heroes at Roncesvalles after shriving the dying Roland (q.v.).

Turpin, RICHARD (1706–39), the famous highwayman, the son of an innkeeper at Hempstead, Essex. He was arrested for horse-stealing and hanged at York. He figures in Ainsworth's 'Rookwood', which gives an account of his great ride to York on Black Bess; but romances connected with his name are legendary.

Turveydrop, father and son, characters in Dickens's 'Bleak House' (q.v.).

Tuscan Order, a simpler form of the Roman Doric order, with only mouldings for ornament.

Tusculum, a town about ten miles SE. of Rome, where Cicero had a villa.

Tusher, THE REVD. THOMAS, chaplain to the Castlewood family in Thackeray's 'Esmond' (q.v.), subsequently a bishop and the first husband of Beatrix Esmond (see *Virginians*).

Tusitála, the 'Teller of Tales', the Samoan name of R. L. Stevenson (q.v.).

Tussaud, MARIE, *Madame Tussaud* (1760–1850), *née* Gresholtz, was born at Berne. She assisted her uncle Curtius in his 'Cabinet de Cire' in the Palais Royal, Paris, and modelled heads of victims of the Terror. She married Tussaud, separated from him in 1800, and, migrating to England, transferred her museum to the Lyceum, Strand, in 1802, and thence to Blackheath. After Blackheath, and until 1884, the Exhibition was at 58 Baker Street; in 1885 it was moved to premises in the Marylebone Road. These, together with many valuable relics and figures, were destroyed by fire in 1925, and the existing building, with the exhibition, was opened on the same site in 1929.

TUSSER, THOMAS (1524?–80), agricultural writer and poet, was educated at Eton and Trinity Hall, Cambridge. He farmed at Cattiwade, Suffolk, and introduced the culture of barley. He published his 'Hundreth good pointes of husbandrie' in 1557 (amplified in later editions) in verse of quaint and pointed expression, many proverbs being traceable to this work. It is a collection of instructions on farming, gardening, and housekeeping, together with humorous and wise maxims on conduct in general.

Tutankhamen (14th cent. B.C.), the son-in-law and successor of the Egyptian heretic king, Amenhotep IV or Akhnaton (q.v.). He reverted to the old religion and was buried in the valley of the tombs of the kings at Karnak, where his tomb, containing a wonderful collection of furniture, jewels, and other relics of the age, was discovered in 1922 by Mr. Howard Carter, excavating on behalf of the earl of Carnarvon.

Tutivillus, see *Titivil.*

Tuyll, ISABELLA VAN, see *Zélide.*

Tvastri, in Hindu theology, the divine builder and smith, the Hindu Vulcan. He is known in post-Vedic writings as *Visvakarma.*

Twa Dogs, *The,* a poem by Burns (q.v.), completed in 1786.

Caesar, the gentleman's dog, and Luath, the ploughman's collie, converse on the comparative happiness of the lives of their rich and poor masters, until the sun goes down,

When up they gat, and shook their lugs,
Rejoic'd they were na men but dogs.

TWAIN, MARK, see *Clemens* (*S. L.*).

Tweedledum and Tweedledee: for the origin of the expression see under *Handel.*

The words were first used in a musical connexion. 'To tweedle' is to produce a succession of shrill musical sounds, to whistle or pipe; and 'tweedledee' and 'tweedledum' were used to suggest the contrast between the sounds of high- and low-pitched musical instruments. [OED.]

Tweedledum and Tweedledee figure in Lewis Carroll's 'Through the Looking-glass', where they engage in a notable battle.

Twelfth Day, 6 Jan., the twelfth day from the Nativity, also called the feast of the Epiphany, was formerly celebrated as the closing day of the Christmas festivities, with special reference, some think, to the Magi (q.v.) or Wise Men of the East. A large cake was served at the festivities, containing a bean or coin, to determine who should be king of the feast.

Twelfth Night, *Or what you will,* a comedy by Shakespeare, produced probably in 1600–1, and first printed in the folio of 1623. The story was probably taken from 'The History of Apolonius and Silla' in 'Riche his farewell to the Military Profession' (1581), an English rendering of a tale in Cinthio's 'Hecatommithi', or from Bandello or Belleforest.

Sebastian and Viola, twin brother and sister, and closely resembling one another, are separated in a shipwreck off the coast of Illyria. Viola, brought to shore in a boat, and disguised as a youth Cesario, takes service as page with Duke Orsino, who is in love with the lady Olivia. The latter rejects the Duke's suit and will not admit him to her presence. Orsino makes a confidant of Cesario and sends her to press his suit on Olivia, much to the distress of Cesario, who has fallen in love with Orsino. Olivia in turn falls in love with Cesario. Sebastian and Antonio, captain of the ship that had rescued Sebastian, now arrive in Illyria. Cesario, challenged to a duel by Sir Andrew Aguecheek, a rejected suitor of Olivia, is rescued from her predicament by Antonio, who takes her for Sebastian. Antonio, being arrested at that moment for an old offence, claims from Cesario a purse that he had entrusted to Sebastian, is denied it, and haled off to prison. Olivia coming upon the true Sebastian, takes him for Cesario, invites him to her house, presses her suit on him, finds him not unwilling, and marries him out of hand. Orsino comes to visit Olivia. Antonio is brought before him, claims Cesario as the youth he has rescued from the sea; while Olivia claims Cesario as her husband. The duke, deeply wounded, is bidding farewell to Olivia and the 'young dissembler' Cesario, when the arrival of the true Sebastian clears up the confusion. The duke, disappointed of Olivia, and becoming conscious of the love that Viola (as Cesario) has betrayed, turns his affection to her, and they are married.

The humour which abounds in the play is chiefly provided by the subordinate characters, who have no essential connexion with the plot: Sir Toby Belch, uncle to Olivia; Sir Andrew Aguecheek, his friend; Malvolio, the pompous conceited steward to Olivia; Maria, her attendant; and the clown, Feste. The play contains one of the most beautiful of Shakespeare's songs, 'Come away, come away, death'.

Twelve of England, THE, in the 'Lusiads' of Camoëns (q.v.), canto VI. xlii et seq. Velloso tells a tale of a tournament arranged by the duke of Lancaster between 'the Twelve of England' and an equal number of Portuguese knights.

Twitcher, JEMMY, in Gay's 'The Beggar's Opera' (q.v.), one of Captain Macheath's associates, who betrays him. The nickname was given to the fourth earl of Sandwich (1718–92), who had been associated with Wilkes in the Medmenham 'brotherhood' and yet, when Wilkes's papers were seized, was active in collecting evidence against him. The allusion is to a line in the play. 'That Jemmy Twitcher should peach me, I own surprised me.'

Two Drovers, The, a short story by Sir W. Scott (q.v.), one of the 'Chronicles of the Canongate', published in 1827.

The story is designed to illustrate the Highland character. Robin Oig M'Combich, a Highland drover of good family, sets out for England with his cattle, in company with his friend, a Yorkshire drover, Harry Wakefield. When they reach Cumberland, the latter, annoyed over some trivial affair of accommodation for the cattle, fixes a quarrel on Robin in an inn, where the whole company join in insulting the Highlander. When Robin refuses to fight with his fists, as beneath the dignity of a Highland gentleman, Wakefield knocks him down. Robin walks twelve miles to fetch his dirk, which he has left with a comrade, returns to the inn, and in the presence of all plunges the dirk in Harry's breast. He then gives himself up to justice, ready to give a life for the life he took.

Two Foscari, The, an historical tragedy by Lord Byron (q.v.), published in 1821.

Jacopo, son of the doge of Venice, Francesco Foscari, has twice been exiled, for venality and for complicity in murder. He has been brought back from exile on a charge of treasonable correspondence, and the play opens with his examination on the rack. The doge, his father, broken-hearted at his disgrace, signs the sentence for his third perpetual exile. But Jacopo's love for Venice is so intense that he expires from dread of leaving it again. The Ten meanwhile decide to require the abdication of the old doge. He at once leaves the palace, and, as he descends the steps and hears the bells of St. Mark's tolling for the election of his successor, falls down and dies.

The play departs slightly from the facts. Jacopo died in exile at Candia, and the doge a few days after his deposition.

Two Gentlemen of Verona, The, a comedy by Shakespeare (q.v.), one of his early works, probably of 1594–5, first printed in the folio of 1623. The story is taken from Montemayor's pastoral romance 'Diana'.

The two gentlemen of Verona are the friends Valentine and Proteus. Proteus is in love with Julia, who returns his affection, Valentine leaves Verona for Milan 'to see the wonders of the world abroad', and there falls in love with Silvia, the duke of Milan's daughter. Presently Proteus is sent also on his travels, and exchanges vows of constancy with Julia before starting. But arriving at Milan, Proteus is at once captivated by Silvia, and, betraying both his friend and his former love, reveals to the duke the intention of Valentine to carry off Silvia. Valentine is banished and becomes a captain of robbers, and Proteus continues his court of Silvia. Meanwhile Julia, pining for Proteus, comes to Milan dressed as a boy and takes service as Proteus' page, unrecognized by him. Silvia, to escape marriage with Thurio, her father's choice, leaves Milan to rejoin Valentine, is captured by robbers and rescued from them by Proteus. Proteus is violently pressing his suit on Silvia when Valentine comes on the scene. Proteus is struck with remorse, and his contrition is such that Valentine is impelled to surrender Silvia to him, to the dismay of Proteus' page, the disguised Julia. She swoons, and is then recognized by Proteus, and the discovery of her constancy wins back his love. The duke and Thurio arrive. Thurio shows cowardice in face of Valentine's determined attitude, and the duke, approving Valentine's spirit, accords him Silvia. Launce, the clownish servant of Proteus, and his dog Crab, 'the sourest natured dog that lives', provide some drollery.

Two Kings of Brentford, see *Rehearsal*.

Two Noble Kinsmen, The, a play by J. Fletcher (q.v.), probably with the collaboration of Shakespeare, printed in 1634.

The play, which deals with the story of Palamon and Arcite, follows fairly closely the story as told by Chaucer in 'The Knight's Tale' (see *Canterbury Tales*), but adds the incidents of the liberation of Palamon from prison by the jailer's daughter, and her going mad for love of him.

Two on a Tower, a novel by Hardy (q.v.), published in 1882.

Lady Constantine, whose notoriously unkind husband has gone to Africa lion-hunting, falls in love with Swithin St. Cleeve, a young astronomer and a man of comparatively humble position. She learns that her husband has died, and marries Swithin secretly. Later she discovers that by doing so she has deprived him of a legacy which would have enabled him to advance in his career; and then that her husband, though now dead, was alive at the time of her marriage with Swithin, which is consequently void.

She insists on his leaving her and accepting advantageous employment in S. Africa. After he has gone, she discovers that she is with child by him. Under pressure from her brother she accepts in haste an offer of marriage from Bishop Helmsdale, and a son is born. Of the arrogant bishop's discovery of her reason for marrying him and of their life together we are told nothing. But the end of the story is illuminating. Swithin returns after the bishop's death. He is disillusioned at finding her an old woman, and is at first cold to her, to her despair; but recovering himself, he says he has come to marry her. The revulsion is too great, and she falls dead of joy. 'The Bishop was avenged.'

Two Years Ago, a novel by C. Kingsley (q.v.), published in 1857.

In this work the author deals with some of the moral problems and material evils of contemporary English life, notably the need for sanitary reform. The central event is the descent of cholera (which was prevalent in England in the middle of the 19th cent.) upon a Cornish village, revealing the self-sacrificing character of some of its inhabitants. Chief among these are the gallant doctor, Tom Thurnall, in whom countless escapes by flood and field have raised self-confidence to the point of arrogance; the nonconformist schoolmistress, Grace Harvey, whose devotion is based on a higher faith; and the high-church curate, Frank Headley, whose grit at last wins the hearts of the dissenting villagers. Contrasted with Tom Thurnall is the effeminate John Briggs, the apothecary's poetic assistant, whose career, based on the assumption of a false name, brings him temporary prosperity, marred by terror of detection, and ended by tragedy. There is a vividly described shipwreck, and a secondary plot involving a denunciation of slavery in the United States. The Crimean War enters slightly into the story, bringing occasion for a crisis in Tom Thurnall's spiritual life, and his final union with Grace Harvey.

Twysden, TALBOT, a character in Thackeray's 'The Adventures of Philip' (q.v.).

Tybalt, a character in Shakespeare's 'Romeo and Juliet' (q.v.). For the allusion in the play to cats in connexion with his name, see *Tibert.*

Tyburn, the name of an ancient manor, north-west of the old city of London, so called from the stream, the Tybourne, which ran through it. Its name was changed to Mary-le-bourne (Marylebone, q.v.) in the 15th cent. The Tybourne flowed south to the Thames through what are now the dips in Oxford Street and Piccadilly, west of Bond Street.

Tyburn is celebrated as the principal place of execution of malefactors until 1783. The gallows, which had formerly stood further east, were moved in the 16th cent. to a point NW. of the present position of the Marble Arch. Here the Tyburn Road turned off from Watling Street, and, following approximately the line of Oxford Street and Holborn, reached the city at Newgate.

Tyburnia, the residential quarter of London in the neighbourhood of Portman Square, so named from its proximity to the ancient Tyburn (q.v.), and frequently mentioned in Thackeray's novels.

Tyler, WAT (d. 1381), the leader of the peasants' revolt of 1381, who with Jack Straw led the peasants of Kent and Essex to London. He was killed by William Walworth, the lord mayor of London, in the course of a discussion with Richard II at Smithfield. He is the subject of a drama by Southey.

TYNDALE, WILLIAM (d. 1536), the translator of the Bible, studied at Oxford and Cambridge. He was preaching in Gloucestershire before 1522 and became involved in disputes with the clergy. He formed the project of translating the Scriptures into the vernacular, but finding difficulties in England went to Hamburg for the purpose. He visited Luther at Wittenberg, and commenced printing his translation of the New Testament at Cologne in 1525. He completed the work at Worms and introduced copies into England, which were denounced by the bishops and destroyed. He himself was ordered to be seized at Worms by Wolsey, but escaped to the protection of Philip, the landgrave of Hesse, at Marburg. He became a Zwinglian and an active pamphleteer, upholding the sole authority of Scripture in the Church and of the king in the State, earning the approval of Henry VIII, which he subsequently lost by opposing the king's divorce. He engaged in controversy with Sir T. More (q.v.) and wrote 'An answere unto Sir Thomas Mores dialoge' in 1531. He was betrayed to imperial officers and arrested for heresy, imprisoned at Vilvorde in 1535, and strangled and burnt at the stake there, in spite of Cromwell's intercession. Tyndale was one of the most remarkable of the Reformation leaders; his original writings show sound scholarship, but his translation of the Bible—consisting of the New Testament (1525), Pentateuch (c. 1530), and Jonah (1531)—the accuracy of which has been endorsed by the translators of the authorized version, is his surest title to fame. He also translated the 'Enchiridion Militis Christiani' of Erasmus (q.v.).

TYNDALL, JOHN (1820–93), professor of natural history at the Royal Institution in 1853 and superintendent there from 1867 to 1887, did much by his investigations to advance and, by his lectures and published works, to popularize science. The following are some of his principal writings: 'The Glaciers of the Alps' (1860), 'Mountaineering' (1862), 'Heat considered as a Mode of Motion' (1863), 'On Radiation' (1865), 'On Sound' (1867), 'On Light' (1869), and 'Lectures on Light' (1873), 'Contributions to Molecular Physics' (1872), 'Floating Matter in the Air' (1881). His famous address to the British Association at Belfast in 1874, on the relation between science and theological opinion, was reprinted in 'Fragments of Science', vol. ii.

Typee, a narrative by H. Melville (q.v.), based on his own experiences in the South Seas, published in 1846. Tom, the narrator, and his companion, Toby, jump ship in the Marquesas and flee to the valley of Typee, where they are entertained hospitably by the savages, though they suspect them of cannibalism. The Typee way of life is described in detail and compared with European civilization, to Europe's disadvantage in many respects. Tom enjoys an affectionate friendship with the beautiful Fayaway, but in spite of every attraction, and fearful of his hosts' ultimate intention, Toby having already left, he makes his escape with difficulty.

Typhon or TYPHOĒUS, in Greek mythology, a terrible monster, son of Tartarus and Gē, and father of various other monsters, such as the Chimaera and the Lernaean Hydra (qq.v.). He had a hundred heads and a tremendous voice. Zeus overthrew him with thunderbolts, set him on fire, and flung him into Tartarus or under Mount Etna or some other volcano. For his identification with the Egyptian god, Set, see *Osiris*.

Tyr, see *Tiu*.

Tyrannic Love, or *The Royal Martyr*, a heroic play in rhymed couplets by Dryden (q.v.), published in 1669.
   Maximin, the Roman emperor, while besieging Aquileia, falls in love with Catharine, the Christian princess of Alexandria, his captive, but is repulsed by her. Catharine converts Berenice the empress to Christianity, and Maximin orders them both to execution. St. Catharine is beheaded, but Maximin is stabbed by Placidius, one of his officers, who loves Berenice.
   The play, which contains some beautiful passages, is marred by absurdities, which provided material for ridicule in 'The Rehearsal' (q.v.).

Tyrrel, FRANCIS, a character in Scott's 'St. Ronan's Well' (q.v.).

TYRRELL, GEORGE (1861–1909), a leader of the modernist movement in religion, joined the Roman Church in 1879 and the Society of Jesus, from which he was dismissed in 1906 for his unorthodox 'Letter to a Professor of Anthropology'. This he published as 'A much abused Letter' with copious annotations. His other published works include: 'Nova et Vetera' (1897), 'Hard Sayings' (1898), 'External Religion' (1899), 'The Faith of the Millions' (1901–2, two series), 'Oil and Wine' (1902), 'Lex Orandi' (1903), 'Lex Credendi' (1906), 'Through Scylla and Charybdis' (an exposition of his religious development, 1907), 'Medievalism' (a reply to Cardinal Mercier's attack on modernism, 1908), 'Christianity at the Crossroads' (1909). 'Essays on Faith and Immortality' (1914) and his 'Autobiography and Life', edited by M. D. Petre (1912), were issued after his death.

Tyrrell, SIR JAMES (d. 1502), a strong adherent of Richard III, and the supposed murderer of the princes in the Tower of London.

Tyrrell or TIREL, WALTER (fl. 1100), son of the lord of Poix in Picardy, was generally believed to have shot the arrow which killed William Rufus, but denied having done so.

TYRTAEUS, a poet who lived at Sparta about the middle of the 7th cent. B.C., and by his war-songs and elegiac lays, fragments of which survive, encouraged his countrymen in their war with the Messenians.

TYRWHITT, THOMAS (1730–86), educated at Eton and Queen's College, Oxford, fellow of Merton and Clerk of the House of Commons (1762–8), is remembered for his edition and exposure of the 'Rowley Poems' (q.v., 1777–8), in the authenticity of which he originally believed; for his 'Observations . . . upon . . . Shakespeare' (1766); and still more for his studies of Chaucer, whose 'Canterbury Tales' he edited in 1775–8, expounding his versification and helping to establish the Chaucer canon.

TYTLER, PATRICK FRASER (1791–1849), joint founder with Sir W. Scott of the Bannatyne Club (q.v.), was author of a 'History of Scotland' from the reign of Alexander III to the year 1603 (1828–43), and a history of 'England under the Reign of Edward VI and Mary' (1839). He also wrote lives of the Admirable Crichton (1819), Wycliffe (1826), Sir Walter Ralegh (1833), and Henry VIII (1837), besides other historical works.

Tzigane, see *Gipsy*.

U

UDALL or UVEDALE, NICHOLAS (1505–56), dramatist and scholar, educated at Winchester, successively head master of Eton and Westminster. He was author of 'Ralph Roister Doister' (q.v.), the earliest known English comedy. He translated selections from Terence and other works, and wrote Latin plays on sacred subjects. Tusser (q.v., 'Five hundreth pointes') complains of having been severely flogged by Udall 'for fault but small or none at all'. Udall got into grave trouble at Eton and was sent to the Marshalsea by the Privy Council. He figures in F. M. Ford's novel, 'The Fifth Queen' (1906).

Udaller, a tenant of land in Orkney or Shetland by the old native form of freehold tenure. The word is connected with 'alodial' as opposed to 'feudal' tenure of land. Magnus Troil, in Scott's 'The Pirate' (q.v.), is frequently referred to as 'the Udaller'.

Udolpho. *Mysteries of,* see *Mysteries of Udolpho.*

Ugolino de' Gherardeschi (*d.* 1289), an Italian Guelph leader, who twice by treachery, in 1284 and again in 1288, made himself master of Pisa. He was finally overthrown, and with his two sons and two of his grandsons was locked up in a tower and starved to death. The episode figures in canto xxxiii of Dante's 'Inferno'.

ULFILAS or WULFILA (A.D. 311–81), a Christian of Cappadocian origin, was consecrated bishop of the Arian Visigoths in 341, and subsequently migrated with them to the neighbourhood of Nicopolis in Moesia. He translated the Bible into Gothic from the Greek, inventing, it is said, an alphabet for the purpose. Fragments of this translation, chiefly of the N.T., survive (e.g. the Codex Argenteus at Upsala), and are of great value to the philological science of the Germanic languages.

Ullin's Daughter, Lord, a ballad by Campbell (q.v.).

ULPIAN (ULPIANUS DOMITIUS), a celebrated Roman jurist, who became secretary and adviser of the emperor Alexander Severus (222–35). He was killed by some soldiers who had entered the palace at night, about 228. He wrote many valuable legal works.

Ulric, in Byron's 'Werner' (q.v.), the son of Werner.

Ulrica, in Scott's 'Ivanhoe' (q.v.), the old sibyl who sets fire to the castle of Torquilstone and perishes in the flames.

Ultima Thule, see *Thule.*

Ultramontane, meaning literally 'beyond the mountain' (i.e. the Alps), a term applied to those who hold extreme views in favour of the papal authority.

Ultrajectum, also *Trajectum ad Rhenum,* in imprints, Utrecht.

Ulysses, see *Odysseus.*

Ulysses, a novel by James Joyce (q.v.), first published in Paris in 1922. Copies of the first English edition were burned by the New York post office authorities, and the Folkestone Customs Authorities seized the second edition in 1923. Various later editions appeared abroad and, after the United States District Court found the book not obscene in 1933, an unlimited edition appeared in America and in England in 1937.

The novel deals with the events of one day in Dublin in June 1904. The principal characters are Stephen Dedalus (the hero of Joyce's earlier, largely autobiographical 'Portrait of the Artist as a Young Man'); Leopold Bloom, a Jewish advertisement canvasser; and his wife Molly. The plot follows the wanderings of Stephen and Bloom through Dublin, and their eventual meeting. The last chapter is a monologue by Molly Bloom. The various chapters roughly correspond to the episodes of Homer's 'Odyssey': Stephen representing Telemachus, Bloom Odysseus, and Molly Penelope. In the course of the story a public bath, a funeral, a newspaper office, a library, public houses, a maternity hospital, and a brothel are visited. A number of other Dublin scenes and characters are introduced. The style is highly allusive and employs a variety of techniques, especially those of the stream of consciousness and of parody, and ranges from extreme realism to fantasy.

Ulyssipo, in imprints, Lisbon.

Uma, in Hindu mythology, a name of the goddess Devi, the wife of Siva.

Umayyads or OMMIADES, a powerful family of the Quraysh tribe (to which the Hashimite family of Mohammed also belonged), which included a series of caliphs, beginning with Moawiyah, the successor of Ali (q.v.). To this family, at a later period, belonged the Arab dynasty that ruled in Spain (8th to 11th cents.).

Umbriel, 'a dusky melancholy sprite' in Pope's 'Rape of the Lock' (q.v.).

Una, in Bk. 1 of Spenser's 'Faerie Queene', typifies the true religion. She is separated from the Red Cross Knight (q.v.) of Holiness (the Anglican Church) by the wiles of

Archimago (q.v.), but meets and is protected by a lion (England), until the latter is killed by Sansloy (q.v.), who carries Una off to a forest. She is rescued by fauns and satyrs, and is finally united to the Red Cross Knight.

UNAMUNO Y JUGO, MIGUEL DE (1864–1936), Spanish writer and philosopher, born at Bilbao. He became professor of Greek at the University of Salamanca in 1892 and later became rector. A bitter and often eccentric critic of Spanish intellectual, social, and political life, he nevertheless opposed thoughtless 'Europeanization'. His greatest work, 'Del Sentimiento Trágico de la Vida' (1912, tr. 'The Tragic Sense of Life', 1921), is concerned with the impossibility of reconciling man's religious aspirations with scientific knowledge. His individualistic philosophy permeates all his work: essays, novels, travel books, and poetry.

Uncial, from the Latin *uncialis*, 'pertaining to the twelfth part', i.e. an inch or an ounce. In connexion with writing, it is applied to letters having the large rounded forms (not joined to each other) characteristic of the chief Greek and Roman book script of the 4th to the 8th cents. The term is commonly explained as meaning originally 'letters of an inch long'. There was also used a slightly less formal script known as half-uncial, which was one of the parents of minuscule script.

Uncle Remus, see *Harris (J. C.).*

Uncle Sam, a jocular name for the government (or people) of the United States, a facetious interpretation of the initials U.S. Various legends connecting the expression with government officials of the name of Samuel appear to be unfounded. [OED.]

Uncle Silas, a novel by J. S. Le Fanu (q.v.), published in 1864.

Maud Ruthyn is the daughter of Austin Ruthyn, a rich eccentric recluse, whose younger brother, Silas, is under suspicion of having murdered in his own house a man with whom he was involved in gambling transactions. Austin Ruthyn, however, believes his brother to be maligned, and at his death leaves his daughter, Maud, to the guardianship of Silas, to whom his fortune will revert in the event of her death. Silas, who is in fact a hypocritical villain, heavily in debt, tries to force a marriage between his niece and his own repulsive son, and when it turns out that his son is married already, plots with him to murder Maud. The author skilfully sets out the various circumstances so as to produce on the reader a sense of terror: the seclusion of Maud from all her friends; the arrival of a sinister French governess, Mme de la Rougierre, an accomplice of the murderers; the description of the spiked hammer with which the murder is to be committed, etc. The murder miscarries, for the governess falls its unintended but deserving victim, and Maud is rescued.

Uncle Toby, MY, Captain Shandy, uncle of the nominal hero of Sterne's 'Tristram Shandy' (q.v.).

Uncle Tom's Cabin, a novel by Mrs. Stowe (q.v.), published in 1852.

Uncommercial Traveller, The, a collection of tales and sketches of places and manners, and of institutions needing reform, by Charles Dickens (q.v.), first published in 'Household Words' and 'All the Year Round', and reissued in 1861 and 1866. It contains some of Dickens's best literary work.

Under the Greenwood Tree, a novel by Hardy (q.v.), published in 1872.

This is an idyll, set in the rustic scene of Mellstock village, of two young lovers, Dick Dewy, son of the local 'tranter' or irregular carrier, and Fancy Day, the schoolmistress, who, after overcoming the usual difficulties in the way of true love, are happily married. The Mellstock musicians, rebellious against their displacement from the church gallery in favour of a harmonium, provided some delightful racy talk. There is a little bitter with the sweet. Fancy Day, engaged to Dick, momentarily yields to the temptation of an offer of marriage by the vicar. She comes to her senses and withdraws, but she will not tell Dick, as the vicar urges.

Understanding, LORD, in Bunyan's 'Holy War' (q.v.), the lord mayor of Mansoul, deposed from his office and imprisoned during the tyranny of Diabolus.

Underwoods, a collection of 'lesser poems' by Jonson (q.v.), first printed in the folio of 1640. It includes the famous poem to Shakespeare, and Whalley's edition (1756) adds the well-known epitaph on the countess of Pembroke ('Sidney's sister, Pembroke's mother') now generally attributed to W. Browne (q.v.).

'Underwoods' is also the name (confessedly adopted from Jonson) of a book of poems by R. L. Stevenson (q.v.).

Undine, a fairy romance published in 1811 by Friedrich, Baron de la Motte Fouqué (1777–1843), German officer of cuirassiers and prolific writer of poetry, drama, and prose fiction. The story was suggested to him by a passage in Paracelsus, and Undine is a sylph, the personification of the watery element. A humble fisherman and his wife have lost their child by drowning, and Undine, a capricious roguish maiden, has come mysteriously to them and been brought up in her stead. A knight, Huldbrand von Ringstetten, takes shelter in their cottage and falls in love with Undine. They are married, and the sylph in consequence receives a soul. But her relations, and particularly her uncle Kühleborn, the wicked water goblin, are a source of trouble. Huldbrand begins to neglect his wife and becomes attached to the haughty Bertalda, who is humbled by the discovery that she is the fisherman's lost child. One day, in a boat on the Danube, Huldbrand, tormented by Undine's kindred, angrily rebukes his wife, and she is snatched away by them into the water and seen no more. Presently Huldbrand proposes to Bertalda, and they are about to be married, when Undine, rising from a well, goes to the knight's room and kisses him, and he dies.

UNDSET, SIGRID (1882–1949), Norwegian novelist, born in Denmark. Her 'Kristin Lavransdatter', which originally appeared in 3 vols. (1920–2), is a work of fiction set in 14th-cent. Norway. This novel, with its successor, 'Olav Audunssön', won her the Nobel Prize in 1928. Both are available in English translations.

Unfortunate Traveller, The, or the Life o Jacke Wilton, a prose tale of adventure by T. Nash (q.v.), published in 1594, the earliest picaresque romance in English, and the most remarkable work of the kind before Defoe. It is dedicated to the earl of Southampton. Jacke Wilton is 'a certaine kinde of an appendix or page' attending on the court of Henry VIII at the time of the siege of Tournay. He lives by his wits, playing tricks on a niggardly old victualler and other gullible occupants of the camp, and gets whipped for his pains. He goes to Münster, which the Anabaptists are holding against the emperor, and sees John of Leyden hanged. The earl of Surrey, the lover of the Fair Geraldine, takes him to Italy as his page. During their travels they meet Erasmus and Sir Thomas More, and Aretino. They hear Luther disputing at Wittenberg. Wilton passes himself off as the earl of Surrey and runs away with an Italian courtesan. There is a pleasant scene where the true earl discovers them and treats the escapade with singular good humour. After a tourney at Florence, where the earl defeats all comers in honour of the Fair Geraldine, Wilton leaves him, and is at Rome during an outbreak of the plague. Here, turning from lighter themes, he depicts scenes of violence and tragedy, rapes, murders, tortures, and executions. Depressed by what he has seen, he is converted to a better way of life, marries his courtesan, and is last seen at the Field of the Cloth of Gold, in the king of England's camp. The whole story is told with much spirit and wit.

Unicorn, a fabulous animal usually regarded as having the body of a horse with a single horn projecting from its forehead; the monoceros of the ancients. Pliny describes it as having, in addition, the head of a deer, the feet of an elephant, and the tail of a lion. Its horn was reputed to have medicinal or magical properties. It has been identified at various times with the rhinoceros, certain species of antelope, etc. See 'The Lore of the Unicorn', by O. Shepard (1930), an interesting piece of research. In Heraldry a unicorn figures as a supporter of the royal arms of Great Britain; the old royal arms of Scotland

had two unicorns for supporters. The narwhal or sea-unicorn has a spirally twisted horn resembling that of the fabulous animal. The word translated 'unicorn' in the O.T. is translated 'wild ox' in the Revised Version.

Uniformity, ACT OF, passed in 1559, forbade the use of any form of public prayer other than the second prayer-book of Edward VI (with some modifications). The Act of Uniformity of 1662 required clergymen and schoolmasters to accept the prayer-book.

Unigenitus Dei Filius, 'The Only-begotten Son of God', a papal bull issued by Pope Clement XI in 1713 condemning the Jansenist (q.v.) heresy. The effect of this bull was felt in all Latin Catholic countries throughout the century; and at last, as Voltaire said, it turned out to the prejudice of the Jesuits, who had driven the pope to issue it.

Unionist, a member of the political party which advocated maintenance of the parliamentary union between Great Britain and Ireland; an opponent of Home Rule. The party was formed in 1886 by the coalition of the Conservatives with those Liberals (Liberal Unionists) who were opposed to Gladstonian Home Rule. While the chief tenet of this party was the maintenance of the union, its general policy and principles gradually became identified with those of the Conservative party.

Unitarian, a member of a religious body that affirms the single personality of the Godhead, as opposed to believers in the Trinity. The distinct English body of Unitarians dates from the secession in 1773 of Theophilus Lindsay from the Anglican Church; and it was to some form of Unitarian Church that the English (as opposed to the Scottish) Presbyterians ultimately turned. It was strong at Manchester and at Norwich in the first half of the 19th cent.

Unities, THE, three principles of dramatic composition, viz. that a play should consist of one main action, occurring at one time (not longer than the play takes to perform), and in one place; expanded from Aristotle's 'Poetics' by 16th-cent. Italian critics, and by French classical dramatists of the 17th cent. The Unities were often modified; e.g. the time-limit was extended to twenty-four hours, and the place to one house or town, rather than one room or street.

University presses. The appointment of printers by European academies to produce learned books under some control and protection was common by the end of the 16th cent. As early as 1470 Jean Heynlin, prior of the Sorbonne, brought printers from Germany to work in the college; but his press had no sanction from the University of Paris and lasted only two years. A printer worked at Oxford from *c.* 1478 until 1486, but his relation to the University is not known.

With the advent of the 'new learning' universities needed new texts and printers needed help and protection for issuing them. The University of Leipzig, devoted to humane studies since 1502, took the lead in attracting printers, directing them to Greek and elegant Latin, and defending their books from attack by conservative authorities. The advantages of printing in a university were exemplified in the polyglot Bible produced in 1502–22 at Alcalá de Henares.

The modern conception of a university press owes much to Leyden. The academy founded there in 1575 appointed an official printer from the first, and was served in that capacity by Christophe Plantin (in 1584–5), by the erudite Raphelengius (*d.* 1595), and three generations of Elzeviers. Their books, edited or approved by the resident professors and well corrected at the press, established the benefits in point of authority, continuity, and universality that a university can bestow in publishing.

In England the University of Cambridge had power by royal charter to appoint printers to work in its precinct and sell books anywhere since 1534, mainly, no doubt, with a view to propagating defence against heresy. It exercised the power from 1583, and Oxford followed the year after (see *Oxford University Press*), apparently with only verbal warrant from the Queen. Costly conflicts with vested interests contesting the universities' right to override private monopolies in such lucrative works as the Bible in English, the Book of Common Prayer, and the Metrical Psalms, induced both universities to forego this privilege in return for money during most of two centuries and to sponsor only works of scholarship.

The press owned, financed, and conducted by a university, as distinct from one censored and protected by it but privately financed and managed, had its origin in England and is still confined to English-speaking countries. Oxford acquired such a press in 1690, when the printing equipment and rights in copy of John Fell (q.v.), came to it by bequest from him. Cambridge took immediate control of its printing in 1698 and exercises it through a board of Syndics.

The style of 'university press' is used by many publishing firms, particularly in Great Britain, the U.S.A., and Canada, some of which also print. They are variously related to the academies from which they take their names. In the U.S.A. Cornell opened a small press in 1869, which lasted until 1894, and Johns Hopkins established an agency for publishing in 1875. The University of Chicago has owned its printing and publishing office since 1894. Harvard, Yale, Princeton, Columbia, California, Toronto, among other North American universities, are equipped to print at least some of their publications.

University Wits, name given to a group of Elizabethan playwrights and pamphleteers, of whom Nash, Greene, Lyly, and Lodge were the chief.

Unknown, THE GREAT, title applied to Sir W. Scott (q.v.) by his contemporaries.

UNO, the Organization of the United Nations (being those which had resisted the Axis powers) for the maintenance of international peace and security. Its Charter was signed at San Francisco on 26 June 1945, and the first meetings of its General Assembly and Security Council were held in London early in 1946.

Unreason, ABBOT OF, see *Misrule.*

Unter den Linden, 'Under the lime trees', the name of a celebrated street in Berlin running eastward from the Brandenburger Thor, and containing the palaces of the former Imperial family, the university, etc.

Unto This Last, four essays on economics by Ruskin (q.v.), published in 1860–2. The publication was begun in 'The Cornhill Magazine', but gave rise to so great an outcry that Thackeray, the editor, discontinued it.

This was the earliest of Ruskin's economic treatises. He first deals with wages and employment, the possibility of fixing wages by legislation, and the maintenance of a regular flow of employment. He then discusses the nature of true wealth, to be distinguished from the riches obtained at the cost of making others poor. He defines the abstract idea of just wages—'that they will consist in a sum of money which will at any time procure for [the worker] at least as much labour as he has given'. He investigates the nature of this 'equivalent', from which the element of 'human capacities and dispositions' must not be excluded, as it is by J. S. Mill. 'The real science of political economy . . . is that which teaches nations to desire and labour for the things that lead to life.' Righteousness and ideals, and not only self-interest and material needs, should be taken by it into consideration. His final plea is for 'Not greater wealth, but simpler pleasure. . . . Care in no wise to make more of money, but care to make much of it; remembering always the great, palpable, inevitable fact—that what one person has, another cannot have.'

Ruskin's views were derided at the time, but many of the reforms that he advocated have since been adopted.

Up, Guards, and at them!, reputed to be the duke of Wellington's order which opened the last stage of the Battle of Waterloo, but Gronow, who claimed to have been lying on the ground close to Wellington immediately before the Guards charged, says that the words actually used were 'Guards, get up and charge!' ('Reminiscences of Capt. Gronow', 1852, p. 101).

Upanishad, see *Veda.*

Upas, a fabulous tree alleged to have existed in Java, with properties so poisonous as to destroy all animal and vegetable life to a distance of fifteen or sixteen miles around it. The account given in 'The London Magazine' of 1783, from which Erasmus Darwin adopted and gave currency to the fiction, professed to be translated from an account by a Dutch surgeon who was at Samarang in 1773. It was apparently the invention of Steevens (q.v.). Darwin ('Loves of the Plants', iii. 238) refers to it as follows:

> Fierce in dread silence on the blasted heath
> Fell Upas sits, the Hydra-Tree of death.

Ur of the Chaldees, the city where, according to the book of Genesis, Abraham settled, and whence he migrated northwards to Haran. It stood on the Persian Gulf near one of the mouths of the Euphrates. Recent excavations have resulted in discoveries of great interest. Ur was the seat of three Sumerian dynasties of which the first came to an end about 3575 B.C., and the third about 2300 B.C. (Peake and Fleure).

Uraeus, a representation of the sacred asp or serpent, employed as an emblem of supreme power and worn on the head-dress of ancient Egyptian divinities and sovereigns.

Urania, the Muse (q.v.) of astronomy.

Uranian Aphrodite or URANIAN VENUS, the 'Heavenly Aphrodite', distinguished from APHRODITE PANDEMOS, the Aphrodite of the World, was the goddess of pure and ennobling love.

Urănus, the personification of the sky, the most ancient of the Greek gods and the first ruler of the universe. He married Gē, the earth, and was father of the Titans, including Cronos, who ousted him from his throne.

The planet *Uranus* was discovered in 1781 by Sir W. Herschel, accidentally.

URBAN, SYLVANUS, the pseudonym of E. Cave (q.v.), and, by succession, of the later editors of 'The Gentleman's Magazine'.

Urbi et Orbi, Latin, 'to the City and the World', an expression used in papal documents to indicate that they are addressed not to the City of Rome alone, but to the whole Catholic world. It was also applied to the blessing given by the pope on exceptional occasions ('Catholic Encyclopaedia').

Urdu. Urdu and Hindi are both literary forms of a dialect spoken in the region of Delhi, and share a common grammatical structure and basic vocabulary. This basic form of the two languages is sometimes called Hindustani, a term which British writers formerly used for Urdu only. Urdu is the language, in the main, of the Muslims of Western Pakistan and of Northern India (though many Hindus and others also speak it). Hindi is the language of the northern Indian Hindus. Urdu is written in the Persi-Arabic script, draws heavily on Persian for its literary vocabulary, and has a literature written, in the main, by Muslims about the life of the Muslim community in the sub-continent. Hindi uses the Devanagari script, draws its literary vocabulary from Sanskrit, and has a literature written mainly by Hindu writers on Hindu themes. Both languages now have many British loan-words and are spoken by large numbers of people far beyond the area where they originated. Hindi is today the national language of India and Urdu one of the two national languages (the other being Bengali) of Pakistan. In drastically simplified grammatical form, sometimes called 'bazaar Hindustani', the common element between Hindi and Urdu serves as a lingua franca all over the north and centre of the sub-continent.

URFÉ, HONORÉ D' (1567–1625), member of an old French family and author of 'Astrée' (1607–28), a long sentimental romance in a pastoral setting presenting an ideal of polite and distinguished living, in which men and women of the world are shown in the guise of shepherds and shepherdesses. The principal substance of the plot, in which the affairs of a multitude of other couples are interwoven, is the love of the shepherd Céladon for the shepherdess Astrée, whose reproaches for his supposed infidelity cause him to throw himself into a river. He is not, however, drowned, as Astrée supposes, and after many trials and adventures regains his mistress's heart. The work was immensely popular and contributed to the refinement of manners and expression.

Urgan, see *Alice Brand*.

Urganda, an enchantress in the romances of Amadis and Palmerin (qq.v.).

Uriah the Hittite, an officer in David's army, the husband of Bathsheba, whom David caused to be killed in battle (2 Sam. xi).

Uriel, one of the seven archangels enumerated in the 'Book of Enoch' (see under *Angel*). Milton ('Paradise Lost', iii. 690) makes him 'Regent of the Sun', beguiled by Satan in spite of his sharp sight.

Urien, see *Ryence*.

Urim and Thummim, certain objects, the nature of which is not known, worn upon the 'breast-plate' of the Jewish high-priest, by means of which the will of Jehovah was held to be declared. They are mentioned in Exod. xxviii. 30; Deut. xxxiii. 8, and other passages.

Urizen, in the mystical poems of Blake (q.v.), a grim old giant, the symbol of restrictive morality, identified with Jehovah. Also a symbol of the bondage of man to the senses.

Urn Burial or *Hydriotaphia*, a treatise by Sir T. Browne (q.v.) published (with the 'Garden of Cyrus', q.v.) in 1658.

The point of departure is the discovery of some ancient sepulchral urns in Norfolk, which leads the author to consider the various modes of disposal of the dead recorded in history and practised in Britain, urns and their contents, funeral ceremonies, and immortality or annihilation. The tone is meditative and mystical, and the style, from the first words of the Epistle Dedicatory, 'When the Funerall pyre was out, and the last valediction over', to the melancholy splendour of the closing passage, 'But the iniquity of oblivion blindly scattereth her poppy', reaches the highest level of rhetorical prose.

URQUHART or URCHARD, SIR THOMAS (1611–60), of Cromarty, educated at King's College, Aberdeen. He fought at Turriff against the Covenanters, withdrew to London, and was knighted in 1641. He followed Prince Charles (later Charles II) to Worcester, where many of his manuscripts were destroyed by the Parliamentarians. He was imprisoned during 1651–2, and died abroad. His best-known work is a translation of the first three books of Rabelais (q.v.) (the first two published in 1653, the third in 1693). He wrote a number of curious treatises on mathematics, linguistics, etc., with strange Greek titles ('Trissotetras', 'Logopandecteision'), collected in 1774 and 1834; among them is his 'Ekskubalauron', which combines an Introduction to his Universal Language with a Vindication of the Honour of Scotland. This contains his well-known account of the 'Admirable Crichton'.

Ursa Major, the Great Bear constellation, see *Callisto*. Also a name given to Dr. Johnson by Boswell's father, Lord Auchinleck.

Ursula, ST., a British saint and martyr, daughter of a 'Christian British King', who, according to legend, was put to death with 11,000 virgins, having been captured by Huns near Cologne when on a pilgrimage. A large number of human bones were discovered when foundations were being dug, in the 12th cent., for the city walls, and these were pronounced to be the bones of the martyrs and venerated in consequence. But bones of men were found among them. One explanation of the legend is that the 11,000 virgins were in reality only one, a certain 'St. Undecemilla'.

There is no mention of St. Ursula before the 10th cent., several hundred years after her supposed martyrdom. Details of the story appear in the 12th cent., and it is told by Geoffrey of Monmouth. Baring-Gould ('Curious Myths') traces St. Ursula to the Swabian moon-goddess Hörsel, the wandering Isis.

USK, THOMAS (d. 1388), the author of 'The Testament of Love', formerly ascribed to Chaucer, was under-sheriff of London by Richard II's mandate in 1387, and was proceeded against by the 'Merciless' parliament in 1388 and executed. 'The Testament of Love' is an allegorical prose work written by Usk in prison to enlist sympathy. Prof. Skeat discovered that the initial letters of the

sections formed an acrostic reading, 'Margaret of virtu, have merci on T S K N V I'. He thought these letters a partial anagram for 'Kitson'. Henry Bradley, as a result of certain rearrangements of the text, found that the last letters should read T H I N U S K, i.e. 'thine Usk.'

Usnach, THE SONS OF, see *Deirdre*.

USSHER, JAMES (1581–1656), a scholar of Trinity College, Dublin, at its foundation, became archbishop of Armagh. He wrote much on theological subjects, and was learned in patristic literature and ancient Irish history. But his chief work is the 'Annales Veteris et Novi Testamenti', a chronological summary in Latin of the history of the world from the Creation to the dispersion of the Jews under Vespasian, of extraordinary critical quality. His dates are still printed in the English Bible. He bequeathed his collection of books and manuscripts to Trinity College, Dublin.

Utgard, in Scandinavian mythology, the outer chaotic world, the residence of the giants, whose chief was *Utgard-Loki*.

Uther Pendragon, in the Arthurian legend, king of the Britons and father of Arthur (q.v.). 'Pendragon' in Welsh means 'chief leader in war'.

Utilitarianism, an essay by J. S. Mill (q.v.), first published as a series of articles in 'Fraser's Magazine' in 1861, and in book form in 1863.

In this work, Mill, while accepting the Benthamite principle (see *Bentham*) that Utility, or the greatest happiness of the greatest number, is the foundation of morals, departs from it by maintaining that pleasures differ in kind or quality as well as in quantity, 'that some *kinds* of pleasure are more desirable and more valuable than others'; also by recognizing in 'the conscientious feelings of mankind' an 'internal sanction' to be added to Bentham's 'external sanctions'. 'The social feelings of mankind, the desire to be in unity with our fellow creatures' constitute 'the ultimate sanction of the greatest happiness, morality'.

Utopia, the principal literary work of Sir T. More (q.v.), is a speculative political essay written in Latin. The work was published in 1516 at Louvain, Erasmus supervising the printing. The form was probably suggested by the narrative of the voyages of Vespucci, printed in 1507. The subject is the search for the best possible form of government. More meets at Antwerp a traveller, one Raphael Hythloday, who has discovered 'Utopia', 'Nowhere land'. Communism is there the general law, a national system of education is extended to men and women alike, and the freest toleration of religion is recognized. The work at once became popular, and was translated into English in 1551, and into French (in

1530), German, Italian, and Spanish. The rapid fame of the book is shown by the reference to Utopians by Rabelais (III. i, published in 1546.)

Utrecht, PEACE OF, the peace concluded in 1713, which terminated the War of the Spanish Succession. By the treaties between France on the one hand and Great Britain, Holland, Prussia, Savoy, and Portugal, on the other, Philip V retained the throne of Spain, but the crowns of France and Spain were never to be united; the Protestant succession was secured in England; the fortifications of Dunkirk were to be dismantled; Spain ceded

her possessions in Italy and the Netherlands to Charles VI, and Sicily to the duke of Savoy; Great Britain retained Minorca and Gibraltar, and acquired Nova Scotia, Newfoundland, and the French part of St. Christopher's. By the BARRIER TREATY the fortresses on the southern frontier of the Netherlands were to be garrisoned by Dutch troops, three-fifths of whose wages were to be paid by the emperor; galling to the latter, and at best a feeble guarantee. See also *Asiento Treaty*.

Uzziel, one of the angels. In Milton's 'Paradise Lost', iv. 781–2, he is 'next in power' to Gabriel.

V

Vae Victis !, Latin, 'Woe to the vanquished !', the exclamation attributed to Brennus, the Gaulish conqueror of Rome (390 B.C.), when, having demanded 1,000 lb. of gold as ransom for the Capitol, he threw his sword into the scales to balance an excess in the quantity delivered (Livy, v. 48).

Vailima, see *Stevenson* (*Robert Louis*).

Vainlove, a character in Congreve's 'The Old Bachelor' (q.v.).

Vaisya, the third of the great Hindu castes, the merchants and the agriculturists.

Vala, see *Blake*.

Valclusa, see *Vaucluse*.

Valdarno (*Val d'Arno,*) the valley of the Arno, in which Florence is situated.

Valence, AYMER DE, in Scott's 'Castle Dangerous' (q.v.), lieutenant to Sir John de Walton.

Valentine, one of the 'Two Gentlemen of Verona' in Shakespeare's play (q.v.).

Valentine and Orson, the subject of an early French romance. Bellisant, sister of King Pepin, is married to Alexander, emperor of Constantinople. The archpriest treacherously accuses Bellisant to her husband and she is banished. A bear carries away one of her children (Orson), who is reared as a wild man. The other (Valentine) is found by Pepin and brought up as a knight. Valentine meets Orson, conquers him, brings him to the court, and tames him. Numerous adventures follow, the principal of which is the imprisonment of Valentine and Orson and their mother Bellisant in the Castle of Clerimond, sister of the giant Ferragus, and their rescue by Pacolet, the dwarf messenger of Ferragus, who has a little magic horse of wood which conveys him instantly wherever he wishes.

The story appeared in English about 1550

as the 'History of two Valyannte Brethren, Valentyne and Orson', by Henry Watson. A ballad in Percy's 'Reliques' deals with it.

Valentine Legend, the hero of Congreve's 'Love for Love' (q.v.).

Valentine Vox the Ventriloquist a novel by Henry Cockton (1807–53), first published in book form in 1840.

Valentine's Day, St., 14 Feb., on which day two martyrs of the name were executed, one a Roman priest, the other a bishop of Terni. There was an ancient practice among young people in England of choosing, by lot or otherwise, on St. Valentine's day, a sweetheart, a lover, or a special friend for the ensuing year, and of sending a present to the person so chosen. John Brand ('Popular Antiquities') quotes 'Paston Letters', ii. 24, as showing that the custom prevailed as early as 1476. Its origin is obscure. A rural tradition that birds choose their mates on the day in question is referred to by Chaucer ('Assembly of Foules', 309), by Shakespeare ('Midsummer Night's Dream', iv. i), and by Herrick in 'Hesperides'. There is a charming essay on St. Valentine's Day in Lamb's 'Essays of Elia'. In Hardy's 'Far from the Madding Crowd', it is the thoughtless sending of a valentine by Bathsheba Everdene to Farmer Boldwood that starts' the train of events leading to the tragedy of the story.

On St. Valentine's Day, 1797, Sir John Jarvis with a fleet of fifteen sail defeated the Spanish fleet of twenty-seven sail off Cape St. Vincent.

Valentinian, a tragedy by J. Fletcher (q.v.), produced between 1610 and 1614.

The play, which includes some beautiful lyrics, deals with the vengeance of Maximus, a general under Valentinian III, for the dishonour of his wife Lucina by the emperor, and her self-inflicted death. To get rid of Aecius, commander of the army and faithful to the emperor, who stands in the way of his vengeance, he causes the emperor's suspicion to fall on Aecius, who takes his own life in consequence. Valentinian is then poisoned by two followers of Aecius. Maximus is proclaimed emperor, takes Eudoxia, Valentinian's widow, as his consort, and reveals to her the part he has played in the deaths of Valentinian and Aecius, even pretending that he has been a party to the ravishment of Lucina. Eudoxia, in abhorrence, poisons Maximus at his inauguration.

'Aecius' is obviously Aëtius (who defeated the Huns at Châlons in 451). Some historical truth underlies the play.

Valerian, the husband of St. Cecilia, whose story is told in Chaucer's 'The Second Nun's Tale' (see *Canterbury Tales*).

VALÉRY, PAUL (1871–1945), French poet, essayist, and critic, an outstanding figure of 20th-cent. French literature. Two famous examples of his obscure but beautiful and musical poetry are 'La Jeune Parque' (1917) and 'Le Cimetière marin' (in the collection 'Charmes', 1922). The latter, translated in 1945 by C. Day Lewis, is a long meditative poem on the theme of death. The 'cemetery' is at the small Mediterranean port of Sète, the poet's birth-place.

Valéry's later writings were almost wholly in prose and include two Socratic dialogues 'L'Âme et la danse' and 'Eupalines ou l'architecte' (1923) and several volumes of criticism, e.g. 'Variété' (1922–44, 5 vols.) etc., 'Monsieur Teste', a sort of intellectual phenomenon, is the name-character of one of his early prose works.

Valhalla, in Scandinavian mythology, a hall in Gladsheim (the residence of Odin), destined for the reception of dead heroes.

Vali, in Scandinavian mythology, the youngest son of Odin, who avenges Balder by slaying Hödur (qq.v.), the two deaths perhaps symbolizing the changes of the seasons. He is one of the survivors of Ragnarök (q.v.).

Valjean, JEAN, an ex-convict, the hero of Hugo's (q.v.) 'Les Misérables'.

Valkyries, THE, in Scandinavian mythology, the messenger maidens of Odin. Their special function was to kill the heroes selected for death in battle, and to conduct them when dead to Valhalla.

Wagner's opera 'Die Walküre' ('The Valkyries'), the second part of the 'Ring der Nibelungen' (q.v.), tells of the flight of Sieglinde, the wife of Hunding, with her brother Siegmund, of their love, and of the fight between Hunding and Siegmund, in which, by the interposition of Wotan, Siegmund is slain. Brynhilde, the Valkyrie, who has endeavoured, contrary to Wotan's order, to protect Siegmund, is degraded and laid to sleep, surrounded by a ring of fire, where

only a hero can enter and awake her. For the continuation see *Siegfried*.

Valley of Humiliation, THE, in Bunyan's 'The Pilgrim's Progress' (q.v.), the place where Christian encounters Apollyon. There is a beautiful description of it in Pt. II, where Mr. Great-heart explains its true character.

Valley of the Shadow of Death, THE, see Ps. xxiii. 4. Christian in 'The Pilgrim's Progress' (q.v.) passes through it, 'a very solitary place', with a dangerous quag on one side and a deep ditch on the other, and the mouth of hell is close by one side of it, from which issue flames and fiends.

Vallombrosa, a valley some twenty miles east of Florence, referred to by Milton in 'Paradise Lost', i. 303.

Vallon, ANNETTE, see *Wordsworth (W.)*.

Vamp, MR., in Peacock's 'Melincourt' (q.v.), a caricature of Gifford (q.v.).

Van Diemen's Land, now called Tasmania, was discovered by Abel Janzoon Tasman in 1642, and so named after Anton van Diemen, governor of the Dutch East Indies, 1636–45.

Van Dyck, see *Dyck (Sir Anthony Van)*.

Van Eyck, JAN, see *Eyck (Jan Van)*.

Van Gogh, VINCENT, see *Gogh (Vincent Van)*.

VAN TUYLL VAN SEROOSKERKEN, see *Zélide*.

VANBRUGH, SIR JOHN (1664–1726), dramatist and architect, was son of a London tradesman, whose father, a merchant of Ghent, had fled to England from Alva's persecutions. In 1691 he was for some time a prisoner in the Bastille as a suspected spy. In 1697 he produced 'The Relapse, or Virtue in Danger' (q.v.) with immense success, and 'The Provok'd Wife' (q.v.) in the same year. His other principal comedies are 'The Confederacy' (q.v., 1705) and 'The Provok'd Husband' (q.v.), which he left unfinished and Cibber (q.v.) completed and brought out in 1728. His collected dramatic works appeared in 1730. As a playwright he offers a strong contrast to his contemporary, Congreve, in that he paid no attention to style. He wrote as he talked, and excelled in caricature. He, together with Congreve, was specially attacked by Collier (q.v.) in his 'Short View'.

Vanbrugh's first building was Castle Howard, 1699–1726. This already shows the grandeur and dramatic quality of his style, which reaches its climax in Blenheim Palace (q.v.). Hawksmoor (q.v.) assisted him in many of his projects. Vanbrugh was Clarenceux king-of-arms, 1704–26.

Vance, PHILO, the detective in a series of stories of crime by the American author, Van Dine (Willard Huntington Wright, 1888–1939).

VANCOUVER, GEORGE (1758–98), explorer, accompanied James Cook on his second voyage, was in Rodney's victory at Les Saintes in 1782, and was subsequently sent on a voyage of discovery to Australia and the North Pacific (1791–5). He surveyed the south-west of Australia and of New Zealand, and the Pacific coast of America, sailing round the island now called after him Vancouver (it had been discovered earlier by Spaniards) and returning by Cape Horn. His 'Voyage of Discovery to the N. Pacific' appeared posthumously in 1798.

Vandals, a Germanic tribe which in the 4th and 5th cents. A.D. invaded western Europe, and established settlements in various parts of it, especially in Gaul and Spain, finally in 428–9 migrating to northern Africa, where they supplanted the old Roman provincial government. In the year 455 their king, Genseric, led a marauding expedition against Rome, which he took and sacked. The Vandals were overthrown by Belisarius (q.v.) in 533, and this was a great misfortune for Christendom, for it let in the Muslims in the 7th cent.; and these, not the Vandals, completed the ruin of Roman Africa and Mauretania.

Vanessa, Swift's name for Esther Vanhomrigh. See *Swift*.

Vanhomrigh, ESTHER (1690–1723), see *Swift*. The name is pronounced 'Vanummery'.

Vanir, in Scandinavian mythology, a race of gods, distinct from the Æsir (q.v.), but who became united to them. They were the gods of the atmosphere, and included Niördr, Frey, Freya, and Heimdal (qq.v.). It is suggested that the Æsir and Vanir were originally the gods of two different races or religions, which coalesced.

Vanity Fair, in Bunyan's 'The Pilgrim's Progress' (q.v.), a fair set up by Beelzebub, Apollyon, and Legion, in the town Vanity, through which pilgrims passed on their way to the Eternal City. The town was so called because it was lighter than vanity, and in the fair were sold all kinds of vanity—houses, honours, kingdoms, and all sorts of delights. There Faithful was burnt to death; but there, in Pt. II, were found some pious persons who could now show their heads, for the blood of Faithful lay as a load upon his oppressors.

Vanity Fair, a novel by Thackeray (q.v.), published in monthly numbers in 1847–8.

The novel is principally concerned with the parallel careers of two strongly contrasted characters: Rebecca (Becky) Sharp, the clever, unscrupulous, and courageous daughter of a penniless artist and a French opera-dancer; and Amelia Sedley, a pretty, gentle, unintelligent creature, whose father is a rich man of business and lives in Russell Square. The pair are brought together as girls at Miss Pinkerton's Academy, where Becky is an articled pupil and teaches French. We follow her through her attempt to capture the fat Jos Sedley, Amelia's brother and ex-collector of Boggley Wallah, to the home of the dirty, cynical, old Sir Pitt Crawley, where she is engaged as governess and captivates Sir Pitt himself and his rich sister Miss Crawley. The baronet on the death of his wife proposes to her, and brings to light the fact that Becky has overreached herself by getting secretly married to Rawdon, Sir Pitt's second son and the favourite of Miss Crawley, cavalry officer, gambler, and duellist; a revelation that infuriates Sir Pitt and Miss Crawley, and loses Rawdon his aunt's inheritance.

Meanwhile Amelia's father is ruined by speculations, and her intended marriage with a young officer, George Osborne, is forbidden by Osborne's purse-proud father. Amelia is heartbroken at the desertion of George, a worthless fellow whom she blindly adores. Captain Dobbin, George's fellow officer, her honest and unselfish worshipper, brings George to a sense of the shabbiness of his conduct, and the marriage takes place in defiance of old Osborne, who utterly repudiates his son. Then follows the campaign of Waterloo, and the chief actors are brought together at Brussels, where George, before being killed in the battle, engages in an intrigue with Becky, now Mrs. Rawdon Crawley.

Much of the remainder of the story is occupied with the skilful generalship by which the undaunted Becky wins her way into the highest society, first in Paris, then in London, in spite of poverty and disadvantages of birth. Unfortunately she does not confine herself to legitimate manœuvres, but compromises her reputation, if not her virtue, by her encouragement of the vicious old Lord Steyne, from whom, without her husband's knowledge, she receives large sums of money. Rawdon, who is devoted to his wife, and in spite of his faults has a high sense of honour, finding her and Lord Steyne together in incriminating circumstances, breaks with her after a furious scene with his lordship.

Amelia, plunged in grief by the loss of the husband she still worships, lives with her shiftless parents a life of poverty and humiliation which the devoted Dobbin has secretly done his best to alleviate. She is even forced to surrender her son to old Osborne, in order to obtain from him some means of support. After ten years Dobbin comes home from India, but though Amelia is grateful to him, the memory of her husband still stands between her and him. It is only after Becky, now a disreputable frequenter of continental haunts, has revealed to her George's infidelity that Amelia's idol is finally shattered, and room is made in her heart for Dobbin, whom she finally marries.

There are many other entertaining characters in the book: Pitt Crawley, the old baronet's pompous elder son; the Revd.

Bute Crawley, the baronet's brother, and his designing wife; Briggs, Miss Crawley's companion and Becky's 'sheep-dog'; Major O'Dowd, his Irish wife, and Glorvina, his dashing sister; the Bareacres family whose rank is the only ground for their arrogance; and the tyrannical Lady Southdown, Pitt Crawley's mother-in-law, who administers tracts and medicine to all her family.

Vanity of Human Wishes, The, a poem by S. Johnson (q.v.), published in 1749. It is an imitation of the Tenth Satire of Juvenal.

The poet considers the various objects of human ambition and indicates their vanity. First, power, which he illustrates by the rise and fall of Thomas Wolsey, of Buckingham, Hyde, and others. Then he points to the dangers attending eminence in learning, and the end of Galileo and Laud. He passes to military glory and the fate of Charles of Sweden; and then to the miseries attending great length of life and the dangers of physical beauty. His conclusion is:

> Still raise for good the supplicating voice,
> But leave to Heav'n the measure and the
> choice.

Varangians, THE, from ON. *Væringi*, apparently from *var-*, plighted faith; the Scandinavian rovers who in the 9th and 10th cents. overran Russia and reached Constantinople; hence the Northmen (latterly also the Anglo-Saxons) forming the bodyguard of the later Byzantine emperors. [OED.] The Varangians figure in Scott's 'Count Robert of Paris' (q.v.).

Varden, GABRIEL, a character in Dickens's 'Barnaby Rudge' (q.v.), father of Dolly Varden.

Variorum or VARIORUM EDITION, an edition, especially of the complete works of a classical author, containing the notes of various editors or commentators [OED.].

Varney, RICHARD, a character in Scott's 'Kenilworth' (q.v.).

Varuna, in early Vedic mythology, the greatest, with Indra, of the Indian gods, the lord and maintainer of the physical universe. The name is perhaps to be identified with the Greek οὐρανός, heaven. In post-Vedic mythology, Varuna appears as the god of the ocean and of the night.

VASARI, GIORGIO (1511–74), Italian painter, architect, and author of 'The Lives of the most excellent Italian Architects, Painters, and Sculptors' (1550 and 1568), for generations the main source for the history of Italian art.

Vasco da Gama, see *Gama*.

Vashti, the rebellious queen of Ahasuerus (see Esther i). She figures in Pt. I of Abercrombie's (q.v.) series of dramatic poems, 'Emblems of Love',

Vatel, FRANÇOIS (*d.* 1671), steward to Fouquet and subsequently to the Prince de Condé. Because he thought the fish would not arrive in time for a Friday's repast given at Chantilly by the prince to Louis XIV, Vatel committed suicide.

Vathek, An Arabian tale, by W. Beckford (q.v.), published in English in 1786.

The work was written by Beckford in French and translated into English, probably by Samuel Henley, the translation being revised by Beckford. It reflects in part a spiritual experience in the author's life, but what precisely this was remains obscure.

The Caliph Vathek, grandson of Haroun-al-Raschid, under the influence of his sorceress mother, the Greek Carathis, and of his own unbounded curiosity and megalomania, becomes a servant of Eblis (the Devil), makes a sacrifice of fifty children, and sets off from his capital, Samarah, to the ruined city of Istakar, where he is promised the sight of the treasures of the pre-Adamite sultans. On the way he falls in love with Nouronihar, the beautiful daughter of one of his emirs, who accompanies him on his quest. Amid various grotesque and extravagant incidents, he obtains admission to the subterranean halls of Eblis, only to discover the vanity of the riches and wonders that he sees there, and to receive the penalty of his crime, in the form of eternal torture. The principal literary merit of the work lies in the description of this inferno and of Vathek's end.

To 'Vathek' Beckford added three 'Episodes' (the last unfinished), also oriental tales, which were only recently published. They were translated from the French by Sir F. T. Marzials (1912).

Vatican, THE, the palace of the pope on the Vatican Hill in Rome. It contains the Sistine Chapel (q.v.), the Stanze (see *Raphael*), the Vatican Library, and galleries of pictures, sculptures, and objets d'art. The Vatican City is an independent sovereign state.

Vatican Decrees, THE, adopted in July 1870 at the Oecumenical Council summoned by Pius IX, laid down a theological definition of the doctrine of papal infallibility.

Vaucluse or VALCLUSA, a village near Avignon in the south of France, famous as the residence of Petrarch, and for the fountain which he celebrated.

Vaudeville, a light popular song or a stage performance of a light and amusing character interspersed with songs, from *vau de vire*, in full *chanson du Vau de Vire*, a song of the Valley of the Vire (in Calvados, Normandy). The name is said to have been first given to songs composed by Olivier Basselin, a fuller of Vire (15th cent.).

Vaudois, see *Waldenses*.

VAUGHAN, HENRY (1622–95), educated at Jesus College, Oxford, is noteworthy for his 'Silex Scintillans', a collection of religious poems (including the magnificent 'They are all gone into the world of light'), of which the first part was published in 1650, and the second in 1655. Of his profane works, 'Poems' appeared in 1646, 'Olor Iscanus' (q.v.) in 1651, and 'Thalia Rediviva' (including a section of 'Pious Thoughts and Ejaculations') in 1678. His 'Collected Works' were published in 1871. He was known as the 'Silurist' because of his love for the country of Brecknock, the county of his birth, which was anciently inhabited by the Silures.

VAUGHAN, THOMAS (1622–66), twin brother of Henry Vaughan (q.v.), alchemical writer, author of 'Magia Adamica', etc. He engaged in controversy with Henry More (q.v.), and was in part an original of Ralpho in 'Hudibras' (q.v.).

Vautrin, the master-criminal, one of the most powerful characters of Balzac's series of novels 'La Comédie humaine'. He makes his first appearance in 'Le Père Goriot'. He may have had a real-life prototype in Vidocq (q.v.).

Vaux, ROLAND DE, the baron of Triermain, see *Roland de Vaux*.

VAUX, THOMAS, LORD (1510–56), a contributor to 'Tottel's Miscellany' (q.v.), principally remembered as the author of 'The aged Lover renounceth Love', the source of the song mumbled by the grave-digger in 'Hamlet'.

Vauxhall or FOX HALL, originally 'Falkes Hall' (said to be from Falkes de Breauté, captain of John's mercenaries, and lord of the manor in the early 13th cent.), famous for the gardens laid out there in the middle of the 17th cent., and at first called 'The New Spring Gardens', because they replaced the old Spring Gardens (q.v.) adjoining St. James's Park. Vauxhall Gardens are frequently referred to from that time by dramatists and other writers, including Pepys. Sir Roger de Coverley visited them with Mr. Spectator (he commented on the scarcity of nightingales in the gardens as compared with less desirable visitors—'Spectator', No. 383). Thackeray in ch. vi of 'Vanity Fair' and Fanny Burney in 'Evelina' describe the visits to them of certain of their characters. The gardens were finally closed in 1859.

Veal, MRS., see *Defoe*.

Veck, TOBY ('Trotty'), a character in Dickens's 'The Chimes' (q.v.).

Vectis or VECTA, the Roman name of the Isle of Wight.

Veda, one or other of the four ancient sacred books of the Hindus (called the Rig-, Yajur-, Sāma-, and Atharva-Veda). Each Veda includes a *sanhita* or collection of *mantras* or hymns, and a *Brahmana* or body of precepts; and to each is attached an *Upanishad* (mean-

ing 'a sitting-down at the feet of an instructor'), a speculative mystical treatise dealing with the Deity, creation, and existence. The date of the Vedas is unknown, but they are among the most ancient literary works of the world.

VEGA, GARCILASSO DE LA, see *Garcilasso de la Vega.*

VEGA, LOPE DE (1562–1635), the founder of the Spanish drama, and the author of a great number of plays, poems, and romances, which have been a source of inspiration to European literature in general, particularly to that of France. A curious testimony to his facility is that he wrote a long continuation of Ariosto while taking part in the expedition of the Armada, from which he returned safely.

Vehmgericht or VEHMIC TRIBUNALS, tribunals that existed in Westphalia for the maintenance of public peace and order, derived from the tribunals of the late Carlovingians. They exercised an extraordinary power, persons of exalted rank being subject to their jurisdiction and frequently punished. They were originally royal tribunals. They rose to importance in the 12th cent., became secret in the 15th cent., and were not suppressed until the 16th. The members of the order were initiated with mystic rites and had secret signs of recognition. They figure in Scott's 'Anne of Geierstein' (q.v.).

Veiled Prophet of Khorassan, The, see *Lalla Rookh.*

Velasquez, DIEGO RODRIGUEZ DA SILVA (1599–1660), Spanish painter, born in Seville. He was appointed Court painter in 1523 to Philip IV, who declared that he would be painted by no one else, and of whom, and his Court, Velasquez painted many portraits. The realism of his early genre and religious scenes was modified by the study of the Italian masters, though it predominated in all his work and influenced the French Impressionist painters of the 19th cent.

VELLEIUS PATERCULUS, see *Paterculus.*

Vendée, LA, a department in the west of France, the scene of civil war during the French Revolution incited by the priests (far more than by the squires) of the region. It was the 'levée en masse' by the decree of the Convention of 23 Feb. 1793 which led to the first insurrection, more against this quasi-conscription than in favour of the *ancien régime*. See also *Chouans.*

Vendémiaire, from Latin *vindemia,* grape-gathering, the first month in the French Republican calendar (see *Calendar.*)

Vendice or VINDICE, the chief character in 'The Revenger's Tragedy', ascribed to Cyril Tourneur (q.v.).

Veneering, Mr. and Mrs., in Dickens's 'Our Mutual Friend' (q.v.), types of flashy social parvenus.

Venetia, a novel by Disraeli (q.v.), published in 1837.

The story is partly based on the life of Byron with some admixture of that of Shelley, but is placed in the latter part of the 18th cent. Venetia is the daughter of Mr. Herbert and Lady Annabel Herbert, who has separated from her husband owing to his subversive views on morality, politics, and religion. He is, however, a man of character as well as ability, joins the American forces in their revolution, and becomes a general. He subsequently lives in seclusion in Italy. Venetia is brought up by her mother in complete ignorance of her father, but grows up with an instinctive devotion to him, which is increased by the discovery of his portrait and of his sonnets. She is also thrown into intimate contact with the young Lord Cadurcis, a youth of brilliant abilities, who presently becomes animated with the same subversive ideas as Herbert. He is in consequence looked upon by Lady Annabel with aversion, his hope of marrying Venetia is frustrated, and he is obliged to leave England owing to a social scandal. Venetia's health is impaired by the troubles of her heart, and mother and daughter travel to Italy. Meeting accidentally her father there, Venetia effects the reconciliation of her parents, and the general happiness appears complete when Cadurcis joins them, at once wins Herbert's affection, and recovers the esteem of Lady Annabel. But at this juncture, when the obstacles to the union of Cadurcis and Venetia have been removed, Cadurcis and Herbert are drowned in a squall in the bay of Spezia.

Veni, vidi, vici, Latin, 'I came, I saw, I conquered', words which Suetonius in 'Lives of the Caesars' (*Julius*, 37) says were displayed before Julius Caesar in his Pontic triumph (after his victory over the rebel Pharnaces II, 47 B.C.). According to Plutarch (Life of Caesar) the three words formed the whole of the account of this victory which he sent to his friend Amintius.

Venice Preserv'd, or a Plot Discovered, a tragedy in blank verse by Otway (q.v.), produced in 1682.

Jaffier, a noble Venetian youth, has secretly married Belvidera, daughter of a proud senator, Priuli, who has repudiated her. Jaffier, reduced to poverty, begs Priuli for assistance, but is met with insults. Pierre, a foreign soldier with a grievance against the Venetian republic, stimulates Jaffier's desire for revenge, confides to him a plot that is hatching against the State, and introduces him to the conspirators. As a pledge of his loyalty to them Jaffier places Belvidera in the charge of their leader, Renault, but without explaining the reason. Renault in the night offers her insult. She escapes to her husband,

who, in spite of his pledge to the contrary, makes known to her the conspiracy. To save her father, who, as one of the senators, is to be killed, she persuades Jaffier to reveal the plot to the Senate, but to claim as reward the lives of the conspirators. These are arrested. Jaffier, loaded by them with insults, is overwhelmed with remorse. The senators, in spite of their promise, condemn the conspirators to death. Jaffier threatens to kill Belvidera unless she secures their pardon from her father. She succeeds, but Priuli's intervention is too late. Belvidera goes mad. Jaffier stabs his friend Pierre on the scaffold and then himself, and Belvidera dies broken-hearted.

The play with Betterton as Jaffier and Mrs. Barry as Belvidera was very well received, and was frequently revived; it was seen at Drury Lane Theatre in 1829, and at Covent Garden under Macready between 1837 and 1839. The senator Antonio is a caricature of Shaftesbury.

Venn, Diggory, the reddleman in Hardy's 'The Return of the Native' (q.v.).

Ventidius, (1) in Shakespeare's 'Timon of Athens' (q.v.), one of the faithless friends of Timon; (2) in Shakespeare's 'Antony and Cleopatra' (q.v.) and in Dryden's 'All for Love' (q.v.), Antony's general.

Venus, identified with the Aphrodite of the Greeks and the Astarte of the Syrians, was the Roman name for the goddess of beauty and love. She sprang from the foam of the sea near the island Cythera (whence the epithets 'Anadyomene' and 'Cytherean'). Zeus gave her in marriage to Hephaestus (Vulcan), the ugliest of the gods. She was unfaithful to him, was found in the arms of Ares (Mars), and was exposed to the ridicule of the gods. By Ares she became mother of Harmonia; by Ares, Zeus, or Hermes, of Eros (Cupid); by Hermes of Hermaphroditus; and by Dionysus (Bacchus) of Priapus. She became enamoured also of Adonis, and of Anchises (by whom she was mother of Aeneas). In the contest with Hera and Athene for the golden apple, the prize was awarded to her by Paris. She was portrayed in antiquity rising from the sea, e.g. 'Aphrodite Anadyomene' by Appelles; with a gesture of modesty, e.g. 'Aphrodite of Cnidos' by Praxiteles and the Hellenistic 'Medici Venus'; or partly draped, e.g. the 'Venus de Milo', c. 100 B.C., found in 1820 in the ruins of a theatre on Melos and now in the Louvre. See *Uranian*.

Venus, the second planet in order of distance from the sun, known as the morning or evening star.

Venus and Adonis, a poem in six-lined stanzas by Shakespeare (q.v.), published in 1593, and dedicated to Henry Wriothesley, earl of Southampton. It was probably Shakespeare's first published work. Venus, in love with the youth Adonis, detains him from the chase and woos him, but cannot win his love. She begs him to meet her on the morrow, but he is then to hunt the boar. She tries in vain to dissuade him. When the morning comes she hears his hounds at bay, and, filled with terror, goes to look for him, and finds him killed by the boar.

Venus, MR., in Dickens's 'Our Mutual Friend' (q.v.), a preparer of anatomical specimens and for a time an ally of Silas Wegg.

Venusberg, or MOUNTAIN OF VENUS, the Hörselberg in Thuringia, in the caverns of which, according to medieval legend, the goddess Venus held her court. See *Tannhäuser*.

Vercelli Book, a codex of Old English manuscripts in the possession of the chapter of Vercelli in N. Italy. It is unknown how it came into their keeping. It contains prose sermons and religious poetry, particularly the 'Andreas' and 'The Dream of the Rood' (qq.v.), and the 'Elene' and the 'Fates of the Apostles' of Cynewulf (q.v.).

Vercingetorix, the chief of the Gallic tribe of the Arverni, who roused his countrymen to resist Julius Caesar and carried on the struggle against him with great ability, as described in Caesar's 'Commentaries' (Bk. VII). He was captured at the taking of Alesia, was brought to Rome for Caesar's triumph, and afterwards put to death.

Verdant Green, The Adventures of Mr., see *Bradley* (E.).

Verdi, GIUSEPPE (1813–1901), the great Italian composer of operas, was the son of a village innkeeper and was trained by the organist of his village. He is said to have been rejected from the Milan Conservatoire for lack of musical talent. His most important works were: 'Ernani' (1844), 'Rigoletto' (1851), 'Il Trovatore' (1853), 'La Traviata' (1853), 'Un Ballo in Maschera' (1859), 'Aïda' (1871), 'Otello' (1887), and 'Falstaff' (1893).

Verdun, a French fortified town on the Meuse, with a long history as an outpost of Lorraine, and an old bishopric of the Holy Roman Empire. It became French in 1552 and guards the straightest and shortest road from central Germany to Paris. It fell to the Prussians in 1792 and was for a time lost to France. During the 1914–18 war it was for several months (1916) the centre of stubborn resistance to German attack. The defence, which later turned to an offensive, was conducted by General (later Marshal) Petain.

Vere, ARTHUR DE, see *De Vere (Arthur)*.

VERE, AUBREY DE, see *De Vere (Aubrey)*.

Vere, ISABELLA, a character in Scott's 'The Black Dwarf' (q.v.).

VERGA, GIOVANNI (1840–1922), Italian novelist, dramatist, and writer of short stories, born at Catania. His finest works portray life at the lower levels of society in his native Sicily. The novels 'I Malavoglia' (1881) and 'Mastro-don Gesualdo' (1889) deal respectively with a family of poor Sicilian fisherfolk and an ambitious master stone-mason in economic competition with the local gentry. The story 'Cavalleria rusticana' ('Rustic Chivalry', 1880), after being dramatized by the author, was adapted as a libretto for Mascagni's opera. True to the principles of *verismo* (an Italian literary movement akin to Naturalism), Verga sought to eliminate from his works all trace of his own personality and outlook, and perfected a unique narrative style, which combined the literary language with idioms and constructions from popular and dialect speech. His English translators include D. H. Lawrence, whose 'Little Novels of Sicily' (1925) and 'Cavalleria rusticana and Other Stories' (1928) contain the best of Verga's tales. Lawrence also translated the second of the great Sicilian novels under the title 'Master don Gesualdo' (1923).

Verges, one of the constables in Shakespeare's 'Much Ado about Nothing' (q.v.).

VERGIL, the Roman poet, see *Virgil*.

VERGIL, POLYDORE (1470?–1555?), a native of Urbino, who came to England in 1502 as sub-collector of Peter's pence, and held various ecclesiastical preferments, being archdeacon of Wells from 1508 to 1554. He published his 'Anglicae Historiae Libri XXVI' in 1534–55, a chronicle of special value for the reign of Henry VII. He was also author of a 'Proverbiorum Libellus' (Venice, 1498), anticipating the 'Adagia' of Erasmus.

Verisopht, LORD FREDERICK, a character in Dickens's 'Nicholas Nickleby' (q.v.).

VERLAINE, PAUL (1844–96), French poet who died in poverty in Paris after a life in which bouts of alcoholism alternated with periods of repentance and religion. His poetic collections include: 'Les Fêtes galantes' and 'La Bonne Chanson' (1870), 'Romances sans paroles' (1874), 'Sagesse' (1881), perhaps his finest lyrics, produced during one spell of repentance, 'Jadis et Naguère' (1884), etc. His verse is evocative, rhythmic, and musical ('De la musique avant toute chose' was his own advice to poets).

Verlaine made more than one stay in England, the first time with the poet Rimbaud, to follow whom he threw up everything—home, wife, and employment. On one occassion he spent nearly two years teaching in English schools.

Vermeer, JAN (1632–75), of Delft, Dutch painter. Only about forty paintings by him are known, mostly interiors in which significance is given to the quiet scenes by the subtle treatment of light and composition.

VERNE, JULES (1828–1905), French novelist, who achieved great and enduring popularity by the combination of adventure with popular science in such books as the 'Voyage au centre de la Terre' (1864), 'Vingt mille lieues sous les mers' (1869), and 'Le Tour du monde en quatre-vingts jours' (1873).

VERNER, KARL ADOLPH (1846–96), a philologist of Copenhagen, the son of a German father and Danish mother. 'Verner's Law', which completes 'Grimm's Law' (see *Grimm, F. L. C.*) of consonantal variations in the Aryan languages, was a notable advance in the science of comparative philology.

Vernon, DIANA, the heroine of Scott's 'Rob Roy' (q.v.).

Veronica, ST., in Christian legend, the woman of Jerusalem whose cloth or kerchief was used to wipe the face of Christ on the way to Calvary, and retained miraculously impressed upon it His features. Whence the word *vernicle*, signifying this cloth (which is preserved at St. Peter's, Rome) or the representation upon it. The name *Veronica* is a corruption of *Berenice* (itself a Macedonic form of the Greek *Pherenice*, 'bringing victory'). *Veronica* suggested *verum icon*, 'true image', and thus perhaps gave rise to the above legend.

Vers libres, verses in which various metres, or various rhythms, are combined, or the ordinary rules of prosody disregarded.

Versailles, a town a few miles south-west of Paris where stands the royal palace built by Louis XIV, c. 1660–1710, round a hunting box built by Louis XIII. The architects were Le Vau and J. H. Mansart; Le Brun supervised the interior decoration, the grandest example of which is the Galerie des Glaces, and Le Nôtre laid out the gardens. Two small palaces were built in the park, the Grand Trianon by Louis XIV for Madame de Maintenon, and the Petit Trianon by Louis XV for Madame du Barry; the latter became the favourite 'rustic retreat' of Marie Antoinette. The Peace of Versailles or Treaty of Paris was signed at Versailles in 1783, by which the independence of the United States was recognized and peace made with France and Spain. In the palace of Versailles King William of Prussia was proclaimed German Emperor in 1871; and here was signed the TREATY OF VERSAILLES, which terminated the war of 1914–18 with Germany, on 28 June 1919.

Vertue, GEORGE (1684–1756), engraver and antiquary, collected in his notebooks materials for a history of art in England. The notebooks were bought by Horace Walpole, and utilized in his 'Anecdotes of Painting'. They have been published by the Walpole Society (1930–47).

Vertumnus, an Italian deity, worshipped as the god of the changing year and the giver of fruits. He became enamoured of the goddess Pomona (q.v.), pursued her in various shapes, and won her in the guise of a beautiful youth. Pope has a poem on the subject, adapted from Ovid's 'Metamorphoses', XIV.

Verulam or VERULAMIUM, the ancient Romano-British town whose modern name is St. Albans, and from which Francis Bacon took his title of Baron Verulam. It has been partly excavated; it stood on the opposite bank of the little river Ver to the modern St. Albans.

Vesey, ELIZABETH (1715?–91), wife of Agmondesham Vesey, a member of the Irish parliament. She was one of the leaders of the Blue Stocking (q.v.) circle.

Vesey, SIR JOHN, a character in Bulwer Lytton's comedy, 'Money' (q.v.).

Vesey-Neroni, SIGNORA, a character in Trollope's 'Barchester Towers' (q.v.).

Vespucci, AMERIGO, see *Amerigo Vespucci*.

Vesta, akin to the Greek goddess Hestia, was worshipped by the Romans in every household as the goddess of the hearth. Her circular temple stood in the forum. In it the sacred fire (supposed to have been brought from Troy) was tended by the VESTAL VIRGINS. These were originally drawn from patrician families and were required to remain celibate for thirty years. They enjoyed great privileges and honour, had the best seats at games and festivals, were chosen as arbiters in cases of moment, and had the power of pardoning criminals whom they met accidentally on the way to execution. In cases of violation of their vow, they were buried alive. The Temple is thought to have represented the house and hearth of the king, as the Vestals represented his daughters.

Vestal Virgins, see *Vesta*.

Vestiges of Creation, see *Chambers* (R.).

Vestris, MADAME, Lucia Elizabeth Mathews (1797–1856), granddaughter of Bartolozzi the engraver, was an unrivalled operatic singer with a contralto voice. She appeared frequently at Drury Lane, Covent Garden, and the Haymarket, London, 1820–31.

Veto, MONSIEUR and MADAME, nicknames given to Louis XVI and Marie Antoinette during the French Revolution, in allusion to the king's right (which he used more than once in 1791–2) of vetoing decrees of the Legislative Assembly.

Vholes, a lawyer in Dickens's 'Bleak House' (q.v.).

Vicar of Bray, The, the title of a well-known song of unknown authorship, dating from the 18th cent. The subject is a time-serving parson, who boasts that he has accommodated himself to the religious views of the reigns of Charles, James, William, Anne, and George, and that whatsoever king may reign he will remain Vicar of Bray.

Various suggestions have been made as to who this vicar was. Haydn ('Dictionary of Dates') quotes Fuller as stating that Symon Symonds, vicar of Bray, Berks., in the reigns of Henry VIII, Edward VI, Mary, and Elizabeth, was twice a Papist and twice a Protestant. When charged with being a time-server he is said to have replied, 'Not so, neither, for if I changed my religion, I am sure I kept true to my principle, which is to live and die the vicar of Bray' (see D'Israeli, 'Curiosities of Literature', *s.v.* Vicar of Bray).

Vicar of Christ, a title first assumed by Pope Innocent III (1198–1216).

Vicar of Hell, see *Bryan.*

Vicar of Wakefield, The, a novel by Goldsmith (q.v.), written in 1761–2 but not published until 1766. Goldsmith received £60 for the manuscript.

The story is told by the Revd. Dr. Primrose, the Vicar, kindly, charitable, devoid of worldly wisdom and not without some literary vanity. His wife, Deborah, is proud of her housekeeping and her children, with aspirations to gentility. Six children, two girls, Olivia and Sophia, and four boys (see *Primrose*), complete the family. At first they are prosperous and contented, but misfortunes presently come upon them thick and fast. The Vicar loses his independent fortune through the bankruptcy of a merchant. They move to a new living under the patronage of a certain Squire Thornhill. Thornhill, who is an unprincipled ruffian, seduces Olivia after a mock ceremony of marriage, and deserts her. She is discovered by her father and brought home, but his humble vicarage is destroyed by fire. He himself is thrown into prison for debt at the suit of Thornhill; and George Primrose, who challenges the latter to a duel to avenge his sister, is overpowered by ruffians and likewise sent to prison. The Vicar's second daughter, Sophia, is forcibly carried off in a postchaise by an unknown villain, and Olivia, who has been pining away since her desertion, is reported to the Vicar to be dead. All these misfortunes he bears with fortitude and resignation.

On their removal to their new vicarage the Primrose family have made the acquaintance of a certain Mr. Burchell, who appears to be a broken-down gentleman, kind-hearted but somewhat eccentric. He occasionally visits them, and offers advice concerning the disposal of the daughters, which, though wise, is unpalatable to the ambitious Mrs. Primrose. This leads to a breach in their relations, and he is even suspected of being Olivia's seducer. By good fortune he is now the means of rescuing Sophia, thereby increasing the regard she already feels for him. It thereupon appears that he is in reality the benevolent Sir William Thornhill, the squire's uncle. The squire's villainy is now exposed, and it appears that the abduction of Sophia was carried out by his design. All now ends

happily. Sir William marries Sophia. Olivia is found not to be dead, and her marriage to the squire is shown to have been, contrary to his intentions, legal. The Vicar's fortune is restored to him, and George marries the young lady of his heart, from whom he had been separated by his father's misfortunes.

In the course of the work are included the famous adventure of Moses Primrose (q.v.) and the gross of green spectacles, as also three well-known poems, 'The Hermit' (q.v.) or 'Edwin and Angelina', the 'Elegy on the Death of a Mad Dog', and the lyric sung by Olivia, 'When lovely woman stoops to folly'.

Vice, The, a fool or buffoon introduced into some of the interludes (q.v.) and later moralities (q.v.). The character was probably evolved from the merry and mischievous devil 'Tutivillus' (see *Titivil*), one of the stock figures of mysteries and moralities.

Vice Versa, a novel by F. Anstey (q.v.), published in 1882, the story of the misadventures of Mr. Bultitude, a father who, by the action of an Indian charm, is transformed into the physical appearance of his schoolboy son, while the son takes the outward form of his father; each retaining their original mental characteristics. Mr. Bultitude has to go to school while Dick remains at home and behaves as a schoolboy might be expected to behave.

'Vicisti, Galilaee', see *Julian the Apostate.*

VICTOR AND CAZIRE, the pseudonyms under which P. B. Shelley (q.v.) and Elizabeth Shelley published 'Original Poetry' in 1810.

VICTORIA, queen of England (1819–1901), reigned 1837–1901. The 'Letters of Queen Victoria' have been issued in three series, 1837–61 in 1907, 1862–85 in 1926–8, 1886–1901 in 1930–2. Her 'Leaves from a Journal of Our Life in the Highlands, 1848–61' appeared privately in 1867, and publicly in 1868. A second part, 'More Leaves', followed in 1883, covering the years 1862–3.

Victoria and Albert Museum, at South Kensington, London, was created out of the surplus funds of the Exhibition of 1851, and was first known as the Department of Practical Art, its guiding principle being the application of art to industry. Its principal collections are of pictures (including the Raphael cartoons belonging to the Crown), textiles, ceramics, furniture. It also contains a large art library.

Victorian, an epithet applied to anything (spiritual or material) or to a person (author, artist, politican, etc.) considered typical of the reign of Queen Victoria. Among the characteristics of the age in allusion to which the term is sometimes used are its improved standard of decency and morality; a self-satisfaction engendered by the great increase of wealth, the prosperity of the nation as a whole, and the immense industrial and scientific development; conscious rectitude and deficient sense of humour; an un-questioning acceptance of authority and orthodoxy.

Victory, The, Nelson's flag-ship at Trafalgar. She was a line-of-battle ship of 100 guns. She is now in Portsmouth harbour.

Vidar, in Scandinavian mythology, a son of Odin, and one of the gods who survive Ragnarök (q.v.). He is the silent god, the god of the forest. It is he who slays Fenrir (q.v.).

Vidocq, FRANÇOIS-EUGÈNE (1775–1857), a famous French criminal who in later life espoused the cause of law and order and became head of a Government criminal-investigation brigade. The 'Mémoires de Vidocq', which have been translated, are probably not by him.

Vienna, THE CONGRESS OF, was held by the principal European powers in 1814–15, after Napoleon's first abdication, to settle anew the boundaries of the European states. Among those who attended it were the emperors of Russia and Austria, the king of Prussia, Wellington and Castlereagh representing Great Britain, and Talleyrand representing France. By its decisions France was con-fined practically to her frontiers of 1792, Prussia was much enlarged, the Austrian Netherlands and the old territories of the Dutch Republic were united as a new king-dom of the Netherlands. Savoy and Nice were restored to the king of Sardinia. Austria received Lombardy and Venetia, and became dominant in Italy. A new kingdom of Poland was formed under the Tsar. The slave trade was declared illegal. The naviga-tion of tidal waters was thrown open.

Vignette, an ornamental design on a blank space in a book, especially at the beginning or end of a chapter, of small size, and unenclosed in a border. The word is a diminutive of the Fr. *vigne*, a vine; originally meaning an ornament of leaves and tendrils.

VIGNY, ALFRED VICTOR, *Comte de* (1797–1863), French poet, dramatist, and novelist, an early leader of the Romantic movement in French literature. His works include: 'Poèmes antiques et modernes' (1826) and the famous collection 'Les Des-tinées' published (1864) after his death; an historical novel of the period of Louis XIII, 'Cinq-Mars' (1826); translations from Shake-speare; the drama 'Chatterton' (1835); and three stories, episodes of the Napoleonic wars, 'Servitude et grandeur militaires' (1835).

Vikings: the Scandinavian adventurers who from the 8th to the 11th cent. practised piracy at sea and committed depredations on land as far as the Mediterranean (Hasting the Viking sacked Pisa). The Old Norse word is commonly regarded as derived from *vik*, a creek. The OED., however, shows reason to think that the word originated in the Anglo-Frisian area and is derived from the Old English *wic*, camp, the formation of temporary encampments being a prominent feature in Viking raids.

Village, The, a poem by Crabbe (q.v.), pub-lished in 1783, in which the poet presents the life of the rustic poor unidealized, in sombre colours.

Village Blacksmith, The, a poem by Long-fellow (q.v.), published in 1841.

Villanelle, a poem, usually of a pastoral or lyrical nature, consisting normally of five three-lined stanzas and a final quatrain, with only two rhymes throughout. The first and third lines of the first stanza are repeated alternately in the. succeeding stanzas as a refrain, and form a final couplet in the quatrain. [OED.]

VILLEHARDOUIN, GEOFFROI DE (*c.* 1152–*c.* 1212), marshal of Champagne, was an eyewitness of the events described in his 'Conquête de Constantinople' or account of the so-called fourth Crusade, the first great literary work in French prose. Villehardouin relates with vigour and picturesqueness the negotiations with the doge of Venice, the departure of the crusading host, its diversion from its proper purpose to various more secular undertakings, including the capture of Constantinople, the subsequent dissensions and intrigues, culminating in the crowning of Baldwin of Flanders as emperor of the East, and the grant of the kingdom of Macedonia to Boniface of Montferrat.

Villette, a novel by C. Brontë (q.v.), pub-lished in 1853.

The story, which is a rehandling of material already dealt with in 'The Professor' (then unpublished), reflecting the personal ex-periences of the authoress, is that of the life of an English girl without beauty, money, or friends, who obtains, in order to support herself, a post as teacher in a girls' school at Brussels. There, by virtue of a strong character, steeled by adversity, she soon establishes her position and wins the respect of the capable, if unscrupulous, headmistress, Madame Beck. She firmly represses a dis-position to fall in love with the handsome John Bretton, the English doctor of the school, in whom she recognizes an acquain-tance of her childhood, the son of her own godmother. She watches with friendly con-cern his infatuation for the worthless flirt, Ginevra Fanshawe, followed by a happier love for the tiny companion of his boyhood, Paulina Home. But the principal theme is the description of the heroine's gradual fascination by the waspish, despotic, but golden-hearted little professor, M. Paul Emanuel, and of the change in him from bitterness and tyranny to esteem and affec-tion. His generosity leaves her mistress of her own school at Brussels when he is called away by business to the West Indies. Whether he shall live to return and marry her is left to the reader to decide. The drabness of the story is redeemed by its biographical aspect and by the drawing of the characters, particularly of Monsieur Paul, Madame Beck, and the heroine herself.

VILLON, FRANÇOIS (*b.* 1431), French poet, a poor scholar of the university of Paris, who spent a riotous life between the tavern and the prison, and narrowly escaped the gallows for theft. Gay, witty, ironic, melancholy, he struck a new note in his lyrics, in which he sang the experiences of his own life. His chief works are the 'Petit Testament', the 'Grand Testament', and a number of *ballades* and *rondeaux*. Among the latter the 'Ballade des dames du temps jadis' and 'La Belle Heaulmière' were translated by D. G. Rossetti and Swinburne (qq.v.) respectively.

VINCENT DE BEAUVAIS, a 13th-cent. Dominican, author of the 'Speculum Majus', an enormous compilation of all the knowledge of the time. He is mentioned by Chaucer in the prologue to the 'Legend of Good Women'.

Vincentio, (1) the duke in Shakespeare's 'Measure for Measure' (q.v.); (2) a character in his 'The Taming of the Shrew' (q.v.).

Vindication of Natural Society, A, a treatise by E. Burke (q.v.) published in 1756.
   This is one of the first of Burke's published writings. It is an ironical answer to Bolingbroke's indictment of revealed religion, in imitation of his style and in the form of a *reductio ad absurdum*. Bolingbroke had pointed to some of the unfortunate results of religious creeds; Burke examines the various forms of artificial society, despotic, aristocratic, and democratic, and shows that they may all result in tyranny. He shows the evils resulting from artificial laws and the division of society into rich and poor. His conclusion is, 'If you should confess all these things, yet plead the necessity of political institutions, I can argue with equal, perhaps superior, force, concerning the necessity of artificial religion. If you say that natural religion is a sufficient guide without the foreign aid of revelation, on what principle should political laws become necessary?'

Vindication of the Rights of Woman, see Godwin (Mrs. *Mary Wollstonecraft*).

Vindice, see *Vendice*.

Vindobona, in imprints, Vienna.

Vinegar Bible, THE, an edition of the Bible printed by Baskett (q.v.) at Oxford in 1716–17, so called from the substitution or misprint of the word 'vinegar' for 'vineyard' in the heading of Luke xx.

VINER, CHARLES (1678–1756), educated at Hart Hall, Oxford, a jurist who published an 'Abridgment of Law and Equity' in twenty-three volumes (1742–53). He was the founder of the VINERIAN PROFESSORSHIP of common law at Oxford, and of various fellowships and scholarships at the same university.

Vinland, the region of North America where, according to the Norse sagas, a settlement was made by Norsemen in the early years of the 11th cent. It appears to have been in the neighbourhood of Cape Cod. The name is derived from the grapes said to have been found there by the discoverers.

Vintry, THE, according to Stow a part of the bank of the Thames in the City of London where the merchants of Bordeaux landed their wines. It gave its name to one of the wards.

Vinum theologicum, a proverbial expression for exceptionally good wine, due to the monks' reputed fondness for good living. (See e.g. Montaigne, III. xiii; Henri Estienne, 'Apologie pour Hérodote', ch. xxii; Holinshed, i. 282; Rabelais in the earlier editions of 'Gargantua' has 'chopiner théologalement', 'to drink freely of the best wine'.)

Viola, the heroine of Shakespeare's 'Twelfth Night' (q.v.).

Violenta, one of the dramatis personae of Shakespeare's 'All's Well that Ends Well' (q.v.) who appears only once (III. v) in the play and does not speak; sometimes referred to as typical of a nonentity.

Violet-crowned City, THE, Athens, so called by Pindar and Aristophanes, perhaps from the beautiful purple colour sometimes to be seen on the mountains round the city. But the epithet is also applied by the Greek poets to Aphrodite, the Muses, and the Graces.

Virelay, a song or short lyric piece, of a type originating in France in the 14th cent., usually consisting of short lines arranged in stanzas with only two rhymes, the end-rhyme of one stanza being the chief one of the next. [OED.]

Virgidemiarum, Sex Libri, by J. Hall (q.v.), a collection of satires on the abuses of the day, in the spirit of Juvenal. The first volume was published in 1597 and the second in 1598. The 'Virgidemiae' ('Virgidemia' means a 'harvest of rods') deal with literary matters, with institutions and conventions, and, in the 'byting' satires of the last three books, with individuals, whose identity under their pseudonyms was probably clear to contemporaries. Among their subjects are the neglect of learning, the impostures of astrology, ostentatious piety, the character of an avaricious squire, and the servile condition of a tutor. The book was condemned by the High Commission to be burnt.

VIRGIL (PUBLIUS VERGILIUS MARO) (70–19 B.C.), the Roman poet, born at Andes, a village near Mantua. His chief works were the 'Aeneid', the epic poem of the Roman people, recounting the adventures of Aeneas and his Trojans and his settlement in Italy; the 'Georgics', a didactic poem on the cultivation of the soil and the rearing of cattle and bees; and the 'Eclogues' or 'Bucolics', imitations of the pastorals of Theocritus. There are also minor poems attributed on doubtful authority to him, such as 'Culex', 'Ciris', 'Moretum', etc. See also *Sortes Virgilianae* and, below, *Virgil's Fourth Eclogue*.

VIRGIL, POLYDORE, see *Vergil* (*P.*).

Virgil's Fourth Eclogue, written in 40 B.C. and hailing the birth of a child who should bring back the golden age, was interpreted by the early Church and in the Middle Ages as a prophecy of Christ; and Virgil and the Cumaean Sibyl (l. 4, 'Ultima Cumaei venit iam carminis aetas') held a special place in medieval belief (e.g. Virgil was Dante's guide to the gates of Paradise: the Sibyl appears in the 'Dies Irae' hymn). The identity of the child to whom Virgil was really referring has not been fully established: it may have been either a son of Asinius Pollio, to whom the poem is addressed, or more probably the expected child of Octavianus and Scribonia (who was, in fact, a girl, Julia).

Virgil's Gnat, a poem by Spenser (q.v.), adapted from the 'Culex' attributed to Virgil. A shepherd sleeping in the shade is about to be attacked by a serpent, when a gnat, to warn him, stings him on the eyelid. The shepherd crushes the gnat, and sees and kills the serpent. The next night the ghost of the gnat reproaches him for his cruelty. The shepherd, filled with remorse, raises a monument to the gnat.

Virgilia, in Shakespeare's 'Coriolanus' (q.v.), the wife of Coriolanus.

Virgin-Martyr, The, a tragedy by Massinger and Dekker (qq.v.), printed in 1622.

The Emperor Diocletian bids his daughter Artemia choose whom she will marry. She chooses Antoninus, a brave soldier, son of Sapritius, governor of Caesarea. He declines the dangerous honour, being moreover devoted to Dorothea, a maid of the Christian sect, who are at the time subject to persecution. Theophilus, a zealous persecutor, and Harpax, 'an evil spirit', his secretary, betray Antoninus and Dorothea to Artemia, who finds them together, and at once orders them to execution, but presently allows Theophilus to send his daughters to Dorothea to convert her to the pagan religion. The daughters, instead, are converted by Dorothea to Christianity, and on their boldly professing it are killed by their own father. Dorothea, attended by her 'good spirit', Angelo, is subjected to extremes of torture and indignity and finally executed, Antoninus dying at her side. In the last act, Angelo and Harpax, the good and evil spirits, contend for the soul

of Theophilus. Theophilus summoned before Diocletian proclaims his conversion to Christianity, courageously suffers torture, and dies. The same story has been treated in poems by Swinburne and G. M. Hopkins.

Virgin Queen, a name for Queen Elizabeth I of England.

Virginia, a daughter of the centurion, Lucius Virginius. Appius Claudius, the decemvir, became enamoured of her and sought to get possession of her. For this purpose she was claimed by one of his favourites as daughter of a slave, and Appius in the capacity of a judge gave sentence in his favour and delivered her into the hands of his friend. Virginius, informed of these proceedings, arrived from the camp, and plunged a dagger into his daughter's breast to save her from the tyrant. He then rushed to the camp with the bloody knife in his hand. The soldiers, incensed against Appius Claudius, marched to Rome and seized him. But he destroyed himself in prison and averted the execution of the law. This incident led to the abolition of the decemviral power. The story (which is in Livy, iii. 44 et seq.) is the basis of Sheridan Knowles's (q.v.) tragedy 'Virginius', and of Macaulay's (q.v.) lay 'Virginia'.

Virginians, The, a novel by Thackeray (q.v.), published in twenty-four serial numbers, Nov. 1857 to Sept. 1859.

The author relates the fortunes of the descendants of Colonel Henry Esmond (see *Esmond*), in particular of the twin sons, George and Henry, of his daughter Rachel. Rachel has married a Warrington (ancestor of the friend of Pendennis) and survived him as owner of an estate in Virginia. George Warrington, the elder twin, disappears in General Braddock's disastrous expedition against Fort Duquesne, and is believed to have perished. His younger brother, now regarded as the heir of a great property, visits England, and is received with questionable cordiality by his cousins of the Castlewood family—Lord Castlewood, a well-bred cardsharper, his brother Will, a cowardly swindler and bully, and their notorious sisters, in particular the elderly Maria, who inveigles Harry into a promise of marriage. With them is the dominating character of the book, Baroness Bernstein, the Beatrix Esmond of the earlier novel, who has buried her first husband, Tom Tusher, the bishop, and the second, the baron, and is now a stout sardonic old lady with a very dark pair of eyes, who conceives a strong affection for Harry, and influences his fortune for good and evil. Harry, who is a frank, open-handed, but stupid fellow, plunges into a course of dissipation which lands him in a sponging-house, whence he is rescued by his brother George, who has survived his wounds and spent eighteen months as a prisoner in French hands. Harry, being no longer heir to the property, escapes from the clutches of the mercenary Maria, enters the army, serves with distinction under Wolfe, returns to Virginia, and marries the daughter of his mother's housekeeper, Mrs. Mountain. George settles in London and leads a struggling life; for his tyrannical mother, whose love is centred on Harry, cuts off supplies when he marries Theo, the daughter of the gallant but impecunious old General Lambert. In time, however, he inherits the Warrington property, and his troubles come to an end.

The book contains a vivid account of the rakish and unprincipled society of the day, and introduces Wolfe and Washington. The latter part deals with the American War of Independence.

Virginie, see *Paul et Virginie.*

Virgins, THE ELEVEN THOUSAND, the companions of St. Ursula (q.v.) who, according to legend, suffered martyrdom at Cologne in 452.

Virgo, a zodiacal constellation and the sixth sign of the zodiac, which the sun enters about 20 Aug. See *Astraea* and *Icarius* for alternative stories of its origin.

Virtues, one of the orders of the celestial hierarchy. See *Angel.*

Virtues, in scholastic philosophy, comprised the three THEOLOGICAL VIRTUES, faith, hope, and charity, and four CARDINAL VIRTUES, justice, prudence, temperance, and fortitude.

Vishnu, in Hindu mythology, the second god in the triad (Brahma, Vishnu, and Siva), regarded as the preserver. He had many incarnations, which were assumed when some disaster threatened the world. One of the most interesting of these is KRISHNA (q.v.). Another is MATSYA, the fish which saves Manu (q.v.) from the deluge by means of an ark; a third is RAMA, whose exploits are told in the 'Rāmāyana' (q.v.). A fourth is BUDDHA, adopted apparently by the Brahmans in order to place Buddhism in what they regarded as the proper relation to their own religion; for they represent Vishnu as adopting the form of Buddha in order to delude by his teaching the enemies of the gods. Vishnu's wife is LAKSHMI (or SRI). Vishnu shares with Siva the principal worship of modern Hindus, Brahma having fallen into the background.

Vision concerning Piers Plowman, The, see *Piers Plowman.*

Vision of Judgment, A, a poem in hexameters by Southey, published in 1821.

The preface, in defence of this metrical innovation, contains, in a digression, a violent attack on the works of Byron, 'those monstrous combinations of horrors and mockery, lewdness and impiety'.

The poet in a trance sees George III, who had died in 1820, rise from the tomb, and, after receiving from the shade of Perceval the latest intelligence about affairs in England, proceed to the gates of Heaven. The Devil,

accompanied by Wilkes, comes forward to arraign him, but retires discomfited, and the king, after receiving a testimonial from Washington, is admitted to Paradise, where he is greeted by previous English sovereigns, the worthies of England, and finally by his family.

The poem was amusingly parodied by Byron in 'The Vision of Judgment' (q.v.).

Vision of Judgment, The, a satirical poem by Lord Byron (q.v.), published in 'The Liberal' in 1822.

In 1821 had appeared Southey's 'A Vision of Judgment' (q.v.), containing in the preface a violent attack on Byron's works. Byron replied in the appendix to 'The Two Foscari' (q.v.) and in the present satire, a travesty of Southey's poem, in which, besides holding up the poet laureate to derision, he treats the subject of the late king's appearance before the tribunal of heaven very disrespectfully if very humorously. Amid the buffoonery the poem includes a splendid stanza (xxxii) on the meeting of Satan and Michael. The publisher was prosecuted for endangering the public peace by a publication calumniating his late majesty, convicted, and fined.

Vision of Mirza, The, an allegory by Addison (q.v.), published in 'The Spectator' (No. 159). Mirza has a vision of human life in the form of a bridge of three score and ten arches, over which the multitudes are passing, some dropping through concealed trap-doors into the flood beneath.

Vision of Theodore, the Hermit of Teneriffe, The, see *Johnson (S.).*

Visions of the Daughters of Albion, see *Blake.*

Visvakarma, see *Tvastri.*

Vita Nuova, see *Dante.*

VITRUVIUS, POLLIO (*fl.* 40 B.C.), Roman architect and author of 'De architectura', the only surviving classical treatise on architecture. It was much studied by Renaissance and later architects; the first printed edition was published in 1486.

Vittoria, a novel by G. Meredith (q.v.), published in 1867.

The scene is laid in northern Italy in the period of the first rising of 1848, at the inspiration of Mazzini, against the Austrian domination. The author depicts the dissensions and suspicions of the period, and the conflict between the republicans and the supporters of Charles Albert. Against this background we have a continuation of the romance of 'Sandra Belloni' (q.v.). The noble-minded singer throws herself with ardour into the movement for Italian independence and places her voice at the service of the cause, singing under the name of Vittoria in the opera at Milan the song which is to be the signal of Italian revolt. But her connexion with her English friends, particularly with

Wilfrid Pole, now an officer in the Austrian army, brings her under the suspicion of a crazy patriot. This, and the enmity of two women, Anna von Lenkenstein and Violetta d'Isorella, involve her, the gallant Carlo Ammiani, whom she marries, and Wilfrid himself, in a series of dangerous situations, from which she emerges widowed. Merthyr Powys reappears in the character of her devoted and self-sacrificing friend and protector.

Vittoria, The, the only one of Magellan's (q.v.) five ships to complete (in 1521, with 18 men out of the original 265 members of the expedition) the first circumnavigation of the globe. Some perplexity was caused by her arriving one day later than her journal indicated—the converse of what happened to Mr. Phileas Fogg (q.v.), who went round the world the opposite way.

Vittoria Corombona, see *White Divel.*

Vitus, St., the son of a Sicilian nobleman, who is said to have suffered martyrdom under Diocletian. His relics were in the 9th cent. removed to the abbey of Corvey in Saxony, where his cult developed. The saint is especially invoked in cases of *chorea*, the disease otherwise known as St. Vitus's Dance.

Vivian Grey, a novel by Disraeli (q.v.), published in 1826–7. This was the first of Disraeli's novels, written when he was only 21, and is based on 'imagination acting upon knowledge not acquired by experience' but from books and the conversations that he heard.

Vivian Grey, a precocious youth of intelligence, charm, and ambition, thinks that he can achieve success by his wits and audacity. He gains great influence over the marquis of Carabas, a selfish disappointed politician, and builds up round him a faction of discontented peers and M.P.s, by skilfully playing on their foibles. His scheme to create a new party is, however, defeated by the machinations of the treacherous Mrs. Lorraine. He is challenged by Cleveland, the designated leader of the new party, who has been led to regard him as a traitor. In the duel Cleveland is killed, and Vivian Grey leaves the country. A succession of adventures on the Continent, in love and politics, leaves him with the 'satisfaction of knowing himself to be the most unfortunate and unhappy being that ever existed'.

Vivien, see *Lady of the Lake.*

Vogelweide, Walther von der, see *Minnesingers.*

Volapük, an artificial language, chiefly composed of materials from European tongues, invented in 1879 by a German priest, Johann M. Schleyer, as a means of international communication.

Volpone, or *The Fox,* a comedy by Jonson (q.v.), first acted in 1606 and printed in 1607.

Volpone, a rich Venetian without children, feigns that he is dying, in order to draw gifts from his would-be heirs. Mosca, his parasite and confederate, persuades each of these in turn that he is to be the heir, and thus extracts costly presents from them; one of them, Corvino, even sacrifices his wife to Volpone in hope of the inheritance. Finally Volpone overreaches himself. To enjoy the discomfiture of the vultures who are awaiting his death, he makes over his property by will to Mosca and pretends to be dead. Mosca takes advantage of the position to blackmail Volpone; and Voltore, a lawyer, who has aided Volpone in the infamous conspiracy against Corvino's wife, finding himself defrauded of his expected reward, reveals the whole matter to the senate; whereupon Volpone, Mosca, and Corvino receive the punishment they merit. Sir Politick Would-Be, the English traveller in Italy, with his absurd schemes for supplying Venice with red herrings and detecting by means of onions and bellows whether there is plague on a ship, and Lady Politick Would-Be, the voluble female pedant, have little connexion with the main plot. The names of the principal characters, Volpone (the fox), Mosca (the fly), Voltore (the vulture), Corbaccio (the crow), Corvino (the raven), are significant of the parts they play.

It was under the name of Volpone that Godolphin was attacked by Dr. Sacheverell in 1710.

Volscius, Prince, a character in the duke of Buckingham's 'The Rehearsal' (q.v.). He is torn between love and honour, and comes on the stage with one boot on and one off, his legs illustrating his distraction.

Volsung, in Icelandic legend, a descendant of Odin, and the father of Sigmund and grandfather of Sigurd. See *Volsunga Saga.*

Volsung, Sigurd the, see *Sigurd the Volsung.*

Volsunga Saga, a prose version of a lost cycle of heroic songs of which fragments survive in the poetic Edda (q.v.), dealing with the families of the Volsungs and the Niblungs. It has been translated by W. Morris and E. Magnusson (1888). For the treatment in it of the story of Sigurd and Brunhild, see *Sigurd the Volsung.*

VOLTAIRE (1694–1778), the name assumed by François Marie Arouet and by which he is generally known. He was born in Paris, was educated by Jesuits, began writing early, and, after two spells of detention in the Bastille, spent the years 1726–9 in exile in England. The chief literary fruit of this sojourn was his 'Lettres philosophiques' (1734) in which he discussed various aspects of English life and criticized, by comparison, French institutions. Being exposed thereby to danger of arrest he took refuge at Cirey near the frontier of Lorraine, at the house of Mme du Châtelet, where he spent the next ten years. In 1750, at the pressing invitation

of Frederick II, he took up his residence at
Potsdam, but king and philosopher soon
disagreed, and in 1753 Voltaire settled at
Ferney close to the Swiss frontier. He
returned to Paris when 84 years old and
enjoyed there a brief spell of glory before his
death.

His literary activity had been prodigious
and varied. He had written philosophical
works, such as the 'Dictionnaire philoso-
phique' (1764), histories such as the 'Siècle
de Louis XIV' (1751), tragedies (the best of
a poor dramatic age, of which 'Zaïre' and
'Alzire' are perhaps the most notable),
philosophical tales (including the famous
'Candide', 1759), an indifferent epic ('La
Henriade'), and an unseemly mock epic on
Joan of Arc, 'La Pucelle', besides innumerable letters, pamphlets, dialogues, and pieces
of light verse, of which his felicity of expression made him a perfect master. He repeatedly condemned Shakespeare for lack of
taste and ignorance of the classical rules of
the drama, notably in his 'Lettre à l'Académie'
(1776; see also *Montagu, Mrs. E.*).

The greater part of his work was made the
vehicle for his philosophical views. While
affirming the existence of the deity, he condemned all dogmatic religions, especially
Catholicism and its priesthood, attributing to
these an intolerance and superstition which
he regarded as the worst scourges of humanity
('*Écrasons l'infâme!*'). The dominant trait
of his writings on political as well as religious
subjects is lack of respect for existing institutions and contempt for authority. He was
thus a dissolvent influence and prepared
the way for the Revolution. His hatred
of intolerance and injustice was shown in
practical form by the arduous campaigns he
undertook for the rehabilitation of Jean Calas
and other victims of religious and political
persecution.

A biography of Voltaire by Lord Morley
was published in 1872.

Volumnia, in Shakespeare's 'Coriolanus'
(q.v.), the mother of Coriolanus.

Volundr, see *Wayland the Smith.*

Voluspa Saga, a poem included in the
Elder Edda (see *Edda*), describing the creation and destruction of the world.

VON HÜGEL, FRIEDRICH, *Baron of the
Holy Roman Empire* (1852–1925), Roman
Catholic theologian and philosopher. He was
born in Florence and after a cosmopolitan
education settled in England in 1867. He
studied natural science, philosophy, and
religious history, adopting the critical views
of the Old Testament. In 1905 he founded
the London Society for the Study of Religion,
which brought him into touch with thinkers
and scholars of the most diverse views. His
works include 'The Mystical Element of
Religion' (1908), 'Eternal Life' (1912), and
'The Reality of God' (published posthumously, 1931).

Voodoo, a body of superstitious beliefs and
practices, including sorcery, serpent-worship,
and sacrificial rites, African in origin, current
among Negroes in the West Indies and
Southern United States.

VORAGINE, JACOBUS A, see *Golden
Legend.*

Vorticism, a literary and artistic movement
based on Cubism (q.v.), founded by Wyndham Lewis (q.v.).

Vortigern, a legendary king of Britain in
the 5th cent., who, it is said, usurped the
crown. About 449 he invited the Jutes to
England to aid him against the Picts, and,
according to legend, married Rowena,
daughter of their leader, Hengist; after which
the Jutes declined to go away again. The
story is in Layamon's 'Brut', ll. 14255–396.

Vortigern and Rowena, a pseudo-Shakespearian play forged by W. H. Ireland (q.v.),
on the story of Vortigern (q.v.).

VOSSIUS, GERHARD JOHN (1577–1649),
and ISAAC (1618–89), his son, eminent
Dutch scholars. The father, who was invited
to England and made a canon of Canterbury,
was professor of history at Amsterdam,
and author of 'Historia Pelagiana'. The
son came to England and was a canon of
Windsor 1673–89. He published editions of
Catullus and Juvenal and 'Observations' on
classical subjects.

Vox Clamantis, a poem of 10,000 lines in
Latin elegiacs by Gower (q.v.), recounting
the Peasants' Rising of 1381 and exposing the
corruption of contemporary society, especially in its political aspect.

Vrain-Lucas, see *Lucas (V.-).*

Vronsky, COUNT ALEXIS, in Tolstoy's 'Anna
Karenina', the lover of Anna.

Vulcan or MULCIBER, the Roman equivalent
of the Greek god HEPHAESTUS. He was the
god of fire and the patron of workers in
metal. Hephaestus is represented as the son
of Hera, and was hurled from Olympus by
Zeus when he took his mother's part in a
conjugal quarrel. He fell for nine days and
dropped on the island of Lemnos, breaking
his leg and remaining thereafter lame. He
erected forges on earth, indicated by the
presence of volcanoes, and wrought many
ingenious pieces of mechanism. He is said
to have made, at the request of Zeus, the first
woman that ever appeared on earth, known as
Pandora (q.v.). Aphrodite (Venus) was given
him for his wife, but she was unfaithful to
him. Her amour with Ares (Mars) was
detected by means of a net prepared by
Hephaestus. In 'Iliad' xviii he forges, at the
request of Thetis, the armour of Achilles.
For Milton's fine lines on his fall from
heaven, see P.L. i. 740 et seq.

Vulgar Errors, the usual name for *Pseudodoxia Epidemica, or, Enquiries into very many*

received Tenents and commonly presumed Truths, a treatise by Sir T. Browne (q.v.), published in 1646.

This was the author's longest work. He first analyses the causes of mistaken popular beliefs, attributing them to the common infirmity of human nature and the inclination of mankind to error, to false deductions, to credulity, to adherence to authority, and finally to the endeavours of Satan. He then ranges over a vast number of legends and beliefs, discussing them with a pleasant irony and quaint fancy; for instance, that crystal is ice strongly congealed, that an elephant has no joints (based 'on the gross and somewhat cylindrical composure of the legs'), that snails have no eyes, and the popular notions about mandrakes and the salutation of a person who has just sneezed.

Vulgate, THE, from the Latin *vulgatus*, 'made public or common', a term applied more particularly to St. Jerome's Latin version of the Bible completed in 405. The CLEMENTINE text of this, a recension made by order of Clement VIII (1592–1605), is the authorized text of the Roman Catholic Church. See *Bible*.

Vye, EUSTACIA, a character in Hardy's 'The Return of the Native' (q.v.).

W

WACE OF JERSEY (*d*. after 1171), wrote *c*. 1154 a 'Roman de Brut' or 'Geste des Bretons', dedicated to Eleanor, queen of Henry II, embodying the Arthurian legends, based on Geoffrey of Monmouth (q.v.). This was one of the sources of Layamon's 'Brut' (see *Layamon*). Wace also wrote a 'Roman de Rou' (i.e. Rollo) or 'Geste des Normands', a history of the dukes of Normandy. He was made canon of Bayeux by Henry II.

Wacht am Rhein, Die, 'The Watch on the Rhine', a German national song of which the words were composed in 1840 by Schneckenburger, and which became very popular during the Franco-German War.

Wackles, MRS. and the MISSES MELISSA, SOPHY, and JANE, in Dickens's 'The Old Curiosity Shop' (q.v.), kept a 'Ladies' Seminary' at Chelsea.

Wade, GEORGE (1673–1748), an Irishman who rose to be field-marshal in 1743. He was commander-in-chief in England in 1745, but he was superseded for failing to stop the advance of Prince Charles Edward. He had been sent to the Highlands in 1724, where he was celebrated for the military roads that he constructed. The famous distich

Had you seen these roads before they were made
You'd hold up your hands and bless General Wade

does not contain a 'bull' (as generally supposed) because a 'made road' differs from a road (G. Sheldon, 'From Trackway to Turnpike', 1930).

Wade, MISS, a character in Dickens's 'Little Dorrit' (q.v.), a suspicious, venomous woman who entices away Tattycoram from the Meagles family.

Wade's boat, in Chaucer's 'The Merchant's Tale' (see *Canterbury Tales*), l. 179:

And eek thise olde widwes, God it woot, They conne so muchel craft on Wades boot.

According to Skeat's note Wade was a famous hero of antiquity who is mentioned in various poems and in Malory's 'Morte Darthur', VII. ix. He was the son of Wayland the Smith (q.v.) and the king's daughter, and had a magic boat called Wingelock (French *Guingelot*, see *Gringolet*). 'Old widows', says Chaucer in effect, 'know too much of the craft of Wade's boat; they can fly from place to place in a minute, and if charged with any misdemeanour, will swear they were a mile away'. A 12th–13th-cent. English reference to Wade is recorded in 'The Academy' (1896), i. 137, 157.

Wadman, WIDOW, in Sterne's 'Tristram Shandy' (q.v.), a comely 'daughter of Eve', who occupies the house and garden next to that of 'my Uncle Toby' and tries to secure him for a husband.

Waft of Death, a phrase used by G. Fox (q.v.) in his 'Journal' for the year 1658. He writes: 'And after this I mett him [Oliver Cromwell] riding into Hampton Court park, and before I came at him he was riding in the head of his life guard, and I saw and felt a waft of death go forth against him that he looked like a dead man.'

Wagg, MR., in Thackeray's 'Vanity Fair' (q.v.), a satellite of Lord Steyne. His name has allusion to Theodore Hook (q.v.).

Waggoner, The, a poem by Wordsworth (q.v.), composed in 1805, and published in 1819 with dedication to Charles Lamb.

It tells how Benjamin the Waggoner, driving home his team of eight horses through the night among the Lakeland hills, escapes the temptation of the Swan Inn, but falls victim to that of the Cherry-Tree, and loses his place in consequence. But no one else can drive the team, and Lakeland loses both waggoner and wain.

Wagner, the attendant of Faust in Marlowe's 'Doctor Faustus' (q.v.) and in Goethe's 'Faust'.

WAGNER, (WILHELM) RICHARD (1813–83), German musician and poet, who by the combination of these twin arts in his great music-dramas ('Der Ring des Nibelungen' (q.v., 1853–70), 'Tristan und Isolde' (1865), the 'Meistersinger' (1868), 'Parsifal' (1882), etc.). and also by his critical work, 'Oper und Drama' (1851), exerted a powerful influence on German music and literature. He created, or at least reformed, musical drama by combining the spoken drama with the old 'opera' in which music was the sole aim. The philosophy underlying his work, which uses myth and legend, was deeply influenced by Schopenhauer (q.v.). A distinguishing characteristic is his exploitation of the *leit-motif*. He wrote his own libretti.

Wahabi, a follower of Abd-el-Wahhab, a Muslim reformer (1691–1787) whose sect flourished in central Arabia.

Wainamoinen, the principal hero of the 'Kalevala' (q.v.), the god of music and poetry.

WAINEWRIGHT, THOMAS GRIFFITHS (1794–1852), wrote art-critiques for 'The London Magazine' during 1820–3 and exhibited at the Royal Academy. He was a forger and a poisoner, and died a convict in Tasmania. He was the original of Varney in Bulwer Lytton's 'Lucretia' and suggested to Dickens his sketch, 'Hunted Down'. He was a friend of C. Lamb and the subject of an essay by O. Wilde (qq.v.).

Wakefield, EDWARD GIBBON (1796–1862), a colonial statesman, who from 1829 devoted himself to the reform of the administration of the Australian colonies. He had been in 1826–9 in prison for abducting an heiress; wrote 'The Art of Colonization' in 1833; and went with Lord Durham to Canada, as unofficial adviser, in 1838; he had some share in writing Lord Durham's famous 'Report'. He opposed the transportation system and procured the discontinuance of the wasteful free grants of land to settlers. Land was to be sold to these at a fairly high price by the Crown, and part of the proceeds employed to assist emigration. He secured the formation of the South Australian Association in 1834, and of the New Zealand Association in 1837, to organize the colonization of those countries. He himself emigrated to Wellington in 1853.

WAKEFIELD, GILBERT (1756–1801), educated at Jesus College, Cambridge, edited the 'Georgics' (1788), 'Horace' (1794),

'Lucretius' (1796–9), and some Greek plays, and published 'Silva critica' in 1789. He was a vigorous controversial writer, and conceived a violent hatred of Pitt and of Porson. He attacked the latter's 'Hecuba' in a 'Diatribe Extemporalis' in 1797. He also edited some English authors, including Pope. He was imprisoned for a seditious pamphlet, 1799–1801.

Wakefield, HARRY, the English drover in Scott's 'The Two Drovers' (q.v.).

Wakefield Plays, see *Mysteries*.

Wakem, MR. and PHILIP, characters in George Eliot's 'The Mill on the Floss' (q.v.).

Walbrook or WALLBROOK, London, a stream that had its source in the fens beyond Moorgate (q.v.), passed through the city wall, and, flowing under many bridges, divided the city in two, issuing into the Thames at Dowgate. The present street called Walbrook roughly follows part of its course.

The name is not taken from the city wall; it is *weall-broc*, the stream of the Britons.

Walcheren Expedition, a disastrous expedition, directed against the French, undertaken in 1809. The British troops under Lord Chatham (eldest son of the great Chatham), with a naval force under Sir Richard Strachan, reached Walcheren, an island at the mouth of the Scheldt, and took Flushing, but failed to achieve anything else, and the expedition was obliged to return after suffering heavy losses from fever. The idea of such an expedition was excellent; it was probably suggested by the French exile, Dumouriez. Antwerp, where a new French fleet was being built, was the objective; and when the expedition was being planned Austria was still holding out on the Danube. But Castlereagh ought to have known that the islands at the mouth of the Scheldt were notoriously unhealthy and that there was no drinkable water there. And the expedition started too late (28 July), when Napoleon had already won Wagram. The incident inspired the well-known epigram (there are various readings of the first line):

The Earl of Chatham, with his sword drawn,
Stood waiting for Sir Richard Strachan;
Sir Richard, longing to be at 'em,
Stood waiting for the Earl of Chatham.

Waldeck, MARTIN, the subject of a legend from the German interposed in Scott's 'The Antiquary' (q.v.), a charcoal-burner enriched by gold obtained from the demon of the Harz Mountains, and brought to an evil end by his wealth.

Waldegrave, HENRY, in Campbell's 'Gertrude of Wyoming' (q.v.), the husband of Gertrude.

Walden, or Life in the Woods, a narrative by H. D. Thoreau (q.v.), published in 1854.

Waldenses or WALDENSIANS, the adherents

of a religious sect which originated in the south of France about 1170 through the preaching of Peter Waldo, a rich merchant of Lyons. They rejected the authority of the pope and various rites, and were excommunicated in 1184 and subjected to persecution. But they survived and eventually became a separately organized church, which associated itself with the Protestant Reformation of the 16th cent. and still exists, chiefly in northern Italy and the adjacent regions. Their persecution by the duchess-regent of Savoy in 1655 led to Milton's noble sonnet, 'Avenge, O Lord, thy slaughtered saints', and caused Cromwell to insist on his new ally, France, putting an instant stop to the massacre. In French the Waldenses are called *Vaudois*.

Waldhere, the name given to two short fragments (11th cent.) of an OE. epic poem preserved in the Royal Library at Copenhagen.

We know from other sources that Waldhere was the son of a king of Aquitaine, who was given up to Attila, king of the Huns, and became one of his generals, but escaped with Hiltgund (daughter of a king of Burgundy), to whom he had been betrothed when young. In the course of their flight they are waylaid, and Waldhere, after slaying his assailants in a first encounter, is surprised and wounded on the following day, but is able to continue his journey and is finally married to Hiltgund. The fragments give speeches that pass just before the second fight.

WALEY, ARTHUR DAVID (1889–1966), poet and authority on Chinese and Japanese literature. He is probably best known for his translations of Chinese poetry which he first published in 1918, and for his translation of the Japanese novel, 'The Tale of Genji' (q.v.). His other works include 'The Nō Plays of Japan' (1921), 'The Pillow-Book of Sei Shōnagon' (1928), 'The Analects of Confucius' (1938), 'Monkey' (1942, tr. of a 16th-cent. Chinese novel), 'The Poetry and Career of Li Po, A.D. 701–762' (1951), and a miscellany, 'The Secret History of the Mongols and other Pieces' (1964).

Walker, HOOKEY, a derisive exclamation expressive of incredulity. It is not unlikely that it was derived from some hook-nosed person of the name of Walker, but the various stories told to explain it have probably no foundation. [OED.]

WALKER, THOMAS (1784–1836), of Trinity College, Cambridge; called to the bar 1812; magistrate of Lambeth Police Court 1829. He is noted as the author of a weekly periodical, 'The Original', of which twenty-nine numbers appeared (20 May to 2 Dec. 1835) up to his death in Jan. 1836. Each number contains short articles on a variety of subjects; its purpose was 'to treat, as forcibly, perspicuously, and concisely as each subject and my own ability will allow, of whatever is most interesting and important

in Religion and Politics, in Morals and Manners, and in our Habits and Customs', and is especially remembered for his admirable papers on health and gastronomy.

Walking Stewart, see *Stewart (F.).*

Walkinshaw, CLAUD, his sons, and his wife LEDDY GRIPPY, characters in Galt's 'The Entail' (q.v.).

Wall, THE ROMAN, see *Hadrian* and *Severus.*

Wall Street, in Lower New York, a short street running from Broadway to the East River, the financial centre of the city, where the principal banks and the Stock Exchange are situated.

WALLACE, ALFRED RUSSEL (1823–1913), was born at Usk in Monmouthshire, and educated at the Grammar School at Hertford. He left school at the age of 14, studied surveying, was for a time apprentice to a watchmaker, and schoolmaster at Leicester, where he made 'the acquaintance of Henry Walter Bates, the naturalist. In 1848 he joined Bates in a trip to the Amazon for the collection of specimens. The expedition, including the destruction of their ship by fire on the homeward voyage, is described in Wallace's 'Travels on the Amazon and Rio Negro' (1853). A further voyage to the Malay Archipelago (1854–62) is described in his 'Malay Archipelago' (1869). It was in 1858 during an attack of fever at Ternate in the Moluccas that the idea of natural selection as the solution of the problem of evolution flashed upon him, and he at once communicated it to Darwin. The outcome, a testimony to the generosity of both the great biologists, was the famous joint communication to the Linnean Society on the theory of evolution. Among numerous works and scientific papers Wallace published in 1876 his 'Geographical Distribution of Animals', in 1889 the semi-popular 'Darwinism', in 1898 'The Wonderful Century', in 1903 'Man's Place in the Universe', and in 1905 his autobiography, 'My Life'.

WALLACE, EDGAR (1875–1932), a very prolific author, one of the masters of the pure 'thriller', among whose numerous works it is almost impossible to select the most notable. A few landmarks for the inquiring social and literary historian are: 'The Four Just Men' (1905) and its followers, 'Sanders of the River', 'The Angel of Terror', 'The Green Archer', 'The Fellowship of the Frog', 'The Dark Eyes of London', 'The Hand of Power' (novels); 'The Terror'(1927), 'The Squeaker' (1927), 'The Calendar', 'On the Spot'(plays).

Wallace, SIR WILLIAM (1272?–1305), the Scottish patriot of the time of Edward I, who devoted his life to resistance to the English and was finally captured by treachery and executed in London, is the subject of a long poem by Henry the Minstrel (q.v.), 'Blind Harry'.

WALLACE, WILLIAM (1844–97), educated at St. Andrews and Balliol College, Oxford, succeeded T. H. Green as professor of moral philosophy at Oxford (1882–97). Wallace devoted himself largely to the elucidation of Hegel's thought, and his principal publications were 'The Logic of Hegel' (1874), translated from Hegel's 'Encyclopaedia', and 'Hegel's Philosophy of Mind' (1894). After his death appeared his 'Lectures on Natural Theology and Ethics' (1898). His 'Life of Arthur Schopenhauer' appeared in 1890.

Wallace Collection, THE, named after Sir Richard Wallace (1818–90), whose widow (d. 1897) bequeathed it to the nation. The nucleus of the collection was formed by his father Richard, fourth marquess of Hertford (1800–70), who lived most of his life in Paris, where he collected particularly French 18th-cent. works of art. Sir Richard added medieval and Renaissance works, and armour and plate. The collection is housed in Hertford House, Manchester Square, London.

Wallenstein, ALBRECHT EUSEBIUS VON (1583–1634), an Austrian general celebrated for his campaigns in the Thirty Years War (q.v.). After many victories he was defeated by Gustavus Adolphus at Lützen in 1632. He now prepared to abandon the Imperial cause; but the emperor, Ferdinand II, suspecting his intention, removed him from his command. Wallenstein was murdered by some of his officers when he was believed to be on the point of going over to the Swedes. His career is the subject of a great historical trilogy by Schiller (q.v.), of which the two last parts were translated by S. T. Coleridge (q.v.).

WALLER, EDMUND (1606–87), inherited Beaconsfield in Buckinghamshire, and was educated at Eton and King's College, Cambridge. In 1631 he married a London heiress, who died in 1634. He entered parliament early and was at first an active member of the opposition. Later he became a Royalist, and in 1643 was leader in a plot ('Waller's plot') to seize London for Charles I. For this he was imprisoned, fined, and banished, but, on betraying his associates, spared execution. He made his peace with Cromwell in 1651 and returned to England. He was restored to royal favour on the Restoration and was again member of parliament. After the death of his first wife he had paid unsuccessful court to Lady Dorothy Sidney, whom he celebrated in poems as 'Sacharissa', and married Mary Bracey as his second wife in 1644. Waller was a precocious poet. He wrote, probably as early as 1625, a complimentary piece on 'His Majesty's Escape at St. Andere' (Prince Charles's escape from shipwreck at Santander) in heroic couplets, one of the first examples of a form that prevailed in English poetry for some two

hundred years. His verse, much of which is occupied with praise of 'Sacharissa' (and also of Lady Carlisle and others), is of a polished simplicity, and was highly commended by Dryden. Some of his best work belongs to his later period: the 'Panegyric to My Lord Protector', the 'Instructions to a Painter' on the battle of Sole Bay, and 'Of the Last Verses in the Book', containing the famous lines,

> The Soul's dark cottage, battered and decayed,
> Lets in new light through chinks that time hath made.

His earlier pieces, 'On a Girdle' and 'Go, lovely Rose!', are also well known. He published six cantos 'Of Divine Love' in 1685.

WALLIS, JOHN (1616–1703), the mathematician, was educated at Felsted School and Emmanuel College, Cambridge, and was Savilian professor of geometry at Oxford, 1649–1703. He was one of the founders of the Royal Society. His famous 'Arithmetica Infinitorum', which contained the germs of the differential calculus, was published in 1655.

WALPOLE, HORACE, *fourth earl of Orford* (1717–97), fourth son of Sir Robert Walpole, was educated at Eton and King's College, Cambridge. He travelled in France and Italy with Gray (q.v.) in 1739–41, and was M.P. successively for Callington, Castle Rising, and Lynn from 1741 to 1767. In 1747 he settled at Strawberry Hill, Twickenham, which he made into 'a little Gothic castle', and in it collected articles of virtu and established a printing-press. Here he printed Gray's two Pindaric odes, in 1758 his own 'Catalogue of Royal and Noble Authors', in 1762–80 his 'Anecdotes of Painting in England' (which still retain importance), and in 1765 his 'Catalogue of Engravers in England'. He also printed a description of his house and collections, and other works (prose and verse) and editions. Walpole visited Paris in 1765, 1767, and 1775. He published 'The Castle of Otranto' (q.v.) in 1764, and 'Historic Doubts on Richard III' and 'The Mysterious Mother' (q.v.) in 1768. He befriended Kitty Clive, the actress, and Mary Berry, the authoress, and her sister Agnes. He succeeded his nephew in the earldom in 1791. His collected 'Works' were published in 1798. Of his voluminous correspondence, a series of 'Miscellaneous Letters' formed vol. v of the 'Works', and collections of 'Letters' appeared in 1820, 1840, 1857–9 (Peter Cunningham), and 1903–5 (Mrs. Paget Toynbee, 16 vols.), with supplementary volumes in 1918 by Paget Toynbee. The Yale edition of Walpole's 'Correspondence', planned for publication in c. 50 vols., began to appear in 1937 (W. S. Lewis et al.). It is on his letters that Walpole's literary reputation principally rests. They are remarkable both for their charm and their autobio-

graphical, social, and political interest. They
extend from 1732 to 1797, and display his
affectionate disposition and cheerful fortitude
in sickness. His principal correspondents
were Sir Horace Mann, his own cousin
Henry Seymour Conway (Field Marshal), the
countess of Upper Ossory, George Montagu,
and, in his later days, Miss Berry. His letters
to Madame du Deffand were destroyed by his
wish. Hers to him were edited by Mrs.
Toynbee in 1912.

WALPOLE, Sir HUGH (SEYMOUR)
(1884–1941), novelist, among whose works
are: 'Maradick at Forty' (1910), 'Mr. Perrin
and Mr. Traill' (1911), 'Prelude to Adventure'
(1912), 'Fortitude' (1913), 'The Dark Forest'
(1916), 'The Green Mirror' (1918), 'The
Cathedral' (1922); and an historical sequence
comprising 'Rogue Herries' (1930), 'Judith
Paris' (1931), and 'The ·Fortress' (1933).

Walpole, Sir ROBERT, *first earl of Orford*
(1676–1745), educated at Eton and King's
College, Cambridge, was M.P. for Castle
Rising (1701–2) and King's Lynn (1702–12
and 1713–42), and was soon recognized as a
great man of business and a leader of the
Whig party. He was secretary of war, 1708–
10, and treasurer of the navy, 1710–11.
After the fall of the Whig ministry he was, in
1712, expelled from the House of Commons
and imprisoned in the Tower on a vexatious
charge of venality in office. He was prime
minister and chancellor of the exchequer,
1715–17, and again 1721–42, during which
periods he did much to encourage trade, both
international and colonial, by removing import and export duties and restrictions. He
followed a policy of union with France and
held the view that England's best interest lay
in European peace. He vainly resisted the
clamour for war with Spain in 1738–9 and
made the mistake of remaining in office when
the demand proved irresistible. Walpole
was the first minister since the Restoration
who made a special study of finance and
commerce; he laid the foundations of free
trade and modern colonial policy. He was the
father of Horace Walpole (q.v.). His grandson sold his fine collection of pictures to the
Tsarina Catherine II.

WALPOLE, Sir SPENCER (1839–1907),
author of a 'History of England from 1815
to 1856' and 'The History of Twenty-five
Years (1856–1880)', a continuation of the
former, published respectively in 1878–90
and 1904–8 (the last-named work was incomplete, only four volumes being published); also of a 'Life of Lord Russell' (1889).

Walpurgis Night, so called from St. Walpurgis (an English nun who in the 8th cent.
helped to convert the Germans to Christianity), the night before 1 May, when, according
to popular superstition in Germany, the
witches and the Devil hold a festival on the
Brocken in the Harz Mountains. It is the
subject of a scene in Goethe's 'Faust', Pt. I.

WALSH, WILLIAM (1663–1708), poet.
His critical judgement was valued by Dryden
and he gave early encouragement to Pope.
'The Despairing Lover' is his best-known
poem.

Walter Lorraine, the name of the first novel
written by Pendennis (q.v.).

Walther von der Vogelweide, see *Minne-*
singers.

WALTON, IZAAK (1593–1683), was born
at Stafford, was apprenticed to an ironmonger in London, and later carried on
trade there on his own account. He was the
friend of Donne, of Sir Henry Wotton, and
of Bishops Morley, Sanderson, and King.
The latter part of his life he spent at Winchester, where his son-in-law was prebendary,
and there he died. He published his biographies, of John Donne (q.v.) in 1640, of
Sir Henry Wotton (q.v.) in 1651, of Richard
Hooker (q.v.) in 1665, of George Herbert
(q.v.) in 1670, and of Bishop Sanderson in
1678. The 'Compleat Angler' (q.v.), by
which he is chiefly known, first appeared in
1653, largely rewritten in the second edition
(1655). See also *Cotton* (*C.*).

Walton, Sir JOHN, in Scott's 'Castle
Dangerous' (q.v.), governor of Douglas
Castle.

Walton, Sir WILLIAM TURNER (1902–   ),
composer, educated at the Cathedral Choir
School and Christ Church, Oxford. He became
closely associated with the Sitwells (qq.v.)
and his early composition 'Façade' (1923), 'an
entertainment for reciting] voice and instruments', consisted of poems of Edith Sitwell
read to the accompaniment of flute, clarinet,
trumpet, saxophone, 'cello, and percussion.
His other works include the overture 'Portsmouth Point' (1926), 'Sinfonia Concertante
for Piano and Orchestra' (1928), 'Belshazzar's
Feast' (1931), an oratorio with text by Osbert
Sitwell based on the Book of Daniel, 'Symphony' (1935), 'Crown Imperial', the well-
known Coronation March (1937), and a
Chaucerian opera, 'Troilus and Cressida'
(1954), as well as a number of concertos and
symphonies. He has also written music for
the screen versions of 'Henry V', 'Hamlet',
and 'Richard III'.

Walwain, see *Gawain.*

Wamba, in Scott's 'Ivanhoe' (q.v.), 'the
son of Witless', the devoted and heroic
jester of Cedric the Saxon.

Wanderer, The, an OE. poem of 115 lines,
included in the 'Exeter Book' (q.v.), telling of
the wanderings of a man who has lost his lord.
He dreams of his former happiness, and reflects on the vicissitudes of human life. See
also *The Seafarer.*

Wanderer, The, a moral and descriptive
poem in five cantos by R. Savage (q.v.),
published in 1729; designed to prove that

man may owe
The fruits of bliss to bursting clouds of woe.

But the execution of the plan is difficult to follow. Johnson, who praises the poem, admits that it is not so much 'a regular fabrick' as 'a heap of shining materials thrown together by accident'.

Wandering Jew, THE, a Jew condemned to wander about the world until Christ's second coming, because, according to the legend, as Christ bore the cross to Calvary, the Jew chid him, and urged him to go faster.

A pamphlet was published at Leyden in 1602 relating that Paulus von Eizen, bishop of Schleswig, had in 1542 met a Jew named Ahasuerus, who admitted that he was the Jew in question. The story became popular, and many instances of the appearance of the Wandering Jew are recorded from the 16th to the 19th cent.

But a somewhat similar story is told by the English chronicler, Matthew Paris (q.v.), at a much earlier date. An Armenian archbishop visited England in 1228, and, while being entertained at St. Albans, was asked if he had ever seen or heard of Joseph, who was present at the Crucifixion, and was said to be still alive, as a testimony to the Christian faith. The prelate replied that the man had recently dined at his own table. He had been Pontius Pilate's porter, by name Cartaphilus, who, when they were dragging Jesus from the Judgement Hall, had struck him on the back, saying, 'Go faster, Jesus, why dost thou linger?', to which Jesus replied, 'I indeed am going, but thou shalt tarry till I come.' This man had been converted soon after and named Joseph. He lived for ever, and was now a very grave and holy person. It is noteworthy that Matthew Paris was a monk at St. Albans at the time of the archbishop's visit. About 1240–50 Philip Mousket, afterwards bishop of Tournay, wrote his rhymed chronicle, which contains a similar account of the Jew, derived from the same Armenian prelate (Baring-Gould, 'Curious Myths').

The legend of the Wandering Jew has been made the subject of many German works, and Goethe designed a poem on the subject. Eugène Sue's 'Le Juif errant' introduces it. There is a ballad in Percy's 'Reliques' in which the Wandering Jew is described as having been a shoemaker, who refused to allow Christ, on the way to Calvary, to rest upon a stone. George Croly (1780–1860) wrote a romance, 'Salathiel' (1829), on the same subject.

Wandering Willie, Willie Steenson, the blind fiddler in Scott's 'Redgauntlet' (q.v.). 'Wandering Willie's Tale' is an episode in the novel, an example of the author's successful use of the supernatural.

'Wandering Willie' is also the name of a song by Burns.

Wanderings of Cain, The, a prose-poem by S. T. Coleridge, written in 1798. The work

was undertaken in conjunction with Wordsworth, who was to have written the first canto. Coleridge wrote the second canto; but the work was then abandoned, and 'The Ancient Mariner' was written instead.

WANLEY, HUMFREY (1672–1726), began life as a draper's assistant at Coventry, but read widely and went to Oxford in 1695, and was an assistant in the Bodleian Library in 1696. He displayed remarkable skill in palaeography and assisted Edward Bernard in the preparation of the 'Catalogi Librorum Manuscriptorum Angliae et Hiberniae' (1697). He produced in 1705 a catalogue of Anglo-Saxon manuscripts, which is still the standard work. He was librarian to the first and second earls of Oxford, and began the catalogue of the Harleian MSS., a work on which he was engaged when he died.

WANLEY, NATHANIEL (1634–80), divine and compiler. He published 'The Wonders of the Little World' (1678, an anecdotal treatise on mankind), and other works. His poems have been edited by L. C. Martin (1928).

Wans Dyke or WODEN'S DYKE, a defensive entrenchment of Roman or Romano-British construction running from Savernake nearly to the Bristol Channel.

Wantley, The Dragon of, see *Dragon of Wantley.*

Wapping, adjoining the Tower of London, 'the usual place of execution for hanging of pirates and sea-rovers, at the low water mark there to remain till three tides had overflowed them', but after the removal of the gallows further off 'a continual street or filthy straight passage, with alleys of small tenements or cottages builded, inhabited by sailors and victuallers, along by the river Thames almost, to Radcliff' (Stow), later known as the Ratcliffe Highway.

War and Peace, a novel by Tolstoy (q.v.).

Warbeck, PERKIN (1474–99), the impostor who gave himself out for Richard, duke of York, son of Edward IV; in fact the son of John Osbeck or De Werbecque, controller of Tournay. He was welcomed in Scotland by James IV, and married Lady Catherine Gordon in 1495. He landed in Cornwall in 1497, proclaiming himself King Richard IV, was taken prisoner, confessed his imposture, and was hanged. For Ford's play see *Perkin Warbeck.*

WARBURTON, BARTHOLOMEW ELLIOTT, see *Crescent and the Cross.*

Warburton, JOHN (1682–1759), herald and antiquary. He was an indefatigable collector and owned many rare manuscripts. Most of the rare Elizabethan and Jacobean plays in his possession were through his own 'carelessness and the ignorance' of Betsy Baker, his servant, 'unluckily burned or put under pye bottoms'. A list in his handwriting of those destroyed, fifty-five in number, and of those saved, three and a fragment, has been preserved. Some of the burnt manuscripts were unique.

WARBURTON, ROWLAND EYLES EGERTON (1804–91), author of 'Hunting Songs and Ballads' (1846), 'Hunting Songs and Miscellaneous Verses' (1859), and of a version of Gray's 'O tu severi Religio loci' (the alcaics written by Gray in the album of the Grande Chartreuse).

WARBURTON, WILLIAM (1698–1779), rose to be bishop of Gloucester in 1759. He was much engaged in theological controversy, writing with vigour and arrogance. His principal works were: 'The Alliance between Church and State' (1736) and 'The Divine Legation of Moses' (1737–41), a paradoxical argument that the very absence in the Mosaic law of any reference to a future life, a necessary element in a scheme of morality, is a proof of the divine mission of the law-giver. His 'Doctrine of Grace', directed against John Wesley's views, was published in 1762. He brought out in 1747 an edition of Shakespeare which was sharply criticized, and in 1751 an edition of Pope's works (he had been left Pope's literary executor). He was a bad scholar, a literary bully, and a man of untrustworthy character.

WARD, ARTEMUS, see *Browne* (*C. F.*).

WARD, EDWARD ('Ned') (1667–1731), tavern-keeper and writer of Hudibrastic doggerel verse and coarse humorous prose, is remarkable for his sketches of London life and characters. Some of the best of these are contained in 'The London Spy' (1698–1709), a simply told tale of a country resident who visits London, meets a cockney acquaintance, and with him ranges about the town, noting sights, sounds, and smells, and odd characters. His 'Hudibras Redivivus' was published in 1705–7.

WARD, MARY AUGUSTA, better known as MRS. HUMPHRY WARD (1851–1920), was granddaughter of Thomas Arnold of Rugby. She wrote her first novel, 'Miss Bretherton', in 1884, and translated Amiel's 'Journal intime' in 1885. She embodied in her most famous novel, 'Robert Elsmere' (1888), her view that Christianity could be revitalized by emphasizing its social mission and discarding its miraculous element. Among her other novels, 'The History of David Grieve' followed in 1892, 'Marcella' in 1894, 'Sir George Tressady' in 1896, 'Helbeck of Bannisdale' in 1898, 'The Marriage of William Ashe' in 1905, and 'The Case of Richard Meynell' in 1911. Besides carrying on much social and philanthropic work, Mrs. Humphry Ward was an active opponent of the extension of the franchise to women.

WARD, WILLIAM GEORGE (1812–82), known as 'Ideal Ward' from his most famous work, was educated at Winchester, and was a scholar of Lincoln College, Oxford, and a fellow of Balliol. He was a keen religious controversialist and capable dialectician, adopted the theological views of Newman (q.v.), and wrote in defence of his Tract XC in 1841. He published 'The Ideal of a Christian Church', a Romanizing treatise, in 1844, in consequence of which he was removed from his degree for heresy. He was lecturer in moral philosophy at St. Edmund's College, Ware, 1851–8, and editor of the 'Dublin Review', 1863–78, writing against liberal theology and in favour of papal infallibility. He was commemorated by Tennyson in the touching poem in which he is described as 'Most generous of all Ultramontanes, Ward'.

Warden, HENRY, in Scott's 'The Monastery' and 'The Abbot' (qq.v.), an earnest Protestant divine.

Warden, *The*, a novel by A. Trollope (q.v.), published in 1855. This was the first of the Barsetshire series, and the first of Trollope's novels that met with success. The idea of it was conceived while Trollope one summer evening was wandering about the neighbourhood of Salisbury Cathedral.

The Revd. Septimus Harding, gentle, retiring, and conscientious, is a widower with two daughters, the elder of whom is married to the Revd. Dr. Theophilus Grantly, son of the bishop, and archdeacon of Barchester. The bishop has made Harding precentor of the cathedral and warden of Hiram's Hospital, a charitable foundation maintaining twelve old bedesmen. The property of the charity, having increased in value, yields enough, after housing the old men in comfort, to provide £800 a year for the warden, who enjoys what is practically a sinecure. This is attacked as an abuse by John Bold, an energetic young surgeon of Barchester, with a passion for reform; the matter is taken up by the 'Jupiter' newspaper (see *Thunderer*), and finally an action is brought against the warden and the bishop's steward, on behalf of the old bedesmen, who it is alleged are being defrauded of their rights. All this causes poor Mr. Harding intense distress, for he is not satisfied that there may not be some ground for the allegation. The situation is complicated by the fact that Bold is in love with Harding's younger daughter, Eleanor, and she with him. In spite of the strenuous opposition of Archdeacon Grantly, a somewhat worldly divine and a vigorous and overbearing defender of the rights of the Church, Harding resigns his wardenship. Meanwhile Eleanor has pleaded with Bold and persuaded him to withdraw his action. There the matter is left. The old bishop, Harding's close friend, refuses to fill the wardenship, the hospital falls into decay, and the bedesmen lose the friendly care of their former warden. Bold marries Eleanor. Harding remains precentor of the cathedral, and obtains a small living in addition. The story is continued in 'Barchester Towers' (q.v.).

Wardle, Mr., a character in Dickens's 'The Pickwick Papers' (q.v.).

Wardour, Sir Arthur, and his son and daughter Captain Reginald and Isabella, characters in Scott's 'The Antiquary' (q.v.).

Wardour Street, the name of a street in London which was formerly occupied mainly by dealers in antique and imitation-antique furniture. Hence 'Wardour-Street English' is applied to the pseudo-archaic diction affected by some modern writers, especially of historical novels.

Ware, The Bed of, see *Bed of Ware.*

Waring, one of the 'Dramatic Romances' of R. Browning (q.v.), published in 1842.

The poem is the reminiscence of a friend, Domett (q.v.), who has left England. The poet's fancy follows Waring in the places where he may now be. Finally he is reported to have been seen off the Illyrian coast in a light bark, sailing away into the sunset.

Warming-pan, a word used with allusion to the story that James II's son, afterwards called the Old Pretender, was a suppositious child introduced into the queen's bed in a warming-pan.

WARNER, WILLIAM (1558?–1609), studied at Oxford and was an attorney in London. He published in 1585 'Pan his Syrinx', seven prose tales, and a translation of the 'Menæchmi' of Plautus in 1595. His chief work is 'Albion's England', a metrical British history, with mythical and fictitious episodes, extending in the first (1586) edition from Noah to the Norman Conquest. It was brought down to James I's reign in 1606; a complete edition appeared (posthumously) in 1612. Meres, in his 'Palladis Tamia' (1598), associated him with Spenser as one of the two chief English heroic poets, and with Spenser, Daniel, Drayton, and Breton as a lyric poet. Drayton also eulogized him.

WARREN, JOHN BYRNE LEICESTER, *Baron de Tabley* (1835–95), educated at Eton and Christ Church, Oxford, published some volumes of verse under the pseudonyms of 'George F. Preston' (1859–62) and 'William Lancaster' (1863–8), and two tragedies, also under pseudonyms, 'Philoctetes' (1866) and 'Orestes' (1868). In 1893 and 1895 he published over his own name two series of 'Poems Dramatic and Lyrical', in which he is at his best; also a 'Guide to Bookplates' (1880). His collected poems appeared in 1903. De Tabley was a botanist, and his poems give proof of his close observation of nature.

WARREN, SAMUEL (1807–77), a student of medicine at Edinburgh, then a barrister, M.P. for Midhurst, and a master in lunacy, and the author of many legal textbooks. He is remembered for his 'Passages from the Diary of a Late Physician' (1838, after having appeared in 'Blackwood'), and for his very popular novel, 'Ten Thousand a Year' (1839),

the story of Mr. Tittlebat Titmouse, a draper's assistant, who comes into a large fortune, thanks to documents forged by the lawyers Gammon and Quirk. Having successfully ousted the rightful owners of the property, Charles Aubrey and his charming sister Kate, the lawyers proceed to blackmail Titmouse, whose unexpected elevation to wealth gives rise to absurd consequences. He marries Lady Cecilia, the daughter of the earl of Dredlington, and is returned to parliament by reckless corruption. Finally the fraud is exposed, Titmouse is discovered to be of illegitimate birth, is imprisoned for debt, goes mad, and is confined in a lunatic asylum, and Gammon commits suicide.

Warrington, George, a character in Thackeray's 'Pendennis' (q.v.), who figures also in 'The Newcomes'. He is a descendant of the Warringtons of 'The Virginians' (q.v.).

Wars of the Roses, The, the prolonged struggle between the houses of York and Lancaster, whose badges were respectively a white and a red rose. The wars began in 1455 in Henry VI's reign and ended with the defeat and death of Richard III at Bosworth in 1485, and the accession of Henry VII, who, by marrying Elizabeth of York, united the two lines.

Wart, Thomas, in Shakespeare's '2 Henry IV', one of the recruits for Falstaff's force.

WARTON, JOSEPH (1722–1800), brother of T. Warton (q.v.), educated at Winchester and Oriel College, Oxford, held various livings and was a conspicuously unsuccessful headmaster of Winchester (1766–93). He was a literary critic of wide knowledge and independent judgement, and is principally known for his 'Essay' on Pope (1756 and 1782), in which he criticized the 'correct' school of poetry and distinguished 'betwixt a man of wit, a man of sense, and a true poet'.

WARTON, THOMAS (1728–90), brother of J. Warton (q.v.), educated at Trinity College, Oxford, was professor of poetry at Oxford (1757–67) and subsequently Camden professor of history, and poet laureate in 1785, an appointment that was celebrated in the 'Probationary Odes' (see *Rolliad*). He was the author of many works, including 'Poems' (1777), notable for their revival of the sonnet; a 'History of English Poetry' (1774–81), a valuable pioneer work; and 'Observations on the Faerie Queene of Spenser' (1754). He edited the early poems of Milton and the famous miscellany of university verse entitled 'The Oxford Sausage' (1764). He was the author of much varied, including humorous, verse. In spite of several sparrings he and Dr. Johnson were warm friends. Warton was a real predecessor of the Romantic school, and a much bigger man than has been (until recently) recognized.

Warwick, Mrs., the heroine of Meredith's 'Diana of the Crossways' (q.v.).

Warwick the King-maker, Richard Neville, *earl of Warwick* (1428–71), instrumental in placing Edward IV on the throne in 1461, and in restoring Henry VI in 1470; killed at Barnet, 1471.

Washington, GEORGE (1732–99), born in Virginia, was General Braddock's A.D.C. in the war with the French and the Indians (1755), and was appointed commander-in-chief of the Continental Forces in the War of American Independence. He compelled the surrender of Cornwallis at Yorktown in 1781. He was president of the American convention of 1787, and first president of the United States (1789). A man notable for his lofty character, self-command, calmness, justice, and wisdom.

George Washington figures in Thackeray's 'The Virginians' (q.v.).

Washington and the Cherry-tree. The story is told in Mason L. Weems's 'A History of the Life and Death, Virtues and Exploits of General George Washington' (1800); the incident is now regarded as apocryphal, but it is frequently quoted.

When George was about six years old he was given a hatchet, with which he amused himself chopping everything that came in his way. One day he unluckily tried its edge on a beautiful young English cherry-tree. The next morning George's father, seeing what had befallen his tree, which was a great favourite, asked George if he knew who had killed it. George staggered under the question for a moment, but quickly recovered himself, and bravely cried out: 'I can't tell a lie, Pa; you know I can't tell a lie. I did cut it with my hatchet.' 'Run to my arms, you dearest boy,' cried his father in transports; 'glad am I, George, that you killed my tree; for you have paid me for it a thousandfold.'

WASHINGTON, BOOKER TALIAFERRO (1856–1915), born of a Negro slave mother on a Virginia plantation, studied at Hampton after the Civil War, and then devoted himself to raising the moral and intellectual status of his fellow Negroes, working out a scheme of education for them and becoming the foremost representative of his race. He was an eloquent speaker and voluminous writer. His works include an interesting autobiography, consisting of two parts: 'Up from Slavery' (1901) and 'Working with Hands' (1904).

Watch on the Rhine, The, see *Wacht am Rhein.*

Watchman, The, a periodical issued by S. T. Coleridge (q.v.) from 1 Mar. to 13 May 1796.

Water Babies, The, A Fairy Tale for a Land-Baby, by C. Kingsley (q.v.), published in 1863.

The story tells, with much pleasant humour, how little Tom, the chimney-sweep, employed by the bully, Mr. Grimes, runs away, falls into a river, and is turned into a water-baby. In the river and sea he makes intimate acquaintance with all sorts of aquatic creatures and learns the wickedness of ill-using efts and the like, and also the necessity of self-sacrifice. The first edition was charmingly illustrated by (Sir) Noel Paton.

Water-Poet, THE, see *Taylor (John).*

Waterloo, a village to the S. of Brussels, where, on 18 June 1815, was fought the battle in which Napoleon was finally and decisively defeated. The allied British, Netherlanders, Hanoverians, and Brunswickers, under the duke of Wellington, held their own until the close of the day, when the Prussian army under Blücher appeared, and took Napoleon in the flank. The French Imperial Guard made a last desperate charge and was repulsed. Wellington then ordered a general advance, before which the French gave way and fled. Wellington had some 70,000 men, Napoleon rather more, Blücher about 40,000. The word 'Waterloo' is used allusively for a decisive contest.

Waters, Childe, see *Childe Waters.*

Waters, Young, see *Young Waters.*

WATERTON, CHARLES (1782–1865), naturalist, of Walton Hall, Yorks., who resided in British Guiana during 1804–12 and subsequently travelled in the Orinoco region, wrote an interesting narrative of his 'Wanderings in S. America' (1825), in which occurs the famous account of his ride on an alligator.

Watier's, a club founded at 81 Piccadilly, at the suggestion of the Prince Regent, by Watier, the prince's chef, as a dinner club, noted for its elaborate cooking. It was frequented by men of fashion (including Beau Brummel, q.v.), became a gambling centre, and was closed about 1819.

Watling Street, one of the great Roman roads of Britain, which ran from Dover, through Canterbury, past the ancient city of London, crossing the Thames by a ford at Westminster, where the river was exceptionally wide and shallow, then along the line of what is now the Edgware Road, through St. Albans and across England to Chester. The name in Old English was *Wæclinga Stræt;* the first word, apparently the genitive plural of the name of a (real or imaginary) family or clan, occurs also in *Wæclinga ceaster* 'the Wæclings' city', the Old English name of St. Albans.

In Chaucer's 'The Hous of Fame', ii. 431, the eagle draws the poet's attention to the Milky Way and says:

> And some, parfay,
> Callen it Watling Street.

Watling Street, London, was probably a diversion to London Bridge of the older Watling Street (see above) that crossed the Thames by the ford at Westminster.

Watson, Dr., in the cycle of stories by Sir A. Conan Doyle (q.v.) relating to Sherlock Holmes, the detective, is a stolid medical man, Holmes's companion and assistant in his adventures, and his chronicler. His stupidity, which is good-humouredly tolerated by his brilliant leader, serves as a foil to set off the qualities of the latter.

WATSON, RICHARD (1737–1816), educated at Trinity College, Cambridge, professor of chemistry, 1764, and Regius professor of divinity, 1771, became bishop of Llandaff in 1782. He wrote a notable 'Apology for Christianity' (1776) in reply to Gibbon, and an 'Apology for the Bible' (1796) in reply to Thomas Paine.

WATSON, THOMAS (1557?–92), was possibly educated at Oxford, and was a law-student in London. He published a Latin version of the 'Antigone' of Sophocles, with an appendix of Latin allegorical poems and experiments in Latin metres, in 1581; and in 1582, 'Ἑκατομπαθία, or Passionate Centurie of Loue', eighteen-line English poems (called 'sonnets'), reflecting classical and French and Italian poems, and being in some cases translations; this is his most important work. He published Latin versions of Tasso's 'Aminta' (1585) and of 'Raptus Helenae' from the Greek of Coluthus (1586); his version of the 'Aminta' was rendered into English, without authority, by Abraham Fraunce (1587). He published 'The first Sett of Italian Madrigalls Englished' (1590) and an 'Eglogue' (Latin and English) on Walsingham's death (1590). His Latin pastoral 'Amyntae Gaudia' appeared posthumously in 1592, and 'The Tears of Fancie', sixty English sonnets, inspired by Petrarch and Ronsard, in 1593; a few previously unpublished poems by him appeared in 'The Phoenix Nest' (1593) and 'England's Helicon' (1600). His sonnets appear to have been studied by Shakespeare and other contemporaries. He was the 'Amyntas' of Spenser's 'Colin Clouts come home againe' (q.v.), and was declared by Francis Meres to be the equal of Petrarch, Theocritus, and Virgil.

WATSON, Sir WILLIAM (1858–1935), poet, born in Yorkshire, whose chief works are: 'Lachrymae Musarum' and 'Lyric Love' (1892), 'The Eloping Angels' (1893), 'Odes and other poems' (1894), 'The Father of the Forest' (1895), 'The Year of Shame' (1896), 'The Heralds of the Dawn' (1912), 'Collected Poems' (1906).

Watsons, The, an unfinished fragment of a novel by Jane Austen (q.v.), written about 1805 and appended by J. E. Austen Leigh to the second edition of his 'Memoir of Jane Austen' (1871); reprinted, Oxford, 1927.

Emma Watson, who has been brought up by a well-to-do aunt, on the latter's re-marriage returns to her family, who live in a modest way in a Surrey village. A pretty, sensible girl, she is here surrounded by persons of inferior minds, her sisters being chiefly bent on the acquisition of husbands. The other principal characters, who are introduced to the reader in a local ball-room scene, are Lady Osborne, handsome and dignified; her son Lord Osborne, a fine young man with an 'air of coldness, of care-lessness, even of awkwardness about him'; Mr. Howard, a gentlemanly clergyman; and Tom Musgrave, a hardened flirt. The intention appears to have been that the heroine should marry Mr. Howard, but the authoress completed little more than the *mise en scène* of the story.

Watt, JAMES (1736–1819), born at Greenock, was son and grandson of mathematicians, and son of a mathematical-instrument maker. He began his career as a mathematical-instrument maker, showing great manual dexterity. While repairing a model of John Newcomen's steam-engine, he discovered the cause of its waste of power (1764), and devised the separate condenser and air-pump to remedy this defect. He was in partnership with Matthew Boulton at the Soho Engineering Works, Birmingham, 1775–1800, and it was owing to this association that he was able to bring his various inventions to such fruit. He patented the 'Watt' steam-engine in 1769, and continued improving it by various mechanical devices down to about 1785. He also projected the screw-propeller, and by his own researches discovered the composition of water. He was about equally devoted to chemistry and music and drawing, and in spite of very poor health, much beloved in every society. He became F.R.S. in 1785.

WATT, ROBERT (1774–1819), author of the 'Bibliotheca Britannica, or a general Index to British and Foreign Literature' (1824), the first great bibliographical work produced in Scotland.

Watteau, ANTOINE (1684–1721), French painter of *fêtes champêtres* and French and Italian comedy characters, expressing, with melancholy undertones, the playful spirit of the rococo. The costumes of his ladies, dressed as shepherdesses, have given his name to various articles of dress, such as the *Watteau hat*.

WATTS, ISAAC (1674–1748), the son of a Nonconformist schoolmaster, is remembered as the author of 'Divine Songs for Children', 1715, containing such well-known lines as:

> Let dogs delight to bark and bite,
> For God hath made them so;

and the lines about the little busy bee. He also wrote a number of hymns, some of which have obtained a wide popularity, including 'O God, our help in ages past', 'When I survey the wondrous Cross', 'There is a land of pure delight', and 'Jesus shall reign where'er the sun'. He published a selection of metrical 'Psalms of David' in 1719, and a number of doctrinal treatises and educational manuals. There is a monument to him in Westminster Abbey.

WATTS-DUNTON, WALTER THEO-
DORE (1832–1914), gave up his profession of
solicitor to devote himself to literary criticism,
on which subject he contributed many
valuable articles to 'The Athenaeum'. He
was much interested in the gipsies, and republished in 'The Coming of Love' (1897) scenes
in verse previously printed in 'The Athenaeum', in which Rhona Boswell, a gipsy girl,
figures prominently. Gipsies again play an
important part in his novel 'Aylwin' (1898),
originally called 'The Renascence of Wonder',
which met with great success. Watts-Dunton
had met Borrow (q.v.) in 1872, and his recollections of him may be read in his editions
of 'Lavengro' (1893) and 'The Romany Rye'
(1900). His best critical work is on 'Poetry'
in the E.B. (9th ed., 1885).

Watts-Dunton befriended Swinburne (q.v.)
in his declining health, took him to his house
at Putney (where Swinburne lived from 1879
until his death), and exercised a devoted and
tactful control over him.

WAUGH, EVELYN ARTHUR St. JOHN
(1903–66), novelist. His work is mainly
satire, sophisticated and witty, and includes
the following novels: 'Decline and Fall'
(1928), 'Vile Bodies' (1930), 'Black Mischief'
(1932), 'A Handful of Dust' (1934), 'Scoop'
(1938), 'Put Out More Flags' (1942), 'Brides-
head Revisited' (1945), 'The Loved One'
(1948), 'Men at Arms' (1952), 'Officers and
Gentlemen' (1955), and 'The Ordeal of
Gilbert Pinfold' (1957). He also wrote a life of
Edmund Campion (1935).

Waverley, the first of the novels of Sir W.
Scott (q.v.), published in 1814. Much of it
had been written, and thrown aside, some
years before.

Edward Waverley, a young man of romantic disposition ('a sneaking piece of imbecility'
Scott himself, with perhaps excessive severity,
called him), has been brought up in part by
his father, a Hanoverian in politics, in part
by his uncle Sir Everard Waverley, a rich
land-owner of Jacobite leanings. Obtaining a
commission in the army in the year 1745, he
joins his regiment in Scotland, and there,
while on leave, visits his uncle's friend, the
baron of Bradwardine, a kind-hearted but
pedantic old Jacobite, and attracts the
favourable notice of the gentle Rose Bradwardine, his daughter. Impelled by curiosity,
he visits Donald Bean Lean, a Highland
freebooter, in his lair, and Fergus Mac-Ivor
Vich Ian Vohr of Glennaquoich, a young
Highland chieftain, active in the Jacobite
interest. While at Glennaquoich, he falls in
love with Fergus's sister Flora, whose beauty
and ardent loyalty to the Stewart cause appeal
to his romantic disposition. These visits, injudicious in an officer of the British army
at a time of acute political tension, compromise Edward with his colonel. He moreover falls a victim to Jacobite intrigues and
finds himself accused of fomenting mutiny
in his regiment, and is finally cashiered and

arrested. From imprisonment he is rescued
by the action of the devoted Rose, and, under
the influence of a sense of unjust treatment,
of Flora's enthusiasm, and of a gratifying
reception by Prince Charles Edward, he joins
the Jacobite forces. At the battle of Prestonpans he has the good fortune to save from
death Colonel Talbot, a distinguished English
officer and friend of his family, and the influence of the latter, after the final defeat and
dispersal of the Pretender's army, is the
means of securing Edward's pardon and the
rehabilitation of the good baron of Bradwardine. Meanwhile Edward has been decisively rejected by the spirited Flora, and has
turned his affections to the milder and more
congenial Rose, to whom in due course he is
married. Fergus is convicted of high treason
and bravely meets his end, and Flora retires
to a convent.

Among the minor characters may be mentioned bailie Duncan Macwheeble, Bradwardine's 'prime minister'; Davie Gellatley, the
'innocent', the mouthpiece of some of Scott's
most beautiful lyrics; and the laird of Balmawhapple, the quarrelsome sportsman who
falls foul of Edward and contributes to his
early discomfiture. For Colonel Gardiner,
Edward Waverley's commanding officer, see
under *Doddridge.*

Way of All Flesh, The, a novel by S. Butler
(1835–1902, q.v.), published in 1903 after
the author's death.

In the form of a novel, brilliant with wit
and irony, Butler here presents a study in one
of his favourite themes, the relations of
parents to children, a study embittered by
some of his own recollections. The idiosyn-
crasy of the Pontifex family is traced from
father to son through several generations: old
John Pontifex, the village carpenter; George
Pontifex, the domineering publisher; Theobald his son, who is bullied into taking orders
and jockeyed into marriage with the smug
Christina; and Ernest, their child, who in turn
suffers cruelly from the pharisaical tyranny of
his father during childhood and schooldays,
until, after his ordination, the reaction from
suppression leads to sudden catastrophe. He
manages to insult a young woman whom he
takes for a prostitute, and is sentenced to six
months' imprisonment. On emerging, ruined,
from prison, he contracts a disastrous union
with Ellen, a former maidservant of his family,
but is released from the incubus of her
drunkenness by the discovery that she is
already married. A fortune inherited from an
aunt permits him to devote the rest of his life
to literature. The gloom and irony of the
work are relieved by the pleasant portrait of
Alethea Pontifex (drawn from Butler's friend,
Eliza Mary Ann Savage) and the 'godless old
sinner', Mrs. Jupp, the landlady.

Way of the World, The, a comedy by Congreve (q.v.), produced in 1700. This is the
most finished of Congreve's comedies, but
it was not very well received and the author

in disgust renounced any further writing for the stage.

Mirabell is in love with Millamant, a niece of Lady Wishfort, and has pretended to make love to the aunt in order to conceal his suit of the niece. The deceit has been revealed to Lady Wishfort by Mrs. Marwood to revenge herself on Mirabell, who has rejected her advances. Lady Wishfort, who now hates Mirabell 'more than a quaker hates a parrot', will deprive her niece of the half of the inheritance which is in her keeping, if Millamant marries Mirabell. The latter accordingly contrives that his servant Waitwell shall personate an uncle of his, Sir Rowland, make love to Lady Wishfort and pretend to marry her, having, however, first married Lady Wishfort's woman, Foible. He hopes by this deception to win Lady Wishfort's consent to his marriage to her niece. The plot is discovered by Mrs. Marwood, and also the fact that Mirabell has in the past had an intrigue with Mrs. Fainall, daughter of Lady Wishfort. She conspires with Fainall, her lover and the pretended friend of Mirabell, to reveal these facts to Lady Wishfort, while Fainall is to threaten to divorce his wife and discredit Lady Wishfort unless he is given full control of Mrs. Fainall's property and Millamant's portion is also handed over to him. The scheme, however, fails. Mrs. Fainall denies the charge against her, brings proof of Fainall's relations with Mrs. Marwood, while Mirabell produces a deed by which Mrs. Fainall, before her last marriage, made him trustee of her property. Lady Wishfort, in gratitude for her release from Fainall's threats, forgives Mirabell and consents to his marriage to Millamant.

Besides the finished portrait of Millamant, finely tempered in sense and intellect, Congreve's most brilliant creation, there are amusing characters in Sir Wilfull Witwoud, Lady Wishfort's boisterous country nephew, and Foible and Waitwell, the servants. The dialogue is exceptionally brilliant and there are some highly entertaining scenes; while Lady Wishfort's display of 'boudoir Billingsgate' (as Meredith called it) when she discovers how she has been tricked is unequalled in its kind.

Wayland or WELAND THE SMITH, a hero of Teutonic myth, known in the Norse version as *Volundr*. According to the Elder Edda, he was one of three brothers settled in Ulfdale and married to Valkyries or war-nymphs. After nine years, these were constrained by fate to leave their husbands. Two brothers departed in search of their partners, but Weland remained at home working at his smith's craft and amassing wealth. Besieged by Nidudr, a Swedish king, he was cruelly lamed by the cutting of the sinews of his knee, and conveyed to a small island where he was forced to work for his captor. Here he murdered the sons of Nidudr, and presented their gold-set skulls to their father,

gems made from their eyes to their mother, and a breast-ornament of their teeth to Bodhilda, their sister, who became his victim. He then entered the palace of Nidudr and recounted to him the fates of his children, afterwards escaping.

He is the *Wieland* of German epics, who fashioned the famous sword Mimung. There are traces of his legend in England. He was supposed to have his forge in a dolmen near the White Horse on the Berkshire Downs (see Scott's 'Kenilworth'). His misfortunes are referred to in the 'Complaint of Deor' (q.v.). King Alfred translates Boethius 'ubi nunc sunt ossa Fabricii' by 'where are now the bones of Weland once the cunning goldsmith of old'.

Wayzgoose, according to the OED. probably a corruption of *waygoose*, arising from an etymological conjecture by Bailey (1731), who connected the word with *wayz-goose*, stubble goose. But it has now been discovered from old records of the Oxford University Press that the word was formerly *wake-goose*. It signified originally an entertainment given by a master printer to his workmen 'about Bartholomewtide', marking the beginning of the season of working by candle-light. In later use it is an annual festivity held in summer by the employees of a printing establishment.

Weak ending, the occurrence of an unstressed or proclitic monosyllable (such as a preposition, conjunction, or auxiliary verb) in the normally stressed place at the end of an iambic line.

Wealth of Nations, Inquiry into the Nature and Causes of the, a treatise on political economy by Adam Smith (q.v.), published in 1776, originally delivered in the form of lectures at Glasgow.

Adam Smith's work is the first comprehensive treatment of the whole subject of political economy, and is remarkable for its breadth of view. Smith shared the objection of the French physiocrats (q.v.) to the mercantile system, but he did not share their view that land is the sole source of wealth. The 'Wealth of Nations' sets out with the doctrine that the labour of the nation is the source of its means of life. It insists on the value of the division of labour. Labour is the standard of value, and originally was the sole determinant of price; but in a more advanced state of society three elements enter into price—wages, profit, and rent—and these elements are discussed separately.

The second book deals with capital, its nature, accumulation, and employment. With the increase of capital there is an increase of productive labour and a decrease in the rate of interest.

After this exposition the author proceeds to an elaborate attack on the mercantile system, and an advocacy of freedom of commerce and industry. His political economy is essentially individualistic; self-interest is the proper criterion of economic action. But the universal pursuit of one's own advantage contributes, in his view, to the public interest.

Wearin' of the Green, The, an Irish national folk-ballad, attributed to the last decade of the 18th cent.

WEBB, MARY (1881–1927), author of Shropshire country novels, including 'Gone to Earth' (1917), 'Precious Bane' (1924), etc.

WEBB, SIDNEY JAMES, *first Baron Passfield* (1859–1947), and MRS. BEATRICE WEBB, *née* Potter (1858–1943), authors jointly and singly of numerous works connected with the investigation of social and economic conditions in England and with the furtherance of a socialist policy; especially associated with the Fabian Society (q.v.).

Webster, DANIEL (1782–1852), born in New Hampshire, in America, rose to great eminence as an orator, both in the practice of the law, in the House of Representatives and Senate, and in discourses to the public, in which he stimulated the idea of union among the American States. He was twice secretary of state. His speeches, even in ordinary criminal trials, show a rare literary quality, comparable to that displayed by the speeches of Burke. Among the best known of them is the Discourse on the 200th anniversary of the landing of the Pilgrims (1820), the Bunker Hill oration (1825), and the Adams and Jefferson speech (1826).

WEBSTER, JOHN (1580?–1625?), the son of a London tailor, and himself a freeman of the Merchant Taylors' Company, collaborated with Dekker and other dramatists in a number of comedies, 'Christmas comes but once a year' (1602), 'Westward Hoe' (q.v.) and 'Northward Hoe' (q.v.) in 1603–4 (printed in 1607), and with Rowley in 'A Cure for a Cuckold' (q.v., printed 1661). He completed for the stage Marston's 'Malcontent' (1604). With Heywood and Tourneur he published elegies on Prince Henry in 1612. His tragedies, founded on Italian *novelle*, show that he approached in tragic power nearest of his contemporaries to Shakespeare; they are 'The White Divel' (q.v.), produced *c.* 1608; 'Appius and Virginia' (q.v., perhaps partly by Heywood), *c.* 1609; 'The Duchess of Malfi' (q.v.), *c.* 1614. His tragi-comedy, 'The Devil's Law Case', was published in 1623. His tragedy on contemporary French history entitled 'Guise' and 'A late Murder of the Son upon the Mother' (written in conjunction with J. Ford, *c.* 1624) are lost. Collected editions of his plays were published (1830) by Alexander Dyce, (1856) by William Hazlitt, and (1927) by F. L. Lucas.

WEBSTER, NOAH (1758–1843), American lexicographer, was educated at Yale University and was subsequently a teacher and a journalist. The chief work by which he is remembered is his great 'American Dictionary of the English Language' (1828), of which there have been several subsequent editions.

Wedding, *Ballad upon a,* see *Suckling.*

Wedgwood, JOSIAH (1730–95), founder of the pottery at Etruria, where he produced 'Queen's' ware, a fine cream-coloured 'useful ware', and 'Black Basalt' and 'Jasper' 'ornamental wares'. He developed large-scale production but maintained a high standard of quality, employing artists to design in the classical taste.

THOMAS WEDGWOOD (1771–1805), son of Josiah, was the first to produce (unfixed) photographs, and was a generous patron of S. T. Coleridge.

Wedmore, TREATY OF, between Alfred and Guthrum, king of the Danes, after the defeat of the latter at Ethandun in 878. The treaty gave Alfred Wessex, Sussex, Kent, and the western half of Mercia. The rest of England as far as the Tees was surrendered to the Danes and became known as the Danelaw. But either by this, or by a treaty two years later, Alfred kept London. Wedmore is at the foot of the Mendips.

Weeping Philosopher, see Heraclitus.

Wegg, SILAS, in Dickens's 'Our Mutual Friend' (q.v.), a one-legged impudent old rascal, with a smattering of education, who becomes reader to Mr. Boffin and attempts to blackmail him.

Weir, MAJOR, in Scott's 'Redgauntlet' (q.v.), Sir Robert Redgauntlet's monkey in 'Wandering Willie's Tale', named after a famous wizard executed at Edinburgh for sorcery and other crimes.

Weir of Hermiston, an unfinished novel by R. L. Stevenson (q.v.), published in 1896. The fragment does little more than set the scene and present the chief characters, but it includes some of Stevenson's finest work.

Archie Weir is the only child of Adam Weir, Lord Hermiston, the lord justice-clerk, a formidable 'hanging judge', grim and stern, wielding with a fierce enjoyment the terrors of the law. His mother, a pale ineffectual woman, dies young, and leaves Archie, 'a fine ardent modest youthful soul' with a taste for letters, to the care of a father whom he both dreads and dislikes. Archie, revolted at the cruel glee with which the old judge hounds to death some wretched criminal at a trial, passes a grave public affront on his father, and is banished by him to the solitude of Hermiston, a remote pastoral village. He shrinks from the uncongenial society of the clodpole lairds of the neighbourhood, and lives a recluse, with Kirstie, his devoted housekeeper and distant relative. She is aunt to four notable brothers, the 'Black Elliotts', famed for their hunting down of their father's murderer. These have a young sister, Christina, whose beauty attracts Archie. The two fall deeply in love and have many meetings, which at last become known to Kirstie and to Archie's disloyal friend and visitor, Frank Innes. Moved by Kirstie's earnest warning and Frank's facetious comments, Archie tells Christina that their secret meetings must cease, and offends her deeply. At this point the fragment ends, but we know that in Stevenson's intention the argument was to proceed as follows. Archie persists in his good resolution of avoiding further conduct compromising to Christina's good name. Taking advantage of this and of the girl's unhappiness and wounded vanity, Frank Innes seduces her. This becomes known to Archie, who has an interview with Frank, which ends in a quarrel and in Archie killing Frank. He is tried before his own father and sentenced to death. Meanwhile Kirstie, who has discovered that Frank, and not, as had hitherto been supposed, Archie, is the author of Christina's betrayal, informs the Four Black Brothers. These gather a following, and after a great fight break the prison where Archie lies confined, and rescue him. He and Christina thereafter escape to America. But the ordeal of taking part in the trial of his own son is too much for the old judge, who dies of the shock. Lord Hermiston is believed to be drawn from Robert Macqueen, Lord Braxfield.

Weissnichtwo('Know not where'; cf. Scott's 'Kennaquhair'), in Carlyle's 'Sartor Resartus' (q.v.), the town where Teufelsdröckh was professor.

Weland the Smith, see *Wayland the Smith.*

Well of St. Keyne, The, a ballad by Southey (q.v.).

The well is in Cornwall. 'Whether husband or wife come first to drink thereof, they get the mastery thereby', says Fuller. The ballad tells how a Cornishman, though he left his bride at the church porch to hurry to the well, was outwitted by her—for she had taken a bottle of the water to church.

Well-Beloved, The, a novel by Hardy (q.v.), published serially in 1892, reissued in revised form in 1897.

The scene is the 'Isle of Slingers', that is, Portland, and the tale deals with the peculiar temperament of its inhabitants. Jocelyn Pierston the sculptor, an 'islander', falls in love successively with three Island women—Avice Caro, her daughter, and her granddaughter, of the same name—seeking in each an elusive ideal Well-Beloved; but the perversity of circumstances prevents him from marrying any of them. In his old age he marries an elderly widow, from whom all pretence of being the Well-Beloved has long since departed.

Wellborn, FRANK, a character in Massinger's 'A New Way to pay Old Debts' (q.v.).

Weller, SAMUEL, in Dickens's 'The Pickwick Papers' (q.v.), Mr. Pickwick's devoted servant, formerly boots at the White Hart in the Borough, a cheerful, facetious, and resourceful character, with an endless store of humorous illustrations apposite to the various incidents of life. The greatest character that Dickens ever drew.

Weller, TONY, in Dickens's 'The Pickwick Papers'(q.v.), a coach-driver, the father of Sam Weller. He has married a widow, who keeps the 'Marquis of Granby' inn at Dorking.

WELLESLEY, DOROTHY, *Duchess of Wellington* (1889–1956), a poet who was admired by Yeats and to whom he wrote letters on poetry (published in 1940). Her collected poems were published under the title 'Early Light' (1956).

WELLS, CHARLES JEREMIAH (1800–79), author of 'Stories after Nature' (1822) and, under the pseudonym of H. L. HOWARD, of 'Joseph and his Brethren: a Dramatic Poem' (1824). In 1876 (and in the World's Classics in 1908) this was republished with an essay by Swinburne. It was greatly admired by Rossetti.

WELLS, HERBERT GEORGE (1866–1946), the son of a small tradesman and professional cricketer, was apprenticed to a draper in early life, a period of which reflections may be seen in some of his best novels ('The History of Mr. Polly', 'Kipps', 'The Wheels of Chance'). He became a teacher at Midhurst Grammar School and subsequently graduated at the Normal School of Science, South Kensington. He followed the teaching profession until 1893, when he definitely adopted that of letters. A vivid light is thrown on the circumstances of his life and mental development by his interesting 'Experiment in Autobiography' (1934).

Wells's novels divide themselves broadly into three groups: (1) fantastic and imaginative romances, in which, after the manner of Swift in 'Gulliver's Travels' (q.v.), the author projects himself to a distant standpoint—the moon, the future, the air—and views our life from outside, e.g. as an angel sees it ('The Wonderful Visit'); (2) novels of character and humour, of which 'The History of Mr. Polly' (q.v., 1910) is the type; (3) discussion novels—discussion, that is, in the main, of human ideals and progress—to which Wells's essay on 'The Contemporary Novel' ('Fortnightly Review', Nov. 1911, reprinted in 'An Englishman Looks at the World', 1914) serves as a general introduction.

Wells's publications include: 'The Time Machine' and 'The Wonderful Visit' (1895), 'The Invisible Man' (1897), 'The War of the Worlds' (1898), 'When the Sleeper Wakes' (1899, revised and reissued in 1911 as 'The Sleeper Awakes'), 'Love and Mr. Lewisham' (1900), 'The First Men in the Moon' (1901), 'Anticipations' (sociological essays, 1902), 'The Food of the Gods' (1904), 'A Modern Utopia' and 'Kipps' (1905), 'The War in the Air' (1908), 'Tono-Bungay' (1909, one of Wells's most remarkable works, a picture of English society in dissolution in the later 19th cent. and of the advent of a new class of rich), 'Ann Veronica' (1909), 'The History of Mr. Polly' (q.v., 1910), 'The New Machiavelli' (1911), 'The Country of the Blind' (short stories, 1911), 'Bealby' (1915), 'Mr. Britling sees it through' (1916), 'The Outline of History' (1920, first issued in fortnightly parts), 'Short History of the World' (1922), 'The World of William Clissold' (1926), 'The Open Conspiracy' (1928), 'The Science of Life' (with Dr. Julian Huxley and Mr. G. P. Wells, 1929), 'The Shape of Things to Come' (1933).

Wemmick, in Dickens's 'Great Expectations' (q.v.), clerk to Mr. Jaggers the lawyer, and Pip's good friend.

Wen, THE, William Cobbett's name for London ('Rural Rides', *passim*).

Wenham, MR., in Thackeray's 'Vanity Fair' (q.v.), a satellite of Lord Steyne.

Wentworth, SIR THOMAS, see *Strafford*.

Werewolf or WERWOLF, a person who (according to medieval superstition) was transformed or was capable of transforming himself at times into a wolf. Lycaon, an impious king of Greek mythology, who served a dish of human flesh to Zeus to test whether he was really a god, and was turned into a wolf as punishment, is an early instance of the superstition, and the ancient writers and Norse mythology afford other examples. The belief in werewolves was widespread in England, Wales, Ireland, and the greater part of the Continent down to the 17th cent., and is hardly extinct everywhere even today, though with the disappearance of the wolf the delusion necessarily loses its basis. Cf. the story of William of Palerne (q.v.). In Scotland hares take the place of wolves.

The first element in the word has usually been identified with the OE. *wer*, man, but the OED. regards this as doubtful.

Werner, a tragedy by Lord Byron (q.v.), published in 1822, founded on 'The German's Tale' in Sophia and Harriet Lee's 'Canterbury Tales'.

The dissolute and outlawed son of Count Siegendorf, bearing the assumed name of Werner, finds himself by accident in the same house as his enemy, Count Stralenheim, and under a sudden impulse robs him. His son Ulric, more determined, murders Stralenheim to conceal his father's dishonour, but without his father's knowledge, and throws the appearance of guilt on the Hungarian, Gabor. Later, when Werner has become Count Siegendorf, he finds himself confronted by Gabor, who accuses Ulric of the crime. Ulric seeks to kill Gabor, but is prevented by Siegendorf, who shrinks from assassination and dies broken-hearted at his own infamy and his son's crime.

Werther, *The Sorrows of Young*, see *Goethe*.
Thackeray wrote a short satirical poem

called 'The Sorrows of Werther' ending with the well-known lines:

> Charlotte, having seen his body
> Borne before her on a shutter,
> Like a well-conducted person
> Went on cutting bread and butter.

WESLEY, CHARLES (1707–88), a brother of J. Welsey (q.v.), founded, while a student at Christ Church, a 'methodist' society of pious young men, who strictly observed rules of fasting and prayer. To this society belonged John Wesley and George Whitefield, and these, with Charles himself, were the principal leaders of the Methodist movement. From a literary standpoint, Charles Wesley is remembered as the composer of a very large number of hymns, including 'Jesu, lover of my soul', many of which are still in use. He left a 'Journal', published in 1849.

WESLEY, JOHN (1703–91), of old Puritan ancestry, was educated at Charterhouse and Christ Church, Oxford. He became fellow and tutor of Lincoln College, and leader of the 'methodist' society of his brother Charles (q.v.) in 1729. He accepted charge of the Georgia mission in 1735 and came under the influence of the Moravians, and after his return to England became a member of the Moravian 'society' at Fetter Lane Chapel. He visited Zinzendorf at Herrnhut in 1738, and was appointed his first lay preacher. He then began field preaching and opened a Methodist chapel at Bristol, and for the remainder of his life showed prodigious activity in his ministry, preaching forty thousand sermons and travelling many thousands of miles, nearly all on horseback. He was a man of real and deep learning, and of autocratic temper. He had a passionate desire to remain a member of the Church of England, but he committed a definite act of schism when, in 1784, he ordained a minister (for one of his American congregations); his brother Charles was bitterly opposed to this. John Wesley published twenty-three collections of hymns (1737–86) and his collected prose 'Works' (1771–4). His 'Journal', of which a standard edition was published in 1909–11, is remarkable not only as a record of his spiritual life and tireless activity, but also for its pathos, humour, and observation of mankind. Southey's 'Life of John Wesley', perhaps one of the best biographies in the language, was published in 1820. See also *Methodism*.

Wessex, the kingdom of the West Saxons, who established themselves in Hampshire early in the 6th cent., and extended their dominion north and west under their kings, Cerdic and Cynric. It included Hants, Dorset, Wilts., Berks., and part of Somerset. Ultimately, under Egbert, Alfred, and their successors, the kingdom of Wessex developed into that of England.

'Wessex' is used by Hardy (q.v.) to designate the south-west counties, principally Dorset, which are the scene of his novels.

WEST, DAME REBECCA (1892–   ), novelist, critic, and political writer. Her novels include 'The Return of the Soldier' (1918), 'The Judge' (1922), 'Harriet Hume' (1929), 'The Thinking Reed' (1936), and 'The Fountain Overflows' (1957). Her other work includes 'The Strange Necessity' (essays and reviews, 1938), 'Black Lamb and Grey Falcon' (a book about Yugoslavia, 1942), 'The Meaning of Treason' (a study of traitors, 1949), and 'The Court and the Castle' (a study of political and religious ideas in imaginative literature, 1958).

West Indian, The, a comedy by Cumberland (q.v.), produced in 1771.

Stockwell, having early in life secretly married in Jamaica the daughter of his rich employer, old Belcour, has had a son by her, who has been passed off on old Belcour as a foundling, brought up by him, and has inherited his property. Young Belcour, as he is called, comes home, but Stockwell postpones recognizing him as his son until he has made trial of his character.

Young Belcour, a generous but harebrained fellow, falls in love at first sight with Louisa, daughter of the impecunious Captain Dudley, tracks her to the lodgings where she lives with her father and brother Charles, and is there beguiled into thinking her the mistress of Charles by the rascally landlord Fulmer and his wife, who hope to profit by the intrigue. Charles is in love with his rich cousin Charlotte, stepdaughter of the avaricious and unscrupulous Lady Rusport, but in his poverty will not confess his love, though it is returned by Charlotte. Belcour generously comes to the assistance of Captain Dudley in his pressing needs, but his impudent addresses to Louisa, under a mistaken idea of her character, and his inconsiderate gift to Louisa—because he happens to have no other present handy—of some jewels entrusted to him for Charlotte, lead to grave complications and a duel with Charles. The imbroglio is cleared up by Charlotte (to whom Belcour frankly confesses his disposal of her jewels) with the help of the amiable Irishman, Major O'Flaherty. Belcour discovers his mistake, is pardoned by Louisa and obtains her hand, and is recognized by his father. Charles is discovered to be the real heir of his grandfather's property, which Lady Rusport had tried to appropriate, and marries Charlotte.

West Point, New York State, on the W. bank of the Hudson, where the U.S. Military Academy trains cadets for army service. It figured in the Revolutionary War: Washington had his headquarters there in 1779, and in 1780 Benedict Arnold endeavoured treasonably to surrender it to the British.

WESTCOTT, BROOKE FOSS (1825–1901), theological scholar, bishop of Durham, famous for his recension, jointly with F. J. A. Hort, of the Greek text of the New Testament (1871). He also wrote commentaries on the Gospel and Epistles of St. John and on the Epistle to the Hebrews.

Western, SQUIRE and SOPHIA, characters in Fielding's 'Tom Jones' (q.v.).

Western Empire, THE, the more westerly of the two parts into which the Roman Empire was divided in A.D. 395. Its capital was Rome. It came to a real end with the deposition of Romulus Augustulus in 476, and its pretended revival by the pope and Charlemagne in 800 was far from being a reality, though it nominally endured as the Holy Roman Empire till 1806.

Westlock, JOHN, a character in Dickens's 'Martin Chuzzlewit' (q.v.), at one time pupil of Mr. Pecksniff.

Westminster Abbey: a monastery dedicated to St. Peter was founded, in the 7th or 8th century, on the island of Thorney in the estuary of the Thames, close to where Watling Street reached the river at Tothill. It was re-founded, after destruction by the Danes, and endowed with a large manor, in the time of Edgar and Dunstan. The river was gradually pushed back and the adjoining land reclaimed. Edward the Confessor passed much of his reign at Westminster and built a great church for the monks. It was rebuilt by Henry III and added to and partly reconstructed in subsequent reigns. Chaucer was clerk of the king's works at the abbey during part of Richard II's reign. 'Poets' Corner' in the S. transept contains the monuments or other memorials of Chaucer, Spenser, Shakespeare, Ben Jonson, Milton, and other British authors. It is in the abbey that the English sovereigns are crowned.

Westminster Hall, a part of the old Westminster Palace, built by William Rufus (perhaps in the place of an earlier hall) and rebuilt, substantially in its present form, by Richard II. The early kings held many of their Christmas and other festivities there. Many of the early parliaments sat in it, and it was the principal seat of justice from the time of Henry III until the 19th cent., and the scene of many great trials, among others of Strafford, Charles I, and Warren Hastings.

Westminster Palace, supposed to date from Edward the Confessor, on the site now occupied by the Houses of Parliament, was damaged by fire in 1512 and ceased to be a royal residence, but a great part of it remained. The Houses of Lords and Commons for a long time sat in buildings of the Palace, until these were destroyed by the fire of 1834. All that now survives of the palace is Westminster Hall (q.v.) and the crypt of St. Stephen's chapel.

Westminster Review, The, was founded in 1824 by Bentham (q.v.), with the assistance of James Mill (q.v.), as the organ of the philosophical radicals. John Bowring was its first editor. In 1851 George Eliot(q.v.) became its assistant editor (under John Chapman).

Westminster School was founded by Queen Elizabeth in 1560. Among its famous pupils have been Ben Jonson, George Herbert, Locke, Dryden, Wren, Bentham, Gibbon, Cowper, and Southey.

Westphalia, THE PEACE OF, concluded in 1648 by the treaties of Osnabrück and Münster, brought to an end the Thirty Years War in Germany. The religious and political equality of the German states was secured; France was granted most of Alsace; Sweden received part of Pomerania and other districts; Holland and Switzerland were declared independent.

Westward for Smelts, a collection of tales borrowed from the 'Decameron' and similar sources, recounted by seven fish-wives who embark after selling their fish in London; by 'Kinde-Kit of Kingston' (1603?, 1620).

Westward Ho!, a novel by C. Kingsley (q.v.), published in 1855.

This was the most successful of the author's novels, and is a patriotic tale of adventure, Jesuit intrigue, and naval enterprise of the time of Queen Elizabeth. The hero, Amyas Leigh, a spirited Devonshire lad, after being disappointed in his desire to sail with John Oxenham on his last ill-fated expedition, has accompanied Drake on his voyage round the world. The story continues with his participation in the military measures against the Spaniards who landed at Smerwick in 1580, in the course of which he takes prisoner a Spanish captain, Don Guzman. The latter, while on parole in Devonshire, falls in love with the beautiful Rose Salterne, and, assisted by Amyas's Jesuit cousin, Eustace, induces her to leave her home, marries her, and carries her off to the Spanish main. Amyas and his brother Frank, and other disappointed suitors of Rose, with Salvation Yeo, 'flower and pattern of all bold mariners', sail in pursuit, but with tragic results. Rose, brought under suspicion by their action, falls a victim to the Inquisition, together with Frank Leigh. Amyas and his ship's crew wander for three years in South America, capture a Spanish galleon, and return to England with the beautiful Ayacanora, whom they have found ruling an Indian tribe. The last chapters of the book are devoted to Amyas's pursuit of his vengeance on Don Guzman, for which the arrival of the Armada provides an opportunity. But Providence takes the vengeance out of his hands. After a long pursuit the Spaniard is wrecked and drowned, and Amyas is struck blind by lightning. He ends by marrying Ayacanora, who has proved to be the daughter of John Oxenham.

Westward Hoe, a comedy by J. Webster (q.v.) and Dekker (q.v.), printed in 1607, but entered at the Stationers' Hall in 1605.

The main plot deals with an escapade of three merry wives and their gallants to Brentford, where their husbands find them at an inn, but their innocence is established. In the sub-plot Justiniano, an Italian merchant, convinced of his wife's infidelity, abandons her and lives disguised, enjoying the comedy of London life. Mistress Justiniano is involved in an intrigue with a profligate earl, but conscience intervenes, and repentance and reconciliation follow.

Weyburn, MATTHEW (MATIE), a character in Meredith's 'Lord Ormont and his Aminta' (q.v.).

WEYMAN, STANLEY JOHN (1855–1928), established his reputation as an historical novelist by 'A Gentleman of France' (1893, dealing with the period of Henry of Navarre, followed by a number of other romances of a similar character, showing imagination based on sound historical knowledge, and including 'Count Hannibal' (1901, the Massacre of St. Bartholomew) and 'Chippinge' (1906, the Reform Bill).

WHARTON, EDITH (1862–1937), American novelist, born in New York. She was a friend of Henry James (q.v.) and deeply influenced by him, but her work is original and of distinct character. She spent much of her life in France, and Europe as often as the United States is the scene of her fiction. She excelled in both the short story and the novel. Her chief books were 'The Valley of Decision' (1902), 'The House of Mirth' (1905), 'Ethan Frome' (1911), 'The Reef' (1912), 'The Custom of the Country' (1913), 'Xingu and Other Stories' (1916), 'The Age of Innocence' (1920), 'Glimpses of the Moon' (1922), 'The Children' (1928), 'Hudson River Bracketed' (1929), 'The World Over' (1936), 'A Backward Glance' (autobiography, 1934).

What you Will, (1) sub-title of Shakespeare's 'Twelfth Night' (q.v.); (2) a comedy by John Marston (q.v.), printed in 1607, of no great importance, except for containing, it is said, some satire of Ben Jonson.

WHATELY, RICHARD (1787–1863), educated at Oriel College, Oxford, of which he became fellow and tutor. He was principal of St. Alban Hall, 1825–31, and professor of political economy at Oxford, 1829–31. He was appointed archbishop of Dublin in the latter year. His 'Historic Doubts relative to Napoleon Buonaparte' (1819) is a clever satire on rationalist criticism of the Scriptures. His Bampton Lectures on 'The Use and Abuse of Party Feeling in Matters of Religion' were published in 1822. But his fame rests chiefly on his 'Logic' and 'Rhetoric', popular expansions of articles in the 'Encyclopaedia' (1826 and 1828). In theology he showed himself a critic of dogma, and was a supporter of the Broad Church views.

WHEATLEY, PHILLIS (1753?–85), Negro poet, born in Africa and shipped as a child to the slave-market of Boston, the first of her race to contribute to American literature. Her poems were first published in London in 1773.

Wheel, in prosody, see *Bob and Wheel.*

WHETSTONE, GEORGE (1544?–87?), author of miscellaneous verse and prose tales, is principally remembered for his 'Promos and Cassandra' (1578), a play in rhymed verse (based on a tale in Cinthio's 'Hecatommithi'), which provided the plot for Shakespeare's 'Measure for Measure' (q.v.) and is an early example of English romantic comedy.

WHEWELL, WILLIAM (1794–1866), the son of a carpenter, educated at Lancaster Grammar School and Trinity College, Cambridge, learned German thoroughly and helped to introduce the analytical methods of continental metaphysicians. He was professor of moral philosophy at Cambridge from 1838 to 1855, and master of Trinity College from 1841 till his death. His principal works were the 'History' (1837) and the 'Philosophy' (1840) 'of the Inductive Sciences', his 'Astronomy and Physics in reference to Natural Philosophy' (1833), and his treatise (published anonymously in 1853) contesting the probability of the 'Plurality of Worlds'. He published and edited many other works in natural and mathematical science, philosophy, and theology, including 'Elements of Morality' (1845) and 'The History of Moral Philosophy in England' (1852).

Whiff of Grapeshot, The, the title of the last chapter of Carlyle's 'French Revolution' in which he describes how Buonaparte with artillery quelled the insurrection headed by the 'Section Lepelletier' against the Convention on the 13th Vendémiaire of the year IV (5 Oct. 1795).

Whig, a word probably shortened from *Whiggamore*, one who urges on a mare, was originally applied to the Covenanters in the west of Scotland who in 1648 wrested the government from the Royalist party and marched as rebels to Edinburgh, and in later years to the extreme section of the Covenanting party. About 1679 it was applied to the Exclusionists, who opposed the succession of James II to the Crown. Hence from 1689 it came to be used for an adherent of one of the two great political parties in England. Since the middle of the 19th cent. the term has been mostly superseded by *Liberal*, but is occasionally used to express adherence to moderate or antiquated Liberal principles. [OED.] It is often applied to the great Whig families who professed a kind of aristocratic or limited fondness for liberty.

Whig Examiner, The, a literary and political periodical published by Addison (q.v.). Five numbers appeared in Sept. to Oct. 1710.

Whisker, in Dickens's 'The Old Curiosity Shop' (q.v.), the Garlands' pony.

Whiskerandos, DON FEROLO, in Sheridan's 'The Critic' (q.v.), the lover of Tilburina.

Whist, the name of the popular card-game developed from the 16th-cent. game called 'Triumph' (whence the word 'trump') or 'Ruff and Honours'. The name may perhaps be due to the silence which prevails during the game, but it was originally 'whisk', and is so called by Taylor the water-poet and by Farquhar.

Whistlecraft, see *Frere.*

WHISTLER, JAMES ABBOT McNEILL (1834–1903), painter and etcher, born at Lowell, Massachusetts. He settled in England in 1866, living in Chelsea. In reaction against Victorian subject pictures, he called his paintings, both portrait and landscape, by such names as 'symphony' or 'nocturne' to emphasize their aesthetic qualities. In 1878 he brought a libel action against Ruskin for condemning his 'Nocturne in Black and Gold' as 'flinging a pot of paint in the public's face' and was awarded a farthing's damages. He was a friend of Oscar Wilde and his equal as a wit, as can be seen in 'The Gentle Art of Making Enemies' (q.v.).

Whit-Sunday, the seventh Sunday after Easter, observed as a festival of the Christian Church in commemoration of the descent of the Holy Spirit on the day of Pentecost. *Whit* is for *white*, and is generally taken to refer to the ancient custom of the wearing of white baptismal robes by the newly baptized at the feast of Pentecost (from which our word 'candidate' is derived).

Whitaker's Almanack, founded in 1868 by Joseph Whitaker (1820–95), a publisher, and at one time (1856–9) editor of 'The Gentleman's Magazine'. It is a compendium of general information regarding the government, finances, population, and commerce of the world, with special reference to the British Commonwealth and the United States, besides being an almanac in the ordinary sense.

WHITE, GILBERT (1720–93), born at Selborne in Hampshire, was educated at Oriel College, Oxford, of which he became a fellow. He spent most of his life as curate of Selborne, refusing various livings in order to remain in his beloved birthplace. He began in 1751 to keep a 'Garden Kalendar' and later a 'Naturalist's Journal'. He made the acquaintance of two distinguished naturalists, Thomas Pennant and the Hon. Daines Barrington, with whom from 1767 he carried on a correspondence which formed the basis of his 'Natural History and Antiquities of Selborne' (published in 1789). He died at his house, 'The Wakes', Selborne. 'A Naturalist's Calendar, extracted from the papers of the late Rev. Gilbert White' appeared in 1795. An edition of his 'Works on Natural History' with notes by Bell, Daniel, Owen, and Yarrell, was issued in 1837. An edition of his 'Journals' by Walter Johnson was published in 1931. The Selborne Society for the preservation of birds, plants, etc., was founded in 1885 in memory of Gilbert White.

WHITE, HENRY KIRKE (1785–1806), the son of a butcher at Nottingham, was articled to a lawyer at Nottingham. By a volume of verses (1803) he attracted the favourable notice of Southey, who thereafter protected him, and wrote a memoir of him in 1807 after his death. White obtained a sizarship at St. John's College, Cambridge, where overwork brought about his death. He was praised by Byron, but little survives of his work except one or two hymns ('Oft in danger, oft in woe').

WHITE, JOSEPH BLANCO (1775–1841), born at Seville, entered Seville University in 1790 and was ordained priest, but abandoned the priesthood, came to England, and studied at Oxford. He published 'Evidences against Catholicism' in 1825, received the degree of M.A. at Oxford in recognition of his services to the Church, and settled at Oriel College. He became a friend of Whately, and, when the latter was appointed archbishop of Dublin, accompanied him there as tutor to his son. His other publications include 'Observations on Heresy and Orthodoxy' (1835), and translations into Spanish of Paley's 'Evidences', etc. He wrote the sonnet on 'Night and Death' (published in the 'Bijou', 1828), which Coleridge declared the finest and most grandly conceived sonnet in our language.

WHITE, PATRICK (1912–), Australian novelist, author of 'Happy Valley' (1939), 'The Living and the Dead' (1941), 'The Aunt's Story' (1948), 'The Tree of Man' (1956), 'Voss' (1957), 'Riders in the Chariot' (1961), and 'The Burnt Ones' (1964).

WHITE, TERENCE HANBURY (1906–64), is best known for his trilogy on the Arthurian legend, published under the title 'The Once and Future King' (1958). He also wrote 'Farewell Victoria' (1933), a novel, and 'The Goshawk' (1951), an account of how he trained a hawk. 'The Book of Beasts' (1954) is a translation from a 12th-cent. Latin bestiary.

WHITE, WILLIAM HALE (1831–1913), known as a writer under the pseudonym MARK RUTHERFORD, was the son of William White, a dissenter, bookseller, and later a well-known doorkeeper of the House of Commons and author of 'The Inner Life of the House of Commons' (1897). Hale White was educated with a view to becoming an independent minister, but in 1854 entered the Civil Service, rising to be assistant director of contracts at the Admiralty.

His literary work began with the publication in 1881 of 'The Autobiography of Mark

Rutherford', followed in 1885 by its sequel 'Mark Rutherford's Deliverance', works of intimate spiritual self-revelation, marked by sincerity and depth of feeling and ironic humour. His other imaginative works were: 'The Revolution in Tanner's Lane' (1887), 'Miriam's Schooling and other Papers' (1890), 'Catharine Furze' (1893), 'Pages from a Journal' (1900), 'More Pages from a Journal' (1910), and 'Last Pages from a Journal' (posthumous, 1915). Under his own name he translated Spinoza's 'Ethic' (1883) and 'Emendation of the Intellect' (1895), and published an 'Examination of the Charge of Apostasy against Wordsworth' (1898) and 'John Bunyan' (1905).

White's, a chocolate-house in St. James's Street, London, started in 1697 by Francis White. The first number of 'The Tatler' announced that accounts of gallantry, pleasure, and entertainment would emanate from White's Chocolate House. It was taken over by Arthur (the founder of Arthur's Club) and converted into a club, which became a celebrated gaming centre. The present clubhouse with its bow-window (associated with Beau Brummel) dates from 1755, though much altered inside and out.

White Company, THE, a body of English mercenaries led by the condottiere Hawkwood (q.v.) about 1360 into Italy, where they took part in the wars then prevailing. They are found fighting for the marquis of Monferrato against Milan, and for Pisa against Florence. Sir A. Conan Doyle (q.v.) wrote a spirited story with this title about a similar company.

White Cross Knights, see *Hospitallers of St. John of Jerusalem.*

White Divel, The, or *Vittoria Corombona,* a tragedy by J. Webster (q.v.), produced *c.* 1608, published in 1612. The play is founded on events that took place in Italy in 1581–5.

The duke of Brachiano, husband of Isabella, the sister of the duke of Florence, is weary of her and in love with Vittoria, wife of Camillo. Flamineo, brother of Vittoria, helps Brachiano to seduce her, and contrives the death of Camillo, while Brachiano causes Isabella to be poisoned. Vittoria is tried for adultery and murder, and in spite of her 'innocent-resembling boldness' sentenced to confinement, whence she is carried off and married by Brachiano. Flamineo quarrels with his young brother, the virtuous Marcello, and kills him. The duke of Florence avenges Isabella by poisoning Brachiano, and two of his dependants kill Vittoria and Flamineo. The play contains many splendid passages, including the famous dirge by Cornelia, the mother of Marcello, over her dead son, 'Call for the robin-red-breast and the wren' (Act v. iv).

White Friars, THE, the Carmelites, whose habit is distinguished by a white cloak and scapular. They had a convent in Fleet Street, London, which gave its name to the adjoining district.

White Hart Inn, THE, in Southwark, is referred to by Shakespeare in '2 Henry VI', IV. viii, as the headquarters of Jack Cade. There, at a later period, Mr. Pickwick first met Sam Weller. It survived until 1889.

White Hoods of Ghent, a name given to members of the popular party in Ghent who led the rebellion against the count of Flanders in 1381. They are referred to in Taylor's 'Philip van Artevelde' (q.v.).

White Horse, THE, the figure of a white horse, reputed (by later writers) to be the ensign of the Saxons when they invaded Britain. Also the figure of a horse cut on the face of the chalk downs in Berkshire and popularly supposed to represent the 'White horse' of the Saxons. There are other 'White Horses' on the Downs, e.g. near Westbury. 'The Scouring of the White Horse', by Tom Hughes (q.v.), was published in 1859.

A white horse is the heraldic ensign of Brunswick, Hanover, and Kent.

White Horse Cellar, THE, stood at the corner of Piccadilly and Dover Street. It was a famous starting-point for coaches.

White House, THE, at Washington, the official residence of the President of the United States.

White Jacket, by H. Melville (q.v.), published in 1850, is a fictional narrative based on the author's life as a common seaman aboard a frigate in the U.S. Navy.

White Knight, THE, one of the chess pieces in Carroll's 'Through the Looking-glass' (q.v.).

White Lady, THE, a character of German folk-lore, appearing in various legends; perhaps a survival of the goddess Holda or Berctha of Teutonic mythology.

White Lady of Avenel, THE, a supernatural being introduced by Scott in 'The Monastery' (q.v.).

White Moon, THE KNIGHT OF THE, in 'Don Quixote' (q.v.), the bachelor Samson Carrasco, who assumes the disguise in order to overcome Don Quixote and oblige him to return to his home.

White Queen, THE, one of the chess pieces in Carroll's 'Through the Looking-glass' (q.v.).

White Rose, THE, the emblem of the House of York in the Wars of the Roses.

White Rose of Raby, THE, Cicely, daughter of Ralph Neville, first earl of Westmorland, wife of Richard, duke of York, and mother of Edward IV and Richard III.

White Ship, The, a poem by D. G. Rossetti (q.v.), included in 'Ballads and Sonnets', published in 1881.

The butcher of Rouen, Berold, tells the story of the sinking of the 'White Ship' in which Prince William, son of Henry I, was returning with his half-sister from France. The ship ran on a reef. The prince was placed in a boat and might have been saved, but returned to the ship to rescue his sister, whereupon the boat was swamped. As none of the courtiers dared to tell the king, a little child was sent to do so.

White Surrey, Richard III's horse (see Shakespeare, 'Richard III', v. iii).

Whiteboy, a member of a secret agrarian association formed in Ireland in 1761, so called from the fact that its members wore a shirt over their clothes to distinguish each other at night. The Whiteboys figure in 'Tales by the O'Hara Family' by Banim (q.v.).

Whitechapel, lying to the east of Aldgate, London, was in Strype's time 'a spacious fair street for entrance into the city eastward', 'a great thoroughfare, being the Essex Road'. The region became one of the worst localities in London, both in respect of its narrow filthy streets and disreputable inhabitants, until the construction of the broad Commercial Road through the centre of it, and better policing, improved its character. It is still a poor quarter and has a large Jewish population.

A WHITECHAPEL SHAVE, according to Dickens ('Uncommercial Traveller'), 'is in fact, whitening, judiciously applied to the jaws with the palm of the hand'.

WHITEFIELD, GEORGE (1714–70), educated at St. Mary de Crypt School, Gloucester, and Pembroke College, Oxford, joined Charles Wesley's 'Methodist Society', and undertook a missionary journey to Georgia in 1738. He subsequently engaged in evangelical preaching in New York, Pennsylvania, and other parts of America, adopting Calvinistic views, so that his followers and those of Wesley separated and formed rival parties. He became domestic chaplain to Lady Huntingdon in 1748, and founder of Lady Huntingdon's Connection, a body of Calvinistic Methodists, whom the countess energetically supported. He compiled a hymn-book (1753) and published sermons and autobiographical writings. Whitefield was ridiculed by Samuel Foote (q.v.) in his play 'The Minor', and was satirized in Graves's 'The Spiritual Quixote' (q.v.). See also *Mesopotamia*.

Whitehall, London, once known as York Place, from the residence of the archbishop of York, passed into the hands of Cardinal Wolsey, who built a palace there, which (like Hampton Court) he had to cede to Henry VIII. The name 'Whitehall' became current in James I's reign, when Inigo Jones designed a new palace, completing only the Banqueting House. The Tudor buildings were destroyed by fire in 1698 and Wren designed a new palace, but nothing was built. The execution of Charles I took place 'in the open street before Whitehall', between the centre of the Banqueting Hall and its north end (Loftie).

'Whitehall' is now the name of the street leading from Trafalgar Square to Westminster and, in a transferred sense, of the government offices which stand on and near the site of the palace.

WHITEHEAD, ALFRED NORTH (1861–1947), educated at Sherborne and Trinity College, Cambridge, professor of applied mathematics in the Imperial College of Science and Technology (1911–24), professor of philosophy at Harvard University (1924–36). He was the author of many important philosophical and mathematical works, including 'Principia Mathematica' (with Bertrand Russell, 1910), 'Science and the Modern World' (1925), 'Religion in the Making' (1926), 'Symbolism' (1927), 'Process and Reality' (1929), 'Adventures of Ideas' (1933).

WHITEHEAD, CHARLES (1804–62), poet, novelist, and dramatist, published in 1831 'The Solitary', a poem, which met with warm approval. His quasi-historical romances, 'Jack Ketch' (1834), 'Richard Savage' (1842), were also successful, as was also his play, 'The Cavalier' (1836). His career was wrecked by intemperance, and he died in Australia.

WHITEHEAD, WILLIAM (1715–85), educated at Winchester and Clare Hall, Cambridge, produced at Drury Lane in 1750 a tragedy, 'The Roman Father' (a version of Corneille's 'Horace'), which was highly successful and was followed by another tragedy, 'Creusa', in 1754, and a comedy, 'The School for Lovers', in 1762. He was appointed poet laureate in 1757. His productions in this capacity met with much unfriendly comment, to which he replied in 'A Charge to Poets' (1762), but his earlier productions are not without merit. His 'Plays and Poems' were collected in 1774, and a complete edition of his poems appeared in 1788.

Whites, THE, a faction in medieval Florence. See *Bianchi.*

Whitford, VERNON, a character in Meredith's 'The Egoist' (q.v.).

WHITMAN, WALT (1819–92), born on Long Island, New York, became an office boy at 11 years of age, and subsequently a printer, wandering school-teacher, and contributor to, and editor of, various magazines and newspapers. Deeply affected by the teachings of Emerson (q.v.), he published his first edition of 'Leaves of Grass' in 1855, twelve poems, saturated, as he describes it, 'with the vehemence of pride and audacity of freedom necessary to loosen the mind of still-to-be-form'd America from the folds, the superstitions, and all the long, tenacious, and stifling anti-democratic authorities of Asiatic and European past'. When Emerson was sent a copy he

replied hailing the work, with good reason, as 'the most extraordinary piece of wit and wisdom that America has yet contributed'. The second edition (1856) added 21 poems and the third edition (1860) 122. The six further editions that appeared in Whitman's lifetime were revised or added to, the work enlarging as the poet developed. During the Civil War Whitman worked as a clerk in Washington, but his real business was as a volunteer hospital visitor among the wounded, an experience which affected him deeply, as can be seen in his prose 'Memoranda During the War' (1875) and in the poems he published under the title of 'Drum-Taps' in 1865. In the 'Sequel' to these poems (1866) appeared the great elegy on Abraham Lincoln, 'When Lilacs Last in Dooryard Bloom'd'. In spite of his achievement, and his efforts at self-publicity, Whitman was disregarded by the public at large. He offended some by his outspokenness on sexual matters, but he also won admirers, some of the warmest being Englishmen, such as Swinburne and W. M. Rossetti (qq.v.). After a paralytic stroke in 1873 he left Washington and lived quietly in Camden, New Jersey, still writing, though without the originality of his earlier years.

WHITTIER, JOHN GREENLEAF (1807–92), American poet, was born of Quaker parents at Haverhill, Massachusetts, where Thomas Whittier, his Puritan ancestor had built the oak farmhouse described in 'Snow-Bound'. He began life as a farmer's boy and supported himself while at Haverhill Academy by shoemaking and teaching. His poetical instincts were aroused by reading Burns's poetry, and he was from early years an industrious writer. He edited various periodicals and became an ardent abolitionist, and secretary of the American Anti-Slavery Society, and was more than once attacked by mobs on account of his political opinions. After 1840 he lived in seclusion at Amesbury, near his birthplace. He has always been a popular poet in America, owing in part to the transparent sincerity and nobility of his character, in part to the appeal to the young made by his ballads. He published many volumes of poems, of which a final collected edition appeared in 1888–9. Among these the best known are 'Snow-Bound' (1866), a description of an old Puritan Colonial interior, and 'The Tent on the Beach' (1867), a cycle of verse tales.

Whittington, RICHARD (*d.* 1423), son of Sir William Whittington, a mercer in London. He rose to be lord mayor of London, 1397–8, 1406–7 (a year of plague), and 1419–20. He was a liberal benefactor of the city, leaving legacies for rebuilding Newgate prison and other purposes (including a city library). The popular legend of Whittington and his cat, the germ of which is probably of very remote origin, is not known to have been narrated before 1605, when a dramatic version and a ballad were licensed for the press. The story of a cat helping its owner to fortune has been traced in many countries of Europe. It is also suggested that it is based on a confusion between 'a cat' and the French *achat*, in the sense of 'trade'. According to the story, Whittington, when in the service of Mr. Fitzwarren, a London merchant, sent his cat, the only thing he possessed, as part of one of the latter's trading ventures; the king of Barbary, who was plagued with rats and mice, purchased the cat for an enormous sum. Meanwhile Whittington, in consequence of ill-treatment by the cook under whom he served as scullion, ran away. He rested at Holloway, and hearing Bow Bells ringing, as he fancied, the words,

> Turn again, Whittington,
> Lord Mayor of London,

returned to Fitzwarren's house.

Who's Who, an annual biographical dictionary of contemporary men and women. First issued in 1849 and now published annually (incorporating since 1901 'Men and Women of the Time').

Whole Duty of Man, The, a devotional work published in 1658, in which man's duties in respect of God and his fellow men are analysed and discussed in detail. The book was at one time attributed to Lady Dorothy Pakington (*d.* 1679). She was, however, probably only the copyist. The book, by internal evidence, is the work of a practised divine, acquainted with Hebrew, Syriac, and Arabic, perhaps Richard Allestree (1619–81), chaplain in ordinary to the king, Regius professor of divinity, and provost of Eton. It had enormous popularity, lasting for over a century; it is comparable in this respect only to the 'Imitatio Christi' and to Law's 'Serious Call'. Some of the injunctions in it belong to a sterner age than the present, e.g. 'But of all the acts of disobedience that of marrying against the consent of the parent is one of the highest.'

WHYMPER, EDWARD (1840–1911), a pioneer of Alpine climbing, who made the first ascent of a number of peaks in the Alps. His first successful ascent of the Matterhorn in July 1865 was followed by a disastrous descent, three of his party being killed. He related his experiences in 'Scrambles in the Alps' (1871). He published in 1892 'Travels among the Great Andes of the Equator'. Whymper was by profession a wood-engraver, and illustrated many books.

WHYTE-MELVILLE, GEORGE JOHN (1821–78), educated at Eton, and a captain in the Coldstream Guards, served in the Crimea as a major of Turkish irregular cavalry. He was killed in the hunting-field. His novels, in many of which hunting figures largely, include 'Digby Grand' (1853), 'Holmby House' (1860), 'Tilbury Nogo' (1861), 'The Gladiators' (1863), 'Contraband' (1870), 'Sarchedon' (1871), 'Satanella' (1872), 'Katerfelto' (1875),

'Roy's Wife' (1878), and 'Black but Comely' (1879). His 'Riding Recollections' appeared in 1878.

WHYTHORNE, THOMAS (1528–96), educated at Magdalen College School and Magdalen College, Oxford. After three years as 'servant and scholar' in the household of John Heywood (q.v.) he became a teacher of music and composer of madrigals. His autobiography, 'A Book of Songs and Sonetts', discovered in manuscript in 1955, was edited by James M. Osborn and published in 1961. It is not only an interesting document of Tudor life and poetry and music, but also, because Whythorne wrote in his own phonetic system, a key to the pronunciation of his day.

Wickfield, MR. and AGNES, characters in Dickens's 'David Copperfield' (q.v.).

WICKLIFFE, see *Wycliffe.*

Widdicombe Fair, the title of a popular song. 'For some reason or other, not exactly known', writes S. Baring-Gould in 'English Minstrelsie', 'this has become the accepted Devonshire song. . . . The date of words and tune is probably the end of the last [18th] cent.'

Tom Pearse lends his grey mare to carry a party (including Old Uncle Tom Cobbleigh) to Widdicome Fair, but the mare takes sick and dies, and is still to be seen haunting the moor at night. Widdicombe or Widecombe-in-the-Moor is near Ashburton.

Widdrington, see *Witherington.*

Widow, WIDDY, or WIDDER, THE, sometimes with the suffix 'of Windsor', soldiers' term of affectionate endearment for Queen Victoria. See Kipling's 'Plain Tales from the Hills', 'Barrack Room Ballads', etc.

Widow of Watling Street, The, see *Puritan (The).*

Widsith, a poem of 143 lines in Old English, so named after its opening word. It is included in the 'Exeter Book' (q.v.).

Widsith, a wandering minstrel, belonging to the Myrging tribe, speaks of his travels and the kings he has heard of. He pretends he was in Italy with Ælfwine (Alboin, 6th cent.), and with Eormanric (Hermanric, 4th cent.) king of the Goths, who gave him a rich bracelet. This he handed over to Eadgils, his own lord, who gave him land, his father's heritage. Thus do minstrels wander over many lands, giving fame and receiving gifts.

The kernel of the poem may belong to the 7th cent. or an even earlier date. It was elaborately edited by R. W. Chambers, 1912.

Wieland, see *Wayland the Smith.*

WIELAND, CHRISTOPH MARTIN (1733–1813), German poet and writer of romances, whose best-known works are light ironic verse-tales, drawn from medieval or oriental sources, of which 'Oberon' (on the story of Huon of Bordeaux, 1780) is a good example. Wieland translated eleven of Shakespeare's plays into German prose, and 'A Midsummer Night's Dream' into verse.

Wife of Bath, (1) see *Canterbury Tales*; (2) the title of an unsuccessful comedy by J. Gay (1713).

Wife of Usher's Well, The, a ballad of the Scottish border. The wife sends her three sons to sea, and soon gets tidings of their death. Their ghosts come back on one of the long nights of Martinmas, and the mother, deceived by the apparitions, orders a feast; but at cock-crow they disappear.

WIGGLESWORTH, MICHAEL (1631–1705), colonial American poet, born in England, who emigrated in 1638, and who is known chiefly for his long Calvinistic poem, 'The Day of Doom' (1662).

WILBERFORCE, WILLIAM (1759–1833), educated at St. John's College, Cambridge, and a M.P. for Yorkshire, devoted himself to the cause of the abolition, first of the slave-trade, then of slavery, and to other philanthropic projects. He published in 1797 'A Practical View of the Prevailing Religious System of Professed Christians', a work that had an immense influence. He was the leading layman in the 'Clapham Sect' (as Sydney Smith nicknamed the Evangelicals), and he just lived to know that the second reading of the Bill abolishing slavery was carried.

WILCOX, MRS. ELLA WHEELER (*née* Wheeler) (1850–1919), American poet and journalist, described ('The Times', 31 Oct. 1919) as 'the most popular poet of either sex and of any age, read by thousands who never open Shakespeare'. She began to publish poems in 1872, and her last volume, 'Poems of Affection', was published posthumously in 1920. Her books of verse include 'Poems of Pleasure', 'Poems of Passion', 'Poems of Hope', 'Poems of Experience', 'Poems of Progress', 'Poems of Love', 'Poems of Cheer', etc. Her 'Collected Poems' were published in 1921.

Wild, JONATHAN (1682?–1725), worked as a buckle-maker in London. He became head of a large corporation of thieves, and opened offices in London for the recovery and restoration of property stolen by his dependants. He gained notoriety as a thief-taker, and was ultimately hanged at Tyburn. His 'Life and Actions' were related by Defoe (1725). For Fielding's satire see *Jonathan Wild the Great*.

Wild Boar of the Ardennes, see *Ardennes*.

Wild-Goose Chase, The, a comedy by J. Fletcher (q.v.), acted with great success in 1621, and printed in 1652.

Mirabell, the 'wild goose', a Don Juan with an aversion to marriage, is 'chased' by Oriana, his betrothed, who tries various

wiles to bring him to the altar. She feigns madness for love of him, but is detected, and finally wins him in the disguise of a rich Italian lady. His two companions, Pinac and Belleur, with less assurance, carry on an amusing courtship of Rosalura and Lillia-Bianca, alternately pursuing and pursued, with ultimate success. Farquhar's comedy, 'The Inconstant', is based on this play.

Wild Huntsman, THE, a spectral huntsman of German folk-lore, the subject of a ballad ('Der wilde Jäger') by Bürger, imitated by Sir W. Scott. Scott's version was included in 'The Chase and William and Helen: two ballads from the German', published anonymously in 1796. The legend is that a wild-grave (keeper of a royal forest), named Falkenburg, not only hunted on the Sabbath but also tyrannized over the peasants under his authority. After his death he continued to haunt the forest, and he and his hounds might be heard, though rarely seen.

Wildair, SIR HARRY, a character in Farquhar's 'The Constant Couple' (q.v.) and in its sequel, which bears his name.

WILDE, OSCAR FINGAL O'FLA-HERTIE WILLS (1854–1900), educated at Trinity College, Dublin, and at Magdalen College, Oxford, gained at the latter the reputation of founder of an aesthetic cult, which was caricatured in Gilbert and Sullivan's comic opera, 'Patience'. In 1895 he was sentenced to two years' imprisonment with hard labour for homosexual practices. After his release he lived abroad and finally settled in Paris, where he died. He published his first volume of 'Poems' in 1881, followed by several works of fiction, including 'The Picture of Dorian Gray' (1891), and several sparkling comedies, of which the best known are 'Lady Windermere's Fan', produced in 1892; 'A Woman of No Importance', in 1893; and 'The Importance of being Earnest', in 1895. His play 'Salomé' (in French, see *Salome*) was published in 1893. But the most remarkable of his works were the 'Ballad of Reading Gaol' (1898) and 'De Profundis' (1905), written during his imprisonment. His 'Letters', edited by R. Hart-Davis, were published in 1962.

Wildenhaim, BARON, a character in Mrs. Inchbald's 'Lovers' Vows' (q.v.).

WILDER, THORNTON NIVEN (1897–   ), American novelist and dramatist, born in Wisconsin. 'The Bridge of San Luis Rey' (1927) is the best known of his novels, but 'Ides of March' (1948), among others, is also notable. He scored considerable success in the theatre with 'Our Town' (1938) and 'The Skin of Our Teeth' (1942).

Wildeve, DAMON, a character in Hardy's 'The Return of the Native' (q.v.).

Wildfell Hall, The Tenant of, a novel by A. Brontë (q.v.), published in 1848.

The tenant of Wildfell Hall is Helen Graham, said to be a widow. Her youth and beauty, her secluded mode of life, and her silence about her antecedents set the tongues of local gossips wagging, and the gossip turns to scandal when it is discovered that she receives secret visits from her landlord, Frederick Lawrence. Gilbert Markham, the narrator of the tale, a young gentleman farmer and her neighbour, who has fallen in love with her, is loyal in his conviction of her innocence until he overhears her in affectionate conversation with Lawrence. The result is a violent scene between the two men.

The threatened rupture of relations between Gilbert and Helen forces the latter to confide her secret to her lover, and this she does in the form of her diary, which occupies a great part of the book. In this she recounts her youthful marriage with Arthur Huntingdon, a drunken profligate, her miserable life with him, and her efforts to reclaim him, until his shameless conduct and corrupting influence on her child force her to seek the asylum of Wildfell Hall, provided for her by Lawrence, who is her brother. Soon after the revelation of her secret to Gilbert, Helen returns to her husband to nurse him in an illness which, aggravated by his intemperance, proves fatal. The discovery that Helen is now wealthy is an obstacle to the renewal of Gilbert's suit, but this is finally overcome.

Wildfire, MADGE, see *Murdockson.*

Wilding and **Mrs. Wilding,** characters in Shirley's 'The Gamester' (q.v.).

Wildrake, ROGER, a character in Scott's 'Woodstock' (q.v.).

Wilfer Family, THE, characters in Dickens's 'Our Mutual Friend' (q.v.).

Wilfrid or WILFRITH, ST. (634–709), bishop of York, of which see he was twice deprived. He was instrumental in winning the adherence of King Oswy of Northumbria to the Roman, as opposed to the Columban, Church (synod of Whitby), and was involved in other ecclesiastical disputes; he was imprisoned by Ecgfrid, king of Northumbria, in 680; and in 681 took refuge in Sussex, where he converted the South Saxons and taught them to fish. He twice appealed successfully to Rome against the deprivation of his functions. He is commemorated on 12 Oct. 'The Conversion of St. Wilfrid' is a beautiful tale in Rudyard Kipling's 'Rewards and Fairies'.

Wilhelm Meisters Lehrjahre and ***Wanderjahre,*** see *Goethe.*

Wilhelmstrasse, often used to signify the German Foreign Office, which stood in that street in Berlin.

WILKES, JOHN (1727–97), the son of a Clerkenwell maltster, was educated at the University of Leyden, and, after marrying an heiress much older than himself, led a life of dissipation and became a member of the Medmenham Abbey (q.v.) fraternity. He was elected M.P. for Aylesbury in 1757 and 1761. He founded in 1762 'The North Briton' (q.v.) in which he skilfully attacked the government of Lord Bute. His prosecution for libel in connexion with No. 45 of this paper and the publication of the obscene 'Essay on Woman' led to the suppression of 'The North Briton' and to his own expulsion from the House of Commons, and outlawry. He retired to Paris, whence he returned in 1768 and was elected M.P. for Middlesex, and his outlawry was reversed. He was again expelled from the House in 1769 for a libel in the 'St. James's Chronicle', and three times re-elected for Middlesex, his elections being each time annulled. He was made sheriff of London and Middlesex, and finally took his seat without opposition in 1774, in which year he was lord mayor of London.

A man of much wit, ability, and determination, though of low moral standard, and an idol of the London mob, he was the means of asserting and securing several of our most valuable political rights.

Wilkins, PETER, see *Peter Wilkins.*

WILKINSON, SIR JOHN GARDNER (1797–1875), educated at Harrow and Exeter College, Oxford, a distinguished Egyptologist, arrived independently at conclusions regarding hieroglyphics identical with those of Champollion (q.v.). He was author of a standard work, 'Manners and Customs of the Ancient Egyptians' (1837–41).

Will's Coffee-house, called after William Unwin, its proprietor, was at No. 1 Bow Street, at the corner of Russell Street. It was frequented in the 17th and 18th cents. by authors (notably by Dryden, Wycherley, Addison, Pope, and Congreve), wits, and gamblers. The first number of 'The Tatler' (q.v.) announced that all poetry appearing in it would be under the article of Will's Coffee-house.

Willbewill, THE LORD, in Bunyan's 'The Holy War' (q.v.), 'as high-born as any man in Mansoul', 'a man of great strength, resolution, and courage', one of the first that went over to Diabolus.

Will-o'-the-Wisp, see *Ignis Fatuus.*

Willet, JOHN, in Dickens's 'Barnaby Rudge' (q.v.), the host of the Maypole Inn, and JOE his son, finally the successful wooer of Dolly Varden.

Willett, WILLIAM (1856–1915), a builder, who with his father established a remarkable reputation for the houses they built in London, Chislehurst, Hove, and other places. He is especially remembered as the pioneer of 'daylight saving', of which he began the advocacy in 1907. The measure, to the furtherance of which he devoted much time, energy, and money, was adopted by parliament in 1916; but Willett did not live to see this.

William I, of Normandy, 'The Conqueror', king of England, 1066–87.

William II, or RUFUS, king of England, 1087–1100.

William III and Mary, king and queen of England from 1689. Mary died in 1694, William in 1702.

William IV, king of England, 1830–7.

William and Helen, see *Lenore.*

William and Margaret, a ballad by Mallet (q.v.), written in 1723, and first published in Aaron Hill's 'Plain Dealer', No. 36, July 1724. It is included in Percy's 'Reliques' under the title 'Margaret's Ghost'.

The ghost of Margaret, who has died before her time, betrayed by William, visits her faithless lover at dead of night, upbraids him, and bids him come and see 'how low she lies' in the grave. He goes to the grave, lays himself down, and never speaks more.

William de la Marck, see *Ardennes.*

William of Cloudesley, see *Adam Bell.*

WILLIAM OF MALMESBURY (*d.* 1143?), historian, was born between 1090 and 1096. He was educated at Malmesbury Abbey, and became librarian. He probably resided some time at Glastonbury, later revisions of his 'Gesta Regum Anglorum' containing notices derived from the history and charters of Glastonbury. His works include 'Gesta Regum Anglorum', covering the period from A.D. 449 to 1127; its sequel 'Historia Novella' dealing with English history to 1142; 'Gesta Pontificum Anglorum', finished 1125; and 'De Antiquitate Glastoniensis Ecclesiae', written between 1129 and 1139. William of Malmesbury is not only an historian of high authority, but a picturesque and vivacious writer, who diversifies his narrative with anecdotes, reminiscences, and comments. The 'Gesta Regum' has two passages about Arthur, whom William regards as a great warrior, while discrediting many of the stories about him (see E. K. Chambers, 'Arthur of Britain').

WILLIAM OF NEWBURGH (1136–98?), educated at the Augustinian priory of Newburgh, Yorkshire, was the author of a 'Historia Rerum Anglicarum' in Latin, covering the period from 1066 to 1198, but mainly devoted to the reigns of Stephen and Henry II. It is the best historical work extant by an Englishman of this period, and earned for its author Freeman's opinion that he was 'the father of historical criticism'.

William of Norwich (1132?–44), saint and martyr, was apprenticed to a tanner of Norwich. He is said to have been murdered when twelve years old by Jews as a victim, in compliance with what was believed to be a

Jewish rite. The resting-place of his body in Norwich Cathedral became a centre of pilgrimage. He is commemorated on 25 March.

William of Palerne, one of the earliest of the 14th-cent. alliterative English romances, of some 5,500 lines and probably of Latin source.

William is prince of Apulia. He is saved from poisoning in childhood by a werewolf (q.v.), who is, in reality, the heir to the kingdom of Spain, but has been enchanted by his stepmother, the queen of Spain. William falls in love with Melchior, daughter of the emperor of Rome, and William, as he flees with her, is again protected by the werewolf. William then fights against the king of Spain, captures him, and forces the stepmother to undo her magic. The werewolf is restored to human form and reveals the identity of William.

William of Wykeham (1324–1404), bishop of Winchester and chancellor of England, obtained a papal bull for the endowment of Winchester College in 1378, and issued the charter of foundation of New College, Oxford, in 1379. His college was built in 1380–6, and his school in 1387–94. He was first employed as clerk of the king's works at Windsor, and it has been suggested that he may have been the architect who planned the castle there.

Williams, CALEB, see *Caleb Williams.*

WILLIAMS, CHARLES WALTER STANSBY (1886–1945), poet, novelist, and theological writer. His novels, which have been described as supernatural thrillers, include 'War in Heaven' (1930), 'Descent into Hell' (1937), and 'All Hallows' Eve' (1944). Of his theological writings probably the most important was 'The Descent of the Dove' (1939). His literary criticism included a study of Dante, 'The Figure of Beatrice' (1943). In verse he wrote a number of plays on religious themes including 'Thomas Cranmer' (1936) and 'Seed of Adam' (1948), but his most original poetic achievement is perhaps his cycle on the Arthurian legend, 'Taliessin through Logres' (1938) and 'The Region of the Summer Stars' (1944). His work as a whole is concerned with the interrelation of romantic and theological ideas.

WILLIAMS, HELEN MARIA (1762–1827), resided chiefly in France after 1788 and wrote from there 'Letters' (1790–5) which contain interesting information on the state of Paris and France just before and during the Revolution.

WILLIAMS, ISAAC (1802–65), educated at Harrow and Trinity College, Oxford, came under the influence of Keble and was one of the participants in the Oxford Movement (q.v.). He contributed No. 80 to the 'Tracts for the Times', on 'Reserve in communicating Religious Knowledge'; also Nos. 86 and 87. He also was author of poems in 'Lyra

Apostolica' (q.v.) signed 'ζ', and of several volumes in prose and verse, notably the volume of poems entitled 'The Cathedral' (1838). His 'Autobiography' (edited by Sir G. Prevost in 1892) is an interesting record of the days of the Oxford Movement.

WILLIAMS, JOHN (1761–1818), satirist and miscellaneous writer, best known by his pseudonym 'Anthony Pasquin'. He was associated with various journals in Dublin and London, and wrote formidable theatrical criticisms. In 1797 he took out a libel action in respect of the poem, 'The Baviad', by William Gifford (q.v.), but failed when it was shown that he had himself libelled every respectable character in the kingdom from the sovereign down. He emigrated to America and died in poverty.

Williams, MICHAEL, in Shakespeare's 'Henry V' (q.v.), one of the English soldiers who converse with the king before the battle of Agincourt.

WILLIAMS, TENNESSEE (1914–), American dramatist, born in Mississippi. He made his reputation with 'The Glass Menagerie' (1945), which is set in the slums of St. Louis, and was even more successful with 'A Streetcar Named Desire' (1947), a violent and effective study of sexual aberration, also set in the South. Among other plays written in a similar evocative style and on related sensational themes are 'Rose Tattoo' (1951) and 'Cat on a Hot Tin Roof' (1955). His other writings include the novel 'The Roman Spring of Mrs. Stone' (1950).

WILLIAMS, WILLIAM CARLOS (1883–1963), American poet, born in New Jersey. He published many volumes of verse, of which the most ambitious is 'Paterson' (in five books, 1946–58). His own city becomes a symbol under which 'the beginning, seeking, achieving and concluding' of a man's life is expressed. His 'Collected Earlier Poems' appeared in 1951, and 'Collected Later Poems' in 1950.

Williamson, SIR JOSEPH (1633–1701), succeeded Arlington as secretary of state in 1674. He was a patron of Muddiman (q.v.), and it was under his direction that Muddiman started 'The Oxford Gazette' (q.v.) in 1665.

WILLIS, NATHANIEL PARKER (1806–67), born at Portland, Maine, American author of plays, essays, and poems. Among his works are: 'Pencillings by the Way' (1835), 'Loiterings of Travel' (1840), 'Letters from under a Bridge' (1840), 'Outdoors at Idlewild' (1854), 'Poems: Sacred, Passionate and Humorous' (1869).

Willoughby, SIR CLEMENT, a character in Fanny Burney's 'Evelina' (q.v.).

Willoughby, SIR HUGH (d. 1554), navigator, despatched by Sebastian Cabot (q.v.) in 1553 as captain-general of an expedition (with Richard Chancellor as pilot-major) which was to endeavour to reach China by the north-east passage. He perished on the coast of Lapland. The story of his great effort is given by Hakluyt (q.v.).

Willoughby, JOHN, a character in Jane Austen's 'Sense and Sensibility' (q.v.).

WILLOUGHBY DE BROKE, RICHARD GREVILLE VERNEY, *nineteenth Baron* (1869–1923), educated at Eton and New College, Oxford, master of the Warwickshire Foxhounds from 1900, was author of the classical 'Hunting the Fox' (1920).

WILMOT, ROBERT (*fl.* 1568–1608), dramatist, rector of North Ockendon, 1582, and of Horndon-on-the-Hill, 1585. He published in 1591 'The Tragedie of Tancred and Gismund' (q.v.), a play based on Boccaccio, and the oldest English play of which the plot is certainly taken from an Italian novel.

Wilmot, the name of the three principal characters in Lillo's 'The Fatal Curiosity' (q.v.).

Wilson, ALISON, in Scott's 'Old Mortality' (q.v.), the housekeeper of Silas Morton of Milnwood.

Wilson, CAPTAIN, in Marryat's 'Midshipman Easy' (q.v.), the captain of the hero's first ship.

WILSON, SIR ARNOLD TALBOT (1884–1940), author, among other works, of 'The Persian Gulf' (1928), two books on Mesopotamia during the War of 1914–18, and 'South West Persia' (1941).

WILSON, SIR DANIEL (1816–92), author of 'The Archaeology and Prehistoric Annals of Scotland' (1851) and 'Memorials of Edinburgh in the Olden Time' (1846–8), and some biographical and other works.

WILSON, EDMUND (1895–), American critic and novelist, born in New Jersey. His critical writings include 'Axel's Castle' (1931), essays on the Symbolist movement, and 'The Wound and the Bow' (1941), essays on Dickens, Kipling, etc. 'To the Finland Station' (1940) is an account of the European revolutionary tradition. His other writings include the novel 'I Thought of Daisy' (1929), and 'Memoirs of Hecate County' (1946), short stories.

WILSON, JOHN (1627?–96), a native of Plymouth, was educated at Exeter College, Oxford, and became a barrister of Lincoln's Inn and recorder of Londonderry. His principal plays are two comedies on the Jonsonian model, 'The Cheats' (1664) and 'The Projectors' (1665), in which sharks, bravoes, usurers, astrologers, and their victims are vigorously and effectively displayed; and a tragedy, 'Andronicus Comnenius' (1664), based on the adventurous career of the Roman emperor Andronicus Comnenus (1183–5). A fourth drama, 'Belphegor, or the Marriage of the Devil', was printed in 1691.

WILSON, JOHN (1785–1854), educated at Glasgow University and Magdalen College, Oxford, was elected professor of moral philosophy at Edinburgh University in 1820 on the strength of his Tory principles. He joined the editorial staff of 'Blackwood's Magazine' (q.v.) in 1817, and contributed to it the greater number of the 'Noctes Ambrosianae' (q.v.), in which he figures as 'Christopher North'. He joined with Lockhart and Hogg in the production of the famous 'Translation from an Ancient Chaldee Manuscript', in which Edinburgh notabilities were satirized in scriptural language ('Blackwood', Oct. 1817). He was author of the poems 'The Isle of Palms' (1812) and 'The City of the Plague' (1816). 'The Recreations of Christopher North' appeared in 1842, and several volumes of his essays in 1866. His 'Works' were edited by Prof. Ferrier in 1855–8. Wilson was one of the first critics to do justice to the poetry of Wordsworth.

WILSON, THOMAS (1525?–81), educated at Eton and King's College, Cambridge, privy councillor and secretary of state in 1578, published the 'Rule of Reason' in 1551, and the 'Art of Rhetorique' in 1553. The latter is noteworthy in the history of English literature; in it the author urges the importance of writing of English matters in the English tongue, avoiding affectations and latinisms.

Wilton, JACKE, see *Unfortunate Traveller.*

Wimble, WILL, in Addison's 'The Spectator' (q.v.), a friend of Sir Roger de Coverley, a good-natured officious fellow, who hunts a pack of dogs better than any man in the country, and is generally esteemed for the obliging services that he renders to all.

Wimsey, LORD PETER, the detective hero of many stories by Dorothy Sayers.

Winchester College, see *William of Wykeham* and *Wykehamist.*

WINCHILSEA, ANNE FINCH, *Countess of* (1661–1720), a writer of pleasant occasional verse (praised by Sir E. Gosse) and a friend of Pope and Rowe (qq.v.). Wordsworth found affinities in some of her work. One of her longer poems, 'The Spleen', contains a couplet about the 'jonquille' and 'Aromatick Pain' of which there are echoes in Pope's 'Essay on Man' and Shelley's 'Epipsychidion'.

WINCKELMANN, JOHANN JOACHIM (1717–68), the son of a German shoemaker, became the founder of the modern study of Greek sculptures and antiquities. By his understanding of the ideal of Greek art, its spiritual quality, its sense of proportion, and its 'noble simplicity and quiet grandeur', he exerted an immense influence on subsequent thought and literature (e.g. on Goethe). His principal works were the 'Gedanken über die Nachahmung der griechischen Werke in der Malerei und Bild-

hauerkunst' (1755), and the 'Geschichte der Kunst des Altertums' (1764). Winckelmann is the subject of an essay by Pater and of 'The Conversion of Winckelmann' by A. Austin.

Windsor, HOUSE OF, since 1917 the official designation of the royal family of Great Britain.

Windsor Castle, in Berkshire, a royal residence, founded by William the Conqueror, and extended by his successors, particularly by Edward III and Charles II. It was rebuilt by Sir Jeffery Wyatville for George IV.

Windsor Forest, a pastoral poem by A. Pope (q.v.), published in 1713, combining descriptions of the English countryside and field sports with historical, literary, and political passages.

Winifreda, *Song to,* a poem published in 1726 and included in Percy's 'Reliques', extolling happy married life on moderate means. The author is unknown.

Winkle, NATHANIEL, in Dickens's 'The Pickwick Papers' (q.v.), one of the members of the Corresponding Society of the Pickwick Club.

Winkle, RIP VAN, see *Rip van Winkle.*

Winner and Waster, *Good Short Debate between,* an alliterative poem composed in the middle of the 14th cent., discussing the economic problems of the day. It perhaps contributed to inspire the 'Vision concerning Piers Plowman' (q.v.).

Winter's Tale, *The,* a play by Shakespeare (q.v.), probably produced in 1609–10, and based on Robert Greene's 'Pandosto' (q.v.). It was not printed until the folio of 1623.

Leontes, king of Sicily, and Hermione, his virtuous wife, are visited by Leontes' friend, Polixenes, king of Bohemia. Leontes, presently filled with a baseless suspicion of the relations of Hermione and Polixenes, attempts to procure the death of the latter by poison, and on his escape imprisons Hermione, who in prison gives birth to a daughter. Paulina, wife of Antigonus, a Sicilian lord, tries to move the king's compassion by bringing the baby to him, but in vain. He orders Antigonus to leave the child on a desert shore to perish. He disregards a Delphian oracle declaring Hermione innocent. He soon learns that his son, Mamillus, has died of sorrow for Hermione's treatment, and shortly after that Hermione herself is dead, and is thereupon filled with remorse. Meanwhile Antigonus leaves the baby girl, Perdita, on the shore of Bohemia, and is himself killed by a bear. Perdita is found and brought up by a shepherd. When she grows up, Florizel, son of King Polixenes, falls in love with her, and his love is returned. This is discovered by Polixenes, to avoid whose anger Florizel, Perdita, and the old shepherd flee from Bohemia to the court of King

Leontes, where the identity of Perdita is discovered, to Leontes' great joy, and the revival of his grief for the loss of Hermione. Paulina offers to show him a statue that perfectly resembles Hermione, and when the king's grief is intensified by the sight of this, the statue reveals itself as the living Hermione, whose death Paulina had falsely reported in order to save her life. Polixenes is reconciled to the marriage of his son with Perdita, on finding that the shepherd-girl is really the daughter of his former friend Leontes. The rogueries of Autolycus, the pedlar and 'snapper-up of unconsidered trifles', add gaiety to the later scenes of the play; and his songs, 'When daffodils begin to peer' and 'Jog on, jog on, the foot-path way', are famous.

Winterblossom, PHILIP, a character in Scott's 'St. Ronan's Well' (q.v.).

Winterbourne, GILES, a character in Hardy's 'The Woodlanders' (q.v.).

WIREKER, NIGEL (*fl.* 1190), precentor of Christ Church, Canterbury, author of 'Speculum Stultorum', a satire on monks, an elegiac poem recounting the adventures of Burnell the Ass (q.v.). It is referred to in Chaucer's 'The Nun's Priest's Tale'.

Wisden, *A Cricketer's Almanack*, first published in 1864 by John Wisden & Co. The first number contains the laws of cricket, scores of 100 and upwards from 1850 to 1863, records of extraordinary matches, etc. The publication still continues.

Wisdom of Solomon, one of the books of the Apocrypha, attributed by tradition to Solomon's authorship, but probably from a Greek original of a period little anterior to Christianity. It is an eloquent eulogy of wisdom, with illustrations of its beneficent influence, and a condemnation of idolatry.

Wise Men of Gotham, see *Gotham.*

Wise Men of Greece, see *Seven Sages.*

WISE, THOMAS JAMES (1859–1937), bibliographer, collector, and editor, who formed the great Ashley Library (q.v.). In 1934 his credit as a bibliographer was gravely damaged by the publication of a book ('An enquiry into the nature of certain 19th-century pamphlets' by J. Carter and G. Pollard, 1934) which proved that a large number of rare pamphlets whose authenticity depended upon Wise's statements were in fact forgeries—in particular an edition of Mrs. Browning's 'Sonnets from the Portuguese' (q.v.) said to have been published in Reading in 1847.

Wishfort, LADY, a character in Congreve's 'The Way of the World' (q.v.).

Wit without Money, a comedy by J. Fletcher (q.v.), written about 1614, printed in 1639.

Witch, The, a play by T. Middleton (q.v.), written before 1627, not printed until 1778.

The principal part of the plot is based on the story of the revenge of Rosamond on Alboin in the history of the kings of Lombardy. In Middleton's play the duchess is obliged by her husband to drink a health at a banquet out of a cup made from her father's skull and, to avenge herself, purchases by her pretended favours the help of a courtier, Almachides, to kill her husband. (The same subject is treated in D'Avenant's 'Albovine' (q.v.) and in Swinburne's 'Rosamund, Queen of the Lombards'.) In this and the subordinate intrigue, the assistance of the witch Hecate is called in, and part of the interest of the play lies in the comparison between Middleton's Hecate and the witches in Shakespeare's 'Macbeth'. Charles Lamb in his 'Specimens' has indicated the difference between them.

Witch of Atlas, The, a poem in *ottava rima* by P. B. Shelley (q.v.), written in 1820.

The poet, in playful mood, invents the myth of a beautiful and beneficent witch, the daughter of Apollo, who tames wild beasts, plays pranks in her magic boat among the clouds, can see the souls of men under their mortal forms, blesses those whom she sees most beautiful, but 'writes strange dreams upon the brain' of those who are less beautiful, and mischievously crosses their purposes.

Witch of Edmonton, The, a tragi-comedy by Dekker, J. Ford, W. Rowley (qq.v.), 'etc.' (as the title states), first performed probably in 1623, but not published until 1658.

Frank Thorney marries his fellow servant Winifred, without his father's knowledge and against his will. To save himself from being disinherited, he, at his father's bidding, also marries Susan Carter, and presently, to extract himself from his embarrassment, murders her and attempts to throw the guilt on her two rejected suitors, but is discovered and in due course executed.

The old woman of Edmonton, who is persecuted by her neighbours until she sells her soul to the devil in order to be revenged on them, and becomes the witch that they have called her, provides the title for the play, but has little connexion with the main plot. This part is notable for the characteristic sympathy shown by Dekker for the poor outcast.

Witch of Endor, THE, see *Endor.*

Witchcraft, The Discoverie of, see *Scott (R.)*

Witches' Sabbath, see *Sabbath (Witches').*

WITHER, GEORGE (1588–1667), was born at Bentworth in Hampshire and educated at Magdalen College, Oxford. His satires, 'Abuses stript and whipt', published in 1613, in spite of the innocuous character of their denunciations of Avarice, Gluttony, and so forth, earned him imprisonment in the Marshalsea. There he wrote five pastorals under the title of 'The Shepherd's Hunting', containing some of his best verse, a continuation of the 'Shepherd's Pipe' which he had written in conjunction with William Browne (q.v.), the 'Willie' of these eclogues. In the second of these, Wither (in the character of Philarete) describes the 'hunting of foxes, wolves, and beasts of prey' (the abuses) which got him into trouble with the government. His 'Fidelia', a poetical epistle from a faithful nymph to her inconstant lover, appeared in 1617 (privately printed, 1615) and again, with the famous song, 'Shall I, wasting in despair', in 1619. His 'Motto. Nec habeo, nec Careo, nec Curo', published in 1621, led again to his imprisonment; it is a pleasant self-eulogy, in three parts, dealing with the three phrases of his motto. In 1622 appeared his 'Mistress of Phil'Arete', a long panegyric of his mistress Arete, a partly real, partly allegorical personage; also the collection of pieces called 'Juvenilia', containing most of his best work. After this he became a convinced Puritan and published principally religious exercises, notably his 'Hymnes and Songs of the Church' (1623) and his 'Heleluiah' (1641). No complete edition of Wither's works has been published, but six collections were published by the Spenser Society, 1872–8. During the Civil War he raised a troop of horse for parliament in 1642, and was captain and commander of Farnham Castle in that year.

Witherington or WIDDRINGTON, in the ballad of Chevy Chase (q.v.), the knight who when his legs were cut off, fought upon his stumps.

Wititterly, MR. and MRS., in Dickens's 'Nicholas Nickleby' (q.v.), typical snobs.

Wits, The, a comedy by D'Avenant (q.v.), published in 1636.

This play is generally considered D'Avenant's comic masterpiece. Young Pallatine, a wit, who lives in London on an allowance, but finds it unequal to his wants, is in love with Lucy, who sells her jewels to provide him with money and is in consequence turned out of doors by her cruel aunt, who suspects her of misconduct. She takes refuge with Lady Ample, the rich ward of Sir Tyrant Thrift, who proposes to force an unwelcome marriage on his ward before he loses control over her. Meanwhile Pallatine's wealthy elder brother comes to town, with old Sir Morglay Thwack, for a spell of dissipation. He tells young Pallatine that he will never more give him money, but that he must live by his wits, as he himself and Thwack propose to do. In pursuit of this purpose they become involved in a series of adventures, are thoroughly fooled, and the elder Pallatine is released from his troubles only on making liberal provision for his brother and Lucy. Thrift is likewise fooled and held to ransom.

WITTGENSTEIN, LUDWIG JOSEF JOHANN (1889–1951), an Austrian Jew by birth, lived most of his adult life in Cambridge, England, where he was professor of philosophy (1939–47). Trained as an engineer, he came to philosophy through the study of the philosophy of mathematics with Bertrand Russell. He himself published only the 'Tractatus Logico-Philosophicus' (1922); in this aphoristic and difficult book he presents the view that the only meaningful use of language is as a picture of empirical, scientific fact; otherwise language will be tautological, as in logic and mathematics, or nonsensical as in metaphysics and judgements of value. About 1930 he began to doubt the correctness of this approach; he gradually developed the view that language had a vast multiplicity of uses, which he likened to the multiplicity of tools in a carpenter's tool-bag, and that the traditional problems of philosophy arose from a misunderstanding of the use of those concepts in terms of which the problems arose; this misunderstanding he likened to mental cramp or bewilderment, and held that the problems could be dissolved by carefully bringing out the true character of the language in which they were framed. Thus there were no philosophical results, in the form of answers to questions, but only the growth and dissolution of philosophical puzzlement. Amongst other posthumously published writings, the 'Philosophical Investigations' contains a full account of this later position.

Wittol, SIR JOSEPH, a character in Congreve's 'The Old Bachelor' (q.v.).

Witwoud, and his half-brother SIR WILFULL WITWOUD, characters in Congreve's 'The Way of the World' (q.v.).

Wives and Daughters, the last and unfinished novel of Mrs. Gaskell (q.v.), published in 'The Cornhill Magazine' 1864–6.

In this novel Mrs. Gaskell's subdued humour and irony are seen at their best. Mr. Gibson is the simple hard-working doctor of the little town of Hollingford. He is a widower at the outset of the story. Molly, his daughter, an honest and unselfish girl, is passionately devoted to her father. Dr. Gibson, partly to protect his growing daughter, partly to please himself, marries a widow, Mrs. Kirkpatrick, formerly governess at 'The Towers', the neighbouring seat of Lord Cumnor, a superficially attractive woman, but with all the petty vices of a shallow, selfish nature, to which Mrs. Gaskell amusingly holds up the mirror. The marriage of her father goes far to spoil Molly's previously happy life, but she loyally strives to accept the new conditions. Her lot is improved when Mrs. Gibson's own daughter, Cynthia, arrives from the Continent, where she has been educated, a fascinating girl without her mother's petty dishonesty, but also without Molly's capacity for deep love and strong sense of principle. She has entangled herself, when 16, with Mr. Preston, Lord Cumnor's clever but ill-bred agent, from whom she has borrowed money and who has availed himself of this to extract a secret promise of marriage from her; him, however, she now hates. Another family enters largely into the drama: Mr. Hamley, a hot-tempered, good-natured old squire; his gentle wife, who presently dies; and their two sons, Osborne and Roger. The parents' hopes are set on Osborne, handsome and clever, who is to distinguish himself at Cambridge and make a brilliant marriage. But he fails miserably at the university, and secretly marries a French governess. The resulting situation produces a bitter estrangement between Osborne and his father. Osborne's health fails and he dies, leaving a baby son, and the squire realizes too late his past harshness and the bitterness of his loss. Roger, the younger son, without his brother's outward charm, is made of sterner stuff, becomes senior wrangler and an eminent man of science. The story is largely occupied with the relations of the Gibson and Hamley families. The Hamleys are devoted to Molly, who falls in love with Roger, as Roger does with Cynthia. Cynthia, although engaged to Preston, accepts Roger, without loving him, to Molly's distress. However, realizing the incongruity of their characters, Cynthia throws him over and marries a man better suited to herself, after Molly has liberated her from the pursuit of Preston. All promises well when the unfinished work closes, for Roger has discovered the worth of Molly and will evidently marry her.

There are many pleasant and amusing subordinate characters: the arrogant Lady Cumnor; her kindly daughter, Lady Harriet; the Misses Browning and Mrs. Goodenough, genteel inhabitants of Hollingford.

Wizard of the North, THE, Sir W. Scott (q.v.).

WODEHOUSE, PELHAM GRENVILLE (1881–   ), humorous novelist, among whose chief works are: 'Uneasy Money' (1917), 'Piccadilly Jim' (1918), 'A Damsel in Distress' (1919), 'The Indiscretions of Archie' (1921), 'The Clicking of Cuthbert' (1922); and the series of Jeeves stories (from about 1911 onwards), which have been collected in 'My Man Jeeves', 'The Inimitable Jeeves', 'Carry on, Jeeves', 'Very Good, Jeeves', and 'The Jeeves Omnibus'.

Woden, the Old English name of the god called in Norse Odin (q.v.), from whom our 'Wednesday' or 'Woden's day' is derived.

WODROW, ROBERT (1679–1734), was minister of Eastwood near Glasgow, and university librarian of Glasgow. His works include a 'History of the Sufferings of the Church of Scotland from the Restoration to the Revolution' (1828–30). He also kept private notebooks (partly in cipher) published by the Maitland Club in 1842–3 as 'Analecta, or materials for a history of remarkable providences'. He was a great book-collector,

and left a valuable collection of broadsides and pasquinades (see J. H. Burton, 'The Book-hunter'). He is commemorated in the Wodrow Society, devoted to the history of Presbyterianism and the works of eminent Presbyterians.

Woeful Countenance, THE KNIGHT OF THE, Don Quixote (q.v.).

Woffington, MARGARET (1714?–60), 'Peg Woffington', the celebrated actress, was the daughter of a bricklayer in Dublin. She was engaged by Rich for Covent Garden in 1740 and was immediately successful, acting in a great number of leading parts. She quarrelled with Mrs. Bellamy and while playing Roxana to Mrs. Bellamy's Statira drove her off the stage and stabbed her. Her amours were numerous and for some time she lived with Garrick. For Charles Reade's novel and the play 'Masks and Faces' concerning her, see *Peg Woffington*.

WOLCOT, JOHN (1738–1819), 'PETER PINDAR', began his career as a physician, in which capacity he was attached to Sir William Trelawny, governor of Jamaica (1767–9). He then took holy orders, but returned to the practice of medicine in Cornwall. He abandoned medicine for literature in 1778 and removed to London with the painter Opie, whom he had helped. He published his satirical 'Lyric Odes to the Royal Academicians' in 1782–5, followed by a mock-heroic poem, 'The Lousiad' (q.v.) in 1785, and various satires on George III. He was attacked by Gifford in 'The Anti-Jacobin' (q.v.). His 'Bozzy and Piozzi', in which Boswell and Mrs. Thrale set forth their respective reminiscences of Dr. Johnson in amoebaean verse, appeared in 1786. He became blind before his death. He had a gift for the comical and mischievous exposure of foibles, but his work suffers from vulgarity of thought and inelegance of style.

Wolf of Badenoch, The, see Stewart (Alexander).

WOLFE, CHARLES (1791–1823), educated at Trinity College, Dublin, was curate of Donoughmore, co. Down, from 1818 to 1821. He was the author of the splendid lines on 'The Burial of Sir John Moore' (apparently based on Southey's narrative in the 'Annual Register', and first published in the 'Newry Telegraph' in 1817). Wolfe wrote no other poem worthy of remark (his 'Remains' were published in 1829).

WOLFE, THOMAS (1900–38), American novelist, born in North Carolina. He made his reputation with his first, largely autobiographical, novel 'Look Homeward, Angel' (1929). Among his other novels is 'Of Time and the River' (1935).

WOLFRAM VON ESCHENBACH (*fl. c.* 1200–20), a Bavarian knight and a great German epic poet, whose principal works were the epics 'Parzival' (q.v.) and 'Willehalm'. He also composed fragments of 'Titurel' (q.v.) and several *Tagelieder* (dawn pieces).

WOLLSTONECRAFT, MARY, see *Godwin (Mrs. M. W.).*

Wolsey, THOMAS, see *Cavendish (G.).*

Wolstan, ST., see *Wulfstan (St.).*

Woman in the Moone, The, a prose play by Lyly (q.v.), published 1597. The shepherds of Utopia ask Nature to provide a woman to 'comfort their sole estate'. Nature creates Pandora, endowing her with the qualities of the Seven Planets. Pandora's moods and actions vary as the planets in turn assume the ascendant, with consequent complications among the shepherds.

Woman in White, The, a novel by Wilkie Collins (q.v.), published in 'All the Year Round' in 1860.

The story is told by several of the characters in succession. Walter Hartright, a drawing-master, is accosted on a lonely road by a woman dressed entirely in white, who shows signs of being partially demented and appears to have escaped from an asylum. He is engaged by Mr. Fairlie, a selfish valetudinarian, to give lessons to his niece, Laura Fairlie, and her half-sister, Marian Halcombe. He falls in love with Laura, who strikingly resembles the woman in white, and she returns his love, but she has promised her father on his death-bed that she will marry Sir Percival Glyde, of Blackwater Park, and Hartright leaves the country in despair. The marriage of Laura to Sir Percival takes place, and it comes to light that Sir Percival, whose affairs are embarrassed, has married Laura to get possession of her wealth, that he is responsible for the confinement of the woman in white, Anne Catherick, in an asylum, and that Anne Catherick and her mother are in possession of a secret concerning Sir Percival, of which he is determined at all costs to prevent the revelation. Unable to obtain Laura's signature to the surrender of her money, Sir Percival and Count Fosco, his friend (a fat, smooth villain, admirably conceived), contrive to get Laura confined in an asylum as Anne Catherick, while Anne Catherick, who dies, is buried as Lady Glyde. The device is discovered by the courage and resource of Marian Halcombe, and Laura is rescued. At this point Hartright returns to England, takes Laura and Marian under his care, and discovers Sir Percival's secret (that he was born out of wedlock and has no right to the title). Sir Percival is burnt to death while tampering with the parish register in a last effort to save his position. Anne Catherick turns out to be Laura's half-sister, and Laura and Hartright are happily married. Fosco is forced to supply the information which restores Laura to her position, and is killed by a member of an Italian secret society that he has betrayed.

Woman Kilde with Kindnesse, A, a domestic tragedy by T. Heywood (q.v.), acted about 1603, printed in 1607.

Frankford, a country gentleman, is the husband of Anne, a 'perfect' wife. But his happiness is ruined by the treachery of Wendoll, a guest to whom Frankford has shown every kindness and hospitality. Frankford discovers Anne in the arms of Wendoll. But instead of taking immediate vengeance on her, he determines to 'kill her even with kindness'. He sends her to live in comfort in a lonely manor-house, only prohibiting her from seeing him or her children again. She dies from remorse, after having sent for Frankford to ask forgiveness on her death-bed, and received it.

This play, in which pathos and manliness are blended, is considered Heywood's masterpiece. It opens with a pleasant hawking scene.

Woman who did, The, a novel by Grant Allen, raising the question of the moral basis of marriage, published in 1895. It is the tragic story of a noble and pure-minded woman of advanced views, who regards marriage as a barbarous institution incompatible with the emancipation of women, courageously follows out her principle in her relations with the man she loves, and suffers the inevitable penalty.

Woman-Hater, The, see *Beaumont.*

Women beware Women, a tragedy by T. Middleton (q.v.), published in 1657, thirty years after his death.

The story involves two interwoven plots. The first is concerned with the guilty love of Hippolito for his niece Isabella. Hippolito's sister, Livia, makes Isabella believe that she is not akin to him and she then consents to marry a foolish young heir as a screen for her own passion for Hippolito.

The second is based on the life of the historical Bianca Capello. Bianca has run away from her father's house and married Leantio, a merchant's clerk. The duke, seeing her at her window, becomes enamoured of her and carries her off to be his mistress. Reproved by the cardinal, his brother, for his sin, he contrives the death of Leantio, and marries Bianca. For this purpose he incites Hippolito to kill Leantio by revealing to him that his sister Livia has become enamoured of Leantio. These various crimes, in the last act, meet with their retribution in a wholesale massacre of the characters.

Wonders of the World, THE SEVEN, see *Seven Wonders of the World.*

WOOD, ANTHONY, or, as he latterly called himself, ANTHONY À WOOD (1632–95), antiquary and historian, was educated at New College School, Oxford, Thame School, and Merton College, Oxford. He prepared a treatise on the history of the University of Oxford, which was translated into Latin and edited (with alterations) by Dr. John Fell (q.v.), dean of Christ Church, and published as 'Historia et Antiquitates Univ. Oxon.' (1674). Of this an English version by Wood, issued by John Gutch, is the standard edition (1786–96). Wood published 'Athenae Oxonienses' (1691–2), a biographical dictionary of Oxford writers and bishops, containing severe judgements on some of these, and was expelled from the University in 1693 at the instance of Henry Hyde, second earl of Clarendon, for a libel which the work contained on his father, the first earl. Several antiquarian manuscripts left by Wood were published posthumously. His 'Life and Times', edited by Andrew Clark, occupy five volumes of the Oxford Historical Society's publications (1891–1900). In the same series A. Clark has edited his 'History of the City of Oxford' (three vols., 1889–99).

WOOD, ELLEN, better known as MRS. HENRY WOOD (1814–87), novelist, among whose best-known works are 'East Lynne' (1861), 'The Channings' (1862), 'Johnny Ludlow' (1874–90), and 'Pomeroy Abbey' (1878).

Wood's half-pence, see *Drapier's Letters.*

Woodcock, ADAM, the falconer in Scott's 'The Abbot' (q.v.).

Woodcourt, ALLAN, a character in Dickens's 'Bleak House' (q.v.).

Wooden Horse, THE, an instrument of punishment, chiefly military, formerly in use. The back of the horse was a sharp wooden ridge, across which the offender was seated, with his hands tied behind his back, and muskets hung to his feet.

The Wooden Horse, Clavileño (q.v.), is the subject of an amusing episode in 'Don Quixote'.

Wooden Horse of Troy, THE, see *Horse (The Trojan)*.

Wooden Spoon, THE, a spoon made of wood, formerly presented by custom at Cambridge to the lowest on the honours list in the mathematical Tripos.

WOODFORDE, THE REVD. JAMES (1740–1803), fellow, and at one time sub-warden, of New College, Oxford, and the holder of livings in Somerset and later in Norfolk, was author of the 'Diary of a Country Parson' (5 vols., 1924–31) which gives a vivid picture of the life of the period in college and country parish, with special reference, incidentally, to what was eaten and drunk.

Woodhouse, MR., in Jane Austen's 'Emma' (q.v.), the father of Emma, an amiably egoistic old valetudinarian.

Woodlanders, The, a novel by Hardy (q.v.), published in 1887.

The scene is the wooded country on the skirts of Blackmoor Vale in Dorset. Honest Giles Winterborne, in the apple and cider

trade, is betrothed to Grace Melbury, daughter of a timber-merchant of Little Hintock. But on her return from the fashionable school to which she has been sent to finish her education, her social superiority to her rustic lover is evident. This and a financial misfortune that at this time befalls Giles induce her ambitious father to bring the engagement to an end, and to hustle his daughter into marriage with Edred Fitzpiers, a fascinating young doctor, a marriage to which she consents in spite of her suspicion of a low intrigue between Fitzpiers and Suke Damson, a village girl. Fitzpiers is presently lured away from his wife by the wealthy widow, Felice Charmond, and the hope of a divorce brings Grace and the faithful Giles together again. But the hope proves illusory. Fitzpiers returns from his travels abroad with Mrs. Charmond, and Grace flies for refuge to Giles's cottage in the woods. Owing to delicacy on his part and respect for the proprieties on hers, she is left alone in the cottage, and the man she loves, though ill, betakes himself to a crazy shelter of hurdles, where after a few days of exposure he dies. Mrs. Charmond being now dead, Grace and Fitzpiers are ultimately reconciled.

Parallel with the devotion of Giles to Grace is the devotion of poor plain Marty South, the typical primitive Wessex girl, to Giles. Marty and Grace meet by his death-bed and pray for his soul; together they regularly visit his tomb. At the end of the book, after Grace has rejoined her husband, Marty stands alone beside the tomb.

Woods of Westermain, The, a poem by G. Meredith (q.v.) included in 'Poems and Lyrics of the Joy of Earth', published in 1883.

Woodstock; or, The Cavalier. A tale of the year 1651, a novel by Sir W. Scott (q.v.), published in 1826. The work was written when misfortunes were heaping themselves upon the author: his financial ruin, the death of his wife, and the grievous illness of his beloved grandson.

The period is that of the Civil War, and the story centres in the escape of Charles II from England after the battle of Worcester. The scene is laid in the royal lodge and park of Woodstock, near Oxford, of which the gallant old cavalier, Sir Henry Lee, is ranger. His nephew, Colonel Markham Everard, has, for reasons of conscience, adopted the parliamentary cause, distinguished himself as a soldier, and earned the favour of Cromwell. On the other hand he has incurred the displeasure of the fiery old Lee, and the course of his love for Lee's daughter, Alice, has been gravely impeded. Parliamentary commissioners are sent to sequestrate Woodstock, but through Everard's influence with Cromwell are withdrawn, for Cromwell hopes that the fugitive Charles II will take advantage of the opportunities for concealment offered by the old lodge, and be captured there. Charles indeed arrives, disguised as the page of Colonel Albert Lee, Sir Henry's son; and during his residence at the lodge makes ardent love to the unwilling Alice, first in the character of page and, when this fails, of king. This brings about a fierce dispute between Everard and Charles, and bloodshed is prevented only by the interposition of Alice. The king, from a generous impulse, relieves the anguish caused to Everard by the preference apparently shown by Alice to his rival, by revealing to him his identity; and Everard promises not to betray him. Cromwell, advised by a spy of the presence of Charles at Woodstock, now arrives with a force to capture him, arrests Everard, and prepares to surround the lodge. During these preparations the king receives warning and flees, leaving Albert to personate him and thus delay the pursuit. After an exciting search, Albert is captured and the escape of the fugitive king is revealed. Cromwell, after having, in his fury, ordered the immediate execution of Everard, Sir Henry Lee, and his other prisoners, presently relents and pardons them. The reconciliation of Everard and Sir Henry, and the marriage of Everard and Alice, are brought about by a parting message from Charles. An important feature in the story is the supposed haunting of Woodstock. The Royalists take advantage of it, by 'playing at ghosts' in the secret passages of the old mansion, in order to defeat the intended sequestration.

The portrait of Cromwell has been criticized; the author makes, it is said, the mistake of representing Oliver as being in supreme power before he became lord protector in 1653. But the work gives a vivid picture of a reckless cavalier, Roger Wildrake; of the Revd. Nehemiah Holdenough, Presbyterian minister of the town of Woodstock; of Puritan soldiers and preachers (including Joseph Tomkins, the steward of the parliamentary commissioners, a mixture of hypocrisy and enthusiasm); and of plotters and spies on both sides.

Wookey Hole, a cavern in the Mendip Hills in Somersetshire, the legendary abode of the Witch of Wokey, a ballad concerning whom is included in Percy's 'Reliques'. She was changed into a stone by a 'lerned wight' from Glaston, but left a curse behind that the maidens of Wokey should find no lovers.

WOOLF, VIRGINIA (1882–1941), daughter of Sir Leslie Stephen (q.v.), author of fiction: 'The Voyage Out' (1915), 'Night and Day' (1919), 'Jacob's Room' (1922), 'Mrs. Dalloway' (1922), 'To the Lighthouse' (1927), 'Orlando: A Biography' (1928), 'The Waves' (1931), 'The Years' (1937), 'Between the Acts' (1941); essays and other works: 'The Common Reader: First Series' (1925), 'Second Series' (1932), 'A Room of One's Own' (1929), 'Flush: A Biography' (1940), 'The Death of a Moth' (1942), 'A Haunted House' (1943), 'The Moment' (1947), 'The Captain's Death Bed'

(1950), 'Granite and Rainbow' (1958). 'A Writer's Diary' (1953) was selected and edited by her husband, Leonard Woolf.

Virginia Woolf contributed to the development of the art of fiction. From 'Jacob's Room' to 'Between the Acts' she continued to experiment with the form of the novel, minimizing the importance of facts, events, and character analysis in order to concentrate on the moment by moment experience of living. She eliminated the author as·narrator or commentator. She was also a distinguished critic who excelled in conveying the impression made by an author or a work upon a receptive and cultivated mind. In 'A Writer's Diary' her reflections upon each of her works from its conception to its accomplishment convey a vivid impression of the joys and the agonies of creative effort.

WOOLMAN, JOHN (1720–72), American Quaker, who travelled during many years preaching the faith, and was author among other works of a 'Journal' (1774) notable for the purity of its style. Charles Lamb wrote, 'Get the writings of John Woolman by heart and love the early Quakers.'

WOOLNER, THOMAS (1825–92), sculptor and poet, one of the original Pre-Raphaelite Brethren (q.v.) and a contributor to 'The Germ' (q.v.). He met with small success and went to the Australian goldfields, his departure inspiring Madox Brown's picture 'The Last of England' (1852). The statue on the Thames embankment of J. S. Mill (q.v.) is by him.

Woolsack, THE, the usual seat, without back or arms, of the lord chancellor in the House of Lords, made of a large square bag of wool and covered with cloth. It is said to have been adopted in Edward III's reign as a reminder to the Lords of the importance to England of the wool trade. The term is often used allusively to signify the lord-chancellorship.

Woolsey, *The Life and Death of Thomas*, see *Cavendish (G.).*

Woolwich, on the Thames below London, often used to signify the Royal Military Academy, where cadets were trained for the Royal Artillery and Royal Engineers. Also a great arsenal. It is now a part of London.

Wooster, BERTRAM (familiarly known as 'Bertie'), an amiable, vacuous young man-about-town in the stories of P. G. Wodehouse (q.v.); the employer of Jeeves (q.v.).

Wopsle, MR., in Dickens's 'Great Expectations' (q.v.), a parish clerk who turns actor and plays Hamlet with indifferent success.

Worcester, THE BATTLE OF, fought on 3 Sept. 1651; the Scottish army with Charles II was utterly defeated by Cromwell, who referred to his victory as 'a crowning mercy'.

Worde, WYNKYN DE (active 1477–1535), printer, born at Worth in Alsace. His real name was Jan van Wynkyn. He came to London *c.* 1477 and became Caxton's (q.v.) assistant, inheriting his press on Caxton's death in 1491. He printed nearly 800 books, including new editions and broadsides. Among the most notable were 'The Golden Legend' (1493), the 'Vitae Sanctorum Patrum' of St. Jerome, translated by Caxton (1495), 'Morte Darthur' (1498), and 'The Canterbury Tales' (1498).

WORDSWORTH, DOROTHY (1771–1855), sister and constant companion of W. Wordsworth. Her 'Journals' were edited by W. Knight, 1896 and 1904. A life and study of her by E. de Selincourt appeared in 1933.

WORDSWORTH, WILLIAM (1770–1850), born at Cockermouth, the son of an attorney of that place, was educated at the grammar school of Hawkshead and St. John's College, Cambridge, leaving the University without distinction. In 1790 he went on a walking tour in France, the Alps, and Italy. He returned to France late in 1791, and spent there a year. The revolutionary movement was then at its height and exercised a strong influence on his mind. While in France he fell in love with the daughter of a surgeon at Blois, Annette Vallon, who bore him a daughter (see Émile Legouis, 'William Wordsworth and Annette Vallon', 1922). The episode is in part reflected in 'Vaudracour and Julia', written in 1805. In 1793 he published 'An Evening Walk' and 'Descriptive Sketches' (of the Alps), his first serious poetical efforts. When the French Revolution was followed by the English declaration of war and the Terror, Wordsworth's republican enthusiasm gave place to a period of pessimism, which manifested itself in his tragedy, 'The Borderers' (q.v.), written in 1795–6. He received in 1795 a legacy of £900, left to him by his friend Raisley Calvert, a mark of Calvert's confidence in Wordsworth's genius. In the same year Wordsworth made the acquaintance of S. T. Coleridge (q.v.). A close and long-enduring friendship developed between the poets, and Wordsworth, his sister Dorothy, and Mr. and Mrs. Coleridge lived for a year in close intercourse at Alfoxden and Stowey in Somerset. Together the poets published in 1798 'Lyrical Ballads' (q.v.), which marked a revival in English poetry, but was unfavourably received. The volume contained the 'Lines written above Tintern Abbey' (written in 1798). Together also, at the end of the same year, the poets went to Germany, Wordsworth and his sister wintering at Goslar. Here Wordsworth began 'The Prelude' (q.v.) and wrote 'Ruth', 'Lucy Gray', 'Nutting', the lines on 'Lucy' (q.v.), and other beautiful poems. In 1799 he settled with his sister at Grasmere, where he spent the remainder of his life (at first at Dove Cottage). In 1800 appeared an enlarged edition of the 'Lyrical Ballads', with

a critical essay named 'Observations', expounding Wordsworth's principles of poetry, to which was added in 1802 an appendix on 'Poetic Diction'. This edition of the 'Lyrical Ballads', and particularly the 'Observations', were received by the critics with extreme hostility, which left Wordsworth unmoved. To the year 1800 belongs 'Michael', one of the most harmonious of Wordsworth's poems. His financial position having been improved by the repayment of a debt on the death of Lord Lonsdale, he married in 1802 Mary Hutchinson of Penrith. He made a tour in Scotland in 1801, a journey to Calais in 1802, and another tour in Scotland in 1803, and began a cordial friendship with Sir W. Scott (q.v.). Events abroad now changed his political attitude to one of patriotic enthusiasm, while the death of his brother John in 1805 and the physical decline of his friend, S. T. Coleridge, deeply affected him. In 1805 he completed 'The Prelude', which, however, was not published until after his death. In 1807 he published poems, including the odes to 'Duty' (written in 1805) and on 'Intimations of Immortality', 'Miscellaneous Sonnets', and 'Sonnets dedicated to Liberty'. To the same year belongs 'The White Doe of Rylstone' (a tragedy of the time of Queen Elizabeth, in which the surviving daughter of a family of Catholic rebels is comforted by the visits of a white doe that she has reared in happier times), published in 1815. In 1813 he was given the office of distributor of stamps for the county of Westmorland, which brought him in some £400 a year. He now moved to Rydal Mount, Grasmere, which he occupied till his death. He again toured in Scotland in 1814, and in that year published 'The Excursion' (q.v.), of which a part, 'The Story of Margaret', had been written many years before (1797). In the same year was written 'Laodamia', on the legend of the wife of Protesilaus, who is allowed by Hermes to converse with the shade of her husband killed before Troy, and dies when the shade disappears. 'Dion' and the 'Ode to Lycoris', further poems on classical subjects, followed in 1816 and 1817. 'Peter Bell' (q.v., written in 1798) and 'The Waggoner' (q.v., written in 1805) appeared in 1819. To this year belong the 'River Duddon' sonnets, published in 1820. The 'Ecclesiastical Sonnets' appeared in 1822. He travelled on the Continent in 1820, 1823, and 1828, publishing in 1822 a volume of poems entitled 'Memorials of a Tour on the Continent'. He went to Ireland in 1829, to Scotland in 1831 (writing 'Yarrow Revisited', published in 1835), and again in 1833. A tour in Italy in 1837 inspired several pieces, published in his last volume, 'Poems chiefly of Early and Late Years' (1842). He resigned his place in the stamp office and received a civil list pension in 1842. In 1843 he succeeded Southey as poet laureate. His later writings show him in politics converted from a revolutionist to an opponent of liberalism. He was buried in Grasmere churchyard.

Mention should be made of two prose works by Wordsworth: his essay 'Concerning the Relations of Great Britain, Spain, and Portugal . . . as affected by the Convention of Cintra', published in 1809, in which he deplores the lack of vigour shown by the English policy; and 'A Description of the Scenery of the Lakes in the North of England', written in 1810 as an introduction to T. Wilkinson's 'Select Views in Cumberland' and republished with additions in 1822, an interesting account of the county and its inhabitants.

Wordsworth's 'Poetical and Prose Works', together with Dorothy Wordsworth's 'Journals', edited by W. Knight, appeared in 1896, and his 'Poetical Works' (ed. E. de Selincourt and H. Darbishire, 5 vols.) in 1940–9 and 1952–4. 'Letters of the Wordsworth Family, 1787–1855' (chiefly of William Wordsworth) were edited by W. Knight in 1907, and 'Letters of William and Dorothy Wordsworth' (ed. E. de Selincourt) appeared in 1935–9.

World, The, a periodical that appeared in 1753–6, owned by Robert Dodsley and managed by Edward Moore. Chesterfield and Horace Walpole were among the contributors.

World's Classics, a series of cheap reprints of standard works of English literature, but including also some translations (e.g. of Tolstoy, Pope's 'Homer', Dryden's 'Virgil', Florio's 'Montaigne', and others). The series began in 1901 and is still in progress; some 600 volumes have been published.

Worldly Wiseman, Mr., in Bunyan's 'The Pilgrim's Progress' (q.v.), an inhabitant of the town of Carnal Policy, who tries to dissuade Christian from going on his pilgrimage.

Worms, Diet of, see *Luther.*

Worthies of the World, The Nine, were 'three Paynims, three Jews, and three Christian men', viz. Hector of Troy, Alexander the Great, and Julius Caesar; Joshua, David, and Judas Maccabaeus; Arthur, Charlemagne, and Godfrey of Bouillon (Caxton, Preface to the 'Morte Darthur'). The list of worthies in Shakespeare's 'Love's Labour's Lost', v. ii, is not quite the same, for it includes Pompey and Hercules.

Worthies of England, The, by Fuller (q.v.), published in 1662, after his death.

The work is a kind of gazetteer of England, in which the author takes the counties one by one, describes their physical characteristics, natural commodities, and manufactures, with quaint comments on each. After these come short biographies, not devoid of humour, of the local saints, martyrs (i.e. persons who suffered for the Protestant faith), prelates, statesmen, judges, notable soldiers, sailors, and writers; and lists of the gentry and sheriffs.

WOTTON, Sir HENRY (1568–1639), was educated at Winchester and New and Queen's Colleges, Oxford, and entered the Middle Temple. He became agent and secretary to the earl of Essex, 1595, and was employed by him in collecting foreign intelligence. He was ambassador at the court of Venice and employed on various other diplomatic missions from 1604 to 1624. While on a visit to Augsburg he wrote in his host's album the famous definition of an ambassador, 'vir bonus peregre missus ad mentiendum Reipublicae causa', 'which he would have been content should have been thus englished "An Ambassador is an honest man, sent to lie abroad for the good of his country" ' (Walton); Scioppius mentioned this in his printed diatribe against James I (1611). Wotton was provost of Eton, 1624–39. He published 'Elements of Architecture' (1624). A collection of his poetical and other writings appeared under the title 'Reliquiae Wottonianae' (containing his famous 'Character of a Happy Life' and 'On his Mistress, the Queen of Bohemia'—'You meaner beauties of the night') in 1651 (enlarged editions, 1672 and 1685). His 'Life' was written by Izaak Walton (1670). His 'Life and Letters', by L. Pearsall Smith, appeared in 1907. There is a handy modern edition of his poems, together with those of other 'courtly poets', by John Hannah (1870).

Would-be, Sir Politick and Lady, characters in Jonson's 'Volpone' (q.v.).

Wragg is in custody: M. Arnold (q.v.) in the first of his 'Essays in Criticism', commenting on the exuberant satisfaction of Mr. Roebuck with the state of England, quotes a newspaper paragraph ending with these words. Wragg was a girl who had left the workhouse with her young illegitimate child. The child had been found strangled.

Wrayburn, Eugene, a character in Dickens's 'Our Mutual Friend' (q.v.).

Wreck of the Hesperus, The, a poem by Longfellow (q.v.), published in 1841.

Wren, Sir Christopher (1631–1723), son of Christopher Wren, dean of Windsor, 1635–58, and nephew of Matthew Wren, bishop of Ely (who was imprisoned in the tower, 1642–60). Wren was educated at Westminster school and Wadham College, Oxford. He became a fellow of All Souls in 1653 and was a prominent member of the circle of scholars who later were founder members of the Royal Society (q.v.). With them he studied anatomy, mathematics, and astronomy, being appointed professor of anatomy at Gresham College, London, in 1657, and Savilian professor of astronomy at Oxford in 1661. His first architectural works were the chapel of Pembroke College, Cambridge (1663–5), and the Sheldonian Theatre, Oxford (1664–9). A few days after the Fire of London in 1666, he presented a plan for rebuilding the City, but it was not adopted. He was, however, made surveyor in charge of the City churches, and designed fifty-two of them. He had prepared a scheme for repairing St. Paul's before the Fire, and when, in 1668, it became clear that it must be rebuilt, he prepared designs. The centrally planned 'Great Model' of 1673 was Wren's favourite, but a more traditional plan was required; work began on the new building in 1675 and it was finished in 1710. Wren became surveyor-general of the king's works in 1668 9; he designed part of Whitehall Palace (destroyed by fire, 1698), Kensington Palace, extensions to Hampton Court, Chelsea Hospital, and part of Greenwich Hospital. His university buildings include the library of Trinity College, Cambridge, and Tom Tower, Christ Church, Oxford. Wren was brought up in the High Church tradition to which his father and uncle belonged. He was buried in St. Paul's. 'Parentalia, or Memories of the Family of the Wrens', published 1750, is a collection of family documents made by Wren's son, Christopher.

Wren, JENNY, the business name of the doll's dressmaker in Dickens's 'Our Mutual Friend' (q.v.). Her real name was Fanny Cleaver.

WREN, PERCIVAL CHRISTOPHER (1885–1941), writer of romantic stories of adventure, the best known being those about the Foreign Legion, 'Beau Geste' (1924) and its sequels.

Wright, FRANK LLOYD (1867–1959), American architect. He developed in his Prairie Houses the open plan in which interior and exterior spaces—rooms, verandahs, etc.—'flow' into each other.

WRIGHT, THOMAS (1810–77), educated at Trinity College, Cambridge, was instrumental in founding the Camden and Percy Societies (qq.v.). He published four volumes of 'Early English Poetry' in 1836, and in 1840 edited 'The Vision and Creed of Piers Plowman'. His 'Biographia Literaria of the Anglo-Saxon Period' appeared in 1842, and 'Anecdota Literaria' in 1844. He published many other works, some in collaboration with J. O. Halliwell (afterwards Halliwell-Phillipps), on subjects connected with the literature, history, and customs of England, including 'Queen Elizabeth and her Times' (1838) and a 'History of Domestic Manners and Sentiments in England during the Middle Ages' (1862).

Wrong Box, The, see *Tontine.*

Wronghead, SIR FRANCIS, a character in Vanbrugh and Cibber's 'The Provok'd Husband' (q.v.).

Wulfila, see *Ulfilas.*

WULFSTAN (*d.* 1023), archbishop of York, author of homilies in the vernacular, including a famous address to the English ('Sermo Lupi ad Anglos'), in which he describes the desolation of the country owing to the Danish raids and castigates the vices and demoralization of the people.

Wulfstan or WOLSTAN, ST. (1012?–95), was educated at the abbey of Peterborough and became a monk of the priory of Worcester, where he was successively schoolmaster, precentor, sacristan, and prior. He was appointed bishop of Worcester in 1062. He assisted Harold on his accession, but subsequently made submission to the Conqueror. He was the only Englishman left in possession of his see by William I. He preached at Bristol in condemnation of the slave trade practised by English merchants against their fellow countrymen, and procured its abandonment. He was buried at Worcester (of which he had rebuilt the cathedral) and is commemorated on 19 January.

Wuthering Heights, a novel by E. Brontë (q.v.) published in 1847.

The central figure of this sombre and highly imaginative story is Heathcliff, a gipsy waif of unknown parentage, picked up by Mr. Earnshaw in the streets of Liverpool and brought home and reared by him as one of his own children. Bullied and humiliated after the elder Earnshaw's death by Earnshaw's son Hindley, Heathcliff's passionate and ferocious nature finds its complement in Earnshaw's daughter, Catherine, and he falls passionately in love with her. Overhearing her say that it would degrade her to marry him, he leaves the house. Returning three years later he finds Catherine married to the insignificant Edgar Linton. Being possessed of money, he is welcomed by Hindley, a coarse-natured gambler, who is now married. Heathcliff's vindictive nature henceforth has full play. His violent love for Catherine brings her to her grave at the birth of her daughter Cathy. He marries Edgar's sister Isabella, not loving her, and cruelly maltreats her. He gets Hindley and his son Hareton completely in his power, brutalizing the latter in revenge for Hindley's treatment of himself when a child. Later he lures the young Cathy to his house and forces a marriage between her and his own sickly and repulsive son, with a view to getting Linton's property eventually into his own power. After his son's death, affection springs up between Cathy and Hareton, and Cathy sets about the latter's education. Heathcliff's nature has now worn itself out. He longs for the death that will reunite him with Catherine. His attempt to destroy the houses of Earnshaw and Linton fails in the end from lack of resolution, and at his death Hareton and Cathy are left to be happy together.

WYATT, SIR THOMAS (1503?–42), was educated at St. John's College, Cambridge. He held various posts at home and abroad, including that of ambassador to Charles V (1537–9), in the service of Henry VIII. He was a lover of Anne Boleyn before her marriage with Henry VIII, and was temporarily imprisoned in the Tower of London in 1536 on the discovery of Anne's alleged post-nuptial infidelities. He was again imprisoned in the Tower as an ally of Thomas Cromwell, but released in 1541. He was a close student of foreign literature, and (with Surrey, q.v.) introduced the sonnet from Italy into England. His first published works appeared as 'Certayne Psalmes . . . drawen into Englyshe meter' (1549), and many of his poems, which include rondeaux, lyrics, and satires in heroic couplets, were issued by Tottel (q.v.) in his 'Miscellany' (1557); his 'Collected Poems' (ed. K. Muir) were published in 1949. He was a lyric poet of the purest note. His portrait after Holbein is in the National Portrait Gallery. He was the father of Sir T. Wyatt, who tried to raise an insurrection against the Spanish marriage of Mary I (1554).

Wybrow, ANTHONY, a character in George Eliot's 'Mr. Gilfil's Love-Story' (see *Scenes of Clerical Life*).

WYCHERLEY, WILLIAM (1640–1716), of a Shropshire family, was educated first in France, then at Queen's College, Oxford. His first play, 'Love in a Wood, or St. James's Park', brought him the favour of the duchess of Cleveland, the king's mistress. Some years'later he secretly married the widowed countess of Drogheda, daughter of the first earl of Radnor, and incurred thereby the displeasure of Charles II, who had offered him the tutorship of his son, the duke of Richmond. Wycherley's first play, 'Love in a Wood', above referred to, a comedy of intrigue of which St. James's Park furnishes the scene, was acted in 1671 and published in 1672. His second play, 'The Gentleman Dancing-Master' (q.v.), was acted in 1671 or 1672 (published in 1673); 'The Country Wife' (q.v.) in 1672 or 1673 (published in 1675); his last play, 'The Plain Dealer' (q.v.), probably in 1674 (published in 1677). His 'Miscellany Poems' (published in 1704) led to a friendship with Pope, who revised many of his writings. His 'Posthumous Works' appeared in 1728. Lamb classes him with Congreve as one of the best masters of 'Artificial Comedy' ('Last Essays of Elia'). Wycherley was labelled by Macaulay as licentious and indecent. The present view of him is that he was a satirist more savage than Congreve, but a poet less sensitive. Contemporaries named him 'manly Wycherley'.

WYCLIFFE, JOHN (c. 1320–84), was born, according to Leland, at Ipreswell or Hipswell near Richmond in Yorkshire, and probably educated at Balliol College, Oxford. There is a tradition also of his being at Queen's and at Merton, and he appears to have been master of Balliol. A realist in philosophy and a religious reformer, he advocated the poverty of the clergy and attacked church endowments. His 'De Dominio Divino' (1376)

expounds the doctrine that all authority is founded on grace; which leads to the idea that wicked kings, popes, and priests should have no power. Wycliffe was in consequence banned by Pope Gregory XI. Moved to bolder defiance, he now attacked the papacy and after the Great Schism (q.v.) of 1378 declared it 'Antichrist itself'. He went on to condemn the whole hierarchy, to deny the doctrine of transubstantiation, and to assert the right of every man to examine the Bible for himself. He was condemned by an ecclesiastical court for his theological doctrines, and retired to Lutterworth, where he died. The Lollards adopted and exaggerated his views. From a literary standpoint he is chiefly notable as having instituted the first translation into English of the whole Bible, himself translating the Gospels, probably the New Testament, and possibly part of the Old Testament. Why he was not burnt alive, no one knows; but his remains were disinterred (by Fleming, bishop of Lincoln, the founder of Lincoln College, Oxford, which was later to be the home of Wesley) and thrown into the river Swift (a tributary of the Avon), whence the prophecy:

> The Avon to the Severn runs,
>   The Severn to the sea,
> And Wycliffe's dust shall spread abroad
>   Wide as the waters be.

The Hussite movement in Bohemia was based on Wycliffe's influence, and Huss's works, which were largely copies of Wycliffe's, in turn influenced Luther. The standard life of Wycliffe is by H. B. Workman (1926). See also *Bible (The English)*.

Wycliffe, OSWALD and WILFRID, characters in Scott's 'Rokeby' (q.v.).

Wykeham, WILLIAM OF, see *William of Wykeham*.

Wykehamist, a member, past or present, of Winchester College. Among Wykehamists famous in a literary connexion may be mentioned Grocyn, Udall, Sir H. Wotton, Sir T. Browne, Otway, W. Somerville, E. Young, William Collins, J. Warton, Sydney Smith, T. Arnold, A. Trollope, F. Buckland, and L. Johnson (qq.v.).

WYLIE, ELINOR HOYT (MRS. W. R. BENET) (1885–1928), American poet and novelist. Her works include 'Nets to Catch the Wind' (poems, 1921), 'The Venetian Glass Nephew' (novel 1925), 'Mortal Image' (novel, 1927), 'Collected Poems' (1932), 'Last Poems' (1943).

Wynd, HAL O' THE, Henry Smith, the hero of Scott's 'The Fair Maid of Perth' (q.v.).

Wynkyn de Worde, see *Worde*.

WYNTOUN, ANDREW OF (1350?–1420?), a canon regular of St. Andrews and author of 'The Orygynale Cronykil', a metrical history of Scotland from the beginning of the world to the accession of James I. He becomes a valuable authority in the later part of the work. Among his stories is that of Macbeth and the witches, Malcolm, and Macduff. The chronicle was first published in 1795 from a manuscript in the Royal Library.

Wyvern, a chimerical animal (in heraldry and romance) imagined as a winged dragon with two feet like those of an eagle and a serpent-like barbed tail. The word is from Old French *wyvre*, a serpent.

X

X-Rays, see *Röntgen.*

Xanadu, in Coleridge's 'Kubla Khan' (q.v.), the place where the Khan decreed 'a stately pleasure-dome'. The name is taken from the passage in 'Purchas his Pilgrimes' which inspired the poem. 'This citie is three dayes journey northeastward to the citie Xandu, which the great Chan Cublay now raigning built.' The passage goes on to describe the enclosure or park with meadows, rivers, deer, and 'a faire wood, in which he hath built a royall House on pillars gilded and vernished' (described in the margin as 'A goodly house of pleasure'). See 'Purchas his Pilgrimes', Hakluyt Soc., 1906, vol. xi, p. 231, 'Marco Polo'. J. L. Lowes in his 'The Road to Xanadu' (1927) reconstructs, with the aid of one of Coleridge's notebooks (of the years probably 1795–8), the process by which the images in the poem were drawn from various sources.

Xanthian Marbles, a collection of sculptures, now in the British Museum, discovered in 1838 by Sir Charles Fellows (1799–1860), traveller and archaeologist, in the ruins of Xanthus, an ancient city of Asia Minor.

Xanthippē, the wife of Socrates (q.v.), said to have been a scold.

Xanthus, one of the horses of Achilles ('Xanthus and Balius of Podarges' strain', Pope's 'Iliad'), who, when chidden for leaving Patroclus dead on the field, warned Achilles of his own approaching death (Homer, 'Iliad', xix, *ad fin.*).

Xanthus, in Homer, is also a name of the river Scamander (q.v.).

Xavier, ST. FRANCIS (1506–52), a Spaniard, one of the founders of the Society of Jesus, and a famous missionary in the Far East. He is commemorated on 3 December.

Xenocrătēs (396–314 B.C.), a native of Chalcedon and a Platonic philosopher, the successor of Speusippus as head of the Academy (q.v.). His character is said to have been in harmony with his philosophy, for when sent on embassy to Philip of Macedon, he refused a present from him of fifty talents.

XENOPHĂNĒS (*c.* 576–480 B.C.), a Greek poet, born at Colophon, who migrated to Elea, and was formerly thought to have been the founder of the Eleatic School of philosophy. He was a satirist who attacked the current religion and asserted the unity of an all-pervading God. He inferred from shells and fossils found in the quarries of Syracuse that the earth had undergone great changes and risen from the sea.

XENOPHON, an Athenian, probably born about 430 B.C., was, when young, a pupil of Socrates. He joined the Greek contingent raised by the younger Cyrus in 401 for his war with Artaxerxes. After the battle of Cunaxa, Xenophon was elected one of the generals of the Greek force, which was left in a dangerous situation between the Tigris and Euphrates, and took a leading part in the memorable retreat thence to the Black Sea. He then accepted service under Agesilaus, king of Sparta, against the Persians in 396, and was present on the Spartan side at Coronea in 394, as a consequence of which his exile was decreed at Athens. After this he settled at Scillus, near Olympia, where some of his works were composed. The sentence of exile was finally revoked, but Xenophon probably died at Corinth about 355.

Xenophon's principal writings include: the 'Anabasis', or history of the expedition of the younger Cyrus and the retreat of the Greeks; the 'Hellenica', a continuation of the history of Thucydides down to the battle of Mantinea (362); the 'Cyropaedia', a political romance based on the history of Cyrus, the founder of the Persian monarchy; the 'Oeconomicus', on the management of a household and property; treatises on 'Horsemanship', on 'Hunting' (authorship doubtful), and on the duties of a cavalry commander; and the 'Memorabilia' of Socrates and the 'Symposium', in which works he expounds the doctrines and character of the great philosopher.

Xerxes, king of Persia (485–465 B.C.), the son of Darius Hystaspes. He bridged the Hellespont with boats, invaded Greece, overcame the resistance of Leonidas and 300 Spartans at Thermopylae (q.v.), but was defeated at Salamis (480 B.C.). He is the King Ahasuerus of the Book of Esther.

Ximena (in French CHIMÈNE), the wife

of the Cid (q.v.). Cibber (q.v.) wrote an adaptation of Cornejlle's 'Le Cid', called 'Ximena, or the Heroic Daughter' (1719).

Ximenes, FRANCISCO (1436–1517), a Span-ish cardinal and statesman, who printed the Complutensian Polyglot Bible (q.v.) and founded the University of Alcalá. But he also destroyed countless Arabic works of learning, especially after the taking of Granada.

Y

Yahoo, see *Gulliver's Travels.*

Yahweh, see *Jehovah.*

Yajuj and **Majuj,** see *Gog and Magog.*

Yale University, originally founded as a school at Saybrook, Connecticut, in 1701, was transferred to New Haven, Connecticut, in 1716 and called Yale College in conse-quence of benefactions received from Elihu Yale (1648–1721), a native of Boston, Massa-chusetts, who came to England, entered the service of the East India Company, and be-came governor of Madras. It received a new charter in 1745 and assumed the name of Yale University in 1887.

Yama, in Hindu theology, the ruler of the world of the dead. In post-Vedic writings he is also the judge of men, who punishes the wicked.

Yankee, a nickname for a native or in-habitant of the United States. During the War of Secession it was applied by the Con-federates to the soldiers of the Federal army. Its origin is uncertain. It has been derived from the Cherokee *eankke,* slave, coward, said to have been applied to the inhabitants of New England by the Virginians for not assisting them in a war with the Cherokees; and explained as an Indian corruption of the word *English.* Perhaps the most plausible explanation is that it comes from the Dutch *Janke,* diminutive of *Jan,* John. [OED.] In America it is used only of the New Englander and New Yorker.

Yankee Doodle, a popular song of the American troops during the War of Indepen-dence. The words are supposed to have been written by a British doctor, Richard Shuckburgh, in derision of some motley American volunteers in 1755, and set to a tune of Cromwell's time. It did not appear in print until about twenty years later.

Yardley Oak, a poem by Cowper (q.v.), written in 1791.

Yarico, see *Inkle and Yarico.*

YARRELL, WILLIAM (1784–1856), zoolo-gist, author of the 'History of British Birds' (1843) and the 'History of British Fishes' (1836).

Yarrow, THE, a river in Selkirkshire that joins the Ettrick near Selkirk. It has inspired many poets, from the author of the ballad 'The Dowie Houms of Yarrow' onwards, in-cluding Hamilton of Bangour, the Revd. John Logan (1748–88),· James Hogg, Scott, and Wordsworth.

Yaughan, 'Go, get thee to Yaughan; fetch me a stoup of liquor' (says the first grave-digger in Shakespeare's 'Hamlet', v. i). 'Yaughan' was perhaps an anglicization of the German 'Johann' and the name of an actual tavern-keeper in London.

Year, THE, *see* Appendix III.

Year Books, reports of English common law cases for the period 1292–1534, of great interest from an historical as well as a legal standpoint. They were succeeded by the law 'Reports'. F. W. Maitland (q.v.) began editing them, and the work is still going on.

Yeast, a novel by C. Kingsley (q.v.), pub-lished in 'Fraser's Magazine' in 1848, and as a separate book in 1851.

This was the first of Kingsley's novels and is crude as a literary work. It deals with some of the social and religious problems of the day (the miserable conditions of the rustic labourer, the game laws, and the Tractarian movement), largely by means of dialogues between the hero and various other charac-ters. The story is that of the reactions of the generous but undisciplined nature of Lance-lot Smith to the influences exercised on him by the philosophical Cornish game-keeper Tregarva, the worldly Colonel Bracebridge, the Romanizing curate Luke, Lancelot's orthodox love Argemone Lavington, and the philanthropic banker Barnakill; he is seen suffering the loss, first of his fortune, and then of Argemone. The story ends in a vague and semi-mystical indication that Lancelot is to seek his salvation in contributing to the regeneration of England.

YEATS, WILLIAM BUTLER (1865–1939), eldest son of J. B. Yeats and brother of Jack Yeats, both celebrated painters, was born in Dublin and educated at the Godolphin School, Hammersmith, and the High School, Dublin. For three years he studied at the School of Art in Dublin, where with a fellow student, George Russell (AE) (q.v.), he developed an interest in mystic religion and the supernatural. At 21 he abandoned art as a profession in favour of literature, writing 'John Sherman and Dhoya' (1891) and editing 'The Poems of William Blake' (1893), 'The Works of William Blake' (with E. J. Ellis, 3 vols., 1893), and 'Poems of Spenser' (1906). A nationalist, he helped to found an Irish Literary Society in London, and another in Dublin; and subsequently applied himself to the creation of an Irish national theatre, an achievement which, with the help of Lady Gregory (q.v.) and others, was partly realized in 1899 when his play, 'The Countess Cathleen' (q.v., 1892), was acted in Dublin. The English actors engaged by the Irish Literary Theatre gave place in 1902 to an Irish amateur company, which produced Yeats's 'Cathleen ni Houlihan' in that year. The Irish National Theatre Company was thereafter created, which, with the help of Miss A. E. Horniman, acquired the Abbey Theatre (q.v.) in Dublin. Yeats's early study of Irish lore and legends resulted in 'Fairy and Folk Tales of the Irish Peasantry' (1888), 'The Celtic Twilight' (1893), and 'The Secret Rose' (1897). Irish traditional and nationalist themes and the poet's unrequited love for Maud Gonne, a beautiful and ardent revolutionary, provided much of the subject matter for 'The Wanderings of Oisin and other Poems' (1889), 'The Land of Heart's Desire' (1894), 'The Wind among the Reeds' (1899), 'The Shadowy Waters' (1900) and such of his later plays as 'On Baile's Strand' (1904) and 'Deirdre' (1907).

With each succeeding collection of poems Yeats moved further from the elaborate, Pre-Raphaelite style of the 1890s. 'In the Seven Woods' (1903) was followed by 'The Green Helmet and Other Poems' (1910), 'Poems Written in Discouragement' (1913), 'Responsibilities: Poems and a Play' (1914), and 'The Wild Swans at Coole' (1917). His mounting disillusionment with Irish politics came to a head in 1912 and 1913 with the controversy over the Lane Bequest of French Impressionist paintings. The Easter Rising of 1916, however, restored his faith in the heroic character of his country. The following year he married Georgie Hyde-Lees, who on their honeymoon attempted automatic writing, an event that exercised a profound effect on his life and work. His wife's 'communicators' ultimately provided him with the system of symbolism described in 'A Vision' (1925) and underlying many of the poems in 'Michael Robartes and the Dancer' (1921), 'Seven Poems and a Fragment' (1922), 'The Cat and the Moon and Certain Poems' (1924), 'October Blast' (1927), 'The Winding Stair' (1929), 'Words for Music Perhaps and Other Poems' (1932), 'Wheels and Butterflies' (1934), 'The King of the Great Clock Tower' (1934), 'A Full Moon in March' (1935), 'New Poems' (1938), and 'Last Poems and Two Plays' (1939). In the poems and plays written after his marriage he achieved a spare, colloquial lyricism wholly unlike his earlier manner, although many

themes of his early manhood reach their full flowering in the later period.

Yeats served as a senator of the Irish Free State from 1922 to 1928; was Chairman of the Commission on Coinage; and in 1923 received the Nobel Prize for Literature. He died in 1939 in the South of France, but in 1948 his body was brought back to Ireland and interred at Drumcliff in Sligo, where much of his childhood had been spent.

Yeats's other publications include such collections of essays as 'Ideas of Good and Evil' (1903), 'Discoveries' (1907), 'Per Amica Silentia Lunae' (1918), 'The Cutting of an Agate' (1919) and 'On the Boiler' (1939). Most important of the many books he edited and introduced was 'The Oxford Book of Modern Verse' (1936). He wrote good letters, and five major collections have been made: 'Letters on Poetry from W. B. Yeats to Dorothy Wellesley' (1940), 'Florence Farr, Bernard Shaw and W. B. Yeats' (1941), 'W. B. Yeats and T. Sturge Moore: Their Correspondence 1901-37' (1953), 'W. B. Yeats: Letters to Katharine Tynan' (1953), and Allan Wade's notable edition of 'The Letters of W. B. Yeats' (1954). Also posthumously published were his 'Collected Poems' (1950), 'Collected Plays' (1952), 'Autobiographies' (1955), 'The Variorum Edition of the Poems' (1957), 'Mythologies' (1959), 'Essays and Introductions' (1961), 'The Senate Speeches of W. B. Yeats' (1961), and 'Explorations' (1962). There are biographies by Joseph Hone, 'W. B. Yeats 1865-1939' (1942) and by A. N. Jeffares, 'W. B. Yeats, Man and Poet' (1949, revised 1962). A second edition of Allan Wade's 'A Bibliography of the Writings of W. B. Yeats' was published in 1958.

Yellow Book, The, an illustrated quarterly which appeared from 1894 to 1897. Many distinguished writers and artists contributed to it, notably Aubrey Beardsley and Max Beerbohm, Henry James, Edmund Gosse, Walter Sickert, etc.

Yellow Dwarf, The, one of the fairy tales of the Comtesse d'Aulnoy (d. 1705).

A queen consults the Fairy of the Desert about the marriage of her daughter, the Princess Toutebelle, who wishes to remain single. The Yellow Dwarf offers himself as suitor, and obtains from the queen the promise of the princess's hand by threats. The princess to escape this fate consents to marry the king of the Gold Mines. But the marriage is prevented by the Yellow Dwarf; king and princess both perish, and are turned into palm trees.

Yellow Journalism, a name given to the sensational journalism of America which developed about 1880. The term is derived from the appearance in 1895 of a number of the 'New York World' in which a child in a yellow dress ('The Yellow Kid') was the central figure of the cartoon, this being an experiment in colour-printing designed to attract purchasers. [OED.] The YELLOW PRESS is a term applied in England to sensational periodicals:

Amid that Press of Yellow hue
One sheet was yellower yet,
It was (Great Heavens!) the Oxford U-
niversity Gazette.
(A. D. Godley, 'In a Strange Land', 1913.)

Yellow Peril, THE, the supposed danger of a destructive invasion of Europe by Mongolian peoples. It was much talked of in the latter part of the 19th cent.

Yellow-backs, cheap editions of novels, so called from being bound in yellow boards. They were the ordinary 'railway novels' of the seventies and eighties of the last century.

Yellowley, TRIPTOLEMUS and BARBARA, characters in Scott's 'The Pirate' (q.v.).

Yellowplush, MR. CHARLES JAMES, a footman, a character assumed by Thackeray (q.v.), as observer of manners and also as literary critic, in several of his earlier works, 'The Yellowplush Correspondence' (1837–8) and 'Mr. Yellowplush's Ajew' (1838), reprinted as 'Memoirs of Mr. C. J. Yellowplush' ('Miscellanies', 1856). The 'Memoirs' contain the story of the Hon. Algernon Deuceace (q.v.). 'Jeames's Diary' was printed in 'Punch', Nov. 1845–Feb. 1846, and was reprinted as 'The Diary of C. Jeames de la Pluche' (see *Jeames*) in 'Miscellanies' (1856).

Yeo, SALVATION, a character in C. Kingsley's 'Westward Ho!' (q.v.).

Yeobright, CLYM, THOMASIN, and MRS., characters in Hardy's 'The Return of the Native' (q.v.).

Yeoman's Tale, The, see *Canterbury Tales*.

Ygerne, see *Igraine*.

Yggdrasil, in northern mythology, the world tree, an ash, representing all living nature, which connects heaven, earth, and hell. Under its branches sit the Norns (q.v.). The dragon Nidhöggr gnaws at its root in Niflheim, an eagle sits at its summit, and the squirrel Ratatösk runs up and down to sow strife between the two. Our maypoles and Christmas trees are said to be derived from this conception. See also *Jack and the Beanstalk*.

Yiddish, derived, either directly or through the German-Jewish *jiddisch*, from the German *jüdisch*, Jewish; the language used by Jews in Europe and America, consisting mainly of German, with Balto-Slavic or Hebrew words, and printed in Hebrew characters.

Ymir, in Scandinavian mythology, the primeval giant who was nourished by the milk of the cow Audhumla; his vast bulk filled a portion of the original abyss. He was the father of the frost-giants.

Yniol, in Tennyson's 'Geraint and Enid' (q.v.), the father of Enid.

YONGE, CHARLOTTE MARY (1823–1901), was born at Otterbourne in Hants, and educated by her father. She came under the influence of John Keble (q.v.), vicar of the neighbouring parish of Hursley, who urged her to expound his religious views in fiction. 'The Heir of Redclyffe' (q.v., 1853) first brought her popular success. 'Heartsease' followed in 1854, 'The Daisy Chain' (of which 'The Trial' is a continuation) in 1856, and 'Dynevor Terrace' in 1857: Her early historical romances included 'The Little Duke' (1854), 'The Lances of Lynwood' (1855), 'The Prince and the Page' (1865), 'The Dove in the Eagle's Nest' (1866), and 'The Caged Lion' (1870). She edited 'The Monthly Packet' from 1851 to 1898, to which she contributed 'Cameos from English History'. She issued in all 160 books, including a life of Bishop Patteson (1874), a 'History of France' (1879), and a 'Life of Hannah More' (1888).

Yorick, (1) in Shakespeare's 'Hamlet' (q.v., v. i), the king's jester, whose skull the gravediggers throw up when digging Ophelia's grave. He is perhaps to be identified with Tarlton (q.v.); (2) in Sterne's 'Tristram Shandy' (q.v.), 'the lively, witty, sensible, and heedless parson', of Danish extraction, and probably a descendant of Hamlet's Yorick. Sterne adopted 'Yorick' as a pseudonym in his 'Sentimental Journey' (q.v.).

Yorkshire Tragedy, A, a play published in 1608 and stated in the title to be written by Shakespeare, but internal evidence and the late date make it extremely improbable that he had any part in its authorship.

The play is based on certain murders actually committed in 1605. The husband, a brutal and depraved gamester, suddenly filled with remorse when he realizes his shame, murders his two children and stabs his docile and devoted wife.

Yorktown, on the shore of the Chesapeake, where, in 1781, the British army under Lord Cornwallis was blockaded by the American army and the French fleet under De Grasse. The capitulation of the former practically brought the American War of Independence to an end.

YOUNG, ANDREW JOHN (1885–   ), honorary canon of Chichester Cathedral, and poet. Most of his shorter poems deal with nature. His 'Songs of Night' were published in 1910 and 'Collected Poems' in 1950. 'Into Hades' and 'A Traveller in Time' are religious poems on a vision of the world after death, published in 1958 under the title 'Out of the World and Back'.

YOUNG, ARTHUR (1741–1820), the son of a Suffolk clergyman, became well known as an agricultural theorist, though unsuccessful as a practical farmer. He wrote a large number of works on agricultural subjects and edited the periodical 'Annals of Agriculture'

(1784–1809), which extended to forty-seven volumes (parts of another volume were published in 1812 and 1813). His power of political and social observation is shown by his 'Political Arithmetic' (1774) and his 'Tour in Ireland' (1780), but his fame rests chiefly on his 'Travels in France' (q.v., 1792). He became secretary to the Board of Agriculture in 1793. Young was connected with the Burneys, and his country house, Bradfield Hall, Suffolk, is described in Fanny Burney's 'Camilla'. He took Fanny Burney to hear Warren Hastings's trial in Westminster Hall and she was charmed with him. He went blind about 1811, and spent a sad old age.

Young, BRIGHAM (1801–77), Mormon (q.v.) leader, first saw the 'Book of Mormon' in 1830, was appointed president of the Mormon Church in 1844, led the Mormons to Utah in 1847, founded Salt Lake City, and was appointed governor of Utah territory in 1851.

YOUNG, EDWARD (1683–1765), born at Upham, near Winchester, and educated at Winchester and New College and Corpus Christi College, Oxford. He received a law fellowship at All Souls College, Oxford, in 1708, and, having been disappointed in his hopes of a parliamentary or professional career, took orders and became rector of Welwyn in 1730, where he spent the remainder of his long life, never receiving the ecclesiastical promotion to which many of his contemporaries thought him entitled. In 1731 he married Lady Elizabeth Lee, daughter of the second earl of Lichfield. His literary work includes two plays, 'Busiris', a tragedy of violence and ungoverned passion, successfully produced at Drury Lane in 1719, and 'The Revenge' (q.v.), another tragedy, produced at the same theatre in 1721. In 1725–8 he published a series of satires under the title 'The Universal Passion' (the Love of Fame), which were witty and brilliant and were much admired until they were thrown into the shade by the satires of Pope. In 1742–5 appeared the work by which he is principally remembered, 'The Complaint, or Night Thoughts on Life, Death, and Immortality' (see *Night Thoughts*), which immediately became very popular. He published 'The Brothers', a tragedy written long before, in 1753, and 'Resignation', his last considerable poem, in 1762. Dr. Johnson winds up his life of Young with the words—'But, with all his defects, he was a man of genius and a poet.'

Young, PATRICK, see *Clement I*.

Young Plan, THE, a financial scheme for the settlement of German Reparations which superseded the Dawes Plan (q.v.). It was evolved by an international committee of experts which sat in 1929 under the chairmanship of Mr. Owen D. Young, an Ameri-

can. It fixed the final figure of German liabilities under the Treaty of Versailles (an average annuity of about £100,000,000 for 37 years, and a maximum of £80,000,000 for another 21 years). The organs of control set up under the Dawes Plan were abolished, and the Bank of International Settlement was created to act as general trustee ('The Times', Annual Review, 1930).

Young Waters, a Scottish ballad, included in Percy's 'Reliques'. Young Waters comes riding into the town and the queen declares his is the fairest face her eyes did ever see. The jealous king has Waters fettered and put to death.

Younger Son, *The Adventures of a*, see *Adventures of a Younger Son*.

Youwarkee, the 'gawrie' whom Peter Wilkins (q.v.) married.

Ysengrin, see *Isegrym*.

Ysolde or YSOUDE, see *Iseult*.

Yuga, in the division of time set out in Hindu mythology, is a period comprising a certain number (1,200 to 4,800) of *divine years*, each divine year being equal to 360 years of mortal men. There are four Yugas, called the Krita, Treta, Dvapara, and Kali Yuga. The first was the golden age and endured for $4,800 \times 360 = 1,728,000$ years of mortals. Each of those which followed showed a decline of righteousness and happiness as compared with its predecessor. The present, the Kali Yuga, is the worst. Its duration is $1,200 \times 360 = 432,000$ years of mortals.

Yule, from the Old English *geol*, Christmas day or Christmastide, corresponding to the Old Norse *jól*, a heathen feast lasting twelve days, and (later) Christmas.

Yule, SIR HENRY (1820–89), see *Cathay*. He was, with Arthur Coke Burnell, originator of 'Hobson-Jobson' (q.v.).

Yvetot, see *Roi d'Yvetot*.

Ywain and Gawain, a verse-romance of the 14th cent., translated from the French of Chrétien de Troyes. Ywain, a knight of the Round Table, is the hero, and Gawain plays a secondary part. Ywain, with the magic help of the damsel Lunet, kills the knight of a castle and falls in love with his mourning widow, Alundyne, whom, again with Lunet's help, he persuades to marry him. At Gawain's instance he leaves her to go in search of fame, assisted by a lion, and forgets his wife. He takes the part of one of Gawain's sisters in an attempt to get all her father's property, while Gawain takes the part of the other. Ywain and Gawain fight without knowing each other. At nightfall they learn each other's name and are reconciled. Lunet effects the reconciliation of Ywain and Alundyne.

Z

Zadig, a satirical tale by Voltaire (q.v.).

Zadkiel, an angel of Rabbinical lore; also the pseudonym of William Lilly (q.v.) and of Richard James Morrison (1795–1874), author of the 'Herald of Astrology' (1831, continued as 'Zadkiel's Almanac').

Zagrēus, see *Orphicism.*

Zâl, in the 'Shahnameh' of Firdusi (q.v.), the father of Rustem (q.v.).

Zambullo, DON CLEOFAS, the hero of Le Sage's 'Le Diable Boiteux' (q.v.).

Zamzummims, giants, 'a people great, and many, and tall, as the Anakims' (Deut. ii. 20–21).

Zanga, a character in E. Young's 'The Revenge' (q.v.).

ZANGWILL, ISRAEL (1864–1926), was a prominent member of Jewish literary society in England, as a lecturer, novelist, and playwright. He was author, among many novels, of 'Children of the Ghetto' (1892, dramatized by him in 1899), 'Merely Mary Ann' (1893), 'Ghetto Tragedies' (1893), 'The Master' (1895), 'Dreamers of the Ghetto' (1899), 'Ghetto Comedies' (1907).

Zany, from the Italian *zani,* the name of servants who act as clowns in the 'Commedia dell' Arte', a comic performer attending on a clown, acrobat, or mountebank, who imitates his master's acts in a ludicrously awkward way. Hence an attendant, follower (almost always in a contemptuous sense); or a buffoon; or a fool, simpleton. The Italian *zani* is the Venetian and Lombardic form of *Gianni = Giovanni,* John. [OED.]

Zanzis, a supposed poet referred to by Chaucer in 'Troylus and Cryseyde', iv. 414. The name perhaps arises from a misreading of Boccaccio's text which Chaucer is translating.

Zapolya, a 'dramatic poem' in humble imitation of 'The Winter's Tale', by S. T. Coleridge (q.v.), published in 1817. Zapolya is a dowager queen of Illyria driven from the throne by the usurper Emerick. After a twenty years' interval she returns to power with her son Bethlen.

Zara, a character in Congreve's 'The Mourning Bride' (q.v.).

Zaraph, the lover of Nama in Moore's 'The Loves of the Angels' (q.v.).

Zarathustra, see *Zoroaster.*

Zarathustra, Thus spake, see *Nietzsche.*

Zastrozzi, see *Shelley* (*P. B.*).

Zeal-of-the-land Busy, a character in Jonson's 'Bartholomew Fayre' (q.v.), a typical religious humbug.

Zegris, see *Abencerrages.*

Zeitgeist, German, the spirit or genius which marks the thought or feeling of a period.

Zelica, the heroine of 'The Veiled Prophet of Khorassan', one of the tales in Moore's 'Lalla Rookh' (q.v.).

Zélide, the name given to herself in a self-portrait by ISABELLA VAN TUYLL VAN SEROOSKERKEN, also known as BELLE DE ZUYLEN, and after her marriage as MME DE CHARRIÈRE (1740–1805), a Dutchwoman of good family, great intelligence and originality, and considerable beauty. She numbered among her many suitors James Boswell, who quickly reconciled himself to her rejection of his hand. Declining more brilliant matches, she married her brother's Swiss tutor, the dull but worthy M. de Charrière. Her unhappy married life was brightened by an ardent intellectual friendship with Benjamin Constant, until she was ousted by Mme de Staël. She wrote in French a number of novels, of which the best known are 'Lettres Neuchâteloises' (1784), 'Mistress Henley' (1784), 'Lettres écrites de Lausanne' (1787). There is an interesting account of her life in Geoffrey Scott's 'Portrait of Zélide'.

Zelmane, in Sidney's 'Arcadia' (q.v.), the name assumed by Pyrocles when disguised as a woman.

Zeluco, a novel by Dr. J. Moore (q.v.), published in 1786.

Zeluco, sprung of a noble Sicilian family, is a thorough-paced scoundrel, actuated in all his doings by lust, cruelty, selfishness, or revenge; his character is redeemed solely by a certain intrepidity. The novel is a long story of his misdeeds. As a child he crushes a pet sparrow to death; he drives his widowed mother to her grave heart-broken; has a slave beaten to death in the West Indies; and engages in various discreditable love-affairs. He sets himself to get possession of a beautiful and high-minded girl, and to effect his purpose stages an attack on her by robbers, from whom she is rescued by himself. He kills their child and drives her mad, finally meeting his own death from a stiletto under scandalous circumstances. In spite of the repulsive and improbable character of much of the tale, it is told with considerable humour. Zeluco sometimes overreaches himself and meets with his deserts. And there are three amusing servants: Dawson, who writes an entertaining description of a visit to Paris, and Buchanan and Targe, the Scotsmen who quarrel about the character of Mary Queen of Scots.

Zend-Avesta, the sacred writings of the Parsees, literally the Avesta (q.v.) with the interpretation. The word *Zend* came to be used to denote the old Iranian language in which the Avesta is written.

Zenelophon, see *Cophetua*.

Zeno, of Citium in Cyprus, the founder of the Stoic school of philosophy (close of the 4th cent. B.C.). He was shipwrecked as a young man on the coast of Attica, while on a trading voyage, settled at Athens, and devoted himself to the study of philosophy. For his ethical teaching see under *Stoics*.

Another Zeno, of Elea (*c.* 450 B.C.), was a disciple of Parmenides (q.v.) and expounded his philosophy. In Dickens's 'Pickwick' (ch. xv) Mr. Leo Hunter, whose wife is going to give a fancy-dress party, suggests Zeno, among other 'founders of clubs', as an appropriate character for Mr. Pickwick to assume.

Zenobia, SEPTIMIA, widow and successor (*c.* A.D. 266) of Odenathus, ruler of Palmyra, a city state in Syria which had enjoyed the protection of successive Roman emperors. Zenobia was an ambitious woman who invaded Asia Minor and Egypt in open hostility to Rome. She was captured and deposed by Aurelian (272), and Palmyra was utterly destroyed.

Zenocratē, the wife of Tamburlaine, in Marlowe's play of that name.

Zephalinda, in Pope's 'Epistle to a Young Lady [Miss Blount], on her leaving the town after the Coronation', the young lady who goes

> from opera, park, assembly, play,
> To morning walks, and prayers three times
> a day

in the country, where she will

> O'er her cold coffee trifle with her spoon,
> Count the slow clock, and dine exact at
> noon.

Zephon, in Milton's 'Paradise Lost', iv. 788, a 'strong and subtle Spirit' charged, with Ithuriel, to search the Garden of Eden for Satan.

Zephyrus, in Greek mythology, the personification of the west wind. He was the father of Xanthus (q.v.) and Balius, the horses of Achilles.

Zerbino, in the 'Orlando Furioso' (q.v.), a Scottish prince and perfect knight, of whom it was said that Nature broke the mould in which he had been fashioned. He was the lover of Isabella (q.v.). He was rescued by Orlando when about to be executed on a false charge, but was killed by Mandricardo when attempting to defend the arms that Orlando in his madness had thrown away.

Zetland, an old name of the Shetland Isles.

Zeugma, a figure of speech by which a single word is made to refer to two or more words in a sentence, especially when properly applying in sense to only one of them; e.g. 'See Pan with flocks, with fruits Pomona crowned'. Cf. *Syllepsis*.

Zeūs, the greatest of the Greek gods, in whom the myths of many different nations centred. The Roman god Jupiter was identified with him, and the Greek myths transferred to him. According to Hesiod, Zeus was the son of Cronos (q.v.) and Rhea; he was saved by his mother from being devoured by Cronos, was entrusted to the Corybantes (q.v.) to educate on Mt. Ida in Crete, and ousted his father from the government of the world. He gave the empire of the sea to his brother Poseidon (Neptune), and of the infernal regions to his brother Hades (Pluto). He repelled the attack of the giants on heaven and destroyed them. He is represented in mythology as marrying his sister Hera (Juno), and also other goddesses such as Themis and Ceres, and as assuming various disguises in his amours with mortals. He introduced himself to Danae (q.v.) in a shower of gold, to Leda (q.v.) as a swan, to Europa (q.v.) as a bull, to Callisto as Diana, and to Alcmena as Amphitryon (q.v.). His worship was widespread and of great solemnity. He was regarded as the king and father of gods and men, with power over all other deities save the Fates.

The colossal chryselephantine statue of Zeus in his temple at Olympia by Phidias (q.v.), was one of the Seven Wonders of the World (q.v.). It was removed to Constantinople in the 5th cent. A.D., where it was destroyed in the great fire of 476.

Zeūxis (late 5th cent. B.C.), Greek painter from Heraclea in Lucania (southern Italy). His most famous painting was an ideal portrait of Helen of Troy. He painted illusionistic still-lifes; it is said that birds pecked at his painting of a bunch of grapes. But in this he was excelled by Parrhasius (q.v.). Zeuxis is said to have died from laughing at a comical picture he had painted of an old woman.

Zimbabwe, a Bantu name given to the extensive ruins near Victoria in Mashonaland discovered in 1868 and described by J. T. Bent in his 'Ruined Cities of Mashonaland' (1871). The ruins are attributed to Bantu builders of the 14th or 15th cents. Their chief features are a roughly elliptical kraal some 800 feet in perimeter, surrounded by a massive stone wall, and an elaborately fortified hill adjoining it. [E.B.]

Zimri, (1) in 1 Kings xvi, the servant of Asa, king of Judah, captain of half his chariots, who conspired against the king, 'drinking himself drunk in the house of Arza steward of his house', and went in and killed him, and reigned in his stead. 'Had Zimri peace, who slew his master?' (2 Kings ix. 31); (2) in Dryden's 'Absalom and Achitophel' (q.v.), in allusion to the above, represents the duke of Buckingham.

Zingano, ZINGARO (plural *Zingani, Zingari*), a gipsy. 'I Zingari' is the name of a famous cricket club.

Zionism, a movement among modern Jews, founded in 1897 by an Austrian, Theodor Herzl, having for its object the assured settlement of their race upon a national basis in the land of Israel.

Zisca or ZISKA, JOHN (1360–1424), a Bohemian nobleman, who, after fighting at Tannenberg (1410), later against the Turks, and for the English at Agincourt, became the leader of the Hussites, built the fortress of Tabor, and gained many victories over the Imperialists. It is related that he ordered his skin after his death to be made into a drumhead. 'Must I be annihilated lest, like old John Zisca's, my skin might be made into a drum?' (Burke, 'Letter to a Noble Lord').

Zobeide, in the 'Arabian Nights' (q.v.), the wife of the caliph Haroun-al-Raschid.

Zodiac, from the Greek ζῴδιον, a sculptured figure (of an animal), a sign of the zodiac; a belt of the celestial sphere extending 8 or 9 degrees on each side of the ecliptic within which the apparent motions of the sun, moon, and planets take place. It is divided in twelve equal parts called *signs*. These are named after the twelve constellations (Aries, Taurus, Gemini, Cancer, Leo, Virgo, Libra, Scorpio, Sagittarius, Capricornus, Aquarius, Pisces) with which at a former epoch they severally coincided approximately. They no longer do so owing to the precession of the equinoxes.

Zohar, see *Cabbala.*

Zohara, see *Harût and Marût.*

ZOÏLUS, a grammarian of Amphipolis, of the period of Philip of Macedon. His name became proverbial as that of a carping critic, on account of his strictures on Homer, Plato, and Isocrates.

ZOLA, ÉMILE (1840–1902), the principal figure in the French school of naturalistic fiction, of which 'Thérèse Raquin' (1867) is his first example. After 1870 he set about his principal work, 'Les Rougon-Macquart', which he termed the 'natural and social history of a family' (the two branches of the Rougons and the Macquarts) whose conduct over five generations could be seen as conditioned by environment and by hereditary characteristics, largely drunkenness and mental instability. In this series of twenty novels he displays a panorama of 19th-cent. French life, studying vice and crime with faithful minuteness and focusing attention mainly on the more animal aspects of human

nature. 'Germinal', for instance, depicts the life of a great mining community, 'La Terre' the life of the agricultural peasant, 'Le Ventre de Paris' the markets of the metropolis, 'L'Assommoir' its taverns. The cynicism and pessimism that characterize these give place to a more romantic mood in 'La Faunte de l'Abbé Mouret', 'La Joie de vivre', and 'Le Docteur Pascal'. 'La Débâcle' deals with the catastrophe of the war of 1870. In his three later works, 'Lourdes', 'Rome', and 'Paris', Zola examines what the religion and social organization of the day have to offer to man. His last works, 'Fécondité', 'Travail', and 'Vérité', are long disquisitions on the subject of their several titles, the last with reference to the Dreyfus case, in which Zola intervened on the side of truth with memorable vigour (notably in his letter to 'L'Aurore', 'J'accuse!').

Zoological Gardens, London: the origin of these is to be found in the 'lions at the Tower'. Wild beasts were kept at the Tower of London (q.v.) soon after it was built. Henry I had a number of lions, leopards, and other animals there, and we hear of a present of three leopards to Henry III, in compliment to the royal arms. A white bear and an elephant were there in the 13th cent., and a very large collection by the middle of the 18th cent. It then dwindled until 1822, when it was once more increased by Mr. Cops, and in 1834 transferred to the present 'Zoo' in Regent's Park, where the Zoological Society, founded in 1826 by Sir Stamford Raffles, had already brought together a certain number of animals. (Loftie, 'History of London'.)

Zophar, one of the three friends of Job (q.v.). The name means 'chatterer'.

Zophiel, in Milton's 'Paradise Lost', vi. 535, one of the 'victor Angels', 'of Cherubim the swiftest wing'.

Zoroaster, the Greek form of *Zarathustra*, the founder of the Magian system of religion, probably an historical personage who has become the subject of legends; a Persian who is believed to have lived in the 6th cent. B.C., during the reigns of Cyrus, Cambyses, and Darius.

The Zoroastrian religion was founded on the old Aryan folk-religion, but the polytheistic character of the latter was completely changed. The essential feature of Zoroastrianism is the existence of two predominant spirits: Ahura-Mazda (Ormazd) the wise one, the spirit of light and good; and Ahriman, the spirit of evil and darkness. The conflict between these two is waged in this world, and centres in man, created a free agent by Ormazd. Zoroastrianism includes the belief in life after death, eternal punishment or eternal death according to the balance of a man's good and evil deeds on this earth.

Zoroaster, who claimed to be the prophet sent by Ormazd, thus raised the ancient

Aryan religion to a higher and more spiritual level. The other deities of the Vedic pantheon, with the exception of the god of fire, and Mithra, the god of day, disappeared or sank to the position of minor evil spirits.

Zuleika, (1) according to Muslim tradition (Sale's 'Koran', xii), the name of Potiphar's wife; (2) the heroine of Byron's 'The Bride of Abydos' (q.v.).

Zuleika Dobson, see *Beerbohm.*

Zürich Bible, THE, a German version of the Bible, printed in 1530, embodying Luther's translation of certain portions and, as regards the rest, the work of other translators.

ZWEIG, ARNOLD (1887–   ), German novelist, known in England as the author of 'Der Streit um den Sergeanten Grischa' (1928, 'The Case of Sergeant Grischa').

Zwingli, ULRICH (1484–1531), a famous Swiss leader of the Reformation. He first found his inspiration in Erasmus and Luther, but soon drew away from the latter, and by 1525 had rejected the mass altogether; and this split Switzerland into Catholic and Protestant cantons. To Zwingli the Eucharist was purely symbolic; there was no 'real presence' at all, not even in the (later) Calvinistic sense, still less in the Lutheran sense of 'consubstantiation'. It ended in civil war, in which Zwingli was killed in battle.

APPENDIX I

CENSORSHIP AND THE LAW OF THE PRESS

§ 1. *The control of the press*

THE introduction of printing immensely increased facilities for the spread of sedition and heresy, grave dangers always threatening the life of government and church, and as the industry of the press developed in the 16th century, we find the publication of subversive matter a cause of increasing concern to the authorities. Proclamations against heretical and seditious books begin under Henry VIII in 1529, and the requirement that books shall be licensed for printing by the privy council or other royal nominees is introduced in 1538. Edward VI in 1547 and 1549 issued orders against the use of popish books of prayer and instruction. Mary, by proclamation in the first year of her reign, forbade the printing of any book or other matter without her special licence for the same, and endeavoured, notably by a proclamation of 1555, to prevent the importation from abroad of the works of the reformers. A notable date in the history of the subject is 1557, when the Stationers obtained a charter of incorporation (see the article below on *Copyright*). Thereafter only members of the Stationers' Company or other persons holding a special patent might print any work for sale in the kingdom.[1] The incorporation was advantageous both to the book trade and the State, for the craft gained in dignity and organization, while the facilities for the supervision of printed matter were improved. The charter did not transfer to the Stationers the responsibility in the matter of undesirable publications, but it seems probable that the wardens exercised some discretion, at any rate before the Star Chamber orders of 1586, as to the need for seeing the 'hand' of an official licenser before recording a copyright. In 1559 Elizabeth, in the first year of her reign, issued 'Injunctions' requiring that no book should be printed unless licensed by her majesty, six of her privy council, or certain specified dignitaries of the Church, and that the names of those licensing the work should be printed at the end of it. The injunction must have proved largely ineffective, for, in spite of renewed orders, a multitude of unauthorized pamphlets continued to issue from the press. In 1586, at the instance of Archbishop Whitgift, a further effort was made to enforce State control: an ordinance of the Star Chamber directed that no printing press should be set up in any place other than London, apart from one in each of the university towns of Oxford and Cambridge, and that no more presses should be set up at all until those already existing had through natural causes been reduced to such number as the Archbishop of Canterbury and the Bishop of London thought sufficient for the needs of the realm. The ordinance again forbade the printing of unlicensed works. In 1588 Whitgift appointed twelve persons to license books for printing; he was especially concerned to check the flow of puritan pamphlets which at this time were attacking the episcopal system. The conflict between bishop and puritan continued, and has left its trace in English

---

[1] The sale in the kingdom of foreign-printed books had been regulated by an Act of 1533. In 1564 Elizabeth addressed a letter to the Bishop of London directing him to make arrangements for the seizure of any subversive books brought from overseas to London or other ports. In 1586 we find the Archbishop of Canterbury issuing to Ascanius de Renialme, merchant bookseller, a licence to bring in from foreign parts some few copies of sundry books, which though popish and seditious, are yet in many respects expedient to be had by some of the learned of this realm; these copies to be delivered to approved persons only.

literature in the Marprelate tracts (see *Martin Marprelate*). In 1599 an edict was issued requiring that certain satirical works, notably those of Gabriel Harvey and Thomas Nash (qq.v.), should be burnt, and that no satires or epigrams should be printed thereafter.

A further stringent decree (1637), imposing severe penalties on offending printers, was among the last measures of the Star Chamber; but the abolition of the Chamber by the Long Parliament in 1641 did not carry with it any liberation of the press. On the contrary, Parliament during 1642 was much occupied with offences by writers and printers, and in 1643 issued an Ordinance requiring that no book should be printed unless previously licensed by an officer named by them, and appointed a licenser. It was this activity which in 1644 called forth Milton's noble protest, the 'Areopagitica' (q.v.). But the protest fell on deaf ears, and the licensing system continued throughout the Commonwealth period; indeed we find Milton himself acting as a licenser in 1651–2.

By this time journalism, a new element in English letters, had come into existence. It had its origin in the manuscript newsletters which, after the introduction of regular postal services, were dispatched to subscribers from the metropolis. The licensing system and the Star Chamber decrees, as well as the royal prerogative in the distribution of news, proved for a long time an impediment to the publication of any sort of printed journal. In 1622 authority was first given to certain stationers for the issue of periodical pamphlets relating the course of foreign wars (the Thirty Years War was then in progress and was being watched with intense interest). Such pamphlets were known as Corantos. In 1632 the Star Chamber prohibited the publication of news from abroad, and the interdict on Corantos was not raised until 1638, when Nathaniel Butler and Nicholas Bourne were granted a monopoly of the printing of foreign news. These later Corantos in turn vanished after a few years, and in 1641 appeared the first authorized 'newsbooks' or printed 'Diurnalls' of parliamentary proceedings and other domestic intelligence. It is not surprising that at this period of political excitement similar but unauthorized newsbooks were soon produced in great numbers, supplementing or replacing the newsletters of the scriveners. These printed newsbooks, unlike the manuscript newsletters, came under the censorship established by the Long Parliament, and we read of many suppressions and imprisonments, until Cromwell in 1655 put an end to all unofficial periodicals. Licensed newsbooks were allowed afresh by the Rump parliament in April 1659, but at the end of the same year permission for their issue was restricted to certain journalists.

Under the Restoration the control and licensing of the press were continued. In 1662 a Licensing Act was passed for two years, then extended to 1679. It forbade the printing of any book or pamphlet contrary to the doctrine and discipline of the Church of England or tending to the scandal of Church or government; and it required that all books and pamphlets should be licensed by persons appointed for the purpose. It empowered the king's messengers by warrant under the sign manual or under the hand of the Secretaries of State or of the Master and Wardens of the Stationers' Company to search houses and shops for unlicensed books and to bring before the authorities any which they suspected to contain seditious or heretical matter. It also regulated the conduct of the book trade.[1] After 1679 came a period during which the press was controlled by the prosecution of offenders

---

[1] Under this Act Roger L'Estrange (q.v.) was in 1663 appointed surveyor of printing presses and licenser.

under the ordinary law. In 1685 the Licensing Act was revived until 1694, in which year Parliament refused to renew it, and the licensing system (so far as the press was concerned) came finally to an end. The case against the Act was prepared by John Locke (q.v.): it was pointed out that the Act had not served the purpose for which it was made, which was to prevent the publishing of seditious matter; it had appointed no penalties for offences, but had left transgressors to the common law, which already had sufficient powers to deal with them; moreover licensers had not been free from partiality. The abandonment of the Act was not due to any change of opinion in Parliament or government in favour of the liberty of expression. Various bills restraining the press were introduced in the following years, but failed to obtain approval. Other measures were resorted to. The detection of the authors and publishers of libels was entrusted to two salaried 'messengers of the press', assisted by informers in the service of the government and by the presentments of grand juries. Both Houses of Parliament were also active in drawing the attention of government to obnoxious publications and even carried out examinations and committed offenders to prison. The Solicitor to the Treasury was charged with the duty of examining alleged libellous matter, which term may be said to have included anything published with the intent of causing a breach of the peace, or likely to bring the king, the government, Parliament, or the administration of justice into contempt, or to incite to the alteration of anything in Church or State by illegal means. Upon the Solicitor's advice the Secretaries of State issued warrants for the arrest of the suspected parties. These were examined, and as a consequence might be committed to prison and prosecuted. The usual punishments were the pillory, imprisonment, fines, and the requirement of security for future good behaviour. But John Matthews was hanged for high treason in 1719 in consequence of his pamphlet 'Vox Populi Vox Dei', in which he asserted that James III was the rightful King of England. Defoe was arrested in 1703 for his pamphlets on ecclesiastical matters, imprisoned and pilloried. Even if prosecution did not follow examination, the power of arrest, accompanied by seizure of papers and type, frequently repeated, enabled the Government to harass and even ruin obnoxious printers. The 'Freeholder's Journal' and the 'True Briton' were thus brought to an end in 1723 and 1724. Ordinary warrants issued by the Secretary of State specified the charge against the person named in them. But in the first half of the 18th century the Secretary of State also issued general warrants, which might authorize the arrest of a person unnamed, and the seizure of unspecified papers. Their use for the former purpose became impracticable owing to a decision of the courts in 1765 and was further declared illegal by the Commons in 1766; their use for the latter purpose was declared illegal by the courts in 1763 in connexion with the case of No. 45 of the 'North Briton'. Wilkes (q.v.) had started this paper in 1762 in opposition to Bute's 'The Briton', and in it had attacked the Government with increasing audacity. No. 45, imputing deliberate untruth to the authors of the recent speech from the throne, gave an opportunity for legal proceedings, and a general warrant was issued for the arrest of the authors, printers, and publishers of the number. When this had been executed, Wilkes brought an action against Wood, the Under-Secretary concerned, on the ground that the seizure of his papers under the warrant had been illegal, and the jury by direction of Lord Chief Justice Pratt (later Lord Camden) returned a verdict in his favour.

Wilkes was concerned in another important reform. In trials for libel the province of the jury was at first restricted to deciding the fact of publication and interpreting the innuendoes that the alleged libels might contain. It was left to the judge to determine whether the publication was libellous or not. This restriction of the jury's province had been questioned from time to time, and the right of the jury to decide the whole issue was asserted by Bolingbroke in the 'Craftsman' (see below), and maintained by Lord Camden and by Wilkes. The restriction was removed by Fox's Libel Act of 1792.

Another of the Government's measures, designed in part to reduce the number of libels, was the Stamp Act of 1712, which imposed a duty of $\frac{1}{2}d.$ on every periodical of half a sheet or less, and of $1d.$ on every whole sheet (altered by an Act of 1725 to a halfpenny on every half-sheet). This for a time lessened the number of periodicals but it discouraged publications favourable to the Government at least as much as those of the opposition; ultimately there was no considerable reduction in the number of papers published.

In general, executive interference with the press diminished in the course of the eighteenth century. The Government relied in part, for meeting the attacks made upon it, on its own pamphlets and journals, notably for a time on the 'London Gazette' (which Steele was appointed to conduct, 1707–10), on Defoe's 'Review' (1704–13), and on the 'Examiner' (to which Matthew Prior and Swift were contributors). At a later period we find Bute's 'The Briton' (edited by Smollett) employed to meet the attacks of 'The Monitor'. The Government sometimes bought up an opposition paper (such as the 'London Journal'), or subsidized pro-government prints (such as the 'Daily Courant' and 'Free Briton', and later the 'Daily Gazetteer') and had these distributed gratis over the kingdom. The ablest of the opposition papers, the 'Craftsman', long defied the resentment of the Government. Bolingbroke and Pulteney were its best-known contributors. Its publisher was tried in 1729 and acquitted, but in 1731 was sentenced to imprisonment and fine.

The attempt of Charles I to arrest the five members had left Parliament disinclined to the publication of its proceedings. It was held accordingly a breach of privilege to print without permission the proceedings of either House or even to mention the names of members of Parliament in the press. A dry summary of the proceedings, known as the 'Votes', was allowed to appear, but it contained no account of the debates and entirely failed to meet the demands of the public at times of political excitement. From the accession of Anne some discreet account of the proceedings was introduced in Abel Boyer's 'The Political State of Great Britain', and from 1716 in the 'Historical Register'. In 1732 the 'Gentleman's Magazine' and the 'London Magazine' began reporting debates (Johnson's editorship of these in the 'Gentleman's Magazine' is famous). In 1738 the House of Commons by resolution reaffirmed its privilege and threatened the utmost severity against offenders. But the reports of debates continued, under such transparent disguises as accounts of proceedings in the senate of Lilliput. A last and unsuccessful attempt to enforce the privilege was made in 1771, when the House of Commons took action against the printers of certain journals. Here again we find Wilkes taking part in the conflict, on the side of the liberty of the press.

The application of the law in the later eighteenth and early nineteenth century in restraint of the press may be illustrated by the cases of Thomas Paine (q.v.), who was brought in danger of arrest by what was regarded as his subversive work, 'The Rights of Man' (q.v., 1791–2), and fled the country in consequence; and of Cobbett (q.v.), who in 1810 received a sentence of two years' imprisonment and a fine of £1,000 for a denunciation of flogging in the army. The last special restriction on the newspaper press, the Stamp Duty, was abolished in 1855; the stamp, for postal purposes, was retained until 1870. With the lapse of the Licensing Act in 1694 the importance of the Stationers' Company in connexion with the control of the press came to an end, though registration at Stationers' Hall continued necessary for certain purposes in relation to copyright (see the article below on *Copyright*.)

§ 2. *Control of dramatic performances*

IN the sixteenth century companies of players were attached to the court and to households of the nobility. Some of these companies travelled about the country giving performances at private houses and to the public. In addition, there were wandering troupes of miscellaneous players under no patronage. In the larger towns the guilds continued to present Corpus Christi plays, and similar performances were given sporadically in smaller places, but the performers of these probably remained amateurs. Some measure of control over stage performances was exercised in the interests of public order from about the middle of the century. The licensing of individual plays, in one form or another, begins in 1549 if not earlier; and the subjection of players, unless 'protected', to the laws relating to vagabonds dates at least from 1554, and was probably enforced in practice even earlier. These measures were re-enacted in the reign of Elizabeth. By the Injunctions of 1559 already referred to she directed that no interlude should be played unless previously licensed by the mayor of the town, or in the country by the lord lieutenant or two justices of the peace; and no plays were to be so licensed which treated of matters of religion or of the governance of the country. By an Act of 1572 all players were to be deemed rogues and vagabonds unless they belonged to a baron of the realm or person of higher degree, or were licensed by two justices. The mayor and corporation of London, who under the Injunctions of 1559 had jurisdiction over stage plays in the city of London, the chief centre of theatrical activity, were in general hostile to dramatic performances, partly from puritan sentiment, partly because the performances were apt to give rise to overcrowding and tumults, and moreover tended to spread infection in the frequently recurring periods of plague. The court on the other hand, and Elizabeth herself, favoured the players, and the grant in 1574 of a patent to the Earl of Leicester's company, authorizing them to play in all towns without hindrance by the local authorities, conflicted with the powers previously conferred on the corporation. The latter retorted with an act of Common Council requiring all players to be licensed by the corporation and all plays allowed by it. The conflict between court and city was keen and prolonged, and during certain periods the corporation prohibited all performances within the city boundaries. In consequence, the first permanent playhouse in London was erected in Finsbury fields, outside the Lord Mayor's jurisdiction. Another issue of the conflict was to bring the players increasingly under the authority of the Master of the Revels, a court official, and from about 1574 no plays might be performed in England without his licence. His authority was gradually extended: in 1581 he was given power to commit offenders to prison; after 1606 he is found issuing licences for the printing as well as the performance of plays; also for various non-dramatic performances, such as those of acrobats and displays of animals. Under James I and Charles I the London companies of players worked under royal patents; companies protected by nobles are still found in the provinces. It should be emphasized that at this time the official control over the drama was directed to the exclusion of matters of religion and government, and was exercised in the interests of Church and State, not of morality. It may be recalled that Jonson came under suspicion of papacy and treason for his 'Sejanus' (q.v.), and (together with Marston and Chapman) got into trouble for disparaging allusions to the Scots in 'Eastward Hoe' (q.v.). Daniel incurred suspicion of allusion to Essex's plot in his 'Philotas' (q.v.). Other famous examples of official interference with the Elizabethan drama may be mentioned. The original name of the fat knight in Shakespeare's 'Henry IV' was Sir John Oldcastle. To avoid offence to members of the family of that name, Shakespeare was required to change it, and substituted Falstaff. In the play 'Sir Thomas More' (q.v.), the part relating to the insurrectionary movement in London was required by the Master of the Revels to be omitted. The performance of Middleton's 'A Game at Chesse' was prohibited on the complaint of the Spanish Ambassador. But the attitude of the puritans to the drama was quite different from that of the Government. They regarded the stage as an immoral institution; the character of their hostility to it may be gathered from 'Histriomastix' (1632), in which Prynne (q.v.) asserted that stage plays, from their origin in the Devil onwards, had been the source of every possible crime. The work was held by the Star Chamber to reflect on Charles I and his queen, and Prynne was sentenced to lose his ears, to imprisonment, and to a heavy fine. The drama, on the other hand, was full of contemptuous references to the puritans. In 1642 the Long Parliament put an end to all dramatic performances. The prohibition was to some extent evaded, was repeated in 1647, and towards the end of the Commonwealth period was in part relaxed, for D'Avenant (q.v.) was then allowed to present certain semi-dramatic entertainments accompanied by music.

After the Restoration Charles II issued patents to D'Avenant and Thomas Killigrew the elder (q.v.), authorizing them to form two companies of actors with exclusive rights of performance in London and Westminster, and enjoining on them to expunge all profaneness and scurrility from the plays that should be acted. But Sir Henry Herbert, who had been Master of the Revels under Charles I, asserted his right to grant licences, and many quarrels resulted. Finally an arrangement was arrived at between Herbert and Killigrew for sharing the control of the stage, and on Herbert's death Killigrew succeeded him as Master of the Revels. In the reaction which followed the period of puritan austerity, the administration of the censorship was very lax. Not only was gross indecency tolerated, but references to political and religious matters were inadequately controlled. In course of time, after the death of Charles II, the public mood changed, and there was a revolt against the previous licentiousness. Jeremy Collier's attack 'on the profaneness and immorality of the stage' (1697) found a wide measure of sympathy. It was followed in 1698 by a royal order prohibiting the acting of anything contrary to religion and good manners and forbidding the Master of the Revels to license plays containing anything of the kind. The attention of the censor was thus specifically directed to moral supervision. But the gradual chastening of the drama which followed and which led to such plays as those of Rowe, Addison, and Steele, may be attributed more to a change of public sentiment than to the action of the censor.

In the early part of the eighteenth century the control of the stage appears to have been exercised largely by the Lord Chamberlain himself. Little of importance in its history is recorded until Rich in 1728 produced Gay's 'Beggar's Opera' (q.v.), a play containing social and political satire and obvious allusions to Walpole and Townshend. The performance of its sequel, 'Polly', was prohibited by the Lord

Chamberlain. In 1736 and 1737 Fielding, in his 'Pasquin' and 'The Historical Register for 1736', carried political satire and personal allusion to greater lengths; and it was no doubt to some extent in consequence of these plays that Walpole took statutory powers, by the Licensing Act of 1737 (10 Geo. II, cap. 28), to control dramatic performances. This Act made the Lord Chamberlain licenser of theatres in London and Westminster and in other places of residence of the sovereign; it imposed penalties on the performance for hire anywhere in Great Britain of plays not licensed by him, and required that a copy of every new play proposed to be performed should be sent to him. For the purpose of his duties under the Act the Lord Chamberlain appointed an Examiner of Plays as his official subordinate. The Act was unpopular with the public and was evaded in various ways. Brooke's 'Gustavus Vasa' (q.v.) was one of the first plays censored, owing to a supposed allusion in it to Walpole; Johnson's ironical 'Compleat Vindication of the Licenser of Plays' on this occasion (1739) reflected the popular resentment. 'Edward and Eleanora', a play about Edward I and Eleanor of Castile, by James Thomson (q.v.), was similarly prohibited on account of its political allusions. It is more difficult to understand why Charles Macklin's 'Man of the World' (q.v.) should for many years have been refused a licence. Another well-known incident was the prohibition of 'A Trip to Calais' by Samuel Foote (q.v.), until he had removed from it the character of Lady Kitty Crocodile, in which the Duchess of Kingston was ridiculed.

The most interesting of the appointments to the post of Examiner of Plays in the early nineteenth century was that of George Colman the Younger (q.v.), who held the office from 1824 to 1836. Some of his plays and poems had shown him no strait-laced moralist, and one of his proposed productions at the Haymarket had even been forbidden by the Lord Chamberlain. The severity with which he now exercised his duties as censor and prohibited expletives and scriptural allusions was therefore a surprise to authors and managers. He tempered this severity, however, by letting his opinion be known that it was no part of his duties to spy on the theatre and to see that plays were performed in accordance with his obliterations. He was succeeded by John Kemble the actor, and the latter in 1840 by his son John Mitchell Kemble. William Bodham Donne was appointed Examiner of Stage Plays in 1857, E. F. S. Pigott in 1874, G. A. Redford in 1895, C. H. E. Brookfield in 1912; Brookfield died in the following year. G. S. Street held the office 1913–36.

In 1832 a Select Committee of the House of Commons was appointed under the chairmanship of Edward Bulwer-Lytton (the future Lord Lytton, q.v.) to consider the working of the Act of 1737. The recommendations of this committee led to the passing in 1843 of an Act (6 & 7 Vict. cap. 68) whose provisions, substantially, are in force at the present day. It left the censorship of the drama in the hands of the Lord Chamberlain and empowered him to forbid the acting for hire of any play or part thereof 'whenever he shall be of opinion that it is fitting for the preservation of good manners, decorum, or the public peace so to do'. The administration of the censorship under this Act has at times given rise to much criticism; in particular the refusal of a licence to certain plays by distinguished authors (such as Maeterlinck, Ibsen, and Bernard Shaw) evoked strong protests. In 1909 the matter was considered by a Select Committee of both Houses. The evidence given before it showed a large measure of agreement among dramatic authors that the censorship should be abolished or modified; among managers of theatres, on the other hand, that some form of licensing plays before their production should be retained. The Committee's principal recommendations were that the Lord Chamberlain should remain the licenser of plays, that it should be optional to submit a play for licence and legal to perform an unlicensed play. The Committee enumerated the various grounds (indecency, offence to the sentiment of religious reverence, offence to a foreign power, etc.) on which the Lord Chamberlain should refuse a licence; and it recommended the action to be taken if a play produced without a licence should appear to the Attorney-General improper to be played on any of these grounds, or to the Director of Public Prosecutions improper to be played on the ground of indecency. No legislative action has followed the report of the Committee.

§ 3. *The present law of the press and drama*

THE following are the chief heads under which the law today punishes the publication of illegal matter:

1. *Libel as a civil injury*, the publication of matter defamatory of the plaintiff, that is, 'calculated to convey to those to whom it is published an imputation on the plaintiff injurious to him in his trade, or holding him up to hatred, contempt, or ridicule',

(*a*) unless it appears that the publication is privileged, either

(i) absolutely (this applies to Reports and Proceedings published under the authority of either House of Parliament, documents used in judicial proceedings, and reports of State officials to their superiors; but not necessarily to the reproduction of any of the above in newspapers);

or (ii) partially (this applies to reports of parliamentary, judicial, or other public proceedings, provided that the report is fair and accurate and was not published maliciously, that the matter is of public concern and its publicity for the public benefit, and that the defendant has not refused on request to publish in the newspaper in which the publication complained of was made a reasonable contradiction or explanation);

(*b*) or unless the defendant can prove the defamatory matter to be true (if a statement of fact) or fair and honest comment on a subject of public interest (if a matter of opinion).

Everyone who is party to producing, printing, and issuing the libel (author, proprietor of a newspaper, printer, publisher, and in certain circumstances the vendor) is liable in respect of it.

2. *Libel as a criminal offence*, i.e. as calculated to provoke a breach of the peace or to outrage public feeling or morality, or to endanger the State:

(*a*) libels defamatory of private character. Here in order to establish justification, it is necessary to prove not only that the defamatory statement is true, but also that its publication is for the public benefit;

(*b*) libels (not in the popular sense of the word, but publications which the State for public purposes prohibits) that are

(i) blasphemous, i.e. written or published with the malicious intent of outraging Christian sentiment or of misleading the uneducated on a sacred subject. 'If the decencies of controversy are observed, even the fundamentals of religion may be attacked without a person being guilty of blasphemous libel' (Lord Coleridge);

(ii) obscene, i.e. matter tending to deprave and corrupt those whose minds are open to such immoral influences, and into whose hands the matter is likely to fall. The Act 20 & 21 Vict. cap. 83 was passed for the purpose of preventing the sale of obscene books, etc. An instance of action by the Government to restrain the sale of printed matter on the score of alleged obscenity is afforded by the well-known case of Joyce's 'Ulysses' (q.v.). An edition of 500 numbered copies, published by John Rodker, Paris, for the Egoist Press, London, in January 1923, was confiscated (with, it is said, the exception of one copy) by the British Customs authorities, and this action effectively prohibited publication in Great Britain so long as the Government's policy remained unchanged. Under the Obscene Publications Act 1959 a book 'is deemed to be obscene if its effect . . . if taken as a whole, is such as to tend to deprave and corrupt persons who are likely, having regard to all relevant circumstances, to read . . . the matter contained . . . in it'. Sect. 2 reads shortly as '. . . any person who, whether for gain or not, publishes an obscene article shall be liable upon conviction' to certain penalties. Sect. 4 reads, 'A person shall not be convicted of an offence against Section 2 if it is proved that publication of the article in question is justified as being for the public good on the ground that it is in the interests of science, literature, art, or learning, or of other subjects of general concern.' Before the passing of the 1959 Statute defendants were not allowed by law to call any evidence with regard to the literary or other merits of the book. Sub-sect. 2 (of sect. 4) reads, 'that the opinion of experts as to the literary, artistic, scientific, or other merits of an article may be admitted in any proceedings under this Act to establish or to negative the said ground.' 'Lady Chatterley's Lover' by D. H. Lawrence (q.v.) was the subject of the case *Regina* v. *Penguin Books Limited*, heard at the Old Bailey in 1960 (20 Oct.–2 Nov.). The case, which resulted in the acquittal of Penguin Books and the release of the book for sale, was interesting because for the first time the defendants were allowed to bring witnesses to give evidence on the literary and moral qualities of the book;

(iii) seditious, i.e. matter tending to bring into hatred or contempt the sovereign, the government and constitution, or either House of Parliament, or to excite to the alteration of anything in Church or State by unlawful means, or to raise discontent and disaffection among the king's subjects, or to promote ill-will and hostility between different classes of them.

In a trial for criminal libel a defendant presumptively responsible for the publication (such as a newspaper proprietor) who is able to prove that such publication was made without his authority, consent, or knowledge, and that the publication did not arise from want of due care on his part, is freed from criminal responsibility.

3. *Infringement of copyright* (see the article on *Copyright* below).

4. *Slander of property*, i.e. the publication of a statement referring to the property or trade of another which is false and is calculated to cause, or has caused, damage.

5. *Contempt of Parliament or Court*, i.e. the publication of matter defamatory of or insulting to either House of Parliament, or reflecting on any member of such House in his character of member, or of any matter reflecting on one of the Superior Courts of Record or referring to the parties concerned in causes therein, if the matter is calculated to prejudice the public against the parties before the cause is heard, or to interfere with the due administration of the law.

The printer is required to put his name and address on every copy of every paper or book printed by him to be published or dispersed (2 & 3 Vict. cap. 12).

Dramatic performances. The Act of 6 & 7 Vict. cap. 68 (1843) requires that a copy of new plays and additions to old plays intended to be acted for hire shall be sent at least seven days before the first acting thereof, together with the prescribed fee (which is not to exceed two guineas in any case), to the Lord Chamberlain, who may forbid the acting of any play or of any part thereof anywhere in Great Britain. Penalties for infringement are prescribed, and the meaning of 'acted for hire' is defined. The Act further requires that theatres shall be authorized either by letters patent or by the Lord Chamberlain or (outside London and other places of royal residence) by justices of the peace (this last provision has been modified by Local Government Acts).

[The following works among others have been consulted in the preparation of §§ 1 and 2 above: the C.H.E.L., Fowell and Palmer, 'The Censorship in England', L. Hanson, 'Government and the Press, 1695–1763'; so much of § 3 as relates to the control of the press is based on Fisher and Strahan, 'The Law of the Press'.]

APPENDIX II

NOTES ON THE HISTORY OF ENGLISH COPYRIGHT

By Sir Frank Mackinnon[1]

'No man but a blockhead ever wrote except for money', said the great man. In order to increase the number of books worth reading, mankind has been concerned to see that writers may get some reward for their industry. And so there came to be devised that security for them which we call Copyright.

The first English Copyright Act was the celebrated Statute[2] of 1709. But something akin to the protection of copyright had existed for at least a century and a half before that date. This had two principal sources and means of support, firstly, the prerogative rights of the Crown, and secondly, the domestic arrangements of London booksellers under the rule of the Stationers' Company.

The action of the Crown was part of its practice to grant monopolies in general, but from an early date after Caxton printed his first book[3] at Westminster in 1477, it claimed especial rights as to printed books. There are indeed traces of a claim that all printing was the king's prerogative. There is, for example, a record[4] of a privilege granted in 1597 to the queen's footman to print certain schoolbooks for 14 years; and as late as 1631 of a grant[5] to one Weckherlin of the sole right to print some of the Latin classics.

But a royal grant of the sole privilege to print new books was much more common. In 1518 Richard Pynson, the second holder of the office of King's Printer, produced the first English book in Roman type, and on its title-page is inscribed, 'Cum privilegio impressa a rege indulto, ne quis hanc orationem intra biennium in regno Angliae imprimat aut alibi impressam et importatam in eodem regno Angliae vendat'. Pynson's later books are only inscribed, 'Cum privilegio a rege indulto'.

The Act[6] of 1623 abolished monopolies; but sect. 5 of it excepts Letters Patent for new inventions, and sect. 10 provides that the Act shall not extend to any Letters Patent that concern Printing, Saltpetre, Gunpowder, and Ordnance.

For more than two centuries after Pynson's grant in 1518 it was common for such a privilege to be obtained from the Crown. For example, Loggan's 'Oxonia Illustrata' (Oxon. e Theatro Sheldoniano, 1675) has printed in it a grant by Charles II giving Loggan 'the sole Priviledge of printing the aforesaid Delineations for the term of 15 years next ensuing the date of this our License'. And the practice became so inveterate that it was often continued after the Act of Anne was passed in 1709. So when in 1741 the bookseller Austin was minded to publish a second edition of Stackhouse's 'History of the Bible' (first published in 1732) he got Letters Patent from George II giving him the sole privilege of printing his edition for 14 years. And the early editions of Warburton's Pope have printed in them a licence

---

[1] The paragraphs concerning the Copyright Act of 1956 and the last two paragraphs under the heading *International Copyright* were contributed by Kenneth Ewart.

[2] 8 Anne, cap. 19.

[3] There exists in the Record Office a lease dated 10 May 1482 of premises in St. Mark's Alley, St. Clement's Lane, to Henry Franckenbergk and Bernard Van Stondo 'merchants of printed books'. The Act of 1483 (1 Rich. III, cap. 9) to prevent aliens trading within the realm, by sect. 12 made an exception in favour of any Artificer or Merchant Stranger bringing into this Realm or selling any Books written or printed. The demand for the new luxury evidently exceeded the native supply. This foreigner's privilege was repealed in 1533 by 25 Hen. VIII, cap. 15.

[4] S. P. Dom. (1595–7), p. 352.   [5] S. P. Dom. (1629–34), pp. 514, 557.

[6] 21 James I, cap. 3.

or grant from George II, dated 24 July 1759, giving Warburton 'our Royal Privilege and License for the sole printing and publishing the said Works' for 14 years.

There was a second way in which the Crown was concerned with copyright. In certain classes of books it claimed an especial prerogative right, and granted the sole privilege of printing them. These were State documents, like Acts of Parliament and Orders in Council, Bibles and Prayer Books, the Year Books, and Almanacs.[1] Except as to the Year Books and Almanacs, this right was a real one, and survives today. The Queen's Printers are still, by Letters Patent, empowered to print Acts of Parliament, Bibles, and Prayer Books. That the University Presses of Oxford and Cambridge share the right with them arises solely from the fact that each of the Universities possesses an early Charter (that of Oxford 1636), which authorizes it 'to print all manner of books'.

A third way in which the Crown may be said to have been concerned in the maintenance of the rights of authors and their publishers was in connexion with the licensing of publications. But this part of the Crown's activity is to a large extent combined with the working of the Stationers' Company as the controlling power over the publication of books.

In 1557 a charter of Queen Mary incorporated 97 named persons to constitute the Company of Stationers. The motive for this creation was very little concerned with the protection of authors and their copyright. It was in fact because 'certain seditious books . . . are daily printed, renewing and spreading great and detestable heresies against the catholic doctrine of the holy Mother Church'. It was ordered that no one should exercise the art of printing unless he was a freeman of the Company, and the Master and Wardens were authorized to seize and destroy prohibited books, and to imprison anyone printing contrary to their orders. The Company was further empowered to make by-laws for regulating the trade.

This charter was confirmed by Queen Elizabeth in 1559; and in the same year a Royal Injunction required that a licence for the printing of any book must be obtained from some authority (see the article on *Censorship* above).

From a very early date after 1557 the Stationers' Company began to keep registers of the proprietors of 'copy', and books were entered in these by the printers to whom authors had sold them. From 1576 to 1595 more than 2,000 'copies' of books were registered, entirely or in shares, as the property of particular members. As only members of the Company could legally print, the entry in the register showed which member had the right to print a particular book, and any infringement of this by another printer-member could be prevented, or remedied, by fines imposed by the Company. Any printing by a piratical printer, not a member, could be stopped by the Company's power to destroy his press altogether. The State Papers of the sixteenth and seventeenth centuries, especially in reference to the Star Chamber and the High Commission Court, contain many references to the activity of the Company in both these ways.

Not unnaturally the richer members of the Company came to own the largest number of 'copies', and this caused discontent among the smaller men. A royal decree of 1585 confirmed the charter of the Company, but recited that many of the richer members[2] had yielded divers of their copies to the Company for the benefit and relief of the poorer members. This process would make the Company itself the proprietor of certain works.

---

[1] The royal claim to almanacs may have been based on their being derived from the Tables in the Prayer Book. That it was without foundation was eventually decided in *Stationers' Co.* v. *Carnan* (1775), 2 W. Bl. 1002.   [2] Mr. Tottell surrendered 'Romeo et Julietta' *inter alia*.

The effect of all this was that by 1600 the sole right of printing a particular book, not yet called 'copyright',[1] was protected in two ways, *first* by virtue of Royal Grants giving the grantee a sole right of printing for a specified number of years, and *secondly* by the rules and by-laws of the Stationers' Company. There is, however, no record of any case in the law courts in which this right was enforced or recognized. The fact that it could be so thoroughly upheld by the domestic powers of the Company is no doubt the reason for this.

These two sources of the sole right to print are recognized by the decree of the Star Chamber in 1637 'touching the Regulation of Printers and Founders of Letters'. That enacted by sect. 2 that every book should be licensed and entered in the Register Book of the Stationers' Company; and by sect. 7 that no person should print or import any copy which the Company of Stationers, or any other person, has by any letters patent, order, or entrance in their Register Book, the right or allowance solely to print.

The Star Chamber having been abolished in 1641, an Ordinance of 1641 prohibited printing without the consent of the owner of the 'copy' of any book. And this was followed by the famous Ordinance of the Long Parliament of 1643. This provided that no book should be printed unless licensed (see the article on *Censorship* above). It also enacted that no book, of which the copy had been granted to the Stationers' Company 'for their relief and the maintenance of their poor', be printed by any one without the licence of the Company. It also renewed to the Company the power to break up unlicensed presses, and to search for, and confiscate, unlicensed books.

But here again, as in Queen Mary's Charter to the Company of 1557, the primary motive was not the protection of authors. For the preamble to the Ordinance recites that 'many false, scandalous, seditious, and libellous' works have been lately published, 'to the great defamation of Religion and Government'; and that many private presses have been set up. It was the part of this Ordinance that required all books to be licensed that gave rise to Milton's 'Areopagitica'. 'For that part', he says, 'which preserves justly every man's copy to himself, or provides for the poor, I touch not, only wish they be not made pretences to abuse and persecute honest and painful men, who offend not in either of these particulars.' And near the end he speaks of 'the just retaining of each man his several copy, which God forbid should be gainsaid'.

There were further Ordinances to the same effect in 1647, 1649, and 1652. And after the Restoration an Act[2] of 1662 was again passed 'for preventing the frequent abuses in printing seditious, treasonable, and unlicensed books and pamphlets'. This again incidentally dealt with copyright. By sect. 3 all books are to be entered in the Register of the Stationers' Company, and by sect. 6 'no person shall print or import any book which any person by virtue of letters Patent, or of entries duly made in the Register Book of the Company . . . has, or shall have, the right, privilege, authority, or allowance solely to print without the consent of the owner or owners'.

In 1684 a new charter was granted to the Company, which recited the ownership of 'copies' according to the Register by members of the Company, and went on, 'We, willing and desiring to confirm and establish every member in their just rights and properties, do well approve of the said Register, and declare that every member of the Company, who shall be the proprietor of any book, shall have and enjoy such

---

[1] The earliest quotation for the word 'Copyright' in the OED is dated 1767 from *Blackstone's Commentaries*.
[2] 13 & 14 Car. II, cap. 33.

sole right, power, privilege, and authority of printing such book or copy as in that case hath been usual heretofore.'

These Licensing Acts were several times re-enacted, but the last of them lapsed in 1694. The effect of this was that there remained no Act of Parliament recognizing the sole right to print, and this was no doubt one of the reasons for the passing of the Act of 1709.

It is of great importance to observe that, though Letters Patent from the Crown used to specify a period, usually 14 years, for the sole right of printing, there is nowhere any trace of any limitation of time in regard to the ownership of 'copy' by registration with the Company. In the year 1700 there can be no doubt that this was universally recognized as a perpetual right. The Tonsons, for example, through most part of the eighteenth century were regarded as the undoubted owners of the copyright in 'Paradise Lost', under an assignment from Milton dated 1667, duly entered in the Register. They were also regarded as the proprietors of Shakespeare's plays, though I do not know that they had any assignment from the author on which to rely. And the Special Verdict in *Millar* v. *Taylor* in 1769 stated 'that before the reign of her late Majesty, Queen Anne, it was usual to purchase from authors the *perpetual* copyright of their books and to assign them from hand to hand for valuable considerations, and to make the same the subjects of family settlements for the provision of wives and children'.

In short, in 1700 it was the universal belief of the trade, and probably of lawyers, that by the common law an author, or his bookseller-assignee, had a perpetual copyright in any book.

The Act of 1709 was probably the result of petitions from the Booksellers in 1703, 1706, and 1709. What they desired was not the creation of copyright—as to that they had no doubt, nor as to its duration—but the provision of machinery by which it could be more readily enforced. This they had enjoyed, under the Licensing Act which expired in 1694, by the power to seize unlicensed and unregistered books.

The title of the Act of 1709 was 'An Act for the encouragement of Learning, by vesting[1] the copies of printed books in the authors or purchasers of such copies during the times therein mentioned'. The Preamble recited that persons have of late frequently taken the liberty of printing books without the consent of the authors, or proprietors, of such books, to their great detriment and too often to the ruin of them and their families. The first section enacted that from 10 April 1710 an author of a book already printed, or the bookseller who had bought his copy, should have the sole right and liberty of printing such book for the term of 1 and 20 years, and no longer; and an author of any book not yet published should have the sole liberty of printing it for the term of 14 years from its publication, and no longer. If anyone printed a book in breach of these rights, the offender should forfeit the book, and be liable to pay a penalty of a penny for every sheet found in his possession. Sect. 2 provided that no offender should be liable to such forfeiture or penalties unless the title to the copy of the book should be entered in the Register of the Stationers' Company. Sect. 4 provided a cumbrous machinery for fixing fair prices for books in case of a complaint by anyone that a bookseller was asking an unreasonable price.[2] Sect. 5 provided for the delivery of copies for certain

---

[1] In the original Bill this was 'securing'.

[2] There was precedent for this in an Act of 1533 (25 Hen. VIII, cap. 15) which provided that if English printers increase the price of books at too high and unreasonable prices the Lord Chancellor, Lord Treasurer, or two Chief Justices may hold an inquiry with 12 jurors and limit the prices. The Act of 1709 in the above clause gave power to limit prices, in England, to the Archbishop of Canterbury, the Lord Chancellor, the Bishop of London, the two Chief Justices, the Chief Baron, and the Vice-Chan-

libraries: I refer to this later. Sect. 7 provided that nothing in the Act should extend to prohibit the importation and sale of any books in Greek, Latin, or any other foreign language, printed beyond the seas.

Sect. 9 was, 'Provided that nothing in this Act contained shall extend, or be construed to extend, either to prejudice or confirm any right that the said Universities, or any of them, or any person or persons have, or claim to have, to the printing or reprinting any book or copy already printed, or hereafter to be printed.' And the final sect. 11 was, 'Provided always that after the expiration of the said term of fourteen years, the sole right of printing or disposing of copies shall return to the author thereof, if they are then living, for another term of fourteen years.'

The great 'Question of Literary Property' which reverberates through the second half of the eighteenth century, and has its echo in the pages of Boswell, was whether the perpetual copyright, at common law, of an author or his bookseller-assignee survived the passage of this Act, or was destroyed by it. Until their final discomfiture in 1774 the Booksellers were confident that it survived. They regarded the Act as only designed to provide, for the periods named, machinery for enforcing the right by forfeiture and penalties; and they relied confidently on the proviso in clause 9. But ultimately the words 'and no longer' in clause 1 proved fatal to them.

The question could hardly arise until the expiration of the 21 years in 1731. And for a time the Booksellers were successful, especially in applications for injunctions in the Court of Chancery. For example, in 1735 the proprietor of 'The Whole Duty of Man', claiming under an assignment of 1657 (from what author is not apparent), successfully restrained a rival from printing it. And in 1736, before Lord Hardwicke, 'Tonson and Others' vindicated their 'copy' in 'Paradise Lost' under the assignment from Milton of 1667.

In 1769 the question came before a Court of Law in the famous case of *Millar* v. *Taylor*. It concerned Thomson's 'Seasons', published 1726–30. Thomson's 28 years under clauses 1 and 11 of the Act of 1709 had therefore expired by 1758. He had sold all his rights to Millar. In 1763 Taylor reprinted the work, and in 1766 Millar sued him in the King's Bench. In 1769 the Court delivered judgement, and it was one of the few occasions on which that Court, during the 32 years of Lord Mansfield's reign as Chief Justice, was not unanimous. Lord Mansfield, Mr. Justice Willes, and Mr. Justice Aston decided in favour of Millar. Mr. Justice Yates (after a 'very decent preface', as the reporter, Burrow, records) delivered a lengthy dissentient judgement in favour of Taylor. So, for the time, the Booksellers won.

The chief source of trouble to the London Booksellers was the activity of printers in Ireland and Scotland. For some reason they do not seem to have attempted to take action in Dublin,[1] and those who read booksellers' catalogues are aware that Dublin reprints of all the important books in the eighteenth century are numerous. But they did attack those whom they no doubt regarded as the Edinburgh 'pirates', and this was eventually their undoing.

The first edition of Stackhouse's 'History of the Bible' was published in 1732. A second edition[2] was published by his assignee, Austin, in 1744. Stackhouse died

cellors of Oxford and Cambridge; and in Scotland, to the Lord President, the Lord Justice General, the Lord Chief Baron, and the Rector of Edinburgh University. Nothing is provided as to Ireland.

[1] One of the pamphlets ('A Letter from a gentleman in Edinburgh to his friend in London concerning Literary Property', 1769) referring to Blackstone's support of the perpetual right at common law ('Commentaries', ii. 406) says, 'His book has been reprinted in Ireland, copies have been smuggled over to Britain, and a good many of them, it is said, were seized some time ago by the Doctor's agents in the port of London; but if he really believes he has any right at common law, why does he not sue the Irish printers for piracy, robbery, or theft, in virtue of this *common law right?*'

[2] It was for this edition that Austin got the Letters Patent from George II, mentioned *supra* p. 921, giving him the sole privilege of printing it for 14 years.

in 1752, so his 28 years under the Act expired in 1760. In 1767 Donaldson, an Edinburgh bookseller, reprinted the book. In 1770 Hinton, a London bookseller, and the assignee of Austin, sued Donaldson in the Court of Session. Ilay Campbell was Donaldson's advocate, and James Boswell was his junior. On 28 July 1773 the Court of Sessions, by eleven to one, decided in favour of Donaldson. The eleven included Lord Auchinleck, Lord Hailes, and Lord Kames: the one dissentient was Lord Monboddo. So the London booksellers had won in London in 1769 and had lost in Scotland in 1773.

In 1774 came *Donaldson* v. *Beckett* in the House of Lords. This again concerned Thomson's 'Seasons'. Beckett had bought from Millar's executors the copyright that had been upheld in *Millar* v. *Taylor* in 1769. And Beckett made his claim in the English Court of Chancery against the Edinburgh 'pirate' Donaldson, who had re-printed 'The Seasons'. Lord Chancellor Bathurst granted a perpetual injunction against Donaldson, whereupon Donaldson appealed to the House of Lords. The hearing began[1] 4 February 1774. The judges, then twelve in number, being summoned, they all attended with the exception of Lord Mansfield: it was not the etiquette for him to advise the House; as a peer himself, if he were present, he would form part of the tribunal. Five questions were submitted to the judges, to which they gave answers by varying majorities. But to the most vital question—'Whether by the Statute of 1709 an author is precluded from every remedy, except on the foundation of the said statute, or on the terms and conditions prescribed therein'—six answered 'Yes', and five answered 'No'.

Lord Mansfield, who might have sat, and upheld the view he had taken in *Millar* v. *Taylor* five years before, did not attend the House. And on the motion of Lord Camden, on 22 February, the House decided in favour of the appellant, Donaldson,[2] and *Millar* v. *Taylor* was overruled. The English booksellers had found their Bannockburn.

They attempted to get relief from Parliament, but a Bill for that purpose, having passed the Commons, was rejected by the Lords. But the Universities of Oxford, Cambridge, St. Andrews, Glasgow, Aberdeen, and Edinburgh, and the Colleges of Winchester, Eton, and Westminster got an Act[3] in 1775 giving them perpetual copyright 'in books given or bequeathed to the said Universities and Colleges for the advancement of useful learning, and other purposes of education'. This was subject to the condition that such books be printed at their own private presses, which Oxford and Cambridge alone possessed!

In 1814 the author's period of 14 years, with a second 14 years, if he was alive at the end of the first, under the Act of 1709 was altered when, by 54 Geo. III, cap. 156, the author was given 28 years, and, if he were living at the end of that period, the term of his life.

So matters remained until Serjeant Talfourd in 1837 began his efforts to secure an increased period of copyright in the interests of authors. He was removed from the House of Commons, by being made a Judge, before his crusade was successful

---

[1] Johnson wrote to Boswell, 7 Feb. 1774: 'The question of Literary Property is this day before the Lords. Murphy drew up the Appellant's case, that is the plea against the perpetual right. I have not seen it, nor heard the decision. I would not have the right perpetual.' Boswell, 'Life', ii. 272.

[2] When Mr. Dempster said, 'Donaldson, Sir, is anxious for the encouragement of literature. He reduces the prices of books so that poor students may buy them', Dr. Johnson said (laughing), 'Well, Sir, allowing that to be his motive, he is no better than Robin Hood, who robbed the rich in order to give to the poor'. Boswell, 'Life', i. 438.

[3] 15 Geo. III, cap. 53. Sect. 33 of the Copyright Act 1911 provides that 'Nothing in this Act shall deprive any of the Universities and Colleges mentioned in the Act of 1775 of any copyright they already possess under that Act.' But the Act of 1775 itself is repealed by the Act of 1911, so that none of the Universities or Colleges can acquire a perpetual copyright in the future.

in 1842. Sixty years was his proposal, in the Bill he introduced without success in 1838. The question was further debated in 1841 and 1842, and was made memorable by two famous speeches of Macaulay. His proposal, supported by a wealth of historical instances, was that the period should be 42 years, or the life of the author, whichever was the longer. The House was convinced by his eloquence. Sir George Trevelyan, in his 'Life of Macaulay',[1] says: 'Never has any public man, unendowed with the authority of a minister, so easily moulded an important piece of legislation into a shape which so accurately accorded with his own views as did Macaulay the Copyright Act of 1842'.

Sir Robert Peel successfully moved one amendment, by which seven years was added to the author's life. In the result the Act[2] of 1842 gave copyright for the period of 42 years from the date of publication, or until seven years after the author's death, whichever was the longer. Sect. 5 of the Act empowered the Judicial Committee of the Privy Council to authorize, after the author's death, the reprinting of a book which the proprietor of the copyright refused to permit. Sect. 11 continued the Registry at Stationers' Hall, and provided that certificates issued there should be *prima facie* proof in any court of the ownership of the copyright. And by sect. 24 no action for infringement could be begun unless the work had been entered in the Registry before the writ was issued. This meant that the Registry was not necessarily a complete record of publications, though the great majority were entered. But a publisher could abstain from registering altogether, unless he came to want to sue for an infringement, when he must register before starting his suit.

This Act, like all previous ones, dealt with copyright as from the time of publication. There never was any doubt that by the common law the author of any writing, or his personal representative after his death, had complete and perpetual power over his work so long as it remained unpublished. This applied to letters. The recipient of a letter had the property in the paper, but, unless he had express or implied authority from the writer (as the Editor of a newspaper, for example), he had no right to publish copies of it. In pure theory the purchaser of an unpublished letter of Samuel Johnson could have been restrained from publishing it by his then personal representative, who would be found in a line of successive executors from Lord Stowell, the survivor of his three executors.[3]

This Act of 1842 provided for English literary copyright until it was replaced by the Act[4] of 1911. This effected three momentous changes. *Firstly*, it increased the period of copyright to the life of the author and 50 years after his death. This got rid of difficult questions that used to arise when the period of copyright began from the date of publication.[5] In the case of a posthumous work, however, copyright was (by sect. 17) to subsist for 50 years from publication. *Secondly*, the Act tacitly abolished the Register at Stationers' Hall, since it no longer made registration there necessary for any purpose. And so those records, which had been kept for three and a half centuries, came to an end.[6] *Thirdly*, the Act altered the nature of the perpetual

---

[1] Vol. ii, p. 132. [2] 5 & 6 Vict. cap. 45.
[3] In the early 20th cent., in litigation between two publishers about some letters of Charles Lamb, one of the parties, in order to strengthen his case, got hold of Lamb's personal representative (in a line from his executor, Moxon), caused him to take out letters of administration *de bonis non*, and took an assignment of the right to publish from him. [4] 1 & 2 Geo. V, cap. 46.
[5] Possibly it was an inducement to the inferior publisher to indulge in that reprehensible practice of putting no date on a title-page.
[6] In fact the registration of books at Stationers' Hall continued until Dec. 1923. This was done with the object of securing copyright in Canada, since the Act of 1911 was not (by sect. 25) to apply to a self-governing Dominion until made to do so by domestic legislation. This was not passed in Canada, but the result of two Canadian statutes of 1921 and 1923 (on similar lines to the English Act of 1911) caused the final closing of the Stationers' Hall Register.

common law right of an author, and his personal representatives, in an unpublished work. For its definition of 'copyright' includes the right, if a work is unpublished, to publish it, or any substantial part of it. Thus the right became part of the personal property of the deceased author.

In regard to the unpublished manuscript of a deceased author two questions may follow: (1) Who is the owner of the manuscript? and (2) Who is proprietor of the right to publish it? As to the latter it was provided by sect. 17 (2) that the ownership of an unpublished manuscript after the author's death, when acquired pursuant to a will made by the author, should be *prima facie* proof of the copyright being vested in the owner of the manuscript. Apart from this, the proprietor was the express devisee of the copyright, or copyrights in general, of the deceased, or his residuary legatee.

By sect. 2 it was an infringement to produce or reproduce a work, or any substantial part thereof, in any material form, without the consent of the owner of the copyright. But a proviso adds that certain acts should not constitute an infringement, in particular (i) any fair dealing with any work for the purposes of private study, research, criticism, review, or newspaper summary; and (ii) the reading or recitation in public by one person of any reasonable extract from any published work.

Sect. 4 of the Act re-enacted the provision of sect. 5 of the 1842 Act as to the power of the Judicial Committee of the Privy Council to authorize the reprinting of a book unreasonably withheld by the owner of the copyright.[1]

A proviso to sect. 3 of the Act introduced a novelty by enacting that on the expiration of 25 years from the death of the author of a published work anyone might reproduce it if he gave notice of his intention to the owner of the copyright, and paid him royalties at the rate of ten per cent. on the price at which he published the book. Another novelty was contained in a clause in sect. 2. It was not to be an infringement of copyright to publish, in a collection mainly composed of non-copyright matter, bona fide intended for the use of schools and so described on the title-page and in any advertisements of the book . . . short passages from published literary works not themselves published for the use of schools . . . provided that not more than two of such passages from works by the same author were published by the same publisher within five years, and that the source from which such passages are taken was acknowledged.

The next milestone was the Copyright Act (1956, 4 & 5 Eliz. II, cap. 74), passed as the result of the labours of the Copyright Committee, set up in 1951, which presented a very valuable report in October 1952. It modified the 1911 Act very considerably to bring it into line with modern conditions and with the requirements of two new international Conventions, viz., the Brussels Convention of 1948, and the Universal Copyright Convention of 1952. Some of the changes introduced by the 1911 Act were themselves swept away, and, in particular, sect. 4 (which had never in fact been used) and the proviso to sect. 3 which have already been noted.

The new Act also recognized that scope should be given to certain libraries to make research and private study easier by providing students with copies of articles in periodicals, and copies of parts of published works (sect. 7)—the 1911 Act would only have protected the student who made his own copies of the extracts he required. But perhaps the most extensive amendment is contained in sect. 7 (6) which provides that where, at a time more than 50 years from the author's death and more than 100

---

[1] The equivalent of this power of a public authority to prevent the suppression of books, or the demand of an excessive price for them, has thus been continuous since 1533. I am not aware that the power has ever been invoked.

years from the time it was made, there is a manuscript or copy of an unpublished work which is open to public inspection then the work may be reproduced 'for purposes of research or private study, or with a view to publication'. The words 'or with a view to publication' have to be considered in the light of subsect. (7); and subsect. (6) does not in any way deprive the owner of the copyright in the document of his rights. Under the provisions of sect. 17(2) of the Copyright Act 1911 (which are substantially re-enacted by sect. 38 of the Act of 1956), for example, the bequest of an unpublished work by Will gave the legatee the copyright in the unpublished work. It follows that there is a mass of historical or literary material, open to inspection by the public, in libraries throughout the country which remains unpublished because it is difficult or impossible to find the owner of the copyright with a view to obtaining permission to publish. Sect. 7(7) of the 1956 Act, read in conjunction with sect. 7(6) seeks to remove the difficulty by providing that where an author seeks to publish a new work in which he incorporates the whole or part of such material he may not publish the new work without satisfying two conditions, viz., (1) he must establish that the identity of the owner of the copyright in the old work is not known to the proposed publisher of the new work and (2) that notice of the intended publication is given in such form as may be prescribed by regulations made by the Board of Trade, called 'The Copyright (Notice of Publication) Regulations, 1957' and contained in 'Statutory Instruments 1957. No. 865', obtainable at HMSO. These conditions are, of course, intended to ensure that only if the copyright owner cannot be traced, and fails to materialize as the result of the publication of the prescribed notice will the publication of the new work be regarded as other than an infringement of copyright. If the owner is thus brought to light the new work can only be published with his consent. However, even though the last words of sect. 7(6) are much modified by sect. 7(7) the result should be to make available to the public generally a mass of material which hitherto they could only see by visiting the appropriate library.

International Copyright

This is a most complicated topic, which can only be noticed very briefly. Following upon an abortive Act[1] of 1838, the Act[2] of 1844 empowered Her Majesty by Order in Council to direct that foreign authors should have British copyright to the same extent as British subjects. Such Orders were issued as to countries which had given, or were prepared to give, similar protection to British authors. Between 1846 and 1886 sixteen Orders in Council were issued as to various European states, and they resulted in considerable complication.

In 1885 the Berne Convention providing for a uniform international system was arranged, and this was given effect to by the Act[3] of 1886. Most States with any pretensions to civilization and culture became parties to the Convention, but the United States (with whom no arrangement under the Act of 1844 had been possible) did not.

The Berne Convention was revised by the Berlin Convention of 1908, again by the Rome Convention of 1928 and finally by the Brussels Convention of 1948. Most civilized States with the exception of the United States were parties to these.

Up to 1891 printers and publishers in the United States dealt as they liked with the works of British authors. In that year the Chace Act was passed, partly in the interests of foreign authors, but at least as much for the benefit of American printers. It enabled a foreign author to enjoy copyright in the United States, provided that he

---

[1] 1 & 2 Vict. cap. 59.   [2] 7 Vict. cap. 12.   [3] 49 & 50 Vict. cap. 33.

delivered two copies of his work on publication to the Librarian of Congress, and provided those two copies were printed from type set within the limits of the United States.

A revised United States law was passed in March 1909. Sect. 15 of this provides that of any printed book, except the original text of a book of foreign origin in a language other than English, the text of all copies accorded protection under this Act . . . shall be printed from type set within the limits of the United States . . . and the printing of the text and binding of the said book shall be performed within the limits of the United States.[1] A noble concession to humanity provides that this requirement shall not apply to works in raised characters for the use of the blind.

Many of the restrictions contained in the United States law were progressively released, particularly after 1945, but a very real step forward in the sphere of international relations was taken with the passing of the Universal Copyright Convention, the product of UNESCO, in 1952. It established the principle of mutual protection of copyright throughout the contracting States, upon the same basis as each contracting State protects the works of its own nationals. Further (and most important) it provides in Article 3 that works first published outside a contracting State are to enjoy protection throughout the remaining contracting States without any formality such as registration, if all copies published 'bear the symbol © accompanied by the name of the copyright proprietor and the year of first publication, placed in such manner and location as to give reasonable notice of claim of copyright'. The U.S.A. joined in 1955;[2] and thus for the first time established really satisfactory arrangements with most of the civilized world.

The Universal Copyright Convention did not abrogate the Berne Union, which continues to operate between the contracting parties, but it did bring in, not only the U.S.A., but a large number of States which had hitherto not entered into copyright relations with the European countries, e.g., most of the South American Republics. A notable exception is Russia, which is a party to no international copyright treaties at all.

Delivery of Copies to Libraries

By an Act[3] of 1666 every printer was required to deliver three copies of the best and largest paper of each book printed by him to the Master of the Stationers' Company for the use of the King's Library, and the two Universities, under a penalty for not doing so.

Bentley, in the Preface to his 'Dissertation on the Letters of Phalaris' (1699), says that as Keeper of the King's Library he procured nearly a thousand volumes under this. But some booksellers refused to comply; and one named Bennet in particular declared that 'he knew not what right the Parliament had to give away any man's property; that he hoped the Company of Stationers would refuse, and try it out at law; that they were a Body, and had a common Purse, and more to this purpose'.

The Act of 1709 by clause 5 required nine copies to be delivered at Stationers' Hall for the Royal Library, the two English and four Scottish Universities, Sion

---

[1] The law of 1891 required the copies to be printed from type set within the limits of the United States. This made it possible for plates to be made there, and the actual printing from them, and the bookbinding, to be done in this country. The law of 1909 effectively puts an end, so far as books in English are concerned, to so nefarious a practice. By sect. 21, as amended in 1919, the deposit within 60 days of publication of one copy printed abroad will secure an interim copyright for four months. If the American printed copies are not deposited within that time all protection will cease.

[2] Great Britain did not join until 1957, but this delay was solely due to the fact that technical amendments to the law, which were embodied in the Copyright Act 1956, were a necessary preliminary.

[3] 17 Car. II, cap. 4.

College, and the Advocates' Library in Edinburgh. According to a Cambridge pamphlet[1] of 1770, under this provision 'very few books of value have been obtained, the booksellers . . . chusing rather to forfeit all the benefit of the Act, and trust one another, by never entering their books in the Register . . .; or when this method is not safe enough, entering only one Volume of each Sett'.

After the Union these nine copies were, by 41 Geo. III, cap. 107, increased to eleven by the addition of Trinity College, Dublin, and the King's Inn, Dublin. Sion College, the four Scottish Universities, and the King's Inn, Dublin, lost this right to copies in 1836, but by other sections of the Act[2] were given an annual payment out of the Consolidated Fund by way of compensation, the money to be spent on books for their libraries. This, I think, they still enjoy.

The Act of 1842 by sects. 6 and 7 required one copy to be delivered at the British Museum, and by sect. 8 four copies at Stationers' Hall, for the Bodleian, the Cambridge University Library, the Advocates' Library, and the Library of Trinity College, Dublin.

Finally the Act of 1911 by sect. 15 requires the delivery of copies for the same five libraries,[3] and a sixth for the National Library of Wales. Every book must be sent to the British Museum, but to the other Libraries only those for which a written demand, by the authorities of any of the libraries, is made within a year of publication. And the books to be delivered to the National Library of Wales shall not include books of such classes as may be specified in regulations to be made by the Board of Trade.

Despite representations made by the publishers to the 1952 Copyright Committee that this compulsory delivery to libraries was unfair the Copyright Act 1956 did not remove the requirement.

[1] 'Observations occasioned by the Contest about Literary Property.'
[2] 6 & 7 Will. IV, cap. 110.
[3] The 'National Library of Scotland' is substituted for the 'Advocates Library' by 15 & 16 Geo. V, cap. 73.

APPENDIX III

THE CALENDAR

ENGLISH historical documents and literary remains are dated in various ways, and the tables below are designed to make it easier to convert their dates into terms of the modern calendar. While the only era that has been in common use has been the era of the Incarnation, popularized by the writings of the Venerable Bede, from the latter part of the twelfth century legal documents, especially those emanating from the royal government, have often been dated, not by the year of Our Lord, but by the regnal year of the ruling monarch; this practice survives in the dating of acts of parliament. Both in narratives and private and public documents of the Middle Ages it was usual to express a particular date within a year by reference to a saint's day or feast of the Church; while in ecclesiastical records the Roman calendar (see below) was sometimes used to indicate the day of the month.

Most of the errors made in translating dates into modern terms arise from doubt about the starting-point of the year of the Incarnation (also known as the Year of Grace, or Year of Our Lord). For there was wide variation of practice until the reform of the calendar introduced in England in 1751 by the Act 24 Geo. II, cap. 23 ('Lord Chesterfield's Act'). Before this time records of different types are found to have employed simultaneously different methods of reckoning. In classical Rome, according to the calendar established by Julius Caesar and known as the Julian calendar, the year began on 1 January. Although, in the Middle Ages, under Christian influences other dates were chosen for beginning the year, the pagan usage survived, the Church calculated its calendar within the framework of a solar year beginning on 1 January, and 'New Year' gifts were given on that day. Early English chroniclers usually preferred a year beginning on Christmas Day. From the latter part of the twelfth century, according to a mode of reckoning which started on the Continent, the feast of the Annunciation ('Lady Day', 25 March) became the starting-point of the year for most purposes in England, and this remained the legal and official mode of reckoning until the reform of the calendar in 1751. Even so, in the Middle Ages Benedictine chroniclers continued to date their year from Christmas, and both then and later a private person, drawing up a will or writing a letter, might use the same method. After 1582 Englishmen had to reckon with the fact that some continental countries (and Scotland, in 1600) had agreed to begin the year on 1 January; and English writers of the next century and a half sometimes give a double year-date for days from 1 January to 24 March. Eventually, Lord Chesterfield's Act, in 1751, provided that the day after 31 December 1751 should be, throughout the dominions of the British Crown, 1 January 1752.

Lord Chesterfield's Act also made a major reform by substituting the Gregorian calendar ('New Style') for the Julian ('Old Style'), so bringing England into line with most European countries, excepting Greece, the Balkans, and Russia. When Pope Gregory XIII ordered this reform in 1582, it had involved the omission of ten days after 4 October 1582 (see *Calendar*). By 1752 the discrepancy between the Old and New Styles had increased, and the Act provided that the eleven days between 2 September and 14 September 1752 should be omitted.

The Roman Calendar. The Julian calendar, like ours, divided the year into twelve months, each containing the same number of days as the corresponding month in our calendar. In each month there were three special days, known respectively as the Kalends, the Nones, and the Ides. The Kalends were the first day of the month; the Nones and Ides were the 5th and 13th respectively, except in March, May, July, and October, when they were the 7th and 15th. The other days of the month were numbered with reference to the Kalends, Nones, or Ides, as being so many days *before* one or other of them, but in this reckoning the first and last days of the series were both included. Thus A.D. (*ante diem*) V Kal. Jun. (the fifth, or as we should say, the fourth day before 1 June) was the designation of 28 May; A.D. IV Id. Jun. = 10 June; Prid. (*pridie*) Id. June. = 12 June. Every fourth year an additional day was introduced by doubling 24 February (the 24th became *bis VI Kal. Mart.*, the 25th became *VI Kal. Mart.*, so that these years were known as 'bissextile' years).

Indictions. The indiction was a fiscal period of 15 years, at the beginning of which the property tax in the Roman Empire was reassessed. It was instituted by the Emperor Constantine and was reckoned from 1 September 312. At a time when other eras were not in use, it was a useful element in dating: the expression 'indiction 5' signified the fifth year in an unspecified cycle of fifteen years. The Papacy maintained the practice of using the indiction for dating, either by itself or in conjunction with the pontifical year or year of grace; some other chanceries used it in the Middle Ages for the elaborate dating of their most formal documents. Their calculations were not always correct, and the historian is sometimes hampered by not knowing whether 1 September, 24 September, or 25 December was chosen as the opening date.

The **Dominical Letter** (from *dies dominica*, Latin for Sunday) is a convention adopted in chronological tables to indicate the day in January on which the first Sunday falls in any particular year; from which the day of the week for every day in that year can readily be found. The letters A to G, corresponding to the numbers 1 to 7, are taken for this purpose, so that if the first Sunday falls on 1 January, the Dominical Letter of the year is A; if on 2 January, the Dominical Letter is B, and 1 January in that year is a Saturday; if on 7 January, the Dominical Letter is G, and 1 January is a Monday. The first day of successive ordinary years falls on successive days of the week, and their Dominical Letters are consequently in the reverse order of the alphabet. In leap years the interposition of 29 February has the effect of making 1 March and the remaining days of the year fall one day later in the week than if the year had been ordinary. Accordingly a leap year is treated as if composed of January and February of an ordinary year, and of March–December of the succeeding ordinary year, and two Dominical Letters are assigned to it, viz. those appropriate to the two years in question. Thus the year 1216, being a leap year, has the Dominical Letters CB, because the first Sunday in 1216 fell on 3 January, while the days of the months from March to December fall on days of the week corresponding to a first Sunday, in an ordinary year, on 2 January.

In TABLE I below, the years in the first, fifth, and sixth columns are 'historical' years (1 January–31 December). The dates of Easter Day and of the beginning[1] and ending of regnal years, from 1066 to 1752 inclusive, are according to the Julian Calendar or Old Style. From 1583 to 1752 the date of Easter according to the Gregorian Calendar or New Style is added in a separate column. From 1753 all

---

[1] From the time of Edward VI a reign was reckoned as beginning on the day of the predecessor's death. For the reigns from Richard I to Henry VIII the date of commencement given below is that on which, according to public records, the reign was regarded as having begun. The practice for the first century after the Norman Conquest, when the regnal year was seldom employed, is uncertain. Here the coronation date is given.

dates are New Style. The date of Easter connects this table with Table III, and the Dominical Letter connects it with Table V.

TABLE II is an abbreviated calendar for 1752, in which year the change from Old Style to New Style was made.

TABLE III gives the dates of the principal movable Feasts according to the various dates on which Easter Day may fall. The Dominical Letter connects this table with Table V.

TABLE IV gives the dates Feasts and Saints' Days most frequently used in dating documents.

TABLE V, used in conjunction with Table I, makes it easy to find the day of the week on which any day of the month fell in any year from 1066 onwards.

TABLE I

Leap years are shown in heavy type and by double Dominical Letter

Year	Dominical Letter	Easter Day	Regnal Years		
			No.	Beginning	Ending
1066	A	16 Apr.	1 Will. I	25 Dec. 1066*	24 Dec. 1067
1067	G	8 Apr.	2 Will. I	25 Dec. 1067	24 Dec. 1068
1068	FE	23 Mar.	3 Will. I	25 Dec. 1068	24 Dec. 1069
1069	D	12 Apr.	4 Will. I	25 Dec. 1069	24 Dec. 1070
1070	C	4 Apr.	5 Will. I	25 Dec. 1070	24 Dec. 1071
1071	B	24 Apr.	6 Will. I	25 Dec. 1071	24 Dec. 1072
1072	AG	8 Apr.	7 Will. I	25 Dec. 1072	24 Dec. 1073
1073	F	31 Mar.	8 Will. I	25 Dec. 1073	24 Dec. 1074
1074	E	20 Apr.	9 Will. I	25 Dec. 1074	24 Dec. 1075
1075	D	5 Apr.	10 Will. I	25 Dec. 1075	24 Dec. 1076
1076	CB	27 Mar.	11 Will. I	25 Dec. 1076	24 Dec. 1077
1077	A	16 Apr.	12 Will. I	25 Dec. 1077	24 Dec. 1078
1078	G	8 Apr.	13 Will. I	25 Dec. 1078	24 Dec. 1079
1079	F	24 Mar.	14 Will. I	25 Dec. 1079	24 Dec. 1080
1080	ED	12 Apr.	15 Will. I	25 Dec. 1080	24 Dec. 1081
1081	C	4 Apr.	16 Will. I	25 Dec. 1081	24 Dec. 1082
1082	B	24 Apr.	17 Will. I	25 Dec. 1082	24 Dec. 1083
1083	A	9 Apr.	18 Will. I	25 Dec. 1083	24 Dec. 1084
1084	GF	31 Mar.	19 Will. I	25 Dec. 1084	24 Dec. 1085
1085	E	20 Apr.	20 Will. I	25 Dec. 1085	24 Dec. 1086
1086	D	5 Apr.	21 Will. I	25 Dec. 1086	9 Sep. 1087
1087	C	28 Mar.	1 Will. II	26 Sep. 1087*	25 Sep. 1088
1088	BA	16 Apr.	2 Will. II	26 Sep. 1088	25 Sep. 1089
1089	G	1 Apr.	3 Will. II	26 Sep. 1089	25 Sep. 1090
1090	F	21 Apr.	4 Will. II	26 Sep. 1090	25 Sep. 1091
1091	E	13 Apr.	5 Will. II	26 Sep. 1091	25 Sep. 1092
1092	DC	28 Mar.	6 Will. II	26 Sep. 1092	25 Sep. 1093
1093	B	17 Apr.	7 Will. II	26 Sep. 1093	25 Sep. 1094
1094	A	9 Apr.	8 Will. II	26 Sep. 1094	25 Sep. 1095
1095	G	25 Mar.	9 Will. II	26 Sep. 1095	25 Sep. 1096
1096	FE	13 Apr.	10 Will. II	26 Sep. 1096	25 Sep. 1097
1097	D	5 Apr.	11 Will. II	26 Sep. 1097	25 Sep. 1098
1098	C	28 Mar.	12 Will. II	26 Sep. 1098	25 Sep. 1099
1099	B	10 Apr.	13 Will. II	26 Sep. 1099	2 Aug. 1100
1100	AG	1 Apr.	1 Hen. I	5 Aug. 1100*	4 Aug. 1101
1101	F	21 Apr.	2 Hen. I	5 Aug. 1101	4 Aug. 1102
1102	E	6 Apr.	3 Hen. I	5 Aug. 1102	4 Aug. 1103
1103	D	29 Mar.	4 Hen. I	5 Aug. 1103	4 Aug. 1104
1104	CB	17 Apr.	5 Hen. I	5 Aug. 1104	4 Aug. 1105
1105	A	9 Apr.	6 Hen. I	5 Aug. 1105	4 Aug. 1106
1106	G	25 Mar.	7 Hen. I	5 Aug. 1106	4 Aug. 1107
1107	F	14 Apr.	8 Hen. I	5 Aug. 1107	4 Aug. 1108
1108	ED	5 Apr.	9 Hen. I	5 Aug. 1108	4 Aug. 1109
1109	C	25 Apr.	10 Hen. I	5 Aug. 1109	4 Aug. 1110
1110	B	10 Apr.	11 Hen. I	5 Aug. 1110	4 Aug. 1111
1111	A	2 Apr.	12 Hen. I	5 Aug. 1111	4 Aug. 1112
1112	GF	21 Apr.	13 Hen. I	5 Aug. 1112	4 Aug. 1113
1113	E	6 Apr.	14 Hen. I	5 Aug. 1113	4 Aug. 1114
1114	D	29 Mar.	15 Hen. I	5 Aug. 1114	4 Aug. 1115
1115	C	18 Apr.			

* Date of coronation.

Year	Domi-nical Letter	Easter Day	Regnal Years		
			No.	Beginning	Ending
1115	C	18 Apr.	16 Hen. I	5 Aug. 1115	4 Aug. 1116
1116	BA	2 Apr.	17 Hen. I	5 Aug. 1116	4 Aug. 1117
1117	G	25 Mar.	18 Hen. I	5 Aug. 1117	4 Aug. 1118
1118	F	14 Apr.	19 Hen. I	5 Aug. 1118	4 Aug. 1119
1119	E	30 Mar.	20 Hen. I	5 Aug. 1119	4 Aug. 1120
1120	DC	18 Apr.	21 Hen. I	5 Aug. 1120	4 Aug. 1121
1121	B	10 Apr.	22 Hen. I	5 Aug. 1121	4 Aug. 1122
1122	A	26 Mar.	23 Hen. I	5 Aug. 1122	4 Aug. 1123
1123	G	15 Apr.	24 Hen. I	5 Aug. 1123	4 Aug. 1124
1124	FE	6 Apr.	25 Hen. I	5 Aug. 1124	4 Aug. 1125
1125	D	29 Mar.	26 Hen. I	5 Aug. 1125	4 Aug. 1126
1126	C	11 Apr.	27 Hen. I	5 Aug. 1126	4 Aug. 1127
1127	B	3 Apr.	28 Hen. I	5 Aug. 1127	4 Aug. 1128
1128	AG	22 Apr.	29 Hen. I	5 Aug. 1128	4 Aug. 1129
1129	F	14 Apr.	30 Hen. I	5 Aug. 1129	4 Aug. 1130
1130	E	30 Mar.	31 Hen. I	5 Aug. 1130	4 Aug. 1131
1131	D	19 Apr.	32 Hen. I	5 Aug. 1131	4 Aug. 1132
1132	CB	10 Apr.	33 Hen. I	5 Aug. 1132	4 Aug. 1133
1133	A	26 Mar.	34 Hen. I	5 Aug. 1133	4 Aug. 1134
1134	G	15 Apr.	35 Hen. I	5 Aug. 1134	4 Aug. 1135
1135	F	7 Apr.	36 Hen. I	5 Aug. 1135	1 Dec. 1135
			1 **Steph.**	22 Dec. 1135*	21 Dec. 1136
1136	ED	22 Mar.	2 Steph.	22 Dec. 1136	21 Dec. 1137
1137	C	11 Apr.	3 Steph.	22 Dec. 1137	21 Dec. 1138
1138	B	3 Apr.	4 Steph.	22 Dec. 1138	21 Dec. 1139
1139	A	23 Apr.	5 Steph.	22 Dec. 1139	21 Dec. 1140
1140	GF	7 Apr.	6 Steph.	22 Dec. 1140	21 Dec. 1141
1141	E	30 Mar.	7 Steph.	22 Dec. 1141	21 Dec. 1142
1142	D	19 Apr.	8 Steph.	22 Dec. 1142	21 Dec. 1143
1143	C	4 Apr.	9 Steph.	22 Dec. 1143	21 Dec. 1144
1144	BA	26 Mar.	10 Steph.	22 Dec. 1144	21 Dec. 1145
1145	G	15 Apr.	11 Steph.	22 Dec. 1145	21 Dec. 1146
1146	F	31 Mar.	12 Steph.	22 Dec. 1146	21 Dec. 1147
1147	E	20 Apr.	13 Steph.	22 Dec. 1147	21 Dec. 1148
1148	DC	11 Apr.	14 Steph.	22 Dec. 1148	21 Dec. 1149
1149	B	3 Apr.	15 Steph.	22 Dec. 1149	21 Dec. 1150
1150	A	16 Apr.	16 Steph.	22 Dec. 1150	21 Dec. 1151
1151	G	8 Apr.	17 Steph.	22 Dec. 1151	21 Dec. 1152
1152	FE	30 Mar.	18 Steph.	22 Dec. 1152	21 Dec. 1153
1153	D	19 Apr.	19 Steph.	22 Dec. 1153	25 Oct. 1154
1154	C	5 Apr.	1 **Hen. II**	19 Dec. 1154†	18 Dec. 1155
1155	B	27 Mar.	2 Hen. II	19 Dec. 1155	18 Dec. 1156
1156	AG	15 Apr.	3 Hen. II	19 Dec. 1156	18 Dec. 1157
1157	F	31 Mar.	4 Hen. II	19 Dec. 1157	18 Dec. 1158
1158	E	20 Apr.	5 Hen. II	19 Dec. 1158	18 Dec. 1159
1159	D	12 Apr.	6 Hen. II	19 Dec. 1159	18 Dec. 1160
1160	CB	27 Mar.	7 Hen. II	19 Dec. 1160	18 Dec. 1161
1161	A	16 Apr.	8 Hen. II	19 Dec. 1161	18 Dec. 1162
1162	G	8 Apr.	9 Hen. II	19 Dec. 1162	18 Dec. 1163
1163	F	24 Mar.	10 Hen. II	19 Dec. 1163	18 Dec. 1164
1164	ED	12 Apr.	11 Hen. II	19 Dec. 1164	18 Dec. 1165
1165	C	4 Apr.	12 Hen. II	19 Dec. 1165	18 Dec. 1166
1166	B	24 Apr.			

* The date of Stephen's coronation according to William of Malmesbury.
† Date of coronation.

Year	Dominical Letter	Easter Day	Regnal Years		
			No.	Beginning	Ending
1166	B	24 Apr.	} 13 Hen. II	19 Dec. 1166	18 Dec. 1167
1167	A	9 Apr.	} 14 Hen. II	19 Dec. 1167	18 Dec. 1168
1168	GF	31 Mar.	} 15 Hen. II	19 Dec. 1168	18 Dec. 1169
1169	E	20 Apr.	} 16 Hen. II	19 Dec. 1169	18 Dec. 1170
1170	D	5 Apr.	} 17 Hen. II	19 Dec. 1170	18 Dec. 1171
1171	C	28 Mar.	} 18 Hen. II	19 Dec. 1171	18 Dec. 1172
1172	BA	16 Apr.	} 19 Hen. II	19 Dec. 1172	18 Dec. 1173
1173	G	8 Apr.	} 20 Hen. II	19 Dec. 1173	18 Dec. 1174
1174	F	24 Mar.	} 21 Hen. II	19 Dec. 1174	18 Dec. 1175
1175	E	13 Apr.	} 22 Hen. II	19 Dec. 1175	18 Dec. 1176
1176	DC	4 Apr.	} 23 Hen. II	19 Dec. 1176	18 Dec. 1177
1177	B	24 Apr.	} 24 Hen. II	19 Dec. 1177	18 Dec. 1178
1178	A	9 Apr.	} 25 Hen. II	19 Dec. 1178	18 Dec. 1179
1179	G	1 Apr.	} 26 Hen. II	19 Dec. 1179	18 Dec. 1180
1180	FE	20 Apr.	} 27 Hen. II	19 Dec. 1180	18 Dec. 1181
1181	D	5 Apr.	} 28 Hen. II	19 Dec. 1181	18 Dec. 1182
1182	C	28 Mar.	} 29 Hen. II	19 Dec. 1182	18 Dec. 1183
1183	B	17 Apr.	} 30 Hen. II	19 Dec. 1183	18 Dec. 1184
1184	AG	1 Apr.	} 31 Hen. II	18 Dec. 1184	18 Dec. 1185
1185	F	21 Apr.	} 32 Hen. II	19 Dec. 1185	18 Dec. 1186
1186	E	13 Apr.	} 33 Hen. II	19 Dec. 1186	18 Dec. 1187
1187	D	29 Mar.	} 34 Hen. II	19 Dec. 1187	18 Dec. 1188
1188	CB	17 Apr.	} 35 Hen. II	19 Dec. 1188	6 Jul. 1189
1189	A	9 Apr.	} 1 Ric. I	3 Sep. 1189*	2 Sep. 1190
1190	G	25 Mar.	} 2 Ric. I	3 Sep. 1190	2 Sep. 1191
1191	F	14 Apr.	} 3 Ric. I	3 Sep. 1191	2 Sep. 1192
1192	ED	5 Apr.	} 4 Ric. I	3 Sep. 1192	2 Sep. 1193
1193	C	28 Mar.	} 5 Ric. I	3 Sep. 1193	2 Sep. 1194
1194	B	10 Apr.	} 6 Ric. I	3 Sep. 1194	2 Sep. 1195
1195	A	2 Apr.	} 7 Ric. I	3 Sep. 1195	2 Sep. 1196
1196	GF	21 Apr.	} 8 Ric. I	3 Sep. 1196	2 Sep. 1197
1197	E	6 Apr.	} 9 Ric. I	3 Sep. 1197	2 Sep. 1198
1198	D	29 Mar.	} 10 Ric. I	3 Sep. 1198	6 Apr. 1199
1199	C	18 Apr.	} 1 John	27 May 1199†	17 May 1200
1200	BA	9 Apr.	} 2 John	18 May 1200	2 May 1201
1201	G	25 Mar.	} 3 John	3 May 1201	22 May 1202
1202	F	14 Apr.	} 4 John	23 May 1202	14 May 1203
1203	E	6 Apr.	} 5 John	15 May 1203	2 Jun. 1204
1204	DC	25 Apr.	} 6 John	3 Jun. 1204	18 May 1205
1205	B	10 Apr.	} 7 John	19 May 1205	10 May 1206
1206	A	2 Apr.	} 8 John	11 May 1206	30 May 1207
1207	G	22 Apr.	} 9 John	31 May 1207	14 May 1208
1208	FE	6 Apr.	} 10 John	15 May 1208	6 May 1209
1209	D	29 Mar.	} 11 John	7 May 1209	26 May 1210
1210	C	18 Apr.	} 12 John	27 May 1210	11 May 1211
1211	B	3 Apr.	} 13 John	12 May 1211	2 May 1212
1212	AG	25 Mar.	} 14 John	3 May 1212	22 May 1213
1213	F	14 Apr.	} 15 John	23 May 1213	7 May 1214
1214	E	30 Mar.	} 16 John	8 May 1214	27 May 1215
1215	D	19 Apr.	} 17 John	28 May 1215	18 May 1216
1216	CB	10 Apr.	} 18 John	19 May 1216	19 Oct. 1216
			} 1 Hen. III	28 Oct. 1216*	27 Oct. 1217
1217	A	26 Mar.	} 2 Hen. III	28 Oct. 1217	27 Oct. 1218
1218	G	15 Apr.			

* Date of coronation.

† John was crowned on Ascension Day 1199; his regnal years run from one Ascension Day to the eve of the next and are therefore irregular.

Year	Dominical Letter	Easter Day	Regnal Years		
			No.	Beginning	Ending
1218	G	15 Apr.	3 Hen. III	28 Oct. 1218	27 Oct. 1219
1219	F	7 Apr.	4 Hen. III	28 Oct. 1219	27 Oct. 1220
1220	ED	29 Mar.	5 Hen. III	28 Oct. 1220	27 Oct. 1221
1221	C	11 Apr.	6 Hen. III	28 Oct. 1221	27 Oct. 1222
1222	B	3 Apr.	7 Hen. III	28 Oct. 1222	27 Oct. 1223
1223	A	23 Apr.	8 Hen. III	28 Oct. 1223	27 Oct. 1224
1224	GF	14 Apr.	9 Hen. III	28 Oct. 1224	27 Oct. 1225
1225	E	30 Mar.	10 Hen. III	28 Oct. 1225	27 Oct. 1226
1226	D	19 Apr.	11 Hen. III	28 Oct. 1226	27 Oct. 1227
1227	C	11 Apr.	12 Hen. III	28 Oct. 1227	27 Oct. 1228
1228	BA	26 Mar.	13 Hen. III	28 Oct. 1228	27 Oct. 1229
1229	G	15 Apr.	14 Hen. III	28 Oct. 1229	27 Oct. 1230
1230	F	7 Apr.	15 Hen. III	28 Oct. 1230	27 Oct. 1231
1231	E	23 Mar.	16 Hen. III	28 Oct. 1231	27 Oct. 1232
1232	DC	11 Apr.	17 Hen. III	28 Oct. 1232	27 Oct. 1233
1233	B	3 Apr.	18 Hen. III	28 Oct. 1233	27 Oct. 1234
1234	A	23 Apr.	19 Hen. III	28 Oct. 1234	27 Oct. 1235
1235	G	8 Apr.	20 Hen. III	28 Oct. 1235	27 Oct. 1236
1236	FE	30 Mar.	21 Hen. III	28 Oct. 1236	27 Oct. 1237
1237	D	19 Apr.	22 Hen. III	28 Oct. 1237	27 Oct. 1238
1238	C	4 Apr.	23 Hen. III	28 Oct. 1238	27 Oct. 1239
1239	B	27 Mar.	24 Hen. III	28 Oct. 1239	27 Oct. 1240
1240	AG	15 Apr.	25 Hen. III	28 Oct. 1240	27 Oct. 1241
1241	F	31 Mar.	26 Hen. III	28 Oct. 1241	27 Oct. 1242
1242	E	20 Apr.	27 Hen. III	28 Oct. 1242	27 Oct. 1243
1243	D	12 Apr.	28 Hen. III	28 Oct. 1243	27 Oct. 1244
1244	CB	3 Apr.	29 Hen. III	28 Oct. 1244	27 Oct. 1245
1245	A	16 Apr.	30 Hen. III	28 Oct. 1245	27 Oct. 1246
1246	G	8 Apr.	31 Hen. III	28 Oct. 1246	27 Oct. 1247
1247	F	31 Mar.	32 Hen. III	28 Oct. 1247	27 Oct. 1248
1248	ED	19 Apr.	33 Hen. III	28 Oct. 1248	27 Oct. 1249
1249	C	4 Apr.	34 Hen. III	28 Oct. 1249	27 Oct. 1250
1250	B	27 Mar.	35 Hen. III	28 Oct. 1250	27 Oct. 1251
1251	A	15 Apr.	36 Hen. III	28 Oct. 1251	27 Oct. 1252
1252	GF	31 Mar.	37 Hen. III	28 Oct. 1252	27 Oct. 1253
1253	E	20 Apr.	38 Hen. III	28 Oct. 1253	27 Oct. 1254
1254	D	12 Apr.	39 Hen. III	28 Oct. 1254	27 Oct. 1255
1255	C	28 Mar.	40 Hen. III	28 Oct. 1255	27 Oct. 1256
1256	BA	16 Apr.	41 Hen. III	28 Oct. 1256	27 Oct. 1257
1257	G	8 Apr.	42 Hen. III	28 Oct. 1257	27 Oct. 1258
1258	F	25 Mar.	43 Hen. III	28 Oct. 1258	27 Oct. 1259
1259	E	13 Apr.	44 Hen. III	28 Oct. 1259	27 Oct. 1260
1260	DC	4 Apr.	45 Hen. III	28 Oct. 1260	27 Oct. 1261
1261	B	24 Apr.	46 Hen. III	28 Oct. 1261	27 Oct. 1262
1262	A	9 Apr.	47 Hen. III	28 Oct. 1262	27 Oct. 1263
1263	G	1 Apr.	48 Hen. III	28 Oct. 1263	27 Oct. 1264
1264	FE	20 Apr.	49 Hen. III	28 Oct. 1264	27 Oct. 1265
1265	D	5 Apr.	50 Hen. III	28 Oct. 1265	27 Oct. 1266
1266	C	28 Mar.	51 Hen. III	28 Oct. 1266	27 Oct. 1267
1267	B	17 Apr.	52 Hen. III	28 Oct. 1267	27 Oct. 1268
1268	AG	8 Apr.	53 Hen. III	28 Oct. 1268	27 Oct. 1269
1269	F	24 Mar.	54 Hen. III	28 Oct. 1269	27 Oct. 1270
1270	E	31 Mar.	55 Hen. III	28 Oct. 1270	27 Oct. 1271
1271	D	5 Apr.	56 Hen. III	28 Oct. 1271	27 Oct. 1272
1272	CB	24 Apr.	57 Hen. III	28 Oct. 1272	16 Nov. 1272

Year	Domi-nical Letter	Easter Day	Regnal Years		
			No.	Beginning	Ending
1272	CB	24 Apr.	1 Edw. I*	20 Nov. 1272†	19 Nov. 1273
1273	A	9 Apr.	2 Edw. I	20 Nov. 1273	19 Nov. 1274
1274	G	1 Apr.	3 Edw. I	20 Nov. 1274	19 Nov. 1275
1275	F	14 Apr.	4 Edw. I	20 Nov. 1275	19 Nov. 1276
1276	ED	5 Apr.	5 Edw. I	20 Nov. 1276	19 Nov. 1277
1277	C	28 Mar.	6 Edw. I	20 Nov. 1277	19 Nov. 1278
1278	B	17 Apr.	7 Edw. I	20 Nov. 1278	19 Nov. 1279
1279	A	2 Apr.	8 Edw. I	20 Nov. 1279	19 Nov. 1280
1280	GF	21 Apr.	9 Edw. I	20 Nov. 1280	19 Nov. 1281
1281	E	13 Apr.	10 Edw. I	20 Nov. 1281	19 Nov. 1282
1282	D	29 Mar.	11 Edw. I	20 Nov. 1282	19 Nov. 1283
1283	C	18 Apr.	12 Edw. I	20 Nov. 1283	19 Nov. 1284
1284	BA	9 Apr.	13 Edw. I	20 Nov. 1284	19 Nov. 1285
1285	G	25 Mar.	14 Edw. I	20 Nov. 1285	19 Nov. 1286
1286	F	14 Apr.	15 Edw. I	20 Nov. 1286	19 Nov. 1287
1287	E	6 Apr.	16 Edw. I	20 Nov. 1287	19 Nov. 1288
1288	DC	28 Mar.	17 Edw. I	20 Nov. 1288	19 Nov. 1289
1289	B	10 Apr.	18 Edw. I	20 Nov. 1289	19 Nov. 1290
1290	A	2 Apr.	19 Edw. I	20 Nov. 1290	19 Nov. 1291
1291	G	22 Apr.	20 Edw. I	20 Nov. 1291	19 Nov. 1292
1292	FE	6 Apr.	21 Edw. I	20 Nov. 1292	19 Nov. 1293
1293	D	29 Mar.	22 Edw. I	20 Nov. 1293	19 Nov. 1294
1294	C	18 Apr.	23 Edw. I	20 Nov. 1294	19 Nov. 1295
1295	B	3 Apr.	24 Edw. I	20 Nov. 1295	19 Nov. 1296
1296	AG	25 Mar.	25 Edw. I	20 Nov. 1296	19 Nov. 1297
1297	F	14 Apr.	26 Edw. I	20 Nov. 1297	19 Nov. 1298
1298	E	6 Apr.	27 Edw. I	20 Nov. 1298	19 Nov. 1299
1299	D	19 Apr.	28 Edw. I	20 Nov. 1299	19 Nov. 1300
1300	CB	10 Apr.	29 Edw. I	20 Nov. 1300	19 Nov. 1301
1301	A	2 Apr.	30 Edw. I	20 Nov. 1301	19 Nov. 1302
1302	G	22 Apr.	31 Edw. I	20 Nov. 1302	19 Nov. 1303
1303	F	7 Apr.	32 Edw. I	20 Nov. 1303	19 Nov. 1304
1304	ED	29 Mar.	33 Edw. I	20 Nov. 1304	19 Nov. 1305
1305	C	18 Apr.	34 Edw. I	20 Nov. 1305	19 Nov. 1306
1306	B	3 Apr.	35 Edw. I	20 Nov. 1306	7 Jul. 1307
1307	A	26 Mar.	1 Edw. II	8 Jul. 1307	7 Jul. 1308
1308	GF	14 Apr.	2 Edw. II	8 Jul. 1308	7 Jul. 1309
1309	E	30 Mar.	3 Edw. II	8 Jul. 1309	7 Jul. 1310
1310	D	19 Apr.	4 Edw. II	8 Jul. 1310	7 Jul. 1311
1311	C	11 Apr.	5 Edw. II	8 Jul. 1311	7 Jul. 1312
1312	BA	26 Mar.	6 Edw. II	8 Jul. 1312	7 Jul. 1313
1313	G	15 Apr.	7 Edw. II	8 Jul. 1313	7 Jul. 1314
1314	F	7 Apr.	8 Edw. II	8 Jul. 1314	7 Jul. 1315
1315	E	23 Mar.	9 Edw. II	8 Jul. 1315	7 Jul. 1316
1316	DC	11 Apr.	10 Edw. II	8 Jul. 1316	7 Jul. 1317
1317	B	3 Apr.	11 Edw. II	8 Jul. 1317	7 Jul. 1318
1318	A	23 Apr.	12 Edw. II	8 Jul. 1318	7 Jul. 1319
1319	G	8 Apr.	13 Edw. II	8 Jul. 1319	7 Jul. 1320
1320	FE	30 Mar.	14 Edw. II	8 Jul. 1320	7 Jul. 1321
1321	D	19 Apr.	15 Edw. II	8 Jul. 1321	7 Jul. 1322
1322	C	11 Apr.	16 Edw. II	8 Jul. 1322	7 Jul. 1323
1323	B	27 Mar.	17 Edw. II	8 Jul. 1323	7 Jul. 1324
1324	AG	15 Apr.			

* The distinguishing numbers of Edward I, Edward II, and Edward III are often omitted. A king described in a document as 'Edward' is not necessarily Edward I.

† Date of proclamation.

Year	Domi-nical Letter	Easter Day	Regnal Years		
			No.	Beginning	Ending
1324	AG	15 Apr.	} 18 Edw. II	8 Jul. 1324	7 Jul. 1325
1325	F	7 Apr.	} 19 Edw. II	8 Jul. 1325	7 Jul. 1326
1326	E	23 Mar.	} 20 Edw. II	8 Jul. 1326	20 Jan. 1327*
1327	D	12 Apr.	} 1 **Edw. III**	25 Jan. 1327	24 Jan. 1328
1328	CB	3 Apr.	} 2 Edw. III	25 Jan. 1328	24 Jan. 1329
1329	A	23 Apr.	} 3 Edw. III	25 Jan. 1329	24 Jan. 1330
1330	G	8 Apr.	} 4 Edw. III	25 Jan. 1330	24 Jan. 1331
1331	F	31 Mar.	} 5 Edw. III	25 Jan. 1331	24 Jan. 1332
1332	ED	19 Apr.	} 6 Edw. III	25 Jan. 1332	24 Jan. 1333
1333	C	4 Apr.	} 7 Edw. III	25 Jan. 1333	24 Jan. 1334
1334	B	27 Mar.	} 8 Edw. III	25 Jan. 1334	24 Jan. 1335
1335	A	16 Apr.	} 9 Edw. III	25 Jan. 1335	24 Jan. 1336
1336	GF	31 Mar.	} 10 Edw. III	25 Jan. 1336	24 Jan. 1337
1337	E	20 Apr.	} 11 Edw. III	25 Jan. 1337	24 Jan. 1338
1338	D	12 Apr.	} 12 Edw. III	25 Jan. 1338	24 Jan. 1339
1339	C	28 Mar.	} 13 Edw. III	25 Jan. 1339	24 Jan. 1340
1340	BA	16 Apr.	} 14 & 1 Edw. III†	25 Jan. 1340	24 Jan. 1341
1341	G	8 Apr.	} 15 & 2 Edw. III	25 Jan. 1341	24 Jan. 1342
1342	F	31 Mar.	} 16 & 3 Edw. III	25 Jan. 1342	24 Jan. 1343
1343	E	13 Apr.	} 17 & 4 Edw. III	25 Jan. 1343	24 Jan. 1344
1344	DC	4 Apr.	} 18 & 5 Edw. III	25 Jan. 1344	24 Jan. 1345
1345	B	27 Mar.	} 19 & 6 Edw. III	25 Jan. 1345	24 Jan. 1346
1346	A	16 Apr.	} 20 & 7 Edw. III	25 Jan. 1346	24 Jan. 1347
1347	G	1 Apr.	} 21 & 8 Edw. III	25 Jan. 1347	24 Jan. 1348
1348	FE	20 Apr.	} 22 & 9 Edw. III	25 Jan. 1348	24 Jan. 1349
1349	D	12 Apr.	} 23 & 10 Edw. III	25 Jan. 1349	24 Jan. 1350
1350	C	28 Mar.	} 24 & 11 Edw. III	25 Jan. 1350	24 Jan. 1351
1351	B	17 Apr.	} 25 & 12 Edw. III	25 Jan. 1351	24 Jan. 1352
1352	AG	8 Apr.	} 26 & 13 Edw. III	25 Jan. 1352	24 Jan. 1353
1353	F	24 Mar.	} 27 & 14 Edw. III	25 Jan. 1353	24 Jan. 1354
1354	E	13 Apr.	} 28 & 15 Edw. III	25 Jan. 1354	24 Jan. 1355
1355	D	5 Apr.	} 29 & 16 Edw. III	25 Jan. 1355	24 Jan. 1356
1356	CB	24 Apr.	} 30 & 17 Edw. III	25 Jan. 1356	24 Jan. 1357
1357	A	9 Apr.	} 31 & 18 Edw. III	25 Jan. 1357	24 Jan. 1358
1358	G	1 Apr.	} 32 & 19 Edw. III	25 Jan. 1358	24 Jan. 1359
1359	F	21 Apr.	} 33 & 20 Edw. III	25 Jan. 1359	24 Jan. 1360
1360	ED	5 Apr.	} 34 & 21 Edw. III	25 Jan. 1360	8 May 1360†
			} 34 Edw. III	9 May 1360	24 Jan. 1361
1361	C	28 Mar.	} 35 Edw. III	25 Jan. 1361	24 Jan. 1362
1362	B	17 Apr.	} 36 Edw. III	25 Jan. 1362	24 Jan. 1363
1363	A	2 Apr.	} 37 Edw. III	25 Jan. 1363	24 Jan. 1364
1364	GF	24 Mar.	} 38 Edw. III	25 Jan. 1364	24 Jan. 1365
1365	E	13 Apr.	} 39 Edw. III	25 Jan. 1365	24 Jan. 1366
1366	D	5 Apr.	} 40 Edw. III	25 Jan. 1366	24 Jan. 1367
1367	C	18 Apr.	} 41 Edw. III	25 Jan. 1367	24 Jan. 1368
1368	BA	9 Apr.	} 42 Edw. III	25 Jan. 1368	24 Jan. 1369
1369	G	1 Apr.	} 43 Edw. III	25 Jan. 1369	10 Jun. 1369
			} 43 & 30 Edw. III§	11 Jun. 1369	24 Jan. 1370
1370	F	14 Apr.	} 44 & 31 Edw. III	25 Jan. 1370	24 Jan. 1371
1371	E	6 Apr.	} 45 & 32 Edw. III	25 Jan. 1371	24 Jan. 1372
1372	DC	28 Mar.			

* Date of deposition.

† In 1340 Edward III asserted his claim to the French crown and added his French regnal years to his English regnal years. In 1360 he undertook to renounce his claim to the throne of France and dropped the French regnal years in dating.

§ In 1369 Edward III resumed his claim to the French crown, counting in the years 1360–9 during which his claim had been in abeyance.

Year	Domi-nical Letter	Easter Day	Regnal Years		
			No.	Beginning	Ending
1372	DC	28 Mar.	} 46 & 33 Edw. III	25 Jan. 1372	24 Jan. 1373
1373	B	17 Apr.	} 47 & 34 Edw. III	25 Jan. 1373	24 Jan. 1374
1374	A	2 Apr.	} 48 & 35 Edw. III	25 Jan. 1374	24 Jan. 1375
1375	G	22 Apr.	} 49 & 36 Edw. III	25 Jan. 1375	24 Jan. 1376
1376	FE	13 Apr.	} 50 & 37 Edw. III	25 Jan. 1376	24 Jan. 1377
1377	D	29 Mar.	} 51 & 38 Edw. III	25 Jan. 1377	21 Jun. 1377
			} 1 **Ric. II**	22 Jun. 1377	21 Jun. 1378
1378	C	18 Apr.	} 2 Ric. II	22 Jun. 1378	21 Jun. 1379
1379	B	10 Apr.	} 3 Ric. II	22 Jun. 1379	21 Jun. 1380
1380	AG	25 Mar.	} 4 Ric. II	22 Jun. 1380	21 Jun. 1381
1381	F	14 Apr.	} 5 Ric. II	22 Jun. 1381	21 Jun. 1382
1382	E	6 Apr.	} 6 Ric. II	22 Jun. 1382	21 Jun. 1383
1383	D	22 Mar.	} 7 Ric. II	22 Jun. 1383	21 Jun. 1384
1384	CB	10 Apr.	} 8 Ric. II	22 Jun. 1384	21 Jun. 1385
1385	A	2 Apr.	} 9 Ric. II	22 Jun. 1385	21 Jun. 1386
1386	G	22 Apr.	} 10 Ric. II	22 Jun. 1386	21 Jun. 1387
1387	F	7 Apr.	} 11 Ric. II	22 Jun. 1387	21 Jun. 1388
1388	ED	29 Mar.	} 12 Ric. II	22 Jun. 1388	21 Jun. 1389
1389	C	18 Apr.	} 13 Ric. II	22 Jun. 1389	21 Jun. 1390
1390	B	3 Apr.	} 14 Ric. II	22 Jun. 1390	21 Jun. 1391
1391	A	26 Mar.	} 15 Ric. II	22 Jun. 1391	21 Jun. 1392
1392	GF	14 Apr.	} 16 Ric. II	22 Jun. 1392	21 Jun. 1393
1393	E	6 Apr.	} 17 Ric. II	22 Jun. 1393	21 Jun. 1394
1394	D	19 Apr.	} 18 Ric. II	22 Jun. 1394	21 Jun. 1395
1395	C	11 Apr.	} 19 Ric. II	22 Jun. 1395	21 Jun. 1396
1396	BA	2 Apr.	} 20 Ric. II	22 Jun. 1396	21 Jun. 1397
1397	G	22 Apr.	} 21 Ric. II	22 Jun. 1397	21 Jun. 1398
1398	F	7 Apr.	} 22 Ric. II	22 Jun. 1398	21 Jun. 1399
1399	E	30 Mar.	} 23 Ric. II	22 Jun. 1399	29 Sep. 1399
			} 1 **Hen. IV**	30 Sep. 1399	29 Sep. 1400
1400	DC	18 Apr.	} 2 Hen. IV	30 Sep. 1400	29 Sep. 1401
1401	B	3 Apr.	} 3 Hen. IV	30 Sep. 1401	29 Sep. 1402
1402	A	26 Mar.	} 4 Hen. IV	30 Sep. 1402	29 Sep. 1403
1403	G	15 Apr.	} 5 Hen. IV	30 Sep. 1403	29 Sep. 1404
1404	FE	30 Mar.	} 6 Hen. IV	30 Sep. 1404	29 Sep. 1405
1405	D	19 Apr.	} 7 Hen. IV	30 Sep. 1405	29 Sep. 1406
1406	C	11 Apr.	} 8 Hen. IV	30 Sep. 1406	29 Sep. 1407
1407	B	27 Mar.	} 9 Hen. IV	30 Sep. 1407	29 Sep. 1408
1408	AG	15 Apr.	} 10 Hen. IV	30 Sep. 1408	29 Sep. 1409
1409	F	7 Apr.	} 11 Hen. IV	30 Sep. 1409	29 Sep. 1410
1410	E	23 Mar.	} 12 Hen. IV	30 Sep. 1410	29 Sep. 1411
1411	D	12 Apr.	} 13 Hen. IV	30 Sep. 1411	29 Sep. 1412
1412	CB	3 Apr.	} 14 Hen. IV	30 Sep. 1412	20 Mar. 1413
1413	A	23 Apr.	} 1 **Hen. V**	21 Mar. 1413	20 Mar. 1414
1414	G	8 Apr.	} 2 Hen. V	21 Mar. 1414	20 Mar. 1415
1415	F	31 Mar.	} 3 Hen. V	21 Mar. 1415	20 Mar. 1416
1416	ED	19 Apr.	} 4 Hen. V	21 Mar. 1416	20 Mar. 1417
1417	C	1 Apr.	} 5 Hen. V	21 Mar. 1417	20 Mar. 1418
1418	B	27 Mar.	} 6 Hen. V	21 Mar. 1418	20 Mar. 1419
1419	A	16 Apr.	} 7 Hen. V	21 Mar. 1419	20 Mar. 1420
1420	GF	7 Apr.	} 8 Hen. V	21 Mar. 1420	20 Mar. 1421
1421	E	23 Mar.	} 9 Hen. V	21 Mar. 1421	20 Mar. 1422
1422	D	12 Apr.	} 10 Hen. V	21 Mar. 1422	31 Aug. 1422
			} 1 **Hen. VI**	1 Sep. 1422	31 Aug. 1423
1423	C	4 Apr.	} 2 Hen. VI	1 Sep. 1423	31 Aug. 1424
1424	BA	23 Apr.	}		

Year	Dominical Letter	Easter Day	Regnal Years		
			No.	Beginning	Ending
1424	BA	23 Apr.	} 3 Hen. VI	1 Sep. 1424	31 Aug. 1425
1425	G	8 Apr.	} 4 Hen. VI	1 Sep. 1425	31 Aug. 1426
1426	F	31 Mar.	} 5 Hen. VI	1 Sep. 1426	31 Aug. 1427
1427	E	20 Apr.	} 6 Hen. VI	1 Sep. 1427	31 Aug. 1428
1428	DC	4 Apr.	} 7 Hen. VI	1 Sep. 1428	31 Aug. 1429
1429	B	27 Mar.	} 8 Hen. VI	1 Sep. 1429	31 Aug. 1430
1430	A	16 Apr.	} 9 Hen. VI	1 Sep. 1430	31 Aug. 1431
1431	G	1 Apr.	} 10 Hen. VI	1 Sep. 1431	31 Aug. 1432
1432	FE	20 Apr.	} 11 Hen. VI	1 Sep. 1432	31 Aug. 1433
1433	D	12 Apr.	} 12 Hen. VI	1 Sep. 1433	31 Aug. 1434
1434	C	28 Mar.	} 13 Hen. VI	1 Sep. 1434	31 Aug. 1435
1435	B	17 Apr.	} 14 Hen. VI	1 Sep. 1435	31 Aug. 1436
1436	AG	8 Apr.	} 15 Hen. VI	1 Sep. 1436	31 Aug. 1437
1437	F	31 Mar.	} 16 Hen. VI	1 Sep. 1437	31 Aug. 1438
1438	E	13 Apr.	} 17 Hen. VI	1 Sep. 1438	31 Aug. 1439
1439	D	5 Apr.	} 18 Hen. VI	1 Sep. 1439	31 Aug. 1440
1440	CB	27 Mar.	} 19 Hen. VI	1 Sep. 1440	31 Aug. 1441
1441	A	16 Apr.	} 20 Hen. VI	1 Sep. 1441	31 Aug. 1442
1442	G	1 Apr.	} 21 Hen. VI	1 Sep. 1442	31 Aug. 1443
1443	F	21 Apr.	} 22 Hen. VI	1 Sep. 1443	31 Aug. 1444
1444	ED	12 Apr.	} 23 Hen. VI	1 Sep. 1444	31 Aug. 1445
1445	C	28 Mar.	} 24 Hen. VI	1 Sep. 1445	31 Aug. 1446
1446	B	17 Apr.	} 25 Hen. VI	1 Sep. 1446	31 Aug. 1447
1447	A	9 Apr.	} 26 Hen. VI	1 Sep. 1447	31 Aug. 1448
1448	GF	24 Mar.	} 27 Hen. VI	1 Sep. 1448	31 Aug. 1449
1449	E	13 Apr.	} 28 Hen. VI	1 Sep. 1449	31 Aug. 1450
1450	D	5 Apr.	} 29 Hen. VI	1 Sep. 1450	31 Aug. 1451
1451	C	25 Apr.	} 30 Hen. VI	1 Sep. 1451	31 Aug. 1452
1452	BA	9 Apr.	} 31 Hen. VI	1 Sep. 1452	31 Aug. 1453
1453	G	1 Apr.	} 32 Hen. VI	1 Sep. 1453	31 Aug. 1454
1454	F	31 Apr.	} 33 Hen. VI	1 Sep. 1454	31 Aug. 1455
1455	E	6 Apr.	} 34 Hen. VI	1 Sep. 1455	31 Aug. 1456
1456	DC	28 Mar.	} 35 Hen. VI	1 Sep. 1456	31 Aug. 1457
1457	B	17 Apr.	} 36 Hen. VI	1 Sep. 1457	31 Aug. 1458
1458	A	2 Apr.	} 37 Hen. VI	1 Sep. 1458	31 Aug. 1459
1459	G	25 Mar.	} 38 Hen. VI	1 Sep. 1459	31 Aug. 1460
1460	FE	13 Apr.	} 39 Hen. VI	1 Sep. 1460	4 Mar. 1461*
1461	D	5 Apr.	} **1 Edw. IV**	4 Mar. 1461*	3 Mar. 1462
1462	C	18 Apr.	} 2 Edw. IV	4 Mar. 1462	3 Mar. 1463
1463	B	10 Apr.	} 3 Edw. IV	4 Mar. 1463	3 Mar. 1464
1464	AG	1 Apr.	} 4 Edw. IV	4 Mar. 1464	3 Mar. 1465
1465	F	14 Apr.	} 5 Edw. IV	4 Mar. 1465	3 Mar. 1466
1466	E	6 Apr.	} 6 Edw. IV	4 Mar. 1466	3 Mar. 1467
1467	D	29 Mar.	} 7 Edw. IV	4 Mar. 1467	3 Mar. 1468
1468	CB	17 Apr.	} 8 Edw. IV	4 Mar. 1468	3 Mar. 1469
1469	A	2 Apr.	} 9 Edw. IV	4 Mar. 1469	3 Mar. 1470
1470	G	22 Apr.	} { 10 Edw. IV	4 Mar. 1470	3 Mar. 1471
			} { 49 & 1 Hen. VI†	9 Oct. 1470	14 Apr. 1471
1471	F	14 Apr.	} 11 Edw. IV	4 Mar. 1471	3 Mar. 1472
1472	ED	29 Mar.	} 12 Edw. IV	4 Mar. 1472	3 Mar. 1473
1473	C	18 Apr.	} 13 Edw. IV	4 Mar. 1473	3 Mar. 1474
1474	B	10 Apr.			

* Date of deposition of Henry VI and recognition of Edward IV.

† The period of the restoration of Henry VI (1 Oct. 1470–11 Apr. 1471) was described as follows: 'Anno ab inchoatione regni nostri quadragesimo nono et readeptionis nostrae regiae potestatis anno primo.' The reckoning of the regnal years of Edward IV was not altered on account of this restoration.

Year	Dominical Letter	Easter Day	Regnal Years		
			No.	Beginning	Ending
1474	B	10 Apr.	} 14 Edw. IV	4 Mar. 1474	3 Mar. 1475
1475	A	26 Mar.	} 15 Edw. IV	4 Mar. 1475	3 Mar. 1476
1476	GF	14 Apr.	} 16 Edw. IV	4 Mar. 1476	3 Mar. 1477
1477	E	6 Apr.	} 17 Edw. IV	4 Mar. 1477	3 Mar. 1478
1478	D	22 Mar.	} 18 Edw. IV	4 Mar. 1478	3 Mar. 1479
1479	C	11 Apr.	} 19 Edw. IV	4 Mar. 1479	3 Mar. 1480
1480	BA	2 Apr.	} 20 Edw. IV	4 Mar. 1480	3 Mar. 1481
1481	G	22 Apr.	} 21 Edw. IV	4 Mar. 1481	3 Mar. 1482
1482	F	7 Apr.			
			} 22 Edw. IV	4 Mar. 1482	3 Mar. 1483
1483	E	30 Mar.	{ 23 Edw. IV	4 Mar. 1483	9 Apr. 1483
			{ 1 Edw. V	9 Apr. 1483	25 Jun. 1483
			1 Ric. III	26 Jun. 1483	25 Jun. 1484
1484	DC	18 Apr.	} 2 Ric. III	26 Jun. 1484	25 Jun. 1485
			3 Ric. III	26 Jun. 1485	22 Aug. 1485
1485	B	3 Apr.	**1 Hen. VII**	22 Aug. 1485	21 Aug. 1486
1486	A	26 Mar.	} 2 Hen. VII	22 Aug. 1486	21 Aug. 1487
1487	G	15 Apr.	} 3 Hen. VII	22 Aug. 1487	21 Aug. 1488
1488	FE	6 Apr.	} 4 Hen. VII	22 Aug. 1488	21 Aug. 1489
1489	D	19 Apr.	} 5 Hen. VII	22 Aug. 1489	21 Aug. 1490
1490	C	11 Apr.	} 6 Hen. VII	22 Aug. 1490	21 Aug. 1491
1491	B	3 Apr.	} 7 Hen. VII	22 Aug. 1491	21 Aug. 1492
1492	AG	22 Apr.	} 8 Hen. VII	22 Aug. 1492	21 Aug. 1493
1493	F	7 Apr.	} 9 Hen. VII	22 Aug. 1493	21 Aug. 1494
1494	E	30 Mar.	} 10 Hen. VII	22 Aug. 1494	21 Aug. 1495
1495	D	19 Apr.	} 11 Hen. VII	22 Aug. 1495	21 Aug. 1496
1496	CB	3 Apr.	} 12 Hen. VII	22 Aug. 1496	21 Aug. 1497
1497	A	26 Mar.	} 13 Hen. VII	22 Aug. 1497	21 Aug. 1498
1498	G	15 Apr.	} 14 Hen. VII	22 Aug. 1498	21 Aug. 1499
1499	F	31 Mar.	} 15 Hen. VII	22 Aug. 1499	21 Aug. 1500
1500	ED	19 Apr.	} 16 Hen. VII	22 Aug. 1500	21 Aug. 1501
1501	C	11 Apr.	} 17 Hen. VII	22 Aug. 1501	21 Aug. 1502
1502	B	27 Mar.	} 18 Hen. VII	22 Aug. 1502	21 Aug. 1503
1503	A	16 Apr.	} 19 Hen. VII	22 Aug. 1503	21 Aug. 1504
1504	GF	7 Apr.	} 20 Hen. VII	22 Aug. 1504	21 Aug. 1505
1505	E	23 Mar.	} 21 Hen. VII	22 Aug. 1505	21 Aug. 1506
1506	D	12 Apr.	} 22 Hen. VII	22 Aug. 1506	21 Aug. 1507
1507	C	4 Apr.	} 23 Hen. VII	22 Aug. 1507	21 Aug. 1508
1508	BA	23 Apr.	} 24 Hen. VII	22 Aug. 1508	21 Apr. 1509
1509	G	8 Apr.	**1 Hen. VIII**	22 Apr. 1509	21 Apr. 1510
1510	F	31 Mar.	} 2 Hen. VIII	22 Apr. 1510	21 Apr. 1511
1511	E	20 Apr.	} 3 Hen. VIII	22 Apr. 1511	21 Apr. 1512
1512	DC	11 Apr.	} 4 Hen. VIII	22 Apr. 1512	21 Apr. 1513
1513	B	27 Mar.	} 5 Hen. VIII	22 Apr. 1513	21 Apr. 1514
1514	A	16 Apr.	} 6 Hen. VIII	22 Apr. 1514	21 Apr. 1515
1515	G	8 Apr.	} 7 Hen. VIII	22 Apr. 1515	21 Apr. 1516
1516	FE	23 Mar.	} 8 Hen. VIII	22 Apr. 1516	21 Apr. 1517
1517	D	12 Apr.	} 9 Hen. VIII	22 Apr. 1517	21 Apr. 1518
1518	C	4 Apr.	} 10 Hen. VIII	22 Apr. 1518	21 Apr. 1519
1519	B	24 Apr.	} 11 Hen. VIII	22 Apr. 1519	21 Apr. 1520
1520	AG	8 Apr.	} 12 Hen. VIII	22 Apr. 1520	21 Apr. 1521
1521	F	31 Mar.	} 13 Hen. VIII	22 Apr. 1521	21 Apr. 1522
1522	E	20 Apr.	} 14 Hen. VIII	22 Apr. 1522	21 Apr. 1523
1523	D	5 Apr.	} 15 Hen. VIII	22 Apr. 1523	21 Apr. 1524
1524	CB	27 Mar.			

Year	Domi-nical Letter	Easter Day	Regnal Years		
			No.	Beginning	Ending
1524	CB	27 Mar.	} 16 Hen. VIII	22 Apr. 1524	21 Apr. 1525
1525	A	16 Apr.	} 17 Hen. VIII	22 Apr. 1525	21 Apr. 1526
1526	G	1 Apr.	} 18 Hen. VIII	22 Apr. 1526	21 Apr. 1527
1527	F	21 Apr.	} 19 Hen. VIII	22 Apr. 1527	21 Apr. 1528
1528	ED	12 Apr.	} 20 Hen. VIII	22 Apr. 1528	21 Apr. 1529
1529	C	28 Mar.	} 21 Hen. VIII	22 Apr. 1529	21 Apr. 1530
1530	B	17 Apr.	} 22 Hen. VIII	22 Apr. 1530	21 Apr. 1531
1531	A	9 Apr.	} 23 Hen. VIII	22 Apr. 1531	21 Apr. 1532
1532	GF	31 Mar.	} 24 Hen. VIII	22 Apr. 1532	21 Apr. 1533
1533	E	13 Apr.	} 25 Hen. VIII	22 Apr. 1533	21 Apr. 1534
1534	D	5 Apr.	} 26 Hen. VIII	22 Apr. 1534	21 Apr. 1535
1535	C	28 Mar.	} 27 Hen. VIII	22 Apr. 1535	21 Apr. 1536
1536	BA	16 Apr.	} 28 Hen. VIII	22 Apr. 1536	21 Apr. 1537
1537	G	1 Apr.	} 29 Hen. VIII	22 Apr. 1537	21 Apr. 1538
1538	F	21 Apr.	} 30 Hen. VIII	22 Apr. 1538	21 Apr. 1539
1539	E	6 Apr.	} 31 Hen. VIII	22 Apr. 1539	21 Apr. 1540
1540	DC	28 Mar.	} 32 Hen. VIII	22 Apr. 1540	21 Apr. 1541
1541	B	17 Apr.	} 33 Hen. VIII	22 Apr. 1541	21 Apr. 1542
1542	A	9 Apr.	} 34 Hen. VIII	22 Apr. 1542	21 Apr. 1543
1543	G	25 Mar.	} 35 Hen. VIII	22 Apr. 1543	21 Apr. 1544
1544	FE	13 Apr.	} 36 Hen. VIII	22 Apr. 1544	21 Apr. 1545
1545	D	5 Apr.	} 37 Hen. VIII	22 Apr. 1545	21 Apr. 1546
1546	C	25 Apr.	} 38 Hen. VIII	22 Apr. 1546	28 Jan. 1547
1547	B	10 Apr.	} 1 **Edw. VI**	28 Jan. 1547	27 Jan. 1548
1548	AG	1 Apr.	} 2 Edw. VI	28 Jan. 1548	27 Jan. 1549
1549	F	21 Apr.	} 3 Edw. VI	28 Jan. 1549	27 Jan. 1550
1550	E	6 Apr.	} 4 Edw. VI	28 Jan. 1550	27 Jan. 1551
1551	D	29 Mar.	} 5 Edw. VI	28 Jan. 1551	27 Jan. 1552
1552	CB	17 Apr.	} 6 Edw. VI	28 Jan. 1552	27 Jan. 1553
1553	A	2 Apr.	(7 Edw. VI	28 Jan. 1553	6 Jul. 1553
			{ 1 **Jane**	6 Jul. 1553	19 Jul. 1553
			1 **Mary**	19 Jul. 1553*	5 Jul. 1554
1554	G	25 Mar.	2 Mary	6 Jul. 1554	24 Jul. 1554
1555	F	14 Apr.	1 & 2 P. & M.	25 Jul. 1554†	5 Jul. 1555
			1 & 3 P. & M.	6 Jul. 1555	24 Jul. 1555
1556	ED	5 Apr.	2 & 3 P. & M.	25 Jul. 1555	5 Jul. 1556
			2 & 4 P. & M.	6 Jul. 1556	24 Jul. 1556
1557	C	18 Apr.	3 & 4 P. & M.	25 Jul. 1556	5 Jul. 1557
			3 & 5 P. & M.	6 Jul. 1557	24 Jul. 1557
			4 & 5 P. & M.	25 Jul. 1557	5 Jul. 1558
1558	B	10 Apr.	(4 & 6 P. & M.	6 Jul. 1558	24 Jul. 1558
			(5 & 6 P. & M.	25 Jul. 1558	17 Nov. 1558
			1 **Eliz. I**	17 Nov. 1558	16 Nov. 1559
1559	A	26 Mar.	2 Eliz. I	17 Nov. 1559	16 Nov. 1560
1560	GF	14 Apr.	3 Eliz. I	17 Nov. 1560	16 Nov. 1561
1561	E	6 Apr.	4 Eliz. I	17 Nov. 1561	16 Nov. 1562
1562	D	29 Mar.	5 Eliz. I	17 Nov. 1562	16 Nov. 1563
1563	C	11 Apr.	6 Eliz. I	17 Nov. 1563	16 Nov. 1564
1564	BA	2 Apr.	7 Eliz. I	17 Nov. 1564	16 Nov. 1565
1565	G	22 Apr.	8 Eliz. I	17 Nov. 1565	16 Nov. 1566
1566	F	14 Apr.			

* Mary reckoned the beginning of her second and succeeding regnal years as though Jane had not been queen.

† Date of Mary's marriage to Philip, king of Naples and Jerusalem and (after 16 Jan. 1556) Spain.

Year	Domi-nical Letter	Easter Day Old Style	Easter Day New Style	Regnal Years No.	Regnal Years Beginning	Regnal Years Ending
1566	F	14 Apr.		9 Eliz. I	17 Nov. 1566	16 Nov. 1567
1567	E	30 Mar.		10 Eliz. I	17 Nov. 1567	16 Nov. 1568
1568	DC	18 Apr.		11 Eliz. I	17 Nov. 1568	16 Nov. 1569
1569	B	10 Apr.		12 Eliz. I	17 Nov. 1569	16 Nov. 1570
1570	A	26 Mar.		13 Eliz. I	17 Nov. 1570	16 Nov. 1571
1571	G	15 Apr.		14 Eliz. I	17 Nov. 1571	16 Nov. 1572
1572	FE	6 Apr.		15 Eliz. I	17 Nov. 1572	16 Nov. 1573
1573	D	22 Mar.		16 Eliz. I	17 Nov. 1573	16 Nov. 1574
1574	C	11 Apr.		17 Eliz. I	17 Nov. 1574	16 Nov. 1575
1575	B	3 Apr.		18 Eliz. I	17 Nov. 1575	16 Nov. 1576
1576	AG	22 Apr.		19 Eliz. I	17 Nov. 1576	16 Nov. 1577
1577	F	7 Apr.		20 Eliz. I	17 Nov. 1577	16 Nov. 1578
1578	E	30 Mar.		21 Eliz. I	17 Nov. 1578	16 Nov. 1579
1579	D	19 Apr.		22 Eliz. I	17 Nov. 1579	16 Nov. 1580
1580	CB	3 Apr.		23 Eliz. I	17 Nov. 1580	16 Nov. 1581
1581	A	26 Mar.		24 Eliz. I	17 Nov. 1581	16 Nov. 1582
1582	G	15 Apr.		25 Eliz. I	17 Nov. 1582	16 Nov. 1583
1583	F	31 Mar.	10 Apr.	26 Eliz. I	17 Nov. 1583	16 Nov. 1584
1584	ED	19 Apr.	1 Apr.	27 Eliz. I	17 Nov. 1584	16 Nov. 1585
1585	C	11 Apr.	21 Apr.	28 Eliz. I	17 Nov. 1585	16 Nov. 1586
1586	B	3 Apr.	6 Apr.	29 Eliz. I	17 Nov. 1586	16 Nov. 1587
1587	A	16 Apr.	29 Mar.	30 Eliz. I	17 Nov. 1587	16 Nov. 1588
1588	GF	7 Apr.	17 Apr.	31 Eliz. I	17 Nov. 1588	16 Nov. 1589
1589	E	30 Mar.	2 Apr.	32 Eliz. I	17 Nov. 1589	16 Nov. 1590
1590	D	19 Apr.	22 Apr.	33 Eliz. I	17 Nov. 1590	16 Nov. 1591
1591	C	4 Apr.	14 Apr.	34 Eliz. I	17 Nov. 1591	16 Nov. 1592
1592	BA	26 Mar.	29 Mar.	35 Eliz. I	17 Nov. 1592	16 Nov. 1593
1593	G	15 Apr.	18 Apr.	36 Eliz. I	17 Nov. 1593	16 Nov. 1594
1594	F	31 Mar.	10 Apr.	37 Eliz. I	17 Nov. 1594	16 Nov. 1595
1595	E	20 Apr.	26 Mar.	38 Eliz. I	17 Nov. 1595	16 Nov. 1596
1596	DC	11 Apr.	14 Apr.	39 Eliz. I	17 Nov. 1596	16 Nov. 1597
1597	B	27 Mar.	6 Apr.	40 Eliz. I	17 Nov. 1597	16 Nov. 1598
1598	A	16 Apr.	22 Mar.	41 Eliz. I	17 Nov. 1598	16 Nov. 1599
1599	G	8 Apr.	11 Apr.	42 Eliz. I	17 Nov. 1599	16 Nov. 1600
1600	FE	23 Mar.	2 Apr.	43 Eliz. I	17 Nov. 1600	16 Nov. 1601
1601	D	12 Apr.	22 Apr.	44 Eliz. I	17 Nov. 1601	16 Nov. 1602
1602	C	4 Apr.	7 Apr.	45 Eliz. I	17 Nov. 1602	23 Mar. 1603
				1 & 36 Jac. I*	24 Mar. 1603	23 Jul. 1603
1603	B	24 Apr.	30 Mar.	1 & 37 Jac. I	24 Jul. 1603	23 Mar. 1604
				2 & 37 Jac. I	24 Mar. 1604	23 Jul. 1604
1604	AG	8 Apr.	18 Apr.	2 & 38 Jac. I	24 Jul. 1604	23 Mar. 1605
				3 & 38 Jac. I	24 Mar. 1605	23 Jul. 1605
1605	F	31 Mar.	10 Apr.	3 & 39 Jac. I	24 Jul. 1605	23 Mar. 1606
				4 & 39 Jac. I	24 Mar. 1606	23 Jul. 1606
1606	E	20 Apr.	26 Mar.	4 & 40 Jac. I	24 Jul. 1606	23 Mar. 1607
				5 & 40 Jac. I	24 Mar. 1607	23 Jul. 1607
1607	D	5 Apr.	15 Apr.	5 & 41 Jac. I	24 Jul. 1607	23 Mar. 1608
				6 & 41 Jac. I	24 Mar. 1608	23 Jul. 1608
1608	CB	27 Mar.	6 Apr.	6 & 42 Jac. I	24 Jul. 1608	23 Mar. 1609
				7 & 42 Jac. I	24 Mar. 1609	23 Jul. 1609
1609	A	16 Apr.	19 Apr.	7 & 43 Jac. I	24 Jul. 1609	23 Mar. 1610
				8 & 43 Jac. I	24 Mar. 1610	23 Jul. 1610
1610	G	8 Apr.	11 Apr.	8 & 44 Jac. I	24 Jul. 1610	23 Mar. 1611
				9 & 44 Jac. I	24 Mar. 1611	23 Jul. 1611
1611	F	24 Mar.	3 Apr.			

* The Scottish regnal year of James I (reckoned from his accession in Scotland on 24 July 1567) is generally given in documents as well as his English regnal year.

Year	Domi-nical Letter	Easter Day Old Style	Easter Day New Style	Regnal Years No.	Beginning	Ending
1611	F	24 Mar.	3 Apr.	9 & 45 Jac. I	24 Jul. 1611	23 Mar. 1612
1612	ED	12 Apr.	22 Apr.	10 & 45 Jac. I	24 Mar. 1612	23 Jul. 1612
				10 & 46 Jac. I	24 Jul. 1612	23 Mar. 1613
1613	C	4 Apr.	7 Apr.	11 & 46 Jac. I	24 Mar. 1613	23 Jul. 1613
				11 & 47 Jac. I	24 Jul. 1613	23 Mar. 1614
1614	B	24 Apr.	30 Mar.	12 & 47 Jac. I	24 Mar. 1614	23 Jul. 1614
				12 & 48 Jac. I	24 Jul. 1614	23 Mar. 1615
1615	A	9 Apr.	19 Apr.	13 & 48 Jac. I	24 Mar. 1615	23 Jul. 1615
				13 & 49 Jac. I	24 Jul. 1615	23 Mar. 1616
1616	GF	31 Mar.	3 Apr.	14 & 49 Jac. I	24 Mar. 1616	23 Jul. 1616
				14 & 50 Jac. I	24 Jul. 1616	23 Mar. 1617
1617	E	20 Apr.	26 Mar.	15 & 50 Jac. I	24 Mar. 1617	23 Jul. 1617
				15 & 51 Jac. I	24 Jul. 1617	23 Mar. 1618
1618	D	5 Apr.	15 Apr.	16 & 51 Jac. I	24 Mar. 1618	23 Jul. 1618
				16 & 52 Jac. I	24 Jul. 1618	23 Mar. 1619
1619	C	28 Mar.	31 Mar.	17 & 52 Jac. I	24 Mar. 1619	23 Jul. 1619
				17 & 53 Jac. I	24 Jul. 1619	23 Mar. 1620
1620	BA	16 Apr.	19 Apr.	18 & 53 Jac. I	24 Mar. 1620	23 Jul. 1620
				18 & 54 Jac. I	24 Jul. 1620	23 Mar. 1621
1621	G	1 Apr.	11 Apr.	19 & 54 Jac. I	24 Mar. 1621	23 Jul. 1621
				19 & 55 Jac. I	24 Jul. 1621	23 Mar. 1622
1622	F	21 Apr.	27 Mar.	20 & 55 Jac. I	24 Mar. 1622	23 Jul. 1622
				20 & 56 Jac. I	24 Jul. 1622	23 Mar. 1623
1623	E	13 Apr.	16 Apr.	21 & 56 Jac. I	24 Mar. 1623	23 Jul. 1623
				21 & 57 Jac. I	24 Jul. 1623	23 Mar. 1624
1624	DC	28 Mar.	7 Apr.	22 & 57 Jac. I	24 Mar. 1624	23 Jul. 1624
				22 & 58 Jac. I	24 Jul. 1624	23 Mar. 1625
1625	B	17 Apr.	30 Mar.	23 & 58 Jac. I	24 Mar. 1625	27 Mar. 1625
				1 Car. I	27 Mar. 1625	26 Mar. 1626
1626	A	9 Apr.	12 Apr.	2 Car. I	27 Mar. 1626	26 Mar. 1627
1627	G	25 Mar.	4 Apr.	3 Car. I	27 Mar. 1627	26 Mar. 1628
1628	FE	13 Apr.	23 Apr.	4 Car. I	27 Mar. 1628	26 Mar. 1629
1629	D	5 Apr.	15 Apr.	5 Car. I	27 Mar. 1629	26 Mar. 1630
1630	C	28 Mar.	31 Mar.	6 Car. I	27 Mar. 1630	26 Mar. 1631
1631	B	10 Apr.	20 Apr.	7 Car. I	27 Mar. 1631	26 Mar. 1632
1632	AG	1 Apr.	11 Apr.	8 Car. I	27 Mar. 1632	26 Mar. 1633
1633	F	21 Apr.	27 Mar.	9 Car. I	27 Mar. 1633	26 Mar. 1634
1634	E	6 Apr.	16 Apr.	10 Car. I	27 Mar. 1634	26 Mar. 1635
1635	D	29 Mar.	8 Apr.	11 Car. I	27 Mar. 1635	26 Mar. 1636
1636	CB	17 Apr.	23 Mar.	12 Car. I	27 Mar. 1636	26 Mar. 1637
1637	A	9 Apr.	12 Apr.	13 Car. I	27 Mar. 1637	26 Mar. 1638
1638	G	25 Mar.	4 Apr.	14 Car. I	27 Mar. 1638	26 Mar. 1639
1639	F	14 Apr.	24 Apr.	15 Car. I	27 Mar. 1639	26 Mar. 1640
1640	ED	5 Apr.	8 Apr.	16 Car. I	27 Mar. 1640	26 Mar. 1641
1641	C	25 Apr.	31 Mar.	17 Car. I	27 Mar. 1641	26 Mar. 1642
1642	B	10 Apr.	20 Apr.	18 Car. I	27 Mar. 1642	26 Mar. 1643
1643	A	2 Apr.	5 Apr.	19 Car. I	27 Mar. 1643	26 Mar. 1644
1644	GF	21 Apr.	27 Apr.	20 Car. I	27 Mar. 1644	26 Mar. 1645
1645	E	6 Apr.	16 Apr.	21 Car. I	27 Mar. 1645	26 Mar. 1646
1646	D	29 Mar.	1 Apr.	22 Car. I	27 Mar. 1646	26 Mar. 1647
1647	C	18 Apr.	21 Apr.	23 Car. I	27 Mar. 1647	26 Mar. 1648
1648	BA	2 Apr.	12 Apr.	24 Car. I	27 Mar. 1648	30 Jan. 1649
1649	G	25 Mar.	4 Apr.			

Year	Domi- nical Letter	Easter Day Old Style	New Style	Regnal Years No.	Beginning	Ending	
1649	G	25 Mar.	4 Apr.	[1 Car. II]*	[30 Jan. 1649]	[29 Jan. 1650]	
1650	F	14 Apr.	17 Apr.	[2 Car. II]	[30 Jan. 1650]	[29 Jan. 1651]	
1651	E	30 Mar.	9 Apr.	[3 Car. II]	[30 Jan. 1651]	[29 Jan. 1652]	
1652	DC	18 Apr.	31 Mar.	[4 Car. II]	[30 Jan. 1652]	[29 Jan. 1653]	
1653	B	10 Apr.	13 Apr.	[5 Car. II]	[30 Jan. 1653]	[29 Jan. 1654]	
1654	A	26 Mar.	5 Apr.	[6 Car. II]	[30 Jan. 1654]	[29 Jan. 1655]	COMMONWEALTH*
1655	G	15 Apr.	28 Mar.	[7 Car. II]	[30 Jan. 1655]	[29 Jan. 1656]	
1656	FE	6 Apr.	16 Apr.	[8 Car. II]	[30 Jan. 1656]	[29 Jan. 1657]	
1657	D	29 Mar.	1 Apr.	[9 Car. II]	[30 Jan. 1657]	[29 Jan. 1658]	
1658	C	11 Apr.	21 Apr.	[10 Car. II]	[30 Jan. 1658]	[29 Jan. 1659]	
1659	B	3 Apr.	13 Apr.	[11 Car. II]	[30 Jan. 1659]	[29 Jan. 1660]	
1660	AG	22 Apr.	28 Mar.			29 May 1660†	
1661	F	14 Apr.	17 Apr.	12 Car. II	[30 Jan. 1660]	29 Jan. 1661	
1662	E	30 Mar.	9 Apr.	13 Car. II	30 Jan. 1661	29 Jan. 1662	
1663	D	19 Apr.	25 Mar.	14 Car. II	30 Jan. 1662	29 Jan. 1663	
1664	CB	10 Apr.	13 Apr.	15 Car. II	30 Jan. 1663	29 Jan. 1664	
1665	A	26 Mar.	5 Apr.	16 Car. II	30 Jan. 1664	29 Jan. 1665	
1666	G	15 Apr.	25 Apr.	17 Car. II	30 Jan. 1665	29 Jan. 1666	
1667	F	27 Apr.	10 Apr.	18 Car. II	30 Jan. 1666	29 Jan. 1667	
1668	ED	2 Mar.	1 Apr.	19 Car. II	30 Jan. 1667	29 Jan. 1668	
1669	C	11 Apr.	21 Apr.	20 Car. II	30 Jan. 1668	29 Jan. 1669	
1670	B	3 Apr.	6 Apr.	21 Car. II	30 Jan. 1669	29 Jan. 1670	
1671	A	23 Apr.	29 Mar.	22 Car. II	30 Jan. 1670	29 Jan. 1671	
1672	GF	7 Apr.	17 Apr.	23 Car. II	30 Jan. 1671	29 Jan. 1672	
1673	E	30 Mar.	2 Apr.	24 Car. II	30 Jan. 1672	29 Jan. 1673	
1674	D	19 Apr.	25 Mar.	25 Car. II	30 Jan. 1673	29 Jan. 1674	
1675	C	4 Apr.	14 Apr.	26 Car. II	30 Jan. 1674	29 Jan. 1675	
1676	BA	26 Mar.	5 Apr.	27 Car. II	30 Jan. 1675	29 Jan. 1676	
1677	G	15 Apr.	18 Apr.	28 Car. II	30 Jan. 1676	29 Jan. 1677	
1678	F	31 Mar.	10 Apr.	29 Car. II	30 Jan. 1677	29 Jan. 1678	
1679	E	20 Apr.	2 Apr.	30 Car. II	30 Jan. 1678	29 Jan. 1679	
1680	DC	11 Apr.	21 Apr.	31 Car. II	30 Jan. 1679	29 Jan. 1680	
1681	B	3 Apr.	6 Apr.	32 Car. II	30 Jan. 1680	29 Jan. 1681	
1682	A	16 Apr.	29 Mar.	33 Car. II	30 Jan. 1681	29 Jan. 1682	
1683	G	8 Apr.	18 Apr.	34 Car. II	30 Jan. 1682	29 Jan. 1683	
1684	FE	30 Mar.	2 Apr.	35 Car. II	30 Jan. 1683	29 Jan. 1684	
1685	D	19 Apr.	22 Apr.	36 Car. II	30 Jan. 1684	29 Jan. 1685	
				37 Car. II	30 Jan. 1685	6 Feb. 1685	
				1 Jac. II	6 Feb. 1685	5 Feb. 1686	
1686	C	4 Apr.	14 Apr.	2 Jac. II	6 Feb. 1686	5 Feb. 1687	
1687	B	27 Mar.	30 Mar.	3 Jac. II	6 Feb. 1687	5 Feb. 1688	
1688	AG	15 Apr.	18 Apr.	4 Jac. II	6 Feb. 1688	11 Dec. 1688	
				Interregnum	12 Dec. 1688	12 Feb. 1689	
1689	F	31 Mar.	10 Apr.	1 Wm. & Mar.	13 Feb. 1689	12 Feb. 1690	
1690	E	20 Apr.	26 Mar.	2 Wm. & Mar.	13 Feb. 1690	12 Feb. 1691	
1691	D	12 Apr.	15 Apr.	3 Wm. & Mar.	13 Feb. 1691	12 Feb. 1692	
1692	CB	27 Mar.	6 Apr.	4 Wm. & Mar.	13 Feb. 1692	12 Feb. 1693	
1693	A	16 Apr.	22 Mar.	5 Wm. & Mar.	13 Feb. 1693	12 Feb. 1694	
1694	G	8 Apr.	11 Apr.	6 Wm. & Mar.	13 Feb. 1694	27 Dec. 1694‡	
				6 Wm. III	28 Dec. 1694		
1695	F	24 Mar.	3 Apr.			12 Feb. 1695	

* Charles II reckoned his regnal years from 30 Jan. 1649 (the date of the execution of Charles I) but did not reign in England and rarely used regnal years in dating until his restoration, 29 May 1660. During the Commonwealth public documents were dated according to the year of our Lord. Oliver Cromwell died 3 Sept. 1658. Richard Cromwell abdicated 24 May 1659, after which the government was carried on by Parliament and the Army until the restoration.

† Date of the restoration of Charles II. ‡ Queen Mary died in the night of 27–28 Dec.

947

Year	Dominical Letter	Easter Day		Regnal Years		
		Old Style	New Style	No.	Beginning	Ending
1695	F	24 Mar.	3 Apr.	7 Wm. III	13 Feb. 1695	12 Feb. 1696
1696	ED	12 Apr.	22 Apr.	8 Wm. III	13 Feb. 1696	12 Feb. 1697
1697	C	4 Apr.	7 Apr.	9 Wm. III	13 Feb. 1697	12 Feb. 1698
1698	B	24 Apr.	30 Mar.	10 Wm. III	13 Feb. 1698	12 Feb. 1699
1699	A	9 Apr.	19 Apr.	11 Wm. III	13 Feb. 1699	12 Feb. 1700
1700	GF	31 Mar.	11 Apr.	12 Wm. III	13 Feb. 1700	12 Feb. 1701
1701	E	20 Apr.	27 Mar.	13 Wm. III	13 Feb. 1701	12 Feb. 1702
1702	D	5 Apr.	16 Apr.	14 Wm. III	13 Feb. 1702	8 Mar. 1702
1703	C	28 Mar.	8 Apr.	1 Anne	8 Mar. 1702	7 Mar. 1703
1704	BA	16 Apr.	23 Mar.	2 Anne	8 Mar. 1703	7 Mar. 1704
1705	G	8 Apr.	12 Apr.	3 Anne	8 Mar. 1704	7 Mar. 1705
1706	F	24 Mar.	4 Apr.	4 Anne	8 Mar. 1705	7 Mar. 1706
1707	E	13 Apr.	24 Apr.	5 Anne	8 Mar. 1706	7 Mar. 1707
1708	DC	4 Apr.	8 Apr.	6 Anne	8 Mar. 1707	7 Mar. 1708
1709	B	24 Apr.	31 Mar.	7 Anne	8 Mar. 1708	7 Mar. 1709
1710	A	9 Apr.	20 Apr.	8 Anne	8 Mar. 1709	7 Mar. 1710
1711	G	1 Apr.	5 Apr.	9 Anne	8 Mar. 1710	7 Mar. 1711
1712	FE	20 Apr.	27 Mar.	10 Anne	8 Mar. 1711	7 Mar. 1712
1713	D	5 Apr.	16 Apr.	11 Anne	8 Mar. 1712	7 Mar. 1713
1714	C	28 Mar.	1 Apr.	12 Anne	8 Mar. 1713	7 Mar. 1714
				13 Anne	8 Mar. 1714	1 Aug. 1714
1715	B	17 Apr.	21 Apr.	1 Geo. I	1 Aug. 1714	31 Jul. 1715
1716	AG	1 Apr.	12 Apr.	2 Geo. I	1 Aug. 1715	31 Jul. 1716
1717	F	21 Apr.	28 Mar.	3 Geo. I	1 Aug. 1716	31 Jul. 1717
1718	E	13 Apr.	17 Apr.	4 Geo. I	1 Aug. 1717	31 Jul. 1718
1719	D	29 Mar.	9 Apr.	5 Geo. I	1 Aug. 1718	31 Jul. 1719
1720	CB	17 Apr.	31 Mar.	6 Geo. I	1 Aug. 1719	31 Jul. 1720
1721	A	9 Apr.	13 Apr.	7 Geo. I	1 Aug. 1720	31 Jul. 1721
1722	G	25 Mar.	5 Apr.	8 Geo. I	1 Aug. 1721	31 Jul. 1722
1723	F	14 Apr.	28 Mar.	9 Geo. I	1 Aug. 1722	31 Jul. 1723
1724	ED	5 Apr.	16 Apr.	10 Geo. I	1 Aug. 1723	31 Jul. 1724
1725	C	28 Mar.	1 Apr.	11 Geo. I	1 Aug. 1724	31 Jul. 1725
1726	B	10 Apr.	21 Apr.	12 Geo. I	1 Aug. 1725	31 Jul. 1726
1727	A	2 Apr.	13 Apr.	13 Geo. I	1 Aug. 1726	11 Jun. 1727
1728	GF	21 Apr.	28 Mar.	1 Geo. II	11 Jun. 1727	10 Jun. 1728
1729	E	6 Apr.	17 Apr.	2 Geo. II	11 Jun. 1728	10 Jun. 1729
1730	D	29 Mar.	9 Apr.	3 Geo. II	11 Jun. 1729	10 Jun. 1730
1731	C	18 Apr.	25 Mar.	4 Geo. II	11 Jun. 1730	10 Jun. 1731
1732	BA	9 Apr.	13 Apr.	5 Geo. II	11 Jun. 1731	10 Jun. 1732
1733	G	25 Mar.	5 Apr.	6 Geo. II	11 Jun. 1732	10 Jun. 1733
1734	F	14 Apr.	25 Apr.	7 Geo. II	11 Jun. 1733	10 Jun. 1734
1735	E	6 Apr.	10 Apr.	8 Geo. II	11 Jun. 1734	10 Jun. 1735
1736	DC	25 Apr.	1 Apr.	9 Geo. II	11 Jun. 1735	10 Jun. 1736
1737	B	10 Apr.	21 Apr.	10 Geo. II	11 Jun. 1736	10 Jun. 1737
1738	A	2 Apr.	6 Apr.	11 Geo. II	11 Jun. 1737	10 Jun. 1738
1739	G	22 Apr.	29 Apr.	12 Geo. II	11 Jun. 1738	10 Jun. 1739
1740	FE	6 Apr.	17 Apr.	13 Geo. II	11 Jun. 1739	10 Jun. 1740
1741	D	29 Mar.	2 Apr.	14 Geo. II	11 Jun. 1740	10 Jun. 1741
1742	C	18 Apr.	25 Mar.	15 Geo. II	11 Jun. 1741	10 Jun. 1742
1743	B	3 Apr.	14 Apr.	16 Geo. II	11 Jun. 1742	10 Jun. 1743
1744	AG	25 Mar.	5 Apr.	17 Geo. II	11 Jun. 1743	10 Jun. 1744
1745	F	14 Apr.	18 Apr.	18 Geo. II	11 Jun. 1744	10 Jun. 1745
1746	E	30 Mar.	10 Apr.	19 Geo. II	11 Jun. 1745	10 Jun. 1746
1747	D	19 Apr.	2 Apr.	20 Geo. II	11 Jun. 1746	10 Jun. 1747
1748	CB	10 Apr.	14 Apr.	21 Geo. II	11 Jun. 1747	10 Jun. 1748
1749	A	26 Mar.	6 Apr.	22 Geo. II	11 Jun. 1748	10 Jun. 1749

Year	Domi-nical Letter	Easter Day Old Style	Easter Day NewStyle	Regnal Years No.	Regnal Years Beginning	Regnal Years Ending
1749	A	26 Mar.	6 Apr.	23 Geo. II	11 Jun. 1749	10 Jun. 1750
1750	G	15 Apr.	29 Mar.	24 Geo. II	11 Jun. 1750	10 Jun. 1751
1751	F	7 Apr.	11 Apr.	25 Geo. II	11 Jun. 1751	10 Jun. 1752
1752*	EDA*	29 Mar.	2 Apr.	26 Geo. II	11 Jun. 1752	21 Jun. 1753†
1753	G	22 Apr,		27 Geo. II	22 Jun. 1753	21 Jun. 1754
1754	F	14 Apr.		28 Geo. II	22 Jun. 1754	21 Jun. 1755
1755	E	30 Mar.		29 Geo. II	22 Jun. 1755	21 Jun. 1756
1756	DC	18 Apr.		30 Geo. II	22 Jun. 1756	21 Jun. 1757
1757	B	10 Apr.		31 Geo. II	22 Jun. 1757	21 Jun. 1758
1758	A	26 Mar.		32 Geo. II	22 Jun. 1758	21 Jun. 1759
1759	G	15 Apr.		33 Geo. II	22 Jun. 1759	21 Jun. 1760
1760	FE	6 Apr.		34 Geo. II	22 Jun. 1760	25 Oct. 1760
				1 Geo. III	25 Oct. 1760	24 Oct. 1761
1761	D	22 Mar.		2 Geo. III	25 Oct. 1761	24 Oct. 1762
1762	C	11 Apr.		3 Geo. III	25 Oct. 1762	24 Oct. 1763
1763	B	3 Apr.		4 Geo. III	25 Oct. 1763	24 Oct. 1764
1764	AG	22 Apr.		5 Geo. III	25 Oct. 1764	24 Oct. 1765
1765	F	7 Apr.		6 Geo. III	25 Oct. 1765	24 Oct. 1766
1766	E	30 Mar.		7 Geo. III	25 Oct. 1766	24 Oct. 1767
1767	D	19 Apr.		8 Geo. III	25 Oct. 1767	24 Oct. 1768
1768	CB	3 Apr.		9 Geo. III	25 Oct. 1768	24 Oct. 1769
1769	A	26 Mar.		10 Geo. III	25 Oct. 1769	25 Oct. 1770
1770	G	15 Apr.		11 Geo. III	25 Oct. 1770	24 Oct. 1771
1771	F	31 Mar.		12 Geo. III	25 Oct. 1771	24 Oct. 1772
1772	ED	19 Apr.		13 Geo. III	25 Oct. 1772	24 Oct. 1773
1773	C	11 Apr.		14 Geo. III	25 Oct. 1773	24 Oct. 1774
1774	B	3 Apr.		15 Geo. III	25 Oct. 1774	24 Oct. 1775
1775	A	16 Apr.		16 Geo. III	25 Oct. 1775	24 Oct. 1776
1776	GF	7 Apr.		17 Geo. III	25 Oct. 1776	24 Oct. 1777
1777	E	30 Mar.		18 Geo. III	25 Oct. 1777	24 Oct. 1778
1778	D	19 Apr.		19 Geo. III	25 Oct. 1778	24 Oct. 1779
1779	C	4 Apr.		20 Geo. III	25 Oct. 1779	24 Oct. 1780
1780	BA	26 Mar.		21 Geo. III	25 Oct. 1780	24 Oct. 1781
1781	G	15 Apr.		22 Geo. III	25 Oct. 1781	24 Oct. 1782
1782	F	31 Mar.		23 Geo. III	25 Oct. 1782	24 Oct. 1783
1783	E	20 Apr.		24 Geo. III	25 Oct. 1783	24 Oct. 1784
1784	DC	11 Apr.		25 Geo. III	25 Oct. 1784	24 Oct. 1785
1785	B	27 Mar.		26 Geo. III	25 Oct. 1785	24 Oct. 1786
1786	A	16 Apr.		27 Geo. III	25 Oct. 1786	24 Oct. 1787
1787	G	8 Apr.		28 Geo. III	25 Oct. 1787	24 Oct. 1788
1788	FE	23 Mar.		29 Geo. III	25 Oct. 1788	24 Oct. 1789
1789	D	12 Apr.		30 Geo. III	25 Oct. 1789	24 Oct. 1790
1790	C	4 Apr.		31 Geo. III	25 Oct. 1790	24 Oct. 1791
1791	B	24 Apr.		32 Geo. III	25 Oct. 1791	24 Oct. 1792
1792	AG	8 Apr.		33 Geo. III	25 Oct. 1792	24 Oct. 1793
1793	F	31 Mar.		34 Geo. III	25 Oct. 1793	24 Oct. 1794
1794	E	20 Apr.		35 Geo. III	25 Oct. 1794	24 Oct. 1795
1795	D	5 Apr.		36 Geo. III	25 Oct. 1795	24 Oct. 1796
1796	CB	27 Mar.		37 Geo. III	25 Oct. 1796	24 Oct. 1797
1797	A	16 Apr.		38 Geo. III	25 Oct. 1797	24 Oct. 1798
1798	G	8 Apr.		39 Geo. III	25 Oct. 1798	24 Oct. 1799
1799	F	24 Mar.		40 Geo. III	25 Oct. 1799	24 Oct. 1800
1800‡	E	13 Apr.				

* See Table II.

† To make up for the eleven days omitted in Sept. 1752, eleven days (11–21 June) were added at the end of the regnal year.   ‡ The year 1800 was not a leap year.

Year	Dominical Letter	Easter Day	Regnal Years		
			No.	Beginning	Ending
1800	E	13 Apr.			
1801	D	5 Apr.	} 41 Geo. III	25 Oct. 1800	24 Oct. 1801
1802	C	18 Apr.	} 42 Geo. III	25 Oct. 1801	24 Oct. 1802
1803	B	10 Apr.	} 43 Geo. III	25 Oct. 1802	24 Oct. 1803
1804	AG	1 Apr.	} 44 Geo. III	25 Oct. 1803	24 Oct. 1804
1805	F	14 Apr.	} 45 Geo. III	25 Oct. 1804	24 Oct. 1805
1806	E	6 Apr.	} 46 Geo. III	25 Oct. 1805	24 Oct. 1806
1807	D	29 Mar.	} 47 Geo. III	25 Oct. 1806	24 Oct. 1807
1808	CB	17 Apr.	} 48 Geo. III	25 Oct. 1807	24 Oct. 1808
1809	A	2 Apr.	} 49 Geo. III	25 Oct. 1808	24 Oct. 1809
1810	G	22 Apr.	} 50 Geo. III	25 Oct. 1809	24 Oct. 1810
1811	F	14 Apr.	} 51 Geo. III	25 Oct. 1810	24 Oct. 1811
1812	ED	29 Mar.	} 52 Geo. III	25 Oct. 1811	24 Oct. 1812
1813	C	18 Apr.	} 53 Geo. III	25 Oct. 1812	24 Oct. 1813
1814	B	10 Apr.	} 54 Geo. III	25 Oct. 1813	24 Oct. 1814
1815	A	26 Mar.	} 55 Geo. III	25 Oct. 1814	24 Oct. 1815
1816	GF	14 Apr.	} 56 Geo. III	25 Oct. 1815	24 Oct. 1816
1817	E	6 Apr.	} 57 Geo. III	25 Oct. 1816	24 Oct. 1817
1818	D	22 Mar.	} 58 Geo. III	25 Oct. 1817	24 Oct. 1818
1819	C	11 Apr.	} 59 Geo. III	25 Oct. 1818	24 Oct. 1819
1820	BA	2 Apr.	} 60 Geo. III	25 Oct. 1819	29 Jan. 1820
1821	G	22 Apr.	} 1 Geo. IV	29 Jan. 1820	28 Jan. 1821
1822	F	7 Apr.	} 2 Geo. IV	29 Jan. 1821	28 Jan. 1822
1823	E	30 Mar.	} 3 Geo. IV	29 Jan. 1822	28 Jan. 1823
1824	DC	18 Apr.	} 4 Geo. IV	29 Jan. 1823	28 Jan. 1824
1825	B	3 Apr.	} 5 Geo. IV	29 Jan. 1824	28 Jan. 1825
1826	A	26 Mar.	} 6 Geo. IV	29 Jan. 1825	28 Jan. 1826
1827	G	15 Apr.	} 7 Geo. IV	29 Jan. 1826	29 Jan. 1827
1828	FE	6 Apr.	} 8 Geo. IV	29 Jan. 1827	28 Jan. 1828
1829	D	19 Apr.	} 9 Geo. IV	29 Jan. 1828	28 Jan. 1829
1830	C	11 Apr.	} 10 Geo. IV	29 Jan. 1829	28 Jan. 1830
			} 11 Geo. IV	29 Jan. 1830	26 Jun. 1830
1831	B	3 Apr.	} 1 Wm. IV	26 Jun. 1830	25 Jun. 1831
1832	AG	22 Apr.	} 2 Wm. IV	26 Jun. 1831	25 Jun. 1832
1833	F	7 Apr.	} 3 Wm. IV	26 Jun. 1832	25 Jun. 1833
1834	E	30 Mar.	} 4 Wm. IV	26 Jun. 1833	25 Jun. 1834
1835	D	19 Apr.	} 5 Wm. IV	26 Jun. 1834	25 Jun. 1835
1836	CB	3 Apr.	} 6 Wm. IV	26 Jun. 1835	25 Jun. 1836
1837	A	26 Mar.	} 7 Wm. IV	26 Jun. 1836	20 Jun. 1837
1838	G	15 Apr.	} 1 Vic.	20 Jun. 1837	19 Jun. 1838
1839	F	31 Mar.	} 2 Vic.	20 Jun. 1838	19 Jun. 1839
1840	ED	19 Apr.	} 3 Vic.	20 Jun. 1839	19 Jun. 1850
1841	C	11 Apr.	} 4 Vic.	20 Jun. 1840	19 Jun. 1841
1842	B	27 Mar.	} 5 Vic.	20 Jun. 1841	19 Jun. 1842
1843	A	16 Apr.	} 6 Vic.	20 Jun. 1842	19 Jun. 1843
1844	GF	7 Apr.	} 7 Vic.	20 Jun. 1843	19 Jun. 1844
1845	E	23 Mar.	} 8 Vic.	20 Jun. 1844	19 Jun. 1845
1846	D	12 Apr.	} 9 Vic.	20 Jun. 1845	19 Jun. 1846
1847	C	4 Apr.	} 10 Vic.	20 Jun. 1846	19 Jun. 1847
1848	BA	23 Apr.	} 11 Vic.	20 Jun. 1847	19 Jun. 1848
1849	G	8 Apr.	} 12 Vic.	20 Jun. 1848	19 Jun. 1849
1850	F	31 Mar.	} 13 Vic.	20 Jun. 1849	19 Jun. 1850
1851	E	20 Apr.	} 14 Vic.	20 Jun. 1850	19 Jun. 1851
1852	DC	11 Apr.	} 15 Vic.	20 Jun. 1851	19 Jun. 1852
1853	B	27 Mar.	} 16 Vic.	20 Jun. 1852	19 Jun. 1853
1854	A	16 Apr.	} 17 Vic.	20 Jun. 1853	19 Jun. 1854
1855	G	8 Apr.	} 18 Vic.	20 Jun. 1854	19 Jun. 1855

Year	Dominical Letter	Easter Day	Regnal Years No.	Beginning	Ending
1855	G	8 Apr.	19 Vic.	20 Jun. 1855	19 Jun. 1856
1856	FE	23 Mar.	20 Vic.	20 Jun. 1856	19 Jun. 1857
1857	D	12 Apr.	21 Vic.	20 Jun. 1857	19 Jun. 1858
1858	C	4 Apr.	22 Vic.	20 Jun. 1858	19 Jun. 1859
1859	B	24 Apr.	23 Vic.	20 Jun. 1859	19 Jun. 1860
1860	AG	8 Apr.	24 Vic.	20 Jun. 1860	19 Jun. 1861
1861	F	31 Mar.	25 Vic.	20 Jun. 1861	19 Jun. 1862
1862	E	20 Apr.	26 Vic.	20 Jun. 1862	19 Jun. 1863
1863	D	5 Apr.	27 Vic.	20 Jun. 1863	19 Jun. 1864
1864	CB	27 Mar.	28 Vic.	20 Jun. 1864	19 Jun. 1865
1865	A	16 Apr.	29 Vic.	20 Jun. 1865	19 Jun. 1866
1866	G	1 Apr.	30 Vic.	20 Jun. 1866	19 Jun. 1867
1867	F	21 Apr.	31 Vic.	20 Jun. 1867	19 Jun. 1868
1868	ED	12 Apr.	32 Vic.	20 Jun. 1868	19 Jun. 1869
1869	C	28 Mar.	33 Vic.	20 Jun. 1869	19 Jun. 1870
1870	B	17 Apr.	34 Vic.	20 Jun. 1870	19 Jun. 1871
1871	A	9 Apr.	35 Vic.	20 Jun. 1871	19 Jun. 1872
1872	GF	31 Mar.	36 Vic.	20 Jun. 1872	19 Jun. 1873
1873	E	13 Apr.	37 Vic.	20 Jun. 1873	19 Jun. 1874
1874	D	5 Apr.	38 Vic.	20 Jun. 1874	19 Jun. 1875
1875	C	28 Mar.	39 Vic.	20 Jun. 1875	19 Jun. 1876
1876	BA	16 Apr.	40 Vic.	20 Jun. 1876	19 Jun. 1877
1877	G	1 Apr.	41 Vic.	20 Jun. 1877	19 Jun. 1878
1878	F	21 Apr.	42 Vic.	20 Jun. 1878	19 Jun. 1879
1879	E	13 Apr.	43 Vic.	20 Jun. 1879	19 Jun. 1880
1880	DC	28 Mar.	44 Vic.	20 Jun. 1880	19 Jun. 1881
1881	B	17 Apr.	45 Vic.	20 Jun. 1881	19 Jun. 1882
1882	A	9 Apr.	46 Vic.	20 Jun. 1882	19 Jun. 1883
1883	G	25 Mar.	47 Vic.	20 Jun. 1883	19 Jun. 1884
1884	FE	13 Apr.	48 Vic.	20 Jun. 1884	19 Jun. 1885
1885	D	5 Apr.	49 Vic.	20 Jun. 1885	19 Jun. 1886
1886	C	25 Apr.	50 Vic.	20 Jun. 1886	19 Jun. 1887
1887	B	10 Apr.	51 Vic.	20 Jun. 1887	19 Jun. 1888
1888	AG	1 Apr.	52 Vic.	20 Jun. 1888	19 Jun. 1889
1889	F	21 Apr.	53 Vic.	20 Jun. 1889	19 Jun. 1890
1890	E	6 Apr.	54 Vic.	20 Jun. 1890	19 Jun. 1891
1891	D	29 Mar.	55 Vic.	20 Jun. 1891	19 Jun. 1892
1892	CB	17 Apr.	56 Vic.	20 Jun. 1892	19 Jun. 1893
1893	A	2 Apr.	57 Vic.	20 Jun. 1893	19 Jun. 1894
1894	G	25 Mar.	58 Vic.	20 Jun. 1894	19 Jun. 1895
1895	F	14 Apr.	59 Vic.	20 Jun. 1895	19 Jun. 1896
1896	ED	5 Apr.	60 Vic.	20 Jun. 1896	19 Jun. 1897
1897	C	18 Apr.	61 Vic.	20 Jun. 1897	19 Jun. 1898
1898	B	10 Apr.	62 Vic.	20 Jun. 1898	19 Jun. 1899
1899	A	2 Apr.	63 Vic.	20 Jun. 1899	19 Jun. 1900
1900*	G	15 Apr.	64 Vic.	20 Jun. 1900	22 Jan. 1901
1901	F	7 Apr.	1 Edw. VII	22 Jan. 1901	21 Jan. 1902
1902	E	30 Mar.	2 Edw. VII	22 Jan. 1902	21 Jan. 1903
1903	D	12 Apr.	3 Edw. VII	22 Jan. 1903	21 Jan. 1904
1904	CB	3 Apr.	4 Edw. VII	22 Jan. 1904	21 Jan. 1905
1905	A	23 Apr.	5 Edw. VII	22 Jan. 1905	21 Jan. 1906
1906	G	15 Apr.	6 Edw. VII	22 Jan. 1906	21 Jan. 1907
1907	F	31 Mar.	7 Edw. VII	22 Jan. 1907	21 Jan. 1908
1908	ED	19 Apr.	8 Edw. VII	22 Jan. 1908	21 Jan. 1909
1909	C	11 Apr.			

* The year 1900 was not a leap year.

Year	Domi-nical Letter	Easter Day	Regnal Years		
			No.	Beginning	Ending
1909	C	11 Apr.	9 Edw. VII	22 Jan. 1909	21 Jan. 1910
1910	B	27 Mar.	10 Edw. VII	22 Jan. 1910	6 May 1910
1911	A	16 Apr.	1 **Geo. V**	6 May 1910	5 May 1911
1912	GF	7 Apr.	2 Geo. V	6 May 1911	5 May 1912
1913	E	23 Mar.	3 Geo. V	6 May 1912	5 May 1913
1914	D	12 Apr.	4 Geo. V	6 May 1913	5 May 1914
1915	C	4 Apr.	5 Geo. V	6 May 1914	5 May 1915
1916	BA	23 Apr.	6 Geo. V	6 May 1915	5 May 1916
1917	G	8 Apr.	7 Geo. V	6 May 1916	5 May 1917
1918	F	31 Mar.	8 Geo. V	6 May 1917	5 May 1918
1919	E	20 Apr.	9 Geo. V	6 May 1918	5 May 1919
1920	DC	4 Apr.	10 Geo. V	6 May 1919	5 May 1920
1921	B	27 Mar.	11 Geo. V	6 May 1920	5 May 1921
1922	A	16 Apr.	12 Geo. V	6 May 1921	5 May 1922
1923	G	1 Apr.	13 Geo. V	6 May 1922	5 May 1923
1924	FE	20 Apr.	14 Geo. V	6 May 1923	5 May 1924
1925	D	12 Apr.	15 Geo. V	6 May 1924	5 May 1925
1926	C	4 Apr.	16 Geo. V	6 May 1925	5 May 1926
1927	B	17 Apr.	17 Geo. V	6 May 1926	5 May 1927
1928	AG	8 Apr.	18 Geo. V	6 May 1927	5 May 1928
1929	F	31 Mar.	19 Geo. V	6 May 1928	5 May 1929
1930	E	20 Apr.	20 Geo. V	6 May 1929	5 May 1930
1931	D	5 Apr.	21 Geo. V	6 May 1930	5 May 1931
1932	CB	27 Mar.	22 Geo. V	6 May 1931	5 May 1932
1933	A	16 Apr.	23 Geo. V	6 May 1932	5 May 1933
1934	G	1 Apr.	24 Geo. V	6 May 1933	5 May 1934
1935	F	21 Apr.	25 Geo. V	6 May 1934	5 May 1935
1936	ED	12 Apr.	26 Geo. V	6 May 1935	20 Jan. 1936
			1 **Edw. VIII**	20 Jan. 1936	11 Dec. 1936
			1 **Geo. VI**	11 Dec. 1936	10 Dec. 1937
1937	C	28 Mar.	2 Geo. VI	11 Dec. 1937	10 Dec. 1938
1938	B	17 Apr.	3 Geo. VI	11 Dec. 1938	10 Dec. 1939
1939	A	9 Apr.	4 Geo. VI	11 Dec. 1939	10 Dec. 1940
1940	GF	24 Mar.	5 Geo. VI	11 Dec. 1940	10 Dec. 1941
1941	E	13 Apr.	6 Geo. VI	11 Dec. 1941	10 Dec. 1942
1942	D	5 Apr.	7 Geo. VI	11 Dec. 1942	10 Dec. 1943
1943	C	25 Apr.	8 Geo. VI	11 Dec. 1943	10 Dec. 1944
1944	BA	9 Apr.	9 Geo. VI	11 Dec. 1944	10 Dec. 1945
1945	G	1 Apr.	10 Geo. VI	11 Dec. 1945	10 Dec. 1946
1946	F	21 Apr.	11 Geo. VI	11 Dec. 1946	10 Dec. 1947
1947	E	6 Apr.	12 Geo. VI	11 Dec. 1947	10 Dec. 1948
1948	DC	28 Mar.	13 Geo. VI	11 Dec. 1948	10 Dec. 1949
1949	B	17 Apr.	14 Geo. VI	11 Dec. 1949	10 Dec. 1950
1950	A	9 Apr.	15 Geo. VI	11 Dec. 1950	10 Dec. 1951
1951	G	25 Mar.	16 Geo. VI	11 Dec. 1951	6 Feb. 1952
1952	FE	13 Apr.	1 **Eliz. II**	6 Feb. 1952	5 Feb. 1953
1953	D	5 Apr.	2 Eliz. II	6 Feb. 1953	5 Feb. 1954
1954	C	18 Apr.	3 Eliz. II	6 Feb. 1954	5 Feb. 1955
1955	B	10 Apr.	4 Eliz. II	6 Feb. 1955	5 Feb. 1956
1956	AG	1 Apr.	5 Eliz. II	6 Feb. 1956	5 Feb. 1957
1957	F	21 Apr.	6 Eliz. II	6 Feb. 1957	5 Feb. 1958
1958	E	6 Apr.	7 Eliz. II	6 Feb. 1958	5 Feb. 1959
1959	D	29 Mar.	8 Eliz. II	6 Feb. 1959	5 Feb. 1960
1960	CB	17 Apr.	9 Eliz. II	6 Feb. 1960	5 Feb. 1961
1961	A	2 Apr.			

Year	Domi-nical Letter	Easter Day	Regnal Years		
			No.	Beginning	Ending
1961	A	2 Apr.	} 10 Eliz. II	6 Feb. 1961	5 Feb. 1962
1962	G	22 Apr.	} 11 Eliz. II	6 Feb. 1962	5 Feb. 1963
1963	F	14 Apr.	} 12 Eliz. II	6 Feb. 1963	5 Feb. 1964
1964	ED	29 Mar.	} 13 Eliz. II	6 Feb. 1964	5 Feb. 1965
1965	C	18 Apr.	} 14 Eliz. II	6 Feb. 1965	5 Feb. 1966
1966	B	10 Apr.	} 15 Eliz. II	6 Feb. 1966	5 Feb, 1967
1967	A	26 Mar.	} 16 Eliz. II	6 Feb. 1967	
1968	GF	14 Apr.			
1969	E	6 Apr.			
1970	D	29 Mar.			
1971	C	11 Apr.			
1972	BA	2 Apr.			
1973	G	22 Apr.			
1974	F	14 Apr.			
1975	E	30 Mar.			
1976	DC	18 Apr.			
1977	B	10 Apr.			
1978	A	26 Mar.			
1979	G	15 Apr.			
1980	FE	6 Apr.			
1981	D	19 Apr.			
1982	C	11 Apr.			
1983	B	3 Apr.			
1984	AG	22 Apr.			
1985	F	7 Apr.			
1986	E	30 Mar.			
1987	D	19 Apr.			
1988	CB	3 Apr.			
1989	A	26 Mar.			
1990	G	15 Apr.			
1991	F	31 Mar.			
1992	ED	19 Apr.			
1993	C	11 Apr.			
1994	B	3 Apr.			
1995	A	16 Apr.			
1996	GF	7 Apr.			
1997	E	30 Mar.			
1998	D	12 Apr.			
1999	C	4 Apr.			
2000	BA	23 Apr.			

TABLE II

ABBREVIATED CALENDAR FOR THE YEAR 1752

THE year was a leap year; 1 January was on a Wednesday, and the first Sunday was 5 January. The eleven days 3–13 September were omitted. The Dominical Letter for January and February was E; for March–2 September it was D; for 14 September–December it was A. Easter Day New Style fell on 2 April.

January	February	March	April
W 1 Circumcis.	S 1	S 1 Lent iii	W 1
M 6 Epiph.	W 12 Ash W.	W 25 Annunc.	
S 26 Septuag.	S 29	S 29 Easter	

May	June	July	August
F 1	M 1	W 1	S 1
Th 7 Ascens.			
S 17 Whit Sun.			

September	October	November	December
Tu 1	S 1 Trinity xvii	W 1	F 1
W 2			
Eleven days omitted			
Th 14			M 25 Christmas

TABLE III

DATES OF MOVABLE FEASTS DEPENDENT ON THE DATE OF EASTER

(The double Dominical Letter indicates leap years)

Dominical Letter	Septuagesima Sunday	Ash Wednesday	EASTER DAY	Ascension Day	Pentecost or Whit Sunday	Trinity Sunday	Advent* Sunday
D	Jan. 18	Feb. 4	Mar. 22	Apr. 30	May 10	May 17	Nov. 29
ED	19	5					
E	19	5	23	May 1	11	18	30
FE	20	6					
F	20	6	24	2	12	19	Dec. 1
GF	21	7					
G	21	7	25	3	13	20	2
AG	22	8					
A	22	8	26	4	14	21	3
BA	23	9					
B	23	9	27	5	15	22	Nov. 27
CB	24	10					
C	24	10	28	6	16	23	28
DC	25	11					
D	25	11	29	7	17	24	29
ED	26	12					
E	26	12	30	8	18	25	30
FE	27	13					
F	27	13	31	9	19	26	Dec. 1
GF	28	14					
G	28	14	Apr. 1	10	20	27	2
AG	29	15					
A	29	15	2	11	21	28	3
BA	30	16					
B	30	16	3	12	22	29	Nov. 27
CB	31	17					
C	31	17	4	13	23	30	28
DC	Feb. 1	18					
D	1	18	5	14	24	31	29
ED	2	19					
E	2	19	6	15	25	Jun. 1	30
FE	3	20					
F	3	20	7	16	26	2	Dec. 1
GF	4	21					
G	4	21	8	17	27	3	2
AG	5	22					
A	5	22	9	18	28	4	3
BA	6	23					

* *Advent Sunday* is Nov. 30 (the feast of St. Andrew) or the nearest Sunday to it before or after.
Sexagesima Sunday is the Sunday next after Septuagesima Sunday.
Quinquagesima Sunday is the second Sunday after Septuagesima Sunday.
Shrove Tuesday is the day before Ash Wednesday.
Passion Sunday is the second Sunday before Easter Sunday.
Palm Sunday is the Sunday next before Easter Sunday.
Good Friday is the Friday before Easter Sunday.
Quasimodo Sunday (so named from the first word of the Introit for the day) or *Low Sunday* is the Sunday next after Easter Sunday.
Corpus Christi is the Thursday after Trinity Sunday.

Dominical Letter	Septuagesima Sunday	Ash Wednesday	EASTER DAY	Ascension Day	Pentecost or Whit Sunday	Trinity Sunday	Advent Sunday
B	Feb. 6	Feb. 23	Apr. 10	May 19	May 29	Jun. 5	Nov. 27
CB	7	24					
C	7	24	11	20	30	6	28
DC	8	25					
D	8	25	12	21	31	7	29
ED	9	26					
E	9	26	13	22	Jun. 1	8	30
FE	10	27					
F	10	27	14	23	2	9	Dec. 1
GF	11	28					
G	11	28	15	24	3	10	2
AG	12	29					
A	12	Mar. 1	16	25	4	11	3
BA	13						
B	13	2	17	26	5	12	Nov. 27
CB	14						
C	14	3	18	27	6	13	28
DC	15						
D	15	4	19	28	7	14	29
ED	16						
E	16	5	20	29	8	15	30
FE	17						
F	17	6	21	30	9	16	Dec. 1
GF	18						
G	18	7	22	31	10	17	2
AG	19						
A	19	8	23	Jun. 1	11	18	3
BA	20						
B	20	9	24	2	12	19	Nov. 27
CB	21						
C	21	10	25	3	13	20	28
DC	22						

TABLE IV

FEASTS AND SAINTS' DAYS FREQUENTLY USED IN DATING DOCUMENTS

Adorate dominum	3rd Sun. after Epiphany
Adrian (of Canterbury)	9 January
Ad te levavi	1st Sun. in Advent
Agatha	5 February
Agnes	21 January
Alban	22 June*
Albert *see* Ethelbert	
Aldhelm	25 May
All Hallows, All Saints	1 November
All Souls	2 November
Alphege	19 April
Ambrose	4 April
Andrew	30 November
Anne	26 July
Annunciation	25 March
Aspiciens a longe	1st Sun. in Advent
Audoenus (Ouen)	24 or 25 August
Audrey *see* Etheldreda	
Augustine (of Canterbury)	26 May
Augustine (of Hippo)	28 August
Barnabas	11 June
Bartholomew	24 August
Bede, Venerable	27 May
Benedict	21 March
His translation	11 July
Birinus	3 December
Blasius	3 February
Boniface	5 June
Botolph	17 June
Bricius (Britius)	13 November
Candlemas	2 February
Canite tuba	4th Sun. in Advent
Cantate domino	4th Sun. after Easter
Cathedra Petri	22 February
Catherine	25 November
Cecilia	22 November
Cena domini	Maundy Thursday
Chad (Cedde)	2 March
Christmas (*Natale domini*)	25 December
Christopher	25 July
Circumcision	1 January
Clausum Pasche	1st Sun. after Easter
Clement	23 November
Cornelius and Cyprian	14 September
Corpus Christi	Thursday after octave of Pentecost
Crispin and Crispinian	25 October
Cross, Holy	
Exaltation of the	14 September
Invention of the	3 May
Cuthbert	20 March
His translation	4 September
Cyprian and Justina	26 September
Daemon mutus	3rd Sun. in Lent
Da pacem	18th Sun. after octave of Pentecost
David	1 March

* 17 June according to the Prayer Book of 1662.

Deus in adiutorium	12th Sun. after octave of Pentecost
Deus in loco sancto	11th Sun. after octave of Pentecost
Deus qui errantibus	3rd Sun. after Easter
Dicit dominus	23rd and 24th Sun. after octave of Pentecost
Dies cinerum	Ash Wednesday
Dies crucis adorande	Good Friday
Dies mandati	Maundy Thursday
Dionysius (Denis), Rusticus, and Eleutherius	9 October
Domine, in tua misericordia	1st Sun. after octave of Pentecost
Domine, ne longe	Palm Sunday
Dominus fortitudo	6th Sun. after octave of Pentecost
Dominus illuminatio mea	4th Sun. after octave of Pentecost
Dum clamarem	10th Sun. after octave of Pentecost
Dum medium silentium	Sun. in octave of Christmas *or*, Sun. after Jan. 1 when this falls on eve of Epiphany
Dunstan	19 May
Eadburga (of Winchester)	15 June
Ecce deus adiuvat	9th Sun. after octave of Pentecost
Editha	16 September
Edmund (archbishop)	16 November
His translation	9 June
Edmund (king)	20 November
His translation	29 April
Edward the Confessor	5 January
His translation*	13 October
Edward (king of W. Saxons)	18 March
His translation I	18 February
II	20 June
Egidius (Giles)	1 September
Enurchus, correctly Evurcius	7 September
Epiphany	6 January
Esto mihi	Sun. before Ash Wednesday (Quinquagesima)
Ethelbert (king)	20 May
Etheldreda	17 October
Euphemia	16 September
Eustachius	2 November
Evurcius	7 September
Exaudi domine	Sun. in octave of Ascension, *or* 5th Sun. after octave of Pentecost
Exsurge domine	2nd Sun. before Ash Wednesday (Sexagesima)
Fabian and Sebastian	20 January
Factus est dominus	2nd Sun. after octave of Pentecost
Faith	6 October
Felicitas	23 November
Franciscus	4 October
Gaudete in domino	3rd Sun. in Advent
Geminianus *see* Lucianus	
George	23 April
Giles (Egidius)	1 September
Gregory	12 March
Grimbold	8 July
Gule of August	1 August
Guthlac	11 April
Hieronymus (Jerome)	30 September
Hilary	13 January
Hugh (bp. of Lincoln)	17 November
Inclina aurem tuam	15th Sun. after octave of Pentecost
In excelso throno	1st Sun. after Epiphany
Innocents	28 December

* Often called the Feast of St. Edward in the quindene of Michaelmas.

Invocavit me	1st Sun. in Lent
In voluntate tua	21st Sun. after octave of Pentecost
Isti sunt dies	Passion Sunday
James	25 July
Jerome (Hieronymus)	30 September
John the Baptist	24 June
His beheading	29 August
John the Evangelist	27 December
Ante Portam Latinam	6 May
Jubilate omnis terra	3rd Sun. after Easter
Judica me	Passion Sunday
Judoc	13 December
Justus es domine	17th Sun. after octave of Pentecost
Lady Day (Annunciation)	25 March
Laetare Jerusalem	4th Sun. in Lent
Lambert	17 September
Lammas	1 August
Laudus	21 September
Laurence	10 August
Leonard	6 November
Lucianus and Geminianus	16 September
Lucian	8 January
Lucy	13 December
Luke	18 October
Machutus	15 November
Margaret (queen of Scotland)	8 July
Margaret (virgin and martyr)	20 July
Mark	25 April
Martin	11 November
His translation	4 July
Mary, Blessed Virgin	
Annunciation (Lady Day)	25 March
Assumption	15 August
Conception	8 December
Nativity	8 September
Purification	2 February
Visitation	2 July
Mary Magdalene	22 July
Mathias	24 February*
Matthew	21 September
Maurice	22 September
Meliorus	1 October
Memento mei	4th Sun. in Advent
Michael	29 September
In Monte tumba	16 October
Mildred	13 July
Miserere mihi	16th Sun. after octave of Pentecost
Misericordia domini	2nd Sun. after Easter
Name of Jesus	7 August
Nicholas	6 December
Nicomedes	1 June
Oculi	3rd Sun. in Lent
Omnes gentes	7th Sun. after octave of Pentecost
Omnia quae fecisti	20th Sun. after octave of Pentecost
Omnis terra	2nd Sun. after Epiphany
Osanna	Palm Sunday
O Sapientia	16 December
Osmund	4 December
Oswald (bp.)	28 February

* 25 February in leap years.

Oswald (king)	5 August
Patrick	17 March
Paul, Conversion of	25 January
Perpetua	7 March
Peter and Paul	29 June
Peter ad Vincula	1 August
Philip and James	1 May
Populus Sion	2nd Sun. in Advent
Prisca	18 January
Priscus	1 September
Protector noster	14th Sun. after octave of Pentecost
Quasimodo	1st Sun. after Easter
Reddite quae sunt	23rd Sun. after octave of Pentecost
Remigius, Germanus, and Vedastus	1 October
Reminiscere	2nd Sun. in Lent
Respice domine	13th Sun. after Pentecost
Respice in me	3rd Sun. after octave of Pentecost
Richard (bp. of Chichester)	3 April
His translation	15 July
Rorate celi	4th Sun. in Advent
Salus populi	19th Sun. after Pentecost
Scholastica	10 February
Si iniquitates	22nd Sun. after octave of Pentecost
Silvester	31 December
Simon and Jude	28 October
Sitientes	Sat. before Passion Sunday
Stephen	26 December
His invention	3 August
Suscepimus deus	8th Sun. after octave of Pentecost
Swithun	2 July
His translation	15 July
Thomas the Apostle	21 December
His translation	3 July
Thomas Becket	29 December
His translation	7 July
Timotheus and Symphorianus	22 August
Transfiguration	6 August
Urban	25 May
Valentine	14 February
Vincent	22 January
Viri Galilei	Ascension Day
Vocem jucunditatis	5th Sun. after Easter
Wilfrid	12 October
Wufstan	19 January

Note. The occurrence on the same day of a movable and fixed feast may cause doubt and difficulty, e.g. if Ash Wednesday coincides with the feast of a patron saint, or Easter with Lady Day. There appear to have been in the Middle Ages no precise rules, observed by the Christian churches at large, for resolving these difficulties. But in England Clement Maydeston (*c.* 1390–1456) drew up a 'Directorium Sacerdotum' or Priests' Guide, based on the Sarum Ordinale, in which he dealt, among other things, with the celebration of feasts in the different contingencies arising from the variations of the calendar. By the end of the fifteenth century this work had obtained wide acceptance in England. Early in the sixteenth century its place was taken by the Sarum Pica or 'Pie', where its rules were adopted, and this was incorporated with the Sarum Breviary. The precise rules may be conveniently found in the 'Directorium' and the 'Tracts' of Clement Maydeston, reproduced in vols. vii and xx of the publications of the Henry Bradshaw Society. Their underlying principle is that when two feasts coincide which cannot conveniently be celebrated on the same day, the inferior feast is transferred to the first unoccupied day.

The Introit to the Mass for each Sunday of the year (e.g. *Adorate dominum*, above) has often been used as a method of dating. It must therefore be noted that liturgical practice has changed since medieval times in respect of the Sundays after Pentecost. In the Roman Missal revised in 1570 each of these Introïts was attached to one Sunday earlier than was usual in medieval practice. In this table the usual medieval practice is followed. Thus, *Da pacem* appears as the 18th Sunday after the octave of Pentecost (= 18th Sunday after Trinity), whereas in modern missals it is the Introit for the 18th Sunday after Pentecost.

TABLE V

DAY OF THE WEEK
ON WHICH THE FIRST OF EACH MONTH FALLS
ACCORDING TO THE DOMINICAL LETTER OF THE YEAR

(The double Dominical Letter indicates leap years)

Dominical Letter	Jan.	Feb.	Mar.	Apr.	May	Jun.	Jul.	Aug.	Sep.	Oct.	Nov.	Dec.
A	Su	W	W	S	M	Th	S	Tu	F	Su	W	F
BA	S	Tu										
B	S	Tu	Tu	F	Su	W	F	M	Th	S	Tu	Th
CB	F	M										
C	F	M	M	Th	S	Tu	Th	Su	W	F	M	W
DC	Th	Su										
D	Th	Su	Su	W	F	M	W	S	Tu	Th	Su	Tu
ED	W	S										
E	W	S	S	Tu	Th	Su	Tu	F	M	W	S	M
FE	Tu	F										
F	Tu	F	F	M	W	S	M	Th	Su	Tu	F	Su
GF	M	Th										
G	M	Th	Th	Su	Tu	F	Su	W	S	M	Th	S
AG	Su	W										

Note. The first and last quarters of the year begin on the same day of the week and the other two quarters a day earlier, except in leap years when all the first three quarters begin on the same day and the fourth quarter a day later.